WHO'S WHO IN ART

36TH EDITION

WHO'S WHO IN ART

36TH EDITION

Biographies of leading Men and Women
in the World of Art in Britain today:
Artists, Sculptors, Designers, Architects, Illustrators,
Critics, Lecturers, Curators and Craftsmen.

Lynda Murray
Editor

Nicky Austin
Assistant Editor

Morven Press
2014

Morven Press
16 Templars Firs
Royal Wootton Bassett
Wiltshire SN4 7EN
Great Britain

ISBN 978 0 9536039 2 3

Distributed exclusively in the United States of America, its Possessions, Canada and Mexico, by:
Cengage Learning Inc.
27500 Drake Road, Farmington Hills,
Michigan 48331 – 3535 U.S.A.

Typeset by Hilary Perry, Bristol, hilary562000@gmail.com
Produced for Morven Press by Kismet, Salisbury, SP5 4EJ
Printed and bound in the UK

To

Tony

ACKNOWLEDGEMENTS

To my Assistant Editor, Nicky Austin, for her sterling effort and fortitude in editing and adding over 250 new artists amongst many other tasks, I extend my gratitude. For all matters technical and artistic regarding our website and our new online Submission process, and for his patience with my endless queries, special recognition goes to Rhys Thomas. My thanks to Sarah Baile de Laperrière for stepping in to lend a hand when it was most needed, and a big thank you to my husband Tony Murray for his continuing support.

I gratefully acknowledge my debt to the officers of the academies, societies, groups, artists clubs and galleries for their continuous co-operation, as well as the numerous individuals who have helped us in this edition, many of them artists themselves.

For the errors and omissions I take full responsibility and I would like to take the opportunity to apologise to those we have inadvertently erroneously recorded, may they rest assured that all corrections notified to me will be included in the next edition.

I am constantly aware in my work of the influence of the previous Editor, Charles Baile de Laperrière, without whom it would not have been possible for me to produce this or the previous edition. I hope that he is looking on and saying 'Bon' as he used to do frequently in the office when he was pleased with the general progress of things.

Lynda Murray

October 2014

EDITOR'S NOTES

In compiling Who's Who In Art it is my aim to produce a comprehensive list of biographical details of living artists of any nationality, active or being represented in the United Kingdom or Ireland today, as well as leading personalities in British Contemporary Art.

Who's Who In Art embraces exponents of all forms of painting, drawing, graphic art and sculpture in their widest forms and any medium.

This edition follows the tradition of the last, with three directory indexes:

- **A** – An Index of over 1400 Alphabetically Indexed Artists' Websites.
- **B** – An Index of over 700 Modern and Contemporary Art Gallery Websites. This will enable the reader to access several thousand illustrated works of artists listed in the book, as well as an innumerable quantity of works recorded on the galleries websites.
- **C** – An Index of Society Websites.

The omission of well-known names is most regrettable, but we are limited to those artists who wish their names to appear. Standard entries are free and merit is the only criterion.

If, by any chance, there are artists of repute who have never been approached, I can only apologise for the oversight and hope, if they should read these editor's notes, they will inform us of the omission so that they may appear in the next edition of Who's Who In Art, which will be published in 2016.

All the entries in the last edition have been submitted to the individuals concerned and any corrections or additions notified have been incorporated in the present edition. We have approached numerous artists and many new names appear for the first time. We always welcome applicants and names of artists recommended by others.

CONTENTS

Who's Who In Art Editions

1st	1927	19th	1980
2nd	1929	20th	1982
3rd	1934	21st	1984
4th	1948	22nd	1986
5th	1950	23rd	1988
6th	1952	24th	1990
7th	1954	25th	1992
8th	1956	26th	1994
9th	1958	27th	1996
10th	1960	28th	1998
11th	1962	29th	2000
12th	1964	30th	2002
13th	1966	31st	2004
14th	1968	32nd	2006
15th	1970	33rd	2008
16th	1972	34th	2010
17th	1974	35th	2012
18th	1977	36th	2014

AN APPEAL

TO

ARTISTS, GALLERIES

AND

AGENTS

Applications for inclusion in Who's Who in Art are always sympathetically considered.

If you know of an artist who you think should be included an entry form will be sent on request. Standard entries are free and there is no obligation whatsoever to purchase a copy of the book on publication. Merit is the only criterion for inclusion.

Any information that should be added to existing entries should be sent to the Editor immediately.

Galleries receive a free listing in the directory. If you would like your gallery to be included in the next edition, please send us your details

Who's Who in Art is revised every two years.

NOTES

AIMS AND ACTIVITIES OF ACADEMIES, GROUPS, SOCIETIES, ETC.

Armed Forces Art Society

Annual Exhibition in Mall Galleries, London. Anyone of any rank who is serving or has served in the Armed Forces (including Reserve Forces and cadets) is entitled to apply to become an Associate of the Society; spouses and widows/widowers of such may also apply for Associateship. The Committee considers applications from eligible personnel. Applicants are accepted if their work is deemed to be of the requisite standard. Once accepted for membership applicants are eligible to submit works for selection for the exhibition.
Chairman: John Ashton. *Membership Secretary*: Martin Balshaw.
Email: www.armedforcesart@yahoo.com *Exhibition Secretary*: Mike Murtagh.

Association of British Naïve Artists

ABNA – The Association of British naïve Artists was founded by British naïve artist Peter Denham in the year 2000. Its aim is to promote Naïve Art in the UK, and to educate and encourage people from all walks of life to express themselves through painting. Sadly Peter died a few years ago, but the Association now has a membership of over 50, and holds regular exhibitions in Cornwall and other counties. Many members selected from the growing website have been asked to exhibit in galleries around the UK and abroad.
Judy Joel of Mousehole is Director and Secretary, and oversees the Association generally. The Association is headed by its Chairman Mervyn Clingan who was a friend of Peter Denham and a Founder Member.
For more information contact Judy Joel at littlepicturegallery@gmail.com or through the *website*: www.britishnaives.co.uk or by writing to ABNA, Noah's Ark, Abbey Place, Mousehole, Cornwall, TR19 6PQ

The Association of Illustrators (AOI)

The Association of Illustrators (AOI) is a not-for-profit trade organization promoting contemporary illustration and maintaining industry standards. Established in 1973 the AOI has worked successfully with businesses and colleges to increase the standing of illustration as a profession and improve commercial and ethical conditions. With a membership that includes freelance illustrators, agents, students and colleges the AOI continues to support and educate future generations at every stage of their career.
Website: http://www.theaoi.com *Email*: info@theaoi.com
Facebook: http://www.facebook.com/theaoi *Twitter*: http://twitter.com/theaoi

Buckinghamshire Art Society

The Buckinghamshire Art Society was founded in 1920 and plays a very active role in promoting visual arts in the county of Buckinghamshire by organizing two exhibitions every year, an open exhibition and a member's exhibition. The member's exhibition incorporates the 'Young Artists Award', introduced in 2006, in order to encourage artistic activities among younger members of the public and to forge links with the art education system.
The objectives of Buckinghamshire Art Society are 'the encouragement of painting, drawing, printmaking and sculpture and related activities within the County of Buckinghamshire'. To achieve this 'the Society shall strive to present and represent the Best of Art in Buckinghamshire'.
If you wish to know more about us and see some examples of work produced by the members, please visit our website at www.bucksart.co.uk , where you will also find a list of current members. You can email us on mail@bucksart.co.uk

The Cartoonists Club of Great Britain

Since its inaugural meeting at The Feathers Pub, Tudor St, London on Friday 1st of April 1960, The Cartoonists' Club of Great Britain has evolved into one of the largest cartoonist's organisations in the world, with a membership of over 200 full and part time Cartoonists in the United Kingdom (and further afield).

Our membership reflects the specialisations within the profession, all aspects of the business being severally represented, from single gags to strips, Caricature and Cartoon illustration. Prominently featured in our constitution are our objectives as an organisation with emphasis on encouraging good social contacts between cartoonists, (who for the most part lead rather more solitary professional lives than most) and to promote the art of the Cartoon.

Many of the great names from the British cartoon fraternity have passed through our portals during the last 43 years and all have contributed something to the organisation. We have collectively been responsible for organising very many local, nationwide and international Cartoon events, from exhibitions and competitions to charitable fund raising events or indeed demonstrating the art of the Cartoon to enthusiastic youngsters at road shows and public exhibitions. Cartooning has fantastic appeal to a wide section of the great British public with a high level of interest and curiosity with the mirth you would expect to be evident at a Cartoon event.

The organisational structure of the Club is fairly informal. The Committee, of 15 members, including The Chairman, Secretary, Treasurer and Projects Officer, meets once a month to conduct our various affairs. We publish internally a monthly newsletter 'The Jester'. The Club also publishes a complete members handbook usually every four years or so and also manages a permanent body of framed Cartoon work on general theme, called 'The Cartoonists' Exhibition'. This exhibition is available for various Club events such as link-ups with other arts organisations and galleries or as a fund raising exhibition at charity auctions.

Chairman: Graham Fowell. *Treasurer*: Jill Kearney. *Secretary*: John Stilgoe.

Email enquiries: secretary@thecartoonistsclub.com. *Website*: www.ccgb.org.uk.

The Chartered Society of Designers

Founded in 1930, CSD is the professional body for designers. It is the world's largest chartered body of professional designers and is unique in representing designers in all disciplines.

CSD is governed by Royal Charter and as such its members are obliged to practice to the highest professional standards. The Society is also a registered charity and adheres to best practice as a membership organization.

Membership is only awarded to qualified designers who must also prove their professional capability during an admission assessment. If a designer has MCSD™ or FCSD™ after their name you can be assured of a professional service.

The Society exists to promote concern for the sound principles of design in all areas in which design considerations apply, to further design practice and encourage the study of design techniques for the benefit of the community. In doing so, it seeks to secure and promote a professional body of designers and regulate and control their practice for the benefit of industry and the public.

With 3000+ members in 34 countries around the world, CSD offers a truly diverse and inclusive base of professional designers, each committed to operating to the highest professional standards in whichever field or country they practice.

Address: 1 Cedar Court, Royal Oak Yard, Bermondsey Street, London SE1 3GA.

Tel: 020 7357 8088. *Fax*: 020 7407 9878. *Email*: csd@csd.org.uk. *Website*: www.csd.org.uk.

Chelsea Art Society

Exhibition held annually at The Main Hall, Chelsea Old Town Hall, Kings Rd., London SW3.

President: Julian Barrow. *Vice-President*: Ann Marvolean. *Hon.Secretary*: Heather Wills-Sandford. *Hon. Treasurer*: William Bale.

Council: Roger Dellar RI PS, John J. Petts, Anne Wright, Katherine Yates, Michael Alford, Marysia Jaczynska, Janet Treloar RWS, Christine E. Ellis, Alison Pullen, Penny Reeve, John Stillman, Gilbert Whyman.

Address: Hon. Secretary, 50 Bowerdean St., London SW6 3TW. *Tel*: 020 7731 3121.
Website: www.chelseaartsociety.org.uk./

The Cheltenham Group of Artists

The Cheltenham Group was founded in 1920 with the aim of bringing together local professional artists from a wide range of disciplines. The group comprises members of all ages working in both contemporary as well as traditional media representing current art directions. The group has never drawn up a formal manifesto: indeed it is a characteristic of the exhibitions that works are widely varied in style, approach and technique.

A regular programme of members' exhibitions is held together with a bi-annual open exhibition. Prizes are awarded for works of special merit in a variety of categories.

Contact: Robert Freeman. *Address*: 59 Cirencester Road, Charlton Kings, Cheltenham, Glos, GL53 8EX. *Tel*: 01242 580506. *Email*: bob@rifreeman.co.uk
Website: www.cheltenhamgroupartists.org

The Colour Group

Founded in 1940 as an interdisciplinary society aiming to bring together those interested in all aspects of colour. Monthly public lectures (October to May) provide a forum for information on colour in the arts and sciences. Admission is usually free. Members receive a regular newsletter. An elected committee administers the biennial Newton Medal and Turner Medal and the William David Wright and David Palmer financial awards. Membership (available online) currently comprises 200 scientists, artists and other interested persons.

Address: The Hon.Secretary, The Colour Group (Great Britain), c/o Applied Vision Research Centre, City University, Northampton Square, London EC1V 0HB.
Website: www.colour.org.uk. *Email*: info@colour.org.uk.

The East Anglian Group of Marine Artists

In 1979 six amateur and professional marine painters met at the famous "Butt and Oyster" pub at Pin Mill on the banks of the River Orwell, Suffolk. Inspired by the surroundings and a shared enthusiasm for depicting the maritime scene, the East Anglian Group of Marine Artists was brought into being. Soon others were invited to join, amongst them being some well-known and highly regarded artists with a leaning towards East Coast subject matter. An inaugural exhibition was held in Ipswich early the following year, since when the group has moved from strength to strength with a steady improvement in standards and diversity.

Candidate members exhibit with the group before being considered for full membership at the annual general meeting. The group has a maximum of 35 full members.

Exhibitions are held several times a year, at galleries such as Mandell's Gallery, Norwich; Thompson's Gallery, Aldeburgh; and Sea Pictures Gallery in Clare.

President: Kenneth Denton RSMA ISMP FRSA PEAGMA.
Chairman: Richard Dack RSMA RWA EAGMA.
Hon. Secretary: Andrew King ROI IEA EAGMA, Pond Cottage, Long Lane, Colby, Norfolk NR11 7EF. *Tel*: 01263 761737. *Email*: info@andrewkingroi.co.uk.
Website: eastangliangroupofmarineartists.org.uk

Federation of British Artists

The Federation of British Artists (FBA) is a registered charity established in 1961 which operates the Mall Galleries. Through its programme of exhibitions, the FBA provides a focal point for contemporary, mainly figurative art by living artists. It aims to promote and encourage the study and practice of the visual arts by showcasing contemporary works in different media and different subjects. Its open submission exhibitions attract both well-established artists and emerging talent.

The FBA is home to eight of this country's most prestigious art societies, each exhibiting annually at the Mall Galleries, and includes: the Pastel Society, New English Art Club, Royal Society of British Artists, Royal Institute of Painters in Watercolours, Royal Institute of Oil

Painters, Royal Society of Portrait Painters, Royal Society of Marine Artists, and the Society of Wildlife Artists.
Mall Galleries also runs The Threadneedle Figurative Prize: Figurative Art Today as well as FBA Futures.
The FBA is entirely reliant for its income on sponsorship, sales commissions and membership fees. It places great importance on its educational activities, which include programmes for children considered at risk and other hard to reach audiences.
Director: Lewis McNaught *Chairman*: The Rt Hon Michael Portillo
Address: Mall Galleries, The Mall, London SW1 *Tel*: 020 7930 6844
Website: wwww.mallgalleries.org.uk

Free Painters and Sculptors (FPS)

This FPS was founded in 1952 when painter members of the ICA formed an individual group devoted to the principle of a 'free association of painters for mutual assistance, without regard to style, with no theory held in common, but believing in vital experiment and friendship'. Initially known as the Free Painters Group, the name was changed in the mid-Sixties to the Free Painters and Sculptors to include sculptors who had become an integral part of the Group.
In 1972 the FPS opened the Loggia Gallery in Buckingham Gate where exhibitions of members' work were held. Group shows were also sent to galleries out of London. Giving up our gallery, in 2000 we moved with SPANA to new premises. From there we send out pictures from our Reserve Collection to galleries in London and around the country.
Membership is £30 annually and Student Membership £15. Persons interested in the visual arts are welcomed and applications will be submitted to the Executive Committee. Full membership is awarded to practising artists whose work is of the required standard.
The Free Painters and Sculptors is an Incorporated body and is registered as an Educational Charity.
Chairman: Penelope MacEwan. *Secretary*: Owen Legg. *Address*: 14 John Street, London WC1N 2EB. *Tel*: 0207 828 5963. *Website*: www.piczo.com/FreePaintersAndSculptors

The Fylingdales Group of Artists

Members are frequently asked the question of what is The Fylingdales Group of Artists, and find it difficult to give a definite answer. We are not an Art Society in the usual sense, and we are not connected in any way to a certain Early Warning Radar Station – as is sometimes thought.
The Group usually hold one Exhibition a year at the Pannett Art Gallery, Whitby, although we occasionally hold other exhibitions at different venues. We meet formally as a group once a year, following our Annual Exhibition. A glance at the list of members will show that we are scattered over a large area, and it is a measure of the strength of the Group that Members are prepared to travel quite long distances to attend our annual General Meeting. The main bond between us is a love of Yorkshire, its coastline, and of painting.
The Group was founded on 25th June 1925 at a meeting held in Mr. Denton Hawley's studio in Robin Hood's Bay. It was to be limited to 12 members although this was increased to the present number of 22 some time later. Dame Ethel Walker, ARA, Owen Bowen and Ulric Walmsley were among the founder members, Denton Hawley became the first Secretary.
Exhibitions were held annually in the Church Rooms, Robin Hood's Bay, until the outbreak of war in 1939. They ceased during the War Years but the Group was brought together again at the end of hostilities by Mr. Harold Todd, who continued to serve the group as Secretary for many years. The Annual Exhibition continued to be held in Robin Hood's Bay until 1952 when it moved to its present venue at the Pannett Gallery, Whitby.
The Group is open to amateur and professional Artists, and when a vacancy occurs, membership is by invitation only.

Charirman: David Allen. *Treasurer*: Don Micklethwaite. *Secretary*: Michael Atkin. *Address*: 'Byways', Low Street, Scalby, Scarborough YO13 0QW *Tel*: 01723 378278 *Website*: www.thefylingdalesartists.co.uk. *Email*: mail@thefylingdalesartists.co.uk

Glasgow Art Club

This Club was formed in 1867 to advance the cause of and stimulate interest in art in all its branches by means of exhibitions of works of art, life classes, the acquisition of Publications on art, lectures on art subjects, and by such other means as the Council may decide from time to time. Consequently, the Club's Membership comprises painters, sculptors, architects and others involved in creative work as Artist Members and ladies and gentlemen interested in art as Lay Members. To be admitted to Artist membership, candidates must submit examples of their work for the approval of the Artist Members. Painters, sculptors and members pay on admission an entry fee.
Secretary: Jonathan Lord, MA, The Glasgow Art Club, 185 Bath Street, Glasgow G2 4SN. *Tel*: 0141 248 5210. *E-mail*: secretary@glasgowartclub.co.uk

Guild of Aviation Artists

The Guild of Aviation Artists, a specially authorised Friendly Society founded in 1971, incorporates the Society of Aviation Artists, which held its first exhibition in 1954 at London's Guildhall. However, by 1958, a number of professional members had become somewhat disenchanted with the Society and turned their attention to a small social club catering for light flying and gliding enthusiasts called the Kronfeld Club, which was keen to put on an exhibition of aviation art at its Victoria premises. So it was that top professionals like Wootton, Turner and Young hung their work alongside artists who actually flew the aeroplanes.
It is the same today, and from these small beginnings, the Guild now has over 450 members including a number of "Friends" who are mostly artists as well. An annual open exhibition, held at the Mall Galleries and entitled 'Aviation Paintings of the Year', is sponsored by, amongst others, Rolls-Royce and Messier-Dowty. It attracts a prize of £1,000, sponsored by BAE Systems, for the artist of what is judged to be the best exhibit.
Other exhibitions are organized to commemorate many of the important events in our aviation history and members' work continues to be sought by historians, publishers and collectors alike. Their paintings are hanging in service messes and clubs, museums, galleries and aviation offices throughout the world.
President: Michael Turner FGAvA (President). *Founder President*: The Late Frank Wootton OBE GAvA *Chairman*: Graham Cooke MBE GAvA. *Treasurer*: Mrs Janet Latham. *Administrator/Secretary*: Mrs Susan Gardner. *Address*: Trenchard House, 85 Farnborough Road, Farnborough, Hants GU14 6TF *Tel*: 01252 513123 *Fax*: 01252 510505 *E-mail*: admin@gava.org.uk

Guild of Railway Artists

The Guild of Railway Artists was formed in October 1979 to forge a tangible link between artists whose interests included the depiction of the railway scene past and present. Amongst the aims of the Guild is the furtherance of the artistic portrayal of railways in its many facets and the staging of railway exhibitions.
Since its formation the Guild has mounted many successful "Railart" exhibitions throughout the United Kingdom showcasing its members works. Its major Annual exhibition for 2014 is to take place at the Kidderminster Railway Museum, Kidderminster. It is hoped to stage the 2015 Annual Exhibition at The National Railway Museum.
The Guild has also produced five fine art books of its members work – "The Great Western Collection" (1985), "To the Seaside" (1990), reprinted as "Great Railway Paintings Inspired by the Seaside" (2005), "A Century of Railways" (1996), "Along Artistic Lines" (2003 GRA/NRM Joint book) and "Emotions of Railway Art" (2011).
Members meet on a regular basis at Members Days, Selection Panel Meetings and the Annual

General Meeting. The Guild has its own website at www.railart.co.uk which gives up to date information about the Guild and its exhibitions, examples of members work and a Print Shop where prints by certain Guild artists can be purchased.
Chief Executive Officer: Frank Hodges, HonGRA. *Address*: 45 Dickins Road, Warwick, CV34 5NS *Tel*: 01926 499246 *Email*: frank.hodges@railart.co.uk

Hesketh Hubbard Art Society

Founded as RBA Art Club under the auspices of the Royal Society of British Artists. Members meet on Monday or Friday evenings to draw from the model throughout the year. New members admitted any Monday or Friday after a folio of work is inspected. No tuition unless specially requested. The Mall Galleries, The Mall, SW1.
President: Simon Whittle. *Hon.Secretary*: Frances Tipton.
Address: 17 Carlton House Terr., London SW1Y 5BD. *Tel*: 020 7930 6844.

The Hilliard Society of Miniaturists

Society founded in 1982 by Sue Burton and miniaturist Rosalind Pierson. Worldwide membership of around 300 artists, sculptors, and Patrons of miniature art. Full exhibiting artists entitled to use HS (HSF – Founder Member). Charter Member of the World Federation of Miniaturists.
Annual Wells exhibition held in June. AGM/awards luncheon, demonstrations. Two excellent social and technically informative newsletters annually. Work accepted and returned by post, worldwide. This friendly society supports and encourages artists, whilst promoting miniature art internationally.
Enquiries: The Secretary, c/o 26 St. Cuthbert Avenue, Wells, Somerset BA5 2JW
Email: hilliardsociety@aol.com *Website*: www.hilliardsociety.org
(Office hours: Tuesday/Wednesday 9.30am-2.30pm).

Ipswich Art Society

Ipswich Art Society was founded in 1874, celebrated its 137th Annual Open Exhibition in 2014. They also hold the Anna Airy Award Exhibition for young artists aged 16-25, and separate exhibitions of work of full members and of Friends of the Society. Annual Open Exhibition June/July.
Address: 89 Bucklesham Road, Ipswich. *Tel*: 01473 711178

The Lake Artists Society

The Lake Artists' Society was founded in 1904 largely on the initiative of W.G.Collingwood, the well known artist and local historian, and secretary to John Ruskin, to promote the work of its members. The first exhibition was held in 1905, and exhibitions have been staged every year since then, except for four years during the Second World War. The Summer Exhibition has become an established event in Cumbria, attracting over 10,000 visitors each year. The Winter Exhibition is held at The Art Gallery, Rheged, Penrith from Nov-Jan.
Membership is limited to 45 and high standards are maintained through careful selection of works and a rigorous procedure for the election of new members.
President: Vivienne Pooley. *Vice-President*: Graham Twyford. *Treasurer*: Peter Lansbury. *Secretary*: Gillian Moore. *Tel*: 01900 827294 *Website*: www.lakeartists.org.uk

The Liver Sketching Club

The Liver Sketching Club was founded on 11 May 1872 - initially as the Liverpool Amateur Sketching Club. In 1874, the club's name was changed to its present one as dropping the word 'Amateur' paved the way for professional artists to become members.
The club was founded by Samuel Burkinshaw, the Art Master at Liverpool College, and ten of his students - Joseph Hetherington, Johnathon Viner Garrett Loney, James Towers, Robert L Farmer, George M Richardson, John C Halfpenny, Albert Sutcliffe, J G Owens, John Skirrow and J B Brew.
The meeting at which the club was founded was held in the Committee Room at St

Augustine's School in Salisbury Street where members initially met. Since then it has been based at various locations around Liverpool - The Palatine, Cable Street [1875]; Pool Buildings, South Castle Street [1878]; 22 Williamson Street [1879]; Cuthbert's Buildings, Clayton Square [1880]; 11 Dale Street [1890]; Bluecoat Chambers [1973]; 36 Seel Street [1993] and, since 2004, in Gostins Building, Hanover Street.
The Liver Sketching Club has now been continuously active in Liverpool for more than 141 years and is busier than ever with about 90 members attending one or more of over 30 regular meetings each month - almost all of them working from the live model.
The club regularly exhibits at various external venues as well as its own gallery next to the studio and holds an Open Night each year in May. It has an extensive library, and interesting archive and a collection of work by past members. The club's Patron is Loyd Grossman OBE, FSA.
Address: Gostins Building, 32-36 Hanover Street, Liverpool L1 4LN.
Email: liversketchingclub@yahoo.co.uk *Website*: www.liversketchingclub.co.uk

The London Group

Founded in 1913 by an amalgamation of the Camden Town Group and the English Vorticists, the London Group is composed of working artists, has a written constitution, annually elected officers, a working committee and a selection committee. There are usually between 90 and 100 members and an annual fee is charged. The London Group aims to support contemporary artists from diverse backgrounds working in a wide range of media. Throughout its lifetime The London Group has given artists a platform to show work to the public without the constraints of commercial, establishment and curatorial censorship.
The Group has just celebrated its centenary, with five major exhibitions spread over the year, receiving both press and television coverage and culminating with an evening reception at Tate Britain on the 100th anniversary of the opening of the Group's first exhibition. The Ben Uri Museum & Gallery marked the Group's centenary with a show entitled 'Uproar! The First 50 Years of The London Group', resulting in its highest ever attendance figures. David Redfern, the Group's archivist, wrote 'The London Group: a history 1913 - 2013' to tie in with the centenary. The book is the first to document its entire history and copies are still available. The Group's biennial Open, in which the work of members is exhibited alongside those selected from open submissions, was reinstated in 2007. The Centenary Open included artists from across the world with prizes worth over £5000. A special prize of a solo show was also awarded. Under the current presidency, the Group has been offered preferential choice for regular exhibitions at The Cello Factory, Waterloo, London, all of which have been staged by an energetic, enthusiastic and committed membership.
Previous members have included Jacob Epstein, Walter Sickert, Wyndham-Lewis, Vanessa Bell, Henry Moore and David Hockney.
Address: The London Group, PO Box 61045, London SE1 8RN *President*: Susan Haire
Website: www.thelondongroup.com *Email*: enquiries@thelondongroup.com

The Master Carvers' Association

The Master Carvers' Association, founded in 1897, is the only Association for professional wood and stone carvers. Originally constituted as an employers association to enable national negotiations with the emerging unions, today the Association has transformed into a forum for professional wood and stone carvers.
The objects of the Association are the promotion, protection and interests of the wood and stone carving trades, and of the Association's members in particular.
There are three categories of membership, Member, Honorary Member and Associate Member. The Committee elects candidates for membership. More detailed information, including a history and the criterion for membership can be found on the website.
Hon. Secretary: Paul Ferguson, Unit 2, 15b Vanduke Road, Leighton Buzzard, Beds, LU7 3HG *Tel*: 01525 851594 *Email*: info@mastercarvers.co.uk.
Website: www.mastercarvers.co.uk

Medical Art Society

The Medical Art Society was founded in 1935 by a distinguished group of 'doctor-artists' who liked to draw, paint or sculpt at leisure. It has continued ever since as an independent society supported by its members, currently about 150, through their subscriptions (£20 annually) and partly by a bequest from the late Baron ver Heyden de Lancey. Administrative support is provided by the Royal Society of Medicine's Academic Department. Membership is open to any doctor, dentist or vet whether qualified, student or retired. A number of events are arranged each year by and for members and their painting friends. Besides painting days and weekends there are life drawing sessions, lectures and painting holidays abroad. The highlight of the year is the Annual Exhibition.
Patron: Mr Thomas Coates RWS NEAC PPRBA RP *President*: Mr Neil Weir
Address: c/o Academic Department, Royal Society of Medicine, 1 Wimpole Street, London W1G 0AE *Tel*: 020 7290 3948

The National Acrylic Painters' Association

This Association, founded in 1985, is for all practising artists and painters, who wish to explore the potential of the acrylic medium. Successful applicants are elected into full membership. It is recognised that acrylic painting is but a medium amongst others, yet that as a painting substance it has a flexibility that renders it extremely versatile. NAPA holds Annual Exhibitions at venues throughout the United Kingdom.
Founder: Kenneth J. Hodgson. *President*: Alwyn Crawshaw. *Director*: David Hillhouse.
The Association's patrons are: Dr. Sally A. Bulgin, Mark Golden – USA, Dr Catherine Marcangeli – France, and The Master of the Fine Art Trade Guild. NAPA has international members in Brazil, Europe and Israel.
Further information and details of membership obtainable from:
Website www.napauk.org or The National Acrylic Painters' Association, 49 Cortsway, Greasby, Wirral, Merseyside, CH49 2NA.

National Society of Painters, Sculptors and Printmakers

The National Society was formed in 1930 to escape rigid traditionalism by allowing Member Artists to exhibit a diversity of the best of creative art with full freedom of expression. The objects of the Society are to advance the awareness of the public by promoting or demonstrating painting, sculpture and printmaking and to hold an annual exhibition in London (and secondary exhibitions from time to time) of the work of artists of every creed and outlook representing all aspects under one roof without prejudice or favour to anyone.
Membership is in two categories: Members (NS) and Associate Members (AMNS). Members are elected on merit from among those Associates who have had at least two works selected for the annual exhibition for three years. Application information may be requested from the Hon. Secretary. A Newsletter is sent to Members and Associates twice a year.
President: Michael Clifford Leman. *Hon. Secretary*: Sarah Elizabeth Beaumont.
Address: PO Box 22894, London NW9 6ZE.

Nature in Art

NATURE IN ART is a museum of fine, decorative and applied art inspired by nature. It opened to the public in May 1988 and in June 1988 HRH Princess Alexandra attended a celebration of the opening. Nature in Art is the first of its kind anywhere in the world. It is housed in a fine, early Georgian mansion set in its own grounds and is owned and managed by Nature in Art Trust, registered charity 1000553.
Nature in Art is readily accessible from M5 (J11 and 11A) and the centre of Gloucester (both 10 minutes by car). The entrance is on A38 in Twigworth, one mile North of A40.
Art inspired by nature, from all periods and parts of the world in any medium, including works by living artists, is included in the permanent collection. All aspects of nature are included (but domestic, farm and sporting animals etc. are excluded). Temporary exhibitions are held regularly and the permanent collection on show is regularly changed.

Nature in Art was twice "specially commended" in the National Heritage Museum of the Year Awards. The museum is fully registered.

Facilities include free car parking, meals and light refreshments all day, library and reference collection of slides and other information, children's play area, shop, studios and nature garden with open air sculptures.The museum is fully accessible to wheelchair users. Different artists are in residence February/November and courses and demonstrations on a wide range of art techniques are arranged. A new conference/education centre opened in 1994. Open Tuesday-Sunday and Bank Holidays 10am-5pm. Closed other Mondays, (except by special arrangement when the facilities of Wallsworth Hall can be privately hired), and on Dec. 24, 25 and 26.

Patron: H.R.H. Princess Alexandra. *President*: Prof. Sir Ghillean Prance.

Chairman: Dr David H. Trapnell *Director*: Simon H. Trapnell.

Address: Wallsworth Hall, Twigworth, Gloucester GL2 9PA. *Tel*: 01452 731422.

Website: www.nature-in-art.org.uk *Email*: enquiries@nature-in-art.org.uk

Nature in Art Trust

Established as a Registered Charity (No. 1000553) in 1982, the Trust owns and manages Nature in Art. This centre has been created to exhibit, study and teach fine, decorative and applied art inspired by nature in all media from all national origins and all historical periods depicting any living (or previously living) wild thing. The facilities of Nature in Art are described under that title.

Friends of the Trust receive a regular Newsletter, *Nature in Art*, free admission to all regular activities of the Society, use of the library etc. Individual and gallery membership (for commercial and institutional galleries) is available. Further details from the Membership Secretary, Nature in Art (q.v.).

Patron: H.R.H. Princess Alexandra. *President*: Prof. Sir Ghillean Prance.

Director: Simon H.Trapnell.

Address: Wallsworth Hall, Twigworth, Gloucester GL2 9PA. *Tel*: 01452 731422.

Website: www.nature-in-art.org.uk *Email*: enquiries@nature-in-art.org.uk

New English Art Club

The New English Art Club was founded in 1886. Its origin was a wave of foreign influence in the person of a number of students who had worked in the Parisian schools. The New English Art Club came into existence as a protest against a false concept of tradition, and it stands today against an equally false rejection of tradition. It holds drawing and observation of prime importance, and has a drawing school teaching these basic principles. The annual exhibition is held in the Mall Galleries, The Mall, SW1, when the work of non-members is considered for display, November/December.

President: Jason Boyer PNEAC, RP, PS. *Hon. Treasurer*: David Corsellis.

Keeper: Charlotte Halliday, NEAC, RWS. *Assistant Keeper*: Bob Brown.

Address: 17 Carlton House Terr., London SW1Y 5BD. *Tel*: 020 7930 6844.

Website: www.neac.co.uk

Oxford Art Society

The Oxford Art Society is one of the oldest in the country. Edward Burne-Jones, Gilbert Spencer, the Carlines, the Nashes and John Piper have all exhibited the Society since its foundation in 1891.

The Society exists to seek exhibition opportunities for its members, holding both annual members' exhibition and an annual open exhibition, in Oxfordshire.

The majority of the Society's members have professional training, a large number exhibit during Oxford Art Weeks, and a number exhibit nationally and internationally.

To become a member of the Society, it is necessary to have had work selected at two of the open exhibitions. It is at the discretion of the Committee to invite new artists to become members.

President: Johannes Von Stumm FRBS. *Chairman*: Peter Farley. *Deputy Chair*: Jane Hope. For further information please visit our *website* www.oxfordartsociety.org.uk

Pastel Society

Founded 1898. Annual exhibition open to all artists who work in any "dry" medium, i.e. pastel, pencil, charcoal, chalk, conté, sanguine, etc., at The Mall Galleries, The Mall, SW1.
President: Cheryl Culver RBA. *Vice-President*: Jeannette Hayes.
Hon. Secretary: Jenny Halstead FMAA. *Hon. Treasurer*: Colin Murfet.
Address: 17 Carlton House Terrace, London SW1Y 5BD. *Tel*: 020 7930 6844.
Website: www.thepastelsociety.org.uk

Penwith Society

The Penwith Society was founded in 1949 by a group of notable contemporary artists in St Ives and its seasonal exhibitions became a national show place for contemporary work. The Society has an elected membership limited to fifty, and an unlimited associated membership. Its aims are to encourage practicing artists and craftworkers in Cornwall and to further public interest in the arts. To this end four members' exhibitions are held a year, also selected artists and exhibitions from both inside and outside the area.The gallery has charity status. It is a unique complex of buildings, including public galleries, book shop, artist's studios and the Print Workshop, with facilities for silkscreen, etching and relief printing and dark room. Eleven studios and two cottages complete this remarkable arts and crafts complex. Open all year, Tuesday to Saturday, 10.00-1.00 and 2.30-5.00.
Curator: Kathleen Watkins *Address*: Back Road West, St Ives, Cornwall.
Tel: 01736 795579

Royal Academy of Arts

The Royal Academy was founded in 1768 under the patronage of George III, as a society for the promotion of the arts of design. Sir Joshua Reynolds was the first President. Since that date it has fulfilled this role through promotion of the work of living artists with an unbroken series of Summer Exhibitions, held annually since 1769. It provides post-graduate training for 60 students in the Royal Academy Schools, which were established at the foundation.
The Academy continues to administer trust funds for the benefit of artists and for the promotion of the visual arts, and has a distinguished Collection and Research Library, and an Archive. Loan exhibitions, of great international importance, date from the 1870s. The Royal Academy receives no direct Government subsidy. It is an independent, self-supporting institution, under the patronage of the Crown, and its activities are directed by its Members (Painters, Engravers, Sculptors and Architects) who serve in rotation on the Council. The President is elected annually.
The Royal Academy is supported by sponsorship, through the subscriptions of its 90,000 Friends, its Patrons and Benefactors, its Corporate Members, an active fundraising programme, retail sales of art books and specially commissioned works.
President: Christopher le Brun *Keeper*: Eileen Cooper.
Secretary and Chief Executive: Dr. Charles Saumarez Smith CBE *Treasurer*: Paul Huxley.
Address: Burlington House, Piccadilly, London W1J 0BD. *Tel*: 020 7300 8000.
Website: www.royalacademy.org.uk

Royal Birmingham Society of Artists

The Royal Birmingham Society of Artists (RBSA) is an artist-led charity, which supports artists and promotes engagement with the visual arts through a range of inclusive activities: exhibitions, workshops, demonstrations and other events.
The RBSA Gallery is owned by the Society, making it one of a few rare galleries to be owned by artists and run for artists. It has a changing programme of exhibitions on two floors, and on the ground floor a café and craft wall spaces. The ground floor also houses the Craft Gallery, which has established a reputation as *the* place to find exciting and unique handmade jewellery. Entrance to the gallery is free.

Address (*Society and Gallery*): The Royal Birmingham Society of Artists, 4 Brook St., St. Paul's, Birmingham B3 1SA. *Tel*: 0121 236 4353.
Website: www.rbsa.org.uk *Email*: secretary@rbsa.org.uk rbsagallery@rbsa.org.uk

Royal Cambrian Academy of Art

The Royal Cambrian Academy of Art was founded in 1881, and granted its Royal Charter in 1882. The Headquarters have been in Conwy since 1886. In 1993 the Academy moved from Plas Mawr to its new purpose built Gallery, where Exhibitions are held throughout the year. The main Exhibition is the Annual Summer Exhibition, and there is also an Open Exhibition held annually.
Forms for this exhibition and membership of the Academy may be obtained from the Gallery and website.
President: Jeremy Yates *Vice-President*: Ann Lewis.
Hon. Secretary: Sonja Benskin Mesher. *Gallery Administrator*: Joan Halliday.
Education Officer: Wendy Couling.
Address: Crown Lane, Conwy LL32 8AN.
Gallery open 11am-5pm Tuesday to Saturday, closed Sunday and Monday.
Tel: 01492 593413. *Email*: rca@rcaconwy.org. *Website*: www.rcaconwy.org

Royal Glasgow Institute of the Fine Arts

This Institute was founded in 1861 and has now over 1,100 Members. Its object is "to promote a taste for art generally and more specifically to encourage contemporary art, to further the diffusion of artistic and aesthetic knowledge and to aid the study, advancement and development of art in its application." Towards the attainment of this object, the Institute holds open annual exhibitions in The Mitchell, Glasgow, and shows approximately 350 works in all mediums. The RGI Kelly Gallery is available for hire. The Membership fee is an initial payment of £35, Annual subscription £25, Corporate Members Scheme £117.50.
Secretary: Mrs. Lesley Nicholl *Address*: 5 Oswald St., Glasgow G1 4QR.
Tel: 0141 248 7411. *Fax*: 0141 221 0417.
Email: rgi@robbferguson.co.uk. *Website*: www.rgiscotland.co.uk

Royal Hibernian Academy

The Academy was incorporated by Charter of King George IV in 1823 with the intention of encouraging the fine arts in Ireland by giving Irish artists the opportunity of exhibiting their works annually. It was reorganized under a new Charter in 1861 and enlarged to thirty Constituent Members, and up to the present time has consistently fulfilled its original aims.
The Academy has encouraged and developed art in Ireland since its foundation. It has given the Irish artist his status; and the present position of Irish Art can be said to be the outcome of the encouragement it has afforded to Irish men and women of talent and the part it has taken in art affairs generally in the country.
There is hardly an Irish artist of note living or dead who has not been a member of the Academy or who has not benefited in one way or another by its activities.
President: Des McMahon RHA. *Secretary*: David Crone RHA.
Treasurer: James English RHA. *Keeper*: Donald Teskey RHA.
School Principal: Mick O'Dea RHA *Address*: 15 Ely Place, Dublin 2.

Royal Institute of Oil Painters

Founded in 1883 as the Institute of Painters in Oil Colours. The annual exhibition, which is open to all artists, subject to selection, is held in the Mall Galleries, The Mall, SW1.
President: Ian Cryer. *Vice-President*: Tim Benson
Hon. Secretary: Luis Morris. *Hon. Treasurer*: Susan Scott.
Address: 17 Carlton House Terr., London SW1Y 5BD.
Tel: 020 7930 6844 *Website*: www.theroi.org.uk

The Royal Institute of Painters in Watercolours

Formed in 1831 as the "New Society of Painters in Water-colours," a title which was afterwards changed to the "Institute of Painters in Water-colours." Shortly after the opening of the 1884 Exhibition the command of Queen Victoria was received that the Society should henceforth be called "The Royal Institute of Water-colours."

The honour of a diploma under the Royal Sign Manual was given to the members on August 29, 1884, by virtue of which they rank as *Esquires*. Members are limited to 100. Annual Open Exhibition, March, at The Mall Galleries, The Mall, SW1.

President: Andy Wood, RBA *Vice-President*: Tony Hunt

Address: 17 Carlton House Terr., London SW1Y 5BD. *Tel*: 020 7930 6844.

Website: www.mallgalleries.org.uk

Royal Scottish Academy

The Royal Scottish Academy (RSA), in the heart of Edinburgh, instructs, inspires, informs and funds artists as well as presenting a year-round programme of exhibitions and events. Founded in 1826 by a group of eminent artists and granted a Royal Charter in 1838, the RSA continues to be led by a body of artists and architects (Academicians) prominent in their field. The RSA remains independent from local or national government funding, relying instead on bequests, legacies, sponsorship and earned income which allows the RSA the autonomy to develop and present a wide range of initiatives, without restriction and remain and independent voice for cultural advocacy.

One of the largest independent supporters of artists in Scotland, the RSA disperses some £200,000 annually through an extensive programme of scholarships, awards and residencies. Relationships with new artists and architects are developed through *RSA New Contemporaries*, the largest exhibition of graduate art which, with the *RSA Annual Exhibition* and the *RSA Open Exhibition*, an open submission opportunity, forms part of the RSA's extensive revolving programme of exhibitions and events.

The RSA also manages an historic collection of Scottish artworks and archive which is recognised by the Scottish Government as being of national significance. Works from the RSA Permanent Collection are available to rent and income from this is directed towards the upkeep and conservation of the collection. This forms part of a fully comprehensive art consultation provided by the RSA which offers advice on building a collection through rental purchases and the commission of new works.

Over the last decade, every aspect of the RSA has been reviewed to ensure that the RSA remains relevant to the needs of today's artists and architects, both nationally and internationally.

President: Arthur Watson PRSA. *Secretary*: Marion Smith RSA

Treasurer: Gareth Fisher RSA. *Librarian*: Will Maclean, MBE, FRSE, RSA.

Keeper: George Donald RSA. *Director*: Colin R Greenslade.

Address: The Mound, Edinburgh, EH2 2EL. *Tel*: 0131 225 6671.

Email: info@royalscottishacademy.org *Website*: www.royalscottishacademy.org.

Royal Scottish Society of Painters in Watercolour

This Society was founded in 1878, and in 1888 Queen Victoria conferred on it the title "Royal." In its first Exhibition twenty-five artists showed their works; today there are 119 exhibiting Members.

The object of the Society is to encourage and develop the art of painting in watercolour and the appreciation of this art, and toward the attainment of that object exhibitions of watercolour painting are held annually. While these are normally held in Edinburgh, they have on occasion been held in Glasgow, Aberdeen, Dundee and Perth. Candidates for Membership must be sponsored by Members of the Society, and must submit works for the consideration of the Members at an election meeting. The entrance fee is £45 and the annual subscription £45.

President: John Inglis RSW *Secretary*: Mrs Lesley Nicholl
Address: 5 Oswald St, Glasgow G1 4QR. *Tel*: 0141 248 7411.
Email: rsw@robbferguson.co.uk *Website*: www.thersw.org.uk

Royal Society of British Artists

This Society was founded in 1823, incorporated by Royal Charter in 1847 and constituted a Royal Society in 1887. Membership is limited to 200. Annual exhibition held each year, when the work of non-members is admitted after selection at The Mall Galleries, The Mall, SW1.
President: James Horton. *Hon. Secretary*: Judith Gardner.
Hon. Treasurer: Colin Gardner. *Keeper*: Julian Halsby.
Address: 17 Carlton House Terr., London SW1Y 5BD. *Tel*: 020 7930 6844.

Royal British of Society Sculptors

Established in 1905 as a not-for-profit company (83239), we are a membership society of 500 + professional sculptors and are a registered charity (212513). We are the oldest and largest organisation dedicated to sculpture in the UK.
Committed to the pursuit of excellence in the art form, we aim to inspire, inform and engage people with sculpture/three dimensional art. We offer opportunities to see and experience the extraordinary diversity of contemporary work and to learn from those who make it through our exhibition programme.
We support sculptors by providing bursaries to newly emergent sculptors, a mentoring scheme and a growing number of awards and residencies. Members benefit from holding an internationally recognised professional accreditation (Associate ARBS and Fellow FRBS), and the shared knowledge and experience of this network of sculptors at all stages of their careers.
RBS invites professional artists who work in three dimensions as a significant part of their practice to apply. Successful applicants will demonstrate a high level of expertise, experience, and contemporary understanding; their work must contribute to the language of sculpture. Applications are via an online form at our website and selection is by peer review by the sculptor members of the Council. Selection meetings are held four times a year in June, September, December, and March.
President: Terry New PRBS *Vice-President*: Clare Burnett VPRBS
Treasurer: Matthew French
Address: 108 Old Brompton Road, London, SW7 3RA. *Tel*: 02073738615
Website: www.rbs.org.uk *Email*: info@rbs.org.uk

Royal Society of Marine Artists

The RSMA was founded in 1939, to encourage the practice and appreciation of marine art in Britain. The first exhibition was in 1946 after WWII ended. Initially known as the Society of Marine Artists, the right to use the title Royal was granted by Her Majesty the Queen in 1966. Membership to the Society can only be achieved by election, initially as an Associate and by subsequent promotion to Member. Before being considered as an applicant artists must demonstrate a consistently high standard of work by being successful in exhibiting regularly at the Society's Annual Open Exhibition, which is held in October at the Mall Galleries in London. There is also a Friends of the RSMA section for anyone who has an interest in marine art and who wishes to support the Society.
President: Elizabeth Smith PRSMA. *Vice-President*: Geoff Hunt PPRSMA.
Hon. Secretary: Margaret Heath RSMA. *Hon. Treasurer*: David Allen RSMA.
Address: 17 Carlton House Terr., London SW1Y 5BD. *Website*: www.rsma-web.co.uk.
Email: info@rsma-web.uk. *Tel*: 0207-930-6844.

Royal Society of Miniature Painters, Sculptors and Gravers

This Society was founded in 1896 and its aim is to promote the fine art of miniature painting or any allied craft. The annual exhibition is held in London at the Mall Galleries. The Gold

Bowl Award was established in 1985 and is one of the highest accolades for miniature art in the world. Non-members may submit work.
Membership is by selection after establishing a consistently high standard of work. (ARMS - Associate Member, RMS - Full Member).
President: Rosalind Pierson. *Executive Secretary*: Claire Hucker, Laurels Studio, Stone, Berkeley, Gloucestershire GL13 9LD *Tel*: 01454 269268
Email: info@royal-miniature-society.org.uk

Royal Society of Painter-Printmakers

The Royal Society of Painter-Printmakers was founded in 1880. The Society was granted a Royal Charter in 1911. Eminent Past-Presidents have been Sir F. Seymour Haden, Sir Frank Short, Malcolm Osborne and Robert Austin. All the well-known printmakers have exhibited with the Society, whose annual exhibition caters for and encourages all forms of printmaking. An election of Associates is held annually.
As part of its aim to promote a knowledge and understanding of original printmaking, the Society organises courses, talks and tours.
President: Mychael Barratt. *Vice President*: Trevor Price.
Hon. Secretary: John Duffin. *Address*: Bankside Gallery, 48 Hopton St., London SE1 9JH. *Tel*: 020 7928 7521. *Website*: www.re-printmakers.com

Royal Society of Portrait Painters

This Society was founded in 1891 and has for its object the promotion of the fine art of portrait painting. The annual exhibition is held during April/May in The Mall Galleries, The Mall, SW1 and non members may submit work in any medium, except miniatures or sculpture, to the Selection Committee.
President: Robin-Lee Hall *Hon. Secretary*: Melissa Scott-Miller RP NEAC.
Vice-President: Simon Davies. *Hon. Treasurer*: Jason Walker.
Address: 17 Carlton House Terr., London SW1Y 5BD. *Tel*: 01932 562368.
Website: www.therp.co.uk

Royal Ulster Academy of Arts

President: Carol Graham, PRUA *Hon.Secretary*: Amanda Croft *Treasurer*: Barbara Killen
All correspondence to: *Secretary*: Kay McKelvey, 57 Ballycoan Road, Belfast BT8 8LL

Royal Watercolour Society

The Royal Water-Colour Society, which is next in seniority to the Royal Academy, was founded in 1804. It has numbered amongst its distinguished Members John Varley, Peter de Wint, David Cox, John Sell Cotman, Samuel Prout, Samuel Palmer, Ambrose McEvoy and D. Y. Cameron to mention but a few. Two exhibitions are held annually - in the spring and autumn. These exhibitions are confined to the works of Members. An annual exhibition open to all water-colour painters is held in the Spring. There is an annual election of Associates.
As part of its educational remit, the Society organises courses, talks, tours and other events on the subject of water-colour.
President: Thomas Plunkett *Vice President*: Wendy Jacob
Address: Bankside Gallery, 48 Hopton St., Blackfriars, London SE1 9JH. *Tel*: 020 7928 7521. *Fax*: 020 7928 2820.

Royal West of England Academy

The Academy was founded in 1844. Election to Membership (R.W.A.) is by postal ballot. The Academy is an independent, self-supporting institution, founded to assist professional artists, sculptors and architects, through exhibitions and other activities. Regular and varied exhibitions are shown at its galleries.
An Open Exhibition is held every autumn; open sculpture, painting and print exhibitions are held triennially; information may be obtained from the office.

President: Janette Kerr, PRWA *Address*: Queen's Rd., Clifton, Bristol BS8 1PX. *Tel*: 0117 973 5129. *Website*: www.rwa.org.uk *Email*: info@rwa.org.uk

St. Ives Society of Artists

Holds Spring, Summer and Autumn Members' Shows in the Main Gallery in the Mariners Church, St.Ives, Cornwall. There is also one invited exhibition, and two Open exhibitions – in September and December.
More information about all the exhibitions will appear on the website which is www.stisa.co.uk
Chairman: John Watson *Administrator*: April Brooks.
Address: Norway Square, St Ives, Cornwall TR26 1NA. *Tel*: 01736 795582.
Email: gallery@stisa.co.uk

Scottish Artists' Benevolent Association

This Association was formed in 1889, and gives assistance to distressed deserving artists, their widows and dependants. Each year it disburses over £10,000.
Life Membership (£25) is open to all. Subscriptions and donations should be sent to the *Secretary*: Mrs Lesley Nicholl *Address*: Second Floor, 5 Oswald St, Glasgow G1 4QR. *Tel*: 0141 248 7411. *Fax*: 0141 248 0417.

The Small Paintings Group

The Small Paintings Group was founded in 1991 by Peter Peterson RBA, Sandra Pepys LPS and Dennis Gilbert NEAC to promote the interest and attraction of small paintings. The Group Membership consists of 35 distinguished artists who also paint large works. The maximum size of the image is 12 x 12 inches or 144 square inches. The Group has an annual exhibition at the Piers Feetham Gallery, Fulham, London and also shows at other galleries including the Russell Gallery in Putney and Highgate Contemporary Art.
President: Anne Wright RBA. *Vice President*: Sandra Pepys LPS. *Hon. Treasurer*: John Paul. *Hon. Secretary*: Barbara Richardson RBA. *Website*: www.thesmallpaintingsgroup.com .

Society of Botanical Artists

The Society of Botanical Artists is an International Society, founded in 1985.
Holds an open exhibition at Westminster Central Hall, Storey's Gate, London SW1H 9NH each year April/May. Combines art and science and strives to enhance botanical art by proper promotion.
President: Sandra Wall Armitage. Enquiries to *Executive Secretary*: Mrs. Pamela Henderson, 1 Knapp Cottages, Wyke, Gillingham, Dorset SP8 4NQ. *Tel*: 01747 825718.

Society of Designer Craftsmen

The Society of Designer Craftsmen was founded in 1888 as The Arts and Crafts Exhibition Society with Walter Crane and William Morris among its most prominent members, each of whom was to serve as President. Its aim is to strengthen the professional standards and status of designer-makers in Great Britain and to stimulate public awareness by bringing works of fine craftsmanship before the public through major comprehensive exhibitions and specialised displays. In 1960 the Society assumed its present title as representative of the largest body of independent professional crafts practitioners in Britain. It lays great emphasis on helping young graduates at the outset of their careers by arranging assessments of their work and offering Licentiateship of the Society (LSDC) to those whose work is of a high standard. Among its other activities, the society mounts an annual exhibition of work by selected fellows, members and licentiates.
Applications for election as Members (MSDC) are considered on a regular basis throughout the year by a Selection Committee, which meets to examine the individual craft pieces submitted. Fellowship of the Society (FSDC) may be awarded by a majority vote of the Fellows on Council.
Annual subscriptions: Fellows and Members £70; Licentiates and Associates, £40.

Tel: 07531 798983. *Website*: www.societyofdesignercraftsmen.org.uk
Email: info@societyofdesignercraftsmen.org.uk

Society of Equestrian Artists

Founded in 1978/79, the Society of Equestrian Artists exists to encourage the study of equine art and, by mutual assistance between members, to promote a standard of excellence in its practice worthy of the subject's importance in British artistic traditions.

Membership comprises Associate and Full Members, who have attained a consistently high standard in their work, as well as Friends, who may be artist or non-artist.

Annual Exhibitions, normally early Autumn at a major central London venue.

President: Sir Mark Prescott Bt. *Chairman*: Mark Heathcote OBE.

Hon Treasurer: James Moor. *Hon Secretary*: Deborah Burt, Sarum, Church Road, Woodborough, Pewsey, Wiltshire SN9 5PH

Email: sec@equestrianartists.co.uk.

The Society of Graphic Fine Art – The Drawing Society

(formerly: The Society of Graphic Artists)

Founded in 1919. The Society exists with the purpose of promoting drawing skills by means of exhibitions for both Members and Non-Members work. Suitable artwork will be drawings in any medium, any original form of printmaking, watercolours and acrylic with evidence of additional drawing, but no oils.

President Roger Lewis SGFA, UKCPS 020 8655 0221

Vice-Presidents: Jo Hall SGFA AOI , Keith M Kennedy SGFA RAS Cert.

Hon. Treasurer:Archie Niven SGFA *Hon. Secretary*: Marie Blake SGFA

PR and Publicity: Geoff Simpson FCIPR 0161 483 1790 *Contact*: www.sgfa.org.uk

Society of Heraldic Arts

Aims to serve the interests of heraldic artists, craftsmen, designers and writers, to provide a "shop window" for their work, to obtain commissions on their behalf and to act as a forum for the exchange of information and ideas. Candidates for admission as Craft Members should be artists or craftsmen whose work comprises a substantial element of heraldry and is of a sufficient high standard to satisfy the requirements of the Society's advisory council.

Founded 1987

President: Anthony Wood NDD, FRSA, FHS, FSSI, FSA (Scot), SHA *Chairman*: Claire Street MSDC, FSHA *Hon. Secretary*: John J. Tunesi of Liongam MSc. FSA Scot.

Membership Secretary: David Hopkinson Hon. FHS, SHA

Website: www.heraldic-arts.com

Society of Portrait Sculptors

The Society of Portrait Sculptors was founded in 1953. It is a registered charity established to promote the art of portrait sculpture, encourage the highest standards, challenge preconceptions and stimulate interest in this timeless yet contemporary art form. This is done primarily through the Society's annual open exhibition held in May at Sladmore Contemporary.

President: Etienne Millner FRBS. *Vice-President*: Olivia Musgrave ARBS.

Hon. Secretary: Robert Hunt. *Hon. Treasurer*: David Houchin.

Address: 50A Hyde Street, Winchester, Hants SO23 7DY. *Tel*: 01962 860904.

Website: http://www.portrait-sculpture.org/ *Email*: sps@portrait-sculpture.org

Society of Scottish Artists

The SSA was founded in 1891 to represent the adventurous spirit in Scottish art. Today the SSA has over 500 members throughout Britain of which 125 are elected Professional members. Associate and Ordinary membership is also available by payment of an annual subscription.

The main focus of the Society is its Annual Exhibition which traditionally takes place in the Royal Scottish Academy in Edinburgh.

Submission of work is open to both members and non members, who undergo the same selection procedures, ensuring that each Annual Exhibition is unique, challenging and innovative.
For details about the Annual Exhibition or about membership, contact the Administrator or visit the website.
President: Gayle Nelson. *Administrator*: Julia Douglas. *Tel*: 07516 034178.
Email: admin@s-s-a.org *Website*: www.s-s-a.org

Society of Wildlife Artists

Founded in 1964, the Society of Wildlife Artists is a registered charity that seeks to generate an appreciation of and delight in the natural world through all forms of fine art based on or representing the world's wildlife. Through exhibitions and publications of fine art, the Society aims to further an awareness of the importance of conservation in order to maintain the variety of the world's ecosystems and its wildlife. The Society also supports and promotes art based objectives of other conservation and wildlife charities.
Through a bursary scheme the Society is able to help young artists keen to develop their knowledge and skills in wildlife art.
The focus of the Society's work is the annual exhibition featuring all media, held in September/October at the Mall Galleries, London. Included with the work of members from the UK and abroad is that of successful Bursary applicants, as well as a selection of work from non-members. The Annual Exhibition of the SWLA is the foremost event in the British wildlife art calendar.
President: Harriet Mead.
Hon. Vice-Presidents: Andrew Stock, Bruce Pearson, Robert Gillmor and Keith Shackleton.
Hon. Secretary: Chris Rose. *Address*: 17 Carlton House Terr., London SW1Y 5BD.
Tel: 020 7930 6844. *Website*: www.swla.co.uk

Society of Women Artists

This Society was founded in 1855 for the encouragement of women painters and sculptors, etc. The Annual Exhibition at the Mall Galleries runs in June and is open to all women artists.
Patron: Princess Michael of Kent. *President*: Sue Jelly. *Vice-President*: Belinda Tong.
Hon. Secretary: Caroline de Peyrecave.
Executive Secretary: Rebecca Cotton, Larchlands, Daisybank Road, Cheltenham GL53 9QQ.
Website: www.society-women-artists.org.uk

The Society of Wood Engravers

The SWE was founded in 1920 by a group of artists which included Philip Hagreen, Robert Gibbings, Lucien Pissarro, Gwen Raverat and Eric Gill; it thrived until World War II and continued in the altered context after it. After a decade in which there were no exhibitions, it was re-formed in the 1980s, with its first new exhibition in 1984 and has steadily built an international reputation for excellence. It now tours its annual exhibition to several venues; organizes regular additional exhibitions; publishes a monthly newsletter and a quarterly journal for members and subscribers; and is an international contact-point for all interested in the subject. The Society also administers The Rawlinson Bequest, through which grants are made to students of wood engraving. Subscription is open to anyone, artist, collector or simple enthusiast. Exhibitions are open to all forms of relief printmaking. Sending-in days are usually in the summer. The work of members and non-members alike is subject to selection. Membership: applications are considered from those who have had their work hung in at least three different exhibitions organized by the Society. Applicants are required to submit a portfolio of work and are elected on merit. Details of all the above are obtainable from the General Secretary.
Chairman: Peter Lawrence. *Secretary*: Geri Waddington, The Old Governor's House, Norman Cross, Peterborough PE7 3TB. *Tel*: 01733 242833.
Website: www.woodengravers.co.uk

Ulster Society of Women Artists

At a time when a woman's sole purpose was to grow up, look after husband, bring up perfect children and run the perfect home it was very difficult for women artists to achieve the recognition or obtain the opportunities to exhibit that their male counterparts enjoyed. Fifty four years ago there was no art society in Northern Ireland that would accept women artists as members. This archaic attitude enraged Gladys Maccabe so much that she decided to do something about it. She invited ten prominent women artists that lived in the province to come together to make up the original membership of The Ulster Society of Women Artists. The first meeting at Gladys' home in Mount Charles, University Road, Belfast, laid the foundation stone for encouragement and new companionship between fellow women artists. By the following year their membership had grown to 60 (with now over 120 members) and their first major exhibition was held at the Belfast Museum and Art Gallery. The Society has continued to have an annual exhibition with The Waterfront Hall, Belfast, being the venue for the last number of years. The Duchess of Abercorn is the Patron of the Society.
Achieving membership is and always has been considered a mark of distinction, and the number of artists trying to achieve membership is increasing each year.
President: Margaret Brand. *Vice-President*: Isabel Strugnell. *Secretary*: Kate Rocks *Treasurer*: Sheena Hughes
Further information about the Society can be found on the *website* www.uswa.co.uk

The United Kingdom Coloured Pencil Society

The Society was founded in 2001 by Bob Ebdon with three aims:
1) To support UK based artists who use, or wish to use, coloured pencils, in any way.
2) To educate artists and the public about coloured pencils.
3) To promote coloured pencils as fine art medium.
The Society has approximately 500 members, the majority in the UK but also internationally within 19 other countries. Members range from beginners to professional artists who have won prizes in other prestigious competitions while using coloured pencils.
Our Open International Exhibition is held annually (September/October) at different venues around the UK to give a valuable opportunity to show the versatility and quality of work which can be achieved using this medium. There is also a non-prejudged annual exhibition in Keswick, hosted by Derwent, at the Cumberland Pencil Museum.
Members are allowed to put UKCPS after their names once they have received signature status, which is earned after they have successfully exhibited in the Open International Exhibition in 3 years – silver and gold signature status is also available. 37 members currently have signature status.
Members receive a fully illustrated quarterly magazine with features on artists, medium, tips and techniques and a list of workshops around the UK. They have access to a lively forum to share their artwork, discuss materials, try the monthly theme and keep in touch with like minded artists. There are several Coloured Pencil Groups around the UK and it is the intention to increase these to cover the whole of the UK. There is also a blog for the latest news, including successes of any members in competitions, exhibitions etc.
The website is a useful gateway both to attract members and as a useful resource to existing members. All the past exhibitions are available to view online featuring all the successful entries. There is a 'gallery' section where members can have their own page to showcase samples of their artwork with a biography.
Website: www.ukcps.co.uk *Email*: secretary@ukcps.co.uk

United Society of Artists

Founded in 1921, the Society aims to exhibit work of professional quality primarily in London but also elsewhere in Britain and in any media. New Members are selected based on work submitted. At least one Open Exhibition is held each year. Artists who are not members of the Society may submit works for exhibition in accordance with the Society's current regulations. Members or Associate Members can submit up to 6 pictures, and shall have specific rights to have their work hung relating to the number of works submitted.

President: Chris Francis *Vice-President*: Ann Whitehead
Secretary: Anthony Goss, 37 Harvard Court, Honeybourne Road, London NW6 1HL
Website: www.united-artists.org.uk

The Wapping Group of Artists

The Wapping Group of Artists is a group of painters dedicated to painting from nature in company with one another on Wednesdays throughout the summer months from the end of April until the end of September. The founding membership was drawn from the Langham Sketching Club - their chosen subject London's river.

Following the 1939-45 war, the founders, meeting in the Prospect of Whitby Public House at Wapping in 1946, decided to paint the Thames from the Pool of London down the dozen reaches to the estuary.

The 21 original members decided on a limited membership of 25 and this is still so, with a maximum of 25 statutory members (who become senior members on reaching the age of 80). The first president was Jack Merriott.

Annual exhibitions were held first at the P.L.A. building on Tower Hill, later at the Royal Exchange, followed by 21 years at St. Botolphs Church, Aldgate. Since 2002 the Group has held its annual exhibition at the Mall Galleries in February or March of each year.

The river has changed amazingly but today's members still have the same love of painting and the same enthusiasm for their subject. The Group's painting venues now extend from Henley-on-Thames (occasionally upstream to Abingdon and Goring) down as far as the Estuary, and up to Wivenhoe and West Mersea in Essex and down the Kent coast as far as Margate. The Group also paint at venues in London, such as Spitalfields or Lincolns Inn.

The Group is now in its 68th year, and in 2006 Seafarer Books in conjunction with Sheridan House published a new hardback, full colour book entitled 'The Wapping Group of Artists –Sixty years of painting the Thames'.

President: Robin Mackervoy ROI
Hon. Sec.: Steven Alexander, PhD, 16 King's Ride, Camberley, Surrey GU15 4HX
Website: www.thewappinggroupofartists.co.uk

NOTES

COMPETITIONS AND ART PRIZES

Parker Harris

Founded in 1990, Parker Harris Partnership specialise in the organisation, administration, promotion, press, and public relations of visual art exhibitions, competitions, and events. Parker Harris also act as consultants in visual arts and sponsorship matters, and project manage public art commissions. The partners are Emma Parker and Penny Harris.

Parker Harris have organised such open exhibitions as the Jerwood Painting Fellowship and The Hunting Art Prizes. They are currently behind the organisation of the long running ING Discerning Eye exhibition, the Sunday Times Watercolour Competition, and the Jerwood Contemporary Painters exhibition.

www.parkerharris.co.uk Parker Harris Partnership, PO Box 279, Esher, Surrey, KT10 8YZ. *Tel*: 01372 462190 *Email*: info@parkerharris.co.uk

The ING Discerning Eye Exhibition

The ING Discerning Eye is a show of small works independently selected by six prominent figures from different areas of the art world including two artists, two collectors and two critics. Each curate their own section, inviting well known artists to exhibit alongside lesser known artists selected from the open competition. Previous selectors have included HRH The Prince of Wales, Sir Peter Blake, and Loyd Grossman. Prizes awarded in a range of categories. Maximum dimensions: 2D – 20" x 20" (including the frame), 3D – 20" x 20" x 20" (including the plinth/stand). Receiving dates nationwide August / September annually. Launched 1990.

2014 exhibition opens to the public at Mall Galleries, November 13 - 23, including weekends. For details visit www.discerningeye.org. *Tel*: 01372 462190 *Email*: de@parkerharris.co.uk

Sunday Times Watercolour Competition

Annual competition with prizes totalling £17,500, promoting and celebrating the diversity and beauty of the medium of watercolour. Abstract, figurative, and landscape pieces in any water soluble medium are considered from nationwide submission. First prize £10,000. Other awards include 2nd Prize £6,000, Smith & Williamson Prize £1500, and Vintage Classics Prize for Cover Art £500 - commission to create the cover art for a Vintage Classic. Works must have been carried out in the last three years and not previously exhibited. Applications are made online at www.parkerharris.co.uk. The 2014 exhibition will take place 15-20 September at the Mall Galleries. *Tel*: 01372 462190 *Email*: watercolour@parkerharris.co.uk

Lynn Painter-Stainers Prize

Created by the Worshipful Company of Painter-Stainers and the Lynn Foundation, this annual prize is to encourage creative representational painting and promote the skill of draughtsmanship. Total prize money: £25,000. First prize is £15,000 and an engraved gold medal. Open to artists born or resident in the UK. Applications are made online at www.lynnpainterstainersprize.org.uk *Tel*: 01372 462190 *Email*: lps@parkerharris.co.uk *Website*: www.lynnpainterstainersprize.org.uk www.parkerharris.co.uk

The National Open Art Competition

Annual Competition with an impressive total prize fund of £60,000, the National Open Art aims to nurture creative talent from emerging and established artists. Mediums include painting, drawing, photography, original prints, wall hung installations and computer generated art. The 2014 exhibition will take place at Somerset House, London 18 September - 26 October. Applications are made online at www.thenationalopenartcompetition.com. *Tel*: 07986 697693 *Email*: secretary@thenationalopenartcompetition.com

The Tiranti Prize for Young Portrait Sculptors

For details of this prize and entry requirements, contact: Alec Tiranti Limited, 3 Pipers Court, Berkshire Drive, Thatcham, Berkshire RG19 4ER, or see www.tiranti.co.uk www.portrait-sculpture.org

The Threadneedle Prize

Championing the most exciting figurative art produced in the UK and Europe today, the Prize offers the winning artist a cash award of £20,000, plus the winner's own exhibition at Mall Galleries in 2015. The competition sets out to promote and encourage excellence. Experienced and emerging artists are encouraged to submit fresh and intriguing works that are strong and topical observations on the world around us, using a variety of mediums, styles and approaches, with an overall focus on the quality and confidence of the finished work.
Submission is open annually from March to May. The exhibition takes place at Mall Galleries in September/October.
For more information visit www.threadneedleprize.com.
Contact: threadneedleprize@mallgalleries.com

ARTISTS' WEBSITES

AARONS, Andrew
www.andrewaarons.com

ABRAHAMS, Ivor
www.ivorabrahams.info

ACKROYD, Jane V.M.
www.janeackroyd.com

ADAIR, Hilary
www.hilaryadair.co.uk

ADAMS, Ken Praveera
www.kenadams.co.uk

ADAMS, Sarah
sarahadamspainting.co.uk

ADAMSON, Crawfurd
www.crawfurdadamson.com

ADLINGTON, Mark
www.markadlington.com

AHMAD, Sophie Maryum
www.rainbirdfineart.com

AIDA, Emiko
www.aidastudios.com

AIRD, Philippe Leigh
www.PhilippeAird.com;
www.phoenix-gallery.co.uk

AKIB, Hashim
www.hashimakib.com

AKROYD, Carry
www.carryakroyd.co.uk

AL-ATTAR, Suad
The Bridgeman Art Library

ALBUTT, Virginia
virginia-albutt.co.uk

ALDOUS, Veronica
www.aldousart.co.uk

ALEXANDER, Gregory
www.gregory-alexander.com

ALEXANDER, Naomi
www.naomialexander.com

ALFORD, Michael
www.michaelalford.co.uk

ALLEN, Ceri
www.ceriallen.co.uk

ALLEN, David
www.davidallenrsma.org.uk

ALLEN, Guy Rupert Stafford
www.guyallenart.com

ALLEN, Martin John
www.martinjallen.com

ALLEN, Roger Michael
www.rogerallen.co.uk

ALLSWORTH JONES, Lucilla Teresa
www.artistlucillajones.com

ALLUM, Avis Elizabeth
www.avisallum.com

ALLWRIGHT, Peter
www.peterallwright.com

ALSOP, William
www.alsoparchitects.com

ALTENBURGER, Ekkehard
www.altenburger.org.uk

ANDERSON, Jennifer
www.jennifer-anderson.co.uk

ANDREWS, Carole
www.carol-andrews.co.uk

ANGELINI, Cristiana
www.blueforce.demon.co.uk/
cristiana.angelini

ANNFIELD, Jill
www.anfieldharris.com

ANSELL, Amanda Louise
www.amandaansell.co.uk

ANTONIOU, Andrew
www.antoniou.com.au

APPLEYARD, Caroline Jane
www.appleyard-art.co.uk

ARCHER, Nicholas Lloyd
www.nicholasarcher.com

ARKINSTALL, Kevin
www.heraldic-arts.com

ARMITAGE, Sandra Wall
www.watercolourflowers.co.uk

ARNOLD, Phyllis Anne
www.portraits-miniaturesandsilhouettes.com

ARNUP, Sally
www.sallyarnup.co.uk

ASH, Lucy
www.lucyash.com

ASHCROFT, Phil
www.philashcroft.com

ASHMAN, Malcolm Paul
www.malcolmashman.co.uk

ASHMAN, Margaret Christina Elizabeth
www.margaretashman.com

ASQUITH, Rosalind Lucy
www.rosasquith.com

ASTBURY, Paul
www.paul-astbury.com

ATHERTON, Barry
www.athertonart.co.uk

ATKIN, Ann Fawssett
www.ann-fawssett-atkin.co.uk
www.ann-fawsett-atkin.com

ATKIN, Michael
www.michaelatkin.co.uk

ATKIN, Ron
www.artwanted.com/RjjA

ATKINS, David Alexander
www.david-atkins.com

ATKINSON, Kim
kimnaturepenllyn.blogspot

ATKINSON, Shelagh
www.shelaghatkinson.co.uk

ATTREE, Jake (Jonathan)
www.jakeattree.co.uk

AUGUST, Lillias Anne
www.lilliasaugust.com

AUSTIN, Franki
www.frankiaustin.co.uk

AUSTIN, Michael J.
www.jonathancooper.co.uk

AVELLINO, Alessia E.R.
www.alessiaavellino.com

AYLES, Debbie
www.debbieaylesartist.co.uk

BACKHOUSE, David John
www.davidbackhousesculptures.com

BAILEY, Caroline
www.carolinebailey.co.uk

BAILEY, Liz
www.lizbailey.org.uk

BAILEY, Susanna
www.susannabailey.com

BAINES, Valerie
www.valeriebaines.com

BAKER, Alix
www.alixbaker.com

BAKER, Christopher William
www.christopherwbaker.com

BAKER, Darren
www.dbfinearts.co.uk

BAKER, Ian David
www.iandavidbaker.com

BALAAM, Louise
www.louisebalaam.co.uk

BALDWIN, Mariella Christina
www.mariellabaldwin.com

BALDWIN, Martyn John
www.martynbaldwin.com

BALDWIN, Peter
www.peterbaldwinartist.co.uk

BALKWILL, Raymond James
www.raybalkwill.co.uk

BANNING, Paul
www.paulbanning.com

BANNISTER, Geoffrey Ernest John
www.geoffbannisterartist.com

BAPTIST, Gerry (Gerald William)
www.gerrybaptist.co.uk

BARANOFF, Elena
www.elenabaranoff.com

BARBER KENNEDY, Mat
www.matbarberkennedy.com

BARKER, Allen
www.allenbarker.com

BARKER, Kathy
www.karhybarker.co.uk

BARKER, Noel
www.noelgallery.ndo.co.uk

BARLOW, Andrew David
http://levenart.org/levenart/members-work/Pages/andrew-barlow.html

BARLOW, Bohuslav
www.bohuslavbarlow.co.uk

BARNES, Maggie (Dorothy Margaret)
www.maggiebarnes.co.uk

BARNES-MELLISH, Glynis Lily
www.barnesmellish.com

BARNETT, Rosemary
www.rosemarybarnett.co.uk

BARÓN, Maite
www.tessabaron.co.uk

BARR, Shona Stewart MacInnes
www.shonabarr.com

BARRATT, Mary H.
axis database

BARRETT, Margaret
www.margaretbarrett.co.uk

BARRON, Robert Hall
www.bobbarron.com

BARROW, David
davidbarrowpaintings.50megs.com

BARTLETT, Paul Thomas
www.royalsocietyofbritishartists.org.uk

BASSINGTHWAIGHTE, Paul
www.basspaul.co.uk

BATE, William Richard
billbate.co.uk

BATES, Andrea Maria
www.andreabates.co.uk

BATES, Patricia Jane
www.patbatesart.co.uk

BATT, Deborah Jane
www.deborahbatt.co.uk

BATTLE, Jay
www.jaybattle.com

BATTYE, Martin
www.targetfollow.com

BAUMFORTH, David John
www.davidbaumforth.com

BAWTREE, John Andrew
www.johnbawtree.com

BAXTER, Denis Charles Trevor
www.rwa Bristol

BAXTER, Richard
www.richardbaxter.com

BAYS, Caroline
www.carolinebays.co.uk

BAYS, Jill
www.jillbays.com

BEALE, Gillian
www.gillianbeale.co.uk

BEALE, Philippa S. Vaux
www.philippabeale.com

BEALING, Nicola Janette
www.nicolabealing.co.uk

BEARD, Peter Fraser
www.peterbeard.co.uk

BEATON, Rosemary
www.rosemarybeaton.co.uk

BEATTIE, Paul
www.paulbeattieart.com

BEAUMONT, Sarah Elizabeth
www.sarahbeaumont.com

BECKER, Haidee
www.haideebecker.com

BECKFORD, Laurence
www.beckfordartworks.co.uk

BEE, Sarah
www.sarahbee-painter.com

BEECROFT, Jane Christine
www.janebeecroft.co.uk

BEER, David
www.penhavengallery.co.uk

BEESLEY, Mark
www.remaginations.com
ipswich-art-society.org.uk

BELDERSON, John Walter (Rev.)
www.beldersonart.com

BELL, Ellen Mary
www.ellenbell.co.uk

BELL, Michael Munro (Mike)
www.mike-bell.artistwebsites.com

BELLAMY, David
www.davidbellamy.co.uk

BELLWOOD, Colin
www.colinbellwood.com;
www.NuMasters.com
www.londonart.co.uk colinbellwood.eu

BELYI, Peter
www.peterbelyi.com

BENDALL-BRUNELLO, Tiziana
www.tizianab-b.co.uk

BENNALLACK HART, Michael John
www.mbhart.co.uk

BENNETT, Margaretann
www.margaretannbennett.co.uk

BENNETT, Terence
www.terencebennett.co.uk

BENSON, Dawn Mary
www.barwellgallery.co.uk

BENTHAM, Martin
www.martinbentham.com

BENTLEY, Raymond NS
raymondbentley.com

BERESFORD-WILLIAMS, Mary E.
axis

BERNSTEIN, Carol
www.carolbernstein.co.uk

BERRY, June
www.juneberrypaintings.eu

BERRY, Peter Leslie
www.peterberry.org.uk

BETOWSKI, Noel Jan
www.noelbetowski.com

BETTNEY, Julian
www.julianbettney.me.uk
facebook julianbettneyfineart

BEVAN, Oliver
www.oliverbevan.com

BEVERIDGE, Philippa Jane
www.philippabeveridge.com

BEVIS, Michael John Vaughan
www.artservegallery.com
www.artinthevillage.info

BEWICK, Pauline
www.paulinebewick.ie

BIALOKOV SMITH, Malgorzata
www.bialokozart.org.uk

BIGMORE, Christine
www.christine-bigmore.co.uk

BINNS, David
www.swla.co.uk

BIRCH, David William
www.davidwbirch.co.uk

BIRCHALL, Christine Winifred
www.chrissiebirchall.com

BIRNBAUM, Aimee
mirabilisart.com
aimeebirnbaum.com

BIRO, Val (B. S.)
www.valbiro.co.uk

BISHOP, Peter Anthony
peterbishoppaintings.com
BISHOP, William Henry
www.bishopmarineart.com
BISSELL, Lauren Hayes
www.lhbissell.com
BLACK, John Frederick
www.johnfblack.webeden.co.uk
BLACK, Simon
www. thomascormanarts.com
BLACKWOOD, Simon Anthony James
www.simonblackwood.com
BLAKE, Adrienne
www.adrienneblake.com
BLAKE, Marie Dora
www.marieblake.com
BLAKE, Quentin
www.quentinblake.com
BLAKER, Michael
www.michael-blaker.co.uk
BLANE, Frances Aviva
www.avivablane.com
BLIK, Maurice
www.mauriceblik.com
BLISS, Ian Reynolds
www.rosalindbliss.co.uk
BLOOMER, Paul
www.paulbloomer.com
BOAG, Francis
www.francisboag.com
BOLAN, Sean Edward
www.seanbolan.co.uk
BOND, Jane
www.TheRp.co.uk
BONE, Tina
www.tinabonedtp.co.uk
BOOKLESS, Sarah Theresa
www.riverbanktreegallery.co.uk
www.tcweb.co.uk/scottish-art-circle
BOOTH, Araceli
www.watercolours-aracelibooth.com
BOOTH, Helen
httl://helenbooth.com
BOOTH, Rosa-Maria
www.rosmarart.com
BOSWELL, Laura
www.lauraboswell.co.uk
BOSWELL, Tim George
www.timboswellglass.kk5 org
BOULTON, Janet
www.janetboulton.co.uk
BOUSFIELD, Neil
www.inkyfingerspress.com
BOWEN-MORRIS
www.nigelbowen-morris.com
BOWLING, Frank
frankbowling.com
BOWMAN, Day
www.daybowman.com
BOWYER, Francis David
www.francisbowyer.com
BOYD, Graham
www.grahamboyd.co.uk
BOYD, Lee John
www.leeboydartist.com
BOYES, Judy Virginia
www.judyboyes.co.uk
BOYT, Judy
www.judyboyt.com
BRADFORD, Shane
www.shanebradford.com
BRADSHAW, Elizabeth Anne Makin
www.lizmakinbradshaw.co.uk
BRAMLEY, Victor
www.st.ivessociety of artists.com
BRANTON, Sam
www.sambranton.com
BRASON, Paul
www.paulbrason.co.uk
BRASSINGTON, Alan Francis
www.alanbrassington.com
BRAYNE, David
davidbrayne.wordpress.com
BRENTON, John
www.johnbrenton.co.uk
BRERETON, James
www.burlington.co.uk
BREWSTER, Claire
clairebrewster.co.uk
BREWSTER, Martyn Robert
www.martynbrewster.co.uk
BRIDGE, Eoghan
www.lindablackstone.com
BRIDGES, Ann Elizabeth
www.ann-bridges.com
BRIDGLAND, Judith Irene
www.jibridgland.com
BRIERTON, Irene Annette
www.irenebrierton.co.uk
BRINDLE, Sharon Elizabeth
www.sharonbrindle.com
BRINDLEY, Robert Edward
www.robertbrindley.com
BRISCOE, Michael J.
www.mikebriscoe.co.uk

BRISTOL, Sophy
www.panterandhall.com

BRIXEY-WILLIAMS, Julie
www.juliebrixey-williams.co.uk

BRODERICK, Laurence John
www.laurencebroderick.co.uk

BROOKES, Gerry
www.gerrybrookes.com

BROOMFIELD, Frances
www.francesbroomfield.co.uk

BROTHERTON, Mollie
www.terrain-vallone.co.uk

BROWN, Bob
www.bobaugurbrown.co.uk

BROWN, Colin
www.colinbrown.eu

BROWN, David
www.wix.com/davidartshed/david-brown

BROWN, Diana Elizabeth
www.swla.co.uk

BROWN, John Robert
www.johnbrown-sculptor.co.uk

BROWN, Keith
www.homepage.ntlworld.com/cyberform

BROWN, Peter Edward Mackenzie
www.Peterbrownneac.com

BROWN, Ralph
www.ralphbrown.co.uk

BROWN, Susan Lee
www.susanleebrown.weebly.com

BROWNE, Piers
www.piersbrowne.com

BRUCE, George J. D.
www.georgebruceartist.com

BRYCE, Gordon
www.gordonbryce.co.uk

BUCHANAN, Hugh Ross
www.hughbuchanan.co.uk

BUCK, Jon
www.jonbucksculpture.com

BUCKLEY, Patricia Ann
www.patriciabuckley.co.uk

BUCKMASTER, Emma Elizabeth
www.emmabuckmaster.com

BUDD, Tiffany Jane
www.tiffanybudd.co.uk

BUHLER, Michael Robert
www.michaelbuhler.org

BURBRIDGE, Claire-Chantal Emma
www.claireburbridge.com

BURGE, Pery
www.chronoscapes.com

BURGESS, Brenda Jean
www.brendaburgessarts.co.uk

BURGESS, Peter
www.rasalumni.org

BURKE, Christopher Paul
www.chrisburke.org.uk

BURKE, Peter
www.peterburke.co.uk

BURKETT, Norman Hittersay
www.burkett.nl

BURNLEY, Heather Wynn
www.heatherburnley.weebly.com

BURR, Lesley Jane
www.lesleyburr.co.uk

BURSNALL, Paul
www.paulbursnall.co.uk

BURTON, Simon
www.simonburton.org

BURY, Carole
www.carolebury.com

BUSBY, John P.
www.thelandgallery.com
www.wildlifeartgallery.com

BUTLER, James
www.jamesbutler-ra.com

BUTLER, Vincent
vincentbutler.co.uk

BUTT, Alistair Neal
www.alistairbutt.co.uk

BUTT, Desiree Jill Mary
www.desireebutt.co.uk

BUTT, Jennifer Gillian
www.jennybutt.com

BUTTERFIELD, Sarah Harriet Anne
www.sarahbutterfield.co.uk

BUTTERWORTH, John Russell
www.jbutterworth.co.uk

BUXTON. Jennifer
www.tigertigerburningbright.com

BYRNE, Andrea
www.andreabyrne.com

BYROM, Gillie Hoyte
www.enamelportraitminiatures.co.uk

CAHILL, John
www.tenbyharbourgallery.co.uk

CAIN, Judith
www.judithcain.blogspot.co.uk

CAINS, Gerald Albert
www.rwa.org.uk

CALLAND, Ruth Elaine
www.transitiongallery.co.uk

CALLAWAY, Sonia Sylvia
www.britishnaives.co.uk Melinsey Mill

CALVER, Michael
www.axisweb.org/artist/michaelcalver
www.goeform.net
www.michaelcalver.co.uk
www.nsanewlyn.com

CAMBRIDGE, Melanie Ann
www.melaniecambridge.com

CAMERON, Zoe Rebecca
www.zoecameron.co.uk

CAMPBELL, Christopher
www.startspace.co.uk

CAMPBELL, Huw Phillip
www.zap-art.f2s.com

CAMPBELL, Stephen Maxwell
www.smcampbell.eu

CANNING, Neil
www.neilcanning.com

CANNON, George Edward
Lake Artists

CANTER, Jean Mary
www.jeancanter.co.uk

CARDEW, Sidney
c/o Mall Gallery, London

CARDNELL, Delia
www.deliacardnell.com

CAREY, Annabel
www.ctcinternationalartists.com

CAREY, Laura
www.special-art-effects.co.uk

CARNIE, Andrew John
www.andrewcarnie.co.uk

CARR, David James
www.davidcarr.me.uk

CARRINGTON-SMITH, Lynette
www.lynettecarringtonsmith.com

CARRUTHERS, Derek William, Prof.
derekcarruthers

CARTER, Beth Arabella
www.bethcarter.co.uk

CARTER, Mary Elizabeth
www.marycarter.co.uk

CARTER, Simon Charles
simoncarterpaintings.co.uk

CARVER, Margaret
www.greatyarmouthartists.co.uk

CARY, Caroline Anne
www.carolinecary.com

CASE, David Charles
www.davidcasefineart.com

CASSELDINE, Nigel
www.romanystudio.co.uk

CASSON, Lucy
www.axisweb.org/artist/lucycasson

CASTLE, James Munro
www.jamescastlesculpture.co.uk

CASWELL, Sarah
www.sarahcaswell.co.uk

CAULKIN, Martin
www.gicleegallery.org.uk

CHAITOW, Michael
www.michaelchaitow.com

CHALMERS, Angela
www.angelachalmers.com

CHANCE, Sula
www.sulaartist.co.uk

CHANCELLOR, Deborah Ann
www.ameliaessex.co.uk

CHAPLIN, Michael James
www.mikechaplin.com

CHAPMAN, John Lewis
www.johnchapman.co.uk

CHEEK, Martin
www.martincheek.co.uk

CHEFFINS, Valma Maud
axisweb.org/artist/valmacheffins

CHERRY, Anne
www.gicleegallery.org.uk

CHERRY, Norman
www.normancherry.co.uk

CHESTERMAN, Merlyn
www.twohartonmanor.co.uk

CHEUNG, Gordon
www.gordoncheung.com

CHEVARIN, Frederic Marcel Jacques
www.frederic-chevarin.com

CHIRINO, Marta
www.martachirino.com

CHITTENDEN, Charlie
http//:charliechittendendaily.blogspot.com

CHRISTOPHER, Ann
www.annchristopher.co.uk

CHUANG, Yaojen
www.yaojenchuang.com

CHUHAN, Jagjit (Ms.)
www.chuhan333.wix.com/paintings#

CHURCHILL, Robert Bruce
www.robchurchill.com

CIRENZA, Lisa
www.cirenza.com

CLARIDGE, Trish
trishclaridge.com

CLARK, Mary
www.printmaker.mary-clark.co.uk

CLARK, Michael Graeme
www.michaelclarkartist.co.uk

CLARKE, Graham Arthur
www.grahamclarke.co.uk

CLARKE, Granville Daniel
www.granvilledclarke.co.uk

CLARKE, Hilda Margery
www.thefirstgallery.com

CLARKE, Jonathan
www.jonathanclarke.co.uk

CLAY, Andie Joy
www.andieclay.com

CLAYDEN, Phillippa
www.phillippaclayden.co.uk

CLAYTON, Inge
www.ingeclayton.com

CLEMENTS, Patricia Kathleen
www.patriciaclementsart.com

CLIFTON-BLIGH, Olivia
www.bullmillarts.co.uk

CLINE, Penelope
www.figtreepress.co.uk

CLOAKE, Beatrice Pierrette Denise
www.beatricecloake.net

CLORAN, Julian Thomas
www.narolc.blogspot.com

CLOSSICK, Peter
peterclossick.com

CLYNE, Thora
www.catpawtraits.co.uk

COATES, Carol
www.carolcoates.co.uk

COATES, Penny
www.pecoates.com

COBLEY, David Hugh
www.davidcobley.co.uk

COBURN, Ivor Basil
watercoloursivorcoburn.com

COCKRILL, Maurice
www.cockrill.co.uk

COHEN, Bernard
Flowers East Gallery

COKER, Norman Richard
www.normancoker.co.uk

COLDWELL, Paul
www.paulcoldwell.org

COLE, Barbara Evelyn (B.E.)
RBS

COLLINS, Clive Hugh Austin
www.clivecollinscartoons.com

COLLINS, Kate
www.katecollinsartist.co.uk

COLLINS, Marjorie
www.marjoriecollins.com

COMBES, Richard A.
www.dukeriesartgallery.com

COMRIE, Rowena Susan
www.rowenacomrie.co.uk

CONNELLY, Roy
www.royconnelly.com

CONNER, Angela
www.angelaconner.co.uk

CONNOLLY, Anthony
www.anthonyconnolly.co.uk

CONWAY-JONES, Richard William
www.conway-jones.co.uk

COODE, Caroline Ann
carolinecoode.co.uk

COOK, Christian Manuel
www.chriscookpaintings2.com

COOK, Ian David
www.ian-cook-art.com

COOK, Jennifer Martin
www.jennycook.net.

COOK, Stephen Thomas
www.stephencookartist.com

COOMBE, Nick
www.coombearchitecture.com

COOPER, Eileen
www.eileencooper.co.uk

COOPER, Jessica
www.jessicacooper.co.uk

COOPER, Julian
www.artspacegallery.co.uk
www.heatoncooper.co.uk

COPPINGER, Sioban
www.siobancoppinger.co.uk

CORBETT, Lily Gloria
www.theartofcreativity.co.uk

CORBETT, Peter George
www.petercorbett.co.uk

CORKREY, Michael
www.michaelcorkrey.com

CORLETT, Roseanne Serena
www.roseannes-art.co.uk

CORNELL, David
www.davidcornell.com

CORSELLIS, Jane
www.newenglishartclub.co.uk

COUDRILLE, Jonathon Xavier
www.coudrille.com

COULOURIS, Mary Louise
www.artmlc.co.uk

COUSINS, Timothy
www.anderssonhall.com

COX, Julian Charles
www.juliancoxartist.co.uk

CRAIG-McFEELY, Joanna
www.botanicalillustration.co.uk
CRAWFORD, Alistair
www.alistaircrawford.co.uk
CRAWFORD, Susan L.
www.slcrawford.com
CRAWSHAW, Donna
www.donnacrawshaw.co.uk
CRAWSHAW, June Eileen
www.crawshawgallery.com
CRESWELL, Alexander Charles Justin
www.alexandercreswell.com
CROFT, Paul John
www.spgw.co.uk
http://users.aber.ac.uk/puc/paulcroft/open.htm
CROOK, P. J.
www.pjcrook.com
CROSBY, Dido
www.didocrosby.com
CROSSLEY, Gordon
www.gtc-art.com
CROSTHWAITE, Sally
www.sallycrosthwaite.co.uk
CROUCH, Helga Ursula
www.wildlybotanical.co.uk
CROW, Becky
www.beckycrow.co.uk
CROWE, Victoria Elizabeth
www.victoriacrowe.com
CROZIER, Philip
www.philipcrozier.com
CROZIER, William
www.williamcrozier.com
CRYER, Ian David
www.iancryer.com
CULLEY, Derek
www.derekculley.com/golgotha
CULLINAN, Edward
http://ecarch.co.uk
CULMER, Matt
www.mattculmer.com
CULVER, Cheryl Vivien
www.cherylculverpaintings.co.uk
CUMING, Fred
www.fredcuming.com
CUMMINGS, Novette
www.novettecummings.com
Saatchi Gallery Online
CUMMINGS, Gus
guscummings.com
CUNNIFFE, Simon David
www.artlondon.com
CURLING, Peter Michael Napier
www.petercurling.com
CURRY, Denis Victor
www.humanpoweredwing.co.uk
CURSHAM, Juliet
www.cursham.co.uk
CURTIS, David Jan Gardiner
www.djcurtis.co.uk
CURTISS-FULLER, Merrie Fleur Blaker
www.merriecf.com
CUTHBERT, Rosalind
www.roscuthbert.co.uk
CUTLER, Sally Ann
www.southbank-printmakers.com
D'ARCY HUGHES, Ann
brightonprintmaking.co.uk
DACK, Tom
northeastartcollective.com
DAKAKNI, Susan Marie Therese
www.susandakakni.com
DALRYMPLE, Neil
www.neildalrymple.com
DANGOOR, Linda
www.lindadangoor.com
DANIELLS, Derek Howard
www.derekdaniells.co.uk
DANIELS, Jase
www.jasedanielsart.com
DARBISHIRE, Stephen John
www.stephen-darbishire.com
DARLOW, Les
www.lesdarlow.com
DARTON WATKINS, Christopher
www.dartonwatkins.com
DAVID-COHEN, Yael
www.yaeldc.co.uk
DAVIDSON, Jennifer Ann
www.walledgarden.co.uk
DAVIDSON , Philomena
www.davidsonarts.com
DAVIDSON, Richard John
www.richarddavidson.co.uk
DAVIES, Heather
www.heatherdavies.co.uk
DAVIS, Cynthia
www.cynthiadavis.co.uk
DAVIS, James Spence
www.jamessdavis.com
www.meadowsfineart.com
DAVIS, Jason Pyper
www.jasonpyperdavis.com
DAVISON, Martin
www.martindavisonart.com

DAWSON, Susan Shepherd
www.stivessocietyofartists.com

DAY, Zoë Claire
www.zoeday.com

de LACY, Ellie
www.elliedelacy.co.uk

DE MEESTER, Angeline
www.contemporarybotanicart.com

de MONCHAUX, Paul
www.pauldemonchaux.co.uk

DEAN, Graham
www.grahamdean.com

DEAN, Margaret
www.studiorogmag.com

DEAN, William Alfred
www.BillDeanROI.com

DEARNLEY, Benjamin Chad
www.bendearnley.com

DEL CAMPO, Michele
www.micheledelcampo.com

DELLAR, Roger
www.rogerdellar.com

DEMPSTER, Justin William
dempsterpaintings.com

DEMSTEADER, Mark
www.panterandhall.com

DENTON, Kenneth Raymond
www.dentonuk.net

DENYER-BAKER, Pauline
www.paulinedenyerbaker.com

DESMET, Anne Julie
www.annedesmet.com

DEVEREUX, Jacqueline
www.watercolour-online.co.uk

DI GIROLAMO, Megan Ann
www.megan-di-girolamo.co.uk/megan htm

DICK, Colin
www.colindick.com

DICKENS, Mark
www.markdickens.net

DICKENS, Pip
www.pip-dickens.com

DICKER, Kate
www.katedicker.com

DICKESON, Gaynor
www.gaynorsflora.com

DIGGLE, Philip
www.philipdiggle.co.UK

DITZ
www.aappl.com

DJORDJEVIC, Jovan
www.jovandjordjevic.com

DMOCH, Paul
http://www.artmajeur.com/aquarelliste

DODD, Alan
www.alandodd.co.uk

DODDS, James
www.jamesdodds.co.uk

DOIG, Maxwell Kirkcaldy
www.maxwelldoig.com

DONALD, George M.
www.georgedonald.com
www.royalscottishacademy.org

DONALDSON, Antony
www.antonydonaldson.com

DONLIN, Martin
www.martindonlin.com

DOREY, Russell Peter
www.russelldorey.co.uk

DOUBLEDAY, John
johndoubleday.co.uk

DOUGLAS, Brian David
RBA, NEAC

DOWE-EDWARDS, Virginia
www.virginiadowe.com

DOWLER, Niggy
www.niggydowler.com

DOWSON, Katharine
www.katharinedowson.com

DRAPER, Kenneth
www.kennethdraper.com

DRAPER, Matthew John
www.matthewjdraper.co.uk

DRING, Melissa Jane
www.totallyessential.com

DRUMMOND, Vicki
www.vickidrummond.co.uk

DRURY, Christopher
www.chrisdrury.co.uk

DU TOIT, Susanne
www.susannedutoit.com

DUBNYCKYJ, Alicia
www.aliciadubnyckyj.com

DUFFIN, Stuart
www.stuartduffin.com

DUFFY, Terry
www.terryduffy.info

DUFORT, Antony
www.antonydufort.com

DUGGAN, Chris
cee-dee.com

DUKES, Robert Laurence
www.browseanddarby.co.uk

DUMITRIU, Anna
www.annadumitriu.com

DUMPER, Bridget Veronica June
www.bridgetdumper.co.uk

DUNCAN, Jean
www.jeanduncan.freeuk.com

DUNCAN MEYER, Mary Elizabeth Anne
http://www.intune.co.uk/Meyer.Duncan

DUNN, Philip
www.windowgallery.co.uk

DUNSEATH, Chris
www.axisweb.org/artist/chrisdunseath

DUPEYRON, Carole
www.caroledupeyron.com

DYRENFORTH, Noel
www.noel-dyrenforth.com

EASTHAM, Tracey
www.traceyeastham.co.uk

EASTOP, Geoffrey Frank
www.bsgart.com

EATON, Paul
www.eatongoldsmiths.com

EATWELL, David
www.gallery-modern-art.com

EDEN, Max Nigel Byron
maxeden.co.uk

EDMANDS, Trevor Parton
trevoredmands.com

EDMONDSON, Stewart
www.sterartedmondson.com

EDWARDS, Alan C.L.
www.alan-edwards-artist.com

EDWARDS, C.C.G.
www.ccgedwards.com

EDWARDS, John
www.johnedwards-artist.com

EDWARDS, John Colin
www.johnedwardsrp.com

EDWARDS, Malcolm
www.malcolmedwardsart.co.uk

EDWARDS, Peter Douglas
www.peteredwards.net

EDWARDS, Sylvia
www.sylviaedwards.com

EGAN, Orla
www.orlaegan.com

EGGLETON, Margaret
www.margareteggleton.co.uk

ELKINS, Bridgette Mary
www.westdean/reclamation.org

ELLIOT, Ian Scott
www.ianelliott.com

ELLIOTT, Chuck (Charles)
www.chuckelliott.com

ELLIOTT, Helen
www.helenelliott.net

ELLIOTT, Paul
www.blacksmithonline.co.uk

ELLIOTT, Susan Jane
susanelliottmosaics.co.uk

ELLIOTT, Walter Albert
www.elliottartgallery.com

ELLIS, Belinda Anne
www.belindaellis.co.uk

ELLIS, Edwina
www.edwinaellis.co.uk

ELLIS, Ian
www.radley.org.uk/ian%27s%20web%20page/ian's%20web%20page.html

ELLIS, Ian Roy
ianellis.weebly.com

ELLMAN, Daphne Ann
www.daphneellman.co.uk

ELMORE, Pat
www.patelmore.co.uk

ELPIDA
www.realartfirst.com

ELRINGTON, Ptolemy Pieter Charles
www.hubcapcreatures.com

ELSTEIN, Cecile
www.cecileelstein.com

ELWELL, Brian
www.phoenixgallery.co.uk
www.brianelwell.co.uk

ELWES, Luke
www.lukeelwes.com

EMANUEL, John
www.johnemanuel.co.uk

ENRIGHT, Mo
www.mo-enright.me.uk

ERLAND, Sukey
www.sukeyerland.me.uk

ERSKINE-JONES, Susan Helen
www.erskine-jones.com

EVANS, Tony
www.turnerfinearts.com
www.ukfinearts.com

EVELEIGH, Aldous
www.aldouseveleigh.com

EVERETT, Julia
juliaeverettgallery.co.uk

FAILES, Colin Michael
www.colinfailes.co.uk

FAIRCLOUGH, Michael
www.michaelfairclough.co.uk

FALCIDIA, Paulette
www.falcidia-art.co.uk

FALLSHAW, Daniel
www.artofcreation.co.uk

FANSHAWE KATO, Jill
www.jillfanshawekato.com

FARMAR, Francis Edmund
www.francisfarmar.com

FARQUHARSON, Linda
www.linocut.co.uk

FARRELL, Anthony
www.anthonyfarrell.co.uk

FARRELL, Odette
www.odettefarrell.com

FARRER, Rosemary Ann
www.rosemaryfarrer.com

FARRINGTON, Karen Lynne
www.britishnaives.co.uk

FARTHING, Douglas Paul
douglasfarthingart.com

FARTHING, Stephen
www.stephenfarthing.com

FAULDS, Robert Gordon
www.gordon-faulds.com

FAULKNER-STEVENS, Debby
www.dabbyfaulknerstevensart.com

FAWCETT, David Noel Lloyd
www.davidfawcett.co.uk

FEDERER, Frances Mary
www.gilding.net

FEIJOO, Fernando
www.fernandofeijoo.com

FELD, Anthony Eric (Tony)
www.tonyfeldpaintings.co.uk

FENNER, Michael James
mike-fenner-paintings.co.uk

FERGUSON, George
www.fm-architects.co.uk

FERGUSON, Paul
www.paulferguson.co.uk

FERGUSON, Shaun
www.shaunferguson.co.uk

FERRAND SCOTT, Victoria Jane
www.axisweb.org/artist/victoriaferrandscott

FILIPE, Paulo Duarte
www.pauloduartefilipe.blogspot.com

FINDLAY, Denise
www.denisefindlay.com

FINER, Stephen
www.stephenfiner.com

FINLATOR, Hannah Verena
www.fairfields.demon.co.uk/onlinegallery/hannah.html

FIRMSTONE, David James
www.davidfirmstone.com

FISHER, John Edward
www.franciskylegallery.com

FLEMING-WILLIAMS, Julia Elizabeth Catherine
www.rooths.co.uk

FLÖCKINGER, Gerda
www.mobilia-gallery.com/artjewel.html

FLOWER, Rosina Margaret
www.rosinaflower.co.uk

FOLAN, Andrew
www.andrewfolan.com

FONTAINE, Fleur
www.artmadness.co.uk

FONTAINE-WOLF, Rebecca
www.rebeccafontain-wolf.com

FORBES, Ronald
www.ronald-forbes.com

FORD, Mary
www.maryford.co.uk

FORD, Noel
www.fordcartoon.com

FORD, Peter Anthony
www.peterford.org.uk

FOREMAN, Margaret
www.margaretforeman.co.uk

FOSTER, Christine
www.lilacarts.co.uk

FOSTER, Richard Francis
www.richardfoster.co.uk

FOUNTAIN, Desmond Hale
www.desmondfountain.com

FOX, Jane Amber
www.janefoxartist.com
www.rbs.org.uk
www.sculpturecymru.org.uk

FOX, Karrie
www.artmaps.co.uk

FOX, Peter
peterfoxartist.co.uk
www.axisartists.co.uk
redwinggallery.co.uk

FOX OCKINGA, Fyne Marianne
www.mariannefoxockinga.co.uk

FRAME, Mary Elizabeth Bruce
www.maryframepaintings.co.uk

FRANKLIN, Linda Ann
www.franklinart.co.uk

FRANSES-BEAN
www.artbag.me

FREARS, Naomi
www.naomifrears.com

FREEMAN, John
www.johnfreemanstudio.co.uk

FREEMAN, Lily
www.happypaintings.co.uk

FREEMAN, Ralph
www.ralphfreeman.co.uk

FREER, Roy
www.royfreer.co.uk

FREW, Hilary
www.hilaryfrew.com

FROEHLICH, Cadi
www.cadifroehlich.co.uk

FRÖHLICH-WIENER, Irene
www.breakingart.com.//:irene

FROST, Anthony
www.galleryonline.org.uk

FRY, Minne
eyestorm.com

FRY, Paul
www.paulfry.co.uk

FULLARTON, James
jamesfullarton.com

FULLER, Martin Elliott
www.martinfuller.net

FURNEAUX, Alan C. George
www.alanfurneaux.com

FURSE, Vikky (Victoria Picton)
www.londonart.co.uk/vikkyfurse
www.society-women-artists.org.uk/vikkyfurse

GABAY, Laurie, L.
www.lauriegabay.co.uk

GADSBY, Betty Patricia
www.bettygadsby.co.uk

GAGE, Anthea Dominique Juliet
www.antheagage.co.uk

GAIT, Judith
www.judithgait.co.uk

GALE, Colin
www.colingale.com

GALE, Jeremy
www.jeremygale.co.uk

GALE, Martin
www.martingale.ie

GALES, Simon
www.simongales.com

GALLOWAY, Richard Andrew
www.RichardGalloway.co.uk

GALT, Cameron
www.bankside.com
www.camerongalt.com

GANTER, Josephine
http://joganter.wordpress.com

GARDINER, Iain
http://www.behance.net/iaingardiner

GARDINER, Vanessa
www.vanessagardner.co.uk

GARDNER, Grace
www.artsake.co.uk
www.falmouthartgallery.com

GARDNER, Judith Ann
www.royalsocietyofbritishartists.org.uk
www.newenglishartclub.co.uk

GARDNER, Reginald Stephen
www.rsgardner.co.uk/com

GARFIT, William
williamgarfit.co.uk

GARNER, Jacki (Jacqueline Anne)
www.jackiegarner.co.uk

GARNER, Todd Russell
members.aol.com/tgarner454

GASKELL, Eric
www.egdesign.co.uk

GATTEAUX, Marcel
www.caeltgallery.com

GELDART, William
www.geldartgallery.com

GELLER, William Jasper
www.williamgeller.co.uk

GEORGE, Andrew Scott
bertramenterprises.co.uk

GEORGE, Brian
briangeorgeart.com

GEORGE, David
www.sculptor.freeserve.co.uk

GERAGHTY, Paul Leo
www.stivespainter.com

GERRIE, Pamela Margaret
office of Benny Wenda

GIBBONS, John
www.johngibbons.org.uk

GIBBS, Stephen Roy
www.londonart.co.uk

GIBSON, Jane Barr
www.cornerwaysart.co.uk

GIBSON-WATT, Marcia Susan
www.gibsonwatt.co.uk

GIFFORD, Andrew John
www.jmlondon.com

GILBERT, Dennis
www.dennisgilbert.net

GILBERT, George
www.georgegilbertrsw.co.uk

GILBERT, Rowena Justine
www.rowenagilbert.com

GILBERT, Terence John
www.terencegilbert.com

GILDER, Russell H.
www.russellgilderpaintings.com

GILI, Katherine
www.katherinegili.com

GILLESPIE, Sarah
www.sarahgillespie.co.uk

GILLICK, James Balthazar Patrick
www.gillick-artist.com
www.jonathancooper.co.uk

GILMOUR, Judith
www.judithgilmour.com

GLANVILLE, Christopher
www.christopherglanville.co.uk

GLASS, Margaret
www.margaretglass.com

GLASSBOROW, Stephen
www.galleryperutz.com

GLASSFORD, Susan Hilary
www.meadowbankfarm.co.uk

GLOVER, Rebecca
www.rebeccaglover.co.uk

GODDARD, Juliette Ingrid
www.cosalondon.com

GODDEN, Nicola Jane Averill
www.nicolagodden.com

GOLDBART, Sarah Rachel
www.sarahgoldbart.com

GOLLON, Chris
www.chrisgollon.com

GOOD, Trudy
www.belgraviagallery.com

GOODFELLOW, Peter George
www.lostgallery.co.uk

GOODHALL, Peter
www.petergoodhall.co.uk

GOODMAN, Ben
www.bengoodman.co.uk

GOODMAN, Pamela Clare
www.claregoodmanartist.co.uk

GOODMAN, Sheila
www.sgart.co.uk

GOODWIN, Diane
included in art-in-miniature.org
leeminiaturecollection.com

GOOSEN, Frederik Johannes (Frits)
www.fritsgoosen.nl

GORDON-LEE, Michael
devonartistnetwork.co.uk/GORDONLEE

GORMAN, Susan Mary
www.sue-gorman-ceramics.co.uk

GOUGH, Paul James
www.amd.uwe.ac.uk/vortex/

GOUGH, Piers
www.czwgarchitects.co.uk

GRAA JENSEN, Lisa
www.lisagraajensen.com

GRADIDGE, Daphne
www.daphnegradidge.co.uk

GRAHAM, David
www.davidgraham-studio.com

GRAHAM-MACKAY, Fiona
www.fionagraham-mackay.net

GRAINGER, Chris Rowan
www.rowangrainger.com

GRANGER-TAYLOR, Nicolas
www.ngrangertaylor.com

GRANT, Kenneth Stephen
www.kenneth-grant.com

GRANT, Marianne
www.swissart.ch/marianne-grant

GRANVILLE-EDMUNDS, Peter Donald
www.artistspace.net

GRAY, Douglas
www.douglasgray.com

GREEN, Anthony
www.anthonygreenra.com

GREEN, Brenda Mary
www.brendagreenart.co.uk

GREEN, Diana
www.thestourgallery.co.uk

GREEN, Gerald
www.ggarts.demon.co.uk

GREEN, Judith Ann
www.judigreen.co.uk

GREEN, Lorna
www.lornagreen.com

GREENHALF, Robert Ralph
www.robertgreenhalf.co.uk

GREENLAND, Martin James Howard
www.martingreenland.co.uk

GREENSLADE, Suzanne Lyon
www.suzgreenslade.com

GREENWELL, Patricia K.
www.tate-it-aint.co.uk

GREENWOOD, Philip John
www.philgreenwood.info

GREGORY, Norma
normagregorybotanicalartist.com

GRENVILLE, Hugo Gerard
www.hugogrenville.com

GREY, Jenni
www.designerbookbinders.org.uk

GRIBBIN, Launcelot Benedict
www.launcegribbin.co.uk

GRICE, David
www.artbydavidgrice.com
GRIFFITH, David Lloyd
www.davidlloydGriffith.co.uk
GRIFFITHS, David
www.david-griffiths.co.uk
GRIFFITHS, Michael
www.michaelgriffithsfineart.com
GRIFFITHS, Simon John
www.simongriffithssculpture.co.uk
GRISLEY, Jackie
www.jackiegrisley.co.uk
GROVES, John Michael
www.johngroves.org
GUDGEON, Simon David
www.simongudgeon.com
GUNNING, David Edward
www.gunningarts.co.uk
GURREY, Charles Stewart
www.charlesgurrey.com
GUSTARD, Tim
www.timgustard.com
HAGGER, Henry Benjamin
camdenprintmakers.co.uk
HAINES, Jean
www.jeanhaines.com
HALL, Caroline
www.carolinehall.net
HALL, Christopher Compton
www.christopherhall-painter.com
HALL, Dennis Henry
www.parrotpress.co.uk
HALL, Sam
www.samhallart.com
HALLAM, Marilyn
www.aptstudios.org/artists
HALLIDAY, Colin Thomas
www.startspace.co.uk
HALLOWES, Veda Nanette
www.vedahallowes.co.uk
HALSBY, Julian
www.newlandgallery.co.uk
HAMBLING, Maggi
www.maggihambling.com
HAMEL, Francis Etienne
www.francishamel.com
HAMILTON, Julia
www.juliahamilton.co.uk
HAMILTON, Katherine
katehamiltonartist.co.uk
HAMILTON, Susie
www.susiehamilton.co.uk
HAMMICK, Tom
www.tomhammick.com
www.hammickeditions.com
HAMPTON, F. Michael
www.michael-hampton.com
HANLEY, James
www.jameshanley.net
HANNAFORD, Elizabeth
www.elizabethhannaford.com
HANSCOMB, Brian
www.brianhanscomb.co.uk
HANSELAAR, Marcelle
www.marcellehanselaar.com
HARBON, Jan
www.janharbon.com
HARDIMAN, Patsy Christine
www.LondonArt.co.uk
HARDING, Alexis
www.mummeryschnelle.com
HARDMAN, Paul Ritson
www.hartoons.co.uk
HARDY, Robert
www.roberthardyartist.co.uk
HARE, Derek Charles
derekhare.co.uk
HARLEY, Alexandra
www.alexandraharley.co.uk
HARMAN, Alice
www.cow-shed-studio.com
HARPER, Alison
www.harperart.com
HARRIS, Jennifer Joy
www.rwa.org.uk
HARRIS HUGHES, Susanna Dioné Neate
www.susannaharrishughes.com
HARRISON, Mark Stephen
www.paintingsbymarkharrison.com
HARRISSON, Tim
www.timharrisson.co.uk
HART, Aidan Christopher
www.aidanharticons.com
HART-DAVIES, Christina Ann
www.christinahartdavies.co.uk
HARTILL, Brenda
www.brendahartill.com
HARVEY, Patricia
www.sgfa.org
HASTE, Kendra
www.kendrahaste.co.uk
HASTINGS, Gerard
www.modernbritishart.net

HAUGHTON, Patrick
www.axisweb.org/artist/patrickhaughton
www.nsanewlyn.com/newlyn-society-of-artists/partick-haughton

HAVSTEEN-FRANKLIN, Eleanor
www.eleanorhavsteenfranklin.com

HAWKES, Ben
www.benhawkes.co.uk

HAWKES, Justin Sheridan
www.justinhawkes.com

HAY, Ian
www.members.aol.com/ianhaygallery

HAYDEN, Toni
www.tonihayden.com

HAYES, Georgia
www.georgiahayes.com

HAYWARD, Louise May
louisehayward.co.uk

HAYWARD, Timothy John
www.jonathancooper.co.uk

HAYWARD-HARRIS, Martin John
www.hayward-harris.co.uk

HAZZARD, Charles Walker
www.charleswalkerhazzard.com

HEADLEY, Catherine Louise
Catherine Headley.co.uk

HEARD, Peter
peterheard.com

HEATH, Crispian
www.crispianheath.com

HEATH, Margaret Felice
www.margaretheath.co.uk

HEATHCOTE, Peregrine
www.peregrineheathcote.com

HEATON-HARRIS, Linda Jacqueline
www.lindaheaton-harris.co.uk

HEINDORFF, Michael
www.londonartscafe.org.uk/shows/mh/index.htm

HELD, Julie
www.julieheld.com

HELLMAN, Louis Mario
www.louishellman.co.uk

HELY HUTCHINSON, Nicholas David
www.nicholashelyhutchinson.com

HEMMANT, Lynette
www.lynettehemmant.com

HEMMING BRAY, Rachel
www.rachelhemmingbray.co.uk

HENDERSON SMITH, Tom
www.hendersonsmith.co.uk

HENON, Sue
www.atelierhenon.de

HEPWORTH, Anthony
www.anthonyhepworth.com

HERBST, Günther Daniel
www.contemporaryartsociety.co.uk

HERICKX, Geoffrey Russell
geoffreyherickx.com

HERIZ-SMITH, Bridget
www.bridgetheriz.co.uk

HERON, Susanna
www.susannaheron.com

HEUGHAN, Christine Joy (Chrissie)
www.chrissieheughanpaper.co.uk

HEVESI, Michael
www.thecorridoroflife.com

HEWITT, John Haslam
www.abstractacrylicart.co.uk

HEWLINGS, Charles
www.charleshewlings.com

HEYWOOD, Denise Suzanne
www.deniseheywood.com

HICKS, June Rhodes
www.trevescanstudio.com

HICKS, Peter Michael
www.petermhicks.co.uk

HICKS-JENKINS, Clive
www.hicks-jenkins.com

HIGGINSON, Clifford Edward
www.cliffhigginson.co.uk

HILLHOUSE, David
www.davidhillhouse.com

HILLS, Dominic
www.edgarmodern.com

HILLS, Jonathan Graham
www.smartshillstudios.co.uk

HIPPE, Susan Kerstin
www.absolutearts.com/portfolio/s/susanhippe

HITCHENS, John
www.johnhitchens.com

HOBBS, Philip Lawrence
www.plhobbs.co.uk

HOCKIN, Julie
www.hockinandroberts.com

HODDER, Monroe
www.monroehodder.com

HOIDA, Peter
www.petehoida.co.uk

HOLD, William Ashley
ashleyhold-artist.info

HOLDEN, John
agnews gallery.com - exhibitions April 2008

HOLMES, Clyde
www.clydeholmes.force9.co.uk
HOLMES, Linda Ruth
www.lindaholmes.co.uk
HOLMES, Walter
walterholmes.co.uk
HOLTOM, Roger
www.rogerholtom.co.uk
HOMES, Ronald Thomas John
ronaldhomes.co.uk
HOOD, Andrew David
www.andrewhoodgallery.com
HOPE, Benjamin
www.benjaminhope.net
HOPKINS, Clyde David F.
APT, SoCo & Advanced Graphics London
HOPKINSON, Sian Carolyn
www.sianhopkinson.com
HORNER, Marguerite
margueritehorner.moonfruit.com
HORNER, Michael Julian Alistair
www.galleryonthenet.com
HORTON, James Victor
www.jameshortonartist.com
HOUGH, Liz
www.art-on-line.co.uk
HOWARD, Ghislaine Marianne
www.ghislainehoward.com
HOWARD, Ken
www.kenhoward.co.uk
HOWARTH, Anna
www.annahowarth.com
HOWARTH, Derek
www.derekhowarth.co.uk
HOWELD, Cheryl
www.ch-fineart.com
HOWELL, David
www.davidhowell.co.uk
HOWELLS, Suzanne
www.suehowells.com
HUFTON, Susan Mary
web.me.com/suehufton/calligraphy
HUGHES, Christine
www.christinehughesimages.co.uk
HUGHES, Kevin Michael
www.kevinhughesri.com
HUGHES, Tom
www.tomhughespainting.co.uk
HUNKIN, Sally Elizabeth
kew-artists.com
HUNT, George Robert
spate-art.co.uk
HUNTER, Alexis
www.alexishunter.co.uk
HUNTER, Christa
www.christahunter.com
HUNTER, Elizabeth
www.ecrhunter.com
HUNTER, Janet Claire (Jan)
www.janhunter.com
HURDLE, Robert Henry
www.roberthurdle.co.uk
HURFORD, John Roger
www.johnhurford.co.uk
HUSON, Cedric Nigel
www.cedrichuson.com
HUXLEY, Jonathan
www.jonathanhuxley.co.uk
I'ANSON, Mari
www.mari-artist.co.uk
IBBOTSON, Pam
www.pamibbotson.co.uk
IMMS, David
www.fossegallery.com
INGLIS, Catherine Elizabeth
www.cathinglis.com
INSOLL, Christopher
www.chrisinsoll.com
IRVIN, Magnus
www.magnusirvin.co.uk
ISHAM, Anthony Ralph
www.themarineartist.com
ISOM, Graham Michael
www.grahamisom.co.uk
IZZARD, Pamela
www.pamelaizzard.eu
JACKLIN, Bill
www.bjacklin.com
JACKSON, Ashley
www.ashley-jackson.co.uk
JACKSON, Bridget H.
www.bridgethjackson.com
JACKSON, Dilys Mary
dilysjackson.co.uk
JACKSON, H. J.
www.norwichprintfair.co.uk/hj_jackson
JACKSON, Kurt Dominic
www.kurtjackson.co.uk
JACKSON, (Penelope) Mary
www.newenglishartclub.co.uk
JACOBSON, Stephen Roy
www.stephenjacobson.co.uk
JACZYNSKA, Marysia
chelseaartsociety.org.uk
apauk.org

JAFAR, Abu
www.abujafar.com

JAFFE, Ilona Lola Langdorf
www.todres.fsnet.co.uk

JAGGER, Janette
www.jaggeronline

JAKOBER, Ben
www.jakobervu.com

JAMES, Andrew John
andrewjamesartist.co.uk

JAMES, Gary M.
www.voyageart.co.uk

JAMES, Janice
www.janicejamesceramics.com

JAMES, Nicholas Philip
www.philipjamestudio.ndo.co.uk

JAMES, Ric
www.jamesfineart.co.uk

JAMES, Roderick Morris
www.jamesfineart.co.uk

JAMESON, Kerry
www.kerryjameson.com

JARAY, Tess
www.tessjaray.com

JASINSKI, Alfons B. RSW
alfjasinski.com

JEFFREY, Jill
www.jilljeffrey.com

JELBERT, Rebecca
www.rebeccajelbert.co.uk

JELBERT, Wendy
www.wendyjelbert.co.uk

JELLEY, Susan Jane
www.suejelley.co.uk

JELLICOE, Colin
www.colinjellicoe.co.uk

JENKINS, Josie
www.rosiejenkins.co.uk

JENKINS, Kate
www.cardigan.ltd.uk

JENKINS, Lawrence Fifield
www.lawrencejenkins.co.uk

JENNISON, Robert William
www.rwa.org.uk

JERVIS, Sharon
www.sharonjervis.com

JIANG HUANG, Limin
www.liminart.com

JOEL, Judy
www.judyjoel.com

JOEL, Timothy Nathan
www.joeljoel.com

JOHANSSEN, Clara
www.clarajohanssen.com

JOHNS, Annie
www.anniejohns.me

JOHNS, Phil
www.philjohns.com

JOHNSON, Annette
www.annettejohnson.co.uk

JOHNSON, Ben
www.benjohnsonartist.com

JOHNSON, Carl
www.numasters.com
oldbakeryartists.com

JOHNSON, Michael Alan
michaeljohnsonart.com

JOHNSON, Tlws
www.tlwsglass.co.uk

JOHNSON, (William) Holly
www.hollyjohnson.com

JONES, Chris
www.chrisjonesart.com

JONES, Colin
www.celjones.co.uk

JONES, Geraldine M.L.
www.amboarts.co.uk

JONES, GRIMES &
www.grimesandjones.co.uk

JONES, Malcolm
http://www.chisenhale.co.uk/chisenhale/studios/malcolm-jones

JONES, Robert William
www.firstlightgallery.co.uk

JONES, Royston
www.pacificstream.info

JONES, Steven
www.stevenjonesartist.com

JONES, Timothy Martin
window135.com
window135.tumblr

JONES, Yvonne
www.yvonnejones.net

JONSSON, Lars Ossian
www.larsjonsson.se

JORDAN, Maureen Ann
www.maureenjordan.com

JOSEPH, Jane
www.janejoseph.co.uk

JOWETT, Jenny Ann
www.jennyjowett.com

JOYCE, Peter Dennis
www.peterjoyce.org.uk

JUILLERAT, Paul
www.hotairdesign.com

KALKHOF, Peter Heinz
www.annelyfineart.co.uk/Gallery-Artists

KALMAR, Janos
www.janoskalmar.com

KANE, Martin
www.martinkane.net

KANTARIS, Rachael Anna
www.kantaris.com

KAPLAN, Krystyna
www.kaplan.4me.pl

KARAS, Vanja
www.vanjakaras.com

KARN, Barbara
www.barbarakarn.co.uk

KARTT, Orson
www.orsonkartt.com

KAVANAGH, Paul
www.paul-kavanagh.co.uk

KEABLE, Karen S.J.
www.ksjkeable.co.uk

KEELEY, Simon Phillip
www.simonkeeley.com

KELLETT, Ursula
www.ursulakellett.co.uk

KELLY, Antoinette Louise
www.saatchiart.com/A.Kelly

KELLY, Brendan
www.brendankellyartist.co.uk

KELLY, Deirdre
deirdrekellydeirdrekelly.com

KELLY, Marty
www.blueleafgallery.com

KELSEY, Robert
www.rkelsey.com

KELSO, James Philip
www.kelsopaintings.com

KENNEDY, Keith Manning
www.sgfa.org.uk

KENNEDY, Margaret
www.margaretkennedyworldpress.com

KENNEDY, Michael Peter
www.michaelkennedy.org

KENNISH, Jenny
www.jennykennish.com

KERMAN, Lesley Frances
www.lesleykerman.co.uk

KERR, Janette
www.janettekerr.co.uk
extremewavetheory.blogspot.com

KERSHAW, Walter
www.walterkershaw

KESTEVEN, Abel
www.ablekesteven.com

KEY, Geoffrey
www.geoffreykey.com

KHETANCHI, Gopal Swami
www.khetanchistudio.com

KIANUSH-WALLACE, Katy
http://www.art-arena.com

KIDBY, Paul James
www.paulkidby.net

KIDD, Alan Hunter
http://www.alankidd.com

KIKI, John
www.johnkiki.co.uk

KIMBLE, Grace
www.gracesart.co.uk

KINAHAN, Lady Coralie
www.coralie-kinahan.com

KING, Andrew Norman
www.andrewkingroi.co.uk

KING, Anna kathleen
www.anna-king.com

KING, Robert
www.robertking.co.uk

KINGSTON, Angela Hoppe
www.angelahoppekingston.com

KINMONT, Andrew
www.andrewkinmont.com

KIPNISS, Robert
rkipniss.net

KITCH, Nate
www.natekitch.com

KLEIN, Anita
www.anitaklein.com

KLEIN, Randy
www.randyklein.co.uk

KNEALE, William Henry (Bill)
www.billkneale.co.uk

KNIGHT, Geraldine
www.geraldineknight.com

KNIGHT, Marguerite
www.guildstudioartists.com

KNIGHT, Sera Manioglu
www.seraknight.co.uk

KNOX, Liz
www.lizknox.com

KOCH, C.-Clarissa
www.c-clarissakoch.com

KORALEK, Paul George
www.abk.co.uk

KOROSHILOV, Valery
www.koroshilov.com

KOWAL POST, Christine
www.christinekowalpost.com

KOZARZEWSKA, Magda
www.magdakozarzewska.co.uk

KUBECKI-PEARCE, Terence Peter
www.terrykubecki.co.uk

KURTZ, Peter Felix Magnus von
www.fetishfoto.co.uk

LAI, William Sui Khee
www.outsidein.org.uk/william-lai

LAKEY, Antony William Albert
www.myspace.com/Antony_Lakey

LAKIN, Michael
michaellakinart.co.uk

LAMB, Thomas
www.thomaslamb.com

LAMB, Yuki
wwww.yukilamb.com

LANCASTER, Maureen (Mo)
www.molancaster.co.uk

LANDERS, Linda Anne
www.lindalanders.co.uk

LANE, Jason
www.jasonlane.org.uk

LANG, Demi
www.demilang.com

LANGFORD, Martin James
www.martinlangford.com

LANGHORN, Doreen M.
www.society-women-artists.org.uk

LARMONT, Eric
larmalone.co.uk

LAST, Bob
www.thepastelsociety.org.uk

LAST, Joanne
www.joannelast.co.uk

LATHAM, Helen
www.lathamhelen.com

LAUBIN, Carl David
www.carllaubin.com

LAUCHLAN, Anya
www.Rolland-Fine-Art.com

LAWRENCE, Amanda
www.amandalawrenceglass.com

LAWRENCE, Peter Alfred
the-art-works.co.uk

LAWRENCE, Sandra
www.sandralawrence.co.uk

LAWRENCE, Tory
www.torylawrence.com

LAWSON, Sonia
www.sonialawson.co.uk

LAWTON, Teresa
www.teresalawton.co.uk

LAYZELL, Peter
www.peterlayzell.com

LE BRUN, Christopher Mark
www.christopherlebrun.co.uk

LE GRICE, Klio
facebook Klio le Grice

LE MARCHANT, Sir Francis
www.francislemarchant.com

LEACH, Jenny
www.j-art.co.uk

LEACH, Ursula Mary
www.ursulaleach.co.uk

LECOURT, Elisabeth
www.elisabethlecourt.com

LEE, Sidney Edward
www.StIvesSocietyofArtists.com

LEES, Caroline
www.carolinelees-icons.co.uk

LEESON, Geoffrey Glynne
www.wobblybridge.co.uk

LEGG, Owen
www.woodcraftpress.co.uk

LEIGH, Michael
laughingshed.blogspot.com

LEMAIRE, Angela Jacqueline
www.angelalemaire.co.uk

LEMAN, Jill
www.jillleman.co.uk

LEMAN, Martin
martinleman.co.uk

LENDIS, John Andrew
www.johnlendis.com

LENNON, Stephen
www.stephenlennon.co.uk

LESTER, James Richard
www.james-lester.com

LETTS, John Barry
www.lettssculptures.co.uk

LEVERITT, Thomas Michael James
www.leveritt.com

LEVIN, Eddy
www.goldenmeangauge.co.uk

LEWIS, Ann
www.annlewis.co.uk

LEWIS, Jane
www.janelewisartist.com

LEWIS, Jane
janelewisart.co.uk

LEWIS, Jo
www.jolewisart.co.uk

LEWIS, Roger Leslie
www.sgfa.org.uk

LEWIS, Sanchia
www.sanchialewis.co.uk
LEWTHWAITE, Paul Frank
www.paullewthwaite.com
LEYSHON-JONES, Steffan
www.urbandecoy.co.uk
LIEN, Natasha
www.natashalien.com
LIGHT, Vivienne Mary
www.viviennelight.co.uk
www.cantertonbooks.co.uk
LIGHTFOOT, Katharine Lucy
www.katlightfoot.com
LIJN, Liliane
www.lilianelijn.com
LIMBREY, John Nigel Stephens
www.fossewayartists.com
LIN, Hsiao-Mei
www.hmlin.co.uk
LIN, Htein
www.hteinlin.com
LINDLEY, Ali (Alison Mary)
alilindleyartist.co.uk
LINDSAY, Alister
alisterlindsay.co.uk
LINDSAY, Rosemary
www.rosemarylindsay.com
LINDSLEY, Kathleen Margaret
www.ravenpressgallery.co.uk
LING, Steven
wwww.picassomio.com/steven-ling.html
LIPTON, Laurie
www.laurielipton.com
LITTLE, Alistair John
wwww.alistairlittle.com
LJUNGDALH, Stine
(in progress) stineljungdalh.com
LLOYD, Rosamond Ann
www.rosamondlloyd.com
LLOYD-JONES, Pamela
www.pamelalloydjones.com
LLYWELYN HALL, Dan
www.danllywelynhall.co.uk
LOCKHART, David
RSW Lockhart
LOGAN, Andrew
www.andrewlogan.com
LOKEN, Julia
www.loken.co.uk
LOKER, John Keith
johnloker.co.uk
LONG, Denny Jane
www.dennylongrwa.co.uk
LONG, Gary Nigel
www.garylongart.com
LONGWORTH, Carl
www.carllongworth.com
LOVEDAY, Ross
rossloveday.co.uk
LOVELL, Margaret
www.margaretlovell.co.uk
LOVETT, Alastair Philip
alovett.co.uk
LOWDAY, Sue
www.suelowday.co.uk
LOWE, Jeff
www.jeff-lowe.com
LOWE, Peter
www.peterllowe.plus.com
LOWRY. John Roger
rogerspaintings.web.com
LUBAR, Katherine
www.katlubar.com
LUCAS, Akemi
www.koshujapaneseart.co.uk
LUKE, John
www.johnlukepaintings.com
LUKIC, Jelena
www.homunculus.co.uk/jelena/
LUMLEY, Thomas Henry
www.thomaslumley.com
LUMSDEN, James
www.axisweb.org/artist/jameslumsden
LYDBURY, Jane Sarah
www.janelydbury.com
LYDIATE, Avril Ann
www.avrillydiate.co.uk
LYFORD, Rosina
www.rosinalyford.com
LYNCH, James
www.james-lynch.co.uk
LYNCH, Kate Mary
www.katelynch.co.uk
LYONS, Joan
www.joanlyons.co.uk
LYWOOD, Sally
www.gallerixia.no
MACALPINE, Jean
www.jeanmacalpine.com
MACARA, Andrew
www.macara.com
MACARTHUR, Susan
www.susanmacarthur.co.uk
MACCORMAC, Sir Richard Cornelius
www.mjparchitects.co.uk

MACDONALD, Alan
www.alanmacdonald.net

MACDONALD, Allan Sween
www.allanmacdonald.co.uk

MACDONALD, Donald
www.donaldmacdonaldspaintings.co.uk

MACDONALD, Frances
www.crinanhotel.com

MacFARLANE, Sheila Margaret
www.aberfeldywatermill.com

MacGREGOR, Moira
www.moiramacgregor.com

MACINTYRE, Hilke
www.macintyre-art.com

MACINTYRE, Ian
www.macintyre-art.com

MACKAY, Jane Elizabeth
http://www.soundingart.com

MacLENNAN, Alastair MacKay
http://www.vads.ahds.ac.uk/collections/maclennan

MADDISON, John Michael
johnmaddison.co.uk

MADDISON, Robert
www.maddisonfineart.co.uk

MAHON, Phyllis Josephine
www.phyllismahon.com

MALCOLM, Bronwen
www.bronwenmalcolm.com

MALENOIR, Mary
www.malenoir.co.uk

MALHOTRA, Sheila
www.sheilazart.com

MALLIN-DAVIES, Joanna
www.mallin-davies.com

MALTMAN, Philip John
www.numasters.com
www.maybole.org/photogalleries

MANIE, Ann Elizabeth
www.annmanie.net

MANLEY, Brett
www.brettmanley.co.uk

MANNING, Baz
www.heraldic-artist.com

MANNING, Julia
www.juliamanning.co.uk

MARCHANT, David Edwin
videoartinbox.com

MARIA, Veronique
www.veroniquemaria.co.uk

MARINE, Tom
www.reltonmarine.com

MARINKOV, Sasa (Alexandra)
www.sasamarinkov.co.uk

MARKEY, Danny
www.redfern-gallery.com

MARLBOROUGH, Rosita
www.rositamarlborough.com

MARLIN, Brigid
www.brigidmarlin.com

MARSH, Robert Burkall
under construction

MARTIN, Barry John
www.barrymartin.co.uk

MARTIN, Blandine
www.blandinemartin.com

MARTIN, Jean B
www.jeanbmartin.co.uk

MARTIN, John Scott
www.johnscottmartin.co.uk

MARTIN, Marie-Louise
wwww.marie-louisemartin.com

MARTIN, Mary Grace
www.marymartin.co

MARTIN, Sonia
www.soniamartin.co.uk

MARTINEAU, Luke
www.lukemartineau.com

MASSIE, Claudia
www.claudiamassie.co.uk

MATHESON, Andrew Kenneth Mackenzie
andrewmatheson.co.uk

MATHEWS, Binny
www.hereasel.com

MATTHEWS, Les
www.lesmatthews.co.uk

MATTHEWS, Sally
www.sallymatthews.co.uk

MAUGY, Sandrine
www.sandrinemaugy.com

MAY, Elsie D.
www.elsiemay.com

MAY, Joanna
www.joannamay.com

MAYES, Emerson
www.emersonmayes.co.uk

McADAM CLARK, Caroline
www.mcadamclark.com

McADAM FREUD, Jane
www.janemcadamfreud.com

McCARTER, Keith
www.keith-mccarter.com

McCARTHY, Peter
www.pmcart.co.uk

McCARTNEY, Jamie
www.jamiemccartney.com

MCCLARY, Louise
www.louisemcclary.com

McCOMBS, John
www.johnmccombs.co.uk

McCOY, Josie
www.josiemccoy.co.uk

McCRUM, Bridget
www.bridgetmccrum.com

McCULLOCH, Ian
www.s-s-a.org/html/featart/mcculloc/index.htm

McDERMOTT, John
johnmcdermottartist.com

McDOWELL, Phyllis Ann Graham
www.phyllismcdowell.com

McEWAN, Angus Maywood
www.angusmcewan.com

McFADYEN, Jock
www.jockmcfadyen.com

McGOOKIN, Colin Trevor
www.colinmcgookin.com

MCGREGOR, Euan Robert
www.euanmcgregorpaintings.co.uk

McGREGOR, Lynn Barbara
www.lynnmcgreagor.co.uk

McGUIGAN, Bernard
www.bernard-mcguigan.co.uk

McINTYRE, Fiona Mary Elspeth
www.fionamcintyre.com

McKAY-KNIGHT, Sophie
wwww.sophiemckayknight.com

McKEAN, Lorne (Miss)
www.lornemckean.com

McKECHNIE, Christine
www.christinemckechnie.co.uk

McKENNA, John Anthony
www.johnmckenna.co.uk

McKENZIE, Mo
www.mo-mckenzie.co.uk

McKERRELL, John
www.artistsandillustrators.co.uk

McKIVRAGAN, Terrence Bernard
www.terrymckivragan.co.uk

McLACHLAN, Edward Rolland
www.edmclachlan.co.uk

McLAREN, Sally
www.sallymclaren.co.uk

McLEAN, Mary
www.paintingsinminiature.com

McMULLEN, Sue
www.suemcmullen.citymax.com

McNAUGHTON, Rachel Patricia
www.artbyrachel.co.uk
www.minigalleryworld.com/Rachel_McNaughton

McRAE, Jennifer
www.jennifermcrae.co.uk

McWILLIAMS, Simon
www.simonmcwilliams.com

MEAD, Harriet Rebecca
www.harrietmead.co.uk

MEDCALF, Gina
www.ginamedcalf.com

MEDWAY, Sarah
www.medwayart.com

MEEK, Elizabeth R.
www.elizabethmeek.com

MEEKS, Sheila Mary
sheilameeks.com

MELAMED-ADAMS, Alicia
www.aliciamelamed.com

MELEGARI, Carl
www.carlmelegari.co.uk

MELROSE, Janet Margaret
www.janetmelrose.com

MELVIN, Johanna Helga
www.johannamelvin.com

MENDELOW, Anne
annemendelow.com

MENDOZA, Edwin
www.mendoart.co.uk

MENDOZA, June
www.junemendoza.co.uk

MENZIES, Gordon William
www.ionagallery.com

MERRICK, Tony
www.tonymerrick.com

MICHAEL, Colin
www.colinmichael.wix.com/colinmichael

MIDDLETON, Michael
www.mikemiddletonartist.co.uk

MIDDLETON, Nicholas
www.nicholasmiddleton.co.uk

MIDGLEY, Julia
www.juliamidgley.co.uk

MIERS, Christopher John Penrose
www.christopher-miers.co.uk

MILBURN, Elizabeth Mary
www.lizmilburn.co.uk

MILLER, Andrew Peter
www.andrewmillerartist.com

MILLER, Colin James
www.colin-miller.co.uk

MILLER, Ingrid
millerkonst.se

MILLER, Ronald George
ronaldmiller.se

MILLER, Shannon
www.shanmiller.com

MILLINGTON, Terence
www.terencemillington.net

MILLMORE, Mark Alexander
www.eyelidproductions.co.uk

MILLNER, Etienne Henry de la Fargue
www.etiennemillner.com

MILLS, Glynis
www.equestrianartists.co.uk

MILLS, John W.
johnwmills.com

MILLS, Teresa Ann
www.teresamills.blogspot.com

MILNE, Judith Erica
www.miart.org.uk

MILNER, Judy
www.judymilner.com

MILO-GRAY, Marcelle Jane
www.milo-gray.co.uk

MINTER, Lynda Maria
www.lyndaminter.com

MIRECKI, Wladyslaw
www.chappelgalleries.co.uk

MISTRY, Dhruva
www.dhruvamistry.com

MITCHELL, Gordon
www.gordonmitchell.co.uk
www.gordonmitchell.net

MITCHELL, Janet Elizabeth
www.janetmitchell.co.uk

MITCHELL, Lewis John
www.rainydaygallery.co.uk
Lewis Mitchell Artist

MITCHELL, Shuna Patricia
www.shoosal.com

MOGER, Jill
www.jillmogersculptures.co.uk

MONROE, Chuck
www.chuckmonroeart.com

MONTAGUE, Lucile Christine
www.axisartists.org.uk

MOORE, Cleland Randolph
www.clelandmoore.co.uk

MOORE, Gabrielle Kaye
www.gabymoore.co.uk

MOORE, Sally
www.artwales.com

MORAN, Carolyne Sandra Anne
www.carolynemoran.com

MORENO, Michel
http://www.michelmoreno.com

MORETON, Nicolas
www.nicholasmoreton.com

MOREY de MORAND, C.
www.cmoreydemorand.co.uk

MORGAN, Dr. Michael
www.marinehouseatbeer.co.uk

MORGAN, Howard James
howard-morgan.co.uk

MORGAN, Mark Andrew
www.markasculptor.com

MORLEY, John
www.johnmorley.info

MORREAU, Jacqueline Carol
www.morreaux.co.uk

MORRELL, Peter John
petermorrell.co.uk

MORRIS, Elizabeth
www.elizabethmorrisprints.co.uk

MORRIS, John Meirion
john meirion morris

MORRIS, Mali
www.malimorris.co.uk

MORRIS, Suzi
www.suzimorrisart.com

MORRISON, Les (Leslie Howard)
www.lesmorrison.co.uk

MORROCCO, Jack Bernard
www.jackmorrocco.com

MORROW, Gary Thomas
www.garymorrowart.com

MORSE, Colin Benjamin Scale
www.bestofruralwales.co.uk
www.welshpictures.co.uk

MORTIMER, Justin Roger
justinmortimer.co.uk

MORTON, Gina
www.ga-morton.co.uk

MOSELEY, Malcolm
www.malcolmmoseley.com

MOSS, Zoë
www.zoemoss.com

MOTT, Miranda J. M.
www.mjmott.co.uk

MOUNTJOY, Robert William
mountjoy-rw.com

MOXLEY, Susan
www.susanmoxley.co.uk

MUIR, Jane
www.janemuir.com

MULCAHY, Bruce
www.brucemulcahy.co.uk

MULLEN, Kay
www.epsomartcourses.co.uk

MULROY, Alison
www.alisonmulroy.com

MUMBERSON, Stephen Leonard
ADRI

MUNDY, William Percy
www.billmundy.co.uk

MUNOZ, Andrew
www.andrewmunoz.co.uk

MUNRO, Barbara
botanicalart-barbaramunro.co.uk

MUNSLOW, Angela E.
www.figurativeart.co.uk

MURLEY, Lawrence Mario
lawrencemurley.co.uk

MURPHY, Richard
www.richardmurphyarchitects.com

MURRAY, Donald
www.donaldmurrayda.co.uk

MURRAY, George Alexander
www.george-murray.co.uk

MUSGRAVE, Olivia Mirabel
www.jmlondon.com

MUSGRAVE, Sally Ann
www.kapiljariwalagallery.co.uk

MYERS, Chris
www.chrismyersart.com

MYERS, Emily Margaret
www.emilymyers.com

MYINT, Khin
www.khinmyint.co.uk

NASH, Elizabeth
www.elizabethnash.co.uk

NASON, Kristine
www.kristinenason.com

NAUMANN, Anuk Danuta Katarzyna
www.anuknaumann.co.uk

NEAL, Arthur Richard
www.arthurneal.co.uk

NEAL, Charles William
www.charlesnealartworks.co.uk

NEAL, Trevor
www.trevorneal.co.uk

NEILAND, Brendan
www.brendanneiland.com

NEILL, Errol James
www.neillfineart.co.uk

NEILL, William Andrew Knight
www.william-neill.co.uk

NESBITT, Mark Alexander
www.CaricaturesByLukeWarm.co.uk

NEWBERRY, Angela
www.angela-newberry.co.uk

NEWMAN, Ros
www.rosnewman.com

NEWSOME, Peter Martin
www.peter.newsome.com

NEWTON, William Alexander
williamnewtonsculptor.com

NICHOLLS, Paul Edward
www.paulnichollsartwork.com

NICKOLLS, Deborah
www.deborahnickolls.com

NIJMAN, Christina Maria
www.tinynijmanart.com

NINNES, Lesley Marian
www.picturefromstives.com

NOAKES, Michael
www.michael-noakes.co.uk

NOBLE, Guy
www.guynoble.com

NOBLE, Jean
www.jeannoble.com

NORRIS, David
www.davidnorris.co.uk

NORRIS, Linda
www.linda-norris.com

NOYES, Margot
www.thesuffolkgroup.co.uk

NUGENT, Lesley
www.nuggletonart.co.uk

O'AIVAZIAN, Edman
www.edmano.com

O'BRIEN, Emer
www.emerobrien.com

O'CARROLL, John Patrick
www.johnocarroll.co.uk

O'DONOGHUE, Declan
www.sffurniture.co.uk

O'HARA, D. Patrick
www.ohara-art.com

O'KEEFE, Kevin
www.kevinokeefe-art.com

O'NEILL, Junko
www.junkooneill.com

O'REILLY, Oran
www.oranoreilly.co.uk

O'RORKE, Robert Ashley
www.robert-ororke.com

ODA, Mari-Ruth
www.mari-ruthoda.com

OLDFIELD, Juliet Jane
www.janeoldfield.co.uk

OLINER, Sheila
http://www.org/artist/sheilaoliner

ONIANS, Richard (Dick) Lathbury
www.dickonianssculptor.co.uk

ONO, Takumasa
www.takumasaono.co.uk

OOZEERALLY, Barbara
www.barbaraoozeerally.co.uk

ORCHARD, Alison
www.alisonorchard.com

ORMELL, Christopher Peter
www.philosophyforeducation.co.uk

ORR, Chris
www.chrisorr-ra.com

ORR, Jacqueline Elizabeth
www.jacquelineorr.com

ORWIN, Carol
www.orwinsculptures.com

OSBORNE, Mark
www.markosborneart.com

OSBORNE, Roy
www.coloracademy.co.uk

OSLER, Anthony John
www.anthonyoslermarineartist.co.uk

OTTEY, Piers Ronald Edward Campbell
www.piersottey.co.uk

OULTON, Therese
Tate, Marlborough & "therese oulton"

OUTRAM, Steven
www.stevenoutram.com

OVERTON, Alan
www.fromcreativenetwork.org.uk

OWEN, Glynis
www.glynisowensculptor.co.uk

PACE, Nicholas
nicholaspace.com

PACKHAM, John Leslie (Les)
www.lespackham.co.uk

PAGE-ROBERTS, James
www.webpageroberts.blogspot.com

PALLISER, Anthony
www.anthonypalliser.com

PALMER, Juliette
www.royalsocietyofbritishartists.org.uk

PALMER, Margaret
Pastel Society

PANCHAL, Shanti
www.shantipanchal.com

PANKHURST, Alvin Ernest
www.alvinpankhurst.com

PANNETT, Denis Richard Dalton
www.denispannett.co.uk

PAPADOPOLOUS, George
www.yorgosglass.com

PARDUE, Prudence
www.pruepardue.com

PARFITT, David Granville
www.newenglishartclub.co.uk
www.messums.com

PARKER, Cornelia
www.frithstreetgallery.com/artists/bio/cornelia_parker

PARKER, Gill
www.gillparker.com

PARKIN, Ione
www.ioneparkin.co.uk

PARKIN, Michael Robert
parkinfineart.co.uk

PARKINSON, Richard Henry
www.richardparkinson.co.uk

PARRISH, Kevin Alun
www.kevinparrish.co.uk

PARRY, Alan
www.alanparryart.com

PARRY, David
www.davidparryart.com

PASKETT, David
www.davidpaskett.co.uk

PASS, Donald James
www.donaldpass.com

PATON, Anne Elizabeth
www.annepaton.com

PATRICK, Emily (Katherine Emily)
www.emilypatrick.com

PATTERSON, Janet
www.janetpatterson.co.uk

PATTON, Marcus
www.operahat.co.uk

PAUL, Sylvia
www.sylviapaul.com

PAVEY, Don
www.coloracademy.co.uk

PAVLENKO, Sergei
www.spavlenko.demon.co.uk

PAYNE, Mandy
www.mandypayneart.com

PAYNE, Michael Gustavius
mgpayne.com

PAYNE, Tom
www.startspace.co.uk

PEARSON, Bruce Edward
www.brucepearson.net

PECKHAM, Barry Arthur
www.barrypeckham.co.uk

PEGLITSIS, Nicolas
www.nicolaspeglitsis.com

PENKETH SIMPSON, Barbara
www.penketh-simpson.co.uk

PERKINS, Marion
www.soc-botanical-artists.org

PERKINS, Shelly Louise
www.shellyperkins.co.uk

PERRIN, Sally Jane
www.saa.co.uk/art/sallyjaneperrin

PERRY, Jayne
www.jaynecperry.com

PERRY, Julian
www.austindesmond.com

PERRYMAN, Margot
www.margot-perryman.co.uk
www.arttolivewith.co.uk

PERSEY, Robert
www.robertpersey.com

PESKETT, Tessa
www.theorangetreegalerie.com

PETHERS, Ian Peter Andrew
www.glenrockstudio.co.uk

PETLEY, Roy
www.petleyfineart.com

PETRITOLI, Alvaro
www.alvaropetritoli.com

PETRY, Nancy Virginie
www.nancypetry.com

PETTERSON, Melvyn Lawrence
www.melvynpetterson.com

PEVERALL, Adrienne
www.stisa.co.uk

PHILLIPS, Anna
wwww.annbrain.co.uk

PHILLIPS, Rex
www.rex-phillips.co.uk

PHILLIPS, Tom
www.tomphillips.co.uk

PHIPPS, Jemma Louise Rose
www.jemmaphipps.com

PICHÉ, Roland
www.rolandpiche.com

PICK, Wayne Erich
www.startspace.co.uk

PICKERING, J. Robin H.
www.robinpickering.co.uk

PIDOUX, Janet Anne
www.janepidoux.co.uk

PIER, Catherine Julie
www.catherinepier.com

PIERCY, Rob
www.robpiercy.com

PIERSE, Simon
www.simonpierse.co.uk

PIESOWOCKI, Leon
www.leonpiesowocki.net

PIG, Christopher Maximillian
chrispig.com
vinsonart.com

PIKE, Jonathan
www.jonathanpike.co.uk

PILLKAHN, Lorna Mary
www.kristelpillkahn.co.uk

PIMLOTT, Geoffrey
http://www.1clikpic.com/geoffreypimlottarws/

PINSCHOF, Maria Flora
pinschofpaintinggallery.com

PINSKY, Michael
www.michaelpinsky.com

PITTAWAY, Neil John
www.njpittaway.co.uk

PLATT, Theo
www.theoplatt.com

POCOCK, Heather
www.franciskylegallery.com

PODBERY, Neil
www.neilpodberyfineart.co.uk

PODESTA, Anthony Andrew
https://sites.google.com/site/aapodesta/

POLAINE, Peter David
www.peterpolaine.com

POLLARD, Brian
www.brianpollard.co.uk

POLLOCK, Sir George F.
www.georgepollock.co.uk

POOK, Graham Arthur
grahampook.co.uk

POOLE, Greg
http://homepage.virgin.net/greg.poole

POOLE, Jonathan
www.jonathanpoole.co.uk

POOLEY, Vanessa
www.vanessapooley.com

POPE, Annabel
www.annabelpope.com

PORTELLI, Guy Anthony
www.portelli.sculptor.co.uk

PORWOL, Steven
www.stevenporwol.co.uk

POTTS, David
www.davidpottspaintings.com

POVEY, Edward
www.edwardpovey.com

POWELL, Adela Margaret
www.adelapowell.co.uk

POWELL, Andy
under construction, see saatchigallery.com

POWELL, Joanne
joannepowellart.co.uk

PRAED, Michael
www.michaelpraed.co.uk

PREST, Kathy
www.kathyprest.co.uk

PRICE, Christopher Francis
www.BibaBook.com

PRICE, Harry
www.harrypriceart.co.uk

PRICE, Richard Evan
www.manyaigelfinearts.com

PRICE, Trevor
www.trevorprice.co.uk

PRING MacSWEENEY, Dale Louisiana
www.rainbowzebra.net/dale_pring_macsweeney/
www.dalepringmacsweeney.com

PROCTER, Alison
www.alisonprocter.co.uk

PROCTER, Brenda
www.brendaprocter.webeden.co.uk

PROUD, Alastair Colm
alastairproud.com

PROWSE, Alexander Reginald
www.alexprowse.co.uk

PUGH, Tim
www.timpugh.co.uk

PULLAN, Tessa
www.tessapullan.co.uk

PURSER, Keith
www.jc-art.com

PYBUS, Michelle Christine
www.pybusfinearts.co.uk

PYE, Chris
www.chrispye-woodcarving.com

PYE, William
www.williampye.com

PYNE, Kenneth John
www.kenpyne.com

PYTEL, Walenty
www.wyebridge.com

QUARTLEY, Freddie
www.freddiequartley.com

QUIGLEY, Thomas Antony Gerard
www.tomquigleyshowcase.co.uk

QUIGLEY, Vlad
www.vladquigley.com

QUINN, Mary P.
www.maryquinnsculptor.com

RAE, Barbara
www.barbararae.com

RAE, John
johnraeartist.wordpress.com

RAE, Robin
www.robinraepaintings.co.uk

RAISON, Jennifer Mary
with ABNA (Association of British Naive Artists)

RAKE, Charles Robert
www.charlesrake.co.uk

RAMSBOTHAM, Meredith
www.meredithramsbotham.com

RANCE, Victoria
www.victoriarance.com

RANDALL, Carl
www.carlrandall.com

RANDALL-PAGE, Peter
www.peterrandall-page.com

RANK-BROADLEY, Ian
www.ianrank-broadley.co.uk

RASMUSSEN, Peter Ole
peterrasmussenpainting.co.uk
peterrasmussenportraits.co.uk

RAWLINGS, Bryan John
www.bryanrawlings.com

RAWLINGS, Raymond
www.rayrawlings.co.uk

READING, Peter William
www.peter-reading.com

REDEMER, Roberta
www.bracknellartgallery.org.uk

REDFERN, June
www.juneredfern.com

REDINGTON, Simon
www.kamikazepress.com

REES (HARRIS), Delphine Valerie
www.delreeswatercolours.com

REES-DAVIES, Kay
www.kay-rees-davies.co.uk

REIS, Klari
www.klarireis.com

REITER, Laura
laurareiter.com

RELTON, Christine
www.reltonmarine.com

RELTON, Maxine
www.maxinerelton.com

REMFRY, David
www.davidremfry.com

RHYS JAMES, Shani
www.axisweb.org/secvpg.aspxartistID67

RICE, Brian Wilfrid
brianrice.info

RICH, Graham Denton
www.faslondon.com

RICHARDSON, Fran
www.franrichardson.com

RICHARDSON, Ilana
www.ilana-richardson.com

RICHARDSON, Michael Peter
www.michaelrichardsonfineart.com

RICHARDSON, Philip David
philip-richardson.com

RICHARDSON, Ray
www.rayrichardson.co.uk

RICKETT, Michael
www.dot-art.co.uk/artist/mike-rickett

RIDLEY, Annabel
www.annabelridley.co.uk

RIDLEY, Virginia
http://www.VirginiaRidley.co.uk

RIGGS, Clive
www.saa.co.uk/art/cliveriggs

RISOE, Paul Schjelderup
www.paulrisoe.com

RITCHIE, Ian
www.ianritchiearchitects.co.uk

RITCHIE, Paul Stephen
www.ritchieart.co.uk

ROBERTS, Richard Travers
www.richardrobertsbronzes.com

ROBERTS, Simon
www.simonroberts.com

ROBERTSON, Saul
www.saulrobertson.com

ROBINSON, Barbara
www.barbararobinsonpaintings.com

ROBINSON, Kay
www.c-a-n.co.uk

ROBINSON, Wayne
www.waynejrobinson.com

ROCHFORT, William
www.williamrochfort.com

ROCK, Jill Elizabeth
www.galleryartist.com/JillRock

RODULFO, Peter
www.rodulfo.deviantart.com

RODWELL, Charles
charlesrodwellarts.com

ROGERS, Carol Ann
www.hvaf.org.uk/gallery/rogers

ROGERS, John Rowland
www.johnrogersartist.co.uk

ROMAIN, Ricky Stuart
www.rickyromain.com

RONA
www.ronapainting.com

ROSE, Christopher Andrew
www.chrisrose-artist.co.uk

ROSE, Juliet Sarah
www.juliet-rose.com

ROSE, Tim Simon
www.timroseartist.com

ROSKELL, Susan Kim
www.kimroskell.co.uk

ROSS, Annie
www.annieross.com

ROSS, John
www.axisweb.org/artist/johnross

ROSS, Michèlle
http://www.michelleross.org.uk

ROSS, Rachel
www.rachelross.co.uk

ROWE, Julian
www.julianrowe.co.uk

ROWLAND, Dawn
www.dawnrowland.com
www.dawnrowland.co.uk

ROWSELL, Joyce
www.joycerowsell.com

RUBIRA, Sue (Susan Debra)
www.suerubira.co.uk

RUDD, Bob
www.bobrudd.com

RUDDUCK, Ron
www.rbs.org.uk;
www.sculpturesales.fsnet.co.uk

RUDDY, Austin
c/o www.art-connections.org.uk

RUNAYKER, Irene
www.runayker.com

RUSHMER, Gordon
www.gordonrushmer.com

RUSPOLI, Francesco Mario Robert
www.francesco-ruspoli.com

RUSSELL, Caroline
www.russellsculptures.com

RUSSELL, Christine Gillian
www.art-christinerussell.co.uk

RUSSON, Bobbie Jane
axis, and Facebook 'Bobbie Russon's Art Page'

RUST, Graham Redgrave
www.grahamrust-murals.com

RUTHERFORD, Iain
www.iainrutherford.com

RUTT, Loraine
www.lorainerutt.net

RUTTER & BENNETT, Christopher & Evelyn
www.rbs.org.uk
rutterandbennett.com

RYDER, Brian Leonard
www.brianryder.org

RYDER, Susan
www.susanryder.co.uk

RYLAND, Christopher
www.christopherryland.co.uk

RYRIE, Jenny
www.jennyryrie.com

SALARZA-GRANT, Chito
www.chitosalarza.com

SALMON, Antonia
www.antoniasalmon.co.uk

SAMUELSON, Becky
www.beckysamuelsonfinearts.co.uk

SANDERS, Rosanne Diana
www.rosiesanders.com

SANDERS, Susan Mary
www.richardparkinson.co.uk

SANDERSLEY, Deborah
www.deborahsandersley.com

SANN, Tin Tin
www.tintinsann.com

SAUNDERS, Anthony James
www.militarygallery.com

SAVIC, Nikola Voin
www.artnet.com

SAVINE, Gerald
geraldsavine.co.uk

SAWYER, David James
http:davidsawyerrba.artweb.com

SCARLAND, John
www.scarland.co.uk

SCHARVERIEN, Pat
www.printmakers3.com

SCHETNEV, Leonid
www.cultinfo.ru/schetnev

SCHILDERMAN, Pamela
www.pamelaschilderman.com

SCHLEE, Nick
www.nickschlee.co.uk

SCHOFIELD, David Owain
www.david-schofield.com

SCHOFIELD, Sara Anne
www.saraschofield.co.uk

SCHUTT, Gisella
www.britishnaives.co.uk

SCOTT, Celia Maxwell
www.celiascott.com

SCOTT, Dafila Kathleen
www.dafilascott.co.uk

SCOTT, Jac
www.jacscott.com

SCOTT, Malcolm
YouTube (Painting Nature and The Bomb)/Google Malcolm Scott Artist

SCOTT, Richard Ridsdale
www.thesuffolkgroup.co.uk

SCOTT, Sally
www.sallyscottartist.co.uk

SCOTT BOLTON, Tim
timscottbolton.co.uk

SCOULLER, Glen
www.glenscouller.com

SCOULLER, Kim
www.kimscouller.com

SCOULLER, Lara
www.larascouller.com

SCULLARD, Susan Diane
www.suescullard.co.uk

SEAGER, Harry Abram
www.harryseagersculptor.com

SEAWARD, Tommy
www.tommyseaward.com

SEE-PAYNTON, Colin Frank
www.see-paynton.co.uk

SEELEY, Eric Charles
www.rasalumni.org

SEGELMAN, Frances Rosaline
www.segelman.com

SEGRAVE, Lydia
www.lydiasegrave.com

SEIJO, Armando
http://armandoseijo.blogspot.com/

SELIGMAN, Lincoln David Madron
www.lincolnseligman.co.uk

SEMMENS, Jennifer Anne
www.jennifersemmens.co.uk

SEMPLE, Kate
www.katesemplesculpture.co.uk

SENFT, Nadin
www.nadinsenft.co.uk

SENIOR, Bryan
www.thecivicsociety.org/gallery.html

SERGEANT, Emma
www.emmasergeant.com

SETCH, Terry
www.terrysetch.co.uk

SEWARD RELFE, Elizabeth Anne Harvey (Liz)
www.sewardart.co.uk

SEXTON, Anthony John
www.jsexton.eu

SHACKLETON, Keith Hope
sarahspackman.com

SHAKESPEARE, Francesca
www.francescashakespeare.com

SHARMA, Alli
www.allisharma.com

SHARP, Elizabeth
www.stantongraphics.co.uk

SHAW, Andrew Stuart Dunlap
www.oio.nu

SHAW, Philip Trevor
www.rebeccahossack.com
www.philshawonline.com

SHAW, Tim
www.timshawsculptor.com

SHEARD, Rosalind Elizabeth Allaway
www.londonart.co.uk

SHEDLEY JORDAN, Tessa
www.tshedleyjordan.co.uk

SHEINMAN, Sally
www.sallysheinma.co.uk
www.wmyy.co.uk

SHEPHERD, David
www.davidshepherd.org

SHEPHERD, Eve
www.eveshepherd.com

SHEPHERD, Gerald
www.ionistart.com
www.ionistart.co.uk
www.ionstart.me.uk
www.geraldshepherd.co.uk

SHERRATT, Matt
www.mattsherratt.com

SHIELDS, Christopher Ronald
www.chris-shields.com

SHIELDS, Mark
www.grosvenorgallery.com

SHIRLEY, Rachel
oil painting medic

SHIRLEY SMITH, Richard Francis
www.richardshirleysmith.co.uk

SHOA, Nahem
http://www.nahemshoa.co.uk

SHORT, Susan
www.susan-short.co.uk

SHOWELL, Billy
www.billyshowell.co.uk

SHURROCK, Christopher
www.rwa.org.uk
www.56groupwalesart.co.uk

SHUTT, David Richard Walter
www.shuttpaintings.com

SIDOLI, Dawn Frances
RWA & NEAC

SIEVEWRIGHT, Dionne Lesley
www.dionnesievewright.co.uk

SILVERTON, Norma
www.normasilverton.com

SIMMONDS, Jackie
www.jackiesimmond.co.uk

SIMPSON, Catherine Anne
www.cathysimpsonillustration.com

SIMPSON, Charles
www.csimpson-art.co.uk

SIMPSON, Leslie
www.britpaint.co.uk
www.britpaint.com

SIMS, Anna
www.annasims.co.uk

SIMS, Ronald Ivan
ronsimsart.com

SINGLETON, Alex
www.saatchionline.com/profile/2533
www.artgallery.co.uk/artist/alex_singleton-2

SINNOTT, Kevin
kevinsinnott.co.uk

SKINNER, John
www.johnskinner.me.uk

SLATER, Paul
www.paulslaterbugle.com

SLATTER, Alexander John
www.alexanderslatter.co.uk

SLATTERY, Nicola
www.nicolaslattery.com

SLOAN, Joseph
www.artvitae.com/sloan

SLOAN, Victor
www.victorsloan.com

SMITH, Barry Edward Jervis
www.barrysmithwork.co.uk

SMITH, C. Philip
philipsmithbookart.com

SMITH, Elizabeth Anne
www.elizabethsmith.co.uk

SMITH, Graham
www.gfsmith.net
SMITH, Jenny
www.jennysmith.org.uk
SMITH, Jonathan
www.jonathansmithart.co.uk
SMITH, Marion
marionsmithsculptor.co.uk
SMITH, Peter Macdonald
www.petermacdonaldsmith.co.uk
SMITH, Richard Michael
www.richardsmith.gallery.btinternet.co.uk
SMITH, Rita
www.ritasmith.org.uk
SMITH, Ronald F
gallery websites
SMITH, Simon
www.simonsmith.plus.com
SMITH POLYBLANK, Emily Elizabeth
www.emilysmithpolyblank.co.uk
SNOWDEN, Matthew
www.matthewsnowden.co.uk
SNOWDEN, Richard Connal
wwww.richardsnowden.co.uk
SOAN, Hazel Penelope
www.hazelsoan.com
SOFILAS, Mark Peter
www.marksofilasart.com
SONGHURST, Anne
www.annesonghurst.co.uk
SOPHIA-WHITE, Elizabeth Mary
elizabethsophia-white.com
SOREL, Agathe
www.agathesorel.co.uk
SORRELL, Julia
www.juliasorrell.ukartists.com
SORRELL, Richard
www.richardsorrell.co.uk
SOSNER, Robert
www.robertsosner.com
SOUTHEY, Marilyn Sylvia April
www.marilynsoutheyshowcase.com
SPACKMAN, Sarah
sarahspackman.com
SPANKIE, Will
www.willspankie.com
SPARE, Richard John
www.richardspare-kayspare.com
SPELLER, Michael Phillip
www.spellersculptures.com
SPENCER, Liam David
www.liamspencer.co.uk
SPENCER, Sarah
www.sarah_spencer.co.uk
SPOWERS, Antonia Caroline
antoniaspowers.co.uk
SPRAKES, John
johnsprakes.com
ST. JOHN ROSSE, Nicholas David
www.nstjohnrosse.com
STANDEN, Peter
www.reubensutton.com
STANFORD, Dee
www.deestanford.com
STANSFIELD, David Paul
www.davidstansfieldartist.co.uk
STATTER, David Harold
www.davidstatter.net
STAUVERS, Feliks
www.feliksstauvers.co.uk
STEPHENS, Roger Madoc
rs-sculpture.net
STEPHENSON, Christine Frances
www.paintingsofplants.com
STEPHENSON, Daphne Eulalia Beatrix Felicia
www.daphnestephenson.com
STEPHENSON, Jack
www.portraitsfromlife.co.uk
STEVENS, Chris
www.chrisstevens.co
STEVENTON, Brian Thomas
briansteventon.co.uk
STEWART, Alan
www.alanstewart.org.uk
STEWART, David
davidstewwwart.com
STEWART, Hannah
www.hannahstewartsculpture.co.uk
STILLMAN, John
www.johnstillman.co.uk
STJERNSWARD, Philippa
www.philippastjernsward.com
STOCK, Andrew Nicholas
www.andrewstock.co.uk
STOCKWELL, Susan
www.susanstockwell.co.uk
STOKER, Richard
www.richardstoker.co.uk; and facebook
STOKES, Jayne Emma
www.jaynestokes.com
STONE, Adam
adamstoneart.com
STONE, Pamela Ann
www.pamstone-artist.co.uk

STONES, Alan
www.alanstones.co.uk

STONES, Anthony
www.sculptor.co.nz

STONES, Leslie W.
www.lesliestones.co.uk

STRAFFORD, Judy
www.judystrafford.co.uk

STRANG, Michael
www.michaelstrang.com

STRANGELOVE, Nikolas Alexander
www.nikstrangelove.com

STREET, Clare
www.handengravers.co.uk/clarestreet
www.heraldic-arts.com/clarestreet

STREETHER, Lila Pauline
www.bsba.co.uk/lilastreether

STREVENS, Bridget Julia
www.bridgetstrevens.com

STRICKLAND, David Robert
www.stricklandsculpting.co.uk

STRINGER, Simon Kenneth
simonstringer.com

STUART, Henrietta Margaret Mercedes
www.heneriettastuart.com

STUART, Robert
www.robertstuartart.com

STUBBS, Michael
www.michaelstubbs.org

STUMMEL, Henning Friedrich
www.henningstummelarchitects.co.uk

STYLES, (Elizabeth) Caroline
www.carolinestyles.com

STYLIANOU, Lorraine
lorrainestylianou.com

SULLIVAN, Benjamin Christian
www.benjaminsullivan.com

SULLIVAN, Wendy
www.wendysullivanartist.com

SUMMERFIELD, Angela Mary
www.angelasummerfield.com

SUMMERFIELD, Janette
www.jls-artist.com

SUMMERS, Haidee-Jo
www.haideejo.com

SUMMERS, Rosalind
ispyart ; www.artistsandillustrators.co.uk/rosalidsummers

SUMNER, Emma Elizabeth
www.emmasumner.com

SUMNER, Josephine Louise
www.josephinesumner.com

SURRIDGE, Mark Steven
www.marksurridge.co.uk

SUTHERLAND, Dianne
www.diannesutherland.com

SUTTON, Jake
www.jakesuttonprints.com

SUTTON, Jilly Bazeley
www.jillysutton.com

SUTTON, Linda Olive
www.lindasutton.com

SWALE, Suzan Georgina
www.susanswale.co.uk
www.thelondongroup.com

SWAN, Ann
www.annswan.co.uk

SWAN, Martin
www.martinswan.com

SWANBOROUGH, Patsy & Janet
www.rosehillstudio.co.uk

SWEENEY, Kevin Michael
www.abstractsculptures.co.uk

SWINFEN EADY, Katherine Anne
www.katherinswinfeneady.com

SYKES, Barbara
www.barbarasykes.com

SYMINGTON, Christy Mary
www.christysymington.com

SYVERSON, Judith
www.MontanaProfessionalArtistsAssoc.com

TABER, Jacqueline
www.jacquelinetaber.co.uk

TAHERIAN, Christine
www.society-women-artists.org.uk
www.christinetaherian.com

TAIT, Wendy Ann
www.wendytait.com

TAMPLIN, Heather
www.heathertamplin.co.uk

TANDY, Bonita Marilyn
www.theinternetartshop.com

TANG, George
www.georgetang.com.hk

TARR, Michael
www.michaeltarr.co.uk

TAYLOR, Alan
www.supercovers.co.uk

TAYLOR, Alan
www.paintingstore.net

TAYLOR, Krista Louise
www.kristataylor.com

TAYLOR, Martin
www.martintaylor.org

TAYLOR, Michael Ryan
www.mrtaylor.co.uk

TAYLOR, Sean
www.softday.ie

TAYLOR, Wendy Ann
www.wendytaylorsculpture.co.uk

TENGBERG, Violet
www.violettengberg.com

TERRY, Karl Elliott
www.karlterry.co.uk

TESIC, Biljana
www.biljanatesic.com

TESKEY, Donald
donaldteskey.com

THOMAS, Chris
www.christhomas.info

THOMAS, Glynn David Laurie
www.glynnthomas.com

THOMAS, Lex
www.lexthomas.co.uk

THOMAS, Robin
wwww.robinthomasart.co.uk

THOMPSON, Kathleen M.
Flickr and Saatchi online

THOMSON, Diana
dianathomsonsculptor.co.uk

THORESBY, Valerie Cecilia
www.valeriethoresby.co.uk

THORN, Richard Charles
www.richardthornart.co.uk

THORNTON, Leslie
www.leslie-thornton.net

THORPE, Hilary
www.hilarythorpe.co.uk

THURGOOD, Gwyneth
www.micro-art.co.uk

THYNN, Alexander (7th Marquess of Bath)
www.lordbath.co.uk

TIDNAM, Nicholas Rye
www.tidnam.com

TIERNEY, Sadie
www.sadietierney.co.uk

TIHOV, Yanko
www.yankotihov.co.uk

TILLYER, William
www.jacobsongallery.com
www.tillyer.com

TIMMIS, Rosemarie
www.rosemarietimmis.co.uk

TINGLE, Michael
www.mike-tingle.com

TITCOMBE, Cedric Anthony
www.bigartweb.net

TODD, Anthony (Tony) John
www.tony-todd.co.uk

TODD, Daphne Jane
daphnetodd.com

TOLLEY, Elinor
elinortolleygallery.co.uk

TOLSTOY, Carolinda
www.carolinda-tolstoy.co.uk

TOOP, Bill
www.billtoop.com

TOVEY, David Charles Wilson
www.stivesart.info

TOWNSEND, Christopher Leonard
www.christophertownsend.co.uk

TOWNSEND, Storm Diana
by name 'Storm Townsend'

TOWSEY, Mary
www.marytowsey.com

TRANT, Carolyn
http://carolyntrantparvenu.blogspot.com

TRATT, Richard
www.richardtratt.co.uk

TRAVERS SMITH, Linda Mary
www.travsart.net

TRAYHORNE, Rex
www.rextrayhorne.co.uk

TREANOR, Frances
www.francestreanor.com

TREASURE, Paul
www.paultreasurepaintings.co.uk

TRELOAR, Janet Quintrell
Royal Watercolour Society Members page & Chelsea Art Society Members page

TREVENA, Shirley
shirleytrevena.com

TROITZKY, Nina
www.artel.org.uk

TUBB, Stephen David
www.tubbart.co.uk

TUCKER, Alistair
www.alistairtucker.com

TUDBALL, Ruthanne Amelia
www.ruthannetudball.com

TURNBULL, Andrew
www.akturnbull.com

TURNER, Anthony Hugh
www.anthonyturner.net

TURNER, Cyril B.
http://miniaturepaintings.mysite.orange.co.uk

TURNER, Jacquie
www.jacquieturner.com

TURNER, Roger
www.rogerturnerart.com

TURPIN, Louis
www.louisturpin.com

TUTE, George William
www.georgetute.com

TUTTIETT, Dora
www.dorat.yourprivatespace.com
www.axisartists.org.uk

TWEED, Jill
www.jilltweed.com

TYLER, Carol
www.caroltylerpaintings.com

UGLOW, Ruth
www.ruthuglow.com

UNDERWOOD, George
www.georgeunderwood.com

UNWIN, Dr. Bren
www.brenunwin.com

UPTON, Mark Lundy
www.markupton.com

URQUHART, Anne
www.nonsafety.co.uk/pauk.html

USHER, Jean
www.jeanusher.com

VAHEY, Lorna
www.neac.co.uk

VALENTINE-DAINES, Sherree E.
www.parklanefinearts.co.uk

VAN BIERVLIET, Emmie
www.emmievb.com

van ZWANENBERG, Miki
www.mikivanzwanenberg.co.uk

VANDER HEUL, Yvonne Christine
www.drawingwaterworks.net

VARELA, Armando
www.armandovarela.net

VEALE, Anthony McKenzie
www.anthonyveale.com

VELAZQUEZ, Fernando
www.fernandovelazquez.co.uk

VERITY, Charlotte Eleanor
www.charlotteverity.co.uk

VICARI, Andrew
www.andrew-vicari.com

VINCENT, John
www.johnvincent.co.uk

VISOCCHI, Michael
www.michaelvisocchi.com

VIZE, Susan Linda (Sue)
www.suevize.com

VOGEL, Paul Sidney
www.paulvogel.com

VON STROPP
www.outsiderart.co.uk

VON STUMM, Johannes
www.vonstumm.co.uk

VOROBYEV, Alexander
www.alexandervorobyev.com

WADDELL, Heather
www.hwlondonartandartistsguide.com

WADDINGTON, Geri
www.geriwaddington.com

WADE, Jonathan Armigel
www.jonathanwade.co.uk

WAGER, Sandy
http://artbysandywager.weebly.com

WAITE, Andrew John
www.andywaite.net

WAKEFIELD, Nicole
www.nicolewakefield.co.uk

WALDEN, Lynne
www.britishnaives.co.uk

WALDRON, Dylan Thomas
www.dylanwaldronartist.co.uk
www.dylanwaldron.co.uk

WALKER, Edward Donald
www.edwalkermarine.com

WALL, Jacy
www.jacywall.co.uk

WALLER, Jonathan Neil
www.geocites.com/jonathanwalleruk

WALTER, Stephen
www.stephenwalter.net

WALTERS, Juliet
www.julietwalters.co.uk

WALTERS, Kate
www.katewalters.co.uk

WALTON, John
www.therp.co.uk/rpartists/artistjohnwalton

WANG, Elizabeth
www.radiantlight.org.uk

WANLESS, Tom
www.t.b.wanless.btinternet.co.uk

WARD, Benjamin Gordon Tobias
www.tobyward.net

WARD, Claire Kathleen
www.claireward.net

WARD, Eric Thomas
www.ericward.org

WARD, Michael Lawrence
michaelwardstuff.com

WARNER, Zheni
www.zheni.co.uk

WARREN, Michael John
www.mikewarren.co.uk

WARREN, Vaughan
www.thepenzanceartgallery.com

WATERS, Jefferson
www.dot-art.co.uk

WATERS, Katherine Mary
www.corpusgallery.com

WATLING, Gareth
www.gwbirdpaintings.co.uk

WATSON, Alan
www.alanwatsonartist.com

WATSON, Thomas Jude (Tomas)
www.jillgeorgegallery.co.uk

WEALLEANS, Jon
www.jonwealleans.co.uk

WEBB, Barbara
www.camdenprintmakers.co.uk

WEBB, Sarah Ann
www.sarahwebb.com

WEBSTER, John Morrison
www.johnwebster.org.uk

WEIR, Linda Mary
www.lindaweir.com

WELCH, Rosemary Sarah
rosemarywelch.info

WELTON, Peter
www.peterwelton.com

WEST, Johe
see Chameleon Gallery

WEST, Keith
art-sacredprofane.com

WESTERGAARD, Hanne
hannewestergaard.co.uk

WESTON, David J.
www.artisticactivities.co.uk

WESTON, Neville Edward
www.nevilleweston.co.uk

WHALLEY, Stella
www.stellawhalley.com

WHEELER, Fiona
www.botanical-artist.com

WHISHAW, Anthony
www.anthonywishaw.com

WHITAKER, Vivien
www.vivienwhitakersculpture.com

WHITCOMBE, Susan Anne Clare
www.susiewhitcombe.com

WHITE, Amanda
amandawhite-contemporarynaiveart.com

WHITE, Donna
www.donnawhite.co.uk

WHITE, Helen Elizabeth
www.helen-white.co.uk

WHITE, Josephine Helen
josiewhiteart.co.uk

WHITE, Lucy Annette
www.cornwallhumanists.org.uk

WHITE, Philippa
www.chelseaartsociety.org.uk

WHITE, Robert Edward
www.robertwhite.info

WHITE, Victoria
www.victoriawhite.co.uk

WHITEHEAD, Steve
www.panterandhall.com

WHITING, Philip John
www.axisartists.org/artistid/9453

WHITMAN, Rosalind Marion
www.rosalindwhitman.com

WHITTAKER, Lucianna
www.luciannawhittaker.com

WHITTEN, Jonathan Philip
www.stkewpottery.co.uk

WHITTLE, Janet
www.janetwhittle.co.uk

WHITTON, Judi
www.watercolour.co.uk

WIGGINS, Toby
www.tobywiggins.co.uk

WILEMAN, Peter
peterwilemanartist.co.uk

WILKIE, Kim
www.kimwilkie.com

WILKINS, William Powell
williamwilkins.co.uk

WILLIAMS, Alex
www.alexwilliams.net

WILLIAMS, Brigitte
www.brigittewilliams.co.uk

WILLIAMS, Charles
www.unclecharles.co.uk

WILLIAMS, Fran
www.franwilliams1310.com

WILLIAMS, Glynn
www.glynnwilliams.co.uk

WILLIAMS, Graham Richard
www.grahamwilliams.co.uk

WILLIAMS, Jacqueline E. E.
www.jacquelinewilliams.co.uk

WILLIAMS, Jane
www.janewilliamsartist.co.uk

WILLIAMS, John
www.freeformphoto.co.uk

WILLIAMS, Martin
www.sculpturaldesignltd.co.uk

WILLIAMS, Nicholas Charles
www.nicholascharleswilliams.co.uk

WILLIAMS, Simon
www.swillustrations.com

WILLIAMS-ELLIS, Bronwyn Mary
www.handmade-tiles.co.uk

WILLIAMS-ELLIS, David Hugo Martyn
www.DWE.com

WILLIAMSON, Geraldine Mooring
www.britishnaives.co.uk

WILLIS, Lucy
www.lucywillis.com

WILLOW, Hannah
www.hannahwillow.com

WILSON, Arthur
www.arthurwilson.co.uk

WILSON, Conor John
www.conorwilson.co.uk

WILSON, David
www.david-wilson.net

WILSON, Douglas
www.highgateart.com

WILSOn, Peter Reid
peterwilson-artist.com

WILSON, Susan
www.susanwilsonartist.com

WILSON, Timothy Hugh
www.ashmolean.org/contact/staffpages/?pid=386

WILSON-DICK, Ian
ianwilson-dick.com

WINDSOR, Alan
www.alanwindsor.eu

WINKELMAN, Joseph William
www.winkelman.co.uk

WINNER, Tolleck
www.tolleck.com
www.tolleckwinner.com
www.artlandfoundation.org.uk

WINSTANLEY, Paul
www.paulwinstanley.com

WINTER, Faith
www.FaithWinter.co.uk

WISE, Gillian
www.gillianwise.com

WNEK-WEBB, Ewa
www.wnek-webb.co.uk

WOOD, Andy
www.andywoodgallery.com

WOOD, Christopher Malcolm Fayrer
www.christopherwood.co.uk

WOOD, Juliet Anne
www.julietwood.co.uk

WOOD, Nigel
www.nigel-wood.co.uk

WOOD, Sarah Diane
www.sarahwoodard.com

WOODFINE, Sarah
www.daniellearnaud.com

WOODMAN, Jim
www.jimwoodman.co.uk

WOODROW, Bill (William Robert)
www.billwoodrow.com

WOODRUFF, "Bronte" Elizabeth
www.h-art.org.uk

WOODS, Alistair
www.alistairwoods.co.uk

WOODS, Michael John
www.michaelwoods.me.uk

WOODWARD, Justine
Hilliard Society website

WOUDA, Marjan Petra
www.marjanwouda.co.uk

WRAITH, Edwin
www.edwinwraith.com

WRAITH, Robert
www.robbiewraith.com

WRAY, Peter
www.peterwrayre.com
www.handprintstudio.co.uk

WRIGHT, Anne
www.annewrightart.co.uk

WRIGHT, Bert
www.bertwright.com

WRIGHT, Jennifer May
www.wrightfineart.co.uk

WRIGHT, Lisa
lisawrightartist.co.uk

WRIGHT, Liz
www.wrightfineart.co.uk

WRIGHT, Roy
roywright.co.uk

WRIGHT, Steve
www.stevewrightart.com

WRIGHT, Stuart Pearson R.
www.stuartpearsonwright.com

YALLUP, Pat
www.patyallup.com

YATES, Alan
www.alanyates-sculpture.com

YOUNG, April
www.aprilyoung.co.uk

YOUNG, Emily
www.emilyyoung.com

YOUNG, Miriam
c/o www.chelseaartsclub.com

YOUNG, Pippa
www.pippayoung.co.uk

YOUNSON, Sydna
www.younson.com

ZACRON
www.zacron.com

ZENIN, Eugene
www.zenin.dk

ZESCHIN. Elizabeth Anne
www.zeschin.com

ZGORZALEK, Jerzy
www.artgallery-reklama.com.pl

ZWART, Valerie
www.valeriezwart.com

ZWOLINSKA-BRZESKI, Teresa
www.theartshopper.com

NOTES

GALLERIES AND WEBSITES

LONDON

A&D GALLERY
www.aanddgallery.com
ABBOTT & HOLDER
www.abbottandholder.co.uk
ACKERMANN & JOHNSON
www.artnet.com
ADAM GALLERY
www.adamgallery.com
ADRIAN SASSOON
www.adriansassoon.com
ADVANCED GRAPHICS LONDON
www.advancedgraphics.co.uk
AFFORDABLE ART FAIR
www.affordableartfair.com
AGNEW'S GALLERY
www.agnewsgallery.co.uk
AINSCOUGH CONTEMPORARY ART
www.acag.co.uk
THE AIR GALLERY
www.farishams.com
ALAN CRISTEA GALLERY
www.alancristea.com
ALBEMARLE GALLERY
www.albemarlegallery.com
ALBION
www.albion-gallery.com
ALISON JACQUES GALLERY
www.allisonjacquesgallery.com
A LITTLE BIT OF ART
www.alboart.co.uk
ALLA BULYANSKAYA GALLERY
www.allabulgallery.com
ALMA ENTERPRISES
www.almaenterprises.com
ANNELY JUDA FINE ART
www.annelyjudafineart.co.uk
ANTHONY REYNOLDS GALLERY
www.anthonyreynolds.com
APT
www.aptstudios.org
ARCHEUS
www.archeus.co.uk
ARCHITECTURAL ASSOCIATION
www.aaschool.ac.uk

ARTANDPHOTOGRAPHS LTD
www.artandphotographs.com
ARTANGEL
www.artangel.org.uk
ARTDOG LONDON
www.artdoglondon.co.uk
ART FIRST
www.artfirst.co.uk
ART LAB
www.artlab-gallery.co.uk
ART LONDON
www.artlondon.net
ART PILGRIM LONDON
www.artpilgrim.co.uk
ART SPACE GALLERY
www.artspacegallery.com
THE ARTS GALLERY
www.arts.ac.uk
THE ARTHOUSE GALLERY
www.lewishamarthouse.co.uk
THE ART MOVEMENT
www.art-movement.com
ASSOCIATES
www.associategallery.co.uk
ATLAS GALLERY
www.atlasgallery.com
ATRIUM GALLERY PRICEWATERHOUSECOOPERS
www.dicksonrussell.co.uk
AUGUST ART
www.augustart.co.uk
AUSTIN/DESMOND FINE ART
www.austindesmond.com
BANKSIDE GALLERY
www.banksidegallery.com
BARBARA BEHAN
www.barbarabehan.com
BARBICAN ART GALLERY & THE CURVE
www.barbican.org.uk/artgallery
BARRETT MARSDEN GALLERY
www.bmgallery.co.uk
BEACONSFIELD
www.beaconsfield.ltd.uk
BEARDSMORE GALLERY
www.beardsmoregallery.com
BEAUX ARTS
www.beauxartslondon.co.uk
BELGRAVE GALLERY
www.belgravegallery.com

BELGRAVIA GALLERY
www.belgraviagallery.com
BEN BROWN FINE ARTS
www.benbrownfinearts.com
BEN URI GALLERY
www.benuri.org.uk
BERNARD CHAUCHET CONTEMPORARY ART
www.chauchet.com
BERNARD JACOBSON GALLERY
www.jacobsongallery.com
BERTRAM
www.bertramenterprises.co.uk
BEVERLEY KNOWLES FINE ART
www.beverleyknowles.com
BHAVAN CENTRE ART GALLERY
www.bhavan.net
BISCHOFF/WEISS
www.bischoffweiss.com
BLOOMBERG SPACE
www.bloomberg.net
BOUNDARY GALLERY
www.boundarygallery.com
BOURLET FINE ART FRAME MAKERS
www.bourlet.co.uk
BROADBENT
www.broadbentgallery.com
BROWSE & DARBY
www.browseanddarby.co.uk
BYARD ART
www.byardart.co.uk
CAMDEN ARTS CENTRE
www.camdenartscentre.org
CAMPBELL'S ART GALLERY
www.campbellsart.co.uk
CAPITAL CULTURE
www.capitalculture.eu
CAROLINE HODGKINSON
www.hodgkinsonart.com
CAROLINE WISEMAN
www.carolinewiseman.com
CATHARINE MILLER
www.catherinemiller.com
CATHERINE PORTER FINE ART
www.catherineportergallery.com
THE CATTO GALLERY
www.catto.co.uk
CELIA PURCELL CONTEMPORARY
www.celiapurcell.com

THE CHAMBERS GALLERY
www.thechambersgallery.com
CHARLOTTE STREET GALLERY
www.r-h-g.co.uk
CHELSEA SPACE
www.chelsea.arts.ac.uk
CHISENHALE GALLERY
www.chisenhale.org.uk
CITY & GUILDS OF LONDON ART SCHOOL
www.cityandguildsartschool.ac.uk
CLAPHAM ART GALLERY
www.claphamartgallery.com
COLEMAN PROJECT SPACE
www.colemanprojects.org.uk
COLLYER BRISTOW GALLERY
www.collyerbristow.com
COLOMB ART GALLERY
www.colomb-art.co.uk
CONNAUGHT BROWN
www.connaughtbrown.co.uk
CONTEMPORARY APPLIED ARTS
www.caa.org.uk
CONTEMPORARY ART SOCIETY
www.contempart.org.uk
CORVI-MORA
www.corvi-mora.com
COSA
www.cosalondon.com
COUNTER
www.countergallery.com
THE COURT GALLERY
www.courtgallery.com
CRANE KALMAN GALLERY LTD
www.cranekalman.com
CREATIVE PICTURE FRAMING
www.creativepictureframing.co.uk
CRICKET FINE ART
www.cricketfineart.co.uk
CROSS GALLERY
www.crossgallerycross.blogspot.com
CUBITT GALLERY
www.cubittartists.org.uk
CURWEN & NEW ACADEMY GALLERY
www.curwengallery.com
THE CYNTHIA CORBETT GALLERY
www.thecynthiacorbettgallery.com
DAIWA FOUNDATION JAPAN HOUSE
www.dajf.org.uk

DANIEL KATZ LTD.
www.katz.co.uk
DANIELLE ARNAUD
www.daniellearnaud.com
DANUSHA FINE ARTS
www.danusha-fine-arts.co.uk
DEBUT ART LTD & THE CONINGSBY GALLERY
www.coningsbygallery.com / www.debutart.com
DESIGN MUSEUM
www.designmuseum.org
DICKSMITH GALLERY
www.dicksmithgallery.co.uk
DOMINIC GUERRINI FINE ART
www.dominicguerrini.co.uk
DOMOBAAL
www.domobaal.com
DOROTHÉE SCHMID ART CONSULTING
www.dorotheeschmid.com
THE DRAWING GALLERY
www.thedrawinggallery.com
THE DRAWING ROOM
www.drawingroom.org.uk
DULWICH PICTURE GALLERY
www.dulwichpicturegallery.org.uk
DUNCAN R MILLER FINE ART
www.duncanmiller.com
DURLACHER FINE ART
www.durlacherfineart.com
THE EAGLE GALLERY
www.emmahilleagle.com
EAST WEST GALLERY
www.eastwestgallery.co.uk
THE ECONOMIST PLAZA
www.contempart.org.uk
ELEVEN
www.elevenfineart.com
ENGLAND & CO.
www.englandgallery.com
ENID LAWSON GALLERY
www.enidlawsongallery.co.uk
ESTORICK COLLECTION OF MODERN ITALIAN ART
www.estorickcollection.com
FAGGIONATO FINE ARTS
www.faggionato.com
FAIRFAX GALLERY
www.fairfaxgallery.com
FIELDGATE GALLERY
www.fieldgategallery.com

FINE ART COMMISSIONS
www.fineartcommissions.com
FINE ART CONSULTANCY
www.fineartconsultancy.com
FIUMANO FINE ART
www.fiumanofineart.com
FLACA
www.flaca.co.uk
THE FLEMING COLLECTION
www.flemingcollection.co.uk
FLOWERS CENTRAL
www.flowerseast.com
FLOWERS EAST / FLOWERS GRAPHIC
www.flowerseast.com
FLYING COLOURS GALLERY
www.flyingcoloursgallery.com
FOSS FINE ART
www.fossfineart.com
FOURWALLS
www.four-walls.co.uk
FRANCIS KYLE GALLERY
www.franciskylegallery.com
FRED
www.fred-london.com
THE FRENCH ART STUDIO
www.thefrenchartstudio.com
FRITH STREET GALLERY
www.frithstreetgallery.com
FROST & REED
www.frostandreed.com
THE FUTURE TENSE
www.thefuturetense.net
GAGLIARDI GALLERY
www.gagliardi.org
GALERIE BESSON
www.galeriebesson.co.uk
GALERIE ENVIE D'ART
www.enviedart.com
THE GALLERIA
www.safinearts.com
THE GALLERY
www.lomaart.co.uk
GALLERY 5
www.natashakumar.co.uk
GALLERY 19
www.gallery19.com
GALLERY 286
www.gallery286.com

GALLERY 320
www.gallery320.co.uk
GALLERY K
www.gallery-k.co.uk
GALLERY PANGOLIN
www.gallery-pangolin.com
GALLERY RICHMOND
www.galleryrichmond.com
GASWORKS
www.gasworks.org.uk
GIMPEL FILS
www.gimpelfils.com
GRAPEVINE IN LONDON III
www.grapevinegallery.co.uk
GREENGRASSI
www.greengrassi.com
GREENWICH PRINTMAKERS GALLERY
www.greenwich-printmakers.org.uk
GROSVENOR GALLERY
www.grosvenorgallery.com
GUILDHALL ART GALLERY
www.guildhall-art-gallery.org.uk
GX GALLERY
www.gxgallery.com
HACKELBURY FINE ART LTD
www.hackelbury.co.uk
HACKNEY FORGE
www.hackneyforge.com
HALES GALLERY
www.halesgallery.com
HAMILTONS GALLERY
www.hamiltonsgallery.com
HANINA GALLERY
www.haninafinearts.com
HARLEQUIN GALLERY
www.studio-pots.com
HART GALLERY LONDON
www.hartgallery.co.uk
HAUNCH OF VENISON LONDON
www.haunchofvenison.com
HAUSER & WIRTH GALLERY LONDON
www.hauserwirth.com
HAY HILL GALLERY
www.hayhill.com/www.sirin.co.uk
HAYWARD GALLERY
www.hayward.org.uk
HENRY SOTHERAN LTD.
www.sotherans.co.uk/prints

HERALD STREET
www.heraldst.com
HICKS GALLERY
www.hicksgallery.co.uk
HIGHGATE FINE ART
www.oddyart.com
HIGHGATE GALLERY
www.hlsi.net
HOLLYBUSH GARDENS
www.hollybushgardens.co.uk
HOOPERS GALLERY
www.hoopersgallery.co.uk
HORSE HOSPITAL
www.thehorsehospital.com
HOTEL
www.generalhotel.org
HOULDSWORTH
www.houldsworth.co.uk
IAP FINE ART
www.iapfineart.com
IBID PROJECTS
www.ibidprojects.com
ICA (INSTITUTE OF CONTEMPORARY ARTS)
www.ica.org.uk
I-CABIN
www.i-cabin.co.uk
IMPERIAL WAR MUSEUM
www.iwm.org.uk
INGO FINCKE GALLERY
www.ingofincke.com
IRAN HERITAGE FOUNDATION
www.iranheritage.org
JAGGEDART
www.jaggedart.com
JAMES FREEMAN GALLERY
www.jamesfreemangallery.com
JAMES HYMAN FINE ART
www.jameshymanfineart.com
JAMES KINMONT FINE ART
www.kfineart.co.uk
JEREMY HAMMICK
www.jeremyhammick.co.uk
JERWOOD SPACE
www.wimbledonarts.ac.uk
JILL GEORGE GALLERY
www.jillgeorgegallery.co.uk
JOANNA BIRD POTTERY
www.joannabirdpottery.com

JOHN IDDON FINE ART
www.johniddonfineart.com
JOHN MARTIN LONDON
www.jmlondon.com
JOHN MITCHELL FINE PAINTINGS
www.johnmitchell.net
JOHNNY VAN HAEFTEN GALLERY
www.johnnyvanhaeften.com
JONATHAN CLARK
www.jonathanclarkfineart.com
JONATHAN COOPER
www.jonathancooper.co.uk
THE JONATHAN WYLDER GALLERY
www.jonathanwylder.com
KATE MACGARRY
www.katemacgarry.com
KINGS ROAD GALLERY
www.kingsroadartgallery.com
THE KOWALSKY GALLERY at DACS
www.dacs.org.uk
LA GALERIE LONDON
www.lagalerielondon.co.uk
LAURA BARTLETT GALLERY
www.laurabartlettgallery.com
LENA BOYLE FINE ART
www.lenaboyle.com
LINDA BLACKSTONE GALLERY
www.lindablackstone.com
LIMEHOUSE GALLERY
www.limehousegallery.co.uk
LISSON GALLERY
www.lisson.co.uk
LLEWELYN ALEXANDER GALLERY
www.LlewelynAlexander.com
LONDON GALLERY WEST
www.wmin.ac.uk
LONDON PRINTWORKS TRUST
www.londonprintworks.com
LONDONPRINTSTUDIO GALLERY
www.londonprintstudio.org.uk
LONG & RYLE
www.longandryle.com
LOUIS T. BLOUIN INSTITUTE
www.ltbfoundation.org
LOUNGE
www.lounge-gallery.com
LUCY B CAMPBELL FINE ART
www.lucybcampbell.com

McHARDY COOMBS SCULPTURE GALLERY
www.mchardy-sculpture.com
MACLEAN FINE ART
www.macleanfineart.com
THE MALL GALLERIES
www.mallgalleries.org.uk
MANYA IGEL FINE ARTS
www.manyaigelfinearts.com
MARK BARROW FINE ART
www.markbarrowfineart.co.uk
MARK GALLERY
www.markgallery.co.uk
MARK JASON GALLERY
www.markjasongallery.com
MARLBOROUGH FINE ART
www.marlboroughfineart.com
MARTYN GREGORY
www.martyngregory.com
MATHAF GALLERY
www.mathafgallery.com
MATTHEW BOWN GALLERY
www.matthewbown.com
MATT'S GALLERY
www.mattsgallery.org
MAUGER MODERN ART
www.maugermodern.com
MAUREEN PALEY
www.maureenpaley.com
MAX WIGRAM GALLERY
www.maxwigram.com
THE MAYOR GALLERY
www.artnet.com/mayor.html
MEDICI GALLERY
www.medicigallery.com
MENIER CHOCOLATE FACTORY
www.edgarmodern.com
MERRIFIELD STUDIOS
www.tommerrifield.co.uk
MESSUM'S
www.messums.com
MICHAEL HOPPEN GALLERY
www.michaelhoppengallery.com
THE MILLINERY WORKS
www.millineryworks.co.uk
MODERN ART
www.stuartshavemodernart.com
MODERN BRITISH ARTISTS
www.modernbritishartists.co.uk

MOONBOW JAKES GALLERY
www.axisweb.org.uk/artist/jonathanpolkest

MORLEY GALLERY
www.morleycollege.ac.uk

MOT
www.motinternational.org

MURPHY MACHIN
www.murphymachinart.net

NAHWHAL INUIT ART GALLERY
www.narwhalgallery.com www.niaef.com

THE NATIONAL GALLERY
www.nationalgallery.org.uk

93
www.ninetythree.co.uk

THE NOBLE SAGE ART GALLERY
www.thenoblesage.com

NOLIA'S GALLERY
www.fotolog.com/alexion555/

NORTHCOTE GALLERY
www.northcotegallery.com

NOVAS GALLERY, CAMDEN
www.novas.org

THE NUNNERY
www.nunnerygallery.com

OCTOBER GALLERY
www.octobergallery.co.uk

OLIVER CONTEMPORARY
www.oliverart.co.uk

108 ROSEBERY AVE
www.windowsoneoeight.com

OPERA GALLERY LONDON
www.operagallery.com

OSBORNE SAMUEL
www.osbornesamuel.com

OSBORNE STUDIO GALLERY
www.osg.uk.com

PAINTBOX FINE ART
www.paintboxfineart.com

PANGOLIN LONDON
www.pangolinlondon.com

PANTER & HALL
www.panterandhall.com

PARADE
www.maureenpaley.com

PARASOL UNIT FOUNDATION FOR CONTEMPORARY ART
www.parasol-unit.org

PATRICK HEIDE CONTEMPORARY ART
www.patrickheide.com

PAUL STOLPER
www.paulstolper.com
PEACE AND COLOUR GALLERY
www.peaceandcolour.info
PEER
www.peeruk.org
PESCALI & SPROVIERI
www.sprovieri.com
PETER NAHUM AT THE LEICESTER GALLERIES
www.leicestergalleries.com
PHOTOFUSION
www.photofusion.org
THE PHOTOGRAPHERS' GALLERY
www.photonet.org.uk
PIANO NOBILE FINE PAINTINGS
www.piano-nobile.com
PIERS FEETHAM GALLERY
www.piersfeethamgallery.com
PLATFORM FOR ART
www.tfl.gov.uk/pfa
PLUS ONE GALLERY
www.plusonegallery.com
POLLOCK FINE ART
www.pollockfineart.com
POND GALLERY
www.pondgallery.co.uk
PORTAL PAINTERS
www.portalpainters.co.uk
PORTLAND GALLERY
www.portlandgallery.com
POUSSIN
www.poussin-gallery.com
PURDY HICKS GALLERY
www.purdyhicks.com
PYMS GALLERY
www.pymsgallery.com
QUANTUM CONTEMPORARY ART
www.quantumart.co.uk
THE RAILINGS GALLERY
www.railings-gallery.com
RAINBIRD FINE ART
www.rainbirdfineart.com
RAQUELLE AZRAN VIETNAMESE FINE ART
www.artnet.com/razran.html
RAW SPACE
www.wadadaw.com
REBECCA HOSSACK GALLERY
www.r-h-g.co.uk

REDFERN GALLERY
www.redfern-gallery.com
RICHARD NAGY
www.richardnagy.com
RIFLEMAKER
www.riflemaker.org
RITTER/ZAMET
www.ritterzamet.com
ROCKET
www.rocketgallery.com
ROKEBY
www.rokebygallery.com
ROLLO CONTEMPORARY ART
www.rolloart.com
ROMAN BLACK GALLERY
www.romanblackgallery.com
RONA GALLERY
www.ronagallery.com
ROSSI & ROSSI Ltd
www.rossirossi.com
THE ROWLEY GALLERY
www.rowleygallery.co.uk
ROYAL ACADEMY OF ARTS
www.royalacademy.org
ROYAL OVERSEAS LEAGUE
www.roslarts.co.uk
THE RUSSELL GALLERY
www.russell-gallery.com
SAATCHI GALLERY
www.saatchi-gallery.com
SADIE COLES HQ
www.sadiecoles.com
ROBERT SANDELSON
www.robertsandelson.com
SARAH MYERSCOUGH FINE ART
www.sarahmyerscough.com
SARTORIAL CONTEMPORARY ART
www.sartorialart.com
SE1 GALLERY
www.se1gallery.com
SERPENTINE GALLERY
www.serpentinegallery.org
SESAME
www.sesameart.com
SHERIDAN RUSSELL GALLERY
www.sheridanrussellgallery.com
SIGNAL GALLERY
www.signalgallery.com

SIMON LEE
www.simonleegallery.com
SKYLARK GALLERIES: Artist-Run
www.skylarkgallery.com
SOUTHBANK PRINTMAKERS
www.southbank-printmakers.com
SOUTH LONDON GALLERY
www.southlondongallery.org
SOVIET CARPET & ART GALLERIES
www.russian-art.co.uk
SPACE
www.spacestudios.org.uk
STANDPOINT GALLERY
www.standpointlondon.co.uk
STARK GALLERY
www.starkgallery.com
STEPHEN FRIEDMAN GALLERY
www.stephenfriedman.com
STERN PISSARRO GALLERY
www.pissarro.net
STOPPENBACH & DELESTRE
www.artfrancais.com
THE STRANG PRINT ROOM
www.art.museum.ucl.ac.uk
THE STUDIO
www.clareinskip.com
THE STUDIO GLASS GALLERY
www.studioglass.co.uk
STUDIO 1.1
www.studio1-1.co.uk
STUDIO VOLTAIRE
www.studiovoltaire.org
SUTTON LANE
www.suttonlane.com
SW1 GALLERY
www.sw1gallery.co.uk
TADEMA GALLERY
www.tademagallery.com
TAG FINE ARTS
www.tagfinearts.com
TANYA BAXTER CONTEMPORARY
www.kingsroadartgallery.com
TATE BRITAIN
www.tate.org.uk
TATE MODERN
www.tate.org.uk
THACKERAY GALLERY
www.thackeraygallery.com

THEOBALD JENNINGS
www.theobaldjennings.com
THOMAS DANE GALLERY
www.thomasdane.com
THOMPSON'S GALLERY
www.thompsonsgallery.co.uk
TIMOTHY TAYLOR GALLERY
www.timothytaylorgallery.com
TONI HEATH GALLERY
www.toniheath.com
TRACEY McNEE FINE ART
www.traceymcnee.com
TRANSITION GALLERY
www.transitiongallery.co.uk
TRICYCLE GALLERY
www.tricycle.co.uk
TURF
www.stephaniecarltonsmith.co.uk
20/21 BRITISH ART FAIR
www.britishartfair.co.uk
UNION
www.union-gallery.com
VICTOR ARWAS GALLERY
www.victorarwas.com
VICTORIA AND ALBERT MUSEUM
www.vam.ac.uk
VICTORIA MIRO GALLERY
www.victoria-miro.com
VILMA GOLD GALLERY
www.vilmagold.com
VINESPACE
www.vinespace.net
WADDINGTON GALLERIES
www.waddington-galleries.com
THE WALK
www.walkgallery.com
WATERHOUSE & DODD
www.modbritart.com
WEBBS ROAD FINE ART
www.thewebbsgallery.co.uk
WHITE CUBE
www.whitecube.com
WHITECHAPEL
www.whitechapel.org
WHITECHAPEL PROJECT SPACE
www.whitechapelprojectspace.org.uk
WHITECROSS GALLERY
www.whitecrossgallery.com

WHITE SPACE GALLERY
www.whitespacegallery.co.uk
WHITEWALL PARTNERS
www.whitewallpartners.com
WHITFORD FINE ART
www.whitfordfineart.com
W H PATTERSON
www.whpatterson.com
WILKINSON GALLERY
www.wilkinsongallery.com
WILL'S ART WAREHOUSE
www.wills-art.com
WIMBLEDON ART STUDIOS
www.wimbledonartstudios.co.uk
WIMBLEDON COLLEGE OF ART
www.wimbledon.arts.ac.uk
WOLSELEY FINE ARTS / MVAC
www.wolseleyfinearts.com
WOOLFF GALLERY
www.woolffgallery.co.uk
ZEBRA GALLERY
www.zebragallery.co.uk
ZEST GALLERY
www.zestgallery.com

PROVINCIAL GALLERIES-ENGLAND

BATH

ADAM GALLERY
www.adamgallery.com

ANTHONY HEPWORTH FINE ART DEALERS LTD
www.anthonyhepworth.com

BATH CONTEMPORARY
www.bathcontemporary.com

BEAUX ARTS BATH
www.beauxartsbath.co.uk

BO LEE GALLERY
www.bo-lee.co.uk

EDGAR MODERN INTERNATIONAL ART
www.edgarmodern.com

GALLERY NINE
www.gallerynine.co.uk

HILTON FINE ART
www.hiltonfineart.com

MAUGER MODERN ART
www.maugermodern.com

ONE TWO FIVE GALLERY
www.carolewaller.co.uk

QUEST GALLERY
www.questgallery.co.uk

ROSTRA & ROOKSMOOR GALLERY
www.rostragallery.co.uk

VICTORIA ART GALLERY
www.victoriagal.org.uk

THE WHITE ROOM GALLERY
www.thewhiteroomgallery.com

BEDFORDSHIRE

BEDFORD STREET GALLERY
www.bedfordstreetgallery.com

EAGLE GALLERY
www.eaglegalleryartists.co.uk

BERKSHIRE

THE BARKER GALLERY
www.thebarkergallery.com

THE BLUE DUCK GALLERY
www.theblueduckgallery.co.uk

THE CONTEMPORARY FINE ART GALLERY ETON
www.cfag.co.uk

JAMES GOURLAY GALLERY
www.jamesgourlaygallery.com

THE LEMON GROVE GALLERY
www.thelemongrovegallery.com
MODERN ARTISTS GALLERY
www.modernartistsgallery.com
STANLEY SPENCER GALLERY
www.stanleyspencer.org.uk

BIRMINGHAM

IKON GALLERY
www.ikon-gallery.co.uk
INTERNATIONAL PROJECT SPACE
www.internationalprojectspace.org
MAC
www.macarts.co.uk

BRISTOL

ALEXANDER GALLERY
www.alexander-gallery.co.uk
ARCHITECTURE CENTRE, BRISTOL
www.architecturecentre.co.uk
ARNOLFINI
www.arnolfini.org.uk
INNOCENT FINE ART LTD.
www.innocentfineart.co.uk
LIME TREE GALLERY
www.limetreegallery.com
ROYAL WEST OF ENGLAND ACADEMY
www.rwa.org.uk
TRANSITOR
www.transitor.uk.com

BUCKINGHAMSHIRE

CARINA HASLAM ART
www.carinahaslamart.com
DADBROOK GALLERY
www.dadbrookgallery.co.uk
RED GALLERY
www.redgallery.co.uk

CAMBRIDGESHIRE

BYARD ART
www.byardart.co.uk
CAMBRIDGE BOOK & PRINT GALLERY
www.cambridgeprints.com
EE FINE ART
www.eefineart.com

KETTLE'S YARD GALLERY
www.kettlesyard.co.uk
WYSING ARTS CENTRE
www.wysingartscentre.org

CHESHIRE

CLARK ART LTD.
www.clark-art.co.uk
THE WATERGATE STREET GALLERY
www.watergatestreetgallery.co.uk

CORNWALL

BESIDE THE WAVE
www.beside-the-wave.co.uk
BEYOND THE SEA
www.beyondthesea.co.uk
CORNWALL CRAFTS ASSOCIATION
www.cornwallcrafts.co.uk
THE DRANG GALLERY
www.thedranggallery.com
KESTLE BARTON
www.kestlebarton.co.uk
MID CORNWALL GALLERIES
www.midcornwallgalleries.co.uk
THE NET LOFT GALLERY
www.cornwall-art.co.uk
OPEN SPACE GALLERIES
www.openspacegalleries.com
OUT OF PLACE GALLERY
www.outofplaceart.co.uk
PADSTOW CONTEMPORARY GALLERY
www.padstowgallery.com
PADSTOW STUDIO
www.padstowstudio.co.uk
PENHAVEN GALLERY
www.penhavengallery.co.uk
THE SALT GALLERY
www.thesaltgallery.co.uk
SCHOOLHOUSE GALLERY, MORVAH
www.morvah.com
THE SQUARE GALLERY
www.thesquaregallery.co.uk
TREGONY GALLERY
www.tregonygallery.co.uk
TRELISSICK GARDEN
www.paulvanstone.co.uk
WATERSIDE GALLERY
www.watersidegallery.co.uk

YEW TREE GALLERY
www.yewtreegallery.com

***Newlyn*:**

BADCOCK'S GALLERIES LTD.
www.badcocksgallery.co.uk

NEWLYN ART GALLERY
www.newlynartgallery.co.uk

***Penzance*:**

THE ALVERTON GALLERY
www.thealvertongallery.co.uk

CORNWALL CONTEMPORARY
www.cornwallcontemporary.com

THE EXCHANGE
www.newlynartgallery.co.uk

GLASS HOUSE GALLERY
www.glasshousegallery.co.uk

LIGHTHOUSE GALLERY
www.lighthouse-gallery.com

NEWLYN ART GALLERY
www.newlynartgallery.co.uk

NEWLYN SCHOOL GALLERY
www.newlynschoolgallery.com

PENLEE HOUSE GALLERY & MUSEUM
www.penleehouse.org.uk

PZ GALLERY
www.pzgallery.com

RAINYDAY GALLERY
www.rainydaygallery.co.uk

***Scilly Isles*:**

GALLERY TRESCO
www.gallerytresco.co.uk

***St.Ives*:**

ART SPACE GALLERY
www.artspace-cornwall.co.uk

BELGRAVE GALLERY ST. IVES
www.belgravegallery.com

MILLENNIUM
www.millenniumgallery.co.uk

NEW CRAFTSMAN GALLERY
www.newcraftsmanstives.co.uk

THE PILCHARD PALACE GALLERY
www.pilchardpalace.co.uk

PORTHMINSTER GALLERY
www.porthminstergallery.co.uk

ST IVES SOCIETY OF ARTISTS
www.stisa.co.uk
TATE ST IVES
www.tate.org.uk/stives
THE WILLS LANE GALLERY
www.willslanegallery.co.uk

***Truro*:**
GLASS HOUSE GALLERY
www.glasshousegallery.co.uk
LANDER GALLERY
www.landergallery.co.uk
LEMON STREET GALLERY
www.lemonstreetgallery.co.uk
LIGHTHOUSE GALLERY
www.lighthouse-gallery.com

CUMBRIA

ABBOTT HALL ART GALLERY
www.abbotthall.org.uk
BECKSTONES ART GALLERY
www.beckstonesartgallery.co.uk
THE BEETROOT TREE
www.thebeetroottree
CASTLEGATE HOUSE GALLERY
www.castlegatehouse.co.uk
HIGHHEAD SCULPTURE VALLEY
www.highheadsculpturevalley.co.uk

DERBY

THE HAYLOFT GALLERY
www.thehayloftgallery.co.uk

DEVON

AINSCOUGH CONTEMPORARY ART
www.acag.co.uk
THE ART ROOM
www.theartroomtopsham.co.uk
THE BURTON ART GALLERY & MUSEUM
www.burtonartgallery.co.uk
COOMBE GALLERY
www.coombegallery.com
DELAMORE GALLERY & SCULPTURE GARDEN
www.delamoregallery.com
THE DEVON GUILD OF CRAFTSMEN
www.crafts.org.uk

HYBRID GALLERY
www.hybrid-devon.co.uk
MARINE HOUSE AT BEER
www.marinehouseatbeer.co.uk
THE MARLE GALLERY
www.themarlegallery.co.uk
METAL PIG FORGE
www.metalpigforge.co.uk
PETE CASWELL CONTEMPORARY GALLERY
www.petecaswell.co.uk
SPACEX
www.spacex.co.uk
STEAM GALLERY AT BEER
www.steamgallery.co.uk
WHITE SPACE ART
www.whitespaceart.com

Exeter:

GALLERY 36
www.gallery36.co.uk
GLOSS GALLERY
www.glossgallery.co.uk
POLKA DOT CONTEMPORARY GALLERY
www.polkadotgallery.com
SOUTHGATE GALLERY
www.southgategallery.co.uk

DORSET

ALPHA HOUSE GALLERY
www.alpha-house.co.uk
THE ART STABLE
www.theartstable.co.uk
THE ARTHOUSE GALLERY
www.thearthousegallery.co.uk
ARTWAVE WEST
www.artwavewest.com
PIERREPOINT GALLERY
www.pierrepointgallery.co.uk
SHERBORNE HOUSE
www.sherbornehouse.org.uk
SLADERS YARD
www.sladersyard.co.uk

EAST SUSSEX

BOXBIRD GALLERY
www.boxbird.co.uk
CHALK GALLERY
www.chalkgallery.co.uk

CAMERON CONTEMPORARY ART
www.cameroncontemporaryart.com
DE LA WARR PAVILION
www.dlwp.com
FOUR SQUARE FINE ARTS
www.foursquarearts.co.uk
NICHOLAS BOWLBY
www.nicholasbowlby.co.uk
SARAH O'KANE CONTEMPORARY FINE ART
www.stannesgalleries.com
THEBES GALLERY
www.emmamason.co.uk

ESSEX

CHAPPEL GALLERIES
www.chappelgalleries.co.uk
FIRSTSITE@THE MINORIES ART GALLERY
www.firstsite.uk.net
GEEDON GALLERY
www.geedongallery.co.uk
HEAD STREET GALLERY
www.headstreetgallery.co.uk
i2 ART
www.i2artgallery.com
NORTH HOUSE GALLERY
www.northhousegallery.co.uk

GLOUCESTERSHIRE

THE ART GALLERY
www.artgallery.co.uk
ASTLEY HOUSE FINE ART
www.art-uk.com
CAMPDEN GALLERY
www.campdengallery.co.uk
CELIA LENDIS CONTEMPORARY
www.celialendis.com
GALLERY PANGOLIN
www.gallery-pangolin.com
HADFIELD FINE ART
www.hadfieldfineart.co.uk
HUGH ANGLE GALLERY
www.hughanglegallery.com
JOHN DAVIES GALLERY
www.johndaviesgallery.com
JONATHAN POOLE
www.jonathanpoole.co.uk
MARTIN'S GALLERY
www.martinsgallery.co.uk

RUSKIN MILL GALLERY
www.joydeberker.com
WETPAINT GALLERY
www.contemporary-art-holdings.co.uk
THE WONDERWALL GALLERY
www.thewonderwallgallery.com

HAMPSHIRE

ASPEX
www.aspex.org.uk
BELL FINE ART
www.bellfineart.co.uk
COURCOUX & COURCOUX CONTEMPORARY ART Ltd.
www.courcoux.co.uk
JANE FUEST GALLERY
www.janefuestgallery.co.uk
JENNA BURLINGHAM FINE ART
www.jennaburlingham.com
JOHN HANSARD GALLERY
www.hansardgallery.org.uk
LACEWING FINE ART GALLERY & STUDIO
www.lacewing.co.uk
MAE GALLERY
www.maegallery.com
THE MINSTER GALLERY
www.minstergallery.com
NEVILLE CONTEMPORARY ART
www.artneville.com
ON LINE GALLERY
www.online-gallery.co.uk
THE SELBORNE GALLERY
www.hampshireartistscooperative.com
SMART GALLERY
www.smartgallery.org.uk

HARROGATE

GODFREY & WATT
www.godfreyandwatt.co.uk
McTAGUE OF HARROGATE
www.mctague.co.uk
108 FINE ART
www.108fineart.com
SMART GALLERY
www.smartgallery.co.uk

HEREFORDSHIRE

GALLERY 54
www.gallery-54.com

MONNOW VALLEY ARTS CENTRE
www.monnowvalleyarts.org
WILTON CASTLE
www.beckfordfineart.co.uk
WOLSELEY FINE ARTS
www.wolseleyfinearts.com

HERTFORDSHIRE

ARTSHED – WARE Ltd
www.artshed-ware.com
COURTYARD ARTS
www.courtyardarts.org.uk
LINDA BLACKSTONE
www.lindablackstone.com

KENT

CASTLE ARTS
www.castlearts.co.uk
FRANCIS ILES GALLERY
www.francis-iles.com
LIBERTY GALLERY
www.liberty-gallery.com
LILFORD GALLERY
www.lilfordgallery.com
REDLEAF GALLERY
www.redleafgallery.com
STRANGE CARGO
www.strangecargo.org.uk

LEEDS

HENRY MOORE INSTITUTE
www.henry-moore-fdn.co.uk

LINCOLNSHIRE

WOODBINE CONTEMPORARY ARTS
www.woodbinecontemporaryarts.co.uk

LIVERPOOL

BLUECOAT GALLERY
www.bluecoatartscentre.com
TATE LIVERPOOL
www.tate.org.uk/liverpool

MANCHESTER

CASTLEFIELD GALLERY
www.castlefieldgallery.co.uk

CORNERHOUSE
www.cornerhouse.org
MANCHESTER ART GALLERY
www.manchestergalleries.org
RICHARD GOODALL GALLERY
www.richardgoodallgallery.com

MERSEYSIDE

LADY LEVER ART GALLERY
www.ladyleverartgallery.org.uk
VIEW TWO GALLERY
www.viewtwogallery.co.uk
WALKER ART GALLERY
www.thewalker.org.uk

MIDDLESEX

LINDA BLACKSTONE GALLERY
www.lindablackstone.com

MILTON KEYNES

MILTON KEYNES GALLERY
www.mk-g.org

NORFOLK

BIRCHAM GALLERY
www.birchamgallery.co.uk
BURNHAM GRAPEVINE
www.burnhamgrapevine.co.uk
DAVID CASE FINE ART
www.davidcasefineart.com
THE FORUM
www.makingfaces.org.uk
GRAPEVINE
www.grapevinegallery.co.uk
KING'S LYNN ARTS CENTRE
www.kingslynnarts.co.uk
NORWICH GALLERY
www.norwichgallery.co.uk
OUTPOST
www.norwichoutpost.org
ST.JUDE'S MODERN BRITISH
www.stjudesgallery.co.uk

NORTHAMPTONSHIRE

FERMYNWOODS CONTEMPORARY ART
www.fermynwoods.co.uk

NORTHUMBERLAND

TALLANTYRE GALLERY
www.tallantyre-gallery.co.uk

NORTH YORKSHIRE

ARTSBANK
www.artsbank.co.uk
BIANCO NERO GALLERY
www.bianconero.co.uk
LINTON COURT GALLERY
www.gavaganart.co.uk
LUND GALLERY
www.bianconero.co.uk
YORKSHIRE SCULPTURE PARK
www.ysp.co.uk

OXFORDSHIRE

ASKEW ART
www.askewart.co.uk
BARN GALLERIES
www.barngalleries.com
BARRY KEENE GALLERY
www.barrykeenegallery.co.uk
BOHUN GALLERY
www.bohungallery.co.uk
BRIAN SINFIELD GALLERY
www.briansinfield.com
EDITION 3
www.edition3.co.uk
IONA HOUSE GALLERY
www.ionahousegallery.org
MODERN ART OXFORD
www.modernartoxford.org.uk
WREN GALLERY
www.wrenfineart.com

RUTLAND

GOLDMARK GALLERY
www.goldmarkart.com
ORANGE STREET GALLERY
www.orangestreetgallery.com
SAMUEL ROBSON FINE ART
www.srfagallery.com
WOODBINE CONTEMPORARY ARTS
www.woodbinecontemporaryarts.co.uk

SHEFFIELD

PENLEY CONTEMPORARY ART
www.penleyart.com
SITE GALLERY
www.sitegallery.org

SCILLY ISLES

GALLERY TRESCO
www.gallerytresco.co.uk
GLANDORE GALLERY
www.glandoregallery.co.uk

SHROPSHIRE

TWENTY TWENTY
www.twenty-twenty.co.uk

SOMERSET / N.SOMERSET

AT THE CHAPEL
www.atthechapel.co.uk
ATKINSON GALLERY
www.atkinsongallery.co.uk
BOWLISH CONTEMPORARY GALLERY
www.bowlishgallery.co.uk
THE DRUGSTORE GALLERY
www.thedrugstoregallery.com
HARLEQUIN GALLERY
www.harlequingallery.co.uk
THE LLOYD GILL GALLERY
www.thelloydgillgallery.com
JANE CARTNEY ART STUDIO & GALLERY
www.regentgallery.co.uk
THE SADLER STREET GALLERY
www.sadlerstreetgallery.co.uk
TOLLHOUSE GALLERY
www.clevedonpier.com

SUFFOLK

THE HUNTER GALLERY
www.thehuntergallery.com
LIME TREE GALLERY
www.limetreegallery.com
SMITHS ROW
www.smithsrow.org
WILDWOOD GALLERY
www.wildwoodgallery.co.uk

SUNDERLAND

NORTHERN GALLERY FOR CONTEMPORARY ART
www.ngca.co.uk

SURREY

CCA GALLERIES
www.ccagalleries.com
CHALK HILL CONTEMPORARY ART
www.chalkhill.co.uk
FOYER/ JAMES HOCKEY GALLERIES
www.ucreative.ac.uk/galleries
GALLERY ONE
www.gallery-one.co.uk
GRANDY ART
www.grandyart.com
GUILDFORD HOUSE GALLERY
www.guildfordhouse.co.uk
JOHN IDDON FINE ART
www.johniddonfineart.com
LIFE - THE GALLERY
www.lifethegallery.com
THE LIGHTBOX
www.thelightbox.org.uk
McALLISTER THOMAS FINE ART
www.mcallisterthomasfineart.co.uk
MITCHELL STUDIO GALLERY
www.mitchellstudiogallery.co.uk
THE ROBERT PHILLIPS GALLERY
www.riverhousebarn.co.uk

TYNE AND WEAR

BALTIC CENTRE FOR CONTEMPORARY ART
www.balticmill.com
THE BISCUIT FACTORY
www.thebiscuitfactory.com
THE GLOBE GALLERY
www.globegallery.org
MUSHROOM WORKS STUDIOS AND GALLERY
www.mushroomworks.com
WORKPLACE GALLERY
www.workplacegallery.co.uk

WALSALL

NEW ART GALLERY WALSALL
www.artatwalsall.org.uk

WARWICKSHIRE

COMPTON VERNEY
www.comptonverney.org.uk
THE GALLERY UPSTAIRS
www.thegalleryupstairstorquil.co.uk
THE STOUR GALLERY
www.thestourgallery.co.uk

WEST MIDLANDS

THE BRITISH GLASS BIENNALE
www.ifg.org.uk
THE NEW ART GALLERY WALSALL
www.artatwalsall.org.uk

WEST SUSSEX

ASKEW ART
www.askewart.co.uk
CASS SCULPTURE FOUNDATION
www.sculpture.org.uk
THE MILL STUDIO
www.themillstudio.com
MONCRIEFF-BRAY GALLERY
www.moncrieff-bray.com
PALLANT HOUSE GALLERY
www.pallant.org.uk
ZIMMER STEWART GALLERY
www.zimmerstewart.co.uk

WEST YORKSHIRE

COLOURBOX
www.reltonmarine.com
YORKSHIRE SCULPTURE PARK
www.ysp.co.uk

WILTSHIRE

BENT ART GALLERY
www.bentartgallery.co.uk
BLUESTONE GALLERY
www.bluestonegallery.com
THE CLARE INSKIP GALLERY
www.clareinskip.com
CROFT GALLERY
www.thecroftgallery.co.uk
GALLERY PERUTZ
www.galleryperutz.com

KATHARINE HOUSE GALLERY
www.katharinehousegallery.co.uk
NEW ART CENTRE
www.sculpture.uk.com

WORCESTERSHIRE

BROADWAY MODERN
www.broadwaymodern.com
THE GALLERY AT BEVERE
www.beverevivis.com
GREENSTAGE GALLERY
www.greenstagegallery.co.uk
PRIORY GALLERY BROADWAY
www.priorybroadway.com

YORK

KENTMERE HOUSE GALLERY
www.kentmerehouse.co.uk
LIQUID AMBER ART GALLERY
www.liquidamberartgallery.com
YORK ART GALLERY
www.yorkartgallery.org.uk

PROVINCIAL GALLERIES – WALES

ANGLESEY

JANET BELL GALLERY
www.janetbellgallery.com
ORIEL COAST GALLERY
www.orielcoastgallery.co.uk
ORIEL TEGFRYN GALLERY
www.orieltegfryn.com
UCHELDRE CENTRE
www.ucheldre.org

CARDIFF

THE ALBANY GALLERY
www.albanygallery.com
KOOYWOOD GALLERY
www.kooywoodgallery.com
MARTIN TINNEY GALLERY
www.artwales.com
OFF THE WALL
www.galleryoffthewall.com
ORIEL KOOYWOOD GALLERY
www.kooywoodgallery.com
ORIEL WASHINGTON GALLERY
www.washingtongallery.co.uk
ST DAVID'S HALL FOYER GALLERIES
www.stdavidshallcardiff.co.uk
THIRD FLOOR GALLERY
www.thirdfloorgallery.com
WASHINGTON GALLERY
www.washingtongallery.co.uk

CARMARTHENSHIRE

THE CORNER HOUSE GALLERY
www.cornerhouse-gallery.co.uk
FOUNTAIN FINE ART
www.fountainfineart.com
ORIEL MYRDDIN GALLERY
www.orielmyrddingallery.co.uk

DENBIGHSHIRE

SANCTUARY GALLERY
www.sanctuarygallerywales.com

GWYNEDD

ORIEL FFIN Y PARC
www.welshart.net
ORIEL PLAS GLYN-Y-WEDDW
www.oriel.org.uk

ORIEL Y MOR
www.tonnau.com
ROYAL CAMBRIAN ACADEMY
www.rcaconwy.org

MONMOUTHSHIRE

THE ART SHOP
www.theartshopandgallery.co.uk
DENISE YAPP CONTEMPORARY ART
www.deniseyapp.com
NEW LEAF GALLERY
www.newleafgallery.co.uk

PEMBROKESHIRE

HARBOUR LIGHTS GALLERY
www.art2by.com
ORIEL Q - QUEENS HALL GALLERY
www.forielqueenshallgallery.org.uk
ORIEL Y PARC
www.orielyparc.co.uk
TENBY MUSEUM & ART GALLERY
www.tenbymuseum.org.uk
WEST WALES ART CENTRE
www.westwalesartcentre.com

PENARTH

FFOTOGALLERY
www.ffotogallery.org
WASHINGTON GALLERY
www.washingtongallery.co.uk

POWYS

MID WALES ART CENTRE
www.midwalesarts.org.uk
MoMA WALES
www.momawales.org.uk
SPECTRUM GALLERY
www.spectrumgallery.co.uk

SWANSEA

ATTIC GALLERY
www.atticgallery.co.uk
ELYSIUM GALLERY
www.elysiumgallery.com
GLYNN VIVIAN ART GALLERY
www.glynnviviangallery.org
MISSION GALLERY
www.missiongallery.co.uk

PROVINCIAL GALLERIES – SCOTLAND

ABERDEENSHIRE

THE CARBYART GALLERY
www.carbyart.co.uk
GALLERY HEINZEL
www.galleryheinzel.com
GALLERY i
www.galleryi.co.uk
LOST GALLERY
www.lostgallery.co.uk
RIVERSIDE GALLERY
www.riversidegallery.com
TOLQUHON GALLERY
www.tolquhon-gallery.co.uk

ARGYLL & BUTE

JUNO DESIGN GALLERY
www.junogallery.com
TIGHNABRUAICH
www.tig-gallery.com

DUMFRIES & GALLOWAY

HIGH ST GALLERY
www.highstgallery.co.uk

DUNDEE

DUNDEE CONTEMPORARY ARTS
www.dca.org.uk

EAST LOTHIAN

STENTON GALLERY
www.stentongallery.com

EDINBURGH

ANTHONY WOODD GALLERY
www.anthonywoodd.com
ATTICSALT
www.atticsalt.co.uk
BOURNE FINE ART
www.bournefineart.com
CITY ART CENTRE
www.cac.org.uk
DEAN GALLERY
www.nationalgalleries.org/summer
DOVECOT STUDIOS
www.dovecotstudios.com

THE FRUITMARKET GALLERY
www.fruitmarket.co.uk
HANOVER FINE ARTS
www.hanoverfinearts.co.uk
JAMIE PRIMROSE
www.jamieprimrose.com
LANDINGS GALLERY
www.roslarts.co.uk
THE LEITH GALLERY
www.the-leith-gallery.co.uk
NATIONAL GALLERY OF SCOTLAND
www.nationalgalleries.org
OPEN EYE GALLERY
www.openeyegallery.co.uk
RIVERSIDE GALLERY at the Dundas Street Gallery
www.riverside-gallery.co.uk
ROYAL SCOTTISH ACADEMY
www.royalscottishacademy.org
ROYAL SCOTTISH ACADEMY BUILDING
www.rsw.org.uk
SCOTLANDART.COM
www.scotlandart.com
THE SCOTTISH GALLERY
www.scottish-gallery.co.uk
SCOTTISH NATIONAL GALLERY OF MODERN ART
www.nationalgalleries.org
SCOTTISH NATIONAL PORTRAIT GALLERY
www.nationalgalleries.org
UNION GALLERY
www.uniongallery.co.uk

FIFE

EAST NEUK OPEN STUDIOS EXHIBITION
www.eastneukopenstudios.org

GLASGOW

ART IN THE CITY
www.art-in-the-city.co.uk
BILLCLIFFE GALLERY
www.billcliffegallery.com
COMPASS GALLERY
www.compassgallery.co.uk
CYRIL GERBER FINE ART
www.gerberfineart.co.uk
EWAN MUNDY FINE ART
www.mundyfineart.com
THE GATEHOUSE GALLERY
www.gatehousegallery.co.uk

HUNTERIAN ART GALLERY
www.hunterian.gla.ac.uk
JOHN GREEN FINE ART
www.fineartscotland.com
MANSFIELD PARK GALLERY
www.mansfieldparkgallery.com
ROGER BILLCLIFFE FINE ART
www.billcliffegallery.com
ROYAL GLASGOW INSTITUTE OF THE FINE ARTS
www.rgiscotland.co.uk
TRACEY McNEE FINE ART
www.traceymcnee.com

INVERNESS-SHIRE

THE CASTLE GALLERY
www.castlegallery.co.uk
INCHMORE GALLERY
www.inchmoregallery.co.uk
KILMORACK GALLERY
www.kilmorackgallery.co.uk
TORE ART GALLERY
www.tore-art-gallery.co.uk

ISLE OF ARRAN

ARRAN ART GALLERY
www.arranartgallery.com
THE BURNSIDE
www.theburnside.com
ISLE OF ARRAN ART
www.isleofarranart.co.uk

PERTH & KINROSS

THE ATHOLL GALLERY
www.athollgallery.co.uk
FRAMES CONTEMPORARY GALLERY
www.framesgallery.co.uk
STRATHEARN GALLERY
www.strathearn-gallery.com

SCOTTISH BORDERS

BROUGHTON GALLERY
www.broughtongallery.co.uk
FLAT CAT GALLERY
www.flatcatgallery.co.uk
REIVER'S MOON GALLERY
www.reiversmoongallery.com
THE SMOKEHOUSE GALLERY
www.smokehousegallery.com

PROVINCIAL GALLERIES – IRELAND

NORTHERN IRELAND

BELFAST

EAKING GALLERY
www.eakingallery.co.uk
GOLDEN THREAD GALLERY
www.goldenthreadgallery.co.uk
MULLAN GALLERY
www.mullangallery.com
ORMEAU BATHS GALLERY
www.ormeaubaths.co.uk
THE TAYLOR GALLERY
www.taylorgallery.co.uk
TOM CALDWELL GALLERY
www.tomcaldwellgallery.com

COUNTY ANTRIM

CASTLE UPTON GALLERY
www.castleuptongallery.com
CHARLES GILMORE FINE ART DEALERS
www.charlesgilmore.com
COLOURED RAIN
www.ColouredRain.com
GRACEHILL GALLERY
www.gracehillgallery.com
LISBURN ART GALLERY
www.lisburnartgallery.co.uk
THROATLAKE
www.throatlake.com

COUNTY DOWN

HENRY GILMORE GALLERY
www.henrygilmore.co.uk

COUNTY LONDONDERRY

LANESIDE GALLERY
www.lanesidegallery.com
VOID
www.derryvoid.com

COUNTY TYRONE

GORMLEYS FINE ART
www.gormleys.ie
IRISH ART SALES
www.irishartsales.com

SOUTHERN IRELAND - EIRE

DUBLIN

APOLLO GALLERY
www.apollogallery.ie
DUBLIN CITY GALLERY THE HUGH LANE
www.hughlane.ie
GREEN GALLERY
www.greengallery.ie
GREEN ON RED GALLERY
www.greenonredgallery.com
THE IRISH MUSEUM OF MODERN ART
www.imma.ie
THE JAMES GALLERY
www.thejamesgallery.ie
KERLIN GALLERY
www.kerlin.ie
SOL ART GALLERY
www.solart.ie

COUNTY CORK

BUCKLEY FINE ART
www.buckleyfineart.com
CRAWFORD ART GALLERY
www.crawfordartgallery.ie
THE LAVIT GALLERY
www.lavitgallery.com
MORGAN O'DRISCOLL ART AUCTIONS
www.morganodriscoll.com
TWENTY TWENTY ART GALLERY
www.2020artgallery.com
THE WARREN GALLERY
www.warren-gallery.com

COUNTY GALWAY

STRONACH GALLERY
www.stronachgallery.com

COUNTY KERRY

BIN BAN GALLERY
www.binbanart.com

COUNTY ROSCOMMON

PURPLE ONION ART GALLERY
www.purpleonion.ie

COUNTY WEXFORD

GREENACRES GALLERY
www.greenacres.ie/art-galleries/

ACADEMY AND ART SOCIETY WEBSITES

Armed Forces Art Society
www.afas.org.uk

The Association of British Naïve Artists
www.britishnaives.co.uk

The Association of Illustrators
www.theaoi.com

Bath Area Network for Artists (BANA)
www.bana-arts.co.uk

Birmingham Artists
www.birminghamartists.com

British Society of Master Glass Painters
www.bsmgp.org.uk

Buckinghamshire Art Society
www.bucksart.co.uk

Candid Arts Trust
www.candidarts.com

The Cartoonists Club of Great Britain
www.ccgb.org.uk

The Chartered Society of Designers
www.csd.org.uk

Chelsea Art Society
www.chelseaartsociety.org.uk

The Cheltenham Group of Artists
www.cheltenhamgroupartists.org

The Colour Group
www.colour.org.uk

East Anglian Group of Marine Artists
www.eastangliangroupofmarineartists.org.uk

Euroart Studios and Galleries
www.euroart.co.uk

Federation of British Artists
www.mallgalleries.org.uk

Free Painters and Sculptors
www.piczo.com/FreePaintersAndSculptors

The Fylingdales Group of Artists
www.thefylingdalesgroupofartists.co.uk

Group 75
www.group75.co.uk

Guild of Aviation Artists
www.gava.org.uk

Guild of Glass Engravers
www.gge.org.uk

Guild of Railway Artists
www.railart.co.uk

Hesketh Hubbard Art Society
www.mallgalleries.org.uk

The Hilliard Society of Minaturists
www.art-in-miniature.org
Independent Artists Network (IAN)
www.independentartists.org.uk
Ipswich Art Society
www.ipswich-art-society.org.uk
Ipswich Arts Association
www.ipswich-arts.org.uk
The Lake Artists Society
www.lakeartists.org.uk
Learning Stone Portland Sculpture and Quarry Trust
www.learningstone.org
The Liver Sketching Club
www.liversketchingclub.co.uk
London Group
www.thelondongroup.com
Manchester Academy of Fine Arts
www.mafa.org.uk
Master Carvers' Association
www.mastercarvers.co.uk
Milton Keynes Society of Artists
www.mksa.org.uk
The National Acrylic Painters Association
www.napauk.org
National Association of Decorative and Fine Arts Societies (NADFAS)
www.nadfas.org.uk
National Association of Master Masons
www.namm.org.uk
National Society of Painters, Sculptors and Printmakers
www.ns.highgrovefinearts.co.uk
Nature in Art
www.nature-in-art.org.uk
New English Art Club
www.neac.co.uk
Newlyn Art Gallery
www.newlynartgallery.co.uk
Newlyn Society of Artists
www.nsanewlyn.com
Nottingham Society of Artists (NSA)
www.nottinghamstudios.org
Nottingham Society of Artists Trust (NSAT)
www.nottinghamstudios.org
Oxford Art Society
www.oxfordartsociety.org.uk
Pastel Society
www.thepastelsociety.org.uk
Phoenix Arts Association
www.phoenixarts.org

Printmakers Council
www.printmaker.co.uk/pmc
Royal Academy of Arts
www.royalacademy.org.uk
Royal Birmingham Society of Artists
www.rbsa.org.uk
Royal Cambrian Academy of Art
www.rcaconwy.org
Royal Glasgow Institute of the Fine Arts
www.rgiscotland.co.uk
Royal Hibernian Academy
www.royalhibernianacademy.ie
Royal Institute of British Architects
www.riba.org
Royal Institute of Oil Painters
www.mallgalleries.org.uk
The Royal Institute of Painters in Watercolour
www.mallgalleries.org.uk
Royal Scottish Academy
www.royalscottishacademy.org
Royal Scottish Society of Painters in Watercolour
www.thersw.org.uk
Royal Society of British Artists
www.the-rba.org.uk
Royal Society of British Sculptors
www.rbs.org.uk
Royal Society of Marine Artists
www.rsma-web.co.uk
Royal Society of Miniature Painters, Sculptors and Gravers
www.royal-miniature-society.org.uk
Royal Society of Painter-Printmakers
www.banksidegallery.com
Royal Society of Portrait Painters
www.therp.co.uk
Royal Ulster Academy of Arts
www.ruaonline.com
Royal Watercolour Society
www.royalwatercoloursociety.co.uk
Royal West of England Academy
www.rwa.org.uk
St.Ives Society of Artists
www.stisa.co.uk
Scottish Sculpture Trust
www.scottishsculpturetrust.org
Society for All Artists (SAA)
www.saa.co.uk
Society of Botanical Artists
www.soc-botanical-artists.org

Society of Catholic Artists
www.catholicartists.co.uk
Society of Designer Craftsmen
www.societyofdesignercraftsmen.org.uk
Society of Equestrian Artists
www.equestrianartists.co.uk
Society of Floral Painters
www.socfp.net
Society of Graphic Fine Art
www.sgfa.org.uk
Society of Portrait Sculptors
www.portrait-sculpture.org/
Society of Scottish Artists
www.s-s-a.org
Society of Scribes and Illuminators
www.calligraphyonline.org/
Society of Wildlife Artists
www.swla.co.uk
Society of Women Artists
www.society-women-artists.org.uk
The Society of Wood Engravers
www.woodengravers.co.uk
Suffolk Art Society
www.suffolkartsociety.org
Ulster Society of Women Artists
www.uswa.co.uk
UK Coloured Pencil Society
www.ukcps.co.uk
United Society of Artists
www.united-artists.org.uk
Visual Artists Ireland
www.visualartists.ie
The Wapping Group of Artists
www.thewappinggroupofartists.co.uk
Watercolour Society of Wales
www.watercolourwales.co.uk

BIOGRAPHIES

A

AARON, Cheryl A., BFA, MFA (1972), DipAT (1982); Awards: Arts Council, London Art Board, Paul Hamlyn Trust, Scottish Arts, Docklands Development Trust. *Medium*: oil, prints, photography. *b*: USA. *Educ*: Art Students League, NYC; Tyler School of Fine Arts, Rome. *Studied*: Ohio University, Pratt Institute, Goldsmiths College, London University. *Exhib*: RA, Discerning Eye, National Theatre, Royal Festival Hall, Whitechapel Art Gallery, Curwen Gallery, Barbican, Camden Art Centre, Air Gallery, Hunting-Observer, Museum of London, Garrick-Milne, Christie's, Morley College, Gallery 24, New Academy Gallery, London; Collins Gallery, Glasgow; Cornerhouse, Manchester; Neatherbow, Edinburgh. *Works in collections*: V&A, Marks&Spencer, St.Thomas' Hospital, Chelsea & Westminster Hospital, LB of Hounslow, Hammersmith, TH; New York Public Library, Manchester City Arts, Gateshead, Suffolk CC, Paintings in Hospitals, London Guildhall. *Commissions*: Aldgate Subways Project, GUS. *Publications*: Cafe, Laundry. *Works reproduced*: Sunday Times Magazine (1998), Evening Standard (1997), The Royal Court Theatre, 'The World is a Text' (Prentice Hall), 'Belly Dancing' (Virago). *Address*: 44 Copperfield Rd, London E3 4RR. *Signs work*: "Cheryl A.Aaron".

AARONS, Andrew, NDD (1958), Postgrad.Dip. Printmaking (1991). *Medium*: painter/printmaker; video installations. *b*: London, 1 Feb 1939. *m*: Paula. one *s*. one *d*. *Educ*: Camberwell School of Art, Junior Dept. (1951-54). *Studied*: Camberwell School of Art (1954-58). *Exhib*: Germany, UK, Canada, USA, Australia. *Works in collections*: CBC Toronto; York University, Toronto; Barclays Bank; Bank of Mexico; Cambridge University; Sternberg Centre, London. *Commissions*: Bodilly Suite; Sporting Etchings: Serigraphs of Newmarket Life; Portraits; Landscapes and Mythology. *Publications*: Two Nations in a New Land; A History of Canadian Painting; Is this Art; Journal of Progressive Judaism: Jewish Quarterly; Kettles Yard Publication. *Principal Works*: Landscapes of Memory; Images of the Shoah; Landscapes of War. *Address*: 16 Huntingdon Rd., Cambridge CB3 0HH. *Email*: alaarons@gmail.com *Website*: www.andrewaarons.com *Signs work*: "AARONS" followed by year.

ABBASSY, Samira, BA (Hons) (1987). *Medium*: painter in oil on paper, canvas and board, gouache on paper, etchings. *b*: Ahwaz, Iran, 29 May 1965. *d of*: Naim and Sonya Abbassy. *m*: Guy Buckles. *Educ*: Hillview School for Girls, Tonbridge; West Kent College of FE. *Studied*: Maidstone College of Art and Design, Canterbury College of Art. *Exhib*: Mercury Gallery, East West Gallery London, Joan Prats Gallery, NY. *Works in collections*: South East Arts, Leicestershire CC. *Publications*: book jackets: Landscape Painted with Tea by Milorid Pavich, The Ice Factory by Russell Lucas. *Clubs*: Rye Soc. of Artists. *Address*: c/o Mercury Gallery, 26 Cork St., London W1X 1HB. *Signs work*: "Samira Abbassy."

ABELL, Roy, RBSA, ARCA (Silver Medal, Painting, First Class Hons. 1957); oils, water-colour, etching; Head of School of Painting, Birmingham College of Art; Course Director BA Fine Art, Birmingham Polytechnic (retd.). *Medium*: oil, watercolour. *b*: Birmingham, 21 Jan 1931. *s of*: Alfred Abell, engineer, and Muriel. *m*: Mary Patricia. two *s* one *d* *Educ*: Waverley Grammar School, Birmingham (Jack Davis). *Studied* Birmingham College of Art (1947-52, Harold Smith, Fleetwood-Walker); Royal College of Art (1954-57, Carel Weight, Ruskin Spear, John Minton). *Exhib* Young Contemporaries, RA, John Moores; one-man exhbns.: National Museum of Wales, Ikon, Oriel (Cardiff), Thackeray (London), Tegfryn (Menai), Birmingham Centenary Artist 1989, Brian Sinfield, Burford; Artifex, Sutton Coldfield. *Works in collections* National Museum of Wales, ACGB, Art Galleries of Birmingham, Bradford, Lichfield, Walsall, University of Wales, University of Central England. *Publibations*: The Birmingham School - The Lavenham Press. *Recreations*: cricket: Moseley C.C.; Warwickshire C.C.Cc. *Clubs*: W.O.C.C.A. - Warwickshire Old County Cricketers Association. *Address*: 236 Green Lanes, Sutton Coldfield, Birmingham B73 5LX. *Signs work* "Roy Abell."

ABBOTT, Paul Philip John, BA (Hons) degree in painting (1986-1989); painter in oil and teacher; currently living and working in the USA. *b*: London, 1960. *m*: Audrey Pietre. one *s*. one *d*. *Studied*: Plymouth Foundation Course, WSCAD Farnham, Surrey under Richard Mann (1973-1978) and Robert Lenkiewicz (1979-1985). *Exhib*: 17 solo and 8 group exhibs. (1979-2002). *Works in collections*: Christian Marquant, Christopher and Dominique Brooks, and throughout Europe and USA. *Commissions*: Include - Kate Mortimer, Micky Burn, Donald Martin Betts, John Ingram, Asia Tanlaw. *Address*: P O Box 96, Skull Valley, 86338 Arizona, USA. *Email*: mail@jonathancooper.co.uk. *Signs work* "P. Abbott.".

ABRAHAM, Lorraine, RSMA (Elected Associate 1997, Member 1998); RSMA Education Officer (2008-); 1st Prize College End of Session Award (1963); Royal National Eisteddfod of Wales (1st Prize 1981, 1982). *Medium*: acrylic. *b*: Bridgend, Glamorgan, 26 Jan 1941. *m*: Robert Abraham (decd). *Studied*: Cardiff College of Art (1959-1964), National Diploma in Design 1963, Art Teacher's Diploma (1964); Univesity of Wales School of Education. *Exhib*: Royal National Eisteddfod of Wales, House of Commons British Women's Art (1981), RI, RBA, RWA. *Works in collections*: Drawings purchased by National Museum of Wales (Education Dept.) 1964. *Commissions*: Glamorgan County Council (scraperboards in perspex on site illustrating Richard Llewelyn's 'How Green was my Valley'); Pen drawing of 'Le Petit Sablons' commissioned by diplomatic wives to present to Lady Jackson, wife of Sir Edward Jackson (British Ambassador) at the end of their tour in Brussels 1984. *Misc*: Full time teaching until 1975 including Head of Dept. posts. Resident in Brussels 1982-1984 - these years resulted in a special study of the shrimp fishing industry of Oostduinkerke (1989-2000). *Address*: 15 Marshalls Close, Epsom, Surrey KT19 8HZ.

ABRAHAMS, Ivor, RA, FRBS, Sir Winston Churchill Fellow (1989); NDD Sculpture (Special Hons); elected Professor of Sculpture, Royal Academy Schols (2008). *Medium*: sculpture and prints / film / ceramics. *b*: Lancs., 10 Jan 1935. *m*: Evelyne. two *s* (one decd). *Educ*: Wigan Grammar School. *Studied*: St. Martin's School of Art (under Frank Martin, Anthony Caro), Camberwell School of Art (Prof. Karel Vogel). *Represented by* Mayor Gallery W1, and Bernard Jacobson Gallery, London W1. *Exhib*: One-man shows: Arnolfini Gallery, Bristol (1971), Aberdeen AG (1972), Mappin Gallery, Sheffield (1972), Ferens Gallery, Kingston upon Hull (1979), Warwick Arts Trust, London (1982); Kölnischer Kunstverein, Cologne (1973), Ikon Gallery, B'ham (1976), Yorkshire Sculpture Park, Wakefield (1984); Henry Moore Institute, Leeds (2008), Canary Wharf (2007), RWA Bristol (2012). *Works in collections*: ACGB; Bibliotheque National, Paris; British Council; Denver Museum, Colorado; Metropolitan Museum, NY; V & A; Wilhelm Lembruck Museum, Duisburg; Boymans Museum, Rotterdam, Tate Britain, etc. *Commissions*: Black Lion House, Whitechapel Rd., E1; 39 Chancery Lane with Brian Clark; Painshill Park, Cobham, Surrey, and Chelsea and Kensington Town Hall. *Publications*: E.A. Poe (1975), Oxford Gardens Sketchbook (1976). *Official Purchasers*: over 40 museums worldwide. *Works Reproduced*: numerous magazines, catalogues, books and newspapers. *Recreations*: reading. *Clubs* Chelsea Arts, Dover St Arts Club W1. *Address*: 133 Artillery Road, Ramsgate, Kent CT11 8PT. *Email*: ivor.abrahams@googlemail.com *Website*: www.ivorabrahams.info *Signs work*: "Ivor Abrahams."

ACKROYD, Jane V.M., ARBS, BA (Hons.), MA, RCA (Sculpture). *Medium*: sculptor in mild steel. *b*: London, 25 Feb 1957. *d of*: John Ackroyd, M.A., Oxford. *m*: David Annesley, (divorced). one *s* *Educ*: Godolphin and Latymer School, London. *Studied*: St. Martin's School of Art (1975-79, Adrian de Montford, David Annesley, Anthony Caro); RCA (1980-83, Philip King, Bryan Kneale). *Exhib*: International Garden Festival Liverpool (1984), Serpentine Gallery (1984), Anti-Thesis Angela Flowers Gallery (1986), RA Summer Exhbn. (1988, 1989, 1995, 1996, 1997, 1998, 2001); one-man shows Anderson O'Day (1988 and 1991), Worcester College, Oxford (1997), Kingsgate Gallery 2002, Northern Spain (2011),

Newhall College, Cambridge (2012). *Works in collections* ACGB, Contemporary Arts Soc., Leics. Educ. Authority, London Docklands Development Corp. *Commissions*: 'Herring Gull' Limehouse, 'Moonlight Ramble' Haymarket London, and others. *Address*: 34, Winton Ave., London N11 2AT. *Email*: jane.ackroyd@blueyonder.co.uk *Website*: www.janeackroyd.com *Signs work*: "Jane Ackroyd."

ACKROYD, Norman, RA (1991); painter/etcher. *b*: Leeds, 26 Mar 1938. *s of*: Albert Ackroyd, master butcher. *Educ*: Cockburn High School, Leeds. *Studied*: RCA (1961-64). *Exhib*: extensively in Europe and USA. *Works in collections*: Tate Gallery, V&A, Museum of Modern Art, NY, National Galleries of Scotland, Canada, S. Africa, Norway, The Rijksmuseum and Stedelijk Amsterdam, The Albertina Vienna, Musee d'Art Historie Geneva, British Council, Leeds, Manchester, Sheffield, Hull, Glasgow, Aberdeen, Norwich, Preston, Bradford, Newcastle, and other city A.Gs. *Publications*: Thirty minute film on etching for BBC, writing for Studio International. *Address*: 1 Morocco St., London SE1 3HB.

ADAIR, Don: see PAVEY, Don

ADAIR, Hilary, NDD (1963), ATC (1965), RE (1991); *Medium*: painter/printmaker in water-colour, acrylic, oil, etching, silkscreen, relief. *b*: Sussex, 29 May 1943. *m*: Julian Marshall. two *s*. *Educ*: Chichester High School for Girls. *Studied*: Brighton College of Art (1960-61; 1964-66, J. Dickson), St. Martin's School of Art (1961-63, F. Gore, A. Reynolds). *Exhib*: British Council, RA, Sue Rankin Gallery, Jill Yakas Gallery Athens, RWA, Concourse Gallery, The Barbican, Bankside Gallery, Museum of Garden History, London, Mall Galleries. *Works in collections*: British Council, Gray's Library, Eastbourne, Lancs., Oldham and Stoke-on-Trent Educ. Authorities, Paintings in Hospitals, Royal Devon and Exeter Hospital, Ashmolean Museum, (RE.Collection) Macmillan/Heineman, Towner Art Gallery. *Commissions*: Hilton and Intercontinental Hotels, Athens, P&O's 'Aurora' four Edns. of etchings. *Publications:* The English Garden (Aug. '98) - Arts Review - The Athenian Magazine, The Artist, The Somerset Magazine, "Printmakers' Secrets" by Anthony Dyson. *Works Reproduced*: "Printmakers' Secrets" by Anthony Dyson. *Address*: Conifers, Clanfield Road, Minehead, Somerset TA24 5PD. *Email*: info@hilaryadair.co.uk *Website*: www.hilaryadair.co.uk *Signs work*: "Hilary Adair" on prints, "Adair" on paintings.

ADAMS, Anna: see BUTT, Anna Theresa.

ADAMS, Ken Praveera, MA (1958), DipFA (1964), DipAT (1986); painter in oil and acrylic, sculptor in bronze and ceramic; formerly lecturer in sculpture at St. Martin's School of Art. *b*: Northumberland, 1 Sep1933. *s of*: Alan Adams. Grandson of Moses James Adams. *Educ*: Balliol College, Oxford. *Studied*: Slade School of Fine Art. *Represented by*: Koukan Gallery, 106a Alexandra Park Road, London N10 2AE, www.koukangallery.com. *Exhib*: London, Suffolk, Amsterdam, Dusseldorf, Paris, New York, R.A. Summer Shows (intermittently). *Works in collections*: Museum Sztuki, Lodz, Poland, and private collections in Europe and USA. *Commissions*: Netherhall Gardens Gable, Wild Boar. *Publications*: Leonardo Vol.12 (1979) Commentary on Sculptures. *Works Reproduced*: Leonardo (above). *Misc*: Figurative work veering to abstraction. Also composes music. *Address*: 19 Dartmouth Park Rd., London NW5 1SU. *Email*: ken33adams@gmail.com *Website*: www.kenadams.co.uk *Signs work*: "Ken Praveera Adams" or "K.A." or intermediate forms.

ADAMS, Marina, Dip LA Reading University 1962. Member Landscape Institute 1968; landscape architect in private practice: drawings in ink, water-colour, gouache, crayon. *b*: Athens, 27 Aug 1940. *d of*: Nicholas Haidopoulos and Maria Stavropoulos. *m*: (1964) Robert John Adams, dissolved (1980). one *s*. one *d*. *Educ*: Pierce College, Athens. *Studied*: Reading University (1959-1962). *Exhib*: RA Summer Exhbn. (1987, 1988, 1989, 1990, 1992, 1993, 1994, 1998). *Address*. 3 Pembroke Studios, Pembroke Gdns., London W8 6HX. *Email*. marinadams@dial.pipex.com *Signs work*: "Marina Adams."

ADAMS, Peter Martin, Master Mariner; Liveryman of Hon. Company of Master Mariners; Freeman City of London. *Medium*: watercolour, drawing. *b*: Notts., 17 Jul 1943. *s of*: Cdr. F C Adams, RN Rtd. *m*: Margaret. two *d*. *Educ*: King Edward VII Nautical College, London. *Studied*: self taught, but studied archive works by Wyllie, Dixon, Spurling etc. at National Maritime Museum. *Represented by* International Maritime Organisation; Warwick Leadley Gallery. *Exhib*: Wyllie Gallery; Gallery Marin, Appledore; numerous charity exhibitions of Marine nature (Mall Galleries, various London City Livery Halls, Lambeth Palace, Hull City Council Sea Fever Festival-annually); RSMA 'Britannia & White Horses Exhibition', Chatham Dockyard (1996) *Works in collections*: HRH Duke of Edinburgh - Admiral of the Hon.Co. Master Mariners (watercolour of HQS Wellington). *Commissions*: shipping companies and individuals with shipping interests. *Works Reproduced*: Book illustrations for Seafarer Books. *Misc*: Younger Brethren of the Corporation of Trinity House. *Address*: 62 Main Street, Lambley, Notts., NG4 4PP. *Email*: p.adams687@btinternet.com *Signs work*: "Peter Adams".

ADAMS, Rosalind Suzanne, *Medium*: pastel, watercolour, drawing. *b*: Frimley, 17 Jan 1939. *d of*: Maj.Gen. L de M Thuillier & Mrs Thuillier. *m*: the late Gilbert Adams FRPS. *Educ*: The Grove School (now Royal School) Surrey (1949-55). *Studied*: Westminster College of Commerce (now Univ. of Westminster) (1957-58); Italy (1956-57); Oxford Polytechnic (1974-75 - City & Guilds Teaching Diploma). *Exhib*: Clarges Gallery, London; Devizes Museum; William Thuillier Gallery, London; Reading Museum. *Works in collections*: Private collections worldwide. *Commissions*: Canada, Australia, USA, Europe and England. *Publications*: "Inspirations" Graham Sutherland (Lutterworth Press, 1982); "Marcus Adams, Photographer Royal" (Aurum Press, 1985); series of articles on painters and sculptors; forthcoming publication on Graham Sutherland. *Works Reproduced*: Study of photographer Bertram Park; study of painter Marc Chagall. *Principal Works*: cataloguing and curating the Adams Photograph Archive (1850-1996). *Recreations*: Literature, writing, gardening, travelling to draw. *Clubs*: In and Out Club, 4 St. James's Square. *Misc*: Languages: Italian, German, French, Greek. *Address*: East Stowell Farm House, Nr Marlborough, Wiltshire, SN8 4JS. *Email*: rosalind8@tiscali.co.uk *Signs work*: "RST" (R.S.THUILLIER).

ADAMS, Sarah, BA (Hons 2:1) Fine Art (1984), MA (RCA) Fine Art Printmaking (1987). *Medium*: oil, watercolour. *b*: Wokingham, 27 Jun 1962. *d of*: Mr & Mrs H H G Adams. *Educ*: Falmouth School of Art (Foundation Course 1980-81). *Studied*: Gloucestershire College of Art and Technology (BA Hons 1981-84); Royal College of Art (MA Fine Art Printmaking 1984-87); University of Mysore (Folklore Studies, 1991-92). *Represented by*: The Maas Gallery, London; The Padstow Studio, Cornwall. *Exhib*: Hunting Art Prize Exhibition (2003); Beyond England, Royal College of Art (1996); The Maas Gallery (2007, 09, 11, 13, 14); The Discerning Eye (prizewinner 2009); RWA (prizewinner 2009). *Works in collections*: Royal College of Art, Crill Canavan, Cater Allen Bank, Bank of America, Ogier and Le Mesurier, Sedgewick Group, Count de Monteluce. *Publications*: Encyclopedia of Drawing Techniques, Ian Simpson, London 1987; Sarah Adams: Land and Sea, monograph and text by Dr. Heather MacLennan (2000); 'Sarah Adams, A Sea View' by Andrew Lambirth, Halstar (2013). *Principal Works*: Buttress series; Spring tide series. *Address*: The Padstow Studio, 30 Duke Street, Padstow, Cornwall PL28 8AB. *Website*: sarahadamspainting.co.uk *Signs work*: "Sarah Adams".

ADAMSON, Crawfurd, DA (1975); painter in oil and pastel. *b*: Edinburgh, 24 Mar 1953. *m*: Mary Phimister. one *s*. one *d*. *Educ*: Royal High School, Edinburgh. *Studied*: Duncan of Jordanstone College of Art (1971-76, Alberto Morrocco, David McLure, Jack Knox). *Exhib*: 24 one-man shows since 1984 (seven in London); group shows in UK, USA, Spain, France, Japan, Monaco. *Works in collections*: Metropolitan Museum of Art, NY. *Publications*: exhibition catalogues (1991, 1995). *Address*: 14 Seddlescombe Rd. Sth. St.Leonards-on-Sea

TN38 0TA. *Email*: crawfurd@gmail.com *Website*: www.crawfurdadamson.com *Signs work*: "Crawfurd Adamson."

ADLINGTON, Mark, *Medium*: oil, watercolour, drawing, prints, sculpture. *b*: Hong Kong, 17 May 1965. *Studied*: Winchester College; University of Edinburgh; City and Guilds of London School of Art (1991-94). *Represented by*: John Martin of London, 38 Albemarle Street, London, W15 4JG; Bridgemen Images. *Exhib*: John Martin; New Grafton Gallery; Jenna Burlingham; Campden Gallery; Origin Gallery, Dublin. *Works in collections*: Private and corporate including the late Sir Paul Getty and Lady Getty, Eric and Suzanne Syz, Jonathon H. Kagan. *Publications*: 'The Horse, 30,000 Years of the Horse in Art' Merrell (2006); A Private View, David Wolfers and The New Grafton Gallery (2002); 'Ring of Bright Water' centenary edition Unicorn Press (2014). *Works Reproduced*: Times Literary Supplement cover no 5447/8. *Clubs*: Chelsea Arts Club. Address: Studio 4, 38 St Oswald's Place, London SE11 5JE. *Email*: mark@markadlington.com *Website*: www.markadlington.com *Signs work*: "Mark Adlington" or "MA" with date.

AHMAD, Sophie Maryum, BA (Hons) Fine Art (Painting). *Medium*: oil. *b*: Essex, 24 Jun 1973. *m*: Glen Goodman *Studied*: The Byam Shaw School of Art (1991-92); Central St.Martin's College of Art and Design (1993-96). *Represented by*: Rainbird Fine Art, London. *Exhib*: Christie's 'Art for Life' (2007), Rainbird Fine Art, London (2005-present), Artlounge Gallery, Birmingham (2004); Contemporary Art Society, Art Futures (1996, 2002, 2003), Affordable Art Fair, London (2003, 2004), Will's Art Warehouse, London (2004), The Hurlingham Club, London (2002), Sloane Graphics, London (1996, 1997, 2001, 2002). *Works in collections*: work held in private collections in the UK, India, Barbados, USA, Japan, including private collection of Raymond Kelvin, Founder and CEO of Ted Baker. *Publications*: features in The Jackdaw, The Lady magazine, and Voyager magazine. *Address*: Flat 1, 3rd Floor, Northwood Hall, Hornsey Lane, London N6 5PH. *Email*: sophieahmad@blueyonder.co.uk *Website*: www.rainbirdfineart.com *Signs work*: "S.M.Ahmed".

AIDA, Emiko, MA Fine Art, MA Printmaking; Awards: The Nordstern Award (RA); Coley & Tiley Prize, RBSA; Purchase Prize, Seoul International Print Biennial. *Medium*: oil on canvas, prints. *b*: Tokyo, Japan. *Studied*: Japan: Tokyo Geijutsu University (1982-84), UK: Royal College of Art (1987-89). *Represented by*: Royal Society of Painters & Printmakers, Art Chinese. *Exhib*: The Biscuit Factory, Newcastle; Gallery West, Tokyo (solo show), The Landau Kunstverein, Germany, Florence Biennale, Italy; Seoul International Print Biennial, Korea; Qijiang International Print Festival, China; The Basement Gallery, USA; Bankside Gallery, London. *Works in collections*: The New York Public Library; Guangdong Museum of Art, China; private and Institutes. *Publications*: 'Printmakers Today' (Schiffer, USA); International Contemporary Artists Vol V. (ICA Publishing, USA). *Address*: Studio 1, Unit 2&4, ACAVA, 11 Colville Road, London W3 9RY. *Email*: studio1@aidastudios.com *Website*: www.aidastudios.com *Signs work*: "Emiko Aida".

AINLEY, John Anthony, retired Head Teacher; Diploma in Child Development; MSc, Diploma in the Visual Arts; water colour painter. *b*: Sheffield, 1931. *m*: Ann. one *s*: Mark. one *d*: Elizabeth. *Works in collections* Self portrait on display in Ruth Borchard's permanent collection of British Self-portraits at King's Place in King's Cross London. *Publications*: features in 'Face to Face: A Collection of 100 20th Century Self Portraits'. *Clubs*: Founder of Leatherhead Art Club. Convenor of "Surrey Painters". *Address*: Bridleside, 1A Yarm Ct. Rd., Leatherhead, Surrey KT22 8NY.

AIRD, Philippe Leigh, BA (Hons); 1st International Video Festival Award. *Medium*: oil. *b*: Manchester, 14 Jul 1961. *s of*: George & Joyce Aird. *Studied*: Salford College of Art; Chelsea School of Art; taught by L S Lowry and Harold Riley. *Represented by*: Farmilo Fiumano. *Exhib*: Sotheby's (Farmilo Fiumano); Affordable Art Fair; New York, Los

Angeles, Glasgow, Stockport Art Gallery. *Works in collections*: MUFC players. *Commissions*: private. *Publications*: Phoenix Gallery brochure; book "Eye of the Beholder". *Works Reproduced*: Vortex Paintings. *Principal Works*: abstract. *Recreations*: tennis. *Address*: Phoenix Studio, 17 Ellesmere St., Castlefield, Manchester M15 4JY. *Email*: phil19@btconnect.com *Website*: www.PhilippeAird.com www.phoenix-gallery.co.uk *Signs work*: 'Philippe'.

AIVALIOTIS, Sharon Firth, RE, BA (Hons.) (1979), Postgrad. Dip. (Printmaking) (1980); artist/printmaker in mezzotint, all intaglio processes and graphite; part-time lecturer, St. Martin's School of Art and Design. *b*: Trinidad, 12 Apr 1951. *m*: Stak Aivaliotis. *Studied*: St. Martin's School of Art (1975-79, Albert Herbert), Slade School of Fine Art (1979-80, Bartolomeo Dos Santos). *Exhib*: solo shows: Jill George Fine Art London since 1985; many mixed shows nationally and internationally. *Works in collections*: V&A, Library of Congress Washington DC, Whitworth Gallery Manchester, Ferens AG Hull. *Publications*: 'The Mezzotint: History and Technique' by Carol Wax (Thames and Hudson) *Address*: 22 Brownlow Mews, London WC1N 2LA. *Signs work*: "Sharon Firth Aivaliotis" or "S. Aivaliotis."

AKIB, Hashim David, Diploma in Art and Design; Higher Diploma in Illustration; Winner of the Society for All Artists (SAA) Artist of the Year (2009); Winner of the Society for All Artists (SAA) Professional Artist of the Year (2005, 2007). *Medium*: oil, acrylic. *b*: Leigh On Sea, 24 May 1967. *Partner*: Marie Antoniou. *Studied*: Southend College (1983-1985); Swindon Scool of Art (1985-1987). *Represented by*: Thompsons Art Galleries, London/Aldeburgh; McNeill Gallery, London; Picturesque, Essex. *Exhib*: Various Mall Galleries open exhibitions; Beecroft Art Gallery, Essex; Buckenham Galleries, Southwold. *Work in collections*: Beecroft Art Collection, Essex; various private collections. *Commissions*: Daler Rowney series of paintings for System 3 Acrylics advertising campaign and branding. *Publications*: 'Vibrant Acrylics' published by Search Press (2012); feature writer for Artists & Illustrators magazine (2012 onwards); contributions to other art publications inc The International Artist, The Artist, Pratique Des Arts, Art of England. *Recreations*: Travel, theatre, books, film, walking. *Address*: 14 Cliffsea Grove, Leigh On Sea, Essex SS9 1NQ. *Email*: hashimakib@yahoo.co.uk *Website*: www.hashimakib.com *Signs work*: "HA".

AKROYD, Carry, MA. *Medium*: watercolour, print. *b*: Devon, 31 Jul 1953. *Studied*: Exeter College of Art; Roehampton Institute; University of Nottingham. *Exhib*: Originals Printshows, SWLA, Jerram Gallery, Robert Fogell Contemporary, CCA Cambridge, Royal Botanic Gardens, Edinburgh. *Work in collections*: Helongjing Art Museum, Harbin, China; Paintings in Hospitals (North); Jesus College, Cambridge. *Publications*: "This Happy Spirit", poems of John Clare (co-edited, designed and illustrated, 2013); "Wildlife in Printmaking" (edited for Langford Press, 2011); "Natures Powers and Spells - Landscape Change, John Clare and Me" (Langford Press, 2009). *Misc*: Illustrated "Tweet of the Day" for John Murray. *Address*: 4 Luddington in the Brook, Oundle, Northamptonshire PE8 5QU. *Email*: carry@carryakroyd.co.uk *Website*: www.carryakroyd.co.uk *Signs work*: "Akroyd".

AL-ATTAR, Suad, BA Fine Art; PG Dip (Printmaking); awards: The CIB Award for Excellence (1999), Honorary Award, 1st International Biennial, Malta (1995), Gold Medal, International Biennial, Cairo, Egypt. *Medium*: oil, prints. *b*: Baghdad, Iraq, 23 Jul 1942. *d of*: Ali Sadiq. *m*: Mr.Jamil Abu-Tabikh. three *d*. *Studied*: A.A.Calif. Polytechnic Univ., Baghdad Univ., Wimbledon School of Art & Central School of Art and Design, London. *Exhib*: solo: Green Art Gallery, Dubai (2006), Leighton House Museum, London (2012, 2006, 1997), Chelsea Art Club (2002, 2004), Westcliffe Gallery, Sheringham, Norfolk (2004), Albemarle Gallery, London (1999), Europ Gallery, Los Angeles (1990), Annex Gallery, London (1981), Gallery ALif, Washington DC (1985). Group: British Museum

(2006, 2009); Dubai Art Fair (2008); Women of the World, New York (2000), 230th Summer Exhbn., Royal Academy of Art (1998). *Works in collections* British Museum, Gulbenkian Collection, Barcelona Museum of Modern Art, Amman, Jordan, Museum of Modern Art, Damascus, Museum of Modern Art, Kuwait, Indira Gandhi private collection, New Delhi, Conference Center, Qatar. *Commissions*: Paintings for the Holland Park 1998 Opera. *Publications*: 'Suad Al Attar' (large book of the artist's works), World Literature Project by McGraw-Hill of New York. *Official Purchasers*: The British Museum, Modern Art Museum, Baghdad, Modern Art Museum, Ammam, Jordan. *Works Reproduced*: by Bridgman Art Library; Greeting card by UNICEF (1975, 1993). *Recreations*: travel. *Clubs*: Chelsea Art Club, Royal Academy of Art, Tate Gallery, Leighton House Museum. *Address*: 18 Fitz James Avenue, London W14 0RP. *Email*: suadalattar@hotmail.co.uk *Website*: The Bridgeman Art Library *Signs work*: "SUAD AL ATTAR".

ALBUTT, Virginia, *Medium*: oil. *b*: 24 Jun 1945. two *s.* one *d. Studied*: Corsham, Bath Academy of Art (1963-67); taught at Cambridge School of Art, Anglia Ruskin University (1972-88). *Exhib*: Kettle's Yard Gallery Cambridge (2000); Fitzwilliam College Cambridge (2004, 2005); New Hall Cambridge (2002, 2003, 2006); San Felipe Gallery, Mexico (2003); Kunst Aus Gallery, Heidelberg, Germany (2005); Anglia Ruskin University Gallery, Cambridge (2008); Llewellyn Alexander Gallery, London (2004-14); Selwyn College, Cambridge (2000-11). *Works in collections*: University of Cambridge; private collections in UK, USA, South Africa, Australia and New Zealand. *Commissions*: house and landscape undertaken. *Publications*: range of Greeting Cards for 'Blossoms & Bows'. *Principal Works*: Landscapes and seascapes inspired by light and colour, Italy, India, St. Ives, Suffolk and Cambridgeshire. *Recreations*: travelling, walking. *Clubs*: Cambridge Drawing Society, Cambridge Open Studios, Society of East Anglian Watercolourists. *Address*: 16 Chaucer Road, Cambridge, CB2 7EB. *Email*: valbutt@gmail.com *Website*: virginia-albutt.co.uk *Signs work*: "V. ALBUTT"

ALDOUS, Veronica, BA (Hons), Cert. Ed. *Medium*: watercolour, drawing, poetry, art criticism. *b*: Herts., 9 Jun 1962. *d of*: Vivienne & Basil Ripley-Duggan. *Educ*: St.Mary's Catholic School. *Studied*: Ravensbourne College of Art. *Represented by* Allied Artists. *Exhib*: Coningsby Gallery, London; Society for Art of the Imagination, Highgate; The Gentle Gallery; Avalon Gallery. *Works in collections*: private collections. *Commissions*: Inn on the Park Hotel, Hyatt Carlton Hotel, Maxwell's Restaurant. *Publications*: Quarto Book of Faeries, Quarto Book of Dragons and Mythical Beasts, HQ Quarterly, Urthona. *Principal Works*: Estella's Song; Mr. Wolfslick; Commuter; Seahenge. *Misc*: art lecturer Beechwood Centre; arts correspondent 'Urthona'. *Address*: 7a Downscourt Road, Purley, Surrey. CR8 1BE. *Email*: veronicaspaintbox@yahoo.co.uk *Website*: www.aldousart.co.uk *Signs work* 'Veronica Aldous'.

ALEXANDER, Gregory, RWS (1984), BA (1981); artist in water-colour and oil. *b*: Ramsgate, Kent, 14 May 1960. *s of*: Chris Alexander, ARE, ARCA. *m*: Francesca Rigoni. *Studied*: Canterbury College of Art (1976-78), W. Surrey College of Art (1978-81). *Represented by* Catto Gallery, London NW3 1DP. *Exhib*: RWS, NEAC, RA Summer shows, and over 25 one-man exhbns. in England and Australia. *Works in collections*: RWS Diploma, ANZ Bank Melbourne, National Gallery of Australia. *Publications*: Kipling's The Jungle Book (Pavilion 1991), Tales from the African Plains (Pavilion 1994), Step by Step Water-colour Painting (Weidenfeld & Nicolson 1994). *Address*: 1/73 Abbott St., Sandringham, Melbourne, Victoria 3191, Australia. *Email*: greg@gregory-alexander.com *Website*: www.gregory-alexander.com *Signs work*: "Gregory Alexander."

ALEXANDER, Naomi, NDD (1959), ROI (1982); British Association of Paintings Conservators-Restorers: Member of Royal Institute of Oil Painters. *b*: 1938. *d of*: John and Hazel Alexander. one *d. Studied*: Hornsey College of Art (1954-59), Central School of Art

(1961-63). *Exhib*: RA (1985-2014), Spink, Mercury Gallery, NEAC, RBA, ROI, RP, Fosse, David Messum, British municipal galleries, Richmond Gallery; one-man shows Ben Uri Gallery, Sheila Harrison, Sheridan Russell Gallery, Buxton Museum, Baker Tilly, Vilna Gaon State Museum, Vilnius, Lithuania, Lithuanian Embassy, London, LJCC London, Society of Portrait Sculptors, University of Leicester, Shipley Art Gallery, Museum of Florida USA. *Works in collections*: V&A; Duke of Devonshire; Japanese Broadcasting; Salomon Bank, Tokyo; Sir Richard Storey; Katharine, Viscountess Macmillan; 2nd Royal Tank Regt; Sultan of Oman; Paintings in Hospitals; Baker Tilly; Europos Parkas, Lithuania, Laing Art Gallery, Ben Uri Museum, Baron Van Dedem. *Publications*: Artist and Illustrator, 'Once Upon a Time in Lithuania' (David Paul Books); Collins, Quorto publications. *Official Purchasers*: see collections. *Works Reproduced*: Royal Academy, Arts Review, Observer, Tableaux, Galleries, Centerpoint (United Nations). *Address*: 6 Bishops Ave., London N2 0AN. *Email*: naomialexander@hotmail.com *Website*. www.naomialexander.com *Signs work*: "Naomi Alexander."

ALEXANDER, Steven, BA, PhD. *Medium*: landscape and townscape in oils and watercolour, and pen & ink. *b*: Margate, 9 Dec 1951. *s of*: Chris Alexander, ARE, ARCA. *m*: Ann. one *s*. one *d*. *Educ*: Simon Langton Grammar School, Canterbury. *Studied*: Kings College, London. *Exhib*: RA Summer Exhbn, RSMA, NEAC, RBA, RWS Open Exhibition, WH Patterson: 'Venice in Peril' Exhibition. *Works in collections*: many private collections in UK, Europe and USA. *Works Reproduced*: Wapping Group of Artists website, and www.pochade.co.uk (interviews). *Recreations*: reading, travelling, writing. *Clubs*: Wapping Group of Artists (secretary), Farnham Arts Society. *Address*: 16, Kings Ride, Camberley, Surrey, GU15 4HX. *Email*: steven.alexander1@hotmail.com *Signs work*; 'STEVEN ALEXANDER'.

ALFORD, John, NDD, ATD, RBA, NEAC; painter in oil and water-colour; Director of Art, Shrewsbury School (retd. 1989). *b*: Tunbridge Wells, 14 Oct 1929. *s of*: Arthur William Alford. *m*: Jean. one *s*. two *d*. *Educ*: Reading School. *Studied*: Camberwell School of Art (1949-53, Gilbert Spencer, Richard Eurich, Bernard Dunstan). *Exhib*: RA, RWA, RBA, RSMA, NEAC; numerous one-man shows in England, S. Africa, France, Canada. *Works in collections*: At home and abroad, Reading A.G., Shropshire C.C. *Commissions*: several for the Royal Navy and Royal Canadian Navy. *Address*: 47 Porthill Rd., Shrewsbury, Shropshire SY3 8RN. *Signs work*: "John Alford.".

ALFORD, Michael, BA Hons; Agnes Reeve Memorial Prize; Green & Stone Prize; Lodi Mural Festival Prize. *Medium*: oil, acrylic, watercolour. *b*: Cookham, 15 Sep 1958. *s of*: Col. J.R. Alford. *m*: Marta Marie Maretich. one *d*. *Studied*: Durham University; Chelsea School of Art; Slade (part-time and extra mural). *Represented by*: Medici Gallery, Highgate Contemporary Art, Blackheath Gallery. *Exhib*: Duncan Campbell; Royal Society of Oil Painters; Chatto Gallery; Kings Road Gallery; Collins & Hastie; Highgate Fine Art; Blackheath Gallery; Panter & Hall; Norton Way Gallery, Letchworth, Medici Gallery. *Works in collections*: San Francisco Museum of Modern Art (Fort Mason). *Commissions*: Chelsea Town Hall; Harold Lancer Corporation; Princess Ayse Osmanoglu; Grenadier Guards; Royal Irish Regiment; Parachute Regiment. *Official Purchasers*: Hill & Knowlton; Grenadier Guards; Claridges; Langham Hotel; Royal Irish Regiment. *Recreations*: painting, walking. *Clubs*: Chelsea Art Society. *Address*: 127 Trentham St., London SW18. *Email*: info@michaelalford.co.uk *Website*: www.michaelalford.co.uk *Signs work*: 'MR' or 'M. Alford'.

ALLBROOK, Colin, RI, RSMA, SEA, SWAC; Awards: Excellence in Watercolour, RWA (three times); Turner Watercolour Award (RI); Cuneo Medal, SEA (twice); Royal Bath and West (twice). *Medium*: watercolour, oils. *b*: Barnet, 8 Mar 1954. *s of*: William P. Allbrook. *m*: Christine. *Partner*: Betty. two *s*. two *d*. *Educ*: Ashmole Secondary Modern. *Studied*: evening classes: St.Martin's School of Art. *Exhib*: RI, RWS, RSMA, RWA, ROI,

PS, SEA; Sunday Times Watercolour Competition; Lynn Painter Stainers Exhbn; Royal Bath & West; NRA Llewellyn Alexander. *Works in collections*: Daler Rowney; Burton Art Gallery & Museum; Marquis of Salisbury. *Publications*: Colin Allbrook's North Devon (Halsgrove, 2002). *Works Reproduced*: by Sally Mitchel Fine Arts. *Address*: Hollycot, Umberleigh, North Devon, EX37 9AS. *Email*: colin@allbrook.fsbusiness.co.uk *Signs work*: 'COLIN ALLBROOK'.

ALLEN, Ceri, 2:1 Diploma Painting, 1st Prize Cumbrian Open; AA2 2010 Residency, University of Cumbria; Residency Corpus Christi College, Oxford (2014); Residency St Petersburg (2014). *Medium*: oil, drawing, prints. *b*: Hethersgill, 4 Feb 1962. *Studied*: City & Guilds School of Art, Kennington. *Represented by*: Lake Artists Society; galleries in Cumbria. *Exhib*: Solo shows include: Castlegate Gallery, Cockermouth (1988); Sark Gallery, Hethersgill (1990, 1993); Upfront Gallery, Penrith (2006); Theatre by the Lake, Keswick (2008); Crown Gallery, Carlisle (2011). Group shows include: Lake Artist's Society (1987-); Stephen Ferris Gallery, Nashville, Tenn, USA (1988); Cotton's Atrium, London (1997); London Zoo (1999); Cumbria Institute for the Arts (2005); C-Art Open Studios, Cumbria (2011); Cumbrian Printmakers Collective (2011); AAF; Contemporary Fine Art, Eton; Bath Contemporary Art Fair; Keswick Museum & Art Gallery; London Art & Antiques Fair. *Works in collections*: Tullie House; Carlisle Museum & Art Gallery; St. Mary's Hospital, Paddington; Corpus Christi College, Oxford. *Commissions*: Lord Inglewood; Margaret Forster (novelist); Corpus Christie College, Oxford. *Principal Works*: 'Waterloo Station', Carlisle City Gallery Collection. *Address*: Quarry Grove, Hethersgill, Carlisle, CA6 6ES. *Email*: cmallen1@hotmail.co.uk *Website*: ceriallen.co.uk *Signs work*: "Ceri Allen".

ALLEN, David Frederick, CEngMICE (1970), RSMA (2006); Frank Herring Award (Pastel Society, 2002), Classic Boat magazine award (RSMA 2005), Conway Maritime Press Award (RSMA 2006); Professional Artist of the Year (SAA 2011); R K Burt Canson and Arches Award (RSMA 2013); Draughtsman and Chartered Civil Engineer. *Medium*: pastel and oil. *b*: Harrogate, 10 Mar 1945. *s of*: Nellie & George Frederick Allen. *m*: Diane. *Exhib*: Laing (1990-97), Walker Galleries (1995-2014), Pybus Fine Art (1998-2007), John Noott Galleries (2001-04), Pastel Society (1997, 98, 2002-05), Eton College, Royal Society of Marine Artists (1995-2013); Trattles and Geal (2007-2014); Staithes Gallery (2006-2014). *Works Reproduced*: A Celebration of Marine Art (Bounty Books), International Artist magazine, Leisure Painter magazine. *Recreations*: hill walking. *Clubs*: Fylingdales Group of Artists (elected 1998). *Address*: 2 Almsford Road, Harrogate, North Yorkshire, HG2 8EQ. *Email*: davidallenart@tiscali.co.uk *Website*: www.davidallenrsma.org.uk *Signs work*: "David Allen".

ALLEN, Guy Rupert Stafford, BA (Hons) Fine Art. *Medium*: prints, etchings. *b*: Norwich, 11 Aug 1987. *Studied*: Central St Martins School of Art; Chelsea School of Art (2007-08). *Represented by*: Grandy Art. *Exhib*: Royal Academy Summer Exhibition (2013, 2014); Affordable Art Fair: Hampstead (2011, 2012) / Battersea (2012, 2013, 2014); Grandy Art (2011-); Solo shows: Norfolk Forms, Wiverton Hall (2013), Grandy Art, London (2014). *Works in collections*: private/corporate. *Address*: Storm Cottage, Holt Road, Langham, Holt NR25 7DA. *Email*: info@guyallenart.com *Website*: www.guyallenart.com *Clubs*: Chelsea Arts Club. *Signs work*: "GUY ALLEN".

ALLEN, Joe, BA Hons, RA Post-Graduate Diploma. *Medium*: oil. *b*: 23 Aug 1955, Airdrie, Scotland. *s of*: Annie Campbell & Laurence Allen. *Partner*: Christine Henn. *Educ*: St. Margarets Secondary School, Airdrie, Scotland. *Studied*: Camberwell School of Arts and Crafts, St. Martin's School of Art, RA Schools, London. *Represented by*: Galerie ClaireFontaine, Luxembourg. *Exhib*: Luxembourg, Vienna, Munich, Cologne, Basel, Paris, all major art fairs in Europe and America since 1986; John Moors Liverpool exhbn, RA

Summer Show, Burlington Fine Art Gallery, London W1; Museum Schloss Moyland, 10 Years Work, Germany. *Works in collections*: Dom Museum, Trier, Germany; Schloss Moyland, Germany. *Publications*: numerous magazines and newspapers in Europe. *Works Reproduced*: catalogues and many websites; major fully illustrated catalogue of the Last Ten Years Work published by Museum Schloss Moyland, Germany. *Principal Works*: series of large 10x9ft paintings produced over last ten years. *Recreations*: playing guitar and piano, writing, reading. *Clubs*: Reynolds Club. *Misc*: works are inspired by French Art History and European & American literature. *Address*: 31 Mansfield Rd, London E11 2JN. *Signs work*: Joe Allen.

ALLEN, Martin John, BSc (Hons) 1991 (Horticulture); Royal Horticultural Society (RHS) Gold Medal (1999-Group, 1997, 1995); Society of Botanical Artists (SBA) - Certificate of Botanical Merit (1998, 1996); Chelsea Physic Garden Florilegium Society - Emeritus Fellow. *Medium*: watercolour. *b*: Sunderland, 22 Jun 1970. *Studied*: Nottingham University (1988-91). *Represented by*: Susan Frei Nathan www.sfnbotanicalart.com. *Exhib*: Forum Botanische Kunst (2014, 2010, 2009); Gallery 27, Cork Street, London (2007); Hortus, London (2001); Royal Horticultural Society, London (1999, 1997, 1995); SBA, London (1998, 1997, 1996). *Works in collections*: Shirley Sherwood Collection, Hunt Institute, Kunstammlung der Volksbank Offenburg. *Commissions*: Collectors' plate series (Autumn - 3 designs); Royal Horticultural Society Enterprises Ltd (1996-98). *Works Reproduced*: Pulsatilla Vernalis; Horse Chestnut. *Principal Works*: 'Seeing Potential' series. *Clubs*: Chelsea Physic Garden Florilegium Society, American Society of Botanical Artists. *Misc*: Consultant in native plant conservation and horticulture. *Address*: 4a Samaria Gardens, Middlesbrough, TS5 8DF. *Email*: paintings@martinjallen.com *Website*: www.martinjallen.com *Signs work*: "M J ALLEN", "MARTIN J ALLEN", or "MARTIN ALLEN".

ALLEN, Roger Michael, Cert.Ed. (Art); Derbyshire Open Art Exhibition Watercolour Prize (2003, 2008, 2012). *Medium*: oil, watercolour, drawing. *b*: Maltby, Yorkshire, 17 Oct 1951. *Educ*: Wellingborough Grammar School (1963-69). *Studied*: Trent Park College of Education (1970-73). *Exhib*: Buxton Museum & Art Gallery (solo, 2010); Royal Watercolour Society Open (2009/10/11/12); Royal Birmingham Society of Artists Open (2009); Royal Academy Summer Exhibition (1993, 2013); RWS/Sunday Times Watercolour Competition (2008, 2012, 2013); Royal Institute of Painters in Watercolours (2014). *Works in collections*: Derbyshire County Council; Wellingborough Borough Council; The Landmark Trust; Sir Paul Smith; private collections. *Official Purchasers*: Derbyshire County Council, Wellingborough Borough Council. *Recreations*: walking (between pubs). *Address*: Hoe Grange, Brassington, Matlock, Derbyshire, DE4 4HP. *Email*: roger@rogerallen.co.uk *Website*: www.rogerallen.co.uk *Signs work*: "Allen" (with date and title, on reverse of painting).

ALLISON, Jane, 1st Class BA Hons (1980), Slade Higher Dip. (1982); portrait painter in oil/pastel. *b*: Woking, 21 Mar 1959. *m*: John Tatchell Freeman. one *s*. *Educ*: Charterhouse. *Studied*: Chelsea School of Art (1977-80, Norman Blamey), Slade School of Fine Art (1980-82). *Exhib*: BP Portrait Award, Royal Library, Windsor Castle, St. Pancras Hospital, University of Surrey, Royal Society of Portrait Painters. *Works in collections*: Royal College of Surgeons, Edinburgh, University of Surrey, Royal Institute, Royal Library, Windsor Castle, Guys Hospital. *Commissions*: Sir George Edwards, OM, FRS, Lord Robens, Lord Mishcon, Sir Christopher Collet, Prof. P.S. Boulter, Lord Nugent, etc. Court of Examiners, Royal College of Surgeons, London, Prof. Nairn Wilson, President of the General Dental Council, Baroness Susan Greenfield. *Address*: 12 Sydney Rd., Guildford, Surrey GU1 3LJ. *Email*: jatatchell@aol.com *Signs work*: "Jane Allison."

ALLSWORTH JONES, Lucilla Teresa, Cert.FA (Oxon); painter in oil, water-colour, mixed media. *b*: Exmouth, 30 Jun 1949. divorced. *d of*: Lt. Col. L.A. Jones DSO MC.

one *s*. *Educ*: St David's Ursuline Convent, Brecon. *Studied*: Ruskin School of Fine Art and Drawing (1968-71). *Exhib*: many solo and mixed shows including Ashmolean Museum, Monaco Fine Arts Monte Carlo, Chapter Gallery Cardiff, Weatherall, Green & Smith, London, Osborne Studio Gallery, London, Julian Davies Gallery, San Diego, Louis C. Morten Gallery, Mexico City, Capriole Gallery, Virginia, Mall Galleries, Inst. of Contemporary Arts, Warwick Arts Trust Galleries, London. *Works in collections*: Royal Artillery and Royal Marines, Brecknock Museum UK, USA, Singapore, S. Africa, Holland, Spain and Ireland including those of Prince Kais al Said, His Royal Highness Prince Charles and Ravi Tikoo. *Commissions*: Royal Artillery, Royal Marines. *Publications*: Horse Breeding in Ireland, Horses, Hounds and Hunting Horns by Dr. Colin Lewis (Allen, 1980). *Official Purchasers*: Royal Marines and Royal Artillery. *Recreations*: Riding, reading, walking, theatre, music. *Address*: Dan-y-Parc, Llandefalle, Brecon, Powys LD3 0UN. *Email*: lucillajones@gmail.com *Website*: www.artistlucillajones.com *Signs work*: "L.T.J." or "Lucilla Jones." or "Lucilla Allsworth Jones".

ALLUM, Avis Elizabeth, BA Hons (Textile Design, Leeds), PG Dip. Textile Art, ATC Goldsmiths College. *Medium*: (now) painting/drawing, figurative work. *b*: London, 27 Nov 1951. one *s*. *Studied*: Leeds University, Goldsmiths College, St. Ives School of Painting. *Exhib*: Mariners Gallery, St. Ives, St. Ives Society of Artists, Truro Museum, Helston Museum, Lizard Art Group. *Works in collections*: private. *Clubs*: St. Ives Society of Artists. *Misc*: costume designer. *Address*: Boderwennack Farm, Wendron, Helston, TR13 0NA. *Email*: avis@wendron.freeserve.co.uk *Website*: www.avisallum.com

ALLWRIGHT, Peter James, *Medium*: oil. *b*: Shoreham by Sea, 2 Nov 1958. *m*: Mandy Allwright. two *s*. *Studied*: self taught artist. *Represented by*: Cloud Gallery, Worthing, Brighton, Chester. *Exhib*: one man show at Ardington Hotel, Worthing. With ABNA at Delamore House, Devon and Mariners Gallery, St. Ives Society of Artists, Cornwall. *Works in collections*: Windlesham House School. *Commissions*: numerous. *Works Reproduced*: Limited Edition prints. *Clubs*: Association of British Naive Artists (ABNA). *Address*: 10 Lancaster Road, Goring by Sea, West Sussex BN12 4BP. *Email*: p.allwright@btinternet.com *Website*: www.peterallwright.com *Signs work*: "PETER ALLWRIGHT".

ALSOP, Roger Fleetwood, SGFA (1991); painter in water-colour, crayon, oil. *b*: Skipton, 1946. *s of*: Alan Alsop, accountant. *Educ*: Queen's Boys' Sec. Mod., Wisbech. *Studied*: Cambridge School of Art (1966-72). *Exhib*: Amalgam Gallery, Barnes, Roy Miles Gallery, Zella Nine Gallery, Old Fire Engine House, Ely. *Commissions*: Medici Soc., Mercedes-Benz, Right Now magazine. *Address*: 17 Cardwell Road, London N7 0NL. *Signs work*: "Roger Alsop.".

ALSOP, William, OBE (2000), RA (2000), Dip-ING (1996), AA DIP (1973), ARB (1978), RIBA (1978); many prizes and awards from 1971 to present, including: Toronto Architecture and Urban Design Award (2005), AJ/Bovis Lend Lease Award for Architecture (2003, 2004). *b*: 12 Dec 1947. *Exhib*: Many UK and overseas exhibitions since 1969, including MoMA New York (2005), Venice Biennale (2000, 2002, 2004), Urbis, Manchester (2005), Sir John Soame Museum, London (2002). *Publications*: Selected publications: 'Supercity' (Urbis, 2004), 'Bruce McLean and Will Alsop' (Wiley Academy, 2002), 'Will Alsop, Book 1 (2001) & Book 2 (2002) (Laurence King Publishing). *Misc*: tutor of Sculpture, Central St.Martins College of Art & Design, London, for several years. *Address*: Parkgate Studio, 41 Parkgate Road, London SW11 4NP. *Website*: www.alsoparchitects.com

ALTENBURGER, Ekkehard, *Medium*: sculpture. *b*: Waldshut, Germany, 9 Nov 1966. *s of*: Peter Altenburger. one *s*. *Educ*: apprentice stonemason. *Studied*: Hochschule für Kuenste, Bremen (Dip-Akad); Edinburgh College of Art; Chelsea College of Art (MA). *Exhib*: 1996 - Richard Demarco, Edinburgh; 1999 - Cambridge Darkroom Gallery; 1999 - Goethe Institute, London; 2000 - Kunsthalle Bremen (Germany); 2001 - Goethe Institute,

Salvador, Brazil; 2001 - Jerwood Sculpture Prize, London; 2002 - Le Confort Moderne, Poitier, France; 2002 - APT Gallery, London; 2005 - Sculpturespace Utica (USA). *Works in collections*: Jerwood Collection, Museu Municipal Caldas da Rahina, Poland; Bridcisso Sculpture Park (Italy); Eglisan Sculpture Trail (Swiss). *Commissions*: 2007 - Flühli, Switzerland; 2007/8 - "Negative Fall" Westminster, London; 2007 - Maidstone, Kent; 2006 - Chelsea and Westminster Hospital; 2004 - Brighton & Hove. *Publications*: 1997 - Schottland Bieder; 2001 - Jerwood Sculpture Prize; 2001 - Flash Art; 2002 - Corporate Mentality, by Alexandra Mir. *Address*: Apt-Studios, 6 Creekside, London SE8 4SA. *Email*: info@altenburger.org.uk *Website*: www.altenburger.org.uk *Signs work*: "E. Altenburger".

AMBRUS, Victor Gyozo Laszio, ARCA (1960), RE (1973), FRSA (1978); Prizes: R.A. Arts' Club Prize (1996) Summer Exhbn.; P.S. Prize (1995); Daler Rowney Prize; World Wildlife Prize (1994); Mall Galleries; Library Assoc., Kate Greenaway Gold Medal (1966 and 1975); book illustrator, graphic designer; visiting lecturer, Graphic Design. *b*:Budapest, 19 Aug 1935. *s of*: Gyozo Ambrus, Dipl. Eng. of Chemistry. *m*: Glenys Rosemary, ARCA. two *s*. *Educ*: St. Imre Grammar School, Budapest. *Studied*: Hungarian Academy of Fine Art, Budapest; R.C.A., London. *Exhib*: R.A., R.E., Biennale: Bratislava; Bologna, Italy, Belgium, Japan, Belgrade, New York. *Works in collections*: University of Southern Mississippi, U.S.A.; Library of Congress, U.S.A.; O.U.P., London. *Publications*: The Royal Navy, British Army, Royal Air Force, Merchant Navy, Three Poor Tailors, Brave Soldier Janos, The Little Cockerell, The Sultan's Bath, Hot Water for Boris, Country Wedding, Mishka, Horses in Battle, Under the Double Eagle, O.U.P.: Dracula (1980), Dracula's Bedtime Storybook (1982), and Blackbeard (1983) author and illustrator. *Address*: 52 Crooksbury Rd., Farnham, Surrey GU10 1QB. *Signs work*: "V.G. Ambrus."

AMERY, Shenda, ARBS (1984); sculptor in bronze; Council mem. RBS. *b*: England, 1937. *d of*: William Garrett. *m*: Sheikh Nezam Khazal. two *s*. *Educ*: Municipal College, Southend-on-Sea (chemistry). *Exhib*: RA, Paris Salon, Mall Galleries, Locus Gallery, Osbourne Studio Gallery, Orangery, Holland Pk., Tehran, Iran, Dorman Museum, Middlesborough, Scottsdale, Ariz. *Commissions*: Portrait bust: John Major, Prime Minister, Baroness Thatcher, Prime Minister, Dr. Lee, President Roh Tae Woo, S. Korea, Baroness Betty Boothroyd, Cherie Booth Blair, Robin Cook, M.P., David Blunkett, M.P., Dame Felicity Lott, opera singer, King Hussein and Queen Noor of Jordan. *Clubs*: Arts. *Address*: 25a Edith Grove, London SW10 0LB. *Signs work*: "Shenda Amery."

ANDERSON, Douglas Hardinge, RP; portrait painter and wildlife artist in oils. *Medium*: oil, pen & ink. *b*: 8 Aug 1934. *m*: Veronica née Markes. one *s*. two *d*. *Studied*: under Pietro Annigoni in Florence. *Exhib*: RP, RA Paintings in private collections worldwide. *Works Reproduced*: many wildlife paintings. *Address*: Luthy, Recess, Co.Galway, Eire. *Signs work*: "Douglas Anderson."

ANDERSON, James, BA; East of England art show Under-30 award (1993); printmaker, painter, writer, teacher. *b*: Cambridge, 3 Mar 1965. *Educ*: Worcester College, Oxford. *Studied*: Central School of Art and Design. *Represented by*: Eagle Gallery. *Exhib*: mixed and solo shows in Oxford, Bristol, London, Svendborg Denmark, Lvov Ukraine. *Works in collections*: Museum of History of Religion, Lvov, Ukraine. *Address*: 18c Digby Cres., London N4 2HR. *Signs work*: "J.W. ANDERSON."

ANDERSON, Jennifer, BA (Hons) Fine Art (painting), Duncan Jordanstone College of Art (Dundee); The Ewan Mitchel Painting Prize; The HSBC Management Investment Award for Artists under 35; The Arts Club Prize. *Medium*: painter in oil. *b*: Glasgow, 24 Oct 1975. *d of*: Anne Anderson (artist). *m*: Patrick Gorevan. *Studied*: Duncan of Jordanstone College of Art (Dundee). *Represented by*: Maclean Fine Art, 10 Neville St., London SW7 3AR. *Exhib*: 2 solo shows in Glasgow (The Gate House Gallery), two in London (McLean Fine Art), RSA, RGI, Royal Society of Portrait Painters, BP Portrait Award, The

British Art Fair, The Noble and Grossart Painting Prize, The National Portrait Gallery. *Commissions*: portraits of Mervyn Rolfe, Lord Provost of Dundee, Dr. Ian Graham-Bryce, principal of Dundee University, Mr Wilson Sutherland, Acting Warden, New College, Oxford. *Address*: 107 Hyndland Rd, Glasgow, G12 9JD. *Email*: janderson@hotmail.com *Website*: www.jennifer-anderson.co.uk *Signs work*: 'JA'.

ANDERSON, Wendy, MA; artist; visiting lecturer, Central/St. Martin's School of Art. *b*: Elgin, Scotland, 10 Feb 1961. *Studied*: Gray's School of Art (1979-83), Birmingham Polytechnic (1983-84). *Represented by*: Eagle Gallery. *Exhib*: 'British Art' Eritrea, Eagle Gallery; 'Self-Contained', The Field Institute, Dusseldorf. *Works in collections*: Arthur Andersen, The Economist, Warwickshire Museum. *Commissions*: Scottish Touring Exhbns. Consortium - Touring Exhbn. (1999-2002). *Publications*: 'Artists Now'; author: Education Guides for R.A. 'Sensation' and 'Joseph Beuys'. *Clubs*: London Group (member). *Address*: 19 Arrow Rd., London E3 3HE.

ANDREW, Keith, RCA (1981); artist, painter/printmaker in water-colour, tempera, etching; elected VP Royal Cambrian Academy (1993). *b*: London, 26 Jan 1947. *s of*: John Albert Andrew, shopkeeper. *m*: Rosemary. two *s*. *Educ*: Picardy Secondary, Erith, Kent. *Studied*: Ravensbourne College of Art and Design (1963-67, Mike Tyzack, John Sturgess). *Exhib*: R.A. Summer Exhbn. (1981), Mostyn A.G., Llandudno, Oriel Cardiff (1982), Bangor A.G. (1982), Aberystwyth Arts Centre (1982), Williamson A.G., Birkenhead (1982), National Eisteddfod Swansea (1982) and Anglesey (1983), Oriel Mold (1983), Tegfryn Gallery, Anglesey (1983); group exhbn. 'Through Artists Eyes'. *Works in collections*: National Library of Wales, Contemporary Art Soc. for Wales, University of Wales, Amoco, Ocean Transport, British Gypsum, Milk Marketing Board. *Address*: Gwyndy Bach, Llandrygarn, Tynlon P.O., Holyhead, Anglesey LL65 3AJ, Wales. *Signs work*: "Keith Andrew."

ANDREWS, Carole, SBA; Founder Presidents Hon. Award SBA (1995); professional artist in water-colour; tutor for mid-Surrey Educ. *b*: Worcester Park, Surrey, 13 Jan 1940. *m*: Peter Leonard. two *d*. *Studied*: Sutton College of Liberal Arts (Philip Meninsky, Ken Bates). *Exhib*: Mall Galleries (1983-86), Westminster Central Hall (1986-2002), The Guildhall, London, Alexandra Palace, Turner A.G., Denver, U.S.A., Christie-Wild, Fifth Ave New York. Work in private collections. *Works Reproduced*: Limited edn. and volume prints, illustration for Coalport and Wedgwood porcelain. *Address*: 129 Chapel Way, Epsom Downs, Epsom, Surrey KT18 5TB. *Email*: carole@carol-andrews.co.uk *Website*: www.carole-andrews.co.uk *Signs work*: "Carole Andrews S.B.A.".

ANDREWS, Marcia Tricker, life member IAA; painter in oils. *b*: London, 1923. *d of*: Walter James Tricker. *m*: Edward Andrews (decd). one *s*. one *d*. *Educ*: St. Andrews, London; New City, London, etc. *Exhib*: London and provinces; Mexico, France, Spain, U.S.A. *Works in collections*: University of Surrey; Medway Council Library Loan Service; private collections at home and abroad. *Principle Works*: Life; Man; Religion. *Recreations*: Reading - history, travel, poetry, biographies. *Address*: 40 Robin Hood La., Walderslade, Chatham, Kent ME5 9LD. *Signs work*: "M. ANDREWS," "M. Andrews" or "M.A.".

ANGELINI, Cristiana, DipFA (1955); Laing Exhbn First Prize for London and South-East (1990); Long Service in Education Award, Bexley Council (2007). *Medium*: oil, drawing, pastels. *b*: Italy, 6 Jun 1937. *d of*: Giovanni Poletti.- Conte di Montecassiano. *m*: Alfred Angelini. three *d*. *Studied*: Carrara School of Art, and Florence (1951-54/5). *Exhib*: RA Summer Show (1997, 1998); Mall Galleries (1976-77, 1988, 2002-05-07), Duncan Campbell Gallery (2008), several London Galleries, solo shows, the most recent being Hall Place and Gardens, Bexley Heritage Trust (2004); over 30 mixed shows since 1976. *Works in collections*: private collections UK, USA, Italy. *Commissions*: several still-life and portrait. *Publications*: The Guardian (1992); The Art of Drawing and Painting (Eagle Moss Ltd.), The Drawing and Painting Course (Amber Books, 1996); La Vie magazine (2000), Artists and Illustrators (2004), Woodhasterne UK Greeting Card 'Sunflowers', The Dictionary of Artists in Britain Since 1945 by David Buckman; Thirty Fifth edition of Dictionary of International Biography; The World Who's Who of Women; Mall Galleries "Critic's Choice" (2013). *Works Reproduced*: several works reproduced in books and magazines. *Recreations*: classical music, opera. *Misc*: 1989-92, part-time lecturer ILEA, 1985-2007 part-time lecturer Bexley College AE. *Address*: 12 Prior Street, Greenwich, London SE10 8SF. *Website*: www.blueforce.demon.co.uk/cristiana.angelini *Signs work*: with monogram of 'CA', or 'Cristiana Angelini'.

ANGUS, Michael Graham, *Medium*: oil, watercolour, drawing. *b*: 1 Dec 1947, Kingston. *Studied*: Kingston School of Art. *Exhib*: RA; local exhibitions. *Works in collections*: private collections *Address*: 27 St.Vincent Road, Walton on Thames, Surrey KT12 1PA.

ANNAND, David, sculptor in clay, bronze resin, bronze, mixed media; Awards: Royal Scottish Academy: Latimer (1976), Benno Schotz (1978), Ireland Alloys (1982); Sir Otto Beit medal, R.B.A. (1987). *b*: Insch, Aberdeenshire, 30 Jan 1948. *s of*: J.S. Annand, bank manager (decd.). *m*: Jean. one *s*. one *d*. *Educ*: Perth Academy. *Studied*: Duncan of Jordanstone College of Art, Dundee (Scott Sutherlands). *Exhib*: Royal Scottish Academy, Open Eye, Edinburgh, etc. *Works in collections*: throughout the world, including Edinburgh, Dundee, Perth, Canberra, Wisconsin, Hong Kong. *Commissions*: "Deer Leap" Dundee Technology Pk.; "Man Feeding Seagulls" Glasgow Gdn. Festival; "Grey Heron" Edinburgh Botanic Gdns.; "Cranes" British High Commission Hong Kong; "Naeday Sae Dark", Perth; "Civic Pride" four life-size lions on pillars of steel, Barnet, London. *Address*: Pigscrave Cottage, The Wynd, Kilmany Cupar, Fife KY15 4PU. *Signs work*: "David A. Annand," a tiny frog on a lily leaf.

ANNEAR, Jeremy, DAAD Scholarship, Germany; Atelierhaus Worpswede, Kreissparkasse, Bremen, Germany. *Medium*: oil, watercolour, mixed, print, construction. *b*: Exeter, 18 Feb 1949. *s of*: Ralph and Joyce Annear. *m*: Judy Buxton. two *s*. three *d*. *Studied*: Shebbear College, Exeter College of Art, Rolle College. *Exhib*: one person and mixed shows in Germany, UK, France, Holland and Australia. *Works in collections*: Lazard Bros, Ionian Trust, London University, Deutsch Bank. *Publications*: Catching the Wave by Tom Cross (Halsgrove Press, 2003); exhbns catalogues 1997, 98, 2000, 01, 02; Drawing Towards the End of the Century, NSA (1996); Innovators and Followers by Peter Davies (Bakehouse Publications 1994); Cat Essays by Norbert Lynton, John Russell Taylor, Rachel Barns. *Works Reproduced*: numerous. *Misc*: Artist/Director of Artsound.co.uk, working with contemporary classical musicians and the composer Jim Aitchison. *Address*: Chapel House, Garras, Helston, Cornwall, TR12 6LN. *Email*: jeremyannear@btinternet.com

ANNESLEY, David Robert Ewart, FRBS (1994); sculptor in welded steel; Senior lecturer, St. Martin's School of Art (1975-95). *Medium*: welded steel. *b*: London. divorced. two *s*. one *d*. *Studied*: St. Martin's School of Art (1958-62, Anthony Caro, Frank Martin). *Represented by*: Wilfred Cass. Sculpture at Goodwood. *Exhib*: Waddington (1966, 1968), Poindexter Gallery, N.Y. (1966, 1968), Anderson O'Day (1989). *Works in collections*: Tate Gallery, Arts Council, British Council, MoMA New York, etc. *Commissions*: Peterborough, Orton Centre, Royal Hampshire County Hospital. *Address*: 80 North View Rd., London N8 7LL. *Signs work*: "David Annesley.".

ANNFIELD, Jill. *Medium*: acrylic. *b*: Hereford. *m*: Peter de Vere Moss. one *d*. *Studied*: Hereford School of Art; St.Martins School of Art; Chelsea School of Art. *Exhib*: Crane Kalman; New Grafton; Llewellyn Alexander; Ainscough Gallery; Chelsea Art Society exhbns, The Russell Gallery, SW15, Peers Feetham Gallery, Rowley Contemporary Art Winchester; Jane Fuerst Gallery, Alresford; RA Summer Exhibition. *Works in collections*: internationally. *Commissions*: portraits: Edgar Bronfman Jnr.; Hume Shawcross; Philip, Lord Netherdene; Dr. Xanthe Moss; Naomi Ruddock; Mrs. Suzannah Franklyn. *Works Reproduced*: Fashion drawings in Vogue, Daily Telegraph, Daily Mail etc. *Recreations*:

travel. *Clubs*: Chelsea Arts Club. *Email*: jillannfield@hotmail.com. *Website*: www.annfieldharris.com. *Signs work*: 'J.A.'.

ANSELL, Amanda Louise, BA Hons Fine Art Painting; MFA Painting. *Medium*: oil. *b*: Sudbury, Suffolk, 29 May 1976. *d of*: Roger & Pauline Ansell. *Studied*: Norwich School of Art and Design (1995-1998), Slade School of Fine Art, UCL, London (1998-2000). *Exhib*: Waterfront Gallery, Ipswich (2014, 2011); Eastern Open, King's Lynn (2013, 2007); RA Summer Exhibition (2012, 2009, 2002, 2001); New Blood Art, Crane Mews, Middx (2009); Artswat, Sway, Hants (2008); Halesworth Gallery, Sufolk (2008); Artist Space, Firstsite, Essex (2006); Kettle's Yard, Cambridge (2006); Vertigo, London (2003, 2002, 2000); Business Design Centre, London (2001, 2000); The Paper Bag Factory, London (1999). *Clubs*: Paint Club East. *Address*: 3 St.Andrews Rd, Gt. Cornard, Sudbury, Suffolk, CO10 0DB. *Email*: amandaansell60@hotmail.com *Website*: www.amandaansell.co.uk *Signs work*: "Amanda Ansell".

ANTONIOU, Andrew, RE; BA, MA Printmaking. *Medium*: etching, drawing, painting. *b*: London, 22 Jun 1951. *m*: Marilyn Puschak. *Studied*: Harrow School of Art, Central School of Art (MA), Winchester School of Art (BA). *Represented by*: Australian Galleries. *Exhib*: Bankside Gallery, London; Sydney, Melbourne, Canberra. *Works in collections*: Art Gallery of NSW; National Gallery of Australia; Ashmolean Museum, Oxford; Microsoft, USA; Canberra Museum, Australia; Larnaca Council, Cyprus. *Publications*: 'An Appreciation of Andrew Antoniou' by Rogar MacDonald (Australian Galleries Press). *Misc*: teaches renowned workshop 'Drawing on Yourself'. *Address*: 1 Buckland Street, Mollymook, NSW 2539, Australia. *Email*: ant51@aapt.net.au *Website*: www.antoniou.com.au *Signs work*: 'A.Antoniou'.

ANTONSEN, Sylvia, NDD (1957), ATD (1958). *Medium*: acrylic painting. *b*: Bournemouth, 30 Mar 1937. two *s*. one *d*. *Educ*: King Alfred School, Plou.Schleswig-Holstein, Germany. *Studied*: Bournemouth College of Art (1953-58). *Exhib*: mixed shows from 1993 onwards: Bow House Gallery, Barnet; Thompson's Galleries - Aldeburgh and London; Fountain Fine Art, Llandeilo; Beatrice Royal, Eastleigh; Open Eye, Edinburgh; Anthony Hepworth, Bath (solo show 1997); Cambridge Contemporary Art (solo show 2004); The Leith Gallery, Edinburgh; Red Rag Gallery (solo show 2007). *Works in collections*: private collection of Women's Art; Norwich Union Collection. *Commissions*: many. *Address*: 3 St. Andrews Road, Deal, Kent CT14 6AX. *Email*: antonsenpaintings@yahoo.co.uk *Signs work*: "SYLVIA ANTONSEN".

ap RHYS PRYCE, Vivien Mary, FRBS; sculptor in modelling clay and wax for bronze. *b*: Woking, 1 Nov 1937. *d of*: Brig. M. H. Ap Rhys Pryce. *Educ*: Claremont School, Esher, Surrey. *Studied*: City and Guilds of London Art School. *Exhib*: RA, RWA, Jonathan Poole Gallery, London, and various provincial galleries. *Works in collections*: National Gallery of New Zealand, Wellington, University of Exeter (water sculpture), Nymans Gdns., Handcross, Sussex (fountain). *Commissions*: War memorial at Royal Wotton Bassett. *Address*: 3 Leighton Home Farm Court, Wellhead Lane, Westbury, Wiltshire, BA13 3PT. *Signs work*: Impress of signet ring (Lion's head).

APPLEYARD, Caroline Jane, ABNA. *Medium*: acrylics, oil, prints. *b*: Sheffield, 14 Sep 1966. *m*: Chris Housley. *Exhib*: Turnstone Gallery, Whitby (2006-2014); Mayne Gallery, Kingsbridge (2007-2014); Church Farm Gallery, Baslow (2005-2014); Cloud Gallery, Brighton (2014); Waterfront Gallery, Stromness (2009-2014); Little Picture Gallery, Mousehole (2010-2014); Gallery 49, Bridglinton (2013-2014). *Commissions*: Handelsbanken, France Magazine, Yorkshire Life & Derbyshire Life magazines, Sheffield Childrens' Hospital. *Clubs*: ABNA. Misc: Also paints underwater, in scuba gear, using oils. *Address*: 66 Church Street North, Old Whittington, Chesterfield S41 9QW. *Email*: appleyard.art@hotmail.com *Website*: www.appleyard-art.co.uk *Signs work*: "C J Appleyard".

ARCHER, Nicholas Lloyd, RP; BA (Hons), Post Graduate Diploma (RA Schools); 1st Prize Hunting Art Prizes (2002). *Medium*: painting (oil on canvas), watercolour, drawing. *b*: Yorkshire, 30 Jun 1963. *s of*: Alec and Beryl Archer. *m*: Jenny Pockley. one *d*. *Educ*: Leeds Polytechnic (1983-85). *Studied*: RA Schools (1996-99). *Represented by*: Sarah Myerscough Fine Art, London. *Exhib*: Sarah Myerscough Fine Art (2001, 2002, 2004), Beaux Arts Bath (2004), Gibsone Jessop Gallery, Toronto, Canada (2005); Jerwood Drawing Prize (2003); BP Portrait Award, NPG (1998, 1999, 2002, 2004). *Works in collections*: London Business School. *Commissions*: The Mill Film Production Co.; many portrait commissions. *Publications*: 'Forever England' catalogue foreword - Martin Gayford. *Works Reproduced*: BP Portrait Award Catalogue (1999, 2002). *Address*: c/o Sarah Myerscough Fine Art. 15-16 Brooks Mews, London W1K 4DS. *Email*: nicholas@archerart.fsnet.co.uk *Website*: www.nicholasarcher.com *Signs work*: 'Archer'.

ARCHER, Patricia Margaret Alice, PhD, DipFA, ATD, FMAA, Hon. FIMI; Head of Dept. of Medical Illustration, Guy's Hospital Medical School (1964-83). *b*: London. *d of*: Henry Patrick Archer. *Educ*: Convent Collegiate School, Sacred Heart of Mary, Chilton, Bucks. *Studied*: Ruskin School of Drawing, Slade School of Fine Art (1944-47), Inst. of Education, London (1947-48). *Exhib*: Medical Artists' Assoc., London (1952, 1964, 1970, 1989, 1993); one-man show, London Hospital (1955), Medical Picture Show, Science Museum (1978); "A Brush With Medicine", Barber-Surgeons' Hall, London (1993). *Publications*: illustrations for teaching the medical sciences. *Clubs*: Fellow, Medical Artists' Assoc., Hon. Sec. (1964-68), Chairman (1984-86) and (1990-93), Vice-Chairman (1986-1988) and (1993-1995), Archivist (1986-); Founder Associate, Inst. of Medical Illustrators (1968). *Address*: Rangemore, 30 Park Ave., Caterham, Surrey CR3 6AH. *Signs work*: "ARCHER."

ARCHER, Peter John, *Medium*: Oil, watercolour, drawing, gouache. *b*: Mitcham, Surrey, 21 Dec 1933. *m*: Mrs Karen Archer. two *s*. *Studied*: Wimbledon Art School (1948), Royal College of Art (1955). *Represented by*: Self. *Exhib*: Royal Academy; Mall Galleries (London and other galleries); France and Amsterdam; Auberterre and Jarozac; Bordeaux; Chalais; Vertoilac, Riberac, etc. *Works in collections*: Sultan of Iman; Brigadier Sir Ian Stuart and others; *Commissions*: 67 regimental British Commissions and one Canadian regt, plus other private commissions. *Works Reproduced*: All 67 paintings commissioned by the military have been printed. *Principal Works*: All my commissioned work from 1980 "Charge of the Light Brigade" to 2008 Afghanistan "Ambush at Nad-e Ali" are principal works. *Recreations*: House restoration, digging, hauling, sawing, banging etc. *Misc*: Apart from military work I have painted 7 portraits, landscape, townscapes, seascapes and illustration in Letraset and books. *Address*: 39 Drew Street, Brixham, Devon TQ5 9LA. *Signs work*: "Peter Archer"; "PETER ARCHER".

ARGYROS, Chrysoula, ARMS, MAA, Signature Member, Hilliard Society; MPSGS (DC); Higher Associate, Watercolour Society of South Africa. Many awards, from Honorable Mention to First Place in national and international exhibitions. *Medium*: oil, watercolour. *b*: Lemnos, Greece, 19 Mar 1954. *m*: George Argyros. two *s*. two *d*. *Exhib*: Exhibits worldwide, including UK; RMS, HS: USA: MPSGS, Miniature Art Society Florida. Miniatures in Mariposa, Northern California, Snow Goose Gallery and Seaside Art Gallery (Annual International Exhibitions). South Africa: Miniature Art Society of South Africa, Watercolour Society of South Africa, Rotary Exhibition, Hellenic Art Exhibition. 1st, 2nd, 3rd, 4th and 5th World Federation of Miniatures (Tazmania, London, Washington, Russia). *Works in collections*: Metropolis of the Greek Orthodox Church, Johannesburg; Bank of Athens, Johannesburg. *Commissions*: 9 portraits of past and present Archbishops of the Greek Orthodox Church; 6 paintings for calendars (1994, 1998); painting of former President F.W. de Klerk, which was presented to him in 1994; portrait, Adv. George Bizos (2008). *Publications*: Modern Masters in Miniature Art in America. *Works Reproduced*:

calendars (1994, 1998). *Recreations*: Theatre, dance, music. *Clubs*: Art Book Club, Lyceum Club of Greek Women, Highveld Forum, Panathanaiki Womens Association. *Address*: 9 St. Paul's Road, Houghton 2198, Johannesburg, South Africa. *Email*: chrysoula.argyros@gmail.com *Signs work*: "Chrysoula Argyros".

ARKINSTALL, Kevin, HSDAD, SHA; heraldic artist, calligrapher and illuminator. *Medium*: gouache, raised gilding on vellum, oil, watercolour, drawing, prints, sculpture. *b*: Shropshire, 8 May 1967. one *s.* two *d. Studied*: Reigate School of Art, under Anthony & Margaret Wood. *Works in collections*: HM The Queen, Windsor Castle, The Royal Horticultural Society, HM Govt UK. *Commissions*: Windsor Castle refurbishment, RHS, HM Govt Ministry of Justice; numerous civil and local authorities, private patrons. *Publications*: articles, essays in "The Heraldic Craftsman", Journal of the Society of Heraldic Arts. *Clubs*: Member of Heraldry Society; Calligraphy & Letter Arts Society. *Misc*: regularly runs courses in the Calligraphic, Heraldic and Manuscript Arts, including raised gilding techniques. *Address*: Corner Cottage, 10-12 Ridgeway, Ottery St.Mary, EX11 1DT. *Email*: k.arkinstall@hotmail.com *Website*: www.heraldic-arts.com *Signs work*: "K.ARKINSTALL".

ARKLESS, Lesley Graham, BA Hons; painter/illustrator in oil, gouache, water-colour; MA Museums and Galleries in Education (1993); Head of Education, Design Museum, London. *b*: Northumberland, 30 Jan 1956. *d of*: Norman G. & Joyce G. Arkless. *m*: John M. Butterworth. two *s.* one *d. Educ*: Church High School for Girls, Newcastle-upon-Tyne. *Studied*: West Surrey College of Art and Design (1974-78). *Exhib*: Ash Barn Gallery, Petersfield, St. Edmund's Art Centre, Salisbury, National Museum of Wales, 'Pictures for Schools', Astoria Theatre, London, Le Havre Municipal Gallery, Sanderson's Gallery, London. *Publications*: author and illustrator: 'What Stanley Knew' (Andersen Press, London). *Address*: 2 Nun's Walk, Winchester, Hants. *Signs work*: "LESLEY ARKLESS."

ARLOTT, Norman Arthur, SWLA; freelance wildlife illustrator in water-colour, author. *b*: 15 Nov 1947. *s of*: R.W.A. Arlott. *m*: Marie Ellen. one *s.* two *d. Educ*: Stoneham Boys School. *Exhib*: Annual SWLA, London, widely in UK, also USA. *Publications*: over 100, including 'Norman Arlott's Bird Paintings', and many Commonwealth stamp issues, i.e. Bahamas, Jamaica, British Virgin Islands. *Address*: Hill House, School Rd., Tilney St. Lawrence, Norfolk PE34 4RB. *Signs work*: "Norman Arlott."

ARMFIELD, Diana M. (Mrs. Bernard Dunstan), ARA (1989), RA (1991), Hon. Rt. RCA (Wales), MCSD, Hon. PS, Hon. NEAC., Hon. Rt. RWA, RWS; painter, retired textile and wallpaper designer; taught at Central School, and Byam Shaw Art School. *Medium*: oils, pastels, watercolours, prints. *b*: Ringwood, Hants, 1920. *d of*: Joseph Harold Armfield. *m*: Bernard Dunstan, R.A. three *s* (one decd). *Educ*: Bedales. *Studied*: Slade School, Central School. *Represented by*: Browse & Darby, London; Albany Gallery, Cardiff. *Exhib*: Festival of Britain; one-man shows, Browse and Darby, Albany Gall, USA, W. Australia etc.; RA with book launch, Holland, RA Summer Exhbns. (1966-), Royal Cambrian Academy, Bankside Gallery, Mall Galleries. *Works in collections*: V&A, RWA, Govt. picture collection, Contemporary Art Soc. (Wales), National Trust, Yale Centre (British Art), HRH Prince of Wales, Lancaster City Gallery, RA Diploma Collection, RWA Talbot Collection. *Commissions*: HRH Prince of Wales, Reuters, Contemporary Art Soc. for Wales, National Trust. *Publications*: The Art of Diana Armfield by Julian Halsby (David & Charles, 1995). Artist in Residence: Perth (1985), Jackson Hole, USA (1989). Mitchell Beazley - "Drawing", "Painting in Oils". Articles: 'The Artist', 'Leisure Painter'. *Official Purchasers*: Gov't Picture Collection. *Works Reproduced*: widespread. *Recreations* music, gardening. *Address*: 10 High Park Rd., Kew, Richmond, Surrey TW9 4BH. *Signs work*: "D.M.A."

ARMITAGE, Ann Susan, BA Hons Fine Art Painting; Elizabeth Foundation for the Arts, Travel Grant; Art Newspaper Award; Northbrook College Award. *Medium*: oil, watercolour.

b: Huddersfield, 10 Nov 1959. *Studied*: Grimsby School of Art (foundation, 1984); Canterbury College of Art (1984-87). *Represented by*: Lynne Strover Gallery, Merriscourt Gallery, Wykesham Gallery, East West Gallery, Langham Fine Art. *Exhib*: regularly with above. Gallery Urd, Bergen, Norway (solo); RA Summer Exhbns 1998, 1999, 2003; Discerning Eye (1995, 2003); Chichester Open (2001, 2002); Mall Galleries - RBA, NEAC, ROI, PS, Laing (2001); Singer & Friedlander (2001); Watercolour C21 RWS (1999, 2001); Royal Overseas League (1994); The Traveller, Wexas International (1995). *Works Reproduced*: Homes and Gardens magazine (May 1998); Art Review, Art for Under £1000 (1995) *Address*: Flat D, 6 Hardel Rise, London SW2 3DX. *Signs work*: "A.S.A."

ARMITAGE, Karen Marie. *Medium*: oil, watercolour, drawing, pastel. *b*: London. *m*: Mark Armitage. four *s*. *Studied*: Chelsea School of Art, Regent St. Polytechnic; 3 years portrait painting with Stanley Grimm (PPRP), Jason Bowyer. *Represented by*: William Paterson Gallery; Oliver Swann Gallery; Bridgeman Art Library since 1985. *Exhib*: RA (7 times) , RP (portraits, first time aged 17), Chelsea Art Society, RI, ROI, RWS, NEAC. *Works in collections*: many originals and reproductions. The Bridgeman Art Library since 1985. *Commissions*: through Oliver Swann Gallery, Bridgeman Art Library, Patterson Gallery, NEAC. *Publications*: Bridgeman Art Library. *Works Reproduced*: over 60 by Bridgeman Art Library; Oliver Swann Gallery, Patterson Gallery. *Recreations*: travel and painting, fishing, dogs, riding. *Clubs*: Chelsea Arts Club; Dover St. Arts Club. *Misc*: Studio Painting in own studio - some teaching. *Address*: Hurst Farm House, Wisborough Green, W.Sussex, RH14 0AH. *Signs work*: "Karen Armitage".

ARMITAGE, Paul, BA Fine Art, MFA Fine Art; Boise Travel Award. *Medium*: oil. *b*: Gillingham, Kent, 22 Mar 1953. *s of*: Roy Armitage. *Studied*: Gloucestershire College of Technology (BA), Reading University (MA). *Represented by*: Innocent Fine Art, Bristol. *Exhib*: generally in Cornwall and Oxfordshire; Affordable Art Fair (2001); Royal West of England Academy. *Works in collections*: Digital Computers. *Commissions*: Digital Computers. *Address*: Trevider Farm, St.Buryan, Penzance, Cornwall, TR19 6BP.

ARMITAGE, Sandra Wall, People's Choice, awards: SBA Annual Open Exhbn. (2006); Daler Rowney Award (Best Painting in Exhibition), SBA Annual Open (2006); SBA Certificate of Botanical Merit (CBM) 2008. *Medium*: water colour & mixed media. *b*: 25 Sep 1943. *m*: Paul Armitage. two *d*. *Educ*: Cheadle Hulme School. *Studied*: Manchester College of Art (1960-64) (Post Grad 1964-65). *Exhib*: SBA Annual Open Exhbn, Central Hall, Westminster (1998-2007); Heal's Gallery (joint shows, 1976-78); The Stable Gallery, Wandsworth (1978-79); Darlington Arts Centre (solo, 1980); Sevenoaks Wildlife Centre (1992-2000) & Florum (2002-2012); Palmengarten, Germany (2010-2012), Luton Hoo Walled Garden Annual Open Exhibition (2010, 2011, 2012). *Works in collections*: internationally. *Commissions*: Todan Co. Ltd., Japan (calendar 2006-2010); Tiffany's NY (1992-96), commissioned on their behalf by Sybil Connolly, International Designer. *Publications*: illustrations for: 'Decoupage-Painted Furniture' by Rubena Gregg (David & Charles); 'Irish Hands' by Sybil Connolly (Hearst); 'The Botanical Palette' (Harper Collins) *Official Purchasers*: Mr.K.Kowaguchi, President: Todan Co. Ltd., Japan (private collection) *Works Reproduced*: as calendars and greeting cards by Gordon Fraser Gallery, Hallmark Cards, Ling Design, Todan Co. Ltd., Japan. *Recreations*: gardening, *Misc*: Past President Rotary Club of Luton Someries (2006-07); exhibition curator for Luton Hoo Walled Garden & Publicity Director Society of Botanical Arts. *Address*: Common Farm, Luton Road, Chalton, Bedfordshire, LU4 9UH. *Email*: sandra@watercolourflowers.co.uk *Website*: www.watercolourflowers.co.uk *Signs work*: 'SANDRA WALL ARMITAGE'.

ARN or ARNEAL, Arthur Richard: see NEAL, Arthur Richard.

ARNOLD, June, PS, FCSD; SWAc; Intermediate NDD; DipAD 1st Class Hons (Interior Design); Dartmoor Artists Public Prize (1992, 1994, 1997); S.W. Academy Public Prize

(2003); Pastel Society, Frank Herring and David Sinfield Fine Art Award (2004); S.W. Academy Prize (2010). *Medium*: pastels, oils, acrylics. *b*: Halifax, 6 Mar 1944. *d of*: James Oliver Sykes. *m*: Christopher George Arnold. *Educ*: Horsham High School. *Studied*: West Sussex College of Art; Kingston College of Art. *Represented by*: Marine House at Beer; FBA Mall Galleries. *Exhib*: PS, SWA; Seymour Gallery, Totnes; Combe Farm Gallery, Dittisham; Wycombe Galleries, Stockbridge; Coves Quay Gallery, Salcombe; Marine House Gallery, Beer; Sarah Samuels Fine Paintings; Thomson's, Aldburgh; Picture Craft Gallery Norfolk; Gloss Gallery Exeter. *Works in collections*: private collections. *Commissions*: interiors, portraits. *Works Reproduced*: Limited edition cards. *Principal Works*: interiors, figurative. *Recreations*: travel, gardening, music (Classical), current affairs. *Address*: 24 Old Manor Close, Holne Close, Ashburton, Devon TQ13 7JF. *Email*: junearnold@tiscali.co.uk *Signs work*: 'June Arnold'.

ARNOLD, Phyllis Anne, RMS (1988), ARMS(1983), SM (1976-86), USWA(1982), PUSWA (1988-91), PUSM (1987-93), UWS (1984), HS (1985); Hunting Group finalist (1980, 1981, 1983), RMS Memorial Gold Bowl (1988); miniaturist. *Medium*: ink, gouache, acrylic and oils. *b*: Belfast, 1938. *d of*: David McDowell, engineer. *m*: Michael J. Arnold, C.Eng. two *s*. *Educ*: Victoria College, Wallace High School. *Studied*: self taught, entered Commercial Art Dept. Short Bros & Harland (1956-58). *Exhib*: SM, RMS, RA, USWA, HS, UWS, RUA. *Works in collections*: Ulster Museum, Belfast. *Commissions*: Ulster Television, Coalport Porcelain. *Works Reproduced*: Felix Rosensteil Widow & Sons. *Address*: Phyllis Arnold Studio, Deepwell House, Lowry Hill, Bangor, Co. Down, N. Ireland BT19 1BX. *Email*: artist@portraits-miniaturesandsilhouettes.com *Website*: www.portraits-miniaturesandsilhouettes.com *Signs work*: "P.A. ARNOLD".

ARNOTT, Ian, DA (Edin); DipTP (Edin); RSA, RIBA, FRIAS; Civic Trust Awards (10); RIBA Award (1); EAA Awards (2); Saltire Society Awards (2); RSA Gold Medal for Architecture. *Medium*: architecture: design and planning. *b*: Galashiels, 7 May 1929. *s of*: Henry & Margaret Arnott. *m*: Stella. one *d*. *Educ*: Galashiels Academy. *Studied*: School of Architecture; School of Town Planning; Edinburgh College of Art. *Exhib*: Royal Scottish Academy, Edinburgh; RIBA, London; RIAS, Edinburgh; Association of Consultant Architects, London; Civic Trust, London. *Works in collections*: 'Timeline': Diploma work, Royal Scottish Academy. *Commissions*: bespoke houses, housing, schools, hospitals/health buildings, theatre/cultural/recreation, commercial/leisure, urban masterplanning. *Publications*: work published in many periodicals and books. *Principal Works*: Saltire Court, Edinburgh; AEU HQ, London; Edinburgh Park; An Carn, Stornoway; The Rink, Gifford. *Recreations*: painting, travelling, music. *Clubs*: New Club, Edinburgh. *Address*: The Rink, Gifford, East Lothian, EH41 4JD. *Email*: iana@therink.fsbusiness.co.uk

AROM-HOBBS, Haika, BA (Hons) Fine Art. *Medium*: own handmade paper, collage and mixed media. *b*: Rishon-le-Zion, Israel, 1946. *d of*: Samuel Arom. *m*: Malcolm. one *d*. *Studied*: School for Applied Art, Tel Aviv (1960-65); Art Teacher Training (1965-67); Ravensbourne College of Art (1969-72). *Exhib*: RA Summer Exhibition (1992, 1995); Ben Uri Gallery (2001); Salon des Arts, London (2000, 2003, 2004); Harrow Contemporary Art (2003); West House, Pinner (2004). Solo exhibitions: St Raphael Gallery, London (1999), Fovea Gallery, London (2005). *Works in collections*: private collections in Israel, England & USA. *Publications*: 'Artist Now' Portfolio (supported by Arts Council). *Address*: 116 Shaftesbury Avenue, South Harrow, Middlesex, HA2 0PW. *Email*: haikaarom@hotmail.com *Signs work*: "H. Arom".

ARNUP, Sally, FRBS, ARCA (1954); sculptor in bronze. *b*: London, 15 Jul 1930. *d of*: L. Baynton-Williams. *m*: Mick Arnup, ARCA. two *s*. two *d*. *Studied*: Kingston School of Art (1943-50, H. Parker), Camberwell School of Art (1951, Dr. Vogel), Royal College of Art (1952-55, John Skeaping). *Exhib*: Tryon Gallery (1973, 1976, 1981), USA (1977, 1980, 1986, 1987), Drobak Norway (1976), Wexford Festival (1974, 1978, 1982, 1986), York

Festival (1969, 1976, 1978, 1980, 1984, 1988, 1992), Florence (1983), Edinburgh Festival (1988), Stamford Art Centre (1987, 1990), Holland & Holland (Paris, London 1994, 1995, 1997), Gainsborough's House, Suffolk (1998), Pyramid Gallery York ('01), Sabin Gallery London ('01, '04), Renishaw Hall Sheffield ('02), Blake Gallery York ('02, '05, '07, '11), Sinfield Gallery, Oxon (1998, '03), Bowes Museum ('10). *Works in collections*: HM The Queen, Burton Agnes, York A.G., Lord Halifax, Lord Middleton, York University. *Commissions*: Robert Fleming, Rowntree Trust, Hartrigg Oaks (1999), Hartlepool (2007), Prince Philip, Duke of Edinburgh (2000). *Principal Works*: William Wilberforce (2007). *Address*: Studios Holtby, Panman Lane, York YO19 5UA. *Website*: www.sallyarnup.co.uk *Signs work*: "ARNUP."

ASH, Lucy, BA (1977), BTechDist. (1995); painter in oils, ink & spray paint, digital artwork; designer; creative director of lucyash.com. *b*: London, 4 Feb 1955. *d of*: Michael and Dulcie Ash (née Orme). *Educ*: Millfield School, Somerset. *Studied*: Central St. Martins, Camberwell College of Art, South Thames College. *Exhib*: Heseltine Masco, Oztenzeki, Austin Desmond, London, Mokotoff, New York, On the Wall, London, RWA, Cork St. Fine Art, London, Heartbreak Gallery, London; William Road Gallery, London. *Works in collections*: private Collections, Bluedoor Ltd. *Commissions*: Bluedoor Ltd., Sony Radio Awards, Microsoft. *Publications*: 'A Taste of Astrology', pub. Alfred A Knopf, New York. (1988), written and illust.; 'The Astrological Cookbook', pub. Sainsbury (1993), written. *Recreations*: walking, swimming. *Clubs*: Chelsea Arts, Grouch Club. *Misc*: Multimedia Digital Artwork. *Address*: 54 Broxash Road, London SW11 6AB. *Email*: la@lucyash.com *Website*: www.lucyash.com *Signs Work*: "AsH" with line through centre joining the A and H, and an arch of dots above the S.

ASHBY, Derek Joseph, DA (Edin.); artist in oil painting and steel and aluminium; lecturer in drawing and painting, Gray's School of Art, Aberdeen. *b*: 24 Jun 1926. *s of*: Oswald Roy Ashby. *m*: Mairi Catriona. one *s*. one *d*. *Educ*: Oldham High School. *Studied*: Edinburgh College of Art (1948-51) under Gillies, Henderson, Blyth; RA Schools (1953-55) under Rushbury. *Exhib*: RSA, Aberdeen Artists, SSA. *Works in collections*: Scottish Arts Council. *Clubs*: A.A.S., S.S.A. *Address*: Old Invery, Auchattie, Banchory, Kincardineshire AB31 6PR. *Signs Work*: "Derek Ashby."

ASHCROFT, Phil, BA Hons Illustration, PGDip Illustration; Finalist, John Moores Painting Prize (2014); Finalist, Celeste Art Prize (2007); Daler Rowney and Liquitex Awards (1998); Royal Society of Art Travel Award to Hong Kong (1991). *Medium*: acrylic, drawing. *b*: Farnham, Surrey, 30 Jun 1970. *Partner*: Mayling To. one *s*. *Studied*: WSCAD, Farnham (Foundation, 1988-89); Harrow College of Art & Design (1989-92); St. Martin's College of Art & Design, London (1992-94). *Exhib*: Selected solo exhibitions: GTD, Edinburgh (2013); Margaret Harvey Gallery, UH Galleries, St. Albans (2006); EXIT, Hong Kong (2005); Deptford X, London (2001). Selected Group Exhibitions: Walker Art Gallery, Liverpool (2014); Blackall Studios, London (2012); Fishmarket Gallery, Nothampton (2011); Deptford X (2009); Concrete and Glass, London (2008); Schwartz Gallery, London (2008); The Collective Gallery (touring Edinburgh, The Lincoln Collection and g39 Cardiff, 2008-9); New Art Gallery, Walsall (2007-08). *Works in Collections*: Levis; New Art Gallery, Walsall; Royal Mail; Sony Archive; Private and corporate collections in Europe, Asia and America. *Commissions*: include: Godzilla (1954) theatrical release film poster, limited edition print and DVD for British Film institute (2005); PSP Presents Cut-Out, customisation project for Sony PSP/Peter Saville Design (2005); Poster and leaflet campaign, Amnesty International UK (1994). Publications: "Phil Ashcroft - Solar System Parameters 2005-2013" (hardback mongraph pub. Gamma Proforma, 2013). *Clubs*: Artist Member, Contemporary Art Society. *Address*: 35 Adagio Point, 1 Bridge Walk, London SE8 3FH. *Email*: info@philashcroft.com *Website*: www.philashcroft.com *Signs work*: "Phil Ashcroft".

ASHE, Faith: see WINTER, Faith

ASHER, James, artist in water-colour, oil, lithograph. *b*: Butler, Missouri, 14 Apr 1944. *s of*: Glenn William Asher. *m*: Joe Anna Arnett. one *s*. one *d*. *Educ*: Central Missouri University. *Studied*: The Art Center College of Design, Los Angeles, Calif. *Exhib*: Catto Gallery, London, Zaplin-Lampert Gallery, Santa Fe, NM, Artists of America, Denver (1991-1997), Gilcrease Museum, Royal Water-colour Soc., London (1992). *Works in collections*: Museum of Fine Arts, Santa Fe:*Publications*: Water-colour Magic (Summer, 1999). *Address*: P.O. Box 8022, Santa Fe, New Mexico 87504-8022, USA. *Signs Work*: "James Asher.".

ASHMAN, Malcolm Paul, RBA, ROI. *Medium*: oil, watercolour, drawing. *b*: Bath, 14 Jul 1957. *Educ*: Keynsham Grammar School. *Studied*: Somerset College of Art. *Represented by*: Brian Sinfield Gallery, Oxon; Denise Yapp Fine Art, Monmouth. *Exhib*: RA Summer Exhbn, RWA Bristol, Mall Galleries, NEAC, ROI, RBA, Victoria Gallery, Bath; Royal Society of Portrait Painters; Holbourne Museum Portrait Prize; Threadneedle, London. *Works in collections*: Wessex Collection, Longleat; Victoria Gallery, Bath, The Royal Bank of Scotland. *Commissions*: Dragon's World publishers 1988-96. *Publications*: 50 Wessex Artists, Evolver. *Clubs*: Bath Society of Artists. *Address*: Bath Artists' Studios, Upper Bristol Road, Bath, BA1 3AJ. *Email*: mail@malcolmashman.com *Website*: www.malcolmashman.co.uk *Signs work*: M.A.

ASHMAN, Margaret Christina Elizabeth, MA Oxon (Physics), Somerville College; MA Brighton (Printmaking and Professional Practice), BA Fine Art Hertfordshire; Julian Trevelyan Memorial Award 2004; University of Herts. Prizewinner 2003; International Print Prize, 3rd Guanlan Print Biennial 2011. *Medium*: printmaking. *b*: Northampton, 19 Sep 1959. *d of*: Patricia and Donald McPhie. *m*: Kevin Ashman. one *s*. three *d*. *Studied*: Universities of Brighton, Hertfordshire and Oxford (Somerville College). *Represented by*: Printroom, Bankside Gallery, Greenwich Printmakers. *Exhib*: Krakow Triennial (2009); Liege Biennial (2009); Guanlan, China (2007, 2009, 2011); Print Triennia Vienna (2010); Tokyo Prints (2012); Global Print, Douro (2013). *Works in collections*: Museum of Graphic Art, Split; Shenzen University; Guanlan Print Base; Ashmolean Museum; The Americas Biennial Exhibition of Contemporary Prints, Iowa; Guandong Museum of Art, China; Penang State Museum, Malaysia' V&A Museum; Kent Print Collection. *OfficialPurchasers*: Lovells, University of Hertfordshire, Citigroup, Art Therapies Centre London. *Works Reproduced*: Printmakers Secrets, A. Dyson 2009. *Principle Works*: A Time to Love, A Time to Mend, Maid of the Mist. *Misc*: member of Royal Society of Painter Printmakers; Chairman Printmakers Council. *Address*: 71 Great Russell Street, London WC1B 3BP. *Email*: margaretashman@btinternet.com *Website*: www.margaretashman.com *Signs Work*: "Margaret Ashman".

ASHMORE, Biba Victoria, DipAD; Awarded David Murray Studentship (1972) by RA. *Medium*: oil, watercolour, drawing. *b*: Trieste, 29 Nov 1952. *d of*: Mr NH & Mrs GM Ashmore. *Partner*: Mr S Campbell. *Educ*: The Town and Country School, London (1964-69). *Studied*: The Camden Arts Centre, London (1969-70), Camberwell School of Arts and Crafts (1970-74). *Exhib*: RA Summer Exhbn (1975, 1976, 1978, 1996, 1997); Mall Galleries (1973); London Group (1975); Llewellyn Alexander Gallery (2000); The Hunting Art Prizes at Royal College of Art (2001); Corpus Christie Church "Disparate Threads" (2009); Tate Library, Brixton (2010); Carnegie Library (2011). *Works in collections*: private. *Commissions*: portrait. *Official Purchasers*: RA/Harrison Weir Fund (1978) for RA Collection. *Recreations*: visiting exhibitions, cooking. *Address*: 134 Leander Road, London SW2 2LJ. *Email*: ashmorebiba@tiscali.co.uk *Signs work*: "Biba Ashmore" or "B.Ashmore" on the front of work, or at/on the back on canvas or stretcher.

ASQUITH, Rosalind Lucy, BA. *Medium*: cartoons/illustrations b & w and watercolour. *b*: Hove, Sussex. *m*: John Fordham. two *s*. *Studied*: Camberwell School of Art. *Represented* *by*: Jodie Hodge and United Agents, www.unitedagents.co.uk. *Exhib*: Drill Hall, Cartoon Art Trust, The Gallery, Brighton Arts Centre, Battersea Arts Centre, numerous travelling exhbns. *Works in collections*: private houses. Murals: York Cathedral, Bath Hafebutsoth Museum, Qatar Museum, Phillips Museum Oslo, Bucks County Museum, Aylesbury. *Publications*: over sixty books, Guardian, Observer, Times, Time Out, City Limits, She, etc. *Works Reproduced*: see publications. *Address*: 51 Muswell Avenue, London N10 2EH. *Email*: rosasquith@mac.com *Website*: www.rosasquith.com *Signs work*: Ros Asquith.

ASTBURY, Paul, MA Hons RCA Dip AD; Awards: Arts Council 1977, Craft Council 1984, British Council 1997. *Medium*: oil, sculpture. *b*: Hough, Cheshire, 11 Dec 1945. *s of*: Elizabeth & John Thomas Astbury. *m*: Lesley. two *s*. one *d*. *Studied*: Stoke-on-Trent College of Art (1961-68); Royal College of Art (1968-71). *Exhib*: Victoria & Albert Museum, Yorkshire Sculpture Park, Museum of Modern Art Oxford, Shigoraki Museum, Japan, Ulster Museum Belfast, Für Angewandekunst, Vienna, Röhsska Museum, Goteborg, Sweden, Musee Ariana Geneva, Aberystwyth Arts Centre; Museum of Fine Arts, Houston, USA. *Works in collections*: V&A, Museum of Fine Arts, Houston, USA, Ulster Museum, Shigaraki Museum, Japan, Rohss Museum, Sweden, York Museums Trust, Aberystwyth Art Centre, Crafts Council Collection, Arizona State Uni Art Museum, USA, North Western Arts Association, Portsmouth Museum and Art Gallery, Mint Museum USA plus private collections. *Publications*: 'Images in Clay Sculpture' Charlotte Speight (Harper & Row 1983), 'Post Modern Ceramics' Mark Del Vecchio (Thames & Hudson 2002); 'Dictionary of International Biography' - 35th Edition (Melrose Press, 2009); 'Postmodernism, Style and Subversion, 1970-1990' (V&A Press, 2011). *Principal Works*: 'Jacket' & 'Trousers', 'Tree in a Landscape', 'Wendy House, Dragon & Machine', 'T.V. Dish', 'Box'. *Address*: 62 Sedgeford Road, Shepherds Bush, London W12 0NB. *Email*: pja_62@hotmail.com *Website*: www.paul-astbury.com *Signs work*: "P.J.A" , "PAUL ASTBURY" or "Astbury".

ATHERTON, Barry, NEAC, SSA; NDD, DA (Manc.) Dist. (1965), Leverhulme Scholarship (1965-66), RASCert. (1969); artist in mixed media; Lecturer in Fine Art, Glasgow School of Art 1973-2003. *b*: England, 1944. *m*: Linda. two *s*. *Studied*: Manchester College of Art and Design (Norman Adams), RA Schools (Edward Bawden). *Exhib*: solo shows: New Academy Gallery, London (1990, 1992, 1994, 1997, 1999, 2002), Mistral Galleries, London (1996), Art Gallery and Museum, Kelvingrove, Glasgow (2003), People's Palace, Glasgow (2007). *Works in collections*: Aberdeen A.G., University of Strathclyde, Glasgow Caledonian University, Paisley University, Glasgow Museums; also private and corporate collections, in U.K., Europe and USA. *Commissions*: University of Strathclyde, Glasgow Caledonian University, Paisley University, Alexon/Vogue, The Crown Estate Millennium Exhbn. *Publications*: 'Interview with the Artist', Pryle Behrman (Artline), 'Reflections in the Glass of History', Ray McKenzie. *Address*: 235 Nithsdale Rd., Glasgow G41 5PY. *Email*: atherton@ymail.com *Website*:www.athertonart.co.uk *Signs work*: no signature, identification on the back.

ATKIN, Ann Fawssett, NDD; Dip. Royal Academy of Arts. *Medium*: acrylic; clay. *b*: Lindfield, Sussex, 1937. *m*: Ron Atkin. two *s*. *Studied*: Brighton College of Art; Royal Academy Schools. *Exhib*: founded in 1979 The Gnome Reserve, Wild Flower Garden, Pixie Kiln and Gallery at West Purford in N. Devon; featured 70+ times on TV and numerous times on radio and in newspapers, magazines and books worldwide. Paintings in mixed and solo exhibitions, including the RA Summer Exhibition. *Works in collections*: Painting in the Dartington Hall Trust Collection; Paintings and limited edition prints in private collections in the UK, Republic of Ireland, France, Guernsey, Switzerland, Denmark, Spain, Holland, Germany, Finland, Austria, Luxembourg, Thailand, Tenerife, Barbados, Sweden, Dubai, Cyprus, South Africa, Australia, New Zealand, Canada and the USA. *Commissions*: many pottery landscape scenes with the people depicted as boy and girl pixies. *Recreations*: gardening, bird watching, walking. *Clubs*: The Reynolds Club. *Address*: Wild Flower

Studios, Abbots Bickington, N. Devon EX22 7LQ. *Email*: paintings@ann-fawssett-atkin.co.uk *Website*: www.ann-fawssett-atkin.co.uk www.ann-fawssett-atkin.com *Signs work*: "Ann Atkin; Ann Fawssett, Ann Fawssett Atkin".

ATKIN, Michael, DipAD, ATD. *Medium*: etcher/printmaker. *b*: Middlesbrough, 13 May 1952. *s of*: Roy Atkin. *Educ*: Middlesbrough Grammar School. *Studied*: Middlesbrough College of Art (1968-71); Maidstone College of Art (1971-74, DipAD); Liverpool University (1974-75, ATD). *Exhib*: 30 one-man exhibitions since 1975. Over 40 mixed exhibitions including: Ferens Exhibition, Hull (1977-2009); Fiac, Paris (1977-1980); Fylingdales Group (1995-2009); Jeunes Graveurs Anglais, Paris (1976, 1980, 1982, 1984); NEAC (1992-94); Scarborough Open (regularly from 1991). *Works in collections*: Leeds City Council, Teesside College of Art, London College of Printing, V&A, British Museum, Bibliotheque Nationale, Paris. *Publications*: 'The Scarborough Tragedy', 'Beggars Bridge', 'Blue' (Bracken Press, founded by Michael Atkin in 1974). *Official Purchasers*: V&A Museum, British Library, Beverley Art Gallery. *Clubs*: Printmakers Council, Secretary, The Fylingdales Group of Artists. *Address*: 'Byways', Low Street, Scalby, Scarborough, YO13 0QW. *Email*: mail@michaelatkin.co.uk *Website*: www.michaelatkin.co.uk *Signs work*: "MICHAEL ATKIN".

ATKIN, Ron, painter in water-colour and oil; Bronze and Silver medallist, RAS. *b*: Leics., 3 Feb 1938. *m*: Ann Fawssett-Atkin. two *s*. *Studied*: Loughborough College of Art (1954-57), RA Schools (1957-61). *Exhib*: regularly at R.A.; mixed shows: Roland, Browse and Delbanco. *Works in collections*: Lincoln College Oxford, Dartington Trust, Devon C.C. Schools Museum Service, Plymouth City Museum and A.G. Shortlisted for a Gulbenkian Printmakers award; featured in first and second edition of Dictionary of British Art Volume VI, 20th century painters and sculptors; also in Debrett's and Dictionary of Artists in Britain since 1945. *Publications*: 20 poems pub 2012 "Ten of the Best" ISBN 978-0-85781-216-2; The White Sea Scrolls ISBN 978-9572099-0-9; Virgin Gives Birth to a Fish with One Way ISBN 0-9538907-9-1. *Official Purchasers*: Plymouth City Museum & Art Gallery. *Works Reproduced*: in Apollo Mag, and in the above books. *Recreations*: walking and observing a two-acre paradisiacal garden. *Address*: Wild Flower Studios, Abbots Bickington, Devon EX22 7LQ. *Email*: wildflower.studios@gmail.com *Website*: www.artwanted.com/RjjA *Signs work*: "Ron Atkin.".

ATKINS, David Alexander, BA (Hons.) Fine Art Painting 1st Class. *Medium*: artist in oil and watercolour. *b*: London, 20 Feb 1964. *m*: Jacqueline. three *d*. *Studied*: St. Martin's School of Art (1982-83), Winchester School of Art (1983-86). *Represented by*: Albemarle Gallery, London. *Exhib*: Discerning Eye, Alresford Gallery, Singer & Friedlander, Albemarle Gallery (2 solo); Fairfax Gallery, Chelsea; Albany Gallery, Cardiff; Beaux Arts, Bath; Stables Gallery, Ireland; Courcoux & Courcoux, Hampshire; Campden Gallery; McAllister Thomas Gallery. *Works in collections*: Creasey Collection, Salisbury; Guildhall, Kingston, Surrey; Hampshire Council Collection. *Commissions*: four murals for GLC. *Publications*: The Public Catalogue Foundation, Hampshire; The Public Catalogue, Dorset. *Address*: 31 Monmouth Rd., Dorchester, Dorset DT1 2DE. *Email*: davidatkins@madasafish.com *Website*: www.david-atkins.com *Signs work*: 'David Atkins'.

ATKINS, Ray, DFA (Lond); painter in 2D-oil, acrylic, drawing mediums, sculptor in 3D-clay, cement, wax. *b*: Exeter, 9 Jul 1937. *Partner*: Hsiao Hwa Li. one *s* (decd). one *d* (decd). *Studied*: Bromley College of Art (1954-56, 1958-61), Slade School of Art (1961-64). *Represented by*: Art Space Gallery, 84 St. Peters St., London N1 8JS. email: mail@artspacegallery.co.uk. *Exhib*: one-man shows: Whitechapel A.G. (1974), RWA Bristol retrospective (1996), and many other one-man and group shows. *Works in collections*: BM, British Council, Arts Council, South West Arts, Somerset CC, and private collections Europe and America. *Publications*: 'Ray Atkins' RWA (1996) ISBN No. 1899525 04 1; Ray Atkins – Paintings of the Figure, Truro (1999); 'Broken Ground' (2001); Ray Atkins-

Paintings 2003 ISBN 09528502-5-7; Ray Atkins-Paintings 2005 ISBN 0-9549623-1-1. *Official Purchasers*: British Museum, British Council, Arts Council. *Address*: Maison de Comminges, 31160 Aspet, France. *Email*: ray.atkins@orange.fr *Signs work*: "Ray Atkins," 2D work is signed on the back.

ATKINS, Rosalind Jane, SWE; Bachelor of Fine Art, Graduate Diploma of Fine Art. *Medium*: printmaking, wood engraving. *b*: Terang, Australia, 20 May 1957. two *s*. *Studied*: Royal Melbourne Institute of Technology University. *Represented by*: Australian Galleries, Melbourne and Sydney. *Exhib*: Australia, United Kingdom, USA. *Works in collections*: Australian National Gallery, Art Gallery of New South Wales, National Library, State Library of Victoria. *Publications*: 'Australian Prints', Art Gallery of NSW 1998, 'Women Engravers' Virago Press 1988. *Works Reproduced*: as above. *Clubs*: Society of Wood Engravers. *Address*: 2 Clive Street, Alphington, Victoria 3078, Australia. *Email*: rosatkins@iprimus.com.au

ATKINSON, Anthony, ARCA (1954); painter in oil; Dean, Colchester Inst. *b*: 1929. *s of*: Claude Atkinson. *m*: Joan Dawson. one *s*. one *s-d*. *Educ*: Wimbledon College. *Studied*: Royal College of Art. *Exhib*: RA, Leicester Galleries RWS; one-man: Minories, Colchester, Leighton House, London, Gainsborough's House, Sudbury, Mercury Theatre, Colchester, British Council, Kuwait, Coach-House Gallery, Guernsey, Highgate Fine Art, Chappel Gallery, John Russell, Ipswich. *Works in collections*: Essex Museum; Ernst & Young; Essex CC; Colchester Hospital, etc. *Works Reproduced*: Shell, London Transport, The Artist, Artist v Illustrators. *Clubs*: President Colchester Art Soc. *Address*: Coach House, Great Horkesley, Colchester, Essex CO6 4AX. *Signs work*: "ATKINSON."

ATKINSON, Eric Newton, NEAC, RCA; painter in oils and collage; Nat. Dipl. (1st hons., painting), RA Drawing Medal, Silver Medal for Painting; Dean, Faculty of Arts, Fanshawe College, London, Canada; Chairman, Fine Art, Leeds College of Art. *b*: W. Hartlepool, 23 Jul 1928. *s of*: James Atkinson. *m*: Muriel H. Ross. one *s*. one *d*. *Educ*: Dyke House, W. Hartlepool. *Studied*: W. Hartlepool College of Art and RA Schools. *Represented by*: Moore Gallery, Toronto; Thielsen Gallery, London, Ontario. *Exhib*: Redfern Gallery, Tate Gallery, Austin Hayes, York, Leeds Univ., Wakefield and Middlesbrough city galleries, Zwemmer Gallery, Corcoran Gallery, Rothman Gallery, Mendelson Gallery, Capponi Gallery, Pollock Gallery, Mendel Gallery, Carnegie Mellon, USA, Tate, St. Ives, Wallace Gallery, Calgary; Beaverbrook Gallery, NB. *Works in collections*: National Portrait Gallery, Contemporary Art Soc., M. of W., Leeds, Leicester, Wakefield, Hereford and Kendal A.G., Leeds City A.G. Collection, McIntosh Gallery UWO, Government Art Collection, UK; V&A Collection. *Publications*: "The Incomplete Circle" Eric Atkinson, Art and Education, ed. David Lewis (Scolar Press, 2000). *Address*: 69 Paddock Green Cres., London N6J 3P6, Ontario, Canada. *Email*: murielatkinson@sympatico.ca *Signs work*: "Eric Atkinson.".

ATKINSON, Kim, MA (RCA) (1987); SWLA (1992); Young Bird Artist of the Year (1992), Royal Society for the Protection of Birds Art Award (2002). *Medium*: artist in water-colour, oil, printmaking, drawing. *b*: Bath, 1962. *d of*: Mr. & Mrs. A. Atkinson. *m*: Gwydion Morley. one *s*. *Studied*: Falmouth School of Art (Foundation); Cheltenham College of Art (BA Painting); Royal College of Art (MA Natural History Illustration). *Exhib*: Wales, England, Europe, America. *Publications*: Birds in Wales (Poyser, 1994) (illustrations); chapter in Water-colour Masterclass by Lawrence Wood (Collins, 1993), work included in Artists for Nature Foundation; publications resulting from projects in Poland, France, Spain, Ireland and India; Drawn to the Forest (2000, Wildlife Art Gallery), Modern Wildlife Painting (Pica Press, 1998); The Forgotten Forest (The Wildlife Art Gallery, 2004). *Recreations*: gardening, Natural History *Misc*: subject matter primarily nature, esp.- birds, plants and insects within the landscape, both abroad and around her Welsh coastal home. *Address*: Ty'n Gamdda, Uwchmynydd, Pwllheli, Gwynedd LL53 8DA. *Email*: kim.atkinson257@btinternet.com *Website*: kimnaturepenllyn.blogspot *Signs work*: "Kim Atkinson." or "KA".

ATKINSON, Shelagh, HND Communication Studies (1988). *Medium*: printmaker and painter. *b*: 1959. *Studied*: Napier University, Edinburgh (1988); Leith School of Art, Edinburgh (2003/2004). *Exhib*: Edinburgh, Japan, London, Bulgaria, Berlin, Chicago, China. *Works in collections*: Scottish National Portrait Gallery, Edinburgh; Scottish National Museum, Edinburgh; New Hall College Art Collection, Cambridge, England. *Commissions*: book cover Heirts Bluid, Chapman Publications, Scotland (1995), Circle the City, Community Project Edinburgh (1995/6), CD cover design Wee Dram Records (2004). *Publications*: catalogues: Footsteps, Panzerhalle Berlin (1998), Harlech Print Biennale, Wales (2000), Print Triennial, Kanagawa Yokohama (2001), Tidaholm Lithographic Symposium, Sweden (2002), Lessendra Print, Sofia, Bulgaria (2004/5), Print Contemporary, Kumming China (2012), Douro Print Biennial (2013). *Official Purchasers*: Scottish National Portrait Gallery, Edinburgh; Scottish National Museum, Edinburgh. *Works Reproduced*: My Ties with Milk - etching in Alistair Findlay's book 'Never Mind the Captions' (Luath Press, 2012). *Recreations*: walking. *Clubs*: Scottish Artists Union, Edinburgh Printmakers Workshop, Visual Artists Scotland (VAS). *Address*: Roberton Cottage, Dolphinton, West Linton, Peebleshire, EH46 7AB. *Email*: art@shelaghatkinson.co.uk *Website*: www.shelaghatkinson.co.uk *Signs work*: "S Atkinson".

ATKINSON, Ted, DFA (Lond., 1952), RE (1988), FRBS, FRSA (1957), Slade Prize Winner (1952); sculptor; Head of Sculpture School, Coventry University (1968-83). *b*: Liverpool, 21 Mar 1929. *s of*: Edward Atkinson, musician. *Educ*: Oulton School, Liverpool. *Studied*: Liverpool College of Art and Slade School, Slade Post-graduate Scholar (1952-53). *Works in collections*: Arts Council, London, Ashmolean Museum, Oxford, Dallas Art Museum, Kunst Academie, Dresden, Fitzwilliam Museum, Cambridge, Museum of Modern Art, N.Y., Seattle Art Museum, etc.; public sculptures in Coventry, Dusseldorf, Hamburg, Univ. Birmingham. *Misc*: One of six sculptors chosen to represent Britain at Expo 88 Brisbane. *Address*: 4 De Vere Pl., Wivenhoe, Essex CO7 9AX.

ATTREE, Jake (Jonathan), DipAD (Painting) (1972), RA Schools Post-Grad. Cert. (1977); Landseer prize, Creswick prize, David Murray Scholarship; painter. *b*: York, 13 Oct 1950. *s of*: Noel and Mary Attree. *m*: Lindsay Knight. *Educ*: Danesmead, York. *Studied*: York College of Art (1966-68), Liverpool College of Art (1969-72), RA Schools (1974-77). *Represented by*: Messums. *Exhib*: regular one person and group shows nationally and internationally. *Works in collections*: Leeds City Council, City of Dortmund, Grays A.G. Hartlepool, Sheffield University, Nuffield Trust, Bradford Museums and Galleries. *Publications*: "Views from a Hill" catalogue (2007); "Marks on a White Ground" catalogue (2008); "St.Nicholas Field" catalogue (2009). "Jake Attree" Messums catalogue. *Misc*: Studio: Dean Clough, Halifax HX3 5AX. *Address*: Studio: Dean Clough, Halifax HX3 5AX. 33 Titus St., Saltaire, Shipley BD18 4LU. *Email*: jakeattree@hotmail.co.uk *Signs work*: usually unsigned, unless requested, then "J. Attree."

AUERBACH, Frank Helmut, painter. *b*: Berlin, 29 Apr 1931. *Educ*: privately. *Studied*: St. Martin's School of Art; RCA. *Exhib*: one-man shows: Beaux-Arts Gallery (1956, 1959, 1961, 1962, 1963); Marlborough Fine Art (1965, 1967, 1971, 1974, 1983, 1987, 1990, 1997, 2004, 2009); Marlborough, NY (1969, 1982, 1994, 1998, 2006); Marlborough Galerie, Zurich (1976); Saint Louis Art Museum, Missouri (1990-91); retrospective, Hayward Gallery (1978), Venice Biennale (1986) (joint winner Golden Lion), Hamburg (1986), Essen, Madrid (1987), Rijksmuseum Vincent Van Gogh, Amsterdam (1989), Royal Academy of Arts, London (2001), Fitzwilliam Museum, Cambridge (2007), Courtauld Gallery, London (2009), Yale Center for British Art, New Haven (1991), National Gallery, London (1995). *Works in collections*: Metropolitan Museum, NY; Museum of Modern Art NY; Los Angeles County Museum; National Gallery of Australia; B.M.; Tate Gallery, London; and many other museums; British Council; Arts Council; Contemporary Art Society, etc. *Address*: c/o Marlborough Fine Art Ltd., 6 Albemarle St., London W1S 4BY.

AUGUST, Lillias Anne, RI; BA Hons (1978), CNAA (1979); RI (2006); RI Prizewinner (2002, 2005, 2006, 2010); Laing Regional prizewinner (2000). *Medium*: painter in watercolour. *b*: Gloucester, 5 May 1955. married. two *s*. *Studied*: Goldsmiths College, London (1973-1977), Birmingham Polytechnic (1977-1978). *Exhib*: Hunter Gallery, Long Melford (2001-09); Singer & Friedlander Sunday Times Watercolour Exhib. (2001); Artworks, Rougham (2000-08); RI (2000-2009); Laing Exhibs. (1992, 1995, 1998, 2000); Firstsite, Colchester (2000); RWS, London(1996, 2002, 2009); Art Auction East (2004, 2005); Langham Fine Art (2006-08); Threadneedle Prize, London (2009); Arlesford Gallery, Hampshire (2009); Russell Gallery, Putney (2009); RI in Landau, Germany (2009); Gallery Lefort, Bath (2010); Mid Cornwall Galleries, Par (2010); Edmund Gallery, Bury St. Edmunds (2011); Minster Gallery, Winchester (2011); RI & RWS, Mall & Bankside Galleries, London (2011). *Works in collections*: Hylands House, Chelmsford; St. Edmunds Cathedral, Bury St. Edmunds. *Commissions*: Chelmsford Borough Council; St. Edmundsbury Borough Council, Suffolk; St. Bartholomew's Hospital, London; The National Trust; project artist, Suffolk Cathedral Millennium Project (2000-2005). *Publications*: Millennium Tower, St. Edmundsbury Cathedral (pub. 2005); Vaulted Ceiling, St. Edmundsbury Cathedral (pub. 2011); The Artist Magazine (2010); L'Art Aquarelle (2010), Watercolour Artist (USA 2011); Artist & Illustrators magazine (2011). *Address*: West Barn, Golden Lane, Lawshall, Bury St. Edmunds, Suffolk IP29 4PS. *Email*: lilliasaugust@btinternet.com *Website*: www.liliasaugust.com *Signs work*: "Lillias August" or "LA.".

AUSTIN, Franki, BA (Hons) Painting, PGDip in Glass, MPhil Fine Art. *Medium*: glass, installation, painting, ceramics. *b*: Middlesex, 30 October 1946. *Partner*: Anthony Amies. *Studied*: University of Hong Kong (1979-1980), Central School of Art & Design (1981-86), Central St. Martins College of Art (1989), University of Plymouth (-2001). *Represented by*: www.beverleyknowles.com. *Exhib*: solo exhibitions include: Camden Arts Centre, London (1988); 4As Gallery, France (1990), Dartington Hall (1997), Brunel University (1999), Canary Wharf (2003), Symphony Hall, Birmingham (2003), Finestra Art Space, Chicago, USA (2006), University of Surrey (2006), Beverley Knowles Gallery (2008), Koukan Gallery (2011). *Works in collections*: including: University of Surrey; The Florence Trust; Visva-Bharati University (India), Royal Free Hospital. *Commissions*: in private collections. *Publications*: include: Her Mind's Eye (1996); On a Process of Influence (1996); Royal Academy Illustrated (2002); Chelsea Arts Club Yearbook (2005); Glass at Central (2011). *Clubs*: Chelsea Arts Club. *Address*: UF15, Barbican Arts Group, Blackhorse Lane Studios, 114 Blackhorse Lane, Walthamstow, London E17 6AA. *Email*: franki.austin@googlemail.com *Website*: www.frankiaustin.co.uk *Signs work*: 'Austin'.

AUSTIN, Michael J., *b*: London, 13 Sep 1959. one *s*. *Educ*: left school at 16. *Represented by*: Jonathan Copper, Park Walk Gallery, London. *Exhib*: solo shows: Park Walk Gallery (1996, '97, '99, 2000, '02, '03, '04, '05). *Works in collections*: Royal Collection. *Commissions*: Tour Artist HRH The Prince of Wales (India/Oman Nov 2003). *Works Reproduced*: prints and posters, The Art Group, London. *Address*: 61 Manstow Road, Exeter, Devon EX1 2QA. *Email*: mail@jonathancooper.co.uk *Website*: www.jonathancooper.co.uk

AVELLINO, Alessia E.R., BA (Hons) Drawing and Painting; Painter-Stainer bursary for Easel painting; Bruce Church Travel Scholarship; Foundation Course Chelsea College of Arts; 'The Drawing Year' - The Prince's Drawing School, London. *Medium*: painter, drawer, charcoal and oil. *b*: Sofia, Bulgaria, 16 Sep 1972. *d of*: Antonio and Concita Avellino. *Studied*: Chelsea College of Art, Camberwell College, The Prince's Drawing School. *Represented by*: Iker Garcia Barrenetyea, The Vyner Studio, 1 Viner Street, E2 9DG. *Works in collections*: BP, Yolles Engineers, ITV Television, Holman, Fenwick & Willan; private collections in the UK and USA. *Commissions*: Yolles Engineers, Canary Wharf.

Publications: Artists Newsletter, Blueprint Magazine, The Times, Lloyd's List. *Address*: 3 Mallard House, Bridgeman Street, London NW8 7AN. *Email*: alessiaavellino@gmail.com *Website*: www.alessiaavellino.com *Signs work*: AER Avellino (A.E.R.A. on paintings).

AYLES, Caroline, Chelsea Art Society Award. *Medium*: oil. *b*: Gartolharn, 2 May 1960. *d of*: Anne and Normile Baxter. one *s*. one *d*. *Educ*: Queensgate, Gordonstoun. *Studied*: South Thames College. *Represented by*: Portland Gallery. *Exhib*: RA Summer Exhbn, Art 2002, Art London (2003), Portland Gallery (2002, 2003, 2004, 2007), Royal College of Art (2006). *Works in collections*: Palace of Westminster. *Clubs*: Chelsea Arts Club, Soho House. *Address*: 28 Crescent Grove, London SW4 7AH. *Email*: caroline.ayles@btinternet.com *Signs work*: Caroline Ayles.

AYLES, Debbie, BA (Hons); Sciart R&D Award, The Wellcome Trust (2004); 1st Prize, Daily Telegraph/Novartis 'Vision of Science' Photographic Awards (2005). *Medium*: acrylic, watercolour, drawing. *b*: London. one *s*. one *d*. *Studied*: Colchester School of Art. *Exhib*: RI (2013, 2014); Lynn Painter-Stainers Prize (2014); RWS (2012, 2013, 2014); East Contemporary Art (2013); NEAC (2011); London Group Open (2008, 2009, 2011); ING Discerning Eye (2010); Art Liberating Lives (2009); RWA (2009); Institut de Cultura de Barcelona, Spain (2006); Science Museum/Glasgow Scientific Centre (2005-06). *Works in collections*: Starbucks; The Wellcome Trust Image Library; Eastern Contemporary Art Collection, Essex County Council; Essex County Hospital; private clients. *Commissions*: private. *Publications*: Magazines: 'Science' (July 2007); 'International Review of Neurobiology' (Vol. 74, 2006); 'The Neurobiology of Painting' (pub. Academic Press, San Diego); 'What it is like to have a migraine'; Debbie Ayles multimedia 'Mig Installation' (D. Ayles, Micola, K. Podoll, paper pub. Confinia Cephalagia, Italy 2004); New York Arts Daily Newsletter webarticle (2003), 'Kaleidoscopic hallucinations as visual aura symptom in migraine' (paper pub. Confinia Cephelagia, Italy (2003), 'Inspired by migraine': Sarah Raphael's 'Strip paintings' (JRSM, 2002). *Works Reproduced*: Jesmond Barn. *Address*: 19 Woodfield Drive, West Mersea, Essex CO5 8PX. *Email*: debbieayles@yahoo.co.uk *Website*: www.debbieaylesartist.co.uk *Signs work*: "Debbie Ayles".

AYRES, Gillian, CBE, OBE, RA; Hon. Doctor Lit., University of London. *Medium*: painter. *b*: Barnes, London, 3 Feb 1930. two children. *Educ*: St. Paul's Girls' School. *Studied*: Camberwell School of Art. *Represented by*: Alan Cristea Gallery. *Exhib*: group shows: Musée d'Art Moderne; Bienale de Paris, Paris (1959); Situation, London (1960-61); one-man shows, Gallery One (1956), Kasmin Gallery (1965-66, 1969), Knoedler London (1979, 1982, 1985, 1987), Knoedler New York (1985), R.A. British Art (1987), London, and Stuttgart, Germany. Awarded Japan International Art Promotion Association Award (1963), Gold Medal Triennale, India (1991). *Works in collections*: Tate Gallery, Museum of Modern Art, NY; Yale Center for Brit Art. *Publications*: 'Gillian Ayers' Mel Gooding (2001) *Misc*: taught at Bath Academy, St. Martin's; Head of Painting, Winchester School of Art (1978-) *Address*: c/o Alan Cristea Gallery, 31 Cork Street, London W1S 3NU. *Email*: info@alancristea.com *Signs work*: "Gillian Ayres."

B

BACKHOUSE, David John, RWA. FRBS, FRSA; sculptor in bronze and stone. *b*: Corsham, Wilts., 5 May 1941. *s of*: Joseph Helme Backhouse. *Partner*: Jennifer Ann Weston. one *s*. two *d*. *Educ*: Lord Weymouth School, Warminster. *Studied*: West of England College of Art. *Exhib*: one-man shows: London, New York. *Works in collections*: RWA, Royal Opera House, Covent Garden, Telford Dev. Corp., City of Bristol and private collections throughout Europe and in USA. *Commissions*: Animals in War, Park Lane, London W1. *Address*: Silenus, 8 Bishop Ken Close, Wells, Somerset BA5 3ND. *Email*: jennieweston@yahoo.co.uk *Website*: www.davidbackhousesculptures.com *Signs work*: "Backhouse".

BAFFONI, Pier Luigi, NS (1975), ROI (1979); artist in oil, water-colour and pastel. *b*: Turin, Italy, 11 Aug 1932. *s of*: Pierpaolo Baffoni, accountant. *m*: Mary Bainbridge. two *s*. *Educ*: College of the Missioni Consolata, Turin. *Studied*: College of Art, Turin (1954-58) under Luigi Guglielmino and privately from Alessandro Pomi of Venice. *Exhib*: one-man shows, Italy, Hertford, Cambridge, Bedford, Hitchin; mixed shows, Biennale of Castelfranco Veneto, Bologna, Mall Galleries, London; Hawker Gallery, Amersham. *Works in collections*: Montebelluna Town Hall, Bedfordshire Educ. Art Loan Service. *Publications*: included in "Modern Oil Impressionists" by Ron Ranson – David & Charles, (1992). *Address*: 140 Station Rd., Lower Stondon, Beds. SG16 6JH. *Signs work*: "P. L. Baffoni."

BAILEY, Caroline, BA (Hons), MA, RSW; Awards: Daler Rowney RWS Open (1994), The Artist Award RWS Open (1997), Glasgow Arts Club Fellowship RSW (1999), NS Macfarlane Charitable Trust Award RSA (1999). Scottish Arts Club Award. *Medium*: artist in water-colour, gouache, acrylic. *b*: Chester, 5 Aug 1953. two *d*. *Educ*: St. Dominics High School. *Studied*: Manchester Polytechnic (1972-76). *Exhib*: John Noott Galleries Worcs., Broadway Modern Worcs., Walker Galleries Harrogate, Colours Gallery Edinburgh, Manor House Gallery Oxon, also Open Exhbns. RSW, RSA, RWS, Ainscough Contemporary Art, London and Dartmouth, ClarkArt, Hale, Cheshire, Denise Yapp Contemporary Art, Albany Gallery, Cardiff. *Works in collections*: Irish Management Inst., Maclay Murray & Spens, Edinburgh Fund Managers, Callscan Ltd, Nynas. *Publications*: Landscape Drawing and Painting by Patricia Monohan. *Clubs*: RSW. *Address*: Heathfields, Dunnockswood, Alsager, Stoke-on-Trent ST7 2XU. *Website*: www.carolinebailey.co.uk *Signs work*: 'Caroline Bailey' (always in pencil).

BAILEY, Julian. NEAC; BFA Oxon.(1985), RA Dip. (MA) (1988); Turner Gold Medal, RA Schools (1987); Landseer Scholarship (1988); David Messum Prize (2011); Manya Igel Prize (2011); elected Member of the New English Art Club (2011). *Medium*: oil and gouache. *b*: Cheshire, 8 Apr 1963. *s of*: Dudley Bailey, artist. *m*: Sophie Cullen, ceramist. two *s*. two *d*. *Educ*: Malvern College. *Studied*: Ruskin School of Art (1982-85), RA Schools (1985-88, Jane Dowling, Norman Blamey, RA). *Exhib*: RA, New Grafton Gallery, Browse & Darby (1997-2014), Slades Yard Gallery, Dorset. *Works in collections*: National Trust (FFA), New College, Oxford, Warbergs, Reed Executive, HRH the Prince of Wales, Dorchester County Council. *Recreations*: sailing. *Clubs*: Chelsea Arts *Address*: The Old Vicarage, Stinsford, Dorchester, Dorset DT2 8PS. *Email*: julian@julianbailey.co.uk *Signs work*: "J.B." or "JULIAN BAILEY."

BAILEY, Liz, BA Hons Fine Art; BSc Hons Anthropology (UCL); MA Visual Anthropology (Distinction) Goldsmiths. *Medium*: oil, photography, video. *b*: Herts., 19 Jan 1951. *m*: Ralph. two *s*. one *d*. *Studied*: Byam Shaw School of Fine Art (1998-2002); UCL (1981); Goldsmiths (2007-2008). *Exhib*: solo exhbn: Tricycle Gallery, London (2006); Group exhbns: 2011: Jerwood Drawing Prize 2011. Borderlines Film Festival - UK; RA Summer Exhbn (2012, 2010, 2008, 2005, 2004); 2010: Secret of England's Greatness Ex - Austria. Columbia Gorge Film Festival USA; 2009: DACS '1984' Exhibition - London; 2008: London Art Fair; 2007: London Group Open exhibition, Lyn Painter Stainers Prize Open Exhibition, Welsh Artist of the Year Exhnb - Cardiff; 2006: Artsway Open, Sarah Myerscough Fine Art, Thompson Gallery London; 2005: Discerning Eye Ex, Vertigo Gallery (2003, 04, 05). *Works in collections*: Esmee Fairbairn Foundation; The McGraw-Hill Companies Ltd; Hangar 7 - Salzburg, Austria; Basis-Wein, Vienna, Austria; private collections UK, Spain, USA, Austria. *Publications*: in RA Illustrated (2005); Celeste Art Prize catalogue (2006); The Secrets of England's Greatness catalogue (2010); Jerwood Drawing prize catalogue (2011). *Works Reproduced*: reviews: a-n magazine (Nov 2006); solo exhibition 'On the Road' review by Roy Exley. *Misc*: residency at The Florence Trust Studios, Highbury, London N5 (Aug 2002-July 2003); lives and works in London and Welsh

Borders. *Address*: 10 Grove Terrace, Highgate Road, London NW5 1PH. *Email*: liz@lizbailey.org.uk *Website*: www.lizbailey.org.uk *Signs work*: 'Liz' and date.

BAILEY, Susanna, BFA Hons, Slade Higher Diploma; Nancy Balfour Award; painter, printmaker, lecturer and writer. *Medium*: painting and printmaking (etching) - oil, acrylic, watercolour. *b*: Lusaka, Zambia, 12 Oct 1953. *d of*: Prof. D.K. Bailey. four *d*. *Educ*: USA, Britain, Eire. *Studied*: Slade School of Fine Art (1975-77) (post graduate). *Represented by*: Tracie Specia, Los Angeles. *Exhib*: Venice Gallery, Los Angeles; Beaux Arts, Bath; nationally and internationally since 1985. *Works in collections*: House of Westminster, London; IBCA, Castle Hotel, Taunton; Sevicor, LA, Chelsea Arts Club London. Personal Collections: Jane Seymore, Michael Goreachor, Sir Charles Marling. *Commissions*: Castle Hotel, Taunton; IBCA, London & Paris. *Recreations*: walking, writing, gardening, still daydreaming. *Clubs*: Chelsea Arts Club. *Misc*: teaches in UK, Italy, France, Spain, USA. *Address*: 2 Chapel Path, Colerne, Wiltshire, SN14 8DL. *Email*: mail@susannabailey.co.uk *Website*: www.susannabailey.com *Signs work*: "Susanna Bailey".

BAILEY, Terence Robert, NDD (1958), ATD(1962), RBSA (1991); painter in oil; Senior lecturer, Northumberland CHE (1962-79). *b*: Wolverhampton, 21 Dec 1937. *m*: Kate (Valerie Ann Browning). three *s*. *Educ*: Wolverhampton Technical High School. *Studied*: Wolverhampton College of Art (1954-58), Bournemouth College of Art (1962). *Exhib*: Northern Painters (1966), Northern Art Exhbn. (1978), prize winner RBSA Open (1986), RP, ROI, regularly at RBSA; several one-man shows. Winner in Alexon "Women on Canvas" portrait competition (1990). *Works in collections*: Northumberland CC, Northern Arts, National Library of Wales, RBSA; many private collections. *Address*: Dovey Studio, Aberdyfi, Gwynedd LL35 0LW. *Signs work*: "Terry Bailey."

BAIN, Julia Mary, MFPS (1985), Mem. Chelsea Art Soc. (1984); Woodrow Award (1986); sculptor in terracotta, wax and bronze. *b*: London, 22 Jun 1930. *d of*: Guy Warrack, conductor and composer. *m*: 1st: David Bain, F.R.C.S.; 2nd Peter Cooke C.B.E. three *s*. one *d*. *Educ*: The Legat School of Russian Ballet. *Studied*: ILEA Chelsea/Westminster (1978-81), Sir John Cass College (1981-83). *Exhib*: FBA (1983-89), RBA, SWA, NS, FPS Trends, Art of Living SPS, Chelsea Art Soc.; one-man shows, Windsor Festival (1981, 1986, 1989), Century Gallery, Datchet (1990, 1995), The Deanery, Windsor Castle (1993, 1995). Work in private collections. *Commissions*: The 'Tablet' Madonna - many portraits and others; The 'Woodrow Award'. *Recreations*: choral singing. *Address*: Oak Lodge, Maltmans Lane, Chalfont St.Peter, Gerrards Cross, Bucks SL9 8RP. *Email*: julia.cooke3@virgin.net *Signs work*: "J.B."

BAINES, Richard John Manwaring, MA, PhD, ROI, RDS, NDD, ATD, V.P.ROI (1997), P.ROI (1998); painter, writer, lecturer, critic, broadcaster (radio & TV); previously Senior lecturer/Head of Academic Studies, London College of Fashion. *b*: Hastings, 1940. *s of*: John Manwaring Baines, BSc, FSA, FMA. *m*: Maureen Gregory. two *s*. one *d*. *Studied*: Regent St. Polytechnic, Goldsmiths' College, Birmingham Polytechnic. *Exhib*: ROI, RBA, NS, RE, Painter-Etchers, London and provinces; one-man exhbns. Hastings (1968, 1987). *Works in collections*: County Borough of Hastings, Manx Museum, London Inst. 'Genesis Triptych' in Fairlight Parish Church. *Commissions*: Royal Arms and mural restorations, All Saints Church, Hastings. *Publications*: Mainly design history. *Clubs*: East Sussex Arts (President). *Address*: Badgers End, Warren Rd., Fairlight, E. Sussex TN35 4AG. *Signs work*: "RJMB" as monogram.

BAINES, Valerie, ARMS (1985), founder-member of SBA (1988), FLS (1991), VPSBA (1996); Botanical artist, miniature painter and natural history illustrator. *Medium*: watercolour, oil. *b*: Romford, 1935. *m*: Brian Norman. one *s*. *Educ*: Roxeth Mead School, Harrow on the Hill; Royal College of Music, London. *Studied*: Harrow Art School. *Exhib*: RMS, RHS, The Royal Academy, Society of Botanical Artists, Westminster Galleries, Mall Galleries, Alpine Gallery, Medici Gallery, 7th Exhbn. of International Botanical Art,

Carnegie Mellon University, Pittsburgh, USA, Memorial University, Botanic Gardens, Newfoundland, Canada, Le Jardin des Cinq Sens, Yvoire, France. *Works in collections*: Carnegie Mellon University Botanical Library, Pittsburgh, USA, Port Lympne, Kent; many private collections world-wide, including U.K., America, India, South Africa, Canada and France. *Commissions*: Oil paintings of houses. Water-colour interiors, flowers, gardens etc. 14 gorilla portraits for John Aspinall 1988/9. *Publications*: The Naturalist's Garden by John Feltwell (Ebury Press, 1987), Botanical Diary (St. Michael, 1989), The Story of Silk, J. Feltwell (Allen Sutton 1990), The Big Book (Collins, 1991), Meadows, J. Feltwell (Allen Sutton 1992), Glorious Butterflies, (Butterfly Conservation 1993), Gardens and Butterflies Calendar (Butterfly Conservation 1998), Mindful of Butterflies, Bernard S. Jackson (The Book Guild 1999), A2 poster for Watch (Wildlife Trusts 2000), Guernsey Sketchbook 2011. *Works Reproduced*: Arte y Botanica. Seleccion de Illustraciones de 'The Society of Botanical Artists' (Caja Madrid Obra Social 2001); The Art of Botanical Painting, Margaret Stevens VPSBA (2004); The Botanical Palette, Margaret Stevens PSBA 2007. *Recreations*: music, gardening. *Misc*: biographical articles in 'The Artist' Nov 1983, 'Kent Life' 1999, 'Magnet' 2007. Butterfly Garden Design, Juniper Hall, FSC Dorking, Surrey. *Address*: 26 Crittle's Court, Wadhurst, E. Sussex, TN5 6BY. *Website*: www.valeriebaines.com *Signs work*: "V.B.", "Valerie Baines" and "V. BAINES."

BAKER, Alix, PCAFAS; several prizes at exhibition; Chairman Armed Forces Art Society (2002-07). *Medium*: most media. *b*: Southborough 26 Jan 1947. *d of*: Field Marshal Sir Geoffrey and Lady Baker. *m*: Brigadier Thomas Bremridge. two *s*. *Educ*: PNEU School, Burgess Hill; Windsor Girls School, Germany. *Studied*: Sir John Cass, Tower Hill, London. *Exhib*: Many galleries at home and abroad including Mall Galleries, Malcolm Innes Gallery, Christie's, Wykeham Gallery, Al Muntasir Gallery Oman. *Works in collections*: Series for HM Sultan Qaboos, Oman; many museums; corporate and private collections; National Collection. *Commissions*: official military, corporate and private; Royal presentations. *Publications*: Specialist journals; artwork for books. *Official Purchasers*: numerous. *Works Reproduced*: numerous. *Principal Works*: landscape, architectural, figurative, marine, military. *Recreations*: skiing, walking, reading. *Clubs*: several Art Societies. *Address*: Applegate, Church Lane, Goodworth Clatford, Andover SP11 7HL. *Email*: art@alixbaker.com *Website*: www.alixbaker.com *Signs work*: AB (monogram).

BAKER, Christopher William, BA Hons (Fine Art, 1978), PGCE (1981), RBA (1981); printmaker, oil on canvas, dramatic landscape paintings; Tutor, West Dean College; David Murray Landscape Scholarship, Royal Academy; Laing Painting Prize Winner; major Award British Arts Council; Wolfers-O'Neill Foundation; Canadian Arts Council: Banff Centre for the Arts. *Medium*: oils, watercolour, printmaking. *b*: Essex, 27 May 1956. *s of*: Mrs. M. Sugden, Capt. D.S. Baker. *Educ*: Kingham Hill School, Oxon. *Studied*: West Surrey College of Art and Design (1974-75, M. Fairclough), Glos. College of Art and Design (1975-78, Prof. D. L. Carpanini), Exeter University. *Represented by*: The New Grafton. *Exhib*: Royal Academy, RWA, RBA, Mall Galleries, Phoenix Gallery, Highgate, Burstow Gallery, Brighton College; Wyckeham Gallery, Stockbridge; Portsmouth Museum of Art; Pallant House Gallery, Chichester; Petworth House Gallery; Oslo Museum of Art, Brighton Museum. *Works in collections*: Coventry Adult Educ., Oundle School, West Dean College, The Royal Mint (London). *Commissions*: The Royal Mint, No1 London Bridge, Hon. Nicholas Soames, Edward James Foundation. *Official Purchasers*: Art Contact, London. *Works Reproduced*: The Artist, Quattro Publications; Encyclopedia of Oil Painting; Encyclopedia of Watercolours; Perspective for Artists; The Watercolour Palette; Oil Painters Masterclass. *Principal Works*: 'Ultimate Thule', 'Terra Incognita'. *Clubs*: Chelsea Arts Club. *Misc*: Research Expedition - Antarctica 2003; Canadian High Arctic 1997; 2000 Banff Centre for the Arts. *Address*: 110 Fitzalan Rd., Arundel, W. Sussex BN18 9JY. *Website*: www.christopherwbaker.com *Signs work*: "Christopher Baker."

BAKER, Darren, Fine Art Trade Guild Best Artist (2003); Yorkshire Young Achiever (2005); Princes Trust celebrate success (2007); Pastel Society Award Winner. *Medium*: oil, drawing. *b*: Huddersfield, 16 Mar 1976. *s of*: John & Carol Baker. *m*: Abigail Baker. *Studied*: Bradford Art College (1995-1998). *Represented by*: Whitewall Galleries. *Exhib*: One-man shows: Haynes Fine Art (2006, 2007); Whitewall Gallery, St. James's, London (2005); Artisan Gallery, London (2003); DFN Gallery, New York (2000); many mixed shows at home, USA and international including Royal Academy Summer Exhibition (2005), Discerning Eye, Mall Galleries (2009), Whitewall Galleries, London (2009). *Works in collections*: Professional Footballers Association, Unilever Plc, Lloyds TSB, House of Lords, St.James's Palace, Peter Jackson (director), George Lucas (director). *Commissions*: Lloyds TSB, Downing Street, English FA, Palace of Westminster Art Collection, Lucasfilms. *Publications*: Still Life in Oils (Rotovision). *Works Reproduced*: several artworks in limited edition prints worldwide. *Address*: 30 Howard Way, Meltham, Huddersfield HD9 4NW. *Email*: admin@dbfinearts.co.uk *Website*: www.dbfinearts.co.uk *Signs work*: "D. Baker".

BAKER, Ian David, *Medium*: acrylic paintings & photographs. *b*: London, 19 Aug 1945. *s of*: adopted: 1st name David Paul Perry. *Studied*: Epsom School of Art (1960-64). *Represented by*: Pyms Gallery (2005-, Paintings). *Exhib*: Group and one-man shows since 1980: Ebury Gallery; 1984: ICAF/1, Barbican invited artist; 1985: Revolt Gallery, Hamburg; 1986: ICAF/2; 1988: St. Judes Gallery; 1991, 1994: Photographs BKK Thailand; 1998: Kensington Library (Photographs); 2001: SEW9 Restaurant/Gallery (Paintings); 2003: Walls Galerie, Amsterdam (Paintings); 2004: 286 Gallery; 2007:Stark Gallery, Canterbury; 2009 RA Summer Exhibition. *Commissions*: family portraits (2004); child portrait, London (2005). *Publications*: Two photography books 'Younger Days' (1993); 'Out of Season' (1987). *Works Reproduced*: 1985: 'The Male Nude' a modern view, Rizzoli;1999: 'Homme' – Carlton. *Recreations*: Arts; World Cinema; music; cycling; swimming. *Address*: 5 Adelphi Court, 2 Augusta Gardens, Folkestone, Kent, CT20 2RR. *Email*: mail@iandavidbaker.com *Website*: www.iandavidbaker.com *Signs work*: "Ian David Baker".

BAKER, Kathleen, BSc; MPhil; PhD; 2 silver medals (RHS); 4 gold medals (AGS); bronze medal at Kirstenbosch Biennale (2013). *Medium*: watercolour. *b*: Ebbw Vale, 29 Mar 1939. *m*: Ronald. *Studied*: Birmingham University (Botany); Newcastle University. *Exhib*: London SBA exhibitions; Botanical Art Exhibitions, Palmengarten Frankfurt; National Botanic Garden, Wales; Kirstenbosch Biennale (2013) bronze medal. *Works in collections*: private. *Works Reproduced*: A painting to illustrate use of brown colour in SBA publication "Botanical Palette"; painting of Magnolia Grandiflora used for publicity of SBA silver jubilee. *Recreations*: photography, travel. *Clubs*: Alpine Garden Society; Society of Botanical Artists. *Address*: Derwen Deg, Llanarthne, Carms SA32 8HL. *Email*: ronbaker777@hotmail.co.uk *Signs work*: "Kath Baker".

BAKERE, Ronald Duncan, MA, FRSA. *Medium*: sculptor in metal and clay. *b*: Lanark, Scotland, 7 Sep 1935. *m*: (1) Dr. Jane Earthy. (2) Macaria Saducos. three *s*. one *d*. *Educ*: Norwich School, Christ Church, Oxford. *Studied*: Putney School of Art, Sir John Cass Dept. of Art at London Guildhall University. *Exhib*: Arts Club, Dover St., Brixton A.G.; South Thames College, etc. *Commissions*: private. *Clubs*: sometime Chairman Brixton Art Gallery, Sussex Arts Club, London Flotilla. *Address*: 11B Sussex Heights, St. Margaret's Place, Brighton BN1 2FQ.

BALAAM, Louise, NEAC, RWA; BA Hons (Fine Art), MA (Fine Art). *Medium*: oil. *b*: Surrey, 7 Feb 1954. *m*: Keith Balaam. two *d*. *Studied*: Kent Institute of Art & Design, Canterbury, Kent (1997-2002); Canterbury Christchurch University, Canterbury (2005-07). *Represented by*: Cadogan Contemporary, SW7; John Davies Gallery, Glos; White Space Art, Totnes, Devon; Fairfax Gallery, Tunbridge Wells and Norfolk; Belgrave Gallery, St. Ives;

Hilton Fine Art, Bath. *Exhib*: Solo shows: Cadogan Contemporary, John Davies Gallery (2012, 2014); Royal Academy Summer Shows, Threadneedle Prize, Lynn Painter-Stainers Prize, Hunting Art Prize, Discerning Eye. *Works in collections*: private collections. *Address*: 81 Brittains Lane, Sevenoaks, Kent TN13 2JS. *Email*: balaam_louise@hotmail.com *Website*: www.louisebalaam.co.uk *Signs work*: "Louise Balaam".

BALDWIN, Arthur Mervyn, NDD (1955), Rome Scholarship, Sculpture, 1960; sculptor in metals and synthetics; self employed artist and restorer; 1978, retired defeated by lack of public appreciation - now restores antique watches for which service people happily pay. *b*: Immingham, Lincs., 1 Feb 1934. *s of*: William Henry Baldwin. *m*: Patrica Mary. two *s*. *Educ*: Humberstone Foundation School, Old Clee, Lincs. *Studied*: Grimsby School of Art, Leicester College of Art. *Works in collections*: National Museum of Wales, Arts Council (Wales); Städtischen Kunstammlungen, Ludwigshafen. *Address*: 18 The Walk, Cardiff CF2 3AF. *Signs work*: sculpture unsigned; drawings etc. signed "MERVYN BALDWIN."

BALDWIN, Gordon, OBE (1992), NDD (1952), Central Dip. (1953); ceramist; Hon. Dr. RCA. *b*: Lincoln, 10 Nov 1932. *s of*: Lewis Nelson. *m*: Nancy Chandler. one *s*. two *d*. *Educ*: Lincoln School. *Studied*: Lincoln School of Art (1949-51, Toni Bartl), Central School of Art and Design (1951-53, Dora Billington). *Works in collections*: V&A; Southampton A.G.; Crafts Council; Leicester Educ. Authority; Usher Gallery, Lincoln; Abbots Hall, Keswick; Paisley A.G.: Boymans van Beuningen, Rotterdam; Bellrive Museum, Zurich; Penn. State University, USA; Gateshead A.G.; Swindon A.G.; Museum of Art, Melbourne; Museum of Art, Perth; Knukke-Heiste, Keramion, W.Germany; Octagon Centre, Idaho, USA. *Address*: Barrett Marsden Gallery, 17-18 Grt. Sutton St., London EC1V 0DN.

BALDWIN, Mariella Christina, MA Diploma Botamical Illustration, English Gardening School. Awards: RHS Silver medal (2009), Vice Chancellor's Prize, University of Sussex (2011). *Medium*: watercolour, drawing. *b*: Dorking, 10 Feb 1958. *Partner*: Christopher Grundy. two *s*. one *d*. *Studied*: English Gardening School, Chelsea Physic Garden (1997), UCA Farnham (BA Hons Fine Art, 2009); West Dean College (PGDip, 2010); University of Sussex (MA Visual Arts 2011). *Exhib*: Hunt Institute for Botanical Documentation, Pittsburgh, USA; Ursus Gallery, New York, USA; Daphne Johns Contemporary Art, London SW1; RHS, Vincent Square, London; Bolton Street Gallery, London; Ebury Gallery, London; Hampton Court Palace and others in UK and USA. *Works in collections*: Hunt Institute for Botanical Documentation, Pittsburgh, USA; Chelsea Physic Garden/Hampton Court Palace. *Publications*: "Botanical Painting" (Crowood Press, 2011). *Works Reproduced*: Flower Paintings from the Apothecaries' Garden (Brown, A., Cribb, P., Barlow, G., 1999); Financial Times. *Principal Works*: Turks Turban Cucurbita Maxima. *Recreations*: gardening, writing, sailing. *Clubs*: Chelsea Arts Club. *Address*: Walton Mill, Walton Lane, Bosham PO18 8QB. *Email*: mariella.baldwin@gmail.com *Website*: mariellabaldwin.com *Signs work*: monogram: M on top of B in centre of the 4 numerals of the year.

BALDWIN, Martyn John, DipAD; BP Portrait Awards (Commended). *Medium*: oil, drawing. *b*: Edgware, 18 May 1959. *s of*: Leslie & Doreen Baldwin. *m*: Christine. *Educ*: Downer Grammar School. *Studied*: Harrow School of Art (1979-83). *Exhib*: RA, NPG, Mall Galleries, Thompson Gallery, London; New Gallery, Walsall; Alton Gallery, Barnes. *Works in collections*: private/corporate, Queens Gallery Belfast. *Publications*: BP Portrait Award (1990-2001); National Portrait Gallery; 500 Portraits National Portrait Gallery. *Works Reproduced*: Star Portraits (Series 1) BBC. *Address*: 13 rue de Petit Puits, 13210 St. Remy de Provence, France. *Email*: info@martynbaldwin.com *Website*: www.martynbaldwin.com *Signs work*: "M. Baldwin" or "BALDWIN.".

BALDWIN, Nancy, painter. *b*: 3 Mar 1935. *d of*: Hayden Thomas Chandler. *m*: Gordon Baldwin. one *s*. two *d*. *Educ*: St. Joseph's Convent, Lincoln. *Studied*: Lincoln School of Art

(1949-52, Toni Bartl), Central School of Art and Design (1952-54, Dora Billington). *Exhib*: Reading Gallery, Thames Gallery, Windsor, The Gallery, Eton College, Cross Keys Gallery, Beaconsfield, Salix, Windsor, Oxford Gallery, City Museum and Gallery, Stoke-on-Trent, Midland Group, Nottingham, Ikon, Birmingham, Holsworthy, London, Carmel College Gallery, Bohun Gallery, Henley, Ellingham Mill, Bungay, prize winner Midland View (1980), Lynne Strover Gallery, Cambridge, Barrett Marsden Gallery, London; Ruithin Centre Wales; Mission Swansea; Eton College Gallery; Jam Eton. *Works in collections*: Ashmolean Museum, Oxford and private collections in UK, Italy, Switzerland, Belgium, Hong Kong, France, USA. *Address*: Rylands House, Greathales St., Market Drayton TF9 1JN.

BALDWIN, Peter, NDD (1962); Guella Purchase Trust Award - Eastern Open. *Medium*: oil. *b*: Aldeburgh, Suffolk, 23 Feb 1941. *s of*: B & K.N. Baldwin. one *s*. one *d*. *Studied*: Norwich School of Art (1958-62 with Jeffrey Camp and Michael Andrews). *Exhib*: Affordable Art Fair, Battersea (2000); Eastern Open (2002, 03, 04, 05); Norwich Castle Open (2005, 2008, 2012); Royal Academy Summer Show (2007, 2008); Retrospective - Gallery 18/21, Norwich; Duncan Campbell Fine Art, London (2010). *Works in collections*: Castle Museum, Norwich; Norfolk County Council; N. Norfolk District Council. *Commissions*: private. *Publications*: 'Wide Skies - A Century of Painters in Norfolk', Dictionary of Artists in Britain, 'Water Marks' art in East Anglia. *Works Reproduced*: Modern Painters, Green Pebble Magazines, oil paintings in public ownership. *Principal Works*: 'Havergate Island' - Castle Museum, Norwich; 'Beeston Hill' - North Norfolk District Council. *Recreations*: sailing. *Clubs*: Norwich 20 Group. *Misc*: Chairman of Norfolk County Council (1995/6). *Address*: 10 Barford Road, Sheringham, Norfolk, NR26 8EQ. *Email*: peterbaldwin@john-lewis.com *Website*: www.peterbaldwinartist.co.uk *Signs work*: "PB".

BALDWIN, Warren, DipAD (1971); Singer & Friedlander/Sunday Times Watercolour Competition (3rd prize 1990, 1992, 1st Prize 1995), The Hunting Art Prize (2nd 1995), The South West Academy of Art Annual Exhbn (1st 2000), The Prince of Wales Award for Portrait Drawing RSPP (2003), The Jerwood Drawing Prize (2008). *Medium*: watercolour, drawing, prints. *b*: London, 7 Apr 1950. *m*: Wilhemina Croonenberghs. *Studied*: Wimbledon School of Art (1967-68), The London College of Printing (1968-71), but mainly self-taught, in self-imposed isolation 1971-81. *Exhib*: RA Summer Exhbn, Mall Galleries, RSPP, Discerning Eye, NEAC, The Jerwood Drawing Prize, National Portrait Gallery Portrait Awards, Offer Waterman & Co, Waterhouse & Dodd (Cork Street), RCA, Holburne Museum of Art Bath, many mixed shows since 1982. *Works in collections*: Singer & Friedlander, Beecroft Art Gallery, many private collections in UK, Europe and Asia. *Address*: 2 Leaphill Road, Bournemouth, Dorset, BH7 6LU. *Signs work*: 'Warren Baldwin' on reverse.

BALKWILL, Raymond James, SWAc (elected Academician of the South West Academy of Fine and Applied Art, 2006); *Medium*: watercolour, pastel, oil. *b*: Exeter, 7 Oct 1948. *m*: Jane. two *s*. *Studied*: Exeter College of Art. *Exhib*: Open shows including RI, RWA, Bristol, South West Academy, Exeter. *Works in collections*: internationally. *Publications*: regular contributor of articles to 'The Artist'. Author of 7 books. 'Ray Balkwill's Exe Estuary', 'Watercolour Plus. . .', 'Coastal Landscapes', 'Painting Landscapes with Atmosphere', 'A Picture of Devon', 'A Picture of Cornwall', 'Travelling Light'. *Clubs*: St. Ives Soc. of Artists. *Address*: 'Thistledown', Marley Rd., Exmouth, Devon EX8 4PP. *Email*: ray@raybalkwill.co.uk *Website*: www.raybalkwill.co.uk *Signs work*: " RAY BALKWILL."

BALL, Gerald, RCA (1979); painter in water-colour and tempera. *b*: Ashton-under-Lyne, 24 May 1948. *s of*: Robert Ball, musician. *m*: Ann Mumford. *Educ*: Hartshead Comprehensive. *Studied*: Ashton-under-Lyne CFE. *Exhib*: RWS, Richard Hagen, Ltd., RI, Manchester Academy, Agnews, Tegfryn Gallery, Bourne Gallery, Catto Gallery, David

Curzon Gallery, Walker Galleries, Crossing Gate Gallery, Brian Sinfield. *Works in collections*: Coleg Harlech. Work in many private collections worldwide. *Commissions*: numerous. *Address*: Old Golderwell, Golderfield, Pudleston, Leominster, Herefordshire HR6 0RG. *Signs work*: "GERRY BALL."

BALMER, Barbara, RSA, ARSA (1973), RSW (1966), RGI (1988); painter in oil and water-colour. *b*: Birmingham 1929. *m*: George Mackie, DFC, RDI, RSW. two *d*. *Studied*: Coventry School of Art; Edinburgh College of Art. *Exhib*: one-man shows: Demarco Gallery, Edinburgh (1965-70), Scottish Gallery, Edinburgh (1975, 1980, 1985, 1988), Posterngate Gallery, Hull (1983), Stirling Gallery (1976), Usher Gallery, Lincoln (1984); Retrospective '55-'95 Touring Exhbn. (1995-96). *Works in collections*: Glasgow Kelvingrove A.G., Edinburgh City Art Centre, Aberdeen A.G., Perth A.G., SNPG, SAC, Usher Gall. Lincoln, Leicester City Museum, Royal Bank of Scotland, Citibank, Coventry Herbert A.G., Dundee McManus A.G., Stamford Museum. *Works Reproduced*: Many catalogues and Giclee prints. *Principal Works*: Large oil paintings of Tuscany/Umbria; posthumous portrait of Donald Dewar, Scotland's 1st 'First Minister'. *Address*: 32 Broad St., Stamford, Lincs, PE9 1PJ. *Signs work*: "Barbara Balmer."

BALMER, Derek Rigby, RWA; painter in oil; President, Royal West of England Academy; RA (Hon.) Pro. Chancellor University of the West of England; Doctor of Arts (Hon) UWE. *b*: Bristol, 28 Dec 1934. *s of*: Geoffrey Johnson Balmer. *m*: Elizabeth Mary Rose. one *s*. one *d*. *Educ*: St. Gabriel's Convent, Waterloo House, Sefton Pk. *Studied*: West of England College of Art (Dennis Darch, Derek Crowe, Paul Feiler). *Represented by*: Anthony Hepworth Fine Art, Bath; Catto Gallery, London. *Exhib*: Arnolfini (four), New Art Centre, Leicester Gallery, RWA Represented by Anthony Hepworth Fine Art Bath, and Gisela Van Beers London, Dutch Dealers: Smelik and Stokking The Hague and Amsterdam; recent one-man shows at Anthony Hepworth, London; Six Chapel Row, Bath. Also RA Summer Show; Retrospective (1950-2007), Royal West of England Academy, Bristol 'Presidents Eye'; Campden Gallery (2005, 2008, 2011); Catto Gallery, London (2010, 2012); Catto Gallery, London (solo 2014); Art Room, Topsham, Devon (solo 2015). *Works in Collections*: RWA Collection; Royal Collection. *Publications*: 'A Singular Vision' published 2012 by John Sansom, a memoir by Derek Balmer and Andrew Lambirth. *Clubs*: Chelsea Arts. *Address*: Mulberry House, 12 Avon Grove, Sneyd Pk., Bristol 9 1PJ. *Signs work*: "Balmer" or "Derek Balmer."

BANKS, Brian, painter in acrylic, oil, mixed media. *b*: London, 21 Oct 1939. *s of*: William John Ralph. *m*: Christine, divorced 1974. two *s*. one *d*. *Educ*: Sir Walter St. John's Grammar School, London. *Studied*: St. Martin's (1956-57), Peter de Francia, Edward Middleditch, James Dring; privately with John Flavin, ARCA (1958). *Exhib*: one-man shows: Colin Jellicoe Gallery, Manchester; Ansdell Gallery, London; Zaydler Gallery, London; Fermoy Art Gallery, King's Lynn; Conway Hall, London; Leigh Gallery, London, (1984, 1985), Trinity Arts Centre, Tunbridge Wells. Represented by Leigh Gallery, Bloomsbury, London. *Works in collections*: Britain, Australia, France, USA, Denmark. *Address*: 8 Ravenet Ct., Battersea Pk. Rd., London SW11 5HE. *Signs work*: "BANKS" (year).

BANKS, Claire Elinor, BA (Hons)1st Class, MFA; Alastair Salvesen Art Travelling Scholarship (administered through RSA) 1995; Rome Scholar in Painting, British School at Rome (1992-3), Anna Miller Trust Scholarship (2001). *Medium*: oil, watercolour, drawing. *b*: Edinburgh, 26 Mar 1967. *Educ*: Craigmount High School. *Studied*: Edinburgh College of Art (1985-91). *Represented by*: Open Eye Gallery, Edinburgh. *Exhib*: 11 solo exhbns in Scotland and Italy, including RSA, Open Eye Gallery Edinburgh, Florence (2), Cremona, Italy (1); many group exhbns including RSA and RSW. *Works in collections*: RSA Archive, City of Edinburgh Council, Paintings in Hospitals Scotland. *Official Purchasers*: RSA Archive, City of Edinburgh Council, Paintings in Hospitals Scotland. *Address*: 2 Grosvenor

Place, Main Street, St. Boswells, Roxburghshire, TD6 0AT. *Email*: cbjb@bosells.fsnet.co.uk *Signs work*: Claire Banks (on reverse of work).

BANKS, Nancy, UA, MFPS; sculptor in bronze, direct plaster, terracotta and mixed media. *d of*: the late W.J. Yates. *m*: John Banks, M.Eng., F.Eng. two *s*. *Educ*: Nutgrove, Rainhill, Lancs. *Studied*: Sir John Cass College of Art, and Eltham Art Institute. *Exhib*: Mall Galleries, RBA, UA, NS, RMS, SWA, SPS, Barbican, Bloomsbury, Guildhall, Alpine, Weighouse galleries, I.E.E., Blackheath, Usher, Lincs., Worthing Museum and A.G., MAS-F. *Works in collections*: UK, USA, Japan, Spain. *Commissions*: several private; trophy for presentation to HMS Brave. *Clubs*: L.L.L.C. *Address*: B.1. Marine Gate, Brighton, E. Sussex BN2 5TQ. *Signs work*: "N. BANKS" or "Nancy Banks" depending on size of work.

BANNING, Paul, RI (2005), RSMA (2004); N.D.D. (Hons.) Furniture Design (1956); painter in watercolour and oil, most subject matter; designed furniture in industry until 1986, now professional painter; Llewellyn Alexander Award, RI Exhibition (2002), RWS C21 Freshfields Prize (2000); AFAS Army Museum Prize (2005, 2007); St. Cuthberts Watercolour prize RSMA (2008); RI Turner watercolour Award (2011). *b*: Port of Spain, Trinidad, 1 Aug 1934. *m*: Margaret. three *s*. one *d*. *Educ*: Clifton College, Bristol. *Studied*: West of England College of Art, Bristol (1953-1957), taught drawing by Victor Passmore. *Exhib*: many. in UK, Holland, Dubai, France, USA and Trinidad; NEAC, RA, Singer and Friedlander Watercolour Competition, Lynn Painters Stainers (2007, 2014); RWS/Sunday Times (2009, 2010, 2011). *Works in collections*: Freshfields. *Publications*: articles for Artists, and Artists & Illustrators Magazine; L'Art de L'Aquarelle France, and Watercolour Artists USA. *Recreations*: Gardening. *Clubs*: Member of Wapping Group of Artists, Chelsea Art Society, Armed Forces Art Society. *Address*: Woodlands Corner, Redlands Lane, Ewshot, Farnham, Surrey GU10 5AS. *Email*: paulbanning@uk2.net *Website*: www.paulbanning.com *Signs work*: Now signs work "PB."

BANNISTER, Geoffrey Ernest John, served Royal Navy Minesweepers (1942-46); EVT instructor in Commercial Art (Royal Navy, 1945-46). *Medium*: artist/designer, figure, scraper-board, water-colour, oils. *b*: Birmingham, 15 Jan 1924. *s of*: Henry J. Bannister. *m*: Beryl Parr Robinson, 1949 (deceased, 1966). one *s*. one *d*; remarried, 1967, Susan Jennefer Peters, 2 *s*. *Educ*: St. Philip's Grammar School. *Exhib*: Walsall Art Gallery; Worcester Cathedral. *Works in collections*: boardrooms, private homes. *Commissions*: chairpersons, directors, general public, portraits, animals, landscapes etc. *Works Reproduced*: all private commissions. *Principal Works*: boardrooms/private homes. *Recreations*: golf - now retired; painting pictures. *Clubs*: Catenian Assoc., Walsall Society of Artists. *Address*: Crossways, 811 Sutton Rd., Aldridge, Walsall, W. Midlands WS9 0QJ. *Email*: geoff_bannister@hotmail.com *Website*: www.geoffbannisterartist.com *Signs work*: "Geoff Bannister."

BAPTIST, Gerry (Gerald William), RE. *Medium*: oil, drawing, print. *b*: India, 16 Sep 1935. *m*: Jean. one *s*. one *d*. Studied: Walthamstow School of Art (1952-53); London School of Printing (1953-56). *Exhib*: regularly in RE shows, Bankside Gallery, London; many one-man and mixed shows. *Works in collections*: Guildford Borough Council; Bank of England; Ashmolean Museum, Oxford. *Commissions*: Rosensteils Publishers, Waitrose, Starbucks, W.H. Smiths, Marks and Spencer, London Contemporary Art and others, including private commissions, particularly portraits. *Recreations*: Sailing. *Address*: White Hollow, Clandon Road, West Clandon, Guildford, GU4 7UW. *Email*: gerry.baptist@gmail.com *Website*: www.gerrybaptist.co.uk *Signs work*: "Baptist".

BARANOFF, Elena, Fine Artist - paintings, portraits, icons, miniatures; Mundy Sovereign Portrait Award (2005); MASF Historical & Mythical Award (2003); MASF Mixed Media Award, (2004); RMS Gold Memorial Bowl Hon. Mention, (1997, 1998, 2002,

2008, 2011); Co-Founder, Egg Tempera Movement. *Medium*: egg tempera. *b*: Ivanovo, Russia, 10 Aug 1960, divorced. one *d*. *Studied*: Masters Diploma in Miniature Painting (1977-1982), Palekh Art College, Russia. *Exhib*: National Portrait Gallery, UK; Dean Gallery, UK; Southampton City Art Gallery, UK; Springfield Art Museum, USA; Smithsonian Institution, USA; Leepa-Rattner Museum, USA; Gulf Coast Museum, USA; Mall Galleries, UK. *Works in collections*: HRH Prince of Wales; His Grace Archbishop Kyrill of San Francisco; Private collections - USA, UK. *Commissions*: Private collectors, art galleries and companies - USA, UK. *Publications*: BBC World News; The Scotsman; Press Association News; Santa Fe New Mexican; Gentry Design. *Works Reproduced*: catalogues, newspapers, magazines. *Address*: 268 Bush Street, # 3625, San Francisco, CA 94104, USA. *Email*: elenabaranoff@elenabaranoff.com *Website*: www.elenabaranoff.com *Signs work*: 'Elena Vladimir Baranoff'.

BARANOWSKA, Janina, artist in oil. *b*: Poland, 28 Oct 1925. *d of*: Josef Zbaraszewski, officer in Polish Army. *m*: Maksymilian Baranowski. one *s*. *Educ*: In Poland, Middle East and Scotland. *Studied*: Borough Polytechnic under Prof. Bomberg (1947-50), School of Art at the Polish University of Stefan Batory in London (1951-54). *Exhib*: One-man shows: Drian Gallery, Grabowski Gallery, Raymond Duncan Galleries, Alwin Gallery, Grand Prix Rencontre Lyon, France, Det Lille Galleri, Norway, State Galleries in Krakow and Poznan, Poland, Royal Festival Hall, London, Dixon Gallery - University of London, Bloomsbury Gallery, Woburn Fine A.G., Polish Cultural Inst. Mixed exhib.: RA, Burlington Gallery, Cassel Gallery, RBA Galleries, New Vision Centre, Walker's Galleries, Whitechapel A.G., Edinburgh. *Publications*: Editor of Contemporary Polish Artists in G.B. (1983), Form and Colour (Congress of Polish Culture). *Clubs*: W.I.A.C., Group 49, I.A.L., I.A.A. - U.K. National Com., A.P.A. in G.B. (Chairman), N.S.P.S. (Mem.). *Address*: 20 Strathmore Rd., London SW19 8DB. *Signs work*: "Baranowska."

BARBER, Raymond, ACFI, AM.II.M., City and Guilds, London Inst. (1943), EMEU (1937), SSIA (1945); Course Tutor at Footwear Dept Wellingborough Technical College; Footwear Section Head (retd.). *b*: 30 Sep 1921. *m*: Eileen. *Educ*: Kettering Rd. Inst., Northampton, College of Technology, Northampton, Leicester College of Technology. *Exhib*: Walsall, London, in conjunction with "Leather, Footwear and Allied Industries" Export Corp., Ltd.; Quality Footwear Exhib., Seymour Hall, London. *Clubs*: N.C.T.S.A., N.G.C., N.S.M.E. *Address*: 10 Wantage Cl., Moulton, Northampton NN3 7UY. *Signs work*: "Renny."

BARBER KENNEDY, Mat, BA (Hons) (1984), MA (1988), RI (1994); painter in mixed media collage using water based media, water-colour, acrylic, ink. *b*: Hornchurch, Essex, 7 Oct 1962. *m*: Sherry Kennedy. three *s*. *Educ*: Coopers Company and Coborn School. *Studied*: Royal College of Art. *Represented by*: Shell House Gallery, Ledbury; Linda Blackstone Gallery, Pinner; E.S. Lawrence Gallery, Charleston S.C. & Aspen, Co. *Exhib*: annual Spring show at Mall Galleries, regular events at galleries in England and America. *Works in collections:* Chicago Public Library, Hertfordshire County Council. *Commissions*: The Marchday Group, Pollard Thomas & Edwards Architects. *Address*: 1706 1/2 S. Halsted St., Chicago, Illinois 60608, USA. *Email*: mbk@matbarberkennedy.com *Website*: www.matbarberkennedy.com

BARFIELD, Mary Lane, President Royal Birmingham Society of Artists (1995-2001); Honorary Doctorate from Aston University. *Medium*: oil, drawing. *b*: Detroit, Mich., USA, 23 Sep 1937. *m*: decd. one *s*. one *d*. *Studied*: Michigan State University, USA; Queen & Adelphi Colleges, NY; Birkbeck, University of London. *Represented by*: RBSA. *Exhib*: RBSA; Mall Galleries, London; Royal West of England Academy, Bristol; various provincial galleries in the West Midlands. *Works Reproduced*: Landscapes - for website and publicity RBSA. *Recreations*: singing in 2 choirs, travel, archaeology. *Clubs*: U3A. *Address*:

14 Blenheim Road, Moseley, Birmingham B13 9YY. *Email*: mary.lane@blueyonder.co.uk *Signs work*: "M.L.Barfield".

BARKER, Allen, HND (1960); artist in acrylic paint; Personal tutor and Specialist lecturer, Central St. Martin's School of Art. *b*: Australia, 11 Mar 1937. *m*: Marilyn Norton-Harvey. one *s*. *Educ*: Lismore High School. *Studied*: art at National Art School, Sydney (1955-60); lithography at Central School of Art, London (1962). *Exhib*: one-man shows: University of Kent (1967), University of Essex (1968), Galerie Junge Generation, Vienna (1969), Lucy Milton Gallery, London (1971, 1973), Galerie Van Hulsen, Amsterdam (1972), Ferens A.G., Hull (1973), City A.G. Manchester (1973), Laing A.G., Newcastle-upon-Tyne (1973), Museum and City A.G., Leicester (1974), City Museum and A.G., Portsmouth (1974), Ikon Gallery, Birmingham (1974), Park Sq. Gallery, Leeds (1974), Kinsman Morrison Gallery, London (1975), Galerie Grafica, Tokyo (1976), ICA (1976), Structured Theatre Co., Nuffield Theatre, Lancaster University (1976), Galerie Grafica, Nasaka (1977), Architectural Assoc., London (1977), Coracle Press, London (1978), Galleri Morner, Stockholm (1978), Gallery Pinc Studio, London (1996), 21st Century Gallery, London (1997), retrospective exhbn. Bonham's Fine Art, London (1998), Cambridge University (Sir Norman Foster Building, Faculty of Law, one-man show, 1998), Carpet designed by Barker produced and made by Mike Evans and showing in London (1999), ArcArt Gallery, London (2004, 2006). Documentation of all exhbns. held in the archives of the Tate Gallery, London (1999); 2010 Ongoing artistic director at La Strada Fasion Circus; Proud2 Gallery at the O2, London (2011); Le Sorelle Gallery, London (2013). *Works in collections*: National Art School Gallery, Sydney, Australia; Sheffield Museum and City A.G., Leicester Museum and City A.G., Manchester City A.G., Galerie Orez Mobile, Den Haag, Holland, AT and T, New York, Museum Boymans Van Beuningen, Rotterdam, Cambridge University, Sir Norman Foster Bldg., Faculty of Law; numerous work in private collections. *Publications*: The Guardian, review by William Valley, Manchester (1973); Financial Times, review by Maria Vaizey, London (1974); L'Art Vivant, colour article by Georgina Oliver, Paris (1974); Studio International Journal of Modern Art, colour article by Jennifer Oille, London (1975); The Daily Telegraph, review of The Structured Theatre by F.H. London (1976); Connaissance des Arts, colour article on young English painters, Paris (1977); Two-page colour article on Boreatton Workshop, Nippon Broadcast Publications, Japan (1992); T.N.T. Magazine, two-page colour article by Tiffany Bakker, London (1996); Evening Standard, review of the Bonhams Exhibition, London (1997); The Australian Magazine, colour article and review by Jane Cornwell titled "London Bridges", (July 2000). *Misc*: Formed: Structured Theatre Co. (1976), Bassett Architectural Constructions and Designs (1984), Boreatton Bat Soc. of Fine Artists and Designers (1990). Travelling Visually - Boreatton Hall, Shrewsbury - Master Classes and Performance Workshops (1991). *Address*: 14 Bassett Rd., London W10 6JJ. *Email*: info@allenbarker.com *Website*: www.allenbarker.com *Signs work*: "Barker."

BARKER, Clive, sculptor in bronze and chrome. *b*: Luton, Beds., 29 Aug 1940. *s of*: F. Barker. *m*: Rose Bruen - divorced. two *s*. *Educ*: Beech Hill Secondary Modern. *Studied*: Luton College of Technology and Art (1957-59) under Clifford Barry, ARCA. *Represented by*: Whitford Fine Art, 6 Duke Street, St. James's, London SW1. *Exhib*: Robert Fraser Gallery, Hanover Gallery, Musee d'Art Moderne, Museum of Modern Art, NY, Palais des Beaux-Arts, Palazzo Strozzi, Whitford Fine Art London, etc. *Works in collections*: Arts Council of Gt. Britain, British Council, V&A, Tate Gallery, British Museum, National Portrait Gallery, Smithsonian Institution, Washington DC; Stadtliche Kunsthalle, Mannheim; Gallery of South Australia, Adelaide. *Publications*: Pop Art Re-defined (Thames & Hudson), Image as Language (Penguin), Pop Art (Studio Vista), Art in Britain 1969-70 (Dent), Objekt Kunst (Dumont); Clive Barker - Catalogue Raisonne 1958-2000 Sculpture. . .Skira 2002 by Anjo Fermon and Marco Livingstone. *Address*: c/o Ms A Fernon, 55 Cadogan Square, London SW1X 0HY. *Signs work*: "Clive Barker."

BARKER, Dale Devereux, RE, BA (Hons) (1984), H DipFA (Slade) (1986); printmaker, public artist. *b*: Leicester, 4 Feb 1962. *m*: Rebecca Weaver. *Educ*: Alderman Newton's Grammar School, Leicester. *Studied*: Loughborough College of Art and Design, Leicester Polytechnic and Slade (Stanley Jones). *Exhib*: 26 solo exhbns. *Works in collections*: Tate Gallery, V&A, Ashmolean, New York Public Library, Harvard University, Yale University, Columbia University. *Commissions*: Clifford Chance, British Rail, Lloyds Insurance, Taylor-Woodrow, Penguin Books, Colchester BC, Wolverhampton BC. *Publications*: Published own collaborative books with poets Martin Stannard (G.B.), Paul Violi (U.S.) and Kenneth Koch (U.S.) *Recreations*: competitive swimming. *Address*: The Bungalow, Capel Grove, Capel St. Mary, Ipswich, IP9 2JS. *Email*: dale.d.b.@talk21.com *Signs work*: "D.D. Barker."

BARKER, David, DipAD (1966), ATC (1967), HonRE (1995), Prof. Lu Xun Academy of Fine Arts, China (1997); Senior lecturer/research translator; Senior lecturer, University of Ulster, Prof., Lu Xun Academy of Fine Arts, Mem. International Exchange Com., China National Academy of Fine Arts; drawing/silk screen. *b*: Dorchester, 11 Jan 1945. *m*: Catherine Elizabeth (née Grover). one *s*. two *d*. *Educ*: University of London (1962-67), University of Leeds (1988). *Studied*: Goldsmiths' College, London. *Publications*: An English-Chinese Glossary of Printmaking Terms (1995), The Chinese Arts Academies Printmaking Exhibition (1993), The Techniques of the Chinese Print (in preparation), The Woodcuts of Zheng Shuang (1999), '30 Years of the Printmaking Workshop' (2001). *Address*: University of Ulster, School of Art and Design, York St., Belfast BT15 1ED. *Signs work*: "David Barker."

BARKER, Jill, BA (1982), SGFA (2001); MA (2004) Printmaking. *Medium*: wood engraving. *b*: Hong Kong, 21 May 1955. *d of*: Professor & Mrs D. Barker. *Educ*: Durham High School. *Studied*: Newcastle-upon-Tyne (1979-1982) under Ralph Sylvester; University of the West of England, Bristol (2002-2004). *Exhib*: national and international events. *Works in collections*: Princeton University, Graphic Arts Library, USA; Wood Engravers Network; Hutton-Wilson Collection, and private. *Commissions*: privately undertaken. *Publications*: Alembic Private Press Guide (1984); Holy Sonnets by John Donne (Alembic Press 1986), Black Goddess (Chiron Press 1991); 'Time Beyond Time' by H.Todd (Sun on Earth Books, 2005); 'Works on Wood' (Chiron Press, 2001); 'Small Blocks' Vols 1, 2, 3, (Chiron Press, 2002). *Official Purchasers*: Taunton & Somerset NHS Trust (2005); Papyrus Ltd. (2005); Sedgemoor District Council (1997); Welsh Development Agency (1992). *Address*: 7 Church House, Churchview, Evercreech, Somerset BA4 6HX. *Signs work*: "Jill Barker."

BARKER, Kathy, ASWA; BA Hons, MA Printmaking; 1999 Florence Trust Studio Award. *Medium*: Portraits - oils & charcoals. *b*: Hayle, Cornwall, 27 Sep 1963. one *d*. *Studied*: Foundation, University of the London Arts (UAL) (1991-92); BA Hons, UAL (1992-95); City & Guilds 7307 Stage 1 Teacher Training. *Exhib*: London: Piers Feetham Gallery (2005), Art Direct Westbourne Studios (2005), Royal Society of Portrait Painting, Mall Galleries (2008), Society of Women Artists, Mall Galleries (2008, 09, 10), Art for Youth, Mall Galleries (2006/7), The Florence Trust Studios (2000), Marks & Spencer Corporate Head Office (2000); Raw Art Gallery (1999); Charles Cecil, Florence, Italy (2009); West Dean College, West Sussex (2006/7); The Beatrice Royal Gallery, Eastleigh (1999). *Works in collections*: private collections. *Commissions*: private portrait commissions, and to write 'Drawing and Painting the Clothed Figure' (2005). *Publications*: 'Drawing and Painting the Clothed Figure' (Crowood Press, 2005). *Principal Works*: Portraits. *Misc*: Murals and landscapes. Tutor: Life drawing and portraiture. Taught at West Dean College (Drawing tutor for Postgraduate Tapestry & Visual Arts (2008/09/10); short course tutor West Dean (2002-08). *Address*: 65 Rosaville Road, Fulham, London SW6 7BN. *Email*: kathy_barker@hotmail.com *Website*: www.kathybarker.co.uk *Signs work*: "KATHY BARKER ASWA".

BARKER, Noël, ABNA Member. *Medium*: oil, acrylic. b: Leeds, 23 Dec 1924. *m*: decd. one *s*. two *d*. *Educ*: St. Leonards at St. Andrews, Fife. *Studied*: self taught. *Exhib*: RONA, Ash Barn, Ann Mei Chadwick, Barbican, Bozman Gallery SA, Crane Gallery, Century Gallery, Festival Theatre, First Floor Gallery Naive, Australia, Harrods, Nankey Gallery Amsterdam, Medici Gallery, Oast House, Round House, Royal Academy, Webbs Gallery, Worlds End Gallery, Wilma Wayne Gallery, Wykeham Gallery, Courcoux & Courcoux, Stockbridge, ABNA. *Works in collections*: nuberous both in UK and abroad - mostly private collections. *Commissions*: mostly private. *Publications*: Encyclopedia of Naive Art (pub. 1984), RONA Guide to Naive Art. *Principal Works*: Naive. *Recreations*: sailing. *Clubs*: Royal Southern Yacht Club. *Address*: 8 College Close, Hamble, Southampton SO31 4QU. *Email*: moorings@btinternet.com *Website*: www.noëlgallery.ndo.co.uk

BARLOW, Andrew David, SM (1990), BWS (1995), ARMS (2012). Selected Finalist, International Artists Competition (2001). *Medium*: oil, watercolour, drawing, prints. *b*: Calcutta, India, 8 Jun 1932. *m*: Joyce Davies Barlow. two *d*. *Educ*: Acklam Grammar School (M'bro), Worksop College, Notts. *Studied*: Constantine College: HND Mechanical Engineering (1955); studied Life Drawing (1950-55). *Exhib*: RMS, Mall Galleries; Cork Street Gallery, London, The International Guild of Artists; Leven Art Society; group and solo exhibitions, NE England. *Works in collections*: in Australia, New Zealand, South Africa, Canada, UK, Japan, India; Ashorne Hill Management College (paintings and prints. *Commissions*: Cleveland Bridge/Trafalgar House; Ashorne Hill Management College. *Works Reproduced*: Limited Edition prints of local watercolours. *Recreations*: photography, cooking, occasional golf. *Clubs*: Leven Art Society, Stokesley. *Misc*: Runs private painting class in the village of Kildale, North Yorkshire. Father was also an engineer and a watercolourist. *Address*: 11 Fanacurt Road, Guisborough, North Yorkshire TS14 8BJ. *Email*: andrew.david.barlow@googlemail.com *Website*: http://levenart.org/levenart/members-work/Pages/andrew-barlow.html *Signs work*: "A.D.BARLOW ARMS".

BARLOW, Bohuslav, DipAD (Hons) (1970), SGFA; artist mainly in oil, some pastel. *b*: Bruntal, Czechoslovakia, 8 Jul 1947. *m*: Karen Barlow. one *s*. one *d*. *Educ*: St. Mary's Grammar School, Blackburn. *Studied*: Manchester (1966), Central School of Art, London (1967-70). *Exhib*: RA, RE, PS, International Contemporary Art Fairs. Work in many Northern municipal collections, Manchester Academy. *Works in collections*: Leeds City Council, Coopers & Lybrand, N.Rothschild, Royal Family of Saudi Arabia. *Commissions*: Four large murals for MEPC plc., Bronte Soc. *Publications*: Visual Alchemy - Bohuslav Barlow; "Charms and Chimera" vols 1-4. *Works Reproduced*: www.penninegallery.co.uk. *Recreations*: running, on fell and road; playing piano. *Clubs*: Manchester Academy. *Misc*: Opened own gallery in Todmorden 1997. *Address*: Shade Studio, 58 Burnley Road, Todmorden, Lancs. OL14 5EY. *Email*: bohuslav12@googlemail.com *Website*: www.bohuslavbarlow.co.uk *Signs work*: "B. Barlow."

BARLOW, Gillian, BA (1970), MA (1971), PGCE (1972), RHS Gold medal (1994, 1997, 1999). *Medium*: artist in water-colour on paper and vellum. *b*: Khartoum, Sudan, 10 Dec 1944. *Educ*: Ashford School for Girls, Kent; University of Sussex. *Studied*: Slade School (1962-63, Patrick George, John Aldridge). *Exhib*: solo shows: British Council, Bombay; Hudson View Gallery, NY; Vassar College, NY; Blond Fine Art, London; Spinks Fine Art, London; numerous mixed shows: Newhouse Galleries, NY; Millbrook Galleries, NY; Mall Galleries, London. *Works in collections*: Hunt Inst. of Botanical Documentation, Pittsburgh, USA; Vassar College, NY; Lady Margaret Hall, Oxford; Boscobel Restoration, NY; British Council, India; Shirley Sherwood Botanical Painting Collection, London; Royal Horticultural Soc. London; Chelsea Physic Garden, London; Royal Botanic Gardens, Kew, London. *Commissions*: numerous private commissions. *Publications*: Plantsman, (1992, 1993); New Plantsman (1994, 1997); Curtis Botanical Magazine, Kew (since 1998 annually). *Works Reproduced*: Contemporary Botanical Artists (RBG Kew, 1996), A Passion for Plants (Cassell 2001), Treasures of Botanical Art (RGG Kew 2008), Losing Paradise? (ASBA, New York, 2009). *Email*: gillianbarlow@btinternet.com *Signs work*: 'G.B.' and 'G.BARLOW'.

BARNARD, Roger, BA Fine Art (1974). *Medium*: participatory set-ups some include video; painting, drawing, photography, holography, writing. *b*: London, 4 Nov 1951. *s of*: E.C. and J.M. Barnard. *Educ*: Chichester High School for Boys. *Studied*: West Sussex College of Design (1970-71), North Staffs. Polytechnic (1971-74). *Exhib*: one-man shows, Tate Gallery, Air, Scottish Arts Council Gallery, Third Eye Centre, South Bank London, Truro, etc.; mixed shows, Tate, Serpentine, Hayward, Air, Holborn Underground Comp., Whitechapel, Arts Council of G.B. touring exhbn., Coventry, Chichester, Third Eye Centre, Osaka Triennale '90' (Painting), '91' (Print) Japan, etc. *Works in collections*: Royal Inst. of Cornwall County Coll., Contemporary Art Centre Osaka, Japan; private collections in UK, USA, France, Germany; UCH London. *Commissions*: Organisations, incl. British Refugee Council, and private individuals. *Address*: Hough Hall, Hough Hall Road, Moston, Manchester, M40 9NJ. *Signs work*: paintings since 1970 unsigned, drawings dated, some signed "R. Barnard."

BARNES, Ann Margaret, B.Ed(Hons) (1973), MFPS (1974), AMNS (1978), FRSA (1995). *Medium*: artist in airbrush, acrylic and mixed media on botanical themes. *b*: London. *d of*: William Barnes, water-colour artist. *Educ*: Wimbledon County School for Girls; Stockwell College of Education, Bromley. *Exhib*: FPS, NS, Soc. of Botanical Artists; one-man shows: London, Chiswick, Leatherhead, Henley, Croydon, Morden. *Address*: 16 Mount Pleasant, Ewell, Epsom, Surrey KT17 1XE. *Signs work*: "A. Barnes."

BARNES, Diane Stephanie, BA (Hons) 3-D design (Jewellery) Sheffield (1973), Leverhulme Travel Scholar (1973-74); printmaker in lino; demonstrator (Art in Action); artist in residence (Nature in Art, various schools, stately homes); part-time teacher of multiply disabled young adults. *b*: London. *m*: Roger (jeweller). two *s*. *Studied*: Sheffield Polytechnic (1970-73). *Exhib*: many, nationally and internationally including Beatrice Royal, Bankside, Mall Galleries. *Works in collections*: Gallup, Royal Marsden Hospital, Provident Bldg. Soc., National Trust, Dewsbury Hospital. *Commissions*: Year 2000 calendar for New Internationalist, which won "Best International Food Calendar 2000" Award. *Misc*: Appeared recently on "Handmade" for Channel 4 T.V. *Address*: 8 Moor Park Mount, Leeds LS6 4BU.

BARNES, Maggie (Dorothy Margaret), National Diploma in Studio Ceramics (Distinction); Rutherford Award (1978/79); Full Member, Society of Designer Craftsmen. *Medium*: sculpture - porcelain & handmade paper. *b*. Scarborough, 15 Aug 1940. d of: Wilfrid & Alice Nellist. *m*: David W. Barnes (divorced). three *s*. Educ: Scarborough Girls High School. *Studied*: Harrogate College of Art & Design (1976-1979); Burg Coraidelstein, Klotten an der Mosel (1987-1991). *Represented by*: Lund Gallery, North Yorkshire; Galerie Bowig, Hannover; Mercer Art Gallery, Harrogate; European Ceramics Gallery (own gallery). *Exhib*: UK, Belgium, Netherlands, Germany, Luxembourg, France; European Ceramics gallery; Gallery Böwig; Galerie 18; Society of Designer Craftsmen; Galerie 'L', Hamburg; Triennale de la Porcelaine 1992; many small exhibitions across UK and continental Europe. *Works in collections*: Kestner Museum, Hannover; Westerwald Museum; Mercer Art Gallery, Harrogate; Little Rock, Arkansas, USA; represented in private collections in UK, USA, Japan, Central Europe and Australia. *Publications*: Studio Ceramics, Contemporary Porcelain, Contemporary Studio Porcelain (all by Peter Lane); Ceramics Manual by Graham Flight. *Official Purchasers*: Kestner Museum, Hannover; Gallery Böwig, Hannover, Mercer Art Gallery, Harrogate; Cochem-an-der-Mosel (Council). *Works reproduced*: Nerikom - Small Publication 2012. *Principal Works*: small sculptures in unglazed porcelain & Nerikomi porcelain. *Recreations*: reading, good film, theatre, gallery visiting. *Misc*: Currently working on a period of research and development to produce body of work & illustrated history of my 30 years porcelain production (continuing). *Address*: Apartment 2, Rear 20 Finkle Street, Knaresborough, N. Yorks HG5 8AA. Email: info@maggiebarnes.co.uk. *Website*: www.maggiebarnes.co.uk *Signs work*: "Maggie Barnes MSD-C".

BARNES-MELLISH, Glynis Lily, SWA; BA Hons Fine Art (1975), Advanced Combined Fine Art Dip. (1983); portrait painter in water-colour. *Medium*: watercolour. *b*: Bromley, Kent, 10 Jun 1953. *d of*: Alan John Mellish. one *d*. *Educ*: The William School, Letchworth. *Studied*: St. Albans School of Art (1971-72, 1981-83), W. Surrey College of Art and Design (1972-75). *Exhib*: annually RI, SWA, PS. *Works in collections*: Self portrait - Lee Valley University. *Publications*: The Artist, Hodder & Stoughton, Penguin Books; DK Publishing; Quarto Books. *Clubs*: Cambridge Drawing Soc. *Misc*: Limited Edition Prints (Solomon & Whitehead Ltd.) *Address*: 44c High Street, Henlow, Bedfordshire, SG16 6AA. *Website*: www.barnesmellish.com *Signs work*: "Mellish."

BARNETT, Rosemary, RASA, FRBS; Founder and Director Frink School of Sculpture; curator Jerwood Sculpture Park (2000-2004); sculptor. *Medium*: stone/wood/bronze. *b*: Kingston-on-Thames, Surrey, Aug 1940. *m*: Nigel John Burfield Holmes. two *s*. two *d*. *Educ*: Queen's Gate, London. *Studied*: art at Kingston School of Art, Royal Academy Schools (Arnold Machin). *Exhib*: RA Summer Exhibitions, 43 Great Russell St., 1, Finsbury Av., Mall Gallery, Royal West of England Academy, Art in Action, Oxford, The Orangery, Holland Park, London W14; Botanical Gardens at Leicester University, Doddington Hall, Coughton Court, Foxlowe Gallery, Western Park. *Commissions*: Royal Mint, London University, Household Cavalry, Coventry Cathedral, Shallowford House Ecumenical Retreat Centre, St.Thomas's Church, Hanwell; St.Giles Church, Hartington, Derbyshire; private commissions. *Principal Works*: Quaker Service Memorial at National Memorial Arboretum. *Recreations*: walking. *Clubs*: Reynolds Club, Royal Society British Sculptors. *Address*: 25 Brookfields Road, Ipstones, Staffordshire, ST10 2LY. *Email*: rosemarybarnett25@hotmail.co.uk *Website*: www.rosemarybarnett.co.uk

BARNETT HUGHES, Emyr, Certificate in Education (1971), Certificate in Carving and Guilding (1983). *Medium*: Wood. *b*: Pentredwr, Llangollen, Wales, 12 Dec 1949. *s of*: Trevor Lloyd Hughes. *m*: Rosemary Hughes. one *s*. one *d*. *Educ*: Trinity College, Carmarthen, South Wales. *Studied*: City and Guilds of London Art School. *Exhib*: Wood carving Exhibitions and Trade Fayres; Eisteddfodau. *Commissions*: Windsor Castle, House of Lords, Madam Tussauds, The College of Arms, local churches, Tom Ford - Ford's Shop in New York, St. Fagan's Museum of Welsh Life, Cardiff (St. Teilo's Church carvings) etc. *Principal Works*: Windsor Castle restoration. *Recreations*: sculpture. *Clubs*: Association of Master Carvers. *Address*: 1 Woodside Cottage, Payford Bridge, Redmarley, Glos., GL19 3HY. *Signs work*: "EBHughes".

BARNHAM, Nicholas, NDD (Norwich), ATD (Southampton). *Medium*: watercolour, drawing, lino cuts. *b*: Walsingham, Norfolk, 12 Jan 1939. *m*: Linnea Birgitta. three *s*. five *d*. *Studied*: Royal Masonic School 1947-56, Norwich School of Art 1956-60. *Represented by*: Baron Art, 17 Chapel Yard, Holt, Norfolk, NR25 6HG; The Shetland Gallery, Sellafirth, Yell, Shetland, ZE2 9DG. *Exhib*: RA Summer Exhibitions (exhib. approx. 12 pictures); seven one-man shows at the Thackeray Gallery, Kensington; Union Society, Cambridge; The Old Fire Engine House, Ely; Gainsborough's House; Halesworth Gallery, DLI Museum & Arts Centre, Durham; Shetland Museum Gallery, Lerwick; Robert Colquhoun Memorial; also in Germany and Sweden. *Works in collections*: Richard Rodney Bennet, Christopher Hogwood, Ruth Lady Fermoy, Pamela Miles & Tim Pigott-Smith, Marks & Spencer, Cleo Lane & Johnny Dankworth, Government Art Collection, Shetland Islands Council etc. etc. *Commissions*: Somerville College, Oxford. *Publications*: Book illustrations include "The Return of the Tide" and "I am Horatio Nelson". *Official Purchasers*: Somerville College,

Marks & Spencer, Sealink, British Rail. *Recreations*: messing about in boats. *Misc*: Taught at Cambridge School of Art 1969-79; Spends part of each year working in Unst, Shetland, painting and printing; Nominated for Associate Membership, Royal Academy, RWS and Royal Society of Painters, Etchers and Gravers. *Address*: 70 Mill Road, Wells-next-the-Sea, Norfolk, NR23 1DB. *Signs work*: "Nicholas Barnham"

BARÓN, Maite, BA Art and Design (Fashion), Interior Design, BTec PDC Interior Decorative Applications, BTec. PDC in Fine Art Management and Professional Practice; Teachers Training City & Guilds 7307, stages 1 & 2; teaching experience - interior design, photoshop and dreamweaver, papermaking and paper products, colour workshops, decorative paint finishes, decoupage, stencilling, drawing; designer, artist and printmaker in drypoint, collograph, etching, screen printing, acrylics, paper making, fibre art. *b*: Barcelona, Spain, 10 Jun 1965. *s of*: Joaquin Baron. *Studied*: International Centre of Art Studies Interart, Barcelona (1985-88), Art and Design School, Barcelona (1984-85), London Print Studio (1999), Kensington and Chelsea College (1999), WAES (1997-01), Central Saint Martin's College; NLP Coaching Certificate; NLP Master Practitioner. *Exhib*: RBA. and National Print Exhbn. at Mall Galleries, Falmouth Arts Centre; UA at Westminster Gallery; Walford Mill (Wimborne); New York Prestige Artists Debut (2000), Manhattan, NY, USA; The Laing Art Competition Exh. (2001); Saatchi & Saatchi, the Art Phoenix Art Auction for the Kosovo children; the Intrinsic Book, the Barbican Library, London; Open Biennale 1999, Whiteley's, London; Freshly Printed, Buckingham Galleries, Southwold, Suffolk; Impact at Spike Island Printmakers, Bristol; Royal Society of British Artists (1998), Mall Gallery, London; National Print Exhibition (1998 & 1999), Mall Gallery, London; The Laing Art Competition Exhibition (2001), The Mall Gallery, London, EWACC 2nd Group Exhbn., La Gallerie Espace City Garden, Paris (2002), Fresh Art, Business Design Centre, London (2002). *Works in collections*: private collections Barcelona, Madrid, Ireland. *Commissions*: available for private commissions in 'Healing' Art/Colour Psychology. *Publications*: Catalogues: 2001 The Laing Art Competition Exhbn., The Mall Gallery London; 2000 National Print Exhibition, The Mall Gallery, London; 1999 United Society of Artists, 78th Annual Exhibition, Westminster Gallery, London; 1999 National Society of Painters, Sculptors and Printmakers, 66 Annual Exhibition, Whiteley's, London. *Clubs*: N.A.A., Printmakers' Council, Paperweight, Axis, N.A.P.A., N.S.A., A.U.A. *Address*: Flat 2, 46 Chiswick Lane, London W4 2JQ. *Email*: maite@tessabaron.demon.co.uk *Website*: www.tessabaron.co.uk

BARR, Shona Stewart MacInnes, BA (Hons), MA. *Medium*: oil, watercolour, drawing. *b*: Glasgow, 25 Aug 1965. *d of*: Prof D.I.H. & Mrs M. Barr. *m*: Nicholas A. Virgo. *Educ*: Laurel Bank School (1970-83). *Studied*: Glasgow School of Art (1984-88); Staten Kunstakademi, Oslo (1988-89); Winchester School of Art (1991-92). *Represented by*: Flying Colours Gallery. *Exhib*: Flying Colours Gallery, Edinburgh and London; Bohun Gallery, Henley-on-Thames; Roger Billcliffe Gallery, Glasgow; Atholl Gallery, Dunkeld; Lillie Art Gallery, Milngavie, and many others. *Works in collections*: Fleming Collection, Lillie Art Gallery, Prior's Court School, Strathclyde University, and others. *Commissions*: Prior's Court School (painting for Parent's Room). *Publications*: 'The Art of Prior's School' ISBN 0-9507212-2-0. *Works Reproduced*: several book covers, including 'The Cry of the Deer' David Adam ISBN 978-0-281-06118-1 *Recreations*: Argentine Tango dancing, Tai Chi, gardening. *Clubs*: Glasgow Art Club. *Address*: Studio 123, Wasps Artists Studios, 77 Hanson Street, Glasgow, G31 2HF. *Email*: shona@shonabarr.com *Website*: www.shonabarr.com *Signs work*: "BARR".

BARRATT, Mary H., BA (1969); part-time art lecturer. *Medium*: painter in oil. *b*: Annesley Woodhouse, Notts., 27 Mar 1948. *d of*: A.H. Fryer, head teacher. *m*: Michael Ian Barratt. *Studied*: Loughborough College of Art and Design (1966-69, Philip Thompson,

Colin Saxton). *Represented by*: Elaine Heane (Worksop); Karen Sherwood (Sheffield). *Exhib*: 359 Gallery, Nottingham, Crucible Theatre, Sheffield, Rufford Country Pk., Ollerton, Merlin Gallery, Sheffield, Pierrepont Gallery Thoresby Park, Newark, The Rebecca Hossack Gallery, Southwell Minster. *Works in collections*: Nottingham University, Leicester Royal Infirmary, Wetherspoon Restaurant chain (5 national venues). *Commissions*: Wetherspoon Restaurant chain. *Publications*: Resurgence Journal. *Official Purchasers*: hospitals, universities. *Works Reproduced*: photographed and recorded by Alfred Rolfe (Halfway - Sheffield). *Clubs*: Worksop Cricket and Sports Club. *Misc*: work moving decisively towards a spiritual content. *Address*: 7 Craigston Rd., Carlton-in-Lindrick, Worksop, Notts. S81 9NG. *Email*: jandmbarratt@hotmail.com *Website*: axis database *Signs work*: "M. Barratt."

BARRETT, Margaret, SEA; NDD, ATD. *Medium*: oil, watercolour, drawing, pastel. *b*: Surrey, England, 1947. *m*: Stan Barrett. one *s*. one *d*. *Educ*: Portsmouth High School GPDST. *Studied*: Portsmouth and Leicester Colleges of Art. *Exhib*: Mall Galleries; Christies, London; Museum of Modern Art, Wales; John Davies Gallery, and others; Society of Equestrian Artists, Royal Birmingham Society of Artists, Pastel Society, Society of Marine Artists, Society of Women Artists. *Works in collections*: private and corporate collections nationally and internationally. *Commissions*: Royal Doulton, Aynsley China, Canon Inc., Gallifords plc, ILPH, Lady Lloyd Webber, many private individuals and various equestrian societies. *Official Purchasers*: World Horse Welfare, SSAFA. *Works Reproduced*: Limited Edition prints by Felix Rosenstiel and Sally Mitchell Fine Art. *Principal Works*: Specialises in Equestrian art and portraiture, also Mediterranean landscapes. *Recreations*: History & archaeology, gardening, travel, bridge. *Address*: 'Springfield', 4 Priory Road, Market Bosworth, Leics., CV13 0PB. *Email*: margaret@margaretbarrett.co.uk *Website*: www.margaretbarrett.co.uk *Signs work*: "Margaret Barrett".

BARRETT, Priscilla, SWLA; freelance illustrator and wildlife artist in water-colour, pastels, pencil, pen and ink. *b*: S. Africa, 4 May 1944. *m*: Gabriel Horn. *Educ*: Universities of Cape Town and Stellenbosch. *Exhib*: solo exhbns. in Cambridge, also exhib. London, Brighton, Lavenham. *Publications*: Collins Field Guide - Mammals of Britain and Europe; European Mammals; Evolution and Behaviour; The Domestic Dog; Running with the Fox; The Wolf; A Year in the Life: Badger; A Year in the Life: Tiger; RSPCA Book of British Mammals; Ecotravellers Wildlife Guides to Costa Rica, Belize, Tropical Mexico, Ecuador; History of British Mammals. *Recreations*: Agility and riding. *Address*: Jack of Clubs, Lode, Cambridge CB5 9HE. *Signs work*: "Priscilla Barrett."

BARRON, Robert Hall, *Medium*: mixed media. b: Birtley, Co. Durham, 23 Jan 1943. *Exhib*: solo: Grey College, Durham University (2013); Civic Centre, Gateshead (2011); The Colne Gallery, Colchester Hospital (2009); Red Box Gallery, Newcastle upon Tyne (2009); Frost and Reed Gallery, London (2008); Edinburgh Festival (2006); Riverside Gallery, Richmond on Thames (2005); The Biscuit Factory, Newcastle upon Tyne (2004); St. Martin in the Bull Ring, Birmingham (2001); Ely Cathedral (2001); Durham Cathedral (2000); Mall Galleries (2000); Durham Art Gallery (1998); Washington Arts Centre, Tyne and Wear (1990); Whitehaven Museum and Art Gallery, Cumbria (1987); Bury Art Gallery (1986); Hereford Museum and Art Gallery (1986); Wolverhampton Art Gallery (1986); Bury St. Edmunds Art Gallery (1985); Chelmsford and Essex Art Gallery (1985); Buddle Arts Centre, North Tyneside (1984); Sunderland Arts Centre (1983); and group shows across the UK since 1978. Works in collections: Bury Art Gallery & Museum, Wolverhampton Art Gallery, Northern Arts. *Commissions*: Barclays Development Capital; Colchester General Hospital; Ernst & Young; Goldmann Sachs International; Investors in Industry Solihull; J D Wetherspoon plc; Sunderland Post Graduate Medical Centre. *Publications*: The Public Catalogue Foundation (Staffordshire & Greater Manchester); The Journal Culture Magazine (2009); Living North Magazine (2003); Fine Art Magazine 'Antique Collecting' (2000); Baltic Art Gallery & Archive, Newcastle upon Tyne; Jerwood Gallery Library & Archive.

Address: 'Oakes', West End Road, West End, Southampton SO30 3BH. *Email*: barron@bobbarron.com *Website*: www.bobbarron.com *Signs work*: "Barron".

BARROW, David. *Medium*: oil, watercolour, drawing, prints, sculpture. *b*: Wigan, 1 Oct 1959. *s of*: Anthony E.Barrow. *m*: Joanne. two *s*. one *d*. *Exhib*: Royal Academy, Royal Scottish Academy, Manchester Academy, Newcastle City Art Gallery, O2 London, Mall Galleries London, Salford City Art Gallery, Turnpike Gallery, Chapple Gallery, Bury Art Gallery, Thomson Gallery London. *Works in collections*: Wigan MBC, Liverpool FC, JJB - Wigan Athletic FC, Tamla Motown Museum, University of Michigan USA. *Commissions*: Ocean Colour Scene album cover "Live at the Jam House", Ocean Colour Scene album cover "Live in Birmingham". *Official Purchasers*: Paul Weller, Martha Reeves, OCS - Steve Craddock. *Misc*: Northern Soul paintings featured in film "Souled Out" - David Barrow Artistic Consultant. *Address*: 8 Wilson Ave, Wigan, WN6 7HD. *Email*: david.barrow2@btinternet.com *Website*: davidbarrowpaintings.50megs.com *Signs work*: "b a r r o w".

BARRY, Jo, RE; BA. *Medium*: watercolour, drawing, prints. *Educ*: Bexley Grammar School. *Studied*: Ravensbourne College of Art and Design. *Exhib*: Royal Academy Summer Show (since 1974); New Academy, London; Bankside Gallery, London; Montpellier Gallery, Stratford-upon-Avon; Gallery Nine, Bath; J&G Gallery, Chichester; H.C. Dickens (Oxfordshire); For Your Walls (Louth); Carmens Gallery, Maryland, USA; numerous galleries in New England, USA. *Address*: Wing House, Milky Down Lane, Hightown Hill, Ringwood, Hants, BH24 3HG. *Email*: barry4lee@aol.com *Signs work*: 'Jo Barry'.

BARTH, Eunice, painter in oil and acrylic in contemporary style. *b*: London, 1937. *m*: Philip Barth MA. two *d*. *Educ*: Neyland House, Sevenoaks; Regent Polytechnic; local Quinton and Kynaston art classes. *Studied*: in England, France and Spain; principal teacher Chris Channing. *Exhib*: FBA, VA, and local venues. *Works in collections*: Stoller Household and various private collections in England. *Clubs*: United Society of Artists. *Address*:53 Charlbert Court, Macrennal St., St. Johns Wood, London NW8 7DB. *Signs work*: "Eunice Barth."

BARTLETT, Adrian, NDD (1961), ATD (1962); artist in painting, etching, lithography. *b*: Twickenham, 31 Mar 1939. *m*: Victoria Bartlett. two *d*. *Educ*: Bedales School. *Studied*: Camberwell School of Art. *Exhib*: British Council, Athens (1985), Morley Gallery (1996), Walk Gallery (1999 and 2003), Piers Feetham Gallery 2007. *Works in collections*: BM, Ashmolean, V&A, Berlin Graphotek, etc. *Commissions*: mural for Anglo American (2000). *Publications*: Drawing and Painting the Landscape (Phaidon, 1982). *Clubs*: Chelsea Arts. *Address*: 132 Kennington Park Rd., London SE11 4DJ. *Email*: ajb.bartlett@virgin.net

BARTLETT, Charles, PPRWS, RE, ARCA. *Medium*: artist in oil and water-colour, printmaker. *b*: Grimsby, 23 Sep 1921. *s of*: Charles Henry Bartlett. *m*: Olwen Jones. one *s*. *Educ*: Eastbourne Grammar School. *Studied*: Eastbourne School of Art, RCA. *Exhib*: solo; John Russell Gallery, Ipswich, (regular exhibitor), Hayletts Gallery, Maldon, Essex; two one-man shows in London; major Retrospective Exhbn. (1997), Bankside Gallery, London, Bohun Gallery, Henley-on-Thames (regular exhibitor). *Works in collections*: V&A Museum, National Gallery of S. Australia, Arts Council of Great Britain, Artothek, Dusseldorf, Albertina Collection, Vienna; numerous public and private collections in Britain and abroad. *Publications*: Monograph: Charles Bartlett, Painter and Printmaker; Starting in Watercolour, Watercolour Expert, The Complete Artist, Watercolour Masters. *Recreations*: music and sailing. *Address*: St. Andrew's House, Fingringhoe, nr. Colchester, Essex CO5 7BG. *Signs work*: "Charles Bartlett."

BARTLETT, Paul Thomas, RBSA (1997), ARBA (1979), RBA (1981); FE/AE Teaching Cert (UCE, 1987), RA Schools PG Cert./MA (1980), PG Dip. hist. art/design (UCE, 1990),

BA Hons. Fine Art (Falmouth 1976). Major Prizes: NOT The Turner Prize 2004; Turner Gold Medal (RA Schools); Stowells Trophy national competition for Art Colleges; Royal Overseas League; Spirit of London; Mid Art; Hunting Group; Alexon Women on canvas; RBSA: Prize Show, & Open Drawing. Awards/Scholarships: Elizabeth Greenshield Foundation; David Murray. *Medium*: painter/draughtsman/printmaker/lecturer. *b*: B'ham, 7 Jul 1955. *s of*: H.T. Bartlett, designer. *Exhib*: RA, NPG, V&A ("Garden Exhibition" 1979), RBA, RBSA, Birmingham Museum and Art Gallery, Petleys (Cork St., London). *Commissions*: articles for 'Artist & Illustrator', 'Art of England', 'Leisure Painter' etc. *Works Reproduced*: Ian Hutchison, Quarto, Dorling Kindersley etc. *Address*: 144 Wheelers Lane, Kings Heath, B'ham. B13 0SG. *Email*: paulbartlettrbsa@btinternet.com *Website*: www.royalsocietyofbritishartists.org.uk *Signs work*: "Paul Bartlett" or " P.T.B."

BARTLETT, Victoria Anne, NDD (1961), ATD (1962). *Medium*: mixed media relief and 3D images, also paper and textile works. *b*: Caterham, 1940. *m*: Adrian Bartlett. two *d*. *Studied*: Camberwell School of Art, and Reading University (1957-62). *Exhib*: solo exhbns: The Egg & The Eye, Los Angeles; Van Doren Gallery, San Francisco; Gallerie Simoncini, Luxembourg. In London: Morley Gallery, Edward Totah Gallery, Camden Art Centre, Benjamin Rhodes Gallery, Peralta Pictures, Piers Feetham Gallery; group exhibitions in Britain, USA, Australia, France, Hungary, Poland and Luxembourg including The Chicago Art Fair 1995 with Browse & Darby, and the London Group since 1978. *Works in collections*: South Bend Regional Museum of Art, USA; Savaria Museum, Szombathley, Hungary; Chelsea and Westminster Hospital; Kroll International; Royal Marsden NHS Foundation Trust, and numerous private collections. *Address*: 132 Kennington Park Rd., London SE11 4DJ. *Signs work*: "Victoria Bartlett."

BARTOLO, Maria, painter in mixed media, including wax and varnish. *b*: Cardiff, 7 Dec 1967. *d of*: N.A. Bartolo. *Educ*: Oaklands R.C. Comprehensive. *Studied*: City and Guilds of London Art School (Roger de Grey). *Exhib*: The Discerning Eye, Mall Galleries, Christie's, Sotheby's, RA Summer Show, Barbican. *Works in collections*: Art Council, De Beers. *Works Reproduced*: RA magazine, CV magazine, Evening Standard Newspaper (four edns.). Winner of Evening Standard prize. *Address*: 23a Milner Sq., London N1.

BARTON, Charlotte, Cecelia, Gillbe, BA Fine Art Painting. *Medium*: oil, watercolour, drawing, prints. *b*: Maidstone, Kent, 24 Aug 1964. *d of*: Robert & Moira. *Educ*: St.Mary's, Shaftesbury; Salisbury College of Technology. *Studied*: Kingston School of Fine Art. *Exhib*: group shows: Fisherton Mill Gallery, Salisbury (2005), Art for UK Youth, Mall Galleries (2004, 2005), The Gallery, Cork Street (2004), Oxford Brookes University (2002), Stanley Picker Gallery, Kingston University (2001), Edinburgh City Art Gallery (2001), The John Ruskin Brantwood Museum (2001); touring group show 'Demarco70/2000/The Road to Meikle Seggie' (2001); solo shows: Michael Tippett Centre, Bath Spa University (2004), Hackney, London (2002). *Official Purchasers*: T.R.H. The Earl and Countess of Wessex *Recreations*: horses, yoga, running. *Address*: Watership Down, Sydmonton, Newbury, Berks RG20 9NJ. *Email*: charliegbarton@aol.com *Signs work*: 'Charlie Barton'.

BARTON, Patricia: see MYNOTT, Patricia

BASSINGTHWAIGHTE, Paul, BA (Hons) Fine Art; Spirit of London (watercolour prize, 1981); Travel Award, Poland (2005). *Medium*: oil, watercolour, prints. *b*: London, 9 Mar 1963. *s of*: Lewin Bassingthwaighte, artist. *Studied*: Chelsea School of Art (1982-86), National Film and Television School (1986-90). *Exhib*: RA, RWS, The London Group, Piccadilly Gallery, Flying Colours Gallery; Art'97, '98, '99, 2000, 2001; Art Expo New York, Lena Boyle, Bohun Gallery, Kato Gallery Tokyo, Ainscough Contemporary, Fish Gallery, Young Masters Atlanta, Christie's, Sotheby's, Bonhams, Thompsons Gallery, Quantum Contemporary Art, New Grafton Gallery. *Works in collections*: Leicestershire

Museums Arts and Records Service, The Permanent Fine Art Collection and 'Artworks' Loan Scheme, Derek Jacobi, Clive Owen, Kathy Burke, Liza Tarbuck. *Commissions*: large painting for Elizabeth Acland. *Publications*: Dictionary of Artists in Britain Since 1945 (David Buckham), Art Review (Oct '99), The Hill Magazine (Sept '99), Illustrator of 'Le Provencal Diet' (2007). *Official Purchasers*: Leicestershire Museum and Art Gallery. *Works Reproduced*: Camden Graphics (2002). *Recreations*: travel. *Misc*: film/video, photography, graphic design/illustration. *Address*: 22 Winscome Street, London N19 5DG. *Email*: pbassingthwaighte@yahoo.co.uk *Website*: www.basspaul.co.uk *Signs work*: 'Paul Bassingthwaighte', on the reverse.

BATCHELOR, Bernard Philip, RWS; painter in water-colour and oil. *b*: 29 May 1924. *Studied*: St. Martin's and City and Guilds of London Art schools gaining City and Guilds Painting medal and a David Murray Scholarship. Subject matter relates mainly to town or landscapes with figures, coastal scenes, etc. *Work in collections:* many in private collections here and abroad; also MOW, Museum of Richmond and Richmond Parish Charity Lands. Painting of HMS Richmond presented to the ship by the Borough of Richmond and Twickenham; etching of Vauxhall bridge (1952) to DCMS. *Address*: 50 Graemesdyke Ave., East Sheen, London SW14 7BJ. *Signs work*: "B.P. BATCHELOR" or sometimes "B.P.B."

BATCHELOR, Valerie, artist in water colour, acrylic and pastel. *b*: 16 Mar., 1932. *m*: John. one *s*. *Studied*: Salisbury College of Art (1947-50). *Exhib*: solo shows: Salisbury Library (1990, 1993, 1996), Salisbury Playhouse (1991-98), R.I. since 1985, RWA since 1990. *Publications*: book illustrations including Collins Artists Manual. *Clubs*: N.A.P.A. *Address*: 'Tresses', Larkhill Rd., Durrington, Wilts. SP4 8DP.

BATE, William Richard, BA Fine Art Painting. *Medium*: oil. *b*: Liverpool, 13 Jul 1962. *Studied*: Central Shool of Art and Design. *Represented by*: Coombe Gallery, Dartmouth; Medici Gallery, London W1. *Exhib*: Gagliardi Gallery, London; Royal Society of British Artists, Mall Galleries; New English Art Club, Mall Galleries; Royal Institute of Oil Painters, Mall Galleries; Thompson's Gallery London; Roy Miles Gallery London; Leighton House London; Affordable Art Fair London; Hicks Gallery London; Quantum Art London; M. Neill Fine Art; Coombe Gallery, Dartmouth; Advocate Gallery, Wimbledon; Medici Gallery London. *Address*: 46 West Street, Dormansland, Lingfield, RH7 6QS. *Email*: bill@billbate.co.uk *Website*: billbate.co.uk *Signs work*: "W.R.Bate".

BATES, Andrea Maria, Elected member of Oxford Art Society (1974), elected member of Fosseway Artists, Cirencester (1981). *Medium*: pastel, oil. *b*: Budapest, Hungary, 11 May 1943. *d of*: Andrew J.A. Bartok. *m*: David N. Bates. two *s*. *Educ*: Paris, Montreal. *Studied*: Academy of Fine Arts, Vienna (1959-62). *Exhib*: solo: Oxford Playhouse (1969, 1984), Phyllis Court Club, Henley (1983), regular solo participant in Oxford Art Weeks since 1985, plus many others. Group: RBA (1980s), ROI (1981), Medici Gallery, Grafton Street (1984-1991), John Noott Gallery, Broadway (1997-2001), Rooksmoor Gallery, Bath (1998-2003), Pastel Society, Mall Galleries (1984, 2000, 2001, 2004-2007), Alexander Gallery, Clifton (1998-2012), Carmel Gallery, Ottawa (2004-present), Woburn Abbey (July 2013). *Commissions*: Portrait of Eric Lane Burslem, Founder of BALPA (hangs in boardroom of BALPA, Heathrow). *Works Reproduced*: illustrations: pen & ink in "The Story of Enstone" (Enstone Local History Circle, 1999); By the Rideau River, in "100 Ways to Paint Favourite Subjects, Vol. 1" (International Artist, 2004); 3 cards by Medici (1993); 2 cards by Hallmark UK (1998). *Recreations*: circle dancing, gardening. *Address*: Hillside, Oxford Road, Enstone, Oxon, OX7 4NE. *Email*: info@andreabates.co.uk *Website*: www.andreabates.co.uk *Signs work*: "A Bates".

BATES, Joan Elliott, DFA (Lond.) 1952; Awards: Laing Painting Competition 3rd prize, Laing Painting Competition 2nd prize, Cornelissen award. *Medium*: oil, watercolour, drawing, printmaking, gouache, ink, charcoal. *b*: Sheffield, 22 Jan 1930. *d of*: John Elliott, solicitor. *m*: John F. Bates. three *s*. *Studied*: Sheffield College of Art (1947-49), Slade School of Fine Art (1949-52, Prof. William Coldstream). *Exhib*: RA Summer Exhbns., The Paris Salon, NEAC, RWS, RBA, ROI, RI, RWA, RE, The Hunting Award, The Laing, Discerning Eye, and in numerous galleries in London and the provinces, including The New Grafton, Cadogan Contemporary, Bohun Gallery, Beaux Arts and New Ashgate Gallery. *Official Purchasers*: Government Art Collection - one oil; Paintings in Hospitals - one watercolour, one gouache. *Works Reproduced*: The Complete Drawing Course, Ian Simpson, Collins Artist's Manual, Collins Artist's Colour Manual, Quarto publications and others. *Address*: 17 Marlow Mill, Mill Rd., Marlow, Bucks. SL7 1QD. *Signs work*: "J. Elliott" or "J.E."

BATES, Patricia Jane, B.Ed (Lond) (1976), MFPS (1980). *Medium*: oil, oil collage, mixed media, sculpture, printmaking. *b*: Surbiton, 8 Jan 1927. *d of*: George and Elsie Simon (decd.). *m*: Martin Colin Bates. one *s*. one *d*. *Educ*: Priors Field, Godalming. *Studied*: Bartlett School of Architecture (1944-46), Epsom School of Art (1947-48), Byam Shaw (1952-53). *Represented by*: FPS, Guildford, Farnham and Chertsey Art Societies, Mill Gallery, Coverack. *Exhib*: one-man shows: Loggia Gallery, London, Guildford Institute, RSCH Guildford, Cranleigh Art Centre; mixed shows: Mall Galleries, London; Lewis Elton, Guildford Univ., Holy Trinity Church, Guildford; Clyde & Co. Solicitors, Guildford; Harvey Gallery, Guildford; 'Vivartis', King Edwards School, Witley, Showcase, Bramley; one-man show Guildford Cathedral - 25 collage and oil paintings (Aug 2010). *Works in collections*: UK, USA, Australia, India, Japan. Collage sold at auction for 'Whitetail' Exhibition in Nairobi for East African Wildlife. *Commissions*: several. *Works Reproduced*: illustrations for Enid Blyton books. *Principal Works*: series of paintings from Bunyan's Pilgrims progress. *Misc*: Art teaching: children in India, Surrey Secondary Schools, Guildford High School Juniors, WEA and other adult groups. *Address*: Brackenhurst, Wonham Way, Gomshall, Guildford, Surrey GU5 9NZ. *Email*: patcobates@supanet.com *Website*: www.patbatesart.co.uk *Signs work*: "PAT BATES" or "PAT SIMON BATES."

BATT, Deborah Jane, artist in acrylic, oil and water-colour. *b*: London, 12 Dec 1966. *Exhib*: Extensively throughout the UK. *Works in collections*: both private and corporate collections in the UK and US. *Clubs*: Fine Art Trade Guild, National Acrylic Painter Association, National Society of Painters, Sculptors and Printmakers. *Address*: 45 The Terrace, Wokingham, Berks. RG40 1BP. *Email*: deborah.batt@virgin.net *Website*: www.deborahbatt.co.uk *Signs work*: "D.J.B."

BATTERBURY, Helen Fiona, self taught artist in water-colour. *b*: Stockton-on-Tees, 30 Jul 1963. *m*: Paul Batterbury. two *s*. one *d*. *Educ*: Durrants School, Watford. *Exhib*: SEA, SWLA, SWA, Wildlife Art Soc., numerous mixed exhbns.: Century Gallery, Thoresby Hall, Newport Gallery. *Commissions*: Commissioned as equestrian artist primarily. *Publications*: wrote and illustrated article The Horse in Watercolour for Leisure Painter magazine (Jan. 1997); paintings reproduced in many sporting magazines as promotions for exhbns. *Clubs*: S.W.A., Wildlife Art Soc. *Address*: Hoveringham Hall, Hoveringham, Notts. NG14 7JR. *Signs work*: "Fergusson."

BATTLE, Jay. *Medium*: sculpture. *b*:Toronto, 20 May 1966. *m*: Chloe Battle. two *d*. *Represented by*: Hart Gallery, Islington, London. *Exhib*: Stockholm Art Fair (1998); Shape of the Century, 100 Years of Sculpture in Britain (Salisbury, Canary Wharf, 1999); Shadows on Stone, Sherborne (2000); Royal West of England Academy, Bristol (2002); Royal British Society of Sculptors, London (2004), Newby Hall Sculpture Park, Ripon, N. Yorks. (2004), Atkinson Gallery, Millfield (2004); Commonground, Artsway, Hampshire (2005), Sculpture in the Garden: a celebration of the Royal Society of Sculptors Centenary, University of Leicester Botanic Garden (2005); Art Loan Collection, University of Winchester Link Gallery (2005); Sculpture in the Planning - Sculpture in the Making, Atkinson Gallery,

Millfield (2005); London Art Fair / Art London, Chelsea (2006), Summer Exhibition, Hart Gallery, Nottingham (2006, 2007, 2008); Line and Boundary, Hart Gallery, London (2007); Royal Academy Summer Exhibition (2008, 2009). *Works in collections*: Canary Wharf PLC, University of Winchester, Bournemouth University. *Publications*: 'Shape of the Century: A Hundred Years of Sculpture in Britain'; 'Shadows on Stone: Sculpture at Sherborne'; 'The Art of Canary Wharf: Conde Nast; Art Loan Collection (University of Winchester/Bournemouth University); Royal Academy Illustrated: 2008. *Clubs*: The Royal British Society of Sculptors (ARBS). *Address*: Pipers Old Drier, Pipers Farm, Clarendon Park, Salisbury, Wiltshire, SP5 3ES. *Email*: info@jaybattle.com *Website*: www.jaybattle.com *Signs work*: "J Battle".

BATTYE, Martin, BA, FRSA, 2003 Watercolour Prize Eastern Open. *Medium*: oil, watercolour. *b*: Woddbridge, 30 Mar 1952. *m*: Hilary. four *d*. *Studied*: Sunderland School of Art. *Exhib*: RA Summer Exhbn; Eastern Open; 12 East Anglian Artists; King of Hearts, Norwich; Chappel Galleries, Colchester; Graham & Oldham, Ipswich; Warehouse, Lowestoft. *Works Reproduced*: cover painting - W.G.Sebald: A Critical Companion. *Misc*: Chairman, Kirton Healthcare Group Ltd. *Address*: Old Forge, Hempnall, Norwich NR15 2AD. *Email*: martinballye@kirtonhealthcare.co.uk *Website*: www.targetfollow.com *Signs work*: Martin Battye

BAUMFORTH, David John, painter of contemporary northern seascapes and landscapes in watercolour, acrylic and oil. *b*:York, 21 Oct 1942. *m*: Jenny. two *d*. *Educ*: Nunthorpe Grammar School. *Represented by*: The Walker Galleries, Harrogate and Honiton; Brian Sinfield, Burford; The Corridor Gallery, Snainton. *Exhib*: RWS Open, RA Summer Exhib., Hunting Prizes, The Daily Mail, Not the Turner Prize, and many national galleries. *Works in collections*: various national and international collections. *Commissions*: Many. *Recreations*: Ferrari driver, motor sport, English Bull Terrier enthusiast. *Clubs*: F.O.C.; BARC. *Misc*: 'Anyone who has an eye for art the deep passionate colour of Turner, the pure loving observations of Constable, must rejoice that our century has David Baumforth. This work is the real thing, wet with sea spray we can feel, fresh with gusts of wind, always mysterious, always beautiful, art to be cherished.' - Sister Wendy Beckett. *Address*: Low Garth, Snainton, Scarborough, N. Yorks YO13 9AF. *Email*: baumforth@lowgarth.fsnet.co.uk *Website*: www.davidbaumforth.com *Signs work*: "D J Baumforth." and monogram.

BAWDEN, Richard, RWS, NEAC, RE (ARCA). *Medium*: engraved glass, mosaic, murals, cast iron, watercolour, drawing, prints. *b*: Braintree, 18 Mar 1936. *m*: Harriet. one *s*. one *d*. Educ: Bryanston. *Studied*: Chelsea School of Art; St. Martin's; National Service RAF; RCA Graphic Design & Printmaking. *Exhib*: NEAC, RWS, RE: Bircham Gallery, Holt; Fry Gallery, Saffron Walden, and many others throughout the UK. *Works in collections*: H.M. The Queen, Prince Charles, Ashmolean Oxford. *Commissions*: Mosaic in swimming pool for John Hedgecoe; Engraved glass screen for Beschamp St. Paul Church three saints, also at Great Bardfield; Prints for Editions Alecto, Monuments of the Industrial Revolution lithographs; Follies lighographs Curwen Studios; Illustrations for "Hammer & Hand" (book on wrought & cast iron in Cambridge); Linocut posters for Gainsborough's house print workshop; tea towels of birds, animals and cats for Stuart Morris Textiles Ltd.; Murals in restaurants in Aldeburgh and Attleborough; private commissions. *Works Reproduced*: Editions of prints; etchings and linocuts sold through galleries mostly in East Anglia, Dorset and the West Country. *Recreations*: gardening, walking, exploring new places. *Clubs*: NEAC, RWS, RE. *Address*: 72 Benton Street, Hadleigh, Suffolk IP7 5AT. *Email*: h.r_bawden@btopenworld.com

BAWTREE, John Andrew, D.Arch. (Kingston, 1977), ARBA (1982), RBA (1984); Greenshield Foundation Award (1978, 1980); painter in oil on canvas. *b*: Cheam, Surrey,

1 Nov 1952. *s of*: Harold Maurice Bawtree. *Educ*: Bradfield College, Berks. (1966-70). *Studied*: Kingston Polytechnic School of Architecture (1970-73, 1975-77). *Exhib*: RA, RBA; one-man: Cambridge, Oxford, Oman, Aldeburgh, Piers Feetham Gallery, London, Melitensia Gallery, Malta, British Embassy, Oman. *Works in collections*: Greenshield Foundation, Montreal, Foreign and Commonwealth Office, Muscat. *Commissions*: Chelsea Financial Services and Grindlays Bank. *Works Reproduced*: prints, cards, calendars. *Clubs*: Chelsea Arts. *Address*: Pine View, Peasenhall, Suffolk IP17 2HZ. *Email*: john@johnbawtree.com *Website*: www.johnbawtree.com *Signs work*: "John Bawtree."

BAXTER, Ann W., NDD (Hons.) (1955), SEA; winner, British Sporting Art Trust Sculpture Prize (1990), joint winner (1986, 1998, 2004) and President's Medal (1994); freelance sculptor in wood, stone and bronze. *b*: Leeds, Nov 1934. *m*: W.L.J. Potts (decd.). one *s*. *Educ*: Leeds Girls' High School. *Studied*: Leeds College of Art (1950-55, Harry Phillips). *Exhib*: SEA annually, Open exhbns.: Leeds City A.G., Cartwright Hall Bradford, Wakefield City A.G., and widely in U.K. in private and public galleries. *Works in collections*: York City A.G., and private collections in UK, USA, Europe and Australia. *Commissions*: presentation pieces for the SEA. *Misc*: breeds Arabian horses. *Address*: Ivy Farm, Roecliffe, Boroughbridge, York YO51 9LY. *Signs work*: "A.W. Baxter."

BAXTER, Denis Charles Trevor, RWA (2002); Royal Society of British Artists (2003), FRSA (1970), Mem. Printmakers Council (1981), NS (1987), President, NS (1989-2001), Society of Graphic Fine Art (2001); awarded the Gold Medal for Graphic Art at the 2nd Biennale Internazionale DellArte Contemporanea in Florence (1999), awarded the Gold Medal for Graphic Art presented by the Spanish Embassy at the Kyoto International Exchange Exhibition, Japan (1999); teacher, lecturer, artist. *Medium*: printmaking, oil and watercolours. *b*: Southsea, 1 Mar 1936. *m*: Diana M.Hawkins, NS, FRSA. *Educ*: Ryde School, I.O.W. *Studied*: Bournemouth and Poole College of Art (1964-65); Stockwell College, Bromley, Kent (1965-68), Bournemouth and Poole College of Art (1969-74) *Exhib*: RA, RWA, RBA, RE, NEAC, PS, NS, UA., Organised the first EuroArt Touring exhbn in the UK at Christchurch, Dorset, before moving on to Ahrenshoop, Germany and Brussels. Organised for the Printmakers Council an exchange exhbn entitled 'Reflections' with printmakers from Landau, Germany. The Mini Print Internacional Barcelona, Spain; Galerie Meier, Arth am See, Switzerland. Euroart Touring Exhibition at La Defense, Paris, Barbizon and in Oosterbeck, Holland. *Works in collections*: Canada, France, Germany, Japan, Switzerland, UK, USA. *Commissions*: Commissioned by an International Finance Company based in Luxembourg to produce a set of etchings asa presentation pack for each of their principal clients. *Publications*: Two articles published for inclusion in the catalogue for 'World Festival of Art on Paper' in Kranj, 2000. An article on etching published in the 'Artist and Illustrator' magazine. *Official Purchasers*: work purchased by four Hampshire hospitals for display in various departments. *Clubs*: Chelsea Arts, Royal Over-Seas League, Royal Society of Arts. *Address*: Knightley House, 54 Anderwood Drive, Sway, Lymington, Hants SO41 6AW. *Email*: mail@the-rba.org.uk *Website*: www.rwa Bristol *Signs work*: "Denis Baxter" or "D.B."

BAXTER, Richard, BA (Hons) (First Class). *Medium*: ceramics. *b*: Westcliff-on-Sea, Essex, 13 Aug 1959. *m*: Kate. one *s*. *Studied*: Loughborough College of Art & Design. *Represented by*: New Ashgate Gallery, Farnham; Rye Art Gallery, East Sussex. *Exhib*: New Ashgate Gallery (2013); Pyramid Gallery, York (2013); Art in Action (2009, 2010, 2012, 2013); Art in Clay, Hatfield (2009, 2012, 2013); Rye Art Gallery, E. Sussex (2013); Bury St. Edmunds Art Gallery (2012); Henry Moore Foundation, Perry Green (2011/12); Appleyard Gallery, Holt (2011/12); Artisan Gallery, Willesden, London (2010); Leigh Art Trail (2009/10/11/12); Pi Kwadraat Gallerie, Erpe, Belgium (2010); TAP, metaculture.org (2009); Catto Gallery, London (2009). *Works in collections*: Ken Stranding Collection, Bristol. *Commissions*: David Chipperfield RA; Heston Blumenthal, BBC; Courtauld Gallery Shop; Stella McCartney; BBC TV; Restaurant Tristan, Horsham, Sussex; Victoria & Albert

Museum; Chernobyl Children's Project; West Stow Anglo-Saxon Village, Suffolk. *Publications*: Colour in Glazes by Linda Bloomfield (A&C Black 2011); The Ceramiocs Book 2006 (Ceramic Review Books); Sopot Ulica Sztuki (2004); 500 Bowls (Lark Books 2003); The Glaze Book. Stephen Murfitt (Krauze 2002); Potters Directory of Shape and Form; From Mud to Music (2006); Potters, Ceramic Review Publishing Ltd (12th Edition 2000, 11th Edition 1997, 10th Edition 1994, 9th Edition 1992); Bury St. Edmunds Art Gallery promotional brochure (Ceramic Musical Instruments degree thesis, 1981); Daily Mail (25/3/2006 gardening page); Grand Designs Magazine Sept 2006; Ceramic Review 217 Jan/Feb 2006: BBC Good Homes magazine, June 2005. *Official Purchasers*: Southend on Sea Borough Council. *Recreations*: semi pro musician. *Clubs*: Anglian Potters. *Address*: Old Leigh Studios, 61 High Street, Leigh on Sea, Essex SS9 2EP. *Email*: richard@richardbaxter.com *Website*: www.richardbaxter.com *Signs work*: "Richard Baxter".

BAYS, Caroline, PS; BA Hons Painting/Printmaking (2006), PGCE (2010), Higher Surrey Diploma – Communication Design (1982). *Medium*: oil, drawing, pastels. *b*: Weybridge, 26 Jul 1960. *d of*: Jill Bays & Bernard Bays (decd). *m*: Mr.A.Williams. *Studied*: Epsom School of Art and Design (1979-82), Roehampton University (2004-06), Brooklands College (2008-10). *Exhib*: Royal Society of Portrait Painters (1998-2012), The Pastel Society (1997-2012), NEAC (1998, 1999, 2005), The Discerning Eye, Mall Galleries (2005), The Hunting Prize, Royal College of Art (2002), The Garrick Milne Prize, Christie's (2000), Waterman Fine Art, London (1999-2000), Century Gallery, Henley (1999-2000), Fosse Gallery, Stow-on-the-Wold, Glos (2001-03), Ruth Borchard Self Portrait Exhibition, Kings Place Gallery, London; solo exhibitions: Paintings & Drawings, The Robert Phillips Gallery, Walton on Thames, Surrey (2002, 2004, 2007, 2012). *Work in collections*: private UK, France, Italy. *Publications*: The Artist (2012). *Address*: The Cottage, 8e Windsor St., Chertsey, KT16 8AS. *Email*: carolinebays@googlemail.com *Website*: www.carolinebays.co.uk *Signs work*: "Caroline Bays".

BAYS, Jill, NDD(1951), BA (Open)(1985); PGCE; artist in water-colour and oil, teacher. Medium: watercolour. *b*: Ambala, India, 24 Nov 1931. *d of*: W.C. Burton, RAF (decd.). *m*: Bernard Bays (decd.). two *d*. *Educ*: Sir William Perkins', Chertsey. *Studied*: Guildford School of Art (1947-51). *Exhib*: RI, SWLA, SWA, numerous shared exhbns. with husband and others. *Publications*: The Watercolourist's Garden (David and Charles, 1993), Flowers in the Landscape (David and Charles, 1995), Drawing Workbook (David and Charles, 1998), The Watercolourist's Nature Journal (David and Charles, 2001); Watercolour in a Weekend (Flowers) (David & Charles, 2004), The Flower Painters Essential Handbook (David & Charles, 2006); Flower Painters Workbook (David & Charles, 2009). *Address*: Bayswater, Hamm Ct., Weybridge, Surrey KT13 8YB. *Email*: jebays@btinternet.com *Website*: www.jillbays.com *Signs work*: "Jill Bays."

BEACH, John, RMS, AMPSGS, MASF; 'Masters Award 2000', Million Brushstrokes Exhbn; First Prize annual 'Lake Oswego Fesival of Art Exhbn', USA; the 'Manny Sullivan Memorial Award for Excellence' and overall 2nd, Miniature Painters Society of Washington DC (2004, Hon. mention 2001); Llewelyn Alexander Award in the Hilliard Society Exhbn (1998); Hon mentions: RMS (1999, 2000); Miniature Art Society of Florida Exhbn (2003). *Medium*: watercolour (miniaturist). *b*: Windsor, 7 Nov 1930. *m*: Marion. *Studied*: Kingstone School of Art (1945-47). *Exhib*: Westminster, London; Llewellyn Alexander; Mall Galleries; Hilliard Society, Bath; Tavistock; Gold Coast, Australia; in USA: Washington DC; Florida; Lake Oswego; Lexington Massachusetts; Bethlehem, PA; Portland, Oregon. *Works Reproduced*: greeting cards. *Recreations*: painting. *Address*: Lyndale, 60 Coppermill Road, Wraysbury, Staines, Middx, TW19 5NS. *Signs work*: 'JOHN BEACH.'

BEALE, Gillian. *Medium*: oil, watercolour, drawing, prints. *b*: Bridlington. one *s*. one *d*. *Studied*: Lincoln College of Art/Swarthmore Leeds; Hull University. *Exhib*: Usher Gallery

Lincoln; Thirsby Hall; Neka Gallery Bali, Indonesia; Scorer Gallery Lincoln; Tatton Park, Patchings Gallery, Notts; NEC Birmingham; Ranby Hall, Lincoln Fine Art; Hemswell Antique Centre; Museum of Art, Orlando USA. *Works in collections*: France, Spain, Japan, Australia, USA etc. *Recreations*: travel, swimming. *Misc*: Art Tutor, Lincoln County Council. *Address*: Paxhaven Studio, Doddington, Lincoln, LN6 4RS. *Website*: www.gillianbeale.co.uk *Signs work*: "GILLIAN BEALE."

BEALE, Philippa S. Vaux, BA (Hons), ATD (1970), MA (1986), PGDip Digital Imaging (2006); Fellow of the Institute of Higher Education (2006). *Medium*: oil or acrylic on canvas. *b*: Winchester, 17 Jan 1946. *d of*: Joseph Vaux-Beale. *m*: David Troostwijk (1929-2009); Christopher Plato m. 2000. one *s*. *Studied*: Winchester School of Art, Goldsmiths' College, University of London, University of Reading, UAL. *Exhib*: Camden Arts Centre, Akumulatory 2 Galleria, Poland; Richard Demarco Gallery, Edinburgh; Flowers East, Acme Gallery, Gulbenkian Gallery, ICA London; The Third Eye, Glasgow; Arnolfini, Bristol; Blue Coat, Liverpool; Danielle Arnaud; The Discerning Eye, Mall Galleries; Station of the Cross at St. Pancras Church, London; Whitechapel Gallery; The LCC Galleries. *Works in collections*: Tate Gallery Archive, National Art Archive, V&A, Camden Council, Southampton City Art Gallery, Angela Flowers, Shur Collection, Johnson Collection, AIR Gallery New York. *Commissions*: Le Chemin de Croix, Church of the Virgin, Poitiers. *Publications*: The Sexual Imagination, edited by Harriet Gilbert (Jonathan Cape), Roszika Parker, Women's Images of Men, edited by S. Kent and J. Moreau (Pandora Press, Unwin Paperbacks), L. McQuiston, Graphic Agitations (Phaidon), D. Postle, The Mind Gymnasium (Gaia Books). State of Art Installation and Site Specific, State of Art, Portrait and Landscape, Bare Hill Publishing; Bluebird and Other Stories; Under the Greenwood. *Works Reproduced*: 'Graphic Agitations' Liz McQuiston, Phaidon, 'outsidedge online magazine' 2002, London Group 90 years of visual arts' 2003. State of Art *Principal Works*: 'Baby Love', 'The Girl in the Red Shoes'; 'Bluebird'; 'The Stations of the Cross. *Clubs*: President, London Group (1995-98); Chelsea Arts Club. *Address*: 2 Route de Couhe, Vaux en Couhe 86799, France. *Email*: philippabealeart@googlemail.com *Website*: www.philippabeale.com *Signs work*: "P.S.B."

BEALING, Nicola Janette, RWA (Royal West of England Academician). *Medium*: oil, prints. *b*: Hertford, 29 Oct 1963. two *s*. *Studied*: Byam Shaw School of Art, London. *Represented by*: Cadogan Contemporary, London; Beaux Arts, Bath; Wills Lane Gallery, St. Ives. *Exhib*: numerous solo and group shows including: Hunting Art Prizes, Discerning Eye, Mall Galleries (Invited Artist 2004, 2008, 2011); Beaux Arts, Bath; Wagner & Schortgen, Luxembourg; BP Portrait Award, NPG; RSBA; Belgrave Gallery, Cornwall; Waterman Fine Art; Cadogan Contemporary; Flowers Gallery; Threadneedle Prize, Mall Galleries. *Works in collections*: Jerwood Contemporary Collection; Unilever; Deutsche Bank; Cliveden; Millfield School; Channel 4 TV; London International Brokers; Royal College of Paediatrics and Child Health; Prudential Plc; Hampshire County Council. *Commissions*: 'Inside Art' Channel 4 (1996). *Official Purchasers*: The Jerwood Foundation. *Works Reproduced*: 'Artist & Illustrator Magazine' (Mar 2000); 10 Years of the BP Portrait Award (NPG, 2001). *Recreations*: travelling, eating. *Clubs*: Chelsea Arts. *Address*: Lower Goonhusband, Debigna Lane, Helston, Cornwall, TR12 7PP. *Email*: bryant.bealing@virgin.net *Website*: www.nicolabealing.co.uk *Signs work*: 'NB.'

BEARD, Peter Fraser, BA (Hons), INAX Design Prize (1996), Pot D'Or Keramisto (2000), Silver Medal XVIII Biennial Vallauris, France. *Medium*: sculpture, ceramic, stone, bronze. *b*: Southport, 5 Nov 1951. *Studied*: Ravensbourne College of Art, London. *Exhib*: taken part in over 100 group exhbns, and 45 solo shows since 1975 in many countries including Japan, Korea, Australia, USA, Europe, Canada, UK (inc.RA). *Works in collections*: Museum Ariana, Geneva; Stoke-on-Trent City Museum; Keramion Museum, Koln Museum and Neue Sammlung, Germany; INAX Corporation, Japan; University of

Kansas, USA; Ichon World Ceramic Centre, Korea; Norwich Museum; Burnley City Art Gallery. *Publications*: author of 'Resist and Masking Techniques'. *Works Reproduced*: in numerous books and magazines since 1973. *Misc*: see website for details. *Address*: Tanners Cottage, Welsh Road, Leamington Spa CV32 7UB. *Email*: peter@peterbeard.co.uk *Website*: www.peterbeard.co.uk *Signs work*: initials 'PFB', and symbol.

BEATON, Rosemary, 1st Class BA Hons Degree and Postgraduate Studies; Winner of National Portrait Award (1984). *Medium*: stained glasss, oil, watercolour, drawing. *b*: Greenock, 6 Jul 1963. *d of*: Mary & Malcolm Beaton. *m*: Paul Doherty. one *s*. three *d*. *Studied*: Glasgow School of Art (1981-86). *Represented by*: Boundary Gallery, London. *Exhib*: Glasgow, London, Shetland, Maastricht, Amsterdam, Aachen, Kendal, Edinburgh, Dunfermline, Leicester, Stirling. *Works in collections*: The National Portrait Gallery, London; The British Broadcasting Corporation. *Commissions*: painter Sir Robin Day for NPG (1985); Stained Glass window (11m x 2.2m) Palisade Properties, Glasgow (2005). *Publications*: '20th Century Portraits', R. Gibson & H. Clerk; Many 'Images of a Queen', I. McFarlane. *Principal Works*: portrait of Sir Robin Day; The West End Window, Glasgow. *Address*: 17 Laighpark Ave, Bishopton, Renfrewshire, PA7 5BH. *Email*: rosemarybeaton1@yahoo.co.uk *Website*: www.rosemarybeaton.co.uk *Signs work*: "Rosemary Beaton."

BEATTIE, Basil, RA; RA Schools Cert, Major Arts Council Award, Athena Awards, John Moores 2nd Prize winner, Nordstern Print Prize (RA). Elected Royal Academician 2006. *Medium*: oil, watercolour, drawing, prints. *b*: West Hartlepool, 9 Jan 1935. three *d*. *Studied*: West Hartlepool College of Art (1950-55); Royal Academy Schools (1957-60). *Exhib*: Selected solo exhibitions: James Hyman Gallery (2011), Abbot Hall, Cumbria (2010), Purdy Hicks Gallery (2009) Two Rooms, New Zealand (2008), BP New Displays, Tate Britain (2007), Marking a Year, Childers Street in association with the Eagle Gallery (2002), Above and Below Sadler's Wells Theatre in association with the Eagle Gallery (2002), Todd Gallery (1998), Angel Row, Nottingham (1995), MAAK Gallery (1993), Drawing on the Interior, Eagle Gallery (1991), Jerwood Gallery, Hastings (2013), Hales Gallery, London (2014). *Works in collections*: RA Collection (Diploma work), Tate Collection, Government Art Coll., Arts Council, CAS, Birmingham City Museum, Whitworth Manchester, Swindon Museum, Deutsche Bank Coll, Southampton City Art Gallery. *Commissions*: Mural for Metro Newcastle (commissioned by Northern Arts). *Publications*: Basil Beattie - Taking Steps. Large Work 1986-2009. *Official Purchasers*: Tate Gallery, Government, Arts Council. *Clubs*: Chelsea Arts Club. *Address*: 1 Village School House, Lower Green West, Mitcham, Surrey CR4 3AF. *Email*: basilbeattie@hotmail.co.uk *Signs as*: "Basil Beattie".

BEATTIE, Paul, unltd.org 2005 Entrepreneurship Award for teaching art in local community. The Arts Council of Wales (2 awards 2007, 2009); Oriel Wrexham Peoples Choice Award (2009); Professional Associate Member, SAA; Member, Associate of Animal Artists. *Medium*: oil, watercolour, drawing, acrylics, sculpture. *b*: Pwllheli, Wales, 25 Apr 1965. *Partner*: Katherine R. Jones. one *s*. two *d*. *Studied*: self taught with over 26 years experience. *Exhib*: A.E. Dutton & Sons, Chester (1996); Black Sheep Gallery, Hawarden (1998); Llanarmon Arts & Crafts Centre (solo, 1999); Oriel Gallery, Mold (1999); Oriel Gallery, Wrexham (2007, 2009); Farndon Arts Centre (1997); Cafe Nero, Wrexham (solo, 2011); Many online sources. *Work in collections*: private collections, UK and internationally. *Commissions*: private sector, UK and internationally. *Principal Works*: Wildlife Art, Landscapes, Native North Americal Art, Fantasy. *Clubs*: Artist Reference Photos (Founder) 2011. *Misc*: Full name Paul Beattie, art tutor, workshop facilitator, and demonstrations for art groups (UK). *Address*: 7 Rose Grove, Rhosnesni, Wrexham, LL13 9DP. *Email*: contact@paulbeattieart.com *Website*: www.paulbeattieart.com *Signs work*: "P Beattie".

BEAUMONT, Jeffrey (Jeff), *Medium*: watercolour (occasionally pen and ink, pencil). *b*: 15 Feb 1949. *s of*: Jack and Hilda Beaumont. *m*: Rose Anne. one *s*. one *d*. *Educ*: Holmfirth High School. *Exhib*:several solo exhbns. Holmfirth Civic Hall, also Holmfirth Artweek for past 20 years, Saddleworth Museum and Art Gallery, Buxton Museum and Art Gallery, Barnard Castle (92 venues), Lupton Square Gallery (Honley), etc. *Works in collections*: worldwide, including America, Canada, Finland, Spain, Australia, Borneo, etc. *Commissions*: considered upon request. *Publications*: several articles in Yorkshire Post, Huddersfield Examiner. *Works Reproduced*: limited edition prints of several Yorkshire scenes. *Recreations*: sport, particularly football (Huddersfield Town FC), long distance walking, outdoor photography. *Clubs*: Yorkshire Watercolour Society. *Address*: 5 Chaucer Close, Honley, Holmfirth, Huddersfield, W. Yorks, HD9 6EN.

BEAUMONT, Sarah Elizabeth, BA (Hons) (1988), PGcert (2011); FRSA (2001), NS.(2000), NAPA (1997); Worshipful Guild of Painter Stainers Prize for Art; Pro Art Prize for Contemporary Painting; Aya Broughton Prize (2008). *Medium*: painter in oil and acrylic. *b*: London, 10 Sep 1966. *Educ*: City of London School for Girls, EC1; University of Lancaster (1985-88). *Exhib*: RA, SWA, NS, NAPA; group shows include London: Westminster Gallery, The Atrium, Whiteley's, Mall Galleries, R.A, Barbican Arts Centre, Lamont Gallery, Art-Islington; The Mariners Gallery, St. Ives; Jersey Gallery, Osterley Park; numerous galleries around the UK; LFI Hadid Pavillion, Weil-am-Rhein, Germany. *Works in collections*: in USA, Canada, Australia, Europe. *Commissions*: various for public bldgs. including the Millfield Theatre, London. *Publications*: Dominatrixes (EPS). *Misc*: Hon Sec National Society of Painters, Sculptors and Printmakers. *Address*: P.O.Box 22894, The Hyde, London NW9 6ZE. *Email*: sarah@sarahbeaumont.com *Website*: www.sarahbeaumont.com *Signs work*: "S.E Beaumont."

BECKER, Bill, BA (Hons) Psychology (Reading University 1971); BA (Hons) Fine Art (2000), MA Fine Art (2002) Lincolnshire and Humberside University; poet, qualified hypnotist and family therapist. *Medium*: oil on canvas. *b*: London, 1 Feb 1932. *m*: multi divorcee. two *s*. two *d*. *Educ*: Chichester High School, Army School of Physical Training. *Studied*: Bognor Regis (Teachers) Training College; Tavistock Institute of Human Relations. *Exhib*: RA Summer Exhbn (2004), Hull, Boston (Lincs), Barton-on-Humber. *Commissions*: do 'negotiated' art, where client and I negotiate a painting through interview/discussion. *Publications*: several poems published. *Principal Works*: landscape - mostly trees with dream-like mystical elements, and old age themes. *Recreations*: Romantic old fashioned music - mainly English and French late 19th-20th century. Romantic poetry. *Address*: 30 Bargate, Grimsby, N E Lincs DN34 4SZ. *Website*: billbecker@btinternet.com *Signs work*: "Bill Becker."

BECKER, Haidee, draughtsman, painter in oil. *Medium*: oil. *b*: Los Angeles, Calif., 13 Jan 1950. *d of*: John Becker & Virginia Campbell. *m*: Clive Sinclair, author. one *s*. one *d*. *Educ*: French Lycée. *Studied*: with Uli Nimptsch, RA, Elizabeth Keys, Adrian Ryan. *Exhib*: RP, HAC, RA, Ben Uri Gallery (The London Jewish Museum), Roland, Browse & Delbanco, New Grafton, C.D. Soar & Son, Odette Gilbert Gallery, Timothy Tew Galerie, Atlanta, Georgia; Anne Berthoud, Redfern Gallery, Byard Art, Thomas Henry Fine Art Ltd., Bourne Fine Art, Fine Art Society, Angela Flowers, Redfern Gallery, Purdy Hicks. *Works in collections*: NPG. *Commissions*: Bocca di Lupo, London. *Address*: 16 Canonbury Grove, London N1 2HR. *Email*: haidee@slopusfilms.com *Website*: www.haideebecker.com *Signs work*: "Becker."

BECKER, Skadi, ARMS, HS, SLm, MASF, RGA; awards: Chairman's Choice (SLm, 2005); Best in Show (SLm, 2006); World Federation of Miniaturist 2008 Best Portrait in any Medium; MASF 2009 Best Portrait. *Medium*: watercolour on ivorine. *b*: Germany, 5 Aug 1937. *d. of*: Maria Reiser. *Partner*: Mr. G .Hammond. two *s*. one *d*. *Studied*: self-taught artist (miniatures). *Exhib*: RMS, HS, SLm, MASF, RGA, SAMAP, Llewellyn Alexander Gallery, World Exhibition of Miniature Art. *Works in collections*: Hilliard Society Travelling Exhibition. *Commissions*: portraits. *Address*: 24 Ullswater Drive, Tilehurst, Reading, RG31 6RS. *Email*: skadibecker@virgin.net *Signs work*: (monogram).

BECKERLEY, Tracy, MA (1989), BA (Hons) (1986), Higher Dip. in Visual Art (1987), Art Foundation Dip. (1983); artist in gouache, paper making, printmaking; visiting lecturer, Lincoln Art School and Brooks University; and psychotherapist. *b*: Bournemouth, 10 Dec 1963. *Studied*: Harrow CHE (1982-83, Brian Pummer), Gwent CHE (1983-86, Roy Ascot), Oxford Polytechnic (1986-87, Ivor Robinson), Chelsea School (1988-89, Tim Mara). *Exhib*: Whitechapel Open (1994); mixed shows in East-West Gallery, Todd Gallery, Concourse Gallery Barbican, Flowers East, Overseas League House, Whitworth Gallery, Business Design Centre. *Address*: Suite 22, Sparkford House, Battersea Church Rd., London SW11 3NQ. *Signs work*: "Beck."

BECKERS, David John. *Medium*: oil, watercolour. *b*: East Sheen, 9 Dec 1944. *Educ*: Twickenham Technical College. *Studied*: St. Martins, London College of Printing & Graphic Art. *Exhib*: Laing Art Competition; Mall Galleries; William Pelly Gallery; Tulip Gallery; Pierrepoint Gallery. *Works Reproduced*: Limited Edition prints. *Recreations*: golf, walking. *Address*: 4 Overton Close, Timber Hill, Lyme Regis, DT7 3HQ. *Email*: beckersart@tiscali.co.uk *Signs work*: "David Beckers."

BECKFORD, Laurence, MCA; Apprentice served 1978. *b*: Exeter, 30 Mar 1961. *Commissions*: Historic buildings, Windsor Castle, Hampton Court Palace, ecclesiastical, cathedrals, private commissions. *Address*: 7 Jury Road, Dulverton, Somerset, TA22 9DX. *Email*: laurence.beckford@sky.com *Website*: www.beckfordartworks.co.uk

BEE, Sarah, PS; DipAD. *Medium*: mixed. *b*: Salisbury, 22 Sep 1951. one *s*. *Educ*: Gillingham Comprehensive, Dorset; Bournemouth Art School. *Studied*: Maidstone School of Art; Heatherley School of Fine Art. *Exhib*: PS, RI, NEAC; Hicks Gallery, Wimbledon; First View, Stourhead; Coombe Gallery, Dartmouth. *Works in collections*: internationally. *Commissions*: Pure Recruitment, The Strand, London. *Address*: 20 Brooklands, Totnes, Devon, TQ9 5AR. *Email*: sarahbee@hotmail.co.uk *Website*: www.sarahbee-painter.com *Signs work*: 'Bee.'

BEECROFT, Glynis: see OWEN, Glynis

BEECROFT, Jane Christine, DipAD, ATC, PGDip HMAD. *Medium*: painting, mixed media, sculpture. *b*: Bristol, 9 Feb 1949. *m*: Richard Cranage. two *s*. one *d*. Studied: Falmouth Art College (1965-67), Cardiff College of Art (1967-70), University of Wales, Cardiff (1970-71), Falmouth College of Arts (1992-94). *Exhib*: solo exhibitions: 10 throughout Cornwall 1998-2014; many Group shows, including: Falmouth Art Gallery (1983, 2000, 2001, 2003, 2004, 2005, 2007, 2009, 2010); Newlyn Art Gallery; Penwith Art Gallery; RWA (2001, 2006); The Crypt Gallery, St. Ives (1999, 2010); Out of Place Gallery, Porthtowan (8); Market St. Mews, Penryn (5); The Poly, Falmouth (11); AAF London (2001).*Works in collections*: Falmouth Art Gallery. *Commissions*: private commissions. *Publications*: Feature in 'Exhibit A' art publication (1998); included in Falmouth Art Gallery catalogue '20 Years of Art in Cornwall' (2000), 'Voyages & Discovery' (2009); 'Beyond Perception - The Art of Jane Beecroft' by Dominique Toure (2012). *Recreations*: travelling, architecture, gardening. *Clubs*: Falmouth Art Club. *Misc*: Taught in Secondary Schools, Abergavenny (1971-73), Falmouth (1976-80); Falmouth College of Arts (1990-96); Founder Member Art Co-op, Art Space Gallery, St. Ives (2000). Previously worked in ceramics - Signed JSC (1970-84). *Address*: 1 Bar Terrace, Falmouth, Cornwall TR11 4BP. *Email*: art@janebeecroft.co.uk *Website*: www.janebeecroft.co.uk *Signs work*: "Jane Beecroft" or monogram of JB.

BEER, David, National Teachers Certificate (main subject Ceramics, 1971); retired from teaching after 27 years in 1998. *Medium*: oil, pastel, acrylics. *b*: Whitstable, Kent, 13 Feb 1943. *s of*: Mr & Mrs H.T. Beer. one *s*. one *d*. *Studied*: Bishop Otter College, Chichester (teaching, ceramics); St. Ives School of Painting. *Exhib*: RWA, Penwith Society St. Ives, Walker Galleries; Gallery Upstairs, Henley-in-Arden, Warwickshire; Mid-Cornwall Galleries; Kendalls Fine Art, Cowes, Isle of Wight; Innocent Fine Art, Bristol; Thomas Henry Fine Art, Nantucket, USA; Walker Galleries, Harrogate; Penhaven Gallery, St. Ives (owned by David Beer himself); Webbs Road Gallery, London; Glasshouse Gallery, Penzance. *Works in collections*: many private collections, both in UK and abroad. *Commissions*: private commissions for life pictures. *Publications*: exhibition catalogues only. *Principal Works*: landscapes/seascapes in oil using palette knife; life drawings (nudes) using pastel and acrylic. *Recreations*: painting! walking the dog! *Address*: Penhaven, 4 St. Peters Street, St. Ives, Cornwall, TR26 1NN. *Email*: beer@penhavengallery.co.uk *Website*: www.penhavengallery.co.uk *Signs work*: David Beer.

BEESLEY, Mark, Datec Diploma in Art and Design. *Medium*: oil, pastel, watercolour. *b*: England, 29 Jan 1953. *Educ*: Burton-on-Trent Grammar School. *Studied*: Nottingham University; Suffolk College, Ipswich. *Exhib*: The Halesworth Gallery (2004), Christchurch Mansion, Ipswich (2004), Peter Pears Gallery, Aldeburgh (2006), The Aldeburgh Gallery (2009, 2013), Re & New Gallery, Woodbridge (2009. 2011, 2013). *Works in collections*: Suffolk County Council; private collections in UK, USA and Australia. *Publications*: article in 'Artist & Illustrators' magazine (October 2003); article in supplement to 'New Statesman' magazine (October 2005); Journal of American Planning Association (cover, 2008). *Works Reproduced*: "The Artist's Sketchbook" (Northlight Books, 2001); "Growing tomorrow's Energy" poster for Shell Wind Energy USA (2007). *Principal Works*: ongoing series of paintings inspired by wind turbines in the landscape. *Clubs*: Ipswich Art Society. *Address*: 45 Old Barrack Road, Woodbridge, Suffolk, IP12 4ET. *Email*: mark.beesley1@virgin.net *Website*: www.remaginations.com or ipswich-art-society.org.uk *Signs work*: "HMB" (monogram) or "HMBEESLEY."

BEESON, Jane, Arnolfini Open Competition prize winner, 1963. *Medium*: oil & PVA on canvas and hardboard. *b*: Weybridge, Surrey, 10 Apr 1930. *d of*: Sir Noel Bowater, Bt. *m*: Christopher Beeson. three *s*. one *d*. *Studied*: Kingston School of Art, Surrey (1949-51); Beaux Arts, Paris (1951-52), under Brianchon; Slade, London (1953). *Exhib*: John Moore's, Liverpool (1961), painting purchased by Ferens Art Gallery, Hull; Richard Demarco Gallery, Edinburgh purchased a painting for their permanent collection (1966); Rowan Gallery, London (1963); Graves Art Gallery, Sheffield (1963); Penwith, St. Ives (1964); Arnolfini, Bristol. 3 prizewinner exhibition (1964); one-woman show (1966); 7 paintings shown in St. Ives Artists exhbn at the RAMM, Exeter (2002). *Works in collections*: "Mauve and Yellow" bought by Director, Ferens Art Gallery, Hull, and in other private collections; also painting in Richard Demarco Gallery Collection, Edinburgh. "Winter I" bought by the Royal Albert Museum, Exeter (2002), "Still Life" bought by the Royal Albert Museum (2002) (both permanent collection). *Publications*: 4 novels, plays for theatre, radio and TV; 2 poetry collections & poems included in various anthologies. *Address*: Ford Farm, Manaton, S. Devon TQ13 9XA. *Email*: jane.beeson@tesco.net *Signs work*: "J. Beeson."

BEESON, Peter, DipAD. *Medium*: oil, casein, watercolour. *b*: London, 29 August 1955. *m*: Joanna Mayes. *Studied*: Sir John Cass School of Art, Whitechapel (1973-77). *Represented by*: Walker Galleries. *Exhib*: RA Summer Exhibition (2009, 2011, 2012); Walker Galleries, Harrogate (solo 2011,13, two-person, 2007, 2009, group 2008); Rowley Contemporary, Winchester (2007-09); Red Rag Gallery, Stow-on-the Wold (2008-2014); Penhaven Gallery, St.Ives (2001-09); Lynn Strover Gallery, Cambridge (2001, 2003, 2007); Langham Fine Art, Bury St.Edmunds (2007); Walker Galleries, Honiton (solo, 2001-06); Rowley Contemporary, London (2003-06), Maltby Gallery, Winchester (2002), Belgrave

Gallery, St. Ives (2011, 2012, 2013). *Works in collections*: international, private and corporate. *Commissions*: The Hare Estate. *Publications*: 'Art About St. Ives'. *Recreations*: surfing. *Address*: 12 Bellair Terrace, St.Ives, Cornwall, TR26 1JR. *Email*: peterbeeson.artist@gmail.com *Signs work*: "Peter Beeson" on back, monogram "pb" on front.

BEHAN, John, RHA, sculptor in metal. *b*: Dublin, 17 Nov 1938. *s of*: Simon and Margaret Behan. one *s*. one *d*. *Studied*: NCAD Dublin (1957-60), Ealing Art College London (1960-61), The Royal Academy, Oslo, Norway (1968). *Represented by*: Kenny's Art Gallery, Middle Street, Galway (contact:Tom Kenny). *Exhib*: all major Irish Exhibitions from 1960 onwards, including IELA, Royal Hibernian Academy, Independent Artists, Group 65, Ruing Ground Project 67, Western Artists. Also Project Gallery, The Taylor Gallery New York, Gordon Gallery Derry, Kenny Gallery Galway, Cork Arts Society, Wagner Gallery Aust. *Works in collections*: National Gallery of Irelend, Hugh Lane Municipal Gallery Dublin, Crawford Gallery Cork, Queen Beatrix of the Netherlands, HMH, Late Samuel Beckett. *Commissions*: 'Arrival' - UN Plaza, NYC; Famine Ship, Murnsk Co Mayo; Wings of the World - Shenzhen, China; Twin Spires, NUIG, Galway; Carlow 1798 Memorial 'The Tree of Liberty' Winged Man - Enrics Co Clare. *Publications*: catalogue, essays, notes by Seamus Heaney, Brian Friel, Poet of Structure by Hayden Murphy. *Official Purchasers*: Galway Corporation, Dublin Corporation, NUIG Galway. *Works Reproduced*: numerous in Bronze Edition since 1970. *Principal Works*: in China, New York, Mayo-Ireland, Dublin. *Recreations*: reading and travel. *Clubs*: Arts Club Dublin, Royal Hibernia Academy since 1990, Aosdana. *Address*: Chestnut Lane, Lower Dangan, Galway, Ireland.

BEILBY, Pauline Margaret, NDD(1950); portrait and equestrian sculptor in clay, textile designer, freelance; water-colour paintings. *b*: Bramcote, Notts., 21 Jun 1927. *d of*: Percy Goold Beilby. *m*: Keith David Barnes, lace manufacturer. two *s*. *Educ*: Nottingham Girls' High School. *Studied*: Nottingham College of Arts and Crafts under A. H. Rodway, ARCA, FRSA, principal. *Address*: Burleigh House, 15 Albemarle Rd., Woodthorpe, Notts. NG5 4FE. *Signs work*: with monogram.

BELCHER, William Leeder, NDD, DesRCA, FCIAD; freelance artist/designer/ illustrator in textiles, graphics and painting. *Medium*: oil, watercolour, drawing. *b*: 2 Jun 1923. *s of*: Sidney Belcher. *m*: Colleen Belcher (Designer/ Painter). *Educ*: Hastings Grammar School. *Studied*: Worthing School of Art (1947-50), RCA (1950-54). *Exhib*:many group exhbns including RA, Gimpel Fils Gallery, AIA Gallery, Jane England Gallery. *Works in collections*: private collections. *Commissions*: illustrations for many publications including IBM, Unilever, Radio Times, The Observer, Punch, The Oldie, Design. *Publications*: The Designer, Art News, The Author, BBC TV2 etc. *Works Reproduced*: in magazines, newspapers and books. *Address*: 304 Kew Road, Kew Gardens, Surrey, TW9 3DU. *Signs work*: 'William Belcher.'

BELDERSON, John Walter (Rev.), B.Arch., BD (Natal and London); Yorkshire Watercolour Society (1981); Minister of United Reformed Church (1965-1998, ret.); watercolour tutor, N.Yorks C. Council (1990-98). *Medium*: watercolour, oils, acrylic. *b*: 27 Aug 1933. *s of*: John Henry Belderson OBE. *m*: Elizabeth. one *s*. two *d*. *Studied*: Hilton College, Natal; Univ. of Natal; London Univ (1947-64). *Exhib*: YW Soc. exhbns.; annual solo (1987-) Yorkshire; South Africa (P.W. Storey prizewinner); USA - Windsor, Conn.; Germany - Stuttgart; Aiton Gallery, Crieff, Scotland. *Works in collections*: various - UK, Germany, South Africa, USA. *Commissions*: 'Harrogate in Bloom' Committee, Cockridge Hospital, Leeds; mural - Halifax Churches Comm. Centre; 'Old and New Testament' - two glass enamel painted windows (Dacre Church). *Official Purchasers*: Leeds (West) United Hospitals; Harrogate in Bloom - Silcoates School; Wakefield. *Works Reproduced*: "Nidderdale Praise, poetry and paintings" (book). *Clubs*: Pateley Bridge Club. *Address*:

27 Grange Road, Dacre Banks, Harrogate, HG3 4HA. *Email*: belderson@onetel.com *Website*: www.beldersonart.com

BELL, Ellen Mary, BA Theatre Design, BA Illustration, MA Fine Art, MA Creative Writing (ongoing); Prizewinner: Paperwork 2005. *Medium*: drawing, installation. *b*: Upton, Cheshire, 16 Sep 1962. *Partner*: Mr. Pip Jones. one *d*. *Studied*: Wimbledon School of Art (1981-84), Manchester Met Uni (1991-94), Norwich School of Art (1999-2001), Dartington College of Arts (2008-10). *Represented by*: Four Square Fine Arts. *Exhib*: solo and group, including: Rebecca Hosscak Gallery (2002-04); SoFA, Chicago (2004); Collect, V&A Museum (2004); b.j.spoke Gallery, New York (2005); Millennium Galleries, Sheffield (2006); City Gallery, Leicester (2007); Redchurch St. Gallery, London (2011); Arnolfini, Bristol (2011). *Works in collections*: V&A Print Collection; Anglia Ruskin University. *Commissions*: private commissions: Mr. David Newel (clock restorer), Mrs. Pam Long. *Publications*: 'Speaking Soul' (City Gallery, Leicester), 'Hard Work' (Four Square Fine Arts); 'Camera Obscura & Other Stories' (Four Square Fine Arts). *Principal Works*: Installations: 'Talk to Me' (Chapel Row, Bath); 'Story' (Bristol Museum & Art Gallery); 'Speaking Soul'. *Clubs*: Design & Artists Copyright Society (DACS), Author Licensing Copyright Soc. (ALCS). *Address*: Cwrt Cenydd, Llanbadarn Road, Aberystwyth SY23 1EQ. *Email*: ellenbell.bell07@gmail.com *Website*: www.ellenbell.co.uk *Signs work*: "ELLEN BELL".

BELL, Michael Munro (Mike), Dip AD Hons Art & Design; Queens Award 1965; American Art Awards (2011, 12). *Medium*: Fine Art, mixed media (painting). *b*: Newcastle upon Tyne, 27 Sep 1942. *m*: Margaret Ann. *Educ*: teaching as Head of Department: 1975-80 Hyton Red House School, 1988-95 Wearside College of FE. *Studied*: Sunderland College of Art & Design 1961-66 (now Univ. of Sunderland). *Represented by*: Biscuit Factory (Newcastle), Artists Haven Gallery (Ft Lauderdale, Florida). *Exhib*: Biscuit Factory, Newcastle; Coningsby Gallery, London; Sheridan Russell Gallery, London; Artists Haven Gallery, Florida; Art Domain Gallery, Leipzig; Caelum Gallery New York; Alpha Art, Edinburgh; John Green Fine Art, Glasgow; Brownston Gallery, Devon; Walker Gallery, Harrogate; AAF London, Bristol, Edinburgh, Newcastle Art Fairs. *Works in collections*: private; Sunderland Education Authority. *Commissions*: Indigo Arts for several hotels, Wetherspoons Hotels, private. *Publications*: Artists Haven Members Spring Edition 2012; 100 Contemporary International Artists 2007, European Community Library. *Official Purchasers*: Sunderland Education Authority. *Works Reproduced*: Limited Ed. Prints, Indigo Arts, Easy Art, Apaw Gallery (China). *Recreations*: walking, reading, music. *Clubs*: Network Artists. *Misc*: www.axisweb.org/artistmikebell. *Address*: Yarrow Cottage, West Woodborn, Northumberland, NE48 2RX. *Email*: mike@annbell48.fsnet.co.uk *Website*: www.mike-bell.artistswebsites.com *Signs work*: "Mike Bell".

BELL, Stanley Fraser, DA (Mural Design) Glasgow (1970); artist in mixed media reliefs and painted murals; former Senior Lecturer, Glasgow School of Art; former Chairman, Glasgow League of Artists. *b*: Glasgow, 12 Jan 1928. *s of*: John Armour Bell. *m*: Catherine MacDonald. one *s*. *Studied*: Glasgow School of Art (1966-70). *Exhib*: Scottish Young Contemporaries (1969, 1970, 1971), The Clyde Group, Edinburgh (1971), John Player Bienalle 2 Touring Exhbn. (1971), 'With Murals in Mind' Acheson House, Edinburgh (1974), 'Un Certain Art Anglais' Paris, Brussels (1979); regular exhibitor in group exhbns. in Scotland and elsewhere. *Works in collections*: large scale exterior murals in Glasgow, National Galleries of Scotland. *Clubs*: Glasgow Art. *Address*: 419 North Woodside Rd., Glasgow G20 6NN. *Signs work*: "Stan Bell."

BELL, Trevor, Hon.RWA; Winner Paris Biennale 1958; Head of Painting Winchester School of Art 1966-70; Professor for Graduate Painting, Florida State University, USA, 1972-1996; awarded Professor Emeritus 1995. *Medium*: painter. *b*: Leeds, 18 Oct 1930. *m*: Harriet. *Represented by*: Waterhouse & Dodd, The New Millennium Gallery - St. Ives,

Lydon Fine Art - Chicago USA. *Exhib*:solo exhibitions: Waddington Gallery, London (1958, '60, '62, '64); Richard Demarco Gallery, Edinburgh (1970); New Millennium Gallery, St.Ives (2001, 2003, 2005, 2007); Gillian Jason, ART2003; Waterhouse & Dodd, London (2006); plus many others at home and in the US. *Works in collections*: Selected Public Collections: Laing Art Gallery, Newcastle; Leeds City Museum and Art Gallery; Museum of Art, Fort Lauderdale, Florida; Phoenix Art Museum, Arizona; Tate Gallery, London; Victoria and Albert Museum, London; Wakefield City Art Gallery; Whitworth Art Gallery, Manchester; numerous private collections in Europe, Canada and the United States. *Address*: Vellyndruchia, Tremethick Cross, Penzance, Cornwall, TR20 8TZ. *Email*: bellstudio@btinternet.com *Signs work*: "TREVOR BELL" (on rear).

BELLAMY, David, self taught artist in water-colour, writer. *b*: Pembroke, 15 Jun 1943. *s of*: Arthur and Edith Bellamy. *m*: Jenny Keal. one *d*. *Educ*: Narberth Grammar School. *Exhib*: Cleveland Gallery, Bath; Lincoln Joyce Fine Art, Gt. Bookham; Albany Gallery, Cardiff; Mathaf Gallery, and many others. *Works in collections*: Berol Ltd., Welsh Development Agency, and worldwide. *Commissions*: army! *Publications*: written and illustrated: Wild Places of Britain; Painting in the Wild; Wild Coast of Britain; David Bellamy's Water-colour Landscape Course, Developing your Water-colours; Images of the South Wales Mines, Wilderness Artist; Learn to Paint Water-colour Landscapes; David Bellamy's Coastal Landscapes; David Bellamy's Pembrokeshire; Painting Wild Landscapes in Watercolour; David Bellamy's Guide to Watercolour Painting; also fine art prints. *Recreations*: mountaineering. *Clubs*: Alpine Club. *Misc*: Produced 6 DVDs on painting in watercolour. *Address*: Maesmawr, Aberedw, Builth Wells, Powys LD2 3UL. *Website*: www.davidbellamy.co.uk *Signs work*: "David Bellamy."

BELLWOOD, Colin, Master of Arts. *Medium*: oil, collage. *b*: Castleford, Yorks, 1 Jul 1949. *s of*: Doreen & William. *m*: Margaret. one *s*. one *d*. *Educ*: Castleford Grammar School. *Studied*: Leeds College of Art, Coventry College of Education, University of Leeds (1950-70). *Exhib*: Royal Academy Summer Exhibition (1989, 1992, 1997 - 2 works hung, 1998, 2000 - 2 works hung); one-man shows: The Coningsby Gallery, London (2003, 2007), The Dundas Gallery, Edinburgh (2005); Galeria Doreen, Los Azahares, Seville (Mar-May 2014). *Works in collections*: works in private collections in London, New York, The Hague, and others in Europe and N. America. *Publications*: a novel "Jack Remnant" pub. 2008, second novel "The Proof of the Soul" pub. 2011; a collection of poems and paintings, "Something in Seville" pub 2012. *Misc*: now works in his studio in Seville, Spain. *Address*: Viriato 14.4, Seville 41003, Spain. *Email*: colinbellwood@yahoo.com.au *Website*: www.colinbellwood.com www.NuMasters.com www.londonart.co.uk colinbellwood.eu. *Signs work*: "COLIN B."

BELSEY, Hugh Graham, MBE (2004); BA (1976), M.Litt. (1981); museum curator; Curator, Gainsborough's House (1981-2004), freelancing thereafter; Senior Research Fellow, Paul Mellon Centre for Study 'British Art ' London (2006-). *b*: Hemel Hempstead, 15 May 1954. *s of*: Graham Miles Belsey, FMICE. *Educ*: University of Manchester and The Barber Inst. of Fine Arts, Birmingham. *Publications*: articles for art periodicals and exhbn. catalogues. Gainsborough at Gainsborough's House; Thomas Gainsborough: A Country Life. *Address*: 7 Rae's Yard, Bury St.Edmunds, Suffolk IP33 3EY. *Email*: h.g.belsey@talk21.com

BELTON, Liam, RHA (1993), ARHA (1991), ANCA (1971); painter in oil, keeper of Royal Hibernian Academy (1995). *b*: Dublin, 1947. *m*: Sharon Lynch. two *s*. one *d*. *Educ*: Synge Street. *Studied*: National College of Art, Dublin (1966-72). *Exhib*: five one-man shows, various group shows throughout Ireland. *Works in collections*: Dept. of Labour, ESB, GPA, National Self-Portrait Collection, KPMG, Craig Gardner, Sisks, Elm Park Hospital, An Post., AIB, OPW, Haverty Trust, Contemporary Arts Soc., Ulster Bank. *Misc*: Member of A.A.I. and S.S.I.; Board mem. N.S.P.C. and R.H.A. Gallagher Gallery. *Address*: 18 Whitethorn Rd., Artane, Dublin 5, Ireland. *Signs work*: "Liam Belton, R.H.A."

BELYI, Peter, MA Printmaking (2000); Birgit Skiold Prize, National Print Exhibition (2003); Gavin Graham Gallery Award, National Print Exhbn (2002); Outstanding Printmaking Award, St.Petersburg Print Biennale (2001), Galleries Magazine Award, National Print Exhbn (2000). *Medium*: oil, prints, conceptual (installation). *b*: St.Petersburgh, Russia, 21 Apr 1971. *m*: Joanna Rogers. two *d*. *Studied*: Camberwell College of Art (1998-2000); Academy of Applied Art Ceramics Dept., St.Petersburg (1990-92); Secondary Art School of the Academy of Arts, St.Petersburg (1982-89). *Exhib*:over 10 solo exhbns in UK and overseas since 1994; RA Summer Exhbn (2001, 2002, 2003, 2004, 2005), My Neighbourhood, Rossia 2, Moscow Biennale (2005); National Print Exhbn, Mall Galleries (2001, 2003), Discerning Eye (2001, 2003), 5th Open Print Exhbn, RWA (2000); over 20 group exhbns in UK and overseas since 1992. *Works in collections*: V&A Permanent Collection; Ashmoloean Museum, RE Diploma Exhbn. *Official Purchasers*: V&A. *Principal Works*: Installations: Dream of a Concierge, Dream of the Dictator, My Neighbourhood, White Project, series of large-scale woodcuts 2000-2005. *Address*: c/o 16 Dartmouth Row, Greenwich, London SE10 8AN. *Email*: pbelyi@hotmail.com *Website*: www.peterbelyi.com *Signs work*: 'Peter Belyi.'

BENDALL-BRUNELLO, Tiziana, BA Joint Hons. (Fine Art/Ceramics) 1994; 1st Prize Winner of 'Terra Piemonte' Prize for Ceramics (Castellamonte Museum, Italy, 2004). *Medium*: porcelain and glass. *b*: Turin, Italy, 8 Feb 1959. *m*: John Bendall-Brunello. *Studied*: Camberwell College of Art (1991-94). *Exhib*: Hayward, Sotheby's, Barbican, Bowes Museum, Kettles Yard, Cambridge; Kunstmuseum, Wolfsburg, Germany; National Glass Centre, CCA Cambridge; Roger Billcliffe, Glasgow; Scottish Gallery, Edinburgh; The Bluecoat, Liverpool; Affordable Art Fair (London & New York), Glasgow Art Fair, Scotland; SOFA Exhbn, Chicago; Art 2000 - International Art Fair, San Francisco International Gift Fair, USA; Chelsea Crafts Fair, London; Castellamonte Museum, Italy, 1st Prize winner of 'Terra Piemonte'; Contemporary Applied Arts, London; Beatrice Royal Contemporary Art and Craft Gallery; Affordable Art Fair, Milan; Affordable Art Fair, Amsterdam. *Publications*: 'Breaking the Mould' - Black Dog publishing (2007). *Address*: 33 Cowper Rd., Cambridge CB1 3SL. *Email*: tiziana@glasspencil.co.uk *Website*: www.tizianab-b.co.uk *Signs work*: "TIZIANA BENDALL-BRUNELLO."

BENGE, Bryan Neil, BA (Hons) (1977), MA (1994); lecturer, conceptual artist; Hon.Sec., London Group (1995-). *b*: Middlesex, 16 Jun 1953. *m*: Maria Wasley. *Studied*: Chelsea School of Art (1973), Kingston Polytechnic (1974-77), Kingston University (1992-94). *Exhib*:Young Contemporaries, RA, American Council for the Arts, NY (Liquitex in Excellence, prize winner 1993); London: Mall Galleries, Barbican Centre, Danielle Arnaud, Morley Gallery, Westminster, Bedford Hill, St. James, Tricycle, London Inst., Central St. Martin's; Europe: Pompidou Centre, Reichstag Germany, Sarajevo, Obala Gallery. *Works in collections*: Tate Gallery London Archives. *Clubs*: London Group. *Address*: 51 Bramble Walk, Epsom, Surrey KT18 7TB. *Signs work*: "BRYAN BENGE."

BENJAMIN, Norman: see IBRAM, Peter B.

BENJAMINS, Paul, BA (1st Class Hons), MA (RCA); artist in oil and acrylic. *b*: London, 18 Oct 1950. *m*: Jacqui. one *s*. one *d*. *Studied*: Camberwell School of Art (1969-73), RCA (1973-75). *Exhib*: solo shows: Thumb Gallery, London (1984, 1986, 1987), Galerie Pascal Gabert, Paris (1989, 1991, 1994), Gallery Cafe Mandy, Bergenz, Austria (1990), Jill George Gallery, London (1991, 1994, 1996, 2000), Champagne Vranken, Epernay (1993), Galerie Wam, Caen (1995), Brighton University Gallery (1998); group shows: numerous including Brighton Polytechnic Gallery, John Moores W.A.G. Liverpool,

Thumb Gallery, International Contemporary Art Fairs (London, Bath, Los Angeles), Galerie Pascal Gabert, Paris, Original Print Gallery, Dublin, etc. *Commissions*: Royal Princess, Rhombert Austria, Herouville-St. Clair, Normandy, France. *Address*: c/o Advanced Graphics London, Ground Floor, 32 Long Lane, London SE1 4AY.

BENNALLACK HART, Michael John, BA; Gold Clio New York 1987, Silver Clio NY 1988, D&AD Award 1988; Andrew Herring Prize, Pastel Society (1995). *Medium*: pastel, oil. *b*: Worthing, Sussex, 4 Aug 1948. *s of*: Major & Mrs N J Bennallack Hart. *m*: Sheila Brownlee. *Educ*: Douai School. *Studied*: Ravensbourne College of Art & Design (1966-70). *Represented by*: Medici Gallery. *Exhib*: Spectrum Gallery, New York (1978-82); Open Eye Gallery, Edinburgh (1996); Royal College of Art (1996); John Mitchell & Son, London (1998-2001); Mall Galleries, London (1995, 2002, 2010); Montgomery Gallery, San Francisco (2001); Rye Art Gallery (2003); Royal Academy, London (2004); Brian Sinfield, Burford (2004); Medici Gallery, London (2003-13); Walton Gallery, London (2003); Collins & Hastie London (2004); Galerie Carla Magna, Paris (2010), Jorgensen Fine Art, Dublin (2011), Langham Gallery, London (2011), Russell Gallery, London (2011); Roland Goslett Gallery, Richmond (2014); Blackheath Gallery, London (2012-2014). *Works in collections*: private, corporate, public. *Commissions*: private, corporate. *Recreations*: Jazz drumming. *Clubs*: Chelsea Arts Club, London. *Address*: 11 St. Pauls Road, Richmond, Surrey, TN9 2HH. *Email*: ben@mbhart.co.uk *Website*: www.mbhart.co.uk *Signs work*: "BH."

BENNETT, Brian Theodore Norton, MA Oxon. (1954), ROI (1973), PROI (1987-94), NS (1985), Hon. UA (1985); landscape painter in oil; Director of Art, Berkhamsted School (1957-8), Governor, Federation of British Artists (1992-98). *b*: Olney, Bucks., 1927. *s of*: Horace T. Bennett. *m*: Margrit Elizabeth Brenner. *Educ*: Magdalen College School, Oxford and Magdalen College, Oxford. *Studied*: Ruskin School of Art, Oxford (1950) part-time; Regent St. Polytechnic (1956) evening classes. *Represented* by: The Hawker Gallery, Amersham Bucks.; Francis Iles, Rochester, Kent. *Exhib*: RA., RBA, ROI, RSMA, etc. *Publications*: Choir Stalls of Chester Cathedral (1965), Oil Painting with a Knife (1993), A Painter's Year; Twelve Months in the Chilterns (2001). *Official Purchasers*: Buckinghamshire County Museum, Aylesbury; Berkhamsted Town Council. *Address*: 18 Upper Ashlyns Rd., Berkhamsted, Herts. HP4 3BW. *Signs work*: "BRIAN BENNETT" on front. Signature on reverse.

BENNETT, David Stuart, BA (Hons) (1992), MA (RCA) (1995), SWLA (1992-present); artist in water-colour and oil. *b*: Doncaster, 11 Dec 1969. *Studied*: Leeds Polytechnic (1989-92), Royal College of Art, London (1993-95). *Exhib*: one-man shows: England; mixed exhbns. America, Holland, Spain, France, Ireland. *Publications*: Artist for nature publications, Flight of Cranes to Extremadura; and Alaska's Copper River Delta; Nick Hammond, Modern Wildlife Painting; Robin Darcy Shilcock: Pintores de la Naturaleza. *Address*: 16 Pearl St., Harrogate HG1 4QW. *Signs work*: "David Bennett."

BENNETT, June, NDD, ATD; painter/jeweller in silver and gold. *b*: Grange over Sands. *d of*: E. B. Steer. *m*: Michael Bennett. two *s*. *Educ*: Ulverston G.S. *Studied*: Lancaster and Leicester Colleges of Art. *Representd by*: Castlegate house Gallery, Cockermouth. *Exhib*: Goldsmiths Hall, Midland Group Gallery, Nottingham, Park Square Gallery, Leeds, Mignon Gallery, Bath, Ashgate Gallery, Farnham; one-man shows, Castlegate House Gallery, Cockermouth (1988, 1989, 1991, 1993, 1994, 1999, 2001, 2003), The Beacon, Whitehaven (2004), Orange Street Gallery, Uppingham (2005), Stronach Gallery, Ireland (2005, 2007). *Works in collections*: Jewellery: Abbot Hall Gallery, Kendal, Shipley A.G.; Paintings: Carlisle Museum and A.G., Copeland CC House of Lords Coll. Painting full time from 1987. *Address*: The Hollies, Port Carlisle, Cumbria CA7 5BU. *Signs work*: "June Bennett," "J.B." and Sheffield Assay Office hallmark.

BENNETT, Margaretann, VAS (1997); RSW (2004); BA (Hons); The William Bowie Award (PAI Exhbn 2006); Langside College Watercolour Award (RGI, 2005); The Armour Award (RGI, 2006); Glasow Art Club Fellowship; The Mabel MacKinlay Award (RGI 2011); The Scottish Arts Club Award (RSW 2010). *Medium*: mixed media. *b*: Belshill, 21 Apr 1968. *d of*: Thomas Gerrard Bennett. *Partner*: Richard Davies (Artist). *Educ*: Uddington Grammar School. *Studied*: Glasgow School of Art (1987-91). *Exhib*: RGI; RSW; RSA; PAI; Panter & Hall, London; London Art Fair, Battersea; Red Rag Gallery, Worcestershire; Gallery Heinzel, Aberdeen; 20/21 British Art Fair; Saffron Gallery, Sussex. *Works in collections*: Paintings in Hospitals; Inverarity Vaults Ltd. *Commissions*: numerous private. *Address*: Flat 3/2, 27 Cartvale Road, Glasgow, G42 9TA. *Email*: margaretannbennett@hotmail.com *Website*: www.margaretannbennett.co.uk *Signs work*: 'Bennett.'

BENNETT, Michael, NDD, ATD; painter in oils. *b*: Windermere, 1934. *s of*: T. W. Bennett. *m*: June Steer. two *s*. *Educ*: Windermere Grammar School. *Studied*: Lancaster and Leicester Colleges of Art. *Represented by*: Castlegate House Gallery, Cockermouth. *Exhib*: one-man shows: Park Square Gallery, Leeds, Mignon Gallery, Bath, Bluecoat Gallery, Liverpool, Ashgate Gallery, Farnham, Abbot Hall, Kendal, AIA Gallery, London; Leeds, Birmingham, Hull and Lancaster Universities, Castlegate Gallery, Cockermouth, Broughton House Gallery, Cambridge, Orange Street Gallery, Uppingham, Stronach Gallery, Ireland. *Works in collections*: Abbot Hall Gallery, Wakefield City A.G., Lincolnshire Arts Assoc., John Player Collection, Leeds Educ. Authority, Kettle's Yard, Univ. of Cambridge and Northern Arts Assoc., House of Lords Collection. *Address*: The Hollies, Port Carlisle, Cumbria CA7 5BU. *Signs work*: "Bennett" and date.

BENNETT, Terence, NDD, FRSA, Yorkshire Television Fine Art Fellowship (1973-74); painter in oil on canvas and water-colour, teacher; Head of Fine Art, Thomas Rotherham College, Rotherham (1976-91); the Sidney Holgate Fellowship, University of Durham (2001). *b*: Doncaster, 7 Nov 1935. two *s*. one *d*. *Studied*: Doncaster School of Art (Eric Platt, T.A. Anderson). *Exhib*: RA, ROI, NEAC, Drian Gallery, Travelling exhbn. Yorkshire, Lincolnshire, NS, British Painting, Mall Galleries. *Works in collections*: Nuffield Foundation, Bank of England, Yorkshire Television, Yorkshire Arts Assoc., Leeds Educ. Authority, Halifax Bldg. Soc., Sheffield University, Cambridge University, Doncaster Borough Council, ICI Ltd., Durham University. *Misc*: Prizes: Singer and Friedlander, Sunday Times Water-colour competition. *Address*: Rambler Cottage, 43 Main St., Sprotbrough, Doncaster, S. Yorks. DN5 7RH. *Email*: tedmbennet@aol.com *Website*: www.terencebennett.co.uk *Signs work*: "Terence Bennett."

BENSON, Dawn Mary, LSIA (1974), Surrey Dip. (1974) Graphic Design; Worked in graphic design business for 16 years. *Medium*: Stylised Figurative Sculptor, producing work in Bronze and Bronze resin; Painter in various media. *b*: Montreal, Canada, 7 Dec 1952. *d of*: Paul R Stephens (decd), Janet Hyde. *Partner*: Lendon Scantlebury. one *d*. *Educ*: Thames Valley Grammar School, Twickenham. *Studied*: Twickenham College (1970-74, Stan Smith and Osmund Caine), Sir John Cass p/t (1976-78), Richmond College p/t (1989-94). *Represented by*: variety of galleries throughout the UK. *Exhib*: London and galleries throughout UK. *Works in collections*: USA, NZ, Australia, UK and Europe, Germany. *Commissions*: portrait sculptures in London, Amsterdam (also sold Sotheby's); paintings in NZ and USA Large commercial project for 8 sculptures for Expo 2000 in Hanover, and for Jordanian Embassy (as part of a team); private commissions. *Publications*: 52 Things to Do ISBN 978-0-9569803-0-4. *Principal Works*: sold in galleries and Affordable Art Fair, London, private commissions. *Recreations*: Gardening, walking, travelling. *Clubs*: Oxford Sculptors. *Address*: 33 Barwell, Wantage, Oxfordshire, OX12 9AZ. *Email*: dawnstephens@yahoo.com *Website*: www.barwellgallery.co.uk *Signs work*: 'DMB', 'Dawn Benson', 'D.M.Benson' or 'D.Benson.'

BENSON, Gordon Mitchell, OBE RA FRACS AADip SADG ARIBA FRIAS; Awards: Bovis Lend Lease & AJ Best Work Award (2004), Stirling Prize Shortlist RIBA (Official named Runner-up 1999, shortlist 2002), RIBA Regional Award (2002), Ediinburgh Architectural Association Centenary medal (2000); Competitions: Kent History Centre (Second place, 2004); Sydney University, Australia (Shortlisted 2003); British Embassy, Warsaw (Shortlisted 2003); Waterford Masterplan (Second Place 2002); Pearse Street Development, Trinity College (Shortlisted 2002); Turner Art Centre, Margate (Shortlisted 2002); Housing, Dublin Docklands Development Authority (Winner 2001); National Gallery of Ireland (Winner 1996); Cowgatehead Library, Edinburgh (Winner 1995); Museum of Scotland (Winner 1991); Glasgow Auditorium (Winner 1989). Projects include: Battersea Power Station Residential (2003-04); Royal College of Surgeons, Edinburgh (2002-03); Quayside Housing Project, DDDA (2001-02); Millennium Wing Extension, National Gallery of Ireland, Dublin (1996-2002); Museum of Scotland, Edinburgh (1992-98); Float Museum & Temple to Time, Jyohanna & Oshima, Japan (1994); Boarbank Hall, Cumbria, Physiotherapy Room & Oratory (1986 & 1985); Isle of Dogs, London Docklands (1985); Housing, Camden (1974-75) and many others. *b*: Scotland, 5 Oct 1944. one *s*. one *d*. *Publications*: numerous. *Clubs*: Arts Club, Highgate Golf Club, Gounock Yacht Club. *Misc*: Diploma Tutor, Diploma Unit 7, Architectural Association, London (1977-86); Chair of Architecture, Strathclyde University (1986-90); Simpson's Professor, Edinburgh University (1991-96). *Address*: 40 Charlton Kings Road, London NW5 2SA.

BENTHAM, Martin, RWA; BA (Hons); 1st Prize, Annual Exhibition Royal Bath & West Show (2007); Daler Rowney Oil Painting Prize, 155th Autumn Exhibition RWA Bristol (2007); 1st and 2nd Prize, Viewers Choice Award 156th Autumn Exhibition RWA Bristol (2008); elected RWA 2009. *Medium*: oil, drawing. *b*: Aldershot, Hampshire, 30 Oct 1961. one *d*. *Studied*: Exeter College of Art & Design (1982-85). *Exhib*: One-man shows: Barn House, Blagdon (1993, 95, 97, 99, 2006, 2008); Royal West of England Academy (2010, 2012). Mixed shows: RA Summer Exhibition (1989); Royal West of England Academy Autumn Exhibition (1987, 88, 89, 90, 92, 93, 94, 95, 2000, 2007, 08, 09, 10, 11, 12, 13); Bath Society of Artists, Victoria Art Gallery, Bath (2005, 11, 12, 13); Atkinson Gallery, Millfield, Street (1994, 2005, 07, 08, 09, 12). *Work in collections*: private/corporate; RWA Permanent Collection, Bristol; Royal Collection. *Commissions*: Mendip Hills Landscape Assessment, Countryside Commission (1998); private commissions. *Publications*: Martin Bentham RWA catalogue (ISBN 978-0-9566408-0-2). *Misc*: Professional artist. Address: 2 Providence Cottage, Street End, Blagdon, North Somerset BS40 7TL. *Email*: info@martinbentham.com *Website*: www.martinbentham.com *Signs work*: "Bentham".

BENTLEY, Raymond NS. Winner, AYA Broughton Painting Prize (NS) 2011, 2013; Member National Society of Painters, Sculptors and Printmakers (NS). *Medium*: oil, watercolour. *b*: Stoke-on-Trent, 27 Nov 1938. *Partner*: Mr JM Lawton. *Educ*: Longton High School. *Studied*: St. Martins School of Art (1956-60); Sir John Cass Faculty of Art, Architecture and Design. *Represented by*: Westside Contemporary Gallery, Northumberland (2012-2014). *Exhib*: Young Contemporaries, Aia Gallery (both 1960); NEAC, NS, RI, ROI, RWS (PASSIM), Trends, Buckingham Gate (date unknown); Teeside Art Gallery (c 1987); Artsbank, Saltburn (2011); Westside Contemporary Gallery (2012, 2013); Studio Eleven Gallery, Hull (2012, 2013); Barefoot Gallery, Boston Spa (2012-2014); Menier Gallery, London (2013); Palace Hub, Redcar (2013, 2014). *Works in collections*: private and corporate. *Commissions*: First National Bank of Chicago, Shand Kidd, University of Maryland. *Works Reproduced*:Chelsea Arts Club Yearbook (2014). *Clubs*: Chelsea Arts Club. *Address*: 3 Bristol Avenue, Saltburn-by-the-Sea, Cleveland, TS12 1BW. *Email*: raymondbentley@hotmail.com *Website*: raymondbentley.com *Signs work*: "R. BENTLEY."

BENTON, Graham, NDD (1964), ARBSA (1986); RBSA (2005); abstract painter/illustrator in oil, gouache, collage, charcoal, pastel; part-time art tutor; Former Sec.

and Chairman Walsall Arts Council and Walsall Soc. of Artists; coordinator Walsall Artists Network; Associate mem. Penwith Soc. of Arts; Mem. NSEAD.; Member of Royal Birmingham Soc. of Artists. *b*: Birmingham, 24 Oct 1934. *s of*: Sidney Benton. *Studied*: Walsall School of Art (1952-56, George Willott, Angus Macauley), Wolverhampton College of Art (1962-64, John Finnie, Bernard Brett). *Exhib*: Stafford A.G., Lichfield A.G., Walsall A.G., Letchworth A.G., 273 Gallery, London, Keele University, Salthouse Gallery, St. Ives, Penlee House, Penzance, RBSA Galleries, Birmingham, Wednesbury A.G., Camborne School of Mines; Solihull A.G., Mid-art, Dudley, Staffordshire Open; Retrospective - New Art Gallery, Walsall "St. Ives to Walsall" (2011). *Works in collections*: Arthur Andersen, London; RBSA Gallery, Birmingham; Walsall New Art Gallery; Private Collections in England. *Address*: 38 Upper Forster St., Walsall, W. Midlands, WS4 2AA. *Email*: graham_benton@hotmail.co.uk *Signs work*: "(Graham) Benton."

BERESFORD-WILLIAMS, Mary E., BA Hons. Fine Art, Reading (1953 Class 1); Cert. Educ. (1954); painter, printmaker and photographer; South-West Arts Major Award (1978); Photographer in Residence, Television South-West (1986-87); First Prize (Purchase) Burton Gallery, Bideford Open Art Competition (1999). *b*: London, 30 Apr 1931. *d of*: F.N.& B.D.Elliott. *m*: David Beresford-Williams. one *s*. *Educ*: Watford Grammar School. *Studied*: painting: Reading University under Prof. J.A. Betts. *Exhib*: Galleries in London and the South-west; solo shows Burton Gallery, Bideford, Devon (1998), Torre Abbey, Torquay, Devon (2000), Greenway Garden Gallery, (NT), Brixham (2002), Devon Guild (Café) (2003, 2007). *Works in collections*: Paintings, photographs and prints in public and private collections. Prints in hospitals. Prints in hotels. *Commissions*: portraits, prints. *Publications*: 1973-1997 made many screen prints, sold in limited editions. 1988 book of photographs: A Portrait of TSW. Since 2000 has been making digital prints. *Official Purchasers*: Torre Abbey, Torquay; Burton Gallery, Bideford; National Trust, Saltram House, Devon. *Principal Works*: 'Summer on the Dart', 'The Lesson', 'The Birthday Party', 'Concert at Saltram'. *Recreations*: reading, travel. *Address*: 11 Langdon Lane, Galmpton, Brixham, Devon TQ5 0PQ. *Email*: beresford-williams@hotmail.co.uk *Website*: axis *Signs work*: "M. Beresford-Williams" , "MBW.", or "M.B.Williams."

BERMANT, Judith Rose, NDD. *Medium*: watercolour, drawing, prints, sculpture. *b*: London, 12 May 1939. widowed. *d of*: Mr & Mrs F Weil. two *s*. two *d*. *Educ*: Avigdor Grammar School. *Studied*: St. Martins School of Art (1955-1958). *Exhib*: 12 solo exhbns; many group shows including RA Summer exhbns, Royal Festival Hall, Mall Galleries, RP, Camden Arts Centre, Bloomsbury Galleries, Barbican Centre, Belgrave Gallery, House of Commons, etc. *Commissions*: many portrait commissions including: Mrs. Ruth Winston-Fox (mother of Lord Robert Winston), Lord & Lady Levene's children, Lord Jakobovits, etc.; stained glass windows: Shomrei Hadath Synagogue. *Publications*: book covers: 'The Patriarch', 'Titch', 'Dancing Bear', 'Genesis', 'On the Other Hand' - biography of Lord Jakobovits *Official Purchasers*: prints bought by Contemporary Arts Society for new BUPA HQ. *Address*: 18 Hill Rise, London NW11 6NA. *Email*: Judy@bermant.com *Signs work*: 'Judy Bermant.'

BERNARD, Mike, BA (Hons) (1978), RAS Dip (1981), R.I. (1997); demonstrator of painting techniques to art societies; painter in mixed media, acrylics, oil, tutor. *b*: Dover, 2 Aug 1957. *m*: Susan. one *s*. one *d*. *Studied*: West Surrey College of Art and Design (1975-78), RA Schools (1978-81). *Exhib*: RA, NEAC, RI, numerous one-man and group exhbns. *Works in collections*: Government Art Collection, Legal and General Assurance, William Garfield Ltd., Crosby Doors. *Commissions*: several mural and large scale works. *Works Reproduced*: writer for art magazine. *Clubs*: Elected member of Royal Institute of Painters in Watercolour (R.I.) *Address*: Nutcombe Farm, Nutcombe Hill, Combe Martin, North Devon, EX34 0PQ.

BERNSTEIN, Carol, NDD, BA (Open University), Post Grad Diploma Goldsmiths; painter and printmaker. *Medium*: oil, watercolour, prints, mixed media work on paper, and photography. *b*: Surrey. *m*: Sidney Bernstein (architect). one *s*. one *d*. *Studied*: Kingston School of Art and Design (now Kingston University); Goldsmiths College. *Exhib*: solo shows: Murray Edwards (New Hall) College Cambridge; Castle Theatre Wellingbrough; Modern Artists Gallery, Whitchurch; Butley Gallery, Butley; Boughton House Gallery, Cambridge; Clare Hall, Cambridge; Wolfson College, Oxford; over 35 group shows including RA Summer Exhbn; J Gallery. *Works in collections*: Murray Edwards (New Hall) College Cambridge; Clare Hall, Cambridge; Wolfson College, Oxford; Many private collections in UK, Europe and USA. *Commissions*: 2 large paintings, Sand Lane Hotel, Barbados. *Publications*: making and editing short films, writing a book on the artist Ernest F Edwards. *Address*: Barn Studios, 71a High Street, Titchmarsh, NN14 3DF. *Email*: carber@btconnect.com *Website*: www.carolbernstein.co.uk

BERRISFORD, Peter, NDD, ATD; painter (oils, water-colours), lecturer: Arts Council, National Trust, NADFAS, Swans (Hellenic). *b*: Northampton, 11 Feb 1932. *s of*: Ernest Berrisford. *m*: Jacqueline. one *s*. *Studied*: Northampton, Chelsea College of Art (Diploma), Bournemouth Art College (Travelling Scholarship 1953), Graduate Southampton University (1954). *Exhib*: Bear Lane, Wildensteins, Piccadilly, Trafford, Leicester, Hahn Galleries, London, RBA, RA, John Moore's, Melitensia Gallery, Malta. *Works in collections*: Hertfordshire, Hull, Surrey, Leicester, Sheffield, Northampton, Wales University, East Sussex CC. *Commissions*: Lithographs: New York Book of Month Club, Curwen Studios. Paintings for BBC's 'The Clothes in the Wardrobe' and 'The House of Eliott' (filmed 1992 and 1993). *Works Reproduced*: 'Young Artists of Promise' (Studio, 1957), 'Dictionary of Artists who Painted Malta' ('SAID' 1988). *Address*: 73 Woodgate Rd., Eastbourne BN22 8PD. *Signs work*: oils "Berrisford," water-colours "Peter Berrisford."

BERRY, June, DFA Lond. (1948), RE (1986), RWS (1993), NEAC (1990), RWA (1993); Vice President RWS 2001-2004; artist in etching, oil and water-colour. *b*: Melbourne, Derbyshire, 10 Aug 1924. *d of*: Edwin Reeve. *m*: John Berry. one *s*. two *d*. *Educ*: Boston Lincs. *Studied*: Slade School of Fine Art (1941-42, 1946-49). *Represented by*: Bankside Gallery, 48 Hopton St., London, SE1 9JH. *Exhib*: RA, RE, RWS, RWA, NEAC, and in Germany and USA. *Works in collections*: Victoria and Albert Museum, Ashmolean Museum Oxford, Royal West of England Academy, Graphotek, Berlin, National Museum of Wales, Kettering A.G., Oldham A.G., HM The Queen, The Government Art Collection, National Art Collection, Malta. *Publications*: Limited Edn. Livre d'Artiste 'Passing Days' (1984), 'Garden Painters' by Ariel Luke (A&C Black 2009); Watercolour Masters (Cassell 2006); The Watercolour Expert (Cassell 2004). *Recreations*: gardens. *Address*: 45 Chancery La., Beckenham, Kent BR3 6NR. *Email*: juneberry@talktalk.net *Website*: www.juneberrypaintings.eu *Signs work*: "June Berry."

BERRY, Peter Leslie, NDD Sculpture, PGDip (Slade School), MA (Art Ed.), M.Soc.Sci.(Cultural Studies). *Medium*: sculpture. *b*: Cheltenham, Glos, 11 Jul 1936. *s of*: E.L.Berry. one *s*. one *d*. *Educ*: Cheltenham Grammar School. *Studied*: Cheltenham College of Art, Slade School (1961-63), University of Birmingham. *Exhib*: Ikon Gallery Birmingham (solo and mixed since 1966); Art Council Gallery Cambridge; Goethe Institute, Glasgow; Modern British Artists Gallery, London (solo, 2007); LCBD Gallery, Leicester (solo 2009); City Gallery, Leicester 19th, 20th, 21st Open Exhibitions (2007-09); The Gallery, Atkins Building, Hinckley (solo, 2011). *Works in collections*: art works in private collections; 'The Meaning of Objects' (Research document), Geffrye Museum, London (2010). *Commissions*: Garden sculpture Malvern (2008). *Recreations*: music, sport, reading. *Misc*: Has studied and taught Yoga (Advanced Teaching Qualification); Lecturer in Art/Sculpture 1963-94. *Address*: 31 Stanton Road, Sapcote, Leics., LE9 4FR. *Email*: p.l.berry@btinternet.com *Website*: www.peterberry.org.uk *Signs work*: "P L BERRY."

BERRY-HART, David James, MA; painter, sculptor and writer; Awards: Arts Council (1975), West Midlands Arts Association (1978). *b*: Trinidad, 1940. *s of*: Ralph and Alice Berry-Hart. two *s.* two *d. Studied*: St. Martin's School of Art (1959-1961), City of Birmingham Polytechnic (1981-83). *Exhib*: one-man shows: AIA Gallery, London (1969), Herbert A.G. Coventry (1970), Camden Arts Centre (1975), University of Warwick (1977), Imperial College (1979), Royal National College for the Blind (1979), Cannon Hill Park (1979), Whitefriars Coventry (1988), mid-Warwickshire College Gallery (1990), Worcester City A.G. (1991), Quaker Gallery, London (1994), Nuneaton A.G. (1996), Brewhouse Gallery, Taunton, (1999); group: Spectrum Central (1971), Art in Steel (1972), Gawthorpe Festival (1974), On the Town sculpture (1987), Cultural Connections (1995), Nottingham Trent University; with "The Firm" exhib. Hampshire (Touring) (1983-4), Carlisle A.G. (1984), Liverpool University (1985), Williamson A.G. (1986), Beecroft A.G. (1987), Chelmsford A.G. (1987), Nuneaton A.G. (1998). *Works in collections*: RNCB Imperial College. *Publications*: Midlands Arts Magazine, Spectrum Central Catalogue. *Address*: 15 Old Forge Road, Fenny Drayton, Nuneaton, Worcs., CV13 6BD.

BERRYMAN, Derek James, NDD (1951), Society of Lithographic Designers (1952), ATD Durham (1955), B.Ed (Hons) (1977), FRSA (1960); Head of Art Dept., Prince Henry's Grammar School, Otley, Yorkshire (1957-1961), lecturer (retd.); Sir John Cass College, Leeds College of Art, Buckinghamshire CHE, Weston-super-Mare School of Art; Graphic Designer, Carlton Studio; Hydrographic Draughtsman., Admiralty, London. *b*: Chingford, Essex, 1926. *s of*: James Berryman, B.A. Manchester. *m*: Irene Metzger, daughter of Peter, architect, Tübingen University, Germany. one *s.* one *d. Educ*: Normanhurst School, Chingford, St Aubyn's School, Woodford, S.W. Essex Technical College. *Studied*: St. Martin's, London; Sir John Cass College; Durham University; Bristol University; Scholarship to Syracuse University, USA. *Exhib*: RA, RBA, ROI, RWA, Scotland, Germany, USA, and provincial galleries in England. *Works in collections*: various USA, Germany and Britain. *Misc*: War service: 1944-48 Air Crew R.A.F.V.R., transferred into Army; Gordon Highlanders, later in Indian Army. *Address*: The Mill House, Wester Tillyrie, by Milnathort, Kinross-shire KY13 0RW. *Signs work*: "Berryman" or initial "B" with date.

BEST, Irene, artist in acrylic. *b*: Sunderland, 3 Jun 1937. *m*: Kenneth. one *s.* one *d. Educ*: New College, Durham. *Exhib*: Witham Hall Gallery, Barnard Castle; Westminster Gallery, London; Darlington A.G.; Durham A.G.; Bede Gallery, Jarrow; RBSA Gallery, Birmingham. *Clubs*: N.A.P.A., Soc. of Amateur Artists. *Address*: 10 Wilbore Croft, Aycliffe, Co. Durham DL5 6TF.

BEST, Ronald O'Neal, RCA, DipFA, Post Dip.; teaches litho at Heatherley School of Fine Art, London; painter and printmaker. *Medium*: oil, etcher, watercolour. *b*: London, 25 May 1957. *Educ*: Sladebrook High School, London. *Studied*: Byam Shaw School of Art; Croydon College of Art; RCA London; Asst. to Winston Branch, painter. *Exhib*: ROI, NEAC, PS, SGA, Salon des National, Paris, Lynn Stern Young Artists, London, Eva Jekel Gallery, Twentieth Century British Art Fair, RCA London, 1492-1992 Un Nouveau Regard sur les Caraibes, Paris, Art House, Amsterdam, President Portobello Group, Pall Mall Deposit Gallery, the Portobello Group, W11 Gallery, Gallery Cafe, Portobello Printmakers. Coordinator, Visual Arts Portobello Festival. Founded the Chelsea Painters and Printmakers (1999), manager, Notting Hill Fine Art Gallery, co-ordinator, Art for the Unemployed, Portobello Academy of Drawing. *Works in collections*: RCA, Croydon College, Grange Museum, London. *Commissions*: London Art Forms. *Clubs*: Portobello Group, Chelsea Printmakers, Portobello Printmakers. *Address*: 19D St. Julian's Rd., London NW6 7LA. *Signs work*: "Ronald Best."

BETOWSKI, Noel Jan, BA Hons Fine Art Painting (1976), ATC London University (1977); John Constable Landscape Competition prize winner 1987 3rd, 1988 2nd. *Medium*: oil and mixed media on canvas. *b*: Essex, 11 Dec 1952. *m*: Pamela Jane Niblett. one *s. Educ*:

St. Mary's RC School, Tilbury, Essex. *Studied*: Thurrock Technical College, Essex (1970-1972), Central School of Art and Design, London (1973-1976), London University, Inst. of Education (1976-1977). *Exhib*: widely, including: NPG, RA New Grafton Gallery, London; Royal Festival Hall; Mercury Gallery, London; Worcester City Art Gallery; Crane Kalman Gallery, London; Camden Arts Centre, Walker Galleries; Highgate Fine Art; Penwith Gallery. *Works in collections*: numerous collections worldwide. *Commissions*: Kinlet Hall School, Bewdley, Worcs., Peters and May Shipping Company, Southampton. *Publications*: include: Noel Betowski (1998), St. Ives 1975-2995: Art Colony in Transition - Peter Davies; Noel Betowski - Illumination (2005); Behind the Canvas S. Britain (2001). *Clubs*: Penwith Society. *Address*: Tregonebris House, Sancreed, Penzance, Cornwall TR20 8RQ. *Email*: pam@betowski.fsnet.co.uk *Website*: www.noelbetowski.com *Signs work*: "Noel Betowski."

BETTNEY, Julian, BTEC, HND. *Medium*: glass, mosaic, collage, oil, drawing, print, sculpture, picture frames. *b*: UK, 2 April 1966. *Studied*: Berkshire College Art and Design. *Represented by*: The Studio Gallery. *Exhib*: One man shows: Hyde Park Gallery (1991), Brading Roman Villa (2003), Conningsby Gallery (2005), Radley College tvada fair (2006), Richard Allan Gallery, Chelsea, Llewellyn Alexander Gallery, Royal College of Art, Mall Galleries, Chelsea Art Society, Esher Fine Art (2010), Globe Gallery. *Works in collections*: private and international private collections. *Commissions*: celebrity commissions UK and international. *Publications*: Real Art Magazine Ltd Editions; Arte TV; Meridien TV news; Gulf State radio; British Airways magazine. *Works Reproduced*: Madeira stones; Hawaii beaches and stones, Waterlillies, Windsor Castle. *Principal Works*: Madeira stones series (Oils) - beach landscapes and stone studies; Waterlillies (Oil) - Abbotsbury Sub Tropical Gardens; Concorde (glass); NYC and London Olympics (glass); Eyes of the Storm (Sculpture); Lovers (sculpture); the kiss (oils), Hawaii stones series (oils) - beach landscapes and stone/coral studies. Windsor Castle series including frogmore series (oils), noctolescent clouds (oils), Figures of the earth series (oils, chalks, charcoal, collage, clay), underwater lovers (mosaic, glass, timber, oil glass, mirror), a tudor forest scene (mosaic, glass, timber, oil glass, mirror), amber falls (mosaic, glass, timber, oil glass, mirror). Misc: looking for representation. *Address*: The Studio Gallery, The Old Bank, The Green, Datchet, Berkshire, SL3 9JH. *Email*: sales@julianbettney.me.uk *Website*: www.julianbettney.me.uk facebook julianbettneyfineart *Signs work*: "julian bettney".

BEVAN, Oliver, ARCA (1964). *Medium*: principally oil, also pastel, lithography. *b*: Peterborough, 28 Mar 1941. *s of*: David Bevan, painter, photographer, garden designer. *m*: Patricia Thornton (artist) (1946-2009). *Partner*: Annick Le Mee. two *s*. three *d*. *Educ*: Eton. *Studied*: RCA (Carel Weight, Colin Hayes, Leonard Rosoman). *Represented by*: Galerie de l'Ancien Courrier, Montpellier, France. *Exhib*: Angela Flowers (1981), Odette Gilbert (1984), Gallery 10 (1991), "City/Two Views", Barbican (1986); exhib. in and curated "The Subjective City" touring exhbn. (1990-91), "Witnesses and Dreamers" touring (1993-94), "The Motor Show" touring (1996-97); solo "Urban Mirror" National Theatre (1997), Hunting Art Prizes, RCA (2000, 2001), Galerie de l'Ancien Courrier, Montpellier, France (2005-2013), Galerie Ducastel Avignon (2008), Galerie Clavreul, Paris (2011), Retrospective Uzes France (2012). *Works in collections*: Contemporary Art Soc., Museum of London, Middlesbrough Art Gallery, Unilever, Sainsbury, Guildhall A.G. *Commissions*: four ptgs for BAA Gatwick (1990), Art on the Underground (1993). *Publications*: "London in Paint" Mus. of London, Modern Paintings in the Guildhall Art Gallery. *Principal Works*: 'Westway Triptych' (Museum of London); 'Walk' Guildhall Art Gallery. *Address*: 9 Rue Grande Bourgade, 30700 Uzès, France. *Email*: oliverb@oliverbevan.com *Website*: www.oliverbevan.com *Signs work*: canvases signed on back "Oliver Bevan" - elongated vertical in "B"; works on paper "OB '87", etc.

BEVAN, Tony, DipAD (1974), HDFA (1976); painter in acrylic and oil. *b*: Bradford, 1951. *Partner*: Glenys Johnson. one *d*. *Studied*: Bradford College of Art (1968-71),

Goldsmiths' College (1971-74), Slade School of Fine Art (1974-76). *Exhib*: ICA London touring Britain (1980-87), Haus der Kunst Munich (1989), Kunsthalle Kiel (1988), Whitechapel A.G. (1993). *Works in collections*: Staats Galerie Moderner Kunst Munich, Kunsthalle Kiel, Metropolitan Museum of Art NY, Yale University, BM, Theo Wormland Foundation Munich, British Council, Arts Council, MOMA (NY), Toledo Museum, Ohio, Wolverhampton A.G. *Address*: Studio 2, Acme Studios, 165 Childers St., London SE8 5JR. *Signs work*: "Bevan."

BEVERIDGE, Philippa Jane, MFA Art in Architecture, BA (Hons) Landscape Architecture. Artist in Residence: Musee-Atelier du Verre, Sars Poteries, France; Catalan Government Grant; Jutta Curry-Franz Memorial New Talent Award, Dusseldorf, Germany. *Medium*: Sculpture in glass and mixed media. *b*: Holbury, 17 Nov 1962. *Partner*: Mark Waudby. *Studied*: Greenwich University, London (1981-84); Massana School of Art, Barcelona (1988-92); University of East London (2005-07). *Exhib*: Solo shows: Tassen Museum, Amsterdam (2013); Musee du Verre, Sars Poteries, France (2010); Museo de Arte en Vidreo, Madrid (2009); FAD Gallery, Barcelona (2008); Artonivo Gallery, Bruges (2004); Barcelona Archaeological Museum (2001); British Council, Barcelona (1995). Selected Group shows: Blackwell House, UK (2013); CAEE Arts Centre, Andorra (2013); The Gallery in Redchurch Street, London (2012); William Morris Gallery, London (2010); CAA, London (2010); Pyramid Gallery, UK (2009); curator and exhibitor, North House Gallery, UK (2007); Mediterranean Biennale finalists' show, Maritime Museum, Barcelona. *Works in collections*: Kunstsammlungen Der Veste Coburg. European Museum For Contemporary Glass. Coburg, Germany; Musée-Atelier du Verre, Sars-Poteries, France; Museo de Arte en Vidrio de Alcorcón (MAVA), Spain; Private collections in Europe, Japan and the United States. *Commissions*: Forty glass panels for the Can Xarina Restaurant in Catalonia; Two glass walls for a private residence/office on Paseo de Gracia, Barcelona; Commission to design and produce prototypes in glass for Avantcraft Lugo, Spain; Fused glass panels for dividing screen in private residence, Costa Brava, Spain; Glass curtains for a Paris-based exhibition by the Enric Miralles Practice; Privately in Japan, Spain and the UK. *Publications*: Authored work: Warm Glass (2003, pub. Lark Books), Mosaic (2004, pub. Barron Books). Selected publications include: New Glass Review 29 & 22; Glass Art from the Kiln by Rene Culler (Schiffer Pub Ltd.); Céramique et Verre, no. 171; Verre & Création, no. 58; Terminal B, Barcelona Creative Database, featured artist (2007); print and Glass by Kevin Petrie (A&C Black). *Official Purchasers*: European Museum For Contemporary Glass. Coburg, Germany; Musee-Atelier du Verre, Sars-Poteris, France. *Principal Works*: Feather Crown Series; Lost and Found; The Human Presence in the absence of a figure 1-VII; Human Shields; Custodian of Memory; 'Longing for the land of your memories...'. *Recreations*: film, reading, walking, music. *Clubs*: Contemporary Glass Society. *Address*: 42 Knox Court, Studley Road, London SW4 6SA. *Email*: philippabeveridge@ya.com *Website*: www.philippabeveridge.com *Signs work*: "PJB" or "PJ Beveridge".

BEVIS, Michael John Vaughan, Cert Ed., AIE, ARPS, FRSA, F.CollP., DFA (Painting); educational art consultant; artist in oil, photographer. *b*: London, 11 Oct 1948. *s of*: Albert John Bevis, actor stage manager. *m*: Marie Janice Gair. two *d*. *Educ*: Clarks College (1960-65). *Studied*: Hornsey College of Art (Foundation, 1966-67), Walthamforest Technical College and School of Art (1967-70), Barking NELP (1970-72), London University Inst. of Educ. (Associateship, 1980-81). *Represented by*: Work on file at: Art Search Ltd., Project Art Ltd., Contemporary Arts Project Ltd., The Antiques and Fine Art Location Agency. *Exhib*: one-man: Loggia Gallery, London (1980); group: Mall Gallery, London. *Works in collections*: gallery and private collections. *Publications*: associateship report 'Some Art activities in Prison'. *Misc*: Director of Artserve Limited, Gallery, Lockram Villas, 7 Collingwood Rd., Witham, Essex CM8 2DY; Director: Schoolserve Ltd. *Address*: 2

Bergen Ct., Maldon, Essex CM9 6UH. *Email*: m.jv.bevis@talk21.com *Website*: www.artservegallery.com www.artinthevillage.info *Signs work*: "M.J.V. BEVIS."

BEWICK, Pauline, RHA, Áosdana; awards: UN Poster (1981), Irish Life Arts (1990); artist in water-colour, tapestry, sculpture, etching, ceramic, etc.; a member of Internat. Womans Forum (Ireland) etc. *b*: Northumberland, 1935. *d of*: Collateral descendant of Thomas Bewick. *m*: Dr. Patrick Melia, psychiatrist. two *d*. *Educ*: progressive schools. *Studied*: NCAD, Dublin. *Exhib*: Taylor Gallery Dublin, Catto Gallery London, Odette Gilbert Gallery London, Guinness Hop Store, Irish Museums, etc. *Works in collections*: in many public and private collections worldwide, including '7 Ages' Permanent Collection Works from 2-70, Waterford, Kerry Council. *Commissions*: latest: 'A Visual Translation - Midnight Court' (2007, The Merriman Co.), Doris Lessing. *Publications*: subject of Painting a Life by James White, former Director of the National Gallery of Ireland, (1985); author and illustrator, Ireland: An Artist's Year (Methuen, 1990); A Boy and a Dolphin (Granada, 1983); illustrated, Irish Tales and Sagas (1994); author and illustrator: The South Seas and a Box of Paints (Art Books Int. London, 1996); The Yellow Man (1996); Seven Ages (Arlen House Galway). *Works Reproduced*: in a number of publications including 'Ireland, an Artists Year' Methuen, 'The South Seas and a Box of Paints' Art Books International, 'Kelly Read's Bewick' Arlen House, 'Seven Ages' works from the life of P.Bewick (Arlen House, 2005). *Clubs*: Chelsea Arts, London; United Arts, Dublin. *Misc*: Documentary: A Painted Diary by David Shaw-Smith, R.T.E., Channel 4, Pompidou Centre Paris, Los Angeles and Chicago film festivals (1994). Two years spent painting and writing in Polynesia, resulting in a book (see above). *Address*: Treanmanagh, Glenbeigh, Co. Kerry, Ireland. *Email*: paulinebewick@eircom.net *Website*: www.paulinebewick.ie

BIALOKOZ SMITH, Malgorzata, Four Counties Open Painting Competition, Second Prize (1988). *Medium*: acrylic, mixed own techniques in 2 & 3D. *b*: Warsaw, 10 Sep 1937. *d of*: Prof. D J Tilgner. one *s*. one *d*. *Studied*: Technical College of Art, Academy of Art, Gdansk, Poland (1951-57); St. Martins School of Art (1957); Trent Polytechnic, Nottingham (1973, FETC). *Exhib*: selected group exhibitions since 1982 include: Museum of Modern Art, Oxford (1983, 1992); Bankside Gallery (1988); touring exhibition Spain/Portugal (1993); Stadt Norderstedt, Germany (1998); RA Summer Exhibition (2000); Said Business School, Oxford (Retrospective, 2005); Reszel Castle Gallery, Poland (2007); Oak Crest Gallery, Victoria, Canada (2008), North Wall Arts Centre, Oxford (2010). *Works in collections*: Poland: Museum of Contemporary Art in Radom; Oxford: Asmolean Museum, St. Cross College, St. James Hospital, Isle of Wight. Private collections in England, Poland, Austria, Israel, USA, Pakistan, Australia, Japan, Canada, Germany, New Zealand. *Recreations*: Photography, gardening. *Address*: Studio 54, 54 Pendennis Road, London SW16 2SP. *Email*: m.bialokozsmith@hotmail.co.uk *Website*: www.bialokozart.org.uk

BICKNELL, John, BA (Hons) (1980), HDipFA (Lond) (1983), Slade prize (1983), Boise Scholarship (1983), Greater London Arts award (1986), John Moores prize (1987), Henry Moore Fellow, Leeds Polytechnic (1989-90); painter. *b*: Surrey, 1958. *s of*: Peter Bicknell. *m*: Christina Dorees. two *d*. *Educ*: Ottershaw School. *Studied*: WSCAD (1975-77), NE London Polytechnic (1977-80), Slade School of Fine Art (1981-83). *Exhib*: numerous group shows, including John Moores, Whitechapel, Christie's, New Contemporaries, RCA, Miro Foundation, Barcelona, Monjuic, Girona, Cleveland International Drawing Biennale, Metathesis Touring Greece, Slow Burn Touring UK; one-man shows: Pomeroy Purdy Gallery, London. *Works in collections*: Nat. West, Reed International, Texaco. *Address*: School of Art, Architecture and Design, Leeds Metropolitan University, Calverley St., Leeds LS1 3HE. *Signs work*:"John Bicknell."

BICKNELL, Les, BA (Hons); book artist, printmaking/sculpture; visiting lecturer, Camberwell College of Art. *b*: Coventry, 4 Mar 1963. *s of*: Tony and Pauline Bicknell.

m: Jayne Knight. two *s*. *Educ*: Binley Park Comprehensive. *Studied*: London College of Printing (1982-85). *Exhib*: over 20 one-man shows since 1985 including Maison du LAC, Domart-en-Pontenthieu, V& A, Nigel Greenwoods. *Works in collections*: Tate Gallery, V&A, Rijkmuseum, Bodleian Library, MOMA, NY Public Library. *Commissions*: Many bookworks, including Eastern Arts Board and Birmingham Libraries. *Publications*: edited: Mapping Knowledge, The Book as Art, Beyond Reading. *Address*: Eva's Place, Sibton Green, Saxmundham, Suffolk IP17 2JX.

BIDDULPH, Elizabeth Mary, ROI (1952), Hon. senior mem. ROI (1982), NDD (1947), Hon.Cert.RDS (1942); painter chiefly in oils, portraits, landscapes, still-life, flowers; judging panel, John Laing Painting Competition (1988); voluntary art teaching to small class of mentally ill patients from 2000, selling work privately. *b*: Port Elizabeth, S.A., 17 Jun 1927. *d of*: A D S Dunn, Comdr. RN. *m*: deceased. one *s*. *Educ*: Hamilton House School, Tunbridge Wells. *Studied*: Wimbledon School of Art (1944-47) under Gerald Cooper, ARCA, Slade School of Fine Art (1949-51). *Exhib*: yearly at ROI; one-man shows, Hornsey Library (1971), Barclays Bank, Egham (1977), Egham Library (1985), murals in shop, Virginia Water (1984). *Commissions*: portraits; repainted and designed ceiling panels for writer Ralph Dutton's home 1961-62 (original ones destroyed by fire). *Publications*: articles for Leisure Painter Magazine (1980-81, 1987). *Recreations*: playing the piano, gardening. *Address*: 74 Clarence St., Egham, Surrey TW20 9QY. *Signs work*: "E. Biddulph."

BIDDULPH, Jacki, BA Fine Art; Print Prize, Arts Club, Dover St. (2007). *Medium*: prints. *b*: London, 19 Jun 1946. *d of*: Norman Hare. *m*: Mike Biddulph. two *s*. *Studied*: St. Martins School of Art; Ravensbourne College of Art. *Exhib*: Royal Academy Summer Show (regularly from 1970s-2007), The New Contemporaries, London Group, Mall Galleries 'Originals', Roman Black Gallery, London; Zella Nine, London; Print Room, Hampstead, Patterson, London; Cubertou Group Show, France; Konstraugarton Group, Sweden. *Works in collections*: Chase Manhattan Bank NY, Lloyds Bank London, Pictures for Hospitals, Peru, Toronto, Sweden, New Zealand. *Misc*: Printmaking instructor - Royal Academy Schools 1968-2000 *Address*:51a Belsize Avenue, London NW3 4BN. *Email*: jackibiddulph@hotmail.com

BIGMORE, Christine. *Medium*: oil, watercolour - specialises in Still Life. *b*: Surrey, 10 Mar 1960. two *s*. *Studied*: Croydon College of Art and Design (1976-78); further studies, (1993-98) Sutton College of Liberal Arts, Mall Galleries, City Literary Guild, Royal College of Art. *Represented by*: Frost & Reed, St. James, London. *Exhib*: Art London 2006. *Works in collections*: private collections in the UK and overseas. *Commissions*: commercial and private. *Publications*: Surrey Occasions Magazine, Country Life Magazine, Artists and Illustrators magazine. *Works Reproduced*: Tiger, A Portrait - limited edition print. *Address*: 18 Bramley Road, Sutton, Surrey, SM1 4NN. *Email*: chris.christine@hotmail.co.uk *Website*: www.christine-bigmore.co.uk *Signs work*: "C BIGMORE."

BILL, Joan Ada, NDD, ATD, UA; painter in all media. *b*: Redcar, 14 Jun 1933. *m*: Frank Bill. one *s*. one *d*. *Educ*: Saltburn High School. *Studied*: Middlesborough Art College; Sheffield Art College, Sir John Cass. *Exhib*: UA, RI, Artists in Essex, Bankside Gallery. *Works in collections*: private collections UK and abroad. *Commissions*: portraits in pastel and oils, landscapes. *Publications*: pen and ink illus. - Farmhouses in an English Landscape by Sir William Addison; Essex Countryside Books. *Address*: 11 Egg Hall, Epping, Essex CM16 6SA. *Signs work*: "JABILL.": "JOAN BILL."

BINGHAM, Janice Elizabeth, ARMS, HS, SLm. Awards: President's Special Commendation Award, RMS (2000); Fred Skipper Award for Best Wildlife Painting, Society of Limners (2009). *Medium*: oil, gouache, watercolour. *b*: Co. Durham, 11 Jan 1948. two *s*. *Studied*: Cleveland College of Art. *Represented by*: RMS, HS, SLm. *Exhib*: Royal

Miniature Society, Hilliard Society, Society of Limners, World Federation of Miniaturists (in Washington DC, and Burnie, Tasmania); Miniature Art Society of Florida, International Art Exhibition, Clearwater, Florida. *Works in collections*: H.H. Shaikh Zayed Bin Sultan Al-Nahyan, United Arab Emirates; The Arab Horse Society, Marlborough, Wiltshire; Colonel E.B. Wilson, Director of the Royal Stud in Abu Dhabi. *Commissions*: H.H. Shaikh Zayed Bin Sultan Al-Nahyan through Colonel E.B. Wilson; The Arab Horse Society, Colonel E.B. Wilson; Colonel B. Lees and his wife; Cleveland Point to Point Committee. *Works Reproduced*: Limited Edition "A Tribute to Shergar" signed by Walter Swinburn. *Principal Works*: Portrait of H.H. Shaikh Zayed Bin Sultan Al-Nahyan upon His Supreme Champion "Vain Huzzar" with a falcon. *Recreations*: walking, gardening, reading and travel. *Clubs*: Leven Art Society. *Address*: "April Rise", 104 Roseberry Crescent, Great Ayton, North Yorkshire, TS9 6EW. *Email*: janice@media-drive.co.uk *Signs work*: "Janice E Bingham".

BINNS, David, NDD (1956), SWLA (1968); RSPB Fine Art Award (1990, 1992, 1993, 1994); awarded Doctor of Letters, Bradford University (2000); freelance artist in water-colour, lino, scraperboard; teacher SP courses. *b*: Sutton-in-Craven, 30 Sep 1935. *s of*: Dan Binns, teacher and artist. *m*: Molly. one *s*. two *d*. *Educ*: Ermysted's Grammar School, Skipton. *Studied*: Skipton Art School (Dan Binns, J. C. Midgley), Leeds College of Art (Pulée). *Represented by*: self. *Exhib*: SWLA, RI, HC Dickens, Bloxham, Oxfordshire, Manor House, Ilkley, Aquarious Gallery, Harrogate, Leigh Yawkey Woodson Museum, Wisconsin, U.S.A., Northern Exh'n wildlife art (Liverpool), NEWA (ABR). *Works in collections*: New Zealand, Australia, USA, Canada, France, UK. *Commissions*: Northumberland NP, RSPB, Country Artists, private commissions. *Publications*: Passion for Puffins, Yorkshire Birds, Birds of the Lake District, author W.R.Mitchell MBE. *Works Reproduced*: Dalesman, childrens animal books, circular jigsaws, print by Soloman & Whitehead, Medici cards, RSPB calendar and cards, Yorkshire Journal, plate and beaker designs for Country Artists Ltd. *Recreations*: bird watching *Clubs*: S.WL.A. *Address*: Holmestead, 9 Boundary Ave., Sutton-in-Craven, Keighley, Yorks. BD20 8BL. *Email*: david@davidbinns.wanadoo.co.uk *Website*: www.swla.co.uk *Signs work*: "David Binns."

BIRCH, David William, painter/printmaker, water-colour and wood engraving; landscape and architectural subjects; St Cuthbert's Mill 1st Prize 21st Century Watercolour Competition, RWS Bankside Gallery. *b*: 28 Jan 1945. *s of*: May and Eric Birch, engineer/designer. *m*: Annabel Carey (artist and art tutor). one *s*. *Educ*: Wellesbourne School, Birmingham. *Studied*: mentors: water-colour - Kay Kinsman, wood engraving - William T. Rawlinson. *Represented by*: The Gallery at the Guild, Chipping Campden. *Exhib*: RA, RI, RWS, RE, SWE, RWA; solo exhibitions: Michael Tippitt, Bath; Gloucester City Art Gallery; Goldsmiths College, London; John Noott Gallery, Broadway, Ombersley Gallery, Worcester, Confederation Life, Bristol; Warwick Museum and Art Gallery; regular in towns and villages of the West of England; Broadway Art Festival Biannual, RWS/Sunday Times Watercolour Competition. *Works in collections*: University of Bristol, Confederation Life Insurance Co., Gloucester City Art Gallery. *Clubs*: Fosseway Artists, Blockley Art Society. *Address*: Croftsbrook, Blind La., Chipping Campden, Glos. GL55 6ED. *Email*: davidwbirch@croftsbrook.co.uk *Website*: www.davidwbirch.co.uk *Signs work*: "David W. Birch."

BIRCHALL, Christine Winifred, VPSWA, SFP. *Medium*: oil, pastel. *b*: Leics., 13 May 1950. *d of*: Mr&Mrs D J Birchall. *m*: Robert King. two *s*. *Studied*: taught to paint by my husband, Robert King RI, RSMA. *Represented by*: Kendalls Fine Art, Isle of Wight. *Exhib*: Alexander Gallery, Bristol; Obliqué Gallery, Honfleur, France; The House of Bruar, Scotland; The Wykeham Gallery, Stockbridge, Hants; Beaulieu Fine Arts, Beaulieu, Hants; Coastal Gallery, Lymington, Hants; Minster Gallery, Winchester. *Works Reproduced*: 'Roses by the Sea' - Artgroup for Laura Ashley – worldwide. *Recreations*: sport and keep-fit, walking. *Clubs*: Vice-President SWA; Past Vice-President SWA. *Address*: 2 Coastguard

Cottages, Lepe, Southampton SO45 1AD. *Email*: chrissiebirchall@hotmail.co.uk *Website*: www.chrissiebirchall.com *Signs work*: 'C.W.Birchall'.

BIRKBECK, Paul. *Medium*: acrylic, oil, watercolour, drawing. *b*: London, 2 Mar 1939. *m*: Sally. three *d*. *Studied*: Epsom and Ewell School of Art and Design (1956-59). *Represented by*: Keith Chapman. *Exhib*: Royal Academy (78, 86, 87, 91, 97), Imperial War Museum (86), Royal Soceity of Painters in Watercolour, Bankside Gallery (87, 88). One-man shows: Chapman Gallery, London (1988), Gallery 27, London (1997). Mixed Shows: South Bank Show, London (1989), Mall Gallery, London (1992), Portal Gallery, London (1997, 98), British Art Fair, London (2000, 2001, 02, 03, 05, 08, 10). *Works in collections*: Newport Museum and Art Gallery, Newport, Wales *Commissions*: Vivienne Rush:- Mural and two paintings. *Misc*: Lectured at: Leicester College of Art, Epsom College of Art, Royal College of Art. *Address*: 81 Pepys Road, London SW20 8NW. *Email*: sallybirkbeck@hotmail.com *Signs work*: "Paul Birkbeck."

BIRNBAUM, Aimee, RI; Elected Member Royal Institute of Painters in Watercolours (2007); Prizes: The Worshipful Company of Painter-Stainers Prize (2007); The June Stokes-Roberts Bursary in Painting in Watercolours (2007); National Print Exhibition Kew Studio Prize (2001); Royal Watercolour Society St. Cuthbert's Mill Award C21 Exhibition (2000); Ben Uri Gallery Printmaking Prize (1995). *Medium*: watercolour, prints; painter and etcher. *b*: New York City, 10 May 1952. *m*: Michael Birnbaum QC. *Studied*: Museum School of Fine Arts, Boston Tufts University (1972-76), Sir John Cass School of Art (1985-86). *Represented by*: Gallery Z, Groznjan, Croatia; Sheridan Russell Gallery, London; Art for Art's Sake, London. *Exhib*: selected: Brunel Museum, London (2012, solo), Gallery Z, Groznjan, Croatia (2011, solo), Art in Action, Waterperry, Oxford (2012), Affordable Art Fair Hampstead Heath (2011), Sheridan Russell Gallery, London (2007, solo), annually since 2007 at Mall Galleries with the RI as member. *Work in collections*: Tony Baldry MP, Kenneth Brannagh actor. *Recreations*: ballet, iyengar yoga. *Clubs*: memberships: Southbank Printmakers, Greenwich Printmakers. *Misc*: Co-founder of Mirabilis Art with Nina Zelenko. *Address*: 12 St Mark's Crescent, London NW1 7TS. *Email*: aimeebirnbaum@talktalk.net *Website*: mirabilisart.com aimeebirnbaum.com *Signs work*: "Aimee Birnbaum".

BIRO, Val (B. S.), illustrator, painter, author. *Medium*: b/w line, watercolour, gouache. *b*: Budapest, Hungary, 6 Oct 1921. *d of*: Dr. B. Biro Balint. *m*. (1) Vivien Woolley. one *d*. (2) Marie-Louise Ellaway. *Educ*: Cistercian School, Budapest. *Studied*: Central School of Arts, London. *Represented by*: David Schutte, Petersfield GU31 4LB. *Exhib*: Budapest, London, Chichester, Bath, Ashmolean, Petworth House, Uppark House, Petersfield Museum. *Works in collections*: V&A Museum, British Museum and private. *Commissions*: from numerous British and foreign publishers. *Publications*: Author of 36 titles in the Gumdrop Series; Hungarian Folk Tales, Rub-a-Dub-Dub and some 40 other books for children; illustrated some 400 books, incl. My Oxford Picture Word Book, Hans Andersen, Aesop's Fables, The Father Brown Stories, The Joking Wolf, American Start with English, Bible Stories for Children, Grimms Fairy Tales, Perrault's Tales of Mother Goose, The Arabian Nights etc. *Works Reproduced*: in all the above books, Radio Times, other periodicals. *Principal Works*: 'Gumdrop' series, Award Giftbook series. *Recreations*: vintage motoring. *Clubs*: Vintage Sports Car, Vintage Austin Register. *Misc*: Lecturer on Art and storytelling. *Address*: Bridge Cottage, Brook Ave., Bosham, W. Sussex PO18 8LQ. *Email*: v.biro@btinternet.com *Website*: www.valbiro.co.uk *Signs work*: "Biro" or "Val Biro."

BISHOP, Peter Anthony, DFA (Lond), ATC, MA, PhD. *Medium*: painter in acrylic and mixed media, printmaker, lecturer in Fine Art/History of Art. *b*: Pembroke, 21 May 1953. *Educ*: Society of Friends School, Sibford; Banbury School of Art (1971-72). *Studied*: Slade School (1972-75), Birmingham Institute of Art and Design (1992-95), Slade School (1996-98), School of Art Aberystwyth (1998-2001). *Exhib*: various group and solo exhbns including Amwell Gallery, London; RA; Laing Landscape; MoMA (Wales); Royal Cambrian Academy; National Library of Wales. *Works in collections*: numerous public and private. *Publications*: "Vision and Revision: Mountain Scenery in Snowdonia 1750-1880" (University of Wales, Aberystwyth 2001); Peter Bishop: Cader Idris (Peter Bishop 2012). *Works Reproduced*: Arts Review, Miller's Picture Price Guide (1994), Royal Academy Illustrated (1998), 'Art for Amnesty' (2001). *Principal Works*: mountain landscape of North Wales with reference to its visual history. *Address*: Old Furnace, Knowbury, Ludlow SY8 3JH. *Email*: peterbishop215@brinternet.com *Website*: peterbishoppaintings.com

BISHOP, William Henry, self taught artist in water-colour and oil of seascapes and landscapes. *b*: Liss, Hants., 21 Jun 1942. *s of*: Henry Bernard Bishop. *m*: Helen Dunkerley. three *s*. *Educ*: King's School, Canterbury. *Represented by*: in America: Quester Gallery, Stonington, Connecticut 06378, and Quester Gallery, 119 Rowayton Ave., Rowayton, CT 06853. *Exhib*: RSMA, Armed Forces, Southampton Maritime Year; one-man show: Royal Exchange Gallery, London (1989). *Works in collections*: USA, Australia, New Zealand, Oman, Singapore, Hong Kong, Falkland Islands, UK, Gibraltar, Germany, South Africa, Minnesota Marine Art Museum. *Commissions*: R.N. Museum, Portsmouth, and Mary Rose Museum, Portsmouth; HMS. Warrior Museum, The Mathew Project, City of Bristol. *Publications*: Dictionary of Sea Painters (E.H.H. Archibald). *Principal Works*: On display in the Minnesota Marine Art Museum, USA, 40"x72" Battle of Trafalgar (oil on canvas). *Address*: West Mill, Mill Lane, Langstone, Havant, Hants. PO9 1RX. *Email*: bill@bishopmarineart.com *Website*: www.bishopmarineart.com *Signs work*: "W. H. Bishop" and "William H. Bishop" in new millenium.

BISSELL, Lauren Hayes, AS, AFC; awards: Mary Scott-Kestin Cup (2004); Wildscape Artist of the Year (2002). *Medium*: watercolour and acrylic, wildlife art and fantasy subjects. *b*: Birmingham. *d of*: Ron Dorman. *m*: Lorne Bissell. one *s*. *Exhib*: Mall Galleries, London; The Canterbury Pilgrim, Canterbury; RBSA; Marwell Zoological Park, Winchester; Wells Town Hall; The Gallery, Ottery St.Mary; Mayfield Gallery, Bournemouth. *Works in collections*: private collections: Canada, USA, Belgium, New Zealand, UK. *Works Reproduced*: for a list of open edition prints see www.lhbissell.com. *Principal Works*: 'Sea Song', 'Girl with the Flaxen Hair', 'The Canterbury Tales' Collection. *Clubs*: Signature Member of 'Art for Conservation'. *Address*: 987a Wimborne Road, Moordown, Bournemouth, Dorset BH9 2BS. *Email*: lhbissell@cwctv.net *Website*: www.lhbissell.com *Signs work*: 'L.B.', 'LHB', 'LAUREN HAYES BISSELL H.S., A.F.C.'

BIZON, Edna, SWA (1987); artist in oil. *b*: 13 Aug 1929. *m*: Ken Bizon. *Educ*: Honor Oak School. *Studied*: St.Martin's School of Art (1943-44), Camberwell School of Art (1944-46, Lawrence Gowing, John Minton, Claude Rogers). *Exhib*: RA from 1974 to 1994; one-man shows: Thorndike, Leatherhead (1970, 1977), Augustine, Holt (1973), Munich, W.Germany (1982), O'Nians King St. Galleries (1987), Look of Helmsley (1988), King St. Galleries (1990), Llewellyn Alexander (1991, 1993, 1995, 1997, 1999, 2001, 2003, 2005, 2007, 2009, 2011, 2013), Guild of Norwich Painters (1993-2013). *Works in collections*: Public Catalogue Foundation; Bowes Museum, County Durham. *Clubs*: Guild of Norwich Painters. *Address*: Drove End, West St., North Creake, Norfolk NR21 9LQ. *Signs work*: "Edna Bizon."

BLACK, Antonia Ninette Hudson, Fine Art Degree (Slade); RBSA (1996-2003); Birmingham Midland Inst. (1992); Singer & Friedlander/Sunday Times (2nd Prize-2003; 3rd Prize-2006), 3rd Prize (2001); Grand Prix Salon International de la Peinture (2003) A L'eau Trégastel, France; RBSA Prize (2003, 2006). *Medium*: watercolour, gouache. *b*: Perth, WA, 9 Jun 1938. *d of*: H & W Hudson Shaw. *m*: R A Jones. one *s*. one *d*. *Educ*: Sydney Church of England Girls Grammar School. *Studied*: National Art School, Sydney; Slade School of Fine Art, London. *Represented by*: Roman Black Gallery, London; Robin Gibson

Gallery, Sydney; Brian Sinfield, Burford. *Exhib*: RWS, RA Summer Exhbn, Art League Washington DC, USA; The Australian Embassy, Washington DC; Robin Gibson Gallery, Sydney; Singer & Friedlander, RBSA, Roman Black Gallery; Gallery 9, Birmingham; Affordable Art Fair, London; RI; Mall Galleries; RWA; Salon International Trégastel, France; London Art Fair, Business Design Centre, Islington; Art London, Royal Hospital Chelsea; Brian Sinfield Gallery, Burford. *Works in collections*: Sydney, New York, London; Singer & Friedlander. *Commissions*: mosaic murals chevron, Hilton Hotel, Sydney; Beckford Silk, Worcs (silk scarves), National Trust (silk scarf); mural after Douanier Rousseau, France. *Official Purchasers*: Singer & Friedlander Bank, 'Uluru' Ayers Rock, Central Australia. *Works Reproduced*: La Tour de l'Abbaye de Hambye, France. *Recreations*: travel, yoga. *Clubs*: Vintage Sports Car Club (own 1923 Peugeot); UCL Women's Dining Club. *Misc*: teaching:Kingston & Richmond Adult Colleges, Torpedo Factory, Virginia USA, 'Brushworks' at home in Gloucestershire; Jack Beck House, Yorkshire; Blockley Art Soc. Glos., North Cotswold Art Soc. *Address*: The Old Rectory, Alderton, Glos GL20 8NR. *Email*: bjab@carsart.co.uk *Signs work*: Antonia Black.

BLACK, John Frederick, MA (Manc.), NDD, DLCA (Hons), ATC (Dist.) FFPAA, FRSA; 2003 Prizewinner of three National Open Competitions. *Medium*: oil, watercolour, drawing, acrylic, gouache. *b*: Appleby Magna, Leics., 2 Jun 1943. *s of*: John Frederick & Doris Black. *m*: Diana. two *s*. one *d*. *Educ*: Loughborough College School. *Studied*: Loughborough College of Art (1959-63); Brighton College of Art (1963); Manchester Polytechnic. *Represented by*: Sportsframe Gallery, Wellingborough; The Dial House Gallery, Kimbolton. *Exhib*: 2004-12 solo exhibitions: London, Riseley, Bedford, Aldeburgh, Florida, Wellingborough, Kettering, Bath & Coggeshall. Group exhbns: Belfast, Winchester, Edinburgh, Northampton. Mall Galleries: RSMA, NEAC, Not the Turner Prize (Highly Commended). *Official Purchasers*: Bedfordshire County Council; Bedford Hospital; Wellingborough Town Council. *Clubs*: Founder of the Fellowship of Amateur & Professional Artists. *Misc*: 1965-68 Head of Art & Design, St. Edmunds School, Canterbury; 1968-1993 Senior Lecturer & Head of Department, Bedford College of F.E.; 1993-97 Head of Art Education, De Montfort University, Bedford; 1995-99 External Examiner for Art, B.Ed & MA, Queens University, Belfast & Anglia University Polytechnic. *Address*: "The Old Bakehouse", 82 Crabb Street, Rushden, Northants, NN10 0RH. *Website*: www.johnfblack.webeden.co.uk *Signs work*: "John Frederick Black."

BLACK, Simon, BA Hons Wolverhampton (1981); Public Art Freeform (1998); First Prize Art Royal Free Project Royal Free Hospital (2001), prizewinner South Bank Picture Show (1989). *Medium*: painter in oils, also works in mixed media. *b*: Salford, 17 Mar 1958. *s of*: Reuben and Phyllis Black. *m*: Raina Sheridan. two *d*. *Educ*: Manchester, Wolverhampton. *Studied*: Stand Grammar School, Bury; Manchester Polytechnic, Wolverhampton Polytechnic. *Represented by*: self and Ruth Corman (Thomas Corman Arts). *Exhib*: many solo and group shows including: Art London 2003, Pivotal Art Glasgow, Irish Art Fair (2002), Woolf Gallery, London (2001), Mercury Gallery, Portal Gallery, RA (1998), Barbican, Merseyside Maritime Museum, Quay Arts Isle of Wight, South Hill Park Arts Centre, Bracknell, Trinity Arts Centre, Tunbridge Wells, Midland Art Centre Birmingham. *Works in collections*: Royal Free Hospital London, Financial Services Authority London, Office for Public Management London, Harbour Vest Partners London, Ben Uri Collection, etc. *Commissions*: Royal Free Hospital (6 paintings), Financial Services Authority, Ascott Mayfair, and a number of private commissions. *Publications*: include 'Galleries Magazine' Oct 2003, Paint it Black (Jewish Chronicle, 1999), Angels and Mechanics Catalogue (1996); 'Artists in the Ben Uri Collection' (1994). *Misc*: Director of 'Designer and Artists Copyright Society' (DACS), trustee of RIVA (Residencies in Visual Arts). *Address*: 11 Wellington Avenue, London N15 6AS. *Email*: siblack@onetel.net.co.uk *Website*: www. thomascormanarts.com

BLACKBURN, David, artist in pastel on paper; awarded Hon D Litt by University of Huddersfield. *Medium*: Pastel. *b*: Huddersfield, 1939. *Studied:* Huddersfield School of Art (1955), Royal College of Art (1959-62, Kenneth Clark, patron and adviser). *Represented by*: Messum's Fine Art, 8 Cork Street, London W15 3LT. *Exhib*: solo shows include: Peter Bartlow Gallery, Chicago; Huddersfield A.G.; Kreis Unna, Germany; Charles Nodrum Gallery, Melbourne, Australia; Hart Gallery, London and Nottingham, Yale Centre for British Art, Dulwich Picture Gallery, Mussums Gallery (2014). *Works in collections*: MOMA (NY), British Council, Leeds City A.G., Queensland A.G.; Ashmolean Museum, Oxford; British Museum, London. *Publications*: 'David Blackburn and the Visionary Landscape Tradition' by Sasha Grishin, 'A Landscape Vision' by Malcolm Yorke (both Hart Gallery Publications). 'David Blackburn: The Sublime Landscape' Charlotte Mullins. *Misc*: Lives and works in Huddersfield. *Address*: c/o Messums, 8 Cork Street, London W15 3LT. *Signs work*: "David Blackburn."

BLACKLOCK, George, DipAD (1974), MFA (1976); painter in oil and wax on canvas; Senior lecturer in painting, Wimbledon School of Art. *b*: Durham, 11 Apr 1952. one *s*. *Studied*: Stourbridge College of Art (1971-74, Barrie Cook), Reading University (1974-76, Terry Frost). *Works in collections*: ACGB. *Address*: 11-31 Oarsmen Rd., London N1. *Signs work*: "George Blacklock."

BLACKMORE, Clive David, painter. *b*: Kingston-on-Thames, 1940. *Studied*: Twickenham and Kingston Schools of Art. *Exhib*: The New Millenium Gallery, St. Ives, Cornwall; Lymne Strover Gallery, Cambridge; regularly in the West Country and London. *Address*: Eastcliff Farm, Rinsey, Ashton, Helston, Cornwall TR13 9TS. *Signs work*: "Clive Blackmore."

BLACKWOOD, Simon Anthony James, DipAd (1970); artist in oil and pastel. *b*: Chelmsford, 17 May 1948. *s of*: H.J. Blackwood, policeman. *m*: Laura C.M. Blackwood. one *d*. *Educ*: Gilberd School, Colchester. *Studied*: Colchester School of Art, Coventry School of Art (Anthony Atkinson, Don Foster). *Exhib*: Art and Mysticism (1975) ICA London; one-man shows: Dundas Gallery 'Bus Stop' Series (1985), Netherbon Arts Centre 'Aquatic Light' Series (1986), Anthony Mould Ltd. London (1989), Michael Parkin Fine Art (1991, 1995), William Hardie Gallery Glasgow (1992), Brian Sinfield Gallery Burford (1992, 1994), Kusav, Istanbul (1994, 1995), Cynthia Bourne, London (1996); Art London (2004, 2005); Glasgow Art Fare (2005); Foss Fine Arts, London (2006); Art Amatoria, Edinburgh (2009); Scottish Borders Council - Scott Gallery (2009); SBC - Peebles Museum (2010). *Works in collections*: Flemings Collection, Nomura International, Sabanci Corporation, Mr & Mrs Ward (UK), Ms Horide Kasan (USA), Mr Sohei Kurita (Japan). *Commissions*: accepted. *Address*: The Studio, Wells Old Lodge, Bedrule, Nr. Hawick, Roxburgh. TD9 8TD. *Email*: simonblackwood@btconnect.com *Website*: www.simonblackwood.com *Signs work*: "S.A.J.B." or "S.B."

BLAKE, Adrienne, NDD, Regional Prize, National Open Art Competition. *Medium*: oil, drawing. *b*: Bristol, 11 Feb 1941. *m*: Brian Blake. two *s*. *Studied*: West of England College of Art (1956-61). *Exhib*: Royal Academy Summer Exhibition (2008-2009); National Open Art (2008, 09, 10); Royal West of England Academy Open (2005-2008); Sunday Times Watercolour Open (2007); Discerning Eye (2006); many others in UK and abroad. *Works in collections*: AXA PPP; Ernst and Young. *Publications*: Art Review; Womens Art; BBC South East, varoius newspapers. *Address*: 6 Eden Road, Tunbridge Wells, Kent, TN1 1TS. *Email*: adrienneblake@btinternet.com *Website*: www.adrienneblake.com *Signs work*: "Adrienne Blake."

BLAKE, Elisabeth, SFP (1997), SBA (2007); DipAD (Fine Art); SFP Presidents Award for Excellence (2007). *Medium*: watercolour. *b*: S.Devon, 3 May 1946. *Studied*: University of London, Goldsmiths College of Art. *Exhib*: Mottisfont Rose Garden, Romsey; Sir Harold Hillier Arboretum, Romsey; Ventnor Botanic Gardens; Jersey; Salisbury (with SFP); SBA Open Exhbns, Central Hall Westminster; Portsmouth City Museum; Southampton City Art Gallery, Stourhead, Chichester. *Recreations*: gardening, swimming. *Clubs*: RHS. *Address*: 3 Gardner Road, Titchfield, Fareham, Hants. PO14 4EF. *Email*: enb:blaki01.myzen.co.uk *Signs work*: 'ELISABETH BLAKE.'

BLAKE, Marie Dora, ASGFA (1994); NDD (1958), ATC (1959). *Medium*: oil, acrylic, watercolour, pastel, printmaking. *b*: London, 12 Mar 1938. *d of*: Eric Blake. *m*: Charles Calcutt Smith. two *s*. one *d*. *Educ*: Richmond and E.Sheen Grammar School. *Studied*: Kingston-on-Thames School of Art (1954-58), London University Inst. of Educ. (1959). *Exhib*: NEAC, ROI, RSMA, SWA, DFN Gallery New York., SGFA. *Publications*: author - "You Can Paint Pastels" Harper Collins U.K., (2000); Watson Guptil, NY (2000); Editions Fleuris, Paris (2001); Artist & Illustrator Magazine (1996); regular contributor Leisure Painter Magazine (1998-2004). *Clubs*: S.W.A. '87-'97. *Address*: Long Close, Clappentail La., Lyme Regis, Dorset DT7 3LZ. *Email*: marie@marieblake.com *Website*: www.marieblake.com *Signs work*: "Marie Blake."

BLAKE, Quentin, CBE, RDI, MA, FCSD; illustrator and teacher; Head of Dept. of Illustration, Royal College of Art (1978-85), Visiting Professor (1988-), Appointed Children`s Laureate (1999); Honorary Doctor of London Institute 2000; Honorary Doctor Royal College of Art 2001; Honorary Fellow Royal Academy 2001; Officier des Arts et des Lettres 2007; Hon D.Litt Cambridge University; Prizes: Maschler Prize 1991, Bologna Ragazzi Prize 1996, Prince Philip Designers Prize 2011. *b*: Sidcup, Kent, 16 Dec 1932. *Educ*: Downing College, Cambridge. *Studied*: part-time, Chelsea School of Art. *Represented by*: AP Watt, 20 John Street, London WC1N 2DR. *Exhib*: one-man shows, Workshop Gallery, Illustrators A.G.; retrospective of illustration work, National Theatre (1983); Chris Beetles' Gallery (1994, 1996, 2002); Somerset House (2003-04); Dulwich Picture Gallery (2004-05). *Publications*: illustrated over three hundred children's books, also books for adults; Mr. Magnolia (Kate Greenaway medal 1981). *Address*: 30 Bramham Gdns., London SW5 0HF. *Email*: zagazoo2002@yahoo.com *Website*: www.quentinblake.com *Signs work*: "Quentin Blake."

BLAKER, Michael, Royal Soc. Painter-Printmakers, Hon. Retd. Fellow. *Medium*: etcher, painter, writer. *b*: Hove, 19 Jan 1928. *m*: Catriona McTurk. *Educ*: Brighton Grammar School. *Studied*: Brighton College of Art. *Exhib*: RA, RE, RWA, RP, etc., and galleries across the UK. *Works in collections*: Tate Gallery (drawing), V&A (etchings). *Publications*: The Autobiography of a Painter-Etcher (1986); M.B. Etchings (1985); A Beginner's Guide to Oil Painting (1994). Editor, Printmaker's Journal (1983-93). Contributor to Printmaking Today. Self-published (Prospect Lodge Publications): comic novellas: Out of Place Angel; An Architect Unleashed; Artists at Large, etc. *Recreations*: early jazz. *Address*: 122 Grange Rd., Ramsgate, Kent CT11 9PT. *Email*: catblake@freeuk.com *Website*: www.michael-blaker.co.uk

BLANE, Frances Aviva, Higher Diploma Fine Art Post Grad; Award winner Jerwood Drawing; International Visitor, Djerassi Foundation, California USA. *Medium*: oil painting, drawing. *b*: London, 14 Sep 1964. *d of*: Sir Sigmund Sternberg. *Studied*: Chelsea School of Art; Byam Shaw School of Drawing; Slade Post Grad. UCL. *Represented by*: De Queeste Art, Belgium. *Exhib*: Curwen Gallery; Galerie Seitz & Partner, Berlin; Painting with John McLean, London (2000); Drawing with Basil Beattie, London (2001); London Architecture Biennale (2004); Usher Gallery; Jesus College Cambridge; Shillam & Smith (2006); Annely Juda Fine Art (2007); London Original Print Fair; Marlborough Fine Art (2006); De Queest Art, Belgium (2010, 2011, 2014), Drawing Breath Jerwood Prize Winners (2006/2007); Kings College, London University (2014). *Works in collections*: London School of

Economics; Sternberg Centre; Blindart; Jesus College, Cambridge; Usher Gallery, Lincoln; Three Faiths Forum, London; Moorfields Collection. *Publications*: various catalogues, Times Newspaper Calendar 2000. *Works Reproduced*: BBC Online. *Recreations*: playing chess, swimming, theatre, reading, walking. *Clubs*: MD America Art Alliance; International Fellowship for Visual Artists; Djerassi Institute California. *Address*: 5 Hill Court, 34 West Road, London NW6. *Website*: www.avivablane.com

BLIK, Maurice, ATC (1968), PPRBS (1997), FRSA (1999); sculptor in bronze. *b*: Amsterdam, 21 Apr 1939. *s of*: Barend & Marie Blik. one *s*. one *d*. *Educ*: Downer Grammar School. *Studied*: Hornsey College of Art (1956-60), University of London (1968-69). *Exhib*: Mall Galleries, Ben-Uri Gallery, Royal Academy, Art for Offices (London, UK), Cavalier Galleries (Conn., USA), Museum Masters (New York), Irving Gallery (Palm Beach, USA), Blains Fine Art (London), Robert Bowman (London), Hooke Gallery Sag Harbor (New York, USA). *Works in collections*: Work in private and public collections. *Commissions*: East India Dock, London; J.P. Morgan, London; Donnington Valley, Newbury, UK; Middlesex University, London; Jersey Museum, Jersey, C.I.; Glaxo Smith Kline HQ, London; Vanderbilt University Hospital, Nashville, Tenn. USA; Regent Quarter, Kings Cross, London; Evacuees Memorial, London. *Clubs*: Chelsea Arts. *Address*: 501 Bunyan Court, Barbican, London EC2Y 8DH. *Email*: mauriceblik@yahoo.com *Website*: www.mauriceblik.com

BLISS, Ian Reynolds, NDD (1954), ATD (1955), RI (1992); artist in water-colour and wood engraving; social worker. *b*: Derby, 2 Apr 1930. *m*: Jill Michelle Cheney. one *s*. three *d*. *Educ*: Repton. *Studied*: Leicester (1950-55). *Exhib*: RA, RI, Piccadilly Gallery, Nevill Gallery Canterbury, Alex Gerard Fine Arts, Fenny Lodge Gallery, Russell Gallery. *Work in Collections*: Lady Victoria Getty Collection, Bridgeman Library. *Works Reproduced*: Dry Red Press. *Recreations*: gardening and reading. *Address*: 10 Vicarage Lane, Wing, Leighton-Buzzard LU7 0NU. *Email*: rosalindbliss@icloud.com *Website*: www.rosalindbliss.co.uk *Signs work*: "IAN BLISS."

BLISS, Rosalind, DA Edinburgh College of Art (1959). *Medium*: oil, gouache, wood engraving, acrylic, lino cut, collage. *b*: London, 2 Sep 1937. *d of*: Douglas Percy Bliss and Phyllis Dodd. *Educ*: St. Bride's School, Helensburgh. *Studied*: Edinburgh College of Art (1955-59, mural painting). *Exhib*: RA, RSA, Glasgow Institute; Oxford Gallery; Derby City Museum and Art Gallery, etc. *Commissions*: murals, screens, book plates for various and private collectors. *Publications*: "Miss Margaret Beardsley of Ivy Cottage" The Bliss Press (2009). *Works Reproduced*: Engravers; Engraved Gardens; Modern British Bookplates. *Clubs*: The Art Workers Guild. *Misc*: 'murals' painted on folding screens. *Address*: Hillside Cottage, Windley, Nr Belper, Derbyshire, DE56 2LP. *Signs work*: Rosalind Bliss.

BLOOMER, Paul, RA postgrad Dip., BA (Hons); artist, lecturer. *Medium*: painting, printmaking, drawing. *b*: Dudley, 1966. two *d*. *Studied*: Royal Academy Schools, Nottingham Polytechnic. *Represented by*: Boundary Gallery, London. *Exhib*: Boundary Gallery, Walsall Gallery, RA Summer Show, Shetland Museum. *Works in collections*: Walsall, Dudley, Shetland Art Galleries, Barnet Council, Grampian Hospitals. *Publications*: The Black Country Man (articles), various newspaper reviews. *Clubs*: RASAA. *Address*: Brake Cottage, Bigton, Shetland, ZE2 9JA. *Email*: paul@paulbloomer.com *Website*: www.paulbloomer.com *Signs work*: "Paul Bloomer."

BLOXHAM, Judith Ann, B.Ed Hons (1985); artist, specialist in painting detailed silks, mainly ties. *b*: Workington, Cumbria, 28 Jan 1961. *d of*: Donald Bone. *m*: David Gerald Bloxham. one *s*. one *d*. *Educ*: Whitehaven Grammar School. *Studied*: Cumbria College of Art and Design, Carlisle, St. Martin's College, Lancaster. *Exhib*: RSMA 4th International

Miniatures Exhbn., Toronto, Fitz Park Museum, Keswick, St. Martin's, Lancaster, Cumberland Pencil Museum, Keswick, Wild ties V&A, Whale tail Nairobi. *Commissions*: Mural commissions in Carlisle City. Specialist tie commissions, including B.P. and Akito Racing. *Misc*: Work in private collections. *Address*: 3 Boston Ave., Carlisle, Cumbria CA2 4DR. *Email*: judybloxham@hotmail.com *Signs work*: "J.A.B." or "J.A. Bloxham."

BOAG, Francis, Diploma in Drawing and Painting; MA Fine Art. *Medium*: acrylic mixed media, watercolour. *b*: Dundee, 14 Sep 1948. *m*: Teresa Margaret Sinclair Boag. two *s*. one *d*. *Educ*: Lawside Academy, Dundee. *Studied*: Duncan of Jordanstone College of Art (1965-69); Robert Gordon's University (1998-99). *Represented by*: Fraser Gallery, St. Andrews; Gallery Heinzel, Aberdeen; Eduardo Alessandro Studios, Dundee; Morningside Gallery, Edinburgh; Dooway Gallery, Dublin. *Exhib*: RSA, RGI, RSW; Berozkina Gallery, Seattle, USA; Ravensbourne and Tay, Palais Royal, Paris; Bridge Gallery, Dublin; Thompsons Gallery, London; Richmond Hill Gallery, London; Falle Fine Art, Jersey; Red Rag Gallery, Stow. *Works in collections*: Public: Aberdeen Art Galleries; Grampian Hospital Trust; Glasgow Airport; Prestwick Airport; Edinburgh Airport; Peacock printmakers, Aberdeen; Ninewells Hospital, Dundee; Dundee University Collection; Aberdeen College; Stirling University; Irish State collection. Corporate Collections: McClay Murray Spens; Scott Fyffe; Acumen Financial Advisors; RBS; Conoco Oil; Wood Group; Simpson & Marwick; Scottish Enterprise, Grampian; Baxter Food Group; Edrington Group; Exxon Mobil. *Commissions*: John Lewis PLC; Digby Brown, Solicitors; Audrey Baxter, CEO Baxter Foods; Dr. Kazem Benbehani, Envoy, W.H.O. *Publications*: Books: "Work Small, Learn Big" (International Artist Publishing Inc., 2003); "Looking Back" (Fraser Gallery, 2008); "Francis Boag" (Gallery Heinzel, 2010); "The Mearns Distilled" (Francis Boag, Andy Hall, 2009); "Dictionary of Scottish Art and Architecture" (Glengarden Press, 2004). Magazines: International Artist (issue 19, 2001; issue 23, 2002); The Scots Magazine (Feb 2014). E-book "Francis Boag" (Gallery Heinzel, 2014). *Official Purchasers*: Royal Bank of Scotland; Stirling University; Eire National Acquisitions; Grampian Hospital Trust. *Works Reproduced*: Greetings cards: Unicef; Scotlands Artists; Kelly Cards, Eire. Book Cover: Robert Louis Stevenson 1 and 2, Ed. Milan Miletic (Published in Serbia). Limited Edition Prints: Eduardo Allesandro Studios, Fine Art Publishing, Ury Fine Art. *Principal Works*: Catterline Reds; Dorsoduro; Manhattan from the east River Ferry; Ury Ramble. *Recreations*: Hill-walking, football. *Misc*: Head of Art & Design, Aberdeen Grammar School (1989-2001). *Email*: boagart@btinternet.com *Website*: www.francisboag.com *Signs work*: "BOAG".

BOCKING, Helen, Harrow Dip. in Illustration (1976); artist in water-colour of wildlife, country sports, animal and equestrian portraits. *b*: Gillingham, 4 Jun 1954. *Educ*: Fort Pitt School, Kent. *Studied*: Goldsmiths' College (1972), Harrow School of Art (1973-76, Sam Marshall, Brian Liddel). *Exhib*: SWLA, RSPB, BFSS, Game Conservancy; various one-man shows. *Works in collections*: S. London A.G., and many private collections. *Address*: 30 Town Dam Lane, Donington, nr. Spalding, Lincs. PE11 4TP. *Signs work*: "H. Bocking."

BOGICEVIC, Mira, BA (Hons) 1984, Arts Council in England Grant 2005, North of England Regional Prize Winner, ING Discerning Eye 2007. *Medium*: Painting, sculpture, textiles. *b*: New Malden, Surrey, 15 Aug 1950. *Studied*: Camberwell School of Art (1980-81); Goldsmiths' College (1981-84); Camberwell School of Art and Design (1985-86). *Exhib*: solo: Cartwright Hall Art Gallery, Bradford (1989); Nicholas Treadwell Gallery, Bradford (1990); Bankfield Museum, Halifax (1991); Quay Art, Hull (1996); Farfield Mill Arts & Heritage Centre, Cumbria (2005); Sheffield University (2007). Open: RA Summer Exhibition (2006, 2007), ING Discerning Eye (2007, 2008), Leeds Artist Open (2007, 2009). Group: throughout the UK. *Works in collections*: Sheffield University Fine Art Society, private collections. *Commissions*: Liberty Studio (1987), Cartwright Hall Art Gallery, Bradford (1989), Nicholas Treadwell (1990), private commissions. *Works*

Reproduced: 'Crafts' May/June 1987, 'The Fabric Decorator' 1988, 'Yorkshire Life' March 2006. *Address*: 3 Newland Park Close, York, YO10 3HW. *Signs work*: "MB", "Mira Bogicevic".

BOLAN, Sean Edward, GRA; artist in oil and water-colour of landscapes, architecture, historical transport and military subjects. *Medium*: Ink, watercolour, gouache and oils occasionally. *b*: Rowlands Castle, Hants., 25 May 1948. *s of*: Edward Bolan, Ex. CQMS, Grenadier Guards. *m*: Raina Marion. two *d*. *Educ*: Warblington Secondary Modern School, Havant, Hants. *Studied*: Portsmouth College of Art (1965-68). *Works in collections*: private, municipal, Science Museum, S. Kensington, Guards Museum, Grenadier Guards, National Railway Museum, Welsh Guards, Scots Guards and Grenadier Guards. *Works Reproduced*: Limited edition prints, book jackets and illustrations, greeting cards, CD covers, etc. *Address*: Drive Cottage, Campden House Estate, Chipping, Campden, Glos. GL55 6UP. *Website*: www.seanbolan.co.uk *Signs work*: "Sean Bolan."

BOLTON, Janet Mary, SBA (1992); Dip.AD (1970), ATD; RHS Gold medallist (1994); teacher, artist in pastel and pencil specialising in botanical subjects; art teacher, Kingsmead Technology College, Hednesford, Staffs. *b*: 26 Sep 1947. *Educ*: Gravesend Girls' Grammar School. *Studied*: Bath Academy of Art (1968-70), Bristol University (1972). *Exhib*: RHS, SBA, Oxford University and numerous shows in Midlands. *Works in collections*: Oxford University and private collections worldwide. *Publications*: 'Fruits' design for Aynsley china 'Grande Tasse' range (1993). *Address*: 7 Raven Cl., Hednesford, Staffs. WS12 2LS. *Signs work*: "Janet M. Bolton," "J.M. Bolton" or "J.M.B."

BONADA, Cinzia, RBA; Awarded first prize for Artistic Excellence (1997/1998) by Kensington/Chelsea Arts Council; painter in oil, pencil and pastel. *b*: Jersey, C.I., 22 Apr 1938. *d of*: Carlile Boyd and Queenie Kitto. *m*: Johnny Bonada. one *s*. two *d*. *Educ*: Jersey Ladies College, Bush-Davies, Royal Ballet School. *Studied*: Richmond Adult College (1975-79, Charles Fowler) and with Peter Garrard (1982-87). *Exhib*: RA, RBA, RP, NEAC, etc. Founder member of Small Paintings Group. *Works in collections*: Drapers' Hall, AWG, Lampeter University, Japan, New Zealand, Europe, USA, Egypt, Australia, HSBC Holdings plc, London, Art Workers Guild, Jersey Museum, C.I. *Commissions*: Trevor Eldrid Past Master/Drapers' Hall, Sir John Hill, F.R.S., Chev. Stephen Weiss, Prof. W. Winklestein, Peter Barker, M.B.E., Valerie Guy, B.E.M., Prof. D. Cohn-Sherbok; Don Weinstein, R.O.H. *Publications*: 'Portraits' by Thomas Coates. *Address*: 9 Alexandra Rd., Twickenham, Middx. TW1 2HE. *Signs work*: "Cinzia."

BOND, Jane, RP, NEAC, City & Guilds School of Art, (Roger de Grey, DipFA 1981), RA Schools (Peter Greenham, Post Grad Dip. F.A. 1984); artist in oil, charcoal and pencil of portraits, still lives, interiors. Formerly theatre, film and TV designer. *b*: Zimbabwe, 1 Apr 1939. *Educ*: Holy Trinity Convent, Bickley; Kinnaird Park School, Bromley, Kent. *Studied*: St Martins School of Art, Royal Academy Schools. *Exhib*: RA, NEAC, Hayward Gall., National Theatre, Glyndebourne Opera House, etc. *Works in collections*: private: England, Europe and USA. *Commissions*: Portraits including; the Rt.Hon.Baroness Boothroyd, Lord Ron Dearing, Sir Aaron Klug.Om, Dr. John Moses, Dean of St.Paul's Cathedral, The Rt. Hon Baroness Perry of Southwark, Mrs. Vivienne Duffield, David Wooton, Lord Mayor of London. *Clubs*: Two Brydges. *Address*: 8 Ceylon Rd., London W14 0PY. *Email*: jane.bond07@yahoo.co.uk *Website*: www.TheRp.co.uk

BOND, Marj, DA (Glas.), SSWA (1974), RSW (1989), SSA (1989); Thyne Scholarship; artist in oil, acrylic, etching. *Medium*: mixed on paper and canvas. *b*: Paisley, Scotland. *d of*: Hubert McKechnie, organist and ships draughtsman. *m*: James A. Gray, architect. one *s*. two *d*. *Educ*: Paisley Grammar School. *Studied*: Glasgow School of Art (David Donaldson, Mary Armour, Benno Schotz). *Represented by*: Open Eye Gallery, Bohun Gallery Henley. *Exhib*: many one-man shows, RSA, SSA, RSW, Scottish Soc. of Woman Artists. *Works in* *collections*: Arts in Fife, Edinburgh University, Dunfermline Building Soc., Perth A.G., Priorscourt School, Paintings in Hospitals, Lillie Gallery. *Commissions*: Paintings in Hospitals, Cunard Liners, Priors Court School, Mary Queen of Scots - 400 Women. *Publications*: Who's Who in Scotland, catalogues. *Official Purchasers*: Edinburgh University. *Clubs*: Scottish Art Club. *Address*: Eden Cottage, Old Town, Gateside, Fife KY14 5SL. *Email*: bondgray@aol.com *Signs work*: "Marj."

BONE, Charles, PPRI, ARCA, Hon FCA (Canada); FBI Award for Design; painter and designer; former Governor, Federation of British Artists (Mall Galleries); Past President, Royal Institute of Painters in Water-colour; Awarded Hunting Group Prize for a British water-colour (1984); artist in water-colour, oil, variety of mediums including ceramic and murals. *b*: Farnham, Surrey, 15 Sep 1926. *m*: Sheila Mitchell, FRBS, ARCA (decd). two *s*. *Studied*: Farnham School of Art; Royal College of Art. *Exhib*: 52 one-man, Spain, Holland, USA, Britain. *Works in collections*: many mural paintings in public buildings and water-colours and oils in private collections, including members of the Royal Family. *Publications*: author, Charles Bone's Waverley; Foreword by H.R.H. Prince of Wales; author, The Authors Circle, Foreword by Sir John Gielgud; Cathedrals, foreword by Archbishop of Canterbury. *Clubs*: Chelsea Arts. *Address*: Winters Farm, Puttenham, nr. Guildford, Surrey GU3 1AR. *Signs work*: "BONE."

BONE, Tina, Assoc. SBA, CBM (2012). *Medium*: oil, watercolour, drawing, letter illuminations, gilding. *b*. Stapleford, Cambs, 30 Apr 1950. *m*: David John Bone. three *s*. *Studied*: self-taught artist. *Represented by*: Darryl Nantais Gallery (www.nantias-gallery.co.uk); wikigallery.org; Frida-kahlo-foundation.org; Toulouse-lautrec-foundation.org. *Exhib*: National Exhibition of Wildlife Art; Marwell International Wildlife Art Soc; Society of Botanical Artists; Natural World Art Group; Assoc of Animal Artists; Cambridge Open Studios; 'Arts Butanica', Luton Hoo Walled Garden. *Commissions*: Five botanical works - prints used as ID cards in Tropical House, Marwell Wildlife, Hants (Original Collection displayed at Marwell). Many private commissions. *Publications*: Forthcoming (with S.M. Haslam) Riparian Loss. Agriculture for Development - 'Fresh Water and Crops in Malta' Eastern Voices - poem, 'I'd rather work from home'; Picture of the Month, Artists and Illustrators Magazine. *Works Reproduced*: 'Canoodling in the Loquats' (592306), White Helleborines and Chiffchaffs (602506); all works in reproduction. *Recreations*: Golf, tennis, badminton, nature, walking, caravanning. Clubs: Cambridge Lawn Tennis Club; Bourn Golf Club, Mid Anglia Centre CC. *Address*: 18 Harbour Avenue, Comberton, Cambridge CB23 7DD. *Email*: tina.bone@tinabonedtp.co.uk. *Website*: www.tinabonedtp.co.uk *Signs work*: "T Bone" as monogram.

BOOKLESS, Sarah Theresa, Diploma of Art (Fine Art)(1972); Maclaine Watters Medal, RSA, Edinburgh (1971); Hospitalfield Award, Arbroath (1971). *Medium*: oils/mixed media, watercolour, acrylics. *b*: Glasgow, 1950. *Educ*: Eastbank Academy (1962-68). *Studied*: Glasgow School of Art (1968-72); Jordanhill College of Education (1972-73). *Exhib*: Royal Academy, London; Royal Scottish Academy; Llewellyn Alexander; Trinity College, Dublin; Kelvingrove Art Galleries, Glasgow; Gold Gallery, Edinburgh; Iona House Gallery, Woodstock, Oxford; University of Glasgow Memorial Chapel (Lentfest Exhibition) The Stations of the Cross. *Works in collections*: Riggs Bank, London; private collections throughout the UK. *Publications*: The First Post (Art in Pictures, 26 Aug 2008); 'Serenade of Spring' (part of the Llewelyn Alexander Gallery mixed Summer Exhibition). *Principal Works*: The Fourteenth Station of the Cross on permanent exhibition in St. Mungo's Church, Parson St., Glasgow. *Misc*: described as an expressive colourist, varied subject matter, inspired by poetry, prose and music. Also strong visionary artist. *Email*: sarahtrese12@yahoo.co.uk *Website*: www.riverbanktreegallery.co.uk www.tcweb.co.uk/scottish-art-circle *Signs work*: 'S.Bookless', 'Sarah Bookless', or 'Sarah T. Bookless.'

BOOTH, Araceli, 2nd Prize, Bockingford Competition, 1993, 1996 Edwin Young Exhibition. *Medium*: watercolour. *b*: Valencia, Spain, 25 Jul 1940. *d of*: Ricardo Quiles, Adela Hoyo. *m*: John Booth. two *d*. *Studied*: Valencia, Spain, 1957 - painting classes by Richard Plincke, courses by Paul Riley, Charles Reid. *Exhib*: RI (1988, 89, 90, 92, 93, 95); SWA (1991, 92, 93): SBA (1992, 93, 94); Laing London (1992); RWS (1996); Salisbury, Winchester, Warminster, Bath, Romsey, Stockbridge (Wykeham), Daler (Bournemouth, Guildford, Tenerife, Valencia); various SFP exhibitions solo and group; international exhibitions at (La Llanca' (Verona), Colombia. *Works in collections*: Wiltshire Art Collection; Marquis of Bath private collection. *Commissions*: Ducal centenary. *Publications*: "History and Dictionary of British Flower Painters" (J. Walpole); "En los albores del siglo XXI." *Clubs*: SFP (Society of Floral Painters); AAV (Agrupacion de acuarelistas Valencianos); Frome Art Society. *Address*: 25 Marleys Way, Frome, BA11 3NG. *Email*: aracelibooth@hotmail.com Website: www.watercolours-aracelibooth.com *Signs work*: "Araceli Booth."

BOOTH, Helen, BA Fine Art Painting (1989); Pollock Krasner Award for Work on Paper (2011). *Medium*: installation, scultpure, drawing, print. *b*: Burton on Trent, 10 Dec 1967. *Partner*: Craig Morrison. two *d*. *Studied*: Wimbledon School of Art. *Represented by*: Cadogan Contemporary, London. *Exhib*: internationally. *Address*: Derw Mill South, Pentrecwrt, Llandysul, Wales, SA44 5DB. *Email*: helenboothartist@gmail.com *Website*: http://helenbooth.com *Signs work*: "Helen Booth".

BOOTH, Rosa-Maria, FRSA (2007), VPRMS (2006-2012), RMS (1999), HS(F) (1983), MASF (1984), Dip. Fashion (1970); 17 awards including 1st Place Drawing & Pastel (1983), and 1st Place Abstract (1984-88) MAS-Florida; painter and miniaturist. *Medium*: oil, acrylic. *b*: Olot, Spain, 9 Nov 1947. *d of*: J.E.Parejo Alonso. *m*: Peter Charles Booth (decd.). *Educ*: Sagrado Corazón de Maria, Olot; Inst. Marti, Barcelona. *Studied*: privately and in Paris under Madeleine Scali; L'Escola Olotina, Spain (Emili Parejo, J.M. Agusti); Thurrock Technical College (M. Martin, K.Walch). *Exhib*: RA, RMS, HS, Mall Galleries, Barbican, Westminster Gallery, Llewellyn Alexander, N. Ireland, Spain, France, Sweden, Canada, USA, Australia and Russia. *Works in collections*: Work in private collections. *Publications*: Works included in the Centenary Book of the RMS, Artistas del Millennium Enciclopedia Europea; Homenaje a la Mujer Artista, El Arte en Su Maxima Expression; Listed in the Dictionary of International Biography, Great Women of the 21st Century (ABI); World Who's Who of Women; Royal Academy Exhibitors Book. *Recreations*: entertaining, studying works at galleries and museums, etc. *Address*: 36 Windsor Ave., Grays, Essex RM16 2UB. *Email*: rosmar.booth@hotmail.co.uk *Website*: www.rosmarart.com *Signs work*: "ROSMAR."

BORELLO, Wendy Doreen, RSMA; Higher Associate, Watercolour Society of South Africa; Awards include: Best in Painting (2008), Best in Show (2010), Botswana Heritage Celebrations; St. Cuthberts Award (2007 & 2008); Caran D'Ache Award (2009); Great Art Award (2012); The Two Rivers Watercolour Prize (2012). *Medium*: watercolour. *b*: Essex, 13 Nov 1947. *d of*: H G R Backshall. *m*: Remigio. *Studied*: Technicon Pretoria (Carl Jeppe, 2001 & 2002). *Exhib*: Botswana National Museum, Gaborone (1986-2013); SADC Festival, Namibia (2000); Manor Gallery, Johannesburg (2000-2009); RSMA, Mall Galleries, London (2003-2013); Patchings Art Centre, Nottingham, UK (2006-2012); Pretoria Art Museum, South Africa; Thapong Art Centre, Gabarone (2008-2013). Solo Exhibitions: Botswana National Museum (1987, 88); Berman Gallery, Johannesburg (1999); Kizo Art Gallery, Durban (2009). *Works in collections*: private, public and corporate including: The Bank of Botswana, Monash University, Botswana National Museum. *Commissions*: include: Anglo American Corporation, Kalahari Conservation Society. *Official Purchasers*: Botswana Government. *Recreations*: include ornithology. *Address*: P O Box 603, Gaborone, Botswana, Africa. *Email*: borello@sharps.co.bw *Signs work*: "WENDY BORELLO."

BORKOWSKI, Elizabeth Irena, DipAD, Prix de Rome, Feodora Gleichen award (1971) Sculpture; Runner-up, design commission by the Fountain Society for the Queen Fountain in Parliament Square (1989); sculptor/painter in clay, bronze, water-colour, charcoal, pencil, art teacher. *b*: Redhill, 7 May 1949. *Educ*: Ursuline High School, Brentwood. *Studied*: Camberwell School of Art and Crafts, British School at Rome (Brian Taylor, Paul de Moncheaux). *Exhib*: RA Summer Show (1973), Palazzo Barberini National Museum of Rome (1973), Chelsea School of Art Rome Scholars (1986), Bates, Baskomb & Bayne Art Restorers, Battersea, London (watercolours/bronzes, 1987), Chelsea Harbour (1993), Chelsea Art Fair (1996), Lapada Fine Art Fair, RCA (1999). Elected ARBS (1992). *Primcipal Works*: Unicorn for Fountain Project, Parliament Square, London. *Address*: 3 High Trees Rd., Reigate, Surrey RH2 7EH. *Signs work*: "Lissa Borkowski."

BOSWELL, Laura, BA Joint Honours Art History/Visual Art. *Medium*: print. *b*: London, 27 Nov 1965. *m*: Ben. one *s*. *Educ*: St. Helens School Northwood. *Studied*: Harrow College of Higher Education (1983-4); Aberystwyth University (1984-7). *Exhib*: Solo shows: One Church Street, Missenden; Quay Arts, Newport; Obsidian Art, Stoke Mandeville. Joint shows: Margate Gallery; West Ox Arts, Bampton; Harris Manchester College, Oxford; Biscuit Factory, Newcastle. Also: Blackheath Gallery, Bankside Gallery, Margate Gallery. *Works in collections*: MI-Lab Mokuhanga Print Collection, Japan; House of Lords; National Print Collection; Buckingham County Museum; Nagasawa Art Park Collection, Japan; National Print Collection of Wales. Commissions: Great Western Street Twin Enamel murals, Bucks CC; Leysdown-on-Sea enamel installation, Swale Council; Healing Arts for NHS Isle of Wight; St. Wilfids Hospice, Eastbourne. *Official Purchasers*: House of Lords; Buckingham County Museum. *Recreations*: Running, spinning and knitting, cookery. Misc: Columnist of "Artist and Illustrators Magazine" on the business side of being an artist. *Address*: 7 Great Horwood Road, Winslow, Bucks MK18 3LY. *Email*: laura@lauraboswell.co.uk *Website*: www.lauraboswell.co.uk *Signs work*: "Laura Boswell".

BOSWELL, Tim George, Best Blown Glass, International Glass Centre (2008); Winner, Art in Action Award for Contemporary Glass, British Glass Biennalle (2010); Winner, Student Award British Glass Bienalle (2008); Worshipful Glass Sellers Bursary Award (2011). *Medium*: glass. *b*: Sheringham, 25 Dec 1961. one *s*. *Studied*: The International Glass Centre, Brierley Hill (2006-2009), Wolverhampton University (2011-2012). *Exhib*: Peter Layton Gallery (Winners, 2012), Birmingham Botanical Gardens (2012); twenty twenty Gallery, Much Wenlock (2012); Art in Action (201); Peter Layton's Gallery (Essence, 2010); Contemporary Glass Society (2010); British Glass Biennalle (2010, 2008); Corning Glass Museum (Collaborations, 2008). *Work in collections*: Glass Dalek, Broadfield House Glass Museum (with Charlotte Hughes Martin). *Commissions*: The Wishing Tree, Norfolk & Norwick Hospital (current project). *Publications*: Neus Glass (2010), Craft & Design Magazine (2011). *Recreations*: music, magic. *Clubs*: Member, Contemporary Glass Society. *Misc*: Formed 'The Bandits of Glass' (2010) - a West Midlands glass blowing demonstration team. *Address*: Flat 2, Molyneux Chambers, 129-135 High Street, Brierley Hill, West Midlands OY5 3AU. *Email*: timboswell@rocketmail.com *Website*: www.tomboswellglass.kk5.org *Signs work*: "Tim Boswell" or "T.G.Boswell".

BOTT, Dennis Adrian Roxby, DipAD (1972), Cert.Ed (1973), ARWS (1981), RWS (1983) AWG (1989-2005); painter in water-colour and oil. *b*: Chingford, 29 Apr 1948. *s of*: Frederick William Roxby Bott. *Educ*: Forest School, nr. Snaresbrook, London E17. *Studied*: Colchester School of Art (1967-69), Norwich School of Art (1969-72). *Exhib*: one-man shows, Ogle Gallery, Eastbourne, Gallery 33, Billingshurst, The Grange, Rottingdean, Ogle Gallery, Cheltenham, Bourne Gallery, Reigate, Worthing Museum and A.G., Canon Gallery, Chichester, Ebury Galleries. *Works in collections*: Towner A.G., Eastbourne, Hove Museum, Brighton Museum. *Commissions*: Wardroom of H.M.Y. Britannia, National Trust. *Clubs*: Arts. *Address*: School House, Bucks Green, Horsham, W. Sussex RH12 3JP. *Signs work*: "Roxby Bott."

BOULTON, Janet, painter, water-colour and paper relief, specialising in still life and landscape gardens. *b*: Wiltshire, 14 Sep 1936. *d of*: E.F. Boulton, farmer. *m*: Keith Baines, poet and translator. one *d*. *Studied*: Swindon and Camberwell Schools of Art (1953-58). *Exhib*: widely in mixed shows including Belfast Arts Council Open, Chichester National, London Group, R.A. Summer Exhbns., The Cairn Gallery, etc.; one-person shows: Mercury Gallery, 26 Cork St. W1, (1988, 1991, 1994, 1997); Redfern Gallery (2001, 2004). *Works in collections*: Southern Arts, Radcliffe Infirmary, John Radcliffe Hospital, I.O.W. Area Health Authority, National Gallery, Ottawa, John Radcliffe NHS Trust, Swindon Museum & Art Gallery. *Publications*: edited and transcribed, Paul Nash Letters to Mercia Oakley 1909-1918 (Fleece Press, 1991), Monograph, Mercury Graphics (1985-91), Homage to Andre Derain, collaboration with Ian Hamilton Finlay (Wild Hawthorn Press, 1998), Monograph, Two Gardens; Monograph, Paper Relief Works. *Misc*: Residencies: Lankmead Comprehensive, Abingdon (1980), Radcliffe Infirmary, Oxford (1986). *Address*: 64 Spring Rd., Abingdon OX14 1AN. *Email*: mail@janetboulton.co.uk *Website*: www.janetboulton.co.uk

BOURDON SMITH, Diana, RWA (1990); painter in oil, water-colour, charcoal and mixed media. *b*: 16 Dec 1933. *m*: Richard (decd.). four *d*. *Studied*: Kingston Art School. *Exhib*: RA, NEAC, RWA. *Works in collections*: Royal West of England Academy. *Clubs*: Chelsea Arts Club. *Address*: 19 Crescent La., Bath BA1 2PX. *Signs work*: "D.M.B.S."

BOURGUIGNON, Doris, (née Blair); ARCA; painter in acrylic, oil, water-colour and gouache. *Studied*: College of Art, Belfast; RCA, London; Wallace Harrison, NY; Fernand Leger, Paris; Andre Lhote, Paris. *Exhib*: one-man and group shows: Belfast, Galerie l'Angle Aigu, Brussels; Museum and A.G., Belfast. *Works in collections*: Museum and A.G., Belfast. *Publications*: illustrated Various Verses by John O'The North. *Address*: 8a Gunter Grove, London SW10 0UJ. *Signs work*: "Doris Bourguignon", "Doris V. Blair" on academic work.

BOURNE, D. Peter, DA (Glasgow), RSW (1982); painter in oil, gouache, water-colour. *b*: Madras, India, 1 Nov 1931. *s of*: D.J. Bourne, BA, MICE. *m*: Marjorie. two *s*. two *d*. *Educ*: Glasgow. *Studied*: Glasgow School of Art (1950-54, David Donaldson). *Exhib*: RSA Edinburgh, RGI Glasgow, RSW Edinburgh. *Works in collections*: City Art (Edinburgh), Pictures for Schools (Edinburgh), paintings in hospitals. *Publications*: Dictionary of Scottish Painters - Paul Harris and Julian Halsby (Cannongate Publishing). *Address*: Tressour Wood, Weem, Aberfeldy, Perthshire PH15 2LD. *Signs work*: "Bourne."

BOURNE, Jean Susan, BA Hons (1971), Dip.Mus.Stud. (1972), AMA (1974), FMA (1992); Museum curator; Curator, Towneley Hall Art Gallery and Museum, Burnley; President, North West Federation of Museums and Art Galleries (1993-94). *b*: Rochdale, 23 Feb 1950. *d of*: Bernard Bourne. *Educ*: Queen Margaret's School, Escrick, Lancaster University, Manchester University. *Publications*: museum guides, exhbn. catalogues, articles on oak furniture. *Address*: 94 Higham Hall Rd., Higham, Lancs. BB12 9EY. *Signs work*: 'J.Susan Bourne.'

BOUSFIELD, Neil, BA (Hons) Animation (1990), MSc Computer Graphics (1997), MA Printmaking (2007) awarded with Distinction; Rebecca Smith Award (2007); awarded Rawlinson Bequest by SWE, *Medium*: engraving, illustration, prints. *b*: Middlesbrough, 18 Dec 1967. *Studied*: Cleveland College of Art and Design (1984-87), West Surrey College of Art and Design (1987-90), Teesside University (1996-97), University of the West of England (2003-07). *Exhib*: New Designers, London (2006), The Society of Wood Engravers Annual Exhbn (2006), exhibitions across the UK, and major Arts/Film Festivals worldwide (1991-98). *Works in collections*: V&A, British Library. *Principal Works*: "Downsized" (2005), "The Cycle" (2007), illustrated artist books. *Address*: 23 Avenue Terrace, Stonehouse, Gloucestershire, GL10 3RE. *Email*: prints@inkyfingerspress.com *Website*: www.inkyfingerspress.com *Signs work*: "NEIL BOUSFIELD."

BOWEN-MORRIS, Nigel Vaughan, MA (Oxon); MFA (NEC). *Medium*: oil, prints, photography. *b*: Barmouth, Gwynedd, 17 Aug 1961. *Studied*: St.Catherine's College, Oxford; New England College, New Hampshire, USA. *Exhib*: RA (2002, 2006); MOMA Wales (solo, 2004); The Gallery in Cork Street (solo, 2002, 2003, 2005, 2006); Agora Gallery, Chelsea, New York (artist in residence, 2005); Art for Life, Christie's, London (group, 2002, 2003, 2004, 2005); Florence Biennale, Italy (2005); Cork Street Annual Open Exhibition (2008); Royal West of England Academy, Bristol (Open Photography 2, 2011); Berlin Biennale, Germany (Open Platform, 2012); Gallerie D'Arte Mentana, Florence, Italy (2012). *Works in collections*: private collection: Florida USA, Australia, Scotland, England. *Publications*: Recent Works (2002). *Works Reproduced*: Bridgeman Art library, London. *Principal Works*: oil on canvas. *Recreations*: Natural History. *Clubs*: FRGS, FLS. *Misc*: Monoprints at the Curwen Studio, Cambridgeshire (2005), Miro Foundation Workshops in Japanese Print and Photographic Text (2005, 2007), Mallorca, Balearic Islands; Photographic Workshop on Art Documentation, Vyner Street Gallery, London (January 2012). *Address*: Panos 22, Athens, Greece 16671. *Email*: recentworks@hotmail.com *Website*: www.nigelbowen-morris.com *Signs work*: 'Nigel Bowen-Morris.'

BOWER, Susan, BSc (1973), MSc (1974), PGCE (1976), ROI, RBA; naive painter in oil. *b*: Tadcaster, Yorkshire, 20 Mar 1953. *m*: Stephen Bower. one *s*. three *d*. *Educ*: Nottingham, Sussex and Leeds Universities. *Exhib*: ROI, RBA, NEAC, RI, RWS, RA Summer exhibitions, Kentmere House Gallery, York; galleries around the country. *Works in collections*: Three works in the 'Anthony Petullo Collection'; works in the Bridgeman Art Library. *Works Reproduced*: cover of 'Time Out'; cover of Penelope Mortimer's novel 'The Pumpkin Eaters'. *Address*: Larchfield House, Church St., Barkston Ash, Tadcaster, N. Yorks. LS24 9PJ. *Signs work*: "BOWER."

BOWEY, Olwyn, ARCA, RA; painter in oil and gouache. *b*: Stockton-on-Tees, Cleveland, 10 Feb 1936. *Studied*: West Hartlepool School of Art, Royal College of Art. *Address*: 4 Peace Lane, Heyshott, Midhurst, Sussex GU29 0DF. *Signs work*: "Olwyn Bowey."

BOWLING, Frank, ARCA, RA, OBE; Guggenheim Fellowships (1967 & 1973); Pollock Krasner Awards (1998 & 1992). *Medium*: acrylic. *b*: Bartica, B.G., 29 Feb 1936. *m*: Rachel Scott. three *s*. *Studied*: Royal College of Art (1959-62). *Represented by*: Spanierman Modern, New York; Emanuel Silberstein, Washington DC; Hales Gallery, London. *Exhib*: Whitney Museum, NYC (1971); Tibor de Nagy, NYC; Serpentine Gallery, London (1986); Tate Gallery, London (2012); Center for Inter American Relations, NYC (1973); Hirschhorn, Washington DC (1976). *Works in collections*: Museum of Modern Art, NYC; Metropolitan Museum, NYC; Tate Gallery, London; Museum of Fine Arts, Boston. *Commissions*: Shakespeare Quatro Centenary (1964). *Publications*: 'Frank Bowling' by Mel Gooding (2011). *Official Purchasers*: Government Art Collection. *Recreations*: watching cricket and athletis. *Clubs*: Chelsea Arts Club, Royal Overseas Club. *Address*: 8A John Islip St., London SW1P 4PY. *Website*: frankbowling.com

BOWMAN, Day, BA; B.Ed (Hons). *Medium*: oil, watercolour, drawing, collage. Widowed. one *s*. *EStudied*: Chelsea School of Art (1977-80); Institute of Education, London. *Represented by*: Jenny Blyth Fine Art, www;jennyblythfineart.co.uk. *Exhib*: Recent exhibitions include: Bluecoat Liverpool (2014); Spacex Exeter (2014); Royal Academy Summer Exhibition (2014); Aesthetica Art prize (2013, 14); Nord Art Germany (2013); Olympic Commission for Weymouth Railway Station (2012); ICCI dome, Weymouth Beach with rock group Phoria (2012); RWA Open (2012). *Works in collections*: St.Vincent and Grenadines Govt.; Bournemouth University; Hilton Hotel Group; Phillip Morris Inc; Actes Sud Publishing; RNLI, ING. *Commissions*: Olympic Commission 2012 for Weymouth Station. *Publications*: Recent publications include: Art Monthly (2014); Guardian Guide

(2014); Aesthetica Magazine (2013, 14); Nort Art 2013 catalogue; The Spectator (2008); The Week (2008); Galleries Guide (2008); Proof Magazine (2008). *Clubs*: Chelsea Arts Club. *Address*: 76a King's Road, London SW3 4TZ. *Email*: day@daybowman.com *Website*: www.daybowman.com *Signs work*: 'Day Bowman.'

BOWNESS, Sir Alan, Kt., CBE, MA; art historian; formerly Director, Henry Moore Foundation, Director of the Tate Gallery, and Professor of History of Art and Deputy Director, Courtauld Inst. of Art, University of London. *b*: London, 11 Jan 1928. *s of*: George Bowness. *m*: Sarah Hepworth Nicholson. one *s*. one *d*. *Educ*: University College School, Downing College, Cambridge, and Courtauld Inst. of Art. *Publications*: William Scott: Paintings (Lund Humphries, 1964); Modern Sculpture (Studio Vista, 1965); Henry Moore: Complete Sculpture 1949-1986 (Five vols. Lund Humphries, 1965-1988); Alan Davie (Lund Humphries, 1968); Gauguin (Phaidon, 1971); Complete Sculpture of Barbara Hepworth 1960-70 (Lund Humphries, 1971); Modern European Art (Thames & Hudson, 1972); Ivon Hitchens (Lund Humphries, 1973); The Conditions of Success (Thames & Hudson, 1989); Bernard Meadows (Lund Humphries, 1994). *Address*: 91 Castelnau, London SW13 9EL.

BOWYER, Francis David, BA Hons (1974), RWS (1991), PPRWS, NEAC (1993); artist in water-colour and oil; part time teacher. *b*: London, 20 May 1952. *s of*: William Bowyer, RA, RWS, NEAC, RP. *m*: Glynis Porter. one *s*. one *d*. *Educ*: St. Mark's School, London SW6. *Studied*: St. Martin's School of Art (1971-75, Ken Roberts, Ken Bale), Hammersmith School of Art (1976-77, Ruskin Spear). *Exhib*: RA Summer Exhbn., NEAC, RWS. *Works in collections*: Royal Watercolour Society, Diploma Collection; HRH Prince of Wales Collection; Arts Club, Dover St, W1; Royal Collection. *Commissions*: National Grid (1993). *Publications*: Art of Drawing and Painting (1995). *Works Reproduced*: RWS Card Collection. *Recreations*: sport. *Address*: 12 Gainsborough Rd., Chiswick, London W4 1NJ. *Email*: francis@bowyerfineart.co.uk *Website*: www.framcisbowyer.com *Signs work*: "Francis Bowyer."

BOWYER, Jason Richard, MA, RP, NEAC, PS; Greenshield Foundation (1983), Daler-Rowney award RA Summer Exhbn. (1986), William Townesend scholarship (1987), 'Changing Faces' Award, RP Annual (2003); Regional award, Hunting Group Prizes, RCA (1999); Critics Prize, NEAC Annual, Mall Galleries; painter in oil and pastel, draughtsman; Founder, New English School of Drawing (1993). *b*: Chiswick, London, 4 Mar 1957. *s of*: William Bowyer, RA. *m*: Claire Ireland (Bowyer). one *s*. *Educ*: Chiswick School. *Studied*: Camberwell School of Art (1975-79), RA Schools (1979-82). *Exhib*: RA (1980-85, 1992-01); one-man show New Grafton (1991, 1995, 1997, 2001), Cedar House Gallery (2004). *Works in collections*: Arts Club, Dover St.; Arthur Andersen, Warburgs; Royal Tank Regiment. *Commissions*: Royal Tank Regiment; Emmanuel School, Fulham FC. *Publications*: Starting Drawing (Bloomsbury Press, 1988). *Recreations*: football, cricket *Address*: Studio No.7, Kew Bridge Steam Museum, Green Dragon Lane, Brentford, Middx. TW8 0EN. *Email*: jasonbowyer@yahoo.co.uk *Signs work*: "J.R. Bowyer." or initials JRB.

BOWYER, William, RA (1981), RWS, NEAC, RP; artist in oil paint, water-colour; Head of Fine Art, Maidstone College of Art (1970-81); Hon. sec. NEAC. *b*: Leek, Staffs., 25 May 1926. *s of*: Arthur Bowyer. *m*: Vera Mary. two *s*. one *d*. *Educ*: Burslem School of Art. *Studied*: RCA (Carel Weight, Ruskin Spear). *Exhib*: RA., NEAC, RWS, many galleries London and provinces. *Works in collections*: RA, RWS, NPG, Sheffield City AG, City of Stoke-on-Trent, many provincial, and private collections home and abroad. *Clubs*: Arts, Dover St. Arts *Address*: 12 Cleveland Ave., Chiswick, London W4 1SN. *Signs work*: "William Bowyer.".

BOYD, Graham, NDD, ATD (1951); Head of Painting, University of Hertfordshire (1976-93) & BA Fine Art course leader. *Medium*: painting, acrylics on canvas and paper. *b*: Bristol, 1928. *s of*: Herbert Leslie Boyd. *m*: Pauline Lilian (decd). one *s*.

one *d*. *Educ*: Watford Grammar School. *Studied*: Watford School of Art and London University. *Represented by*: The Campden Gallery, Chipping Campden, Glos, www.campdengallery.co.uk. *Exhib*: include London Group, RA, John Moores, Belfast 68, Triangle Artists, NY, London and Barcelona, Atlantic Fusion: Lisbon, Madrid, Paintings from the 70s, Piper Gallery, London; one-man shows: AIA (1962, 1967), Molton Gallery (1963), Oxford Gallery (1969, 1971, 1982), University of Hertfordshire (1980, 1988, 1994-2001), Spacex 1983, Sandra Higgins Fine Arts (1991), Harriet Green (1997), deli Art, Smithfield (1999, 2004), Pilgrim Gallery, WC1 (2003), Salt Gallery, Hayle (2004, 2006), Bushey Museum (2004); Courtyard Gallery, Hertford (2007), NI Gallery (2007); Parndon Mill Gallery, Harlow (2008), The Campden Gallery, Glos (2009); Watford Museum (2011); Hertford Theatre Gallery (2013); Gibberd Gallery, Harlow (2014). *Works in collections*: Walker Gallery, Trinity College, Oxford, Triangle Trust, New York, City of Barcelona, University of Hertfordshire, BMW Financial Services, The Landmark Trust, Bushey Museum. *Publications*: 'Disruptive Tendencies' recent paintings by Graham Boyd, Cuillin Bantock, University of Hertfordshire; Picturing the Sublime in the recent work of Graham Boyd; (Richard Dyer) Campden Gallery; The Public Art Catalogue. *Works Reproduced*: Aquarelle prints. *Address*: Blackapple, 54 Scatterdells Lane, Chipperfield, Herts. WD4 9EX. *Email*: graham.boyd54@gmail.com Website: www.grahamboyd.co.uk *Signs work*: "Graham Boyd" or "G. BOYD."

BOYD, Lee John, BA Hons Fine Craft Design; Kilfedder Award. *Medium*: oil, scuplture. *b*: Middlesbrough, England, 11 Jan 1971. one *s*. *Studied*: Cleveland College of Art & Design; University of Ulster. *Represented by*: 19 Karen, Australia; Canvas Gallery, Belfast; Arbourey Gallery, Belfast. *Exhib*: 'Art for Nothing', Slovenia & Hoxton Square Gallery, London (2007); 'Small Rays of Hope' Rhonda Schaller Gallery, New York (2007); 'What a Dream', Estonia (2008); 'Ship of Fools', Yara Sculpture Gallery, Australia (2008); 'Big Sky', Northern Ireland (2008); BBC 'Wildlife Artist of the Year' finalist (2009); Royal Ulster Academy Show (2009); '8x8', Canvas Gallery (2010); Saatchi Online 'Artist of the Week' (2011); BBC 'Show Me the Monet' finalist and exhibitor at RCA (2011); 'i art' Sync Space (2012); 'Artigram' Sync Space (2012). *Commissions*: National Trust. *Publications*: The Culture Cave - 'Is it a bird? Is it a plane? No it's Art and a Rabbit' www.culturecave.com. *Official Purchasers*: North Down Borough Council. *Works Reproduced*: Indigo Salon - Paris Fashion Show 'She Had a Nose for Trouble'. *Clubs*: Member of Visual Arts Ireland. *Misc*: Founder Member of an independent arts group "Firsty?". Tutor Northwest Regional College (2006-09). *Address*: 54 Drumawhey Gardens, Bangor, County Down, Northern Ireland BT19 1SR. *Email*: lee1boyd@yahoo.co.uk *Website*: www.leeboydartist.com *Signs work*: "LEE".

BOYD-BRENT, James, ARE (1988), BA(Hons.) (1988), MFA Univ. of Minnesota (1994); artist/printmaker in etching, woodcut, water-colour; Asst. Professor, University of Minnesota, Minn. USA. *b*: Solihull, England, 10 Aug 1954. *m*: Mary. one *s*. *Educ*: Selborne College. *Studied*: Anglia Polytechnic (1984, Walter Hoyle), Central/St. Martin's School of Art (1985-88, Norman Ackroyd, Bernard Cheese, David Gluck), University of Minnesota (1991-94, Malcolm Myers). *Exhib*: UK and USA. *Works in collections*: work in public and private collections in UK and USA. *Publications*: "Here by Design" (pictorial survey of design) published by Goldstein Museum of Design, U.S.A. *Clubs*: A.R.E., Mem. Southern Graphic Council, U.S.A. *Address*: 2231 Scudder St., St. Anthony Park, St. Paul, MN 55108, USA. *Email*: jboydbre@umn.edu *Signs work*: "James Boyd-Brent."

BOYDEN, Ann, nee COWLEY; SWA; portrait painter in oil, water-colour, pastel, teacher; art teacher for Adult Educ.; British School, Brussels and South Somerset. *b*: London, 1 Jun 1931. *d of*: Dr. Anthony Beach Cowley and Mary Mabel Cowley. *m*: Alan Boyden (deceased). three *s*. *Educ*: Godolphin School, Salisbury. *Studied*: Southern College of Art, Bournemouth (1948-52). *Exhib*: SWA Nottingham Castle Gallery, Dillington House;

solo shows: Ancaster Gallery, British Council, Brussels, Bath Literary Society Gallery, Artists 303, Mall Gallery London. *Works in collections*: international. Works Reproduced: Gordon Fraser Greeting Card Company. *Clubs*: Dillington Water-colour Soc., Artists 303 Group, Sherborne Arts Society. Group. *Address*: Brambleside, 52, Beechwood Drive, Crewkerne, Som., TA18 7BY. *Email*: ann920@btinternet.com *Signs work*: "Ann F. Boyden."

BOYDEN, John, BA (Lond), DipAGMS (Manc), AMA, Cert.Theol. (Wales); teacher at The Old Grammar School, Lewes (1991-2001); Curator, Hove Museum and Art Gallery, Sussex (1973-86); painter in oil and acrylic, and woodcarver. *b*: Tunbridge Wells, 1942. *s of*: G J Boyden, MA, HMI. *m*: Christine Portsmouth. two *s*. *Studied*: Northbrook College, Worthing (foundation). *Exhib*: Brighton Festival (2001), Northbrook College (2003), Adur Festival (2007-2014). *Publications*: Edited 'German Lyric Poetry' (2011). *Address*: 3 Rosslyn Rd., Shoreham-by-Sea, W. Sussex BN43 6WL. *Signs work*: "John Boyden."

BOYES, Judy Virginia, SWA (1984), BWS (1985); self taught landscape painter in water-colour. *Medium*: watercolour. *b*: Alton, Hants., 1 Jul 1943. *d of*: S.D. Potter, art teacher. *m*: John Boyes. two *d*. *Educ*: Eggars Grammar School, Alton. *Exhib*: RI, Mall Galleries, SWA, Westminster Gallery; one-man shows: Liverpool University, Atkinson A.G., Southport, Guildford House A.G., Forest Gallery, Guildford. *Publications*: front cover of Artist Magazine, features and articles on water-colour technique in Artist. *Address*: Crag House, Grasmere, Cumbria, LA22 9QA. *Email*: judy.boyes@btinternet.com *Website*: www.judyboyes.co.uk *Signs work*: "Judy Boyes."

BOYT, Judy, MA, FRBS, SEA; awarded RBS medal Rebellion; British Sporting Art Trust and Sladmore Awards. *Medium*: bronze, resins, silver, steel, drawing. *b*: 7 Jun 1954. *Educ*: Oxford High School, West Oxon College, Witney. *Studied*: Oxford, Wolverhampton, North Staffs. Universities. *Exhib*: UK, USA, Jersey, Switzerland, France, Saudi Arabia, Oman. *Works in collections*: Japan; The National Racing Museum, Newmarket; Cheltenham Racecourse; Princeton University, USA; Wildenstein; HM The Queen, HH The President of the United Arab Emirates, Sheikh Hamdan al Maktoum, UAE; The Royal Palaces, Oman. *Commissions*: 'Rebellion' - Standard Life; Mitsubishi Motors Trophy, Badminton Horse Trials; Golden Miller, Cheltenham racecourse; 'Up to the Line', Windsor; The Working Horse Monument - Liverpool, 'Stretton' lifesize equine, Yorkshire; Epsom Town 'Evocation of Speed'; 'Attraction', Duke of Roxburghe; 'JCB', Sir Anthony & Lady Bamford, 'The Black Prince', Morpeth, 'The Watchkeeper', The Royal Navy College, Dartmouth, 'Herons', Oman, 'Masked Marvel' St Leger Winner. *Works Reproduced*: 'Going for Bronze', documentary; Sculpting the Equestrian bronze 'Up to the Line', HTV; The book: 'The Alchemy of Bronze' -Tony Birks. *Address*: Westwood, Easterton Sands, Devizes, Wilts. SN10 4PY. *Email*: judy@judyboyt.com *Website*: www.judyboyt.com *Signs work*: "Judy Boyt."

BRADFORD, Shane, BTEC HND, BA (Hons). Winner, Celeste Painting Prize (2007). *Medium*: oil, gloss paint, drawing, sculpture. *b*: London, 3 Oct 1971. *s of*: Annie Inman, Robert Bradford. *m*: Olivia Bradford. one *d*. *Educ*: Holland Park Comprehensive. *Studied*: Chelsea College of Art (1990-92), Brighton University (1992-95). *Represented by*: V1 Gallery, Copenhagen; Conagh Young Gallery, Dublin; Home from Home, Munich. *Exhib*: Discerning Eye (2001), Space Gallery (2003), M&R Gallery (2003, 04, 05, 06), Stiftelsen 3.14 Museum, Norway (2004), M.K.Ciulion's Museum, Lithuania (2005), Artsway (2005) , Celeste Painting Prize (2006, 2007-winner, 2009), Haunch of Venison (2007), Campbell Works (2007), Rod Barton (2007), CTRL, Houston (2008), Vegas Gallery (2009), V1 (2008-9). *Works in collections*: Stiftelsen Museum, M.K.Ciulionis Museum. Many private collections. *Works Reproduced*: Art Review, Art World, Art of England, Elle, Tatler, Contemporary. *Address*:15 Tanner House, Tanner Street, London SE1 3LL. *Email*: studio@shanebradford.com *Website*: www.shanebradford.com *Signs work*: "SHANE BRADFORD."

BRADLEY, Marion. *Medium*: acrylic. *b*: Darwen, Lancs, 21 Apr 1946. *m*: James Ingham Riley. *Studied*: self taught. *Exhib*: Many galleries in the North West of England. Member of the Lake Artists Society since 1983, exhibits annually; Wolf House Gallery, Silverdale, Lancs. with husband James Ingham Riley. *Works in collections*: many private and corporate collections here and abroad. *Principal Works*: mountain landscapes. *Recreations*: climbing and walking. Semi-retired now. *Clubs*: Lake Artists Society (1982), Ambleside Art Society, Lancaster Art Society. *Misc*: Paints mostly flowers in landscapes, and botanical studies. *Address*: Gale House Villa, Low Gale, Ambleside, LA22 0BB. *Email*: mail@marionbradley.plus.com *Signs work*: "Marion Bradley".

BRADSHAW, Bronwen Jeanette, BA (Hons.) (1966), RWA (1988); artist in etching, silkscreen, oil, tempera, musician, artists' books. *b*: London, 7 Sep 1945. divorced. *Partner*: Roger Frood. one *d*. *Educ*: Sutton High School GPDST. *Studied*: University of London. *Exhib*: RA, RWA, RE, New Munich Gallery, many group shows in the South-West. *Works in collections*: RWA. *Clubs*: Spike Island Printmakers; Royal West of England Academy. *Address*: The Dove, Butleigh, Glastonbury, Som. BA6 8TL. *Email*: bronbradshaw@yahoo.com *Signs work*: "Bronwen Bradshaw," "Bradshaw" or "B.B."

BRADSHAW, Elizabeth Anne Makin, SWA (1997), LSIA; Surrey Diploma in Art and Design: Illustration and Typography First Class (Hon.). *Medium*: oil, watercolour, etchings, prints. *b*: Bovingdon, 1 Jan 1953. *d of*: Maurice J.Makin BICC. *m*: Christopher Bradshaw. one *s*. two *d*. *Studied*: Twickenham College of Art and Design; LSIA (1970-74). *Exhib*: London, Camberley, Sunningdale, Wokingham, Reading, and across UK. *Works in collections*: Surrey Heath Museum, Camberley. *Commissions*: private individuals; commissions include wildlife botanical, abstract, portraiture. *Clubs*: Camberley and Frimley Society of Arts, Sunningdale Art Society. *Misc*: an experimental printmaker skilled in the art of etchings and mezzotint. *Address*: 1 Abingdon Road, Sandhurst, Berks GU47 9RN. *Email*: liz@heatherbradshaw.co.uk *Website*: www.lizmakinbradshaw.co.uk *Signs work*: 'E.A Makin Bradshaw', 'E.A.Bradshaw.'

BRADSHAW, Peter, freelance artist in oils and gouache. *b*: London, 23 Oct 1931. divorced. *s of*: Billing A. Bradshaw, telephonist. one *d*. *Educ*: Kingsthorpe Grove, Bective. *Studied*: Northampton School of Art (1945-47) under F. Courtney, E. Goodson. *Exhib*: United Artists, ROI, Northampton Town and County and local exhbns. *Works in collections*: various UK, worldwide. *Commissions*: various private collections. *Publications*: Railway Art. *Works Reproduced*: various Christmas and greetings cards. *Address*: 4 Bective Rd., Northampton NN2 7TD. *Signs work*: "P. Bradshaw" (cat and robin featured in work).

BRAIN, Ann: see PHILLIPS, Anna.

BRAMER, William, MA, RCA (1968), gold medal, RCA (1968); printmaker, etcher; visiting lecturer, RCA, Kingston University, head of painting, University of Northumbria, fellow in creative arts, Trinity College, Cambridge (1970-1972). *b*: Nottingham, 14 May 1943. one *s*. *Educ*: Loughborough Grammar School. *Studied*: Nottingham College of Art (1960-1965), RCA (1965-1968). *Exhib*: numerous exhibs. internationally, including galleries in Paris, Berne, Zurich, London, New York. *Works in collections*: Arts Council, Queen Elizabeth College, London University, Trinity College, Cambridge, Leicester Education Authority, RCA, IBM, and others. *Misc*: Studio and editions printed at Atelier Lacourière et Frèlaut, Paris; studio in St. Ives, Cornwall. *Address*: 11 Maryon Mews, Hampstead, London NW3 2PU. *Signs work*: "William Bramer."

BRAMLEY, Victor, painter in oil, watercolour and acrylic. *b*: Sheffield, 16 Nov 1933. *s of*: family name: Oliver. *m*: Jacque Moran. *Partner*: Bernadette Contrino. *Educ*: Firth Park Grammar School, Sheffield. *Studied*: self taught. *Exhib*: British Landscape Society (Mall Galleries), London, Exeter University, Cornwall, Cumbria. 30 one-man shows. *Works in* *collections*: many private collections. *Clubs*: senior member of St. Ives Society of Artists. *Misc*: Studio/Gallery: Princes St. Gallery, Penzance, Cornwall. *Address*: 13 St. Warren St., Penzance, Cornwall TR18 2DW. *Website*: www.st.ivessociety of artists.com *Signs work*: "VICTOR BRAMLEY."

BRAND, Margaret Mary Madeleine, AIMBI (1968), MMAA (1969); medical artist, figurative and expressionist painter in oil, water-colour and mixed media; founder associate of IMBI. *b*: London, 1938. *Educ*: Stella Maris Convent, Devon. *Studied*: Reigate and Redhill School of Art; Post-grad. diploma in medical illustration, Guy's Hospital Medical School (1961); Deputy Head of Dept. of Medical Illustration, Guy's Hospital (1963-69). *Exhib*: RA, RMS, London and provincial societies and galleries. *Works Reproduced*: illustrations in medical and scientific books and journals. *Address*: 'Whitecot', Doctors Lane, Chaldon, Surrey CR3 5AF. *Signs work*: "M. Brand" or "M.B."

BRANDEBOURG, Margaret, (previously listed as M.E.Winter); part-time teacher in adult educ. for ILEA. *b*: Surbiton, Surrey, 28 Apr 1926. *d of*: Eric Brandebourg, solicitor. *m*: Deryck William Winter. two *s*. three *d*. *Educ*: Tiffin Girls' School. *Studied*: Kingston Art School and RA Schools. Since 1976 has worked in textiles. *Exhib*: British Crafts Centre, Seven Dials Gallery, etc. *Works in collections*: Private Collections. *Commissions*: in Portsmouth Museum. *Publications*: book on Seminole Patchwork (Batsford, 1987). Lectures and demonstrates on this subject. *Clubs*: Quilter's Guild (founder mem.). *Address*: 3 Cedars Rd., Hampton Wick KT1 4BG. *Signs work*: Margaret Winter.

BRANTON, Sam, BA Hons Fine Art. *Medium*: drawing. *b*: Oxford, 28 July 1985. *Studied*: Norwich School of Art & design (2004-07). *Represented by*: James Freeman Gallery. *Exhib*: Voyages Extraordinaires, James Freeman Gallery, London (2011); Erotica Beastia, James Freeman Gallery, London (2009); Metro-land, Flora Fairbairn Projects, Oxford (2009); Whispers of Immortality, Natalia Goldin Gallery, Stockholm (2008); Faux Pas de Deux, Signal Gallery, London (2008); Hollywood Apocalypse, Black Maria Gallery, Los Angeles (2008). *Works in collections*: The Kabin Contemporary Art Collection. *Email*: sam.branton@hotmail.com *Website*: www.sambranton.com *Signs work*: "SAM BRANTON".

BRANSCOMBE, Dianne Lois, RMS (1996), SWA (1994), ARMS (1993), HS (1991); Masters Award for Best Set of Larger Paintings (A.Milliem Brushstrokes Exhbn, Llewelyn Alexander Gallery, 1999); Best Set of Miniatures, RMS Exhbn. (2000); teacher. *Medium*: water-colour and oil. *b*: Norwich, 1 Oct 1949. *m*: Robert. two *d*. *Educ*: Norwich City College. *Studied*: Goldsmiths' College (1969-72). *Represented by*: Llewellyn Alexander Gallery, London; Tudor Gallery, Norwich; Westcliffe Gallery, Sheringham. *Exhib*: RMS, SWA, HS, RA Summer show, Mandell's Gallery Norwich, Llewellyn Alexander Gallery London; The Guild of Norwich Painters, and many mixed shows. *Works Reproduced*: International Artist Magazine (Aug/Sep 2004); book 'Wide Skies' by A.May & B.Watts; cards, Medici and Clover greetings. *Address*: Bangala, 27 The Green, Surlingham, Norfolk NR14 7AG. *Signs work*: "D.L. Branscombe."

BRASIER, Jenny, RHS Gold medals: for pencil drawing (1982, 1989), for paintings in water-colour on vellum (1988, 1994), for paintings on paper (2000); botanical artist and illustrator in water-colour on vellum and paper. *b*: Worcs., 9 Aug 1936. two *s*. *Educ*: Sir James Smith's Grammar School, Camelford; University of Nottingham, School of Agriculture. *Exhib*: RBG Kew, RHS, SBA, V&A, Natural History Museum, Hunt Inst. Pittsburgh, Smithsonian Inst. Washington, The Linnean Society, worldwide with The Shirley Sherwood Collection, etc. *Works in collections*: V&A, Natural History Museum, Nature in Art, Hunt Inst. for Botanical Documentation, Carnegie-Mellon University Pittsburgh, The Shirley Sherwood Collection, The Highgrove Florilegium. *Commissions*: numerous. *Works Reproduced*: numerous, including The Cyclamen Society Journals, Hosta, the Flowering

Foliage Plant, The Art of Botanical Illustration, The Highgrove Florilegium, etc. *Address*: Bridge Cottage, Camelford, Cornwall PL32 9TL.

BRASON, Paul, RP (1994); portrait painter in oil. *b*: London, 17 Jun 1952. two *s*. one *d*. *Educ*: King James I Grammar School, I.O.W. *Studied*: Camberwell College of Art (1970-74). *Exhib*: NPG, RP, RWA, RA. *Works in collections*: NPG, Royal Collection Windsor Castle, Government Art Collection, Eton College, Trinity and Balliol Colleges, Oxford; Duke of Westminster; Goodwood House; Lady Lever Art Gallery, Liverpool; Merton College; RAF; RAC Club; Grosvenor Museum, Chester; University of Wales; private collections: UK, USA, France, Italy. *Clubs*: Arts Club, Chelsea Arts Club. *Address*: Blakeley's House, Beechen Cliff, Bath, BA2 4QT. *Email*: paulb@paulbrason.co.uk *Website*: www.paulbrason.co.uk *Signs work*: "P.B." or "BRASON" and date.

BRASSINGTON, Alan Francis. *Medium*: oil, watercolour, drawing, sculpture. *b*: Zimbabwe, 18 Mar 1960. *s of*: Trevor Brassington. *m*: Lisa Jane Brassington. one *s*. one *d*. *Educ*: Ireland, Dublin. *Studied*: Glasgow School of Art. *Represented by*: Andrew Esson. *Exhib*: Contemporary Art, Manchester; Maggy Kay Cheshire - Liverpool; LPC Manchester; Theo Waddington, London; Ian Peck, New York. *Works in collections*: Sony, Cartier, Saudi Arabian Royal Family, HRH Queen, Ralph Lauren. *Commissions*: Sony, Cartier, Duke of Devonshire. *Publications*: Daily Telegraph, Telegraph Magazine, Field, Country Life, Daily Mail, House & Garden. *Recreations*: old cars. *Address*: 5 Edwards College, South Cerney, Cirencester, GL7 5TR. *Email*: alan.brassington@tiscali.co.uk *Website*: www.alanbrassington.com *Signs work*: "A.BRASSINGTON."

BRATBY, Dayan Eduardo Joachim Jesse, *b*: 7 Mar 1968. *s of*: John Bratby RA & Jean Cooke RA. *Partner*: Marina Stradomska. one *d*. *Studied*: studied under mother and father. *Exhib*: Royal Academy. *Principal Works*: "Incredible Hulk." *Address*: 110 Tunnel Avenue, East Greenwich, London SE10 0SD. *Signs work*: "Dayan Bratby."

BRAVEN, Angela, NDD; Qualified Art Therapist; taught at Chelsea Art School for 24 years, and Ravensbourn and Hastings Art School. *Medium*: oil, watercolour, drawing, prints. *b*: 2 Jul 1947. *d of*: Olive and Arthur Braven. *m*: Gus Cummings, RA. two *s*. one *d*. *Studied*: Hammersmith Art & Buildings. *Exhib*: RA; Angela Flowers Gallery; Battersea Arts Centre; Odette Gilbert Gallery, Cork Street (solo show); Easton Rooms, Rye; Hastings Museum (solo show); Coastlines-Kent Inst. of Art and Design; (Braven & Bratby) Terrace Gallery, Worthing; Invited artist for Exhibition organised by the Arts Trust, Mumbai. *Works in collections*: Everard Reid Gallery, Atlanta, USA; Hastings Museum; Mumbai, India. *Commissions*: two 15ft murals for the Conquest Hospital, Hastings. *Publications*: featured on BBC TV abroad in Britain. *Works Reproduced*: many watercolours for Athena Publications. *Recreations*: jazz blues, tango, reading, swimming in sea, gardens. *Clubs*: Chelsea Art Club. *Misc*: I paint landscapes, interiors, gardens, dreams and autobiographical paintings using strong colours, so a lot of work is sold abroad. *Address*: Harpsichord House, Coburg Place, Hastings, TN34 3HY. *Signs work*: 'ABraven' or 'AB'

BRAYNE, David, RWS (2000); BA Hons (1977); B.Phil (1985). *Medium*: water based paintings. *b*: Wolverhampton, 10 Aug 1954. *m*: Jane Brayne. one *s*. one *d*. *Educ*: Kitwood Boys Secondary Modern (Boston), *Studied*: Trent Polytechnic (1973), Gloucestershire College of Art (1977), University of Exeter (1985). *Represented by*: RWS - Bankside Gallery, London. *Exhib*: all over the place. *Misc*: (Anthony David Brayne). *Address*: 4 Enfield Terrace, Weymouth Road, Evercreech, Somerset BA4 6JE. Email: d.a.brayne@gmail.com *Website*: davidbrayne.wordpress.com *Signs work*: "BRAYNE".

BRAZIER, Connie, Hon.RSWA (2001); artist in water-colour, and engraved glass; Glass Engraving Tutor (retd.), Sutton College of Liberal Arts. *b*: Croydon. *d of*: Arthur Philip Guerrier, solicitor. *m*: Desmond Brazier. two *s*. *Educ*: Stamford High School for

Girls, Lincs. *Studied*: Croydon School of Art (Reginald Marlow, Frederick Hinchliffe, Michael Cadman). *Exhib*: Europa Gallery, Sutton (1977, 1979, 1981, 1983, 1984), Whitehall, Cheam (1986), Fairfield Halls (shared) (1987), Civic Centre A.G., Tunbridge Wells (1987), Playhouse, Epsom (1991), RI, RMS, SBA. Invited to exhibit in Paris and New York. *Clubs*: Lewes Art. *Address*: 27 Sadlers Way, Ringmer, Lewes, East Sussex BN8 5HG. *Signs work*: "CMB."

BREEDEN, Keith James, RP (1999); self taught painter and sculptor in oil, water-colour, pencil, wood and metal. *b*: Cheshire, 25 Mar 1956. *m*: Helen. one *s*. two *d*. *Exhib*: MoMA Wales, Hamiltons London, Arts Connection, Llanfyllin, RP at Mall Galleries, BP Awards, NPG, London. *Works in collections*: private collections internationally, RLC Bicester, Oundle School. *Commissions*: Maj. Gen. G.W. Field, CB, OBE, Resident Governor HM Tower of London; Jack and Morley Richards, Ty Nant; Maj. G. Crook & Smuts; H. Lloyd, QC; David McMurray. *Works Reproduced*: record sleeves for Pink Floyd, Fine Young Cannibals, ABC, The Cult, Scritti Politti, etc. *Address*: Fronheulog, Llanfihangel, Llanfyllin, Powys, Cymru SY22 5HZ.

BRENT, Isabelle, designer/painter/illustrator specialising in water-colour and gold leaf. *b*: Caversham, 17 Mar 1961. *d of*: Norman Edmund Brent. *Studied*: Loughborough College of Art and Design; further studies in France and Italy; Employed in academic research and study in the Dept. of Decorative Arts, Leicester Museums and Art Galleries. *Exhib*: RA, London and other provincial galleries in Britain; Paris, Tokyo, New York, Michigan and Indianapolis etc. *Works in collections*: private throughout the world. *Commissions*: Specially commissioned by the MCC - a commemorative print depicting the evolution and development of cricket at Lords. *Publications*: illustrated: The Christmas Story (8 foreign editions, miniature editions and 3 reprints), Noah's Ark, A Cat for all Seasons, Cameo Cats, A Christmas Record Book, An Alphabet of Animals, All Creatures Great and Small, The Complete Just So Stories (4 reprints, described as 'The Definitive edition of Kiplings' great work'), Fairy Tales of Oscar Wilde (3 reprints), Grimm's Fairy Tales, Fairy Tales of Hans Christian Andersen, The Little Mermaid and Other Fairy Tales, Christmas Fairy Tales, Celtic Fairy Tales, Cats Love Christmas Too, The Golden Bird, King Midas, Best Loved Poems, Noah and the Devil, In the House of Happiness, Fairy Tales of Hans Christian Andersen for the Readers Digest. The attention to detail in the books and the academic research behind each illustration sets the work apart from other artists. Also well-known in America since 1992 for sophisticated and beautifully designed complete ranges of stationery for Marcel Schurman Company, San Francisco. Gift wrap, tissue, bags, boxes, Christmas and greeting cards, books, etc. Much sought after for miniature paintings on vellum in antique gold lockets and antique frames. *Recreations*: lives with a dalmatian, cat and Belgium hare - all have the run of the house and garden and frequently appear in the books. Main interests are classical music, Egyptology, Saxon History and theatre. *Address*: The Galandiere, 4 Road Tollent, 62410 Caumont, France.

BRENTON, John, BA (Hons). *Medium*: oil, sculpture. *b*: Plymouth, 13 Aug 1964. *m*: Gail. one *s*. one *d*. *Educ*: Brannel School, Cornwall (1975-80); St. Austell VI Form College (1980-83). *Studied*: Aslager College (now part of Manchester Municipal University), 1983-86. *Exhib*: solo shows since 2002 at: Panter & Hall, Mayfair; Fowey River Gallery; The Biscuit Factory, Newcastle upon Tyne; Tregony Gallery; John Noott, Broadway. *Work in collections*: private and corporate, worldwide. *Commissions*: many private and corporate. *Publications*: 'International Artist Magazine', 'The Artist', 'Leisure Painter'. *Works Reproduced*: Limited Editions of a number of originals. *Principal Works*: Oil paintings of Cornwall, various, painted en plein air. *Recreations*: surfing, walking, photography. *Clubs*: Newquay Velo. *Address*: 29 Shackleton Drive, Newquay TR7 3PE. *Email*: mail@johnbrenton.co.uk *Website*: www.johnbrenton.co.uk *Signs work*: "JB" as monogram.

BRERETON, James. *Medium*: oil, drawing. *b*: Derby, 16 Oct 1954. *s of*: James Brereton (Snr) & Margaret Myers. *Studied*: The Joseph Wright Art School, Derby (1968-69). *Exhib*: one-man shows in Derbyshire since late 1970s; RSMA, London, since 1979; Burlington Paintings, London. *Works in collections*: private collections. *Works Reproduced*: greeting cards / book covers and illustrations. *Address*: 37 Quarn Gardens, Quarn Street, Derby, DE1 3HJ. *Website*: www.burlington.co.uk *Signs work*: "JAMES BRERETON."

BRETT, Simon, SWE, ARE (1986); wood engraver; Chairman, S.W.E. (1986-92). *b*: Windsor, 27 May 1943. *s of*: Antony Brett, hospital administrator. *m*: Juliet Wood. one *d*. *Educ*: Ampleforth College. *Studied*: St. Martin's School of Art (1960-64, as a painter; learned engraving from Clifford Webb). *Exhib*: SWE, RE, RA, and occasional one-man shows; retrospective 'An Engraver's Progress' Bankside, London (2013); Oxford and Bath (Holbourne Museum). *Works in collections*: The Royal Collection, Windsor Castle; Royal Academy Library. *Commissions*: over forty books illustrated, mainly for Folio Society and Fine Print Publications. *Publications*: 'Wood Engraving - How to do it' (3rd revised edition 2010), 'An Engraver's Globe' (2002); other books, essays and articles on wood engraving. *Address*: 12 Blowhorn St., Marlborough, Wilts. SN8 1BT. *Signs work*: "Simon Brett."

BREVANT, Grisot, BEPC; Artiste peintre. *Medium*: gouache, pastel, dessins, oils. *b*: Paris, France, 26 Sep 1947. *d of*: Pierre et Andrée Grisot. *m*: Patrick Girard. *Educ*: Ecole Freinet (Vence AM) et (Cannes AM) Lyceé. *Studied*: Entreé a l'Ecole des Arts Decoratifs de Nice a 14ans avec dispense (4 ans) d'études examen et Diplôme (CAFAS), Zatkine (Sculpteur et Peintre). *Represented by*: France: Galerie 'Albane', Nantes; Galerie Le 'Sagittaire', Annecy; Galerie Cimaise, Besancon; Japan: Galerie Daimaru, Tokyo; London: Bernard Chauchet. *Exhib*: Paris: galeries: Guigné Universite, Carre d'Or; Province: Etats Unis (Cannes) Sagittaire (Annecy); Chifflet, Contemporaine, Cimaise (Besançon); Saluden (Brest) Mas d'Artigny (St. Paul de Vence). *Works in collections*: Galeries Etrangèrs: Daimaru (Tokyo), Lambertini (Rome), Atelier 5 (Amsterdam). *Commissions*: Collectionneurs: Privés (Munich, Paris, Buenos Aires), Fresques Commandeés par une Grande Banque Suisse. *Publications*: catalogues et plaquettes faites lors de plusieurs expositions. *Works Reproduced*: Télévision: 1995 Compte Rendu Exposition (Monaco) AM. *Principal Works*: Jeux de Lumière; Atmosphère d'Eté; Le Printemps. *Address*: 318 Route des Valettes Sud, 06140 Tourettes sur Loup, France

BREWSTER, Claire, BA (Hons) Textiles/Fashion. *Medium*: mixed paper/media. *b*: Lincolnshire, 22 Jul 1968. *Studied*: Lincoln College of Art (1986-87), Middlesex Polytechnic (1987-1990). *Exhib*: London Transport Museum, Tag Fine Arts, Posted Projects, Jagged Art, Hastings Museum and Art Gallery, Flow Gallery, National Craft Gallery Ireland, Houston Centre for Contemporary Craft, Royal London Hospital, London Art Fair, Gallery Sbensimmon Paris. *Works in collections*: London Transport Museum, Bury Museum and Art Gallery, Corinthia Hotel. *Commissions*: Corinthia Hotel. *Publications*: Paper; Tear, Fold, Rip, Cut (2009); World of Interiors; Vogue; Inside Out. *Address*: 13 Westcliff House, Baxter Road, London N1 3HS. *Email*: mail@clairebrewster.co.uk *Website*: clairebrewster.co.uk *Signs work*: "Claire Brewster".

BREWSTER, Martyn Robert, BA (1974), Post. Grad. Dip. in Printmaking (1975), ATC (1978); Eastern Arts award (1977), British Council Award (1991); painter in oil and acrylic, drawings, printmaking. *b*: Oxford, 24 Jan 1952. *s of*: Robert Brewster. *Educ*: Watford Boys' Grammar School. *Studied*: Herts. College of Art (1970-71), Brighton Polytechnic (1971-75), Brighton Art Teachers' Centre (1977-78). *Represented by*: Waterhouse and Dodd - London/New York. *Exhib*: one-man shows: Jill George Gallery London (1988-2010); Waterhouse and Dodd (2012-present). *Works in collections*: Russell-Cotes A.G. and Museum, Dorset. Many public and private collections U.K. and abroad. V&A Museum, Arts Institute, Bournemouth, Bournemouth University. *Publications*: Monograph on artist by

Simon Olding (Scolar Press, 1997). *Address*: 15 West Rd., Boscombe, Bournemouth, Dorset BH5 2AN. *Email*: martynbrewster@btinternet.com *Website*: www.martynbrewster.co.uk *Signs work*: "Brewster" either on front or back of work with date.

BRIDGE, Eoghan, 'Ireland Alloys Award' for Most Promising Young Artist (RSA, 1989). *Medium*: sculpture. *b*: Edinburgh, 1963. *s of*: Thomas James Joseph Bridge. *m*: Angela. two *s*. one *d*. *Studied*: Harrogate College of Art; Leeds Polytechnic. *Represented by*: Linda Blackstone. *Exhib*: Leith Gallery (2001-2004); Bohun Gallery, Henley-on-Thames (1999-2004); Cambridge Contemporary Art (1997-2004); Open Eye, Edinburgh (1990-2004); RSA (1989, 90, 92); AAF London (1999-2004); Mall Galleries, (1991); and extensively across UK. *Commissions*: public: designed and produced 'The Yorkshire Television Press Awards' (1988); Rutland Court 'Horse & Rider' bronze, Baillie Gifford, Rutland Court, Edinburgh; Silvermills 'Horse-Rider-Eagle', bronze, Silvermills Residential Dev., Edinburgh; 'Horse-Rider-Eagle', Prior's School, Newbury. *Address*: c/o Linda Blackstone Gallery, r/o 13 High Street, Pinner HA5 5QQ. *Email*: linda@lindablackstone.com *Website*: www.lindablackstone.com *Signs work*: 'EOGHAN BRIDGE.'

BRIDGE, Muriel Elisabeth Emily, (Mrs. Millie Taylor); NDD; BA Fine Art (1983); First Prize, Chichester Open (1996); *Medium*: collage, watercolour, mixed media. *b*: Rome, 1934. *d of*: Robert N. Bridge. *m*: John R. Taylor (decd). one *s*. two *d*. *Studied*: (graphic design) at St. Martin's School of Art (1950-54). Southampton College (1980-83). *Exhib*: regularly with SWA Westminster; RI exhbn. at Mall Galleries; Whiteleys, Queensway; One-man shows: West Dean College, New Grafton Gallery, also Lanzarote. Locally: Brighton Museum, Portsmouth Museum, Bishops Palace Chichester, Centre of Arts Chichester. Paintings in private collections worldwide. *Commissions*: 8ft. mural for travel agents in Regents St.; Brochure cover for Chichester Festivities. *Publications*: Art in Nature. *Official Purchasers*: Pallant House, Chichester. *Works Reproduced*: Art in Nature. *Recreations*: travel, painting in India every winter. *Clubs*: Founder mem. New Park Artists. *Misc*: Head of Art Dept. at Grammar school for 17 yrs.; Art Lecturer, Chichester College. *Address*: The Mews, 22 Victoria Rd., Chichester, W. Sussex PO19 4HY. *Signs work*: "M. Bridge."

BRIDGES, Ann Elizabeth, BA (Hons) Design (1st class Hons. 1999), R.Cam. A. (2000); monoprint (printmaker); artist in residence Chester Zoo (1999-2001); Arts Council Awards (2000, 2004, 2005, 2006). *Medium*: drawing, painting, printmaking. *b*: London, 27 Apr 1960. *d of*: Martin Matthews (goldsmith, watchcase maker) and Margaret Matthews. one *s*. two *d*. *Educ*: Thomas Peacocke Comprehensive, Rye. *Studied*: Yale College, Wrexham (1995-6), North Wales College of Art and Design, Glydwr University (1996-1999). *Exhib*: London, Wales (National Eisteddfod), UK and USA. *Works in collections*: private collections, Art for Health (Glan Clwyd cancer unit), Paintings in Hospitals (Wales), Hilton Hotel, Prague, DCI Ltd, Dhaka. *Commissions*: Chester Zoo, Rowan Foods, Private Commissions. *Publications*: Debretts Guides to Etiquette (1999); Included in Monoprint Printmaking Handbook (2006); New York Arts annual catalogue (2006). *Official Purchasers*: paintings in hospital, FCI Ltd Dhaka. *Works Reproduced*: Indigoart Ltd. *Principal Works*: large images of Aquariums, 'Shoal', wildlife ponds. *Recreations*: walking, theatre, swimming. *Clubs*: Arts Centre Group. *Misc*: Freedom of the City of London (1993). *Address*: 58 High Street, Otford, Sevenoaks, Kent TN14 5PQ. *Email*: abridges@gotadsl.co.uk *Website*: www.ann-bridges.com *Signs work*: "AB" or "Ann Bridges."

BRIDGLAND, Judith Irenè, MA (Hons) (1984); Macroberts Open Prize (1999), Royal Glasgow Institute (2009); Scottish landscape painter. *Medium*: oil, watercolour, drawing, prints. *b*: Australia, 1962. *Studied*: University of Glasgow (1980-84). *Represented by*: Duncan & Miller Fine Arts, St. James's, London. *Exhib*: Glasgow Royal Concert Hall (1991); Demarco European Art Foundation (1993); Collins Gallery, University of

Strathclyde (1994); McLean Art Gallery & Museum, Greenock (1995); RGI (1996-2003, 2008-10, 2013); Laing (1997, 1998); Scottish Drawing Competition (1997-2011); SAAC (1998); Veem Gallery, Philadelphia, USA (1998); PAI (1995-2014); St. Petersburg, Russia (2003); Upplands Vasby Art Museum, Stockholm, Sweden (2003); Lille Art Gallery, Milngavie (2005); Maclaurin Art Gallery, Ayr (2009, 2013); RSW (2001, 2013). Solo shows: Duncan R Miller Fine Arts, London (2006-present). *Works in collections*: The Royal Bank of Scotland, University of Strathclyde; Glasgow Caledonian University, British Midland. Address: The Studio, 1430 Pollokshaws Road, Glasgow, G41 3SN. *Email*: judith@jibridgland.com *Website*: www.jibridgland.com *Signs work*: "J.I.BRIDGLAND".

BRIERTON, Irene Annette, SWA (1988), HS (1997); HRH Princess Michael of Kent Watercolour Award, SWA (2004); Llewelyn Alexander Masters Award (2004) for a Most Outstanding set of 6 miniature paintings of birds in watercolour on paper; ARMS (2006), RMS (2008). *Medium*: painter of wildlife in water-colour. *b*: Belper, 10 Dec 1948. *d of*: William Gibson, MBIM. *m*: Robert Brierton. one *s*. one *d*. *Educ*: Burnham Grammar School, Bucks. *Exhib*: RI (1985-88), SWLA (1985), SWA, Llewellyn Alexander (Fine Paintings) Ltd., London, RMS (1996-99, 2005, 2006, 2008, 2009), National Exhibition of Wildlife Art (NEWA, 2001-2009), Alexander Gallery, Bristol (2006-2007), British Birdwatching Fair (1996-2009). *Works Reproduced*: paintings by WWF as cards. *Recreations*: actively involved in wildlife conservation. *Misc*: Chair: Mid-Derbyshire Badger Group since 1990. *Address*: 17 St. Michael's Cl., Crich, Derbyshire DE4 5DN. *Email*: irene_brierton@btopenworld.com *Website*: www.irenebrierton.co.uk *Signs work*: "Irene Brierton."

BRIFFETT, Susan Joyce, painter of landscapes in pastels and murals and scenery in acrylic, and biblical-based work. *b*: London, 10 May 1960. *m*: Geoffrey Hewlett. two *s*. *Educ*: Kingsbury High School, London. *Exhib*: Stanmore Library, Harrow Art Centre and with UA, Westminster Central Hall, London. *Commissions*: various, locally. *Clubs*: United Society of Artists, Society of Equestrian Artists. *Misc*: Briffett is the painting name of Mrs Susan J. Hewlett. *Address*: 39 Wemborough Rd., Stanmore, Middx. HA7 2EA. *Signs work*: "S.J.BRIFFETT."

BRIGHT, Madge, AROI (1990); winner, ROI award Cornellissen prize; self taught artist in oil and mixed media. *b*: S. Africa, 15 Feb 1939. *m*: P.S. Johnson. three *s*. *Educ*: Chaplin Gwelo, Rhodesia. *Exhib*: ROI Mall Galleries, SBA, Britain's Painters, Hertford-Century Gallery Henley-on-Thames, Iwano Gallery Osaka Japan, Noor Gallery Bahrein, Look Out Gallery Plettenberg Bay S. Africa, Llewellyn Alexander Fine Art. *Works in collections*: National Gallery Zimbabwe. *Clubs*: S.B.A., Hertford Art Soc., Five Women Artists Plus. *Address*: 1 Great Ash, Lubbock Rd., Chislehurst, Kent BR7 5JZ. *Signs work*: "Madge Bright."

BRIGSTOCK, Jane Lena, ARE, BA Hons. (Painting) (1979), MA (Printmaking) (1980), British Institution Fund Printmakers award (1981); guest artist, California College of Art and Crafts (1981-82); painter in pastel, water-colour, printmaker; lecturer, Nene College, Northampton; Maidstone School of Art; Chelsea School of Art. *b*: 28 Mar 1957. *d of*: Michael John Brigstock. *m*: Michael Addison. one *s*. two *d*. *Educ*: Wellingborough County High School for Girls. *Studied*: Maidstone School of Art, and Chelsea School of Art. *Exhib*: RA, Cleveland Drawing Bienale, Royal Overseas League, Drew Gallery, Canterbury, Bankside Gallery. *Works in collections*: Northampton CC. *Misc*: Mem. Soc. of Painter-Printmakers. *Address*: 76 West Hill Rd., St. Leonards on Sea, E. Sussex TN38 0NE. *Email*: jane.brigstock@btinternet.com *Signs work*: "J.L. Brigstock."

BRINDLE, Sharon Elizabeth, BA Hons; BP Portrait Award (1997, Special Commendation). *b*: Staffs., 20 Dec 1958. *d of*: Danny & Muriel Brindle. *Educ*: Haglay Park Comp., Rugeley, Staffs. *Studied*: Camberwell School of Arts (1979-82). *Represented by*: Falle Fine Art, Jersey. *Exhib*: solo: Falle Fine Art, Jersey (1998, 2007); Judges Exhibition,

Jersey Art Centre (2004); Stephen Lacy Gallery, London (2003); Portland Gallery, London (1992); Boundry Gallery, London (1992). *Works in collections*: Bill Hopkins; Paul Abbott; Jane Asher; John Falle; Ron Bowen. *Commissions*: Stanley Spencer Society, copy of 'Last Supper' by Stanley Spencer (1984, now in Cookham Church). *Publications*: The Dictionary of Artists in Britain since 1942 - David Buckram. *Works Reproduced*: Ron Bowen - Drawing Masterclass, p.133 (Ebury Press, 1992). *Principal Works*: 'Warrior', 1991 pastel & conté. *Recreations*: travel, reading, yoga. *Address*: 17 Ion Court, 280 Columbia Road, London E2 7RW. *Email*: brindle_sharon@yahoo.co.uk *Website*: www.sharonbrindle.com *Signs work*: 'Sharon Brindle.'

BRINDLEY, Donald, ARCA Sculpture (1951), FRBS (1973); sculptor in clay, bronze, ceramics of portraiture, equestrian subjects; Consultant to Josiah Wedgwood & Sons, Royal Worcester Porcelain Co., and continental and American businesses. *b*: Penkhull, Stoke-on-Trent, 22 Feb 1928. *s of*: Albert Brindley, pottery manager. one *s*. one *d*. *Educ*: Burslem College of Art. *Studied*: RCA (1948-51, Profs. Frank Dobson and John Skeaping, RA). *Works in collections*: HM The Queen, the late Lord Mountbatten. *Address*: Fernlea, Leek Rd., Stockton Brook, Staffordshire Moorlands ST9 9NH *Signs work*: "D. BRINDLEY"

BRINDLEY, Robert Edward, RSMA (1997) - Archivist (2004-present). *Medium*: watercolour, oil, pastel and acrylic. *b*: Burton on Trent, Staffs. 11 Feb 1949. *m*: Elizabeth Brindley (née Brooke). one *s*. one *d*. *Exhib*: Mall Galleries (RSMA and ROI); Ferens Hull; Carrisbrooke Gallery; Mercer Gallery, Harrogate; Houses of Parliament; Pure Watercolour Society. *Works in collections*: 'Royal Society of Marine Artists' Diploma Collection, National Maritime Museum, Falmouth, Cornwall. *Commissions*: paintings for "Allied Breweries UK Ltd." Burton on Trent. *Publications*: Author: Painting Boats and Coastal Scenery, Painting Landscapes in Oils, Painting with Pastels. Readers Digest: How to Paint Watercolours. Various contributions for The Artist and The Artist & Illustrator. Instructional painting DVDs. *Address*: Sundial Cottage, Sleights, Whitby, N. Yorks. YO22 5EQ. *Email*: mail@robertbrindley.com *Website*: www.robertbrindley.com *Signs work*: "Robert Brindley."

BRISCOE, Michael J., BA (Hons), RCamA; artist in oil and acrylic on canvas. *b*: Colwyn Bay, 11 May 1960. *s of*: T.J. Briscoe. three *s*. one *d*. two *s-d*. *Educ*: Eirias High School. *Studied*: Wrexham College of Art (1978-79, David Cooper), Sheffield City Polytechnic (1979-82, Brian Peacock, Terry Lee). *Represented by*: Martin Tinney Gallery. *Exhib*: Sheffield National (1980), Stowells Trophy (prize winner), Wales '83 Travelling Exhbn., RA Summer Exhbn. (1983-85), Through Artists Eyes Mostyn A.G., Paris Salon des Nations (1984), Blackthorn Galleries, Birkenhead (1998), Quay Arts, Kingson upon Hull (1999); mixed shows, Piccadilly Gallery (1984-85), RCA Conwy (2000), Martin Tinney Gallery; Dealer Plus One Gallery. *Works in collections*: Welsh Contemporary Art Soc., MOMA Wales. *Misc*: Selling paintings in Holland, Germany in 1995. *Address*: 81 Coed Coch Rd., Colwyn Bay, Clwyd LL29 9UW. *Website*: www.mikebriscoe.co.uk *Signs work*: "Mike Briscoe.".

BRISTOL, Sophy. *Medium*: oil. *b*: Brighton, 1973. *m*: Harry Darrell-Brown. *Studied*: Surrey Institute of Fine Arts. *Represented by*: Panter and Hall, London. *Exhib*: worldwide. *Address*: c/o Panter & Hall, 11-12 Pall Mall, London SW1Y 5LU. *Email*: enquiries@panterandhall.com *Website*: www.panterandhall.com *Signs work*: 'Sophy Bristol'.

BRIXEY-WILLIAMS, Julie, RBS; MA; Birgit Skiold Memorial Trust Award (2007); Leverhulme Trust Award (2003). *Medium*: sculpture, drawing, performance, collaborative practice. *b*: Leigh-on-Sea, 8 Jun 1961. *m*: Andrew. two *s*. *Studied*: Kingston University (1998-2000), (2000-2001). *Exhib*: Victoria & Albert Museum (2002); Mottisford Abbey (2013); The Strand Gallery, London (2013); Frost Museum, Miami (online curation, 2012); Dundee Contemporary Arts (2011); Collyer Bristow Gallery, London (2010); Glasgow

International Artist' bookfair (2008); Heriot Watt University (2004); Dartington College Gallery (2006); Barbican Library, London (2010); Orleans House Gallery, Twickenham (2004); Business Design Centre, London (2001). *Works in collections*: Tate Gallery Artists' Book Archive; Yale Centre of British Art; Birmingham Museum of Art Library; Association of Anaesthetists of GB & I; Queen Charlotte's Hospital, London; Laban Centre, London. *Commissions*: 'Arabesque' for the Campaign for Drawing (V&A, 2002). Publications: "Drawing Now: Between the Lines of Contemporary Art" (Tauris, 2007), "Step Feather Stitch: An Unfaithful Reading" (Choreographic Practices Vol 3 2012), "locationotation" (Art and Space, 2001), "point and place" (Art and Space, 2007), "Equals: Exploring Feminism through Art and Conservation" (Boobis, Kershaw eds. 2013), "From Portrait to Self-Portrait" (Antonio Nodar), "Magic Power Presence" (Iris, 2012). *Misc*: Founder Member of collaborative group "Point and Place" (6 artists), also collaborates with performer Libby Worth. *Address*: 27 St. James Avenue, Ealing, London W13 9DL. *Email*: juliebw@hotmail.com *Website*: www.juliebrixey-williams.co.uk *Signs work*: "Julie Brixey-Williams" and "JBW".

BROAD, Ronald Arthur, freelance artist in oil and water-colour specialising in winter landscape and line drawing. *b*: Crookham, Berks., 2 Sep 1930. *s of*: A.B. Broad, farmer and landowner. *Educ*: Newbury Grammar School, St. Aidan's College (C. of E.), Birkenhead. *Studied*: tutored by George Bissill. *Exhib*: regularly at RA. *Clubs*: Hockley Golf. *Address*: Belmont, Orchard Rd., S. Wonston, Winchester, Hants. SO21 3EX. *Signs work*: "Ronald A. Broad.".

BROBBEL, John Christopher, RBA, WCSI, PGCE, RAS (Cert.); awards, RAS silver medal for fig. drawing, David Murray studentship (1975-1976), British Inst. Fund award, Richard Jack prize, Landseer Scholar (1976-1977), Vincent Harris mural design prize, Painter Stainers bursary, Spirit of London prizewinner, RUA William Connor award; teacher and author. *Medium*: oil. *b*: Hartlepool, 16 Dec 1950. *m*: Rosemary Stapleton. *Studied*: Byam Shaw School of Art, under Peter Garrard PPRBA, RA Schools, under Peter Greenham RA. *Represented by*: Solomon Gallery, Dublin; James Wray, Belfast. *Exhib*: RA, RHA, RUA, RBA, NEAC, Cleveland International Drawing Biennial; solo exhibs.: Kilcock Gallery, Kildare, Jorgensen Fine Art, Dublin, Grant Fine Art, N. Ireland; William Franks, Monkstown, Co.Dublin. *Works in collections*: Sir Brinsley Ford, OPW, Dublin, Masonic Museum, Dublin, Trinity College, Dublin, St. James's Hospital, Dublin. *Commissions*: Masonic Museum, Dublin, Trinity College, Dublin. *Publications*: 'Drawing With Ink', and 'Pencil Drawing', F Warne, London (1981); articles, reviews for Artist magazine. *Official Purchasers*: Dept. Environment, N.Ireland. *Clubs*: United Arts, Dublin, Friends of National Gallery, Ireland. *Address*: 14 Lansdowne Park, Ballsbridge, Dublin 4, Ireland. *Signs work*: "John C. Brobbel.".

BRODERICK, Laurence John, ARBS, FRSA; NDD. *Medium*: bronze and stone, figurative esp. otter carvings and portrait heads. *b*: Bristol, 18 Jun 1935. *s of*: John Leonard Broderick. *m*: Ingrid. three *s*. *Educ*: St. Nichol's, Clifton, Bristol; Bembridge School, I.O.W. *Studied*: Regent St. Polytechnic (1952-57), Hammersmith School of Art (1964-65). *Exhib*: Royal Academy, Royal Scottish Academy, Royal Society of British Artists, Contemporary Portrait Society, Society of Wildlife Artists and the Royal West of England Academy, Exhibitions in Scotland, England, Jersey, France, Monaco, Germany, USA and Canada. *Commissions*: include The Bull, Birmingham; Leaping Salmon, Chester Business Park; Annual World Champion Trophies, International Tennis Federation; Goddess Athena and the Owl, Royal Caribbean International; Family of Otters, EON UK plc, Coventry; Turtle, Prudential plc Art Collection, London; Mother and Child, Diageo plc, Perth; Indian Elephant Calf, Royal Caribbean International; Teko, Kyleakin, Isle of Skye; Madonna and Child, All Saints, Weston-super-Mare; Tortoise, Turtle and Mayan Figures, Vision of the Seas; Crucifix, The Priory, Christchurch; Madonna of the Magnificat, The Priory, Dunstable; St

Mark and the Lion, St Mark's, Mansfield; Sir Roy Calne, Addenbrookes Hospital, Cambridge; June Marchioness of Aberdeen and Temair, Haddo Arts Trust; Philippe Chatriet, International Tennis Federation, Roland Garros, Paris. *Address*: Thane Studios, 10 Vicarage Rd., Waresley, Cambridgeshire SG19 3DA. *Email*: info@laurencebroderick.co.uk *Website*: www.laurencebroderick.co.uk *Signs work*: "Laurence Broderick.".

BROGAN, Honor, BA (English and French), DipEd (1967 and 1968, Cardiff). *Medium*: charcoal, oil, water-colour, clay, pastel. *b*: Welshpool, 26 Jan 1946. *m*: Diarmuid Brogan (decd). one *s*. *Educ*: Welshpool High School, University College, Cardiff. *Studied*: Morley College (Peter Richmond, Alan Thornhill and Tatiana Litvinov). *Exhib*: Artist in Residence, Lichfield Festiveal (1996, 2001); Celtic/Uzbek Exchange at Tashkent Artists Union (1995); RA Summer Exhbn (1997, 2008); Belgrave Hall Painters at Pump House, Battersea Park; BACF Royal Cambrian Academy (1999); Chelsea Arts Soc.; Sculpture for Rumania; GLC Peace Exhbn.; Not the Royal Academy; Albany, Cardiff (2000, 2002, 2005); Tabernacyl Machynlleth Summer Shows; Tenby Museum and Art Gallery (2007); Artist in Residence, Dore Abbey (2007); Dylan Thomas Museum, Swansea (2003); Fretwork Drawings at Sprout Contemporary Art (2011); Denise Yapp Contemporary Art - various exhibitions; Glyndebourne Opera Gallery (2008, 2010). *Works in Collections*: Slaughter and May Collection; Tenby Museum and Art Gallery. *Recreations*: walking, swimming, travelling, choral singing. *Misc*: Hugh Casson Drawing Prizes special commendation at RA Summer Show (2008). *Address*: 12 Westover Road, London SW18 2RG. *Email*: honorbrogan@hotmail.co.uk *Signs work*: "Honor Brogan", small works "H.B."

BROOKE, David, BA Hons (1978), SGFA (1993), UA (1994), NAPA (1997); Society for Art of the Imagination (1998); artist in oil, acrylic, pen and ink; President Soc. of Graphic Fine Art. *b*: Yeovil, 24 Nov 1956. *Studied*: Yeovil School of Art (1972-75), Hull College of Art (1975-78). *Exhib*: ROI, UA, SGFA, RWA, NAPA, South West Academy, plus fourteen one-man shows and many mixed exhbns. in England. *Works in collections*: Longleat House, Wilts. *Clubs*: S.G.F.A., U.A., N.A.P.A., Society for Art of the Imagination. *Misc*: Administrator, Yeovil Arts Centre, 80 South Street, Yeovil, Som. BA20 1QH. *Address*: 15a Severalls Park Ave. Crewkerne, Som. TA18 8DW. *Signs work*: "D. Brooke" or "David Brooke.".

BROOKES, Gerry, BA Hons Fine Art; RGN; BTEC Company Director Qsand Ltd, Morecambe; SAA Professional; FPS London. *Medium*: mixed media. *b*: Redditch, Worcs, 1944. divorced. *d of*: Clifford & Marion Harris. one *s*. two *d*. *Educ*: Bridley Moor, Redditch. *Studied*: North East Worcestershire College (1982-84); Margaret St. Birmingham University (1984-87). *Represented by*: Qsand Arts, Morecambe. *Exhib*: Piece Hall Gallery, Halifax; Royal Hallamshire Hospital, Sheffield; Cleveland International Drawing Biennale, Middlesborough; Brighton Women's Exhbn, Pankhurst Centre, Manchester; Book Project: Bromham Mills, Beds.; Westbury Farm Studios, Milton Keynes; Genesis Gallery, Norfolk; USA 2000 (ongoing); St.Peters UCLA, Preston; Bentham Gallery; Gregson Arts Centre, Lancaster; Folly Gallery, Lancaster; Creative Consultants Gall, Manchester; Frederick Finelines, USA; Maiden Bridge, Lancaster; Mid-Penning Gallery, Burnley; Inner City Living, Preston; Bankside Gallery, London; Jersey Gallery, London; Artshed, Leicester; Art Interiors-Internet Gallery, Qsand Arts, Morecambe (ongoing). *Commissions*: The Mariners, Lancaster; Wichfield Mural, Morecambe; Crufts Winner; various portraits, mural signposts (Morecambe). *Publications*: Freshfield Advertising Campaign, Lancashire. *Official Purchasers*: Nashbrooks, USA; Queen Alexander Hospital, Redditch; private collections. *Works Reproduced*: Freshfield Ad Campaign (Pearce Group). *Recreations*: Qsand Arts Project, Morecambe. *Misc*: Lecturer in art: Lancaster and Morecambe College; Cumbria Adult Education; WEA Liverpool. *Address*: 26a Lister Grove, Heysham, Lancs, LA3 2DF. *Email*: gerrybrookes26a@hotmail.co.uk *Website*: www.gerrybrookes.com *Signs work*: 'GMV BROOKES'.

BROOKES, Malcolm John, ATD (1964), RBSA (1974), RCA (1995); teacher, painter in gouache, oil and pastel. *b*: Birmingham, 11 Jul 1943. *s of*: William Brookes, telephone engineer. *m*: Norma Turner. one *s*. one *d*. *Educ*: Moseley School of Art. *Studied*: Birmingham College of Art and Crafts (1959-64, Gilbert Mason). *Exhib*: RBSA, Worcester A.G., Lichfield, Malvern, Stoke-on-Trent A.G., Dudley A.G., Icon Gallery, Birmingham, Royal West of England Academy, Mall Galleries, Royal Cambrian Academy. *Clubs*: R.B.S.A., RCamA, Birmingham and Midland Pastel Society. *Address*: 3 Clive Rd., Bromsgrove, Worcs. B60 2AY. *Signs work*: "M.J. Brookes.".

BROOKS, Alan Spencer, HS, SLm, ARMS. *Medium*: dry watercolour/ goache on watercolour paper. A very colourful, long lasting, photographic effect. *b*: Slough, 18 Oct 1960. *s of*: Dr.G.T.Brooks. *Exhib*: Mall Galleries (RMS); Adventureres Art Club, Hampstead Heath; Weald of Sussex Art Club (Burgess Hill), Adur Art Club (Shoreham-by-Sea). *Works in collections*: over 4000 paintings sold to general public in Shoreham/Worthing, Somerset, Lindfield, Haywards Heath, London, Lewis, Chichester. *Commissions*: accepts commissions of Landscape views of Sussex, and pet portraits in dry watercolour/gouache. *Publications*: RMS, HS, SLm catalogues. *Works Reproduced*: none. *Principal Works*: 3x4 painting of Jesus in the Garden of Gethsemany; miniatures in dry watercolour/gouache. *Clubs*: Abur Art Club, WOSAC, Adventurers Art Club. *Address*: The Dolphins, 40 Wykeham Way, Burgess Hill, RH15 0HF. *Signs work*: 'Alan S Brooks SLm, H.S., ARMS'.

BROOKS, Brenda, self taught artist specialising in oil - beach scenes/seascapes. *b*: London, 1932. *m*: William (decd). two *d*. *Educ*: Middleton College, Purley, Surrey. *Exhib*: Mall Galleries, various solo and mixed shows in London and South East. *Works in collections*: NatWest, Paintings in Hospitals. *Works in collections*: NatWest, Paintings in Hospitals. *Commissions*: Brighton Museum, CD covers for Voiceprint. *Misc*: owns Brooks Studios, 2 Heene Road, Worthing, Sussex, BN11 3SD for workshops in all aspects of art, and exhibitions to promote Sussex Artists. *Address*: The Pointed Gable, 35 West Parade, Worthing, Sussex BN11 5EF. *Email*: brendabrooks@tiscali.co.uk *Signs work*: "B.B.".

BROOMFIELD, Frances, BAHons; Awards - North West Arts (1989); Pollock Krasner Foundation Award, New York (1991); Oppenheim - John Downes (1993); London Arts Board (1995). *Medium*: Oils and tempera. *b*: Warrington, 29 Aug 1951. *m*: Terry Taylor. *Studied*: Warrington Art College (1967-1969); Newport Art College (1969-1972); studied life drawing with Cecil Collings 1980s Central School of Art. *Represented by*: Portal Painters, London since 1980. *Exhib*: Portal Gallery, London; Steinway Gallery, North Carolina, USA; Portals, Chicago, USA; Bremen Art Gallery; London Art Fair; Affordable Art Fair; Art London; C20/21 Art Fair, Birmingham City Art Gallery; Towner Gallery, Eastbourne; Bath Arts Festival; Warrington Museum. *Works in collections*: Warrington Museum and Art Gallery, Fairfield House Museum, Bath; Glasgow Museums; Guildford Musem and private collections. *Commissions*: A series of paintings of composers for a private client; illustration work including Russell Hoban's 'Medusa Frequency' book cover. *Publications*: 'A Singular Vision' (Wilder) Prestel (2009); 'The Lexicon Der Phantastischen Kunstler' (Habarta (2009)); 'The Dictionary of Artists in Britain since 1945' (Buckman) Art Dictionaries Ltd (1998). *Works Reproduced*: With Bridgeman Art Library several images reproduced, special interest in Lewis Carroll subjects. Also book covers for Colin Dann's 'Animals of Farthing Wood' series (Randon House). *Misc*: Worked with Ivor Cutler on an illustrated alphabet project. My painting 'George Formby - Speed Ace' projected onto 28 landmarks UK wide as part of BBC/PCF collaboration February 2013. *Address*: 107 Lord Street, Crewe, Cheshire CW2 7DP. *Email*: portalartist@btinternet.com *Website*: www.francesbroomfield.co.uk *Signs work*: "FB" as monogram inside a diamond shape.

BROTHERTON, Benjamin David, BA (Hons); MA; 2002 Graduation prize; 2005 Juliet Gomperts Trust; 2002-06 Artist in Residence, Kings School, Canterbury. *Medium*: oil, drawing. *b*: Cuckfield, 6 Oct 1978. *m*: Mollie Brotherton. two *s*. one *d*. *Studied*: Foundation: Reigate School of Art (1998); BS (Hons) 2002 & MA 2004 Canterbury Christ Church University College. *Represented by*: Grandy Art. *Exhib*: Chapel Gallery, Ormskirk (2004); Royal Society of British Artists Open (2005); Discerning Eye (2005); Royal Society of Oil Painters Open (2005); Grandy Art mixed shows (2006-12); Grandy Art solo shows (2008, 2010); Primavera Artistica del Gers, Calatayud, Spain (2010); The Little Gallery mixed shows, St. Emilion, France (2009-10); Jazz in Marciac, France (2007-present); Society of Wildlife Painters Open (2012); Ashdown Gallery, Sussex (2014). *Works in collections*: private & corporate. *Commissions*: private. *Official Purchasers*: Calatayud City Collection. *Address*: A Sansoulet, Sadeillan, France 32170. *Email*: ben_brotherton@hotmail.com *Signs work*: "B. Brotherton".

BROTHERTON, Mollie, BA, MA; 2010: Prix de Sculpture, St. Sever de Rustan Salon des Arts. *Medium*: ceramics, collage, drawing. *b*: Taunton, 25 Jan 1975. *m*: Ben Brotherton. two *s*. one *d*. *Studied*: Canterbury Christchurch University College (1994-7, 1999-2001); Somerset College of Art and Technology (1993-4). *Represented by*: Ashdown Gallery, Forest Row; Walford Mill Craft Centre, Wimbourne; New Ashgate Gallery, Farnham. *Exhib*: Jazz in Marciac, France (2009-2014); Salon des Arts, St. Sever de Rustan, Fr. (2011); Primavera Gersois, Calatayud, Spain (2010); Affordable Art Fair, London (2007); Art in Clay, Glasgow (2005, 2006); Rufford Craft Centre, Nottinghamshire (2003); Lie of the Land, Coombe Farm Gallery, Dartmouth (2002); Johnnies Art House, Whitstable (2001); Sarah Wiseman Art Gallery, Oxford. *Works in collections*: private and corporate, in UK, France and USA. *Commissions*: private. *Official Purchasers*: Reading City Council; Kings School, Canterbury. *Address*: A Sansoulet, Sadeillan, 32170 France. *Email*: mollie.brotherton@hotmail.com *Website*: www.terrain-vallone.co.uk *Signs work*: "MB".

BROWN, Alan Holtby. *Medium*: oil, watercolour. *b*: London, 16 Mar 1936. *m*: Jean. two *s*. *Studied*: London College of Printing; Ealing College of Art. *Represented by*: Alexander Miles Gallery Ltd., St.Katherine Docks, London. *Exhib*: Royal Academy Summer Exhibitions, Portal Gallery, Guildhall Art Gallery; Royal Exchange, London; Linda Blackstone, Pinner, Cockermouth, Castlegate House, Jersey Gallery, Osterley House, Sheen Gallery, Richmond; RBA, Mall Galleries (2003-2008); Royal Society of Portrait Painters (2008); Spencer Coleman, Stamford; Meller, Merceux, Oxford; Dolphin House Gallery, Colyton, Devon. *Works in collections*: throughout the world; Bolton Museum Art Gallery. *Publications*: Northern Editions. *Official Purchasers*: S.I.V.Cooke Fund; London Borough of Hillingdon. *Recreations*: drawing, music, walking, travel, woodwork. *Misc*: Have painted extensively in the Yorkshire Dales, Devon and London. *Address*: 29 Manor Way, Ruislip, Middx, HA4 8HE. *Signs work*: "Alan".

BROWN, Bob (Robert Auger), NDD (1956), NEAC (1964); painter in oil; Assistant Keeper, NEAC (1990-2007); Hon.Mem. NEAC (2001). *Medium*: oil. *b*: London, 10 Feb 1936. *m*: Susan. two *s*. *Studied*: Croydon College of Art (Fred Dubury, Lionel Bulmer). *Exhib*: usual mixed and private. *Works in collections*: private/corporate. *Misc*: Full name is Robert Auger Brown but known as Bob Brown *Address*: The Barn, 29 Park Road, Worthing BN11 2AS. *Email*: bob.augur@btinternet.com *Website*: www.bobaugurbrown.co.uk *Signs work*: "Brown.".

BROWN, Colin, BA (Hons) Painting (1986); Post Grad Diploma (1987); Pollock-Krasner Award, New York (1996); Scottish Arts Council Award (1998, 2001). *Medium*: paint and collage. b: Dundee, 16 Feb 1962. *Studied*: Duncan of Jordanstone College of Art, Dundee (1982-1987). *Represented by*: Fraser Gallery, St Andrews, Scotland; Icon Gallery, Singapore. *Exhib*: Includes solo: Panter & Hall, London (2010); Galerie Bongartz, Hanover (1998); Inverness Museum and Art Gallery (1997); Galerie Kulturfabrik, Krefeld (1993). Group: Kelvingrove Art Gallery, Glasgow (2011); Richard Hagen Gallery, Broadway (2006 to present); Landes Museum, Dusseldorf (1993). *Work in collections*: Private collections in UK, Italy, Germany, Netherlands, Denmark, Luxembourg, USA, Japan, Singapore. *Commissions*: Stadt Kramer Museum, Kempen, Germany (1994). *Publications*: Cutting Edges, Contemporary Collage, Berlin (2001); Collage: Assembling Contemporary Art, London (2008). *Works Reproduced*: In previously stated publications and other varied books and art magazines. *Misc*: Lived in Florence (1987) and Dusseldorf (1991-95); studio in Scotland since 1996. *Address*: 19 Bridgefield, Stonehaven, AB39 2HY. Email: colinbrown77@yahoo.co.uk *Website*: www.colinbrown.eu *Signs work*: "COLIN BROWN".

BROWN, David, President, Liver Sketching Club (2013, 2007, 2005; Past Secretary; Archivist). *Medium*: oil, pencil and ink, sculpture. *b*: Wirral, 14 Mar 1944. m: Susan Lee Brown. one *s*. one *d*. *Exhib*: Royal Cambrian Academy; Royal Birmingham Society of Arts; Liverpool Biennial/Independents; Williamson Art Gallery, Birkenhead; The Artists' Club, Liverpool; Holmfirth Art Week; Liverpool Cathedral; Pannett Art Gallery, Whitby, North Yorkshire; Highton Gallery, St. Paul's, London; Hanover Gallery, Liverpool; Heswall Arts Festival; The Gallery, Liverpool; Liverpool Academy of Art; etc. *Works in collections*: Private collections throughout the UK, plus USA (4), France (5), Spain (3), New Zealand (2), Australia (1) and Ukraine(1). *Commissions*: Various portrait commissions. A series of paintings depicting shop windows in Liverpool. *Recreations*: Collector of painting and drawings. *Clubs*: Liver Sketching Club; Wirral Society of Arts (Past Hon Sec); Two Rivers Art Group. *Misc*: Author of "The History of the Liver Sketching Club" (2013). Biographer of 1000+ artists linked to the Liver Sketching Club since it was founded in 1872. Curator. U3A Art Appreciation Co-ordinator; Qualified YachtMaster Offshore. Fellow of the Institute of Credit Management. *Address*: 105 Mark Rake, Wirral, CH62 2DJ. *Email*: davidartshed@yahoo.co.uk *Website*: www.wix.com/davidartshed/david-brown *Signs work*: "DAVID BROWN".

BROWN, Diana Elizabeth, SWLA (1967); painter in pen and ink, oil and watercolour; wildlife and animal artist and illustrator, specialises in deer and British wild mammals. *b*: Cambridge, 16 Apr 1929. *m*: Ian Alcock. *Educ*: Perse, Cambridge. *Studied*: Tunbridge Wells School of Art, and in Denmark. *Exhib*: SWLA, PS. *Works in collections*: private collections worldwide. *Commissions*: various books, animal portraits, wildlife paintings. *Publications*: Wildlife, deerstalking and scientific books, magazines and newspapers. *Recreations*: watching the abundant wildlife surrounding her home. *Clubs*: S.W.L.A., friend S.E.A., U.D.A.S., A.A.A. *Address*: Shannel, Ballogie, Aboyne Aberdeenshire AB34 5DR. *Website*: www.swla.co.uk *Signs work*: "Diana E Brown" and monogram of "DEB."

BROWN, Doris, SWA (1987); freelance landscape artist in water-colour and ink, tutor and lecturer. *b*: Newcastle under Lyme, Staffs., 17 Apr 1933. *d of*: Cecil Brown. *Educ*: Burslem College of Art, Stoke-on-Trent. *Studied*: Burslem and Stoke Schools of Art and privately under Reginald G. Haggar, RI, FRCA. *Exhib*: RI, BWS, SWA, and numerous one-man shows. *Works in collections*: Hanley Museum, Stoke-on-Trent and Newcastle Fine A.G., University of Keele; paintings in private collections in England, America, Italy, S. Africa. *Clubs*: President and tutor to: Newcastle Water-colour Soc., Blythe Bridge Water-colour Soc., Oulton Water-colour Soc. *Address*: 86 Dunbrobin St., Longton, Stoke-on-Trent, Staffs. ST3 4LL. *Signs work*: "Doris Brown S.W.A.".

BROWN, John, DA, RSW; Royal Academy Landscape studentship; Royal Scottish Academy Macaline Walters Bronze Medal; Glasgow SA Post.Dip. Highly Commended; Cargill Travel Scholarship, RSA; Carnegie Travel Scholarship; RGI James Torrance Award; SSAC Arts Club Award; Scottish Provident Award; Heinzel Gallery Award; RSW Alexander Munro Award. *b*: Irvine, Scotland, 19 Oct 1945. *s of*: Alexander Brown. *m*: Elizabeth (decd). three *s*. *Educ*: Ardrossand Academy. *Studied*: GSA. *Represented by*: Duncan Miller Fine Arts; Scottish Gallery. *Exhib*: DMFA; Scottish Gallery; Green Gallery; Heinzel Gallery;

John Davis, Richmond Hill, Thompsons, Stenton, Open Eye Gallery, Red Barn, London Art Fair, Glasgow Art Fair, 20/21 British Art Fair, RGI, RSW, Torvance Gallery, Moray House Chessel Gallery. *Works in collections*: Robert Fleming Holdings Ltd., Scottish Life Assurance Co. Ltd., Scottish Provident, John Menzies plc, Korean Embassy, Willie Art Gallery, University of Edinburgh, Kuwait Royal Family, Hugh Martin Partners, RBS. *Commissions*: portraits: Hugh McDiarmuid, Viscount Arbuthnot, Chenevix-Trench, British Steel Chairman, Royal Archers. *Official Purchasers*: Craigie College. *Works Reproduced*: A History of Scottish Art; Compendium of Scottish Art; Who's Who Scotland. *Principal Works*: 'Journey's End'. *Recreations*: gardening. *Address*: 92 Trinity Road, Edinburgh, EH5 3JU. *Signs work*: 'JOHN C. BROWN'.

BROWN, John Robert, formerly FRBS; sculptor in bronze and stone; formerly Head of Art, Hampstead Garden Suburb Inst. *b*: London, 7 Jul 1931. *s of*: Robert Brown. *m*: Pauline Brown. one *s*. one *d*. *Educ*: Queen Elizabeth's, Barnet. *Studied*: Hornsey School of Art, Hampstead Garden Suburb Inst. (Howard Bate, RA). *Works in collections*: Prudential Art Collection, Glaxosmith Kline Collection. *Commissions*: 'Joy of the Family', Priors Court School, Thatcham (2000); BBC People's Award Trophy (2000); 'Tête à Tête', Harpenden (2001); 2 sculptures for Central Middx. Hospital (2001), 2 sculptures for Crowne Plaza Hotel, Marlow (2003); 'Mother and Child' for St. John the Baptist, Chipping Barnet (2004); 2 Sculptures for Leconfield House, Curzon Street, London, W1 (2006); sculpture for Darent Valley Hospital, Kent (2014); Celebration II for Upper Chesapeake Medical Center, Bel Air, Maryland, USA (2013). *Address*: The Bow House, 35 Wood St., Barnet EN5 4BE. *Email*: info@johnbrown-sculptor.co.uk *Website*: www.johnbrown-sculptor.co.uk *Signs work*: "J.R. Brown.".

BROWN, Julian Seymour, ATD, NDD; painter and graphic designer in water-colour, acrylic and oil. *b*: Swansea, 3 Jul 1934. *s of*: Grandson of Seymour Brown, A.T.C. *m*: Gillian Thomas. two *s*. two *d*. *Educ*: Swansea Grammar School. *Studied*: Swansea College of Art (1950-55, Howard Martin), University College of Wales (1955-56). *Exhib*: one-man shows: WWAA Gallery, Henry Thomas Gallery, Trapp Art Centre (1989, 1990, 1991), The Session House Gallery (1991, 1992, 1993, 1994, 1995, 1996, 1997, 1998, 1999, 2001, 2002), The Abulafia Gallery (1998); work exhib. throughout the Principality. Bridge Gallery (1999, 2002), Goscar Gallery (2002), Patio Galler (2002), Oriel Emrys Gallery (2001), work accepted for 'Welsh Artist of the Year' (2001, 2002). *Works in collections*: Dyfed C.C. *Commissions*: 10 paintings for New Artists cards, Pembrokeshire; Paintings for Carmarthenshire Life Magazine. *Address*: Penyrallt, Alltycnap, Johnstown, Carmarthen, Carmarthenshire SA31 3QY. *Signs work*: "Julian Brown.".

BROWN, Keith, DipAD (First Class Hons), HDA, MA(RCA), Sir James Knott's Scholarship. *Medium*: Sculpture, Digital Sculpture, Computer Arts. *b*: Hexham, 29 Jan 1947. *m*: Jenny Brown. one *s*. two *d*. *Studied*: RCA; Cheltenham Fellow in Sculpture (1995/96); Junior Fellow in Sculpture Cardiff College of Art (1996/97). *Exhib*: SigGraph 2004, Art Gallery USA; St@rt_up 'Moving Sculpture' Museum of New Zealand; RA Summer Exhbns (2002, 2003, 2005); ISEA 2002 Artworks, Nagoya, Japan; 'Made Known' UTS Australia; 'Digital Art Exhibition' ISIMD3 2005, Turkey. *Works in collections*: International Print Collection, Krakow, Poland; Icondata World Print 2006. *Commissions*: Sale Leisure Centre, Sale, Cheshire. *Publications*: Rapid Prototyping Casebook 'Sculpture for the New Millennium'. *Official Purchasers*: Trondheim Kunstforening Norway; Welsh Arts Council. *Works Reproduced*: 'Outdoor Sculpture in Britain' RA Illustrated 2003. *Clubs*: MAFA. *Misc*: Director of Art and Computing Technologies Miriad M/C Met.Uni.; founder and president, Fast-UK (Fine Art Sculptors and Technology in the UK). *Address*: 18 Westfield Road, Chorlton-cum-Hardy, Manchester M21 0SP. *Email*: cyberform@ntlworld.com *Website*: www.homepage.ntlworld.com/cyberform *Signs work*: 'J.K.Brown'.

BROWN, Lucy, MA (Hons) Fine Art (1991); tutor; artist in mixed media installations and video. *b*: Herts., 4 Aug 1967. *Educ*: Haberdashers' Aske's School for Girls, Elstree. *Studied*: Edinburgh University and Edinburgh College of Art (1986-91). *Exhib*: SSA, group and solo shows in Scotland, UK and abroad. *Work in collections*: Edinburgh City Arts Centre, Glasgow Museums and Galleries. *Address*: 48 Montrose Terr., Edinburgh EH7 5DL. *Signs work*: "Lucy Brown" or not at all.

BROWN, Peter Edward Mackenzie, BA (Hons) Fine Art (1990), PGCE (FE) 1993, NEAC, PS, ROI; RP, Hon.RBA; Le Clerc Fowle Medal; Critic's Choice (NEAC: 2009, 2011, 2013);Lynn Painter Stainers Prize Runner Up (2012); Prince of Wales Award for Portrait Drawing 2008; Artist in Residence, Savoy Hotel (2006); Hunting Art Prize: Drawing Prize (2005); Crossgate Gallery Purchase Prize (2005); Arts Club Award (2001, 2002, 2008), W. H. Patterson Memorial Award (2000), Llewelyn Alexander Award (1999), Bristol Fine Art Prize, RWA (1998), St. Cuthbert's Mill Award (1997), Pastel Society Non-Members Award (1996); artist in oil, pastel and charcoal. *b*: Reading, 28 Jul 1967. *m*: Lisa Maria. three *s*. two *d*. *Studied*: Bath CHE (1986-87), Manchester Polytechnic (1987-90). *Represented by*: Messums, 8 Cork Street, London W1. *Exhib*: regularly with NEAC, ROI, PS, RA Summer Exhibition, Messums London, W.H. Patterson Fine Art Ltd. London, Victoria Art Gallery, Bath and Albany Gallery, Cardiff. *Works in collections*: National Library of Wales, Victoria A.G., Bath, Holburne Museum, Bath; Target Corporation; RAC Club; The Drapers Company; Howard de Walden Estate. *Commissions*: RAC Club, Pall Mall. *Publications*: "Brown's Bath: The Work of Peter Brown" pub. 2008, ISBN 978 0 95599727 06; "My Indian Travels" pub 2013 ISBN 978 19084864 17; 13 x exhibition catalogues. *Address*: 52 Combe Park, Bath BA1 3NH. *Email*: Peter@Peterbrownneac.com *Website*: www.Peterbrownneac.com *Signs work*: "Peter Brown" in handwriting.

BROWN, Philip, AMGP, former VPSIAC, former VPSCA; painter, stained glass artist, author. *b*: London, 4 Nov 1925. *s of*: Leslie Norman Brown, MA & Marjorie Brown. *m*: Gounil Hallin. five *d*. *Educ*: St. Paul's School, London. *Studied*: Slade School of Fine Art, Ateliers d'Art Sacré, Paris. *Exhib*: one-man shows: London, Brighton, Oxford, Paris, Carmargue, Madrid, Malaga, Alicante, Sweden, Japan. Art Underground, Eastbourne (Oct 2013). *Works in collections*: 15 books in Library, Sussex Downs College, Eastbourne; Prize painting Picasso's 90th Birthday Exhibition, Malaga. *Commissions*: stained glass in St. John's Cathedral, Umtata, S.A., many churches in England. *Publications*: Essentials of Drawing and Painting; Picture Making; Painter in Spain; Never Mind Picasso, Create Your Own World; Pen Drawing and Art of Hatching; Pages from Our Life; nine local history books (Ratton and Norman Trilogy) 3 A1 Millennium Maps for Willingdon, Jevington; 'Stained Glass'; 'The Quest' (Michelam Priory); Psychic books (2007-9) with Gounil from The Other Side: Life After Life, Into the Unknown; Thinking Ahead; The Next Stage; Happiness Over 400 Years (Reincarnations). *Address*: 1 Huggetts La., Lower Willingdon, Eastbourne, E. Sussex BN22 0LZ. *Email*: philipbrowniconpress@yahoo.co.uk *Signs work*: "Philip Brown.".

BROWN, Stephen Edward, RBA (1998). *Medium*: oil. *b*: Chard, 20 Dec 1947. *m*: Kathleen Irene. one *s*. one *d*. *Studied*: Somerset College of Art (1969-71), and privately with Patrick Larking, RP, ROI. *Exhib*: RWA, RBA, ROI, RA Summer Exhbn., Thompson's Gallery, Ainscough, Contemporary Art, all in London; Red Rag Gallery, Stow-on-the Wold; The Spa Galleries, Tunbridge Wells; The Minster Gallery, Winchester. *Address*: Apple Orchard, 63 Woolbrook Road, Sidmouth, Devon EX10 9XB. *Email*: sebrba98@aol.com *Signs work*: "S.B.".

BROWN, Susan Lee. *Medium*: oils, printmaking, conceptual - multi-discipline. *b*: 22 Jun 1949. m: David Brown. *Studied*: mainly self taught, with some fine art training at University of California. *Exhib*: Royal Cambrian Academy; National Exhibition of Wildlife Art;

Liverpool Biennial/Independents (solo and group shows); Williamson Art Gallery, Birkenhead; Liverpool Open; Liverpool Open Editions; Holmfirth Art Week; Liverpool Cathedral; Manchester Ary Fair; Heswall Arts Festival; House of Lords, London; the Gallery, Liverpool; Liverpool Adacemy of Art; Sefton Park Lodge, Liverpool; Dot-Art, varoius group and solo exhibitions. Visual Arts Director Heswall Arts Festival (2011); Advisor, Visual Arts Heswall Arts Festival (2012-13); Curator, Exhibition of 14 Artists Art in Wirral Left Bank of the Mersey; Heswall Arts Festival (2013); Curator, exhibition of artists from With These Hands (2011-12); Wirral Society of Arts Exhibition, Williamson Art Gallery (2009-2013); Wirral Open, Williamson Art Gallery (2008-2014); Wirral Spring, Williamson Art Gallery (2008-2013); De Junk - Re Junk Exhibitions (2010-2013); Liverpool Open, Editions Gallery Liverpool (2013); Liverpool Spring Open, Baltic Triangle Liverpool (2011-2014); National Exhibition of Wildlife Art (2011-2013); Liverpool Biennial Independents, Solo and Group shows (2008, 2010 and 2012). *Works in collections*: Private collections thorughout the UK, Europe and USA. *Comissions*: Hoylake mural commissioned by Wirral Borough Council Art and Culture Trail (2013). *Clubs*: Art on the Wirral; Wirral Society of Arts; Two Rivers Art Group; Dot-Art; Friends of the Williamson Art Gallery and Museum (Membership Secretary). *Address*: 105 Mark Rake, Wirral, CH62 2DJ. *Email*: brownds@talktalk.net *Website*: www.susanleebrown.weebly.com *Signs work*: "SUSAN LEE BROWN".

BROWN, Robert Auger. see Brown, Bob.

BROWNE, Piers, RA Schools Certificate (1975); John Player Portrait Prize (2nd, 1987); Artichoke Printmaking Prize (London, 2008); Painter of the North (Discerning Eye Show, London 2011). *Medium*: oil, etchings. *b*: London, 8 Sep 1949. *m*: Charlotte (decd). one *s*. two *d*. *Educ*: Byam Shaw 1968-70. *Studied*: RA Schools 1972-75. *Represented by*: Walker Contemporary Art, Harrogate; Highgate Contemporary Art, London; Pyramid Gallery, York. *Exhib*: RA Summer Shows, NEAC. *Works in collections*: Shore Capital, John Mortimer, HRH Prince Charles, Edward Guinness CVO, Julie Andrews, Julie Christie etc. *Commissions*: Christopher Andrew's houses, Richard Hall's portrait, Rick & Dida Lamb's Cornish Beach (2009) for example. *Publications*: A Shropshire Lad (1988); An Elegy in Arcady (1990); Wordsworth: A Lakeland Anthology (winner, WHSmith Illustrated Book of the Year '91); Wensleydale (1994); The Glorious Trees of Great Britain (2002); Sonnets for a Siren (2008). *Official Purchasers*: York City Art Gallery, Plymouth Art Gallery, V&A, British Museum, Bodleian, Cambridge University libraries. *Principal Works*: 'Return of the Boats' (etching, 2004); Ancient Pine:Rothiemurchas (oil, 2000), and seascape oils (2004-09). *Recreations*: walking, writing poetry, playing piano, travelling. *Clubs*: CPRE, Greenpeace. *Address*: Heugh, Nappa Scar, Askrigg, Leyburn, N Yorks DL8 3JY. *Email*: piersbrowne@btinternet.com *Website*: www.piersbrowne.com *Signs work*: 'PIERS BROWNE'.

BROWNING, Mary Helena, NDD (1956), ATD (1957), SEqA (1988); animal artist in pastel specialising in horses and dogs. *Medium*: Pastel. *b*: Watford, 15 Mar 1935. *Educ*: East Haddon Hall School, Northants. *Studied*: Southampton College of Art (1953-56), Leicester College of Art (1956-57). *Exhib*: SEA (annually since 1985); awarded President's Medal (1991). *Works in collections*: Kennel Club Gallery. *Publications*: Coursing - The Pursuit of Game with Gazehounds (Standfast Press, 1976), Rebecca, the Lurcher. *Works Reproduced*: Christmas cards each year for the JR Whippet Rescue and Italian Greyhound Rescu - Patron of both rescues. *Recreations*: riding. *Address*: Parish House, Greatworth, Banbury, Oxon. OX17 2DX. *Signs work*: "MARY BROWNING."

BROWNSWORD, Neil Joseph, MA (RCA), PhD; Winner of the British Ceramic Biennial (2009) Award. *Medium*: sculpture/installation. *b*: Stoke-on-Trent, 25 Nov 1970. two *s*. one *d*. *Studied*: University of Wales Cardiff (BA (Hons) Ceramics), London (MA

Ceramics and Glass), Brunel University (PhD). *Represented by*: Contemporary Applied Arts. *Exhib*: Ting, Thang, Trash, Permanenten, The West Norway Museum of Decorative Art, Bergen (2011); Relic, Brighton & Hove Museum (solo, 2011); Contemporary British Studio Ceramics, The Mint Museum of Art, USA (2010); Possibilities and Losses, Middlesborough Institute of Modern Art (2009); Elegy, Blås & Knada, Stockholm (solo, 2009). *Work in collections*: Victoria & Albert Museum, London; Middlesbrough Institute of Modern Art; Brighton & Hove Museum; National Public Art Council, Sweden. *Publications*: Whiting, D., 'Relic', Brighton & Hove Museum catalogue (2011). *Principal Works*: Salvage Series (2005); Relic (2011); Elegy (2009). *Address*: 294 Princes Road, Penkhull, Stoke-on-Trent ST4 7JP. *Email*: n.b@ntlworld.com

BRUCE, George J. D., PPRP (1991-94); elected RP (1959), Hon. Sec. (1970-84), Vice President (1985-90); portrait painter and painter of landscapes, still life, flowers etc. in oil; runs studios in London and Suffolk. *Medium*: oil and pencil. *b*: London, 28 Mar 1930. *m*: Jeanne C. Fleischmann (decd). *Educ*: by my portrait sitters. *Studied*: Byam Shaw School of Drawing and Painting (Brian D. L. Thomas, OBE, Patrick Phillips, RP, Peter Greenham, RA). *Exhib*: Royal Society of Portrait Painters, RA, David Messum Galleries. Over the years has painted and exhibited many flower pieces, still lifes, landscapes, etc. in the UK and abroad. *Works in collections*: Scottish National Portrait Gallery; numerous private. *Commissions*: has painted many private and official portraits male and female for the Church, City institutes, Colleges and businesses. *Principal Works*: three official portraits of Archbishop Ramsey for the Church of England, and Speaker George Thomas for the House of Commons. *Recreations*: skiing, windsurfing. *Clubs*: Athenæum. *Address*:6 Pembroke Walk, Kensington, London W8 6PQ. *Website*: www.georgebruceartist.com *Signs work*: 'George J.D. Bruce'.

BRUNSDON, John Reginald, ARCA (1958), RE (1995); full time artist in etching. *b*: Cheltenham, 1933. *m*: Ibby. one *s*. four *s-s*. one *s-d*. *Educ*: Cheltenham Grammar School. *Studied*: Cheltenham College of Art (1949-53, R.S.G. Dent, K. Oliver), RCA (Julian Trevelyan, Alastair Grant, Edwin Ladell). *Exhib*: one-man shows, England, USA, Canada, Australia, Sweden, Belgium. *Works in collections*: Arts Council, Tate Gallery, British Council, V&A. *Publications*: Technique of Etching and Engraving (Batsford, 1964). *Address*: Old Fire Station, Church St., Stradbroke, nr. Eye, Suffolk IP21 5HG. *Signs work*: "John Brunsdon.".

BRUNSKILL, Ann, Assoc. of Royal Society of Painter Etchers (1969); painter and printmaker. *b*: London, 5 Jul 1923. *d of*: Hugh George Edmund Durnford, M.C. *m*: John Brunskill. two *s*. one *d*. *Educ*: Langford Grove School. *Studied*: Central School of Arts and Crafts, Chelsea College of Art. *Works in collections*: V&A, Bibliothèque Nationale, University College, Oxford, South London Collection of Original Prints, Lib. of Congress, Washington, USA, J. Lessing Rosenwald Alverthorpe Coll., USA, Universities of Princeton, Yale, USA, National Library of Australia, Canberra. *Address*: Star & Garter Cottage, Egerton, Ashford, Kent TN27 9BE. *Signs work*: "Ann Brunskill" and "AB" with date on paintings.

BRUNWIN, David Martin, MA, D.Phil.(Oxon); painter in water-colour and oil. *b*: Banbury, Oxon, 27 Nov 1939. *m*: Margaret. one *s*. one *d*. *Educ*: Oxford University. *Exhib*: RSMA, RI. *Publications*: pages in 'The Wapping Group of Artists -Sixty Years of Painting by the Thames' (Oct 2005), ISBN 0-9547062-5-0. *Clubs*: Wapping Group of Artists. *Address*: 40 Snells Wood, Cokes Lane, Little Chalfont, HP7 9QT. *Email*: david@brunwin.com *Signs work*: "David Brunwin" or "DMB."

BRYANT-DUNCAN, Enid Dena, (née Bond); artist in oils, scraper-board, water-colour; retired gallery owner and restorer. *b*: Gloucester, 19 Mar 1930. *m*: Terry Duncan. three *s*.

Educ: Red Maids' School, Westbury-on-Trym, Bristol. *Studied*: Royal West of England Academy of Art. *Exhib*: St. Albans Gallery (1975), St. Albans Museum (1970), Paris, Salon de Nations (Jan. 1983), R.H.S. International Exhbn. (Mall Galleries, 1984), St. Albans Gallery (1987), Paris (1987), Galerie Salammbo, Paris (1988), St. Albans Abbey (1991), Luton Hoo Station House (1996, 1998), Artists Corner, Chepstow (1999), Newnham Art Exhbn. (2001), The Manse, Westbury-on-Severn (2002). *Works in collections*: St. Albans, South Africa, Canada, America, France *Commissions*: mural in local church 'Healing Angel' (2004). *Publications*: True Ghost Stories (Hamilton); 'True Ghost Stories of the Forest of Dean' (A Manse Publication, 2008); 'Fairies Angels and Beasts of the Forest of Dean; Old and New Family Recipes from the Forest of Dean; Dena;' Herbal Remedies (illustrated); Dena's Country Cakes. *Recreations*: gardening, patchwork, church, painting, writing. *Misc*: 3 TV appearances, radio, magazine articles, newspapers. *Address*: The Manse, The Village, Westbury-on-Severn, Glos. GL14 1PA. *Signs work*: "D.B.", "Dena" or a snail.

BRYCE, Gordon, ARSA (1976), RSA, RSW (1976); Diploma in Art; numerous awards since 1965 including Chalmers Bursary, RSA; Keith Prize , RSA (1965), 1st Prize Pernod Scottish Academy Competition (1967); Arts Council Awards (1968, 1971, 1980), Latimer Award, RSA (1969), May Marshall Brown Award (1977), Educational Institute of Scotland Award (1981), Shell Expo, Premier Award (1982), Sir William Gillies Travelling Scholarship (1984). *b*: Edinburgh, 30 Jun 1943. *s of*: George and Annie Bryce. *m*: Hilary. three *s*. two *d*. *Studied*: Edinburgh College of Art under Sir Robin Philipson and Sir William Gillies (1965). Appointed lecturer in printmaking, Grays School of Art, Aberdeen; Head of Fine Art, Grays School (1986-1995). Currently painting full-time. *Represented by*: Thackeray Gallery, London. *Exhib*: 50 one-man shows throughout Britain, USA and Ireland 1955-2011. *Works in collections*: private collections throughout Britain, Ireland, USA, Canada, Europe, Australia and the Far East. *Recreations*: fishing. *Address*: 2 Culter House Road, Milltimber, Aberdeen, AB13 0EN. *Website*: www.gordonbryce.co.uk

BRYCE, Hazel Virginia, (previously FOSTER); Diploma Foundation Studies Art and Design (2000); Winner, Pen Ink (Artists & Illustrators Magazine, 1996); mainly self-taught. *Medium*: drawing, prints, sculpture, specifically papier mâchè sculpture. *b*: Henley-on-Thames. *d of*: Professor Bryce-Smith. one *s*. *Studied*: Reading College and School of Arts and Design (2000). *Exhib*: RA Summer Exhbn (1999); Beatrice Royal, Eastleigh, Natural World Exhbn (2000); Christie's 'Art for Life' (2001, 2002); Oxfordshire Open Art Weeks (2002, 2003). *Commissions*: Reading Museum (to make papier mâchè figures for Reading Rock Festival Exhbn, 2004) *Principal Works*: 'The Sea Horse' (papier mâchè). *Address*: 7 Elm Court, Sonning Common, Reading RG4 9ND. *Email*: hazel@hazelbryce.wanadoo.co.uk *Signs work*: 'H.Bryce' or 'Hazel Bryce'.

BRYCE, John Dunbar, BSc (Eng) in Engineering, SWE, GAvA, RE. *Medium*: watercolour, wood engraving, oils. *b*: 17 Nov 1934. *m*: Ann Margaret. one *s*. one *d*. *Educ*: Glyn Grammar School 1946-53. *Studied*: Kings College London 1953-56 (Mechanical Engineering); self-taught in art. *Exhib*: Bankside Gallery, Mall Galleries, Guildhall Winchester, Wapping Group of Artists, Guild of Aviation Artists, Royal Academy, Guildhall London. *Works in collections*: Science Museum, Museum of Flight Scotland, RAF Museum, Ashmolean Museum, Cutty Sark Trust. *Commissions*: 'Thrust' World Land Speed Record. *Publications*: Printmakers Secrets, Wapping Group of Artists - Sixty Years of Painting by the Thames. *Official Purchasers*: Rolls-Royce, British Aerospace, Messier-Dowty, RAF Museum Hendon, Museum of Flight Scotland, Farnborough Air Sciences Trust. *Principal Works*: Cutty Sark Conservation Bomb Aimer; Thames Barrier. *Clubs*: Royal Society of Painter-Printmakers, Society of Wood Engravers, Farnham Art Society, Wapping Group of Artists, Guildford Art Society. *Address*: 37 Copse Ave, Weybourne, Farnham, Surrey, GU9 9EA. *Email*: scorperjohn@btinternet.com *Signs as*: "John Bryce".

BRYON, Dilys Muriel, *Medium*: oil, watercolour, drawing, prints, ceramic. *b*: West Bridgford, Nottingham, 27 Sep 1930. *m*: Derek Banham. three *d*. *Educ*: Wesbridgeford High School, Nottingham High School for Girls. *Studied*: Wimbledon School of Art (1947-51), London University of Education (1951-2), London University Birkbeck College (1997-2001), Morley College London (Etching/Mezzotint 1974-9), Atelier Contrepoint Paris (1991, 3 months). *Represented by*: Musée Adzak, Paris; Printmakers Council London. *Exhib*: Bankside Gallery, London (2010, mixed, PMC); Vyner St. Gallery "Untitled" (2011, mixed, PMC); 'Acquire Art' Gallery, London (group, 2011); 'Originals '04', Mall Galleries, National Society of Painters Sculptors & Printmakers, Westminster Gallery, London (2002); Pump House, London (solo, 1995), The First Gallery, Southampton (2014 solo). *Work in collections*: Embragel University, Cabo Frio, Brazil; Scarborough Art Gallery; Brunel University, London; Tamar Art University, Japan; Musée Adzak, Paris. *Publications*: "The World Who's Who of Women" (1990/91 p.120), "Dictionary of Artists in Britain since 1945", David Buckman (p.206). Article in 'Printmaking Today' by Dilys Bryon relating to Hayter Method print 'Molten Sea and Sky' - etching, "Outside Eye, Inside Eye" (booklet, illustrated) by Derek Banham and Dilys Bryon, "Idea and Process" (booklet by Dilys Bryon illustrated). *Works Reproduced*: "Throughout the Laurels", "Through the Walnut Tree", "Maize Field". *Principal Works*: "Trapped Bird" oil (1968), "Dorset August" monoprint (2000). *Recreations*: reading, theatre, concerts, languages (especially French). *Address*: Monks Green Farm, Cobham Road, Fetcham, Surrey KT22 9RU. *Email*: dilysbryon@tecres.net *Signs work*: "Dilys Bryon".

BUCHANAN, Hugh Ross, *Medium*: watercolour. *b*. Edinburgh, 29 May 1958. *m*: Ann de Rohan. three *d*. *Studied*: Wellington College, Edinburgh College of Art (1976-81). *Represented by*: Francis Kyle Gallery. *Exhib*: Henderson Gallery Edinburgh (1982), Cale Art London (1982), Scottish Gallery (1984 etc.), Francis Kyle Gallery (1986 etc.), Bilbao Art Gallery (1987), Lincoln Center New York (1991), Petworth (1994), National Gallery of Wales (1998), National Theatre (1998), Queens Gallery (2005), University of Aberdeen (2009), Summerhall, Edinburgh (2013). *Works in collections*: HM The Queen Mother, HRH The Prince of Wales, Victoria & Albert Museum, National Trust, City of Edinburgh, Deutsche Bank, Flemings Bank. *Commissions*: Palace of Westminster, Bank of Scotland, University of Edinburgh, University of Aberdeen *Publications*: 'The Eloquence of Shadows' (1994), Winter Light (2010). *Official Purchasers*: HM Queen Mother Lying in State (House of Lords 2002). *Recreations*: motorcycle maintenance. *Clubs*: BSA Owners Club. *Misc*: Board Member: Govt. Arts & Heritage Committee (1989), Scottish National Trust (1990-92), Dundee Contemporary Arts (1996), Scottish Arts Council (1997-2000). Address: Woodhall, Pencaitland, East Lothian, EH34 5DH. *Email*: hughbuchananartist@gmail.com *Website*: www.hughbuchanan.co.uk *Signs work*: "Buchanan".

BUCK, Jon, MA, RWA, ARBS; sculptor in bronze. *b*: Bristol, 8 Sep 1951. *m*: Jane Buck. two *d*. *Studied*: Trent Polytechnic (1976-79), Manchester Polytechnic (1979-80), Fellow at Cheltenham College of Art and Design (1980-81). *Represented by*: Gallery Pangolin. *Exhib*: one-man shows: 2011 'Making a Point: The Point of Making' Gallery Pangolin; 2009 'Behind the Lines' Pangolin, London; 2005 'Odd Birds & Other Selves' Gallery Pangolin; 2000 'Intimate Connections' Gallery Pangolin. *Commissions*: 1995: 'Stret Beacon' Porthcawl; 'On Our Heads' Harlesden; 1996: 'New Age' British Consulate, Hong Kong; 1997: 'Common Knowledge' Merthyr Tydfil; 1998: 'Embracing the Sea' Deal; Returning to Embrace', Canary Wharf,; 2000: 'In the Swim' West Quay, Southampton; 2001: 'Family' and 'Equilibrium' Milton Keynes General Hospital; 2002: 'Family', Paddington Central; 2004: 'Flat Out', Bristol University; 2007: 'From Ship to Shore', Portishead Marina. *Publications*: 'Jon Buck Making a Point: The Point of Making' 2011 ISBN 978-0-9570417-0-7. *Address*: Luther Cottage, 619 Wellsway, Bath BA2 2TY. *Email*: jondbuck@hotmail.com *Website*: www.jonbucksculpture.com

BUCKLEY, Patricia Ann, BA (Hons) 1987. *Medium*: oil, watercolour, drawing, prints. *b*: Sussex, 23 Jul 1947. *d of*: Tom & Gladys Buckley. *Studied*: Kingston University, Surrey (1984-87). *Exhib*: Lynn Painter-Stainer Prize/Exhibition (2009); Royal Academy Summer Exhibitions (1965, 1966, 1979, 1984, 1985, 1986, 1992, 1995, 1998, 2000, 2004, 2009). Mixed exhibitions: Piccadilly Gallery, W1 (1982, 1983, 1987); Francis Kyle (1988); Belgrave Gallery NW3 (1997): Hunting Group Nat. Art Comp. (1987, 1990); Discerning Eye Nat. Comp. (1991, 2003, 2004). *Works in collections*: University of London (Institute of Education), private collections UK and USA, *Commissions*: book jacket "The Duke of Danzig" by Alan Truex (2005) Visited Gdansk to sketch the Golden Gate entrance 1988. *Publications*: Medici Society greetings card (Window painting, oils). *Recreations*: walking, writing, reading, cinema, travelling. *Misc*: Solo exhibition: The Art Centre, Institute of Education, University of London (1979) reviewed in Arts Review, Dec 1979. *Address*: 8 Kingfisher Lodge, Strawberry Vale, Twickenham, TW1 4SL. *Email*: patriciabuckley@uk2.net *Website*: www.patriciabuckley.co.uk *Signs work*: "P.B." (post 1979, minus etchings).

BUCKMAN, David John, qualified teacher, history specialist; full-time journalist for 50 years, since 1998 exclusively on art. *b*: Ringmer, Sussex, 20 Jun 1936. *s of*: Ernest Perceval Buckman & Dorothy Buckman. *Educ*: College of St. Mark and St. John, Chelsea (1957-59); Portsmouth Training College/Southampton University (1959-60). *Studied*: history. *Publications*: 'Dictionary of Artists in Britain since 1945'; contributed to Macmillan's 28-vol 'Dictionary of Art', and Brian McFarlane's 'The Encyclopedia of British Film'. Artists' monographs include J B Manson, Leonid Pasternak, Jonathan Clarke, Mary Griffiths, Martin Leman, Roderic Barrett, Katherine Hamilton, Glyn Morgan; 'Mixed Palette' a study of Frank Ward and Kathleen Walne; 'Charles Debenham's East Anglia'; biography of sculptor A.H. Gerrard; 'From Bow to Biennale: Artists of the East London Group'; contributor to The Independent, The Guardian and The Jackdaw; advisor, The Public Catalogue Foundation. *Clubs*: The Critics' Circle. *Address*: 2 Ufton Grove, London N1 4HG. *Email*: dbuckman@writer1.plus.com

BUCKMASTER, Emma Elizabeth, MA. *Medium*: prints. *b*: UK, 13 May 1957. *m*: Simon. three *s*. one *d*. *Studied*: Exeter University (1976-79); Essex University (2000-03); Cambridge School of Art (ARU, 2006-09). *Exhib*: Royal Academy Summer Exhibition (2013); Norwich Castle (2012); Art in Action, Waterperry (2014). *Address*: Moores Farm, Felsham, Bury St. Edmunds, Suffolk IP30 0PU. *Email*: emmabuckmaster@btinternet.com *Website*: www.emmabuckmaster.com *Signs work*: "EMMA BUCKMASTER".

BUDD, Rachel, RCA, BFA (Hons), MFA (Hons); painter in oil on canvas; part-time lecturer, Cheltenham College of Art and Design, and Central St. Martin's School of Art. *b*: Norwich, 6 Mar 1960. *d of*: David John Budd. *Studied*: University of Newcastle upon Tyne (1978-82, Prof. Rowntree), RCA (1983-86, Peter de Francia). *Exhib*: one-man shows: Purdy Hicks (1991), '3 Ways' British Council travelling show, Hungary, Poland, Czechoslovakia (1990), Athena Art Awards (1987), London Group (1987), Lloyds Bldg. Art for the City (1987), RA Summer Exhbn. (1987), Contemporary Arts Soc. Market, Covent Gdn. (1987). *Works in collections*: County Nat.West. London, IBM, Contemporary Art Soc., Lloyds of London, Arthur Anderson Collection, ICI. *Address*: The Padstow Studio, 30 Duke Street, Padstow, PL28 8AB.

BUDD, Tiffany Jane, BA Hons Textile Design; Signature status of UKCPS; Finalist, New Artists Competition, Demontfort Fine Art Publishers (2005), second in Caran D'ache competition. *Medium*: watercolour, drawing, acrylics, pastels. b: Kingston upon Thames, 30 Mar 1973. one *d*. *Studied*: Wimbledon School of Art (Foundation, 1991-92); University of Plymouth (1992-95). *Represented by*: Image by Design, The Art Bay Gallery, Arte Arts, Fiesta Collectables. *Exhib*: Cranleigh Arts Centre (2012), Thames Ditton Library Gallery

(2012); UKCPS Annual Exhibition, Westminster (2011); Inchmore Gallery, Inverness (2011); Gallery on the Square, Usk, Wales. *Work in collections*: numerous in private collections. *Commissions*: 'The Beehive', Wetherspoons Group at Gatwick South Terminal; Derwent Pencil Company (four tin lids commission); Marks & Spencer (Wall Art Department). *Official Purchasers*: Wetherspoons Pub Chain; Dembies Wine Estate, Dorking, Surrey. *Works Reproduced*: mainly through Image by Design. *Principal Works*: A style the artist has developed called 'fractured', using light perspective and movement as its key source using lines. *Recreations*: demonstrations for Art Societies and Clubs. *Clubs*: Member, Fine Art Trade Guild. *Address*: 2 Westbrook, 13 Portsmouth Road, Thames Ditton, Surrey KT7 0SY. *Email*: tiffanydowling@wall-power.co.uk Website: www.tiffanybudd.co.uk *Signs work*: "Tiffany Budd".

BUHLER, Michael Robert, ARCA; Rowney Award, Royal Academy (1984); artist in oil and acrylic. *b*: London, 13 Jun 1940. *s of*: Robert Buhler, RA. one *s*. one *d*. *Educ*: Bryanston School. *Studied*: Royal College of Art (1960-63, Carel Weight, Roger de Grey, Ruskin Spear, Colin Hayes). *Exhib*: Galeria Boitata, Porto Alegre, Brazil, Museo do Estado da Bahia, Brazil, Eastern Arts Assoc., New Art Centre, RA, England Gallery, Chappel Gallery. *Works in collections*: Liverpool University, Carlisle City A.G., BM, Arts Council, RA, DOE. *Commissions*: Posters for British Museum (1979); UFO illustrations, Mary Evans Picture Library. *Publications*: Tin Toys 1945-1975 (Bergstrom and Boyle). *Clubs*: Chelsea Arts. *Misc*: "Abductees" animated film (1994). *Address*: 6 Cavell St., London E1 2HP. *Website*: www.michaelbuhler.org *Signs work*: "Michael Buhler."

BULBROOK, Kaija. SWA (Council); BA (Hons). *Medium*: pastel, acrylic, oil, charcoal, etching, aquatint, monoprints. *b*: London. *m*: Stephen. one *s*. one *d*. *Studied*: Kingston College of Art. *Represented by*: Red Leaf Gallery, Tunbridge Wells; Nick Hills. *Exhib*: Mall Galleries, London (PS, SWA); The Red Leaf Gallery, Tunbridge Wells; Bay Art Gallery, Margate; Picturecraft Gallery, Holt, Norfolk; various other venues in the S.E. of England. *Address*: Rogley Farm, Cranbrook Road, Biddenden, TN27 8ET. *Email*: bulbrook@rogley.wanadoo.co.uk *Signs work*: 'Kaija Bulbrook'.

BULGIN, Sally, BA (Hons), MA, PhD (History of Art); painter in acrylic; Editor, The Artist magazine. *b*: Ashford, Kent, 8 Nov 1957. *d of*: Ernest Bulgin. *Educ*: Highworth School for Girls, Ashford. *Studied*: Reading University (1977-81, Terry Frost), Courtauld Inst., London (1981-91). *Exhib*: RA Dip Galleries, NAPA, Clare College, Cambridge. Work in private collections. *Publications*: author of Acrylics Masterclass (1994); Oils Masterclass (1996); Lucy Willis: Light in Watercolour (1997), (all Harper Collins); Ken Howard: Inspired by Light (David & Charles, 1998); Consultant editor Collins Art Class (1999, Harper Collins). *Clubs*: Patron, National Assoc. of Painters in Acrylics; Hon. Vice-Pres., Royal Birmingham Soc. of Artists. *Address*: Clougy House, Canterbury Road, Brabourne, Ashford, Kent, TN25 6QP. *Signs work*: "Sally Bulgin."

BULL, Anne, SWA, ASEA. *Medium*: figurative painter in oils, pastels, acrylic and watercolour. *b*: Ealing, W. London, 22 Jul 1940. *d of*: Oliver Hamilton Bull, BA (Hons), Artist. *m*: Geoffrey William Bull, CEng, FRACS. one *s*. *Studied*: Ealing School of Art, National Portrait Gallery w/shop, London Sketchclub, Mary Ward Centre Holborn. *Exhib*: Mall Galleries, London with: RSMA, RP, PS, SWA, SEA, Art for Youth; Chelsea Arts Society; Webbs Gallery; Llewellyn Alexander; St. Ives Soc Artists; Carlyle Gallery; Fowey River Gallery; Gallery 12, Cheltenham; Long Curve Gallery, Glos; Wymore Assoc. Cincinnati, USA; Battersea Affordable Art Fairs, Chelsea Arts Fair, Neville Fine Art. Solo exhbn: Mariners Gallery, St. Ives. *Works in collections*: UK and internationally. *Commissions*: Earls Court Boat Show for Cosmos Int.; British Airways (Operation Happy Child); BA Publicity Open Days. *Publications*: 'Chelsea Morning' in Leisure Painter mag.; '100 Ways to Paint People' via International Artist; Millers Art Guide, Paintings 18th

Century to Present (2005). *Principal Works*: figurative oils. *Clubs*: mem. Chelsea Art Soc. St. Ives Soc. of Artists; Fellow, Moseley Art Society. *Address*: The Cow Barn, Trevithal Farm, Paul, Penzance, Cornwall, TR19 6UQ. *Email*: annesstudio@aol.com *Signs work*: 'Bull'.

BULLIVANT, Tina, BA Hons; artist in water-colour, mixed media, oil. *b*: Brighton, 25 May 1958. *m*: Clive Bullivant. one *s*. *Educ*: Lourdes Convent. *Studied*: Brighton University (1976-80, Luther Roberts, Robert Birch). *Exhib*: SWA Sussex Open, Guild of Sussex Artists Open Exhbn., many mixed exhbns. *Works in collections*: Crawley Arts Council. *Clubs*: Artists of the Weald. *Address*: 110 Streatfield Rd., Uckfield, E. Sussex TN22 2BQ. *Signs work*: "T. Bullivant, S.W.A."

BULLOCK, Hazel, MFPS (1970); painter in oil and acrylic. *Studied*: St. Martins School of Art, Sir John Cass School of Art (1962). *Exhib*: RBA, FPS, HAC, Browse and Darby, Whitechapel; one-man shows, Loggia Gallery (1973), Judd St. Gallery (1985), Phoenix Gallery, Highgate (1989), Phoenix Gallery, Lavenham (1989), dn Gallery New York (2000), Loggia Gallery, London (2001), mixed exhibitions. *Works in collections*: private collections in England and Spain. *Clubs*: Arts. *Address*: 32 Devonshire Pl., London W1G 6JL. *Signs work*: "H. Bullock."

BUMPHREY, Nigel, schoolmaster, goldsmith, and furniture maker; Diocesan adviser to Diocese of Norwich for Church Plate; Freeman of the Worshipful Company of Goldsmiths & The City of London; Fellow of the Royal Society of Arts; Fellow of the Society of Antiquaries (FSA). *b*: Norwich, 22 Feb 1928. *s of*: Herbert Bumphrey. *m*: Eileen. *Educ*: The City of Norwich School and Loughborough College (now Loughborough University). *Studied*: Central School of Arts and Crafts and Norwich Art School. *Exhib*: Norfolk Contemporary Crafts Soc., and others, Goldsmiths' Hall. Works mainly on commissions. *Works in collections*: Norwich City Collection. *Commissions*: Badges of office for various societies - British Association of Occupational Therapists, Travelling Club of Surgeons of Gt. Britain et al. *Principal Works*: Domestic Plate and Church Silver. *Clubs*: Royal Overseas League. *Address*: 28g Jessopp Rd., Norwich NR2 3QB.

BURBRIDGE, Claire-Chantal Emma, BA (Hons) Fine Art and History of Art (Oxon), MA Printmaking; fine artist in sculpture, printmaking and painting. *b*: London, 14 Dec 1971. *m*: Joby Talbot (Composer). one *s*. *Studied*: Magdalen College, Oxford, Ruskin School of Fine Art (1990-93), Camberwell College (1993-95). *Represented by*: USA: Toomey Tourrell Gallery, San Francisco; Davis and Cline Gallery, Ashland, Oregon. *Exhib*: Toomey Tourrell Gallery, San Francisco, USA; Davis and Cline Gallery, Ashland, Oregon, USA; Coram Gallery London, Mall Galleries, Collyer Bristow, RWA, St. John's College Oxford, M.W. Contemporary Art, Hanging Space London, Attendi London, etc. *Works in collections*: Ashmolean Museum, Oxford, Herts.CC Art Collection. *Address*: 16 Denman Rd., Peckham, London SE15 5NP. *Email*: claire-burbridge@hotmail.co.uk *Website*: www.claireburbridge.com

BURGE, Pery, BA (Hons) Mus Ed (1970); Cert Higher Ed Pass Graphic Arts (1994); Full Member National Society (NS) (2009). *Medium*: Ink on paper; ink in water photography. *b*: Launceston, 26 Feb 1955. *Studied*: Gipsy Hill College, Kingston (1973-79); Anglia Polytechnic University (1992-4). *Exhib*: Opens: Air Gallery, London; Phoenix, Exeter; Whiteleys, London; Gallery 47, London; Simpleward, Exeter. Solo: Chenies St, London; West Dean, Chichester; Merlin, Sheffield; Innovation Centre, Exeter. Conferences: ISFV Gottingen (2006); ISFV Nice (2008). *Work in collections*: Exeter University Library; Harrison Building and Centre for Business and Climate Solutions. *Publications*: Full papers: Journal of Visualization 10:2 April 2007 pp.171-178 'Hidden Patterns: Creating Radial Spreads of Ink in Water'; Leonardo 40:5 October 2007 'Looking Beneath the Surface; The

Radial Spread of Ink in Water'; Journal of Visualization 12:2 April 2009 pp. 173-180 'Patterns of Ink in Water and Air: Creating Radial Spreads of Ink in Water'. *Recreations*: Photography; music, walking. *Misc*: Artist in residence, Exeter University, funded by The Leverhulme Trust, studying artistic flow visualization (2011-2012). *Address*: Old Meeting Hall, Winters Lane, Ottery St Mary, Devon EX11 4AW. *Email*: pery@mac.com *Website*: www.chronoscapes.com *Signs work*: "PERY BURGE".

BURGESS, Brenda Jean, BA (Hons). *Medium*: oil, prints, sculpture. *b*: Merseyside, 3 May 1961. *d of*: Jean and David Pennington. *m*: Ian. two *s*. *Educ*: Astor of Hever. *Studied*: Kent Institute of Art & Design; University College, Christ Church, Canterbury. *Exhib*: Mall Galleries (2007); Marlowe Gallery, Canterbury (2004/05); Bentliff Gallery, Maidstone (2001/02); RA (2001); Johnnie's Art Warehouse, Whitstable (2000); Ayres Gallery, London (1997); Bowe House, Canterbury (1997); Gallery on the Green, Bearsted (1994/96). *Works in collections*: Alan Wisket (Deal), William Smith (Sussex), Delyss Byrd (Lenham), Annie Gardner (Otham), Jon Graham (Leeds), Paula Tresnan (Cranbrook), T. Scrivens (Weavering), V. White (Yalding), R. Hurst (Kent). *Commissions*: many portrait sculptures, including: Oliver, Georgie, Charlie, Jack, Harry, Toby, Sasha, Luke, Kathleen, Delyss, Alan Hurst, Alan Wisket, Ruby through Blue, Rainforest Girl. *Principal Works*: portrait sculptures/oil paintings. *Misc*: committed community artist working with Kent CC, Maidstone BC, Stately homes, museums, schools and adult groups providing quality art workshops; Leeds Castles artist/educator (2007). *Address*: Downslee, Grove Green Road, Weavering Street, Maidstone, Kent, ME14 5JX. *Email*: brendaburgess@brendaburgessarts.co.uk *Website*: www.brendaburgessarts.co.uk *Signs work*: 'Burgess'.

BURGESS, Howard John, ACII. *Medium*: oil. *b*: Kensington, 3 May 1954. *Educ*: Buckhurst Hill County High School. *Represented by*: Thompson's Gallery, Aldeburgh; The Russell Gallery, Putney; Coastline, Aldeburgh. *Exhib*: RA (1998, 2001, 2006), NEAC (2001), RSMA (2002), Thompson's Galleries, Guildhall Art Gallery, London. *Works in collections*: Epping Forest District Museum. *Commissions*: various private. *Recreations*: following cricket, painting. *Address*: 37 Greenhill, High Road, Buckhurst Hill, IG9 5SH. *Signs work*: 'HB'.

BURGESS, Peter, painter in oil and watercolour. *b*: 1952. *m*: Catherine (decd. 2003). *Studied*: Wimbledon School of Art (1972-74), R.A. Schools (1974-77). *Exhib*: RA, etc.; one-man shows: Thackeray Gallery, etc. *Works in collections*: Contemporary Art Soc., Derby City A.G., The Harborough Museum, Nottingham City Council, Leics. Educ. Authority, S. Derbyshire Health Authority, S. Nottingham College, Adam and Co., The Boots Co. plc; many private collections in Britain, USA and Europe. *Address*: 28 North Fen Road, Helpringham, Lincolnshire NG34 0RR. *Email*: peter.burgess99@btinternet.com *Website*: www.rasalumni.org *Signs work*: "Peter Burgess" on reverse of painting, "PB" (in box) on front.

BURKE, Andrew, DA (Edin.), David Murray Landscape Studentship RA, London; Travelling Scholarship from Edinburgh School of Art (Summer 1970). *Medium*: acrylic. *b*: Glasgow, 7 Apr 1947. *Studied*: Carlisle College of Art and Design (1967-68); Edinburgh School of Art (1968-71); Post-Diploma in Drawing and Painting, (1971-72). *Exhib*: many group exhbns including RA Summer Exhbns, RSW; regular exhibitor RSA, RGI. *Works in collections*: HRH The Duke of Edinburgh. *Address*: 82 Lennox Ave., Scotstoun, Glasgow G14 9HG. *Email*: andrewburke47@yahoo.com *Signs work*: 'Andrew Burke'.

BURKE, Christopher Paul, BA (Hons) 1st Graphic Design and Art History; Cartoonist of the Year 2000; Creative Circle Gold Medal. *Medium*: illustrator, caricaturist and cartoonist. *b*: London, 4 Oct 1955. *m*: Amanda Doran. two *s*. *Studied*: St. Martin's,

London 74, Canterbury College of Art 75/8. *Exhib*: one man shows: Roughs Gallery (1984), Conningsby Gallery (2002); two-man show - David Austin Gallery (1993); Mayfield Music Festival (2008). *Works in collections*: V&A, London Transport Museum and many private collections. *Commissions*: Welsh National Opera, BBC, Marks and Spencer, Menhuin School, Tatler, Virgin, Vogue, Tesco, London Review of Books, Sony, Dawn French (theatre drawings). *Publications*: Dictionary of Twentieth Century British Cartoonists and Caricaturists; Dictionary of British Cartoonists and Caricaturists 1730-1980; The British Art of Illustration 1780-1993; regular contributor to The Times, FT, Punch, Radio Times, Sunday Times, Sunday Telegraph. *Works Reproduced*: Penguin, Pan, Guardian, Observer, Evening Standard, Economist, Sunday Telegraph, etc. *Principal Works*: over 80 murals for Ottakar's Bookshops and Christmas catalogues, posters and p.o.s.; Wine Cellar Off Licences and Parisa Wine Bars corporate identity, posters, catalogues. *Misc*: two children's books with Lenny Henry: Charlie and the Big Chill; Charlie Queen of the Desert; stamps for Barbados and Malaysia; animated TV ad for Irish Tourist Board. *Address*: 54 St. James Road, Tunbridge Wells, Kent, TN1 2LB. *Email*: christopher.burke@btclick.com *Website*: www.chrisburke.org.uk *Signs work*: 'Burke'.

BURKE, Peter, sculptor. *b*: London, 29 Feb 1944. *m*: Wendy. two *d*. *Educ*: Bristol Technical School and Rolls Royce Bristol. *Studied*: Bristol Polytechnic (1972). *Exhib*: galleries in UK, USA, Europe, Korea. *Works in collections*: Contemporary Art Soc.; Beradi Collection, Portugal. *Commissions*: Large scale works in UK, USA, Portugal, Korea. *Publications*: The Class Sculpture Foundation: www.sculpture.org.uk. *Address*: 9 Woolley Green, Bradford on Avon, Wilts. BA15 1TZ *Email*: peter@peterburke.co.uk *Website*: www.peterburke.co.uk *Signs work*: "P. Burke," "PB." or not at all.

BURKETT, Norman Hittersay, RA (1974), painter in oil and pastel, sculptor. *b*: Dublin, Ireland, 23 Sep 1942. three *s*. two *d*. *Studied*: at Royal Academy under Peter Greenham. *Exhib*: all over Holland. *Works in collections*: private. *Commissions*: Diverse councils, cities, institutions. *Clubs*: RASAA. *Address*: Stepelerveld 50, 2151 JN-Nieuw Vennep, Holland. *Email*: norman@burkett.nl *Website*: www.burkett.nl

BURMAN, Chila Kumari, BFA (Hons) (1982), MFA (1984); mixed media artist, printmaker, photographer. *b*: Liverpool, 17 Jan 1963. *s of*: Bachan Singh Burman, ice cream vendor. *Studied*: Southport College of Art, BA. Leeds Polytechnic (1st Class Hons. in Printmaking and MFA), and Slade School of Fine Art, University College of London. *Exhib*: Internationally and nationally - widely, e.g New York, Canada, Cuba, India, S.Africa, Europe. *Works in collections*: V&A, Arts Council of England, Birmingham City Museum and Art Gallery, Walsall Art Gallery, British Council, Devi Foundation, India, Tate Gallery, Wellcome Trust, London and private collections world-wide. *Publications*: Own monograph 'Beyond two Cultures' by Lynda Nead (Kala Press); contributed to Framing Feminism, Visibly Female, Women and Self - Portraiture by Francis Barzello (Thames & Hudson). Currently represented by the Andrew Mummery Gallery, London. *Address*: 20 Woodview Cl., Hermitage Rd., London N4 1DG. *Signs work*: "C.K. Burman."

BURN, Hilary, BSc.Hons. (Zoology) (1967), SWLA (1983); freelance wildlife artist/illustrator in gouache, specialising in birds. *b*: Macclesfield, Ches., 8 Apr 1946. *d of*: Colin Barber, engineering draughtsman. *Educ*: Macclesfield High School, and University of Leeds. *Exhib*: SWLA Annual, regularly with RSPB, Wildfowl Trust, Wildlife A.G., Lavenham, Nature in Art, Glos. *Publications*: illustrated, R.S.P.B. Book of British Birds (1982); Wildfowl: An Identification Guide to the Ducks, Geese and Swans of the World (1987); Crows and Jays: An Identification Guide (1993); The Handbook of Bird Identification (1998); Handbook of the Birds of the World (1994-2011). *Clubs*: S.WL.A. *Address*: Huish Cleeve, Huish Champflower, Taunton, Som. TA4 2HA. *Signs work*: "Hilary Burn."

BURNLEY, Heather Wynne, CAS, FPS, SWA; Cert Ed. (Art & Drama). *Medium*: paint in oils, sculpt in clay which is cast in resin or bronze. *b*: Theydon Bois, Essex, 11 May 1937. *d of*: Bernard & Winifred Burnley. *Educ*: Upholland Grammar School, Wigan. *Studied*: Bath Academy of Art; L'Accademia delle Belle Arti, Florence. *Represented by*: CAS & SWA. *Exhib*: Hanley, Stockport, Leek, London, Corwen, Llangollen, Art Parks International, St. Martin, Guernsey; Mid Wales Art Centre. *Works in collections*: Hanley Museum and Art Gallery. *Commissions*: 4 sculpture portraits, 2 portrait in oils, 1 seated figure of Cardinal Newman (18" high), 1 seated figure of Owain Glyndwr for Corwen Library, bas relief portrait of Sir Henry Walford-Davies. *Official Purchasers*: Trustees of Glastonbury Abbey, The Society of the Work (for the chapel at) Cardinal Newman Centre, Littlemore, Oxford. *Principal Works*: Sculpture Group in bronze: Sigeric Riding Mule at Glastonbury Abbey. *Misc*: currently working on 'The Visitation'. *Address*: Pen-y-Foel Isaf, Gwyddelwern, Denbighshire, LL21 9DU. *Email*: burnleyh@hotmail.co.uk Website: www.heatherburnley.weebly.com *Signs work*: 'Heather Burnley, CAS, SWA'.

BURR, Lesley Jane, BA (Hons); MA (1997); 1st Prize Laing Art Competition (1992); Scottish Prize and National Commended - Laing (1994); Ruth Davidson Memorial Scholarship - France (1997); Hi-Arts (2002 & 2008); Faroe Islands Lithographic workshop (2003). *Medium*: oil; pastels; prints; tiles. *b*: St. Bees, Cumbria, 15 Jan 1963. *m*: Fergus Murray, Town Planner. one *d*. *Studied*: Glasgow School of Art (1981-85); Duncan of Jordanstone, Dundee (Public Art & Design, 1985-87). *Represented by*: Compass Gallery (Cyril & Jill Gerber). *Exhib*: McGill Duncan Gallery; 400 Women, London & Edinburgh Festival 2011; Mystical landscapes, Tighnabruich Gallery; Compass Gallery; Glasgow Print Studio; RGI; RA; Vaila Fine Art, Shetland; Boundary Gallery, London; The Shetland Museum. *Works in collections*: Smith Museum, Stirling; The Shetland Museum; Shetland Arts Trust; Stobhill Hospital and Royal Jubilee Hospitals, St.Andrews College. *Commissions*: Site specific mosaic and tile commissions in Glasgow, Dundee, East Kilbride, Shetland, Argyll. *Principal Works*: Shetland Silent Bird series; symbolic landscapes. *Recreations*: walking, gardening, travel, practising Buddhist. *Clubs*: Artmap Argyll, RGI. *Misc*: Co-founder of Veer North; Artmap Argyll. Known as one of the "Glasgow Girls". Lecturer at Argyll College UHI (present); Buddhist. *Address*: 73 Argyll Street, Lochgilphead, Argyll, PA31 8NE. *Website*: www.lesleyburr.co.uk *Signs work*: "BURR".

BURROWS, Geoffrey Norman, mem. East Anglian Group of Marine Artists. *Medium*: oil, watercolour. *b*: St. Faiths, Norfolk, 16 May 1934. *s of*: Alfred Norman Burrows, automobile engineer. *Educ*: The Paston Grammar School, N. Walsham, Norfolk. *Studied*: Norwich Technical College, full C&G Certificate in Telecommunications Engineering. *Exhib*: RA, RWA, RBA, ROI, RSMA, NEAC, RI, Paris Salon, various solo and mixed exhbns at home and on the continent. *Works in collections*: Atkinson AG, Southport; Norfolk CC; Norwich Union Insurance Co.; Post Office Archives; Zenith Corporate Communications. *Works Reproduced*: in 'Wide Skies - A Century of Painting and Painters in Norfolk'. *Clubs*: Norfolk and Norwich Art Circle; East Anglian Group of Marine Artists. *Address*: 84 Crostwick Lane, Spixworth, Norwich NR10 3AF. *Signs work*: "Geoffrey Burrows".

BURSNALL, Paul, Finalist, Aesthetica Journal Annual Competition. *Medium*: acrylic. *b*: Hayes, Middx, 17 Mar 1948. *s of*: George Bursnall. *m*: Deirdre. two *s*. *Studied*: Full Tech Cert. HND Product Design, Slough College. *Represented by*: Indigo Gallery, Brackley; Art at 88; Reg Rag, Bath; Taurus, Oxford; Primrose, Northampton; Picture Parlour, Boscastle; Curator Art, Stow. *Exhib*: Alfred East Gallery; Artshed, Ware; Stowe School Heseltine Gallery; Banbury 400; Swan, High Wycombe; Mariners Gallery, St. Ives; Delamore Gallery, Cornwood; Salon des Artistes, Mouvaux, France. *Works in collections*: private collectors in UK and Ireland. *Commissions*: several. *Publications*: featured in Daily Mail 4/7/08, Buckinghamshire Life May 2009; Aesthetica Works Annual; ABNA Book 2012; Several editions of Cornwall Today. *Works Reproduced*: limited editions. *Misc*: Founder member of Jailhouse Art; Member of ABNA (Association of British Naive Artists); Member of BAFA (Bucks Art for All); Bucks Art Society. *Address*: Old Stocks House, New Inn Lane, Sawcott, Bucks, MK18 4HP. *Email*: pbursnall@msn.com *Website*: www.paulbursnall.co.uk *Signs work*: "BURSNALL (with year)".

BURTON, Charles William, Hon. Doctor of Letters; Gold Medal, Eisteddfod of Wales; painter in oil and water media. *b*: Treherbert, 17 Aug 1929. *s of*: Charles and Eurlys Burton. *m*: Rosemary (children from former marriage to Jean Francis). two *s*. one (decd.) *d*. *Studied*: Cardiff College of Art, Royal College of Art. *Represented by*: Martin Tinney. *Exhib*: one-man shows: British Council Brussels, Welsh Arts Council, Cardiff, Brecknock Museum, Martin Tinney Gallery. *Works in collections*: BBC Wales, Welsh Arts Council, Contemporary Arts Soc. of Wales, DOE, National Museum of Wales, Newport Art Gallery, House of Lords, et alia. *Publications*: A Taste of the Belgian Provinces. *Clubs*: CASW. *Address*: 12 Plymouth Rd., Penarth CF64 3DH. *Signs work*: "BURTON".

BURTON, Philip John Kennedy, BSc (1958), PhD (1967), SWLA; painter in acrylic; retired scientific civil servant, British Museum (Natural History). *b*: London, 9 Jan 1936. *m*: Jennifer Mary. one *s*. one *d*. *Educ*: Finchley Catholic Grammar School, University College, London. *Exhib*: SWLA. *Publications*: Birds of the Western Palearctic, various field guides, Identification Guide to Raptors of the World. *Address*: High Kelton, Doctors Commons Rd., Berkhamsted, Herts. HP4 3DW. *Email*: pjkburton@supanet.com *Signs work*: "Philip Burton."

BURTON, Simon, MA (RCA), BA (Hons) Fine Art Painting. *Medium*: oil, watercolour, drawing, prints. *b*: Doncaster, 10 Apr 1973. *Partner*: Ms Graziella Belli. *Studied*: Royal College of Art (1995-97), Brighton University (1992-95). *Represented by*: Arch 402/Joanna Foster Fine Art, London; Artary Galerie Stuttgart. *Exhib*: 'Between Cave and Gate', Artary Gallery (solo, 2012); 'Nowhere Men', Arch 402 Gallery (solo, 2011); 'Black Swan, Blue Woman' (solo, 2010); Huddersfield Art Gallery; 'Under the Sign of Saturn', Kookmin University Gallery, Seoul (solo, 2007); 'A Sort of Night to the Mind' & 'Generations', Arch 402; RA Summer Exhibition (2010, 2012). *Works in collections*: Royal College of Art Collection, Aldrich Collection, PWC Collection, Robert & Susan Kasen Summer Collection, Dimensional Media, Kirklees, William Louis-Drefus Collection, Falmouth Art Gallery Collection, Swindon Museum and Art Gallery, Abbot Hall Collection. *Publications*: 'Simon Burton Paintings' Arch 402 ISBN 978-0-9570574-1-8; 'A Sort of Night to the Mind' Arch 402 ISBN 978-0-9570574-0-1; 'Generations' Arch 402. *Works Reproduced*: Royal Academy Summer Exhibition Catalogue (2010). *Address*: 51 Talfourd Road, London SE15 5NN. *Email*: simonburton@live.com *Website*: www.simonburton.org *Signs work*: "Simon Burton".

BURTON-RICHARDSON, David, First Prize, Landscape painting, Nuneaton Festival of the Arts (1984). *Medium*: oil, acrylic, drawing, sculpture. *b*: Leicesterm 13 Jan 1961. *s of*: Sheila & Arnold Burton. *Educ*: Mkt Bosworth High School, Bosworth College, Leics. *Studied*: self-taught. *Exhib*: Nuneaton Museum and Art Gallery; Oddfellows Gallery of Contemporary Art, Kendall; Tenby Museum and Art Gallery; Pontypool Museum and Art Gallery; Scolton Manor Museum; Llantarnam Grange Arts Centre, Cwmbran; Lyth Gallery; Washington Gallery, Penarth; Mariners Gallery, St. Ives, Cornwall; Norwegian Church, Cardiff. *Works in collections*: Tenby Museum and Art Gallery; Pontypool Museum and Art Gallery; Pembrokeshire County Council Art Collection; Prince Phillip Hospital, Llanelli; Pembrokeshire and Derwen Health Authority; Carmarthen Health Authority; Bloomfield Centre, Narberth, Nuneaton Museum and Art Gallery; many major works in museums and private collections. *Commissions*: Night Club Murals (1998); 'Homage to Van Gogh' (private collector, 1997). *Publications*: 'From Now to Zero: The Work of David Burton' (2005) (Pembrokeshire County Museums). *Works Reproduced*: numerous in books, catalogues, posters, magazines. *Recreations*: art history, history, walking, reading. *Clubs*:

NAPA full member. *Misc*: The David Burton-Richardson Collection and Archive is housed at Scolton Manor Museum; Signature 'dB R' (d and B joined) is an abbreviation of D.B.R. The 'R' is artists' mothers maiden name of Richardson. Only recent works (2005-) are signed in this way. *Address*: Glan Preseli, Efailwen, Clynderwen, Pembs. SA66 7UY. *Email*: david@burton6838.fsworld.co.uk *Signs work*: 'David Burton.R' or 'dBR', often signed on reverse of works.

BURY, Carole, BA (Hons) Textiles: Fine Art Embroidery (1981). *Medium*: oil, drawing, paper textiles. *b*: Gloucestershire, 17 January 1959. two *d*. *Studied*: Cheltenham College of Art (1977-78); Manchester Polytechnic (1978-81). *Exhib*: Exhibiting Member of '62 Group of Textile Artists' 1981-1995; Papua New Guinea and Australia 1985-88; Regular exhibitions in Kent, Gloucestershire and Yorkshire 1992-2012; RWA Bristol 2007; Nature in Art 2005-2012. *Works in collections*: private. *Commissions*: private. *Address*: 2 Hill View, Elkstone, Cheltenham GL53 9PB. *Email*: carole@carolebury.com *Website*: www.carolebury.com *Signs work*: "Carole Bury".

BUSBY, John P., RSA, RSW, SWLA; lecturer, Edinburgh College of Art (1956-88); Master Wildlife Artists medal for 2009 from Leigh Yawkey Woodson, Art Museum, Wisconsin, USA. *b*: Bradford, 2 Feb 1928. *s of*: Eric Busby, MBE. *m*: Joan. one *s*. two *d*. *Educ*: Ilkley Grammar School. *Studied*: Leeds Art College (1948-52), Edinburgh Art College (1952-54); Post Grad. (1954-55), major travel scholarship (1955-56). *Represented by*: The Land Gallery, Lockington; The Wildlife Art Gallery, Lavenham; Society of Wildlife Artists. *Works in collections*: SAC, Flemmings Bank, Bradford, Glasgow and Wakefield A.Gs., Yorks Arts Assoc.; many private collections including HRH The Duke of Edinburgh. *Publications*: The Living Birds of Eric Ennion (Gollancz), Drawing Birds (RSPB), Birds in Mallorca (Helm), Nature Drawings (Arlequin), Land Marks and Sea Wings (The Wildlife Art Gallery, Lavenham), many illustrated books, Looking at Birds (Layford Press). *Recreations*: bird watching, music. *Address*: Easter Haining, Ormiston Hall, Tranent, E. Lothian EH35 5NJ. *Email*: johnbusbyartist@btinternet.com *Website*: www.thelandgallery.com www.wildlifeartgallery.com *Signs work*: "John Busby."

BUSTIN, Jane, BA (Hons) Fine Art; painter. *b*: Borehamwood, Herts., 11 May 1964. *m*: David Gryn. one *s*. *Educ*: Nicholas Hawksmoor School, Herts. *Studied*: Hertfordshire College of Art, Portsmouth Polytechnic. *Exhib*: solo exhibs.: John Jarves Gallery (1995), Eagle Gallery (1998/2000); group exhibs. include British Abstract Painting (2000), Flowers East, Chora - touring exhib. (1999). *Works in collections*: Unilever, British Land, United Overseas, DLA Solicitors, KIAD Canterbury, V&A Museum, Goldman Sachs. *Commissions*: private commissions. *Publications*: "And a Year Ago, I Commemorated a Missed Encounter . . .", collaboration with writer Andrew Renton, pub. E.M. Arts; catalogues: Nameless Grace, Eagle Gallery; Chora, by Sue Hubbard and Simon Morley; British Abstract Painting, by Mathew Collins. *Address*: Artprojx, 1 Hillside Gardens., London N6 5SU. *Email*: janebustin@hotmail.com *Signs work*: "Jane Bustin."

BUTCHER, Sue, UEI Cert.AD (1979); artist in acrylic and plant fibres. *m*: Edward Butcher. two *s*. *Educ*: Penarth Grammar School. *Studied*: Hereford College of Art (1977-80). *Exhib*: regular exhibitor RA and West of England, winner, Sainsbury's National Touring Exhib. (1982-83), Japan (1987, 1993), SWA (1987), various mixed and one-man shows. *Works in collections*: Tayor Gallery, London, Hereford City A.G., Hereford Council Offices. *Publications*: poetry in various magazines. *Misc*: B.B.C. and I.T.V. television programmes (1990), radio broadcasts to U.S.A. and Canada. *Address*: Litley Orchard, Gorsty La., Hereford HR1 1UN. *Signs work*: "S. Butcher."

BUTLER, Elizabeth A., RWS (1999), BA, MA (RCA). *Medium*: watercolour, prints. *b*: Brampton, Cumbria, 12 Jun 1948. *m*: Ingram Pinn. one *s*. *Studied*: Liverpool College of

Art; RCA. *Represented by*: Francis Kyle Gallery, London since 1979. *Exhib*: Christie's, London (2004); Discerning Eye, Mall Galleries (2001, 2003); National Theatre (2001); Arts Club, London (1987), New York (1984). *Works in collections*: Government Art Collection; Abbot Hall Gallery, Kendal; Queen Mother's Art Collection, Windsor; Royal Watercolour Society Diploma Collection. *Commissions*: set of stamps commemorating British gardens for the Post Office (1983); series of paintings of Harewood House and grounds for Earl of Harewood. *Publications*: 'The Seasons' (William Collins, 1982); 'Watercolour Expert' (Cassells, 2004). *Principal Works*: landscape. *Misc*: taught at Colchester School of Art (1973-83); Camberwell School of Arts and Crafts (1982-92); Dulwich Picture Gallery continuously since 1988. *Address*: 33 Alexandra Road, Chiswick, London W4 1AX. *Email*: lizbutlerpinn@gmail.com *Signs work*: 'liz Butler' on reverse of painting, or 'LB' (with B inverted) on front.

BUTLER, James, MBE (2009); RA (1972), RWA (1980), FRBS (1981). *Medium*: sculptor in bronze and stone. *b*: Deptford, 25 Jul 1931. *s of*: Walter Arthur Butler. *m*: Angela Berry. five *d*. *Educ*: Maidstone Grammar School. *Studied*: Maidstone School of Art (1948-50); St. Martin's School of Art (1950-52). *Exhib*: Royal Academy, Richard Hagen, Richmond Hill Gallery. *Commissions*: Major commissions: portrait statue of President Kenyatta of Kenya, Nairobi; monument to Freedom Fighters of Zambia, Lusaka, Zambia; sculpture of The Burton Cooper, Burton-upon-Trent; memorial statue of Richard III, Castle Gardens, Leicester; statue of Field Marshal Earl Alexander of Tunis, Wellington Barracks, London; Dolphin fountain, Dolphin Sq., London; statue of John Wilkes, New Fetter La., London; bronze sculpture of the Leicester Seamstress, Hotel St., Leicester; statue of Thomas Cook, London Rd. Leicester; memorial statue to Reg Harris, N.C.C. Manchester; statue of Billy Wright, Wolverhampton; statue, James Greathead, Cornhill, London; D-Day Memorial to Green Howards, Crépon, Normandy; statue of James Brindley, Coventry Canal Basin, Fleet Air Arm Memorial, Embankment, London, portrait statue Jack Walker, Blackburn Rovers F.C., bust of Robert Beldam, Corpus Christi College, Cambridge, Royal Seal of the Realm, statue of Stan Cullis, Wolverhampton F.C.; busts of Sir Frank Whittle, R.J. Mitchell, Roy Chadwick - RAF Club Piccadilly; cellist, harpist in music annexe Marlborough School, portrait bust of Queen Elizabeth the Queen Mother, Butchers' Company, London; Rainbow Memorial, Fere en Tardenois, France. *Publications*: James Butler, An extended personal view of a Collector, by John Meulkens. *Clubs*: Arts. *Address*: Valley Farm Studios, Radway, Warwicks. CV35 0UJ. *Email*: info@jamesbutler-ra.com *Website*: www.jamesbutler-ra.com *Signs work*: surname and year e.g. "Butler '09".

BUTLER, Vincent, sculptor, figurative, bronzes; mem. Royal Scottish Academy, Royal Glasgow Inst. *b*: Manchester, 1933. *m*: Camilla. two *s*. *Studied*: Edinburgh College of Art; Academy of Fine Art, Milan. *Exhib*: numerous one-man shows in various parts of the country. *Works in collections*: 5 bronze portrait busts in The Scottish National Portrait Gallery; private collections in Britain, U.S.A., Germany, Italy, Israel, etc. *Commissions*: Portrait of H.R.H. Duke of Edinburgh, bronze (2002); large bronze 'family group' at Waterfront, Edinburgh (2004). *Publications*: Casting for Sculptors (A&C Black, 1997). *Address*: 17 Dean Park Cres., Edinburgh EH4 1PH. *Email*: vincentbutler@talktalk.net *Website*: vincentbutler.co.uk

BUTT, Alistair Neal, RSMA. *Medium*: Oil; watercolour. *b*: Umtata, South Africa, 7 May 1963. *Studied*: Worksop College (Art and Design) (1976-79); Blackpool and the Fylde College (Technical Illustration) (1979-83). *Represented by*: Lincoln Joyce Fine Art; Beckstones Art Gallery; Jack Fine Art; Sea Pictures Gallery. *Exhib*: Solo, joint, mixed at Lincoln Joyce Fine Art; Beckstones Art Gallery; Jack Fine Art; Sea Pictures Gallery. Plus: Granby Gallery, Bakewell; Mall Galleries, London; Duckeries Art Gallery, Worksop; Pybus Fine Art, Whitby; The Wykeham Gallery, Stockbridge; The Little Picture Gallery, Mousehole. *Address:* 25 Searby Road, Sutton-in-Ashfield, Nottinghamshire, NG17 5JQ.

Email: artist@alistairbutt.co.uk *Website*: www.alistairbutt.co.uk *Signs work*: "ALISTAIR BUTT".

BUTT, Desiree Jill Mary, *Medium*: watercolour, acrylic. *b*: Uffculmebutt, 26 Apr 1935. *m*: William James. *Educ*: Mount St Mary's Convent, Exeter. *Studied*: Somerset College of Art and Technology, Taunton (as mature student 2001-2003). *Represented by*: herself. *Exhib*: As member of Tiverton Art Society, at: Tiverton Hospital, Golf Club, East Devon Arts Festival, Tiverton Library and Council Offices, Hofheim Germany, South West of England Academy Exeter, Royal West of England Academy Bristol. *Commissions*: many and varied. *Principal Works*: midnight (2008, no. 52 at SWAc); Retail Therapy (2008, no. 134 at RWA). *Recreations*: walking, art galleries, visiting old buildings, cooking. *Clubs*: Tiverton Art Society.*Address*: Tilthen House, The Square, Uffculme, Devon EX15 3AA. *Email*: desireebutt@btinternet.com *Website*: www.desireebutt.co.uk *Signs work*: "Desiree Butt".

BUTT, Jennifer Gillian, Diploma in General Art and Design (merit), BTEC. *Medium*: acrylic. *b*: Sidcup, 13 Jun 1968. *d of*: Patricia Butt. *Partner*: Paul. one *d*. *Educ*: Falmouth School of Art, Falmouth, Cornwall. *Studied*: National Diploma in Art and Design (Foundation). *Represented by*: Lander Gallery, Truro; New Craftsman, St. Ives; Round House Gallery, Sennen Cove, Cornwall. *Exhib*: Royal West of England Academy, Bristol (RWA) 150th Autumn Selected Exhibition; group shows: Mid-Cornwall Galleries, St.Blazey, Truro Museum, Trebah Garden Gallery. *Commissions*: various private commissions throughout the UK; Sydney, Australia and New York. *Publications*: Wavelength (Surf magazine), West Briton, Inside Cornwall, Cornwall Arts. *Works Reproduced*: limited edition prints of 'Flooded Surface' and 'Trevaunance'; Oceans Edge, Sandpods and Lone Limpet. *Recreations*: surfing; walking and sketching along coastal footpaths. *Clubs*: Truro Art Society, Penzance Art Club. *Misc*: all my works are based on the beauty of the North Coast of Cornwall, with its surreal and serene ever changing images. *Address*:2 Crown Terrace, Perranwell Station, Cornwall, TR3 7JZ. *Email*: jennybutt@postmaster.co.uk *Website*: www.jennybutt.com

BUTT, Laurence Arnold, BA (Hons.) Fine Art (1998); artist in oil, acrylic, charcoal, and sculpture. *b*: London, 9 Sep 1954. *m*: Tatiana. three *s*. one *d*. *Studied*: Surrey Inst. of Art and Design, Farnham. *Exhib*: Whiteley's London, RA, Brighton, Russia, New Masters London. *Works in collections*: Surrey Institute of Art & Design. *Commissions*: still life, portraits, abstract art, spiritual paintings, landscape and prints. *Works Reproduced*: R.A. Abstract. *Clubs*: Sussex Art Club. *Misc*: varied commissions welcomed. *Address*: 9 Southdown House, 2 Silverdale Lane, Eastbourne, E.Sussex BN20 7AL. *Email*: lauriebutt@aol.com *Signs work*: "Laurence A. Butt.".

BUTTERFIELD, Sarah Harriet Anne, B.Soc.Sci. Architecture Edin. (1975) 'Magna cum Laude', Cert. Fine Art Ruskin School of Fine Art, Oxford (1978), Distinction; qualified as architect 1983; self employed as artist since 1986; Official Tour Artist, on Royal Tour by HRH Prince of Wales to Egypt, Saudi Arabia and India. Awards: Egerton Coghill Landscape prize (1977), Winsor and Newton award, Hunting Group Competition finalist, commendation Spectator Magazine Three Cities Competition, art reviewer, LBC Arts & Entertainment Sunday Program. *b*: London, 28 Aug 1953. *m*: David Willetts. one *s*. one *d*. *Exhib*: Judd St. Gallery, London (1987), Agnew's Young Contemporaries (1988), Richmond Gallery, Cork St. (1990), Roy Miles Gallery (1991); Discerning Eye (1997); dfn Gallery New York (2000); one-man show: Cadogan Contemporary (1991, 1994, 1997), 27 Cork St., London (2001), Albemarle Gallery, London (2005), Frost and Reed (2011, 2012). *Works in collections*: British Airways: Terminal 4 Departure Lounge, Gatwick Airport; Jerry's Home Store, Chelsea, London; David Lloyd Slazenger Racquet Club; Trusthouse Forte Hotels in Yorkshire and Exeter; Wimbledon Lawn Tennis Museum; 'Davies', Gt. Newport St., London. Private collection of HRH Prince of Wales. *Recreations*: tennis, running, films, music. *Clubs*: mem., Equity. *Address*: 21 Ashchurch Grove,. London W12 9BT. *Email*: sarah.butterfield@mac.com *Website*: www.sarahbutterfield.co.uk

BUTTERWORTH, John Malcolm, MA(Ed.), FRSA, NDD, ATD; artist in oils, water-colour, etching, silkscreen and lithography, paper; Fine Art Degree Course Leader, Design Faculty, Southampton IHE (retd. from post 1997). *b*: Lancs., 16 Jul 1945. *s of*: Jonathan and Annie (Tilling) Butterworth. *m*: Lesley G. Arkless, B.A.Hons. two *s*. one *d*. *Educ*: Rochdale Technical School for Boys. *Studied*: Rochdale College of Art (1961-63), Newport College of Art (1965-66), Cardiff College of Art (1965-66), David Murray Scholarship (R.A.) 1965. *Exhib*: Wills Lane Gallery, St. Ives, University of Surrey, Southampton Civic A.G. (one-man shows), Pictures for Schools Exhbn., National Museum of Wales, Cardiff, Midsommergarten Gallery, Stockholm, Cleveland, Drawing Biennale, International Print Biennale, Monaco, "Outpost" Venice Biennale (1995). *Works in collections*: Bristol Educ. Authority, Kent Educ. Authority, Surrey University, Hampshire C.C. *Address*: 2 Nuns Walk, Winchester, Hants. SO23 7EE. *Signs work*: normal signature for prints, "J.M.B." monogram for paintings.

BUTTERWORTH, John Russell, BA (Hons) Fine Art, MA Painting; Northern Young Contemporaries Prizewinner (1985); travel scholarship at Winchester SOFA (awarded by Albert Irwin). *Medium*: oil, prints. *b*: Malvern, Worcs, 22 Feb 1962. *s of*: Janet Mathilde Leyen-Decker. *Partner*: Denise Eileen Twomey. *Educ*: Kelsey Park Boys School, Beckenham, Kent. *Studied*: Winchester School of Art (1980-83), Chelsea School of Art and Design (1983-84). *Represented by*: various galleries in Kent and London. *Exhib*: RA Summer Exhbn (1999, 2001), Beardsmore Gallery London 4 Artists (2001), Canterbury Museum and Gallery 'Passing Tales' (2000). *Works in collections*: private collections London, Kent, France, Kuala Lumpar, Winchester SOFA Collection. *Commissions*: 'Sartorial Art' for Maurice Sedwell Ltd., Savile Row London; 'Creative Vista' album sleeve Mr Ben Cooper. *Works Reproduced*: Poetry Review Magazine Vol 92 No 3 Autumn 2002. *Principal Works*: 'Seasalter', 'Falling Down' (The Descent). *Recreations*: keen club cricketer. *Clubs*: Whitstable CC, Contemporary Arts Group (Whitstable). *Misc*: 'making connection with the human spirit through art'. *Address*: 51a Cromwell Road, Whitstable, Kent, CT5 1NW. *Email*: john.butterworth@tinyworld.co.uk *Website*: www.jbutterworth.co.uk *Signs work*: John Butterworth.

BUXTON, Jennifer, HRMS (retd.), Hon.Sec.RMS (1980-87), Hilliard Soc.; portrait, animal and landscape painter in water-colour, silverpoint, pastel, oil, gouache and acrylic; first winner of RMS Gold Memorial Bowl Award for best miniature (1985). *Medium*: watercolour, pastel, carbon drawings, oil, acrylic and coloured pencils. *b*: Hornsey, 12 Apr 1937. *d of*: N. Pearson, company director. *m*: Captain Vic (RN). two *s*. *Educ*: Northfield School, Watford. *Studied*: Frobisher School of Animal Painting (1948-53, Marguerite Frobisher), Byam Shaw School of Art (1954-57, Dunstan, Phillips, Mahoney). *Exhib*: Watford, Manchester, Bath, Wells, Paris Salon, Kendal, Ulverston, Ilkley, Toronto, annually RMS London. *Commissions*: numerous. *Misc*: now painting wild tigers in India, selling prints, all profits to building a school in Indian village, tree-planting in India, protection of tigers and the forest. *Address*: Windy Ash Barn, Ulverston, Cumbria LA12 7PB. *Email*: jen@windyashbarn.com *Website*: www.tigertigerburningbright.com *Signs work*: "jb", "Jen Buxton" or "J. Buxton."

BUXTON, Judy, BA (Hons) Fine Art, RA Dip Fine Art; Nat West Art Prize finalist and prizewinner (1997), Cyril Sweet Award (1996), Gold Medal The Worshipful Company of Painter-Stainers, Royal Watercolour Award (1996), David Murray Travel Scholarship; Hunting Art Prize (2nd Prize). *Medium*: oil, watercolour. *b*: Sydney, 16 Dec 1961. *d of*: John and Leonore Buxton. *m*: Jeremy Annear. *Studied*: Falmouth College of Art (1987-90), Royal Academy of Art (1990-93). *Represented by*: New Millennium Gallery, St. Ives, Cornwall. *Exhib*: Hunting Art Prizes, RCA 98/99/00/02/03/04/05, New Millennium Gallery 1997-03,

Messums 1998-03, Beaux Art Gallery Bath 2001, Newlyn Art Gallery 1994-03, Royal Academy Summer Exhbn. 91/92/93/98. *Works in collections*: Falmouth College of Art, Guinness Collection, Swiss Bank. *Commissions*: The Crystal Serenity. *Publications*: Catching the Wave by Tom Cross (Halsgrove Press 2003), Newlyn Society of Artists Members Book (NSA Pub. 2000), exhbn.cat. Messums (foreword by William Packer), exhbn. cat. New Millennium Gallery (2002), Nat West Art Prize catalogue, exhbn. catalogue New Millennium (2004, foreword by William Packer). *Works Reproduced*: Royal Overseas League cat. (1997), Drawing the Nude by Diana Constance (Apple Press 1994), London Underground poster campaign for RA Summer Exhbn (1993). *Recreations*: travel, piano. *Clubs*: Reynolds Club RA Alumni. *Misc*: Freedom of the City of London, Hon.Freeman of the Worshipful Company Painter Stainers. *Address*: Chapel House, Garras, Helston, Cornwall, TR12 6LN. *Signs work*: J Buxton.

BYRNE, Andrea, BA (Hons) Fashion & Textiles, MA Fine Art, MA Aural & Visual Cultures; Drapers Record 'Graduate Award' Winner (1984), The Guardian Fashion Illustrated Award (1987). *Medium*: painting, watercolour, installations. *b*: Islington, London, 9 Jun 1962. *Partner*: Simeon Farrar. *Studied*: Liverpool John Moores University (1981-84); Central St. Martins Art College, University of the Arts (2004-2006); Goldsmiths College, The London University. *Exhib*: Solo shows and group shows including: The East Wing Collection, The Courtauld; Hicks Gallery London; 20 Hoxton Square Gallery London; Islington Arts Factory; Resonance Radio - Painting for Radio. *Works in collections*: private and corporate collections nationally and internationally. *Commissions*: Rimmel London; Saatchi & Saatchi; Island Records; MC Art Private and corporate commissions. *Address*: Studio 308, Erlang House, 128 Blackfriars Road, London SE1 8EQ. *Email*: info@andreabyrne.com *Website*: www.andreabyrne.com *Signs work*: "Andrea Byrne".

BYROM, Gillie Hoyte, RMS, HS, BSOE, MEd (Exeter), BEd (Cambridge); portrait miniaturist working in vitreous enamel on copper or gold. *Medium*: vitreous enamel paint. *b*: Ceylon, 5 Nov 1952. *m*: Peter Byrom, OBE. *Educ*: Llotja School, Barcelona. *Exhib*: numerous. *Works in collections*: Wimbledon Lawn Tennis Museum, Diploma Collection of RMS. *Commissions*: numerous. *Publications*: The Royal Miniature Society 100 Years; The Techniques of Painting Miniatures; Macmillan Dictionary of Art: Limoges. *Clubs*: Royal Society of Miniature Painters, Sculptors and Gravers, Hilliard Society, British Soc. of Enamellers, Devon Guild of Craftsmen, Guild of Enamellers. *Address*: Studio 268, Dartington Space, Dartington Hall, Totnes, Devon TQ9 6EN. *Website*: www.enamelportraitminiatures.co.uk

C

CAHILL, John, BA (Hons) Fine Art (1976), MA Painting (1980); painter in oil and water-colour, printmaker, etcher; professional artist and gallery owner. *b*: 19 Nov 1954. *m*. Gillian. one *d*. *Studied*: Portsmouth Polytechnic (1976), Royal College of Art (1980). *Exhib*: RA Summer Shows; one man shows: Harris Museum, Preston, St. David's Hall, Cardiff. Sunday Times Watercolour Competition (2012); Lynn Painters-Stainers Prize (2012, 2014). *Works in collections*: Lord Bath, Longleat House; Welsh Assembly, Cardiff. *Commissions*: many private commissions. *Works Reproduced*: fine art prints, calendars, cards. *Address*: The Harbour Gallery, 1 St. Julian St., Tenby, Pembrokeshire, SA70 7AY. *Email*: tenbyharbgallery@aol.com *Website*: www.tenbyharbourgallery.co.uk

CAINS, Gerald Albert, NDD (Painting S.L.1953), ATD (1957), ARWA (1971), elected RWA (1978), ADAE (University of Wales, 1975); RWA Finalist Hunting Group Prizes (1984). *Medium*: oil and water-colour. *b*: Stubbington, Hants., 11 May 1932. *s of*: Albert George Cains. *m*: Ruth Lillian Blackburn. one *s*. one *d*. *Educ*: Gosport County Grammar School. *Studied*: Southern College of Art, Portsmouth (1949-53). *Exhib*: mixed: RA; RWA;

ROI; RBA; Football and Fine Arts, London 53: Pics for Schools (Cardiff); Euro '96 London; Wessex Artists, Southampton 78 (2nd prize). Selected for Touring Exhbn. ACGB, Art Federations Bureau, Millfield Open (2003, 04, 05); Discerning Eye, Mall Galleries (2003); "One Love - Football", Lowry Gallery, Salford, Manchester (2007). *Works in collections*: Lancashire Museum Service, RWA, Walsall Museum Service, Wessex Longleat House, Victoria Art Gallery Bath. *Commissions*: mural: Southmead Hospital, Bristol. *Works Reproduced*: in 'Acrylic School' Hazel Harrison (Readers Digest), 'How to Paint and Draw' Hazel Harrison (Quarto), 'Oil Painters' Pocket Palette' Rosalind Cuthbert (Batsford), Complete Painter, Brian Gorst, Watson Guptill, NY; The Oil Painters Bible, Quarto 2005, Marglin-Scott. *Principal Works*: 'The Miner in his Garden', oil (Wessex Coll., Longleat House). *Clubs*: R.W.A., Bath Soc. of Artists. *Address*: 1 Broadway Cottages, Broadway Lane, Clandown, Radstock, Somerset BA3 2XP. *Website*: www.rwa.org.uk *Signs work*: "G. A. CAINS."

CAINS, Judith, NDD, ATC; Harewood Award, Landscape Open (1995); 1st Prize, Laing Regional (1995); Major Prize Laing Regional (1995); Arts Council Award (2003), 'The Discerning Eye', London - Northern Regional Prizewinner (2010). *Medium*: acrylic. *b*: England, 10 May 1944. *Studied*: Leeds College of Art (1960-64); Goldsmiths College (1964-65). *Represented by*: Thackeray Gallery, London. *Exhib*: solo shows: Thackeray Gallery; Myles Meehan Gallery; Royal Botanical Gardens, Kew; Palo Alto, California; Leeds City Art Gallery, mixed shows including Belgium International Biennale (2002); RA Summer shows. *Works incollections*: public and private collections UK and abroad. *Commissions*: NHS Trust: floor piece and ten paintings for St James Hospital, Leeds. *Publications*: 'Judith Cain "Being in Place" Landscapes of Central Asia (2003)'; 'Judith Cain, Thackeray Gallery' (10 catalogues 1996-2014). *Works Reproduced*: on numerous occasions in national press and magazines. *Clubs*: Chelsea Arts Club, London. *Address*: 30 Grove Road, Headingley, Leeds LS6 4EE. *Email*: judithcain1@gmail.com *Website*: www.judith-cain.blogspot.co.uk *Signs work*: 'Judith Cain'.

CAINES, Ronal Arthur, National Diploma Design (Painting); ATD. *Medium*: oil. *b*: Bristol, 13 Dec 1938. *m*: Susan Caines. one *s*. two *d*. *Educ*: Bristol Cathedral School. *Studied*: West of England College of Art (1955-61). *Represented by*: Levent Gallery, London, Rob Whittle Fine Art. *Exhib*: RA, RWA, NEAD, Mall Galleries, Discerning Eye, Arnolfini (Bristol), Brighton Art Gallery, Chichester Open; solo exhbns: Alpha House Gallery, Sherbourne; Levent Gallery. *Works in collections*: West of England College of Art; Lord Gosford; Lord Rees; John Fortune; Ron Weldon. *Misc*: began playing saxophone at art school, founded East of Eden in 1967, performed throughout Europe. Later career as free jazz musician. *Address*: 36 Titian Road, Hove, E. Sussex BN3 5QS. *Signs work*: 'R.Caines'.

CAINES, Susan Mary, RWA (1995); NDD painting, ATD. *Medium*: painter in oils. *b*: Bristol, 1 Feb 1935. *d of*: Bertie Weaver and Dorothy Shepstone. *m*: Ronald Caines. one *s*. two *d*. *Educ*: St. George's Grammar School. *Studied*: West of England College of Art, ATD awarded by Bristol University 1956. *Represented by*: Lena Boyle Fine Art, London; Ainscough Contemporary, London; Alpha House, Sherborne; RWA. *Exhib*: since 1989, including one-person shows annually since 1990. Royal Academy Summer Exhbn 1993-2003. One-person show Royal West of England Academy Galleries 1999. *Works in collections*: Royal West of England Academy, West of England College of Art, private collections. *Official Purchasers*: RWA Talboy Bequest for the RWA Collection. *Works Reproduced*: illustrated catalogues of RA and RWA, and 'Pictures in an Academy'. *Recreations*: travelling in Italy, photograpy, reading. *Clubs*: RWA, Bath Society of Artists. *Address*: 36 Titian Road, Hove, E. Sussex BN3 5QS. *Email*: susan.caines@ntlworld.com

CALLAGHAN, Dora, née BEST. *Medium*: oil. *b*: Wimbledon, London 20 Jul 1931. *d of*: George & Dora Best. *m*: Edward Ronald Callaghan. two *s*. one *d*. *Educ*: Bromley High

School. *Studied*: studied art with Mrs. Doris Cox until the end of WWII. *Exhib*: Royal Academy (1982, 1983, 1992, 1993); Mall Galleries: Laing (1981), RBA (1981), ROI (1987, 1990, 1994, 1995, 1997), SWA (1979, 2007). Westminster Hall: SWA (1989, 1990), SBA (1988). Mixed exhibitions: Lewisham, Blackheath and Chelsea Societies of Art. *Recreations*: listening to classical music and drama. *Address*: 35 Northbrook Road, Lewisham, London SE13 5QT. *Signs work*: "DORA'C".

CALLAND, Ruth Elaine, MA, MSc; Awards: Arts Council (2007); Art 4 All (1998); Boise Travelling Scholarship (1987); Fellowship in Painting, Gloscat, Cheltenham (1987). *Medium*: Live Art, oil, drawing. *b*: Scunthorpe, 8 Apr 1963. *d of*: John & Christine. *m*: Jonathan Waller. two *d*. *Educ*: Lanchester Polytechnic (Coventry, 1982-85). *Studied*: Chelsea School of Art (1986-87); Birkbeck College (1986-87). *Represented by*: Transition Gallery, London. *Exhib*: Rational Rec, Bethnal Green (2007); Transition Gallery (2005, 2007); Hastings Museum & Art Gallery (2007); Three Colts, London (2006); The Residence, London (2006); Vestry House Museum, London (2005, 2006); The Foundry, London (2005); Temporary Contemporary, London (2005); Flowers East (2003); Derby Museum and Art Gallery (1998); Paton Gallery (1987, 1989); New Contemporaries, ICA (1986). *Works in collections*: Leicestershire Collection, Coventry University, British Gas Plc, Slade School of Art. *Commissions*: Hastings Museum and Art Gallery (2007), Transition Gallery (2007), Arty Magazine (commissioned drawings, issues 14, 17). *Misc*: also known as: Radmilla Click, Hepsibah, Countess Euphoria, Professor Timecreep, Dame Batlove. *Address*: 35 Campbell Road, Walthamstow, London E17 6RR. *Email*: ruth8@tinyworld.co.uk *Website*: www.transitiongallery.co.uk

CALLAWAY, Sonia Sylvia. *Medium*: Acrylic on wood and canvas, linoprints. *b*: Plymouth, 6 May 1962. *m*: Ian. one *d*. *Studied*: TAFE, Perth, W. Australia (1988-90); Perth Technical College (1977-80). *Represented by*: The Association of British Naive Artists. *Exhib*: St. Ives, and locally. *Works in collections*: Australia, America, UK, Europe. *Commissions*: various corporate. *Works Reproduced*: Pagan Dawn, Springboard Stones (magazines). *Recreations*: swimming, music, walking, travel. *Clubs*: Catweazle Fan Club, Friend of the Witchcraft Museum. *Address*: 49 Roseland Gdns, Veryan, Nr. Truro, Cornwall TR2 5QR. *Email*: callawayhouse@freenetname.co.uk *Website*: www.britishnaives.co.uk Melinsey Mill *Signs work*: S followed by outline of fish bones then C.

CALLMAN, Jutta Gabrielle: see SAUNDERS, Jutta Gabrielle.

CALVER, Michael, BA (Hons) Fine Art (1971); Arts Council Grants (2003, 2005); Pollock Krasner Foundation Grant (2007). *Medium*: painter, printmaker. *b*: Kent, 6 Apr 1942. *m*: Megan. one *s*. two *d* . *Studied*: St.Martins (1958-59), East Ham Tech. (1967-68), Winchester School of Art (1968-71), Brighton Polytechnic (1971-72). *Exhib*: Solo Shows: Wolf at the Door, Penzance (1987); Exeter and Devon Arts Centre (1996); University of Bath (1997); Black Swan Guild, Frome (1999); Exeter Phoenix (2004); Brewhouse, Taunton (2007); Manu Chhabria Gallery, Dubai (2008). Group shows: RWA Bristol (1989, 90, 97, 99, 2000, 2009), William Desmond, Exeter (1991), Gordon Hepworth, Exeter (1991, 1992), Newlyn Art Gallery (1997, 99, 2001, 03, 04), Campden Gallery, Glos (2005), Sherborne House (2006), Tokyo (2002), Bad Homburg (2005). Art Fairs: London, Bristol, Bath, Glasgow (1999-2005), The Exchange, penzance (2011), Bucca Ballery, Newlyn (2012, 2013). *Works in collections*: private and corporate, UK/Japan/Dubai. *Publications*: Illustrated catalogue 'Silent Moves', The Brewhouse, Taunton (2007); Illustrated catalogue, 'Full Spectrum', Sherborne House, Sherborne (2006). *Clubs*: Member of Newlyn Society of Artists. *Address*: 3 Twyford Place, Tiverton, Devon, EX16 6AP. *Website*: www.axisweb.org/artist/michaelcalver www.geoform.net www.michaelcalver.co.uk www.nsanewlyn.com *Signs work*: "M.Calver".

CALVERT, Diana, NEAC (1979); artist in oil. *b*: Capel, Surrey, 7 Oct 1941. *m*: Richard Martineau. *Educ*: Benenden School, Cranbrook, Kent. *Studied*: Byam Shaw (1959-63, Charles Mahoney). *Exhib*: RA, RP, RBA, NEAC. *Address*: The Lawn, Walsham-le-Willows, Bury St. Edmunds, Suffolk IP31 3AW. *Signs work*: "D.C."

CALVOCORESSI, Richard, BA, MA; Director (since 2007) Henry Moore Foundation; Director, Scottish National Gallery of Modern Art, Edinburgh (1987-2007); research asst., Scottish National Gallery of Modern Art (1977-79); research asst., Modern Collection, Tate Gallery (1979-82), asst. keeper (1982-87). *b*: Westerham, Kent, 1951. *m*: Francesca Temple Roberts. one *s*. two *d*. *Educ*: Magdalen College, Oxford; Courtauld Inst. of Art, University of London. *Publications*: author, Magritte (1979, 1984, 1990, 1994, 1998, 2000), Lee Miller: Portraits from a Life (2002), 'Lucien Freud on Paper' (2008); exhbn. catalogues: Tinguely (1982), Reg Butler (1983), Cross Currents in Swiss Art (1985), Oskar Kokoschka 1886-1980 (1986), Early Works: Lucian Freud (1997), Le Miller Portraits (2005), Francis Bain: Portraits and Heads (2005); Anselm Kiefer: Morgenthall Plan (2013), Georg Baselitz: Farewell Bill (2014); and catalogue essays on Miró, Klee, Penck, Baselitz, Lüpertz, von Motesiczky, Gormley, Picabia, Gabrielle Keiller Collection etc.; various articles and reviews; co-curator, 'Vienna 1908-1918', 'Century City', Tate Modern, (January-April 2001). *Address*: Henry Moore Foundation, Dane Tree House, Perry Green, Much Hadham, Herts, SG10 6EE.

CAMBRIDGE, Melanie Ann. *Medium*: oil. *b*: Stockport, 19 Jul 1963. *m*: Peter. *Represented by*: The Wey Gallery, 44 Bridge Street, Godalming, Surrey. *Exhib*: Mall Galleries; Gallery 54, Mayfair; RAC Club, Pall Mall; various other South East venues. *Commissions*: all to private individuals. *Publications*: Art Instruction books for Harper Collins: 'Success with Oils'; 'Learn to Paint Landscapes in Oils'; 'You can Paint Acrylics'; '30-Minute Oils'. *Recreations*: skiing, narrowboating. *Clubs*: Maritime Art Group (Founder Member & Hon Sec). *Address*: 17 Derwent Drive, Purley, Surrey, CR8 1ER. *Email*: art@melaniecambridge.com *Website*: www.melaniecambridge.com *Signs work*: "MELANIE CAMBRIDGE".

CAMERON, Ronald, NDD (1951); sculptor in bronze, terracotta, pewter and silver. *b*: London, 8 Oct 1930. *m*: Dorothy. two *d*. *Educ*: Wilson's Grammar School. *Studied*: Camberwell School of Art (1947-51). *Exhib*: bronzes at Bruton Street Gallery, Mayfair, London; also galleries in Europe and N. America. *Address*: 9 Morecambe St., London SE17 1DX. *Signs work*: "R. Cameron."

CAMERON, Zoe Rebecca, BA Hons Degree in Fine Art. *Medium*: painter in oils and acrylics. *b*: Havant, UK, 29 Jan 1959. *Educ*: Cranford House School, Moulsford, Oxon. *Studied*: Maidenhead Coll. of Art (Foundation), Glos. Coll. Art and Design 1977-80. *Represented by*: Avalon Gallery, Marazion; Square Gallery, St. Mawes. *Exhib*: Newlyn Orion, Penzance; Spacer Gallery, Exeter; Tate Gallery, St. Ives; Cadogan Gallery, London; David Messum Gallery, London; Saltrum House, Plymouth. *Works in collections*: Longleat House, Warminster; Dolphin House, Barbican, Plymouth. *Commissions*: Tate Gallery St. Ives - mug design; Lord Bath - portrait; PLM Estates, Barbican Plymouth, 9 paintings; private portrait commissions; Truro Cathedral, paintings for Saints Chapel. *Publications*: 'Living on the Line' - catalogue, ARTNSA, The Female Perspective - Chapel Gallery Gulval. How to live a good life and Aesop's Fables.The Stations of the Cross in Truro Cathedral. *Principal Works*: series: Mrs. Morris's Companions, Truth and Lies, Finding and Losing, Fragile Lives. How to live a good life and Aesop's Fables, Stations of the Cross. *Clubs*: associate mem. Newlyn Gallery. *Misc*: studied Italy 1993, '97, '98., Malta 1995-6 Studio Italy Florence 1994, taught Venice Academy 2000, Portrait of a Punk - Youtube films 2013. *Address*: Bluebell Cottage, St.Martins Green, St.Martins, Helston, TR12 6BW. *Email*: zoe@zoecameron.co.uk *Website*: www.zoecameron.co.uk *Signs work*: "Z Cameron".

CAMP, Ann, ARCA (1946), FSSI; freelance calligrapher and lettering designer; lecturer at Digby Stuart College, Roehampton Institute; retd. from teaching (1990). *b*: London, 1924. *d of*: Leonie Camp and Instructor Capt. John Camp, R.N. *Studied*: Hampstead Garden Suburb Inst. and RCA. *Works in collections*: loan collections of V&A, LCC and National Museum of Wales; Book 4, RAF Book of Remembrance in St. Clement Dane's Church; lettering on stamps, murals, etc. *Publications*: Pen Lettering (first published 1958 by Dryad Press; republished by A&C Black, 1984). *Clubs*: Soc. of Scribes and Illuminators. *Address*: 115 Bridge La., London NW11 9JT. *Signs work*: "Ann Camp."

CAMP, Jeffery, RA (1984); artist; lecturer, Slade School. *Educ*: Edinburgh College of Art, DA (Edin.). *Exhib*: one-man, Galerie de Seine (1958), Beaux Arts Gallery (1959, 1961, 1963), New Art Centre (1968), Serpentine Gallery (1973), S. London A.G. (retrospective, 1973), Bradford City A.G. (1979), Browse and Darby (1984, 1993), Nigel Greenwood Gallery (1986, 1990); retrospective, Royal Albert Memorial Museum, Exeter, Royal Academy of Arts, London, Manchester City A.G., Laing A.G., Newcastle (1988-89); group shows: Hayward Annuals (1974, 1982, 1985), British Council Touring Exhbns. to China and Edinburgh (1982) and to India (1985), Chantrey Bicentenary, Tate Gallery (1981), Narrative Painting I.C.A., London Arts Council Touring, The Hard Won Image Tate Gallery (1984); Twining Gallery, N.Y. (selected by William Feaver 1985), Peter Moores Liverpool Exhbn. (selected by William Feaver 1986); Athena Art Awards, Barbican Centre, London (1987), Land: Sea: Air, Herbert Read Gallery, Canterbury and tour (1987), 'The Self Portrait' Artsite Gallery, Bath and tour (1987). *Publications*: Draw (1981). *Address*: 27 Stirling Rd., London SW9 9EF.

CAMPBELL, Alex, professional artist in acrylic paint; Adviser NAPA. *b*: Dukinfield, Ches., 5 Apr 1936. *m*: Anne. one *s*. one *d*. *Educ*: Hyde County Grammar School, Ches. Worldwide private collections and commissions. *Address*: Wern Mill, Nannerch, Mold, Flints. CH7 5RH. *Email*: huwpc@hotmail.com

CAMPBELL, Christopher. *Medium*: oil. *b*: Birmingham, 26 Sep 1975. *Studied*: Leeds Metropolitan University, UK. *Represented by*: Start Space, London. *Exhib*: Start Space, Catto Contemporary, Leeds, Metropolitan Gallery, Paton Gallery, New Academy Gallery. *Works in collections*: Lodeveans Collection. Private collections in the UK include: Damien Whitmore, Scott Capurro. Other private collections in Europe, Middle East, Asia and America. *Publications*: 'Epoch', Christopher Campbell ISBN 978-0-948413-1-7. *Address*: c/o Start Space, 150 Columbia Road, London E2 7RG. *Email*: contact@startspace.co.uk *Website*: www.startspace.co.uk *Signs work*: "CHRISTOPHER CAMPBELL".

CAMPBELL, Huw Phillip, BA Graphic Art and Design (1977); artist/graphic designer in acrylic paint. *b*: Madagascar, 27 Feb 1955. *Studied*: Newport College of Art (1974-77). *Exhib*: UK and USA with NAPA including: Westminster Gallery, London, and the first International Open Long Beach Arts Gallery, Calif.; 'Vital Art 1993', Atlantis Gallery, London, 'Lyrical Orientations', Beatrice Royal Contemporary A.G., Eastleigh, British Work House Gallery, Dallas, Tex., Clifton Arts Club annual Open, Bristol, Cheltenham Group of Artists Summer Open, Society for Art of Imagination, NAPA 2002 The Mariners Gallery St. Ives, The Tobacco Factory Bristol. *Clubs*: N.A.P.A., Design and Artists Copyright Soc., Society for Art of Imagination. *Address*: Flat 3, 3 Priory Street, Monmouth, Monmouthshire NP25 3BR. *Email*: huwpc@hotmail.com *Website*: www.zap-art.f2s.com *Signs work*: "H.P.C."

CAMPBELL, James Alexander, ARCA (1964); Crafts Council index of selected makers. *Medium*: ceramic, charcoal, pastel, watercolour. *b*: Cawdor, Scotland, 1942. five *d*. *Educ*: Eton (1955-60) (Gordon Baldwin). *Studied*: RCA (1960-64 David Queensberry). *Exhib*: Oxford Gallery, Aberystwyth Arts Centre, The Stour Gallery, West Wales Arts

Centre, Amalgam, London, Brewery Arts, etc. *Works in collections*: National Gallery of Victoria, Australia, Manchester City A.G., Dundee A.G., Aberdeen A.G., National Library of Wales, National Museum and Gallery of Wales, Tokoname Inst. of Ceramic Art, Japan. *Commissions*: illustrations for 'Cofio' ('Memory'), interactive CDR for Pembrokeshire CC; illustrations for 'Thistles in Aspic' by Hugh Cawdor. *Publications*: Collector's History of English Pottery by Griselda Lewis, Painted Ceramics by Brenda Pegrum, The Potter's Dictionary of Shape and Form by Neal French, Pembrokeshire Art, ed. David Lewis. *Official Purchasers*: The National Trust. *Recreations*: music. *Email*: jamescampbellart@hotmail.com *Signs work*: 'James Campbell' or 'Campbell' or 'JC'.

CAMPBELL, Joan Betty, RMS (1980), SWA (1975), Retd. Hon. RMS (1995), HRSWA (1994); artist in water-colour, oil and acrylic; teacher of miniature painting, private tuition. *b*: London, 4 May 1923. *d of*: Joseph Longhurst. *m*: Archie Campbell. one *d*. *Educ*: Loughton County High School for Girls, Essex. *Studied*: Ilford Evening Institute (mostly self-taught). *Exhib*: Westminster Galleries, Llewellyn Alexander Gallery, MAS-F (Florida), Paris Salon (1973, 1974), Bilan l'Art Contemporain of Paris (1978). *Commissions*: Franklin Mint 'Birds of the World' Miniature Porcelain Plates (1983) RSA. *Publications*: Art Editor, Hillingdon Writer. *Clubs*: Member U3A; Water Colour Tutor. *Address*: 21, Cole Court, Reservoir Road, Kettering, Northants. NN16 9QN. *Signs work*: miniatures "J.B.C." or "JC" entwined; larger works "Joan Campbell."

CAMPBELL, Lee, BA (Hons) Fine Art (1991), MA History and Theory of Art (1993); professional artist and lecturer, painter in oil, drawings in charcoal; first Artist-in-Residence, King's School, Canterbury (1994-95), Artist-in-Residence, St. Saviour's Church, Pimlico; Winner of Worshipful Co. of Painters Stainers Award (1993). *b*: New Zealand, 25 Feb 1951. *Studied*: Chelsea School of Art, Canterbury College of Art, University of Kent. *Exhib*: Solo show: Fairfax Gallery, Tunbridge Wells (1997); Albemarle Gallery, London (1997 gallery artist). *Works in collections*: USA, Scandinavia, Australia. *Commissions*: mural: Space Science Dept., University of Kent. *Clubs*: F.P.S. (Hon. Sec.). *Address*: 212 Hood House, Dolphin Square, London SW1V 3NQ. *Signs work*. "Lee Campbell."

CAMPBELL, Raymond, self taught artist in oil and acrylic, known for still life subjects. *b*: Morden, Surrey, 2 Apr 1956. *Educ*: Garth High, Morden. *Exhib*: RA, etc. *Works in collections*: England, Germany, Austria, Australia. *Works Reproduced*: limited edn. Prints. *Address*: 63 Courtnay Rd., Woking, Surrey GU21 5HG. *Signs work*: "Raymond Campbell."

CAMPBELL, Stephen Maxwell, BA (Hons) Interactive Art. *Medium*: oil. *b*: Manchester, 1985. *Partner*: Angelika. one *s*. *Studied*: Manchester School of Art (2001-2007); Escola de Belles Arts Barcelona (2006); Nikolaus Copernicus University Torun (2008). *Represented by*: Clark Art Ltd, Hale, Cheshire. *Exhib*: Group exhibitions: The Etihad Stadium, Manchester (2014); Clark Art Gallery, Cheshire (2013); The Corn Exchange, Bristol (2013); The Octagon, Bath (2011); Buxton Museum, Derbyshire (2010); The Bath Gallery, Bath (2010); Temporary Art Space, Halifax (2009); Obsidian Art, Buckinghamshire (2008); Brighton Art Fair, Sussex (2008); Studio Art Gallery, Warrington (2007); Holden Gallery, Manchester (2007). One man shows: Sandbar, Manchester (2012); Brantwood, Coniston (2012); The Station Hotel, Manchester (2011); The Albert Club (2011) From Space, Salford (2010); Gallery Od Nova, Torun, Poland (2008); Night and Day, Manchester (2007). *Works in collections*: Kelloggs, Chetham's School of Music, Automet, Wythenshawe Hospital. *Commissions*: Smooth FM, Wythenshawe Hospital, Chetham's School of Music. *Address*: 47 Ashbourne Road, Eccles, Manchester M30. *Email*: stephen@smcampbeell.eu *Website*: www.smcampbell.eu *Signs work*: "SMC".

CANNING, Neil, Hon Doctorare, University of Exeter. *b*: Enstone, Oxon., 28 Apr 1960. *s of*: Gerald Canning. *Partner*: Paul Marston. *Educ*: Spendlove School, Charlbury, and

Chipping Norton School. *Studied*: privately with Betty Bowman (1978-81). *Exhib*: numerous including: RA Summer Show, NPG, Europart Geneva, London Contemporary Art Fair, 20th Century Art Fair, Art London. *Works in collections*: HM Customs and Excise, Rolls Royce, Eagle Star, Smithkline Beecham, University of Wales, NatWest Bank, London Insurance Investment Trust, ICI, Paintings in Hospitals, Unilever. *Publications*: illustrated Skylighters (Methuen). *CAddress*: Orchard Court, Relubbus, Penzance, Cornwall TR20 9EN. *Website*: www.neilcanning.com *Signs work*: "NEIL CANNING" (verso).

CANNON, George Edward, Elected Member Lake Artists Society; Bronze Medal for Painting, Regent School of Art, London. *Medium*: oil, watercolour, drawing. *b*: Staveley, 4 Jan 1930. *m*: Dorothy. two *s*. one *d*. *Educ*: Windermere Grammar School. Studied: Regent Street School of Art, London (1948). *Exhib*: New Art Centre, London; RBA Gallery, London; Walker Art Gallery, Liverpool; Abbott Hall, Kendal; Theatre in the Forest, Grisedale; St. Martin's College, Lancaster; Charlotte Mason, Ambleside; Castle Gate House, Cockermouth; Fairfield Mill, Cumbria; Lake Artists Annual Summer Exhibition, Grasmere, Cumbria; Retrospective, Oddfellows Contemporary, Kendal; Corke Art Gallery, Liverpool. *Works in collections*: Abbott Hall; Mary Birkes; James Naughtie; Peter Talbot. *Publications*: Lake Artists catalogues. *Recreations*: music, fell walking, theatre. *Address*: Gowan Studio, 29 Fairfield Close, Staveley, Cumbria LA8 9RA. *Website*: Lake Artists *Signs work*: "GEORGE CANNON".

CANTER, Jean Mary, Elected Associate Member: Royal Society of Miniature Painters, Sculptors and Gravers 2008; Full member 2011; Society of Graphic Fine Art 1977, President 1994-1999, Honorary 2006; UK Coloured Pencil Society 2003, Gold Signature Member 2012. *Medium*: watercolour, coloured pencil, drawing. *b*: Epsom, 18 Mar 1943. *d of*: Major Henry Canter. *Educ*: Convent of the Sacred Heart, Epsom (1948-1956). *Studied*: 13+ Junior Art Award to Epsom School of Art (1956-61); Wimbledon School of Art (1961-63). *Exhib*: SGFA, RWS, UKCPS, RI, RMS, Landscape Society, Chelsea Art Society, Llewellyn Alexander; Medici Gallery, London; many local and provincial galleries. Prizes: SGFA 1983, 1984, 1985, 1990, 1993, 1996x2, 1997, 2006, 2007; UKCPS 2006, 07, 10, 12, 13; Recommended UKCPS 2006; Llewellyn Alexander 'A Million Brushstrokes' 2004, 2007; RMS Gold Memorial Bowl Honourable Mention 2008. *Works in collections*: Bourne Hall Museum Collection, Ewell. *Commissions*: some private commissions. *Publications*: articles and demonstrations for "Artist's and Illustrator's", "Eaglemoss", "Painting with Watercolours" and a regular feature "The Drawing Class" for "Painting World" magazines. *Works Reproduced*: Drawings, paintings and step-by-step demonstrations for many 'How-to' art books (Quarto). *Recreations*: music. *Clubs*: ARMS, UKCPS, SGFA. *Misc*: Colourist for Baynton-Williams, Antique Print Dealers 1968-72; Part-time Art Tutor for mid-Surrey Adult Education 1972-2007 running classes in Watercolours, Drawing Techniques, Gouache and Flower Painting. *Address*: 7 Cox Lane, Ewell, Epsom, Surrey KT19 9LR. *Website*: www.jeancanter.co.uk *Signs work*: "JEAN CANTER." (& year).

CAPRARA, Julia Rosemary, NDD, ATC Lond. (1961), MSDC, Hon. Exhibiting mem. 62 Group (1970); designer in embroidery, textile artist; co-principal, Opus School of Textile Arts. *b*: London, 27 Feb 1939. *d of*: John I. L. Jenkins. *m*: Alex. Caprara. one *s*. *Educ*: Perse School for Girls, Cambridge; Henrietta Barnett School, Hampstead. *Studied*: Hornsey College of Art (1955-61). *Exhib*: one-man show of Embroidery at Commonwealth Institute A.G.; 62 Group shows: Guildford House, National Museum of Wales, Congress House, Foyle's A.G., Australia, USA, Japan. *Works in collections*: National Museum of Wales, Cardiff; Holocaust Museum, Israel; private collections. *Commissions*: Wall panel, City Technology College, Bradford, Braintree Art Collections; private commissions. *Publications*: The Magic of Embroidery (B.T.Batsford). *Address*: 20 Crown St., Harrow-on-the-Hill, Middx. HA2 0HR. *Signs work*: "Julia Caprara."

CARDEW , Sidney, RSMA; senior design engineer, Ford MC (retd.); Ranelagh Press Award (RSMA, 2009) to the Artist of an Outstanding Marine Watercolour; self taught marine artist in water-colour and oil. *b*: London, 1931. *m*: Eunice. one *s*. one *d*. *Educ*: S E Essex Technical College. *Exhib*: RSMA, RWS, London galleries. Work in collections internationally. *Commissions*: Large marine water-colour for London offices. *Publications*: article on Wapping Group, Calendar 1992, Articles in Wapping Group of Artists, Watercolour Skies & Clouds Techniques, RSMA Book, Celebration of Marine Art. *Clubs*: Wapping Group, London Sketch, Essex Art, Chelsea Arts. *Address*: 38 Repton Avenue, Gidea Park, Essex RM2 5LT. *Website*: c/o Mall Gallery, London *Signs work*: "Sidney Cardew."

CARDNELL, Delia, RI (2000); Stokes-Roberts Bursary, Worshipful Company of Painter Stainers (1995); RI Winsor & Newton Young Artist (1999); National Young Artist, Laing Art Competition (1999); RI Frank Herring Award (2000), council of the Royal Institute of Painters in Water-colours, 2001-2006 & 2010-2014. *Medium*: watercolours and oil. *b*: London, 14 Oct 1974. *Educ*: Francis Holland School (Clarence Gate), (1986-91); South Hampstead High School, (1991-93). *Exhib*: Exhibitions include: RP, NEAC, RBA, Laing Art Competition, Sunday Times Watercolour Competition, SWA; South West Academy of Fine and Applied Arts, Royal Water-colour Society, Royal Society of Portrait Painters and their 2001 exhibition of selected paintings held at the National Portrait Gallery; work exhibited at various galleries and held in many collections. *Commissions*: accepted. *Works Reproduced*: Cards for The Artists General Benevolent Institution and Medicin Sans Frontieres, 2009-. *Address*: c/o 26 Ockendon Rd., Islington, London N1 3NP. *Website*: www.deliacardnell.com *Signs work*: "Delia Cardnell."

CAREY, Annabel, BSc Hons, PGCE. *Medium*: acrylic, oil, watercolour, batik. *b*: 1953. *d of*: Pam and Eric Luke. *m*: David W. Birch (artist). two *s*. one *d*. *Studied*: Durham University, Nottingham University (1971-75). *Represented by*: Christine Talbot-Cooper - International Artists. *Exhib*: RWA; RWS; solo exhbns: Michael Tippett Centre, Bath; Goldsmiths College, London; Gloucester City Museum and Art Gallery; solo touring exhbns: 'Spirit of Stones', Marischal Museum, Aberdeen; Lotherton Hall, Leeds; Hereford Art Gallery; Royal Cornwall Museum and Art Gallery, Truro (2003-06); Newport City Musum and Art Gallery (2009); Winds of Change Gallery, Winchcombe (2010). *Works in collections*: Gloucester City Museum and Art Gallery. *Works Reproduced*: Limited edition prints of 'Spirit of Stones' available. *Address*: Croftsbrook, Blind Lane, Chipping Campden, Glos GL55 6ED. *Email*: talbotcooper@onetel.com *Website*: www.ctcinternationalartists.com *Signs work*: 'A.Carey' or 'A' within larger 'C'.

CAREY, Laura. *Medium*: sculpture. *b*: Scotland, 2 Nov 1955. *m*: Paul Carey. one *d*. *Studied*: City & Guilds of London Art School (1975-79); Goldsmiths College University of London (1993-94, PGCE in Art & Design); City University 1995-96, MA in Art Policy; Christies Education, RSA Fine and Decorative Arts Professional Diploma. *Exhib*: private and corporate, commercially. Worked for Madame Tussauds Studios as a freelance sculptor after leaving arts school. *Works in collections*: private and corporate. *Commissions*: Various private and corporate. Public works: Tobacco Docks, London; Dunn & Bradstreet Headquarters. International private commissions in Switzerland, Australia, Turkey, North America, Scotland and England. *Official Purchasers*: Collaborative Sculpture for the World Cup 2010 - The Ultimate Performing Player. *Works Reproduced*: private and corporate, recently Greenwich University. *Recreations*: exhibition, theatre and film goer. *Misc*: Taught at Wimbledon School of Art and South Bank University. Collaboratives with husband Paul with the London Group. Professional experience: Film, Television - figurative effects, working with directors such as Stanley Kubrick. *Address*: Greenwich, London SE10 0JZ. *Email*: laura@special-art-effects.co.uk *Website*: www.special-art-effects.co.uk *Signs work*: "Laura Carey".

CARNEY, William Davies: , BA Hons; Charles Pears Award for Best Painting in RSMA Exhbn (2003). *Medium*: oil, watercolour, drawing. *b*: Stockton-on-Tees, 18 Aug 1943. *s of*: Walter Carney. one *s*. *Studied*: Hornsey School of Art, London (1976). *Represented by*: RSMA. *Exhib*: RA, ROI, NEAC, RBA, NEAC, RSMA, private galleries, Royal Navy venues, Herts. Art Society, Llewellyn Alexander Gallery, The Cut (London), Waterloo SE1 8UN. *Works in collections*: private collections in UK, USA, Yugoslavia, Canada. *Publications*: International Artists (Painting Still Life and Florals). *Principal Works*: oil painting 'Old Harry's Rock' (Charles Pears Award). *Recreations*: travel, history. *Clubs*: RSMA. *Address*: 75 Baker Street, Potters Bar, Herts EN6 2EX. *Email*: wdcarney@yahoo.com *Signs work*: 'W.Carney, ARSMA'

CARNIE, Andrew John, BA (1982), RCA (1986); painter, sculptor, photographer and new media artist. *b*: 8 Jan 1957. *s of*: Dr. and Mrs. J.M. Carnie. *m*: Judith Mary Wallas. two *s*. one *d*. *Educ*: Lakes School, Windermere. *Studied*: Goldsmiths' School of Art, London, Royal College of Art, London. *Represented by*: SCICULT. *Exhib*: many mixed person shows including 'Head On' Science Museum, London; International Film Festival, Rotterdam; 'Disperse', Amnesty International HQ, London; Whitechapel Open, Mostyn Open, John Moores; and one-person shows including Girray Gallery, London, Flowers Gallery, London, Winchester Gallery, Bracknell Gallery, Plymouth Art Centre, Tram Gallery, London, and Columbus Gallery, Georgia, U.S.A., Millais Gallery, Southampton. *Works in collections*: Unilever London, Chase Manhattan Bank London, Coopers and Lybrand London, Kaempher Corp., Washington, U.S.A., Prudential Collection, London. *Commissions*: DC Dance Company., Arts Humanities Board, Wellcome Trust. *Publications*: Andrew Carnie (Winchester Gallery). ISBN 1 873451 45 8. *Address*: 5 Powell Rd., London E5 8DJ. *Email*: andrewcarnie@tram.ndo.co.uk *Website*: www.andrewcarnie.co.uk *Signs work*: "ANDREW CARNIE" or not at all.

CARPANINI, David Lawrence, Prof, PRE (1995-2003), Dip.AD, MA (RCA), ATC, Hon.RBSA., RCA, RWA, RE, NEAC, Hon RWS; painter, printmaker; British Inst. Awards Committee Sch. Engraving (1969). *b*: Abergwynfi, Glam., 1946. *s of*: Lorenzo Carpanini. *m*: Jane Carpanini. one *s*. *Educ*: Glan Afan Grammar School, Port Talbot. *Studied*: Gloucestershire College of Art (1964-68), Royal College of Art (1968-71), University of Reading (1971-72). *Exhib*: RA, RBA, RWA, RE, NEAC, Bankside Gallery, New Academy Gallery, Agnews, Piccadilly Gallery, Attic, Albany, Mostyn, Fosse and Brandler Galleries, Welsh Arts Council, etc. *Works in collections*: National Library and National Museum of Wales, Contemporary Art Society for Wales, Newport A.G., Glynn Vivian A.G., Dept. Environment, RWA, NCB, ASTMS, Glam., Glos., Clwyd., Avon, Yorks. Educ. Authorities, and private collections in UK, USA, Canada, Europe, Australia, etc. Television Films: C4 (1984), HTV (1987, 1997, 1998). *Publications*: numerous articles and pictures have been published in various art periodicals and reference books; reproductions, cards, catalogues etc. *Address*: Fernlea, 145 Rugby Rd., Milverton, Leamington Spa, Warwickshire CV32 6DJ. *Signs work*: "David L. Carpanini."

CARPANINI, Jane, DipAD, ATC, RWA, RWS, RCA; artist in water-colour and pencil. *b*: Luton, 1949. *d of*: Derrick Stanley Allen. *m*: David L. Carpanini. one *s*. *Educ*: Bedford High School. *Studied*: Luton College of Art (1967-68), Brighton Polytechnic (1968-71), University of Reading (1971-72). *Exhib*: RA, RWA, RBA, RWS, Bankside Gallery, Attic, New Academy Gallery, Fosse and Brandler Galleries, Welsh Arts Council, Mostyn, Albany, etc. Winner of Hunting Group prize Watercolour of the Year (1983). *Works in collections*: National Library and National Museum of Wales, Burnley Building Soc., etc., and private collections in UK, USA, Europe. TV films, HTV (1997). *Publications*: has contributed to various art periodicals; numerous reproductions; cards, prints, calendars, catalogues, etc. *Address*: Fernlea, 145 Rugby Rd., Milverton, Leamington Spa, Warwickshire CV32 6DJ. *Signs work*: "Jane Carpanini."

CARR, David James, BA Fine Art; Slade School Painting prize, Steer prize, Nettleship prize, David Murray Landscape Scholarship, Boise Scholarship UCL; painter and printmaker. *b*: Middlesbrough, 15 Mar 1944. *m*: Marie Wylan. one *d* (from first marriage). *Educ*: Sir William Turners Grammar School, Coatham, Yorkshire. *Studied*: Slade School (1962-66), John Aldridge, Auerbach, Coldstream, Uglow. *Represented by*: London-Rowley Gallery, Adam Butler Fine Art, The Walk SE1; San Francisco, Calif. - Thomas Reynolds. *Exhib*: RA, London Group, Cleveland Biennale, Laing, Hunting Group, Singer & Friedlander. *Works in collections*: London Heritage, Royal Free, Wesleys Chapel, Ford Motors, UCL, local authorities; private collections: UK, USA, Japan. *Commissions*: Wesley Chapel, London (millennial); Ford Motors. *Publications*: Introduction to Painting the Nude (Quarto). *Works Reproduced*: London Group Year Book 2003, www.thomasreynolds.com. *Clubs*: London Group. *Address*: 22 Minton Mews, London NW6 1XX. *Email*: artdcuk@yahoo.co.uk *Website*: www.davidcarr.me.uk *Signs work*: "DAVID CARR." or 'David J.Carr.'

CARRINGTON-SMITH, Lynette, DipAD, SM, SLM (RHS); three Silver Medals & the Silver Lindley (for Special Scientific Interest) for 3 collections of botanical paintings at RHS. *Medium*: watercolour. *b*: Bath, 9 Oct 1946. two *s*. one *d*. *Studied*: West of England College of Art (textiles). *Exhib*: Royal Horticultural Society, Westminster Hall (SBA), USA, Spain and France. *Commissions*: UK greeting card collections, mual designs for private client. Spain: 1998-2012. commissions for Mayor of Principality of Tivissa, and large private collection of still lifes for restauranteur and private commissions. *Works Reproduced*: greetings cards and limited artist prints. *Clubs*: SBA. *Misc*: currently working on large collection of paintings for future exhibitions, on commissions, completing the 'Far East' Collection, and collection of paintings of Canadian flora, birds and insects. *Address*: 2052 Forestry Farm Road, RR1 Delhi, Norfolk County, Ontario N4B 2W4, Canada. *Email*: lynettecarrington9@gmail.com *Website*: www.lynettecarringtonsmith.com *Signs work*: "L.C.K." or "Lynette Carrington-Kerslake" or "L.C.S."

CARROLL, Leo, Chartered Civil Engineer, Academician Royal Cambrian Academy(1980); Member National Society of Painters, Sculptors & Printmakers (1974); award Paris Salon (1974). *Medium*: painter in oils, acrylics, watercolour, pastel. *b*: St. Helens, 30 Dec 1932. *m*: Dorothea. two *d*. *Studied*: self-taught. *Exhib*: Royal Cambrian Academy, RA, Manchester Academy of Arts, Royal Society of British Artists; National Society of Painters, Sculptors and Printmakers; regularly over 25 years with Royal Institute of Oil Painters. One-man exhbns in London, North Wales, Cheshire, Lancashire, Shropshire. *Works in collections*: work on regular show in commercial galleries Lancashire, North Wales, Cheshire. *Commissions*: Concrete Society, and numerous private collections. Portraits/landscapes. *Official Purchasers*: Liverpool University. *Misc*: Landscape paintings convey the visual image freely interpreted with close tonal values. Other subjects vary from groups of figures to single figure studies. *Address*: Romany, Plough Lane, Christleton, Chester, CH3 7PT. *Email*: leo@leocarroll.plus.com *Signs work*: 'CARROLL'.

CARRON, William John, WCSI (1977); ARHA (1996); acrylic marine and landscape painter; tutor. *b*: Dublin, 28 July 1930. *m*: Barbara Warren, RHA. one *d*. *Educ*: Bolton Street School of Education and Technology. *Studied*: NCAD, Dublin. *Exhib*: RHA and WSI; one-man shows in Dublin. *Works in collections*: RHA and WSI collections; Nat. self-portrait (Limerick University); private collections in Ireland, UK and USA. *Publications*: 'A Painter in the West', (poems and pen and ink drawings), 'In Roundstone Church Yard', (poems and pen and ink drawings). *Clubs*: Royal Dublin Society. *Address*: "Matakana", Grey's Lane, Howth, Co. Dublin, Eire. *Signs work*: "W. CARRON."

CARRUTHERS, Derek William, Prof, (Emeritus Professorship - Nottingham Trent), BA; artist in various media, mainly oil painting. *Medium*: constructions, paintings etc.

b: Penrith, Cumbria, 1935. *s of*: William Edward Carruthers. *m*: Eileen. one *s*. one *d*. *Educ*: Royal Grammar School, Lancaster. *Studied*: Durham University, King's College (now Newcastle University) (Victor Pasmore, Richard Hamilton, Lawrence Gowing). *Exhib*: John Moores Liverpool, 'Structure' Bradford Arts Festival, Midland View, Open Drawing Show, Cheltenham, Sunday Times RWS Exhibition. *Works in collections*: Northern Arts, Leics. Educ. Authority, Bradford A.G., Abbot Hall Gallery Kendal, Leicester University, Leeds City Gallery. *Commissions*: Relief for Attenborough Building, Leicester University. *Publications*: Artisan (1979), Haunting Monuments (1985), Recent Paintings (1985-88), Figuring Art (2004). *Works Reproduced*: in publications *Address*: The School House, Harston, nr. Grantham NG32 1PS. *Email*: derekcarruthers@btinternet.com *Website*: derekcarruthers *Signs work*: "CARRUTHERS" and "Derek Carruthers."

CARSWELL, Fiona Charis, BA Hons (1983); artist in water-colour, mixed media and book binding. *b*: Scotland, 10 Mar 1960. *m*: Richard Hackett. one *s*. two *d*. *Educ*: Rugby High School. *Studied*: Oxford Polytechnic (1980-83, Ivor Robinson). *Exhib*: various exhbns. showing book work and paintings in London, Brussels, Oxford and USA. *Address*: Windrush Cottage, Fulbrook, Oxon. OX18 4BL. *Signs work*: "Fiona Charis Carswell" or "F.C.C."

CARTER, Alexander Peter, BA (1986), MA (1989); painter in oil and watercolour. *b*: Epsom, Surrey, 12 Sep 1951. *m*: Sorrel Scott-Carter. two *s*. *Educ*: Wellington College, Berks. *Studied*: art Camberwell (1983-86), Royal Academy (1986-89). *Exhib*: Highgate (1995), Plough Terrington (2000). *Clubs*: RASAA. *Address*: 26 Station Rd, Okehampton, Devon EX20 1EA.

CARTER, Beth Arabella, BA (Hons) Fine Art; award: 1st prize Northern Graduates Show (1995) Royal College of Art; Cyprus College of Art, Paphos. *Medium*: sculpture, bronze and drawing (charcoal). *b*: Derbyshire, 25 Oct 1968. *d of*: Roy Carter. *Studied*: Sunderland University UK (1992-95), Bath College Further Education (1990-91), Academy Fine Arts Bulgaria (1991-92). *Represented by*: Bertrand Delacroix Gallery, New York; Axelle Fine Art, New York. *Exhib*: The above New York galleries, also View Art Gallery, Bristol, UK; Bo-Lee Gallery, Bath, UK. *Works in collections*: private collections UK, Cyprus, Bulgaria, Monte Carlo, USA. *Commissions*: lifesize bronze, private commission (2002), numerous private; site specific installation 'Beauty and the Beast' Show (2006), National Trust, Stourhead, Wiltshire, UK. *Address*: 38 Chatsworth Rd, Bristol, BS4 3EY. *Email*: bethcarter@tantraweb.co.uk *Website*: www.bethcarter.co.uk *Signs work*: 'BC'.

CARTER, Derek Ronald, SGFA, painter in black and white media, watercolour, pastel, acrylic and oil; cityscape artist. *b*: London, 1930. *m*: June. two *s*. one *d*. *Educ*: Clarks College, London. *Studied*: with Brian Gallagher PS (1990-1993), Slade Summer School (1991-1993) under Jo Volley. *Exhib*: ROI, Pastel Society, Society Graphic Fine Art, and various in South East England. *Works in collections*: private collections in UK and USA. *Address*: 5 Park Lawn Rd., Weybridge, Surrey KT13 9EU. *Signs work*: "CARTER."

CARTER, Joan Patricia, RMS(1986), SWA (1985); Gold medallist Paris Salon (1974), finalist Hunting Group prizes (1980), Hon. men. Gold Bowl RMS; freelance portrait painter, book illuminator, illustrator and calligrapher in water-colour, pastel, acrylic and silverpoint; writer. *b*: Vancouver, BC, Canada, 11 Mar 1923. *d of*: Major G.F.B. Willcox, RA (India), soldier and artist. *m*: Alan Henry Carter. two *s*. *Educ*: Lord Selkerk School, Vancouver, Canada. *Studied*: CFE, Longbridge Rd., Ilford; Havering CFE, Hornchurch (A' level Art and Art History). *Exhib*: Schweinfurt, Germany, Paris Salon, R.A., numerous one-man shows etc., MAS-F. *Works in collections*: miniature portrait (1.5" x1") of Mrs. S. Lucas on gold bowl, RMS (1985). *Publications*: Uncle Bill and Aunt Ethel, Allergy Cooking (Ian Henry Pub.), Solo Cooking on a Shoe String (Ian Henry Pub.), Illuminated Calligraphy (Search

Press), Illuminated Alphabet (Search Press), Illuminated Design: The Art of Illumination (Search Press), Silverpoint (Search Press), numerous Remembrance books - thirteen in England, one Normandy, France, one Tristan da Cunha, various talks and broadcasts, and articles; art work for book cover (Fowler Wright); book: 'Vegan Veggie Cookbook', 'Tessie Bear's Country Week-end'. *Address*: 4 Osprey Close, Hoveton, Norwich, Norfolk NR12 8DR. *Signs work*: art books: "Patricia Carter"; other books: "J.P. Carter".

CARTER, John, RA (elected 2007); Leverhulme Travelling Scholarship (1963); Peter Stuyvesant Foundation Travel Bursary (1966); Arts Council of Britain Award (1977); Arts Council Purchase Award (1979: Prizewinner, Tolly Cobbold Eastern Arts 3rd National Exhibition (1981). Medium: sculpture. *b*: Hampton Hill, 3 Mar 1942. *m*: Belinda Cadbury. *Studied*: Twickenham School of Art (1958-59), Kingston School of Art (1959-1963), British School at Rome (1964). *Represented by*: Redfern Gallery, London; Galerie Hoffmann, Friedberg, Germany. *Exhib*: Solo exhibitions include: Redfern Gallery, London (1968, 1971, 1974, 1977, 2010, 2013); Galerie Hoffman, Friedberg, Germany (1998, 2008, 2014); Tennant Gallery, Royal Academy of Arts, London (2013) and many more throughout Europe, Japan and USA. Group exhibitions include: New Generation (1966); Hayward Gallery, London (1974); Southampton City Art Gallery (2008) and many others in UK and abroad. *Works in collections*: Work in many public and corporate collections in Britain and abroad. *Recreations*: Hill walking in Wales. *Clubs*: Chelsea Arts. Misc: Part time lecturer in various art schools from 1965 inc Chelsea College of Art and Design until 1999. *Address*: 71A Westbourne Park Road, London W2 5QH. *Email*: west2studios@waitrose.com *Signs work*: "John Carter".

CARTER, Lucille Anne, SBA (2004); BTech National Diploma for Art & Design; Margaret Grainger Memorial Bowl (SBA 2004), SBA Highly Recommended (2005). *Medium*: watercolour. *b*: Melbourne, Australia, 8 Jun 1944. *m*: Barry Carter. one *s*. one *d*. *Studied*: Echuca, Bendigo Teachers College (Art Teaching, 1961-62); Melbourne University College (Arts, 1963). *Exhib*: Riverside Mansions, Wapping, London (1997); SBA, Westminster Gallery (annually since 1999). Solo shows: Ascougphee Hall, Spalding, Lincs (2000). *Works in collections*: many via SBArt@Central Hall. *Commissions*: Leverington Hall, Wisbech, Cambs; Frettenham Mansion, Norwich. *Publications*: calendars, postcards, greetings cards. *Misc*: Sold most of the 40 exhibited platters and wallplates at End of Course exhibition (2002). Qualified Art Teacher. *Address*: 81 Goodwins Road, Kings Lynn, Norfolk PE30 5PE. *Email*: bcarter188@yahoo.co.uk *Signs work*: "Lucille".

CARTER, Mary Elizabeth, MA, ARCA; painter in oil of miniatures, portraits, rural and domestic scenes; Princess of Wales Scholarship. *Medium*: Oil. *b*: London, 1947. *d of*: H.E. Carter. *m*: J. B. Hiscock, painter. two *s*. one *d*. *Educ*: Ursuline Convent, Wimbledon. *Studied*: Kingston School of Art, Royal College of Art (Carel Weight, Roger de Grey). *Exhib*: Zaydler Gallery, R.W.A., Llewellyn Alexander Gallery, Richard Hagen Gallery, Miniaturist for New Grafton Gallery, R.A. Summer Exhbn. since 1968, Hestercombe House. *Works in collections*: Southend-on-Sea Library, R.A., Camden Council. *Publications*: The Dog Who Knew Too Much. *Address*: 2 Hodges Cottages, Hemyock, Cullompton, Devon EX15 3RW. *Email*: mary@marycarter.co.uk *Website*: www.marycarter.co.uk *Signs work*: "Mary E. Carter."

CARTER, Rita Violet, (nee DUNNING); NDD (1964), ATD (1965), Cert. RAS (1968); previously art lecturer West Sussex Colleges, presently painter, poet, illustrator. *Medium*: painter in watercolour, acrylics, oil; Illustrations pen and ink. *b*: London, 3 Jun 1944. *m*: Derek. two *s*. three *d*. *Educ*: Ifield Grammar School. *Studied*: West Sussex College of Art & Crafts (1960-64), London University (1964-65), RA Schools (1965-68). *Exhib*: Surrey, Sussex, Midlands (Worcs. and Shropshire). *Works in collections*: America - EMI (Capital Records), various private in UK. *Commissions*: illustration, painting. *Publications*: anthologies- 'One for Jimmy', 'Along the Line', 'Trees at the World's Edge', 'Path to the

Year's Height', 'Lodestones', 'A Brush With Words' Painting and Poetry book (2005). *Clubs*: Shropshire Border Poets, RASAA. *Misc*: involved with preparing poetry/painting exhbn. with Border Poets and RASAA/Reynolds Club at Martin's Gallery, Cheltenham, Glos, in Oct 2005. *Address*: 17 Bowling Green Close, Burford, Tenbury Wells, WR15 8RD. *Email*: atir_49@yahoo.co.uk

CARTER, Roy. *Medium*: sculpture. *b*: London, 11 Apr 1938. one *s*. two *d*. *Studied*: self-taught. *Exhib*: RA (2007), RWA (2006, 2007), Discerning Eye (2007). *Address*: The Chimneys, Dauntsey Lock, nr. Lyneham, Wiltshire, SN15 4HE. *Email*: roycarter10@btinternet.com *Signs work*: "R.C." (with year).

CARTER, Simon Charles. *Medium*: acrylic, watercolour, drawing. *b*: Chelmsford, Essex, 28 Nov 1961. *s of*: Colin Carter, Architect. *m*: Ruth. two *s*. *Educ*: Colchester Royal Grammar School. *Studied*: North East London Polytechnic (1981-84). *Represented by*: Messum's; Walton Fine Art. *Exhib*: Firstsite, Essex; Hastings Museum & Art Gallery; Waltons Fine Art, Suffolk; Great Eastern Hotel, London; Agnews, London; Messum's, London; London Art Fair; Toronto Art Fair. *Works in collections*: private/school/hotel collections in England & USA. *Publications*: 'Another Day on the Beach', Firstsite, Essex (2003); 'Get Constable', Ipswich Town Hall Galleries (2008) Borderlines, Messums (2011). *Works reproduced*: WaterMarks, Art in East Anglia, Black Dog Books 2010. *Recreations*: gardening. *Misc*: Won RHS Gold Medal for a show garden at Hampton Court Show 2006 in collaboration with designer Thomas Hoblyn. *Address*: 4 Buckfast Ave., Kirby Cross, Essex, CO13 0PU. *Email*: simon@simoncarterpaintings.co.uk *Website*: simoncarterpaintings.co.uk *Signs work*: "SIMON CARTER".

CARTWRIGHT, Richard Saint George, painter in pastel and oil. *b*: Epsom, Surrey, 30 Sep 1951. *Studied*: self taught. *Exhib*: solo shows every two years at John Martin, London and Adam Gallery, Bath. *Works in collections*: private collections. *Address*: 9 Woolcot St., Redland, Bristol BS6 6QH. *Email*: rsgcartwright@hotmail.com *Signs work*: "Richard Cartwright."

CARVER, Margaret, RMS (1995), SWA (1997); artist in oil, pastel, water-colour, pencil; Chairperson, Gt.Yarmouth Soc. of Artists for 23 years; Certificate of Excellence for 6 miniature landscapes - Llewelyn Alexander. *b*: Caister-on-Sea, 10 Sep 1941. *m*: Richard Carver. two *s*. *Educ*: Caister High School; Gt. Yarmouth CFE. *Studied*: evening classes and part-time courses. *Exhib*: Westminster and Mall Galleries with SWA and RMS, Norwich, Gt. Yarmouth. World Exhibitions of Miniature Art in London, Tasmania and Washington DC; Llewelyn Alexander, London; Medici Galleries, London; Bath, Canterbury, Wells. Five solo exhibitions in East Anglia. *Works in collections*: Gt. Yarmouth and District Society. Two watercolours in book of original paintings accepted by H.M. Queen Elizabeth II commemorating her Diamond Jubilee in library at Sandringham House. *Publications*: SWA Exhibitors. RMS 'One Hundred Years' vellum bound copy in Queen's library at Windsor. *Misc*: promoted art at local hospital for 21 years. *Address*: 3 Orchard Cl., Caister-on-Sea, Gt. Yarmouth,. Norfolk NR30 5DS. *Email*: ra.carver@btinternet.com *Website*: www.greatyarmouthartists.co.uk *Signs work*: "M. CARVER."

CARY, Caroline Anne, FPS; Palet Prize for Mixed Media; Purchase Prize Painting Royal London Hospital. *Medium*: painter in acrylic and mixed media. *b*: 28 Jul 1940. *m*: Lucius Cary (divorced). one *s*. three *d* (one decd). *Educ*: Convent of the Sacred Heart, Woldingham. *Studied*: Camberwell and Chelsea Colleges of Art under Lawrence Gowing. *Represented by*: Studio 106, Piers Feetham. *Exhib*: Clarges Gallery, Jonathon Poole, Clark Fine Art, Gallery Zol, Bruton St. Gallery, Austin Desmond Fine Art, William Desmond Fine Art, Devon, etc.; solo exhibitions: London: Loggia Gallery, New Grafton Gallery, Langton Gallery, Lord Leighton's Studio, Leighton House, Sue Rankin Gallery; Watatu Gallery, Nairobi, Century Gallery Henley, Galerie Souham, Paris, Z Gallery, N.Y., The Millinery Works, London; The

Royal London Hospital - Sam Pease; Corporate Connoisseurs; Piers Feetham; Collaboration ICG Paintings Laser Nightfilm, Cary & Webb; Trinity Buoy Wharf, Docklands. *Works in collections*: private collections: R. Agnew, J. Agnew, K. Shapland, M. Fisher; public collections: The Royal London Hospital, Whitechapel, London. *Commissions*: several. *Official Purchasers*: The Royal London Hospital, Whitechapel. *Recreations*: films, reading, walking. *Clubs*: Chelsea Arts. *Address*: The Studio, 14 Gunter Grove, London SW10 0UJ. *Email*: caroline@carocary.co.uk *Website*: www.carolinecary.com *Signs work*: "C.A.C."

CASDAGLI, Daphne Catherine, RE, MA (RCA); Print-technician (1972-73), then visiting lecturer at the Byam Shaw School of Art (1973-84); lecturer for Foundation, Printmaking & Illustrative Arts at the City & Guilds of London Art School (1973-1998); Elected Associate Royal Society of Painter Printmakers (1998), Fellow RE (2003), appointed Honorary Curator (2003). *Medium*: oils, watercolour, printmaking, drawing. *b*: Cairo, 11 Dec 1946. *d of*: Emmanuel Casdagli. *Educ*: in Cairo, Paris and England. *Studied*: Beaux Arts de Versailles(1964-1965), Guildford and Farnham Schools of Art(1965-69), RCA under Prof. Carel Weight and Sir Roger de Grey (Masters degree, 1969-1972). *Represented by*: Bankside Gallery (RE). *Exhib*: The British Council, Athens; RA Summer Exhibition, Arts Club, Bankside Gallery, Mall Galleries, London; Jonleigh Gallery, Guildford; Chichester Centre of Arts. *Works in collections*: UK, Europe, America, Venezuela. *Commissions*: Murals for Greek restaurant; St. Quinterie Press portfolio. *Publications*: illustrations for books on techniques. *Recreations*: piano playing, gardening. *Address*: Newark Farmhouse, Chichester Rd., West Wittering, W.Sussex, PO20 8QA. *Signs work*: "D. Casdagli."

CASE, David Charles, MA (1966), Hon. RE; publisher. *b*: 18 Oct 1943. *m*: Anthea. two *d*. *Educ*: Oakham School, Oxford University. *Address*: The Old Rectory, Church Road, Brockdish, Norfolk IP21 4JJ. *Website*: www.davidcasefineart.com

CASSELDINE, Nigel, ARWA (1985), RWA (1991), Brandler Painting prize (1988); artist/painter in oil on gesso/drawing; Council mem. RWA (1990-93, 1996-98); Mem. AOI. *b*: Havering, Essex, 1947. *s of*: G E Casseldine and P W M Lovesy. *m*: Jenny Partridge. one *s*. one *d*. *Educ*: N. Romford Comprehensive School. *Studied*: Camberwell and Sir John Cass Schools of Art (1966-68, part-time); studio assistant to F.V. Magrath (1969-72). *Exhib*: RA, RWA, Bath Festival, Edinburgh Festival, Medici Gallery, Gloucester A.G. and Museum, Bruton Gallery, Penwith Galleries (St. Ives), etc. *Works in collections*: RWA, Cheltenham and Gloucester, Lord of Bath. *Publications*: 20th Century Painters and Sculptors by F. Spalding; Light by L. Willis; 'Pictures in an Academy' (Redcliffe Press). *Official Purchasers*: Royal West of England Academy. *Works Reproduced*: Oil paintings in publich ownership, Bristol; BBC Your Paintings. *Principal Works*: 'Shingle Street'; portrait of John Burzynski. *Address*: Romany Studio, Woodbridge Rd., Tunstall Woodbridge Suffolk IP12 2JE. *Website*: www.romanystudio.co.uk *Signs work*: "CASSELDINE" in red.

CASSON, Lucy, BA Hons. *Medium*: sculpture. *b*: Buckinghamshire, 20 Mar 1960. *Partner*: Tod. *Educ*: Gt Missenden Secondary Modern, Hereford Art Foundation. *Studied*: Camberwell School of Art, London 1978-81. *Exhib*: Velvet Da Vinci San Fran USA, Scottish Gallery, Rebecca Hossack Gallery, Ruthin Arts Centre Tour, Contemporary Applied Art, Montbeliard France, Craft2eu Hamburg Germany, Found Gallery Tokyo, Diorama Gallery, Nancy Margolis Main USA, Blickling Hall, Eastnor Castle, Oriel Davis Newport, Medi. *Works in collections*: British Council, Crafts Council, V&A Museum, Anthony Petullo Collection Milwaukee USA. *Commissions*: Moorfields Eye Hospital, Devonport Dental Hospital, Woodstock Museum, Hull Festival, Lieux Publics France, Newcastle Metro, Evelina Childrens Hospital, Look Ahead Housing Ilford, Sustrans - Oxon, Chess Set Crafts Council, Aberdeen Hospital, Theatre Design - Monster Productions, Likewater Company Tokyo, Foxes and Cheeries Brixton London, Bronze Seating Leeds, Co-op

Headquarters, Yorkshire Dance Centre, Russel-Cotes Art Gallery. *Publications*: Lucy Casson - Ruthin Arts 2001. *Address*: 22 Combermere Rd, London SW9 9RF. *Email*: lucycasson@hotmail.co.uk *Website*: www.axisweb.org/artist/lucycasson *Signs work*: "Lucy CASSON".

CASSON, Simon John, ARE (1992), RAS(MA) (1994), Central Printmaking Dip. (1990), BA (Hons.) Fine Art (1988); painter in oil, printmaker in etching. *b*: York, 17 May, 1965. *Educ*: Rose Avenue School, Zambia, Cumbria, Penistone Grammar School, Sheffield. *Studied*: Barnsley College of Art (1985), Exeter College of Art and Design (1985-87), Central St. Martin's (1988-90, Norman Ackroyd), Royal Academy of Arts (1991-94, Prof. Norman Adams). *Exhib*: Regular solo shows at Long & Ryle Gallery, London. *Works in collections*: Private collections home and abroad. *Address*: 87a Albion Rd., Stoke Newington, London N16 9PL.

CASTLE, James Munro, BA Hons (Sculpture); Associate Royal British Society of Sculptors (2004); Elected Royal Scottish Academician (2008). *Medium*: sculptor - painted wood, bronze, plaster, mixed media drawing. *b*: Aberdeen, 14 Dec 1946. *s of*: Johann & James Castle. *m*: Susan Harrison. one *s*. one *d*. *Studied*: Ealing School of Art (1967-68); Winchester School of Art (1968-71); Royal College of Art (Foundry Course, 1980). *Represented by*: Compass Gallery, Glasgow. *Exhib*: selected one-man shows: Artspace Galleries, Aberdeen; Crawford Centre, St.Andrews University; Open Eye Gallery, Edinburgh; Compass Gallery, Glasgow; Pier Art Gallery, Orkney; Bohun Gallery, Henley-on-Thames; Swindon Art Gallery and Museum; Gallery Oldham. Group exhibitions throughout UK and Germany 1984 to present. Curator: Sculpture at Gloucester Cathedral and Malmesbury Abbey (2001); co-curatore, 186th Annual Exhibition Royal Scottish Academy, Edinburgh (2012). *Works in collections*: public and private. *Publications*: 'James Castle - Sculpture and Drawing' (Peacock Printmakers, Aberdeen). *Works Reproduced*: solo and group exhibition catalogues. *Recreations*: cycling. *Misc*: Senior Lecturer in Sculpture at the University of Gloucestershire, appointed 1988-2009. *Address*: 'Newlands', Kings Walk, Malmesbury, Wilts. SN16 9DB. *Email*: castleharrison@tiscali.co.uk *Website*: www.jamescastlesculpture.co.uk *Signs work*: 'James Castle'.

CASTLE, Roger Bernard, UA (1988); landscape marine artist in oil; council mem. UA. *b*: Dartford, 30 Apr 1945. *m*: Brenda. two *s*. one *d*. *Educ*: Dartford. *Studied*: under the late William Walden, RBA. *Exhib*: RA, ROI, NEAC, RBA, UA; gallery artist at Century Gallery Henley, Roger Freen Fine A.G. Kent, Blackheath Gallery, F. Illes, Rochester. *Works in collections*: KCC Ashford. *Misc*: studio: Hales Pl., High Halden, Kent. *Address*: 38 Harvey Road, Willesborough, Ashford, Kent TN24 0AG. *Signs work*: "R.B. CASTLE."

CASWELL, Sarah, SBA; SBA People's Choice Award 2012; Finalist BBC2 TV Show Me the Monet 2012. Mall Galleries Exhibition. *Medium*: oil, acrylic, non-ferrous metals (i.e. silver). *b*: Bristol, 16 Apr 1966. *Studied*: Sir John Cass School of Art, London (1985-89). *Exhib*: solo: RHS Chelsea Flower Show, London (2011-2014); Oxo Gallery, London (2009); Red Dot Gallery, Holt, Norfolk (2008). Mixed: Catto Gallery London (2010); John Noott, Broadway (2012 onwards). Various other solo and mixed exhibitions. Works in collections: private and corporate. *Commissions*: P&O Cruises, Oriental Restaurant, Azura; Waterbabies Ltd, Head Office boardroom; various private. *Works Reproduced*: by Rosenstiel's. *Clubs*: Member, Society of Botanical Artists. *Address*: Great Walsingham Barns, Hindringham Road, Gt. Walsingham, Norfolk NR22 6DR. *Email*: sarah@sarahcaswell.co.uk *Website*: www.sarahcaswell.co.uk *Signs work*: "S. Caswell".

CATCHPOLE, Heather O., RMS, PPHSF; National Dip. in commercial and Applied Art (1962). *Medium*: portrait and dog artist in pastel; miniatures in watercolour on ivorine. *b*: Winnipeg, Canada, 26 Aug 1942. *d of*: Kenneth Siddons Osler, MA. *Educ*: Durban Girls'

High School. *Studied*: Natal School of Arts and Craft, RSA. *Exhib*: RMS, RA, Hilliard Soc. MASF, MAS.SA. *Works in collections*: Hilliard Soc. Permanent Collection. *Publications*: author/illustrator 'Heidi, Holly and other dogs'. In various books on techniques of miniature painting. *Misc*: 2001-2004 President of Hilliard Society of Miniaturists. *Address*: Heelers, Fitzhead, Taunton, Som. TA4 3JW.*Email*: heather.catchpole42@gmail.com *Signs work*: "Heather O. Catchpole," miniatures: the letter O with H inside with the year underneath it.

CATLOW, Geoffrey. *Medium*: acrylics, paper constructions, oil, drawing. *b*: Colne, Lancs., 1 May 1948. *s of*: Renee Maxfield. *m*: Jenni. one *s*. *Studied*: Burnley School of Art 1964-66 (Pre Diploma); Portsmouth College of Art 1966-69 (Diploma in Art and Design); Chelsea School of Art 1969-70 (Post Graduate). *Represented by*: The Art Movement. *Exhib*: RA Summer Exhibition (2008), Art London (2008, 2009), The London Art Fair, Islington (2007, 2008), Art Space, Portsmouth (2001, 2002, 2005, 2009), Affordable Art Fair, New York (2005, 2006); Spectrum Fine Art, London (2004), The Gallery, Cork Street, London (2004). Solo exhibitions include: The Beatrice Royal Gallery, Eastleigh, Hants (2003), The Brompton Gallery, Southampton (2000). Installation in the Round Tower at entrance to Portsmouth Harbour (1999). *Works in collections*: Portsmouth City Council Collection; private collections in Germany, USA and UK. *Publications*: cover design for 'Autism Spectrum Disorders' by Dermot Bowler (Wiley). *Misc*: Chair and Trustee of Art Space in Portsmouth. *Address*: 3 Albert Road, Southsea, Portsmouth, PO5 2SE. *Email*: geoff.catlow@talk21.com *Signs work*: "Geoff Catlow" or "GC".

CATTRELL, Annie Katherine, BA (Hons) Fine Art (1984), MA Fine Art (1985); artist in glass, paper and mixed media; lecturer, Sculpture Dept., Cheltenham School of Art. *b*: 15 Feb 1962. *Studied*: Glasgow School of Art (1980-84, Sam Ainsley), University of Ulster (1984-85, Alistair MacLennan). *Exhib*: Collins Gallery Strathclyde University (1989), 369 Gallery 'Artist's Choice' (1990), Artist in Residence, Chessel Gallery (1991), Paperworks, Seagate Gallery (1992). *Works in collections*: SAC, MacManus A.G. and Museum Dundee, City Art Centre Edinburgh. *Publications*: reviews, Edinburgh Medicine vol.65, Alba (1991) Mar./Apr., etc. *Clubs*: Collective Gallery, Edinburgh. *Address*: 11 Anderton Close, London SE5 8BU. *Signs work*: "Annie Cattrell."

CAUDWELL, Celia, NDD (1995), SWA (1993), SBA (1994), AUA (1994); artist in water-colour, oil, pen and ink, pottery/ceramics; gallery owner, mem. FATG. *b*: Ewell, Surrey, 11 Jul 1943. *m*: John Caudwell. two *s*. *Educ*: Upper Chine School, Shanklin, IOW. *Studied*: Winchester School of Art (1961-64), Goldsmiths' College School of Art (1964-65). *Exhib*: Ryde Library/Gallery IOW, Boldrewood Gallery, Southampton University, Seely Gallery, Newport IOW, Westminster Gallery, Mall Galleries, Omell Gallery, Laing Art Competition Winchester. *Publications*: A Brief History of Winkle Street IOW. *Address*: Brookside Cottage, Winkle St., Calbourne, I.O.W. PO30 4JF. *Signs work*: "Celia Caudwell."

CAULKIN, Martin, RI (1983), RBSA (1983); Royal Birmingham Society of Artists, Certificate of Merit 1(979); Hunting Group Art Prizes, Finalist (1983); Award for Outstanding Watercolour, Paper Mill (2001). *Medium*: watercolour, tempera, oil. *b*: B'ham, 12 Feb 1945. *s of*: Howard Caulkin, Grandson of F.E.H. Caulkin, Hon. RBSA. *m*: Anne Cherry, SWA. one *d*. *Educ*: Great Barr Comprehensive, Sutton Art College (1958-1961). *Studied*: B'ham College of Art (1962-65, Glyn Griffiths). *Exhib*: RWS, RBSA, RI, RA Summer Show, Singer and Friedlander water-colour exhbn., Shell House Gallery, Ledbury, Worcs., Manor House Gallery, Chipping Norton, Linda Blackstone Gallery, Pinner, London, Rona Gallery, London, Hillier Gallery, Stratford-upon-Avon. *Publications*: Landscape in Watercolours (Studio Vista); Paintings from Photographs (Harper Collins); Contemporary British water Colour Artists (Shandong Fine Arts Publishing House). International Artist: Oct/Nov 2001. *Official Purchasers*: 1) 1978-82: Brunot Productions; Prints (Americana, Fantasy, Landscape. 12 in all). *Principal Works*: Landscape, figurative, abstract.

Recreations: reading, gardening, films. *Clubs*: Royal Institute of Painters in Watercolour. *Address*: September Cottage, Naunton, Upton upon Severn, Worcester WR8 0PY. *Website*: www.gicleegallery.org.uk*Signs work*: "Martin Caulkin."

CAVACIUTI, Peter, painter on handmade paper from China, Korea, Japan and Nepal using Chinese ink and traditional pigments and has developed methods of mixing colours from 17th c. Chinese recipes. *b*: London, 13 May 1952. *Studied*: seven years with Prof. Fei Cheng Wu, continued with Prof. Bao at the Central Academy of Art, Beijing. *Exhib*: Urasenke Foundation, Kyoto, Japan; Salon de l'Aquarelle de Belgique, Belgium; RA Summer Show, London; RWS; SGFA; The Discerning Eye, London; Kettles Yard, Cambridge; recent solo shows: Daiwa Foundation, London (1999) and Galerie Leda Fletcher, Geneva (2001). Demonstrations include Kettle's Yard and the Victoria and Albert Museum. *Works in collections*: Urasenke Foundation; Clare Hall College, Cambridge. *Publications*: illustrated: 'Taoist Wisdom' by T. Freke (Godsfield Press, 1999), 'The Japanese Tea Ceremony' (Element Books, Ltd.); included in 'Dictionary of Painters in Britain since 1945' (1998). *Works Reproduced*: Millennium calendar for IKEA Ltd.; posters and cards, Art Group Ltd.; calendar for W.H.Smith Ltd. (2002). *Clubs*: Far Eastern Painting Soc., Kaetsu Chado Soc. *Address*: 2 Oxford Rd., Cambridge CB4 3PW.

CAYLEY, Jeanette Ann, MSc MB BS (London) FFSRH, mem. Inst. Psychosex. Med.; Patrons Prize, Medical Art Society (2007). *Medium*: pen and ink, watercolour, acrylic, oil, wood engraving. *b*: Plymouth, 4 Sep 1947. *m*: Charles Cayley. three *s*. *Educ*: Middlesex Hospital and University College, London. *Studied*: Plymouth College of Art. *Exhib*: Medical Art Society (1970-2009), Chelsea and Westminster Hospital Gallery (one-woman show) (2002); West Oxfordshire Artweeks (2003-2008), Bateman Buildings, Covent Garden (one-woman show, 2006); Linacre College, Oxford (one-woman show, 2008); Student work exhibited at Society of Wood Engravers 2008 Show, Bankside Gallery. *Misc*: lectures in Interface between Medicine and Art. *Address*: Oakleigh Cottage, The Green, Leafield, OX29 9NP. *Signs work*: 'J A Cayley'.

CECIL, Roger, artist in oil and oil pastel; David Murray Award (1966). *b*: Abertillery, 18 Jul 1942. *Studied*: Newport College of Art. *Exhib*: Howard Roberts Gallery, Cardiff (1966), R.A. Summer Exhbn. (1987, 1989); one-man shows, New Academy Gallery, London (1988, 1989, 1991, 1993, 1995-97), Cleveland Drawing Biennale (1989). *Publications*: B.B.C. documentary The Gentle Rebel. *Address*: c/o The New Academy Gallery, 34 Windmill St., London W1P 1HH. *Signs work*: "Roger Cecil."

CEMBROWICZ, Cordelia, BA (Hons), MA. *Medium*: drawing, prints, sculpture. *b*: Bristol, 5 Jul 1983. *Studied*: Royal College of Art (2008-2010); University College of Art (2003-2006); Central St.Martins (2001-2002). *Exhib*: Northern Print Biennale (2009); RA Summer Show (2009); RCA Secret (2009); Battle of Ideas, RCA (2009); Cafe Gallery (2009); East London Printmakers (2007); RWA Autumn Show (2007); Bluecoat Display Centre (2007); Simple Galerie, Gstaad (2007); Artonomy Gallery Truro (2006-2007). *Address*: 3 Sion Hill, Clifton, Bristol, BS8 4BA. *Signs work*: "CORDELIA CEMBROWICZ".

CHAITOW, Michael, BA Fine Art (Painting and Printmaking); Llewelyn-Smith Prize for Painting. *Medium*: oil, watercolour, drawing, prints. *b*: Herts., 3 Aug 1944. *s of*: Boris Chaitow. *Educ*: Lancing. *Studied*: Central St.Martins; Commonwealth Painting Scholarship, Baroda, India 1971-73. *Exhib*: British Art: New Directions, Puck Building New York (1982); Piccadilly Gallery, Cork Street, London (1987); First Cardiff Festival, St.David's Hall (1990); Merz Contemporary Art (1991); Art '97 London Contemporary Art Fair (1997). *Works in collections*: Dr.William Johnson (collector, Guernsey, 53 paintings). *Commissions*: St. John's Church, Hampstead Parish, London - memorial painting (2005). *Publications*:

Arts Review (1979, 1984); Marxist Review (1991). *Official Purchasers*: cover: 'Lifestream' by David Boadella (1987) (Routledge & Kegan Paul). *Works Reproduced*: 'Dawn I', 'Avenue of Trees', 'Cornfield-Ely'. *Address*: 'Caersalem', Commercial Street, Abergwynfi SA13 3YH. *Email*: michaelchaitow@hotmail.com *Website*: www.michaelchaitow.com *Signs work*: 'Michael Chaitow'.

CHALKER, Jack Bridger, Hon.MA, ARCA, RWA, ASIA, Hon FMAA; painter in oils, illustrator, medical/surgical artist, illustrator in oil, gouache, pen and wash etc.; Consultant, Birmingham University (art and design); War artist with Australian Army, Bangkok (1945). *b*: 10 Oct 1918. three *s*. one *d*. *Educ*: Alleyn's School, Dulwich. *Studied*: Goldsmiths' College (1936-39), RCA (1946-49). *Exhib*: RBA, RWA, RP, London galleries; mixed shows: London, Cheltenham; one-man shows: Dixon Gallery London, RWA, Australia, Japan (Peace Museum, Kyoto), Holland and Thailand. *Works in collections*: Cheltenham, Imperial War Museum London, Army Museum London,War Memorial Canberra, Australia, Holland, Japan and in many films UK, USA, Australia; Work in private collections, U.K. and Abroad. *Commissions*: Range of Portraits/Landscapes/Genre paintings. *Publications*: author and illustrator: Burma Railway Artist (Leo Cooper, 1944, and Viking O'Neil Australia), 'Burma Railway. Images of War' (Mercer Books, 2007), Japanese publication 'Burma Railway. Images of War' (Asahi Shimbun, Japan, 2008); wide range of surgical/medical publications, UK, America and Australia. *Official Purchasers*: Army Museum, Imperial War Museum London, War Memorial Museum, Canberra, Australia. *Works Reproduced*: In some 34 Books, Films etc. *Principal Works*: Millfield School, Army Museum London (Oil Paintings). *Recreations*: horse-riding, gliding. *Clubs*: Arts, Lansdowne. *Address*: Bleadney Mill, Bleadney, Wells, BA5 1PF. *Email*: chalker@ic24.net *Signs work*: "Jack Chalker."

CHALLINOR, Trevor, RWA (1992); Cheltenham Group (1964)-Hon.Sec.1980-85; NDD (Painting); Slade Dip FA UCL London; Leverhulme Research Award (1958/59); David Murray Award (1951); Cornelissen W/c Prize RWA (1987). *Medium*: watercolour, acrylic, oil. *b*: Edgebaston, B'ham, 17 Mar 1938. *s of*: Ralph Clifford & Jessie (Fryer). *m*: Patricia Christine (divorced). two *s*. one *d*. *Educ*: Moseley School of Art; Aston Tec. College, B'ham. *Studied*: Birmingham College of Art & Crafts (1954-58); Slade School UCL (1959-61). *Exhib*: RA Summer exhbns (1984/85/86/88); RWS (1984/85/86/90); RWA (1986-2002); Singer & Friedlander Watercolour exhbns (1986/88), many provincial galleries; group shows: Bristol, Cheltenham, Gloucester, Cardiff, France and Germany. *Works in collections*: various private and public collections in the UK and worldwide, including Cheltenham Museum Art Gallery, C&G Building Society Collection. *Works Reproduced*: RWS Watercolour catalogues; Annecy (France) catalogue. *Principal Works*: watercolour: interior/exterior, still life, landscape, and figure images. *Address*: 49b Ryeworth Road, Charlton Kings, Cheltenham, Glos. GL52 6LS. *Signs work*: 'Challinor'

CHALMERS, Angela, First Class BA Fine Art. *Medium*: watercolour, photograms, Alternative Process. *b*: Stoke-on-Trent, 4 Jan 1963. *m*: David. *Studied*: University of Hull (2002-2005). *Exhib*: Usual, mixed and solo. *Works in collections*: private collections. *Address*: Woodend Creative Workspace, The Crescent, Scarborough, N. Yorkshire YO11 2PW. *Email*: studio@angelachalmers.com *Website*: www.angelachalmers.com *Signs work*: "Angela Chalmers".

CHAMBERLAIN, Trevor, ROI (1972), RSMA (1970); Past President of the Wapping Group of Artists; Past President of Chelsea Art Society; Chris Beetles award, Winner at 1987 RWS Exhbn. *Medium*: marine, town, figure and landscape painter in oil and water-colour. *b*: Hertford, 13 Dec 1933. *s of*: Frederick Joseph Chamberlain. *m*: Elaine Waterfield. one *s*. *Educ*: Ware Central School. *Exhib*: London and abroad, R.A. Summer Exhbns. *Works in collections*: Guildhall A.G., London, Hertford Museum, Government Art Collection,

National Maritime Museum, Falmouth; Hertford Town Council; Ware Museum. *Publications*: The Connoisseur, Studio International, Dictionary of Sea Painters, 20th Century Marine Painting, Water-colour Impressionists; Author of 'Oils', 'Trevor Chamberlain - A Personal View' and 'England and Beyond' and 'Oil-Painting, Pure & Simple'. *Official Purchasers*: GPO Headquarters, Taylor Woodrow, Hampshire Regiment, Winsor & Newton, Marks & Spencer, The Caravan Club, Guildhall Art Gallery, London. *Works Reproduced*: Royle Publications, BBC TV, Connecticut TV. *Recreations*: music, travelling. *Address*: Braeside, 1 Goldings La., Waterford, Hertford, Herts. SG14 2PT. *Signs work*: "T. Chamberlain."

CHAMBERS, Stephen Lyon, BA Hons, MA, Rome Scholarship; painter in oil on canvas. *b*: London, 20 Jul 1960. *m*: Denise de Coruova. two *s*. *Educ*: Holland Park Comprehensive. *Studied*: Winchester School of Art (1978-79), St. Martin's School of Art (1979-82), Chelsea School of Art (1982-83). *Represented by*: Flowers East, London. *Exhib*: widely in Europe, USA and UK. *Publications*: Strange Smoke by John Gillett; Paintings 1988-89 by Gerard Wilson; Felonies and Errors by Isabella Oulton. *Address*: 129 Offord Rd., London N1 1PH. *Signs work*: paintings on canvas only signed on reverse.

CHANCE, Sula, President's Award, NAPA National Ehibition 2002; President's Award, NAPA International Exhibition 2005. *Medium*: oils & acrylics on canvas. *b*: Trinidad. *Exhib*: Platform for Art, Piccadilly Circus 2002, NAPA International Exhibition, USA, 2003; 'Closing the Door', Jewish Museum, Camden (2005). *Works in collections*: private collections. *Misc*: her work is inspired by the Caribbean of her childhood, showing the colours and rhythms of Caribbean flora, fauna, and Carnival life; featured BBC1 TV (Jun 2003), featured BBC radio (July 2003), BBC London TV (2005). *Address*: 9 Widley Gardens, Waterlooville, Hants, PO7 5RB. *Email*: sulaartist@aol.com *Website*: www.sulaartist.co.uk *Signs work*: 'sula'.

CHANCELLOR, Deborah Ann, BA Hons Fashion Design with Marketing. *Medium*: acrylic. *b*: Coventry, 25 Jul 1966. *d of*: William Walsh. *m*: James. two *s*. *Educ*: University of East London 1985-89. *Commissions*: Corporate clients: Courvoisier, Perrier, London Clubs International (Ritz, Les Ambassadeurs), UBS, Sears Plc, Viyella Greeting Card publisher. Amelia Essex 'Vintage Collection'. *Recreations*: caring for my boys and dog, music and cooking. *Address*: 23 Colebrooke Avenue, Ealing, London W13 8SZ. *Email*: info@ameliaessex.co.uk *Website*: www.ameliaessex.co.uk *Signs work*: "D.Chancellor".

CHANDLER, Cynthia Ann, landscape and coastal scene painter in water-colour and oil and portrait painter in oil, pastel and water-colour. *b*: Isleworth, Middx., 1 Jan 1937. *d of*: Thomas Joseph Wilfred Elliott. *m*: Frank Chandler. two *s*. one *d*. *Educ*: Hampton High School. *Studied*: Twickenham School of Art (Mr. Duffy, Mr. Kane, Miss Palby). *Exhib*: UA, PS, and several Midland exhbns. *Works in collections*: Nuneaton Art Gallery (3). *Clubs*: President, Rugby and District Art Soc., Coventry and Warwickshire Soc. of Artists, Banbury and District Art Soc. *Address*: 36 Dunsmore Ave., Rugby, Warwickshire CV22 5HD. *Signs work*: "Cynthia Chandler," "CYNTHIA CHANDLER."

CHAPLIN, Michael James, NDD, RE, RWS, FRSA; printmaker, water-colourist; Past Vice-Pres. Royal Soc. of Painter-Printmakers. *b*: St. Neots, 19 Sep 1943. *m*: Gay Lloyd. one *s*. one *d*. *Educ*: St. Albans Boys' Grammar School. *Studied*: Watford College of Art (1961-64), Brighton College of Art (1966-67), post-graduate. *Exhib*: RWS, RA Summer Shows, Tate Britain - Film on Turners Techniques. *Works in collections*: Ashmolean and Fitzwilliam museums; public and private collections worldwide, Royal Collections. *Commissions*: mural for Express Newspaper's boardroom; United Arab Shipping. *Publications*: regular contributor to Artist Magazine. Resident art expert on Channel 4 TV 'Water-colour Challenge'; "Mike Chaplin's Expressive Watercolours" published Oct. 2001, Harper

Collins. *Address*: Suffield, Orchard Drive, Weavering, Maidstone, Kent ME14 5JG. *Website*: www.mikechaplin.com *Signs work*: "Michael Chaplin, R.W.S."

CHAPMAN, Christopher Benedict, British Council Scholarship to Milan. *Medium*: oil, prints. *b*: St.Albans, 22 Mar 1943. *Partner*: Louise. one *d*. *Studied*: Hornsey College of Art (1960-64); Kings College, Cambridge (1973-76). *Exhib*: including: Libri Einaudi, Milan (1979/1983); Galleria Delle Ore, Milan (1984, 1987, 1990); 'Associations', Jill George Gallery (1998); 'Old Contemporaries' Islington Arts Centre (2011). *Works in collections*: private collections in Italy, USA, UK, Ireland, France. *Publications*: including: 'Mostra di Graphica di Christopher Chapman', Libri Einaudi, Milan (1979); Galleria Delle Ore, Milan, catalogues (1984, 1987, 1990); L'Unita: 1993; La Gazetta delle Arti: 1997; Il Giorno: 1987; 'Memory & Reality' by Jonathan Falla (1995); Drawings for '21 Poems by Velarde' (2011). *Recreations*: travelling. *Address*: 58 Burma Road, London N16 9BJ. *Signs work*: "CHAPMAN".

CHAPMAN, John Lewis, Matthew Brown Trophy; BAS Portfolio Award; artist in water-colour, gouache, oil, acrylic. *b*: Blackburn, 11 Sep 1946. *Studied*: Blackburn Art College (James Dolby). *Exhib*: RA Summer Exhbn., Patersons, London, Lewis Textile, Blackburn, Haworth Art Gallery, Accrington, Jersey, Birmingham, Warrington, Newcastle, Harrods, London, Unicorn Gallery, Wilmslow; Art Decor, Whalley. *Works in collections*: Blackburn Art Gallery. *Publications*: "John Chapman's Lancashire" (pub. Halsgrove); International Artist magazine; 22 signed Limited Editions (published by Miss Carter Publications, Bolton). *Address*: 25 Silverwell St., Bolton BL1 1PP. *Email*: info@johnchapman.co.uk *Website*: www.johnchapman.co.uk *Signs work*: "J.L. CHAPMAN."

CHAPMAN, Mark, BA (Hons) Fine Art: 1st Class (1982), MA Fine Art (1983); artist in water-colour, metal and wood construction; Teacher of Art: Sherbourne School for Girls, Dorset. *b*: Cuckfield, Sussex, 30 Jan 1958. *Studied*: Sunderland (1979-82), Birmingham (1982-83). *Exhib*: Leicestershire Schools Exhbn. (1983-90); Sculpture in the Garden, Deans Court, Wimborne (1991, 1993, 1995). *Address*: Marnel Cottage, Church Lane, Osmington, Dorset DT3 6EW. *Signs work*: "M. Chapman."

CHART, Helga, RSW (1994), DA (Edin) Post Grad.; artist in oil and mixed media; lecturer in art and design, Edinburgh's Telford College (retired). *b*: Edinburgh, 31 Aug 1944. *m*: H. Robertson. one *s*. *Educ*: Edinburgh. *Studied*: Edinburgh College of Art (1962-66, Sir Robin Philipson, David Michie, John Houston). *Exhib*: mixed shows 1968-95; three solo shows Edinburgh; RSA, RSW, SAAC, SSA. *Works in collections*: British Rail, IBM, Edinburgh schools, Pictures in Hospitals (Scotland). *Address*: 19 Dalrymple Cres., Edinburgh EH9 2NX. *Email*: helgachart@btopenworld.com *Signs work*: "Helga Chart."

CHATER, A.J., ERAC Diploma in Print and Illustration; Cert. in Advertising; Cert. Education. *Medium*: prints. *b*: London, 21 Apr 1953. *Studied*: Southend College of Technology. *Exhib*: RA Summer Show (2002, 2004). Many mixed shows, 1st and 2nd International Alternative Photo Art, 3d International Photo Alternative; Waverley City Gallery, Melbourne, Australia. *Commissions*: painting and 100 prints for British Army. *Publications*: Alternative Photography, Art & Artists Edition One. *Misc*: involved with the invention and development of temperaprint. *Address*: 13 Winton Avenue, Westcliff-on-Sea, Essex SS0 7QU. *Email*: alex.chater@macunlimited.net *Signs work*: 'A J Chater'.

CHATTEN, Geoffrey, RBA (1992); RBA G.Vivis Memorial Award, RBA Frinton-on-Sea Gallery Award; self taught painter of E. Anglian life and landscape, figures and marine subjects in oil. *b*: Gorleston, Norfolk, 20 Sep 1938. *s of*: one of 11 children of Frederick William & Edith May Chatham. *m*: Patricia Chatten. one *s*. one *d*. *Exhib*: RA, RBA, ROI, Southwell Brown Gallery, Richmond, Surrey, John Noott Gallery, Broadway, Fosse Gallery, Fosse on the Wold, Waterman Gallery, London, Dassin Gallery, Los Angeles, Gt. Yarmouth

Galleries, John Gardner Gallery, Uppingham. *Works in collections*: Maritime Trust, many private collections throughout Britain and overseas. *Publications*: Lydia Eva (Maritime Trust). *Clubs*: Hon. Member Gt. Yarmouth Society of Artists. *Address*: 82 Suffield Rd., Gorleston, Great Yarmouth, Norfolk NR31 7AL. *Signs work*: "Chatten."

CHAUCHET, Claude, President of the UNAID (union nationale des architects d'interieur et décorateurs); President of firm Dekoras (1966). *Medium*: painting: oil, gouache; furniture design: glass, steel, wood, carpet and fabric design. *b*: St. Maurice, France, 21 May 1935. *m*: Irina Nano. two *s*. one *d*. *Educ*: studied painting with Pierre Grisot, ecole Boulle (1950), and ateliers Beaux Arts de Paris. *Represented by*: Bernard Chauchet. *Exhib*: furniture: 'Salon International du Meuble, Paris' (1969-75), Spring Fine Art and Antiques Fair, Olympia, London (Feb 2003), Affordable Art Fair London & NY (2003). *Works in collections*: Centre Creation Industrial, Pavillon de Marsan, Musée Arts Décoratifs. *Publications*: Collection Connaissance des Arts 'Decoration' Hachette (1973) (table basse (low table) 1969, page 201, Appartment Mr. Boccaro, Dekoras p.25); l'oeil, Plaisirs de France, Maison et Jardin. *Clubs*: Art Connaissance, Tradition (ACT), UNAID. *Misc*: worked for Jansen as interior decorator and in 1966 founded his own decorating firm (Dekoras) under which he edited furniture and fabrics. *Address*: 50 bis rue Madeleine Michelis, 92200 Neuilly/Seine, France. *Email*: cchauchet@free.fr

CHEEK, Martin, CNAA, BA Hons Graphic Design. *Medium*: mosaic. *b*: Birmingham, 6 Jan 1959. *s of*: Fred & Beryl Cheek. *m*: Margaret Foreman. one *s*. one *d*. *Studied*: Exeter College of Art & Design. *Exhib*: Solo exhibitions since 1993 include: Chelsea Arts Club (1998, 2000), Gallery of Mosaic Art & Design (2001-05), Fish Slab Gallery, Whitstable (2002), Old Town Gallery of Contemporary Art, Margate (2004). Group exhibitions across the UK regularly since 1995. *Commissions*: Public Commissions include Museum of Modern Art Wales. *Publications*: Martin Cheek: 'Fused Glass Mosaics' (Schiffer 2012); 'Mosaic Craft' (Collins & Brown/Anova Books, 2007); 'The Art of Mosaic' (New Holland, 2002); 'Making Mosaics' (New Holland, 2000); 'Design Source Book: Mosaics' (New Holland, 1998); 'Mosaics in a Weekend' (New Holland, 1995). *Works Reproduced*: in many magazines including: Art & Craft Magazine, Artists & Illustrators, Country Life, Homes and Gardens, The Lady, The Sunday Times Style Magazine, The Telegraph, Woman & Home. *Clubs*: Chelsea Arts Club. *Misc*: Was for many years a part-time lecturer in Animation at The Royal College of Art, and a former art critic for the Daily Express. Now works full time as a mosaic artist. *Address*: Flint House, 21 Harbour Street, Broadstairs, Kent CT10 1ET. *Email*: cheekmartin@hotmail.co.uk *Website*: www.martincheek.co.uk *Signs work*: "MARTIN CHEEK".

CHEESE, Bernard, RE (1988), ARCA (1950); printmaker in lithography and water-colour. *b*: London, 1925. *s of*: Gordon William Cheese, taxi driver. three *d*. *Educ*: Beckenham Grammar School. *Studied*: Beckenham School of Art (Edward Bawden), Royal College of Art (Edwin Ladell). *Exhib*: Bankside Gallery, Zwemmer Gallery (1965), R.A., John Russell Gallery, Ipswich, Thompson Gallery, Aldeburgh, Fry Gallery, Saffron Walden, Royal Academy, University of Wales. *Works in collections*: Library of Congress, Washington, Cincinnati Museum, NY Public Library, Leeds Library, V&A (Print Room), Government Art Collection, University of Wales, Hunterian Museum Glasgow, Ashmolean Oxford, Fry Art Gallery, MoMA. *Publications*: illustrated many music books for A&C Black. *Address*: 2 High St., Nayland, Colchester CO6 4JE. *Signs work*: "Bernard Cheese."

CHEFFINS, Valma Maud, (nee Toplis); artist/printmaker in etching and aquatint; former teacher. *b*: Maidenhead, 18 Jun 1946. *d of*: Thomas Oldfield Jones Toplis. *m*: Frank Cheffins. *Educ*: Clark's College, Ilford; Beal Grammar School for Girls. *Studied*: St. Osyth's Training College (1964-67, Graham Eccles, Michael Kaye), Barking Technical College (1967-80, Harry Eccleston, OBE). *Exhib*: Loggia Gallery, Bankside Gallery, RE, The

Barbican, International Print Triennial, Japan (2001), Country Living Magazine Fairs (2000-2005); Society of Women Artists, Mall Galleries (2009. 2010, 2012). *Works in collections*: Britain, America, Europe, Ireland, Australasia. *Commissions*: Architecture in France; Architecture - Gloucester Cathedral. *Publications*: The Artist, May 2008 p.20. *Official Purchasers*: Marks and Spencer. Professor Ken Howard RA. *Clubs*: Ilford Art Soc., Essex Art Club, Essex Craft Society, Essex Guild of Craftsmen. *Address*: 62 Chadville Gdns., Chadwell Heath, Romford, Essex RM6 5UA. *Email*: frank.cheffins@bt.internet.com *Website*: axisweb.org/artist/valmacheffins *Signs work*: "VALMA CHEFFINS."

CHERRY, Anne, MA (RCA) (1973), SWA (1987), ARBSA (1990); Princess Michael of Kent Award for Best Work in Show (SWA, 2002); Royal Society of Arts Travel Bursary 1970; Harris Tweed Award 1972 (Jean Muir). *Medium*: watercolour. *b*: Isle of Sheppey, 16 Oct 1948. *d of*: George William Cherry, MA, MSc (Oxon). *m*: Martin Caulkin, RI, RBSA. one *d*. *Educ*: John Willmott Grammar School. *Studied*: Sutton Art College (1967-68), B'ham College of Art (1968-71), RCA (1971-73, Joanne Brogden, Zandra Rhodes). *Exhib*: RBSA Galleries, RWS, RI, SWA, Shell House Gallery, Ledbury, Manor House Gallery, Chipping Norton, Neville Gallery, Canterbury, Linda Blackstone Gallery, Pinner, London; Birties of Worcester; Hillier Gallery, Stratford-upon-Avon. *Commissions*: House portraits, gardens, portraits, landscapes, femmes fatales. *Publications*: "Landscape in Watercolour", Patricia Monahan, (Studio Vista), Beginner's Guides. *Works Reproduced*: Most works available as Giclée prints. *Principal Works*: landscapes, still life, femmes fatales. *Recreations*: gardening, music, tailoring. *Clubs*: Society for the Protection of Ancient Buildings, Civic Society. *Address*: September Cottage, Naunton, Upton upon Severn, Worcester WR8 0PY. *Email*: caulkintowers@hotmail.com *Website*: www.gicleegallery.org.uk *Signs work*: "Anne Cherry."

CHERRY, Norman, PhD, DA, MCSD, FRSA; designer - jeweller and silversmith, precious and non-precious metals; academic: formerly Pro Vice Chancellor, University of Lincoln. *b*: Airdrie, Lanarkshire, 2 Aug 1949. one *s*. *Studied*: Glasgow School of Art (1966-70, J. Leslie Auld). *Exhib*: Facèré, Seattle; Scottish Gallery, Edinburgh; Alternatives, Rome; Lesley Craze, London. *Works in collections*: Dundee Museums and Art Galleries, Tennessee Technological Univ., USA, British Museum, Birmingham Museum, Royal Museum of Scotland. *Commissions*: 1973: Silver Centrepiece, KOSB; 1977: Chalice & Paten, St. Mary's Bishohphill Junior, York; 1997: Freedom casket for Sir Simon Rattle, City of Birmingham; 2006: Crozier for Bishop of Lynn; 2009: Rosewood Processional staves & Chancellor's Medal, University of Lincoln. *Publications*: work discussed or illustrated in several, including "Textile Techniques for Jewellers" by Arline Fisch (Lark Books); several conference papers; recent curatorial projects: "Transplantation", "Masters and Proteges"; 'Jewellery Design & Development: from Concept to Object' published by Bloomsbury. *Misc*: Churchill Fellow (1983). Work executed in precious & non-precious materials, includes woven metals. Research into subversion of biomedicine for extreme Body Modification. *Email*: norman.cherry@uwclub.net *Website*: www.normancherry.co.uk *Signs work*: Sponsors mark: N.C. inside lozenge struck on all precious metalwork and assayed and hallmarked @ Edinburgh and Birmingham.

CHESTERMAN, Merlyn, BA Hons in Fine Art, Dip.Ed.; Council member of the Royal Society of Painter-Printmakers. *Medium*: woodblock printmaker. *b*: London, 18 Jun 1949. *d of*: Prof.W.D. & Mrs Chesterman. one *s*. one *d*. *Educ*: King George V School, Hong Kong. *Studied*: Bath Academy of Art, Corsham, Wilts.; Bath University. *Exhib*: The Royal Academy, Bankside Gallery, The Mall Galleries, London Original Print Fair. *Works in collections*: City Hall Museum of Art Permanent Collection, Hong Kong; V&A, Ashmolean. *Misc*: two residencies at St. Croix Watershed Research Station, Science Museum of Minnesota, USA; teaches short courses in woodcuts at West Dean College, Chichester, and runs printmaking courses in North Devon. *Address*: 2 Harton Manor,

The Square, Hartland, Devon, EX39 6BL. *Email*: merlyn@twohartonmanor.co.uk *Website*: www.twohartonmanor.co.uk *Signs work*: "MC".

CHEUNG, Gordon, BA Fine Art Painting (1998), MA Fine Art Painting (2001); British Council International Arts Award (2003), Arts Council of England International Award (2003), Lexmark Painting Prize finalist (2003); John Moore's Painting Prize 24 (2006). *Medium*: paint, multimedia. *b*: Lambeth, London, 13 Sep 1975. *s of*: Lawrence Cheung. *m*: Rui Matsunaga. *Educ*: Central St. Martin's (CSM), Royal College of Art. *Exhib*: Nunnery Gallery, London (2003), John Hansard Gallery, Southampton (2003), Eyestorm Gallery, London (2003), British Art Show 6 (2005), Tour UK beginning at Baltic Centre of Contemporary Art. Solo show: 'Paradise Lost', Laing Art Gallery (2007); RA Summer Exhbn (2007). *Works in collections*: Museum of Senegallia, Italy; Royal College of Art, London; London Institute, London; Arizona State Museum, USA; Hirshhorn Museum, USA. *Address*: 6 Beverley Hyrst, Addiscombe Road, Croydon, CR0 6SL. *Email*: gordon.cheung@lineone.net *Website*: www.gordoncheung.com *Signs work*: 'GORDON CHEUNG'.

CHEVARIN, Frederic Marcel Jacques, ARBS; MEng; Member, Oxford Art Society. *Medium*: sculpture. *b*: Lisieux, France, 20 Jul 1971. *m*: E. two *s*. *Studied*: ESITC, Caen, France (1995-98); Mentored by Vasco Montecchi (2005-06), and Helaine Blumenfeld OBE FRBS (2008-09). *Exhib*: onform, Burford (2010, 2012); onform, London (2013); Royal West of England Academy, Bristol (20130); Chelsea Flower Show (2013, 2014); Woburn Abbey (2012); Winchester Cathedral (2012); University of Leicester (2011); RBSA (2010). *Works in collections*: Private collections in UK, Switzerland, France, Italy. Sculptures in the public domain: Highgate Cemetery, London; Willen park, Milton Keynes. *Publications*: interview published by the art magazine Duemila (Matteo Editore, Italy, nov 2010). *Principal Works*: Limestone, marble, alabaster, onyx and bronze scultures. *Address*: 154 Oxford Road, Oxford OX3 0RF. *Email*: f.chevarin@tiscali.co.uk *Website*: www.frederic-chevarin.com *Signs work*: "F.Chevarin".

CHILTON, Elizabeth Carlyle, Ruskin Cert. Fine Art and Design (1964-67); artist in oil, some etching and sculpture. *Medium*: oils, pen and ink, watercolours. *b*: Darlington, 1 Mar 1945. *d of*: E. R. Chilton, FRIBA, FTPI. *m*: R. G. Denning, D.Phil., Oxon. two *s*. *Educ*: Headington School for Girls, Oxford. *Studied*: Ruskin School, Oxford University, University of Illinois, U.S.A., Mem. of the Italian Academy. *Exhib*: R.A., Paris Salon, Oxford University Colleges, N.E.A.C., R.O.I., Southwark Cathedral. *Works in collections*: Town Hall, Whitchurch, Hants., Magdalen College, Oxford, Wadham College, Oxford. *Commissions*: private individuals. *Works Reproduced*: prints of Oxford Colleges. *Recreations*: gardening, walking. *Address*: Purlin House, Toot Baldon, Oxford OX44 9NE. *Email*: denning_elizabeth@hotmail.com *Signs work*: "Chilton."

CHIPP, Beverley, versatile artist in eclectic media including: photograpic, literary, graphic and 3D art; specialises in thought provoking pieces on many issues. Current work in oils has a surreal and visionary nature, focusing on cosmic phenomena. *b*: 1964. Yorkshire. Arts and crafts family. *Studied*: self-taught. *Exhib*: "It's a Fine Line" and "Angeltoad Landing", Lauderdale House (2001), "All Stars", Union Chapel, London (2001). "Diorama" and "The Wagon & Horses Show", The Establishment (2002). *Commissions*: specialising in non-profit organisations, charities and ethical companies. *Publications*: "Occasional Sights" curated by Anna Best, published by the Photographers Gallery; "Going to Court, Not War", an introduction to the International Court of Justice. Various poems in a number of anthologies published by Forward Press. *Misc*: Member of The House of Wheat Art Collective. *Address*: 10 Chenies St. Chambers, 9 Chenies St., London WC1E 7ET. *Email*: angeltoad@aol.com *Signs work*: "angeltoad."

CHIPP, Terry, MA (1994); painter and mixed media constructor; artist and art education adviser, tutor to individuals and small groups. *b*: Yorkshire, 1949. *Studied*: Doncaster and

Durham (1967-1971). *Exhib*: four solo exhibs. and many group exhibs., including Doncaster Artists, touring exhib. in Kentucky, USA. *Works in collections*: private collections across UK and ten countries worldwide. *Commissions*: many private commissions for landscapes and house portraits. *Address*: 250 Sprotbrough Rd., Doncaster, S. Yorks. DN5 8BY. *Email*: terry@chippco.co.uk *Signs work*: "T CHIPP."

CHIRINO, Marta, OVSBA (1998); RHS Gold Medal (1999); BSc (1986). *Medium*: pencil on paper, and ink for scientific illustration. *b*: Madrid, 12 Jun 1963. *d of*: Martin Chirino & Margarita Argenta. *m*: Eduardo Rodriguez. two *d*. *Educ*: Nuestra Señora Santa Maria (Madrid). *Studied*: Universidad Autonoma, Madrid; Universidad Complutense, Madrid. *Represented by*: Madrid: Galeria Bat; Galeria Pelayo 47; Canary Islands: Galeria Cuadro, Galeria Magda Lazaro. *Exhib*: solo: Galeria Magda Lazaro (Sta. Cruz de Tenerife); Galeria Delayo47, Madrid (2006); Museo Nestor, Gran Canaria (2006/7); group: annually with SBA since 1998 except 3 yrs; Galeria Cuatrodiecisiete, Madrid (2003); Galeria BAT, Madrid (2006, 2009). *Works in collections*: Museo Postal y Telegrafico, Madrid. *Commissions*: Real Jardin Botanica de Madrid, and several other official institutions around Spain. *Publications*: Main publications - Scientific Illustrations for: Flora Iberica Vols V, VI, VII; Flora Acuatica Castilla-La Mancha; Alimentos Sillestres Comunidad de Madrid; Marta Chirino: De Botanica (catalogue, 2007); Libro de Los Mojos (author Marta Chirino); 'Marta Chirino: Sobre la Naturaleza y el Arte'. *Works Reproduced*: all botanical drawings since 1987; commissions by the Botanical Gardens, Madrid; several aquatic plants posters, and pencil drawings in various catalogues and books. *Misc*: graphic designer. *Address*: C/Reyesmagos 18 (9 Lz), 28009 Madrid, Spain. *Email*: martachirino@hotmail.com *Website*: www.martachirino.com *Signs work*: 'CHIRINO ARGENTA'.

CHITTENDEN, Charlie, *Medium*: oil. *b*: 27 May 1960. *Represented by*: www.nicholasbowlby.co.uk. *Exhib*: Affordable Art Fair, Battersea Park, London (2010, 2011, 2012); Red Leaf Gallery, Royal Tunbridge Wells, Kent (Summer Exhibition 2011). *Works in collections*: over 200 purchases worldwide. *Email*: Radkachittenden@yahoo.co.uk *Website*: http//:charliechittendendaily.blogspot.com *Signs work*: "Charlie Chittenden".

CHRISTIE, Janet Mary, DA (Edin.) (1961), FSBA (1986 resigned 1997); RHS Silver medal (1982), Grenfell medal (1985); former founder mem. Soc. of Botanical Artists; painter in water-colour. *Medium*: Watercolour. *b*: Kampala, Uganda, 12 Mar 1939. two *s*. one *d*. *Educ*: Cranley, Edinburgh. *Studied*: Edinburgh College of Art (1957-61, Robin Philipson, Gillies, John Maxwell, John Houston). *Exhib*: RSSW, SAAC, RHS, also various mixed exhbns.; solo shows: Norwich, London, and Edinburgh area; Royal Academy Summer Exhibition (2001, 2004, 2005, 2006), several RSA exhbns Edinburgh; several RGI exhbns, Glasgow. *Address*: Marbert, Springhill Rd., Peebles EH45 9ER. *Signs work*: "J.M.C."

CHRISTOPHER, Ann, RA, FRBS, RWA, BA; sculptor. *b*: Watford, Herts., 4 Dec 1947. *d of*: Wm. Christopher. *m*: K. Cook. *Educ*: Watford Girls' Grammar School. *Studied*: Harrow School of Art (1965-66), West of England College of Art (1966-69). *Represented by*: Pangolin, London. *Exhib*: Redfern Gallery, London; Ann Kendall Richards Inc., New York; RA. *Works in collections*: Bristol City A.G., Contemporary Arts Soc., Chantrey Collection, London, Glynn Vivian A.G., Royal Academy, Corcoran A.G., Washington DC, British Museum. *Commissions*: 1997 Linklaters & Paines, London, 1998 Gt. Barrington, USA, 2001 Port Marine, Bristol, 2002 Albi, France. *Publications*: Ann Christopher 'Sculpture 1969-89'. also 'Sculpture 1989-94. *Address*: c/o Royal Academy of Arts, Burlington House, Piccadilly, London W1J 0BD. *Website*: www.annchristopher.co.uk *Signs work*: "AC."

CHUANG, Yaojen, BSc Arch, Dip Arch, ARB RIBA Part II. *Medium*: sculpture, drawing, prints. *b*: Taipei, 12 Feb 1982. *Studied*: Bartlett School of Architecture, University College London (2001-2004); Bartlett School of Architecture, University College London (2006-2008). *Exhib*: Royal Academy London (2009, 2010), Venice Architecture Biennale (2010),

Christ Church, Spitalfield, London (2010), easaHQ, Manchester (2010), Candid Arts Centre, London (2010, 2011), Zilouf's, London (2011), Dreamspace Gallery, London (2009), Slade School Gallery, London (2007, 2008), ETSAM, Madrid (2008), Vojtech Museum, Kosice, Slovakia (2006), Academy of Fine Arts and Design, Bratislava, Slovakia (2005), FCU, Taichung, Taiwan (2005), Galerie Jaroslava Fragnera, Prague (2004), Stazione Leopolda, Florence (2003). *Works in collections*: Entwistle Gallery, New Bond Street, London; Leaf Gallery, Maidstone, Kent. *Publications*: "Exubernace" AD Architectural Design (March/April 2010), Blueprint (June 2009), "Contemporary Digital Architecture: Design and Techniques" (Links), "Building Design" (July 2008), "La Vie" November 2010. *Works Reproduced*: "The Euphoric Field", "Opium is a Season", "Infiltration", "Actaeon". *Principal Works*: "The Euphoric Field", "Opium is a Season". *Address*: Flat 2, Peridot Court, 63 Virginia Road, London E2 7NF. *Email*: hello@yaojenchuang.com *Website*: www.yaojenchuang.com

CHUHAN, Jagjit (Ms.), DFA (Lond) (1977); artist in oil on canvas; lecturer, curator. *b*: India, 10 Jan 1955. *Studied*: Slade School of Fine Art (1973-77). *Exhib*: Solo shows: Ikon Gallery, B'ham (1987), Commonwealth Inst., London (1987), The Lowry, Manchester (2002), Watermans Arts Centre, London (2004); Victoria Gallery, Liverpool (2013); Mixed shows: Barbican Centre, London (1988), Tate Gallery, Liverpool (1990-91), Galeria Civica, Marsala, Sicily (1991), Arnolfini, Bristol (1991); Asia Triennial, Manchester (2011). *Works in collections*: Arts Council Collection; North West Arts Board; Usher Gallery, Lincoln; Grosvenor Museum, Chester; Cartwright Hall, Bradford; Tameside Museum & AG; University of Liverpool. *Publications*: 'A Long Way from Home' (Lowry Press, 2002); Parampara Portraits (Shisha, 2004); 'J Chiham; Recent Paintings' (Victoria Gallery and Museum, (2013). *Address*: Liverpool Art School, John Moores University, 68 Hope St., Liverpool L1 9EB. *Email*: j.chuhan222@btinternet.com *Website*: www.chuhan333.wix.com/paintings#

CHUIKOV, Valeriy, painter in oils on canvas. *b*: Zaporozhie, Ukraine, 27 Mar 1949. *s of*: Eugenie Chuikov. *m*: Elena Chuikov. one *s*. *Educ*: Kiev State Art Institute. *Studied*: Kiev Republican Special Art College, Kiev State Art Institute, Academy of Art, Moscow. *Represented by*: Garden of Eden Art Gallery. *Exhib*: Roy Miles Gallery, Alberti Gallery, Omell Gallery, New Grafton Gallery, The Leith Gallery, Blackheath Gallery, Gallery on the Green, Francis Iles, The Rochefort Gallery, Garden of Eden and others. *Works in collections*: National Ukrainian Art Museum, The Russian Ministry of Culture Collection, The State Art Collection of the Moscow Art Academy, British Embassy in Kiev. *Commissions*: for Archbishop of Ukraine Philaret, Chairman of FIFA Joseph Beatter. *Publications*: more than 30 sources including books, catalogues, albums, articles. *Works Reproduced*: by Rosenstiel's. *Principal Works*: portrait of Che Guevara, Tragedy of Chile, Grand Prince Vladimir. *Clubs*: mem. Union of Artists of the Ukraine and USSR. *Address*: Flat 3, The Vale, Broadstairs, CT10 1RB. *Email*: e.chuikov@ntlworld.com *Signs work*: 4.B. (early works), V.Chuikov.

CHURCHILL, Martin, DA (Edin); DFA (Painting) Post Grad.; Guthrie Award RSA, Hunting Group Art Prize (1st Prize), Elizabeth Greenshields Award, Canada; BP Portrait Award (2nd Prize), Morrison Scottish Portrait Award Winner; David Cargill Award RGI. *Medium*: oil, drawing. *b*: Glasgow, 18 Nov 1954. *Educ*: Wick High School (1967-72). *Studied*: Edinburgh College of Art: DA (Edin) with Distinction (1976); Post Graduate Diploma In Fine Art (Painting) with Distinction (1977); Fellow in Painting, Gloucester College of Art (1981-82). *Represented by*: The Fine Art Society (London). *Exhib*: RA, RSA, RGI, NPG, RP, RCA (London), Mall Galleries, The Fine Art Society, Grosvenor Gallery London. *Works in collections*: The Fleming Wyfold Art Foundation, Deutsche Bank, IBM, BP International, Hove Art Gallery, City Art Centre Edinburgh, Hunterian Gallery, University of Glasgow, Scottish Arts Council,Scottish Life Assurance, Nuffield Foundation, Robert Fleming Holdings Ltd. *Commissions*: University of Edinburgh (print). *Publications*:

FAS Now, 125 Yrs (1876-2001); A History of Scottish Art; The Fleming Collection. *Official Purchasers*: Scottish Arts Council; Hove Art Gallery; Hunterian Glasgow University; City Art Centre, Edinburgh; The Nuffield Foundation, Hospitals in Scotland. *Works Reproduced*: print of Edinburgh University to commemorate their 400th Anniversary. *Principal Works*: 'Palace Hotel (Edinburgh)'-Guthrie Prize (stolen 1981). *Recreations*: listening to classical music, making sculpture, photography. *Clubs*: Scottish Arts Club, Edinburgh. *Address*: 69 Fillebrook Road, Leytonstone, London E11 4AU. *Signs work*: 'Churchill'.

CHURCHILL, Robert Bruce, BA (Hons) Architecture; PGCE (Art). *Medium*: oil, watercolour, drawing, prints, pastels, etchings, collage. *b*: Vancouver, BC, 22 May 1965. *s of*: Alexandra Churchill (Artist). *m*: Serena Churchill. one *s*. one *d*. *Educ*: Vancouver. *Studied*: University of British Columbia (Art History); Oxford Polytechnic (Architecture); University of Gloucestershire (PGCE). *Exhib*: RI; RWA; Museum of Oxfordshire; Cheltenham Art Gallery and Museum; The Foreign Press Assoc., London; The White Room Galleries (Leamington Spa and Bath); Brian Sinfield (Burford); also, works selected by the Emily Carr College of Art for touring exhbn. of British Columbia; La Chapelle des Capucins (Turenne, France); Riva D'Arno Gallery (Florence, Italy). *Works in collections*: private collections internationally. *Commissions*: The Royal Shakespeare Company, Stratford-upon-Avon; The Watermill Theatre, Newbury. *Works Reproduced*: watercolours of various subjects published by H.M. Graphics as limited editions. *Recreations*: surfing, travelling, cooking, music. *Address*: Court Lodge, Overbury, nr. Tewkesbury, Glos. GL20 7PH. *Website*: www.robchurchill.com

CIOBOTARU, Gillian Wise: see WISE, Gillian.

CIREFICE, Vittorio Antonio, FRSA (2005); Dip. Ad. Chelsea, Post Dip. RA Schools; painted professionally since leaving RA Schools. *Medium*: egg tempera, oil. *b*: Bangor, N. Wales, 19 Apr 1949. *s of*: Marco Cirefice. *m*: Heather Grills. two *d*. *Educ*: Holyhead Comprehensive. *Studied*: RA Schools under Peter Greenham (1971-74). *Represented by*: Emer Gallery, Belfast. *Exhib*: various. *Works in collections*: private collections including: John Hulme, MEP; Brindslie Ford (Courtauld Inst.); Mary McAleese (President Ireland); Public collections: National Gallery Wales (Cardiff), Down Civic Museum (Downpatric), Queen's Collection. *Commissions*: Stations of the Cross, for St.Bartolo Casalattico, Italy (2004). *Publications*: TV appearances - 'Songs of Praise', 'Awash with Colour', 'Fathom Line', 'Scene Around 6'. *Principal Works*: Gaelic sports, festivals and fairs. *Recreations*: the mountains. *Clubs*: RASAA. *Misc*: lives, works and exhibits exclusively in rural environments. *Address*: Ballymagart Mill, Ballyardle Rd., Kilkeel, Co. Down, BT34 4JX. *Email*: cirefice@btopenworld.com *Signs work*: 'V Cirefice'.

CIRENZA, Lisa, BA Hons (1985), MA (1987). *Medium*: oil, drawing, acrylics and digital, mixed media. *b*: USA, 1963. *m*: Peter. three *s*. one *d*. *Studied*: Stanford University, also Princes Drawing School, Central St. Martins, The Art Academy, Norfolk School of Painting, Jean-Pierre Brazs Atelier. *Exhib*: Art of Angel, Art Below - Candid Arts Trust - Hackney Wicked - Drawn Together - Gallery K - World Wide Arts LA. *Works in collections*: Tottenback Collection, Floyd Collections, private/corporate. *Commissions*: private/corporate. *Recreations*: Pianist, linguist, writer. *Address*: 26 Willoughby Road, London NW3 1SA. *Email*: art@cirenza.com *Website*: www.cirenza.com *Signs work*: "L Cirenza".

CLARIDGE, Trish. SWA; BA Hons Fine Art; PGDip Theatre Design. *Medium*: Egg tempera, pastels, oil. *b*: Middlesex, 1953: *m*: John Thompson. two *d*. *Studied*: Cheltenham Art School, Bristol Old Vic School. *Represented* by: Mo at Fish Out of Water Gallery, Wotton Under Edge, Glos. *Exhib*: Solo exhibitions: National Trust House, Newark Park: Under the Edge Arts, Glos; Gelbe Gallery, Baltimore, Ireland. Group shows: Pastel Society,

Royal Society of Portrait Painters, Society of Women Artists, Mall Galleries, London, and widely in the UK. *Works in collections*: private collections. *Commissions*: portrait and individual commissions, specialist decorative Fine Art work. *Publications*: Magazines and catalogues. *Address*: Melrose House, 6 Long Street, Wotton under Edge, Gloucestershire GL12 7EP. *Email*: jtpc2@tiscali.co.uk *Website*: trishclaridge.com *Signs work*: Early work "P Claridge", now a square enclosing combined initials "TC".

CLARK, Bruce Michael, MA, DAE, Cert. Ed.; painter in oil. *b*: Bedfont, 17 Jul 1937. *s of*: William Clark, artist in watercolour. *m*: Jill Clark. two *s*. *Educ*: Strodes School. *Studied*: Bath Academy of Art, Corsham (1958-60) under Howard Hodgkin, Gwyther Irwin, William Crozier. *Represented by*: NuMasters.com. *Exhib*: eleven one-man shows including Chiltern Gallery, London; Compendium Galleries, Birmingham; Worcester City A.G.; One Off Gallery, Dover; Tabor Gallery, Canterbury; numerous group shows including Walker's Gallery; Woodstock Gallery; Kootenay Gallery, Canada; Festival de Provence, France; Minotaur Gallery, Toronto; Royal Academy, Rowley Gallery, London; Cambridge Contemporary Arts, Rye Art Gallery; Stark Gallery, Canterbury. *Publications*: included in 'Dictionary of Artists in Britain since 1945'. *Address*: Mingladon, Manns Hill, Bossingham, Canterbury, Kent CT4 6ED. *Signs work*: "Clark."

CLARK, Mary. *Medium*: stone lithography, prints. *b*: London, 9 Nov 1952. *Studied*: Swansea College of Art (1971-75). *Represented by*: myself. *Exhib*: Private galleries in Bradford on Avon, Wilts; Royal Academy Summer Show (2009); Print Room Gallery, Widcombe, Bath. *Works in collections*: private collections: UK, France, Australia, Republic of Ireland. *Clubs*: Member of Frome Artist Printmakers. *Address*: 11, Tory, Bradford on Avon, Wiltshire, BA15 1NN. *Email*: maryclarkcopywriter@btinternet.com *Website*: www.printmaker.mary-clark.co.uk *Signs work*: "MARY CLARK".

CLARK, Michael Graeme, PAI; BA (Hons); The Jamieson Award (2011); Winsor & Newton Award, RSW (2010); Wren Gallery Award, PAI (2007, 2008); Art Hire Prize, PAI (2005, 20070); Selected, Sunday Times/Singer Friedlander Watercolour Prize (2007). *Medium*: oil, watercolour. *b*: Ayr, 25 Jan 1959. *m*: Karen. one *s*. two *d*. *Studied*: Edinburgh College of Art (1979-83). *Represented by* :Thompson's, Marylebone, London; Lime Tree Gallery, Bristol; Doubtfire Gallery, Edinburgh; Lemond Gallery, Glasgow; Roger Billcliffe Gallery, Glasgow. *Exhib*: Solo shows include: Doubtfire Gallery, Edinburgh (2012); Bath Contemporary (2011); Lime Tree Gallery, Bristol (2011); Thompson's, Marylebone (2011); RGI Kelly Gallery, Glasgow (2010); Randolph Gallery, Edinburgh (2005, 2006); Sally Hunter Fine Art, London (1996, 1998); Chelsea Flower Show (1997/8). Group exhibitions include: RSW (2010, 2012), VAS Annual (2012); Panter and Hall, London (2012); RGI (2011); NEAC (2010); PAI (2011). *Works in collections*: Royal Bank of Scotland. *Works Reproduced*: various publications; Wild Apple Graphics USA; Woodmansterne UK. *Recreations*: cooking, wine, golf. *Clubs*: Glasgow Art Club, Prestwick St. Nicholas Golf Club. *Address*: 4 Mount Charles House, 36 Mount Charles Crescent, Alloway, Ayrshire KA7 4NY. *Email*: michaelclarkartist@googlemail.com *Website*: www.michaelclarkartist.co.uk *Signs work*: "Clark".

CLARK, Peter Christian, Oxford University Certificate of Fine Art; professional painter of abstract paintings in oil, acrylic and gouache; hand-made prints and wallpaper, bas-relief constructions. *b*: Bradford, Yorks., 19 Apr 1950. *s of*: T. H. Clark, ACP, ARDS, FRSA. *Educ*: Clifton House School, Harrogate, HMS Conway, Anglesey, N. Wales. *Studied*: Ruskin School of Drawing and Fine Art under Richard Naish, MA. *Exhib*: mixed shows: Ashmolean Museum, Oxford, Museum of Modern Art, Oxford, Llewellyn Alexander Gallery, London. Private commissions. *Address*: 40 Delancey St., London NW1 7RY. *Signs work*: "Peter Clark", "Christian Clark" and "P.C.C."

CLARKE, Edward, RAS PG Dip, BA (Hons); figurative portrait and landscape artist painting in oils and drawing in charcoal; RA Schools Prizes for landscape and portraiture (1986). Antique Collector Magazine's Annual Prize for Figurative Painting and Drawing (1987); Wise Speke Prize for Best Drawing in 'Up Close and Personal' Exhibition, Hatton Gallery, Newcastle (2006). *b*: Hartlepool, 1962. *Educ*: Manor School, Hartlepool. *Studied*: Cleveland College of Art (1980-81), Sheffield Hallam University (1982-85), R.A. Schools (1985-88). *Exhib*: RA Summer Exhbn. and RA Dip. Galleries, London (1986, 1987, 1988), NPG, London (1988, 1991), Agnews, London (1990), Centro Modigliani Gallery, Florence (2002), Burlington Fine Arts, London (2005), Red Box Gallery, Newcastle (2007); Royal Society of Portrait Painters Exhibition, Mall Galleries, London (2007). *Works in collections*: various, including National Trust's Foundation for Art. *Clubs*: Royal Academy Schools Alumni Member. *Address*: 304 Catcote Rd., Hartlepool, Cleveland TS25 3EF. *Signs work*: "Edward Clarke."

CLARKE, Graham Arthur, Hon.MA Kent Ambassador, ARCA Chevalier de la Confrerie du Cep Ardechois, Hon. Associate KIAD, President CPRE (Kent); artist in etching and water-colour, author. *b*: Chipping Norton, Oxon., 27 Feb 1941. *m*: Wendy. one *s*. three *d*. *Educ*: Beckenham Grammar School. *Studied*: Beckenham School of Art, RCA. *Exhib*: Wildenstein & Co., Bond St., London; Henie-Onstadt, Oslo. *Works in collections*: V&A, British Museum, Tate Gallery, National Libs. Scotland, Ireland and Wales, Hiroshima Peace Museum, National Lib. Congress (USA). *Publications*: Graham Clarke's History of England, Graham Clarke's Grand Tour, Joe Carpenter and Son - English Nativity, W. Shakespeare (Gent.) actual notte booke, The World of Graham Clarke (Japanese), A Norwegian Sketchbook, Graham Clarke's Kent 'Baitboxstew' - Graham Clarke's Cornwall; Octopolis to Halki, Vinerelles. *Address*: White Cottage, Green Lane, Boughton Monchelsea, Maidstone, Kent ME17 4LF. *Email*: info@grahamclarke.co.uk *Website*: www.grahamclarke.co.uk *Signs work*: "Graham Clarke."

CLARKE, Granville Daniel, FRSA, YWS (1989-2005); professional artist in water-colour and pencil. *b*: Keighley, Yorks., 26 Oct 1940. *s of*: James Edward Clarke. *Educ*: Cudworth, Secondary Modern School of Life. *Studied*: Barnsley School of Art (1955-60). City & Guilds 1st Class Hons. (1957), Full Tech. Cert. (1959). *Represented by*: Jacquie Evans Management, London 0208-699-1202. *Exhib*: numerous one-man exhbns. since 1977; Westminster Gallery, London, Salford A.G., Mercer Gallery Harrogate, Doncaster A.G., Sir William Russell Flint Gallery Guildford, Laing at Mall Galleries London, Barnsley to Bombay Round the World Exhbn., Cooper Gallery Barnsley. Royal Society of British Artists Exhbn., London (2000), Open College of the Arts (2005). *Works in collections*: Michael Parkinson, Christine Foyle Estate, Countess of Wharncliffe (Estate). *Commissions*: P&O Cruise Lines, Mercedes Benz, Guardian Newspapers, Yorkshire Water. *Publications*: 'Sketches and Expressions' (1991). Listed in: Millers Art Guide (2005), International Biographical Dictionary (2005). *Works Reproduced*: many limited editions. *Principal Works*: commissioned to commemorate UK's first motorway Toll as a Limited Edition Print (2004). *Recreations*: cricket. *Misc*: 36 national TV appearances Channel 4 artist in residence/commentator 'Water-colour Challenge' (1998); uniquely interprets the musical classics through his art in live performance. Professional musician/writer/performer with 'Foggy Dew-O' (1965-76). *Address*: Huskar Cottage Studio, Silkstone Common, nr. Barnsley, S.Yorks. S75 4RJ. *Email*: g.danny.clarke@virgin.net *Website*: www.granvilledclarke.co.uk *Signs work*: "Granville D. Clarke"

CLARKE, Hilda Margery, BA (Hons.), FRSA; Director, 'The First' Gallery. *Medium*: artist in oils and other media. *b*: Manchester, 10 Jun 1926. *d of*: Frank Thompson. *m*: Geoffrey Clarke. two *s*. *Educ*: Eccles Secondary School. *Studied*: privately in Manchester (Master: L. S. Lowry) and Hamburg; Southampton Art College, Ruskin School Print Workshop, Oxford (Chris Orr, Norman Ackroyd); B.A. Southampton. *Exhib*: London Galleries: John Martin, Albermarle Street and Chelsea; FPS, Buckingham Gate; The Mall

Galleries; Camden Town. New Ashgate, Farnham; Bettles Gallery, Ringwood. One-man shows, Hamwic, Southampton; Westgate Gallery, Winchester; Hiscock Gallery, Southsea; Turner Sims Concert Hall Foyer Inauguration; Southampton University; Ramsgate Library Gallery, Kent; Southampton City Art Gallery. *Works in collections*: Southampton University, South East Arts, (RAB) St. Mary's Hospital, I.O.W., Felder Fine Art (42), London; Mrs.Angela Hunt (35), Southampton; Lady Lucas, Stockbridge; Robert Miles, London etc. *Commissions*: 'To the Sea' Lady Lucas. *Recreations*: music, literature. *Address*: 'The First' Gallery, 1 Burnham Chase, Bitterne, Southampton SO18 5DG. *Email*: margery@thefirstgallery.com *Website*: www.thefirstgallery.com *Signs work*: "H.M. Clarke."

CLARKE, Jeff, RE, NDD, Rome Scholarship (1956-58), British Inst. Fund Scholarship. *Medium*: painting, drawing, etching. *b*: Brighton, 1935. *Studied*: Brighton College of Art (1952-56). *Represented by*: Elizabeth Harvey-Lee. *Exhib*: Oxford Bear Lane Gallery, Oxford Gallery, Museum of Modern Art Oxford, Christ Church Picture Gallery, RE, RA Summer shows, National Print shows Mall Galleries, London, Discerning Eye, NEAC. *Works in collections*: Ashmolean Museum, Universities of Oxford, Cambridge, Reading. Many private collections in Europe, USA and Australia. *Address*: 17 Newton Rd., Oxford OX1 4PT. *Signs work*: "Jeff Clarke".

CLARKE, Johnnie. *Medium*: oil, watercolour, drawing, prints, sculpture. *b*: Tanzania, 3 May 1940. *Studied*: Academie de la Grande Chaumière, Bideford, Camberwell. *Represented by*: Toby Clarke. *Exhib*: RA. *Commissions*: Wetherspoons Liverpool: sculpture. *Publications*: War Child Art Auction (Feb 2004) Christie's. *Misc*: BBC2 The Apprentices. *Address*: High House, 1 Castle Hill, Dunster TA24 6SQ. *Signs work*: 'Clarke'

CLARKE, Jonathan. *Medium*: aluminium sculpture. *b*: Suffolk, 14 May 1961. *s of*: Geoffrey & Bill Clarke. *m*: Joanne. one *s*. *Educ*: Sudbury Upper School. *Studied*: studied under father. *Represented by*: Ron Howell, The Strand Gallery, Aldeburgh, Suffolk. *Exhib*: RA Summer Exhbn (1989, 91, 92, 95, 96, 98, 99); Chappel Galleries Essex; Strand Gallery Aldeburgh; Byard Art, Cambridge; Art London; Lena Boyle Fine Art; Metropolitan Museum, Tokyo; Belgrave Gallery, St. Ives; Open Eye, Edinburgh; Galeria Carezzonica, Venice; Pallant House, Chichester; Snape Maltings, Suffolk; Trinity Hall, Cambridge; North House Gallery, Manningtree. *Works in collections*: Christchurch Mansions, Ipswich; Britten Pears Library, Aldeburgh; Trinity Hall, Cambridge; Gateway Foundation, St. Louis, USA. *Commissions*: 'The Way of Life', Ely Cathedral; 'Stations of the Cross' 'Emaaus', Southwell Minster; P&O Lines, Asda, Tesco; Notley Bird, Notley; 'Browsers' New St Square, London; 'Gateway' New Fetier Lane London; Chichester Cathedral. *Publications*: 'Sea Legs' National Maritime Museum, Cornwall; Strand Gallery. *Principal Works*: 'The Way of Life' Ely Cathedral; 'Gateway' New Fetier Lane. *Address*: Stowe Hill, Hartest, Bury St.Edmunds IP29 4EQ. *Email*: jc@jonathanclarke.co.uk *Website*: www.jonathanclarke.co.uk *Signs work*: 'JC'.

CLARKE, Pat, Surrey Dip. (1969); artist in water-colour, oil, pastel; printmaker; Adult Education teacher, and special needs teacher (1970-80); since 1984, joint owner with husband of art gallery, Oriel y Odraig, Blaenau Ffestiniog, N. Wales. *b*: Banstead. *d of*: Samuel Clarke. *m*: Peter Elliott. *Studied*: Reigate Art School (1966-69). *Exhib*: Loggia Gallery, Gallery of Modern Art, London, Hereford City A.G., Rhyl and Denbigh Arts Centres, etc; 45 one-woman shows. *Works in collections*: Hereford City A.G. *Publications*: To the Mountain (1994). *Works Reproduced*: 12 artists cards. *Clubs*: N.S., F.P.S., Royal Cambrian Academy, Conwy, Watercolour Soc. of Wales. *Address*: 4 Bryn Dinas, Rhiwbryfdir, Blaenau Ffestiniog, Gwynedd LL41 3NS. *Signs work*: "Pat Clarke."

CLARKE, Ronald Aquilla, BA (Hons). *Medium*: oil, drawing. *b*: Leicester, 17 Mar 1950. *Educ*: City Boys Grammar School, Leicester. *Studied*: University of East Anglia (UEA),

1968-71. *Exhib*: Native American Arts Movement (NAPCAM) Exhibitions at Nuneaton, Riversley Park, and elsewhere (1980s), Maddermarket Theatre and other venues in Norwich (1970s). *Publications*: Author of art catalogues in capacity as an art historian (1970s-1980s, published by Herbert Art Gallery). *Misc*: Keeper of Art at the Herbert Gallery, Coventry April 1974-May 2009. Resumed practice as artist in 2006 after a gap of twenty years. Recent art projects: "Drawn to St.Ives" 2007; "The End of the Vacuum" 2009; Black Country Paintings 2011. Living in Plymouth from 2012. *Address*: 18 David Road, Coventry, CV1 2BW. *Signs work*: "Ron Clarke"; also "R.Aquilla Clarke".

CLARKE, Sheena Elizabeth Brough, NDD Illustration; Head of Art, St.Paul's Prep School, London (1968-2001); teaching in USA (1981-83). *Medium*: batik, wood engraving, acrylic, calligrapher. *b*: London, 15 Apr 1942. *Partner*: Philip Berg (Musician). *Studied*: Winchester Art School (1958 -1962). *Exhib*: RA (1968, 1969); RA British educational tour (1969-70); group and solo in UK, Southern Yemen, Kenya. *Works in collections*: in the USA. *Commissions*: private and commercial: book illustrations, portraits, calligraphy, murals. *Works Reproduced*: greeting cards; book jackets. *Principal Works*: illustrated five books by Don Pavey (2006). *Misc*: studio: 30 Wayside, Sheen, SW14 7LN. *Address*: 38a Dancer Road, Richmond, Surrey TW9 4LA. *Email*: sheena.clarke@virginmedia.com *Signs work*: Sheena Clarke.

CLAY, Andie Joy, BA (Hons) 1975; Society of Women Artists - St Cuthbert's Mill Award (2011); 2013 elected as Member, Society of Women Artists. *Medium*: mixed media, acrylic, pastel. *b*: Surrey, 13 Apr 1954. *m*: Dave Clay. *Studied*: London College of Printing, London (1971-75). *Exhib*: ING Discerning Eye Exhibition - Mall Galleries 2011; from 2011 Society of Women Artists, Mall Galleries; 159th Autumn Exhibition, RWA Bristol; Sea Pictures Gallery, Clare, Suffolk; Friends Room Gallery, RWA Bristol; The Albany Gallery, Cardiff; Off the Wall Gallery, Cardiff; Denise Yapp Contemporary Art, Monmouth; Oriel Ynys Mon, Anglesey; Oriel Plas Glyn y Weddw, N. Wales; Oriel Ceri Richards, Swansea; Fine and Contemporary Gallery, Suffolk; Artist in Residence, Rhosygilwen, Pembrokeshire. *Publications*: 'Paint! Landscapes (RotoVision)'. *Address*: Porth, Blaenporth, Cardigan, Ceredigion SA43 2AP. *Email*: andie@andieclay.com *Website*: www.andieclay.com *Signs work*: "Andie Clay."

CLAYDEN, Phillippa, BA Hons; RA Post-Graduate Diploma; Landseer Prize; Dorothy Morgan Prize. *Medium*: oil, watercolour, collage. *b*: London, 4 Aug 1955. *d of*: Pauline & Alan Clayden. *Partner*: Denzil Forrester. *Studied*: Central School of Art and Design; RA School. *Represented by*: Boundary Gallery (1989-2002). *Exhib*: RA, Whitechapel, Royal overseas League, Orangery, Southampton Art Gallery, ICA, Business Design Centre, Bilim Sanat Gallery, Plymouth Museum Gallery, Commonwealth Inst., The Gallery in Cork Street, Wallspace Gallery. *Works in collections*: TSB, Freshfields, various private. *Commissions*: various private. *Publications*: 3 catalogues for boundary gallery. *Works Reproduced*: in 'Landscape Painting' by Kimm Stevens. *Recreations*: walking. *Clubs*: Penwith Society of Artists, Plymouth Society of Artists, Chair of RASA - Royal Academy Schools Alumni. *Address*: 68 Woodland Rise, Muswell Hill, London N10 3UJ. *Email*: phillippa-c@hotmail.co.uk *Website*: www.phillippaclayden.co.uk

CLAYTON, Inge, FRSA. *Medium*: oil, watercolour, drawing, prints, sculpture, collage and assemblage. *b*: Salzburg, Austria. *d of*: Josef Fagerer. *m*: Anthony Clayton. one *s.* one *d.* *Educ*: Austria. *Studied*: Camden Arts Centre; Camden School of Art (largely self-taught). *Represented by*: Catto Gallery, Hampstead, London; Maurice Sternberg, Chicago, USA. *Exhib*: Affordable Art New York (2002), Art on Paper RCA (2003); solo: Ana Mei Chadwick Gallery, Boundary Gallery, St. Judes Gallery, Centaur Gallery, Enid Lawson Gallery, Zella Gallery, Proud Gallery, Blackheath Gallery, Maurice Sternberg Gallery (Chicago), The Orange Gallery (Rutland), Wiseman Gallery (Oxford), Adze Gallery (York), Metal Gallery (London) and many more. *Commissions*: Four Seasons Hotel, Jeremy Irons, Stephen

Berkhoff. *Publications*: Jack Yates 'Collage'; Jack Yates 'Fragments'. *Works Reproduced*: Homage to Picasso 'Demoiselles d'Avignon' on glass painting filmed and edited. *Recreations*: classical music, film, walking (to Birmingham on Grand Union Canal). *Clubs*: Chelsea Arts Club, Fellow Royal Society of Art. *Misc*: biographical film 30 mins. (Japan); advisory artist in 'Young Gifted and Broke' featured in erotic documentary. *Address*: 5 Randolph Ave., London W9 1BH. *Website*: www.ingeclayton.com *Signs work*: 'CLAYTON'.

CLEGG, Margrit, BA Hons Fine Art, Postgraduate Diploma in Printmaking. *Medium*: mixed media painting and printmaking (etching). *b*: Bremen, Germany, 18 Oct 1941. *d of*: Walter Arno Oestmann. *m*: R.S. Clegg. one *s*. *Educ*: Oberschule Bremen, Germany. *Studied*: Wimbledon School of Art, London. *Exhib*: solo: New Millennium Gallery, St.Ives (2001-03); selected: RA, Morley Gallery, Westminster, Tate St. Ives, Newlyn Art Gallery, Penwith Art Gallery St. Ives, Printmakers Gallery St. Ives, Lemon Street Gallery Truro, Art-Fair London 2001-2005 (New Millennium Gallery), Stoneman Gallery, Penzance; Gallery 49, Falmouth; Westcotts Gallery, St. Ives; Porthminster Gallery, St. Ives; Miar Ceramics & Arts, Brighton. *Works in collections*: private collections in Britain, Germany, USA and Canada. *Publications*: 'Drawing Towards the End of the Century 1996' (Newlyn Art Gallery); 'Another View' Marion Whybrow (1996), 'ARTNSA' (Newlyn Artists Publications, 2001). *Misc*: work is inspired by archaeology, ancient architecture and the signs and symbols carved in rocks, temples and city walls. *Address*: 6 Academy Flats, Academy Place, St. Ives, Cornwall, TR26 1LD. *Email*: margritclegg@yahoo.co.uk *Signs work*: Margrit Clegg.

CLEMENTS, Jeff, MBE (2007); Hon Fellow MDE (Meister der Einbandkunst) (2007); NDD (1955), Fellow Designer Bookbinders; artist in acrylic, fine bookbinder; partner with Katinka Keus, Restauratie atelier Meridiaan, Amsterdam; formerly Dean, Faculty of Art and Design, University of the West of England (-1988). *b*: Plymouth, 23 Feb 1934. *Partner*: Katinka Keus. two *s*. *Educ*: Devonport High School for Boys. *Studied*: Plymouth College of Art (1950-55), Central School of Arts and Crafts (1956-57). *Exhib*: from 1955 Daily Express Young Artists to recent ones in the Netherlands, Estonia, UK. *Works in collections*: fine bindings in: Royal Library, V. & A., London; Royal Library, The Hague; The Museum of the Book, The Hague; Texas University; University of Indiana; Röhsska Museum, Sweden; The National Library of Estonia, Tallinn; The Keatley Trust; The John Paul Getty Jr. Trust, The Rylands Library, Manchester etc.; paintings in private collections: Nice, Geneva, London, Birmingham, Bristol, Exeter, Oxford, York, The Hague, Amsterdam, Washington D.C., Tallinn. *Commissions*: The Clothworkers' Company (2009). *Publications*: Book Binding (Arco, 1963), Ambachtelijk Boekbinden (Gaade, 1991); articles in 'The New Bookbinder' etc. *Address*: Jan Luijkenstraat 38II, 1071 CR Amsterdam, Holland. Email: clementskeus@yahoo.com. *Signs work*: "Jeff Clements" with 'J' and 'e' forming an monogram, and the 'ff' incorporated in the 'C' of 'Clements'.

CLEMENTS, Patricia Kathleen, SWA (2006), ASWA (2005); NDD; St.Cuthberts Mill Award - winner Best Painting on Paper; Artist in Residence, Agora Gallery, New York, USA (2006-07). *Medium*: oil, pastel, prints. *b*: Epping, 19 May 1953. *d of*: John Dart. *Educ*: Midhurst Grammar School. *Studied*: Worthing College of Arts & Crafts; Central School, London (Life & Fine Art). *Exhib*: RA Summer Exhbn (1980-94); Llewellyn Alexander (1991); Brighton Lanes (1985); Battersea Webbs Gallery (2002, 2004); SWA (2003, 2004); Pastel Society, Mall Galleries (2003); Society of British Landscape (2004); Parkside Gallery, Sheen (2005); solo shows: Bartley Drew Gallery, Bloxham Gallery (2000). *Works in collections*: TUC Headquarters, Congress House, London; Art Directors, TV Times & Hello Magazines; private collections at home and abroad. *Works Reproduced*: Giglee Prints, Art Decaf. *Recreations*: interior design, outdoor sketching in South of France. *Address*: 2 Cornwall Road, Twickenham, Middx TW1 3LS. *Email*: 2003@patriciaclements.com *Website*: www.patriciaclementsart.com

CLIFTON, David James, ARCA, MA; professor fine art; exhbn. artist, painter in watercolour and oil, mixed media. *b*: Derby, 10 Jul 1938. *s of*: S. J. Clifton. *Educ*: at private and public schools; sometime placed Truro's (Eton). *Studied*: Bournville School of Art (Ruskin Hall), Birmingham College of Art (1956-58), Royal College of Art (1958-61). *Exhib*: Bourneville, Birmingham, Young Contemporaries, Royal College of Art, and London shows. Possible retrospective hung at Tate: withdrawn. *Commissions*: private. *Publications*: Contemporary Situation; New Wave Writing; Poetry; Serious Matters; Existential Surreal Metaphysical Metaphor Ethic Image and Criterion. *Misc*: Sometime: guest invitation National Liberal Club in London. *Address*: Flat 8, 63 Fountain Rd., Edgbaston, Birmingham B17 8NP. *Signs work*: "D. J. Clifton." Ref: no third party agent.

CLIFTON-BLIGH, Olivia, ARBS (2004); BA (Hons)(1993); Winner of the Althea Wynne Award for Sculpture (2014). *Medium*: Sculptor in bronze, plaster and paper. *b*: Wiltshire, 11 Oct 1971. *m*: Daniel Petkoff. one *s*. one *d*. *Educ*: Downe House, Berks. *Studied*: Goldsmiths' College, London University (1990-1993), Brighton Polytechnic (1989-1990). *Represented by*: King's Road Gallery, London. *Exhib*: solo and group exhibs., London and various galleries in British Isles; R.A. Summer Exhib. (1996-1998), Artist in Residence, (North Foreland Lodge, 1997), Delamore Arts, Devon (2004-14 Kings Road Gallery, London (2000-14), Long & Ryle, London (2010-12). *Works in collections*: Lord Bath's Wessex Collection. *Publications*: 'A Birthday Book' by Kate Holland (2009). *Address*: 2 Bull Mill, Crockerton, Warminster, Wilts. BA12 8AY. *Website*: www.bullmillarts.co.uk *Signs work*: "OLIVIA CLIFTON-BLIGH."

CLINE, Penelope, Cert. of Art, Cert. of Printmaking; artist in oil and acrylic. *b*: London, 27 Apr 1947. *d of*: Arthur Walters, Elizabeth W. *m*: Keith Richard Cline. one *s*. two *d* (one decd). *Educ*: Deepdene School. *Studied*: Brighton Polytechnic. *Exhib*: SWA (1994-97), NAPA (1994-96, 1998-99), Brighton Open (1993, 1996), Chichester Open (1995); solo shows: Brighton Festival and local socs. annually. *Works in collections*: UK, USA and S. Africa. *Publications*: contributed to 'Her Mind's Eye', 'Bonfire Magazine', 'Gator Springs Gazette', and 'The Writers' Muse', some book covers for Flame & Littoral Press and others. *Works Reproduced*: The Introduction. *Clubs*: N.A.P.A., Assoc. Sussex Artists. *Address*: 23 Brangwyn Drive, Westdene, Brighton BN1 8XB. *Email*: pennycline@hotmail.com *Website*: www.figtreepress.co.uk *Signs work*: "Penelope Cline" or "P. Cline."

CLOAKE, Beatrice Pierrette Denise, NAPA. *Medium*: oil, watercolour, acrylic; landscape, still life, wildlife, portrait. *b*: Amiens, France, 21 Nov 1946. *d of*: Pierre Pasquier, artist. *m*: Burton Cloake. one *s*. two *d*. *Educ*: Amiens. *Studied*: under father. *Represented by*: DACS. *Exhib*: Westminster (1995); Black Sheep Gallery, Hawarden (NAPA, 2001); Nevill Gallery, Canterbury (NAPA, 2003); Henley Royal Regatta (Summer 2006); Obsidian Art Gallery (NAPA, 2008); View Two Gallery, Liverpool (NAPA 2009); Folkestone (mixed, 2010); Watercolour (solo exhibition, 2012). *Works in collections*: private, corporate. *Commissions*: Bank of Scotland Corporate, design Burns Night (2006, 2007), Clydesdale Bank; and private. *Publications*: Hythe & Romney Life. *Official Purchasers*: Clydesdale Bank. *Works Reproduced*: prints by artist. *Clubs*: NAPA, Portrait Society of America, FFC, DACS. *Address*: 6 Alexandra Corniche, Hythe, Kent CT21 5RN. *Email*: beatrice_cloake@btinternet.com *Website*: www.beatricecloake.net *Signs work*: 'B.Cloake' and 'Beatrice Cloake'.

CLORAN, Julian Thomas, NAPA (1998); self taught artist in acrylic and felt-tip pens. *Medium*: Acrylic. *b*: Brighton, 10 Mar 1967. *Educ*: self taught from eleven years old. *Studied*: home, briefly Ruskin College, Oxford, 1999. *Exhib*: numerous local and national shows since 1987, including Westminster Gallery, NAPA London show (1999), Fiveways Artists' Open Houses (2000), The Biscuit Factory, Hove (2001), Williamson Art Gallery, Birkenhead (2011). *Commissions*: series of posters advertising exhbns., cabaret and other events for Brighton venues including 'One Off Gallery'. *Publications*: 'The Sage of Aquarius' (Authorhouse 2006) a novel. *Works Reproduced*: line drawings in small press magazines. *Address*: 1 Treyford Close, Woodingdean, Brighton BN2 6NP. *Email*: artworker1@yahoo.com *Website*: www.narolc.blogspot.com *Signs work*: "Julian Cloran."

CLOSSICK, Peter, BBSI (1969), BA (Hons) Fine Art (1978), ATC (1979); Elected London Group (1999). President London Group (2001-2005), Vice President London Group (2008-2010); President Blackheath Art Society (2008-2010); Elected New English Art Club (2011-); artist in 2D painting and drawing, lecturer/fine art; Elected Freeman Painter-Stainers Guild (2012). *Medium*: oil and water-colour. *b*: London, 18 May 1948. *s of*: Peter & Edith Clossick. *m*: Joyce. one *d*. *Educ*: Finchley Catholic Grammar School 1959-65. *Studied*: Leicester College of Art and Design (1966-69), Camberwell School of Art (1974-78, Antony Eyton, David Hepher, Gary Wragg), Goldsmiths' London University (1978-79). *Represented by*: Gallery Duncan Terrace, London; Boundary Gallery, London NW8. *Exhib*: John Moores, London Group, RA, Whitechapel Open, PS, ROI and National Portrait Gallery - John Player Award, Cooling Gallery, Cork St., Gallery Duncan Terrace, London, Woodlands Art Gallery, London, Sweet Waters Gallery, London, Phoenix Gallery, London, Bow House Gallery, Herts., Pelter Sands, Bristol, The Solomon Gallery, London, Arti et Amicitiae, Amsterdam, Basle Miami, USA. *Works in collections*: Corpus Christi College, Oxford, Working Men's College, London; Greenwich Community College, Life Long Learning, UK; private and international. *Commissions*: John Byrt, QC, Trevor Aston, Oxford Fellow. *Publications*: The New Painting Course (Quarto plc). Painting Without a Brush (Studio Vista), The London Group - 90th Anniversary. *Official Purchasers*: Life Long Learning, UK. *Works Reproduced*: The London Group 90th Anniversary ISBN 0-9545238-0-6. *Recreations*: reading and travel. *Address*: 358 Lee High Rd., Lee Green, London SE12 8RS. *Email*: peter.clossick@gmail.com *Website*: peterclossick.com *Signs work*: 'Peter Clossick'.

CLOUGH, Carolyn Stafford: see STAFFORD, C. Carolyn.

CLOUGH, Pauline Susan, PS (1982); artist in pastel, acrylic and oil. *b*: 16 Oct 1943. *d of*: Lesley J. Bird and Millie F. Bird. *m*: Peter Clough. one *s*. one *d*. *Educ*: Sharmans Cross High School. *Studied*: Bourneville School of Art, Birmingham (Phyllis Devey). *Exhib*: RA, RI, PS, SWA, RBSA and many provincial galleries. *Works in collections*: Hove Museum. *Clubs*: mem. Pastel Soc. *Address*: 'Sundown', 103 Allington Rd., Newick, Lewes, E. Sussex BN8 4NH. *Signs work*: "P.S. Clough" and "Clough."

CLUR, Elizabeth Mary, Diploma Witwatersrand School of Art (1941), 4 years Chinese study; 1st Annual Award Best Painting on Show, Brush and Chisel Club; W.H. Coetzer Prize (1984). *Medium*: oil, watercolour, pastel, pen & ink, pencil. *b*: Benoni, 2 Oct 1920. *d of*: British parents C.E. Bailey (Cornwall), Daisy Roberts (Leeds). *m*: Leonard Clur, Engineer. one *s*. one *d*. *Educ*: Durban Girls College; Parktown Convent Joh'burg. *Studied*: Witwatersrand School of Art (1937-41) Johannesburg, S. Africa; Chinese art under Prof. Fok (KAM). *Exhib*: solo exhbns Vryburgher Hall Linden, Jhb, SA, Rosebank gallery. Many group exhbns. all over South Africa 1954-1998; Brush and Chisel Club, SA Watercolour Society, Artists Under the Sun. *Works in collections*: Directors Collection Ltd. *Commissions*: paintings sold worldwide. *Publications*: The Collectors Guide to Art and Artists in South Africa (Oct 1998); illustrated all work in 'South African Handbook Concrete Technology' by F.S.Fulton (1957); illustrations, Macmillan Anthology of Verse. *Works Reproduced*: calendars, 1980s,1990s; illustrations, two books. *Clubs*: Brush and Chisel Club SA, SA Watercolour Society, Artists under the Sun Soc. *Misc*: teaching adults and children for 45 years, preparing many for entry into Schools of Art. *Address*: 7 Keepers Coombe, Crown Wood, Bracknell, Berks, RG12 0TN. *Signs work*: 'E.M.Clur'.

CLUR, Paddy June Gillian, BSc Hons (Zoology, Botany). *Medium*: pastels, watercolours, pencil. *b*: Johannesburg, SA, 1 Jun 1949. *d of*: Elizabeth Clur. *Educ*: Witwatersand University, Johannesburg. *Studied*: no formal training in art, but always interested in wildlife conservation. *Exhib*: Everard Read Gallery, Johannesburg, Natural History Exhibition (1995), annual exhbns at the Brush and Chisel Club of SA; The Directors Collections. *Works in collections*: private collections in UK and abroad. *Publications*: 'A Collectors Guide to Art and Artists in Southern Africa' (1998). *Recreations*: reading, travel, wildlife conservation. *Clubs*: Brush and Chisel Club of S.Africa; Associate mem. Artists Under the Sun. *Misc*: now living permanently in Britain. *Address*: 7 Keepers Coombe, Bracknell, Berkshire, RG12 0TN. *Signs work*: 'P Clur'.

CLUTTON-BROCK, Eleanor, BA Hons; Member of Oxford Art Society. *Medium*: sculpture and painting. *b*: 19 Jun 1946. *d of*: Alan Clutton-Brock, Slade Prof. of Fine Art, Cambridge. two *s*. *Studied*: Goldsmiths, London: pupil of Annie Wootton and Peter Rush. *Represented by*: Stour Gallery. *Exhib*: RA Summer Exhbn (2002, 2003, 2004); RWA Autumn Exhbn (2004, 2005, 2010, 2011, 2012, 2013); 'David Remfrey Selects' at Bohun Gallery, Henley-on-Thames; mixed shows include Banbury Mill, Bampton, Stour Gallery, Shipton-on-Stour, Modern Art Oxford (2005), Bankside Gallery, Henley Royal Regatta, Linacre College, Oxford, Bucks County Museum, Sewell Gallery, Chastleton House, Oxford Art Society, Oxford Sculptures, North Wall Gallery, Oxford. *Works in collections*: Linda Sutton, David Remfry, Lady Pilling, Bill Woodrow RA, Nicholas Mynheer, Briony & Andrew Lawson, Mrs Joyce Weil, Mrs. T Boswood. *Commissions*: Dr. Marvin Weil: portrait sculpture, Dr. Clifford Weil, Mr. Paul Lee, Danielle de Niese, Mrs. Tricia Duggan, Mr. Alan Trump, Mr. Freddie Jones. *Recreations*: writing fiction and reading, walking. *Clubs*: Member of Oxford Art Society and Oxford Sculptors. *Address*: Stable End, Church Road, Northleigh, OX29 6TX. *Email*: eclepaper@hotmail.com *Signs work*: 'Eleanor Clutton-Brock' 'E.C-B'.

CLYNE, Thora, MA Hons in Fine Art (1960); Special Prize (SSWA, 1984); Anne Redpath Award (SSWA, 1979); Andrew Grant postgrad. Scholarship and Travel Fellowship (1960-61); artist in oil, water-colour, pastel, pen and ink, printmaking. *b*: Wick, Caithness, 10 Nov 1937. *m*: G. Clemson, composer. *Educ*: Edinburgh University; Edinburgh College of Art (1955-61). *Exhib*: Morrison Portrait Competition, Royal Scottish Academy (1991, 1995, 1997); International Lithographic Symposium, Tidaholm, 2002; 2nd Print Open, DCA, 2002; Highlands, Views & Visions, RSA (2007); Edinburgh Art Fair, Hanover Fine Arts (2010, 2011); Stirling Art Gallery, FDPW (2009); Silver Prints, Fifespace (2011); Hong Kong Print Fair, FDPW; London Lives Travel, Bankside Gallery (2011); Bon Papillon Gallery, Edinburgh (2012); Impact 8, Dundee; RSA Open (2013). *Works in collections*: Edinburgh City Art Centre, Ross & Cromarty Educ. Authority, First Scottish-American Trust Co., Ltd., Gillies Bequest, RSA, Ciba Geigy, Coopers & Lybrand. *Works Reproduced*: "Stone Lithography" , "Plate Lithography" by Paul Croft. *Clubs*: Fife Dunfermline Printmakers Workshop, Perthshire Open Studios. *Address*: Tillywhally Cottage, Milnathort, Kinross-shire KY13 0RN. *Email*: thora@catpawtraits.co.uk *Website*: www.catpawtraits.co.uk *Signs work*: "Thora Clyne."

COATE, Peter, RWA, ATD, Chelsea Dip. (1950); painter in oil, water-colour, and teacher; Director, Mendip Painting Centre (1974-86). *Medium*: oil and watercolour. *b*: Nailsea, Som., 9 Mar 1926. *s of*: Redvers Coate, cidermaker. *m*: Margaret Bickerton (died 1978). Pamela Somerville (1980). one *s*. one *d*. *Educ*: Sherborne and New College, Oxford. *Studied*: Chelsea under Robert Medley, Claude Rogers and Ceri Richards. *Exhib*: London Group, RA, NEAC, SWLA, RWA, ROI, Bath Society of Artists; and many one-man shows in West Country galleries including The Patricia Wells Gallery, The Mignon Gallery, The Mall Gallery, The Ginger Gallery, Bristol Guild, The Court Gallery, and The Albany Gallery,

Cardiff and Wells and Mendip Museum. *Works in collections*: RWA, Hertfordshire and Cumberland County Councils, Nuffield Foundation, Wells and Mendip Museum. *Works Reproduced*: Wells Cathedral, The West Front. *Principal Works*: The Grand Pier, Weston-super-Mare (1980). *Misc*: Painter of wild landscape, birds, old buildings, many Somerset churches. Has made many painting excursions to Wales - Brecon Beacons, Pembrokeshire (Skokholm and St.Davids), North Wales around Cader Idris, the Lleyn Peninsula, and to Tuscany. Made two invited visits to Cill Rialaig in Western Ireland. *Address*: Orchard Lodge 2A Ash Lane Wells Somerset BA5 2LU. *Signs work*: "Peter Coate."

COATES, Carol, BA Hons, PGCE. *Medium*: drawing, print, acrylic. *b*: Kingston Upon Thames, 18 Jul 1955. two *s*. *Studied*: Buckinghamshire Chiltern University College (1999-2004), Reading University (2004-2005). *Exhib*: Artonomy Fine Art, Truro (2006); Et Cetera Gallery, Hackney (2007); Candid Arts, Islington (2007); Cass Business School, London (2008); Slough Museum (2009); Brick Lane Gallery, London (2010); Lloyd Gill Gallery, Weston Super Mare (2010); South Hill Park Arts Centre, Bracknell (2011). Solo shows: Progress Theatre, Reading (2012); Gallery@49, Bracknell (2012). *Works in collections*: private. *Publications*: Illustrations for 'Behind the Laughing Mask' John Griffin. *Works Reproduced*: 'Woman, No cry' (acrylic on canvas) selected to illustrate Axisweb 21 new artist's page. *Misc*: Teaches at The Reading School. Member of ReOrsa, artist-run gallery and studios (2011-2013). *Address*: 8 Queens Ride, Crowthorne, Berkshire RG45 6LG. *Email*: cagscoates@btinternet.com *Website*: www.carolcoates.co.uk *Signs work:* 'Carol Coates'.

COATES, Penny, HS, RMS. *Medium*: watercolour/mixed media. *b*: Norwich, 12 Mar 1938. *m*: David. one *s*. two *d*. *Educ*: Wombwell Technical College. *Studied*: with Elizabeth Woods, past curator, Grundy Museum, Lytham St.Annes; Janet Sheath, RMS, SWA. *Exhib*: Llewellyn Alexander Fine Paintings Ltd., Royal Miniature Society, Hilliard Society, The Society of Women Artists. *Works in collections*: HRH Princess Michael of Kent. *Commissions*: locally and through the RMS Exhibition at the Mall Galleries. *Principal Works*: Miniature work mostly galleons and tall ships. The Royal Yacht Squadron; Cowes Waterfront; East Cowes Waterfront; Farringford Manor, IOW (the home of Lord Tennyson). *Clubs*: West Wight Painting Circle; SAA. *Address*: 27 Forest End, Camphill, Newport, Isle of Wight PO30 5PG. *Email*: coatesforestend@talktalk.net *Website*: www.pecoates.com *Signs work*: 'Penny Coates'.

COATES, Thomas J., PNEAC, PPRBA, RWS, RP; awarded De Lazlo Medal, 1st and 3rd prizes in Sunday Times Water-colour Exhbns. (1988, 1989); Past President Pastel Society; RWA, membre de Honneur French Pastille., Hon. RBSA, many other awards; painter of landscapes, townscapes and portraits in oil and water-colour. *b*: 1941. *Studied*: Bournville and Birmingham Colleges of Art (1956-61), RA Schools (1961-64). *Exhib*: RA, RBA, and many one-man shows including New Grafton Gallery, Cross Gate Gallery, Ky., USA, W.H. Patterson, Mall Gallery, Alresford Gallery. *Works in collections*: HM The Queen. HRH Prince of Wales. Many other private collectors. *Publications*: Creating a Self Portrait. *Recreations*: golf, walking the dog. *Clubs*: Dover Street Arts Club, Chelsea Arts Club, Hampshire Golf Club. *Address*: Bladon Studio, Hurstbourne Tarrant, Hants. SP11 0AH.

COBLEY, David Hugh, RP (1997), RWA (2001); NEAC (2004); portrait and figure painter in oil, charcoal, pencil, pen. *Medium*: oil. *b*: Northampton, 27 Jun 1954. three *d*. *Studied*: Northampton and Liverpool. *Represented by*: The National Portrait Gallery, Royal Society of Portrait Painters. *Exhib*: RA, BP Portrait Award, RP, RWA, Hunting Art Prizes, Discerning Eye, New English Art Club. *Works in collections*: throughout the UK and abroad. *Commissions*: National Portrait Gallery, English National Ballet, Royal Engineers, Royal Marines, many Oxofrd and Cambridge colleges, Westminster Abbey, etc. *Publications*: The Portrait Now, Nairne & Hargate. *Works Reproduced*: in The Artist, Artists and Illustrators, International Artist, Art Class (Harper Collins) magazines. *Principal Works*: HRH The Princess Royal Princess Anne, Ken Dodd OBE, Sir Martin Evans. *Recreations*: sculling. *Clubs*: ACRC. *Address*: Bath Artists' Studios, The Old Malthouse, Comfortable Place, Bath BA1 3AU. *Email*: mail@davidcobley.co.uk *Website*: www.davidcobley.co.uk *Signs work*: monogram.

COBURN, Ivor Basil, DA.(1955), UWS, NDD (1956), WCSI, ARUA, FSBA; RHS six Gold and two Silver medals, two Grenfell; Royal Ulster Academy Gold medal (perpetual); artist in water-colour and oil. *b*: Belfast, 10 Apr 1934. *s of*: Alfred and Margaret Coburn. *m*: Patricia. one *s.* three *d. Educ*: Grosvenor High School, Belfast. *Studied*: Belfast College of Art, Leeds College of Art, and University. *Exhib*: one-man shows: Belfast, Dublin, Newcastle, Londonderry, Glasgow, London, Antwerp, Brussels, Paris, Annecy, Compiegne, Wexford Galway (2003), Dublin; group shows: London, Belfast, Brussels, Paris, Dublin, Rochester, Windsor. *Works in collections*: USA, Canada, France, Belgium, Holland, Australia, New Zealand, Israel, Sweden, England, Ireland, Scotland, Wales, Germany. *Commissions*: self-portrait, National Collection Ireland. *Publications*: Flower Painting Techniques by Sue Burton. *Official Purchasers*: NUU (New University, Ulster), UCD (University College, Dublin), QUB (Queen's University, Belfast). *Works Reproduced*: limited edition Siamese Cats 'Watchful' and 'Sleeping Ching', 2 paintings of Monet's Garden, 850 limited ed. black cat 'Malt'. *Clubs*: S.B.A. (Founder mem.)., UWS (Founder mem.). *Address*: The Springs, 50 Megargy Rd., Magherafelt, Co. Londonderry BT45 5HP, N. Ireland. *Email*: ivorcob@hotmail.com *Website*: watercoloursivorcoburn.com *Signs work*: "Ivor B. Coburn."

COCKER, Doug, DA, ARSA, FRBS; sculptor. *b*: Alyth, Perthshire, 1945. *m*: Elizabeth. two *s.* one *d. Educ*: Blairgowrie High School. *Studied*: Duncan of Jordanstone, Dundee (1963-68). *Exhib*: RSA, Yorkshire Sculpture Pk., The British Art Show, Air Gallery London, Serpentine Gallery London, Fruitmarket Gallery, Edinburgh, Third Eye Centre, Glasgow. *Works in collections*: Arts Council, Scottish Arts Council, Contemporary Art Soc., Kelvingrove A.G., Glasgow, Peterborough A.G., Greenshields Foundation, Montreal, Leicester University, Hunterian A.G., Glasgow, Essex CC, Staffs. CC, MMA Sarajevo. *Address*: Lundie Mill, Lundie, Angus DD2 5NW. *Signs work*: "DOUG COCKER."

COCKRILL, Maurice, RA (1999); Elected Keeper of Royal Academy of Arts (2004). *Medium*: artist in oil on canvas and other media. *b*: England, 1936. *s of*: William Cockrill and Edith Godfrey. three *s. Studied*: Wrexham School of Art and University of Reading (1960-64). *Exhib*: one-man shows: Edward Totah Gallery (1984, 1985), Kunstmuseum, Düsseldorf (1985), Bernard Jacobson Gallery (1987, 1988, 1990, 1992, 1994, 1995), Retrospective '1974-94' Walker A.G. (1995) (illus. cat.), Galerie Clivage, Paris (1995), Annandale Galleries, Sydney (1995), Galleri Clivage, Paris (1997), Galerie Helmut Pabst, Frankfurt (1997), Royal West of England Academy (1998), Purdy Hicks Gallery, London (1998), Archrs Fine Art, London (2002), Galerie Vidal-St.Phalle, Paris, 2003. Hillsboro Fine Art, Dublin 2005. Galerie Alders, St. Tropez, 2006. Cheltenham Museum, 2007. *Works in collections*: ACGB, Walker A.G., Unilever, BM, Contemporary Art Soc., Centro Cultural Arte Contemporaneo, Polanco, Mexico, Kunstmuseum, Düsseldorf. *Publications*: monograph, authors, Marco Livingstone and Nic. Alfrey, pub. Merrett 2002. *Principal Works*: "Four Seasons", oil. Walker Art Gallery, Liverpool, 1991. "Divided # 83", Royal Academy, diploma work, 2000. *Clubs*: Chelsea Arts, Dover Street Arts Club, Lansdowne Club. *Address*: 78b Park Hall Rd., London SE21 8BW. *Email*: admin@cockrill.co.uk *Website*: www.cockrill.co.uk *Signs work*: full signature on back.

CODNER, Stephen Milton, painter in oil, pastel, portrait, landscape, still life, etcher. *b*: Clevedon, Som., 1952. *s of*: John Codner, RWA. Grandson of Maurice Codner, RP, ROI. *m*: Carolyn Hamilton. three *d. Educ*: Bryanston School Dorset. *Studied*: Camberwell School of Art and Crafts, City and Guilds Art School. *Exhib*: RA. RP, RWA, ROI, 'Discerning Eye.' *Address*: 33 Whyke Lane, Chichester, PO19 7US. *Signs work*: "S. M. CODNER" or "STEPHEN CODNER."

COHEN, Bernard, Slade Dip.; professional artist in painting and printmaking; Slade Professor and University of London Chair in Fine Art; Director of Slade School, UCL; Emeritus Slade Professor (1988-2000), Fellow of University College, London. *b*: London, 28 Jul 1933. *s of*: Victor Cohen. *m*: Jean. one *s.* one *d. Studied*: Slade School of Fine Art (1951-54, Sir William Coldstream). *Exhib*: Major retrospective: Hayward Gallery (1972 touring), Kasmin Gallery (1963-1967), Waddington Galleries (1972, 1974, 1977, 1979, 1981, 1990), Flowers East (1998), Flowers West, L.A. (1999), 'Artist in focus', Tate Gallery (1995), British Pavilion Venice Biennale (1966), 'Work of Six Decades' Flowers East Gallery (2009). *Works in collections*: Arts Council, MoMA (NY), Tate Gallery, V&A, etc. *Publications*: Hayward Retrospective 1972 - Arts Council GB, Waddington Galleries (1974-1990), Bernard Cohen, Paintings from the 90s - Flowers East Gallery; Paintings from the 60s - Flowers East Gallery (2007); book 'Work of Six Decades', Lynton-McKay Flowers. *Address*: 80 Camberwell Grove, London SE5 8RF. *Email*: bwc44@hotmail.com *Website*: Flowers East Gallery *Signs work*: "Bernard Cohen" on works on paper only.

COKER, Norman, Richard, City & Guilds of London Inst. FETC (1974), FSBA (1986); art teacher Adult Educ. Centres; Founder mem. SBA (Society of Botanical Artists); awarded the Founder President's Honour in the year 2000 and 2004; artist in oil, lecturer. *b*: Grays, Essex, 27 Jan 1927. *m*: Doreen Anne. *Educ*: Park Secondary School, Grays. *Studied*: Thurrock Tech. College. *Exhib*: Nairobi, Kenya (wild life), The McEwan Gallery, Scotland (British Flower Painters), The Veryan Gallery, Cornwall, Singapore, London, Amsterdam, The Frinton Gallery; one-man show at Beecroft Gallery, Westcliff-on-Sea (1991). *Works in collections*: many private collections worldwide including HRH The Princess Anne, The Princess Royal, an equestrian portrait of HRH with her horse Doublet. *Commissions*: James Last (orchestra leader) a painting of the Royal Albert Hall. *Publications*: work included in "The Encyclopedia of Flower Painting Techniques" by Sue Burton (Quarto, 1997); work in print with Rosentiel's of Chelsea, Medici; 'Dictionary of International Biography 31st Ed.'; 'The Cambridge Blue Book' (International Biographical Centre, Cambridge, England); autobiography, 'A Brush with my Palette' published 2005. Copies in the National Published Archive, The Universities of Oxford, Cambridge, Trinity College Dublin, and the National Libraries of Scotland and Wales. *Works Reproduced*: Jason Productions, New Zealand; Paper Rose of Nottingham. *Address*: "Tensing", Muckingford Rd., Linford, Stanford-le-Hope, Essex SS17 0RF. *Website*: www.normancroker.co.uk *Signs work*: "Norman R. Coker."

COLDWELL, Paul, BA Fine Art; Slade Higher Diploma; Professor of Fine Art, University of the Arts, London. *Medium*: drawing, prints, sculpture. *b*: London, 8 Nov 1952. *m*: Charlotte Hodes. one *s.* one *d. Studied*: Bristol Polytechnic (1972-75); Slade School of Fine Art (1975-77). *Represented by*: Eagle Gallery, London. *Exhib*: solo: Kettle's Yard, Cambridge (2008); Eagle Gallery (2007); Edinburgh Printmaker (2005); London Print Studio, Queen's Gallery-Delhi (2002); Arthouse, Dublin (1999); Freud Museum, London (1996); numerous group shows including biennales at Ljubljana, Macau, Cairo and New York. *Works in collections*: Tate Gallery, Arts Council of England, V&A, Imperial War Museum, MoMA New York, British Museum. *Publications*: Finding Spaces Between Shadows (2005, Camberwell Press); Printmaking: A Contemporary Perspective (2010 Black Dog). *Clubs*: AICA. *Address*: 86 Oakfield Road, London N4 4LB. *Email*: p.coldwell@chelsea.arts.co.uk Website: www.paulcoldwell.org *Signs work*: 'PAUL COLDWELL'.

COLE, Barbara Evelyn (B.E.), ARBS (2003); BA (Hons) Sculpture; MA (Sculpture). *Medium*: drawing; sculpture (bronze, aluminium, stone). *b*: Newport, Gwent, 14 May 1952.

d of: Jack and Sylvia Vickery. *Partner*: Roger Wilson. one *s*, Andrew Cole. *Educ*: Croesyceiliog Grammar School, Cwmbran. *Studied*: Nottingham Trent University, Rochdale College of Art, Sheffield Hallam University. *Represented by*: Belgrave Gallery, St. Ives; Colin Jellicoe, Manchester. *Exhib*: RA (1994, 95, 98, 2000, 02, 06); Triennial Sculpture Exhbn. RWA (1999); Wales Drawing Biennale (1997/8, 1999/2000); Jerwood Drawing Prize (2004/5); Solo: Holden Gallery, Manchester (2000); B.E. Cole New Work, Chichester (2004); Group: Rural Central, LCF (2006); Sir Harold Hillier Gardens, Hampshire (2009); RBS (2008) London *Works in collections*: London College of Fashion; private collections UK, USA and WA. *Commissions*: private (1994-2007). *Official Purchasers*: LCF, London. *Works Reproduced*: Royal Academy Illustrated, 2002; Jerwood Drawing Prize, 2004/5. *Principal Works*: Form (aluminium); Untitled (boulder) (aluminium); Sea Form (gold on bronze). *Misc*: exhibits as B.E. Cole; also Associate, Penwith Gallery, St.Ives, Cornwall. *Address*: Meadowhead Farm, Lobden, Whitworth, Lancs., OL12 8XJ. *Website*: RBS *Signs work*: 'B.C.'; 'B.E.C.'

COLEMAN, Brian, Mem. Pastel Soc.; painter in water-colour; Art Director/Graphic Designer, advertising. *b*: Cheam, Surrey, 3 Sep 1935. *m*: Joan Coleman. *Educ*: Stoneleigh Secondary Modern. *Exhib*: Kingsmead Gallery, Bookham, Surrey. *Address*: 2 Sheraton Drive, West Hill, Epsom, Surrey KT19 8JL. *Signs work*: "Brian Coleman".

COLLETT, Paula, BA (Hons); public/community artist in textile/soft sculpture; workshop leader. *b*: Wakefield, 16 Jul 1969. *Educ*: Woodkirk High. *Studied*: Chelsea School of Art and Design (1989-92, Roger Hoare). *Exhib*: tree art: Oakwell Hall. *Works in collections*: Huddersfield Royal Infirmary, Airville Leisure Centre. *Address*: 11 Boldgrove St., Earlsheaton, Dewsbury, W. Yorks. WF12 8NA. *Signs work*: "P. Collett."

COLLINGBOURNE, Stephen, painter, sculptor; prize winner, RSA, and John Moores; Awards: Welsh Arts Council, Scottish Arts Council, Arts Council GB, British Council. *Medium*: 3D steel, bronze, copper; 2D collage, printing, drawing and painting. *b*: Dartington, 15 Aug 1943. *s of*: J.C. and A.M. Collingbourne. *m*: Aileen Keith (artist). one *s*. one *d*. *Studied*: Dartington College of Art (1960-61); Bath Academy, Corsham (1961-64). *Exhib*: British Council, Malaya; Chapter, and Oriel, Cardiff; Camden Arts Centre, Zella 9, Fisher Gallery and Serpentine, London; Kettles Yard, Cambridge; MacRobert Arts Centre, Stirling; Third Eye Centre, Glasgow; City Art Centre and Talbot Rice, Edinburgh; Nykarleby, Kokkola and Helsinki, Finland. *Works in collections*: Leicester Art Gallery, Devon, Leicestershire and Hertford Educ. Authorities, Edinburgh City Art Centre, Motherwell Council, Art in Hospitals. *Commissions*: Welsh Arts Council, Leicester University, Livingstone, Edinburgh. *Publications*: Drawing Comparisons (ISBN 0-9531180-0-2). *Works Reproduced*: 'Open Air Sculpture in Britain' by W J Strachan. *Principal Works*: '4Fold', Leicester University. *Address*: Tofts, Blyth Bridge, West Linton, Peeblesshire EH46 7AJ. *Email*: collingbourne@talktalk.net *Signs work*: 'Stephen Collingbourne' or 'Collingbourne'.

COLLINGE, Robert Anthony, NDD (1955), ATD (1956), Blond Travelling Scholarship (1957), Slade Dip. (1959); artist in collage and construction; taught at: Canterbury College of Art (1961-63), London College of Printing (1962-63), Goldsmiths' School of Art (1963-96, working with Anton Ehrenzweig and Harry and Elma Thubron); mem. London Group; Vice President London Group (2000-2001). *b*: Cheshire, 28 Jul 1934. *Educ*: King's School, Chester. *Studied*: Liverpool College of Art (1951-56), British School at Rome (1957), Slade School (1957-59). *Exhib*: Northern Young Artists; Five Painters, Sandon Studios, Liverpool; Young Contemporaries; Drian Gallery; Hope Hall Gallery, Liverpool; New Art Centre, London; London Group's 75th Anniversary Exhbn. RCA (1988), Storey Inst., Lancaster, Invited Artists Exhbn. (1993), London Group's 80th Birthday Open Exhbn., Concourse Gallery, Barbican (1993), Joint exhbn. with Elma Thubron, Storey Inst., Lancaster (1994);

London Group's Biennial Open Exhbn., Concourse Gallery, Barbican (1995), 'Musée Imaginaire' group exhbn. Museum of Installation, Deptford (1997); solo show: Woodlands Gallery, Blackheath (1995), The Walk Gallery, London (Mar. 2001), Stark Gallery, London (2001).*Works in collections*: Arts Council, Goldsmiths' College Gallery, Archive of the Museum of Installation; various private collections. *Publications*: in collaboration with Anton Ehrenzweig a booklet 'Towards a theory of Art Education (Goldsmiths' College, 1964). *Address*: 32 Prior St., Greenwich, London SE10 8SF. *Signs work*: "TONY COLLINGE."

COLLINGS, David, Dip. (1969), ATD (1972); artist in oil on board, canvas; teacher of mentally handicapped. *b*: London, 1949. *s of*: Robert Collings. *Studied*: Redruth School of Art (1965-69), Berks. College of Education (1969-72). *Exhib*: widely in SW England, Brittany and Ireland. *Works in collections*: Contemporary Art Soc. *Clubs*: Newlyn Soc. of Artists. *Address*: 3 Lyn Terr., Newlyn, Penzance, Cornwall. *Signs work*: "David Collings."

COLLINS, Clive Hugh Austin, Awards: Romania, Knokke-Heist, Netherlands, Macedonia, Japan, Canada, Germany, UK. *Medium*: brush and pens, gouache, mainly AppleMac. *b*: Weston-Super-Mare, Avon, 6 Feb 1942. *s of*: Greville and June Collins. *m*: Lynne; one *s*. & one *d*. by previous marriage. *Educ*: Shene Grammar School. *Studied*: Kingston Art College, England. *Exhib*: Cartoon Gallery, London (1993), The Barbican, London (1993), Zagreb, Croatia (1987). *Works in collections*: Museum of Cartoon Art, Basel; Cartoon Art Trust, GB. *Publications*: Dictionary of Twentieth Century Cartoonists and Caricaturists (ed. Mark Bryant); Handbook of Sailing and Watersports (Mondria), Montreal Catalogue of Cartoons, Funny Book of ... Sex, Motoring, Work; The Idiots Guide to Sex. *Works Reproduced*: Punch (1964-2003), Playboy (1972-date), current newspapers and magazines. *Recreations*: drawing, meeting friends, music and films. *Clubs*: The British Cartoonists Association, NCS. *Address*: Mead Cottage, 77 Woodfield Road, Hadleigh, Essex, SS7 2ES. *Email*: collinscartoons@aol.com *Website*: www.clivecollinscartoons.com *Signs work*: 'Clive Collins'.

COLLINS, Kate, ABNA; Buxton Open Exhibition Medal, Great British Art Show G-Mex Manchester Prize. *Medium*: oil, watercolour, ceramic art & egg tempera. *b*: Macclesfield, Ches, 22 Jul 1948. *m*: Geoff Collins. *Studied*: self-taught. *Exhib*: solo: Tib Lane Art Gallery, Manchester, Hamster Gallery, Preston; Medici Gallery (Liverpool, London); Accrington Art Gallery (Howarth), Stockport Municipal Art Gallery. Mixed: Buxton Art Gallery, ABNA Exhibition Cornwall, Society of Tempera Paintings Exhibition London. *Works in collections*: Saddleworth Museum; the late Helen Bradley's collection; various private collections at home and abroad. *Commissions*: Medici Society; Camden Graphics; Arthur Kaplans Fine Art Prints. *Publications*: Medici Cards; Camden Graphics cards. *Official Purchasers*: Saddlworth Art Gallery, Lancashire. *Principal Works*: "Girls with geese", "Three pigs". *Clubs*: ABNA; Saddleworth Group of Artists. *Address*: 'Moss Lawn', Middlewood Rd., Hr Poynton, Cheshire, SK12 1TU. *Email*: katengeoff@ntlworld.com *Website*: www.katecollinsartist.co.uk

COLLINS, Marjorie, SWA (1994); SBA (2008); Winsor & Newton Grand Prize Award 'The Artist' Celebration 2000 Competition; St. Cuthbert Mill Runner Up Award (SBA 2007); Daler Rowney Choice Award (SWA 2008); St. Cuthbert Mill 3rd Prize (RWS 2009); Winsor & Newton 1st Prize (RWS 2011); Daniel Smith Award for Excellence in Colour (SWA 2011); shortlisted Artist of the Year (2013) Artists and Illustrators Magazine. *Medium*: watercolour and acrylic. *b*: Chicago, USA, 24 Feb 1941. *m*: Professor Michael Collins. one *s*. one *d*. *Studied*: University of Michigan (BSc Design), and Art Institute of Chicago. *Exhib*: RA Summer Exhbn, Hunting Prizes, Sunday Times Watercolour Competition; ROI, RWS, RI; solo shows: Joy Horwich Gallery, Chicago; Barbican Centre, London; many group shows in London and UK. *Works in collections*: USA, UK, Australia. *Publications*: Artists

& Illustrators Magazine (1995); 'Painting Great Pictures from Photographs (1999); 'Inspiration to Paint' (2002); How Did You Paint That? (2004); Painting Light and Shadow (2004); Different Strokes (2007); International Artist Magazine (2009). *Works Reproduced*: 1987 HM Government Office of Arts and Libraries. *Recreations*: playing bridge. *Clubs*: Oxford Art Society. *Address*: 28 Hayward Road, Oxford OX2 8LW. *Email*: mac@marjoriecollins.com *Website*: www.marjoriecollins.com *Signs work*: 'M.Collins'.

COMBES, Richard A., ROI (2004); BA & BArch (Hons) in Architecture; MA Fine Art (Cum Laude), New York Academy of Art; Cornelissen Prize for Outstanding Work (ROI, 2003); Stanley Grimm Award (ROI, 2005) - Visitors Vote 1st & 2nd Prize; The Menena Joy Schwafe Memorial Award - Outstanding Painter (ROI, 2006). *Medium*: oil and charcoal. *b*: Manchester, 28 May 1963. *m*: Luna. *Educ*: Retford, N. Notts., England. *Studied*: University of Liverpool; New York Academy of Art. *Represented by*: Mike Levers; Dukeries Art Gallery. *Exhib*: RA Summer Exhbn (2006, 2007); ROI (2003-07); RP (2001-04); National Portrait Gallery, BP Awards (1996-2003); Harley Gallery, Welbeck, Notts (2005, 2008); Whittington Fine Art, Henley on Thames; permanent at Dukeries Art Gallery, Worksop. *Works in collections*: Barbara Streisand, Jeffrey Epstein, Leslie Wexner, John Major (former PM). *Commissions*: portraits of: Sir Hugh Neill KCVO, CBE, Ex Lord Lieutenant of South Yorkshire, Master Cutler of Sheffield; Sir Andrew Buchanan, Lord Lieutenant of Nottinghamshire. *Recreations*: swimming, reading, old films. *Address*: Dukeries Art Gallery, 88 Gateford Rd., Worksop, N.Notts., S80 1TY. *Email*: mike@dukeriesartgallery.com michael.levers@ansbronze.com *Website*: www.dukeriesartgallery.com

COMRIE, Rowena Susan, BA (Hons) Fine Art. *Medium*: oil, watercolour, drawing, print, sculpture. *b*: Southend-on-Sea, Essex 30 Sep 1959. one *s*. one *d*. *Studied*: University of Reading (1978-92). *Represented by*: Rendezvous Gallery, Aberdeen. *Exhib*: Selected Solo Shows: Rendezvous Gallery, Aberdeen (2011, 2014); House for an Art Lover, Glasgow (2013); Ivy Tech John Waldron Arts Centre, Bloomington Indiana, USA (2013); Hughson Gallery, Glasgow, Spring Line (2011); The Arches Glasgow (2011); Meffan Museum, Forfar (2010); Tolbooth Art Centre, Kirkcudbright (2010); Angus Digital Media Centre, Brechin (2003); Gracefield Arts Centre, Dumfries (1999); Aberdeen Maritime Museum (1999/2000); Demarco European Foundations, Edinburgh (1996); Aberdeen City Art Gallery (1996). *Works in collections*: Aberdeen City Art Gallery & Museum, Iona Abbey Trust Ltd, Grampian Hospitals Art Trust, Paintings in Hospitals, Edinburgh, University of Aberdeen, Deloitte & Touche, J.D. Wetherspoon plc. Logica plc. Cabot plc. The Iris Archive, Fareo Petroleum, Aspect Capital, New Hall Art Collection, Murray Edwards Hall, University of Cambridge. Walter Scott Global Investment Management, "100 Flowers" Collection, New South Glasgow Hospitals; New Hall Art Collection, Murray Edwards College, Cambridge Unviersity. *Commissions*: BBC TV (Jonathan Meades: Off Kilter Titles Art Work, 2009). *Official Purchasers*: Aberdeen Art Gallery, Grampian Hospitals Trust. *Works Reproduced*: in: Aberdeen Art Gallery Magazine, Glasgow Herald, Herald Arts Magazine, Scottish Himes Magazine. *Principal Works*: "Capsize", "Glasgow Colours" (shortlisted for Aspect Prize). *Recreations*: sailing. *Clubs*: Professional Member of Society of Scottish Artists (elected), President Scottish Artists Union (2011-2014). *Address*: Flat 2.1, 2 Garrioch Drive, Glasgow G20 8RP. *Email*: info@rowenacomrie.co.uk *Website*: www.rowenacomrie.co.uk *Signs work*: "Rowena Comrie".

CONLON, Elizabeth, self taught part-time painter in oil, water-colour, egg tempera and embroidery. *b*: Dublin, 1938. *m*: Norman Rogers. one *s*. one *d*. *Exhib*: annually at SBA, RSMA, ROI, etc. *Publications*: author and illustrator: Learn to Paint Flower Portraits in Water-colour. *Address*: 61 Orchard Ave., Poole, Dorset BH14 8AH.

CONN, Roy. *Medium*: oil, gouache, mixed media, photography. *b*: London, 19 Jan 1931. *Educ*: Westminster College. *Studied*: early training Structural Engineering-mainly Self-taught as a painter. Elected member of Penwith Society in 1959. Moved to St.Ives Oct. 1958. *Exhib*: solo exhibitions at the Rowan Gallery, London and Arnolfini Gallery, Bristol. Numerous group exhbns and mixed shows including: London Group, New Vision Centre, John Moores, Liverpool, Bradford City Art Gallery, Penwith Gallery, Tate St.Ives, etc. *Works in collections*: public collections include: Contemporary Arts Society, Arts Council of Northern Ireland, V&A Museum, Cornwall Education Authority, The Ind Coope Collection. Work also in many private collections in UK and abroad. *Clubs*: Penwith Society of Arts, Country Club UK. *Address*: 1 Porthmeor Studios, Back Road West, St.Ives, Cornwall TR26 1NG. *Signs work*: Roy Conn.

CONNELLY, Roy. *Medium*: oil. *b*: London, 1966. *m*: Victoria. *Represented by*: various commercial galleries. *Exhib*: Royal Academy of Arts, New English Art Club, Royal Society of British Artists, Royal Society of Marine Artists, Discerning Eye - invited artist, Venice in Peril - W.H. Patterson; Royal Institute of Oil Painters. *Works in collections*: private and corporate. *Commissions*: Ardington House, Oxfordshire. *Publications*: Art in Devon, The Artist. *Misc*: Plein Air Brotherhood - Founder Member. *Address*: Mulberry Cottage, Partridge Row, Assington, Suffolk Co10 5LP. *Email*: mail@royconnelly.com *Website*: www.royconnelly.com *Signs work*: "ROY CONNELLY".

CONNER, Angela, FRBS, American Inst. Architects Award; sculptor in stone, bronze, water, light, wind; competition winner, Economist Plaza, London, Aston University, de Gaulle, London, Cambridge, Lexington Airport, Kentucky etc. *b*: London. *m*: John Bulmer. one *d*. *Represented by*: Rebecca Townshend (Australia); Peggy Townsend (USA); A.Conner Ltd. (UK). *Exhib*: Metropolitan Museum, NYC; Jerwood Foundation; Sothebys; Lincoln Center, N.Y., Browse & Darby; Hirschl Gallery, Cork St., London; Solomon Fine Arts, Ireland; Galerie Piece Unique, Paris; Friends of the Tate, London; Gimpel Fils Gallery, NY; Royal Academy Summer Show; V&A Museum; Temple Gardens, London; Carnegie Museum of Modern Art; Washington Museum; Sculpture by the Sea, Sydney, Australia, etc. *Works in collections*: Arts Council GB, National Portrait Gallery, Pittsburgh Museum of Modern Art, Jewish Museum, NY, Musee de l'Armee, Paris, V&A Museum, House of Commons, National Trust, etc.; private collections, HRH Prince of Wales, Paul Mellon, Dr. Roy Strong, President Chirac, John Major, Crown Prince of Saudi Arabia, Duke of Devonshire, Lord Sainsbury, Dame Drew Heinz, Gunter Sachs, Lord Rothschild, Mrs. Henry Ford, Viscount Salisbury, French Embassy, etc *Commissions*: largest outdoor sculpture in Europe, Dublin; city centre pieces for Heinz Hall Plaza, Pittsburgh, U.S.A.; Horsham, Surrey, Chesterfield, Derbyshire; largest indoor sculpture, Lovells, London, Mobile Arch, Longleat, Wessex and some 100 others. Many bronze portraits - H.M. The Queen, Prime Ministers, Tom Stoppard, Lucien Freud, Dame Janet Baker, John Betjeman, Lord Rothschild etc *Works Reproduced*: various books and magazines in UK, Australia & USA *Principal Works*: Largest outdoor sculpture in Europe, tallest indoor mobile in Europe, gold and silver water mobile for State dining table, UK; Memorial to Victims of Yalta outside V & A, London, etc. *Recreations*: Breeding and showing Morgan Horses, Equitation etc. *Address*: George and Dragon Hall, Mary Pl., London W11 4PL. *Email*: angela.conner@tiscali.co.uk *Website*: www.angelaconner.co.uk *Signs work*: Conner.

CONNOLLY, Anthony, RP (2009), BA Hons; Prince of Wales Award for Portrait Drawing (2004 & 2012), The Changing Faces Prize (2009). *Medium*: oil, pencil. *b*: Huddersfield, 2 Jun 1957. *m*: Josephine Edmondson. *s* four. *d* six. *Educ*: St. Peter Claver College. *Studied*: Goldsmiths 1978-81. *Exhib*: selected exhibitions include: RP (1997-2014), NEAC (2013); Royal Hibernian Academy (2011, 12, 13); Discerning Eye (2002); Garrick Milne Prize Exhbn (2003); RWA (2004); Artexpo, Antwerp (2005); GMAC, Paris (2006), Battersea Art Fair (2006), Kitsch Biennale Munich (2008); solo shows: London Oratory (2001), Century House, Salisbury (2005); Summerleaze Gallery (2009), ABA Gallery London (2008); Editions Picard, Paris (2011); 'Broken Meats' Kings College, Cambridge

(2013). *Works in collections*: Campion Hall, Oxford; Irish Guards; Royal Artillery. *Publications*: Painting Portraits 2011. *Address*: Old Bridzor, Wardour, Tisbury, Wiltshire, SP3 6RG. *Email*: mail@anthonyconnolly.co.uk *Website*: www.anthonyconnolly.co.uk *Signs work*: 'Anthony Connolly'.

CONNON, William John, DA (1959), post-Dip. (1960); painter, draughtsman; retd. lecturer in drawing and painting at Grays School of Art, Aberdeen. *b*: Turriff, 11 Dec 1929. *m*: Margaret Reid Mair. one *s.* one *d. Educ*: Turriff Academy. Gordon's Technical College, Aberdeen. *Studied*: Grays School of Art, Aberdeen; Hospitalfield, Arbroath. *Exhib*: Aberdeen Artists' Society, McBey Printroom (AAG), Peacock Printmaker/ Edinburgh: Society of Scottish Artists; Royal Scottish Academy; Danish Institute; The Scottish Gallery ('Northern Lights'). *Works in collections*: Aberdeen Art Gallery, City of Edinburgh Art Centre, RSA (Muirhead Bequest), Grampian Hospitals Art Trust; Duke of Edinburgh. *Works Reproduced*: 'Oil Paintings in Public Ownership' (Aberdeen vol). *Address*: 8 Fonthill Rd., Aberdeen AB11 6UB. *Signs work*: "wjconnon."

CONSTABLE, Richard Golding. *Medium*: mixed media. *b*: Lewes, 8 Jun 1932. *s of*: Lt. Col. John Constable, RA. *m*: Valerie Zelle. two *s.* four *d. Educ*: Marlborough College, Millfield School, Cambridge University. *Exhib*: London, Ipswich, Bath, Norwich, Lincoln, Woodbridge, Halesworth, Hereford, Spanish Biennale, Versailles, Singapore, W. Germany, Eire, Glasgow, New York, Cincinnati, Dubai, Al Ain, Abu Dhabi, Muscat. *Works in collections*: worldwide. *Clubs*: Butterfly Conservation. *Address*: The Old Smithy, Hayne, Blackborough, East Devon EX15 2JD. *Signs work*: "R. Constable."

CONTRACTOR DORAB DADIBA. Dadiba Cowasji Contractor; NS; sculptor; part-time instructor for creative wood and stone carving at several Adult Education Centres in Essex. Employed by the Government of India to restore the famous rockcut sculptures of India; Awards: Special Award for Wood Sculpture, Bombay State (1958, 1959); First Prize and Premier Award with Trophy for the most outstanding Exhibit for Chalkstick Sculpture, London (1969); 'Dennis Price Challenge Trophy' for the best wood Sculpture, London (1970-77) and awards from different Boroughs, London. *Medium*: wood and other mediums. *b*: Bombay, 13 Feb 1929 Naturalised British Citizen. *Educ*: Dr.Antonio Da Silva High School. *Studied*: Sir J.J. School of Art, obtained Government Diploma (1957). *Exhib*: Guggenheim Gallery, London (1970); Romford (1972); Euro Arts and Crafts, Birmingham (1976), Mall Gallery, London (1978-81), Paris (1983); India House, London (1972), Woodstock Gallery, London (1975), Queen's Theatre, Hornchurch (1977), Romford (1982), Kenneth More Theatre, Ilford (1988). *Works in collections*: Private Collections in the Royal Family, late Dame Barbara Hepworth, late Henry Moore; private collections worldwide. *Misc*: Parsee Zoroastrian parents, Dadiba Cowasji Contractor (violin and cello restorer). *Address*: 10 Elizabeth House, Durham Avenue, Gidea Park, Romford, RM2 6JU. *Signs work*: "DORAB" or "D.C."

CONWAY, Bryan, SEqA; artist in oil and water-colour. *b*: Derbyshire, 3 Jan 1932. married. four *s. Educ*: Becket School, Nottingham. *Studied*: Arthur Spooner's studio and Nottingham College of Art. *Exhib*: Christie's of London annually, and many provincial galleries. *Works Reproduced*: calendars British Coal, British Steel publications, numerous cards. *Address*: 14 Ellesmere Drive, Trowell, Nottingham NG9 3PH. *Signs work*: "Bryan Conway."

CONWAY, Jennifer Anne, RMS (1979), SM (1981), Dip.BCPE (1957); painter and miniaturist in water-colour and oils. *b*: Brecon, 6 Oct 1935. *d of*: Ernest Brookes. *m*: John F. Conway. one *s.* one *d. Educ*: Brecon Girls' Grammar School; Bedford College of Physical Education (1954-57). *Exhib*: RA, Paris Salon, RMS, SWA, Mall Galleries, Westminster Gallery, Bankside Gallery, Woburn Abbey, Miniature Art Soc. Florida, Soc. of Miniature Painters, S and G, Washington, USA; solo shows: Brecknock Museum (1980, 1989, 1993,

1998), Lion House Gallery (1988), Sable & Hogg Gallery, Brecon (2001). *Works in collections*: Marchioness of Tavistock. *Works Reproduced*: Welsh Crafts, Brecon 900 commemorative plate Royal Doulton, greetings cards, post cards, series of prints 'Country Collection', 'Brecon Cathedral', 'Brecon Beacons'; illustrated book 'A Pocketful of Posies' by J. & J. Conway. *Address*: Copper Beech, Maescelyn, Brecon, Powys, Wales LD3 7NL. *Signs work*: "Jennifer Conway".

CONWAY-JONES, Richard William, BA Hons Photography, Film & TV; Datec Diploma Graphic Design. *Medium*: oil, watercolour, drawing, prints, scultpture, film & music. *b*: Slough, Berkshire, 28 Jun 1964. *Studied*: Haileybury College, Hertford (1977-1982); Berkshire College of Art & Design (1982-84); Harrow Technical College (1984-87). *Exhib*: Long & Ryle Gallery (1989); Norden Farm Arts, Maidenhead, Berkshire; Museum of River & Rowing, Henley; Alphabet Bar, Soho; Dinton Pastures House, Berkshire. *Works in collections*: Tate Birtain; many private collections in UK and abroad (Sweden, Italy). *Principal Works*: Ivy paintings/seascapes/outsider art/ figures/goldfish/cats. *Recreations*: sailing. *Clubs*: Henley Sailing Club. *Address*: 7 Lansdowne Terrace, Twyford, Berkshire RG10 9DY. *Email*: englandsgreatestlivingpainter@gmail.com *Website*: www.conway-jones.co.uk *Signs work*: "RW Conway-Jones".

CONWAY-SEYMOUR, Frances. RWA; Bristol 600; painter in oil, conté, water-colour, collage. *b*: Bristol. *m*: Robert Hurdle; John Seymour. two *s.* two *d. Studied*: West of England College of Art, Bristol, under George Sweet, Robert Hurdle, Francis Hoyland, William Townsend, Peter Lanyon. *Exhib*: England and France. *Works in collections*: Lord Bath's collection of Wessex Painters at Longleat; Royal West of England Academy. *Recreations*: reading, travel. *Misc*: Opened an Art Gallery in Liverpool in 2006 - The Lark Lane Atelier. *Address*: 37 Cornwallis Cres., Clifton, Bristol BS8 4PH. *Email*: frances110@btinternet.com *Signs work*: 'Frances Conway-Seymour'.

COODE, Caroline Ann, Dip AD (Printmaking). *Medium*: printmaker, lino and woodcut, collagraph, etching, wood engraving. *b*: Wimbledon, 26 Jul 1938. *d of*: Lt.Col. & Mrs. I.A.Peachell. *m*: Mark (divorced). five *s. Educ*: The Mount School, Mill Hill. *Studied*: Sir John Cass College of Art, Whitechapel (1984-88). *Exhib*: 7 solo; 2 two-man; 6 three-man; 3 four-man (2005/6); group shows in UK, Germany, Nepal and Israel, including: Royal Academy Summer Show (2003, 2010); Society of Wood Engravers (2002/3, 2009/10); Hanover Fine Arts, Edinburgh (2009); Biscuit Factory, Newcastle (2012). *Works in collections*: Artspace, Richmond, Surrey; Council for the Arts, Hounslow, Middlesex; Kingston University, Surrey; Ministry of Education and Culture, Landau, Germany; Malone House, Belfast; Royal Victoria Infirmary, Newcastle upon Tyne. *Commissions*: P & O 'Oriana'- 2 landscape collagraphs of 50 each. *Publications*: articles in 'Printmaking Today' and 'The Artist'. *Works Reproduced*: City Information Centre, Newcastle-upon-Tyne tourist leaflet, Hatton Gallery Bulletin, Newcastle-upon-Tyne. *Recreations*: gardening, DIY, theatre, classical music. *Misc*: organiser of 'Namaste' touring exhbn of British and Nepalese Artists (2000-02); Committee Member of Friends of the Hatton Gallery, Newcastle-upon-Tyne' North East co-ordinator for Quaker Arts Network. *Address*: 74c St.George's Terrace, Newcastle-upon-Tyne, NE2 2DL. *Email*: cacoode@phonecoop.coop *Website*: carolinecoode.co.uk *Signs work*: "Caroline Coode".

COOK, Christian Manuel, NDD (1965); *Medium*: artist in acrylic, gouache, pastel, water-colour, collage and drawing media, also prints, linocuts. *b*: Grossenhain, Germany, 26 Jun 1942. *s of*: Werner von Biel & Uschi Cook. *Partner*: Marni Bloor. one *s. Educ*: Kent College, Canterbury. *Studied*: Camberwell School of Art (Robert Medley, Frank Auerbach, Frank Bowling), London College of Printing. *Exhib*: Kingsgate Gallery, Hornsey Library (New Gallery), HAC (Camden Arts Centre), City Literary Inst., Loggia Gallery. *Works in collections*: Westminster City Council and private collections. *Works Reproduced*: in

"Drawing Matters" by Jane Stobart. *Misc*: Organised painting holidays in the UK and France. *Address*: 77 Cumbrian Gdns., London NW2 1EH. *Email*: chrismcook@mac.com *Signs work*: "C.M. Cook" or "Chris Cook".

COOK, Ian David, RI, RSW (1978); Post. Grad. Fine Art, Glasgow; Hutcheson Drawing Prize, Cargill Travelling Scholarship to Spain/N. Africa, Arts Council Travel Award to Central Africa; RI Award (2000), Winsor & Newton Award, RI (2005); RGI Fellowship of Glasgow Art Club (2011). *Medium*: mixed media/sculpture. *b*: 1950. *s of*: the late William Cook, shipyard manager, and Margaret Falconer. *m*: Elaine. two *s*. one *d*. *Educ*: Camphill High School, Paisley. *Studied*: Glasgow (1969-72). *Exhib*: Royal Glasgow Concert Hall, (1996); major exhibition on hist./contemporary aspects of American West; Scottish Gallery ('80, '81); Scottish Contemp. shows, RGI, RSW; various London galleries; Dublin; European and American venues; Edinburgh Festival; Manorhouse Gallery. *Works in collections*: Trainload Freight, Lloyds Bank, BBC. *Commissions*: decor. work/ Stakis PLC, Crest Hotels, Continental Hotels. *Publications*: Dorling Kindersley/ Watercolour Techniques series. *Address*: 3 Falside Rd., Paisley PA2 6JZ. *Email*: idcook@talktalk.net Website: www.ian-cook-art.com *Signs work*: "Cook."

COOK, Jennifer Martin, NDD, ATD; painter; carved and painted wood. *b*: Preston, Lancs., 10 Nov 1942. *d of*: Jane and Albert J. Heathcote. *Educ*: Casterton School. *Studied*: Harris College, Preston (1960-65); Leicester College of Art (1965-66). *Exhib*: RA (1975, 1976, 1981, 1982, 1983); one-man shows: Mercury Gallery, London (1976, 1978), Leics. Museum and A.G. (1982), City Gallery, Leicester (1997); group shows: Yew Tree Gallery, Oxford Gallery, Gallery on the Green, Lexington, Mass., USA, Shipley Art Gallery. *Works in collections*: Middlesbrough, Leics., Oxfordshire. *Address*: 17 Brookhouse Ave, Leicester LE2 0JE. *Email*: jenny-cook@ntlworld.com *Website*: www.jennycook.net *Signs work*: "Jenny Cook."

COOK, Richard, DipAD (Painting), MA (RCA) Painting; artist. *b*: Cheltenham, 31 Oct 1947. *s of*: Richard Leonard Cook. *m*: Parton Zia. one *s*. *Educ*: Salesian College, Oxford. *Studied*: St. Martin's School of Art (1966-70), R.C.A. (1970-73). *Represented by*: Art First, London; Wills Lane, St. Ives, Cornwall. *Exhib*: House Gallery, London (1981), Hayward Gallery, London (1976, 1980), Artists Market, London (1976-80), Serpentine Gallery, London (1987), Odette Gilbert Gallery, London (1989, 1991), Austin/Desmond (1995, 1997, 2000, 2003), "Luminous", Tate St. Ives (2001), Art First 2007, 2008; Exchange, Penzance (2010). *Works in collections*: B.M., Arts Council, Manchester City A.G., Deutsche Bank, Barclays Collection, Slaughter & May Collection, Tate Collection, London. *Publications*: "Luminous", Tate St. Ives catalogue. *Address*: 13 North Corner, Newlyn, Penzance, Cornwall TR18 5JG.. *Email*: richardvfcook@blue-earth.co.uk *Signs work*: "Richard Cook."

COOK, Richard Peter, RBA, Dip.A.D. Maidstone (1971), Post Grad. Royal Academy Schools (1975), ATC (1977), RBA (1978), E.T. Greenshield Travelling Scholarship (1972), Richard Ford Spanish Scholarship (1981); landscape and portrait painter in oil, water-colour, gouache. *Medium*: oils and watercolour. *b*: Grimsby, 27 Feb 1949. *s of*: Richard & Marie Antoinette. *m*: Christine. two *d*. *Educ*: Grimsby College of Art, Maidstone College of Art (1968-71). *Studied*: Royal Academy Schools (1972-75). *Represented by*: Mall Galleries, London: Royal Society of British Artists. *Exhib*: one-man show, RA Schools (1980); RBA (1977-); RA Summer Shows (1975-81, 1983, 1993); Art in Action (1988-93); NEAC; Royal Portrait Soc.; NPG in 1984 John Player Award Show; Singer & Friedlander Water-colour Exhbns. and commercial galleries. *Works in collections*: Public Catalogue Foundation Collection; UK and overseas. *Commissions*: Dame Beryl Paston Brown. Jean Holme: commissioned by Homerton College, Cambridge. *Works Reproduced*: BBC Public Art Collection. *Recreations*: holidays, golf. *Address*: 17 Windlesham Gdns., Brighton BN1 3AJ. *Email*: cookrichard@sky.com *Signs work*: "Richard P. Cook RBA".

COOK, Stephen Thomas, BA (Hons); Art Teaching Certificate. *Medium*: oil, watercolour, pastel, drawing. *b*: Romford, 8 Aug 1952. *s of*: Edward & Angela Cook. *m*: Pauline Anne Cook. one *s*. *Educ*: The Campion School, Hornchurch (1963-70). *Studied*: Hornsey College of Art (1970-71); North East London Poly (1971-73); Institute of Education (1977-80); Goldsmiths College (1982-83) ATC. *Represented by*: Brandler Galleries, Brentwood, Essex. *Exhib*: Brandler Galleries; Beecroft Gallery, Westcliff-on-Sea; Society of Equestrian Artists, Christies; Equus Gallery, Newmarket; Heath Gallery, Ascot; Osborne Studio Gallery; Caxton Gallery, Frinton, Essex. *Works in collections*: numerous private collections throughout UK, also Dublin, Mebourne, Lexington, Santa Monica, Toulouse. *Commissions*: regular commissions, mainly horseracing paintings/pastels. *Works Reproduced*: Injured Jockeys Fund promotional material, range of catalogues. *Principal Works*: horseracing paintings/ pastels. *Recreations*: walking, reading, racing. *Misc*: taught in Adult Education for 25 years. Runs regular classes/workshops at Arts Centre in Hornchurch, Essex, and monthly one-day workshops in watercolour. *Address*: 7 Austral Drive, Hornchurch, Essex RM11 1JJ. *Email*: stevecook852@msn.com *Website*: www.stephencookartist.com *Signs work*: 'Cook'.

COOKSON, Delan, FSDC, Gold Medal (Vallauris, 1974), Churchill Fellow (1966); Senior Lecturer in ceramics at Buckinghamshire College of Higher Education. *b*: Torquay, 13 Sep 1937. *s of*: W. R. Cookson. *m*: Judith. *s* two. *Educ*: Bournemouth School. *Studied*: Bournemouth College of Art, Central School of Arts and Crafts. *Exhib*: Oxford Gallery, British Crafts Centre, Craftsman Potters Assoc., Design Centre, Midland Group Gallery, Whitworth Art Gallery, New Craftsman, St. Ives; one-man shows: Salix, Windsor, Bohun Gallery, Henley, Peter Scott Gallery, Lancaster and Galerie an Gross, St. Martin, Cologne. *Publications*: Ceramic Review, Studio Porcelain and Studio Ceramics by Peter Lane. *Clubs*: Cornwall Crafts Assoc., C.A.C. Index of Selected Members. *Address*: 3 King George Memorial Walk, Phillack, Hayle, Cornwall TR27 5AA. *Email*: delancookson@hotmail.com

COOMBE, Nick, MA, RCA, RIBA; RIBA Award (1997, 2004); D&AD Award (2004), RSA 'Art for Architecture' Award (2001). *Medium*: architect and exhibition designer. *Studied*: Royal College of Art (1980-83). *Exhib*: RA (2004); RIBA (1997, 2000); RCA (1996), Mackintosh Museum, Glasgow (1990); Camden Arts Centre (1989). *Commissions*: 'The Heart' (Wellcome Collection), 'Posh' (The British Council); 'Abracadabra' (Tate Britain); 'This Was Tomorrow' (Barbican Arts Centre); 'Mixed Belongings', 'Beauty and the Beast', 'Out There', 'Solid Air', 'Approaching Content' (Crafts Council); 'Shift' (Arts Council England). *Publications*: works in The Guardian, The Independent, The Times, The Telegraph, Sunday Times, RIBA Journal, RSA Journal, etc. *Address*: The Tea Building, Shoreditch High Street, London E1 6JJ. *Email*: nick@coombearchitecture.com *Website*: www.coombearchitecture.com

COOMBS, Jill, 3 Gold Medals (RHS); botanical illustrator in water-colour. *b*: Horsham, 1935. *m*: Bernard Coombs. one *s*. one *d*. *Educ*: High School for Girls, Horsham. *Studied*: West Sussex College of Art (1952-55), botanical illustration under Mary Grierson at Flatford (1976-79). *Exhib*: Kew Gdns. Gallery, National Theatre, RHS, Broughton Gallery, Arundel Festival, Chelsea Physic Gdn., Carnegie-Mellon University USA, Horsham Museum. *Works in collections*: USA, Australia, Japan, UK, Shirley Sherwood Collection, Kew, RHS, Chelsea Physic Gdn., Horsham Museum, Highgrove Florilegium. *Commissions*: Crabtree & Evelyn, Readers' Digest, RHS Kew. *Publications*: illustrated: Plant Portraits by Beth Chatto, Herbs for Cooking and Health by C. Grey-Wilson. *Works Reproduced*: in: Country Life, Curtis Botanical Magazine, Flora Iraq, Flora Qatar, Flora Egypt, The Crocus, Flower Artists of Kew. *Recreations*: gardening, mountain walking. *Clubs*: Association of Sussex Artists, Chelsea Physic Garden Florilegium Society. *Address*: Weald House, Handford Way, Plummers Plain, Horsham, W. Sussex RH13 6PD. *Signs work*: "Jill Coombs."

COOPER, Eileen. DipAD, MA, RCA, Elected RA (2001). artist in oil and works on paper, prints, ceramics. *b*: Glossop, 10 Jun 1953. *m*: M. Southward. two *s*. *Studied*: Goldsmiths' College and RCA (1971-77). *Exhib*: numerous solo and group shows, RA Summer Exhib. (2001). Recent solo shows: 'Time of Your Life', Art First, London (2005), Eileen Cooper 50, Art First, London (2003), Passions, New Work on Paper, Art First, London/ New York (2002), Raw Material, Dulwich Picture Gallery, London (2000), Raw Material II, Art First, London. *Works in collections*: Arts Council, British Council, Whitworth Art Gallery, Yale University, Kunsthalle, Nuremberg,, New Hall, Cambridge, British Museum, V&A. *Commissions*: 1982-Staircase Project, ICA, London; 1992 - The Art, television programme for BBC Education; 1994 - Inside Art, Channel 4 documentary; 1999 - cover and illustrations for Carol Ann Duffy's childrens' poetry book 'Meeting Midnight'. *Address*: Art First, 9 Cork St., London W1X 1PD. *Email*: eileen@eileencooper.co.uk *Website*: www.eileencooper.co.uk *Signs work*: "Eileen Cooper" on reverse.

COOPER, Emmanuel, PhD; potter stoneware and porcelain, writer and broadcaster; editor of Ceramic Review; member of Arts Council England, London; visiting Professor, Royal College of Art. *b*: Derbyshire, 12 Dec 1938. *Educ*: Tupton Hall Grammar School, Derbyshire. *Studied*: Middlesex University (PhD). *Exhib*: Contemporary Applied Arts, London, many other one-man and mixed exhbns. here and abroad. *Works in collections*: V&A, Royal Museums of Scotland. *Publications*: 10 Thousand Years of Pottery (British Museum Press); Bernard Leach: Life and Work (Yale University Press). *Recreations*: theatre, dance, South Coast. *Clubs*: Chelsea Arts Club. *Address*: 38 Chalcot Rd., London NW1 8LP. *Email*: emmanuelcooper@lineone.net

COOPER, Jessica, RWA (2007); BA Hons (Textiles/Fine Art); Foundation Course Diploma; Newlyn Society of Artists; Penwith Society of Artists. *Medium*: painter. *b*: Bristol, 1967. *d of*: Mr & Mrs L E Cooper. *m*: Benjamin Yarwood. one *s*. one *d*. *Studied*: Falmouth College of Art; Goldsmiths College, London. *Represented by*: Edgar Modern, Bath; Belgrave, Cornwall. *Exhib*: RWA Bristol; Newlyn Art Gallery, Cornwall; Tate St. Ives; Sherborne House, Dorset; The Stour Gallery, Warwickshire; The Exchange, Cornwall. *Works in collections*: Hypatia Trust, Cornwall; Slaughter & May, London; RWA Bristol; Newlyn Art Gallery, The Exchange, St. Enodoc Hotel - Cornwall; Kestle Barton, Cornwall. *Publications*: Tate Publishing; Halsgrove; Newlyn Society of Artists; Truran; St. Ives Publishing; Art Press. *Address*: Foundry House, 1 Tregeseal Terrace, St. Just, Penzance, Cornwall TR19 7PL. *Email*: jessicacooper@blueearth.co.uk *Website*: www.jessicacooper.co.uk *Signs work*: 'Jessica Cooper'.

COOPER, Josephine Mary, SM (1974), RMS (1983), UA (1975), SWA (1988); Silver Medallist, Paris Salon (1974), Prix Rowland (1977); artist in oil and water-colour, also drypoint engravings and monotypes. *b*: Brighton, 8 Aug 1932. *d of*: Everard Frisby. *m*: Tom Cooper. one *s*. one *d*. *Studied*: St. Albans School of Art under Kathleen Pargiter; Mid-Herts. College of Further Education under Kenneth Haw; Hertfordshire College of Art and Design under Peter Jacques; Will Raymont, privately. *Exhib*: RMS, UA, SM, RI, RSMA, RBA, Laing, SGA, Britain in Water-colour, Bilan de l'Art Paris and Quebec, Liberty of London, Medici Gallery, RA Summer Exhbn. (1980-85); one-man shows throughout mid-Herts area, also Liberty of London. *Publications*: included in 20th Century Marine Paintings. *Clubs*: Welwyn Garden City Art, Hertford Art Soc. *Address*: 27 Parkfields, Welwyn Garden City, Herts. AL8 6EE. *Signs work*: "Jo Cooper" and "JMC" (miniatures dated).

COOPER, Julian, BA (Hons) Fine Art; painter in oil, water-colour, pastel. *b*: Grasmere, 10 Jun 1947. *s of*: William Heaton Cooper, landscape painter. *m*: Linda. *Educ*: Heversham Grammar School. *Studied*: Lancaster Art College (1963-64), Goldsmiths' College (1964-69), Boise Travelling Scholarship (1969-70). *Represented by*: Art Space Gallery, 84 St. Peters St., London N1 8JS. *Exhib*: London Group, Serpentine Gallery, JPL Fine Art, Paton

Gallery, V&A, Laing A.G., University of Durham, Flowers East, Art Space Gallery, Wordsworth Trust, Grasmere, Brewery Arts Centre, Kendal, Hartlepool Art Gallery, Wolverhampton Art Gallery, Tate Britain, Museo Nazionale della Montagna, Turin. *Works in collections*: ACGB, Laing A.G., Bolton A.G., Lancaster University, Northern Arts, ILEA, Abbot Hall A.G., Reuters, Unilever, Pentagram, Davy Offshore Modules, Ferguson Industrial Holdings, Bankers Trust, Air U.K., Mountain Heritage Trust, Brathay Hall Trust, Tullie House Museum, Carlisle; Museo Nazionale della Montagna, Turin. *Commissions*: County Hall, Durham, Theatre by the Lake, Keswick, Kendal Magistrates Court, Mountain Heritage Trust. *Official Purchasers*: Arts Council of England. *Works Reproduced*: book cover for Fleur Adcock's Under Loughrigg. "Mind Has Mountains" pub: Wordsworth Trust; 'Cliffs of Fall' (pub. ArtSpace Gallery); 'Pareti, Ghiacci, Precipici' (pub: Museo Nazionale della Montagna). *Recreations*: climbing, walking. *Clubs*: Chelsea Arts, Alpine Club. *Address*: Manor House 23 St. Helen's St., Cockermouth, Cumbria CA13 9HX. *Email*: juliancooper@talk1.com *Website*: www.artspacegallery.co.uk www.heatoncooper.co.uk *Signs work*: "Julian Cooper."

COOPER, Philippa , Slade Diploma (1954). *Medium*: watercolour and oil, etcher. *b*: 30 Mar 1934. *d of*: Phyllis Bray/ John Cooper. - artists. two *d*. *Educ*: South Hampstead High School. *Studied*: Slade School, UCL, Gower St., London. *Exhib*: solo exhbn. Judd Street Gallery (1987, 1990); mixed shows: Young Contemporaries, A Family of Painters - 3 Generations, Queen Mary College (1978, organised by artist), Sally Hunter Fine Art (1997), Collyer-Bristow Gallery (1997), Millinery Works, Chappel Galleries (2005). *Works in collections*: Strang Print Room, University College, London (etchings); John Weeks, Architect; Eric Phillips, and others. *Recreations*: looking at paintings, exploring landscapes. *Clubs*: Twentieth Century Society, Plantlife. *Address*: 13 Denton House, Halton Road, Canonbury, London N1 2AE.

COOTE, Michael Arnold, painter in oils, water-colour, acrylic, oil and soft pastel, charcoal, pencil; Freeman of the City of London (1977). *b*: London, 18 Mar 1939. *m*: Anita Davies. two *s*. one *d*. *Studied*: mainly self taught; Sir John Cass (sculpture and life class). *Exhib*: PS, ROI, Mall Galleries, Alpine Gallery, many provincial galleries including John Noott Gallery and Barry Keene Gallery, Henley on Thames. *Works in collections*: London, Bath, America, Germany, Italy. *Address*: 1 Tadlows Cl., Upminster, Essex RM14 2BD. *Signs work*: "M Coote".

COPPINGER, Sioban, BA Hons (1977), ARBS (1991), FRBS (1995), FRSA (1999) *Medium*: sculptor in bronze, copper, silver, concrete. *b*: 20 May 1955. *m*: Peter Penfold. *Educ*: New Hall School, Boreham, Essex. *Studied*: Bath Academy of Art (1975-77). *Exhib*: 2006: Morgan Boyce, Marlborough (Solo); Puthall Sculpture Park, Wiltshire; RWA Bristol; 2005: Watermill Theatre, Newbury, Berkshire (Solo); 2001: Art in Prospect, Ramsbury, Wiltshire; ArtParks International, Guernsey. *Works in collections*: British Rail Board: 'Tempus Fugit' (National Garden Festival Gateshead '90); 'The Jolly Fisherman', 'The Gardener and the Truant Lion' (Paul Temple Ltd); Nottinghamshire County Council: 'The Beeston Seat' (Broxtowe Borough Council); 'Man & Sheep on a Park Bench' (East Midlands Arts, Arts Council of Great Britain). *Commissions*: Work in public places: 'Mrs Hedges', Great Notley, Essex; 'Birmingham Man', Chamberlain Square, Birmingham; 'Elephant's Waterworks', Basingstoke Hospital, Hants.; 'Tempus Fugit' (National Garden Festival Gateshead '90), Templecombe Station, Somerset; 'The Beeston Seat', Beeston, Notts.; The Gardener and the Truant Lion' (Chelsea Flower Show & National Garden Festival, 1986), Stoke Mandeville Rail Station, Bucks; 'Man & Sheep on a Park Bench', Rufford Country Park, Notts. *Address*: The Muse, 23 Oxford Road, Lambourn, Berkshire, RG17 8XS. *Email*: sioban@coppinger.fsnet.co.uk *Website*: www.siobancoppinger.co.uk *Signs work*: "S. Coppinger."

CORBETT, Lily Gloria, MA in Sacred and Traditional Art (The Princes School of Traditional Art). *Medium*: oil, watercolour, drawing, sculpture, egg tempera and gilding on gesso ground. *b*: Hampshire, 22 May 1945. *Studied*: The City Literary Inst. with Cecil Collins (1976-86); The Princes School of Traditional Art, London. *Exhib*: RA, Cheniel Galleries, London, Piers Feetham Gallery, Richard Philp Gallery, RCA, The Princes Foundation, 'Shakespeare and Islam' at Shakespeares Globe (2004), Timothy Hobart Fine Art. *Works in collections*: many private collections. *Commissions*: private. *Recreations*: singing Rabindranath Tagore songs and Indian ragas. *Clubs*: Chelsea Arts Club. *Misc*: I teach drawing and painting based on Cecil Collins' teaching, and also teach egg tempera, gilding, gesso and oil painting. *Address*: c/o Chelsea Arts Club, 143 Old Church Street, London SW3 6EB. *Email*: lilycorbett@waitrose.com *Website*: www.theartofcreativity.co.uk *Signs work*: 'L.C.' or 'Lily Corbett'.

CORBETT, Peter George, BA Hons (1974); artist in oil on canvas; awards: 2000 - Vincent Van Gogh Award, St. Lukas Academy, Memmelsdorf, Germany; 2000 - Albert Einstein International Academy Foundation, honour in recognition of outstanding achievements; 1998 - Merseyside Contemporary Artists Exhibition, Purchase Prize, Liverpool; 1993 - Honorary Professor, Académie des Sciences Humanie Universelles, Paris, France. 2000 - Hon. Prof. Honoris Causa (Painting), St. Lukas Academy, Germany; 2000- International Peace Prize, United Cultural Convention, U.S.A.; 2002 - World Lifetime Achievement Award, American Biographical Institute, U.S.A.; 2004 - Lexmark European Art Prize (Northwest Regional Winner). *b*: Rossett, N. Wales, 13 Apr 1952. *s of*: John Hotchkins Corbett, G.P. *Educ*: Liverpool College. *Studied*: Liverpool College of Art and Design (1970-71, Maurice Cockrill), Manchester Regional College of Art and Design (1971-74, Brendan Neiland, Keith Godwin). *Exhib*: Please see website. *Works in collections*: Great Britain, America and Australia, Netherlands, West Germany, Spain. Founder Mem. Chair, Merseyside Visual Arts Festival (1989-90). International German Art Prize, St. Lukas Academy, Memmelsdorf, Germany (Painting and Poetry) Grand Diploma (1998). Public collections: Atkinson Gallery, Southport, The University of Liverpool Art Gallery, Hope University Liverpool. *Recreations*: playing the piano, yoga, meditation. *Clubs*: Design and Artists Copyright Society, London (life member), Maison Internationale des Intellectuels, Paris, France (1994). *Misc*: Galleries, Slide libraries: Museum of Modern Art, New York, U.S.A. *Address*: Flat 4, 7 Gambier Terr., Hope St., Liverpool L1 7BG. *Website*: www.petercorbett.co.uk

CORETH, Mark Rudolf, self taught sculptor in bronze (wildlife). *b*: London, 5 Sep 1958. *m*: Seonaid. one *s.* two *d. Educ*: Kenya, Herefordshire (St. Richards Prep.). Ampleforth College. *Represented by*: Sladmore Gallery, 32 Brutin Place, Berkeley Square, London W1J 6NW. *Exhib*: Sladmore Gallery, London W1. (1986, 1990, 1992, 1994, 1996, 1998, 2000, 2002), Galerie la Cymaise, Paris (1993, 1995, 1997, 1999, 2001), Sydney (1996), Geneva (1997), New York (1999, 2001). *Commissions*: life-size Cheetah Group, Dubai; Drinking fountains at Globe Theatre and National History Museum. *Recreations*: flying, shooting, fishing, riding, travel. *Address*: c/o Sladmore Contemporary, 32 Bruton Place, off Berkeley Square, London W1J 6NW. *Email*: markcoreth@tiscali.co.uk

CORKREY, Michael, First Prize Hunting Art Prizes (1994). *Medium*: Oil. *b*: St Albans, 24 Nov 1962. *Studied*: Leeds Polytechnic (1982-85), Royal Academy Schools (1986-89). *Represented by*: Sarah Myerscough Fine Art, London. *Exhib*: Solo shows: Sarah Myerscough Fine Art (2004, 2006, 2007, 2008), selected mixed shows: Hunting Art Prizes (1993/94/95/96/99); John Player/BP Portrait Awards, NPG (1986/86/89/90/91/92); London Art Fair (2002-2012); British Art Fair (2009-2011); Toronto Art Fair (2006/07/08); Chelsea Art Gallery, Palo Alto USA (2006). *Work in collections*: Private/corporate, internationally. *Commissions*: Private portrait commissions. *Address*: 75 Kennington Park Road, London SE11 4JQ. *Email*: michaelcorkrey@hotmail.co.uk *Website*: www.michaelcorkrey.com *Signs work*: "MICHAEL CORKREY".

CORLETT, Roseanne Serena, (was GARDNER). *Medium*: oil, sculpture, acrylic. *b*: Hong Kong, 30 Jan 1948. *d of*: Mr & Mrs C.A.N. Walker. *m*: Anthony Corlett. *Educ*: St. James's, West Malvern. *Studied*: Sorbonne, Paris. *Exhib*: RA Summer Exhbn (2000); solo shows: Shepherd Market (2001), Playhouse Salisbury (2003); Chelsea Art Society (1997, '98, '99); Christies 'Art for Life' (2006, 2007); ABNA (2012). Solo shows: Tisbury (2012). *Work in collections*: M. Etherington-Smith, Editor Arts Review. *Commissions*: for outdoor temple ceiling. *Publications*: 3 pages in Woman & Home (June 2001). *Works Reproduced*: Bronze torso. *Principal Works*: La Dame aux Violettes, and lifesize self-portrait. *Recreations*: gardening. *Clubs*: Boodles. *Misc*: member of Association of British Naive Artists (ABNA); member of Dorset Art Week. *Address*: Dunworth House, Donhead St. Mary, Shaftesbury, Dorset SP7 9DQ. *Email*: roseanne21@btinternet.com *Website*: www.roseannes-art.co.uk *Signs work*: "Roseanne".

CORNELL, David, FRSA (1970), FRBS (1971), VPSPS (1977), PSSMCE (1995); sculptor in bronze. *b*: Enfield, 18 Sep 1935. *s of*: Henry Arthur Cornell. *m*: Geraldine. four *s*. *Educ*: Essendene. *Studied*: Central School of Art, London and Harrow School of Art (1952-62, Friend, Fryer and Philip Turner) Engraving and Sculpture; Academy of Fine Art, University of Pennsylvania (1968-70, Robert Beverley Hale) Anatomy. *Exhib*: London: RA, Mall Galleries, Guildhall, RBS Hall Place, Pavlova Soc., Park Walk Galleries, Plazzotta Studio, Edith Grove Gallery, Harrods; Iberian Bronze Gallery, London and Dublin, Newmarket Gallery, Newmarket, Royal Fine Art, Tunbridge Wells, Armstrong-Davis Gallery, Arundel, Scone Palace Scotland, English Gallery, Beverly Hills, USA, LCA Chelsea, Royal West of England Academy, Bristol, Alwin Gallery, Tunbridge Wells, Wales Fine Art - Chepstow. *Works in collections*: Wellcome Foundation, London. Recent works include portrait of Princess Diana and Queen Mother. *Commissions*: Life-size: Sir Arthur Conan-Doyle, numerous coins for world mints, latest being first official Royal mint coin of Prince William. *Address*: Barcombe Manor, Innhams Wood, Crowborough, E. Sussex TN6 1TE. *Email*: davidcornell1@aol.com *Website*: www.davidcornell.com *Signs work*: "David Cornell."

CORSELLIS, Jane, NEAC, RWS, RCA; artist in oil, water-colour, etching, lithography. *b*: Oxford, 1940. two *s*. *Studied*: Byam Shaw School of Art. *Exhib*: RA, RBA, NEAC, RWA, RWS, RCA; one-man shows: Hong Kong, Ottawa, Kuala Lumpur, Upstairs Gallery, New Academy Gallery, London (1988, 1990, 1992, 1994, 1996, 1998, 2000, 2002, 2004), Hollis Taggart Gallery, NY (1998), Messums London (2006, 2008, 2010, 2012). *Works in collections*: Canada, USA, Italy, France, Germany, Australia, Malaysia, Singapore and UK. *Publications*: Painting Figures in Light; Watson Guptill, A Personal View (David and Charles). Landscapes in Oils (APV Films Ltd.), Coastal Watercolours (APV Films Ltd.). *Clubs*: Chelsea Arts. *Address*: 54 Strand on the Green, London W4 3PD. *Website*: www.newenglishartclub.co.uk *Signs work*: "Corsellis."

COSMAN, Milein, Slade Diploma Fine Art; painter, graphic artist. *b*: Gotha. *d of*: Hugo Cosmann. *m*: Hans Keller. *Educ*: Düsseldorf; International School, Geneva. *Studied*: Slade School. *Exhib*: one man shows: Berkeley Galleries, Matthiesen, Molton Gallery, City of London Festival, Aldeburgh Festival, Stadtmuseum, Düsseldorf, Dartington, Belgrave Gallery, Palais de Beaux Arts, Brussels; The Wigmore Hall, Austrian Cultural Forum. *Works in collections*: e.g. NPG, British Museum, V&A, Ashmolean, The Hunterian (Glasgow), British Academy, Britten-Pears Foundation, Stadtmuseum Dusselford, Kupferstichkabinett (Berlin), Wigmore Hall, Palais des Beaux Arts. *Publications*: Musical Sketchbook (Bruno Cassirer, Faber & Faber, 1957), Stravinsky at Rehearsal (Dobson, 1962), Strawinsky Dirigiert (Ullstein, 1962), Stravinsky Seen and Heard (Toccata Press, 1982); books illustrated: Penguin Music Magazine, A Composer's Eleven (Cardus, Cape, 1975), Stravinsky The Music-Maker (Toccata Press, (2010), Milein Cosman: Lebenslinien (*Lifelines*) (Edition Memoria 2012) etc. *Misc*: Work repro.: Radio Times and other national and foreign press, art and musical magazines. Series of Educational Programmes on Drawing for ITV. *Address*: 3 Frognal Gdns., Hampstead, London NW3.

COTTON, Alan, DLitt (Honorary Doctor of Letters, Univ. of Exeter); NDD, ATD (B'ham), FRSA, M.Ed.; painter in oil, water-colour and pastel; works on art films for television; Executive Com., Phoenix Arts Centre, Exeter; President Emeritus SWAc (South West Academy of Fine & Applied Arts); Hon Professor of Art, University of Bath. *b*: Redditch, 8 Oct 1938. *m*: Patricia Esmé. two *s*. two *d*. *Educ*: Redditch County High School. *Studied*: Redditch School of Art, Bournville College of Art, B'ham College of Art, Universities of B'ham and Exeter (Research Fellow). *Represented by*: David Messum Galleries in Cork Street, London since 1983: annual exhibitions. *Exhib*: over 50 one-man shows in U.K., Canada, France and the U.S.A. including Hammer Galleries N.Y. (1993). *Works in collections*: City of Exeter A.G., City of Plymouth A.G., Carlton Television, Royal Marines, Lympstone, Universities of Southampton and Exeter, Queen Mary II, University of Surrey, University of Bath. *Publications*: "Alan Cotton On a Knife Edge". Biography by Jenny Perry, pub. Halsgrove, 2003. "Alan Cotton Giving Life a Shape" Biography by Jenny Perrry pub Halstar. *Clubs*: Chelsea Arts Club. *Address*: Brockhill Studio, Colaton Raleigh, nr. Sidmouth, Devon EX10 0LH. *Signs work*: "Alan Cotton."

COUDRILLE, Jonathon Xavier, SWAc; Childrens Book of the Year (1976). *Medium*: oil, ink. *b*: Landewednack, 20 Nov 1945. *s of*: Francis Coudrille. *m*: one decd; one divorced. one *s*. one *d*. *Studied*: everything of worth learned from private tutors. *Represented by*: Mann-Rennick +447545431822. *Exhib*: Royal Academy; Harrogate Festival; Albemarle St., Hoxton; Boundary Road Clerkenwell; Public galleries: Falmouth, Southampton, Penwith, St. Ives, The Byram, Newlyn, Salon des Arts, South-West Academy, The Walker (Liverpool Biennial); regular exhibitor in artist members shows at The Arts Club. *Works in collections*: The Marquis of Bath, Bank of Nova Scotia, Abel Herrero-Ducloux Esq., Diocese of Truro, Falmouth Gallery, Arts Club, etc. *Commissions*: portraits. *Publications*: 'A Beastly Collection'; 'Farmer Fisher'; 'Vulgar Frog'; 'The Surrealists in Cornwall', Stuckist Publications. *Official Purchasers*: Bank of Nova Scotia; Falmouth Council. *Works Reproduced*: by Saatchi. *Principal Works*: Metathesis Series, Biomorphic Series, Fallen Angel Series, The Harbinger, The Analogues. *Clubs*: The Arts Club, London. *Address*: Cliff House Studio, Cadgwith, Helston, Cornwall TR12 7LB. *Email*: coudrille@gmail.com *Website*: www.coudrille.com *Signs work*: early works (1950s/60s): 'JXC'; (1970s/80s): 'Jonathon Coudrille'; later oils with monogram, graphics 'Coudrille'.

COUGHLAN, Shirley Lyall, County Major Award - Essex County Council 1953; Intermediate Exam; National Diploma in Design 1953; Art Teachers Certificate 1954. *Medium*: printmaking, drawing, painting, ceramics, photography, textiles, collages. *b*: 26 Feb 1932. *Educ*: Colchester County High for Girls, Colchester School of Art 1949-53. *Studied*: London University - Institute of Education 1953-54; taught by John O'Connor, Blair Hughes Stanton, Carel Weight, and others; courses at Wymondham and Loughborough. *Exhib*: Young Contemporaries Exhibitions (London & touring); Laing Exhibitions; 'Eastern Open', King's Lynn, 1999; 'Drawings for All', Gainsborough's House, Sudbury, Suffolk (2000, 2002); Leicester, King's Lynn, Colchester, Ipswich, Bury St. Edmunds; Member and Exhibitor, Ipswich Art Society. *Works in collections*: Diana Quick, and various other private collections. *Recreations*: music, gardening, natural history, crosswords, collecting. *Clubs*: Suffolk Craft Society; Suffolk Art Society. *Misc*: spent 34 years in Art Education in Leicestershire, Norfolk and Suffolk. *Address*: 26 Warrington Road, Ipswich, Suffolk, IP1 3QU. *Signs work*: "SLC" or "S.L.Coughlan".

COULING, Paula, SWA (1993); landscape painter in acrylic; no formal art training. *b*: Birmingham. *d of*: James Frederick Rogers (decd.). *m*: Robert H. Couling. two *s*. *Exhib*: SWA Westminster Gallery; solo shows: Christchurch. *Publications*: greetings cards by the

Medici Soc. *Clubs*: Romsey Art Group, Hengist Group of Artists. *Address*: 201 Salisbury Rd., Burton, Christchurch, Dorset BH23 7JT. *Signs work*: "Paula Couling."

COULOURIS, Mary Louise, RE (2000), ARE (1973); DipAD (London) (1961); Post Grad. Scholarship, Slade School (1962); French Government Scholarship (1963); Churchill Fellowship in USA and Mexico (1993); artist and printmaker; Artists Exchange, Athens for Glasgow Year of Culture (1990). *Medium*: watercolour, oil, printmaking. *b*: New York, 17 Jul 1939. *d of*: George Alexander Coulouris, actor. *m*: Gordon Wallace. one *s.* one *d. Educ*: Parliament Hill School, London, Chelsea School of Art. *Studied*: Slade School, London University (1958-62) under Antony Gross; Ecole des Beaux Arts, Paris (1963-64); Atelier 17, Paris (1963-64) under William Hayter. *Represented by*: Bankside Gallery, London; William James Gallery, Athens. *Exhib*: RA (1966, 1971, 1972, 1973); one-man shows: London, Oxford, Paris, Aberdeen, Glasgow, Athens. Artists Exchange: Athens for Glasgow Year of Culture (1990). Sainsbury Wine Label Competition Winner (1997), Purdue University, USA (1999), Circle Gallery, Edinburgh (2003), Melina Mercouri Gallery, Greece (2005), Just Scottish, Edinburgh (2007), William James Gallery, Athens (2007). *Works in collections*: London Weekend TV, Bibliotheque Nationale, Paris, New York Public Library, Nuffield Trust, Trinity College, Oxford, Bank of Scotland, Edinburgh District Council, Hambros Bank, Sainsbury PLC, Scottish Natural Heritage, House of Lords, Graphothek, Berlin Museum. *Commissions*: Scottish Poetry Library 3 Carpets (1999); mural: British Rail (1985); print: British Healthcare Arts (1993), Tapestry, Yale College, Wrexham, N.Wales 2003. *Publications*: 'Techniques to Trigger the Mind' Printmaking Today Vol.7 No. 4 (1998). *Official Purchasers*: House of Lords. *Works Reproduced*: 2 wine labels for Sainsbury's - 60,000 bottles. *Principal Works*: Mural: Linlithgow Rail Station, 1985; Tapestry, Yale College, N. Wales. *Recreations*: cycling, reading. *Address*: 5 Strawberry Bank, Linlithgow, West Lothian EH49 6BJ. *Email*: strawberrybanks@yahoo.co.uk *Website*: www.artmlc.co.uk *Signs work*: "Mary Louise Coulouris."

COULSON, Nancy Diana, (née Hibbert), sculptor stone, alabaster, marble, clay, wood, bronze; subjects: animals, portrait heads in terracotta, clay for bronze. *b*: Kenilworth, 6 Mar 1926. *d of*: JPM Hibbert MC. *m*: Robert Coulson. two *s.* one *d. Educ*: Kingsley School, Leamington Spa. *Studied*: Chelsea Art School (1946-48), Chelmsford (under Ivor Livie). *Exhib*: RA, FPS, SCA, Vaughan College Leicester, Bury St. Edmunds, Aldeburgh, Chelmsford, Westcliff-on-Sea. *Works in collections*: Chapter House, Chelmsford; Mansion House, London; Broomfield Hospital; Lord St. John Fawsley; Abe Lerner, N.Y.; Sir Alastair Stewart, Bt.; Baroness Platt of Writtle; Daniela Landschuetz, Munich; Mrs. Martin Read (Felsted); St. John Baptist Church Loughton. *Commissions*: Madonna (for Bishop of Chelmsford) St. Barnabus; sundials: St. Mary Great Warley, and Broomfield Hospital, Chelmsford. *Official Purchasers*: Chelmsford Cathedral: Broomfield Hospital. *Principal Works*: 'The Human Condition' carved pearwood(2005); 'Great Seal' Chelmsford Cathedral Chapter House 45"dia.; Bronze Portrait heads of Bishop Neville Welch, Professor Emeritus Richard Gregory C.B.E., Mrs. Dawn Arthur, Herr Walter Carlein, Mayor of Baden-Baden, Sir Alastair Stewart Bart, Bishop of Chelmsford, John Trillo; Connie Hawker (2014). *Recreations*: gardening, family and friends. *Address*: Medlars, Mounthill Ave., Chelmsford CM2 6DB. *Email*: nancy.coulson@tesco.net *Signs work*: "N.C."

COURTNELL, Louise, BA (Hons) Fine Art - Painting, studied under Robert Lenkiewicz 1987-94. Plymouth Foundation Course. *b*: Plymouth, 24 Apr 1963. *d of*: Derek and Lesley Courtnell. *Studied*: Bristol Polytechnic 1982-85. *Represented by*: independent. *Exhib*: National Portrait Gallery, BP Portrait Award 1991, '92, '93, '94, '97, '98, 2000, '0 Cooling Gallery, Cork Street - 'Brian Sewell's Choice', Mall Galleries - RS Portrait Painters and Discerning Eye. *Works in collections*: Royal Holloway College. *Official Purchasers*: Church in Wales, Feb 2002 (Dr. Rowan Williams, Archbishop of Wales). *Principal Works*: self-portraits - National Portrait Gallery, BP Portrait Award. *Misc*: specializes in portraiture in oils, also landscape and still life. Teaches teachings of Robert Lenkiewicz. *Address*: Vista Hermosa, Rame, Torpoint, PL10 1LG. *Signs work*: l. Courtnell.

COUSENS, Ruth Margaret, FSAI; Medaille d'Or, Paris Salon (Tricentenaire 1973) T.C., Women of the Year Luncheon; artist in water-colour; art teacher of history, architecture and painting: St. George's Ramsgate, Maidstone Technical High, Sittingbourne Girls' Grammar, pupils of Wilmington Grammar Schools, St. Olaves' Boys' Grammar School, Orpington; Day Courses Director and Tutor 'The Architectural Heritage of Thanet Towns of Ramsgate, Broadstairs, Margate; Rutherford College School of Continuing Education, University of Kent at Canterbury; Founder-Project Director, Castle Trust Arts Centre, Ramsgate. *b*: London, 1930. *d of*: Abbot Winstanley Upcher (Burke's Landed Gentry), Pioneer Missionary to Arabia, and Ruth Wingate, niece of Sir George Pirie, late Pres. Scottish R.A. *m*: Stanley G. Cousens. one *s*. *Educ*: St. George's Ramsgate, and Clarendon Malvern. *Studied*: Rolle College, Exeter (1948-50, E.T. Arnold). *Exhib*: Paris Salon, RA, RI, RIBA, etc.; one-man shows, 'Regency Ramsgate', Townley House, Ramsgate (1973), Royal Museum, Canterbury (1978), Geneva (1985), Westend, London (1986); by invitation: 'La Femme Creatrice d'Art', Monte Carlo (1976) (Brit. rep.), 'British Artists', Paris (1979), Expo Quebec, Canada (1980). *Works in collections*: Thanet Council, Ramsgate Charter Trustees; private: Sir Robert Bellinger, Rt. Hon. Edward Heath, MP. *Commissions*: book jackets, retail postcards; booklet 'Regency Ramsgate'. *Address*: 17 Spencer Sq., Ramsgate, Kent. *Signs work*: "R.M. COUSENS."

COUSINS, Timothy, BA (Hons) Fine Art; PGCE (Art Teaching). *Medium*: oil, watercolour, acrylic and gouache. *b*: Weston-super-Mare, 29 Jul 1952. *s of*: Constance Chapman. *m*: Angie Cousins. two *d*. *Educ*: Christ's Hospital, Horsham, Sussex. *Studied*: Exeter College of Art and Design; Ravensbourne College of Art and Design. *Represented by*: Anderssonhall; Ginette Kentish. *Exhib*: solo exhbns: Colston Hall, Bristol (1977); Deli Art London (2000); two-person, with Germaine Dolan, Diorama Gallery, London (1998); numerous group shows at APT Gallery London; Belgrave Gallery, London; Belgrave Gallery, St.Ives; Huddersfield Art Gallery; Derby Museum and Art Gallery. *Works in collections*: Rowing Museum, Henley-on-Thames; Whitstable Museum and Art Gallery; Huddersfield Art Gallery; Goldsmiths' College, London; Lewisham College, London; London Borough of Greeenwich. *Commissions*: fourteen paintings for offices - The Easton Corporation. *Official Purchasers*: Goldsmiths College, London. *Works Reproduced*: 'Sharing a View' catalogues, and numerous others. *Principal Works*: 'Eltham Bus Stop'; 'Bandstand'. *Recreations*: playing and watching cricket. *Address*: 1 Chestnut Rise, Plumstead, London SE18 1RJ. *Email*: aandtcousins@aol.com *Website*: www.anderssonhall.com *Signs work*: 'Timothy Cousins'.

COUTU, Jack, ARE, ARCA; printmaker and sculptor; etching and engraving on copper, miniature carving in boxwood and ivory; netsuke. *b*: Farnham, Surrey, 13 Sep 1924. *s of*: Herbert Coutu. *Educ*: Farnham Grammar School. *Studied*: Farnham School of Art (1947-51), RCA (1951-54). *Exhib*: travelling exhibition of Netsuke and Prints (2004 & 2005). *Works in collections*: King Gustave of Sweden, Museum of Fine Art, Boston, Mass., Bradford City Art Gallery, V&A, Arts Council of Great Britain, Government Art Collection. *Publications*: articles in "International Netsuke Society Journal" (1996). *Address*: Bramblings, 22 Quennells Hill, Wrecclesham, Farnham, Surrey GU10 4NE. *Signs work*: "Coutu"

COWAN, Judith, BA Fine Art (1977), MA Sculpture (1978), Gulbenkian Rome Scholarship (1979); Henry Moore Bursary (1992). *b*: London, 8 Dec 1954. *Studied*: Sheffield Polytechnic (1974-77); Chelsea School of Art (1977-78). *Exhib*: solo exhbns. include: 'from life', Museo Laboratorio di Arte Contemporanea, Rome (2005); 'present, passing' Angel Row Gallery, Nottingham (touring, 1999), 'Passages and Incidents', Kettles Yard Gallery, Cambridge(1996), 'Sex, Birth, Sex, Death', Stefania Miscetti, Rome (1995), 'Water rises'

Camden Arts Centre (1993), 'a line of blue and a pool of red' Yorkshire Sculpture Park (1992), 'New Sculpture' Oriel Mostyn, Llandudno (1989-90) (touring). *Works in collections*: ACGB, London Borough of Tower Hamlets, Leics. Educ. Authority, New Hall, Cambridge; Hechinger Collection. *Publications*: 'the capacity of things: from life, monograph, Gangemi Editore (2005) ISBN 88-492-0861-8. *Address*: 2a Culford Mews, London N1 4DX.

COWDY, Richard Davenport, NDD, ATC. *Medium*: bronze sculpture. *b*: London, 18 Sep 1937. *s of*: Bernard Cowdy. *Partner*: Helen Simmonds. two *s.* two *d. Educ*: Alleyns Grammar School. *Studied*: Camberwell Art School. *Exhib*: London Group, RA, Marlborough Gallery, Burford Gallery, Dulwich Gallery. *Works in collections*: London Stock Exchange, Sydney, Paris, Amsterdam, Hong Kong. *Commissions*: Sainsbury's Calne Shopping precinct (sheep bronze), Calne Precinct (pigs bronze), various portraits, John Bentley School Calne: bronze boy and girl, and abstract bronze for language college; New Hospital at Newbury, Bronze fish on Jurassic rock; Bronze Pyramid in Public Square, Devizes. *Official Purchasers*: Colmans Mustard Norwich (large bronze bull's head). *Recreations*: music. *Misc*: visiting lecturer at the Slade, London, Guildford Art School, Camberwell Art School. *Address*: 18 Wood St., Calne, Wilts, SN11 0DA. *Email*: richardcowdy@yahoo.co.uk *Signs work*: R D Cowdy

COX, Julian Charles, ARBS (2006); Diploma in Sculpture Restoration; Post Grad Teaching Certificate. *Medium*: indian ink drawings, sculpture: wood, bronze, stone. *b*: 25 Jan 1961. *s of*: Ken & Audrey Cox. *Educ*: Colston's Boys School, Bristol. *Studied*: City & Guilds of London Art School (1983-86); University of London, Goldsmiths College (1988-89). *Represented by*: Jonathan Poole-Compton Cassey Gallery; Innocent Fine Art, Clifton, Bristol. *Exhib*: RWA; C20th Art & Design Fair, London; 20/21 British Art Fair, London; Olympia Affordable Art Fairs; Art Ireland, Dublin; Art London. *Publications*: 'Naked Lines' ibook of ink drawings published in 2010. *Misc*: 1986-88 - Sculpture Restorer (Plowden & Smith International Conservators). Now, part-time teacher of Design & Technology, and Art. *Address*: 14 Phoenix Grove, Westbury Park, Bristol BS6 7XY. *Email*: e@juliancoxartist.co.uk *Website*: www.juliancoxartist.co.uk *Signs work*: 'COX' ('O' incised with barbed 'J').

COX, Paul, BA (Hons) (1996), MA, RAS (1999); sculptor. *b*: Shoreham-by-Sea, 28 Jan 1975. *Educ*: Steyning Grammar School. *Studied*: BA - Winchester School of Art, MA - Royal Academy Schools. *Works in collections*: Gazely Properties, Surrey Institute of Art. *Commissions*: Gazely Properties, Surrey Institute of Art. *Clubs*: RASAA. *Address*: 426 South Coast Rd, Telscombe Cliffs, Peacehaven, E.Sussex, BN10 7BE.

COX, Stephen B., BA Hons, British Council Research Scholar, PGCE (Merit); artist, interior designer, teacher; director, 'Club Anglia' international summer school; taught art: Wellington College, Reading Grammar, Langley College; arts organiser, Hexagon Reading; founder, Regional Secretary Artists Union; production manager independent British films (1977-80); promoter pop groups/artists; fashion model photographer; sponsor, Manpower Services Commission YTS. *s of*: the late Bernard Cox. *Educ*: Grange and Kingswood Grammar Schools. *Studied*: Reading University; Researched: Bucharest Fine Arts University. *Exhib*: now average four one-man shows and group shows annually UK and Europe. *Works in collections*: UK, Europe, USA. *Commissions*: painting/sculpture England. *Works Reproduced*: many catalogues, radio, TV interviews U.K. and Europe. Council mem./Head of Westminster lobby: Design and Artists Copyright Soc. *Misc*: Events: produced/performed (as Nevetz) Germany, France, U.K., Romania.; (studio) Chalkpit Farm, Englefield, Berks. *Address*: 60 Elmhurst Rd., Reading RG1 5HY. *Signs work*: "STEPHEN".

COYNE, Douglas, Hon.FRCA, NDD (Illustration) (1950); painter in oil and water-colour. *b*: Newark-on-Trent, 6 Jun 1930. *m*: Dinah Wood. *Studied*: Newark School of Art (1944-48),

Nottingham College of Art (1948-50). *Exhib*: one man shows: Chipping Campden (1988, 1990, 1993, 1998, 2000); mixed shows: with Oxford Art Soc. and Blockley Art Soc. *Works in collections*: Newark Museum. *Address*: Mill Cottage, Calf Lane, Chipping Campden, Glos. GL55 6JQ. *Signs work*: "COYNE" (oils), "DOUGLAS COYNE" (water-colours).

CRAIG-MARTIN, Michael, Millard Professor of Fine Art, Goldsmiths' College. *b*: Ireland, 28 Aug 1941. one *d*. *Studied*: Yale University (1961-66). *Address*: c/o Gagosium Gallery, 17 Davies St., London W1K 3DE. *Signs work*: "Michael Craig-Martin."

CRAIG-McFEELY, Joanna, Director SBA, SFP, FCPGFS, ASBA Associate Member AFAS; awards: Joyce Cummings Presentation Award (SBA, 2004); 5 RHS Silver Gilt Medals (1999, 2002, 2003, 2006, 2008), SFP Presidents Award for Excellence (2009). *Medium*: watercolour on paper and vellum. *b*: Beckenham, 2 May 1934. *d of*: Mona & Douglas Jenkins. *m*: Gerald Craig-McFeely. two *s*. two *d*. *Educ*: Mayfield Convent; St.Mary's Hospital, Paddington. *Studied*: master classes Jenny Phillips (Venice). *Exhib*: SBA (1998-2014); SWA; American Society of Botanical Artists, New York (2005); Chelsea Physic Garden Florilegium Society, Munich (2002); RHS (1999, 2002, 2006, 2008); selected for 13th International Exhibition of Botanical 'Art & Illustration', Pittsburgh USA (2010); Palmengarten Frankfurt Germany (2010, 2012, 2014); AFAS Mall Galleries (2011-2014). *Works in collections*: Chelsea Physic Garden Florilegium; Highgrove Florilegium; Hunt Institute of Botanical Documentation USA. *Works Reproduced*: in 'The Art of Botanical Painting' and on cover (2004); 'The Apothecaries Garden' (2005). *Principal Works*: botanical. *Recreations*: skiing, silver smithing. *Misc*: State Registered Physiotherapist (retd.). *Address*: Tintern, Hillbrow Road, Liss, Hampshire, GU33 7QA. *Email*: info@botanicalillustration.co.uk *Website*: www.botanicalillustration.co.uk *Signs work*: 'JCMcF'.

CRAMP, Jonathan David, ATD, RWS; painter; Head of Art Dept., Fishguard C.S. School (1954-81). *b*: Ninfield, Sussex, 29 Jan 1930. *s of*: David Cramp. *m*: Elizabeth (painter) (decd). *d* one. *Educ*: Huish Grammar School, Taunton, Bexhill Grammar School. *Studied*: Hastings School of Art (1946-51) (Vincent Lines). *Represented by*: Bankside Gallery. *Works in collections*: Arts Council of Wales, Contemporary Art Society for Wales, Pembrokeshire County Museum, Schools Service, National Museum of Wales, Shell Oil (UK) Ltd., National Grid Co., Cartrefle and Caerleon Colleges of Education, various education authorities, the Government Art Collection, Providence Museum, Rhode Island, USA, British Steel, National Library of Wales. *Commissions*: Shell Oil (UK) Ltd, National Grid Co. *Address*: Heatherdene, Windy-Hall, Fishguard, Pembs. SA65 9DU.

CRAWFORD, Alistair, (Professor), DA (1966), ATC (1968), MCSD (1973-86), MSTD (1977-97), Fellow, Printmakers Council (1978-93), Churchill Fellow (1982), FRPS (1991-98), RCA (1994-2010), Hon.RE (2000); Balsdon Senior Fellow, British School at Rome (1995-96); Hon. member European Society for the History of Photography (2009); painter, printmaker, photographer, art historian and exhibition curator; writer, performer. *b*: Fraserburgh, 25 Jan 1945. *Studied*: Glasgow School of Art (1962-66). *Exhib*: 56 solo, over 200 joint and selected exhibitions throughout Britain and abroad. Recent solo: 'Landscape Capriccios' University of Wales, Aberystwyth (2005), Denbighshire Arts Touring (2006) 'North By Northwest', Jersey Arts Centre (2006), 'Made from Wales', Brecknock Museum, Brecon (2007); 'Rretrospective 1963-2009 National Library of Wales (2009) . Awards including Welsh Arts Council, British Council, British Academy, Gold Medal Fine Art, Royal National Eisteddfod of Wales (1985); performance: 'An Evening with Eugenie Strong' (1996-) and 'Brief Exposure' (2001-); curated exhibitions shown throughout Britain and Ireland, Austria, Italy, Sardinia, Switzerland, U.S.A. *Works in collections*: 470 works in public and corporate collections throughout Britain and USA and private collections worldwide. *Publications*: Over 150 publications in English, French, Italian including:

Mario Giacomelli (1983, 1985); Elio Ciol, Italia Black and White (1986); Elio Ciol, Assisi (1991); Kyffin Williams (1995); Alistair Crawford Collected Photographs (1995); Robert MacPherson 1814-72 , Father P. P. Mackey (1851-1935) Photographer (2000); Mario Giacomelli (2001, 2002, 2005, 2006). Erich Lessing Reportage - Photography 1948-73 (2002, 2003, 2005); Robert MacPherson 1814-1872, The Final Proof (2008); column: 'Brief Exposure' for Inscape Magazine 1999-. *Address*: 64 Dove House, Great Cornard, Sudbury, Suffolk CO10 0GF. *Email*: info@alistaircrawford.co.uk *Website*: www.alistaircrawford.co.uk *Signs work*: "Crawford" followed by the last two digits of the year.

CRAWFORD, Anne Menzies Hamilton, Professional Member: Scottish Society of Artists; Visual Artists of Scotland; Awards: The Royal Scottish Academy Ottile Helen Scholarship Fund Prize for best work by a woman sculptor; Finalist, Morrison Portrait Award. *Medium*: sculpture, watercolour, drawing. *b*: Penang, Malaysia, 29 Aug 1932. *d of*: Francis Charles Bruce. *m*: Hunter Ralston Crawford (deceased). two *s*. *Educ*: Tanglin School, Cameron Highlands, Malaysia; Frensham, NSW, Australia; Roedean, Brighton. *Studied*: Chelsea School of Commercial Art (1951-53); Studio assistant to Bernard Adams for 6 months (1953/4). *Exhib*: RSA, RGI, SSWA, SSA, Scottish Society of Visual Artists; Open Eye Gallery, Edinburgh; Crawford Centre of the Arts, St.Andrews; Aberdeen Art Gallery; Lille Art Gallery, Strathclyde; Thompson's, the City/ Marylebone; Demarco Gallery, Edinburgh. *Works in collections*: Sculpture: University of Paisley. Paintings: Vanderbilt Foundation, New York; St. Thomas' Hospital, London. *Commissions*: approx. 25-30 portrait heads, and 20 dogs & cats. *Publications*: 'Working as an Artist'. *Works Reproduced*: St.Thomas' from Lollards Tower, Lambeth Palace. *Principal Works*: Portrait heads. *Recreations*: grandchildren. *Clubs*: New Club, Edinburgh (Associate). *Address*: Old Brambletye House, Forest Row, East Sussex, RH18 5EH. *Email*: annecrawford111@gmail.com *Signs work*: "AHC" or "Anne Crawford" (watercolours).

CRAWFORD, John Gardiner, DA, Post Dip., RSW, RBA, RI; painter in water-colour, acrylic; Awards: Gray's School of Art, First Prize for Painting (1962); Governor's Award for Painting, Hospitalfield College of Art (1963); Royal Scottish Academy, Bursary Award (1964); First Prize, Scottish Arts Council Open Exhbn. (1969); Scottish Arts Council, Bursary Award (1981); Hunting Award, First Prize for Water-colour (1982); RI Medal (1983); Hunting Award, Second Prize (1984). *b*: Fraserburgh, 1941. *s of*: John Gardiner Crawford, fisherman. *m*: Elspeth Younger. one *s*. one *d*. *Educ*: Fraserburgh Academy. *Studied*: Gray's School of Art, Aberdeen. *Exhib*: internationally. *Works in collections*: worldwide. *Address*: Dunedin, 34 Strachan St., Arbroath, Angus DD11 1UA. *Signs work*: "CRAWFORD."

CRAWFORD, Susan L., equestrian artist and portrait painter in oil. *b*: Scotland, 11 May 1941. *d of*: H.Com. WH Crawford and Mrs P.M. Crawford, neé McCosh. *m*: Jeremy Phipps. one *s*. one *d*. *Educ*: Priors Field, Godalming. *Studied*: Studio Simi, Florence (1968-70). *Exhib*: solo show at Tryon Gallery (2001); part of large shows at NPG, Royal Scottish Academy, Queen's Gallery, V&A, RA, National Gallery of Penang, RP, National Horseracing Museum, Newmarket, Cross Gate Gallery, Kentucky USA. *Works in collections*: HM The Queen, HM Queen Elizabeth the Queen Mother, HRH The Prince of Wales, the late Paul Mellon, HM Sultan Qaabos of Oman, The Sultan of Brunei, Prince Khalid Abdulla, The Duke of Devonshire, Sir Arnold Weinstock, Kerry Packer, etc. *Commissions*: 21 Derby winners; Royal portraits. *Publications*: included in Stella Walker's 'Sporting Artist of the 20th Century', '100 Years of British Farming Livestock'; etc. *Works Reproduced*: Rosenstiels, Fine Art Publishers, 33-35 Markham St., Chelsea Green, London SW3 3NR and own studio. *Misc*: mother of Jake Phipps, designer & Jemma Phipps, portrait painter, *Address*: Heathfield House, Bonchester Bridge, Hawick, TD9 8JB. *Website*: www.slcrawford.com *Signs work*: "S.L. Crawford."

CRAWSHAW, Alwyn, SEA, BWS, PNAPA, FRSA (1978), UA (Hon.) (2000); artist in acrylic, water-colour and oil; director (partner), Russell Artists Merchandising Ltd., Kingston-upon-Thames, Surrey (1957-80); Lecturer and demonstrator on acrylic, oil and water-colour painting for Daler-Rowney & Co., Ltd. Bracknell Berks.; President, National Acrylic Painters Assoc.; Founder, Soc.of Amateur Artists (1992). *b*: Mirfield, Yorks., 20 Sep 1934. *s of*: Fred Crawshaw. *m*: June Crawshaw. one *s.* two *d. Educ*: Hastings Grammar School for Boys. *Studied*: Hastings School of Art (1949-51) under Vincent Lines. *Exhib*: RBA; one-man shows: Harrods, St. Paul's Gallery, London, Marina Gallery, Weybridge, Barclay A.G., Chester, Guildford Galleries, Guildford, Mensing Gallery, Germany; joint exhbn. with June Crawshaw, St. Helier Gallery, Jersey, C.I. (1992), Patricia Wells Gallery, Bristol (1989) and Tokyo, Japan (1998, 2001). *Publications*: Pub. by Harper Collins: Alwyn Crawshaw's Oil Painting Course (1992), A Brush with Art (1991), Alwyn Crawshaw Paints Oils (1992), Alwyn Crawshaw Paints on Holiday (1992), Alwyn Crawshaw's Acrylic Painting Course (1993), Alwyn Crawshaw's Watercolour Painting Course (1991), Crawshaw Paints Acrylics (1994), Crawshaw's Sketching and Drawing Course (1995); Crawshaw Paints Constable Country (1996); Alwyn and June Crawshaw's Outdoor Painting Course (1997); Learn to paint with Acrylic Colours (Collins); Learn to paint with Watercolours (Collins); Learn to paint landscapes (Collins); Learn to paint boats and harbours (Collins); Learn to Sketch (Collins); Learn to Paint Still Life (Collins); Learn to Paint Outdoors in Watercolour (Collins); Learn to Paint in Oils for the Beginner (Collins); The Artist at Work - Alwyn Crawshaw (Collins); Sketching with Alwyn Crawshaw (Collins); The Half-Hour Painter (Collins); "You Can Paint Watercolour" pub. 2000, Harper & Collins. Guest on BBC Radio, BBC T.V., Independent Radio, discussing painting techniques; guest on the 'Gay Byrne Radio Show' R.T.E. Ireland (Mar. 1991), T.S.W. television series 'A Brush with Art' by Alwyn Crawshaw, 12 half hour programmes, 'Crawshaw Paints in Oils', 8 half hour programmes, 'Crawshaw Paints on Holiday', 6 half hour programmes (1992), 'Crawshaw's Watercolour Studio' 8 half hour programmes (1993), 'Crawshaw Paints Acrylics', 8 half hour programmes (1994), 'Crawshaw's Sketching and Drawing Course', 10 half hour programmes (1995), 'Crawshaw Paints Constable Country' T.V. for Anglia and Channel 4, 6 half hour programmes. All TV series screened network by Channel 4, and screened by P.B.S. America from April 1993, and Japan. TV series – 8 half hour programmes "Crawshaw's Watercolour Cruise" (2000), 'You Can Paint Landscapes in Watercolour' pub. Harper Collins (2003); 'Alwyn Crawshaw's Ultimate Painting Course' pub. Harper Collins (Sep.2006); '30 Minute Sketching' pub. Harper Collins (2008). *Address*: 21 Beckmeadow Way, Mundesley, Norwich, Norfolk NR11 8LP. *Email*: a.crawshaw@btconnect.com *Signs work*: "ALWYN CRAWSHAW."

CRAWSHAW, Donna, SWA, SEA; animals and landscape painter in acrylic and water-colour. *Medium*: acrylic. *b*: Woking, Surrey, 16 Mar 1960. *d of*: Alwyn Crawshaw. *m*: Andrew G.L. Goolding (Fine Art Dealer). two *d. Studied*: West Surrey College of Art and Design. *Exhib*: Omell Galleries, London; Ascot, Forest Gallery Guildford; Mall Galleries and Westminster Hall (various); Clifton Gallery, Bristol; Grimes House Gallery, Cotswolds; Wellington Gallery, Ballymena; Cheng-Kim Loke Gallery, Slimbridge; Valley Art Gallery, N.Ireland; Tallantyre Gallery, Morpeth, Northumberland; Cotswold Galleries, Stow-on-the-Wold; Whibleys, Worthing; Kingfisher Gallery, Cowbridge; Triton Gallery, Torquay. *Works Reproduced*: Country Fine Arts and Solomon & Whitebread - Fine Art Prints; Royal Worcester Porcelain by Bradford Exchange; greetings cards by various. *Address*: Rhiwe Farm, Llanddeusant, Llangadog, Carms. SA19 9SS. *Email*: donnacrawshaw@email.com *Website*: www.donnacrawshaw.co.uk *Signs work*: "Donna Crawshaw."

CRAWSHAW, June Eileen, BWS (1987), SWA (1988), NAPA (1997); artist in water-colour, oil and acrylics, potter in ceramics, porcelain. *b*: Woking, Surrey, 20 Jun 1936. *d of*: Ernest Bridgman, mechanical engineer. *m*: Alwyn Crawshaw. one *s.* two *d. Educ*: Kingfield Secondary School, Woking. *Studied*: painting under Alwyn Crawshaw, SEA, BWS, PNAPA,

FRSA (1970-87); ceramics at Danefield College, Woking (1975-80, June Duckworth). *Exhib*: joint exhbns. with Alwyn Crawshaw, Donna Crawshaw, SWA, Godalming Galleries (1985), Yorkshire Artists (1987), Sidmouth Visual Arts Festival (1981-87), BWS (1987), joint exhbn. with Alwyn Crawshaw Harrods (1986), SWA Annual Exhbn., BWS Annual Exhbn., joint exhbn. with Alwyn Crawshaw at The Patricia Wells Gallery, Bristol (1989), St. Helier Gallery, Jersey, C.I. (1992), and Tokyo, Japan (1998, 2001); teaches with Alwyn Crawshaw on painting courses every year since 1982. *Publications*: 'You can Paint Seashore in Watercolour' (Harper Collins, 2004), Watercolour Made Easy (Harper Collins, 1995); Alwyn and June Crawshaw's Outdoor Painting Course (1997). Featured in TV series: 'Crawshaw Paints on Holiday' Channel 4 (1992) and P.B.S. America (1993) and book of series; 'Crawshaw Paints Acrylics' Channel 4 (1994) P.B.S. America (1994) and book of series; 'Crawshaw's Sketching and Drawing Course' Channel 4 (1995) P.B.S. America and book of series. All three series in Japan. *Address*: 21 Beckmeadow Way, Mundesley, Norwich, Norfolk NR11 8LP. *Website*: www.crawshawgallery.com *Signs work*: "June Crawshaw" (paintings).

CREBER, Frank, BFA (1981), MFA (1987); artist in oil on canvas, water-colour, pen and ink. *b*: Amersham, Bucks., 12 Jan 1959. *m*: Marguerite. two *s*. *Studied*: Newcastle University (Roy Kitchen), Chelsea School of Art (Ian Stephenson). *Exhib*: Sue Williams, Portobello Rd. (1988, 1989, 1991), Barclays Bank Young Painters £10,000 competition, Henry Moore Gallery, RCA. London (awarded joint winner 1987), Paton Gallery, London (1990), Artist of the Day, Flowers East, London (1989). *Works in collections*: Unilever, Arthur Andersen & Co.,Art for Hospitals, Leics. Schools Coll., Stanhope Construction Ltd. *Address*: 49 Darnley Road, Hackney, London E9 6QH.

CREFFIELD, Dennis, *b*: London, 29 Jan 1931. four *s*. seven *d*. *Educ*: Colfes Grammar School, London. *Studied*: Borough Polytechnic, London with David Bomberg (1948-51), Slade School of Fine Art, London (1957-61); Gregory Fellow in Painting at the University of Leeds (1964-68). *Represented by*: James Hyman Gallery, 5 Savile Row, London W15 3PD. *Exhib*: many mixed and one-man exhbns; A Retrospective Exhibition, Flowers East Gallery, London (2005). *Works in collections*: include: Tate Britain, Contemporary Art Soc., National Trust, House of Commons, Arts Council of Gt. Britain, Government Art Collection, Imperial War Museum, The Contemporary Art Soc., The British Museum (Dept of Prints and Drawings). *Commissions*: include: South Bank Board – Medieval English Cathedrals (1987); The National Trust Foundation for Art – Petworth (1990) and Orford Ness (1994); The House of Commons Fine Art Commission (1990). *Address*: 3/45 Marine Parade, Brighton BN2 1PE. *Signs work*: Dennis Creffield.

CRESWELL, Alexander Charles Justin, artist in water-colour, author; Knight of the Order of Francis I (KFO). *b*: Helsinki, 14 Feb 1957. *m*: Mary Curtis Green. one *s*. two *d*. *Educ*: Winchester College. *Studied*: Byam Shaw School of Art (1976), W. Surrey College (1976-78). *Exhib*: Portland Gallery, London; Hirschl & Adler Galleries New York; John Martin of London, Spink & Son, Cadogan Gallery, New Academy London, also Europe, Hong Kong and S. Africa. *Works in collections*: Palace of Westminster, The Royal Collection, The Frick Museum, Forbes Collection. *Commissions*: Royal Collection, Royal Bank of Scotland, English Heritage, BBC, Duchy of Cornwall, HSBC Bank Middle East, HM The Queen; HRH The Prince of Wales. *Publications*: The Silent Houses of Britain (1991), Out of the Ashes (1999). *Clubs*: INTBAU, A.W.G., Institute of Classical Architecture, Royal Cornwall Yacht Club. *Address*: Copse Hill, Ewhurst, Surrey GU6 7NN. *Website*: www.alexandercreswell.com *Signs work*: "Alexander Creswell."

CREW, Rowan Alexander, ARBA (1987), RBA (1988); self taught artist in water-colour, acrylic and oil. *b*: Woodchurch, Kent, 31 Dec 1952. *s of*: Alfred Crew, teacher. *m*: Linda Bannister. three *d*. *Educ*: Homewood Secondary Modern. *Exhib*: RI, RBA, ROI, NEAC.

Works in collections: KCC, and private collections. *Address*: Brook Farm House, Brook St., Woodchurch, Ashford, Kent TN26 3SP. *Signs work*: "Rowan Crew."

CREWE, Pamela Ann Row, BA Hons (Fine Art), PGCE. *Medium*: oil, watercolour, drawing, prints. *b*: Newcastle-upon-Tyne, 31 Jan 1939. *d of*: R S G Row. one *s*. *Educ*: Dame Allan's Girls' School, Newcastle-upon-Tyne. *Studied*: Reading University 1957-61, London University Institute of Education 1961-62. *Exhib*: Longden Gallery, Macclesfield; Ancient High House, Stafford; Northumbria University, Stafford Shire Hall, Open Studios, Wedgwood, Barber Institute, Stoke-on-Trent Open, Society of Staffordshire Artists, The Hepworth Gallery Longden, Englands Gallery (Leek) in Italy, Walsall Art Gallery, Dame Catherine Harpur School Ticknell, SWE, SWA, RBSA, Keele University, The Forest Gallery Staffs, Cannock Museum, Hednesford, Aurora Fine arts, Cannock, Royal Academy Summer Exhibition, MS Trust, New Mills Heritage Centre, Duchess Gallery, Kielder, Melbourne Arts Festival, Derbyshire (2013). *Publications*: illustrated "Nasen" educational publications. *Address*: 13 New Street, New Mills, High Peak, Derbyshire SK22 4PE. *Email*: pam@becksbridgestudio.co.uk *Signs work*: "P. Crewe", "Pamela Crewe" or "Pamela Row Crewe".

CRISFIELD CHAPMAN, June, DA (Glasgow) (1955); National Award - Garrick/Milne Competition (portrait). *Medium*: wood engraving, portraiture, illustration. *b*: Kent, 4 Jun 1934. *m*: William Woodside Chapman, D.A. two *s*. *Educ*: Kilmarnock Academy. *Studied*: Glasgow School of Art. *Exhib*: solo: National Theatre London, Shakespeare's Globe London, Glasgow City A.G. Kelvingrove, Palace of Westminster, Natural History Museum at Water Rothschild Museum, Chelsea Physic Garden, Royal Botanic Garden Edinburgh; group: Edinburgh International Festival, Royal Scottish Academy, Royal Society of Painter Printers' Opens, Chaucer/Caxton, Westminster Abbey. *Works in collections*: engravings - Glasgow City, Edinburgh City, Ashmolean Museum, Oxford, Fitzwilliam Museum Cambridge, Fleming Scottish, London; portraiture - Theatre Museum (V&A), Paisley Museum, William Morris Society, Royal Academy Dramatic Art, National Trust. *Commissions*: theatre portraits, illustrative engraving, theatre gouaches - 'Tribute to Scottish Theatre', 'Entertainment' panel, private portraiture, engravings. *Publications*: engravings Folio Book Society's Shakespeare (1988), 'The Countryman' ('87-'98), illustration in Radio Times. *Official Purchasers*: Garrick Club, London, Flemings Bank, Glasgow Corporation, Faculty of Public Medicine, Aberdeen Hospital, Essex Education Authority, V&A, Morris Society. *Works Reproduced*: engravings Folio Book Society, The Countryman Magazine, Radio Times, Engravers' Globe. *Misc*: talks, demonstrations, including British Library, V. & A. Museum. *Address*: 23 Smythe Rd., Billericay, Essex CM11 1SE. *Signs work*: "CRISFIELD" or "CRISFIELD CHAPMAN."

CROFT, Ivor John, CBE, MA (Oxon. and Lond.); painter and former civil servant. *b*: 6 Jan 1923. *s of*: Oswald Croft. *Educ*: Westminster School; Christ Church, Oxford; Institute of Education, University of London; London School of Economics. *Exhib*: group shows: various, 1958 onwards including Camden Arts Centre (Survey of Abstract Painters, 1967); John Player Open Exhbn. (1968, 1969); Covent Garden Gallery (Critical Discoveries, 1973); Lorient, Brittany (Festival Interceltique, 1993); Anthony Hepworth (2002/14); one-man shows: Gardner Centre for the Arts, University of Sussex (1970); University of Warwick (1971), Reform Club (2007/8). *Works Reproduced*: Art and Artists, postcard. *Clubs*: Reform. *Address*: 15 Circus Mews, Bath BA1 2PW. *Signs work*: "John Croft" on back.

CROFT, Maria Danuta, Ministry of Education Arts & Crafts National Diploma in Design (1953); Diploma Painting and Printed Textile (Hand) (1955). *Medium*: palette knife work, oil, watercolour, drawing, prints, pen and ink. *b*: Poland, 15 Jun 1932. *d of*: Rafal Kornel Ryzenski, officer/teacher. *m*: Arthur Jack Croft, ex. RN. three *s-s*. two *d*. *Studied*:

Plymouth College of Art (under Lewis Duckett, Mr.Pickup, Mr Herman, Mis Lee). *Exhib*: Art Frame Gallery, Tavistock and Plymouth; Tavistock Town Hall Art Society; Liskeard, Cornwall; Holiday Inn, Plymouth; and across the West Country; winner of Best Painting in the Show 3 times with TGA Society. *Works in collections*: Baroness Thatcher (private collection); Tavistock Town Hall (Mayor's Parlour); private. *Commissions*: Polish Maritime Training Ship 'Jan Turlejski'; moorland ponies, dogs, portraits, etc. Works sold in US, Canada, Australia, Poland, Belgium, Germany, Spain, Ireland and UK, over 200 paintings. *Publications*: Leisure Painter; (featured in) WWII story of Poles in India (12 Dec 2009), and contribution to 'Finding Poland' by Dr. Matt Kelly (Feb. 2010). *Principal Works*: 'Baroness Thatcher, Iron Lady'; Town Criers; scenes of Moorlands. *Recreations*: flower display for exhibitions, shop windows, theatre scenery, floats. G&S make-up artist, Plymouth Society. *Clubs*: Tavistock Group of Artists. *Address*: Barley House, 2 Barley Market, Street, Tavistock, Devon PL19 0JF. *Signs work*: 'Maria D.Ryzewska', 'Maria D.Skalski', 'Lynx', 'Lynx Skalski', 'Lynx Croft', 'M.D.Croft' or 'Maria Danuta Croft'.

CROFT, Paul John, ARE (2005), TMP; BA Hons Drawing & Painting (Printmaking), PGDip Drawing & Painting (Printmaking), PGCE (Art & Design); many awards including: Elizabeth Greenshields Foundation award (1992, 1994), Arts Council Awards (1997, 1998, 2005), AHRC award (2006); Lecturer in Fine Art Printmaking, Aberystwyth School of Art. *Medium*: printmaking - lithography. *b*: Belfast, 14 May 1963. *s of*: Richard Croft, PPRUA. *Studied*: Edinburgh College of Art (1981-86), University of Ulster, Belfast (1989-90), Tamarind Institute, University of New Mexico, USA (1994-96). *Exhib*: Selected exhibitions include: Bankside Gallery (2007); Wrexham Print International (2007); Contemporary Welsh Printmakers, Lahore, Karachi, Pakistan (2007); Prints of Wales, Kansas City (2007); RE Bankside Gallery (2006); Affordable Art Fair, Battersea (2006); Wales Drawing Biennale (2005); Stark Gallery, London (2005); Attic Gallery, Swansea (2004-07); Royal Ulster Academy, Belfast (2004); many others since 1998. *Works in collections*: The Royal Society of Painter Printmakers (2005), University of Wales, Aberystwyth (2000), The Allied Irish Bank Print Collection, Dublin (1999), Arts Council of Northern Ireland (1998). *Works Reproduced*: "Stone Lithography" (A&C Black, 2001); "Plate Lithography" (A&C Black, 2003); "Collecting Original Prints" Rosemary Simmons (A&C Black, 2005); and various articles and catalogues. *Recreations*: reading, travel. *Clubs*: Aberystwyth Printmakers. *Address*: 10 Green Gardens, Trefechan, Aberystwyth, Ceredigion, SY23 1BB. *Email*: puc@aber.ac.uk *Website*: www.spgw.co.uk http: //users.aber.ac.uk/puc/paulcroft/open.htm *Signs work*: (printers chop mark)

CROFT, Richard John, RUA (1967); President, Royal Ulster Academy of Arts (1997-2000); Founder Member of Group 63; Print Fellowship Ulster Polytechnic (1977); RUA Gold Medal (2000). *Medium*: artist in oils/print. *b*: London, 1935. *m*: Helen Kerr, RUA. one *s.* one *d. Studied*: Bromley, and Brighton Colleges of Art. *Exhib*: Ireland, England and abroad; retrospective exhbn. Queens University Belfast (2003), and Touring, Lisburn, Downpatrick, Armagh; RUA Belfast, RHA Dublin. *Works in collections*: public and private, N.I. Arts Council, Government of NI, Queen's University Belfast, Oxford University, London University, Irish Embassy Beijing, Ulster Television, National Self-Portrait Collection of Ireland etc. *Publications*: Mike Catto Art in Ulster 2 (1977), RUA Diploma Collection (2000). *Address*: The Lodge, 187 Main St., Dundrum, Co. Down N.I. BT33 0LY. *Email*: croftlodge1@btinternet.com

CROKER, Valerie, SBA (1987), HS (1994) SFP (2001); artist in water-colour, pen and ink. *b*: Cardiff, 19 Aug 1931. one *s.* one *d. Educ*: Abbey School, Reading. *Studied*: Maidenhead Art School (1950), Reading University (1951-53, Prof. Betts). *Exhib*: SWLA, UA and SWA; solo shows: Henley, Bath, Wells, Winchester; and many other mixed shows in UK and abroad. *Commissions*: Coalport plates for British Wildlife appeal. *Publications*: illustrated: People and Places by J H B Peel, Old Wives Tales by Eric Maple, The Secret

Lore of Plants and Flowers by Eric Maple, Still Waters by Margaret Cornish. *Recreations*: conservation, gardening and crafts. *Misc*: Work used for cards, tableware, etc. *Address*: Jessamine Cottage, 7 Lower Rd., Edington, Westbury, Wilts. BA13 4QW. *Signs work*: "Valerie Croker" or "V.C."

CROOK, P.J., MBE (2011), Hon Doctor of Art 2010 Univeristy of Gloucestershire. RWA (1993), MAFA; painter; Awards: RWA (First Prize, 1984); Cheltenham Group (First Prize, 1990); Gift of Life (Prizewinner, 1993); Royal Bath & West (First Prize, 1978). *b*: Cheltenham, 28 Jun 1945. *m*: Richard Parker Crook. one *s*. one *d*. *Studied*: Gloucestershire College of Art (1960-65). *Represented by*: Brian Sinfield; Galerie Alain Blondel, Paris; Loch Gallery, Toronto; Panter and Hall, London. *Exhib*: One Person Shows: Panter and Hall (2014); Alpha Gallery, London (2012, 2013); Galerii Vaal, Tallinn, Estonia (2010); Brian Sinfield Gallery, Burford (1997, 99, 2004, 07, 09); Galerie Alain Blondel Paris (1991,93, 95, 97, 99, 2002, 08); Loch Gallery, Toronto (1998, 2007); Draakoni Galerii, Tallinn, Estonia (2006); Cheltenham Art Gallery and Museum (2006, 1996, 86); Morohashi Museum of Modern Art-Japan (2001, 06), City Museum and Art Gallery, Gloucester (2002, 06); Robert Sandelson, London (1994-2003); Theo Waddington Fine Art, Boca Raton, Florida (2000); Barry Friedman Ltd., New York - Art 1998, Chicago 1998; Royal West of England Academy, Bristol (1997); Portal Gallery, London (1980-1994); Lee Drexler, New York (1989). Selected group exhibitions: Royal Academy of Arts (1978-83, 1985, 1987, 1988, 1990, 1991, 1995, 2008, 2009, 2010, 2011); RWA annually since 1978; 2002- Rugby Art Gallery and Museum; 2001- The Holburne Museum; 2000- Melton Carnegie Museum; 2000- Women beyond Borders - London & San Francisco; 1997- Women light up the night - Berlin; 1996 - Die kraft der bilder Realismus der gegenwart - Berlin; 1996- Imperial War Museum; 1995 - Murs peints, Mairie de Paris; 1994- VIII Salon International de l'affiche et des arts de la rue - Paris; 1993-4- Lincoln Museum and Art Gallery; 1993- The Gift of Life - London; 1992- Royal Albert Memorial Museum, Exeter; 1991- Leicester Museum and Art Gallery; 1990- Brighton Museum and Art Gallery; 1998- British Figurative Painting since 1945' British Council tour of Far East; 1986- National Portrait Gallery; 1982- World of Newspapers prizewinner; Sotheby's; RA; 1980- City Museum and Art Gallery, Stoke on Trent. *Works in collections*: King Abdullah; ALJ, Jeddah; BDO, London; Can West Global Communications, Toronto; Centrica; Cheltenham Art Gallery and Museum; Cheltenham Racecourse; City Museum, Gloucester; Daniel Owen Community Centre, Mold; Department for Transport, London; El Mundo, Madrid; Ha'aretz, Tel Aviv; Imperial War Museum; JP Morgan Inc,; Morohashi Museum of Modern Art, Japan; Murray Edwards College, University of Cambridge; Open Museum, Leicestershire; Ville de Paris; Paintings in Hospitals; Presidential Palace, Estonia; Ralli Museum, Ceasaria; Royal Hospital, Gloucester; Royal West of England Academy; Sagitta, London; Standard Chartered Bank, London; Templeton Asset Management, Toronto. *Commissions*: ALJ Saudi Arabia; Daniel Owen Centre; Gloucestershire College; JP Morgan; Standard Chartered Bank; Bishop of Gloucester; Cheltenham Music Festival; Alderman Knight Special School Tewkesbury. *Publications*: PJ Crook: Peintures (Editions Ramsay, Paris, 1993); PJ Crook: A Retrospective (Cheltenham AG&M,1996); PJ Crook (Artemesia Press, London, 2003). *Official Purchasers*: Cheltenham Art Gallery & Museum; Morohashi Museum of Modern Art; Welsh Arts Council. *Works Reproduced*: reproduction handled by Bridgeman Art Library. *Clubs*: Chelsea Arts, London. *Misc*: Patron, National Star College; President, Friends of Cheltenham Art Gallery & Museum; a Gloucestershire Ambassador; Patron Cheltenham Open Studios; Patron, Artshape Patron, Linc. *Address*: The Old Police Station, 39 Priory Lane, Bishop's Cleeve, Cheltenham GL52 8JL. *Email*: pj@pjcrook.com *Website*: www.pjcrook.com *Signs work*: "P.J. Crook."

CROSBY, Dido. *Medium*: sculpture. *b*: London, 9 Dec 1961. *d of*: Theo Crosby and Anne Buchanan. one *s*. *Educ*: Bedales School, Oxford University (Zoology) 1981-1984, BA.

Studied: Central St.Martins (Sculpture) 1991-1996, BA. *Exhib*: Jagged Art, London; Campden Gallery, Chipping Campden, Glos. *Works in collections*: 'White Gazelle' Winner of the Bernard Noble Sculpture Prize 2010, Colletta, Liguria, Italy; 'Pair of Indian Runner Ducks' 2007, The Prudential Art Collection, London. *Commissions*: Globe Theatre (four Falcon finials, 1996); Acton Court, Iron Acton, Bristol (cast iron Cow, Sow and Piglets, 2003, and Pair of Barn Owls in Bronze, 2004); Dunderave Castle, Loch Fyne, Argyll (large bronze Horse, 2005). *Address*: 52 Thorne Road, London SW8 2BY. *Email*: dido@didocrosby.com *Website*: www.didocrosby.com *Signs work*: "Dido Crosby" or "Dido".

CROSS, Richard Henry, BA (Hons) 1980, PG Dip RAS 1984; lecturer Blackburn College. *Medium*: figurative painter. *b*: Derby, 19 Jan 1958. *m*: Sarah O'Regan. one *s.* one *d. Educ*: Heanor Grammar School, Derbyshire. *Studied*: Liverpool College of Art (1977-80), Royal Academy Schools (1981-84). Work influenced by Peter Greenham and Norman Blamey. *Exhib*: Northern Young Contemporaries (1981), Royal Overseas League (1984), National Portrait Gallery (1986), BP Portrait Award (2010), Royal Academy Summer Exhbn (1985, 86, 90, 91, 2012). *Works in collections*: many private collections. *Publications*: '500 Portraits' NPG 2010. *Clubs*: RASAA (Reynolds Club). *Misc*: figurative painter producing work based on analytical drawing from direct observation. *Address*: 10 Fort St, Clitheroe, Lancs, BB7 1BY. *Email*: richardcross247@aol.com *Website*: www.richardcrossgallery.com

CROSS, Roy, RSMA (1977), SAA (1952), GAvA (1998); historical marine and aviation painter in gouache, acrylic and oils. *b*: London, 23 Apr 1924. *m*: Rita May (decd.). one *s. Exhib*: Malcolm Henderson Gallery, St. James's, (1973); one-man shows: Börjessons Gallery, Gothenborg, Sweden, (1975 and 1977); Marine Arts Gallery, Salem, Massachusetts (1976, 1989, 1999, 2003). *Works in collections*: National Maritime Museum; Constitution Museum, Boston, USA; Peabody Museum, Salem, USA and UK. *Publications*: many limited edition prints of marine pictures signed and numbered by the artist (1977-1999) published in Sweden (2), USA (7) and Britain (3), plus art prints by Franklin Mint, Rosenstiel's, plates by Hamilton Collection, etc. *Works Reproduced*: many periodicals (marine, aviation) and own books. Autobiographies: Celebration of Flight (2004), Celebration of Sail (2005), Vintage Years of Airfix Art (2010). *Address*: Squirrels, 4 Hither Chantlers, Langton Green, Tunbridge Wells, Kent TN3 0BJ. *Signs work*: "Roy Cross ©" and usually dated.

CROSSLEY, Gordon, painter in oil; Retd. Senior lecturer in Art and Design, Barking College of Technology. *b*: Surrey, 6 Dec 1929. *s of*: Fred Eric Crossley. *m*: Jo Glosby (decd). one *s.* three *d. Educ*: Rutlish School, Merton. *Studied*: Wimbledon School of Art. *Exhib*: RA, RBA, NEAC, PS, NS, Madden Gallery; one-man shows, Phoenix Gallery (1984), Gainsborough Gallery, Beecroft Gallery, Thompson's Gallery Aldeburgh; Aubley Art Gallery, Dunmow (Gallery Artist), Dictionary of International Biography (2009). *Works in collections*: Essex Museum, 2 paintings. *Misc*: gives painting demonstrations to Art Groups, Galleries and Schools. *Address*: The Sanctuary, Sheering, nr. Bishop's Stortford, Herts. CM22 7LN. *Website*: www.gtc-art.com

CROSTHWAITE, Sally, SBA; RHS Gold medal; botanical illustrator. *Medium*: watercolour. *b*: Woking, Surrey, 14 Apr 1944. *m*: Patrick Crosthwaite. one *s.* two *d. Studied*: English Gardening School, Chelsea Physic Garden (Distinction, Diploma Course, Botanical illustration). *Exhib*: Malcolm Innes Gallery, London, SBA Open, etc., also in USA and numerous mixed exhibitions. *Works in collections*: Hunt Institute of Botanical Documentation, Carnegie Mellon University, USA, Chelsea Physic Garden, Lindley Library, Royal Horticultural Society, Royal Botanic Gardens, Kew, Highgrove Florilegium. *Commissions*: numerous private in UK and USA. *Publications*: various illustrations in books. *Works Reproduced*: fruit and tulip designs on plates. Limoges dinner service. *Address*: Lynchmere Farmhouse, nr. Haslemere, Surrey GU27 3NG. *Email*: sallycrosthwaite@supanet.com *Website*: www.sallycrosthwaite.co.uk

CROUCH, Helga Ursula, Cert.AD (Dist.) (1962), Dip.AD (graphics) (1964), FSBA (1986), FLS (2001); RHS Silver-Gilt Medal, Certificate of Botanical Merit. *b*: London, 18 Jan 1941. *d of*: Clifford L.B. Hubbard, FIAL, ABA. *m*: Julian Terence Crouch M.I.L.T. one *d*. *Educ*: Willoughby H.S. High School, Sydney, Australia. *Studied*: Cardiff College of Art (1959-62, A.T. Kitson), Central School of Arts and Crafts (1962-64, P. Kitley). *Exhib*: mixed shows: Mall Galleries, Westminster Gallery, Linnean Soc., RHS, Hunt Inst. Botanical Documentation, Pittsburgh, Kew Gardens, The Discerning Eye, Old Fire Engine House, Ely, Ashmolean Museum, Oxford, Cambridge Drawing Society; Shirley Sherwood Gallery, Kew; Forum Botanische Kunst, Germany; Fry Art Gallery, Saffron Walden; solo shows: Dorking Hall, Cambridge Open Studio, Little Sampford, Jonathan Cooper Gallery, London. *Works in collections*: The Shirley Sherwood Collection of Contemporary Botanical Art, Mr. & Mrs. Peter Warne, Windlesham Arboretum, Surrey. *Publications*: Kew Magazine, Arte y Botanica, The Art of Botanical Painting, Contemporary Botanical Artists, A New Flowering - 1000 Years of Botanical Art, The Art of Plant Evolution, Country Living, Country Homes and Interiors, Artful Nature. *Recreations*: Conservation gardening, topiary. *Clubs*: Linnean Society, Society of Botanical Artists, Cambridge Open Studios, European Boxwood and Topiary Society, Cambridge Drawing Society. *Address*: The Mill House, Little Sampford, nr. Saffron Walden, Essex CB10 2QT. *Email*: helga.crouch@wildlybotanical.co.uk *Website*: www.wildlybotanical.co.uk *Signs work*: "Helga Crouch" hidden in work.

CROW, Becky, BA (Hons) Three Dimensional Crafts. *Medium*: Jewellery. *b*: London, 18 Mar 1977. *m*: Jude Godden. *Studied*: University of Brighton (1996-99); Camberwell College of Art & Design (Foundation, 1995-96). *Exhib*: Chelsea Craft Fair (2001, 2002, 2003); The Contemporary Craft Fair, Bovey Tracey, Devon; 'Made' (London, Brighton); Newcastle Arts Centre; Leeds City Gallery; Yorkshire Sculpture Park; Ruthin Gallery; The Steensons, Belfast; Art in Action; Old Courthouse Gallery, Cumbria. *Works in collections*: Brighton and Hove Museum Collection. *Commissions*: The Wildlife Trust; various private. *Official Purchasers*: The Wildlife Trust; National Trust of Scotland; V&A; British Museum; Brighton and Hove Museum. *Clubs*: The Sussex Guild; British Jewellers Association. *Address*: Rosehill Workshop, 13a Rose Hill, Brighton, BN2 3FA. *Email*: thebrightoncrow@yahoo.com *Website*: www.beckycrow.co.uk *Signs work*: "BECKY CROW" or "B CROW".

CROWE, Victoria Elizabeth, OBE, FRSE, DHC, RSA, RSW; MA(RCA). *b*: 1945. *Studied*: Kingston College of Art (1961-65), R.C.A. (1965-68). *Represented by*: Scottish Gallery, Edinburgh; Browse & Daarby, London. *Works in collections*: National Portrait Gallery London; Scottish National Portrait Gallery; Scottish National Gallery Modern Art; Glasgow Museums and Art Galleries; Danish National Portrait Gallery; City Art Centre, Edinburgh; Universities of Aberdeen, Cambridge, Edinburgh, Heriot-Watt, Newcastle, Oxford; Royal Academy; Royal Scottish Academy; Royal College of Art; National Museums of Scotland. *Commissions*: Portrait Galleries of London and Scotland; Boots PLC; Royal College of Surgeons, Edinburgh; Royal College Physicians, Edinburgh; Dept. Neuro Science, Edinburgh University; Royal Society, Edinburgh; Worshipful Company of Leathersellers, London. *Publications*: 'Painted Insights' Victoria Crowe, pub. A.CC. (2001); 'A Shepherd's Life' pub. National Galleries of Scotland (2000); Victoria Crowe, Duncan MacMillan pub ACC (2012). *Address*: The Bank House, Main St., W. Linton, Peeblesshire EH46 7EE. *Website*: www.victoriacrowe.com *Signs work*: "Victoria Crowe."

CROWTHER, Michael, Welsh Arts Council Bursary (1977); Resident Artist, Alayrac, Le Havre, France 2009. *Medium*: oil, drawing. *b*: St.John's Chapel, Co.Durham, 9 May 1946. *m*: Celia Davies, jeweller. two *s*. *Studied*: Leeds College of Art (1964-68); retired as Head of Painting, University of Wales Institute Cardiff, 2006. *Exhib*: Serpentine Gallery, London (1975); Twelve Brit Painters, Reyjavik, Iceland (1977); British Art Show (1979,

1980); Benjamin Rhodes Gallery, London (1987, 1988); 11th Paris Biennale (1980); Sara Hilden Museum, Tampere, Finland (1981); John Moores Exhbn. (1982, 1985); Martin Tinney Gallery, Cardiff; HAPPYtheworldsomade, Nunnery Gallery, London (curated by Peter Jones, 2001); 'Drawn from the Hatton' - Exhibition of drawings spanning four centuries from the Hatton Gallery Collection, Univ. of Newcastle upon Tyne (2008); Precious Things, Highlanes Gallery, Drogheda, Ireland (curated by Graham Crowley, 2008); Leeds College of Art Gallery (2012). *Works in collections*: National Museum of Wales, Arts Council of Great Britain, Welsh Arts Council, Contemporary Arts Society for Wales, Leicester Education Authority, Univ. of Newcastle-upon-Tyne, Southern Arts Assoc., Russell Coates Museum, Bournemouth. *Address*: 112 Kimberley Road, Cardiff, CF23 5DN. *Signs work*: "Michael Crowther" or "M.C."

CROZIER, Philip, MA (Fine Art), DipAD. *Medium*: oil. *b*: Kent, 26 Dec 1947. *s of*: Kathleen Crozier (artist). *m*: Jane. one *s.* three *d. Studied*: Bath Academy of Art, Corsham; Goldsmiths. *Represented by*: The London Group. *Exhib*: Royal Academy, South Bank Centre, Kettle's Yard, Brighton Art Gallery, Bankside Gallery, Cork Street Gallery, Sussex University, Camden Art Centre, South London Art Gallery etc. *Works in collections*: Goldsmiths Collection, East Sussex County Council, Private Collections UK/USA. *Works Reproduced*: "Oil Paintings in Public Collections in Sussex", "The London Group Catalogues 2001-Present", "An Andrew Crozier Reader. 2012". *Clubs*: London Group. *Address*: Morven, High Street, Queen Camel, Somerset, BA22 7NQ. *Email*: pjkcrozier@hotmail.com *Website*: www.philipcrozier.com *Signs work*: "CROZIER".

CROZIER, William, Premio Lissone, Milan (1960), Visiting Fellowship, New York Studio School (1979), Prof. Emeritus, Winchester School of Art (1987); Elected member, Aosdana (1991); The Gold medal for painting of The Oireachtas, Dublin (1994); Honorary Member, Royal Hibernian Academy (2001). *Medium*: painter in oil on canvas. *b*: Glasgow, 1930. *m*: Katharine Crouan. one *s.* one *d. Educ*: Marr College, Troon (1942-48). *Studied*: Glasgow School of Art (1949-53), David Donaldson, Mary and William Armour. *Represented by*: The Taylor Galleries, Dublin. *Exhib*: Drian Galleries London (1958-70); Arthur Tooth & Sons, London (1961-64); Serpentine Gallery, London (1978); Richard Demarco Gallery, Edinbugh (1965, 69, 83); Angela Flowers (1985, 2007); Bruton St. Gallery, London (1995, 96); Taylor Galleries, Dublin (1990, 1998, 2004). *Works in collections*: National Gallery of Australia; National Gallery of Canada; Museum of Modern Art, Copenhagen; Carnegie Museum of Art, Pittsburgh; Scottish National Gallery of Modern Art; City Art Gallery, Gdansk; National Museum of Art, Warsaw; V&A Museum; ACGB, London; IMMA, Dublin; Crawford Art Gallery, Cork, etc. etc. *Commissions*: BNP Paribas, London. *Publications*: "William Crozier" ed. Crouan, K., with essays by Kennedy, SB and Vann, P.208 pages (Lund Humphries, London 2007). *Official Purchasers*: Allied Irish Banks, Dublin; Office of Public Works, Dublin; Bank of Ireland; Credit Lyonnais, London; BP Plc; Arthur Anderson Plc; Merrill Lynch; Channel 4 TV. *Recreations*: Listening to jazz, reading Proust. *Clubs*: The Arts Club, London; The Chelsea Arts Club, London; The Groucho Club, London. *Address*: c/o The Taylor Galleries 16 Kildare Street Dublin 2. *Website*: www.williamcrozier.com *Signs work*: "CROZIER" lower left or right of canvas.

CRYAN, Clare, ATC, DA; artist specializing in water-colour; Tutor-in-Charge, The Blue Door Studio. *b*: Dublin, 3 Nov 1935. *Educ*: Dominican Convent, Sion Hill. *Studied*: National College of Art, Dublin; Ulster College of Art, Belfast and with Kenneth Webb in The Irish School of Landscape Painting. *Represented by*: Kenny Gallery, Galway; James Gallery, Dublin. *Exhib*: RHA, RUA, NS, Salon d'Automne, Festival International Paris, Osaka, Brussels, Luxembourg, Hong Kong. *Works in collections*: Killiney Castle, Dublin, H.M. Queen Beatrix of the Netherlands. *Recreations*: horse riding, cross country. *Clubs*: European Inst. of Water-colours. *Address*: c/o The Kenny Gallery, Liosbán Retail Park, Tuam Road, Galway, Ireland. *Signs work*: "Clare Cryan."

CRYER, Ian David, ROI; painter in oils, visual celebrator of all things English. *b*: Bristol, 1959. *m*: Wendy Patricia. one *s*. one *d*. *Educ*: Ridings High School, Bristol. *Studied*: part-time Bristol Polytechnic (1978-82); and in Kensington under Leonard Boden, RP (1978-81). *Exhib*: Bristol Art Centre (1976), P. Wells Gallery (1983), Linfield Galleries (1984, 1985), RA, RSMA, GRA, RBA, RWA, ROI, NEAC, Hunting Group finalist (1990), Discerning Eye (1991), Cooling Gallery (1992), 1st International Art Biennial, Malta (1995), NRM York. *Works in collections*: many private collections including Price Waterhouse, Longleat House, Bass Museum, Burton-on-Trent, Wadworth & Co., Bristol Rovers FC, EWS Railway Co., Crossrail, House of Lords, Royal Mail. *Clubs*: Royal Institute of Oil Painters. *Address*: 93 Bath Rd., Willsbridge, Bristol BS30 6ED. *Email*: ian.cryer@btinternet.com *Website*: www.iancryer.com *Signs work*: "Ian Cryer."

CULLEN, Patrick, NEAC, artist in oil, watercolour, and pastel. *b*: 8 Aug 1949. *m*: Sally. two *d*. *Studied*: Camberwell 1973 -1976.. *Exhib*: The Thackeray Gallery, Kensington, London W8. *Works in collections*: RA, Sheffield City Art Gallery. *Clubs*: New English Art Club and Pastel Society. *Address*: 19, Mount Pleasant Cres., London N4 4HP. *Signs work*: "Patrick Cullen."

CULLEY, Derek, BA, MA; Awards: Art Colony Galicnick residency, Macedonia (1994); BIRD2005 International Art Award. (Special Award by Jury); Pollock-Krasner Foundation Grant (2006-2007); The Cill Rialaig Project Ireland (2008). *Medium*: oil, drawing, print. *b*: Dublin,Ireland, 12 Sep 1952. *m*. Eilish Elizabeth Culley. four s. one *d*. Educ: Pearse College, Clogher Road, Dublin. *Studied*: Open University (BA); Brunel University (MA European Marketing & Business Studies). *Represented by*: Gallery Different, London; Carrie Neely - Northern Ireland and internationally. *Exhib*: Recent one man shows: ALT ENTS Art Group, Civic Centre, Tallaght, Dublin (2008, 2011); Pro Arts, Oaklands, USA (2009); The Tea Rooms, Birkdale, UK (Cill Rialaig Series: 2010, 2011, 2012); Independents Biennial, Liverpool (2010, 2012); Liverpool Anglican Cathedral (2011); Prayer Room, IEC 2012 Congress RDS, Dublin; Parallax Art Fair 9, London (2013); Editions Gallery, Liverpool (2014). *Works in collections*: Private collections in UK, Ireland, Canada, USA, Germany, Mexico, Brazil. Skopje Museum of Contemporary Art, Republic of Macedonia; Wolfson College, Oxford; Bede Gallery, Jarrow; Beijing Natural Culture Centre, Beijing, China. *Commissions:* private commissions. *Publications*: various. *Recreations*: work and family. *Clubs*: United Arts Club, Dublin, Ireland. *Address*: 7 Burlington Road, Southport, Merseyside, PR8 4RX. *Email*: funkypaddy@btinternet.com *Website*: www.derekculley.com/golgotha *Signs work*: "Derek Culley".

CULLINAN, Edward, CBE, RA, FRSA; architect, artist; has taught and lectured in Canada, USA, Australia, NZ, Norway, Malta, Japan, Eire, etc. and many places in England, Wales and Scotland; Founder and principal architect, Edward Cullinan Architects, authors of many modern bldgs. and receivers of many awards. *b*: London, 17 Jul 1931. *m*: Rosalind. one *s*. two *d*. *Studied*: architecture: Architectural Assoc., Cambridge and Berkeley, Calif. *Publications*: Edward Cullinan Architects by Kenneth Powell (Academy Editions, 1995); Edward Cullinan, Architects (RIBA Publications, 1984); Ends, Middles, Beginnings (Black Dog, 2005). *Address*: Edward Cullinan Architects, 1 Baldwin Terrace, London N1 7RU. *Website*: http://ecarch.co.uk *Signs work*: "E.C." or "Edward Cullinan Architects."

CULMER, Matt, *Medium*: mainly paints outdoors. *b*: London, 15 Feb 1973. *Partner*: Liza. *Educ*: self taught. *Exhib*: various private and public exhibitions. *Works in collections*: private/corporate. *Address*: Sidmouth, Devon. *Email*: mattculmer@me.com *Website*: www.mattculmer.com *Signs work*: "M. CULMER".

CULVER, Cheryl Vivien, RBA(2003); PS(2004); Diploma in Art & Design, Fine Art; Willi Hoffman-Guth Award; Brian Sinfield Gallery Award; Henri Roche Pastel Award; Girault Pastel Award. *Medium*: pastel. *b*: Almondsbury, nr. Bristol, 12 Jan 1947. *d of*:

Frederick & Patricia Gould. *m*: John Culver. *Educ*: Thornbury Grammar School. *Studied*: Leicester Polytechnic/College of Art. *Exhib*: Mall Galleries with Pastel Society and RBA since 2001. Galleries across UK. *Works in collections*: private collections UK and abroad. *Commissions*: private. *Publications*: The Artist Magazine 2002*, The Pastel Journal, Cincinatti USA December 2008, The Artist Magazine March/April 2009*, The Artist Magazine March 2010*, Pratique des Arts Feature article October 2010, The Artist Magazine September, October and November 2010*, The Leisure Painter 2011, The Artist Magazine January, February and March 2012*, The Artist Magazine Sep 2013*. *These articles were created and written by Cheryl. 'Green Art; Trees, Roots and Leaves' by E Ashley Rooney. *Recreations*: walking. *Address*: 9 Stone Cross Lees Sandwich Kent CT13 0BZ. *Email*: cherylvculver@btinternet.com *Website*: www.cherylculverpaintings.com *Signs work*: 'Cheryl Culver'.

CUMING, Fred, ARCA, ARA (1969), RA (1974), NEAC, Hon ROI, Hon RBA; D.Litt Kent University (2004). *Medium*: oil. *b*: London, 16 Feb 1930. *m*: Audrey Lee. two *s*. *Studied*: Sidcup School of Art (1945-1949), RCA (1951-1955) under John Minton, Carel Weight, Rodrigo Moynihan, Ruskin Spear, Colin Hayes, Robert Buhler. *Represented by*: Manya Igel, London; Sinfield, Burford, Oxon; Adam Gallery, Bath. *Exhib*: UK, USA, Argentina, Ireland and Europe. *Works in collections*: RA, National Portrait Gallery, Canterbury, Scunthorpe, Preston, Eastbourne, Brighton, Hove, Salford, Monte Carlo, Worcester Coll., Oxford, St. John's Coll., Oxford, Lloyds of London, W.H.Smith, Farendon Trust, LWT, Nat. Trust Foundation for Art, University of Kent, etc., also USA and South America. *Publications*: Figure in the Landscape, Unicorn Press; video, The Art of Fred Cuming R.A., R.A. collection and "Atmosphere of Landscape, Fred Cuming". *Clubs*: Chelsea Art Club, Dover Art Club. *Address*: The Gables, Wittersham Rd., Iden, Rye, E. Sussex TN31 7UY. *Website*: www.fredcuming.com *Signs work*: "Cuming."

CUMMINGS, Albert Arratoon Runciman, UA (1973), FSA (Scot) (1973); painter in tempera, oil and water-colour, book illustrator, picture restorer. *b*: Edinburgh, 20 Aug 1936. *m*: Marjorie Laidlaw. one *s*. one *d*. *Educ*: Edinburgh. *Studied*: apprentice stage designer under William Grason, Edward Bowers, painting under Charles Napier, Robert Jardine. *Exhib*: UA, Scottish Gallery, Fine Art Soc., Edinburgh Gallery, Open Eye Gallery. *Works in collections*: Leeds Educ. authorities, Edinburgh Hospital Board. *Publications*: Dictionary of Scottish Art and Arch (Pub. Antique Collectors Club). *Clubs*: Scottish Arts. *Address*: 4 School Rd., Aberlady, E. Lothian.

CUMMINGS, Ann. *Medium*: painter in oil, pastel and egg tempera. *b*: Edinburgh, 12 Dec 1945. *d of*: Alexander Cummings (engineer). *m*: Dr. Laurie Jacobs, BSc, MBChB. three *s*. *Educ*: Stamford College (1989-91) and under Albert A.R. Cummings (1991-94). *Exhib*: Edinburgh, Glasgow, Dunkeld, Stamford, London, Eton and Peterborough. *Clubs*: Welland Art Soc. *Address*: Hollywell, 38 Church St., Werrington, Peterborough, Cambs. PE4 6QE. *Signs work*: "A.C."

CUMMINGS, George Reid, L. Bryne Waterman Award (1995) Boston, USA for work in preserving the history of the modern whaling industry. *Medium*: oil. *b*: Edinburgh, 11 May 1932. *m*: Mabel A. one *s*. one *d*. *Studied*: studied the use of oil painting by Joan Renton, RSA Edinburgh (1985). *Exhib*: RSMA (1988); permanent exhbns.: Kendall Whaling Museum, Sharon Boston, Massachusetts; Sandefjord Whaling Museum, Sandefjord, Norway; Tonsberg Maritime Museum, Tonsberg, Norway; Grytviken Whaling Museum, South Georgia, Falkland Islands; Chr. Salvesen plc., Edinburgh, Scotland. *Commissions*: from Sir Gerald Elliott, Past Chairman Chr. Salvesen plc., Sir Maxwell Harper Gow, and numerous private individuals worldwide. Specializes in recording accurate details of the modern whaling industry ships and general maritime art. Paintings are technically correct giving very accurate detail of the vessel painted for historic purposes. *Clubs*: Chairman Salvesen's ex Whalers Club, Edinburgh. *Address*: 19 Blackford Hill View, Edinburgh EH9 3HD. *Signs work*: "George R. Cummings, Edinburgh" and year completed.

CUMMINGS, Novette, BA (Hons) Visual Arts. *Medium*: Acrylic, Mixed media. *b*: England. *Studied*: University of London Goldsmiths. *Exhib*: Meiner Gallery (2009), Brighton Gallery, (1990), Royal Academy (2009), London College of Printing (1999/2000), Brixton Art Gallery (1985/86), Goldsmiths (1987), Whitechapel Open (1988). *Publications*: Summer Exhibition, Royal Academy. *Principal Works*: Tightly Packed. *Address*: 16 Leysfield Rd, London W12 9JF. *Website*: www.novettecummings.com Saatchi Gallery Online *Signs work*: "N. Cummings".

CUMMINS, Gus, RA (1992); NDD (1963), MA (RCA)(1967); Henry Moore Prize (London Group, 1982), 'Spirit of London' (Second Prize, 1983), Daler-Rowney Prize (RA, 1987), Hunting Group (First Prize : Mall Galleries1990, RCA1999), House and Garden Prize and Blackstone Award (RA, 1992), Royal Watercolour Society Prize (2001), Jack Goldhill Award for Sculpture (RA, 2005). *Medium*: oil, gouache, water-colour, sculpture. *b*: London, 28 Jan 1943. *m*: Angela Braven, painter. two *s*. one *d*. *Educ*: Sutton and Wimbledon Art School and RCA. *Exhib*: extensively, seven solo shows since 1990. Widely throughout the UK and in Norway, Holland, United Arab Emirates, USA, Ireland. *Works in collections*: RA, RCA, Contemporary Arts Soc., Towner Coll., Hastings Museum Coll., Hastings Library, Freshfields plc., FT Coll., House of Commons, A.T.Kearney (London & Chicago), National Trust, Costain plc, ICI. *Clubs*: Chelsea Arts, The Arts Club (Dover Street). *Address*: Harpsichord House, Cobourg Pl., Hastings, Sussex TN34 3HY. *Email*: gus@guscummins.com *Website*: guscummins.com *Signs work*: "Gus Cummins."

CUNNIFFE, Simon David, BA Joint Hons, PGCE. *Medium*: Oil, Drawing, Prints. *b*: Lincoln, 1974. *m*: Kelly. one *d*. *Studied*: De Montfort University, Leicester, Fine Art & History of Art (1996), Canterbury Christ Church University PGCE (1998). *Represented by*: artlondon.com. *Exhib*: Royal Academy Summer Exhibition 2007, Canterbury Festival 2008, William Harvey Hospital Fine Art, Horsebridge Gallery, Canterbury Musuem and Art Gallery, Hampshire Art Fair. *Works in collections*. Private/Corporate. *Commisions*: Corporate. *Misc*: Founding member of William Harvey Hospital Fine Art. *Address*: 11 Fordwich Rd, Sturry, Canterbury CT2 0BW. *Email*: cuniffes@towers.kent.sch.uk *Website*: www.artlondon.com *Signs work*: SIMON CUNIFFE.

CURLING, Peter Michael Napier, *Medium*: oil, watercolour, drawing. *b*: Waterford, 13 Jan 1955. *s of*: Edward & Norah Curling. *m*: Louise Curling. one *s*. two *d*. *Educ*: Stonyhurst & Millfield. *Studied*: Signorina Simi in Florence (1972-74), John Skeaping, RA (1975). *Exhib*: First one-man show in Lambourne aged 14. First exhibition at Combridges, Dublin (1972), London (1976) followed by regular exhibitions at Tryon Gallery; Kentucky USA; Saratoga; Cork Street, London (2003); Merrion Square, Dublin (2004); Studio exhibition on Co. Tipperary (2009). *Works in collections*: of numerous Irish collectors. *Commissions*: painted horse portraits of leading racehorses in Ireland, UK and USA but has not taken commissions for a number of years. *Publications*: 'The Owner', written and illustrated by Peter Curling; 'Hot Cherry' written by Marcus Armytage, illustr. by P. Curling. *Works Reproduced*: numerous limited edition prints since 1972. *Recreations*: country pursuits. *Clubs*: Kildare Street Club; Chelsea Arts Club; Turf Club. *Address*: Skehanagh, Goolds Cross, Cashel, Co. Tipperary, Ireland. *Email*: petercurling@eircom.net *Website*: www.petercurling.com *Signs work*: "P. CURLING".

CURRY, Denis Victor, Hon.RWA (2009); Dip.FA (Slade) painting (1950) sculpture (1951), RCA.(1992); Associate, Royal Aeronautical Society (1975); artist/scientist. *Medium*: oil, water-colour, bronze, stone, kinetic. *b*: Newcastle-on-Tyne, 11 Nov 1918. *m*: Jennifer Coram. *Educ*: Durham Johnson School. *Studied*: Durham - Architecture(Kremer), Slade School of Fine Art (Schwabe, Coldstream). *Exhib*: London

Group, RA, RWA, Slade Bi-Centenary, Oriel, Cardiff, Residency - sculpture, St. David's (1991), RCamA, Sculpture at Margam, National Eisteddfod (1994, 2003); many group and one-man shows U.K. and abroad. *Works in collections*: Pembrokeshire Museum and A.G., Tunnicliffe Museum, Anglesey, Chatsworth House, Contemporary Art Soc., Wales. *Commissions*: numerous public and private, inc. 2 x life-size bronze eagles, swans, horses, fig (Processional Cross). *Publications*: Poetry Wales, This Land is Our Land (B.M. Nat.Hist. 1989), Laying Out the Body (Seren 1992), R.Ae.Soc. Symposium - Man-powered Aircraft Group (1975) (Elected Associate 1975); own publication: Denis Curry Painting Sculpture Images (1985). *Principal Works*: initiation of thrust with a prototype human-powered ornithopter-cf. website. *Recreations*: research - wing kinetics in nature; judo; chess. *Address*: Fron, Llanycefn, Clynderwen, Pembrokeshire SA66 7XT. *Email*: curry2@totalserve.co.uk *Website*: www.humanpoweredwing.co.uk *Signs work*: "Denis Curry," "D. Curry" , "D.C." or "D.V.Curry".

CURSHAM, Juliet, SEqA; self taught sculptor in bronze of equestrian subjects, animals and figures; SEqA Sculptor Award. *Medium*: Bronze, Silver, Gold. *b*: Nottingham, 23 Aug 1960. *d of*: J.C. and E.J.Cursham., niece of Diccon Swan, portrait painter. *m*: Edward Packe-Drury-Lowe.. one *s* and one *s-s.* one *d. Exhib*: Van Dell Gallery, Palm Beach, Florida; Tryon Gallery, London; Osbourne Studio Gallery; Royal Hong Kong Jockey Club; Brandy Wine Polo Club, Pennsylvania; Newmarket Racecourse; Hong Kong Jockey Club, Beijing. *Works in collections*: Life-size horse and jockey for the Hong Kong Jockey Club; collections in America, Japan, Brunei, Canada. *Commissions*: Dancing Brave, Generous, Venture to Cognac, Ryadian, Best Mate, Aztec Warrior, numerous polo pony studies and life size bronze of the stallion Monsun and life size horse and jockey in Beijing; Life size of Silent Witness with Felix Coetsee Sha Tin racecourse, unveiled November 2009. *Principal Works*: Life size sculptures in Hong Kong, Beijing, Germany and at Prestwold Hall, Leicestershire. *Recreations*: hunting, gardening, eventing, skiing, polo. *Address*: Prestwold Hall, Loughborough, Leics. LE12 5SQ. *Email*: juliet@cursham.co.uk *Website*: www.cursham.co.uk *Signs work*: "Juliet Cursham."

CURTIS, Anthony Ewart, DipAE (Lond), RWA; experimental and landscape artist; served R.N. (1946-48); Mail Marketing International Prize (RWA, 2002); Hon. BSc Loughborough University. *Medium*: watercolour, gouache (often combined), oils. *b*: Wakefield, 7 Jul 1928. *s of*: G. E. and G. L. Curtis née Provis. *m*: Joyce Isabel Yates. three *s.* one *d. Educ*: Kingswood Grammar School, Loughborough (1948-50); London University (1974-76). *Studied*: Bath Academy, Corsham (1950-51, Potworowski, Scott, Armitage, Lanyon, Wynter). *Represented by*: Mark Barrow Fine Art, Griffiths Road, Wimbledon SW19 1SP. *Exhib*: (1952-): Redfern, Zwemmers, Daily Express Young Painters, London Group, R.W.A. (1952 to date), Arts Council Modern Stained Glass (1960-61), R.I. (1983), R.W.S. (1984), 'Migraine Images' at St. Martin-in-the-Fields (1993). One-man shows include Bear Lane, Oxford (1959), Reading (1961), Cookham (1964), R.W.A. (1995); ceramic sculpture: Scopas, Henley (1975), Century, Henley (1980), Recent and Retrospective Work, Bloomsbury Gallery, University of London (1987), Retrospective shows 'Recollections', Wooburn Festival (1992); Australian Works, Methuen Gallery, R.W.A. (1995), Art on Paper Fair, R.C.A. (Julian Lax, 2000-2004), British Art Fair (Julian Lax, 2001-2004), Bucks 21 Group (2001-3, later resigning); Mark Barrow Fine Art (2006 to date). *Works in collections*: RWA, Bristol Educ. Com., sand-blasted screen, St. Andrew's, Hatter's Lane, High Wycombe. *Works Reproduced*: Young Artists of Promise (1957); contributor: A Celebration of Bath Academy of Art at Corsham. Entry in 'Artists in Britain since 1945'. *Clubs*: FPS ('50s-'70s - lapsed membership). *Misc*: Working visits to Australia (1988-89); Oregon, USA.(1990, 1993), S.Africa (1996, 2000, 2002). *Address*: 11 Meysey Close, Meysey Hampton, Glos., GL7 5LL. *Signs work*: "Anthony Curtis," ("AC" on small works).

CURTIS, David Jan Gardiner, ROI (1988), RSMA (1983); artist in oil and water-colour. *b*: Doncaster, 15 Jun 1948. *s of*: Arthur Gardiner Curtis, writer. *Partner*: Susan Scott. one *s*. *Educ*: Doncaster Grammar School. *Represented by*: Richard Hagen Ltd, Yew Tree House, Broadway, Worcs. 01386 853624 *Exhib*: RA, RSMA, RI, RWS, RBA, NEAC ROI, RP Singer Friedlander/Sunday Times water-colour competition 1st prizewinner (1992), 2nd prizewinner (1997). *Works in collections*: Doncaster Museum and A.G., Ferens Gallery, Hull, Sultanate of Oman, Rockefeller Institute, New York, Cusworth Hall Museum, Doncaster; Pannect Museum, Whitby. *Commissions*: Include: HM Crown Commissioners, Cavalry & Guards Club, Piccadilly, Duke of Lancaster's Regiment - Official painting H.M. The Queen, Presentation of the Colours 2008. *Publications*: author, A Light Touch - The Landscape in Oils and The Landscape in Water-colour - a Personal View and films of the same titles; also 'Light effects in Water-colour' (video) 1997. Author: 'Light and Mood in Watercolour' (2005) and DVD (same title) 2005. Author: 'Capturing the Moment in Oils' (2007) and film of the same title; 'Paiting with Impact' and film of same title 2009; 'Painting on Location' and film of the same title (2013). *Address*: Gibdyke House, Gibdyke, Misson, Doncaster, S. Yorks. DN10 6EL. *Email*: david@djcurtis.co.uk *Website*: www.djcurtis.co.uk *Signs work*: "D.J. Curtis."

CURTIS, Joyce, DipAE (Lond.); artist and children's book illustrator in water-colour, gouache, oil, pencil; former Organiser (S.Bucks.), Bucks. Art Week Visual Images Group. *b*: Sulhamstead, 5 Aug 1934. *d of*: H.J. Yates. *m*: Anthony Curtis. three *s*. one *d*. *Educ*: Faringdon Grammar School; Post-grad. Dip., London (1985-86). *Studied*: Bath Academy of Art, Corsham (1952-54, Potworowski, Litz Pisk, Frost, Meadows, Armitage, Ellis). *Exhib*: solo shows, Dixon Gallery, University of London (1986), Corsham (1990), High Wycombe Museum (1993); three joint exhbns. with husband; mixed shows including R.W.A. *Publications*: contributor: A Celebration of Bath Academy of Art at Corsham. *Address*: 11 Meysey Close, Meysey Hampton, Glos., GL7 5LL. *Signs work*: "Joyce Curtis."

CURTIS, Roger, NDD (1965), ATD (1966); painter in oil, watercolour and acrylic; paints beaches, harbours and landscapes of the far South-West of Cornwall, has also painted in Italy and New Zealand. *Medium*: oil, acrylic, watercolour. *b*: Birmingham, 9 Apr 1945. *m*: Christine. one *s*. one *d*. *Educ*: George Dixon Grammar School.. *Studied*: Birmingham College of Art and Design (1961-1965). *Exhib*: various group exhibs. including RI, RSMA and RWA; currently at a number of small galleries in the West Country and London. *Works in collections*: The National Collection, and private collections in Britain, USA, Europe, Japan, New Zealand and Australia. *Official Purchasers*: Wellingborough Council. *Clubs*: St. Ives Society of Artists. *Address*: 2 Coombe Vale, Newlyn, Cornwall TR18 5QU. *Signs work*: "ROGER CURTIS".

CURTISS-FULLER, Merrie Fleur Blaker, BA Fine Art, MA Fine Art; Winner of 3rd Prize, Winsor & Newton Young Artist of the Year, ROI (2002); Winner of the Winsor & Newton Young Artist Award, SWA (2007). *Medium*: oil, watercolour, drawing, prints. *b*: Maidstone, 31 Jul 1981. *d of*: Peter. *m*: Simon Dadd. *Studied*: Christchurch University, Canterbury, Kent (2002-2005). *Exhib*: Royal Institute of Painters in Watercolours (2009, 2008, 2007); The Women's Art Show, Fairfields Art Centre (2009, 2007); Society of Women Artists (2008, 2007, 2010); Royal Watercolour Society (2008, 2011); Royal Society of British Artists (2000); Royal Institute of Oil Painters (2004, 2002, 2001); Discerning Eye (2004, 2003), Royal Society of Portrait Painters (2012). *Works in collections*: Maidstone Museum. *Commissions*: private commissions/portrait commissions. *Address*: 31 Sandling Lane, Maidstone, Kent, ME14 2HS. *Email*: merriecf@yahoo.co.uk *Website*: www.merriecf.com *Signs work*: "MCF".

CUTHBERT, Rosalind, RWA (1998); MA (RCA)(1977); BP Portrait Award (National Portrait Gallery, 1981, 2nd Prize); painter-engraver in gouache, oils, mixed media and wood engraving. *b*: Weston-super-Mare, 1951. *d of*: Rev L.V. & Mrs D. Payne. *m*: David. one *d. Studied*: Central School of Art and Design (1971-74), RCA (1974-77). *Exhib*: mainly in the South-West and London, also France and USA. *Works in collections*: NPG, National Poetry Library, National Art Library (V&A), Contemporary Art Soc. *Commissions*: various portraits and other commissions. *Publications*: Founded Yellow Fox Press (1993). Publish handmade books of poetry and wood engravings: 'Islands' (1993), 'Birdsong and Water' (1994), 'Nature Studies' (1995), 'Bouncing Boy' (1999), 'HLEP!' (2001). *Principal Works*: portrait of Cecil Collins at the Central School of Art 1983. *Clubs*: R.W.A., Fine Press Book Assoc. *Address*: Winscombe Farm Studio, Parsons Way, Winscombe, N. Somerset BS25 1BT. *Email*: roscuthbert@hotmail.com *Website*: www.roscuthbert.co.uk

CUTLER, Sally Ann, BA (Hons) Graphic Design/Illustration. *Medium*: prints. *b*: Buckinghamshire, 1969. *Studied*: Liverpool - John Moores University 1988-1991. *Represented by*: Southbank Printmakers Gallery, London. *Exhib*: Royal Society of Portrait Painters, Mall Gallery (2007-2012); 5th, 6th & 7th International Mini Print Exhibition (2004-10); Royal Academy Summer Exhibition (2006, 2007, 2012, 2013); Southampton City Art Gallery (2007); Bite/Originals, Mall Gallery (2005-07, 2010-11); Society of Wood Engravers (2011-12); Discerning Eye (2010). *Works in collections*: National Library of Wales; Milly Althorp Collection, Barnet; Ashmolean Museum, Oxford; private collections. *Commissions*: Tate Gallery, Liverpool; BBC. *Misc*: Art teacher at Dulwich Picture Gallery since 2000. *Address*: 25a Gairloch Road, London SE5 8NG. *Website*: www.southbank-printmakers.com *Signs work*: "SALLY CUTLER".

CZERWINKE, Tadeusz, NDD (1957), ATC (1973), SPS (1976), DAE (1981); sculptor, carver, modeller and potter in stone, wood, perspex, bronze and terracotta; Head of Arts and Crafts Dept., Shoeburyness Comprehensive School. *b*: Poland, 19 May 1936. *s of*: Sylvester Czerwinke, industrial thermal design engineer. *m*: Ewa. one *s*. one *d. Educ*: St. Peter's Winchester. *Studied*: Winchester School of Arts and Crafts (1957, Norman Pierce, FRBS). *Exhib*: regularly at SPS, Mall Galleries, Federation of British Artists, APA in GB., Salon des Nations, Paris; one-man portrait sculpture exhbn. Posk Gallery (1987) and at the Polish Hearth, London. *Works in collections*: Church of Czestochowa, Huddersfield; Kosciuszko Museum, Rappersville, Switzerland; St. Peter's Hinkley, Leics.; Les Laurents, Dordogne, France; St. Catherine's Dock, London; Our Lady of Lourdes Convent, Kent; Town Hall, Monte Cassino, Italy; Parish Church, Devonia Rd., London; St. Sebastian & John the Baptist, Preston; Andrzej Bobola Church, London; Memorial, Eaton Pl., London; General Sikorski Museum, London; Memorial, Marshal J. Pilsudzki Inst., London; Posk (Centre of Polish Culture, London); Dom Narodowca, London; S. Michalowski, Shute House, nr. Honiton; sculptures and portraits in private collections in U.K. and overseas. *Address*: 20 Whitehouse Way, Southgate, London N14 7LT. *Signs work*: "Tad. Czerwinke."

D

D'AGUILAR, Michael, gold, silver and bronze medals, Royal Drawing Soc., Armitage and silver medal, R.A. (1949); artist in oil and pastels. *b*: London, 11 May, 1922. *Educ*: privately and in Spain, Italy and France. *Studied*: RA Schools under Henry Rushbury, RA, Fleetwood-Walker, ARA, William Dring, RA (1948-53). *Exhib*: RA, RBA, NEAC, Irving Galleries, Gimpel Fils, Leicester Galleries, Young Contemporaries; one-man shows, Gimpel Fils, Irving Galleries, New Grafton Gallery, Bruton St. Gallery (annually), Redfern Gallery. *Publications*: work repro.: Artist, Studio, La Revue Moderne des Arts; articles in Diario de Tarragona. *Clubs*: Chelsea Arts, Arts Dover St., London Sketch, Reynolds. *Address*: Studio 4, Chelsea Farm House, Milmans Street, London SW10 0DW. *Signs work*: "M. D'Aguilar."

D'AGUILAR, Paul, artist in oil, water-colour; 1st prize for drawing at RA Schools (1949); gold, silver and bronze medals, RDS. *b*: London, 9 Sep 1927. *Educ*: privately in

Spain, Italy and France. *Studied*: RA Schools (1948-53) and with Prof. Barblain (Siena). *Exhib*: RA, Redfern, Young Contemporaries, Leicester Galleries, Daily Express Young Artists, RBA, NEAC, Sindicato de Iniciativa (Spain), Irving Gallery (1952), Temple Gallery (1960), New Grafton, Canaletto (1971), Southwell Brown Gallery (1974), Langton Gallery (1973, 1976); Carlyle Gallery, Old Church St., Chelsea (April/May 2003), The Dover Street Arts Club (2008). *Works in collections*: Lord Rothermere. *Works Reproduced*: in Artist, Studio, Collins Magazine, La Revue Moderne, Drawing Nudes (Studio Vista). *Clubs*: The Arts Club, 40 Dover Street. *Address*: 11 Sheen Gate Gdns., London SW14 7PD. *Signs work*: "P. D'Aguilar."

D'AMOUR, Viola, art nouveau co-collaborator with Vlad Quigley; model and ballerina. *Educ*: Charterhouse, Orpington College. *Exhib*: pop art nouveau portraits of Viola D'Amour, Vampyria, Damned US tour Ad2000, The Big Draw, Vampire Viola, Shock/Anglo-French Aubrey Beardsley centenary. *Publications*: Viola D'Amour, Viola D'Amour's Phantom Sword, Evlalie, Vampire Viola, Varney the Vampyre, 21st. Century Ghouls, Viola and the Vampires, Crimson, Demeter, Betty and the Boobies; advertising, catwalk, films, T.V. *Address*: c/o 276a Lower Addiscombe Rd., Croydon, Surrey CR0 7AE. *Signs work*: "Viola D'Amour."

D'ARBELOFF, Natalie, painter, printmaker, book-artist, writer. *b*: Paris, 7 Aug 1929. divorced. *d of*: Alexandre d'Arbeloff, Prince (Russian). *Educ*: Marymount School, NY. *Studied*: Art Students' League, NY, Central School of Art, London. *Exhib*: numerous group shows; solo shows include: Museum Fine Arts, Colorado Springs, Camden Arts Centre, Victoria & Albert Museum, Rijksmuseum, Meermano-Westreenianum, The Hague. *Works in collections*: V&A, Manchester Polytechnic Library, Library of Congress, Washington DC, NY Public Library, Harvard, Princeton, Newberry Library, Humanities Research Center, Austin, National Library, Australia, and many more. *Commissions*: murals: Asuncion, Paraguay and London. *Publications*: Creating in Collage (Studio Vista), An Artist's Workbook (Studio Vista), Designing with Natural Forms (Batsford), Livres d'Artiste (own NdA Press), Augustine's True Confession, The Augustine Adventures. *Address*: c/o Society of Design Craftsmen, 24 Rivington St., London EC2A 3DU.

D'ARCY HUGHES, Ann, NDD Graphic Design; Industrial Arts Scholarship, Coventry; Lucy Clayton Travelling Scholarship; Slade Fine Art Bk.Ass. Illustration Award 1st Prize (2004); lecturer in Printmaking University of Brighton. *Medium*: prints. *b*: Paignton, 19 May 1945. one *s*. one *d*. *Studied*: Lanchester College of Art, Coventry; Brighton School of Art; Atelier 17 Paris; assistant Anthony Gross for Slade School University of London for 4 years. *Works in collections*: University of London, University of Sussex, University of Brighton, Xerox , BBC. *Commissions*: 70-minute video for the Open College of Arts; Hay Management: Drawing for Westminster Hall Conference. *Publications*: University of Brighton: Technical booklet on Lithography to go with Art Video. *Misc*: founder and co-director of Brighton Independent Printmaking (BIP) 5 yrs, a fine art, open access printmaking workshop. *Address*: 13 Hampstead Road, Brighton BN1 5NG. *Email*: bip@brightonprintmaking.co.uk *Website*: brightonprintmaking.co.uk

D'VATZ, Timur, Guinness Prize for 'First Time Exhibitor' at Royal Academy of Arts Summer Exhbn, London 1994; A.T. Kearney Prize - Degree Show Royal Academy of Arts 1996. *Medium*: painter in oil. *b*: Russia, 16 Apr 1968. *Educ*: Lycee in Tashkent. *Studied*: Republican College of Art, Tashkent, Uzbekistan (1983-87); Post-Grad Royal Academy Schools (1993-96), awarded Jack Goldhill Scholarship. *Exhib*: Cadogan Contemporary, London (2000, 2002); Bruton Street Gallery (2001), BP Portrait Award (2002), National Portrait Gallery, London, Aberdeen Art Gallery, Scotland (2002). *Works in collections*: Tretyakov National Gallery, Moscow: Guinness PLC, in private collections in UK, USA, Russia. *Commissions*: 1994 - work commisssioned by Guinness PLC; private commissions.

Publications: illsutrations for 'The Resurrection of the Body' by Maggie Hamand (Penguin Books Ltd.). *Works Reproduced*: by Senecio Editions. *Clubs*: Royal Academy Schools - Alumni Association (Reynolds Club). *Address*: 84 Galloway Road, London W12 0PJ. *Email*: timur.d'vatz@virgin.net

DACK, Richard, DipAD (Hons); BEd (Hons); ATD; Worshipful Company of Shipwrights Award; Maimeri Award. *Medium*: oil, prints. *b*: 27 Sep 1944. *Educ*: Lowestoft County Grammar School. *Studied*: Camberwell School of Art (1963-67); Reading University ('67-68); Sussex University (1974-75). *Represented by*: Coves Quay Gallery, Salcombe; Buckeham Galleries, Southwold. *Exhib*: RA, RSMA, RWA, NEAC, ROI, Llewellyn Alexander, Messums. *Works in collections*: Worshipful Company of Shipwrights; many private collections. *Commissions*: several undertaken privately. *Publications*: 'An Affair with the Sea': The Artist (Aug 2005). *Address*: 12 Mirbecks Close, Worlingham, Beccles NR34 7RS. *Signs work*: 'R.Dack'.

DACK, Tom, artist in water-colour, oils, gouache, pastel and line, specialises in marine, aviation and landscape, as well as industrial scenes of the north east, particularly mining subjects; 'Classic Boat' Award, RSMA 2004 Open Exhbn. Mall Galleries, London. *b*: Newcastle Upon Tyne, 26 May 1933. *m*: Catherine. one *s*. one *d*. *Studied*: Newcastle College of Art and Industrial Design. *Exhib*: solo shows; Patricia Wells Gallery (Bristol), Oddfellows, Kendal, Darlington A.G., Trinity Maritime Centre, Newcastle, Bryam Gallery, Huddersfield, South Shields Art Gallery, Durham Light Infantry Museum and Gallery, Durham, Sally Port Gallery, Berwick-on-Tweed, Osborne Gallery, Corbridge on Tyne. Participated: 'Journal Open, Newcastle; RSMA Open Exhbn, Mall Galleries, London. *Works in collections*: South Shields Museum & Art Gallery, and Tyne & Wear Museums. *Commissions*: Several private. *Publications*: 'Oil Paintings in Public Ownership in Tyne & Wear Museum', 'The Artists of Northumbria' - Marshall Hall. *Official Purchasers*: Tyne & Wear Museums. *Recreations*: reading, classical music. *Address*: 13 Selwyn Ave., Whitley Bay, Tyne & Wear NE25 9DH. *Email*: tomdack21@yahoo.co.uk *Website*: northeastaartcollective.com *Signs work*: 'Tom Dack'.

DAINES, Deirdre, NEAC; RA Silver medal, bronze medal and Greenshields Award, RA Cert, Eric Kennington prize for drawing, Winsor and Newton prize; painter in oil drawing and pastel, mainly figure paintings; teacher; etchings, portrait commissions. *b*: Ware, 2 May 1950. *d of*: Laurie Daines. *Educ*: Tottenham High Grammar School. *Studied*: RA Schools (1970-73, Peter Greenham). *Exhib*: New Grafton, RA Summer Exhbn., RP, Agnew's, Watermans, Petley Fine Art, Cork Street; one-man shows, Thos. Agnew (1988), Cale Art (1982), one-man show Royal Academy's School 1981. *Works in collections*: Guinness, Nuffield Trust, Pole Carew, Bonham Carter. *Commissions*: Studio 3, Muspole Workshops, Muspole St, Norwich. *Address*: 114, Desmond Drive, Old Catton, Norwich, Norfolk. *Signs work*: "Daines."

DAKAKNI, Susan Marie Thérèse, (nee QUINE); PS (2003); Frank Herring Award, Pastel Society (2002); Hon. Mention for The Founder Presidents Honour (SBA, 2003); Purcell Paper Award, Pastel Society (2012). *Medium*: pastel and charcoal. *b*: Calcutta, India, 17 Sep 1934. *d of*: Mr John & Rita Quine. *m*: Matt Dakakni. one *s*. *Studied*: Regent Street Polytechnic (1951-53); Central School of Arts and Crafts (1953-55). *Exhib*: Pastel Society Annual; Society of Wildlife Artists; Society of Botanical Artists; Westminster Gallery; Mercer Art Gallery, Harrogate; Alresford Gallery, Hants; St.Davids Hall Gallery, Cardiff; Southampton City Art Gallery; The Watercolour and Drawing Exhibition, London; group exhbns abroad and locally in Surrey and Sussex. *Commissions*: private, portraiture. *Publications*: article in Artist Magazine, March 2010 by Ken Gofton; article in "Making a Mark" review by artist & writer Katherine Tyrrell for PS exhibition 2011. *Clubs*: Sussex County Arts Club Brighton & ASA Horsham. *Misc*: taught part-time-Lincoln School of

Art; worked in a commercial art studio in London for a number of years. *Address*: 'Carmel Cottage', 33 Church Street, Steyning, W.Sussex, BN44 3YB. *Website*: www.susandakakni.com *Signs work*: 'S Dakakni'.

DALBY, Claire, RWS, RE, SWE.; Vice-Pres. RWS (1994-98); E.T.Greenshields Schol. (1962), D.Murray Studentship (1966); J Smythies Prize for Botanical Illustration (1994); Shackleton Schol to paint Landscapes in Falkland Is. (2000); *Medium*: watercolour, wood-engraving. *b*: St. Andrews, 20 Nov 1944. *d of*: Charles Longbotham, RWS. *m*: D. H. Dalby, PhD. *Educ*: Haberdashers' Aske's Girls' School Acton. *Studied*: City and Guilds of London Art School (1964-67). *Exhib*: RA, RWS, RE SWE, RWS regularly. Solo exhibitions London (1981, 1982. 1988), Lerwick, Shetland (1988, 1991, 1995, 2000). Numerous group exhibitions all over UK also Sweden, Australia, US. *Works in collections*: Fitzwilliam Museum, Cambridge; many private collections worldwide. *Commissions*: four wild plants for Surrey CC's Norbury Park Project (1996), "Charity" rose for National Gardens Scheme (1997). *Publications*: "Claire Dalby's Picture Book" (Carr, Kettering 1989); Wallcharts: "Lichens and Air Pollution" , "Lichens on Rocky Seashores" (Natural History Museum, London, 1981, 1987); "Shetland Lichens" with D.H.Dalby (Shetland Heritage Publications, 2005). *Official Purchasers*: Ashmolean Mus., Oxford; Natural History Mus., London; National Museums and Galleries of Wales, Cardiff; Shetland Mus., Lerwick, Hunt Institute for Botanical Documentation, Pittsburgh, USA. *Works Reproduced*: 'Women Engravers' by P.Jaffé (Virago Press, London 1988); 'An Engravers Globe' by Simon Brett (Primrose Hill Press, London 2000); 'Voyages of Discovery' by Tony Rice (Scriptum Editions London 1999); 'The Watercolour Expert' (Cassell Illustrated, London 2004). *Address*: 2 West Park, Stanley, Perthshire PH1 4QU.*Signs work*: 'Claire Dalby'.

DALE, Tom, DA (1958), HRMS, HSF; artist in water-colour. *b*: Greenock, 23 Jun 1935. *m*: Myra. two *d*. *Exhib*: Glasgow School of Art. *Works in collections*: private in Europe and N.America. *Address*: Woodbourne House, West Shepton, Shepton Mallet, Som. BA4 5UN. *Signs work*: "Dale."

DALRYMPLE, Neil, DipAD (1971), ATC (1972), SWLA, FBA; ceramic sculptor. *b*: 16 Jun 1949. one *s*. three *d*. *Educ*: Cardiff University (1971-1972), post grad. *Studied*: Loughborough College of Art and Design (1968-1971). *Represented by*: Compton Cassey Gallery, Withington, Cheltenham, Glos. *Exhib*: Mall Galleries, Nigel Stacey Marks Fine Art Gallery, Perth, Henry Brett Gallery, Stow-on-the-Wold, Slimbridge Wildfowl and Wetlands Trust, Glos. *Works in collections*: Canada Art Bank, Greater Victoria Art Gallery, Nature in Art, Wallworth Hall. *Commissions*: numerous, incl. Salmon and Trout Assoc., Atlantic Salmon Trust, two life size salmon presented to Orri Vibusson by HRH Prince Charles. *Clubs*: SWLA. *Address*: 20 Maes-y-Dre, Ruthin, Denbighshire LL15 1DB. *Website*: www.neildalrymple.com *Signs work*: "Neil Dalrymple."

DANGOOR, Linda, MA Honours Graphic Design; London Certificate in Painting. *Medium*: Drawing; ceramic sculpture; mixed media painting. *b*: Baghdad, Iraq, 4 Jun 1949. *Studied*: Byam Shaw (1969-71); Central School of Art (1971-73); Central School (1979-80); Professional Development Diploma (Ceramics). *Exhib*: Galleri Herder (1971); Gallery 5, London (1976); Ateliers d'Art (1986, 1990); Affordable Art Fair (2000); Patricia Fairfield (2000); Gallery 27, Cork Street (2001); Robert Phillips Gallery (2002); Gavin Graham (2002); 54 The Gallery (2008); Art in Action (2010, 2011, 2012); The Gallery London (2011). Publications: Ceramic Review (2010). *Recreations*: Photography; cooking. *Misc*: Have written a cookery book, "Flavours of Babylon". *Address*: 18-19 Kingsgate Workshops, 116 Kingsgate Road, London NW6 2JG. *Email*: lindadangoor@gmail.com *Website*: www.lindadangoor.com *Signs work*: "LD".

DANIELLS, Derek Howard, Daler Rowney Painting Award, RBA Exhibition, Mall Galleries, Londond 2009; Member of The Wapping Group of Artists. *Medium*: oil, pastel, acrylic. *b*: Stony Stratford, 22 Nov 1949. *m*: Caroline Daniells. one *s*. *Studied*: self taught. *Represented by*: various galleries (see below). *Exhib*: W.H. Patterson Fine Art, London; Oakham Gallery, London; John Noott Gallery; Royall Fine Art, Tunbridge Wells; Hawker Gallery, Amersham; Island Fine Art, IOW. Mall Galleries, London regularly with: RBA, ROI & Wapping Group of Artists. *Works in collections*: Henrietta Duchess of Bedford; Dr. Vijay Mallya. *Publications*: Personal Impressions - The Work of Derek Daniells; Contributed to several books and many magazine articles both in the UK and abroad. *Works Reproduced*: many works reproduced in books and magazines worldwide. *Clubs*: Wapping Group of Artists. *Address*: 71 Clarence Road, Stony Stratford, Milton Keynes MK11 1JF. *Email*: cdl.daniells@sky.com *Website*: www.derekdaniells.co.uk *Signs work*: "Derek Daniells".

DANIELS, Alfred, RWS, RBA, ARCA; Prizes: Lord Mayor's Award 1966, Spirit of London 1979-80-81, De Lazio Medal; Knapping Prize Football and the Fine Arts Lord Mayors Award Spirit of London Exhibition 1979, 1980, 1983. *Medium*: watercolour, acrylic, alkyd, oil. *b*: London, 8 Oct 1924. *s of*: Samuel Daniels. *m*: Margot Hamilton Hill ARCA. *Educ*: George Greens School. *Studied*: Woolwich Polytechnic, Royal College of Art. *Exhib*: RA, Rona Gallery, Mall Gallery, Bankside Gallery, Manya Igel Fine Arts, Russel Gallery, Gimpel Fils, Zwemmer Gallery, ICA Gallery, Redfern Gallery, Whitechapel Art Gallery. *Works in collections*: Cambridgeshire Educ. Com., Leicester Educ. Com., Leeds University, Nottingham Museum, Guildhall Museum, Graves Gallery, Tate Gallery. *Commissions*: Hammersmith Town Hall, British Rail, O.U.P., St. Fergus Gas Terminal, Shell Oil, Glaxo, British Transport Training School, Wembley, Mercantile Credit Bank, London; triptych, St.Nicholas Church, Rotherfield, Greys, Henley, Oxford University Press. *Publications*: Drawing and Painting (1961), Drawing Made Simple (1963), Enjoying Acrylics (1975), Painting with Acrylics (1988). *Official Purchasers*: Nuffield Foundation; GLC. *Works Reproduced*: Studio International, The Artist, Art and Artists, R.A. Illustrated, Arts Review, Nuffield Foundation, The Times. *Recreations*: drawing. *Clubs*: Langham. *Misc*: elected Keeper of the RBA, 1992. *Address*: 24 Esmond Rd., London W4 1JQ. *Signs work*: "Alfred Daniels."

DANIELS, Jase, BA Hons Animation; Award: South West Undergraduate Animator of the Year (Royal Television Society). *Medium*: illustration, mixed media, drawings, prints, sculpture, animation, Sound Art. *b*: UK. *Educ*: Helston Community College. *Studied*: Surrey Institute of Art & Design; Cornwall College. *Exhib*: Conway Hall, London (2012, with FoolishPeople). *Commissions*: "How to Become a Guitar Player from Hell", Jason Earls; "Kim Chi Flying Fish", D.W.Green; "Princess Crocodile", D.W.Green; "This City is Alive" with Forrest Armstrong; "Undermind" , Martin Heaviside; "The Village Tales of Fekenham Swarberry 1-3", Russell C.J. Duffy; "Virulant Experience" FoolishPeople. *Publications*: The Swallows Tail - Cover Art; Bust Down the Door and Eat All the Chickens - Cover Art; "The Grubby End" by Jase Daniels (pub. Crossing Chaos/Enigmatic Ink, www.crossingchaos.com); Trespass Magazine 'Americana' issue (2009); contributes to 'Discharge Art Blog/collective'. *Works Reproduced*: Artwork and composition for 'Vomitus Skink'. *Recreations*: musician, wrestling cats, zooming on my scooter. *Misc*: available for commissioned work. *Address*: Reading, UK. *Email*: jason2019@hotmail.com *Website*: www.jasedanielsart.com. *Signs work*: "J.Daniels".

DARBISHIRE, Stephen John, B.Ed (1971), RBA (1983); painter in oil, water-colour, pastel. *b*: Greenodd, Cumbria, 9 Dec 1940. *s of*: Dr. Stephen Bright Darbishire. *m*: Kerry Delius. two *d*. *Educ*: Ulverston Grammar School, Cumbria. *Studied*: Byam Shaw School of Art (1958-59). *Exhib*: RA, RBA, RP, RIO, NEAC, Richard Hagen Gallery, Broadway. *Works Reproduced*: as limited editions, open editions, greetings cards, etc. *Address*: Agnes

Gill, Whinfell, Kendal, Cumbria LA8 9EJ. *Email*: stephen@stephen-darbishire.com *Website*: www.stephen-darbishire.com *Signs work*: "Stephen J. Darbishire," "Darbishire".

DARBY, Philip, self taught artist in oil. *Medium*: oil. *b*: Birmingham, 14 Jun 1938. *s of*: Wilfred Darby. *m*: Susan. two *s*. *Exhib*: Newlyn Orion, Penwith Soc., Galerie Artica, Cuxhaven, Germany, RWA, Polka.Gallery, Exeter. *Works in collections*: Open University. *Address*: Flat 6, 36 Morab Road, Penzance, Cornwall TR18 4EX. *Signs work*: "Phil Darby."

DARLOW, Les, City & Guilds, Technical & Scientific Illustrations. *Medium*: pastel, oil, watercolour, drawing, print. *b*: Blackpool, 22 Jun 1961. *m*: Karen. three *s*. *Educ*: Warbreck High School, Palatine Art College. *Studied*: Palatine and Fylde College, Blackpool (1980-83). *Exhib*: Grundy Art Gallery. *Commissions*: Worldwide. Various. *Publications*: Leisure Painter (July 2014). *Clubs*: Member of Northern Artists Group. *Misc*: Specialises in teaching Pastel and Pastel techniques. *Address*: 43 Plovers Way, Blackpool, Lancashire FY3 8FD. *Email*: lesdarlow@sky.com *Website*: www.lesdarlow.com *Signs work*: "Les Darlow".

DARTON WATKINS, Christopher, MA (Oxon) (1951); painter in oil, wax, collage and mixed media; British Open Painting Competition, Arnolfini Gallery Bristol (2nd Prize). *b*: Hants., 1928. *s of*: Ricard Watkins, sculptor. *m*: Torun. one *s*. *Educ*: Ampleforth College and Oxford. *Studied*: Ruskin School of Art, and privately. *Exhib*: Bear Lane Gallery, Oxford, Arnolfini Gallery, Bristol, Gallery Aix, Stockholm, Seifert-Binder Gallery, Munich, Alwin Gallery, London, Indar Pasricha Fine Art, Anthony Dawson Fine Art, Edwin Pollard Gallery, David Curzon Gallery, Gerard Peters Gallery, Santa Fe, Original A.G., Båstad, Sweden, Galleri Tersaeus, Stockholm Art & Form, Stockholm, Sweden. *Works in collections*: Linacre and Hertford Colleges, Oxford, Liverpool University, Royal Hospital, Chelsea, S.N.E.E., Lisbon, Soc. of Apothecaries, Stockholm, Svenska Handsbanken, Stockholm, Charterhouse Bank, London. *Commissions*: received a Pollock Krasner Foundation Award, N.Y., USA. *Clubs*: L'Association Internationale des Arts Plastiques, UNESCO. *Address*: No.1 Dawes Cottages, Putney Bridge Road, London SW15 2PR. *Website*: www.dartonwatkins.com *Signs work*: "C. Darton Watkins."

DARWIN, Thomas Gerard, FRBS (1978), B.Ed. (1976); sculptor in resins and metal powders. *b*: Standish, Lancs., 10 Jun 1928. *s of*: Thomas Darwin, coal miner. *m*: Marie Agnes (decd.), remarried Bridget. three *s*. two *d*. *Educ*: St. Peter's College, Freshfield. *Studied*: St. Mary's College, Strawberry Hill (1951-53, L. de C. Bucher, KSS, ARCA), Wigan School of Art (1955-57, Woffenden). *Exhib*: one-man show: Rural and Industries Bank, Perth, WA; numerous joint shows. *Works in collections*: Several religious works in churches and schools in England and Australia, busts in private collections and public places in Swaziland and Australia. *Commissions*: Monument (Warrior and Maiden), Manzini, Swaziland; Bust of Queen Labotsibeni for King Sobhuza of Swaziland; Bust of Blessed Mary Mackillop for Pope Benedict XVI. *Principal Works*: Stations of the Cross for St. Mary's Cathedral, Perth, Australia. *Address*: Ezulwini, 34 Croyden Rd., Roleystone, WA 6111. Australia. *Email*: t.gdarwin@bigpond.com.au *Signs work*: "G. Darwin."

DAVID-COHEN, Yael, BA. *Medium*: painting in mixed media on found fabric, printmaking, artists books. *b*: Jerusalem, 28 Apr 1942. *s of*: Joseph and Thea David. *m*: Dr. S.L.Cohen. three *d*. *Educ*: University of Tel Aviv. *Studied*: Tel Aviv School of Art; St.Martin's School of Art. *Exhib*: selected solo: Institute of Education, London (1982, 86, 87, 90), Jerusalem Theatre, Jerusalem, Israel (1992, 95), The Coningsby Gallery, London (1997, 2000, 02, 04), Galerie Le Cocon, Hamburg, Germany (2007); since 1983, group exhibitions worldwide. *Works in collections*: Victoria and Albert Museum, British Museum (prints), British Library, Museum of Art and Design New York, Museum of Fine Art Philadelphia. *Publications*: Book of Ruth (Limited Edition). *Official Purchasers*: Book of Ruth (Yale University, British Library, National Library of Israel, JTS New York, Hebrew

Union College Cincinnatti). *Principal Works*: "Sightline" - USA. *Address*: 175 West Heath Road, London NW3 7TT. *Email*: mail@simonyael.co.uk *Website*: www.yaeldc.co.uk

DAVIDSON, Jennifer Ann, BA (Hons) Fine Art; won several 'Best Landscape' awards in National Competitions; finalist in Laing Art Competition. *Medium*: acrylic, pastel, mixed media. *b*: Stanmore, Middlesex, 2 Oct 1938. *d of*: Frank and Nora Nelson. *Partner*: Peter Johnston. one *d*. *Educ*: Grammar School, Stratford-on-Avon. *Studied*: Mid-Warwickshire School of Art (1954-57); University of the West of England (1992-95). *Exhib*: RA Summer Exhbn, RWA, Mall Galleries, Discerning Eye; Westminster Central Hall, Olympia; Business Design Centre, Islington; Rooksmoor Gallery, Bath; Templeton College, Oxford; John Noott, Broadway; The Norwegian Arts Centre, Cardiff; Black Swan, Frome, and many others. *Works in collections*: Japan, Spain, Moscow, Monaco, Portugal, many in the UK, also the Governor of the Bank of Jamaica. *Commissions*: private commissions undertaken. *Works Reproduced*: Giclée prints of most popular paintings available. *Principal Works*: paintings of The Ridgeway (Ancient track across England). *Recreations*: dogs and horses, walking, sewing and embroidery. *Clubs*: Bath Society of Artists, Clifton Arts Club, Clevedon Art Club, Friends of the RWA. *Address*: Leighbrook House, Sutton Lane, Redhill, North Somerset BS40 5RL. *Email*: jenniferdavidson@leighbrook.wanadoo.co.uk *Website*: www.walledgarden.co.uk

DAVIDSON, Philomena, PPRBS, RWA, FRSA; sculptor. *b*: Westminster, 1949. *d of*: Thomas Davidson, violinist. *m*: divorced. two *d*. *Educ*: Convent of Jesus and Mary, Willesden. *Studied*: sculpture: City and Guilds, London (1967-70, James Butler, RA), RA Schools (1970-73, Willi Soukop, RA). *Exhib*: RA Summer Show, RWA Bristol, sculpture at Margam, Chelsea Harbour Sculpture (1993, 1996). April 1990 elected first woman President Royal Society of British Sculptors (1990-96), Managing Director, The Sculpture Company (1995-1998). *Works in collections*: life-size bronzes Queens Ct., Milton Keynes Shopping Centre; Lady Henry Somerset Memorial, Victoria Embankment Gdns., London; "Fairway" a large outdoor sculpture for Donnington Valley. Hotel and Golf course, Newbury, Berks. *Misc*: Managing Director, The Davidson Arts Partnership (1999-present day). *Address*: 4 Church Walk, Bletchingley, Surrey, RH1 4PD. *Email*: phil@davidsonarts.com *Website*: www.davidsonarts.com

DAVIDSON, Richard John, BA (First) Fine Art. *Medium*: oil. *b*: Newcastle on Tyne, 2 Sep 1946. *s of*: May & Arthur Davidson. *m*: Alison. two *s*. *Educ*: Fettes College (1959-64), Worcester College, Oxford (1964-67). *Studied*: Wimbledon School of Art. *Represented by*: Zimmer Stewart Gallery, Arundel. *Exhib*: Zimmer Stewart Gallery, Arundel (2007, 08, 09); Eyesform Britart Gallery, Maddon Street (2005); Groucho Club, Soho (2002); Chichester Open (2007, 08, 09); Riverside Gallery, Richmond (2001); Biscuit Factory (2005, 2008, 2013); Clapham Art Gallery (2000); Royal Academy Summer Exhibition (2003). *Works in collections*: Taylor Wessing, Baker & McKenzie, Hg Capital, Pivot Design Inc. Private collections in USA, Argentina, Norway, Italy, Canada and UK. *Commissions*: numerous private commissions. Painting to commemorate 50th Anniversary of Baker M. McKenzie (International Law Firm). *Publications*: 'Artists Eye' Art Review (Sept 2000); 'Object of the Week', Daily Telegraph (9 Jan 2001). *Address*: Brookdene House, Graffham, Petworth, GU28 0NL. *Email*: Richard.davidson@btinternet.com *Website*: www.richarddavidson.co.uk *Signs work*: "R.J.Davidson".

DAVIES, Brian. *Medium*: oil. *b*: Isleworth, Middx, 23 Feb 1942. *s of*: Daniel Martin & Elizabeth Anne Davies. *Educ*: Latymer. *Studied*: London. *Represented by*: John Adams Fine Art Ltd @ Ebury Galleries. *Exhib*: Group Exhibitions: London & provincial galleries, Bermuda, Dusseldorf, Paris Salon; Royal Academy Summer Exhibition (1974, 1978, 1982, 1984, 1985, 2000, 2002). Solo exhibitions: Nishiki Gallery, Hong Kong; Granby Gallery, Derbyshire (1992, 1994, 1996, 1998, 2000, 2002, 2004); John Adams Fine Art at Ebury

Galleries (1996, 2000, 2001, 2002, 2003, 2011). *Works Reproduced*: reproductions as prints. *Recreations*: bicycles. *Address*: 57A York Street, Twickenham, Middx, TW1 3LP. *Signs work*: "Brian Davies".

DAVIES, Gareth, Hon. SGFA; artist in pencil, black ink, coloured pens. *b*: St. Asaph, N. Wales, 10 Feb 1972. *Educ*: Gogarth School/TVEI Centre Gogarth. *Exhib*: SGFA, Botanical Fine Art Soc. *Publications*: Heroes All: The Story of the RNLI, by Alec Beilby. *Address*: Bryn Awelon, Pentywyn Rd., Deganwy, Gwynedd, LL31 9TL. *Signs work*: "G.P. Davies."

DAVIES, Heather. *Medium*: mixed media, watercolour, drawing. *b*: Stockton, 10 Sep 1953. one *s*. *Studied*: Fine Art, Printmaking & Textiles: Hartlepool College of Art, Loughborough College of Art. *Exhib*: Royal Watercolour Society, London; Royal Scottish Society of Painters in Watercolour; Adam Gallery, Bath; Castlegate Gallery, Cumbria; London Stock Exchange; Ruthven Gallery, Perthshire; Brian Sinfield Gallery, Oxfordshire; Turnstone Gallery, N. Yorks; Broughton Gallery, Edinburgh. *Works in collections*: Offices of The Cumbria newspaper; Lord Egremont, Petworth, Sussex. *Publications*: "The Lake Artists - A Centenary Celebration" (2004). *Official Purchasers*: Cumberland Newspapers Group Ltd. *Recreations*: horse riding, walking. *Address*: Parkhead Byre, Parkhead, Renwick, Penrith, Cumbria CA10 1JQ. *Email*: heather@heatherdavies.co.uk *Website*: www.heatherdavies.co.uk *Signs work*: "HD" as monogram.

DAVIES, Ivor, NDD (1956), ATD (1957), PhD (Edin.) (1975), VPRCA (1993); artist/painter in oil, tempera, water-colour, gouache, crayon. *b*: Wales, 9 Nov 1935. *Studied*: Cardiff (1952-56) and Swansea (1956-57) Colleges of Art, Lausanne University, Edinburgh University. *Exhib*: over 50 one-man shows worldwide since 1963, also Multi-media Destruction in Art 1960s, including National Museum of Wales; retrospective Brno, Czech Republic (2006); 'Blast to Freeze' 20c British Art, Wolfsburg and Toulouse; 'Art and the Sixties', Tate (& Australia and NZ tour, 2004-2005). *Works in collections*: Deal Coll. Dallas, ACGB, WAC, SAC, National Museum of Wales, etc. *Publications*: articles on Modern Art History, others in Welsh language journals; illustrations: Spirit (1971), Rubaiyat (1981), Science and Art (1981), 'The Age of the Vanguards' (in Italian, UTET, Turin, 2002), 'Discovering Welsh Art' (in Welsh, Univ. Wales, Cardiff, 1999). *Recreations*: languages. *Address*: 99 Windsor Rd., Penarth CF6 1JF. *Signs work*: "Ivor Davies."

DAVIS, Cynthia, self taught artist in oil. *b*: Allahabad, India. *m*: Eric Bernard Davis (decd). *Exhib*: St Ives Soc. of Artists, Mariners Gallery, Penwith Gallery. *Address*: 1 Bay Villas, St. Ives Rd., Carbis Bay, St. Ives, Cornwall, TR26 2SX. *Email*: cynthiadavis@sky.com *Website*: www.cynthiadavis.co.uk *Signs work*: "Cynthia Davis."

DAVIS, James, LIFA; Freeman the Worshipful Company Painter-Stainers (1972); Freeman of the City of London (1973); sculptor, carver and restorer in stone, marble. *b*: London, 16 Jul 1926. *s of*: James E. Davis, engineer. *m*: Joan Davis. *Educ*: Eastbrook Boys School, Dagenham, Essex. *Studied*: Sir John Cass School of Art (1949-53) under Bainbridge Copnal. *Exhib*: Guildhall; Leighton House, Royal Exchange, Mall Galleries. *Works in collections*: Painters Hall, Chelsea and Kensington Town Hall, Community Centre, Shoeburyness, Barclay International, Gracechurch St., St. Nicholas Church, Elm Park, Essex, St. Nicholas Church, Canewdon, Essex, Hyde Park Corner, London W1, Town Centre, Chelmsford, Essex. *Address*: Studio Workshop, 39a West Rd., Shoeburyness, Essex, SS3 9DR. *Signs work*: "J. Davis."

DAVIS, James Spence, DA, RSW; David Cargill Award, RGI; Reid Kerr Painting Award, PAI. *Medium*: oil, watercolour, drawing. *b*: Glasgow, 2 Jul 1944. *s of*: Hugh & Mary Davis. *m*: Doreen Elizabeth Davis. one *s*. one *d*. *Studied*: Glasgow School of Art (1963-67). *Represented by*: Eton Contemporary Fine Art; Red Rag Gallery; The Wren Gallery;

Gatehouse Gallery; John Davies Gallery; Morningside Gallery. *Exhib*: Royal Glasgow Institute of the Fine Arts; The Royal Scottish Academy; The Royal Scottish Society of Painters in Watercolour; Paisley Art Institute. *Works in collections*: The Royal Collection, Holyrood Palace; Glasgow City Chambers; The Vatican; The Feisal Royal Family Collection; Arisaig Holdings, Singapore; Cargill Thomson Bequest. *Commissions*: portrait commission for The Vatican, and many others. *Official Purchasers*: Duke of Edinburgh; Glasgow City; The Vatican. *Works Reproduced*: by Meadows Fine Art (www.jamessdavis.com). *Principal Works*: portrait of Bishop of Paisley; 'Staffa' at Royal Glasgow Institute of Fine Arts (2005); Arisaig Series Singapore. *Clubs*: Glasgow Art Club. *Address*: The Meadows, 25 Arran Crescent, Beith, Ayrshire, KA15 2DU. *Website*: www.jamessdavis.com www.meadowsfineart.com

DAVIS, Jason Pyper, BA (Hons) Fine Art; Mayfest Prize 1997; The Royal Glasgow Insititute Award 1998; 1st Prize, MacRobertson Open 2003; City of Glasgow Award 2003. *Medium*: jewellery, oil, drawing, sculpture. *b*: Paisley, 17 Feb 1973. *s of*: James & Doreen Davis. *m*: Denise Findlay. *Studied*: Glasgow School of Art (1992-96). *Represented by*: Morningside Gallery, Edinburgh; Contemporary Fine Art, Eton; Lime Tree Gallery, Suffolk; Arteries Gallery, Glasgow. *Works in collections*: Costley & Costley Hotels, Troon, Scotland; The City Chambers, Glasgow; Merk Finance, Glasgow; International Law Courts, The Hague, Amsterdam (Judges Chambers). *Commissions*: commissioned to produce a series of seven heads for Precious Records, Glasgow (1996). *Official Purchasers*: The City Chambers, Glasgow. *Address*: 15 St. James Terrace, Lochwinnoch Road, Kilmacolm, Inverclyde, PA13 4HB. *Email*: jason@pyperdavis.co.uk *Website*: www.jasonpyperdavis.com *Signs work*: "PYPER".

DAVIS, Kate, BA (1982), H.Dip. (1986), MA (Status) Oxon. (1992), Stanley Picker Fellow (1986-87), Whitechapel Young Artist of Year (1988), Sargant Fellow, British School of Rome (1998); subject-led sculpture, video, photography and drawing; sculpture tutor, Royal College of Art; Jerwood Drawing 1st Prize, 2001; Sydney Water Sculpture Prize, 2002. *b*: Chesham, Bucks., 23 Feb 1960. one *d*. *Studied*: Herts. College of Art and Design (1978-79), Falmouth School of Art (1979-82), Slade School of Fine Art (1983-86). *Represented by*: Fred (Ltd), London. *Exhib*: solo: Milch, Newlyn A.G., University Gallery, Fred (Ltd), London, Whitechapel A.G., group shows in Britain and abroad. Rhodes & Mann, Gutleut 15. *Works in collections*: National Sculpture Centre, Oronsko, Poland; British Land, Middlesborough Art Gallery., British Museum, Campbelltown Art Gallery, Sydney. *Commissions*: Economist Plaza. *Publications*: Kate Davis (Milch, 1997); as if (University of Essex, 2001) (Crossing-Closing) Gutleut Verlag 2002. *Address*: 56 Nelson Rd., London N8 9RT. *Signs work*: "K.A. DAVIS."

DAVIS, Michael Robert, NDD, MA (RCA); artist in charcoal conté (drawing), lecturer; Principal Lecturer (Painting), Kent Inst. of Art and Design. *b*: Birmingham, 11 Sept., 1943. *m*: Susan Davis. one *d*. *Educ*: Birmingham College of Art (1959-64), Royal College of Art (1964-67). *Exhib*: RA Summer Exhbn. since 1986, Hayward Annual (1982), 15 British Painters, British Council, Barcelona, 5 British Artists - de Grey, Davis, Hockney, Freud, Weight, Alabama USA, Mike Davis (drawings El Palau Valencia), Cassian de Vere Cole, London. *Works in collections*: Arts Council, and private. *Publications*: Guardian Arts Review, Contemporary Arts Review Guardian, Times Arts Review, 5 British Artists Honouring England, Alabama Times, Panning for Gold - George Melly (1993), Andrew Lambirth review or show at Cassian de Vere Cole (1996). *Address*: 5 Elmers End Rd., London SE20 7ST.

DAVIS, Pamela, VPRMS (1979), FSBA (1985), SWA (1977), HSF (1983); Awards: Gold Memorial Bowl (RMS 1991), Llewelyn Alexander Gallery (Subject Award 1993, Masters Award 1998-2003); Masters Award 2008 miniaturist (group); miniaturist and flower painter. *Medium*: oil, acrylic, gouache. *b*: Molesey, 27 Aug 1927. *m*: Ronald. two *s*. *Educ*: Ashford

County School. *Studied*: Twickenham School of Art (1942-45, Dorothy Parlbey). *Exhib*: Westminster Gallery, London: RMS, SWA, SBA; Llewellyn Alexander Gallery, London. *Address*: Woodlands, Pond Copse Lane, Loxwood, W. Sussex, RH14 0XF. *Signs work*: "Pamela Davis."

DAVIS, Simon, HND Art and Design (1988); RBSA (2005), HonSec RBSA (2007). *Medium*: gouache, oil. *b*: Stratford-upon-Avon, 8 Jun 1968. *m*: Sarah. *Studied*: Mid-Warwickshire College of Art and Design (1984-86), Swindon School of Art and Design (1986-88). *Represented by*: Red Rag Gallery, Stow-on-the-Wold; Wonderwall, Cirencester. *Exhib*: Mall Galleries (2006, 2007), RBSA ,Birmingham (2004 onwards), Clifton Gallery, Bristol (2004), Beaux Arts, Bath (2004). *Works in collections*: RBSA Permanent Collection. *Publications*: various collections of comic strip work worldwide. *Misc*: illustrates comic strips for British comic 2000AD since 1994. *Address*: Leasowes Cottage, Leasowes Road, Offenham, Worcs., WR11 8RQ. *Email*: simsal20@tiscali.co.uk *Signs work*: "S B DAVIS".

DAVISON, Martin, MA (1958); SGFA (2000). *Medium*: painter, designer and sculptor in all media. *b*: Birmingham, 19 Dec 1931. *s of*: Geoffrey and Molly Davison. *Partner*: Patricia Starr. *Educ*: King Edward's School, Birmingham; New College, Oxford. *Studied*: Ruskins Schools (Oxford) and St.Martin's (London) (part-time). *Exhib*: ROI, PS, SGFA, UA, NEAC, Chelsea Art Society, Richmond Art Society, Society of Feline Artists, Llewellyn Alexander, Orleans House Gallery, Riverside Gallery (Richmond); one-man shows: Riverside Barn (Walton); Post Nostalgia Gallery (Teddington); Bumbles Gallery (East Sheen); Orange Tree Theatre (Richmond). *Publications*: "Rubik's Magic Strategy Game" by Martin Davison. *Recreations*: playing jazz clarinet and piano. *Address*: 89 Ashleigh Road, Mortlake, London SW14 8PY. *Email*: martin.mortlake@talktalk.net *Website*: www.martindavisonart.com *Signs work*: "M.DAVISON".

DAVISON, Robert (Bob), BA Fine Art, MA Fine Art; Course Leader Fine Art, Painting & Drawing, Associate Senior Lecturer: School of Art, Media & Design, University of Gloucester (1981-). *Medium*: acrylics, watercolour, drawing. *b*: Worstead, Norfolk, 1954. *m*: Lucy. three *s*. *Studied*: West Surrey College of Art & Design (1972-76); Chelsea School of Art (1977-78). *Exhib*: Solo exhibitions: Mace Ltd., London; The Rangers House, Blackheath; The Helenic Centre, London; The JKing of Hearts, Norwich. RWA, Bristol (2005, 2006, 2007), Mall Galleries (2001). Numerous mixed exhibitions in Norfolk, Gloucestershire and London. *Works in collections*: include: Eastern Arts Association; Sealink UK; Bank of Switzerland; Private Bank & Trust; Simmons & Simmons; University of Gloucestershire; Gloucester Royal Hospital. *Commissions*: Sue Chappel Trust; Gloucestershire Royal NHS Trust. *Misc*: Since 1980s has worked for numerous galleries, companies and private collectors as organiser and advisor. *Address*: The Change, Randwick, Stroud, Gloucestershire GL6 6EU. *Email*: bob.davison@talktalk.net *Signs work*: "R Davison".

DAWKINS, Ann. *Medium*: oil. *b*: Salisbury, 24 Mar 1948. *m*: Richard Dawkins. *Exhib*: Royal Academy Summer Exhibition (1996, 1997). *Works in collections*: private. *Address*: 161 Castle Street, Salisbury, SP1 3TB. *Email*: ann_dawkins@hotmail.com *Signs work*: "AD".

DAWSON, Susan Shepherd, BA (Hons) fine art (painting); painter of landscapes and garden scenes in oil, watercolour, and charcoal drawings en plein air; also maker of silver jewellery. *b*: Ponteland, Northumberland, 18 Feb 1955. one *s*. two *d*. *Educ*: Church High School, Newcastle-upon-Tyne. *Studied*: Bath Lane School of Art, Newcastle, Liverpool Polytechnic. *Exhib*: St. Ives Society of Artists and various exhibs. in Cornwall. *Works in collections*: various collections in Europe and New Zealand. *Address*: c/o Westwood House Townsend, Hayle, Cornwall, TR27 6AQ. *Email*: suesdawson@hotmail.com. *Website*: www.stivessocietyofartists.com. *Signs work*: "Sue Dawson."

DAY, Daphne P.A., Prof., AGPP (1979); artist in oil and water-colour. *b*: London. *Educ*: private. *Studied*: Chelsea School of Art, St. Martin's Lane for stone-carving, Camberwell School of Art for bronze-casting. *Exhib*: Mall Galleries, Knapp Gallery, Art Connoisseur Gallery, Westminster Gallery and Lauderdale House; one-man show: Durban and Johannesburg (1954); Heraldic portrait of Sir Winston Churchill exhib. for 6 years at Blenheim Palace from 1967. *Address*: 20 The Avenue, Bedford Pk., Chiswick, London W4 1HT. *Signs work*: "Daphne Day."

DAY, Jane, B.Ed (Hons) (1989); smoke-fired ceramics; Subject Leader (ceramics), City of Bath College. *b*: Cambridge, 18 Jun 1966. *Educ*: Bath College of Higher Educ., but largely self taught. *Commissions*: Selfridges, London (Smokefired Vessel Forms). *Publications*: Ceramic Review. *Principal Works*: smoke-fired vessel forms. *Recreations*: oil painting. *Address*: 38 Cossham Rd, St. George, Bristol BS5 8DL. *Email*: janecday@hotmail.com

DAY, Zoë Claire, Short listed Royal Society Portrait Painters Annual Exhibition (2012, 2014); Bafa "Winner, Best in Show" (2009, 2011, 2013). *Medium*: oil. *b*. Aylesbury, 17 Jun 1974. *m*: Mark. two *s*. *Educ*: Royal Latin Grammar School, Buckingham. *Studied*: Nene College of Art, Northampton (Foundation in Art and Design); Nottingham Trent Univeristy (Fashion and Textiles); Ruskin School of Art, Oxford (Anatomy and the Figure 2012); Heatherleys School of Art, Chelsea, London (Portraiture 2011). *Represented by*: The Portrait Guild, www.portraitguild.com; Stani Art House, Stony Stratford, Buckinghamshire. *Exhib*: Aim Gallery, Milton Keynes; 'Not the Royal Academy', Llewellyn Alexander Gallery, Waterloo, London; Orleans House Gallery, Richmond, London; Woburn Abbey, Bedfordshire; Stowe School, Buckinghamshire; Stani Art House, Stony Stratford, Buckinghamshire. *Works in collections*: Rt Hon John Bercow MP; Brain Tumour Research Trust. *Publications*; "Someone Has To Die" series by Richard Hallows 8 volumes front and back cover illustrations. *Principal Works*: Portrait of Rt Hon John Bercow MP presented at Speakers House. *Recreations*: Grade 6 Cellist. *Address*: Pipers, Main Street, Akeley, Bucks MK18 5HW. *Email*: z.day@btinternet.com *Website*: www.zoeday.com *Signs work*: "Zoe Day".

DAYKIN, Michael, MA (RCA); artist, curator. *b*: Yorkshire, 1947. *Studied*: Watford School of Art (1970-71), St. Martin's School of Art (1971-74), RCA (1974-77). *Exhib*: City University Gallery, Cleveland College of Art Gallery, XO Gallery, The Figure of Eight Gallery, Gallery K, Attache Gallery. *Works in collections*: Northern Arts, Brown and Wood, Musee d'Art Contemporaire, Skopje, Macedonia. *Commissions*: Benchmark Holdings, Quaglino's. *Address*: 9 Lowder House, Wapping Lane, London E1W 2RJ. *Signs work*: "Daykin."

de DENARO, Furio, Historian of Art, Artist, Printmaker, teacher at University of Trieste (from 1996), il Bisonte (from 1998), Institut of Art Trieste (1978-81, and from 1996), Scuola Liberadell Acquaforte, Trieste (from 2002); National Drawing Comp. Award (1973); Regione FVG (1982); Torinotortona Award (1991); Rotary Award (1992); Varese Award (2002). *Medium*: wood engraving, copper engraving, etching, drawing, watercolour. *b*: Trieste, 3 Sep 1956. *s of*: Fabio and Brunetta Bruno. *m*: Roberta Dittura. one *s*. *Studied*: Institut of Art Trieste (MA 1974, Art Degree 1976) Camden School of Art (1979-80), London Camberwell College of Art, (Summer 1989), il Bisonte, Florence (1988-90), BA (Hons) University of Trieste (1991). *Represented by*: il Bisonte, Firenze; Society of Wood Engravers. *Exhib*: Trieste, Monfalcone, Milano, Ortona, Pisa; Great Britain, Schwetzingen, New York, New Caanan, Toronto, Monchengladbach, Firenze, Venezia, Urbino, Genova. *Works in collections*: New York City Public Library; University Barcelona; Rijeka; Malbork Genova (Villacroce); Ortona; Firenze; Trieste (Museo Civico). *Commissions*: Comune di Varese, Ex Libris Museum, A.i. Ex Libris. *Publications*: Domenico Tempesti: i Discorsi

Sopra l'Intaglio (Firenze 1994), Omaggioa Gabor Peterdi (Monfalcone 2004); portfolio: Presenze Incise a Trieste (1996); Ilsegno Inciso (2001); Ex Libris Biblioteca CMSATS (2005); Pinicchio Xilografico. *Works Reproduced*: Ex Libris (Milano 1991), Grafica d'Arte (Milano 1996), Encyclopedia Bio-Biblio Contemporary Ex Libris (Portugal 1996), An Engravers Globe (UK 2002) by Simon Brett, and many others. *Recreations*: judo, cycling and mountain biking. *Clubs*: il Bisonte, Society of Wood Engravers. *Misc*: Artistic Co-ordinator: Centro Culturale Tranquillo Marangoni. *Address*: salita di Gretta 33, 34136 Trieste, Italy.

de GRANDMAISON, Constance, HS (2003), ARMS (2004); awards: winner Bidder & Bourne Award for Best Sculpture (2003). *Medium*: miniature portraits in relief - wax, metal, terra cotta, perspex. *b*: Canada. *m*: Nicolas. one *s*. *Studied*: self-taught, and various art and sculpture courses. *Exhib*: Mall Galleries, HS, RMS. *Works in collections*: D.Heathcote; E.J. Pyke bequest to V&A and Fitzwilliam College, Cambridge. *Commissions*: E.J. Pyke, D. Heathcote, Mrs E. Milling, C. James, and others. *Publications*: Biographical Dictionary of Wax Modellers (as Constance Sykes) by E.J. Pyke. *Address*: 2604-1850 Cornox Street, Vancouver, BC V6G IR3, Canada. *Email*: burkinholdings@shaw.ca *Signs work*: 'Constanza'.

DE LA COUR, Brian David, M.Des. RCA; works on paper in oil bar, acrylic, charcoal and pastel; brooches in steel, acrylic and paint. *b*: Bushey, Herts, 4 Apr 1946. *s of*: Alfred Cour. *m*: Dora. two *s*. *Educ*: Harrow School of Art. *Studied*: Royal College of Art. *Represented by*: Benjamin C. Hargreaves. *Exhib*: Group shows: The Gallery, London; Diorama, London; Logos Gallery, London; Gallery Fresh, London; Tom Blau Gallery, London; Mark Senior Gallery, London; Mall Galleries, London; Aspects Gallery, London; Contemporary Applied Arts, London; Wakefield Art Gallery, One Aldwych Hotel, London; Kunstgwebe Museum, Berlin; Stadt Museum, Munich; Shipley Art Gallery and Museum. *Publications*: Brit Art Directory. *Recreations*: photography, walking. *Address*: 60 Bonnersfield Lane, Harrow, Middlesex, HA1 2LE.

de LACY, Ellie, HS. *Medium*: gouache and watercolour. *b*: Walsall, 5 Nov 1966. *Studied*: self-taught. *Exhib*: HS. *Works in collections*: national and international. *Commissions*: national and international. *Works Reproduced*: limited edition prints. *Principal Works*: equine, wildlife, and pet portraits in miniature; Replicas (in miniature) of animal art, for example, the work of George Stubbs. *Clubs*: Three Oaks Art Club. *Address*: Salehurst, Butchers Lane, Three Oaks, E.Sussex TN35 4NG. *Email*: ellie@elliedelacy.co.uk *Website*: www.elliedelacy.co.uk *Signs work*: 'E de LACY'.

DE MEESTER, Angeline, BA Hons; FLS; SBA; RHS Gold (2007); RHS Silver Gilt (2010, 2013); CBM. *Medium*: watercolour. *b*: London, 15 Jul 1969. *m*: Charles. two *s*. one *d*. *Studied*; Epsom College of Art (1987-88); Central St Martins (1988-91); English Gardening School (2005-07). *Exhib*: RHS Exhibition Halls (2007, 2008, 2010, 2013); Society of Botanical Artists Annual London Exhibition (2008-2014); Botanische Kunst, Germany (2011, 2014); Ebury Street Fine Art Gallery (2011); Waddesdon Manor (2009); Haampton Court Palace (2010); Cumberland Lodge (2010); Palmengarten, Germany (2010, 2012); Hunt Institute, USA (2010). *Works in collections*: Inc. RHS Lingley Library, Hunt Institute Pittsburgh USA, Dr Shirley Sherwood, Hampton Court Palace. *Publications*: Surrey Life, July 2007; SBA catalogue cover (2014). *Address*: Larkbarrow, Southdown Road, Wolkingham, Surrey CR3 7DP. *Email*: info@contemporarybotanicart.com *Website*: www.contemporarybotanicart.com *Signs work*: "ANGELINE DE MEESTER" or "A M DE MEESTER".

de MEO, Pamela, *Medium*: oil or watercolour. *b*: London, 2 Sep 1920. *d of*: Dr. Boris Vinyk, Sybil Moody. *m*: Major Brian Synge. three *s*. *Educ*: Cheltenham Ladies' College. *Studied*: St. Martin's College of Art, Chelsea School of Art, Heatherleys (1953). *Exhib*: RA (1988, 1994, 1996), Paris Salon, RBA Galleries, Chelsea Artists, Bankside Gallery (GB,

USSR Assoc., 1985), Mall Galleries, Bowmore Gallery, Halkin St., W1 (1989), Charity Exhbn. for Red Cross (1991), Gagliardi Gallery, Chelsea (1993), Patterson Gallery, Albemarle St. (1994), Chelsea Arts Soc. (1993, 1994, 1996, 1999, 2003), Britain-Russian Assoc. (1995); one-man show: Tradescant Trust Museum (1988); The Mall Galleries (1996); Arts Club (1994-1998); one man show at home address - June 19th; Chelsea Festival (1999, 2001-2003); 150th anniversary of the Heatherley School of Fine Art; Chelsea Art Exhibitions (1994-1999); Edith Grove Gallery (1995). *Commissions*: A portrait of the late Col. Oliver Berger - commissioned by his wife Lady Rose Berger. *Publications*: Belgravia magazine. *Official Purchasers*: Sultan of Brunei. *Works Reproduced*: In the Chelsea Festival magazine - A Russian Rose View & Flowers. *Recreations*: singing & dancing. *Clubs*: Dover St. Arts, Chelsea Arts. *Address*: 4 Pembroke Close, Grosvenor Crescent, London SW1X 7ET. *Signs work*: "P. de Meo."

de MONCHAUX, Paul, Arts Council Major Award (1980); Purchase Award Contemporary Art Society (1982); The Northern Electric Environmental Award (1990); Civic Trust Award with Townshend Associates for design of Oozells Square, Birmingham (2000). *Medium*: sculpture. *b*: Montreal, 20 May 1934. *s of*: Emile de Monchaux. *m*: Ruth. one *s*. three *d*. *Studied*: Art Students League, New York (1952-54); Slade School of Fine Art (1955-58). *Represented by*: Megan Piper Ltd. *Exhib*: RA; ICA; Serpentine Gallery; John Moores Liverpool; Whitechapel Gallery; Piper Gallery. *Works in collections*: Contemporary Art Society; Colchester District Hospital; BBC. *Commissions*: Euston Station (benches, 1990); 'Basilica', Coventry Crown Court (1991); Wilfred Owen Memorial, Shrewsbury (1993); Oozells Square, Birmingham (1998); 'Enclosure' West Park Southampton; Brunswick Square, Birmingham (2001)' 'Song' BBC Memorial to Winston Churchill (2005); 'Silence' memorial to WWII Jersey Slave Workers (2007); 'Breath' Norwich Memorial Gardens (2011); 'Girton Column' Girton College Cambridge (2012). *Misc*: lecturer Goldsmiths College (1960-65); Head of Sculpture and Head of Fine Art, Camberwell School of Art (1965-86). *Address*: 56 Manor Avenue, London SE4 1TE. *Email*: p.demonchaux@btinternet.com *Website*: www.pauldemonchaux.co.uk *Signs work*: 'Paul de Monchaux'.

de SAULLES, Mary, ARIBA, (1948), AAdip (1947), FCSD (1959), FRSA (1981); architect and designer, interior, exhbn., display; deputy to chief officer of specialized design section, LCC Architects' Dept. (1950-52); partnership with John Lunn, FSIA (1951-55); Industrial Designer, BEA (1959); private practice (1960), interiors, exhbns., housing, etc. Conservation consultant. *b*: Westcliff-on-Sea, 1925. *m*: Patrick de Saulles, A.A.dip. (d. 1997). two *s*. *Studied*: architecture: Architectural Assoc. School of Architecture, London. *Publications*: The Book of Shrewsbury (Barracuda Books Ltd.; revised, updated "The Story of Shrewsbury", and published by Logaston Press, Nov 2013 - available on Amazon). Designers in Britain, Nos. 4 and 5, Architectural Review. *Clubs*: Architectural Assoc. *Address*: Watergate House, St Mary's Water Lane, Shrewsbury SY1 2BX. *Signs work*: "Mary de Saulles."

DE STEMPEL, Sophie, Cristina. *Medium*: oil. *b*: Hythe, 31 Dec 1960. *m*: Sir Ian Holm. *Educ*: Sacred Heart Convent. *Studied*: City & Guild School of Art (1978-81). *Represented by*: Browse & Darby. *Exhib*: Houldsworth Fine Art (1990, 92, 94).*Publications*: Harper & Queen, Vanity Fair. *Official Purchasers*: Barclays Bank. *Clubs*: none. *Misc*: Lucien Freud model (1980-91). *Address*: 46 Bassett Road, London W10 6JL. *Signs work*: 'Sophie de Stempel'

de VERE COLE, Cassian, art dealer; Director, Cassian de Vere Cole Fine Art (since 1993) specialising in twentieth century British and Irish paintings and drawings, and international contemporary art; Previously: Christie's, London (1990-92), freelance London and New York (1988-90), Michael Parkin Gallery, London (1986-88). *b*: London, 1966. *Clubs*: Chelsea Arts, Garrick. *Address*: c/o Cassian de Vere Cole Fine Art 50 Elgin Cres., Notting Hill, London W11 2JJ.

DEAKINS, Sylvia, ATD (1946), SGFA (1986), CDS (1987); painter and illustrator in oil, gouache, pastel, ink, collage. *b*: Eccleshill, W. Yorks., 18 Oct 1924. *d of*: A.N. Leeming. *m*: C.E. Deakins (decd.). one *s*. one *d*. *Educ*: Hendon County Grammar. *Studied*: Hornsey College of Art (1941-46, Douglas Percy Bliss, Russell Reeve, Francis Winter). *Exhib*: RA, RBA, NEAC, and numerous galleries in E. Anglia. *Publications*: illustrated many for OUP Longmans, Ward Lock, including A Beginner's Bible (1958), and Listening to Children Talking (1976). *Address*: 1 Mill Lane, Gt. Dunmow, Essex CM6 1BG. *Signs work*: "Sylvia Deakins," or "S.D."

DEAKINS, Thomas William (Tom), BA (Hons) (1980), ATC (1982), Charles Spence Memorial prize (1977); painter in oil. *Medium*: Oil. *b*: Barnet, 8 Dec 1957. *s of*: Cyril Deakins, ARE. *m*: Ann Logan. two *s*. *Educ*: Newport Grammar School, Essex. *Studied*: University of Newcastle upon Tyne (1976-80, Kenneth Rowntree, Derwent Wise). *Represented by*: Aubrey Art Gallery, Gt. Dunmow, Essex. *Exhib*: RA Summer Shows since 1983, Medici Gallery (1989), William Hardy Glasgow (1991), Chappel Gallery, Colchester (1995, 2000, 2006), Bruton St. Gallery (1999), Royal Institute of Oil Painters (2005-2007), Aubrey Art Gallery, Dunmow, Essex (2010-2014), Dunmow Art Gallery, (2014). *Works in collections*: Hatton Gallery, University of Newcastle, Epping Forest District Museum, Beecroft A.G. Westcliff on Sea; The Gardens of Easton Lodge, nr. Dunmow, Essex, Chelmsford and Essex Museum; Fry Art Gallery, Saffron Walden, Crown Estate. *Commissions*: "Sacred Grove" - large drawing on wood to commemorate 60th Anniversary of end of WWII, at the gardens of Easton Lodge. *Address*: 31 The Causeway, Gt. Dunmow, Essex CM6 2AA. *Email*: Tom.deakins@btinternet.com *Signs work*: "Tom Deakins"

DEAN, Dorothy, SWA; artist in gouache, oil, pastel. *b*: 14 May 1920. *d of*: A.J. Dean, *m*: K.W. Howard. one *s*. *Educ*: Bromley County School, Kent. *Studied*: Goldsmiths' School of Art (1936-39), Eastbourne Art School, Guildford (part-time post war). *Exhib*: RI, ROI, RBA, RPS, PS, numerous solo and shared exhbns. in London, S. England and Bedford, private galleries Hampshire. *Works in collections*: private collections: France, Germany, Switzerland and Canada. *Address*: Ashley Cottage, Bentworth, Alton, Hants. GU34 5RH. *Signs work*: "Dorothy Dean" and "D. Dean."

DEAN, Graham, BA Art & Design; Abbey Award, British School, Rome (1992), Trivanorum Art Centre, India (2000), International Fellowship at the Vermont Studio Centre, USA. *Medium*: watercolour on handmade indian paper, prints, acrylic on canvas. *b*: Birkenhead, Merseyside, 5 Dec 1951. *s of*: Mr & Mrs L.L. Dean. *m*: Denise Dean. one *s*. one *d*. *Studied*: Laird School of Art, Birkenhead (1968-70); Bristol Poly, Faculty of Art and Design (1970-73). *Represented by*: Waterhouse & Dodd, Galerie Frans Jacobs/ Judith Bouwknegt/ Amsterdam, Salamatina Gallery, New York. *Exhib*: solo: Balse Art Fair(1987), 20th C Art, The Armoury New York (2004); semi-retrospective, Brighton Art Gallery and Museum (1996), Williamson Museum and Art Gallery (1995), Triumph Gallery, Moscow (2013). *Works in collections*: V&A Watercolour Coll.; Ferens Museum and Art Gallery, Hull; Williamson Museum and Art Gallery, Birkenhead; Ing Collection, Amsterdam*ublications*: 'Art Today', Phaidon. *Works Reproduced*: 'Foreign Correspondent' (1987); 'Compartments' (1974); 'Nightswimming' (2000). *Principal Works*: 'The Kiss' (1987); 'Foreign Correspondent' (1987); 'Compartments' (1974); 'Nightswimming' (2000). *Recreations*: tennis. *Address*: 17 Norfolk Road, Brighton, East Sussex BN1 3AA. *Email*: grahamdean472@btinternet.com *Website*: www.grahamdean.com

DEAN, Margaret, NDD Painting; ATD; Liverpool City Council Travelling Scholarship. *Medium*: oil, acrylic, drawing. *b*: Liverpool, 8 Jan 1939. *m*: Roger Dean. one *s*. one *d*. *Studied*: Liverpool College of Art (1955-60); Liverpool University (1960-61). *Represented by*: The Art Room Gallery, Topsham. *Exhib*: Public collections; France, USA, London, Liverpool, Keele University, Bowes Museum, County Durham, Birmingham. *Works in* *collections*: Public Collections; Liverpool Ciy Council, Walker Art Gallery, Associated Printing Services, New Jersey, USA, Manchester City etc. *Commissions*: Exeter City Swimming Pool; Commando Training Centre, Lymstone, Deven; RNAS Culdrose Naval Station, Cornwall; Oxford Architects etc. *Publications*: inclusion in Catalogue of British Painting, Walker Art Gallery, Liverpool. *Official Purchasers*: Liverpool City Council, Manchester City Council, Exeter City Council, Oxford Architects Partnership. *Works Reproduced*: Catalogue of British Paintings; Devon Life; Evolver; Exeter Living; Watherston inc New York, USA; Associated Printing Services, New Jersey, USA. *Recreations*: Reading, swimming, walking, sewing, languages. *Clubs*: Exeter Twinning Circle. *Misc.* Art lecturer and demonstrator. Address: 25 Culverland Close, Exeter EX4 6HR. *Email*: studiorogmag@msn.com *Website*: studiorogmag.com *Signs work*: "MD" monogram

DEAN, Roger, National Diploma (Sculpture) (1957); British Council Scholarship (1959); Gulbenkian Travelling Scholarship (1959). *Medium*: Sculpture. b: Warrington, 8 Mar 1937. *m*: Margaret. *Studied*: Liverpool College of Art (1953-59), Brera Academy, Milan (Jun-Dec 1959). *Represented by*: The Art Room Gallery, 8a The Strand, Topsham, Exeter EX3 0JB. *Exhib*: Lane Gallery, Bradford; Bowes Museum, Co Durham; Compendium Gallery, Birmingham; Walker Art, Liverpool; Liverpool University; Exeter University; John Moores Sculpture Competition (prizewinner); Exe Gallery, Exeter; Bluecoat Gallery, Liverpool; Keele University, Staffordshire; most recent exhibition Art Room, Topsham (2012). *Works in collections*: Walker Art Gallery, Liverpool; Keele University; Atkinson Art Gallery, Southport; Gulbenkian Foundation, London. *Commissions*: Public Art for: Exeter City Council; South West Arts Assn; North Devon Council; Teignbridge Council. *Publications*: Ancient and Modern, The Art and Architecture of Princesshay, Exeter. *Works Reproduced*: Arts International; Guardian; Devon Life. *Principal Works*: Princesshay Development Exeter; Hatherleigh Cattle Market. *Misc*: Finalist Prix de Rome (1958); Gulbenkian Fellow in Fine Art, Keele University (1965-66). *Address*: 25 Culverland Close, Exeter, Devon EX4 6HR. *Email*: studiorogmag@msn.com *Signs work*: "RD".

DEAN, William Alfred, ROI (2010), NDD (1953), ATC (1956). *Medium*: oil. *b*: London, 1 Mar 1932. *m*: Gloria (decd). one *s*. *Studied*: The Latymer School - Hornsey College of Art (1948-53, 1955-56). *Represented by*: A & K Wilson Gallery, Harpenden, Herts. *Exhib*: one-man shows: A & K Wilson; mixed shows: RA Summer Exhibition; RSMA; RBA; NEAC; Disc. Eye.; ROI at the Mall; Priory Gallery, Broadway; Francis Iles, Rochester; Hawker Gallery, Amersham. *Works in collections*: Palace of Westminster. *Commissions*: Palace of Westminster; private in America, England, Greece, Australia. *Publications*: Medici Society, Artists and Illustrators. *Works Reproduced*: Medici Society. *Recreations*: golf, music, theatre. *Clubs*: Wapping Group of Artists *Address*: 3 Willowside Court, 31 Waverley Road, Enfield, Middlesex, EN2 7BP. *Email*: deanwaroi@btinternet.com *Website*: www.BillDeanROI.co.uk *Signs work*: "Dean", catalogue entries "Bill Dean".

DEANE, Frederick, RP (1972); painter in oil, gouache, pastel. *b*: Manchester, 1924. *m*: Audrey Craig. two *s*. one *d*. *Studied*: Manchester College of Art (1940-43), R.A. Schools (1946-51, Philip Connard). Served with Para Regt. 1st Airborne Div. (1943-45). Visiting tutor: Manchester College of Art (1952-60), City of London Polytechnic (1970-82). *Exhib*: RA, RP, Ebury Gallery. *Works in collections*: Chatsworth; Oxford, Cambridge, Manchester, Rhodes, McGill and Kent Universities; Manchester City A.G. *Commissions*: 11th Duke of Devonshire, Lord Florey, Mrs. Peter K. Roosevelt, Princess Dadiani, Lord Denning. *Clubs*: Chelsea Arts. *Address*: Penrallt Goch, Llan Ffestiniog, Gwynedd, LL41 4NS. *Signs work*: "Deane."

DEANE, Jasper, Cert.FA.(Oxon) (1971), MA (RCA) (1978); PGCE Greenwich University (2001); artist in water-colour and oil. *b*: Ches., 15 Jul 1952. *Educ*: Bryanston

School, Blandford. *Studied*: Ruskin School of Drawing (1969-71), RCA (1975-78), Greenwich University (2000-2001). *Exhib*: numerous exhbns. of paintings, drawings and water-colours in London & Paris, including RCA, Cadogan Gallery and Royal Festival Hall; Man & Eve Gallery. *Works in collections*: many private collections including Peter O'Sullivan, Martin Mills, Fiona Spencer-Thomas, Julian Wilson, Brian Patten. *Commissions*: include paintings for Martin Mills and Dr. Claudia Pacheco. *Publications*: includes work for the Folio Society and RCA; 'Colour Research' pub. Man & Eve Gallery (2006). *Official Purchasers*: Oxford University, Wadham College JCR (1970). *Principal Works*: 'Colour Research' (2006). *Recreations*: playing the guitar. *Clubs*: RCA Alumni, Chelsea Arts. *Address*: 13c St. Stephens Ave., London W12 8JB. *Email*: jasper.deane@googlemail.com *Signs work*: "J.D." or "Jasper Deane."

DEARDEN, Chris, NDD, ARUA, UWS, WCSI (Ireland); painter in water-colour, art teacher; Council mem.: RUA, and UWS. *b*: Halifax, 27 Dec 1941. two *d*. *Studied*: Huddersfield College of Art. *Exhib*: Mall Gallery, London (1991-1996), Royal Hibernian (1979-98), Royal Ulster (1978-99), Laings, Cavehill Gallery, Belfast, etc. *Works in collections*: BBC, UTV, DOE, Albert Reynolds (Irish Prime Minister), HRH Prince Charles, National Trust, USA and Russia. *Commissions*: MOD, Palace Barracks, Belfast, BBC. *Address*: 4 Knockagh Terr., Greenisland, Co. Antrim, N.I. BT38 8RN. *Signs work*: "Chris Dearden."

DEARNLEY, Benjamin Chad, BA (Hons) Sculpture. *Medium*: sculpture. *b*: Salisbury, Wilts, 29 Feb 1964. *s of*: Dr.Christopher H & Bridget D. Dearnley. *m*: Sr. Lynn B. Parr. two *d*. *Studied*: Camberwell College of Arts (2003-2006). *Represented by*: The Belgravia Gallery, Mayfair, London. *Exhib*: Saatchi Gallery (2011), Salisbury Cathedral, solo show (2012), RHS Chelsea (2012-13), Queen Elizabeth Hall, Truman Brewery, Brick Lane. The Girkin, BT Tower, Art at the Edge, Olympia (2012-13), Trafalgar Square (2012), Henley Royal Regatta (2011-12), Vienna, Haus Wittgenstine (2013), NSW Australia. *Works in collections*: Lionel Tertis (1876-1975) bust, RAM York Gate Gallery; Dr.C.H.Dearnley bust (1940-2000), RSCM, Salisbury; Lillian Tertis, Erin Arts Centre. *Commissions*: Olympian, Bath. The Tennis Girl (2011). Law courts London, Zephyrus Bath. Princes Trust, The Gift, Festival of Stone, Bristol (2013). Various bronze and alabaster portraits. *Official Purchasers*: BT Head Office, Aviva London, Dunhumby London, Belgravia Gallery, Bath City. *Principal Works*: Olympian 2012, Bath, Father of the Bicycle, Bristol, Talking Stone, Caerwedros, Wales. *Clubs*: Clifton Arts Club. *Address*: Pensarn Chapel House, Caerwedros Road, llandysul, SA44 6BH. *Email*: info@bendearnley.com *Website*: www.bendearnley.com *Signs work*: "BCD" (as monogram) and "B.C.DEARNLEY".

DEBENHAM, Charles, NDD. *Medium*: oil. *b*: Colchester, 9 Aug 1933. *m*: Eilish. two *s*. one *d*. *Educ*: Colchester Royal Grammar School. *Studied*: Colchester School of Art. *Exhib*: Royal Academy (1980-2009 - with one or two gaps); Royal West of England Academy (1988-2013 occasional gap); South West Academy of Fine Arts (2000-2008); Minories Colchester & Chappel Galleries (one-man exhibitions, five and four respectively); Gainsborough House, Sudbury (1970). *Works in collections*: Colchester Museums, Epping Forest District Museum, East Contemporary Art - University Campus Suffolk. *Commissions*: London Electricity, National Grid. *Publications*: Charles Debenham's East Anglia (2000); From the Other Side of the Street (2006). *Works Reproduced*: as above plus oil paintings in public ownership (Essex). *Address*: Little Simons, Oldhouse Road, Great Horkesley, CO6 4EQ. *Signs work*: "Chas Debenham".

DEES, Stephanie Jane, RSW (2004), BA (Hons); MFA/The Scottish Arts Club Award (RSW, 2007); Cuthbert Young Artist Prize (RGI, 2006); Alexander Graham Munro Travel Award (RSW, 2002); Scottish International Education Trust Award (1998); Andrew Grant Bequest (ECA, 1997). *Medium*: acrylic/ mixed media. *b*: Hexham, 29 Mar 1974. *d of*: James

& Angela Dees. *Partner*: Peter Fortune. *Educ*: North Berwick High School. *Studied*: Edinburgh College of Art. *Represented by*: Scottish Gallery; Lemon Street Gallery. *Exhib*: The Scottish Gallery, Edinburgh since 1997; Lemon St. Gallery, Truro; White Space Gallery, Devon; Red Rag Gallery, Glos.; Red Rag Gallery, Bath. *Works in collections*: Paintings in Hospitals, Scotland; Chartered Surveyors of Scotland; Caledonian Hotel, Edinburgh; Edinburgh College of Art; Bank of Scotland; Scottish Courage; Royal College of Physicians. *Commissions*: many private. *Publications*: many brochures for solo shows at Scottish Gallery and Lemon Street. *Official Purchasers*: Alastair Salvesen, Eastern General Hospital. *Recreations*: RSW Council Member 2004-07. *Clubs*: Scottish Arts Club. *Address*: 20/6 Boat Green, Edinburgh, EH3 5LW. *Email*: stephaniedees@hotmail.co.uk *Signs work*: 'Stephanie Dees'.

DEL CAMPO, Michele. *Medium*: oil, prints. *b*: Sannicandro Garganico, Italy, 3 Aug 1976. *m*: Amparo Tarazona. one *d*. *Educ*: 2001: BA (Hons) in Illustration, Duncan of Jordanstone College of Arts, Dundee (UK); 2007: Fine Arts Degree, Universidad Complutense, Madrid (Spain). *Represented by*: Mark Jason Gallery, London; Jorge Alcolea Gallery, Madrid; Enlace Arte Contemporaneo, Lima. *Exhib*: one-man shows: Alpha Gallery, Gork Street, London (2013); Imago gallery, Lugano (2012); Enlace Arte Contemporaneo, Lima (2011); Mark Jason Gallery at The Gallery in Cork Street, London (2010); Mark Jason Gallery, London (2008); Galeria Jorge Alcolea, Madrid (2004, 2005, 2007); Galeria Fernando Alcolea, Barcelona (2005-2006); Galeria American Prints, Valencia (2004); Villa Zoya, Milano (1998). *Works in collections*: Standard Chartered Bank, London; BMW, Spain; Peugeot, Spain; Unipublic, Spain; Museo San Clemente, Spain. *Address*: Islington, London. *Email*: michele@micheledelcampo.com *Website*: www.micheledelcampo.com

DELAHAYE, Muriel, DA (Manc); teacher's certificate. *Medium*: Paintings - oil on canvas, Drawings - charcoal, pastel (figurative, local coastline, people on beach, fishermen and folklore). *b*: Lancs., 18 Feb 1937. one *s*. *Studied*: Regional College of Art, Manchester; Victoria College, Unversity of Manchester. *Represented by*: Oriel Tir a Mor, Borth; www.lpdelahay@yahoo.co.uk. *Exhib*: numerous, six solo shows; 1994 – 1st prize winner, Museum Modern Art, Wales; 2000 – 1st prize winner, 'Art West 2000 – Wales, Land and People'. Aberystwith Arts centre, Ceredigion Museum; Tabernacle Museum Modern Art, Machynlleth; Drawing Biennale; Attic Gallery, Swansea; Washington Gallery, Penarth; St. David's Hall, Cardiff; Civic Hall, Stuttgart, Germany; Albany Gallery, Cardiff; Kyffin Williams Drawing Prize, Anglesey; Nick Holly Gallery, Swansea; Oriel Tir a Mor, Borth; Studio 8 Gallery, Ruthin, Wales. *Commissions*: numerous - Families on Beach - seascapes - children. *Works Reproduced*: Limited edition, signed Giclee prints on cotton rag paper of 20 paintings; Book cover - Honno Publishers. *Address*: 'Efailwen', High St., Borth, Ceredigion, SY24 5JQ. *Email*: lpdelahaye@yahoo.co.uk *Signs work*: "M. DelaHaye".

DELHANTY, Denys, ATD (1949), RWA (1963); artist in collage, oil, water-colour, gouache; past Hon. Sec. and council mem. R.W.A.; Head of Art, Cheltenham Ladies College (1951-64), Senior Lecturer, Rolle College, Exmouth and Gloucester (1964-81). *b*: Cardiff, 13 Oct 1925. *m*: Kate Ormrod. three *s*. one *d*. *Educ*: St. Illtyd's College, Cardiff. *Studied*: Cardiff College of Art (1942-44, 1947-50, Ceri Richards). *Exhib*: RWA, etc. *Works in collections*: RWA, Welsh Arts Council, Cheltenham A.G., National Gallery of Wales. *Publications*: articles in Leisure painter magazine. *Recreations*: gardening, collecting ceramics. *Clubs*: Fosseway Artists, Cheltenham Group, Royal West of England Academy. *Address*: Combe House, Sheepscombe, Stroud, Glos. GL6 7RG. *Signs work*: "Denys Delhanty."

DELHANTY, Kate Elisabeth, DFA (Slade); artist in oil; artist mem. R.W.A.; taught art at Cheltenham Ladies College (1953-60). *b*: London, 8 Nov 1928. *d of*: Frank Ormrod, artist/lecturer. *m*: Denys Delhanty. three *s*. one *d*. *Educ*: Downe House, Newbury, Berks.

Studied: Reading University, Slade School of Fine Art (1950-53, Prof. Coldstream). *Exhib*: RA, Bristol (RWA), Cheltenham A.G., Bristol Guild, etc. *Works in collections*: RWA, Cheltenham A.G. *Publications*: articles in Leisure Painter Magazine. *Clubs*: Fosseway Artists, Cheltenham Group, Royal West of England Academy. *Address*: Combe House, Sheepscombe, Stroud, Glos. GL6 7RG. *Signs work*: "Kate Delhanty."

DELLAR, Roger, PS, RI, ROI; self taught artist in all media; A winner of 16 National Painting Awards including The Anthoy J Lester Art Critic's Award and the Le Clerc Fowle Medal. *b*: St.Albans, 29 May 1949. *m*: Lynda Ann Dellar. one *s.* one *d. Exhib*: RWS, PS, RSMA, NEAC, RI, ROI, RWA, RBA, RA, RP; Peninsula Gallery, USA; John Noott Gallery, Broadway; Fine Art UK, Ledbury; Whittington Gallery, Henley. *Works in collections*: internationally, University of Surrey. *Commissions*: Sir Donald Limon, Clerk of House of Commons. *Publications*: featured in: 'Watercolour Innovations' by Jackie Simmonds; 'The Wapping Group of Artists, the First Fifty Years'; 'The Artist' Magazine; 'The Wapping Group of Artists Sixty Years of Painting the Thames'. *Clubs*: Wapping Group of Artists, Langham Sketching Club, Chelsea Arts Society. *Misc*: Artist in Residence for Guildford International Music Festival, Petersfield Music Festival, Petworth House, and Festival of the Sea, Portsmouth. *Address*: Nutcombe Hill Cottage, Hindhead Rd., Hindhead, Surrey, GU26 6AZ. *Email*: rogerdellar@btinternet.com *Website*: www.rogerdellar.com *Signs work*: "ROGER DELLAR".

DELLER, Jeremy, Turner Prize (2004), Appointed Trustee Tate Gallery (2007); Awarded Albert Medal (RSA, 2010); Represented Great Britain at the Venice Biennale (2013). *Medium*: installation. *b*: London, 1966. *Studied*: Courtauld Institute of Art. *Represented by*: The Modern Institute, Glasgow; Art Concept, Paris; Gavin Brown's enterprise, New York. Exhib: "Open Bedroom" (1993); EAST International (1995); Centre for Visual Arts, Cardiff (1999); Wattis Institute for Contemproary Arts, San Francisco (2002); Centre Pompidou, Paris & Barbican Art Gallery, London (2004); Kunstverein, Munich (2005); Palais de Tokyo, Paris (2008); Creative Time and New Museum, New York/Hammer Museum, LA/Museum of Contemporary Art, Chicago (2009); Cornerhouse, Manchester (2009); Hayward Gallery (retrospective, 2012). *Commissions*: 2009: Manchester International Festival & Cornerhouse ("Procession"); 2009: The Three M Project ("It Is What It Is: Conversations About Iraq"). *Publications*: "The English Civil War; Part II" by Jeremy Deller (pub. Artangel, 2002); "The Uses of Literacy" by Jeremy Deller (pub. Book Works, 2004); "Folk Archive: Contemporary Popular Art from the UK" by Jeremy Deller & Alan Kane (pub. Book Works, 2006); "Marlon Brando, Pocahontas, And Me" by Jeremy Deller (text by Heidi Zuckerman Jacobson, pub. Aspen Art Press, (2009); "It Is What It Is. Conversations About Iraq" by Jeremy Deller (text by Nato Thompson, pub. Creative Time Books, 2009); "Procession" by Jeremy Deller (ed. Lesley Young, pub. Cornerhouse Publications, 2010); "Jeremy Deller: Social Surrealism" (ed. Robert Eikmeyer, Alistair Hudson, pub. Moderne Kuknst Nürnberg, 2012); "Joy in People" by Jeremy Deller (text by Stuart Halll, Ralph Rugoff, Rob Young, pub. Hayward Publishing, 2012); "Sound in Z: Experiments in Sound and Electronic Music in Early 20th Century Russia" (ed. Jeremy Deller, David Rogerson, Matt Price, 2013); "All That Is Solid Melts into Air" by Jeremy Deller (pub. Hayward Publishing, 2013); "Jeremy Deller: English Magic - Venice Biennale" (text by Chris Dercon and Hal Foster, pub. Biennale di Venezia, British Pavilion, 2013). *Principal Works*: projects include: "Acid Brass" (1997); "Unconvention" (1999); "The Battle of Orgreave" (2001); "After the Goldrush" (2002); "Memory Bucket" (2003); "Folk Archive" (2005); "Our hobby is Depeche Mode" (2006); "It Is What It Is" (2009); "So Many Ways to Hurt You" (2010); "Sacrilege" (2012); "Posters" (2012); "Joy in People" (2012); "The Bruce Lacey Experience" (2012); "English Magic" (2013); "Speak To The Earth" (2007-2017). *Misc*: instigated The Bat House Project in 2006, the result of which was a London bat facility at the Westlands Centre, Barnes. *Email*: jeremydeller@yahoo.co.uk *Website*: www.jeremydeller.org

DEMARCO, Richard, OBE, l'Ordre des Arts et Lettres de France, Cavaliere de la Reppublica d'Italia, Gold Order of Merit Republic of Poland, Hon. FRIAS, Hon.DFA (ACA), RSW, SSA, RSA; water-colourist/printmaker in water-colour, gouache, pen and ink, screen printing, etching; Professor Emeritus of European Cultural Studies, Kingston University; Artistic Director, Demarco European Art Foundation; Hon. Royal Scottish Academician (HRSA). *b*: Edinburgh, 9 July, 1930. *m*: Anne Muckle. *Educ*: Holy Cross Academy, Edinburgh. *Studied*: Edinburgh College of Art (1949-54, Sir William Gillies, Sir William MacTaggart, Leonard Rosoman). *Exhib*: over sixty one-man shows including Third Eye Centre (Glasgow), Aberdeen Artspace, Editions Alecto Gallery (London), Octagon Gallery (Belfast). *Works in collections*: SNGMA, Dundee City A.G., V&A, Aberdeen A.G., Hunterian Museum Glasgow, SAC, Edinburgh City A.G., Citibank, Chemical Bank, Bank of Scotland, Royal Bank of Scotland, Clydesdale Bank, HRH Prince Philip, HRH Prince Charles, The British Government Art Collection. *Publications*: The Road to Meikle Seggie - The Artist as Explorer, A Life in Pictures. *Recreations*: exploring 'The Road to Meikle Seggie' from Scotland to the Mediterranean. *Clubs*: hon. mem. Scottish Arts, hon. mem. Chelsea Arts. *Misc*: (office) Demarco European Art, New Parliament House, 5 Regent Road, Edinburgh EH7 5BL. *Address*: 23a Lennox St., Edinburgh, EH4 1PY. *Signs work*: "Richard Demarco."

DEMPSTER, Justin William, BA Hons (1995); East Sussex Travel Award (1996). *Medium*: oil, acrylic. *b*: Luton, 6 Dec 1972. *m*: Vanessa Meintjes. *Educ*: Icknield High School, Luton. *Studied*: University of Brighton. *Exhib*: RA Summer Exhbn (2004); Hunting Art Prizes, RCA (2002); Discerning Eye, Mall Galleries (2004); other mixed shows: Hall Gallery, Leonard Street, London (1992); Mall Galleries (1994); East Sussex Arts Winners, Gardners Arts Centre, Sussex (1996). *Publications*: cover Hunting Art Prizes Catalogue (2002). *Works Reproduced*: 'Gorgewalk', advertisement for Hunting Art Prizes. *Address*: 23 Honeygate, Luton, Beds LU2 7EP. *Website*: dempsterpaintings.com *Signs work*: 'Justin Dempster'.

DEMSTEADER, Mark, The Lyceum Prize; The Sidney Andrews Scholarship; The Public Eye Prize, The Affordable Art Fair. *Medium*: oil, watercolour, drawing. *b*: Manchester, 1963. *Studied*: Rochdale College, Oldham College; Slade School. *Represented by*: Panter & Hall, London. *Exhib*: Panter & Hall, London. *Address*: c/o Panter & Hall, 11-12 Pall Mall, London SW1Y 5LU. *Email*: enquiries@panterandhall.com *Website*: www.panterandhall.com *Signs work*: 'M.Demsteader'.

DENISON, David, surrealist artist in acrylic and oil; tutor, Prison Staff College, Wakefield. *b*: Wakefield, 21 May 1939. *s of*: Ernest Denison. *m*: Linda. one *s*. two *d*. *Educ*: Snapethorpe Secondary Modern School, Wakefield. *Studied*: Doncaster College of Art (1972). *Exhib*: Wakefield, Skipton, London, Keighley, Bradford, Camden Arts Centre; one-man shows: Manor House Public A.G., Ilkley (1970, 1977), Goole Museum and A.G. (1971), Wakefield Museum and A.G. (1972, 1974), Leeds City Gallery (1973), Doncaster A.G. (1973), Arthur Koestler Exhbn. London (1977), Bradford Cartwright Hall (1980), Angela Flowers Gallery, Arts Council of Gt. Britain. *Works in collections*: Brighton Museum and A.G., Sir Roland Penrose Collection. *Publications*: illustrated The Battle of Wilderness Wood by R. Adams. *Address*: 58 Station Rd., Burley in Wharfedale, W. Yorks. *Signs work*: "D. Denison."

DENNING, Antony, C&G Dip. (1988); sculptor and carver in wood, stone, welded steel. *b*: Berks., 1 Nov 1929. *m*: Mary Denning. three *s*. three *d*. *Educ*: Clayesmore. *Studied*: Horsham School of Art, Weymouth College (1985-86), City & Guilds Art School (1986-88). *Exhib*: Cumberland Lodge, Windsor (1965), Blythes, Edinburgh (1966), Hambledon, Blandford (1971), Nuffield, Southampton (1972), Museum, Dorchester (1977), Arts Centre, Salisbury (1979), Honiton Festival (1994), etc. *Works in collections*: Southampton

University; private collections in UK, Europe, USA, Canada. *Commissions*: Fishmongers' Co., Grocers' Co., St. Peter's Boyatt Wood, All Saints' Wardour, St. Mary's School, Highgate School, and private commissions. *Publications*: The Craft of Woodcarving (Cassell, 1994), Woodcarving - Two Books in One (Sterling, U.S.A, 1999; Apple Press, U.K., 2000). *Clubs*: Soc. of Heraldic Arts. *Address*: 42 Nettlecombe, Shaftesbury, Dorset, SP7 8PR. *Signs work*: "Antony Denning."

DENNIS, Christopher John, SLm, ASEA; artist in water-colour and oil of equestrian, countryside and dogs art, abstract and miniatures. *b*: Derby, 10 Feb 1946. three *s.* one *d. Educ*: Ushaw College. Taught by artist mother B.C. D'Oyly Aplin. *Exhib*: exhbns: Chelsea, Mall Galleries, Alexander Llewellyn, Royal Miniature Soc., Society of Equestrian Artists, Hilliard Soc. *Works in collections*: Queen's miniatures. *Commissions*: York Race Committee, Racecourse Association. *Address*: 3 The Cottages, Aldfield, Ripon, N.Yorkshire HG4 3BE.

DENT, Ann, mem. Chelsea Art Society. *Medium*: oil, watercolour. *b*: Kensington, 30 Jul 1924. *d of*: Dr. John Yerbury Dent & Alma Dent. *m*: widow. one *s.* two *d. Studied*: Coventry Art School; St.Martin's School of Art; Ecoles des Beaux Artes, Paris. *Exhib*: RA; National Portrait Gallery; Mall Galleries; Sunday Times Water Colour Exhibition (Mall Galleries, 2007 - by selection); Manchester Town Hall. *Works in collections*: National Portrait Gallery; Huntings Ltd; Leicester Art Gallery; Aldeburgh Festival Marland Gallery (1998). *Commissions*: portraiture and landscape commissions, at home and abroad; Laing Calendar 1983. *Official Purchasers*: National Art Collections Fund. *Works Reproduced*: by NPG. *Principal Works*: portrait of Sir Angus Johnson Wilson (NPG). *Recreations*: drawing, reading. *Misc*: appeared on Japanese TV in 1993. *Address*: 12 Smith Street, Chelsea, London SW3 4EE. *Signs work*: 'Ann L.Dent'.

DENTON, Kenneth Raymond, RSMA, FRSA, ISMP, President East Anglian Group of Marine Artists; landscape and marine artist in oil, Royal Society of Marine Artists, International Society of Marine Painters. Fellow: Royal Society of Arts. Hunting Group Art Awards. *Medium*: oils. *b*: Chatham, 20 Aug 1932. *s of*: Stanley Charles Denton. *m*: Margaret Denton (decd.). three *s. Educ*: Troy Town School, Rochester. *Studied*: Rochester School of Art and Technical School, Medway College of Art for decorative design and painting, landscape painting with David Mead. *Exhib*: York, Rochester, London, Eastbourne, Thames Ditton, Stratford-on-Avon, Norwich, Los Angeles, Mystic, Vancouver, San Francisco, Pennsylvania, Washington D.C., Tunbridge Wells; 45 one-man shows, ROI, RBA, etc. *Works in collections*: world-wide. *Commissions*: many, private. *Official Purchasers*: Financial Institutions, Banks, etc. *Works Reproduced*: hundreds: cards, calendars, prints, books, etc. Medici Soc., Royles, Artists Britain, Yachting Monthly, Yachting World, Connoisseur, Guild Prints. *Recreations*: music, classical piano. *Clubs*: R.S.M.A. *Address*: Priory Farm Lodge, Sporle, Kings Lynn, Norfolk, PE32 2DS. *Website*: www.dentonuk.net *Signs work*: "Kenneth Denton."

DENTON, Raymond, NDD (1960); The Charles Pears Prize; winner of 'Best in Show' Prize 2004 St. Ives Society of Artists 1st Open Exhibition. *Medium*: oil, pastel. *b*: Lambeth, London, 4 Sep 1939. *m*: Anne. one *s.* one *d. Educ*: Leeds College of Art. *Studied*: book illustration. *Exhib*: Royal Academy, The Royal Society of Marine Artists, The Laing Art Exhbn, also Yorkshire Artists Exhbn Bradford, Cardiff, Penzance, Falmouth, St. Ives, Cheltenham, Fowey and many London galleries. *Publications*: Artist and Illustrators, Cornwall Today. *Clubs*: St. Ives Society of Artists. *Misc*: Featured on west country television. *Address*: Trebartha Place, 26 Fore Street, St. Erth, Cornwall, TR27 6HT

DENYER-BAKER, Pauline, Des RCA, RMS, HS, MASF, SLm; Intermediate NDD in Design; Silver Bowl RMS (World Exhibition of Miniatures, 1995); Best Traditional Portrait

Miniature (MASF, 2001, 2007); Washington Award for Still Life (World Exhibition of Miniatures, 2004); Bell Award (HS, 2004). *Medium*: oil and watercolour on ivorine, portraits in miniature. *b*: Hove, Sussex. *d of*: RCW Sheppard. *m*: Brian Denyer-Baker, ARCA. two *s*. *Educ*: Brighton and Hove High School. *Studied*: Brighton College of Art; Royal College of Art. *Represented by*: commissionaportrait.com. *Exhib*: RA Summer Exhbns (1989-2004); World Exhibition of Miniatures, Tasmania (1990); World Exhibition of Miniatures, London (1995). *Works in collections*: Europe, America, Canada, Australia, Austria, Japan, UK. *Commissions*: Earl of Buchan (2004); ten miniature portraits for Hancock family (2006). *Official Purchasers*: Earl of Buchan. *Works Reproduced*: 'Eye of the Artist', William Feaver (Observer, Jun 1993). *Principal Works*: 'Michelle' Summer Exhibition RA 1996; 'Sam' Summer Exhibition RA 2005; 'Eye of the Artist' Summer Exhibition RA 1993. *Recreations*: music, gardening, swimming. *Clubs*: Royal Miniature Society full member; Hilliart Society; Society of Limners. *Address*: Pollards Farm Cottage, Ditchling Common, Burgess Hill, W.Sussex RH15 0SE. *Email*: paulinedenyerbaker@gmail.com *Website*: www.paulinedenyerbaker.com *Signs work*: 'Pauline Denyer-Baker Des R.C.A.'

DESMET, Anne Julie, RA (2011), RWA (2009), MA(Oxon) (1991), RE (1991), Rome Scholar in Printmaking (1989-90); SWE; BA (Oxon) 1986; Editor of 'Printmaking Today' (1998-2013). Hon Fellow, Aberystwyth University. *Medium*: wood engraving, linocut, collage. *b*: Liverpool, 14 Jun 1964. *m*: Roy Willingham. one *s*. one *d*. *Educ*: Sacred Heart High School, Liverpool. *Studied*: Worcester College, Oxford (1983-86), Central School of Art, Printmaking (1987-88). *Represented by*: Hart Gallery, London. *Exhib*: group shows: worldwide; selected solo shows UK: Hart Gallery, London (2004-2012); Whitworth Art Gallery (1009, touring UK in 2010); Ashmolean Museum (1998, touring UK in 1999); Duncan Campbell Gallery (1991-2002) Royal Overseas League (1992), Godfrey & Watt Gallery (1993, 1995, 2009); Ex Libris Museum Moscow, Russia (1995). *Works in collections*: Ashmolean Museum, BM, V&A, Whitworth, Fitzwilliam, National Art Library; H.M.The Queen, Ex Libris Museum, Moscow; museums in France, Finland, Brazil, Poland, Italy. *Commissions*: Sotheby's, British Museum, British Library, 'The Times', V&A. *Publications*: 'Primary Prints' (A&C Black 2010); 'Handmade Prints' (A&C Black, 2000); 'Anne Desmet: Towers and Transformations' (Ashmolean Museum 1998); 'Anne Desmet - Urban Evolution' (Whitworth 2009). *Address*: 22 Queen Anne Road, Hackney, London E9 7AH. *Email*: anne.desmet@btinternet.com *Website*: www.annedesmet.com *Signs work*: "Anne Desmet".

DESOUTTER, Roger Charles, RSMA; painter in oil. *b*: London, 21 Mar 1923. *m*: Mary Elizabeth. one *s*. one *d*. *Educ*: Mill Hill School and Loughborough College. *Exhib*: RSMA, Stacy-Marks Galleries, ROI, GAvA, Lloyds, Mystic Seaport, Forbes Gallery, New York, Marine Arts Gallery, Salem, Kirsten Gallery, Seattle. *Works in collections*: US Mercantile Marine Academy. *Commissions*: Shipping Companies, Banks, Insurance Companies, Lloyds Agents. *Publications*: 20th Century British Marine Painting, Liners in Art, A Celebration of Marine Art; paintings reproduced as greeting cards, calendars and fine art prints. *Address*: Copshrews, Amersham Rd., Beaconsfield, Bucks, HP9 2UE. *Signs work*: "ROGER DESOUTTER."

DEVEREUX, Jacqueline, Patchings 2001 & 2002; Beaux Arts de Beziers, France; Elected President of the Society of Graphic Fine Art, London, Feb 2014.. *Medium*: watercolour. *b*: London, 16 Mar 1948. *d of*: George Alexander Allen. *m*: Barry Devereux, photographer. one *d*. *Studied*: St.Albans Art School (Fine Art Printmaking). *Represented by*: Society of Graphic Fine Art. *Exhib*: Mall Galleries (RI, SWA); Bankside Gallery (RWS); Cork Street (SGFA); Menier Gallery (SGFA); Chelsea Art Society; Tore Gallery, Inverness; La Jolla, USA; Tokyo, Japan; RK Burt Gallery, London; Barbican Library, London. *Works in collections*: Esso, London; College Paul Bert, Beziers, France. *Commissions*: BRL Hardy Wines, Adelaide; Oriel House Hotel, N.Wales; Posford Duvivier, Peterborough; BP Sanders

& Co Ltd, Hertfordshire. *Publications*: "Watercolour Innovations" by Jackie Simmonds (Harper Collins); The Artist, Leisure Painter. Book "A Private View - an artist's world" by Jackie Devereux (Jacaranda Publishing). *Recreations*: travel, writing. *Address*: 47 West Street, Crowland, PE6 0EE. *Email*: jb.devereux@btinternet.com *Website*: www.watercolour-online.co.uk *Signs work*: "J.B.DEVEREUX".

DEVLIN, George, RSW (1964); painter in oil, water-colour, etching and ceramics. *b*: Glasgow, 8 Sep 1937. *s of*: George Devlin. *Studied*: Glasgow School of Art (1955-60). *Exhib*: many one-man shows; Belfast Open 100, 2nd British Biennale of Drawing, Contemporary Scottish Painting (Arts Council), etc. *Works in collections*: HM The Queen, Scottish National Gallery of Modern Art, Arts Council, Aberdeen A.G., Essex County Council, Leicester and Strathclyde Universities, Edinburgh City Collection, Argyle County Council. *Publications*: illustrations for Scotsman and Maclellan Publishers. Designed set and costumes for new ballet by Walter Gore (1973) and presented by Scottish Ballet. *Address*: Rosebank, 6 Falcon Terr. Lane, Glasgow, G20 0AG. *Signs work*: "Devlin."

DEWSBURY, Gerald, RCamA (2003); BA; landscape, architecture and natural history painter in oil and water-colour. *b*: Dartford, 11 Jan 1957. *s of*: John Russell Dewsbury, engineer. *m*: Kim Rolling. one *s.* one *d. Educ*: King Edward VI Grammar School, Retford. *Studied*: Falmouth School of Art (1977-80). *Exhib*: RA, London; John Noott Gallery, Broadway; St. David's Hall, Cardiff; Theatr Clwyd, Mold; Alderley Gallery, Alderley Edge; Y Capel, Llangollen; Ffin y Parc, Llanrwst; RCA, Conwy; Twenty-Twenty Gallery, Much Wenlock; plus numerous others. *Works in collections*: Stowells of Chelsea; Grosvenor Museum, Chester; Soc. for Contemporary Art in Wales; Tabernacle Museum of Modern Art, Wales - Machynlleth; Sultan of Oman; plus numerous other private collections. *Commissions*: regularly works to commission. *Address*: Tyn-Y-Ffridd, Llangwm, nr. Corwen, LL21 0RW. *Signs work*: "Gerald Dewsbury" or "G.D."

DI GIROLAMO, Megan Ann, FRBS, RBA, SPS; MA Ceramics (1987), ATC (Lond.) (1963), NDD (1962); awards: De Laszlo Medal (R.B.A.), 1996; Silver Medal (R.B.S.), 1997; Frink Sculpture School Award, 1999; Potclays Award, 2000; Scott Goodman Harris Award 2001; UBS Award 2004; ceramic sculptor – stoneware and raku, casting – bronze and resin; Artist in Residence, Astor College for the Arts. *b*: New Delhi, 13 Jan 1942. *d of*: Robert & Mavis Surdivall. *m*: Romeo di Girolamo PRBA. two *d. Educ*: Aylesbury Grammar School. *Studied*: High Wycombe College; Hornsey School of Art; South Glamorgan Institute of Higher Education. *Exhib*: The Mall Galleries Royal Society of British Artists (1987-2001), Royal Academy (1993, 1996, 2005), Royal West of England Academy (1996-7), Society of Portrait Sculptors (1999-2001), RBS Summer Exhibition (2000), Albemarle Gallery London, The Gallery Manchester, Art in Action, Waterperry. *Commissions*: Great Missenden Church (Dunford), Villa Scalabrini (Vatican), Harris – sculpture, Bennet – sculpture, Dr. Riley – Wendover Health Centre, Trilogy – St. Mary's Church, Aylesbury (Fairclough). *Publications*: features in "Modern British Sculpture" by Guy Portelli (2005). *Address*: Sandrocks Studio, Sandrocks Hill, Sedlescombe, Battle, E.Sussex TN33 0QR. *Email*: megan@di-girolamo.co.uk *Website*: www.megan-di-girolamo.co.uk/megan htm *Signs work*: 'Megan di Girolamo'.

DI GIROLAMO, Romeo, RBA, NDD; artist in oil; Bucks. Architectural Competition (1953, 1954); Bucks. Art Scholarship (1954-59); Granada Theatre National Painting Prize (1957); David Murray Travelling Scholarship awarded by R.A. (1959); formerly Head of Art Depts., Gt. Marlow Secondary, Slough Grammar for Boys, The Radcliffe Comprehensive; at present Head of Painting Dept., Amersham College of Further Education and School of Art (formerly High Wycombe School of Art); mem. of the Academic Board and Governor of the College. *b*: Civitella Casanova, Italy, 1939. *s of*: Paolo Emilio di Girolamo. *m*: Megan, A.T.C. *Educ*: Quainton and Waddesdon secondary schools. *Studied*:

High Wycombe School of Art (1954-59). *Exhib*: RA, RBA, Art Bureau Travelling exhbns. and many one-man shows. *Works in collections*: private collections in many countries. *Address*: Sandrocks Studio, Sandrocks Hill, Sedlescombe, Battle, E.Sussex TN33 0QR. *Signs work*: "Romeo di Girolamo."

DI STEFANO, Arturo, MA Fine Art (1981); painter in oil on linen, woodcuts, etchings. *b*: England, 25 Feb 1955. *s of*: Salvatore and Nicolina Di Stefano. *m*: Jan Di Stefano. one *s*. *Studied*: Goldsmiths' College, University of London (1974-77, Jon Thompson), R.C.A. (1978-81, Peter de Francia). *Exhib*: Kettle's Yard, Cambridge (1988), Serpentine Gallery (1989), John Hansard Gallery (1989); one-man shows, Oxford O4 Gallery, Pomeroy Gallery, London (1987), Woodlands Gallery (1987), Fasolino Gallery, Turin (1987), Pomeroy Purdy Gallery, London (1989), Purdy Hicks (1991,1993,1996), Walker A.G. (1993). *Works in collections*: Unilever, Arthur Andersen, Museum of London, N.P.G. London, Government Art Collection, Walker A.G., L'pool, Barclays Bank, Leicester Museum, Harris Museum, Preston. *Commissions*: Portrait of Sir Richard Doll for National Portrait Gallery, London. *Publications*: The School of London: A Resurgence in Contemporary Painting (Alistair Hicks, Phaidon 1989); four catalogues: 1989, 1991, 1993, 1995. *Address*: 92 Fairfoot Rd., Bow, London E3 4EH. *Signs work*: "A. Di Stefano."

DICK, Colin, NDD (1951); figurative painter in oil, water-colour, stoneware sculpture, retd. teacher; former Head of Art, Campion School, Royal Leamington Spa. *b*: Epsom, Surrey, 28 Feb 1929. *m*: Delia D., MA. one *s*. two *d*. *Educ*: Wennington School, and Leighton Park. *Studied*: St. Martin's (1947-1951, Frederick Gore, RA, R.V. Pitchforth, RA). *Represented by*: Hobbs McLaughlin. *Exhib*: 'Romanies, Fairs and local customs' Nuneaton Riversley Gallery (1995), Herbert A.G. Retrospective, Christchurch JCR Oxford, Musée Boulogne sur Mer, Biarritz Galerie Municipal, 'Coventry between Bombing and Reconstruction' Herbert A.G. (1997), RA Summer Exhbns. (seven oil paintings). *Works in collections*: Herbert A.G. and Museum, Coventry (35 paintings). *Commissions*: Midland waterways and traditional gatherings commissions accepted, portraits of people of ephemeral lifestyles in unusual beautiful settings, multi-cultural musicians. *Publications*: "Colin Dick: Seeing Life" by Richard Yeomans PhD (pub. Hobbs McLauglin) - on sale at Herbert Art Gallery, Coventry and from www.collindick.com (£30 post free). *Works Reproduced*: 'Last of the Horsedrawn Narrowboats - Coventry Canal' Bridgeman Art archiveonline/Herbert Art Gallery section; 'Horizon' Arts Magazine Issue No. 1 "17 Paintings by C.D." www.saltpublishing.com/horizon/issues/01; Art Space magazine of Leamington Spa Society of Artists Issue 2010. *Recreations*: painting at horse fairs. *Clubs*: Umbrella for the Arts, Coventry; University of the Arts, London. *Address*: Stoke Green Studio, 98 Binley Rd., Stoke, Coventry CV3 1FQ. *Email*: colindick@gmail.com Website: www.colindick.com *Signs work*: "Colin Dick."

DICKENS, Mark, Post-Grad Diploma (Italy), BA (Hons). *Medium*: painting, mixed media. *b*: London, 18 Jul 1963. *Studied*: 'Il Bisonte' School of Graphic Art, Florence, Italy (1988); Maryland Institute College of Art, Baltimore, USA (1984); Central School of Art and Design, London (1983). *Represented by*: Stephen Lacey Gallery, London. *Exhib*: 2003: 'Art London' Artfair, Chelsea, Stephen Lacey Gallery, London Group 90th Anniversary Show, Cork St., Artfair 2003, Islington. 2002: Gallery Artists, Stephen Lacey Gallery, International Arts Festival, Prague, Gallery Fine 2, London. *Works in collections*: Banca Toscana, Italy. *Commissions*: Kuwait Petroleum (Europe). *Works Reproduced*: Media Contacts - Quarterly 'Art London' (2003). *Clubs*: elected mem. 'London Group of Artists'. *Address*: Space Studios, 142 Vauxhall Street London SE11 5RH. *Email*: markdickens14@hotmail.com *Website*: www.markdickens.net

DICKENS, Pip, BA (Hons) Fine Art Painting, (First Class); MFA. *Medium*: oil. *b*: Fiskerton-cum-Morton, Nottinghamshire, 14 Jun 1962. *m*: Brian. *Studied*: Harrogate

College of Art & Technology (BTEC ND), (1993); Leeds Metropolitan University (1966); Slade School of Fine Art, London (2000). *Represented by*: Renee Pfister, London; Artzu Gallery, Manchester; David Knowles/Atelier, Leeds/London; Alan Kluckow, Berkshire; Campden Gallery, Glos; Festival Gallery (online). Exhib: Solo shows: Rugby Art Gallery, Rugby (2013); Campden Gallery, Glos. (2013); The Brindley Arts Centre (2012); Daiwa Anglo-Japanese Foundation, London (2012); Stanley & Audrey Burton Gallery, University of Leeds (2012); Creative Arts Building, University of Huddersfield (2011); Cartwright Hall Art Gallery, Bradford (2010); Brahm Gallery, Leeds (2008); Cassian de Vere Cole Fine Art, London (2000). Group shows include: Islington Mill, Salford (2012); Beldam Gallery, London (2011); Brass Gallery, Leeds (2010); Monika Bobinska Gallery, London (2007). *Works in collections*: Cartwright Hall Art Gallery, Bradford; The Stanley & Audrey Burton Gallery, University of Leeds, Numerous Private Collections UK and overseas. Corporate Collections: Doyle Caygill Capital SA, Geneva, Switzerland; The Arch Hotel, London; Sovereign Capital, London. *Commissions*: Commissioned Residency at The Stanley and Audrey Burton Gallery, University of Leeds; Leverhulme Artist in Residence at University of Huddersfield, Department of Music; Research in Japan (part of Leverhulme project); Artist in Residence, Cartwright Hall Art Gallery, Bradford, Yorkshire; Research in Iceland - Edna Lumb Art Travel Award; Design for Integral external public art commission Piccadilly, London (MAKE architects). *Publications*: "Shibusa - Extracting Beauty" by Pip Dickens & Professor Monty Adkins (pub. Univ. of Huddersfield Press, 2012); Exchange Magazine; The Leeds Guide 2004; Exhibition catalogues. *Misc*: Full name is Philippa Anne Dickens but known as Pip Dickens to avoid confusion with another UK British painter of same name. Lecturer in Fine Art at Lancaster University since 2013. *Address*: 15 Thornfield, Ashton Road, Lancaster LA1 5AG. *Email*: pip@pip-dickens.com *Website*: www.pip-dickens.com *Signs work*: "P A DICKENS".

DICKER, Kate, Elected Member of Society of Wood Engravers and The Royal Society of Painter-Printmakers (2007); BA Hons (1979-80), Postgrad Dip: History of the Modern Period (1992-94); MA Fine Art Printmaking (2004). *Medium*: wood engraving, painting and printmaking. *b*: Southsea, 15 Nov 1953. *d of*: Molly Dicker (painter and etcher, 1924-2000). *Studied*: Camberwell College of Art (John Lawrence), Winchester School of Art. *Exhib*: Southampton City Art Gallery (2004), Society of Wood Engravers, Royal Academy (1998), The Bankside Gallery, London; Portsmouth University. *Works in collections*: Royal County Hospital, Winchester, Hampshire County Council, Winchester City Council, Kensington & Chelsea Borough Council, Hampshire County Council Archive & Museum Services. *Commissions*: illustrations for: Weald & Downland Open Air Museum Medieval Cookery Book by Maggie Black (1993); In the Valley of The Fireflies by Peter Hobday (1995); Tales from a Village School by Miss Read (1995). *Publications*: Articles: 'Artists' Books, Microbes and Mechanical Trolls'; 'Printmaking Today' (Nov 2000); 'Wood Engraving in Britain's Art Schools' Printmaking Today (Nov 1998), 'Metro Links from Rivers to the Sea' Printmaking Today (Autumn 2004). *Clubs*: The Society of Wood Engravers, The Society of Painter-Printmakers. *Misc*: in 2002 awarded Southern Arts Colle Verde Residency, Italy. *Address*: 6 Rosewarne Court, Hyde St, Winchester, SO23 7HL. *Email*: kd-zappypod@talktalk.net *Website*: www.katedicker.com *Signs work*: "Kate Dicker".

DICKERSON, John, MFA, (1968), Dr.RCA (1974); artist and lecturer. *Medium*: painting, ceramics, sculpture, drawing. *b*: Swaffham, Norfolk, 11 Oct 1939. *s of*: F.E. Dickerson, businessman. *m*: Mary Robert. one *s*. *Educ*: Hammond's School, Swaffham. *Studied*: Goldsmiths' College, Art Students' League, NY, Pratt Inst., NY (1966-68), RCA (1971-74). *Works in collections*: Japan, USA, UK, Taiwan, Malaysia, Sweden, Australia, Serbia, Hong Kong, Spain, Montenegro, Canada, Saudi Arabia, Switzerland. *Publications*: author: Raku Handbook; Pottery Making - A Complete Guide; Aspects of Raku Ware;

Pottery. *Misc*: currently on the faculty of Syracuse University: London programme. *Address*: 47 Creffield Rd., London W5 3RR. *Email*: johndickerson4@gmail.com *Signs work*: some ceramics and sculpture carry "JD" monogram; other works signed "John Dickerson."

DICKESON, Gaynor, SRN, MmedSci (in OH), DipSBA (Dist), SBA, SFP, RHS Silver medal for Magnolia x Solangeana Series (2011), SBA CBM (2009, 2012); Botanica 2010 Lucca Silver Gilt. *Medium*: watercolour, colour pencil, drawing. *b*: Rugby, 12 Apr 1947. *m*: Robin. two *s*. two *d*. *Studied*: QE Hospital Birmingham (1965-68); SRN, Birmingham (1968); Psychology, OH & Business, Norway (1980-91); MmedSci Birmingham (1996); SBA distance learning botanical art (2007-09). *Exhib*: LA, California (1984); Stavanger (1990); Westminster Central Hall (2007-); Lucca, Italy (2010); Palmengarten, Frankfurt (2010, 2012); Cumberland Lodge (2010); Hunt Institute, Pittsburgh (2013); other exhibitions. *Works in collections*: Saga Petroleum - Stavanger, Cumberland Lodge - Windsor Park, Hunt Institute, private collections. *Commissions*: Esso Norge (1994); private commissions. *Principal Works*: Mallards (1990); Savoy Cabbage (2009); Magnolia Series (2011). *Recreations*: gardening, walking. *Clubs*: Society Botanical Artists, Society Floral Painters, Society for All Artists, American Society of Botanical Artists. *Address*: Saltings, Windmillfield, Bosham, Chichester, W. Sussex PO18 8LH. *Email*: gaynorsflora@mac.com *Website*: www.gaynorsflora.com *Signs work*: until 2000 "Gaynor Houghland", since 2000 "Gaynor Dickeson".

DICKSON, James Marshall, DA (Edin, 1964), RSW (1972); artist in ink, gouache, PVA; Head of Art, Lochgelly Centre. *b*: Kirkcaldy, 31 Jul 1942. *s of*: James Dickson, driver. *Educ*: Beath High School. *Studied*: Edinburgh College of Art (1960-64, Stuart Barrie). *Exhib*: RSW (Edin), RGI (Glasgow), Kirkcaldy A.G., Perth A.G., Loomshop Gallery. *Works in collections*: Banff County, Angus County, Aberdeen, Tayside, Leeds Educ. *Address*: 44 Main St., Lochgelly, Fife. *Signs work*: "James Marshall Dickson, R.S.W."

DICKSON, Jennifer, RA, RE, LLD (1988), CM (1995); printmaker and photographer. *b*: Piet Retief, S. Africa, 17 Sep 1936. *Studied*: Goldsmiths' College School of Art (University of London, 1954-59) and Atelier 17, Paris, under S. W. Hayter. *Works in collections*: V&A; National Gallery of Canada; Hermitage, Leningrad; Cleveland Art Institute, etc. *Publications*: 30 major suites of original prints. *Address*: 20 Osborne St., Ottawa, Ontario K1S 4Z9, Canada.

DIGGLE, Philip, painter in oil on canvas. *b*: 30 Dec 1956. *s of*: Dedalus Diggle, B.A., M.A., Ph.D. *Educ*: Ancoats Manchester Grammar; Trinity College Oxford. *Exhib*: Bede Gallery, Jarrow, Warwick Arts Trust (1985), Angela Flowers Gallery (1986, 1987), Art Now, London (1986, 1987, 1988), Festival of the 10th Summer, Manchester (1986), Barcelona Workshop (1988), Flowers East (1989, 1991); one-man shows: Rochdale A.G. (1985), Angela Flowers Gallery (1985), Warwick Arts Trust (1985), Some Bizarre Gallery Piero(1988, 1989), Barbizon Gallery, Glasgow (1989, 1990, 1991), Barcelona Workshop (1989), Flowers East (1991); Granada/LWT (1988), B.B.C. Playbus (1990), Piroque NY, NY. *Works in collections*: Chase Manhattan Bank, NY, Rockerfeller Centre. For information see www.philipdiggle.com. *Works Reproduced*: Film: Philip Diggle (35 mins), released July 2003. *Address*: 498 Archway Rd., London N6 4NA. *Website*: www.philipdiggle.co.uk

DINN, Catherine Margaret, BA (1979), MA (1980), Dip. Art Gallery and Museum Studies (1981); Curator, Falmouth Art Gallery (1981-92); freelance writer and lecturer. *b*: Norfolk, 4 Sep 1957. *d of*: Dr. & Mrs. A.J. Dinn. *m*: Michael E. Richards. two *d*. *Educ*: Walthamstow Hall, Sevenoaks. *Studied*: History of Art and English, University of Nottingham (1976-79), Courtauld Inst. of Art (1979-80), University of Manchester (1980-81). *Publications*: Co-author (with David Wainwright) of biography of Henry Scott Tuke, R.A. (Sarema Press, 1989; reprinted 1991). *Address*: Boscolla, Florence Pl., Falmouth, Cornwall, TR11 3NJ.

DITZ, professional photographer (info@aappl.com). *Medium*: acrylic. *b*: Vienna, Austria, 9 Oct 1945. *m*: Cameron Brown. one *d. Represented by*: The Bridgeman Art Library; london@bridgeman.co.uk; Artists and Photographers Press Ltd, info@aappl.com. *Exhib*: RA (1982, 84, 85, 89, 90, 91, 92, 93, 97, 2000, 2001); Hillside Gallery, London (1989 -97, 2003); Fosse Gallery, Stow-on-the-Wold (1985-88); Mall Galleries (1983, 84, 90); many more across UK and in France. *Publications*: 'A Collection of Cat's Tales' (pub. AAPPL, 2003); 'What is It? Photographs to Keep You Guessing' (pub.AAPPL, 2005). *Works Reproduced*: many worldwide. *Principal Works*: animal 'spreads'-single pictured comprising multiple images of animals. *Recreations*: riding, photography, gardening. *Address*: Church Farm House Wisley Surrey GU23 6QL. *Email*: ditz@aappl.com *Website*: www.aappl.com *Signs work*: 'Ditz'.

DIXON, Jo, Society of Woman Artists (SWA); South West Academy of Fine & Applied Arts (SWAC); Thelma Hulbert Gallery's Open Art Exhib (2002); SWAC (2004) Marine House at Beer Award; Black Swan Guild Open Exhib (2002); SWA (2009) Barbara Tate Award at Mall Galleries. *Medium*: Oil, charcoal. *b*: Gainsborough, 24 Apr 1950. *m*: Dr. Michael Dixon. one s. two *d. Educ*: Wycombe Abbey School. *Studied*: Hammersmith College of Art. *Represented by*: Priory Gallery Broadway; Marine House at Beer. *Exhib*: Solo exhibitions: St John's Smith Square (1994), Ross-on-Wye Festival (1999). Royal West of England Academy Autumn Exhibitions, Royal Academy, South West of England Academy, Platform 100-Discerning Eye, Bridport Arts Centre (2012). Priory Gallery, Broadway; SWA Mall Gallery. *Works in collections*: Exeter Healthcare Arts. *Commissions*: Many private commissions. *Publications*: Marie Claire; Devon Life; International Artist; Bristol Magazine. *Official Purchasers*: Exeter Healthcare Arts. *Works Reproduced*: Bristol Magazine front cover (Nov 2004). *Principal Works*: Mainly figurative. Recreations: Music. *Address*: Culmside, Mill St., Uffculme, Devon EX15 3AT. *Email*: jana.hodixon@gmail.com *Signs work*: "JO DIXON".

DJORDJEVIC, Jovan, BA Hons Fine Art (First Class) 1980. *Medium*: Stamp design & manufacture, oil, watercolour, drawing, prints, sculpture. *b*: Rochdale, Lancashire, 25 May 1957. *s of*: Zinadin & Ewa Djordjevic. one *s.* one *d. Educ*: Greenhill School, Rochdale. *Studied*: Rochdale College of Art (Foundation, 1975-76); Lanchester Polytechnic, Coventry (1976-80). *Represented by*: Nick Diggory Illustration. *Exhib*: Recent exhibitions include: Arthaus Open Studios 12, Wivenhoe (2009); Colchester Art Society Summer Open Exhibition (2009); Kowalsky Gallery, London (2009); Printmakers Council 7th International Mini Print Exhbn (2009); Royal Academy Summer Exhibition (2008); Digby Gallery, Mercury Theatre, Colchester (2008); Association of Illustrators (national venues, 1996-2008). *Works in collections*: Waltham Forest Council; Lambeth Council; Labour Museum, Manchester; Bernd Laygaff. *Commissions*: Coventry City Council; Ikon Gallery, Birmingham; Peoples March for Jobs, Liverpool to London 1981. *Publications*: "Giant Leap" by Adrian Berry (ISBN 0312877854). *Official Purchasers*: Lambeth Council; Waltham Forest Council. *Works Reproduced*: 'Box Clever', 'Wivenhoe International Clock', 'Food for Thought'. *Principal Works*: 'Box Clever' a set of 25 miniature prints (Limited Edition). *Recreations*: printmaking, reading, cooking, foraging, gardening. *Clubs*: Colchester Art Society; Association of Illustrators; DACS. *Address*: 56 Rosabelle Avenue, Wivenhoe, Essex, CO7 9NZ. *Email*: jovan@jovan.demon.co.uk *Website*: www.jovandjordjevic.com

DMOCH, Paul, self taught artist in water-colour, architect; 3rd prize winner in The International Artist magazine competition (2002). *b*: Warsaw, 22 Sep 1958. *m*: Grazyna. one *d. Studied*: Polytechnic of Warsaw (architecture). *Exhib*: RI (1997 winner Frank Herring award, 1998-99), RBA (1997-98), NEAC (1997), Singer and Friedlander/Sunday Times Water-colour Competition (1996-00, '06), RWS (1997, winner Daler-Rowney Premier and Saunders Waterford awards) (1999-00); Albermarle Gallery, London (2001). *Works in* *collections*: Vatican and private collections worldwide. *Address*: 5 Cherry Close, South Wonston, Winchester, Hants. SO21 3HU. *Email*: pauldmoch@hotmail.com *Website*: http://www.artmajeur.com/aquarelliste *Signs work*: "PaDmoch".

DOBSON, Mary: see THORNBERY, Mary

DOCHERTY, Michael, RSA (2005); DA (Edin.) (1968), Post-Grad. Dip. (1969), ARSA (1984); artist in oil/acrylic on canvas/wood, ink/graphite on paper/card; lecturer, Edinburgh College of Art; senior lecturer/ course leader in painting, ex-Dean of Faculty, Heriot-Watt University. *Medium*: mixed media. *b*: Alloa, 28 Dec 1947. *s of*: George Docherty. *m*: Odette Dominique Vitse. one *s*. one *d*. *Educ*: St. Modan's High School, Stirling. *Studied*: Edinburgh College of Art (1964-68, 1968-69); Moray House College 1969-70, Post-graduate course. *Exhib*: Richard Demarco Gallery, New 57 Gallery, Fruitmarket Gallery, French Inst., National Gallery of Modern Art, Fremantle Art Centre, Western Australia, RSA, RSW, Air, London, Fine Art Soc., France, Brazil, Hungary, Poland, Finland, USA, Spain, Germany, Latvia, Lithuania; Invited exhibitions: various venues. *Works in collections*: Contemporary Art Soc., Scottish National Gallery of Modern Art, Scottish Arts Council, Edinburgh College of Art, Royal Scottish Academy, City of Edinburgh Art Centre, National Library of Scotland. *Commissions*: various national and international. *Publications*: various. *Works Reproduced*: various surveys of contemporary art/ catalogues. *Address*: 20 Howard Pl., Edinburgh, EH3 5JY. *Email*: mike_doc@hotmail.com *Signs work*: "Michael Docherty" on reverse.

DODD, Alan, NDD (1963), Cert. RAS (1966); painter, interior designer, muralist. *b*: Kennington, Ashford, Kent, 23 Nov 1942. *Educ*: Ashford Grammar School. *Studied*: Maidstone College of Art, Royal Academy Schools. *Exhib*: RA Bicentenary Exhibition (1968); one-man shows: New Grafton Gallery (July, 1969, Nov., 1970, Oct., 1972), 'Four English Painters' Galleria Estudio Cid, Madrid (Nov., 1970); Baroque & Gothick: architectural studies from the Grand Tour (The Georgian Group, Nov 2004); 'Pangea' Gallery, Yoxford, Suffolk: Grand Tour Paintings (Aug 2005). *Works in collections*: V&A, Sir John Soane's Museum; also in private collections in England, USA, Australia, Spain, Portugal. *Commissions*: V&A: The Painted Room (1986), Alexandra Palace: Murals (1988), Spencer House: Trompe l'oeil work (1990), Sir John Soane's Museum: Pompeiian ceiling (1992), Home House: re-creation of three lost works by Zucchi (1998), set designs for Opera Omnibus: "Masked Ball" (2000), designed the Westminster Millennium Cross, memorial to the late Cardinal Hume (2000); Tusmore Park, Bicester: two large grisaille panels of classical figure groups for the rotunda of the new house (2004); Gothick dining room, Brompton Square (2006); Backdrop for the new Cavalry at Brompton Oratory (2011); 'Facade', a 50ft garden mural, Eye, Suffolk (2013). *Misc*: alternative address: High Hall, Weston, Beccles, Suffolk NR34 8TF. *Address*: 295 Caledonian Rd., London N1 1EG. *Website*: www.alandodd.co.uk *Signs work*: "Dodd" with date.

DODDS, James, Doctor of the University of Essex: DU (Essex) 2007; Shipwright (1976), BA (1980), MA (1984); artist in oil and linocut. *b*: Brightlingsea, 3 May 1957. *m*: Catherine. one *s*. one *d*. *Studied*: Colchester School of Art (1976-77), Chelsea School of Art (1977-80), R.C.A. (1981-84). *Exhib*: National Maritime Museum Cornwall (2003), National Maritime Museum Greenwich (2003), Tide & Time Museum, Yarmouth (2004), Messum's, London (2004, 2006, 2007, 2009, 2011), Dowling Walsh, Rockland, Maine, USA (2010, 2012). *Works in collections*: Britten-Pears Library, Ipswich and Horniman Museums, National Maritime Museum. *Commissions*: National Trust, Lloyds Register. *Publications*: Peter Grimes, The Wanderer, The Shipwright Trade, Wild Man Of Orford, Wild Man of Wivenhoe, Alphabet of Boats, Black Shuck, James Dodds paintings, ABC of Boat Bits, The Song of the Waterlily, Longshore Drift, "James Dodds and the Jardine Press", River Colne Shipbuilders, 'Tide Lines' by Ian Collins (biography). *Address*: Barnacle House, 20 St.

John's Rd., Wivenhoe, Colchester, Essex, CO7 9DR. *Email*: james@jamesdodds.co.uk *Website*: www.jamesdodds.co.uk *Signs work*: "James Dodds" or "J.D."

DOGGETT, Susan Marguerite, BA (Hons); WCC award for Contemporary Craft (1994); book artist and bookbinder in mixed media; Lecturer in book arts, Croydon College; M.A. (design by independent project). *b*: Reading, 24 Sep 1960. *d* one. *Educ*: Waingel's Copse School, Woodley, Reading. *Studied*: Oxford Brookes University and Brighton University. *Exhib*: Festival Hall London, Royal Library Copenhagen, Angel Row Gallery Nottingham, Crafts Council, London, American Crafts Museum, NY, Washington DC Centre for Book Arts Minnesota. *Works in collections*: Tom Phillips, private libraries USA. *Commissions*: Booker Prize bindings (1996, 1998, 1999). *Publications*: 'Bookworks' (Apple Press, 1998). *Clubs*: Fellow of Designer Bookbinders. *Address*: 4 Lancaster Ct., Lancaster Ave., London SE27 9HU. *Signs work*: "S.D." or "Sue Doggett."

DOIG, Maxwell Kirkcaldy, BA (Hons) Fine Art, Post Grad Diploma Fine Art, Joseph Webb Drawing Prize, Laura Ashley Scholarship, Villiers David Prize. *Medium*: mixed media on canvas on panel. *b*: Huddersfield, 21 Feb 1966. *s of*: David, Thomas Doig & June Doig. *Educ*: Salendine Nook High School, Batley Art College, Manchester School of Art, Slade School of Art UCL. *Studied*: drawing, painting, etching, lithography, life drawing, anatomy. *Represented by*: Albemarle Gallery, 49 Albemarle St, London. *Exhib*: Albemarle Gallery , Hart Gallery (one man and group shows); Christies, Ettinger Gallery New York (group); various London Art Fairs; touring exhbn: 'Painting and Drawings 87-97' Huddersfield AG, Harrogate AG, Wakefield AG and Salford AG, Forni Gallery in Bologna and Milan. *Works in collections*: Prudential plc, Provident Financial Group, University of London, Mercer Gallery Harrogate, Huddersfield Art Gallery, Holman Fenwick & Willan; many private collections. *Publications*: fully illustrated exhibition catalogues for solo exhibitions at Albemarle Gallery. *Official Purchasers*: Prudential plc (2003), Provident Financial Group (1991), Huddersfield AG (1997), Mercer Gallery, Harrogate (1995). *Works Reproduced*: 'Paintings and Drawings 87-97' Exhibition catalogue, 'Villiers David' Prize Exhbn. Calatogue (1999), Albemarle Gallery Exhbn. Catalogue (2003). *Principal Works*: 'Self Portrait Drawing, A Textile Worker' (1996), 'Figure in a Boat' (2001), 'Teabreak' (2001), 'White Boat, Self Portrait' (2003), 'Figure in Moorland Water' II (2010). *Recreations*: collector of paintings and ceramics. *Clubs*: none. *Address*: 63 Birch Road, Berry Brow, Huddersfield HD4 7LR. *Email*: maxwelldoig@hotmail.co.uk *Website*: www.maxwelldoig.com *Signs work*: Maxwell Doig.

DOKOTLIVER, Miriam, MA Fine Art & Design; BA Hons Fine Art. *Medium*: mixed media, watercolour, oil. *b*: Ukraine. one *s.* one *d. Studied*: Glasgow School of Art; Gray's School of Art. *Exhib*: Mall Galleries; RSA; Compass Gallery, Glasgow; Roger Billcliffe, Glasgow; Jonathan Shore, New York; The Hanover Galleries, Liverpool; The Talbot Rise Gallery, Edinburgh; McLellean Galleries, Glasgow. *Works in collections*: Cameron Mackintosh, UK; Kan & Law Design Consultants, Hong Kong; Aberdeen Art Gallery & Museum; Conoco UK, Scotland; University of Aberdeen, Scotland. *Address*: 41 Kelvinside Gardens, Glasgow G20 6BQ. *Email*: dokotliver@yahoo.co.uk *Signs work*: 'Miriam Dokotliver', 'Dokotliver'

DONALD, George M., DA (1967), ATC (1969), MEd. (1980), RSA (1993), RSW (1976); artist in painting & printmaking; former lecturer in drawing and painting, Edinburgh College of Art; Summer School Director, Centre for Continuing Studies. *Medium*: Painting. *b*: Ootacamund, S. India, 12 Sep 1943. one *d. Studied*: Edinburgh College of Art; Hornsey College of Art; Edinburgh University. *Represented by*: Open Eye Gallery, Edinburgh; Bohun Gallery, Henley-on-Thames; Edinburgh Printmakers Workshop. *Exhib*: annually. *Works in collections*: V&A, RSA, SAC, Aberdeen A.G., SNGMA, Hunterian Museum; and in public and private collections in UK, USA, Europe, Far East. *Commissions*: worldwide.

Publications: Anatomia (Artists book) pub. Flying Horse Press, University of Central Florida (2004). *Works Reproduced*: www.georgedonald.com. *Misc*: teaches anatomy drawing at 'The Princes Drawing School' London, University of Florida, USA. *Address*: Bankhead, By Duns, Berwickshire TD11 3QJ. *Email*: g.donald@surfree.co.uk *Website*: www.georgedonald.com www.royalscottishacademy.org *Signs work*: "George Donald."

DONALDSON, Antony, Post Grad Scholarship in Fine Art (1962-3); Harkness Fellowship to USA (1966-68). *Medium*: oil, drawing, prints, sculpture. *b*: England, 2 Sep 1939. *s of*: John William Donaldson. *m*: Patricia Anne. two *s*. *Studied*: Slade School of Fine Art; London University. *Exhib*: Solo: first one-man show at the Mayor Rowan Gallery London followed by several other (1965-82, 1989, 2004), Felicity Samuel Gallery, London, many overseas including Galerie Alain Blondel, Paris; Corcoran Gallery, Los Angeles; group exhbns: over thirty worldwide since 1958 inc. RA. *Works in collections*: Gulbenkian Foundation, Lisbon; Tate Gallery, London; Ulster Museum, N. Ireland; Walker AG, Liverpool, Arts Council GB, plus many UK and worldwide. *Commissions*: Park Hyatt, Tokyo; Victoria Mills, London; Tower Bridge Piazza; Anchor Court, London. *Works Reproduced*: 'Pop Art' Lucy Lippard (pub.Frederick Praeger, NY, 1966); 'Movements in Art since 1945', Edward Lucie-Smith (pub. Thames & Hudson 1969); 'Pop Art', Michael Compton (pub.Hamlyn, 1970); Art and the Sixties, This Was Tomorrow, ed. Chris Stephens and Katherine Stout (Tate Gallery, 2004), and numerous other publications. *Address*: 91a Pimlico Road, London SW1W 8PH. *Email*: info@antonydonaldson.com *Website*: www.antonydonaldson.com *Signs work*: 'Antony Donaldson'.

DONALDSON WALTERS, Sheila, FRSA; Council Member Chelsea Art Society; Royal Scholarship RCA (wartime); later calligrapher for Historical Section War Cabinet Offices. *b*: London, Oct 1920. *d of*: James Alexander Donaldson. *m*: Nigel Vincent Walters (decd). one *s* (decd). three *d*. *Educ*: Royal Masonic School. *Studied*: Bromley & Beckenham Art Schools, Chelsea and Royal College of Art; SIAD, BTEC, DATEC Committees. *Exhib*: Chelsea Art Society (1980-); Queen's University, Belfast. *Works in collections*: private collections in England, France, Portugal & USA; Imperial War Museum, London. *Commissions*: Designed 'Joseph's' first shop in Kings Road, Salon 33; Consultant designer for World Congress of Anaesthesiologists, London (1968). *Principal Works*: Education - encouragement of the arts a lifetime occupation. *Recreations*: reading, listening to music, meeting friends. *Clubs*: Chelsea Arts Club SW3. *Address*: Studio 6, Chelsea Farmhouse Studios, Milmans Street, London SW10 0BY. *Signs work*: 'Sheila Donaldson Walters' or 'SDW'.

DONLIN, Martin, HND Architectural Glass; Recent awards include: Royal Society of Arts Award (Belfast Project, 2010); Art in Airports Award, Indianapolis, USA (2009); Public Art Award, Poole (2008); Art in Health Award, Belfast (2006); Art for Architecture Church Award, Frankfurt, Germany (2004). *Medium*: architectural glass. *b*: Hockley, Essex, 1959. *m*: Laura Windle. *Studied*: Medway College of Design (1977-78); Swansea (1984-87). *Commissions*: include: Coleridge College, Cambridge; MediCo Centre, Paderborn; Dallas Love Field; Michigan State University; Indianapolis Airport: Empire Theatre, Liverpool; Rhondda Hospital; City Hall, Belfast; Queen Alexandra Hospital; New Apostolic Church, Frankfurt; San Antonio Hospital, USA; Washington Metro, USA; Raleigh Durham Airport, North Carolina, USA; Belfast City Hall; Manchester Police Force; Hammersmith Hospital; Aberdeen Dental School, and many others worldwide. *Principal Works*: Architectural stained glass. *Address*: 438 South Coast Road, Telscombe Cliffs, East Sussex BN10 7BE. *Email*: martin@martindonlin.com *Website*: www.martindonlin.com

DONOVAN, Patrick Richard. *Medium*: oil, watercolour, pen & graphite. *b*: Frimley, Surrey, 19 May 1944. *m*: Marilyn. two *s*. *Exhib*: N. Wales in conjunction with the Arts Council for Wales. Various one-man exhibitions in the UK and France. Royal Society of Marine Artists (2004-2009), Maritime Gallery Mystic Seaport USA (2006-2009), Modern

Marine Masters, Mystic Seaport (2007-2009). *Works in collections*: private UK and abroad; National Museum of Wales; Local Authority museums. *Commissions*: Shipping Companies, Armed Services, RNLI, private collectors. *Address*: Clare House, 41 The Droveway, St.Margarets Bay, Dover, CT15 6BZ. *Signs work*: "PATRICK R. DONOVAN".

DOREY, Russell Peter, BA Hons (Painting), PGDip. RA Schools. *Medium*: oil on canvas, pencil drawings. *b*: Chelmsford, Essex, 26 Mar 1961. one *s.* one *d. Educ*: Felsted School, Essex. *Studied*: Maidstone College of Art (1979-82, John Titchell, ARA), RA School (1983-86, Norman Blamey, RA). *Represented by*: Curwen and New Academy Galleries, 34 Windmill Street, London W1T 2JR. *Exhib*: RA Summer Exhbns. (1985-86), Agnews Young Contemporaries (1988), Burlington Gallery; Spa Galleries, Tunbridge Wells; Abbott and Holder, London; Curwen Gallery, London. *Address*: 31 St. Thomas Rd., Hastings, E. Sussex TN34 3LG. *Email*: russelldorey@hotmail.co.uk *Website*: www.russelldorey.co.uk *Signs work*: "Russell Dorey."

DORMENT, Richard, BA (1968), MA (1969), MPhil (1975), PhD (1975); art critic, Daily Telegraph; Hawthornden Prize for Art Criticism in Britain (1992); Critic of the Year, British Press Awards (2000). *b*: USA, 15 Nov 1946. *m*: Harriet Waugh. one *s.* one *d* (by a previous marriage). *Studied*: Princeton University (1964-68), Columbia University (1969-75). *Publications*: Alfred Gilbert (1985); Alfred Gilbert, Sculptor and Goldsmith (exhbn. catalogue, RA London, 1986); British Painting in the Philadelphia Museum of Art, From the Seventeenth through the Nineteenth Century (1986). *Address*: Daily Telegraph, 1 Canada Square, Canary Wharf, London E14.

DOS SANTOS, Bartolomeu, Emeritus Prof. in Fine Art, University of London, Fellow (UCL), RE; artist and printmaker, public art, ceramic tiles, etched stone; taught at Slade School of Art (1961-1996). *b*: Lisbon, 24 Aug 1931. *Studied*: Lisbon Art School (1950-1956), Slade School, under Anthony Gross (1956-1958). *Exhib*: 87 solo exhibs. worldwide, retrospective, Gulbenkian Foundation, Lisbon (1989), Retrospective - The London Institute (2001). *Works in collections*: British Museum, V&A, MOMA NY, Bibliotheque Nationale, Paris. *Commissions*: include, etched stone decoration for Entre Campos tube station, Lisbon, Nihonbashi station, Tokyo, Macau Museum. *Publications*: Pas Memorial, by J. Saramago, Koron Verlag, Zurich (1999). *Address*: 57 Talbot Rd., London N6 4QX. *Signs work*: "B Dos Santos."

DOUBLEDAY, John, sculptor. *Medium*: mainly sculpture cast in bronze - also works in two dimensions. *b*: Langford, Essex, 1947; *s of*: G. V. Doubleday, farmer. *m*: Isobel J. C. Durie. three *s.* (one decd). *Educ*: Stowe. *Studied*: Goldsmiths' College (1965-68). *Exhib*: one-man shows in London, New York, Amsterdam, Cologne. *Works in collections*: include Charlie Chaplin (1981) Leicester Square; Isambard Kingdom Brunel (1982) Bristol and Paddington; The Beatles (1984) Liverpool; Commando Memorial CTCRM (1986); Sherlock Holmes (1991) Switzerland; Graham Gooch (1992) Chelmsford; J.B. Pflug (1994) Braith Mali Museum, Biberach, Nelson Mandela (1997) UWC in Italy, UK, USA, Singapore; Gerald Durrell (1999) Jersey; Sherlock Holmes (1999) Baker St. Station, London; The Dorset Shepherd (2000) Dorchester; 'Jimmy' Jabara (2004); USAF Academy, Colorado Springs, Nelson (2005); Gibraltar (Bicentennial Memorial); Battle of Maldon Monument, Essex (2006); Lord Woolf and Rt Hon. Selwyn Lloyd, Fettes College (2009); Guruji Chichalkar (Indore) (2010); Museums include: Ashmolean Museum, BM, V&A, and Tate. *Commissions* HM The Queen, Gibraltar (2012); Pte Herbert Colombine VC, Walton (2014). *Address*: Goat Lodge, Great Totham, Maldon, Essex, CM9 8BX. *Email*: i.doubleday@btinternet.com *Website*: johndoubleday.co.uk

DOUGLAS, Brian David, NEAC, RBA; BA (Fine Art), RAS. *b*: 8 Jul 1948. *s of*: David Douglas. *Educ*: Maidstone, RA Schools. *Studied*: RAS (1973). *Exhib*: RBA, NEAC, RA.

Works in collections: Brinsley Smith. *Publications*: RBA; entry in 'Dictionary of International Biography' 32nd Edition (Nov 2005). *Works Reproduced*: RBA. *Recreations*: reading, music. *Clubs*: RBA, NEAC. *Address*: 26 Whitestone Drive, York, YO31 9HZ. *Website*: RBA NEAC *Signs work*: 'Brian Douglas'.

DOUGLAS, Jean Mary, Dip.AE (1979), SBA (1991); artist in pastel and oil, school teacher (retd.). *b*: London, 26 Sep 1927. *d of*: Sidney and Margaret Elgie. *m*: Frank Douglas. two *d*. *Educ*: Loughton County High School and Teacher Training College, Portsmouth. *Studied*: London University Art Diploma (1976-79). *Exhib*: Royal Exchange, Guildhall, Mall Galleries, Central Hall Westminster, and mixed exhbns. E. Anglia, S. England and Wales, also Sweden and Austria. *Publications*: Reproduction rights of paintings sold to Royle and Medici, etc. *Address*: 'Crossways', Main Road, Westfield, E.Sussex, TN35 4QH. *Signs work*: "J.M.D."

DOVER, Peter Charles, BA (Hons) Graphic Design (1984), MA (RCA) Fine Art (1988), ARE (1995); printmaker, painter, maker in relief printmaking on paper, found objects and materials; also musician. *b*: Merseyside, 10 Apr 1954. *Educ*: Wallasey Grammar School. *Studied*: Wallasey College of Art (1980-81), Leeds Metropolitain University (1981-84), RCA (1986-88, under the late Alistair Grant). *Exhib*: Curwen, New Academy Gallery, London. *Works in collections*: Tate Gallery, Ashmolean, Dudley Museum, Plymouth Museum, London Hospital, St.Thomas's, Estonia National Museum. *Commissions*: I.T.U. Floor of Gt. Ormond Street Hospital for Sick Children, silkscreen mural 'The Sea' (1990-91). *Address*: 8 Betts House, Betts St., London E1 8HN. *Signs work*: "P.C. Dover" usually verso.

DOWDEN, Joe Francis, painter in watercolour. *b*: Wimbledon, London, 16 Jun 1958. *m*: Ruth. *Exhib*: Singer & Friedlander, Sunday Times watercolour competition (1998, 2000), Laing art competition (1998, 1999, 2000), RI (1998), RSMA (1998), Chichester Open (1998), eleven solo exhibs., yearly exhib. in Surrey. *Publications*: Water in Watercolour (Search Press), Two in One Watercolour (David & Charles), regular articles for Artists & Illustrators magazine; videos: Make it Look Real, Volumes 1&2 (Teaching Art). *Address*: 91 Downlands Ave., Worthing, W. Sussex BN14 9HF. *Email*: joedowden@yahoo.co.uk *Signs work*: "Joe Francis Dowden."

DOWE-EDWARDS, Virginia, BA Hons. *Medium*: ceramics. *b*: Ipswich, Suffolk, 9 May 1974. *m*: Adam Edwards. two *d*. *Studied*: BA Hons 3D Design: Ceramics, University of Wolverhampton (1994-97); BT Tech Art & Design, Suffolk College, Ipswich (1992-94). *Represented* by: OCG, Ambleside; CCA, Cambridge; The Cupola Gallery, Sheffield. *Exhib*: Shire Hall, Stafford; Leith Gallery, Edinburgh; Imagine Gallery, Long Melford; Pyramid Gallery, York; Mid Cornwall Gallery, Parr; Rostra Gallery, Bath; Wills Art Warehouse, Putney; Fenwick Gallery, Warkworth; Cecilia Colman Gallery, St. Johns Wood; Serena Hall, Southwold; Baxters, Dartmouth; Craft Centre, Leeds; Torquil, Henley in Arden. *Commissions*: private. *Publications*: New British Design 1998 by Peta Levi (pub. Mitchell Beazey). *Principal Works*: Hand-built ceramic smoke-fired dogs. *Address*: Old Newton House, 16 Main Street, Newton, Rugby, Warwickshire CV23 0DY. *Email*: virginiaedwards@btinternet.com *Website*: www.virginiadowe.com *Signs work*: monogram with paw symbol stamped onto base of paw

DOWLER, Niggy. *Medium*: oil. *b*: London, 9 Jul 1990. *Studied*: self taught. *Represented by*: Hybrid Gallery, Honiton; Redrag Gallery, Bath. *Exhib*: Solo: Hybrid Gallery (2014); various group (2012-2014). *Works in collections*: private collections. *Commissions*: Lady Ursula D'Abo (2013); Tom Meyer (2013); Nick Meyer (2014). *Publications*: International Artist. *Address*: Knyftons Farm, Old Ditch, Westbury-sub-Mendip, Wells, Somerset BA5 1HN. *Email*: niglydowler@gmail.com *Website*: www.niggydowler.com *Signs work*: "Niggy D", "ND".

DOWLING, Jane, Hon. RBA, BA (Oxon) Hons. (1946), MA (Oxon.) (1977); painter, etcher, engraver; drawing tutor, Ruskin School of Drawing for over 30 years and currently, and taught for over 30 years at RA schools. *b*: Dec 1925. *d of*: Dr G.B. Dowling, M.D., F.R.C.P. *m*: Peter Greenham, (decd.). one *s*. one *d*. *Educ*: St. Anne's College, Oxford. *Studied*: Slade and Ruskin; Byam Shaw; Central School (Gert Hermes). *Represented by*: Bridgeman Art Library. *Exhib*: New Grafton Gallery, RA Summer Exhbn. since 1954; many mixed exhbns., Travelling Arts Council exhbn. with Peter Greenham (1984), 'The Glass of Vision' at Chichester Cathedral, 'The Long Perspective' Agnews (1987), 'A Personal Choice' Kings Lynn (1988), 'Art in Churches' Tewkesbury and Worcester (1991), retrospective, Mompesson House, Salisbury (1992), Leighton House (2001) Tempera Society, Stations: The New Sacred Art, Bury St. Edmunds Art Gallery Trust, (Lent 2000), Chappell Gallery (2002), small retrospective, Antony House Cornwall (2009); St.Peters College, Oxford, Queens College, Oxford. *Works in collections*: HRH The Prince of Wales, The late Sir Brinsley Ford, Judy Egerton, Dr. Nicholas Penny, Sir Richard Carew Pole, Farringdon Trust Buscot House, Southampton City A.G., Ashmolean Museum and loans to Churchill Hospital and John Radcliffe Hospital. *Commissions*: small mural: Edwin Abby Mural Fund for the Oxford Oratory Church (1995). *Publications*: various articles. *Official Purchasers*: The Faringdon Trust; Lady Margaret Hall, Oxford, and see above. *Recreations*: drawing. *Clubs*: Oxford Union. *Address*: The Old Dairy, opp. St Mary's House, Charlton-on-Otmoor, nr. Islip, Oxon., OX5 2UQ. *Signs work*: "J.D."

DOWLING, Tom, artist in oil. *b*: Dublin, 23 Jun 1924. *s of*: G.B. Dowling, M.D., FRCP, Consultant Dermatologist. *Educ*: Royal Naval College, Dartmouth. *Studied*: City & Guilds of London Art School (1963-67, Gilbert Spencer, Rodney Burn, Bernard Dunstan). *Exhib*: RA, RBA, NEAC, ROI, RP, RE, Richard Allen Gallery, New Grafton Gallery, Pictures for Schools exhbn. *Works Reproduced*: "Cowes Week". *Clubs*: Emsworth Sailing. *Address*: 31 Slipper Rd., Emsworth, Hants. PO10 8BS. *Signs work*: "TOM DOWLING" or "T.B.D." (on small paintings).

DOWNIE, Kate, DA, Post Dip.F.A.; artist/lecturer in acrylic, collage, printmaking, photography; part-time tutor, Fine Art Dept., Edinburgh College of Art. *b*: N. Carolina, USA, 7 Jun 1958. *m*: Peter Clerke. one *d*. *Educ*: Ellon Academy, Aberdeenshire. *Studied*: Gray's School of Art, Aberdeen (1975-80, Alexander Fraser, Francis Walker). *Exhib*: Collins Gallery, Glasgow (1991), Talbot-Rice Gallery, University of Edinburgh (1992), Amsterdam, Brussels, Utrecht, Cardiff, Aberdeen. *Works in collections*: Aberdeen A.G., Aberdeen University, Edinburgh University, Kelvingrove A.G., Peoples Palace Glasgow, Allied Breweries, Cleveland A.G., SAC, BBC Scotland. *Clubs*: Scottish Arts, Edinburgh. *Address*: 20 Boswell Avenue, Edinburgh EH5 2EB. *Signs work*: "Kate Downie."

DOWSON, Katharine, Princess of Wales Scholarship RCA, IIRG Research Fellow. *Medium*: sculpture. *b*: London. *Studied*: Heatherley's (1984-85); Camberwell BA (1985-88); Royal College of Art MA (1989-92). *Represented by*: GV Art London. *Exhib*: 'Brains: The Mind as Matter', 'Medicine Now', 'Images of the Mind', The Glass Delusion, Gregor Mendel: Planting the Seeds of Genetics, Head On, Spectacular Bodies, Myriad, Mitosis, Relics of the Mind, British Glass Biennial x2, RA Summer Exhibition x5. Shows in UK, Europe, S. Korea, Brazil, Singapore, USA. *Works in collections*: Arts Council; Wellcome Collection; Ulster Museum; Aberdeen Art Gallery; Institute of Neuroscience Newcastle University. *Commissions*: Cultura Inglesa, Newcastle University, Wellcome Collection, Biomechanical Society. *Publications*: Brains: The Mind as Matter, Images of the Mind, Relics of the Mind, Glass North East, Head On, Spectacular Bodies, Myriad, Shark Infested Waters Saatchi Collection. *Principal Works*: Myriad, Pia Mater, My Soul. *Clubs*: Chelsea Arts Club, Royal British Society of Sculptors. *Website*: www.katharinedowson.com *Signs work*: 'Katharine Dowson', 'K.Dowson'.

DOYLE, John, MBE (1994), RWS; 3rd prize Singer & Friedlander; artist in water-colour and aquatint; past President, Royal Water-colour Soc. (1996-2000). *b*: London, 15 Feb 1928. *s of*: Eric Doyle. *m*: Elizabeth two *s.* two *d. Educ*: Sherborne School. *Studied*: Maidstone College of Art, part-time. *Exhib*: Canterbury Cathedral (1973, 1976, 2008), RA, RWS, Spinks (1981, 1983, 1990), Catto Gallery, Hampstead (1989), exhibition to mark 1400th anniversary of Foundation of Cantebury Cathedral (1997), Chris Beetles Gallery (2002), Sissinghurst Castle (2010), Paintings of Mount Athos, Hellenic Centre (2014). Exhibits twice a year with the Royal Watercolour Society, Bankside Gallery. *Works in collections*: The Vatican. *Publications*: An Artist's Journey down the Thames (Pavilion Books, 1989). *Clubs*: Garrick. *Address*: Church Farm, Warehorne, Ashford, Kent, TN26 2LP. *Signs work*: "J.D." on small works, "John Doyle" on large works either pencil or water-colour.

DRAPER, Kenneth, MA (1969), RA (1992); sculptor and painter; Mark Rothko Memorial Scholarship (1971); Arts Council Major Award (1977). *b*: Killamarsh, Sheffield, 19 Feb 1944. *m*: Jean Macalpine, photographer/artist. one *s. Educ*: Killamarsh Secondary Modern. *Studied*: Chesterfield School of Art, Kingston College of Art and RCA (Bryan Kneale). *Exhib*: one-man shows: Redfern Gallery, Royal Academy, Hart Gallery, Islington, Peter Bartlow Gallery, Chicago, Adelson Gallery, N.Y.; Glen Greene Gallery, Santa Fe; Austin Desmond Gallery, London; Louise Hallett Gallery, London; Quest Gallery, Bath; New Academy Gallery, London. *Works in collections*: Arts Council of Great Britain, Contemporary Arts Soc., Fitzwilliam Museum, Ashmolean Museum Courtauld Inst., Mappin Art Gallery, Sheffield, Usher Gallery Lincoln, Lloyds of London, International Bank of Japan, London, ICI London, McCrory Corporation NY USA, Harris Museum Preston. *Publications*: The Life and Art of Kenneth Draper by Roger Bertoud. *Address*: Carrer Gran 55a, 07720 Es Castell, Menorca, Spain. *Email*: drapermacalpine@gmail.com *Website*: www.kennethdraper.com *Signs work*: "Kenneth Draper."

DRAPER, Matthew John, BA (Hons) Fine Art. *Medium*: drawing. *b*: Stone, Staffordshire, 21 Mar 1973. *s of*: Jean Draper. *Studied*: Walsall College of Art (1991-92), Falmouth School of Art and Design (1992-95). *Represented by*: Open Eye Gallery, Edinburgh; Lemon Street Gallery, Truro. *Exhib*: Open Eye Gallery (2000, 2002, 2004, 2006, 2008), Lemon Street Gallery (2005, 2007, 2009, 2009), Beaux Arts Bath (2004, 2006), Jerwood Drawing Prize (2006), Hunting Art Prize (2002, 2004), Royal Scottish Academy (2003, 2006), Royal Scottish Society of Painters in Watercolour (2001, 2002), Cheltenham Open Drawing (1999), Art Miami (2006), Chelsea Art Fair (2001, 2003), Art London (2003), Affordable Art Fair (2001, 2002, 2005), From Castle to Palace, City Art Centre, Edinburgh (2007), Royal Glasgow Institute (2002, 2006). *Works in collections*: City of Edinburgh, Glasgow Museum and Art Gallery, Bank of Scotland, Paintings in Hospitals Scotland. *Commissions*: The Calledonia Hotel, Edinburgh. *Publications*: "Nostalgia", Lemon Street Gallery (2005), "January Light" Lemon Street Gallery (2007), "In Series" Lemon Street Gallery (2009). *Address*: 15/5 Chancelot Terrace, Edinburgh, EH6 4SS. *Email*: matt.draper@hotmail.co.uk *Website*: www.matthewjdraper.co.uk *Signs work*: "MATTHEW J. DRAPER".

DRING, Melissa Jane, BSc (Hons.) 1989, PS, ARBSA, FBI. Dip. (1988); police forensic artist, portrait painter in pastel and oil, freelance courtroom artist. *b*: Winchester, 1 Apr 1944. *d of*: William Dring, RA RWS RP. *m*: Michael Little. two *s. Educ*: St. Swithun's, Winchester. *Studied*: Winchester School of Art, R.A. Schools. *Exhib*: RA, RP, RBA, PS. *Works in collections*: Northampton Central Museum and A.G., Jane Austen Centre, Bath, Czech Embassy London, Northampton Guildhall. *Commissions*: portraits in private and public collections in oil and pastel; forensic art facial recreations for TV programmes on C4, BBC1, BBC4, ITV3, Open University. *Publications*: Pastel Artist International, The Artist, Jane Austen's Regency World; articles on forensic artwork in Police Review, and The Journal of Audiovisual Media in Medicine. *Principal Works*: New speculative likeness; a forensically researched portrait of Jane Austen, commissioned by the Jane Austen Centre, Bath, 2002. *Address*: 10 St. George's Pl., Northampton, NN2 6EP. *Email*: m.a.m.j.little@btinternet.com *Website*: www.totallyessential.com *Signs work*: "Melissa Dring."

DRIVER, James, BA Hons History of Art. *Medium*: wood engraver, prints. *b*: Romsey, 2 Jan 1955. *m*: Nicky. two *s*. *Studied*: University of Manchester (1977). *Exhib*: Royal Society of Miniature Painters, Sculptors and Gravers (2002, 2003, 2004, 2006); Worthing Art Gallery Open Exhibition (2005, 2008, 2013); 'Bite', Mall Galleries (2013); Society of Wood Engravers (2013-2014). *Works in collections*: private. *Publications*: 'Animals in Art', 'Huge Art' both pub. Oxford University Press, (2105). *Works Reproduced*: 'Animals in Art' (OUP, 2015). *Recreations*: Bee-keeping, fishing, gardening, walking. *Address*: An Skyber, Tregongen, Ruan High Lanes, Cornwall, TR2 5LD. *Email*: handforged99@hotmail.com *Signs work*: "A. JAMES DRIVER".

DRLJACHA, Zorica, ARBS; awarded First Prize British Institute in Sculpture (1961), anatomy drawing competition (1962), Landseer Scholarship, first prize and silver medal (1963), Catherine Adeline Sparkes prize; sculptress in bronze, aluminium, resin, ciment fondu. *b*: Yugoslavia, 14 Jul 1942. *d of*: Rajna and Ilija Drljacha, detective sergeant. *m*: Mladen. two *d*. *Educ*: Grammar school (Yugoslavia), Luton College of Technology. *Studied*: Goldsmiths' College under H. W. Parker, FRBS, R. Jones, RA; RA Schools under C. Mahoney, RA, Sir Arnold Machin, OBE, RA, Sir Henry Rushbury, KCVO, CBE. *Exhib*: RA summer exhbns., RBS, Alwyn, Chelsea, Forty Hall, Portrait Society, open-air Holland Park, Davies St., Ealing, Chiswick, etc. *Works in collections*: England, USA, Yugoslavia, Germany, Italy, France. *Commissions*: figures for "Battle of Trafalgar" at Madame Tussauds (1966), Expo '67 (Canada). *Address*: 152 Sutton Ct. Rd., Chiswick, London W4 3HT.

DROUGHT, George James, RCamA; NDD Graphic Design (1960). *Medium*: watercolour, oil, etching. *b*: St.Helens, 14 Jun 1940. *s of*: Jane & Samuel Drought. *m*: Mary. one *s*. *Educ*: Liverpool College of Art, LCC Central School. *Exhib*: RA Summer Exhbn (twice), RI Painters in Watercolour, Royal Hibernian Academy, University of Liverpool, etc. *Works in collections*: Birkenhead Art Gallery, University of Liverpool Art Gallery, many private collections as small watercolours. *Commissions*: steady stream of private commissions. *Works Reproduced*: The Public Catalogue. *Recreations*: walking. *Clubs*: Royal Cambrian Academy, Wirral Society of Arts. *Misc*: now working as self-employed artist. *Address*: 46 East Lancashire Road, St Helens, Merseyside, WA11 9AB.

DRUMMOND, Vicki, ABNA. *Medium*: gouache, acrylics. *b*: Totnes, 12 Apr 1961. *m*: Neil Drummond. *Educ*. Falmouth Comprehensive School. *Studied*: No formal study just lots of looking at paintings, travel and appreciation of art. *Commissions*: Lake Lugano, Lucerne (1981). *Publications*: Postcard from an Artist, Cornwall Today, June 2011. *Clubs*: member of the Association of British Naive Artists (joined June 2014). *Address*: 15 Waterloo Road, Falmouth, Cornwall TR11 3NU. *Email*: animations@macace.net *Website*: www.vickidrummond.co.uk

DRURY, Christopher, Artists and Writers programme - Antarctica; sculptor, land artist, works on paper, photography. *b*: Colombo, Ceylon, 8 Jun 1948. *Partner*: Kay Syrad. two *d*. *Educ*: Canford School. *Studied*: Camberwell School of Art. *Represented by*: Browngrotta, USA. *Exhib*: London, Los Angeles, Leeds, Dublin, Edinburgh, San Jose, San Francisco, Reno, De La Warr Pavilion, Mostyn Art Gallery; mixed shows: Europe, America and Japan. *Works in collections*: British Museum, CAS, Leeds City A.G., Whitworth A.G. Manchester, Henry A.G. Seattle, Towner A.G. Eastbourne, British Government Collection, Wellcome Trust, Nevada MA. *Commissions*: Site specific works in Britain, Europe, America and Japan. *Publications*: Songs of the Earth-T&H; Chris Drury 'Silent Spaces' - monograph

Thames & Hudson, 'Mushrooms/Cluds' Nevada Museum of Art. *Official Purchasers*: V & A , British Museum. Whitworth Art Gallery, Leeds City Art Gallery, Henry Art Gallery-Seattle, S.E. Arts & Arts Council England collections, Nevada Museum of Art. *Principal Works*: Medicine Wheel, Cloud Chambers, Mushroom Clouds. *Address*: Buckle Cottage, Park Lane, Laughton BN8 6BP. *Website*: www.chrisdrury.co.uk *Signs work*: "Chris Drury."

DRY-PARKER, Linda Joan, BA (Hons) Fine Art, Post Graduate Printmaking; Alice Bales Award. *Medium*: oil, watercolour, drawing. *b*: Essex, 16 Jul 1951. *d of*: J.A. Dry-Parker. *m*: S.A. Glassborow. one *s.* one *d.* *Studied*: Kingston Poly-Newcastle upon Tyne; Brighton School of Art & Design. *Represented by*: Gallery Perutz (UK); Wentworth Gallery (Aus). *Exhib*: Art Asia (HK); Ronald Coles Gallery, Sydney (Aus); Port Jackson Fine Art (USA); L'Attitude Gallery, Boston (USA). *Works in collections*: Walt Disney (HK), Holmes A Court, Mandarion Hotel, Phillipines. *Commissions*: St.Vincents Hospital, Shangri La Hotels, Australian Cancer Council. *Address*: Talycoed Court Lodge, Talycoed, Monmouth NP25 5HR. *Email*: glass@iinet.net.au *Signs work*: 'Linda Dry-Parker'.

DU TOIT, Susanne, BAFA (Pretoria, SA), MFA (Massachusetts, Boston USA). *Medium*: oil, etching. *b*: S. Africa, 5 Mar 1955. *d of*: Wes & Elise Boshoff. *m*: Pieter. two *s.* two *d.* *Studied*: University of Pretoria; Massachusetts College of Art, Boston USA. *Exhib*: RA; RWA; in England several galleries, many mixed shows; widely in S. Africa, USA, France. *Works in collections*: private collections internationally. *Address*: Le Bosquet, Wellingtonia Ave., Crowthorne, RG45 6AF. *Email*: susannedt@hotmail.com *Website*: www.susannedutoit.com *Signs work*: 'Susanne du Toit'.

DUBNYCKYJ, Alicia, BA (Hons). *Medium*: Gloss paint. *b*: Scunthorpe, 19 May 1979. *Studied*: Birmingham Institute of Art (1998-2001); Royal College of Art (2001-2002). *Represented by*: Sarah Myerscough Fine Art, London; Helpe Gallery, San Francisco; Hubert Gallery, NYC; Artitled, Netherlands. *Exhib*: With galleries listed in Birmingham, London, Glasgow, Edinburgh, Nottingham, Paris, New York, San Francisco, Toronto, Holland. *Works in collections*: British Airways; University of Central England; Rover; DSI Pharmaceuticals; Modus; Maersk. *Commissions*: Princess of Kuwait; Ron Dennis (Head of McLaren), Sir David Tang. *Publications*: NY Arts Magazine; Esquire Magazine; The Independent; The Sunday Times; Ten4. *Address*: 14 Selsey Road, Edgbaston, Birmingham B17 8JS. *Email*: alidub19@hotmail.com *Website*: www.aliciadubnyckyj.com *Signs work*: "ALICIA DUBNYCKYJ".

DUCKER, Catherine, BA (Hons) Fine Art, RWS; painter in water based and oil paints: subject focus is colour and abstracted forms from flowers and the natural landscape. *b*: Wallingford, 24 Apr 1973. *Studied*: Central St. Martin's (1990-91, 1992-96). *Exhib*: Contemporary Art Soc. (1996), Royal Water-colour Soc. (1997), Henley Festival (1997), Royal Academy Summer (2001), Singer and Frielander (2000/2001). *Works in collections*: private collections. *Commissions*: Henley Festival, and various private garden commissions. *Address*: Littlestoke Farm, Littlestoke, Wallingford, Oxon. OX10 6AX. *Email*: catherineducker@hotmail.com

DUDLEY NEILL, Anna, DFA (Lond., 1957), RI (1980); artist in water-colour and oil. *b*: Merton, London, 26 Jul 1935. *d of*: Arthur Leonard Dudley, flooring specialist. *m*: Michael A. Neill. two *s.* *Educ*: Tolworth Secondary School. *Studied*: Winchester School of Art (1950-54), Slade School of Fine Art (1954-57). *Exhib*: Deist, Belgium (1977, 1979), RI, Cahors, France (1992), Mall Galleries, London (Royal Institute of Painters in Watercolour). Royal Watercolour Society. *Works in collections*: RI. *Clubs*: R.I. *Address*: 15 Putney Heath Lane, London SW15 3JG. *Signs work*: "Anna Dudley."

DUFFIN, Stuart, SSA, RSA; artist in etching, mezzotint, oils, digital; Etching Master, Glasgow Print Studio; Artist in Residence, Moscow, Jerusalem, Belfast. *b*: Windsor, 13 Jun

1959. *Studied*: Grays School of Art, Aberdeen (Dip.Fine Art Printmaking). *Represented by*: Glasgow Print Studio Gallery. *Exhib*: USA, Europe, Israel, Russia, Japan, India, New Zealand. *Works in collections*: Scottish Arts Council, Jerusalem Foundation, Glasgow City Council, BBC, Glasgow University, Karkov Museum. *Commissions*: "Last Supper" oil on canvas for Langside Parish Church, Glasgow. *Address*: 40 Cromarty Ave., Glasgow G43 2HG. *Email*: info@stuartduffin.com *Website*: www.stuartduffin.com

DUFFY, Stephen James, artist, potter, printmaker in linocuts, screen-print, lithography, water-colour, ceramics. *b*: Winchelsea Beach, E. Sussex, 5 Feb 1962. *s of*: James Duffy. *Educ*: Rye Comprehensive. *Exhib*: Rye Soc. of Artists, Fremantle Print Biennial, W.A., Farnham Maltings Gallery, Modern Print Gallery, Wirksworth, Ormond Rd. Printmakers, Grundy A.G., Blackpool, Rye A.G. Easton Rooms, U.A., various mixed exhbns. *Publications*: Rye Nature Reserve, Irish Folk Tales (to be published). *Clubs*: Printmakers Council, U.A., Rye Fishheads. *Address*: c/o Rye Society of Artists, Romney House, Saltbarn Lane, Rye, E. Sussex TN31 7PH.

DUFFY, Terry, BA Hons, MA; painter of abstract art in oils on canvas and board, also photography and glass; Chair: British Art and Design Assoc.; Founder: Arena Studios, Liverpool. *b*: Liverpool, 25 Mar 1948. *m*: Angela. one *s*. one *d*. *Exhib*: London, Paris, Berlin, New York, Venice, Cape Town. Presently a major touring exhibition of the painting "Victim, no resurrection"; Monuments, Liverpool Biennial (sponsored by Barclays Bank, 2008); Palazzo Contarini, Venice Biennial (sponsored by Sotheby's, 2009); Brunswick Centre, London (2012). *Works in collections*: corporate and private collections in Europe and U.S.A., including Sainsbury, Bosch, Panasonic, BBC, AON, Welsh National, Liverpool University. *Commissions*: Platform 7 "Silent Cacophony" other projects with Camden Council London re WW1. *Misc*: Reviews, media coverage: Studio International, The Guardian, Time Out, B.B.C. World News, Art Review, Art World U.S.A., The TUBE, The Independent, etc. *Address*: 6 The Kings Gap, Hoylake, CH47 1HE. *Email*: info@terryduffy.info *Website*: www.terryduffy.info *Signs work*: "TERRY DUFFY".

DUFORT, Antony, MA Fine Art (1975), DipAD (1974) Chelsea School of Art. *Medium*: public sculptor, painter, printmaker, draughtsman, author, filmmaker. *b*: Belfast, 12 Jun 1948. *d of*: Timothy Nesbitt-Dufort, MA Grandson of Doris Travis (Dorothea . e Halpert) painter, pupil of Sickert. one *s*. *Educ*: Ampleforth College, New College Oxford. *Studied*: Central School of Art (1971) under Norman Ackroyd, Winchester School of Art (1971) under John Bellany, Chelsea School of Art (1972-74) under Norman Blamey, painting; Edinburgh School of Art (1974-75) under Dick Hart, printmaking. *Exhib*: RA, NEAC, RWS, RBA, ROI, RP; one-man shows: Leighton House Museum (1988), Maas Gallery (1990), Artbank Gallery, Glasgow (1994), Knöll Gallery, Basel (1994), Milne & Moller, London (1997). *Works in collections*: Permanent collection of The House of Commons, Marylebone Cricket Club, Nottinghamshire County Council, London Oratory School, Eton College, Oriel College, Ampleforth College, Forest of Dean District Council, Hard Rock Café Los Angeles, Brook's Club. *Commissions*: Pope John Paul 2 for the City of Caen, Normandy (2005/06); Baroness Thatcher (full length) for Members' Lobby of the House of Commons (2005/06); 'Testing for Gas', Miners' Tribute Sculpture for Nottinghamshire at Silverhill near Teversal (2004/05). Bust of Cardinal Hume for Ampleforth College (2002/03). 'Fast Bowler' for the MCC at Lord's Cricket Ground (2001/02). Tribute Sculpture for the Miners of the Forest of Dean Cinderford, Glos (1999/2000); Mother and Child, London Oratory School (1995/96). *Publications*: Ballet Steps, Practice to Performance. Clarkson N. Potter, NY and Methuen (1985), revised edition (1991), paperback edition, Hodder & Stoughton (1993). Awarded 'Best Book for Young Adults' (1985, 1991) by New York Public Library. *Principal Works*: see commissions. *Email*: antony@dufort.com *Website*: www.antonydufort.com *Signs work*: "Antony Dufort" or "Dufort." (with date).

DUGGAN, Chris, BA Fine Art. *Medium*: Oil; watercolour; drawing. *b*: Hillingdon, 19 Mar 1956. *m*: Janet Folland. *Studied*: St Martin's (1974-5); Goldsmith's College (1975-78). *Exhib*: Showroom Gallery, Bethnal Green; Political Cartoon Gallery, Bank of England Museum; Museum of National History, Paris ('un nouveau monde'); Coningsby Gallery Cartoon Museum; Chris Beetles Gallery; Greenwich Visitors Centre; London Art Fair. *Works in collections*: Bank of England Museum; Archer Cartoon Collection; British Cartoon Archive; Kent University; Monnow Valley. *Commissions*: Several satirial portraits. *Publications*: Pictures appeared in many newspapers and magazines. *Official Purchasers*: Bank of England Museum. *Recreations*: Art galleries; music; cycling. *Address*: 10 Hilly Fields Crescent, London SE4 1QA. *Email*: dugganillustration@dsl.pipex.com *Website*: cee-dee.com *Signs work*: "CD" circled.

DUKES, Robert Laurence, Boise Travel Scholarship (1988); NPG Portrait Award (2006). *Medium*: oil. *b*: Hull, 14 May 1965. *Studied*: Grimsby School of Art (foundation) 1981-84; Slade School of Art, 1984-88. *Represented by*: Browse and Darby, 19 Cork Street, London W1S 3LP. *Exhib*: RA Summer Exhbn (2000-08, 2011, 2012); Critic's Choice, Wales (ed. A Lambirth) (2006); one-man shows: Browse and Darby (2005, 2008, 2011). Lynn Painter Staines (2013) Runner-up prize. *Works Reproduced*: RA Illustrated 2004, 2006, 2008. *Misc*: Lecturer at National Gallery, teaches at Prince's Drawing School. *Address*: 72 Parkside Estate, Rutland Road, London E9 7JU. *Website*: www.browseanddarby.co.uk

DUMITRIU, Anna, BA (Hons), MA Fine Art; Year of the Artist Award (2000), Brighton Festival Arts and Business Award (2001), Personal Development Award-Arts Council (2003), Project Development Grant-Arts Council (2003). *Medium*: watercolour, bioart, installation performance. *b*: Shoreham-by-Sea, 24 Mar 1969. *d of*: Alan and Joyce Presence. *m*: Dan Dumitriu. one *s*. *Studied*: University of Brighton (1990-6) studying Fine Art Painting; 2005. *Represented by*: Phoenix Gallery, Brighton; Scicult.com. *Works in collections*: Science Museum; State Museum, Novorsibirsk, Siberia, Russia. *Commissions*: The Wellcome Trust, Brighton and Hove City Council. *Principal Works*: Normal Flora Project, The Institute of Unnecessary Research. *Address*: Phoenix Brighton, Brighton, BN2 9NB. *Email*: annadumitriu@hotmail.com *Website*: www.annadumitriu.com

DUMPER, Bridget Veronica June, BA Hons (Fine Art); MA (Sculpture); SWA Mayfair & Cavendish Sculpture Award (2008). *Medium*: Drawing, prints, sculpture, acrylic painting. *b*: Romsey, 27 Jun 1949. *m*: John H W Dumper. two *s*. *Educ*: Priestland Secondary Modern, Romsey. *Studied*: Farnham College of Art and Technology (1991-94); Winchester School of Art and Design (1995-96). *Exhib*: The Mall Galleries, London; Southampton City Gallery, Southampton; The Discovery Centre, Winchester; Tour de Mole, Sauve, France; Grounds of Beaulieu Motor Museum, Beaulieu, Five Arrows Gallery, Exbury Gardens, Beaulieu. *Works in collections*: Sculpture "New Beginnings" City Gallery, Winchester. *Commissions*: Numerous/private collections. *Principal Works*: Sculpture. *Recreations*: Reading, walking, swimming, music. *Clubs*: Drama. *Address*: Beech House, Romsey Road, Broughton, Stockbridge, SO20 8DB. *Email*: bridgetdumper@hotmail.com *Website*: www.bridgetdumper.co.uk *Signs work*: On sculpture "BVJD" monogram; on paintings "BD" or "Bridget Dumper" or "B. Dumper".

DUNBAR, Lennox, Professor; RSA (2005), ARSA (1990); artist in drawing, painting and printmaking; Head of Printmaking, Grays School of Art, Aberdeen. *b*: Aberdeen, 17 May 1952. *s of*: Lennox Dunbar. *m*: Jan Storie. two *s*. one *d*. *Educ*: Aberdeen Grammar School. *Studied*: Grays School of Art, Aberdeen (1969-74). *Exhib*: New Scottish Prints (1983, NY and touring USA), Bradford Print Biennale (1984), Cleveland Drawing Biennale (1989), Intergrafik, Berlin (1990), International Print Biennale Cracow Poland (2000), and many group exhbns. national and international. *Works in collections*: Aberdeen, Paisley, Middlesbrough A.Gs., Portland Museum, Oregon, USA, BBC, Mobil Oil, Royal Scottish

Academy, Contemporary Art Soc., HRH Princess Royal; Chancellor of the Exchequer. *Address*: West Denmore, Auchnagatt, Ellon, Grampian, AB41 8TP. *Email*: l.dunbar@rqu.ac.uk *Signs work*: "Dunbar" or "L.R. Dunbar."

DUNCAN, Clive Leigh, FRBS (1983), RBA (1984), SPS (2005); NDD (1966); sculptor; Principal lecturer and Head of Sculpture, London Guildhall University, Sir John Cass Faculty of Art (1973-93); President, Thomas Heatherly Educational Trust (1974-94). *b*: London, 1944. *s of*: the late John Charles Duncan. *m*: Janet McQueen, painter. one *s.* one *d. Educ*: John Colet School, Wendover. *Studied*: High Wycombe College of Art (1961-64), Camberwell School of Art (1964-66 under Sidney Sheppard), City and Guilds School of Art (1966-68 under James Butler, RA). *Exhib*: RA, RBA, Guildhall, London, G.I., Nicholas Treadwell, Portland Sculpture Pk., Playhouse Gallery, Harlow. *Works in collections*: Britain, inc. Reading Museum and Art Gallery; Spain, USA. *Commissions*: Trafalgar Crown, Royal Mint (VC, Fifty Pence, Iraq Civilian Medal); The Snowdrop Garden Figure, Child Bereavement Trust. *Address*: Holme Cottage, Shiplake, Henley on Thames, Oxon. RG9 3JS. *Signs work*: "DUNCAN."

DUNCAN, Jean, RUA, USW, DA (Edin) 1955, Advanced Dip. printmaking University of Ulster (1981); artist in painting, video and printmaking; Hon. Trustee, Seacourt Print Workshop; Tokyo International Mini-Print Triennial 2005-Jury Award. *Medium*: painting & printmaking. *b*: Edinburgh, 27 Dec. 1933. *d of*: A D Fraser & Rhoda Cameron. *m*: Roderick. two *s.* two *d. Educ*: James Gillespie's High School, Edinburgh. *Studied*: Edinburgh College of Art (William Gillies, Leonard Rosoman), University of Ulster (David Barker). *Represented by*: Caldwell Gallery, Belfast; Graphic Studio Gallery, Dublin. *Exhib*: solo shows: Guiness Gallery, Dublin, One Oxford St. Gallery, Belfast, Waterfront Hall, Belfast, Hillsboro Fine Art, Dublin., Naughton Gallery, Queen's University, Belfast; Farmleigh Gallery, Dublin. *Works in collections*: Arts Council of NI, UCD Dublin, UTV Belfast, Northern Bank, AIB Bank, Dept. of Arts, Culture and the Gaeltacht, Irish National Self-portrait collection, Office of Public Works, Dublin, Limerick University, Dundee City A.G., Queen's University, Belfast, Bank of Ireland, UTV Belfast, Irish Intercontinental Bank. *Principal Works*: 'Still Dancers' with composer Piers Hellawell; 'The Fly' with composer Deirdre McKay; 'a pale yellow sky' with Deidre McKay. *Recreations*: reading, walking. *Address*: 15 Rugby Court, Belfast, N.I. BT7 1PN. *Email*: jeaniduncan@hotmail.com *Website*: www.jeanduncan.freeuk.com *Signs work*: Jean Duncan.

DUNCAN, Jeremy John, BA Hons Fine Art. *Medium*: oil. *b*: Exeter, 15 Sep 1964. *s of*: Mrs.C.E.Duncan. *Educ*: Exmouth School. *Studied*: Exeter College of Art and Design (1983-4); Gloucestershire College of Art and Design (1984-7). *Represented by*: Waterhouse & Dodd, 26 Cork Street, London W1S 3ND and 104 Greene Street, New York NY10012 www.waterhousedodd.com. *Exhib*: Waterhouse & Dodd; RA Summer Exhbn; ROI; RWA. *Commissions*: Thomas Cole Kinder, Sasha Waddell Associates. *Official Purchasers*: Scheringa Museum, Spanbroek, Holland. *Works Reproduced*: in 'Homes and Gardens', 'The Complete Oil Painter'; Italian Architectural Digest, Artknowledge News. *Principal Works*: London, Paris and New York series. *Recreations*: reading, visiting country houses. *Clubs*: Associate of the Society of Architectural Illustrators. *Misc*: lecturer in drawing and painting, Stroud College. *Address*: 6 Royal Parade, Bayshill Road, Cheltenham, GL50 3AY. *Email*: jeremyduncan5@gmail.com *Signs work*: 'J Duncan'.

DUNCAN, Terence Edward, specialist in display service for museums and personal collections. *Medium*: artist in oil and water-colour. *b*: Harpenden, Herts., 17 Aug 1947. *m*: Mrs. E.D. Bryant-Duncan. three *s-s. Educ*: Manland Secondary Modern, Harpenden. *Studied*: St. Albans School of Art; Harpenden Art Centre. *Exhib*: St. Albans Gallery (1971), Amateur Artists' Exhbn., London (1967), Batchwood Hall, St. Albans. *Works in collections*: permanent collection Red Lion Inn, Westbury-on-Severn. *Publications*: article,

Hertfordshire Countryside; woodwork projects Guild of Mastercraftsmen; Traditional Woodworking Tools (Eddington Press, 1989). Lecturing on: woodwork, Oaklands College, Harpenden (1993-97), picture framing, Oaklands College Hatfield Campus (1993-98), antique furniture restoration, Stanmore College, Middx. (1996-98). *Misc*: Teaching own workshop. *Address*: The Manse, The Village, Westbury-on-Severn, Gloucs. GL14 IPA. *Signs work*: "Terry" with date.

DUNCAN MEYER, Mary Elizabeth Anne, ASGFA; Diploma in Figurative Sculpture (2006-06); fine art tutor; trained as printmaker and painter. *Medium*: watercolour, drawing, prints, sculpture. *b*: London, 27 Jun 1942. *d of*: Daphne Pearson Andrew. *m*: divorced. three *s.* one *d. Educ*: Queens Gate School. *Studied*: Regent St. Polytechnic, Central School of Art (1960-63); Beaux Arts, Paris. *Represented by*: Ian Irving (Agent). *Exhib*: RA (2000); Atrium Library, Cork St., London (1999), Workhouse Gallery (2000), Start Gallery (2003), Cromwell Hospital (2002); Edith Grove Gallery; Stephen Bartley Gallery; Fulham Society of Artists and Potters (2007); Chelsea and Westminster Hospital (2007); Soc. Graphic Fine Arts (2007). *Works in collections*: Art in Hospitals; bronze sculpture Mother and Child, oil painting Majorca - Doctor Hamami, Head Consultant, Cromwell, and private collections. *Commissions*: Carnavalle Restaurant; portraits (pastel). *Works Reproduced*: Kew Gardens watercolour. *Recreations*: theatre, concerts, opera. *Clubs*: Chelsea Arts Club. *Address*: 49 Prothero Rd., Fulham, London SW6 7LY. *Email*: elizabeth.duncanmeyer@yahoo.com *Website*: http://www.intune.co.uk/Meyer.Duncan *Signs work*: "Elizabeth Duncan Meyer."

DUNCE, Brian Redvers, PS (1992); painter and draughtsman in all media; has taught at Chelsea School of Art; Corsham Bath Academy; Middlesex University; Yehudi Menuhin Music School. *b*: Godalming, 29 Apr 1937. *m*: Veronica. one *d. Studied*: Guildford School of Art, Salisbury School of Art, Reading University, under Jack Rodway, John Kashdan, Peter Startup. *Exhib*: major galleries in UK, France, Germany, Switzerland, USA. *Works in collections*: Royal Brunei Collection, V&A Prints and Drawings, McColls, Pricewaterhouse Coopers, and private collections in UK, France, Canada. *Commissions*: Arts Council, National Trust, Oxford University, ICA, Poetry Society, Cambridge University. *Works Reproduced*: The Pastel Society 1898-2000 Centenary book ISBN 0 9537927 0 6 and many catalogues. *Principal Works*: Preludes and Interludes Debussy Performance Installation 6 x 54ft (1.83 x 16.47m). *Recreations*: walking, swimming. *Address*: The Studios, Wonersh Court, The Street, Wonersh, Guildford, Surrey, GU5 0PG. *Email*: bdunce437@btinternet.com *Signs work*: "Brian Dunce."

DUNIGAN, Anthony Gordon, SWE; Diploma in Painting (City and Guilds of London Art School, 1974); David Murray Scholarship 1972 and 1974; Philip Connard Award (1973); Oppenheim-John Downes Memorial Trust Awards (2003, 2004). *Medium*: oil, wood-engraving. *b*: Skegness, Lincs., 3 Aug 1946. *s of*: Albert & Dorothy Dunigan. *Educ*: George Mitchell School, Leyton, London E10. *Studied*: Hastings School of Art (1968-70), City and Guilds of London Art School (1971-74). *Exhib*: Royal Academy Business Art Galleries (1981); Ernst and Young Exhibitions, Cambridge (1993-94); Mall Galleries; The Moseley Gallery (1998); St. Edmundsbury Cathedral (2002); Fry Gallery, Saffron Walden (2002); Irma Stern Museum, Capetown (2003); Galleria Communale d'Arte Contemporanea, Italy (2005); annual touring shows with SWE. *Works in Collections*: The Ashmolean Museum, Oxford; SWE Archive, Manchester Metropolotan University. *Publications*: 'An Engraver's Globe' by Simon Brett (2002). *Clubs*: Society of Wood Engravers. *Address*: 5 Whiting Road, Oulton, Lowestoft, Suffolk, NR32 3QA.

DUNLOP, Alison M., BA(Hons.) (1980), RSW (1990); Greenshield Foundation award (1982, 1986); painter in water-colour, oil; President, SAAC. *b*: Chatham, Ontario, Canada, 24 Mar 1958. *d of*: M.E. Dunlop (decd.). *m*: R.F. Hood. *Studied*: University of Western Ontario, London (1976-78), L'Ecole des Beaux-Arts, Besançon, France (1978-79),

University of Guelph, Canada (1979-80), Edinburgh College of Art (1982-83). *Exhib*: Canadian Soc. of Painters in Water-colours, Gallerie Rochon, Toronto, RSW, SAAC, Scottish Gallery, Thackeray Gallery, Kingfisher Gallery, Bruton Gallery. *Works in collections*: Canada, USA, GB. *Address*: Croft Cottage, Crichton, By Pathhead, Midlothian, EH37 5UZ. *Signs work*: "DUNLOP" and year.

DUNN, Alfred, ARCA (1961), Hon FRCA; artist. *b*: Wombwell, Yorks, 4 Oct 1937. *s of*: George Simeon Dunn. *m*: Maureen Angela Dunn. one *s*. one *d*. *Educ*: Wath-upon-Dearne Grammar School. *Studied*: Royal College of Art (1959-61). *Exhib*: Galerie Buchhandlung Claus Lincke, Dusseldorf (1976), Monika Beck Gallery, Hamburg (1976, 1993), Redfern Gallery, London (1965, 1966, 1969, 1971, 1975, 1978, 1983, 1993), L'Umo del Arte, Milan (1971), Atlantis Gallery (1982), Galarie Julia Philippi, Heidelberg (1994); Das Druckgraphisce work retrospective 70er bis 90er Jahre (1995); Peter Scott Gallery, Lancaster University (2007). *Works in collections*: Manchester City A.G., Cadillac Co., Houston, General Hardware Manufacturing Co., New York, Monika Beck Gallery, Germany, L'Umo del Arte, Milan, Yorkshire Sculpture Park, V&A, Arts Council, London. *Commissions*: Concourse - Macau Ferry Terminal, Hong Kong; Hotel Victoria, Hong Kong; 574nd Dorothy Weinstein, New York, USA. *Recreations*: Bowling (Crown Green). *Clubs*: Trawden Forest Bowling Club. *Address*: Little Moss Farm, Trawden, nr. Colne, Lancs. BB8 8PR. *Signs work*: "Alf Dunn."

DUNN, Anne, painter, all mediums. *b*: London, 4 Sep 1929. *d of*: Sir James Dunn, Bt. *m*: (1) Michael Wishart, 1950. one *s*. (2) Rodrigo Moynihan, 1960. two *s*. 1951 Francis Wishart (etcher); 1959 Daniel Moynihan (painter). *Studied*: Chelsea, Academie Julian, Paris. *Exhib*: one-man shows, Leicester Galleries (8); Redfern Gallery, London; Fischbach Gallery, NY (8); Philadelphia; Ville de Paris (2); Gallery 78, Fredericton, Canada (2); many group shows worldwide, RA (1978-93), Dactyl Foundation New York (1999, 2001), Gallery 55, Mercer Street NY (2005) (5); Tibor de Nagy Gallery NY (2005); Retrospective 1976-2008 Gallery 78, Fredericton, Canada (2009); Retrospective 1949-1968, Redfern Gallery, London (2010). *Works in collections*: Arts Council, M of W., Carlisle City A. G., Columbus Gallery of Fine Arts, US, Beaverbrook A.G., NB, Financial Times Inc. GB, Commerce Bankshares, Kansas City, Mo., Amerada Hess Corp. NY, Xerox Corp. NY, Chemical Bank NY, Bank of Nova Scotia, Canada, New Brunswick Provincial Art Bank, Canada, The Art Centre, University of New Brunswick, Canada. *Commissions*: numerous, portraits, book illustrations, book jackets. *Publications*: Editor, Art and Literature (1964-68). *Official Purchasers*: numerous. *Works Reproduced*: numerous. *Clubs*: W.I.A.C., Chelsea Arts. *Address*: Domaine de St. Esteve, Lambesc, B.D.R. 13410, France. *Signs work*: "Anne Dunn."

DUNN, Philip, DipAD (Fine Art) (1968), ATC (1969); painter/printmaker in acrylic, oil, gouache, screenprinting; Founder Member. Fiveways Artists' Open Houses. *b*: London, 26 May 1945. *m*: Carole-Anne White (deceased). *Educ*: Chiswick Grammar School, London. *Studied*: Twickenham College of Technology (1964), Hornsey College of Art (1964-68), Brighton College of Art (1968-69). *Exhib*: many including London, NY, Brighton, Bath, Cheltenham, also twenty solo exhbns. since 1968. Exhib. exclusively through Window Gallery, Brighton since 1982. *Works in collections*: Brighton Centre, NHS. *Official Purchasers*: Brighton Health Care NHS Trust. *Works Reproduced*: many, all published by Window Gallery, mainly of Brighton and Hove seafront with or without deckchairs. *Recreations*: gardening. *Address*: c/o Window Gallery, Studio 9, Turner Dumbrell Workshops, Northend, Ditchling, Hassocks, W. Sussex BN6 8TJ. *Email*: info@windowgallery.co.uk *Website*: www.windowgallery.co.uk *Signs work*: "Philip Dunn."

DUNNE, Berthold, Mem. Water-colour Soc. of Ireland (1951); artist in water-colour; 1st prize watercolour section, National CDL art competition (1981); Amarach Consultants award, Watercolour Society of Ireland (2006). *b*: Dublin, 21 Sep 1924. *s of*: Michael D. Dunne. *m*: Barbara Kelly. two *d*. *Educ*: Christian Brothers Schools, Synge Street. *Studied*: National College of Art, Dublin, under John Keating, PRHA, and Maurice MacGonigal, RHA (1946-51). *Exhib*: RHA, Oireachtas Art Exhbn., Water-colour Soc. of Ireland., RHA Banquet exhbn., Case 99, Case 2000 and Case 2004 Lavit Gallery Cork. *Works in collections*: Self-portrait in the National Self-Portrait Collection; one painting in Water-colour Soc. of Ireland Coll.; University of Limerick; watercolour "Low Tide Howth" acquired by Office of Public Works, Dublin; watercolour "House on the Cliff, Spanish Point, Co. Clare" acquired by the Department of Foreign Affairs, Dublin. *Address*: Goa, 29 Shrewsbury Rd., Shankill, Co. Dublin, Eire. *Signs work*: "Berthold".

DUNSEATH, Chris, RWA, FRBS; BA (Hons); HDipFA (Lond). *Medium*: sculpture. *b*: Bangor, N.Ireland, 3 Mar 1949. *m*: Pip. one *s*.two *d*. *Studied*: Yeovil School of Art (67-68); Gloucestershire College of Art, Cheltenham (68-71); Slade School of Fine Art (71-73); Sculpture Fellow, Cardiff College of Art (73-74); Winston Churchill Travelling Fellowship for Sculpture (92). *Exhib*: London: Royal Academy Summer Exhibition, New Art Centre, Barbican, Warwick Gallery, Serpentine Gallery, Butler's Wharf, Sotheby's Grosvenor Gallery, Flow Gallery, RBS, Mall Galleries, Rollo Gallery. Regional: Oriel Cardiff, Parnham House, Ikon Birmingham, YSP, Oxford Gallery, Hannah Peschar, Phillips Gallery (Taunton), Brewery Arts (Cirencester), RWA, Met Office, Devon Guild, Botanic Gardens (Edinburgh), International: Museo, Seattle, USA; Sanyi, Taiwan. *Works in collections*: Arts Council England; The Royal Collection; Ackerman Foundation, NY, USA; McDermott Collection, Dallas, USA; RWA Bristol; Dame Stephanie Shirley; The Met Office; University of Leicester; Robert Redford, California, USA; SPP Foundation, USA. *Commissions*: West Bromwich, Sandwell; The Waterfront, Dudley. *Address*: Primrose Cottage, East Street, Chiselborough, Stoke Sub Hamdon, Somerset TA14 6TW. *Email*: CChrisDunseath@aol.com *Website*: www.axisweb.org/p/chrisdunseath *Signs work*: 'CD; CHRIS DUNSEATH; C.DUNSEATH'.

DUNSTAN, Bernard, RA (ARA 1959: Trustee 1990-95), NEAC, RWA (President 1980-84). *Medium*: painter in oil and pastel. *b*: 19 Jan 1920. *s of*: the late Dr. A. E. Dunstan. *m*: Diana Armfield, R.A. three *s*. *Educ*: St. Paul's School. *Studied*: Byam Shaw School, Slade School of Fine Art. *Represented by*: Thos. Agnew & Sons, Bond St., London. *Exhib*: RA, NEAC etc., one-man exhbns. at Roland Browse & Delbanco, Agnew's, etc. *Works in collections*: Bristol, Rochdale, Coventry, National Gallery of New Zealand, London Museum, National Portrait Gallery, Royal Collection, Contemporary Art Soc., Arts Council, etc. *Commissions*: many portrait commissions. *Publications*: Painting Methods of the Impressionists, The Paintings of Bernard Dunstan (1993), ed. Ruskin's Elements of Drawing, etc. *Recreations*: music. *Address*: 10 High Park Rd., Kew, Richmond, Surrey TW9 4BH. *Signs work*: "B.D."

DUPEYRON, Carole. *Medium*: oil, photography. *b*: Caen, France, 31 Mar 1970. *d of*: Jean-Claude Deveze & Catherine Delage. *m*: Laurent Dupeyron. two *s*. one *d*. *Studied*: Columbia University, New York (1989-1992), HEC, France (1992-1994). *Exhib*: Carpenter's Workshop, London (2005); Royal Thames Yacht Club, London (2006); Royal Academy Summer Exhibition (2008); New HeArt City Gallery (2011). *Commissions*: private commissions. *Clubs*: Stade Francais. *Address*: 50 rue Perronet, 92200 Neiully-sur-Seine France. Email: caroledupeyron@mac.com Website: www.caroledupeyron.com *Signs work*: "Carole D."

DURBIN, Eleanor Mary, BA (Hons.) (1972), MPhil (1984); artist/teacher in painting in acrylic, gouache, water-colour, printmaking: etching, woodcut; Head of Art Dept., Guildford High School; Teacher: Godolphin and Latymer School; from 2009, full time artist/printmaker. *b*: London, 11 Jun 1949. *d of*: Leslie Durbin (silversmith). *m*: Martin

Henley. one *s.* one *d. Educ*: Twickenham County School, Middx. *Studied*: Hornsey College of Art (1967-68), Leeds University (1972) BA Hons, (1984) MPhil. Fine Art, Central School of Art and Design (1977-79). *Exhib*: Cleveland Drawing Biennale (1975, 1977); Chenil Galleries, Young British Printmakers (1978); Printmakers Council National Touring exhbn. (1979); RWS, Bankside Gallery, Contemporary Water-colours (1983); Tradescant Museum of Garden History (1986); National Print Exhbn. Mall Galleries (1999, 2000, 2004); 2001 BITE Print Exhibition, Mall Galleries. *Address*: 89 Park Rd., Teddington, Middx. TW11 0AW. *Email*: eleanorhenley@yahoo.co.uk *Signs work*: "Eleanor Durbin."

DYNEVOR, Lucy, (née Rothenstein), painter in oil and pastel, and formally conservator of works of art; Graduate Diploma, Garden Conservation. *b*: Sheffield, 1934. *d of*: Sir John Rothenstein. *m*: Lord Dynevor; (divorced), husband Simon Carter (decd). one *s.* three *d. Educ*: The Old Palace, Mayfield, Sussex. *Studied*: Ruskin School of Fine Art in Oxford and conservation of art with Dr. Helmuth Ruhemann; Architectural Assoc., London 1991-4. *Exhib*: one-man shows: University College of Swansea, New Grafton Gallery, London (1991); mixed shows include Crane Kalman Gallery (1995). *Works in collections*: UK, Canada, USA. *Clubs*: Chelsea Arts Club. *Address*: Higher Easthams House, Crewkerne, Somerset, TA18 7QQ. *Signs work*: "L.D." or "Lucy Dynevor."

DYRENFORTH, Noel, artist in batik. *b*: London, 17 Jun 1936. *s of*: Harold and Rachel Dyrenforth. *Partner*: Andrea Tierney. one *s. Educ*: St. Clement Danes, London; CAC Bursary (1977); Craftsmen-in-residence Arts Victoria '78, Toorak State College; study/travel in USA, Indonesia, India, China. *Studied*: Goldsmiths' College of Art, University of London, Central School of Art, London. *Exhib*: one-man shows: 1965-2003: Cambridge, London, Coventry, Bradford, Loughborough, Oxford, Nottingham, LA (USA), Lincoln, Hull, Halifax, Melbourne (Australia), Bremen and Cologne (Germany), Banbury, Tokyo & Kyoto (Japan), Indonesia, Guizhou University (China), Boston USA and over 130 mixed exhbns. *Works in collections*: Victoria & Albert Museum London, and six others. *Publications*: Batik with Noel Dyrenforth by J. Houston (Orbis Publications, London); The Technique of Batik by Noel Dyrenforth (Batsford Publishing Co. 1988), new paperback issue (1997), Batik - Modern Concepts and Techniques by Noel Dyrenforth (Batsford, London 2003), 'Art Textiles of Great Britain' (Telos Publications 2006). *Address*: 11 Shepherds Hill, Highgate, London N6 5QJ. *Email*: Noel.dyrenforth@hotmail.com *Website*: www.noel-dyrenforth.com *Signs work*: 'NDyrenforth'.

E

EADES, Patricia, HS. *Medium*: watercolour, pastels, oils. *b*: Esher, Surrey, 17 Mar 1936. *d of*: Mr & Mrs L R Randall. *m*: Edwin John Eades. one *d. Educ*: St.Joseph's Convent, East Molesey, Surrey. *Studied*: mainly self-taught. *Exhib*: HS, Wells; SWA; Llewellyn Alexander Gallery; Robin McInnes, Island Landscapes, IOW; various island exhibitions. *Publications*: IOW County Press calendar 2006. *Recreations*: reading, gardening. *Clubs*: Island Art Groups. *Address*: 'Serendip', Fine Lane, Shorwell, Isle of Wight PO30 3JY. *Signs work*: 'PE' (monogram), 'P.A.EADES', 'Patricia Eades'.

EALES, Elisabeth Jennifer, SWA; SFP(retd). *Medium*: watercolour. *b*: Exeter, Devon, 29 Dec 1934. *d of*: Mr & Mrs Richard Tadman. *m*: Paul Eales, LLB (solicitor). one *s.* one *d. Educ*: Clifton High School, Bristol. *Studied*: mainly self-taught; also attended SCOLA, Sutton, Surrey, Adult Education Classes. *Exhib*: Westminster Gallery, Mall Galleries; Le Mur Vivant Gallery, London; Sofiero Castle, Helsingborg, Sweden; SBA, and other galleries in UK. *Works in collections*: many private individuals in UK and abroad, including USA, Holland, Kenya, East Africa, New Zealand. *Commissions*: private commissions. *Recreations*: gardening, grandchildren and family, cooking, theatre and history of art. *Address*: Park Cottage, Park Road, Banstead, Surrey SM7 3DL. *Signs work*: 'EJE'.

EAMES, Angela, BA Hons, HDFA, MA (Computing in Art and Design); artist/lecturer in drawing/electronic media. *b*: Malmesbury, Wilts., 28 May 1951. *m*: Bill Watson. *Educ*: Woking County Grammar School. *Studied*: Bath Academy of Art (1971-74, Michael Kidner), Slade School of Art (1974-76, Tess Jaray, Noel Forster), Middlesex University (1991-92, John Lansdown). *Exhib*: widely, including London, Berlin, Linz, Bratislava and the USA. *Misc*: Work commissioned and in private collections. Lectures: Associate Senior Lecturer in Computer Aided Studies, University of Wolverhampton. *Address*: 15 Chapter Rd., Kennington, London SE17 3ES. *Signs work*: "A. Eames."

EASTHAM, Tracey, BA (Hons) Fine Art Painting, MA Fine Art Painting. *Medium*: collage. *b*: Lancashire, 28 Apr 1983. *m*: Christopher. *Studied*: Loughborough University. *Exhib*: Solo Shows: Airspace Gallery (2012), Cornerhouse Gallery: Projects (2010). Selected Group Shows; Aid & Abet (2013); Transition Gallery, Mermaid & Monster, D21 Gallery (Leipzig), Bureau Gallery (2011); Exeter Phoenix, Talbot Rice Gallery, Wolverhampton Art Gallery (2010); Harris Museum & Art Gallery, Cynthia Corbett Gallery (2009); Project Space Leeds (2008). Across the UK, and in Europe. *Works in collections*: The Co-operative Group Corporate Collection: the NHS, various private collections. *Commissions*: The Co-operative Group (2013), Arts & Business (2011), NHS Guild Lodge Unit (2008). *Principal Works*: "Secret Britain" (2010). *Clubs*; A-N, Axis Web, Kids of Dada. *Misc*: Edited and produced "The Liverpool Art Journal" (2009-2009). *Address*: 300 Chorley Road, Westhoughton, Greater Manchester BL5 3NS. *Email*: tracey_eastham@yahoo.co.uk *Website*: www.traceyeastham.co.uk *Signs work*: "Tracey Eastham".

EASTON, Arthur Frederick, Surrey Dip. (1964), ROI (1979), NS (1980); Dip. of Merit for Painting, University of Arts, Italy (1982); Pres. Reigate Soc. of Artists; artist in oil and water-colour, art teacher. *b*: Horley, Surrey, 9 Feb 1939. *s of*: Frederick William Easton. *m*: Carolle. three *d*. *Studied*: Reigate School of Art and Design (1961-64). *Exhib*: RA, ROI, RBA, NS, RP, NEAC; 20 one-man shows; 14 shared shows; 36 mixed shows. Prize winner Upper St. Gallery (1973), Hunting Art Prize exhbn. (1990), International Arts Fair, Olympia (1991). *Works in collections*: Museum of British Labour. *Works Reproduced*: in The Artist, Quarto Publishing, Leisure Painter; posters, Ikea of Sweden; greetings cards, Les Editions Arts et Images du Monde. *Clubs*: Reigate Soc. of Artists. *Address*: 4 Winfield Grove, Newdigate, Surrey RH5 5AZ. *Signs work*: "A. Easton."

EASTON, Bella, Postgraduate Diploma (2000), BA (Hons.) (1993), Fine Art painting; BTec Nat. Dip. (1990) Art and Design; painting in oil, printmaker in etching and silkscreen. *b*: Epsom, Surrey, 28 Dec 1971. *m*: Daniel Wray. two *s*. *Studied*: Suffolk CFE (1988-90), Winchester School of Art (1990-93), Fellowship in Printmaking, City & Guilds of London Art School (2000-02), Royal Academy of Art (1997-2000). *Exhib*: Panter & Hall, London (2002), Japan (2001), event; John Russell Gallery, Suffolk (2002), 401½ Open Studio (2001), Curwen Gallery, London (2001), Summer Show (2001, 2000, '99, '98), Thompson's Gallery, London ('99), NEAL, London ('98, '97), Discerning' Eye, London ('98). *Works in collections*: M&G Ltd., RWA, Tesco's, San-Ei Gen FFI (UK), BMW (GB) Ltd., Rover Group. *Commissions*: Tesco's 'a bag for life'; Rover Group Motor Show. *Publications*: limited edition books: English Fish in Foreign Lands, Japan (2001), Alf'n'Betty, (1998), Royal Academy Summer Exhibition illustrated catalogue (2001), R.A. Magazine (June 2000 issue), Royal Academy greeting card published by Canns Down Press. *Misc*: Awards: Japan 2001 subsidy (2000), R.O.S.L. Arts travel scholarship (2001), MacFarlane Walker Trust (2000), David Murray Prize (2000), The Gen Foundation for research in Japan (2000), The Worshipful Company of Painters/Stainers ('97-'00), Lever Hulme Scholarship, ('97-'00), M&G Purchase Prize, ('98), R.W.A. – Bursary, ('98), etc. *Address*: 33 Jansen Walk, Battersea, London SW11 2AZ. *Email*: bella.easton@virgin.net *Signs work*: "Bella Easton."

EASTON, David William, RI (1985), NDD (1956), BEd (1976); painter in water-colour, pastel, acrylics, gouache. *b*: Leicester, 29 Aug 1935. *s of*: John Donald Easton. *m*: Shirley.

two *s.* one *d. Educ*: Wyggeston School, Leicester. *Studied*: Leicester College of Art (1952-56). *Exhib*: RA, PS, RI, and many galleries throughout the UK. *Publications*: Watercolour Flowers (Batsford, 1993), and Watercolour Inspirations (Batsford, 1997), both re-issued in paperback (2001). *Address*: 9 Evington La., Leicester, LE5 5PQ. *Email*: eastonart9@gmail.com *Signs work*: "David Easton."

EASTON, Frances, 1st Class Dip. (Florence, 1960); painter of landscapes, nudes and still life in oil. *b*: Kenya. *d of*: Brig. G.L. Easton, MC (decd). *m*: Keith Stainton. three *s-s.* three *s-d. Educ*: Wycombe Abbey. *Studied*: Accademia di Belle Arti, Florence (1957-60, Prof. Giovanni Colacicchi). *Exhib*: one-man shows: London, Paris, Rome, most FBA Socs., Paris Salon (1977), Laing Competition (1986), Venice - Treviso (award). *Works in collections*: UK, France, Canada. *Commissions*: Kennedy Inst., London (Founder's portrait); Suffolk/W. Germany 'Twinning' landscape of Gainsborough's birthplace. *Clubs*: Hesketh Hubbard Art, Hurlingham, The Arts. *Address*: 5 Chelsea Studios, 410 Fulham Rd., London SW6. *Signs work*: "Frances Easton (Stainton)."

EASTON, Shirley, SWA (1988-92), NDD (1956), ATD (1957); painter in water-colour and acrylic. *b*: Leicester, 28 Apr 1935. *d of*: Herbert A. Swift. *m*: David Easton, R.I. two *s.* one *d. Educ*: Gateway Girls' School, Leicester. *Studied*: Leicester College of Art (1952-57, D.P. Carrington). *Exhib*: RA (1986), RI (1985-2001), SWA (1988, 1990, 1991). *Address*: 9 Evington La., Leicester LE5 5PQ. *Signs work*: "Shirley Easton."

EASTON, Timothy, Heatherley's Scholarship, London (1966), Elizabeth Greenshields Memorial Award, Montreal (1973); Winston Churchill Travelling Fellowship (1996); painter in oil on canvas, sculptor in bronze. *b*: 26 Aug 1943. *s of*: Dendy Bryan Easton, MIHort., DHRU. *m*: Christine Darling. two *d. Educ*: Christ College, Brecon. *Studied*: Kingston School of Art (1960-64), Heatherley School of Art (1966-67). *Exhib*: Chicago, Kansas, Los Angeles, Washington, New York and various Art Expos in America between 1968 and 1987; London and provinces from 1970 onwards; Germany, Luxembourg and Jersey 1984-1987 *Works in collections*: Hereford City A.G. *Publications*: John Hedgecoe's Nude Photography (Ebury Press, 1984), Timothy Easton, Oil Painting Techniques (Batsford, 1997). *Address*: Bedfield Hall, Bedfield, Woodbridge, Suffolk IP13 7JJ. *Signs work*: "Timothy Easton" or "Easton."

EATON, Paul, VPRMS - Vice President Royal Miniature Society for Sculpture (2013); RMS (2012); MMA (2013); HS (2012); MASF (2013); MPSGS - Washington DC (2013). Awards: MASF - 1st prize 'Sculpture and Scrimshaw Award' with 'Family of Warthogs' (2011); MPSGS - Best New Artist with 'African Elephant' (2011); MASF 1st prize 'Sculpture and Scrimshaw Award' with 'Northern Bobcat' (2012); World Federation Miniaturists Best Sculpture with 'Lookout' (20112); MPSGS First Place Sculpure Award with 'Family of Spoonbills' (2012); MASF 1st prize 'Sculpture and Scrimshaw Award' with 'Splash' (2013); MPSGS 'Second Place Sulpture Award' with 'I was here first' (2013); Seaside Art Gallery Best in Show with 'Where are you going?'. *Medium*: Sculpture. *b*: London, 23 Apr 1955. *m*: Jacqui. two *s.* one *d. Educ*: Ottershaw Boys School. *Exhib*: Royal Miniature Art Society; Hilliard Society; Miniature Artist Society of Florida; Miniature Society of Painters, Sculptors and Gravers, Washington DC; World Federation of Miniaturists; Snow Goose Gallery, Pennsylvania, USA; Seaside Art Gallery, North Carolina; Stock Exchange, London; Lemon Tree Gallery, Englewood, Florida. *Works in collections*: private collections. *Commissions*: Dating from 1980 to present including yachts, helicopters, cars, animals, birds and humans. *Official Purchasers*: Hawk Conservancy, Gloucester; presentation to Princess Anne of 'Golden Eagle'; P&O Cruises; Princess Diana - Presentation of 'Spindrift'; Young Envonmentalist of the Year - four years running - Osprey and Salmon, Humpback Whale and Calf, Barn Owl in Flight and Otter; Encyclopedia Brittanica - British Garden Bird Collection in sterling silver; Encyclopedia

Brittanica - British Owl Collection; Franklin Mint - Lords of the Air. Principal Works: Wildlife and ongoing collections. *Recreations*: falconry, cars, travelling. *Clubs*: North American Falconry Association, AC Owners Club; Goodwood Road Racing Club. *Address*: 161 High Street, Cranleigh, Surrey GU6 8BB. *Email*: info@eatongoldsmiths.com *Website*: www.eatongoldsmiths.com *Signs work*: "Paul Eaton VPRMS MAA MASF MPSGS HS",

EATWELL, David, painter in oil, landscape, abstract and cubism. *b*: 1 Jun 1960. *Educ*: Hereford High School. *Exhib*: Lower Nupend Gallery, one man shows - Wood for the Trees, Lees (1996), Recent Paintings (1997, 1998), Recent Paintings - Christmas (1998), 5th Exhibition (1999). His paintings are on permanent exhibition at the Lower Nupend Gallery, 6' Exhibition 2000, 7' Exhibition 2002. *Address*: c/o Lower Nupend Gallery, Cradley, Nr. Malvern, Worcs. WR13 5NP *Website*: www.gallery-modern-art.com *Signs work*: "DAVID EATWELL."

EAVES, John, ATC (1952). *b*: Bristol, 10 Nov 1929. *m*: Cecily Edith (decd). two *s*. two *d*. *Educ*: Bembridge School, Bembridge, IOW. *Studied*: Bath Academy of Art, James Tower (ceramics), William Scott (painting) (1949-52). *Exhib*: throughout GB, Germany and USA. *Works in collections*: Arts Council of GB; City A.G., Bristol; Royal West of England Academy; South West Arts; Victoria A.G., Bath; University of Bath; Prediger, Schwäbisch Gmünd, G.; City of Braunschweig, G.; private collections in G.B., Germany and USA, & Target Collection. *Commissions*: mural entitled "Horizons" completed January 2001 for Hotel Barcelona, Exeter. *Publications*: in Henry Cliffe's Lithography (Studio Vista, 1965). Awarded Winston Churchill Travelling Fellowship to U.S.A. (1966), Print and Water-colour Prizes, Westward T.V. Open Competition (1973, 1975), Leverhulme Emeritus Fellowship (1986) to study painter Emil Nolde, 'A Cast of Stones' by Philip Gross 1996 (drawings), John Eaves, The Colour of Music (monograph) pub. 2000. *Address*: 2 Belgrave Pl., Bath, Avon BA1 5JL. *Signs work*: "Eaves '98."

ECCLESTON, Margaret, NDD (1954), ATD (1955), BA Hon Ed (1955); painter in oil, pastel and watercolour; retired from full time education, now giving private workshops, invited tutor at St. Ives School of Painting. *b*: Worcestershire, 30 Mar 1934. two *d*. *Educ*: Holy Trinity Convent, Kidderminster, Worcs. *Studied*: Birmingham College of Art, under Marion Mackay (textile design). Also studied textiles, painting and pottery for ATD; BA Hons Child Psychology (Birmingham University). *Exhib*: recent exhibs. include - Contemporary Print Show, Barbican Centre, London; Mariners Gallery, St. Ives, Penhaven Gallery, The New Craftsman, Printmakers Gallery; St. Ives Soc. of Artists,: solo exhib. St. Ives 1999 & 2002, Gordes, Provence, France, 2000. Group exhibitions with St. Ives Society of Artists. *Works in collections*: New York and Paris. *Commissions*: private in England, Guernsey and USA. *Publications*: History of Moseley, Birmingham, St. Ives Illustrated Diary 2004 & 2005, St. Ives Illustrated Diary St.Ives Publication; book - Days in St. Ives (fully illustrated); St. Ives Address Book (2003). *Principal Works*: Landscapes, Sea Scapes, Figure Drawing, Still Life. *Clubs*: Porthmeor Printmakers, St. Ives, Dartmouth Art Soc., South Hams (Devon) Arts Forum. *Address*: Chatwell House, 9 Tuckers Brook, Modbury, S.Devon PL1 0TX. *Signs work*: "Margaret Eccleston."

EDE, Basil, South Eastern Wildlife Exposition Lifetime Achievement Award; founder member SWLA. *Medium*: oil. *b*: Fetcham, Surrey 12 Feb 1931. *s of*: Guy R. Ede. *m*: Daphne Shiela. two *s*. *Educ*: St.Johns School, Leatherhead, Surrey. *Studied*: Kingston Art School 1947/48. *Represented by*: self. *Exhib*: solo shows include: The Rowland Ward Gallery, London (1958); The Tryon Gallery (1960, '62, '64, '65, '68, '75, '80); Kennedy Galleries, New York (1966, 1971, 1979); The Palm Springs Desert Museum, California (1987); Wimborne Arts Festival (1993); also extensively across the USA. *Works in collections*: The Collection of HRH The Duke of Edinburgh (Buckingham Palace and other Royal palaces); The Warner Collection (USA); The Annenberg Collection; The Ulster Museum (Belfast,

Northern Ireland). *Publications*: 'Birds of Town and Village', Country Life (1965); 'Basil Ede's Birds' (1980); 'Wild Birds of America - The Art of Basil Ede' (1991). *Address*: Mark Cross House, Mill Lane, Laughton, Lewes, East Sussex, BN8 6AN. *Email*: basilede1@aol.com *Signs work*: "Basil Ede".

EDEN, Max Nigel Byron, NDD (1950), ATD (1951); painter in oil, acrylic, water-colour. *b*: St. Helens, Lancs., 12 Nov 1923. *s of*: Isaac Eden. *m*: Valerie. one *s*. one *d*. *Educ*: Cowley School, St. Helens (1928-41), Borough Rd. College, London (1942-43, 1947-48). *Studied*: Liverpool College of Art (1948-51), Ecole des Beaux Arts de Paris (1951-52), Copenhagen Academy (1954-55). *Exhib*: In France, Denmark, England, USA, Canada and Spain. Retrospective, 50 works (6 Oct-25 Nov 2005, Liverpool University). *Works in collections*: Southport Atkinson Gallery; private collections: Leo and Jilly Cooper, also in Europe, UK, USA, and Canada. *Address*: 7 Baker's Lane Churchtown Southport Merseyside PR9 9RN. *Email*: max.eden@btinternet.com *Website*: maxeden.co.uk *Signs work*: "Eden."

EDGERTON, Charmian, BA (Hons) (Graphic Design), SBA, SWA; painter in pastel. *b*: 16 Sep 1944. *m*: Nick Edgerton, psychologist. one *d*. *Educ*: Hillcourt School, Dublin. *Studied*: Zurich Kunstgeverbe Schule (1961), Dublin (1962, K. McGonigal), Stoke-on-Trent Polytechnic (1967, graphic design/illustration). *Exhib*: Medici (1991), Alresford Gallery (1993), Gallery Artist of John Thompson Gallery and Alresford Gallery, Aldburgh and Albemarle St., assorted Opens, Barry Keene Gallery, Henley, Blackheath Gallery SE3, John Noott Gallery, Broadway, Pheasantry Fine Arts, Headcorn, Kent, 20th Century Gallery, Windsor, John Falle, Jersey. *Commissions*: Pastel Painting, and Flowers and Plants Ed. Jenny Rodwell (Cassell, 1993); author, Learn to Draw Flowers (Harper Collins); regular contributor to Leisure Painter magazine, and demonstrator for Rowney's Pastels. *Address*: 13 Camden Row, London SE3 0QA. *Signs work*: "Charmian" and "C.P.E."

EDMANDS, Trevor Parton, MA, NDD (Painting Special), PGCE; figurative Sculpture Award BI. *Medium*: assemblages/constructions - oil, watercolour, drawing, prints, sculpture. *b*: Leeds, 23 Apr 1936. *m*: Ursula. two *d*. *Studied*: Leeds College of Art (1953-57), Leeds University Institute of Education (1958), Leeds Metropolitan University (1997-98). *Exhib*: Too numerous to list but include Europe, USA, Japan and UK. Solo exhibitions include Leeds City Art Gallery; Malton Gallery, Cincinnati, USA; Padden Gallery, Munster, Germany; Palazzo Communcale, Camerino,Italy. *Works in collections*: numerous. *Publications*: Triquarterly, The Signal and other notable US journals. Panerge. Chapman Woodman Press UK. *Recreations*: sports, walking, literature, film. *Clubs*: Hallamshire Tennis & Squash. *Address*: 80 Brookhouse Hill, Sheffield, South Yorkshire S10 3TB. *Email*: trevoredmands@yahoo.co.uk *Website*: trevoredmands.com

EDMONDS, Angela, BA Hons Fine Art (1990), MA (1997); artist in mixed media drawing, assemblage, photoworks; part-time lecturer. *b*: London, 26 Nov 1946. *m*: Brian. one *s*. one *d*. *Educ*: Hendon County Grammar School. *Studied*: Watford College of Art (1985-86), University of Herts. (1986-90), Middlesex University (1995-97). *Exhib*: solo shows: Ten Year Retrospective, Attenborough Centre, Leicester (2004); Moor Park Mansion (1989), Flower Gallery, London (1991), Harlequin Centre (1992); 'Landmarks', Cyberaxis, curator (2000); The Bull Gallery, Barnet (2001), Hertford Museum (2001); two-person show: Knapp Gallery, London (1995); group shows: (1988) Camden Art Centre, Wexner Center, U.S.A., R.A.; Ikon Gallery, B'ham, Conference Centre, Brighton (1991), Business Design Centre; (1994): Arts - Fife Touring; (1995): Leicester City Gallery, Kettles Yard, Cambridge; (1996): Stoke Newington Gallery; (1997): Contact Gallery, Norwich; (1999): Bilston Gallery, Osterley Park (2001); Ferens Gallery, Hull, Margaret Harvey Gallery (2000), Mainzer Kunstpreiz (2001); The Place, Letchworth (2002); Essex University, Colchester (2005), The Courtyard, Hertford (2006); Faith House Gallery, Dorset (2007), Parallel Visions, Wilmington USA and touring. *Works in collections*: Glaxo Plc., Aldenham

School, Watford Museum, Capital & Counties Plc., Bushey Museum, Ruskin Museum, and many private collections. *Commissions*: 1989-92: drawings on site - The Harlequin Centre Development. Prizes: 1989: 1st Prize 'Hertfordshire Open' touring, 'Hunting Group Art prizes' touring; 1992: 1st Prize 'Drawings for All' Gainsborough House, touring. *Publications*: awards: Paul Hamlyn 1997, Year of the Artist 2000. *Address*: 102 Oaklands Ave., Oxhey, Watford, Herts. WD19 4LW. *Signs work*: "Angela Edmonds" or not at all.

EDMONDSON, Stewart, BA (Hons) First Class Landscape Architecture. *Medium*: Watercolour; drawing; mixed media. *b*: Leeds, 23 Aug 1965. *Partner*: Fenella Brown. one *s*. *Studied*: Leeds Metropolitan University. *Represented by*: Beaux Arts, Bath; D'Art Gallery, Dartmouth. *Exhib*: Solo Show: Beaux Arts, Bath, D'Art Gallery, Dartmouth. Mixed shows: London Art Fair; 2020; Battersea Affordable Art Fair. *Works in collections*: Private; corporate. *Commissions*: Ilsington Country House Hotel. *Publications*: 'Wild Land, Wild Hearts - Poetry & Paintings' Meridian Press. *Works reproduced*: Prints with D'Art Gallery, Dartmouth. *Address*: Wooton, Holne, Ashburton, Devon TQ13 7RU. *Email*: stewartedmondson@freeuk.com *Website*: www.stewartedmondson.com *Signs work*: "S.A. EDMONDSON".

EDWARDS, Alan C.L., BA (Hons) (1982), PGCE (1983), ATD (1983), MEd (1990); painter/teacher; Chair NAPA. *b*: 1947. *s of*: C.L. Edwards. *m*: Carmel Wood. two *s*. two *d*. *Studied*: Laird School of Art (1965-67), Liverpool Polytechnic (1979-83), Liverpool University (1986-90). *Exhib*: Royal Academy London (Stowells Trophy); Walker Art Gallery, Liverpool; Ainscough Gallery, Liverpool; Hanover Gallery, Liverpool; Williamson Art Gallery, Birkenhead; Black Sheep Gallery, North Wales; Theatre Clwyd, North Wales; Durham Museum and Art Gallery; RBSA Galleries, Birmingham; Westminster Gallery, London; Grosvenor Museum, Chester; Long Beach Arts, California, USA; The Mariners Gallery, St. Ives; Gold Gallery, Edinburgh. *Works in collections*: England, NZ and Ireland. *Publications*: Visual Resource Packs for Teachers, International Artist Oct/Nov 2001. *Address*: 6 Berwyn Boulevard, Bebington, Wirral, Merseyside CH63 5LR. *Email*: alan.edwards420@ntlworld.com *Website*: www.alan-edwards-artist.com *Signs work*: Alan Edwards."

EDWARDS, Benjamin Ralph, C&G Dip. (1972), RAS Cert. (1977), ATC P/G Goldsmiths' College (1978); painter/etcher in black and white etching, drawing, charcoal and pencil, lecturer; painting tutor P/T City and Guilds Art School, London. *b*: London, 11 Dec 1950. *s of*: Eric Fredrick Edwards. *m*: Ylva. one *s*. *Educ*: St. Christopher School, Letchworth, Herts. *Studied*: pre college with Capt. P.J. Norton, DSO, RN; City and Guilds Art School (1968-72, Eric Morby), Atelier 17, Paris (1972-73, S.W. Hayter), RA Schools (1973-77, Roderick Barret). *Exhib*: RA Summer Exhbn. (1977 onwards), Kanagawa Prints, Okohama, Japan (1982-84), RE (1969-75). *Works in collections*: V&A, Wellesley College Library, Mass., Newberry Library, Chicago, Bridwell Library, Dallas, Texas. *Publications*: illustrated, The Four Seasons at Parkgate Cottages (Parkgate Press), A Fox under my Bed (Macmillan). *Address*: The Parkgate Press, 7 Argyle Rd., N. Finchley, London N12 7NU

EDWARDS, Brigid, BSc (Hons); artist in water-colour on vellum; photography. *b*: London, 16 Feb 1940. *m*: R.J. Edwards. *Educ*: Our Lady of Sion, London, University College, London *Studied*: Central School of Art (1960-63). *Represented by*: Thomas Gibson Fine Art Ltd. *Exhib*: RHS, RBG Kew, RA, Thomas Gibson Fine Art, Beadleston, NY, S. H. Ervin, Sydney, Yasuda Kasai Museum of Art, Tokyo; National Gallery of Modern Art, Edinburgh; The Ashmolean Museum, Oxford; Wills Lane Gallery, St. Ives, Cornwall (2009, photographs). *Works in collections*: Hunt Inst., Carnegie Mellon University, Penn., RBG Kew. *Publications*: illustrated: 'Primula' monograph (Batsford). *Address*: 72 Clarence Way, London NW1 8DG. *Signs work*: "Brigid Edwards" or not at all.

EDWARDS, C.C.G. *Medium*: sepia, watercolours and silverpoint, drawing, prints, oil; new work on English oak panels and handmade paper. *b*: London, 3 May 1936. *m*: Georgina. two *s*. *Educ*: Sir George Monoux Grammar School, London. *Studied*: attached to studio of Thomas Kennedy, London, for ten years. *Exhib*: RA, Paris Salon, Royal Cambrian Academy, Royal institute of Oil Painters, numerous galleries. *Works in collections*: private collections in USA, Canada, France, Germany and Australia. *Publications*: cover of Wessex Magazine and Dorset Magazine; La Revue Moderne, Paris. *Address*: Burlton Cottage, Shillingstone, Dorset DT11 0SP. *Website*: www.ccgedwards.com *Signs work*: 'Edwards'.

EDWARDS, Gareth, RWA, NSA, BA Hons Art History. *Medium*: painting and sculpture. *b*: Berkshire, 31 Mar 1960. *m*: Rachael Reeves. two *d*. *Educ*: Kennylands Boarding School, Berkshire. *Studied*: London University (Art History); Goldsmiths (ATC). *Represented by*: Hart Gallery, London; Caelum Gallery, New York. *Exhib*: RA; Campden Gallery; Hart Gallery; Lemon St. Gallery, Truro; Bird & Davis, London; RWA Bristol; Newlyn Art Gallery, Newlyn; NSA; National Maritime Museum, Falmouth; Caelum Gallery, New York, USA; Art Fairs: London, Miami, Geneva, Nimes. *Works in collections*: Falmouth Art Gallery; Dr John & Kit Hart Collection, Nottingham; international. *Commissions*: Holmes Place Fitness; Dr John & Kit Hart Collection, Nottingham; Anne O'Brien; Saatchi & Saatchi. *Publications*: 'Painting in St. Ives since 1960' by Peter Davis (St. Ives Press, 2007). *Works Reproduced*: in Cornwall Today, Inside Cornwall, Galleries mag, RA magazine. *Principal Works*: Luxe Eterna (Frankie & Jackson), Emotional Weather. *Recreations*: poetry, interior and garden design; collects contemporary ceramics. *Clubs*: Newlyn Society of Artists. *Misc*: runs 'Gareth Edwards Painting School'. *Address*: 'Valley View', Lamorna Cove, Penzance, Cornwall TR19 6XN. *Email*: gaz.ed@talktalk.net *Signs work*: 'gareth edwards' or 'GARETH EDWARDS'.

EDWARDS, John, ARBS; painter and sculptor; Head of Painting, Sculpture, St. Martin's School of Art (1980-88). *b*: London, 3 Mar 1938. *Studied*: Hornsey School of Art, Leeds University Inst., and L'Cambre Brussels. *Works in collections*: Arts Council, British Council, Belgian Government, CAS, CNAA, Govt. Art Collection, Gulbenkian Foundation, Solomon R. Guggenheim Museum, NYC. *Commissions*: Southampton University, Hackney Council, etc. Fellowships: British Council Scholarship Brussels, Winston Churchill Fellowship, Leverhulme Fellowship, London Arts Board, Pollock-Krasner Foundation Grant. *Address*: (studio) 52 Isledon Rd., London N7 7LD. *Email*: johnedwards.artist@btopenworld.com *Website*: www.johnedwards-artist.com *Signs work*: "John Edwards."

EDWARDS, John Colin, RP, Cert. RA Schools; Silver and Bronze Medallist RA Schools; Elizabeth T. Greenshield Art Foundation Award, Canada (1970, 1972); World Wildlife Fund Art Award (1986). portrait, nude painter. *Medium*: oil, pencil, chalk, charcoal. *b*: Kidderminster, 23 Aug 1940. *s of*: William Edwards. *m*: Patricia Rose, M.Sc. two *d*. *Educ*: Sladen School, Kidderminster (1951-53), Stourbridge Art School (1953-55). *Studied*: Pietro Annigoni in Florence; RA Schools. *Represented by*: Royal Society of Portrait Painters. *Exhib*: Tate Gallery, NPG, RA, RP, Windsor Castle, SWLA, Tryon, Malcolm Innes and Solent Galleries. *Works in collections*: HM The Queen; Baroness Thatcher, OM; Royal Collection, Windsor; Adjutant General's Corps; Royal College of Radiologists; The Law Society; Carpenters Company; Cambridge, Oxford, Aston, Leicester Universities, Tate Gallery, Ashmolean Musuem, etc. *Commissions*: Oxford University Press; Taylor Hackford; Edmund de Rothschild; Penelope Keith; Helen Mirren; The Hon. William Hague, MP; Institute of Civil Engineers; Lord Mar and Killie; Institute of Structural Engineers; Lord Ali; Royal College of Pathologists. *Publications*: Tate Gallery, Mitchell Beazley, Collins Publications, etc. *Official Purchasers*: Royal Collection Windsor; House of Commons; Tate Gallery; Sultanate of Oman. *Works Reproduced*: Mitchell Beazley, Paper House, Cosmopolitan, Tatler. *Principal Works*: H.M. The Queen; Baroness Thatcher, O.M.; William

Hague, M.P. *Recreations*: classical music. *Address*: Chesterville Gallery and Studio, 163 Chester Rd. North, Kidderminster, Worcs. DY10 1TP. *Email*: holbine@aol.com *Website*: www.johnedwardsrp.com *Signs work*: "John Edwards" and "Edwards."

EDWARDS, Karen, RWA; BA Hons Fine Art. *Medium*: oil on canvas. *b*: London, 8 Jan 1961. *d of*: Douglas Roopnarine. *m*: Simon Edwards. one *s.* two *d. Studied*: University of Newcastle upon Tyne. *Represented by*: Cube Gallery, Bristol. *Works in collections*: University of Newcastle upon Tyne. *Clubs*: mem. Royal West of England Academy. *Address*: 6 Ninetree Hill, Cotham, Bristol BS1 3SG. *Email*: karenedwards@blueyonder.co.uk

EDWARDS, Malcolm, RCA, B.Arch, RIBA. *Medium*: watercolour and mixed media. *b*: Liverpool, 24 Jan 1934. *m*: Elizabeth. *Educ*: Hawarden Grammar School. *Studied*: Liverpool University. *Exhib*: Pastel Society; RI; St.Davids Hall, Cardiff; Tegfryn Gallery, Menai Bridge; Hen Capel Gallery, Llangollen; John Davies Gallery, Stow on the Wold; Pen y Fan Gallery, Brecon; Kooywood Gallery, Cardiff; Ffin y Parc Gallery, Llanwrst. *Works in collections*: National Library of Wales; Clwyd Fine Arts Trust; Contemporary Art Society for Wales; National Museum & Gallery of Wales; international. *Commissions*: Clwyd Fine Arts Trust. *Address*: Caeronwy, Rhosemor Road, Halkyn, Holywell, Flintshire, CH8 8DL. *Email*: malcolmedwards@mac.com *Website*: www.malcolmedwardsart.co.uk *Signs work*: "Malcolm Edwards".

EDWARDS, Mary Elizabeth. *Medium*: mixed media, acrylic/pastel, oil. *b*: Coventry, 7 Mar 1943. *d of*: James and Hilda O'Nions. *m*: David Edwards. one *s.* two *d. Studied*: self taught. *Exhib*: RA Summer Exhbn; Herbert Art Gallery Open, Coventry; Llewellyn Alexander, London; RWA Bristol Open; St. David's Hall, Cardiff. *Clubs*: Wye Valley Art Society; Glos Society of Artists. *Misc*: Committee Member Forest of Dean Open Studios, Art Trail. *Address*: Lindor's Farm, St. Briavels, Lydney, Glos GL15 6RP. *Signs work*: 'M.E.'

EDWARDS, Peter Douglas, BA Hons Fine Art; BP Portrait Award First Prize (National Portrait Gallery). *Medium*: painter, oils. *b*: Chirk, 20 Nov 1955. *s of*: Harry William Edwards. *m*: Lesley Sutherland. three *s.* one *d. Educ*: Oswestry School (1964-74). *Studied*: Foundation Shrewsbury School of Art (1974-75), Cheltenham GCAD (1975-78). *Represented by*: Beadleston Gallery, New York, Britart.com. *Exhib*: one-man: Contemporary Poets, National Portrait Gallery exhbn and tour; widely UK and abroad. *Works in collections*: National Portrait Gallery, Metropolitan Museum New York, Ulster Museum, National Museum of Wales, National Museums and Galleries on Merseyside, Ferens Hull. *Commissions*: Sir Bobby Charlton (NPG, 1991), Sir Peter Middleton (Chairman of Barclays, 1994), Kazuo Ishiguro (NPG, 1994), Baroness Tessa Blackstone. *Official Purchasers*: NPG London, Liverpool Poets, Willy Russell, Seamus Heaney. *Works Reproduced*: Seamus Heaney, Sir Bobby Charlton. *Principal Works*: as above. *Recreations*: gardening, running. *Clubs*: Chelsea Arts Club. *Address*: 10 Upper Brook Street, Oswestry, Shropshire, SY11 2TB. *Email*: artyedwards@btinternet.com *Website*: www.peteredwards.net

EDWARDS, Sylvia, artist, printmaker, painter in water-colour, oil, acrylic. *Medium*: watercolour. *b*: Boston, Mass *d of*: Junius Griffiths Edwards, music impressario (decd), and Sylvia E. Mailloux (decd). *m*: Sadredin Golestaneh. one *s.* two *d. Educ*: Boston public schools. *Studied*: fine art at Massachusetts College of Art, Boston, Mass. (1956-60, Prof. Lawrence Kupferman), Boston Museum of Fine Arts. *Exhib*: consistently in one-woman and mixed shows and international art expositions; London: Berkeley Sq. Gallery, CCA Gallery and Christopher Hull Gallery; Tokyo, Bankamura, Mitsukoshi Mihonbashi Branch; Osaka, Nii Gallery (1989); Alexandria, Egypt, Alexandria Museum of Fine Arts (1980); Mediterranean Biennale (1980); Munson Gallery, Chatham, Mass. (1992); Morehead Planetarium, Chapel Hill, NC; Natalie Knight Gallery, Johannesburg, SA (1991); Singapore,

Art Base Gallery (sponsored by Citibank, 1989); Bankamura, Tokyo (1991); CCA Gallery Oxford (1996); The Galleria, Boca Grande Florida (2000), CCA Gallery, London (2003); Grovesnor Gallery, London (2003); State of the Art Gallery, Sarasota, Fla (2007). *Works in collections*: Tate Gallery, London; Boston University Special Collections; Mugar Memorial Library; National Museum of Women in the Arts, Washington, D.C.; Alexandria Museum of Women in the Arts; Alexandria Governorate, Egypt; Cape Museum of Fine Arts, Dennis, Mass.; Midwest Museum of American Art, Elkhart, Indiana. *Publications*: 'The Nucleus' narrative book of drawings; 'The Undoing of the Square' 'Painters' Wild Workshop'; Sylvia Edwards 'Works on Hand Cast Paper'; work widely published by UNICEF, Coriander Studios and CCA Galleries, London for limited editions in silkscreen, and the London Art Group for prints and Bruce McGaw graphics; numerous gallery handbooks and catalogues; articles and television talks 'Sylvia Edwards Talks with Mel Gooding'. Monograph "Sylvia Edwards" published London Pallas Athene (introduction by Mel Gooding and David Elliot). *Clubs*: Chelsea Arts. *Address*: 14 Cadogan Sq., London SW1X 0JU. *Website*: www.sylviaedwards.com *Signs work*: "Sylvia Edwards."

EDWARDS, Yvonne Sylvia, SBA, CBM (1997, 2000 & 2008); artist in water-colour; RHS Silver Gilt Medal. *b*: S. Australia, 28 Nov 1942. *m*: Malcolm Edwards two *s*. *Exhib*: SBA since 1994. *Works in collections*: Shirley Sherwood and Lindley Library. *Address*: Lodge Farm, Moot Lane, Dowton, Wilts. SP5 3LN. *Email*: yvonneedwards2005@tiscali.co.uk

EGAN, Órla, Four awards, The Office of Public Works Gallery, Donegal; Donegal Arts Festival Award. *Medium*: oil. *b*: Dublin, 25 Apr 1947. one *s*. one *d*. *Ed*uc: Largely self taught. *Represented by*: Dublin: Leinster Gallery, Sandford Gallery; McKenna Gallery, Omagh, Northern Ireland. *Exhib*: RHA, Dublin (1998, 1999, 2002, 2003, 2004, 2006, 2008, 2012); RUA (2002, 2004); Sligo Art Gallery, The Crawford Gallery, Cork. UK Galleries: Thompsons Gallery, London; Wren Gallery, Burford, Oxfordshire; The Crypt Gallery, St. Ives, Cornwall (2013, 2014). *Works in collections*: Michael D. Higgins (The Irish President); Mrs Jean Kennedy Smith (former American Ambassador to Ireland); Melita Danaro; Martin Mooney. *Commissions*: private commissions. *Publications*: A Buyers Guide to Irish Art, Belfast Telegraph and local papers. *Official Purchasers*: The Electricity Supply Board, Head Office, Dublin; The Office of Public Works, Great Blasket Centre, Kerry; The Office of Public Works, Glebe Gallery, Co. Donegal. *Misc*: 12 paintings accepted into the RHA, and two into the RUA. Picture featured on Irish TV with HRH Prince Charles and Tony O'Malley. *Address*: Gartan, Church Hill, Letterkenny, Co. Donegal, Ireland. *Email*: martinjegan@eircom.net *Website*: www.orlaegan.com Signs work: "Orla Egan".

EGGLETON, Margaret, SWA, SBA, SGFA (Council Member); 2003 SBA Highly Commended; 2007 SGFA Highly Commended for Chiaroscuro Theme; 2009 SWA Prize for Most Original Painting. *Medium*: ink, watercolour, mixed media, pastel. *b*: Sale, Cheshire, 20 Feb 1943. d of: Stanley and Winifred Irving. *m*: Stuart. one *s*. one *d*. *Educ*: Sale Grammar School. *Studied*: Trent Park Teacher Training College (main subject Art). *Exhib*: RWS, RI, Mall Galleries, Cork Street, Menier Gallery. *Works in collections*: private collections in many countries. *Publications*: Drawing Masterclass Flowers (Search Press, May 2012), Drawing Masterclass Landscapes (Search Press, May 2014). *Works Reproduced*: Medici Cards, Giclee Prints. *Principal Works*: Oxford High Cityscape, Gherkin Cityscape, Evening Light (London Cityscape). *Recreations*: music, walking, photography, reading. *Clubs*: Croydon Art Society, Epsom and Ewell Art Group. *Misc*: teaches Watercolour & Mixed Media, organises painting holidays, demonstrations, Art Group critic. *Address*: 82 Tabor Gardens, Cheam, Sutton, Surrey, SM3 8RY. *Email*: eggleton.art@btinternet.com *Website*: www.margareteggleton.co.uk *Signs work*: 'M.EGGLETON'.

ELFORD, Norman, NDD, ATD, GRA; artist in oil, acrylic, alkyd. *b*: Portsmouth, 6 Jul 1931. *m*: Dorothy one *s*. one *d*. *Educ*: Portsmouth Northern Grammar School. *Studied*:

Southern Colleges of Art, Portsmouth (1947-51), Bournemouth (1951-52) *Exhib*: NRM York; Hexagon, Reading; two one-man shows: Stroud Festival, Gloucs.; regular exhbns. G.R.A. Work in private collections. *Commissions*: designs for Royal Doulton and Spode Fine China plates; calendars and greetings cards, fine art marine prints. *Clubs*: G.R.A., President, Portsmouth & Hampshire Art Soc. *Address*: 36 Torrington Rd., North End, Portsmouth PO2 0TP. *Signs work*: "NORMAN ELFORD."

ELGAR, Juliet Jane, BA (Hons) Art/Teaching; painter; arts crafts tutor in drawing and painting, now independent. *b*: Wiltshire, 18 Mar 1942. three *s.* two *d. Educ*: La Retraite Convent, Salisbury, Wilts. *Studied*: Bath Academy of Art under J. Hoskin sculptor, H. Hodgekin and M. Hughes, painters. *Exhib*: Westminster Gallery, London, Arthouse, Richmond, Gallery at Dauntsey's School, Wilts. *Commissions*: various landscape, portrait and design. *Misc*: Would like to be commissioned in aid of environmental charities on 50/50 profit. *Address*: 22 St. Mary's Grove, Richmond, Surrey TW9 1UY. *Email*: j-elgar@hotmail.com *Signs work*: "Jane Elgar."

ELIAS, Ken, BA Hons Fine Art (1969), MA Fine Art (1987), RCA; painter in acrylic on paper; Royal Cambrian Academician. *b*: Glynneath, West Glamorgan, 9 Nov 1944. *Studied*: Cardiff College of Art (1965-66, 1985-87), Newport College of Art (1966-69), University of Wales, Cardiff (1969-70). *Exhib*: regularly in solo and group shows in UK and abroad. *Works in collections*: National Museum of Wales, National Library of Wales, Arts Council of Wales, Contemporary Art Society for Wales, Newport Museum and Art Gallery, Bangor College Normal, Brecknock Museum & Art Gallery, University of Glamorgan, School of Art, University of Wales Aberystwyth, Editions Alecto and private collections U.K. and abroad. *Publications*: 'Ken Elias: Thin Partitions' (Monograph ISBN 978-1-85411-501-0) published by Seren Books 2009 (www.seren-books.com). *Clubs*: Welsh Group, R.Cam.A., 56 Group Wales. *Address*: 29 Park Ave., Glynneath, West Glamorgan SA11 5DP. *Email*: elias734@btinternet.com

ELKINS, Bridgette Mary, Post Grad Dip. Painting and Drawing (2005). *Medium*: oil, acrylic, mixed media. *b*: Didsbury, 11 Jun 1937. *d of*: Wilfrid Morley. *m*: widow. two *d. Educ*: Haunton Hall, nr.Tamworth. *Studied*: with professional painters in Cyprus, Bermuda and England; Slade Summer School; West Dean College/Sussex University (2005). *Represented by*: Red Biddy Gallery, Shalford, Surrey. *Exhib*: RA Summer Exhbns; numerous open exhbns and group shows in UK and overseas, including: Mall Galleries and London Art Fairs (2008); St.Botolph's Club, Boston, Mass. USA; The Studio Gallery, Midhurst (2004); Reclamation, Post Graduate Show, West Dean College. *Works in collections*: CMC Head Office, California, USA; several private UK and European, Canadian and Australian collections. *Official Purchasers*: Cyprus Mines Corp.HQ, California, USA; Bermuda Govt. Premier's Office. *Recreations*: Visiting art galleries, overseas travel, horse racing, theatre. *Misc*: tour guide lecturer, Pallant House Gallery, Chichester. *Address*: Bex Mill House, Heyshott, nr. Midhurst, W.Sussex GU29 0DQ. *Email*: belkins@bexmill4.freeserve.co.uk *Website*: www.westdean/reclamation.org *S igns work*: 'BM Elkins' or 'BME' (on paper). Early work 'BM Jemal' or 'BMJ' (until Dec 1980).

ELLIOT, Ian Scott, Diploma in Art (GSA). *Medium*: oil/canvas. *b*: Glasgow, 12 Aug 1946. *m*: widowed. one *s. Educ*: Bellahouston Academy, Glasgow (1958-64). *Studied*: Glasgow School of Art (1964-68); Jordanhill Education Centre (1968-69). *Exhib*: Institute shows: PAI, RSW, RGI, Aberdeen Artists Society. Solo shows: Gatehouse Gallery, Glasgow; Barker Gallery, Eton; Scotlandart.com, Glasgow; Framework Gallery, Troon; Rowan Gallery, Helensburgh; Torquhoun Gallery, Tarves. Two person shows: Marine House Gallery, Beer; Strathearn Gallery, Crieff; Green Gallery, Aberfoyle. Group shows: Thompson's, Aldeburgh; Red Rag, Stow; Corte-Real, Algarve, amongst many others up and down Britain. *Works in collections*: Turnberry Hotels; corporate groups; private collections in Spain, France, Italy, USA. *Commissions*: in general private collectors, corporate and local businesses. *Publications*: 'International Artist' magazine, full 10-page spread on technique, etc (Volume 60). *Works Reproduced*: Tartan 2CV (cards); Hopscotch (cards); Next (Home) Stores; Art from Scotland (prints). *Principal Works*: Tuscan, Mallorcan, Scottish landscapes and seascapes. *Recreations*: photography, plants, golf, walking. *Clubs*: haggs Castle GC. *Misc*: Principal teacher of Art & Design (King's Park Secondary School, Glasgow, til 1997). Won gold, bronze medals on four occasions for art; Finalist in a global art landscape competition (International Artist magazine). *Address*: 18 Midlothian Drive, Glasgow, G41 3QX. *Email*: ianscottelliot@gmail.com *Website*: www.ianelliot.com *Signs work*: "ELLIOT".

ELLIOTT, Chuck (Charles), BA (Hons) Graphic Art, First Class. *Medium*: drawing, prints, digital. b: London, 15 Jul 1967. *Partner*: Dr. Jessica Harris. two *s*. *Studied*: Middlesex University (1988-1992). *Represented by*: Beaux Art Gallery, Bath; Catto Gallery, London. *Exhib*: Beaux Art Gallery, Bath; Catto Gallery, London; Bristol Gallery, View Gallery; Close House. Group shows: RA, RCA, Southbank Centre, London Art Fair; Art London; AAF London/NYC and many more. *Works in collections*: The Met Building, London; Greater London House; many other corporate spaces. *Publications*: CODA at Close; Synaesthetic; Beaux Art catalogue; Catto Gallery catalogue. *Principal Works*: Flow; Revolver; Halcyon; Radial. *Recreations*: Gardening. *Address*: 10 Southfield Road, Cotham, Bristol BS6 6AY. *Email*: chuck.elliott@btinternet.com *Website*: www.chuckelliott.com *Signs work*: "Chuck Elliott" and "C. Elliott" and monogram.

ELLIOTT, Helen, ABNA. *Medium*: Acrylics and Oil Pastels. *b*: Hull, Yorkshire, 14 May 1964. *d of*: Peter & Margaret Brown. *m*: David Elliott. two *d*. *Studied*: self-taught naive artist. *Represented by*: Fountain Fine Art; Galeri Betws-y-Coed; The Narberth Gallery; Penore Art, Cardigan. *Exhib*: solo show: Oriel Ceri Richards, Swansea (2009). Represented Wales at the International Festival Exhibition of Naive Art, France (2008, 2009); Fountain Art, Llandeilo (solo 2008, joint 2005-09); Pendre Art, Cardigan (solo exhibition 2007 - a 10 year Retrospective). *Works in collections*: private and corporate. *Commissions*: murals for local and national schools and private commissions. *Publications*: "Pembrokeshire - A Look upon the Land and Sea", Celtic Horizons (pub.2003). *Clubs*: ABNA; Founder Member, NAOW (NAive Artists of Wales). *Address*: Toll Gate House, Carmarthen Road, Newcastle Emlyn, Carmarthenshire, SA38 9DA. *Email*: mail@helenelliott.net *Website*: www.helenelliott.net *Signs work*: "ELLIOTT".

ELLIOTT, J. see BATES, Joan.

ELLIOTT, Mary E. see BERESFORD-WILLIAMS, Mary.

ELLIOTT, Paul, FWCB (Fellow Worshipful Company of Blacksmiths); Award: WCB bronze medal. *Medium*: metal - artist blacksmith. *b*: Harrow, 10 Apr 1968. *s of*: J Barrow & R.Elliott. *m*: J.M.Elliott. two *d*. *Studied*: City & Guilds Blacksmithing and Engineering; COSIRA (Rural Development Commission). *Commissions*: of sculptures, arbours, bridges, pergolas, staircases, water features, benches etc. for public and private, including Harrow Park, Scottish Arts Council, Sainsbury's, City Livery Companies, National Theatre, London, Chelsea Show Gardens, National Trust, religious bodies, Flying Hill Estate, Hampshire, Chisenbury Priory, Exbury Estate. *Works Reproduced*: in Metal Design International (2005); regularly featured in BABA; Contemporary Ironwork (2006). *Recreations*: artist blacksmithing, sailing. *Address*: Hammer & Tongs, Bulbourne Forge, Tring, HP23 5QF. *Email*: info@blacksmithonline.co.uk *Website*: www.blacksmithonline.co.uk

ELLIOTT, Susan Jane, BA Hons Textile Design. *Medium*: recycled ceramic & mosaic. *b*: Brighton, 16 Dec 1959. *m*: John Knowles. two *s*. *Studied*; Ravenbourne College of Art &

Design, Chislehurst, Kent (1979-81). *Represented by*: Mauger Modern, London; Cube Gallery, Bristol/London. *Exhib*: Art Fairs London/New York, Tokyo/New York, Tokyo, Toronto, Los Angeles, Amsterdam (2005-2012); Mixed gallery shows: Mauger Modern, Cube gallery (2005-2012), Byard Fine Art Cambridge. One woman show: 'The Crypt Gallery, London (2010). Whitechapel Open, & Festival Hall London (1989, 1990). *Works in collections*: private, corporate. *Commissions*: private, public - Asda Supermarket, Ship Bar Winchelsea, St. Leonards on Sea, 'Lions of Bath' charity auction. *Publications*: magazine/newspaper. *Works Reproduced*: Mosaic flag 'Best of British' - Woodmansterne cards. *Misc*: Worked as community artist with 'Freeform Artworks' Hackney London (1987-1998). *Address*: The Foresters Arms, 2 Shepherd Street, St. Leonards on Sea TN38 0ET. *Email*: susanonsea@yahoo.com *Website*: susanelliottmosaics.co.uk Signs work: "SUSAN ELLIOTT".

ELLIOTT, Walter Albert, FBIS, LFIBA, SGFA, PS; artist in pastel, oil, water-colour, acrylic; mem. Academy of Italy, Pres. Ilfracombe Art Soc., mem. International Assoc. of Art. *b*: Wembley, 24 Oct 1936. *s of*: Albert Elliott. *m*: Beryl Jean (decd). one *s.* one *d. Educ*: Pinner Grammar School; de Havilland Aero College. *Studied*: Hammersmith Polytechnic, Harrow College of Art. *Exhib*: PS, SGFA, UA (Mall Galleries), Pilton Arts Exhbn., Ilfracombe Art Soc.; Burton Gallery, Bideford, Salon de Paris (1984), Torbay Guild of Artists. Permanent exhbn. of artwork at the Elliott Gallery, Hillsview, Braunton, N. Devon. EX34 9NZ. *Works in collections*: 'The Ascent of Man' (N. Devon Atheneaum 1970-81, now along with many other paintings by Walter A. Elliott on exhibition at The Elliott Gallery, Braunton); Europe, Geneva, Canada, Australia, USA. *Publications*: articles, Spaceflight, British Interplanetary Soc. 'The Dream of Gotama', a recently published 320 page book written and illustrated by Walter A .Elliott (21 fine art illus.). *Works Reproduced*: numerous. *Principal Works*: Triptych - 'The Ascent of Man' Triptych - 'Man a Share-Time Bubble', 'The Arising of Intelligence', 'Searching for the Temple of Man's Heart', 'The Caress', 'Easter Bonnet', 'Refugees', Little Deaf Girl Learning to Speak', 'Young Mankind on the Threshold', 'Einstein', 'Time Tried', 'Earth's Human Flowers', 'Compassion', The Lake of Venus', 'Human Symphony', 'Old George', 'Moonlight over Venice', 'Caftane Walk', 'Japanese Family', Japanese Tea Party', 'Enchanted Ballroom', 'Woolacombe Beach', 'Devonshire Walk', 'Amour Maternal', 'The Sea Captain', 'Peace', 'Homeless', 'The Drop is in the Ocean, the Ocean is in the Drop', 'The Eternal Artist', 'The Warrior', 'The Favourite Hat', 'The Healing', 'The Sermon', 'The Bluebird', 'Charleston', 'Two Little Clowns', 'Durham Cathedral', 'The Shepherdess', 'The Birth of Mother Nature' (triptych), 'Love Duet' (triptych), Love Duet with Wings and Flowers, 'Cosmic Wings', 'The Potter'. *Clubs*: President of the Ilfracombe Art Society. *Address*: Sollake Studio, Warfield Villas, Ilfracombe, N. Devon EX34 9NZ. *Email*: artform222@aol.com *Website*: www.elliottartgallery.com *Signs work*: "Walter A. Elliott."

ELLIS, Belinda Anne, A for E Lottery Grant. *Medium*: acrylic, watercolour, drawing, oils, etching, monoprinting. *b*: London, 16 Apr 1949. *m*: Colin Challenger. one *s.* two *d. Studied*: Sir John Cass College, London (1967-69); North East London Polytechnic (1969-72); St.Martin's School of Art (1972-73). *Exhib*: RA Summer Exhbn, Royal Festival Hall, Whitechapel Open, Air Gallery, Warwicks Arts Trust, Woodlands Gallery, Harlech Biennale (1996), Banbury and Woodstock Museums, 'deliArt' Smithfield, Lab Gallery New York, Said Business School Oxford, Mall Galleries. *Works in collections*: Triangle Arts Association; L'Art en vie Collection, France; Vara Komum Concert Hall, Sweden. *Commissions*: murals, Polytechnic of Central London (1974). *Publications*: Women Artists Slide Library Journal (1987). *Works Reproduced*: RA Illustrated (2004); House and Garden (1982). *Misc*: Triangle Artists' Workshop, New York (1986); 'Art in Situ' Project, Drôme, France (2001, 2006). *Address*: St. Mary's Lodge, Church Street, Bloxham, Oxon OX15 4ES. *Email*: mail@belindaellis.co.uk *Website*: www.belindaellis.co.uk *Signs work*: 'Belinda Ellis' or 'B.Ellis'.

ELLIS, Christine Elizabeth, ADB (1960), AOI (1990); landscape and portrait artist in pencil, ink, water-colour and oil; illustrator; writer; Brian Sinfield Fine Art Award (2005); Purcell Papers, Pastel 2006; CAS Sculptors' Own 2007; ROI Art Events (2007 & 2009). *Educ*: Sacred Heart High School. *Studied*: Maria Assumpta College, Rose Bruford College. *Exhib*: solo exhibition: 2012 Garrick's Temple, Hampton; 1999 Buckingham Galleries, Southwold; mixed exhibitions: RI, RBA, Discerning Eye, Pastel Soc., ROI, SWA, Lynn Painter/Stainers, NEAC; annually with CAS. *Works in collections*: Life-size sculpture at Bursledon Brickwork's Museum; Paper based Sculpture of Jane Carlyle with National Trust at Carlyle House, Chelsea. *Commissions*: Cover illustrations 1997 Egon Ronay Guides. Landscapes and portraits: Martina Navratilova; Damon and Georgie Hill; All England Club, Wimbledon; Equitable Life, and for private individuals in many countries. Illustrations: St. George's; La Prairie; Keymer Tiles; Wates; Squires. *Publications*: 2012 "Poems and Such-like" (poetry and illustrations), illustrations to "To ja, Dawid" by Anne Holm; illustrations for "Pull's Ferry" (Norwich, 1998), BBC short stories for children broadcast (1979-82). *Address*: North Cottage, 6 High St., Hampton on Thames, Middx. TW12 2SJ. *Signs work*: "C.E. Ellis."

ELLIS, Edwina, RE (1987), SWE (1984); MA Fine Art (2004), Hon MA (2003); PhD Fine Art (2010). *Medium*: engraving. *b*: Sydney, Australia, 14 May 1946. *m*: P.J.N. Ellis. *Educ*: Manly Girls, Sydney. *Studied*: National Art School, Sydney, Aberystwyth University. *Represented by*: Hart Gallery, London. *Exhib*: RA, RE, Duncan Campbell (1988-97), Godfrey and Watt (1987-2001), NSW State Library, Australia, Fine Art Soc., London, Ashmolean Museum, Redfern Gallery London, V&A (1994), Hart Gallery London (2012). *Works in collections*: V&A, University Library of California, Australian National Library Canberra, Ashmolean Museum Oxford, Fitzwilliam Museum Cambridge, Art Gallery of N.S.W. Australia, London Transport Museum, Museum of London, NSW State Library, University of Wales, Aberystwyth University, NSW University. *Commissions*: London Transport: 'Art on London Transport' poster (1996); Royal Mint : Four One Pound Coin designs (2003); The Times Masthead (2008). *Publications*: Planned Spontaneity - Aberystwyth University (2010). *Official Purchasers*: Royal Mint, British Museum, Museum of London. *Works Reproduced*: 'Handmade Prints', 'Relief Printmaking', 'Printmaking for Beginners', 'Engravers Globe'. *Principal Works*: Bridge pound coin designs Times masthead. *Clubs*: Chelsea Arts *Address*: Rhyd Goch, Tyn-y-Graig, Ystrad Meurig, Ceredigion SY25 6AJ. *Website*: www.edwinaellis.co.uk *Signs work*: "E.N. Ellis."

ELLIS, Ian, BA (Hons), Post Grad Painting, Royal Academy of Arts; awarded Landseer Scholarship whilst at RA; Director of Fine Art, Radley College, Oxfordshire. *Medium*: fine art mixed media. *b*: Manchester, 1961. *m*: Valerie. two *s*. *Educ*: Rochdale College of Art, Loughborough College of Art. *Studied*: Royal Academy of Art (Peter Greenham, Norman Blamey). *Exhib*: The Sewell Centre Gallery, Oxfordshire. *Works in collections*: public and private collections. *Publications*: Mentioned in Christopher Hiberts book 'Radley - No Ordinary Place'. *Clubs*: RASAA. *Address*: The Sewell Centre Gallery, Radley College, Oxfordshire, OX14 2HR. *Email*: ipe@radley.org.uk *Website*: www.radley.org.uk/ian%27s%20web%20page/ian's%20web%20page.html

ELLIS, Ian Roy, BA (Hons) Painting, MA Painting; New Art in Yorkshire Painting Prize (1987, Leeds City Art Gallery). *Medium*: oil paint. *b*: Sheffield, 16 Oct 1962. *s of*: Jo & Roy Ellis. *m*: Maud Gambier-Ellis. one *s*. one *d*. *Studied*: Sheffield (Foundation), Coventry (BA), Manchester (MA). *Exhib*: Discerning Eye, Mall Galleries (2000), APT Gallery (1997), Herbert Museum & Art Gallery (1991), The Mappin Art Gallery (1989), Graves Art Gallery, Sheffield, Intercity 1988 Birmingham & Sheffield, New Art in Yorkshire (1987), Leeds City Art Gallery. *Works in collections*: Sheffield City Art Galleries. *Commissions*: British Steel, Brooke Tool Engineering, Lyons Bakery. *Publications*: Review: Guardian (1990, by Robert Clarke). *Official Purchasers*: Sheffield City Art Galleries. *Works Reproduced*: Dinosaur's

Blood (1997, APT Gallery, Pale Green Press, London). *Principal Works*: Fear (1987), Monster (1996), The Sting (2000), The Accident (2000), Perfectly Ordinary Homes (2004), Still Life Series (2008), A Gripping Tale (2013). *Misc*: Inventor of the Ellis Colour Mixing Systems (2011) and (2013). *Address*: 48B Vardens Road, Battersea, London SW11 1RH. *Email*: eillisian51@yahoo.com *Website*: ianellis.weebly.com *Signs work*: "IRE".

ELLIS, John Colin, UA (1988), MBIAT (1971), MIPD (1973); artist/architectural illustrator in water-colour, oil, acrylic; artist working mainly on architectural subjects, plus land and town scapes developing into abstract art; designer/illustrator within retail commercial and residential sectors. *b*: Fleetwood, Lancs., 1945. *m*: Penny. one *s*. one *d*. *Educ*: Bailey Secondary, Fleetwood. *Studied*: Blackpool School of Art (1961-67). *Exhib*: one-man shows: N.Wales, Stamford, Peterborough, London. *Works Reproduced*: housing sale illustration and brochure design. *Clubs*: U.A. *Address*: The Gallery, Braceborough, Stamford, Lincs. PE9 4NT. *Signs work*: "John C. Ellis."

ELLIS, Katy, RI (2003), RBA (2007); BA Hons; John Kinross Scholarship (1995); Baker Tilly Prize (2004); Treg' Aquarelle: Watercolour and Gouache Award (2003), Gouache Award (2004), Le Prix Maimeri (2005). *Medium*: watercolour and gouache. *b*: Greenwich, 20 Feb 1973. *d of*: Shirley Felts. *Partner*: Colin Grant. *Educ*: Haberdashers Askes Hatcham School for Girls (1984-1990). *Studied*: Blackheath School of Art (Foundation Course, 1990-91); Glasgow School of Fine Art (1991-95). *Exhib*: RWS Open (1992-2007); RI Open (1993-2007); Singer Friedlander/Sunday Times (2003, 2004); Scotlandart.com Gallery, Glasgow; Red Rag Gallery, Stow-on-the-Wold; The Sheen Gallery, Richmond; The Medici Gallery, London; Bell Fine Art, Winchester; Stark Gallery, London & Canterbury; Morninside Gallery, Edinburgh; Haddenham Gallery, Haddenham; The Old Fire Engine House, Ely; Baker Tilly offices, London. *Works in collections*: private collections, and ongoing exhbns at Scotlandart.com & The Old Fire Engine House. *Commissions*: several private commissions. *Publications*: Premier Magazine (1996/97); 'Water' by Chris Mulhern (Acorn Book Co., 1996); 'Paint' by Betty Hosegood (RotoVision Pub., 1998); The Artist magazine (1998, 2005) etc. *Address*: 20 Fairycroft Road, Saffron Walden, Essex, CB10 1LZ. *Email*: elliskaty@hotmail.com *Signs work*: 'Katy Ellis RI, RBA'.

ELLIS, William John, FRSA; artist in oil, water-colour, crayon; author/artist. *b*: Rhyl, 21 Sep 1944. *s of*: John Ellis. *m*: Gaynor Ellis. one *s* .one *d*. *Educ*: Glyndwr Secondary Modern, Rhyl. *Studied*: Glyndwr Secondary and later under Robert Evans Hughes RA. *Exhib*: Rhyl Town Hall and Holywell Library. *Publications*: author of Seaside Entertainments 100 Years of Nostalgia; Rhyl in old Picture Postcards; Entertainment in Rhyl and N. Wales (published July 1997); 'The Spirit of Rhyl' (pub. Landmark Publishers, 2004). *Recreations*: jazz, collecting theatre memorabilia. *Clubs*: Clwydian Art Society, Clwyd Assoc. for the Visual Arts, Mem. of Rhyl Liberty Players, Abergele Players, British Music Hall Soc., Manchester Music Hall Soc., Derbys. and Notts. Music Hall Soc. *Misc*: Has own music hall company 'The Spotlights'. *Address*: 2a Carlisle Ave., Rhyl, Denbighshire, LL18 3UD. *Email*: rhylbillellis@yahoo.co.uk *Signs work*: "B. Ellis."

ELLMAN, Daphne Ann, SWA, SFP (Society of Floral Painters); Winner, Isle of Wight Landscape Award (1999, 2005). *Medium*: acrylic and mixed media. *b*: Herne Bay, Kent, 20 Jul 1952. *d of*: Margaret & Ivor Lear. *m*: Mel Ellman. one *d*. *Educ*: Southport High School; Eastbourne High School. *Studied*: self-taught. *Exhib*: Mall Galleries; Westminster Hall; Clairmonte Gallery; First Floor Gallery, Romsey; Exbury; Sir Harold Hilliers Arboretum; Ventnor Botanic Garden; Burley, New Forest; Wight Light Gallery. *Works in collections*: The Wakeham Collection, and private collections internationally. *Publications*: Leisure Painter publications; 'Start with Art'; included in 'How to Create Textures in your Paintings' and '50 Years of the Undercliff'. *Works Reproduced*: through Libra Jones Associates Ltd. *Clubs*: Romsey Art Group; Marwell Art Society.

Address: 3 Wollescote House, 37 Spring Hill, Ventnor, Isle of Wight, PO38 1PF. *Email*: daphne@daphneellman.co.uk *Website*: www.daphneellman.co.uk *Signs work*: 'D.E.'

ELLWOOD, Derek, Laing Award, London; Barnes, Willis & Howard Award. *Medium*: ceramics, oil, watercolour, drawing, prints, sculpture. *b*: Rochdale, 7 Feb 1931. *s of*: H & A Ellwood. *m*: Joan Ellwood. one *s*. *Studied*: Rochdale School of Art, Lancs.; Bath Academy of Art, Corsham, Wilts; tutors: Sir Terry Frost, William Scott, Peter Lanyon, Bryan Wynters, James Tower (ceramics). *Exhib*: RA Summer exhbns, Daily Express Young Artists; AIA Gallery, London; Redfern Gallery, London; Inst. of Contemporary Artists; ROI; Laing Exhbns, Mall Gallery; 'Discerning Eye'; NEAC; Royal Society of British Artists; RP; Hunting Group; Garrick-Milne, Christie's, London; Crossgate Gallery, USA; Singer Friedlander/Sunday Times, London; Rowley Contemporary Art, Winchester. *Works in collections*: private & corporate. *Commissions*: portraits; Rev. William T. Atkins; Sir Robin & Lady Saxby & family; Sir George Solti; Jean Muir; Quentin Crisp; Barbara Cartland. *Works Reproduced*: limited edition prints; bronze sculpture; fabric designs. *Recreations*: music. *Clubs*: Arts Club, Dover St., London; Chelsea Arts Club, London. *Address*: 2 Warren Mews, London W1T 6AL. *Email*: derek.ellwood@gmail.com *Signs work*: 'ELLWOOD'.

ELMORE, Pat, RBA (1996); Showborough Sculpture Prize; sculptress in stone and wood, also portraits and ceramics. *Medium*: Wood, stone, ceramics. *b*: Rugby, 10 Sep 1937. *d of*: William Lomas. four *s*. two *d*. *Exhib*: solo shows, Bampton Arts Centre, Bedford Central Library, Swindon Links Library, Wantage Museum, The Stable Gallery at Green College Oxford; group shows: RBA, Mall Galleries, RWA, Cheltenham Art Soc., Syon Lodge London, Salammbo Galerie Paris, Gloucester Museum, Jersey (Village Gallery); Galerie D/Art Roquebrune, Monaco; Black Swann Gallery, Woodstock. *Works in collections*: . Permanent sculpture garden and gallery, and ongoing sculpture tuition at Nutford Lodge. *Commissions*: Thamesdown Arts, Abingdon Town Council, The Church Army Exeter, Magdalen College Oxford. *Official Purchasers*: Royal Berkshire Hospital. *Address*: Nutford Lodge, Longcot, nr. Faringdon, Oxon. SN7 7TL. *Email*: pat@patelmore.co.uk *Website*: www.patelmore.co.uk *Signs work*: "P.A. Elmore".

ELPIDA, (née Georgiou), B.A.Hons. (1986), M.A. (1990); artist in oil on canvas. *b*: London, 23 Sep 1958. *d of*: Lucas Georgiou (decd). *m*: Herbert Capelle. two *d*, Alesya and Luca. *Educ*: St Marylebone School for Girls. *Studied*: St Martin's School of Art (1983-86), RA Schools (1987-90). *Exhib*: ROI at Lloyd's, Royal Overseas League (prizewinner), 'New Generation' Bonham's, RA Summer Show (1991) (prizewinner, Guinness award), RA Premium Show (Winsor and Newton award), Berlin Academy of Art; one-man shows: Christopher Hull Gallery, Lynne Sterne Gallery, 'The Leicestershire Collection', Leicester, 'East End Open Studios', Acme Studios, London, Whitechapel Open. *Works in collections*: Unilever plc, Guinness Collection. *Address*: 26 Ellesmere Rd., Chiswick, London W4 4QH. *Website*: www.realartfirst.com *Signs work*: "Elpida."

ELRINGTON, Ptolemy Pieter Charles, BA Art and Design. *Medium*: Sculpture. *b*: London, 4 Sep 1965. *m*: Eva Garay. one *s*. *Studied*: Lincoln College of Art (1985-86), Bradford and Ilkley Community College (1987-1990). *Exhib*: London, Athens, Barcelona. *Work in collections*: Prudential. *Commissions*: RSPB, MAFF, Essex County Council, Brighton County Council, Environment Agency, Ronseal, Kenwood, Ecover. *Publications*: Furniture for the Future - Tristan Titeaux; Shark A Visual History - Richard Ellis. *Address*: The Forge, Coombe Farm, Westfield Avenue North, Saltdean, East Sussex BN2 8HP. *Email*: ptolemy@hubcapcreatures.com *Website*: www.hubcapcreatures.com *Signs work*: "P Elrington".

ELSTEIN, Cecile, MA, FRSA (1997); NW Arts Bursary Award 1993; Colour Prize - 9th British International Print Biennale (1986). *Medium*: drawing, print, sculpture and video.

b: Cape Town, S.Africa, 8 Feb 1938. *d of*: Michael and Ruth Hoberman. *m*: Max Elstein. one *s* (decd). one *d*. *Educ*: Private pupil of Catherine Yarrow artist/potter 1965-9. *Studied*: Sculpture & Printmaking, West Surrey College of Art and Design (1975-1977); MA Art as Environment, Manchester Metropolitan University (1996). *Represented by*: Wendy J Levy Contemporary Art Ltd *Exhib*: nationally, internationally. *Works in collections*: in UK and abroad. *Commissions*: Portrait sculpture, landscape sculpture, prints, drawings. *Publications*: DVD and companion booklet. 'Tangents, a mindscape in a landscape' 2003-4. *Official Purchasers*: Whitworth Art Gallery, Manchester; Clare Hall Cambridge. Alsager/Massachusetts Fine Art Collection. *Works Reproduced*: in 'A colourful canvas twelve women artists in the North West' by Judy Rose & Wendy J. Levy (2006); Exhibiting Gender by Sarah Hyde (1997). *Principal Works*: View website. *Clubs*: RSA, LAN, PMSA, MAFA, Didsbury Drawing. *Address*: 25 Spath Rd., Didsbury, Manchester M20 2QT *Email*: cecile@cecileelstein.com *Website*: www.cecileelstein.com *Signs work*: 'Cecile Elstein'.

ELWELL, Brian, MA Fine Art; Post-Grad Diploma Printmaking; Chelsea Dip. Fine Art; National Dip. in Design. *Medium*: oil. *b*: Jersey, 28 Nov 1938. *s of*: Frank Elwell. *Partner*: Emma Greeley. three *s*. two *d*. *Studied*: Chelsea School of Art; Birmingham Polytechnic; Wimbledon School of Art. *Represented by*: Phoenix Gallery, Bath. *Exhib*: selected solo exhbns: Bath Artists Studios (2008); Fusion Gallery, Bristol (2005); Rooksmoor Gallery, Bath (2003); Jelly Gallery, Reading (2001); Victoria Art Gallery, Bath (2000), Black Swan Guild, Frome (1996), etc.; selected group shows: Phoenix Gallery, Bath (2005), Fusion Gallery (2005); Grand Designs Live, London (2005); Hot Bath Gallery, Bath (2004); Leith Gallery, Edinburgh (2004); Red Rag Gallery, Stow (2004), Holborne Portrait Prize Exhibition (2008), etc.; Art Fairs across UK, including Affordable Art Fair (2000, 01, 03, 04). *Works in collections*: Marquis of Bath, David Messum, Southern Arts Assoc., Southampton University, Salisbury Dist. Hospital; Charles Pettiward; Linda Saunders; Brian Roper; David Messum. *Commissions*: portraits: Stephanie Cole, John Sergeant, Val Hepplewhite. *Publications*: 'Meetings with Remarkable People' - A Book of Portraits. *Principal Works*: portraits: Desmond Tutu, John Simpson, Sir Patrick Moore, Sir Derek Jacobi, etc. *Address*: 1 Tennyson Road, Bath, BA1 3BG. *Email*: info@phoenixgallery.co.uk *Website*: www.phoenixgallery.co.uk www.brianelwell.co.uk *Signs work*: 'Elwell'.

ELWES, Luke, BA, MA. *Medium*: oil, watercolour. *b*: London, 26 Jul 1961. *Studied*: Camberwell School of Art; Bristol University; Birkbeck. *Represented by*: Adam Gallery, Cork Street, London W1. *Exhib*: Solo show: Adam Gallery London (2011, 2012, 2014); Art First, London and New York (1998, 2000, 2002, 2004, 2007); Broadbent, London (2004, 2005); Young Gallery, Salisbury (2013); North House Gallery, Essex (2012); Galerie Marceau-Bastille, Paris (2009); Galerie Vieille du Temple, Paris (1993, 2000); Rebecca Hossack, London (1990, 1991, 1993, 1995); Group shows include: RA (1995, 1998, 2003, 2005, 2007, 2009, 2011); Estorick Collection, London (2010); Browse & Darby, London (2010); Galerie Ceribelli, Bergamo (2007, 2008); and many more. *Works in collections*: public and private in Europe and USA. *Commissions*: National Trust, Imperial College, Christie's, Bayer, Royal Military Academy, Worth Abbey. *Publications*: all publications listed on website. *Works Reproduced*: listed on website. *Address*: 23 Lawford Road, London NW5 2LH. *Email*: luke.elwes@blueyonder.co.uk *Website*: www.lukeelwes.com *Signs work*: 'Luke Elwes'.

EMANUEL, John. *Medium*: ink and gouache; oils; mixed media; prints. *b*: Bury, Lancs., 13 Feb 1930. *s of*: John and Beatrice. *Partner*: Janet Axten. one *d*. *Represented by*: Belgrave Gallery, St. Ives; Manya Igel Fine Art, London; Thompson Gallery, London; Stour Gallery, Shipston-on-Stour. *Exhib*: Gilbert Parr Gallery, London (1979); Montpelier Studio, London (1979-98); Beaux Arts, Bath (1988, 1992); Artist Market Warehouse, London(1978); Hayward Annual, London (1982); Cleveland International Drawing Biennale (1979); TSW Open Touring Exhbn. (1984-5); Royal West of England Academy, Bristol (1992, 1995);

Mall Galleries, London (2002); The Stour Gallery, Shipton on Stour (2003, 2005, 2007); Penwith Gallery St.Ives (2005). *Works in collections*: Cornwall County Council, Truro; Slaughter and May, London; Tesco plc.; Crown Courts, Truro; Evans & Shalev, Architects, London. *Commissions*: Tate St. Ives to make an etching for the opening of the gallery in 1993 as one of the Porthmeor Printmakers. *Publications*: Dictionary of Artists in Britain since 1945 (David Bucknan, 1998). *Works Reproduced*: 'Catching the Wave - Contemporary Art and Artists in Cornwall from 1975 to the Present Day' (Tom Cross, 2002). *Recreations*: walking. *Clubs*: Chelsea Arts Club, London; Penwith Society of Arts. *Misc*: moved to Cornwall 1964, lived in St.Ives since 1983. *Address*: 3 Fore St., St. Ives Cornwall TR26 1AB. *Email*: jhnemanuel@yahoo.co.uk *Website*: www.johnemanuel.co.uk *Signs work*: John Emanuel.

EMERY, Edwina, ARBS (1984); Freeman of Worshipful Company of Goldsmiths (1986); sculptor and designer in chalk, oil and acrylic; retained exclusively by Garrard, the Crown Jewellers, animalier, portrait and design since 1982. *b*: Huntingdonshire, 10 May 1942. divorced. two *s*. two *d*. *Educ*: Grammar School and privately. *Exhib*: permanently at Garrard, Regent St., Oscar and Peter Johnson Gallery. Work collected by Royalty and Heads of State worldwide, also private collectors. *Commissions*: include prestigious confidential commissions, also racing, polo, portraits Lester Piggott and Willie Shoemaker, many for industry and commerce. *Publications*: Commercial Art in Youth. *Clubs*: The Farmers, Whitehall Court. *Address*: Little Manor, Ibberton, Dorset DT11 0EN.

EMMERICH, Anita Jane, (née POLLOK), International member and exhibitor: RMS, SWA, HSF; miniature painter specializing in contemporary and historical portrait, profiles and silhouettes in oil on vellum or old ivory; RMS Group Award Winner (2004); the President's Special Commendation Award for all miniature paintings submitted, RMS Exhibition, London (1998), the Master's Award for the Most Outstanding Set of Miniatures at The Llewellyn Alexander Gallery, London (1996, 2006), Judges Choice, GMAS, Atlanta, USA (1997). Individual Member's Award Certificate, WFM, Tasmania (2000), plus numerous awards UK and USA; donates and judges the 'Anita Emmerich Presentation Award'. *b*: London, 3 Feb 1938. *m*: W. M. Ernst. two *s*. *Educ*: Sydenham High School for Girls (GPDST), London. *Studied*: self taught miniature painter *Exhib*: London, the South East, and various overseas galleries; England, Jersey, N. Ireland, France, Germany, USA, Australia, Japan. *Works in collections*: Work in private collections, RMS Diploma Collection, can be seen at the Llewellyn Alexander Gallery, London. *Commissions*: for collectors and private requests. *Publications*: 'RMS 100 Years'. *Works Reproduced*: in Art Magazines. *Recreations*: Woodland garden preservation, Wild Life, Family. *Misc*: 1993 Contemporary Art Consultant, Diocese of Rochester Kent. Previously mem. of S.M., S.Lm., A.S.M.A. (Q). (T). (N.S.W.)., G.M.A.S., MASF, WFM, MPSGS, ASOFA; Keeper of the RMS Diploma Collection 2001-2010. *Address*: 'Fielder's Folly' Cherry Garden Lane Wye, Ashford, Kent TN25 5AR. *Email*: e.emmerich@sky.com *Signs work*: 'AJE' (as monogram).

ENGLAND, Frederick John, NDD, ATC (Lond), IAG, MFPS, Norwegian Scholarship (1960), Medaille d'Argent, Paris Salon (Gold Medal, 1975), Diploma d'Honneur, International Arts Guild, Monte Carlo; painter in oil, lithograph, etching, water-colour; ex-lecturer in painting and design at Leek School of Art; ex Pres. Soc. of Staffordshire Artists; director, England's Gallery, Leek. *b*: Fulham, London, 5 Mar 1939. *s of*: Frederick Thomas England. *m*: Sheelagh Jane. *Educ*: Deacons School. *Studied*: Brighton College of Art and Crafts (1956) under Sallis Bonney, ROI, RWS, Charles Knight, ROI, RWS, R T. Cowen, Principal; Hardanger Folkschule, Norway (1960) under Oddmund J. Aarhus; London University (1961) under Ronald Horton. *Exhib*: Paris Salon, Arts Council of N. Ireland, RBA, RI Summer and Winter Salon, RBSA, Manchester Academy, Bradford Open Exhibition, Trends Free Painters and Sculptors, RWA, SIA (travelling shows included). Open Exhibition Stafford, Society of Staffordshire Artists; one-man shows:

Galerie Helian, Montreux, England's Gallery, Burlington Gallery, Buxton Schaffer Gallery, Market Drayton, Galerie für Zeitgenössische Kunst, Hamburg, Galerie Bernheim-Jeune, Paris, I.A.G. Monte Carlo, Zilina, Czechoslovakia, Octagon Gallery, Bolton, University of Keele, Gallerie Helion, Montreux, Holstebro, Denmark. *Works in collections*: Nicholson Institute, Goritz Coll., Fenning Coll., Geneva, City of Stoke-on-Trent Art Gallery. *Commissions*: R. Breeze murals, 'Homage to Monet', 'Homage to Hirsage' (30m x 8m). *Official Purchasers*: City of Stoke on Trent Museum and Art Gallery. *Works Reproduced*: Art of England. *Clubs*: Past President Society of Staffordshire Artists (Hon Life Member). *Misc*: Reviewed work in La Revue Moderne, Les Journal des Jeunes, Boomerang (Paris Salon Edition of One Hundred Young European painters), Dictionnaire des Artists, Repertorium Artis, Dictionnaire International d'Art Contemporain. *Address*: Ball Haye House, 1 Ball Haye Terr., Leek, Staffs ST13 6AP. *Email*: englands.gallery@anstrad.co.uk *Signs work*: "England."

ENGLISH, Bill, NDD (First Class), Cert RAS, ATC; Head of Fine Art Derby 1964-67, Head of Fine Art Nottingham 1967-72, Principal Norwich School of Art 1972-88. *Medium*: paint, collage. *b*: Houghton-Le-Spring, 12 Dec 1931. *m*: Helen (deceased). two *s.* two *d. Educ*: Reed's School, Cobham, Surrey 1942-48. *Studied*: art Sunderland 1948-52, RAS 1952-56, Leeds 1956-57. *Exhib*: one-man shows in York (1964), Norwich (1979), Chelsea (1989), Ipswich (1990), Peralada (1992), Espolla (1998). Mixed shows: Norwich (1975-2014). *Works in collections*: private, UK and abroad. *Clubs*: Chelsea Arts Club (Chairman 1989), RASAA. *Address*: 185 Newmarket Rd, Norwich, NR4 6AP.

ENRIGHT, Mo, BA (Hons), MA; NS. *Medium*: oil, prints. *b*: North Yorkshire, 9 Jul 1953. *Studied*: Art Foundation Course, Warwickshire College, Leamington Spa; BA (Hons) Fine Art, Coventry University; MA History of Art & Design, Birmingham University of Central England. *Represented by*: Fumano Fine Art, London. *Exhib*: The Public, West Bromwich (2012); Rugby Art Gallery & Museum (2012), Affordable Art Fair, Battersea (2012); Flanders International Fusion Art Expo, Belgium (2011); Fiumano Fine Art, London (2010); Lewis Gallery, Rugby School, Warks (solo, 2009); Art Show, Amsterdam (2009); St Mary's Church, Warks (solo, 2002); Galerie am Schloss, Brühl, Germany (1986); Leamington Spa Art Gallery & Museum (solo, 1983). *Works in collections*: Potterton-Baxi International, Warwick; Motor Panels, Coventry; Rubery Holding, West Midlands; Rutland Sixth Form College. *Commissions*: St Mary's Church, Leamington Spa; Potterton International Portobello Works, Warwick. *Publications*: Catalogue for Peter lanyon Exhibition (commissioned by Gimpel Fils Gallery London). *Official Purchasers*: Major Award & Purchase Prize Winner, by main sponsors of Midland View II - Arts Council Touring exhbn to 6 venues. *Works Reproduced*: 'Cathedral' Durham Cathedral - A Celebration 1093-1993 (Macdonald Press, 1993); 'The Easter Story' Art & Christianity Bulletin, Eye to Eye, Eye 21 (2013). *Principal Works*: 'Tread Softly With Me', 'The Easter Story Panels', 'Cathedral Interior'. *Recreations*: travelling to interesting places. *Clubs*: National Society, LSA, Axis. *Misc*: President of Flag (2013). *Address*: Art-E Studios UK, 96 Telford Avenue, Leamington Spa CV32 7HP. *Email*: info@mo-enright.me.uk *Website*: www.mo-enright.me.uk *Signs work*: "M. Enright".

ERLAND, Sukey, SPS; Lecturer 3D Studies; Royal Western Academy, John Brandler Award. *Medium*: sculpture (bronze, resin bronze, stoneware). *b*: Farnham, Surrey, Aug 1927. *d of*: Col. & Mrs. C.F.King DSO. MC *m*: John Erland. three *s. Educ*: St. Nicholas, Fleet; Chatelard, Switzerland. *Studied*: Farnham School of Art; Chelsea School of Art with Willi Soukop. *Represented by*: Artparks International Garden Gallery, Broughton; Mythic Garden, Devon; First Sight Fine Art, Bath, Albany Gallery, Cardiff, Bowlish Contemporary Gallery, Shepton Mallet. *Exhib*: Broadway Modern, Cotswolds, Guernsey, Royal Academy, Royal West of England Academy, Society of Portrait Sculptors, Artists 303, Atkinson Gallery, Millfield Art Centre, East Lambrook Manor, Albany Gallery. *Works in collections*: in USA,

Japan, Australia, Great Britain. *Commissions*: Brotherhood of Man, New York; Rover Motor Co. commissioned portrait of Ben Hervey Bathurst, many portrait commissions. *Publications*: featured in Somerset Magazine, Historic House Magazine. *Official Purchasers*: 'Pelicans' purchased by Bristol Zoo. *Principal Works*: figurative bronzes of people and animals. *Recreations*: gardening, riding. *Clubs*: Society of Portrait Sculptors, Artists 303. *Address*: The Malthouse, Totterdown Lane, Pilton, Shepton Mallet, Som. BA4 4EA. *Website*: www.sukeyerland.me.uk *Signs work*: 'SE'.

ERSKINE-JONES, Susan Helen, *Medium*: oil, prints. *b*: Cape Town, 9 Mar 1963. *m*: Gareth Erskine-Jones. two *s*. *Studied*: Micheallis, University of Cape Town (1986), Post Graduate Fine Art - Cape Technicon (1988). *Represented by*: House Gallery, Olney. *Exhib*: Karen Taylor Gallery, Twickenham; Stroud House Gallery, Stroud; The Red Gallery, Thame. *Principal Works*: Investigate and use eco-friendly materials in printmaking and painting. *Address*: 96 South Street, Leighton Buzzard LU7 3PA. *Email*: susan@erskine-jones.com *Website*: www.erskine-jones.com *Signs work*: "Erskine-Jones".

ESPLEY, Tom, NEAC; NDD, DFA London; 1st Prize 'Spirit of London' (1984). *Medium*: oil, watercolour, tempera, etc *b*: 24 Jul 1931. *s of*: Mr. & Mrs. T.H. Espley. *m*: Maureen. two *s*. *Educ*: The Downs School and Bryanston. *Studied*: Camberwell School of Art, Slade School, University College, London. *Represented by*: Gallery Duncan Terrace. *Exhib*: Mitsukoshi Tokyo, Hayward Annual 1982, Royal Academy (1965-96), NEAC since 1999. *Works in collections*: Guinness, Chase Manhattan Bank, Eagle Star, Jesus College Oxford, Ondaatje Collection, the late King Hussein of Jordan, Cheltenham And Gloucester Building Society. *Publications*: photographs for catalogue Bonnard Exhbn. Hayward Gallery (1994). *Official Purchasers*: British Rail, Full Sutton Prison. *Address*: 24 Duncan Terrace, London N1 8BS. *Signs work*: 'T E', 'T ESPLEY', 'TOM ESPLEY', 'ESPLEY'.

EUSTACE, Eric George, HS (1991), ARMS (1993); painter in water-colour and acrylic. *b*: Dunstable, 14 Jan 1925. *m*: Edna Roberts. *Studied*: art at Luton College (1953-55). *Address*: 28 Buttercup Close, Dunstable, Beds. LU6 3LA. *Signs work*: "Eric G. Eustace."

EVANS, Brenda Jean, BA Hons. (1976), RAS (1979), SWA (1986); artist in water-colour and oil painting. *b*: Birmingham, 6 Jun 1954. *d of*: Alfred John Evans. *Educ*: Aldridge Grammar School. *Studied*: Sutton Coldfield School of Art, Loughborough College of Art, RA Schools. *Exhib*: RA Summer Shows, Highgate Gallery, Tenterden, SWA, Grape Lane Gallery, York, Edinburgh, New Grafton Gallery, Business Art Galleries, Singer and Friedlander, Kentmere House Gallery, New English Art Club. *Works in collections*: HRH Princess Michael of Kent, Mr. and Mrs. Ronnie Corbett. *Works Reproduced*: Medici Cards, Canns Down Press, Ranelagh Press. *Recreations*: gardening. *Address*: Oystercatcher, 31 Beresford Road, Whitstable, Kent CT5 1JP. *Signs work*: "Brenda Evans."

EVANS, David Arthur, NDD, ATD; Emlyn Roberts' Memorial Awards (3); Edith Lodwick Award CSC; Ken Etheridge Award CSC. *Medium*: watercolour, acrylic. *b*: Burry Port, Wales, 9 Aug 1932. *s of*: Mervyn James Evans & Adeline Jane Evans. *m*: Audrey. one *s*. one *d*. *Studied*: Llanelli School of Art; Swansea College of Art. *Exhib*: RA (1992, 1994, 2001, selected 1993, 1983); RWA (1990, 92, 93, 94, 96, 97, 98, 2000, 03, 04); RSMA (1993-2004, except 2002); RI (1993, 98, 99, 2000, 01, 02, 03, 04, 05); Waterman Fine Art, London; Llewellyn Fine Art, London; Chelsea Art Society; series of one-man exhbns in Cardiff, Camarthen, Llandeilo, Swansea, Lesneven (Brittany). *Works in collections*: Brandler Galleries, London; Peter Hedley Gallery, Dorset; National Library of Wales. *Commissions*: Royal British Legion, Burry Port. *Publications*: work included in 'Art School' Acrylics/Paint Landscapes (Winsor & Newton). *Official Purchasers*: National Library of Wales; Llanelli Town Council. *Works Reproduced*: RA; European Art '96; Paint Landscapes. *Principal Works*: marine paintings. *Recreations*: travelling abroad, and local history. *Clubs*: CAS. Misc: Served in the Royal Marines 1952-1954. *Address*: 24 The Crescent, Burry Port, Camarthenshire SA16 0PP. *Signs work*: 'David Evans'.

EVANS, David Pugh, ARCA (1965), RSW (1975), RSA (1989); artist in oil and acrylic. *b*: Abercarn, Gwent, 20 Nov 1942. *s of*: John David Charles Evans, lorry driver. *Educ*: Newbridge Grammar School, Gwent. *Studied*: Newport College of Art (1959-62, Thomas Rathmell), R.C.A. (1962-65, Prof. Carel Weight). *Exhib*: Fruit Market Gallery, Edinburgh, University of York, Mercury Gallery, London, Open Eye Gallery, Edinburgh. *Commissions*: Carlisle A.G., SAC, Hunterian Museum, Glasgow, Glasgow A.G., Royal Scottish Academy, RA, City A.G., Edinburgh, Aberdeen A.G., Scottish Television, Government Art Collection, Royal Bank of Scotland, Readers Digest, First National City Bank of Houston. *Address*: 17 Inverleith Gdns., Edinburgh EH3 5PS. *Signs work*: "D.P. Evans."

EVANS, Eurgain, NDD (1958), RA Schools Cert. (1961); painter in oil and water-colour; retd. lecturer, Faculty of Art and Design, W. Glamorgan Inst. of Higher Educ., Swansea. *b*: Betws y Coed, Gwynedd, 28 Mar 1936. *d of*: Tom Wern *Educ*: Llanrwst Grammar School. *Studied*: Wrexham College of Art; RA Schools *Exhib*: Pritchard Jones Hall, Bangor University Wales, London Welsh Assoc. Young Contemporaries, RA, FPS, etc. *Works in collections*: National Museum of Wales, Aberystwyth, and many private collections. *Address*: 24 Masefield Way Parc Beck, Sketty Swansea, S. Wales SA2 9FF. *Signs work*: "Eurgain."

EVANS, Margaret Fleming, DA, ATC, UA; portrait painter in oils and pastels, art tutor; teacher in adult education in Kent. *b*: Glasgow, 9 Apr 1952. *d of*: Thomas Carswell. *m*: Malcolm William Evans. one *s*. one *d*. *Educ*: Whitehill Senior Secondary School, Glasgow. *Studied*: Glasgow School of Art (1970-74, Dr. David Donaldson, RP, A.Goudie, RP, L. Morocco, J. Robertson, ARSA). *Exhib*: London and S.E. England. *Address*: Larasset, High Halden, Ashford, Kent. TN26 3TY

EVANS, Marlene Elizabeth, SWA (1990), ABWS (1987), AYA (1989); artist of botanical studies and landscapes in water-colour, ink, mixed media. *b*: Barking, Essex, 17 Feb 1937. *d of*: J.B. Stringer, taxi business proprietor (decd). *m*: Lyn Evans (decd). one *s*. one *d*. *Educ*: Racecommon Rd. School, Barnsley. *Studied*: Barnsley School of Art (textile design, L.H.H. Glover, ARCA, ATD, R. Skinner, ATD). *Exhib*: one-man shows: Cawthorne S.Y. (1990), Ossett, W. Yorks. (1991), annually SWA and BWS, also various mixed exhbns. *Works in collections*: private. *Recreations*: countryside, walking, etc. *Address*: 14 Spencer St., Barnsley, S. Yorks. S70 1QX. *Email*: marlene.evans99@gmail.com *Signs work*: "M.E. Evans."

EVANS, Peter John, 2nd prize open comp at Museum Modern Art, Machynlleth. *Medium*: Oil. *b*: Neath, 27 Oct 1950. *m*. Carole Patricia. two *s*. two *s-d*. *Educ*: Basic secondary school education. *Studied at*: Mainly self taught; part-time student at Swansea University; extra mural and WEA under Mike Freeman. *Represented by*: Brian Sinfield. *Exhib*: Brian Sinfield Gallery, Burford; Kooywood Gallery, Cardiff; Albany Gallery, Cardiff; Nick Holly Gallery, Swansea; The Museum of Modern Art, Machynlleth; Queens Hall, Narberth; The Glyn Vivian Gallery, Swansea; Ceri Richards Gallery, Swansea University; The Art Shop, Abergavenny. *Works in collections*: Various private collections both in Wales and abroad. *Commissions*: Portrait of retiring president of the WEA. *Recreations*: Fishing; walking. *Clubs*: Member of "Friday Group" South Wales artists. *Address*: 2 Allister Street, Neath, W. Glam SA11 1EN. *Email*: peterevans1950@hotmail.co.uk *Signs work*: "P.J. Evans".

EVANS, Tony, BA (Hons) Fine Art; Wirral Met Coll. Fellowship Award. *Medium*: unique sculptures and architectural panels, drawing. *b*: Liverpool, 19 Nov 1944. *s of*: John Evans (saddler), Alice Evans (kitchen maid). *m*: Brenda. one *s*. one *d*. *Educ*: De La Salle Grammar School (1955). *Studied*: Liverpool Community College (1997); Wirral Met College (1999).

Represented by: 'Turner Fine Arts' Art Agency. *Exhib*: Williamson Art Gallery, Birkenhead (2000); Brindley Gallery, Runcorn (2004); Cork Street Gallery, London (2004); Mall Galleries, London (2003); Pacific Road Art Centre (1999); Angela McAlpine Gallery, Chester Racecourse (2005); Atkinson Art Gallery & Museum, Southport (2001); Sheridan Russell Gallery, London (2005); UK Fine Arts, Birmingham (2009); Watergate Gallery, Cheshire (2009); Turner Fine Art Show, travelling nationwide annually. *Works in collections*: Lever-Fabergé Collection, Port Sunlight, Wirral; life-size animal sculptures for UK Fine Arts Gallery. Private clients nationwide and Far East. *Official Purchasers*: Atkinson Art Gallery, Southport; Delamere Forestry Commission, Cheshire. *Address*: Unit 6, 27 Warstone Road, Hockley, Birmingham B18 6JQ. *Email*: info@turnerfinearts.com *Website*: www.turnerfinearts.com www.ukfinearts.com *Signs work*: 'Tony Evans'.

EVELEIGH, Aldous, *Medium*: oil, watercolour, drawing, prints, film & video. *m*: Stephanie Williams. *Educ*: Harvey Grammar School, Folkestone. *Studied*: Folkestone School of Art, foundation (1976, 1981); Bristol Polytechinc, BS (1970-73); Royal College of Art, MA (1981-84). *Exhib*: Some solo shows: New Metropole Arts Centre, Folkstone (1976-1981); Abbot Hall Art Gallery, Kendall (1985); Coventry Gallery, Sydney, NSW 1987); Long Gallery, Woolongon, NSW (1988); Diorama Art Gallery, London (1985, 1987); Galerie Rauber, Gutersloh, Germany (1992); Galerie Dialoog, Ostend, Belgium (1992 annually until 2001); Casa Fernando Pessoa, Lisbon (1996); Epal Museu, Lisbon (1998); Centre d'Art Actuel, Brussels (1998); Elspeth Kyle Gallery, London (2006); Artane Gallery, Istanbul (2007, 2008); Salon Schmitz, Cologne (2010), Fabrica Braco de Prata, Lisbon (2013), Casa Fernando Pessoa, Lisbon (2014). *Works in collections*: University of Woolongon; University of London; Casa Fernando Pessoa. *Misc*: Artist's films: New York New Work; Short Stretch of the Thames; Aldous in Istanbul; Warping on Water; Aldous in London. *Address*: 4 Monmouth Place, London W2 5SA. *Email*: aldouseveleigh@yahoo.com *Website*: www.aldouseveleigh.com *Signs work*: "ALDOUS"; "AE" monogram or "ALDOUS EVELEIGH".

EVELEIGH, John, DipFA (Lond) (1951), FRSA (1965), elected Fellow (W,gong) (1988), DCA (W,gong) (1991), Aust. WCI (1991), SWLA (1995), Professorial Fellow James Cook (1992-1994); practicing artist using mixed media; Hon. Founder Arts Director, New Metropole Arts Centre (1961), Hon. Founder Arts Director, The Long Gallery University of Wollongong, Australia (1984); Hon. Director of the University of Wollongong Art Collection); Hon. Director of the James Cook Art Collection. *b*: London, 15 Dec 1926. *s of*: William and Josephine Eveleigh. *m*: Margarete (Gretl). *Educ*: Clayesmore School, Dorset (1940-44). *Studied*: Canterbury College of Art (1944-45), The Slade - London University (1948-52), University of Wollongong (1986-90). *Exhib*: one-man shows include: Wildenstein, Piccadilly, South London, Nevill, Abbot Hall, Morley College, Posk, Drew & Marsh Galleries, Metropole Arts Centre (6), University of Wollongong and Perc Tucker – Australia. *Works in collections*: Camberwell, Herts. and Kent County Councils, Welsh Contemporary Arts Soc., Wollongong City Gallery, Wollongong University, James Cook University, Metropole Arts Centre. Private collections: Australia, Europa, China, South Africa, UK, USA. *Commissions*: public and private, portrait, landscape and wildlife. *Works Reproduced*: books, magazines. Published over 150 catalogues. *Misc*: Directed video art documentaries. *Address*: 4 Broadfield Rd., Folkstone, Kent CT20 2JT. *Signs work*: "John Eveleigh."

EVERETT, Julia, BA Hons Fine Art. *Medium*: Abstract landscape painter in oil. *b*: Wolverhampton, 30 Mar 1967. *Partner*: John O'Sullivan (musician). *Studied*: Brighton University (1986-89). *Represented by*: Julia Everett Gallery; Art Star; The Funky Art Gallery. *Exhib*: Affordable Art Fair, London & New York (2003-2013), Funky Art Gallery, Oxford (2012); Free Space Gallery (2012); Horsebridge Arts Centre, Whitstable (2009); Lacy Road Gallery, Putney (2007); Waterloo Gallery (2006), plus various group exhibitions from 1990-2013. *Works in collections*: St. Mary's Hospital, Paddington and many private and corporate collections. *Commissions*: many private commissions. *Recreations*: Facebook and Twitter. *Misc*: West London Thame based artist. *Address*: Acava Palace Wharf Studios, 56 Rainville Rd., Hammersmith, London W6 9HN. *Email*: juliaeverettgallery@tesco.net *Website*: juliaeverettgallery.co.uk *Signs work*: "J. EVERETT" (on the back of canvas).

EWING, John, RAS Cert (1951), ATD (1954), DAE (1970), BA (Hons) OU (1977); retired art teacher (was a full time arts and crafts teacher for forty years); paints mainly landscape home counties and a wide range of subject matter. *Medium*: oil and mixed media. *b*: Paris, 29 Jul 1929. *m*: Barbara. one *s*. *Educ*: Hove County Grammar. *Studied*: Croydon and Malvern Art Schools, Royal Academy Schools. *Exhib*: Mall Galleries, Piccadilly Gallery, etc *Works in collections*: various, mainly oils. *Clubs*: RASAA. *Address*: 44 Norfolk Ave Sanderstead, Surrey, CR2 8BP. *Email*: j.b.ewing@btinternet.com

F

FABER, Rodney George, self taught artist in water-colour and pen and ink drawing; mem. SGFA 1987-98. *b*: Liverpool, 8 Jun 1935. *s of*: Leslie Faber. *m*: Asne Wainer. *Educ*: Hasmonean Grammar School. *Exhib*: SGFA Annual exhbns. and mixed exhbns. in various galleries in London and the Home Counties. Commission and other works in numerous private collections both in UK and abroad. Rexel prizewinner SGFA (1992). *Address*: Studio: 37 Darwin Ct., Gloucester Ave., London NW1 7BG. *Signs work*: "FABER."

FAILES, Colin Michael, City & Guilds Dip. (Sculpture) (1972), Beckworth travel scholarship to Egypt (1972), Postgrad. (Sculpture) Cert. R.A. Schools, Silver medal (Sculpture) (1975), bronze medal (Sculpture) (1976). *Medium*: mural artist and sculptor. *b*: Farnborough, Kent, 2 Oct 1948. *s of*: Ceril Walter Failes. *Educ*: Arle School, Cheltenham. *Studied*: City & Guilds of London Art School (1969-72, James Butler, RA), RA Schools (1973-76, Willi Soukop, RA). *Exhib*: RA Summer Exhbns. (1976, 1980, 1987, 1988). *Works in collections*: London, Monaco, Luxembourg, Malta. *Commissions*: murals: "Oriana" P&O; Vintners' Hall, City of London; Bridge Housing Assoc., London, Worshipful Company of Distillers, London, Claridge's Hotel, London; A member of the Armada Project Painting Team, Palace of Westminster; Ceiling Painting Everyman Theatre, Cheltenham. *Works Reproduced*: in "Painting Murals" (MacDonald Orbis), and "Murals" (New Holland). *Clubs*: R.A. Schools Alumni Association. *Address*: 6 Elfindale Rd., London SE24 9NW. *Email*: colinfailes@btinternet.com *Website*: www.colinfailes.co.uk *Signs work*: "COLIN FAILES" or "C.M. Failes."

FAIRCLOTH, Shireen, Full School Drawing Certificate (1950); Intermediate Examination in Arts & Crafts (1953); City and Guilds Pattern Cutting & Dressmaking (1953). *Medium*: drawing, painting, sculpture. *b*: East Sheen, Surrey, 6 Jan 1936. *Educ*: St.Joseph's Convent, Sidcup, Kent. *Studied*: Sidcup School of Art (1951-53). Subsequently painting at Adult Education classes. *Exhib*: one-man show 1984 - Torrington, North Devon, paintings of 'Tarka' country to co-incide with opening of film. Twice in Royal Academy Summer Show also mixed shows at Chenil Galleries, Chelsea Art Society & Fulham Art Society; 3 person show at 'Old Sorting Office Arts Centre', Barnes (2005). *Commissions*: private commissions for child and pet drawings, paintings of horses and prize farm animals. *Works Reproduced*: cover of a cookbook (lemon painting) (2006). *Recreations*: learning the flute (and to read music); swimming. *Misc*: worked as commercial artist 1966-1980 specialising in birds, animals and illustrations for encyclopedias; 'Halcyon Days' enamel boxes - flowers and birds. *Address*: 42 Anselm Road, London SW6 1LJ. *Email*: shireenfaircloth@gmail.com *Signs work*: 'SF'.

FAIRCLOUGH, Michael, RE (1964), Rome Scholar in Engraving (1964-66), NEAC (1995); painter/printmaker; lecturer, Belfast College of Art (1962-64); West Surrey College of Art (1967-79). *b*: Blackburn, 16 Sep 1940. *s of*: Wilfred Fairclough. *m*: Mary Malenoir. two *d*. *Studied*: Kingston School of Art (1957-61); British School at Rome, (1964-67); Atelier 17, Paris (1967). *Exhib*: one-man shows Henley-on-Thames, Farnham, Toronto, Auckland, Berkeley Square Gallery, London (2000), Osborne Samuel, London (2004); Royal Academy Summer Exhibitions c.50 works. *Works in collections*: V&A, Ashmolean, Usher Gallery, Bowes Museum, Royal Albert Museum, New York Public Library. *Commissions*: mural, Farnham Post Office (1970), Post Office 'National Trust' issue of five stamps (1981), Meteorological Office, Exeter (2004). *Official Purchasers*: Government Art Collection, Post Office, Meteorological Office. *Works Reproduced*: 'Complete Guise to Prints and Printmaking'. *Recreations*: gliding. *Address*: Tilford Green Cottages, Tilford, Farnham, Surrey GU10 2BU. *Email*: info@michalfairclough.co.uk *Website*: www.michaelfairclough.co.uk *Signs work*: "Michael Fairclough." or MF.

FAIRFAX-LUCY, Edmund, painter of interiors, still-life and landscapes in oil. *b*: Oxford,1945. *Studied*: City & Guilds of London Art School, and R.A. Schools (1967-70) winning David Murray Travelling Scholarship (1966, 1967, 1969). *Exhib*: RA since 1967, New Grafton Gallery since 1971. *Works in collections*: Brinsley Ford. *Misc*: information on date painting commenced/ time of year, time of day and sometimes place inscribed on reverse of painting or frame. *Address*: Charlecote Park, Warwick CV35 9EW. *Signs work*: work unsigned.

FAIRGRIEVE, James Hanratty, DA (Edin), RSW, RSA; Gillies award, RSW (1987); retd. lecturer, painter in acrylic. *b*: Prestonpans, E. Lothian, 17 Jun 1944. *s of*: Andrew & Helen Fairgrieve. *m*: Margaret Fairgrieve. two *s*. one *d*. *Educ*: Preston Lodge Senior Secondary School. *Studied*: Edinburgh College of Art. *Exhib*: Hawarth A.G. (1974), Triad Arts Centre (1974), Scottish Gallery (1974, 1978), Scottish Arts Club (1973, 2013), New 57 Gallery (1969, 1971), Edinburgh University (1975), Mercury Gallery, London (1980, 1982, 1987), Macauley Gallery (1983), Mercury Gallery, Edin (1984), Stichill Gallery (1990), Maclean Fine Art, London (2002, 2005), Open Eye Gallery (2001, 2010, 2014), Fosse Gallery (1992), Pontevedra, Spain (1995), Roger Billcliffe (1997), Edinburgh City Art Centre (1998), Portland Gallery (1999), Albemarle Gallery (1999), Frank T Sabin Gallery (2000), Fosse Gallery (2000), Compass Gallery (2000), Noble Grossart Prize Exh (2001), New Grafton Gallery (2002, 2003), Origin Art Gallery (2002), Leith Gallery (2003), Thompsons Gallery, London (2004), Medici Gallery, London (2004), Randolph Gallery, Edin (2004), Gothenburg Prestopans (2005), Art, London (2010). *Works in collections*: Edinburgh Corp., Scottish Arts Council, National Bank of Chicago, Milngavie A.G., HRH The Duke of Edinburgh, Argyll Schools, RCP, Perth A.G., Lord Moray, Leeds Schools, Ian Rankin, J.K. Rowling. *Publications*: 'Eye in the Wind' - Edward Gage; 'Scottish Water-colour Painting' - Jack Firth; 'A Picture of Flemings' - B. Smith; 'Dictionary of Scottish Art and Architecture' - P. McEwan. *Recreations*: fly-fishing. *Address*: Burnbrae, Gordon, Berwickshire, Scotland TD3 6JU. *Email*: Meggrieve@hotmail.com *Signs work*: "J. Fairgrieve."

FAIRHURST, Miles Christopher, painter in oil; painter of East Anglian landscape in tradition of Edward Seago and Arnesby-Brown, and abstracts; former owner of Fairhurst Gallery, London. *b*: Norwich, 3 Dec 1955. *Educ*: Gresham's School, Holt, Norfolk. *Studied*: largely self taught; studied under father, Joseph Fairhurst and at University of Aix-en-Provence, France. *Exhib*: RSMA, Mall Galleries, Park Grosvenor Galleries, London, Barnes Gallery, London, and various London and provincial galleries. *Works in collections*: private collections in UK, USA, Australia, New Zealand, Europe. *Commissions*: oil painting for TV commercial for Volkswagen (1987). *Publications*: illustrations for Millers Picture Price Guide (1994 onwards), 'Of Skies and Landscapes' - article for 'The Artist' magazine (2010). DVD - 'Edward Seago Oil Landscape Techniques with Miles Fairhurst' - Town House Film (2009). *Works Reproduced*: dust jacket illustration for 'Gypsy Jib-A Romany Dictionary' by

James Haywood (2003). *Address*: Turkey Hall, Metfield, Suffolk, IP20 0JX. *Signs work*: "M. Fairhurst." and 'MCF' on abstracts.

FAKHOURY, Bushra, BA, MA, PhD (Lond.); sculptor in bronze, stone. *b*: Beirut, 1 Apr 1942. *d of*: Bachir Fakhoury, chemist. two *s*. *Educ*: St. Paul's, Wimbledon School of Art and Emanuel. *Studied*: Beirut University College, American University of Beirut, University of London. *Exhib*: Bloomsbury Galleries (1986), Mall Galleries (1986), Jablonski Gallery (1987), Ashdown Gallery (1988), Kufa Gallery (1989). *Publications*: Art Education in Lebanon. *Address*: 57 Madrid Rd., Barnes, London SW13 9PQ.

FALCIDIA, Paulette. *Medium*: acrylic, oil pastels, carving, installation, assemblage. *b*: Monyash, 27 Aug 1946. *m*: divorcee. one *s*. one *d*. *Educ*: Highfield School for Girls (1958-63). *Studied*: Chesterfield College of Art (1963-65); self-taught, studied under: Nasing Das, Disangen, Rajistan, India (1996); Hillsborough College (2005-2007) Access Art & Design. *Exhib*: RA (2000); Dept. Psychiatry, Sheffield University (1996); S10 Gallery, Sheffield (1998); Haitch's Bakewell (1998); Rowland Gallery Sheffield (1997); Ranmoor Church, Sheffield (1997); Blue Moon Cafe, Sheffield; Park View, Sheffield; Sheffield Wednesday Conference Room. *Commissions*: Regional Engineering and Computing Technology (Rotherham). *Publications*: Telegraph and Star, Sheffield; Focus Magazine; Westside Magazine. *Official Purchasers*: Regional Engineering and Computing Technology (Rotherham). *Principal Works*: large body of work conceived by dredging the subconscious. *Recreations*: self-analysis through art. *Misc*: wood carving, finding inspiration from its natural form; art therapy for Stocksbridge Rehab Centre. *Address*: Cliffe House, Flat 4, 10 Whitworth Road, Ranmoor, Sheffield S10 3HD. *Website*: www.falcidia-art.co.uk *Signs work*: (drawing of eye) and RIS.

FALCONBRIDGE, Professor Brian, PPRBS; DipAD (Fine Art) (1973), HDFA (Slade) (1975), elected FRBS (1997), President of the Royal British Society of Sculptors (2004-09); Professor of Visual Arts, Goldsmiths'; Dean: Sir John Cass Faculty of Art, Media & Design, London Metropolitan University (2005-2010); sculptor in bronze and wood. *b*: 1950. one *s*. one *d*. *Educ*: Fakenham Grammar School. *Studied*: Canterbury College of Art (1968-69), Goldsmiths' College School of Art (1970-73), Slade School of Fine Art (1973-75). *Exhib*: numerous mixed and solo exhbns. in UK, Europe and Far East. *Works in collections*: ACE, University of East Anglia and private collections in UK and abroad. *Clubs*: Chelsea Arts. *Address*: c/o Royal British Society of Sculptors, 108 Old Brompton Road, South Kensington, London SW7 3RA. *Signs work*: "Brian Falconbridge."

FALLA, Kathleen M., MBE; FFPS(1985); relief printmaker and sculptor in wood. *Medium*: mostly wood. *b*: Guernsey, C.I., 25 Jan 1924. *d of*: John Hocart Falla. *m*: Kenneth R. Masters (decd). one *s*. one *d*. *Educ*: Ladies College, Guernsey. *Studied*: Guildford School of Art and Morley College, London. *Exhib*: solo shows: Lauragais, France, University of Surrey, Godalming Museum; shared shows: Loggia Gallery, Farnham Maltings; group shows: Barbican, West of England Academy, Brighton Polytechnic Gallery, Bloomsbury Galleries, Yvonne Arnaud Art, Guildford, etc. *Works in collections*: Guildford University. *Misc*: Awarded MBE for work with 'Conquest Art', a society enriching the lives of people with disabilities. Awarded under married name of Kathleen Masters. *Address*: Old Barn Cottage, Church La., Witley, Surrey GU8 5PW. *Signs work*: "Kit Falla." or "KMF".

FALLSHAW, Daniel, painter in oil acrylic and light, also pastel, charcoal, pen & ink, and pencil, sculptor in various media; Former M.D. of Creative Media Communications design consultants. *b*: London, 17 Nov 1946. *s of*: George James Fallshaw. *m*: Elizabeth Mary. two *d*. *Educ*: Broxhill, Romford and privately. *Studied*: under Arnold Allerbach (1966-68) Portraiture and painting under Leonard Boden, FRSA; sculpture under Jack Gillespie and Edmund Holmes; graphic design at the London College of Printing under Leonard Cusdens and Don Smith. *Exhib*: Mall Galleries, NS, UA, numerous London and UK galleries nationwide. *Works in collections*: National Collection. *Publications*: "Art of Creation – inspired images". *Official Purchasers*: Dover Museum; HM Government. *Works Reproduced*: 'Web of Life' painting published by Benedictine Sisters of Erie, Pennsylvania USA; Bluebell Wood, limited edition to launch 'Prince of Peace' website. *Address*: Meadow Farm Cottage, Broad End, Elsworth, Cambridge CB23 4JD. *Email*: fallshaw11@yahoo.com *Website*: www.artofcreation.co.uk *Signs work*: "Fallshaw" – sculpture "DF."

FANSHAWE KATO, Jill, NDD, ATC. *Medium*: Ceramics. *b*: Nottingham. *m*: Setsno Kato. *Educ*: Torquay Girls Grammar School, Devon. *Studied*: Chelsea School of Art, London; Brighton Art Teachers Training Course. *Represented by*: Scottish Gallery, Edinburgh; Yew Tree Gallery, Cornwall; Beaux Arts, Bath; Keio Department Store Gallery, Tokyo. *Exhib*: refer to website. *Works in collections*: Aberystwyth Arts Centre, Wales; World Ceramics Expo, S. Korea; Taurus Crafts, Glos; Nature in Art, Gloucestershire. *Commissions*: Yokohama National Museum, Japan; Asada House, Japan; 1BJ Bank, London. *Publications*: 'Source of Inspiration' Carolyn Genders; 'Ceramic Surfaces' Jo Connell; 'Colour in Glazes' Linda Bloomfield. *Official Purchasers*: see work in collections. *Works Reproduced*: Ceramic Review 3-09 'The Kimono of Food'; 'Jill Fanshawe Kato' Craft and Design Magazine 8/2011; 'Jill Fanshawe Kato' Craft Arts International 80 (2010). *Principal Works*: Yokohama National Museum, Japan; Asada House, Japan; 1BJ Bank, London. *Recreations*: Birdwatching; walking; gardening; travel; painting. Misc: 43 exhibitions in Japan includes 11 solo shows Keio Department Store Gallery, Tokyo. *Address*: 58 Beechfield Road, London N4 1PE. *Email*: jillfanshawekato@talktalk.net *Website*: www.jillfanshawekato.com *Signs work*: "Jill Fanshawe Kato" or name stamp.

FARLEY, James Osmer, ARBS (1990), ANSS (1985); portrait and architectural sculptor in clay, wax, direct metal, steels, bronze, copper. *b*: Cleveland, Ohio, 10 Apr 1935. *s of*: Wayne B. Farley, mechanical process engineer. *m*: Gillian Lewin. one *d*. *Studied*: Pennsylvania Academy of Fine Art (1952-56, Walker Hancock, Harry Rosin, Andrew Wyeth), Chicago Art Inst. (1957-59, Edvard Chaisang). *Exhib*: Art and the Corporate Image (1981). *Works in collections*: Arizona: Bell Center, Sun City; City Hall, Glendale; Centennial Hall, Mesa; St. Luke's Hospital, Phoenix; Hanna Boys Center, Sonoma, Calif. *Clubs*: F. & A. Masonic Lodge. *Misc*: other address: 4718 E. Portland, Phoenix, AZ. 85008, U.S.A. *Address*: 150 Scott Ellis Gdns., St. John's Wood, London NW8 9HG. *Signs work*: "James Farley."

FARMAR, Francis Edmund, Diploma in Art and Design. *Medium*: painting in watercolour, oil and acrylic. *b*: Cheam, Surrey, 8 May 1948. *s of*: Hugh Farmar. *m*: Jane Lamb. 1 *s-d*. *Educ*: Eton College. *Studied*: Simi Academy Florence, St.Martin's College of Art London, West of England College of Art Bristol. *Represented by*: Flying Colours Gallery, London. *Exhib*: several solo and mixed exhibitions since 1990, including Chelsea Arts Club (1992), Coleherne Road, London (1996), Duncan Campbell (1997-2006), Angel Lane Gallery, Shaftesbury (2000, 01), John Noot Galleries, Broadway, Worcs (2001), RCA (2002), Wren Gallery, Burford (2004-5); The Gallery, Tresco (2005); Hankyu, Osaka, Japan (2005); Flying Colours Gallery, Edinburgh (2006); Flying Colours Gallery, London (2008-10); Fosse Gallery, Stow-on-the Wold (2011). *Works in collections*: Duke of Devonshire; Marquis of Bath, Longleat; Drapers Company London; numerous private collections in UK, USA and Europe. *Commissions*: Unicef Christmas card (1998), and numerous private. *Publications*: Carlos Nadal. *Works Reproduced*: various national magazines. *Recreations*: cooking, gardening. *Clubs*: Chelsea Arts Club. *Address*: The Old Rectory, Sedgehill, Shaftesbury, Dorset, SP7 9JH. *Email*: francis.farmar@btconnect.com *Website*: www.francisfarmar.com *Signs work*: Francis Farmar.

FARQUHARSON, Alex, MA (Dist) Arts Critic, BA English/Art Comb. Hons.; curator; Exhbn. Officer, Spacex Gallery, Exeter. *b*: Chalfont St. Giles, 26 Sep 1969. *Educ*: Exeter

University, City University, London. *Studied*: Exeter College of Art and Design (now Plymouth University) (1988-91). *Publications*: numerous catalogue texts. *Address*: c/o Spacex Gallery, 45 Preston St., Exeter EX1 1DF.

FARQUHARSON, Andrew Charles, artist in water-colour. *b*: Johannesburg, S. Africa, 14 Dec 1959. *s of*: Margaret Irene Chadwick Arridge, NS, FSBA, ARMS. *Educ*: St. John's College, Johannesburg. *Studied*: under his mother. *Exhib*: group show Johannesburg. *Misc*: Lectured: University of Wales, Anglo Spanish Soc., Inst. of Spain. *Address*: 80b Naylor Rd., Peckham, London SE15. *Signs work*: "A.C. Farquharson."

FARQUHARSON, Linda, BA Hons Design, PDGip; Awards: Sekalski Prize for Printmaking. *Medium*: prints, linocuts, wood engraving. *b*: Aberdeen, 22 Apr 1963. *Studied*: Duncan of Jordanstone College of Art (1981-85, 1985-86). *Exhib*; SWE, RGI, Visual Arts Scotland. Private galleries include: Castle Gallery, Inverness; Mansfield Park Gallery, Glasgow; Open Eye Gallery, Edinburgh; Scottish Gallery, Edinburgh. *Works in collections*: RA Library; Manchester Metropolitan University; Trinity College Library, Hartford USA; Lillie Gallery. *Publications*: "Irish Folk and Fairy tales" (Folio Society, 2007); "Lady of the lake" (The ASS for Scottish Literary Studies, 2007). *Address*: Borelick Farmhouse, Dunkeld, Perthshire PH8 0BX. *Email*: linda@linocut.co.uk *Website*: www.linocut.co.uk *Signs work*: "Linda.M.Farquharson" or"LM Rarquharson" or "LMF".

FARR, Colleen, Des RCA, *Medium*: oil, watercolour, egg tempera. *b*: London, 24 Nov 1931. *d of*: D.H. Farr. *m*: William Belcher. *Studied*: Harrow School of Art, RCA. *Exhib*: RA Summer Exhbn, RWS Bankside Gallery, Mall Galleries: Society of Landscape Painters, Sunday Times Watercolour Competition. *Recreations*: gardening. *Address*: 304 Kew Road, Kew, Richmond Surrey TW9 3DU. *Email*: colleen.farr@btinternet.com *Signs work*: 'Colleen Farr'.

FARR, Dennis Larry Ashwell, CBE, MA, HonDLitt., FRSA, FMA; Director, Courtauld Institute Galleries (1980-93); Director, Birmingham Museums and Art Gallery (1969-80); Senior Lecturer in Fine Art, University of Glasgow (1967-69); Curator, Paul Mellon Collection, Washington, D.C. (1964-66); Asst. Keeper, Tate Gallery, London (1954-64). *b*: 3 Apr 1929. *m*: Diana Pullein-Thompson, writer. one *s.* one *d. Educ*: Luton Grammar School. *Studied*: Courtauld Inst. of Art, University of London (1947-50). *Publications*: William Etty (1958), Catalogue of the Modern British School in the Tate Gallery (with M. Chamot and M. Butlin, 1964-65), English Art 1870-1940 (1978), Lynn Chadwick, Sculptor (with Eva Chadwick, 1990), etc. *Address*: Flintlock Cottage, Weydown Rd., Haslemere, Surrey GU27 1DS.

FARRELL, Alan Richard, painter in water-colour and oil, miniaturist and member of RMS, MAA, HS, MPSGS and MASF; chartered engineer and member of Institution of Electrical Engineers; Has received several awards in U.K. and overseas including Best of Show in MPSGS Washington DC, 1st in International category in Washington, Gold for best painting in any traditional medium in Ottawa and 1st in Watercolour (MASF, Florida). *b*: London, 17 May 1932. married. two *d. Studied*: S.E. Essex Technical College and School of Art (1953-56). *Exhib*: RA, RMS, RI, RSMA, RBA, UA, International Boat Show, Britain in Water-colours, and several international exhibitions overseas including World Exhibition in the Dillon Ripley Centre (Smithsonian Museum) Washington DC, and Gallery of Russian Academy Art, Moscow. *Address*: The White House, Whitesmith, nr. Lewes, E. Sussex BN8. *Signs work*: "ALAN FARRELL" printed bottom right or left-hand corner; paintings dated on reverse.

FARRELL, Anthony, NDD (1965), RA Dip. (1968); artist in oil, etching. *b*: Epsom, 28 Mar 1945. *s of*: William Farrell. *m*: Sarah. one *s.* three *d. Educ*: Belfairs High School. *Studied*: Camberwell School of Art (1963-65), RA Schools (1965-68). *Exhib*: RA Common

Room, Minories, Colchester, RA Summer Exhbns., Serpentine Gallery, Christchurch Mansions, Ipswich, Gainsborough House, Sudbury, Arts Space, London. *Works in collections*: ACGB, The Minories, Colchester, Epping Forest Museum, Manchester City A.G., Beecroft A.G., Westcliff-on-Sea, Borough of St. Edmundsbury and Suffolk CC, Essex Health Authority, Ipswich Borough Council. *Clubs*: Royal Academy Alumni Association (Reynolds Club). *Address*: 6 Avenue Rd., Leigh-on-Sea, Essex SS9 1AX. *Email*: anthonyfarrell45@yahoo.com *Website*: www.anthonyfarrell.co.uk *Signs work*: "Anthony Farrell."

FARRELL, Don, RI (1984), RBA (1985), SFCA; RI medal (1984); Daler Rowney award RBA Exhbn. (1992); painter in water-colour and mixed media. *b*: Vancouver, BC, 3 Oct 1942. *m*: Margaret. two *s*. *Represented by*: Adam Gallery, 24 Cork Street, London. *Exhib*: RA Summer Exhbn (2004, 2005), RI (1984-01), RBA (1983-01), Vancouver International Arts Fair (1998), 20/21 British Arts fair (2000, 2002), The Gallery in Cork St. (2000), London Contemporary Art Fair (2001, 2002, 2003, 2004), Adam Gallery, London (solo, 2002), Royal College of Art, London (2002, 2003), Works on Paper, The Park Avenue Armory, New York (2002, 2003). *Works in collections*: HRH The Prince of Wales; private and corporate collections: Britain, Canada, USA and Europe. *Address*: 521 Maquinna Place, Qualicum Beach, B.C., V9K 1B3., Canada. *Signs work*: "Don Farrell." and "FARRELL".

FARRELL, Odette, Honourable Mention at Bird International Award, Beijing, China; Awarded at Watercolour National Competition, Mexico City, Mexico. *Medium*: Oil, watercolour, drawing, sculpture, mixed media. *b*: Mexico City, 6 Apr 1967. *m*: Luis Alberto Torres. one *s*. one *d*. Studied: Universidad Metropolitana, Mexico City - BA Architecture. *Represented by*: Highgate Contemporary; Bowlish Art. *Exhib*: La Galleria Pall Mall, London; Cadogan Contemporary, London; Highgate Contemporary; Urban Retreat Gallery, Dublin; Museo Dolores Olmedo, Mexico City; Atenea Gallery, San Miguel Allende, Mexico; Academy of Fine Art, Beijing, China; Europaische Akademie, Berlin; Arte In, Rome. *Works in Collections*: Natural Culture Centre, Beijing, China; Europaische Akademie, Berlin, Germany; Soqquadro, Rome, Italy; private collections. *Publications*: Dublin News; Irish Art Review; Oggi Newspaper; Reforma Mexico. *Works Reproduced*: Man on Couch (book cover). *Principal Works*: The Road; 9 Flamingoes. *Clubs*: Free Painters and Sculptors, Hesketh, Hubbard. *Address*: 17 Datchworth Ct, 30 Queens Drive, London N4 2XB. *Email*: odettefarrell@gmail.com *Website*: www.odettefarrell.com

FARRER, Rosemary Ann. *Medium*: oil, watercolour, drawing, prints. *b*: Minehead, Somerset, 12 Nov 1956. *m*: Adrian Lyons. one *d*. *Studied*: Camberwell School of Arts and Crafts (1974-75); Ruskin School of Drawing (1975-1978). *Exhib*: solo shows: Newman Rooms, Oxford (1978), Brew House Gallery, Taunton (1979), Chelsea Town Hall, London (1980, 1981), John Hancock Centre, Chicago USA (1983, 1984), Clarendon Gallery, London (1983), Studio Show, London (1986, 1988, 1993), The Talent Store, London (1990), Picture This, London (1991), Evere Gallery, Brussels (1998), Marlborough Open Studios (2003, 2005, 2007, 2008). Mixed shows: Royal Academy Summer Exhibition (3 times, most recently 2009), Greenwich Printmakers Association (member from 1985-1995). *Recreations*: reading, walking, gardening, thinking. *Address*: Stoke Farm, Beechingstoke, Pewsey, Wilts, SN9 6HQ. *Email*: rosemaryfarrer@aol.com *Website*: www.rosemaryfarrer.com *Signs work*: "R.A.Farrer".

FARRINGTON, Karen Lynn, ABNA. *Medium*: acrylic, gouache - mixed, watercolour, drawing. *b*: Leicester, 28 Dec 1954. one *s*. one d. *Studied*: BEd Hons, Bishop Otter College, Sussex (1977); OCA Drawing (2003); Drawing in Colour (2007); NCFE Textile (2008). *Exhib*: Alley Gallery, Launceston (2010); Upton Cross Arts Festival (2011-); Charles Caisley Festival,Launceston (2011, 2013); Orchard Learning Studios, Gunnislake (2012, 2013); More Than Art, Saltach (2013-2014); Solo: Cowslip Workshops, Launceston. *Works in collections*:

private and corporate in UK, Europe, Australia, Canada and USA. *Commissions*: Lawrence House Museum, Launceston; Tippetts of Cornwall; Launceston Town Council Town Guide; Ann's Gallery, Lostwithiel; Levannick School; Lifton Community Hall. *Principal Works*: Launceston Town Guide 2013. *Recreations*: walking, travel, gardening, local events. *Clubs*: ABNA. *Misc*: Known as Karen Farrington Launceston Artist on Facebook and Pinsinterest. *Address*: 2 St. Johns Road, Launceston, Cornwall PL15 7DA. *Email*: karen_farrinton@yahoo.com *Website*: www.britishnaives.co.uk *Signs work*: "K7" or "K.L.Farrington", dated.

FARROW, Kieron, BA (Hons) Fine Art (1982); artist, painter and printmaker in oil, monoprints. *b*: Barnsley, Yorks., 25 Aug 1949. *m*: Megan Farrow. two *s*. *Studied*: Middlesex University. *Exhib*: group shows: Ikon Touring Exhbn. (1985, 1986), Present Prints, Royal Festival Hall London; one-man shows: Curwen Gallery (1999), Museum of Archaeology, Valletta, Malta (1985). *Works in collections*: JP Morgan, Wall St., NY; Lake Point Tower, Chicago; Royal British Legion, Malta; Royal Borough of Kensington and Chelsea, London; Norwich Castle Museum; Scarborough A.G. *Address*: c/o Curwen Gallery, 4 Windmill St., London W1P 1HF.

FARTHING, Douglas Paul, MBE Military Division; QCVS. *Medium*: oil, watercolour, print, drawing. *b*: Gt Yarmouth, 12 Jun 1967. *m*: Julia. two *d*. *Studied*: Self taught. Princes Drawing School (Post Grad course 2014-15). *Represented by*: Mandells Gallery, Norwich http://www.mandellsgallery.co.uk/ *Exhib*: Armed Forces Art Society, Mall Galleries; Mandells Gallery, Norwich; Norwich Cathedral; National Arboretum, Staffordshire; commercial galleries across the UK. *Works in collections*: National Army Museum; 4th Battalion Parachute Regiment; 3rd Battalion Royal Anglian Regiment; Snibston Museum, Leicestershire; BBC Your Paintings www.bbc.co.uk/arts/yourpaintings/artists/farthing-douglas-sergeant-major-b-1967 *Official Purchasers*: as above, and museum collections NAM/Snibson. *Works reproduced*: NAM the fourth man in Kabul Afghanistan www.nam.ac.uk/online-collection/detail.pho?acc+2005-07-766-1 *Principal Works*: "The fourth man". *Clubs*: Armed Forces Art Society. *Address*: 44 The Street, Corton, Lowestoft, Suffolk NR32 5HT. *Email*: douglasfarthing@yahoo.co.uk *Website*: douglasfarthingart.com *Signs work*: "Douglas Farthing".

FARTHING, Stephen, RA (1998); Emeritus Fellow St. Edmund Hall, University of Oxford (2000); Honorary Curator of Collections, Royal Academy of Arts (2000). *Medium*: painting and drawing. *b*: London, 16 Sep 1950. one *d*. *Studied*: St.Martins (1969-73); Royal College (1973-76); British School in Rome (1975). *Represented by*: Frost and Reed, London & New York. *Exhib*: Paris Biennale, France (1982); S.Paulo Biennale, Brazil (1989); Edward Totah Gallery (1985-1990); National Museum of Modern Art, Kyoto (1994); Chelsea Future Space, London (2006); Gus Fischer Gallery, Auckland, NZ (2007). *Works in collections*: Arts Council of England, British Council, British Museum. *Commissions*: Ashmolean; Government Art Collection fund; Walker Gallery, Liverpool; Otemar University, Japan. *Publications*: Intelligent Persons Guide to Modern Art (Duckworth, 2002); 1001 Paintings You Must See Before You Die (Cassell, 2006). *Works Reproduced*: on RA website. *Recreations*: watercolour painting; tennis. *Clubs*: Chelsea Arts Club. *Address*: c/o The Royal Academy, Burlington House, Piccadilly London W1J 0BD. *Website*: www.stephenfarthing.com *Signs work*: "STEPHEN FARTHING".

FAULDS, James Alexander, DA.; artist in water-colour and oil; art teacher. *b*: Glasgow, 15 Jan 1949. *s of*: Alexander Faulds. *Educ*: Knightswood Secondary School. *Studied*: Dundee College of Art (1968-72). *Exhib*: Dundee under 30s, RSA, SSA, Colquhoun Memorial, Group 81, Glasgow, Eden Court Gallery, Contemporary British Water-colours, Festival Theatre, Pitlochry, RSW, John Laing, London, Nürnberg, Germany. *Clubs*: Glasgow Art; founder mem., Group 81, Glasgow. *Address*: 3 Camphill Ave., Glasgow G41 3AV.

FAULDS, Robert Gordon, *Medium*: oil, watercolour, drawing. *b*: Paisley, Scotland, 24 Jan 1957. *Partner*: Elizabeth Earley. *Studied*: Bath Academy of Art (1976-77); Preston Polytechnic (1977-80). *Exhib*: Royal Academy Summer Exhibition (2008, 2009); National Open Art, Chichester (2008, 2009, 2010, 2011); Jerwood Drawing Prize (2007). *Works in collections*: Hestercombe Gardens, BBC Open University; private collections UK, ROI, USA, Japan. *Address*: Coles Building, Hamp Street, Bridgwater, TA6 6AR. *Email*: studio@gordon-faulds.com *Website*: www.gordon-faulds.com *Signs work*: "GORDON FAULDS".

FAULKNER, Amanda, BA (Hons) Fine Art (1982), MA Fine Art (1983); artist in charcoal and pastel on paper, acrylic on canvas, lithography and etching; Senior lecturer in Fine Art, Chelsea College of Art and Design, University of the Arts, London. *b*: Poole, 5 Dec 1953. *d of*: Richard Faulkner, B.Sc. & Gillian Hopkinson (née Park). *Partner*: Christopher Coe. one *s*. *Studied*: St. Anthony's, Leweston, Dorset, and Canford School, Dorset. *Studied*: Bournemouth College of Art (1978-79), Ravensbourne College of Art and Design (1979-82), Chelsea School of Art (1982-83). *Exhib*: regularly at Angela Flowers Gallery and Flowers East since 1983; and in UK and internationally. *Works in collections*: including ACGB, Unilever plc, V&A, Contemporary Art Soc., Whitworth A.G., Silkeborg Kunstmuseum, Denmark. *Address*: 131 Listria Pk., London N16 5SP. *Email*: amandafaulkner@blueyonder.co.uk *Signs work*: "Amanda Faulkner."

FAULKNER, Iain, BA Hons (Fine Art). *Medium*: oil. *b*: Glasgow, 28 Jul 1973. *s of*: John and Janet Faulkner. *m*: Laura. *Studied*: Glasgow School of Art (1991-96). *Represented by*: Albemarle Gallery, London. *Exhib*: Albemarle Gallery, London; Eleanor Ettinger Gallery (New York); Sammer Gallery (Spain). *Works in collections*: The Prudential; private collections in Europe, USA, Japan. *Commissions*: portraits commissioned by Glasgow Chambers of Commerce, Royal College of Pharmaceutical Medicine, St.Andrews Society, private collectors. *Address*: c/o Albemarle Gallery, Albemarle Street, London W15 4JR. *Signs work*: IF.

FAULKNER, Robert Trevor, ARCA (1955), FRBS; figurative sculptures in bronze, terracotta and direct metal; specialist in polychrome metal wild-life and aeronautical subjects. *b*: 17 Sep 1929. *m*: Brenda Mabel (Flowers). one *d*. *Educ*: Penistone Grammar School. *Studied*: Sheffield School of Art (1946-50); RCA (1952-55). *Represented by*: Derwent-Wye, Rowsley, Derbyshire DE4 2EB. *Exhib*: Moorland, Alwin (London), John Noott Galleries, Broadway, Worcs; Renishaw Art Group; Derwent Wye Gallery. *Works in collections*: Ulster Museum, Derbys.; Oxford and Lancs.Educ. Authorities; Pewterers Company, London, Sir Reresby Sitwell. *Commissions*: medals for Virginia Air and Space Museum; trophy, Royal Aero Club; medals for BMFA, Golfing figures for Jack Spencer (Goldsmiths'); Samuel Fox & Co. (Steelworks) Sheffield; Molins Ltd.: WVEC (Virginia). *Publications*: Manual of Direct Metal Sculpture (Thames & Hudson, 1978). *Recreations*: swimming, model engineering. *Clubs*: Sheffield S.M.EE.E., Sheffield S.A. *Address*: 4 Birchitt Cl., Bradway, Sheffield S17 4QJ. *Signs work*: "TREVOR FAULKNER" or "T.F."

FAULKNER-STEVENS, Debby, RMS, SWA, HS; Awards: Alexander Gallery Award, HRH Princess Michael of Kent Award, Llewellyn Alexander Masters Award for Miniature Painting. *Medium*: miniature painter in watercolour. *b*: Newport Pagnell, Bucks, 1954. *m*: Alan. one *d*. *Educ*: Radcliffe Grammar School, Wolverton (A Level Art). *Studied*: self taught. Exhib: Society of Women Artists and Royal Miniature Society at the Mall Galleries; Llewellyn Alexander Gallery; Southwold Gallery; Chris Beetles Ltd.; Fine Art UK; B&W Thornton, Stratford upon Avon; World Miniature Exhibition, Smithsonian, Washington, USA. *Works in collections*: private collections. *Publications*: Illustrator - "A Midsummer Mouse" by Barry Thornton (pub. 2014). *Recreations*: history, architecture, writing, fashion. *Misc*: Works on calfskin vellum for the miniature painting. *Address*: 32 Summerhayes, Great

Linford, Milton Keynes, MK14 5EU. *Email*: faulknerstevens@btinternet.com *Website*: www.debbyfaulknerstavensart.com *Signs work*: "DFS" (and year, ie. '04, '12, '14 etc.).

FAUST, Pat, artist in oil, water-colour, pastel, theatrical designs, murals. *Studied*: Crescent Theatre, Birmingham. *Exhib*: RGI, Manchester Academy, Birmingham A.G., Sewerby Hall, Bridlington, Scarborough A.G. and Town Hall, Ferens A.G., Hull, Beverley, Cartwright Hall, Bradford, Pannett, Whitby, RA, RBA, SWA, RCamA, UAS, Leeds City A.G., Paris Salon, Gallery Vallombreuse Biarritz, Brye A.G., Glaisdale, City Gallery, Darlington, Francis Phillips Gallery, Sheffield, Northern Academy of Art, Harrogate A.G., Guildhall, York, Yorkshire Artist Biennal, City A.G. York, Yorkshire Pastel Soc., Haworth, Cliffe Castle Museum and A.G. Keighley, Yorks.; one-man shows: Marshalls, Scarborough, Hull University, Yorkshire Pastel Soc., Dewsbury A.G. and Museum, Scarborough Scene, Scarborough Art Gallery (2001); joint exhbn. March-May 1998 Sewerbury Hall, Bridlington, Walker Gallery, Harrogate. *Works in collections*: Scarborough A.G., Scarborough Town Hall, Menston Hospital and private collections. Official purchases: painting of Scarborough A.G. (hung R.A.) by Scarborough Corp. Winner shield best medium (1992) and award (1993, 1994) Sewerby Hall, Bridlington. *Signs work*: "Pat Faust."

FAWCETT, David Noel Lloyd, *b*: Southport, 15 Apr 1965. *m*: Jacqueline. three *s*. *Studied*: Self-taught. *Represented by*: The Enid Lawson Gallery; Nichlas Bowlby (dealer); Mid Cornwall Gallery; Green Tree Gallery. *Works in collections*: The Open University Collection and private. *Publications*: The Public Catalogue Foundation Catalogue (Berkshire, Buckinghamshire, Oxfordshire). *Works Reproduced*: The Royal Academy (postcard); an album cover for The Bluetones. *Recreations*: Drumming, football coach, keep fit. *Address*: 6 Queens Road, Tunbridge Wells, TN4 9LU. *Email*: davidf@depinna.co.uk *Website*: www.davidfawcett.co.uk *Signs work*: "DF".

FAWLEY, Charlotte Audrey, NDD Illustration (1957); painter/designer in oil, pastel, water-colour. *b*: Blackpool, 6 Dec 1934. *Educ*: Arnold High School, Blackpool. *Studied*: Blackpool School of Art (1953-57), Camden Arts Centre, London (1964-66, Aubrey Williams). *Exhib*: Royal Opera House, Covent Garden; Royal National Theatre, South Bank; Primrose Hill Gallery; Soar Gallery Kensington; Chelsea Arts Club; RAC Club, Pall Mall; Bafta, Piccadilly, etc. Work in collections internationally. *Commissions*: Design of backcloth and costumes for ballet 'Serpentime' for Royal Ballet tour Kenya (1996). BBC2 Series 'Making their Mark' (R. Foster) 6 artists on drawing in different mediums. BBC2 Newsnight - graphics for Falklands War (1981) and Gulf War CNN. *Publications*: illustrated: 'Thinking About God' (HarperCollins). *Clubs*: Chelsea Arts, BAFTA, Piccadilly, London. *Address*: 56 Holley Rd., Wellington Court, London W3 7TS. *Email*: Acfawley@aol.com *Signs work*: "CHARLOTTE FAWLEY."

FAWSSETT, Ann: see ATKIN, Ann

FEASEY, Judith Mary, Cert. RAS (1976), ATC (1977); MA Fine Art (2000); 1976 Turner Gold Medal Landscape Painting; 1975/76 - David Murray landscape Scholarships; 1976 - British Institution Fund award for painting. 1976 - Arthur Hacker silver medal portrait painting; 1979 - Austrian Government Scholarship to attend International summer academy in Salzburg. *Medium*: painting in oil & watercolour, printmaking *b*: Southgate, 3 Sep 1945. *d of*: Cyril Feasey, mechanical engineer. *Educ*: St. Maurs Convent, Weybridge, Surrey. *Studied*: Guildford School of Art (1965-69), RA Schools (1973-76) UCL Goldsmiths (1976-77), East London University (1998-2000). *Exhib*: Four-man show, Alfred East Gallery, Kettering. Two Man show Rotherhithe Community Centre. Open exhibitions include Royal Academy Summer shows, Royal Society of Portrait Painters, Spirit of London and Mall Galleries, London, etc. *Clubs*: Royal Academy Schools Alumni. *Address*: 90 Webster Rd., London SE16 4DF. *Email*: judyfeasey@yahoo.co.uk *Signs work*: "J. Feasey" or "J.M.F."

FEDERER, Frances Mary, BA in Book Illustration; MPhil - Glass, Gold and the Image. *Medium*: Gilding and painting on glass. *b*: London, 6 May 1946. *m*: Stefan Majka. one *s*. *Studied*: Camberwell Shool of Art (1962-1967); Royal College of Art (2007-2009). *Represented by*: Self. *Exhib*: Various group shows: Coburg Glass Exhibition, Germany (2005); World Exhibition of Glass Art, Stenige, Sweden (2008); British Glass Biennale (2010); The Glass Canvas, Glazenhuis, Commel, Belgium (2011); Glass Inspirations, Burgdorf, Switzerland (2011); IVth International Glass Festival, Luxembourg (2011); The Goldsmiths Company, London (2012); British Glass Biennale (2012). *Works in collections*: 'Annie Get Your Gun' in permanent collection, V&A. *Publications*: Gold Leaf, Print and Glass, (pub. 2012, book). *Recreations*: Member, Art Workers Guild. *Address*: 20 Valonia Gardens, London SW8 1PY. *Email*: francesfederer@gmail.com *Website*: www.gilding.net *Signs work*: "FRANCES FEDERER"; "F. Federer".

FEIJOO, Fernando, RE Council Member; Gwen May Student Printmaker (2003); Winner, Design a Book of Fables (FPBA, 2004); BA (Illustration, 1st Class Hons); MA Fine Art (Distinction). *Medium*: relief printing, lithography, screen printing. *b*: Cambridge, 26 Sep 1978. *m*: Pilar Munoz. *Studied*: KIAD, Maidstone; Winchester School of Art. *Represented by*: Vinson Gallery, USA; Eyestorm Gallery, London; Bankside Gallery. *Exhib*: Bankside Gallery; MoMA Wales; Eyestorm Gallery; Vinson Gallery USA; Estonia Print Triennial; Fry Art Gallery, Saffron Walden; International Print Triennial Vienna, Oldenburg, Poland; 2nd Qijiang International Print Exhibition, China; RWA Open Print Exhibition, Bristol. *Works in collections*: MoMA Wales; Ashmolean Museum, Oxford; V&A, London. *Commissions*: Dolphin Hotel. *Publications*: Ambit, Printmaking Today, inspiring writing in 'Art & Design', 'Printmakers Secrets', 'Printmaking on a Budget', 'Graphic Art Magazine' (Estonia, Tallin). *Works Reproduced*: book published by FPBA, Cracks Progress & Charlies Progress. *Recreations*: sport, travelling. *Misc*: works at the Curwen Studio as Master Printer, and visiting lecturer at universities around the country. *Address*: 80 Union Lane, Cambridge, CB4 1QB. *Email*: feijoo@talk21.com *Website*: www.fernandofeijoo.com *Signs work*: 'Feijoo'.

FELCEY, Trevor, ARCA (MA); Lorne Award (1991). *Medium*: oil, drawing, prints. *b*: Sussex, 25 Aug 1945. *Studied*: Grimsby School of Art; Camberwell School of Art; RCA. *Represented by*: Chris Insoll (01872-580445). *Exhib*: many mixed shows. Principal one-person shows: Brunel University Gallery (1976); Ian Birksted Gallery, London (1982); Concourse Gallery, Byam Shaw School of Art (1993); Plough Arts Centre, Devon (1999); Galerie Hofmann and Kyrath Berlin (2001); Royal Albert Memorial Museum Exeter, Beldam Gallery Brunel University (2005). *Works in collections*: Chantrey Bequest (University of Liverpool Collection), Nuffield Foundation; Franklyn Memorial Collection, South Humberside; Leicester Education Authority; Brunel University Collection. *Address*: Church House, Throwleigh, Devon EX20 2HU. *Signs work*: 'T.Felcey'.

FELD, Anthony Eric (Tony), *Medium*: Oil. *b*: London, 1 Sep 1956. *m*: Jill Feld. one *s*. one *d*. *Educ*: Foundation course, Chelsea School of Art (1975-76). *Exhib*: Brighton Art Fair (2009, 2010); Untitled Art Fair (2011); Parallax Art Fair (2011); Royal Institute of Oil Painters Annual Exhibition (2010, 2011); Cork St Open Exhibition (Aug 2011, 2012); Cork St Prizewinners Exhibition (Feb 2012); DSWF Wildlife Artist of the Year (2010, 2011, 2012, 2013); Currently showing at Number Four Gallery, St Abbs amd Look Gallery, Helmsley. Also exhibited at Natural Nature exhibition, Staphorsius Gallery, West Zaan, Netherlands. *Works in collections*: Private. *Address*: 55 Ashurst Avenue, Saltdean, East Sussex BN2 8DR. *Email*: tonyfeldpaintings@gmail.com *Website*: www.tonyfeldpaintings.co.uk *Signs work*: "T. FELD".

FELL, Michael Anthony, FSDC, LRE; painter/printmaker; former Head of Foundation, City & Guilds London; visiting tutor, Prince of Wales Inst., London. *b*: London, 31 Jan

1939. *s of*: Sir Anthony Fell. *m*: Maureen. two *s*. *Educ*: St. George's, Weybridge. *Studied*: St. Martin's, City & Guilds London. *Exhib*: Jordan Gallery (1972-84), Halesworth Gallery (1972-85), Mall Galleries, Clementi House Gallery (1991), Gallery Renata, Chicago, Belanthi Gallery, New York, Chappel Galleries, Essex (1993, 1999), Comteroux Perpignan (1993), Flaran, France (1996), Grosvenor Gallery, London (1996). *Works in collections*: BM; Arts Council; Victoria National Gallery University Melbourne, Australia; Churchill Library, Massachusetts; Michael Estorick Collection. *Clubs*: Asylum, Charlotte St. *Address*: 17 Fonnereau Rd., Ipswich, Suffolk IP1 3JR. *Signs work*: "Michael Fell."

FELLOWS, Elaine Helen, BA (Hons) (1981), HS (1987), SWA (1988), RMS (1992), USM (1990); professional painter of portraits and still life in miniature in water-colour on vellum or ivorine. *b*: Walsall, 27 Nov 1959. one *s*. *Studied*: Walsall College of Art (1977), Wolverhampton Polytechnic (1978-81). *Exhib*: RMS (Hon. mention 1989, 1991), SWA, Hilliard Soc. (Bell award 1990), Ulster Soc. of Miniaturists (Madam MacCarthy Mór Memorial Award 1991), Llewellyn Alexander Award (1993), Suzanne Lucas Award (1995), Llewellyn Alexander Gallery, Linda Blackstone Gallery, France, Hong Kong, USA. *Works in collections*: GB, USA, France, Germany. *Publications*: The Techniques of Painting Miniatures; contributor to The Magic of Miniatures. *Address*: Bwlch House, Beguildy, Knighton, Powys LD7 1UG. *Signs work*: 'ehf'.

FENNER, Michael James, BA (Hons), ATD (Dist); painter in acrylic. *Medium*: acrylic. *b*: Liverpool, 5 Jan 1952. *m*: Alison. one *s*. two *d*. *Studied*: Laird School of Art, Newport College of Art. *Exhib*: group and one-man shows: Birkenhead, Liverpool, Durham., USA, Ireland, London. *Works in collections*: Williamson A.G., Birkenhead, Dee Fine Art, private collections in Britain, Ireland and Europe. *Commissions*: portraits, England and Holland. *Publications*: magazine articles. *Principal Works*: Series of Urban Landscapes, 'Orpheus' and 'Dante' series. *Recreations*: Slide guitar *Clubs*: N.A.P.A. *Address*: la Charlesville, Oxton, Birkenhead CH43 1TP. *Email*: tonybaudelaire@yahoo.com *Website*: mike-fenner-paintings.co.uk *Signs work*: "M.J. Fenner."

FERGUSON, George, CBE, BA, BArch, PPRIBA, RWA, Hon MA Univ. of Bristol (2001); Hon. Doctorate of Design, University of West of England (2003); President Royal Institute of British Architects (RIBA) (2003-05). *Medium*: people, pencils and oils *b*: Winchester, 22 Mar 1947. one *s*. two *d*. *Educ*: Wellington College. *Studied*: University of Bristol and RWA. *Exhib*: RWA; Director, Ferguson Mann Architects; Director, Bristol Brewing Co Ltd; Director, Tobacco Factory Enterprises Ltd; Partner, Bristol Collective (art collectors). *Commissions*: various architectural. *Publications*: Races against Time (1984). *Principal Works*: Tobacco Factory Arts Centre, Bristol. *Recreations*: theatre, travel, making things happen. *Clubs*: Chelsea Arts Club. *Address*: 18 Great George St., Bristol BS1 5RH. *Email*: gf@fm-architects.co.uk *Website*: www.fm-architects.co.uk

FERGUSON, Paul, ACR (Accredited Conservator/Restorer); Member of the Mastercarvers' Association (Hon. Secretary 1992-present, President 1999-2002); Liveryman of the Worshipful Company of Turners; Freeman of the City of London; Established the Paul Ferguson Workshop, Fine Wood Carving & Guilding, 1978. *Medium*: wood/gold. *b*: London, 17 Oct 1950. *m*: Jessie Ferguson. one *s*. two *d*. *Studied*: Kingston College of Art. *Represented by*: Accredited Member of The Institute of Conservation. *Commissions*: Restoration or new commissions: Windsor Castle, Osborne House, Osterley Park, Lancaster House, Admiralty House, Palace of Westminster, Kensington Palace, Woburn Abbey, Renishaw Hall, Victoria & Albert Museum, National Portrait Gallery, The Wallace Collection, The Imperial War Museum, The Army Museum, Royal Academy, Goldsmiths Hall, Drapers Hall, Stationers Hall. *Clubs*: The Georgian Group, Folly Fellowship. *Address*: Workshop 20, 21 Wren Street, London WC1X 0HF. *Email*: pf@paulferguson.co.uk *Website*: www.paulferguson.co.uk

FERGUSON, Shaun, BA Hons; Post-Graduate Diploma; The Richard Ford Award (Spain Scholarship 1988); The Discerning Eye 'New Discovery Award' (1990). *Medium*: acrylic and oil. *b*: Crewe, 8 Aug 1963. *Studied*: Royal Academy of Arts (1985-88); Trent Polytechnic, Nottingham (1982-85); Chester College of F.E. (1981-82). *Represented by*: Fairfax Gallery. *Exhib*: various group and one-man shows at Fairfax Gallery in London, Tunbridge Wells and Burnham Market (1998-2009); Glasgow International Arts Fair (2006-09); London Art Fair, Islington (2005-09); 'Art London' (2003, 2004); The Discerning Eye (1991, 92, 96, 2003); RA Summer Exhbn (1992, 2001); 'Aspects of Irish Art 1960-90'; Dublin Museum of Modern Art (1994); Henry Wyndham Fine Art, London (1990, 91); one-man show, Solomon Gallery, Dublin (1991). *Works in collections*: Durban Museum, S. Africa; Dublin Museum of Modern Art; Ulster Museum, N. Ireland; Lloyds Bank. *Clubs*: Reynolds Club. *Misc*: Fine Art lecturer, City College, Brighton. *Address*: Flat 9, 33 Compton Avenue, Brighton, BN1 3PT. *Website*: www.shaunferguson.co.uk *Signs work*: 'S.M.FERGUSON'.

FERGUSSON, Helen: see BATTERBURY, Helen Fiona.

FERRAN, Brian, BA, DBA, HRHA, HRUA; painter in acrylic and oil; artist and former chief executive of the Arts Council of N. Ireland. *b*: Derry, Ireland, 19 Oct 1940. *m*: Denise. one *s*. one *d*. *Studied*: Courtauld Inst., London University, Brera Academy, Milan, Queens University, Belfast. *Exhib*: regularly in Ireland, USA, Switzerland and Mexico. *Works in collections*: Ulster Museum, Arts Council of N. Ireland, Arts Council of Republic of Ireland, Allied Irish Bank, Gordon Lambert Collection, Crawford Municipal Gallery, Cork. *Publications*: exhib. catalogues and Basil Blackshaw - painter, a monograph published 1995. *Address*: Goorey Rocks, Malin, Inishowen, Co.Donegal, Eire. *Email*: brian.ferran@aol.com *Signs work*: "Brian Ferran."

FERRAN, Denise, PhD(1997); Hon MFA (1996), University of Ulster; BA (Hons), Diploma in Advanced Studies in Education; Awards include: Ulster Academy Silver medal (1974), Ulster Academy Watercolour Prize (1991), Fulbright Fellowship for research, Boston College USA (2001); Fulbright Scholar, Minnesota, USA (2006-07). *Medium*: oil, watercolour. *b*: Saintfield, Co.Down, 19 Nov 1942. one *s* (decd). one *d*. *Studied*: St.Mary's University College, Belfast; Queens University, Belfast; Trinity College, Dublin; Courtauld, University of London. *Exhib*: Glebe Gallery, Donegal (2008), McGilloway Gallery, Derry (2006), Riverview Gallery, Enniskillen (2000), Tower Museum/McGilloway Gallery (1999), Cavehill Gallery (1992), Ulster Arts Club, Belfast (1991), Fendersky Gallery (1986), Gordon Gallery, Derry (1982/85/89/92), University Gallery, Queens University, Belfast (1977), Keys Gallery, Derry (1977). *Works in collections*: Arts Council of Northern Ireland, Haverty Trust, Ulster Television, Ulster Bank, First Trust Bank, Bank of Ireland, Northern Bank, Dept. of Environment (NI). *Commissions*: Novotel, Belfast; Boardroom of Northern Bank, Belfast; National Bank of Australia. *Publications*: W.J. Leech, An Irish Painter Abroad (1996), F.E. McWilliams (2008), The Sculptor F.E. McWilliam (2012). *Works Reproduced*: Novotel "Fermanagh Childhood", prints and paintings. *Clubs*: Fulbright Alumni, Council of Royal Ulster Academy, Board IUSA. *Address*: Goorey Rocks, Malin, Inishowen, C. Donegal Ireland. *Email*: drdeniseferran@aol.com *Signs work*: "Denise Ferran".

FERRAND SCOTT, Victoria Jane, Associate Member Royal British Society of Sculptors; BA (Hons) 1978 & 2002, MA 2004. *Medium*: sculpture, drawing, prints. *b*: Grays, Essex, 15 Mar 1958. *Studied*: University of Manchester (1975-78), Leeds College of Art (1996-98), Bretton Hall (1999-2002), University of Leeds (2002-04). *Exhib*: one man show: Brahm Gallery, Leeds (2007). Royal Academy Summer Exhibition (2008), Royal West of England Academy Autumn Exhibition (2008, 2009); Royal Society of Sculptors (2010); Leeds Fine Artists (2011). *Publications*: 'The Naked Quarry' Yorkshire Quarry Arts

(2008). *Clubs*: Yorkshire Sculptors Group. *Misc*: Artist in Education at the Yorkshire Scuplture Park. *Address*: Field Head, Smaws, Tadcaster, North Yorkshire LS24 9LP. *Email*: vferrandscott@smaws.fsnet.co.uk *Website*: www.axisweb.org/artist/victoriaferrandscott

FERRY, David Dawson, RE (2011); FRSA; BA (1979), HDFA (Lond.) (1981); printmaker/collagist; lecturer, Camberwell/Canterbury/Winchester Art Schools; Pollock/Krasner Award, New York (2002), bronze medal, First International Artists Book Competition, Seoul, Korea (2005); Appointed Professor of Printmaking, Cardiff (2010). *b*: Blackpool, 5 Feb 1957. *s of*: Brian Ferry. *Studied*: Blackpool College Tech. (1975-76), Camberwell School of Arts and Crafts (1976-79, Mario Dubsky, Agathe Sorell), Slade School of Fine Art (1979-81, Stanley Jones). *Represented by*: Booklun New York, Roe & Morgan London *Exhib*: Photomontage exhbn. in Dresden, New York (2002) Roe & Moore, London (2003), Berlin (2005), Seoul (2005), Chelsea Arts Club, London (2005), Laurence Graham, London (2006); Sandra Higgins London (2012); Chart Gallery, London (2014). *Works in collections*: Ashmolean; Grundy A.G., University College, St.Thomas Hospital, Maidstone A.G., Nuclear Electric, Marconi Instruments U.K., British Airways, Art Institute of Chicago, USA, University of Oxford, University of Southampton, Museum Modern Art, V&A, National Art Library. *Commissions*: GEC, UK. *Publications*: author, Painting Without a Brush, U.K. (1991), U.S.A. (1992), France (1994); 'Aspects of our National Heritage', 'From the Window Seat' (2002), 'Montage Pictures' (2010). *Works Reproduced*: Dictionary of Modern British Painters, Frances Spalding. *Clubs*: Chelsea Arts Club. *Misc*: Formed video production titled 'Lost Shoe Productions'. *Address*: c/o Cardiff School of Art and Design, Cardiff CF24 0SP. *Email*: dferry@carfiddmet.ac.uk *Signs work*: "D.D. Ferry" or "D.D.F."

FESTING, Andrew Thomas, MBE; RP (1992); President, Royal Society of Portrait Painters (2002-2008); Honorary Doctorate of Literature, Northumbria University; portrait painter in oil. *b*: Chalford, 30 Nov 1941. *m*: Virginia Fyffe. one *d*. *Educ*: Ampleforth College *Exhib*: RP. *Works in collections*: National Gallery Dublin, Royal Coll., National Portrait Gallery, Palace of Westminster. *Address*: Fawcett, Colwell, Hexham, Northumberland NE46 4TP. *Signs work*: "A.T. Festing."

FFYFFE, Terrance Michael, Winner, Discerning Eye (1995), Eastern Open (1997); artist, figurative painter of nudes, religious paintings and portraits in oil. *b*: Melbourne, Australia, 21 Dec 1957. *Educ*: St.Joseph's College, Melbourne. *Studied*: Prahran College now Swineburne University (1975-77). *Represented by*: Andrew Lamont Gallery, London. *Exhib*: numerous selected exhbns. *Works in collections*: internationally, mainly UK, Australia and USA. *Commissions*: private portrait and mural commissions. Commissioned by London Borough of Havering for Murals in Upminster and Gidea Paek Libraries. *Address*: c/o 51 Billet Lane Hornchurch, Essex RM11 1AX. *Email*: TerryFfyffe@aol.com

FILIPE, Paulo Duarte, NAPA; writer and painter in acrylic. *b*: Portugal, 3 Sep 1962. one *d*. *Exhib*: Teatro Lethes, Faro, Portugal (1990); Galeria "O Arco", Faro, Portugal (1991); 2nd Forum, da AMI, Lisbon, Portugal (1997); IP.3, Faro, Portugal; Vilamoura Marinotel, Portugal (1998); Centro Cultural, Lagos, Portugal (1998); Black Sheep Gallery, Hawarden, N. Wales (1999); Westminster Gallery, London (1999); Art Show, Manchester; Art Centre, Los Angeles, USA; Galerie Not, London (1999), Art Expo, New York (2000), Limelight Gallery, London (2000), Conservatorio Regional do Algarve, Portugal (2004), Artists Gallery of Seattle, USA (2005), Gallerie Dina Brito, Olhao, Portugal (2005), Galeria Municipal Albufeira (2005); Galeria de Arte Samora Barros, Albufeira (2006); Galeriea de Arte Praça do Mar, Quarteira (2006). *Publications*: Art Guide '92, Art Guide 95/96, Contemporary Art Year Book 98, Art 2001.com Guide. *Clubs*: Bromley Art Society, NAPA, ISAP. *Misc*: For Paulo Duarte Filipe, painting never is nor has been an amorphous or even ambiguous act. His painting does not allow any distraction nor even the slightest hint of indifference. As if we were induced, for a time undefined, into a curious and bizarre hypnotic state. His phone no is 00351 966 303772. *Address*: Apartado 970, 8000 Faro, Portugal. *Email*: pauloduartefilipe@hotmail.com *Website*: www.pauloduartefilipe.blogspot.com *Signs work*: "Paulo Duarte Filipe."

FILIPOV, Stanislav Nikolov, The Society of Wood Engravers Prize for Outstanding Print from Overseas (70th Annual Exhibition). *b*: General Toshevo, 17 Aug 1969. *Studied*: University of Veliko Tarnovo, Bulgaria (1996). *Exhib*: Society of Wood Engravers, UK (since 2006). *Works in collections*: "Ex Libris P Jonker", Pieter Jonker, The Netherlands; "Adam and Eve", Rabbi F.R. Berry, UK; "The Seagull", Loek Aarsen, The Netherlands; "Ex Libris Bilge", Muhsin Bilge, Turkey. *Address*: Ul. 'Pirin Planina' 4A, Grad General Toshevo 9500, Oblast Dobritch, Bulgaria. *Email*: stanifil2005@abv.bg

FINCH, Julie, Director of Bristol Museums, Galleries and Archives. *Studied*: University of Hull BA (Hons) Heritage Studies; University of Leicester MA Museum Open University - PG Dip Senior Management; FRSA; AMA. *Address*: City of Bristol Museum and Art Gallery, Queens Road, Bristol BS8 1RL.

FINDLAY, Denise, BA (Hons) Fine Art (Drawing and Painting); Elizabeth Greenshields Award (1998, 2001, 2002), Kennox Prize (runner-up). *Medium*: oil, drawing, figurative painter, portrait artist. *b*: Glasgow, 14 Dec 1973. *d of*: Gordon & Vivien Findlay. one *d*: *Studied*: Glasgow School of Art (1992-96). *Represented by*: The Scottish Gallery; Lemon Street Gallery; Thompsons. *Exhib*: solo exhbns: The Scottish Gallery (1999, 2001, 2004); Portland Gallery (2003); Kennox Prize, Thompsons (2005); Lemonstreet Gallery (2006), selected and participant in Sky Arts Portrait Artist of the Year (2013). *Works in collections*: HRH The Prince of Wales; Picardy Television, Sir David Murray. *Commissions*: Picardy Television; many private; Costley & Costley Hotels. *Publications*: catalogues for solo exhbns, article in 'Homes and Interiors Scotland' (1999, Issue 12). *Clubs*: The Glasgow Art Club. *Address*: Nittingshill, Port Glasgow Road, Kilmacolm, Inverclyde, PA13 4SG. *Email*: info@denisefindlay.com *Website*: www.denisefindlay.com *Signs work*: 'FINDLAY'.

FINDLAY, Sheila Anne Macfarlane, RWS, DA(Edin.), Post-Grad.(1950), Travelling Scholar (1951); artist and illustrator in water-colour and oil. *b*: Auchlishie, Kirriemuir. *d of*: William R. Findlay, farmer. *m*: Alfred Hackney, RWS, ARE, DA(Edin). two *d*. *Educ*: Webster's Seminary. *Studied*: Edinburgh College of Art (1945-51) under John Maxwell, Penelope Beaton, Sir William MacTaggart, Leonard Rosoman. *Exhib*: RA, RWS, Catto Gallery, R.A. Prizewinner (1993). *Works in collections*: Department of the Environment, MacFarlanes, Alan Howarth CBE, MP. *Publications*: children's books illustrated for Faber & Faber, Adprint, Harrap, Odhams, Medici Soc. *Address*: Barnside, Lodge La., Cobham, nr. Gravesend, Kent DA12 3BS. *Signs work*: "Sheila Findlay."

FINEGOLD, Stephen M., BA (Hons) 1st class, Postgrad. (Dip.); artist in oil, acrylic, pastel, collage, print; Artistic Director, FCA Gallery. *b*: London, 17 Jun 1959. *m*: Josephine. two *s*. *Educ*: Beal Grammar School, Ilford. *Studied*: Bradford College, Central School. *Exhib*: London, Salisbury, Yorkshire. *Works in collections*: FCA Gallery, UK, Spain, France, Australia, South Africa, USA. *Commissions*: private, CAB. *Misc*: also actor, director, writer. *Address*: 2 Savile Glen, Halifax, W. Yorks., HX1 2BH. *Email*: stephenfinegold@hotmail.com *Signs work*: "Finegold."

FINER, Stephen, artist. *Medium*: oil etc. *b*: London, 27 Jan 1949. *Studied*: Ravensbourne College of Art (1966-70). *Represented by*: www.artspacegallery.co.uk. *Exhib*: one-man shows: Four Vine Lane, London, Anthony Reynolds Gallery, Berkeley Sq. Gallery, Bernard Jacobson Gallery, Woodlands A.G., Agnew's, Six Chapel Row, Bath, Pallant House Gallery, Charleston, ArtSpace Gallery; selected mixed shows: British Art 1940-1980, from the Arts Council Coll., Hayward Gallery (1980), Collazione Ingleze 2, Venice Biennale (1984), The

Portrait Now, NPG (1993), Men on Women (1997-98), '50 Contemporary Self-Portraits', Six Chapel Row, Bath (1999), 'British Art 1900-1998' Agnews (1998), 'Painting the Century 101 Portrait Masterpieces 1900-2000', N.P.G. (2000-01), The Art of Giving, Towner (2011), 'People and Portraits', Towner (2013), 'Artists Make Faces', Plymouth AG (2013). *Works in collections*: ACGB, British Council, Contemporary Arts Soc., Atkinson A.G., NPG (David Bowie), Los Angeles County Museum of Art; Magdalene College; Pallant House Gallery, Towner, Tullie House, University of Sussex. *Publications*: 'Painting the Century 101 Portrait Masterpieces', NPG etc. *Works Reproduced*: www.npg.org.uk, 'The Portrait Now' (Marlene Dietrich), 'Painting The Century' (David Bowie and Iman) etc. *Address*: 20 Kipling St., London SE1 3RU. *Email*: londonpainting@tiscali.co.uk *Website*: www.stephenfiner.com *Signs work*: "S.A. Finer" on reverse.

FINLATOR, Hannah Verena, BA (Hons); residency abroad. *Medium*: oil. *b*: North Carolina, 28 Nov 1977. *d of*: Wallace Finlator. *Educ*: BFA, MFA. *Studied*: Corcoran College of Art Mons.; Newcastle University. *Represented by*: Henshelwood Gallery. *Exhib*: Société Imaginaire, Germany; Hemicycle Gallery, Washington DC; Corcoran Museum, Washington DC; Center St. Arts, Virginia, USA; Hatton Gallery, Newcastle and across UK. *Works in collections*: Henshelwood Gallery, Newcastle; Andrew Heard (dir. Shipley Gallery, UK) .*Commissions*: private. *Works Reproduced*: in gallery catalogues. *Address*: Templestr, 45, 50668 Cologne, Germany. *Email*: hannahverena@yahoo.com *Website*: www.fairfields.demon.co.uk/onlinegallery/hannah.html *Signs work*: 'Hannah Finlator'.

FIRMSTONE, David James, MBE, RWS; Vice-President RWS; NDD, ATD; Recent prizes: Hunting Art Prize, short listed for 1st prize (1993), Hunting Art Prize, prizewinner (1998, 1999, 2001), St. Helens Open, prizewinner (1994, 1995), Manchester Academy, painting prize (1996), Chichester Open, prizewinner (1998), Chester Open, 1st prize (1999), Laing Open, prizewinner (1999), RWS Bankside, Water-colour: Century 21: Daler Rowney 1st prize/The Artist Prize/The Ashdown Gallery prize, for best landscape (1999), Prizewinner Sunday Times/Singer & Friedlander Watercolour (2006). *Medium*: landscape painter in water-colour, tempera, acrylic, oils and mixed media. *b*: Middlesbrough, 28 Apr 1943. *m*: Jean Gilbert-Firmstone. two *s*. *Studied*: Middlesbrough College of Art, Birmingham University. *Represented by*: James Huntington Whiteley. *Exhib*: Galleries 1995-99: The Piccadilly, Waterman Fine Art, Warrington Art, Manchester Art, Royal College Open, The Mall, British Art Show, Gallery 27, International Art Show, RA; one-man show: Gallery 27, Cork Street April (2002, 2004), RWS Gallery, Bankside, London, New Ashgate Gallery, Farnham, NEAC, 2005 Sunday Times Watercolour Invited Artist. *Works in collections*: The British Museum (The Grosvener Collection), Singer & Friedlander, Freshfields. *Commissions*: Est, est, est Restaurants: Chester, Alderley Edge, Edinburgh, Formby, Knutsford, Shrewsbury, Newcastle, Harrogate, Chiswick, Notting Hill Gate, Liverpool, Glasgow. *Publications*: 'Cheshire in Tuscany', 'Watercolour Expert'. *Official Purchasers*: Singer & Friedlander; Freshfields Bruckhaus & Deringer. *Works Reproduced*: Parker Harris. *Clubs*: Vice-President Royal Watercolour Society. *Address*: Orchid House, Old Park, St. Laurence, Ventnor, Isle of Wight PO30 1XR. *Email*: firmy.gilby@virgin.net *Website*: www.davidfirmstone.com *Signs work*: "David J. Firmstone," "David Firmstone," "D.Firmstone," "Firmstone."

FISHER, John Edward, BA Hons Fine Art; Fellow, Ravensbourne College of Communication. *Medium*: oil. *b*: Coventry, 7 Jul 1938. *s of*: Charles Sidney Fisher. *m*: Janet Mary Fisher. three *s*. *Educ*: Cheylesmore Secondary School; Coventry College of Art Junior Art Dept. *Studied*: Camberwell School of Arts and Crafts. *Represented by*: The Francis Kyle Gallery. *Exhib*: Group shows: The Italian Journey: Footsteps of J W Goethe (1987), Paradise is Here (1989), Mozart's Travels (Lincoln Centre, New York) and others. One-man shows (Francis Kyle Gallery) Villages and Valleys of the Ardeche (1988), Provence and Pamphylia (1989), Egypt and Italy (1991), Jordan and Italy (1993), Central Asia (1996), In Mongolia

(1998), Writers' rooms (2002), Writers' rooms II (2006), Writers' Rooms 3 (2008), Writers' Rooms 4 (2011) and Writer's Rooms 5 (2013). Lair of the Leopard: Twenty artists go in search of Lampedusa's Sicily (2005), Everyone Sang: A View of Siegfried Sassoon and his world by twenty five painters today (2006), That gong tormented sea: contemporary painters pursue the idea and reality of Byzantium (2009) and This twittering world: contemporary painters celebreate TS Eliot's Four Quartets. *Works in collections*: many private collections thoughout Europe and USA. *Commissions*: portraits in America and Saudi Arabia; The Guardian; The Artist. *Publications*: The Lair of the Leopard books. *Works Reproduced*: Writers' Rooms - i.e. Robert Graves museum. *Recreations*: fly fishing, clay pigeon shooting. *Clubs*: CPSA. *Address*: 88 Lee Road, Blackheath, London SE3 9DE. *Email*: j.fisher8@btinternet.com *Website*: www.franciskylegallery.com *Signs work*: "John Fisher".

FITZGERALD, Susan Margaret, BA (1978), MA (1988); full-time painter in water-colour and oil. *b*: Linc., 8 Jan 1946. *m*: Edward Michael Fitzgerald. two *s*. *Educ*: Boston Girls' Grammar School. *Studied*: York School of Art (1962-64), Sunderland College of Art (1964-67). *Exhib*: Chris Beetles Ltd., London; The Catto Gallery, London; World of Drawings and Water-colours, London; Adam Gallery, Bath; Bourne Gallery, Reigate; Medici Gallery, London; Nevill Gallery, Canterbury. *Commissions*: Medici Gallery, London, Nevill Gallery, Canterbury. *Misc*: Much time spent painting in France in her studio nr. Montpellier. Has lived/worked in Middle East and Far East. *Address*: Paragon House, 3 Stone Rd., Broadstairs, Kent CT10 1DY. *Signs work*: "Sue Fitzgerald."

FLEMING, James Hugh, BA Hons (1987); printmaker, painter, illustrator, lecturer, poet. *b*: Barrow in Furness. *s of*: James Arthur Fleming. *m*: Norma. one *s*. one *d*. *Studied*: Open University, Liverpool Polytechnic. *Exhib*: Acorn Gallery, Bluecoat Gallery, Hanover Gallery, Davey Gallery, Williamson A.G., Dee Fine Arts, Marie Curie Foundation, Merseyside Artists Touring Exhbn., Heffers, Oriel Mostyn, Cadaques Mini Print, Intaglio Mini Print, Manchester Academy, Humberside Printmaking Exhbn., Theatre Clwyd, Ruthin Craft Centre, Broekman A.G. *Clubs*: N.A.P.A., Wirral Soc. of Arts, A.B.W.S., Bluecoat Studio Printmakers' Group. *Address*: 19c Church Rd., West Kirby, Wirral, Merseyside L48 0RL. *Signs work*: "Jim".

FLEMING-WILLIAMS, Julia Elizabeth Catherine, Gilder. *Medium*: oil. *b*: Bournemouth, 10 Dec 1946. *d of*: Ian and Barbara Fleming-Williams. *m*: Edward Rooth. two *s*. one *d*. *Studied*: Farnham Art College; Hammersmith College of Art. *Represented by*: Rooths of Bradford-on-Avon. *Exhib*: RA, RWA, Chomé Gallery, Rooths Gallery, White Exmead. *Works in collections*: private. *Recreations*: keeping chickens. *Address*: 18 Market Street, Bradford-on-Avon BA15 1LL. *Email*: jecr@rooths.co.uk *Website*: www.rooths.co.uk *Signs work*: 'JFW' (and date).

FLEMMING, Anthony, First Class Hon Degree, Goldsmiths College, London. *Medium*: oil, watercolour, drawing, prints. *b*: London, 17 Apr 1936. *m*: Heather. three *d*. *Educ*: Frensham Heights. *Studied*: Goldsmiths College under Sam Rabin, Roberts Jones, Ken Martin, Rowland Hilder. *Exhib*: RI, RSMA, New Grafton, Duncan Campbell, Francis Iles, and in USA, Netherlands, France, Spain and Japan. *Works in collections*: Shell, BP, Woolwich BS, Bank of Bermuda, Shipowners Protection. *Commissions*: Shell, BP, Woolwich BS, Robotham Shipping, Shipowners Protection, Nat West Bank. *Recreations*: sailing. *Clubs*: MYC, Weald of Kent (President). *Address*: Four Winds, Beechenlea Lane, Swanley Village, Kent BR8 7PR. *Email*: tonyflemming@msn.com *Signs work*: 'Anthony Flemming'.

FLEMONS, David John. *Medium*: oil, watercolour, drawing, prints, airbrush. *b*: Portchester, 29 Mar 1938. *m*: Elaine Flemons. two *s*. *Studied*: Portsmouth Art College (1956-60); Municipal College, Portsmouth (1958 & 1959). *Represented by*: Goldfield Gallery, 24 High Street, Old Portsmouth. *Exhib*: since 1994; Alicante, Spain; Gaudamar &

Dolores; Open Air Shows (12 works sold) (2005-2006); One-Day Show for charity, Ingoldfield Farm (23 Feb1997), 1 mt showing, 10 works hung, Alexander Palace London (1994), Art in the Park (Summer 1994, 2 works sold). *Works in collections*: private (Close-up Poppy), Salisbury collector. *Commissions*: for Chicilian Restaurant, Portdown Hill Top (1961); Seascape 2 (16' x 18"oil), private. D.Day - One. *Publications*: Mail on Sunday, Print Sales 1994: oil 'Sound on Vision' After Evening Dinner with Elizabeth Quin, Actress, 'Children of a Lesser God' Lord Mayor Show, Portsmouth (1994). *Works Reproduced*: Storm over Isle of Wight Sands; Squall at Sally Port; Bluebell Woods; Tomatoes; Metal Fatigue; Womans Scorn, Party Poppers, Dark Side of Pale, Elements Meet, City Girls, Rainman Series, Old Portsmouth. *Recreations*: cars, horseriding. *Misc*: Specialist Renovation of Listed Buildings; Planning and Recording visual systems - sold worldwide to United Nations, UNICEF, etc. *Address*: Ingoldfield Farm, Ingoldfield Lane, Soberton, Hants., SO32 3QA. *Email*: DavidJFlemons@hotmail.com *Signs work*: "David J. Flemons".

FLETCHER, Adelene, NDD (1960), SBA (1989); artist in water-colour. *b*: Stockport, 6 Aug 1940. *m*: A.J. Fletcher. one *s.* one *d. Educ*: Fylde Lodge High School. *Studied*: Stockport Art School (1956-58), Manchester Regional College of Art (1958-60). *Exhib*: RI, RWS, SBA, and many mixed exhbns. *Publications*: author of books on flower painting, work is published in print, including limited editions. *Address*: 20 Alexandra Rd., Warlingham, Surrey CR6 9DU. *Signs work*: "A. Fletcher."

FLETCHER, Alistair Richard, BA Hons (1985), RE (1985), British Inst. award (1983), Commendation Stowells Trophy (1984), Garton and Cook award (1985); teacher, artist in etching, drawing and painting. *b*: Gosforth, Northumberland, 25 Jan 1963. *s of*: Gordon Richard Fletcher, B.A.Hons. *m*: E.M. Fletcher. two *s.* two *d. Educ*: Henry Smith School, Hartlepool. *Studied*: Cleveland College of Art and Design (1981-82), Kingston Polytechnic (1982-85), Bretton Hall (1986-87). *Exhib*: RE, Lowes Court Gallery, Egremont. *Address*: 8 John St., Moor Row, Cumbria CA24 3ZB. *Signs work*: "Alistair R. Fletcher."

FLÖCKINGER, Gerda, CBE; Freeman of the Goldsmiths Company; Honorary Fellow, University of the Arts. *Medium*: precious metals, inks, monotypes, photography, enamels. *b*: Innsbruck, Austria, 8 Dec 1927. *d of*: Anna Frankl & Karl Flöckinger. *m*: divorced. *Studied*: St.Martin's School of Art (1945-50), Central School of Arts and Crafts (1950-52 (etching), 1952-56 (jewellery techniques)). *Represented by*: Electrum Gallery; Adrian Sassoon; Mobilia Gallery. *Exhib*: solo exhibitions: The Crafts Centre of Great Britain (1968), V&A (1979, 1986, 2006), Bristol City Art Gallery & Museum (1971), Dartington Cider Press Gallery (1977), Crafts Council shop at the V&A (to celebrate her CBE, 1991), Electrum Gallery (2007). Group exhibitions worldwide since 1961. *Works in collections*: Bristol City Museum & Art Gallery, The Crafts Council, Royal Scottish Museum, Edinburgh, Schmuckmuseum Pforzheim, Germany, V&A, Centre Georges Pompidou, Paris, France, The Goldsmiths' Company, Boston Museum of Fine Art, USA, and many private collections. *Publications*: included in many publications worldwide since 1963. *Recreations*: Hybridising Iris Germanica, fashion, Siamese cats, driving. *Clubs*: University of the Arts. *Address*: c/o Catherine Williams, The Crafts Council, 44a Pentonville Road, London N1 9BY. *Email*: gerdaline@btconnect.com *Website*: www.mobilia-gallery.com/artjewel.html *Signs work*: "GF" on gold disc/more important pieces: "GF" plus flower - both on separate discs (gold).

FLOWER, Rosina Margaret, SAF, FPS; painter. *Medium*: oil, watercolour. *b*: London. *m*: Michael (decd). one *s.* one *d. Educ*: London and Headley. *Studied*: 1971-75 with Dennis Syrett (PROI), Bassetsbury Manor (Tom Coates PRBA, NEAC, RWS, RP), Burleighfield House (Anne Bruce). *Exhib*: RBA, ROI, Paris Salon, RSMA; Britains Painters, RWS; Galerie Hautefeulle, Paris; Bloomsbury Gallery; Langham Fine Art; Medici Gallery, Roy Miles Gallery; solo shows: Loggia Gallery, SW1; The Talent Store, Belgravia; Osterley Park

House, London; The Gallery, Henley Management College. *Works in collections*: in private hospitals and private collections. *Works Reproduced*: greetings cards, Daler Rowney catalogue. *Clubs*: FPS, SAF (Paris Salon), Visual Images Group. *Address*: 132 Roberts Ride, Hazlemere, Bucks. HP15 7AN. *Email*: rosina@rosinaflower.co.uk *Website*: www.rosinaflower.co.uk *Signs work*: "Flower," "R. Flower" or "Rosie".

FLUDGATE, Robert, artist in oil, pen and ink, pastel; specialising in pictures inspired by music and musicians; lovers and flowers; still life, portraits; also writes plays, poems, short stories. *b*: Islington, London, 18 Oct 1950. one *d. Educ*: Highbury Grove Grammar School. *Works in collections*: Channel Islands and London. *Address*: 15 St Mildreds Road, Ramsgate, Kent CT11 0EQ. *Signs work*: "Bob Fludgate," "R.E.G. Fludgate" or "R.E.G."

FLYNN, Dianne Elizabeth, DipAD (1973), ATC (1974); artist in oil, acrylic and water-colour; 1st Prize, Royal Overseas League. *b*: Yorkshire, 11 Oct 1939. *m*: Paul Hedley, painter. *Studied*: Manchester School of Art (1970-73), Leeds Polytechnic (1973-74). *Exhib*: Priory Gallery, Broadway; Walker Galleries, Harrogate; Galerie Chaye, Honfleur; MacConnal-Mason Gallery, London; Art Gallery Gérard, Wassenaar; Victorian Gallery, Dallas; Odon Wagner Gallery, Toronto; Thompson's Gallery, Aldeburgh & London; Wren Gallery, Burford; Gallery Joniskeit, Stuttgart; Jonathan Grant Galleries, Aukland, NZ. *Publications*: 'Portrait Drawing Techniques' (Batsford, 1979). *Recreations*: Reading, music. *Address*: 6 Powderham Cres., Exeter EX4 6DA. *Email*: dianne@dfph.elipse.co.uk *Signs work*: 'D.E.Flynn'

FOLAN, Andrew, RHA; ANCAD, HDFA; Douglas Hyde Gold Medal (1984). *Medium*: digital media, prints, sculpture. *b*: Donegal, 1956. *s of*: Peter Colm Folan. *m*: Dr Roisin Kennedy PhD. one *s.* one *d. Educ*: Mount St.Joseph's College, Roscrea, Tipperary, Ireland. *Studied*: National College of Art and Design, Dublin; Slade School of Fine Art, London. *Represented by*: Royal Hibernian Academy, Dublin. *Exhib*: solo exhbns: Ashford Gallery, Dublin (2002); Triskel Arts Centre, Cork (2000); Original Print Gallery, Dublin (1995); Project Arts Centre, Dublin (1982). *Works in collections*: Irish Museum of Modern Art, Trinity College Dublin, University College Dublin, The Irish Arts Council. *Commissions*: The Royal Hospital, Belfast; The Central Bank of Ireland; Temple Bar Properties, Dublin; The Mater Hospital, Dublin. *Publications*: The Works series (Gandon Editions, 1991); Profile (Gandon, 2002). *Address*: 45 Lower Mount Pleasant Avenue, Ranelagh, Dublin 06 Ireland. *Email*: andrewfolan@eircom.net *Website*: www.andrewfolan.com *Signs work*: 'Andrew Folan'.

FOLKES, Peter Leonard, ATD, RWA, RI, Hon FCA, Hon UA; painter in oil, water-colour and acrylic; Lecturer; Awarded a 'Mention in Dispatches' for Distinguished Service, 1946, by the Secretary of State for War. *b*: Beaminster, 3 Nov 1923. *s of*: Leonard Folkes. *m*: Muriel Giddings. two *s. Educ*: Sexey's School Bruton. *Studied*: West of England College of Art, Bristol (1940-42 and 1947-50). *Exhib*: RA, RWA, RI.; one-man shows: Crespi Gallery, New York (1965), University of Southampton (1965, 1973), Barzansky Gallery, New York (1967), Alwin Gallery, London (1970), Gainsboroughs' House Gallery, Sudbury (1977), RWA Galleries, Bristol (1986), Guildhall Gallery, Winchester (2001). *Works in collections*: Arts Council of Great Britain; RWA; Southampton Solent University; University of Southampton; private collections in Europe and America. *Commissions*: London Contemporary Art (2002). *Official Purchasers*: Arts Council of Great Britain, Royal West of England Academy. *Address*: 61 Ethelburt Ave., Swaythling, Southampton, SO16 3DF. *Signs work*: "Folkes."

FONTAINE, Fleur, SAI (1998); writer, painter in oil. *b*: Denmark, 25 May 1941. *m*: John Warren (divorced). one *s.* one *d. Studied*: Hørsholm Højskole (1959-60, Helge Ernst) and Skoulunde Stage Art (Knud Hegelund), Sorø Ungdom Skole (1958-59), South France

(1995-97 Pierre and Michel Mira). *Exhib*: The Mall Gallery, Orland House Gallery, Quaker Gallery, and others. *Works in collections*: throughout the world. *Commissions*: Euston Sq. Hotel. *Publications*: The Book of Life (1995). *Works Reproduced*: cards, booklets, teeshirts. *Clubs*: Danish Club (part of Dover St. Arts), Soc. for Arts of The Imagination. *Address*: 6 Pointers Cottages, Wiggins Lane, Ham, Richmond, Surrey TW10 7HF. *Website*: www.artmadness.co.uk *Signs work*: "FLEUR' FONTAINE."

FOINTAINE-WOLF, Rebecca, BA (Hons); ASWA (Associate Member of Society of Women Artists); Winsor & Newton Young Artists Award (2011). *Medium*: Oil, drawing, prints, mixed media. *b*: Southport, Australia, 16 Mar 1982. *Studied*: Surrey Institute of Art and Design (2000-2004) BA (Hons) Fine Art. *Exhib*: The Mall Galleries; The V&A; RCA; Cork Street; Meller Merceux Gallery; The Affordable Art Fair; The Chelsea Arts Club; MC & Saatchi; The County Hall Gallery; Opera Gallery, Budapest; The Paintworks, Bristol. *Works in collections*: Private/corporate. *Commissions*: Private. *Clubs*: The Chelsea Arts Club. Misc: Winner/finalist on BBC2's 'Show Me The Monet' (2011). *Address*: 33 Morrish Road, Brixton, London SW2 4EE. *Email*: info@rebeccafontaine-wolf.com *Website*: www.rebeccafontaine-wolf.com *Signs work*: "RFW".

FOORD, Susan Jane, BA (Hons) Fine Art (1983), RWA (1997); Granada Foundation Award, MAFA (1993). *Medium*: mixed media. *b*: London, 9 Jul 1945. two *s*. *Educ*: Manchester High School of Art (1958-60). *Studied*: Jacob Kramer College of Art, Leeds (1977-80), Leeds Polytechnic (1980-83). *Represented by*: Cube Gallery, London & Bristol. *Exhib*: solo: Adam Gallery (1998, 2000, 2001, 2003, 2005), RWA (1999); Offer Waterman & Co. Fine Art (1997); Old Town Hall, Havant (1993); mixed: RA Summer Show (1993-2003, 2007), RWA Autumn Exhbn. (1993-2011), Gallery 7, Hong Kong (1994-97); Art International, New York; EuropArt, Palexpo, Geneva; Musee du Prieure, Harfleur, France; Northern Young Contemporaries (1981); Aspex Gallery, Portsmouth (1990); Dean Clough, Halifax; two-person shows: Foss Fine Art, London (2006, 2008); The Manor House, Ilkley. *Works in collections*: RA., Arts Club, RWA Bristol, Provident Financial, Talbots, Leicestershire Collection for Schools and Colleges; private collections UK, Europe, USA., Asia. *Official Purchasers*: RA Arts Club; RWA; Provident Financial; Leicester Collection for Schools & Colleges. *Works Reproduced*: RA Illustrated (1994-5;1998; 2000); Pictures in an Academy, RWA; The Public Catalogue Foundation, Bristol. *Address*: 17 Downfield Rd., Clifton, Bristol BS8 2TJ. *Email*: sjfoord@hotmail.com *Signs work*: 'S.Foord', 'Susan Foord' or 'S.J.Foord'.

FORBES, Christine, ALAM (Hons); BA (Hons); Anthony Amies Award for Painting (2003). *Medium*: watercolour, drawing, acrylic and ink. *b*: 3 May 1951. *m*: Paul Martin. one *d*. *Educ*: private. *Studied*: Northbrook College, Worthing, W.Sussex. *Represented by*: www.numasters.com. *Exhib*: RA Summer Exhbn (2004); Worthing Art Gallery (mixed, 2003, 2004); The Capitol, Horsham (solo, 2004); Chequer Mead, E.Grinstead (2004). *Works in collections*: Ms. Stephanie Morgan. *Commissions*: various private. *Address*: 48 Forest Road, Worthing, W.Sussex BN14 9LY. *Email*: forbesart@aol.com

FORBES, Ronald, mem. Royal Scottish Academy, mem. Royal Glasgow Institute of the Fine Arts (RGI). *Medium*: painter. *b*: Perthshire, 22 Mar 1947. *m*: Sheena H. Bell. one *s*. two *d*. *Studied*: Edinburgh College of Art. *Represented by*: Sonia Zaks Gallery, Chicago; Hamnavoe Gallery, Aberdeen. *Exhib*: solo exhbns in Scotland, England, Ireland, Netherlands, Australia, USA. *Works in collections*: museums of Cork, Dundee, Perth, Smith/Stirling, Hunterian/Glasgow, Narodowego/Gdansk, State Library Queensland; Royal Scottish Academy; Universities of Strathclyde, Dundee and Abertay Dundee. *Publications*: most recent: 'Ronald Forbes: Riddles and Puzzles' (2002) with essay by Dennis Adrian, 'Ronald Forbes: (Mind) Games' with essay by Dr. Peter Hill (2005); 'Ronald Forbes: De Rerum Natura: The Nature of Things' (2009). *Misc*: visiting Professor at University of Abertay, Dundee. *Address*: 13 Fort Street, Dundee, DD2 1BS, Scotland. *Email*: ronnieforbes@blueyonder.co.uk *Website*: www.ronald-forbes.com *Signs work*: forbes.

FORBES COLE, Joy, NDD, Kingston (1958); landscape painter in oil; tutor in painting at Chiswick and Isleworth Polytechnics; Tutor Co-ordinator and founder member of Kew Studio. *Medium*: oil, watercolour and prints. *b*: London, 19 Dec 1934. *d of*: Frances Forbes Cole. *m*: Alban Clarke. *Educ*: Northlace School, Cheam. *Studied*: Sutton School of Art (1950-1953), Kingston College of Art (1956-1958) under Reginald Brill. *Exhib*: solo and group exhibs., London, Surrey, Hampshire and Kent. *Works in collections*: Lord Beaumont of Whitley, Dr. G.V. Planer. *Commissions*: CIBA (ARL) Ltd., G.V. Planer Ltd., Jermyn Industries. *Recreations*: music, reading, the countryside. *Clubs*: Richmond Art Society. *Address*: Flat 1, 24 Lambert Ave., Richmond, Surrey TW9 4QR. *Email*: joyforbes24@gmail.com *Signs work*: "J Forbes Cole."

FORD, Mary. *Medium*: paintings. *b*: London, 7 Jun 1944. *d of*: Mary & Anthony Ford-Whitcome. one *s*. one *d*. *Studied*: Byam Shaw School of Art (1970-73); Royal Academy Schools (1973-76). *Represented by*: Oliver Contemporary, London. *Exhib*: New Contemporaries (1972); CCA Galleries London (1976/86); RA Summer Exhbn (1977/79); Pallant House, Chichester (1985); Easton Rooms, Rye Art Gallery (1986); Roy Miles, London (1994); Wills Lane Gallery, St. Ives (1995-2006); Falmouth Art Gallery (2004); Oliver Contemporary, London (2002-14); solo exhbns: Sadlers Wells Theatre (1975); Eastgate Gallery, Chichester (1983); Oliver Contemporary, London (2003, 2008, 2010); Belgrave Gallery, St.Ives (2009-2013). *Works in collections*: Tate, London; Slaughter and May Art Collection, London. *Commissions*: private and business. *Works Reproduced*: Tate Publishing. *Clubs@* Penwith Society. *Address*: 69 Trevethan Road, Falmouth, Cornwall TR11 2AT. *Email*: mary@maryford.co.uk *Website*: www.maryford.co.uk *Signs work*: 'Mary Ford' or 'MF' (monogram).

FORD, Noel, Dog-Cartoonist of the Year-United Nations (Cartoonists Against Drug Abuse); Lindsay Awards (Australia); Yomiyori Shimbun (Japan). *Medium*: digital. *m*: Margaret. one *d*. *Educ*: Kegs Grammar School, Nuneaton. *Studied*: Birmingham College of Art (briefly). *Exhib*: many exhbns in UK, USA, Europe. *Works in collections*: Cartoon Arts Trust, The National Cartoon Archive - University of Kent, The Nuneaton Museum and Art Gallery. *Commissions*: all work is commissioned. *Publications*: UK national newspapers and magazines, various USA and Europe. *Recreations*: films, playing guitar, reading. *Clubs*: British Cartoonists Assoc., Cartoonists Club of GB, Professional Cartoonists' Organisation. *Misc*: professional cartoonist since 1975 (Feb). *Address*: Ty Rhyd, Ystrad Meurig, Ceredigion, SY25 6AX. *Email*: noel@fordcartoon.com *Website*: www.fordcartoon.com *Signs work*: Noel Ford.

FORD, Peter Anthony, Sen. Fellow RE (1990), VPRWA (2007), RWA (2000); artist, independent exhibition organiser and writer; co-proprietor of Off-centre Gallery, Bristol. Designer of bookplates (ex libris). *b*: 17 Apr 1937. *Partner*: Christine Higgott. one *s*. *Educ*: Hereford High School, St. Mary's College, Twickenham, Brighton College of Art, London University (Diploma in special education). *Studied*: Brighton College of Art (1960-1961) under Michael Chaplin RE, RWS (tutor in etching). *Exhib*: Create Centre Gallery, Bristol (2001), Daiwa Anglo-Japanese Foundation, London (2001), The New Gallery, RWA, Bristol (2007). *Works in collections*: Tate Gallery (Artists' Books Collection), Nat. Art Library, V&A Museum, Bibliotheque National, Paris, Ashmolean Museum, Oxford, Bristol City Museum; also public collections in Poland, Russia, Spain etc. *Publications*: A Time of Transition - Contemporary Printmaking In Russia and Ukraine; articles in A.N. (Artists' Newsletter); Printmaking Today; Grapheion. *Clubs*: member of The Bookplate Society. *Address*: Off-Centre Gallery, 13 Cotswold Rd., Bedminster, Bristol BS3 4NX. *Email*: offcentre@lineone.net *Website*: www.peterford.org.uk *Signs work*: "Peter Ford."

FOREMAN, Margaret, Winner, BP Portrait Award, National Portrait Gallery (1980); Royal Overseas League; Commonwealth Prize; Landseer Prize. *Medium*: oil, drawing. *b*: Kuala Lumpur, Malaysia, 27 Apr 1951. *d of*: J.E.A. Foreman & Kitty Whitehead. *m*: Martin Andrew Cheek. one *s.* one *d. Educ*: Bishops High School Guyana, Ladies College, Guernsey. *Studied*: Goldsmiths College (1969-73. 1973-76); Royal Academy Schools. *Represented by*: Martin Cheek. *Exhib*: Royal Academy Summer Show since 1972, also at the RBA Mall Galleries. Exhibited in Public and Private Galleries in London and Canterbury since 1976. *Works in collections*: National Portrait Gallery (Tulle House Carlisle Carel Weight Bequest), Royal Museum, Canterbury. *Commissions*: over 70 portrait commissions including: National Portrait Gallery, Rab Butler, Sir Richard Southern - St. John's College Oxford; Sir John Butterfield, Downing College Cambridge; Pears Soap Collection of Portraits; Lord Edmund Davies, University of Cardiff. *Principal Works*: Sir Richard Southern, St. Johns Oxford; The Follett family, private. *Recreations*: travel. *Clubs*: RBA (lapsed). *Misc*: It is important to the artist that she always paints from life, and for her portraits requires sittings. *Address*: Flint House, 21 Harbour Street, Broadstairs, Kent CT10 1ET. *Email*: maggiecheek@tiscali.co.uk *Website*: www.margaretforeman.co.uk

FORREST, Martin Andrew, BA (Hons), Dip Hist. Art, FSA (Scot.); artist in oil, art restorer, art historian, editor. *b*: Musselburgh, E. Lothian, 7 Jan 1951. *m*: Helen Forbes. one *s.* one *d. Educ*: Musselburgh Grammar School. *Studied*: Wimbledon School of Art (Maggie Hambling and David Poole) and post graduate Birmingham Polytechnic. *Exhib*: Royal Scottish Academy, RGI, Open Eye Gallery Edinburgh, Kemplay and Robertson, Edinburgh. *Works in collections*: private: UK, USA, France. public: University of Surrey, Serres Castet, France. *Commissions*: private figure, landscape, decorative art and portrait commissions. *Publications*: numerous publications and exhbn. catalogues; Introduction to 'The House that Jack Built' by Robert Burns; contributor to Grove's Dictionary of Art. *Address*: 10 Langtongate, Duns, Berwickshire, TD11 3AE.

FORRESTER, Denzil, BA Hons Fine Art, MA Fine Art; Korn Ferry International Award, RA Summer Show; Rome Scholarship; Harkness Fellowship. *Medium*: oil, drawing. *b*: Grenada, 12 Jan 1956. *Educ*: Stoke Newington Comprehensive, London. *Studied*: Hackney & Stoke Newington FE College, Central School of Art, Royal College of Art. *Exhib*: selected solo shows: Commonwealth Institute, London (1986); Limelight Club, New York (1987); 'Dub Transition' Touring Exhibition (1990-94); 'Farewell to Shadowland', 198 Gallery, London (1995) 'Memory and Images', Peterborough Museum & Art Gallery (1996); 'Two Decades of Painting' The Edward Wilmot Blyden Project (2002); The Cork Street Gallery, Mayfair (2008). *Works in collections*: Freshfields, London; Arts Council of Great Britain; Harris Museum & Art Gallery, Preston; Katie & Ian Walker, Atlanta, USA. *Publications*: 'Dub' (1990-94); Two Decades of Painting (2002). *Official Purchasers*: ACGB - Witch Doctor diptych (oil on canvas 304x396cm). *Works Reproduced*: Bag Bag (oil on canvas, 183x122cm). *Principal Works*: Funeral of Winston Rose (1982, oil on canvas 204x280cm). *Recreations*: travel. *Address*: 68 Woodland Rise, Muswell Hill, London N10 3UJ. *Email*: denzil@fsmail.net

FOSTER, Christine, SBA; painter in water-colour. *b*: Winsford, Ches., 16 Jul 1947. *m*: Stuart. *Exhib*: local and London. *Address*: 133 Swanlow Lane, Over, Winsford, Ches. CW7 1JB. *Email*: fostatwins@aol.com *Website*: www.lilacarts.co.uk *Signs work*: C and F intertwined.

FOSTER, Judith, NDD, ARCA; painter/printmaker in oil, water-colour, pastel, etching. *b*: 19 Oct 1937. *m*: Richard Pinkney. two *s. Educ*: Bath High School GPDST. *Studied*: Ipswich School of Art (1955-59, Philip Fortin, Colin Moss), RCA (1959-62, Carel Weight, Ruskin Spear, Ceri Richards), Abbey Minor Scholarship (1962). *Exhib*: one-man shows: Ipswich, Bath, Peterborough, Edinburgh, Northampton; group shows: UK, Belgium,

Finland, and RA, RCA. *Works in collections*: local authority collections; private collections UK, USA, Europe. *Clubs*: Suffolk Group, Ipswich Art Soc., Bearing 0900. *Address*: 10 The Street, Bramford, Ipswich, Suffolk IP8 4EA. *Signs work*: "J. Foster" or initials on small works.

FOSTER, Lord Norman Robert (Foster of Thames Bank), Baron 1999 (Life Peer), Kt. 1990, OM, RA, RDI Dip.Arch. (Manc.), M.Arch. (Yale), RIBA, FCSD, Hon. FAIA, Hon.BDA.; Chairman, Foster and Partners Ltd. *b*: Reddish, 1 Jun 1935. *s of*: Robert Foster. four *s*. one *d*. *Educ*: Burnage Grammar School, Manchester. *Studied*: architecture: Manchester University School of Architecture and Dept. of Town and Country Planning, Yale University School of Architecture. *Exhib*: RA, London, Paris, Bilbao, Barcelona, Seville, Tokyo, Florence, Nimes, Norwich, Manchester, Milan, New York, Zürich, München, Madrid, Hong Kong. *Works in collections*: Museum of Modern Art, N.Y., Centre Georges Pompidou, Paris. *Publications*: Norman Foster: Buildings and Projects Vols. 1, 2 & 3 (1990), Vol. 4 (1996). *Address*: Foster and Partners, Riverside Three, 22 Hester Rd., London SW11 4AN.

FOSTER, Richard Francis, RP; Lord Mayor's award for London Views (1972); painter in oil. *b*: London, 6 Jun 1945. *s of*: William Foster, M.A. *m*: Sally Kay-Shuttleworth. one *s*. two *d*. *Educ*: Harrow and Trinity College, Oxford. *Studied*: Signorina Simi, Florence (1963-66), City and Guilds, London (1967-70). *Exhib*: RA, RP; one-man shows, Jocelyn Feilding Gallery (1974), Spink & Son (1978, 1982, 1984, 1991, 1997); Portrait Retrospective "So Far" with Rafael Valls (1999), 'Further' with Partridge Fine Art (2003), 'Home and Away' with Indar Pasricha Gallery (2005); 'Just Now' The Gallery, Cork Street (2008), 'Still At It' Cork Street (2013). *Works in collections*: Royal Collection, National Portrait Gallery. *Clubs*: A.W.G., Chelsea Arts. *Misc*: Vice President R.P. (1991-1993), Hon Treasurer (2003-2006). Went with HRH The Prince of Wales to South America 2009 as official artist. *Address*: 5a Clareville Grove, London SW7 5AU. *Website*: www.richardfoster.co.uk *Signs work*: "Richard Foster."

FOUNTAIN, Desmond Hale, FRBS (1986), Pre-dip. (Stoke-on-Trent 1966), DipAD (Exeter), ATD/Cert.Ed. (Bristol 1970); sculptor, female nudes and life-size children, bronze editions of nine.*b*: Bermuda, 29 Dec 1946, divorced. *s of*: D.O.T. Fountain, accountant and Ruth Masters Fountain, artist. *m*: Egonora 'Luli'. one *s*. one *d*. *Educ*: Normanton College, Buxton, Derbys. *Exhib*: one-man shows (1980-96): Alwin Gallery, London; Coach House Gallery, Guernsey; Sally le Gallais, Jersey; Windjammer Gallery, Bermuda; Renaissance Gallery, Conn., USA; Cavalier Galleries, Conn., USA; The Sculpture Gallery, Bermuda; Falle Fine Art, Jersey; Bermuda National Gallery, The Desmond Fountain Gallery, newly opened in Hamilton, Bermuda; Royall Fine Art, Tunbridge Wells, Kent; Chasen Galleries, Richmond, Virginia, USA. *Works in collections*: throughout USA, Canada and Europe, numerous hotels, banks, public sites, corporations and Bermuda National Gallery. Founded the vehicle for Bermuda National Gallery (1982). *Publications*: 'Desmond Fountain: Sculptor' ISBN 09531 07019. *Address*: P.O. Box FL317, Flatts FLBX, Bermuda. *Email*: sculpture@ibi.bm, desfountain@logic.bm *Website*: www.desmondfountain.com *Signs work*: "Desmond Fountain" or "Fountain."

FOX, Jane Amber, ARBS (2007); MA Sculpture, BA Fine Art, BSc.Psychology, nurse, midwife, health visitor; Awards: The Welsh Poetry Competition (Specially Commended) (2007); Oppenheim Downes Memorial Trust Award (2003); ACAVA Studio Award (2002); MA Scholarship, RCA, London (1999-2001); The Prankard Jones Memorial Prize, Slade School, UCL (1997); The Monnington Prize, The Slade, UCL (1996); Entry Scholarship, The Slade, UCL (1995); Third and First Painting Prize, The Gwynedd Open, Holyhead, Wales (1994, 93). *Medium*: oil, drawing, sculpture, writer/poet/filmmaker. *b*: Tredegar, Wales. one *s*. *Studied*: RCA (1999-2001), The Slade School of Fine Art, UCL (1995-99); University College

Cardiff (1982-85). *Exhib*: 2008: Labyrinths in Europe, with Cynefin Theatre Company; 2007/2008: DACS-Politics Pays Back: Images of Political life in the UK and around the world; film showing of 'Where Now (An Eye for an Eye, and We're All Blind), Kowalsky Gallery, London; 2004: Raindance East Film Festival, Experimental Shorts, London; 2002: Experimentica, Chapter, Cardiff; 2002: Arcadia in the City, London. *Commissions*: 2000: Underground Movement, Feeringbury IX, Colchester; 1999: New Contemporaries on Tour, Liverpool Biennial and Beaconsfield Gallery, London. *Publications*: 2007: Cold and Conflict, Sex and Solar Plexus (published in Literary Pocketbook); 2006: White Rabbit (published in poetry anthology 'Routemasters and Mushrooms'); 2002: Arcadia in the City; 1999: New Contemporaries. *Principal Works*: Black Forms (1997); Forget your Perfect Offering (2000); Intimate Immensity (2001); Getting Ready, Never Ready, Ever Ready (2002); Where Now (An Eye for an Eye and We're All Blind) (2006); Microscope (2007). *Misc*: Sports Diver (BSAC). *Email*: info@janefoxartist.com *Website*: www.janefoxartist.com www.rbs.org.uk www.sculpturecymru.org.uk

FOX, Karrie, full membership NAPA; BA (Hons) Illustration. *Medium*: acrylic-semi abstract. *b*: Eastbourne, 13 Feb 1951. *d of*: Mrs. Barbara Fletcher. *m*: Dr. Simon Fox. three *s.* one *d. Educ*: St. Austell Grammar School. *Studied*: Falmouth College of Art, Cornwall. *Represented by*: various galleries throughout the UK including Chase Art, Wadebridge, Atishoo, St. Austell, Fisherton Mill, Salisbury. *Exhib*: National Acrylic Painters Association; Westminster Gallery; Falmouth Arts Centre; Obsidian Art, Stoke Mandeville; Otterton Gallery, Devon. *Works in collections*: Toshio Sakai, Japan. *Works Reproduced*: in Koi Keepers (front cover), Koi Ponds and Gardens, Koi Carp Magazine; limited editions prints on fine art paper, Giclee prints on Canvas, greeting cards. *Recreations*: running, yoga, skiing. *Clubs*: Falmouth Fine Arts. *Address*: Toll Lowarn, Penelewey, Truro, Cornwall, TR. *Email*: karriefox@me.com *Website*: www.artmaps.co.uk *Signs work*: karrie (lower case, on front of work), Karrie Fox on back of canvas

FOX, Peter, BA (Hons) Degree Fine Art. *Medium*: painting, printmaking, sculpture and assemblage. *b*: Kettering, 12 Apr 1952. *Educ*: Kettering School for Boys. *Studied*: Falmouth College of Arts 1979-82 under Francis Hewlett. Printmaking under Norman Ackroyd (Winchester). *Exhib*: Oriel 31 Gallery, Powys; Yew Tree Gallery, Morvah; Newlyn Art Gallery (Critic's Choice - Joan Bakewell); Royal Cornwall Museum, Truro; England & Co., London; Mall Galleries, London; Provincetown, New England, USA; 'Insiders: Art and the Box' touring UK (Arts Council, England); Atlantic Gallery Falmouth; Rowley Gallery London. *Works in collections*: Dartington Hall Trust, Schumacher College, Falmouth Art Gallery. *Publications*: ARTNSA (2002); 'St.Ives and Cornish Art 1975-2005' by Peter Davies (pub. 2007); Revolver: Art Cornwall by Jesse Leroy Smith. *Official Purchasers*: Falmouth Art Gallery *Principal Works*: Petroglyphs - series utilising slate and oil painted panels, gouache paintings, woodcut prints. *Recreations*: Latin American Percussionist with Quijada. *Misc*: Director of Redwing Contemporary Art, Penzance. *Address*: Little Treskello, Plain an Gwarry, Penzance, Cornwall TR17 0DU. *Email*: peter.fox400@gmail.com *Website*: peterfoxartist.co.uk www.axisartists.co.uk redwinggallery.co.uk *Signs work*: 'Peter Fox'.

FOX OCKINGA, Fyne Marianne. *Medium*: woodcut, drawing, watercolour. *b*: Baarn (Netherlands), 6 Feb 1943. *d of*: Willem Hendrik Okkinga. *m*: Robert Fox (journalist). one *s.* one *d. Educ*: MMS Hengelo (O) Netherlands. *Studied*: Bath Academy of Art, Corsham, Wilts (1960-63); Rijksakademie van Beeldende Kunsten, Amsterdam (1963-66). *Exhib*: from 1976 regularly in England and the Netherlands; RA Summer Exhbns; Barbican; Royal Festival Hall; Geffrye Museum; CTRL Visitor's Centre St.Pancras; Mall Galleries: 'Originals', 'Discerning Eye'; Open Studio shows since 1994 every year in Islington; and the Chocolate Factory; Galerie Van Heyningen, Den Haag; Netherlands: Galerie Petit Amsterdam, Rosa Spier Huis Laren (NH), Galerie Den Andel Groningen; Galerie Visée Diepenheim, Galerie "Leesbibliotheek" Zutphen, Galerie Koopmans, Eernewoude; Stadsmuseum Woerden 2012;

Buro Happold 2010; Stratford Old Town Hall 2012; Kingsgate Gallery 2012; Dutch Centre, Austi Friars 2013. *Works in collections*: ABN-AMRO Bank; Pilkington Corporate Collection; McAlpine; many private collections. *Commissions*: Arsenal-Emirates Stadium 2004-2005 Scenes of Construction; since 2001 a historical record of the changes at King's Cross St.Pancras with a second sponsored exhbn. in the LCR Visitor's Centre (2005); Kings Place construction, Olympic Stadium site 2009-2011; Graphic Calendar 2013 (Netherlands). *Publications*: illustrations for "Once More with Feeling", a book of classic hymns (Short Books, 2007); Logo for London Farmers' Market. *Recreations*: music, vocal and instrumental (piano, recorder). *Address*: 6 Thornhill Square, London N1 1BQ. *Email*: fmfoxockinga@gmail.com *Website*: www.mariannefoxockinga.co.uk *Signs work*: 'Marianne Fox Ockinga' or 'Marianne Ockinga'.

FRAME, Mary Elizabeth Bruce, BA Fine Art (Dunelm). *Medium*: oil, pastel, watercolour. *b*: Newcastle-upon-Tyne, 30 May 1936. *d of*: Thomas Bruce Frame. *m*: James Attree. one *d* from previous marriage. *Educ*: Rutherford High School, Newcastle-upon-Tyne. *Studied*: King's College, Durham University (1954-58). *Exhib*: mixed exhibitions: Royal Institute of Painters in Watercolour; Pastel Society; Royal West of England, Bristol; Fosseway Artists, Helios Group. one-man: Braemar, Ullapool, London, Durham, Isle of Colonsay. *Works in collections*: Westminster Council. Private collections in the UK, USA and Europe. *Commissions*: private. *Recreations*: drawing, travel, walking. *Address*: Fordhill Lodge, Temple Guiting, Cheltenham, Glos. GL54 5XU. *Email*: frameattree@btinternet.com *Website*: www.maryframepaintings.co.uk *Signs work*: "MARY FRAME".

FRAME, Roger Campbell Crosbie, CA (1973); Secretary of: RSW; Chartered Accountant. *b*: Glasgow, 7 Jun 1949. two *s.* one *d. Educ*: Glasgow Academy. *Clubs*: Glasgow Art. *Address*: 29 Waterloo St., Glasgow G2 6BZ.

FRANC, Barbara, sculptor in wire. *b*: London, 27 Oct 1954. *m*: Philip Sindall. one *d. Studied*: Morley College of Art (John Bellany, Maggie Hambling). *Exhib*: Phillips International Auctioneers, Molesey Gallery, Roy Miles Gallery, Fitch's Ark, Usiskin Contemporary Art, Worthing Museum; Sculpture Prize, Chelsea Art Soc., Linley & Co., Pimlico. *Commissions*: d.p.ua advertising agency - 6' fish for their offices, group of birds for LCA. *Publications*: Garden Crafts by Geraldine Rudge, Country Living, Homes & Gardens, Painting World, Country Homes & Interiors magazines. *Clubs*: Nine Elms Group of Artists. *Address*: 11 Queen's Gdns., Ealing, London W5 1SE. *Email*: barbara.franc@btinternet.com *Signs work*: "Babara Franc."

FRANCYN, (Dehn Fuller), FFPS, WIAC, NS; painter in oils and gouache. *b*: Portsmouth. *d of*: Walter Henry Fuller, lecturer. *m*: Curt Dehn. one *s.* one *d. Educ*: at home. *Exhib*: one-man shows: Paris, The Hague, Utrecht, Sydney, London; group shows: Free Painters and Sculptors, WIAC, Hampstead Artists, NS, etc. *Works in collections*: Holland, Germany, USA, Australia. *Publications*: Poems, Man's Moment (USA), portfolio of folk-songs, collection of poems. *Clubs*: I.C.A., Hampstead Artist. *Address*: 6 Elsworthy Ct., Elsworthy Rd., London NW3.

FRANK, Dianne, SBA, OAS. *Medium*: coloured pencil, watercolour, gouache, pencil. *b*: Vancouver, 11 Oct 1950. *m*: Robert C.Allen, FBA. one *s. Studied*: UBC (BA, 1994); self-taught artist. *Exhib*: SBA Annual Exhbns (2004, 2006, 2007, 2008, 2009, 2010, 2011, 2012); Oxford Artweeks (2003-12); Broad Face & St. Nicholas Church, Abingdon; University of Oxford, Dept. of Economics; Oxford Art Society (2007, Said Bus. School; 2008, Woodstock, Oxon). *Address*: 9 Salisbury Crescent, Oxford, OX2 7TJ. *Email*: diannelfrank@hotmail.com *Signs work*: 'D.FRANK', 'D.F.', 'DIANNE FRANK'.

FRANKLIN, Annette Winifred, HS; artist in water-colour, oil, pastel, pen and ink, and gouache; miniature portraitist, Poole Pottery paintress (1945-50); CSA. *b*: 28 Jan 1932;

Adopted from orphanage 1936. Blood father Lesley Rex Ferguson, blood mother Winifred E.Ballard. *m*: Stanley Franklin. *Educ*: St. James and Henry Harbin Schools, Poole. *Studied*: mainly self taught, some tuition - pottery painting: (John Adams, Ruth Pavley); oil painting: (Leonard and Margaret Boden). *Exhib*: RMS & RWS at Mall Galleries., Westminster Hall, Hilliard Society, Gatcombe Farm, Royal School of Needlework, Foyles London, College of Fashion and Design, Wallsworth Hall. *Works in collections*: UK, USA, Australia, Bahrain, Abu Dhabi, NZ, The Princess Royal & Capt. Mark Phillips. *Publications*: Quilting and Design by M. McNeal; articles for Poole Pottery Collectors Club and Hilliard Society Magazine. *Official Purchasers*: portraits in oil of Sir Peter Scott, Simon Combes (wildlife artist), Peter Scott (Gliding Club Nympsfield), President of World Wide Helicopters (Mr Arnie Sumarlidison, USA), various commissions. *Works Reproduced*: painted own designs on vases and plaques, also on china and wooden boxes. *Principal Works*: The United Arab Emirates Emblem (for the Ruler of Sharja). *Recreations*: gold and silver embroidered on wild silk. *Clubs*: Fine Art Promotions, Poole Pottery Artist Collectors Club, Lansdown Art, Fosseway-Artist. *Address*: 'Sunnymead', 15 Marsh Lane, Leonard Stanley, nr. Stonehouse, Glos. GL10 3NJ.

FRANKLIN, Linda Ann AFAS, BA (Hons) Visual Arts AFAS; Artist in residence Lansdowne Club, Mayfair, London (2008-09), full member AFAS. *Medium*: Mixed media; acrylic; enamel. *b*: Naples, 30 Dec 1955. *m*: Simon Franklin. one *s*. one *d*. *Educ*: Holy Cross Convent. *Studied*: Elizabeth Gaskell College Speech Therapy (1974-75); Army Officer (1976-79): Winchester School of Art (2000-2004). *Represented by*: Jenny Weinberger Gallery, Wilts. *Exhib*: Society of Women Artists, Mall Galleries, London (2012); Armed Forces Art Society, Mall Galleries, London (2009, 2010, 2011); Discerning Eye, Mall Galleries, London (2010); Chelsea Art Society, London (2009, 2010, 2011); Lansdowne Club, Mayfair, London (2008); solo show; Chanly Gallery, Kensington, London (2006, 2008). solo shows; local Wiltshire exhibitions. New York 11th Avenue (2012), Edinburgh Art Fair (2013), Mall Galleries, London (2013), Bristol Art Fair (2013), New Chelsea Art Gair, London (2013). *Works in collections*: Lansdowne Club, Mayfair, London. *Official Purchasers*: Lansdowne Club, Mayfair, London "The Heart of Battle" work in their collection. *Recreations*: Tennis, riding. *Clubs*: AFAS. *Address*: Castleton House, Donhead St Mary, Shaftesbury, Dorset SP7 9DQ. *Email*: linda@franklinart.co.uk *Website*: www.franklinart.co.uk *Signs work*: "L A Franklin".

FRANSES-BEAN, Debra, Student of the Year (2004) Digitex Print Prize; Edward James Bursary, Sculpture (2003). *Medium*: Oil; sculpture; wallpaper. *b*: London, 9 Dec 1967. *m*: Jonathan. one *s*. *Studied*: Kennington City & Guilds (2001-2002); Central Saint Martins (2002-2005). *Represented by*: Mark Jason Gallery, London; Wanrooij Gallery, Holland. *Exbib*: Art Chicago; Art London; 20/21 Royal College of Arts; Engrave Danger, Venice (2004); London Design Festival (2010, 2011); Artware Editions, New York; Manart, Paris. *Works in collections*: Misc. private and corporate in UK, Europe, USA. *Commissions*: Private. *Publications*: Artists Kitchens and various magazines. *Works Reproduced*: Sculptures available in editions of eight. *Principal Works*: Sculptures of resin handbags containing recycled objects. *Recreations*: Cycling, yoga, travel. *Clubs*: Broadwater Sailing; Dover Street Arts Club. *Address*: The Red House, Summerhouse Lane, Harefield, Uxbridge UB9 6HX. *Email*: dfbean3@mac.com *Website*: www.artbag.me *Signs work*: "D F BEAN".

FREARS, Naomi, *Medium*: Painter and printmaker. *b*: Leicestershire, 3 Mar 1963. *m*: John. one *d*. *Studied*: Loughborough, foundation (1981-82); Sunderland, BA and printmaking prize (1982/6). *Represented by*: Beaux Arts, Bath; Millennium Gallery, St Ives. *Exhib*: Solo shows at Beaux Arts, Bath and Millennium Gallery, St Ives. Group Shows include Tate, St Ives; Newlyn Art Gallery; The Exchange, Penzance; Falmouth Art Gallery; Royal West of England Academy. *Works in collections*: Including The Wilson Collection; Slaughter and May; Falmouth Art Gallery; Sunderland University; Falmouth College of Art;

Cornwall County Council. *Publications*: Art Now Cornwall, Tate Publications; Artists Studios, MJ Long. *Recreations*: Cinema, motorcycling. *Clubs*: Ladies and Gentlemen of the Arts Walking Club. *Misc*: Member - Newlyn Society of Artists; Founder member - Porthmeor Printmakers. *Address*: 4 Fern Glen, St Ives, Cornwall TR26 1QP. *Email*: naomifrears@hotmail.co.uk *Website*: www.naomifrears.com *Signs work*: "NAOMI FREARS".

FREEMAN, Janet A., B.Ed (Hons), BSA. *Medium*: painting/oils. *b*: Bedford, 5 Dec 1933. *m*: Richard Freeman. three *s*. one *d*. *Studied*: Goldsmiths' School of Art, University of London; Bath Academy of Art, Bath Spa University. *Represented by*: Duncan Campbell Fine Art, London.; Gallery Nine, Bath. *Exhib*: Duncan Campbell, London, Royal Academy Summer Exhibition, NEAC London, Millfield Open, RWA, Annual Bristol, School House Gallery Bath, Laing Open, Black Swan Guild Frome, Bath University, Rob Whittle Fine Art, Birmingham, Victoria Art Gallery, Bath yearly; Gallery Nine, Bath. *Works in collections*: Marquis of Bath, Leonard Mannaseh PPRWA. *Publications*: The Duncan Campbell Collection, Bloomsbury Auctions, London, 'Bath Society of Artists - a history' (2013). *Clubs*: Bath Soc. of Artists. *Address*: 7 Portland Terrace., Bath BA1 2SH. *Signs work*: "J.A. Freeman."

FREEMAN, John, NDD, ATD (Sheffield, 1965); Taught Armthorpe School (1963-69). *Medium*: watercolour, drawing, prints. *b*: Doncaster, 12 Jul 1942. *s of*: Tom Freeman. one *s*. *Educ*: Doncaster Technical High School (1954-59). *Studied*: Doncaster School of Art (1959-63); Sheffield (ATD Course 1964-65). *Exhib*: Whitby (1967), Doncaster (1968, '69, '74), Leeds (1969); Stoke-on-Trent, Harrogate, York, Guildford, Leeds, Darlington, Ibiza, Middlesborough, Jersey (1985, '87, '89, '91, '95, '97), Beverley Darlington, Scarborough (1989, 1991); RSMA (1999); permanent exhibition of work in Whitby studio. *Commissions*: RCA Ltd., British Steel Corporation; RAF Fylingdales, British Coal, The Ogden Group Cater Allen Bank Jersey, Abbey National Overseas, Jersey Telecom, Studio 18 St. Helier, Hargreaves Quarries, Bradford Exchange, ICI Wilton, Wentworth Puzzles Ltd., plus many private commissions. *Publications*: 2 instructional DVDs. *Works Reproduced*: over 60 limited edition prints, self-published. *Principal Works*: "The Pull"; "The Launch" - epic Lifeboat studies. *Clubs*: Vice President, Whitby Art Society; Fylingdales Group of Artists. *Misc*: 4 TV appearances, images used by RNLI, now well known for nocturne watercolours - specialises in the Whitby area. *Address*: Studio of John Freeman, 9 Market Place, Whitby, YO22 4DD. *Email*: john@johnfreemanstudio.co.uk *Website*: www.johnfreemanstudio.co.uk *Signs work*: "J. FREEMAN".

FREEMAN, Lily, FPS, BA Hons (1978); painter in oil and water-colour; lectured on Modern Art, Univ. of 3rd Age for 15 years. *b*: Vienna, 7 Feb 1920, widow. *d of*: Hans Fischer. one *d*. *Educ*: Realgymnasium, Vienna. *Studied*: Vienna, Arthur Segal School, Hampstead (A. Segal, Marianne Segal). *Exhib*: NY Expo (1985), Barbican (1982), Orangery, Holland Pk. (1979, 1981-85), Alicante, Spain (1983), Loggia Gallery (1978, 1982, 1984), Cockpit Theatre, Odeon Marble Arch, Hampstead Town Hall, New Art Theatre, Alpine Club, Hampstead Art Centre, Ben Uri Gallery (The London Jewish Museum), Royal Overseas League, Guildhall, London, Tradescant Trust, Leighton House, Burgh House. *Works in collections*: Dr. Lansky, Vienna; Hendon School, London. *Publications*: Preparation for publication of total life's work is in progress. *Address*: 65 Dunstan Rd., London NW11 8AE. *Website*: www.happypaintings.co.uk *Signs work*: "Freeman".

FREEMAN, Michael John, NDD, ATD. *Medium*: oil, watercolour, drawing, prints. *b*: Swansea, 10 Apr 1936. *s of*: John Stanley Freeman. *Partner*: Shirley Duckfield. *Educ*: Bishop Gore Grammar School, Swansea (1947-55). *Studied*: Swansea School of Art (1955-58, Teaching Diploma). *Represented by*: Fountain Fine Art, Llandeilo; West Wales Art Centre, Fishguard. *Exhib*: Welsh Group; MoMA Machynlleth; National Museum of Wales;

The Bar Covent Museum, York (1993); Retrospective 1964-84: Glynn Vivian Art Gallery & Museum (1985), Queens Hall, Narbeth (2001); also organised 32 annual public student shows (extra-mural Uni & WEA) of paintings, drawings and prints (1971-2003). *Works in collections*: Welsh Arts Council; Glynn Vivian, Swansea; Bangor College, and numerous private collections in UK, Germany, Sweden, USA & Canada. *Commissions*: not accepted. *Publications*: Dictionary of British Artists since 1945 by David Buckman. *Works Reproduced*: booklet covers on Marco Polo & Naxos CDs; in exhibition catalogues and reviews. *Principal Works*: Series 1 Shipwrecks; 2 Crabsongs; 3 Canute; 4 Via Crucis (14 Stations). *Recreations*: music, but also published musicology - writings chiefly on Joseph Holbrooke (1878-1958) and other British composers, mainly in British Music Society and 'Welsh Music'. *Clubs*: British Music Society (retd), Welsh Group. *Misc*: My best teacher was the composer Edmund Rubbra. *Address*: 11 Walters Street, Manselton, Swansea, SA5 9PL. *Signs work*: "FREEMAN" and date (e.g. FREEMAN '08) on verso.

FREEMAN, Ralph. *Medium*: painting and construction. *b*: London, 15 Jan 1945. *m*: Catherine. two *d. Studied*: Harrow and St.Martin's Schools of Art (1961-65). *Represented by*: Thackeray Gallery, London. *Exhib*: Tate St. Ives, Freud Museum, Camden Arts Centre, Royal Cornwall Museum, Gardner Arts Centre, Artspace, Millennium Gallery, Wordsworth Trust, Edinburgh Festival, Falmouth Arts Gallery, Maidstone Museum, Chicago Expo, Newlyn and Penwith Galleries, Thackeray Gallery. *Works in collections*: Yad Vashem Museum, Israel, Freud Museum, London, Falmouth Art Gallery. *Commissions*: 'Man, Spirit, Energy' Albion Project. *Publications*: Foundations & Fragments, Tate Gallery St. Ives, D Cohen Freud Museum, Foundations and Fragments by E. Davies; More Than the Message, M. Bird, New Millennium Gallery; The Book Show; Journal of History of Modern Art, G. Morra. *Recreations*: Jazz pianist and composer. *Misc*: Visiting lectureships: Central St Martins, Falmouth University, Sussex University, University of Central England, Bournemouth College of Art. *Address*: 52 Canfield Gardens, London NW6 3EB. *Email*: ralph@ralphfreeman.co.uk *Website*: www.ralphfreeman.co.uk *Signs work*: Freeman or RF.

FREEMAN, Richard, M.Ed, RWA; BS Artists; Morris Singer Award, RWA (1997); sculptor in clay, plaster, bronze. *Medium*: ceramic sculpture, bronzes, mixed media, paint/acrylic on board. *b*: Windsor, 12 Apr 1932. *m*: Janet Freeman. three *s.* one *d. Studied*: Goldsmiths' College, Univ. of London, Chelsea Art School, London, University of Bristol. *Exhib*: recent shows include McHardy Sculpture Co. London, Wills Lane Gallery St. Ives, Anthony Hepworth Fine Art Bath, School House Gallery Bath, RWA Annual Bristol (1992-2009), Victoria Art Gallery, Bath; Duncan Campbell Fine Art, London; Gallery Nine, Bath. *Works in collections*: Royal West of England Academy, Bristol; The Ken Stradling Collection, Bristol; internationally, Derek Balmer, RWA. *Publications*: RWA magazines, 'Bath Society of Artists - a history'. *Clubs*: RWA Bristol, Senior Academician; Bath Society of Artists. *Address*: 7 Portland Terrace., Bath BA1 2SH. *Signs work*: "FREEMAN" or "R.F."

FREER, Roy, NDD, ATD, ROI, RI, NEAC; artist in oil and water-colour; art course tutor and organiser, demonstrator, lectures on appreciation of painting and drawing. *Medium*: oil and watercolour. *b*: Birmingham, 1938. *m*: Sally Freer. two *s. studied*: Bournville School of Art, and Birmingham College of Art. *Represented by*: Federation of British Artists, Mall Galleries, London. *Exhib*: The Callo Gallery, London; Anna Mel Chadwick Gallery, London; The Ceddar House Gallery, Surrey; The Chappel Gallery, Essex; Barry Whittlington Fine Art, Henley-on-Thames *Clubs*: Societies: New English Art Club, Royal Institute of Painters. *Address*: 5 Bridgefoot, Cross Street, Sudbury CO10 2DG. *Email*: royfreer@btinternet.com *Website*: www.royfreer.co.uk *Signs work*: "ROY FREER".

FREETH, Peter, RA, RE; Dip. Fine Art Slade School (1960), ARA, (1990), Elected RA (1990), RE (1989); printmaker in etching, aquatint, water-colour, teacher; Tutor of Etching, RA Schools, London; Awards: Prix de Rome, Engraving (1960), RA Summer Exhbn: Best

Print (1986), Hunting Art Prizes: Drawing/Print Prize (2002, 2004). *b*: B'ham, 15 Apr 1938. *s of*: A.W. Freeth. *m*: Mariolina. two *s*. *Educ*: KEGS Aston, B'ham. *Studied*: Slade School of Fine Art (1956-60, Antony Gross, William Coldstream); British School in Rome. *Represented by*: Beardsmore Gallery, London NW5. *Exhib*: RA, RE, Christopher Mendez, London SW1, Bankside Gallery (2001), London SE1, Beardsmore Gallery, London NW5, City Gallery, EC3, Mary Kleinman Gallery, N1, Christchurch College Picture Gallery, Oxford (2005); 'My Affairs with Resin', Retrospective, Royal Academy, Tennant Room (2008-9). *Works in collections*: V&A, BM, Arts Council, Fitzwilliam Cambs., Metropolitan Museum, NY, National Gallery, Washington, Ashmolean, Oxford, Govt. art collection, Hunterian Museum, Glasgow. *Recreations*: music, reading. *Address*: 83 Muswell Hill Rd., London N10 3HT. *Signs work*: "P. Freeth."

FREUNDLICH, Grace Ruth, Travelling Fellowship, Scottish Arts Council (1979), Fellowship, Provincetown Workshop (1976); artist in acrylic, ink, oil, graphite; instructor; exhbn. com., Provincetown Art Assoc. and Museum. *b*: New York, 6 May 1939. two *s*. *Educ*: University of Wisconsin, Madison (1964), art & art history; CUNY (NY); HS of Music & Art, NYC. *Studied*: Hunter College Graduate School (Bob Swain), Provincetown Workshop (Leo Manso, Victor Candell). *Exhib*: Gallery Matrix, Provincetown (1993, 1994), Foundry Gallery, Washington, D.C. (1981), Demarco Gallery, Edinburgh (1980), Provincetown Workshop (1976), Provincetown Art Assoc. and Museum (1986-96); solo show, Roosevelt House of Hunter College, N.Y. (1975), Galerie Henri, Boston, Mass. (1961). *Works in collections*: University of Wisconsin, Hunter College, Histadrut, Israel, American Forum, National Press Bldg., Washington D.C.; and Ilana Soesman, Israel, Marion Namenwirth, St. Paul, Minn., A&S Hoffman, Jerusalem, Israel. *Commissions*: The Land meets the Sea, The Sea meets the Land, American Forum, Washington DC. *Publications*: Precis, with Robert E. Miller on exhbns. at Gallery Matrix, Provincetown. *Clubs*: College Art Assoc., National Women in the Arts Museum, Washington, D.C. Provincetown Art Assoc. and Museum. *Misc*: Scottish Arts Council fellowship/travelling, through Richard Demarco. *Address*: 200 W. 93rd St. 4J, New York, N.Y. 10025 USA. *Email*: graciousf@earthlink.net *Signs work*: "G.F." or "G. Freundlich."

FREW, Hilary, FRBS (1960), RBA (2000), Cert RAS, ATD, PGCE; Leverhume Award (1961); sculptor in Portland stone; design technology teacher (1979-1993), now freelance sculptor; Mem. Sec. RASA/Reynolds Club at Royal Academy; De Lazlo Award 2009. *Medium*: stone carving, modelling for bronze, silver work. *b*: Essex, 30 Mar 1934. *m*: G.R. Bonye. one *s*. one *d*. *Educ*: convents in Buckingham, Felixstowe and Bedford, St. Andrews University. *Studied*: S.E. Essex School of Art (1954-1957) (under T.B.Huxley Jones), Royal Academy Schools (1957-1961) (Maurice Lambert, and Arnold Machin); Stockwell College (1972-1973), Goldsmith's College (1978-1979). *Exhib*: Mall Galleries, Royal British Society of Sculptors, numerous group society exhibitions in Trails and Garden Galleries in London and the S.E. as well as Florence and USA. *Works in collections*: Bromley Educ. Authority and many private collections. *Commissions*: Many private commissions including portraits. *Recreations*: photography, sculpture, swimming. *Address*: Dees Holt, Raggleswood, Chislehurst, Kent BR7 5NH. *Email*: info@hilaryfrew.com *Website*: www.hilaryfrew.com *Signs work*: "H F." as monogram.

FRIEDEBERGER, Klaus, painter. *b*: Berlin, 1922. *m*: Julie. *Educ*: Quakerschool Eerde, Netherlands. *Studied*: E. Sydney Tech. College. *Exhib*: one-man shows: Belfast (1963); Aberystwyth School of Art (2009); London 1963, 1986, 1990, 1992, Works 1940-1970 (2007); group shows since 1944. Europe Prize, Ostende 1964 (Gold Medal), National Gallery of Australia, 'Surrealism' (1993), 'The Europeans' (1997). *Works in collections*: private: Australia, England, Europe, U.S.A. Official purchases: Mosman Art Prize 1949, National Gallery of Australia, British Museum, University of Wollongong. *Publications*: Encyclopedia of Australian Art, Twenty Five Years Annely Juda Fine Art (London 1985),

Surrealism (Canberra 1993), The Dictionary of Art /Grove Art Online (OUP), The Europeans (Canberra 1997), Dictionary of Artists in Britain since 1945, Klaus Friedeberger Works 1940-1970 (London 2007), Recent Work (Aberystwyth 2009); Australian Art and Artists in London 1950-1965 (2012). *Address*: 16 Coleraine Rd., London SE3 7PQ. *Signs work*: "Friedeberger."

FROEHLICH, Cadi, BA Hons, MA Fine Art, Awards: Jerwood Drawing Prize, 2nd (2010), Red Mansion Prize (2014). *Medium*: sculpture. *b*: Portsmouth, 17 May 1973. *Studied*: University of Birmingham (1995); San Jose State University (Certification, 1999); Brighton University (FdA, 2011); Camberwell & Chelsea (2013). *Represented by*: Made in Arts, London (MiAL). *Exhib*: Brixton East (2014); Dalston Point Zero, London (MiAL, 2014); Creekside Open, APT (2013); Space Station 65, London (2013); John Hansard Gallery, Southampton (2012); Beaconsfield Arts, London (2012); Hannah Barry, London (2012); Peckham Open (2011); Daily-Weekly, Brisbane, Australia (2011); Tenderpixel (curated, 2011); Jerwood Drawing Prize (2010); Without Borders, San Jose, California (1998). Solo shos: (o)ccupant #7, Grey Area Gallery, Brighton. *Works in collections*: Chelsea College Library Special Collection. *Commissions*: Grey Area Gallery, Brighton; White Night 2011, Brighton. *Publications*: 2014 Axis Web MA Stars digital publication; JAWS UAL first edition (2013); Expedition, CCW, London (2012). *Address*: 313 Ditchling Road, Brighton BN1 6JJ. *Email*: now@cadifroehlich.co.uk *Website*: www.cadifroehlich.co.uk *Signs work*: "CF".

FRÖHLICH-WIENER, Irene, sculptress in bronze, stone, wood, fibreglass, cement. *b*: Luzern, Switzerland, 26 Aug 1947. *d of*: Sigmund Wiener. *m*: Josef Fröhlich. two *d*. *Educ*: Kantons-Schule, Luzern (Matura), Institut Maïeutique (Art-therapy). *Studied*: Centre de la gravure Contemporaine, Geneva (1969), Marylebone Inst. (1973-74, carving under E. Mehmet), HGS Inst. (John Brown), Sir John Cass School of Art (Clive Duncan). *Exhib*: RBA, Royal Festival Hall, Camden Art Centre, Woodstock Gallery, Smee Gallery, Norfolk, Ben Uri Gallery (The London Jewish Museum), Mall Galleries, Old Bull Art Centre, Draycott Gallery, Blenheim Gallery, Cecilia Coleman Gallery, October Gallery, dfn Gallery, USA (New York). *Works in collections*: Helmut Stern Collection, Michigan, McHardy Sculpture Co., London, Gold Art, Haifa. *Commissions*: Rank Xerox (1996) award. Hertsmere: Bushey Park (1998), 'Tree of Life' Finchley Synagogue (1999), Florida Parc, Lugano (2001). *Clubs*: H.V.A.F. and Royal Soc. of Sculptors, F.P.S. *Address*: Via Cassarinetta 2, CH 6900 Lugano, Switzerland. *Website*: www.breakingart.com.//:irene *Signs work*: "Irène."

FROST, Anthony, DFA (1973); South West Open Prizewinner; artist in acrylic paint on canvas. *b*: St. Ives, Cornwall, 4 May 1951. *s of*: Terry Frost, artist. *m*: Linda Macleod. two *s*. *Educ*: North Oxon. Technical College and School of Art, Banbury. *Studied*: Cardiff College of Art (1970-73). *Represented by*: Advanced Graphics London, The Somerville Gallery Plymouth, Beaux Arts London. *Exhib*: Four Young Artists, Penwith Gallery, St. Ives; John Moores, Liverpool; Public Hanging, St. Ives; Dangerous Diamonds, Hull; Anthony Frost - on Colour, Newlyn Gallery; "Viva Blues" Newlyn Gallery (1996), touring Birmingham, Darlington and London (1997); The Belgrave Gallery, London (1997); King's University, Cambridge (1998); Corporate Connoisseurs, London (1999); Jersey Arts Centre, Jersey (1999), Hilsboro Fine Art, Dublin (2001); Corporate Connoisseurs, London (2001); Advanced Graphics, London (2001); The Original Print Gallery, Dublin (2002), 'Big Colour in Space' Space Gallery Penzance (2003), 'Zig Zag Wanderer' The Somerville Gallery, Plymouth (2004); 'Lunar Notes Neon Dreams' Advanced Graphics, London (2005). *Works in collections*: John Moores, Liverpool, Nuffield Trust, Contemporary Arts Soc., Cornwall C.C., Kasser Foundation, New York, Whitworth Gallery Manchester, The Bank of America, Canary Wharf London, Addenbrooks NHS Cambridge, Truro Museums and Art Galleries, Devon CC, Contemporary Irish Art Society, Limerick Museum and Art Gallery.

Commissions: UNESCO Paris, CDC IXIS Bank of France, Mutuelle Générale Assurance corporation Paris, The Eden Project - planting design for fodder crops exhibit in the roofless biome. *Publications*: "Viva Blues", 'Zig Zag Wanderer'. *Clubs*: Subbuteo Football, Petangue, Boule. *Misc*: performance "The Fast and Bulbous" Show Painter, Poet Head to Head! - Anthony Frost and Phil Bowen. Also "The Stand Upslide Show"- Anthony Frost. *Address*: Rosemergy Cottage, Morvah, Penzance TR20 8YX. *Website*: www.galleryonline.org.uk *Signs work*: "Anthony Frost."

FROST, Michael John, LLCM (1947), BA English Hons (1951), MA Politics (1969), AFAS. *Medium*: oil, pastel and acrylic. *b*: Burton-on-Trent, 8 Apr 1930. *Educ*: Burton Technical High School, Leeds University, Lancaster University. *Studied*: Glasgow School of Art (1963-1966), more recently taught by Rod Williams, Victor Ambrus, Brian Gallagher and Salliann Putman. *Exhib*: PS, RWA, The Armed Forces Art Society; numerous art groups and societies. *Address*: 2 Bedford Ave., Frimley Green, Surrey GU16 6HP. *Signs work*: "FROST."

FRY, Minne, BA (1953); painter and printmaker in oil, water-colour, etching. *b*: Johannesburg, 20 Dec 1933. *d of*: J.S. Zidel, MRCS, LRCP. *m*: Lionel Fry. one *s.* two *d. Educ*: University of the Witwatersrand. *Studied*: Central School of Art (1955, Cecil Collins, Denis Bowen, Mervyn Peake), Morley College (Adrian Bartlett, Frank Connelly). *Represented by*: eyestorm.com. *Exhib*: New Vision Centre (1958), Camden Galleries (1989), Green Room (1995), Coningsby Gallery (2000). *Works in collections*: CAS. *Clubs*: National Society of Painters, Sculptors & Printmakers. *Address*: 16 Caroline Pl., London W2 4AN. *Email*: minnefry@dsl.pipex.com *Website*: eyestorm.com. *Signs work*: "Minne Fry."

FRY, Paul, BA Fine Art. *Medium*: sculpture, oil, drawing, print. *b*: Somerset, 26 Feb 1972. *Partner*: Susanna Bauer. one *s*. *Studied*: Falmouth College of Art. *Represented by*: Ren Fine Art, Badcocks Gallery, Padstow Fine Art. *Exhib*: with Badcocks Gallery: AAF Hampstead (2014), Tremenheere Sculpture Garden (2013), AAF Battersea (2013, 2012). The Rose Theatre, Ascot (Ren Fine Art, 2013); Turners Warehouse, Newlyn (2013); Limbo, Truro (2013); Bucca Gallery, Newlyn (2013); Quidigy Gallery, Andover (2012); Padstow Fine Art (2012); Open Space Gallery, Falmouth (2012); Pydar Gallery, Truro (2012); Chapel Gallery, Gulval, Penzance (2012); Hilton Fine Art, Bath (2012); Badcocks Gallery, Cornwall (2011); Josie Eastwood Fine Art, Winchester (2011). *Address*: Penzance, Cornwall. *Email*: p.fry@live.co.uk *Website*: www.paulfry.co.uk *Signs work*: "Paul Fry".

FULLARTON, James, Diploma - DA (Drawing and Painting) Glasgow. *Medium*: oil, watercolour, drawing. *b*: Glasgow. *Exhib*: RSA, RGI, Roger Billcliffe Fine Art. *Clubs*: Glasgow Art Club. *Address*: Craigengower, Straiton, Ayrshire, KA19 7NG. *Email*: james_fullarton@talk21.com *Website*: jamesfullarton.com *Signs work*: "FULLARTON".

FULLER, Martin Elliott, Discerning Eye Modern Painters Prize (1996); First Prize, Hunting Art Prizes (1987); Guggenheim-McKinley Scholarship (American Art Workshop Italy, 1964); Artist-in-residence Santa Fe, New Mexico (1991-2). *Medium*: oil, watercolour, drawing, prints. *b*: Leamington Spa, 9 Feb 1943. *s of*: Sidney Fuller. *m*: Margaret Rand. one *d. Studied*: Mid-Warks College of Art; Hornsey College of Art. *Represented by*: Studio II, 2 Blenheim Gardens, London SW2. *Exhib*: over twenty solo exhbns inc.: Arnolfini, Bristol City Art Gallery, Camden Arts Centre; RZA Galerie, Dusseldorf; Austin Desmond Fine Art; Adam Gallery, Cork Street, London (2005); over twenty group exhbns inc: Redfern Gallery, Angela Flowers, Michael Parkin, V&A, Barbican Centre, National Theatre, Jonathan Clark Fine Art (with Edward Burra); Retrospective, Leamington Spa Art Gallery & Museum (curated by William Packer, 2001). *Works in collections*: Bristol City Art Gallery and Museum; Trinity College, Oxford; Unilever; Chelsea and Westminster Hospital; Railtrack; Bank of America; Leamington Spa Museum. *Commissions*: Waldorf Hotel, London; Radisson Hotel, Cork and Glasgow; Malmaison Hotel, London. *Publications*: numerous, inc. 'The Guardian', 'Arts Review', 'Spectator', 'Modern Painters', 'The Times', 'Ambit', 'Apollo'.

Works Reproduced: Ambit, Erotic Review, Modern Painters, Arts Review, Observer etc. *Recreations*: modern opera, jazz, Wagner. *Clubs*: Garrick, Chelsea Arts, Groucho, Academy. *Misc*: BBC Radio 3, 'Private Passions' with Michael Berkeley. *Address*: Studio 2, Blenheim Studios, 29 Blenheim Gardens, London SW2 5EU. *Email*: martin@martinfuller.net *Website*: www.martinfuller.net *Signs work*: 'Martin Fuller'.

FULLER, Peter Frederic, RAI (1976), AAH(1976), FPS(1991); Whatman prize; painter in water-colour; art historian. *b*: Ramsgate, 10 Apr 1929. *s of*: Frederic Fuller, RAF. *m*: Rosemary Blaker. one *d*. *Educ*: John Hezlett School. *Studied*: Maidstone College of Art. *Exhib*: RA, RBA, RPS, RWS (Open), RI, NEAC, FPS, RSMA, The Discerning Eye, KCC 'Kent Artists', Britain in Water-colours, Towner A.G., E. Stacey-Marks Gallery Eastbourne, Arts Centre Folkestone, Arune Arts Centre Arundel, Roger Green Fine Art High Halden, Bakehouse Gallery Sevenoaks, Cloisters Gallery Canterbury, Leeds Castle, KCC County Gallery, Redleaf Gallery Tunbridge Wells, finalist in the Laing Art Competition. *Works in collections*: America, Australia, Canada, France, Germany. *Commissions*: for landscapes and portraits from various distinguished people including the former Bishop of Southwark. *Works Reproduced*: in "The Artist". *Recreations*: music and reading. *Misc*: teacher of water-colour painting. *Address*: 29 Sandling La., Penenden Heath, Maidstone, Kent ME14 2HS. *Signs work*: "Peter Fuller."

FURLONG, Gillian, David Murray Landscape Prize (RA) (1968). *Medium*: oil. *b*: Kingston, Surrey, 1 May 1948. *d of*: Betty Ryder. *m*: Edward Dawson, NEAC (decd). one *s*. three *d*. *Studied*: Epsom School of Art (1965-67); Camberwell School of Arts and Crafts (1967-70). *Exhib*: RA Summer Exhbn (1972-74, 1978-85, '87-'89, 2001); Affordable Art Fair, Battersea (1999-2012); David Curzon (1996-2012); Discerning Eye (1997, '99, 2000, '02); Francis Iles (1998-2011); Lincoln Joyce Fine Art (1994-2014); Rowley Gallery (1996-2006); Russell Gallery, Putney (2004-14); 'Not the RA', Llewellyn Alexander (1997-2004, 2007-2014); RBA (2009), Island Fine Arts, Bembridge, Isle of Wight (2014). *Works Reproduced*: 'Early Morning: Crete', Getty Images; 'Sunday Morning: Newlyn', Kunstverlag Weingarten; through Bridgeman Art Library; "Saturday Morning: Georgina" Kalenderverlag Mannheim; "Saturday Afternoon: Tallulah Reading" Kalenderverlag Mannheim. *Address*: 4 Warwick Court, 4 Lansdowne Road, London SW20 8AP. *Email*: gillianfurlong@gmail.com *Signs work*: 'G.F.'

FURNEAUX, Alan C. George, PG Dip. *Medium*: acrylic. *b*: London, 6 Feb 1953. *m*: Lorraine. one *s*. two *d*. Educ: De Burgh Secondary, Tadworth, Surrey. *Studied*: Reigate School of Art. *Represented by*: Thompsons Gallery, Aldeburgh. *Exhib*: Thompsons Gallery; David Curzon, Wimbledon; Black Heath Gallery, Tranquil Vale, Blackheath; Market House Gallery, Marazion, Cornwall. *Works in collections*: Hampshire Water Board. *Commisions*: Royal Caribbean Cruiseliners, Hampshire Water Board. *Publications*: "How I See it" blurb. *Works Reproduced*: Medici, Solomon & Whitehead, Met Colours, Marks & Spencers, Robertsone, Art Cards Cornwall, Clare Maddicott Designs and many more. *Recreations*: music, playing guitar. *Address*: 1 Carminone Crescent, Penzance, Cornwall TR18 2RH. *Email*: alan@alanfurneaux.com *Website*: www.alanfurneaux.com *Signs work*: "Alan Furneau".

FURNESS, Valerie Jane, NDD (Painting), ATD; taught at Falmouth College of Art; Head of Art at Redmaids School; Senior Art Award, Wimbledon School of Art (now Wimbledon College of Art). *Medium*: mixed media/collage, oil, watercolour, drawing, oils. *b*: Devon, 23 Aug 1931. *d of*: Paul Jacob Furness. *Partner*: Trevor Graves (decd) writer/poet. one *s*. *Educ*: Barnstaple Girls Grammar School, Devon; Upper Tooting High School, London. *Studied*: Wimbledon School of Art; University of London. *Exhib*: Newlyn Art Gallery, Cornwall; Penwith Society of Art, St. Ives; Penlee Museum, Penzance; Oxford College & RWA, Bristol; Humanist Association, London; New Gallery, RWA Bristol (2-man show with Peter Morrell, 2007); Wills Lane Gallery, St. Ives; Quest Gallery, Bath; Katharine House

Gallery, Marlborough. *Works in collections*: James Brockbank & Louise Ronane, Islington; Mrs Rudman, Penzance; Mr & Mrs Stanley; Nina Zborwska ('Woman with Irises'), Painswick, and other private collections. *Commissions*: mural: Dawsons, Bristol; portraits including Prof. Richard Gregory; 'Dwarf Juggling', Jonathan Dawson, Tangier. *Publications*: 'Morocco-Paintings and Poems' by Jane Furness & D. Enay; The Dictionary of Artists in Britain Since 1945; St. Ives Art Colony 1975-2007. *Official Purchasers*: Henry Gilbert ('The Red Chair'), Wills Lane Gallery; Chris Gange; Katharine House Gallery. *Works Reproduced*: many Moroccan paintings and drawings. *Principal Works*: 'Woman with Irises' (oil); 'Girl Catching Wasps'; 'The Red Chair'; portrait of Prof. Richard Gregory. *Recreations*: literature, music, travel, theatre. *Clubs*: Penwith Society of Artists (1959-66). *Misc*: Works in Morocco every year. Studio in Bristol House. *Address*: 8 Camden Terrace, Clifton, Bristol BS8 4PU. *Email*: jane.furness@talktalk.net *Signs work*: "V J Furness".

FURSE, Vikky (Victoria Picton), SWA . *Medium*: pastel, acrylic, collage etc. *b*: Bath, Somerset, 7 Mar 1945. *m*: Chris Furse. *Studied*: St. Martin's School of Art 1962-1964; Ravensbourne College of Art; Hornsey College of Art 1968. *Represented by*: Paul Wynter, London Art. *Exhib*: Pastel Society & SWA. Mall Galleries; Many group shows London, Scott Polar Research Institute, Cambridge; Nature in Art Gallery Museum etc. *Works in collections*: Kecskemet, Hungary; Scott Polar Institute, Camb. (Sketchbooks, requested for archive). *Commissions*: Many portrait commissions including by Sir Donald Sinden. *Publications*: Funds Europe; Artists & Illustrators (4-page feature); The Artist; Featured 'Acrylic Workshop' by Phyllis McDowell (D&K). *Principal Works*: Specialises paintings of polar regions, particular travelling with Inuit hunters and their dog teams in NE Greenland. *Clubs*: Arctic Club (elected). *Misc*: Residencies: Nature in Art Gallery Museum, Glos; Antarctica International Arts Programme; Gordonstoun School Scotland. Lecture, M/V Polar Star Expedition Tour Ship Arctic/Antarctic. *Address*: Hegg Hill Oast, Smarden, Kent TN27 8NX. *Email*: fursesofhegg@uwclub.net *Website*: www.londonart.co.uk/vikkyfurse www.society-women-artists.org.uk/vikkyfurse *Signs work*: "V.FURSE" or "V.P.FURSE".

G

GABAY, Laurie, L., BA (Hons) English, BA (Hons) Fine Art. *Medium*: oils, acrylics, mixed media. *b*: Paris, 14 Dec 1963. *Studied*: Paris, finished BA year at Wycombe College (Bucks). *Exhib*: Battersea Art Fair, Affordable Art Fair, Henley, Teddington Art Fair, Danceworks, Sandelson Gallery Cork Street, Millennium Hotel, Knightsbridge; theatres and colleges in Bucks., and venues relating to my theme 'dance and movement' semi-abstract to abstract. *Address*: 94 Highworth Road, London N11 2SH. *Email*: laulise09@gmail.com *Website*: www.lauriegabay.co.uk

GADSBY, Betty Patricia, SBA; Dip SPA (Dist, 2011); RHS Silver Medal, Malvern Spring Show (2013). *Medium*: watercolour, coloured pencils. *b*: Galley Common, 24 Dec 1960. *m*: Edward Chesney. *Studied*: North Warwickshire College of Technology and Art (2002/2006); Distance learning course, SBA (2009-1011). *Exhib*: SBA Annual Exhibition, Westminster, London (2013, 2014); Pittenweem Arts Festival, Fife (2009, 2010, 2011, 2014). *Commissions*: De Jager Bulb catalogue front cover, Spring 2013 - Lily "Anastasia". *Recreations*: Banger and stock car racing (watching, not participating!) *Clubs*: Birmingham Society of Botanical Artists. *Address*: Kindar, Hickman Road, Galley Common, Nuneaton, Warwickshire CV10 9NG. *Email*: gadgetrad2@aol.com *Website*: www.bettygadsby.co.uk *Signs work*: "BPG" or "BPGadsby".

GAGE, Anthea Dominique Juliet, SSA, RSW; The May Marshall Brown Award (2006); art teacher, artist in gouache and water-colour. *Medium*: gouache. *b*: Edinburgh, 21 Mar 1956. *d of*: Edward A. Gage, PPSSA, RSW. *m*: David Dunlop. *Educ*: John Watsons School, Stevenson's College of Educ. *Studied*: Edinburgh College of Art (Dip. 1974-78, Post. Dip.

1978-79, David Michie, George Donald). *Represented by*: self. *Exhib*: annually at SSA, RSW; various mixed exhbns. *Publications*: Who's Who in Scotland. *Principal Works*: "So Many Arks", "Guess", "What an Eye", "Bergen". *Recreations*: singing, gardening, kite flying. *Email*: anthea.gage@mypostoffice.co.uk *Website*: www.antheagage.co.uk *Signs work*: "Anthea Gage."

GAINSFORD, Sylvia Petula, NDD, ATD; painting and illustrating. *Medium*: acrylic. *b*: 1942. *m*: Leon Olin. *Studied*: Royal Tunbridge Wells (1962, painting and wood engraving). *Exhib*: numerous. *Works in collections*: Kallis Foundation, Beverly Hills. *Commissions*: numerous, both private and civic. *Publications*: Food from the Countryside (Leon and Sylvia Olin); The Country Kitchen (Della Lutes); Just Like You and Me (Johnny Morris); Divination card designs, commissioned & published by A.G.Muller/Urania are: Tarot of the Old Path (4th World best seller), Tarot of Northern Shadows & Kabbalah; Rune Vision with Anova Books; A Strange Way to Make a Living (Leon and Sylvia Olin) 319 pages, includes 49 colour plates of artist' work. Reviewed on Amazon.co.uk. *Works Reproduced*: Limited Edition Prints (Buckingham Fine Art), Cards (Society Cards, Medici, Bishopsgate). *Misc*: T.V. Film on work & lifestyle. Divination card designs featured in Hollywood documentary film. *Address*: Fron Haul, Rhos-y-Caerau, Goodwick, Pembrokeshire SA64 0LB. *Signs work*: "Sylvia P. Gainsford."

GAIT, Judith, Bachelor of Fine Art, Lottery Award, arts projects with elderly benchmarked by Health Education Authority, Masters Degree in Fine Art Research. *Medium*: wall-hangings, mixed media drawings, paintings. *b*: Michigan, 4 Dec 1948. two *s.* three *d. Educ*: California College of Arts and Crafts; Ruskin School of Drawing; University of California; Instituto Dante Alighieri, Florence; Royal Miniature Society. *Studied*: University of the West of England. *Exhib*: numerous craft-council galleries; Invited Guest Maker American Museum in Britain; Southwest Academy of Art; Invited guest maker Stroud Bienniale, Bankside Gallery, Gallery 286, Royal College of Pathologists. *Works in collections*: Paintings in Hospitals; Salisbury District Hospital; Bristol Care and Repair Housing Agency; Bristol Special Care Baby Unit. *Commissions*: numerous private commissions. *Official Purchasers*: Norton-Radstock Town Council, NHS Trusts. *Works Reproduced*: Encyclopedia of Quilting Techniques; Waistcoats; Patchwork Pocket Pallet. *Recreations*: visiting museums, walking. *Address*: St Mary's Cottage, Hemington, Bath, BA3 5XX. *Email*: gaitlaan@gmail.com *Website*: www.judithgait.co.uk

GALE, Colin David, BA Hons Fine Art; MA Printmaking. *Medium*: prints. *b*: London, 10 Sep 1965. *m*. Erika Turner-Gale. two *s*. *Studied*: Camberwell School of Arts and Crafts (1981-87). *Represented by*: Artichoke Print Workshop, London. *Exhib*: Bankside Gallery, Royal Academy of Arts (2009, 2010). *Publications*: 'Etching & Photopolymer Techniques' (A&C Black, 2006); Practical Printmaking (A&C Black); Printmakers Bible (Bloomsbury, 2012). *Recreations:* Tae Kwondo. *Misc*: Co-founded Artichoke Print Workshop, Brixton, London - etching lithography and relief printing. *Address*: 161 Hollydale Road, Nunhead, London SE15 2TF. *Email*: colingale@btinernet.com *Website*: www.colingale.com

GALE, Jeremy, BA (Hons) 1st (1984). *Medium*: mixed media, oil, drawing, prints. *b*: Congo, 24 Dec 1961. *s of*: J.W.L.Gale CBE, & Eunice Gale. *Studied*: Central School of Art and Design, London (1981-84), Scuola Lorenzo de Medici, Florence (1984). *Exhib*: RIBA Summer Exhibition (1985); The Julius Gottlieb Exhibition Centre, Oxon (1986); Cromwell Gallery, London (1988); The Lethaby Gallery, London (1990, 1993); Burgh House, London (1992); Manor Gallery, London (1997); Chequer Mead Art Gallery, Sussex (1998); The Barn, Hawaii (2002). *Publications*: Contributor to 'In Celebration of Cecil Collins: Visionary Artist and Educator' (2008). *Address*: The Studio, Flinders, Henfield Road, Upper Beeding, West Sussex BN44 3TF. *Email*: pjeremygale@hotmail.com *Website*: www.jeremygale.co.uk *Signs work*: "Jeremy Gale".

GALE, Martin, ANCAD (1973), RHA (1996); Degree in Painting. *Medium*: oil, watercolour, drawing, prints. *b*: Worcester, 20 Mar 1949. *s of*: John and Joan Gale. two *s*. one *d*. *Educ*: Newbridge College, Co. Kildare. *Studied*: National College of Art and Design, Dublin. *Represented by*: Taylor Galleries, Kildare St., Dublin; Johon Martin Gallery, Albemarle Street, London. *Exhib*: RHA (1990-2005); Martin Gale Retrospective, RHA Dublin and Ulster Museum Belfast (2004-05); numerous solo and group exhibs. in Ireland, group exhibs. in Britain and USA, alos XI Biennale de Paris (1980-1981); International Connection - 'Sense of Ireland' Festival, London (1980); Images from Ireland, Brussels (1989); NCAD '250 Drawings 1746-1996'. *Works in collections*: Irish Museum of Modern Art; Arts Council of Ireland; European Parliament, Strasbourg; all major public and private collections in Ireland and Britain. *Commissions*: National Self Portrait Collection, European Parliament, Strasburg, ESB Municipal Gallery, Waterford, and others. *Publications*: Exhib. catalogues, catalogue essays. Gandon Editions - Works 19, Martin Gale in conversation with Brian Fallon; Martin Gale - Work in Progress. *Official Purchasers*: Dept. of Finance & Personnel, Belfast; Crawford Municipal Gallery, Cork; Office of Public Works; National Self-Portrait Collection. *Misc*: member of AOSDANA, Royal Hibernian Academy (RHA). *Address*: Coughlanstown, Ballymore Eustace, Co. Kildare, Ireland. *Email*: martinjgale@gmail.com *Website*: www.martingale.ie *Signs work*: "Martin Gale."

GALE, Richard John, DipAD (1968), MA (RCA, 1973); artist in oil. *b*: Bristol, 8 Feb 1946. *s of*: C. L. Gale. *m*: Frances Joan. *Educ*: Weston-super-Mare Grammar School. *Studied*: Kingston upon Thames School of Art (1965-68), RCA (1970-73). *Address*: 5 Hillside Rd., Clevedon, North Somerset. *Signs work*: "R. Gale."

GALES, Simon, B/Tec.Dip (Dist) (1985), BA (First Class Hons) Fine Art (1988); painter in oil on linen or canvas. *b*: 1964. *s of*: Frederick & Antonia Gales. *m*: Susanne (née Folke). two *s*. one *d*. *Educ*: The Kings School, Ely. *Studied*: Ipswich School of Art (1983-85), Goldsmiths' College, London (1985-88). *Exhib*: Solo exhibitions: Bruton St. Gallery (1999, 2001, 2003), Albemarle Gallery (2008), "Focus Unfocus", The Eyeline Series, Park Walk Gallery (2011, 13). Selected group shows: Berkeley Square Gallery (1988), Christie's New Contemporaries (1989), Gillian Jason Gallery (1991), Waterman Fine Art (1995), Jill George Gallery (1990), Art Chicago, Park Walk Gallery, Chicago USA (2010), Art Toronto, Park Walk Gallery, Toronto, Canada (2011, 12, 13). *Works in collections*: Colchester and Ipswich Museums, The Ipswich Collection; London Underground Museum, Covent Gdn., Robert Holmes à Court Museum, Perth, Australia, Accenture PLC, private collections worldwide. *Commissions* London Transport (for the Museum of Childhood, Bethnal Green, 1990). *Publications*: 'Guilded Gutter Life of Francis Bacon', Millers Price Guide for Pictures 1983. *Works Reproduced*: 'Childhood' 1990 London Transport Museum. *Misc*: painter of metaphysical imagery on 3D panels. *Address*: La Symeronie, Coulaures 24420 France. *Email*: susanne.folke@orange.fr *Website*: www.simongales.com *Signs work*: "SIMON GALES" (on reverse).

GALLAGHER, Brian, artist in water-colour, pastel and pencil; Secretary and Council mem. Pastel Soc; tutor to painting courses. *b*: Chester, 31 May 1935. *s of*: Frederick Alexander Gallagher, musician. *m*: Rosemary June Webb. one *s*. *Studied*: Portsmouth College of Art, privately under Herbert Green. *Exhib*: PS, SWLA, Porthill Gallery London, Anna-Mei Chadwick Gallery, London, RBSA Galleries, Birmingham, John Nevill Gallery, Canterbury, Cowleigh Gallery, Malvern, Mercer Art Gallery, Harrogate, Southampton City Art Gallery, and many provincial galleries. *Publications*: 'Step-by-Step Guide to Pastel Techniques'. *Works Reproduced*: contributor to art magazines. *Clubs*: London Sketch. *Address*: 99 Gilmore Cres., Ashford, Middx. TW15 2DD. *Signs work*: "Brian Gallagher."

GALLOWAY, Richard Andrew, BTEC Diploma Art Foundation; BA Hons Painting/Printmaking; MA Printmaking (RCA); Bazil Alkazzi Award RCA (2004); Augustus

Martin Prize RCA (2004). *Medium*: drawing, prints, linocut. *b*: Kettering, 18 Jun 1980. *s of*: David Galloway. *Studied*: RCA; Northumbria University; Nene University. *Exhib*: Wyer Gallery, St.John's Hill (2006); 200 Art Fair (2005); 'The Great Unsigned', 47 Great Eastern Street (2005); The New Academy Gallery, London (2005); AAF Recent Graduates, Battersea (2004). *Works in collections*: Saatchi Collection, London; Ben Alkazzi Collection, London. *Publications*: Le Gun Magazine, RCA. *Address*: 50c Elderfield Road, Hackney, London E5 0LF. *Email*: info@RichardGalloway.co.uk *Website*: www.RichardGalloway.co.uk *Signs work*: Richard Galloway.

GALT, Cameron, BA (Hons) Fine Art; Elizabeth Greenshields Award; RWS/Sunday Times Prize (2008). *Medium*: oil, watercolour, drawing. *b*: Greenock, 1964. *s of*: Hugh Galt. *Partner*: Caroline Mansell. one *s.* one *d. Studied*: Duncan of Jordanstone, Dundee (1984-88). *Represented by*: Bankside Gallery. *Exhib*: various group and solo shows, UK. *Works in collections*: numerous corporate and private, including the Duchess of Westminster Collection. *Commissions*: numerous private, including portraits of the late Amschel Rothschild for Anita Guinness, and Geraldine Ogilvy for the late Viscount Rothermere. *Clubs*: The Royal Watercolour Society. *Address*: 19 Edward St., Walsall, WS2 8RS. *Email*: camerongalt@live.co.uk *Website*: www.bankside.com www.camerongalt.com *Signs work*: Artist's monogram comprises of the initials 'C.G.'

GAMBLE, Tom, RWS; painter in oil and water-colour; Mem. AWG; senior lecturer, Art and Design, Loughborough College of Art (1952-84); Freeman of City of London, Gold Medallist and Liveryman of the Worshipful Company of Painter/Stainers; Winner, Turner Medal & Award for Painting in Watercolour 2012. *b*: Norton-on-Tees, 6 Feb 1924. married. *s of*: Thomas Gamble, engineer. one *s. Studied*: Constantine College, Middlesbrough. *Exhib*: RA, RWS, Bankside Gallery London, Royal Festival Hall, Mall Galleries, Singer & Friedlander/Sunday Times Exhibitions; Hunting Group Prizes, Brian Sinfield, Milne & Moller, Woodgates Gallery, East Bergholt, Burlington Gallery, London; Leicester A.G., Middlesbrough A.G., Exposicion International de Acuarela Barcelona, American and Canadian Water-colour Socs., and various provincial galleries. *Works in collections*: HM Queen; Lloyds of London, University of Loughborough, Notts CC, Leics.CC, Crathorne Collection, Worshipful Company of Painter/Stainers, Intelligence Corps HQ; private collections in Europe, USA, Canada. *Works Reproduced*: 'Artists of Northumbria' (2005), 'Visions of Venice', 'The Story of Watercolour', 'Expostion Internacional de Acaurela', 'Old Watercolour Society's Club Vol.63', 'Watercolour Masters', 'Watercolour Expert'; International Watercolours, Drawings and Prints. *Recreations*: music & travel. *Clubs*: Arts. *Address*: 10 Blythe Green, East Perry, Huntingdon, Cambs. PE28 0BJ. *Signs work*: "Tom Gamble."

GANJEI, Parastoo, BA Graphic Design, Advance Cert. in Animation. *Medium*: acrylics, watercolour. *b*: Tehran, Iran, 1 May 1952. *Studied*: University of Decorative Arts (Graphic Design), Croydon College of Art and Design (Animation), Bournemouth and Poole University (Graphic Design). *Represented by*: NAPA; Allied Artists of America. *Exhib*: SWA, Winchester City Hall, Arlsford Gallery, Salisbury City Hall, Wetminster Gallery (London), The Beatrice Royal Gallery (Eastleigh), Black Sheep Gallery (Chester), Hawker Gallery (Amersham), Modern Artist Gallery (Berks). *Works in collections*: The Princess of Brunei. *Commissions*: private clients (USA, Asia, Europe). *Publications*: Leisure Painters Magazine, International Artist Magazine. *Works Reproduced*: Medici (London) greeting cards. *Misc*: still life painter mainly in acrylic, lots of details, patterns, bold and beautiful colours. *Address*: 117 Lowther Road, Bournemouth, Dorset, BH8 8NP. *Email*: parastooganjei@aol.com

GANTER, Josephine, MA (Hons) Fine Art; John Kinross Scholarship (1988); Rome Scholarship in Printmaking (1989); Boise Scholarship (1994); Sir William Gillies Award (2005). *Medium*: printmaking, etching, digital print, photography. *b*: Yorkshire, 12 Nov

1963. *Studied*: Edinburgh University. *Exhib*: Hart Gallery, London; Glasgow Print Studio Gallery; AIR Gallery, New York; Open Eye Gallery, Edinburgh. *Works in collections*: Edinburgh City Art Centre; Jane Vorhees Zimmerli Collection, Rutgers University, USA; New York Public Library; Museum of Fine Art, Antwerp; Hunterian Art Gallery and Museum, Glasgow, Pallant House. *Publications*: Talbot Rice Gallery, Edinburgh University - catalogue "Cardinal Glimpses", Glasgow Print Studio - catalogue - "Forms of Being". *Address*: 68 Murano St., 3/1, Glasgow G20 7RX. *Email*: josephine.ganter@ntlworld.com *Website*: http://joganter.wordpress.com *Signs work*: "JO GANTER".

GARDINER, Iain, RMS, Dip Graphic Design; BP Portrait Award (2006, second in Visitors Choice); RMS Gold Memorial Bowl Award (2010); RMS Presidents Special Commendation for Large Work; RMS Mundy Sovereign (2011); RMS Presidents Special Commendation (2013); on the Council of the RMS. *Medium*: Computer Art (Photoshop), oil, drawing, print, sculpture. *b*: Chorley, Lancashire, 14 Feb 1969. *Educ*: Sea Point Boys High School. *Studied*: University of Cape Town (1988-91). *Exhib*: BP Portrait Award 2006 finalist, NPG; Aberdeen Art Gallery (2006); Royal West of England Academy (2006-7); Mall Galleries: Royal Society of Portrait Painters (2007), Royal Society of Miniature Painters, Sculptors and Gravers (2007-2013); NEAC (2010, 2011), The Art Critics Circle's Secret Centenery Exhibition (2013); *Works in collections*: The Sue Lee Collection of Contemporary Miniature Art, and numerous other private collections around the world. *Publications*: 500 Portraits, National Portrait publications (book, 2011): BP Portrait Award 2006 catalogue; Royal Society of Miniature Painters and Gravers catalogue (2008-2011); Artists & Illustrators Magazine (July 2007, 250th issue); The Artist Magazine (Oct 2010). Online: ArtnSpire; Wall Street International Magazine (10 June 2013); Kensington and Chelsea Today. Mall Galleries catalogue (Jul-Dec 2013), Galleries Magazine (Oct 2013), The Saturday Times Newspaper (12 Oct 2012). *Works Reproduced*: Mr & Mrs Gardiner (oil on canvas board) printed by NPG into posters; 'Reflection 4' (oil on canvas) printed onto postcards by the RMS; Reflection from the Portrait Restaurant (oil on canvas), and 'Girl in a Regent Street Window 1' (oil on canvas) used as promotional advertising for RMS and Mall Galleries. *Clubs*: Royal Society of Miniature Painters Sculptors and Gravers. *Address:250* Park Road, Kingston-upon-Thames, Surrey KT2 5NA. *Email*: iaingardiner1969@yahoo.co.uk *Website*: http://www.behance.net/iaingardiner *Signs work*: "Iain Gardiner".

GARDINER, Jeremy, Churchill Fellowship (1984); Harkness Fellowship (1984); New York Foundation for the Arts Fellowship (1987); AHRC Grant (2007); Ace Award (2010). *Medium*: Prints, acrylic. *b*: Munster, Germany, 26 Apr 1957. *m*: Veronica. one *s*. one *d*. *Studied*: Newcastle University (1975-79); Royal College of Art (1980-83). *Represented by*: Paisnel Gallery, St Jame's, London. *Exhib*: Museu d'Art Moderna de la Ville de Paris (1983); Museu de Arte Moderna, Sao Paolo (1990); Fine Arts Museum, Long Island (1991); Belgrave Gallery (2000); Paisnel Gallery (2008); Chelsea Arts Museum, New York City (2009); Pallant House Gallery (2010); Kings Place Gallery, London (2013). *Works in collections*: BNP Paribas; Gaz de France; Government Art Collection; Imperial College Art Collection; Victoria and Albert Museum. *Commissions*: General Electric. *Publications*: Jeremy Gardiner: The Origins of Landscape, Lund Humphries (2013). *Misc*: Taught at MIT, Pratt Institute of Art and Design, Royal College of Art, Ravensbourne. *Address*: 2 Audley Avenue, Bath BA1 3BL. *Email*: mail@jeremygardiner.co.uk *Signs work*: "JEREMY GARDINER".

GARDINER, Vanessa, BA (Hons) (1982); Awards: South West Arts-Fine Art (1999, 2003); Prince of Wales Bursary, British School at Athens (2009-10). *Medium*: painter in acrylic, on plywood/hardboard. *b*: Oxford, 7 Apr 1960. *d of*: Patrick Lancaster Gardiner. *Partner*: Mr. A. Lowery, painter. one *d*. *Studied*: Oxford Polytechnic (1978-79), Central School of Art and Design, London (1979-82, David Haughton). *Represented by*: Thackeray

Gallery, London. *Exhib*: solo shows: Quercus Gallery, Bath (2014); Campden Gallery, Glos (2013); Sladers Yard, Dorset (2012); Hart Gallery, London, (2011, 2009, 2007, 2005, 2003, 2001); British School at Athens (2010); Duncan Campbell, London (2000, 1998, 1996, 1992, 1991). Recent group shows: Thackeray Gallery, London (2014); Sladers Yard, Dorset (2014); RA Summer Exhibition (2013, 2003); Lynn Painter-Stainers, London (2013). *Works in collections*: Bournemouth University. Carlow Art Collection; Ballinglen Arts Foundation Archive, Ireland; Magdalen College, Oxford 2008; Fidelity International; New Hall, Cambridge; Huddersfield City Art Gallery, British School at Athens, Athens (2010). *Works Reproduced*: Modern Painters Magazine,1996 Elizabeth James. 'Reinventing the Landscape: Vivienne Light, Canterton Books; 'Landscape and Architecture' Hart Gallery (2005), text by Judith Bumpus; Hart Gallery 'Linear Coasts' (2007); Hart Gallery 'Connecting Lines' (2009) text by Julian Bell; Hart Gallery. *Misc*: Fellow, Ballinglen Arts Foundation, Co.Mayo, Ireland (2003, 2007). *Address*: Lilac Cottage, Fernhill, Charmouth, Dorset DT6 6BX. *Email*: vanessa.gardiner@tiscali.co.uk *Website*: vanessagardner.co.uk *Signs work*: "Vanessa Gardiner."

GARDNER, Grace. *Medium* oil, etching, collage, drawing, monoprints. *b*: Grand Rapids, Michigan, USA 27 Jul 1920. *m*: widow of William. *Studied*: Art Institute of Chicago (1950s). Privately with Frances Richardson (1950s), Rudolf Pen (1960s), Kwok Wailau (1970s). *Represented by*: Agent: Dr. Helen V. Andrew; Gallery: The New Gallery, Portscatho. *Exhib*: Falmouth Art Gallery (since 1985, ten exhibitions, three solo); The Mariner's Gallery, St.Ives (Retrospective, 2004, New Works 2007); The New Gallery, Portscatho (since 1999 to present); Driang Galleries, London (1972, 1974, 1976); New Craftsman, St.Ives; Penwith Gallery, St.Ives; Newlyn Gallery; Online Gallery, Southampton. *Works in collections*: public and private collections in America, Britain, Europe and the Far East. *Publications*: 'Grace Notes, A Life in Art' (2009, Halsgrove); 'Once More from the Beginning' (2002). *Works Reproduced*: in many newspapers and periodicals worldwide. *Recreations*: reading, writing, travel. *Address*: 17 Kersley Road, Flushing, Falmouth, Cornwall, TR11 5TR. *Website*: www.artsake.co.uk www.falmouthartgallery.com *Signs work*: "GRACE GARDNER".

GARDNER, Judith Ann, BA Hons Fine Art (1974); RBA (2000); Small Painting Group (2003); NEAC (2009); painter in oil; de Laszlo Medal Winner at RBA (2003). *Medium*: oil, pastel. *b*: Kent, 15 Apr 1952. *m*: Colin. two *d*. *Studied*: Maidstone College of Art under principal, William Bowyer R.A., tutor, Frederick Cuming RA and David Winfield (1970-1974). *Exhib*: RA, RBA, NEAC, ROI, Discerning Eye, Russell Gallery Putney; Geedon Gallery Fingringhoe; Island Fine Arts Gallery IOW; Josephine Harpur Gallery Bury St Edmunds; Art in Action Waterperry and other galleries. *Works in collections*: private collections in UK, USA and Australia. *Publications*: Artist Magazine (October 2002, April 2006); Kent Life Magazine (Jan 2011); Artists and Illustrators (Mar 2013). *Address*: 41 Willowbank, Sandwich CT13 9QA. *Email*: judithgardner01@btinternet.com *Website*: www.royalsocietyofbritishartists.org.uk www.newenglishartsclub.co.uk *Signs work*: "J Gardner."

GARDNER, Peter Colville Horridge, ROI (1977), ATD (1951), FRSA (1969); *Medium*: oil. *b*: London, 25 Oct 1921. *s of*: Ronald E. Gardner. *m*: Irene (decd 2008). *Educ*: St. Matthias C. of E. School, London SW5. *Studied*: Hammersmith School of Art (1935-38, 1946-50), London University Inst. of Educ. (1950-51, 1971-72). *Exhib*: RA, RBA, ROI, NEAC. *Works in collections*: Nuffield Foundation, York University. *Address*: 11 Pixmead Gdns., Shaftesbury, Dorset SP7 8BZ. *Email*: gardnermead@gmail.com *Signs work*: "Peter Gardner."

GARDNER, Reginald Stephen. *Medium*: oil. *b*: Prestwich, Bury, 24 Apr 1948. *s of*: Charles Everard Gardner. *m*: Beryl Claire Gardner. two *s*. *Studied*: Manchester High School of Art. *Represented by*: Bill Clark of Clark Ltd, Hale Cheshire & Bond Street London; Dave Gunning, Todmorton Fine Art, Lancashire. *Exhib*: Chenil Gallery, London; Colin Jellicoe

Gallery, Manchester (solo and mixed); National Theatre, London; Lincoln Gallery; Great House Gallery, Norwich; Turtle Creek, Texas, USA; Watermill, Hampshire; Preston Harris Museum & Art Gallery; Collect art.com; Clarke Art, Bond St., London. *Works in collections*: private, national and international, including USA, Belgium, Russia, Bermuda, New Zealand, France. *Publications*: "Northern School" (p.89), Peter Davies (Redcliffe Press), Peter Brook & Reg Gardner. Art and Soul - Live Names. *Works Reproduced*: Wilson's calendar 1978. *Principal Works*: painted and sold over 2,000 works over 40 years. *Address*: 68 Sandyhill Road, Blackley, Manchester, M9 8GL. *Email*: reginald.gardner@btinternet.com *Website*: www.rsgardner.co.uk/com *Signs work*: "R.S.GARDNER" or "RSG".

GARDNER, Roseanne Serena: see CORLETT.

GARFIT, William, RBA.; ILEA Dip with hon., Byam Shaw School Cert. with Distinction, RAS Cert.; artist in oils, specialising in River Landscapes and pen and wash illustration work. *b*: Cambridge, 9 Oct 1944. *m*: Georgina Joseph. one *s*. two *d*. *Educ*: Bradfield College. *Studied*: Cambridge School of Art (1963), Byam Shaw (1964-67), RA Schools (1967-70). *Exhib*: one-man shows, Waterhouse Gallery (1970, 1972, 1974), Mall Galleries (1976), Stacey Marks, Eastbourne (1978), Tryon and Moorland Gallery, London (1981, 1983, 1985, 1988, 1991), Holland & Holland Gallery (1994), Tryon Gallery (2009). *Commissions*: many in private collections. *Publications*: illustrated: Dudley Worst Dog in the World, Amateur Keeper, Your Shoot, The Woods Belong to Me, The Fox and the Orchid, Prue's Country Kitchen, Cley Marsh and its Birds, The Game Shot, How the Heron got Long Legs, The Woodpigeon; Author of: 'Will's Shoot' (1993), 'Will's Shoot Revisited' (2005), 'Will's Shooting Ways' (2009), 'Will's Pigeon Shooting' (2012). *Recreations*: shooting, bird watching, botany. *Address*: The Old Rectory, Harlton, Cambridge CB3 7ES. *Email*: william.garfit@btinternet.com *Website*: williamgarfit.co.uk *Signs work*: "William Garfit."

GARLAND, Nicholas Withycombe. *Medium*: pen and ink, oil paint, woodcuts, gouache, watercolour. *b*: London, 1 Sep 1935. *s of*: T O Garland and M Withycombe. *m*: Priscilla Roth. three *s*. one *d*. *Studied*: Slade School of Fine Art (painting and etching). *Exhib*: Fine Arts Society, Bond St.; Grosvenor Gallery; The Cartoon Museum, Museum of London. *Works in collections*: British Museum, V & A, Imperial War Museum, Museum of London, Ashmolean. *Commissions*: A boxed set of Linocuts for Mark Birley of Annabel's Nightclub, commissioned by the Mayor of London to make a graphic record of the 2012 Olympic Games. *Publications*: "I Wish..." Waywiser Press; "Drawing the Games" published by the Greater London Authority. *Address*: 12 Parkhill Road, London NW3 2YN. *Email*: nicholasgarland@blueyonder.co.uk *Signs work*: 'Nicholas Garland' or 'Garland'.

GARNER, Jackie (Jacqueline Anne), *Medium*: watercolour; acrylic. *b*: Gloucestershire, 2 Sep 1964. *Studied*: Medway College of Design (1984-87). *Exhib*: Society of Wildlife Artists, Mall Galleries, London (2005-11); Royal Institute of Painters in Watercolours, Mall Galleries, London (2011); National Exhibition Wildlife Art (2010, 12, 13). Solo exhibitions: Cheng Kim Loke Gallery, Glos (2006, 2010); Falkland House, Westminster, London (2007); Coningsby Gallery, London (2009). *Works in collections*: private/corporate. *Commissions*: Corporate. *Publications*: Author and illustrator of "The Wildlife Artist's Handbook". Pub. 2013. *Misc*: Education officer and artist in residence at Nature in Art Museum and Art Gallery, Glos (1993-2008). *Address*: Old Cider House Studio, Humphires End, Randwick, Stroud, Glos GL6 6EW. *Email*: artist@jackiegarner.co.uk *Website*: www.jackiegarner.co.uk *Signs work*: "GARNER".

GARNER, Todd Russell, AA (Illustration), BA (Painting), MFA (Ceramics). *Medium*: acrylic, sculpture. *b*: Pasadena, Calif., USA 20 May 1953. *s of*: Donald E.Garner. *m*: Angela. *Studied*: Pasadena City College (1971-75), California State Polytechnic University (1979-83), California State University, Long Beach (1986-88). *Represented by*: Tracey McNee Fine Art, Glasgow/London. *Exhib*: Selected solo exhbns: Rio Hondo Community College

Gallery, Whittier, California (1984); Lillie Art Gallery, Milngavie (1994); Callender House Gallery, Falkirk (1995); T Garner Gallery, Glasgow (1996); Lloyd Jerome Gallery, Glasgow (1999); Art Exposure Gallery, Glasgow (2000, 2001, 2003); Henshelwood Gallery (2005); selected group exhbns: Glasgow Art Fair (2000-05), AAF London (2000-05); London Art Fair Dublin Art Fair (Tracey McNee Gallery, 2006). *Publications*: Ceramics Monthly, The List, Glasgow Herald, Scotland on Sunday, The Califonia Art Review, Studio Pottery, Uptown. *Recreations*: travel. *Address*: Flat 1-4, 148 Hill Street, Garnethill, Glasgow G3 6UA. *Email*: tgarner454@aol.com *Website*: members.aol.com/tgarner454 *Signs work*: "T.Garner".

GARRETT, Roger MacLean, artist in oil; University Lecturer; Senior Lecturer, University of Bristol. *b*: Nairn, Scotland, 10 Feb 1942. *m*: Bertha Garrett. one *s.* one *d. Exhib*: RWA (1995, 1997, 1998), RA (1997, 1998), School House Gallery, Bath (1997), RBSA (1998), Chichester, Open Exhbn. (1998). *Address*: 38 Holmes Grove, Henleaze, Bristol BS9 4EE. *Signs work*: "R.G." and "Roger Garrett."

GARTON, Michael, NDD (1956), DFA (1959), RWA (2000); painter in oil; retired lecturer in painting. *b*: Reading, Berks., 5 Jun 1935. *m*: Antonia. one *s.* four *d. Educ*: Reading, Berks. *Studied*: Guildford (1950), Exeter (1956), Slade School (1959). *Exhib*: RA Summer Exhib (1977, 1987, 1997), RWA (1997-2001). *Works in collections*: private collections. RWA public collection. *Publications*: Landscape Research (1984), Art in Nature (1996). *Clubs*: Kenn Group of Artists. *Address*: 5 Silver Terr., Exeter, Devon EX4 4JE. *Signs work*: "M Garton."

GASKELL, Eric, ASGFA; BA (Hons) Fine Art; Backhouse Fine Art Prize, *Medium*: oil, acrylic. *b*: Wigan, 21 Oct 1957. *s of*: Eric Shurrock Williams. *m*: Susan. one *d. Studied*: Sunderland College of Art (1977-80); Wigan (1976-77). *Exhib*: Norwich Arts Centre (1980/1); Sunderland Arts Centre (1980/1); Alnwick (1981); Hull City Gallery (1981); Middleborough (1981); Luton (1989); AoI (1990); Pentagon Type Gallery (1992); Rugby Gallery (2000, 01, 02, 05); Rugby School Gallery (2001, 03); The Wonderwall, Cirencester (2004); SGFA (2003, 04); SGFA, London (2005, 06); Montserrat, New York (2004); The Salon, New York (2005); Ghent Expo (2004); RBSA (2006). *Works in collections*: International private collections. *Publications*: International Artist (July 2003); Computer Arts Projects Guide (Feb 2007). *Recreations*: genealogy. *Address*: 6 Gold Avenue, Cawston, Rugby, CV22 7FB. *Email*: eric@agdesign.co.uk *Website*: www.egdesign.co.uk *Signs work*: "E GASKELL' or "EG".

GASSON, Barry, OBE, Professor, Dip.Arch, MS, MA, ARIAS, RIBA, RSA; awarded Royal Scottish Academy Gold Medal, Royal Academy Premier Award, Museum of the Year Award, Gold Medal 4th World Bienale of Architecture. *Medium*: architecture. *b*: Westcliffe-on-Sea, 27 Aug 1935. *s of*: Gladys and Stanley Gasson. *m*: Rosemary Gasson. one *s.* two *d. Studied*: Birmingham School of Architecture; Columbia University New York City. *Publications*: contributor to: John Julius Norwich 'The Burrell Collection' (1983). *Principal Works*: major work: architect for the galleries for the Burrell Collection, Glasgow (won in open competition and opened by HM the Queen, 1983). *Recreations*: biodynamic farming, photography. *Address*: Lagard, 82110 Bouloc, France. *Email*: gassonbarry@free.fr *Signs work*: "Barry Gasson".

GATHERER, Stuart Luke, MA in Fine Art. *Medium*: oil painting. *b*: Nocton Hall, 19 Aug 1971. *m*: Annabel Gatherer. *Studied*: Edinburgh University, Edinburgh College of Art. *Represented by*: Albemarle Gallery, 49 Albemarle Street, London W1S 4JR. *Exhib*: McEwan Gallery, Scotland (2000), Portland Gallery, London (1997), Eleanor Ettinger Gallery, New York (1999), Albemarle Gallery, London (exclusive representation) (1998, 99, 01, 03). *Works in collections*: Standard Life. *Principal Works*: 'The Cutting Edge' 74x84in (2002); 'Danae's Consumation Party' 60x70in (2002), 'The Unveiling' 60x80in (2001), 'The

Optimism of Contemporary Life' 56x72in (1999), 'Anatomy Lesson of the On-Line Doctor' 72x80in (2001). *Clubs*: Chelsea Arts Club. *Address*: Beacon Cottage, Eastnor, HR8 1EP

GATTEAUX, Marcel, landscape and still-life artist in oil. *b*: Mitcham, Surrey, 1 Oct 1962. *Studied*: Camberwell School of Art (1980-81, Dick Lee, Sargy Mann); then studied restoration for a number of years before redirecting his attention to painting. *Exhib*: one-man shows, Caelt Gallery (1997-2005). *Works in collections*: Churchill Hotel, London; Cliveden and private collections in the UK and USA. *Publications*: Millers Picture Price Guide. *Address*: 182 Westbourne Grove, London W11 2RH. *Email*: art@caeltgallery.com *Website*: www.caeltgallery.com

GEARY, Robert John, MSIA (1967); FCSD (1980-2007); FRSA (1981); Hon SGFA (1994). *Medium*: editorial illustration (mainly satirical humour) in line and wash. *b*: London, 15 Jan 1931. *s of*: Robert & Ada Florence Geary. *m*: Hazel Mair Plant (decd). one *d*. *Studied*: Hammersmith School of Arts and Crafts (1945-48). *Exhib*: SGFA, Chelsea Art Society. *Works in collections*: work in private collections: The Saatchi Gallery, Museum of London. *Works Reproduced*: 'The Oldie' magazine; The Independent; The Sunday Telegraph; Punch (1978-81), and Private Eye publications. *Principal Works*: Character portraits. *Clubs*: SGFA. *Address*: 70 Felton Lea, Sidcup, Kent DA14 6BA. *Signs work*: "Robert Geary" or "R.G."

GEDDES, Stewart John, MA Arts Criticism (1997), BA (Hons.) Fine Art (1983), RWA (1996), M.Phil (Royal College of Art) (2007); preferred medium - acrylic; University tutor; Vice President, Royal West of England Academy 2002-2005. *b*: Maidstone, Kent, 4 Mar 1961. *s of*: Brian Malcolm Geddes. *m*: Juliet Simmons. two *s*. *Educ*: Maidstone School for Boys. *Studied*: Canterbury College of Art (1979-80, Eric Hurran), Bristol Polytechnic (1980-83, Alf Stockham), City University, London (1996-97, Professor Eric Moody); Royal College of Art (2004-07, John Stezaker). *Exhib*: RA, RWA, Cadogan Contemporary, London; Jersey Arts Centre; Advanced Graphics, London; Hockney Gallery, RCA, London. *Works in collections*: House Of Commons, RWA Permanent Collection, Landmark Plc. *Publications*: Research RCA 2007. *Clubs*: Chelsea Arts Club. *Address*: 49 Noyna Rd., Tooting Bec, London SW17 7PQ. *Email*: s.geddes1@ntlworld.com *Signs work*: "S.J. GEDDES" on back of work.

GEDEN, Dennis John, D.Litt (Hons); painter. *Medium*: oil. *b*: Ontario, Canada, 25 Apr 1944. *m*: Sandie. *Studied*: Sir George Williams', Montreal. *Represented by*: The Redfern Gallery. *Exhib*: exhibits internationally. *Works in collections*: Tate, London, MacLaren Art Centre, Barrie, Canada, Simon Fraser University, Vancouver, Canada, Anderson Collection, Buffalo, USA, Government of Ontario Art Collection, Canada, Bibliotheque Nationale, Paris. *Commissions*: Canada Council, Ontario Arts Council, Art Gallery of Ontario. *Address*: c/o Redfern Gallery, 20 Cork St., London W1S 3HL. *Email*: gedensan@vianet.on.ca *Signs work*: "D Gedden."

GELDART, William, artist/illustrator in pencil, pen and ink, scraperboard, pen and wash, water-colour. *b*: Marple, Ches., 21 Mar 1936. *s of*: William Edmund Geldart. *m*: Anne Mary. one *s*. one *d*. *Educ*: Hyde Grammar School. *Studied*: Regional College, Manchester (1956-57). *Exhib*: RA, Manchester Fine Arts, Chris Beetles and various others. *Works in collections*: worldwide. *Commissions*: Hallé Orchestra, Manchester International Airport, Ciba Geigy, ICI, Rolls Royce, CJS, ICL, Reynolds Chains, Manchester Grammar School, Chetham School of Music, Astra Zeneca, Hodder & Stoughton, Gallimard (Paris), and others. *Publications*: written and illustrated: Geldart's Cheshire; illustrated many books for leading publishers. *Address*: Geldart Gallery, Chelford Rd., Henbury, nr. Macclesfield, Ches. SK11 9PG. *Email*: william.geldart@virgin.net *Website*: www.geldartgallery.com

GELLER, William Jasper, FRSA, Hon SGFA; designer; Past Pres., Soc. of Graphic Fine Artists. *Medium*: pen and ink. *b*: London, 21 Dec 1930. *s of*: Henry Geller, master butcher.

m: widower. *Partner*: Leonie Mott. two *d*. *Educ*: Loughton School. *Studied*: City of London, Apprentice in Art, Central School, Regent Polytechnic (1947-52). *Exhib*: RSMA Annual show, SGFA Annual show, FBA Touring Exhbn, UA Annual Show, Essex Art Club, Maldon Art Club. *Works in collections*: Port of London Authority and private collections. *Official Purchasers*: Port of London, Essex County Council. *Works Reproduced*: 20th Century British Marine Painting. *Principal Works*: Drawings of working sailing vessels. *Recreations*: sailing. *Clubs*: Rotary International, Old Loughtonians H.C., Maldon Art Club, Essex Art Club *Address*: 26 Wellington Road, Maldon, Essex CM9 6HL. *Email*: w.geller@talktalk.net *Website*: www.williamgeller.co.uk *Signs work*: "William Geller."

GENTLEMAN, David, RDI (1970); ARCA; Prince Philip Designers Prize (2007). artist and designer: illustration, stamps, posters, etc. *Medium*: watercolour, lithography, wood engraving. *b*: London, 11 Mar 1930. *s of*: Tom & Winifred Gentleman. *m*: Susan (née) Evans. one *s*. three *d*. *Educ*: Hertford Grammar School. *Studied*: St. Albans School of Art (1947-48), R.C.A. (1950-53, Edward Bawden, John Nash). *Exhib*: solo exhbns. at Mercury Gallery, London (1970-2000), Fine Art Society (2004, 2007, 2010, 2012, 2014). *Works in collections*: BM, V&A, Tate Britain, Fitzwilliam Museum, National Maritime Museum, and in private collections. *Commissions*: Murals at Charing Cross Underground Station (1979). *Publications*: David Gentleman's Britain, - London, - Coastline, - Paris, - India, - Italy (1982-97); A Special Relationship (1987); Artwork (2002); London You're Beautiful (2012); In the Country (2014) and many illustrated. *Address*: 25 Gloucester Cres., London NW1 7DL. *Email*: d@gentleman.demon.co.uk *Signs work*: "David Gentleman."

GEORGE, Andrew Scott, DA (Edin.); Prizes: SWA Exeter, RWA (twice). *Medium*: egg tempera. *b*: Newcastle upon Tyne, 13 Aug 1952. *s of*: Marcus George. *m*: Valerie George. one *s*. one *d*. *Studied*: Edinburgh College of Art (1970-74); Moray House, Edinburgh. *Represented by*: Bertram Enterprises. *Exhib*: Anthony Hepworth, Marine Gallery, Affordable, Glasgow Art Fair, Art London, Portal Gallery, Sadler Gallery, Gallery Lefort, High Street Gallery - Kirkcudbright, Royal Academy, Portland Gallery, Panter and Hall, Lime Tree Gallery, Albany Gallery, Sladres Yard.. *Works in collections*: Flemming Collection, Sherrier Centre, Leicestershire, Dorsey & Whitney. *Commissions*: mainly private. *Publications*: Butterfly Friendly Garden. *Official Purchasers*: Leicestershire County Council. *Clubs*: Butterfly Conservation. *Misc*: Habitat Creation - large earthworks - dragons etc. (see butterfly friendly garden). *Address*: Noone Cottage, Springers Hill, Coleford, Radstock, BA3 5LN. *Email*: valgeorge52@btinternet.com *Website*: bertramenterprises.co.uk *Signs work*: "Andrew George".

GEORGE, Brian, RBA, AROI, FRSA, MPhil. (Loughborough), MEd (Nottingham), Hons. BEd (Loughborough); painter in oil and acrylic; hard edge abstracts based on decay, dereliction and Suffolk coast sea defences; part-time lecturer at Nottingham and Derby Universities. *b*: Ripley, Derbyshire, 7 Jun 1945. *m*: Joan (née Smith). *Educ*: Queen Elizabeth's Grammar School for Boys, Mansfield; Loughborough and Nottingham Universities; Cambridge Institute of Education. *Exhib*: RBA, ROI, Laing; exhibited one-man and with groups throughout Great Britain and Europe. *Works in collections*: Nottinghamshire Library Service, Heiligenhaus Civic Collection, Nottingham University and numerous private collections. *Clubs*: President, Mansfield Society of Artists. *Address*: Westfield House, 251 Alfreton Rd., Blackwell, Alfreton, Derbyshire DE55 5JN. *Email*: beageart@aol.com *Website*: briangeorgeart.com *Signs work*: "B GEORGE."

GEORGE, David, wood sculptor, mostly fine-finished for interior display, abstract, curvacious beautiful woods; walnut, yew, cherry, etc., copper water features, sculptures. *Medium*: wood. *b*: Winchester, 20 Feb 1952. *Educ*: Andover Grammar School, Salisbury College, Basingstoke College. *Studied*: botany, zoology, holistic therapist. *Exhib*: various shows, galleries, South England. *Commissions*: oak troll for Test Valley Borough Council, depicting "Billy Goats Gruff" story; 'Celtic Art' sculpture for Andover Museum. *Principal Works*: 'Spiritual Growth' on display T.V.B.C. H.Q., Andover. *Misc*: fully qualified holistic therapist, and acoustic guitarist. *Address*: Little Park Studio, Little Park, Andover, Hants SP11 7AX. *Email*: davidgeorge@sculptor.freeserve.co.uk *Website*: www.sculptor.freeserve.co.uk *Signs work*: Unsigned.

GEORGE, Patrick, artist. *b*: Manchester, 1923. *m*: 1st 1955 June Griffith (dissolved 1980); 2nd 1981 Susan Ward (dissolved 2009). *Partner*: Susan Engledow. four *d*. *Educ*: Edinburgh College of Art, Camberwell School of Art; taught, Slade School, University College London (1949-88); Slade Professor (1985-88). *Exhib*: Gainsborough's House, Sudbury (1975); retrospective, Serpentine Gallery (1980); Browse and Darby. *Works in collections*: Arts Council, Tate Gallery, etc. *Recreations*: Veg Gardening. *Misc*: Dealers: Browse and Darby. *Address*: Grandfathers, Great Saxham, Bury St. Edmunds IP29 5JW. *Signs work*: 'Patrick George'.

GEORGIOU, Elpida: see ELPIDA.

GERAGHTY, Martin Peter, *Medium*: Drawing, mixed: Traditional/digital. *b*: Warrington, 13 Dec 1968. *Partner*: Claire L Hand. one *d*. *Studied*: North Cheshire College (1985-87); Salford Polytechnic (1987-89). *Represented by*: Freelance. *Exhib*: The Cartoon Museum, London; Mixed and private. *Works in collections*: The Cartoon Museum Archive; various private/corporate. *Commissions*: BBC; Panini; numerous corporate/private. *Publications*: Numerous graphic novels (pub: Panini); The Flood; The Crimson Hand. *Recreations*: Walking, photography, antiquaria books, real ale. *Misc*: Younger brother of Cornish landscape painter, Paul Geraghty. *Address*: Warrington, Cheshire WA4 1QD. *Email*: martin.geraghty1968@btinternet.com *Signs work*: "Martin Geraghty".

GERAGHTY, Paul Leo, BA (Hons) Fine Art, ATC; Adrian Henri Memorial Award (2003, 2004, 2005), NAPA President's Award (2004); Fine Art Trade Guild Award (2005); Daler Rowney, Best British Painting (2006); 'The Artist', Best Painting Award (2007); Adrian Henri Memorial Award (2009). *Medium*: acrylics. *b*: Warrington, 18 Jun 1954. *m*: Katrina. one *s*. *Educ*: Stockton Heath County Secondary School. *Studied*: North Staffordshire Polytechnic, Goldsmiths College, University of London. *Exhib*: St. Ives Library (2003), Mariners Gallery (2003), 'Out of the Blue' , Marazion (2003), Williamson Gallery (2004), Gateway Gallery, Shrewsbury (2004), Cube3, University of Plymouth (2005), Falmouth Municipal Art Gallery (2004); Rathaus Stuttgart (2005), Mariners Gallery, St. Ives (2006), Waterside Gallery, St. Ives (2007); La Figura Gallery, Windsor (2008); Obsidian Gallery, Bucks (2008); View Two Gallery, Liverpool (2009). *Works in collections*: Inverliever Lodge Trust. *Clubs*: NAPA. *Address*: 2 Belmont Place, St. Ives, Cornwall, TR26 1DT. *Email*: pg@minerslamp.freeserve.co.uk *Website*: www.stivespainter.com *Signs work*: Paul Geraghty or P.G.

GERRIE, Pamela Margaret, BA Hons Fine Art Sculpture, PGCE; Special Entry to Kingston School of Art; President Cambridge University Pottery Society (1996); Arts Council Award (Nov 2000). *Medium*: sculpture, ceramics, fire. *b*: Chelsea, London, 1 Feb 1952. *d of*: Robert Gerrie and Margaret Alston. *Partner*: Phil Humphreys. one *s*. one *d* and two *s-d*. *Studied*: Kingston School of Art; K.O.T. Garnett College of Education. *Represented by*: Gail Olding, "Edge of Ordinary", Espacio Gallery, Shoreditch, London. *Exhib*: RA Summer Show 2004, Discerning Eye, London 2008; numerous mixed shows. *Works in collections*: public collections: Butterly tile, Oncology Dept, Bristol Royal Infirmary; private collections Washington DC, USA, UK and Europe. *Commissions*: coldcut fire sculpture logos, Lee Scratch Perry Meltdown Festival, Royal Festival Halls (2003); Strawberry Fair Festival, Grand Finale Fire Sculpture (1998); British red Cross Performance and Bodyart, Guildhall, London (1994); and many others. *Principal Works*: "Window", Peacock butterfly tile. *Recreations*: driving around in a camper van. *Misc*: TV-1996 Fire

Sculpture construction, Wysing Arts Cambridge (ITV, Anglia); 1997 1st American/British Contemporary Sculpture Iron Pour (ITV, Suffolk); 2013 ongoing: Collaboration with Benny Wenda (Nobel Peace Prize nominee (2013) for "Free West Papua" Tribal Peoples' Campaign. *Address*: c/o 8 Walpole Road, Cambridge CB1 3TJ. *Email*: pamela.gerrie@gmail.com *Website*: office of Benny Wenda *Signs work*: "PMG" (earlier work as P.Smith).

GETHIN, Jackie, CIC, SBA. *Medium*: watercolour. *b*: Brikendon, Herts., 14 May 1949. *m*: Richard. three *d*. *Educ*: Effingham House School, Cooden, Sussex. *Studied*: Southampton College of Art, Bournemouth and Poole College of Art (Keith Rennison). *Exhib*: numerous mixed shows including SBA. *Works in collections*: Francis Iles, Rochester. *Works Reproduced*: by The Medici Society Ltd. *Recreations*: walking. *Clubs*: Soc. of Botanical Artists. *Address*: Trotts Ash, Sole Street, nr. Gravesend, Kent DA12 3AY. *Email*: rjgethin@aol.com *Signs work*: "Jackie Gethin."

GIBB, Avril V.: see WATSON STEWART, (Lady) Avril Veronica.

GIBBONS, Jeff, BA (Hons.), MA; prizewinner John Moores (1995). *Medium*: oil, watercolour, drawing. *b*: London, 9 Nov 1962. *m*: Joanna Melvin. one *s*. one *d*. *Studied*: Ravensbourne (1980-1981), Middx. Polytechnic (1981-1984), London University (1989-1991). *Exhib*: various exhibs including, Morley Gallery, London (1994), Bede Gallery, Jarrow (1996), John Moores (1995 - prizewinner & 1999), Natwest Gallery (1997 & 1998), Art Business Design Centre (1999-2001); RA Summer Exhbn (2002); selected solo shows: 2005: St.Giles, Cripplegate, Barbican; Art Space Gallery, London; Gloucester Cathedral; Emma Hill Fine Art, London (1999, 2001); Art Space Gallery & Project Space (2007, 2009); Annunciation, Oxley, Herts (2010); Ladder, Testbed 1 (2011); NOT Flowers, London (2012); 100 Plus, Zurich (2014). *Works in collections*: Special Collections at: Henry Moore, Tate, Chelsea College of Art. *Publications*: Walking Paintings 2012, Negative Enthusiasm 2013, NOT Flowers with essay by C. Philpott. *Works Reproduced*: catalogues, John Moores (19 & 21), Natwest (1997 & 1998), British Library Report (2000-2001), RA Summer Show (2002). *Address*: 123 Evering Road, London N16 7BU. *Email*: gibbonsjef@gmail.com *Signs work*: "Jeff Gibbons."

GIBBONS, John, BA Hons. (Sculpture); Head of Sculpture, Winchester School of Art, elected Prof. (1995). *b*: Ireland, 1949. *Educ*: Ireland. *Studied*: St. Martin's School of Art. *Represented by*: Flowers East London; Taylor Galleries, Dublin. *Exhib*: solo exhibitions: International Arts Centre, London (1975), Project Gallery, Dublin (1979), Nicola Jacobs Gallery, London (1981), Triangle Center, N.Y.C. (1984), Serpentine Gallery (1986), John Hansard Gallery, Southampton University (1986), Galerie Wentzel, Köln (1987), Madeleine Carter Fine Art, Boston, Mass. (1988), Flowers East (1990, 1992, 1994, 1997, 1999, 2003), Flowers Graphics, London (1996), Butler Gallery, The Castle, Kilkenny Ireland (1996), Whitworth A.G. Manchester (1997), Kettles Yard, Cambridge (1997), Lothbury Gallery, London (1998), Temple Bar Gallery, Dublin (1998), Crawford Municipal A.G., Cork (1998), Nograd History Museum, Salgotorjan, Hungary (1999), Endre Horvath Gallery, Balassagyarmat, Hungary (1999), The Napolean Garden, Holland Park, London (2002), Taylor Galleries, Dublin (1999, 2005), Flowers Central, London (2001, 2007), One Canada Square, Canary Wharf, London (2005), Canem Galeria, Castello, Spain (2006). *Works in collections*: Tate, London; Arts Council England; Edmonton Art Gallery, Alberta, Canada; The Modern Art Centre/Calouste Gulbenkian, Lisbon; The Museum of Contemporary Art, Barcelona, Spain; The Czech Museum of Fine Arts, Prague; The Whitworth Art Gallery, Manchester; Jesus College, University of Cambridge; Syracuse University, New York, USA; OPW, Environmental Protection Agency, Johnstown Castle, Co. Wexford, Ireland; The National Self-Portrait Collection, University of Limerick, Ireland; Nograd History Museum, Salgotorjan, Hungary; Contemporary Arts Society, Dublin; Contemporary Art Society,

London; The Comino Foundation; Sculpture at Goodwood; The Ballinglen Archive, The Ballinglen Arts; Foundation, Ballycastle, County Mayo, Ireland; Imperial College Healthcare Charity Art Collection, London; Cork County Council, Cork, Ireland. *Commissions*: sculpture at Goodwood. *Publications*: Gonzalez: A Legacy; Introduction to catalogue, South Bank Centre, Whitechapel. *Misc*: Visit website for a comprehensive view of CV and images. *Address*: 14 Almond Rd., London SE16 3LR. *Website*: www.johngibbons.org.uk *Signs work*: "J.G." welded on.

GIBBS, Mavis, Dip.SLm, HS. *Medium*: watercolours - miniatures (portraits, flowers, animals). *b*: London, 10 Aug 1939. *m*: George Gibbs. two *d. Studied*: self-taught. *Exhib*: SLm, Chichester (annually); HS, Bath (annually); World Exhibition of Miniatures (Tasmania, 2007). *Works in collections*: various private collections in USA, Japan, South Africa, UK. *Commissions*: via recommendation. *Clubs*: Willesborough Art Fellowship (Founder Member). *Address*: 33 Cherry Glebe, Mersham, Ashford, Kent, TN25 6NL. *Email*: mavisgibbs@gznet.co.uk *Signs work*: 'Mavis Gibbs' or 'MJG' (monogram).

GIBBS, Stephen Roy, SGFA; London Diploma in Design (LDAD, 1980); Cert Ed. (1996); BA Hons Education and Training (Greenwich, 1999). *Medium*: watercolour, drawing, prints, sculpture. *b*: Southend-on-Sea, 10 May 1957. *s of*: Roy Frederick Gibbs and Pauline Jean Gibbs (nee Fraser). *Educ*: Cecil Jones High School, Southend-on-Sea (1968-75). *Studied*: Southend College of Arts and Technology (Foundation, 1975-77); London College of Printing (1977-1980); South East Essex College (1994-99). *Represented by*: www.londonart.co.uk. *Exhib*: RA, RWA, Discerning Eye, Singer & Friedlander/Sunday Times Watercolour Competition, RI, Beecroft Art Gallery (Southend-on-Sea), Estuary Art Gallery (Leigh-on-Sea), Menier Gallery, London, United Society of Artists. *Works in collections*: Beecroft Art Gallery. *Commissions*: sculptures commissioned for charity Childline. *Publications*: featured on page 264 of 'Oil Paintings in Public Ownership in Essex', The Public Catalogue Foundation, ISBN 1-904931-15-4, first published 2006. *Official Purchasers*: Beecroft Art Gallery (paintings, permanent collection); many paintings and linocuts in private collections. *Works Reproduced*: in The Times, The Echo (Basildon & Southend-on-Sea). *Principal Works*: linocuts, Seaside paintings, Topiary paintings. *Recreations*: photography, exhibitions, music. *Misc*: Society of Graphic Fine Artists. *Address*: 11 Stanfield Road, Southend-on-Sea, Essex SS2 5DQ. *Email*: stephen.gibbs@southend.ac.uk. *Website*: www.londonart.co.uk. *Signs work*: 'Stephen Gibbs' or 'Stephen R.Gibbs' on earlier works. Now signs as 'S.G.', and in all cases followed by the year work was produced.

GIBILARO, Jason, painter in oil and acrylic. *b*: London, 25 Aug 1962. *Studied*: St. Martin's School of Art and Design (1980-81), Brighton School of Art and Design (1981-84). *Exhib*: RA Summer Show, Peterborough Museum and Gallery, Christopher Hull Gallery London. *Works in collections*: University of London Picture Club. *Commissions*: Hazard Evaluation Laboratory. *Address*: 62 Kemble House, Barrington Rd., London SW9 7EF.

GIBSON, Jane Barr, RMS, HS; BA, artist in oil, pastel, water-colour of miniatures and larger works; Artist in Residence, Dorothy L. Sayers Soc.; Llewelyn Alexander Gallery Award 2011 at Hilliard Society Exhibition, Wells. *b*: Smithton, Tasmania, 14 Sep 1954. *Studied*: Carlisle College of Art and Design, Norwich School of Art. *Exhib*: RMS Westminster Gallery London, H.S. Wells, Medici Gallery London, Polak Gallery London, Malcolm Innes Gallery, London and Edinburgh, Samap, France (miniature soc.), Smithsonian Institute, Washington DC, Hobart & Burnie, Tasmania. *Works in collections*: Capitol Hill, Washington DC, USA. *Commissions*: "Lockerbie Remembered" (commissioned by Dumfries & Galloway Constabulary). *Publications*: illustrated: To Those Who Love - poetry book by Jo McNaught. *Works Reproduced*: by Hockin & Roberts Ltd. (Cornwall). *Address*: 'Cornerways', 7 Selkirk Rd., Kirkcudbright DG6 4BL. *Email*: jane@cornerwaysart.co.uk *Website*: www.cornerwaysart.co.uk

GIBSON, Veronica, BA (Hons); painter in oil, private teacher. *b*: St. Albans, Herts., 15 Apr 1954. *Educ*: Loretto College. *Studied*: Hertfordshire College of Art (1972-73), Canterbury College of Art (1978-81, Thomas Watt, DA Edin.). *Exhib*: RA, NEAC, ROI, RWA, Cardiff. *Works in collections*: S. Glamorgan; private: France and Sweden. *Address*: Ty Coed, Chapel St., Bedlinog, Mid Glamorgan CF46 6TS.

GIBSON-WATT, Marcia Susan, BA Graphic Design. *Medium*: acrylic, pastel and recently oil. *b*: London, 12 Sep 1949; 4 grandchildren. *d of*: Sir Roger Cary. *m*: Robin Gibson-Watt. three *s.* one *d. Educ*: St.Mary's Convent, Ascot. *Studied*: Studio Simi Florence (1966-67); Kingston Art College (1967-71). *Exhib*: RA Summer Exhbn (several times, most recent 2005); The Gallery in Cork Street (1999, 2001, 2004); Alpine Gallery, London (1986, 87); solo: Memphis Botanic Gardens, Tennessee, USA (2003), Fosse Gallery (2007); Gallery 27, Cork Street (2008); La Galleria, Pall Mall (2009). *Works in collections*: Terry Wogan, D Barbour, the late Sir Geraint Evans. *Commissions*: label for English and Californian Vineyard; Betty Parsons retirement present, presented at RA; Robin Price: Welsh Black Cattle, a large Swiss landscape for private client in Switzerland. *Publications*: has illustrated two privately published (Bluestone Books) prayer books: 'The Four Graces' and 'A.C.T.S. I', and now 'Hope in the Valley' a paperback bereavement book with black & white illustrations to be published in USA. *Principal Works*: 'Tea Pickers in Sri Lanka' and Lumle village, Nepal (6'x4' gouache/pastel). *Recreations*: travel. *Clubs*: Chelsea Arts Club. *Address*: Gelligarn, Llanyre, Llandrindod Wells, Powys LD1 6EY. *Email*: robin.gibson1@btconnect.com *Website*: www.gibsonwatt.co.uk

GIFFORD, Andrew John. *Medium*: oil paint, also neon and all forms of artificial light. *b*: Sheffield, 26 Mar 1970. *s of*: John and Kay Gifford. *m*: Rosie. one *s.* one *d. Educ*: Foundation, York Tech., first class BA Hons Newcastle University. *Studied*: Fine Art. *Represented by*: John Martin of London, 38 Albemarle Street, London W1X 3FB. *Exhib*: solo: Art London, Chelsea Barracks (2003), John Martin of London (2002); group (2000): 'Blue', The New Art Gallery, Walsall, French Paintings, Art 2000, BDC, Islington; (1997) Northern Lights, Fruit Market Gallery, Edinburgh. *Works in collections*: Walsall, New Art Gallery; Middlesborough Art Gallery. *Recreations*: 1996-97 part-time lecturer/ Newcastle and Aberdeen University. *Misc*: Documentaries: Date with an Artist BBC2 (1997); Don't Look Down, Scottish TV (1997). *Address*: 35 Addinson Road, Hove, BN3 1TQ. *Email*: rosieinfrance@hotmail.com *Website*: www.jmlondon.com

GILBERT, Dennis, NEAC; portrait and landscape painter; formerly senior lecturer, Chelsea School of Art; all conventional media (oil, watercolour, pastel). *b*: London, 7 Jan 1922. *s of*: Gordon S. Gilbert. *m*: 1st Joan Musker; 2nd (2000) Ann Kodicek. three *s.* one *d. Educ*: Weston-super-Mare. *Studied*: St. Martin's School of Art (1946-51). *Exhib*: RA, Paris Salon, RP, RBA, NEAC, Soc. of Landscape Painters, Small Paintings Group (Past President), Browse & Darby, Leicester Galleries, Redfern, W.H. Patterson Fine Art, Thompsons Gallery, Duncan Miller and Zwemmer Galleries, etc.; one-man shows: F.B.A. Gallery (1968), Langton Gallery (1982), Gill Drey Gallery (1989), Highgate Fine Art (1997 and 2002), Piers Feetham Gallery (2002, 2005), Chambers Gallery (2007). *Works Reproduced*: The Artist (periodical). *Clubs*: Arts, Chelsea Arts, London Sketch Club. *Address*: Top Studio, 11 Edith Gr., Chelsea, London SW10 0JZ. *Email*: dennis@dennisgilbert.net *Website*: www.dennisgilbert.net *Signs work*: "Dennis Gilbert."

GILBERT, George, RSW (1973), DA (Glasgow) 1961, Post. Dip. (1962); Art Store award PAI (1992); WG Gillies Award, RSW (1993); RCPSG award, RGI (2006); RSW Council award (2007); Strathearn Award (RGI, 2007); Artstore Award - Scottish Drawing Competition (2009). *Medium*: water-colour, acrylic, pen and wash. *b*: Glasgow, 12 Sep 1939. *s of*: Samuel Gilbert, railwayman. *m*: Lesley. three *s. Educ*: Glasgow. *Studied*: Glasgow School of Art (1957-61): Guthrie Book Prize (portraiture). *Exhib*: one-man shows:

Kelly Gallery, Glasgow (1967), Byre Theatre, St. Andrews (1979), Loomshop Gallery, Lower Largo (1981, 1988, 1990), Torrance Gallery, Edinburgh (1991); several joint shows in Glasgow and Edinburgh; regular exhibitor at RSA, RSW, etc., also Commonwealth Arts Festival, Bath Art Fair, Cleveland International Drawing (90). One man shows: The Gatehouse Gallery, Glasgow (1996), The Open Eye Gallery, Edinburgh (1994), The Courtyard Gallery, Crail (1996, 1997), Pittenweem Arts Festival (2003, 2004, 2005), Roger Billcliffe Gallery (2008). *Works in collections*: Nuffield Foundation, Fife Regional Council; Heritage collection, St. Monans; Royal College of Physicians & Surgeons, Glasgow; many private home and abroad. *Address*: 282 Ferry Road, Trinity, Edinburgh EH5 3NP. *Email*: enquiry@georgegilbertrsw.co.uk *Website*: www.georgegilbertrsw.co.uk *Signs work*: "George Gilbert."

GILBERT, John Stewart, Cert.Ed.(1955), Art teaching Cert. (1964); taught in Cheltenham, then Sheffield as Head of Art and Crafts Dept., Abbeydale Grange School; examiner A level Art (practical and Art history); silver medal Paris Salon (1965), first prize International Competition for Professional Artists Still Life in Oils (1999); Prize Winner Great Sheffield Art Shows. *Medium*: painter in oil, watercolour, acrylic and pastel. *b*: 25 Apr 1933. *m*: Helena Rosemary. one *s*. one *d*. *Educ*: St. Paul's College Cheltenham under George W. Sayer 1953-55. *Studied*: Bournemouth and Poole College of Art under E.D'Arcy Lister 1963-64. *Exhib*: RA, Paris Salon, RWA, RI, ROI, RWS, BSP, etc. *Works in collections*: America, Sweden, Finland, Spain, New Zealand, Derbyshire County Council, Lady Wortley, Lord Ingoldsby. *Commissions*: court artist for YTV since 1992; Group portraits: Officers' Mess 2nd Battalion Royal Fusiliers; Leeds coroner's court, and other individuals. *Publications*: illustrations for Phasmid Society, entry in La Revue Moderne des arts et de la vie September 1963, entry Repertorium Artis 1969 (International Arts Guild) and Christmas cards. *Works Reproduced*: Rotherham City Centre (Going Home). *Recreations*: art, family, gardening and music. *Clubs*: Associate of the Societe des Artistes Francais since 1966. Chairman, Yorkshire Watercolour Society, also Cheltenham Art Club, Hallam Art Group, President of Underbank Art Group. *Address*: 4 Oakbrook Rd, Sheffield, S11 7EA.

GILBERT, Rowena Justine, BA (Hons) Three Dimensional Crafts (2002): 'Best Up and Coming Local Artist Award 2002' (Brighton & Hove), Craft & Design Selected Award Finalist - Ceramics 2011. *Medium*: painting, sculpture, ceramics. *b*: Taplow, Berkshire, 24 Nov 1979. *d of*: Terence Gilbert. *Educ*: 3D Crafts-University of Brighton (specialising in ceramics and plastics). *Studied*: Art and Design Foundation- Brighton College of Technology; A'levels (Fine Art, Fashion & Textiles, Design and Technology, Mathematics) Christs Hospital School, Horsham. *Exhib*: New Ashgate Gallery, Farnham; Royal Exchange Theatre Craft Shop, Manchester; The Biscuit Factory, Newcastle upon Tyne; Northern Lights Gallery, Keswick; Henry Paddon Contemporary Art, Eastbourne; Bluemoon Gallery, Tunbridge Wells; Bell Fine Art, Winchester. *Address*: Studio 3, Level 5 (North), New England House, New England Street, Brighton, E.Sussex, BN1 4GH. *Email*: info@rowenagilbert.com *Website*: www.rowenagilbert.com

GILBERT, Terence John, SEA. *Medium*: oil, watercolour, pastel. *b*: London, 14 Oct 1946. *s of*: J.S.Gilbert. *m*: Pamela Gilbert. one *s*. one *d*. *Educ*: London. *Studied*: Camberwell Arts School, London. *Represented by*: Mathaf Gallery, W.H.Patterson, London; Osborne Studio Gallery. *Exhib*: Mathaf Gallery, London, Dubai, Jordan, Saudi Arabia, Oman, Society of Equestrian Artists, Osborne Studio Gallery, London (2004); one-man shows Bruton Street Gallery (1995-2002) London, Mathaf Gallery (2010). *Works in collections*: former President Reagan, Charlton Heston, Sheikh Mohammed al Maktoum, Sir Peter O'Sullevan, Sultanate of Oman, J.P.MacManus, Frankie Dettori, Mr & Mrs J Magnier. *Commissions*: Royal Blackheath Golf Club, Racehorse Owners Association, Derby Winners Nashwan and Generous, Royal Palace of Jordan, British Airways, The Ashes at the Oval 2005, James D. Jameson, Coolmore Stud. *Publications*: Punch Magazine, Golf Monthly, ES Magazine, exhibition catalogues. *Official Purchasers*: Royal Palace Amman, Jordan. *Works Reproduced*: limited editions of sport and landscapes. *Principal Works*: H.M. The Queen, and President Reagan riding at Windsor. *Address*: Wisteria Cottage, 27 Rushington Avenue, Maidenhead, Berks, SL6 1BY. *Email*: info@terencegilbert.com *Website*: www.terencegilbert.com *Signs work*: 'T.J.Gilbert'.

GILDEA, Paul Rudolph, BA Hons. Fine Art; artist in oil on canvas; part time tutor, Fulham and Chelsea AEI. *b*: London, 3 Jan 1956. *s of*: John Robert Denis Gildea, BA Hons. *Educ*: Dulwich College. *Studied*: Camberwell School of Arts and Crafts (1975-76), Middlesex Polytechnic (1976-79). *Exhib*: Serpentine Summer Show (1982), Whitechapel Open (1987), Riverside Open (1987), RA Summer Show (1987). *Address*: 41 Ballater Rd., Brixton, London SW2 5QS. *Signs work*: "Gildea."

GILDER, Russell H., Awards: Lynn Painter-Stainers Prize Finalist (2007), Discerning Eye Finalist (2004), Hunting Prize Finalist (2003). *Medium*: oil, drawing, prints. *b*: Plymouth, 20 May 1966. *Partner*: Caroline McRae. two *d*. *Studied*: Birmingham City University (School of Fine Art, 1993-96), Greenwich University (2000-01). *Represented by*: British Art Portfolio, Guilsborough Court, Guilsborough, Northants. *Exhib*: RA Summer Exhibition (2014), RWA Bristol (2008, 2012), RBSA Birmingham (2008), BSA, Bath (2006), Glasgow Art Fair (2006), Discerning Eye (2004). *Works in collections*: Birmingham City University; Aomori Contemporary Arts Center, Japan. *Commissions*: private commissions. *Publications*: "The Mountains of Snowdonia in Art" by Peter Bishop (pub. Gwasg carreg Gwalch, 2015). *Works Reproduced*: A View at: Pont Aberglaslyn (drawing - charcoal on paper, 2013). *Principal Works*: paintings and drawings of the ancient border landscape of England and Wales. *Address*: 20 Broadlands, Shaldon, Devon TQ14 0EH. *Email*: russgilder@gmail.com *Website*: www.russellgilderpaintings.com *Signs work*: "R H G".

GILDER, Theresa, Dip. Art & Craft. *Medium*: sculpture. *b*: Manchester, 26 Sep 1935. three *s*. *Studied*: Penzance School of Art (1956-59). *Exhib*: Thompsons City Gallery, London; Courcoux & Courcoux, Stockbridge; Penwith Gallery, St. Ives; Trelissick Gallery, Truro; Gordon Hepworth Gallery, Devon; Royal West of England Academy, Bristol; Trelowarren Gallery, Helston; New Craftsman, St. Ives; Lighthouse Gallery, Penzance; Coach House Gallery, Guernsey; Summerhouse Gallery, Marazion; Marsdon Fine Art, London; Truro Museum. *Works in collections*: Lord Jeffrey Archer; Truro City Museum. *Commissions*: Control Tech HQ, Powys, Wales; Home Farm Trust; Mermaid Centre, Truro. *Publications*: Front covers: "Women Before God" (Lavinia Burn, 1988), "A Referred Pain" (Penny Snow, (1997), Womens Institute Art Diary 1993. *Recreations*: walking, reading, singing, gardening. *Misc*: 3 year Apprenticeship with J.S. Design, Manchester. Mother of Lawrence Murley, stone carver. *Address*: 24 Kings Road, Penzance, Cornwall TR18 4LG. *Email*: theresa.gilder@talktalk.net *Signs work*: "T.G", "t.gilder" or "Theresa Gilder".

GILES, Peter Donovan, PhD (Middx) (2000), NDD (Special level Illustration) (1959), ATC (Lond) (1960), FRGS; painter, illustrator and sculptor; countertenor; teaches part-time, workshops. *Medium*: mixed. *b*: Perivale, Middx., 15 Feb 1939. *s of*: Donovan Eric Giles and Evelyn Mary Sherlock. *m*: Elizabeth Ann Broom (decd). one *s*. one *d*. *Educ*: Castlehill College, Ealing. *Studied*: Ealing School of Art (1954-59), Hornsey College of Art (1959-60). *Exhib*: All Hallows on the Wall, EC2; provincial one-man shows; lecture tours, USA and Canada. *Works in collections*: Lichfield City A.G., War Memorial Ely Cathedral. *Commissions*: various. *Publications*: novels, non-fiction, cartoons, board games. *Address*: Filmer House, Bridge, Canterbury, Kent CT4 5NB. *Email*: petergiles@filmer-house.co.uk *Signs work*: "Peter Giles."

GILI, Katherine, FRBS; BA (1970); Advanced Dip. (1973); Elephant Trust Award; Jack Goldhill Award (2013). *Medium*: Sculpture. *b*: Oxford, 6 Apr 1948. *d of*: J.L. & E.H.Gili.

m: Robert Persey. one *s*. *Studied*: Bath Academy of Art (1966-70), St Martin's School of Art (1971-73) . *Exhib*: solo shows: Salander/O'Reilly NY, Serpentine Gallery; Poussin Gallery; mixed shows: Tate Gallery, Hayward Gallery, Serpentine Gallery, RA, Conde Duque Centre Madrid, Battersea Park, Flowers East, New Art Centre Sculpture Park, Pride of the Valley Sculpture Park, Poussin Gallery. *Works in collections*: Arts Council of England, and private collections in Britain, Spain and USA; City of Lugano Switzerland; General Electric, USA; Railtrack; Cartwright Hall Museum, Bradford. *Publications*: numerous exhbn. catalogues, reviews, articles. *Clubs*: Anglo-Catalan Society. *Misc*: selector for New Contemporaries, Serpentine Summer Show, 'Have you Seen Sculpture from the Body' Tate Gallery. *Address*: 7 The Mall, Faversham, Kent, ME13 8JL. *Email*: katherine@persey.plus.com *Website*: www.katherinegili.com *Signs work*: some work signed.

GILLARD, Charles Richard, NDD (1961) (Illustration), Cert RAS (Painting) (1964), Leverhulme Scholarship (1964); part-time lecturer, senior lecturer, workshop director for drawing, London and University of Wales (1965-95). *Medium*: oil, egg tempera, drawing, prints. *b*: Southampton, UK, 11 Sep 1940. *Studied*: Southampton College of Art (1957-61), Royal Academy Schools (1961-64). *Exhib*: RA, Christie's etc. *Commissions*: private commissions for paintings, still lifes and portraits. *Publications*: London Parks 1976. *Clubs*: RASAA. *Address*: Flat 3, 1-3 Little Titchfield St, London W1W 7BU. *Signs work*: 'CRG', 'CRGillard'.

GILLESPIE, Sarah, BFA (Oxford); Egerton Coghill Award (1983); Elizabeth Greenshield International Award (1984). *Medium*: oil, drawing. *b*: Winchester, 27 Jun 1963. *d of*: David Gillespie ARCA & Ann Gillespie ARCA. *Partner*: Paul Kirkup. one *s*. one *d*. *Studied*: Atelier Neo-Medici, Paris (1981/1982), Ruskin School of Drawing and Fine Art, Oxford (Pem.Coll., 1982-85). *Represented by*: Waterhouse & Dodd, London. *Exhib*: solo: Thursday Gallery, Bath (1989), Ombersley Gallery, Worcs. (1997), New Street Gallery, Plymouth (2003), Waterhouse & Dodd (2005, 2007). Selected group shows (since 1982): Weir Gallery, Bath (1988), Gallery Revel, New York (1990), Cheltenham Open (1997), RWA Open (1999), Thompson's Gallery, Stow on the Wold (2001, 2002), Art London (2005), The London Art Fair (2006, 2007, 2009, 2010), Coombe Gallery, Dartmouth (2006); Beaux Arts Bath (2008). *Works in collections*: Merryl Lynch Bank, Rolls Royce, Victoria Gallery Bath, Government Offices (SW). *Publications*: "Sarah Gillespie. The Slapton Ley Project", White Lane Press (2007); "View from the Boat House Window" with Brian Patten (2009). *Official Purchasers*: Victoria Gallery, Bath; Government Offices (SW). *Address*: Clover Cottage, Blackawton, Totnes, Devon, TQ9 7BN. *Email*: studio@sarahgillespie.co.uk *Website*: www.sarahgillespie.co.uk *Signs work*: "GILLESPIE".

GILLICK, James Balthazar Patrick, BA (Hons). *Medium*: painter in oil, drawings, drypoint, portraits, still lifes, figures. *b*: Kings Lynn, 8 Feb 1972. *m*: Miriam. three *s*. three *d*. *Educ*: Ratcliffe College, Wisbech Grammar School. *Studied*: C&G CHE. *Represented by*: Jonathan Cooper: Park Walk Gallery. *Exhib*: numerous exhibs., London and nationally. *Works in collections*: Baroness Thatcher. *Commissions*: portraits: Baroness Thatcher (1998), Rt. Rev. M. Couve de Murville, Archbishop of Birmingham (1999); His Holiness Pope John Paul II (2004/05). *Clubs*: Chelsea Arts Club. *Address*: c/o Jonathan Cooper, Park Walk Gallery, 20 Park Walk, London SW10 0AQ. *Email*: james@gillick-artist.com *Website*: www.gillick-artist.com www.jonathancooper.co.uk *Signs work*: monogram - G bisected by J.

GILLIMAN, Tricia, BA (Hons) Fine Art, MFA Fine Art; artist in oil on canvas; Senior lecturer, Central/St. Martin's School of Art, London Inst. *b*: 9 Nov 1951. *m*: Alexander Ramsay. one *s*. *Studied*: Leeds University, Newcastle University. *Exhib*: Benjamin Rhodes (1985, 1987, 1993), Arnolfini (1985), Gardner Centre, Brighton (1993), Jill George (1997-99), John Moores (1983, 1985, 1989, 1991), etc. *Works in collections*: Contemporary Art Soc., Unilever PLC., New Hall Cambridge, University of Liverpool, Herbert A.G. Coventry,

University of Leeds, Stanhope Properties Ltd., Television South West, The Stuyvesant Foundation. *Commissions*: BBC Film: The Colour Eye: The Dynamics of Paint. *Address*: 149 Algernon Rd., London SE13 7AP.

GILLMOR, Robert, NDD (1958), ATD (1959); freelance illustrator, designer, painter in water-colour, black and white, lino-cut prints; Director Art and Craft, Leighton Park School (1959-65); President, S.WL.A.(1984-94), President, Reading Guild of Artists (1969-84). *b*: Reading, 6 Jul 1936. *s of*: Gerald Gillmor. *m*: Susan Norman, painter. one *s*. one *d*. *Educ*: Leighton Pk. School, Reading. *Studied*: School of Fine Art, Reading University (1954-59, Prof. J.A. Betts, William McCance, Frank Ormrod, Hugh Finney). *Exhib*: SWLA. *Works in collections*: Ulster Museum and A.G., Belfast, Reading Museum and A.G. *Publications*: 150 books illustrated. Author: 'Cutting Away', Langford Press (2006); Joint author: 'Art of the New Naturalists', Collins (2009); Author: 'Birds, Blocks & Stamps', Two Rivers Press (2012); Author: 'Cover Birds', Two Rivers Press (2013). *Address*: North Light, Hilltop, Cley, Norfolk NR25 7SE. *Signs work*: "R.G." or "Robert Gillmor."

GILLMORE, Olwen Nina, SWA; sculptor in clay and bronze. *b*: Zimbabwe, 19 Mar., 1936. *d of*: John Henry Forsyth. *m*: Charles Gillmore. two *s*. three *d*. *Educ*: USA (1980-82), London Karin Jonzen (1983-90). *Exhib*: Chelsea; SWA London; Chichester Cathedral; USA; Guernsey, CI. *Commissions*: Chase Hospice Service for Children, Cotswold Wildlife Park; King Edward VII School, Whitley, Surrey; private commissions. *Address*: Sarnesfield, Lurgashall, Petworth, W. Sussex GU28 9EZ. *Email*: olwen.gillmore@tiscali.co.uk *Signs work*: "Olwen."

GILMOUR, Judith, DA (Glas); ceramist in stoneware and porcelain thrown and assembled. *b*: Edinburgh, 2 Oct 1937. one *d*. *Studied*: Edinburgh College of Art, Glasgow School of Art. *Exhib*: Roger Billcliffe Glasgow, Scottish Gallery and Open Eye Gallery, Edinburgh, R.A. Summer Show, Crafts Council Contemporary Applied Arts. *Works in collections*: Royal Museum Edinburgh, Art Galleries Glasgow and Aberdeen, Wustum Museum Wisconsin, Graz Museum Austria. *Commissions*: wall panel: Diaspora Museum, Tel Aviv; entry hall: Canada Life Assurance Head Office. *Clubs*: Chelsea Arts. Selected makers Inex Crafts Council, Mem.: Contemporary Applied Arts, Assoc. of Applied Arts (Scotland). *Address*: 52 Bronsart Rd., London SW6 6AA. *Website*: www.judithgilmour.com

GIRLING, Angela Marie, Silver Gilt Medal from RHS, joint gold plus bronze and silver. *Medium*: watercolour. *b*: Southend-on-Sea, 1952. *m*: Revd Ian Gilring. one *s*. one *d*. *Studied*: Sutton College of Liberal Arts. *Exhib*: RHS Vincent Square, Sutton, Surrey, Hunt Institute of Botanical Illistration Pittsburgh, Sir Harald Hillier Gdns, Sofiero Sweden, National Botanical Gdns of Wales, Patent Office Munich, Jersey, Royal Victoria Pk Southampton, Mottisfont Gdns, Bath, Bradford on Avon, Gardeners World Live, Nant-y-Coy Mill Pembs, Centre of Alternative Technology, Malvern Show. *Works in collections*: various private collections. *Commissions*: various private individuals. *Works Reproduced*: Lings Cards, stationery by Robert Fredericks, National Trust. *Clubs*: President of the Bath Society of Botanical Artists, Society of Floral Painters, Chelsea Physic Gdns. Florilegium Society, Emeritus member. *Email*: angiemgirling@ymail.com *Signs work*: "ANGIE GIRLING".

GIRVIN, Joy, BA Hons. Fine Art (1984), Post Grad.Dip. in Painting (1987); artist in oils and pastels; Art Tutor. *b*: Herts, 15 Nov 1961. *Educ*: University of Northumberland (1984), Royal Academy Schools of Art (1987). *Exhib*: regularly at Cadogan Contemporary Gallery, London. *Works in collections*: Barings Bank, National Trust Foundation for Art, Paintings in Hospitals, London Weekend TV, Manchester City A.G., Exeter Museum and A.G. *Commissions*: Gardens, Italian landscape. *Clubs*: A.C.G and Sailing, member of Chisendale Studios. *Address*: 4 Dellsome Lane, Wellham Green, Herts AL9 7NF. *Signs work*: "Joy Girvin."

GLANVILLE, Christopher, RWA; David Murray Landscape Scholarship (1968, 1970); landscape painter in oil on canvas, oil on panel; Vice-President RWA (1992-97). *Medium*: oil and watercolour. *b*: London, 10 Aug 1948. *s of*: Roy Glanville, RBA, RSMA, marine artist and illustrator. *m*: Zelda Glanville, potter and painter. one *s*. *Educ*: St. Clement Danes Grammar School, London. *Studied*: Heatherley School of Art (1965), Byam Shaw School of Art (1967-70, B. Dunstan, M. de Sausmarez), RA Schools (1970-73, P. Greenham). *Exhib*: RA, RWA, Bruton Gallery, Kaplan Gallery, Woburn Abbey, NEAC, Alresford Gallery, Sinfield Gallery, Wykeham Gallery, W.H. Patterson, Frost & Reed, Jerram Gallery, Mandells Gallery. *Works in collections*: RWA, Richmond Museum, Kingston Museum, MBNA Bank. *Publications*: Dictionary of British Artists Since 1945; RA Exhibitors. *Works Reproduced*: BBC - Your Paintings - in association with the Public Catalogue Foundation. *Address*: Galveston, Giggs Hill Road, Thames Ditton, Surrey, KT7 0BT. *Website*: www.christopherglanville.co.uk *Signs work*: "GLANVILLE." or "G."

GLASS, Margaret, PS, Membre Société des Pastellistes de France; landscape and marine artist. *Medium*: pastel and oil. *b*: Chesham, Bucks., 1950. *m*: Mr.Brian Smith. *Address*: Hill Cottage, Needham Road, Barking, Suffolk IP6 8HP. *Email*: margaret.glass@btinternet.com *Website*: www.margaretglass.com *Signs work*: "M.R.G."

GLASSBOROW, Stephen, BA (Hons) Fine Art; BA (Hon) Sculpture. *Medium*: sculpture. *b*: London, 10 Mar 1951. *s of*: Maurice Glassborow. *m*: Linda Dry-Parker. *Studied*: Brighton College of Art. *Represented by*: Gallery Perutz (UK); Wagner Gallery (Sydney, Australia). *Exhib*: Makers Mark Gallery, Sydney; Art International, Hong Kong; L'Attitude Gallery, Boston; Port Jackson Fine Art, Los Angeles. *Works in collections*: KPMG Sydney, Qantas, Bank of New Zealand, Walt Disney, McDonalds Group, Remy Martin. *Commissions*: Hastings City Council, Hilton Shanghai, Boston City Council, Apollo Group Singapore, Star City Casino. *Official Purchasers*: Whitehorse City Council, Victoria; Rochester City Council. *Address*: Talycoed Court Lodge, Monmouth, NP25 5HR. *Email*: glass@iinet.net.au *Website*: www.galleryperutz.com *Signs work*: 'STEPHEN GLASSBOROW'.

GLASSFORD, Susan Hilary, Diploma of Art. *Medium*: etching, engraving, oil, watercolour, drawing, prints. *b*: London, 11 Mar 1946. *grand-d of*: George Herbert Peet (artist). *m*: John Glassford. one *s*. one *d*. *Educ*: Queen Anne Grammar School for Girls, York. *Studied*: I.M.Marsh College, Liverpool (1964-7, teacher training); Cumbria College of Art & Design (1980-3). *Exhib*: RA Summer Exhbn; RBA Mall Galleries; Laing Exhbn; various group exhbns since 1982. *Works in collections*: The British Embassy, Madrid. *Commissions*: private. *Publications*: The Lake Artist Society - A Centenary Celebration. *Principal Works*: landscape and travel subjects, painter and printmaker. *Recreations*: travel. *Clubs*: The Lake Artist Society (1992). *Misc*: shows work in own gallery. *Address*: Meadowbank Farm, Curthwaite, Wigton, Cumbria CA7 8BG. *Email*: sueglassfordart@aol.com *Website*: www.meadowbankfarm.co.uk *Signs work*: 'Susan H Glassford' or 'SHGlassford'.

GLAZEBROOK, Christina Fay, Hon.SGFA (1987); artist in pastel, water-colour; teacher of art for Herts. CC, and Watford Borough Council. *b*: Watford, 1 Apr 1934. *d of*: George Cornish. *m*: Charles Michael Glazebrook. two *s*. *Educ*: Watford Technical College of Art. *Studied*: Cassio College, Watford (1976) and St. Alban's College of Art (1981). *Exhib*: PS (1980-81), Liberty's (1982), SGA (1985, 1987), Herts. in the Making (1986-87), UA (1998), Mall Galleries, Knapp Gallery, London, and many one-man shows. *Address*: 10 Monkshood Cl., Highcliffe, Christchurch, Dorset BH23 4TS. *Signs work*: "Fay Glazebrook.".

GLIDDEN, Brian. Prize winner (2nd prize) Ferens Open Exhibition 2012. *Medium* oil, watercolour, drawing. *b*: Skellow, nr. Doncaster, 27 Nov 1936. *m*: Betty Rose. one *s*. one *d*. *Studied*: Doncaster College of Art (mid 60s/early 70s); Doncaster Technical College (1952-55, part-time student); toolmaker. *Exhib*: Royal Institute Painters in Watercolour (1981-

1985); Royal Society of Marine Artists (1981-83, 1991-92, 2005); Singer & Friedlander/Sunday Times Watercolour Competition (1990-91); Ferens Open Exhibitions 1970s onwards; Fylingdales Group Artist, Doncaster Open Art (2000 onwards). *Recreations*: drawing, painting, militaria, gardening, model making. *Address*: 15A Grange Lane, Burghwallis, Doncaster, S. Yorks, DN6 9JR. *Email*: betbri@btinternet.com *Signs work*: "B. GLIDDEN".

GLOVER, Rebecca, BA (Hons). *Medium*: Oil, drawing, sculpture, installation. *b*: UK, 2 0 Jan 1984. *Studied*: The Art Academy, London; St Oswalds School of Painting, London; Edinburgh College of Art. *Exhib*: Solo: Goat Major Projects, Cardiff (2012); Koukan Gallery, London (2011); PM Gallery & House, London (2011). Selected Group: Ovada, Oxford (2012); Chelsea Art Fair, London (2012); Departure Foundation, Birmingham (2012); Cafe Gallery Project, London (2011); Grosvenor Gallery, London (2010); Market Estate Project, London (2010). *Works in collections*: Private. *Commissions*: 10th Anniversary Sculpture, Greatmore Studios, Cape Town, South Africa. *Address*: 75 Kenworth Road, London E9 5RB. *Email*: rebecca@rebeccaglover.co.uk *Website*: www.rebeccaglover.co.uk *Signs work*: "R GLOVER".

GODDEN, Nicola Jane Averill, BA (Hons) Sculpture; MRBS (1993). *Medium*: sculpture. *Studied*: West Surrey College of Art & Design (1978-81). *Represented by*: Hay Hill Gallery, London; The Sculpture Park, Surrey. *Exhib*: Hay Hill, London (2012-14); The Sculpture Park (2005-2014); Imagine Gallery, Sussex (2014); EDS Gallery, Edinburgh (2014); Wykeham Gallery, Stockbridge; Tom Caldwell Gallery, Belfast (1990-2014); Hannah Peschar Sculpture Garden, Surrey (1990-96, 2007-09); Sarah Wiseman Gallery, Oxford (2005); Hiscox Art Cafe, London (2000). *Works in collections*: The Vincent Ferguson Collection; The Eric and Jean Cass Collections. *Commissions*: 'Icarus', Olympic Village (2012); "Sir Peter Scott", WWT & Berkeley Homes; Nene University; Eastman Kodak, Philadelphia; Mount Row Properties; Albion Properties; British & Commonwealth Properties plc. Speyhawk plc. *Principal works*: "Icarus"; "Peter Scott". *Recreations*: Flying light aircraft (Pilot) PPL. *Address*: Hampton House, Dockenfield, Surrey GU10 4HX. *Email*: nicolagodden@aol.com *Website*: www.nicolagodden.com *Signs work*: "GODDEN".

GODDARD, Juliette Ingrid, BA (Hons) Fine Art, Middlesex University; MA (RCA) Fine Art Printmaking at the Royal College of Art; Henry Moore Bursary RCA. *Medium*: acrylics, ceramics, drawing, prints, sculpture. *b*: Kent, 13 Mar 1959. *d of*: Peter Goddard. *m*: Charles Scott. *Educ*: Magna Carta Secondary School; Ashford Sixth Form College. *Studied*: Epsom School of Art and Design. *Represented by*: Cosa London (Gallery). *Exhib*: RA Summer Exhbn; Crafts Council, London; Christie's; Swiss Embassy, London; Basel, Switzerland; Chateau de Penthes, Geneva; Chapter Arts Centre, Wales; Aberystwyth University, Wales; Fifty Years of Printmaking - Australian Touring Exhbn; Hot off the Press - Ceramic and Print. *Works in collections*: Switzerland: Davidoff/Lang & Partners, Basel; Kecskemet: International Ceramic Collection, Budapest; Crawley Museum Collection; private Swiss collections and collectors. *Commissions*: Davidoff for Lang & Partners Architects. *Publications*: books: 'Printed Clay', 'Ceramic & Print' (A&C Blacks), 'Potters Guide to the Ceramic Surface'; '100 Years of the Royal College of Art'; magazines: Ceramic Review - UK, Ceramic Technical, Ceramic Monthly; 'Allegemeines kunstlerlexikon' (world biography). *Works Reproduced*: catalogues for solo exhbns; in '100 Years of the Royal College of Art', 'Printmaking at the Royal College of Art' catalogue. *Recreations*: music, sports, skiing, travel. *Clubs*: RCA Society, London; Le Club Francais - Swiss Club. *Address*: 9 Dingle Close, West Green, West Sussex RH11 7NG. *Email*: juliette13_uk@yahoo.com *Website*: www.cosalondon.com *Signs work*: 'Juliette Goddard'.

GOGOLIUK, Gennadii, Maud Hutchinson Gemmel Prize, RSA (2001). *Medium*: oils. *b*: Russia, 25 Mar 1960. *s of*: Vladimir Gogoliuk. *m*: Rose France. two *s.* three *d. Educ*: St.Petersburg Academy of Arts. *Studied*: Faculty of Painting, Studio of Moeseenko

Represented by: John Martin of London. *Exhib*: Russia, Finland, Germany, Denmark (1990-95), Scottish Society of Artists (2000), Royal Scottish Academy (2001, 2003, 2008); solo shows: John Martin of London (2000, 01, 03, 05, 07, 09); Scotland-Russia Institute, Edinburgh (2009). *Commissions*: private commissions. *Publications*: Exhbn. catalogues: Stubnitz (1993) Manege Biennial Exhbn, St.Petersburg (1994). Published by John Martin of London: solo show (2001), 'On the Edge of Things' (2003), 'Waves of Time' (2005), 'Pursuing the Ideal' (2006), 'Silver Threads' (2007), 'A Thousand and One Mornings' (2009). *Recreations*: writing the eternal book with Pan Pesochnyi. *Address*: 32 Sciennes Rd, Edinburgh, EH9 1NT. *Signs work*: Gogoliuk.

GOLDBACHER, Fiona C., water-colourist, sculptress in marble. *b*: London, 1935. *d of*: Donald Robertson. *m*: Rodolfo Goldbacher. one *s.* one *d. Educ*: Iona College, NZ. *Studied*: under Ruth Liezman. *Exhib*: Chiba Museum,Tokyo; Tanja Flandria, Morocco; Blackheath, Bow House, Heiffer, Thompsons, Gagliardi Galleries, London; Turtle Gallery, Sussex. *Works in collections*: Sanyu Art Japan, Blackheath, Gagliardi, Thompsons Galleries, London, John Noott, Broadway, Cotswolds, Turtle Gallery, Sussex. *Works Reproduced*: various cards and prints. *Misc*: other address: 43 via Borgo 2, Strettoia (Lucca), Tuscany. *Address*: 14 Edmunds Walk, London N2 0HU. *Signs work*: "Fiona C. Goldbacher."

GOLDBART, Sarah Rachel, BA (Hons). *Medium*: painter in acrylics. *b*: Watford, Herts, 26 Jul 1964. *d of*: Leonard and Sheila Goldbart. *Studied*: Middlesex Polytechnic (Foundation Course); Loughborough College of Art and Design (Degree). *Represented by*: Michael Wood Fine Art Gallery, Plymouth; The Square Gallery, St. Mawes, Cornwall. *Exhib*: Lander Gallery, Truro; Mariners Gallery, St. Ives; Lennox Gallery, London; London Contemporary Art Gallery, London; Smiths Gallery, London; Stark Gallery, London; New Gallery, Birmingham; Falmouth Art Gallery, Cornwall. *Works in collections*: IBM, Sir William Mather, Countess of St. Germans, The Lithuanian Embassy, The Ukrainian Embassy. *Commissions*: P&O Developments, J.D.Wetherspoon, Stakis Hotels, Radisson Edwardian Hotels, Architects and Interior Designers; private commissions. *Publications*: Gallery West Catalogue, 'Optimum Light' (A Celebration of Works Old and New). *Works Reproduced*: limited edition Giclee prints. *Principal Works*: semi-abstract still life/portraits/abstract. *Address*: London. *Email*: sarah@sarahgoldbart.com *Website*: www.sarahgoldbart.com

GOLDSMITH, Patricia, NDD (1950), ATD (1951), Post Graduate RA Schools (1951). *Medium*: painter in oil and watercolour, monotypes, drypoint etchings, collagraphs and collage. *b*: Hove, Sussex, 27 Mar 1929. *d of*: Mr & Mrs R.H.Kerley. *m*: Colin. one *s.* four *d. Educ*: Brighton and Hove High School. *Studied*: Brighton (1947-51), RA (1951-55). *Exhib*: Sussex Artists, Royal Portrait Society, RA, RWA, Marlborough Artists, S. West Academy of Fine Art and with Marlborough 'Open Studios'. *Address*: 15 Hyde Lane, Marlborough, Wilts, SN8 1JL. *Email*: colingol@colingal.demon.co.uk

GOLLON, Chris, Finalist: The Spectator Prize (1989); Fellowship, Institute of Advanced Study, Durham University (2008-09). *Medium*: acrylic on canvas, printmaking, film making. *b*: London, 1953. *m*: Anne. one *s.* one *d. Studied*: autodidact. *Represented by*: IAP Fine Art, London. *Exhib*: solo shows: Ferens Gallery (1993), Bretton Hall, W.Yorks (1994), Huddersfield Art Gallery (2001, 2005), River & Rowing Museum, Henley (2002, 2008), Gallery Simoncini, Luxembourg (1995), Domo Gallery, New Jersey; Thompson's Gallery, London (2006), IAP Fine Art, London (2007, 2008, 2009). Mixed shows: Spink & Son, London (1989), ART'97, Chicago, Connaught Brown, London (1998), Sotheby's, London (2001), St.Paul's Cathedral (2004), New Jersey Center for Visual Art (2005). *Works in collections*: Church of England, River & Rowing Museum, Henley (purchased with aid from V&A Museum, London), Huddersfield Art Gallery, Institute of Advanced Study, Durham, University of Hull. *Commissions*: 14 Stations of the Cross (200-2008) for St.John on Bethnal Green, London, a grade-one listed church designed by Sir John Soane. 'Gollon at

Henley', painting commissioned by River & Rowing Museum, Henley (2008). *Publications*: 'Presence: Images of Christ for the Third Millennium' (2004, Biblelands); 'Stations of the Cross', Chris Gollon & Sarah Maitland (Continuum, 2009); 'Being Human' catalogue, pub. Institute of Advanced Study (2009); 'Chris Gollon: Humanity in Art' by Tamsin Pickeral (Hyde & Hughes, 2010). *Clubs*: The Union. *Address*: c/o IAP Fine Art, P O Box 2253, Iver, Bucks, SL0 0DF. *Website*: www.chrisgollon.com *Signs work*: "Chris Gollon" on front of canvas.

GOLPHIN, Janet, RWS (1992), VPRWS (1998), RBA (1993); artist in water-colour, oils, mixed media. *b*: Pontefract, 7 Nov 1950. one *s*. *Exhib*: Bankside Gallery, London, Medici Soc., London, Thompsons Gallery, London, Mall Galleries, Richmond Hill Gallery, Richmond, Surrey, RA Summer Exhbn., Manor House Gallery, Chipping Norton, Oxon, Ashdown Gallery, Haywards Heath, Albany Gallery Cardiff. *Works in collections*: HM The Queen, Provident Financial, Brodsnorth Hall, M. Doncaster, Johnson and Johnson, John Lewis Partnership. *Commissions*: John Lewis Partnership. *Clubs*: R.W.S., R.B.A., Manchester Academy of Fine Art, Leeds Fine Art. *Address*: 6 Orchard View, Darrington, W. Yorkshire WF8 3AZ. *Signs work*: "Janet Golphin."

GOOCH, Wendy, (nee ALLEN), HS. *Medium*: watercolour, oils, acrylic. *b*: Gorleston-on-Sea, Norfolk, 7 Sep 1939. *d of*: Mr & Mrs Cyril Frederick Allen. *m*: Paul Bernard Gooch. *Educ*: Gt.Yarmouth Technical High School. *Studied*: self-taught artist in all media and sizes. *Exhib*: HS, Wells; Mall Galleries, London; RMS, Westminster Galleries, London; Crome Gallery, Norwich; Tudor Gallery, Norwich. *Works in collections*: private collections in UK, USA and New Zealand. *Commissions*: pet portraits in various mediums. *Principal Works*: wild and domestic animals, countryside, marine. *Recreations*: music, drama, walking. *Clubs*: Gt.Yarmouth Gilbert and Sullivan Society and Norwich Gilbert and Sullivan Society. *Address*: 3 Robinson Road, Scole, Diss, Norfolk IP21 4EF. *Signs work*: 'W.G.' (miniatures), 'W.Gooch' (others).

GOOD, Trudy, self taught. *Medium*: oil, watercolour, drawing. *b*: Farnborough, Hants, 30 Aug 1967. *Educ*: Farnborough Sixth Form College. *Studied*: Winchester School of Art. *Represented by*: Belgravia Gallery, Mayfair. *Exhib*: one-man shows: Belgravia Gallery, Llewellyn Alexander Gallery, Bell Fine Art Winchester, Desmoulin Gallery. *Works in collections*: Lenny Goodman (judge on Strictly Ballroom), and many other private collections. *Commissions*: commissioned to draw the Collection of Lindka Cierach, fashion designer, for London Fashion Week. *Works Reproduced*: posters by 'The Art Group', limited edition prints of the 'Ballroom Series'. *Principal Works*: figurative, specialising in pastel and charcoal. *Address*: c/o Belgravia Gallery, 45 Albemarle Street, Mayfair, London W1S 4JL. *Email*: trudy2socksgood@tesco.net *Website*: www.belgraviagallery.com *Signs work*: 'TMG'.

GOODALL, Oscar Ronald, RSW; Dip.& PD, Dundee College of Art. Lectured for Scottish Arts Council, Chairman of Scottish Advisers in Art and Design, Adviser in Art/Design Central Region Scotland. Lectured for Extra-Mural Depts. of Dundee, St. Andrews and Stirling Universities, Art Education St.Lucia. *Medium*: oil, water-colour, acrylic, pastel; abstract, landscape, drawings. *b*: S.Australia, 30 Jun 1924. *m*: Janet M.Goodall (née Wylie) DA (Glas.). one *s*. one *d*. *Educ*: Perth Academy, RAFVR (Royal Air Force Volunteer Reserve) 1942. *Studied*: Dundee Col. of Art, and Hospitalfield, Arbroath. *Exhib*: Major Scottish Exhibitions, RSA, RSW, SSA, Scottish Gallery, Colours & 41 Galleries, Edin. etc. British Council and Arts Council, The Scottish Gallery, Eduardo Alessandro Studios, The Wren Gallery, The Green Gallery. *Works in collections*: Perth Art Gallery, Dundee Art Gallery, Scottish Arts Council. *Official Purchasers*: Scottish Arts Council, Dundee, Perth Art Galleries. *Works Reproduced*: 'Golden River', 'Fragments'. *Recreations*: fishing, gardening, good company, travel, talking, looking. *Misc*: co-founder of 'The Dollar Summer School', & Dollar Civic Trust. *Address*: 27 Drummond St., Muthill, Perthshire, PH5 2AN. *Signs work*: Goodall.

GOODE, Mervyn, landscape painter best known for his oil paintings of the English countryside – featuring mainly the landscape close to his main home in Hampshire, as well as seascapes/estuary subjects inspired by the landscape close to his second home in South Devon, and also known for his landscapes produced from his travels in the South of France. *b*: 1948. *m*: Stephanie. *Educ*: Gloucestershire College of Art. *Exhib*: has exhib. widely through the U.K. and also in the USA; one-man exhbns.: Highton Gallery, EC4 (1970), Alpine Gallery, W1 (1970, 1971), King St. Galleries, SW1 (1974), Furneaux Gallery, SW19 (1975), Southwell Brown Gallery (1976, 1984), Fraser Carver Gallery (1977), Reid Gallery (1978, 1981, 1983, 1985, 1987, 1989, 1991, 1993), Windsor and Eton Fine Arts (1978, 1980), Century Gallery (1982, 1984, 1985), David Messum (1982), Medici Gallery, W1 (1983, 1985, 1990), H.C. Dickins, W1 (1987, 1989), Arun Art Centre (1987), Bennet Galleries, U.S.A. (1988), Bourne Gallery (1992, 1994, 1995, 1996, 1998), David Messum W1 (1993, 1994), John Noott (1995, 1997), Nevill Gallery (1998), Jerram Gallery (1999); mixed exhbns.: Medici Gallery, W1; H.C. Dickins, W1; Mall Galleries (ROI); Royal Academy Business Art Galleries, W1; Southampton A.G.; Bruton Gallery, Somerset; Southwell Brown Gallery, Richmond; Bourne Gallery, Reigate; David Curzon Gallery, London SW19; Century Galleries - Hartley Wintney and Henley-on-Thames; Nevill Gallery, Canterbury; Omell Galleries - London W1 and Ascot; Kingsmead Gallery, Bookham; Wykeham Gallery, Stockbridge; H.C. Dickins, Bloxham; David Messum, Cork St. W1; Burlington Paintings, W1; John Noott, Broadway, Worcs.; Ashgate Gallery, Farnham; Jerram Gallery, Salisbury; D'Art Gallery, Dartmouth; Walker Gallery, Honiton; Alexander Gallery, Bristol; W.H. Patterson, London, W1. *Works in collections*: private collections in U.K. and world-wide. *Commissions*: not accepted. *Works Reproduced*: by the Medici Society, Kingsmead Publications, Bucentaur Gallery, Royle, Rosenstiel's, Almanac Gallery and Country Cards; in numerous periodicals and books; on ITV and BBC TV, etc. *Address*: Lane Copse, Hawkley, Hants. GU33 6NS. *Signs work*: "Mervyn Goode."

GOODFELLOW, Peter George, 2nd Class Honours, Central School of Art, London. *Medium*: collage, oil, watercolour, prints. *b*: Middlesbrough, 14 Jun 1950. *s of*: Tommy & Joan Goodfellow. *m*: Jean. *Educ*: Bede Hall Grammar School, Billingham. *Studied*: Middlesbrough College of Art, Central School of Art, London. *Exhib*: V&A, Duncan Miller, Osbourne, Lennox (London); Open Eye, Edinburgh; Art from Scotland (New York, USA); Riverside, Lost, Duff House (N.E. Scotland); Iona House (Oxfordshire); Biscuit Factory (Newcastle); Tracey McNee (Glasgow); Leith Gallery (Edinburgh). *Works in collections*: Conoco, Cidel Bank, Saab-Scania, BTelecom, Penguin, Saatchi & Saatchi, Qantas, V&A, Collins, Glenfiddich, BBC, BASF. *Commissions*: private chapel for Philip Astor (Hon); 24 panel paintings and 3 stained glass windows, Migvie, Aberdeenshire. *Publications*: various publications, periodicals, etc. *Official Purchasers*: many. *Works Reproduced*: many. *Principal Works*: Currently large scale expressionist oil landscapes. *Recreations*: painting, stamp collecting, watching football, driving. *Address*: The Lost Gallery, Strathdon, Aberdeenshire AB36 8UJ. *Email*: Jean@lostgallery.co.uk *Website*: www.lostgallery.co.uk

GOODHALL, Peter, BA (Hons). *Medium*: oil, drawing. *b*: 1957. *Studied*: Exeter College of Art & Design (1976-79). *Exhib*: First solo exhibition: Northcott Theatre, Exeter (1980); West Country, Home Counties, Covent Garden shows; RSMA; Mystic Maritime Museum, USA; RWA; Antiques of the Orient, Singapore; Affordable Art Fairs (2002-); Cork Street, London; Contemporary Art Fairs; SWAc.. *Works in collections*: private and corporate worldwide including RAF and Royal Navy. *Works Reproduced*: widely published. *Address*: 30 North Street, Ottery St. Mary, Devon, EX11 1DR. *Email*: petergoodhall@live.com *Website*: www.petergoodhall.co.uk *Signs work*: "PETER GOODHALL".

GOODMAN, Ben, SWE; BA Hons Illustration (First Class); Best New Exhibitor Award, SWE 75th Annual Exhibition. *Medium*: wood engraver, prints. *b*: Birmingham, 20 Oct 1987. *Partner*: Laurie Stansfield. *Studied*: University of the West of England (2008-11). *Exhib*:

BITE: Artists Who Print (2012); SWE Annual Exhibition (2012, 2013); RA Summer Exhibition (2013); RWA Annual Autumn Open (2013), and various other venues. Solo show: Christmas Steps Gallery, Bristol (2014). *Works in collections*: private. *Commissions*: Das Kabinet des Dr. Calgari (Palgrave Macmillan, 2012 - front cover). *Publications*: "Keepers" Artist Book (self published, 2011); *Principal Works*: "Jungle Gardener" (wood engraving, 2012). *Clubs*: Society of Wood Engravers. *Address: BV Studios, 37 Philip Street, Bristol BS3 4GA. Email:* contactne@bengoodman.co.uk *Website*: www.bengoodman.co.uk *Signs work*: "BEN GOODMAN".

GOODMAN, Pamela Clare, BA Hons Fine Art; City & Guilds Cert. in Teaching Adult Education. *b*: Ottery St.Mary, Devon, 13 Jun 1963. *d of*: Mr. V. Uren & Mrs. M.L. Bale. *m*: divorced. *Studied*: Winchester School of Art. *Exhib*: Exeter Cathedral, Winchester Guildhall, Bell Fine Art Gallery Winchester, numerous open studio shows, touring exhibition with www.littlevangogh.co.uk. *Works in collections*: UK, Canada and USA. *Commissions*: horses, boats/marine work, and many landscape commissions. *Official Purchasers*: many restaurants and Southampton Hospital, mayor of Winchester, Hampshire public ownership. *Works Reproduced*: Cathedral magazine, and cards, prints. *Principal Works*: Princess Anne being given the 'freedom' of Winchester on Guildhall steps. *Misc*: demonstrations for art societies. *Address*: 5 West End Close, Winchester, Hampshire, SO22 5EW. *Email*: claregoodmanartist@gmail.com *Website*: www.claregoodmanartist.co.uk

GOODMAN, Sheila, PS (2011), SWA (1995); Dip AD (Graphic Design); Most Popular Painting, SWA (2008); Unison Pastel Award, Pastel Society (2009). *Medium*: oil, acrylic, pastel. *b*: Bolton, 1949. *m*: Philip. *Studied*: High Wycombe College of Art (1966-69). *Exhib*: RA, RWA, Mall Galleries. *Works in collections*: Hunting Management Services Group Ltd., Hampshire County Council, Russell-Cotes Museum. *Publications*: The Artist Magazine; Leisure Painter; Pastel Journal. *Works Reproduced*: prints made by Rosenstiels and Dayfold. *Address*: Chapel House, Kingston, Ringwood, Hants BH24 3BJ. *Email*: enquiries@sgart.co.uk *Website*: www.sgart.co.uk *Signs work*: 'Sheila Goodman'.

GOODWIN, Diane, HS, SLm; self taught painter of miniatures specialising in portraiture in water-colour on ivorine/polymin. *b*: Brighton, 31 May 1954. one *s.* one *d. Exhib*: RMS, SAMAP, Hilliard & Limners Societies, World Federation of Miniaturists exhibitions in London, Washington and Tasmania; several galleries etc. Work in collections internationally. *Commissions*: taken. *Publications*: Former Editor of The Hilliard Society Newsletter. *Misc*: formerly exhibited uner PAVITT. *Address*: 2 North Head, Milford on Sea, Lymington SO41 0LX. *Email*: dianna@tiscali.co.uk *Website*: included in art-in-miniature.org leeminiaturecollection.com *Signs work*: "DG" (monogram).

GOODWIN, Leslie Albert, MBE, RI, ROI, RWA; artist in oil, water-colour, pastel, book illustrator; Chairman, Leicester Soc. Artists. *b*: Leicester, 13 Jun 1929. *s of*: Joseph Henry Goodwin. *m*: Elizabeth Whelband. one *s.* one *d. Studied*: Leicester College of Art (1949-55). *Exhib*: RA, RWA, RI, PS; six one-man shows, Vaughan College, Leicester University; mixed shows, Leicester A.G. *Works in collections*: English Electric - Nuclear Power Division; Bristol Old Vic Co.; Leicester Royal Infirmary; various public collections; NHS Founder 'Asterisk' Soc. of Artists; broadcaster/art critic for BBC, Art Critic for 'The Leicester Mercury'. *Commissions*: several for 'Geest'. *Works Reproduced*: The Artist, Artist and Illustrators, 'The Wednesday Painter'. *Address*: The Studio, 28 Lubbesthorpe Rd., Braunstone, Leics. LE3 2XD.

GOOSEN, Frederik Johannes (Frits), VBKH'sum (1981), RSMA (1990), EKC (1992), KV Gooi & Vechtstreek (1993); artist in oil and water-colour; 1988 Award of Excellence - Mystic Seaport; 2001 Rudolph J Schaefer Award - Mystic Seaport; 2002 The Peoples Choice Award - City of Enkhuizen. *b*: Hilversum, 13 Dec 1943. *m*: M.R. Bekenkamp. two *s. Educ*: self-taught. *Exhib*: Great Britain, Switzerland, Norway, USA, Germany, The

Netherlands. *Works in collections*: Mystic Seaport Museum, CT; Diploma Collection RSMA; Maritime Museum, Falmouth UK, and several public bldgs. in Holland. *Address*: Waterschapslaan 14, Blaricum, Holland. *Email*: frits.goosen@tele2.nl *Website*: www.fritsgoosen.nl *Signs work*: "F.J. Goosen."

GORDON-LEE, Michael, A.L.I. (1977); Member of Somerset Guild of Craftsmen and South-West Sculptors Association; landscape architect, designer, artist and sculptor. *Medium*: works in pastel, oil, and sculptures in plaster, wood and bronze. *b*: Harrow, 1943. *s of*: John Desmond Gordon-Lee. *m*: Gordon-Lee, Pamela. one *s*. one *d*. *Educ*: Whitehawk Boys School, Brighton Art College. *Studied*: Hammersmith College of Art and Building, Chester Art College, Liverpool, West Dean College. *Represented by*: Courthouse Gallery, Somerton; Riverside Gallery, Barnes. *Exhib*: Manchester Academy, Pastel Soc. (Mall Galleries), RWA, Theatr Clwyd, Mold, Merseyside Artists, Frodsham Arts Centre, Hanover Gallery, Grosvenor Museum Chester, Dartington, Somerset Guild, Ilminster Arts Centre, Gloss Gallery, Exeter, Sidmouth and Southern France, John Leach Gallery. *Works in collections*: Grosvenor Museum, Chester; and public and private collections worldwide. *Commissions*: Grosvenor Museum, Chester; Rexel Ltd.; private. *Official Purchasers*: Grosvenor Museum, Chester; Rexel Ltd. *Works Reproduced*: Grosvenor Museum, Chester; Rexel Ltd.; exhibition catalogues. *Principal Works*: landscapes, historic gardens and bronze sculptures. *Recreations*: coastal walking, music, the arts. *Clubs*: Exmouth Art Society. *Address*: 12 King Charles Way, Sidmouth, Devon, EX10 9JX. *Email*: michaelgordon-lee@hotmail.com *Website*: devonartistnetwork.co.uk/GORDONLEE *Signs work*: "GORDON-LEE" (paintings), "MGL" (sculptures).

GORMAN, Susan Mary, BA (Hons) Ceramica; 3 year research studentship, School of Art and Design, Loughborough. *Medium*: Ceramics. *b*: Dartford, 22 Feb 1951. *m*: Warwick Gorman. two *s*. *Studied*: Chesterfield College of Art and Design (2001-3); Loughborough University (2003-9). *Exhib*: Buckenham Gallery, Southwold (2009, 2011); Warwick Gallery, Warwick (2010); Derby Museum and Art Gallery (2012); Opus Gallery, Ashbourne (2012). *Works in collections*; Private international collections. *Publications*: Negotiating Thesis and Practice Through Pottery; Sixth Sense Awareness; Transcending Technique. *Recreations*: walking; theatre. *Misc*: Member of Peak District Artisans; specialises in 'neriage' porcelain. *Address*: 94 Malthouse Lane, Ashover, Derbyshire S45 0BU. *Email*: suegorman@btinternet.com *Website*: www.sue-gorman-ceramics.co.uk *Signs work*: "Sue Gorman".

GOUGH, Paul James, MA (1985), PhD (1991), RWA (1998); artist in pastel and chalk; Dean, University of West of England, Bristol; Head of Painting, Bristol Polytechnic. *b*: Plymouth, 27 Mar 1958. *m*: Kathleen. one *s*. two *d*. *Studied*: Wolverhampton Polytechnic (1976-79), RCA (1980-85). *Exhib*: Watermans Centre, Solomons, London; Bristol, Lancaster, Swindon, Manchester, Harlech biennale, Ottawa, Paris. *Works in collections*: Imperial War Museum, Royal Marines, Royal Artillery, Pirelli, Lord Rothermere, Canadian War Museum. *Publications*: articles and chapters in numerous academic journals. Television presenter: Art Show (BBC2 1998), Canvas (HTV 1995-99). *Address*: 136 Stackpool Rd., Southville, Bristol BS3 1NY. *Website*: www.amd.uwe.ac.uk/vortex/ *Signs work*: "P.J. Gough."

GOUGH, Piers, CBE (1998); RA (2001); RIBA; FRIAS; AA DIP; Hon.Fellow, Queen Mary, Univ. of London (2001); D. Univ. Middlesex (1999); FRSA. *Medium*: architect. *b*: Brighton, 24 Apr 1946. *s of*: Peter & Daphne Gough. one *s*. *Educ*: Uppingham School. *Studied*: Architectural Association School (1965-71). *Exhib*: Luryens Exhibition (1982); Victorian & Early 20th Century Galleries; Regency Galleries (2003); National Portrait Gallery; 'Saved' Exhibition, Hayward Gallery (2003). *Works in collections*: Royal Academy; V&A. *Commissions*: China Wharf (1988); The Circle, Bermondsey (1990); Street-Porter House (1998), Westbourne Grove Public Lavatories (1993); Camden Wharf,

Camden Lock (1996-2002); Green Bridge, Mile End Park (1997-2000); Bling Bling Building, Liverpool (2006); Arsenal on the Move (2001-14). *Publications*: English Extremists (1998); Shock of the Old (Ch4 TV series, 2000); CZWG Brochure (2006). *Recreations*: swimming, parties. *Clubs*: Shoreditch House. *Address*: CZWG Architects LLP, 17 Bowling Green Lane, London EC1R 0QB. *Email*: p.gough@czwgarchitects.co.uk *Website*: www.czwgarchitects.co.uk *Signs work*: "Piers Gough".

GOW, Neil, *Medium*: sculptor in wood, small and large scale (outdoor). Abstract and semi figurative. *b*: Greenford, Middx., 22 Mar 1940. *s of*: Herbert Nelson Gow (decd). *m*: Jean. one *s* (decd). one *d*. *Educ*: Fitzgeorge, Malden, Kingston Technical College. *Exhib*: RWA, SWA, Amnesty International Sculptures (Bristol and London), Henry Brett Gallery, 5D Gallery, Kennys Galway, etc. *Commissions*: Monmouthshire Council (outdoor figures at Tintern and Abergavenny); various Monmouthshire schools and day centres; Ballard School; Sustrans; Wotton-under-Edge Town Council; Forestry Commission; Brecon Beacons National Park; various private individuals. *Clubs*: Glos. Soc. of Artists. *Misc*: participate in demonstration/display sculpting. Studio visits by appointment. *Address*: Brownshill Cottage, Brownshill, Stroud, Glos. GL6 8AG. *Email*: neil.gow3@googlemail.com

GRAA JENSEN, Lisa, BA (Hons) (1978), RI (1996), AOI (1994); illustrator and painter in acrylic inks. *b*: Copenhagen, Denmark, 2 Mar 1953. *m*: J.A. Hendrich, MA. one *s*. one *d*. *Studied*: Sir John Cass School of Art (1974-75), Camberwell School of Art (1975-78, John Lawrence). *Represented by*: Llewellyn Alexander Gallery, London; Bridgeman Art Library; Hillier Gallery, Stratford on Avon. *Exhib*: RI, Mall Galleries mixed shows, CCA Galleries, numerous exhbns. in South East, work available at Llewellyn Alexander Gallery, London, Russell Gallery, Putney, London, Stephen Jack Fine Art. *Works Reproduced*: Fine Art prints for Rosenstiels and CCA Galleries, cards for Royle, Paperhouse, Kingsmead, Royal Academy Enterprises, Medici, Cambridge University Press; Kestral Books, Hamlyn, BBC Publications, Radio Times, Heinemann Macmillan; Fine Art UK, Hopscotch Cards, Henley Regatta Cards. *Recreations*: Travels with narrowboat, renovating old French cafe. *Address*: 32 The Crescent, Wimbledon Park, London SW19 8AN. *Email*: lisa@lisagraajensen.com *Website*: www.lisagraajensencom. *Signs work*: "GRAA JENSEN."

GRACIA, Carmen, RE; etcher and engraver in colour, painter in oil. *b*: Mendoza, Argentina, 18 May 1935. *m*: E.T. Rockett (decd). one *s*. *Educ*: Escuela de Bellas Artes, Mendoza, Argentina. *Studied*: L'Atelier 17, Paris, under Stanley Hayter (1960-1964), Slade, London, under Anthony Gross (1965-1966). *Exhib*: 32 solo, and 300 group exhibs. *Works in collections*: 30 in museums and public collections. *Official Purchasers*: Museums and Public Collections: London: Victoria and Albert Museum; British Museum; Slade School of Art; Dulwich Library; St Pancras Library; The Government Art Collection. Paris: La Biblioteque Nationale; Collection du Musee de la ville. Skopje: Musee d'art Contemporaine. Oslo: National Gallery. U.S.A.: Public Gallery, New York; Pan American Union Collection, Washington; Public Library, Boston; University of Alberta Print Center. South London Art Gallery. City Literary Institute. Sao Paolo: Musee d'Art Contemporaine. Worcestershire: Dudley Art Gallery. Leicester: City Art Gallery; Royal Infirmary. Lancashire: Oldham Art Gallery. Berlin: The Graphotek. Yorkshire: Wakefield Art Gallery; Scarborough Art Gallery. Wales: Newport Art Gallery. Gloucestershire: Cheltenham Art Gallery and Museum. Oxford: Ashmolean Museum. Cambridge: Fitzwilliam Museum. Buckinghamshire: County Museum. *Clubs*: Art Societies: Greenwich Printmakers Assocn.; Fellow, Royal Society of Painters Printmakers. *Address*: 65 Westover Rd., High Wycombe, Bucks. HP13 5HX. *Signs work*: "CARmen GRAcia."

GRADIDGE, Daphne. *Medium*: painter in oils and water based media. *b*: Salisbury, 19 Sep 1953. *Studied*: theatre design at Nottingham School of Art and at The Slade. *Represented by*: Anthony Hepworth Fine Art. *Exhib*: Solo: Anthony Hepworth Fine

Art; Park Walk Gallery. Mixed: The Discerning Eye; Sunday Times Watercolour Competition; Oakham Gallery; London Art Fairs at Islington, Olympia and RCA. *Works in collections*: Shirley Sherwood Collection; RHS Lindley library and private collection in Britain and abroad. *Commissions*: mural paintings for the Chelsea and Westminster Hospital and other hospitals in London, Hampshire and Wiltshire. *Misc*: Member of the Art Workers Guild. *Address*: Ashlands Southampton Road Landford, Salisbury Wiltshire, SP5 2EQ. *Email*: mail@daphnegradidge.co.uk *Website*: www.daphnegradidge.co.uk *Signs work*: "DG."

GRAHAM, Brian Kenneth Frederick, inaugural Bournemouth International Festival Artist (1994); first prizewinner, Royal West of England Academy's annual exhibition (1992); painter in oil/acrylic. *b*: 26 Aug., 1945. *m*: Carol. two *s*. *Educ*: Poole Grammar School. *Studied*: part time at Bournemouth College of Art (1960-1962), but mainly self taught. *Exhib*: over twenty solo exhibitions, (two in Cork Street); many group shows. *Works in collections*: Dorset County Museum; Skandia Life Assurance Company; Poole Borough Council; Parnham House, Bournemouth University. *Publications*: Ochre and Ice. Brian Graham. Essay by Paul Hyland. *Misc*: Represented by Hart Gallery, Islington, Cornwall and Nottingham. *Address*: Central House, Mount Pleasant Lane, Swanage, Dorset BH19 2PN. *Signs work*: "Brian Graham."

GRAHAM, Carol, DipAD; artist in oil; Council mem. RUA. *b*: Belfast, 17 Apr 1951. one *s*. one *d*. *Studied*: Belfast College of Art and Design (1969-74). *Exhib*: Ulster Museum, NI Arts Council, Tom Caldwell, The Engine Room, The Guinness Hopstore Gallery, Elaine Somers Hollywood. *Works in collections*: Trinity College Dublin, National Self-portrait Collection Limerick, Ulster Television, Ulster Museum, Belfast City Council, DoE, NIE Veridian. *Commissions*: portraits: Dr. Mary Robinson (President), James Galway (Flautist), Lord Grey (Governor NI), Lord Lowry, Sir Ian Frazer. *Publications*: cover, Bernard McLaverty Secrets; cover, The Blue Globe (poetry). *Clubs*: R.U.A. *Address*: 1 Glenmore Terr., Lisburn, N.I. BT27 4RW. *Signs work*: "CAROL GRAHAM."

GRAHAM, David, RP, ARCA, RBA; Prizes: Spirit of London Competition; Lord Mayors Art Award (twice); painter in oil. *b*: London, 20 May 1926. *m*: Martha Graham. *Studied*: Hammersmith School of Art, St. Martin's School of Art, Royal College of Art (1948-1951, 1st Class Degree). *Exhib*: RA (1951-2001); RP; Paris Salon, Grand Palais; Christies, Sothebys, Bonhams; Fosse Galleries, Stow-on-the-Wold. Retrospective at Mall Galleries (1990) Solo shows include: Herbert Art Gallery and Museum, Coventry - 100 Paintings of Israel (1987), Mall Galleries (1971), Bruton St. Gallery (1997). *Works in collections*: London Museum, Barbican, Guildhall Art Gallery, Arts Council, Belgrave House Art Collection, Coca Cola Ltd, National Hospital for Neurology and Neurosurgery, etc. also overseas: New York, Paris, Switzerland, Germany, Ghana, Greece, Bermuda, South America. *Commissions*: Spanish & Portuguese Synagogue; National Hospital for Neurology. *Publications*: video - A Painters View. 'Face to Face' - Philip Vann. *Works Reproduced*: Royal Academy Illustrated. *Recreations*: painting, travel. *Clubs*: Chelsea Arts. *Misc*: Head of Painting, Sir John Cass School of Art. *Address*: 2 Curran Studios, Lucan Place, Chelsea, London SW3 3PQ. *Email*: davidgrahamRP@gmail.com *Website*: www.davidgraham-studio.com *Signs work*: "David Graham."

GRAHAM, Peter, BA Hons (1980), ROI. *b*: Glasgow, 17 Feb 1959. *m*: Valerie. one *s*. *Studied*: Glasgow School of Art (1976-80). *Exhib*: Bourne Gallery Reigate, Llewellyn Alexander Ltd, London, many mixed shows including RSA, ROI, RSMA, and RI. *Works in collections*: British Council, Nan Yang Academy, Singapore, Lord Morton, Lord Max Rayne, Lady Graham, Lady Nairn, Ernst & Young, Glasgow. *Publications*: 'An Introduction to Painting Still Life' (Apple, 2004). *Clubs*: Glasgow Art Club. *Address*: 57 Kirklee Rd., Glasgow G12 0SS, Scotland. *Signs work*: "Peter Graham" or "Graham."

GRAHAM-CAMPBELL, Robert Dugald, Fellow of the Chelsea Physic Garden Florilegium Society. *b*: 16 Feb 1944. *Studied*: St.Martins School of Art. *Exhib*: Moorland Gallery, London; Fortescue Swann, London; Malcolm Innes, London; Royal Watercolour Society. *Commissions*: for botanical paintings, architectural and landscapes accepted. *Address*: Flat 4, 35 Cheyne Place, London SW3 4HL. *Email*: d.grahamcampbell@btinternet.com

GRAHAM-MACKAY, Fiona, BA (Hons); MA. *Medium*: Oil; drawing. *b*: Hawick, 24 Feb 1961. *m*: Christopher Lee, Writer. three *s*. one *d*. *Educ*: Scottish Highers; privately (Africa and Belize); Galashiels Academy. *Studied*: Royal College of Art; Maidstone College of Art; Newcastle Art College. *Exhib*: Mall Galleries, London; RSPP Spring Exhibition; regional galleries; RCA; Thumb Gallery; Illustrators Gallery, Eindhoven, Holland. *Works in collections*: Carrington Family; Richards Family; Royal Southampton Yacht Club. *Commissions*: Lord Carrington; HRH Prince Michael of Kent; Private Patron Antigua; Penguin Books, book jacket. *Works reprocuced*: magazines; greetings cards; book illustrations, including Penguin. *Recreations*: Sailing, windsurfing, skiing. *Misc*: Artist in residence, Royal Southampton Yacht Club. *Address*: Bayford Studios, Woodside, Stoddards Lane, Beckley Nr Rye, East Sussex TN31 6UE. *Email*: fgraham1@mac.com *Website*: www.fionagraham-mackay.net *Signs work*: "F G-M".

GRAINGER, Chris Rowan. *Medium*: oil, watercolour, drawing, sculpture. *b*: Epsom, Surrey, 17 Jan 1936. *s of*: Geoffrey Grainger. *m*: Juliet Grainger. two *s*. one *d*. *Educ*: Farnham School of Art. *Studied*: Bath Academy, Bristol Old Vic School. *Represented by*: Llewellyn Alexander Gallery, London. *Exhib*: Alwin Gallery, London, Royal Festival Hall; Llewellyn Alexander, Royal Academy, London Group, Ben Uri Gallery, Boundary Gallery, Anthony Hepworth, Cork Street Gallery; Chapel Row Gallery, Bath. *Works in collections*: Health Trusts, LAMDA, private worldwide. *Commissions*: several private. *Publications*: "The Gate" (2006); "Talking Amongst Myself" (2010); "The Divine Springtime" (2010); "Rowan Grainger" (2009); "Colours Rising" (2010). *Works Reproduced*: Arts Review, Daily Telegraph, Galleries magazine; Rowan Grainger catalogue 2009; Publications. *Principal Works*: "The Rehearsal"; "Seated Mother and Child" (carving); "Conversations" (series). *Recreations*: theatre. *Address*: 3 The Old Batch, Ashley Road, Bradford-on-Avon, BA15 1TL. *Email*: chrisrgrainger@btinternet.com *Website*: www.rowangrainger.com *Signs work*: "ROWAN GRAINGER".

GRANGER-TAYLOR, Nicolas, BA (Hons) Fine Art; PGDip Painting (RA); *Medium*: oil on canvas. *b*: London, 18 Jun 1963. *Educ*: Latymer Upper School, Hammersmith. *Studied*: Kingston Polytechnic (1981-82), Bristol Polytechnic (1982-85), R.A. Schools (1987-90). *Exhib*: Royal Academy Summer Exhbn. (1987, 1989, 1992, 2006, 2008, 2009, 2010) John Player Portrait Award (1987), BP Portrait Award (1990, 1995); Metropolitan Museum of Art, New York (1996); one-man shows Cadogan Contemporary (1988), Waterman Fine Art (1991, 1993), Offer Waterman (1999, 2003); Jonathan Cooper (2011, 13). *Works in collections*: Metropolitan Museum of Art, New York; Nat West; The Duke of Devonshire; Barry Humphries CBE; Steve Martin Collections, USA. *Commissions*: Luton University; The 2nd Royal Tank Regiment; Latymer Upper School. *Works Clubs*: Chelsea Arts Club. *Misc*: Grandson of the artist Edith Granger-Taylor (1887-1958). *Address*: 11 Brierley, London SW12 9LY. *Email*: ngrangertaylor@hotmail.com *Website*: www.ngrangertaylor.com *Signs work*: "N. Granger-Taylor" or "NGT".

GRANT, Keith Frederick, ARCA; landscape and portrait painter. *b*: Liverpool, 10 Aug 1930. *m*: Hilde Ellingsen-Grant. one *s* (decd). two *d*. *Educ*: Bootle Grammar School, Lancs. *Studied*: Willesden School of Art, Royal College of Art. *Represented by*: Chris Beetles Gallery, London; Galleri Arctandria, Oslo. *Exhib*: Fitzwilliam Museum, Cambridge; National Gallery of Iceland, Reykjavik; National Gallery of Modern Art, Edinburgh;

Municipal Museum of Madrid; Hayward Gallery, London, and elsewhere. *Works in collections*: Mural/mosaics, Charing Cross Hospital, London (1979), Gateshead Metro Station (1981/83), Beaverbrook Foundation, Peter Stuyvesant Coll., Arts Council of G.B., Contemporary Art Soc., V. & A., Fitzwilliam Museum, Cambridge, Manchester City A.G., National Gallery of N.Z., Government Art Collection, London, and other public and private collections at home and abroad. *Commissions*: paintings and stained glass – Charing Cross Hospital, London (2000); 2004 winner of competition to execute a new altarpeice for Kopervik Church, Karmoy, Norway 'Triptych of The Lamb', 2005 altarpiece installed and dedicated; 2001/2002 co-inaugurated Artists and Writers programme of the British Antarctic Survey. *Works Reproduced*: 'Art in Design', London, Harper-Collins Publishers, London. *Clubs*: Garrick. *Address*: P.B. 7, 3834 Gvarv, Norway. *Email*: kefreg@online.no *Signs work*: "Keith Grant" or "K. F. Grant."

GRANT, Kenneth Stephen, *Medium*: oil, watercolour, drawing, prints. *b*: London, 7 Apr 1934. *s of*: Donald Grant & Maryne Jaginger. *m*: Pamela. one *s*. *Studied*: self taught artist, son of seafaring family. *Represented by*: Mandell's Gallery, Norwich. *Exhib*: RSMA (late 1960s and 1980 at London Guildhall); with N R Omell for past 20 years; with Mandell's Gallery for past 10 years. *Works in collections*: marine and aviation works in private collections in UK, USA, Europe and Australasia. *Commissions*: Musical company: CD covers, light music. *Publications*: US Naval Institute Press - 'History of the USS Constitution'. *Official Purchasers*: Institution of Marine Engineers - RNLI Lifeboat 'Marine Engineer'. *Works Reproduced*: Marine History, and Aviation (Battle of Britain & USAAF), landscape. *Principal Works*: Maritime History; recently North Sea Working Sail, Locomotives (North Norfolk Railway), Landscape, Coastal Scenes. *Recreations*: walking, and on-the-spot sketching; the study of Maritime/Aviation/Railway history. *Address*: 14 Edgebrook, off Holway Road, Sheringham, Norfolk, NR26 8HA. *Website*: www.kenneth-grant.com *Signs work*: "Kenneth Grant" (some landscapes as "Grant").

GRANT, Marianne, NS (1977), FRSA (1975); painter in oil. *b*: St. Gallen, Switzerland, 1931. widowed. one *s*. one *d*. *Educ*: High School, Zürich. *Studied*: Art Colleges in Zürich and Geneva. *Exhib*: one-man shows BH Corner Gallery, Cooling Gallery, Century Galleries, Henley-on-Thames, East London Gallery, El Greco Gallery, Royal Northern College of Music, Debenhams of Romford, Austria, Germany, Switzerland. *Works in collections*: Ernst Waespe (Zürich), Standard Telephone and Cables Ltd., Arts Centre Hornchurch. *Works Reproduced*: Fine Art Prints for 'Prints for Pleasure' and Peinture. *Clubs*: N.S., Essex Art. *Address*: Erlenwiesenstrasse 18, 8152 Glattbrugg (Zürich), Switzerland. *Email*: jagra@bluewin.ch *Website*: www.swissart.ch/marianne-grant *Signs work*: "Marianne Grant."

GRANVILLE, artist in acrylic. *b*: Liverpool, 12 Jul 1945. *Studied*: Northwich College of Art (1961-65), Southport College of Art (1980-82). *Exhib*: Over sixty exhbns. in England and Spain since 1967. *Works in collections*: Museo de la Real Academia de Bellas artes de San Fernando, Madrid. *Works Reproduced*: various exhbn. catalogues, articles and reviews; painting reproduced as cards and prints around the world. *Misc*: Work inspired by Spain and all things Spanish. *Address*: 14b Derwent Ct., Troutbeck Rd., Liverpool L18 3LF.

GRANVILLE-EDMUNDS, Peter Donald, 1st Class BA (Hons); MA Fine Art; 'Highly Commended' RBSA. *Medium*: oil, watercolour, drawing, mixed media. *b*: Hertford, 22 Sep 1931. *s of*: A.D.Edmunds & G.Edmunds. *m*: Erica M.Granville-Edmunds. one *s*. one *d*. *Educ*: Malven House, Herts; Cooper School, Herts. *Studied*: St.Albans School of Art (now Univ.of Hertfordshire); Cheltenham & Glos. College of Higher Education; University of Gloucestershire. *Represented by*: Design and Artists Copyright Society; The Art Group; Saatchi and Saatchi. *Exhib*: University of London; Queen Elizabeth Conference Centre, London (2000); Mall Galleries (2001, 2004); Cheltenham Open (2002, 2004); Royal West of England Academy (2005); RBSA (2005); Martins International Fine Art Gallery/Ovada

Gallery, Oxford (2005); Mariners Gallery, St. Ives, Cornwall. *Works in collections*: University of London, Deutsche Bank, Writers Guild London, Glos. National Health Trust; private collections in USA, Europe and Switzerland. *Commissions*: Martins Fine Art Gallery. *Works Reproduced*: numerous catalogues. *Recreations*: influences of music and zen, calligraphy, English History. *Clubs*: Cheltenham Group of Artists. *Misc*: selected for Biennale de'll Arte Contemporania, Florence, Italy. *Address*: The Old Stables, 156 Hewlett Road, Cheltenham GL52 6TT. *Email*: peter@artistspace.net *Website*: www.artistspace.net *Signs work*: 'PETER D. GRANVILLE-EDMUNDS'.

GRAY, Douglas, RMSA; HND in Advertising & Illustration; figurative painter, seascapes, cityscapes; Winsor & Newton Best Oil Painting Award 2011 (RSMA); Elected Associate Member Royal Society of Marine Artists 2013; Winner of Russel & Chapel Best Oil (2012, 2013). *Medium*: oil. *b*: Wetherby, 18 Apr 1965. *s of*: Alwyn Gray. *m*: Margaret Mason Gray. *Studied*: Doncaster College of Art (1983-85). *Represented by*: Spencer Coleman Fine Art; Blake Gallery; John Noott Galleries; Whittington Fine Art. *Exhib*: selected exhibitions: Catto Gallery, London (2005); RBA (2007); ROI (2007); Blake Gallery, York, UK (2005-solo, 2006, 2007, 2008); W H Patterson, London (2008); Oakham Gallery, London (2009); W H Patterson, London (2010); John Noott Gallery, Broadway (2010); RSMA (2005-2013); Whittington Fine Art (2012); Thompsons Fine Art London (2013, 2014). *Works in collections*: National Westminster Bank, Pan Macmillan, Royal Mail, Universal Studios; Warner Brothers; William Hague, MP; Savoy Hotel London. *Commissions*: private/corporations. *Publications*: International Artist Magazine; Artists & Illustrators Magazine; Picture Business Magazine. *Clubs*: RSMA. *Address*: 3 Sea Cliff Road, Scarborough, N. Yorks, YO1 2XU. *Email*: douglas.gray14@btinternet.com *Website*: www.douglasgray.com *Signs work*: "Douglas Gray".

GRAY, Euan, Alexander, Alastair Salvesen Travel Scholarship (2004); Cuthbert New Young Artist Award, RGI (2003); British Institution Award Fund, RA (1996); Nat West Prize for Art Shortlist (1994, 1996); Aeneas Travel Award, RA (1995); Alexander Grahame Munro Travel Award (1995); RSA Morrison Portrait Award (1993). *Medium*: oil, watercolour, drawing, etching. *b*: Aberdeen, 13 Jun 1973. *Studied*: Slade (MFA, 1995-98); Edinburgh School of Art (BA First Class Painting and Drawing, 1991-95). *Exhib*: solo: RSA 'Journey' (2005); mixed: The Hunting Art Prizes (2004); Transmission Expo (2003); the 228th RA Summer Exhbn (1996); BP Portrait Exhbn, NPG (1994). *Misc*: BBC Radio Scotland: 'The Arts Show' (26 May 2005). *Address*: 27 Marchbank Road, Bieldside, Aberdeen AB15 9DJ. *Email*: euan_a_gray@yahoo.co.uk *Signs work*: 'Euan Gray'

GRAY, Jane Campbell, ARCA, FMGP; stained glass artist; Liveryman, Worshipful Company of Glaziers (1983). *Medium*: stained glass. *b*: Lincoln, 1931. *d of*: Archibald Denison Ross, M.A. *m*: Kiril Gray. two *d*. *Studied*: Kingston School of Art (1949-52); Royal College of Art (1952-55) under Lawrence Lee and assisted him with Coventry Cathedral nave windows (1955-58). *Exhib*: Examples of work: Uxbridge - St. Margaret's; Civic Centre entrance screen and Alphabet of Flowers in Marriage Room; Hillingdon Hospital Chapel (26 panels); St. Peter's, Martindale, Cumbria (15 windows); Pitminster, Somerset (East window, 1989); Shrewsbury Abbey (1992, 1997); Apothecaries' Hall; Glaziers Hall, London Bridge; Christchurch Priory (1999); St. Sarkis Armenian Church, London, 2000; St Nicholas, Blakeney, Norfolk (2002); St. Oswald's Oswestry (2004); St. Petroc, Inwardleigh, Devon (2005); Holy Nativity, Knowle, Bristol (2006). *Publications*: "Playing with Rainbows" published by Ellingham Press 2011. *Misc*: Over 160 lights in 83 churches; coats-of-arms, domestic windows. *Address*: Ferry Cottage, Shrawardine, Shrewsbury SY4 1AJ. *Signs work*: "Jane Gray".

GRAY, Leonard I.H., DA (1952), RSW (1968); John Laing (London) Landscape Painting Award (1996, 97, 98); Major Award RSW (1995); May Marshall Brown Award,

RSW (1984); Stirling University Award (1981); Educational Institute of Scotland, Award (1980). *Medium*: gouache and mixed media. *b*: Dundee, Scotland, 21 Apr 1925. *s of*: Edward E.M. Gray. *m*: Alexina. one *s*. one *d*. *Educ*: Harris Academy, Dundee, Scotland. *Studied*: Edinburgh College of Art (1952) Post-Grad. Scholar (1952-53). *Exhib*: RA London, RSA, RSW Edinburgh, Glasgow Institute, Mall Galleries London, Aberdeen Gallery, Scottish Arts Council, Edinburgh, London. *Works in collections*: HRH the Duke of Edinburgh's Collection Edinburgh, Royal Scottish Academy, Edinburgh's City Gallery, Greenock Art Gallery, National Trust, Regional Authorities of Aberdeen, Edinburgh, Dundee and Highland, Heriot Watt and Aberdeen Universities, Royal Bank of Scotland, Clydesdale Bank, Royal Hospitals, Edinburgh and Aberdeen. *Publications*: 'Scottish Water-colour Painting' (1979), 'Dictionary of Scottish Art' (1994 & 2006). *Official Purchasers*: see work in collections. *Address*: 27 Marchbank Road, Bieldside, Aberdeen, AB15 9DJ. *Signs work*: 'Leonard Gray'.

GREAVES, Derrick Harry, ARCA (1952). *Medium*: acrylic, oil, watercolour, drawing, prints, collage. *b*: Sheffield, 5 Jun 1927. *s of*: Harry Greaves, steel worker. *m*: Sally. two *s*. one *d*. *Educ*: apprentice signwriter (1943-48). *Studied*: RCA (Carel Weight, John Minton, 1948-52); British School, Rome (1952-54). *Represented by*: James Hyman Fine Art, London. *Exhib*: Contemporary Art Soc., Venice Biennale, Pushkin Museum Moscow, John Moores, Carnegie International Pittsburgh, R.A., Mall Galleries; one-man shows: Beaux Arts, Zwemmer, Inst. of Contemporary Arts, Bear Lane Oxford, Belfast and Dublin, Whitechapel Gallery, Cranfield Inst. of Technology, Monika Kinley, City Gallery Milton Keynes, Hart Gallery London, Galerie Daniel Wahrenberger, Zurich, James Hyman Gallery. *Works in collections*: ACGB; Bank of Ireland, Dublin; NY Public Library; Leeds, Reading, Sheffield, Southampton and Walker A.Gs.; Wesleyan University, Chicago; Tate Gallery; British Museum and worldwide. *Publications*: folios and books: Also (with Roy Fisher) 1971; Songs of Bilitis (1977); Sanscrit Love Poems (1987); 'From Kitchen Sink to Shangri-La' by James Hyman (2007). *Address*: The School, Weston Longville, Norwich, Norfolk NR9 5JU. *Signs work*: "Derrick Greaves".

GREEN, Anthony, RA (1977), DipFA Slade (1960), Harkness Fellow (1967-69); elected Fellow of University College, London (1991); painter in oil; trustee Royal Academy (2001-2008). *b*: Luton, 30 Sep 1939. *m*: Mary Cozens-Walker. two *d*. *Educ*: Highgate School, N6. *Studied*: Slade School of Fine Art. *Exhib*: over 100 one-man shows worldwide since 1962. *Works in collections*: Tate Gallery, Arts Council, museums and art galleries in USA, Japan, Brazil, etc. *Publications*: A Green Part of the World (Thames and Hudson). *Principal Works*: Resurrection - A Sculpture, RA 2003. *Address*: 40 High St., Little Eversden, Cambs. CB23 IHE. *Website*: www.anthonygreenra.com *Signs work*: "Anthony Green," "A. Green," "Anthony," "A.G." or not at all.

GREEN, Brenda Mary, SBA; Dip.Ed. Ceramics; Hon.Sec. SBA. *Medium*: coloured pencil, also stonewear pottery. *b*: Chingford, 4 Apr 1947. *Educ*: Colchester County High (1958-65); Colchester School of Art (1965-67). *Studied*: St. oOsyth's Training College, Clacton-on-Sea, Essex (1967-70). *Exhib*: Local County shows and own exhibitions. Society of Botanical Artists, Methodist Central Hall, Westminster. *Commissions*: mainly local. *Publications*: Work shown in "Botanical Painting with Coloured Pencils" by Ann Swan. *Works Reproduced*: Prints and cards reproduced from originals. *Recreations*: badminton. *Clubs*: Honorary member, Anglian Potters. Misc: Also a potter. Examples of her work can be seen on the website. *Address*: Hardy's, School Lane, Gt. Horkesley, Colchester, Essex CO6 4BL. *Email*: bm.green19@btinternet.com *Website*: www.brendagreenart.co.uk *Signs work*: "BM Green".

GREEN, David John, ROI; landscape painter in water-colour and oil. *b*: London, 23 Feb 1935. *m*: Eileen Ann. two *s*. *Educ*: Goldington Rd. Secondary Modern, Bedford. *Exhib*: RI, RBA, ROI; one-man shows: London, Cambridge, Bedford. *Works in collections*: Luton

Museum, Boston English Gallery. *Commissions*: undertaken. *Address*: The Wilden Gallery, Wilden, Beds. MK44 2QH. *Signs work*: "DAVID GREEN."

GREEN, Diana. *Medium*: oil, pastel and etching. *b*: Warks., 17 Aug 1945. *m*: Michael Green. one *s.* one *d.* *Studied*: Birmingham College of Art (Graphics and Illustration). *Represented by*: The Stour Gallery, Shipston on Stour Warwickshire CV36 4AJ. *Exhib*: various mixed exhibitions, London, since 1989, including RA Summer Exhbn (2001, 03); Singer and Friedlander; Discerning Eye; Pastel Society, Mall Galleries; solo shows: Islington, London (2000), Tokyo (2003), Southwell Minster, Notts (series 21 etchings 'Creation and Fall', 2004), St.Alban's Cathedral, Hertfordshire (2006), Gloucester Cathedral (2008); Southwark Cathedral, Stour Gallery Winter Exhibition (2011); Bankside Gallery, London Lives, Little Buckland Gallery, Broadway Festival & RWS Open (2012). *Works in collections*: Pilkington Collection. *Publications*: entry in 'Artists in Britain Since 1945', David Buckman; Bristol Art Dictionaries. *Misc*: 'Artist in Residence' Bourton House, Moreton-in-Marsh, Glos (2004). *Address*: Odd House, Oddington, Glos GL56 0UP. *Email*: dianagreeninteriors@googlemail.com *Website*: www.thestourgallery.co.uk *Signs work*: 'DG' or 'Diana Green'.

GREEN, Gerald, Dip.Arch. (1978); *Medium*: water-colour, oil and acrylic. *b*: Nuneaton, 22 Jun 1947. *m*: Diana. one *s.* one *d.* *Educ*: King Edward VI Grammar School, Nuneaton. *Studied*: Leicester Polytechnic (Architecture, 1973-77). *Represented by*: several commercial galleries in UK, see website. *Exhib*: ROI, RI, PS, Mall Galleries, London; Glos. City Art Gallery; Granada Television; Shanghai International Watercolour Biennial China; Sunday Times Watercolour Exhibition; 'Not the Turner Prize' Exhibition. *Works in collections*: private clients in UK, Russia, USA and Germany. *Commissions*: over 1500 architectural illustration commissions undertaken for both national and international clients. *Publications*: regular contributor to Arts magazines; work featured in ten books, most recently 'Artists Essential Guide to Watercolour' (David & Charles, 2008). *Official Purchasers*: Coventry Building Society. *Address*: 211 Hinckley Rd., Nuneaton, Warwickshire CV11 6LL. *Email*: ggarts@btinternet.com *Website*: www.ggarts.demon.co.uk *Signs work*: 'Gerald Green'.

GREEN, Judith Ann, BA (Hons) Graphic Design. *Medium*: oil, drawing, prints. *b*: Hampstead, London, 28 May 1956. *d of*: Jack Cooper. *m*: Brian James Green. two *d.* *Educ*: Kingston School of Art. *Studied*: Slade School of Fine Art (1997-2000), The Prince's Drawing School, The Drawing MA Programme (2001-2002). *Represented by*: Medici Gallery, 5 Cork Street, London W1S 3LQ. *Exhib*: RA Summer Exhibition (2003, 2006, 2008, 2013), Lynn Painter's Stainers Prize (2008, 2009, 2010), The Threadneedle Prize (2009), Discerning Eye (2004, 2005), RP (2003, 2004), ROI (2002, 2003), Slade Gallery (2000, 2003). Group Show Medici Gallery (2013, 2012, 2011, 2010), The New Gallery (Cornwall) (2011, 2012), Royal West Academy (158, 159); Two man show Medici Gallery (2010). Solo shows 2008: Highgate Gallery, Musee de Batille de Tilly, Normandy. *Works in collections*: HRH the Prince of Wales, Mr. Anthony Van Laast MBE, Sir Clive Woodshaw OBE, Lenny Henry CBE, Dawn French. *Commissions*: Founders portrait commissioned by The Prince's Drawing School, Mr J Whittaker CBE. Awarded 2009. Residency at Kensington Palace, various private. *Publications*; exhibition catalogues x 8; The Spectator, 'Scan and Pounce' Andrew Lambirth, 15 Jun 2013; The 245th Summer Exhibition at RA. *Works reproduced*: Artists & Illustrators (March 2012) 'The Best of British', interview with Judith Green 'Painting Perceptions' September 2010. *Clubs*: Groucho Club, Dean Street. *Address*: Little Rock, 30 Tregony Hill, Tregony, Truro, TR2 5RV. *Email*: judigreen@btopenworld.com *Website*: www.judigreen.co.uk *Signs work*: "J.G" or "Judith Green" known as Judi.

GREEN, Kate (Kathlene Roche), SBA (2014); ARMS (2011); HS (2008). Awards: Suzanne Lucas Award (2007). *Medium*: miniatures in watercolour. *b*: Gateshead, 25 Nov

1946. *m*: Bill. one *s*. one *d*. *Studied*: Open University Degree: BA Hons First Class in Art History and the Philosophy of Art. Durham University (1991-96). *Exhib*: Solo shows include: The Georgian Theatre Royal, Richmond; The McGuinness Gallery, Bishop Auckland. Group shows include: RMS, Mall Galleries; SBA, Central Hall, Westminster; HS, Wells, and local galleries. *Works in collections*: private and corporate. Commissions: private and corporate. *Publications*: British Watercolour Society catalogue (cover for Christmas Exhibition 2003); Swaledale Woollens - painting and commemorative cards. *Misc*: Full name: Kathleen Roche Green. Specialities: Botanical Art and Still Life in large scale and miniature. *Address*: 12 High Garth, Richmond, N. Yorkshire DL10 4DG. *Email*: kateandbill@talktalk.net *Signs work*: "KATE GREEN" (but in very early work sometimes "K.R.Green").

GREEN, Lorna, BA Hons.(1982), MPhil (1991), FRBS (2001); site specific environmental sculptor; permanent and temporary projects using varied relevant materials. *b*: Manchester. *m*: David Rose FRCS (Ed). two *d*. *Studied*: Manchester Polytechnic, Leeds University. *Exhib*: throughout U.K., Australia, Austria, Bosnia, China, Germany, Hungary, Ireland, Israel, Japan, Korea, New Zealand, Holland, France, Italy, Lithuania. *Commissions*: Leeds University; Cribb's Causeway Shopping Centre, Bristol; Kraftplatzroas, Irdning, Austria; Rochdale Partnership/Canalside SRB; Changchun, China; Beer-Sheva, Israel; Monash University, Melbourne, Australia; Penticton, BC, Canada; South Gloucestershire Council; The Hamptons, Worcester Park, Surrey; Queen Elizabeth Hospital, Gateshead NHS Trust; Newall Green High School, Manchester; Wharton Junior School, Winsford, Green Heart Partnership, Herts; Windmill Hill Primary School, Runcorn; Cheshire County Council; York Art Gallery; Darwen Borough Council; Kelloe, Durham; Co-operative Financial Services, Manchester; Bollington, Cheshire; Nord-Pas de Calais, France and Savoie, France; Gangelt, Germany. *Clubs*: Royal British Society of Sculptors. *Address*: Mount Pleasant Farm, 105 Moss Lane, Bramhall, Cheshire SK7 1EG. *Email*: lg@lornagreen.com *Website*: www.lornagreen.com *Signs work*: "Lorna Green."

GREEN, Peter, OBE (1988); Senior Fellow RE; Head of Post Graduate Art Teacher Training, Hornsey College of Art; Dean Faculty of Art and Design Middlesex University; Member (Council) Crafts Council of GB (1985-91); Emeritus Professor Middlesex University (Art & Design). *Medium*: relief printmaker; linocut, woodcut, paper stencil. *b*: London, 10 Jun 1934. *m*: Linda Green. one *s*. *Studied*: Brighton College of Art; University of London Inst. of Education. *Exhib*: solo: London Graphic Arts (1969-72); Crafts Centre of GB (63); Gallery 273 (63); National Art Gallery of Malaysia, KL (98); major group shows: Zwemmers New Editions (62, 63); London Graphics (68-72); Edinburgh Festival (67); Portfolio Gallery (81); Geffrye Museum (72); Pictures for Schools (60-80); Artmonsky Gallery (99); Gorstella Gallery (06); Bankside Gallery, RE; RA Summer Shows (94-2007); Harley Gallery (07). *Works in collections*: Welsh Arts Council, Walker Art Gallery, Bradford City A.G., Univ. of Wales, Laing A.G., South London A.G., Graves A.G., Towner A.G., Birmingham City Gallery, Cecil Higgins Museum, Bedford, Oldham A.G., Exeter City A.G., National A.G. Malaysia; Museum Education Depts. in Detroit, Seattle & Pittsburgh, USA. *Publications*: Creative Printmaking (Batsford, 1964); Introduction to Surface Printmaking (Batsford, 1967); Design Education, Problem Solving and Visual Experience (Batsford, 1975, 77); Working in Art Design (Batsford, 1983); commissioning Editor, Pembridge Press Design History series (1985). *Address*: 38 De Walden House, Allitsen Road, St. John's Wood, London NW8 7BA. *Email*: plgreenart@waitrose.com *Signs work*: 'Peter Green'.

GREEN, Richard, Dip.AD (1968), MA (1970), FRSA (1988); Curator, York City Art Gallery (since 1977); previously Keeper of Fine Art, Laing Art Gallery, Newcastle upon Tyne (1971-77). *b*: 12 Oct 1946. *s of*: George William Green. *Educ*: Palmer's School, Grays. *Studied*: S.W. Essex Technical College and School of Art; Bath Academy of Art; Goldsmiths' College School of Art (1964-68) studied history of art at University of London,

Courtauld Inst. of Art (1968-70). *Publications*: numerous exhbn. catalogues, articles and reviews. *Address*: c/o York City Art Gallery, Exhibition Sq., York YO1 2EW.

GREENBURY, Judith Pamela, RWA (1979); painter in oil, water-colour. *b*: Bristol, 17 Feb 1924. *d of*: Bernard Spielman. *m*: C. L. Greenbury, M.D. (decd). three *s*. *Educ*: Badminton School, Westbury-on-Trym, Bristol. *Studied*: West of England College of Art (1943-46) under George Sweet, Slade School (1946-47) under Prof. Schwabe. *Exhib*: RA, RWA, RSPP, NEAC, Bear Lane Gallery, Oxford, Mall Galleries, London, Alpine Gallery, London, Phyllis Court Club, Henley-on-Thames, Gallery Piano Nobile, Holland Park, London. *Works in collections*: RWA, and many private collections. *Commissions*: many portraits of mothers and children. *Publications*: "Spey Portrait: A Memoir of Fishing and Painting on the Spey 1974-1989"; "George Sweet, Painter, Teacher and Friend"; "Piers and Seaside Towns An Artist's Journey", (published June 20 2001). "Jeanne, A Long Farewell" (June 2003). *Works Reproduced*: in all four of my books. *Recreations*: painting and gardening, previously fly-fishing. *Address*: Clarence House, 11 New St., Henley-on-Thames, Oxon. RG9 2BP. *Signs work*: "J.G."

GREENHALF, Bette, BSc (Econ) Hons. London University, MA Multimedia (computer); Postgraduate Printmaking; Dip. Higher Education Fine Art; artist, writer, poet. *b*: London, 28 Dec 1932. *d of*: Archie and Maud Harmer. *m*: Tom Greenhalf (decd). *Partner*: Alan Tham. *Studied*: London University; University of the Arts, London. *Exhib*: London - Royal Academy, Festival Hall, Mall Galleries, Camden Art Centre, Chaucer Festival, Barbican, Artists for Nuclear Disarmament, Gallery of the Future, Loughborough University, Midlands Art Centre, Centre Culturel C.P. Paris, ICA, Venice Biennale, Salon des Artistes Brussels. *Works in collections*: Nelson Mandela, Tony Blair, John Major, Chaucer Heritage Trust, War Child Bosnia, Ken Livingstone, Artists for Nuclear Disarmament, Terry Waite, Tate and National Art Libraries. *Publications*: Who's Who in International Art, British Contemporary Art (1993); artist's books: Punch and Judy; Venice Biennale 1895-1995 (a socio-political history); Etchings & poems: World War I, Tiananmen Square, Chaucer, Hampstead. *Address*: 91 Greenhill, Hampstead High St., London NW3 5TY. *Signs work*: "Bette Greenhalf."

GREENHALF, Robert Ralph, RBA (1982), S.WL.A. (1981), DipAD(Graphics) (1971); artist in woodcut, water-colour and oils. *b*: Haywards Heath, 28 Jun 1950. *s of*: Robert Henry Taylor Greenhalf. *m*: Sally Grace. one *s*. *Educ*: Haywards Heath Secondary Modern School. *Studied*: Eastbourne School of Art (1966-68), Maidstone College of Art (1968-71). *Exhib*: RA, RBA, S.WL.A., many mixed exhbns. and one-man shows London, England and Wales, Switzerland, Holland, USA, France, Spain, Germany. *Works in collections*: South East Arts, Hastings Museum, Government Art Collection. *Publications*: "Towards The Sea" (Pica Press, 1999), "Baie de Somme and Rye Bay" (Punch Editions 2007). *Recreations*: bird watching, walking. *Address*: Romney House, Saltbarn La., Playden, Rye, E. Sussex TN31 7PH. *Website*: www.robertgreenhalf.co.uk *Signs work*: "Robert Greenhalf."

GREENLAND, Martin James Howard, BS (Hons) 1st Class Fine Art (Painting); First prizewinner John Moores 24 Exhibition of Contemporary Painting, Liverpool (2006). *Medium*: Oil, drawing. *b*: Marsden, Yorkshire, 21 Mar 1962. *m*: Carole. one *s*. one *d*. *Studied*: Exeter College of Art (1983-85). *Exhib*: includes mixed shows: Whitworth New Contemporaries (1985); Abbot Hall, Kendal (1987); John Moores Exhibition (1989, 91, 93, 95, 2006); Syongnam Art Centre, Korea (2010); Ferens Art Gallery, Lincoln (2011). Includes solo shows: Ainscough Gallery, Liverpool (1993, 1996, 1998); Piccadilly Gallery, London (1997, 2000); Huddersfield Art Gallery (1999); Bruton St Gallery (2002); Cumbria University, Lancaster (2008); Brantwood, Coniston (2008); Hope Univeristy, Liverpool (2010); Art Space Gallery, Islington, London (2009, 11); Corke Art Gallery, liverpool (2012); Tullie House Museum and Art Gallery, Carlisle (2014). *Works in collections*: Walker

Art Gallery, Liverpool; Tullie House Museum and Art Gallery, Carlisle. *Commissions*: Painting of Paternoster Square, presented by Mitsubishi Corp to Lord Mayor of London (2003) currently at Mansion House, London. *Publications*: Gallery catalogues Art Space Gallery (Arrangements of Memory (2009); Uncharted Land (2011)); catalogue Tullie House Museum and Art Gallery (Second Novels (2014)). *Official Purchasers*: Walker Art Gallery, Liverpool; Tullie House Museum and Art Gallery, Carlisle; Painting of Paternoster Square, presented by Mitsubishi Corp to Lord Mayor of London (2003) currently at Mansion House, London. *Principal Works*: Before Vermeer's Clouds (Walker Art Gallery); National Park (Tullie House). *Clubs*: Lake Artists Society. *Address*: 44 Craig Walk, Bowness-on-Windermere, Cumbria LA23 2JT. *Email*: martingreenland@hotmail.co.uk *Website*: www.martingreenland.co.uk *Clubs*: Lake Artists Society. *Signs work*: Occasionally as "MARTIN GREENLAND".

GREENSLADE, Suzanne Lyon, BA (Psychology), MA Fine Art. *Medium*: photography. *b*: Atlanta, USA, 24 Jul 1952. *d of*: Barbara & Sam Hirsch. *Partner*: Tony Bestwick. two *d*, two *s-d*. *Studied*: BA, Psychology - Tulane University, New Orleans, USA (1974); PostGrad Dip, Photography - South Eastern Center for the Arts, Atlanta (1985), MA Fine Art - Howard Gardens, Cardiff (1993). *Exhib*: solo exhibitions: Front Street Gallery, North Carolina, USA (1982), Watershed Media Centre, Bristol (1997), Casa Americana, Valencia, Spain (1999), Tuskegee University, Alabama, USA (2000), University of Salamanca, Spain (2001), Tulane University, New Orleans, USA (2003), Washington Gallery, Penarth, S.Wales (2004), Light House, Wolverhampton (2007), Butetown History & Arts Centre, Cardiff (2009). Selected group exhibitions: Univ. of Alabama, USA (1985), Oriel Mostyn (Touring, 1991), Chapter Arts Centre, Cardiff (1992), Impressions Gallery, York, UK (1993), Zelda Cheatle Gallery, London (1993), Noosa Regional Gallery, Queensland, Australia (1996), Howard Gardens Gallery, Cardiff (2006), Eisteddfod Genedlaethol Cymru, Swansea (2006). *Publications*: selected publications: 'Discovering Welshness' (photographs plus one chapter, Gomer, 1992); 'I Spy: Representations of Childhood' (14 photographs, I.B.Tauris, 1999); 'Under the Magnolias: Growing up white in the South' (text plus 85 black and white photographs, Univ. of Valencia, 2004), 'My Other Mother' (2009). *Principal Works*: "My Other Mother (A Tribute to Willie)", 'Waking from the Long Sleep'. *Misc*: Taught at Swansea Metropolitan University 1986-96. Speaks Spanish, Japanese, Italian and some Welsh. *Address*: 3 Plasturton Place, Cardiff, CF11 9HP. *Email*: suzgreenslade@hotmail.com *Website*: www.suzgreenslade.com *Signs work*: "S.Greenslade".

GREENSMITH, John Hiram, NDD (1955), ATD (1956), ARWS (1976), NEAC (1978), RWS(1983), A.RCamA (1986), RCamA (1996); painter in water-colour; former Head of Fine Art, All Saints School, Sheffield. *b*: Sheffield, 22 Apr 1932. *s of*: John Herbert Greensmith, clerk. *m*: deceased. one *s*. one *d* (by previous marriage). *Educ*: De la Salle College, Sheffield. *Studied*: Sheffield College of Art. *Exhib*: RA, RWS, RBA, RCA, NEAC, MAFA. *Recreations*: bowls. *Misc*: accordion playing. *Address*: 77 Whirlowdale Cres., Sheffield S7 2ND. *Signs work*: "John Greensmith."

GREENWELL, Patricia K., BA (1960); artist in water-colour, acrylic, pastel. *b*: Liverpool, 5 Jul 1937. *m*: Alan. three *s*. *Studied*: Durham University (1956-60, Pasmore, Gowing, Stephenson, Hamilton). *Exhib*: local and regional. *Works in collections*: several in national and international private collections. *Publications*: article - Pastel Artists International. Oct/Nov 2001. *Clubs*: N.A.P.A. *Address*: 3 The Mews, Cherry Orchard, Highworth, Wilts. SN6 7TL. *Website*: www.tate-it-aint.co.uk

GREENWOOD, Maurice Arthur, RCA (1996), Associate (1988); artist in water-colour and oil; art tutor; part-time lecturer Llandaillo College, Dept. of Lifelong Learning, University College, N. Wales since 1982; Life President of Denbighshire Art Society, now retired from teaching, part time tutor on Fred Olsen Cruise Ships. *b*: Rochdale, 12 Dec 1930.

s of: Frank and Lily Greenwood. *m*: Joan. two *s*. *Studied*: part-time Rochdale Art School (1946-48) (Peter Burgess Shorrock, 1960-65). *Exhib*: RCamA; St. Davids Hall, Cardiff; National Library of Wales, Aberystwyth; Ectarl, Llangollen; Plas Glyn-y-Weddw, Venue Cymru, Llandudno; and many open and one-man shows. *Works in collections*: Gwynedd Library Services; private collections in USA, British Columbia, Australia, UK. *Address*: Woodlands, 12 Shaftesbury Ave., Penrhyn Bay, Llandudno, N. Wales LL30 3EH. *Email*: mauriceagreenwood@gmail.com *Signs work*: "Maurice A. Greenwood, R.C.A."

GREENWOOD, Philip John, NDD (1965), ATC (1966), RE (1982); printmaker in etching and painter. *b*: Dolgellau, N. Wales, 20 Nov 1943. *s of*: John Edward James Greenwood, R.A.F. *m*: Valery Ratcliff (decd), Sally Dear. four *s*, two *s-s*. *Educ*: Dolgellau Grammar School. *Studied*: Harrow College of Art (1961-65), Hornsey Teachers Training College (1965-66). *Exhib*: RA, RE, Tate Gallery, RGI, 'Printmaking in Britain', Sydney; British Council Gallery, Athens; British Printmakers, Melbourne; Galerie Tendenz, Germany; J. One Fine Arts, Tokyo; Galerie Deux Tetes, Canada; 'Overseas Printmakers', Auckland, NZ; Galerie Beumont, Brussels. *Works in collections*: Tate Gallery, Arts Council, British Council, Derby Museum, Greenwich Museum, Oldham A.G., Graves A.G., Warwick Museum and A.G., Lincoln A.G. and Museum, etc. *Address*: 3 The Square, Elham, Kent, CT4 6TJ. *Email*: art@philgreenwood.info *Website*: www.philgreenwood.info *Signs work*: "Greenwood."

GREETHAM, Robert Michael, BA (Hons) Art; MA (Art and Art History); three awards/grants from Arts Council of Wales. *Medium*: photography, acrylic, mixed media. *b*: Cardiff, 7 Apr 1957. *s of*: Kathleen P. Davies (née), Stanley Greetham. *Studied*: University of Wales School of Art, Aberystwyth. *Exhib*: RA; School of Art Gallery and Museum UWA Aberystwyth; The Gate, Cardiff; Washington Gallery, Penarth; Aberystwyth Arts Centre; St.David's Hall, Cardiff; Ffotogallery, Cardiff; Christie's, London; Oriel Mostyn, Llandudno. *Works in collections*: National Library of Wales; University of Wales Aberystwyth; South Glamorgan County Council. *Commissions*: 'On the House' Chapter Arts Centre; 'Just Another Day' and 'Barrage' Ffotogallery, Cardiff. *Publications*: 'Robert Greetham Photographs 1978-1998' - UWA School of Art Press. *Address*: 902a Newport Road, Rumney, Cardiff CF3 4LL. *Email*: robert.greetham@btopenworld.com *Signs work*: 'R.M.Greetham'.

GREGORY, Annabelle, SWA (2000). *Medium*: oil, drawing, collage, pastel. *b*: Richmond, 29 Sep 1941. *m*: Robert Barry. two *s*. one *d*. *Educ*: Carlyle Grammar School for Girls, Chelsea. *Studied*: St.Martin's School of Art (1958-60); Camden Art Institute (Camden). *Exhib*: Oxford Art Society (1983-98); MoMA, Oxford (1991); Royal Birmingham Society of Artists (1997, 98); SWA (1998-2008, 2010/2012); Brownstone Gallery, Mudbury (2008-2009); Harbour House, Kingsbridge, Devon (2009); St. Ives Crypt Callery with ABNA (2011); Delamore House with ABNA (2012); St Ives Society of Artists Gallery (2013) with ABNA. *Works in collections*: worldwide. *Commissions*: mostly local. *Publications*: ABNA (published Jan 2012). *Principal Works*: mainly collages of botanical form, now painting large 'modern' oils of Marine Subjects and Landscapes. *Recreations*: walking, swimming, yoga & gardening. *Misc*: Now teaching life drawing. *Address*: 35 Church Street, Modbury, Devon PL21 0QR. *Email*: annabellegregory35@gmail.com *Signs work*: 'Gregory', 'GREGORY'.

GREGORY, Norma, TD, Dip AD Ed; Fellow Chelsea Physic Garden. Awards: RHS Gold Medals (2006, 2008, 2011), Silver Gilt (20080), Florilegium Society Margaret Granger Memorial Silver Bowl (SBA 2013), Cert. of Botanical Merit (SBA, 2013, 2014). *Medium*: watercolour. *b*: Yorkshire, 1942. *Studied*: Edge Hill College, Ormskirk (1960-63), Leeds University (1971-72). *Exhib*: RHS Botanical Shows; Museum of Garden History; Hunt Institute of Botanical Documentation, Pittsburgh USA; Chelsea Physic Garden; Brooklyn Botanic Gardens, New York; Westminster Gallery. Numerous UK locations with Leicester

Society of Botanical Ilustrators. *Works in collections*: RHS Lindley Library, Kew Archives, Hunt Institute USA, Chelsea Physic Garden Archives, Natural History Museum. Private collections. *Commissions*: numerous. *Official Purchasers*: Royal Horticultural Society (RHS), Kew Garden Archives. *Works Reproduced*: in "Women Artists" Natural History Museum (2014). *Recreations*: gardening, teaching, reading, painting. *Clubs*: Leicester Society of Botanical Illustrators. *Email*: normagregorybotanicalartist@gmail.com *Website*: normagregorybotanicalartist.com *Signs work*: monogram "NG" with G joined to N.

GRENVILLE, Hugo Gerard. *Medium*: oil, gouache, distemper, ceramics. *b*: London, 5 Aug 1958. *s of*: Gerard Morgan Grenville. *Partner*: Lisa Takahashi. two *s*. *Educ*: p/t Chelsea and Heatherley's Schools of Art. *Represented by*: Wally Findlay Galleries, New York and Palm Beach. *Exhib*: RBA, RI, ROI, Arts Club; seven one-man shows at Messums from 1995; one-man show 2006 in New York at Wally Findlay Galleries; one-man show 2007 Josie Eastwood Fine Art, London; one-man show 2008 & 2009 in Palm Beach at Wally Findlay Galleries, and New York in 2011 and 2013. *Works in collections*: Ministry of Defence; Worshipful Company of Ironmongers, The China Club, Hong Kong; Edinburgh City Council; the late Duke of Devonshire; The Tresco Estate. *Commissions*: War Artist, Bosnia 1995; portraits include: the late Archbishop of Canterbury, Right Rev. Lord Runcie; the late General Sir Willaim Rous; the Countess of Verulam; Michael Chance as Orpheus at the ENO. *Publications*: regular contributor to the Artist Magazine; 'Songs of Light' with Philip Wells (Feb 2006), 'Art & the Gardener' by Gordon Hayward (2008). *Works Reproduced*: Country Life magazine Oct 2007; Artists & Illustrators Oct 2006; The Artist 2005. 06, 07, 08, 09. *Principal Works*: still life with figure, landscapes in the Romantic idiom; also narrative subjects. *Recreations*: books, music, gardening. *Clubs*: Chelsea Arts Club. *Misc*: Runs the Grenville School of Painting in Bristol. *Address*: 18 Tyne Road, Bristol BS7 8EE. *Email*: hugo@hugogrenville.com *Website*: www.hugogrenville.com *Signs work*: 'Hugo Grenville' or 'H.G.'

GRETTON, Keith, NDD, ATC; Awards: London Potters Open Sculpture. *Medium*: prints, acrylics, ceramic sculpture. *b*: Rugeley, Staffs, 24 Dec 1934. *s of*: William Gretton. *m*: Penelope Warner Gretton. two *s*. two *d*. *Studied*: Stafford Art College, London University. *Exhib*: RA Summer Show; Society of Painters, Etchers and Engravers; Barbican (solo); Durham University; RBSA; West of England Academy; Cambridge Contemporary Art, Barn Gallery, Aston; New Ash Gate, Farnham; Brighton Art Fair; regular solo exhbns in UK. *Works in collections*: Chelsea and Westminster Hospital, Homerton Hospital Trust, Lambeth Community Care, private collections worldwide. *Commissions*: founder of Battersea Contemporary Artists Art Fair from 1993-2002; commissions all private. *Official Purchasers*: Department of Trade and Industry. *Works Reproduced*: Studio Magazine, London Potters magazine No 109 profile, The Independent (Oct 06), Art Review, Sunday Times, Building Design, Ceramic Review. *Recreations*: working. *Clubs*: London Potters; (ex-Free Painters). *Misc*: Sale work by Sotheby's. *Address*: 26 Honeywell Road, London SW11 6EG. *Email*: keithgretton34@gmail.com *Signs work*: 'Keith Gretton', 'K' (in circle) or 'G' impressed on clay pieces.

GREY, Jenni, BA (Hons), MA, Fellow, Designer Bookbinders; fine binder and book artist; part-time tutor, University of Brighton. *b*: London, 3 Jul 1950. *m*: Anthony Belfield. one *d*. *Educ*: Bexley Grammar School. *Studied*: Brighton Polytechnic. *Exhib*: regularly since 1982 in England, Europe and America. *Works in collections*: National Poetry Library (England), Koninklijke Bibliotheek (Holland), University of Georgia and Wellesley College (USA), Les Amis de la Reliure d'Art (France), Biblioteca Wittockiana (Belgium), The British Library (England), The John Rylands Library (England), The Library of Congress (USA). *Commissions*: Winchester Cathedral (England). *Publications*: The New Bookbinder (Article 'Progress Making') 2006. *Address*: 26 St. Lukes Rd. Brighton BN2 2ZD. *Email*: jennigrey@btinternet.com *Website*: www.designerbookbinders.org.uk

GRIBBIN, Launcelot Benedict, ATD (1949); BA (Hons.) Hist. of Art (1953); painter in oil, photographer; lecturer, Victoria and Albert Museum; former principal lecturer, London College of Printing; sometime tutor, Messrs. Sotheby's Institute; International freelance lecturer in History of Architecture and Decorative Arts. *b*: Gateshead-on-Tyne, 7 Nov 1927. *s of*: L. B. Gribbin (senior), pharmacist. *m*: Joanna Mary Satchell (decd 2010). two *s*. two *d*. *Educ*: Dartford Grammar School. *Studied*: Sidcup School of Art under Ruskin Spear, A.R.A., Robin Guthrie, William Clause; Courtauld Inst. of Art. *Exhib*: RA, NEAC, London Group, National Soc.; one-man shows, Artists' House, Manette St., etc. *Address*: 8 Mile House La., St. Albans, Herts. AL1 1TB. *Email*: launcegribbin@gmail.com *Website*: www.launcegribbin.co.uk *Signs work*: "L. B. GRIBBIN" (written with brush).

GRICE, Carol Ann. *Medium*: oil, watercolour, acrylics, drawing, prints. *b*: Bingley, W. Yorks, 7 Sep 1949. *m*: David Grice. two *d*. *Educ*: Bingley Grammar School. *Studied*: Bradford Regional College of Art. *Represented by*: Titus Gallery: Saltaire, Antwerp, Malaga. *Exhib*: Lane Gallery, Bradford (1967-68); Anthony Parton, Bradford (1968); Titus Gallery: Saltaire, Antwerp, Malaga (1986-1999); Sigi Krause Gallery, London (1967, 1971); Park Sq. Gallery, Leeds (1972); Bradford City Art Gallery (1992-93); Bart Wouters Gallery, Ekgren, Belgium (2003, 04, 06); Phantom Gallery, Antwerp, Belgium (2006); Amazing Art Gallery, Antwerp, Belgium (20006); Ronda Space Art, Spain (2008-2014); Lecrin Gallery, La Heradura, Spain (2008-09); Anedo Centro Cultural Villa de Nerja, Spain (2009, 10, 11, 12); Aneda Calle de Mercado, Nerja, Spain (2008, 09, 10, 12). *Works in collections*: Corporate and private collections: Europe, USA, Australia. *Commissions*: various private commissions. *Recreations*: Animal charity work. *Clubs*: Aneda, Malaga, Spain. *Misc*: mother to the artist Klio le Grice, and Professor Kliti Grice. *Address*: Apartado de Correos 507, Nerja, Malaga 29780, Spain. *Email*: artistica77@yahoo.com *Signs work*: "Carol".

GRICE, David, painter, sculptor, maker of constructions and mixed media artist; winner, national prizes for painting from age 6; teacher, Bradford School of Art (1971-72). *b*: Saltaire, 1 Oct 1946. *m*: Carol Ann. two *d*. *Studied*: Bradford School of Art (1962-66). *Exhib*: ICA (1969), Angela Flowers Gallery (1970); group shows: worldwide; one-man shows: Titus Gallery, W.Yorks (1988-2000); Gallery Johanna de Poorter, Antwerp (2002-2003); SAG Contemporary Art, Antwerp (2005); Amazing Art Gallery, Antwerp (2004); Phantom Gallery, Antwerp (2006). *Works in collections*: private, corporate and institutional collections inc. Prof. David Sharpe: Prof. Micheal Levi; Prof. Karen U Schallreuter: Prof. Paul Walton; Dr. J. M. Braganza; Peter Black plc; Robert Heller; Prof Kliti Grice; Angela Flowers; Dr Ian Wellings.Bernard Bergman collection, Antwerp. *Commissions*: Fine Art Developments plc, etc. *Principal Works*: "The Fishmongers Wedding" canvas 190cmx190cm; "Children and Animals Exploited for Greed and Vanity sculpture h203cm w69cm d47cm. *Address*: Apartado de Correos, 507, 29780, Nerja, Malaga, Spain. *Email*: artistica77@yahoo.com *Website*: www.artbydavidgrice.com *Signs work*: "DG" as monogram or "David Grice".

GRIDNEV, Valeriy, PS, ROI, ARP; prizes include: Gold Medal, USSR Academy of Arts (1990); Frank Herring Award, PS (2000, 2003); Winsor & Newton/ Daily Mail finalist prize (2004); Winsor & Newton Award, ROI (2005); The Arts Club Award, PS (2006); The Arts Club Award, RP Mall Gallery (2006); portrait painter. *b*: 1 Jan 1956. *s of*: Fedor Gridnev. *m*: Gridneva Ekaterina. one *s*. *Studied*: Sverdlovsk College of Art (1976-1980); St.Petersbyrg Academy of Arts (1983-90); Creative Studio St.Petersbyrg Academy of Arts. *Represented by*: John Noot Galleries; Fine Arts Commissions Ltd; FBA Mall Gallery; Cross Gate Gallery, USA; Whittington Fine Arts. *Exhib*: Mall Gallery (2000-2007), Michael Simpson Gallery (1995); Alberty Gallery (1998-2002); Arndean Gallery (2003, 2005); Langham Fine Art (2002-2007); Brian Sinfeld Gallery (2003); John Noot Galleries (2003, 2004); Cross Gate Gallery (1999-2007). *Commissions*: Henry, 7th Earl of Carnarvon; Jean Wallop, Countess of Carnarvon; Lord Porchester; Mrs. Harry Vane; Louis Frosio, leader of the

Monte-Carlo Orchestra; Lester Piggott; Mrs Charles Brocklebank; Mrs Sheran MacDonald-Buchanan; Mr, Mrs Compton; Mr, Mrs Whitley, Lord Clifford of Chudleigh. *Clubs*: The Arts Club, London. *Address*: 88 Drapers Court, 59 Lurline Gardens, London SW11 4DF. *Email*: valeriygridnev@yahoo.com *Signs work*: 'VALERIY GRIDNEV'.

GRIFFIN, Alison Mary, RMS, SLM, BA Art and Design (1974); minature painter, and landscape and interior artist in water-colour and acrylic. *Medium*: acrylic and watercolour. *b*: Sutton Coldfield, 23 May 1953. *d of*: Charles Green (decd). *m*: Mark Upton Yonge. one *s*. one *d*. *Educ*: Boldmere High School for Girls, Sutton Coldfield. *Studied*: Sutton College of Art (1969-71), Bath Academy of Art (1971-74). *Represented by*: Image Source; Francis Iles. *Exhib*: Francis Iles Gallery, Rochester, Mall Galleries, London. *Works in collections*: private collections. *Works Reproduced*: Limited Edition Prints, Rosenstiels, Medici Cards. *Recreations*: opera, classical music, swimming. *Address*: Wisteria House, 68 North St., Barming, Maidstone, Kent ME16 9HF. *Signs work*: "Alison Griffin."

GRIFFITH, David Lloyd, RCamA (1996), Associate (1988); Certificate Open College (1993); Teaching experience: life drawing, RCA Conwy (1992-96) and Mostyn Gallery Llandudno (2003-2007), Basic art, WEA Coleg Harlech (1998-2008). *Medium*: oil and watercolour. *b*: Colwyn Bay, 30 Mar 1956. *s of*: Roy Lloyd Griffith. *Educ*: Ysgol Emrys Ap Iwan, Abergele, Clwyd. *Studied*: N.E. Wales Inst. (1975-76, N.D. Mackinson, R. Hore), Open College of the Arts (1989-93, E. Williams, H. Bowcott, N. Griffiths). *Represented by*: recent work can be seen at: 'Ffin y Parc' Gallery, Llanrwst; 'Oriel y Bont', Aberystwyth; 'Y Capel', Llangollen. *Exhib*: Rhyl Arts Centre (1997, 1999, 2004), "Land of my Fathers", Oglivy & Estil (1998); selected group shows Royal Cambrian Academy, "I Know what I like, or do I?", Kings College, Cambridge (1997), The Pure Landscape, John Davies Gallery, Stow on Wold (2001). "Moments", Denbigh Museum & Gallery (2001). Two man show at Royal Cambrian Academy, Plas Glyn y Weddw and Theatre Clwyd (2002); Llanrwst Museum (2003). National Library of Wales, Aberystwyth (2004); Y Tabernacl, Machynlleth (2005), Plas Glyn y Weddw (2005); 'Welsh Painters Past and Present', John Davies Gallery (2005); 'Wales Works', Kooywood Gallery, Cardiff (2007); selected artists - 'Gorstella Gallery', Chester (2007), Royal Cambrian Academy (2009); solo 'Y Galeri', Betws y Coed - 2008; solo 'Ffin y Parc' Llanrwst. *Works in collections*: Hospitals in Wales. *Misc*: interviewed for BBC 'Wales Today' in connection with RCamA 125th Anniversary (March 2007). *Address*: 35 Glan y Fedw, Betws Yn Rhos, Abergele, LL22 8AP. *Website*: www.davidlloydGriffith.co.uk *Signs work*: "D.L.G."

GRIFFITHS, David, DFA (Slade); portrait painter in oils; RCA. *b*: Liverpool, 1939. *s of*: Frederic & Muriel Griffiths. *Educ*: Pwllheli Grammar School (1951-57). *Studied*: Slade School of Fine Art (1957-61, Sir William Coldstream). *Exhib*: Royal National Eisteddfod; Retrospective exhibition, National Library of Wales (2002). *Works in collections*: American Embassy, London; Linnean Society, London; Cardiff and County Club; City Hall, Cardiff; Museum and A.G., Newport; Croydon Town Hall; House of Lords; Eton College; National Library of Wales; University of Wales, Cardiff, Swansea and Aberystwyth; Llandovery College; Trinity College; Assoc. of Anaesthetists; Speaker's House, Westminster; Liverpool University; Assoc. of Chartered Surveyors; several public and private collections throughout the country. *Publications*: 'Portraits' David Griffiths (National Library of Wales, 2002). *Address*: Westville House, 49 Westville Rd., Cardiff CF23 5DF. *Email*: dg@david-griffiths.co.uk *Website*: www.david-griffiths.co.uk *Signs work*: "David Griffiths."

GRIFFITHS, Michael, ARE, BA (Hons), Post Grad. Cert. in Printmaking; painter and printmaker; now retired from course leader post at Arts University, Bournemouth. *b*: London, 27 Sep 1951. two *s*. *Studied*: Brighton Polytechnic (1973-1977). *Exhib*: 20 solo exhibs. throughout UK, and numerous group exhibs., UK and abroad. *Works in collections*: numerous private and public collections, including Ashmolean Museum, Oxford, South East Arts,

University of Kent. Victoria & Albert Museum. *Clubs*: Newlyn Society of Artists: Fellow Royal Society of Painter Printmakers (RE). *Address*: 44 Kimberley Road, Bournemouth, BH6 5EX. *Email*: mgriff@live.co.uk *Website*: www.michaelgriffithsfineart.com *Signs work*: "Michael Griffiths" or "MG."

GRIFFITHS, Michèle (Helen Françoise), MA Cantab, Diploma in Modern Social and Cultural Studies, BA Hons Fine Art: Painting, Wimbledon. *Medium*: oil. *b*: London, 8 Aug 1951. *d of*: Robert and Pierrette Hoare (school teachers). *m*: David Griffiths. *Educ*: Blackheath High School. *Studied*: Girton College Cambridge (modern languages degree), Putney School of Art (1990-92); Wimbledon School of Art (1992-95) under Michael Ginsborg and Prunella Clough. *Represented by*: Stour Gallery (Warks) www.thestourgallery.co.uk. *Exhib*: AAF, London (2004, 05); Stour Gallery (2002-07); Hicks Gallery (2004, 05); Mall Galleries, selected for Discerning Eye (2003); Christie's Art for Life (2002, 2004-07); RA Summer Exhbn (1997); Art 2001 with Vertigo Gallery, Hoxton; Art 2000; Turin Art Fair and Art Brussels with James Colman Fine Art; British Art Fair, RCA (2000); and many more. *Works in collections*: works including commissions in private collections in the UK, France, USA and Japan. *Publications*: Feature article in 'Artists and Illustrators' magazine (April 2007) short editorial review in Galleries Magazine (Jul 05); article on 'The Influence of Medical Imaging' in The Lancet (Feb 1997). *Recreations*: walking, sailing, yoga, travel, literature, singing. *Misc*: interest in religions. *Address*: 154 Elborough Street, Southfields, London SW18 5DL. *Email*: michegriffiths@aol.com *Signs work*: 'M.Griffiths'.

GRIFFITHS, Simon John, BA (Hons). *Medium*: Sculpture. *b*: Kingston upon Thames, 25 Nov 1971. *m*: Heather. one *s*. one *d*. *Studied*; Ripon and York St John (1990-94). *Exhib*: Bonhams (Sep 2009); Society of Wildlife Artists (2010, 2011); Art in Clay (2008-12); Potfest (2001-12); Earth and Fire (2011-12). *Works in collections*: Museum of Nature in Art; Newcastle College of Art. *Commissions*: many private and corporate. *Address*: 28 Church Street, Castleside, Co. Durham DH8 9QW. *Email*: s.griffithssculpture@icloud.com *Website*: www.simongriffithssculpture.co.uk *Signs work*: "GRIFFITHS".

GRIFFITHS, Tom, painter, designer and illuminator on vellum; Senior lecturer, Norwich School of Art (1942-49); chairman, Norfolk and Norwich Art Circle (1957, 1958, 1978), President (1983-). *Educ*: City of Norwich School. *Studied*: Norwich School of Art, Heatherleys' and The Grosvenor (London). *Exhib*: RA, ROI, NS and provincial art galleries; one-man shows of townscapes (Norwich). *Works in collections*: many illuminated vellums include Loyal Address (Norwich); Freedom Scrolls for HM Queen Elizabeth the Queen Mother, Sir John Barbirolli (King's Lynn); the Royal Air Force and Regimental presentations and the County War Memorial Book of Remembrance, Norwich Cathedral. *Address*: 15 Essex St., Norwich. *Signs work*: "Tom Griffiths."

GRIGSBY, John Higham, NDD, ATD, ARE (1973), RE (1978). *Medium*: etching. *b*: Staffs., 18 Dec 1940. *Studied*: Stoke and Leicester Colleges of Art. *Exhib*: Young Contemporaries, RA, NEAC, RWA, RWS Galleries, Mall Galleries, FBA Touring Exhbns., Woburn Abbey, Glasgow Institute, London Group, Buenos Aires Print Biennale, Bankside Gallery; solo shows: Hampstead, Exeter, Henley, Beckenham, Bedford School. *Works in collections*: Reading Museum; Whitgift Foundation; Graves Gallery, Sheffield; Open University; National Museum of Wales; Williamson Gallery, Birkenhead; Portland State University (USA); Camden and Greenwich Councils; Hertfordshire, mid-Glamorgan and Sheffield Education Authorities; Exeter University; Bedford School; Fylde Arts Assoc; Imperial College; Fitzwilliam Museum. *Commissions*: Two murals for Trust Houses (1962); Limited edition etching for Unistrut U.K. (1978) and the PCC (1982). *Official Purchasers*: University of Wales. *Address*: 152a Mackenzie Rd., Beckenham BR3 4SD. *Signs work*: "John Grigsby."

GRISLEY, Jackie, SWA. *Medium*: watercolour. *b*: London, 18 Sep 1956. *Partner*: Kim Roskell SWA. *Exhib*: Fine Art UK; Picturecraft, Norfolk; Signature, Kendall; McNeill, Arkhangel, Ireland; various local galleries; Mall Galleries, London (SWA); Westminster Methodist Central Hall, London (SWA); 'Eclipse' (joint watercolour exhibition), Hertford County Hall; Broxbourne Civic Hall (Joint Exhibition). *Works in collections*: private & international. *Publications*: International Artist Magazine 2011 (10 page article). *Principal Works*: Coast and lakeland scenes with dramatic skies. *Misc*: Self-taught watercolourise, career background in graphic design and typography for national newspapers, later as an architectural scenic model maker & watercolour painter. *Address*: 2 Cheapside, Anstey, Buntingford, Herts SG9 0BL. *Email*: jackiegrisley@aol.com *Website*: www.jackiegrisley.co.uk *Signs work*: "J. GRISLEY".

GROARKE, Michael, MA, MCSD chartered designer; BEDA Cert. (Registered European designer); wallpaper/textile/ceramics designer, painter in water-colour and oil. *b*: Manchester, Oct 1943. *m*: Prudence J. Hyde. two *s*. *Educ*: Manchester High School of Art. *Studied*: Calico Printers Assoc. Design School, Manchester Polytechnic Faculty of Art and Design, Manchester Met University, Rochdale College of Art. The Slade. *Exhib*: RA, RWS, RI, RCamA; design work/exhb. Britain, Europe, America and Far East. *Address*: Fourways, 2 Grosvenor Rd., Marple, Stockport SK6 6PR. *Signs work*: "M.G." or "Michael Groarke."

GROSVENOR, Stella Athalie (Mrs.), RBS, Slade Dip. Fine Art (1937); sculptor in bronze, resin, stone, wood, painter in oil. *b*: Beaconsfield. *d of*: Sidney Henderson. *m*: Hugh N. W. Grosvenor, ARIBA. *Educ*: St. Margaret's School, Hampstead. *Studied*: Slade School under Prof. Schwabe and Prof. Gerrard. *Exhib*: group shows, Society Portrait Sculptors, Hampstead Artists Council, R.A., Travers Gallery, Erica Bourne Gallery; one-man show, Foyles, London (1968). *Works in collections*: Dixons. *Publications*: Art Editor, National Trade Press; Illustrated, Caxton Publishing Co. *Clubs*: Hampstead Artists Council, R.B.S. *Address*: 35 Flask Walk, London NW3 1HH. *Signs work*: "A. Grosvenor."

GROVES, Janet B., BA (Hons). *Medium*: oil, watercolour, pastel. *b*: Birmingham, 7 Jul 1942. *m*: Reg Beach. one *s*. one *d*. *Educ*: OU (1984-91). *Exhib*: RA; RBSA; RWA; South West Academy. *Works in collections*: Penzance, Camborne, Liverpool, Manchester, Bristol, London; Sevenoaks, Kent; Brussels, Aix-en-Provence, Reims, Vienna, Sweden. *Clubs*: Birmingham Art Circle. *Address*: 19 Polwithen Road, Penzance, Cornwall TR18 4JW. *Email*: jaybea@beeb.net *Signs work*: 'J.B.Groves'

GROVES, John Michael, RSMA (1977), NDD (Illustration, 1957); Derek Gardner 'Deep Seas' Award, Conway Maritime Award. *Medium*: pastel, oil, pen and ink. *b*: Lewisham, London, 9 Mar 1937. *Educ*: Kilmorie Secondary School, London. *Studied*: Camberwell School of Arts and Crafts (1953-57). *Exhib*: RSMA, Mall Galleries, London. *Commissions*: five (3'x 5') historical oils for this country and abroad, commissioned by Shell. *Publications*: The Tall Ship in Art – Cassell; A Celebration of Marine Art - Bounty Books. *Address*: 114 Further Green Rd., Catford, London SE6 1JQ. *Email*: john@johngroves.org *Website*: www.johngroves.org *Signs work*: "J. Groves."

GRUFFYDD, Pegi, BA (Hons.) (1982), ARCA (1985), Dip.RA (1986); painter/printmaker in oil, water-colour, etching, lithography. *b*: Pwllheli, N. Wales, 28 Apr 1960. *d of*: Morris Griffiths. *Educ*: Ysgol Glan-y-Môr, Pwllheli. *Studied*: Manchester Polytechnic (1978-79), Wolverhampton Polytechnic (1979-82), R.A. Schools (1983-86). *Exhib*: RA Summer Exhbn. (1984-85), Royal National Eisteddfod of Wales (1980-88), Young Artists Forum, Cardiff University, Wales '83, the Welsh Group Touring Exhbn., Midwales Open, Aberystwyth, North Wales Open, Llandudno; one-man show, Theatre Gwynedd, Bangor; group show, Oriel, Bangor. *Misc*: Gallery: Oriel Glyn-y-Weddw, Llanbedrog. *Address*: Llymgwyn Farm, Chwilog, Pwllheli, Gwynedd LL53 6HJ. *Signs work*: "Pegi Gruffydd" or "P.G."

GUARNORI, Jacky, (née Truelove), FSBA (1985), SLm (1986); self taught flower painter in water-colour. *b*: Surrey, 1943. *m*: Peter Truelove. two *s*, one *s-s*. two *s-d*. *Educ*: Grey Coat Hospital, London. *Exhib*: SBA; solo shows: Bromley (4), Croydon (2), Cranbrook (1), Group exhibitions: Francis Iles Fine Art, Sevenoaks Wildfowl Trust, Soc. of Limners, Samlesbury Hall, The Lake Artists, North Wales Soc.of Arts. *Works in collections*: Orpington Library, Shell U.K. *Commissions*: Shell U.K., Dr. Barnados. *Works Reproduced*: greetings cards and calendars. *Clubs*: Ambleside Art Society. *Address*: Oak Bank, Hill Top, Windermere, Cumbria LA23 2HG. *Email*: jacpet@truelove4.wanadoo.co.uk *Signs work*: "Jacky Guarnori" or "J.G."

GUDGEON, Simon David, SWLA; ARBS; Hunting in Art Prize 2007 (International Council for Game and Wildlife Conservation). *Medium*: sculpture in bronze, drawing. *b*: Sherriff Hutton, 4 Oct 1958. *s of*: Tom & Olwen Gudgeon. *m*: Monique. *Exhib*: SWLA (2000-2014); Wykeham Gallery, Stockbridge; Birds in Art, Wisconsin, USA (2005-2014); Simon Gudgeon one-man exhibition, Halcyon Gallery, London (2007); NMWA, Sofa Chicago (2013); SAA, Jerram Gallery, Diehl Galleryl; Holland & Holland (2014). *Works in collections*: Woburn Abbey, Beds.; Amhunnsuide Castle, Isle of Harris; Matthew Gloag Ltd., Perthshire; HRH Duke of Edinburgh; HRH Prince of Wales; Duke and Duchess of Cambridge. *Publications*: 'A Passion for Grouse' (2002); 'Woodcock, Artists' Impressions' (2006); 'Grouse, Artists' Impressions' (2007); SBTL (2013-2014) *Address*: Sculpture by the Lakes, Pallington Lakes, Pallington, Forchester DT2 8QU. *Email*: sg@simongudgeon.com *Website*: www.simongudgeon.com *Signs work*: 'Simon Gudgeon' and 'SG'.

GUISE, Christopher John, MA, RMS; marine painter in oil on wood panels, miniaturist in oil on ivorine; formerly on staff, Hurstpierpoint College. *b*: Darjeeling, India, 19 Jun 1928. *m*: Phyllis Gibson. one *s*. one *d*. *Educ*: Charterhouse and Brasenose College, Oxford. *Exhib*: RMS since 1983, Brighton, Washington, NY, Boston, Toronto, Maritime and Sailing Centres. *Address*: Carys, West Furlong La., Hurstpierpoint, W. Sussex BN6 9RH. *Signs work*: "C.J. GUISE."

GUNNING, David Edward, BA (Hons) Fine Art; PGCE Art Education. *Medium*: Oil, drawing, prints, steel etched images. *b*: Bilston, 30 Jan 1954. *m*: Lizzy Gunning. two *d*. *Studied*: Liverpool Art College (1974-77); Birmingham Art College (1977-78). *Represented by*: The Contemporary Art Gallery, Ebury St, London (1990-99); Shropshire Fine Arts (2005-present day). *Exhib*: The artist has had over sixty solo exhibitions and exhibited in many mixed exhibitions. *Works in collections*: The Royal Collection; The Palace of Westminster; The National Museum of Wales; Devizes Museum; Birmingham Museum and Art Gallery; Walsall New Gallery. *Commissions*: The Area Museum Authority for the South West of England (1986-88); National Museum of Wales (1991-93). The Palace of Westminster (1996). Devizes Museum (2006). *Publications*: Art in Parliament; Art in Wiltshre (2005). *Principal Works*: Ancient Sites - etchings; large steel etched images. Industrial and rural images. *Misc*: 110 small etchings into the Royal Collection in 2005 and 2012. *Address*: 28 Church Hill, Ironbridge, Shropshire TF8 7PZ. *Email*: davegunning@gunningarts.co.uk *Website*: www.gunningarts.co.uk *Signs work*: "DAVID GUNNING".

GURREY, Charles Stewart, BA (Oxon) 1979; MPhil (Cantab) 1981. *Medium*: sculpture. *b*: Thurso, Scotland, 20 Mar 1953. *m*: Doreen Gurrey. four *s*. one *d*. *Studied*: PPE Balliol Colege, Oxford (1976-79); St. John's College, Cambridge (1979-81); Apprenticeship as architectural sculptor, York (1982-97). *Exhib*: Whitworth Gallery, Manchester; Wolseley Fine Arts, London; The New Art Centre, Roche Court, Wiltshite. *Commissions*: include:Guildford Cathedral (West Front); Bletchley Park (Monument); York Minster (Figures and Font); Vale of Glamorgan Civic Offices (Textwork); Bradford Cathedral (Signage); Tunbridge Wells (V.C. Memorial); Ripon Cathedral; Grimsthorpe Castle; Eastback Court (Glos); Blackburn Cathedral; Bootham Arts Centre, York; Leicester

Cathedral. *Principal Works*: West Front carving, Guildford Cathedral; Monument at Bletchley Park. *Clubs*: Art Workers Guild, London; York Artworkers Association. *Misc*: majority of work is done to commission. Exhibits only when invited. *Address*: 238 Beckfield Lane, York YO26 5QS. *Email*: c.gurrey:btinternet.com *Website*: www.charlesgurry.com

GUSTARD, Tim, BA (Hons); Finalist, W&N Young Painter of the Year, ROI (1984); MASF June & Ben Gelbert Award (1998); Jane Blake Award (2001). *Medium*: acrylic. *b*: Louth, Lincolnshire, 24 Oct 1954. *s of*: Reg Gustard. *m*: Marion. *Studied*: North Staffs Polytechnic/Stoke City Art School (1974-77, under Arthur Berry). *Represented by*: Beckstones Gallery, Greystoke; Jack Fine Art. *Exhib*: RA (1981, 2009); ROI (1983, 84, 91, 2005); RSA (1987-97 inc.); RI (1991, 2014); RGI (1994, 95); RSW (1992-96 inc.); solo shows include: John Noott (1999, 2001, 2003, 2005, 2007, 2009); F.T.Sabin, Mayfair (2000, 2001); John Williams, Mayfair (2003); Beckstones (2002, 2004, 2006, 2008, 2010. 2012, 2014). *Works in collections*: Duchess of Buccleuch; MASF; Lord Hothfield; Sir Sandy Crombie. *Publications*: Profiles and features in 'The Artist', 'Leisure Painter', 'Cumbria Life'. *Principal Works*: Still Life paintings in acrylic on paper. *Recreations*: angling. *Misc*: TV appearance: profiled on 'The Dales Diary' (Dec 2008). *Address*: 'Silverdale', St.John's Road, Stainton, Cumbria, CA11 0EQ. *Email*: tim.gustard@btinternet.com *Website*: www.timgustard.com *Signs work*: "Gustard".

GWYNNE-JONES, Emily, ARCA (1970); Mem. Contemporary Portrait Soc.; painter in oil and water-colour. *b*: 7 Jul 1948. *d of*: Allan Gwynne-Jones, DSO, CBE, RA, and Rosemary E. Allan, painter. *m*: M. Frank Beanland, painter. one *s*. two *d*. *Studied*: RA Schools, RCA (1966-70), NE London Polytechnic (textiles), Central School (etching) (1977-78). *Exhib*: RA (1966-90), Mayor Gallery, New Grafton Gallery, Pigeon Hole Gallery, Brotherton Gallery, Discerning Eye, Mall Galleries (1991-92), NEAC; one-man show, Michael Parkin (1977). John Player Award NPG (1987-88). *Works in collections*: RA, Nuffield Trust, National Trust, Eton College, Paintings for Hospitals, BSI. *Publications*: illustrated, Pavane for a Dead Infanta by Hugh Ross Williamson. *Address*: Metfield Lane Farm, Fressingfield, Eye, Suffolk IP21 5SD. *Signs work*: "E.G.J." or "E. Gwynne-Jones."

GYLES, Pauline Yvonne, ARMS (1981), RMS (1985), FSBA (1986); self taught miniature painter in water-colour; Hon. Sec., Royal Miniature Soc. (1987-2001) Vice President (2003); mem. Hilliard Society of Miniaturists; Awarded the RMS Gold Bowl (1994). *Medium*: watercolour. *b*: Bournemouth, 31 Aug 1931. *d of*: E. Stoddart Fox, FRICS, FAI. *m*: Brian Gyles. *Educ*: private schools England and Switzerland. *Exhib*: Medici, Liberty's, Llewellyn Alexander, London, Linda Blackstone, Pinner, Peter Hedley, Wareham. *Works in collections*: Russell Cotes A.G. and Museum, Bournemouth, Soc. of Apothecaries. *Commissions*: Art work for a portrait of Lord Nelson used for Commonwealth stamps. *Address*: 3 Old Coastguard Rd., Sandbanks, Poole, Dorset BH13 7RL. *Signs work*: "Pauline Gyles."

H

HABGOOD, Yvonne: see WALCOTT-YATES, Yvonne.

HACKMAN, David Charles, NDD, ATC, SWE. *Medium*: lino - wood engraving (previously painting). *b*: Southall, Middx, 12 Oct 1936. *s of*: Alfred Wallace Hackman. *m*: Jeanette Rosa. one *s*. one *d*. *Educ*: Southall Grammar School. *Studied*: Ealing School of Art; Hornsey College of Art (Pedagogy course). *Exhib*: one man exhibition at Bignor, W.Sussex; annual SWE exhibitions and local venues, etc. *Works in collections*: Ashmolean Museum, Oxford; Hunt Institute for Botanical Documentation, Pittsburgh, USA. *Commissions*: various paintings over the years. *Publications*: personal brochures for lino and wood engraving. *Recreations*: all things practical. *Clubs*: SWE. *Address*: 18 Eve Road, Isleworth, Middx., TW7 7HS. *Signs work*: 'D.C.Hackman'.

HACKNEY, Isla Katrina, MA Hons. (Edin.) (1985), RWS (1993); artist in water-colour, acrylic, oil, lecturer in art and visual theory. *b*: Wrotham, Kent, 6 Jun 1962. *d of*: Sheila Findlay, RWS and Alfred Hackney, RWS, ARE. *Educ*: Gads Hill Place School, Kent, and Gravesend Grammar School. *Studied*: Edinburgh College of Art (Elizabeth Ogilvie, Robert Callender, William Baillie), Edinburgh University (specialized in British art (Martin Hammer) and Scottish art (Duncan MacMillan)). *Exhib*: RWS, regularly at Bankside Gallery, London; Lynne Strover Gallery, Cambridge. *Works in collections*: Freshfields, Fleet Street, Lord & Lady Sainsbury. *Publications*: author: 'Charles Rennie Mackintosh' and 'A History of Water-colour Painting'. *Address*: 5 Randolph Cres., Edinburgh EH3 7TH. *Signs work*: "Isla K. Hackney."

HADDRELL, Trevor, BA Hons (OU); SWE (2006); RWA (2007); CertEd. *Medium*: painting, print-making. *b*: Rotherham, S.Yorkshire. *s of*: Albert Haddon Haddrell. *Educ*: Oakwood Technical High School, Rotherham. *Studied*: Bath Academy of Art; Open University. *Exhib*: various venues in SW including: Royal West of England Academy of Art; Theatre Collection, University of Bristol; City Museum and Art Gallery, Bristol; The Records Office, City of Bristol. *Works in collections*: Theatre Collection, University of Bristol; City Museum and Art Gallery, Bristol; Hunt Institute, Carnegie Mellon University, Pittsburgh, USA. *Commissions*: several for panoramic engravings of City of Bristol. *Publications*: 'Panoramic Bristol' (2002); 'Asparagus and Other Friends' (2005); 'Bristol and Beyond' (Redcliffe Press, 2006). *Official Purchasers*: University of Bristol; City Museum & Art Gallery Bristol; Hunt Institute, Carnegie Mellon University, Pittsburgh, USA. *Works Reproduced*: over 100 b/w relief engravings of Bristol, also 60 engravings of flowers, fruits and vegetables. *Principal Works*: Black and White engravings up to eight feet six inches in length; watercolours, acrylics. *Recreations*: Opera (listening) especially Wagner. *Clubs*: Society of Wood Engravers, Wagner Society. *Misc*: retired teacher of Art and Design. *Address*: Woodwell Cottage, White Hart Steps, Clifton Wood, BS8 4TQ. *Signs work*: "Trevor Haddrell".

HAGGER, Henry Benjamin, RIBA; Laing Landscape Competition (5 times finalist); Sunday Times/Singer & Friedlander (twice finalist); prizewinner Arts Council 'Art into Landscape' Competition (with sculptor Michael Wright); Discerning Eye. *Medium*: oil, watercolour, pastel, acrylic, printmaking. *Studied*: Hornsey School of Art; University of Newcastle-upon-Tyne; Thames Polytechnic. *Exhib*: L'Orangerie & L'Ecole des Beaux Arts, Paris; RA, RBA, PS, SGFA, NEAC, RWS; Whitechapel Gallery, Serpentine Gallery, Mall Galleries. *Works in collections*: Wendy Brooks and Tim Medland; private collections in Austria, Australia, Cyprus, Denmark, France, Hong Kong, India, Indonesia, Japan, Lebanon, Malaysia, Norway, Portugal, Saudi Arabia, Spain, Sweden, USA UK. *Commissions*: The Wine Society, Emilio Lustau S.A. *Works Reproduced*: contributing artist 'The Art of Drawing and Painting' Readers Digest Association Ltd. *Misc*: teaches at The Institute, London, N2 0GA and privately. *Address*: 3 Vallance Road, Alexandra Park, Wood Green, London N22 7UD. *Email*: henryhagger@yahoo.co.uk *Website*: camdenprintmakers.co.uk *Signs work*: 'HBH'.

HAGUE, Jonathan, NDD, ATD, Netherland State Scholarship. *b*: Llandudno, 18 Nov 1938. *Studied*: Liverpool College of Art (1957-63), Royal Academy of Fine Art, The Hague (1964-66). *Exhib*: one-man shows: The Germeente Museum, The Hague; The Royal Institute Gallery, Piccadilly; sponsored John Lennon. *Address*: 2 Regent St., Leamington Spa, Warwicks CV32 5HW. *Signs work*: "HAGUE."

HAINES, Jean, SWA, SFP, FAS; Anthony J. Lester Art Critic Award. *Medium*: watercolour. *b*: Cardiff, 10 Jun 1951. *m*: John Haines. two *s*. one *d*. *Educ*: Penarth Grammar School. *Studied*: under various artists in Asia and Dubai. *Represented by*: Wey Gallery, Surrey; Lyndhurst Gallery/The Frame Gallery, Hants. *Exhib*: David Shepherd WAY

Exhibition, Mall Galleries, London (2009/2010/2011/2012); SWA, Mall Galleries, London (2009/2010/2011/2012); Solo exhibitions include: Wey Gallery, Godalming (2011, 2012), The Frame, Odiham, Hants (2009/2010/2011/2012); variety of galleries in UK and Dubai. *Works in collections*: British Embassy in Turkey. *Commissions*: £3000 private commission via The Wey Gallery. *Publications*: "How to Paint Colour & Light in Watercolour", "Atmospheric Watercolours". *Principal Works*: Horse Racing scenes. *Recreations*: gardening, walking. *Misc*: Book signing tour of USA in October 2012. Workshops attended by artists worldwide. *Address*: Poulters Bridge Cottage, Crookham Village, Hampshire GU51 5SX. *Email*: jeanhaines@hotmail.com *Website*: www.jeanhaines.com *Signs work*: "JEAN HAINES SWA, SFP".

HAINES, Nick, MA; PGCert (Hum.); LSIA (1974); JNC Professional Qualification in Youth Work; PG Cert (AH); PG Cert (Phil); PG Dip (AH); Association of Art Historians (AAH); Artists and Illustrators prize NAPA (1997), Fine Art Trade Guild prize NAPA(1999), Pro Arte Prize, NAPA (2006). *Medium*: artist in acrylic, oil and mixed media. *b*: Essex, 1952. *m*: Diane. two *s*. four *d*. *Educ*: Wells Blue Grammar. *Studied*: Somerset College of Art. De Montfort University, Open University. *Represented by*: NAPA (National Acrylic Painters Association). *Exhib*: annually with NAPA, NAPA (USA), RBSA Birmingham; Westminster Gallery, London, Bath Fringe Festival, Mariners Gallery, St Ives, Hotbath Gallery, Bath, Black Sheep Gallery, Harwarden, Salthouse Gallery St. Ives, regularly at Millfield Summer Show, etc. *Works in collections*: many private throughout Britain and Europe, including Lord Bath, Longleat House. *Commissions*: private commissions undertaken. *Publications*: Hoarse Trilogy. *Works Reproduced*: Disparate Remedies (A&I). *Clubs*: Retired Chairman of Northeast Somerset Arts, mem.NAPA, mem. Sheridan Club. *Misc*: one grandson, nine grand-daughters. *Address*: Danecott, Leigh High Street, Leigh upon Mendip, BA3 5QQ. *Email*: nick.haines@mail.com *Website*: nickhaines.@mail.com *Signs work*: "Nick Haines".

HAINSWORTH, George, Slade Dip., Gulbenkian Scholar (Rome); artist in oil paint, variety of sculptural media; retired Prof. of Fine Art, Leeds Metropolitan University. *b*: Leeds, 15 Dec 1937. *m*: Lucy M. Rogers. one *s*. one *d*. *Studied*: Leeds College of Art (1955-60), Slade School of Fine Art (1960-62, William Coldstream), British School at Rome (1962-63). *Exhib*: one-man shows: Serpentine Gallery, Ikon Gallery B'ham, Spacex Gallery Exeter, Sue Rankin Gallery, Ainscough Contemporary Art, London; two-person (with Lucy): Cartwright Hall Bradford, Dean Clough Halifax, Doncaster City A.G., ongoing display at Biemen de Haas Gallery, Amsterdam (now closed). *Works in collections*: Leeds University, Hammond Suddard, Baring Investors, Provident Financial Group plc, many private collections. *Clubs*: Yorkshire Sculptors Group, Leeds Fine Art. *Address*: 10 High Road, Everthorpe, East Yorks HU15 2AP. *Email*: lucym.hainsworth@gmail.com *Signs work*: "G. Hainsworth."

HALE, Helen Margaret, ROI, NS, FPS. *Medium*: oil (painting); marble, stone, wood, etc (sculpture). *b*: Harpenden, 18 Apr 1936. *d of*: Robert Hale. *m*: Horne Shepherd (decd). *Partner*: Michael C. Leman. *Educ*: St. George's School, Harpenden. *Studied*: St. Martin's School of Art and Sir John Cass School of Art. *Exhib*: group shows: London, Edinburgh, Paris, Munich. One/two person shows: Bromley, Farnham, Amersham, London. *Address*: Atheldene, Loxwood Rd., Rudgwick, Horsham, W. Sussex RH12 3DW. *Email*: atheldene@btopenworld.com *Signs work*: "HALE."

HALL, Caroline, BA Visual Arts (First Class Hons), MA Painting. Awards: Shortlisted, Threadneedle Prize (2011); Finalist: Fringe MK Painting Prize (2010), Alpan International, New York (2008), Agora International Fine Art Competition, New York. *Medium*: oil. *b*: London, 8 Sep 1959. *Partner*: Lucy Barraclough. two *s*. one *d*. *Studied*: Winchester School of Art (2001-2007). *Exhib*: 2014: Winchester Cathedral; ESPACIO Gallery, London;

The Other Art Fair, London. 2013: Carre d'Artistes, Utrecht (Artist in Residence); Winchester Cathedral; Winchester School of Art Alumna (solo show); The Other Art Fair (Regent's Park & Brick Lane); South Kensington Tube (3m solo banner, tube journey paintings). 2012: The Granary, Weston Park. Solo shows include: DegreeArt, Vyner Street, London. Group shows include: The Ark, Basingstonke; Halls Fine Art, Shropshire; Art in the Garden, Hilliers Arboretum, Hampshire; Greenham Arts, Newbury. *Works in collections*: Carnival Headquarters, Southampton. *Commissions*: Private collectors. Two London Underground paintings on aluminium (2014). *Publications*: Fringe MK catalogue (2010); Hampshire Chronicle (2010); FAD contemporary art website (featured artist, 2009); Artis Spectrum magazine (2008). *Principal Works*: Tube Journeys (Circle Line): Aldgate to Liverpool St., Sloane Square to South Kensington, Tower Hill to Aldgate, Leaving Liverpool St. (oil on aluminium); Attempt to capture moving pixels (acrylic on canvas nos 1-53); Pixels paused (1-14); views from a window - Autumn, Bluebells and Long Walk, Spring; Train Journeys - Beaulieu to Brockenhurst 1&2. *Recreations*: tennis, golf, sailing. *Address*: The Winchester Studio, 23 Little Minster Street, Winchester, Hampshire SO23 9HB. *Email*: carolinehall.art@me.com *Website*: www.carolinehall.net *Signs work*: "caroline hall".

HALL, Christopher Compton, RBA (1988), DFA (1954), RCamA (1994); De Laszlo Medal (1996); painter in oil. *b*: Slaugham, Sussex, 25 Dec 1930. *s of*: Donald John Hall. *m*: Maria Galassi. three *s*. *Educ*: Bedales School. *Studied*: Slade School of Fine Art (1950-54). *Represented by*: The Rona Gallery, Russell Gallery. *Exhib*: Portal Gallery, New Grafton Gallery, RA, Waterman Fine Art, Lynne Stern Assoc., Rona Gallery, Russell Gallery, Thompson's (Marylebone). *Works in collections*: London Museum, National Library of Wales, Reading A.G., Arts Council, OUP, The Ashmolean. *Commissions*: various, mainly of buildings. *Works Reproduced*: "Young Artists of Promise" - Jack Beddington (1957), "20th Century painters and sculptors" - Frances Spalding, "London in paint" - oil paintings in the collection of the Museum of London - Mirielle Galinou & John Hayes, "The Eclipse of a great power" - Keith Robbins, "Variations in an English dialect" - Jenny Cheshire, "London in paint" - David Piper. *Misc*: Local Councillor (Liberal) 1961-76 Mayor of Newbury 1967-68. *Address*: Catherine Villa, Station Rd., Newbury, Berks. RG14 7LP. *Website*: www.christopherhall-painter.com *Signs work*: "C.C. Hall."

HALL, Dennis Henry, ARCA (1955); graphic designer and producer/publisher of Illustrated Limited Edition Books. *b*: Caterham, 1927. *m*: Sylvia Stokeld, ARCA (decd). *Educ*: Lancing College. *Studied*: Chelsea School of Art (Brian Robb), RCA (John Lewis). Taught design: Norwich, Leeds and Oxford Schools of Art or Polytechnica. Founded and ran The Inky Parrot Press at Oxford Polytechnic (1981-87) and now runs another Inky Parrot Press. *Represented by*: and is partner in, publishers Artists' Choice Editions (with Carol Manheim). *Misc*: Books in: V. & A., Cambridge University Library, National Library of Scotland, Rijksmuseum, Columbia and Harvard Libraries, Brookes Oxford University Library, Royal Academy Library. *Address*: The Foundry, Church Hanborough, nr. Witney, Oxon. OX29 8AB. *Website*: www.parrotpress.co.uk

HALL, Jo, BSc.(Hons) Botany (1967), PhD (1971); Past President, Society of Graphic Fine Art, Association of Illustrators; freelance artist and illustrator; formerly biologist in water industry. *Medium*: All drawing media, charcoal, pastel and watercolour/acrylic. *b*: Sidcup, Kent, 31 Jan 1946. *m*: Geoffrey Hall. two *s*. *Educ*: Exeter University, Imperial College, London. *Exhib*: SGFA members and open (1996-2014), Not the Royal Academy (1997-2002), Medici Miniatures (1997-1998); solo exhib. by invitation of the European Space Agency's Fine Art Club (2001); RAC Club Pall Mall (2007); RI Mall Galleries (2005); SWA Mall Galleries (2008). *Works in collections*: ESA's fine art collection, Noordwijk, Holland. *Commissions*: corporate including, Southern Electric, Gardens of Woolley Hall, Assoc. Aviation Inc. (Space Division), The Creation Portfolio, a series of impressions of four galaxies; also private commissions, landscape and portrait. *Publications*: Drawing features for 'Artists and Illustrators' magazine (2008/9). *Address*: Morar, Altwood Close, Maidenhead, Berks. SL6 4PP. *Email*: johall@mhstudios.co.uk *Signs work*: "Jo Hall."

HALL, Nigel John, RA (2003); M.Art RCA. *Medium*: sculptor. *b*: Bristol, 30 Aug 1943. *s of*: H.J. Hall. *m*: Manijeh (née Yadegar). *Educ*: Bristol Grammar School. *Studied*: West of England College of Art (1960-64), Royal College of Art (1964-67), Harkness Fellowship (1967-69). *Exhib*: one-man shows, Galerie Givaudan, Paris; Wilder Gallery, Los Angeles; Galerie Neuendorf, Hamburg and Cologne; Serpentine Gallery, London; Juda Rowan Gallery, London; Nishimura Gallery, Tokyo; Elkon Gallery, NY, Galerie Maeght, Paris; Galerie Mayer, Dusseldorf, Galerie Christian Scheffel, Bad Homburg, Galerie Andreas Thalmann, Zurich; Yorkshire Sculpture Park, Royal Academy, London, Churchill College, Cambridge. *Works in collections*: Tate Gallery, V&A, Arts Council of Great Britain, National Galerie, Berlin, Dallas Museum of Fine Art, Tokyo Metropolitan Museum, Chicago Art Institute, Kunsthaus, Zurich, Museum of Modern Art, NY. *Commissions*: Australian National Gallery, Canberra; IBM, London; Museum of Contemporary Art, Hiroshima; Clifford Chance, London; Bank for International Settlements, Basel; Bank of America, London and Paris; Said Business School, Oxford University. *Publications*: 'Nigel Hall, Drawings and Works on Paper', Royal Academy Publications. *Address*: 11 Kensington Pk. Gdns., London W11 3HD. *Signs work*: "NIGEL HALL."

HALL, Sam, Self taught artist specialising in hyperrealistic landscapes and vignettes of nature. *Medium*: Acrylic; pen and ink paintings. *b*: Stockport, 5 Sep 1936. *m*: Susanna. two *s*. one *d*. *Educ*: Westminster Abbey Choir School; Chorlton High School. *Exhib*: North Norfolk Art Centre (2004); The Business Design Centre, London (2004); Summers Art Loft, Dorking (2004); The Mall Galleries, London (2006); Gallery 47, Bloomsbury (2006); Diamond Air VIP Lounge, Heathrow Airport (2007); The Leatherhead Theatre (2007); The Blue Door Gallery, London (2007, 2008); Bankside Gallery, London (2008). *Works in collections*: The Lloyd Gill Gallery, Weston-Super-Mare (2009); Chartwood Studio, Dorking (2009-2012). *Commissions*: The Dales; Svolvaer Lofoten. *Works Reproduced*; Prints available of all works. *Principal Works*: The Majesty of Sienna; Gaza; path to Park Farm; Exodus; Muggeridge's Farm, Brockham. *Recreations*: Walking, photography, painting, cruise ships. *Misc*: Artworks haning in private collections in the UK, Sweden, Germany, Italy and the USA. *Address*: Chartwood Cottage, Punchbowl Lane, Dorking, Surrey RH5 4ED. *Email*: samhallart@gmail.com *Website*: www.samhallart.com *Signs work*: Monogram "SH" and full signature on reverse.

HALLAM, Marilyn, BA (Hons) Fine Art (1965-69) and MFA (1970-72); Boise Travelling Scholarship (1969). *Medium*: Oil, watercolour, drawing. *b*: Sheffield, 1947. *m*: Clyde Hopkins, artist. *Studied*: University of Reading. *Represented by*: Smith Jariwala (1990-96); Andersson Hall Contemporary Art (2000-05). *Exhib*: Solo include: Bakehouse (GLAA assisted) Vortex London; Towner Eastbourne; Smith Jariwala x 3, London. Group include: Platform 72 MoMA Oxford; Corated N. Serota; Whitechapel Open; Contemporary Art Society Market; Spirit of London; Castlefield Manchester; Art London Olympia; Hastings Museum and Art Gallery; Watercolour Curwen Gall; Advanced Graphics, RA Summer Shows; Clifford Chance. *Works in collections*: Art in Hospitals Hastings, Lewisham, Southwark, University of Reading. other private and corporate Europe, USA. *Address*: Flat 2, 63 Warrior Square, St Leonards-on-Sea TN37 6BG. *Email*: aptlondon@btconnect.com *Website*: www.aptstudios.org/artists *Signs work*: "MARILYN HALLAM".

HALLIDAY, Charlotte Mary Irvine, RWS (1976), NEAC (1961); topographical artist; Keeper, New English Art Club since 1989. *b*: Kensington, 5 Sep 1935. *d of*: Edward Halliday, C.B.E., PPRP, PPRBA, ARCA. *Educ*: Wester Elchies, Francis Holland. *Studied*:

RA Schools (1953-58). *Exhib*: RWS, RBA, NEAC etc. *Commissions*: Salisbury Cathedral, Selfridges, Lord's Pavilion, the Monument, London Clubs, City Banks and many private houses. *Publications*: Illustrations for Dictionary of Edwardian Architecture by A. Stuart Gray (1985) and co-author, with him, of "Fanlights", a visual architectural history (1990). *Recreations*: walking in the Downs, and choral singing. *Address*: 36a Abercorn Pl., London NW8 9XP. *Signs work*: "Charlotte Halliday" or "CMIH."

HALLIDAY, Colin Thomas, BA (Hons) Painting. *Medium*: oils, acrylic, mixed media. *b*: Carlisle, 19 Jan 1964. *s of*: John Andrew Halliday. *m*: Anne. two *d*. *Educ*: Appleby Grammar School, Penrith Grammar School. *Studied*: Cumbria College of Art and Design (1987-88), University of Plymouth (Exeter Campus) (1989-92). *Represented by*: Start Space, 150 Columbia Road, London E2 7RG. *Exhib*: Dulwich Picture Gallery, Lake Artists Society Grasmere, Carnegie Arts Centre Workington, Blyth Gallery Manchester, Grey College Durham, Walk Gallery London, Karen Taylor London, Will's Art Warehouse London, Thomas Corman London, numerous art fairs in London, Glasgow, New York and Miami with Start Space, The Hayloft Gallery, Tregoning Fine Art, GX Gallery. *Works in collections*: Adrian Lester, Grey College Durham, Ashurst Morris and Crisp, NHS Foundation, Brady & Mackenzie, private collections worldwide. *Commissions*: Rotherham NHS Foundation Trust. *Recreations*: DJ. *Address*: c/o Eduardo Sant'Anna, Start Space, 150 Columbia Road, London E2 7RG. *Email*: contact@startspace.co.uk *Website*: www.startspace.co.uk *Signs work*: "Colin Halliday".

HALLIDAY, Irene, DA (1952), Scholarship (1953), Travelling Scholarship (1954), RSW (1955); artist in gouache, acrylic, oil paint. *b*: Kingsmuir, Angus, Scotland, 26 Sep 1931. *d of*: Andrew Halliday, School master. *Educ*: Arbroath High School. *Studied*: Dundee College of Art (1948-53, Alberto Morrocco, RSA, RSW). *Exhib*: 42 one-man shows, Arbroath, Dundee, Edinburgh, Manchester, Salford, New York State. *Works in collections*: art galleries of Arbroath, Bolton, Dundee, Glasgow, Greenock, Salford; education authorities of Dundee, Dunbartonshire, Edinburgh, Fife, Manchester, Wigan; Granada TV., British National Oil Co., Shell Centre, London, Manchester Ship Canal Co., Pilkingham Glass plc. St. Helens, Bowrings and Co. London. *Commissions*: Aumbry Door, St. John's Church, Moston, Manchester (1992), Reredos Wall, St. Christopher's Church, Withington, Manchester (1999), Reredos Wall, St. Chad's Church, New Moston, Manchester (2000). *Address*: 46 Highfield Dene Rd., Didsbury, Manchester M20 2ST. *Signs work*: "Halliday."

HALLOWES, Veda Nanette. *Medium*: sculptor in bronze, also some resin and ceramics teacher. *b*: Johannesburg, 16 Jan 1941. *d of*: Jo'an and Heather Couzyn. *m*: George Richard Hallowes. two *d*. *Educ*: Waverley Girls High School, Johannesburg. *Studied*: Wandsworth Adult Educ. under Molly Ruddle (1988-1999), Wandsworth Adult College (1992-1994); Advanced course in ceramics, Lima, Peru (1975). *Exhib*: two pieces in RA Summer Exhib. (2001); Peru, Hong Kong, Pakistan, London, Newcastle. *Works in collections*: Charing Cross Hospital, London; private collections in UK and worldwide. *Commissions*: various in UK. *Works Reproduced*: usually in editions of nine. *Principal Works*: fruits and anthropomorphic fruits. *Misc*: Has lived in England since 1971. Registered nurse and midwife, for eleven years before training as ceramicist and sculptor; co-founder: Kaleidoscope Arts. *Address*: 1A Avenue Road, West Wimbledon, London SW20 0QR. *Email*: info@vedahallowes.co.uk *Website*: www.vedahallowes.co.uk *Signs work*: 'VH' with year and number in series.

HALSBY, Julian, MA(Cantab.), RBA (1994), FRSA (1997); painter in oil, art historian, critic; Mem. International Assoc. of Art Critics; Critics Circle. *b*: London, 1948. *m*: Miranda Halsby, printmaker. one *s*. one *d*. *Studied*: Emmanuel College, Cambridge (art history). *Exhib*: RBA, NEAC, ROI, many mixed exhbns. in the UK and France, Patterson Fine Art, New Grafton, Wykeham, Century Gallery, Datchett; one-man show: Abbott and Holder

(1998); Russell Gallery, Putney; Sadler Street Gallery, Wells; Newland Gallery. *Publications*: include: Scottish Watercolours 1740-1940 (Batsford, 1986), Dictionary of Scottish Painters 1600-2000 (with Paul Harris) (Canongate, 1995, 4th Edition 2010), Venice: The Artists' Vision (Batsford, 1990), The Art of Diana Armfield, R.A. (David & Charles, 1995); plus exhbn. catalogues and articles for "The Artist."; "A Private View" Lund Humphries (2002). *Address*: Old Hall, 101 Newland, Sherborne, DT9 3DU. *Website*: www.newlandgallery.co.uk *Signs work*: "Halsby."

HALSBY, Miranda, RBA (2001). *Medium*: etchings and aquatints, watercolour. *b*: London, 13 Apr 1948. *m*: Julian Halsby RBA. one *s*. one *d*. *Studied*: Kingston College of Art (1966-67); Hornsey College of Art (1967-68 - left due to student sit-in); London S chool of Occupational Therapy (1968-71); studied etching at Hampstead School of Art. *Represented by*: Newland Gallery, www.newlandgallery.co.uk RBA, www.royalsocietyofbritishartists.org.uk *Exhib*: Abbott and Holder (solo, 2001, 2007); National Print Exhbn, Mall Galleries; work continually in group exhibitions in London and Home Counties. *Works in collections*: work in private collections in England, France, Holland, Japan and USA. *Misc*: Partner in Highgate Gallery, dealing in 19th C. watercolours, art nouveau decorative arts, pottery and jewellery, contemporary painters (1980-88); returned to practising as an artist in 1990. *Address*: Old Hall, 101 Newland, Sherborne, Dorset DT9 3DU. *Email*: halsby2000@halsby.com *Signs work*: 'MIRANDA HALSBY'.

HAMBLING, Maggi, OBE (1995), CBE (2010), Boise Travel award, NY (1969), Arts Council award (1977), Artist in Residence, National Gallery (1980-81); Jerwood Painting Prize (1995), Marsh Award for Excellence for 'Scallop' (2005). *Medium*: oil on canvas, water-colour, drawing, sculpture in bronze and steel, printmaking. *b*: Suffolk, 23 Oct 1945. *d of*: Harry Hambling and Marjorie Hambling (decd). *Studied*: Camberwell School of Art (1964-67), Slade School of Fine Art (1967-69); studied with Lett Haines and Cedric Morris (1960). *Represented by*: Marlborough Fine Art, London & www.maggihambling.com. *Exhib*: solo shows: National Gallery (1981), National Portrait Gallery (1983), Serpentine Gallery (1987), Arnolfini Gallery, Bristol (1988), Yale Center for British Art (1991), National Portrait Gallery (1997), Yorkshire Sculpture Park (1997), Marlborough Fine Art, Morley College Gallery (2001), Sotheby's, Aldeburgh Festival Gallery (2003), Fitzwilliam (2006), Marlborough Fine Art (2005, 2008, 2010), Abbot Hall (2007), Walker Art Gallery, The Lowry (2009), Fitzwilliam (2010), SNAP (2012), SNAP, The Hermitage, USSR (2013). *Works in collections*: include Tate Collection, Whitworth A.G., ACGB, National Gallery, British Museum, NPG, Gulbenkian Foundation, Australian National Gallery, Yale Center for British Art, V&A. *Commissions*: Sculpture for Oscar Wilde, London (1998); 'Scallop', Sculpture for Benjamin Britten, Aldeburgh (2003), The Brixton Heron (2010), The Winchester Tapestries, Winchester Cathedral (2013). *Publications*: 'Maggi and Henrietta' Drawings of Henrietta Moraes by Maggi Hambling, with a preface by John Berger. Bloomsbury 2001; 'Maggi Hambling The Works, and Conversations with Andrew Lambirth' (Unicorn Press, 2006), 'The Sea', Lowry Press (2009), 'George Always', Walker Art Gallery (2009), 'The Aldeburgh Scallop', Full Circle Editions (2010). *Recreations*: tennis. *Clubs*: Chelsea Arts, The Ivy. *Address*: c/o Marlborough Fine Art, 6 Albemarle St., London W1S 4BY. *Website*: www.maggihambling.com *Signs work*: surname on back.

HAMEL, Francis Etienne. *Medium*: oil, drawing. *b*: Coventry, 4 Oct 1963. *s of*: Christopher & Mary Hamel-Cooke. *m*: Rachel Hamel-Cooke. one *s*. one *d*. *Educ*: Summer Fields, Oxford; Marlborough College; Magdalen College, Oxford. *Studied*: Ruskin School of Drawing & Fine Art, Oxford. *Represented by*: John Martin of London, 38 Albemarle Street, London W1. *Exhib*: John Martin (1995, 1997, 2000, 2003, 2004, 2006, 2008); Art 2002 (Design Centre, London), Art London (2009), Said Business School (2004). Mixed Shows include: RA Summer Exhibition (2005, 2006, 2007), Hirschl & Adler, New York

(2007). *Works in collections*: Oxford University Press, Noel Coward Theatre, Rolls Royce, Fortnum & Mason, Sir Cameron Mackintosh. *Commissions*: Oxford University Press, Goldman Sachs, Prince of Wales Theatre, Wyndhams Theatre, Lady Margaret Hall, Farrer & Co., Delfont Mackintosh theatres. *Works Reproduced*: numerous. *Principal Works*: 12 large paintings on permanent view at Fortnum & Masons and in Wyndhams & Prince of Wales theatres. *Recreations*: cooking, reading, walking. *Clubs*: Chelsea Arts Club. *Misc*: Lives mainly at Rousham in Oxfordshire and in Le Marche, Italy for 3 or 4 months a year. *Address*: Garden Cottage, Rousham, Bicester, Oxon OX25 4QU. *Email*: francis.hamel@francishamel.com *Website*: www.francishamel.com *Signs work*: "HAMEL".

HAMILTON, Colin Reginald, MSIA General Illustration; Daily Mail 'Not the Turner Prize' Finalist (2003). *Medium*: oil, watercolour, acrylic. *b*: London, 2 Jan 1950. *m*: Christine. two *s*. *Studied*: East Ham Art School (at 16, 3-year diploma course in Graphic Deisgn, but qualified at 19 as an illustrator - had a London agent). *Exhib*: RA Summer Exhbn (2000), Whitechapel Gallery (1977), Discerning Eye (2000), AAF Battersea (2000), Llewellyn Alexander Gallery 'Not the Royal Academy Show' (2002-2014), Daily Mail 'Not the Turner Prize' (2003, 2004); show at the Kaleidoscope Gallery (2004), Beacroft Gallery (2001-2014), Singer & Friedlander/Sunday Times Watercolour Exhibition (2006, 07), Sherwin Gallery. *Works in collections*: paintings requested and donated to Cancer Research UK, Art4Life auction at Christie's (2002, 03, 04, 05, 06, 07). Private collections England, Greece, Germany, USA. *Commissions*: painted and sold commissions from the age of 12. All commissions taken. Produced the artwork for stage production of 'Gulliver's Travels' The Mermaid Theatre, London. *Publications*: request from 'The Artist Magazine' for an article on my work. *Works Reproduced*: Medici Card Co. *Recreations*: travel, exhibitions. *Misc*: I paint mainly landscapes but have covered almost all subjects in my career. *Address*: 202 Collier Row Lane, Collier Row, Essex RM5 3JB. *Email*: colinhamiltonart@yahoo.co.uk *Signs work*: 'Colin Hamilton', very small, right bottom corner.

HAMILTON, Julia, BA (Hons) Fine Art Painting; BA (Hons) English Literature and Fine Art; Post Grad Printmaking. *Medium*: painting, printmaking. *b*: London, 27 Mar 1962. *d of*: Tom Hamilton (architect). *Educ*: Francis Holland School, London. *Studied*: Exeter University (Fine Art & Eng. Lit, 1980-83); City & Guilds School of Art (Painting, 1999-2002), Central St.Martins. *Exhib*: Royal Academy, Sarah Myerscough, NEAC, Laing Open, New Ashgate Gallery, Gainsboroughs House, National Print Exhibition, Collyer-Bristow, Discerning Eye, Originals - Mall Galleries, Transition, Sarah O'Kane. *Works in collections*: Geffrye Museum. *Clubs*: ICA, Dover Street Arts Club, East London Printmakers. *Address*: 128 Middleton Road, London E8 4LP. *Email*: julia.hamilton3@btinternet.com *Website*: www.juliahamilton.co.uk *Signs work*: 'JULIA HAMILTON'.

HAMILTON, Katherine, Dip. (Byam Shaw) (1974), Dip. Dance and Choreography (1977); painter in oil on canvas, pastel. *b*: 1954. divorced. two *s*. *Educ*: Dartington Hall School. *Studied*: Byam School of Art (1971-74, Diana Armfield); London School of Contemporary Dance (1974-77). *Exhib*: solo shows: Christopher Hull Gallery, Sue Rankin Gallery (1993), Thackeray Gallery (1994), Chappel Galleries (1998), Chappel Gallery (2001); mixed exhbns.: Piccadilly Gallery, New Academy Gallery (1996), Chappel Gallery (1997), R.A. Summer Show (1997), Cambridge Contemporary Art (1998), Woodgates Gallery East Bergholt (1999), mixed show - Chappel Gallery (2002, 2004, 2007), Messum's (2003), Anglia Television 'Coastal Inspirations' (Apr 2006), Anglia Television/Sky Arts 'A Life on Canvas' (documentary on Seago, 2008); Salthouse 2008 Annual Exhibition; 2010: Time and Tide Museum - Circus Exhibition; 2011: 'Inspirations' organised by jarrolds, Norwich; 2012: Solo show Mandell's Gallery, Norwich; Southwold 2010-2012. *Works in collections*: private collections. *Misc*: previously known as Kate Gault. *Address*: Hill House, 61 Covert Rd., Reydon, Southwold, Suffolk IP18 6QE. *Email*: hamilton553@btinternet.com *Website*: katehamiltonartist.co.uk *Signs work*: "Katherine Hamilton."

HAMILTON, Susie, DipAD; BA(Hons); PhD. *Medium*: oil, acrylic, watercolour. *b*: London, 10 Aug 1950. *m*: Peter Hamilton. *Educ*: St.Mary's, Calne. *Studied*: St. Martin's School of Art (1968-72); Univ. of London (1978-87); Byam Shaw School of Art (1989-92). *Represented by*: Paul Stolper. *Exhib*: Paul Stolper; RA Summer Show; John Moores, Liverpool; St. Edmund Hall, Oxford; St. Paul's Cathedral; Voges & Partner, Frankfurt (2005); Ikon Gallery, Birmingham; Whitechapel Art Gallery, London; The Hallion, Edinburgh; Ferens, Hull; St. Giles Cripplegate, London; Babington House, Somerset; Galleri Trafo, Oslo; Gallerie Hugo Opdal, Flo, Norway; Triumph Gallery, Moscow; WW Gallery at Venice Biennale; Jerwood Drawing Prize. *Works in collections*: Murderme; The Economist; Deutsche Bank; The Groucho Club; New Hall Art Collection; Methodist Art Collection; House of St. Barnabas. *Publications*: "Riddled with Light" (Paul Stolper, 2006); "World of Light" (Triumph Gallery, Moscow). *Works Reproduced*: 'Art Works 1960-2000' (Deutsche Bank); 'Monoprinting' (AC Black, 2005); 'Cambridge Companion to Postmodernism', (CUP). *Principal Works*: figures in wilderness. *Recreations*: reading. *Clubs*: Groucho *Address*: 23 Rhondda Grove, London E3 5AP *Email*: susie.hamilton@virgin.net *Website*: www.susiehamilton.co.uk *Signs work*: 'Susie Hamilton'

HAMMICK, Tom, BA (Hons) Ist Class (1990), MA Printmaking; Jerwood Drawing Prize (2004); London Original Print Fair Prize, RA Summer Exhibition (2005); Nexus Prize (2010); artist in residence end 2014-2015. *Medium*: oil, pencil, etching, woodcut. *b*: Tidworth. *m*: Martha one *s* two *d* *Studied*: Camberwell School of Art (1987-92) *Represented by*: Flowers, London, New York. *Exhib*: Selected solo exhibitions: Eagle Gallery, London (1995-2008); Brighton Museum & Art Gallery (2012); Rabley Drawing Centre (2012); Where Where Gallery Beijing (2010); Flowers, New York (2014). *Works in collections*: include Biblioteque Nationale Paris, Library of Congress, USA, British Museum, Yale Center British Art, V&A, Towner Eastbourne, Deutsche Bank, Brighton Museum & Art Gallery. *Publications*: include: 'Never Far Inland' (2009, ISBN 09813756), 'Dreams of Here' (2012, ISBN 978-1-908593-81-1, monograph on the work to be published by Lund Humphries 2015 texts by Julian Bell. *Recreations*: squash, tennis, football, opera, theatre, cycling. *Clubs*: Groucho, Arsenal FC. *Address*: West Beam, Henley Down, Battle, E.Sussex, TN33 9BN. *Email*: hammick@btinternet.com *Website*: www.tomhammick.com www.hammickeditions.com *Signs work*: "Hammick"

HAMMOND, Hermione, Rome Scholar (Painting, 1938). *Studied*: Chelsea Polytechnic, R.A. Schools (Dip.) *Exhib*: one-man exhbns.: Bishopsgate Institute (1956); Colnaghi's (1957); Arthur Jeffress (1961); All Hallows, London Wall (1965); New Grafton (1970); Great King St. Gallery, Edinburgh (1972); Six Portfolios, Chelsea (1973); Hartnoll & Eyre Iran & Cyprus (1978), Michael Parkin and University of Hull (1993); Michael Parkin (2000). *Works in collections*: ceiling decoration, University of London, Guildhall collection, Museum of London, Fondation Custodia, Institut Néerlandais, Paris, Fitzwilliam Museum, Hunterian A.G., Glasgow, Brymor Jones Library, University of Hull, Whitworth, Manchester *Publications*: Oxford Almanack, Arts Review, R.I.B.A. Journal, Country Life *Address*: 2 Hans Studio, 43a Glebe Pl., London SW3 5JE *Signs work*: "Hermione Hammond."

HAMMOND, John Leonard, BA (Hons); mem. South West Academy of Fine and Applied Arts (Chairman Exhibition Committee, 2004, 2005); M.Baker Award South West Academy. *Medium*: acrylics *b*: Woodford Green, 15 Oct 1961 *m*: Dr. Kate Luck *Studied*: Wimbledon Art School; Bath Academy of Art. *Exhib*: John Noott Galleries, Broadway; Marine House at Beer; Montpellier Contemporary Art, Stratford-upon-Avon; Victoria Art Gallery (Bath Soc. of Artists); Mall Galleries (ROI); Albemarle Gallery, London; Rooksmoor 'Best of Bath'; Wykeham Gallery, Stockbridge. *Works in collections*: private collections internationally, Palace of Westminster. *Publications*: 'International Artist' (2000, 2001), 'Leisure Painter' (2000, 2004), 'The Artist' (2001, 02, 03), 'Art in Devon' (2005);

'Capturing Light in Acrylics' co-author Robin Capon (pub. Batsford); 'Capturing Light in Acrylics' APV Films Ltd, 'Free Expression in Acrylics' co-author Robin Capon (Batsford 2008). *Address*: 138 Eastern Ave, Chippenham, Wilts. SN15 3XT *Signs work*: 'J L Hammond'

HAMPSON, Linda Ann, SBA (2013). *Medium*: coloured pencil, pastel. *b*: Zambia, 18 Jun 1959. *Educ*: Higher Diploma in Education, Edgewood College of Education, South Africa (1977-80). *Studied*: self taught artist. *Exhib*: Individual and group exhibitions: Kirstenbosch Botanical Biennale, South Africa (2002, 2004, 2006, 2008, 2010); Society of Botanical Artists, Westminster, London (2011-); Palmengarten, Germany (2012, 2014); NEWA (2014); Focus on Nature, New York State Museum (2010, 2014); South West Society of Botanical Artists (2011-). *Works in collections*: Visitors Centre, Durban Botanic Gardens, South Africa; Head Office, South African National Biodiversity Institute; private collections. *Commissions*: private. *Principal Works*: Botanical and Natural History. *Address*: 6 Rhododendron Avenue, Dunkeswell, Honiton, Devon EX14 4UT. *Email*: linda.hampson702@btinternet.com *Signs work*: "LA Hampson".

HAMPTON, F. Michael, SWLA wildlife artist in water-colour, scraper-board and acrylic; SWLA-WWFN Fine Art award (1988). *b*: Croydon, 29 May 1937. *s of*: Francis Wilkie. *Partner*: Mrs. S.P.France. one *s*. *Studied*: Croydon Art School *Exhib*: RSPB, Sandy, Blackheath Gallery SE3, Mall Galleries, London, Port Lympne Zoo Park, Hythe, Kent, Ringstead Gallery, Hunstanton, Cotswold Wildlife Gallery, Lechlade, Glos; Sun Lounge, Fairfield Halls, Croydon; Eye of the Wind Gallery, Arundel, WWT; Bromley Library, Kent. *Works in collections*: Mr. John Aspinall, The Sultan of Oman. *Works Reproduced*: three jackets of 'British Birds', two jackets of R.S.P.B. 'Birds', (1980-1983), Calendar for Sussex Fine Arts, S.WL.A. Calendars (1987, 1988), S.WL.A.-R.S.P.B. Calendar (1990, 1991, 1992), B.B.C. Wildlife Magazine (Aug. 1992). *Recreations*: DIY, collecting CDs *Clubs*: S.WL.A., Croydon Art *Address*: 13 Sandy Way, Shirley, Croydon, Surrey CR0 8QT. *Website*: www.michael-hampton.com *Signs work*: "M" and "H" with grebe's head.

HANDLEY, Paul, BA(Hons.) 1987, ATC (1991); painter in oil, lecturer; Art History lecturer, Itchen College, Soton. *b*: Newark, Notts., 29 Jun 1964. *Studied*: Norwich School of Art (1984-87, John Wonnacott, John Lessore), Goldsmiths' College (1990-91). *Exhib*: Spectator 1st prizewinner (1992), Hunting Group, NEAC, Discerning Eye, RP, Royal Overseas League, New Grafton Gallery, Alresford Gallery, Quantum Contemporary, Rowley Gallery London, etc. Work in private collections internationally. *Clubs*: N.E.A.C. *Address*: Brook House, 58 Upper Brook St., Winchester, Hants. SO23 8OG. *Signs work*: "P.H."

HANKEY, Christopher Dominic, BA (Hons), MA Fine Art, Postgraduate Diploma; Polish Government 10 month postgraduate scholarship. *Medium*: oil on canvas, board. *b*: Lancaster, 15 Feb 1963. *Partner*: Julia Robinson. one *s*. two *d*. *Studied*: Wolverhampton Polytechnic (1984-87), Academy of Fine Arts Krakow, Poland (1991-92), University of Wales Institute, Cardiff. *Represented by*: Will's Art Warehouse London, Innocent Fine Art Bristol, Rainyday Gallery Penzance, Pydar Gallery Truro, Tregoning Fine Art Ashbourne, International Art Consultants 'Art for Offices' London. *Publications*: Cornishman, Inside Cornwall, Arts Review, Country Home. *Publications*: Cornishman, Inside Cornwall, Arts Review, Country Home. *Works Reproduced*: Arts Review. *Recreations*: astronomy, chess, mountaineering, snowboarding. *Clubs*: Planetary Society, SETI at Home. *Address*: Chy Essack, Boswarthen, Newbridge, Penzance, Cornwall, TR18. *Email*: dom598@aol.com *Signs work*: Christopher D.Hankey.

HANLEY, James, RHA (2001); Secretary RHA (2001-); ARHA (2000); BA History of Art and English (1987), BA Fine Art Painting (1991). *b*: 8 Nov 1965. *m*: Orla Dukes. *Studied*: University College Dublin; National College of Art and Design, Dublin. *Represented by*: RHA, and Solomon Gallery, Dublin. *Exhib*: RHA; Walker Art Gallery,

Liverpool; Germinations VIII Breda, Holland, and tour, Lubeck, Germany; Solo exhbns: Riverrun Gallery, Hallward Gallery & Solomon Gallery, Dublin. *Works in collections*: National Gallery of Ireland; Irish Museum of Modern Art; Arts Council of Ireland; National Self-Portrait Collection; Office of Public Works; European Parliament. *Commissions*: portraits: State portrait of Taoiseach Bertie Ahern T.D., Ronnie Delany, Olympic Gold Medallist. *Official Purchasers*: Office of Public Works, Irish Defence Forces, Royal College of Surgeons in Ireland, Allied Irish Banks. *Works Reproduced*: AN Post, Abbey Theatre, National Lottery. *Address*: 12 Leinster Avenue, North Strand, Dublin 3, Ireland. *Email*: jameshanleyrha@eircom.net *Website*: www.jameshanley.net *Signs work*: 'HANLEY'.

HANLEY, Liam Powys, self taught painter in oil on board, gouache and tempera. *b*: S. Kensington, 4 Apr 1933. *s of*: James Hanley, novelist. *m*: Hilary Hanley, etcher. one *s.* one *d. Educ*: Wrekin College, Salop. *Exhib*: Stone Gallery, Newcastle, Mermaid Theatre, Thackeray Gallery, London, RA, Abbot Hall A.G., Kendal, Phoenix Gallery, Lavenham, Suffolk, Beardsmore Gallery, London, Crane Kalman Gallery. *Publications*: The Face of Winter by James Hanley. *Official Purchasers*: National Library of Wales, Graves Art Gallery Sheffield, Abbot Hall Gallery, Kendal, Leicester, East & West Riding, Yorkshire, Lancashire, Sussex, Camden local authorities. *Recreations*: reading 20th Cent. fiction. *Address*: 21 Woodsome Rd., London NW5 1RX. *Signs work*: "Hanley, L."

HANN, Priscilla, BA, SEqA; sculptor. *b*: Pattingham, nr. Wolverhampton, 11 Oct 1943. *m*: Patrick Kennedy (decd). *Educ*: Downe House, Newbury. *Studied*: Wolverhampton College of Art (1961-65, Ron Dutton), Tyler School of Art, Philadelphia (Dean Le Clair). *Works in collections*: 'Natives of Furlong', Ringwood, Hants. *Clubs*: S.Eq.A., Friend of R.A., British Sporting Art Trust, Public Sculpture and Monuments Assoc. *Address*: Tetstill, Neen Sollars, Cleobury Mortimer, Worcs. DY14 9AH. *Signs work*: "P. Hann."

HANNAFORD, Elizabeth. *Medium*: oil, watercolour, drawing, prints, new media. *b*: Exeter, Devon, 7 Aug 1944. *d of*: Herbert Henry Hannaford. *m*: Dr. Peter John Gorley. one *s.* one *d. Studied*: Leeds University LLB (Hons) (1965), University of Herts PG DIp Art Therapy (1994), re. art: Camden Institute London (Peter Freeth RA, Chris Billett), National Academy, New York USA (William Behnken). *Exhib*: Kings Place, London (2011); Art First Contemporary Art, Cork Street, London (2 solos 2005, group shows 2005-2008), Royal Academy of Arts (2003), Royal College of Art (1998), Collyer Bristow Gallery, London (1997-2008), Newport Museum & Art Gallery (1998) and many others between 1991 and present. *Works in collections*: private/corporate. *Commissions*: private. *Publications*: see website. *Principal Works*: 'Rock (Iceland)' and 'Duets & Canons' (after music by Christopher Bowers-Broadbent). *Misc*: My work is broadly divided between abstracted landscape and music inspired. *Address*: 62 Park Avenue South, London N8 8LS. *Email*: e.hannaford@btinternet.com *Website*: www.elizabethhannaford.com *Signs work*: "E.HANNAFORD" and "EH".

HANSCOMB, Brian, RE (1997); self taught artist. *Medium*: copperplate engraving, pastel and mixed media. *b*: Croxley Green, Herts., 23 Sep 1944. *m*: Jane. two *d. Educ*: Rickmansworth Grammar School *Exhib*: RA Summer Exhibition; RWA Open; RE; NEAC; Clarges Gallery; Crane Kalman Gallery; Lemon Street Gallery, Truro. One-man shows: Beaux Arts, Bath; Royal Cornwall Museum; Royal Albert Museum, Exeter; Hertzbrock, Germany; John Leach Gallery, Somerset; Brook Gallery, Budleigh Salterton. *Works in collections*: GAC, V&A National Art Library, Science Museum, Royal Cornwall Museum and Art Gallery, Bodleian Library, New York Public Library, National Gallery of Australia. *Commissions*: Bowes & Bowes; Merivale Editions; Folio Society (On the Morning of Christ's Nativity) .*Publications*: Sun, Sea and Earth (Whittington Press, 1989); Cornwall - An Interior Vision (Whittington Press, 1992); Matrix (Whittington Press, 1995); The Phoenix (Whittington Press, 2005). *Recreations*: cycling, walking *Clubs*: Cyclists' Touring

Club (CTC). *Address*: Tor View, Limehead, St. Breward, Bodmin, Cornwall PL30 4LU. *Email*: brian@brianhanscomb.co.uk *Website*: www.brianhanscomb.co.uk *Signs work*: "B. Hanscomb" or "B.H."

HANSELAAR, Marcelle, RE; 'Presse Papier Award', Biennale International d'estampe, contemporain, Quebec, Canada (2003), UWA purchase prize, Originals '06, London (2006); Residency, Frans Masereel Center, Be (2008). *Medium*: oil painting, etching, lithography. *b*: Rotterdam, Holland, 23 Mar 1945. *d of*: Visser Hanselaar. *Studied*: Royal Academy of Art, The Hague, Holland (1962-64); Chelsea and Kensington College, London (B-Tech Printmaking, 2001). *Represented by*: De Queeste Art, Belgium; East West Gallery, London; Millennium Gallery, St.Ives; Eyestorm, London. *Exhib*: solo: East West Gallery (2001, 03, 05, 08); De Queeste Art (2004, 05, 06, 07); Stephanie Burns Fine Art (2004, 06); Galerie de Buytensael, Arnhem (2003, 2008); RM Art, Essen (2003); The Millinery Works, London (1999), SNAp Gallery, Edmonton (2009). *Works in collections*: British Museum Prints & Drawings, London; Ashmolean Museum, Oxford; University of Wales Print Collection, Aberystwyth; Clare Hall, Cambridge; New Hall, Cambridge; Rabo Bank, London; Merrill Lynch, London; Mitsukoshi Ltd., London; AMC, Holland; Amsterdam Arts Council; Risk Publications, London; Paintings in Hospitals, London; Sakima Art Museum, Okinawa; Museum of Cont. Engraving, Alijo, Portugal. *Publications*: 'La Petit Mort' (2005), 'Notes from an Incomplete Journey' (2005), 'The weight of smoke' (2007). *Works Reproduced*: catalogues of most solo and group exhibitions. *Clubs*: Arti & Amicitae, Amsterdam; The London Group; Royal Society of Painter Printmakers. *Misc*: taught at: Central School of Art and St.Martin's, London (1987-88); Sotheby's Educ. Inst. (1989-99); Art Dept. SW Teachers Univ., Chongqing, China (1993, 1995, 96); Sichuan Inst. of Fine Art, Chongqinq (1993, 1995, 96); Neijiang Teachers College, Sichuan (1995). *Address*: 58 Eccleston Sq., London SW1V 1PH. *Email*: maha@marcellehanselaar.com *Website*: www.marcellehanselaar.com *Signs work*: 'Marcelle Hanselaar'

HANSELMAN, Keith, Regional Winner, Laing Landscape Competition (1997); St.Cuthbert's Mill Award, Outstanding Watercolour (RI, 2006). *Medium*: acrylic. *b*: Halifax, Yorkshire, 21 Apr 1931. *s of*: Robert Hollins Hanselman. *m*: Cleonicia. three *d*. *Educ*: Royds Hall Grammar School, Huddersfield. *Studied*: Textile Department & School of Art, Huddersfield Tech. College (1954). *Represented by*: Bath Fine Art. *Exhib*: RBA, NEAC, RI, ROI, Mall Galleries; Thompsons Gallery, London; Hagen-Aria Gallery, London; Singer & Friedlander Watercolour Competition; RA (1997, 1998, 2006). *Works in collections*: Royal London Free Hospital; John Lewis Restaurants, Oxford Street, London. *Works Reproduced*: Hawkins Fine Art, Bath. *Address*: 3 Marling Road, Birchencliffe, Huddersfield, HD2 2EE. *Email*: keith@keithhanselman.com *Signs work*: "Keith Hanselman".

HARBON, Jan, SFP, SBA; Presidents Award SFP (2005), SBA (2007); Certificate Botanical Merit SBA (2006); Silver Gilt Medal RHS. *Medium*: watercolour, mixed media. *b*: London, 5 Jun 1948. *d of*: Tom & Jean Braund. *m*: Geoffrey. one *s*. one *d*. *Studied*: London College of Printing - Illustration. *Exhib*: Chelsea Flower Show (2004-2007); SFP, SBA, RHS Winter Shows, London; Hampton Court Palace Flower Show; Southampton City Art Gallery. *Works Reproduced*: limited edition prints. *Address*: Old Pastures, Passfield Road, Passfield, Liphook, Hampshire GU30 7RU. *Email*: janharbon@btinternet.com *Website*: www.janharbon.com *Signs work*: 'JAN HARBON'.

HARCUS, Robert, ASEA, painter in oil; AAEA: first Irish artist to attain Associateship of Society of Equine Art; Gold Medal and Diploma, Salon 2007, Nantes; First Prize Medal: Salon La Rochelle 2009; Medal D'Honneur, Salon La Rochelle 2004-2008. *b*: 1 Sep 1939. *m*: Ethna. *Educ*: St. Vincent's CBS, Glasnevin. *Studied*: completely self-taught. *Exhib*: RHA, the Oireachtas, SEqA; annual solo exhibs. at Kilkenny Arts Festival since 1981; Society of Equestrian Artists, London and Newmarket; American Academy of Equine Art,

Kentucky; Salon D'Arts, La Rochelle; International Salon of Fine Arts, Argeles-sur-Mer; Columbia Arts League, Missouri; Wildlife Experience Museum, Denver, Colorado; Salon D'Arts, Nantes; also extensively throughout Ireland and Great Britain. *Works in collections*: corporate collections in Ireland and USA, including banking institutions and embassies, offices of Government Ministers, and private collections worldwide. *Clubs*: Artists Assoc. of Ireland. *Address*: St. Endas, South Quay, Arklow, Co. Wicklow, Eire. *Email*: RobertHarcus@eircom.net *Signs work*: "Robert Harcus."

HARDAKER, Charles, ARCA (1958), NEAC (1969), RBA (1984). *b*: Oxford, 1 May 1934. *s of*: Charles Hardaker, businessman. *m*: Annick née Pouletaud. *Educ*: Wellesbourne School, B'ham. *Studied*: B'ham College of Arts and Crafts (1949-53), RCA (1955-58). *Exhib*: RA, NEAC, RBA, RP, five one-man shows, San Francisco (2), London (3). *Works in collections*: Tate Gallery (Chantrey Bequest), Guildhall of London, National Library of Wales, Northumbria Water, BP, ICE, Townley Hall, Eire. *Address*: Studio 1, St. Oswald's Studios, Sedlescombe Rd., Fulham, London SW6 1RH. *Signs work*: "Hardaker."

HARDCASTLE, Audrey, SBA (1991); SFP (1996); Certificate of Botanical Merit, SBA (1995); St.Cuthberts Mill Award (1997). *Medium*: watercolour. *b*: 2 Aug 1934. *m*: John. two *d*. *Studied*: University of Southampton School of Education (Certificate in Art & Craft, and Education). *Exhib*: group: SBA, Westminster Gallery (1990); SFP (1996); The Garden Exhibition, Wales (1992); Everard Read Gallery, Johannesburg (1992); The Linnean Society (1991); The Hunt Inst. 8th International Exhbn. *Works in collections*: Hunt Institute for Botanical Documentation (Slipper Orchid). *Commissions*: various in UK. *Works Reproduced*: in 'The Origin of Plants'; 'The Art of Botanical Painting'; 'A History and Dictionary of British Flower Painters'; 'Collins Flower Guide'. *Address*: Compton, 129 Bouverie Avenue South, Salisbury, Wilts, SP2 8EA. *Email*: hard.castles@virgin.net *Signs work*: 'A Hardcastle'.

HARDIE, Gwen, Richard Ford award, RA (1982), Hons. Degree (1983), Daad Scholarship, W. Berlin (1984), Edward 7th British-German Foundation, W. Berlin (1986); painter in oil, sculptor in cement, plaster. *b*: Newport, Scotland, 7 Jan 1962. *d of*: Anne Livingstone and James Hardie. *Educ*: Inverurie Academy. *Studied*: Edinburgh College of Art (1979-84, John Houston), HDK, W. Berlin (1984-85, Baselitz). *Exhib*: solo shows: Fruitmarket Gallery, Edinburgh (1987), Fischer Fine Art, London (1989), SNGMA (1990), Talbot Rice A.G., Edinburgh, Annely Juda, London (1994), Jason & Rhodes, London (1996), Peterborough Museum and Fine A.G. (1997); group shows: Vienna (1986), American tour (1989-92), Frankfurt (1993), Jason & Rhodes, New Artists: Hardie Colvin & Boyd (1995). *Works in collections*: SNGMA, Metropolitan Museum N.Y., Gulbenkian Museum Lisbon, Arts Council, etc. *Commissions*: Portrait of Jean Muir (1985). *Address*: 201W 77th Street, '5D, New York, NY 10024 USA. *Signs work*: "G. HARDIE" or "G.H."

HARDIMAN, Patsy Christine. *Medium*: oil. *b*: Amersham, Bucks, 3 Dec 1946. *d of*: George & Johanna Stevenson. *m*: Stanley. one *s*. *Educ*: Our Lady & St.Anselms, Middx; Paddington Polytechnic, London. *Studied*: Shaftesbury Centre, Richmond, Surrey; FE Centre, Chertsey, Surrey. *Represented by*: LondonArt.co.uk. *Exhib*: RA Summer Exhbn (2000); Llewellyn Alexander (2002/9); Christie's, London, Art for Life (2002/6); Whittlesford Gallery, Cambridge (2002/6); Arndean Gallery, London (2004), Resurrection Exhibition, Bury St. Edmunds (2010), The Brompton Oratory, London (2012), Brentwood Cathedral (2013). *Works in collections*: in Europe and USA. *Recreations*: writing, music, poetry. *Clubs*: Society of Catholic Artists; Christian Arts. *Address*: 7 chemin des Essartis, 17100 Saintes France. *Email*: patsyhardiman@aol.com *Website*: www.LondonArt.co.uk *Signs work*: 'Patsy H'.

HARDING, Alexis, BA (Hons); First Prize, John Moores 23, Walker Art Gallery (2004). *Medium*: oil and gloss paint. *b*: London, Aug 1973. *Studied*: Goldsmiths College (BA Hons)

1992-95. *Represented by*: Mummery & Schnelle, London; Rubicon Gallery, Dublin; Marella Gallery, Milan. *Exhib*: first one-person exhibition: Galerij 565, Aalst, Belgium (1997). Other solo shows include: Andrew Mummery Gallery, Rubicon Gallery Dublin, Galeria Pedro Cera -Portugal, Krohn Galerie -Basal, Marella Arte -Milan, Allerart -Bludenz, Austria (2006), Patricia Sweetow Gallery - San Francisco (2007). Since 1995, he has shown extensively in two-person and group exhibitions internationally. *Works in collections*: Arts Council of England, Bank of Spain, Irish Musum of Modern Art - Dublin, National Museums Liverpool - The Walker, Caldic - Rotterdam. *Publications*: New British Art, Chris Townsend (Thames & Hudson, p.40-48), Twisting into True (text by Martin Holman, Rubicon Gallery), John Moores 23 (Walker Art Gallery, Liverpool), Painting by the Skin of your Eyes, JJ Charlesworth (Andrew Mummery Gallery), Alexis Harding 'Unloosing Control' (text by Caoimhin Mac Giolla Leith), Shimmering Substance (Arnolfini Gallery, Bristol). *Address*: Mummery & Schnelle, 83 Great Titchfield St., London W1 6RH. *Email*: hardingalexis@hotmail.com *Website*: www.mummeryschnelle.com

HARDING, Jane Mary, SWA (1982); artist in line, water-colour and mixed media. *b*: London. *d of*: Edwin Harvey, civil servant. *m*: David Harding (decd). *Educ*: Haberdashers' Aske's Girls' School. *Studied*: Lytham St. Annes School of Art (1940-41). *Exhib*: SWA annually, Britain in Water-colour, Ealing Art Group. *Works in collections*: London Borough of Ealing Central Library, St.Benedicts Church, Ealing Abbey and in private collections in the UK and abroad. *Publications*: editorial illustrations for Amalgamated Press, Odhams, Franey's London Diary, Grolier Press, Sunday Times, Ward Gallery. *Clubs*: Ealing Arts. *Address*: Melvin House, 13 Hartington Rd., Ealing, London W13 8QL. *Email*: jan@janemharding.plus.com *Signs work*: "jane harding." or jh.

HARDISTY, Jan. *Medium*: photography, prints. *b*: Guildford, 23 Jan 1948. one *s*. *Studied*: Central School of Art, London (graphic design); self-taught photography. *Exhib*: RA Summer Show (2004); Merz Gallery, Edinburgh (2005); studio shows, London (1996, 2005). *Works in collections*: Citibank (London) Permanent Collection; international private collections; Celebrity Cruises permanent collection. *Commissions*: Conran shops, London. *Works Reproduced*: internationally by 'The Special Photographers Company Picture Library'. *Address*: Flat 21 5-7 Lambolle Road London NW3 4HS. *Email*: janhardisty@btinternet.com *Signs work*: 'Jan Hardisty'.

HARDMAN, Paul Ritson, B.Ed. *Medium*: cartoonist and illustrator, inks or computer generated colour. *b*: Liverpool, 21 Jan 1947. *m*: Mary. two *s*. *Educ*: De La Salle College, Liverpool; St.Mary's College, Twickenham; London Inst. of Ed. (London Univ.), studying Educational Psychology, Art, Maths. *Exhib*: many cartoon exhbns around Europe and Western Asia. *Works in collections*: FECO Collections. *Commissions*: for film and TV (many); Channel Four Racing. *Publications*: Daily Mirror, Sunday Mirror, Sporting Life. *Clubs*: Cartoonists Club of GB; Federation of Cartoonists Organisations; The British Cartoonists Association; Cartoonists Guild. *Address*: 37 Beach Priory Gardens, Southport, Lancs, PR8 2SA. *Email*: mail@hartoons.co.uk *Website*: www.hartoons.co.uk *Signs work*: Hardman

HARDY, Robert, BA (Hons); MA; ATC; New Contemporaries Prizewinner (1976). *Medium*: oil. *b*: Salford, 13 Aug 1952. *s of*: Eddie and Vera. *m*: Margaret. *Educ*: Salford Grammar School (1963-70). *Studied*: North Staffs Polytechnic (1971-74); Chelsea School of Art (1974-5); London University Institute of Education. *Exhib*: RA Summer exhbn; 20/21 Air Fair, London; Long & Ryle Art Gallery; The Discerning Eye Exhibition; Harriet Green Gallery; Sally Hunter Fine Art; Llewellyn Alexander Gallery; London Art Fair; Open Eye Gallery, Edinburgh; Cambridge Contemporary Art; St.Paul's Cathedral; Tavistock Inst., Reading Art Centre, England & Co, Bury St. Edmunds Cathedral; Ministry of Gozo, Govt. of Malta; The Sheen Gallery; Rudolph Steiner Centre; Sherwin Gallery. *Works in* *collections*: Govt. of Malta. *Publications*: About My Work; Times of Malta; The Tablet; Church Times; Sunday Telegraph; The International Dictionary of Artists who Painted Malta - Nicholas de Piro (AVC Publishers). *Works Reproduced*: RA Summer Exhbn. Catalogue (1998); 'Presence', St.Paul's Cathedral Catalogue (2004). *Recreations*: walking, reading, praying. *Address*: 24 Albemarle Road, East Barnet, Herts EN4 8EG. *Email*: hardyrobert@btinternet.com *Website*: www.roberthardyartist.co.uk *Signs work*: 'HARDY'

HARE, Derek Charles, FRSA. *Medium*: oil, watercolour, drawing, prints. *b*: South Shields, Co.Durham, 24 May 1945. *s of*: Charles W. & Jessie Hare. *m*: Ludmilla Karpoff (divorced). *Partner*: Anne Bachmann. two *s*. *Studied*: Sunderland College of Art (1962-65, Commercial Art). Self taught as a painter. Professional Artist since 1965. *Represented by*: Frost and Reed, London. *Exhib*: since 1967, in UK and overseas, include: Mystic Seaport Gallery, CT, USA (1988-2006); Piano Nobile, London (1989); RSMA (1998); Chelsea Art Fair (1999, 2001, 2002); Arndean Gallery, London (2002, 2003, 2005-08); Biscuit Factory, Newcastle upon Tyne (2003); Burg Galerie 25th Anniversary (2005); Nehru Centre, London (2007); Piers Feetham Gallery, London (2007). *Works in collections*: include: HRH The Duke of Kent, HH Sheikh Maktoum al Maktoum, Sir John Major, Sterling Winthrop Laboratories, NFU, Legal & General, Barclays Bank, Deutsche Bank etc. *Commissions*: Maktoum al Maktoum; John Major; Janus (US); Merck Fink (Germany); Barclays Bank. *Works Reproduced*: by Ecosse Fine Art, Edinburgh Arts. *Recreations*: travel, reading, Jazz, Theatre. *Address*: 6 Stag Lane, Buckhurst Hill, Essex, IG9 5TD. *Email*: info@derekhare.co.uk *Website*: derekhare.co.uk *Signs work*: "HARE" (& date); Limited Edition Prints "Hare".

HARGAN, Joseph R., DA (1974), Glasgow Group (1996), Stirling Smith award (1978), Cargill award (1980), Torrance award (1982), Meyer Oppenheim prize RSA (1985), Hunting Group prizewinner, London (1988), Paisley Art Inst. award (1993), CFAG Award (2001); Founder Mem. and Chairman of Group 81; elected Pres. PAI (1989-2001), elected PAI (1996); William Bowie Award 2002, Maude Gemmell Hutchison Award, Royal Scottish Academy 2002, Richmond Hill Gallery Award 2005, Reid Kerr College Award 2007. *b*: Glasgow, 23 Jan 1952. *s of*: Patrick Joseph Hargan, postman and Elizabeth Scott. *m*: Anne Louise Clarke. two *s*. one *d*. *Studied*: Glasgow School of Art (1970-74, Danny Ferguson, Drummond Bone, David Donaldson). *Exhib*: RSA, RGI, RSW, Art Club, Group 81, RA, PAI, BWS, SSA, etc *Works in collections*: New Zealand, Brazil, USA, Europe and S. America. *Clubs*: Glasgow Art. *Address*: 40 Oakshaw St., Paisley PA1 2DD. *Signs work*: "Hargan."

HARLAND, Inga. *Medium*: mixed. *b*: Victoria West, 6 Feb 1932. *m*: George Rowlands. one *s*. *Studied*: BA (French and English), Univ. College of Rhodesia (1965-67); MA Fine Art, Coventry University (1997). *Exhib*: RA Summer Show (1992, 1998, 2001); Royal West of England Academy (1991, 1993, 1997). Solo exhibition, Library Gallery, Univ. of Warwick (2004); Manchester Academy of Fine Arts Annual Open (1990). *Publications*: RA Illustrated Catalogue (1992, p.54, also in frontispiece). *Recreations*: tennis, walking, bridge. *Clubs*: Association of Midland Artists; Warwick Boat Club; Stratford upon Avon Bridge Club. *Address*: 111 Bridge End, Warwick, CV34 6PD. *Email*: inga.harland@virgin.net *Signs work*: "Inga Harland"

HARLEY, Alexandra, Associate Member of Royal British Society of Sculptors, Free Painters & Sculptors Society. *Medium*: sculpture. *b*: Essex, 13 Aug 1958. *Partner*: Francis Blake (illustrator). two *d*. *Studied*: Wimbledon School of Art (1978-82), St. Martin's School of Art (1982-84). *Exhib*: solo exhibitions: Eger Gallery, London; Chelmsford Library, Essex. Selected exhibitions: Tate Gallery, London; Royal British Society of Sculptors; Poussin Gallery, London; Horb, Germany; Cork Street Gallery, London; Andres Institute, New Hampshire, USA; Bath Society Open; Jarfo Gallery, Koyoto; Janyi Museum, Taiwan. *Works* *in collections*: private. *Commissions*: Broadstairs Folkweek; Gate Theatre, London; BBC 'Charlie's Garden Army', Chinbrook Meadows Peace Garden to commemorate Archibishop Desmond Tutu, Globe Primary School and others. *Works Reproduced*: 'Sculpture', Jane Hill (Hodder & Stoughton, 1998). *Recreations*: traditional music. *Address*: 182 Downhills Park Road, London N17 6AP. *Email*: alexharley@btinternet.com *Website*: www.alexandraharley.co.uk *Signs work*: "A.H."

HARMAN, Alice,: SBA; awards: RHS - Silver Gilt (2000), Silver (2000), Silver (2006). *Medium*: botanical watercolours on paper and vellum. *b*: South Africa, 1 Sep 1957. *d of*: Fredrick & Susan Milton. *m*: Peter Harman. one *s.* one *d. Educ*: Kilgraston School, Perthshire. *Studied*: self-taught. *Exhib*: RI (2003); Pastel Society (2012); RHS (2000, 2006); SBA (1998-2012); Chichester Open Art (1999-2001); Cow Shed Studios, Steyning; North East Open Studios, Kemnay, Inverurie. *Misc*: Classes held at Cowshed Studios, Steyning. *Address*: Hammes Barn, Washington Road, Steyning, West Sussex, BN44 3DA. *Email*: peter.harman@virgin.net *Website*: www.cow-shed-studio.com *Signs work*: 'ALICE HARMAN'.

HARPER, Alison, BA (Hons) Fine Art (1985); Post Grad year (1986); Post-Diploma (Baroda, India, 1995); Norwegian Govt. Scholarship (1986); Commonwealth Scholarship (1993); Ruth Davidson Memorial Award (1998); The Prince of Wales Drawing Studio Bursary (2001); Lady Artists' Trust Award (1988). *Medium*: oil, drawing, prints. *b*: Glasgow, 25 Feb 1964. *d of*: Prof. Alexander M. Harper & Charlotte Harper. *m*: Andrew Wamae. one *s. Studied*: Glasgow School of Art (1981-85); Kunstakademie Oslo (1986); M.S. University, Baroda (1993-95); Prince of Wales Drawing Studio (2001-02). *Represented by*: Boundary Gallery, London (also known as one of 'The Glasgow Girls'). *Exhib*: selected solo & group shows: RA; RSA; NPG; Collins Gallery; Leicester City Art Gallery; Nairobi Museum; Shetland Museum; Stirling Museum; India Today Gallery, New Delhi; Iwate Arts Festival, Kyoto, Japan; National Autumn Exhbn, Oslo; City Arts Centre, Edinburgh; Compass Gallery; Sahmet, New Delhi; Cheltenham Open Drawing (prizewinner). *Works in collections*: Strathclyde University; Museum & Arts Loans Service; BBC Scotland; Glasgow School of Art. *Publications*: 'Angels Wear Silver' (Alison Harper); Sandy Moffatt Catalogue Introduction for Compass Gallery Show (1995); 'Tongues of Diamond' (Collins Gallery catalogue, 1999); 'Restoring Female Identity, Strategies by Scottish Female Artists' (dissertation). *Works Reproduced*: 'Scottish Paintings: 1837 to the Present' (William Hardie, 1990). *Principal Works*: 'Burning Woman'; 'Mother Goddess with Seven Yellow Suns'. *Misc*: ordained Buddhist, lecturer at Glasgow School of Art 1995-2001. *Address*: 47 Radbourne Crescent, London E17 3RR. *Email*: alison@alisonharper.com *Website*: www.harperart.com

HARPER, Charles, ANCA (Hons) ATC, AOSDANA, RHA; painter; head of fine art department, Limerick School of Art and Design. *b*: 30 Jul 1943. one *s.* one *d. Educ*: Crescent College, Limerick. *Studied*: Limerick School of Art, National College of Art, Dublin. *Works in collections*: Arts Council of Ireland, P J Carroll & Co., Irish Museum of Modern Art, Hugh Lane Municipal Gallery, San Francisco Museum of Modern Art, Limerick City Gallery of Art, University of Limerick. *Publications*: Profile: Charles Harper, Gandon Editions, 1998. *Address*: Woodstown House, Ballyvara Rd., Lisnagry, Co. Limerick, Ireland. *Email*: charlesharper600@hotmail.com *Signs work*: "Charles Harper."

HARPER, Edward Lawrence, MA Fine Art, BA (Hons) Fine Art; UK Finalist Lexmark European Art Prize (2003). *Medium*: acrylic on canvas. *b*: Southampton, Hants, 4 Mar 1970. *s of*: Norman and Eileen Harper. *m*: Sarah Jarman. one *s.* one *d. Educ*: Merryoaks Boys, Southampton; Itchen College, Southampton. *Studied*: Goldsmiths College (1996-98), Brighton Polytechnic (1989-92). *Exhib*: solo: 'Systemax', Millais Gallery, Southampton (2005); 'Superdrive' Project Space, Northern Gallery of Contemporary Art, Sunderland

(2004); Mobile Home Gallery, London (2001, 02); group shows: 'Yes, I'm a Long Way From Home' Wolverhampton Art Gallery and touring England; Espace Fauriel, St.Etienne, France (2002), Buro Friedrich, Berlin (2001), Goma, Glasgow (1999). *Works in collections*: Gun St. (213x152cm Acrylic on cotton, 2000), Tyne and Wear Museums Collection Newcastle; Sebert Road (213x152cm Acrylic on cotton, 2005), Southampton City Art Gallery. *Address*: 35 Leighton Avenue, Leigh-on-Sea, Essex, SS9 1QB. *Email*: edharper@waitrose.com *Signs work*: "E Harper".

HARRIGAN, Claire, BA Hons. (1986), RSW (1992); painter in water-colour, acrylic, gouache and pastel. *b*: Kilmarnock, 8 Nov 1964. *d of*: James Harrigan and Elspeth McLaren. *Educ*: Sacred Heart Academy, Girvan. *Studied*: Glasgow School of Art (1982-86, Peter Sumsion, Neil Dallas-Brown, Barbara Rae). *Exhib*: solo shows: Christopher Hull Gallery, London; Gatehouse Gallery, Glasgow; Open Eye Gallery, Edinburgh; Macaulay Gallery, Stenton; Bruton St. Gallery, London; Flying Colours Gallery, London. *Publications*: "Abstract and Colour Techniques in Painting" (Batsford, 2007). *Address*: 83 Dalhowan St., Crosshill, Ayrshire, KA19 7RN. *Email*: claireeharrigan@yahoo.co.uk *Signs work*: "Claire Harrigan."

HARRIS, Alfred, ARCA, FRSA; artist in acrylic and oil; Chairman (retd), Dept. of Art & Design, University of London Inst. of Educ.; Mem. London Group. *b*: London, 21 Jul 1930. *m*: Carmel. one *s.* two *d. Studied*: Willesden School of Art (1952), RCA (1955). *Exhib*: numerous group exhbns. and 15 one-man shows in U.K. and abroad. *Works in collections*: 57 in public and corporate including: Ben Uri A.G.; Bradford University; Sweden: Dalarnas Konstnamind, Dalarnas Museum, Falun Museum, Gothenburg Hospital, Konsthallen Uppsala, Ministry of Culture, Scania Valis, Sodertalje Town Council, Uppsala Museum; G.L.C.; Leics. Educ. Authority; London University; Oxford University; R.C.A.; St. Thomas' Hospital, London; Tate Gallery; Tel Aviv Museum, Israel; Tokai Bank, Japan; Warwick University. *Commissions*: Alfred Harris "A Decade in Retrospect" by Pierre Rouue, University of London Institute of Education (1979); 12 drawings by Alfred Harris, Ben Uri Gallery (The London Jewish Museum) (1959). *Publications*: "Portrait of the Artist" edited by Sarah Fox-Pitt, Tate Gallery Publications (1989); "Modern British Painters 1900-1980" edited by Alan Windsor, Scolar Press (1992); "Dictionary of British Artists Since 1945" edited by David Buckman, Art Dictionaries Ltd (1998), The London Group, The London Group, (2003). *Principal Works*: 3 Series: 1. Playing Cards; 2. Journey of the Dove; 3. Kite Flying. *Address*: 66-70 Camden Mews, London NW1 9BX.

HARRIS, Jennifer Joy, NDD (1955), RWA (1981); etcher and painter in water-colour and acrylic; display designer (1957-1965), art technician in college of education (1966-1977), and faculty of education, Bristol (1977-1978). *b*: Bristol, 8 Apr 1935. *m*: Cyril Cave (decd) *Educ*: Duncan House School, Clifton, Bristol. *Studied*: West of England College of Art, Bristol (1951-1955). *Exhib*: RA, RWA, Nat. Exhib. of Modern British Prints, Blackpool (1979 & 1986); Internat. Mini-Print Exhib. (1997); Nat. Print Exhib., London (1997); and many other exhibs. nationwide and in Paris and New York. *Works in collections*: Print Archive, Scarborough Art Gallery. *Address*: Berry House, Cheriton Fitzpaine, Nr. Crediton, Devon EX17 4HZ. *Website*: www.rwa.org.uk *Signs work*: "J.J.Harris."

HARRIS, Josephine, RWS, NEAC, FGE.; artist in water-colour, drawing and engraved glass. *d of*: P. A. Harris. *Educ*: privately. *Studied*: Plymouth College of Art (1948-52) under William Mann, ARCA, gained NDD. *Works in collections*: Plymouth A.G., Graves A.G., Sheffield, South London A.G., ILEA, KCC. *Misc*: Work to commission for public companies and private individuals in engraved glass. *Address*: Workshop No. 2, 46-52 Church Rd., Barnes, London SW13 0DO *Signs work*: "Josephine Harris" or "J.H."

HARRIS, Marguerite, Fellow of Institute of Medical Laboratory Scientists (retd); ASBA; SFP; RHS Silver Gilt Medal (2002); RHS Silver Medal (2004). *Medium*:

watercolour. *b*: Winchester, 14 Oct 1941. two *s*. *Educ*: Winchester County High School. *Studied*: tutored 1997-2002 by Joan Osborne SBA SFP. *Exhib*: SBA; SFP (Mottisfont Abbey, Hilliers Arboretum); Edinburgh Airport Gallery; Pitlochry Festival Theatre Gallery; Stages Gallery, Machynlleth. *Address*: 40 Kinloch View, Blackness Road, Linlithgow, H49 7HT. *Email*: marguerite.harris55@gmail.com *Signs work*: 'M HARRIS' (with date in Roman numerals from 2000).

HARRIS, Phyllis, SWA, NDD, SGFA (Resigned), AUA; artist in water-colour and pen, lithography, linocut, school teacher (retd). *b*: London, 3 Aug 1925. *m*: Cyril David Harris. one *s*. one *d*. *Educ*: Brondesbury High School, London and Abbey School, Reading. *Studied*: Reading University School of Art (1945-47), Brighton School of Art (1947-48), Camberwell School of Art (1948-50), Harrow School of Art (lithography). *Exhib*: SWA, Brent and Harrow, London. *Works in collections*: locally in Harrow & Wembley. *Clubs*: S.W.A., Wembley Art Soc., Harrow Art Soc., U.A. *Address*: 55 Slough Lane, Kingsbury, London NW9 8YB. *Signs work*: "Phyl Harris."

HARRIS, Roger, RE; Kent County Council Purchase Prize; University of Wales Purchase Prize; Pollock-Krasner Art Foundation Award, New York; 2nd Prize Cleveland International Drawing Biennale. *Medium*: printmaker, painter. *b*: Plymouth, Devon, 18 Feb 1942. *m*: Katherine. one *s* (from previous marriage). one *d*. *Studied*: Kingston College of Art (NDD, 1957-61); Richmond College of Art (Printmaking, 1974-78). *Represented by*: Bankside Gallery, Royal Society of Painter-Printmakers. *Exhib*; Royal Academy Summer Exhibitions; Royal West of England Academy; Printmakers Council; Mall Galleries; Hunting Art Prizes; Sunday Times Watercolour Competition; Society of Wood Engravers; Bath Artist Printmakers Exhibition (invited artist); International Miniature Print Exhbn., Connecticut USA; Society of Graphic Fine Art, Bath; Originals; Art in Action. Solo shows: Wrexham Art Centre; Leeds Museum Design & Craft Gallery. *Works in collections*: Ashmolean Museum, Oxford; Cheltenham Hospital; Cleveland Gallery & Museum; Cornwall Hospital; University of Wales; Kent County Council; Nature in Art, Gloucestershire. *Publications*: Best of International Printmaking; Printmakers' Secrets; Printmakers The Directory; Nocturne Print & article in 'Wohnen' Germany. *Official Purchasers*: Cleveland Gallery & Museum; University of Wales; Kent County Council. *Address*: Springhill Cottage, Quarhouse, Brimscombe, Stroud, Gloucestershire GL5 2RS. *Email*: roger@inkyfingers.myzen.co.uk *Signs work*: "ROGER HARRIS".

HARRIS, Rosemary, MA (Hons.) History of Art; Curator, NatWest Group Art Collection. *b*: Guildford, Surrey, 1 Dec 1962. *m*: Paul Moorhouse. *Studied*: University College, London. *Address*: Royal Bank of Scotland Group Art Collection, 12 Throgmorton Ave., London EC2N 2DL.

HARRIS HUGHES, Susanna Dioné Neate, BA (Hons) Fine Art (1993); MA Printmaking (1998). *Medium*: painter/printmaker/installations. *b*: Kent, 2 Mar 1947. *d of*: Lt. Cdr. Richard Colville MBE DSC, & Mrs Dioné Colville. *m*: Howell Harris Hughes CBE. two *s*. *Studied*: West Surrey College of Art & Design, Farnham (1988-93); Wimbledon School of Art (1995-98). *Exhib*: RA Summer Exhibition (1994, 95); RWA Bristol (1991, 93, 96); Cheltenham Open (1996); Chelsea Arts Club (2000); Fishbourne Roman Palace (2001); Millinery Works, London (2003); Orleans House, Twickenham (2004); St.Mary's Church, Guildford (2004); Discerning Eye (2005); MOMA Wales (2007); Footprint International, Norwalk USA (2008); The Womens Art Show, Basingstoke (2008); Gloucester Print Makers; Stroud (2009), Spike Island Bristol (2009); Visual for Business, Arts & Business (online); Haslemere Museum (2011) St. Giles Cripplegate, London (2014). *Works in collections*: University of Aberystwyth (National Print Collection); Guildford Borough Council; KPMG and various other corporate/private collections. *Commissions*: Worshipful Co. of Barbers (Print) (2011). *Works Reproduced*: The Public Catalogue Foundation, Surrey;

Visual (Arts & Business) Catalogue of Artists. *Recreations*: gardening, tennis. *Clubs*: Chelsea Arts Club. *Address*: Lotisford House, Wonersh, Nr. Guildford, GU5 0QY. *Email*: susannahh@susannaharrishughes.com *Website*: www.susannaharrishughes.com *Signs work*: "SUSANNA HARRIS HUGHES" or "SHH"

HARRISON, Christopher David, BA (Hons), ATC; artist in water-colour, collage, oils, and photographer; Director, Bircham Art Gallery. *b*: Gt. Yarmouth, 21 Oct 1953. *m*: Deborah Margaret. two *s*. *Educ*: Bromley Grammar School, Kent, Boston Grammar School, Lincs. *Studied*: Jacob Kramer College of Art, Leeds (1973-74), Reading University (1974-78), London University Inst. of Educ. (1978-79). *Exhib*: RBA, RA, RI, RWS; many mixed exhbns. throughout England; regular one-man shows Norfolk. *Address*: Alton House. 6 Alexandra Road, Sheringham, Norfolk NR26 8HU. *Email*: chrisharrison2@gmail.com *Signs work*: "Christopher Harrison."

HARRISON, Mark Stephen, BSFA Best Artwork of 1991; John White Memorial Prize 2012. *Medium*: Oil. *b*: Leicester, 27 Feb 1951. *Educ*: Loughborough Grammar School. *Studied*: Trent University (1970-73); Wimbledon School of Art (1974). *Represented by*: Medici Gallery, London; Hicks Gallery, Wimbledon; and three others. *Exhib*: Solo at Broadway Modern (2011); Mall Galleries, London; Hicks Gallery, Wimbledon; Art in Action; WH Patterson, London; Edinburgh Festival; Broadway Modern, Cotswolds; Llewellyn Alexander, London; Gallerina Darlington; Jenggalla, Pranoto and Ubuo Galleries, Bali, Indonesia. *Works in collections*: Private collections in UK, USA and Europe. *Commissions*: 484 book jacket illustrations; private commissions. *Publications*: "Mark Harrison's Dreamlands" Paper Tiger (1990); many art magazines. *Works Reproduced*: 484 book jacket illustrations; "Mark Harrison's Dreamlands"; magazines. *Recreations*: Travel; music. *Clubs*: Sussex County Arts Club. *Misc*: Please see biography page on my website for a more complete summary. *Address*: Flat 5, 13 Palmeira Avenue, Hove, East Sussex BN3 3GA. *Email*: msj.harrison@tiscali.co.uk *Website*: www.paintingsbymarkharrison.com *Signs work*: Initials and roman numerals.

HARRISON, Stephanie Miriam, NDD, HRMS; painter, book illustrator, graphic designer. *b*: Kings Lynn, 10 Dec 1939. *d of*: Cyril Gurr. *m*: John Harrison. *Studied*: Medway College of Art, Rochester (1955-60). *Exhib*: Westminster Gallery, Mall Galleries, The Royal Academy, Linda Blackstone Gallery, Florum, Sevenoaks, Rye A.G., Kent Painter's Group and galleries throughout the U.K.; several one-woman shows. *Works in collections*: Science Museum, BM (Natural History), and private collections. *Publications*: Wild Flowers of Britain, Marine Life, Handbook of British Mammals, Private Life of a Country House, greetings cards. *Address*: Iden Cottage, Wittersham Rd., Iden, nr. Rye, E.Sussex TN31 7XB *Signs work*: "Stephanie Harrison," "S. Harrison" or "S.M.H."

HARRISSON, Tim, BA (Norwich School of Art); Diploma in Post Graduate Studies. *Medium*: sculpture in stone, prints. *b*: Quendon, 14 Jun 1952. *s of*: P.D. & E.H. Harrisson. *m*: Joanna Still. two *s*. *Studied*: Hammersmith College of Art; Byam Shaw School of Art; Norwich School of Art. *Represented by*: The New Art Centre, Rabley Drawing Centre. *Exhib*: Royal Academy; New Art Centre,Salisbury (1990-2010); Ulm, Germany; Russell-Cotes Museum, Bournemouth; Winchester Cathedral; The Eagle Gallery (2007); Rabley Contemporary Drawing Centre (2009); Salisbury Museum (2009); Bournemouth University (2010); Creswell Grays Museum (2011); Rabley Drawing Centre (2012). *Works in collections*: Southern Arts (Arts Council); Winchester Cathedral; Red House Museum, Christchurch. *Commissions*: Southampton Airport; Sea Edge, Southampton City; Russell-Cotes Museum; The New Art Centre. *Publications*: 'Tim Harrisson Carved Time' by Andrew Wilson; Contemporary Art Vol.3, no.4. *Principal Works*: Rotherley Stones I & II. *Recreations*: philosophy. *Clubs*: Royal West of England Academy (2012). *Address*: 4 Beckford Cottages, Hindon, Salisbury, Wilts. SP3 6ED. *Email*: tim@timharrisson.com *Website*: www.timharrisson.co.uk *Signs work*: 'TIM HARRISSON'.

HART, Aidan Christopher, BA, DipEd. *Medium*: sculpture, fresco, icons. *b*: Surrey, 18 May 1957. *s of*: Maxwell Bryce Hart & Shirley Hart. *m*: Sarah Hart. one *s*. one *d*. *Studied*: Auckland University NZ (1975-78); Auckland 2 School Teacher Training College (1979); University of Thessalonika (1987, 88). *Exhib*: one man: Outreach, NZ (1978), Vision Gallery, NZ (1979); Pumphouse, NZ (1999); group: Denis Cohen, NZ (1980); Barry Stern, Sydney (1982); Oriel 31, Wales (1991); Victoria, Bath (1991); Blackburn Museum (1991); Perides Gallery, Athens (2000); Art in Essence, London (2004); Long & Ryle, London (2005); Minneapolis Museum (2005); V&A (2006); Library of Congress, Washington (2006). *Works in collections*: HRH The Prince of Wales; cathedrals of Lichfield, Hereford, Newcastle, Carlisle, Greek Cathedrals of Birmingham & Camberwell etc. *Commissions*: as for collections, plus Shrewsbury School Chapel, St. John's Abbey & University, Minnesota; fresco at Katounia, Evia, Greece; etc. *Publications*: numerous articles; "Techniques of Icon and Wall Painting" (2011); "Sacred Icons" (2000); "Paradise Regained" (1991). *Works Reproduced*: numerous. *Principal Works*: St. Nicholas Church, Amsterdam; frescoes at Evia, Keswick, Stiperstones Monastery, Shrewsbury School, St. John's Bible. *Recreations*: walking. *Address*: 4 Station Road, Pontesbury, Shrewsbury, Shropshire, SY5 0QD. *Email*: mail@aidanharticons.com *Website*: www.aidanharticons.com *Signs work*: "A.HART" (icons unsigned).

HART-DAVIES, Christina Ann, BA Hons.; botanical artist and illustrator in watercolour; 4 RHS Gold medals. *b*: Shrewsbury, 1947. *Studied*: fine art, typography at Reading University (1966-70). *Exhib*: Brisbane, London, RBG. Kew, USA. *Works in collections*: Hunt Inst. Botanical Documentation, Pittsburgh; Shirley Sherwood Collection Contemp. Botanical Artists; Royal Botanic Gardens, Kew. *Address*: 31 Shaftesbury Rd., Poole, Dorset BH15 2LT. *Website*: www.christinahartdavies.co.uk *Signs work*: "CHRISTINA HART-DAVIES," "CH-D" (miniatures).

HARTILL, Brenda, RE, Dip.FA Hons. (1964); New Zealand Queen Elizabeth II Arts Council Study Award (1965-66); UK Arts Council Award in Theatre Design, seconded to Young Vic Theatre (1971). *Medium*: etchings and collographs, collage and painting. *b*: London, 27 Feb 1943. *m*: Harold Moores. one *s*. one *d*. *Educ*: Kings School, Ottery St. Mary; Kelston High, Auckland, NZ. *Studied*: Elam School Fine Art, NZ.; Central School of Art (theatre design, Ralph Koltai). *Represented by*: New Academy Gallery, 34 Windmill Street, London W1T 2JR. *Exhib*: RA Summer Show, RE Bankside Gallery, over 50 galleries worldwide; solo shows: New Academy Gallery and galleries in Australia, NZ, USA, Barbican Centre. *Works in collections*: Bank of England, BP, Amoco, BT. *Commissions*: Morgan Stanley, The Independent newspaper. *Publications*: Printmaking Today. Author of 'Collographs and Mixed-Media Printmaking' (pub. A&C Black), Instructional DVD 'Collagraph, a sculptural approach to printmaking'. *Clubs*: Royal Society of Painter Printmakers. *Address*: Brenda Hartill Prints, Pound House, Udimore, nr. Rye, East Sussex TN31 6BA. *Email*: brenda.hartill@gmail.com *Website*: www.brendahartill.com *Signs work*: "Brenda Hartill."

HARVEY, Jake, DA (1972), RSA(1989); sculptor, carver of limestone/granite, and forger of iron/steel; Professor, Head of Sculpture, Edinburgh College of Art. *b*: Yetholm, Kelso, Roxburghshire, 3 Jun 1948. *m*: Penny Harvey. one *s*. two *d*. *Educ*: Kelso High School. *Studied*: sculpture: Edinburgh College of Art (1966-72) Postgraduate (1971-72), Travelling Scholarship to Greece (1971-72), William Gillies Bursary Research Travel in India (1989). *Exhib*: RSA, Talbot Rice A.G., City Art Centre (Edinburgh), Third Eye Gallery (Glasgow), Camden Arts Centre, Leinster Gallery, Houldsworth FA, Art First (London), Pier Art Centre (Stromness), Aberdeen A.G., Seagate (Dundee), Maclaurin (Ayr), Stavanger (Norway), Lulea (Sweden), Kemi (Finland), Morioka (Japan), National Museum of Scotland (Edinburgh). *Works in collections*: Scottish Arts Council, Edinburgh Museums and Galleries, University of Edinburgh, Contemporary Art Soc., Aberdeen Art Gallery,

Hunterian Museum, Kulturoget, Lulea Sweden. *Commissions*: Hugh MacDiarmid Memorial, Langholm; Compaq Computers Commission, Glasgow; Newcraighall Mining Commission, Edinburgh; Poachers Tree, Maclay, Murray and Spens; Motherwell Heritage Centre; Hunterian A.G., Glasgow; Aberdeen City. *Address*: Maxton Cross, Maxton, St. Boswells, Roxburghshire TD6 0RL. *Signs work*: "Jake Harvey".

HARVEY, Michael, Winsor & Newton Prize. *Medium*: oil, drawing. *b*: Bristol, 7 Oct 1946. *s of*: adopted. *m*: Alison. three *d*. *Educ*: I was exposed to education, left with no qualifications at 15. *Studied*: Royal West of England Art School (Commercial Art, for two years). *Exhib*: RA Summer Exhbn; Arnolfini Gallery, Bristol; RWEA Autumn Exhbn.; 6 Chapel Row Gallery, Bath; private exhbn in London. *Works in collections*: London, Germany, Rome. *Works Reproduced*: in exhibition catalogues. *Recreations*: music, gardening, architecture, books. *Misc*: I work as a general builder/plaster and carpentry. *Address*: Goulters Mill, Nettleton, Chippenham SN14 7LL. *Signs work*: 'M.Harvey'.

HARVEY, Michael Anthony, NDD (1957), FRSA (1972), Linton prize (1973); artist in oil, pastel; journalist and art critic; mem. SGFA, Reigate Soc. of Artists, life mem. IAA (Unesco). *b*: Kew. divorced. *s of*: E.C. Harvey, solicitor. one *s*. *Educ*: Bryanston. *Studied*: Wimbledon School of Art (1955-57). *Exhib*: Whibley, Rutland, Fine Arts, Qantas and Connoisseur Galleries W1., Brighton Pavilion, Portsmouth Museum, and Melbourne, Oslo, Dortmund; fourteen one-man shows. *Works in collections*: Johns Hopkins University, Camden Council, E. Sussex Council. *Works Reproduced*: BBC TV, The Times, Standard, Artist. *Clubs*: Royal Society of Arts, London. *Address*: 15 Waterloo Sq., Bognor Regis, W. Sussex PO21 1TE. *Signs work*: "Michael" or "Michael A. Harvey."

HARVEY, Pat: see YALLUP, Pat .

HARVEY, Patricia, BA, SGFA. *Medium*: watercolour and mixed media. *b*: Isleworth, London, 18 Jun 1942. *m*: Ralph Harvey. *Studied*: Sussex University; Kingston School of Art (part-time). *Exhib*: Royal Institute of Painters in Watercolour; Brighton Festival; Menier Gallery; Arundel Festival. *Works in collections*: France, UK, Middle East, Sweden, USA. *Commissions*: EMI 'Continental Collection' (illustration); ASU Records (France), Marianne Melodie Records (France, illustration). *Publications*: Artists & Illustrators. *Recreations*: networking. *Clubs*: Arts Centre Group. *Misc*: writer and researcher, television arts documentaries. *Address*: 2 Britannia Quay, River Road, Littlehampton, W.Sussex, BN17 5DB. *Email*: patkayharvey@talktalk.net *Website*: www.sgfa.org *Signs work*: "PAT HARVEY".

HASTE, Kendra, BA (Hons) Illustration, MA Natural History Illustration; BBC Wildlife Art Award (1999); Artists for Nature Foundation Award (1997). *Medium*: sculpture. *b*: London, 25 Jan 1971. *d of*: David Haste MA RCA. *Studied*: Wimbledon School of Art (1989-90); Foundation, Camberwell College of Art (BA, 1990-93); RCA (MA, 1996-98). *Represented by*: Patrick Davies Contemporary Art. *Exhib*: solo shows: The Air Gallery, London (2003); Midlands Art Centre, Birmingham (2003); Gloucester Road Tube Station; Beaux Arts, Bath; The Burrell Collection, Glasgow; Kelvingrove Museum & AG, Glasgow; Waterloo Station; Harvey Nicholls; 'Royal Beasts' exhibition at the Tower of London (2011). *Works in collections*: Eric & Jean Cass Collection; London Underground; The Tower of London; many private collections. *Commissions*: private commissions in Europe and USA. *Publications*: 'Modern British Sculpture' by Guy Portelli; 'Animals -A First Art Book' (Francis Lincoln); 'Tigers - Artists for Nature in India'; 'Bleep - The Eric and Jean Cass Collection'. *Official Purchasers*: London Underground; historic Royal palaces. *Address*: 2 Chalk Lane, Epsom, Surrey KT18 7AR. *Email*: kendra.haste@ntlworld.co.uk *Website*: www.kendrahaste.co.uk *Signs work*: 'K Haste' or 'KH'.

HASTINGS, Gerard, MA. Awards: Francis Williams Prize: Fine Art (UCW, 1981); Sir Ben Bowen-Thomas Prize: Art History (UCW, 1981); MacFarlane Walker Bursary for

Painting (1984); Edward Albee Foundation Scholarship (1985); Head of History of Art Department: Brixton College (1984-91), Head of History of Art, MPW College, South Kensington (1991-2009); Painter: acrylic, collage. Also photographer, collector, writer, curator, lecturer, art historian. *b*: Gateshead, 15 Jan 1960. *Partner*: David Evans. *Exhib*: selected solo exhibitions include: 273 Gallery, London (1984), Ashawagh Hall, Long Island, New York (1985), Osborne Gallery, London (1987); Consort Gallery (1991), Globe Centre Gallery, Whitechapel, London (2001-08). Selected group exhibitions since 1980 include: National Library of Wales (1980), Oriel, Cardiff (1982), Consort Gallery, Imperial College, London (1983, 1984), Printmakers Council (1985), Peter Loonam Gallery, New York (1985, 1986), Royal Overseas Leaugue (1984, 1991), ICA, London (1991, 1992), Inaugural Exhibition, MoMA, Machynlleth, Wales (1992), The Gallery, Old Burlington Street (1995), Art Forum (1996); Osborne Samuel, Bruton Street, London (2009); Jonathan Clark Fine Art Gallery, London (2009). *Works in collections*: private and public (UK, Europe, USA). *Publications*: 2011: 'Keith Vaughan: Gouaches, Drawings and Prints' (Osborne Samuel); 2012: 'Drawing to a Close: The Final Journals of Keith Vaughan (Pagham Press); 'Keith Vaughan' (with Philip Vann) (Lund Humphries). *Recreations*: Opera, Ballet, Food. *Misc*: Artist-in-Residence, Salisbury Festival (collaboration with and designs for Sir Alan Bates "A Muse of Fire" (1988). Lives in London. *Email*: gerard_hastings@yahoo.co.uk *Website*: www.modernbritishart.net *Signs work*: "Hastings".

HAUGHTON, Patrick, Cert.Ed., NSA (member 1996). *Medium*: drawing, painting. *b*: Devonport, 27 Dec 1942. *s of*: Thomas Haughton. *m*: Suki (née Dullea). two *s*. one *d*. *Educ*: Barnstaple Grammar School, Devon. *Studied*: Exeter College of Art (1963); West of England College of Art (Bristol, 1964-67). *Represented by*: Market House Gallery, Marazion; Grapevine Gallery, Norfolk. *Exhib*: solo and group exhbns: Falmouth Art Gallery, Cornwall (1997); Michael Wright Fine Art, Bristol (1998-2001); Minster Fine Art, York (2004); Royal West of England Academy "Cornish Perspective" (2009). *Works in collections*: collection 'La Grande Vigne' Dinan, France; private collections Europe, USA and South Africa. *Commissions*: Cornish Theatre Collective (2001-2007): set designs. *Publications*: 'Another View: Art in St.Ives' by Marion Whybrow (1996); St.Ives 1975-2005, 'Art Colony in Transition' by Peter Davies (2005). *Works Reproduced*: '20 Years of Contemporary Art' (Falmouth Art Gallery, 2000); 'Drawing to the End of the Century' (Newlyn Society of Artists, 1996). *Recreations*: travel, music. *Misc*: Artist-in-Residence - Les Amis de la Grande Vigne, Dinan, France (2004). *Address*: 'Elusive Cottage', 74A Lower Market Street, Penryn, Cornwall TR10 8BH. *Email*: patrick.haughton@talktalk.net *Website*: www.axisweb.org/artist/patrickhaughton www.nsanewlyn.com/newlyn-society-of-artists/patrick-haughton *Signs work*: 'Patrick Haughton'.

HAVSTEEN-FRANKLIN, Eleanor, MA Printmaking, PgDip Art Therapy; 3rd Prize Eastern Open (2009) & Bainbridge Open (2011); BITE (2012); Pushing Print (2012); Eastern Approaches (2012, 2013). *Medium*: prints. *b*: Aeroskobing, Denmark, 1973. *d of*: Alan & Collette Havsteen-Mikkelsen. *m*: Dominik. two *s*. one *d*. *Studied*: Chester Univeristy (BA (Hons, 1st Class Art with Psychology 1997); Hertfordshire University (PgDip Art Therapy, 1999); Camberwell College of Arts (MA Printmaking, 07). *Represented by*: The Print Room, London; Art Dog, London; Bircham Gallery, Norfolk. *Exhib*: selected group: Northern Print Biennale 2009, Newcastle; Guanlan International Print Biennale, Shenzhen, China (2009 2013); 'Travelling Light', WW Gallery, London & Venice Biennale, Italy (2009); Originals, London (2008-2012); Royal Academy (2008, 2009, 2010, 2013); Open West 2010, Summerfield Gallery, Cheltenham; 6th International Kyoto Hanga, Kyoto Art Museum, Japan 2012); De Queeste Gallery, Abele, Belgium (2014). Solo: 'Inside out' Watford Museum (2012); 'Corpus', Pie Factory, Margate (2013). *Works in collections*: private collections, and Committee of Guanlan International Print Biennale. *Publications*: Royal Academy Illustrated 2010, 'Northern Print Biennale' 2009, Guanlan Print Biennale, 8th International Kyoto Hanga Exhibition, Japan (2012). *Works Reproduced*: Ex nihilo.

Address: 50 Marshall Avenue, St. Albans, AL3 5HS. *Email*: eleanorhavsteen@yahoo.co.uk *Website*: www.eleanorhavsteenfranklin.com *Signs work*: "Eleanor Havsteen-Franklin'.

HAWDON, Paul Douglas, BA (Hons.) (1982), Dip.RA Schools, RE; painter/printmaker in oil, watercolour, etching. *b*: Manchester, 13 Oct 1953. *s of*: Joseph Douglas Hawdon. *m*: Helena Earl. one *d*. *Educ*: Hyde County Grammar School. *Studied*: St. Martin's School of Art (1978-82), RA Schools (1982-85), Rome Scholar, British School (1988-89). *Exhib*: RE, London Group, Twelve Contemporary Figurative Artists, RA, Christie's Print prize (1985, 1990), 11th International Print Biennale, Bradford, Wrexham Print International (2001, 2003), International Print Triennial Cracow (1994). *Works in collections*: Metropolitan Museum of Fine Art, NY; University of Wales, Aberystwyth. *Publications*: Printmaking Today Vol.4 No.2. *Clubs*: Chelsea Arts. *Address*: 9 Worts Causeway, Cambridge CB1 8RJ. *Signs work*: "Paul Hawdon" or "P.D.H."

HAWKEN, Anthony Wellington John, ARBS (1979), Cert. RAS Sculpture (1971); sculptor in plastics and stone, etcher. *b*: Erith, Kent, 4 Jul 1948. *s of*: Ronald Hawken, FCA., FICA. *m*: Deirdre Bew. two *s*. *Educ*: Northumberland Heath Secondary Modern School. *Studied*: Medway College of Art (1965-68, John Cobbett), RA Schools (1968-71, Willi Soukop). *Exhib*: Hammersmith Summer Exhbn., RBS, Chichester, Stratford upon Avon; one-man show, Blackheath Gallery. *Address*: Studio 74b, Lee High Road, London SE13 5PT. *Signs work*: "A. Hawken."

HAWKES, Ben, BA Hons Illustration. *Medium*: mixed media. *b*: Norwich, 22 Mar 1979. *Studied*: North Oxfordshire School of Art and Design. *Represented by*: Private View Illustrations Agency. *Commissions*: Bloomsbury Picture Book "Bad, Bad, Dog", Random House Picture Books "London A, B, C" & "What is a Crocodile's Favourite Thing?"; The Times; Specsavers; Thomas Pink; FHM; Shell; GQ. *Address*: Flat 5, Herne Hill Mansions, Herne Hill, London SE24 9QN. *Email*: benhawkes1@gmail.com *Website*: www.benhawkes.co.uk

HAWKES, Justin Sheridan, Byam Shaw Diploma, London Diploma, Graham Hamilton Drawing Award. *Medium*: oil, watercolour, drawing, prints. *b*: Cambridge, 7 Oct 1955. *s of*: Leo & Violet Hawkes. *m*: Laura Charles. two *d*, Amelia & Olivia. *Educ*: Foundation Cambridge Art School (1978-79). *Studied*: Byam Shaw (1979-82). *Represented by*: Oeno Gallery PEC Ontario. *Exhib*: Oeno Gallery, PEC Ontario, Canada (2006), Edogawa Cultural Centre, Tokyo (1990), Gallery Iseyoshi Ginza, Tokyo (1990), Bodily Gallery, Cambridge (1994), Amalgam Gallery, London (1995), Royal Watercolour Society, London (1999-2005), Royal Society of British Artists, Mall Galleries (2010), RBSA (2011, 2012), RWS (2012, 2013, 2014). *Works in collections*: Suginoko Yo Chien Kindergarten, Japan. *Commissions*: Cambridge Camerata UK; Chilford Hall, Linton, UK. *Official Purchasers*: Suginoko Yo Chien Kindergarten, Japan; Edogawa Cultural Centre, Tokyo. *Works Reproduced*: Chilford Hall wine label; Camerata Concert programmes. *Recreations*: jazz, piano, cycling. *Misc*: painting conservator, City Desk Publications. *Address*: 2A The Old Rectory Drive, Dry Drayton, Cambridge, CB23 8BU. *Email*: hawkes@justinhawkes.com *Website*: www.justinhawkes.com *Signs work*: "JUSTIN HAWKES".

HAWKINS, Barbara, *Medium*: ceramics, porcelain, jewellery; artist in acrylic, watercolour and oil. *b*: Yorks., 18 Oct 1952. *m*: Michael Hawkins. two *d*. *Studied*: St. Albans and Bristol. *Exhib*: Port Isaac Pottery and Gallery. *Works in collections*: internationally. *Clubs*: Fellow, Craft Potters Assoc. *Address*: Port Isaac Pottery, Roscarrock Hill, Port Isaac, Cornwall PL29 3RG. *Signs work*: " MBH."

HAWKINS, Diana, NS, NAPA, FRSA; Euro-Art; (Village's Europeens d'Artistse's); work inspired by light and atmosphere; Stephen Martin Award, Best Oil; Rural/Landscape painter. *Medium*: paints in oil - acrylic. *m*: Denis Baxter, RWA, RBA. *Exhib*: RWA, RBA,

SWA, "Not the Royal Academy", "A Million Brushstrokes" (annual miniature exhibition), Llewellyn Alexander Gallery London; .Bath Society of Artists. Euro-Art. Brussels - Worpswede - Ahrenshoop - Kronberg - also with National Society - Munich - Euro-Art. Barbizon, France. La Defense, Paris, 1st Euro-Art Exhibition, Christchurch, England, 1st Salon Municipal "La Roche Bernard En Quatre Saisons" Hotel de Ville, Brittany. 2003; Winchester Art Gallery - Southampton Art Gallery; St. Barbes Art Gallery; Webbs Road, Fine Art Gallery, London and Euro Art (touring) Ousterbeck, Holland. *Works in collections*: private collections in England, Germany, France, Australia, Switzerland, South Africa, America. *Commissions*: many for private individuals. *Publications*: Royal Publications; recorded artist in 'The Society of Women Artists List of Exhibitors Book 1855-1996' (4 works hung in 2004 SWA Exhibition at Mall Galleries). *Works Reproduced*: in Robert Cole's "Artists and Illustrators around the New Forest and Solent"; 'Home Interiors' magazine. *Principal Works*: landscapes & rural buildings, large skies. *Recreations*: landscape photography. *Clubs*: Royal Overseas, London, RSA House, London. *Misc*: National Trust Workshops for school children; council member, National Society; made Fellow of the Royal Society of Arts (2000). *Address*: Knightley House, Middle Road, Sway, Lymington, Hants., SO41 6AT. *Email*: ruralart.knightley@btinternet.com *Signs work*: 'Diana Hawkins' (and year).

HAWKINS, Michael, potter. *b*: 2 Aug 1950. *m*: Barbara. two *d*. *Studied*: Redruth School of Art, Cornwall. *Exhib*: London, Edinburgh, Bath, etc. Work in collections internationally. *Clubs*: Fellow, Craft Potters Assoc. *Address*: Port Isaac Pottery, Roscarrock Hill, Port Isaac, Cornwall PL29 3RG. *Signs work*: "MBH."

HAWKINS, Philip Dennis, FGRA; artist in oil, pencil; President, Guild of Railway Artists (1988-98). *b*: B'ham, 26 Sep 1947. *s of*: Dennis Walter Arthur Hawkins. *m*: Sonya. one *s*. one *d*. *Educ*: Lordswood Boys' Technical School, B'ham. *Studied*: B'ham College of Art (1964-68). *Exhib*: NRM York, Science Museum, B'ham, Festival Hall London, regularly with GRA. *Works in collections*: B'ham Post and Mail Ltd., Bristol United Press, BBC, Docklands Light Railway, European Passenger Services, Railfreight, Freightliner, Midland Metro, Royal Mail. *Publications*: Fine art prints, work featured in calendars, greetings cards, magazines, books, etc.; book: (autobiography and paintings, etc.) Tracks on Canvas (1998). Co-director, Quicksilver Publishing. *Address*: 112 Chaffcombe Rd., Sheldon, Birmingham B26 3YD. *Signs work*: "Philip D. Hawkins."

HAY, Ian, NDD (1960), ARCA (Painting 1963); awarded the Andrew J. Lloyd prize for landscape painting; artist in pastel, water-colour, etching, art lecturer; Senior Lecturer in drawing, Colchester School of Art, retired from teaching (2000); awarded Hon. Doctorate (2009) by Essex University for his contribution to East Anglian Art. *b*: Harwich, 25 Jan 1940. *s of*: the late John Hay. *m*: Teresa Sliska. two *s*. *Educ*: Harwich School. *Studied*: Colchester School of Art (1955-60, Hugh Cronyn), RCA (1960-63, Ruskin Spear). *Exhib*: RA Summer Exhbn, Craftsman Gallery and Minories, Colchester, Sandford Gallery, London, Phoenix Gallery, Lavenham, Wivenhoe Arts Centre, Patisserie Valerie, London SW3, Highgate Fine Art, London N6, Digby Gallery, Colchester, Hayletts Gallery, Maldon, major retrospective exhibition 'A Life Drawing' held at Minories Gallery 2010. *Works in collections*: Doncaster City A.G., The Guildhall A.G., Graves A.G., Sheffield, Essex University, Essex County Council, Colchester Borough Council. *Commissions*: A series of paintings commissioned by Ernst & Young for their office space in Birmingham (1996). *Recreations*: pottering. *Clubs*: Colchester Art Soc., Hon. Member. *Address*: 32 Tall Trees, Mile End, Colchester, Essex CO4 5DU. *Website*: www.members.aol.com/ianhaygallery *Signs work*: "Ian Hay."

HAYDEN, Toni, SBA (1985), FLS (1995), ASBA (1995), St. Cuthbert's Mill Award (1995), RHS medals: SGM (1981), GRM (1982), SM (1984, 1995); artist and calligrapher, graphite figure drawings, animal and flower paintings in gouache, pencil portraits; professional artist and tutor; BA Linguistics. *b*: Woodbridge, Suffolk, 22 Aug 1938. *m*: Anthony Hayden (divorced). two *s*. *Educ*: Notre Dame High School. *Studied*: Norwich School of Art (1954-55, Noel Spencer, Alan Webster). *Exhib*: Yasuda Kasai, Tokyo, RHS Westminster, SBA Mall Galleries, Hunt, USA. *Works in collections*: Hunt Inst. for Botanical Documentation, BM (NS), V&A, London University (QMC) Shirley Sherwood, John Innes Centre. *Commissions*: Specialises in magnolia paintings, animal portraits, personalised calligraphy. *Publications*: in progress: 'How to Paint Flowers', 'San Francisco to Go' and 'A Hole New Way of Drawing'. *Address*: 6 Belvedere Pl., Norwich NR4 7PP. *Email*: tonihayden@ntlworld.com *Website*: www.tonihayden.com *Signs work*: "Toni Hayden".

HAYES, Georgia, painter in oil; shortlisted for Wollaston Prize (2000, 2003, 2006). *b*: Aberdeen, 1946. *m*: Robert. one *s*. two *d*. *Studied*: under Roy Oxlade (1977-1982). *Represented by*: Sardac, Lectoure, France. *Exhib*: Towner Gallery, 1991; John Moores 1993, 2008; Oriel Mostyn 1993; Flowers East, London; Harlech 94 International; Maidstone Museum 1995; Brighton Museum; Maidstone Museum 1996; Art First, London 2001; Royal Academy Summer Ex: 1990, 94, 96, 98-2008. 2010. 2013; Transition, London 2009; Turner, Margate 2009; Aberystwyth Arts Centre; Galerie d'Ys, Brussels 2011; Solo Exhibitions; Riviera Gallery, Hastings 1995; Harriet Green Gallery, London 1997; Maidstone Library Gallery 1999; Aberdeen Art Gallery 2000; San Francisco MOMA Artists' Gallery, USA 2002; Cafe Gallery Projects, London; Fred Spratt, San Jose, USA 2003, National Gallery Costa Rica 2006; HQ Lewes 2008; Transition, London (2013). *Works in collections*: National Gallery of Costa Rica; New Hall, Arts Council Collection. *Clubs*: Chelsea Arts Club. *Address*: Diamonds, Bells Yew Green, E. Sussex TN3 9AX. *Email*: georgiahayes@googlemail.com *Website*: www.georgiahayes.com *Signs work*: "Georgia Hayes."

HAYNES, Alexandra, BA; artist in oil and water-colour. *b*: 17 Mar 1966. *Educ*: New Hall, Boreham, Chelmsford, Essex. *Studied*: Shrewsbury Foundation Course, Cheltenham Art College (Michael Hollands, Leslie Prothero). *Exhib*: Mail on Sunday, Dover St. (1988), Contemporary Fine Art Gallery, Eton; one-man shows: Soloman Gallery, London (1988), Mistral Gallery, London (1989, 1990, 1991), Flying Colours Gallery, Edinburgh (1990), Bruton Street Gallery (1992). *Publications*: A Life with Food, Peter Langan by Brian Sewell. *Address*: Edgcote, Banbury, Oxon. OX17 1AG. *Signs work*: "A. Haynes."

HAYWARD, Louse May, RE, SWE; BA (Hons) Fine Art/Painting; MA Printmaking. *Medium*: prints. *b*: London, 17 Apr 1963. *m*: Chris Hall. one *s*. *Studied*: Wimbledon College of Art (1983-86); Camberwell College of Arts (1991-93). *Exhib*: RA Summer Exhibition (2013); Society of Wood Engravers 76th Annual Exhibition, Bankside Gallery and touring (2013); Print of the Month at the V&A (2013); RE Summer Exhibition Bankside Gallery (2013).*Works in collections*: Victoria and Albert Museum, Ashmolean Museum, many private collections. *Clubs*: Fellow of the Royal Society of Painter-Printmakers, Member of the Society of Wood Engravers. *Address*: 284 Queen's Road, New Cross Gate, London SE14 5JN. *Email*: louise.hayward1@btinternet.com *Website*: louisehayward.co.uk *Signs works*: "LOUISE HAYWARD".

HAYWARD, Timothy John, painter in water-colour, oil and gouache; freelance illustrator (1975-2000). *b*: Weybridge, Surrey, 24 Dec 1952. *m*: Catherine. three *d*. *Educ*: King's College, Taunton. *Studied*: Somerset College of Art. *Represented by*: Jonathan Cooper, Park Walk Gallery. *Exhib*: solo exhibs. Park Walk Gallery, London (2001, 2003, 2005, 2007, 2009), Fine Art Fair, Olympia (2002); BADA Antiques Fair (2005, 2006, 2007); Chomé Gallery, Bath (2004); Form Art Fair, London (2007); IV Centuries of Birds, New York (2004). *Commissions*: many private. *Publications*: many natural history books and publications. *Works Reproduced*: 8 limited edition prints: see www.haywardeditions.com/

5 limited edition prints/ Wildlife and sporting prints. *Address*: c/o Jonathan Cooper, Park Walk Gallery, 20 Park Walk, London SW10 0AQ. *Email*: mail@jonathancooper.co.uk *Website*: www.jonathancooper.co.uk *Signs work*: "Tim Hayward."

HAYWARD-HARRIS, Martin John, DIPAD, SIAD, artist and sculptor of wildlife subjects in oil, water-colour, etchings, bronze. *b*: Reading, 28 Oct 1959. *s of*: John Stanley Harris. *Educ*: Maiden Erlegh Comprehensive. *Studied*: Berks. College of Art and Design (1978-84). *Represented by*: Birdscapes Gallery; Anthony Woodd Gallery. *Exhib*: SWLA, BTO, RSPB, WTNC; one man show: Phyllis Court Club, Henley-on-Thames (1990, 1993), East African Wildlife Soc, DSWF AFC Vancouver, Henley Festival (2014). *Works in collections*: Natural History Museum London, Zoologisk Museum, Copenhagen; Gilded Tiger 2063; Nature in Art Museum, Gloucestershire; The Woburn Collection. *Publications*: Bird Art and Photography Artists for Conservation (2009,13); The Chase, Arab Horse Society. *Works Reproduced*: etchings published by H.C. Dickins, auctioned at Sotheby's; Birding World; cover illustration 'In Search of Stones' M. Scott Peck, M.D. auctioned at Christie's. *Principal Works*: Jewel in the Crown; Spirit of Freedom. *Address*: 36 Underhill, Moulsford, Wallingford, Oxfordshire OX10 9JH. *Website*: www.hayward-harris.co.uk *Signs work*: "Martin Hayward-Harris."

HAZLEWOOD, Robin, RI, NDD. *Medium*: watercolour and gouache. *b*: Meriden, Warks., 18 Mar 1944. *s of*: E.R.Hazlewood & N.Parker. *m*: Pauline (1st, decd), Harriett (2nd). one *s*. *Educ*: King Henry VIII School, Coventry. *Studied*: Coventry College of Art (1960-65); Liverpool College of Art (1965-66). *Exhib*: Royal Academy; Mall Galleries; South London Art Gallery; Camden Art Centre; RWS Galleries; Bankside; Conningsby Gallery, London; Workhouse Gallery, London; Chelsea Arts Club Gallery; RAC Pall Mall; The Little Gallery, London. *Works in collections*: in Britain, France, Spain, USA, Hong Kong and Australia. *Publications*: 'Introduction to Drawing' (Arcturus, 2004). *Works Reproduced*: magazines related to water colour painting. *Recreations*: reading, walking, and looking. *Clubs*: Chelsea Arts, Two Brydges. *Misc*: Freedom of the City of London (1994), the Goldsmiths' Company; Head of Putney School of Art (1972-83); Head of Sir John Cass Faculty of Art (1983-86); Vice Provost London Guildhall University (1986-95); mem. RI (2002). *Address*: 16 Beverley Path, Barnes, London SW13 0AL. *Email*: robin@hazlewood-art.com *Signs work*: 'Robin Hazlewood'.

HAZZARD, Charles Walker, FRBS; BA (Hons.) Fine Art (1987), Sir Henry Doulton School of Sculpture (1988-90), Postgrad. H.Dip. Sculpture (1991); sculptor and fabricator in wood; Brother, Art Workers' Guild (1996); Sculpture Fellow, Loughborough University School of Art and Design (1996-98, 1998-99); Arts Council Awards for Individuals (2003, 2007); Elmkey Foundation Arts Award (2007). *b*: B'ham, 5 Feb 1964. *s of*: Frank Hazzard, architect. *Studied*: Cheltenham University (1984-87, Roger Luxton), Sir Henry Doulton School of Sculpture (1988-90, Colin Melbourne), City and Guilds of London (1990-91, Allen Sly). *Exhib*: national shows. *Publications*: books illustrated: Encyclopedic Techniques of Sculpture (1995); monograph: Charles Walker Hazzard, Sculpture, Structures, Drawing (pub. 2009). *Address*: 6 Clydesdale Road, Droitwich. Worcs. WR9 7SA. *Email*: studio@charleswalkerhazzard.com *Website*: www.charleswalkerhazzard.com *Signs work*: "C.W.H." or not at all.

HEADLEY, Catherine Louise, BA (Hons) Fine Art. *Medium*: oil, printmaking. *b*: Leicester, 13 Apr 1948. *d of*: Sidney W.Headley. *m*: Trevor Tanser. *Studied*: Somerset College of Art; Bath Academy of Art, Corsham. *Represented by*: Bircham Gallery, Holt, Norfolk; Stoneman Gallery, Penzance, Cornwall; Stour Gallery, Shipton-on-Stour, Glos; Leicester Print Workshop; Belgrave Gallery St. Ives, Cornwall. *Exhib*: RA Summer Exhbn (1987, 89, 92, 94, 95, 97, 98, 2003, 06); Singer & Friedlander British Watercolour (1998); RI (1988, 90, 95, 96, 97, 98); Royal Society of Painters in Watercolour (1990, 91, 92, 95).

Address: 12 Wheel Lane, Barrowden, Rutland LE15 8ER. *Email*: headleycatherine@aol.com *Website*: Catherine Headley.co.uk *Signs work*: 'Headley'.

HEALER, George, ARBS (1974); sculptor in clay, plaster, wood, cast aluminium, brass and bronze. *b*: 25 Sep 1936. *s of*: John Healer. *m*: Brenda Maureen Healer. one *s*. two *d*. *Educ*: Bullion Lane School. *Studied*: Sunderland College of Art (1952-56) under Harry Thubron, ARCA, and Robert Jewell, ARCA. *Exhib*: RA, RGI, Commonwealth Institute, Woolgate House, London, D.L.I. Durham City, Gulbenkian Gallery, Newcastle-upon-Tyne. *Works in collections*: life-size figures of John and Josiphe Bowes, Bowes Museum, Barnard Castle, Co. Durham. *Publications*: article, Aluminium for Schools for the British Aluminium Federation. *Address*: 12 Melville St., Chester-le-Street, Co. Durham DH3 6JF. *Signs work*: "HEALER" hammered into metal with flat chisel.

HEALER, Reuben John, HND (1984); graphic designer/illustrator. *b*: Gateshead, 17 Dec 1963. *s of*: George Healer, ARBS, NDD. *Educ*: Hermitage Comprehensive. *Studied*: graphic design: New College, Durham (NDAD 1980-82); Cumbria College of Art and Design (HND 1982-84). Graphic designer for: Newcastle Architecture Workshop (1984-85), Pendower Hall, EDC (1985-88), By Design, Seaham, Co. Durham (1988). *Address*: 21 Bede Terr., Chester-le-Street, Co. Durham.

HEARD, Peter. *Medium*: acrylic, watercolour. *b*: London, 31 Aug 1939. *Partner*: Mary King. two *d*. *Studied*: self taught. *Represented by*: John Noott Gallery; Bell Fine Arts Gallery; Dot Rouge Ltd. *Exhib*: solo exhibitions: Portal Gallery, London (1978, 1980, 1982, 1985, 1989); Central Square Gallery, New Jersey, USA (1990); Artists Harbour Gallery, Portsmouth (2004, 2006); John Noott Gallery, Worcs. (2007, 2009); group exhibitions: British Primitives, IKON Gallery (1977); Naivi 77, Zagreb (1977); Art Expo, New York (1989-91); Floren Gallery, Poole, Dorset (2008). *Works Reproduced*: Limited Edition Prints by Dotrouge Ltd., London. *Address*: Lings Cottage, Stogumber, Taunton, Somerset, TA4 3SZ. *Email*: peterheard.art@btinternet.com *Website*: peterheard.com *Signs work*: "Peter Heard".

HEARSON, Susan: see VOGEL, Suzi.

HEAT, Ann Olivia, Gordon Hulson award (2007) RBA; Russell Gallery award (2007) RBA; De Laszlo Medal (2011). *Medium*: oil. *b*: Esher, Surrey, 30 Jul 1945. *d of*: Edward Charles Telling. *m*: Trevor Harvey Heat. *Educ*: Waynfleet, Surrey. *Studied*: The Kathleen Browne School under Kathleen Browne and her Polish husband Marian Kratochwil. *Exhib*: RA, RBA, RP, ROI, NEAC. *Clubs*: R.B.A. *Address*: Stumps Grove Farm, Whitehill La., Ockham, Ripley, Surrey GU23 6PB. *Signs work*: "A.H."

HEATH, Crispian, Craft and Design selected 2013 Gold Award Glass. *Medium*: Sculpture, cast glass. *b*: Cuckfield, 29 Jan 1958. *m*: Wendy. two *d*. *Studied*: Plymouth College of Art and Design (2003-07); Sunderland University, MA Glass (2007-09). *Exhib*: Throughout the UK and Washington DC. *Works in collections*: Private. *Publications*: Kiln Forming Glass; Craft & Design Magazine: issue 229: Sep/Oct 2013. *Clubs*: Contemporary Glass Society. *Address*: 86 Queen Alexandra Road, North Shields, Tyne & Wear NW29 9AR. *Email*: mail@crispianheath.com *Website*: www.crispianheath.com *Signs work*: "Crispian Heath".

HEATH, Margaret Felice, NSS (1964); RSMA (2010); Rowland Hilder Prize (1998). *Medium*: Oil, watercolour. *b*: Oxford, 13 Jul 1944. *m*: Trevor Heath. two *d*. *Studied*: Wimbledon School of Art 1960-64). *Represented by*: FBA; Mall Galleries, London; Llewellyn Alexander Gallery, London. *Exhib*: Mall Galleries, London: RSMA (1999); RI (1998-2007); Laing (2000, 2001); SWA (1999, 2000, 2010); Linda Blackstone Gallery, Pinner (2002-08); Watercolour and Drawings Fair (2004-08); Affordable Art Fair (2005-08);

Lincoln Joyce Fine Art, Surrey (2001-11); Llewellyn Alexander Gallery, London (2003-); WH Patterson Gallery, London (2011, 2012). *Works in collections*: Private collections in Britain and worldwide. *Commissions*: private commissions. *Works reproduced*: By The Art Group (2006); Laing Calendar (2001); Artists and Illustrators (2003); Oxford University Press (1992-97); Pyramid Posters (2011-); Salmon Coast Calendar (2015). *Recreations*: Walking, gardening. *Misc*: Worked as illustrator for advertising and educational books until 1995. Elected RSMA Associate (2006-09); Full member (2010); Hon Secretary (2011-). *Address*: 65 Downs Road, Epsom, Surrey KT18 5JT. *Email*: margaretheath@ntlworld.com *Website*: www.margaretheath.co.uk *Signs work*: "M. HEATH".

HEATH, Michael John, MBE (services to journalism) 2001; 'What the Papers Say' Cartoonist of the Year (1982); Glen Grant Cartoonists of the Year (1978); Pocket Cartoonist of the Year, Cartoonist Club of GB (1977). *Medium*: pen and ink. *b*: London, 13 Oct 1935. *s of*: George Henry Heath/Alice Bremner. *m*: Martha Swift. four *d*. *Studied*: Brighton Art College; trained as animator, Rank Screen Services (1955). *Works in collections*: Saatchi Gallery. *Publications*: Private Eye Cartoon Library (1973, 2nd ed. 1975), Punch Cartoons of Michael Heath (1976), Book of Bores (1976), Star Bores (1979), Bores Three (1983), Love All (1982), Best of Heath (1984), Welcome to America (1985), Heath's Nineties (2000). *Works Reproduced*: weekly in The Spectator, Mail on Sunday, The Sunday Times, Private Eye, Independent. *Recreations*: walking, listening to jazz. *Address*: 6 Chamberlain Street, London NW1 8XB. *Signs work*: Heath.

HEATHCOTE, Peregrine. *Medium*: oil, watercolour, charcoal, drawing, prints. *b*: UK, 10 May 1973. *m*: Louise. one *s*. one *d*. *Educ*: Cheam, Stonyhurst, Harrow. *Studied*: Heatherley School of Art; Florence Fine Art Academy. *Represented by*: Albemarle Gallery; RP. *Exhib*: RA, RP, RBA, Albemarle Gallery, Christie's King Street, Olympia, Guildhall, Hampton Court, Goodwood, Selective Eye. *Works in collections*: McGraw Hill; countless private. *Commissions*: Sultan of Oman; Prince Jeffrey of Brunei; Cilla Black; Julian Fellows; Captains of industry and nobility, livery companies. *Publications*: 'Art of England' (Jul 05); BBC1 documentary 'Star Portrait' (Jun 05). *Works Reproduced*: several - "Supercharged", "Ready to Go", and "Big Easy". *Clubs*: Chelsea Arts Club. *Address*: Flat 11, 85 Cadogan Gardens, London SW3 2RD. *Email*: peregrineheathcote@hotmail.com *Website*: www.peregrineheathcote.com *Signs work*: 'PEREGRINE HEATHCOTE'.

HEATON-HARRIS, Linda Jacqueline. *Medium*: sculpture. *b*: London. *Educ*: Coombe County Girls School. *Studied*: Shenstone Teacher Training College; self-taught, no formal art training. *Exhib*: Liberty's; Wildlife & Wetlands Trust; Art in Action; Gilbert White Museum Selborne Bi-centenary Exhibition; SWA; Swaine & Adeney, London; Christies Wildlife Auction; United Arab Emirates, Abu Dhabi; Holland & Holland, London, New York; Hammond Innes Gallery, St. James. *Works in collections*: Nature in Art, International Centre for Wildlife art, Glos.; private collections throughout the world. *Commissions*: Phillip Astor, Hever Castle; William Douglas-Hume; Prince Sat Jem Sahib of Nanagar; Clerk of Works, St. Paul's Cathedral. *Publications*: "The Woodcock", Colin McKelvie. *Recreations*: travelling; field trips Africa/Central America; gardening; surfing; music; reading. *Misc*: Artist in Residence, Nature in Art, Wildlife Museum, Glos. *Address*: Upper Oakwood, Honey Lane, Selborne, nr. Alton, Hampshire, GU34 3BS. *Website*: www.lindaheaton-harris.co.uk *Signs work*: monogram (plus year).

HECHLE, Ann, FSSI; calligrapher in vellum, water-colour, gold leaf. *b*: 31 Dec 1939. *d of*: James Hechle, stockbroker. *Studied*: Central School of Art and Crafts (1957-60, Irene Wellington). *Exhib*: many group exhbns. *Works in collections*: Minnesota Manuscript Initiative, USA, V&A, Crafts Study Centre, Farnham, Surrey; Fitzwilliam Museum, Cambridge. *Commissions*: 19 calligraphic panels for St. Mary's Hospital, Isle of Wight. *Publications*: co-author: More than Fine Writing (Life and work of Irene

Wellington). Film: In the Making (B.B.C. 1979). *Address*: The Old School, Buckland Dinham, Frome, Somerset BA11 2QR.

HEDLEY, Paul, DipAD (1971); artist in oil, acrylic and chalks. *b*: 19 Dec 1947. *m*: Dianne Flynn, painter. *Studied*: Medway and Maidstone. *Exhib*: Priory gallery, Broadway; Thompson's Gallery, Aldeburgh & London; Walker Galleries, Harrogate; Jonathan Grant Galleries, Auckland NZ; Morningside Gallery, Edinburgh; Red Rag Gallery, Bath. *Works in collections*: London Borough of Camden, Queen Mary College. *Address*: 6 Powderham Cres., Exeter EX4 6DA. *Email*: paul@dfph.eclipse.co.uk *Signs work*: "Paul Hedley."

HEINDORFF, Michael, MA (1977), Fellow, RCA(1988), Hon. Fellow RCA(2001); painter in oil, water-colour, pencil, print; senior tutor, R.C.A. (1980-99). *b*: Braunschweig, Germany, 26 Jun 1949. *s of*: Hans Heindorff. *m*: Monica Buferd (decd). one *s*. one *d*. *Educ*: Wilhelm Gymnasium, Braunschweig. *Studied*: Braunschweig University (1970-75), RCA (1975-77, Peter de Francia, Philip Rawson). *Exhib*: Bernard Jacobson Gallery, London, New York, Los Angeles (1978-92), RA (since 1988) and others internationally. *Works in collections*: Herzog Anton Ulrich Museum, ACGB, Museum of London, Imperial War Museum; Museum of Modern Art, NY; Tate Gallery; National Gallery, Washington. *Commissions*: Imperial War Museum (1986); Designers Guild (1992). *Publications*: CD-ROM of drawings (1995) and others (1996, 1998, 1999). *Official Purchasers*: Tate, London; MoMA, New York; National Gallery, Washington; V&A London; IWM, London; HAU-M, Braunschweig. *Principal Works*: Drawings *Recreations*: Walking. *Clubs*: Chelsea Arts. *Address*: 2 Shrubland Rd., London E8 4NN. *Email*: heindorff@aol.com *Website*: www.londonartscafe.org.uk/shows/mh/index.htm *Signs work*: "M. HEINDORFF."

HELD, Julie, The Royal Watercolour Society (AMRS) elected 2003, The London Group (elected member 2002); BA (Hons.) (1981), RA Schools Postgrad. Dip. (1985); painter in oil on canvas and water-colour on paper; part-time tutor/lecturer. *b*: 25 Mar 1958. *Studied*: Camberwell School of Art (1977-81, Philip Mathews), RA Schools (1982-85, Peter Greenham). *Exhib*: Piccadilly Gallery, Boundary Gallery, Frank Kafka Gallery (Prague), Leipzig, Hayward Gallery, Cheltenham Open Drawing Exhbns., RA Summer Shows, The Royal Watercolour Society. *Works in collections*: amongst others; Nuffield College, Oxford University, New Hall Cambridge University, Usher Gallery, LSE Open University, Ben Uri Gallery (The London Jewish Museum), Baker McKenzie Corporate. *Commissions*: 1. Chichester 750th Anniversary St Richard of Modern Time "Pilgrimage" catalogues 2. private portraits and paintings commissions. *Publications*: various book covers. *Works Reproduced*: Bridgeman Slide Library. *Address*: 48 Barrington Rd., London N8 8QS. *Email*: info@julieheld.com *Website*: www.julieheld.com *Signs work*: "J. HELD" or "J.H." on small works.

HELLER, Rachel Pearl, painter in oil, pastel, charcoal. *b*: London, 15 Sep 1973. *Studied*: Byam Shaw School of Art, Slade, Prince's Foundation, Hammersmith and W. London College. *Exhib*: John Jones Art Centre (1997), Flowers East Gallery (1998-2000). *Works in collections*: various, private. *Address*: 53 Fitzroy Park, London N6 6JA. *Signs work* "Rachel Heller."

HELLMAN, Louis Mario, MBE (1993), B.Arch (1962); Hon. Doc. Oxford Brookes Univeristy (2002), architect, designer, cartoonist, painter in acrylic, water-colour and collage. *b*: 19 Mar 1936. *m*: Maria. one *s*. one *d*. *Studied*: Bartlett School of Architecture, University College, London, Ecole des Beaux Arts, Paris. *Exhib*: Architectural Assoc. (1978), Interbuild (1991-1993), Cambridge (1996), Sir John Soane's Museum (2000); Barcelona (2001), Shrewsbury (2006). *Works in collections*: RIBA Drawings Collection, V&A, London, Sir John Soane's Museum. *Publications*: Architecture for Beginners (1986), Do It With an Architect (1999), Archi-Têtes (2000), Architecture A to Z (2001). *Recreations*: music, cinema, theatre, travel. *Clubs*: Cartoonists Club of Great Britain. *Address*:

6 Montague Gardens, London W3 9PT. *Email*: info@louishellman.co.uk *Website*: www.louishellman.co.uk *Signs work*: "L Hellman."

HELY HUTCHINSON, Nicholas David. *Medium*: oil, gouache, pastel, prints. *b*: London, 30 Apr 1955. one *s*. one *d*. *Educ*: Harrow School. *Studied*: St.Martins School of Art (1975); Bristol Polytechnic (Faculty of Art & Design, 1975-78). *Represented by*: Portland Gallery. *Exhib*: Montpelier Studio, London (1984, 1986, 1988, 1990, 1992, 1994, 1996); Gallery Svetlana, Munich (1987); Solomon Gallery, Dublin (1989, 1991, 1993); Wattis Gallery, Hong Kong (1992, 1994, 1996, 1998); Frederick Gallery, Dublin (2000, 2002, 2004); Jorgensen Fine Art - Dublin (2008); Portland Gallery, London (1997, 1998-Edinburgh Festival, 1999, 2001, 2003, 2005, 2006-Art London, 2007, 2009). *Works in collections*: Unilever, Prudential and many more. *Commissions*: Berkeley Hotel, Thames River Capital and others. *Official Purchasers*: Government Art Collection. *Recreations*: art galleries, tennis, squash. *Clubs*: Chelsea Arts Club, Beefsteak Club. *Address*: Little Tredington, Church Road, Pimperne, Dorset, DT11 8UB. *Email*: info@nicholashelyhutchinson.com *Website*: www.nicholashelyhutchinson.com *Signs work*: "NHH".

HEMBLEY, Stephen James, SGFA; Founder of Shire Studios; part-time tutor. Medium: oil colour, pen and ink, acrylics, mixed media. *b*: Bournemouth, 21 Jul 1957. *s of*: Reginald James Hembley. *m*: Rachel Crawford. *Educ*: Winton School. *Studied*: under George Denham at Bournemouth. *Represented by*: Shire Studios. *Exhib*: one-man shows: London, Telford, Shrewsbury, NEC Birmingham, Bournemouth, Lichfield; numerous group shows. Work in private collections worldwide. *Works in collections*: The Webb Collection; Dr & Mrs Crawford. *Commissions*: The Chapel Frescos of The Wrekin Rose Garden, Shropshire; Sherbrook Industries; KRH Precision Engineering; The Christadelphian Church; Russell Cotes Art Gallery & Museum. *Publications*: books illustrated for Tamarisk. *Official Purchasers*: Tamarisk Publishers, Sherbrook Industries, Greenpeace, Amnesty International, Roden Hall, Norton Motorcycles, St. Mary's Church, Lichfield. *Principal Works*: "The Prize Bull", "The Chapel" - Wrekin Rose Garden. *Address*: c/o Shire Studios (Telford), 25 Bishopdale, Telford, Shropshire TF3 1SA. *Email*: shirestudios@virginmedia.com *Signs work*: "S.J. HEMBLEY."

HEMMANT, Lynette, NDD (1958); landscape, gardens and still-life painter in oil, mixed media, black and white drawing, etching and general illustration; International research Fellow of the International Centre for Fine Art Research of Birmingham University. *b*: London, 20 Sep 1938. *m*: Jüri Gabriel, literary agent. *Studied*: St. Martin's School of Art (1954-58, Roger Nicholson, Bernard Cheese, Vivian Pitchforth). *Exhib*: ROI, and various solo and mixed shows in London, Home Counties, Italy and Australia since 1984. *Commissions*: large pieces for private clients. *Works Reproduced*: Heinemann Group, Hamish Hamilton, Random House, O.U.P., I.P.C. magazines, various US publishers, and through Art Archive photo-library. *Address*: 35 Camberwell Grove, London SE5 8JA. *Website*: www.lynettehemmant.com *Signs work*: "HEMMANT."

HEMMING BRAY, Rachel, *Medium*: Oil, watercolour, drawing, prints, pastel, acrylic. *b*: London, 20 Jun 1947. one *s*. *Educ*: St Christopher School, Letchworth, Herts. *Studied*: Central School of Art, London (1965-66); College of St Matthias, Bristol (1966-96). *Exhib*: Larger solo exhibitions: Bristol City Museum and Art Gallery; BBC (Bristol) Broadcasting House; Bristol Old Vic; Theatre Royal; Rugby Museum & Art Gallery; National Theatre, South Bank, London; and mixed exhibitions including RA and RWA. *Works in collections*: Bristol City Museum & Art Gallery; University of Bristol Theatre Collection; BBC Art Collection; The Warwickshire Police Force; The Nat West Art Collection. *Commissions*: Many portrait commissions including bishops, surgeons, actors, film makers, writers and many musicians, geologists etc. *Official Purchasers*: Bristol City Museum & Art Gallery, purchased 9 works; University of Bristol Theatre Collection, purchased 5 works; BBC Art Collection, purchased 40 works of Sir David Attenborough's work in Bristol; The Warwickshire Police Force, purchased 31 works; The Nat West Art Collection, purchased 1 work. *Works Reproduced*: In books: Bristol's Theatre Royal, Old Vic; Moths of the Bristol Region; Berthold Luberkin; Introduction to Painting Portraits by Rosalind Cuthbert; George Street by Judy Greenbury. *Principal Works*: Musicians esp. string quartets including Britten, Allegri and Skampa quartets; Sir David Attenborough and the making of, "Trials of Life" behind the scenes; Subjects at Bristol Museum; Doris Lessing, Author. *Recreations*: Walking, gardening and enjoys music. *Address*: 10 Southernhay Avenue, Clifton Wood, Bristol BS8 4TJ. *Email*: rachelhemmingbray@gmail.com *Website*: www.rachelhemmingbray.co.uk *Signs work*: "RACHEL HEMMING BRAY" or sometimes "RHB".

HEMPTON, Paul Andrew Keates, MA, RCA; artist in oil paint, water-colour, and etching; Fellow in Fine Art, University of Nottingham (1971-73). *b*: Wakefield, Yorks., 3 Oct 1946. *s of*: Revd. Canon G. B. Hempton, B.A. *m*: Margaret Helena. one *s*. two *d*. *Educ*: King's School, Chester. *Studied*: Goldsmiths' College School of Art (1964-68), RCA (1968-71) under Prof. Carel Weight. *Exhib*: 'British Painting' 74, Hayward Gallery, London; 'John Moores', XI, XIII; '11th Biennale de Paris', MOMA, Paris; Serpentine Gallery, London; Ikon Gallery, Birmingham; Arnolfini Gallery, Bristol; Laing Gallery, Newcastle; 20th Century Watercolour, V&A. *Works in collections*: Arts Council, British Council, V&A, Contemporary Arts Soc., Arnolfini Trust, South West Arts, Leicester Educ. Authority, Nottingham University, Bury, A.G., Newport A.G., Wakefield A.G., Whitworth A.G., Nottingham Castle A.G., Wolverhampton A.G., Wiltshire C.C., Arthur Andersen, London, Campden LBC. *Publications*: 'Dictionary of Twentieth Century British Painters and Sculptors', Frances Spalding. *Works Reproduced*: The Public Catalogue Foundation. *Address*: 9 West End, Minchinhampton, Stroud, Glos. GL6 9JA. *Signs work*: "P.H."

HEMS, Margaret, FSBA, SFP; Royal Drawing Soc. (1940-43), Grenfell Medal RHS (1984-86), Founder mem. FSBA (1985); botanical artist in water-colour and pencil. *b*: Fyfield, Essex, 1 Jan 1931. *m*: John Hems. one *s*. one *d*. *Educ*: Clark's College, Ilford. *Studied*: a period of art classes at Minehead (1981, Sylvia Cave), botanical illustration under Mary Grierson at Flatford Mill. *Exhib*: SBA, HS, Westminster Gallery, Mall Galleries, galleries, West Country, East Anglia, and other mixed exhbns. in England and Wales, Denmark and Austria. *Works in collections*: private: Britain, Europe, USA, Australia. *Commissions*: wrapping paper (Medici); many private commissions. *Publications*: greetings cards for Medici and Parnassus Gallery, numerous exhbn. catalogues. Work featured in 'A History of British Flower Painters 1650-1950', 'Arte Y Botanica' and 'The Art of Botanical Painting' by Margaret Stevens. *Works Reproduced*: Limited edition prints and cards, published by the artist. *Address*: Daubeney Cottage, Water St., Barrington, Somerset TA19 0JR. *Signs work*: "M. Hems" or "M.H." joined.

HENDERSON SMITH, Tom, BA Fine Art; PGCE. *Medium*: drawing, acrylic. *b*: Halifax, 2 Sep 1949. *m*: Gabrielle Hawkes. one *s*. *Educ*: King James's Grammar School, Huddersfield. *Studied*: Newcastle University; Bristol University. *Represented by*: Visions and Journey's Gallery, St Just, Cornwall (1986-1993). *Exhib*: Solo exhibitions: Mariners Gallery, St Ives (2001, 03, 06); Bodmin Shire Hall (2006); Falmouth Poly (2008); Chapel Rowe Gallery, Bath (2010); Trereife House, Penzance (2010); Morvah Gallery, Penzance (2012); Gallery on the Corner, London (2012). Group exhibitions include: Torre Abbey, Devon (2013); Castle Heritage Centre and Art Gallery, Bude (2011); Broadway Gallery, New York (2011); Durham University (2011); Camen Art Gallery, London (2010); Truro Museum, Truro, Cornwall (2002); The Camelford Gallery, Cornwall (2001); Great Atlantic Mapworks Gallery, Cornwall (1998); Newlyn Orion Gallery, Newlyn, Cornwall (1981); Federation of British Artists (1978); Royal Academy Summer Exhibition (1977). *Works in collections*: Private collections in the UK, Europe, USA and Canada. *Commissions*:

Occasional portrait commissions. *Publications*: 'Contemporary Painters' Schiffer (2014); New York Arts Magazine (May 2010). *Works Reproduced*: 'Contemporary Painters' Schiffer (2014). *Principal Works*: Ten Years of Festival Paintings collection (2002-2012); The Turning Year Collection (2012); Lived-in Landscapes collection (2010); In the Ocean Light collection (2008); Shaping a Vision of Cornwall collection (2006); Valleys and Horizons collection (2003); Peninsula Suite collection (2001). *Recreations*: practicing Nichiren Buddhist. Clubs: SGI-UK (Nichiren Buddhist Association); National Acrylic Painters Assocation. *Address*: Berkana, Old Rectory Drive, Bridge Hill, St Columb, Cornwall TR9 6BY. *Email*: tomhendersonsmith@tiscali.co.uk *Website*: www.hendersonsmith.co.uk *Signs work*: "Henderson Smith".

HENOCQ, Ron, Slade Dip. (1973), San Carlos Escuela del Arte MA (1976); artist, Gallery Director, Cafe Gallery since 1984. *b*: 22 Mar 1950. *Address*: Cafe Gallery, Southwark Park, Bermondsey, London SE16 2UA. *Signs work*: "R.Henocq."

HÉNON, Sue, SBA; Owner of Art School in Germany. *Medium*: coloured pencil, oil, watercolour. *b*: Hayes, Middlesex, 8 Jan 1961. *d of*: Derek Bodley. *m*: Sylvain Hénon (artist). *Educ*: Dorcan Comprehensive School, Swindon. *Studied*: Open College of Arts. *Represented by*: SBA. *Exhib*: SBA, Westminster Galleries; Exbury Gardens Five Arrows Gallery; Palmen Garten, Frankfurt; Prinz Georg's Garten, Darmstadt; Schloss Fasanerie, (Besitz-Landgraf Morritz von Hessen); Schloss and Museum Fechenbach-Dieburg; Hofgut Gallery, Reinheim; Darmstadt Kunst Archiv; Museo Centro Gaiàs, Santiago de Compostela, Spain. *Works in collections*: Ratskeller Hausbrauerei GMBH; Sabine Schröder SPD Party; International Women's Club, Frankfurt; Bücher Insel; Kunst Archiv. Darmstadt, Museum Schloss Fechenbach, Town of Dieburg. *Commissions*: The Shah's Jasmine, Orchids, Lotus, Karins' Roses, Isatis tinctoria, Indigofera tinctoria. *Publications*: 'Marianne's Garden'; 'Artists & Illustrators'; Frankfurt Allegemeine; Frankfurt Rundshau, Main-Echo, Darmstadter Echo, Dieburger Anzeiger, Fuldaer Zeitung, Hünfelder Zeitung, Say It With Flowers, Das Blaufärberhandwerk. *Official Purchasers*: Town of Dieburg, Gewo Bau Russellsheim, Förderverein Museum Schloss Fechenbach. *Works Reproduced*: 'Tulip'; 'Spring Tulips'; 'Es War Einmal..', Isatis tinctoria, Indigofera tinctoria, Arctic Poppy. *Principal Works*: 'Tulip'; 'Promises'; 'Pretty Maids in a Row'; 'Pandora's Box'. *Clubs*: Kunst Archiv Darmstadt, The Society of Botanical Artists. *Misc*: Council Member FFMSF. *Address*: Atelier Hénon, Steinstrasse 23, 64807 Dieburg, Germany. *Email*: sue.henon@gmail.com *Website*: www.atelierhenon.de *Signs work*: 'SUE HÉNON SBA'.

HENRIQUES, Benedict James, BA Hons. Fine Art (1986-1990); painter in oil. *b*: 14 Oct 1967. *Studied*: Newcastle-upon-Tyne University. *Exhib*: William Hardie, Glasgow; Browse and Darby, London; National Portrait Gallery (1993, 1998, 1999); Jonathan Cooper Gallery (2001). *Works in collections*: numerous. *Commissions*: assorted. *Address*: 160-162 Old South Lambeth Rd., London SW8 1XX. *Email*: ben.henriques@virgin.net *Signs work*: "B Henriques."

HENTHORNE, Yvonne, Professor, NDD (Painting 1965), ATC (1966), FRSA (1967), Italian Government Bursary (1969), Brazilian Government Scholarship (1971), W. German Research Grant (1974-75); constructed painting; Head of Foundation Studies Dept., Wimbledon School of Art. *b*: Wetherby, Yorks., 1942. *d of*: Leslie Henthorne. *m*: Gary Crossley, Professor, Surrey Institute. one *d*. *Educ*: Grey Coat Hospital, Westminster. *Studied*: London University Goldsmiths' College of Art (1961-66, Patrick Millard, Albert Irwin, Andrew Forge). *Exhib*: open, Young Contemporaries, Tate, Birmingham Festival, Midland Group Gallery, Sheffield Open National, SWA, RBA; one-man shows, Ikon Gallery, Birmingham; Belgrade, Coventry; Laing Gallery, Newcastle-on-Tyne. *Works in collections*: UK, Europe, USA. *Address*: 37 Duke Street, St. James, London SW1Y 6DS. *Signs work*: "Yvonne Crossley."

HEPWORTH, Anthony, BA Hons (1976), Central School. Post Grad Diploma Fine Art (1977). Worked at British Museum 1978-80. Since 1981 has been a dealer. Opened first gallery in Bath in 1985, specialising in 20th Century British painting and sculpture; A Specialist in the work of Keith Vaughan; until recently based in Kensington London SW8. *b*: Wakefield, Yorks, 30 Mar 1952. *s of*: Raymond Hepworth. *m*: Rose. one *d*. *Educ*: South Featherstone Secondary Modern. *Studied*: Pre-Dip & Foundation (Blackpool), BA Hons Fine Art (Bristol) and Central School Post Grad Sculpture. *Exhib*: Acquavella Gallery, New York (1980, sculpture & drawings). *Publications*: compiled Catalogue Raisonne "Keith Vaughan: The Mature Oils 1946-1977" published Sansom & Co, Bristol 2012. *Recreations*: good food and wine, collecting tribal art. *Address*: 16 Margaret's Buildings, Bath BS1 2LP. *Email*: anthony.hepwor@btconnect.com *Website*: www.anthonyhepworth.com

HERBERT, Barry, artist/printmaker, drawings and prints; Head of Fine Art Dept., University of Leeds (1985-92). *b*: York, 19 Mar 1937. *m*: Janet. one *s*. one *d*. *Educ*: Archbishop Holgate's School, York. *Studied*: James Graham College. *Exhib*: 39 one-man shows include: Serpentine Gallery, London (1971), Mappin Gallery, Sheffield (1972), Galerie Brechbühl, Switzerland (1972, 1976, 1979, 1982, 1984), Galerie Steinmetz, Bonn (1979, 1984, 1993, 1995), Karl-Marx-Universität, Leipzig, (1980), Gilbert Parr Gallery, London (1982), Richard Demarco Gallery (1992). *Publications*: 30 editions of prints published in Germany, Switzerland and England; "Barry Herbert - Künstler-Grafiker" (1979); "Barry Herbert" - Drawings and Etchings (1997); 'Barry Herbert- an Argosy of Beauty' (2004- Hirten Presse, Bonn/Berlin). *Address*: 43 Weetwood Lane, Leeds LS16 5NW. *Email*: barryherbert@talktalk.ne. *Signs work*: "Barry Herbert."

HERBST, Günther Daniel, MA Fine Art; Observer Award for New British Artists (2002); IGI Life Vita Art Now - first quarterly award, jointly with William Kentridge (1992). *Medium*: oil, acrylic. *b*: Pretoria, S. Africa, 25 Apr 1963. one *s*. one *d*. *Studied*: Goldsmiths College, Univ.of London (2000-02); Johannesburg Univsity, South Africa (1998-1991, National Higher Diploma Fine Art). *Exhib*: Galerie de L'esplenade, Paris ('Un Art Contemporain d'Afrique de Sud', 1994); Linda Goodman Gallery, SA (1992); Into and Out of Abstraction, Lubomirov-Easton (2014); The Man Who Wasn't There, Gallery AOP, South Africa (2012). Two solo shows with One in the Other (2007, 2009). *Works in collections*: Johannesburg Art gallery, Collection William Kentridge; Iziko National Gallery; Cambridge University Anglo America, Gencor, The New Art Gallery, Walsall. *Publications*: RA Catalogue Summer Exhbn (2003); RA Magazine no.79 (Summer 2003); Observer Magazine (8 Sep 2002); Art Forum (October 2009). *Works Reproduced*: RA Catalogue Summer Exhbn (2003). *Address*: 16b Petticoat Tower, Petticoat Square, Middlesex Street, London E1 7EF. *Email*: guntherdh63@hotmail.com *Website*: www.contemporaryartsociety.co.uk *Signs work*: 'G.Herbst'.

HERICKX, Geoffrey Russell, RMS, HS; Awarded 'Gold Memorial Bowl' at Royal Miniature Society Annual Exhibition (2009), 'Best in Exhibition' Hilliard Society Exhibition (2000); painter in oil and water-colour; teacher, specialist in painting miniatures – all subjects. *b*: Birmingham, 1939. *m*: Maureen. one *s*. one *d*. *Studied*: Birmingham College of Art (1956-58). *Exhib*: three one-man shows in Leicester, work in many private collections, annually at Royal Miniature Soc. and Hilliard Soc. exhibitions. *Publications*: illustrated: Naturalist Summers. *Address*: 33 Ash Tree Rd., Oadby, Leicester LE2 5TE. *Email*: geoffreyherickx@talktalk.net *Website*: geoffreyherickx.com *Signs work*: "G.R. HERICKX."

HERIZ-SMITH, Bridget, BFA (Hons.); award with commendation, History of Art (1977), prizewinner SGA. (1985); part-time tutor Clock House Studios (1979-86); Otley College; UEA; sculptor, figurative. *Medium*: bronze, stone, cement, terracotta. *b*: Hamburg, 13 Dec 1949. *d of*: Audrey Pilkington, painter. one *s*. one *d*. *Educ*: Framlingham Mills Grammar School. *Studied*: Goldsmiths' College, Ravensbourne College (1974-77, Eric

Peskett). *Represented by*: Chalk Hill Contemporary Art, Guildford; Mandell's Gallery, Norfolk. *Exhib*: Sculpture in Anglia (1978, 1981, 1989), R.A. Summer Show (1988, 1992), Musée Lanchelevici, Belgium, Dialogues, St Petersburg, Mercury Gallery, Discerning Eye (1997) Christchurch Mansion, Ipswich, Salthouse 06, Norfolk (2006), Inspirations (2011), Jarrold's Norwich. *Works in collections*: Women's Art, New Hall, Cambridge, Ipswich Borough Council, Norfolk Museums Art Collection. *Commissions*: OOCL Monument, Levington, Suffolk (stone carving); Mother and Child, Cobholm and Lichfield Resource Centre, Great Yarmouth (stone carving). *Publications*: Making the Connection (2002, ISBN 0 948252 13 8); New Hall Art Collection (2003, ISBN 0 9507108 4 9); Artist in our Midst, Green Pebble (2008, ISBN 978-0-9558174-0-9). *Clubs*: groups: Norwich 20, ARC (Gt.Yarmouth). *Address*: 145 Southtown Road, Gt Yarmouth, Norfolk, NR31 0LA. *Email*: b.herizsmith@btinternet.com *Website*: www.bridgetheriz.co.uk *Signs work*: "B.Heriz."

HERON, Susanna, BA (Hons), FRSA, Hon. FRIBA; sculptor. *b*: England, 22 Sep 1949. *Exhib*: solo shows since 1985 include Whitechapel A.G., Camden Arts Centre, Newlyn A.G., Mead Gallery, University of Warwick. *Works in collections*: Stedelijk Museum, Arts Council of England, V&A, CAS, etc., museums in Europe, USA and Australia. *Commissions*: Major public commissions: Consilium European Union, Brussels (1995), sole British representative; front British Embassy, Dublin (1995); Shoreditch Campus, Hackney Community College (1997); Phoenix Project, Priory Place, Coventry City Council (1998-2003); Arnolfini Bristol (1999-2005); Marunouchi Building, Mitsubishi, Tokyo (2002), City Inn, Westminster (2001-2003), Brunswick Centre London (2003-2006); 'Still Point' Metropolitan Cathedral, Liverpool (2003-2007); 'Roche' facade of House of Fraser, Bristol (2008); Sainsbury Laboratory, University of Cambridge 2008-2010. *Publications*: photographs/text: Shima: Island and Garden (Abson, 1992); Stills from Sculpture (Abson, 1999); 'Elements' (Mead Gallery, University of Warwick) published 2003; 'Volume' Stanton Williams (Black Dog Publishing, 2009). *Address*: 39 Norman Gr., London E3 5EG. *Website*: www.susannaheron.com

HERRIOT, Alan B. artist/sculptor in cold cast GRP, painting in oil, acrylic and water-colour; Proprietor, Endeavour Art Studios, Edinburgh. *b*: 20 Feb 1952. *Studied*: Duncan of Jordanstone, Dundee (1969-74, Scott Sutherland, James Morrison). *Exhib*: Aros Centre Skye, Whisky Heritage Centre Edinburgh, Inverary Court House, Fighting Ships (Hartlepool). *Works in collections*: Miner's Monument, Newtongrange, Horse and Figure, Loanhead; 51st Highland Division Liberation Monument, Schijndel (Holland) and Perth (Scotland). *Commissions*: 'Ancient Mariner' 7' statue, Watchet, Somerset. *Publications*: The Foundling; Christmas is Coming; Travellers Tales; Broonies, Silkies and Fairies; Quest for a Kelpie. *Works Reproduced*: military prints. *Principal Works*: Highland Division Memorial. *Recreations*: music. *Address*: Endeavour Art Studios, 75 Trafalgar La., Leith, Edinburgh EH6 4DQ. *Signs work*: "Alan B. Herriot".

HESELTINE, John Robert, B of E.Drawing (1941), B of E Pictorial Design TD (1941), scholarship, Royal College (1942); artist in oil and water-colour, portrait artist; leading name in British illustration (1950s-1970s); descendent of John Postle Hestletine, artist, famous collector, early trustee of National Gallery, a founder of RCA and friend and student of James McNiell Whistler; also related to Peter Worlock, composer. *b*: Ilford, Essex, 14 Sep 1923. *m*: Pam Masco. one *s*. one *d*. *Studied*: SE Essex College of Art (Francis Taylor, ARCA, Allen Wellings, ARCA). *Exhib*: V&A, RWS, RPS, London galleries, including David Messum and W.H. Patterson, and USA Studio and Gallery at East House Petworth. *Works in collections*: Dartmouth Naval College and Museum, Fleet Air Arm Officer's Mess, Yeovilton; private and corporate collections. *Commissions*: many portraits including HM Queen Elizabeth and HRH Duke of York for Royal Naval Air Station, Yeovilton, officers mess, investiture of HRH the Prince of Wales, Bernard Gallagher, Ryder Cup captain for Wentworth golf club. *Publications*: Odhams Press, Fleetway, IPC, London Times, London

Standard, Harpers & Queen, Wentworth Magazine, Surrey Magazine, Twentieth Century Artists by Frances Spalding, Dictionary of British Artists since 1945 by David Buckman. *Clubs*: Wentworth. *Address*: East House, East St., Petworth, W. Sussex GU28 0AB. *Signs work*: "John Heseltine."

HEUGHAN, Christine Joy, (known as Chrissie), BA Hons Fine Art, Drawing and Printmaking; elected professional member Society of Scottish Artists (1996) SSA; Scottish Arts Council (Creative Scotland) Awards (1999, 2006. 2010); Edinburgh Council (2002, 2005); Friends of the Royal Scottish Academy Award (2007); Residency, Mino City, Japan (2001); Fellowship Vermont Studio Centre, USA (2002); The Worshipful Company of Founders, London, Bronze casting. *Medium*: drawing, print, sculpture, artisan paper. *b*: Chelsea, 11 Dec 1950. two *s*. *Studied*: Dumfries and Galloway College, Art and Design, Folio Fine Art (1988-1991); Edinburgh College of Art (1991-1995). *Exhib*: Exhibits UK and internationally: Japan, USA, Hong Kong; regularly exhibits with Society of Scottish Artists; Royal Scottish Academy Open. *Works in collections*: Public and private. *Commissions*: International Design Awards (1998-2003); Curtis Fine Papers; Royal International Caribbean Liners (2000). *Publications*: Susan Wright, Paper Europe, April, pp.64/65 (1999); Jennifer Shaw, Printmaking Today, vol 9, no 4, p.19 (2000). *Official Purchasers*: Dumfries and Galloway Council. *Recreations*: music, watching tennis, garden looking. *Misc*: Lecturer Edinburgh College of Art (1997-2011), Centre for Continuing Studies, mixed media, drawing, sketchbook, paper. *Address*: The Bill Scott Sculpture Centre, Edinburgh Sculpture Workshop, Newhaven, Edinburgh, Scotland EH6 4JT. *Email*: info@chrissieheughanpaper.co.uk *Website*: www.chrissieheughanpaper.co.uk *Signs work*: "Chrissie Heughan".

HEVESI, Michael, BA (Hons) Social Anthropology. *Medium*: photography, sculpture, prints. *b*: Petach Tikva, Israel, 4 Aug 1952. *s of*: Hans Hevesi. *Educ*: Kingston Grammar, Holland Park. *Studied*: Ealing Art School (for 3 weeks); University of Kent, Canterbury (1972-76). *Exhib*: Since 1979 in the UK, Spain, France, Utrecht. *Works in collections*: Spain, UK, USA, Eire, Israel. *Publications*: Gallery Magazine, Western Daily Press, Hampshire Chronicle, Richmond, Sheen & Mortilake Times. *Official Purchasers*: Venezuela, London (Barnes & Fulham). *Works Reproduced*: "Mime in Ballet" Woodstock Winchester Press (2000). *Recreations*: reading, walking, philosophy, poetry, transactional analysis. *Address*: Highfields, 7A Greenway Park, Chippenham, Wiltshire, SN15 1QG. *Email*: m.hevesi@yahoo.co.uk *Website*: www.thecorridoroflife.com *Signs work*: MICHAEL HEVESI, M.HEVESI, M.Hevesi, Womba C.Jester.

HEWITT, John Haslam, BA in Fine Art (Reading) Cert. Ed. ATD. *Medium*: Acrylic 3D painting. *b*: London, 15 Jun 1949. *Educ*: Barrow in Furness Grammar School for Boys. *Studied*: Reading University (Peter Kalkhof, Terry Frost). *Represented by*: Gallery Bastillen, Fredriksberg, Denmark. *Exhib*: Full list of exhibitions on website. *Works in collections*: Greg Arbene Collection, California. *Commissions*: Jorcue Andelmann, Buenos Aires, Argentina; Ernst and Young, London; Mike Boyd, Cumbria; Image Cure, Colorado. *Address*: 21 Festival Road, Millom, Cumbria LA18 5AN. *Email*: johnhewitt99@btinternet.com *Website*: www.abstractacrylicart.co.uk *Signs work*: "J.H. HEWITT" also logo small z within A.

HEWLINGS, Charles, Arts Council Major Award (1979); Wilhelm Lehmbruck Scholarship, Duisburg, Germany (1982); Pollock-Krasner Foundation Grant (2001). *Medium*: sculpture. *b*: Bromsgrove, 8 Aug 1948. *m*. Gina Medcalf. *Studied*: University of Newcastle Upon Tyne (1967-71); St Martin's School of Art, London (1971-73). *Exhib*: Acme Gallery, London (1976); Smith-Jariwala Gallery, London (1990, 1992); Kapil Jariwala Gallery, London (1995); New York Studio Gallery, New York (2002); McLaren Art Centre, Barrie, Ontario Canada (2002); One Canada Square, Canary Wharf, London (2006);

The Cut Arts Centre, Halesworth, Suffolk (2012). *Works in collections*: Arts Council of England; Wilhelm Lehmbruck Museum, Duisburg; Yuzi Paradise Sculpture Park, Guilin, China; private collections in Great Britain, Germany and USA. *Commissions*: George Hormann, Albany NY, USA. *Address*: 64 Acre Lane, London SW2 5SP. *Email*: hewlings@gmail.com *Website*: www.charleshewlings.com *Signs work*: "C.P. HEWLINGS".

HEYWOOD, Denise Suzanne, BA Hons Textile Design, RMS, Assoc SBA, member of Royal Society of Miniature, Painters, Sculptors and Gravers. *Medium*: Watercolour, drawing. *b*: Cheshire, 10 Jan 1960. *m*: David Mills. *Studied*: Loughborough University (1972-1982). *Exhib*: Llewellyn Alexander (Fine Paintings) Ltd, London; Florida, USA; The Mall Galleries, London; Royal Society of Miniature Painters, Sculptors and Gravers; The Westminster Gallery, London; Palmengarten, Frankfurt: Galleri 61, Gothenburg, Sweden. *Commissions*: private and corporate collections internationally. *Works Reproduced*: Fine art prints worldwide. *Misc*: Botanical artist. *Address*: Old Leasowes Farm, Norbury, Bishops Castle, Shropshire SY9 5EA. *Email*: denise@denise-heywood.co.uk *Website*: www.deniseheywood.com *Signs work*: "DENISE HEYWOOD"

HEYWORTH, James Charles, LDAD distinction University of London (1982); illustrator/painter in gouache, water-colour, pen and ink, airbrush. *b*: London, 28 Feb 1956. *s of*: James Heyworth. *Educ*: Wandsworth School. *Studied*: Putney School of Art (1975), Byam Shaw School of Drawing and Painting (1976, D. Nixon), Goldsmiths' College (1979-82, Bernard Cheese). *Exhib*: Battersea Arts Centre, Ripley Arts; one-man Bury Metro Arts Assoc. *Works in collections*: private. *Clubs*: Assoc. of Illustrators. *Address*: 99 Sutton Common Rd., Sutton, Surrey SM1 3HP. *Signs work*: "James Heyworth."

HICKS, Anne Marguerite Christine, RWA, DFA Slade; RWA Prize Winner (with Jerry Hicks) of three dimensional mural competition for Bristol Gas Showroom. *Medium*: oil, gouache, acrylic for portraits; murals; theatre costume design; environmental concepts; the active human figure; and wildlife. *b*: London, 19 Jan 1928. *m*: Jerry Hicks (dec'd). one *s*. one *d*. *Educ*: Hampstead and Minehead. *Studied*: Slade School Schwabe and Coldstream. *Exhib*: RWA annually, British Women Painters at Musée de l'Art Moderne, Paris (1967); Biannual two-person shows with Jerry Hicks; Inaugural exhibition for Grant Bradley Gallery Bristol (2005). *Works in collections*: private collections worldwide. *Publications*: 'A Place for People' - illustrated proposals for Bristol City Docks. *Works Reproduced*: 'An Introduction to Portrait Painting' by Ros Cuthbert; works for RWA. *Principal Works*: Tiled mural for Bristol University Pool; SS Great Britain Hayward Saloon mural (with Jerry Hicks) 1997, 2009; Cast concrete and glass screen entrance Bristol Health Dept. (with Jerry Hicks). *Recreations*: painting and family. *Address*: Goldrush, Gt. George St., Bristol BS1 5QT. *Signs work*: "Anne Hicks."

HICKS, June Rhodes, BA (Hons) (1956), MA (1960); printmaker in etching, and painter; former teacher. *b*: Yorks., 5 Jun 1935. *m*: J. Michael Hicks. two *s*. one *d*. *Educ*: Universities: Leeds, Belfast. *Studied*: Penzance School of Art (Bouverie Hoyton, John Tunnard, Joan Whiteford). *Exhib*: solo shows in Cornwall. *Works in collections*: galleries in Cornwall and elswhere; and in private collections. *Publications*: co-editor Ten Penwith Printmakers (1998). *Clubs*: Founder mem. Penwith Printmakers (group disbanded Sep 2013), mem. St. Ives Soc. of Artists. *Address*: Vingoe Cottage, Travescan Sennen, nr. Penzance, TR19 7AQ. *Email*: jrjmhicks@tiscali.co.uk *Website*: www.trevescanstudio.com *Signs work*: "June Hicks."

HICKS, Nicola, MBE, RWA, FRBS, MA, RCA; sculptor in plaster and straw, bronze; *b*: London, 1960. *m*: Daniel Flowers. one *s*. one *d*. *Studied*: Chelsea School of Art (1978-82), Royal College of Art (1982-85). *Exhib*: numerous solo exhbns. in UK and abroad. *Commissions*: monument to the Brown Dog, Battersea Park, London. *Publications*: 'Nicola Hicks' (Momentum, 1999). *Address*: c/o Flowers East, 82 Kingsland Road, London E2 8DP. *Signs work*: "HICKS."

HICKS, Peter Michael, NDD, ATD, MA Distinction (1990). *Medium*: oil, watercolour, acrylic. *b*: Osgodby, Selby, E.Yorks, 29 Sep 1937. *s of*: Bill Hicks. two *d*. *Studied*: Middlesbrough College of Art (1959); Leeds College of Art (1960); Northumbria University (1988-90). *Exhib*: solo: University of Picardy, Amiens, France (1988); MacLaurin Galleries Ayr (1993); Castlegate House, Cockermouth (1994); Stonegate Gallery, York (1995); Myles Meehan Gallery, Darlington (1996); Brian Sinfield Gallery, Burford (2001); group shows: British Art Month; Roy Miles, Mayfair (1991); Turners Legacy, Contact Gallery, Norwich (1994); Yorkshire Artists, York City Gallery (1998); Messum's, Cork St. (2005, 2010, 2012); Inspired Landscape - 60th Anniversary of North Yorks Moors National Park - 2012. *Works in collections*: Museum of Art, Amiens, France; West Yorkshire Education Authority; Darlington Corporation; work in private collections home and abroad. *Official Purchasers*: Pannett Gallery, Whitby (for permanent collection), and as above. *Works Reproduced*: in 'Living North' regularly, The Spectator (Nov 2005, 2012), Country Life (Nov 2005, 2012). Article on work in 'Living North' (April 2004). *Misc*: appeared in BBC series "Dales Diary", ITV Friday Live (talking about my work). Monograph is in preparation, and short film for TV. Film on my practice by Nick Turner 'Dawn to Dusk'. *Address*: 19 Briar Hill, Danby, Whitby, N.Yorks., YO21 2LZ. *Website*: www.petermhicks.co.uk

HICKS, Philip, Dip. RAS; painter in oil, acrylic and water-colour; Past Chairman, Vice Pres. AGBI. *b*: England, 11 Oct 1928. *s of*: Brig. P H W Hicks, CBE, DSO, MC. *m*: Jill. one *s*. one *d*. *Educ*: Winchester College. *Studied*: Chelsea School of Art and RA Schools. *Represented by*: Messum's Fine Art, Cork Street, London W1. *Exhib*: one-man shows, Marjorie Parr, Robert Self, Hoya, New Art Centre Galleries, Gallery 10, London, Oxford Gallery, VECU Antwerp, Engström Galleri, Stockholm; retrospective, Battersea Arts Centre, London, Bohun Gallery, Henley, 1977 British Council award, David Messum Fine Art, London, John Davies Gallery, Stow-on-the-Wold, Alpha House Gallery, Sherborne. *Works in collections*: Tate Gallery, V&A, Contemporary Art Soc., Imperial War Museum, Nuffield Foundation, RCM, De Beers, Mirror Group, Wates Ltd., NatWest. Bank, BP, APV Holdings, Chandris Shipping. *Commissions*: Wates Ltd., Control Data Corporation, Chandris Shipping. *Publications*: 'Philip Hicks': monograph 160pp: hardback, by John Russell Taylor, pub Oct 2013, Studio Publications. *Works Reproduced*: Imperial War Museum Catalogue of Paintings. *Clubs*: Chelsea Arts, Royal Overseas League. *Address*: Radcot House, Buckland Rd., Bampton, Oxon. OX18 2AA. *Signs work*: "Philip Hicks" (often on reverse) or "HICKS."

HICKS-JENKINS, Clive, Hon.Fellow School of Art, University of Aberystwyth (2004); Creative Wales Award, Arts Council of Wales (2002); Gulbenkian Welsh Art Prize (1999). *Medium*: acrylic, drawing, printing. *b*: Newport, Mon., 11 Jun 1951. *s of*: Trevor and Dorothy. *Partner*: Dr. Peter Wakelin. *Educ*: Italia Conti School. *Studied*: no formal art training. *Represented by*: The Martin Tinney Gallery, Cardiff. *Exhib*: Attic Gallery, Swansea (2005); Martin Tinney Gallery, Cardiff (2004-ongoing); Christ Church Picture Gallery, Oxford (2004), MOMA Wales (2004); Anthony Hepworth Fine Art, Bath (2002); Brecknock Museum & Art Gallery, Brecon (2002); Newport Museum & Art Gallery (2001). *Works in collections*: MOMA Wales; Newport Museum & Art Gallery; Brecknock Art Trust; National Library of Wales; National Museum of Wales; Llandaff Cathedral. *Commissions*: Artists' books for The Old Stile Press (1997-2005). *Publications*: 'The Temptations of Solitude: Paintings by Clive Hicks-Jenkins' (Cardiff, 2004); 'Clive Hicks-Jenkins' (published by Lund Humphries 2011). *Works Reproduced*: British Art Journal Vol.3 (2004) p.68; Art Review (May 2001) p.48; Modern Painters (Summer 2001) p.104. *Address*: Ty Isaf, Llanilar, Aberystwyth, SY23 4NP. *Email*: clive@hicks-jenkins.fsnet.co.uk *Website*: www.hicks-jenkins.com *Signs work*: 'Hicks-Jenkins'.

HIGGINS, John, self taught artist in water-colour and drawing, mixed media; private tuition, tutor for H. F. Holiday Group, Peligoni Painting Holidays and others. *b*: Carshalton,

10 Jul 1934. *m*: Nicola. two *s*. *Exhib*: various exhibitions: solo exhibitions; St. Ives "In All Directions"; St. Ives Society of Artists, Penwith Gallery, St. Ives. *Works in collections*: various private buyers. *Publications*: article for Artist magazine Oct. '99 "Mixing the Media", BBC television short film on Godrevy Lighthouse, April 2000. *Clubs*: St Ives Art Club. *Address*: 6 Richmond Place, St. Ives, Cornwall TR26 1JN. *Signs work*: "J D Higgins."

HIGGINS, Nicola, artist in water-colour; private water-colour tutor, tutoring for H. F. Holiday Group, Peligoni Holidays Greece, and others. *b*: Rustington, Sussex, 1 Mar 1943. *m*: John. one *s*. *Educ*: City and Guilds teachers certificate. *Exhib*: St. Ives Society of Artists; various exhibitions and galleries. *Works in collections*: Various private patrons. *Publications*: article for Artist magazine Dec. '99 "Adventures in Watercolour", short film for BBC Pebble Mill "Which Craft" on water-colour painting Sept. '99. *Clubs*: St. Ives Art Club. *Address*: 6 Richmond Place, St. Ives, Cornwall TR26 1JN. *Signs work*: "Nicola H."

HIGGINSON, Clifford Edward, *Medium*: oil, watercolour. *b*: Salford, 10 Mar 1939. *s of*: Albert Edward & Hilda Higginson. *m*: Vivienne Jean Higginson. three *s*. *Studied*: College of Art, Salford (1957-60), Faculty of Tech and Science, Manchester (1960-64). *Represented by*: Colin Jellico, Colin Jellico Gallery, Manchester. *Exhib*: in one-man shows and joint exhibitions at: Black Sheep Gallery, Hawarden; Bolton Gallery; Central Gallery, Manchester; Colin Jellicoe Gallery, Manchester; Derby City Art Gallery; Hillgate Gallery, Stockport; Lantern Gallery, Worsley; Mariners Gallery, St. Ives, Cornwall; Newa, Liverpool; Salford Art Gallery; Swinton Art Gallery; The Calvery Gallery, Helensburgh; Tib Lane Gallery, Manchester; Torr Top Gallery, New Mills; Vernon Mill Gallery, Stockport. *Works in collections*: in Australia, Switzerland, Scotland, France and Belgium. *Commissions*: over seventy privately commissioned portraits, plus numerous other scenes, animals, etc. *Works Reproduced*: various paintings in local magazines and newspapers. *Recreations*: writing poetry, ballet, theatre, music. *Address*: 82 Malmesbury Road, Cheadle Hulme, Cheadle, Cheshire. SK8 7QL. *Email*: cliffhigginson@talktalk.net *Website*: www.cliffhigginson.co.uk *Signs work*: "CLIFF HIGGINSON".

HIGSON, John, MFPS; self taught sculptor in wood and ceramic, painter in water-colour and pastel. *b*: 30 Oct 1936. *s of*: Albert Edward Higson. *Educ*: Malden West County Secondary. *Exhib*: one-man shows: Bourne Hall, Ewell, Russell Studio, Wimbledon, Malden Centre, New Malden. *Address*: 22 Croxton, Burritt Rd., Kingston upon Thames, Surrey KT1 3HS.

HILL, Anthony, artist, plastician and theorist: works in industrial materials; awarded Leverhulme Fellowship, Hon. Research Fellow, Dept. Mathematics, University College, London (1971-73). *b*: London, 23 Apr 1930. *s of*: Adrian Hill, RBA. *m*: Yuriko Kaetsu, ceramicist. *Educ*: Bryanston. *Studied*: St. Martin's (1947-49), Central School (1949-51). *Exhib*: Kasmin Gallery (1966, 1969, 1980); retrospective exhbn. Hayward Gallery (1983), ICA (1958); Mayor Gallery (1994); Austin Desmond Fine Art (2003). *Works in collections*: Tate Gallery, V&A, British Museum, provincial galleries; Museum of Modern Art, Grenoble, Tel Aviv and Santiago, Louisiana Museum Denmark, Gulbenkian Museum Lisbon, Stuki Museum, Lodz (Poland), Kroller-Muller (Holland). *Publications*: edited Data Directions in Art Theory and Aesthetics (Faber, 1986), Duchamp-Passim (Gordon and Breach 1995). *Works Reproduced*: in English, Continental and American publications since 1950. *Address*: 24 Charlotte St., London W1T 2ND. *Signs work*: "Anthony Hill." or "AH" (as monogram). Since 1975 has made works signed "Rem Doxford", "Achill Redo" and "Redo."

HILL, Carol Elizabeth, SWA; SFP, ARBSA; qualified teacher in Adult Education. *Medium*: oil, watercolour. *b*: Warlingham, Surrey, 23 Jul 1946. *d of*: Mr & Mrs F.C.Matthews. *m*: Michael Hill. one *s*. one *d*. *Educ*: St.Georges School, Hong Kong. *Studied*: oil painting and watercolours under various tutors in UK and abroad. *Represented by*: Little

London Gallery, Derbyshire. *Exhib*: Westminster Gallery; Mall Galleries; Mottisford Abbey, Hampshire; in York, Hull, Harrogate, Sheffield, Nottingham, Derby, Norfolk, Lincoln and Matlock. *Commissions*: many over the years - mainly landscape, seascape and flowers. *Publications*: several articles in magazines. *Works Reproduced*: Limited Edition prints and cards. *Recreations*: gardening, walking, reading. *Clubs*: President of the Matlock Art Society. *Misc*: I also organise demonstrations, workshops and teaching sessions around the UK. *Address*: 'Ashleigh', Yew Tree Hill, Holloway, Matlock, Derbyshire DE4 5AR. *Email*: carolhill@mailauth.co.uk *Signs work*: 'Carol Hill'.

HILL, Charles Douglas, artist in oil. *b*: Dewsbury, W. Yorks., 16 Jun 1953. *m*: Jennifer Haylett, singer. *Educ*: Dewsbury, England, and Sqaumish, Canada. *Exhib*: worldwide; and Longships Gallery, St. Ives. *Works Reproduced*: book cover (Black Swan Pub.), articles 'Cornish World', 'Inside Cornwall'. *Clubs*: St. Ives Soc. of Artists. *Address*: Longships Gallery, St.Andrew's St., St. Ives, Cornwall TR26 1AN.

HILL, Ronald James, UA, SGFA, FSAI; freelance artist in oil, water-colour, pen and ink. *b*: London, 19 Oct 1933. *s of*: James George Hill. *m*: Betty Bunn (decd). *Educ*: Willesden Technical College. *Studied*: Heatherley's School of Art (1958-65, Jack Merriot, Patrick Larkin, Harry Riley). *Exhib*: Paris Salon (1966-69), RBA, UA; one man shows, Brent, Wantage. *Commissions*: Landscapes and architectural subjects in all media. *Address*: Orpheus Studio of Fine Art, Pound Cottage, Kingston Lisle, Wantage, Oxon. OX12 9QL. *Signs work*: "RONN."

HILL, Sonia Geraldine, painter in oil; grant to Maidenhead Art College, Berks (1955). *Medium*: oil. *b*: London, 26 Sep 1939. *d of*: John Alfred England. *Partner*: Major G.H. Clark (decd). *Educ*: Dorchester Abbey School, Oxon. *Studied*: Maidenhead Art College, Berks.; Zambia (pupil with Andrew Hayward). *Exhib*: RA (3 hung-3 passed between 1993 and 2000, including portrait of Quentin Crisp, which now hangs in Vancouver); Christies 'Art 4 Life' (2000-2004); Exh. Richmond Art Gallery (1999, 2003); Paris (2000, 2008); Menorca, Mahon Gallery (2013). *Publications*: R.A. Illustrated (1993) Jack the Lad. *Clubs*: Friend of the RA. *Misc*: three oil portraits of celebrated artist Tracey Emin (2005); Boris Johnson (2012). *Address*: 6a Warfield Rd., Hampton, Middx. TW12 2AY. *Signs work*: "S.G. Hill."

HILLHOUSE, David, Hon. RCamA; BA(1969), ATD(1971), RCA (1979), AMA (1982); artist in water-colour and egg tempera. *b*: Irby, Wirral, 19 Jun 1945. *s of*: Harry Hillhouse. *m*: Paula Lane. two *s*. *Educ*: Birkenhead Institute. *Studied*: Laird School of Art (1964-66), Liverpool College of Art (1966-69). *Exhib*: Merseyside, Wales and Bristol, USA, Germany, France. *Clubs*: Wirral Soc. of Arts, Deeside Art Group, National Acrylic Painters' Association (NAPA). *Address*: 49 Cortsway, Greasby, Wirral CH49 2NA. *Email*: hillhouse_david@hotmail.com *Website*: www.davidhillhouse.com *Signs work*: "David Hillhouse."

HILLI: see THOMPSON, Hilli.

HILLIER, Matthew, SWLA, SAA (USA); wildlife artist in acrylic, pastel and water-colour; Council mem. SWLA. *b*: Slough, 7 May 1958. *Studied*: Dyfed College of Art. *Exhib*: Christie's Wildlife Auction (1994-97), Pacific Rim Wildlife Art Expo (1994, 1995) Tacoma, Vancouver, Soc. of Animal Artists (1995, 1996), Birds in Art, Wisconsin (1993, 1994, 1996), Florida Wildlife Art Expo (1997), Friends of Washington Zoo Wildlife Art Show (1996, 1997). *Commissions*: Ambleside Studio, Michigan. *Publications*: Fine Art Limited Edition prints (Millpond Press, Florida); illustrated: The Rhinocerous, a Monograph (Basilisk Press Limited Edition book). *Address*: 166 Elemr Rd., Middleton-on-Sea, W. Sussex PO22 6JA. *Signs work*: "Mathew Hillier."

HILLIER, Susan Patricia, FBSA; SY.Dip (Fine Art) 1969. *Medium*: watercolour, acrylic, oil, pencil, gouache, etc. *b*: Surrey, 8 Sep 1949. *d of*: Margaret and Frank Hillier. *Educ*:

Mickelham Primary, Mowbray Girls School, Dorking. *Studied*: Reigate School of Art (1964-70). *Represented by*: Lander Gallery, Truro. *Exhib*: 7 solo and 20+ group exhibitions (London, Surrey, Cornwall and Lincolnshire) including Plymouth Municipal Gallery, NT, RHS, Kew Gardens, Tresco Estate. *Works in collections*: throughout the world. *Commissions*: British Rail, Tesco, McMullen's Brewery, Law Society, Police College, Scout Assoc., Royal Horticultural Society etc. *Publications*: illustrated numerous gardening books, scientific botanical publications and natural history subjects. *Official Purchasers*: see commissions. *Works Reproduced*: various magazines. *Principal Works*: drawings for 'Kew', and botanical paintings. *Recreations*: gardening, walking, cooking. *Misc*: founder member and hon. mem. Society of Botanical Artsits, RHS medallist, scientific illustrator Royal Bot. Gdns., Kew. *Address*: 6 Poltair Crescent, St. Austell, Cornwall PL25 4LX. *Signs work*: Susan Hillier.

HILLS, Dominic, BA (Hons) Fine Art. *Medium*: oil on canvas, prints. *b*: Brighton, 10 Aug 1975. *s of*: Michael Hills; Jennifer Fouracres. *Partner*: Nerys Williams. one *s*. one *d*. *Educ*: Brighton School of Art and Design (Foundation). *Studied*: BA Fine Art, John Moore's University, Liverpool; Fresco, Trivandum School of South Indian Mural Painting, India. *Represented by*: Edgar International Modern Art, Bath. *Exhib*: The Menier Gallery, London & Edgar Modern, Bath, solo show "Laughing Pictures" (2007); Edgar Modern Mixed Summer Show (2004, 2005, 2007); RWA 2007; Edgar Modern solo show (2006); Jubilee Gallery, Devon (2005); Innocent Fine Art, Bristol (2005); Fact, Liverpool (2004); Adams Gallery, Wellington, New Zealand (2003); Te Aro Gallery, Wellington (2003); Parking Space Gallery, Liverpool Biennial (2003); LAF (2006, 2007); AAF (2005-07); Art London (2007); Art Ireland, Dublin (2007); Toronto Int. Art Fair (2007); Cambridge '07. *Works in collections*: private. *Commissions*: Buckfastleigh Mural (2005); Inverteign Mural (2005); Teignbridge Mural (2004); Oktober commission, Wellington, NZ (2003). *Publications*: "Dominic Hills: Laughing Pictures" (Foreword by Anne L.Cowe) Bath, 2007. *Address*: c/o Edgar Modern International Art, Bartlett Street, Bath, BA1 2EE. *Website*: www.edgarmodern.com *Signs work*: "Dominic Hills" or "Dominic".

HILLS, Jonathan Graham, MA (Cantab); Prix Italia. *Medium*: oil, drawing. *b*: London, 9 Mar 1954. *s of*: Sir Graham Hills. *m*: Lucy Makin. two *d*. *Educ*: Winchester College and Queens College, Cambridge. *Represented by*: Erika Brandt, 20th Century Gallery, Unit 3U, 2 Michael Rd., London SW6 2AD. *Exhib*: RA Summer Exhbn (2004, 05). *Works in collections*: private, UK and overseas. *Commissions*: Abingdon School. *Clubs*: London Sketch Club (President). *Address*: Longwall House, Penshurst, Kent TN11 8EE. *Email*: jonathanhills@mac.com *Website*: www.smartshillstudios.co.uk *Signs work*: 'J Hills'.

HILTON, Bo, MA Print (1998), BSc Biology (1984); artist in oil on canvas. *b*: London, 9 Nov 1961. *m*: Alice. one *s*. one *d*. *Studied*: Brighton (1985-88). *Exhib*: Cassian de Verre Cole (1995-96), Arthur Anderson (1998). *Clubs*: N.E.A.C. *Address*: 23 St. Luke's Terr., Brighton BN2 2ZE.

HILTON, Rose, Julia, ARCA. *Medium*: oil and watercolour. *b*: Kent, 15 Aug 1931. *d of*: Robert Charles Phipps. *m*: widow of Roger Hilton (d.1975). two *s*. *Educ*: Bromley Technical School for Girls. *Studied*: Beckenham Art School (1948-53), Royal College of Art (1953-57), British School in Rome (1958-59). *Represented by*: David Messum, 8 Cork Street, London W1. *Exhib*: Huddersfield North Light Gallery (1988, '90, '93, '95, 2000, 2002), showing at Tate St. Ives January 2008 and frequently shown in RA Summer Show. *Works in collections*: Plymouth County Museum, Truro County Museum, private collections throughout UK, British Museum Collection. *Recreations*: music, singing. *Clubs*: Chelsea Arts Club. *Address*: Botallack Moor, St.Just, Cornwall, TR19 7QH. *Email*: rose.hilton@tesco.net

HINCHCLIFFE, Michael, artist in water-colour, designer. *b*: London, 25 Apr 1937. *s of*: Tom Hinchcliffe. *m*: Gillian. two *d*. *Educ*: St. Marylebone Grammar School. *Studied*:

St. Martin's School of Art. *Exhib*: RI, UA; many one-man shows. *Works in collections*: Weybridge Museum. *Address*: 37 The Furrows, Walton on Thames, Surrey KT12 3JG.

HIPKINS, Michael William, ARBS; NDD (1964), ATD (1976); artist in oil and water-colour, sculptor in alabaster and marble. *Medium*: fine art. *b*: Blackpool, 21 Jun 1942. *m*: Pauline Ashton. two *s*. one *d*. *Studied*: Blackpool College of Art, S.W. Hayter's Studio 17, Paris. *Represented by*: Belgravia Gallery, London; Artparks International; Sausmarez Manor, Guernsey, C.I.; Walker Galleries, Harrogate; Jo Bennett Originals, Cheshire; Linton Court Gallery. *Exhib*: Blackheath Gallery, The Gallery Manchester's Art House, RSA, Colours Gallery, Warstone Gallery, London Art Fair, Art on Paper Fair. *Works in collections*: Grundy A.G. Blackpool, Lancaster A.G. *Commissions*: series of murals: Blackpool Zoo, several stone carving commissions. *Publications*: included in British Contemporary Art (1993). *Works Reproduced*: greetings cards and prints; Lancashire Life 2002, Lancashire Life 2011. *Address*: Driftwood, Ash Rd., Elswick, Preston, Lancs. PR4 3YE. *Signs work*: "Michael Hipkins."

HIPPE, Susan Kerstin, SGFA; BA (Hons), Roehampton Inst. University of Surrey; progressive drawing; drawing combined with mixed media; tutor. *b*: Johannesburg, S. Africa, 28 Nov., 1966. *Educ*: schools in Denmark, Germany and France. *Studied*: art schools in France (Troyes, Le Havre, Mulhouse), and London (Roehampton Inst.). *Exhib*: solo exhibs. in London and group exhibs. in UK, London, Paris, New York, Spain. *Works in collections*: private. *Commissions*: private. *Publications*: Painting World 2001, Wandsworth Guardian 2001, TNT Magazine 2000. *Clubs*: E.W.A.C.C., Society of Graphic Fine Art. *Address*: 29 Glimpsing Green, Erith, Kent DA18 4HA. *Email*: s-hippi@yahoo.co.uk *Website*: www.absolutearts.com/portfolio/s/susanhippe *Signs work*: "SUSAN HIPPE" or "S.H."

HIRST, Barry Elliot, NDD Painting (1956), DFA (Lond.) (1958), FRSA (1989); painter; Emeritus Prof. of Fine Art, University of Sunderland. *b*: Padstow, Cornwall, 11 Jun 1934. *m*: Christine. one *s*. two *d*. *Educ*: Alleyns School, Dulwich. *Studied*: Camberwell School of Art (1950-52, 1954-56), Slade School (1956-58, Keith Vaughan, Claude Rogers). *Represented by*: Mercury Gallery, London; Thos. Deans Gallery, Atlanta & Tallahassee. *Exhib*: over eighteen one-man shows, including Hanover Gallery, London (1963, 65); Central St. Gallery, Sydney, NSW (1966); Byron Gallery, NY (1968); Compass Gallery, Glasgow (1982); Mercury Gallery, London (1986-99); Latvian State Academy, Riga (1989); Vardy Gallery, Sunderland University (1994); Thos. Dean Gallery, Atlanta (2000); Bourne Gallery, Edinburgh. *Works in collections*: Contemporary Arts Soc., British Council, Sunday Times, Croydon Educ. Com., Northern Arts Assoc., Tyne & Wear Museums, University of Sunderland, Darlington Memorial Hospital, Olinda Museum Brazil, Derby Museum and A.G., HRH Duchess of Kent, Latvian National Museum Riga, Latvian Academy of Art Riga, RAC, Sunderland and Portsmouth Newspapers, Sao Paulo Museum Brazil, BP, A & M Univ. Texas, Royal Bank of Scotland, Macquarie Univ. NSW. *Publications*: illustrations for poetry by: R.S. Thomas, Roy Fuller, George Barker, C.Day Lewis, Alistair Eliot, Rodney Pybus. *Clubs*: Sunderland Assoc. Football Club. *Address*: 12 Bondgate Without, Alnwick, Northumberland NE66 1PP. *Email*: profbehirst@btconnect.com *Signs work*: "BARRY HIRST" or "B.E. HIRST."

HIRST, Derek, ARCA; artist. *b*: Doncaster, 11 Apr 1930. *Studied*: Doncaster School of Art (1946-48), RCA (1948-51). *Exhib*: Drian Galleries (1961), Tooth's Gallery (1962-63), Stone Galleries, Newcastle upon Tyne (1962), University of Sussex (1966), Towner A.G. (1966), Angela Flowers Gallery (1970, 1972, 1975, 1979, 1984, 1987, 1989), Victorian Centre for the Arts, Melbourne, Australia (1980), Pallant House Gallery, Chichester (1987, 1991), Flowers East (1991, 1995), Flowers East at London Fields (1993, 1999), Flowers West, Santa Monica, USA (2001). *Works in collections*: Tate Gallery, V&A, National

Gallery of Canada, ACGB, Contemporary Art Soc., DOE, Fundaçao dos Museus Regionaise de Bahia, Brazil, Bank of Ireland, Dublin, Universities of Sussex and Southampton, Art Inst. of Detroit, Brooklyn Museum, NY, Arizona State University, Phoenix Art Museum, etc. *Address*: 3 The Terrace, Mill La., Sidlesham, Chichester, W. Sussex PO20 7NA. *Signs work*: "Derek Hirst."

HISLOP, Helga: see CROUCH, Helga.

HITCHENS, John, Painter. Compositions evolved from aerial view of landscape. *b*: Sussex, 1940. *s of*: Ivon Hitchens, painter. Grandson of Alfred Hitchens, painter. *m*: Rosalind. two *s* . *Educ*: Bedales School. *Studied*: Bath Academy of Art. *Exhib*: Regular London exhbns. since 1964. *Works in collections*: public and permanent collections UK and abroad. 1979: 52ft. mural, "A Landscape Symphony". *Commissions*: Design for stained glass window (1990); Eight-foot sculpture in cedar wood (1998). *Official Purchasers*: Three paintings as limited edition prints by the Cavendish Collection (1978). *Address*: The Old School, Byworth, Petworth, Sussex GU28 0HN. *Email*: info@johnhitchens.com *Website*: www.johnhitchens.com *Signs work*: "John Hitchens."

HOARE, Diana C., BA Hons; lettering designer, calligrapher, letter carver, carving on stone and slate, calligraphy. *b*: London, 10 Feb 1956. *d of*: Reginald Hoare, picture restorer. *m*: William Taunton. one *s*. two *d*. *Educ*: Godolphin and Latymer; University of Kent, Canterbury. *Studied*: privately with Vernon Shearer, Ievan Rees, Heather Child, Sam Somerville. *Exhib*: solo exhbns. in Dorset, London and B'ham. *Works in collections*: two MS. books at University of Austin, Texas. *Publications*: Advanced Calligraphy Techniques (Cassells), Everybodys Wine Guide (Quarto). *Address*: 73 Nun Street, St.Davids, Pembrokeshire SA62 6NU.

HOBART, John, BSc (Lond), RCA; self taught artist in oil and water-colour; past Vice-Pres. Royal Cambrian Academy; Fellow, University College of N. Wales, Bangor. *b*: London, 27 May 1922. *s of*: Percy John Hobart. one *s*. two *d*. *Educ*: St. Dunstan's College and University College, London. *Exhib*: one-man, Theatre Gwynedd; group shows, Plas Mawr, Conway, Tegfryn Gallery, Cambrian Academy, RI, N.Wales Group, Newlyn, Penwith, Kings College, Cambridge. *Works in collections*: University College of N. Wales, Bangor; private collections in USA, Canada, Australia, UK, Ireland, Holland, Germany. *Address*: Buswisnan, Ludgvan, Penzance, Cornwall TR20 8BN. *Signs work*: "J. Hobart."

HOBART, Lady Caroline Fleur: see LEEDS, Caroline.

HOBBS, Philip Lawrence, President Lake Artists Society 2005; Cert. in Education Art (Teaching Cert) 1975. *Medium*: oil, watercolour, drawing. *b*: New Farnley, Yorks, 1 Nov 1953. *s of*: Lawrence Hobbs & Marie Hobbs nee Webster. *m*: Joan Elizabeth (nee Eastwood). one *s*. *Educ*: Birkenshaw County Secondary / Whitcliffe Mount Grammar. *Studied*: Charlotte Mason College 1972-75. *Represented by*: Hobbs Gallery, Ambleside; Ambleside Gallery, North Carolina, USA. *Exhib*: RI Mall Galleries, Singer & Friedlander/Sunday Times Laing Gallery; group and solo shows UK, USA and Europe; Lake Artists Society annually since 1980. *Works in collections*: many private UK, USA and Europe. *Commissions*: private UK, USA and Europe. *Publications*: magazine articles: The Artist; Artist & Illustrator; International Artist; books featured: Watercolour Landscapes of 23 International Artists (2003), The Lake Artists, A Centenary Celebration (2004); catalogue: P L Hobbs (2009 Retrospective). *Works Reproduced*: limited edition prints, prints, posters, cards, etc. *Principal Works*: in watercolour, workshop interiors, city and landscapes. *Clubs*: elected member Lake Artists Society 1982. *Address*: The Copse, Old Hall Road, Troutbeck Bridge, Windermere, Cumbria, LA23 1JA. *Email*: hobbs.gallery@virgin.net *Website*: www.plhobbs.co.uk *Signs work*: "P.L.HOBBS".

HOCKIN, Julie, SOFA (1996); self taught professional artist working in water-colour, graphite and coloured pencils. Her pictures range from botanical and wildlife subjects to very detailed cat paintings and drawings; Creative Director, Hockin and Roberts Ltd, St Austell. *b*: St. Austell, 3 Feb 1937. one *d*. *Educ*: St. Austell Grammar School. *Exhib*: National Trust Cotehele, Lanhydrock, Marwell Zoological Pk. Winchester, Carlyon Bay Hotel, St. Austell, Llewellyn Alexander Gallery, London, RMS, HS, Cornish Studies Centre, Redruth, Trebah Garden Gallery, Cornwall. *Misc*: Gives talks, demonstrations and teaches. *Address*: Cedar Lodge, Trevarth, Mevagissey, St. Austell, Cornwall PL26 6RX. *Email*: Jrainbowlight@aol.com *Website*: www.hockinandroberts.com *Signs work*: "Julie Hockin" or "JH" joined.

HODDER, Monroe, BA, MBA, MFA; Semi-finalist, Jerwood Painting Prize, London (2001); Art Academician, Kazakh Academy of Arts, Kazakhstan (2007). *Medium*: oil, monotype. *b*: Baltimore, MD, 15 Oct 1943. *d of*: James Mumford Sawhill. *m*: R. Frederick Hodder. *Studied*: MFA, San Francisco Art Institute; MBA, Stanford University; BA, Vassar College. *Represented by*: Belgravia Gallery, Mayfair, London; Vertigo Gallery, Shoreditch, London; Havu Gallery, Denver, Colorado; Butters Gallery, Portland, Oregon; SFMOMA Artists' Gallery, San Francisco, CA, Elin/Eagles Smith Gallery San Francisco; Darnell Fine Art, Santa Fe, New Mexico. *Exhib*: Selected recent exhibitions: solo: Belgravia Gallery, Mayfair, London (2007); Toomey Tourell Gallery, San Francisco, CA (1999, 2000, 2002, 2004, 2006); Vertigo Gallery, London (2003); Tengri Umai Gallery, Almaty, Kazakhstan (1997); Jan Baum Gallery, Los Angeles (1996). International Art Biennale, Kazakhstan (2002); Lindenburgh Gallery, New York (2000); Miami Basel Art Fair (2009); William Havu Gallery (2009); Belgravia Gallery (2008); Galerie La Courette (2008); Butters Gallery (2008). *Works in collections*: Tom Cruise & Katy Holmes, Linklater, Bank of America; over 300 public and private collections internationally. *Publications*: several catalogues. *Official Purchasers*: The Kasteev Museum of Almaty, Denver Art Museum, Palo Alto Art Museum, San Jose Museum of Art. *Works Reproduced*: several catalogues. *Principal Works*: "Stairs of the Sea", "Trees of Russia", "Mysteries". *Recreations*: travel. *Misc*: Art critic for several art magazines in London and Colorado; Studios in UK and US. *Address*: 50 Gordon Place, London W8 4JF. *Email*: monroe7777@aol.com *Website*: www.monroehodder.com

HODGES, Gillian Mary, SWA (1987), HS, SLm, portrait painter in oil and pastel; portraits and character studies from Shakespeare in miniature, oils, acrylic and water-colour; Tutor for adult education, Hants & Surrey (1976-1996), SLm Brian Bull Award for Best Modern Portrait Miniature 2009. *b*: Twickenham, Middx. *d of*: Harry Leslie Snook. *m*: Peter Steer Hodges. two *s*. *Educ*: Richmond School of Art under Jack Fairhurst, ARCA, Salisbury School of Art and Heatherley School of Art (part time). *Exhib*: SWA, various societies in S. and SW of England, Northern Ireland, RMS, HS, SLm, World Federation of Miniaturists, Tasmania (2000); Washington DC (2004), Tasmania (2008), Moscow (2012). Llewellyn Alexander (Fine Paintings) Ltd. (2005, 2006, 2007, 2008). *Works in collections*: 'The Pageant' in Farnham (Surrey) Public Library; Officers' Mess QARANC, Aldershot; Inst. of Aviation Medicine, Farnborough, Regtl HQ 4/7 Dragoon Guards, York. *Commissions*: portraits: Field Marshall Sir Nigel Bagnall, Lt-General Sir Peter de la Billiere, Major-General Tony Jeapes. *Works Reproduced*: QARANC - A day in the Cambridge Military Hospital (1994), The Life of Mary Queen of Scots (1998). *Address*: 2 Abbey Mill, Church St., Bradford-on-Avon, Wilts. BA15 1HB. *Signs work*: "G. M. Hodges."

HODGKINS, Barbara, sculptor in marble, bronze. *b*: USA. *Educ*: Wellesley College, Columbia University, USA. *Studied*: Chelsea School of Art, London. *Works in collections*: Sculpture in corporate collections: Prudential, Bank of China, Bank of Denmark, BP, Reynolds, Hewlett-Packer, Foote, Cone, Belding, MCL (Art and Work award 1987) and in private European, Asian and American collections. *Clubs*: Mem. Royal Soc. of British Sculptors. *Address*: 5 Hurlingham Ct., Ranelagh Gdns., London SW6 3SH.

HODGSON, Carole, FRBS, HDFA (1964); sculptor in cement, bronze, wax, ceramics, lead; Professor of Sculpture, Kingston University. *b*: London, 1940. two *d*. *Studied*: Wimbledon School of Art (1957-62), Slade UCL (1962-64). *Represented by*: Angela Flowers Gallery. *Exhib*: Angela Flowers Gallery, Flowers East, ACGB, WAC, Wustum Museum, USA, Whitefriars Museum, Coventry, New Ashgate, Farnham, Llanelli Festival, Christie's Fine Arts, Buenos Aires, Argentine, Santiago, Chile, Haggerty Museum, USA, Flowers West, LA, USA, Turin Italy. *Works in collections*: Welsh Contemporary Arts, ACGB, WAC, British Council, DOE, Contemporary Arts, Unilever House, Universities of Wales, London, Wisconsin USA, British Medal Soc., Manpower. *Publications*: From the Sea to the Wall (Kingston U. Press), Carole Hodgson by Mary Rose Beaumont (Momentum), British Sculptors of the Twentieth Century (Ashgate), From City to Lake (Angela Flowers), Modern British Sculpture (Schiffer Press) . *Address*: c/o James Ulph, Flowers Central, 21 Cork Street, London W1S 3LZ. *Signs work*: "Carole Hodgson."

HODGSON, Kenneth Jonah, BA, GOE Dip. SW CQSW, PTA; artist in acrylic, oil and water-colour; Exec com. mem., Merseyside Arts (1985-87); Steering com. sec., Merseyside Contemporary Artists (1988-89); Hon. Vice President ISAP-USA (1985). *b*: Liverpool, 2 Aug 1936. *s of*: Jonah Hodgson. two *d*. *Educ*: Liverpool, Herts, Oak Hill College, London, The Open University, NEWI Wrexham Cymru, Liverpool John Moore's University. *Exhib*: RCamA, Williamson A.G., various Liverpool and Chester galleries; collective exhbns. in Newcastle-Staffs, Ludlow, Crosby, RBSA Gallery B'ham and NAPA, USA; individual exhbns. on Merseyside and Wirral. Daylight Group - a Tate Liverpool/Metropolitan Borough of Wirral SSD Arts Project, Art Forum - MBW - SSD (1993). *Works in collections*: paintings in private and public collections in U.K. and other countries. *Clubs*: Sec., Wirral Soc. of Arts (1983-87); Founder, National Acrylic Painters' Assoc. (1985). *Address*: N.A.P.A., 134 Rake La., Wallasey, Merseyside CH45 1JW. *Signs work*: "Kenneth J. Hodgson."

HODSON, John, sculptor in stone and bronze. *b*: Oxford, 19 Aug 1945. *s of*: Frank George Hodson, toolmaker. *Educ*: Willesden R.C. *Studied*: Courtauld Inst. of Art, London. *Exhib*: one-man show Woodstock Gallery, London (1973), Paris Salon, Salon des Independants, Haas Gallery, Albemarle Gallery, Galerie Modern, Berlin, and other international exhbns. *Works in collections*: Berlin Kunst Haas. *Commissions*: Dancing Girl, Midland Bank (large bronze). *Works Reproduced*: in Modern Art Revue, Witt Library Courtauld Inst. of Art, London, The Dictionary of Artists in Britain since 1945. *Address*: 40 Clement Cl., London NW6 7AN. *Signs work*: "Hodson."

HOGAN, Prof. Eileen, MA (RCA), RWS; painter. *b*: London, 1 Mar 1946. *m*: divorced. *Educ*: Streatham Hill and Clapham High School. *Studied*: Camberwell School of Art and Crafts (1964-67), British School of Archaeology at Athens, Royal College of Art (1971-74, Carel Weight). *Exhib*: regularly at the Fine Art Soc., numerous one-man shows in Europe and America. *Works in collections*: V&A, Imperial War Museum, RA, and overseas museums and galleries. *Publications*: Under The Influence: catalogue to accompany retrospective, 1997, and numerous others. *Clubs*: Chelsea Arts, Double Crown. *Address*: 13 Wythburen Place, London W1H 7BU. *Signs work*: "Eileen Hogan."

HOIDA, Peter, *Medium*: Drawing; acrylic on canvas. *b*: Birkenhead, 13 Aug 1944. *Studied*: Cheltenham School of Architecture and Landscape, Gloucester College of Art (1962); Hammersmith College of Art and Building, Goldsmiths College School of Art (1969). *Represented by*: c.hislam@yahoo.co.uk. *Exhib*: Solo exhitions since 1975 include: Guildhall Arts Centre, Gloucester (1987, 1992); The Living Room, London (1994); deliArt, London (2000); Sandra Higgins Fine Art at SE1 Gallery, London (2008). Group exhibitions include: Oriel Senig, Harlech, Wales (1994); Ikon Gallery, Birmingham (2000); RWA Autumn Exhibition, Bristol (2002, 2003); Gallery 6, Chelsea (2009); Gallery 27, Cork Street (2009); Affordable Art Fair, London (2010). *Publications*: see info on website. *Address*:

Cedarwood, Brown's Hill, Stroud, GL6 8AS. *Email*: pete@petehoida.co.uk *Website*: www.petehoida.co.uk *Signs work*: "Pete Hoida".

HOLD, William Ashley, RWA: BA Hons. Fine Art; PGCE; MA 20th Century Art & Design. *Medium*: oil. *b*: Cornwall, 5 Aug 1964. *Educ*: Truro School. *Studied*: Falmouth School of Art. *Exhib*: BP Portrait Award (1994, 1999), Hunting Art Prizes (1996, 1998), Royal Society of Portrait Painters (1995), The Discerning Eye (1999, 2002), Beside the Wave Gallery. *Works in collections*: Falmouth Art Gallery; Truro School Collection; Marjon College. *Commissions*: Grand Sec. General for the Freemasons (Jim Daniel), Principal of the College of St Mark & St John, Plymouth. *Publications*: How To Paint Skin Tones by James Horton (c Quarto Publishing 1993). *Recreations*: climbing, hiking, music, reading. *Address*: 5 Harbour Terrace, Falmouth, Cornwall TR11 2AN. *Email*: ahold@live.co.uk *Website*: ashleyhold-artist.info

HOLDEN, John, Cert RA Schools (distinction); NDD (painting) Special. *Medium*: Acrylic on canvas, drawing, mixed media. *b*: Medway, Kent, 24 Jun 1942. *m*: Liz. *Studied*: Medway College of A&D, Rochester (1959-63); RA Schools (1963-66); Mural decoration with the late Edward Bawden, CBE RA (1966-67). *Represented by*: Agnews Gallery. *Exhib*: RA Summer Exhibition (1988/90/93/95-2002/2005-09); Looking Forward, 30 Contemporary Artists, Agnews Gallery, London (2007); 'A Tradition of Excellence' Agnews Gallery (2008); 'John Holden Recent Works', Agnews (2008); Jerwood Drawing Open, Jerwood Gallery & Tours (2004/2007); Discerning Eye (Invited, 6 works, 2005); Fermyn Woods Contemporary Art (two-man show with Paul Mason, 2004); WitteZaal, Ghent Belgium (two-man show with David Morris, 1998). *Works in collections*: Dept. of Environment; Leicester Education Dept.; Bury Art Gallery; Taylor Vintners; John Moore's University Liverpool; Gough Hotels; Fermyn Woods Contemporary Art and private individuals in Europe, Australia and USA. *Commissions*: Sabbatical Fellowship from the Vice Chancellor's Office, John Moore's University. Large triptych. *Publications*: cat Witte Zaal Ghent by Nicholas Usherwood,1998; The Guardian Guide (Feb 2004); Architectural Journal 2004, RA Illustrated 1995/98/2008; 'Looking Forward 30 Contemporary Artists' Agnews (2007); 'Recent Works' 2008 Agnews; Art in England Issue 45 May 2008/ Galleries April 2008. *Works Reproduced*: in all publications listed. *Principal Works*: Large Triptych John Moores University 1998. *Clubs*: Chelsea Arts; member London Group since 2002. *Address*: 61 High Street, Long Buckby, Northampton NN6 7RE. *Website*: agnews gallery.com - exhibitions April 2008. *Signs work*: 'John Holden' (on the reverse).

HOLLAND, Claerwen Belinda, NDD (1964); David Murray landscape studentship (1963); artist in ink, water-colour, pastel and oils; Principal's Prize Byam Shaw. *b*: Cwmdauddwr, 4 Mar 1942. *d of*: Sir Jim Sothern Holland, Bt. *Educ*: Miss Lambert's School, Queens Gdns., London. *Studied*: Byam Shaw School of Art (1960-64, Maurice de Sausmarez). *Exhib*: RA, NEAC, Bath Contemporary Art Fair (1991); one-man shows: Sue Rankin Gallery, Countryworks Gallery, Montgomeryshire, Thackeray Rankin, Thackeray Gallery. *Works in collections*: The Library, University College, Cardiff; National Library of Wales Aberystwyth. *Commissions*: various. *Publications*: illustrations to A Year and a Day by J.L.G. Holland (Hodder and Stoughton). *Address*: Dderw, Cwmdauddwr, Rhayader, Powys LD6 5EY. *Email*: belindaholland22@btinternet.com *Signs work*: "C.B. Holland."

HOLLAND, Frances, HS, SLm; self taught artist in all media. *b*: Petworth, Sussex, 22 Oct 1939. *d of*: Lillian Holmes. one *d*. *Exhib*: Llewellyn Alexander, London, RA Summer Show (1997, 2001, 2006), RMS Westminster, all local venues. Work in collections internationally, Mall Gallery. *Principal Works*: portrait Miniatures. *Clubs*: 2006 Chairman Royal Tunbridge Wells AS; from 2000 Hon Secretary Tonbridge Art Group, Hilliard Society of Limners, Royal Miniature Society. *Address*: 107 London Rd., Southborough, Kent TN4 0NA. *Email*: frans.art@virgin.net

HOLLAND, Harry, artist in oil on canvas, printmaking. *b*: Glasgow, 11 Apr 1941. *m*: Maureen. two *d*. *Educ*: Rutlish School, Merton. *Studied*: St. Martin's School of Art (1964-69). *Exhib*: extensively in Britain, France, Belgium, U.S.A.; one-man shows: Jill George Gallery (1988, 1990, 1992, 1994, 1996); retrospective travelling Britain Nov. 1991 - Jan. 1993. *Works in collections*: Newport Museum and A.G., National Museum of Wales, Tate Gallery Print Coll. *Commissions*: portrait of Lord Callaghan (1990). *Publications*: Painter in Reality (1991). *Clubs*: Chelsea Arts. *Address*: c/o Jill George Gallery, 38 Lexington St., London W1R 3HR. *Signs work*: "Harry Holland."

HOLLANDS, Lesley Elizabeth, Dip AD; ATC. *Medium*: oil, watercolour. *b*: Kent, 17 Dec 1950. *m*: Peter Gooding (decd). one *s*. one *d*. *Studied*: Brighton College of Art; West Surrey College of Art and Design. *Exhib*: Westminster Gallery, Bankside Gallery, Mall Galleries, Southampton City Museum, Gateway-Shrewsbury, West Dean College (one-woman show). *Works in collections*: in New Zealand, USA, Belfast, Brighton, Highfield School. *Commissions*: Hughfield. *Publications*: articles for 'Leisure Painter'; contribution to 'Leisure Painter Projects Book' (Collins). *Recreations*: gardening. *Clubs*: Petersfield Art Soc.; Bramshott & Liphook Arts and Crafts Soc. *Address*: Griggs Green Cottage, Longmoor Road, Liphook GU30 7PB. *Email*: lesleyhollands@hotmail.com *Signs work*: 'Lesley E.Hollands'.

HOLLEDGE, Bryan Raymond, ARCA, FRSA, AFBA; part-time lecturer, Hammersmith School of Art (1949); part-time teacher, St. Hubert's Special School, Brook Green; lecturer, London School of Printing and Graphic Arts; part-time teacher, Chelsea School of Art; graphic designer, Metal Box (1955); Head of Graphics, Swiss Co. Sulzer Bros. (1958); freelance corporate design/mural, Chelsea Arts Club (1950). *b*: Ealing, Middx., 30 Apr 1919. *s of*: Raymond John Holledge, interior designer and decorator. *m*: Maria Haid. two *d*. *Educ*: Ealing College. *Studied*: Ealing College of Art (1937-40); H.M.F. 1940-46; Royal College of Art (1946-49). *Exhib*: painting in National Gallery Exhbn. for Young Artists, Whitechapel Gallery (1953), Arts Council UK tour, Mural painting, Shipping Co. and Theatres joint exhbn., London (1984); one-man show, London (1955) in assoc. with Atomic Energy Soc. Exhib. regularly at London galleries for painting/etching/wood engraving; recent exhbn. of wood engraving at Syon House, Isleworth. A Companion of Western Europe Dip., Certificate of Merit, Biographical Centre Cambridge (1998). *Publications*: poems. *Misc*: Graphic Consultant to Science (education) Company (2000), wood engraving for Country Life. *Address*: 5 The Green, Feltham, Middx. TW13 4AF. *Signs work*: "Bryan R. Holledge."

HOLLIDAY, S. J., RBA; sculptor, ceramicist and muralist. *b*: Portsmouth, 10 Apr 1955. *Studied*: Portsmouth Polytechnic & ECAT. *Exhib*: Kutani Decorative Ceramics Exhib., Japan; Keramion, Keramik 25th Exhib., Frechen, Germany; European Ceramics, Germany; Westerwald Kreis Exhib., Germany; solo exhib. "Look and Like", Bern, Switzerland, Solo Exhibition Switzerland. *Works in collections*: Kaufmann Collection, Bern, Switzerland. *Address*: 11 The Down, Trowbridge, Wilts. BA14 8QN. *Email*: usram@freenet.co.uk marus@freeuk.co.uk *Signs work*: "SJH" (sculpture) and "S J Holliday" (mural).

HOLLOWAY, Douglas Raymond, ARIBA, RWA; architect retd.; artist in water-colour, pen and wash. *b*: W. Hampstead, London, 25 Aug 1923. *s of*: Raymond Holloway & Norah Gertrude Wells. *m*: Marjorie Cynthia. three *s*. *Educ*: Haberdashers Aske's Hampstead, and Reading School. *Studied*: Royal West of England Academy School of Architecture. *Exhib*: RCamA, various mixed and one-man exhbns. in England and Wales and New York. *Works in collections*: RWA. *Commissions*: on behalf of the people of Lancashire, Douglas Holloway presented a watercolour of the River Hodder at Whitewell in The Forest of Bowland to H.M. The Queen on the occasion of her Golden Jubilee visit to The Guildhall in Preston, 5th August 2002. *Official Purchasers*: The Queen's Lancashire Regiment, Preston. *Address*: Longton Forge, 61 Liverpool Rd., Longton Preston, Lancs. PR4 5HA. *Signs work*: "D.R. Holloway."

HOLLOWAY, Laura Ellen, SWA (1994), Post DipFA (RA), SBA (1999); painter in water-colour and tempera. *b*: Worcester, 1960. *d of*: Jack and Joyce Holloway. *Educ*: Worcester Girls' Grammar School. *Studied*: Glos. College of Art (1978-82), RA Schools (1985-88, Norman Blamey, RA, Jane Dowling). *Exhib*: solo shows at Mason-Watts Fine Art, Warwick (1992); mixed shows in London and Birmingham. *Publications*: Medici Soc. Ltd. (greetings cards). *Address*: 404 Wyld's Lane, Worcester WR5 1EF. *Signs work*: "L.H."

HOLMES, Clyde, RCA Conway, National Diploma of Design (NDD) 1965. *Medium*: oil. *b*: Friern Barnet, London, 20 Oct 1940. *s of*: Charles Sydney Holmes. *Partner*: Cathy Knapp. one *s*. two *d*. *Studied*: Hornsey College of Art, London; St.Martin's School of Art (1961-65). *Represented by*: Henry Boxer Gallery. *Exhib*: Fine Art Society, London (2002), Crane Kalman Gallery, London (2004), The Commonwealth Institute (2002), Saatchi & Saatchi, London (2000), MoMA Wales (1999), National Museum of Wales, Cardiff (1991), Victoria & Albert Museum, London (1990), York City Art Gallery (1991), Abbot Hall Art Gallery, Kendal (1994), Gashall Gallery, Birmingham (1992), Huddersfield Art Gallery (1993), Stafford Art Gallery (1993). *Works in collections*: National Library of Wales; Museum of Modern Art Wales, European Culture Centre - Cologne; private and corporate collections. *Address*: Cwm Hesgin, Frongoch, Bala, Gwynedd, LL23 7NU. *Email*: cwmhesgin@hotmail.com *Website*: www.clydeholmes.force9.co.uk *Signs work*: "C Holmes".

HOLMES, Linda Ruth, BA (Cantab), SWE (1994). *Medium*: painting, printmaking (wood engraving). *b*: Sutton Coldfield, Warks, 5 Jun 1950. *d of*: Mr & Mrs G.L. Kirk. *m*: David Holmes. *Educ*: Weston-super-Mare Grammar School. *Studied*: Newnham College, Cambridge, Camberwell College of Art Summer School. *Exhib*: with Society of Wood Engravers Annual Exhibitions, UK, and in USA. *Works in collections*: British Library, V&A, Penn State University, PA, USA. *Commissions*: Penn State University, PA, USA; The Whittington Press; The Press of Appletree Alley, PA, USA. *Address*: 5 Salters Lane, Walpole, Suffolk, IP19 9BA. *Website*: www.lindaholmes.co.uk

HOLMES, Walter, artist/illustrator in oil, acrylic, pastel and water-colour. *b*: Wallsend on Tyne, 21 Aug 1936. *m*: Helen. two *s*. *Studied*: Newcastle University Evening School, Beamish College, Durham. *Exhib*: Gulbenkian Gallery, Newcastle; Queen's Hall, Hexham; Mall Galleries London; The Art Connection, Eton; The Blake Gallery, York; The Biscuit Factory, Newcastle; Off-the-Wall, Corbridge; The Blagdon Gallery, Morpeth; North East Art Collective, Newcastle; Robinson-Gay Gallery, Hexham. *Works in collections*: PricewaterhouseCoopers, Bank of England, Royal Navy. *Commissions*: Swan Hunter Shipbuilders, N.E. Shipbuilders, Northern Sinfonia, Marie Curie. *Publications*: Newcastle Breweries, Laing Calendar Competition 2nd prize, greetings cards for Kingsmead Publications plc and 4C, Quarto Publishing plc., Artists of Northumbria. *Address*: Eastern Way Farm, 4 Queensway, Darras Hall, Ponteland, Newcastle NE20 9RZ. *Email*: mail@walterholmes.co.uk *Website*: walterholmes.co.uk *Signs work*: "W. HOLMES".

HOLTAM, Brenda, RWS, BFA Hons (1983), RA Schools Postgraduate Dip. (1986); painter in oil, gouache, water-colour; figurative painter of still life, interiors, portraits and landscape; Tutor in water-colour. *b*: Whiteway, Glos., 2 Oct 1960. *m*: Howard Vie. two *s*. one *d*. *Educ*: Stroud Girls' High School. *Studied*: Glos. College of Art and Design (1979, T. Murphy), Falmouth School of Art (1980-83, F. Hewlett), RA Schools (1983-86, Peter Greenham, CBE, RA). *Exhib*: RA Summer Exhbn., NEAC Annual Exhbn., RP, RWS Members Exhbn. Bankside Gallery; two-person exhbn. Cadogan Contemporary (1994). *Misc*: Elected A.R.W.S. (1987), elected to full membership (1992). *Address*: 39 Ashburnham Rd., Richmond, Surrey TW10 7NJ. *Signs work*: "Brenda Holtam" or "Holtam."

HOLTOM, Roger, BA; Cert Ed. *Medium*: Mixed media. *b*: Sheffield, 10 Apr 1961. *Studied*: Leeds University (1979-82); Huddersfield Polytechnic (1987-89); Royal College of

Music (1982-84). *Represented by*: Fiumano Fine Art, London. *Exhib*: London Art Fair; Art London; AAF (London, New York, Singapore); Laborato Rio Aperto; Bussana, Italy; Albatros Studios, Sydney, Australia; Molde Jazz Festival, Norway; Holland House, London. *Commissions*: Slug and Lettuce Restaurants Group. *Official Purchasers*: Champions Real Estate, Chelsea, London; Chestertons Real Estate, Chelsea, London. *Recreations*: Classical chamber music (cello). *Misc*: Works in Bussana Vecchia, Italy. *Address*: 128 Wellmeadow Road, Hither Green, London SE6 1HP. *Email*: rogerholtom@gmail.com *Website*: www.rogerholtom.co.uk *Signs work*: "ROGER HOLTOM".

HOMES, Ronald Thomas John, DFC, FCSD; A.GAvA artist/industrial designer; winner of RSA industrial design bursaries (1948-49); Central School of Arts and Crafts Dip for Industrial Design. *Medium*: various. *b*: London, 3 Oct 1922. *s of*: Arthur Leopold Homes. *m*: Ione Winifred Amelia. two *d*. *Educ*: Willesden Technical College. *Studied*: Central School of Arts and Crafts. *Exhib*: Mall Galleries, London; Aldeburgh, Suffolk; Shaftesbury, Dorset. *Address*: 69 Linden Pk., Shaftesbury, Dorset SP7 8RN. *Email*: ronald.homes@care4free.net *Website*: ronaldhomes.co.uk

HONE, David, PPRHA, Hon. RA, HRSA; ex-officio portrait and landscape painter in oil. *b*: Dublin, 1928. *s of*: Joseph M. Hone, biographer. *m*: Rosemary D'Arcy. two *s*. one *d*. *Educ*: St. Columba's College; Univ. College, Dublin. *Studied*: National College of Art, Dublin (1947-50), under J. Keating and M. MacGonical. *Works in collections*: Portrait Collection, National Gallery, Dublin, Cork Municipal Gallery. *Address*: 4 Ailesbury Gardens, Dublin 4, Eire. *Signs work*: "D. Hone."

HOOD, Andrew David, BA Hons Illustration. *Medium*: acrylic. *b*: Kingston-upon-Thames, 19 Aug 1964. *s of*: John Hood. *Educ*: Stewerts Melveille College Edinburgh; Wilmslow Grammar School. *Studied*: Mid-Cheshire College of Art and Design; Stockport College; John Moores university, Liverpool. *Represented by*: Washington Gallery, Penarth; Moya Bucknall Fine Art, Birmingham. *Exhib*: RWA Autumn Show; SWA Summer Exhibition; solo shows, Washington Gallery (2000, 2002), Battersea Contemporary Art Fair, Colyer Bristow Gallery London. *Works in collections*: work held in private collections throughout the UK and abroad. *Commissions*: Wetherspoons plc; BBC; Woman's Weekly. *Works Reproduced*: works published by the Art Group, Prime Arts Ltd. *Address*: 141 Somerset Road Knowle Bristol BS4 2JA. *Email*: andy.hood@fineartimages.freeserve.co.uk *Website*: www.andrewhoodgallery.com

HOOKE, Robert Lowe, Jr., sculptor of figures, wild animals and birds in bronze; art dealer; investment adviser; Managing Director: Research Vision Ltd. *b*: Canton, Ohio, 12 Sep 1942. *s of*: Robert Hooke, industry executive. *Educ*: Bowdoin College, Brunswick, Maine (B.A.); Columbia University, NY (MBA). *Studied*: NY School of Visual Arts (1973-75, Herbert Kallem). *Exhib*: one-man shows: London, Geneva, Basel, Baden-Baden, Sydney, Johannesburg, Cape Town; group shows: Paris, Zurich, Amsterdam, San Francisco. *Works in collections*: Compton Acres, Poole; Oppenheimer Collection, S. Africa. *Commissions*: various private, Bowdoin College (USA). *Clubs*: Hurlingham, Royal Ocean Racing, Ascot Park Polo, Annabels. *Address*: 61 Holland Pk., London W11.

HOPE, Benjamin, Runner up, Lynn Painter Stainers Prize (2014); Jackson's Prize, United Society of Artists (2014). *Medium*: oil, drawing. *b*: Warrington, 26 Dec 1976. *Studied*: University of Cambridge (2001-2007: PhD in Theoretical Nanoscience, Certificate of Advanced Study in Mathematics (Merit)); University of Warwick (1996-2000: Master of Physics 1st Class, Joint Honours in Maths and Physics). *Exhib*: United Society of Artists (2014), Lynn Painter Stainers Prize (2014); Royal Society of British Artists (2014); Royal Institute of Oil Painters (2013); Royal Society of Miniature Painters, Sculptors & Gravers (2013); Royal Academy Summer Show (2013); Blackheath Art Society (2013); Oxford Art Society (1998, 1999, 2001, 2013). *Works in collections*: Private collections in the UK,

Australia, Italy, Switzerland and the USA. *Commissions*: Duke Humfrey Still Life commemorating the 400th anniversary of its opening, Bodleian Library, Oxford (2001). *Address*: 157 Langton Way, London SE3 7JS. *Email*: ben.hope@cantab.net *Website*: www.benjaminhope.net *Signs work*: "BH".

HOPE-KING, Christopher Stewart, ARMS (1993), RMS (1998), SM (1991), HS (1994), Gold Bowl Hon. mention RMS (1993), Fairman Members subject miniature award (1995); miniaturist in water-colour and acrylics (paints unique duck miniatures) of still life and landscapes; RMS President's Special Commendation, particular mention 2001. *b*: Leeds, Yorks., 16 Sep 1951. *Educ*: Homefield School, Bournemouth. *Studied*: with grandfather, Hector King. *Exhib*: RA Summer Show, Mall Galleries, British Painters, Westminster Gallery (RMS); many one-man shows. *Publications*: included in: Techniques of Miniature Painting (Sue Burton, Batsford), R.M.S. One Hundred Years (Suzanne Lucas, Lucas Art). *Address*: Staddle Cottage, 1 Mill St., Corfe Mullen, Wimborne Minster, Dorset BH21 3RQ. *Signs work*: "H.K."

HOPKINS, Clyde David F., BFA (Hons.) (1969); painter; Professor; Head of Painting, Chelsea College of Art (ret'd 2007); Emeritus Professor, University of the Arts, London (UAL); Chair of the E.A.Abbey Council (British School in Rome). *Medium*: normally oil on linen, or screen prints. *b*: Sussex, 24 Sep 1946. *s of*: F.P & I. Hopkins. *m*: Marilyn Hallam. *Educ*: Bexhill-on-Sea and Barrow-in-Furness, Cumbria. *Studied*: University of Reading (Claude Rogers, Terry Frost). *Represented by*: Advanced Graphics, London (Fine Art Printmakers). *Exhib*: Serpentine Gallery, Hayward Gallery, Ikon Gallery, Francis Graham-Dixon Gallery, Joan Prats Gallery, NYC, USA and many UK and European galleries. Curator exhibition 'Same As It Ever Was..', Mall Galleries, London (2008). *Works in collections*: ACGB, etc. *Commissions*: Arthur Andersen Consulting. *Publications*: various articles and catalogues (1976-2014). *Works Reproduced*: in Royal Academy Summer Show catalogue 2009, for example. *Clubs*: Chelsea Arts. *Misc*: Studios: London and Hastings. *Address*: 55 Marischal Rd., London SE13 5LE. *Email*: clydehopkins@talktalk.net. *Website*: APT, SoCo and Advanced Graphics London. *Signs work*: "Clyde Hopkins."

HOPKINSON, Sian Carolyn, BA (1989). *Medium*: painter in oil. *b*: 17 Apr 1967. *Studied*: Wimbledon School of Art. *Represented by*: Panter & Hall, London. *Exhib*: one-man shows: John Bennett Fine Paintings, London (2000); Rafael Valls, London (2003, 2005). Joint shows: Oakham Contemporary (2009-2011), Panter & Hall (2009-2012). *Publications*: illustrations for 'The Mysterious Fayum Portraits: Faces from Ancient Egypt' by Euphrosyne Doxiadis (Thames and Hudsons, London 1995). *Address*: Barnet, Hertfordshire. *Website*: www.sianhopkinson.com *Signs work*: "SH".

HORE, Richard Peter Paul, ARCA (Painting 1959, Mural Painting, Silver Medal 1960), NDD (Illustration 1955), FRSA (1964), RCA (Cambrian 1978); painter in gouache and mixed media. *b*: Clacton-on-Sea, 1935. *m*: Janice Hart. one *s*. one *d*. *Educ*: Colebaynes High School, Clacton. *Studied*: Colchester School of Art (1951-55, John O'Connor), RCA (1956-60, Carel Weight, Ruskin Spear, Leonard Rosoman). *Exhib*: RA; Welsh Arts Council; WAG, Birkenhead; Mostyn, Llandudno; Mall Galleries; Oriel, Theatre Clwyd; Muse, Philadelphia, USA, Stellenbosch, South Africa. *Works in collections*: RCA, Cheshire County and Chester City Councils, Dept. of the Environment, various private collections. *Commissions*: Chester City Council. *Publications*: Picturesque Chester by Peter Boughton (illustrations). *Address*: 12 Dee Fords Avenue, Chester CH3 5UP. *Signs work*: "RICHARD HORE."

HORNER, Marguerite, BA Hons, MA; Kidd Rapinet Award for Outstanding MA Show 2004. *Medium*: oil, watercolour, drawing. *b*: Lincoln, 18 Jul 1954. *d of*: Dr. & Mrs. E.T. Nix. *m*: Grenville. one *s*. three *d*. *Studied*: BA & MA in Fine Art Painting, Sheffield University 1973-76, City & Guilds of London Art School 2001-04; BBC Scenic Art Dept 1977-80

(BBC trained). *Represented by*: Beverley Knowles Fine Art 2004-09; Knowles/Gresle 2009-. *Exhib*: one-man shows: The Star Gallery, Lewes, East Sussex 2006; Usher Art Gallery, Lincoln 1977; Mappin Art Gallery, Sheffield 1977 (as née) Marguerite Nix; group shows: RA Summer Exhibition 1981, 2005, 2008; Discerning Eye 2005; RSMA 2005; AAF 2005; Art London 2006; London Art Fair, Chelsea 2005, 2007; Beverley Knowles Fine Art 2005, 06, 07. *Works in collections*: Graves Art Gallery, Sheffield (as née Marguerite Nix); private: Simon Draper and others in England, Ireland, Switzerland, Spain, New Zealand. *Commissions*: murals painted for architects Spiromega and Powell-Tuck, Connor and D'Orfelt in the 1980s. *Publications*: 'Arts Review' and many others . *Official Purchasers*: Graves Art Gallery, Sheffield. *Works Reproduced*: 'Until She Listens', Guardian G2: 2006; and The Times T2 2006. *Principal Works*: 'Ever Deeper', 'Faith Pours', 'To be where you really are'. *Recreations*: swimming, walking, reading, films. *Clubs*: Chelsea Arts Club, Esporta Health Club. *Misc*: Founding Member with Sir Peter Blake of 'The Iffley Rd Life-drawing Group of 6 artists in 1996. *Address*: 65 Rusthall Avenue, Chiswick, London W4 1BN. *Email*: margueritehorner@googlemail.com *Website*: margueritehorner.moonfruit.com *Signs work*: "Marguerite Horner" (and sometimes 'Nix' or 'Marguerite Nix' in the early years).

HORNER, Michael Julian Alistair, UA (1999); painter in soft pastel; Council mem. UA. *b*: Amersham, Bucks., 1 Jul 1975. *Educ*: Egerton-Rothesay School, Berkhamsted. *Exhib*: UA Annual - Westminster, Autumn Art Show - Sussex, Artists & Illustrators Exhibition - London, Lingfield Surrey, Penhurst Place Kent, Tunbridge Wells Art Society, Sundridge, Cowden, Kent. *Commissions*: Past include millenium map, Derwent Water from 1000ft up, takes many for portraits of animals and people, gardens. *Works Reproduced*: for publicity online. *Principal Works*: Swiss and Austrian Alpine. *Misc*: teaches and runs workshops. *Address*: The Rectory, Church St., Cowden, Edenbridge, Kent TN8 7JE. *Email*: michael@galleryonthenet.com *Website*: www.galleryonthenet.com *Signs work*: "MICHAEL HORNER."

HOROVITZ, Isabel, BA (Hons) (1978), Dip.Cons. (1982); paintings conservator; freelance conservator and consultant to Royal Academy of Arts. *b*: London, 1957. *m*: Jonathan Blake. three *s*. one *d*. *Educ*: St. Paul's Girls' School. *Studied*: University of London (History of Art), Courtauld Inst. of Art (Conservation of Easel Paintings). *Exhib*: Conservator for RA Loans Exhbns. *Publications*: contributions to various catalogues and conservation literature. *Misc*: Special interest in history, techniques and conservation of paintings on copper supports. *Address*: The Painting Conservation Studio. *Email*: isabelhorovitz@compuserve.com

HORTON, Antony Brian, landscape painter in oil and gouache. *b*: Birmingham, 21 Aug 1933. *s of*: E. Victor Horton, MC, JP. *m*: Sheila Horton. three *d*. *Educ*: Shrewsbury School and Exeter College, Oxford. *Studied*: Cheltenham College of Art (R.S. Dent). *Exhib*: RWS, RA, David Messum Gallery, West Wales Art Centre and local exhibitions. *Clubs*: MCC. *Address*: The Old Rectory, Taplow, Bucks. SL6 0ET . *Signs work*: "A. B. Horton" or "Brian Horton."

HORTON, James Victor, MA (RCA) (1974), RBA (1979); Prize Winner 'Discerning Eye' (1992). *Medium*: oil, water-colour and pastel. *b*: London, 24 Jul 1948. *m*: Rosalind. two *s*. *Studied*: Sir John Cass School of Art (1964-66), City & Guilds Art School (1966-70), Royal College of Art (1971-74) . *Exhib*: widely in Britain and abroad, eleven man shows. *Works in collections*: Girton, Newnham and Trinity Colleges, Cambridge. *Commissions*: extensive portraits. *Publications*: ten books on painting and drawing; numerous articles for art magazines. Taught in art schools and summer schools in Britain and abroad. *Works Reproduced*: many books and magazines. *Misc*: artist in residence to HRH Prince Charles Mt Athos; currently President, Royal Society British Artists. *Address*: 11 Victoria Rd., Cambridge CB4 3BW. *Email*: jamesvhorton@gmail.com *Website*: www.jameshortonartist.com

HORWITZ, Angela Joan, Professor; NS(1982), RAS (1983) FABS (2005); Associated Academician (Arts) Accademia Internationale Greci-Marino, Italy (1999); steward, AGBI (1985-86); Member Beaux-Arts, Cannes, South of France (1996-2007); Academical Knight, Dept. of Arts; Ordine Accademico Internazionale, Italy; Fellow of American Biographical Society; Order of the International Ambassadors; MD Eminent Fellow FABI of the American Biographical Institute; sculptress in stone, bronze, painter in oil and pastel. *b*: London, 14 Oct 1934. *d of*: M. Carson. two *s*. one *d*. *Educ*: Colet Court Girls' School, Rosemead Wales, Lycée Français de Londres. *Studied*: Marylebone Inst. (1978-1990), Sir John Cass College (1983-1985), Hampstead Inst. (1990-92). *Exhib*: Grand Palais, Paris (1985, 1986), RBA, NS, SWA (Mall Galleries), Civic Centre, Southend, City of London Polytechnic, Whitechapel, (1985), SEFAS, Guildhall, Ridley Soc., City of Westminster Arts Council, Alpine Gallery, Smiths Gallery Covent Gdn., Wintershall Gallery, nr. Guildford, The Orangery, Holland Pk. W8, Hyde Park Gallery (Winchester Cathedral, 1993), Beaux Arts, South of France (1997), Salon International du Livre et de la Presse à Genèva (1997), Miramar Hotel Beaux Arts (1998) Association Beaux Arts (1999), Antrum Gallery Bayswater (2000), Carre D'Or Gallery, Paris (2000), Association des Beaux-Arts, Cannes (2007), Raymond Gallery, Beaux Arts (2000); Plaisterer's Hall in aid of Red Cross (2005, 2014); Gallery Saint Sauveur Le Cannet, South of France (2005-2008); Lansdowne Club, Mayfair (2005-2008, 2009. 2011). *Works in collections*: Sculpture in stone for Winchester Cathedral; Well Woman Centre, The United Elizabeth Garrett Anderson Hospital for Women, London; Zurich Switzerland private collection, London private collection, France; Centre Hospitalier de Cannes (2011). *Clubs*: Lansdown. *Misc*: Listed Who's Who in International Art, Dictionary of International Biography, Cambridge Blue Book, Great Women of the 21st Century. *Address*: 6 Wellington House, Aylmer Drive, Stanmore, Middx. HA7 3ES. *Signs work*: "A.H." or "Angela Horwitz".

HOSKINS, Stephen, MA (1981), ARE (1989), RE (1995), BA (Hons) (1977); printmaker in silkscreen, lithography and drawing. *b*: Eastleigh, Hants., 31 Aug 1955. *m*: Dr. Sandy Budden. one *d*. *Educ*: Barton Peveril Grammar School. *Studied*: W. Surrey College of Art and Design (1974-77), RCA (1978-81). *Exhib*: RA, RE, mixed exhbns. worldwide. *Works in collections*: V&A, Tate Gallery. *Publications*: 3D Printing for Artists, Designers and Makers (Bloomsbury, 2013), Inks (A&C Black, 2004), Water-Based Screenprinting (A&C Black (001). *Address*: c/o Centre for Fine Print Research, UWE Bower Ashton Campus, Kennel Lodge Rd, off Clanage Road, Bristol BS3 2JT. *Email*: Stephen.Hoskins@uwe.ac.uk *Signs work*: "S. Hoskins."

HOUCHIN, David John, Silver Medal 2002. *Medium*: sculptor in clay and bronze. *b*: London, 20 Jun 1935. *m*: Katie. two *d*. *Educ*: Eastbourne College. *Studied*: Farnham School of Art (1955-57). *Clubs*: Treasurer of Society of Portrait Sculptors. *Address*: Farm Place, Isfield, Uckfield, E.Sussex, TN22 5TY.

HOUGH, Liz, BA (Hons) Fine Art (1988); Post Grad Dip in Painting (1991); RA Summer Exhbn Artist Under 30 Years of Age, Lanseer Scholarship. *Medium*: oil, drawing, mixed media, collage. *b*: Wolverhampton, 31 Jan 1966. *m*: James Barry. one *d*. *Studied*: Manchester (1985-88); RA Schools (1988-91). *Represented by*: Oliver Contemporary-Carolyn Oliver. *Exhib*: Piccadilly Gallery, Cadogan Contemporary, Offer Waterman Fine Art, RA Summer Exhbn, Belgrave Gallery (St. Ives); New Grafton Gallery. *Works in collections*: Bank of China, TSB, USA, Paintings in Hospitals, Blackwell Group, ATM New York. *Commissions*: London Contemporary Arts. *Address*: 10 Sandows Lane, St. Ives, Cornwall TR26 1QW. *Email*: lizhough@email.com *Website*: www.art-on-line.co.uk *Signs work*: 'LIZ HOUGH'.

HOUSE, Ceri Charles, artist in oil; gilding restorer. *b*: London, 20 Mar 1963. *Partner*: Amanda Wainwright. one *d*. *Educ*: St. Christopher School, Herts. *Studied*: with father, Gordon House. *Exhib*: NPG, BP Portrait awards (1994), RA Summer Shows (1992, 1993,

1995, 2000, 2001), one man show "Personal Pictures" at The Millinery Works 1999, mixed show Millinery Works 2000, 2001, 2002, 2003. *Commissions*: Numerous private commissions. *Publications*: R.A. Illustrated catalogue (1993), RA Illustrated 2000. *Address*: 109 Highbury New Park, London N5 2HG. *Email*: cerihouse@lineone.net

HOUSTON, Ian, ARCM, Member of Guild of Norwich Painters, FRSA; Silver medal, Paris Salon, Gold medal, FNCF. *Medium*: oil and water-colour. *b*: Gravesend, Kent, 24 Sep 1934. *s of*: Angus Houston. *m*: Ingrid. one *s*. one *d*. *Educ*: St. Lawrence College, Royal College of Music, St. Martins School of Art. *Represented by*: Portland Gallery. *Exhib*: over 90 one-man shows UK, USA, Australia. *Works in collections*: The Usher Gallery, Lincoln; Guernsey Museum and Falkland Islands Collection; UK and abroad. *Commissions*: include: Official Artist and Sponsor to the sail training ship "Young Endeavour", The UK Bicentennial Gift to Australia (1987); Painting presented to HM the Queen by the Company of Watermen and Lightermen to mark their 400th Anniversary (1989). *Works Reproduced*: Colour print of "Young Endeavour" - some signed by the Prime Ministers of UK and Australia for fund raising. *Address*: c/o Portland Gallery, 8 Bennet Street London SW1A 1RP. *Signs work*: "Ian Houston."

HOWARD, Diana Rosemary, RA Schools Diploma; Surrey Diploma (Hons); Bronze medal Painting, RAS (1971). *Medium*: oil, watercolour, mixed media. *b*: Wallington, Surrey, 31 Mar 1947. *d of*: Cyril & Grace Howard. *m*: John Morley. one *d*. *Educ*: eccentric private schools. *Studied*: Sutton School of Art; Epsom and Ewell School of Art; RA Schools (1969-71). *Exhib*: RA Summer Exhbns; Piccadilly Gallery; Arnolfini Gallery; Birmingham Museum and Art Gallery; Fine Art Society, London; National Trust Exhbn, Agnews (2000); David Messum AG; Cork Brick Gallery, Suffolk. *Works in collections*: private collections. *Commissions*: mural: Epsom and Ewell Polytechnic (1969). *Publications*: 'Great Ten' poetry by Simon Rae (pub. Brotherhood of Ruralists, 1989); 'Nine Poems' poetry by Eve Machin (pub. Brotherhood of Ruralists, 1987). *Works Reproduced*: 'The Ruralists' Chistopher Martin (Academy Pub., 1991). *Principal Works*: 'Dancer in the Garden'; coll. Caroline Odgers; ruralist paintings. *Recreations*: writing, poetry, eastern mysticism. *Misc*: early member of Brotherhood of Ruralists before name change (known as Broadheath Brotherhood). *Address*: North Green, Stoven, Beccles NR34 8DG. *Signs work*: 'Diana Howard'.

HOWARD, Ghislaine Marianne, BA Hons Fine Art; named 'Woman of the Year' 2008. *Medium*: oils, acrylics, drawings, watercolours, etchings. *b*: Eccles, nr. Manchester, 21 Jun 1953. *d of*: Martin and Maureen Dobson. *m*: Michael Howard. one *s*. one *d*. *Educ*: Adelphi House Grammar School, Salford. *Studied*: University of Newcastle-on-Tyne. *Represented by*: The Cynthia Corbett Gallery, 15 Claremont Lodge,The Downs, Wimbledon. *Exhib*: numerous solo and group shows in UK and abroad, including Manchester Art Gallery, The Whitworth Art Gallery, Liverpool Cathedral, Canterbury Cathedral, St. Paul's Cathedral, York Minster, Imperial War Museum North. *Works in collections*: The Royal Collection, Manchester Art Gallery, The Whitworth Art Gallery. *Commissions*: A Shared Experience (1993), The St. Anthony Sequence (2001), The Stations of the Cross (2000), The Visitation altarpiece (2003). *Publications*: featured in various publications and articles including 'Stations of the Cross: The Captive Figure (2000). *Official Purchasers*: Her Majesty's Prison Service, Methodist Art Collection, British Medical Association, Manchester Metropolitan University. *Works Reproduced*: on website and various publications. *Principal Works*: A Shared Experience; Stations of the Cross; St. Anthony sequence; Visitation altarpiece; 365 Series. *Misc*: widely acclaimed as a painter of shared human experience. *Address*: The Bridge House, 1 Collier Street, Glossop, Derbyshire, SK13 8LS. *Email*: ghislaine.howard@btinternet.com *Website*: www.ghislainehoward.com *Signs work*: usually signs oils and acrylics on the reverse.

HOWARD, Ian, MA (Hons), RSA; artist in acrylic, oil, mixed media, printmaking; Prof. and Principal of Edinburgh College of Art. *b*: Aberdeen,1952. *s of*: H.G. Howard. *m*: Ruth

D'Arcy. two *d*. *Educ*: Aberdeen Grammar School. *Studied*: Edinburgh University, Edinburgh College of Art (1970-76). *Exhib*: numerous one-man and group exhbns. *Works in collections*: SAC, ACGB, Aberdeen A.G., Dundee A.G., Hunterian A.G., City Art Centre Edinburgh, Contemporary Art Soc., Warwick University Art Centre. *Publications*: 'Ian Howard, Painting, Prints and Related Works' (Third Eye Centre Glasgow/Peacock Printmakers, Aberdeen), Heretical Diagrams (Peacock Printmakers, Aberdeen 1997). *Address*: c/o Edinburgh College of Art, Lauriston Place, Edinburgh EH3 9DF. *Signs work*: "I.H." or "Ian Howard."

HOWARD, Ken, (Professor) OBE, RA (1992), Hon.RBSA (1991), RWS (1983), RWA (1981), ROI (1965), NEAC (1961); Appointed Official Artist Northern Ireland Imperial War Museum (1973-78); President, New English Art Club (1998). *Medium*: oil. *b*: London, 26 Dec 1932. *s of*: Frank Howard. *m*: Dora Bertolutti. *Educ*: Kilburn Grammar School. *Studied*: Hornsey College of Art (1949-53), Royal College of Art (1955-58). *Represented by*: Richard Green, 147 New Bond St., W1S 2TS. *Exhib*: New Grafton Gallery (1971, 74, 76, 78, 81, 83, 86, 88, 90, 93, 95, 97, 99), Manya Igel Fine Art (1987-97), Richard Green (2002-09). *Publications*: 'The Paintings of Ken Howard' (David & Charles, 1992), 'Ken Howard, A Personal View' (David & Charles, 1998), 'Light & Dark' (Royal Academy 2011). *Clubs*: Chelsea Arts. *Address*: 8 South Bolton Gdns., London SW5 0DH. *Website*: www.kenhoward.co.uk *Signs work*: "Ken Howard."

HOWARTH, Anna, BA (Hons); Postgraduate Diploma. *Medium*: Paper (paper cutting). *b*: Manchester, 7 Dec 1964. *Educ*: Highfield, Cheshire. *Studied*: Salford University (1996-99); Chelsea (2010); Royal Academy of Dramatic Art (1990-91). *Exhib*: Bluecoat Display Centre, Liverpool; White Space, Totnes; The New Craftsman Gallery, St. Ives; Kestle Barton, Cornwall; Jody Maxwell Gallery, Chicago, USA; Rice Polak Gallery, Massachusetts, USA; Accesso Galleria, Italy; ICA, London; Black Swan Arts, Frome; South London Gallery, London; Rebecca Hossack Gallery, London; Oriel Mostyn, Llandudno, Wales; Beaumaris Festival, Wales; The Barn Gallery, Massachusetts, USA; International Art Fairs (Florida, Amsterdam, Miami, Toronto, Melbourne, Singapore, San Francisco, New York, Santa Fe, Moscow). *Commissions*: Ikea 2011; Mural artist Trafford Centre; Earls Court Exhibition Centre, London. *Publications*: Bridgeman Art Library (2010); Annual Wales View Brochure (2011). *Works Reproduced*: Ikea 2011. *Misc*: Black Swan Arts Public Choice Award (2008). *Email*: anna-howarth@hotmail.co.uk *Website*: www.annahowarth.com *Signs work*: "ANNA HOWARTH".

HOWARTH, Derek, NDD (Hons); ATD; ARBS; former assistant to Henry Moore. *Medium*: sculpture. *b*: Hyde, Cheshire, 20 Aug 1939. *s of*: William and Edith Howarth. *m*: Margaret. one *s*. one *d*. *Studied*: Manchester College of Art and Design; Bournemouth College of Art; . *Exhib*: RA, Leicester University, Abbotsbury Gardens, Renishaw, Long Island USA, Adam Gallery Penarth, Olympia Gallery at St. Brides, Pride of the Valley Sculpture Park, 28 Cork Street, Artshed, many mixed shows including Parndon Hill, Hatfield House, Woburn Abbey (2012). *Works in collections*: Athens Museum, Scottish Museum, Mr & Mrs J.J. Bash, 'Catchi'-Long Island USA, Mr & Mrs P. Ellwood, Mr & Mrs W. Fallis USA, Mr & Mrs D. Mann. *Commissions*: Bluewater, Mr & Mrs P. Ellwood, Athens Museum. *Recreations*: sculpture, sculpture, sculpture! *Address*: Colney Park House, Harper Lane, Radlett, Herts. WD7 9HG. *Email*: Howarthcolneyprk@ad.com *Website*: www.derekhowarth.co.uk *Signs work*: "Howarth", with line across joining centre of 'H's'.

HOWELD, Cheryl. *Medium*: painter, sculptor. *b*: St.Albans, 1944. *s of*: D.A. Freeman. two *s*. *Studied*: Hornsey College of Art under John Hoyland RA and Fred Cuming RA. Private periods of study 74-78 (Charles Hardaker NEAC, Nathan David FRBS) and then in Moscow 92-95 (I. Dmitriev). *Exhib*: PS; RBA; NEAC; Parkwalk Gallery; Stephanie Knight Gallery, (Knightsbridge and Fort Lauderdale); Richmond Gallery, Cork Street;

Glyndebourne Opera House Gallery; Churzee Gallery (Wandsworth and Wimbledon); Wimbledon Fine Art; Sculpture at the Sir Harold Hillier Garden and a series of sculptures for Denmans Garden. Frequently works to commission including one for HRH The Prince of Wales. *Works in collections*: numerous private collections in UK, America, Australia and Europe. *Commissions*: HRH The Prince of Wales; private commissions. *Misc*: opened the Churzee Gallery in London (1988-2006) beside her studio. It showed contemporary paintings and sculpture with Russian art a speciality. *Address*: Field House, Field Road, East Wittering, Chichester PO20 8NN. *Email*: cheryl@howeld.com *Website*: www.ch-fineart.com *Signs work*: 'C.Howeld'.

HOWELL, David, RSMA President (2008-2013); self taught painter in water-colour, oil and pastel. *b*: Markyate, 14 Jul 1939. *m*: Jenny. one *d*. *Educ*: St. Albans Grammar. *Exhib*: RSMA, SEA., many mixed and one-man shows in London and the UK, Middle East, USA, Hong Kong, Japan and Australia. *Works in collections*: United Biscuits, Provident Financial, Charterhouse Bank, Albank Alsaudi Alhollandi, H.R.H. Sultan Qaboos of Oman. *Publications*: City of the Red Sea (Scorpion, 1985); Painting with Oils (Crowood Publishing 2014); Just Watercolour (Ari Films (2013). *Works Reproduced*: LE Prints, magazine articles, fine art cards. *Address*: Stearsby Hall, Stearsby, N. Yorks YO61 4SA. *Email*: dh@davidhowell.co.uk *Website*: www.davidhowell.co.uk *Signs work*: "David Howell."

HOWELLS, Suzanne, ABRSA, SWA, MFPS. *Medium*: watercolour. *b*: Birmingham, 26 Jan 1948. *d of*: Anne & James Keliher. *m*: Gareth. two *d*. *Educ*: Harborne Hill School, Birmingham. *Studied*: self-taught. *Represented by*: Alpha Marketing Ltd., Unit 9, Links BC, Bishops Stortford. *Exhib*: Mall Galleries: RI, NEAC; Victoria Gallery, Derby; Bowl Gallery, London; A.Frame Gallery, Brecon; Westminster Gallery, London; Lawson Gallery, Cambridge; Quay Gallery, Guernsey; Helios Gallery, Birmingham; Templeman Gallery, Saffron Walden; Laing Exhbn, London. *Commissions*: work provided for: film 'The Queen'; TV series: Vicar of Dibley, Eastenders, Little Britain, Dangerfield, My Family. *Publications*: in Artists and Illustrators Magazine; Art of England Magazine. *Official Purchasers*: 250 galleries in the UK; Lynne Rogers MP. *Works Reproduced*: series of 150 limited edition prints. *Recreations*: gardening. *Address*: 28 Bull Street, Harborne, Birmingham B17 0HH. *Email*: garyhow@hotmail.com *Website*: www.suehowells.com *Signs work*: 'S.F.H.' or 'S.F.HOWELLS'.

HOWSON, Peter, DLitt., Honoris Causa, Strathclyde University, BA (Hons.), GSA; painter in oil. *b*: London, 27 Mar 1958. *s of*: Tom William Howson. *m*: Terry (divorced). one *d*. *Educ*: Prestwick Academy. *Studied*: Glasgow School of Art (1975-77 and 1979-81, Alexander Moffat). *Exhib*: widely in Europe and the USA. *Works in collections*: Tate Gallery, V&A, Metropolitan Museum of Modern Art, NY, MoMA, NY, Oslo Museum of Modern Art, Glasgow Art Galleries. *Commissions*: Official war artist, Bosnia (1993). *Publications*: many publications, including 'Peter Howson' by Robert Heller (Momentum, 2003). *Clubs*: The Glasgow Art Club, The Caledonian Club. *Address*: c/o Flowers East, 82 Kingsland Road, London E2 0PP. *Signs work*: "Howson."

HOYLE, Jonathan Martin, BA (Hons) Fine Art, First Class Postgrad. Dip. Painting. *Medium*: painter in oil, gouache. *b*: Rochdale,10 Jul 1957. *Studied*: Gloucestershire College of Art and Design (1976-79), Royal Academy Schools (1979-82). *Represented by*: Abbott and Holder, 30 Museum Street, London, WCIA 1LH. *Exhib*: Discerning Eye, Laing Art Exhibition. *Works in collections*: HRH The Prince of Wales, St.Peter's College, Oxford. *Clubs*: RASAA. *Address*: 91 Millfield, New Ash Green, Longfield, Kent DA3 8HN. *Email*: jonathanhoyle1957@googlemail.com

HUCKVALE, Iris, RMS, SBA., SM; miniaturist in oil on wood and polymin; Silver Gilt Medalist RHS, Certificate of Botanical Merit SBA. *b*: Northampton, 27 Sep 1930. *d of*: Herbert Leeding. *m*: John Huckvale, OBE. one *s*. one *d*. *Educ*: Northampton Grammar

School for Girls. *Studied*: Nottinghamshire Evening Inst., but mainly self taught. *Exhib*: RA, RMS, SWA, SBA, SWLA, Medici, SM, MAS-F, MAS-NJ; one-man show, Coach House Gallery, Guernsey. *Works Reproduced*: Medici greetings cards. *Address*: 4 Heath Green, Heath and Reach, Leighton Buzzard, Beds. LU7 0AB.

HUDSON, Eleanor Erlund, ARCA (1937); graphic artist, portraitist, figure subjects, water-colourist; costume designer, artistic adviser to former Brooking Ballet School of Marylebone. *b*: S. Devon. *d of*: Harold Hudson and Helen Ingeborg Olsen. *Educ*: Wentworth Hall, Surrey. *Studied*: RCA (School of Engraving) under Professors Malcolm Osborne, RA, R. S. Austin, RA, Drawing Prize, 1936, Continuation Schol. (4th year) 1938, Travelling Schol. 1939. *Exhib*: RA, Bankside Gallery, London and international. *Works in collections*: Boston Pub. Library, Fogg Museum, USA, Imperial War Museum, London, War Artist's Advisory Comm. *Misc*: other address: Meadow House, Old Bosham, Sussex PO18 8JF. *Address*: 6 Hammersmith Terr., London W6 9TS. *Signs work*: "ERLUND HUDSON."

HUDSON, Thomas Roger Jackson, Teachers' Cert. (1951), Teachers' Dip. (1961), M.Coll.H. (1962), Mem. AWG; self employed furniture maker and designer. *b*: Bicester, Oxon., 24 Jul 1929. *s of*: Frederick Thomas John Hudson. *m*: Ragnhild Ann Schanche. one *s*. two *d*. *Educ*: Bicester Grammar School. *Studied*: Oxford School of Art (1947), Shoreditch College (1949-51), Camberwell School of Art (1961), Goldsmiths' College (1962). *Works in collections*: private houses, churches, schools, boardrooms. *Publications*: Wheelstocks and Ploughshares (Tabb House, 1988), Gunstocks and Dovetails (Tabb House, 2000), A Carthorse for Miss Crichton (Kindle). *Address*: The Barn, 117 High St., Odell, Bedford MK43 7AS. *Signs work*: carved into all major works (cow).

HUFTON, Susan Mary, B.Ed (Hons) (1980); Certificate and Diplomas in Calligraphy and Bookbinding (1983-86); Fellow of the Society of Scribes and Illuminators (FSSI) (1987); Full member of Letter Exchange. *Medium*: calligraphy, lettering, letter carving. *b*: Worcester, 1 Oct 1957. *d of*: David Kearley. *m*: Robert Hufton. two *s*. *Educ*: Kettering High School for Girls. *Studied*: Roehampton Institute (Southlands College 1976-80; Digby Stuart College 1983-86). *Represented by*: Ann Camp. *Exhib*: Society of Scribes & Illuminators Exhibitions 1991-2012, exhibitions at Chepstow Museum, Ditchling Museum, Wolesey Fine Arts; Crafts Council Touring Exhbn: Minneapolis Institute of Art and many USA venues; V&A (as part of St.John's Bible team, 2005-2012). *Works in collections*: Crafts Study Centre, Farnham. *Commissions*: West Dean College, World Methodist Council. Private commissions: St.John's Abbey Minnesota - the Saint John's Bible, Cambridge Colleges, Oundle School. *Publications*: Step-by-Step Calligraphy (Weidenfeld & Nicholson, 1995); various journals. *Works Reproduced*: in calligraphic journals and books. St. John's Bible. *Recreations*: reading, sewing, music and theatre, outdoors. *Clubs*: Society of Authors. *Address*: 14 Well Street, Bury St Edmunds, Suffolk IP33 1EQ. *Email*: suehufton@me.com *Website*: web.me.com/suehufton/calligraphy *Signs work*: 'SUSAN HUFTON'.

HUGHES, Christine, DipEd (1968), DipFA (1994); painter in oil, printmaker, teacher; watercolour. *b*: London, 20 Feb 1946. *m*: D C C Hughes. two *d*. *Educ*: Homerton College, Cambridge. *Studied*: Southampton College of Art (1989-94). *Exhib*: many mixed and solo shows in S.W. England and Cumbria. Castlegate House, Cumbria; Gallery 2, Ringwood, Hampshire. *Works in collections*: NZ, Australia and widely across Europe. *Official Purchasers*: Hampshire County Council. *Recreations*: sailing, mountain walking. *Address*: Linmoor Cottage, Highwood, Ringwood, Hants. BH24 3LE. *Email*: cchughes@waitrose.com *Website*: www.christinehughesimages.co.uk *Signs work*: "C. Hughes" or H within a C.

HUGHES, Jim, DA (1954), SGA (1972), ATC (1955), TGC (1956); artist/designer/calligrapher; former teacher of art and design, Adult Educ. Dept., University of Glasgow. *b*: Glasgow, 1934. *s of*: Janet Orr, craftswoman, and Edward Hughes. *Educ*: Ayr

Academy. *Studied*: Glasgow School of Art (1950-54); Jordanhill College (1954-56) under Sam Black, DA, RSW. *Works in collections*: Glasgow Art Gallery, National Trust for Scotland, Royal Burgh of Ayr, other work in private collections throughout the world. *Publications*: Graphic Design for S.S.A.E. and Ayr Adult Educ. Booklets. Work featured in B.B.C. TV series "The Quest"(1989). *Address*: 32 Macadam Pl., Ayr KA8 0BZ. *Signs work*: initials on work, name on back.

HUGHES, Kevin Michael, BSc (1969), ALA (1971), RI (2000); Prize for Best Watercolour in 1997 Discerning Eye Exhbn., Benton/Humphries Prize in 1999 Discerning Eye; Third Prize Singer & Friedlander/Sunday Times Watercolour Competition; Ranelagh Press Award, 2006 RI Exhibition; Rowland Hilder Award, 2007 RI Exhibition; artist in watercolour, oil and pastel. *b*: Colwyn Bay, 4 Sep 1947. *m*: Kate Skillington. one *s*. one *d*. *Educ*: Reading University, Polytechnic of N. London. *Exhib*: RI, NEAC, Discerning Eye, RWS, RWA; one-man shows: many since 1980 including several at the Alresford Gallery. *Works in collections*: Wessex Collection, Longleat. *Clubs*: Royal Institute of Painters in Watercolour. *Address*: Edge Hill, Helscott Rd., Marhamchurch, Bude, Cornwall EX23 0JE. *Email*: kevihug@hotmail.com *Website*: www.kevinhughesri.com *Signs work*: "Kevin Hughes."

HUGHES, Marcia, SWA; Awards: Princess Michael of Kent Award for Most Outstanding Watercolour in Show (SWA, 2002); finalist, 'Not The Turner Prize' (2003); Arthur Henderson Hall Award (2004 & 2005). *Medium*: watercolour. *b*: Surbiton, Surrey, 12 Dec 1943. *d of*: Ethel & Roy Beck. *m*: Fenton Hughes. two *s*. one *d*. *Educ*: Coombe County Girls School. *Studied*: self taught. *Exhib*: Mall Galleries: SWA, SBA, 'Not The Turner Prize'; Picturecraft, Holt, Norfolk; Savoy Hotel Gift Shop; Aberfeldy Gallery, Perthshire; Selwyn Smith Studio, Teddington; The Old Post Office, Barnes; Wadhurst, E.Sussex; Vivartis, Godalming. *Works in collections*: internationally. *Commissions*: 'The View from Richmond Hill', for presentation by the Mayor to the warship 'The Richmond'. *Official Purchasers*: The Mayor of Richmond on Thames. *Principal Works*: 'A Fishermans Lot' Newlyn, 'A Fishermans Lot' Aldeburgh. *Clubs*: Molesey Art Society; Teddington Riverside Artists. *Misc*: tutor in art at Richmond Adult Comm. College, Landmark Arts Centre and privately. *Address*: 100 Shacklegate Lane, Teddington, Middx., TW11 8SH. *Email*: marciahughesart@gmail.com *Signs work*: 'Marcia Hughes'.

HUGHES, Tom, BA Hons. *Medium*: Oil. *b*: Colchester, 12 Dec 1979. *Exhib*: RA Summer Show (2013); BP Portrait Prize (2014); Lynne Painter Stainers prize (2013, 14). *Publications*: Leisure Painter (2013); Clifton Matters (2013); Plein Air Magazine (2013). *Address*: Hall Floor Flat, 63 Redland Road, Bristol BS6 6AQ. *Email*: mail@tomhughespainting.co.uk *Website*: www.tomhughespainting.co.uk *Signs work*: "Hughes" old works signed as "H".

HUME, Robin, RGI. *Medium*: oil, clay and bronze. *b*: Airthrey Castle, Bridge of Allan, 1943. *Studied*: Glasgow School of Art. *Exhib*: The Royal Glasgow Institute of the Fine Arts; The Royal Scottish Academy of Painting, Sculpture and Architecture; Glasgow Art Club; Talbot Rice Gallery, University of Edinburgh. *Works in collections*: private collections. *Misc*: taught drawing and painting at Glasgow School of Art 1972-2003. Paid to stop 2003. *Address*: Ashpad, Kirkoswald, Ayrshire, KA19 8JB.

HUMPHREYS, David, BA (Dunelm); Thomas Penman Scholar and State Scholar at Durham University (1958-62); painter and constructor. *b*: London, 27 Oct 1937. *s of*: J.H.Ll. Humphreys. *Educ*: Battersea Grammar School and King's College, Durham University (Dept. of Fine Art). Elected mem. Royal Cam. Academy (1994). *Works in collections*: Arts Council, Leicester, Newcastle, London Universities, Ministry of the Environment, Bishop Otter College, Ashridge College, Nuffield Foundation, ICI, J. Sainsbury, Shell, American Express Bank (London and NY), P&O, Financial Times, HM the Queen Mother, HRH the Prince of Wales, National Library of Wales, UK Government. *Publications*: 'A Painter's

Notes'(1999), A further view (2002), Heaven on Earth (2003). *Address*: Maudlin Hill House, Sopers La., Steyning, W. Sussex BN44 3PU. *Signs work*: "Humphreys." or "dh".

HUNDLEBY, A. R., designer-packaging and graphics, artist in water-colour. *b*: 15 Aug 1923. *m*: Marion Smallshaw, A.T.D. one *s*. two *d*. *Studied*: Lincoln and Leicester. *Address*: 35 Kelross Rd., London N5 2QS; and Hill House, Binham, Norfolk NR21 0DW. *Email*: Ahundleby@aol.com *Signs work*: "HUNDLEBY."

HUNKIN, Sally Elizabeth, artist in etching, water-colour and oils, gardener; Artists Books. *Medium*: principally etching. *b*: Herts. 29 Jun 1924. *m*: Oliver Hunkin, ex-TV producer (decd). one *s*. one *d*. *Educ*: St. Mary's Calne; Dartford College. *Studied*: Richmond Adult College. *Exhib*: solo shows locally and in Suffolk and Manchester; group shows include Royal Soc. of Artist Printmakers, and RA. *Works in collections*: St. Thomas's Hospital. *Commissions*: two friezes for St. Thomas's Hospital. *Works Reproduced*: posters and cards for Kew Gdns. *Address*: 31 Leyborne Pk. Kew, Richmond, Surrey TW9 3HB. *Email*: sallyhunkin@gmail.com *Website*: kew-artists.com *Signs work*: "Sally Hunkin."

HUNT, Emma, BA (Hons), MA; Sen. lecturer, Art and Design History; Course Director, Cultural Studies, Bournemouth and Poole College of Art; adviser to Southern Arts. *b*: Bideford, 27 July 1962. *m*: Martin. two *s*. *Educ*: Leicester and Birmingham. *Exhib*: curated small college exhbns. and at Russell-Cotes Museum. *Publications*: contributor to design history articles. *Address*: c/o Arts University Bournemouth, Wallisdown, Poole, Dorset BH12 5HH. *Signs work*: "E.F. Hunt."

HUNT, Geoffrey William, Past-President RSMA; Wapping Group of Artists; marine artist and illustrator in oil and water-colour. *b*: Twickenham, 11 Mar 1948. *s of*: Eric William Hunt. *m*: Vivienne Anne Hobbs. two *s*. *Educ*: Hampton Grammar School. *Studied*: Kingston School of Art (1966-67), Epsom School of Art (1967-70). *Exhib*: RSMA since 1977; Mystic Seaport Gallery, USA. *Works in collections*: Royal Naval Museum, Portsmouth; R.N. Submarine Museum, Gosport; H.M.S. Neptune, Faslane; Mariner's Museum, Newport News, USA; RSMA Diploma Collection; The Mary Rose Trust. *Publications*: illustrated many book covers including complete series of Patrick O'Brian's Aubrey/Maturin novels; compiler: 'A Celebration of Marine Art' (Blandford, 1996); 'The Tall Ship in Art' (Blandford, 1998); 'The Marine Art of Geoff Hunt' (Conway, 2004); 'The Wapping Group of Artists' (Seafarer, 2005). *Works Reproduced*: print editions by Mystic Seaport; Richard Lucraft; Art Marine. *Recreations*: sailing. *Address*: Dalton House, 60 Windsor Avenue, Wimbledon, London SW19 2RR. *Signs work*: "Geoff Hunt."

HUNT, George Robert, B.Ed. (Hons); PPUA; Awards: Courage Cornishman Picture Competition ref: Wedding of Duke of Cornwall & Lady Diana Spencer. *Medium*: oil, watercolour. *b*: London, 12 May 1934. *m*: Shirley M. Hunt. one *s*. one *d*. *Educ*: self-taught. *Studied*: of St. Mark & St. John, Plymouth (1982-86). *Represented by*: spate-art.co.uk. *Exhib*: Beatrice Royal Gallery, Eastleigh; Chichester Open Art Exhibition; US (United Society of Artists) Open Exhibition, Westminster; Chapter House Exhibition, Gloucester Cathedral; Solo exhibitions at Denbies, Dorking & Chertsey Windor St. Gallery. *Works in collections*: private collections. *Commissions*: private commissions in oils, pastel, sketches. *Official Purchasers*: Social groups. *Recreations*: Mountain walking, swimming, reading, writing. *Address*: Knott's Berry, 17 Ashton Road, Eye, Suffolk IP23 7LF. *Email*: grhunt@btinternet.com *Website*: spate-art.co.uk *Signs works*: "Spate Huntermann".

HUNT, Susie, BA (Hons.) Fine Art (1980); MFA Aberdeen (2007). *Medium*: water-colour and mixed media. *b*: Fareham, Hants., 18 Dec 1957. *m*: Anthony Paul Duley. one *s*. one *d*. *Studied*: Canterbury College of Art (1976-77), West Surrey College of Art (1977-80), Grays School of Art (2006-7). *Exhib*: many mixed and solo shows in London and Home Counties, R.W.S. Awards (1997), R.I. Open (1997, 1998, 2000), Aberdeen Artists (2001), annual Kent

Painters Group charity exhibition, Art for Youth North 2003, Art for Youth London October 2003, Society of Scottish Artists (2006), RSW (2009). *Works in collections*: Wallacespace - London; Grampian Hospitals Arts Trust, Aberdeen; Aberdeen College. *Commissions*: Wallace City Training. *Clubs*: Reigate Soc. of Artists, nominated professional member Aberdeen Artists (2002); Founder 'North East Open Studios' (NEOS). *Address*: Mill Farm, Aquhythie, Invervrie, Aberdeenshire AB51 5NY. *Email*: susiejhunt@hotmail.com *Signs work*: "Susie Hunt."

HUNTER, Caroline, MA Hons History of Art; James Torrance Memorial Award 1999 most Promising Young Painter at Glasgow RGI. *Medium*: acrylic. *b*: Edinburgh, 9 Dec 1964. *d of*: James and Margaret Hunter. *m*: William Self. *Educ*: Stromness Academy, Orkney; Aberdeen University. *Studied*: History of Art. *Exhib*: five solo shows (3 with Mainhill Gallery, Ancrum; prop: Diana Bruce); over 20 mixed shows; regular contributor to RGI and RSA Shows; shortlisted for Noble Grossart Prize (1997); Laing Seascape and Landscape Competition, Mall Galleries 2002 (shortlist). *Publications*: Mainhill Gallery Exhbn. catalogue 2003. *Works Reproduced*: 'Christmas Day' print, 'Field, August' print. *Recreations*: fashion, camping. *Misc*: started painting in 1994, previously cartoon work, illustration and archaeological fieldworker. *Address*: Dunbhronaig, Carsaig, Tayvallich, Argyll PA31 8PN. *Email*: caroline@hunter339.fsnet.co.uk

HUNTER, Christa, SWA; sculptor in terracotta, porcelain, bronze resin, bronze. *b*: Stuttgart, Germany, 18 Aug 1943. one *s*. one *d*. *Educ*: Ostheim Stuttgart. *Studied*: Sculpture course by Major Tugwell/Judy Cousins (1983). *Exhib*: regularly with art socs. in Berks. and Surrey, annually S.W.A. at Westminster Hall and Mall Galleries, Harrods Picture Gallery, Medici Gallery (1994), annually Surrey Sculpture Soc. Sculpture Trail Wisley, Chelsea Flower Show (1998), Art Parks International Sausmarez Manor Guernsey, Belvoir Castle (2001), Druidstone Wildlife Park (2001), Savill Garden, Borde Hill, Kingsmead Gallery Great Bookham, Century Gallery Datchet, and Affordable Art Fair with Linda Blackstone Gallery Pinner, The Gallery Virginia Water, Holme Grange Gallery Wokingham. *Works in collections*: Lincoln Joyce Fine Arts, Great Bookham; Art Parks International, Guernsey; Linda Blackstone Gallery, Pinner. *Commissions*: several private Foundry Bronze. *Address*: 1 Eliot Close, Camberley, Surrey GU15 1LW. *Email*: christahunter@hotmail.co.uk *Website*: www.christahunter.com *Signs work*: "C.H." or "Christa."

HUNTER, Elizabeth, RWA; NDD, ATD, Slade Diploma (Lond); painter and printmaker. *Medium*: oil, prints. *b*: Bristol, 8 Jun 1935. one *s*. *Educ*: Kingswood Grammar School. *Studied*: West of England College of Art (1951-56); Slade School of Fine Art (1956-58, Special Commendation 1958). *Represented by*: Belgrave Gallery, St. Ives; Penwith, Cornwall. *Exhib*: solo shows: Arnolfini, Bristol; Coopers Gallery, Theatre Royal Bristol; Art Garden, Bristol; Trereife Gallery, Penzance (2007). Mixed shows: Newlyn and Penwith Societies, Cornwall, Royal Academy, RWA, Belgrave St. Ives, Badcocks Newlyn, Cube Gallery Bristol, Studio Fusion, Oxo Tower Wharf, Saltgrass, Hamps; The Art Room, Topsham. *Works in collections*: RWA. *Recreations*: opera, gardening. *Clubs*: Newlyn Society of Artists, Penwith Society of Artists. *Address*: 5 Regent Square, Penzance, Cornwall, TR18 4BG. *Website*: www.ecrhunter.com *Signs work*: "HUNTER" or "E.H."

HUNTER, Henry Hay, UA (2000); artist in oil. *b*: Beal, Northumberland, 4 Mar 1934. *m*: Kathleen. *Educ*: St. Peter's School, York. *Studied*: Buckinghamshire College (1995-97). *Exhib*: RDS (1949, 1950), UA (1994-2000). *Works in collections*: private: England, S. Africa, NZ, Germany. *Publications*: Fine art prints. *Clubs*: Southwold Art Circle, Beccles Soc. of Artists. *Address*: 11 Fairmile Close, Worlingham, Beccles, Suffolk NR34 7RN. *Signs work*: "Henry Hay Hunter" or monogram of three H's.

HUNTER, Janet Claire (Jan), BA (Hons) Fine Art (2007); SWA (1997), FETC (1987), Dip. in Advertising and Design (1965); photographer, printmaker and artist in oils and water-colour, dry and acrylic media. *Medium*: digital photography, oils, watercolours. *b*: Reading, Berks., 2 Jul 1946. *m*: Ian Hunter. one *s*. one *d*. *Educ*: Westwood Grammar School, Reading. *Studied*: Berks. College of Art, Reading (1962-65),University College for the Creative Arts, Farnham (2002-2007). *Exhib*: RA Summer Exhibition; Mall Galleries, London; Bankside Gallery, London; Truman Brewery, London; Gallery One, Greyshot; The Lightbox, Woking. *Recreations*: walking, garden design, music, singing, reading. *Clubs*: Guildford Art Society. *Address*: Greatwood, 209 Brox Rd., Ottershaw, Surrey KT16 0RD. *Email*: janhunter1000@yahoo.co.uk *Website*: www.janhunter.com *Signs work*: "Jan Hunter" or "JH".

HUNTERMANN, Spate: see HUNT, George Robert.

HUNTINGTON-WHITELEY, James, BA (Hons) Manchester (1985); Modern British and Contemporary Art Exhbn. Organizer. *b*: 14 Aug 1963. *m*: Magdalen Evans. one *s*. one *d*. *Address*: 38 Hopefield Ave., London NW6 6LH.

HUNTLY, Moira Gay, ATC (Lond), PS (1978), RI (1981), RSMA (1985), RWA (1995); artist in acrylic, oil, pastel, water-colour; President, Pastel Society. *b*: Motherwell, Scotland, 7 Nov 1932. *d of*: G.L.R. Watkins. *m*: Ian E. Buchanan Huntly. one *s*. two *d*. *Educ*: Wirral County School for Girls, Harrow Weald County School. *Studied*: Harrow School of Art (1948-53), Hornsey College of Art (1953-54). *Exhib*: Young Contemporaries, ROI, NEAC, RI, PS, RWA, RSMA, FCA, Pastellistes de France; numerous solo shows, Mystic Maritime Museum, USA, Mercer Art Gallery, Southampton City Art Gallery. *Works in collections*: Maritime Museum, Falmouth (RSMA Coll.). *Commissions*: for international companies. *Publications*: 'Imaginative Still Life', 'Painting and Drawing Boats', 'Painting in Mixed Media', 'Learn to Paint Gouache', 'Learn to Paint Mixed Media', 'The Artist's Drawing Book', 'Learn to Draw Boats', 'Moira Huntly's Sketchbook Secrets'. *Official Purchasers*: Hampshire County Council, National Library of Wales. *Clubs*: The Arts Club, London. *Address*: "Alpha", Collin Cl., Willersey, Broadway, Worcs. WR12 7PP. *Signs work*: "Moira Huntly."

HURDLE, Robert Henry, RWA Hon; painter; senior lecturer until 1981, Faculty of Fine Art, Bristol Polytechnic. *b*: London, 9 Aug 1918. *s of*: Arthur E. Hurdle and Flora Bensted. two *s*. one *d*. *Studied*: Richmond School of Art (1935-37), Camberwell School of Arts and Crafts (1946-48) under Coldstream. *Exhib*: one-man shows, University College of Swansea (1973); Albany Gallery, Cardiff (1974); New Ashgate Gallery, Farnham (1977); City A.G., Bristol (1977); Pao Sui Loong Galleries, Hong Kong Arts Centre (1978); King St. Gallery, Bristol (1982); Farnham Maltings (1983); Pelter/Sands Gallery (1988); Cleveland Bridge Gallery, Bath (1989); Retrospective exhbn. R.W.A. (1995), Robert Hurdle at 80, R.W.A. (1998), Drawings Past and Present, Rood Gallery (2002), Meetings with Trees, RWA (2003). Selective Retrospective, New Gallery RWA (2008); Early Work, Art Room, Topsham (2012). *Works in collections*: Queens Collection; University College, Swansea; RWA Permanent Collection; City Art Gallery, Bristol; Bath University; Hong Kong Arts Centre; Wessex Collection, Longleat and various private collections. *Publications*: 20th Century Painters & Sculptors, Dictionary of Britisl Art vol.vi by Frances Spalding. *Address*: 14 Oxford St., Kingsdown, Bristol BS2 8HH. *Website*: www.roberthurdle.co.uk *Signs work*: signature or seal.

HURFORD, John Roger, SWAC; Artists of the Year (2013); SGFA Presidents Award (2013). *Medium*: oil, watercolour, drawing, acrylics. *b*: Chulmleigh, Devon, 8 Jun 1948. *Studied*: self-taught. *Exhib*: RCA; Burton Gallery, Bideford, Devon; Witney; New York; Tate Liverpool; Mall Gallery, London; SCREAM, London; Menier Gallery, Southwark, London. *Works in collections*: V&A Museum, London. *Commissions*: portraits (local people), theatre design (Mad and her Dad). *Publications*: illustrations in over 40 books. *Works Reproduced*: posters (1967-76); books (1974-2000). *Address*: Wixon Cottage, Chulmleigh, Devon EX18 7DS. *Website*: www.johnhurford.co.uk *Signs work*: 'John Hurford'.

HURN, Peter Henry Charles. *Medium*: oil, watercolour, drawing. *b*: Bristol, 29 Dec 1942. *Educ*: Patchway Secondary Modern, Perth Boys School, W. Australia. *Studied*: Perth Technical College, Perth Faculty of Arts (1959); Birkbeck College, University of London (1969); St. Martin's School of Arts (1970). *Exhib*: Australia, Italy, Switzerland (1960-70s); Mixed shows, Royal Academy (1976); Royal Exchange (1977); "Il Galeone" Cevvo Liguria, Italy (1966); John Moores, Liverpool (1978); Chateau d'Allaman Suiss (1981). *Works in collections*: Switzerland, UK, France, Italy. *Publications*: Who's Who in International Art; The Royal Exchange catalogue; Royal Academy Exhibition (1971-89); Who's Who in Art 24th Ed; John Moores cat. (1978); Il Galeone cat. (1966). *Works Reproduced*: Who's Who in International Art p.6 Suiss. 91-92 ed., 87-88 ed. *Principal Works*: "The Circus of Life", "Patrizia", "Nacht", "Garden of Delight". *Recreations*: art, music, theatre, reading. *Address*: 19 Stuart Court, Recorder Road, Norwich NR1 1NP. *Email*: peternewtonassetmanagement@yahoo.com *Signs work*: "HURN" or mono of H in circle.

HURST, Stephanie, Dip. in illustration (1974), RA Dip. of advanced studies - BA equivalent (1984); painter in oil on board with gesso ground. *b*: Wimborne, Dorset, 3 Jul 1952. *d of*: James Hurst, Chartered architect (retd.). *Educ*: Convent of the Sacred Heart, Weymouth. *Studied*: Bournemouth and Poole College of Art (1970-71), Hornsey College of Art (1971-74), Byam Shaw School of Painting and Drawing (1976-77), R.A. Schools (1981-84). *Exhib*: R.A., Royal Festival Hall, Spirit of London Competition (awarded prize), South Bank Show, Camden Arts Centre - Druce Competition (awarded prize), Bath Contemporary Arts Fair, Elgin Fine Art, Bath, Jonathan Poole Gallery, London. *Address*: 3 King's Ave., Muswell Hill, London N10 1PA. *Signs work*: "S. Hurst" on back of painting.

HUSON, Cedric Nigel, DipAD Painting/Printmaking (1973), RA Schools Post. Grad. Cert. (1978); ING Purchase Prize 2008. *Medium*: Painting. *b*: Salop, 1 Jun 1951. *s of*: Eric & Frances Huson. *m*: Kitta Potgieter. *Educ*: Marlborough Grammar School, Wilts. *Studied*: Salisbury School of Art (1967-68), Swindon School of Art (1968-69), Winchester School of Art (1970-73), Royal Academy Schools (1975-78). *Exhib*: Group shows: Piccadilly Gallery (1987-99), Lamont Gallery (1994-95), RA Summer Exhbn. (1988-94, 1997-98, 2000, 2002, 2004-09, 2011), Hunting Group Open (1989, 1990, 1994), Cleveland Bridge Gallery, Bath (1990), The London Group Open (1990, 1992, 1993), The Discerning Eye (1992, 1995, 1999, 2000, 2001), National Trust Centenary Exhbn. (1995), Everard Read Gallery, Cape Town (1997), Southwark Festival (1997), Everard Read Gallery, Johannesburg (1998), Chambers Gallery (2006), Medici Gallery (2006, 2007), Lost Gallery (2008-14), Discerning Eye (2008 - awarded ING Purchase Prize), Glasgow Art Fair (2009). *Works in collections*: Southampton City Art Gallery; ING Collection UK. *Address*: Sunnyside Croft, Overbrae, Fishrie, Nr. Turriff, Aberdeenshire AB53 5SL. *Email*: cedric.huson@gmail.com *Website*: www.cedrichuson.com *Signs work*: "Cedric Huson."

HUSSEY, Audrey, graduate in Fine Art and Theatre Design, West Country Award (1972); F.P.S. (2000), NAPA (2001); painter in acrylic, theatre design, scenic painting. *Medium*: oil, pastel, mixed media. *b*: Kent, 24 Nov 1945. *m*: Noel Geaney. *Educ*: Maidstone Grammar School, Kent. *Studied*: St. Martin's and Chelsea, London, under Michael Browne, and Alan Cooper (1968-1972). *Represented by*: London Art. *Exhib*: various galleries in London and elsewhere. *Works in collections*: private. *Commissions*: nationally and internationally. *Recreations*: interest in theosophy encompassing metaphysics, cosmology, classical music. *Address*: 25 Brent Lea, Brentford, Middx. TW8 8JD. *Email*: healingart@hotmail.co.uk *Signs work*: "Hussey." or "Audrey [Hussey]".

HUTCHINSON, Keith MacPherson, NS. *Medium*: oil, watercolour; currently painting landscapes and portraits in oil. *b*: East Sheen, 1 Sep 1929. *m*: Christine Hutchinson. *Educ*: Kings College Schools, Wimbledon. *Studied*: Kingston School of Art (1945-50) - Interior Design and Mural Painting. *Exhib*: National Society, RBA, ROI, London Sketch Club,

Highgate Gallery London, Kingston School of Art Retrospective; Hiscock Gallery, Portsmouth; and various galleries in and around London. *Misc*: Managed and set up exhibitions Camden Art Centre; taught painting and drawing, Richmond Adult Community College (1991-2006, p/t); now runs own classes teaching Life, Portrait and Still Life painting and drawing. Long standing involvement in developing the use of the arts. *Address*: 25 Park Drive, East Sheen, London SW14 8RB. *Email*: kandc.hutchison@btinternet.com *Signs work*: "Keith Hutchison" or "KH".

HUXLEY, Jonathan, BA (Hons); RA (Dip); Hunting Art Prizes. *Medium*: oil, watercolour, drawing, ultraviolet paint. *b*: Woking, 10 Nov 1965. *s of*: John and Patricia Huxley. *m*: Estelle Huxley. one *s*. *Studied*: Trent Polytechnic, Nottingham (1987-89); RA (1989-92). *Represented by*: Crane Kalman Gallery, London; Waltman/Ortega Fine Art, Miami; Galerie Olivier Waltman, Paris. *Exhib*: Art Basil, Miami; RA Summer Exhbn; 'Sense and Sensuality' RCA; Nagoya City Art Museum, Japan; Hayashibara Museum of Art, Okayama, Japan; ICA London; Crane Kalman Gallery; FIAC Paris; Galerie Ariel Sibony, Paris. *Works in collections*: UBS Bank, Goldman Sax, Arthur Anderson, Lord Foster of Thames Bank, Swiss Embassy Washington DC, EMI, Channel 4, Met Bar London, Barclays Plc, The American Ambassador to the Court of St James. *Commissions*: Met Bar London; UNESCO Publications, Paris; Tunnel Club, New York (for Grace Jones' birthday party), Red Bull HQ, EMI HQ, London. *Publications*: The Guardian, The Independent, Channel 4 website (The Ideas Factory). *Works Reproduced*: various. *Principal Works*: Saturday Night Special, Met Bar London; Red Route, collection of Norman Foster. *Clubs*: Reynolds Club (RA). *Address*: 96 Raven's Way, London SE12 8HA. *Email*: jonathan@jonathanhuxley.co.uk *Website*: www.jonathanhuxley.co.uk *Signs work*: 'Huxley'.

HUXLEY, Paul, RA, Cert.RAS (1960), Harkness Fellow (1965-67); painter in acrylic, oil, printmaking; Professor Emeritus, Royal College of Art. *b*: London, 12 May 1938. *m*: Susie Allen. two *s*. *Studied*: Harrow School of Art (1951-56, Edward Middleditch), RA Schools (1956-60, Peter Greenham). *Exhib*: numerous solo exhibitions, represented Britain internationally in Biennales and many major group shows. *Works in collections*: Tate Gallery, V&A, plus various museums in the UK, Europe, USA and Australia. *Publications*: Exhibition Road - Painters at the Royal College of Art. *Clubs*: Chelsea Arts. *Address*: 2 Dalling Rd., London W6 0JB. *Email*: paulhuxley@aol.com *Signs work*: "Paul Huxley" in bottom margin of prints and some works on paper, verso on other works on paper and all canvases.

HYATT, Derek James, ARCA; painter/writer. *b*: Ilkley, Wharfedale, Yorkshire, 21 Feb 1931. *m*: Rosomond. one *d*. *Educ*: Ilkley Grammar School. *Studied*: Leeds College of Art (1948-52), Royal College of Art (1954-58). *Exhib*: London one-man shows include Austin Desmond/Gillian Jason Gallery (1987, 1989), Waddington Galleries (1974, 1977), New Art Centre (1960, 1961, 1963, 1966); group shows include John Moores, Cincinnati Bienniale, Arts Council Travelling Exhbns., and two Critics Choice exhbns., Meetings on the Moor (70 paintings), retrospective Bradford Art Gallery (Spring 2001). *Works in collections*: Museum of Modern Art, New York, Contemporary Art Soc., Carlisle, Hull, Bradford, Sheffield and Bootle Art Galleries and Nuffield Foundation. *Publications*: Edited ARK (1958); articles Modern Painters (1987-2002); Alphabet Stone (1997); "Stone Fires Liquid Clouds" The Shamaric Art of Derek Hyatt (2001). *Misc*: 1. Video "Circles on the Dark Rock" Dean Clough Gallery, Halifax(1995). 2. Video "Meetings on the Moor" 70 paintings (1hr 20mins) Bradford 2001. *Address*: Rectory Farm House, Collingham, Wetherby LS22 5AS.

HYMAN, Timothy, RA (Elected 2011); National Portrait Gallery Travel Award 2007; Residencies: Lincoln Cathedral, Sandown Racecourse, Maggie's Cancer Caring Centres. *Medium*: painter in oil, pastel and drawing, writer. *b*: Hove, 17 Apr 1946. *m*: Judith

Ravenscroft. *Educ*: Charterhouse. *Studied*: Slade (1963-67). *Exhib*: Narrative Paintings (I.C.A., Arnolfini, 1979), Blond Fine Art (1981, 1983, 1985), Austin Desmond (1990), Flowers East (1994), Austin Desmond (2000, 2003, 2006, 2009). *Works in collections*: Arts Council, British Museum, British Council, Museum of London, Contemporary Art Soc., Government Art Collection, Los Angeles County Museum, etc. *Publications*: Bonnard (Thames & Hudson, 1998); Bhupen Khakhar; Stanley Spencer (Tate 2001); Sienese Painting (Thames & Hudson, 2003); British Vision (Ghent, 2007). *Recreations*: Italian Cinema, The Novels of John Cowper Powys, Travel. *Address*: 62 Myddelton Sq., London EC1R 1XX. *Signs work*: "T.H."

I

I'ANSON, Mari, artist and tutor. *Medium*: UA; watercolour, oil, acrylic, paintings and illustration. *b*: London, 5 Sep 1932. one *s*. one *d*. *Studied*: School of Science and Art, Weston-super-Mare (1947-1950), (now Technical College); St. Martins and Chelsea, London. *Exhib*: over 30 solo shows - St. John's , Smith Sq., Lauderdale House N6, Burgh House NW3, Foyles Art Gallery, Bridgwater Art Centre, Bull Gallery, Barnet; mixed shows - Central Hall, Westminster; Swiss Cottage Library NW3; Alexandra Palace; Lucy-Kemp-Welch Memorial Gallery, Bushy; Bangkok Patana School, Thailand; Tavistock Centre; Chorak Pattisserie, N2; artsdepot, North Finchley N12; St. George's Hospital, Tooting; The Picture Factory, N12; St. Miguel de Allende, Mexico. *Works in collections*: world-wide. *Commissions*: Octavia Hill Museum, Wisbech, London Borough of Barnet, The Finchley Society, Isgara Restaurant N3; commissions for house portraits and children's portraits. *Publications*: Artists and Illustrators, Daler Rowney Art News, The Encyclopedia of Drawing Techniques, 'Mari I'Anson's Finchley Sketchbook - 2009'. *Clubs*: United Society of Artists; East Finchley Open Group of Artists; Highgate Watercolour Group. *Misc*: Artist in residence at Bangkok Patana International School four times (1994-1997), Deansbrook Junior School, Mill Hill (1999 - 2001, 2010). *Address*: The Studio, 5 The Grove, Finchley, London N3 1QN. *Email*: mari.artist@uwclub.net *Website*: www.mari-artist.co.uk *Signs work*: "Mari I'Anson" or "Mari."

IBBOTSON, Pam, BA (Hons) Fine Art; PGCE; Manchester Academy of Fine Art (MAFA) Major Award (1988), Runner Up Award (1990); National Westminster Bank Award (1991). *Medium*: oil, watercolour, drawing. *b*: Manchester, 26 Sep 1950. *d of*: Stanley Edmondson. one *d*. *Educ*: Marple Hall Grammar School. *Studied*: Sheffield Hallam University (1987); School of Art, Psalter Lane. *Exhib*: RA Summer Exhbn; MAFA; City Art Gallery, Manchester; Quaker Gallery, London; Bonhams, London (Painting Today); Tatton Park (Prize Winning Artists); Stockport Art Gallery; Mappin Art Gallery, Sheffield. *Works in collections*: private collections. *Misc*: mem. MAFA (elected 1988). *Address*: 5 Mill Pond Avenue, New Mills, High Peak, Derbyshire SK22 4HL. *Email*: pam@ibbotson75.freeserve.co.uk *Website*: www.pamibbotson.co.uk *Signs work*: 'Pam Ibbotson'.

IBRAM, Peter B., artist in oil and water-colour; composer of jazz and classical music; Associate, Nottingham Society of Artists. *b*: Manchester, 15 Dec 1937. one *d*. *Educ*: Burnage Grammar School. *Studied*: self taught. *Exhib*: mixed shows: Chenil Gallery, London; Leslie Jones Gallery, St. Albans; Stockport A.G., Oldham A.G., Buxton A.G., Ross Gallery, Manchester; Salon des Independentes-Paris; Museum of Modern Art Wales; Nottingham; one-man show: Portico Gallery Manchester. *Works in collections*: private: America, France, Spain, Italy, Germany, Portugal, Switzerland; public: Portico Gallery, Art in Hospital, Wales, GDS Rugby, GDS Milton Keynes. *Commissions*: Portico Library, Art Gallery, Manchester; Paintings in Hospitals, Wales; GDS Rugby, GDS Milton Keynes. *Publications*: Who's Who in Art. *Clubs*: Nottingham Society of Artists. *Address*: c/o 24 Prestwich Hills, Prestwich, Manchester M25 9PY. *Email*: pibram@hotmail.com *Signs work*: "Norman Benjamin."

IKEDA, Chuya, Master of Arts Communication Design. *Medium*: Pin & paper. *b*: Japan, 27 Nov 1972. *Studied*: Central Saint Martins College of Art & Design. *Exhib*: Future Map 07; Shape of Things to Come (2008); Royal Academy of Arts Summer Exhibition (2008); Jerwood Drawing Prize (2008); Homemade (2009). *Works in collections*: University of Arts London Collection. *Publications*: 'Lead Between the Line' (pub. Graffa Ltd) Jerwood Drawing Award 08. *Address*: 79 Clovelly Way, London E1 0SF. *Email*: psnv4606@hotmail.com

IMMS, David, Dip AD; Central Dip., Northern Arts Purchase Award, Humberside Purchase Award etc. *Medium*: oil, watercolour. *b*: Derby, 24 Sep 1945. *m*: Patricia. one *s*. one *d*. *Educ*: Derby College of Art 1962-64. *Studied*: Central School of Art 1964-67 (Llewellyn Smith Scholarship: Neurath Prize). *Represented by*: Fosse Gallery Fine Art; John Iddon Fine Art. *Exhib*: one man shows include: New Grafton Gallery (1987, 1989, 1992); Dorset County Museum (1995); Wiltshire Heritage Museum (1995, 2001); Fosse Gallery Fine Art (2007). Mixed Exhibitions include RA Summer Exhibition, Llewelyn Alexander Gallery, John Iddon Fine Art. *Works in collections*: include: Victoria and Albert Museum; London Borough of Camden; Paintings in Hospitals; Universities of London, Glasgow, Cambridge, Surrey; Dorset County Library; Wiltshire Heritage Museum; Wessex Collection, Longleat House; Rank Xerox Collection: Northern Arts Association Bolton, Bradford, Leicester, Derby, Northampton, Sheffield Art Galleries. *Clubs*: walking and drawing. *Address*: 6 Church Street, Finedon, Northants, NN9 5NA. *Website*: www.fossegallery.com *Signs work*: "IMMS", "DAVID IMMS".

INCHBALD, Michael, FCSD; Architectural and Interior Designer; twice married. one *s*. one *d*. *Studied*: AA. *Commissions*: include: 1st Class Lounge "Queen's Room" and Library on QE2, and other Liners; Ballroom, banquet areas and suites at Berkeley Hotel, Post House, Heathrow, Claridges' Penthouse, Savoy's River Room and Lincoln Room, Crown Commissioners' HQ, Carlton House Terr., Banks of America and Trust Hanover, Player's and Plessey's HQ Offices, Justerini and Brooks, Boardroom etc. for Imperial Group, Law Society's Lady's Annexe, Dunhill's, Jermyn Street and Worldwide; Residential: Duc de la Rochefoucauld, Duke of St. Albans, Marquess of Ailesbury, Earls of Dartmouth and St. Aldwyn, Countess of Lonsdale, etc. *Address*: Stanley House, 10 Milner St., London SW3 2PU.

INGLIS, Catherine Elizabeth, SWA; Founder Mem. The East Yorkshire Pastel Society; York Art Society; Professional Assoc., Promoter and Demonstrator for The Society of All Artists; Founder Member, East Riding Artists (ERA); Frank Herring Award; Society of Women Artists Peoples Award. *Medium*: soft pastel. *b*: Yorkshire, 18 Jul 1952. *d of*: Jane & Kenneth Ainsworth. *m*: Ron Inglis. two *d*. *Studied*: student of Kenneth Jackson ARCA, and of Jane Parkin SWA, SEA. *Exhib*: SWA; London, Harrogate, Hull, Kennel Club, London and solo exhbns. *Works Reproduced*: limited edition Gicleè prints. *Address*: The Old Granary, Skirpenbeck, York YO41 1HF. *Email*: cath.inglis@btinternet.co.uk *Website*: www.cathinglis.com *Signs work*: 'Catherine E.Inglis'.

INGLIS, John, RGI (2009), PRSW (2005), RSW (1984), FSA (Scot) (1983), DA (1974), Post. Grad. (1975), Travelling scholar (1976); painter in water-colour, oil, lecturer. *b*: Glasgow, 27 Jul 1953. *s of*: Thomas Inglis. *m*: Heather Binnie. two *s*. two *d*. *Educ*: Hillhead High School, Glasgow. *Studied*: Gray's School of Art, Aberdeen (1970-75, William Littlejohn, Frances Walker, Alexander Fraser). *Exhib*: RSA, RSW, RGIFA, SSA, Compass Gallery, Glasgow, Edinburgh, Leeds, Venice, Rome, Canada, Regensberg, Illinois, U.S.A., London. *Works in collections*: Aberdeen A.G., University of Aberdeen, Argyll and Bute Educ. Authority, Scottish Television, Inst. for Cancer Research, Aberdeen Hospitals Collection, Clackmannan District Council Collection, Royal Scottish Academy, Clackmannan College, Scottish Arts Club, Heartland College, Ill., McLean County Arts

Centre, Bloomington, Ill., Scottish Arts Club, Edinburgh. *Address*: 84 Burnhead Rd., Larbert, Stirlingshire FK5 4BD. *Signs work*: "John Inglis" usually on back.

INSALL, Sir Donald W., CBE, LL.D, FSA, RWA, FRIBA, FRTPI (Retd.), SPDip(Hons); architect; Founder-Director, Donald Insall Assocs. (Architects and Planning Consultants), London W1G; Founder-Commissioner, English Heritage, Visiting Prof. University of Leuven, service as Consultant to City of Chester in National Pilot City Conservation Programme; Architects for post-fire Restoration of Windsor Castle; awarded the Medal of Honour (2000) by Europa Nostra; Plowden Medallist; Royal Warrant Holders Association; Harley J. McKee Award, Association for Preservation Technology International. *Medium*: architecture, watercolour. *b*: Clifton, Bristol, 7 Feb 1926. *s of*: William R Insall. *m*: Amy Elizabeth. two *s*. one *d*. *Studied*: RWA School of Architecture, Royal Academy School of Architecture, School of Planning and Research for Regional Development; and SPAB Lethaby Scholar. *Exhib*: RA, RWA, RIBA. *Commissions*: Council of Europe and European Commission Committees. *Publications*: The Care of Old Buildings Today (Architectural Press); 'Architectural Conservation' Encyclopaedia Britannica; Conservation in Action; 'Living Buildings: Architectural Conservation - Philosophy, Principals and Practice (Images Publishing). *Principal Works*: Restoration of Windsor Castle interiors and of the Lords' Chamber ceiling, Palace of Westminster. *Recreations*: visiting, photographing, drawing and enjoying places. *Clubs*: Athenaeum. *Misc*: Consultancy has received over 150 Conservation and Craftmanship Awards/Commendations. *Address*: 73 Kew Green, Richmond, Surrey TW9 3AH. *Signs work*: 'DWI' (with dots beneath letters), or 'Donald W Insall'.

INSHAW, David. *Medium*: painter. *b*: Wednesfield, Staffordshire, 21 Mar 1943. *Studied*: Beckenham School of Art (1959-63); Royal Academy Schools (1963-66); French Government scholarship (1964); taught at West of England College of Art (1966-75), Fellow Commoner in Creative Art, Trinity College Cambridge (1975-77). *Exhib*: one-man shows: Arnolfini Gallery, Bristol (1969, 1971), Waddington Galleries (1975, '80, '84,'89), Wren Library, Trinity College Cambridge (1976, '77) ,Theo Waddington Fine Art (1995, '98), Royal Pavilion Brighton (1978), Nishimura Gallery Tokyo (1987), Annandale Gallery Sydney (1996), RWA Bristol (2003), Agnews (2005), 6 Chapel Row Gallery Bath (1998, 2001); Sladers Yard Dorset (2007), Millinery Works, London (2008). *Works in collections*: including: Arts Council, British Council, City of Bristol Museum and Art Gallery, Dept of Environment, Sunderland Art Gallery, Devizes Museum, Tate Britain London. *Clubs*: Chelsea Arts Club. *Misc*: formed the Brotherhood of Ruralists with six other artists (1975). *Address*: 23 High Street, Devizes, Wilts, SN10 1AT. *Email*: davidinshaw@hotmail.com *Signs work*: "David Inshaw" (on back of paintings).

INSOLL, Christopher, BA (Hons) Fine Art. *Medium*: oil, watercolour, drawing. *b*: London, 28 Jun 1956. *s of*: Deb and Garth Insoll. *m*: Andrea. one *s*. one *d*. *Educ*: Haileybury, Herts. *Studied*: Chelsea Camberwell (exchange); Falmouth School of Art. *Represented by*: New Gallery (Cornwall); Belgrave Gallery London/St. Ives. *Exhib*: RA; RWA; Paris Salon; Newlyn Art Gallery; Truro City Museum; Penwith Soc.Arts; Falmouth Art Gallery. *Works in collections*: Falmouth Art Gallery; Truro Museum. *Commissions*: various private. *Publications*: 'Paintings about Painting, Chris Insoll' by Sarah Drury; Portscatho, Portrait of a Cornish Art Colony, by Chris Insoll (pub. Halsgrove, 2006). *Works Reproduced*: widely. *Recreations*: wine, walking. *Clubs*: Chelsea Arts Club. *Address*: The New Gallery, Portscatho, Cornwall TR2 5HW. *Email*: chrisinsoll@gmail.com *Website*: www.chrisinsoll.com *Signs work*: 'INSOLL' (oils); 'Chris Insoll' (drawings).

INWARD, Jean Mary, MBBS, MRC Psych, AUA; painter in oil and acrylic; psychiatrist (retired). *b*: Bromley, Kent, 9 Sep 1939. two *s*. one *d*. *Educ*: Guy's Hospital, London University. *Studied*: evening classes. *Exhib*: UA, SWA. *Works in collections*: private. *Commissions*: private. *Clubs*: Local. *Address*: 5 Birchdale, Gerrards Cross, Bucks. SL9 7JA. *Signs work*: "Jeanie."

IRENE: see FRÖHLICH-WIENER, Irene.

IRVIN, Magnus, DipFA (1973), RE (1993); artist in woodcuts, short animated films, etching, mixed media, shoes made from bananas and ectoplasm sculptures; founder member of London Institute of Pataphysics. *Medium*: print, sculpture, film, publications. *b*: London, 6 Dec 1952. one *s*. *Educ*: Creighton School, Muswell Hill. *Studied*: Hornsey Art College (1970), NELP Walthamstow (1971-74). *Exhib*: Redfern Gallery, Whitechapel Open, Cleveland Drawing Biennale, Bradford Print Biennale, Ljubljana Print Biennale, Xylon Museum Germany, Art Cologne, Anthony Hancock Retrospective-Foundry Gallery, London E2 (2002). *Works in collections*: ACGB, BM, V&A, International Centre of Graphic Art, Slovenia, Imperial War Museum. *Commissions*: Tunstall Western Bypass, Stoke on Trent - concrete aeroplanes to bypass environment. *Publications*: 'Bananas at War' and 'Chairs and Fleas' - Limited Edition Books, Daily Twit newspaper (for 30 yrs), 'Toilets and Cupboards of South America', 'Toilets and Cupboards of East Africa'. *Works Reproduced*: in Arts Review, Printmaking Today, Sight and Sound, Vertigo, Bizarre. *Recreations*: fishing, travelling, sleeping. *Clubs*: Tesco. *Address*: 17A Ellingfort Road, London E8 3PA. *Email*: magno@pig.abelgratis.com *Website*: www.magnusirvin.co.uk *Signs work*: "M. Irvin."

ISHAM, Anthony Ralph, MRIN, ISMP. *Medium*: oil, watercolour, drawing. *b*: Melksham, Wilts, 26 May 1944. *m*: Lindy née Holme. two *d*. *Educ*: self taught. *Represented by*: Gallery 58, Topsham; Gallerie Lawrence-Arnott, Marrakech; Gallery Hemisphere, Abu Dhabi; Grand Galerie Civray, France. *Exhib*: Acropolis, Nice (one-man, 2004); Oregon, USA (joint, 2005); Paris, Tennessee, USA; Ventura Museum, California, USA (2006); Open Arts, Exeter, UK (2007, 2008, 2009, 2010); Galerie Grande, Civray, France 2009. *Works in collections*: Bernard Stamm (Around the World yachtsman); Minnesota State University Collection; Ship Owners Club of London; Saatchi; Pearson Corporation. *Commissions*: Shipowners Club of London; various private yacht owners; rulers of Abu Dhabi & Oman. *Publications*: Book cover 'Taking the Helm'. *Official Purchasers*: Shipowners Club of London, Pearson Corporation, USA. *Works Reproduced*: various paintings in Limited Edition format. *Principal Works*: "Vigilance & Provident"; "Thomas Fortesque"; "Waiting for the Breeze", "Taking the Helm". *Recreations*: sailing, travelling. *Misc*: International Consultant in Navigation, also painter of portraits by commission. *Address*: 58 Fore Street, Topsham, Devon, EX3 0HW. *Email*: info@themarineartist.com. *Website*: www.themarineartist.com *Signs work*: "Tony Isham".

ISITT, Samuel John, BA (1958), MBIM (1968), MInst.M (1970), IPM (1960); RLSS (Instructor,1952); artist in oil. watercolour, prints, writer, Actor; mem. Equity and Writer's Guild; Director, Oxbridge Artists and Writers. *b*: Newport, Mon., 9 Feb 1935. *m*: Ann (divorced). three *s*. one *d*. *Educ*: Newport High School. *Studied*: Chelsea. *Exhib*: recent exhibs. at Mary Magdalene's Church, Oxford (1997), Oxford Playhouse (1998), Oxford University Club (2001), Nice, France (2005). *Works in collections*: Drs T. and K. Isitt, Vera Chock and others worldwide. *Commissions*: Shirley Knowlton, Hayley Bentley, Sue Walker and others. *Publications*: Mary's Song , and The 7 Deadly Sins (both illustrated by Tania Holland). *Clubs*: Newport R.F.C., Royal Overseas League, Writers' Guild, U.K. Calligraphers, member of Equity (TV and Films). *Address*: 24 Jericho St., Oxford OX2 6BU. *Email*: taff.isitt@yahoo.co.uk *Signs work*: "John Isitt."

ISOGAI, Noboru, SBA; Certificate of Botanical Merit, SBA; Joyce Cuming Presentation Award, SBA; Silver Grenfel Medal, RHS; Judges Special Prize, Japan Seiko Art Association. *Medium*: watercolor. *b*: Gumma, Japan, 30 Jun 1935. one *s*. *Studied*: University of Tokyo (BA, Precision Mechanical Engineering). *Exhib*: SBA Annual Exhibition; Japan Seiko Association Exhibition. *Works in collections*: Shirley Sherwood Collection (2007). *Publications*: Arte Y Botanica SBA (Caja, Madrid); The Art of Botanical Painting (SBA, Collins); Flowers and Gardens (SBA Annual Exhbn catalogue); Hunt 11th International

Exhibition of Botanical Art . *Address*: 6-14-1 Maebara-Higashi, Funabashi-Shi, Chiba-Ken, Japan 274-0824. *Signs work*: 'N.Isogaï'.

ISOM, Graham Michael, NDD (1965), AAEA, SEA; equestrian artist. *Medium*: oils. *b*: Kent, 5 Mar 1945. married. one *s*. two *d*. *Educ*: Dartford. *Studied*: Ravensbourne College of Art (1961-65). *Exhib*: worldwide. *Works in collections*: Kentucky Derby Museum of Racing, Churchill Downs, Louisville. *Commissions*: Household Cavalry (Officer's Mess); large calendar of 12 paintings, 12 Limited Edition equestrian beakers, several Christmas cards. *Publications*: . Racing in Art/ John Fairley; numerous Limited Edition Prints. *Recreations*: garden design. *Address*: 2 Neville Pk., Baltonsborough, Somerset, BA6 8PY. *Email*: graham.isom@virgin.net *Website*: www.grahamisom.co.uk

IZZARD, Pamela, DipAD; artist in oil, acrylic and mixed media, etching, water-colour and pastel, and wood. *b*: London, 14 Nov 1926. *d of*: Charles G.Izzard. *m*: (1) K. Lucas. two *s*. one *d*. (decd). (2) Jack Millar (decd). one *s-s*. two *s-d*. *Educ*: Old Palace School, Croydon, Torquay Grammar School. *Studied*: Beckenham, Bromley and Croydon Schools of Art. *Exhib*: RA, London Group, NEAC, RBA, Curwen Gallery, Linton Ct. Gallery, Ashgate Galleries and various provincial galleries. One-man shows, Ashgate Galleries, Abbot Hall, Kendal, Duncan Campbell Gallery, London, Chelsea & Westminster Hospital, SE1 Gallery. Has taught in art schools in London and the provinces. *Works in collections*: local authorities and private collections in this country and abroad. *Works Reproduced*: RA Illustrated Catalogues, London Illustrated News. *Recreations*: gardening, films, reading, music. *Address*: 10 Overhill Rd., Dulwich, London SE22 0PH. *Website*: www.pamelaizzard.eu *Signs work*: "P. Izzard" or "Izzard" on back.

J

JACKLIN, Bill, RA (1990), MA, RCA (1967), ARA (1989); artist in oil paintings, etching. *b*: London, 1 Jan 1943. *s of*: Harold Jacklin, M.C. *m*: (1) Lesley (divorced). (2) Janet Russo. one *d*. *Educ*: Walthamstow Technical College. *Studied*: Walthamstow School of Art (1962-64), RCA(1964-67, Carel Weight). *Exhib*: one-man shows, London: Nigel Greenwood (1970, 1971, 1975), Hester Van Royen Gallery (1973, 1977), Marlborough Fine Art (1980, 1983, 1988, 1992, 1995, 1997, 2000, 2002, 2004, 2008), Marlborough Gallery, N.Y. (1985, 1987, 1990, 1997, 1999, 2002, 2007, 2012), MoMA Oxford (1992), Museo de Pobo Galego, Santiago de Compostela, Spain (1993), University of Northumbria, Newcastle upon Tyne, England (1994, 2008), Hong Kong Arts Centre, Hong Kong (1995), l'Ecole de Londres Museé, Maillol, Paris (1998-99); Marlborough Monaco (2009); numerous group shows. *Works in collections*: ACGB, British Council, B.M., Government Arts Coll., Metropolitan Museum, NY, MoMA (NY), Museum Boymans-Van Beuningen, Rotterdam, Tampa Museum, Museum of NSW, V&A, Tate Gallery, Yale Centre for British Art. *Commissions*: by Bank of England for painting (Futures Market, London) (1988); Ivy Restaurant in London for painting (The Ivy) (1988); De Beers for Tapestry - "The Park" - 6ft. x 17ft. (1993); Metropolitan Washington Airport Authority for new terminal at Washington National Airport (1994-97); Design Architect, Cesar Pelli & Ass.; mural - "The Rink" - 6ft. x 25ft. (1997). Artist in Residence, British Council Hong Kong (1993-94). *Publications*: Monograph: Bill Jacklin by John Russell-Taylor (Phaidon Press, London, 1997); gallery catalogues and numerous articles and broadcasts. *Clubs*: Chelsea Arts. *Address*: Twin Beeches, 38 Catherine Street, Newport Rhode ISland 02840, USA. *Email*: billjacklin@mac.com *Website*: www.bjacklin.com *Signs work*: "Jacklin."

JACKSON, Ashley, FRSA, UA; Yorkshire Arts and Entertainment Personality of the year (Yorkshire Awards 1996); Freedom of the City of London (2005); Vice President, Yorkshire Society; Yorkshire Lifetime Achievement award (Yorkshire Awards 2006); artist in water-colour; lecturer and demonstrator in w/c throughout Britain, USA, Valencia, Milan and

Madrid. *b*: Penang, Malaysia, 22 Oct 1940. *s of*: Norman Valentine Jackson. *m*: Anne. two *d*. *Educ*: St. Joseph's, Singapore, Holyrood, Barnsley, Hon D. Univ (Huddersfield). *Studied*: Barnsley School of Art (1955-60). *Exhib*: RI, RBA, RWS, Britain in Water-colour, UA; one-man shows: including Upper Grosvenor Gallery, Mall Galleries, Cartwright Hall, Bradford (1998), Armouries, Leeds (2000), etc. *Works in collections*: Royal Navy, Sir Harold Wilson, Sir Yehudi Menuhin, Lord Mason of Barnsley, Rt. Hon. Edward Heath, Yorkshire Bank, Yorkshire Television, N.C.B., Rt. Hon. John Major, Sir Bernard Ingham, President Bill Clinton, NATO HQ Brussels, Rt Hon Lord George Robertson of Port Ellen, The late L.S. Lowry. *Publications*: numerous including: autobiography "My Brush with Fortune" (Secker and Warburg, 1982); "Painting in the Open Air" (Harper Collins 1992); "A Brush with Ashley" (Boxtree 1993); "Painting in the British Isles" (Boxtree 1994); "Ashley Jackson's Yorkshire Moors – A Love Affair (Dalesman, 2000), "50 Golden Years with My Mistress and I" (Dalesman 2006) etc. Featured on YTV documentary – Some Days are Diamond; 2001 – New TV series "In a Different light"; 10 series of "A Brush with Ashley" YTV (1990-2001); own series on BBC, Channel 4, YTV Founder Mem. Yorkshire Watercolour Soc; "An Artist's Life" biography by Chris Bond (2010), My Yorkshire Sketchbook (Dalesman 2012). *Misc*: October 2011 - Grand Central name train "Ashley Jackson - The Yorkshire Artist" with 8 carriages depicting his work. Framing the Landscape - project in partnership with the National Trust (launched 2014). *Address*: Ashley Jackson Galleries, 13-15 Huddersfield Rd., Holmfirth, Huddersfield HD9 2JR. *Email*: ashley@ashley-jackson.co.uk *Website*: www.ashley-jackson.co.uk

JACKSON, Bridget H., *Medium*: Oil, drawing, sculpture. *b*: Cambridge, 2 Feb 1978. *Studied*: Ruskin School of Drawing and Fine Art, Oxford (1998-2000). *Exhib*: Royal Academy Summer Exhibition (2008, 2009); Art Swap, August Art, London (2009). *Principal Works*: Das Ziel (2008); Penelope (2009). *Address*: 11 Parliament Court, Parliament Hill, London NW3 2TS. *Email*: bridgethjackson@yahoo.co.uk *Website*: www.bridgethjackson.com *Signs work*: "BHJ".

JACKSON, Dilys Mary, ARBS; DFA (Lond.), DSE, ATD, MA (FA) Cardiff, BA (Psych). *Medium*: sculpture, drawing. *b*: Badulla, Sri Lanka, 10 Mar 1938. *d of*: Mary & John Jackson. two *s*. *Studied*: Slade School of Fine Art, Swansea College of Art, Swansea University, OU, University of Wales Institute Cardiff. *Represented by*: Campden Gallery, Chipping Campden; Kooywood Gallery, Cardiff. *Exhib*: Solo (2014): Cyfartha Castle Gallery, Merthyr Tydfil; Oriel Canfas, Cardiff. Galleri Brinken, Stockholm; University of Glamorgan; St. Davids Hall, Cardiff; Cowcross Gallery, London; New Hall, Cambridge; Arts Centre, Otzenhausen, Germany; Gordy Gallery, Muncie, Indiana; Maurie, Landivisiau, Brittany; Franconia Sculpture Park, Minnesota; College of Art, Aberystwyth; Royal Academy, London. 2014: Sculpture Cymru, Aberystwyth; Art Central Barry; Futures Gallery, Cardiff.. *Works in collections*: Contemporary Art Society for Wales, Salem Art Works Park, NY, USA; Franconia Sculpture Park, Minnesota, USA; New Hall Cambridge. *Commissions*: Millennium Sculpture, Greenfield Valley; Brick Benches, Ogmore Valley; Railings, Penlan. *Publications*: 'Dilys Jackson: Sculptor' 2003 ISBN: 0-9544439-0-X. *Official Purchasers*: Contemporary Art Society for Wales, National Library of Wales. *Works Reproduced*: 'Stream' in Mapping the Welsh Group at 60. *Principal Works*: Millennium Sculpture, Greenfield Valley. *Clubs*: Memberships: Welsh Group, 56 Group Wales; Sculpture Cymru: Sculptors in Wales; Royal British Society of Sculptors. *Address*: 29 Ilton Road, Penylan, Cardiff CF23 5DU. *Email*: dilysjackson@yahoo.co.uk *Website*: dilysjackson.co.uk *Signs work*: "DILYS JACKSON".

JACKSON, H. J., RE, SWE, NDD, The 2013 Norfolk Arts Award - Winner of 'The Lifetime Contribution to the Arts' award. *Medium*: full-time printmaker using lino - printing entirely by hand, burnishing using a tobacco tin. *b*: Kings Lynn, Norfolk, 7 Dec 1938. *s of*: D S B Jackson. *m*: Maggie Jackson. one *d*. *Educ*: Melton Constable. *Studied*: Norwich

School of Art (1954-58) printmaking under G. Wales, RE. *Exhib*: Touring: Print Exhbns. America and United Kingdom; one-man and mixed group shows throughout East Anglia; work in Print Exhbns. in London, New York and Bombay. Curator of and shows work in the annual Norwich Print Fair each September. Exhibition '60 Years at the Cutting Edge', celebrating 60 Years of Printmaking, Gallery Plus (2013). Prints at Bircham Gallery, Holt, Norfolk (ongoing). *Works in collections*: work selected by The Print Collector's Club (1967 and 1988); designed the 'John the Baptist Tapestry' for Worstead Church, Norfolk (1979); print to commemorate the Centenary of the Avenue Schools, Norwich (1994). *Commissions*: linocuts of 6 Norwich scenes for Hotal, Norwich (1972/3). *Publications*: work included in 'The Complete Manual of Relief Printmaking' (1988), 'Printmakers - The Directory' (2006), 'Printmaker's Secrets' (2009), 'Water Marks - Art in East Anglia' (2010). *Misc*: Work included in a number of public collections, and private collections worldwide; and various educational authorities. *Address*: 12 Whitehall Rd., Norwich NR2 3EW. *Email*: hjjackson@norwichprintfair.co.uk *Website*: www.norwichprintfair.co.uk/hj_jackson *Signs work*: "H. J. Jackson."

JACKSON, Kurt Dominic, BA Oxon (1982); RWA; DLitt (Hon) from Exeter University; Honorary Fellow of St Peter's College, Oxford University. *Medium*: painter in all media, printmaker, etc. *b*: Dorset, 21 Sep 1961. *m*: Caroline. one *s.* two *d. Educ*: Francis Bacon Comprehensive, Herts. *Studied*: St.Peters College, Oxford University. *Represented by*: The Redfern Gallery, 20 Cork St, London W1S 3HL. *Exhib*: numerous solo shows internationally both in public and commercial galleries since 1985. *Works in collections*: numerous municipal and private. *Publications*: 'Kurt Jackson, Cornwall and the Scillies' (1999, White Lane Press ISBN 0953 137 015); 'The Cape' Kurt Jackson and Ronald Gaskell (2002, Truran ISBN 1 85022172 3); 'Sketchbook 2003-2004' (ISBN 1 85022190 1); 'Kurt Jackson - A New Genre of Landscape Painting' (2010, Lund Humphries, ISBN 13:978-184822 1024); 'Kurt Jackson - Sketchbooks' (2012, Lund Humphries, ISBN 13:978-184822 1109). *Clubs*: Royal West of England Academy. *Address*: Seacroft, Kenython Lane, St. Just, Penzance, Cornwall TR19 7PT. *Email*: info@kurtjackson.com *Website*: www.kurtjackson.com *Signs work*: 'Kurt J.'

JACKSON, Maz, BA (Hons) (1976); artist in tempera, water-colour, drypoint, charcoal and line. *b*: Norwich, 6 Aug 1953. *m*: Paul Hill. two *s.* one *d. Educ*: Notre Dame High School, Norwich. *Studied*: Norwich School of Art (1972-76, Edward Middleditch). *Exhib*: dfn Gallery, Manhattan, New York; MONA Fund Raiser, Detroit; Royal Academy, London; Mall Galleries, London; Llewellyn Alexander Gallery, London; Art Connoisseur Gallery, London; Birmingham Art Centre, Hotbath Gallery, Bath, Stroud House Gallery, Stroud; Fermoy Art Centre, Kings Lynn; Primavera Gallery, Cambridge; Chimney Mill Gallery, West Stow; Thompson's Gallery, Aldeburgh, Assembly Rooms, Norwich; Gissing Hall Art Centre, Norfolk; Grapevine Gallery, Norwich. *Works in collections*: Permanent Public Archive Collection, Museum of New Art, Detroit. *Publications*: Painting World magazine. *Clubs*: S.G.F.A., E.W.A.C.C. Artworks. *Misc*: 1998 Artist in Residence at Bressingham Gardens. *Address*: Friends House, Church Rd., East Harling, Norwich NR16 2NB. *Email*: mazjackson@aol.com *Signs work*: "MAZ."

JACKSON, (Penelope) Mary, RWS, NEAC; Fine Art College Diploma; Critics Award NEAC, Agnews. *Medium*: fine art. *b*: Sussex, 15 Dec 1936. *d of*: Ronald and Dorothy Perkins. *m*: Tom Coates. one *s.* two *d. Educ*: Froebel School. Ibtock Place, Sherborne School for Girls. *Studied*: mature student Southampton and Winchester. *Exhib*: Alresford Gallery (two-person), New Grafton, Mall Galleries, Sinfield Gallery (solo), RA Summer Exhbn, Watermans (2 solo), WH Patterson, Royal West Academy, Cross Gate Gallery Kentucky (two person), Royal Watercolour Society, Bankside; Russell Gallery (2 solo). *Works in collections*: Lord Weymouth (Bath), Lady Getty, permanent collection 2nd Battalion REME, Garsington Opera, TH Gunnersen, Marbut Gunnersen, Melbourne, Australia. *Commissions*:

worked as Artist in Residence for Glyndebourne Opera, Garsington Opera. REME commission in Fallingbostal, Germany, David Hunting family portrait. *Publications*: various articles in magazines and books, Artist Illustrator, Leisure Painter, Richard Pikesley Oils Workshop, Tom Coates Self Portraits. *Official Purchasers*: 2nd Battalion REME, Garsington Opera. *Works Reproduced*: cards by 'Rembrants Hat'. *Recreations*: theatre, opera, tennins, ski-ing, swimming. *Address*: Bladon Studio, Hurstborne Tarrant, Hampshire SP11 0AH. *Email*: bladonstudios@mac.com *Website*: www.newenglishartclub.co.uk *Signs work*: 'MaryJackson'.

JACOB, Wendy, ARWS (2005); painter and printmaker in oil, water-colour, gouache, etching. *b*: Wigan, 1941. *m*: Robin Jacob. three *s*. *Educ*: North London Collegiate School. *Studied*: Hammersmith College of Art. *Exhib*: RWS, NEAC Open, Singer & Friedlander, R.A., Laing, Discerning Eye. *Publications*: illustrated: English Bread and Yeast Cookery by Elizabeth David; North Atlantic Seafood by Alan Davidson. *Address*: 8 Ripplevale Grove, London N1 1HU.

JACOBSON, Ruth Taylor, AMGP (2001), DFA Lond (1963); Central St. Martins Post Graduate, Architectural glass; 1st prize, figure drawing at the Slade (1961); painter/printmaker/stained glass artist. *Medium*: painting, printmaking, stained glass. *b*: London, 18 Aug 1941. *d of*: Dr. Henry Taylor, MRCS, LRCP. *m*: U. Jacobson, FRCS, MRCOG. two *s*. one *d*. *Studied*: Slade School of Fine Art (1959-63, Peter Brooker, Andrew Forge). *Exhib*: Agnews, Wildenstein, Royal Festival Hall, Barbican Centre; solo shows: Camden Arts Centre, Poole Arts Centre, Zionist Confederation House, Jerusalem, Stained Glass Museum, Ely Cathedral; Stadtische Galerie Hans Seel, Siegen, Germany. *Works in collections*: Panstwowe Muzeum Oswiecim Brzezinka, Poland, Yad Vashem Museum, Israel, Ben Uri Gallery, London, Victoria & Albert Museum, London. *Commissions*: portrait of H.M. Queen Elizabeth the Queen Mother for the Museums Association; window for Sacred Silver and Stained Glass Galleries, V&A. *Publications*: Journal of Stained Glass. *Principal Works*: 'The Eternal' (V&A). *Clubs*: British Soc. of Master Glass Painters (elected Associate Member 2001). *Address*: 25 Sylvan Avenue, London NW7 2JH. *Email*: ruth@jacobson.plus.com *Signs work*: "Ruth B. Jacobson."

JACOBSON, Stephen Roy, RWA: DipAD (1970); Royal Academy Schools Certificate (1973) (Connoisseur Prize). *Medium*: Oil, drawing, prints. *b*: Manchester, 6 Sep 1946. *m*: Janet Haigh. *Educ*: Manchester High School of Art (1957-63). *Studied*: Manchester College of Art (1963-64); Liverpool College of Art (1964-70); Royal Academy Schools (1970-73). *Exhib*: RA (1972-75); Trafford Gallery, London (1976); Bristol City Museum (1977); Festival Gallery, Bath - two man show (1977); Portal Gallery, London (1979); Piccadilly Gallery, London (1990); Art Connoisseur Gallery, London (1996); RWA New Gallery - solo show (2005); Rebecca Hossack Gallery, London (2006); RWA New Gallery - 2 man show (2010). *Commissions*: Howard Jacobson and Rosalin Sadler portrait (1986); The Mercer Family portrait (1998); The Owen Family portrait (2001). *Recreations*: playing piano. *Misc*: Elected council member for Royal West of England Academy (2011). *Address*: 46 Beach Road West; Portishead BS20 7HV. *Email*: sjacobson@talktalk.net *Website*: www.stephenjacobson.co.uk *Signs work*: "STEPHEN JACOBSON RWA".

JACZYNSKA, Marysia, NDD (1960), ATC (1961); sculptor in wood, stone and bronze, models in clay. *b*: Warsaw, Poland, 30 Sep 1937. *d of*: Henryk Glass-Jankowski. *m*: Kazimierz Jaczynski. one *s*. one *d*. *Studied*: St. Martin's School of Art (1956-60, Anthony Caro), Hornsey College of Art (1960-61), Academie Julien, Paris (1963-64). *Exhib*: regularly in England; solo shows: Poland, France, England. *Works in collections*: private: England, France, Switzerland, USA and Poland. corporate: London, England. *Commissions*: private commissions including portraits. *Publications*: see entry on apauk.org website. *Works Reproduced*: (in bronze) 'Tears', 'Man & a Woman', 'Lullaby', 'Repose',

'Stretching'. *Principal Works*: 'Tears', 'Silent Scream', 'Man & a Woman', 'Wind in her Hair', 'Saved from Drowning', 'Bird of Prey', 'The Secret', 'Hidden Thoughts', 'Stretching 2'. *Recreations*: reading and travelling. *Clubs*: C.A.S., A.P.A., Trinity Arts & Crafts Guild. *Address*: 27 Cascade Ave., London N10 3PT. *Email*: marysiajaczynska@hotmail.com *Website*: chelseaartsociety.org.uk apauk.org *Signs work*: 'Marysia Jaczynska', 'M.Jaczynska', previously 'M.Jankowska', 'MJ' or 'Maria Jankowska'.

JAFAR, Abu, ARBS; acclaimed leading artist and Philosopher of the arts. *Medium*: visual artist and sculptor. *b*: Jhilna, Patuakhali, Bangladesh, 1968. *s of*: Muhammad Sekander Ali (decd) &Sufia Khatun. *Studied*: Institute of Fine Arts, University of Dhaka, Bangladesh (1984-89, Fine Arts, Painting & Drawing); Guildhall University, London (1989-90, Master Drawing of the human figure); Goldsmiths College, University of London (1991-92, Art and Art History); Open University (1997, Philosophy of Arts). *Exhib*: widely in the UK and abroad, including: Burghley Sculpture Garden, Stamford, Lincolnshire (2007); Asia House, London (2007); Aubourn Hall & Gardens, Lincoln (2007); Margaret Harvey Gallery, University of Hertfordshire (2006); Brick Lane Gallery, London (2006); The Brownston Gallery, Modbury, Devon (2006); Designers Week, Leeds (2006); The Sir Harold Hillier Gardens, Romsey (2006); Artshed, Herts. (2005); New London Glass, London (2005); McDowell Modern Art, London (2001); Trafalgar Square, London (2002); The Whitechapel Open (1998); The Changing Room Gallery, London (1995); Brockhall Village, Lancashire (1996); The Concourse Gallery, Barbican Centre, London (1993); The British Council, Dhaka Bangladesh (1990), and many more. *Address*: Explosion Arts International, 22 Blackwell Road, Kings Langley, WD4 8NF. *Email*: info@abujafar.com *Website*: www.abujafar.com

JAFFE, Ilona Lola Langdorf, artist in monotype (oil), tapestries. *b*: Krakow, Poland. *d of*: Sydonia Klausner. two *d*. *Studied*: PE Art College, S. Africa under Joan Wright. *Exhib*: solo shows: Orchid Fine Arts, Lymington, Swanage, Berlin, Johannesburg, Munich, Boston, Freising, Cape Town Eching, Sasolburg, Rustenburg, Antwerp, Van Eck Gallery; group shows: Johannesburg, Paris, London; chosen for 'Mandela's Day', Port Elisabeth, South Africa (2005), Metropolitan Art Museum (poster from painting in their collection). *Works in collections*: King George VI A.G. and Museum, Port Elizabeth, Pretoria A.G. and Museum, Pretoria, RAU Johannesburg, Dom Gymnasium, Freising, Franz Mark Gymnasium, Markt Schwaben, Germany; also private collections and institutions. *Commissions*: Prof. Dr. Maximilliane Kriegsbaum, University Bochem, Kriegsbaum, present Dean of Hamburg University,Germany (2003); St. Mary's Church, Slough (2004). *Address*: Flat 3, 5 St. Winifred's Rd., Meyrick Pk., Bournemouth BH2 6NY. *Email*: lovisetodres@hotmail.com *Website*: www.todres.fsnet.co.uk

JAGGER, Janette, ABNA. Medium: acrylic, oil, watercolour, prints. *b*: Broken Hill, Australia, 9 Dec 1938. two *s*. one *d*. *Educ*: Broken Hill High School. *Studied*: Adelaide School of Arts (1956). *Exhib*: Harbour House, Kingsbridge; Gallery 5 and Loft Studio, Salcombe; Whitechapel, London; Worcester City Library; Birdwood House, Totnes. Works in collections: private. P*rincipal Works*: Village, Brazil; Life in Uganda; Holiday at Bigbury. *Recreations*: writing, gardening. *Clubs*: ABNA, Salcombe Art Club, Press Gang Printmakers. *Misc*: South Hams Art Forum (SHAF). *Address*: 15 Glebeland, Churchstow, Devon TQ7 3RD. *Email*: janettejagger@hotmail.com *Website*: www.jaggeronline *Signs work*: "JANETTE" (paintings), monogram of "JJ" (prints).

JAGO, Joan E., FRSA (1989-2005), FFPS (1992), Wilfred Sirrell Award (City of Westminster Arts Council) 1989, Dip. in Creative Textiles (1985); fibre artist/paper maker. *Medium*: handmade paper. *b*: Leeds, 22 Mar 1930. *d of*: Charles E.D. Burrell. *Educ*: Aireborough Grammar School, W. Yorks. *Studied*: London College of Furniture. *Exhib*: solo shows: Marks & Spencer plc H.Q. Bldg., London (1993); The Media Centre, London

(2003); two-artist shows: Sheridan Russell (2002) Curwen (2004); group shows: 119 including London, Hong Kong and USA. Liverpool Biennale (2005), London Biennale (2006), Curwen Christmas Exhibitions (1997-). *Works in collections*: Wilfred Sirrell Collection. *Works Reproduced*: in 'The Crafter's Complete Guide to Collage' (Watson-Guptill Publications, New York, 1996). *Address*: 606 Nelson House, Dolphin Sq., London SW1V 3NZ. *Email*: joanjago@ntlworld.com *Signs work*: "Joan Jago."

JAIDINGER, Judith, Fellow of the Royal Society of Painter-Printmakers/Society of Wood Engravers. *Medium*: wood engraving, watercolour. *b*: Chicago, Illinois, USA, 10 Apr 1941. *m*: Gerald Szesko. one *d*. *Educ*: School of the Art Institute of Chicago, BFA (1970). *Studied*: drawing, painting, printmaking. *Represented by*: Bankside Gallery, London. *Exhib*: Taipei Fine Arts Museum, Taiwan ROC (1987), San Diego Art Institute, CA (1992), University of Hawaii at Hilo (2000), Esther Allen Greer Museum of Fine Art, OH (1999), 'Wood Engraving Here and Now', Ashmolean Museum, Oxford (1995), Muskegon Museum of Art (solo exhbn.) Michigan (2005). *Works in collections*: Purdue University, West Lafayette, IN; Ashmolean Museum, Oxford; National Museum of American History, Smithsonian Institution; Portland Art Museum, Oregon; Springfield Art Museum, MO. *Commissions*: Face to Face, Penmaen; Busyhaus Publications (1985). *Publications*: 'Lancelot and the Lord of the Distant Isles' (pub. David R.Godine, 2006). *Official Purchasers*: The State Foundation on Culture and the Arts, Honolulu, HI; Illinois State Museum, Springfield, IL. *Works Reproduced*: End Grain Contemporary Wood Engraving in North America (Barbarian Press, 1994); An Engraver's Globe by Simon Brett (Primrose Hill Press, London 2002); Relief Printmaking by Ann Westley (A & C Black, 2001). *Address*: 6110 N Newburg Avenue, Chicago, Illinois 60631, USA. *Email*: jaidinger@sbcglobal.net *Signs work*: 'JAIDINGER'.

JAKOBER, Ben, FBRS; sculptor in stone, iron, bronze; winner of Miro Foundation Prize (1993). *b*: Vienna, 31 Jul 1930. *s of*: Henry Jakober. *m*: Yannick Vu, with whom he now works and signs jointly. one *s*. *Educ*: Mill Hill School; La Sorbonne, Paris . *Exhib*: 1982: Fundación March, Palma; 1984: Palais des Beaux Arts, Brussels; Louisiana Museum, Humlebaek; Städtische Kunsthalle, Mannheim; Museum Moderner Kunst, Vienna; 1985: Recklinghausen Museum; 1986: XLII Biennale di Venezia; 1988: Olympiad of Art, Seoul; 1990: Jeune Sculpture, Paris; 1991: MVSEV, Palma; Musée d'Art Moderne, Pully (VD); 1992: EXPO 92, Seville; 1993: Arnolfini, Bristol; Museum Moderner Kunst Stiftung Ludwig Palais Liechtenstein, Vienna; "MEDIALE", Hamburg; XLV Biennale di Venezia; 1994: Fundació Pilar i Joan Miró a Mallorca, Palma de Mallorca; 1995: Salle delle Reali Poste, Gli Uffizi, Firenze; 1996: Istituto Italiano di Cultura, Paris; Galerie Pièce Unique, Paris; XXIII Bienal International de São Paulo, Brazil; 1998: "Disidentico" Palermo, Mücsarnok Budapest; 2001: Bienal of Valencia; 2002: Castillo St. Barbara Alicante; 2002: Palacia Sastago, Zaragoza; 2008: Museo Arts San Jose. *Works in collections*: Museo Nacional Centro de Arte Reina Sofia, Madrid; Musée d'Art Moderne, Brussels; Museum of Modern Art, Palais Liechtenstein, Vienna; Museum of Austrian Art of the XIX and XX Centuries, Vienna; Kunsthalle Bremen; Kunsthalle, Hamburg; Musée d'Art Moderne F.A.E., Pully (VD); Colombe d'Or, St Paul de Vence; Fattoria di Celle, Pistoia; E.P.A.D., Paris; Seoul Olympic Park; Fondation Vincent Van Gogh, Arles; Fundació Pilar i Joan Miró a Mallorca, Palma de Mallorca; Gabinetto Disegni e Stampe degli Uffizi, Firenze; Museum Beelden aan Zee, Scheveningen; Ludwig Museum Budapest; Museum Fine Arts Budapest. *Commissions*: Peninsula Hotel, Tokyo (2007), Peninsula Hotel, Shanghai (2009), Palace of Justice, Salerno (2007), Gran Hotel Floerida, Barcelona (2006), Gran Hotel Miramar, Barcelona (2007). *Publications*: "Ben Jakober'Yannick Vu" by Achille Bortio Oliva (2006). *Address*: 24 Calle Puente Real, La Pacifica, Canas Guanacaste, Costa Rica. *Email*: ben@jakaobervu.cr *Website*: www.jakobervu.com *Signs work*: "B.J."

JAMES, Andrew John, VPRP, Vice President Royal Society of Portrait Painters; Carroll Foundation Award (1998); The Changing Faces Portrait Prize (2013). *Medium*: oil, visual arts. *b*: Reading, Berks, 6 Aug 1969. *s of*: Dennis James. *m*: Derly Eliana. *Educ*: Battle and Langton Primary School; Claverham Community College, Battle, E.Sussex. *Studied*: self taught. *Exhib*: NEAC; RBA; NPG; RP; solo show Mall Galleries (2003). *Works in collections*: 'People's Portraits' Girton College, Cambridge; Tunbridge Wells Museum and Art Gallery. *Commissions*: BBC TV, Rolf on Art: David Dickinson, General Yakubo Gowon. *Misc*: twin brother of Paul Henry James, visual artist, New York, USA. *Address*: 21 Dorking Road, Tunbridge Wells, Kent TN1 2LN. *Email*: andrewjamesrp@yahoo.co.uk *Website*: andrewjamesartist.co.uk *Signs work*: 'A.JAMES' with date.

JAMES, Donald, BSc (Honours), MA (Art); Awards: Commonwealth of Massachusetts-PE, Australia-MIE; painter, designer; exhibits internationally. *b*: New York, 1932. *s of*: Adolph. *Educ*: San Francisco Art Institute, California School of Fine Arts, Cocoran School of Art, University of California, University of New York, University of London. *Exhib*: San Fransisco, New York, Boston, London, Paris, Vienna, Rome, Sydney, Hong Kong. *Works in collections*: worldwide. *Commissions*: cultural portraits. *Publications*: contributions to Celare Artem. *Principal Works*: wall paintings for Chapel of St. Ursula. *Clubs*: Societies: Ars Ad Summum. *Address*: The Studio, 47 Chelsea Manor St., London SW3 5RZ. *Signs work*: "Don Ald," earlier "James."

JAMES, Gary M., MMAA (Member of the Medical Artists' Association of GB). *Medium*: Acrylics and sculpted frames. *b*: Slough, 22 Sep 1941, raised in Kenya. *s of*: L W R & D M James. *m*: Paulette. two *s*. *Educ*: Duke of York School, Nairobi (1953-60). *Studied*: St.Martins School of Art (1960-64), Med. Artists Ass. of GB (1964-66). *Represented by*: principal outlet: The Everard Read Gallery, Johannesburg. *Exhib*: Royal West of England Academy, Bristol City Museum & Art Gallery, Royal Academy, Paddington Gallery ('81), The Mall Gallery ('81), The Royal Observatory Herstmonceux, Bath Contemporary Art Fair ('93), Bath Society of Artists (2003). One-man shows: The Everard Read Gallery, Johannesburg (singly thereafter), Joint exhibition with son Alex, ERG, (2008). *Works in collections*: Anglo American Mining Corp. *Publications*: RA Illustrated (1980, 90, 91); 'The Egyptian Timescale' (1996), 'The British Timescale' (2000) (principal retailers: The British Museum). *Official Purchasers*: Press & magazines (Principally in South Africa). *Works Reproduced*: (In the RA): Capt. Maltravers Voyage to the Interior (1980), River Market (1990), Forecast (1991). (at Art London): Soko La Pango (2001). *Principal Works*: tightrope walking (ret'd), keeping an illustrated journal. *Address*: 123 Abbey Road, Westbury on Trym, Bristol, BS9 3QJ. *Website*: www.voyageart.co.uk *Signs work*: "Gary M.James".

JAMES, Janice. BA (Hons) Ceramics. *Medium*: Sculpture in clay. *b*: Neath, 10 Dec 1954. *m*: Julian James. one *s*. one *d*. *Educ*: Sandfields Comprehensive School. *Studied*: Swansea Institute of Higher Education (1999-2002). *Exhib*: Broadway Modern, Worcestershire; Kooywood Gallery, Cardiff; RVB arts, Rome; Fisherton Mill Gallery, Salisbury; Russell-Coates Art Gallery and Museum, Bournemouth. *Address*: 35 Gwar-y-caeau, Port Talbot, W. Glamorgan SA13 2UR. *Email*: jj@janicejamesceramics.com *Website*: www.janicejamesceramics.com *Signs work*: "JJ." on the inside of the work.

JAMES, Nicholas Philip, ROI; BA Fine Art; MA History of Art; Slade Scholarship; Trevelyan Goodall Scholarship. *Medium*: oil painting. *b*: Bromley, Kent, 13 Nov 1948. *s of*: Fritz & Janet Wegner. *m*: Sarah Anne. three *d*. *Studied*: UCL (1957-66); Slade School of Art (1966-70). *Represented by*: The Turner Gallery, 88 Queen Street, Exeter, EX4 3RP. *Exhib*: RA Summer Exhibition; The Wold Gallery, Glos.; Manor House Gallery, Chipping Norton; Beaulieu Fine Art, Hants; Courcoux & Courcoux, Hants; RBA, ROI, Whittington Fine Art, Henley; Bourne Gallery, Reigate; Peter Pears Gallery, Aldeburgh; regularly at Turner Gallery, Exeter; RAC Clubs Epsom & Pall Mall (2012/13). *Works in collections*: private collections in UK, Europe & USA; prints in Tate archive (Curwen Gallery gift); CD Roms and publications, media collection of The British Library. *Commissions*: The Guinness

Portrait (200th Anniversary, 1981); Inch Cape plc boardroom portrait; Gutman family portrait, Versa Manos and others. *Publications*: For AN Publications (1996) with Anna Douglas - Artists Stories; for CV Publications: interviews-artists; Small Histories; Studies of Western Art, Curators and Collections *Works Reproduced*: Moorland Views, in 'Dartmoor Artists' by Brian Le Mesurier (Hallsgrove Publishers, 2003). *Principal Works*: The Square Mile; views of the City of London 1999-2004. *Recreations*: cycling. *Misc*: Proprietor of CV Publications. Born Nicholas James Philip Wegner: name changed by deed poll 2002 to Nicholas Philip James. *Address*: Albion House, 49 Park Road, Hampton Wick, Kingston-upon-Thames, Surrey KT1 4AS. *Email*: cvpub@ision.co.uk. *Website*: www.philipjamestudio.ndo.co.uk *Signs work*: 'PHILIP JAMES'.

JAMES, Ric, NDD, ATD, BA; DAE MA; travelling scholarship, Rome; International Lighting Award for Design of 'Manhattan Lamp' in stainless steel (2005). *Medium*: Oil, prints, sculpture, design, photography and furniture design. *b*: Torquay, 23 Oct 1943, married. two *s*. one *d*. *Studied*: Birmingham University; Gloucestershire College of Art. *Represented by*: James Fine Art. *Exhib*: Simic Gallery, California; Rowles Fine Art; Priory Gallery. *Works in collections*: Europe, USA and Japan. *Commissions*: Sculpture, painting and design commissions undertaken for both private and corporate. *Publications*: Biography of sculpture and design being compiled at present. *Works Reproduced*: Paintings, sculpture and design. *Principal Works*: Series on dance - ballet figurative studies - plus abstract bronzes. *Recreations*: Squash and tennis. *Misc*: Head of Art at Cheltenham Grammar School (1969-1979). *Address*: 14 Presbury Road, Cheltenham GL52 2PW. *Email*: ric@jamesfineart.co.uk *Website*: www.jamesfineart.co.uk *Signs work*: "RM JAMES", "Ric" or "RMJ".

JAMES, Roderick Morris, NDD, ATD, DAE, MA; Travelling Scholarship, Rome; International Lighting Award for design of 'Manhattan Lamp' in stainless steel (2005). *Medium*: sculptor. *b*: Torquay, 1943. *m*: divorced. two *s*. one *d*. *Educ*: Gloucestershire College of Art. *Studied*: Birmingham University. *Represented by*: James Fine Art. *Exhib*: Rowles Fine Art, Priory Gallery, Callaghan Fine Art, Olympia Fine Art, Chelsea 20th Century Art, Simic Fine Art USA, Cheltenham Art Gallery. *Works in collections*: numerous collections in Britain, Europe, Japan and USA. *Publications*: biography of Sculpture and Design being compiled at present. *Works Reproduced*: paintings, sculpture and design. *Principal Works*: series on dance - ballet & figurative studies. *Recreations*: squash and tennis. *Misc*: Head of Art at Cheltenham Grammar School from 1969-1979. *Address*: 1 Pitville Court, Albert Rd., Cheltenham, GL52 3JA. *Email*: ric@jamesfineart.co.uk *Website*: www.jamesfineart.co.uk *Signs work*: 'Ric James'.

JAMES, Simon, MA (RCA) (1989); artist in oil, charcoal and printmaking. *b*: 22 Jan 1965. *Educ*: Northampton School for Boys. *Studied*: RA Schools (1984-87), RCA (1987-89). *Exhib*: RA, NEAC, Marks and Spencer Young Artist award (1992), prizewinner in the 10th Cleveland International Drawing Biennale (1991), numerous exhbns. in England, USA, and Berlin. *Works in collections*: Lloyd's of London, Cleveland CC, The Foreign Office. *Address*: Houseboat Clifton, Blomfield Rd., London W9 2PB. *Signs work*: "SIMON JAMES" or "S.J."

JAMESON, Kerry, BA (Hons). *Medium*: sculpture. *b*: London, 1 Nov 1969. *Studied*: Central St.Martin's College of Art and Design; Royal College of Art. *Represented by*: Medici Gallery; Adrian Sassoon; Snyderman-Works, USA. *Exhib*: RA; V&A; SOFA, New York; Artform, Florida, USA; The Geffrye Museum, London. *Works in collections*: David Hockney, Ronnie Wood, Russell Crowe, Valentino, Lord Rothschild, Malcolm McDowell. *Publications*: 'Ceramics: Art and Perception'; The Guardian; The Times; The Independent. *Principal Works*: works in clay and other materials. *Address*: Phipps Bridge Studios, Phipps Bridge Road, Merton, CR4 3PL. *Email*: info@kerryjameson.com *Website*: www.kerryjameson.com *Signs work*: 'Kerry Jameson BA'

JAMESON, Norma Marion, RBA, ROI, NDD, ATD, Goldsmiths' Advanced Dip.; painter, lecturer. *Medium*: works in oils and ceramics. *b*: Burslem, 18 Jan 1933. *d of*: Frank Bertram Salt. *m*: Kenneth Ambrose Jameson (decd). *Educ*: Thistley Hough Grammar School, Stoke-on-Trent. *Studied*: Bath Academy of Art (1951-55); Liverpool University (1955-56); Goldsmiths' College (1978). *Exhib*: RA; various one-man shows in London and the South East. Mem. Royal Society of British Artists and The Royal Inst. of Oil Painters, exhibits annually in South East Open Studios. *Works in collections*: private in the UK and abroad. *Publications*: articles on drawing for "Canvas" and "Leisure Painter", "Batik for Beginners" – Studio Vista. *Works Reproduced*: by Medici, Lings and Elgin Court. *Address*: 111 Hayes Way, Beckenham, Kent BR3 6RR. *Signs work*: "Norma Jameson."

JAMIESON, Susan McDonald, painter in oil and acrylic. *b*: Newbury, 5 Jul 1942. *m*: Andrew. two *s*. one *d*. *Exhib*: RA Summer Show, ROI, New English, Britain's Painters, Medici Gallery, Thomson's Gallery, Dover Street, Wykeham Gallery, Stockbridge. *Clubs*: Arts, Dover St. *Address*: Minstrel House, The Croft, Kintbury, Nr. Newbury, Berks. RG17 9TJ.

JAMISON, Paul, BAHons (1979), PGCE/ATD (1982); artist in oil and water-colour. *b*: Middlesbrough, 16 Sep 1954. *s of*: John Jamison. *Educ*: St. Mary's College, Middlesbrough. *Studied*: University of Newcastle upon Tyne (1975-79), University of Bristol (1981-82). *Exhib*: Hatton Gallery, Newcastle (1979), Alpine Gallery, London (1980, 1983), Bayswater Gallery (1987, 1989, 1991). Work in private hands throughout the world. *Address*: 16 Cosway St., London NW1 5NR. *Signs work*: "Jamison" with year, i.e. '98.

JAMMET, Lin, painter in gouache on paper, oil on canvas. *b*: 22 May 1958. *s of*: Michel Jammet, architect, and Dame Elisabeth Frink, R.A. *m*: Valerie Jammet. two *s*. *Educ*: French Lycée, London; C.E.G. d'Anduze, France; Millfield, Somerset. *Studied*: Chelsea School of Art (sculpture course 1976). *Exhib*: one-man shows: Beaux Arts Gallery, Bath, St. Jude's Gallery, London, Contemporary Fine Art Gallery, Eton, Bohun Gallerie Henley, Beaux Arts Gallery, London. *Clubs*: Chelsea Arts. *Address*: The Print Studio, Building 10, Michael Young Centre, Purbeck Road, Cambridge CB2 8HN. *Signs work*: "Lin Jammet."

JARAY, Tess, DFA (Lond., 1960), FRIBA; painter and etcher, environmental artist; Reader in Fine Art. *Medium*: painting, printmaking *b*: Vienna, 31 Dec 1937. *d of*: Francis F. Jaray, M.I.Chem.E. two *d*. *Educ*: Alice Ottley School, Worcester. *Studied*: St. Martin's School of Art (1954-57), Slade School of Fine Art (1957-60). *Exhib*: solo exhbns.: Whitworth A.G., Manchester, Ashmolean Museum, Oxford, Serpentine Gallery, London, The Djanogly Gallery, Nottingham (2014). *Works in collections*: Stadtisches Museum, Leverkusen, Walker Art Gallery, Liverpool, Arts Council of Gt. Britain, Tate Gallery, Graves Art Gallery, Sheffield, Warwick University, British Museum, V&A Museum. *Commissions*: Floor for Victoria Station, London, Centenary Square, Birmingham, Cathedral Precinct pedestrianisation, Wakefield, St. Mary's Church, Nottingham (floor). *Publications*: 'Painting: Mysteries and Confessions' Published by Lenz Books; monograph: 'The Art of Jess Jaray' Published by Ridinghouse Books. *Address*: 29 Camden Sq., London NW1 9XA. *Email*: email@tessjaray.com *Signs work*: "Tess Jaray."

JARVIS, Gloria, NDD; Médaille d'Argent Paris (1976); artist in oil, water-colour, pastel, ink, gouache; lecturer on historic costume and instructor in costume drawing, Polytechnic, Regent St. (1950-63). *b*: London. *d of*: R. V. Jarvis, artist. *m*: Raymond Smith, B.A. *Educ*: Heathfield School, Harrow; Aylesbury Grammar School. *Studied*: St. Martin's School of Art, London, under James Bateman, RA, the history of art at Florence University. *Exhib*: RA, NEAC, Leicester Galleries; one-man show, Brussels (1970-1982). *Works in collections*: Abbot Hall A.G., Kendal; Museum of the Dynasty, Brussels; International Museum of Carnival and Mask, Binche, Belgium; Museum of Dockland, U.K and private collections. *Commissions*: numerous portraits and genre paintings, Brussels and U.K. *Publications*:

A Jarvis Tapestry, An Easel in the Family, Rose in the Martyrdom. *Works Reproduced*: Macmillan, Brussels Times. Short stories; broadcast by BBC; family and social histories. *Clubs*: Soc. of Women Writers and Journalists. *Address*: Chantry Court, 38 St. Radigund's Street, Canterbury, CT1 2AA. *Signs work*: "Gloria Jarvis."

JASINSKI, Alfons B., RSW (1978), Latimer award RSA (1975), DA Travelling scholar (1969). *Medium*: artist in oil, acrylic, water-colour, pastel (seashore/figure/landscape/ flowers/plant life). *b*: Falkirk, 1945. *s of*: Alfons B. Jasinski. *m*: Ann Conlan. one *s*. two *d*. *Studied*: Edinburgh College of Art (1964-68). *Exhib*: RSA, RSW, ESU, Edinburgh, M. Murray Gallery, London; Artspace, Aberdeen; RGI; Aberdeen City Art Gallery; Fair Maids, Perth; Portfolio 4, Linlithgow; Mercury, Edinburgh; Roseangle, Dundee; Pictures in Hospitals; Loomshop Gallery, Lower Largo, Scottish Gallery, Kirkcaldy A.G., Artis: Flying Colours, Stenton, Peter Potter, Haddington; Ben Papillon & Morningside Gallery, Edinburgh; Greens/Blues, N. Berwick; Jerdan Gallery, Crail; Leith Gallery, Strathearn Gallery. *Works in Collections*: SAC, Edinburgh Schools Collection, Aberdeen City A.G., Duke of Devonshire, PIH Scotland. *Address*: 4 Morven Park, Glenrothes, Fife KY6 3PX. *Email*: alfjasinski@yahoo.co.uk *Website*: alfjasinski.com *Signs work*: "A. B. Jasinski."

JASON, Gillian, Art Gallery Director, Gillian Jason, Modern & Contemporary Art, P.O.Box 35063, London NW1 7XQ. *b*: UK, 30 Jun 1941. *m*: Neville. one *s*. one *d*. *Educ*: Dominican Convent School for Girls, Brewood. *Studied*: Royal Ballet School/London Opera Centre. *Misc*: Director of Gillian Jason Gallery, London, (1981-1994); Jason & Rhodes, London, (1994-1999); Gillian Jason, Modern and Contemporary Art (private dealer representing artists), 1999 onwards. *Address*: 40 Inverness St., London NW1 7HB. *Email*: art@gillianjason.com

JEBBETT, Clive Alexander. *Medium*: acrylic, watercolour, drawing. *b*: Enfield, 28 Aug 1951. *Studied*: Colchester School of Art. *Represented by*: The Wine Street Gallery at No 10 (Devizes). *Exhib*: Unilever - Fabergé (9 works), plus private and corporate collections in England, France, Germany, Spain, Ireland, Canada and America. *Address*:22 High Street, Devizes, Wiltshire, SN10 1AT. *Signs work*: "JEBBETT".

JEFFERSON, Annelise, MA (1990); fine art painter in oil on canvas. *b*: Pembury, 1965. *Educ*: Chichester High School. *Studied*: West Surrey College of Art and Design (Stephen Farthing), Royal Academy (Norman Adams). *Exhib*: RA Summer Exhbn. (1988, 1989, 1990, 1991), Bonhams: The New Generation (1990), Royal Overseas League (1990), Rubicorn Gallery, Dublin (1991), The Hunting Art Prizes finalist (U.K. and Paris, 1991), NEAC, Mall Galleries (1991-92). *Works in collections*: South East Arts, Lloyds of London, Leics. CC; also private collections in UK, Eire, Canada. *Address*: Maycotts Lodge, The Green, Matfield, Tonbridge, Kent TN12 7JU.

JEFFERY, Juliet, NDD, FSSI, SEA; President's medal SEA (1993) watercolour and gouache, and calligrapher. *b*: Bognor Regis, 5 Mar 1943. *Educ*: Warren, Worthing. *Studied*: Brighton College of Art and Crafts (Dennis Flanders, RWS). *Exhib*: SEA Annual, RWS Open, locally and Cumbria, SSI and Portsmouth Museum. *Commissions*: specialises in illustrated and calligraphic house or animal histories (pedigrees); animal portraits. *Publications*: Gypsy Poems and Ballads by Lavengro; Appley Fair; Bender Tents; A Tiny Tale and Sarah's Tales. *Recreations*: gardening, old buildings, animals and my work. *Clubs*: S.Eq.A., Fellow S.S.I., Brother Artworkers Guild. *Address*: 23a Mill Street, Ludlow, Shropshire SY8 1BG. *Email*: juliet@johndiamond0wanadoo.co.uk.co.uk *Signs work*: "Juliet Jeffery."

JEFFREY, Jill, ATD, NDD, ARBSA (1996), PS (1997); designer (theatre) retd. 1991; Awards: Arts Council Design Award (1965), Royal Shakespeare Theatre Design Award (1964), Pastel Society, Mall Galleries, London. *Medium*: oils, pastels, mixed media.

b: Chesterfield, 30 Jul 1940. *d of*: G.R. Clarke. *m*: Peter (decd), Actor. one *s.* three *d. Educ*: St. Joseph's Convent, Chesterfield; St. Martins, Solihull. *Studied*: Coventry College of Art (1957-59, David Bethel), B' ham College of Art (1959-61, Roy Abel). *Represented by*: Stour Gallery, Shipston; FBA Mall Gallery, London; Workshop Wales, Fishguard. *Exhib*: solo shows: Solihull, Chipping Norton, also Mall Gallery, London, National Theatre, London. *Works in collections*: UK, Europe, USA, Canada, Japan, New Zealand. *Commissions*: private commissions undertaken. *Official Purchasers*: Royal Shakespeare Theatre. *Works Reproduced*: for Royal National Theatre, London. *Recreations*: walking, swimming. *Clubs*: Blockley Society of Arts. *Misc*: Artist on Tour – National Theatre (1991 world tour), Artist in Residence R.S.T. Stratford Upon Avon (1993). *Address*: The Hayloft, Crockwell Street, Long Compton, Warwickshire CV36 5JN. *Email*: mrs.jillfjeffrey@btinternet.com *Website*: www.jilljeffrey.com

JELBERT, Rebecca, BA Hons (1st Class). *Medium*: painter in acrylics and watercolour. *b*: Bristol, 30 Mar 1967. *d of*: Wendy Jelbert. *m*: Adam Walker. one *s.*two *d. Studied*: University of the West of England (1987-90); Portsmouth College of Art & Design (1985-87). *Exhib*: one-man shows: C.R.A. Gallery, St.Albans (3 shows); First Floor Gallery, Romsey; Beau Monde, Soho, London; two-man shows: Wykeham Galleries, Stockbridge; The Chettle Gallery, Dorset; mixed: Bonhams, Knightsbridge; Christie's, London; Mall Galleries, London; The Contemporary Art Group, London; The Laing Collection, Winchester; The National Art Collection Fund Exhibition, Kent, and in numerous galleries throughout the South of England in solo, two-man and mixed exhibitions. *Works in collections*: Lord Bath's 'Wessex Art Collection' at Longleat House. *Commissions*: many private. *Works Reproduced*: in 'The World's Stage' poetry book (Ginn), also shown on BBC TV. *Address*: 7 Hartington Park, Redland, Bristol, BS6 7ES. *Email*: info@rebeccajelbert.co.uk *Website*: www.rebeccajelbert.co.uk *Signs work*: "R. JELBERT".

JELBERT, Wendy, SWA, SFP; Teaching/Drama Diploma and medals; Best Painting Awards, London and provinces. *Medium*: mixed media; pen, line and wash, watercolour, acrylics, pastels. *b*: Redhill, Surrey 8 Feb 1943. *m*: Paul Robinson. one *s.* four *d. Studied*: Southampton University. *Exhib*: RI, SWA, Oxford, Cornwall, St. Ives Society of Artists; 1st Floor, Romsey, Hants; Carlseen Gallery, Lymington, Hants; Little Picture Gallery, Mousehole, Cornwall; Mall Galleries & Westminster Galleries, London. *Works in collections*: all over the world. *Commissions*: all over the world. *Publications*: 39 art books-Batsford, Harper Collins, Search Press, David & Charles. *Works Reproduced*: calendars, cards, prints - all over the world. *Recreations*: cycling, swimming, gardening, and looking after 14 grandchildren. *Clubs*: Society of Woman Artists; St. Ives Society of Artists; Marwell Wildlife Society; Society of Floral Painters. *Misc*: has made 12 DVDs. Teacher at West Dean College (Chichester, Sussex), Denman College (Abingdon, Oxford) and locally in Romsey. *Address*: La Palette, 25 Richmond Lane, Romsey, Hants., SO51 7LB. *Email*: art@wendyjelbert.co.uk *Website*: www.wendyjelbert.co.uk *Signs work*: Wendy Jelbert

JELLEY, Susan Jane, SWA, SFP. *Medium*: pastel work, oil, watercolour, drawing, prints. *b*: London, 29 Jun 1945. *d of*: Mollie Marie Wright. *m*: Roger Jelley. two *s. Educ*: Fairfield Grammar, Bristol. *Studied*: Bristol College of Commerce (Business Diploma); West Surrey College of Art (Fine Art, with James Hockey). *Represented by*: C2 Gallery, Bucks (Nicki Clark); Kathi Rodgers, Arizona. *Exhib*: Federation of British Artists; PS; SWA; French Pastel Society; Paris, Limoges, Arizona; Menier Gallery, Southwark; Yvonne Arnaud Summer Festival, Guildford, Farnham; Mayfair Gallery 54; AAF Battersea; C2 Bucks. *Works in collections*: Country Club, Guildford, Surrey; King Edwards School, Witley (Music Dept.); Foxhills Country Club, Chertsey, Surrey. *Commissions*: private: portrait, landscape, in Australia, America, Europe and UK. *Official Purchasers*: Country Club, Guildford, Surrey; King Edwards School, Witley (Music Dept.); Farnham Castle (CD cover); Foxhills Country Club. *Works Reproduced*: 'Dance'. *Principal Works*: dance, jazz, figurative. *Recreations*: travelling, reading, wines/champagnes of France. *Clubs*: The Country Club, Guildford, Surrey. *Misc*: interested in writing and languages. *Address*: Brook House, Upper Birtley, Haslemere Road, Brook, Surrey GU8 5LB. *Website*: www.suejelley.co.uk *Signs work*: 'Jelley'.

JELLICOE, Colin, painter in oils and acrylics; art gallery director. *b*: 1 Nov 1942. *Educ*: Heald Place School. *Studied*: Manchester Regional College of Art. *Exhib*: one-man shows: Monks Hall Museum, Eccles (1970), Stockport A.G. (1981), Salford A.G. (1981), Jellicoe Gallery (1974, 83, 84, 85, 90, 95, 00), Buxton Museum and A.G. (1997); group shows: Northern Images Manchester (1974), North West One Chenil Galleries, London (1976), North West Two National Theatre, London (1979), Contemporary Art Fair, Bath (1981, 82, 83), with Michael Goddard Royal Exchange Theatre Manchester (1985), Edinburgh Festival Fringe (1983, 84, 85), Contemporary Art Fair, London (1984, 85, 86); Open shows: Manchester Academy City A.G. (1970, 73, 75, 76, 81, 84, 85, 88, 92, 95, 2004, 05), R.A. Summer Exhbn. (1981, 2004), Discerning Eye (2000, 01); many others in Preston, Accrington, Bolton, Southsea, Wimbledon and Manchester. *Works in collections*: Granada Television, Manchester; Abbey National Didsbury; Withington Hospital, Manchester. *Recreations*: history of American West; history of American Western films; history of British and American illustrators. *Address*: 82 Portland St., Manchester M1 4QX. *Website*: www.colinjellicoe.co.uk *Signs work*: 'Colin Jellicoe'.

JENKINS, Christopher, Slade Dip. (Painting) (1957), ATC (1958); Fellow CPA, mem. NPA. *Medium*: potter in thrown and glazed oxidised stoneware and wood fired domestic ware; artist in water-colour. *b*: B'ham, 1933. divorced. *s of*: Lincoln and Phyllis Jenkins, artists. one *s*. one *d*. *Educ*: Harrogate Grammar School. *Studied*: Harrogate School of Art (1949-52), Slade School of Fine Art (1952-54 and 1956-57), London Institute of Education (1957-58), Central School (ceramics, 1957-59). *Exhib*: V&A, Crafts Centre, CPA, London, York, Scarborough, Kendal, Nottingham, Manchester, Liverpool, Tokyo, Copenhagen, Paris. *Works in collections*: North West Arts, LEAs: London, Leicester, Bucks., N. Yorks, Kirklees, Hanley, York. *Address*: 19 Towngate, Marsden, Huddersfield HD7 6DD. *Email*: chris@towngatepottery.co.uk

JENKINS, Heinke, RBSA (1967), RBA (1977); Printmaker of the Month, Leicester (1997), Tanner Charitable Trust Prize (1998), Colex and Tilley Prize (2000), T.N. Lawrence Couterory Print Prize (2004); RBSA 1st Prize in Contemporary Prints; tutor for the Open College of the Arts in painting and drawing. *Medium*: printmaker in linocut. *b*: Heilbronn, W. Germany, 2 Jul 1937. *d of*: Dr. Mayer. one *s*. *Educ*: Heilbronn Grammar School. *Studied*: Stuttgart Academy of Arts (Prof. Henninger), Stuttgart College of Graphic and Illustration (Prof. Leo Schobinger). *Exhib*: Germany, USA, England. *Works in collections*: Heilbronn A.G., Stuttgart A.G. *Commissions*: 1993: drawings and linocuts for B'ham University Maternity Hospital in Memory of the old Sorrento Maternity Hospital, B'ham. Now permanent display at Queen Elizabeth University Maternity Hospital, Birmingham. *Publications*: illustrated, Arts Review, 'Ambit' poetry magazine, 'Circle' poems, M. Armstrong. *Recreations*: music, walking. *Clubs*: R.B.S.A., R.B.A., Heilbronn Kunstler Bund. *Address*: 26 Allesley Cl., Sutton Coldfield, Birmingham B74 2NF. *Signs work*: "HEINKE."

JENKINS, Josie, BA Hons Fine Art (Painting). *Medium*: oil, drawing. *b*: Beverley, 8 Feb 1980. *Partner*: Andrew Kynman. *Studied*: Norwich School of Art and Design (1999-2002). *Exhib*: Solo shows: Cork Art Gallery, liverpool (2014); Dot Art, Liverpool (2013); Bridewell Studios and Gallery, Liverpool (2012). Group shows: The Biscuit Factory, Newcastle (2014); Mercer Gallery, Harrogate (2013); Corke Art Gallery, Liverpool (2013); Castlegate House Gallery, Cockermouth (2012); Chapel Gallery, Ormskirk (2012); 3 Bedforbury Gallery, London (2011); The Royal College of Art, London (2011); Nottingham Castle,

Nottingham (2010). *Works in collections*: private. *Commissions*: Liverpool Independant Music Restival (2014). *Address*: 9 St Michaels Road, Aigburth, Liverpool L17 7AN. *Email*: info@rosiejenkins.co.uk *Website*: www.rosiejenkins.co.uk Signs work: "Josie Jenkins".

JENKINS, Kate, BA (Hons) Fashion Textiles with Business Studies. *Medium*: Crochet. *b*: Newport, Gwent, 17 Sep 1971. *Educ*: Our Ladys Convent School, Cardiff. *Studied*: University of Brighton (1992-95). *Represented by*: Rebecca Hossack Gallery, London. *Exhib*: London; New York; Toronto; Amsterdam; Paris; Australia; Brighton. *Works in collections*: Brighton Museum; Crafts Council; private collectors worldwide. *Commissions*: Pommery Champagne; Tesco; Penguin Books. *Publications*: Indie Craft (Jo Waterhouse). *Misc*: Set up her label Cardigan in 2003, designing knitted fashion and homeware. *Address*: Unit 5, Arundel Mews, 13-18 Arundel Place, Brighton BN2 1GG. *Email*: kate@cardigan.ltd.uk *Website*: www.cardigan.ltd.uk *Signs work*: "Kate Jenkins".

JENKINS, Lawrence Fifield, RAS Cert (1972), ATC (Goldsmiths 1973). *Medium*: painter-printmaker. *b*: Sevenoaks, Kent, 7 Oct 1944. *m*: Brigitte. two *s*. *Studied*: Maidstone College of Art (1962-64, David Hockney, Bill Bowyer), Nottingham College of Art, Royal Academy of Art (E. Bawden). *Exhib*: RA, RP, RWS. *Works in collections*: Royal Collections, National Museum of Wales. *Commissions*: Victory Services Club, Trust House Forte, Crown Court, Maidstone. *Clubs*: RASAA. *Misc*: runs Seal Chart Etching Studio, Sevenoaks, TN15 0ES. *Address*: Seal Chart Studio, Chart Farm, Seal Chart, Sevenoaks, TN13 3QJ. *Email*: lawrence.jenkins@wanadoo.fr *Website*: www.lawrencejenkins.co.uk

JENKINS, Thomas Raymond, artist in water-colour; former Chairman Civil Public Service Artists, and President Boreham Art Circle; Mem. Islington Art Society. *b*: London, 24 Jun 1928. *m*: Margaret. one *s*. one *d*. *Studied*: Chelmsford, and St. Ives School of Painting under Roy Ray. *Exhib*: Council of Europe Exhbn., Strasbourg (1979, premier prize), HS Annual at Wells, Montelimar Festival, Barbican Arts Centre 10th Anniversary Exhbn., Llewellyn Alexander Gallery, London. *Works in collections*: private: USA, Canada, Europe, NZ, Australia, Scandinavia, Russia and Japan. *Misc*: teaches student groups, demonstrates to art clubs. *Address*: 28 Butterfield Rd., Boreham, Chelmsford, Essex CM3 3BS. *Signs work*: "Ray Jenkins".

JENNISON, Robert William, RWA, NDD (1954), ATD (1958); painter in oil, occasional printmaker, lecturer (Exeter University). *b*: Grantham, 8 Jun 1933. *m*: Angela Cook (decd). one *s*. two *d*. *Educ*: Grammar School, Weston super Mare. *Studied*: West of England College of Art, Bristol (1950-54, 1957-58, Paul Feiler). *Represented by*: Royal West of England Academy; The Art Room, Topsham, Exeter. *Exhib*: frequent solo and group shows since 1962: London, Wales, South-West, N. Ireland, including RWA, RUA, Milan, Italy., own gallery at Gittisham Studio WEF May 2003, Retrospective exhibition planned at RWA Nov 2010. *Works in collections*: public and private collections in Britain, Europe, USA etc. *Commissions*: mural, Torbay Hospital 1968; two portraits. *Publications*: featured in '50 Wessex Artists' pub. Evolver Books, 'A Picture of Devon' pub. Halsgrove. *Official Purchasers*: Exeter University, RWA, 'Paintings in Hospitals', Royal Devon & Exeter Hospital, Ulster TV, Ulster Bank. *Address*: The Studio, 6 Town Farm Buildings, Gittisham, Honiton, Devon, EX14 3AL. *Website*: www.rwa.org.uk *Signs work*: "Robert Jennison," "R. Jennison" or "R.J."

JERVIS, Sharon, Dist. Wildlife Illustration (1978), MA Graphic Design (1982), MSIAD (1980), ARSM (1996); artist in water-colour and gouache; M.D. Sharon Jervis Ltd. *Medium*: watercolour, gouache. *b*: Leicester, 5 May 1956. one *s*. one *d*. *Studied*: Dyfed College of Art (Wildlife Illustration), Leicester Polytechnic (now De Montfort University), MA. *Commissions*: Many varied license contacts for a variety of publishers and manufacturers in the UK and worldwide. My paintings are used on a diversity of products including diaries, cards, framed and limited edition prints, table top products, mugs, rugs, tapestries, pillows, trays, flags, ceramics, giftware, stationery items and fabrics. *Address*: Farndon Grange, East Farndon, Market Harborough, Leics. LE16 9SL. *Email*: sharon@sharonjervis.com *Website*: www.sharonjervis.com

JESTY, Ronald, artist in water-colour and acrylic, part-time lecturer; Pres. Somerset Soc. of Artists, elected mem. RBA (1982) resigned (1990). *Medium*: Watercolour. *b*: Weymouth, Dorset, 7 May 1926. *s of*: Cyril Benjamin & Violet Jesty. *m*: Margaret Johnson. *Educ*: Weymouth Grammar School; no formal art training. *Represented by*: Newland Gallery, Sherborne, Dorset; Quarr Gallery, Swanage, BH19 2LP quarr@operamail.com; Cove Gallery, Weymouth DT4 8TW. *Exhib*: RI, RWA, RWS, RBA, RA, Singer & Friedlander/Sunday Times water-colour competition, Millfield Open; nine one-man shows. *Works in collections*: Somerset CC. *Publications*: "Learn to Paint Seascapes" (Harper Collins, June 1996). *Works Reproduced*: Seascapes and Waterways (Rotovision SA); Painting Still Life (David & Charles); Vibrant Watercolours (Collins); Painting Workshop (Collins) etc. *Clubs*: Artists 303, Somerset Soc. of Artists. *Address*: 11 Pegasus Court South Street Yeovil, Somerset BA20 1ND. *Signs work*: "R. Jesty" and year.

JIANG HUANG, Limin, MA; artist in oil and water-colour, designer. *b*: 14 Aug 1952. *m*: Gouping Jiang. *Studied*: St. Martin's College of Art and Design. *Exhib*: International Maritime Organization Hall, London, Arts and Science Form, America, France, Swiss, Manchester, Australia, Japan, Belgium, Shanghai. *Works in collections*: Queen Elizabeth II, The Prince of Wales, Museum of Western Art, Japan, Art Modern of City of Paris, Association of China Art, Swiss Art, Japan Fan Art, Tokyo. *Publications*: Taiwan Art Almanas (1994, 1995), International Fan Art (1989-96), Dictionary of International Biography - 28th, Century Appreciate - Chinese Artists Works, The Radiance of Oriental-Chinese Artist in 21st Century, New Century Contemporary Artist Biography, China Contemporary Artist Works Appreciate, Dictionary of China Outstanding Artist, Dictionary of World Calligrapher-Painter 3rd edition, World Outstanding Specialists, Brilliant Accomplishment Century Light of Dawn (1999), Huaxia Chinese Outstanding Talents, China Famous Brush and Ink Artists Works Show. *Principal Works*: oil on canvas (abstract, impressionism). *Misc*: Awarded the Gold Cup Award (2000) China, the World Gold Award (2000) Hong Kong. *Address*: P.O. Box 4595, 9 Howick Pl., London SW1P 1AA. *Email*: liminjh@talk21.com *Website*: www.liminart.com *Signs work*: "LIMIN J.H."

JOEL, Judy, self taught artist; Secretary of Association of British Naive Artists. *Medium*: gouache, acrylic, oil. *b*: Putney, London, 30 Aug 1946. *d of*: Dr. & Mrs. Reginald Glanvill. *m*: Paul. one *s.* one *d. Educ*: Villa Maria Servite Convent School, Bognor Regis. *Represented by*: own gallery: The Little Picture Gallery, Mousehole, Cornwall; Wren Fine Art Gallery, Burford; Clare White Gallery, Yorkshire. *Exhib*: solo shows: London, Surrey, Sussex and Cornwall; Melbourne, Australia. *Works in collections*: Simon Weston, BBC, DTI. *Commissions*: BBC, Simon Weston, Nerys Hughes, Ian Lavender, Jilly Cooper, James Grout. *Publications*: featured in 'The Innocent Eye' by Marion Whybrow; many charity Christmas cards. *Works Reproduced*: several as cards, prints, limited editions. *Principal Works*: BBC, and commissions of life stories. *Recreations*: skiing, swimming. *Clubs*: Moseley Art Society, Association of British Naive Artists. *Address*: Noah's Ark Studio, Abbey Pl., Mousehole, Cornwall, TR19 6PQ. *Email*: littlepicturegallery@gmail.com *Website*: www.judyjoel.com *Signs work*: "J.S Joel." and a little mouse.

JOEL, Timothy Nathan, BTEC Diploma Art and Design; BA (Hons) Photography & Film; ABNA. *Medium*: oil, black ink. *b*: Isleworth, 23 Apr 1971. *s of*: Mr & Mrs Paul Joel. *Studied*: Epsom School of Art & Design (BTEC); Napier University (BA Hons, 1995-99). *Represented by*: The Little Picture Gallery, Mousehole. *Exhib*: various group and solo shows throughout England, Germany, USA, Thailand and Taiwan since 2000. *Works in collections*: private collections worldwide. The Lewenhagener Stuckists Permanent Exhibition Site,

Germany. *Commissions*: private. *Publications*: "Poet Painter" (Wisdom and Knowledge publishers, Taiwan, 2005). *Clubs*: mem. ABNA; Co-founder, The Lewenhagener Stuckists. *Misc*: Owned and ran my own Art Studio Gallery in Taipei City "Beat Studio". Organised many exhibitions there. Now runs (I Studio. *Address*: PO Box 30, Dulan Post Office, Danghe Township, 959-41 Taitung, Taiwan, ROC. *Email*: poetpainter@gmail.com *Website*: www.joeljoel.com *Signs work*: "JOEL" (monograph).

JOHANNESON, Steven Thor, RSMA; artist of land/sea-scapes and nature in most painting mediums, but especially in water-colour; has work published including many Limited Edition Prints; Recipient of "St. Cuthbert's Mill Award", at RSMA (1999). *Medium*: watercolour, gouache, pastel & oil. *b*: Minneapolis, Minn., 16 Jun 1948. *m*: Cybthia Joan Maurer. *Educ*: Menominee High School, Michigan; Bethel College, St. Paul, Minn. *Studied*: Heatherley School of Art, London (1970-73). *Represented by*: Stephen Jack Fine Art (www.jackfineart.com). *Exhib*: RSMA, SWLA, various mixed and one-man shows; galleries include Gallerie Marin Appledore; Arty Crafts, Wadebridge; Chagford Gallery, Dartmoor; The Hawker Gallery, Old Amersham. *Works in collections*: The Sultan of Oman. *Address*: P.O.Box 636, Yamhill, Oregon 97148 USA. *Email*: ThorshavnStudios@aol.com *Signs work*: "S.T. Johanneson" in vermilion.

JOHANSSEN, Clara. *Medium*: acrylic. *b*: Leicester, 12 Oct 1976. *Studied*: self-taught. Studied English and Renaissance Studies at the University of Sussex. *Exhib*: Obsidian Art, Buckinghamshire; Mariner's Gallery, St.Ives; Clare White Gallery, Elsecar; Delamore Arts, Devon. *Works in collections*: various private. *Commissions*: 'Once Upon a Story' for Scholastic UK Ltd (2011). *Publications*: appears in 'Contemporary Painters' by Danijela Kracun & Charles McFadden (Schiffer, 2012) and 'The Association of British Naive Artists' by Daphne Stephenson & Judy Joel (ABNA 2012). *Works Reproduced*: numerous available as Giclee prints. *Clubs*: Association of British Naive Artists. *Address*: Catford, London SE6. *Email*: clarajohanssen@yahoo.co.uk *Website*: www.clarajohanssen.com *Signs work*: prints: "Clara Johanssen"; originals vary.

JOHNS, Annie, BA (Hons) (1989). *Medium*: Drawing; installation. *b*: London, 27 Apr 1945. one *s*. one *d*. *Studied*: Cheltenham College of Art (1963-65); Central St Martins (1984-89). *Exhib*: Cello Factory, London (2010/11); Menier Gallery (2004, 08, 09); Guildhall Art Gallery (2007); Bankside Gallery (2005, 06); Gallery 27, Cork St (2003); Cafe Gallery, Southwark (2003); Athens Art Fair (1997); Antonia Havani, Greece (1996); Dean Clough, Halifax (1992); Castle Museum, Nottingham (1991); Watermans Art Gallery (1988); Henley Festival (1986); Pomeroy Purdy, London (1988). *Works in collections*: Hackey Museum. *Commissions*: Castle Museum, Nottingham (1991). *Recreations*: Gardening. *Misc*: Taught at University of the Arts, Farnham (2008-2010) and City and Islington College (1988-2008). Member of The London Group since 2000. Worked with adults with mental health issues/learning difficulties. *Address*: 11 Bellevue Place, London E1 4UG. *Email*: annie@theendhouse1.demon.co.uk *Website*: www.anniejohns.me *Signs work*: "ANNIE JOHNS".

JOHNS, Phil, elected member of Royal Society of Arts (2002); MA Fine Art; artist in water-colour and oil; Director of Art Publishing Co. *b*: Brentwood, Essex, 15 Feb 1950. *m*: Anna Louise. one *s*. two *d*. *Studied*: Southend Art School, Royal Wanstead School, Canterbury Christ Church University. *Exhib*: over fifteen one-man shows since 1989 worldwide. *Works in collections*: British Petroleum; Forest Healthcare Trust; Intercontinental Hotel, Park Lane. *Commissions*: numerous. *Works Reproduced*: Limited Editions. *Address*: 11 St.Jacob's Place, Canterbury, Kent CT1 3TU. *Website*: www.philjohns.com

JOHNSON, Annette, SWA (1987), NS; painter-etcher in water-colour, oil and etching; mem. National Soc. of Painters, Sculptors and Printmakers, and Soc. of Women Artists.

Medium: oil painting, printmaking. *b*: London, 24 Mar 1943. *m*: Alan. one *s.* one *d. Studied*: etching at Morley College; painting at Sir John Cass College of Art. *Works in collections*: NSPS (1985), RSMA (1985), RI (1981), RA (1985, 2007), SWA annually, NS annually. *Official Purchasers*: painting used in 'The Centenary Book of the Newlyn Gallery, Cornwall'. *Clubs*: The Arts Club, Dover Street. *Address*: 24 Kellerton Rd., Lee, London SE13 5RD. *Email*: annettejohnson1@btinternet.com *Website*: www.annettejohnson.co.uk *Signs work*: "Annette Johnson."

JOHNSON, Ben, MA (RCA); Hon.FRIBA. *Medium*: acrylic, drawing, prints. *b*: Llandudno, 24 Aug 1946. *s of*: Harold & Ivy. *m*: Sheila Johnson. two *s. Studied*: RCA (1965-69). *Represented by*: Alan Cristea Gallery. *Exhib*: Solo shows London: Fischer Fine Art (1975, 84, 86, 92), Blains Fine Art (2002) Alan Cristea Gallery (2010, 2014) National Gallery (2012/11); Dublin: Chester Beatty (2001); Liverpool: The Walker (2008). Worldwide numerous group shows. *Works in collections*: London: British Council, Tate, Contemporary Art Society, De Beers/CSO, RIBA, V&A, BP, Deutsche Bank, British Museum, Guildhall, Government Art Collection. Glasgow City Art Gallery; Whitworth, Manchester; National Museums Liverpool. Rotterdam: Boymans-van Beuningen, Paris: Centre Georges Pompidou. *Commissions*: Numerous public and private including Millennium Jerusalem panorama for Khalili Family Trust; National Museums Liverpool Cityscape for 2008 European Capital of Culture. *Publications*: Numerous. *Official Purchasers*: IBM, Deutsche Bank, HSBC, National Museums of Liverpool, BP, Special Administrative Government of Hong Kong, Cable & Wireless plc, British Steel, British Museum. *Address*: 4 St. Peter's Wharf, Hammersmith Terr., London W6 9UD. *Email*: benjohnson@benjohnsonartist.com. *Website*: www.benjohnsonartist.com. *Signs work*: "Ben Johnson."

JOHNSON, Brian Robert, RI (1988) Bronze Medal Award (1987), Hon. Citizen, Victoria BC; Graduated with distinction from The Art Center College of Design, Los Angeles, Calif. with a Bachelor of Professional Arts (1962); artist in water-colour. *b*: Victoria, B.C., Canada, 4 Apr 1932. married. two *s.* one *d. Educ*: Victoria High School, Victoria College; Art Center College of Design, Los Angeles. *Exhib*: RI, RBA, AWS, FCA, CSPWC, NWWS, CSMA, numerous one-man and group exhbns. in Canada and US. *Works in collections*: Canada, US, Australia, U.K. and Europe. *Address*: 1766 Haultain St., Victoria, B.C., V8R 2L2, Canada. *Email*: brjohnsonri@shaw.ca *Signs work*: "Brian R. Johnson."

JOHNSON, Carl, BA (1971), Post grad. Ateliers 63 Holland (1973), ATC (1975); Prizewinner 2011 Guanlan International Print Biennial, China. *Medium*: painter in oil pastel, drypoint print. *b*: Warwickshire, 5 Dec 1946. *s of*: John Johnson & Marion Drummond. *Partner*: Mrs. K. Johnson. two *s.* one *d. Studied*: B'ham College of Art (1964-65), Solihull Technical College (1965-68), Newport College of Art (1968-71), Ateliers 63, Haarlem, Holland (1971-73), Goldsmiths' College (1974-75). *Exhib*: RA Summer Show (1998, 1999, 2002, 2003), RWA (97, 98, 99, 00, 09), Cuprum, Poland; Produzenten Galerie, Germany; Leicester City A.G.; National Print, Mall Galleries (99, 01, 02, 03, 05); Kunsthalle Giessen, Germany; Guildhall Gallery, Winchester (2000, 2003, 2004, 2005); University College, Winchester (05/06); National Theatre Printmakers Council, Harley Gallery; Miniature Print Exhbn (2003-07); Mini Print Cadaques Spain (2007); Art for Life, Bath (2007, 2008, 2009); Leeds City Art Gallery (2006/07); Yorkshire Sculpture Park (2008); Theatre Royal Bath (2009); Bath Society of Artists (2008, 2009, 2010, 2011); Guanlan Print Centre, China (2011). *Works in collections*: UK, Amsterdam, Germany, Austria, Australia, Poland, New York, Texas, Florida, California, S.Carolina, Gulf States, China. *Commissions*: many private commissions. *Clubs*: walking, weight-lifting. *Clubs*: Old Bakery Artists *Address*: 12 Alexandra Park, Paulton, Bristol, BS39 7QS. *Email*: carljohnson.artist@yahoo.co.uk *Website*: www.numasters.com oldbakeryartists.com *Signs work*: 'Carl Johnson'

JOHNSON, Colin Trever, MAFA; artist in oil, collage, water-colour and inks, principal themes: coastline, harbours, Venice, street markets, windows studio still-life. *b*: Blackpool, 11 Apr 1942. *Studied*: Salford School of Art, Manchester College of Art. *Exhib*: one-man shows: City of London Festival, Liberty's London, Barbican Art Centre London; Derby, Oldham, Bolton, Harrogate, Salford, Scarborough, Buxton, Falmouth, Blackburn, Ayr, Bideford, Margate, Blackpool, Accrington, Ashton-under-Lyne, Stockport, Warrington, and Bury Public A.Gs.; Winchester, Manchester and Leicester Cathedrals; Salford, Manchester and Exeter Universities; Taunton, Stamford and Bridgewater Arts Centres; National Touring Exhibition (1995-97), Royal Northern College of Music, Royal Exchange Theatre. *Works in collections*: Salford, Southport, Manchester, Derby, Torquay and Worthing Public A.Gs., Exeter University, BBC Artist in Residence: Manchester (1980), City of London (1984) and Wigan International Jazz (1986, 1987) Festivals. Directed Festivals of: Bolton (1979), Swinton (1973), Teignmouth (1996), St. Ives Fringe 1999-2007. *Commissions*: Granada Television, B.B.C. North West, Royal Exchange Theatre, Manchester. *Recreations*: collector of: books, tiles, jugs. *Clubs*: Manchester Academy, Morrab Library. *Address*: 27 Bedford Rd., St. Ives, Cornwall TR26 1SP. *Email*: ctj.stives@amserve.com *Signs work*: "Colin T. Johnson."

JOHNSON, Joy Alexandra, BFA (Hons.) (1980), Higher Dip. (Lond.); artist in oils, water-colour. *b*: Hull, 26 Aug 1958. *d of*: Arnold Johnson. *Educ*: Hatfield High School, Yorks. *Studied*: Newcastle upon Tyne Polytechnic (1977-80), Slade School of Fine Art (1982-84, Lawrence Gowing). *Exhib*: Northern Young Contemporaries (1979), Sainsbury Centre (1980), Mappin Gallery Open Art (1984, 1985), RA Summer Exhbn. (1985), several solo exhbns. in London. Received award from Swiss based Vordemberge Gildewart Foundation (1986). *Address*: 17 Bempton La., Bridlington, E. Yorks. YO16 5EJ. *Signs work*: "J.A. Johnson."

JOHNSON, Michael Alan. *Medium*: oil, watercolour, drawing, prints, egg tempera. *b*: Minehead, 25 May 1962. *Partner*: Jill Walker. *Studied*: Reading University (1980-84), Byam Shaw School of Art (1985-6). *Exhib*: Royal Academy Summer Exhibition, Discerning Eye, Silk Top Hat Gallery, Ludlow, Michael Richardson Fine Art, Fosse Gallery, Stow-on-Wold; Shell House Gallery, Ledbury. *Works in collections*: Museum of London. *Publications*: Public Art Foundation Catalogue, City of London, 'Country Life' 25 Jan 2012 'My Favourite Painting'. *Works Reproduced*: 'Viaduct'. *Address*: 15 Elsing Drive, Kings Lynn, PE30 3UT. *Email*: michaelalanjo@hotmail.co.uk *Website*: michaeljohnsonart.com *Signs work*: "MICHAEL JOHNSON".

JOHNSON, Ronald Henry. *Medium*: oil, watercolour, drawing. *b*: London, 23 Dec 1930. *m*: Beryl. *Studied*: Hornsey School of Art (1944-46); Reading University (1949-51). *Represented by*: The Gallery, Chelmsford; Walkern Gallery, Herts. *Exhib*: RSMA regular exhibitor (1958-2001); RI Watercolours (1960-90); RA, RBA, ROI, NEAC, Britain in Watercolours. Various commercial galleries, one-man and group shows, touring exhibitions in UK and overseas (organised by Art Exhibitions Bureau); Paris Salon (1958-73), Hamburg, Munich, Gothenburg, Los Angeles, Bermuda. *Commissions*: include paintings of yachts. *Publications*: listed in "20th Century British Marine Painting", "La Revue Moderne" (1960, Paris), "Cent Artistes du Monde" (1964, Paris), "Flammes Vives" (1967, Paris). *Official Purchasers*: Durham County Museum "The End of the Day" (watercolour) through Teesdale Gallery. *Recreations*: sailing. *Clubs*: Charlton Sailing Club (1961-72); Hertford County Yacht Club; Walton-on-Thames Sailing Club. *Address*: The Limes, Epping Road, Roydon, Harlow, Essex, CM19 5HT. *Signs work*: "R. JOHNSON".

JOHNSON, Rosalie, SWA (1991), SWLA (1990); Awards: Crown Commissioners (1991, 1994); Anthony J Lester Art Critic Award (2005). *Medium*: sculptor in clay, bronze, silver and rusty iron. *b*: South Africa, Oct 1930. *m*: widowed. one *s*. one *d*. *Educ*: St. Cyprian's

School, South Africa. *Studied*: Putney School of Art; Manresa House, Roehampton (pottery and sculpture). *Exhib*: SWLA, Mall Galleries (1990- present); SWA, London (1991-present); RA Summer Exhbn (1991); McGrath Gallery, Chelsea, London (1991-2003); Llewellyn Alexander Gallery, Waterloo, London (1991-present); Cricket Fine Art, Hampshire and Chelsea (1993-present); Louise Sinclair, Walton Street, London (1998-2001); Lady Daphne, Sloane Square, London (1998-2002). *Works in collections*: Dr Vivienne and Daniel Isaacson, Washington, USA; Elizabeth R. Meek, Isle of Wight, UK; Christopher and Shane Wrinch-Schulz, Cape Town, South Africa; Mr & Mrs Hugo Pratt, Hampshire; Mr & Mrs Nigel Goodhew, London. *Commissions*: "Huberta" 7 foot hippo in pool (bronze) for Imperial Place, Capital & Counties Office Complex. *Address*: 18 Clevedon Road, Richmond Bridge, East Twickenham, TW1 2HU. *Signs work*: "ROSALIE JOHNSON".

JOHNSON, Tlws, BAHons Ceramics with Glass; member of the Buckinghamshire Visual Images Group (1980-2014); member of the Buckinghamshire Art Society (1997-2014); member of the Oxfordshire Craft Guild (2002-2014 at present Chairman); member of the Contemporary Glass Society (1996-2014). *Medium*: sculpture. *b*: Birmingham, 14 Jul 1941. *m*: Ron. two *s*. *Studied*: University of Buckignhamshire, High Wycombe. *Exhib*: Open Studio in June; Obsidian Gallery, Stoke Mandeville; Pyramid Gallery, York; Garden Gallery, Woodstock; Court Barn, Chipping Campden; International Festival of Glass, Stourbridge, Worcs. *Commissions*: Jubilee Window, St Lawrence Church, Winslow, Bucks; sculpture and window, Waddesdon School, Bucks; Glass Eisteddford Chair, Crubin, Carms; many private commissions. *Official Purchasers*: Retirement gift, Aylesbury Vale Arts Council. *Works Reproduced*: 'Studio Glass 1960-2000' by David McLaren, Shire Books (2002); '50 Distinguished Contemprary Artists in Glass' The Intelligent Publishers Ltd (2006); 'Kiln Forming Glass' by Helga Watkins-Baker, The Crowood Press (2010). *Recreations*: drawing and photography. Address: The Old Stores Workshop, Main Street, Gawcott, Buckingham MK18 3DZ. *Email*: tlsw.j@sky.com *Website*: www.tlwsglass.co.uk *Signs work*: "Tlws Johnson".

JOHNSON, (William) Holly, Ivor Novello Award (Best Contemporary Song, 1984); Brit Award (Best Single 'Relax', 1984). *Medium*: oil, watercolour, drawing, prints, sculpture, performance, film. *b*: Liverpool, 9 Feb 1960. *s of*: Eric & Pat Johnson. *Partner*: Wolfgang Kuhle. *Educ*: St.Mary's Primary School; Liverpool Collegiate Grammar School. *Studied*: RCA. *Represented by*: Wolfgang Kuhle Artist Management fax: 0207 736 9212. *Exhib*: RA Summer Show (2001, 02, 03, 04, 05); RCA Secret (2000-05); The House of Holly: The Gallery, Cork Street, London (1996); Warchild, Artaid (2002); Tate, Liverpool (2000); Hanover Gallery, Liverpool - Biennial (2002); Norwich Fringe (2005). *Works in collections*: various private, including Marc Almond, Roland Orzabal, Barry Dickens. *Commissions*: illustrations for 'Details' (Condé Nasté); Kirsty MacColl 'Angel' (record Sleeve); 'Carlos' (John Brown Citrus Publishing). *Publications*: RA postcard (2001); House of Holly, catalogue (1996); A Bone in My Flute (autobiography, Random House, 1994). *Works Reproduced*: in Modern Painters, The New Statesman, Tatler, DACS. *Principal Works*: 'Waterfront' (1989); 'UK After the Rain' (2004); 'Balls of Gold and Dick of Diamond' (2005). *Recreations*: musician and reader, poet, nocturnal activities. *Clubs*: Chelsea Arts Club, DACS, RCA Senior Common Room. *Misc*: Multi-media artist, author, poet, singer, songwriter, iconoclast, HIV Positive activist, art journalist. *Address*: P.O.Box 425 London SW6 3TX. *Email*: getdown@thepleasuredome.demon.co.uk *Website*: www.hollyjohnson.com *Signs work*: 'Holly Johnson'.

JOHNSTON, George Bonar, DA (Edin), RSW; artist in oil, gouache and water-colour; formerly adviser in art, Tayside Region Educ. Authority. *b*: Edinburgh, 14 Jun 1933. one *s*. one *d*. *Educ*: Bathgate Academy. *Studied*: Edinburgh College of Art (1951-56) under William Gillies, PPRSA, RSW, and Robin Philipson, PPRSA, ARA, RSW. *Exhib*: regular exhibitor RSA, RSW, RGI; one-man shows: Perth, Kirkcaldy, Glasgow, Dundee; mixed shows: Edinburgh, Aberdeen, London, Paris, Toronto, New York. *Works in collections*: Glasgow, Strathclyde, Edinburgh, Dundee, London, Toronto, USA, France, Australia. *Official Purchasers*: McManus Art Gallery, Dundee; Lillie Art Gallery, University of Dundee; Dundee College of Education, Strathclyde Region, Edin Educ committee etc. *Address*: 10 Collingwood Cres., Barnhill, Dundee DD5 2SX. *Signs work*: "Johnston."

JONES, Allen Christopher, NDD (1959), ATD (1960), RA (1984); painter, sculptor, printmaker; Trustee, British Museum (1990-99); Emeritus Trustee British Museum, ongoing; Doctor of Arts (Honoris Causa), Southampton University, 2007; Prix des Jeunes Artistes, Paris Biennale, 1961; Heitland Foundation Prize, Celle, Germany, 1995. *b*: Southampton, 1 Sep 1937. *s of*: William & Madeline Jones. *m*: Deirdre Morrow. two *d*. *Studied*: Hornsey College of Art (1955-59), RCA (1960-61). *Represented by*: Thomas Levy, Hamburg; Ernst Hilger, Vienna; Kaj Forsblom, Helsinki; Galerie Wetterling, Stockholm & Gothenburg; Lorenzelli Arte, Milan. *Exhib*: since 1961 numerous museum and group shows. *Works in collections*: public museums and private collection worldwide. *Commissions*: public sculpture commissions in the U.K. and Hong Kong; private sculpture commissions in the UK, USA and Europe. *Publications*: "Figures"; "Projects"; "Allen Jones"; "Sheer Magic"; "Prints"; "Sculptures 1965-2002", "Allen Jones Works" (Royal Academy Publications, 2005). *Recreations*: gardening. *Clubs*: Chelsea Arts, Garrick, Arts Club. *Address*: 41 Charterhouse Sq., London EC1M 6EA. *Signs work*: "Allen Jones."

JONES, Aneurin M., NDD (1950), ATD (1955); artist in oil, acrylic, mixed media; retd. Head of Art Dept., Preseli Comprehensive School, N. Pembrokeshire. *b*: 18 May 1930. *m*: Julie Jones. one *s*. one *d*. *Studied*: Swansea College of Art (Principal: Kenneth Hancock, ARCA, Head of Fine Art: William Price, ARCA), Prix de Rome Scholar. *Exhib*: numerous one-man and mixed shows England and Wales. Welsh representative at the Celtic Festival, Lorient, Brittany. *Works in collections*: National Library of Wales, Aberystwyth; Welsh Arts Council; West Wales Assoc. for the Arts; Dyfed County Council; Ceredigion County Council; The Welsh Office, Cardiff. *Commissions*: three full-length studies of Welsh Archdruids for Gorsedd of Bards permanent collections; mural to commemorate 'Owain Glyndwr' the last native Prince of Wales's struggle for independence in the 13th Century; painting to celebrate Aberaeron's 200th Anniversary as a town; painting to celebrate Ceredigion's 2010 Royal Agricultural Show. *Publications*: numerous Welsh/English periodicals, magazines and books. A comprehensive book based on the artists' work "Aneurin"- two editions are sold out, and second book based on artists' work. *Works Reproduced*: in countries such as Finland, Sweden and Holland. *Clubs*: lecturer for various clubs, societies and educational establishments. *Address*: Heulwen, Aberystwyth Rd., Cardigan, Ceredigion SA43 1LU. *Signs work*: "ANEURIN M. JONES"; 1993 onwards "ANEURIN."

JONES, Barry Owen, RWS, RE, NDD; artist in water-colour, etching/aquatint; Gallery Director. *b*: London, 11 Sep 1934. *m*: Alexandria Virginia, née Parsons. one *s*. one *d*. *Educ*: Friern Barnet Grammar School. *Studied*: Hornsey College of Art (1950-55). *Exhib*: RWS, RE, Coach House Gallery, Guernsey, Bankside Gallery. *Works in collections*: Guernsey Museum and A.G., South London A.G. *Commissions*: National Grid Calendar (1993). *Publications*: The Watercolour Expert (RWS); Watercolour Secrets (RWS) due Summer 2014. *Address*: Le Chevalerie, Les Douvres Vineries, La Fosse, St. Martin, Guernsey C.I. GY4 6EF. *Signs work*: "BARRY OWEN JONES".

JONES, Chris, SAA International Young Artist of the Year (1998); Wildlife Artist of the Year (2007). *Medium*: Oil. *b*: Poole, 7 Jun 1974. *m*: Julie. two *d*. *Studied*: ND (1992-94) and HND (1994-96) in Natural History Illustration, Bournemouth and Poole College of Art and Design. *Represented by*: Jerram Gallery, Sherborne, Dorset; John Davies Gallery, Moreton-in-Marsh, Glos. *Exhib*: Christies and Sothebys Auctions (1998-2000); Mall Galleries, London, Society of Wildlife Artists (2000+); Royal Institue of Oil Painters (2006, 2009); RWA, Bristol (2004); Art and the Animal, USA, (2004, 2007); Birds in Art, USA (2005); Cheng-Kim Loke Gallery, Slimbridge (2003, 2008); Art in Action, Oxford (2011). One man shows: John Davies Gallery (20008); Guggleton Gallery (2005). *Works in collections*: Port Lympne and Howletts Estates, Kent; Nature in Art, Twigworth, Glos; various private. *Misc*: Specialises in poultry and wildlife subjects. *Address*: 47 Church Lane, North Bradley, Trowbridge BA14 0TE. *Email*: info@chrisjonesart.com. *Website*: www.chrisjonesart.com. *Signs work*: "CHRIS JONES" pre 2004 work initialled with monogram resembling the profile of an elephant's head.

JONES, Colin. NDD (painting); ATD (University of London). *Medium*: Oil, watercolour, drawing, sculpture, relief constructions. *b*: Worcester, 14 Mar 1934. widowed. one *d*. Educ: Royal Grammar School, Worcester; Rudolph Steiner School, Gloucester. *Studied*: Malvern School of Art, Worcestershire (1955-57); Goldsmith's School of Art, London (1957-60). *Exhib*: Abstract Art, Portland Gallery, London; A Rational Aesthetic, Southampton Art Gallery (2008); Diverse Approaches to a Structured Art (1986); Sequences, Germany (1976); Dusseldorf International Art Fair (1975/6); Systems, Whitechapel Gallery, London and UK tour (1972); Construction England (1963). *Works in collections*: Arts Council of Great Britain; private collections. *Commissions*: Neon sculpture, Nottingham (1985); Wall relief, Leicester University (1982); Neon sculpture, Leicester (1981); 2nd Prize Sculpture Competition, Leeds (1964). *Publications*: 'Artist as Designer' De Montfort Uni, Leic (1982); 'Structure, Series 6, No 1 & 2', Netherlands (1964). *Principal Works*: Oil paintings; relief constructions. *Address*: 153 Glenalmond Avenue, Cambridge CB2 8DH. *Email*: colin@celjones.co.uk *Website*: www.celjones.co.uk *Signs work*: "Colin Jones".

JONES, Doreen, SBA; B.Ed, Cert. Botanical Illustration Birmingham; RHS Gold Medal. *Medium*: watercolour. *b*: Wrexham, 17 Jan 1945. *d of*: Flora & Stan Williams. *m*: A.D. Jones. *Educ*: Grovepark Girls Grammar School. *Studied*: Bangor University. *Exhib*: Central Hall, Westminster since 2000; Royal Horticultural Society (2004, 2005); St.David's Hall, Cardiff; Oriel Gallery, Ynys Mon; various smaller galleries and exhibitions. *Works in collections*: Kew Gardens, Lindley Library, private collections. *Commissions*: private, Wild Flowers for 'Gentleman's Tour of Countryside'. *Publications*: 'Botanical Illustration' (pub. Society of Botanical Artists). *Works Reproduced*: prints and cards. *Principal Works*: collection of rare Cotone Aster; collection of Viburnums. *Recreations*: walking, reading. *Clubs*: Chelsea Physic Garden Florigeum Society; North Wales Society Fine Arts. *Address*: Tophill, Maelor Court, Overton, Wrexham, LL13 0HE. *Email*: jones17maelor@tinyworld.co.uk *Signs work*: 'DJones'.

JONES, Edward Scott, RCA (1964); artist in oil, water-colour, gouache, acrylic. *b*: Liverpool, 6 Jun 1922. *m*: Althea (decd). one *s*. one *d*. *Educ*: Anfield Road Elementary School. *Studied*: Liverpool College of Art. *Exhib*: RCA, Williamson A.G., Bluecoat A.G., RI, RSMA. *Works in collections*: Merseyside Council Libraries, Blackpool Corp. A.G., Salford A.G., Bolton A.G., Williamson A.G., Birkenhead, also works in private collections. *Recreations*: swimming. *Clubs*: City of Liverpool Masters. *Address*: 18 The Fairway, Knotty Ash, Liverpool L12 3HS. *Signs work*: "E. Scott Jones."

JONES, F. Julia, RCA (elected member 2001). *b*: Darton. *m*: A. Neville Jones. two *s*. *Studied*: University of Wales, Aberystwyth; Bangor Technical College. *Exhib*: Royal Cambrian Academy, Conwy; RI Watercolours, London; Society of Botanical Artists, London; Royal National Eisteddfod. *Works in collections*: Hotels in Wales Art; various private collections. *Commissions*: Welsh Water Authority. *Works Reproduced*: in "1882-2002 Royal Cambrian Academy" (RCA, 2002). *Address*: Rhos Cottage, Llanfaes, Beaumaris, LL58 8LR. *Email*: fjanjones@aol.com *Signs work*: "Julia Jones" or "J. Jones".

JONES, Geraldine M.L., DipAD (Hons) (1972), Post Grad. Cert. RA Schools (1975); freelance artist and illustrator in water-colour, oil, pencil, charcoal. *b*: Ampleforth College, Yorks., 23 Nov 1949. *m*: Nigel Jones. *Educ*: The Bar Convent, York. *Studied*: Hull Regional College of Art (1969-72, John Clarke, Michael Chiltern), RA Schools (1972-75, Peter Greenham, Anthony Eyton). *Exhib*: York, Hull, Peterborough, Oxford, London, Norwich, Lincoln, Huddersfield. *Works in collections*: Bradford Cathedral Chapter House. *Commissions*: Bradford Cathedral. *Publications*: 'Stories from Yorkshire Monasteries' (J. & B. Spence). 'The Yorkshire Journal', 'Against the Tide', Marjorie Bourne. *Clubs*: S.G.F.A., Royal Academy Schools Alumni Association. *Address*: Fleet House, Hoffleet Stow, Bicker, Boston, Lincs. PE20 3AF. *Website* www.amboarts.co.uk *Signs work*: "G. Jones."

JONES, GRIMES &, BA (Hons) Animation; BSc (Hons) History & International Relations. Awards: Barracuda Award, St James, Bath (1995); Artist of the Week, Salon Contemporary, London (2011); Ant Tanquary Gin Award for Bad Art, Southbank Centre, London (2011); Bad Artist Peoples Choice award, London (2012). *m*: Acrylic, spray paint, Oilstick, Candle wax and foodstuffs. *b*: Doncaster, 13 Apr 1988. *m*: Nelson Romance. *Partner*: Little Erica Serious. *Educ*: McAuley Catholic High School, Doncaster. *Studied*: University of Lincoln; Nottingham Trent University. *Represented by*: self. *Exhib*: Vintage Festival, Goodwood (2010); The Art Corner, Manchester (2011); Transition Gallery, London (2011); 46 New Broad Street, London (2011); Bad Art Salon, Royal Festival Hall, London (2011); Edinburgh Art Festival, (2011); Monks Gallery, Lincoln (2011); The Betsy Trotwood, London (2011); Patrick Studios, Leeds (2012); LAB, Leeds (2012); Bad Art Salon, Oxford, Vintage at Wilderness (2012); Doncaster Museum (2012); Left Bank, Leeds (2012); Bank Street Arts, Sheffield (2012); Vantage Art Prize, Ellingdon House, Leeds (2013); Westgate Studios, Wakefield (2014); Hepworth Gallery, Wakefield (2014). *Works in collections*: "Hench" - Max Bergius Collection. *Publications*: Manchester Mule; Art Licks magazine (Issue 3, 2011); "The Hemisphere of Liars" by Grimes & Jones (pub. 2013). *Principal Works*: "God's Fridge"; "Hench"; "Mum"; "Listening to Bid Freedia"; "Miniature Heroes" (ongoing). *Clubs*: T'art Group, Idle Working Mens Club. *Address*: Flat 4, 15 Bennetthorpe, Doncaster, South Yorkshire DN2 6AA. *Email*: lewisgrimes88@gmail.com *Website*: www.grimes&jones.co.uk *Signs work*: "Grimes & Jones".

JONES, Heather Edith, HS; artist in water-colour, silver point, pencil; tutor (retd.); specialises in miniature portraits. *b*: Cardiff, 23 May 1930. *m*: Ivor Jones (decd). one *s*. one *d*. *Studied*: Newport School of Art. *Exhib*: RA Summer Show, RMS, HS, LA Gallery, Glyn Vivian Gallery, Swansea, Barbican and Pall Mall Galleries, and privately owned galleries in England, France and USA. Work in private collections. *Commissions*: undertaken by request. *Publications*: illustrations for book of ghost stories, and a children's book and book cover for novel. *Address*: 25 Spencer Gdns., Eltham, London SE9 6LX. *Email*: HeatherSJ@aol.com *Signs work*: "H" and "J" joined

JONES, Helen Coline, HS, ARMS, MAS-F; HND (Natural History illustration), 1st prize MAS-F (animal and birds category), 2nd Prize MAS-F (2001); illustrator/artist in water-colour. *b*: Hereford, 18 Feb 1971. *Studied*: Bournemouth and Poole College of Art and Design (1990-92). *Exhib*: HS, RMS, MAS-F, Canada, Marches Artists, international miniature exhibition Tasmania, Llewellyn Alexander Gallery, London. Work in collections internationally. *Publications*: illustrated: An Identification Guide to Dog Breeds by Don Harper. *Works Reproduced*: greetings cards and wrapping paper. *Clubs*: Marches Artists. *Address*: The Croft, 96 Penn Grove Rd., Hereford HR1 1BX.

JONES, Hywel Wyn, BA (Hons) 1979, M.A. (1980); sculptor. *b*: Aberystwyth, 17 Nov 1956. *Educ*: Cambridge School of Art. *Studied*: Central School of Art, Chelsea School of Art. *Exhib*: War Rooms (2011), Danielle Arnaud, London. Buitendoor Andromeda, Ostend (2009), Hackney Wicked Mission Arts Club (2009), Outdoors (2006), Sense and Nonsense,

Outdoors (2006); Danielle Arnaud, London (2003). *Address*: 37 Tregerddan, Bow Street, Ceredigion SY23 5AU. *Email*: HWJones@hotmail.com *Signs work*: "Hywel Wyn Jones."

JONES, Ian, BFA (Hons) (1979), MFA (1982); artist; lecturer in Fine Art. *b*: B'ham, 3 Jul 1947. *m*: Carole A. Jones. two *s*. *Educ*: Queensbridge Secondary Modern, Moseley. *Studied*: B'ham Polytechnic School of Fine Art (1975-78, Roy Abel, Trevor Halliday), RCA (1979-82, Peter de Francia). *Exhib*: regular exhbns. since 1981, group and individual shows. *Works in collections*: Britain, Europe, America. *Address*: Anderson O'Day Gallery, 255 Portobello Rd., London W11 1LR. *Signs work*: "Ian Jones."

JONES, Karen, SEA; equine water-colourist. *b*: 11 Aug 1942. *d of*: Glyn Jones and Mardorie Meggitt, Sculptor. *m*: Mike Eaton. two *d*. *Educ*: Godolphin and Latymer. *Exhib*: RA, England, Wales and USA. *Works in collections*: England, Wales, Scotland, Ireland, USA, Canada, France, Italy, Germany, Portugal, Holland, W.I., New Zealand, Spain, Australia. *Misc*: Gallery at home: open Summer. *Address*: Blaenllyn, Llangolman, Clunderwen, Pembs. SA66 7XR. *Signs work*: "K.J. '98."

JONES, Lee, self taught fine artist in acrylic. *b*: Liverpool, 26 Aug 1968. *m*: Denise. one *s*. *Exhib*: England, America, etc. *Works in collections*: England, America, Canada, Australia. *Clubs*: N.A.P.A., South Sefton Artists. *Address*: 18 College Rd., Great Crosby, Merseyside L23 0RW.

JONES, Lucy, BA 1st class BA Hons Fine Art, MA (RCA); painter in oil. *b*: 1955. *Studied*: Camberwell School of Art, RCA. *Exhib*: over 16 solo exhibs. at Flowers East Gallery, London, and many group exhibs. including Whitechapel Art Gallery, Camden Arts Centre, RA, Metropolitan Museum of Art, New York. *Works in collections*: Arts Council, Deutsche Bank A.G., London, Government Art Collection, Sheffield City Art Gallery, Usher Gallery, Lincoln. *Address*: c/o University Gallery, Northumbria University, Sandyford Road, Newcastle upon Tyne NE1 8ST. *Email*: gallery@flowerseast.com *Signs work*: "Lucy Jones."

JONES, Malcolm, HDipAD (1973), BA (Hons) (1971); artist in painting, installation, construction. *b*: Merseyside, 12 May 1949. *Studied*: Chelsea School of Art (1972-73), University of Reading (1967-71). *Exhib*: ten solo shows in London public galleries since 1980, internationally in group exhbns. since 1972. Work reviewed in Art Forum, The Architects Journal, The Times, Neue Bildende Kunst, Neues Deutschland, The Guardian, Artscribe, BBC Critics Forum, Arts Review, NRC Handelsblad, Der Tagesspiegel, Frankfurter Rundschau, Het Parool and TV Times. *Works in collections*: Bette Midler, New York. *Publications*: Tolly Cobbold Eastern Arts 4 (1983), Watercolour C21, Bankside Gallery (1999), Singer & Friedlander Exhibition, Mall Galleries (2003). *Works Reproduced*: Whitechapel Gallery Exhibtions Leaflet (March 1993); Architects Journal, Exhibtions Update (March 1997); Artscribe no.50, p.66-67; Artline (June 1984); Tolly Cobbold Eastern Arts 4, Fitzwilliam Museum, catalogue. *Address*: 64 Chisenhale Rd. London E3 5QZ. *Email*: malcolmjones@chisenhale.com *Website*: http: //www.chisenhale.co.uk/chisenhale/studios/malcolm-jones

JONES, Margaret Mary, Dip SBA, Assoc SBA, CBM '12. *Medium*: watercolour, drawing. *b*: Grimsby, Lincolnshire, 29 Aug 1944. *Studied*: no formal art education. *Exhib*: SBA Westminster Central Hall (2011, 2012); Local exhibitions in Lincolnshire. *Clubs*: Lindsy Art Society, North Lincs Art Society, Sheffield Florilegium Society, Society of Botanical Artists. Address: Meadow Farm, 17 Great Coates Road, Healing, N.E. Lincs DN41 7QS. *Email*: margaretmj2@btinternet.com *Signs work*: "Margaret Jones".

JONES, Martyn Vaughan, BA Hons (Illustration). *Medium*: painter in acrylic, oil, mixed media. *b*: Coventry, 26 Oct 1957. *s of*: John and Jean Jones. *Educ*: Blackwood Comprehensive School (1971-75). *Studied*: Newport (Gwent) College of Art (1975-79).

Represented by: Benjamin C.Hargreaves, Fulham, London; Washington Gallery, Penarth; Albany Gallery, Cardiff; Art Matters, Tenby. *Exhib*: Benjamin C.Hargreaves (1997-present). Group shows: Albany Gallery and Three Man Exhibition (Spring 2001); two-man show: Washington Gallery (1998, 2003), also many shows throughout South Wales. *Works in collections*: Mr Victor Spinnetti, Mr Geraint Davies (Head BBC Wales), Mr Chris Segar (tv presenter), many private. *Commissions*: sleeve cover for recording by Philip Madoc of Work of Dylan Thomas, sleeve for 'Was There a Time' (1990). *Works Reproduced*: mainly gallery promotions. *Principal Works*: 'Severn Estuary' series (ongoing project). *Misc*: currently working from narrowboat studio on the Gloucester-Sharpness canal, overlooking River Severn. *Address*: Yew Tree Cottage, Stenders, Mitcheldean, Glos, GL17 0JE. *Email*: martynvaughanjones@hotmail.com

JONES, Mary Lloyd, NDD (1955), ATD (1956); artist in water-colour and oil; Chairman, Wales Artists Development Centre Assoc.; External examiner; BA(Ed.) Art & Design, Trinity College, Carmarthen. *b*: Devil's Bridge, Ceredigion, Wales, 21 Aug 1934. *m*: John Jones. two *d*. *Educ*: Ardwyn Grammar School, Aberystwyth. *Studied*: Cardiff College of Art (1951-56, Eric Malthouse). *Represented by*: Martin Tinney Gallery, Cardiff. *Exhib*: Montserrat Gallery, NY, Martin Tinney Gallery, Cardiff, Gallery of Modern Art, London, John Martin Gallery, Albemarle St., London, Oriel Tegfryad, Menai Bridge. *Works in collections*: National Museum & Gallery of Wales, Cardiff; Tabernacle Museum of Modern Art, Wales, WAC, Crawford Museum and Gallery, Cork, Tyrone Guthrie Centre, Ireland, BBC Wales, Ceredigion CC, S4C Centre, Cardiff Arena/World Trade Centre. *Commissions*: Earth Works, Wales Garden Festival, Ebbw Vale. *Publications*: The Mountains of Wales (Univ. of Wales Press), Our Sisters Land (Univ. of Wales Press). *Clubs*: Gweled (Welsh Artists Assoc.), Water-colour Soc. Wales, R.Cam.A. *Misc*: First Prize, Wales Open Exhbn., Aberystwyth Arts Centre (1997). *Address*: c/o Martin Tinney Gallery, 18 St.Andrews Crescent, Cardiff CF10 3DD. *Signs work*: "Mary Lloyd Jones."

JONES, Megan, NDD (1956) ATD; BA (1957); artist in oil, mixed media, gouache, charcoal, conté; Arts Council of Wales travel grant, Newfoundland (1994). *b*: Neath, S. Wales, 6 Jul 1936. *m*: Derrick Jones. two *s*. *Studied*: Swansea College of Art (1952-57, Alfred Janes). *Exhib*: widely solo and group shows in Britain and abroad. *Works in collections*: Brecknock Museum and Gallery, Brecon; University of Newfoundland, Canada; Nippon-Sieke, Japan; County Hall, Carmarthen; Prince Philip Hospital, Llanelli; British and Continental Fuels, Belgium; Rhondda Heritage Park Gallery; Lidice Community, Czechoslovakia; University College, Swansea; Dr. Rowan Williams; Contemporary Art Society for Wales. *Commissions*: design for sculpted stone marker for Brecon Beacons Way (2005). *Publications*: Essay 'Ceri Richards' (University of Wales Press, 1999), cover 'Songs of Silence' by Patricia Barrie (Honno Press, 1999), Pastel Artists International, 'Drawn from Wales', a history of Swansea Art College; '8 Stones, 8 Artists' (Exploring the Beacons Way Art Trail). *Clubs*: The Welsh Group. *Address*: 9 Heol Derwen, Ystradgynlais, S. Wales SA9 1HL. *Signs work*: "Megan Jones."

JONES, Olwen, RAS (1968), RE (1978), RWS (1989); VPRWS (2004 -07); painter in oil and water-colour, printmaker. *b*: London, 1 Mar 1945. *d of*: William Jones. *m*: Charles Bartlett. *Educ*: Harrow School of Art (1960-65). *Studied*: Royal Academy Schools (1965-68). *Exhib*: first one-man: Zaydler Gallery, London (1971). (1975) Oldham Art Gallery; Wrexham and Lewis Art centres; (1984) Minories Colchester, Usher Gallery Lincoln, University of Durham, Bohun Gallery Henley; (1999) Chappel Galleries Essex; (2000) John Russell Gallery Ipswich. *Works in collections*: National Museum of Wales, Norwich Castle Museum, Reading Museum, Nuffield Foundation, Museum of London, Department of the Environment, Graves Art Gallery Sheffield, Usher Art Gallery Lincoln, Greenwich Library. *Commissions*: Set of nine mural paintings for TrustHouse Forte; Triptych for Priors Court School for Autism. *Official Purchasers*: painting for National Grid; painting for Lloyds of

London. *Works Reproduced*: painting in The National Statistics 'Britain' 1998. *Recreations*: walking. *Address*: St. Andrews House, Fingringhoe, Colchester, Essex CO5 7GB. *Signs work*: "Olwen Jones."

JONES, Robert William, NDD, ATC; painter in oil; full-time artist; former lecturer, Falmouth College of Art. *b*: Newquay, Cornwall, 22 Mar 1943. *m*: Susie Jackson. three *s.* two *d. Educ*: Tretherras School, Newquay. *Studied*: Falmouth Art School. *Exhib*: numerous throughout S. West, London, Cotswolds etc. *Works in collections*: mainly private, museums, S.W. Arts, Plymouth Museum. *Publications*: 'Robert Jones' by Jenny Pery, pub. Halsgrove Press, 'Alfred Wallis Artist & Mariner' by Robert Jones (2001), 'Reuben Chappell Pierhead Painter' by Robert Jones (2006). *Address*: Bodrigey Farm, 23 Sea Lane, Hayle, Cornwall TR27 4LQ. *Email*: robertjonesfirstlightstudio@btinternet.com *Website*: www.firstlightgallery.co.uk *Signs work*: "Robert Jones" on back or "R.J." usually in red on painting.

JONES, Rosamund, RE, Painting NDD; D.Murray Travelling Award, St.Cuthberts Mill Prize, National Print Exhibition; artist in etching, water-colour; shepherd; original work of wildlife, countryside scenes, cockerels, animals, and trout in watercolours. *Medium*: etching on metal. *b*: Harrogate, 1944. *m*: Martin. one *s.* three *d. Educ*: Harrogate. *Studied*: Harrogate, Leeds Colleges of Art. *Exhib*: Cartwright Hall Bradford, Edinburgh, London, Scottish Royal Academy, Royal Academy, London. *Works in collections*: Bankside Gallery. *Publications*: Homes & Gardens. *Principal Works*: etching: 'On My Way to a Party'. *Address*: New Bridge Farm, Birstwith, Harrogate , HG3 2PN. *Signs work*: "Rosamund Jones."

JONES, Royston, Dip.AD (1968), MFA (Illinois, 1971); advisor for the creative industries; Director, Pacific Stream. *b*: Wolverhampton, 15 Jan 1947. *s of*: Percy Jones. one *d. Studied*: Birmingham College of Art and Design (1965-68, John Walker, Trevor Halliday), University of Illinois (1969-71, Jerome Savage, Art Sinsebaugh, Bart Parker). *Exhib*: regularly in Britain and USA. *Address*: Pacific Stream, Basecamp 3, 25-31 Parliament Street, Liverpool L8 5RN. *Email*: roy@pacificstream.info *Website*: www.pacificstream.info

JONES, Stanley Robert, ATD (1950), FSA.; printmaker and archaeologist. *b*: Birmingham, 9 Jun 1927. *s of*: George Jones, brewery departmental manager. two *s.* one *d. Educ*: Elementary School; Yardley Grammar School, Birmingham. *Studied*: Birmingham College of Art under Harold Smith, B. Fleetwood-Walker, ARA (1942-45, 1948-50), RA Schools under B. Fleetwood-Walker, ARA, Henry Rushbury, RA (1950-55). *Exhib*: RA, RBSA, Printmakers' Council Venues, South Yorkshire Open. *Works in collections*: Graves Art Gallery, Sheffield. *Address*: 118 Totley Brook Rd., Sheffield S17 3QU.

JONES, Steven, Dip. in Illustration (1981); artist/illustrator in oil. *b*: Chester, 5 Apr 1959. *s of*: Peter Jones. *m*: Sian. one *s.* two *d. Educ*: Colwyn High School, Colwyn Bay. *Studied*: Wrexham College of Art (1976-81, Keith Bowen). *Exhib*: one-man show: Oriel Môn, Anglesey (1996), Penrhyn Castle, Bangor (1998). *Works in collections*: Bryn Terfel, Dafydd Iwan, Scott Quinell, Dafydd Wisley. *Publications*: Specialises in figures in landscape scenes particularly beach scenes, golf scenes and views of Snowdonia. Many paintings sold through auctions in Britain including Christies, Bonhams and Chrystals. Limited Edition Prints and greetings cards sold throughout Britain and the U.S.A. *Address*: The Steven Jones Gallery, The Bulkeley Hotel, Castle St., Beaumaris, Anglesey, N. Wales LL58 8AW. *Email*: info@stevenjonesartist.com *Website*: www.stevenjonesartist.com *Signs work*: "Steven Jones."

JONES, Timothy Martin, BA Fine Art; MA; Mark Rothko Memorial Trust Travel Award to USA (1980); Calouste Gulbenkian Printmaker Award (1982). Artist in residence: Lewisham (1982-3), WAIT (1984). *Medium*: oil, various. *m*: Meena Chodha. four *s. Studied*: St. Martins School (, 1969-72); RCA (Painting, 1977-80). *Represented by*: Window 135. *Exhib*: Royal Academy Summer Exhibition (1979, 1980, 2008); John Moores (prizewinner,

1980); Nigel Greenwood (1980); Bluecoat Gallery (1982); Whitechapel Open (1983, 1984); Gallery of NSW, Australia (1985); Tate Britain 'St. Martins' (2007). Solo exhibitions include: ICA, Concourse Gallery (1983); Dusseldorf Gallery, Perth, WA (1984); Gallery 24 (1987). *Works in collections*: Bradford Art Gallery; Brunel University; Western Australian Institute of Technology. *Commissions*: 1981 - Brunel University; 1983. *Recreations*: pianist. *Address*: 135 New Cross Road, London SE14 5DJ. *Email*: tmjc@btinternet.com *Website*: window135.com window135.tumblr *Signs work*: "T.M.Jones".

JONES, Trevor Grenville, NDD (1965), MA (1968); painter/printmaker in oil, wax, ink. *b*: 4 Feb 1945. one *s.* one *d. Studied*: Stourbridge College of Art (1960-63), B' ham College of Art (1963-65), RCA (1965-68). *Exhib*: numerous including solo shows: Flowers Graphics, London (1992, 1993), Flowers East, London (1995), Glass Mountain Gallery, Connecticut, USA; group shows: '30 Years of Printmaking' Advanced Graphics London Anniversary Show, Berkeley Sq. Gallery, London (1997), Original Print Gallery, Dublin (2000). *Works in collections*: Scottish National Gallery of Modern Art, Unilever, V&A, BP Group, Johannesburg A.G. and Melbourne A.G., Office of National Statistics, Lasmo UK. *Address*: c/o Advanced Graphics London, B206 Faircharm, 8-12 Creekside, London SE8 3AX.

JONES, Yvonne, PhD., MA Dist.Fine Art. *Medium*: video installation and painting. *b*: Holywell, N. Wales, 9 Oct 1946. *d of*: Joan & Cecil Evans. *m*: Peter M. Jones. two *s. Educ*: Holywell Grammar School. *Studied*: Liverpool College of Art, Winchester School of Art, Southampton University. *Exhib*: Mall Gallery, Liverpool Festival of Arts, Wrexham Arts Centre, R.A. Summer Exhbns. (1989, 1990), Portsmouth City Gallery, Doncaster City Gallery; European tour: Aspex Gallery; Quay Arts Centre; New Contemporaries 2004; Leeds Met Gallery; Winchester Gallery; Barbican Gallery London; Brick Lane London. *Works in collections*: Welsh Arts Council, Merseyside Arts Trust, New Hall, Cambridge, Contemporary Women Artists; private collections: U.K. and Germany. *Address*: 84 New Forest Drive, Brockenhurst, Hants., SO42 7QW. *Email*: yvonnejones@mac.com *Website*: www.yvonnejones.net

JONES, Zebedee, BA (Hons) Fine Art (1992), MA (Hons), Fine Art (1993); painter in oil on canvas and board. *b*: London, 12 Mar 1970. *Partner*: Hatty Lee. *Studied*: Norwich School of Art and Design, Chelsea College of Art and Design. *Represented by*: Hester Van Roisen. *Exhib*: Arts Council, Southampton City A.G., Leeds City A.G., Unbound at the Hayward Gallery (1994), Real Art (Southhampton 1995, Leeds City A.G. 1996); two solo exhbns. (1995, 1997), Dawese Gallery, New York (1999, 2002, 2005); Slewe Gallery, Amsterdam (1998, 2001, 2004). *Works in collections*: Southampton City Art Gallery, Leeds City Art Gallery. *Publications*: 'Affective Light' Rear Window (1994), Unbound Possibilities in Painting, Hayward Gallery (1994), From Here Exhbn. Cat., Essay by Andrew Wilson, Waddington Galleries (1995), Foundations for Fame, The London Inst. (1997), 'Zebedee Jones New Paintings' Catalogue Waddington Gallery, 1999; 'Zebedee Jones Green on Red Gallery, Dublin (1999). *Address*: 1 Albert Bridge Rd., London SW11 4PX.

JONSSON, Lars Ossian, Honorary Doctorate, Uppsala University (2002). *Medium*: watercolour, oil, graphic art. *b*: Stockholm, 22 Oct 1952. *s of*: Sven & May *m*: Ragnhild. two *s.* two *d. Educ*: Autodidact. *Represented by*: Gerald Peters Gallery, Santa Fe, USA; Wildlife Art Gallery, Lavenham. *Exhib*: National Gallery, Stockholm; galleries and museums in Sweden, UK, France, USA etc. *Works in collections*: National Museum of Wildlife Art; The Natural History Museum, Stockholm; Leigh Yawkey Woodson Art Museum. *Publications*: eleven books, including 'Birds and Light' (A&C Black, 2002). *Works Reproduced*: Audubon Magazine. *Principal Works*: works mostly with birds and their habitats. *Recreations*: music. *Misc*: leading authority in field identification of birds. *Address*: Norrgarde, Hamra, S-62010 Burgsvik Sweden. *Website*: www.larsjonsson.se

JOPE, Anne, BA Hons. (1970), ARE (1979), RE (1984), Central Postgrad. Printmaking Dip. (1981), SWE (1984), AOI (1994); painter in oil paint and water-colour, printmaker in wood engraving, woodcut and linocut, illustrator. *b*: Corfe Mullen, Dorset, 31 Jan 1945. *d of*: William John Purrington. *Studied*: Ealing Art College (1966-67), Central School of Art and Design (1967-70, 1980-81). *Exhib*: twelve one-man shows, RA, NEAC, RBA, Camden Arts Centre, Ferens AG, Graffiti, Morley Gallery, Royal Western Academy, St. David's Hall, Cardiff. *Works in collections*: Liverpool public libraries, BM, Malcolmson Collection at Hereford City AG, Ashmolean Museum, Leics. Educ. Com., NPG. *Publications*: The Song of the Reeds and Rushavenn Time, The Honey Gatherers, Animals at the Table, Nightlife Poems. *Address*: 13 Park Street, Woodstock, Oxon OX20 1SJ. *Signs work*: "Anne Jope."

JORDAN, Maureen Ann, NDD, SBA, many awards at the Society of Botanical Artists. *Medium*: pastel, watercolour, acrylic. *b*: 14 Apr 1941. *m*: N.D.H. Jordan. *Educ*: Escourt High School, Kingston upon Hull. *Studied*: Kingston upon Hull College of Art and Crafts. *Exhib*: The Royal Academy, Watercolour and Drawings Fair, Solo exhibitions in Suffolk, Pastel Society, Society of Botanical Artists, New Trends Hong Kong, Art Mart; one woman show New York, Affordable Art Fairs annual show at Llewellyn Alexander Gallery, London; various shows at Frances Iles Gallery, Rochester, also in many galleries around the country. *Works in collections*: around the world. *Commissions*: various private commissions of flowers or gardens. *Publications*: art magazines, art books, greetings cards, prints and limited editions, calendars, stationery products and cards printed in the USA. *Works Reproduced*: many. *Misc*: Organizes pastel workshops and demos in Suffolk. *Address*: 43 Marlborough Road, Ipswich Suffolk IP4 5AX. *Email*: maureen.jordan@btinternet.com *Website*: www.maureenjordan.com *Signs work*: "M.A.JORDAN".

JOSEPH, Jane, painter, printmaker; Leverhulme Travelling Award (1965-66); Abbey Award in Painting (British School at Rome, 1991,1995). *b*: Surrey, 7 Jun 1942. *d of*: L. Joseph. *Studied*: painting: Camberwell School of Art and Crafts (1961-65, Robert Medley, E. Uglow, F. Auerbach, R. Kitaj, R.D. Lee, F. Bowling). *Exhib*: solo shows: Morley Gallery (1973, 1997, 2000), Minories, Colchester (1982), Angela Flowers (1987), Flowers East (1989, 1992), Edinburgh Printmakers (1994), Worcester City Art Gallery (2001), Victoria Art Gallery, Bath (2002), School of Art Gallery, Aberystwyth (2004). Group exhibitions includ: Biennal of Graphic Arts, Ljubljana (2005); RA Summer Exhibitions; Artists and Morley, 40 Years, Morley College (2009); Eagle Gallery, London (2002, 2007, 2008 & 2009, 2013); New Hall, Cambridge (2013). *Works in collections*: Brecknock Museum and Art Gallery, Government Art Collection, Castle Museum, Norwich, Unilever House, Imperial College, London, University of Northumbria, Chelsea and Westminster Hospital, British Museum, Paintings in Hospitals, New Hall, Cambridge, Fitzwilliam Museum, Cambridge, Ben Uri Art Gallery, Hebrew Union College, New York, Worcester City Art Gallery, Lindley Library, London, Ashmolean Museum, Oxford; The National Art Library (V. & A. Museum), London, Yale Center for British Art, New Haven, CT; School of Art Gallery, Aberystwyth; Birmingham City Museum & Art Gallery; The British Library, London; The Whitworth Art Gallery, Manchester; Royal Botanic Gardens, Kew; Morley College, London; Southampton City Art Gallery. *Commissions*: Chelsea and Westminster Hospital, drawings (1994); The Folio Society, etchings to accompany "If This is a Man" and "The Truce" by Primo Levi. *Publications*: 'A Little Flora of Common Plants' with text by Mel Gooding; 'Kinderszen' with text by Anthony Rudolf; 'Seeds & Fruits' with text by Mel Gooding. *Recreations*: walking, and observing life of all kinds. *Address*: 6a Eynham Road, London W12 0HA. *Email*: janejoseph42@gmail.com *Website*: www.janejoseph.co.uk *Signs work*: "Jane Joseph" or "JEJ."

JOWETT, Jenny Ann, NDD (Dairying, 1957), (Lithography, 1982), FSBA (Founder mem.), FSBA; botanical painter in water-colour, teacher; Tutor, Flatford Mill; President SFP; RHS Gold Medals (4), Silver Gilt (4), Silver (1). *b*: 15 Mar 1936. one *s*. one *d*. *Educ*:

Bromley High School, GPDST. *Studied*: Studley College. *Exhib*: West Mills Newbury, Bladon Gallery, Packhouse Bath, John Magee Belfast, The Chelsea Garden London, Interiors of Ascot, Ewhurst Park Hants., Kew Gardens Gallery, Tryon Gallery London, Dr. Shirley Sherwood's Travelling Exhbn; West Silchester Hall; The Said Business Schol, Oxford; annually at Westminster Hall for SBA & SFP. *Works in collections*: Lindley Library, London, Hunt Inst. for Botanical Documentation Pittsburgh, USA, Dr. Shirley Sherwood, Royal Botanic Gardens Kew, Highgrove Florilegium. *Commissions*: Chelsea Plate, Shell UK. *Publications*: Limited edn. prints, cards, calendars; White Garden RHS Plantsman, Curtis Magazine Kew, The Art of Botanical Painting, The Botanical Palette, Treasures of the Royal Horticultural Society. *Address*: West Silchester Hall, Silchester, nr. Reading, Berks. RG7 2LX. Website: www.jennyjowett.com *Signs work*: "JENNY JOWETT."

JOYCE, Peter Dennis, BA (Hons) Fine Art (1985); BA (Hons) History of Art (1985). *Medium*: Acrylic. *b*: Poole, 23 June 1964. *Studied*: Stourbridge College of Technology and Art (1982-85); Bournemouth and Poole College of Art and Design (1980-82). *Represented by*: Anthony Hepworth Fine Art Dealers. *Exhib*: UK: Solo exhibitions and all major London art fairs since 1990 with Anthony Hepworth Fine Art, London and Bath; Samuel Robson Fine Art; Jenna Burlingham Fine Art; Russell Cotes Museum; Lynne Strover Gallery; Cyril Gerber fine Art, Scotland. France: Galerie Bourreau Ravier. USA: Art fairs and exhibitions with Brickwalk Fine Art, Connecticut. *Works in collections*: Includes: Southampton City Art Gallery; Russell Cotes Museum; University of Liverpool; University of Hull; Middlesborough Institute of Modern Art; Bournemouth University; Marlborough College; St George's Hospital, London. *Address*: 6 Springdale Grove, Corfe Mullen, Wimborne, Dorset BH21 3QT. *Email*: peter@peterjoyce.org.uk *Website*: www.peterjoyce.org.uk *Signs work*: "PDJ" with date.

JUILLERAT, Paul, BA (Hons) Fine Art; MA. *Medium*: sculpture in stainless steel and perspex. *b*: London, 8 Mar 1962. *Studied*: Winchester School of Art, Hants (1986-89, BA), Chelsea College of Art, London (2002-03, MA). Taught at: Shrewsbury College of Art (1990-95); Hereford College of Art and Design (1991-93); Winchester School of Art (1993-2001). *Exhib*: various group and solo shows. *Works in collections*: private and corporate. *Commissions*: broad range of private, corporate and large scale commercial commissions. *Principal Works*: 'Needle Point' Worcester (2001), 'Sails' Millennium Point, Birmingham (2001). *Address*: 102 Wellsway, Bath, BA2 4SD. *Email*: paul@hotairdesign.com *Website*: www.hotairdesign.com *Signs work*: "P. JUILLERAT"

K

KALKHOF, Peter Heinz, painter, lecturer in fine art (retired 1999). *Medium*: painting/acrylic on canvas. *b*: Stassfurt, Germany 20 Dec 1933. *s of*: Heinz Kalkhof, company secretary. *m*: Jeanne The (decd). one *s*. *Educ*: Germany. *Studied*: School of Arts and Crafts, Braunschweig; Academy of Fine Art, Stuttgart; Slade School of Fine Art, London; Ecole des Beaux Art, Paris (1954-62). *Exhib*: Annely Juda Fine Art (1970-79, 1990, 1997), Scottish Arts Council, Edinburgh, Glasgow, Juda-Rowan Gallery (1983), Landesmuseum Oldenburg (1988), Camden Arts Centre (1989), Galerie Rösch, Neubrunn (1993)/Karlshruhe (1994), Germany, St. Hugh's College, Oxford (1998), Galerie Planie, Reutlingen (1998), Gallery Roech, Houston/Texas (2000), Annely Juda Fine Art (2002); Gallery +1+2 Artspace, London (2004); Annely Juda Fine Art (2007); Royal Academy Summer Show, London (2004, 2007). *Works in collections*: Northern Ireland Trust, Arts Council of Gt. Britain, Leics. Educ. Authority, European Parliament, Landesmuseum Oldenburg, Ostpreussen Museum, Lüneburg, University of Reading, Museo Salvatore Allende/Chile, Imperial War Museum, London. *Commissions*: 1987 Treaty-Centre: Mural (Taylor Woodrow), Hounslow, London. *Publications*: Catalogue: Oldenburg Landesmuseum, 1988; Catalogue: Galerie Planie, 1998 Reutlingen; Catalogue: Annely Juda Fine Art, 2002 London; Catalogue: Galerie Roesch, 1994

Karlsruhe/Durlach; catalogue, Annely Juda Fine Art (2007). *Recreations*: travelling, museum visits, listening to music, reading. *Misc*: Associate Member of the British Museum; Friend of the Victoria & Albert Museum; Friend of the Royal Academy. *Address*: c/o Annely Juda Fine Art, 23 Dering St., London W1R 9AA. *Email*: p.kalkhof@virgin.net *Website*: www.annelyfineart.co.uk/Gallery-Artists *Signs work*: "Peter Kalkhof."

KALMAR, Janos, RBS; Hungarian Society of Fine and Applied Arts; Art Association of Hungarian Artists; Hungarian Sculptors Society; International Kepes Society; British Art Medal Society; Prizes and scholarships include: Derkovits Scholarship (1983-86); Biennial of FIDEM prize FIBRU (1994); Great Prize of the II. International Biennial of Contemporary Medal-Seixal (PO) (2001); Scholarship of the Hungarian Academy in Rome (2004/5). *Medium*: sculpture. *b*: Budapest, 23 Jul 1952. one *s*. one *d*. *Studied*: Academy of Fine Arts, Warsaw, Poland (1973-78); Academy of Fine Arts, Budapest; Paris (1983), London (1984), Switzerland (1989), India (1990). *Exhib*: Major one-man shows. Group exhibitions. *Works in collections*: British Museum, City of Bath, British Art Medal Society (UK); American Numismatic Society; Graf-Zeppelin-Haus (Germany); Museum of Fine Arts, Poznan (Poland); Skironio Museum, Athens (Greece), and major museums and galleries across Hungary. *Commissions*: Public sculptures for Bath (UK), Kisoros and Fehérgyarmat (Hungary). Hauser Arnold monument, Farkasréti cemetery, Budapest (1981); Ferenc Rózsa portrait, Press Centre, Budapest (1982); Mihály Vörösmarty portrait, Bácsalmás (1983); H.H.Foundation, Germany (2000). *Publications*: include: 'Janos Halmar 1978-2003' (ISBN 963 430 773 6); 'Janos Kalmar' by Abody Rita (Könyvtáros, 1986); The Medal (1987, 1994, 1996); Mozgó Világ (1985, 1987); Art Today (1994). *Address*: Solymarvolgyi, u.132, H-1037 Budapest , Hungary. *Email*: studio@janoskalmar.com *Website*: www.janoskalmar.com *Signs work*: "Janos Kalmar".

KANE, Martin, BA (Hons) (Edin. 1987). *Medium*: oil/canvas, pastel. *b*: Cardiff, 3 Jun 1958. *s of*: Bernard Kane, B.Ed. *m*: Sharon Goodlet. one *s*. *Educ*: St. Andrew's High School, Clydebank, Glasgow. *Studied*: Glasgow School of Art (1981-82), Edinburgh College of Art (1982-87, David Michie). *Exhib*: Angela Flowers Gallery (1988), Jill George Gallery (1990), Thumb Gallery, Atlanta, USA (1990), Kasen Summer Coll., NY; one-man shows: Jill George Gallery (1992, 1993), Beaux Arts, London (1996), Child, Gredden, Lewis, London (2001), 'Scottish Art', Art Association, Old Lyme, Connecticut, USA (2007). *Works in collections*: Cleveland, Middlesbrough; Cleveland, Ohio; Glasgow Museums and A.Gs.; Unilever PLC; Gartmore Investments; Harry Taylor of Ashton, Kasen Summer New York, Campbell Town Museum, Scotland. *Recreations*: reading, music. *Clubs*: Glasgow Art Club. *Misc*: alt. addresses: Beaux Arts Gallery, 22 Cork St., London W1X 1HB; 47 Hawthorn Avenue, Bearsden, Galsgow, G61 3NG. *Address*: Dovehill Studios, 15 East Campbell St., Glasgow G1 5DT. *Email*: martin3658@tiscali.co.uk *Website*: www.martinkane.net *Signs work*: "Martin Kane."

KANTARIS, Rachael Anna, Foundation Dip., BA Hons visual and performing arts, MA Printmaking, artist and freelance tutor in printmaking and colour etching; currently runs Porthmeor Print Workshop, St. Ives, Cornwall; teaches regularly for schools, Newlyn School of Art, Tate Gallery St. Ives, and at Cornwall College on Fine Art Foundation Degree courses. *Medium*: etching and painting. *b*: Brisbane, Australia, 19 May 1967. *m*: Christian Guerrini. two *d*. *Educ*: Helston School, Cornwall. *Studied*: Falmouth School of Art (1985-1986), Brighton University degree (1986-1989) and MA (1990-1992). *Represented by*: Hilton Fine Art, Bath and Penwith Gallery, St. Ives. *Exhib*: British Council Exhib., Ayala Museum, Manila, Philippines; supplies around twenty galleries in U.K; exhibits regularly at Thompson in the City Gallery, London, Affordable Art Fairs, Battersea and Bristol, Belgrave Gallery, St. Ives, Cornwall Contemporary, Penzance, Hiilton Fine Art, Bath, Penwith Gallery, St. Ives. *Works in collections*: British Council, Hong Kong and Manila; Bank of England; Allner Castle, Bonn, Germany. *Publications*: 'Behind the Canvas', by Sarah

Brittain and Simon Cook. An V Gunn,, published by Truran (2001). Featured in 'The Prints of Wilhelmina Barns-Graham' Lund Humphries (2007). 'St Ives The Story of Porthmear Studios' Marion Whybrow, Halstar (2013). *Address*: 3 Parc Bean, St. Ives, Cornwall TR26 1EA. *Email*: rachael@kantaris.com *Website*: www.kantaris.com *Signs work*: "Rachael Kantaris."

KAPLAN, Krystyna, Received Award of Excellence in Video Publishing for a film she directed ('Look Great, Fel Fantastic'); Certificate of Meris at the Chicago International Film Festival; nominated Best Editor at BISFA, etc. *Medium*: batik on paper, cotton & silk & textile collages ('Art Protis'). *b*: Elk, Poland, 11 Mar 1951. *d of*: Henryka & Marian Nosarzewski. *m*: Jan Kaplan, Filmmaker, photographer. *Studied*: MA Diploma at the University of Warsaw; taught by Noel Dyrenforth & Jill Denton at Kingsway College; learned 'Art Protis' at the Studio in Brno, Czech Republic. *Exhib*: solo: 1994 - The Polish Cultural Centre in Prague (batiks on paper, silk, cotton & textile collage), 1995 - The Art Centre in Elk (batiks and collages), 2001 - The Posk Gallery in London (batiks & Fashion accessories), 2002 - The Pygmalion Gallery in Prague, Czech Republic (batiks on paper), 2003 - The Posk Gallery ('Art Protis' collages). Group exhibitions 2004-07 with APA (Association of Polish Artists in Britain). *Publications*: 'Batik on Paper' by Krystyna Kaplan (only publication on the subject so far in the world). *Works Reproduced*: in various magazines and on the internet. *Recreations*: walking, history. *Clubs*: BAFTA. *Email*: kkaplan@4me.pl *Website*: www.kaplan.4me.pl *Signs work*: "KRYSTYNA KAPLAN". Batiks on paper, signature and medieval stamp with letters KK).

KAPOOR, Anish, CBE (2003); 'Premio Duemila' award Venice Biennale (1990), Turner Prize award (1991), Hon. Fellow, London Inst. (1997); Hon. Fellowship Royal Institute of British Architecture (2001). *b*: Bombay, 1954. *Studied*: Hornsey College of Art (1973-77), Chelsea School of Art (1977-78). *Exhib*: numerous solo shows including Patrice Alexandre, Paris (1980), Lisson Gallery (1982-), W.A.G. Liverpool, Barbara Gladstone Gallery, N.Y. (1986), Tate Gallery London, Tel Aviv Museum of Art (1993), Scai The Bathhouse, Tokyo (1999), Baltic Centre for Contemporary Art (2000), Gateshead, as well as many group exhbns. from 1975 to date. *Works in collections*: Tate Gallery, London; Hirshhorn Museum and Sculpture Garden, Washington DC; MOMA, (NY); Weltkunst Foundation, Zurich; Rijksmuseum Kroller-Muller, Holland; Auckland City A.G. (NZ); Vancouver A.G., Canada, etc. *Publications*: many including Breaking the Mould, British Art of the 1980s and 1990s (Weltkunst Coll., London 1999), Vision - 50 years British Creativity (Thames & Hudson, 1999), etc.; numerous exhbn. catalogues. *Address*: c/o Lisson Gallery, 67 Lisson St., London NW1 5DA.

KARAS, Vanja, MA. *Medium*: photography. *b*: Belgrade, Serbia, 5 Oct 1967. *Educ*: BA University of Arts, Belgrade; BA Royal Academy of Dramatic Arts (RADA); Kings College London. *Exhib*: Group and solo exhibition: Royal Academy Summer Exhibition (2009); Siddhartha Art Gallery, Kathmandu (2009); London: Chelsea Arts Club (2009); Portobello Film Festival (2009); Viewfinder Gallery (2009); Royal Overseas League (2008); St.Matthews Gallery (2008); Willesden Gallery (2008); Phtotgraphers Gallery (2007); Association of Photographers (2007); London Independent Photography (2005, 2006); Dissenters Gallery (2005). *Works in collections*: Private and Corporate collections including: De Vere, Searcy's, St.Mary's Hospital. *Clubs*: London Independent Photography, Royal Photographic Society, Association of Photographers, Chelsea Arts Club. *Address*: 144 Holland Road, London W14 8BE. *Email*: vanja@vanjakaras.com *Website*: www.vanjakaras.com *Signs work*: "Karas Vanja".

KARN, Barbara, BA (Hons) Fine Art. *Medium*: Oil; watercolour; drawing; prints; sculpture. *b*: Wootton Bassett, 8 Mar 1949. two *s*. one d. *Educ*: Arts Foundation, Trowbridge College (1982-84). *Studied*: Gloucestershire College of Arts and Technology, Cheltenham

(1984-87). *Represented by*: Open Space Galleries, Falmouth; Bluestone Gallery, Devizes. *Exhib*: Newlyn Society of Artists; St Ives Society of Artists; Devizes Library (1988); Exeter University Geological Museum, Camborne, Cornwall (1988); Truro Cathedral (2003); Lang Gallery, London (2004); Wine Street Gallery, Devizes (2004). *Works in collections*; Private collections in Europe, Australia and USA. *Commissions*: Regularly commissioned by private individuals to draw animals, figures and landscape. *Publications*: Another View, Art in St Ives, Marion Whybrow; Drawing Towards the End of a Century, Newlyn Society of Artists; St Ives 1975-2005; Peter Davies 2007. *Misc*: Resident West Cornwall (1992-2011); Somerset from 2011. *Address*: 2 Rookery Farm Cottages, Lottisham, Glastonbury, Somerset BA6 8PF. *Email*: mail@barbarakarn.co.uk *Website*: ww.barbarakarn.co.uk *Signs work*: "B.KARN" and "KARN".

KARTT, Orson, BAHons. *Medium*: Mixed media. *b*: London, 14 Mar 1954. one *s*. one *d*. *Studied*: West Surrey College of Art and Design. *Represented by*: Panter and Hall, 27 Bury St, London SW1Y 6AL. *Exhib*: London, Hong Kong. *Works in collections*: Private. *Commissions*: Private. *Address*: 28 Comercial Road, Lowestoft NR32 2TD. *Email*: orson@orsonkartt.com *Website*: www.orsonkartt.com *Signs work*: "Orson Kartt".

KAUFFMANN, C. Michael, PhD (1957), FBA (1987), FMA, FSA; Art historian and museum curator (formerly V&A); Emeritus Prof. of the History of Art, and former Director; Courtauld Inst., University of London. *b*: Frankfurt a/M, 5 Feb 1931. *s of*: Arthur Kauffmann. *m*: Dorothea (decd). Dorothea (decd). two *s*. *Educ*: St. Paul's School; Merton College, Oxford (1950-53); Warburg Inst., London (1953-57). *Publications*: The Baths of Pozzuoli: medieval illuminations of Peter of Eboli's poem (1959); An Altarpiece of the Apocalypse (1968); V. & A. Catalogue of Foreign Paintings; British Romanesque Manuscripts 1066-1190 (1975); Catalogue of Paintings in the Wellington Museum (1982); John Varley (1984); Studies in Medieval Art (1992); Biblical Imagery in Medieval England 700-1550 (2003). *Address*: 53 Twyford Ave., London W3 9PZ.

KAVANAGH, Paul, B.Ed (1975); painter in oil on canvas; freelance lecturer at The National Gallery, London. *b*: Liverpool, 8 Jan 1947. one *d*. *Educ*: Nottingham University. *Studied*: Folkestone, under Fred Cuming RA (1980). *Exhib*: London, Linda Blackstone Gallery, Pinner; various galleries in UK. *Works in collections*: in USA, Germany and France. *Commissions*: various nationally and internationally. *Official Purchasers*: Washington Green Fine Art, 44 Upper Gough Street, B'ham B1 1JL. *Works Reproduced*: as limited edition prints by Washington Green. *Address*: 22 Tennyson Ave. Wanstead London E11 2QN. *Email*: paulkavanagh@ntlworld.com *Website*: www.paul-kavanagh.co.uk *Signs work*: "Paul Kavanagh."

KAY, Janet, DipAD, HS, ARMS, SLm. *Medium*: watercolour, gouache. *b*: London, 4 Apr 1943. *d of*: J.A. and Mrs D.H.M. Ogilvie. *m*: John Kay. one *s*. one *d*. *Educ*: Brondesbury and Kilburn High School. *Studied*: Hornsey College of Art (1962-66). *Exhib*: Llewellyn Alexander Gallery, Mall Galleries, Wells Town Hall; Oxmarket Gallery, Chcihester (miniature paintings); Worthing Museum, Horsham Museum, Towner Museum (Eastbourne) (hand painted pebbles). *Works in collections*: Horsham Museum. *Recreations*: tennis, music. *Address*: 22 Church Road, Tarring, Worthing, W.Sussex BN13 1EU. *Email*: jankay@gmail.com *Signs work*: 'JANET KAY'.

KAY, Nora, ARCA, MCSD; decorative studio pottery, lino-cuts, book jackets; designer for Yardley's, Jenners Ltd.; teacher at St. Martin's School of Art, Newland Park College, Maltman's Green School. *Educ*: Wycombe High School, St. Martin's School of Art, RCA. *Exhib*: RBA, NEAC. *Publications*: children's books. *Works Reproduced*: general advertising work, London Transport posters, Christmas cards, book jackets. *Address*: Flat 5, Ethorpe Cres., Gerrards Cross, Bucks. SL9 8PW. *Signs work*: "N.K."

KEABLE, Karen S. J. *Medium*: acrylic. *b*: Great Yarmouth, 12 May 1966. *m*: Kevin B P Keable. one *s*. one *d*. *Educ*: Great Yarmouth Grammar School. *Studied*: Grays School of Art at Robert Gordon University, Aberdeen. *Exhib*: Southwold Gallery; Thompson Gallery, Aldeburgh; Mall Galleries; Hunter Gallery, Long Melford. *Works in collections*: House of Lords Art Collection, and internationally. *Publications*: Making Waves - Artists in Southwold (2005); Acrylic Workshop II (Dorling Kindersley, 2008). *Official Purchasers*: Lord Redesdale. *Clubs*: East Anglian Group of Marine Artists. *Address*: Bracon Lodge, Bracon Ash, Norwich, Norfolk, NR14 8EH. *Email*: karenkeable@btinternet.com *Website*: www.ksjkeable.co.uk *Signs work*: 'K.S.J.KEABLE'.

KEANE, John, BA (1976); painter in oil and mixed media on canvas, PVA and mixed media on paper; Official War artist, Gulf (1991). *b*: Herts., 12 Sep 1954. *m*: Rosemary McGowan. one *d*. *Studied*: Camberwell School of Art (1972-76). *Exhib*: twenty five one-man shows in UK, Europe and USA since 1980. *Works in collections*: Imperial War Museum, Contemporary Art Soc., Rugby Museum, Cleveland Gallery, Harris Museum, Preston, Glasgow Museum and A.G., Aberdeen A.G., Wolverhampton Museum and A.G., Christies Corporate Collection, British Coal, Financial Times, Unilever PLC, Detroit Art Inst. *Publications*: Conflicts of Interest by Mark Lawson (Mainstream Pub. 1995). *Clubs*: Groucho, Chelsea Arts. *Address*: c/o Flowers East, 82 Kingsland Road, London E2 8DP. *Signs work*: "John Keane."

KEARNEY, Joseph, DA Glas. (1961); painter in various media, sculptor, poet. *b*: Glasgow, 14 Sep 1939. *s of*: Joseph Kearney. *Educ*: St. Aloysius' College, Glasgow. *Studied*: Glasgow School of Art. *Exhib*: several one-man shows in Glasgow. *Works in collections*: Glasgow A.G. and Museum and in many private collections. *Commissions*: Portrait of Most Rev. J.D. Scanlan, Archbishop of Glasgow, and many other private commissions. *Official Purchasers*: Kelvingrove Art Gallery & Museum. *Address*: 97 Elmore Ave., Glasgow G44 5BH. *Signs work*: "Kearney."

KEAYS, Christopher, NDD (1960), RA Cert. (1966); elected ROI, 2001; landscape painter in oil; Alan Gourley Memorial Prize (2004). *Medium*: oil. *b*: Caterham, Surrey, 26 May 1937. *m*: Mary. two *d*. *Studied*: Wimbledon School of Art (1957-60, sculpture: Elisabeth Frink), Chelsea School of Art (1960-62, painting: Robert Buhler, Ruskin Spear), R.A. Schools (1962-66, Peter Greenham, Charles Mohoney). Work in collections internationally. *Exhib*: Royal Academy, Federation of British Artists, Llewellyn Alexander, ROI, RBA, NEAC, RSPP, etc. *Works in collections*: Sir Martin Jacomb. *Publications*: Allen Burtram Ltd. *Recreations*: painting. *Clubs*: Reynolds. *Address*: 21 Cope Place, Kensington, London W8 6AA. *Email*: cfkeays@gmail.com

KEELEY, Simon Phillip, MA Art in Architecture; Diploma/Degree Eq. City & Guilds of London Art School; Ray Finnis Trust Award (2003); Craftex 2000 (NAMM) (2000); Basic Heraldry Certificate - Royal College of Arms (2000); The David Ballardie Memorial Award (2000). *Medium*: stone, bronze, resin. *b*: Bolton, Lancs., 28 Dec 1962. *s of*: Christine & Christopher Keeley. *m*: Shelley Rachel Day-Keeley. one *d*. *Studied*: University of East London (2001-3); City & Guilds of London Art School (2001-3). *Represented by*: Garden Architecture Gallery, London (2006); Pond Gallery, London (2004-5). *Exhib*: Affordable Art Fairs: stone carving demonstrations and group exhbn with Kaleidoscope Arts (2003, 2004); National Sculpture Festival, Art Parks International Guernsey (2003); 'Art for the Park', Café with Park (2003); Basquist Selected Graduates Exhbn, Air Gallery, London (2001). *Commissions*: Heraldic Plaque for The Worshipful Company of Skinners (2000); 5 & half stone roses for Westminster Abbey (2002); Corbel Angel for Westminster Abbey (2006). *Works Reproduced*: Head of Antonio Canovas '3 Graces' (plaster, marble, 2006 - measurements taken from orignal plaster of Canovas 3 Graces, Canovas Museum, Possagna, Italy). *Misc*: continually developing carving ideas, both classical and contemporary in an increasing variety of stones. Also looking to increase demonstration, exhibition and teaching opportunities. *Address*: 53 Beulah Grove, Croydon, Surrey CR0 2QW. *Email*: simon@simonkeeley.com *Website*: www.simonkeeley.com

KEIR, Sally, BA (Hons) (1984), MSBA (1989), MSFP (1998); botanical artist in gouache. *b*: Guildford, 29 Sep 1938. *m*: Peter Benson. two *d*. *Educ*: Sydenham School, Devon. *Studied*: Hereford College of Art (1979-81), Duncan of Jordanstone College of Art (1981-84). *Exhib*: RHS gold, silver gilt and silver medals, SBA (1989-97), Linnean Soc. (1990-91), Discerning Eye (1991), Del Bello Gallery, Toronto (1988-90), RSM (1990), Tregaquelle (1994), SWA (1991), Tryon Gallery (1998). *Works in collections*: Hunt Inst. of Botanical Art, Chicago, Shirley Sherwood Coll. *Publications*: Collin's Artists Manual, Contemporary Botanical Artists, Drawing and Painting Course. *Address*: "Maes Yr Haf", 8 Gorlan, Conwy LL32 8RS. *Signs work*: "S.A.K."

KELLETT, Ursula, MA. *Medium*: acrylic, sand, earth, metal. *b*: Frankfurt, Germany, 6 Apr 1952. *m*: Dr. Michael Kellett. one *s*. one *d*. *Studied*: Byam Shaw School of Art (1993-98, Diploma); London School of Art (2000-01). *Exhib*: A Gallery (2001-04); Hudson Gallery (2004-05); Betty Morton Gallery (2004-07); Toyota Museum, Tokyo (2004); Cast Iron Gallery, New York (2003); London Art Fair, London (2010); Chelsea Art Fair (2006); AAF London (2006-09, 2013, 2014). *Works in collections*: in Germany, UK, USA, France. *Works Reproduced*: as poster. *Principal Works*: "Ways of the World", "Snapshots", "Urban Totems" (sculpture). *Recreations*: travel, fitness, cinema, food. *Misc*: Work focusses on the confrontation of natural and urban, reflected in the materials used: sand, earth, pigments, plastics, metal. *Address*: 1A Sheldon Avenue, London N6 4JS. *Email*: contact@ursulakellett.co.uk *Website*: www.ursulakellett.co.uk *Signs work*: "URSULA KELLETT".

KELLY, Antoinette Louise, BA Hons. *Medium*: acrylic. *b*:Epsom, Surrey, 28 Jul 1973. *Studied*: Epsom School of Art & Design (1991-93); Southampton Institute (1995-98). *Exhib*: The Mall Galleries, London (2002, 2004); Gloss Gallery, Exeter, Devon (2012); Lacy Road Gallery, London (2008); Wimbledon Art Studios, Open Studios London (1999, 2000, 2001); Mariners Gallery, St. Ives, Cornwall (2013). *Works in collections*: private collections. *Publications*: ABNA. *Clubs*: Member of The Association of British Naive Artists. *Address*: Le Bourg, Vieux Mareuil, 24340, France. *Email*: antoinette4@gmail.com *Website*: www.saatchiart.com/A.Kelly *Signs work*: "A. Kelly".

KELLY, Brendan, RP; Awards: Hunting Observer Student Prize (1991); BP Portrait Award (Commended 1992, 93, Second Prize 2001); McFarlane Painting Prize, RSA (1995); De Laszlo Prize, RP (2004); HSBC Prize, RP (2006); Changing Faces Prize, RP (2007). *Medium*: oil, watercolour, acrylic. *b*: Edinburgh, 13 May 1970. *s of*: Tom & Philomena Kelly. *m*: Kim Lansdown. *Educ*: Ampleforth College. *Studied*: Camberwell School of Art (1988-9); Slade School of Fine Art (1989-93). *Exhib*: Mall Galleries; National Portrait Gallery; Royal Society of Portrait Painters; Royal Scottish Academy; The Jerwood Space; Treasures of the National Portrait Gallery (tour in Japan). *Works in collections*: Royal Bank of Scotland; Marylebone Cricket Club; Baker and Mackenzie; High Court, Edinburgh; collection of Blair Atholl Castle; National Portrait Gallery; British Army. *Commissions*: Duke of Atholl; Sir Vivian Richards; Kate Adie; Inziman Ul Haq; the Generals of ISAF IX - Afghanistan; General David Richards. *Misc*: Head of Drawing at The Art Academy, London. *Address*: 149 Providence Square, London SE1 2ED. *Email*: bkellyartist@btinternet.co.uk *Website*: www.brendankellyartist.co.uk *Signs work*: 'KELLY'.

KELLY, Deirdre, B.Ed. (Hons) (1984), MA (1987), RE; printmaker. *b*: London, 1 May 1962. one *s*. *Studied*: Wimbledon School of Art. *Exhib*: BP International, Contemporary Art Soc., Galerie Luc Queryel, Harriet Green Gallery. *Works in collections*: Sedgewick Gp. International, Atlantis Paper Co., King's College School, Museuda Gravura, Brazil

Ballingen Arts Foundation. *Commissions*: Reuters (UK) Ltd. *Works Reproduced*: Big Issue (1995), Arts Review (2000). *Address*: 5 Pages Lane, London N10 1PU. *Email*: deidrek99@yahoo.co.uk Website: deirderkellydeirdrekelly.com *Signs work*: "Deirdre Kelly" or "D.K."

KELLY, Fowokan George, sculptor in resins, bronze and wood; trying to recapture lost African elements through art. *b*: Kingston, Jamaica, 1 Apr 1943. *m*: Margaret Andrews. one *d*. *Educ*: East Queen St. Elementary Baptist School, Kingston, Jamaica. *Studied*: self taught. *Exhib*: Brixton Art Gallery (1983), Black Art Gallery (1983), Harley Studio Museum (1997), Assoc. Portrait Sculptors (1999), RA (1991, 2000, 2001). *Works in collections*: London Borough of Hammersmith and Fulham, WEB Du Bois Institute, Harvard University, Unilever, University of West Indies, and private collections. *Commissions*: African People's Historical Foundation, London Borough of Hammersmith and Fulham and private portraits. *Address*: 20 Veda Rd., Ladywell, London SE13 7JF. *Email*: fowokan@hotmail.com *Signs work*: "F G Kelly."

KELLY, Jane Mary, BA (Hons) History with History of Art, Advanced Dip. in Fine Art (Painting). *Medium*: oil, mixed media, drawing. *b*: London, 7 May 1956. *d of*: Ernest Francis Kelly (adopted). *Partner*: (Icat, Brenda). *Educ*: St. Peter's Collegiate School for Girls, Wolverhampton; Penderford High School. *Studied*: Stirling University; The Univ. of Sosnowiec, Poland; The Central School of Speech and Drama. *Represented by*: Stuckism International. *Exhib*: RA Summer Show (2000); Wolverhampton Art Gallery Schools Exhbn (1972); McRobert Centre, Stirling (1976); mixed show at Metropole Arts Centre, Folkestone (2000); 'West London Artists' Show, Sackville Gallery (2000); Liverpool Biennial (2004) WAG; Musee Adzac, Paris (2005); Sotheby's Action, Belfast (2006). *Works in collections*: private collections; EU, based in Luxembourg and Belfast. *Commissions*: Portraits for prisoners in Wormwood Scrubs. *Publications*: work mentioned in several magazines dealing with 'The Struggle Between Painting and Conceptualism'. *Works Reproduced*: portrait of Ken Livingstone for RA Catalogue; Liverpool paintings; portrait of Myra Hindley in numerous newspaper. *Principal Works*: 'If We Could Undo Psychosis'; 'Anne at the Beach'. *Recreations*: growing vegetables, worrying, visiting theatre, radio drama. *Clubs*: The Groucho Club, The Stuckist Painters. *Address*: The Garden Flat, 5 Larden Road, London W3 7ST. *Email*: janekelly@dsl.pipex.com stuckism@yahoo.co.uk *Signs work*: 'JK'.

KELLY, John, BA (1985), MA.(1996); artist in oil on linen, bronze, mixed media. *b*: Bristol, 12 Apr 1965. *m*: Christina Todesco. *Studied*: Rmit University, Melbourne, Australia, (1983-85, 1992-96), Slade School of Art, London (1996-97). *Exhib*: ten one-man shows with Niagara, Melbourne, and Piccadilly Galleries, London. Work in collections internationally. *Clubs*: Colony Room, London. *Address*: Reen Farm, South Reen, Union Hall, West Cork Ireland. *Signs work*: "Klly" and year.

KELLY, Marty, Awards: Donegal County Council (2006, 2001), Arts Council of Ireland (2005). *Medium*: oil. *b*: Carndonagh, Co.Donegal, Ireland, 10 Feb 1979. *Educ*: BTEC Art & Design NWIFHEN, Ireland (1996-97). *Studied*: University Ulster, Belfast (1997-2000). *Represented by*: Blue Leaf Gallery. *Exhib*: "Postmemory", Blue Leaf Gallery, Dublin (2007), "New Paintings", Blue Leaf Gallery, Dublin (2005); "Elsewhere Chronicles", Townhouse Gallery, Belfast (2004), "Steady Gazing, Outward Looking" Townhouse Gallery, Belfast (2003); RUA, Belfast (2007), AAF London (2007, 2002-04), Iontas, Sligo, Ireland (2007), Woolf Gallery, London (2003), Steading Gallery, Kirkcudbright, Scotland (2003). *Works in collections*: Dept of Environment, N. Ireland, Irish Contemporary Arts Society, Bank of Ireland, Mandate Trade Union, Lavelle Coleman Solicitors, Wedgewood Inc, Los Angeles, USA. *Publications*: Buyers Guide to Irish Art 2008, Oxfam Calendar '07 & '08. *Address*: Blue Leaf Gallery, 10 Marino Mart, Fairview, Dublin 3, Ireland. *Email*: info@blueleafgallery.com *Website*: www.blueleafgallery.com *Signs work*: 'MK'.

KELLY, Peter J., RBA, NEAC (elected 2007). *b*: Ilford, Essex, 11 Dec 1931. *s of*: Cyril & Christina Kelly. *m*: Brenda. two *s*. *Educ*: Loxford Central School. *Studied*: Central School of Art and Design. *Represented by*: John Adams Fine Art. *Exhib*: Mall Galleries, John Adams Fine Art, W.Patterson Fine Art, Bankside Gallery, Thompsons Gallery, Waterman Fine Art, Royal Academy Summer Exhbn, and many more. *Works in collections*: HSBC; ING Barings Charterhouse Securities, Ford Motor Company, Higgs and Hill, Kennedy's Solicitors. *Publications*: "How to Create Light in your Painting" (pub.New Holland); "Artist's Guide to Exeptional Colour" (pub. Quarto); "How to Paint from Photographs" (pub. New Holland Press), also in "House and Garden", "The Artist". *Recreations*: classical music. *Clubs*: Small Paintings Group. *Address*: 'The Chestnuts' The Square, Stock, Essex, CM4 9LH. *Email*: kellypeterartist@aol.com *Signs work*: "PJK".

KELSEY, Robert, DA (Glasgow School of Art 1966-70), PAI (Diploma, Paisley Art Institute); FRSA (Fellowship of the Royal Society of Arts); MUniv (2010, Honorary Degree from University of the West of Scotland). *Medium*: oil painter of landscapes and marine subjects. *b*: Glasgow, 4 Apr 1949. *s of*: Alfred, Joseph Kelsey and Ann (nee Cook). *m*: Jean Simpson. one *d*. *Studied*: Glasgow School of Art; The Painting School. *Represented by*: Thompson's Galleries, London and Aldeburgh. *Exhib*: RSA, RGI, RSW, ROI, PAI; one-man shows with Thompson Gallery (1994-2012); John Martin of London (1996-2000), Walker Galleries Harrogate (2003, 2005). *Works in collections*: Paisley Art Gallery and Museum, The Fleming Collection; His Grace the Duke of Bedford; Lord McFarlane of Bearsden; Sir Arnold Clark. *Publications*: Artist and Illustrator Magazines; book, 'Robert Kelsey - The Artist' (pub. 2004). *Official Purchasers*: Credit Lyonnais; Scottish Friendly Assurance; Enterprise Oil. *Works Reproduced*: limited edition prints. *Recreations*: golf, classical music. *Clubs*: Glasgow Art Club, President 2012. *Misc*: television documentary, BBC Breakfast (November 2004). *Address*: Ranfurly, 18 Newtyle Rd, Paisley, PA1 3JU. *Email*: robert@rkelsey.com *Website*: www.rkelsey.com *Signs work*: "Kelsey".

KELSO, James Philip, painter in acrylic. *b*: London, 6 Jul 1934. *m*: Marianne. one *s*. one *d*. *Educ*: Sloane School, Chelsea. *Studied*: self taught. *Exhib*: RA Summer Exhibs. *Works in collections*: private collections in UK, USA, Sweden. *Address*: The Well House, Christmas Common, Watlington, Oxon. OX9 5HJ. *Email*: jim@kelso.co.uk *Website*: www.kelsopaintings.com *Signs work*: "James Kelso."

KENNEDY, Keith Manning, Hon SGFA; RAS Cert.; presently Webmaster, Honorary Member of Society of Graphic Fine Art. *Medium*: painting. *b*: Ewhurst, Surrey, 28 Aug 1941. *m*: Rosemary. *Educ*: Reigate and Redhill School of Art & Craft. *Studied*: West Sussex College of Art; Royal Academy Schools. *Exhib*: Ditchling Gallery (1968); Hove Museum of Art (1982); Towner Gallery, Eastbourne (with Eastbourne Group); Woodstock Gallery, London (1983); Brighton Festival Open Houses (2002/5); RWS Open (1989/96); Bourne Hall, Ewell (2005/6/7). *Works in collections*: Ernst & Young Private Patient Plan; private collections. *Commissions*: mural painting for Metway Electrical (1996). *Publications*: Included in 'New Encycolpedia of Watercolour Techniques'. *Clubs*: elected Member of Sussex Watercolour Society in 2006. *Address*: 10 Furzedene, Furze Hill, Hove, E.Sussex, BN3 1PP. *Email*: keithmkennedy@clara.co.uk *Website*: www.sgfa.org.uk *Signs work*: 'K M Kennedy' or 'K M K'.

KENNEDY, Margaret, Prizewinner Carlow 'Eighse' Arts Festival; 1st & 3rd, Moyglare Stud Kildare Art Comp. (1983, 84); Highly Commended Texaco Childrens Art Comp. (1968). *Medium*: oil. *b*: Dublin, 5 May 1950. *d of*: Michael & Josephine Kennedy. *Educ*: Crumlin & Tallaght National Schools. *Studied*: studied horse anatomy with Iris Kellett, former World Champion rider. *Represented by*: Abbey Gallery, Drogheda. *Exhib*: Mall Galleries, London (2003-5); S.E.A. Exhbn, Christies, London (2002); Irish National Stud; American College Dublin (solo, 1997); Dublin Horse Show RDS (2002, 2005); SEA Exhbn,

Newmarket (2005); Emo Court, NAAS Co.Kildare. *Commissions*: 'History of Tallaght Area' (South Dublin County Library, oil); 10 pictures for 'Partas' Business Enterprise Center. *Publications*: 'All Roads Lead to Tallaght', British Horse Society Christmas Catalogue (1998). *Official Purchasers*: Dublin South County Library. *Works Reproduced*: 'Gentle Giants' by British Horse Society; 'Racing Legends'; 'Arkle'. *Principal Works*: specialises in equestrian paintings in oil. *Recreations*: horse riding, writing, photography. *Clubs*: Associate Member of Society of Equestrian Artists, England. *Misc*: author of children's book 'Mr Luggie Tatters'. *Address*: Tallaght, Dublin, Ireland. *Email*: margaretkennedy50@gmail.com *Website*: www.margaretkennedyworldpress.com *Signs work*: 'M Kennedy' (in red).

KENNEDY, Michael Peter, DFA (Slade); Slade Prize for Lithography (1966). *Medium*: painting, drawing, printmaking. *b*: Dartford, 1943. *Studied*: Bromley School of Art (1960-62); Ravensbourne College of Art and Design (1962-64); Slade School of Fine Art (1964-66). *Exhib*: RA Summer Exhbn (2004, 2006, 2008, 2009, 2010, 2012, 2013); RWA Open Print Exhbn (2004, 2009); Originals 2004, 05, 06, 07, 09; 5th, 6th, 7th & 8th British International Miniature Print Exhbn. *Commissions*: Art @ the Centre, 2007. *Works Reproduced*: catalogues to: 19th-23rd Miniprint Internacional; 1º, 2º, & 3º, Muestra Miniprint; 5th, 6th, 7th & 8th British International Miniprint; Small Print/Big Impression; Printmaking Today Vol 18 No 2 2009. Royal Academy notecard range (2014). *Address*: 107 Knights Croft, New Ash Green, Longfield, Kent DA3 8HY. *Email*: kennedymp@aol.com *Website*: www.michaelkennedy.org *Signs work*: 'Kennedy' or 'MK' (followed by date).

KENNISH, Jenny, RMS (1985), SWA, FSBA; self taught sculptress in porcelain of wild flowers and animals; school teacher; Marwell International Wildlife Art Society, winner of 'Paws' Competition (mixed media); 'Wildscape' Runner-up (2005). *Medium*: porcelain, oils, c. pencils, acrylic and mixed media. *b*: England, 11 Mar 1944. *d of*: William J. Otway, Dorothy L. Cutting. one *s*. one *d*. *Educ*: Nonsuch County Grammar School for Girls; Whitelands Teacher Training College. *Studied*: Zoology, botany and art. *Exhib*: Westminster Galleries with the RMS, SBA, SWA and local societies; Marwell International Wildlife Art Society National Exhibition of Wildlife Art. *Address*: Wychwood, Silchester Rd., Little London, Tadley, Hants. RG26 5EP. *Email*: jenny@jkennish.com *Website*: www.jennykennish.com *Signs work*: "J.K." and "Jenny Kennish".

KENT, Colin, RI (1971); self taught painter in water-colour, acrylic, mixed media; Buzzacott Award; Linda Blackstone Award. *b*: 10 Feb 1934. *m*: Joan. *Educ*: Romford County Technical School; S.W. Essex Technical College and School of Art. *Exhib*: RA, RI, Mall Galleries, Shell House Gallery, Ledbury, Adam Gallery, Bath, London, Blackstone Gallery, Pinner, Manor House Gallery, Chipping Norton, Geneva, New York. *Works in collections*: in Britain, USA, France, Germany, Finland. *Address*: 64 Forest Rd., Romford, Essex RM7 8DT. *Signs work*: "Colin Kent."

KEON, Gerald, NDD Painting (1963). *Medium*: oil, watercolour, drawing, sculpture, constructions. *b*: England, 19 Dec 1942. *Educ*: Tollington Grammar School (1954-59). *Studied*: Hornsey College of Art (1959-62); Byam Shaw School of Art (1962-63). *Exhib*: RA (2003, 2004); Discerning Eye (2003); Sunday Times Watercolour Show (2002, 2003); Francis Kyle Gallery (four one-man shows, five group shows: 1990-98); Yorkshire Artists; Leeds Polytechnic; Air Gallery, London. *Works in collections*: Arts Council; Guildhall Gallery, Corporation of London; private collections. *Works Reproduced*: Francis Kyle Catalogues; RA Catalogues. *Address*: 28 Chelverton Road, London N19 3AY. *Signs work*: 'Keon' (on reverse of work).

KERMAN, Lesley Frances, FRSA; BA Hons Fine Art; Arts Council Major Award 2000; Fellow of the University of Plymouth. *Medium*: oil, watercolour, drawing, prints, bronze and resin. *b*: Middx, 31 Jul 1942. *d of*: R V & P M Kerman. *m*: Graham Rich. one *s*. one *d*.

Studied: University of Durham (BA Hons Fine Art); Newcastle 1960-64 (Victor Pasmore, Richard Hamilton). Taught at Newcastle College of Art, Brighton College of Art (1964-70), Exeter College of Art and Design, University of Plymouth (1970-92). *Exhib*: Young Contemporaries,1962, 1963, Gallery 273 Queen Mary College, 1985, Exe Gallery, Exeter, 1992, Brewhouse, Taunton,1996, represented the UK at the Biella Etching Biennale, Italy1998, World Print Exhibition, Slovenia, 2000, Nature Culture, Ann Lantair, Stornoway, 2002, Science Museum London, 2005, Spike Open, Spike Island, Bristol, 2008 - Paint to Print. I-storm Exeter 2011 Falmouth Art Gallery 'Fishwick and Friends', 2012 Goldsmiths University of London 'Advice to Women in Management'. *Works in collections*: Victoria and Albert Museum London, Tate Archive. *Commissions*: 'The Secrets of Bideford' Public sculpture, The Environment Agency; 'The Secrets of Nuneaton', SUSTRANS. 3 Ways School, Bath; 2009: Devonport Hospitals: 'The Secrets of Devonport' (2012); 'The Secrets of Cardiff' St. Davids. Commissioned by SAAFLE for Land Securities (2011); 'The Secret of St. Annes' commissioned by the Arts Council (2012); Secrets of Venice' Whitehead (2013). *Publications*: 'The Secrets of Cardiff' pub. University of Plymouth, 'Fictions' pub. University of Plymouth, 'The Secrets of Bideford' published by Devon County Council & Little Silver, 'The Secret of St. Anne's Barnstaple' Little Silver 2012; 'Advice to Women in Management' published by Little Silver 2012, 'The Memory of Art School' published by Little Silver 2013. *Official Purchasers* Victoria & Albert Museum, London, Artist's Books Collection. *Address*: 13 Riverside Road, Topsham, Devon, EX3 0LR. *Email*: lesleykerman@blueyonder.co.uk *Website*: www.lesleykerman.co.uk *Signs work*: "Lesley Kerman".

KERN, Doreen, sculptor in bronze; Gold Medal from the Emperor Haile Selassie; consultant to B.M. Replica Dept. *Medium*: bronze. *b*: 9 Aug 1941. divorced. two *s*. *Educ*: Hampstead Garden Suburb Institute; studio assistant at the Morris Singer Art Bronze foundry. *Studied*: under Howard Bates, RA. *Exhib*: Waterloo Fine Arts, Talma Gallery, Tel-Aviv, Ryder Gallery, LA., Galerie Nichido, Tokyo, London University, Bath Festival, National Museum of Archaeology, Valletta, Malta, Design Centre, St. Paul's Cathedral, Edinburgh Festival (1995), Millennium Dome (July 2000), British Library, London. *Works in collections*: Dr Kwame Nkrumah, Guyana, Emperor Haile Selassie (Palace of Addis Ababa), Anne Frank for Anne Frank house, Amsterdam also British Library, Clint Eastwood, Alistair McLean, Miss Bluebell, Chaim Topol; Former Israeli Prime Minister Ariel Sharon and Former Prime Minister of Israel Golda Meir. *Commissions*: all of above portraits in bronze. *Recreations*: theatre critic and features writer, lecturer. *Address*: The Studio, 38 Canons Drive, Edgware, Middx. HA8 7QT. *Email*: doreenkern@onetel.com

KERR, Janet, RWS (1997); painter in water based mixed media on paper, semi abstract work mainly concerned with W. Yorkshire landscape. *b*: Hornchurch, Essex, 20 May 1947. *m*: divorced. one *d*. *Educ*: Palmers Girls School, Barking Regional College (Graphics). *Studied*: painting privately with Charles Bartlett PPRWS. *Exhib*: Bankside Gallery, London, and throughout Britain. *Works in collections*: Museum of Foreign Art, Japan. *Publications*: 'The Watercolour Expert' (Cassells, 2004); 'Watercolour Masters, Then and Now' (Cassells, 2005). *Recreations*: playing traditional American folk music on fiddle. *Address*: 11 New Longley, Norland, Sowerby Bridge, W. Yorks. HX6 3RR. *Email*: janet.kerr@talktalk.net *Signs work*: "JanetKerr."

KERR, Janette, President, Royal West of England Academy; Visiting Research Fellow, UWE; PhD Fine Art (2005); ACE Research & Development Awards (2010/2012); Visiting Artist, Bergen Meteorological Insitution (2012); Windle Trust Bursary (2000); David Murray Studentship Award Royal Academy Schools (1999); Ruskin/Colle Verde Travel Bursary (1996). *Medium*: oil, 2D. *b*: Blairgowrie, 14 Sep 1957. *Partner*: Dr. Steve Poole. one *s*. *Studied*: UWE, Bristol. *Represented by*: Cadogan Contemporary (London); Stour Gallery (Shipston-on-Stour). *Exhib*: RA Summer Shows, London; RWA, Bristol; Cadogan

Contemporary; Hilton Fine Art, Bath; Slader's Yard, Bridport; Workshop Wales, Fishguard; Bonhoga Gallery, Shetland; Museum Vest Ovagen, Norway. *Works in collections*: Dublin Office of Public Works; RWA Permanent Collection; Royal Collection. *Publications*: 'The Power of the Sea: Making Waves in British Art 1790-2014', Samson & Company (2014); 'Night: A Time Between', RWA (2008); 'Fifty Wessex Artists', Evolver Books (2006) *Address*: Hill House, Church Street, Coleford, Somerset BA3 5NA. *Email*: janettekerr2@gmail.com *Website*: www.janettekerr.co.uk extremewavetheory.blogspot.com

KERSHAW, Walter, BA Hons. Fine Art (Dunelm); mural painter and freelance artist in oil, water-colour, mosaic; occasional visiting lecturer in Environmental Art at Universities in the UK, Brazil and W. Germany. *b*: Rochdale, 7 Dec 1940. *s of*: Walter Kershaw. *Partner*: Gillian Halliwell. one *s*. one *d*. *Educ*: De la Salle College, Salford. *Studied*: Durham University (1958-62). *Exhib*: Large scale, public, external murals in Manchester, Trafford Park and N.W. Museum of Science and Industry; Norwich; Brazil, São Paulo and Recife. Internal murals for British Aerospace, Manchester United FC, P&O, Sarajevo International Arts Festival, Salford University, the CEGB, Hollingworth Lake Visitors Centre and Italian Consulate Manchester, Leonard Cheshire Foundation (2003). *Works in collections*: V&A, British Council, Arts Council, Gulbenkian Foundation, 'Cultura Inglesa', Museum of Art, São Paulo; National Collection of Brazilian Art, and other public galleries in the UK. *Works Reproduced*: Photos of murals at the Serpentine, Whitechapel and Tate galleries. *Misc*: Films: 'Terra Firma' BBC 2 (1976), 'First Graffiti Artist' (1977), 'Nationwide' (1982), '5 x 5' W. Germany (1984), 'Folio' Anglia TV (1987), Bosnia T.V. (1996). International Arts Festival. Recorded: 'Conversation Piece' with Sue MacGregor, Radio 4 (1983), 'Kaleidoscope' Radio 4 (1986). *Address*: 193 Todmorden Rd., Littleborough, Rochdale OL15 9EG. *Website*: www.walterkershaw *Signs work*: "Walter Kershaw."

KESTEVEN, Abel, BTEC Illustration; HND Illustration. *Medium*: Drawing; prints; sculpture; acrylic. *b*: Newton Abbott, 5 Sep 1969. *Educ*: O level Art; A level Art. *Studied*: Medway College of Art (1987-89); Kent Institute of Art and Design (1989-91). *Exhib*: Blackheath Gallery, London; Mine Gallery, Carshalton; Alphabet Bar, Beak Street, London; Mall Gallery, London; Cross Gate Gallery, Lexington, USA (Royal Pastel Society); Chelsea Art Society Summer Exhibition. *Works in collections*: In private collections throughout London and the Home Counties. *Commissions*: Various commissions through London galleries. *Publications*: Design Weekly (1997); various illustrations used commercially including Southwark Council. *Works Reproduced*: Some limited editions produced of recent pastel drawings. *Address*: 263 Carshalton Road, Carshalton SM5 3PT. *Email*: abel@abelkesteven.com *Website*: www.abelkesteven.com *Signs work*: "A. KESTEVEN".

KETCHER, Jean, BA Hons. Fine Art Painting (1976); painter in oil, water-colour, etc. art teacher, Copleston High School, Ipswich. *b*: 6 Jul 1955. *Studied*: Ipswich School of Art (1971-73), Maidstone College of Art (1973-76). *Exhib*: Halesworth Gallery, Ellingham Mill, Bungay, Corn Exchange, Ipswich. *Address*: 46 Sandown Rd., Ipswich IP1 6RE. *Signs work*: "Jean Ketcher."

KEY, Geoffrey, NDD, DA Manc. Heywood Medal, Guthrie Bond Scholarship. *Medium*: painter in oil and other media; sculptor. *b*: Manchester, 13 May, 1941. *s of*: George and Marion Key. *Partner*: Judith M O'Leary. *Educ*: High School of Art, Manchester. *Studied*: Regional College of Art, Manchester (1958-61), under Harry Rutherford, William Bailey, Ted Roocroft. *Represented by*: a number of galleries in the UK and abroad; no sole representative. *Exhib*: extensively in the UK, Europe and the Far East, most recently in Hong Kong, London and Dublin. *Works in collections*: Salford A.G., Manchester City Gallery, Bolton A.G., Granada Television, University of Manchester, Manchester Museum of Science and Industry, Victoria and Albert Museum, Wigan Metropolitan Borough, North West Arts Board, Jockey Club of Hong Kong, Society Roquefort, Mandarin Oriental, Hong

Kong, Chateau de St. Ouen, Chateaux Relais, Perrier. *Publications*: G.Key: Drawings (Margin Press), Clowns (Sansom and Company), Geoffrey Key Twentieth-Century Drawings (Sansom and Company), Dictionary of British Art (Collectors Club Press), European Painters (Clio Press), Images (Nicholson & Bass Ltd), Geoffrey Key Paintings, JMOL Publishing. *Official Purchasers*: see collections. *Works Reproduced*: see publications. *Recreations*: collecting European works of art. *Clubs*: President, Salford Art Club. *Address*: 59 Acresfield Rd., Pendleton, Salford M6 7GE. *Email*: enquiries@geoffreykey.com *Website*: www.geoffreykey.com

KHALIL: see NORLAND (NEUSCHUL), Khalil.

KHAN, Keith Ali, BA (Hons.); sculptor in large scale exterior/interior constructions, using fabric and many people; Director, Carnival Designer. *b*: Trinidad, 4 Dec 1963. *s of*: Faiz Khan. *Educ*: King's College, Wimbledon. *Studied*: Wimbledon School of Art, Middlesex Polytechnic (Dante Leonelli), The Street, Port of Spain, Trinidad. *Exhib*: Houston International Festival, Harris Museum, Preston, Arnolfini, Bristol; one-man shows: Bluecoat Gallery, Liverpool, Greenwich Citizen Gallery; on the streets of Notting Hill, as well as numerous designs on TV and stage. *Address*: 79 Grand Drive, Raynes Pk., London SW20 9DW. *Signs work*: "Khan."

KHANNA, Balraj, MA; Winnifred Holtby prize by RSL; painter in acrylic, novelist. *b*: 4 Oct 1939. *s of*: Amar Nath. *m*: Francine Martine. two *d*. *Educ*: Punjab University. *Exhib*: fifty one-man shows: Ashmolean Museum, Oxford, City A.G., Bristol, Galerie Transposition, Paris, Herbert Benevy Gallery, N.Y., Serpentine Gallery, Richard Demarco, Royal Festival Hall, Arnolfini, MOMA Wales, Berlin and Frankfurt, De La Warr Pavilion, Oldham Gallery, MAC Birmingham; Foster Art London; Cartwright Hall Bradford; Arushi Arts, Delhi; Sixty Years of British Art, Hayward Gallery. *Works in collections*: Arts Council; Musee d'Art Moderne, Paris; Ville de Paris; Ashmolean Museum; National Gallery of Modern Art, New Delhi; City A.G., Bristol; City A.G., Bradford; V. & A.; Calouste Gulbenkian Foundation, Lisbon; Hippodrome Theatre, Birmingham. *Commissions*: Birmingham Hippodrome safety curtain, MOMA Wales Mosaic Mural. *Publications*: Nation of Fools (Michael Joseph, Penguin), Sweet Chillies (Constable), Kalighat, Popular Indian Painting, 1800-1930 (Redstone Press), Krishna - The Divine Lover, Art of Modern India (Thames & Hudson, 1998), Human & Divine, The Mists of Simla, Indian Magic (Hope Road). *Address*: 3a Pindock Mews, London W9 2PY. *Email*: balrajkhanna@btinternet.com *Signs work*: "Khanna."

KHANNA, Krishnen, BA (Hons) - Oxford & Cambridge School Certificate. Awards: Bombay Art Society, Lalit Kala Akademy, New Delhi - all India Fine Arts and Crafts Society, New Delhi; Padma Bhusan by Govt. India. *Medium*: painting: oils. *b*: Lyallpur, pre-partitioned Punjab, India, 5 Jul 1925. *m*: Renuka Khanna. one *s*. two *d*. *Educ*: Cathedral City School, Lahore (1932-36); Government High School, Multan (1936-37). *Studied*: Imperial Service College, Windsor UK (1938-42, as Kipling Scholar); Government College, Lahore (1944-45). *Represented by*: Saffron Art, Bombay. *Exhib*: Bombay Art Society; Lalit Kala Akademy; Kumar Gallery, New Delhi; Sakshi Gallery, Bombay; Pundole Gallery, Bombay; Saffron Art, Mumbai; Leicester Gallery, London (3 shows); New Art Centre, London; Berkeley Square Gallery, London; Egan Gallery, New York, Saffron Gallery, New York. *Work in collections*: Yadvisham, Jerusalem; Museum of Modern Art, New York; National Gallery of Modern Art, New Delhi; Roopankar Museum, Bhopal, etc. *Commissions*: by ITC Ltd: Chola mural (80' long drawing); ceiling of Maurya Hotel (4000 sq.ft.); World Wildlife Fund (circular platform in ceramic tiles approx 35' diameter). *Publications*: Principal publications: "Krishnen Khanna - A Critical Biography" by Gayatri Sinha; "Collections of National Gallery Modern Art, New Delhi", Lalit Kala Akademy, ND. "The Great Procession, a mural by Krishnen Khanna"; "Images in my Time"; "The Chola Migrations";

"The Embrace of Love" by Gayatri Sinha. *Works Reproduced*: by Lalit Kala Akademy and Saffron Art, Mumbai. *Principal Works*: NGMA New Delhi, Maurya mural "The Great Procession". *Recreations*: reading, mainly poetry. *Clubs*: India International Centre, New Delhi. *Address*: A48/11A DLF Phasel, Gurgaon 122002, Haryana, India. *Email*: krishenkhannaartist@gmail.com *Signs work*: "K. KHANNA".

KHETANCHI, Gopal Swami, BA. *Medium*: oil. *b*: Sardarshahar (Raj) India, 2 Feb 1958. *s of*: Khetaram Swami. *m*: Indu Bala Swami. one *s*. one *d*. *Studied*: University of Rajasthan, Jaipur (1979). *Represented by*: Mrs. Elizabeth Marie Mitchell-D'Anna. *Exhib*: La Galleria, London (2008); Jawahar Kala Kendra, Jaipur (2002-04, 2006, 2008); Nehru Centre, Mumbai (2005, 2007); Museum Gallery, Mumbai (2006); Rajputana Sheraton, Jaipur (2005). *Works in collections*: personal and corporate. *Works Reproduced*: Mayur Pankh, Ghoomar (by All India Arts, London). *Principal Works*: Shringaar, Vatsalya, Apsara, Ubtan. *Recreations*: music. *Misc*: Khetanchi is focused on communicating the essence of rural India and Indian traditions through his paintings. *Address*: E-4/74A Chitrakoot, Vaishali Nagar, Jaipur, Raj 302021, India. *Email*: khetanchi@gmail.com *Website*: www.khetanchistudio.com *Signs work*: "KHETANCHI".

KIANUSH-WALLACE, Katy, self taught professional artist and illustrator in acrylic, water-colour, pen and ink, pencil, pastel; Owner of Art Gallery and Cultural Website Art Arena; Member of the Executive Council of NAPA, directed the first London exhibition of NAPA at Westminster Gallery, July/Aug. 1999. *b*: Tehran, Iran, 12 Apr 1964. *m*: Jim Wallace. *Educ*: Acton, London. *Exhib*: over sixty solo and group shows during last eight years: Westminster Gallery; RBSA (winner, Royal Sovereign (Rembrandt) Award 1998); Victoria A.G., Bath; Black Sheep Gallery, Hawarden (winner, Daler-Rowney International Award 1999); Mariners Gallery St. Ives (Artists and Illustrators Award 2002); Handel House Gallery, Devizes; The Guildhall, Salisbury; Crosfield Hall, Romsey; Wyvern Theatre, Swindon; BBC World Service, London; National Power, Swindon, etc. Work on permanent exhbn. on Internet galleries worldwide. *Works in collections*: private collections: U.K. and abroad. *Publications*: illustrated children's poetry books, published in Iran, at age ten; covers, two books of poems, 'Closed Circuit' by Shadab Vajdi (Forest Books), and 'As Long As the Moon Shall Rise' by Ellen Moore Anderson (Holy Cow Publications). *Clubs*: NAPA, Wessex Artists. *Address*: 4 Bennett Hill Close, Wootton Bassett, Wiltshire SN4 8LR. *Website*: http://www.art-arena.com

KIDBY, Paul James, *Medium*: oil, watercolour, drawing, sculpture. *b*: London, 24 Jun 1964. *m*: Vanessa. two *s*. one *d*. *Represented by*: Art of the Imagination; Daniel Magmen Gallery, Paris. *Exhib*: Various inc: Chris Beetles Gallery; Air Gallery, London; Science Museum; Royal Academy; Salisbury Museum; St Barb Gallery, Lymington (solo retrospective 2012); Russell Cotes Museum; Willis Museum (solo retrospective (2013). *Works in collections*: Private and commercial. *Publications*: The Art of Discworld; The Last Herd; Le Royaume Enchante; The Pratchett Portfolio; The Charmed Realm etc. *Address*: PO Box 2116, Fordingbridge, Hampshire SP6 2WU. *Email*: info@paulkidby.net *Website*: www.paulkidby.net *Signs work*: "P.J. KIDBY" or initials monogram.

KIDD, Alan Hunter, NDD (1965). *Medium*: oil, watercolour, drawing, print, sculpture. *b*: Glasgow, Scotland, 18 Nov 1943. *m*: Elaine. one *s*. one *d*. *Educ*: Churchill High School, Salisbury, Rhodesia. *Studied*: Walthamstow School of Art Walthamstow, Essex (1961-1965, Peter Blake, Ken Howard, Fred Dubery, Anne House). *Exhib*: UK, Belgium, Rhodesia. *Works in collections*: Worldwide Private and Public collections including Stoke Mandeville Hospital, House of Lords, Aylesbury Vale District Council. *Commissions*: Aylesbury Vale District Council. *Recreations*: Mountain Biking. *Clubs*: Oxfordshire Art Society, Buckingham Art Society. *Address*: 9 Naseby Close, Thame, Oxfordshire OX9 3WA. *Email*: alankidd@macace.net *Website*: http://www.alankidd.com *Signs work*: "Alan H Kidd".

KIKI, John, NDD, RA Diploma. *Medium*: oil, acrylic, drawing, prints. *m*: Mary. two *d*. *Studied*: Camberwell Arts School; Royal Academy Schools. *Represented by*: O.K. Harris Gallery, NYC, USA; Arts Space Gallery, London; St.Giles Gallery, Norwich. *Works in collections*: National Gallery of Wales; The Saatchi Collection; Gallop Finland; Siemans PLC; Chantrey Bequest; University Gallery, Liverpool; Art Esprit; Norwich Castle Museum. *Recreations*: painting. *Address*: 51 Middlemarket Rd, Gt.Yarmouth, Norfolk NR30 2BZ. *Email*: johnkiki@hotmail.com *Website*: www.johnkiki.co.uk *Signs work*: 'John Kiki'.

KILLEEN, Bruce, MA Oxon (1950), RWA (1963), AIA (1964); Painter in oil and watercolour; formerly, senior lecturer, Colchester School of Art, tutor, RA Schools; Art Correspondent, The Guardian. *b*: Warwickshire, 22 Jan 1926. *m*: (1) Angela Fry, artist/potter (died 1997) one *s*., two *d*.; (2) Julie Wroughton, ARCA, RWA (died Dec 2010). *Educ*: Merton College, Oxford. *Exhib*: one-man: Artists International Galleries, Drian Galleries, London; Minories, Colchester; Chappel Galleries, Essex; Alpha House, Sherborne; Malcolm Innes Gallery, Edinburgh; Circle Gallery, Edinburgh, An Tobar Gallery, Tobermory; mixed: RA, RWA, Bruton Street Gallery, Cheltenham Group, Penwith Gallery, St. Ives, Di Rollo Gallery, Anthony Woodd Gallery, Edinburgh etc. *Publications*: Arts Council Art Films (1978-80), 'Evocations', 'Digressions' and 'Collusions' (wood engravings, drawings and poems), with Julia Wroughton (Strathmore Publishing, London, 2007, 2008 and 2010). *Address*: 37 rue Nationale, Lectoure, 32700 France. *Signs work*: "B.A. Killeen" or "B.K."

KIMBLE, Grace, FZS (London); PGCE-Primary (Arts); MA (Cantab) Natural Sciences (Zoology) (bursary 2005/06); SWLA Commended; Nina Mosali Prize (FPS). *Medium*: oil, acrylic, watercolour. *b*: Oxford, 5 Jul 1982. *d of*: Dr Bob Sim & Prof Edith Sim. *m*: Pete. *Studied*: Pembroke College, University of Cambridge; Inst. of Education, University of London. *Exhib*: Gasworks, Birmingham; Magdalen College, Oxford; Whitechapel Galleries, London; Gaskin & Davis, Harrow; Sarian Gallery, Pinner; The Cottons Atrium, London; Mall Galleries (SWLA); Blythe Gallery, Manchester; Bankside Gallery, London (FPS); Osterley House, London; Old Truman Brewery, London. *Works in collections*: Tottenham Hotspurs Football Club. *Commissions*: numerous business, including: The Positive Internet Co., Cafe Cocoa. *Works Reproduced*: Biodiversity: Africa; Zebras; Penguins. *Recreations*: running. *Misc*: Outreach Officer-FPS. *Address*: 1 Mead Villas, Roxeth Hill, Harrow, Middx, HA2 0JY. *Email*: grace@gracesart.co.uk *Website*: www.gracesart.co.uk

KINAHAN, Lady Coralie, USWA, UWA, RUA; artist in oil and water-colour; Lady Mayoress of Belfast (1959-62). *b*: Surrey, 16 Sep 1924. *d of*: Capt. C. de Burgh, DSO, RN. *m*: Sir Robin Kinahan. two *s*. three *d*. *Educ*: 14 governesses and 4 schools. *Studied*: John Hassall, and Chelsea Schools of Art (1943-46); private portrait classes under Sonia Mervyn, A.R.A. (1946-49). *Exhib*: RA, RP, ROI, SWLA, RSA, RUA; solo exhibitions England and Ireland. Opened own gallery 1985 exhibiting landscapes, horses and portraits. *Commissions*: Portraits include Lord Bishop of Durham, Rt. Hon. Humphrey and Mrs. Atkins, General Sir Ian Freeland and Rt. Hon. James Prior. Other commissions for various Regiments and Imperial War Museum. Sporting paintings for Mr. Victor McCalmont and others. *Publications*: Two historical novels and Memoirs. *Works Reproduced*: Limited editions (200) Belfast Harbour; Army Patrol looking over Belfast, and hunting scenes. *Recreations*: painting, travelling, nature, history. *Misc*: Husband made H.M.'s Lord Lieut. for Belfast County (1985). *Address*: 19 Abbey Mews, Amesbury, Wilts. SP4 7EX. *Website*: www.coralie-kinahan.com *Signs work*: "C. de B.K." oils; "Coralie Kinahan" water-colours.

KING, Andrew Norman, ROI, BA (Hons.) (1978), NS (1984), ROI (1992); David Murray Scholarship, RA Schools (1978); Finalist, Winsor and Newton Young Artists award (1985); landscape and marine artist, interested in light and atmosphere in landscape.

Medium: oil and water-colour. *b*: Bedford, 8 Mar 1956. *Partner*: Jane Cort. *Educ*: Barnfield College. *Studied*: Hornsey College of Art, London. *Represented by*: Thompson's Gallery, Aldeburgh; Flint Gallery; A&K Wilson Gallery; Hawker Gallery; Mandell's Gallery. *Exhib*: Britain in Water-colour, RI, NEAC, NS, RSMA, ROI, RWS, RP, Laing; one-man shows: Hunter Gallery, Long Melford; Hawker Gallery, Amersham; A&K Wilson Gallery, Harpenden; Thompsons Gallery, Aldeburgh. *Works in collections*: Luton Arts Council, Beds. C.C., Eagle Star Offices, and in private and royal collections in Britain and abroad. House of Lords (2003) (3 works). *Official Purchasers*: Luton and Beds Arts Council, House of Lords Collections 2003; Norwich Charitable Trusts (2008). *Works Reproduced*: East Anglia Daily Times magazine. *Recreations*: sailing, natural history. *Clubs*: East Anglian Group of Marine Artists. Reynolds Club (RA). *Address*: Pond Cottage, Long Lane, Colby, Norwich, NR11 7EF. *Email*: info@andrewkingroi.co.uk *Website*: www.andrewkingroi.co.uk *Signs work*: "Andrew King."

KING, Anna Kathleen, BA (Hons); Jolomo Lloyds TSB Scottish Landscape Painting Award (2007). *Medium*: Oil. *b*: Lerwick, 27 Feb 1984. *m*: James Knowles. *Studied*: Duncan of Jordanstone College of Art, Dundee (2001-05). *Exhib*: Gallery Heinzel, Aberdeen; Open Eye Gallery, Edinburgh; Beaux Arts, Bath; 108 Fine Art, Harrogate. *Works in collections*: Private; corporate. *Address*: Waukford, Kirk Yetholm, Kelso TD5 8PG. *Email*: ak@anna-king.com *Website*: www.anna-king.com *Signs work*: "AK".

KING, Christabel Frances, BSc Hons (Lond) (1971), FSBA; Linnean Society Jill Smythies Award (1989); botanical artist in water-colour; part-time lecturer. *b*: London, 11 Mar 1950. *d of*: Prof. George King Reeves Research Fellow Surrey University. *Educ*: Sherborne School for Girls. *Studied*: scientific illustration: Middlesex Polytechnic (1973-74). *Exhib*: Messrs. Agnew (1980), Kew Gdns. Gallery (1993); Shirley Sherwood Gallery (2008-). *Works in collections*: RBG Kew, Hunt Botanical Institute, Shirley Sherwood. *Publications*: illustrations in Curtis's Botanical Magazine since 1975; also Flowering Plants of the World, ed. V.H. Heywood (Elsevier 1978); Kew Magazine Monographs: Echinocereus (1985), Pleione (1988, 2nd ed. 1999), Lewisia (1989), Galanthus (1999),Epimedium (2002), Lavandula (2004), Roscoea (2007), Hardy Heathers (2011); Africa's Mountains of the Moon by Guy Yeoman (Elm Tree Books 1989); Flowering Plants of the Falkland Islands by R.W. Woods (Falklands Conservation 2000); Edible Wild Plants and Herbs by Pamela michael (Grub Street 2007). *Clubs*: S.B.A. (Founder mem. 1985), F.L.S. *Address*: 149 Fulwell Park Ave., Twickenham, Middx. TW2 5HG. *Signs work*: "C.F.K." or "C.F. King."

KING, Gordon Thomas, FATG (Guild published Artist of the Year 1999-2000); artist in water-colour, oil; Chairman, FATG Artist Com. *b*: London, 6 Jun 1939. *m*: Mary. two *s*. one *d*. *Studied*: Carlton Studios, Reading University. *Exhib*: RA Summer Show, RI, Halcyon Gallery (ICC, Birmingham), Singer & Friedlander/Sunday Times, retrospective exhibition at Halcyon Gallery (London) March 2002. *Commissions*: 'Romance with Art', 'Drawn to Life'; over 60 limited edn. prints published; 3 special limited edition prints of Darcey Bussell, signed by both dancer and artist, published in aid of Alzheimer's Society. *Clubs*: Fine Art Trade Guild. *Address*: The Hollies, 21 Copthall Lane, Chalfont St. Peter, Bucks. SL9 0BY.

KING, John Gregory, SEA; artist in oil, water-colour, bronze. *b*: West Tytherley, 16 Apr 1929. *m*: Mary Rose. one *s*. one *d*. *Educ*: Canford School. *Studied*: briefly at Salisbury Art College. *Represented by*: The Osborne Studio Gallery, London; Ackermann and Johnson. *Exhib*: seventeen one-man shows in London. *Works in collections*: Alnwick Castle, Goodwood House, Gordon Highlanders Museum, Perth, Royal Fusilier Museum, Tower of London, HM The Queen, Lord Biddulph, Duke of Northumberland, Lord Radnor, Berkeley Castle. *Commissions*: Badminton, Royal Tournament, Sheik Mohamed, Tattersalls,

Ironmongers Co., Royal Bodyguard, Palace of Westminster, Household Cavalry, etc. *Publications*: illustrated: They Meet at 11, They Still Meet at 11, The Golden Thread, The Fox and the Orchid, Gallant Horses and Horsemen. *Official Purchasers*: Newbury Racecourse; The Palace of Westminster. *Works Reproduced*: Horse and Hound; I.P.C.Magazines; Illustrated London News. *Principal Works*: Dubai Millennium (Lifesize); H.M. The Queen Mother Lying in State. *Recreations*: hunting and shooting. *Clubs*: The Arts, The Farmers. *Address*: Church Farm House, West Tytherley, Salisbury, Wilts. SP5 1LB. *Email*: mek@chfarm.freeserve.co.uk *Signs work*: "John King."

KING, Phillip, CBE (1974), PRA, RA; sculptor in steel, bronze, fibreglass; Prof. of Sculpture, Royal Academy of Art, Prof. Emeritus, Royal College of Art. *b*: Tunis, 1934. married; one *s*. (decd). *Educ*: Mill Hill School; Christ College, Cambridge. *Studied*: St. Martin's School of Art. *Exhib*: Rowan Gallery London, Richard Fergen Gallery N.Y., Venice Biennale, Whitechapel Gallery London, Kunsthalle Mannheim. *Works in collections*: Tate Gallery, MOMA (NY), National Gallery of Australia, Kroller Muller Museum, New Museum of Contemporary Art Hiroshima, Yorkshire Sculpture Pk., Kunsthalle Mannheim, etc. *Publications*: The Sculpture of Phillip King by Tim Hilton. *Address*: c/o New Rowan Gallery, 25 Dover St., London W1X 3PA.

KING, Robert, RI (1970), RSMA (1985); Mem. Leicester Soc. of Artists (1960). painter in oil, water-colour; etcher and lithographer. *b*: Leicester, 28 Jun 1936. *s of*: Joseph T. King, engineer. *m*: Christine James. *Educ*: Fosse Boys' School, Leicester. *Studied*: Leicester College of Art (1956-58). *Exhib*: one-man shows, six at Gadsby Gallery, Leicester (1970-80) and Medici Gallery (1980-89); nine with Burlington Paintings (1989-2007); annually with RI, RA, RSMA, Leicester Soc. of Artists. *Works in collections*: Nottingham Educ. Com., Leicester Royal Infirmary, Leicester University, Fishmongers Hall London, Royal Yacht Squadron, Cowes, IOW. *Publications*: illustrated Denys Brook-Hart's 20th Century British Marine Painting; E.H.H. Archibald, The Dictionary of Sea Painters of Europe and America. *Address*: 2 Coastguard Cottages, Lepe, Exbury, Hants. SO45 1AD. *Website*: www.robertking.co.uk *Signs work*: "ROBERT KING."

KINGS, Tarka Huxley, MA; painter/printer in oil, silkscreen. *b*: London, 24 May 1961. *d of*: John Kings, literary editor, and Ann Huxley, author. *Educ*: St. Paul's Girls School. *Studied*: City and Guilds, RA Schools (1982-87, Peter Greenham, Norman Adams). *Exhib*: Creative Salvage (1985), RA, Gallery 24, Phoenix Gallery, Langton Gallery, St. Paul's, Cadogan Contemporary (1988), Bill Thomson Gallery, Rebecca Hossack Gallery (1991, 1993, 1994, 1995). Asst. to Leonard Rosoman, Lambeth Palace Chapel ceiling. *Works in collections*: private collections in USA and England. Artwork for films: 'Secrets' (Dir. Phillip Savile), 'The Dream' (Dir. Con Mulgrave). *Clubs*: Congress. *Address*: 61 Moscow Road, London W2 4JS. *Signs work*: "THK."

KINGSNORTH, Jean, NDD Painting and Lithography, BA Hons History of Art, Post-Grad Diploma in Embroidery and Textiles (Goldsmiths). *Medium*: watercolour, drawing, prints, paintings. *b*: London, 9 Apr 1933. *d of*: Percival Fraser. *m*: Tony Kingsnorth. one *d*. *Educ*: Tonbridge Girls Grammar School. *Studied*: Maidstone School of Art; Courtauld Institute, Goldsmiths College. *Exhib*: RA Summer Show; Camden Arts Centre; Anderson O'Day; Drew Gallery; Brewhouse Gallery (Taunton); University of Kent; Intertext (New Zealand); Commonwealth Inst.; Helios Galerie (Calais); Piece Hall Gallery (Halifax); Battersea Contemporary Art Fair; Orleans House, Hebden Bridge, Salisbury House, Enfield. *Works in collections*: private collections Britain, France, New Zealand, Egypt, Australia, USA, Japan. *Commissions*: Nokia; Royal Caribbean Cruise Line; Peter Millard & Ptnrs. *Publications*: 'Papermaking' by John Plowman (Apple). *Works Reproduced*: various paperpieces in John Plowman's 'Papermaking'; some catalogues. *Principal Works*: Tiryns; Winter Fields, Argos Fragment, Coastal Chart (multi-media). *Recreations*: gardening, travel, history. *Address*:

45 Edenbridge Rd, Enfield, Middx EN1 2LW. *Email*: jeanandtony.kingsnorth@yahoo.co.uk *Signs work*: 'JK' or 'JEAN KINGSNORTH'.

KINGSTON, Angela Hoppe, painter; Travelling Scholarship Corsham, Bath Academy of Art. *Medium*: oil, gouache, watercolour, pastel. *b*: Mumbles, nr. Swansea, 1936. *d of*: Hubert and Lottie Hoppe. *m*: Dr. Gordon (Ph.D.). three *s*. two *d*. *Educ*: Llwyn y Bryn High School, Swansea. *Studied*: Bath Academy of Art, Corsham, Wilts. (1955-58, Adrian Heath, Martin Froy, William Scott). *Exhib*: solo shows: Wolfson College, Oxford (2009); New Hall Art Collection, Murray Edwards College, Cambridge, Waterloo Gardens Tea House, Cardiff, RHS Flower Show Cardiff (2011); Aberglasney House, Aberglasney Gardens, Carmarthen, Wales (2012); Mother and Daughter, St Donats Arts Centre (2014); Taliesin Gallery, Swansea (2002), Mistral Gallery, London (1992), St. David's Hall, Cardiff (1991), University College, Cardiff. Group shows: Welsh Artist of the Year (2013), Royal Watercolour Society Wales (1973-present), Welsh Group (1975-present). *Works in collections*: Glynn Vivian A.G., Swansea, Cork University. *Clubs*: W.S.W., V.O.G.A.,The Welsh Group. *Address*: Monks, Dimlands Rd., Llantwit Major, Vale of Glam. CF61 1SJ, Wales. *Email*: angelakingston1@talktalk.net website: www.angelahoppekingston.com *Signs work*: "A. Hoppe Kingston."

KINMONT, Andrew, BAHons Fine Art 1st Class; associate member of Royal Birmingham Society of Artists (ARBSA). *Medium*: oil, acrylic, mixed media. *b*: Johannesburg, 8 June 1972. *m*: Sandra. two *d*. *Studied*: University of Wales (2004-2007); St Martins College, London (2009). *Represented by*: Royal Birmingham Society of Artists; Cloud Galleries (Chester, Brighton, Worthing); No Naked Walls Galleries (Chertsey, Bramley); Dot Art (Liverpool); Contemporary Art Holdings (Cirencester). *Exhib*: Royal Insitute of Oil Painters, Mall Galleries, London (2012, 2013, 2014); Royal Birmingham Society of Artists, Birmingham (2012, 2013, 2014); Palace Art Fair (2011, 2012); Great North Art Fair (2011, 2013); Windsor Art Fair (2012); Liverpool Art Fair (2012, 2013); One man shows: Yoredale Gallery, Bainbridge (2012); Queen Avenue Gallery, Liverpool (2012). Numerous group exhibitions. *Publications*: Cover of the prestigious "RISK" magazine (Nov 2011). *Principal Works*: Canyon Hues, Pale Light, Turners Pool. *Clubs*: Cheshire Artists Network. *Address*: Chester, CH4 9ES. *Email*: andrewkinmont@hotmail.co.uk *Website*: www.andrewkinmont.com *Signs work*: "KINMONT".

KINMONT, David Bruce, Was Senior member of the University of Bristol where, in 1971, he delivered the George Hare Leonard Memorial Lecture. Visiting professorships: George Washington University, Washington D.C. (1974); universities in Beijing, Shanghai (1986), and Hebei (1989), in China; and at the University of St. Petersburg in 1990, and the Gulbenkian Museum, Lisbon (1996); oil paintings, drawings and silk screen prints; sole dealer: J. K. Contemporary, 3 Cheyne Walk, London. *b*: Kent, 1932. *Educ*: St. John's College, Cambridge. *Exhib*: one-man shows include, Ferens City A.G., Hull (1963); City A.G., Bangor (1960); St. John's College, Cambridge (1969); Churchill College, Cambridge (1976); University of Durham (1981); University of Exeter (1986); Georges, Bristol (1987). *Address*: The Lent House, Clevedon Rd., Flax Bourton, Bristol BS48 1NQ. *Email*: andlent@btinternet.com

KIPNISS, Robert, Elected National Academy of Design, NYC; Royal Society of Painter-Printmakers, London; artist; Honorary Doctorates: Wittenberg University, Springfield, Ohio, USA (1979), Illinois College, Jacksonville, Illinois, USA (1989); Lifetime Achievement Award, Society of American Graphic Artists, NYC (2007). *Medium*: painter in oil, and printmaker. *b*: NYC, USA, 1 Feb 1931. *m*: Laurie Lisle. three *s*. one *d*. *Studied*: self-taught. *Exhib*: Old Print Shop, NYC; Redfern, London; Franklin Riehlman Gallery, NYC. *Works in collections*: The Metropolitan Museum NYC; Whitney Museum, NYC; The British Museum, London; The Fitzwilliam Museum, Cambridge, UK, Pinakotech der Moderne,

Munich; Biblioteque National de Paris; Victoria and Albert Museum, London etc. *Principal Works*: "Robert Kipniss: A Working Artists' Life", a memoir, published 2011 University Press of New England; "Robert Kipniss: Paintings & Poetry, 1950-1964" published The Artists Book Foundation (2013). *Clubs*: The Century, NYC, USA. *Address*: P.O. Box 112 Ardsley-on-Hudson, NY10503, USA. *Email*: rkipniss@msn.com *Website*: rkipniss.net

KIRBY, Michael, MFPS; fine art restorer, artist in oil. *b*: Farnham Common, Bucks., 30 Dec 1949. married. *s of*: H.Kirby, M.I.Nuc.E., LRSH. two *s*. two *d*. *Studied*: High Wycombe School of Art (1967-71) under G. G. Palmer, Romeo Di Girolamo, RBA, Eric Smith, RBA, RWS, Henry Trivick, RBA. *Exhib*: RBA, Open Salon, FPS, HUAS. *Address*: 30 Sycamore Rise, Bracknell, Berks. RG12 3BU. *Signs work*: "M. Kirby."

KIRK, Barry, NDD (1954), ARCA (1959), FRSA (1989); Travelling scholarship RCA (1959); painter, draughtsman; Canterbury College of Art 1959-1988 (Vice-Principal 1974-87, Principal 1987-88); thereafter full-time art practice. *Medium*: oils, watercolour. *b*: Deal, Kent, 17 Feb 1933. *s of*: Dr. Dudley Kirk, MB, ChB. *m*: Pleasance Kirk, ARCA, MSDC. two *s*. *Educ*: Westminster School. *Studied*: Canterbury College of Art (1950-54), RCA (1956-59). *Represented by*: Francis Kyle Gallery, W1. *Exhib*: RA, RWS, Francis Kyle Gallery (1997, 2001, 2004, plus 10 'theme' shows); Alwin Gallery (5 solo shows); Harley Gallery, Notts (2006); Emma Mason Gallery, Sussex (prints, 2012). *Works in collections*: V&A, Kent C.C., Canterbury C.C., Glasgow C.C. *Commissions*: private collectors. *Works Reproduced*: 'Etching', Julian Trevelyan (Studio); 'The Lair of the Leopard', Francis Kyle Gallery (Third Millennium Publishing). *Address*: 13 High St., Bridge, Canterbury, Kent CT4 5JY. *Signs work*: "Barry Kirk."

KIRKMAN, Susan, BSc Physics; no recognised qualifications in art. *Medium*: oil, pastel, etching. *b*: London, 13 Jan 1931. *d of*: Eleanor and Robert Downes. *m*: John Kirkman. *Educ*: Open College of the Arts; Filton College, Bristol (etching), and private tutor Robin Child. *Exhib*: National Print exhbns, Pastel Society, Discerning Eye, Royal West of England Academy, South West Academy, Victoria Gallery Bath, Wine Street Gallery Devizes, and many more. *Works in collections*: Textile Council, Welsh School of Architecture, private collections UK, USA, France, Holland, Germany. *Address*: Witcha Cottage, Ramsbury, Wilts, SN8 2HQ. *Signs work*: S.K. (paintings), S. Kirkman (prints).

KIRKPATRICK, Aidan, LTCL, FRSA; Goldsmiths' Travel Award (1976). *Medium*: pen and watercolour, oils, etching. *b*: Norwich, 13 Mar 1932. *m*: Frances Mary. two *s*. two *d*. *Educ*: Ulverston Grammar School, Glasgow School of Art. *Studied*: St.Benedicts Abbey, Fort Augustus. *Exhib*: RBA, RI, RSMA, Hesketh Hubbard, EAGMA (Mall Galleries); in Belgium at Ghent and Bruges (Oude Huis Longville). *Works in collections*: worldwide. *Commissions*: numerous. *Official Purchasers*: Barclays Bank, Local Government. *Recreations*: Chamber music playing (violin), and sailing. *Clubs*: East Anglian Group of Marine Artists (20 yrs Chairman). *Misc*: Aidan Kirkpatrick Studio, Langley Forge, Langley, Norwich NR14 6BW. *Email*: kirkpatricks@langleyforge.wanadoo.co.uk *Signs work*: 'AIDAN KIRKPATRICK'.

KIRKWOOD, John Sutherland, artist, mixed media, photography and etching. *b*: Edinburgh, 6 Apr 1947. *s of*: J. E. Kirkwood. *m*: Ines Santy. *Educ*: George Watson College, Edinburgh. *Studied*: Dundee College of Art; University of Edinburgh; Moray Ho Institute; Open University. *Exhib*: one-man shows: 57 Art Gallery, Edinburgh Printmakers Workshop, AIR Gallery, Talbot Rice Art Centre, Demarco Gallery, "Scottish Art Now"; Divided Selves - Scottish Self-Portraits 17th c. to Present, Wyfold Art Foundation 2006. *Works in collections*: SAC Loan, Hunterian Museum, University of Glasgow, Scottish Museum of Modern Art, Imperial War Museum, Edinburgh City Arts Centre, University of Edinburgh. *Publications*: Contemporary Paintings in Scotland (1995) - Bill Hare. *Address*: 15 Leopold Pl., Edinburgh EH7 5LB. *Signs work*: "J. S. Kirkwood."

KITCH, Nate, BS Hons Illustration (First); AOI Illustration Award (2013). *Medium*: Digital Collage & Illustration. *b*: Winchester, 27 Jan 1990. *Partner*: Elizabeth Batt. *Studied*: Southampton School of Art & Design (2009-2012). *Exhib*: Guildford House Gallery (2014); Nuneaton Museum and Art Gallery (2014); Blackpool and Fylde College (2014); AOI Illustration Awards - Swansea Metropolitan University & Somerset House (2013); Transmission - Quay Art (2013); Solent Showcase (2012); D&AD New Blood - Spitalfields Market (2012); Twenty Twelve Degree Show (2012); Pointless Posters (2012); Work in Progress - Bargate Gallery (2012); The Brooks - 10 days (2011). *Works in collections*: Oliver Sacks Series - AOI awards collection 2013. *Commissions*: Ted Baker; New Scientist; The Guardian; Times Higher Education; Wired; Shortlist; Globe & Mail; Four Four Two; Professional Manager; Ingenjören; Sekret Firmy. *Address*: 2 Wychwood Place, Winchester SO22 6BE. *Email*: nate@natekitch.com *Website*: www.natekitch.com *Signs work*: "Nate Kitch".

KITSON, Linda Francis, BA (1967), MA, RCA (1970); official war artist, Falkland Islands Task Force (1982); artist/tutor; Pres. Army Arts and Crafts Soc. (1983). *b*: London, 17 Feb 1945. *m*: Hon. Barnaby Howard (1996). *Educ*: Tortingdon Pk., nr. Arundel, Sussex. *Studied*: St. Martin's School of Art (1965-67), RCA (1967-70). *Exhib*: Workshop Gallery, Illustrators A.G., Imperial War Museum (Falkland's War Exhbn. UK tour), National Theatre, RA. *Works in collections*: Imperial War Museum, Fleet Air Arm Museum. *Publications*: Picnic (Jill Norman); The Falklands War, a Visual Diary (Mitchell Beazley); The Plague; Sun, Wind, Sand and Stars (Folio Soc.). *Clubs*: Chelsea Arts, Dover St, Arts Club. *Address*: Flat 3, 25 Onslow Sq., London SW7 3NJ. *Signs work*: "Linda Kitson."

KLEIN, Anita, BA Hons. (1983), MA (1985), RE (1991); Elected President of Royal Soc. of Painter Printmakers 2003; painter/printmaker. *Medium*: oil on board, drypoint, woodcut, acrylic on canvas, linocut, lithography. *b*: Sydney, Australia, 14 Feb 1960. *d of*: Prof. A.G. Klein. *m*: Nigel Swift. two *d*. *Educ*: Hampstead School. *Studied*: Chelsea School of Art (1978-79), Slade School of Fine Art (1979-83, Mick Moon, Paula Rego; 1983-85, Barto dos Santos, Stanley Jones). *Represented by*: Eames Fine Art, London, Advanced Graphics London. *Exhib*: ICA, Hayward, RI, Blond Fine Art; one-man shows: Eames Fine Art, London (main dealer), Cambridge Contemporary Art, Beaux Arts, Bath, Boundary Gallery, London, Advanced Graphics, London, Bankside Gallery, London, JBM Art Australia, Editions Vulfovitch, Sweden. *Works in collections*: ACGB, RE, Ashmolean Museum, University of Wales, British Museum, British Library. *Publications*: "20 Years of Printmaking" catalogue published by Advanced Graphics 2002; 'Anita Klein, Painter Printmaker' pub. Five Leaves Pub. (2006), 'Italian Angels' pub. Five Leaves Pub. (2009), 'Through the Loooking Glass' pub Five Leaves (2011). *Recreations*: studios in London and Tuscany. *Clubs*: Chelsea Arts Club. *Address*: 3 Vesta Court, City Walk, London SE1 3BP. *Email*: anita@anitaklein.com *Website*: www.anitaklein.com

KLEIN, Randy, ACGB. *Medium*: oil, prints, sculpture, artists' books. *b*: New York City, 14 May 1949. *s of*: Hyman Klein. *m*: Jennefer Klein. two *d*. *Educ*: Art Student League, New York, Pratt Institute . *Studied*: ASL of New York (1972-75), University of Chicago (1969-73), City & Guilds Welding and Foundry. *Represented by*: Artbridge, London . *Exhib*: include: Royal Academy, GX Gallery, Classense Ravenna, Midlands Art Centre (MAC), Windsor Arts Centre, Beaux Arts, Massimo Carasi (Milano), Galerie Jean-Pierre Lavignes, European Academy, Palazzo Vernazza, Lecce, St Giles Cathedral, Edinburgh, Rochester Cathedral. *Works in collections*: Tate, MoMA New York, New York Public Library Print Collection, British Library, V&A, Brooklyn Museum. *Commissions*: Giant Leaves, Peckham (2013), Nunhead Rail Station (2009), Paterson Park (2006), Friary Estate (2006), Gallions Mount School (2004), Mozart Estate (2002). *Publications*: Artists books include: 'Road', 'Inner Cities', 'Coney Island', 'Tales of N.Y.', 'Florida'. *Works Reproduced*: RIBA Public Sector Report, RIBA Housing, BBC News, BBC Scotland. *Principal Works*: Tree for

New Cross, London; Paterson Parasol; large scale public works. *Recreations*: music. *Address*: 30 Homeleigh Road, London SE15 3EE. *Email*: info@randyklein.co.uk *Website*: www.randyklein.co.uk *Signs work*: "KLEIN".

KNAPP-FISHER, John, RCA (1992); painter. *b*: London, 2 Aug 1931. *s of*: Prof. A.B. Knapp-Fisher, F.R.I.B.A. *m*: Sheila Basset (divorced). one *s*. one *d*. *Educ*: Eastbourne College. *Studied*: Maidstone College of Art (1951-53), Designer in Theatre. *Exhib*: extensively, England and Wales. *Works in collections*: National Museum of Wales, National Library of Wales, Tenby Museum, Beecroft A.G., Haverfordwest Museum, prize winning panel, Withybush Hospital Haverfordwest, Contemporary Art Soc. for Wales, major private collections worldwide. *Publications*: many Welsh publications. Featured on Welsh radio and television; wrote and illustrated John Knapp-Fisher's Pembrokeshire (Senecio Press, 1995, 2nd edition 2003). *Recreations*: boating. *Address*: Trevigan Cottage, Croesgoch, Haverfordwest, Pembrokeshire SA62 5JP. *Signs work*: "John Knapp-Fisher."

KNEALE, Bryan, RA Rome Scholar; sculptor in steel and all metals, wood, etc.; Mem. CNAA Fine Arts Panel, Royal College of Art, Professor of Sculpture, Royal Academy (1980-83), Head of Sculpture RCA (1985-90), Professor of Drawing (1990), Chairman ASG. *b*: Douglas, IOM, 19 Jun 1930. *s of*: W.T. Kneale, newspaper editor. *m*: Doreen Kneale. one *s*. one *d*. *Educ*: Douglas High School. *Studied*: Douglas School of Art (1947) under W. H. Whitehead; RA Schools (1948-52) under Philip Connard, Henry Rushbury. *Exhib*: John Moores, Art d'aujourd'hui, Paris, Battersea Park, Whitechapel Retrospective, Cardiff, Leics. Educ. Com., Whitechapel, City of London, Peter Stuyvesant, Southampton, British Sculptors, RA Holland Park, Royal Exchange Sculpt., Hayward Gallery, RA, London Group, Redfern Gallery, New Art Centre. *Works in collections*: Tate, Arts Council, CAS, WAG, Fitzwilliam Museum, BM, City Art Galleries of Manchester, Birmingham, Sheffield, Bradford, Wakefield, Leicester, York and Middlesbrough, Sao Paulo, Brazil, Museum of Modern Art, NY, National Galleries of NZ, Queensland and S. Australia, Manx Museum and A.G., Abbot Hall Gallery, Cumberland, Beaverbrook Foundation, Frederickton, Bochum Museum, W. Germany, Bahia Museum, Brazil. *Clubs*: Chelsea Arts. *Address*: 10a Muswell Rd., London N10 2BG. *Signs work*: "BRYAN KNEALE" (die stamp), "Bryan Kneale" (drawings, etc.).

KNEALE, William, Henry (Bill), DipAD, ATD, NAPA; Winner of Clwyd, North Wales and Oswestry Opens, NAPA International Louisiana-Col Art America Award, Prizewinner NAPA Open (2008, 2009); WSA Open (2010). *Medium*: acrylic paint, figurative impressions of people, places visited, landscapes and shorelines. *b*: Crewe, 19 Nov 1945. *s of*: Charles Henry Kneale. *m*: Dilys. one *s* (Dylan). one *d* (Lowri). *Studied*: Flint School of Art, Manchester and Liverpool Universities, studying art, industrial design and art education. *Exhib*: solo: Telford Town Centre, Theatre Clwyd, Royal Pavilion Llangollen, Rhyl Arts Centre, Oriel Ynys Môn Llangefni, and North Wales Hospital Artist Touring Show. Group: NAPA Opens in Durham, St.Ives and Liverpool, Glasgow Art Exposure Gallery; WSA Opens in Williamson Birkenhead. *Works in collections*: private collections Wales, England and Sri Lanka. *Commissions*: Impressions artists for Denbighshire's Heather and Hillforts Project. *Principal Works*: winning Open paintings: Pant March, Llandudno Promenaders, Barmouth, Barmouth Boats, Dee Salt Marsh-Edge, Sea Birds. *Clubs*: NAPA, WSA. *Address*: 12 MossleyMount, Penrhyn Bay, Llandudno, Conwy LL30 3HF. *Email*: bill_kneale@hotmail.com *Website*: www.billkneale.co.uk *Signs work*: 'W.H.Kneale'.

KNIGHT, Clifford (Edgar Levi), FRSA, PVPUA, AFAS; painter in oil, water-colour and mixed media, lecturer/demonstrator. *b*: Kempston, Beds., 8 Mar 1930. *s of*: the late H.R. Knight. *m*: Sherri. three *s-s*. two *s-d*. *Educ*: Kempston Secondary Modern School. *Studied*: under William Twybel, ARCA (1948-54), LCC Central School (1955-57, William Roberts, Merlyn Evans, Paul Hogarth, S.R. Badmin). *Exhib*: UA, NEAC; one-man shows, Upper St.

Gallery (1973), Carlton House Terr. (1983), Bedford, Luton, Letchworth, Northampton, Retford, Wellingborough, Welwyn Garden City, Abbotsholme School, Bedford School. *Works in collections*: Northampton, Luton and Letchworth A.Gs, Crown Commissioners, Texas Instruments, Beds. CC; private collections: USA, S. Africa, Paris, Canada. *Commissions*: Bedford, USA, Paris, London. *Works Reproduced*: Leisure Painter; London Today, TV. *Recreations*: looking at churches. *Misc*: studio address: Roe Farm, Cogenhoe, Northants, NN7 1LL. *Address*: 20 Hearnden Court, Henshaw Road, Wellingborough, Northants NN8 2BH. *Signs work*: "Clifford Knight."

KNIGHT, David Spencer, BA Fine Art; Best Painting, 9th Annual Xmas Exhibition, St.David's Hall; People's Choice, Welsh Artist of the Year (2000). *Medium*: oil, drawing, sculpture. *b*: Essex, 2 Mar 1965. *s of*: John Knight. *Educ*: Comp. *Studied*: University of Wales, Cardiff (1993-96). *Represented by*: Albany Gallery, Cardiff; Denise Yapp Fine Art, Monmouth. *Exhib*: Albany Gallery, Oriel Tri Penarth, Denise Yapp Gallery, Bay Art Gallery, Cardiff, St. David's Hall Cardiff, Campden Gallery, Glos., Wiseman Gallery, Oxford. *Commissions*: private, portraits. *Address*: 16 Larch House, Hollybush Est., Whitchurch, Cardiff, CF14 7EA. *Signs work*: "D.KNIGHT".

KNIGHT, Geraldine, National Diploma, Sculpture; RA Schools Cert.; Prix de Rome Sculpture. *Medium*: sculpture, casting in bronze, figurative, mostly animals. *b*: Horsham, Sussex, 8 Nov 1933. *d of*: Mr & Mrs Knight. *m*: Mark Churchill. *Educ*: Horsham High School for Girls. *Studied*: RA Schools; in Italy. *Represented by*: Sladmore Gallery, Bruton Place, London W1. *Exhib*: RA; Discerning Eye (exhbn. work chosen by W. Packer, also Prince of Wales); West of England Academy; Holly Snapp Gallery, Venice and others. *Works in collections*: worldwide. *Commissions*: mostly private. *Recreations*: travel, and visiting museums. *Clubs*: Chelsea Arts Club, Reynolds Club, RA Schools. *Misc*: overseas address: 595 Guidecca, Venice, Italy. *Address*: The Studio, Overford Farm, Wyham, Oxford OX2 8QN. *Email*: geraldine.knight@appleinter.net *Website*: www.geraldineknight.com *Signs work*: 'Geraldine Knight'.

KNIGHT, Marguerite, ASNS, BANA; DipFA (1969); BA (Hons) (1975); MFA (1981). *Medium*: mixed media, watercolour, acrylic, batik. *b*: Boston, MA, USA, 1946. *m*: Graham. one *s*. one *d*. *Studied*: Vesper George School of Art, Boston (1966-69); Aegean School of Fine Art, Greece (1969); Coleg Harlech, Wales (1970-71); University College of Wales (1972-75); Univ. of North Dakota (1978-81). *Exhib*: solo: Artifact, NYC (2013); Third Street Gallery, North Dakota, US (2007); Woolston Gallery, Bradford, UK (2002); Rood Contemporary Fine Art, Bristol (2002); Creative Space, Worthing (2002), and various group exhibitions in the UK and US. *Works in collections*: North Dakota Museum of Art permanent collection (2007). *Official Purchasers*: Minister of Culture, Greece. *Works Reproduced*: 'Modern Painters'; 'Aesthetica magazine' (2011, 2012). *Clubs*: National Society of Painters, Sculptors and Printmakers, Bath Area Network of Artists. *Misc*: Founder Member of the Bristol Folk House Co-operative (1996); Part-time lecturer at Bristol School of Art (painting, RWA building) since 1984, also other places in Bristol and Bath including the Open College of the Arts. *Address*: 13 Manor Court, Stapleton, Bristol BS16 1SY. *Email*: margueriteknight@talktalk.net *Website*: www.guildstudioartists.com *Signs work*: "M. KNIGHT".

KNIGHT, Sera Manioglu, BA Arch (1977); NAL (1989); SWA (2009); Frank Herring Award at SWA (2010). *Medium*: Watercolour, drawing, acrylic, mixed media. *b*: Ankara, Turkey, 9 Jun 1964. *m*: Duncan Knight. *Studied*: Architecture in Ankara, Turkey (1972-77). *Represented by*: several online galleries. *Exhib*: Numerous joint and solo exhibitions in UK, Turkey and Norway. *Works in collections*: Private and corporate collections in UK, Norway, Turkey, USA, Belgium, France and Australia. *Commissions*: Portraits and buildings. *Publications*: Featured in 'Women in Art' by Reinhard Fuchs. *Official Purchasers*: Garanti

Bankasi (Turkish Bank) purchased paintings for London office. *Works Reproduced*: Prints and cards in UK (www.redbubble.com); calandar and prints in USA; works used by advertising and charity organisations in USA, Brazil, Argentina and UK. *Clubs*: SWA - Society of Women Artists; WSA - Woking Society of Arts; SAS - Sunningdale Art Society; GAS - Guildford Art Society; FAS - Farnham Art Society; NAL - Norwegian Institute for Architetcts. *Misc*: Sera teaches drawing and painting and gives demos and workshops. *Address*: Springfield, Carthouse Lane, Horsell, Woking, Surrey GU21 4XS. *Email*: info@seraknight.co.uk *Website*: www.seraknight.co.uk *Signs work*: "SERA M. KNIGHT".

KNIGHT, Sophie, RWS(1992), ARWS (1990), BA (Hons.) Fine Art (1986), Post Grad. Dip. (1989); Ian Tragarthen Jenkins award (1986), David Murray Scholarship (1988), Erik Kennington award (1989), Hunting Group Student prize (1989), RWS award (1989); painter in water-colour and acrylic. *b*: London, 20 Mar 1965. *d of*: Terence Knight, art director/painter. *Educ*: The New School, Kings Langley. *Studied*: Herts. School of Art, St.Albans (1982), Camberwell School of Art and Design (1983-86), RA Schools (1986-89). *Exhib*: numerous exhbns. including RA Summer Exhbn. (1988), RWS Bankside Gallery SE1 (1988), Mall Galleries (1989), Whitechapel Open (1994); solo shows include Cadogan Contemporary (1991, 2000), Waterman Fine Arts (1993), The Unicorn Gallery, London SW10, Reutlingnen Gallery, Germany (1996). *Works in collections*: BM, The House of Lords, The New Parliamentary Building W1, TSB Bank. *Address*: 36 Ivinghoe Rd., Bushey, Herts., London WD2 3SW. *Signs work*: "Sophie Knight."

KNOWLER, Ann Patricia, SWA (1993); artist in oil and soft pastels; past member of SWA Council. *b*: Pinner, 3 Jun 1940. *m*: Jonathan Knowler. one *s*. one *d*. *Educ*: Northwood Secondary Modern School. *Studied*: F.E. classes and privately under Claude Murrills. *Exhib*: SWA Westminster Gallery. *Works in collections*: several private collections both in UK and abroad. *Commissions*: Artists' Impression-Ventnor Haven, commissioned by Mr. R.G. McInnes for IOW Council. *Publications*: 'Leisure Painter', and limited edition books: '50 Years Along the Undercliffe' of the IOW, by Robin McInnes, 'The Book of the Isle of Wight Coast'. *Clubs*: Weald of Sussex Art, The Adventurers Art, Assoc. of Sussex Artists. *Address*: Sundown, 7 Western Rd., Newick, E. Sussex BN8 4LE. *Email*: ann.knowler@talk21.com *Signs work*: "Ann Knowler."

KNOX, Jack, RSA (1979), RGI (1981), RSW (1987), Hon RIAS (1997), D.Litt (2004); painter in oil; Head of Painting, Glasgow School of Art (1981-92). *b*: Kirkintilloch, 1936. *s of*: Alexander Knox, tailor. *m*: Margaret. one *s*. one *d*. *Educ*: Lenzie Academy. *Studied*: Glasgow School of Art (1952-58, William and Mary Armour). *Exhib*: one-man shows: Scottish Gallery (1966, 1989), Demarco Gallery, Edinburgh (1969), Serpentine, London (1971), Glasgow School of Art (1982), Retrospective (1983), Glasgow A.Gs. (1990), Open Eye Gallery, Edinburgh (1991), Festival Exhbn., Open Eye Gallery, Edinburgh (1993, 1999, 2003). *Works in collections*: Scottish National Gallery of Modern Art, Manchester City A.G., Scottish National Portrait Gallery, Glasgow A.Gs., Arts Council, Otis Art Inst., Los Angeles. *Publications*: The Scottish Bestiary by George Mackay Brown (Charles Booth-Olibborn/Paragon Press, 1986), Lapotiniere and Friends by David and Hilary Brown (Century Editions/Random Century Group Ltd., 1990). *Address*: 66 Seafield Road, Broughty Ferry, Dundee DD5 3AQ. *Signs work*: "Jack Knox."

KNOX, Liz, PAI, PPAI; Diploma of Art (DA Edin. 1971), Diploma of Paisley Art Inst. (PAI, 2005); Winner of Aspect Prize (2003), University of Paisley Award (2006), The Bessie Scott Award (2004), Blythswood Square Quaich GSWA (2007); The Arnold Clark Award (2010); lecturer in Fine Art in Further Education (1983-2003); Concept Gallery Award (2013). *Medium*: gouache, oil, watercolour drawing. *b*: Glasgow, 20 Jan 1945. *m*: Peter Whittle. two *s*. *Educ*: Glasgow and Paisley. *Studied*: Edinburgh College of Art (graduated in Drawing and Painting, 1971). *Exhib*: House of Scientists, St.Petersburg, Russia;

Contemporary Fine Art, Eton; Medici Gallery, London; Royal Glasgow Institute of the Fine Arts; Paisley Art Institute; Duncan Campbell, London; The Edinburgh Gallery; Glasgow Art Club; Retrospective Exhibition, MacLaurin Art Galleries, Ayr (2012); Kelvingrove Art Galleries, Glasgow; Catto Gallery, London; Smithy Gallery, Glasgow. *Works in collections*: Paisley Museum & Art Galleries; The Royal Bank of Scotland, Edinburgh; Aspect Capital Ltd., London; ARA Interior Architectural Design, London; Biggart Baillie, Solicitors, Glasgow and Edinburgh, and private collections internationally. *Works Reproduced*: 'Retrospection' on cover of poetry book 'Paraphernalia' pub. Bloodaxe Books (2007). *Clubs*: Glasgow Art Club. *Misc*: painter of still life and land/townscape. *Address*: Jesmond, High Street, Neilston, Glasgow, G78 3HS. *Email*: lizknox1@ntlworld.com *Website*: www.lizknox.com *Signs work*: "L Knox".

KOCH, C.-Clarissa, ROI (2009), AROI (2006). *Medium*: painter (oils and classical drawing media). *b*: Austria, 13 Oct 1972. *Studied*: initially self-taught, 1997 UCL Medical School Anatomy for Artists, 1997-1999 Florence Academy of Art, Italy, 2001-2004 Summer Student with Nerdrum, Norway. *Exhib*: W H Patterson Fine Arts, London; Whittingdon Fine Art, Henley; Jonathan Cooper's Park Walk Gallery, London (solo and mixed); Solomon Gallery, Dublin; Anderson Fine Arts, Georgia; Panorama Museum, Germany; Palazzo Corsini, Florence. *Works in collections*: private/corporate. *Publications*: "Realism Revisited", catalogue, Panorama Museum, Germany (2003); "Tretyakov Gallery Magazine", Russia (02/2004); "Malenwie die Alten Meister", Die Salzburgerin, Austria (7/8, 2003). *Clubs*: Arts Club - Dover Street. *Address*: Unit 142, Battersea Business Centre, 99-109 Lavender Hill, London SW11 5QL. *Email*: cck_clarissa@hotmail.com *Website*: www.c-clarissakoch.com *Signs work*: "CCK" as monogram with Roman numerals, or "C.-CLARISSA KOCH".

KOJIMA, Yuriko, SBA; President of 'Atelier Bleuet' China Painting Club; Special Art Teacher of High School National Diploma 2006 SGM (RHS). *Medium*: water colour, china painting and instructor. *b*: 19 Apr 1949. *m*: Nobuo Kojima. one *s*. one *d*. *Studied*: Ekota Western Art Institute, Okura China Painting School; National Tokyo Liberal Arts University. *Exhib*: Nakayama Gallery (1999-2002); The Banquet of Flora (2000, 2002, 2004); SOGEI (2002); SBA (2003, 2004, 2006, 2007); Orpa Gallery (2003); RHS Lily Convention (2004); RHS Show (2006). *Publications*: The New Collection of Helleborus (Illust.); Christ Rose Gallery (Illust.); Musashin Rose Society's Quarterly Magazines (cover and column, 2000-2001); Ibaraki Rose Society's magazine (cover). *Principal Works*: Research and painting of Helleborus Species in Europe, Lilium. *Recreations*: gardening, reading, cinema, VTR. *Misc*: Volunteer of Hino City Rose and Hellebore Garden; Director of Japan Christmas Rose Society. *Address*: 20-17-2 Matsuyaga, Hachioji-shi, Tokyo 192-0354, Japan. *Email*: kojima@ttv.ne.jp *Signs work*: 'YURIKO'.

KOLAKOWSKI, Matthew Edmund Czeslaw, BA (1978), MA (1979); artist/painter in oil, sculptor mixed media; Foundation tutor, Woolwich College, and Central St. Martin's; visiting lecturer, Ravensbourne College; Head of Fine Art & Photography, Kensington & Chelsea College (2008-). *b*: Ruislip, Middx., 12 Mar 1956. divorced. one *s*. *Educ*: Douay Martyrs School, Ickenham. *Studied*: Watford School of Art (Michael Werner, Peter Schmidt, Charles Harrison), Ravensbourne College of Art (Brian Fielding, Victor Kwell, Kit Twyford), Chelsea School of Art (Anthony Wishaw, Ian Stevenson). *Exhib*: London Group since 1989; one-man show: Duncan Campbell Gallery (1993, 1995), Mid Pennine Art Centre (1997). *Clubs*: London Group (Vice-Pres. since 1996), elected President (1998). *Address*: Brightside Studios, 9 Dartford St., London SE17 3UQ. *Email*: matthewkolakowski@yahoo.co.uk *Signs work*: "M" in circle or triangle.

KONDRACKI, Henry Andrew, MA Fine Art. Selected Slade Prize in Fine Art (1984, 1985, 1986), South Bank Board Prize (1987), John Moores, LIverpool (second prize 1995),

Cheltenham Drawing Prize 1999, Hunting Group 2000, Hunting Art Prize 2004, Singer Friedlander Prize (second 2004). *Medium*: oil on canvas. *b*: Edinburgh, 13 Feb 1953. *s of*: Pavel Kondracki. *m*: Sara. three *s*. *Educ*: Bellevue School, Edinburgh. *Studied*: Slade School of Fine Art (1982-1986). *Exhib*: Vanessa Deveureux Gallery (1987, 1989), William Jackson Gallery (1991, 1994), Flowers East Gallery (1995, 1996, 1998, 2001), Flowers West Gallery, California (1998, 2000), Flowers Central (2003), Flowers New York (2007), Open Eye Gallery, Edinburgh (2004, 2009), Lemon Street Gallery, Cornwall (2008), Art Space Gallery, London (2008), Scottish Gallery, Edinburgh (1995, 2010, 2012). *Works in collections*: British Council, ACGB, Guildhall, London, Granada Foundation, Manchester, University College London, Manchester A.G., City Art Centre, Edinburgh, Glasgow Museums. *Commissions*: private commissions. *Publications*: Contemporary Scottish Painting by Bill Hare, Paint by Jeffrey Camp. *Works Reproduced*: University of Edinburgh, catalogues. *Address*: 20 Marchmont Cres., Edinburgh EH9 1HL. *Signs work*: "H. Kondracki."

KORALEK, Paul George, CBE, RA, RIBA, FRIAI, AADipl (Hons); architect; Director, Ahrends Burton and Koralek. *Medium*: architecture. *b*: 7 Apr 1933. *s of*: Ernest Koralek. *m*: Jennifer Chadwick. one *s*. two *d*. *Educ*: Aldenham. *Studied*: architecture: Architectural Assoc. *Exhib*: Heinz Gallery, RIBA (1982), RA Summer Show (annually since 1987). *Publications*: Monograph "Ahrends Burton and Koralek". "Collaborations. The Architecture of ABK". *Address*: Unit 1, 7 Chalcot Rd., London NW1 8LH. *Email*: abk@abklondon.com *Website*: www.abk.co.uk

KOROSHILOV, Valery, winner: Artist of the Year (2010). *Medium*: oil. *b*: Chelabinsk, Russia, 1961. *m*: Heleni Tsosko. two *s*. *Represented by*: Casa del Arte Gallery, London. *Exhib*: Artuur Baldinger Gallery, Amsterdam (1992); Albemarle Gallery, London (1997); International Art Expo, New York (2003); International Kunar Even, Antwerp (2005); Colomb Art Gallery, London (2010). *Works in collections*: The Slade and University College, London; Standard Chartered Bank, UK. *Commissions*: P&O Cruises, UK; Smith & Williamson, UK. *Official Purchasers*: Law Chambers, 39 Essex Street, UK; Castle D'Aertrycke, Belgium. *Works Reproduced*: Brit Art Directory (2001). *Principal Works*: "The Day of the Interview" private coll, UK. *Address*: 3 Ashbrook Road, London N19 3DF. *Email*: valery@koroshilov.com *Website*: www.koroshilov.com *Signs work*: "VK".

KOWAL POST, Christine, RCamA (2005); BA (Joint Hons); prizewinner, John Moore's Liverpool. *Medium*: sculpture: polychromed woodcarvings. *b*: Nigeria, 31 Dec 1951. *s of*: Jan Kowal O.B.E., Pamela Dunroe. *m*: Rory Post. *Educ*: Brigidine Convent, Denbigh. *Studied*: University College of Wales, Aberystwyth; Accademia Delle Belle Arti, Florence. *Exhib*: widely in Britain and abroad, including RA; Walker Art Gallery, Liverpool; Manchester and Brighton City Art Galleries; Tate Liverpool; Kiss Untergroeningen and Stadtmuseum, Beckum, Germany. *Works in collections*: Walker Art Gallery, Liverpool; Williamson Art Gallery, Birkenhead; Manchester City Art Gallery; Liverpool University; Villa Merkel Esslingen. *Commissions*: Ashworth Hospital, Merseyside; Glan Clwyd NHS Trust; Wrexham Maelor NHS Trust; Broomfield Hospital, Essex. *Publications*: catalogues of solo and group exhibitions. *Email*: ckowalpost@talk21.com *Website*: www.christinekowalpost.com *Signs work*: 'C.Kowal Post'.

KOWALSKY, Elaine Gloria, Dip of Art, MA; artist in relief, litho, ceramics; Henry Moore Fellow in Printmaking, Leeds Polytechnic. *b*: Winnipeg, Manitoba, 24 Sep 1948. *d of*: Rosemary A. Kowalsky, abstract painter. *m*: Elton Bash, painter. *Educ*: Charleswood Collegiate, Winnipeg. *Studied*: University of Manitoba, St. Martin's School of Art, Brighton Polytechnic; MA Visual Theory University of East London. *Exhib*: RA, and numerous one-man shows. *Works in collections*: V&A, Birmingham A.G., Worcester A.G., Leeds A.G., Manchester A.G., Canada Council Art Bank, University of Manitoba, National Gallery of

Australia, Smithsonian Inst. *Commissions*: banners, Dover Castle. *Publications*: Wood engraving and the Woodcut in Britain c.1890-1990, J. Hamilton (Barrie & Jenkins Ltd. 1994). *Address*: 27 Aberavon Rd., London E3 5AR. *Signs work*: "Elaine Kowalsky."

KOZARZEWSKA, Magda, LCAD (1977), SIAD (1977), B.A.Hons. (1981); artist in oil, charcoal, pencil. *b*: Warsaw, 7 Oct 1952. *d of*: Zbigniew Kozarzewski. *m*: Jonathan Goldberg. one *s*. *Educ*: Grammar School, Warsaw. *Studied*: Chelsea School of Art (1974-77), Slade School of Fine Art (1977-81, Prof. Sir L. Gowing, Patrick George, Euan Uglow). *Exhib*: solo shows: Polish Cultural Inst. (1975), Sue Rankin Gallery (1988), Thackeray Gallery (1991); major retrospective, Polish Cultural Inst. (1991), Thackery Gallery (1993), Duncan Campbell Fine Art (1995, 1997), Konrad Bayer Gallery, Munich (1996); group shows: Hayward Gallery (1982), N.P.G. (1986), Zacheta Gallery, Warsaw (1991), RA (1995), Konrad Bayer Gallery, Munich (1995), Polish Cultural Inst., London (1996). *Works in collections*: UK, Europe, USA, Canada, S. Africa. *Address*: 6 Lidcote, Dunton, Buckingham MK18 3RY. *Email*: magdakoza52@yahoo.co.uk *Website*: www.magdakozarewska.co.uk *Signs work*: "M.K." or "Kozarzewska."

KREYMANN, Ute-Marie, MA Fine Art. *Medium*: mixed media, sculpture. *b*: Leipzig, 24 May 1958. *m*: John Sexton. *Studied*: MA Fine Art UEL 1998; Middlesex University: 1989 BA Interior Design, 1990, transferred to Fine Art BA, 1993. *Represented by*: Wiebke Morgan Gallery, 6 Cyprus Street, London E2, www.wiebkemorgan. *Exhib*: solo: London 2010 67A Gallery; 2003 Wiebke Morgan; 2002 St. Leonards Church, Spitalfields festival; 1995 Berlin: Gallerie Unwahr. Group: 2011 67A Gallery, 2008 Grand Valley University USA; 2011-2002 Wiebke Morgan; 2000 Avivson Gallery, Paris; Hackney Empire Theatre; 1998 St. Pancras Chambers; National Trust, Sutton House; 1997 Southgate Studios, London, Artists Printing; Round Chapel London; Waterman's Art Gallery; 1996 Mall Gallery. *Works in collections*: private. *Commissions*: private. *Publications*: 'Time Out' December 2002, Martin Herbert; 1998 Catalogue Essay Tom McCarthy; 1995 Berliner Zeitung. *Official Purchasers*: Hurlingham & Chelsea School (2004); Winton School (1999) Outdoor sculpture, permanent. *Misc*: 1991-1997 'Art & Place' Founding Member, projects relating to environmental and cultural issues, formed after 1989 Landscape & Sculpture Symposium, Manchester. *Address*: City Studios, 67a Dalston Lane, London E8 2NG. *Email*: ute.kreymann@talk21.com *Signs work*: "UTE KREYMAN".

KRUT, Ansel Jonathan, MA (1986), BFA (1982); painter in oil; awarded Rome prize (1987). *b*: Cape Town, 1959. *s of*: Dr. Louis Harold Krut. *m*: Felicity Powell. two *d*. *Studied*: University of the Witwatersrand (1979-82), RCA (1983-86). *Exhib*: RA, John Moores, London Group, Cité des Arts, Paris; one-man shows Fischer Fine Art (1989, 1990), Gillian Jason Gallery (1994), Jason and Rhodes Gallery (1995, 1996). *Works in collections*: Arts Council London, British Council, Government Art Collection, Harris Museum of Art Preston, Mercer A.G. Harrogate, Ben Uri Collection, Johannesburg A.G. *Address*: c/o Jerwood Gallery, Roack-a-Nore Road, Hastings, East Sussex TN34 3DW. *Signs work*: "A. Krut."

KUBECKI-PEARCE, Terence Peter, DipAD. *Medium*: oil, acrylic, drawing, prints (etchings). *b*: Chingford, Essex, 11 Nov 1947. *s of*: Mary Kubecki & Harry Pearce. *m*: Cherry Storer. two *s*. two *d*. *Educ*: McEntee School, Walthamstow. *Studied*: Walthamstow School of Art: Painting (main), Printmaking/Lino (secondary); Camden Evening Inst (now Westminster Kingsway College, 1993, studied etching with Peter Freeth). *Exhib*: RA Summer Exhbn (1991, 93, 94, 97, 98, 2000, 01, 04, 07, 08); RWA (1994, 95, 97, 98, 2000, 01, 02, 03, 05, 06, 07, 08); National Print Exhbn. (1995, 2002, 03, 04); Discerning Eye (1997, 2001, 2003-09); NEAC (1998, 2001, 02); Hunting Prize (RCA, 1999, 2000, 01, 04, 05); RWA Print Open (1997, 2004); Originals (2006, 2008, 2009); Laing Landscape Exhbn (2001, 02); Lynne Painter Stainers Prize Exhbn. (2009); one-man show Beecroft Gallery,

Westcliff-on-Sea, plus many other exhibitions, most recently of prints. *Recreations*: astronomy and optics. *Clubs*: invited to join 12PM (East Anglian Print Makers Group) 1999, joined Camden Print Makers (2004). *Misc*: continued painting after art school, taught in secondary school for a while then turned to making and selling astronomical reflecting telescopes; since 1994 has concentrated on exhibiting prints and developing etching style. *Address*: 66 Barrett Rd., Walthamstow, London E17 9ET. *Email*: enquiries@terrykubecki.co.uk *Website*: www.terrykubecki.co.uk *Signs work*: 'Terence Pearce' (paintings); 'Terry Kubecki (prints); 'TKP' (drawings/sketches).

KUELL, Victor John, ARCA (1950), Hon. Mem. London Group (elected 1980, Honorarium 1998); RCA Awards: Perspective Drawing Prize; Air Malta Award, 1st International Biennale, Malta. *Medium*: artist in acrylics and water-colour. *b*: Andover, Hants, 28 Aug 1924. *s of*: Ernest Hector & Clarissa Kuell. *m*: Margaret. one *s*. one *d*. *Educ*: Simon Langton, Canterbury. *Studied*: Bromley School of Art (1938-42), RCA (1947-50). *Exhib*: London Group (1977-2012), RA (1987-2003), Galerie Espace Laser, Paris (1990), Galerie Metropolis, Geneva (1985), Société de l'Art Contemporain, Paris (1984), International Biennale of Malta (Award winner, 1995), Galerie Carre D'Or Paris (2000), The Green Space, Dulwich, London; Centre Culturel Christiane Peugeot (Paris, 2005), Chateau D'Auvers (2008), Highgate Scientific and Literary Institute, London (2009), Galerie Mouvances, Paris (2010), Topphoto Gallery, Edenbridge, Kent (Retrospective (2011), Who's Who Art Club International, Galerie 60, Giverny (2012). *Works in collections*: James Capel, N.Y., Mitsui London. *Publications*: Les Editions Art et Image du Monde, The London Group - Visual Arts from 1913. *Address*: 45 Hever Rd., Edenbridge, Kent TN8 5DH. *Email*: margaret_kuell@yahoo.co.uk *Signs work*: "Vic Kuell."

KUHFELD, Peter, BA, NEAC; artist in oil, pencil and charcoal. *b*: Glos., 4 Mar 1952. *m*: Cathryn Showan, artist. two *d*. *Educ*: Gateway School, Leicester. *Studied*: Leicester College of Art (1972-76), R.A. Schools (1977-80, Peter Greenham, Norman Blamey). *Exhib*: RA, NEAC, RP, RBA, RWA, NPG, Windsor Castle, Hampton Court Palace, Accademia Italiana, New Grafton Gallery, Agnews, W.H. Patterson, Christie's, Fine Art Soc., National Gallery of Wales, Cardiff, Brian Sinfield Fine Art, Petley Fine Art; Crossgate Gallery, Kentucky; Everard Read Fine Art, Johannesburg, South Africa. *Works in collections*: HM The Queen, HRH Prince of Wales, Baring Bros., Lazards, Cable and Wireless, Hammerson Group, National Trust, Elizabeth Greenshield Foundation, Hambros, Mercury Asset Management, Sabanci Bank. *Address*: The Corner House, Upper Bridge St., Wye, Kent TN25 5AW. *Signs work*: "Kuhfeld."

KURTZ, Peter Felix Magnus von, MA, BA (Hons), FRSA. *Medium*: photography, installation, multimedia, paint. *b*: Berlin, 15 Mar 1969. *Studied*: University of Lancaster. *Represented by*: Highgrove Fine Arts, London. *Exhib*: UK, Germany, Australia, USA. *Works in collections*: UK, Germany, Switzerland, Australia, USA. *Commissions*: private collectors. *Publications*: (books, magazines, internet) including: Skin Two, Marquis, EPS, 'A' Magazine, Secret Fetish Photo Anthology, Bloody & Dishonour (Satanic Sluts), Arena. *Clubs*: Fine Art Trade Guild. *Address*: Highgrove Fine Arts, PO Box 22894, London NW9 6ZE. *Email*: pfkproductions@yahoo.com *Website*: www.fetishfoto.co.uk *Signs work*: 'Peter Felix Kurtz', 'Peter Kurtz', 'Kurtz', 'PFK'.

KYNOCH, Kathryn Marie, RGI (1994); Latimer Award, RSA; Armour Award, PAI; artist in oil and pastel. *b*: Portobello, Midlothian, 18 Aug 1941. *m*: Michael Andrew Tribe. *Studied*: Glasgow School of Art (1959-64). *Exhib*: RGI, RSA, PAI, RSPP. *Works in collections*: Glasgow A.Gs, Kelvingrove, Hunterian Art Gallery, Glasgow University, Dover House, Whitehall; private collection in Britain and USA. *Commissions*: include RSA Music and Drama, Glasgow, Edinburgh, Stirling, Strathclyde and Leicester Universities. *Clubs*: Glasgow Art. *Address*: 2/L, 12 Clouston St, Glasgow G20 8QT.

KYRIAKIDES, Yvonne, MPhil (RCA); BA (Hons) Fine Art; Saatchi & Saatchi Prize for Painting. *Medium*: drawing, prints, photography, text. *b*: London, 25 Oct 1950. *d of*: Nicholas Christopher Kyriakides. one *s*. one *d*. *Studied*: University of Nottingham (English); Goldsmith's College, London (Fine Art); RCA (Painting). *Exhib*: RA; ICA London; Whitechapel Gallery; Eagle Gallery; Drawing Research Centre, RCA; Queen's Theatre, London; Peterborough Museum and Art Gallery; Sainsbury Centre for Visual Arts, UEA; Kunstlerwerstatt Barnhofwestend, Berlin; Sharjah Biennale, UAE. *Works in collections*: RCA; St.Anne's College, Univ. of Oxford; Peterborough Museum; Annenberg Rare Book & Manuscript Library, PA, USA. *Publications*: 'My Czech Grandmother. A Story' imprint by ImageWord with EMH Arts, London. Commentary for 'Media, Culture and Society' Vol 27 No3. *Principal Works*: drawing series 'Heads' and 'Rivers'; Complicite Sketchbook project; Artist books. *Recreations*: swimming, sailing, choral singing, cinema, theatre. *Misc*: conference profile; drawing collaboration with Theatre de Complicite', 'Streets of Crocodiles' and 'Mnemonic'. *Address*: St.John's College, University of Oxford, OX1 3JP. *Email*: y.kyriakides@blueyonder.co.uk

L

LABAN, Keith Maurice, Surrey Dip. (1970); artist in water-colour; Sir Alec Issigonis Prize for Art (1969). *b*: London, 22 May 1949. *m*: Vivienne Jane Laban (née Ferne). *Studied*: Reigate College of Art (1996-70). *Exhib*: mixed exhbns. London, UK, Holland. *Address:* 2 Bolsover Grove, Merstham, Redhill, Surrey RH1 3NU. *Signs work*: "Laban."

LAGADEC, Jean, Brevet-Mart. *Medium*: acrylic and sculptured paper. *b*: Paris, 12 May 1941. *s of*: Francois & Ruth Lagadec. two *s*. one *d*. *Educ*: Niveau Brevet. *Studied*: College Jean-Saures. *Represented by*: Quayside Gallery. *Exhib*: worldwide. *Works in collections*: private and corporate (Regency, Genesis, etc.) in Africa, Europe, Australia and USA. *Commissions*: private and corporate. *Publications*: Art East; Sticks, etc. *Works Reproduced*: in magazines and newspapers. *Principal Works*: Salomé; Discobolus; Kouros; Ophelia. *Recreations*: martial arts; travelling. *Misc*: autodidact. *Address:* 87 High Street, Ramsey, Cambs. PE26 1BZ *Email*: j.lagadec@talktalk.net *Signs work*: 'Jean Lagadec'.

LAGO, Darren, BA (Fine Art), MA (Fine Art); sculptor in installation and object based artworks; Tutor, Kingsway College, London. *b*: 22 Sep 1965. *Educ*: King Edward VI School, Lichfield. *Studied*: Portsmouth University (Don Hopes), Chelsea School of Art and Design (Shelagh Cluett). *Exhib*: New Contemporary ICA London, Annely Juda Gallery. *Works in collections*: Annely Juda Fine Art Gallery, Unilever House, Unilever plc. *Address:* c/o Annely Juda Fine Art, 4th Floor, 23 Dering Street, London W15 1AW.

LAI, William Sui Khee, RMN; Special Distinction at International Art Biennale, Malta (1999); Prizewinner, International Amateur Art Exhbn, London (1976) The Artist; Short-listed from 10,000 entries for Art from the Heart (News of the World) (1992). *Medium*: oil, watercolour, sculpture, drawing, gouache, chinese ink, acrylics, pastel, mixed media, sculpture: stone & wood. *b*: Singapore, 14 Sep 1941. *s of*: Lai Chek Meng & Lim Kim Hoon. *m*: Maria Encina Gomez Robles. two *s*. *Educ*: St.Andrew's, Singapore. *Studied*: self-taught; evening classes (Adult Education), A Level Art. *Exhib*: RA (1993, 2001); Ann Bellion Gallery (1994, 1995); Malta International Biennale (1995, 97, 99); Library/Museum Surrey 3-man Show (William Lai, Nai Swee Leng, Lye Swee Koon) (1996); Nanyang Academy, Singapore, solo show (1997); Oriental City, London (2001); group shows: AOI, Mall Galleries (1998, 99, 2000, 2007); Goldmark Gallery, Leics. (2002); The Gallery, Cork St., London (2002, 03); Galleriat Art, Kirkcudbright, Scotland (2003); Brave Destiny: Williamsburg Historical Art Centre, NY (2003); Diego Victoria Fine Art, Miami, USA (2003); Lauderdale House, Highgate, London (2004); Obsidian Art Centre, Bucks (2005); Riva Museum, Italy (2005); solo exhbn, paintings and sculptures, Windsor St.Gallery, Chertsey, Surrey (2006); Lofthouse

Gallery, Germany (2005); Mall Galleries (sculpture, 2007); Newdays Gallery, New Malden, Surrey (2008); Harvey Gallery, Guildford, Surrey (2009); Borde Hill Garden, Surrey (2009); Denbies, Dorking, Surrey (2009); Polesden Lacey, Great Bookham, Surrey; Art in the Park, Weybridge, Surrey (2009); Artful Gallery, Surrey (2010); Beaulieu, Hampshire (2011); Outsidein online gallery(2012), Talk at RA, London, Outsidein, West Sussex Open, Pallant House Gallery, Chichester; Galleri Vox, Norway touring to Netherland and Sweden (2013). *Works in collections*: private in UK, USA, Peru, Spain, Norway, Singapore. *Commissions*: none taken. *Publications*: RA Catalogues (1993, 2001); Malta International Biennale catalogues (1995, 97, 99); Malta Biennale Dictionary, Malta Biennale Book 1 (2001); Inscape, AOI (2005). *Principal Works*: Nude Candle Dance; Rehearsal; Shepherdess; Head (Sculpture). *Recreations*: walks, reading, swimming, chess, travels. *Clubs*: Society: Art of Imagination (AOI) (2002-07), Surrey Sculpture Society (2009-2012). *Address:* 276 Woodham Lane, New Haw, Addlestone, Surrey KT15 3NT. *Email*: william_suikhee_lai@yahoo.co.uk Website: www.outsidein.org.uk/william-lai *Signs work*: 'William Lai', 'W.Lai'.

LAIN, Graham E.W., SGFA; retired architectural technician and self taught artist in water-colour, pen and ink. *b*: Wymondham, Norfolk, 18 Sep 1938. *m*: Betty. one *s-s*. one *d*; one s-*d*. *Exhib*: one-man shows biennially. *Address:* Nesbit Cottage, 2 Granary Loke, Spooner Row, Wymondham, Norfolk NR18 9JW. *Signs work*: "G.L."

LAKE, C. Elisabeth Matheson, RMS (1989), HSF (1982-95), NDD (1960); miniature painter (subject, interiors). *Medium*: watercolour and oil. *b*: Norwich, 12 Apr 1939. *d of*: James Matheson Fleming, MRCS, LRCP. *Partner*: James Hearfield. one *s*. three *d*. *Studied*: West of England College of Art (1957-60). *Exhib*: HS (1982-95), RA Summer Exhbn. (1986), many N. American and Canadian exhbns. (1985-89), RMS (1984-). *Works in collections*: England, Scandinavia, N. America. *Publications*: Books, magazines. *Works Reproduced*: RA Christmas card 1986. *Address:* White Cottage Hollow Marsh, Farrington Gurney, Somerset BS39 6TX. *Signs work*: "CEML" (monogram).

LAKEY, Antony William Albert, BA (Hons) Fine Art, Painting. *Medium*: photography and film, oils, drawing. *b*: Elgin, Scotland, 11 May 1981. *s of*: Michael & Elisabeth Lakey. *Partner*: Amanda Dobratz. *Studied*: Northbrook College of Art and Design (2000-2003), Maidenhead College of Art and Design (1999-2000). *Exhib*: 2006: RSA Building, Edinburgh, SSA Group Show; Threshold Artspace, Perth, Group Film Show; Glasgow Film Theatre, Glasgow; Cameo Cinema, Edinburgh; Peacock Visual Arts, Aberdeen. 2005: Bistro du Sud, Glasgow; Transmission Gallery, Glasgow; Kazoo Club, Bar Fly, Glasgow. *Works in collections*: private collections of Oxford University Air Squadron, The Beales family, Henley-on-Thames, Clive Hemsley. *Commissions*: Oxford University Air Squadron, the Beales family, Clive Hemsley, the Corcoran family. *Publications*: The Henley Standard, The Worthing Herald. *Principal Works*: "I Think..." (2003), "Madison" (2004), Film. *Address:* 2/2, 70 Landressy Pl., Bridgeton, Glasgow G40 1HF. *Email*: awalakey@hotmail.com *Website*: www.myspace.com/Antony_Lakey *Signs work*: "LAKEY".

LAKIN, Michael, SBA, SFP; Society of Botanical Artists Diploma; RHS Silver Medal (2014). *Medium*: watercolour. *b*: Melbourne, 27 Oct 1948. *m*: Linda Jane Lakin. one *s*. *Studied*: private tuition by Anne Marie Evans. *Exhib*: SBA (2003-2010, 2012, 2013); SFP (2011, 2012); Royal Horticultural Society, London (2014); Silver Medal - Palmengarten, Germany (2010). *Works in collections*: private collections in France, South Africa, Australia. *Commissions*: private commissions. *Publications*: Author: "A-Z of Botanical Flowers"; "Ready to Paint Botanical Flowers" (pub. Search Press). *Address*: 1 Whitehollows Cottage, Box Lane, Ticknall, Derbyshire DE73 7JN. *Email*: michael.lakin579@btinternet.com *Website*: michaellakinart.co.uk *Signs work*: "Lakin".

LALLY, Richard, painter in oil, pastel and water-colour. *b*: London, 2 Oct 1928. *s of*: A. R. Lally. *Educ*: Brixton College of Building and Architecture (1942-45). *Studied*:

Hammersmith School of Art (1955-59, Leon Underwood, Dennis Gilbert). *Exhib*: one-man shows, Real Club Nautico, Tenerife (1961), Manolette Gallery, Richmond (1977); ROI, NS, UA, SWLA. *Works in collections*: private collections in Rio de Janeiro, Scotland, Zurich, England, USA, Isle of Man. *Commissions*: Many private. *Principal Works*: animals and landscapes, themed abstracts. *Address*: Strathcroy Studio, Drumbeg, Lairg, Sutherland, Scotland IV27 4NG. *Email*: r.lally30@yahoo.com *Signs work*: "LALLY."

LAMAN, Amanda Karen Kirkland, Dip SLm, MCMI. *Medium*: miniatures & silhouettes, oil, watercolour. *b*: Newcastle, 23 Oct 1951. *d of*: A.C.K.Laman, Naval Commander. *Studied*: private tuition. *Exhib*: RA Summer Exhbn (1996, 97, 2001, 2006); Mall Galleries; Gallery 47; Chichester, Preston, Leeds, Kent, Aberdeen, Japan, Tasmania, Washington USA. *Works in collections*: private collections UK and overseas. *Commissions*: commissions undertaken. *Principal Works*: still life and animal portraiture. *Recreations*: ceramic repair, gardening. *Address:* 2a Callow Street, Chelsea, London SW3 6BE.

LAMB, Elspeth, DA (Glas.) (1973), HDipAD (Manc.) (1974), ARSA (1990); lecturer/printmaker in printmaking, papermaking, drawing; Lecturer in drawing and painting, Edinburgh College of Art. *b*: Glasgow, 28 Mar 1951. *d of*: John Cunningham Lamb, accountant. *Educ*: Kings Pk. Senior Secondary School, Glasgow. *Studied*: Glasgow School of Art (Philip Reeves), Manchester Polytechnic, The Tamarind Inst. of Lithography, University of New Mexico, U.S.A. (Lynn Allen). *Exhib*: Mercury Gallery (1988, 1990), Conservative Management (1990), Marlborough Graphics (1991), Glasgow Print Studio (1990). *Works in collections*: SAC, British Council, Japanese Consular Coll., Perth A.G., Glasgow A.G., City Arts. *Address:* Bon a Tirer Editions, 15 E. Campbell St., Glasgow G1 1DG.

LAMB, Thomas, BA Fine Art Painting, MA Fine Art Drawing; Sainsbury Scholarship Painting and Sculpture (2001-2003, BSR). *Medium*: painter. *b*: Lincolnshire, 4 Apr 1978. *s of*: Michael and Anne Lamb. *m*: Yuki Lamb. *Studied*: Wimbledon School of Art, London (1997-2001). *Represented by*: Browse & Darby, London. *Exhib*: British School at Rome (2003); Braccio di Carlo Magno, Piazza San Pietro, Vatican City (2002), Lethaby Gallery, London (1999), Fukuoka Asian Art Museum, Japan (2005), Hyogo Prefectural Museum of Art, Japan (2005), Estorick Collection of Modern Art (2006), Browse & Darby (2008, 2011, 2014), Mall Galleries (2013), The Collection, Lincoln (2012), RWS Bankside Gallery (2013). *Works in collections*: private collections. *Publications*: The British School at Rome Fine Arts (2001-02, 2002-03), Accademia di Bella Arti 'O' Europa (2002), 'Renascence' Hyogo International Competition of Painting (2005), Yomiuri Times (13 May 2005). *Address:* Rose Cottage, Belleau, Lincolnshire, LN13 0BW. *Email*: lambthomas@gmail.com *Website*: www.thomaslamb.com

LAMB, Yuki, BA (Hons) Fine Art Painting, MA Fine Art. *Medium*: painter. *b*: Fukuoka, Japan, 4 Jun 1977. *d of*: Haruo and Kuniko Abe. *m*: Thomas Lamb. *Studied*: Wimbledon School of Art (1997-2000); Chelsea College of Art (2000-2001); Fukuoka Asian Art Museum (2005). *Exhib*: Lexmark European Art Prize, Eyestorm Gallery, London (2003); British School at Rome (2002, 03); Brecce, Rome, Italy (2003), RWS Bankside Gallery (2013, 2014), The Collection, Lincoln (2012), Abbey Walk Gallery (2013). *Address*: Rose Cottage, Belleau, Lincolnshire, LN13 0BW. *Email*: yukilamb@hotmail.com; yukilamb@gmail.com *Website*: www.yukilamb.com

LAMBERT, Colin Joseph, sculptor in bronze and stone. *b*: Guantanamo Bay, Cuba, 17 Jan 1948. *s of*: Virgil Mangus-Colorado, American Indian poet. *m*: Catherine Finn. *Studied*: Chouinard Art Inst., Los Angeles (1966-68); apprenticed with Karl Gomez in Amsterdam (1980-83). *Works in collections*: Stamford Forum, Stamford, Conn.; London United Bldg., London; Renaissance Vineyard and Winery, Calif.; Warminster Market Centre, Warminster, Wilts. *Address:* 11547 College Street, Petaluma, CA 94952, USA.

LAMBERTH, Brian, B Ed (Hons). *Medium*: oil. *b*: London, 28 Jul 1930. *s of*: Edwin Lamberth. *m*: Ruby. two *s*. one *d*. *Educ*: Kingston Grammar School. *Studied*: Michaelis School of Fine Art, University of Cape Town (1956-59); Institute of Education, London University (1969-72). *Represented by*: International Graphics, Walmsley GmbH, Junkersring 11, 76344 Eggenstein, Germany. *Exhib*: London, various galleries; Paris, Rotterdam, Montpellier (France), Cape Town. *Publications*: Book of Flower Paintings. *Principal Works*: landscapes and Thames river scenes, flower still-lifes. *Recreations*: travelling. *Address:* 29 Priory Road, Hampton, Middlesex, TW12 2NS. *Email*: blamberth@hotmail.com *Signs work*: "BRIAN LAMBERTH" or "B. LAMBERTH".

LAMBIRTH, Alan, RBA (1986), RA Gold medal (1982), RA Schools Advanced Dip. (1983), Higher Surrey Dip AD (1980), De Laszlo medal awarded by RBA (1991); artist in oil, pastel, gouache and water-colour, ink. *b*: Cuckfield, 19 Feb, 1959. *s of*: Ivor Edward & Joyce Lambirth. *Educ*: Hazelwick School, Crawley. *Studied*: W. Sussex College of Design (1975-77), Epsom School of Art (1977-80, Peter Peterson), RA Schools (1980-83, Peter Greenham, RA). *Exhib*: RA, RBA, NEAC, Soc. of Landscape Painters; one-man shows: Odette Gilbert Gallery (1984, 1986), Solomon Gallery (1988), Sheila Harrison Fine Art (1989, 1991), Enid Lawson Gallery (1997); four-man show: Hallam Gallery (1990). *Address:* 22 Brushwood Rd., Roffey, Horsham, W. Sussex RH12 4PE. *Signs work*: 'Alan Lambirth' or 'ALAN LAMBIRTH'.

LAMONT, Ian James, painter in oil. *b*: Streatham Vale, 16 May 1964. *s of*: John Lamont, scenic artist. *Educ*: Nork Pk. School; N.E. Surrey College of Technology; Sutton College of Liberal Arts. *Studied*: Kingston Polytechnic School of Art and Design; also portrait painting under Ronald Benham, NEAC, RBA (1982-86). *Exhib*: RA, NEAC, RBA, ROI (Winsor and Newton Young Artist award finalist 1983-88), Royal Portrait Soc., Lynn Painter-Stainers Prize (Exhibition), National Portrait Gallery (BP Award Finalist). *Works in collections*: United Racecourses. *Works Reproduced*: "500 Portraits" (National Portrait Gallery). *Address:* 25 Woodgavil, Banstead, Surrey SM7 1AA. *Signs work*: "Ian Lamont." or "Lamont" or "IL".

LAMPUTT, Norman Howard, NDD (1965). *Medium*: oil, watercolour, drawing. *b*: Much Wenlock, 7 Mar 1943. *s of*: Gordon & Kathleen. *Educ*: Wenlock Edge School. *Studied*: Shrewsbury School of Art (1961-65). *Represented by*: Twenty Twenty, Much Wenlock. *Exhib*: widely throughout the UK. *Works in collections*: private collections in the UK, USA and Europe. *Address:* Flat 5, Lower Bromdon Farm, Wheathill, Burwaton, Bridgnorth, WV16 6QT. *Email*: lamputt755@btinternet.com *Signs work*: "N.H.LAMPUTT".

LANCASTER, John Maurice, NDD, MPhil, PhD, FSAED; painter, calligrapher, heraldic artist, author. *Medium*: watercolour, oil, acrylic, gold, heraldic colours, vellum. *b*: Wigan, 29 May 1930. *m*: Janet Lancaster. *Studied*: Leeds College of Art (1946-51), advanced painting with Victor Pasmore. *Exhib*: sixteen one-man shows in the UK and USA including: Leicester, Nottingham, London, Keele, Bristol, Decatur, USA, Columbus, USA, Thatcher, Az., USA, Cheltenham, Stowe, Wadhurst; group shows: RWA, RBA, Hesketh Hubbard, Mod. Art in Yorkshire, W. Riding Artists, John Noott 20th C. Gallery, Kenulf Galleries, Bristol, and other galleries. *Works in collections*: world-wide. *Commissions*: private, public bodies, City of London institutions, the Church. *Publications*: 18 books. Visiting Prof. and Visiting Artist U.S.A. *Recreations*: golf. *Clubs*: Naval and Military, S.H.A. Liveryman and Court Member Worshipful Company of Gardeners, Freeman City of London. *Address:* 10 Walnut Cl., Cheltenham, Glos. GL52 3AG. *Email*: johnmlanc@aol.com *Signs work*: "John Lancaster."

LANCASTER, Mo, SWA; NDD, ATD. *Medium*: linocut, prints. *b*: Bridgwater, Somerset, 5 Feb 1945. *m*: Ron (Potter). one *s*. one *d*. *Educ*: Secondary, Bridgwater. *Studied*: Somerset

College of Art (1960-65); University of Wales (1966-). *Represented by*: The Watergate Gallery, Leicester; Off the Wall, Cardiff. *Exhib*: Brewhouse Theatre, Taunton (solo 1979, 1993); Arts Centre, Bridgwater (solo 1980, and mixed); RA Summer Exhibition (2006, 2010, 2013); SWA, annually at Mall Galleries, London; RWA (annually since 2006); Leicester Print, Small Print (2007, 2010, 2011); Royal Birmingham (2005, 2006, 2007, 2008, 2009); Victoria Art Gallery, Bath (annually). *Works in collections*: private collections internationally. *Commissions*: illustrating various publications, Somerset. *Official Purchasers*: Somerset County Council presentations. *Works Reproduced*: Society catalogues - SWA & Bath; RA Summer Exhibition Postcard 'We Love London' (2013); Bath Society poster 'Ascot Ladies' (2013); Leisure Painter. *Principal Works*: Linocuts - "Confidences", "Connoisseurs", "We Love London". *Recreations*: reading, music, architecture. *Clubs*: SWA, Bath Society of Artists. *Misc*: Still teaching part-time, and running print-making workshops in Taunton. *Address*: Rose Cottage, Bishops Lydeard, Taunton, Som TA4 3LR. *Email*: molancaster@hotmail.co.uk *Website*: www.molancaster.co.uk *Signs work*: "MO LANCASTER".

LANDERS, Linda Anne, BA (Hons) (1986), RE; Mall Galleries prize for Printmaking (2001). *Medium*: wood engraving, printmaking, handmade books, oils, watercolour, film, theatre, performance, writing. *b*: Herts., 27 Dec 1959. *d of*: Harry Landers (Engineer - Concorde). two *s*. *Studied*: Central St.Martin's School of Art; Desmond Jones Mime and Physical Theatre, Laban Dance Centre. *Exhib*: 'Fine Press' book fairs and exhibitions; RA Summer show; Saatchi & Saatchi; Icehouse Gallery. *Works in collections*: British Art Library, V&A, Ashmolean Museum, RCA, Musuem Van Het Boek, Netherlands, University of California LA, University of Plymouth, USA collections, Longleat House Library. *Commissions*: wood engraving (Circle Press) and Delos and Redlake Press. *Publications*: published 23 Limited Edn. artists books under imprints: Spoon Print Press/'Merlin's Grail'. Inclusion in: 'An Engraver's Globe', 'The Printmaker's Directory'. *Official Purchasers*: Lord Bath. *Works Reproduced*: Woman on a Lion. *Principal Works*: Woman on a Lion, Book large format, Longleat Library. *Clubs*: CAA. *Misc*: musician, filmaker, poet, sculptor, playwright. *Address:* 1st Floor, 68 Elsham Road, London W14 8HD. *Email*: lindalanders87@hotmail.com *Website*: www.lindalanders.co.uk *Signs work*: "Linda Anne Landers" Signature varies according to size of work.

LANE, Christopher Owin, BA Fine Art; MA Fine Art. *Medium*: oil. *b*: London, 24 Apr 1977. *s of*: Chris & Patricia Lane. *Studied*: Barnet College (1995); Northbrook College, Worthing (1996-99); University of Wisconsin (1998); University of East London (2001-02). *Exhib*: with 'SAFE' Studios, Spitalfields Gallery (2001, 02, 04, 05, including solo show in 2002); O2 Brasserie, Bethnal Green Road (2003); St.Martins Church, Plaistow (2003, 2004); Spitalfields Community Festival and Eco Fun Fair (2005). *Works in collections*: St. Martin's Church, Plaistow (painting of 'St.Martin Clothing the Beggar', blessed in 2003, now on permanent display). *Publications*: Christian Arts Journal (Winter, 2003), review. *Recreations*: sport, music, art. *Misc*: travelled extensively in Italy during degree courses. Volunteer for Crisis, working in the Skylight building helping homeless people with their art. *Address:* 9 Prospect Place, Tottenham, London N17.

LANE, Jason, Royal West of England Academician (2004); Year of the Artist Award (2000); Morris Singer Bronze Casting Award (1998). *Medium*: reclaimed steel (sculptor). *b*: Leamington Spa, 28 Oct 1970. *Partner*: Polly Lewis. one *s*. one *d*. *Studied*: Hereford College of Art and Design (1989-90), Exeter Faculty of Art and Design (1990-93); Dublin NCAD (1991). *Exhib*: RWA, Spike Island, Bristol; Workshop Wales Gallery; Jokelson Gallery, Dunkirk; Honiton Arts Festival; The Thelma Hulbert Gallery, Honiton; Hot Bath Gallery, Bath; Contemporary Arts Society, Festival Hall. *Works in collections*: Royal West of England Academy. *Commissions*: Ox for Persimmon Homes, Portishead; St. Pauls Gateway Sculpture (2007); Art Car for Art Car Parade, Manchester (2007); Guard Dog for

Blake Castle Estate (2005); Sustrans Residency-Dewsbury Cycle track (2000); solid fuel vending machine for Crest Homes (2002); Red Bull ship (2004); Mechanical Hammock for Kevin McCloud's Man Made Home series (2013); Mechanical Sound Sculpture for Para Olympics closing ceremony (2012). *Principal Works*: Human hamster wheel; mechanical rocking horse; mechanical drawing machine, Ox, mechanical sound sculpture. *Address:* 18 The Yard, Mina Road, St.Werburghs, Bristol, BS2 9YR. *Email*: jason@jasonlane.org.uk *Website*: www.jasonlane.org.uk *Signs work*: 'Lane'.

LANG, Demi, 2nd, 3rd, 4th and Commended, Much Hadham Art Society Annual Exhibition. *Medium*: Watercolour, drawing, prints, acrylic. *b*: Shoreditch, London 10 Mar 1969. *m*: Stephen Lang. two *d*. *Studied*: Ware College (1985-97) BTEC Diploma Graphic Design. *Represented by*: West Berks Open Studios; www.artgallery.co.uk; www.minigallery.co.uk. *Exhib*: Much Hadham Art Society Annual (2007, 2008, 2009, 2010, 2011, 2012); Hertford Art Society Members Show (2007) and Annual (2007); 'Insight' (2009, 2010, 2011, 2012); Artex (2010, 2011, 2012); Newbury Art Group (2009, 2010); plus many others.*Works in collections*: Numerous works in private collections across UK, Europe, USA and New Zealand. *Commissions*: Seven in private collections. *Works reproduced*: Numerous giclee prints. *Recreations*: Running, reading, music, sketching. *Clubs*: Much Hadham Art Society. *Misc*: Participates in West Berks Open Studios Scheme and sells direct from studio. *Address*: Trelawney, Chapel Lane, Hermitage, Berkshire RG18 9RP. *Email*: demi@demilang.com *Website*: www.demilang.com *Signs work*: "DEMI LANG".

LANG, Wharton, RSMA (1948), now Hon Mem FRSA (1983); sculptor in wood; ex Mem. SWLA; Gold Citation for Best Sculpture at Wildlife Art Society International (2006, 2008). *Medium*: wood sculpture. *b*: Oberammergau, Bavaria, 13 Jun 1925. *s of*: Faust Lang, wood sculptor. *m*: Ingrid. *Educ*: Newquay Grammar School. *Studied*: Leonard Fuller School of Painting (1946) and privately under Faust Lang (1946-49). *Exhib*: St. Ives Society of Artists,, Society of Wildlife Artists, Royal Society of Marine Artists, Wildlife Artists International, also private exhibitions. *Works in collections*: Ulster Museum, Belfast, RSMA Diploma Collection, National Maritime Museum, Greenwich, Carving in Relief 'Castle of Mey' presented to H.M. Queen Mother (1967). *Commissions*: many private. *Address:* Fauna Studio, Mount Zion, St. Ives, Cornwall TR26 3HA. *Signs work*: "W. LANG", "Wharton Lang".

LANGFORD, Martin James, RE. *Medium*: mezzotint, etching. *b*: Kingston upon Thames, 2 Jun 1970. *m*: Therese Langford. one *s*. one *d*. *Studied*: University of Plymouth (BA (Hons) Fine Art 1993); Post Grad. Advanced Printmaking, Central St. Martin's College of Art (David Gluck, RE). *Exhib*: annually at Originals, Affordable Art Fair and Urban Art. *Works in collections*: For Art's Sake, Ealing, W. London; Will's Art Warehouse, Barnes, London; Cupola Gallery, Sheffield; Bankside Gallery, London; South Bank Printmakers, Gabriel's Wharf, London. *Publications*: Selected for Best of International Printmaking book, whole page coverage (Rockport Publishers, U.S.A., 1997); featured in 'Printmaking Today' (Into the Labyrinth' article July 07). *Works Reproduced*: none. *Address:* 2 Norfolk House, The Farmlands, Northolt, Middx. UB5 5EU. *Email*: martinlangford70@hotmail.com *Website*: www.martinlangford.com

LANGHORN, Doreen M., SWA; Awards: Highly Commended RBSA (2004); Harper Collins Prize (1993); Harper Collins Pastel Prize (1994); Daler Rowney Prize at SWA, Mall Galleries (2006); Fine Art UK Award for Creativity (2010); Pastel Society Vice President's Choice (2012). *Medium*: pastel, watercolour, drawing. *b*: Evesham, Worcs., 23 Mar 1946. *d of*: John Bennett Martin. *m*: John A. Langhorn. one *s*. *Educ*: Southend-on-Sea Grammar School for Girls. *Studied*: studied the works of Ruskin Spear and Lucien Freud. *Exhib*: RWA; RSMA; RBSA; SWA; Salon International de la Peinture a L'Eau, Tregastel, France; The Biennial Portrait Exhibition of the RBSA; La Societe des Pastillistes de France; Le Salon du Pastel en Bretagne; Pastel Society; Royal Institute of Painters in Watercolour.

Works in collections: UK, USA, Sweden, Australia, France, Holland, Japan, Belgium. *Publications*: in The Artist Magazine; Fact & Fantasy, United Press Ltd.; listed in the Dictionary of the RSMA and the archives of SWA; book cover for novel by W. Turner-Webster. *Clubs*: SWA, Birmingham & Midlands Pastel Society. *Misc*: specialises in painting people - not just formal portraits, but undertaking daily activities of life. In particular children. Work known for its strong, vibrant colours and luminous quality of light. *Address:* 6 High Street, Chipping Campden, Glos GL55 6AT. *Email*: jodo@talktalk.net *Website*: www.society-women-artists.org.uk *Signs work*: 'DML' or 'D.Langhorn'.

LANGLEY, Siddy. *Medium*: blown glass. *b*: Withnell, Lancs., 2 Feb 1955. *m*: Michael Crane. one *d*. *Studied*: Apprenticed to Peter Layton at London Glassblowing Workshop (1979-81). *Exhib*: Rosengalerie, Amsterdam; 'Glaskunst aus Grossbritannien' Lucerne and Frankfurt; Broadfield House Glass Museum, Dudley; Coleridge of Piccadilly, London and Edinburgh; Musée des Beaux Arts, Rouen; Kringel Gallery, Switzerland; Museu de Arte de São Paulo, Brazil; Neville Pundole Gallery, Canterbury, etc. *Works in collections*: Musée du Verre, Liege, Belgium and Sars Poteries, France; Turner Glass Collection, Sheffield; Norwich Castle Museum; B'ham Museum and A.G.; Leics. Collection for Schools and Colleges; The Glass Museum, Ebeltoft, Denmark. *Commissions*: font for Methodist Church, Winchester. *Address:* The Longhouse, Plymtree, nr. Cullompton, Devon EX15 2JW. *Email*: mail@siddy.com *Signs work*: "Siddy Langley" and year.

LARGE, George Charles, RI (1986), RBA (1997), ATC; artist in oil and water-colour; Awards: Winsor Newton Award, RI Singer Friedlander/Sunday Times, Llewellyn Alexander Award RI St. Cuthbert's Mill Paper Award. *b*: London, 20 Jan 1936. *m*: Pamela Parkinson-Large. one *s-s* two *s*. one *s-d* one *d*. *Educ*: Downhills Central School, Tottenham. *Studied*: Hornsey College of Art (1958-63, Maurice de Sausmarez, John Titchell, Alfred Daniels). *Exhib*: RI, RBA, SWE; one-man shows, Mall Galleries, National Gallery Malta, Duncan Campbel Fine Arts, Melitensia A.G., Malta, Llewellyn Alexander, Goldmark Gallery. *Works in collections*: Ralli Foundation, British Rail, National Gallery Malta, British Consulate Malta, Cranfield Inst., ICI. *Commissions*: Chesterfield Corporation murals. *Publications*: illustrated, Laughter in the Kitchen, and various magazines, Taste of History, Food of the Knights of Malta, Pamela Parkinson-Large; The Cartographer, David Mackenzie; 'Large in Malta', Peter Apap Bologna. *Address:* Affric Cottage, 33 South View, Uppingham, Rutland LE15 9TU. *Email*: george_largo@btopenworld.com *Signs work*: "LARGE 98."

LARMONT, Eric, NDD, ATC; painter in oil, etcher; part-time art lecturer; Prizes and awards: Reeves Bi-centenary Premier Award (1966); Second Non-purchase Prize, Northern Painters Exhibition (1966). *Medium*: oil painting, printmaking & metal sculpture. *b*: South Shields, 27 Sep 1943. *Studied*: Sunderland College of Art (1963-65); Goldsmiths' School of Art (1965-66), Post-grad. Belgian Scholarship (1968-69). *Exhib*: one-man shows, London: 273 Gallery (1969), Scribes Cellar (1978), Holsworthy Gallery (1981), Galerie Blankenese, Hamburg (1983), Pump House Gallery, London (1997); two-man show, Jonathan Poole Gallery (1986); 3 man show; Studio Gallery, London (1999); Putney School of Art (one-man, 2004). *Works in collections*: Carlisle Corporation; private collections: various. *Address:* 20 Rainville Rd., London W6 9HA. *Email*: larmalone@tiscali.co.uk *Website*: larmalone.co.uk *Signs work*: "E.Larmont" or monogram "EL".

LARUSDOTTIR, Karolina, RE, RWS, NEAC; painter in oil and water-colour, etcher and printmaker. *b*: Reykjavik, Iceland, 12 Mar 1944. *Studied*: Ruskin School of Art, Oxford University, Barking College of Art. *Represented by*: www.lindarichardson.co.uk. *Exhib*: Bankside Gallery, RE, RA, RBA; one-man shows: Kjarvalsstadir Reykjavik (1982, 1986), Gallerie Gammelstrand, Kobenhagen, Gallery 10 (1984, 1987, 1991), Cambridge Contemporary Art (from 1994). *Works in collections*: Cartwright Hall Musuem, Bradford; The Vatican Collection, Rome; Nelson Atkin Museum, Kansas City, USA; British Musuem,

London; Ashmolean Museum, Oxford; Fitzwilliam Museum, Cambridge. *Misc*: Prizes: The Dicks and Greenbury Award, Bankside Gallery (1989). Special award: Premio Internazionale Biella per l'incisione, Italy. *Address:* c/o Linda Richardson, 1 Styles, Little Bardfield, Briantree, Essex CM7 4TP. *Email*: linda@lindarichardson.co.uk *Signs work*: "LARUSDOTTIR."

LAST, Bob, NDD, MSIAD, PS. *Medium*: all mediums. *b*: Surrey, 1932. *s of*: Victor Last. *m*: Miriam. two *d*. *Studied*: Sutton School of Art. *Exhib*: Mall Galleries. *Works in collections*: private only. *Commissions*: 1973 St. Mary Magdalene Church, Cowden, Kent (sculpture). *Publications*: 'The Artist' (Jan 2003); 'Artist & Illustrators' (June 2006); 'Artist & Illustrators' (July 2007). *Clubs*: Pastel Society. *Address:* 27 Tate Road, Sutton, Surrey, SM1 2SY. *Website*: www.thepastelsociety.org.uk

LAST, Joanne, GRSM, ARCM. *Medium*: oil, watercolour, mixed media & pastel. *b*: Sutton, Surrey, 29 Apr 1962. *d of*: Bob Last. *Studied*: Royal College of Music (1980-84)*; Putney School of Art (1990-92). *Represented by*: Bernard Chauchet, Thirteen Langton Street. *Exhib*: Thirteen Langton Street Gallery; Pastel Society, Mall Galleries; Royal Institute of Painters in Watercolour, Mall Galleries; Royal Academy of Arts Summer Exhibition; Royal Institute of Oil Painters, Mall Galleries. *Works in collections*: private/corporate. *Commissions*: Sandy Lane Hotel, Barbados; Carlton Tower Hotel, Knightsbridge; Churchill Hotel, London. *Official Purchasers*: 'Tuscan Landscape' - Ikea, worldwide. *Misc*: also known as Jo Last. *Originally trained as Classical pianist. *Address:* 32 Wavertree Court, Streatham Hill, London SW2 4TN. *Email*: jo@joannelast.co.uk *Website*: www.joannelast.co.uk *Signs work*: "J. LAST".

LATHAM, Helen, BA Colour Chemistry. *Medium*: oil. *b*: Stafford, 19 Dec 1954. *m*: Roberto. *Studied*: Jacob Kramer, Leeds (Art Foundation); University of Leeds; Current student, Turps/Banana Painter's correspondence course (2013-14). *Represented by*: Guerilla Galleries, Shoreditch, London; Arts International. *Exhib*: Sainsbury Art Centre, Norwich (2014); Guerilla Galleries - Daniel Liberskind Space, London (2013, 2014); Williams Art, Cambridge (2013); Tatler Magazine (2013-); Burwash Manor - Cambridgeshire Artist's Marquee (2011, 2012); Parallax Art Fair, Old Chelsea Town Hall, London (2012); Norwich Forum Gruop show (2011/2012); Changing Spaces, 75 Regent Street, Cambridge (2011); La Dante, Cambridge (2009); Walls Gallery, Amsterdam (2005, 2007); De Vrijplaats, Amsterdam (2005). *Works in collections*: Private collections. *Commissions*: Private commissions. *Publications*: Art! East Anglia (pub. Green Pebble). *Address*: Great Shelford, Cambridge, CB22 5JL. *Email*: helenla@virginmedia.com *Website*: www.lathamhelen.com *Signs work*: "H.Latham" (verso).

LAUBIN, Carl David, B.Arch. *Medium*: oil. *b*: New York, 8 Dec 1947. *s of*: Alfred & Lillian Laubin. *m*: Christine Creighton-Laubin. one *s*. two *d*. *Studied*: Cornell University College of Art, Architecture & Planning. *Represented by*: Plus One Plus Two Galleries. *Exhib*: RA; Centre Pompidou; Musée d'Aquitaine; Frankfurt Architecture Museum; Museum of London; V&A; Sotheby's Johannesburg; Petworth; Christie's; Thomas Agnew; Castle Howard; St. Paul's Cathedral. *Works in collections*: Museum of London, Castle Howard, Linklaters, National Trust, London Borough of Richmond, Anglo-American Corp. *Commissions*: Castle Howard, Royal Opera House, Royal Armouries, National Trust, Centre Pomidou, Duchy of Cornwall; University of Notre Dame. *Publications*: 'Carl Laubin Paintings' pub. Philip Wilson. 'Exactitude: Hyperrealist Art Today' pub. Plus One Publishing, Thames & Hudson. *Official Purchasers*: Museum of London; London Borough of Richmond; Grosvenor Museum, Chester. *Works Reproduced*: 'London in Paint: Paintings in the Collection of the Museum of London', 'The Architectural Capriccio'. *Principal Works*: 'Hawksmoor', 'Canary Wharf', 'Si Monumentum Requiris', 'Vanbrugh Fields', 'Vanbrugh's Castles'. *Recreations*: gardening. *Address:* 74 Lancaster Road, Hitchin, Herts SG5 1PE. *Email*: carl@carllaubin.com *Website*: www.carllaubin.com *Signs work*: 'Laubin' or 'CL'.

LAUCHLAN, Anya, MA, FFPS; painter/illustrator in oil, acrylic, watercolour. *b*: 6 Apr 1948. *m*: Peter Rolland Lauchlan. one *s*. two *d*. *Studied*: Pushkin Museum of Fine Art, and Moscow Polygraphic - Art and Design (1963-75, Basov, Goncharov, Chazanov, Burdjelian). *Represented by*: Atelier Art International, NY, USA. *Exhib*: Loggia Gallery, Westminster, Leighton House Museum, Menier Gallery, Garden of Eden and various commercial London galleries. *Works in collections*: work in private collections internationally. *Commissions*: Painting scenes from English National Ballet (1998-2000). *Publications*: illustrator of more than 50 books. *Works Reproduced*: "Blue Mountain", "Dance of Spring", "Villa Christina", "Le Buffon", "Golden Roses", "Delphiniums", "White & Gold", "Black Unicorn". *Clubs*: F.P.S. *Address:* The Studio, 2 Grovehill Rd., Redhill, Surrey RH1 6PJ. *Email*: rolland.art@btopenworld.com *Website*: www.Rolland-Fine-Art.com *Signs work*: "Anya Lauchlan," "A. Lauchlan" or "Anya" and dated.

LAWRENCE, Amanda, BA (Glass Design) 1st Class; Fellow, Guild of Glass Engravers. *Medium*: Glass, Kiln-formed and engraved. *b*: Bath, 22 Aug 1963. *m*: Andrew Dickinson. *Educ*: Tunbridge Wells Girls Grammar School. *Studied*: University of Oxford; Wolverhampton University (1998-2001); International Glass Centre, Brierley Hill (2001-2001). *Exhib*: Various including: New Designers (2001-02); Cecilia Colman Gallery, London (2001-08); Art in Action (2005-09); British Glass Biennale (2004); Cheltenham Museum and Art Gallery (2009-11); Nature in Art, Gloucester (2003-11); Society of Designer Craftsmen(2002, 2006-7); Guild of Glass Engravers (1997-2012); Broadfield House Glass Museum (2012); Obsidian Arts (2007-12). *Works in collections*: Private. *Commissions*: Various private. *Recreations*: Walking, wildlife-watching. *Address*: 5 Spring Cottages, The Vatch, Stroud GL6 7JY. *Email*: info@amandalawrenceglass.com *Website*: www.amandalawrenceglass.com *Signs work*: "AJ LAWRENCE".

LAWRENCE, John Wilfred, RE, SWE; winner, Francis Williams Book Illustration award (twice), New York Times Certificate Of Excellence; freelance illustrator in wood engraving and water-colour; part time lecturer, Camberwell School of Art (1960-93); external assessor, Bristol College of Art, Exeter College of Art, Duncan of Jordanstone College of Art, Brighton College of Art, Edinburgh College of Art; Kingston School of Art (various appointments between 1978-94); Visiting Professor in illustration at the London Inst.; part-time lecturer MA Childrens' Book Illustration, Anglia Ruskin University. *Medium*: wood engraving, pen and watercolour. *b*: Hastings, 15 Sep 1933. *s of*: Wilfred James Lawrence and Audrey Constance (née) Thomas. *m*: Myra. two *d*. *Educ*: Salesian College, Oxford. *Studied*: Hastings School of Art (1951-53),and Central School of Art and Design (1955-57). *Exhib*: SWE, Royal Society of Painter Printmakers, Fry Art Gallery, Sir Kenneth Greene library (MMU). *Works in collections*: V&A, Ashmolean Museum, National Museum of Wales, several provincial galleries, and in several collections in USA. *Commissions*: book illustraions with many publishers, also ephemeral work in advertising and design. *Publications*: over 150 books, including recently 'The Once and Future King' by T.H. White (Folio Soc.); 'Lyra's Oxford' by Philip Pullman (David Ficking Books); 'This Little Chick' by J.L. (Walker Books); 'Tiny's Big Adventure' by Martin Waddell (Walker Books); 'Sea Horse' by Chris Butterworth (Walker Books); 'Treasure Island' (Walker Books); 'The Arthur Trilogy' by Kevin Crossley Holland (Folio Society); 'Wayland' by Tony Mitton (David Fickling Books). *Recreations*: piano. *Clubs*: AWG (Master, 1990), SWE (Double Crown, President 2005), Wynked de Worde. *Address:* 6 Worts Causeway, Cambridge CBI 8RL. *Email*: johnlawrence326@btinternet.com *Signs work*: "John Lawrence."

LAWRENCE, Peter Alfred, DipAd (Bristol, 1973), SWE (1998), ARE (2003); winner SWE Prize at National Print Exhibition, Open Printmaking Prize at NPE, Rachel Reckitt Prize for UK Wood Engraver (2003); Printmaking Today Prize at RE Annual Exhibition (2007); Managing Director Oxford Designers and Illustrators. *Medium*: wood engraving and other printmaking. *b*: Hornchurch, Essex, 30 Aug 1951. *s of*: Mr & Mrs A Lawrence. *m*: Cathryn. two *s*. *Studied*: Bristol Polytechnic, Faculty of Art and Design. *Exhib*: Society of Wood Engravers and in group shows. One-man exhbn. at Henman's, Oxford (1999), The Little Gallery, Oxford (2005). *Works in collections*: Ashmolean Museum, Oxford, private collections. *Publications*: featured in 'An Engraver's Globe' (Primrose Hill Press, 2002), Printmakers - The Directory (A&C Black 2006). *Clubs*: Society of Wood Engravers, Royal Society of Painter-Printmakers, Oxford Art Society, Oxford Printmakers Co-operative. *Address:* 48 Lonsdale Road, Oxford, OX2 7EP. *Email*: pete@odi-design.co.uk/ www.woodengravers.co.uk *Website*: the-art-works.co.uk

LAWRENCE, Sandra. ROI (1980); Certificate of Appreciation awarded by the Pentagon 2009. *Medium*: pastels, oil, watercolour, drawing, prints. *b*: London, 2 Jan 1945. *d of*: Brig. Roderick Lawrence OBE & Gillian Bishop. *Educ*: St.Mary's Wantage 1955-1960. *Studied*: St.Martins School of Art 1962-64, The Byam Shaw School of Art 1964-65, Simi's Acedemy, Florence 1966-67. *Exhib*: Solo exhibitions: Peter Hyde Fine Arts, London; The Gallery Mundi, Caracas; Harkness House Gallery, New York; The Cafe Royal, London; Overlord cartoons at Dover Castle; Hamilton Gallery London; Halander Gallery, Palm Beach; Fischer Fine Art, London. Selected group shows include: Mall Galleries: ROI, RSMA, PS, RP; Royal Academy Summer Exhibitions; Singer/Friedlander Sunday Times Watercolour Competition, Glasgow Institute; Hunting Art Prizes, Grosvenor Gallery London, Tryon and Swann Gallery London. *Works in collections*: private/corporate. *Publications*: 'Operation Overlord: the History of D-Day and the Overlord Embroidery' by Stephen Brooks & Eve Eckstein (pub. Ashford, 1989). *Principal Works*: Cartoons for 'The Overlord Embroidery' commissioned by Lord Dulverton. Paintings 272ft long - now hanging in the Pentagon (1968-1972). *Clubs*: Chelsea Arts Club. *Address:* 12 Paultons House, Paultons Square, London SW3 5DU. *Email*: sandratheartist@gmail.com *Website*: www.sandralawrence.co.uk *Signs work*: "Sandra Lawrence".

LAWRENCE, Tory, winner Spink Prize for Painting (1996); Royal Bath & West Soc. (1997); finalist Spink Prize for Painting (1998); finalist Hunting Art Prize (2000, 2001); winner, Drawing for All, Gainsborough's House Museum (2002). *Medium*: oil, watercolour, drawing, prints. *b*: London, 2 Apr 1940. *d of*: John & Nancy Dennistoun. *m*: div. *Partner*: Maggi Hambling. one *s*. one *d*. *Educ*: East Haddon Hall School, Northants. *Studied*: Morley College, Westminster (painting and printmaking). *Represented by*: various galleries. *Exhib*: Royal Academy; National Racehorse Museum, Newmarket; Town Hall Galleries, Ipswich; 12 Star Gallery, European Commission. *Works in collections*: Abacus Electronic Holdings Ltd; All Saints Church, Oaksey, Wilts; Chelsea & Westminster Hospital; de Wiersse Collection, Holland; Ipswich Borough Council Collection - Colchester & Ipswich museums; work in many private collections in UK, USA, Australia and Europe. *Commissions*: Mrs. A. Boulton; Mrs.Simon Burne; Mr M. Bradstock; Sir Edward Cazalet; The late Duke of Devonshire; Mrs. Peter Gatacre; Sir Mark Palmer; Lady Reay; Mr.Martin Scott; Riding for the Disabled; Mr Francis Nicholls; Mrs E. Bracey. *Publications*: Artist's Manual (Harper Collins, 1995); The Week "Where to Buy" Jan 2012; How Artists See Nature (Green Pebble Publications, 2011/12); A Celebration of Cultural History of Coastal Suffolk by Peter Willsher (2013); Vogue Magazine April 2012. *Works Reproduced*: Artists & Illustrators; Galleries Magazine; Modern Painters; The Spectator; The Week. *Recreations*: gardening, cooking, travelling. *Address*: The White House Rendham Saxmundham Suffolk IP17 2AZ. *Email*: tory@torylawrence.com *Website*: www.torylawrence.com *Signs work*: 'Tory Lawrence' (with date), sometimes 'TL' (with date).

LAWRENSON, Diane M., RCA (2000), SWA (2006); sculptor in bronze and bronzed resin; SWA Peter Hambro Sculpture Award (2004); SWA America Square Conference Centre Sculpture Award (2009); SWA Alec Tiranti Sculpture Award (2012); SWA London Art Special Sculpture Award (2013). *b*: Liverpool, 5 Sep 1946. *m*: Kevin A.Howley. two *s* (one now dec'd). one *d*. *Educ*: Keighley College. *Studied*: West Yorkshire. *Represented by*: Royal Cambrian Academy, Mall Galleries, various. *Exhib*: public and private collections. *Address:* Barker House, Winton, Kirkby Stephen, Cumbria CA17 4HS. *Email*: Diane.Lawrenson@yahoo.co.uk *Signs work*: "LAWRENSON."

LAWSON, Gillian, painter in water-colour and oil, printmaker in etching. *b*: 6 May 1936. married. *d of*: Oliver Massingham, director. one *s*. two *d*. *Educ*: Parliament Hill Grammar School. *Studied*: Camden Institute (silkscreen printing, Ingrid Greenfield), Camden Art Centre (1971-75, etching, Dorothea Wight). *Exhib*: Cape Town, SA, Georgetown, Washington, USA, RA, Halesworth Gallery, Burgh House, Hampstead, The Ice House, Holland Park, Hinton Gallery, nr. Horley, Ninth British International Print Biennale. *Address:* 7 Oak Hill Way, Hampstead, London NW3 7LR. *Signs work*: "Gillian Lawson."

LAWSON, Simon Nicholas, BA Hons (1985), RA Post Grad. Dip. (1998); winner, Curwen Print Prize for best non-digital print (RA Summer Exhbn, 2005). *Medium*: oil, watercolour, etching. *b*: Waltham, Lincs., 2 Aug 1964. *s of*: David Lawson, graphic designer. *Partner*: Ann Cansfield Hobson. one *d*. *Educ*: Waltham Toll Bar Comprehensive. *Studied*: Grimsby School of Art (1980-82, Peter Todd), Wimbledon School of Art (1982-85, Bernard Cohen), RA Schools (1985-88, Norman Adams). *Represented by*: Print (vb.n)- 8 Huguenot Place, Wandsworth, SW18 2EN. *Exhib*: Royal Festival Hall (1986), Mall Galleries (1986, 2004, 2005), RA (1987-92, 1998-2007). *Works in collections*: Royal Caribbean Cruise Line, Cabinet Office. *Commissions*: Cabinet Rooms Admiralty Arch. *Works Reproduced*: Royal Academy Summer Exhibition Illustrated Catalogue 2000, 04, 06; Printmaking Today Vol 16 no.2 Summer. *Recreations*: jazz musician. *Address:* Flat One, 20 Allfarthing Lane, Wandsworth, London SW18 2PQ. *Email*: simon_ann.lawson@virgin.net *Signs work*: "S. Lawson."

LAWSON, Sonia, RA, RWS, Hon RWA, RCA, MA (1st) (1959); artist in oil, water-colour, etching; visitor RA Schools 1985-2003. *b*: Wensleydale, Yorks., 2 Jun 1934. *d of*: Fred Lawson and Muriel Metcalfe, artists. *m*: Charles Congo. one *d*. *Studied*: Royal College of Art (1956-59, Prof. Carel Weight), Post-graduate year (1959-60), Travelling Scholarship, France. *Exhib*: solo exhibitions, retrospective tour, Leicester Polytechnic, Mappin Gallery Sheffield, Ferens Hull, Cartwright Bradford, Central Gallery Milton Keynes (1982-83); selected solo exhbns. Kirklees (1985), Manchester (1987), Wakefield (1988), Bradford (1989), London, Boundary Gallery (1989, 1995, 1998, 2000-2003, 2005), retrospective, Dean Clough Gallery (1966-96), Halifax, Stafford 1999 R.W.A. Bristol (2000), Vertigo Gallery, London 2002, Aylesbury Museum and Gallery (2006); mixed shows, New York, Fragments against Ruin tour, China, British Council tour, Arts Council, Tolly Cobbald, John Moores, Edinburgh, R.A. London, Haywards Annual London, Subjective Eye, Midland Group Nottingham. *Works in collections*: Arts Council, Sheffield, Carlisle, Belfast, Bradford, Middlesbrough, Bolton, Harrogate, Rochdale, Wakefield and Huddersfield A.G.s, Open University, M. of W., Leeds University, R.C.A., Nuffield, Cranfield, Imperial War Museum, R.A., Vatican, Chatsworth, RWA Bristol, University of Birmingham, University of Brisbane, University of Queensland, Australia. *Commissions*: Imperial War Museum (1984), Lambeth Palace/Vatican (1989), various portraits. *Publications*: Modern Painters, Summer '96; Art Review, July '96, Galleries Mag Nov 2003, 2005, 2006. *Clubs*: Overseas League. Arts. *Address:* c/o Royal Academy of Arts, Piccadilly, London W1V 0DS. *Email*: art@sonialawson.co.uk. *Website*: www.sonialawson.co.uk *Signs work*: "S. Lawson," "Sonia Lawson" or "Lawson."

LAWSON, Thomas. *Medium*: oil, watercolour, drawing. *b*: Newcastle-upon-Tyne, 8 May 1922. *Studied*: Studied Art, Kings College (1950) & Newcastle-upon-Tyne Certificate in Fine Art; College of Art, Newcastle Certificates in Design & Craft (1980) and Window Display (1960). *Exhib*: Local galleries: Laing Art, Halton, Northumbria; Group Exhibitions:

Royal Society of Portrait Painters, 2006 Newcastle. *Publications*: Listed in 'Artists of Northumbria since 1945', Marshall Hall. *Recreations*: Classical music. *Clubs*: North of England Art Club, Newcastle-upon-Tyne. *Address:* 13 Tweedmouth Court, Newcastle-upon-Tyne, NE3 1YP. *Email*: tomlawson62@yahoo.com *Signs work*: "Tom Lawson".

LAWSON-BAKER, Auriol, muralist, sculptor in bronze; Director, LBP Sculpture and Design; owner "Scene Inside" Mural Co. *b*: 7 Sep 1963. *m*: Neil Lawson-Baker. one *s*. *Educ*: Ditcham Park, Petersfield, Hants. *Exhib*: RA, sculpture project managed throughout UK and Europe including Houses of Parliament Arts Com.; London International Financial Futures Exchange; British Gas plc., etc. *Address:* Graingers, West Ashling, W. Sussex PO18 8DN. *Signs work*: "A. Lawson-Baker."

LAWSON-BAKER, Dr. Neil, MB, BS (Lond), BDS, LDS (Lond.), LDS, RCS (Eng); dental surgeon and sculptor in bronze; Director, LBP Sculpture and Design; Chairman, Chichester Art Trust; Organiser of the National Open Art Competition www.thenationalopenartcompetition.com. *b*: Watford, 8 Nov 1938. *m*: Grace Louise Lawson Baker. one *s*. *Educ*: Merchant Taylors and London University. *Studied*: Guys Hospital (Dental Surgery), St.Georges Hospital (Medicine & Surgery). *Exhib*: one-man shows: Watermans Gallery, London (1991); abstract paintings: The Arts Club, Dover Street, London W1 (June 2005). *Commissions*: Sterling House, Albert Bridge, London, SW11; Entrance and trading floor at London International Financial Futures Exchange; British Gas plc, 7 metre bronze flame, Reading and Loughborough; Entrance Hall, 1 Parliament Street, London SW1; Entrance Gibran Library, Beirut University, Lebanon; Inauguration Sculpture for Channel Tunnel, Eurotunnel plc; Magna Carta Fountain, Runnymead Borough Council, Egham; 14 metre Keris, National Stadium, Kuala Lumpur, Malaysia. *Publications*: Visual Times, a private Journal of sculpture. *Clubs*: Arts. *Address:* Graingers, West Ashling, W. Sussex PO18 8DN. *Email*: neillawsonbaker@aol.com *Signs work*: "Neil Lawson-Baker."

LAWTON, Teresa, BA (Hons) Fine Art (1994). *Medium*: Oil. *b*: Poole, 27 Dec 1952. one *s*. *Studied*: Winchester College of Art (1991-94). *Represented by*: Shirley Crowther Contemporary Art, Ditchling, Sussex. *Exhib*: The London Art Fair (1999-2012); The Affordable Art Fair (1999-2014); The New York Art Fair (2003); The Singapore Art Fair (2011); The Royal Academy Summer Exhibition (2000, 2005, 2006); The Discerning Eye, London (1997); The Laing Exhibition, London (1998); The Millfield Arts Project, Somerset (1998); Highgate Contemporary Art, London (2000-2014); Belgrave Gallery, St Ives (2005-2012); Cadogan Contemporary, London (2000); Flint Gallery, Norfolk (2011, 2014); Lena Boyle Fine Art, London (1999-2011); Gordon Hepworth Fine Art (2000-2007); Bournemouth University Arts Loan Collection (2002-2008); Adanthus Gallery, Wareham, Dorset (2012-2014); Art 20/21 British Art Fair (2001-2014). *Address*: Upwey, Weymouth, Dorset. *Email*: contact@teresalawton.co.uk *Website*: www.teresalawton.co.uk *Signs work*: "T. LAWTON".

LAYCOCK, Allan Bracewell, ATD (1951), FSAI (1975), RWA (1986); landscape painter in acrylic, in situ; lecturer in graphics and illustration. *b*: Sutton-in-Craven, 4 Jun 1928. *Educ*: Keighley Grammar School. *Studied*: Keighley School of Art (1945-46, 1948-50), Sheffield College of Art (1950-51), Norwich School of Art (1951). *Exhib*: one-man and group shows in eastern and S.W. England. Work in private collections in UK and overseas. *Clubs*: President, The Cotswold Art Club. *Address:* Tararua, Broad St., Hartpury, Glos. GL19 3BN. *Signs work*: "Allan Laycock."

LAYZELL, Peter, BA (Hons) Fine Art; artist in oil; Head of Foundation in Art at Blackpool College (2004-). *Medium*: oil. *b*: Hitchin, Herts., 1962. *Partner*: Joanne Bushell. one *s*. one *d*. *Studied*: Mander College, Bedford and Coventry Polytechnic (1981-84). *Represented by*: Portal Gallery, London. *Exhib*: RA Summer Exhbn. from 1986-'00 (prizewinner, 1990); various group exhbns. in London, Solo shows every two years at Portal Gallery, London.

Works in collections: Morgan Grenfell, St. Martin's College, Lancaster, Warrington Arts Council, Southport Art Gallery. *Commissions*: numerous. *Publications*: numerous. *Address:* 26 Bare Avenue, Morecambe LA4 6BE. *Email*: petelayzell@hotmail.com *Website*: www.peterlayzell.com *Signs work*: "P. Layzell" on reverse.

LE BAS, Rachel Ann, RE, NEAC; Mem. AWG, Somerset Guild of Craftsmen; painter, line-engraver, etc. *b*: 9 Apr 1923. *d of*: Capt. R. S. Le Bas, Somerset Light Infantry (retd). *Educ*: W. Heath School, Sevenoaks. *Studied*: City and Guilds of London Art School (A.R. Middleton Todd, RA, RWS, RE, NEAC). *Exhib*: NEAC, RE, RA, etc. *Works in collections*: Ashmolean Museum, Exeter Museum, Southampton Civic Centre, RA Graphics. *Commissions*: Bishop of Bath & Wells; Royal Academy Graphics. *Clubs*: Arts, Dover St. *Address:* Winsford, nr. Minehead, Som. TA24 7JE. *Signs work*: "R. A. LE BAS."

LE BRETON PARKER, G., BA (Hons). *Medium*: oil, prints, sculpture. *Studied*: Warwick University; Central St.Martins. *Exhib*: RA; Smith's Galleries, Covent Garden; Printmakers' Council; London Print Studio; Christie's. *Works in collections*: UK, USA, E. Europe, Canada, France, Italy. *Address:* The Old White Horse, The Street, Little Waldingfield, Sudbury, CO10 0SQ. *Signs work*: 'G.Le Breton Parker'.

LE BRUN, Christopher Mark, DipFA Slade (1974), MA Chelsea (1975), RA (1996); painter, printmaker, sculptor; Trustee National Gallery (1996-2003), Trustee Tate Gallery (1990-95), Trustee Dulwich Picture Gallery (2000-2005), Trustee Prince of Wales's Drawing School (2003-), Professor of Drawing, RA (2000); President of the Royal Academy (2011-). *b*: Portsmouth, 20 Dec 1951. *m*: Charlotte Verity. two *s*. one *d*. *Studied*: Slade School of Fine Art, Chelsea School of Art. Slade School of Fine Art, Chelsea School of Art. *Exhib*: numerous mixed exhbs., one-man shows worldwide since 1978. *Works in collections*: Tate, V&A, BM, MOMA New York, Arts Council, Fitzwilliam Museum, Courtauld, Oslo, Sydney, Yale, SNGMA, Edinburgh, Whitworth, Southampton, etc. *Commissions*: The Parables, Liverpool Cathedral (1996), Portrait of George Steiner, National Portrait Gallery, Monument to Victor Hugo, St. Helier, Jersey 2011. *Publications*: 'Christopher Le Brun' Booth-Clibborn Editions (2001); 'Christopher le Brun Fifty Etchings' Paragon Press (1991). *Clubs*: Chelsea Arts, The Arts Club. *Address:* 8 Love Walk, London SE5 8AD. *Website*: www.christopherlebrun.co.uk

LE GRICE, Klio, BA Hons Silversmithing, Jewellery & Design; BTec Dip. Art & Design. *Medium*: Mixed media 2D paintings and collages plus small pieces of mixed media jewellery, also gouache and acrylic. *b*: Bradford, 19 Feb 1968. *Studied*: Southgate College, London; Sir John Cass College of Art & Design. *Exhib*: Saatchi & Saatchi Advertising, (2001, 2001); Design Centre, Islington, London (2001); Group Expos: Gallery Vertebrae, Vorst, Brussels (2003); Gallery No Soap, Schaarbeek, Brussels (2004); Lambermontmartre, Antwerp, Belgium (2004-); Indiancaps, Antwerp, Belgium (2008), Werkhuys, Borgerhout, Antwerp (2013). Titus Gallery. Solo: Langeleemstraat, Antwerp, Belgium. *Works in collections*: private collections. *Recreations*: cycling, art, kinitting, travelling, films and music. *Misc*: only makes one off pieces. *Address*: Bisschopstraat 9 bus 2, Antwerp, 2060 Belgium. *Email*: klio2002@hotmail.com *Website*: facebook Klio le Grice *Signs work*: "Klio" and date.

LE MARCHANT, Sir Francis, Bt., Cert RAS, Bilan de Paris silver medal; 2 David Murray Studentships; landscape and portrait painter/farmer. *Medium*: painter in oils/watercolours. *b*: Hungerton, 6 Oct 1939. *Educ*: Gordonstoun. *Studied*: art Byam Shaw School, Royal Academy Schools. *Exhib*: Agnews, Roy Miles Fine Art, Sally Hunter Fine Art, Museum of Arts and Science Evansville USA, ING Bank (sponsored by Barings Asset Management). *Works in collections*: Government Art Collection, Financial Times, Evansville Museum of Arts and Science, Barings Asset Management, University of Evansville. *Commissions*: portraits - watercolours/drawings for the Wine Society, private portrait and landscape, houses. *Official Purchasers*: Government Art Collection. *Works Reproduced*: two works on website. *Recreations*: Music, Reading. *Clubs*: Savile Club. *Address:* Hungerton Hall, Grantham, Lincs. NG32 1AJ. *Website*: www.francislemarchant.com *Signs work*: 'Le M', or 'Le Marchant'.

LEACH, Jenny. *Medium*: etching, engraving, prints, oil, drawing. *b*: London, 25 May 1966. *Studied*: Camberwell Art School (1987-91). *Exhib*: solo: Broadway Bookshop (2009). Group: Millinery Works Gallery, London (2008, 2009), Contemporary Print Show, Barbican Centre, London (2000, 1999, 1998), Artichoke Print Workshop Show, Sweet Briars College, Virginia, USA (1999), Gallery Jeanne, Munich, Germany (1997, 1995). *Works in collections*: private. *Misc*: Teaches Diploma, Etching & Life Painting at Putney School of Art & Design. *Address:* Thistleworth Marine, Railshead Road, Isleworth, TW7 7BY. *Email*: jenny@j.art.co.uk *Website*: www.j-art.co.uk *Signs work*: "JL" (Paintings), "Jenny Leach" (Etchings).

LEACH, Ursula Mary, RE, BA (Hons) (1992); printmaker/painter in etching and oil paint. *b*: Woking, 14 May 1947. *m*: John Leach (divorced). *Partner*: Julian G ordon-Watson. one *s*. one *d*. *Studied*: Winchester, Wimbledon and Farnham Schools of Art. *Exhib*: Mall Galleries, London, Redfern, London, Southampton City A.G., Oliver Contemporary, London, Dorset County Museum, Arflex, Osaka & Tokyo, Japan; The Art Stable, Blandford, Dorset. *Works in collections*: Ashmolean Museum, Oxford, Royal Hospitals NHS Trust, Dorset County Hospital; The Curwen Archive; The House of Lords, The Creasey Collection, Kirklees Museums. *Commissions*: Worthing Hospital Postgraduate Medical Centre, Artsreach. *Works Reproduced*: review: Contemporary Art Vol. 2. No.3., ISBN 0-86080-426-7,Growing Concerns - Touring Show Catalogue; Collagraphs and Mixed-Media Printmaking (ISBN 0-780713-6296-0); Elemental Insight Touring Show catalogue reviews, Galleries Magazine May 2006, The Week 2006, 2008; 50 Wessex Artists (ISBN 978-0955-450306); Circles & Tangents, Art in the Shadow of Cranborne Chase, Printmakers Secrets, www.axisweb.org.uk - open frequency (2013). *Address:* 14 The Square, Cranborne, Dorset BH21 5PR. *Email*: ursulaleach@hotmail.com *Website*: www.ursulaleach.co.uk *Signs work*: "U.Leach."

LEAPER, Landreth Francis, RWA; self taught artist in water-colour and mixed media. *b*: Horsham, 22 Dec 1947. *s of*: Landreth E Leaper, Author. *Exhib*: numerous in South and S. West England. *Address:* 28 Gerald Rd., Ashton, Bristol BS3 2DN. *Signs work*: "LEAPER" or "L. LEAPER" or double LL within a circle, sometimes above the year.

LECOURT, Elisabeth, MA; Post Grad Diploma; BAHons; BTEC; BIDA Award for Best Newcomer (2004). *Medium*; oil, watercolour, drawing, sculpture, dresses made out of maps. *b*: Oloron St Marie, 31 Dec 1972. one *d*. *Studied*: Royal College of Art, London (1999-2001); Central Saint Martins, London (1997-1999); Kingston University (1994-1997); Hereford College (1993-1994). *Represented by*: Byard Art. *Exhib*: Europe, Asia, Canada, the USA, Mexico, Hong Kong. *Works in collections*: Art Council, London, England; paintings in Hospitals; Eric Franck Fine Art. *Publications*: Published in Europe, Asia, Canada, the USA, Mexico, Brazil, Hong Kong, Japan, Australia, Russia, Poland. *Recreations*: yoga, travels. *Clubs*: Soho House. *Address*: Studio Voltaire, 1a Nelson's Row, London SW4 7JR. *Email*: studio@elisabethlecourt.com *Website*: www.elisabethlecourt.com *Signs work*: "Elisabeth Lecourt".

LEDER, Carolyn, MA (1968); Curator, Old Speech Room Gallery, Harrow School (1989-2011); Trustee, Stanley Spencer Gallery, Cookham (1978-90, 2004-); formerly Lecturer in History of Art, University of London, Dept. of Extra-Mural Studies (1972-88). *b*: Melbourne, 5 Mar 1945. *d of*: Harold Beck, violincellist. *m*: Professor Malcolm Leder. two *s*. *Studied*: Courtauld Inst. of Art, University of London. *Publications*: book, Stanley Spencer: The Astor Collection (1976); articles; numerous catalogues on English watercolourists including ' Watercolours at Harrow' (2007), and key figures in British Art. Historical Adviser, BBC 2 Television, 'Stanley', drama-documentary on Stanley Spencer (1988). Specialist commentator in Stanley Spencer Gallery's video 'Stanley Spencer: A Painter in Heaven' (1996). Article 'Old Speech Room Gallery' in 'Harrow: Portrait of an English School' (2004). Recent catalogues include 'Spencer's War: The Art of Shipbuilding on the Clyde' (2011); 'Spencer's Earthly Paradise: Stanley Spencer Gallery - 50th Anniversary Exhibition' (2012); 'Perspectives on Love' (2013). She is regularly interviewd about Spencer on radio and television. *Address:* The Steps, Hill Close, Harrow on the Hill, Middx. HA1 3PQ. *Email*: carolyn.leder@brinternet.com

LEDGER, Janet, Hon. Citizen of Dallas; painter in oil of landscapes, townscapes, beach scenes. *Medium*: oil on board - acrylic on board. *b*: Northampton, 22 Jul 1931. *m*: H.E. Clements (decd). two *d*. *Studied*: Northampton School of Art. *Represented by*: Red Rag Gallery. *Exhib*: Dallas Texas, RA Summer Show, Mall Galleries, SWA, Century Gallery, Henley, Medici Gallery, London, Edwin Pollard Gallery, Linda Blackstone Gallery since 1985, 9 Solo Exhibitions 1985-2003 with Linda Blackstone Gallery. *Works in collections*: HRH Princess Margaret, Tate Gallery, National Westminster Bank, Marks & Spencer Plc, National Coal Board, McDonalds Plc. *Works Reproduced*: Sunday Times colour supplement Editions of 250; 'Nuns on the Beach (eating Candyfloss)'; 'Waves'. *Address:* c/o Red Rag Gallery, 5-7 Church Street, Stow on the Wold, Glos GL54 1BB.

LEE, Christine Mary, BA (Hons) Fine Arts, Sculpture (1981); sculptor in various medias; Artistic Director, Ragley Hall Sculpture Park, Warwickshire (1994-95), Artistic Director, Westonbirt Arboretum Sculpture Park, Glos. (1996). *b*: Bucks. *m*: Douglas May. one *s*. one *d*. *Studied*: privately under Ulrica Seaton-Lloyd, Oxford; Banbury Art College (1977-78); St. Martin's School of Art (1978-81); Central School of Art (1981-83, painting and drawing: Cecil Collins). *Exhib*: Spain, USA, UK, Channel Islands. Work in collections worldwide. *Commissions*: numerous including 17 ft. fountain, Stratford-upon-Avon, inaugurated by H.M. The Queen. *Clubs*: F.P.S., Fountain Soc. *Address:* Beechwood House, High Bickington, Devon EX3 9BQ. *Signs work*: "Lee."

LEE, Debbie, 1st Class BA(Hons), Glasgow; Post Baccaluareatte, Chicago; MA, RCA; Commonwealth Universities Research Scholar (India); Sir William Gillies Bursary (RSA). *Medium*: drawing and painting. *b*: Leicester, 15 Jun 1967. *m*: Paul Jefferis. one *s*. *Studied*: Glasgow School of Art (1989); Art Institute of Chicago (1990); Royal College of Art (1992). *Exhib*: Boundary Gallery, London (1997, 2002); Institute of Psychiatry (2004); Budapest Art Expo, Hungary (1994); Cafe Gallery, London (2002); Opus Gallery, Nicosia (1993); Collins Gallery, Glasgow (1999); Gallery 2, Chicago (1990); Peacock Gallery, Aberdeen (1995, 2002); Jerwood Drawing (2002); City Gallery, Leicester (1993, 99); Royal Overseas League (1998). *Works in collections*: British Library, RSA, Aberdeen Library, Indian Center for Public Relations, Aberdeen Royal Infirmary. *Commissions*: Aberdeen Royal Infirmary (mural); St.Mary's of Rotherhithe (Stations of the Cross). *Publications*: 'Tongues of Diamonds' (Collins Gallery catalogue). *Works Reproduced*: in the following catalogues: Jerwood Drawings (2002); Royal Overseas League (1998); Fine Art Society (1998). *Principal Works*: drawings and paintings. *Recreations*: etching. *Clubs*: Bermondsey Artists' Group. *Address:* 29 Admiral Street, Deptford, London SE8 4HZ. *Email*: pauljefferis@ntlworld.com *Signs work*: 'DEBBIE LEE'.

LEE, Sara Charlotte, BA (Hons); National Eisteddfod Highly Commended, TWASI Highly Commended and Bronze medal, Adrian Henri Memorial Award, Lady Scott Award, NAPA 'The Artist' Award, TWASI David Shepherd Award. *Medium*: artist in acrylic, watercolour, graphite, print, paper. *b*: Harwell, 31 Dec 1969. *Studied*: CCTA, Huddersfield University. *Exhib*: WWF Search for an Environmental Sculptor, Welsh National Eisteddfod, BP Portrait Award, TWASI, Hilliard Society, SWLA, NAPA, RMS, Falmouth Art Gallery,

SWA, Welsh Artist of the Year, SOFA, MIWAS, NEWA, RSMA, RBA. *Works in collections*: Falmouth Art Gallery's Permanent Collection; private collections. *Commissions*: gallery and private commissions. *Clubs*: NAPA, FWASI, HS, SOFA. *Address:* 17 The Cleave, Harwell, Oxon, OX11 0EL. *Signs work*: 'Sara C.Lee' or 'S L'.

LEECH, Raymond Ian, RSMA (1986), LSIAD (1969); mem. E. Anglian Group of Marine Artists; landscape and seascape painter in oil and water-colour; partner in a design group, Pencil Point Studio. *b*: Gt.Yarmouth, 1949. *s of*: Gordon William Leech (decd). *Educ*: Edward Worledge School, Alderman Leach High School. *Studied*: Gt.Yarmouth College of Art and Design (1965-69). *Exhib*: RSMA, Hunting Group, Mystic USA, Assembly Rooms Norwich, Ladygate Gallery, and other provincial galleries. *Works in collections*: National Maritime Museum, The Sheik of Oman, Mystic Maritime Gallery USA, etc. *Publications*: represented in Tonal Painting (Quarto). *Address:* 1 The Staithe, Oulton Broad, Lowestoft, Suffolk NR33 9AF.

LEES, Caroline, AFAS; CAS, BAI. *Medium*: watercolour interiors; oil landscapes; egg tempera/gold leaf: Icon painting . *b*: Shropshire, 14 Apr 1940. *d of*: John H. Everall. *m*: Brian Musson Lees. two *d*. *Studied*: Corcoran Gallery School of Art , Washington DC(1982/84); Slade School of Art (Master Classes). *Represented by*: Rafael Valls Ltd, SW1Y 6QB. *Exhib*: Ebury Galleries (1995); Atlantic Gallery, Washington DC (1983, 84); Mathaf Gallery, Knightsbridge (1986, 92, 98, 2000); Henry Brett, Stow-on-the-Wold (1988, 89); RSMA, Mall Galleries (1992); Watermans (1992); Laing Art Group (1996); RA Summer Exhbn (1995, 97, 2005); Rafael Valls Ltd (2001, 2003-06); Indar Pasricha Fine Arts (2005); BADA Chelsea (2008); Rafael Valls Ltd, SW1Y 6QB (2002-2007). *Works in collections*: National Trust; Adam Co. Bank. *Commissions*: F&CO: watercolour for presentation to HRH The Prince of Wales; St.Catherine's Monastry, Sinai, Egypt. *Publications*: Watercolours of Shropshire; The Way to Life (Icons) (UK, 2006; USA, 2007). *Works Reproduced*: Garsington Opera Company; Stacy International 'Oman Today'. *Address:* 14 Ringmer Avenue, London SW6 5LW. *Email*: caroline_lees@talk21.com *Website*: www.carolinelees-icons.co.uk *Signs work*: 'C LEES'.

LEES, Irene, SWA (2007); BA (Hons) Drawing and Applied Art (2005); Martini Prize, Cheltenham Art Festival (2006); Cliff Moss Memorial Award (2005); shortlisted, Jerwood Drawing Prize (2005-06). *Medium*: pen and ink, and drawings in all media. *b*: Oldham, 11 Feb 1943. *d of*: Irene Leghorn. *m*: Harry. three *s*. one *d*. *Studied*: UWE, Bristol (2002-05). *Exhib*: RWA Bristol (2003, 2006); Iguana Gallery, Stroud (2003); RWA (2004); Octagon Visual Arts Centre (Draw Group) (2004); Stroud House Gallery (2005); Sherwell Gallery, Plymouth; London Art Fair; SWA, Mall Galleries (2006); Smithfield Gallery, London (2006); Full Circle, London (2006-07); Holt Gallery, Norfolk (SWA, 2006); Foyer Gallery, UWE, Bristol (2002-06); Wells Gallery, St.Ives (2007). *Commissions*: for private collections in Spain & Australia. *Address:* 5 Bos Vean, The Lizard, Helston, Cornwall TR12 7RU. *Email*: irene17lees@aol.com *Signs work*: 'Irene Lees'.

LEES, Susan Jane, artist in gouache, acrylic, pastel, batik, oil; Wildlife illustrator at Bristol Zoo since 1995. *b*: Bristol, 23 Jun 1961. *Educ*: Hengrove Comp. Bristol. *Studied*: Glos. College of Art and Design (1980-82). *Exhib*: Soc. of Amateur Artists, Soc. of Women Artists, British Soc. of Painters, The Wildlife Art Soc., and local exhbns, National Exhbn. of Wildlife Art. Christies & Sotheby's Wildlife Art Auction. *Clubs*: Soc. of Amateur Artists '93, Wildlife Art Soc. '94, Soc. of Women Artists '95-'96, British Soc. of Painters '94-'95, Whitchurch Art Club '92. *Address:* 163 Avonvale Rd., Redfield, Bristol BS5 9RY. *Signs work*: "Susan Jane."

LEESON, Geoffrey Glynne, NDD, BA. *Medium*: acrylic on canvas, oil, watercolour, drawing, prints. *b*: Sutton, Surrey, 20 Mar 1942. *s of*: G.W.J. Leeson. *m*: Kay. two *s*. *Educ*: London Nautical School (1952-58). *Studied*: Camberwell School of Arts and Crafts (1958-

62, painting and printmaking). Studied under Michael Rothenstein. *Represented by*: Peter Weaver. *Exhib*: solo exhibitions: Scunthorpe Art Gallery (1964), Canaletto Gallery, London (1980), Gallery 21, Tonbridge, Kent (1982), Tunbridge Wells Art Gallery (1990), Ripley Arts Centre, Bromley, Kent (2006, 2007, 2008, 2009, 2012, 2014), Wobblybridge Art Gallery, Tunbridge Wells (2012-2013). *Works in collections*: Kent Clocks, Red Boat Design, private and corporate. *Commissions*: Kent Clocks, Red Boat Design, private and corporate. *Publications*: The Sledge (1987), Jenny Ingham Publications. *Misc*: Known as Geoff Leeson. Taught Art in various schools to include Winterton Comp, Scunthorpe, Oakwood Park Grammar, Maidstone, currently The Priory, Orpington. *Address:* 256 Downham Way, Bromley, Kent, BR1 5NS. *Email*: leeson@wobblybridge.co.uk *Website*: www.wobblybridge.co.uk *Signs work*: on prints "GEOFFREY LEESON", on paintings "LEESON".

LEGG, Owen, FFPS, MBBS; printmaker and artist in oil on board, lino-cut prints, abstract constructions, sculpture in plywood. *b*: London, 1 Aug 1935. *Educ*: Alleyns School, Dulwich; Guy's Hospital, London. *Studied*: Tunbridge Wells Adult Education Centre. *Exhib*: York University, Tunbridge Wells Library, Loggia Gallery, St Martin-in-the-Fields, Oxford, Newcastle - USA, ICA London. *Works in collections*: Greenwich Library; Graphotek, Berlin; Columbia University, NY. *Publications*: Cut in the Chalk, Rubaiyyat of Omar Khayaam; The Garden by V. Sackville West (1989), On First Seeing Iceland (1992), Christmas letters from a Friend (1997), Advice to a Young Explorer (1999), Egily Head Ransom (2001), Battle of Maldon (2003), The Gardens of Stowe (2006), Danse Macabre (2009). *Recreations*: gardening. *Clubs*: Past Honorary Secretary to Free Painters & Sculptors (1999-2009). *Address:* Woodcraft Press, 152 Hadlow Rd., Tonbridge, Kent TN9 1PB. *Email:* owenandhelen.woodcraft@btinternet.com *Website*: www.woodcraftpress.co.uk *Signs work*: "Owen Legg."

LEIGH, David Roy, MA (Oxon) (1972), FSBA (1986); botanical artist in water-colour; former official artist to the Orchid Com. of the RHS. *b*: Leeds, 2 Jun 1945. one *s*. one *d*. *Educ*: City of Leicester Boys' School, and Oxford University (Worcester College). *Exhib*: SBA at Mall Galleries, RHS. *Publications*: illustrated Aroids (Century, 1988), author: Orchids (Cassell, 1990), Growing Your Own Orchids (Salamander) 1982, Field Guide To Wild Flowers (Collins 1989). *Recreations*: golf. *Address:* 5 Ringhill Street, Poundbury, Dorchester, Dorset DT1 3TL. *Signs work*: "David R. Leigh" or more often "D.R.L." with year.

LEIGH, Michael, Post Graduate Degree in Fine Art MA. *Medium*: Oil, watercolour, drawing, prints, collage. *b*: London, 1947. *m*: Hazel Jones. one *s*. *Studied*: Southend School of Art (1963-67); Manchester College of Art and Design (1967-70); Chelsea College of Art (1970-71). *Represented by*: A1 Waste Paper Co Ltd. *Exhib*: Walsall Art Gallery, 'Weirdorama' with Hazel Jone 91995); 'Networking' Arts Council Touring Exhibition (1997); Worcester Art Gallery 'Recycled Postcards' (1997); 'Stick' Southern Arts Touring Exhbition (1998); 'Ray Johnson Retrospective' Whitney Museum, New York (1999). *Work in collections*: Many private collections; Tate Gallery archive. *Commissions*: Boomerang Postcards. *Publications*: Artists Postcards - Jeremy Cooper (2012); Modern Vintage Illustration, Martin Dawber (2012). *Works Reproduced*: Boomerang Postcards (1995-2005). *Recreations*: Walking; collecting. *Misc*: Discovered International Mail Art Network in 1980. Has produced many handmade postcards, publications and rubber stamps. Also known as Wastedpapiers, A1 Waste Paper Co Ltd and Kollage Kid. *Address*: 33 Shipbrook Road, Rudheath, Cheshire CW9 7EX. *Email*: wastedpapiers@yahoo.co.uk *Website*: laughingshed.blogspot.com *Signs work*: "MICHAEL LEIGH".

LEIGH, Michelle Beverly, BA (1st Class) Hons, Fine Art, Painting, MA Painting; British Academy Major State Studentship Award (1986-88). *Medium*: oil, watercolour, prints.

b: Manchester, 20 Apr 1964. *Studied*: Manchester Polytechnic (1982-3), Medlock Fine Art Centre (1983-6), University of Newcastle upon Tyne (1986-88). *Represented by*: Wendy J Levy Contemporary Art, Manchester; Steve Marsling Fine Arts Ltd. *Exhib*: Wendy J Levy Contemporary Art, Manchester (2001, 03, 05, 06), The New Grafton Gallery, London (2005), Firbob & Peacock Contemporary Art (2002, 03), The Whitworth Art Gallery, Manchester (2000), Liverpool Biennial (1999), Reynolds Fine Art, London, Castlefield Art Gallery, Manchester (1991, 99), Salford Museum & Art Gallery, Manchester Academy of Fine Arts (1991), Ben Uri Gallery (1988). *Works in collections*: Rutherstones Loan Collection, Manchester City Art Gallery, Manchester Airport, Harvard University. *Commissions*: Robert J Duncan. *Publications*: 'A Colourful Canvas' 12 Women Artists in the North West, by Wendy J Levy & Judy Rose. *Official Purchasers*: Manchester City Art Galleries, British Midland (for Manchester Airport). *Recreations*: languages, travelling, walking, writing, baking. *Misc*: Draws upon two cultures: her Jewish background, and modern life. *Address:* 229 Hulme St., Hulme, Manchester, M15 5EF. *Email*: michellebleigh@hotmail.com *Signs work*: "M. LEIGH".

LEK, Karel, MBE, RCA, ATD; artist in oil, water-colour and graphic media. *b*: Antwerp, 7 Jun 1929. married. *s of*: Hendrick Lek, artist. one *s*. one *d*. *Studied*: Liverpool College of Art. *Exhib*: National Museum for Wales, RA, RCA, Cardiff, Albany Gallery, Cardiff, Arts Council, Bangor Gallery, Mostyn Gallery, Llandudno, Retrospective (1994) Oriel Ynys Môn, Anglesey, Breknock Museum Brecon (1997); Retrospective RCA (2004); Martin Tinney Gallery, Cardiff. *Works in collections*: University Coll. of N. Wales, Contemporary Art Soc. for Wales, National Library of Wales, Anglesey CC Welsh Collection, Michael Forte Collection, Breknock Museum, Brecon; Curwen Studio. *Official Purchasers*: Nat.Library of Wales: 7 works, 2 sketch books (2005) 16 prints. *Misc*: Documentaries: "Prime Time" HTV (9 May & 9 Oct. 1994), "My Story" BBC2W (19 June 2007). *Address:* Studio House, Beaumaris, Anglesey LL58 8EE.

LEMAIRE, Angela Jacqueline, DipAD (1967); The Society of Wood Engravers (Member). *Medium*: mixed media. *b*: Burnham, Bucks., 27 Sep 1944. *Partner*: Ian Howel. one *s*. *Educ*: Sydney, Australia. *Studied*: Chelsea School of Art; Camberwell School of Arts and Crafts. *Exhib*: 4 solo shows: Open Eye Gallery, Edinburgh (1977); Stadia Graphics, Sydney, Australia (1975); Edinburgh Music School (1993); Grey College, Durham (Retrospective Prints, 2001). Many group shows. *Works in collections*: private collections and national libraries. *Commissions*: The Folio Society, Scottish Borders Council, many others. *Publications*: Artists books, books with The Old Stile Press and others. *Official Purchasers*: The National Libraries and others. *Works Reproduced*: "Forty Five Wood Engravers" (Whittington Press); "An Engravers Globe" (Primrose Hill Press, 2002); "International Contemporary Bookplates" (Portugal, 2007); "Scottish Bookplates" (Bookplate Society, Brian North Lee, 2007), many others. *Principal Works*: 7 books with Old Stile Press. *Address:* The Studio, The Friars, Jedburgh, Roxburghshire, Scotland, TD8 6BN. *Email*: angelamaire2004@yahoo.co.uk *Website*: www.angelalemaire.co.uk *Signs work*: "A.Lemaire" and "AL" on prints, drawings and paintings.

LEMAN, Jill, ARWS (2009); RBA (2011); RWS (2012); DipAD Graphics. *Medium*: acrylic, watercolour, drawing. *b*: USA, 2 Nov 1946. *d of*: H.D. & Elizabeth Winthrop. *m*: Martin Leman. *Educ*: St.Annes School, Chelmsford, Essex; Benenden School, Kent. *Studied*: Colchester School of Art (1963-65), Central School of Art and Design (1965-68). *Exhib*: solo exhibitions: John Russell Gallery, Ipswich (2004, 2007), RONA Gallery, London (2005), Russell Gallery, Putney (2010). Selected Group exhibitions: RWS Open (1996, 2002, 2004-09) , RI Open annually 1997/2009, Singer Friedlander (2006, 07), RBA, RWS, RA Summer Exhbn. (2009); Millinery Works; The Ruth Borchard Self Portrait Competition, King's Place, London. *Publications*: Many books in conjunction with Martin Leman. *Recreations*: painting, drawing, people, books and reading, gardening, walking, writing. *Address:* 1 Malvern Terrace, London N1 1HR . *Email*: jill.leman@yahoo.co.uk *Website*: www.jillleman.co.uk *Signs work*: "Jill Leman" or "JL" (in box, on paintings).

LEMAN, Martin, ARWS, RBA; artist in oil; former graphic design teacher, Hornsey College of Art (1961-77). *Medium*: oils, acrylic, watercolour, etching. *b*: London, 25 Apr 1934. *s of*: Arthur Leman & Eileen (nee Mahoney). *m*: Jill. *Educ*: Royal Masonic School. *Studied*: Worthing School of Art, and Central School of Arts and Crafts. *Exhib*: Selected solo shows: Portal Gallery, London (1971, 94, 98); RONA Gallery, London (1999, 2001, 2002, 2004); Wren Gallery, Burford (1999, 2001); The Russell Gallery, Putney (2010); Many mixed exhibitions including: RA Summer Exhibitions (most recent 2011); Discerning Eye, Chris Beetles; Royal Society of Portrait Painters; Grays Inn at the Langham Gallery, London; Millinery Works, London; The Royal Institute of Painters in Watercolours; The Sunday Times Watercolour Competition; The Royal Society of British Artists; The Royal Watercolour Society. *Works in collections*: Sir Roy Strong & many private collections. *Commissions*: many cat portraits. *Publications*: twenty-six books, mainly cat paintings. *Recreations*: chess, swimming, gardening, walking. *Address:* 1 Malvern Terr., London N1 1HR. *Email*: jill.leman@yahoo.co.uk *Website*: martinleman.co.uk *Signs work*: "Leman."

LENAGHAN, Brenda, RSW (1984). *Medium*: oil and watercolour. *b*: 10 May 1941. *Partner*: Fergus Lenaghan, Architect. one *s*. *Studied*: Glasgow School of Art Dip (1963). *Exhib*: RSA, RA, RSW, RGI; Peter Potter McCauley Gallery; Caltac Gallery, Gerber, Glasgow; William Hardie, Glasgow; Duncan Campbell, London; Christopher Hull, London; Open Eye (Edinburgh); Edin Gallery; Rendezvous, Aberdeen; Richard Hagen, Japan. *Works in collections*: private in USA, Japan, Scandinavia, Australia. *Commissions*: portraits, all work. *Recreations*: painting furniture. *Address:* 'Clouds', 3, The Green, Tyninghame, East Lothian, EH42 1XL. *Email*: brenlen@live.co.uk *Signs work*: 'Brenda Lenaghan'.

LENDIS, John Andrew, MFA. *Medium*: Oil. *b*: Nottingham, 25 March 1950. *m*: Celia Lendis. one *s*. one *d*. *Educ*: BA (Hons); MFA. *Studied*: University of Tasmania, Hobart, Australia. *Represented by*: Handmark Gallery, Hobart, Aus; Celia Lendis Contemporary, Cotswolds. *Exhib*: Australia, Russia, UK - over 30 solo exhibitions. *Works in collections*: Govt House, Tasmania; Scott Polar Research Institute, Cambridge; State Govt of Tasmania; University of Tasmania, private collections. *Publications*: Various. *Works Reproduced*: Magazines, books etc. *Principal Works*: Jane Franklin series. *Recreations*: Children. *Address*: The Mushroom House, Hatherop, Gloucestershire GL7 3NA. *Email*: johnlendis@me.com *Website*: www.johnlendis.com *Signs work*: "J.A.H.L" monogram in box.

LENEY, Sheila, SBA (1987); floral artist in water-colour and embroidery. *b*: London, 23 Nov 1930. *d of*: William W. Davis, insurance surveyor. *m*: Edward W. Leney (decd). two *s*. one *d*. *Educ*: St. Helen's School, Streatham. *Studied*: Croydon School of Art (1947-49), Epsom AEC (1982). *Exhib*: Mall Galleries; Outwood Gallery, Surrey; Linnean Soc.; Lannards Gallery, Sussex; Westminster Gallery, Knapp Gallery, London; McEwan Gallery, Scotland; work in private collections. *Publications*: greetings cards for Medici Soc. *Address:* Invermene, 107 Newton Wood Rd., Ashtead, Surrey KT21 1NW. *Signs work*: "Sheila Leney."

LENNON, Stephen, FIGA (1995), BWS (1994), YWS (1997); artist in water-colour and mixed media. *b*: Burnley, Lancs., 10 Mar 1953. *m*: Laila (née Wesenlund). one *s*. one *d*. *Studied*: mostly self taught, life classes in Burnley in the 1970s. *Exhib*: Laing Finalist (1989); one-man show: Bradford University (1990); mixed shows: Mercer Harrogate, Ginnel Manchester, Salford City A.G., Chantry House Gallery, Ripley, many private collections. *Commissions*: eight paintings for the Marquess of Hartington. *Works Reproduced*: BWS catalogue (1997), articles in the Yorkshire Journal. *Clubs*: Yorkshire Water-colour Soc., Leeds Fine Art Club. *Address:* 24 Ickornshaw, Cowling, nr. Keighley, W. Yorks. BD22 0DE. *Email*: ste@stephenlennon.co.uk *Website*: www.stephenlennon.co.uk *Signs work*: "Stephen Lennon."

LEONARD, (Douglas) Michael, painter and illustrator. *b*: Bangalore, India, 25 Jun 1933. *s of*: Maj. D. G. R. Leonard, IXth Jat Regt. *Educ*: Stonyhurst College. *Studied*: St. Martin's School of Art (1954-57). Worked as an illustrator from 1957-72 and subsequently as a painter. *Exhib*: one-man shows: Fischer Fine Art London (1974, 1977, 1980, 1983, 1988), Harriet Griffin, New York (1977), Gemeentemuseum, Arnhem (1977-78) (retrospective), Artsite, Bath (1989) (retrospective), Jonathan Edwards College, Yale University (2007) (Retrospective), Stiebel Modern New York (1992), Thomas Gibson Fine Art, London (1993, 1997, 2004), Forum Gallery, New York (1999, 2009); mixed shows: "Realismus und Realitat" Darmstadt (1975), John Moores, Liverpool (1976, 1978), "The Craft of Art" Walker A.G. (1979), "Nudes" Angela Flowers, London (1979/80), "The Real British", Fischer Fine Art (1981), "Contemporary British Painters", Museo Municipal, Madrid (1983), "Self Portrait: A Contemporary View", Artsite, Bath (1987), "In Human Terms", Stiebel Modern, New York (1991), 'Its Still Life', Forum Gallery, New York (1998), 'Between Earth and Heaven', Museum of Modern Art, Ostend (2001), "Artists of the Ideal-New Classicism", Palazzo Forti, Verona (2002). *Works in collections*: The Boymans Van Beuningen Museum Rotterdam, De Beer/CSO, NPG, V&A, British Museum, Fitzwilliam Museum Cambridge, Ferens A.G., Hull, Arnot Art Museum, Elmira, NY. *Commissions*: Painted H.M. Queen Elizabeth II for Readers Digest (1986) now in N.P.G. *Address:* 3 Kensington Hall Gdns., Beaumont Ave., London W14 9LS. *Signs work*: "Leonard" or "ML."

LESTER, Anthony John, AICA, Critics' Circle, Hon. RMS, Companion of the Pastel Society, FRSA, art critic, writer and broadcaster. Since 1975 has written many hundreds of articles on British art for publications such as Antique Collecting, Antique Dealer & Collectors Guild, Galleries, Antiques Trade Gazette, Art in London. In the late 1980s/early 90s, picture expert with the Antiques Roadshow and over subsequent years has taken part in BBC programmes such as Going for a Song. Has made over 250 radio broadcasts, and since 2003 been off-screen valuer for BBC's Flog It! Judge for many national art competitions and selector in 2002 for The Discerning Eye. Chairman of the Vetting Committee for the 20/21 International Art Fair. Deputy Chairperson, Exhibitions Committee, Federation of British Artists. *b*: Oxford, 15 Sep 1945. *s of*: Donald James Lester. *m*: Elizabeth Meek, PRMS, PPSWA, HS, FRSA. *Publications*: The Exhibited Works of Helen Allingham; The Stannards of Bedfordshire (1984); Antiques Roadshow: Experts on Objects (1987); George Large (1998); The Pastel Society: Pastel Painting and Drawing 1898-2000 (2000); Pure Gold: 50 Years of the FBA (2011). *Clubs*: Chelsea Arts Club, Royal Society of Arts. *Address:* Firle House, 75 Firls Road, Seaford, East Sussex BN25 2JA. *Email*: anthonylester@fsmail.net

LESTER, James Richard, NDD (1955), SBA (1986). SWAc (2004); artist in water-colour, oil, pastel. *b*: Dover, 18 Dec 1932. one *s*. three *d*. *Studied*: Dover School of Art (1951-53), Canterbury College of Art (1953-55). *Exhib*: RA, RWA, RBA, RI, SBA, SWAc.; one-man show: Tenterden and Otterton. *Works in collections*: many private collections. *Commissions*: accepted for portraits, landscapes and figurework. *Publications*: co-author and illlustrator: 'Painting the Secret World of Nature'. *Clubs*: Society of Botanical Artists, South West Academy of Arts (SWAc). *Address:* Rydon Farm, Ottery St., Otterton, Devon EX9 7HW. *Email*: jim,pessers@btinternet.com *Website*: www.james-lester.com *Signs work*: "James Lester."

LETTS, John Barry, sculptor in clay for casting in bronze. *b*: Birmingham, 20 Aug 1930. *s of*: Joseph Omer Letts, graphic designer. *m*: Patricia Letts. two *s*. one *d*. *Educ*: Sharman Cross Senior School, Birmingham. *Studied*: Birmingham College of Art (1945-49) under William Bloye. *Exhib*: London, Birmingham, Nuneaton, Solihull, Stratford-upon-Avon, Stoke-on-Trent. *Works in collections*: Nuneaton and Stratford-upon-Avon galleries. *Commissions*: one and a half times life-size statue of George Eliot (authoress) for Nuneaton Town Centre (1985); 1994: portrait bust of H.M. The Queen, unveiled by Her Majesty

8 Dec. 1995, commissioned by Warwickshire Health Authority. *Address:* 160 Tilehouse, Green Lane, Knowle, Solihull, W. Midlands B93 9EJ. *Website*: www.lettssculptures.co.uk *Signs work*: "John Letts."

LEVEN, Marian, DA (1966), RSW (1993), RSA (elect, 2005); artist in water-colour, acrylic; Winner, Noble Grossart/ Scotland on Sunday Painting Prize (1997), Saltire Society Art in Architecture Award. *b*: Edinburgh, 25 Mar 1944. *m*: Will MacLean. two *s*. one *d*. *Educ*: Bell-Baxter, Cupar, Fife, Auchtermuchty Primary. *Studied*: Gray's School of Art, Aberdeen (1962-66), Moray House College. *Exhib*: RSA, RSW, RGI, Aberdeen Artists, RA, RWA. *Works in collections*: Arts in Fife, Paintings in Hospitals, Lillie Gallery, Milngavie, Kirkcaldy Museum and A.G., University of Dundee, University of St Andrews, RSA, Demacco Foundation, Fleming Wyfold. *Commissions*: Portraits, sculpture, prints. *Publications*: Various catalogues and art books. *Address:* Bellevue, 18 Dougall St., Tayport, Fife DD6 9JD. *Email*:marianleven@hotmail.com *Signs work*: "Marian Leven."

LEVERITT, Thomas Michael James, MA (Hons) Cantab.; Carroll Award for Portraiture (2000). *Medium*: oils and acrylics. *b*: Glasgow, 16 Jan 1976. *s of*: T C M Leveritt, Esq. *Educ*: Peterhouse, Cambridge. *Studied*: self-taught. *Represented by*: Sara Stewart Fine Art, 107 Walton St., London. *Exhib*: BP Exhbn. (2000, 2001); RP (1999, 2000, 2001); ROI (1998, 2003). *Works in collections*: Somerville College, Oxford. *Commissions*: Simon Thurley; Lord and Lady Northbrook; Rt. Hon. John S. Gummer; Dean and Christi Jernigan. *Address:* 17a South Audley St., London W1K 2NT. *Email*: thomas@leveritt.com *Website*: www.leveritt.com *Signs work*: leveritt.

LEVI, Edgar: see KNIGHT, Clifford.

LEVI, Judy Julia Miriam, MBBS, DPH; Medical Art Society Prize x 3. *Medium*: watercolour, oil. *b*: London, 26 Jun 1930. *d of*: David Levi MS FRCS, Vera Hemmens (journalist, first woman lobby correspondent in House of Commons). three *s*. one *d*. *Educ*: Northwood College, St. Mary's Hospital Medical School. *Studied*: Josh Partridge (watercolour), Robin Child, Lydgate Research Centre, Wiltshire. *Exhib*: Medical Art Society, Royal College of Physicians, Highgate Gallery, Rosvik Gallery. *Works in collections*: Northwick Park Hospital. *Recreations*: family, painting, gardening. *Address:* 103 Swains Lane, London N6 6PJ. *Email*: judlevi.b@btinternet.com

LEVIN, Eddy, B.C.H.D. (Dental), U.Pret., Diploma in Applied Kinesiology. *Medium*: drawing, sculpture, design. *b*: South Africa, 20 Mar 1932. *m*: Jeanette Levin. two *s*. *Studied*: University of Pretoria, S.Africa. *Exhib*: Art in Action, Waterperry (2011, 2012, 2013, 2014); numerous art and craft exhibitions; Demonstrations internationally of The Golden Proportion and Fibonacci Series. *Commissions*: Design and fabrication of Golden Mean Gauges. *Publications*: Mainly in dental journals and lay press. *Recreations*: sailing. *Clubs*: Royal Society of Medicine, Wembley Sailing Club. *Misc*: 50 years General Dental Practice in Harley Street, London, designing and proto-typing new instruments. *Address*: 23 Church Vale, London N2 9PB. *Email*: eddylevin@blueyonder.co.uk *Website*: www.goldenmeangauge.co.uk *Signs work*: "Eddy Levin".

LEWIS, Ann, RCA, BA; printmaker, linocut artist/illustrator in gouache, water-colour, mixed media, pencil, ink. *b*: St. Asaph, N. Wales, 29 Aug 1962. *Studied*: Exeter College of Art and Design (1985-88). *Exhib*: Royal Cambrian Academy - Conwy, WAC, National Library of Wales, Mostyn Gallery, Wales Open, Clwyd Open, Albany Gallery - Cardiff, Tegfryn Gallery - Anglesey, Hanover Galleries - Liverpool, Royal Exchange Theatre - Manchester, Plas Glyn y Weddw -Llyn, Oriel y Môr - Pwllheli,, Lion Street Gallery - Hay on Wye, Martin Tinney Gallery - Cardiff, Cablava Farm Gallery - Hay on Wye, White Lion Street Gallery - Tenby. *Works in collections*: National Library of Wales (2006), UK Government Collection of Art (2012). *Publications*: books illustrated: eight children's books, one collection of poetry, numerous illustrations for published articles. *Address:* 6 Well St. 2, Gerlan, Bethesda, Gwynedd LL57 3TW. *Email*: ann@annlewis.co.uk *Website*: www.annlewis.co.uk *Signs work*: "Ann Lewis."

LEWIS, Christopher Conrad Strafford, RCA, NDD (1950), ATD (1951), RCA (1964); sculptor in clay, woodcarver and printmaker; lecturer in art history & drawing, Chester School of Art, visiting lecturer - North Wales, Liverpool. *b*: Woodford, Essex, 15 Jul 1922. *s of*: Dr. J.B.S. Lewis MD. *m*: Marjory Rae. two *s*. three *d*. *Educ*: Epsom College, Royal Signals 1942-46. *Studied*: Ealing (1946-1950) under Tom Bayley, Hornsey (1951). *Represented by*: Royal Cambrian Academy. *Exhib*: Chester, Liverpool, London, St. Albans, Amsterdam, Wales. *Works in collections*: many private & public collections. *Commissions*: various, including Chester Canoe Club, Queens School, British Legion. *Publications*: Songs of William Shakespeare. *Recreations*: Modern Art, travelling, watching rugby and cricket matches, literature. *Clubs*: Royal Society Art Education (Retired Member). *Address:* Appletrees, 19 Fish St., Redbourn, Herts. AL3 7LP. *Signs work*: "CONRAD LEWIS."

LEWIS, Cynthia, ASWA (2007); DipHE Art & Design. *Medium*: Sculpture: animals and birds in bronze and stone carvings. *b*: Finchley, 14 Sep 1937. three *s*. *Educ*: Henrietta Barnet School; Clarks College. *Studied*: Camden School of Art; NE London Poly (now University); The Institute School of Art. *Exhib*: SWA (2000, 2002, 2005, 2007); Wildlife Society (2005, 2007); Chelsea Art Society (2007); The Institute Annual Show (1994-2002, 2004-2007). *Recreations*: reading, making patchwork quilts, 3D decoupage. *Address:* 15 Kenver Avenue, Finchley, London N12 0PG. *Email*: cynthialewis@sculptures.demon.co.uk *Signs work*: 'C.L.', or 'C.LEWIS', or 'CL' (monogram).

LEWIS, Dennis, RWA (1979), FCSD (1986); artist in oil, acrylic, water-colour; Design Group Chairman (retd). *b*: Bristol, 2 Apr 1928. *s of*: Francis George Henry Lewis. *m*: Irene Margaret. one *s*. two *d*. *Educ*: FAS Bristol. *Studied*: No. 3 Army College (1948, Mervyn Levy), West of England College of Art (1948-52). President, Bristol Savages (1972, 1979, 1989). *Works in collections*: Royal West of England Academy; Bristol Savages. *Clubs*: Bristol Savages. *Address:* 4 Oatley House, Cote Lane, Bristol BS9 3TN. *Signs work*: "Dennis Lewis."

LEWIS, Jane, Dip AD (1974), Slade Higher Diploma (1977), Slade Prize (1977), Artist in Residence Kent Opera (1985), Henry Moore Fellowship in Drawing (1992-03), Oppenheim-John Downes Memorial Trust (2006-7), Arts Council England Grant (2006-08). *Medium*: oil on canvas, pastel, conte, watercolour. *b*: London, 23 Feb 1953. *Represented by*: Red Dot Gallery, Norfolk. *Exhib*: Solo and group exhibitions throughout UK, occasionally Europe. *Works in collections*: University College London; Unilever; Manchester City Art Galleries; Trinity Arts Centre, Tunbridge Wells; Leicester Schools & Colleges Collection; Royal Museum Canterbury; Provident Financial Art Collection; Brown's Hotel London; Sheffield University Fine Art Society; Towner Gallery Eastbourne; Standard Chartered Bank; numerous private collections. *Publications*: 'A Singular Vision - 50 Years of British Painting at the Portal Gallery' (2009). *Works Reproduced*: Bloodaxe Books; Mslexia Magazine; Obsession Publishing; Christie's Contemporary Art; Bridgeman Art Library. *Address:* 11 Jackson Avenue, Leeds, LS8 1NP. *Website*: www.janelewisartist.com *Signs work*: "Jane Lewis".

LEWIS, Jane, BA Hons (Fine Art). *Medium*: oil, watercolour, drawing. *b*: Bedfordshire, 3 Oct 1951. *d of*: Marjorie & Sylfanus Lewis. *Partner*: Robert Estall. two *s*. *Educ*: University College of Wales (Aberystwyth). *Exhib*: RA; NEAC; Fry Gallery, Saffron Walden; Mall Galleries; Bury St.Edmunds Gallery; North House Gallery, Manningtree; Castle Museum, Norwich; solo exhbns: (Andrew) D'Arcy Gallery, Ipswich; widely exhibited in East Anglia and UK. *Publications*: included in: 'Artists at Walberswick' by Richard Scott (2002). *Works Reproduced*: East Anglian Daily Times; Suffolk Journal; Green Pebble Magazine. *Clubs*:

Hollyfarm Studio. *Address:* 12-14 Swan Street, Boxford, Sudbury, Suffolk CO10 5NZ. *Email*: jalewis@mac.com *Website*: janelewisart.co.uk *Signs work*: 'JLewis'.

LEWIS, Jo. *Medium*: Watercolour. *b*: Bristol, 6 May 1967. *m*: Andrew Frood. one *s*. one *d*. *Studied*: University of Edinburgh (1986-90); Leith School of Art (1990-1); Ecole des Beaux-Arts, Valence, France. *Represented by*: Serena Morton www.londonart.co.uk. *Exhib*: City Hall, London; RCA Secret; Serena Morton Gallery; Morton Metropolis; Pump House Gallery; Musee de Valence, France. *Works in collections*: Ashstead Hospital; More London; The Twickenham Experience; The Quad Residential, Twickenham. *Commissions*: Hermes UK; Ashstead Hospital; Taylor Howes Interior Designs; International Art Consultants; Barclays Bank UK, Beaufort Park, London; Brompton Place, London; Lancelot Place. *Address*: 6 Woodsyre, Sydenham Hill, London SE26 6SS. *Email*: jo@jolewisart.co.uk *Website*: www.jolewisart.co.uk *Signs work*: "J LEWIS".

LEWIS, Roger Leslie, Honorary Member and Past President of The Society of Graphic Fine Art (SGFA). Tutor in Fine Art at the Ripley Arts Centre, Bromley, Kent, since 2001 (part-time), 'Signature' member of the United Kingdom Coloured Pencil Society (UKCPS); Awarded 'Annie Longley' Award, 2005, Pastel Society Exhibition, Mall Gallery, London. *Medium*: all media. *b*: Strood, Kent, 2 Sep 1939. *s of*: Winifred and Leslie Lewis. *m*: Elaine Lilian. one *s*. one *d*. *Educ*: Rochester (Kent) Technical College, Medway Art College. *Studied*: Sutton and Cheam School of Art (full-time, 1954-59). *Represented by*: self. *Exhib*: With the Society of Graphic Fine Art at the Menier Gallery, Mall Gallery, London. *Works in collections*: private collections. *Commissions*: portraiture. *Works Reproduced*: In "International Artist" book "How Did You Paint That?", "Painting World" magazine. *Principal Works*: pastel paintings, scraperboard drawings, coloured pencil works, portraiture. *Recreations*: photography, art lectures/critiques. *Misc*: writes features and demonstrations for the art press. *Address:* 27 Lorne Avenue, Croydon, Surrey, CR0 7RQ. *Email*: rogerlewissgfa@tiscali.co.uk *Website*: www.sgfa.org.uk *Signs work*: "ROGER LEWIS".

LEWIS, Sanchia, Cert. Printmaking and Cert. Advanced Printmaking (Distinction 1982); 1st prize Portobello Open Exhib. (1993), Marlborough Gallery Prize,National Open Print Exhib. (1994); etcher and painter in oil. *b*: London, 31 Mar 1960. *m*: Jeremy Youngs. *Studied*: City and Guilds School of Art, London. *Represented by*: The Arterie, East Dulwich, London; Brumfield's Gallery, Boise, Idaho, USA; Weekend Gallery, Hastings, East Sussex. *Exhib*: Serena Hall Gallery, Southwold, Suffolk; RA Summer Exhbn (2006); Originals 05 & 06, Mall Gallery, London; Affordable Art Fair, Battersea (2000-04); Art on Paper Fair, RCA (2001-02). *Publications*: The Art World Directory (pub.Art Review, 2002-); in Dictionary of International Biography, International Biography Centre, Cambridge; featured in 'The Printmakers Gat' by Alan Marshall, published Mascot Media Ltd (2013). *Works Reproduced*: in Dictionary of International Biography, International Biographical Centre, Cambridge. *Address:* 50 Cheltenham Rd., Peckham Rye, London SE15 3AQ. *Email*: sanchia@sanchialewis.co.uk *Website*: www.sanchialewis.co.uk *Signs work*: "Sanchia Lewis."

LEWIS, Stephen, BFA (Hons); sculptor in steel. *b*: 11 Jan 1959. *Educ*: Deyes High School, Maghull, Merseyside. *Studied*: Southport College of Art (1976-77), Manchester Polytechnic (1977-80), Jan van Eyck Academie, Maastricht, The Netherlands. *Exhib*: New Contemporaries, ICI London (1979), Kunst Europa, Germany (1991); one-man shows: Francis Graham-Dixon Gallery (1988, 1990, 1993), Holden Gallery, Manchester (1990). *Address:* 76 Royal Hill, Greenwich, London SE10 8RT. *Signs work*: "Stephen Lewis."

LEWTHWAITE, Paul Frank, ARBS. *Medium*: Sculpture. *b*: Douglas, Isle of Man, 10 Dec 1969. *s of*: Frank Charles & Edith Patricia. *m*: Sarah. *Educ*: Ballakermeen High School, Douglas. *Studied*: Isle of Man College of Further Education (1989-90); University of Sunderland (1990-93). *Represented by*: Transplant (Live) Norway; Nela Alberca Galeria, Madrid. *Exhib*: solo and group shows including venues in UK, New York, Madrid, Barcelona, Bergen and Vienna. *Works in collections*: Geldards Art at the ARC, Nottingham. *Commissions*: Wrightington Hospital, Wigan; Chesterfields Magistrates Court; Greenfields Arts Centre; UMIST, Manchester; Warwickshire College. *Principal Works*: The Generation of Possibilities (1999); A System of Support and Balance (2004). *Recreations*: music, film, literature, sport. *Address:* 80 Melton Road, West Bridgford, Nottingham, NG2 7NF. *Email*: info@paullewthwaite.com *Website*: www.paullewthwaite.com *Signs work*: 'Lewthwaite' (and date).

LEYSHON-JONES, Steffan, BA Hons Graphic Design with Illustration (1997); visual designer; Laing National Under 25 winner 2001; photographer, artist and graphic designer. *Medium*: photo montage; oil & ink. *b*: Slough, 3 Aug 1975. *Educ*: Windsor Boys. *Studied*: Degree, Bath College of Higher Education; Central, St. Martin's, (Foundation). *Exhib*: Laing, Mall Galleries, (2000, 2001); Cabaret Voltaire, Edna Galleria, Buenos Aires (2003); Print Room, London (2000-); Cafe Corridor, Hong Kong (2004), Islington Art & Design Fair, London; West Wing Arts Centre, Berkshire; People's Bookstore, Hong Kong; various smaller exhibs. *Works in collections*: Beckford's Tower Trust, Bath, Great Western Trains, Raleigh International Chile. *Commissions*: Beckford's Tower Trust, Bath, Raleigh International Expedition artist, Chile (2002), Bath and West, www.bleep43.com. *Publications*: 'Words' -bilingual poetry and photography collaboration, with poet Ana Lema, Buenos Aires (pub. 2007, UK and Argentina); Raleigh International Calendar 2003 (Chile); Lantigua.com.ar. *Clubs*: Professional Photographers File, BANA. *Misc*: web gallery: www.untitled.co.uk. *Address:* 7 Colenorton Cres., Eton Wick, Windsor, SL4 6NW. *Email*: colenort@dircon.co.uk *Website*: www.urbandecoy.co.uk *Signs work*: "S L Jones."

LIEN, Natasha, PostGrad Certificate in Drawing; Awarded a Drawing Scholarship with NEAC 2006-2007. *Medium*: oil, drawing, prints. *b*: Hertfordshire, 21 Nov 1977. *Studied*: Central Saint Martin's College of Art and Design (Foundation and BA course, 1996-2000); The Prince's Drawing School (PostGrad Drawing year, 2005-06). *Represented by*: Cambridge Book and Print Gallery. *Exhib*: Dulwich Picture Gallery, Bicentenary Exhibition (2011); Tetbury Music Festival (2009); Chase Exhibition, Royal College of Art (2008); RA Summer Exhibition (2004, 2007, 2008); NEAC, Mall Galleries (2007, 2010, 2011, 2012); Solo exhibition, Pearson Gallery, Slade, UCL (2003); Chateau de Balleroy (2002) . *Works in collections*: (private) HRH The Prince of Wales; Kevin Spacey. *Commissions*: Drawing of The Old Vic Theatre 2007 for Kevin Spacey. *Publications*: Royal Academy Illustrated Catalogue (2007), featured in The Artist magazine (Feb 2007, June 2008). *Misc*: Artist's Residency: 2008 Tetbury Music Festival. *Address:* 10 Cowper Road, Berkhampsted, Herts., HP4 3DE. *Email*: ART@natashalien.com *Website*: www.natashalien.com *Signs work*: "NATASHA LIEN".

LIGHT, Vivienne Mary, Cert.Ed. (1970), MA (1995), Fellow of the Royal Society of Arts (1995). *Medium*: mixed media and constructions, including hand-made plant papers. *b*: Dorchester, Dorset, 9 Nov 1947. *m*: Prof. Paul Light. one *s*. two *d*. *Studied*: Dartington College of Arts. *Exhib*: University of Southampton; Paintings in Hospitals; Natural History Museum, Tring; Theatre Royal, Winchester; Maltby Fine Art; Bristol Guild Gallery; Salisbury Arts Care Trust; Russell Cotes Gallery, Bournemouth; RWA Autumn exhibitions; Salisbury Museum; Mino City Paper Museum, Japan; Southampton Art Gallery, Mall Galleries. *Commissions*: Internationally. *Works Reproduced*: Fifty Wessex Artists (2006); Bournemouth University Art Loan Catalogue (2007/8); University of Winchester Art Loan Catalogue (2005). *Clubs*: Founder Member of 'Paperweight' (1994); 2D3D South Contemporary Art (2001-05, including Chair); Chair of Walford Mill Crafts Centre (2002-07); Committee 'Link Gallery' University of Winchester (2000); Arts Committee, Dorset County Museum (2006-2011). *Misc*: Curator, author of six art books; and publisher:

Canterton Books. *Address*: Canterton House, Pitmans Lane, Morcombelake, Bridport, Dorset DT6 6EB. *Email*: vivienne_light@hotmail.com *Website*: www.viviennelight.co.uk www.cantertonbooks.co.uk *Signs work*: "Vivienne Light".

LIGHTFOOT, Katharine Lucy, BA Hons Fine Art . *Medium*: oil on canvas. *b*: Launceston, Cornwall, 24 May 1972. *d of*: Mr & Mrs D Lightfoot. *m*: Mark Hildyard. one *s*. *Educ*: Kingsbridge School, Devon. *Studied*: Plymouth College of Art and Design (1989-91), University of Plymouth, Exeter Faculty (1992-95). *Exhib*: Arndean Gallery, Cork St., London; Lemon Street Gallery, Truro; Smithfield Gallery, London; Lenox Gallery, Fulham, London; Chomè Gallery, Bath; Air Gallery, London. *Official Purchasers*: 608. *Works Reproduced*: 710. *Address:* 3 Granary Mews, Parliament St., Crediton, Devon, EX17 2BJ. *Email*: info@katlightfoot.com *Website*: www.katlightfoot.com *Signs work*: "K.Lightfoot".

LIJN, Liliane, Honorary Degree of Doctor of Letters, University of Warwick (2005); International Fellowship, Arts Council of England (2005) . *Medium*: sculpture, video. *b*: New York, 22 Dec 1939. *d of*: Herman Segall & Helena Kustanowicz. *Partner*: Stephen Weiss. two *s*. one *d*. *Studied*: École du Louvre Sorbonne, Paris. *Exhib*: has exhibited extensively worldwide, both solo and group exhibitions. *Works in collections*: British Museum, London; Tate Gallery, London; Musée de la Ville de Paris, France; MoMA, New York; Chicago Institute, USA; V&A, London; Bibliotheque National, Paris; Museum of Fine Arts, Bern (Switzerland); Glasgow Museum; Museum of NSW (Australia); City Art Gallery, Manchester; Henry Moore Foundation, Leeds. *Commissions*: many commissions across UK. *Publications*: 'Liliane Lijn: Works 1959-80' (2005); 'Light and Memory' (2002); 'Her Mother's Voice' (1996); 'Crossing Map' (1982); 'Cosmic Dramas' (2012); 'Power Poem Oracle Game' (2014). *Recreations*: cooking, walking, gardening, travelling. *Misc*: films: 'What is the Sound of One Hand Clapping?' (1975); 'Cosmic Dramas' (2012). *Address:* 28 Camden Square, London NW1 9XA. *Email*: liliane@lilianelijncom. *Website*: www.lilianelijn.com *Signs work*: 'LILIANE LIJN'.

LILLFORD, Ralph, PhD, ARCA, NDD; GSM Suez (1952-54). *Medium*: drawing and painting. *b*: Doncaster, 6 Nov 1932. *s of*: W & W Lillford. two *s*. three *d*. *Studied*: Doncaster Coll. of Art & RCA. *Exhib*: Houses of Parliament, European Parliament, Science Museum, St. Lawrence University, USA, Schick Gallery, Saratoga, USA, Channel Tunnel Exhbn., Universities of Bradford, Durham, Brunel and Imperial College. Retrospective Exhbn. Doncaster (1972-92), National Army Museum, Coffs Harbour Gallery, South London Gallery, Russell Coates, Morley College, Cheltenham College, London University, Richmond University. *Works in collections*: RCA, RA, BM, V&A, Nat. Science Museum, Nat. Army Museum, Pushkin, Moscow, State Heritage, St. Petersburg, Dunedin, NZ, Imperial War Museum, The London Museum, Doncaster Art gallery, Slough College; private collections in China, Japan, Australia, Sweden, Holland, France, Spain, Hungary, Dubai, USA, Canada. *Commissions*: 'Crucifixion' mural, Mudgereeba Church, Queensland, Australia; Melbourne Gold Cup; portraits: David Doyle, Gary Neihl; Gary Baildon, Mayor, Gold Coast; Donald Jackson, ATC, MVO; Clara Rodriguez; David Helfgott. *Publications*: unpublished PhD thesis 'A Method of Establishing the Sequence of Printing William Hogarth's Hudibras Prints'. *Works Reproduced*: in catalogues. *Misc*: Taught: Richmond University (1983-98), and in U.S.A., Russia, Holland, France, Italy, Aborigine Centres in Australia. *Address:* 47 Creffield Rd., Ealing, London W5 3RR. *Email*: ralphlillford@hotmail.com

LIMBREY, John Nigel Stephens, NDD (1953), MCSD (1969); Freeman of the Worshipful Company of Goldsmiths, City of London; silversmith and product designer; artist in water-colour and oil; landscape, architectural and marine subjects. *b*: Hatfield, 2 Feb 1933. *Educ*: King Edward's School, B'ham. *Studied*: B'ham College of Art (1949-53). *Exhib*: RI, RWS, RSMA. *Works in collections*: worldwide. *Address:* Silk Mill

Cottage, Chipping Campden, Glos. GL55 6DS. *Website*: www.fossewayartists.com *Signs work*: "Limbrey."

LIN, Hsiao-Mei, BA (1994), MA (1997); Crabtree & Evelyn Scholarship, Taipei City Museum of Fine Arts, Taiwan; Tony Smith Landscape Prize; David Murray Landscape Scholarship; Winsor & Newton Young Artist Award. *Medium*: painter in oil. *b*: Taiwan, 7 Oct 1971. *Educ*: Royal Academy Schools of Art, London (Norman Adam); University of Brighton; Fu Hsin School of Arts, Taipei, Taiwan. *Exhib*: solo shows: Adam Gallery, London, (1999-2014), University of Oxford St. Anne's College (1999), Bohun Gallery, Henley. Group shows: Arts Fair, London (1997-2007), Artfair 20th Century, New York (2002, 2006), Artfair Palm Beach, Miami USA (2003), art4life, Christie's (2002-03), Singer and Friedlander (2002), Royal Academy Summer Shows and many more in UK and abroad since 1988. *Works in collections*: USA, UK, Europe and Far East, corporate and private. *Publications*: Art Review '97, Autumn RA Magazine, Spectator. *Clubs*: RASA (Royal Academy Schools Alumni). *Address:* 9 Southcote Road, London N19 5BJ. *Email*: lin.hm@hotmail.com *Website*: www.hmlin.co.uk

LIN, Htein, *Medium*: Acrylic, performance, installation. *b*: Myanmar, 31 Dec 1966. *m*: Vicky Bowman. two *d*. *Studied*: Rangoon University (1984-88, 1994-5). *Exhib*: Asia House, London (2007); Tasneem Gallery, Barcelona (2009); Thavibu Gallery, Bangkok (2011); Karin Weber Gallery, Hong Kong (2008); Northern Illinois University (2008); Singaport Fringe (2010, 2012); North Wall, Oxford (2011); Kochin Biennale (2012); Dhaka Art Summit (2014); River Gallery Yangon (2014). *Works in collections*: US Embassy, Yangon and private collections in UK, US, Singapore, Hong Kong, Malaysia, Belgium. *Official Purchasers*: US Embassy, Yangon. *Works Reproduced*: 235 Series limited prints. *Principal Works*: 235 Series from prison; Saffron Revolution series; A Show of Hands. *Recreations*: Meditation. *Misc*: Spent almost seven years as a political prisoner in Burma. *Address*: 13 Palfrey Place, London SW8 1PB. *Email*: artisthteinlin@gmail.com *Website*: www.hteinlin.com *Signs work*: "HTEIN LIN".

LINDLEY, Ali (Alison Mary), ASWA, SFP. *Medium*: watercolour. *m*: Nigel. one *s*. two *d*. *Studied*: self taught. *Exhib*: usual mixed and Open; private. *Works in collections*: private UK and overseas. *Clubs*: Romsey/Chandlers Ford Groups. *Misc*: Exhibits as part of three woman group 'Inspired by Nature' at Sir Harold Hillier Gardens (2006-) annually. *Address*: 74 Thornbury Wood, Chandlers Ford, Eastleigh, Hants SO53 5DQ. *Email*: alilindley@hotmail.co.uk *Website*: alilindleyartist.co.uk *Signs work*: "ALI LINDLEY".

LINDSAY, Alister, Diploma in Art (drawing and painting (1983)). *Medium*: oil, drawing, print. *b*: Dundee, 1 Aug 1962. *Studied*: Duncan of Jordanstone College of Art. *Represented by*: Eduardo Alessandro Studios, Dundee. *Exhib*: One man shows: Arbroath Library (1988); Dundee Repertory Theatre (1989); Eduardo Alessandro Studios, Dundee (1992); Atholl Gallery, Dunkeld (1996, 1997). Two man shows: Atholl Gallery (1989, 1991); Eduardo Alessandro Studios (1993); Tolquhon Gallery, Tarves, Ellon (1995). Three man shows: Ninewells Teaching Hospital (1984); The Edinburgh Gallery (2001); Eduardo Alessandro Studios (2003, 2008). *Works in collections*: McManus Gallery Collection, Dundee; Robert Flemming Holdings of London Ltd; Highland Springs Ltd, Blackford. *Address*: 1 Boniface Gardens, Invergowrie, Dundee DD2 5RS. *Email*: alindsay88@blueyonder.co.uk *Website*: alisterlindsay.co.uk *Signs work*: "A.L."

LINDSAY, Rosemary, SBA; Fellow of the Chelsea Physic Garden Florilegium Society; botanical illustrator in water-colour, pen and ink. *b*: Croydon, 22 Jun 1939. *d of*: Douglas & Georgina Gough. *m*: Crawford Lindsay. one *s*. one *d*. *Educ*: Croydon High School. *Studied*: Kingston School of Art (1957-60, architecture: Eric Brown), Morley College (botanical illustration: Margaret Merrett). *Exhib*: Society of Botanical Artists yearly, British Council

Travelling Exhbn., Morley College, Horniman Museum, Battle Gallery, The Other Dulwich Picture Gallery, Limpsfield Gallery, Art in Action at Waterperry, Oriel Ynys Môn Anglesey, Everard Read, Johannesburg, SA, Pashley Manor, Brooklyn Botanic Garden New York; Florum yearly; many private collections. *Works in collections*: Archive of the Florilegium Society of The Chelsea Physic Garden; many private. *Commissions*: RHS. *Publications*: illustrations in R.H.S. Journals and Herb Soc. Journals. *Works Reproduced*: cards and prints published by Aria Cards. *Recreations*: music, reading, travel, gardening, galleries. *Address:* 5 Burbage Rd., London SE24 9HJ. *Website*: www.rosemarylindsay.com *Signs work*: "Rosemary Lindsay."

LINDSLEY, Kathleen Margaret, BA Hons Fine Art (1976). *Medium*: wood engraving. *b*: Gibraltar, 26 Jul 1951. *d of*: Richard Harford Lindsley. *m*: Nicholas Carter. one *s*. one *d*. *Educ*: Burford Grammar. *Studied*: Newcastle-upon-Tyne Polytechnic. Introduced to wood engraving by Leo Wyatt. *Represented by*: self. *Exhib*: London, Oxford, York, Leeds, Halifax, Kendal, Edinburgh, Glasgow, Inverness, Orkney. *Works in collections*: V&A, Manchester Metropolitan University. *Commissions*: illustration, design, bookplates, architecture. Private press work: Perpetua, Black Pennel, Partick, Wild Hawthorn, Whittington, Fleece. *Publications*: Collins Love Poems, Folio Golden Treasury, An Engravers Globe, Woodlanders, Wildlife in Printmaking. *Clubs*: Society of Wood Engravers. *Address:* Raven Press Gallery, Colbost, Dunvegan, Isle of Skye, IV55 8ZS. *Email*: kathleen@ravenpressgallery.co.uk *Website*: www.ravenpressgallery.co.uk

LINES, John, RSMA; Awards: Museum of Modern Art, Wales (1st Prize); RBSA Daler Rowney winner (three times); RSMA (1st Prize); Wellingboro Arts Festival (1st Prize). *Medium*: oil. *b*: Rugby, 3 Aug 1938. *s of*: Mr & Mrs E E Lines. *Educ*: Rugby College. *Studied*: York Art School. *Represented by*: RSMA, RBSA, Red Rag Gallery; Tyler/White Gallery, USA. *Works in collections*: P&O Ships; Fisher Everard Ships; Rugby Council; Nuneaton Council; Birmingham Civic Society. *Publications*: RSMA Marine Art; Millers Art Guide 2003. *Recreations*: cycling, walking. *Clubs*: Rugby Arts Soc., Kineton Arts Soc. *Address:* 12 Wesley Road, Hillmorton, Rugby, CV21 4PG. *Signs work*: 'J.W. Lines'.

LING, Steven, BA (Hons) Fine Art. *Medium*: Painter. *b*: Aldershot, 21 Dec 1966. *Studied*: The Surrey Institute of Art and Design University College (1997-2000). *Represented by*: www.picassomio.com. *Exhib*: Solo exhibitions: The West End Centre, Aldershot (2000); Group exhibitions: The Atrium Gallery, Whiteleys, London (2000); The Affordable Art Fair, Battersea, London (2001); British Society of Graduate Artists and Designers Exhibition, Mall Galleries, London (2002); The Arthouse, Westbourne, Hampshire (2004); Surface Gallery, Nottingham (2005); RCA Secret, Royal College of Art, London (2003-). *Works in collections*: Frimley Park Hospital; Bracknell Forest Borough Council; Rushmoor Borough Council and private collections in UK, Australia, Gibraltar, Ireland and USA. *Commissions*: June 2001: Year of the Artist commission to design the planting for three flowerbeds in Jubilee Gardens, Bracknell Berkshire. *Recreations*: Collector of post war ceramics and glass. *Clubs*: The Organ Club. *Address*: 67 Ashley Road, Farnborough, Hampshire GU14 7HB. *Website*: www.picassomio.com/steven-ling.html *Signs work*: "STEVEN LING".

LINNELL, Judith Anne, BA (Hons) Fine Art; Post Graduate Certificate of Art Education; Award: 2001 Buzzacott Award at the Royal Institute of Painters in Watercolour, Mall Galleries, London. *Medium*: Oil, watercolour, drawing, mixed media. *b*: Kent, 25 Jan 1948. *m*: Stuart Komaromy. one *s*. one *d*. *Educ*: Dr Williams' School, Dolegellau, North Wales (1956-66). *Studied*: University of Leeds (1966-1971). *Represented by*: West Wales Art Centre, Fishguard, Royal Watercolour Society of Wales. *Exhib*: Royal Institute of Painters in Watercolour (1997-2000) Buzzacott Award (2001) Mall Galleries, London; Royal Watercolour Society, Bankside Gallery, London (2005, 06, 07); Affordable Art Fair,

Battersea, Bristol (from 2001); Watercolour Drawings Fair, London (from 2001); The Linda Blackstone Gallery; The West Wales Arts Centre, Fishguard (2009); Royal Watercolour Society of Wales (2010-). *Works in collections*: Leeds University Art Collection purchased by Sir Lawrence Gowring. *Commissions*: Many private collections. *Publications*: Quarto and Eaglemoss publications. *Official Purchasers*: Work for University of Leeds Art Collection purchased by Sir Lawrence Gowing. *Recreations*: Walking; films; reading; travel. *Misc*: Runs her own gallery/studio near Fishguard. Has taught painting to adults for 30 years, runs own workshops. Tutor on painting holidays in Corsica, Crete, Yorkshire Dales and Pembrokeshire. *Address*: Rhosycaerau Farmhouse, St Nicholas, Goodwick, Pembs SA64 0LB. *Email*: judy.linnell@o2.co.uk *Signs work*: "Judy Linnell".

LIPTON, Laurie, BA Fine Art (Hons). *Medium*: drawing. *b*: New York, 11 Nov 1953. *Studied*: Carnegie-Mellon University, Pittsburgh, USA. *Represented by*: Henry Boxer Gallery, Copro Nason, Los Angeles; Billy Shire Fine Art, Los Angeles; Cabinodd, Holland. *Exhib*: recent selected solo shows: Espacio para el Arte, Madrid (2007), mixed shows include: American Visionary Art Museum, Baltimore (2006, 2007), Giger Museum, Zurich (2006), East West Gallery, London (2005), Casa-Decor, Valencia (2004), Orleans House Gallery, Twickenham (2004), Freud Museum, London (2006). *Commissions*: Illuminated manuscripts include: "Splendor Solis", "Mutus Liber" and "Atalanta Fugiens" (for Bibliotheca Philosphica Hermetica, Amsterdam). *Publications*: Juxtapoz Magazine, Du Fantastique Au Visionaire, Metamorphosis ("50 Contemporary Surreal, Fantastic and Visionary Artists"), The Art and Meaning of Women's Altars. *Works Reproduced*: in many lit. magazines and art magazines. *Address:* 12 Steeple Court, Coventry Road, London E1 5QZ. *Email*: laurielipton@yahoo.co.uk *Website*: www.laurielipton.com *Signs work*: "LLipton".

LISTER, Caroline Nicola Josephine, BA Hons (1980), ARBA; painter and printmaker; printmaking tutor, Guildford College of Art (1980); Director and tutor, Tyger, Tyger Printmaking, Cambridge (Intaglio Printmaking Workshop); Steering Group mem. Cambridgeshire Regional College (1989). *b*: Cambridge, 30 Mar 1958. *d of*: Brian Lister, designer of Lister-Jaguar racing car. *Educ*: Perse School, Cambridge. *Studied*: Cambs. College of Arts and Technology (1976-77), W. Surrey College of Art and Design (1977-80). *Exhib*: RBA, RE, RI, PS, RWS, SWA, CDS. *Misc*: studio: Tyger, Tyger Printmaking, Studio One, 37 City Rd., Cambridge CB1 1DP. *Address:* 79 St. Philips Rd., Cambridge CB1 3DA. *Signs work*: "Nicola Lister."

LITTLE, Alistair John, *Medium*: Oil. *b*: Chertsey, 26 Nov 1974. *m*: Victoria Little. *Represented by*: Tiffany Panter, Matthew Hall (Panter & Hall Ltd). *Exhib*: Caelum Gallery, NY (2003); Apart Gallery, London, mixed (2004, 2005); Panter & Hall mixed (2005, 06, 07, 08, 09, 10, 11, 12); Ashurst Lawyer's Show, London (2005, 06, 08); The Affordable Art Fair (2006, 07, 08, 09, 10, 11); The London Air Fair (2006, 07, 08, 09). Solo shows: Panter & Hall (2008, 2011); two person shows (2006, 2010 Panter & Hall/Mausfield Park, Glasgow). *Works in collections*: Jack Vettriano; Ashurst; Xcite Oil, Aberdeen. *Commissions*: Edward Woodward and Michele Dotrice; Xcite Oil, Aberdeen; numerous private. *Publications*: Artists and Illustrators Magazine; Classic and Sports Car Magazine. *Works Reproduced*: Several works printed by, 'The Art Group' and 'Panter and Hall'. *Address*: c/o Panter & Hall, 11-12 Pall Mall London SW1Y 5LU. *Email*: al-ambition@hotmail.com *Website*: www.alistairlittle.com *Signs work*: "ALISTAIR".

LJUNGDALH, Stine. *Medium*: prints, sculpture, photography. *b*: Denmark, 4 Mar 1969. *s of*: Jorgen & Jytie Ljungdalh. *Studied*: Royal College of Art (MA 2003-2005). *Exhib*: include: RA Summer Exhibition (2009, 2005), Royal College of Art (2005), Schwartz Gallery, London (2009), I-MYU Gallery, London (2009), The Dazed Gallery, London (2008), many other London galleries, also UK, Denmark, Switzerland. Solo show: Gallery Project 2006 (Copenhagen). *Works in collections*: Royal College of Art, Institute of

Education and private collections Japan, USA and UK. *Publications*: 'Exhibitions, Politikken' (17 May 2008), 'The Guardian Guide' (8 March 2008, p.37), 'Weekendavisen Culture nr.19' by Mette Sandbye (2007), 'Military' (art publication, 2007), NY Arts Magazine (2006) plus catalogues. *Address:* Unit B, Rollins House, Rollins Street, London SE15 1EP. *Email*: stineljungdalh@hotmail.com *Website*: (in progress) stineljungdalh.com

LLOYD, Reginald James, RI; self taught artist in water-colour, oil, acrylic. *b*: Hereford, 21 Dec 1926. *m*: (1) Diana van Klaveren (decd) (2) Louise MacMillan. three *s*. four *d*. *Educ*: Dawlish Boys and County Senior School. *Exhib*: 'Portrait of the Artist' Tate Gallery, etc. *Works in collections*: Tate Gallery, V&A, National Maritime Museum, Hatton Gallery Newcastle, Burton Gallery Bideford. *Publications*: illustrated: What is the Truth by Ted Hughes, The Cat and the Cuckoo by Ted Hughes, The Mermaid's Purse by Ted Hughes. *Address:* Iffield, North Rd., Bideford, Devon EX39 2NW. *Signs work*: "R.J. LLOYD," "R.J.L." or "R.J. Lloyd."

LLOYD, Rosamond Ann, BA Hons, HND Illustration; Nominated, David Shepherd Wildlife Artist of the Year (2011). *Medium*: sculpture. *b*: Bournemouth, Dorset, 4 Apr 1973. one *s*. *Studied*: London University (Royal Holloway, 1991-4); Swindon College of Art (2000-01). *Exhib*: Art in Action, Waterperry (2012-14); Whittington Fine Art Gallery, Henley-on-Thames (2010); Real Wood Furniture Company, Woodstock (2011-13); Mall Gallery, London (2011); Royal Opera Arcade Gallery, Pall Mall, London (2013). Solo show: Claridges, London (2014). *Works in collections*: includes: Cotswold Wildlife Park, International Rhino Foundation (USA). Private and corporate collections in Europe and USA. *Commissions*: Cotswold Wildlife Park, numerous private. *Clubs*: Surrey Sculpture Society, Marwell International Wildlife Artists Society, Oxfordshire Sculptors Group. *Misc*: Affiliated to Tusk Trust as Official Sculptor. *Address*: Farthynge Cottage, Holcombe Lane, Newington, Oxon OX10 7AJ. *Email*: info@rosamondlloyd.com *Website*: www.rosamondlloyd.com *Signs work*: "R L".

LLOYD-JONES, Pamela, DipArt Ed. (Sydney) 1968, BA Fine Art (Sydney); artist in mixed media and acrylic; specialising in portraiture. *b*: Australia, 4 Jan 1947. one *s*. one *d*. *Exhib*: Australia, France, Canada, USA, Great Britain. *Address:* 7 Roman Close, Acton, London W3 8HE. *Email*: pamelalloydjones@hotmail.com *Website*: www.pamelalloydjones.com *Signs work*: "P. Lloyd-Jones."

LLYWELYN HALL, Dan. BA (Hons); Sunday Times Artist of the Year 2003. *Medium*: oil, watercolour, drawing, prints. *b*: Cardiff, 18 Aug 1980. *s of*: Bridget & Timothy Hall. *Partner*: Aurélie Derguesse. *Studied*: Cardiff UWIC (Wales) - Foundation Diploma; University of Westminster, Harrow Campus (BA (Hons) Illustration). *Represented by*: Roman Black Gallery, London; Washington Gallery, Wales. *Exhib*: Roman Black Gallery, London (2007); Washington Gallery, Wales (2005, 2004), Martin Tinney (2005), The Art Shop (2005), Brecknock Museum, London Art Fair (2007, 2006), Wales Millennium Centre (2006), Albemarle Gallery (2005), Mall Galleries (2006, 2003), St. Davis's Hall (2006, 2004), The Albany Gallery (2004). *Works in collections*: MoMA Wales (Tabernacle Collection), Newport Museum and Gallery, Tenby Museum and Gallery, Houses of Parliament, BT Corporate Collection, Barclays Bank. *Publications*: Matter of Time catalogue, Culture magazine (Times, Sept 2003), Western Mail (numerous). *Principal Works*: Sunday Times, 'Ship Hotel de Splash', 'Fan Hir', 'The Palace of Westminster as a Party Goes By'. *Address:* 22 Stanley Road, South Harrow, Middx., HA2 8AZ. *Email*: danllywelynhall@yahoo.co.uk *Website*: www.danllywelynhall.co.uk *Signs work*: "DLH" or "Dan Llywelyn Hall".

LOBANOV-ROSTOVSKY, Princess Roxane. SWA; water-colourist sculptor in alabaster, marble. *b*: Athens, 3 Oct 1932. *d of*: R. Bibica-Rosetti, Greek Ambassador. two *s*. one *d*. *Educ*: St. George's Ascot, Pretoria Girls High School. *Studied*: Carlton University,

Ottawa; Brighton Polytechnic (Norma Weller, Norman Clarke, RWS). *Exhib*: numerous exhbns. RI, RWS, ROI, RSMA, SWA; one-man shows: The Grange, Rottingdean (1987), Art Gallery, Kettering. *Works in collections*: in USA, Austria, France, Italy, UK, India. *Commissions*: Dream of Gerontius for P. Foss Esq., Standing Stones for B. White Esq. *Publications*: mentioned in D. Rook-Hart 20th C. Marine Painting. *Works Reproduced*: limited edition prints of all watercolours. *Principal Works*: Dream of Gerontius, Othello, Ophelia, Prince Ieor. *Recreations*: Opera, Classical Music, Sailing, Climbing. *Address:* Swallowdale, 67 Woodruff Ave., Hove, E. Sussex BN3 6PJ. *Signs work*: "R. Lobanov-Rostovsky."

LOCKWOOD, Arthur, RBSA (1994); RBA (2001); NDD (1954); ARCA (1959); ARWS (2006); RWS (2009). *Medium*: watercolour. *b*: Birmingham, 27 May 1934. *s of*: Frank T.Lockwood. *m*: Gillian Newing. two *s*. *Studied*: Birmingham College of Art; RCA. *Exhib*: RBA, Mall Galleries; RBSA, RBSA Galleries, Birmingham; RWS Bankside Gallery. *Works in collections*: Walsall Museum & Art Gallery; National Coal Mining Museum; Birmingham Museum and Art Gallery; Museum of Richmond. *Publications*: 'Change in the Midlands' (2007). *Address:* Kingswood Hollow, Mill Lane, Lapworth B94 6HT. *Email*: paulrlockwood@gmail.com *Signs work*: 'Arthur Lockwood' or 'AL'.

LODGE, Jean, RE, BA (Miami), MA (Oxon.); painter/printmaker; Emeritus Fellow of New College, Oxford. *Medium*: colour woodcuts, collages. *b*: USA, 1941. *d of*: Cora Stier Lodge. *Educ*: Miami University, Ohio, Oxford University. *Studied*: Beaux Arts de Paris, Atelier 17 with S.W. Hayter. *Represented by*: Galerie Lucien Schweitzer, Luxembourg. *Exhib*: solo shows: Europe, Japan, India, Argentina, Venezuela, USA, etc.; numerous international print shows. *Works in collections*: Museums in Europe and N. and S. America; Galerie Schweitzer, Luxembourg; Bankside Gallery, London. *Commissions*: Editions of woodcuts for "La Gravure Originale" and Le Trait "Gravure Contemporaine", portraits for New College and Bailliol College, Oxford. *Publications*: 'Printmakers' Secrets' by Anthony Dyson (A&C Black). *Works Reproduced*: 'Bois de Fil, Bois de Bout... La Gravure Sur Bois (pub. Musée des Arelines, St.Cloud, 2009). *Address:* 52 Granville Ct., Cheney Lane, Headington, Oxford OX3 0HS. *Signs work*: "JEAN LODGE".

LOFTHOUSE, Hermione Thornton, NS; painter in water-colour, oil and pastel; tutor, Moor Park College (1968-82); Master Classes for Richmond-upon-Thames Arts Council (1982, 1983), Adult Educ.; UA (1975-2002), VP Ridley Art Soc. *b*: Chelsea. *d of*: Prof. Charles Thornton Lofthouse, musician. *m*: F.H. Lockyer. three *s*. *Educ*: St. Paul's Girls' School. *Studied*: Heatherleys' (1946-50) under Iain Macnab, Académie Julian and La Grande Chaumière (1950); cert. History of Art, Courtauld Inst. *Exhib*: Paris, Germany, NZ Academy, Bombay Museum, WAG, Artists of Chelsea, RBA, ROI, etc.; eleven solo shows, Upper St. Gallery, Mall Galleries, Ice House - Holland Park, Surrey Univ. *Works in collections*: Richmond Parish Charity Lands, RAM, Surrey Univ., Guildford House Museum etc. *Publications*: The Art of Drawing and Painting. *Address:* 48 Compton Way, Farnham, Surrey GU10 1QU. *Email*: htl@amserve.com *Signs work*: "H. Thornton Lofthouse."

LOGAN, Andrew, Dip.Arch.(Oxon.); sculptor in glass. *Medium*: glass. *b*: Witney, 11 Oct 1945. *s of*: William Harold Logan. *Educ*: Lord Williams' Grammar School; Burford Grammar School. *Studied*: architecture: Oxford School of Architecture (1964-70). *Exhib*: ICA (1970), Whitechapel AG, Beverly Hills, LA, Ebury Gallery, Space Gallery, Faerie Fair, Norfolk, Crafts Council, Sandbeck Hall, Yorks., Sculpture Pk., Portland Bill, Commonwealth Inst., German Film Museum, Frankfurt, Hotel Meridian, Singapore, Botanical Gdns., Rome, Angela Flowers (Ireland) Inc., Flowers East (1991), Old Library, Cardiff (1991); first one-man show: New Art Centre, London (1973); retrospective: Museum of Modern Art, Oxford (1991), 'The Happy Heart show', Manchester City Art

Galleries (1995), Moscow Art Fair (1996), 'Reflections of the Heart' Show, Monterrey, Mexico (1997), 'Love' AVAM Baltimore, USA, 'Magic Moments' Ruthin, British Figurative Art, Flowers East, 'Britain in Russia', Ekaterinburg, Russia (1998), 'Universe of Smiles' Expo 2000, Hanover, Germany; 'Glittering Glass' Cheltenham Museum (2000); Summer Exhibition RA (2001); Alternative Miss World Film Show, Norwich (2002); 'Universe of Smiles', Flowers West, LA (2003). *Works in collections*: Andrew Logan's Museum of Sculpture, Berriew, Powys; NPG; Australian Gallery of National Art; Arts Council of Britain; Warner Bros UK; Costume Inst.; MoMA, New York; Curzon Tussaud, London; Cleveland Jewellery Collection, Middlesbrough; Museo de Vidrio, Mexico; HM Queen Elizabeth the Queen Mother; Brian Eno; Derek Jarman; Julie Christie; Zandra Rhodes; Elton John. *Commissions*: Dudley Council; Cheltenham Art Museum; P&O; American Visionary Art Museum, Baltimore USA. *Principal Works*: 'Alternative Miss World' 1972, 1975, 1978, 1981, 1985, 1986, 1991, 1995, 1998 and 2004. *Address:* The Glasshouse, Melior Pl. London SE1 3SZ. *Email*: andrewl@andrewlogan.com *Website*: www.andrewlogan.com *Signs work*: Andrew Logan.

LOKEN, Julia, SBA. *Medium*: watercolour. *b*: Worthing, 28 Oct 1939. *d of*: John & Norah Petty. *m*: James. one *s*. one *d*. *Educ*: Faringdon Grammar School. *Studied*: self-taught. *Exhib*: solo: Oxford area, 21 exhibitions (1982-2014); Geneva, Switzerland (1986, 1990, 1995, 1999); Dijon, France (1990); Gerald Peters Gallery, Santa Fe, USA (2005, 2007, 2009, 2014). *Works in collections*: in Switzerland, France, England, USA. *Commissions*: Sultan of Oman, 2005. *Recreations*: gardening, walking, travel. *Address:* Myrtle Cottage, Tanner's Lane, Eynsham, Oxon, OX29 4HJ. *Email*: julia@loken.co.uk *Website*: www.loken.co.uk *Signs work*: 'Julia Loken'.

LOKER, John Keith, DA Graphic Design (1958), ARCA Fine Art (1963); Nordstein Print Prize - Royal Academy (1994); painter in oil. *b*: Leeds, 15 Sep 1938. *m*: Emily Mayer, sculptor. two *s*. *Studied*: Bradford Regional College of Art (1954-58), Royal College of Art (1960-63). *Represented by*: Flowers East. *Exhib*: over 30 one-man exhbns. in UK and abroad. *Works in collections*: Tate, Arts Council, Power Inst., etc. *Commissions*: Watmough Holding, Bradford, Essex General Hospital, ITN Building (Norman Foster). *Publications*: Monograph published Arnolfini (1981); Thriding published Watmouth Holdings (1984); Monographs published Flowers East (1990/1998/2009). *Clubs*: Chelsea Arts. *Address:* Union Workhouse, Guilt Cross, Kenninghall, Norfolk NR16 2LJ. *Email*: john@flyingbear.co.uk *Website*: johnloker.co.uk *Signs work*: "John Loker," occasionally "J.L."

LONG, Denny Jane, RWA; MA, DipAD, BEd, ATD, NSA (Newlyn Society of Artists) Penwith Printmakers. *Medium*: acrylic & collage, drawing, prints, installation. *b*: Bristol, 4 Nov 1948. *d of*: Harold & Linda Johnston. *m*: Richard Long (1969-98). *Partner*: Jonathan Grimble. two *d*. *Educ*: Redland High School, Bristol. *Studied*: West of England College of Art (now UWE) (1963-67, DipAD Ceramics); Falmouth College of Art (MA Fine Art, 1996-2001). *Represented by*: Jonathan Grimble Modern Art. *Exhib*: RA, RWA, Penwith Gallery St. Ives, Plymouth Arts Centre, Spacex Exeter, Watershed Media Centre Bristol, Bristol Museum and Art Gallery, DeptfordX, Porthminster Gallery St. Ives, Falmouth Art Gallery and Arts Centre, Mid Cornwall Gallery, Chipping Campden Gallery, St. Ives Society of Artists, St. Ives Arts Club, Mall Galleries, London, Helen Feiler Gallery Newlyn, Newlyn Art Gallery, The Exchange Penzance, Yew Tree Gallery Morvah. *Works in collections*: Wilhemina Barns-Graham, Sandra Blow, private collections. *Publications*: 'The Leach Pottery, St. Ives, and the Influence of Bernard Leach' (2005); Mixed Messages, The Versatility of Collage by Anne Manie (2012). *Principal Works*: 'The Fabrics of Life' (1996); 'Original?' (1996); 'Evidence' (2000); 'Rawhide' (2005), 'Morne Jaloux' (2006); 'Tregerthen Springtime (2009); 'Enough Blue to Make a Sailor a Pair of Trousers' (2009); 'Zennor Springtime 2010'. *Recreations*: travel, gardening, vegan cooking, dog walking, yoga, pilates. *Misc*: zen buddhist and UK representative of the Tibetan Buddhist Nuns

Project. *Address:* Lower Tregerthen, Zennor, St. Ives, Cornwall TR26 3BP. *Email*: djdenzen@hotmail.com *Website*: www.dennylongrwa.co.uk *Signs work*: japanese seal: DEN-É.

LONG, Gary Nigel, MA by Research (ADF (Manc). *Medium*: mixed media, oil, drawing. *b*: Birmingham, 10 Feb 1945. *s of*: Nigel and Irene Long. *m*: Patricia Ann Long. one *d*. *Educ*: Hodge Hill School, Birmingham. *Studied*: Birmingham College of Art, Margaret Street (1962-65), Manchester College of Art (School of Advanced Study, 1969). *Represented by*: Lighthouse Gallery, Penzance. *Exhib*: Society of Illustrators, E 63rd Manhattan; Webbs Road Gallery, Battersea, London; Map Works Gallery, Cornwall; Stour Gallery, Shipston-on-Stour; extensively in England, New England and British Columbia. *Commissions*: six paintings for Queen Mary II cruise liner; numerous landscape and portrait commissions. *Publications*: "The Essence". *Official Purchasers*: Slate Valley Museum, Granville, NY; Granite Museum, Barre, Vermont. *Works Reproduced*: short run from 6 paintings on Queen Mary II. *Recreations*: modern jazz, St. Ives, Jazz Club. *Clubs*: member, Society of Illustrators, New York, USA. *Misç*: part-time lecturer, Falmouth College of Art. Featured in BBC Countryfile, painting around St. Ives. *Address:* 3 Restcot, Tyringham Road, Lelant, St. Ives, Cornwall, TR26 3LJ. *Email*: garylong3@aol.com *Website*: www.garylongart.com *Signs work*: "Gary Long" or "Long".

LONG, John Cecil, RHA (2010); BA Slade (1988), Higher Dip. Slade (1990), Artist in Res., Byam Shaw (1990-1991), ARHA (1995); painter in oil; lecturer at NCAD, Dublin (1994-1995), lecturer at Canterbury, Christchurch University (1998-). *b*: Portadown, N. Ireland, 30 Aug 1964. *Educ*: St. Patrick's Boys Academy, Dungannon. *Studied*: Slade School of Fine Art (1984-1990) under Euan Uglow. *Represented by*: Jorgensen Fine Art. *Exhib*: European Modern Art, Dublin (1993); Twentieth Century British Art Fair, London (1996); Theo Waddington Fine Art, London (1998); Jorgensen Fine Art, Dublin (1999, 2003); London Contemporary Art Fair (2001). *Works in collections*: Haverty Trust, Allied Irish Bank. *Publications*: exhib. catalogue, Jorgensen Fine Art (1999, 2003, 2009, 2013), 'British Art' (Southbank Publishing, 2006), prints and posters. *Address:* c/o Jorgensen Fine Art, 14 Royal Hibernian Way., Dublin 2, Eire. *Signs work*: "LONG".

LONGUEVILLE, James, PS (1983), RBSA (1989); landscape painter in oil, pastel and water-colour; lecturer and demonstrator. *b*: Waverton, Chester, 22 Sep 1942. *s of*: Charles Longueville Willding-Jones, B.A. *m*: Elizabeth Mary Smith. two *s*. one *d*. *Educ*: Sedbergh School, Cumbria. *Exhib*: ROI, PS, RI, RCA, RBSA, galleries in UK, Eire, Australia, Canada. *Address:* The Studio, Shocklach, Malpas, Cheshire SY14 7BW. *Signs work*: "James Longueville."

LONGWORTH, Carl, *Medium*: Sculpture. *b*: Gloucester, 7 Feb 1979. *Partner*: Rachel Ann Talbot. *Studied*: Gloucester College of Art (1993-97); The Oval, Stafford (1997-2000). *Represented by*: The Priory Gallery, Broadway; Calken Gallery, London; Plumb Fine Art, Newport; Iona House Gallery, Oxford; The Bath Gallery, Bath; Artifex, Sutton Coldfield; Ingleby Gallery, Derbyshire; Minerva Gallery, Bath; Little London Gallery, Bath/Matlock; Leek Gallery, Staffordshire; Clerkenwell Fine Art, London; Trinity, Cotswolds. *Exhib*: Windsor Horse Show (2011); Olympia Kensington (2010); Chelsea Flower Show (2011, 2012); CLA Game Fair (2012); The Cotswolds Fair, Westonbirt (2010); Tatton Park Fair (2010); Harrogate Art Fair (2010-2011); Buxton Art (2010-2011); NEC Birmingham AAF (2009-2012); Stonyhurst Art (2010-2011); Powderham (2010-2011); Naworth Castle Fair (2010-2012); AAF, London (2009-12); Scone Palace (2010-12). *Principal Works*: Barn owls with distinct silver gray patination. *Misc*: Specialises in synthesized animal sculpture with unique patinations and colours. *Address*: Treetops, Elkstones, Longnor, Buxton, Derbyshire SK17 0LU. *Email*: info@carllongworth.com *Website*: www.carllongworth.com *Signs work*: "LONGWORTH".

LOUDON, Irvine Stewart Lees, ARE (1995) RE (1999), BMBCh (1951), DM(Oxon.) (1973), DRCOG (1961), FRCGP (1976); medical practitioner, medical historian, artist in etching and drawing; Annual Purchase Prize by 'Paintings in Hospitals' at Annual Exhibition by RE, Bankside Gallery (2005). *b*: Cardiff, 1 Aug 1924. *m*: Jean Loudon. two *s*. three *d*. *Educ*: Dauntseys School, Oxford University. *Studied*: Oxford Printmakers Co-operative (1983). *Exhib*: mixed shows with Oxford Art Soc., Oxford Printmakers Co-operative, Bankside Gallery, London; one-man shows in Oxford and London. *Works in collections*: Ashmolean Museum, Oxford. *Publications*: Medical Care and the General Practitioner 1750-1850 (O.U.P. 1986), Death in Childbirth (O.U.P. 1992), Western Medicine: An Illustrated History (O.U.P. 1997), The Tragedy of Childbed Fever (OUP 2000). *Address:* The Mill House, Locks Lane, Wantage, Oxon. OX12 9EH.

LOVEDAY, Ross, self taught artist. *Medium*: acrylic, prints. *b*: Bargoed, S.Wales, 26 Oct 1946. *m*: Christine. two *s*. *Educ*: Bargoed Grammar School. *Studied*: Cardiff University (Optometry). *Represented by*: Eames Fine Art, Bircham Gallery. *Exhib*: RA, Originals, Eastern Art, Laing, RWA, Salthouse, Discerning Eye, Sunday Times Watercolour, Royal Institute of Watercolours, Fermoy Gallery. *Works in collections*: HRH Prince of Wales, Essex CC, Beecroft, Addenbrooks, House of Lords, Celtic Manor. *Publications*: Printmaking Today, Sunday Times, Colour Supplement. *Clubs*: Arts Club, Dover Street. *Address:* Fairfield, Silver Street, Stansted, Essex, CM24 8HE. *Email*: rossloveday@btinternet.com *Website*: rossloveday.co.uk *Signs work*: "Loveday".

LOVELL, Margaret, DipFA (Slade, 1962), FRBS (1973), RWA (1972); sculptor in bronze, marble, slate. DLitt Hon, awarded Honorary Doctor of Letters by University of Leicester (2013). *b*: Bristol, Mar 1939. *m*: Edward. two *s*. two *d*. *Studied*: West of England College of Art, Bristol, Slade School of Fine Art, Academy of Fine Art, Florence (Italian Scholarship 1962-63), Greek Government Scholarship (1965-66). *Represented by*: Katharine House Gallery, Marlborough; Porthminster Gallery, St. Ives. *Exhib*: City Art Gall., Bristol, RA, Marjorie Parr Gall., London (4 one-man shows); one-man shows inc. Park Square Gall., Leeds, Fermoy A.G., King's Lynn, Univ. of Bath , Bruton Gall., Somerset; 1st retrospective Plymouth City A.G. (1972), McHardy Sculpture Co. London, Bruton St. Gallery, London; Sausmarez Sculpture Park, Guernsey; Red Rag Group, Stow-on-the-Wold, R.W.A., Katharine House Gallery, Marlborough; Porthminster A.G., St.Ives; Victoria A.G., Bath. *Works in collections*: public & private collections in UK, Europe, USA, New Zealand and Australia. *Commissions*: Barclays Bank, Bristol; Grafham Water, Hunts. *Publications*: "Margaret Lovell Sculptor" pub. Sansom & Company Ltd. (2009). *Address:* 14 Creswickle Avenue, Hanham, Bristol BS15 3HD. *Website*: www.margaretlovell.co.uk *Signs work*: "M. Lovell."

LOVETT, Alastair Philip, SWE. *Medium*: oil, prints. *b*: Stockton-on-Tees, 8 Aug 1968. *m*: Elizabeth. *Studied*: York University (1987-1990); Durham University (2000-2003). *Represented by*: Zillah Bell, Thirsk; The Sutton Gallery, Edinburgh. *Exhib*: Independent Group Exhibitions (2008-2010); Society of Wood Engravers Annual Exhibitions (2010-2014); Davidson Galleries International Wood Engraving Invitational (2013-14). *Works in collections*: Durham University Permanent Collection, private. *Commissions*: private. *Works Reproduced*: Regional press articles. *Principal Works*: "Sea Coaling Cycle" (oils and engravings); "Slipstream Series" (in progress). *Clubs*: Society of Wood Engravers (Elected). *Misc*: Learned to draw by pavement drawing as a student (i.e. large scale copies of well-known works). *Address*: 1 Plantation Avenue, Littletown, Durham DH6 1PY. *Email*: via website *Website*: alovett.co.uk *Signs work*: "Alastair Lovett".

LOWDAY, Sue, Yorkshire Arts Award/Arts Council Awards (2000, 2002, 2003, 2004, 2006), The Cutlers Company/Armourers and Brasiers (1999). *Medium*: sculpture, leatherwork. *b*: Hull, 26 Mar 1956. *Studied*: Sheffield Polytechnic School of Art & Design

(1974-78); Sheffield Hallam University (2001); Leather conservation: Theo Sturge (2009). *Exhib*: Origin, Crafts Council (2006-2009); Art in Action (2003-2014); Roger Billcliffe Gallery, Glasgow (2002-2009); Walsall Leather Museum (2007); British Library, London Architecture Biennale (2006); Bankside Gallery (2005); The International Art and Design Fair, The Armoury, Manhattan (2004); The Metal Gallery (2004-05); Chelsea Craft Fair (2000-2003); Goldsmiths Hall (1980, 1982, 1985). *Works in collections*: Sheffield Assay Office; City of Sheffield Collection, Town Hall; Millennium Galleries, Sheffield Museums; Manchester City Galleries; Goldsmiths Hall, London; University of Sheffield; Walsall Leather Museum. *Commissions*: Lord Dainton; Sheffield Assay Office. *Publications*: Art Workers Guild 125 Years (pub. Unicorn Press). *Clubs*: Art Workers Guild. *Address*: Rock Villa, Bonchurch Village Road, Ventnor, Isle of Wight PO38 1RG. *Email*: questions@suelowday.co.uk *Website*: www.suelowday.co.uk *Signs work*: Sue Lowday. Hallmark SL.

LOWE, Adam, MFA (Oxon), MA (RCA); artist in oil, printmaking. *b*: Oxford, 18 Feb 1959. *m*: Yuka. *Studied*: Ruskin School of Drawing, Oxford; RCA (Peter de Francia). *Exhib*: regularly at Pomeroy Purdy Gallery, also exhbns. in England and America. Commissioned work in Japan. *Works in collections*: Contemporary Art Soc., Atkinson A.G. *Publications*: A Resurgence in Contemporary Painting (Alistair Hicks, Phaidon 1989). *Address:* Reeds Wharf, Mill St., London SE1. *Signs work*: "ADAM LOWE."

LOWE, Jeff. *Medium*: drawing, prints & sculpture. *b*: Lancashire, 14 May 1952. *Studied*: Leicester College of Art (1970-71); St.Martins School of Art (1971-75). *Represented by*: various galleries worldwide. *Exhib*: Recent Sculpture & Drawings, Glynde House, London (2009); 'Journeys', Sidney Cooper Gallery, Canterbury (2008); 'Drawn Out', Robert Steele Gallery, New York (2008); RA Summer Show (2005) and many more solo and group exhibitions worldwide. *Works in collections*: Leicester Education Authority; North West Arts Association; Arts Council of Great Britian; Contemporary Arts Society; Government Art Collection; Channel 4 Television; Hunterian Art Gallery; Atkinson Gallery Collection, Southport; National Gallery, Australia. *Address:* The Red Wing, 6A Havelock Walk, Forest Walk, London SE23 3HG. *Email*: jeff@jeff-lowe.com *Website*: www.jeff-lowe.com *Signs work*: "JEFF LOWE".

LOWE, Peter. *Medium*: reliefs, drawing, prints, sculpture. *b*: London 1938. one *s*. one *d*. *Studied*: Goldsmiths (1954-60). *Exhib*: see website. *Works in collections*: Arts Council, London; V&A; Musée de Grenoble; Museo de Arte Moderno, Fundacion Soto, Cuidad Bollvar, Venezuela; University of East Anglia; National Museum Warsaw; Peter Stuyvesant Foundation Amsterdam; Kemin Kaupunki Taidesmuseo, Kemi, Finland; Stedelijk Museum, Schiedam; Alvar Alto Foundation, Pino Torinesi, Turin; Museum of Modern Art, Zagreb; Commanderie Sint Jan, Nijmegen; Museum of Art, Chelm, Poland; Tate Britain; Southampton City Art Gallery; Modriaanhuis, Amersfoort; Peter C. Ruppert Collection, Wurzburg; Henry Moore Institute, Leeds; also see website. *Publications*: 'Notes on Plus Minus. A Dialogue with Colin Jones', Structure 6/1 ed Joost Baljeu, Amsterdam (1963); 'Thoughts on Construction' Structure 6/2 ed Joost Baljeu, Amsterdam(1964); 'Statements' Systems catalogue, Whitechapel Art Gallery, Arts Council (1972); 'Engelse en Nederlandse Rationale Tekeningen' De Volle Maan Gallery, Delft, Netherlands (1976); 'Notes on Horizontal Relief Construction' Constructive Context. Arts Council (1979); 'Un pas vers la composition Sereille dans la peinture de Theo van Doesburg, Ed. S. Lemoine. Philippe Sers, Paris (1990); 'Notes on Exhibited Drawings' Peter Lowe Serial Drawings, Clare Hall Gallery, Cambridge (1994); 'Concrete Art, some pros, some cons' KunstKonkret 6. Saarbrücken Ed.S.Rompza & J.Enzweiler (1999); 'On Construction' KunstKonkret 6. Saarbrücken Ed.S.Rompza & J.Enzweiler (2002); 'A Missing Force', KunstKonkret 9. Saarbrücken Ed.S.Rompza & J.Enzweiler (2003); ' Mary Martin as Teacher' KunstKonkret 10. Saarbrücken Ed.S.Rompza & J.Enzweiler (2004); 'Atelierportrait' KunstKonkret 11.

Saarbrücken Ed.S.Rompza & J.Enzweiler (2006). *Official Purchasers*: see website. *Clubs*: The London Group; 'Systems Group'. *Address:* 27 Lanercost Road, London SW2 3DP. *Email*: peterloweuk@yahoo.com *Website*: www.peterllowe.plus.com *Signs work*: "Peter Lowe".

LOWERY, Alex, BA (Hons), Art Council Award. *Medium*: oil, watercolour, drawing. *b*: London, 3 May 1957. *Partner*: Vanessa Gardiner. one *d*. *Educ*: Addey & Stanhope Grammar School, SE14. *Studied*: Bath Academy of Art, Corsham (1976-77); Central School of Art & Design, London (1979-82). *Represented by*: Art First, London. *Exhib*: Gordon Hepworth Gallery, Exeter (1993); County Museum, West Bay, Dorset (1994); Rocket Gallery, London (1995); Art First, London (2002, 2004, 2007). *Commissions*: Dorset County Hospital. *Publications*: 'Re Inventing the Landscape' book by Vivienne Light (2001); 'Re Making Reality' catalogue, Kettle's Yard, Cambridge (1996). *Works Reproduced*: in Modern Painters, Art Review, Galleries, London Magazine, Whats On. *Recreations*: piano, travel. *Address:* Lilac Cottage, Fernhill, Charmouth, Dorset, DT6 6BX. *Email*: alexlowery@tiscali.co.uk *Signs work*: "ALEX LOWERY".

LOWRY, John Roger, ABNA. *Medium*: acrylic. *b*: Kent, 27 May 1945. *m*: Anne Blackmore. two *s*. *Educ*: Crayford School for Gentlefolk. *Studied*: Cornwall College, Penwith College. *Represented by*: ABNA. *Exhib*: Devon, Yorkshire, Surrey, Penzance, St. Ives, etc. *Works in collections*: private collections. *Publications*: ABNA. *Recreations*: sailing, walking, reading, festival organising. *Clubs*: PZHUA, West Cornwall Horticultural Society, Friends of Jubilee Pool, CPRE. *Misc*: Chair, Penzance Harbour Users Association, Golowan Maritime Festival. *Address*: 62 High Street, Penzance, Cornwall TR18 2SU. *Email*: rogerlowry@talktalk.net *Website*: rogerspaintings.webs.com *Signs work*: "Lowry".

LUBAR, Katherine, Shortlisted Celeste Art Prize (2007); Special Reserve, 'About Vision' (2002). *Medium*: acrylic and oil. *b*: Washington DC, USA, 29 Aug 1969. *Studied*: PGDip in Painting: City & Guilds of London Art School (1999); BA in Music Theory, with Minor in Fine Art (1993): Meadows School of Fine Arts at SMU; High School Diploma - Concentration Visual Arts: Arts Magnet High School for the Performing and Visual Arts (1987). *Exhib*: 2012: Victory Gallery, Portland, USA; 2009: WW Gallery, London; Tactile Bosch, Cardiff. 2008: London Art Fair. 2007: Ferreira Projects, London; John Jones, London; Vegas Gallery, London. 2006: Residence Gallery, London; Royal Academy, London; Broughton Gallery, Scotland; Square One Gallery, London. 2005: Signatures Gallery, London; Salon Borbonico de San Nicola la Strada, Naples. 2004: Museum of MADI and Geometric Art, Dallas, USA. *Works in collections*: Museum of MADI and Geometric Art, Dallas, USA; Dept. of Education and Employment, UK. *Clubs*: The Colour Group of Great Britain. *Address:* Basement, 19a, Sutherland Place, London W2 5BZ. *Email*: katherine@katlubar.com *Website*: www.katlubar.com *Signs work*: "Katherine Lubar".

LUCAS, Akemi, Apprenticed to Mr. Seizan Fujimoto for 16 years (since 8), became a named Master, Koshu in 1991. Qualified as Calligraphy teacher specialising in brushes and pen by Bunka Calligraphy School, Japan. *b*: Japan, 18 Jul 1967. *Partner*: Steve Howie. two *d*. *Exhib*: Solo exhibitions: The Gallery, Yamaguchi Chamber of Commerce & Industry; Centre Gallery, Bletchingley, Surrey; Frameless Gallery, London. Group exhibitions include: Nakano Gallery, & Gallery Akarenga, Yamaguchi, Japan. *Commissions*: Maki Restaurant, Richmond; Mokyo Printing Company, Japan; Mitsubishi Automobile Company; Barnart & Westwood; Libra Group. *Publications*: "LOVE and DREAM" by Koshu (2013). *Official Purchasers*: Amazon; Guardian Bookshop; Waterstones; Nakano Gallery, Japan. *Principal Works*: "Meaning of Life", "Love", "Dream". *Recreations*: ballet, zumba. *Misc*: Teaches calligraphy to students in Japan and UK. *Address*: 2 Beckingham House, Portesbury Road, Camberley GU15 3TD. *Email*: akemilucas@gmail.com. *Website*: www.koshujapaneseart.co.uk *Signs work*: "Koshu".

LUKE, John, National Diploma in Design; Higher Diploma in Design Education. *Medium*: oil, drawing, prints. *b*: Co.Durham, 12 May 1944. *s of*: the late John Luke. *m*: June Luke. one *s*. one *d*. *Studied*: Sunderland College of Art (1960-64, NDD); Sunderland University (1990, Dip. Design Ed.). *Exhib*: group exhbns: Seaton Holme Gallery, Easington; Hartlepool Art Gallery; across UK; Major exhibition Mazarron, Spain (2009) (100 pieces of work). *Works in collections*: thoughout UK. *Commissions*: private and business in UK and Spain, including portrait of retiring Lifeboat Coxwain; created visuals for Top Shop's catwalk, Oxford Street, London, Ipswich Town Football Stadium, and refurbishment of the British Telecom Tower (1999); large mural overlooking Canadas, Provence of Murcia, Spain. *Publications*: featured in 'Shafts of Light' mining painting publication by R. McManners & Gillian Wales. *Official Purchasers*: Peterlee Tertiary College (2 mining paintings); several offical purchases. *Works Reproduced*: limited edition prints mining theme, sold in DCC libraries. *Principal Works*: large mining paintings. *Misc*: taught at Hartlepool College of Art (1964-80); Head of Faculty of Exp. Arts, County Durham School until 2002. Works between studio in Spain and home in UK. *Address:* Pippin Barn West, Folly Lane, Copdock, Ipswich, Suffolk IP8 3JQ. *Email*: john.luke544@googlemail.com *Website*: www.johnlukepaintings.com *Signs work*: 'John Luke'.

LUKIC, Jelena, BA (Hons) Sculpture 1st (1987), RA Post Grad RA DipHE (1990); Contemporary View Postgraduate winner, (1990), 'The Hunting Group' Student Prize (1990), Landseer Scholarship (1990), Commonwealth Scholarship Belgrad Univ. (1990), Andre Dunoyer de Segonzac travelling schol. (1990), Bolton House Trust award (1988). *Medium*: painter in oil. *b*: Peterborough, 4 Apr 1962. *m*: Seamus More. one *s*. one *d*. *Studied*: Cambridge College Art and Technology (1982-83), Sheffield City Polytechnic (1983-87), RAS (1987-90). *Exhib*: RA Summer Show (1989, '90, 2000, '01), art4life (2002), various London and regional galleries in UK. *Clubs*: RASAA. *Address:* 3 Clare Court, Thaxted, Essex CM6 2RN. *Email*: jelenalukic@hotmail.com *Website*: www.homunculus.co.uk/jelena/

LUMLEY, Thomas Henry, The Prince of Wales Drawing School Prize, Royal Society of Portrait Painters Annual Show. *Medium*: oil, drawing. *b*: Sheffield, 6 Feb 1980. *s of*: The Earl of Scarbrough. *Studied*: Charles Cecil Studios, Florence (1999-2003). *Exhib*: Royal Society of Portrait Painters (2006, 2007); solo exhibition at Ramsay, Pimlico Road, London; Gallery 27, Cork Street, London (2008). *Works in collections*: private. *Commissions*: private portrait commissions. *Clubs*: Chelsea Arts Club, Blacks. *Address:* 14 Offley Road, London SW9 0LS. *Email*: tom@thomaslumley.com *Website*: www.thomaslumley.com *Signs work*: "THL".

LUMSDEN, James, Royal Scottish Academy Residences for Scotland Award (2010). *Medium*: Painter. *b*: Inverness, 30 Jun 1964. *Partner*: Seonaid McDonald. two *s*. *Studied*: Cardonald College, Glasgow (1983-85) Dip Graphic Design. *Represented by*: Sarah Myerscough Fine Art, London; Paul Kuhn Gallery, Calgary, Canada. *Exhib*: Solo exhibitions include: Sarah Myerscough Fine Art, London (2011, 2009, 2005, 2004, 2002); Paul Kuhn Gallery, Calgary, Canada (2012, 2010); Amber Room Contemporary Art, Edinburgh (2007); Atticsalt, Edinburgh (2006); MAC, Birmingam (2006); Triskel Arts Centre, Cork, Ireland (2001). *Works in collections*: Royal Bank of Scotland; HBOS; Mastercard; Ballinelen Art Foundation; Aalbore Komune. *Misc*: Fellow of Ballinelen Arts Foundation, County Mayo, Ireland. *Address*: Wasps Studio, Patriot Hall, Hamilton Place, Edinburgh EH3 5AY. *Email*: jlummy@aol.com *Website*: www.asixweb.org/artist/jameslumsden *Signs work*: "J. LUMSDEN".

LUSTY, Elfrieda, ARBS (2005); Chelsea Arts Council Prize (2003); Chelsea Arts Society Prize (1997). *Medium*: steel - applied resin, mixed media. *b*: Vienna, 11 Jun 1925. *d of*: Hans & Anna Salzer. *m*: Gordon. two *s*. one *d*. *Educ*: Twickenham County High School; Birkbeck College, London. *Studied*: St. Martins School, London; Kensington & Chelsea College; Richmond College of Art & Vienna. *Exhib*: Mall Galleries (2006); Battersea

Affordable Art Fair (2006); Trinity Arts Guild (1998-2009); Chelsea Art Society (1990-2009); Ealing Art Society (1995-99); one-man exhbn Trinity Arts, Sloane Square (2006). *Works in collections*: mainly private collections. *Commissions*: Holy Trinity, Sloane Street; many private commissions. *Works Reproduced*: collagraphs, sculptures, oil paintings. *Principal Works*: steel, brass, copper, mixed media abstract sculptures. *Recreations*: opera, tennis. *Clubs*: Ealing Art Club, Associate Society of British Sculptors, Chelsea Arts Society, Trinity Arts Guild. *Address:* Flat 10, Thames Reach, Rainville Road, London W6 9HS. *Email*: elfrieda.art@virgin.net *Signs work*: LUSTY (with L running below name, on sculptures), 'Elfrieda Lusty (paintings).

LYDBURY, Jane Sarah, BA Hons English Literature, BA Hons Illustration; wood engraver and illustrator in black and white, and watercolour. *b*: London, 11 Aug 1953. *m*: divorced. two *d*. *Educ*: Newnham College, University of Cambridge, Camberwell School of Art (1978-81). *Represented by*: regularly with Greenwich Printmakers, and Society of Wood Engravers. *Commissions*: occasional private press commissions. Has illustrated for Folio Society, OUP, BBC Publications, Simon and Schuster etc. *Publications*: Goodnight Stories (Piccolo), The Oxford Book of Christmas Poems-(with others) OUP; Ghostly Companions (Methuen); A Book of Christmas Carols (Simon & Schuster); The Norse Myths (Folio Society); This Solid Globe (Camberwell Press) etc. *Address:* 101 Humber Road, London SE3 7LW. *Email*: janelydbury@hotmail.com *Website*: www.janelydbury.com *Signs work*: Jane Lydbury.

LYDIATE, Avril Ann, *Medium*: oil, watercolour, drawing. *b*: Beckenham, Kent, 5 May 1945. *d of*: Audrey & Frederick Lydiate. *m*: Derek Osborne. one *s*. one *d*. *Educ*: Henrietta Barnet, London; Stoke Girls School, Coventry. *Studied*: Coventry College of Art; St.Martin's School of Art. *Exhib*: RA; Coventry Art Gallery; Rugby Art Gallery; Ashbarn, Hampshire; Look Gallery, York; Portal Gallery , London; Peephole Gallery, Long Buckby, Northants. *Commissions*: many. *Misc*: I describe my work as rural fantasy. *Address:* 16 Well Hill Close, Crick, Northants NN6 7TB. *Email*: avril@lydiate1.fsnet.co.uk *Website*: www.avrillydiate.co.uk *Signs work*: 'A.Lydiate'.

LYELL: see ROBINSON, Peter Lyell.

LYFORD, Rosina, Founder Member 'Group Nine Plus' (1973). Prize winner of GLC Spirit of London Competition (1983). *Medium*: acrylic, mixed media, pastel, print. *b*: London, 11 May 1936. two *s*. *Studied*: I left school at fifteen, and was sponsored by J Lyons to study Fine Art with Adrian Heath, Hammersmith (1952-54). Studied at Chelsea School of Art (1957-58). *Exhib*: Selected solo & group exhibitions: 1969: Richmond Hill Gallery, 'Young Contemporary Artists' showed paintings on Bayswater Road. 1972: 'Art goes to Industry'. 1973: 'Chennel Gallery' London. 1974: Caracas, Venezuela. 1975: Seen Gallery, London. 1976: Bauhouse 2', Connecticut, USA. 1979: 'New York Women in Communication', TWA, New York. 1981: Caracas, Venezuela. 1982: Major exhibition Gallery Hormansben, Oslo; RA Summer Show; 1994: Major Exhibition Kunst-Invest. 2002: Webersters Gallery, Surrey. 2007: Robert Philip Gallery, Surrey. *Works in collections*: private collections worldwide. *Commissions*: Lithographs for Gallery Kunst-Invest., Norway. *Works Reproduced*: Posters, prints, cards, film of work in progress. *Recreations*: Theatre, friends, books, walking, garden and music. *Misc*: History is included in the Archives of the National Gallery of Women in Art, Washington DC. Degree course in Jungian psychology. One of sixteen poets to be selected for the Dillon Book Prize. Backpacked alone around Australia. *Address:* 14 Hamhaugh Island, Shepperton, Middx., TW17 9LP. *Email*: art@rosinalyford.com *Website*: www.rosinalyford.com *Signs work*: "Lyford".

LYNCH, James, Greenshield Foundation Award (1983), Pimms Prize, R.A. (1986), Spectator prizewinner (1993). *Medium*: painter in egg tempera. *b*: Hitchin, 12 Jul 1956. *s of*:

Ronald Lynch, ATD. *m*: Kate (nee Armstrong). two *s*. one *d*. *Educ*: Devizes School. *Exhib*: RA, RWS, Portal, Bath Festival Art Fairs; one-man shows: Linfields, Bradford-on-Avon (1982-83), Nevill, Bath (1984), Odette Gilbert, London (1988), Maas Gallery, London (1991, 1993, 1995, 1997, 1999, 2001, 2003), Jonathan Cooper (Park Walk Gallery), London (2008-9). *Works in collections*: Longleat House, Chatsworth House, National Trust, Foundation for Art. *Publications*: illustrated "Wind in the Willows" (Folio Soc., 1995). *Recreations*: paragliding and motorcycling. *Address:* Four Chimneys, High Ham, Langport, Som. TA10 9BB. *Email*: james@lynchmail.fsnet.co.uk *Website*: www.james-lynch.co.uk *Signs work*: "J. Lynch."

LYNCH, Kate Mary, (née ARMSTRONG), BA Hons History of Art, Essex University (1975), PGCE / ATD Bristol University (1976), Post Grad. Diploma in Fine Art, University of West of England (1992) Academician, Royal West of England Academy (RWA). *Medium*: oil, pastel, willow, charcoal. *b*: London, 17 Aug 1949. *d of*: John & Patricia Armstrong. *m*: James Lynch. two *s*. one *d*. *Studied*: University of Essex, Bristol University, University of West of England. *Exhib*: Beaux Arts, Bath (1993, 1996, 1998); Alpha House, Sherborne, (1998, 2000, 2005); Touring Exhibition "Willow" (2003) to Brewhouse, Taunton; Somerset Rural Life Museum; Norfolk Rural Life Museum; Platform Gallery, Clitheroe; Somerset Art Weeks (2000, 2002, 2004, 2006); Touring exhibition "Sheep - from Lamb to Loom" (2009 - Brewhouse, Taunton; New Brewery Arts, Cirencester; Museum of North Craven, Settle; Black Swan Arts, Somerset; Heritage and Arts Centre, Dulverton. *Works in collections*: Wessex Collection, Somerset Museums Collection; Talboys Collection; St.George's Hospital, London. *Publications*: Willow - paintings, drawings and voices ISBN 0-9544394-0-6; 'Sheep - from Lamb to Loom' ISBN 9780954439422. *Address:* Four Chimneys, High Ham, Langport, Somerset TA10 9BB. *Email*: kate.lynch@virgin.net *Website*: www.katelynch.co.uk *Signs work*: "K. Lynch" or "Kate Lynch."

LYONS, Joan, SFP; Prizes: Portrait (SWA 2007); Peoples Choice (SWA 2009); Artist of the Year (SAA 2004). *Medium*: acrylic and pastel. *b*: Isleworth, 4 Oct 1940. *m*: John. two *s*. *Educ*: no formal education. *Exhib*: RWA, National Trust, SWA (2005/7/8/910/11/12, Mall Gallery); South West Academy of Fine Art (Phoenix Gallery, Exeter); Victoria Art Gallery (Bath Society of Artists, 2007/8/9); Compton Acres, Montisfont Abbey, & Hilliers (SFP). *Works in collections*: private. *Commissions*: private. *Clubs*: Fossway Society of Artists; Reading Guild of Artists; West Oxfordshire Arts. *Misc*: weekly Art Club for the village (Kempsford Art) from my studio & gallery, and monthly workshops. *Address:* Oak Cottage, High Street, Kempsford, GL7 4EQ. *Email*: joanlyons1@hotmail.com *Website*: www.joanlyons.co.uk *Signs work*: "Joan Lyons".

LYWOOD, Sally, FPS; BA Art & Design; ATC; Runner-up, Nina Hosali Award (2007). *Medium*: pastel, charcoal, watercolour, acrylic, collage. *b* Exmouth, 7 Mar 1950. *d of*: John & Pamela Lywood. one *s*. *Studied*: Newton Abbott College of Art; Loughborough College of Art; Leeds Polytechnic. *Represented by*: various galleries in Norway (Rogaland). *Exhib*: National Museum, Raratonga, Cook Islands (1998); one woman show, Fotland Mill, Rogaland (2000); group exhbns: Rogaland (2001-07); Painted Penguin Gallery, Caldbeck, Cumbria (2003); Nordic Pastel Forum, Falkenburg, Sweden (2006); Bankside Gallery, Hopton St., London (2007); Osterley House, London (2007). *Works in collections*: private collections in Britain, USA, Australia, Norway, Denmark and Cook Islands. *Commissions*: Stavanger County Council, Norway; British School, Stavanger, Norway; *Publications*: Norwegian Flower Book. *Official Purchasers*: Stavanger Town Council, Stavanger, Norway. *Principal Works*: portraits, nudes, abstract paintings. *Recreations*: walking, dancing, reading. *Address:* c/o Deer Park, Caldbeck, Cumbria, CA7 8EW. *Email*: lywood@c2i.net *Website*: www.gallerixia.no *Signs work*: 'S.Lywood'.

M

MABBUTT, Mary, BA (Hons) Loughborough College Art and Design, RAS PostGrad Cert; part-time lecturer; TSWA National Art Competition; John Moores Exhbn (1995); Major Award South West Arts. *Medium*: painter. *b*: Luton, 2 May 1951. *m*: Joe Coates. one *s*. one *d*. *Studied*: Luton School of Art, Loughborough College of Art and Design, Royal Academy Schools. *Exhib*: solo shows: Paton Gallery, New Grafton Gallery, Newlyn Gallery. *Works in collections*: Metropolitan Museum of Art, New York; Arts Council, London; Coopers and Lybrand, Unilever, Bankers' Trust, Usher Gallery, Lincoln, Pentland Industries, Robert and Susan Summer, New York, Slaughter and May. *Works Reproduced*: The New British Painting: Phaidon. *Clubs*: RASAA. *Address*: 6 Wood Lane, Falmouth, Cornwall, TR11 4RF. *Email*: marymabbutt@btconnect.com

MAC ARTHUR, Paula, post-Grad Diploma RA Schools. *b*: Enfield, 13 Mar 1967. *m*: Matthew Ashby. two *s*. *Studied*: Royal Academy Schools (1990-93), Loughborough College of Art and Design (1987-90). *Exhib*: Whitworth Young Contemporaries, John Player Portrait Award (1st prize), Royal Academy Summer Exhbn., John Moore's Exhibition. *Works in collections*: National Portrait Gallery. *Commissions*: Frederick Sanger (biochemist) for NPG, Baroness von Oppenheim, and President RICS, etc. *Clubs*: RASAA. *Address*: 83 Shrubland Rd, London E8 4NH.

MACALPINE, Jean, BA Fine Art (1976). *Medium*: hand toned and inkjet photographs. *b*: Ribble Valley, Lancs., 1953. *m*: Kenneth Draper, R.A. *Studied*: Bristol College of Art (1973-76), Camberwell College of Art (1976-77). *Exhib*: RA Summer Show; Hart Gallery, London; Flowers East, London; Leeds University Art Gallery; Europ'Art, Geneva; Art London; Clifton Studio NY, USA; Bridport Art Centre, Dorset; On Line Gallery, Southampton; Cleveland Bridge Gallery, Bath; New Academy Gallery, London; Louise Hallett Gallery, London; Sheila Harrison Gallery, London; Quest Gallery, Bath; Castlegate House Gallery, Cumbria; Sa Nostra Foundation, Menorca. *Works in collections*: ICI London; Leicestershire Education Authority; Welsh museums and schools; Leeds University Collection. *Commissions*: West Dorset General Hospital. *Publications*: Jean Macalpine: 'Intervals in Light' by Mary Rose Beaumont (Hart Gallery). *Address*: Carrer Gran 55a, 07720 Es Castell, Menorca, Spain. *Email*: drapermacalpine@gmail.com *Website*: www.jeanmacalpine.com *Signs work*: photographs signed on back "JEAN MACALPINE."

MACARA, Andrew, RBA (1983), NEAC (1984); self taught figurative painter in oil. *b*: Ashbourne, Derbyshire, 4 Apr 1944. *m*: Ann. two *s*. *Educ*: Derby College of Technology. *Studied*: St. Ives School of Painting. *Exhib*: Red Rag Gallery, Stow on the Wold, Glos; Fosse Gallery, Stow-on-the-Wold; Contemporary Fine Art Gallery, Eton; Tarpey Gallery, Castle Donington, Derby. *Works in collections*: Derby Museum and A.G, many private collections in UK and worldwide. *Commissions*: Palace of Westminster (Paintings for Members Dining Room). *Publications*: Quarto Publishing; Pearson Education. *Misc*: many paintings sold by Sothebys and Christies. *Address*: Aberfoyle, 32 Farley Rd., Derby DE23 6BX. *Email*: andrew@macara.com *Website*: www.macara.com *Signs work*: "Andrew Macara."

MACARTHUR, Susan, Fellow of Society of Designer Craftsmen. *Medium*: drawing, textiles, acrylic painting. *b*: Eastbourne, 4 Sep 1952. *d of*: Anthony and Pauline Fishenden. *m*: James D.Macarthur. *Studied*: Laguna Beach School of Art; California State Long Beach University (US: B.A General Art; Associated Arts Degree). *Exhib*: Mall Galleries, London; Affordable Art Fair, Battersea; Star Gallery, Lewes; Byard Art, Cambridge; Linda Blackstone, Pinner; Art in Action, Waterperry; Brighton Art Fair; Bournemouth University Atrium Gallery; Artspace, Henley; Contemporary Textile Fair; Landmark Arts Centre. *Commissions*: private and business. *Publications*: 'L'aura di Giorgio de Chirico' Klaus Podoll; various textile magazines. *Address*: Bena Cottage, South Street, Broad Chalke, Wilts. SP5 5DH.

Email: susanmacarthur@btinternet.com *Website*: www.susanmacarthur.co.uk *Signs work*: 'SMacarthur'.

MACCABE, Gladys, MBE, HROI, M.A. (Honoris Causa), FRSA; Founder and Past-Pres. Ulster Society of Women Artists; Academician with gold medal Italian Academy; Diploma of Merit, University of Arts, Parma; Hon. Academician, Royal Ulster Academy; Hon. Mem. Ulster Water-colour Soc.; Hon. Mem. Ulster Soc. of Miniaturists, Mem. Water-colour Soc. of Ireland; painter in oil and water-colour and various other media; art lecturer, writer and broadcaster; pianoforte soloist. *b*: Randalstown, N. Ireland. *d of*: George Chalmers, army officer and artist. *m*: Max Maccabe. two *s*. *Educ*: Brookvale Collegiate School, Ulster College of Art, France and Italy. *Exhib*: London, Dublin, USA, Canada, Belfast, Scotland, France, etc. *Works in collections*: Irish National Self-portrait Collection, Limerick University (3 works), Imperial War Museum, Ulster Museum, Arts Council of Northern Ireland, The Queen's University, Belfast, Ulster Office, London, Longford County Library, Thomas Haverty Trust, County Dublin Educ. Authority, BBC, Cyril Cusack, Esq., Miss Beatrice Lillie, Lady Wakehurst, the late Adlai Stevenson, Esq., Dr. James White, Director, National Gallery of Ireland, BBC (NI), Royal Ulster Academy, Crawford Municipal A.G., Cork. *Commissions*: numerous. *Publications*: Many important publications; T.V. programmes at home and abroad. *Address*: c/o The Eakin Gallery, 237 Lisburn Road, Belfast BT9 7EN. *Signs work*: "GLADYS MACCABE."

MACCORMAC, Sir Richard Cornelius, Kt 2001: CBE 1994; RA 1993; PPRIBA; Chairman, MacCormac Jamieson Prichard Ltd (incorporated in 2002), formerly a partnership since 1972; President, Royal Institute of British Architects, 1991-93; Taught in Dept. of Arch., Cambridge Uni. (1969-75 and 1979-81), Univ. Lectr. (1976-77); Studio Tutor, LSE (1998). Visiting Professor: Univ. of Edinburgh, Dept of Architecture (1982-85); Hull Univ. (1998-99). Dir. Spitalfields Workspace (1981-); Chm., Good Design in Housing Awards, RIBA London Region (1977); Mem., Royal Fine Art Commn (1983-93); Comr, English Heritage (1995-98). Royal Academy: Chairman: Architecture Committee (1997-); Exhibitions Cttee (1998-); Council (1998-); Advisor: British Council (1993-); Urban Task Force (1998-); Pres., London Forum of Amenity and Civic Soc. (1997-); Trustee, Greenwich Foundation for RNC (1998-2002); FRSA 1982. *b*: 3 Sep 1938. *s of*: the late Henry MacCormac, CBE, MD, FRCP and Marion Maud, d. of B.C.Broomhall, FRCS. *m*: 1964, Susan Karin Landen (separated in 1983). one *s*. (and one *s*. decd). *Educ*: Westminster School. *Studied*: Trinity College, Cambridge (BA 1962); University College London (MA 1965). RIBA 1967. Served RN 1957-59. Proj. Archt, London Borough of Merton, 1967-69; estabd private practice 1969. *Publications*: articles in Architectural Review and Architects Journal. *Principal Works*: major works include: Cable & Wireless Coll., Coventry (Royal Fine Art Comm/Sunday Times Bldg of the Year Award, 1994); Garden Quadrangle, St John's Coll., Oxford (Ind. On Sunday Bldg of the Year Award, 1994); Bowra Building, Wadham Coll., Oxford; Burrell's Fields, Trinity College, Cambridge; (RIBA Regional Award 1997, Civic Trust Award 1997); Ruskin Library, Lancaster Univ. (Ind. On Sunday Bldg of the Year Award, 1996; RFAC/BSkyB Bldg of the Year, Universities Winner, 1998; Millennium Products status awarded by the Design Council 1999); Southwark Stn, Jubilee Line Extension (Millennium Bldg of the Year Award, RFAC Trust/BSkyB 2000); Wellcome Wing, Science Mus. (Celebrating Construction Achievement, Regional Award for Greater London 2000). *Recreations*: sailing, music, reading. *Address*: MacCormac, Jamieson, Prichard Architects, 9 Heneage Street,. London, E1 5LJ. *Website*: www.mjparchitects.co.uk

MACDONALD, Alan, BA (Hons) Fine Art 1984, Post Dip (1985). *Medium*: painter in oil on linen and board. *b*: Malawi, 1962. *s of*: Donald & Margaret Macdonald. *m*: Carolynda. one *s*. *Studied*: Duncan of Jordanstone College of Art, Dundee; Cyprus College of Art, Paphos. *Represented by*: Beaux Arts, Bath; Stewart Gallery, Boise, Idaho, USA. *Exhib*: 1987: Stirling Biennale, Scotland; 1992: 'Far Horizons' Kyoto, Japan; 1995 & 1997:

Hunting Group prizes competition exhbn. RCA London; 1997: John Moores 20, Liverpool; 2000-07: England and Co., London; Caldwell Snyder Galleries, New York & San Francisco; Smelik & Stokking Galleries and Galerie Rademakers, Netherlands; Stewart Gallery, Boise, Idaho, USA; PM Gallery, Ealing, London; Royal Scottish Academy, Edinburgh: 183rd Annual Exhibition, 2009, 'Palate': Scion Installation Space, Los Angeles, 2010; Steward Gallery, Boise, Idaho, USA (2011-13); Beaux Arts, Bath (2013); Royal Scottish Academy, Edinburgh (2013). *Works in collections*: EMI, Old Mutual, Leeds Education, Kailey Hong Kong, Prudential, Worldcom, Corinthia Hotel London. *Commissions*: Corinthia Hotel, London, 2011. *Publications*: Yummy Magazine, Paris, 2009, Art Investor Magazine 2012. *Address*: 46 High Street, Carnoustie, Angus, DD7 6AH. *Email*: alanmacd@globalnet.co.uk *Website*: www.alanmacdonald.net *Signs work*: "Alan Macdonald" and dated on back.

MacDONALD, Alastair James Henderson, Hon. RMS, FRSA, Hon.UA; Gold Bowl Hon. Men. (1991, 1992, 1993, 1998); Llewellyn Alexander Masters Award (1995); miniature painter; Hon. Treas. RMS (1981-2004). *b*: Tighnabruaich, Argyll, 5 Jul 1934. *s of*: Angus Graham MacDonald, licensed master grocer. *m*: Juliet Anne Mead. two *s*. three *d*. *Educ*: Pope Street School, New Eltham. *Studied*: Woolwich Polytechnic School of Art and Crafts. *Exhib*: RMS, UA, MASF, ASMA (Vic), Miniature World Exhibitions I and II. *Works in collections*: RMS 'Diploma' and Sue Lee (USA). *Publications*: Hundredth Anniversary Book, Royal Society of Miniature Painters and Australian Miniatures Past and Present. *Address*: 63 Somers Rd., North Mymms, Herts. AL9 7PT.

MACDONALD, Allan Sween, GP Culloden General Practice; BA (Hons) Degree in Drawing and Painting. *Medium*: oil, drawing. *b*: Inverness, 13 Nov 1965. *s of*: Iain MacDonald. *m*: Zena MacDonald. *Studied*: Edinburgh College of Art, Edinburgh (1983-87). *Exhib*: Duncan Campbell Gallery, London; Lennox Gallery, London; Kilmorack Gallery, Inverness; Brown's Fine Art, Tain. *Publications*: 'As Others See Us' - Scottish Portrait Show. *Recreations*: playing fiddle, song writing. *Address*: 24 Caulfield Gardens, Cradgehall, Inverness-shire, IV2 5GE. *Email*: macdonald_art@yahoo.co.uk *Website*: www.allanmacdonald.co.uk *Signs work*: "A MacDonald".

MACDONALD, Donald, BA (Hons). *Medium*: Oil; drawing. *b*: Stornoway, 5 Apr 1976. *Partner*: Deborah Cruden. one *s*. *Studied*: Grays School of Art (1995-99). *Represented by*: Panter and Hall, London. *Exhib*: Scotlandart.com (2000-07); Edinburgh Art Fairs; Glasgow Art Fairs; London Art Fairs; Panter and Hall Scottish Show; Battersea Art Fair; Singaport Art Fair; Morven Gallery, Isle of Lewis; BP Portrait Award (2009). *Works in collections*: Mead Johnson International Collection (Scottish Representative); Imperial War Museum, Manchester (2012) 'The Quiet Battle'. *Address*: 38 South Dell, Ness, Isle of Lewis, HS2 0SP. *Email*: donaldmacdonaldart@yahoo.co.uk *Website*: www.donaldmacdonaldspaitings.co.uk *Signs work*: "Donald Macdonald" usually on reverse of canvas.

MACDONALD, Frances, SSWA, RGI, Rennie MacIntosh Residency, Colliovre, May 2013; Shortlisted for Noble Grossart Art Prize. *b*: Glasgow, 7 Oct 1945. *d of*: Donald & Frances Macdonald. *m*: Nick Ryan. one *s*. one *d*. *Exhib*: Selected solo exhibitions: Gallery Paton, Edinburgh (1975), Shore Gallery, Edinburgh (1977); Macauley Gallery, Stenton (1988), Sue Rankin Gallery, London (1989), RGI Kelly Gallery, Glasgow (1993, 94, 95), Scottish Arts Club, Edinburgh (1996), Open Eye Gallery, Edinburgh (1997, 99, 2003), Cyril Gerber Fine Art (1998, 99), Portland Gallery, London (2002, 03, 05, 06, 07, 08), Scottish Gallery Edinburgh (2008, 2010). Selected mixed exhibitions: Aberdeen Art Gallery, RSA, RGI, VAS, RSW. *Works in collections*: Gleneagles Hotel, Halifax, Fred Olsen Shipping Line, Royal Bank of Scotland, First National Bank USA, and many other corporate and private collections worldwide. *Recreations*: gardening, sailing, travelling. *Clubs*: Scottish Arts Club. *Address*: The Cottage, Crinan, Argyll, PA31 8SR. *Email*: francesmacdonald@live.com *Website*: www.crinanhotel.com *Signs work*: "Macdonald".

MACDONALD, Robert James, MA, RCA (1976-1979), Dip. LCSAD (1982); printmaker and painter in oil, acrylic, water-colour; trained as a journalist before studying art; prizewinner Singer and Friedlander Watercolour Exhibs. (1994 & 1998); First Prize, Winsor & Newton Award, RWS, 21st Century Exhbn (2005). *b*: Spilsby, Lincs., 1935. *m*: Annie Merrill. two *d*. *Educ*: Te Awamutu College, NZ. *Studied*: RCA (1976-1979), London Central School of Art (Special Advanced Printmaking Studies 1981-1983). *Exhib*: exhibits widely in Wales and London. *Works in collections*: V&A Print Collection, Ferens Gallery, Hull, Brecknock Museum and Art Gallery, Contemporary Art Society for Wales. *Commissions*: private. *Publications*: author and illustrator 'The Fifth Wind' (Bloomsbury 1989); illustrator 'Where Many Shipwrack' (John Donnes Poems), Old Stile Press (2004). *Clubs*: Welsh Group, and Watercolour Society of Wales. *Address*: Abersefin House, Penpont, Brecon, Powys LD3 8EU. *Email*: Abersefin@aol.com *Signs work*: "Macdonald" or "Macd" on early pictures.

MACEY, Julian Bernard, RMS (1995); retired Divisional Youth and Community Officer; self taught artist in oils, water-colour, pastel, pencil; Hon. Life Mem. (1991) and President Gt.Yarmouth and District Soc. of Artists (1994-). *b*: Minehead, Som., 13 Apr 1920. widower. one *s* (decd). *Educ*: Duke of York's Royal Military School, Dover. *Exhib*: Westminster and Mall Galleries with RMS; Tasmania and Washington DC in the World exhibitions of Miniature Art. *Works in collections*: Gt. Yarmouth and District Soc. of Artists. Two drawings in a Diamond Jubilee gift book for Her Majesty Queen Elizabeth II by Great Yarmouth Society of Artists. *Publications*: R.M.S. Centenary Book "One Hundred Years". *Address*: 119 Beccles Rd., Bradwell, Gt. Yarmouth, Norfolk NR31 8AB. *Signs work*: J. B. MACEY or J. B. Macey.

MACEY, Leo, CBE (1979), HS (1988); picture restorer, painter of miniatures in oil on ivorine and board; painter of oleographs. *b*: Minehead, 23 Feb 1922. *s of*: William Henry Macey. two *s*. one *d*. *Educ*: English Military School, Cairo and DYRMS. *Studied*: Frobisher School of Painting (1964-66, Lucy Frobisher). *Exhib*: RWA, HS, Armed Forces Art Soc. *Works in collections*: Sultan of Negri Sembilan, Malaysia and others. *Clubs*: Professional/Businessmen, Warminster. *Address*: 56 Upper Marsh Rd., Warminster, Wilts. BA12 9PN. *Signs work*: "LFM".

MacFARLANE, Sheila Margaret, DA (Edin.) 1964; artist, printmaker and engraver; lecturer in printmaking, Duncan of Jordanstone College of Art, Dundee (1970-76); founder and director, Printmakers Workshop at Kirkton of Craig (1976-90). *b*: Aberdeen, 2 May 1943. *d of*: Alexander Stewart MacFarlane. one *d*. *Studied*: Edinburgh College of Art; Atelier 17 Paris. *Exhib*: 'Tangleha to Bars Nab' touring exhbn. (1999-2004); 'The Finella Prints' Welsh Museum Modern Art (2005-6); The Aberfeldy Watermill & Wall Projects (2009-10). *Works in collections*: national and private collections in UK and private collections Overseas. Previously worked with children with special needs and now as a freelance artist. *Commissions*: 6th Bradford International Prints Exhibition. *Official Purchasers*: include: Kelvingrove Art Gallery, Glasgow; Arts Council of GB; Scottish National Gallery of Modern Art. *Address*: 1 Tangleha', St. Cyrus, Montrose DD10 0DQ. *Website*: www.aberfeldywatermill.com *Signs work*: "Sheila M. MacFarlane."

MacGREGOR, Moira, Diploma Drawing and Painting (1954); awarded Travelling Scholarship (1954). *Medium*: oil, watercolour. *b*: Dundee, 7 Dec 1931. *m*: John McConnell one *s*. one *d*. *Educ*: Harris Academy, Dundee. *Studied*: Dundee College of Art (Alberto Morrocco Head of the Painting School). *Exhib*: RA Summer Exhbns; RWS Open Exhbns; Singer & Friedlander/Sunday Times Watercolour; NEAC; RBA; RI; mixed shows: Cadogan Gallery, London (Spring 1984); solo show: Pentagram Gallery, London (1998, 2003); Retrospective at England & Co Gallery (2011). *Official Purchasers*: set of 12 silk screen prints of fruit bought by Chelsea & Westminster Hospital Arts Programme (1996). *Works*

Reproduced: RA Summer Exhbn postcard (1987); Unicef cards (2); RA Summer Exhbn (2008) card & mini print. *Address*: 12 Orme Court, London W2 4RL. *Email*: studio@moiramacgregor.com *Website*: www.moiramacgregor.com *Signs work*: 'MM'.

MacGREGOR, (Robert) Neil, MA, Ll.B.; Director, British Museum 2002-present, Director National Gallery 1987-2002, Editor Burlington Magazine 1981-86, lecturer in art history and architecture at the University of Reading and the Courtauld Institute 1975-1981. *b*: 16 June, 1946. *Educ*: New College, Oxford: BA French and German (1967); University of Edinburgh: Law (1970); Courtauld Institute of Art: MA History of Art (1975). *Publications*: 'Seeing Salvation: Images of Christian Art' (2002); 'Britain's Paintings' (2003); 'A History of the World in 100 Objects' (2010); 'Shakespeare's Restless World' (2012). *Address*: Director, The British Museum, Great Russell Street, London WC1B 3DG. *Signs work*: "Neil MacGregor."

MACINNES, Jock, RGI; DA in Art and Design, Post Graduate (Highly Commended); Cargill Award (RGI); Scottish Amicable Award (RGI). *Medium*: oil on gesso panel. *b*: 23 Aug 1943. *s of*: John Allan MacInnes. *m*: Elspeth Stirling MacInnes. one *d*. *Educ*: Alloa Academy. *Studied*: Glasgow School of Art. *Exhib*: Portland Gallery, London; Thompsons Gallery, London; Richmondhill Gallery; Open Eye Gallery, Edinburgh; Roger Billcliffe Gallery, Glasgow; Redrag Gallery, Stow-on-the-Wold; Lemon St. Gallery, Truro. *Works in collections*: Dick Institute, Kilmarnock; Paisley Art Institute; Strathclyde University; Glasgow University; Royal Bank of Scotland; Misys Plc; Dumbartonshire Education Authorities; Robert Fleming Holdings; Nationwide Building Society; Scottish Amicable; Royal Bank of Scotland, Sweden, C R Mackintosh Ass. France. *Works Reproduced*: prints: The Art Group, London; Studio Sixty Six, Glasgow. *Address*: Tawthorn Smiddy, Nr. Kilmarnock, Scotland KA3 6HU. *Website*: jaamrgi@sky.com *Signs work*: 'JM'.

MacINTYRE, Hilke. *Medium*: ceramic reliefs, watercolour, print. *b*: Kiel, Germany, 22 Mar 1964. *m*: Ian MacIntrye. one *s*. one *d*. *Educ*: Klaus Harms Schule, Kiel, Germany. *Studied*: Muthesius Schule, College for Art and Architecture, Kiel, Germany (1983-90, Diploma in Architecture). *Represented by*: many galleries. *Exhib*: Solo/2 person show (with husband, artist Ian MacIntyre): Weem Gallery, Pittenweem, Fife (2000), Dundee Contemporary Arts Centre (2005), Bircham Gallery, Holt, Norfolk (2008), East Neuk Festival Exhibition, Fife (2012). Annually in various group shows around the UK including RSA, Edinburgh. *Works in collections*: Private collections in Britain, Europe and worldwide. *Commissions*: East Neuk Festival; National Youth Choir of Scotland; various private commissions for portaits of houses and locations. *Works Reproduced*: lino/woodcuts for illustration and greetings cards. *Principal Works*: Labrynth Floor design, 6x13m (map of East Neuk) commissioned by the East Neuk Festival; "Blackbird in the Rain", "Orange Garden", acrylic on canvas. *Address*: Rinkmuir, Arncroach, Anstruther, Fife KY10 2RL. *Email*: hilke@macintyre-art.com *Website*: www.macintyre-art.com *Signs work*: "Hilke MacIntyre".

MACINTYRE, Ian, BA (Hons) 1st Class painting; Edinburgh College of Art Painting/Drawing Prize. *Medium*: oil, watercolour, gouache, prints. *b*: Aberfeldy, 10 Feb 1958. *m*: Hilke (Rackow). one *s*. one *d*. *Studied*: Edinburgh School of Art (1976-81). *Exhib*: include: RSA; SSA; British Print Show, Mall Galleries; Perth Museum and Art Galleries; RGI Glasgow. *Works in collections*: Perth Museum and Art Galleries; Edinburgh City Art Centre; Edinburgh Hospitals Collection. *Works Reproduced*: in books and magazines, most recently "Jackdaw" magazine. *Principal Works*: 4m long relief print "Think Tank"; "Reality Redesigned by An Artist". *Recreations*: cycling, walking, watching football. *Clubs*: Arncroach Bowling Club. *Misc*: Carnbee and Arncroach Community Council - Chair. *Address*: South Rinkmuir, Arncroach, Anstruther KY10 2RL. *Email*: mail@macintyre-art.com *Website*: www.macintyre-art.com *Signs work*: "Ian Macintyre".

MACKAY, Jane Elizabeth, MB.BS (London) 197; MRC GP. *Medium*: watercolour, oil, mixed media, silkscreen prints. *b*: UK, 1947. *d of*: Barry Sloan Mackay. *Educ*: Perse, Cambridge (1958-65). *Studied*: King's College, London & Westminster Medical School (1965-70), Art courses at West Dean College, Slade, Camberwell. *Represented by*: Benjamin Hargreaves. *Exhib*: solo shows include: Salisbury, Aldeburgh, Dulwich festivals; Wigmore Hall, Royal Northern College of Music; St.John's, Smith Square. Mixed shows include: Florence Biennale (2003), Art on Paper, Watercolours and Drawings Fair. *Works in collections*: Women's Art Collection, New Hall, Cambridge. *Commissions*: paintings of classical music; stained glass design, illustrations for books and CDs. *Publications*: CD cover designs for Hyperion, Collins Classics, Vasari Singers; Boosey & Hawkes; Synesthesia by Robertson & Sagiv (cover); 'The Turn of the Screw' - visual responses to Britten's opera. *Works Reproduced*: 'Britten Series' paintings. *Recreations*: choral singing, oboe, wildlife, gardening. *Misc*: Much of Jane Mackay's art is based on images of synaesthetic images of classical music. *Address*: 60 Cambria Road, London SE5 9AS. *Email*: janemackay@btinternet.com *Website*: http://www.soundingart.com

MACKAY CLARK, Deirdre, NDD; Pimms Prize for Drawing RA (1985); painter in oil, mixed media; tutor. *b*: Ilford, 18 Sep 1937. *d of*: David Mackay Edward, restorer, carver. *m*: John Clark. three *s*. one *d*. *Educ*: Copthall Grammar. *Studied*: Hornsey College of Art (1954-59, Alfred Daniels, Colin Sorensen). *Exhib*: Minories, Colchester, RA Summer Exhbns., RWS, RI, MoMA (Wales), Old School Gallery, Bleddfa, H'Art 2003. Work in private and business collections. Designed/painted ceramics (1977-82). *Work in collections*: Sir William Crawshay. *Publications*: Artists Cards (1984), RA Pubs. (1985), card and print; book jackets (1988), range of Fine Art cards and prints (1989-90). *Misc*: Family ran BOURLETS - 1965. *Address*: Brierley Cottage, Brierley, Leominster, Herefordshire HR6 0NT. *Signs work*: "D.M." or "Deirdre Mackay."

MacKEOWN, Martin Graham Clarke, DA (Edin) (1952); painter in oil. *b*: Belfast, 14 May 1931. *m*: Ann Carr. four *s*. two *d*. *Educ*: Campbell College, Belfast. *Studied*: Belfast College of Art (1948-50), Edinburgh College of Art (1950-52). *Exhib*: numerous. *Works in collections*: National Self-Portrait Collection of Ireland, Clare College Cambridge, Arts Council (N. Ireland), Ulster Television. *Publications*: illustrated several, including ten of his wife's cookery books, e.g. 'Ann Carr's Recipe Collection' (1987). *Address*: Manor House, Itteringham, Norfolk NR11 7AF. *Signs work*: "M. MacKeown."

MACLAURIN, W. Patricia, Annie Longley Award, Pastel Society (2002); Dover St. Arts Club Award MAS (2005); Fine Art Award UK, ROI (2009). *Medium*: oil and pastel. *b*: Christchurch, NZ, 10 Oct 1933. *m*: James (decd). two *s*. two *d*. *Educ*: Convent of the Sacred Heart, Timaru, NZ. *Studied*: Canterbury College School of Art, Christchurch, NZ. *Exhib*: RA Summer Exhbns, Royal Society of Portrait Painters, New English Art Club, Pastel Society, Royal Institute of Oil Painters, Discerning Eye, New Grafton Gallery, Llewellyn Alexander. solo: Sadlers Wells Theatre, Russell Gallery, Geedon Gallery, Lyric Hammersmith and others. *Commissions*: various families. *Works Reproduced*: TSB Lloyds. *Principal Works*: portraits, figurative works. *Recreations*: music, dance. *Clubs*: Arts Club, Dover St. *Address*: 6 Burnside Close, Twickenham, TW1 1ET. *Email*: pat.maclaurin@gmail.com *Signs work*: Maclaurin.

MACLEAN, William J., MBE, DA, RSA, RGI, RSW; Professor, fine art, Dundee College, Univ. of Dundee; Hon D.Litt, University of St.Andrews; Hon D.Litt, University of Aberdeen. *b*: Inverness, 12 Oct 1941. *s of*: John Maclean, master mariner. *m*: Marian Leven. two *s*. one *d*. *Educ*: Inverness Royal Academy, H.M.S. Conway, N. Wales. *Studied*: Grays School of Art, Aberdeen (1961-66); British School at Rome (1966). *Exhib*: one-man shows: Edinburgh, New 57 Gallery, Richard Demarco Gallery, R.H.W. London; group shows: Scottish Arts Council, Art First, London, 3rd Eye Gallery. *Works in collections*: Aberdeen

A.G., Scottish Arts Council, Contemporary Art Society, Scottish National Gallery of Modern Art, Hull A.G., Fitzwilliam Museum, Cambridge, B.M. *Address*: 18 Dougall St., Tayport, Fife DD6 9JD, Scotland. *Signs work*: "W. J. Maclean."

MacLENNAN, Alastair MacKay, MFA (1968), DA (1965); intermedia artist in mixed media installations, actuations, time-based work, conceptual orientation; Prof. of Fine Art, University of Ulster (1992-); Lifetime Achievement Award from TRACE, Cardiff Art in Time, Cardiff. *b*: Blairatholl, Scotland, 3 Feb 1943. *s of*: Christopher MacLennan. *Educ*: Perth Academy, Scotland. *Studied*: School of the Art Institute of Chicago, USA (1966-68), Duncan of Jordanstone College of Art, Dundee, Scotland (1960-65). *Exhib*: national and international festivals of performative and time-based work throughout America, Canada, Britain, E. and W. Europe, Asia. *Works in collections*: British Arts Council; private collections in Britain, America, Canada, Germany, Switzerland and Poland. *Commissions*: Representing Ireland at the Venice Biennale (1997), with 'Body of (D) earth'. *Publications*: reviews and interviews in art publications and periodicals. *Misc*: MacLennan has lived in Belfast since 1975. He is known for long, durational performances, and performance/installations, or 'actuations'. From the seminal work 'Days and Nights' (1981), a 144 hour non-stop actuation, to 'No Nemesis' (2000), his Zen-informed practice has been constant. His concerns include ethics, aesthetics, religious/political bigotry, inclusive tolerance, oppositional or consensus means of political/social improvement, death, decay, new life and mutation, transformation. An enthusiastic and influential artist and educator, he has exhibited extensively nationally and internationally. In 1989 he joined the innovative European performance art group, Black Market International. *Address*: c/o University of Ulster, School of Art and Design, York St., Belfast BT15 1ED, N. Ireland. *Email*: a.maclennan@ulster.ac.uk *Website*: http://www.vads.ahds.ac.uk/collections/maclennan

MACLEOD, Duncan, DA (1974), RSW (1980); artist in mixed media, water-colour, school teacher; SAC Lecturers Panel. *b*: Glasgow, 5 Apr 1952. *m*: Maretta Macleod, artist (divorced). one *s*. one *d*. *Educ*: Clydebank High School. *Studied*: Glasgow School of Art (1970-74, David Donaldson). *Exhib*: RSA, RSW, RGI, and many mixed and one-man shows in Britain. *Works in collections*: UK, USA, France, Sweden, and the Far East. *Address*: 13 Miltonhill, Milton, By Dumlarton. *Signs work*: "Duncan Macleod."

MACMIADHACHÁIN, Pádraig, RWA (resigned 1996); artist, Travelling Prize to Moscow (1957), winner, Laing National Painting Competition (1991), winner Daler Rowney award in Royal West of England Academy (1992), Polish Govt. to Poland (1961). *b*: Downpatrick, Ireland, 2 Mar 1929. *m*: Hazel McCool. two children. divorced. *m*: Ann Slacke. one child. divorced. *m*: Charlotte Kockelberg. divorced. *m*: Bonnie Brown, painter. divorced. *m*: Jane Hobday, painter. *Educ*: Bangor Grammar School; Portora Royal School, Enniskillen. *Studied*: Belfast College of Art (1944-48), National College of Art, Dublin (1948-49), Academy of Art, Krakow, Poland (1960-61). *Exhib*: one-man: Belfast, Dublin, London, Madrid, Krakow, Seattle, Los Angeles, Vancouver, Las Palmas; group shows: RA, RWA, RUA, Gorky Park, Moscow, Irish Exhbn. Living Art, Discerning Eye, Thompson Gallery, Crane Kalman, Cadogan Contemporary City Gallery, Curwen Gallery, New Academy Gallery - all London, Penwith Soc. of Art, St. Ives, Mullan Gallery, Belfast; Stronach Gallery, Co.Galway. *Works in collections*: in many private and public collections throughout the world, among them Hertford College, Oxford; Sussex University; The Bank of China; Irish Allied Bank; West Merchant Bank; Office of Public Works, Ireland; Dept. of Finance & Personnel, Govt. of N. Ireland. *Publications*: three collections of poems. *Misc*: Works always in New Academy Gallery, 34 Windmill Street, London; New Craftsman, St. Ives; Cornwall and Mullan Gallery, Belfast. *Address*: Wharf House Studio, 4 Commercial Lane, Swanage, Dorset BH19 1DE. *Misc*: Work always in New Academy Gallery, 34 Windmill St., London, New Craftsman, St. Ives and The Molesworth Gallery, Dublin.

MACQUEEN, Charles Thomas Keane, DA (1962), RGI (1985), RSW (1984); painter in water-colour, acrylic and oil; lecturer in Art Education at Moray House Inst. of Educ. – retired. *b*: Glasgow, 23 Feb 1940. *Partner*: Christine Woodside RSW, RGI. two *d*. *Educ*: St. Aloysius College. *Studied*: Glasgow School of Art. *Exhib*: numerous exhibs. including RSA, RSW, RGI. *Works in collections*: Royal Scottish Academy, Paisley Museum and Art Gallery, The Royal Bank of Scotland. *Commissions*: two murals for the new Cunard liner, Queen Victoria. *Clubs*: Scottish Arts club. *Address*: Tower View, 1 Back Dykes, Auchtermuchty, Fife KY14 7AB. *Signs work*: "MACQUEEN."

MACRAE, Tom. *Medium*: oil, watercolour, drawing, sculpture. *b*: Rhodesia, 31 Mar 1959. one *s*. one *d*. *Studied*: Northwich School of Art; Stockport School of Art. *Represented by*: Theo Waddington, and self. *Exhib*: RA Summer Exhbns; Hunting Art Prize; Discerning Eye; Jerwood. *Works in collections*: Ericsson, Baker Tilly, Ruan Milborrow Collection, Robertsons. *Works Reproduced*: Royal Academy Summer Exhibition Catalogue (full page). *Clubs*: guitars, automobilia. *Address*: 7 Edwards College, South Cerney, Cirencester GL7 5TR. *Signs work*: 'Tom Macrae'.

MacSWEENEY Dale Louisiana; see PRING MacSWEENEY, Dale Louisiana.

MADDISON, Eileen, NDD (1955), ATD (1956), SBA (1998); botanical artist in water-colour. *b*: Lancs., 22 Aug 1934. *m*: Colin Maddison. one *s*. two *d*. *Studied*: Central School of Art (1953-55), Liverpool College of Art (1955-56). *Exhib*: SBA, Westminster Gallery, Guildford House Gallery, American Daffodil Soc., Pashley Manor, work in private collections internationally. *Address*: 5 Ampfield Court, Baddesley Road, Chandlers Ford, Eastleigh, Hampshire SO53 5EP. *Signs work*: "Eileen Maddison" or "E.M."

MADDISON, John Michael, BA (1974), PhD (1978), FSA (1991); Hon Doctor of Arts (2008). *b*: St. Andrews, 17 Nov 1952. *m*: Jane Kennedy. two *s*. *Studied*: University of Manchester. *Represented by*: The Jerram Gallery, Sherborne. *Exhib*: RA, RI, many mixed exhbns. and one-man shows. *Works in collections*: Lady Margaret Hall, Oxford; Sainsbury Centre, Norwich; Nationwide Building Society. *Commissions*: distemper panels for National Trust restaurant Felbrigg Hall; reredos for Bishop Alcock's Chapel at Ely Cathedral; design of reredos and altar in wrought iron for the Lady Chapel at Ely Cathedral; painted panels and ceiling at St Albans Cathedral; recreation of imagery in the Egyptian Hall at Stowe House. *Publications*: articles and books on medieval architecture and books on country houses. *Address*: 88 St. Mary's St., Ely, Cambs. CB7 4HH. *Website*: johnmaddison.co.uk *Signs work*: "JM" or "John Maddison".

MADDISON, Robert , MENSA. (1987); painter in water-colour, pastel, graphite, metalpoint. One of the few professional artists that concentrates on the technique of metalpoint using pure gold and silver. *b*: Newcastle upon Tyne, 6 May 1946. *s of*: Robert Maddison. *m*: Elizabeth Finch. one *s*. one *d*. *Educ*: Heaton Grammar School. *Studied*: Newcastle College of Art (1962-64, John Crisp), Manchester College of Art (1964-65). *Exhib*: SGFA, NS; numerous one-man shows, Durham University, Tully House Carlisle, Laing Art Gallery Newcastle. *Works in collections*: Durham University; numerous private collections including HRH The Prince of Wales. *Commissions*: Two watercolour paintings commissioned by Northumberland Council to be presented to HRH Prince Charles. *Publications*: The Northern Pennines - An Artist's Impressions; articles; television broadcasts, "The Artist", "International Artist"; a chapter in the book, "Different Strokes". *Misc*: Artist in residence "Prudhoe Community Arts", Artist in Residence "Newcastle Opera House", artist in residence Starbucks. *Address*: Spring Cottage Studio, Dovespool, Allenheads, Northumberland NE47 9HQ. *Email*: rmaddisonfineart@btinternet.com *Website*: www.maddisonfineart.co.uk *Signs work*: "R. Maddison.".

MADDOX, Ronald, PRI, Hon. RWS, Hon. RBA, Hon.PS, Hon.SGFA, Hon.WGA, FCSD, FRSA; illustrator, consultant Designer, artist in water-colour, line, gouache, specialising in architecture and landscape; British stamps Design Council Award (1972); Isle of Man Europa stamps Prix de l'Art Philatelique (1987); Winsor & Newton RI. Award (1981,1991); finalist Hunting Group Art Prizes (1980-81-83); RI Rowland Hilder Award (1996, 2000); Elected President RI (1989) re-elected (1994,1999, 2004, 2009), Governor FBA (1989-2002), AGBI Council/Hon Secretary. *b*: Purley, Surrey, 5 Oct 1930. *s of*: H. G. Maddox. *m*: (1st) Camilla Farrin. 1958 (decd. 1995); two *s*. (2nd) Diana Goodwin (1997). *Studied*: St Albans School of Art, Hertfordshire College of Art and Design, London College of Printing and Graphic Arts. Design/Art Direction 1951-61, freelance from 1962. *Exhib*: RA, RI, RBA Mall Galleries, Bankside Galleries - national and provincial exhbns., one-man shows. *Works in collections*: Britain, USA, Canada, Germany. Designer - British Commemorative stamps (1972/78/84/89). *Publications*: national and international publications. *Clubs*: The Arts Club. *Address*: Herons, 21 New Rd., Digswell, Welwyn, Herts. AL6 0AQ. *Signs work*: "RONALD MADDOX."

MAECKELBERGHE, Margo Oates, artist. *Medium*: painter. *b*: Penzance, Cornwall. *d of*: Mr. & Mrs. E.O. Try. *m*: Dr. one *s*. one *d*. *Educ*: Penzance Grammar School. *Studied*: Penzance School of Art, Bath Academy of Art, Corsham. *Represented by*: various galleries. *Exhib*: London Group, Leicester Galleries, Penwith Gallery, Newlyn Gallery, Plymouth City Art Gallery and Museum, Peter Hyde Fine Arts, London (1968), Ewaston Gallery, Durham University, Edinburgh University, Exeter University, Festival Exhbns. Aldeburgh, Black Swan Gallery, Frome, Kunsthalle Munich, Kursaal Ostend, etc. *Works in collections*: significant representation in private and public collections in Britain and throughout the world. *Publications*: 'The Timeless Land' Denys Val Baker; 'St.Ives Revisited' Peter Davies; 'St.Ives, Portrait of an Art Colony' Marian Whybrow; 'Catching the Wave' Tom Cross; 'Behind the Canvas' S.Cook, S.Britain, etc. *Official Purchasers*: Contemporary Art Society, V. & A. Museum, Plymouth Museum and City Art Gallery, Toronto University, Exeter University, Durham University, Kunst Museum, Berlin, British Council, Cornwall Collection, Devon County Council, etc. *Recreations*: reading, exploring! *Clubs*: Chelsea Arts, Chairman Penwith Society of Artists, Newlyn Society of Artists. *Misc*: elected Bard of Cornish Gorsedd 1997. *Address*: 'Roscadghill' Penzance, Cornwall, TR20 8TD. *Signs work*: Maeckelberghe.

MAGIS, Pascal, Dip. National des Beaux Arts (1976); abstract artist in acrylic and oil and tapestry designer. *b*: Aurillac, France, 1 Apr 1955. *m*: Lilou Magis. *Educ*: Ecole St. Joseph de Sarlat, France. *Studied*: Ecole Nationale des Arts Decoratifs de Limoges, France. *Exhib*: Wimbledon Fine Art, Galerie Lewis Guy, Holland, Galerie Inuit, Denmark, Galerie Briand, France. *Works in collections*: Glaxo Smith Kline, Rabo Bank, A.M.B. Amro. *Commissions*: RA Christoforides Collection. *Address*: c/o Wimbledon Fine Art, 41 Church Rd., Wimbledon Village, London SW19 5DQ. *Email*: magis.art@wanadoo.france

MAHON, Phyllis Josephine, BA Hons (1976); H.Dip.Fine Art (1977); Arts Council Northern Ireland Award (1977); Arts Council East Midlands Award (2004). *Medium*: painting, stonecarving. *b*: Omagh, Co.Tyrone, NI. *d of*: Joseph & Alice Mahon. *m*: (1977-92) Brian Campbell; (2000) Robert Willmington. 2 *s*., 2 *s-s*. 1 *d*., 1 *s-d*. *Educ*: Strabane Convent Grammar (1965-71). *Studied*: Belfast College of Art (1971-6). *Exhib*: solo exhbns: UK and Irish galleries including Belfast, Chester, Dublin, Lincoln, London, Taunton, Worcester, Mount Berry College - Georgia,USA; group exhbns include: RA Summer Show; Curwen gallery; England & Co.; Fung Ping Shan Museum, Hong Kong. *Works in collections*: Arts Council N. Ireland; Belfast Telegraph; UTV; Bedfordshire & Somerset Councils; private collections worldwide. *Commissions*: private commissions: Finland, Germany, Japan, USA, UK. *Publications*: editorial illustrations. *Works Reproduced*: Rouge Press Portfolio (1986); Arts Council Editioned Prints (1989). *Principal Works*: Pietas (1987). *Recreations*: reading, travelling, swimming. *Address*: The Studio, Joll's Lane, Greetham, Horncastle LN9 6NT. *Email*: phyllis.mahon@googlemail.com *Website*: www.phyllismahon.com *Signs work*: 'Phyllis Mahon'.

MAI, Jinyao: see MAK, Kum Siew.

MAINE, John Kenneth, RA; Awards and prized include RCA Drawing Prize, The Bence Pritchard Bequest, Walter Neurath Prize, Mark Rothko Memorial Trust Award; awards from: Henry Moore Foundation, Elephant Trust, Arts Council, British Council, Japan Foundation. *Medium*: sculpture. *b*: Bristol, 31 Oct 1942. *m*: Cilla Maine. two *s*. *Educ*: Bristol Grammar School. *Studied*: West of England College of Art (1960-64); Royal College of Art (Sculpture, (1964-67). *Represented by*: Royal Academy of Arts. *Exhib*: Serpentine Gallery, Hayward Gallery, South Bank Centre, British Museum, Royal Academy. *Works in collections*: includes: Councils of: Aberdeenshire, Cardiff, Dorchester, Howden, Isle of Wight, Kilkenny, Newcastle, North Somerset, Peterborough, Portland. ACGB; Bharat Bhavan Bhopal, India; British Council; British Museum; Hagi City Japan; Hue City, Vietnam; King James' School, Knaresborough; London Boroughs of: Camden, Islington, Lewisham; Middlesbrough Art Gallery; National Gallery of Victoria, Australia; Portsmouth City Museum; RA; Royal Bank of Scotland; Royal Collection; Ruygasaki Town Council, Iberaki Prefecture, Japan; Sharjah Art Museum; Standard Life; Transport for London; Westminster Abbey; Yorkshire Sculpture Park. *Commissions*: Government Art Collection (for British High Commission, Canberra, Australia); London Borough of Islington (War Memorial); North Somerset Council (for Weston-super-Mare promenade); and many others. *Publications*: Royal Academy: 'After Cosmati' Artists' Laboratory 4 (2011). *Official Purchasers*: Arts Council, Government Art Collection, British Museum, British Council. *Principal Works*: 'Arena' South Bank, Memorial - Islington Green, 'Sea Strata' Green Park Tube Station, 'Chiswell Earthworks', The Howden Sequence, 'Pyramid' Peterborough, 'Strata' Iberaki Japan. *Recreations*: interested in music, archaeology, cathedrals and architecture. *Address*: Old School, East Knoyle, Salisbury, Wiltshire SP3 6AE. *Email*: johnmaine@hotmail.com *Signs work*: "John Maine".

MAK, Kum Siew, (Mai, Jinyao), ARCA (1967); full-time artist in Chinese and Western media. *b*: Singapore, 21 Apr 1940. two *s*. *Educ*: Singapore. *Studied*: St. Martin's School of Art (1961-64) under Frederick Gore, RCA (1964-67) under Carel Weight. *Exhib*: RA, ICA, RCA, Serpentine Gallery, Tate Gallery, Whitechapel Gallery. *Works in collections*: Tate Gallery, London; National Gallery, Singapore; Museum of Modern Art, Hyogo, Japan; Arts Council of GB. *Publications*: Talking Pictures, The Best of Friends. *Address*: Derrylehard, Ballydehob, Co. Cork, Eire.

MAKEPEACE, John, OBE (1988), FCSD, FIMgt., FRSA; designer and furniture maker since 1961; Founder and Director: The Parnham Trust (1977-2000). *b*: 6 Jul 1939. *m*: 1983 Jennie Moores. two *s*. *Works in collections*: Cardiff; Fitzwilliam; Leeds; Frankfurt; Art Institute, Chicago; Lewis Collection, Richmond, Va.; V&A; Royal Museum of Scotland. *Commissions*: Furniture commissions for Nuffield Foundation; Post Office; Royal Society of Arts; Boots plc; Banque Generale du Luxembourg. *Publications*: "A Spirit of Adventure in Craft and Design" by Jeremy Myerson. *Clubs*: The Athenaeum, London. *Misc*: Study/Consultancy Tours: Scandinavia; N. America; W. Africa; Australia and Japan. Featured in numerous books, articles and films internationally. *Address*: Farrs House, Beaminster, Dorset DT8 3NB.

MAKLOUF, Raphael, sculptor in bronze; painter. *b*: Jerusalem, 10 Dec 1937. *Studied*: Camberwell School of Art (1953-58) under Dr. Karel Vogel. *Works in collections*: Life-size bronze bust of HM Queen Elizabeth II for Royal Society of Arts, John Adam St., London (1986); life-size bronze bust of General Sir John Mogg for Army Benevolent Fund (1987); Tower of London; Carnegie Hall, NY, etc. New portrait effigy of HM The Queen on all U.K. coinage from 1985; bronze of HM The Queen, National Theatre; 15 Stations of the Cross, for Brentwood Cathedral (architect Quinlan Terry). *Address*: 3 St. Helena Terr., Richmond, Surrey TW9 1NR.

MALCOLM, Bronwen, BA Hons. Fine Art; painter in oil. *b*: London, 31 Jul 1963. *m*: Stephen Ackhurst. one *s*. one *d*. *Studied*: Wimbledon School of Art (1981-1982),

St. Martins School of Art (1982-1985) under Eileen Cooper and Albert Herbert. *Exhib*: Discerning Eye; RA Summer Show; Crickethill NYC, NY ,USA; Thackery Gallery; Gallery 286, London. *Works in collections*: Unilever. *Commissions*: Merrill Lynch, U.K. *Publications*: Arts Review, (Oct. 1987, Dec. 1988), Company, (Jan. 1989), Soloarte 1st issue. *Works Reproduced*: RA Summer Show 2001 catalogue, Soloarte magazine 1st issue. *Clubs*: Chelsea Arts, Alberg Ski Club. *Address*: 19 Crescent Grove London SW4 7AF. *Email*: bronny@ackhurst.com *Website*: www.bronwenmalcolm.com

MALENOIR, Mary, RE (1984); RA Schools Dip. (1964), Rome Scholar in Engraving (1965-67); Prizewinner in: PMC National Print Competition (1987), Huntin Group Competition (1987), Humberside Printmaking Competition (1987), Bankside Gallery Open Print Competition (1989), Arts CLub Prize (1998), RA Summer Exhibn; artist in mixed media. *b*: Surrey, 29 Jul 1940. *d of*: W. E. Malenoir. *m*: Michael Fairclough, artist. two *d*. *Studied*: Kingston School of Art (1957-61), RA Schools (1961-64), SW Hayter's Atelier 17, Paris (1967). *Exhib*: Bohun Gallery Henley-on-Thames, New Ashgate Gallery, Farnham, Discerning Eye London (invited artist), national Open Competition Chichester (Commended), Royal Academy Summer Exhibitions (over 50 works since 1960) etc. *Works in collections*: Ashmolean Museum, Ipswich Museum, Graves A.G. Sheffield, Stephanie Shirley Collection, Prior's Court. *Address*: Tilford Green Cottages, Tilford, Farnham, Surrey GU10 2BU. *Email*: info@malenoir.co.uk *Website*: www.malenoir.co.uk *Signs work*: "MALENOIR." or "m.m."

MALHOTRA, Sheila, BA (1963); Certificat de Langue Francaise (1977); Diplome de Langue Francaise (1979); at Arts College won Scholarship for Outstanding Work. *Medium*: oil, collage, acrylic, mixed media. *b*: Lahore (India), 6 Feb 1943. *d of*: Champa Stokes & Manmohan Nath. *m*: Capt. Sutikshan Malhotra. one *s*. one *d*. *Studied*: Government College of Arts, Chandigarh, India (1963-66). *Exhib*: London Auctions: Christies (2002); Bonhams (2002); One-man shows: Nehru Centre, Mayfair (2001, 05). London Group Shows: Edith Grove Gallery, Fulham (1999); BBAC Edgeware (1999); Sports Academy, Potters Bar, Barnet Cancer Care (2000); East Finchley Library (2000); Indian Institute of Art and Culture, Kensington (2000); London Sketch Club in conjunction with Chelsea Festival (2000); St.Martins in the Field, Trafalgar Square (2000); M P Birla Gallery, Kensington (2002); Hill Rise Gallery, Richmond (2006, 2007). India One-man Shows: Conclave Gallery, Calcutta (1991); ANZ Grindleys Bank Calcutta (1993); Taj Art Gallery, Mumbai (1995); Birla Academy of Art and Culture, Calcutta (1996); Jehangir Art Gallery, Mumbai (1998, 2009/2010). India Group Shows: Govt. Museum & Art Gallery, Chandigarh (1965), Birla Academy, Calcutta (1992, 1993); Academy of Fine Art, Calcutta (1994); Jharok Art Gallery, Dlehi (1994); Century Gallery (1997) etc. *Works in collections*: London: Foresight Ltd., Tatra Sipox, CNN South Asia, Colebrand, Ramon International Insurance Brokers. India: Minister for Backward Classes; Governor Himachal Pradesh; Vice-Admiral RKS Ghandi; Chairman SCI; Vice-Admiral Vishnu Bhagwat; many private and corporate collectors. *Publications*: Art reviews for Confluence (newspaper). *Misc*: Organised Womens Art Show, Mumbai, India (1997), Annual Exhibition, Bombay Art Society at Jehangir Art Gallery (1998); Annual Exhibition, Academy of Fine Arts (1990); invited as Special Judge for Inter-School Art Competition, Calcutta, India. *Address*: 1A Stanley Road, South Woodford, London E18 2NR. *Email*: sheila_malhotra@hotmail.com *Website*: www.sheilazart.com *Signs work*: "SHEILA K MALHOTRA".

MALI, Yashwant, RBS; General Diploma in Fine Art; Gold Medal, Bombay Art Society. *Medium*: mixed media. *b*: Mumbai, India 20 Oct 1934. *Studied*: JJ School, Bombay (1956); St. Martin's School, London (1962). *Represented by*: Mr Tolleck Winner. *Exhib*: India, Paris, Italy, London, Manchester, Oxford, Brighton; 156 group shows, most recent Coningsby Gallery, London (2006); 29 solo shows inc. James Colman, London, Gallery Different (2013). *Works in collections*: Air India, Godreg, Mrs. Profulla Dahamukar, Mrs. Savita Apte, Mrs. Vaishali Thakkar, James Colman, New Malden Art Gallery and Gallery Different.

Publications: Art Review, Art News, Time Out, Christie's London, Confluence of South Asian Perspectives, Network of Richmond & West Arts Magazine, Dictionary of Indian Arts & Artists, Galleries Magazine. *Works Reproduced*: Brain-wave from JJ (Times Review, 1996). *Principal Works*: Pencil Yard (2005); After Dali (1998). *Clubs*: Watemans Art Centre, Brentford; Whitechapel Gallery; Richmond Art Soc.; Twickenham Art Circle; Royal Academy; Tate Gallery. *Address*: 13 Crestwood Way, Hounslow Heath, Middlesex, TW4 5EQ. *Email*: maliart2010@yahoo.co.uk *Signs work*: 'Mali'.

MALIN, Suzi, Slade Post. Grad. (1975); painter in tempera. *d of*: Michael Malin, textile designer. *m*: David Hames. one *s*. one *d*. *Educ*: Badminton, Bristol. *Studied*: Slade School of Art (1969-75, John Aldridge, R.A.). *Exhib*: one-man shows, JPL Fine Arts, London (1977), Achim Moeller, London (1978), Coe Kerr, NY (1978), Galerie d'Eendt, Amsterdam (1983), Gimpel Fils, London (1982). *Works in collections*: NPG; Raby Castle; Gt. Hall, Christchurch, Oxford; Hull University; East Anglia University; Midland Bank. *Commissions*: Lord Home, Alistair Morton, Queen of Greece, Elton John. *Clubs*: Chelsea Arts. *Address*: The Meeting Hall, 158a Mill La., London NW6. *Signs work*: "S. Malin."

MALLIN-DAVIES, Joanna, ARBS; BA Ceramic Design. *Medium*: bronze, clay, misc. *b*: Llwynypia, S.Wales, 2 Dec 1965. *Studied*: South Glamorgan Inst. HE, Howard Gardens, Cardiff. *Represented by*: DBS, Dawlish Society of Sculptors. *Exhib*: Thompson's Galleries (2001-present); Hannah Peschar (1991-93); Mandarin Oriental Fine Art, Hong Kong (1994-2003); Broomhill Art Park (1997-present); Morsø Kunstforening, Denmark (1999), Badcock's Gallery, Cornwall, Open Eye Gallery, Edinburgh (1996-2005). *Works in collections*: Aberystwyth Arts Centre, Broomhill Art Park, Devon, Kirsten Kjaers Museum, Denmark. *Commissions*: Brockhall Village Estate, Lancashire. *Publications*: Encyclopedia of British 20th Century Sculpture; Metamorfoser (Danish Landar Publication). *Official Purchasers*: Welsh Arts Council. *Recreations*: yoga, films, books. *Address*: c/o 31 High Street, Addlestone, Surrey, KT15 1TT. *Email*: Joanna@mallin-davies.com *Website*: www.mallin-davies.com *Signs work*: "J-D", "JM-D".

MALTMAN, Philip John, BA Hons Fine Art. *Medium*: oil, watercolour, drawing, prints. *b*: Irvine, Scotland, 9 Mar 1950. *m*: Stephanie. two *s*. *Educ*: Carrick Academy, Kingsdale School. *Studied*: Hornsey College of Art (1968); Ravensbourne College of Art (1968-71). *Exhib*: Angela Flowers; Bernard Jacobson; London Group; Cheltenham Open Drawing; John Moores Contemporary Painting; Contemporary Art Society; RA Summer Exhbn; 'MAL' Birmingham; Glasgow Print Studio; Bede Gallery, Jarrow; Piers Feetham, London; Hunting Group Art Prizes. *Works in collections*: in USA, Switzerland, Austria, UK. *Commissions*: private and business. *Recreations*: books, beach, garden. *Misc*: on-going work with Katy English on 'My Shore-Your Horizon'; 1996-joint exhibition, 'Beginning and Ending on the Shore'. *Address*: The Mount, 23 Thurlow Park Road, London SE21 8JP. *Email*: philip.maltman@btinternet.com *Website*: www.numasters.com www.maybole.org/photogalleries *Signs work*: 'Philip Maltman'.

MANCHOT, Melanie, MA Fine Art (Photography) (1992); artist/part-time lecturer/photographer; works with video, photography and film. *b*: Germany, 7 Jul 1966. *Studied*: Royal College of Art (1990-92). *Represented by*: Galerie M, Bochum, Germany. *Exhib*: England and abroad, regularly, solo and group shows. 52nd Biennale, Italy; 1st Moscow Biennale; Whitechapel Gallery, London. *Works in collections*: Saatchi, National Art Collection, The Mead Gallery Collection, University of Warwickshire, DG Bank Collections, Germany, Portland Museum, USA, Staedtische Galerie Wolfsburg, Germany, Unilever Collection, London. *Commissions*: Film & Video Umbrella, London (amongst others). *Publications*: Moscow Girls, Haus an Waldsee, Berlin; Love is a Stranger, Prestel Verlag; Look at You Loving Me, Friedrich Reinhardt Verlag, Zurich. *Address*: 33 Dunloe St., London E2 8JR. *Email*: mel@melaniemanchot.net

MANDL, Anita, RWA (1978), FRBS (1980), PhD (1951), DSc (1960); sculptress, formerly University Reader, Medical School, Birmingham; carvings in wood and stone (alabaster, soapstone); also bronzes from carvings cast exclusively by Pangolin Editions. *b*: Prague, 17 May 1926. *d of*: Dr. B. Mandl. *m*: Dr. Denys Jennings (decd). *Studied*: part-time at Birmingham College of Art. *Exhib*: RA, RWA, RSMA, Curwen-New Academy Gallery, Alresford Gallery, Falle Fine Arts, Brian Sinfield Gallery, Wykeham Gallery, Gallery Pangolin, Martin's Gallery, Moncrieff-Bray Gallery, Red Rag Gallery, Jerram Gallery, Pangolin London, John Davies Gallery, Moreton-in-the-Marsh. *Works in collections*: Ulster Museum; Royal West of England Academy; National Maritime Museum. *Commissions*: Zoological Society of London. *Address*: 21 Northview Rd., Budleigh Salterton, Devon EX9 6BZ. *Email*: anitama@onetel.com *Signs work*: Mostly unsigned. (Highly polished carvings are marred by signature). Bronzes marked A.M.

MANGAN, Stephen, BA (Hons) Drawing and Painting; various awards: Saltive Society purchase for RSA; Guthrie Medal for Painting, RSA; Citysites Estates Award, RGI, etc. *Medium*: oil, watercolour. *b*: Musselburgh, 29 Dec 1964. *s of*: Edward and Janet Mangan. *Studied*: Duncan of Jordanstone College of Art, Dundee (1984-89). *Represented by*: Flying Colours Gallery, London; Richard Hagen Gallery, Broadway, Cotswolds. *Exhib*: RSA Annual Exhibition (1994 to present); Royal Academy Annual Exhbn (1998); Royal Glasgow Institute Annual Exhbn (2003 to present); Flying Colours Gallery, London; Richard Hagen Gallery, Broadway; various art fairs in London, New York, Hong Kong, Glasgow etc. *Works in collections*: Royal Scottish Academy, Edinburgh; Metropolitan Museum of Modern Art, New York; private collections in UK, USA, Canada, Holland, Germany, etc. *Address*: 15 James Street, Joppa, Edinburgh, EH15 2DT. *Signs work*: "Mangan".

MANIE, Ann Elizabeth, Dip Fine Art, MA; Lowes Dickinson Scholarship (1982); Debenhams Golden Jubilee Prize (2002); John & Elizabeth Smith 'New Discovery Prize', Discerning Eye (2006). *Medium*: mixed media in paper collage and acrylic, etching & chine collé prints (landscape and still life). *b*: Bromley, Kent, 19 Jan 1954. *m*: Barry John Manie. *Studied*: City & Guilds of London Art School, Kingston College. *Exhib*: RA Summer Exhbn (1988, 93, 97, 2003, 2007. 2011, 2013); Pumphouse Gallery, London (1996, solo exhbn); Waterman Fine Art Ltd., London (1993-2001); Medici Gallery, London (1996); CCA Galleries (1997), SWI Gallery (2006), Discerning Eye (2005, 2006), SWA (2006), RSMA (2006), Langham Fine Art Autumn Exhibition (2007), Christie's Cancer Research Appeal Exhibition (2007); various other group exhbns incl., Business Design Centre; Wills Gallery, St. Ives; Salthouse Gallery, St. Ives; Westcotts Gallery St. Ives; DIAC, Dubai (2010); Agora Gallery, New York, USA (2013). *Works in collections*: private and business. *Commissions*: private and business. *Publications*: 'Collage in the Classroom' pub. A&C Black (2008); 'Mixed Messages, The Versatility of Collage' pub. A&C Black Bloomsbury Publishing. *Official Purchasers*: City & Guilds; The Leyland Collection; Development Securities Ltd. *Clubs*: Penwith Society of Artists; Freeman of the Worshipful Company of Painter-Stainers. *Misc*: Teaching Certificate (FAETC); Collage workshops with children and adults; wall murals. *Address*: Charleston House, Higher Trewidden Road, St.Ives, Cornwall TR26 2DP. *Email*: manies@ntlworld.com *Website*: www.annmanie.net *Signs work*: 'A.M.'

MANLEY, Brett, PG Certificate Glass and Fine Art; PG Cert Glass and Architecture. *Medium*: Glass. *b*: Bedford, 11 June 1957. *Studied*: Wornington RBK&C Adult Ed College (1999-2005); Central Saint Martins (2003-2005); Amberley, Westminster AEC (2008-11). *Represented by*: Zest Contemporary Glass Gallery; Cecilia Coleman Gallery. *Exhib*: Affordable Art Fair; British Glass Bienalle; Central Saint Martins; Cochrane Gallery; Ely Stained Glass Museum; CGS website; International Festival of Glass, London; Glassblowing; National Museums of Scotland; Origin; Bilston Craft Gallery. Solo show: Blackwell Arts and Crafts House. *Works in collections*: Central Saint Martins; The National Museums of Scotland; Dan Klein and Alan J Poole Collections. *Commissions*: Langham

Hotel; Richmond International, London; Redesign and install entrance, Clydesdale House, Kensington. *Publications*: S Bruntnell 'Objects of Desire' (cover); BSMGP: '30cm2', '40cm2'. *Principal Works*: 'Blue Glassscape' RBK&C large outdoor installation. *Recreations*: Allotments; ceramic restoration; collecting. *Misc*: Teaches at Carlton Vale, Brent and her own studio. *Address*: 46b Stoneleigh Street, London W11 4DU. *Email*: info@brettmanley.co.uk *Website*: www.brettmanley.co.uk *Signs work*: "BRETT MANLEY" some work labelled with a BM logo.

MANLEY, Jim, ARUA; Patron's prize, EVA Limerick (1984), Elmwood, Belfast Smallworks (1997) Painting Prize, Iontas (1999), RUA, Ross' Watercolour Prize (2005); painter in water-colour, pastel, collage. *b*: St. Helen's, 1934. *m*: Margaret. three *s*. *Educ*: West Park Grammar School, St. Helen's; De La Salle College, Middleton. *Studied*: Diploma in Special Education, Manchester College of Educations. *Exhib*: over twenty exhbns. in Ireland and England, including London Gallery, Duncan Campbell Fine Arts, Dublin, Solomon Gallery. *Works in collections*: Abbot Hall Kendal, UTV Belfast, Walker Liverpool, Bank of Ireland Dublin, National Self-Portrait Collection, Limerick. *Clubs*: United Arts, Dublin. *Address*: Coastguard Station, Killough, Downpatrick, Co. Down BT30 7QS, N. Ireland. *Signs work*: "J. Manley."

MANN, Caryl J., SWA (1994), NDD (1960); artist in water-colour, pastel, acrylic. *b*: London, 31 Mar 1938. *m*: Christopher Mann. one *s*. *Educ*: Eastbourne High School. *Studied*: Eastbourne School of Art (1956-60). *Exhib*: SWA annually since 1991, David Curzon Gallery since 1988; various mixed and solo shows in Sussex. *Address*: Six Birches, Upper Hartfield, Hartfield, E. Sussex TN7 4DT. *Signs work*: "C. Mann."

MANN, Sargy, HND Mech (1958), NDD (1964); painter. *b*: Hythe, Kent, 29 May 1937. *m*: Frances Carey. two *s*. two *d*. *Educ*: Dartington. *Studied*: Camberwell School of Arts and Crafts (1960-64, Frank Auerbach, Euan Uglow, Dick Lee) (1967, Francis Hoyland). *Exhib*: RA, Hayward Annual (1983), London Group, International Drawing Biennale; one-man shows, Salisbury Festival of Arts, Cadogan Contemporary. *Works in collections*: Arts Council of GB, Contemporary Art Soc., Cleveland CC. *Publications*: Drawings by Bonnard (Arts Council, 1984), Pierre Bonnard Drawings (JPL Fine Art, 1981), Pierre Bonnard Drawings Vols. 1-2 (JPL Fine Art, 1987), Raoul Dufy (JPL Fine Art, 1987), Pierre Bonnard (Nottingham Castle Museum, 1984), Introduction Past and Present (Arts Council, 1987), Bonnard Drawings (John Murray JPL Fine Arts, 1991), Introduction to Bonnard at Le Bosquet Southbank Centre (1994, co-curator); 'Sargy Mann: Probably the Best Blind Painter in Peckham' by Peter & Sargy Mann. *Address*: Lawn Meadow, Bridge St., Bungay, Suffolk. *Signs work*: "Sargy Mann" or "Sargy."

MANNING, Baz, SHA; C&G (London Inst.) in Signwork etc.; Burnett Weston Award for Excellence in Heraldic Art, Canada 1996. *Medium*: Heraldic Artist in enamel, gold leaf, gouache on wood, metal, glass and stone. *m*: married. *Studied*: Hammersmith and West College 1985-87. *Exhib*: The Crusades, Winchester, 1989 (commissioned works); North Wales Tourist Board Travelling Exhibition, based on local heraldry (1990-92); Beaminster 1993, one-man; Canadian Museum of Civilisation (1996), joint; Society congresses. *Works in collections*: Windsor Castle; House of Lords; Speakers House; Palace of Westminster; Goldsmiths Hall; Gunmakers' Proof House; Lincolns Inn; Gray's Inn; Oxford Crown Court (Collection of the Coats of Arms of all High Sherriffs of Oxon). *Commissions*: Royal Household; Curator, Palace of Westminster; Royal Air Force (Empire Test Pilot's School); British Army. *Publications*: Signwork, A Craftsman's Manual (contributor); The Complete Book of Heraldry (contributor); The Heraldic Armory of Lincoln's Inn (e-book); Editor of The Heraldic Craftsman c.1993-96. *Works Reproduced*: Coachmakers Guild: Bournemouth (numerous locations). *Recreations*: Radio 4. *Misc*: Craft member of the Society of Heraldic Arts since 1989. *Email*: heraldicartist@hotmail.co.uk *Website*: www.heraldic-artist.com *Signs work*: dated monogram.

MANNING, Julia, ARE; BA (Hons) Fine Art. *Medium*: artist/printmaker. *b*: London, 8 Dec 1952. two *d*. *Educ*: Notting Hill and Ealing High School. *Studied*: Bath Academy of Art, Corsham, Wilts (1970-74). *Represented by*: Brook Gallery, Budleigh Salterton. *Exhib*: 11 solo shows; many mixed shows. *Works in collections*: Lord Bath, Longleat House; Palace of Westminster (House of Lords); British Embassy Collection, Paris; Aberystwyth University Print Collection; Nature in Art. *Commissions*: many for painted tapestries, murals and trompe l'oeil throughout UK, Europe and USA (1984-2000). *Official Purchasers*: House of Lords, British Embassy Paris, Art in Hospital. *Principal Works*: etchings, collographs and limited edition relief prints. *Recreations*: gardening. *Clubs*: Devon Guild of Craftsmen; Royal Society of Painter Printmakers; Associate Member, Society of Wildlife Artists. *Misc*: 'Makers'- Taunton (Gallery Co-operative) Somerset Printmakers. *Address*: 2 Rosebank, Queen St., Keinton Mandeville, Somerset, TA11 6EQ. *Email*: julia@juliamanning.co.uk *Website*: www.juliamanning.co.uk *Signs work*: "Julia Manning".

MANNOCCI, Lino, BA, MA. *Medium*: oil, drawing, prints. *b*: Viareggio (Italy), 13 Apr 1945. *s of*: Oreste Mannocci. two *s*. one *d*. *Studied*: Camberwell School of Art; Slade (UCL). *Represented by*: Art First, London; Galleria Ceribelli, Bergamo, Italy. *Exhib*: over thirty solo exhbns since 1981 worldwide, most recently, Museo H.C. Andersen, Rome (2005); The Mead Art Museum, Amherst , USA (2009); The New York School of Painting, NY (2010); The Fitzwilliam Museum, Cambridge (2010). *Publications*: Catalogue Raisonné of Claude Lorraine (Yale U.P., 1988); Madre India, Padre Barbiere. *Official Purchasers*: British Museum; Jewish Museum, Vevey; Ludwighaffen Museum, Mead Art Museum, Amherst , USA; The Fitzwilliam Museum, Cambridge. *Clubs*: Chelse Art Club. *Address*: 119 Elgin Avenue, London W9 2NR. *Email*: lino.mannocci@virgin.net

MANOUK: see BAGHJIAN, Manouk.

MANUEL, Sylvia, artist in water-colour, acrylic, pastel; tutor. *b*: London. *Exhib*: England, France, Jersey C.I. *Commissions*: B.B.C., etc. *Address*: Wall Cottage, Leicester Sq., Penshurst, Kent TN11 8BJ. *Signs work*: "Sylvia Manuel" or "S. Manuel."

MARA, Pam, MCSD (1970), NDD (1958), FFPS (1997); illustrator, designer, painter, printmaker in oil, pastel, acrylic, water-colour, lithography. *b*: London, 12 May 1928. *d of*: Harold Faulkner Mara, FIBD. *Educ*: Henrietta Barnett School, London. *Studied*: Willesden School of Art, Central School of Art. *Exhib*: mixed shows: Mall Galleries, Barbican, National Theatre, Bloomsbury Gallery, Loggia Gallery, St. Martin in the Fields Gallery, Royal Festival Hall, Holland Park Orangery, Menier Gallery. Solo Exhibition: Royal Commonwealth Society. *Publications*: illustrated over 100 books, work published in England, America, several European countries, W. Africa, Near and Far East, South Africa and Australasia. *Address*: 5 Gloucester St., London SW1V 2DB. *Signs work*: "Pam Mara."

MARCH, Ann Patricia, DipAD Graphic Design. *Medium*: etching, lithographs, painting, drawing. *b*: Worthing, Sussex, 18 May 1948. *d of*: S.H. & Mildred March. *m*: Ian Stevenson. one *s*. one *d*. *Studied*: Worthing Art College (Pre-Dip, 1965-66), Newport Art College, Wales (DipAD, 1966-69), Brighton Art College. *Exhib*: Royal Academy Summer Show (1986, 1994, 2000), Athena Art Award, Barbican, London (1987), Pallant House, Chichester (1986), Hunting Group Art Prizes, Mall, London (1986), Sussex Open (1986, 1988, 1990, 1995), Painters, Etchers, Bankside (1986), Brighton Festival, North Star Studios, Brighton (annually), Art4Life, Christies (2002). Permanent exhibition at 39 Kensington Gardens, Brighton BN1 4AL. *Clubs*: North Star Studio Cooperative Printmaking Studios, Brighton BN1 4SD. *Address*: 37 Warleigh Road, Brighton, Sussex, BN1 4NT. *Email*: annpmarch@yahoo.co.uk *Signs work*: "Ann March."

MARCHANT, David Edwin, BA (Hons); Arts Council of Wales Award to make film 'Spaceman' (2009); Welsh Artist of the Year Prizewinner (2003). *Medium*: digital video and audio. *b*: Swansea, 26 Jul 1966. *s of*: T.E.&V.S.Marchant. *m*: Lisa Simons. two *s*. one *d*. *Studied*: Caerleon College, University of Wales. *Exhib*: RA Summer Show (2007, 2008, 2009); Chapter Arts, Cardiff; G39 Cardiff; Oriel Myddin, Camarthen; Mall Galleries, London; Wolstern Holme projects, Liverpool; Tactile Bosch, Cardiff; Oriel Llin, Pontadawe; The Chalk House, St. Ives; Center Space, Bristol; Glyn Vivian, Swansea. *Works in collections*: various. *Commissions*: Welsh Arts Council (film commission 'Spaceman', 2009); MGB PR (video art commission - winner of Best Outdoor Marketing Award, 2007), MGB PR - 'The Mask' (Chartered Institute of PR Gold Award, Consumer Campaign 04/5; Chartered Institute of PR Grand Prix Award 04/05). *Publications*: various ed. calendars, Buz, Axis, A-N, One in the Other (book), G39. *Works Reproduced*: 'Burst', 'Not Quite in Control', 'Two Pathways' (all DVDs). *Address*: 128 Overland Rd, Mumbles, Swansea, SA3 4EU. *Email*: videoart@inbox.com *Website*: videoartinbox.com *Signs work*: D.E.MARCHANT".

MARDEL-FERREIRA, Elizabeth Gilchrist, painter in acrylic, ink and wash, printmaker. *b*: Nottingham, 5 May 1931. *s of*: John G. McMeeking, CBE, JP, lace manufacturer. *m*: Joseph Charles Mardel-Ferreira. one *s*. two *d*. *Educ*: Headington School, Oxford. *Studied*: Nottingham College of Art (1949-53). *Exhib*: RA (1978); SWA Work in private collections. *Publications*: Illustrations for Warblington Church guide. *Address*: 15 Warblington Ave., Havant, Hants. PO9 2SD. *Signs work*: "E. Mardel" or "Elizabeth G. Mardel.'

MAREK, Jerzy, self taught primitive painter. *Medium*: oil. *b*: Poland, 22 Apr 1925. *m*: Margaret Baird. *Partner*: Jeanette Lassen (painter) (decd). one *s*. *Represented by*: McCrea Gallery, 298 Portobello High Street, Edinburgh EH15 2AS. *Exhib*: Portal and Grosvenor Galleries, London, also in a number of International and Arts Council Exhbns. for primitive painters. *Works in collections*: Bolton City A.G., Abbott Hall Museum, Kendal, Lancaster City Museum, Glasgow Gallery of Modern Art, Sydney Janis Coll., N.Y., Salford City Art Gallery, Manchester City Art Gallery. *Publications*: Naive Kunst by Ida Niggli, The Rona Guide to the World of Naive Art, Twentieth Century British Naive and Primitive Artists by E. Lister and S. Williams, A World of Their Own by J and M Leman; World Encyclopedia of Naive Art by Oto Bilhaji-Merin; many postcards. *Address*: 7 Pittville St., Portobello, Edinburgh EH15 2BZ. *Signs work*: "J. Marek."

MARGRIE, Victor, CBE, FCSD; potter; Associate Editor, Studio Pottery (1993-2000), Ceramics in Society (2000-2005); Visiting Prof. University of Westminster (1992-96); Director, Crafts Council (1977-84); Mem. Advisory Council, V&A Museum (1979-84); Mem. of Board of Studies in Fine Art, University of London (1989-1994); Mem. UK National Commission for UNESCO (1984-85); Fine Art Advisory Committee British Council (1983-86). *b*: London, 29 Dec 1929. *Works in collections*: V&A, Ashmolean and private collections. *Publications*: contributed to: Oxford Dictionary of Decorative Arts (1975); Europaischt Keramik Seit (1950, 1979); Lucie Rie (1981); contrib. specialist publications and museum catalogues. *Address*: 15 Telegraph Street, Shroton, Iwerne Courtney, Dorset DT11 8QQ.

MARIA, Veronique, BA (Hons) Art and Design; MA Applied Psychosyntheses Psychology Applied to Fine Art Practice; Graduate Leadership, CTI USA. *Medium*: installation, live art, performance, video, sculpture, drawing, print. *b*: London, 28 Mar 1959. one *s*. *Studied*: Northbrook College, Worthing; Brighton University; Middlesex University; CTI USA. *Represented by*: Sheridan Russell Gallery, Borehamwood. *Exhib*: R Space, Belfast (2014); 20th World Congress of Soil Science, Jeju, Korea (2014); Fabrica, Brighton (2013); Cass Sculpture (2013); Pallant House (2013); Bedales Gallery, Hampshire (2004, 2011); RCA (2011); Arlington Arts Centre, Berkshire (2010); Eldfjallasafn Museum, Iceland (2010); Tate Modern (2010); Aspex Portsmouth (2009); Arizona State Museum, USA (2009); Annaghmakerrig, Co. Monaghan, Ireland (2007); Otter Gallery, Chichester (2006);

Louderdale House, Highgate, London (2005); Pallant House Garden Gallery, Chichester (1999); Whitworth, Manchester (1996); House of William Blake, London (1005); Horsham Art Centre (2004). *Works in collections*: Helene Wurlitzer Foundation, Taos, New Mexico, USA; Baer Art Centre, Hosfos, Iceland; Aldridge Foundation; Cass Sculpture, Goodwood; Arizona Art Museum USA; Hollingbery, Alresford, Hampshire. *Commissions*: 40 foot earth and fibre work - permanent, Hollingbery, Hampshire. *Publications*: Dirt Dialogues (Soil Science Society of America, 2015); The Best 500 Ceramic Sculptures (Lark, USA, 2012); 21st Century Ceramics (Lark, 2011); 500 Ceramic Sculptures (Lark, 2009); a-n UK periodical; Contemporary Gardens by Penelope Hill (Birkhauser, 2004); Garden Design by A Maynard & A de Verteuil (Conran Octopus, 2004); Jardins d'Aujord'hui en Europe: Entre Art et Architecture by P Hill (Fonds Mercator, 2002); Gardens Illustrated Journal (2000); New Eden Magazine (1999). *Official Purchasers*: Aldridge Foundation, London; Hollingbery, Alresford, Hampshire. *Principal Works*: The Mound; Orogeny; Moving Practice; Vanitas; 'I Cannot Help What My Heart Feels'. *Misc*: makes work from a psycho-spiritual context with earth at the centre, with unique work being 'ceramics on canvas'. *Address*: 3 Birch Close, Arundel, West Sussex BN18 9HN. *Email*: veroniquemaria@btinternet.com *Website*: www.veroniquemaria.co.uk *Signs work*: "veronique maria".

MARINE, Tom, *b*: Hartlepool, 6 May 1956. *Partner*: Christine Relton. one *d*. *Studied*: Hartlepool Art College; Byam Shaw School of Drawing and Painting; Chelsea School of Art (1974-78). *Represented by*: Galleries throughout the UK. *Exhib*: Many exhibitions and art fairs in UK, Europe, Asia and USA. *Works in collections*: House of Lords, London: five paintings. *Commissions*: Many: both private and corporate. *Publications*: 'Artists in Britain since 1945' 2006 edition. *Official Purchasers*: House of Lords. *Works Reproduced*: Prints from Winn Devon, USA and International Graphics, Germany. *Principal Works*: Landscapes, still life and travel based paintings. *Recreations*: travel; music. *Misc*: Paints in collaboration with Christine Relton since 1996. They run the Colourbox gallery as well as painting together. *Address*: 9 Carr Bank, Otley, West Yorks LS21 2AE. *Email*: colourbox.reltonmarine@btinternet.com *Website*: www.reltonmarine.com *Signs work*: "C. RELTON & T. MARINE" on reverse of canvas.

MARINKOV, Sasa (Alexandra), Fellow of Royal Society of Painter Printmakers (RE); Awards: GLC, South Bank Picture Show, RA Summer Show (twice), Ministry of Transport, London Arts Board; artist in schools. *Medium*: printmaking. *b*: Belgrade, Yugoslavia, 12 Jan 1949. *d of*: Dr. C.B. Marinkov and Mary Lishman. *m*: Michael Jones. one *d*. *Studied*: Fine Art: Leeds University, PGCE London University, Advanced Dip. Printmaking: Central St. Martin's. *Exhib*: Biennales: Cleveland, Bradford, Brazil, Korea, Spain, Xylon 13 & 14, Whitechapel and Riverside Open, London Group, Kunsthaus Zug, Prints from Wood (Arts Council), Royal Academy, RE, SWE, one-man shows. *Works in collections*: Leeds, London & Cambridge Universities; Brazil; Skopje; London and Winchester Hospital; British Rail Freight; Bank of China; Winchester Hospital; Dept. of Transport; Arts Council/South Bank Centre; Ashmolean; Clifford Chance. *Commissions*: British Railways Board; Winchester Hospital. *Publications*: 2001 "Sasa Marinkov's picture book", Quince Tree Press. *Works Reproduced*: 1990-98 Royal Academy Summer Show catalogue; 1994 "Wood engraving and the woodcut in Britain c 1890-1990", James Hamilton; Four A&C Black Printmaking Books (2001-6). *Address*: Woodcut, Riverside, Twickenham TW1 3DJ. *Email*: sasamarinkov@hotmail.co.uk *Website*: www.sasamarinkov.co.uk *Signs work*: "S. Marinkov."

MARJ: see BOND, Marj.

MARKEY, Danny, RWA; painter. *b*: Falmouth, 9 Jun 1965. *Educ*: Falmouth School. *Studied*: Falmouth School of Art and Camberwell School of Art. *Exhib*: Redfern Gallery,

London Group, RA, RWA, South Bank Picture Show (First Prize) Discerning Eye, Newlyn Gallery, Royal Overseas League, Charleston Farmhouse Sussex. *Works in collections*: various private and Old Jail House Museum and Gallery, Texas. *Address*: c/o Redfern Gallery, 20 Cork St., London W1X 2HL. *Email*: art@redfern-gallery.com *Website*: www.redfern-gallery.com *Signs work*: "Danny Markey."

MARKS, Laura Anne Celia, Greenshields Foundation award (1982, 1983); artist in oil, water-colour and pencil. *b*: Toronto, Canada, 1954. *d of*: Benjamin Marks, chemical engineer. *Educ*: Forest Hill Collegiate, Toronto. *Studied*: Central Technical School, The Three Schools of Art, Art's Sake, and Ontario College of Art (1971-80, Paul Young). *Exhib*: one-man shows: Evans Gallery, Toronto (1973), Prince Arthur Gallery, Toronto (1980), October Gallery, London (1982), Alberta House, London (1982), Gallery Gabor, Toronto (1984), International Exhbn., Monte-Carlo (1985), John Denham Gallery, London (1991). *Works in collections*: Ontario House, London. *Address*: 26 West End La., London NW6. *Signs work*: "MARKS."

MARLBOROUGH, Rosita. *Medium*: oil, sculpture. *b*: Madrid, Spain, 26 Sep 1943; divorced. *d of*: Carl Ludwig Douglas. one *s*. one *d*. *Educ*: Konstfack, Stockholm. *Studied*: Ecole Nationale Superieur des Arts Decoratives, rue D'Ulm, Paris. *Exhib*: solo: Museum of South Vermont, USA (2006), Hamiltons Gallery, London (2005), The Fleming Collection, London (2005), Lars Bolander (New York, 2004/Palm Beach, 2001), Hahn Fine Art, London (1998, 1995). Group Exhibitions: Royal Academy Summer Exhibition (2005, 1995), Lighthouse Art Centre, Florida, USA (2004), The Gallery, Blenheim, Oxfordshire (1999, 1998), Cork Street Gallery, London (1997), Central Library, Oxford (1996), High Point, North Carolina, USA (1994), Magdalen College, Oxford (1992). *Address*: Lee Place, Charlbury, Oxon, OX7 3SD. *Email*: rm@rositamarlborough.com *Website*: www.rositamarlborough.com *Signs work*: "R.M." (year).

MARLIN, Brigid, Founded the Society for Art of Imagination. Awards: International Art Appreciation Award for Outstanding Contribution to the Arts, USA (1988); International Painting Competition, Dublin, Ireland (1988); Upper Street Gallery Sculpture Competition, London (1990). *Medium*: oil, watercolour, drawing, prints. *b*: Washington DC, 16 Jan 1936. *d of*: Mr E.R.Marlin & Hilda Van Stockum. three *s*. *Studied*: National College of Art, Dublin; Andre L'Hote Studio Centre d'Art Sacre, Paris; Art Students League, New York. *Exhib*: Selected exhibitions: Mall Galleries (1998, 1999, 2000, 2007), The Gallery in Cork Street (2002, 2003), Brave Destiny, Brooklyn, New York (2003), Diego Gallery, Miami, Florida (2004), SAI European Tour (2004), HR Giger's Castle Museum and Art Gallery (2006); works exhibited in Museums and Art Galleries worldwide. *Works in collections*: National Portrait Gallery; House of Lords Art Collection; National Museum of American Artists & Illustrators. *Official Purchasers*: National Portrait Gallery, London; House of Lords Art Collection, London. *Works Reproduced*: many. *Principal Works*: portraits and fantastic art. *Address*: 28 Castle Hill, Berkhamsted, Herts., HP4 1HE. *Email*: brigmarlin@aol.com *Website*: www.brigidmarlin.com *Signs work*: "Brigid Marlin".

MARR, Leslie, MA (1947); painter and draftsman in oil, water-colour, etc.; Secretary, Borough Group (1947-50). *b*: Durham, 14 Aug 1922. *s of*: Col. J. Lynn Marr, O.B.E., TD. *m*: Maureen Marr. two *d*. *Educ*: Shrewsbury, Pembroke Coll. Cambridge. *Studied*: Borough Polytechnic under David Bomberg. *Represented by*: Piano Nobile Fine Paintings, 129 Portland Rd., London W11 4LW. *Exhib*: one-man shows: Everyman Gallery, Drian Galleries, Laing A.G., Newcastle upon Tyne, Woodstock Gallery, Maddermarket Norwich, Fermoy Gallery, Kings Lynn, "Bomberg and the Family" exhbn. Ben Uri Gallery (The London Jewish Museum), London, Catto Gallery, London; major retrospective, Durham City, 'Piano Nobile' London, Mercer Art Gallery Harrogate, Northumbria University Gallery, Newcastle-upon-Tyne. *Works in collections*: Laing A.G., Newcastle upon Tyne,

University of Haifa, Graves A.G., Sheffield, St. Mary Abbots Hospital, London, Mercer Art Gallery Harrogate, Pallant House, Chichester, Ruth Borchard Collection of self portraits, Kings Place, London. *Publications*: From My Point of View (photographs) (Acorn Editions 1979), 2 albums of piano solos (Seresta Music). *Official Purchasers*: Laing AG Newcastle-on-Tyne, Graves AG Sheffield, Mercer AG Harrogate, Pallant House A.G., Chichester, Ruth Borchard Collection. *Works Reproduced*: Jarrold's Calendar of Norfolk Artists (2004). *Address*: Blandings Cottage, Mill Street, Gimingham, Norfolk NR11 8AB. *Email*: leslie.marr2@gmail.com *Signs work*: 'Marr'.

MARRIOTT, Michael, FRBS (1974), NDD (1960); sculptor in stainless steel, glass, GRP, stone, clay, plaster, bronze. *b*: London, 3 May 1940. *Educ*: Latymer Foundation and Christopher Wren Secondary. *Studied*: St. Martin's School of Art (1956-60, Elizabeth Frink, Anthony Caro, Edward Paolozzi). *Exhib*: one-man shows: Cockpit Theatre, London (1971), Alwin Gallery, London (1976); two-man show: Europa Gallery, Surrey (1978); group exhbns.: annually all over UK since 1960, Margam Park, S. Wales, Barbican Centre, Hannah Peschar Gallery, Surrey; also in USA and Europe. *Works in collections*: IBM Cosham, Hunting Engineering Bedford, Heron House London, Crown House London. *Address*: 16 Seymour Rd., London SW18 5JA.

MARSH, Robert Burkall, MA in Painting (Royal College of Art). *Medium*: Oil; drawing. *b*: Cardiff, 4 May 1950. four *s*. *Studied*: Auckland University; Royal College of Art, London (1975-78). *Represented by*: Bridgeman Art Library. *Exhib*: New Contemporaries; John Moores; Liverpool (prizewinner); Mertz Gallery, London; Cadogan Gallery; Guardian Art for Sale; Royal Academy Summer Exhibition; Royal College of Pathologists, and in New Zealand. *Work in collections*: Granada Foundation; Royal College of Art; Andre Deutsche Publishing. *Commissions*: Portraiture (various). *Works Reproduced*: Bridgeman Library. *Principal Works*: Paintings in oil. *Clubs*: Chelsea Arts Club; London Sketch Club. *Misc*: Teacher and painter. *Address*: 5a Peacock Yard, London SE17 3LH. *Email*: burkallmarsh@aol.com *Website*: under construction. *Signs work*: "ROBERT BURKALL MARSH" or "RBM".

MARSH, Vickie, JP; President SBA (2010); Cert.HE in Botanical Illustration; RHS Silver Gilt Medals (2001, 2004). *Medium*: watercolour, graphite. *b*: Bridgworth, Shropshire, 4 May 1944. *m*: John Haydn Marsh. one *s*. one *d*. *Studied*: Birmingham University (2000-2002). *Exhib*: London Westminster annually (2001-2010); Victoria Gallery and Museum, Liverpool; N. Wales, Penrhyn Castle, Oriel-ynys Mon, Erddig, Ness Botanical Gardens, Liverpool University; Palmengarten, Frankfurt. *Works in collections*: Victoria Gallery and Museum, Liverpool 'Art and Heritage'. Holly Collection, Ness Gardens. *Commissions*: Charles Coates; private. *Publications*: included in: The Art of Botanical Illustration; Wildflowers of Britain and Ireland; Plant Forms for Botanical Artists. *Principal Works*: Development of Plants from the Ice Age 'Moss Lake'. *Clubs*: North Wales Society of Fine Art; Botanical Artists of Ness Gardens. *Address*: "Minas Tirith" Ruthin Road, Coedpoeth, Wrexham, LL11 3US. *Email*: jhandcv@btinternet.com *Signs work*: "Vickie Marsh".

MARSHALL, Maria Heléne, BAHons. (1986); sculptor in steel, stone, wood and canvas. *b*: India, 14 Feb 1964. married. *d of*: Samuel Marshall. *Educ*: Millfield School, Somerset, Ardingly College, Sussex. *Studied*: Chelsea Foundation (1982), Wimbledon School of Art (1986, Glyn Williams), Ecole des Beaux Arts, Geneva. *Exhib*: Gallerie Eric Frank (Geneva, Chicago, Basel); one-man shows: Odette Gilbert Gallery (London and Madrid), Crucral Gallery. Public sculpture 'Goddess' Princes Ct., Brompton Rd. *Address*: The Workshops, 23 Theatre St., London SW11. *Signs work*: "Maria Marshall."

MARSHALL, Richard, PS (1983); painter in oil, pastel, gouache, part-time lecturer; demonstrator. *b*: Goring, Sussex, 29 Jan 1943. *s of*: Phillip James Marshall. two *d*. *Educ*: West Sussex College of Art. *Studied*: under William Cartledge, RI, RSMA (1969-72), Gyula

Sajo (1973-89), former Professor of Applied Art, Budapest Academy, Hungary. *Exhib*: internationally; mixed shows, France, London and Sussex; one-man show, Croydon and Littlehampton; two-man show, Arundel and Worthing. *Works in collections*: UK, Europe and North America. *Publications*: Pastel Artist International, Leisure Painter. *Clubs*: Worthing Atelier Art Group. *Address*: 17 Harsfold Cl., Rustington, W. Sussex BN16 2QQ. *Signs work*: "R. Marshall."

MARSHALL, Steven, BA Hons Fine Art; painter in oil and enamels on glass. *b*: Dover, 10 Apr 1967. *m*: Michèle. *Educ*: Kings School, Wessex. *Studied*: Wolverhampton University. *Exhib*: Future Famous, London; Modern Art and Modernisms, London; View of the New, London; Contemporary Art Soc; RA. *Works in collections*: Ernst and Young, Unilever, Eversheds, Manorca Services. *Publications*: co producer of film for Picasso Pictures, 'In Flight', Readers Digest Award (1990). *Address*: c/o Wimbledon Fine Art, 41 Church Rd., Wimbledon Village, London SW19 5DQ. *Email*: stevenmarshall@virgin.net *Signs work*: "S.M." or "Steven Marshall."

MARTIN, Barry John, Intermediate exam. Arts & Crafts (1963), NDD Painting (1965), Post Dip. (1966), Post Grad. (1967); painter, sculptor, draughtsman, printmaker, acrylic, stainless steel, bronze, electricity, charcoal; former lecturer numerous colleges. *b*: Amersham, Bucks., 20 Feb 1943. *m*: Sarah Anne. one *d*. *Studied*: University of London Goldsmiths' College (1961-66), St. Martin's School of Art (1966-67). *Exhib*: one-man shows: Arts Council, Serpentine Gallery (1970), Richard Demarco Gallery (1971), Newcastle upon Tyne Polytechnic A.G. (1977), Goya Gallery, Zaragosa, Spain (1980), 'Look - Reflections on Structure and Meaning' Olympia (1999), Riverside Studios (2000), Gallery Rigo, Citta-Nova, Croatia (2003), 'Zest Gallery' London (2004), Inaugural Exhibition 'The Drawing Gallery' (2004) etc; group shows: Northern Young Contemporaries, Whitworth A.G. (1965), Young Contemporaries, London (1966), Manifestation of Light - Light Artist's, Bromsgrove Festival, B'ham (1968), Gelsen Kirchen Museum, Berlin (1969), Onnasch Gallery, Berlin (1970), ACGB Hayward Gallery Kinetics (1970), ICA Electric Theatre (1971), Arts Council, Spectrum, Alexandra Palace (1972), Harlow, Essex Movements (1973), 12 British Painters, Arts Council and British Council Exhbn. for Iceland (1977), Beaux Art Gallery, Brussels (1995), Mus. of Modern Art, Paris (2000), Tate Gallery 'New Acquisitions' (2000), Royal Academy Summer Show (2003), 'The Art of Chess', Somerset House, London (2003), S.O.F.A., Chicago Art Exhbn., International (2004); V&A (2011); Henry Moore Institute, Leeds, 'United Enemies' 2011-12. *Works in collections*: numerous public and private including Science Museum, Tate Gallery, NPG, BM, ACGB, Mus. of Modern Art, Paris, Government Art Collection, Deutsche Bank, Victoria & Albert Museum; The British Council, Royal College of Art; Monograph: 'The Tomorrow of My Yesterday' (The Complete Works of Barry Martin) by Julius Bryant (pub.Veeman Press, Rotterdam, 2008). *Commissions*: Howard Staunton Memorial, Kensal Green Cemetery; Mr. Resistor, New King's Rd. London; English Heritage (2005). *Publications*: Light and Movement (1985); Comp. with Red, Mondrian (1986); Chess for Absolute Beginners, with Keene; The 'G' Spot, Lord Burlington (1998); '...au pied de la lettre' (2001); 'Meaning, Movement' (2003) 'The English Grand Tour'. *Recreations*: chess. *Clubs*: A.R.B.S., Chelsea Arts Club, R.A.C., Pall Mall. *Misc*: Studio: South Lodge, Chiswick House Grounds, Chiswick, London W4 2RP. *Address*: 98 Cole Park Rd., Twickenham, Middx. TW1 1JA. *Email*: bsjmartin@btinternet.com *Website*: www.barrymartin.co.uk

MARTIN, Blandine, BA Hons Interior Design & Architecture; First prize for best Painting Cork Street Open Exhibition, 2009, Second prize Portrait of Churchill 2010 presented by Lady Barbara Hamilton. *Medium*: painter & sculptor. *b*: Aix-en-Pce France, 21 Mar 1970. *d of*: Yann Martin (painter) & Danielle Martin. one *s*. one *d*. *Studied*: Metropolitan University, London. *Exhib*: 2012: The big egg hunt 2012 February-April sponsored by Faberge-London; The Cork Street Past Winners Show; October 2011: PROVOK exhibition @ The Catherine Peugeot Cultural Centre, Paris, France; 2010: Windsor Contemporary Art Fair; 2008-2010: B-Uncut launch, Westbourne Studios, London; The 28 Gallery Cork Street, Mayfair; 3 Bedfordbury Gallery, Covent Garden, London; The Kowalski Gallery, East London; The Visual art centre, Essex; The Eaton Terrace gallery, Belgravia, London; Le pavillon de l'Art Contemporain, Paris; The Stroud House gallery, Gloucester; Le carrousel du Louvre art fair, Paris, Fance; Untitled 2008 Chelsea Art Fair, London; The Artspace Gallery, Mayfair, London; The Horsebridge Art Centre, Kent; untitled gallery, the Strand, London; Reference Gallery, 10013 NY USA; 2006-2007: The art house Lewisham, London; Reference Gallery, 10013 NY USA; Battersea Contemporary Art Fair; La petite gallery, Limousin, France; 2004-2005: The Royal National Theatre, South Bank, London; Serena Hall Gallery, Suffolk; Yann Martin Gallery, Marseilles, France; The Euroart Gallery, Tottenham, London; The Hype Gallery, Brick Lane, London. *Misc*: designed posters for the Cherwell Theater Company, Stratford upon Avon. Worked at The National Theatre production office. *Address*: 132 Maiden Lane, Camden Town, London NW1 9UQ. *Email*: blandinemartin@hotmail.com *Website*: www.blandinemartin.com *Signs work*: "BLANDINE MARTIN".

MARTIN, David McLeod, RSW, RGI, DA (Glasgow) (1948), Hon. Professional Mem. SSA (1949), Past Vice-Pres. RSW; David Cargill Award (RGI, 1995), Special Award of Merit, Robert Coloquhoun Memorial Art Prize exhbn., Kilmarnock (1974); Prizewinner, Friends of the Smith Art Gallery, Stirling (1981); May Marshall Brown Award, RSW Exhbn. (1984); Mabel McKinlay Award, RGI (1990); Prizewinner, Laing Exhbn., Mall Gallery, London (1990, 1993); RSW Council Award (2003). *b*: Glasgow, 30 Dec 1922. *s of*: Allan McLeod Martin. *m*: Isobel A.F. Smith (decd). four *s*. *Educ*: Glasgow. *Studied*: Glasgow School of Art, 1940-42 (RAF1943-46), 1946-48. *Exhib*: RA (1984), Bath Contemporary Art Fair (1987), numerous group shows; one-man shows in Glasgow, Edinburgh, Perth, Greenock, Stone Gallery, Newcastle and London. featured artist, Perth Festival (1999), Perth Museum & Art Gallery Retrospective; 'Themes & Variations', John Martin of London (2000), Rhythm & Hues, John Martin (2004); solo show Roger Billcliffe (2005, 2009), with Carlo Rossi (2007), Miami Art Fair (1996), Art International New York (1998). *Works in collections*: Work in numerous public and private collections. *Address*: The Old Schoolhouse, 53 Gilmour St., Eaglesham, Glasgow G76 0LG. *Signs work*: "DAVID M. MARTIN."

MARTIN, Jean B., RSW; DA (Glasgow School of Art); PGTC (Aberdeen College of Education); Hospitalfield Scholarship; International Artist Award; Anne Redpath Award; Morton Fraser Award; Sir William Gillies Award. *Medium*: mixed media; watercolour. *b*: 5 Aug 1947. *d of*: Henry Campbell. *m*: John Martin. one *s*. one *d*. *Represented by*: Flying Colours, London; Richard Hagen Fine Art. *Exhib*: Gatehouse Gallery, Glasgow (1997, 2001); Flying Colours, Edinburgh (1991, 94, 98); Flying Colours Gallery, London (2005, 2009); Queens Gallery, Dundee (2002, 2005); Frames Gallery, Perth (2007); Richard Hagan (2008, 2009, 2012). *Works in collections*: McManus Galleries, Dundee; private collections UK, USA, Australia. *Commissions*: private portrait commissions. *Publications*: Structure and Expression for Flowers in Watercolour, ISBN 1 9219834 22 5. *Works Reproduced*: in 'International Artist' magazine, Art Aquarelle. *Address*: Alma Cottage, 4 Queen Street, Tayport, Fife DD6 9NS. *Email*: jeanmartin@mail2artist.com *Website*: www.jeanbmartin.co.uk *Signs work*: 'Jean B Martin'.

MARTIN, Jenny, MA (Hons) Fine Art; MFA; The Aspect Prize (runner-up, 2005); Fenton Arts Trust Award (2005); Russell Trust Award (2005); Outstanding Print Award, Univ. of Aberystwyth, Nat. Print Exhbn (2003); Frank Herring Award RI (2002); John Kinross Scholarship (RSA, 1997); DM Hall Painting Prize (1997); Andrew Grant Bequest Awards (1994, 96); James Torrance Award (RGI 2006); The RE Prize (Originals 07). *Medium*:

mixed media and printmaking. *b*: Dundee, 23 Sep 1973. *d of*: John & Jean Martin. *m*: Stephen Long. one *s*. *Educ*: Madras College, St. Andrews. *Studied*: University of Edinburgh; Edinburgh College of Art. *Represented by*: Ewan Mundy Fine Art, Glasgow. *Exhib*: RA (2000, 04, 05), RSA (1999-2000), RI (2001-05), RSW (1995-2003), NEAC (2001, 03), RBA (2000, 05), Discerning Eye (2002, 03) W21 Bankside Gallery (2003, 05); Leith Gallery, Edinburgh; Mall Galleries, etc.; solo exhbns include: Ewan Mundy Fine Art , Glasgow (2004), University of Aberystwyth (2006), Edinburgh Printmakers Workshop (2007). *Works in collections*: RSA; Edinburgh College of Art; University of Wales; Royal Bank of Scotland; Paintings in Hospitals. *Publications*: 'Crucial Colour', The Artist Magazine (Dec 2004); 'Artist Masterclass', The Artist Magazine (Sep 2003); fully illustrated catalogue, Ewan Mundy Fine Art (2004). *Misc*: professional member and Council member Visual Arts, Scotland; lecturer at Leith School of Art, Edinburgh; Board Member, Edinburgh Printmakers Workshop. *Address*: 7 Esplenade Terrace, Edinburgh EH15 2ES. *Email*: jmartin9@tiscali.co.uk

MARTIN, John, RBA, BA(Hons.), RA Post Dip. (1983); painter in oil, gouache and water-colour. *b*: London, 25 Jan 1957. *s of*: Robert Albert Martin, gardener. *Educ*: Houndsfield School, London. *Studied*: Exeter College of Art (Micheal Garton, Alexander MacNeish), R.A. Schools (Peter Greenham). *Exhib*: numerous one-man shows in England; mixed shows in France and Canada. *Works in collections*: Norfolk County Collection, Art in Hospital Fund. *Address*: 70 Florence Rd., Brighton BN1 6DJ. *Signs work*: "J.M."

MARTIN, John Scott, NDD (1963). *Medium*: painter, marine artist, printmaker. *b*: Nottinghamshire, 5 Mar 1943. *m*: Hilary. one *s*. one *d*. *Studied*: Nottingham College of Art (1959-63). *Represented by*: Image by Design hugh@ibd-licencing.co.uk. *Exhib*: RBSA, RSMA, RWA, PS. *Works in collections*: RBSA. *Commissions*: National Trust; English Nature. *Works Reproduced*: 'Images of Cornish Tin' (2001). *Address*: Millbank, Mill Lane, Aston Cantlow, Henley-in-Arden B95 6JP. *Email*: info@johnscottmartin.co.uk *Website*: www.johnscottmartin.co.uk *Signs work*: "JSM" or "JOHN SCOTT MARTIN".

MARTIN, Marie-Louise, DFA (1982), BFA (1983); artist printmaker in etching; Past Director, Black Church Print Studio, Dublin; on the Board of Friends of National Collection; Established print studio for Airfield Trust, Dundrum, Co. Dublin 1999-2000; Elected Member of Watercolour Society of Ireland (WCSI) 2009. *Medium*: etching. *b*: Dublin, 29 Mar 1960. *m*: Marcus Casey. *Studied*: National College of Art, Dublin (1978-83). *Exhib*: RA (1987, 1988), RHA (1985-10), RUA (1987-10), An tÓireachtas (1984-02), EVA (1984, 1986, 1988); print exhbns. in Ireland, England, Japan, America, Germany, Spain, Taiwan, Bulgaria, Australia, Italy; exchange print exhbns. to China, Finland, Cuba. Print prizewinner RHA (1989), RUA (2001, 2003). *Works in collections*: BP Oil (Brussels); Kilkenny Castle; Guinness Peat Aviation; National Self portrait Coll.; Contemporary Arts Soc.; Office of Public Works; Stormont Castle, Belfast; Microsoft. *Official Purchasers*: Arts Council, Ireland *Clubs*: United Arts, Dublin. *Address*: 110 Merrion Road, Ballsbridge, Dublin 4. Ireland. *Email*: printmaker@marie-lousemartin.com Website: www.marie-louisemartin.com

MARTIN, Mary Grace, Dip AD (1972); Post Grad. (Painting) RAS (1975); Bard of Cornish Gorsedd; professional painter, landscape and seascape, garden and still-life artist. *Medium*: oil and watercolour. *b*: St.Dominic, 24 May 1951. *m*: James Evans. *Educ*: Callington Grammar. *Studied*: West of England College of Art, Bristol; Gloucester College of Art, Cheltenham; Royal Academy Schools under Peter Greenham. *Exhib*: London, Bristol, Cornwall, etc. Numerous one-man shows. *Works in collections*: National Trust; National Maritime Museum, Greenwich; Plymouth City Museum; Hotel de Ville, Lorient, France. *Publications*: 'A Wayward Genius', Lodenek Press (1978). Illustrated 'Burcombes Queenies and Colloggetts' by Virginia Spiers (1996); 'Olives, Lavender and Vineyards' by Mary Martin and Virginia Spiers (2002) West Brendon; documentary film made for BBC1

'Daffodils, Bullions and Steam' (1984), 'Look Stranger' series. 'Silver Rising' by Virginia Spiers and Mary Martin (2010). *Recreations*: collection and maintainence of West Country apple and cherry varieties. *Clubs*: RASAA. *Address*: Ash Barn, Bury, Callington, Cornwall, PL17 8BP. *Website*: www.marymartin.co *Signs work*: "Mary Martin".

MARTIN, Nicholas Gerard, BA (Hons) (1980); artist in oil-stained acrylics, paper collage and paper mosaics, mural mosaics; educational project artist, Glyndbourne Touring Opera (1987): music and composition for four part choirs. *b*: Edinburgh, 5 Jul 1957. *s of*: James Martin. *m*: Marion Brandis. two *s*. *Educ*: Edinburgh Academy. *Studied*: Edinburgh College of Art (1975-80, Ian Davidson). *Exhib*: RSA, Traverse Theatre, Gardner Art Centre, Brighton Polytechnic A.G., Royal Pavilion A.G., Brighton, Dryden St. Gallery, Horsham Arts Centre, Royal Festival Hall A.G., Ramsgate Library Gallery, Booth Natural History Museum, Brighton, Mason's Law Firm, Sussex Watercolour Society, Ditchling. *Works in collections*: SE Arts, Royal Pavilion A.G., Forestry Commission, Edinburgh, Royal Festival Hall, Towner A.G., mosaic mural for Channel Tunnel, Ashford Library (1990), Herne Bay Sea Front Mosaic Fountain (1993), Govan Shipyard Mural, Glasgow (1993), Queen Elizabeth Queen Mother Hospital Mural (1996), Maps for Rochester City Council, University of Surrey Roehampton, Mosaics 2002-3. *Recreations*: Music Certificate Sussex University. *Misc*: Educational residencies with: Glyndebourne Touring Opera, Destafford School, Hextable School, Spinney School; programme convenor for 'Art for Public Space' degree course at University of Roehampton, Surrey. Since 1999, has combined composition for voices with visual art. *Address*: 2 Baron's Walk Lewes E.Sussex BN7 1EX. *Email*: n.martin@roehampton.ac.uk *Signs work*: "Nicholas Martin."

MARTIN, Sonia, Byam Shaw Diploma; City & Guilds Post Graduate Diploma in Painting; MA Printmaking. *Medium*: Oil; watercolour; drawing; prints. *b*: London. *Studied*: Byam Shaw (1981); City & Guilds Art School (1988); Camberwell College of Art (1988). *Exhib*: Contemporary Art Society; Royal Academy; Barbican Arts Centre; National Theatre; Royal Society of British Artists; New English Art Club; Royal College of Art; New Hall College, Cambridge. *Works in collections*: University of the Arts; Southampton City Art Gallery; Southwark Council; New Hall College, Cambridge. *Commissions*: Private commissions UK and abroad. *Address*: 63B Kennington Park Road, London SE11 4JQ. *Email*: info@soniamartin.co.uk *Website*: www.soniamartin.co.uk *Signs work*: "SONIA MARTIN".

MARTINA, Toni, BA (Hons) (1978), Prix de Rome scholar (1987), RE (elected 1992); many prizes and awards including 1st prize Dept. of Transport National Art Competition (1992), Christie's Contemporary Art award at RA (1987), NY National Academy of Design Summer Exhbn. (1986), Lloyds Bank Printmakers award at RA (1986), prize, London Print Fair, Air Gallery London (1997), Birgit Skiold Prize (2003). *Medium*: painter/printmaker. *b*: London, 7 Mar 1956. *m*: Tessa. one *s*. one *d*. *Studied*: Harrow College of Art (1974-75), Kingston Polytechnic (1975-78), Central School of Art (1986). *Exhib*: Europe and the U.K. including RA Summer Show, RE, Rome, New York, Florida, Czech Republic, India. *Works in collections*: Cambridge libraries, Plymouth Museum, Rochdale Museum, Oldham Museum, Dept. of Transport, Museum of London, The London Hospital, Ashmolean Museum, New York Public Library, US Airways. *Publications*: "Citybites" (TNT Publications). *Address*: 85 Harold Road, Hastings, East Sussex TN25 5NJ. *Email*: t.martina@btinternet.com *Signs work*: "T. Martina.", or "Toni Martina".

MARTINEAU, Luke, Garrick/Milne Portrait Prize, Runner-Up (2003). *Medium*: oils, acrylic. *b*: 27 Mar 1970. *m*: Bella Martineau. one *s*. one *d*. *Educ*: Eton College; Magdalen College, Oxford. *Studied*: Heatherley School of Fine Art. *Represented by*: Panter and Hall, 11-12 Pall Mall, London SW1Y 5LU *Exhib*: Royal Society of Portrait Painters, Mall Galleries (1997-2005, 2009); NEAC, Mall Galleries (2008-2011); Oakham Gallery (2008);

Chelsea Art Society (2000-2014); Panter and Hall (2001, 02, 04, 06, 08, 10, 11, 12); Thompson's Gallery, Dover Street (1997, 99). *Works in collections*: Royal Collection, Middle Temple, Oundle School, Eton College, Magdalen College, Clifton College, Bradfield College. *Commissions*: Accompanied Their Royal Highnesses The Prince of Wales and The Duchess of Cornwall to the Republic of India October 2010 as Official Royal Tour artist. *Clubs*: President, Chelsea Art Society. *Address*: 77 Pennard Road, London W12 8DW. *Email*: luke@lukemartineau.com *Website*: www.lukemartineau.com

MASCO, Pam, artist in oil and water-colour, mixed media. *b*: Springfield, Mass., 19 Mar 1953. *m*: John Heseltine. *Studied*: School of the Boston Museum of Fine Art, U.S.A. (Grad. Dip.) 1976. *Exhib*: Clarendon Gallery, London (1986), David Messum, London (1990), RBA (1992), RWS (1992), Sunday Times Singer & Friedlander Water-colour (1992), W.H. Patterson, London. Studio and Gallery at East House, Petworth., US galleries. *Works in collections*: private and corporate collections; other collections Wentworth Club, Barings Bank. *Commissions*: portrait painting commissions. *Publications*: Dictionary of British Artists Since 1945 by David Buckman. *Address*: The Old Tavern Studio, Petworth W. Sussex GU28 0AH. *Email*: pm.hestletinemasco@virgin.net *Signs work*: "P. MASCO."

MASON, Michael, ATD, DA (Manc) (1956), Fellow in Sculpture British School at Rome (1976), FRBS (1992); sculptor in ceramics/bronze; former PR/lecturer sculpture, Manchester University. *b*: Lancs., 1 Jun 1935. *m*: Barbara. one *s*. one *d*. *Studied*: Manchester College of Art, British School, Rome. *Exhib*: Whitworth A.G., Serpentine Gallery, Yorkshire Sculpture Park, Galleria Bass Caracas, Bloomberg Space, Manchester Art Gallery. *Works in collections*: V&A, ACGB, Zagreb A.G., AVAF Caracas. *Commissions*: Manchester Business School, Hackney Empire. *Publications*: Art International, Ceramic Review. *Official Purchasers*: Juan Carlos Lancara, Cathy Willis, V&A. *Recreations*: T'ai Chi Chuan. *Address*: Lower Woolston Barn, North Cadbury, Yeovil, Somerset TA22 7BW. *Signs work*: "Michael Mason" or "M.M." in rectangle.

MASON, Richard, sculptor of constructions in metals, wood and perspex, painter in oil and acrylic. *b*: Ipswich, 20 June, 1931. *Educ*: Ipswich Grammar School. *Exhib*: one-man show: Woodbridge A.G. (1967); regular exhib. with Ipswich Art Club and Felixstowe Art Group. *Clubs*: Ipswich Art, Felixstowe Art Group. *Address*: Upland Gate, 39 Bishops Hill, Ipswich 1P3 8EW. *Signs work*: "Richard Mason."

MASSEY, Carole Margaret, DipAD; painter/illustrator in acrylic, water-colour, pastel, pencil; art tutor. *b*: Hertford, 8 Jan 1948. *m*: Eric. one *s*. one *d*. *Educ*: Welwyn Garden City Grammar School, Leicester School of Art. *Studied*: St. Albans (John Brunsden), Leicester School of Art (Edward Bawden, David Howells). *Exhib*: Cambridge, London, Hong Kong, Bury St Edmunds. *Commissions*: portraits - people, animals. *Publications*: books – Water-soluble Pencils (Search Press); video – Water-colour Pencils (Teaching Art), Figures in watercolour (Search Press). *Official Purchasers*: Born Free Foundation. *Principal Works*: Rolf Harris, Joanna Lumley portraits. *Clubs*: N.A.P.A., P.A.S.A.A., Bury Art Society. *Address*: Fyletts Barn, The Green, Hawstead, Bury St Edmunds, Suffolk IP29 5NP. *Email*: carole@massey-art.fslyc.co.uk *Signs work*: "CAROLE MASSEY."

MASSIE, Claudia, BA (Hons) Drawing and Painting; shortlisted for Jolomo Landscape award (2009). *Medium*: Oil, watercolour, drawing, prints. *b*: Perth, 15 July 1978. *m*: Dr Matthew Gibson. one *s*. one *d*. *Studied*: Edinburgh College of Art (1996-2000); University of Salamancia, Spain; Facultad de Bellas Artes (1999), Erasmus scholarship. *Exhib*: Ruthven Gallery, Auchterader; AAF Bristol/London (Frames Gallery); Royal Scottish Academy; Flaubert Gallery, Edinburgh, Iona House Gallery, Woodstock, Oxon. *Works in collections*: Jolomo Foundation Collection; private and corporate collections. *Commissions*: Private and corporate. *Misc*: Writes for 'The Spectator' on the arts blog. *Address*: North

Cottage, Glenalmond, Perth PH1 3RY. *Email*: claudiamassie@gmail.com *Website*: www.claudiamassie.co.uk *Signs work*: "MASSIE".

MASSON, Linda, DA, Post Grad Dip.; Travelling Scholarships (2). *Medium*: sculpture, mainly ceramic. *b*: Aberdeen, 27 Jul 1948. *Studied*: Gray's School of Art. *Represented by*: Riverside Gallery, Stonehaven. *Exhib*: Riverside Gallery; Heinzel Gallery, Tolquhon, Aberdeen; RSA, Edinburgh; RGI, Glasgow; Mall Galleries, London; Braemar; Inverurie. *Works in collections*: Royal College of Physicians and Surgeons, Glasgow. *Commissions*: various, private. *Address*: 30a Skateron Road, Newtonhill, Aberdeenshire AB39 3PT. *Signs work*: 'L Masson'.

MASTER, Jean, ROI (1987); painter in oil and acrylic. *b*: London, 25 Feb 1934, married. two *s*. one *d*. *Educ*: St. Joan of Arc Convent, Rickmansworth, Herts. *Studied*: St. Martin's School of Art (Kenneth Martin), also in Hamburg under Prof. Karl Kluth. *Exhib*: Royal Academy, London, Royal West of England, Bristol, Mall Galleries London, solo exhibition Edinburgh and many other mixed exhibitions. *Address*: 16 Hillside Rd., Redcliffe Bay, Portishead, N. Somerset BS20 8EW.

MATHESON, Andrew Kenneth Mackenzie, DA, RBSA, Cert Ed; artist/potter and teacher works mainly in stoneware/porcelain - from Rose House Pottery, 13 Tamworth St, Lichfield, Staffs; thrown or handbuilt pieces reduction fired to 1280°C. *b*: Edinburgh, 22 Jul 1949. *s of*: Farquhar Mackenzie Matheson, accountant. *Educ*: Riland Bedford High School, Sutton Coldfield. *Studied*: Madeley College of Education (1968-71), Grays School of Art, Aberdeen (1974-79), Dip. in Art (1978), postgrad. Dip in Art (1979). *Exhib*: in Scotland and England. *Works in collections*: RBSA, permanent collection, Grays School of Art, Aberdeen, North Ayrshire Museum, work in various private collections in UK and abroad. *Official Purchasers*: in 2000, work purchased by HRH, Prince of Wales. *Works Reproduced*: studiopottery.co.uk. *Principal Works*: Stoneware & porcelain. *Clubs*: Member of: Midland Potters Association; RBSA (Hon Treasurer since (1987); Birmingham Art Circle. *Address*: Driffold, Sutton Coldfield, W. Midlands B73 6HE. *Email*: akmmatheson@googlemail.com *Website*: andrewmatheson.co.uk *Signs work*: "Andrew K.M. Matheson" and work stamped (with monogram symbol).

MATHEWS, Alister, BSc; botanical painter in water-colour. *b*: Prestbury, 25 Feb 1939. *m*: Carl Mathews, Ph.D. one *s*. one *d*. *Educ*: James Allen's Girls' School, Dulwich; University of Wales. *Exhib*: SBA, SWA, Malcolm Innes; solo show: Hitchin Museum, Westminster Gallery annually, National Gallery of Wales, Linnaean Society, Piccadilly, London, Durham Museum, Hunt Institute for Botanical AA & Illustration 8th International Exhibition. *Works in collections*: Hunt Inst. for Botanical Illustration, Carnegie Mellon University, Pittsburg, Shirley Sherwood Collection, National Museum and Gallery of Wales, Cardiff. *Recreations*: gardening. *Address*: 4 Bramshott Close, London Rd., Hitchin, Herts. SG4 9EP. *Signs work*: "Alister Mathews."

MATHEWS, Binny, Elizabeth Greenshield Foundation Award (1989); painter in oil, specialising in portraiture, tutor. *b*: Dorset, 25 Jun 1960. *m*: Stuart Martin, architect. two *s*. *Studied*: Bournemouth and Poole College of Art (1977-78), West Surrey College of Art (1978-81), Brighton Polytechnic (1981-82). *Exhib*: NEAC, Hunting Award, RP, Mall Galleries, NPG (1981, 1982 1985, 1988, 1990, 1993), RA, etc., numerous one-woman shows in the provinces and London. *Works in collections*: La Sainte Union College, Southampton; National Trust, Castle Drogo; Seagrams; British Gas; Carpenters Hall; American Embassy. *Commissions*: John Fowles, Donald Swan, Baroness Cox of Queensbury, The Countess of Normanton, Anthony Little - Headmaster Eton, Fi and Guy Sangster, john Illseley, Louise and Theo Fennell, Vicompte Hugh le Hardy de Beaulieu, Oakham School Heads x 4, Former American Ambassador to London - The Hon Raymond

Seitz, jasper Ridley - Past Master of Carpenters Hall. *Clubs*: Chelsea Arts. *Address*: Lewcombe Woods Farmhouse, Evershot, Dorset DT2 0PH. *Website*: www.hereasel.com *Signs work*: "Binny Mathews.".

MATSUNAGA, Rui, BA Fine Art Painting(1999), MA Fine Art Painting (2002); Lexmark European Painting Prize finalist (2003), May Cristea Award for Painting (2002), Royal Academy Schools of Art Fellow (2002-3), Landseer Award (2001). *Medium*: oils. *b*: Japan, 17 Oct 1968. *d of*: Masahiro Matsunaga. *m*: Gordon Cheung. *Educ*: Central St.Martin's. *Studied*: RA Schools. *Exhib*: Lexmark European Prize (2003), Kyoto Art Centre (2003), Studio J, Osaka, Japan (2003), Michael Goedhuis Gallery, London (2002). *Works in collections*: Museum of Senegallia, Italy; London Institute, London. *Address*: 6 Beverley Hyrst, Addiscombe Road, Croydon, CR0 6SL. *Email*: rui.matsunaga@ukonline.co.uk

MATTHEWS, Les, MA Art (RCA), BA Hons (1st); Galleries Magazine prizewinner, Andrew Brownsword Award. *Medium*: oil painting cityscapes. *b*: 19 Apr 1946. *s of*: Reg and Violet Matthews. *m*: Anthea Matthews. one *s*. one *d*. *Studied*: Gloucestershire College of Art, Royal College of Art; student restorer National Gallery London. *Represented by*: Alan Morgan. *Exhib*: numerous mixed shows including RA, RWA, Athena, Saunders & Bockingford, Sunday Times, Bath Society of Artists, Laing, etc.; Shared and one-man shows: Will's Art Warehouse London, Clifton Gallery Bristol, Europe, Middle East. *Works in collections*: MO, MA, Canberra Australia; many private and public collections including museums, National Trust and universities, HRH Prince Michael of Kent KCVO. *Commissions*: Open University, Hawkwood College, etc. *Publications*: Oxford University Press, Transworld Corgi, Galleries Magazine, RWA publications. *Works Reproduced*: various range of paintings in print form. *Principal Works*: American, European and Far East cityscapes. *Recreations*: travel and wine, intense interest in European Art History. *Clubs*: Bath Society of Artists. *Address*: 16 Streamside, Clevedon, North Somerset, BS21 6YL. *Email*: les@lesmatthews.co.uk *Website*: www.lesmatthews.co.uk *Signs work*: Les Matthews.

MATTHEWS, Sally, BA Hons. *Medium*: sculpture and drawing. *b*: Tamworth, 30 Dec 1964. *m*: Richard Harris (sculptor). one *s*. one *d*. *Studied*: Loughborough College of Art 1983-86. *Exhib*: Tullie Hse Carlisle, Oriel Mostyn Gallery Touring Exhbn., Peggy Guggenheim Collection Venice with sculpture at Goodwood, Collins Gallery Glasgow, Robert Sanderson Cork Street. *Works in collections*: Prudential Corp. London, Shipley Art Gallery Gateshead, National Museum of Wales, Contemporary Arts Society of Wales, Brecknock Museum and Art Gallery. *Commissions*: Grizedale Forest, Gateshead Riverside, Sustrans, Arte Sella Italy, Bialowieza Poland, Sti for Oye, Norway, Botanic Gardens Montreal. *Publications*: 'With Animals', 'Sentient Beings', & 'Gathering'. *Address*: The Castle, Rhosgoch, Builth Wells, Powys, LD2 3JU. *Email*: 2sculptors@freeuk.com *Website*: www.sallymatthews.co.uk

MATTHEWS, Sharyn Susan, SWA; self taught artist in water-colour, acrylic, gouache, oil. *b*: Bristol, 13 Jan 1951. *d of*: Ralph Valentine-Daines, stonemason. one *s*. one *d*. *Exhib*: numerous one-man shows at home and abroad, including Mall Galleries. Work permanently on show Park Lane Fine Arts, Ashtead, Surrey. *Address*: 19 Longdown La. North, Ewell, Surrey KT17 3HY. *Signs work*: "Sharyn Matthews."

MATTHEWS, Zara, MA, RCA (1999); painter in oil, artist printmaker, digital artist. *b*: London, 6 Jun 1960. *Educ*: St Paul's Girls School, Hammersmith, London. *Studied*: Goldsmiths College (1979-1980), Kingston Polytechnic (1980-1983), Royal College of Art (1997-1999). *Exhib*: Flowers East (1991), Eagle Gallery, London (1992, 1996, 2001), Harewood House, Leeds (1996), Kunst Zurich (2004). *Works in collections*: DLA Art Collection, British Land, RCA Print Archive, V&A Print Collection, British Museum. Private collections in Switzerland, Italy and Great Britain. *Principal Works*: 'Self Portrait:

1st Edition' (1999), 'Fold' (2001), 'State of Play' (2004). *Address*: 73-75 Cressy Court, London E1 3JQ. *Email*: zaram@talk21.com *Signs work*: "Zara Matthews."

MAUGY, Sandrine, SFP; MA; CertHE Community Work; Cert. Botanical Illustration; awards: Hillier Legacy Award (SFP, 2003); Silver Medal (RHS, 2004); Popular Choice Runner Up (SFP, 2004); Miggy & Gordon Bath Award for Oil Painting, Runner Up (SFP 2005, 2007); Certificate of Botanical Merit (SBA 2007). *Medium*: watercolour, oil. *b*: Rouen, France, 1969. *Studied*: University of Caen, France. *Exhib*: Mottisfont Abbey, Hampshire; Westminster Gallery, London; Southampton City Art Gallery; The Sandra Whitman Gallery, San Francisco, USA; RHS Hall, London. *Works in collections*: internationally. *Commissions*: Roy Lancaster. *Publications*: Artists & Illustrators Magazine (since 2006). *Recreations*: ballet, gardening. *Address*: Southampton. *Email*: sandrine@sandrinemaugy.co.uk *Website*: www.sandrinemaugy.com *Signs work*: 'SANDRINE MAUGY'.

MAY, Elsie D. *Educ*: Sydney, London, Tunbridge Wells. *Exhib*: Sydney, Melbourne, Bristol, London, Tunbridge Wells, East Grinstead, Cranbrook. *Works in collections*: Australia, USA, UK, Canada, Japan, Netherlands and Switzerland. *Publications*: 'Community Paediatrics' (1981), 'Our Guardian Angels' (2001), 'Sophie and her Star (2003). *Recreations*: walking, theatre, music, yoga. *Address*: 13 Forge Rd, Tunbridge Wells, Kent, TN4 0EU. *Email*: edangel@waitrose.com *Website*: www.elsiemay.com

MAY, Joanna. *Medium*: liquid acrylic through an airbrush, and gouache, also works in oil. Paints wildlife subjects (specialising hare). *b*: Tonbridge, 22 May 1965. *d of*: Mr & Mrs Peter Cowne. three *d*. *Studied*: 2 years technical illustration Bournemouth College, 2 years further study General Illustration Falmouth College graduating 1991. *Exhib*: Christie's Contemporary Art Auction (2001), Westminster Gallery Society of Women Artists (2002/3), Readers Digest Exhbn (1991), AOI Exhbn (1990), Gallery One Barnes (solo show 'The Call of the Wild', 2005), Christie's St. James (2004/05/06) Charity Auction Cancer Research; Brian Sinfield Gallery, Burford (2001, and solo show 2006); 2008 Solo Show - Raymond Blanc's Le Manoir Hotel, 2009 Solo Show - Longleat House Orangery. *Commissions*: paintings commissioned by Raymond Blanc for the Lemongrass Suite at Hotel Le Manoir de Quat'Saison (2007). *Works Reproduced*: by Animal World Magazine (2 yrs), Kingfisher Books. *Misc*: also published under name Joanne Cowne. Life and Works featured on BBC's Spring Watch series (June 2006). Invited to speak about work on BBC's Radio Wiltshire (2005/06); 2010 opened new gallery in Marlborough. 2010 'Elephant parade London' painted elephant, auctioned Elephant Family Charity. 2010 Solo Exhibition 'Year of the Tiger' held at own gallery with speeches by WWF and TV Wildlife Presenter Chris Packham for Save the Tiger, WWF. 2011 Married David Ladd, wedding and career covered by 'Wiltshire Life'. 2011 Solo Exhibition held at home in Wiltshire, opened by Chris Packham, painting of a Lion auctioned to raise money for Tiger conservation at the Isle of Wight Zoo. 2012 Home and Work published in 25 Beautiful Homes magazine. 2012 Solo Show at The Savoy Hotel London, opening speech by Michaela Strachan, paintings based on Iconic Animals of London Zoo, raising awareness for the ZSL London Zoo 'Tiger SOS' charity. 2012 closed gallery in Wiltshire to concentrate on Solo Shows and to place work in galleries in the UK and abroad. New Studio Gallery as listed below. *Address*: Studio Gallery, Chapel House, 77 Main Street, Keevil, Wiltshire BA14 6ND. *Email*: joanna@joannamay.com *Website*: www.joannamay.com

MAYER, Charlotte, ARCA(1952), FRBS(1980); RBS Silver Medal (1991). *Medium*: sculpture in bronze and steel. *b*: Prague, 4 Jan 1929. *d of*: Frederick Mayer. *m*: Geoffrey Salmon. one *s*. two *d*. *Studied*: Goldsmiths' College School of Art (1945-49, Wilson Parker and Roberts Jones), RCA (1949-52, Frank Dobson). *Represented by*: Gallery Pangolin 004(0) 1453 886527; Garden Gallery 01794 301144; Pangolin London 0207 520 1480.

Exhib: RA, RWA, V&A.; Selected Galleries: Belgrave, Pangolin, Sladmore, Berkeley Sq., Garden Gallery Hants; New Academy; Cass Sculpture Foundation; Pangolin, London. *Works in collections*: Wadham College Oxford; The Wirral Autistic Society; Basingstoke and N. Hants. Health Authority; Banque Paribas; Bledlow Manor; J C Decaux, France; St. Ethelburgas Centre for Reconciliation and Peace. *Commissions*: Tree of Life, North London Hospice; Ascent, Barbican, City of London; Journey 2 Nene College, Northants.; Wind and Fire, Marylebone Gate, London; Sea Circle, Liverpool; 'Moon Arch', Prior's Court School, Berkshire. *Publications*: The Mystery of Creation, Lealman and Robinson; Patronage and Practice, Tate Gallery Liverpool; Liverpool Seen, Peter Davis; The Alchemy of Sculpture, Tony Birks, The Art of Prior's Court School, Ann Elliott; Sculpture at Goodwood by Ann Elliott; 'Modern British Sculpture',Guy Portelli; 'Charlotte Mayer in Essence' Tom Flynn. *Recreations*: friends. *Address*: 6 Bloomfield Rd., Highgate, London N6 4ET. *Email*: charlottemayer@talktalk.net *Signs work*: "C.M." or "Mayer."

MAYES, Emerson, BA Hons, Graphic Arts, Leeds Metropolitan University (1994); painter/printmaker and draughtsman of British landscapes. *b*: Harrogate, N. Yorks., 22 May 1972. *Partner*: Melanie Wilkins. *Educ*: St. Aidans C.of E. High School, Harrogate. *Studied*: Harrogate College, Leeds Metropolitan University. *Exhib*: NEAC, Discerning Eye, Laing Landscape prize, numerous solo exhibs. including London and Edinburgh, represented by Gascoigne Gallery, Harrogate. *Works in collections*: N.Yorks. County Council, Harrogate Borough Council, Provident Financial Plc and numerous private collections. *Address*: 5 Cliff View Terrace, Glasshouses, Harrogate, N.Yorks HG3 5QU. *Email*: emerson@mayes100.fsnet.co.uk *Website*: www.emersonmayes.co.uk *Signs work*: "Emerson Mayes."

MAZ: see JACKSON, Maz.

MAZZOLI, Dino (Leopoldo), artist in oil and water-colour. *b*: Terni, Italy, 10 May 1935. *s of*: Gino Mazzoli, artist. one *s*. one *d*. *Educ*: Oriani College, Rome. *Studied*: Villa Massimo, Rome (1953-54, Renato Guttuso), Villa Medici, Rome (1954-56), Eastbourne College of Art, and with Dorothy Swain, R.C.A. *Exhib*: Don Orione, Farnesina, Rome, Heathfield A.G., E. Grinstead Autumn Show, Towner Museum and A.G., Eastbourne, Brighton Museum and A.G., Star Gallery, Lewes, Blackheath Gallery, London; also in Dusseldorf, Germany, St. Laurent en Grandvaux, France, Birmingham, Alabama U.S.A., etc. *Works in collections*: La Charbonniere, St. Laurent en Grandvaux 39150 France. *Principal Works*: has copied out the complete text of the bible and illustrated it with approximately 5000 illustrations in 23 volumes. *Address*: 33 Cavalry Cres., Eastbourne, E. Sussex BN20 8PE. *Signs work*: "D. Mazzoli."

McADAM CLARK, Caroline, RBA, RWS (2008); MA Hons Fine Art; painter in oil, gouache, printmaking; co-Director, Piers Feetham Gallery. *b*: London, 18 Jan 1947. *d of*: James McAdam Clark MC, CVO. *m*: Piers Feetham. one *s*. one *d*. *Studied*: MA at Edinburgh College of Art, Edinburgh University (1965-70). *Represented by*: Thackeray Gallery; Lena Boyle Fine Art; Piers Feetham Gallery. *Exhib*: Highgate Fine Art, Chappell Galleries, Messums London, Thompson's Gallery, Discerning Eye, Lynn Painter-Stainers, various UK art fairs. *Works in collections*: private: France, UK, USA, Netherlands. *Commissions*: illustrator of "Three Fairy Tales" by Oscar Wilde (pub. The Winged Lion, 1995); mural paintings London & Venice. *Publications*: co-author with P. Feetham 'The Art of Framing' (1997). *Official Purchasers*: West Deutches Landesbank; Archant Group; Firmdale Hotels; UCS. *Works Reproduced*: 'Covehithe' oil on paper, illustrated in 'Making Waves' by Ian Collins (pub. Black Dog Books, 2006). *Principal Works*: "The Shipping Forecast" private collection 2007; "On the Road" Arizona 2012. *Recreations*: sailing. *Clubs*: Chelsea Arts. *Address*: Hill Lodge, Church Walk, Aldeburgh, Suffolk IP15 5DU. *Email*: cmcadamclark@hotmail.com *Website*: www.mcadamclark.com *Signs work*: "McAdam Clark."

McADAM FREUD, Jane, MA (1995), FRBS (1994), Freedom of the City of London (1991); Board Member of Scienar 2009. *Medium*: Sculpture. *b*: London, 24 Feb 1958. *d of*: Lucian Freud. *m*: Peter Henson. two *s-s*. *Studied*: Central School of Art (1978-81), Scholarship(1986-89), RCA (1993-95). *Represented by*: Gazelli Art House, Mayfair; Whitelabs, Milan. *Exhib*: Royal Academy Summer Show, Freud Museum, National Arts Club, New York; Sandaram Tagore, NY, USA; Gazelli Art House, Mayfair. 1996-2012. *Works in collections*: include: V&A, BM, Pulitzer Foundation USA, National Gallery Archives, Yorkshire Museum, HRH Queen Elizabeth, National Gallery of Greece. *Commissions*: recent: Oxford & Cambridge Universities. *Publications*: include: Sculpture: On the Edge (1995), 'Relative Relations 2007', 'Inside Out' Paper for Oxford University (2007), 'Old Dreams, New Interpretations' Lung Yingtai Foundation, Taipei (2009). *Official Purchasers*: include: British Museum, V&A, Fitzwilliam Museum, Ashmolean Museum, Berlin State Museum, National Museum of Ireland, Rijksmuseum Leiden. *Clubs*: Associate Lecturer: CSM. *Address*: 4 Elm Close, North Harrow, Middlesex HA2 7BT. *Email*: mail@janemcadamfreud.com *Website*: www.janemcadamfreud.com *Signs work*: "J.Mc.A.F." or "J. McA. Freud."

McARTHUR, Christine Louise, Awards: Travelling Bursary (1975 & 1976); SAC (1980 & 2004); Glasgow Soc. of Women Artists Trust Fund Award & GSWA Lauder Award; RGI NS MacFarlane Award; Alexander Munro Award RSW; resigned from RSW and RGI in 2009. *b*: Kirkintilloch, 14 Mar 1953. divorced. *m*. Roger Billcliffe (2004). two *d*. *Educ*: Lenzie Academy, Glasgow. *Studied*: Glasgow School of Art (1971-1976). *Represented by*: Roger Billcliffe, Glasgow; Lemon St., Truro; Thackeray, London; Ainscough, Dartmouth. *Exhib*: Gertsev Gallery, Moscow and others. *Works in collections*: Royal Bank of Scotland, Clydesdale Bank, John Lewis Partnership, Amerada Hess, Scottish Nuclear plc, Caledonian University, Macfarlane Group, Allied Distillers, Argyll Group plc, Craig Capital, University of Strathclyde, Gertsev Collection. *Commissions*: John Lewis, Glasgow and Peter Jones, London. *Works Reproduced*: Vases on a High Table; Dark Pansies; Hans, May You Always Have Quail's Eggs. *Address*: 190 West George Street, Glasgow G2 2NR. *Email*: christinemcarthur@me.com *Signs work*: "Christine McArthur."

McCARTER, Keith, DA(Edin.) (1960), FSIA (1968), FRSA (1969), ARBS (1991); Sir Otto Beit Medal (RBS, 1992). *Medium*: sculptor in bronze, stainless steel, concrete. *b*: Edinburgh, 15 Mar 1936. *s of*: Peter McCarter. *m*: Brenda Schofield. one *s*. one *d*. *Educ*: Royal High School, Edinburgh. *Studied*: Edinburgh College of Art (1956-60, Eric Schilsky, Helen Turner). *Represented by*: Open Eye Gallery, Edinburgh. *Exhib*: RA, Monaco, Burleighfield Gallery, Alwin Gallery, Berkeley Sq. Gallery, Blains Fine Art. *Works in collections*: Numerous countries worldwide. *Commissions*: many public sited sculptures in UK, USA, Europe, Africa. *Address*: 10 Coopersknowe Crescent, Galashiels, Scotland TD1 2DS. *Email*: keith@keith-mccarter.com *Website*: www.keith-mccarter.com *Signs work*: "McCarter"; small works.

McCARTHY, Lee Thomas, ABNA. *Medium*: acrylics, oil. *b*: 28 Sep 1974. *Partner*: Michelle Padmore. one *s*. *Studied*: Liverpool College of Arts. *Represented by*: ABNA. *Exhib*: Liverpool Art Gallery, Madeleinarts, Editions Gallery, St. Georges Hall. *Works in collections*: private, corporate; Whistlefish Galleries, Cornwall. *Commissions*: private and corporate. *Publications*: Milkwood Publishing, ABNA British Naives. *Works Reproduced*: Milkwood Publishing, Inc Whistlefish Galleries. *Misc*: mostly self taught. *Address*: 53 Haven Road, Fazakerley L10 1LR. *Email*: lee.mccarthy6@btinternet.com *Signs work*: "L McCarthy".

McCARTHY, Peter. *Medium*: acrylic, oils, watercolours. *b*: Westcliff-on-Sea, Essex, 30 Aug 1955. *Studied*: Suffolk College; Colchester School of Art. *Exhib*: The John Russell Gallery, Ipswich (1997-2012), White Space Gallery, London (2005-2006), The Nevill

Gallery, Canterbury (2000-2003), Galerie Not, London (1986), The Mall Galleries, London (1985), Brighton Art Fair (2011, 2013), Art Open Barbican Trust, London (2010), Suffolk Showcase Smiths Art Gallery (2009, 2010, 2011, 2013), Aldeburgh Gallery, Suffolk (2014). *Commissions*: a few. *Clubs*: Ipswich Art Society. *Address*: 35 Orford Street, Ipswich, Suffolk, IP1 3PE. *Email*: P.McCarthy1@ntlworld.com *Website*: www.pmcart.co.uk *Signs work*: "McCarthy".

McCARTNEY, Jamie, BA (Fine Art) (1991); Erotic Signature Prize (2006); The Kyoto Prize, Art Car Parade (2007), *Medium*: sculpture. *b*: Marylebone, London 9 Oct 1971. *Educ*: Westminster School. *Studied*: London College of Printing (Art Foundation, 1986); Hartford Art School, Connecticut (-1991). *Represented by*: JAG Gallery, Brighton; Gallery Kaleidoscope, London; Sheridan Russell Gallery, London; Garden Architecture, London. *Exhib*: Recent exhibitions: AMORA, London (Academy of Sex and Relationships); Body of Work, Lewes (group show, 2007); Peter Jones, London (2007); Arts Club, Mayfair (2007); JAG Gallery, Brighton (2007); Unitarian Church, Brighton (group show, 2007). *Publications*: The World's Greatest Erotic Art of Today Vols I & II. *Official Purchasers*: Public: steel sculpture, Runnymeade Council, Egham, Surrey (1999); Art Car Parade, Blackpool (2007); AMORA: seven sculptures commissioned 2006/2007. *Principal Works*: The Impossibility of Passion (2007). *Address*: Brighton, UK. *Email*: jamie@jamiemccartney.com *Website*: www.jamiemccartney.com

McCAUSLAND, Christine, BA (Fine Art), RASC (Post Graduate in Painting). *Medium*: oil, drawing, prints. *b*: Scotland, 17 Feb 1944. *Educ*: Harrogate School of Art (1969-70) Pre-Diploma (Award for Drawing). *Studied*: Camberwell School of Arts and Crafts BA (Commendation in Art History) under Anthony Eyton and Francis Hoyland (1970-73), Royal Academy Schools (Prize for Draughtsmanship, 1973-76) under John Lessore and Michael Salaman. *Exhib*: Kelvingrove Art Galleries & Museum, Glasgow; 'New Voices' Gowdoc Gallery, Glasgow; Festival Club 'Celtic Images', Edinburgh; Festival Hall, Grafton Gallery, Alexandra Palace, Royal Academy, South London Art Gallery, Pall Mall Gallery, Saint-Mary-in-the-Castle, Hastings, etc. *Works in collections*: Royal Livery Company of Painters and Stainers, private collections. *Address*: 88 Clarendon Road, London W11 2HR. *Signs work*: "CHRISTINE M^{C}CAUSLAND" on prints and drawings. Sometimes on back of paintings.

MCCLARY, Louise, Arts Council of England Award 2003. *Medium*: Watercolour; drawing; prints; acrylic. *b*: Penzance, 3 Dec 1958. *m*: Mat Robinson (architect). two *s*. *Studied*: Penzance School of Art (1975). *Represented by*: Adam Gallery, Bath; Wills Lane, St Ives; Bohun, Henley. *Exhib*: Solo shows: Beaux Arts, Bath (1991, 92, 93, 95); Stations of the Cross, Southwell Minster (2003); Truro Cathedral (2005), 'Presence' St Pauls Cathedral (2004); Waterhouse & Dodd, Cork St, London (2006); Bohun Gallery, Henley (2009); Millennium, St Ives (2010); Adam Gallery, Bath (2010); Adam Gallery, London (2012); Kestle Barton, Cornwall (2012). *Works in collections*: Plymouth University; Cornwall County Council; Treliske Hospital; Truro School. *Publications*: Catalogue Essays by Michael Bird and Nicholas Usherwood; St Ives Colony in Transition by Peter Davies. *Official Purchasers*: Plymouth University. *Works Reproduced*: Resurgence Magazine, Church Times. *Misc*: Head decorator, Troika Pottery (1976-82). *Address*: Caevallack, St Martin, Helston TR12 6DF. *Email*: studio@louisemcclary.com *Website*: www.louisemcclary.com *Signs work*: "Louise McClary".

McCLURE, Daphne Quintrell. *Medium*: acrylic, gouache. *b*: Helston. *d of*: Jane Quintrell Treloar. *m*: George McClure. one *s*. one *d*. *Studied*: Hornsey College, Central School, London. *Exhib*: Thompsons, Cadogan, Archeus, London galleries. Penwith Gallery, St.Ives; Lemon St Gallery, Truro; Cornwall Contemporary, Penzance; Badcocks, Newlyn, Cornwall. *Works in collections*: Newlyn Gallery Cornwall, Germany, Australia, America.

Commissions: Accepted a residency at the Josef Albert Foundation, Conneticut USA (2005); commissioned to design the first Tate mug, St. Ives. *Publications*: monograph -1997 'A Cornish Journey from Porthleven to Penzance'. *Address*: Lower Foys, Alverton Road, Penzance, Cornwall TR18 4DZ.

McCOMB, Leonard William, RA, RE (1993), Slade Dip. (1960); artist-painter, sculptor, printmaker; visiting teacher: RA Schools. *b*: Glasgow, 3 Aug 1930. *m*: Barbara Elenora. *Studied*: Manchester School of Art (Harry Suttcliffe), Slade School (Sir William Coldstream, Prof. A.H. Gerrard). Removed Golden Man sculpture - Lincoln Cathedral Travelling Exhbn. *Works in collections*: Tate Gallery, Arts Council Collection, V&A, BM, Towner A.G., Belfast A.G., B'ham, Manchester, Sheffield, Swindon and Worcester city galleries. *Commissions*: commemorative plaque bronze gold leaf Brookes University, Oxford (1993); tapestry 'Fishes and Invertebrates in the Sea' Boots plc (1994). *Publications*: Arts Council Catalogue (1983), Painting from the South Catalogue (1989), Catalogue Drawings and Paintings, Browse and Darby Gallery (1993), Gillian Jason Gallery; Video Film Arts Council 'Flow of Life' (1983). *Address*: 6 St. Saviours Rd., Brixton Hill, London SW2 5HD. *Signs work*: "McCOMB" and "L.M" within circle and date.

McCOMBS, John, NDD, ROI, RBA, FRSA, MAFA; landscape and figure artist in oil. *b*: Manchester, 28 Dec 1943. *s of*: John McCombs (Snr). *Educ*: Manchester High School of Art (1957-62). *Studied*: St. Martin's School of Art (1962-67) under F. Gore, Reynolds, Kossoff. *Exhib*: RA, Mall Galleries, Manchester City A.G., Saddleworth Museum, John McCombs Gallery. R.A. Scholarship and 'College prize' St. Martin's (1966); Stanley Grimm prize ROI (1990); 'People's prize' Manchester Academy (1991), Alan Gourley Memorial Award ROI (2001). *Works in collections*: Manchester, Salford, Oldham A.G.'s, Saddleworth Museum. *Publications*: articles for 'Leisure Painter' 'International Artist' magazines. *Clubs*: R.O.I., R.B.A., M.A.F.A. *Address*: 12 King St., Delph, Oldham OL3 5DQ. *Website*: www.johnmccombs.co.uk *Signs work*: "J. McCombs," sometimes "J.Mc."

McCOY, Josie, MA Fine Art, BA Fine Art; Woo Charitable Foundation Arts Bursary (2002), Royal West of England Academy Open Painting Exhbn, commended (2001), 1st Prize The Centre of Attention Painting Prize (2001). *Medium*: oil on canvas. *b*: Plymouth, Devon, 14 Nov 1969. *d of*: Keith and Janet McCoy. *Partner*: Andrew Cummings. one *s*. *Studied*: Central St.Martins, Solihull College, & Plymouth College of Art and Design. *Exhib*: solo exhbns: DF Arte Contemporanea, Santiago de Compostela, Eyestorm Gallery, Milan and London, Notting Hill Arts Club, London, Centre of Attention, London; and group shows including Metropole Galleries, Folkestone, The Fieldgate Gallery, London and BP Portrait Award (2000-04), NPG, DA2 (Domus Artium), Salamanca. *Works in collections*: BBC, Collection of University of Wales, Jeremy Mogford Collection, The Borchard Collection of British Self-Portraits in the 20th Century, The Centre of Attention Permanent Collection. *Publications*: The Guardian, Art Review, Art Monthly, Dazed and Confused, Tema Celeste Contemporary Art. *Principal Works*: series: Eastenders, The Royle Family, Contemporary Icons. *Address*: Calle Alfonso de Cordoba 8-3, 46010 Valencia, Spain. *Email*: josie@josiemccoy.co.uk *Website*: www.josiemccoy.co.uk *Signs work*: Josie McCoy.

McCRUM, Bridget, RWA, FRBS; sculptor in stone, bronze-abstracted figurative. *b*: Yorks., 27 Apr 1934. *d of*: Patrick Bain. *m*: Robert McCrum (decd). three *d*. *Studied*: painting at Farnham (1951-55, Musjynski; 1980-82 stone carving). *Represented by*: Messum's Fine Art. *Exhib*: solo shows: St James Cavalier, Malta, Vanessa Deneveux, Phoenix, Plymouth School of Architecture, Dartington Hall Gdns., Wattis Fine Art, Hong Kong, Messums Fine Art; mixed shows: RA, RSA, RWA, New Art Centre at Roche Court, Bohun, Deans Court, University of Surrey, Chelsea Harbour, Plymouth Museum, Concepts Gallery, Sculpture at Goodwood, Onform. *Works in collections*: Frink, Golden Door Foundation, National Trust, Charterhouse Bank, Lismore Castle, Priors Court School,

Spencer Stuart, Tresco, Minnesota Landscape Arboretum. *Commissions*: Hambledon Church, Dittisham; The Homewood, Greenway, Coleton Fishacre, University of Surrey; The Knightsbridge, London; Rolls-Royce A38 Bristol. *Publications*: 'Touch & Time- The Sculpture & Drawings of Bridget McCrum' by Ann Elliot; The Art of Priors Court School; Modern British Sculpture by Guy Portelli; Birds Through Space & Time; Dartmout, An Enchanted Place by J Fiennes. *Clubs*: RBS, RWA. *Address*: Hamblyns Coombe, Dittisham, Dartmouth, Devon TQ6 0HE. *Website*: www.bridgetmccrum.com *Signs work*: "Bridget McCrum" or "McC.".

McCULLOCH, Ian, DA (1957), SSA (1964), ARSA (1989), RSA (2005); painter, printmaker; Fine Art Fellow, Strathclyde University (1994-2009); winner of Glasgow International Concert Hall Mural Competition (1989/90). *b*: Glasgow, 4 Mar 1935. *m*: Margery Palmer. two *s*. *Educ*: Glasgow School of Art (1953-57). *Exhib*: solo exhbns.: Collins Gallery, Glasgow (2009), Royal Scottish Academy, Edinburgh (2007), Peacock Printmakers, Aberdeen (1995), Aberdeen A.G. (1992), Aberystwyth A.C. (1991), Camden A.C. (1986); group exhbns.: New North, Tate Gallery Liverpool (1990), Leabhar Mòr and tour Glasgow (2001/2), The Drawn Figure, University of N.S.W., Australia (2001); Leabhar Mòr - book, exhibition and tour, Stornoway, Isle of Lewis (2002/03).*Works in collections*: Saatchi Collection, Glasgow A.G., Dundee A.G., Edinburgh City A.G., Pallant House A.G., Chichester, Perth A.G., Stirling A.G., R.S.A. Collections, Glasgow, Strathclyde and Liverpool Universities. *Commissions*: mural for Italian Centre, Glasgow (1989). *Publications*: The Artist in his World (Argyll, 1998). *Address*: 51 Victoria Rd., Lenzie, Glasgow G66 5AP. *Email*: IMcCstudio@waitrose.com *Website*: www.s-s-a.org/html/featart/mcculloc/index.htm *Signs work*: "Ian McCulloch."

McDERMOTT, John, Scholarship to Glasgow School of Art. *Medium*: mixed media. *b*: Blantyre, Glasgow, 18 Feb 1957. *Educ*: St. Joseph's RC School, Glasgow (1962-72). *Studied*: Glasgow School of Art (1972); Open University (1981-85); Studied with John Craxton, RA, Crete 1985. *Represented by*: self. *Exhib*: Museum of London, Royal Albert Memorial Museum (RAMM) Exeter; Old Bailey, London; Port Stanley, Falkland Islands; John Creasey Museum & Art Gallery, Salisbury; Exeter Castle; Barbican Centre, London. *Works in Collections*: London AD240, Old Bailey, London/Museum of London; various, Falkland Islands. *Commissions*: London AD240, Common Language. *Publications*: Art as a Language (theoretical paper). *Official Purchasers*: City of London Corporation, Falkland Islands Government. *Principal Works*: Eden Series of Paintings from 2005 to 2009. *Recreations*: Art and ancient civilisations; providing abstract art workshops. *Address*: 13 Wear Barton Road, Countess Wear, Exeter, Devon EX2 7EH. *Email*: john.mcdermott10@hotmail.co.uk *Website*: johnmcdermottartist.com *Signs work*: "John McDermott" - full signature on reverse, initials on front.

McDOWELL, Phyllis Ann Graham, NDD (1958), ATD (1959). *Medium*: oil, watercolour, drawing, prints. *b*: Kent, 19 Mar 1937. *d of*: Thomas Holder. one *s*. three *d*. *Educ*: Chislehurst Grammar. *Studied*: Bromley College of Art (1953-58), Brighton Art Teachers' Training College (1958-59). *Exhib*: 'Retrospective 1953-2007 solo exhibition, The Grand, Folkestone (2007); RA Summer Exhibition; Royal Institute of Painters in Watercolour, Mall Galleries; Society of Botanical Artists, Westminster Galleries. *Works in collections*: British Council - Ghana, Zambia; Africa Centre - Covent Garden. *Commissions*: Saga Rose cruise Liner; postage stamp, Ghana. *Publications*: 'Acrylics Workshop' (Dorling & Kindersley, 2006); 'Just Lay it On' instructional videos and DVDs. *Works Reproduced*: Leisure Painter, Kent Life, 'Watercolour Workshop' (D&K). *Misc*: Founder Member of Folkestone Artists' Cooperative. Monthly article on art in 'Folkestone Herald'. *Address*: 8 Myrtle Road, Folkestone, Kent, CT19 6EE. *Email*: phyllismcd@live.com *Website*: www.phyllismcdowell.com *Signs work*: "Phyllis McDowell".

McEWAN, Angus Maywood, RWS; RSW; Awards: Alasdair Salvesen Award (RSA) (1996); The John Blockley Prize (RI) (2004); 2nd Prize, Kaupthing Singer & Friedlander Watercolour Competition (2007), Bronze Award - Shewzhen Watercolour Bienual, China (2013). *Medium*: water-colour and mixed media. *b*: Dundee, Scotland, 19 Jul 1963. *s of*: Neil and Doreen McEwan. *m*: Wendy Ann Bell McEwan. three *s*. *Studied*: Duncan of Jordanstone College of Art. *Represented by*: Thompson's, London; Aldeburgh; Open Eye, Edinburgh. *Exhib*: Thompson's of Marylebone, London; Open Eye Gallery, Edinburgh; Jerdan Gallery, Crail; RSA; RGI, RSW (Royal Scottish Society of Painters in Watercolours); many countries around the world. *Works in collections*: Duncan of Jordanstone College of Art; Dundee Art Galleries and Museums; Dundee City Council Chambers; Paintings in Hospitals; RSA Collection; Qatar Royal Family; Ernst & Young. *Publications*: International Artist Magazine; Who's Who Scotland; The Watercolour Skies and Clouds Techniques of 23 International Artists; 100 Ways to Paint Still-Life and Florals; 100 Ways to Paint Seascapes, Rivers and Lakes. *Misc*: part-time lecturer, Dundee College. *Address*: 7 Glenleven Drive, Wormit, Newport-on-Tay, Fife, DD6 8NA. *Email*: art@angusmcewan.com *Website*: www.angusmcewan.com *Signs work*: Angus McEwan.

McEWEN, Elizabeth Alexandra, NDD (1960), ATD (1961), USWA (1980), UWS, RUA (1990), SBA (1987); RUA Gold medallist (1991). *Medium*: water-colour, gouache and acrylic. *b*: Belfast, 13 Dec 1937. *m*: James A. Nelson. *Educ*: Belfast Royal Academy. *Studied*: Belfast College of Art (1956-60), Reading University (1960-61). *Exhib*: many mixed and solo shows throughout N. Ireland, SBA London, Laing London. *Works in collections*: Royal Ulster Academy, National Self Portrait Collection, Limerick University, Dept. of Finance, Stormont. *Address*: Bell Rotary House, 10/12 Kings Road, Belfast BT5 6JJ. *Signs work*: "E.A. McEwen."

McFADYEN, Jock, BA, MA; artist in oil on canvas; Arts Council Film Award (1978); Arts Council Major Award (1979); Prizewinner, John Moore's 17 (1981). *Medium*: painting. *b*: Paisley, 18 Sep 1950. *s of*: James McFadyen & Margaret Owen. *m*: (1) Carol (divorced) (2) Susie Honeyman. two *s*. one *d*. *Educ*: Renfrew High School. *Studied*: Chelsea School of Art (BA 1973-76, MA 1976-77, Anne Rees Mogg, Ron Bowen, Ian Stephenson). *Represented by*: The Fine Art Society, London www.faslondon.com. *Exhib*: 36 one-man shows including Blond Fine Art, Imperial War Museum, William Jackson Gallery, Camden Arts Centre, Talbot Rice, Agnew's (2001), Rude Wercs (2005), Fine Art Society (2012). *Works in collections*: 32 public collections including British Council, Imperial War Museum, Kunsthalle Hamburg, National Gallery, V&A., Tate Gallery. *Commissions*: Artist-in-Residence The National Gallery (1981). Designed sets and costumes for Sir Kenneth McMillan's last ballet 'The Judas Tree', Royal Ballet, Royal Opera House, Covent Gdn. (1992). *Publications*: 'Jock McFadyen – A Book about a Painter' monograph by David Cohen, published by Lund Humphries (2001). 12 Exhibition Catalogues. *Works Reproduced*: Art magazines, covers for Penguin, Bloodaxe, Museum Cards, etc. *Principal Works*: large urban landscapes. *Address*: 15 Victoria Park Square, Bethnal Green, London E2 9PB. *Email*: info@jockmcfadyen.com *Website*: www.jockmcfadyen.com *Signs work*: "Jock McFadyen".

McGOOKIN, Colin Trevor, BA (Hons), ARUA; Artist in Residence, Down Lisburn Trust. *Medium*: acrylic, oil, collage, assemblage. *b*: Belfast, 4 Jun 1958. *m*: Punam. one *s*. one *d*. *Educ*: Belfast. *Studied*: Belfast College of Art (now Univ. of Ulster). *Represented by*: Engine Room Gallery, Belfast. *Exhib*: UK, Ireland, Europe, N.America. *Works in collections*: Ireland, UK, USA. *Commissions*: local councils, Ireland. *Publications*: 'Beyond the Partitions', 'From Tradition into the Light', 'Works on Paper', 'Glimpse', 'Thinking Long'. *Official Purchasers*: Arts Council of N. Ireland. *Works Reproduced*: 'Thinking Long' by Liam Kelly (Gandon Editions). *Address*: 28 Belmont Ave., Belfast BT4 3DD Northern Ireland. *Email*: colin.mcgookin@ntlworld.com *Website*: www.colinmcgookin.com *Signs work*: 'C.T.McGookin' (with year, e.g. '05).

MCGREGOR, Euan Robert, BA (Hons) Printmaking; PGCE Secondary Education; RGI Fine Art Travelling Award; RGI Cuthbert Award; RGI David Cargill Award; PAI GAC Fellowship; PAI Arnold Clark Award. *Medium*: Acrylic. *b*: Paisley, 30 Jun 1976. *m*: Emily McGregor. one *s*. two *d*. *Studied*: Glasgow School of Art. *Exhib*: Lime Tree Gallery, Bristol (2012); Roger Billcliffe Fine Art, Glasgow (2012); Oakham Contemporary, London (2011); The Smithy Gallery, Blanefield (2012); Scotlandart.com; McGill Duncan, Castle Douglas. Regular exhibitor: RGI Annual Exhibition; RSA Annual Exhibition; PAI Annual Exhibition; Affordable Art Fairs, Battersea, Cambridge, Bristol, Hampstead. *Works in collections*; Paintings in hospitals. *Clubs*: Glasgow Art Club. *Misc*: Teacher of Art at Johnstone High School. *Address*: 27 Happy Hills, West Kilbride, KA23 9EP. *Email*: euan@chromesun.co.uk *Website*: www.euanmcgregorpaintings.co.uk *Signs work*: "E. MCGREGOR".

McGREGOR, Lynn Barbara, RSW, SSA, VAS; BA (Hons) degree in Drawing and Painting (1984-88), Post-Graduate Diploma in Painting and Printmaking (1989); Awards: Mabel McKinley Art Prize, Royal Glasgow Inst., McLellan Galleries (1999), Eli Lilly Purchase Prize (1996), Scottish Society of Women Artists Special Award, Scottish Arts Club Award (1991). *Medium*: painter in acrylic. *b*: Pittenweem, Fife, Scotland, 21 Aug 1959. *m*: The Hon Michael Faulkner. *Educ*: Waid Academy, Fife, Scotland; Telford College of FE, Edinburgh, Scotland. *Studied*: Edinburgh College of Art. *Exhib*: The Scottish Gallery, Edinburgh; Thompsons, Marylebone, London; Heinzel Gallery, Aberdeen; Strathern Gallery, Crieff; Ardquin Gallery, Haselmere, Surrey. *Works in collections*: Robert Fleming Holdings Ltd., London; Eli Lilly Industries, Surrey; Morrison Construction; Bank of Scotland; Edinburgh College of Art; BBC/Public Catalogue Foundation. *Clubs*: mem. RSW; mem. SSA & VAS. *Misc*: currently living and working on otherwise uninhabited island on Strangford Lough, N. Ireland. *Address*: 35 Farranfad Rd, Downpatrick, Co. Down, NI BT30 8NH. *Email*: lynnmcgregor@elite.com *Website*: www.lynnmcgreagor.co.uk

McGREGOR, Mhairi Patricia, RSW, BA (Hons) Fine Art. *Medium*: oil and watercolour painting. *b*: Paisley, 10 Sep 1971. *d of*: Alastair and Marilyn McGregor. *m*: Graham Batin. one *s*. one *d*. *Studied*: Glasgow School of Art, under J.D. Robertson and Barbara Rae (1989-1993). *Represented by*: Roger Billcliffe Gallery, Glasgow; Thompson's Gallery, London. *Exhib*: 11 solo shows (1993-2005). *Works in collections*: Fleming Collection, London, John Rae Collection, Scotland. *Clubs*: Royal Scottish Society of Painters in Watercolour. *Address*: 33 Park Gardens, Kilbarchan, PA10 2LR.

McGUIGAN, Bernard, RBS; British Interior Design Association Gold Medal 2006. *Medium*: sculpture. *b*: Essex, 16 May 1956. *s of*: Mr & Mrs T F McGuigan. *Partner*: Kate Burton. *Studied*: self taught. *Represented by*: Lucy B Campbell Fine Art, London W8. *Exhib*: Art London (2004-06); RA Summer Exhibition; Bruton Street Gallery; Art Dublin; Art for Offices; Langham Fine Art; Manchester Art House; Bohun Gallery; Saltbox Gallery. *Works in collections*: Bank of India; Aspen Insurance, Bermuda; Lady Lewington. *Commissions*: Sir Sydney & Lady Lipworth; Cambridge Housing Association; Sir Christopher Ondaatje. *Publications*: Modern British Sculpture; Evening Standard; House and Garden. *Recreations*: reading, walking. *Address*: The Annexe, 1B Lady Margaret, London NW5 2NE. *Email*: bernardmcguigan@yahoo.co.uk *Website*: www.bernard-mcguigan.co.uk *Signs work*: "BM^{c}".

McGUINNESS, Michael, RWS (1993); painter in water-colour and oil; Senior typographic and book designer with Readers Digest and, subsequently, Art Editor of The Independent and The Independent on Sunday (1986-91). *b*: Essex, 20 Mar 1935. *Studied*: S.E. Essex Technical College (illustration and typography, Harry Eccleston, OBE), Royal Academy Schools (painting, Fleetwood Walker, RA), Walthamstow School of Art (Stuart Ray). *Publications*: The Encyclopaedia of Water-colour Techniques (two paintings), Einstein for Beginners (illustration), Jung for Beginners (illustration). *Clubs*: Wynken de Worde Soc. *Address*: 4 Denmark Rd., London W13 8RG. *Signs work*: "McG."

McINTOSH, Iain, ARSA; sculptor. *b*: Peterhead, 4 Jan 1945. *s of*: James McIntosh, cabinet maker. *m*: Freida. two *d*. *Educ*: Peterhead Academy. *Studied*: Gray's School of Art (1962-67). *Address*: 53 Kilrymont Rd., St. Andrews, Fife, Scotland KY16 8DQ. *Signs work*: "I.M." plus year.

McINTYRE, Fiona Mary Elspeth, MA European Fine Art, BA Hons Drawing and Painting, Dip. Fine Art Printmaking; Bath Printmakers Award, ProSigns Graphics Award. *Medium*: oil, drawing, print. *Studied*: Winchester School of Art, Barcelona (1992-93); Grafikskolan Forum Malmo Sweden (1989-1992); Edinburgh College of Art (1982-85). *Represented by*: D'Arcy Gallery, Cheltenham. *Exhib*: One Person Shows: Montpellier Gallery Cheltenham 2012, 8 Reece Mews Kensington 2001. Two Person Shows: Wetpaint Gallery Cirencester 2013, Quest Gallery Bath 2011, D'Arcy Gallery Cheltenham 2010. Museum Curated Group Shows: Gerald Moore Gallery London Touring Exhibition 2014, Lymington Museum & Art Gallery 2013, Corinium Museum Cirencester 2013. Group Shows: Bath Contemporary 2013, Moncrieff Bray Gallery Sussex 2012, Montpellier Gallery Cheltenham 2011. *Works in collections*: Sweden, Norway, Iceland, Germany, Britain, Israel, America. *Publications*: Under the Greewood: Picturing the British Tree by Ann Anderson & Ian Massey, pub Sansom & Company; New British Art by Jacob Sutton; A History of Bath Society of Artists by Peter Davies. *Works Reproduced*: in several books and publications. *Principal Works*: "New Fallen" oil on linen; "Reflections in Flooded Field, Yanworth" oil on linen; "Being or Nothingness - Homage to Satre" graphite on paper. *Clubs*: Founding Member: The Arborealists 2014. *Address*: 5 Ampney Mill Cottage, Ampney Crucis, Cirencester, Glos GL7 5RS. *Email*: fiona.me.mcintyre@gmail.com *Website*:www.fionamcintyre.com *Signs work*: "Fiona McIntyre".

McKAY-KNIGHT, Sophie, MA (Hons) Fine Art; Hope Scott Trust Award; Scottish Arts Club Award; RSA Best Painting Award. *Medium*: Drawing; prints; acrylic; mixed media. *b*: Edinburgh, 16 Mar 1973; *m*: Richard Baillie. one *d*. *Studied*: Edinburgh College of Art and Edinburgh University (1992-97); Wirral Metropolitan College. *Exhib*: Solo: Bianco Nero Gallery; The Randolph Gallery; The Campden Gallery; The Leith Gallery; Amber Arts. Mixed include: Royal Scottish Academy, Edinburgh; Colours Gallery; Cyril Gerber Fines Art; The Union Gallery; Red Rag Gallery. *Works in collections*: many private collections in the UK, USA, Canada, New Zealand, Germany. *Commissions*: Private (portrait) Edinburgh, London, York. *Misc*: Worked professionally with Art in Healthcare, Dundee Contemporary Arts, Tate Liverpool. *Email*: sophieelizabeth29@yahoo.co.uk *Website*: www.sophiemckayknight.com *Signs work*: "SMK" and date.

McKEAN, Lorne (Miss), FRBS; sculptor; Silver Medal for sculpture combined with architecture; Feodora Gleichen and Leverhulme Scholarships; Best British Sporting Sculpture. *Medium*: bronze. *b*: 16 Apr 1939. *m*: Edwin Russell, FRBS. two *d*. *Studied*: Florence Guildford School of Art; Royal Academy Schools. *Exhib*: four one-man shows, London W1. *Works in collections*: Portrait sculptures include: the late Marquess of Salisbury, Hatfield House; HRH Prince Philip on polo pony 'Portano', HM The Queen's personal Silver Wedding gift to her husband; the late Prince William of Gloucester, Kensington Palace; Earl of Lichfield for BBC programme 'Portrait'; Prince Charles on 'Pans Folly'. Public works: A.A. Milne public memorial of bear cub at London Zoo; Shearwaters, Shearwater House, Richmond Green; Girl and Swan 17 ft. bronze in Reading; 'Galoubet' French show jumping stallion; H.M. The Queen, Drapers Hall; Flight 27 Feet Bronze, City Square Leeds; half-lifesize bronze HRH Duke of Edinburgh on Portano at Guards Polo Club. *Recreations*: animals. *Clubs*: Guards Polo Club. *Address*: Lethendry, Polecat Valley, Hindhead, Surrey GU26 6BE. *Website*: www.lornemckean.com *Signs work*: "Lorne McKean.".

McKECHNIE, Christine, NDD; Royal Academy of Art Special Award (1983); SGFA Award (2005); Awards for All (2001, for Maze Project). *Medium*: paper collage.

b: Bursledon, 7 Jan 1943. *d of*: Anita & Douglas McGibbon. *m*: Ian James McKechnie. one *s*. one *d*. *Studied*: Southampton School of Art; Kingston School of Art. *Exhib*: RA Summer Show; Royal College of Art; Anna Mel Chadwick, New Kings Road; Bury Walk Gallery, Modern Gallery, Goodge Place; The Market Cross Gallery, Bury St. Edmunds; SGFA, Mall Galleries, NEAC, Thompson Gallery; Chelsea Arts Club, Artworks, Bury St. Edmunds; Suffolk Open Studios, Glyndebourne Festival Opera. *Commissions*: too many to list. *Publications*: Paper Collage (Search Press); articles - The Artist - Leisure Painter. *Works Reproduced*: 'A Celebration of Autumn' (David Adam), prints (Pauntley Press). *Principal Works*: Lake District, Italy, Morocco, Far East, USA, Suffolk. *Recreations*: opera, gardening, walking. *Clubs*: Chelsea Arts Club. *Address*: Cornerways, Southolt, Eye, Suffolk, IP23 7QJ. *Email*: christinemckechnie@suffolkonline.net *Website*: www.christinemckechnie.co.uk *Signs work*: "C Mc Kechnie".

McKENNA, John Anthony, ARBS. *Medium*: sculpture, drawing. *b*: Manchester, 18 Jan 1964. *m*: Claire Suzanne. two *s*. one *d*. *Educ*: Royal Grammar School, Worcester; The Victorian Institute, Worcester. *Studied*: Sir Henry Doulton School of Sculpture (1987-990); Middlesex Polytechnic (1984-85). *Exhib*: various in UK, including London, Birmingham, Glasgow, Channel Islands. *Works in collections*: States of New Jersey, Cunard, Sainsbury, Tesco, Pepsi Fritolay, MEPC, Centro, Ibstock, Warwickshire CC, Leeds City, Haringey BC, Wolverhampton MBC, Havant BC. *Commissions*: numerous public art commissions including bronze statues and relief artworks throughout the United Kingdom commissioned by local government and corporate bodies. *Official Purchasers*: The Crown Estate. *Principal Works*: The Colossus of Brownhills (12+m high); Jersey Cattle Group (St.Helier); The Knight of the Vale (Castlevale); Queen Mary 2 bronze relief panel (7m sq). *Recreations*: kite flying, bronze founding. *Misc*: sculptor specialising in large scale public art projects in fabricated steel and casting bronze statues, and smaller gallery artworks at his studio foundry. *Address*: High McGowaston, Turberry, Ayrshire, KA26 9JT. *Email*: johnmckthesculptor@mac.com *Website*: www.johnmckenna.co.uk *Signs work*: 'JMC' or 'JOHN MCKENNA SCULPTOR'

McKENNA, Laurence, artist in oil, water-colour, pastel and pencil. *b*: 20 Nov 1927. *s of*: Charles J. McKenna. *m*: Carmel Beattie. two *s*. one *d*. *Educ*: St. Kevin's, Belfast. *Studied*: 1965-68 under John Luke, RUA. *Exhib*: Belfast, Dublin, Cork, London, USA. *Works in collections*: private collections: Ireland, Gt. Britain, Italy, USA. *Works Reproduced*: Revue Moderne, Paris (drawing, 1947), Sunday Independent, Dublin (drawing, 1956), Irish News (drawing, 1958), Ulster Illustrated (drawing, 1958), Sunday Independent (drawing, 1965), Ulster Tatler (pastel, Jan '01). *Address*: 23 Grangeville Gdns., Belfast BT10 0HJ. *Signs work*: "LAURENCE McKENNA."

McKENZIE, Mo, ASWA; Teaching Diploma (TMHA); Management Diploma (DMS); Cert. in Fine Art (HNC); Diploma in Fine Art (HND); Artist of the Year Award, Havering (2004); Barbara Tate Award (2008). *Medium*: oil on board/canvas; acrylic. *b*: Buckinghamshire, 1943. *d of*: Anthony Athol Cathcart. *m*: William. *Educ*: Vauxhall Manor School for Girls (1956-61). *Studied*: Brighton College of Art & Craft (1961-63); University of E.London (1992-94). *Represented by*: Studio Eleven Gallery, Essex; Society of Women Artists (SWA). *Exhib*: The Islington Art Circle (1982-83); Royal Festival Hall, London (1961); Eastern Open Exhbn, King's Lynn (1998); Mall Galleries, London (annually since 2001); Beecroft Art Gallery, Essex (annually since 2000); solo exhbns locally at Studio Eleven Gallery and local Essex venues. *Official Purchasers*: Bachorski Gallery, Essex. *Recreations*: Mosaic design, piano, garden. *Clubs*: British Assoc. for Modern Mosaic (BAMM). *Address*: Hornchurch, Essex. *Email*: mo.mck@virgin.net *Website*: www.mo-mckenzie.co.uk.co.uk *Signs work*: 'McK'.

McKENZIE SMITH, Ian, CBE, OBE, DA, PPRSA, Hon RA, Hon RHA, Hon RUA, HRWA, PPRSW., RGI, LL.D. (Aberdeen University, 1991), D.Art (Robert Gordon

University 2000), FRSA, FRSE, FSS, FMA, FSA Scot; ASIAD; artist in oil and watercolour; Commissioner, Museums and Galleries Commission; Trustee, National Galleries of Scotland Museums Director. *b*: Montrose, 3 Aug 1935. *s of*: James McKenzie Smith. *m*: Mary Rodger Fotheringham. two *s*. one *d*. *Educ*: Robert Gordon's College, Aberdeen. *Studied*: Gray's School of Art (1953-59) under Ian Fleming and R. He nderson Blyth; Hospitalfield College of Art, Arbroath (1958 and 1959). *Exhib*: Royal Scottish Academy, Royal Academy, Fine Art Soc., Royal Glasgow Inst., Scottish Gallery, Ingleby Gallery, Open Eye Gallery, Gerber Fine Art. *Works in collections*: Scottish National Gallery of Modern Art, Scottish Arts Council, Abbot Hall Gallery, Kendal, Aberdeen A.G., Glasgow A.G., City Arts Centre, Edinburgh, Perth A.G., Royal Scottish Academy, Arts Council of Northern Ireland, Contemporary Art Soc., IBM, Robert Fleming Holdings, Deutsche Bank, The Robert Gordon University. *Clubs*: Royal Northern, Scottish Arts, Royal Overseas League. *Address*: Heron House, Montrose, Angus DD10 9TJ. *Website*: i.mckenziesmith@btinternet.com *Signs work*: normally unsigned, labelled on reverse.

MCKERRELL, John, Diploma in Art (Ed.Coll.Art) Post Grad (Highly Commended); Helen Rose Travelling Scholarship (Ed.Coll.Art) to Paris; Abbott & Holder Award, RWS (2002); RWS Council Award (1996); Alexander Stone Foundation Award RGI (1988); Tregastelle International Watercolour Award (France, 2000), Daler Rowney Award, RWS (2007), David Gluck Award RWS (2010). *Medium*: watercolour, acrylic, gouache. *b*: Falkirk, 12 Jan 1947. *s of*: William McKerrell. *Educ*: Marr College, Troon. *Studied*: Edinburgh College of Art (1965-70). *Represented by*: self and DACS. *Exhib*: Royal Scottish Academy, Royal Glasgow Institute of the Fine Arts, Royal Scottish Society of Painters in Watercolour, Scottish Society of Artists, Royal Watercolour Society, Royal Insititute of Painters in Watercolour, Sunday Times/Singer Friedlander Comp., Royal Society of Marine Artists. *Clubs*: DACS. *Misc*: Art teacher, Prestwick Academy (1972-1997). *Address*: c/o Summers, 36 Main Street, Symington, Ayrshire KA1 5QF. *Website*: www.artistsandillustrators.co.uk

McKIVRAGAN, Terrence Bernard, RI, NDD; artist in water-colour, acrylic and oils. *b*: Wallasey, 22 Jul 1929. two *s*. *Educ*: Wallasey Grammar School. *Studied*: Wimbledon School of Art (1947-51). *Exhib*: RI annually, Laing, Hunting Group, RA Summer Show, Singer & Friedlander/Sunday Times, NEAC, RBA, RSMA; galleries: Llewellyn Alexander, Manor House Chipping Norton, Alresford Hants., K.D. Fine Art, Guildford, Rowley, Winchester, Peninsula USA, Little Picture, Mousehole, Jerram, Sherborne, Dorset. *Commissions*: Baltic Exchange, Daily Express, Samsung, British Medical Assoc., Abbey National, Deutsch Financial, R.A.C. Pall Mall. *Publications*: Acrylic Masterclass - 9 featured artists, Paint Seascapes & Waterways - 14 artists; Watercolour Skies and Cloud Techniques - 23 International artists; Watercolour Innovations - 8 artists. *Clubs*: Chelsea Art Soc. *Address*: The Old Pottery Bldg., Down Lane, Compton, Guildford, Surrey GU3 1DQ. *Email*: studio@terrymckivragan.co.uk *Website*: www.terrymckivragan.co.uk

McLACHLAN, Edward Rolland, Cartoonist of the Year (4 times). *Medium*: ink and wash. *b*: Leicester, 22 Apr 1940. *m*: Shirley Ann. one *s*. three *d*. *Educ*: Humberstone Village Junior School, Wyggeston Grammar. *Studied*: Leicester College of Art. *Represented by*: Folio; Oxford Designers and Illustrators; Cartoon Stock; Cardmix. *Exhib*: Chris Beetles Gallery; London Cartoon Gallery. *Works in collections*: Chris Beetles Gallery; London Cartoon Gallery. *Commissions*: publishers: Methuen, Macmillan, Profile, Pearson, John Wiley, Oneworld, Oxford University Press; too many Ad agencies to mention. *Publications*: Punch, Private Eye, Spectator, Saga Magazine, Oldie, Salisbury Review. *Recreations*: weight training, cycling, gardening, pubs. *Address*: 3 Spinney View, Coverside Road, Great Glen, Leics, LE8 9EP. *Email*: mail@edmachlachlan.co.uk *Website*: www.edmclachlan.co.uk *Signs work*: McLachlan.

McLAREN, Sally, RE. *Medium*: painting, etching, drawing. *b*: London, 21 Sep 1936. *m*: D. MacLaren Webster. three *s*. *Studied*: Ruskin School of Art, Oxford University (1956-59), Central School of Art, London (1959-61), French Government Scholarship: Atelier 17, Paris (1961, S.W.Hayter). *Represented by*: Bankside Gallery, London. *Exhib*: worldwide. *Works in collections*: worldwide, including New York Public Library, Skopje Museum of Modern Art, Macedonia, etc. *Commissions*: P&O Oriana, National Grid, Printmakers Council Print Club, Print Collectors Club, etc. *Publications*: Printmakers Journal (1989), Water-colours, Drawings and Prints Magazine (1992), Printmaking Today (1996). Featured Artist, Art for Sale in The Guardian, 50 Wessex Artists (2007); Printmakers Directory; Printmakers Secrets. *Official Purchasers*: Government Art Collection; New York Public Library; Devizes Museum; Olivetti; J Walter Thomson; City of Norwich Museum; Edwin Young Collection; Paintings for Hospitals: Scottish Arts Council. *Works Reproduced*: The Response of Landscape - published 2010, edited by Silvie Turner. *Recreations*: sailing, walking, theatre, gardening, music. *Address*: Steeple Close, Milton, East Knoyle, Salisbury, SP3 6BG. *Email*: sally.mclaren@btinternet.com *Website*: www.sallymclaren.co.uk *Signs work*: "Sally McLaren" or "McLaren."

McLEAN, John, self taught painter; Brian Robertson Trust Award (2008); Lorne Award (1993); Arts Council Major Award (1980). *b*: Liverpool, 10 Jan 1939. *s of*: Talbert McLean. *m*: Janet. *Educ*: Reform Street School, Kirriemuir. *Studied*: St. Andrews University; Courtauld Institute. *Exhib*: over fifty solo shows worldwide. *Works in collections*: Tate Gallery, Scottish National Museum of Modern Art, Fitzwilliam Museum, Hunterian Collection, Glasgow University, Swindon, Southampton, Dundee, Glasgow, Edinburgh City and Whitworth Art Galleries, Boca Raton Museum of Art, USA; Yale Centre for British Art, USA. *Commissions*: Edinburgh University; Hairmyres Hospital, East Kilbride; Scottish Equitable H.Q; Strawberry Hill, London; Norwich Cathedral (stained glass). *Official Purchasers*: Arts Council of Great Britain, Scottish Arts Council, British Council. *Address*: 704 Mountjoy House Barbican London EC2Y 8BP. *Signs work*: "John McLean" or "J.M."

McLEAN, Mary, RMS (1994), PVPRMS, Hon. Retired RMS (2009); HS (1990); miniature painter in water-colour; Gold Bowl Hon. Mention (1997); Llewellyn Alexander Award (2000). *b*: Farnborough, Kent, 1944. *m*: John S. McLean. two *s*. one *d*. *Educ*: Marion Vian School, Beckenham. *Studied*: privately with Ronald Jesty, ARBA. *Exhib*: RA, RMS, Llewellyn Alexander (Fine Arts), The Market Cross Gallery, Sturminster Newton, Dorset, Japan and USA, Lannards Gallery, Billingshurst, Sussex, Hilliard Soc. Work in private collections. *Publications*: front cover illustration for specialist poultry magazine, Artist and Leisure Painter magazines, Royal Miniature Society, 100 years book. *Address*: 35 Old Station Gdns., Ashvale, Henstridge, Templecombe, Som. BA8 0PU. *Email*: marysmclean@btinternet.com *Website*: www.paintingsinminiature.com *Signs work*: "Mary McLean."

McLEOD, Ian, DA (Edin), RSW, FFCS; tutor in Life Drawing and Painting, Glenrothes College of Further Education. *Medium*: painter in acrylics on board. *b*: Port, Glasgow, 27 Jun 1939. *m*: Mary Rintoul. one *s*. one *d*. *Educ*: Burntisland Primary/Secondary School, Kirkcaldy High School. *Studied*: Edinburgh College of Art 1961-65; Regent Road Institute for Adult Education; Moray House College, Edinburgh. *Exhib*: 10 solo exhibitions; 3 two-person exhbns.; 56 group exhbns. *Works in collections*: Aberdeen University; Maclean Art Gallery, Greenock; Hamilton City Art Gallery, Ontario; IBM; The Arts in Fife, Fife Council; Edinburgh City Council; Dunfermline Museums and Art Galleries; private collections in the UK, France, Germany and USA. *Commissions*: portraits, drawings, photography for books and videos. *Publications*: Scottish Realism, Alan Bold; The Eye in the Wind: Contemporary Scottish Painting since 1945, Edward Gage; Glasgow League of Artists Yearbook 1978; Roots in the '80s', Emilio Coia, Stan Bell, Duncan MacMillan, Jim Waugh; Dictionary of Scottish Art and Architecture, Peter McEwan; The Paintings of Stephen Campbell, Duncan MacMillan; Scottish Art in the 20th Century, Duncan MacMillan. *Official Purchasers*: see work in collections. *Recreations*: reading, walking, music. *Clubs*: Scottish Arts Club, RSW. *Address*: 3 Craigkennochie Terrace, Burntisland, Fife, Scotland, KY3 9EN.

McMULLEN, Sue, DipAD; PG Cert. of RAS; PG Cert of Educ; lecturer at Salisbury College of Art (1974-1982); RA Schools Turner Gold Medal for Painting; freelance artist. *Medium*: painter in oil, draughtsperson in pen and ink, & mixed media artist. *b*: Yorks., 7 Oct 1948. *d of*: Patrick & June McMullen. *m*: Andrew. one *s*. one *d*. *Educ*: Hull High School for Arts and Crafts. *Studied*: Hornsey; Loughborough; Royal Academy of Arts Schools; The Victoria University of Manchester. *Exhib*: 70+ solo/mixed exhibitions since 1996, including RP (Mall Galleries 2003, 04), RSMA (2004) Art 4 Life, Christie's, Burlington Fine Art, The Athenaeum, Loggia Gallery, London; RA Summer Exhibs.; Upstream Galleries, London; Cathedral Church of St. Nicholas, Newcastle; Ferens Art Gallery, Hull; Crook, Co. Durham; Art Exhib. Grenville Court, Burnham, Bucks; The Westminster Gallery, London. *Works in collections*: slide collection Staffordshire University; private collections UK, USA, Australasia, Netherlands, Switzerland, Europe & Ireland. *Commissions*: Cedric Messina (BBC producer), Sq. Ldr. Revd. Davies, Dr. R. Langford, John Curtis (structural engineer), Christopher Seward, Producer. *Publications*: images for Thea P. Hilcox, Inspirational Art Books pub. Ava/Rotovision (2001), reviews and interviews in art publications and various newspapers. *Official Purchasers*: Cambridge Education Authority. *Principal Works*: Pen & ink drawings of the terrace and gardens, oil paintings of the Messina's London garden, The Tulgy Wood, & The Mallorn Trees. *Clubs*: R.A.S.A.A. *Misc*: Biography in The Dictionary of International Biography (2008), and in The World's Who's Who of Women (2009). *Address*: 36 Whenby Grove, Huntington, York YO31 9DS. *Email*: sue_mcmullen@hotmail.com *Website*: www.suemcmullen.citymax.com *Signs work*: "Sue Mc." and "Sue McMullen".

McNAUGHTON, Rachel Patricia. *Medium*: watercolour and pastel. *b*: 26 May 1952. *d of*: Mr & Mrs R.J.Wilson. *m*: Robert McNaughton. one *s*. one *d*. *Educ*: Leeds Girls High School, Eaton Hall Coll. of Ed. *Studied*: English Theatre Arts. *Exhib*: widely in Yorkshire and N.England; 1 solo show Harlow Carr (Harrogate), 6 solo shows at Wetherby (Yorks). *Publications*: 'Putting Colour into Watercolour' instructional video; 'From Flower to Watercolour' instructional video. *Works Reproduced*: cards & prints by Claughton Images, Wellington Place, Harewood Road, Leeds, www.claughtonphotography.co.uk. *Misc*: runs own classes/workshops in watercolour and pastel; Professional Associate of S.A.A. (Society for All Artists). *Address*: Stonethwaite, Scarsdale Ridge, Bardsey, Leeds, LS17 9BP. *Email*: rachelm@artbyrachel.co.uk *Website*: www.artbyrachel.co.uk www.minigalleryworld.com/Rachel_McNaughton

McNIVEN, Peter Alister, French Govt.Scholarship Cité International des Arts (Paris) (1986) returned (2009, 2011); NPG Portrait Award prizewinner. *Medium*: oil, watercolour, drawing. *b*: Edinburgh, 28 Feb 1952. *m*: Helen (BA Fashion, Kingston). two *s*. one *d*. *Educ*: George Watson's College, Edinburgh. *Studied*: Liverpool Coll. Art; Manchester School of Art. *Exhib*: RA, RP, NEAC, RCA, NPG; Hayward Gallery (British Drawing); Sunday Times Watercolour Competition; various commercial galleries London, South East, Edinburgh, Brittany. *Works in collections*: Queen's Collection, Windsor (O.M drawing); Imperial War Museum (8 portrait drawings); private collections. *Commissions*: Margaret Thatcher; John Nott for Imperial War Museum; Sir George Edwards O.M.; numerous private portrait. *Publications*: First Arts and Crafts with Helen McNiven (Four Art Books for Children). *Principal Works*: portrait, landscape and still life. *Recreations*: music, cooking, art history France/Italy. *Address*: Old Farm Barns, Stovolds Hill, Cranleigh, GU6 8LE. *Email*: pamcn@cranleigh.or *Signs work*: on back 'McNiven', oil & title & date.

McPAKE, John A., NDD, ATD, RE, IPP.MAFA; painter/printmaker working in acrylic painting and etching. *b*: Lancs., 1943. *s of*: Nicholas McPake. *m*: Anne Genner Crawford

M.A.F.A. *Educ*: St. Anselm's College, Birkenhead.*Studied*: Wallasey School of Art and Crafts (1961-65), Liverpool Polytechnic (1965-66), Birmingham Polytechnic (1966-67), Leeds Polytechnic (1977-78). *Exhib*: various group shows including RE's Bankside Gallery, RA Summer shows, Seoul Print Biennale (1986, 1988), MAFA, various one and two person shows, including "Two Artists" at St. George's Chapel, Windsor Castle; Central Art Gallery, Ashton Under Lyne, and The Portico Library and Gallery, Manchester. *Works in collections*: Bankside Gallery (RE's); Colin Jellicoe Gallery, Manchester; various public and private collections in the U.K. and abroad, including Westcote Bell, La Have, Nova Scotia; Cooper Gallery, Barnsley, S. Yorks. *Commissions*: various, including commemorative etching for "Wakefield in the '80's", Print Collector's Club, Commemorative Print, Leeds Art Fair. *Address*: 21 Ingbirchworth Rd., Thurlstone, nr. Sheffield S36 9QN. *Email*: john.mcpake1@btinternet.com *Signs work*: "John A. McPake."

McRAE, Jennifer, NEAC; BA (1st class hons), Higher Diploma Post Grad. Painting/Fine Art; Awards: Hunting Art Prizewinner (1st, 1998; 2nd 1992; Regional 2001), Singer & Friedlander (2nd, 2001 & 2002) etc. *Medium*: painter. *b*: 1959. *d of*: Evelyn & Douglas McRae. *m*: David McLean. one *d*. *Educ*: North Berwick High School. *Studied*: Grays School of Art. *Exhib*: solo: Anthony Hepworth Gallery, Bath (1992, 1994), Open Eye, Edinburgh (1993, 1996), Beaux Arts Bath (1997, 2001, 2003), Scottish Gallery (2000), Scottish Arts Club (2002); Bohun Gallery (2002); Group: Royal Scottish Academy, Edinburgh (1993), National Portrait Gallery (1995, 1996, 1998), Singer & Friedlander, Mall Galleries (1998, 2001, 2002), Discerning Eye, Mall Galleries (2002), National Print Exhibition, Mall Galleries (2003). Also Cricket Hill Assoc. NYC, USA, Aberdeen Art Gallery, Mall Galleries, Contemporary Art Fairs, London, etc. *Works in collections*: Scottish National Portrait Gallery, National Portrait Gallery, Aberdeen Art Gallery, Reading Museum, Clare Hall, Cambridge. *Publications*: Self Portraits by Women, NPG London. *Official Purchasers*: Dame Gillian Beer (Clare Hall Cambridge), Alan Caiger Smith (Reading Museum), Thelma Holt (NPG), Robin Jenkins, (SNPG), Tom Fleming (SNPG, drawing), Paul Anderson (Aberdeen Art Gallery) Michael Frayne (NPG) and many more. *Works Reproduced*: 'Double Exposure' repro. in 'Mirror Mirror'. *Principal Works*: Thelma Holt, portrait (NPG), Robin Jenkins (SNPG), Paul Anderson (Aberdeen Art Gallery), 'Double Exposure', self portrait, Alan Caiger Smith (Reading Museum). *Recreations*: printmaking, running, socialising, travelling, theatre, reading. *Clubs*: Chelsea Arts Club. *Misc*: awarded a scholarship place on the Drawing Year, The Prince's Foundation (2002-3), member of Edinburgh Printmakers since 1993. *Address*: Garden Flat, 3 Spencer's Belle Vue, Bath, BA1 5ER. *Website*: www.jennifermcrae.co.uk

McSLOY, Jane A.C., BA (Hons), MA, HS, SOFA (Assoc.). *Medium*: w/c on ivorine, w/c and gold leaf on vellum (miniatures). *b*: Leicester, 1962. *d of*: W. and R.F. McSloy. *Educ*: BA (English and History of Art) 1981-4 University College, London University; MA (Mediaeval Studies) 1992-4 Birkbeck College, London University; Montefiascone (medieval pigments) 2000. *Exhib*: London; Peterborough City Art Gallery; King's Lynn; Chichester; Wells; Tasmania; Austen Texas. *Works in collections*: University of Austen Texas (illumination to illustrate Gerard Hopkins' poem). *Commissions*: D & S Hughes, N. Bate, H. Lushington, D. Bromilow. *Publications*: Hopkins Quarterly. *Principal Works*: heavily detailed feline subjects and mediaeval illumination using gold and traditional materials. *Recreations*: running (1990 London Marathon), researching Victorian Papier Mache. *Misc*: works as gilder/ furniture restorer; teaches widely, including Geffrye Museum and Victoria and Albert Museum. *Address*: Studio 2F Cockpit Workshops, Cockpit Yard, Northington St., London WC1N 2NP. *Email*: jmcsloy@britishlibrary.net *Signs work*: J McS.

McWILLIAMS, Simon, RUA; BA (Hons) Fine Art; PgDip.RAS; Guinness Award RA; British Institute Award for Painting; award winner at RA, RUA and RHA, major award NI Arts Council, Gold Medal RWA. *Medium*: oil. *b*: Belfast. one *d*. *Studied*: RA Schools,

London. *Represented by*: Skotia Gallery, Santa Fe. *Exhib*: Art Space Gallery, London; RA; RUA; RHA; Cavehill Gallery; Hunting Art Prizes; John Martin Gallery, London; Katzen Gallery, Washington DC; Skotia Gallery, Santa Fe, New Mexico, Los Angeles. *Works in collections*: Arts Council NI; Guinness Plc; Ulster Museum; Queen's University; University of Ulster; AIB Bank; Ulster Television; The Haverty Trust; ESB, Irish Permanent; NI Govt. *Commissions*: ESB Ireland; National Self-Portrait Collection, Ireland; Centrum Kunstlicht in de Kunst (Eindhoven); UNISON for NI. *Publications*: Abstract Armature, Naughton Gallery, Belfast. *Official Purchasers*: Arts Council NI; Guinness; Ulster Museum; Queens University; as collections. *Works Reproduced*: Ulster Museum; Allied Irish Banks; Bank of Ireland; Naughton Gallery. *Principal Works*: 'Church' (Ulster Museum); 'Greyhound Track' (Allied Irish Bank); 'Scaffolding'. *Address*: 4 Grasmere Gardens, Belfast BT15 5EG N.Ireland. *Email*: info@simonmcwilliams.com *Website*: www.simonmcwilliams.com *Signs work*: 'Simon McWilliams'.

MEAD, Harriet Rebecca, SWLA (Assoc. 2000, Full Member 2001, Council 2004, President 2009); ING Discerning Eye 2011 winner Humphreys Prize and joint winner Founders Prize; 2007: Capmark Europe Art Award (Mall Galleries) Winner; 2006: ANF Young Artist 2004; Runner-up Capmark; 2001: Gavin Graham Gallery Award. *Medium*: welded sculptures of wildlife subjects in found objects or sheet steel. *b*: Tring, 2 Sep 1969. *Studied*: 1989 Foundation at Herts College of Art & Design (St.Albans); 1990-93 BA (Hons) Fine Art Sculpture, Norfolk Institute of Art & Design. *Exhib*: SWLA, Mall Galleries; Wildlife Art Gallery, Lavenham; Pinkfoot Gallery, Cley, Norfolk. *Works in collections*: Life sized public art pieces: Suffolk Trinity, Suffolk Showground (2006); Man & Horse, Dromore, Northern Ireland (2007); Red Deer Stag & Two Hinds, Euston Hall, Suffolk (2009); Irish Moiled Cow, Ranfurley House Museum, Northern Ireland (2012). *Publications*: The Great Fen (Artists in Nature for England), Chris Gerrard (2006, ISBN 1904078133). *Recreations*: riding my horses in local Breckland countryside. *Address*: End Cottage, 24 Westgate St, Hilborough, Norfolk, IP26 5BN. *Website*: www.harrietmead.co.uk *Signs work*: "HARRIET MEAD".

MEADOWS, Anthony William, ARMS (1984); self taught painter and illustrator in oil, wood engraving. *b*: Aldershot, 28 Aug 1957. *m*: Dawn Hardy (jeweller). *Educ*: Fanshawe School, Ware. *Exhib*: RA, RI, RMS and several one-man shows. *Works in collections*: Hertford Museum. *Address*: 27 Victoria Rd., Oswestry, Salop. SY11 2HT. *Signs work*: "A. W. Meadows".

MEDCALF, Gina, Italian Govt. Research Grant (1969); NEA Research Grant, New York (1983); NYSCA Research Grant, New York (1984); Pollock-Krasner Foundation Award (2009); Abbey Fellowship (2014). *Medium*: painter. *b*: Llandudno, 12 May 1941. *m*: Charles Hewlings. *Studied*: St. Martins School of Art (1965), Central School of Art and Design (1966-69). *Exhib*: Sound Shore Gallery, Portchester, New York (1987, 1992); Smith Jariwala Gallery (1990, 1991), Chelsea College of Art & Design Gallery (1999); The Cut Art Centre, Halesworth (2009); Chelsea Future Space (2009). Group: Serpentine Painting '73 (1973), Abstract Painting & Sculpture, Stockwell Depot (1986), John Moores 16 (1989), Benjamin Rhodes Gallery (1994), British Abstract Painting, Flowers East (2001). *Works in collections*: private and corporate, London and New York. *Address*: 64 Acre Lane, London SW2 5SP. *Email*: ginamedcalf@gmail.com *Website*: www.ginamedcalf.com *Signs work*: "JEAN M MEDCALF".

MEDHURST, Doreen, RMS (1993), SBA (1989), SWA (1989); Llewelyn Alexander Gallery Master Award Commendation of Excellence - six paintings 'Scenes of Rye' (April 2002), single miniature 'Haymaking' (April 2001); self taught painter in acrylic and oil. *b*: London, 5 Aug 1929. *d of*: Sydney Holmes. *m*: Cyril Medhurst. two *s*. *Educ*: Sydenham High School. *Exhib*: RMS, SBA, SWA, Llewellyn Alexander Gallery, Alfriston Gallery,

Elan Art Centre, Limpsfield Gallery, Cherry Creek Gallery, Oxted, Florum Exhibition, Sevenoaks, and several one-man shows. *Publications*: Greetings cards, Lings, "Penshurst, Kent". *Address*: c/o Mr T Medhurst, Old School House, 5 West Street, Hothfield, Kent TN26 1ET . *Signs work*: "D. Medhurst.".

MEDWAY, Sarah, BA (Hons). *Medium*: abstract painter in oil, watercolour, drawing, prints. *b*: Seaton Carew, Co.Durham, 9 Jul 1955. *d of*: Michael Hilborne-Clarke. *Partner*: Michael Heindorff. one *s*. *Studied*: after early career as ladies' shoe designer 'Sarah Medway Couture Shoes, Piccadilly & Knightsbridge': Chelsea School of Art, Byam Shaw School of Art (1991-94); ICA London (Modern Art Studies- Distinction). *Represented by*: Vertigo Gallery, Hoxton, London. *Exhib*: since 1994, 15 solo exhbns in London (Vertigo) and Milan (Vertigo), Thailand (Chateau de Bangkok) Bangkok, Magdeburg, Frankfurt and Heidelberg, Germany; over 100 group exhbns in the UK and abroad including RA Summer Exhbns; Vertigo Gallery London; Flowers East and Central, London; Tate Britain; South London Gallery; Bloomberg Space, London; Gallery Seven, Hong Kong; Schwetzingen Castle, Germany; Forum Galerie, Usingen; Stephen Lacey Gallery, London. *Works in collections*: numerous corporate collections, and public collections including Nord LB, Germany; Municipal Hospital, Brunswick, Germany; St.Thomas' Hospital; Paintings in Hospitals. *Commissions*: private commissions in UK, Thailand, New York, Belgium, Germany, Italy & Spain. *Works Reproduced*: in catalogues UK and Italy, and Catalogue Triangle Artists Workshop, New York. *Recreations*: theatre, opera, dance, walking, poetry and Shakespeare. *Clubs*: Groucho Club, London; Chelsea Arts Club, London; Soho House; Shoreditch House. *Address*: 509 Union Wharf, 23 Wenlock Road, London N1 7TD. *Email*: medwayart@aol.com *Website*: www.medwayart.com *Signs work*: 'S.Medway' (back of canvas).

MEEK, Elizabeth R., MBE, HPRMS, PPSWA, FRSA; portrait artist; Past President of Society of Women Artists (2000-2005); President Royal Society of Miniature Painters Sculptors & Gravers (2005-); Patron of The Society of Limners; Awards: winner, RMS Gold Memorial Bowl (1995); The Bell Award (1992, 1997), 2008 (best portrait in exhbn.); HS (1993, 1994) (best in exhbn. twice); RMS (1992, 1994) (runner-up for Gold Memorial Bowl, twice); RMS (1993) Gold Bowl hon. mention, The Mundy Sovereign Award (1995, 1999, 2004), Best Set RMS (1999), RMS (2002) Presidents Special Commendation, The Peter Charles Booth memorial Award (RMS, 2005), Daler Rowney Choice Award (2006); Barbara Tate Award for Best Oil, SWA (2004); Joyce Rowsell Award, Hilliard Society (2008), Anita Emmerich Award, RMS (2008), People's Choice SWA (2009); Bonhams Portrait Award, RMS (2009); Llewelyn Alexander Award, RMS (2009); Anthony J. Lester Art Critic Award (2010); The Prince of Wales Award for Outstanding Miniature Painting (2012 RMS); The Arturi Philips Award (2013 RMS). *Medium*: oil and pencil. *b*: London, 7 May 1953. *m*: Anthony J.Lester AICA, HonRMS, FRSA. two *d*. *Educ*: Beaconsfield High School. *Exhib*: RMS, Hunting/Observer, Mall Galleries, Smith Gallery, Yorks., L'Espace Pierre Cardin, Paris, British Painters, Barbican Centre, SWA, HS, Llewellyn Alexander Gallery, RA Summer Exhbn., Royal Portrait Society, Chelsea Art Society; one-woman show in Valletta, Malta, Africa '97 London, Soc. of French Miniature Artists, France, Jersey Arts Centre, Australia & others. *Works in collections*: National Museum of Fine Art, Valletta, Malta; HRH The Prince of Wales; HRH Princess Michael of Kent; The Clockmakers Museum; The Apothecaries Hall. *Publications*: 'The Techniques of Painting Miniatures' by Sue Burton; '100 Years of Miniatures' by Suzanne Lucas; Art in London, Antique Collecting, Londons Evening Standard, Artists & Illustrators. *Clubs*: Fellow Royal Society Arts. *Misc*: media: Interviewed on Radio 4's Woman's Hour, participator on BBC's 'Rolf on Art' and BBC2 'Flog It', BBC World Service, Radio Essex, PBS Television, America, Malta TV & radio, BBC2 Antiques Roadtrip. *Address*: Firle House, 75 Firle Road, Seaford, East Sussex BN25 2JA. *Email*: elizabethmeek@msn.com *Website*: www.elizabethmeek.com *Signs work*: "E.R. Meek.".

MEEKS, Sheila Mary, BA Honours Degree in Fine Art (1977), Post Graduate Certificate in Education (1981), Picker Travel Scholarship (to visit New York, 1977), Royal Bank of Scotland Award, Manchester Academy Show (1996). *Medium*: oil, watercolour, drawing. *b*: Stalybridge, 15 Mar 1955. one *s*. *Educ*: Harrytown Convent School, Romily, Cheshire; Foundation Course, Tameside College, Lancashire. *Studied*: Kingston University, Surrey (1974-77), Cyprus College of Art (1979), Manchester University (1981). *Exhib*: British Council, Nicosia, Cyprus; Castlefield Gallery, Manchester; 20thC British Art Fair (RCA); Chelsea Art Fair; Discerning Eye Exhibition, Mall Galleries, London; Cornerhouse 10th Anniversary Exhibition, Manchester; Royal Academy of Fine Arts Summer Show; Wendy J Levy Fine Art, Manchester; New Grafton Gallery, Barnes, London; Firbob & Peacock, Knutsford, Cheshire. *Works in collections*: Rutherston Collection, Manchester Art Gallery; Readers Digest Corporate Collection, New York. *Publications*: A Colourful Canvas. *Principal Works*: Generally, landscapes and still life paintings. *Address*: 26 Chamberlain Road, Heyrod, Stalybridge, Cheshire, SK15 3BR. *Email*: sheilameeks@fsmail.net *Website*: sheilameeks.com *Signs work*: "S M Meeks".

MEHTA, Sharda, Post Grad Fine Art. *Medium*: etching, collagraph, oil, watercolour, drawing, prints. *b*: Tanzania, 12 Jun 1937. *d of*: B.N. Uohara. *m*: A.K. Mehta. *Studied*: Byam Shaw School of Art. *Exhib*: many in London UK including Royal Academy, also in France. *Clubs*: Alumni Association. *Address*: 4 Fitzroy Close, Highgate, London N6 6JT. *Email*: shardamehtaarts@gmail.com *Signs work*: 'S.Mehta'.

MELAMED-ADAMS, Alicia, UA (1965), Gold medallist, Academie Italia Belle Arti el Lavore (1981), Art in Edinburgh (1984), Gallery Internationale, Paris - Artist in Oil (1984). *Medium*: oil. *b*: Poland, 26 Sep 1927. married. *d of*: Jzydore Goldschlag, oil mining engineer. one *s* *Studied*: (1960-63) St. Martin's School of Art. *Exhib*: Galleries: Solambo Paris (1988); Royal Academy Summer Exhibition (1988); The Mall Gallery (1990, 1991); Mermaid Theatre (1993); Intaglio Manchester (1993); Leicester City (1998); Patron Art-T Centre; Patron Bishop Harris of Oxford Holocaust Exhibition; Hanover Gallery Liverpool International (2000); Cork Street (2003); The Library at the University of Sheffield (2003); Sheffield University 'Soul Survivor'; 'The Art of a Holocaust Survivor' Northwood (2005); Imperial War Museum (2009); Poppies (Women and War) Oxford University (2014) . *Works in collections*: Ben Uri Gallery, The Imperial War Museum London. *Commissions*: Book covers:- Histories of the Holocaust - Stone; Justice and Politics After Second World War Vol 1 & 2 - Bardgett - Cesarani - Reinisch - Steinart. *Publications*: Editions Arts et Images du Monde (1989), British Contemporary Art (1993), Brit Art (2000), The Cambridge Blue Book (2005), Justice and Politics After Second World War (2012). *Official Purchasers*: Imperial War Museum, Ben Uri Gallery. *Works Reproduced*: 8 Paintings Justice and Politics After Second World War Chapter 13. *Principal Works*: Holocaust paintings, flowers, still-lifes, figures and painted pottery. *Address*: 17 Edmunds Walk, London N2 0HU. *Email*: cjadams1@o2.co.uk *Website*: www.aliciamelamed.com *Signs work*: "Alicia Melamed."

MELEGARI, Carl, BA (Hons) Illustration; I Trufeo VR Auto, Soave, Italy; X Mostra du Pitura, S Bonifacio, Italy; Vi Premio Internationale Citta di Soave, Italy. *Medium*: Oil. *b*: Denbigh, Wales, 9 Jan 1958. *m*: Jacqui. one *s*. one *d*. *Educ*: St Davids Comprehensive, Wrexham. *Studied*: Bristol Polytechnic (1977-1980). *Represented by*: Kooywood Gallery, Thompsons Gallery. *Exhib*: Galleries: Kooywood; Thompsons; Balman; Courcoux & Courcoux; Hadfield; Artifex; Ginger; Open Space; Gallerina; Architects; RWA; Artzu; Twenty Twenty; View; Innocent Fine Art; Claremont; Iona House; McAllister Thomas; The Salon des Nations, Paris; Art London; London Art Fair. *Works in collections*: Private; corporate. *Commissions*: Private; corporate. *Publications*: Include: The Artists Pocket Pallette, North Light; The Perfect Drawing, Harper Collins; The Sketching and Drawing Bible; The Encyclopedia of Drawing Techniques, Running Press. *Clubs*: pochade.co.uk; pleinairsociety.co.uk. *Address*: 23 Priory Court Road, Westbury-on-Trym, Bristol BS9 4DB.

Email: carlmelegari@tantraweb.co.uk *Website*: www.carlmelegari.co.uk *Signs work*: "C. MELEGARI".

MELLAND, Sylvia, RE; painter-etcher.. *b*: Altrincham. *d of*: Brian Melland, MD, MB (Lond). *m*: Brian Mertian Melland. one *s*. *Educ*: Altrincham Grammar School. *Studied*: Manchester College of Art, Byam Shaw, London, Euston Road, Central School (Graphics). *Exhib*: one-man shows, Wertheim and Jackson's Galleries, Manchester, Zwemmer Gallery, London, Galleria S. Stefano, Venice, Galerie Maurice Bridel, Lausanne, Galerie Bürdeke, Zürich, Agi Katz Fine Art, London. *Works in collections*: Rutherston Collection, S. London A.G., NY Library, Leeds A.G., Brighton Museum, Coventry Educ. Council, Twickenham Educ. Council, Greenwich Library, Ferens A.G., Hull, V&A, RA (Stott Foundation), Talmuseum des Münstertals, Switzerland, New Hall College, Cambridge and in private collections here and abroad. *Address*: 68 Bedford Gdns., London W8. *Signs work*: prints, "Sylvia Melland," oils, "S.M."

MELLOR, Daphne Elisabeth, BA, FA Dip., MM. *Medium*: oil, watercolour, design (and previously sculpture, fabric & thread, ceramics). *b*: Mansfield, Notts., 15 Sep 1927. *d of*: Mr & Mrs J Caldwell. *m*: (decd). one *s*. one *d*. *Educ*: Convent; Warwick and Solihull High Schools for Girls. *Studied*: Birmingham; London Poly, Architecture; Loughborough, Ceramics; Reading University, Fine Art. *Exhib*: Mall and Llewellyn Alexander Galleries, London; Bedford and Luton Libraries. *Works in collections*: Bedford Library; F.L. Bernard (France); I. Elliot (Zimbabwe); J. Faulkner (Texas); J. Sharp (Australia); G.D. Snedden (Texas); Mrs. Plotkin (USA); G. Woodfine (Bedford), and others. *Commissions*: Banners, cards, cartoons, designs, flip charts, house 'portraits', book illustrations, models, posters. *Publications*: book illustrations for H.Darbon. *Official Purchasers*: Bedford Library (painting); Denman College (model). *Works Reproduced*: magazine cover and tail piece (University magazine, 1947); posters, handbills, logos, housemarks. *Principal Works*: paintings; designs; fabric and thread. *Recreations*: crosswords, gardening, reading, piano, guitar, French. *Clubs*: MENSA, art, French. *Misc*: Won Competition for: Design for Model Youth Club (1944, aged 16); Christmas card (Bedford Art Society, 1986); Best in Show, Painting (Bedfordshire Music & Arts Club); logo for disabled sport. *Address*: 18b Park Avenue, Bedford, MK40 2LB. *Signs work*: "Mellor" (paintings); "Mel" (cards).

MELLOR, Mary, LLB, AKC (1961), Called to Bar (1962), BA Graphics (1984); artist in oil and mixed media; teacher. *b*: Swansea, 1939. *d of*: David M. Clement, CBE, FCA. *m*: His Hon. Judge David Mellor. two *d*. *Educ*: King's College, London, Inner Temple. *Studied*: Norwich School of Art and Design (1979-84). *Exhib*: Norwich Castle Museum, Advice Arcade Gallery etc. King's Lynn Eastern Open, Figurative Painting Prize (1996), Mall Galleries, NEAC (1998), New York Expo. (1999), Sheringham Little Theatre (1999); solo exhbn. Bergh Apton Sculpture Trail, Norfolk (3-Dimensional work). *Address*: The Old Hall, Mulbarton, Norwich NR14 8JS. *Signs work*: "Mary Mellor."

MELLOR, Pamela, FRSA; painter in oil, writer; Hon. Sec., Chelsea Art Society (1971-1978); Com., Armed Forces Art Society. *Medium*: oil. *b*: Sydney, Australia. *d of*: Capt. R C F Creer, RN retd. and Eulalie Henty. *m*: Lt.Col. Gerard Mellor, Royal Signals, retd. *Educ*: at home and abroad. *Exhib*: UA, RWS, RMS, Artists of Chelsea, Chelsea Art Soc., Leighton House, Ridley Art Soc., Armed Forces Art Soc., Dowmunt Gallery, Qantas Gallery. *Works in collections*: HRH The Prince of Wales, The Agent General of NSW, The Agent General of Queensland and other private collections. *Publications*: author, The Mystery of X5 (pub. William Kimber). *Official Purchasers*: HRH The Prince of Wales. *Clubs*: Huntingham Club. *Address*: 44 Stanford Rd., Kensington, London W8 5PZ. *Signs work*: "Pam Mellor."

MELROSE, Janet Margaret, BA (Hons); PGCE; RSW; SSA; VAS (professional member); shortlisted Aspect Prize 2008; Dorothy Duff Memorial Prize VAS. *Medium*: Watercolour, drawing. *b*: Edinburgh, 22 May 1964. *m*: Sott John Morris. two *d*. *Educ*: Royal

High School, Edinburgh. *Studied*: Edinburgh College of Art (1982-86); Moray House College of Education (1988-89). *Represented by*: Josie Eastwood Fine Art; The Union Gallery, Edinburgh. *Exhib*: RSA (2000-07); RSW (2000-12); SSA (2007-12); VAS (2007-12); RGI (2007-11); PAI (2005). *Works in collections*: Art in Hospitals; The Festival Fringe Society; The Bonham Hotel; Rt Hon Alistair and Mrs Darling. *Commissions*: The Royal Air Force; St Ninians Scottish Episcopal Church; Santa Maria Degli Angell, Tripoli, Libya. *Publications*: Drawing Birds, John Busby; Eight by Eight, Harlequin Press. *Official Purchasers*: Grampian Hospital Trust; Angus College Purchase Prize; *Works reproduced*: 'Snowy Owls', Drawing Birds by John Busby. *Recreations*: Horse riding; reading. *Address*: Halley's Yard, Earnbank Road, Crief PH7 3HL. *Email*: janetmelrose@btinternet.com *Website*: www.janetmelrose.com *Signs work*: "Janet M Melrose RSW".

MELVIN, Johanna Helga, BA Hons; Painting of the Month, Russell & Chappel. *Medium*: acrylic and cutout work, watercolour, drawing. *b*: London, 12 Jul 1951. *d of*: Ellen Sömme & John P. Dennis. *m*: Rod Melvin. three *s*. *Educ*: Convent of Our Lady; Convent of St.Agnes and St.Michael. *Studied*: Sir John Cass Faculty of Fine Art, London. *Exhib*: RA; Contemporary Art Society; Mall Galleries; Flowers East Gallery; Spitz Gallery; RCA; The Groucho Club; Stenersen Museum, Oslo; The Barbican; Whitechapel Library; Dover Street Arts Club. *Works in collections*: John Cass Faculty of Fine Art Print Collection; Groucho Club Collection, Colony Room. *Commissions*: Marie Lloyd Wing, Hackney Empire Theatre. *Publications*: Arty Magazine. *Clubs*: The Groucho Club. *Misc*: appointed Limited Editions Assistant at the Whitechapel Gallery, London (2006). *Address*: 20 St.Barnabas Road, Walthamstow, London E17 8JY. *Email*: johanna_melvin@hotmail.com *Website*: www.johannamelvin.com *Signs work*: 'Johanna Melvin'.

MENDELOW, Anne, BSc; artist in oil and pastel; gallery owner promoting Scottish artists. *Medium*: Pastel, oil and printmaking. *b*: Johannesburg, 1 Apr 1947. divorced. two *s*. one *d*. *Educ*: in S.Africa. *Studied*: Wits Pharmacy School (1964-69). *Exhib*: RGI, SAAC, and galleries in Edinburgh, Glasgow and England. *Works in collections*: private galleries in Edinburgh, Glasgow and England. *Recreations*: Bridge, photography. *Address*: Flat 4, 18/19 Adelaide Crescent, Hove, East Sussex BN3 2JF. *Email*: art@annemendelow.com *Website*: annemendelow.com *Signs work*: "Anne Mendelow."

MENDOZA, Edwin, portrait painter, landscape and still life paintings in the Impressionist/Expressionist styles, Matisse, Derain, Bonnard, Jawlenski, member of Federation of British Artists FBA. *Medium*: Oil painting on canvas. *b*: Alexandria, Egypt. *m*: Katherina. two *d*. *Studied*: Fontainbleu, France and St. Martin's School of Art. *Exhib*: in Spain, France, England, Scotland, USA and Canada. *Works in collections*: clients in USA, France, Malaysia, Switzerland, Canada. *Commissions*: Portraits in California, USA and England. *Principal Works*: In Malaysia, 6m x 2m. *Recreations*: Swimming. *Address*: Flat 1, 32 Abbotts Road, London EN5 5DP. *Email*: edwinmendoza_painting@yahoo.co.uk *Website*: www.mendoart.co.uk *Signs work*: "Mendoza".

MENDOZA, June, AO, OBE, RP, ROI, SWA (Hon. Mem.); portrait painter. *b*: Melbourne, Australia; musician parents. *m*: Keith Mackrell. one *s*. three *d*. *Educ*: Lauriston Girls' School, Australia. *Studied*: St. Martin's School of Art. *Exhib*: various galleries internationally, esp. London. *Works in collections*: government; HM Forces; industry; commerce; medicine; academic and legal professions; theatre; sport, and private collections internationally. Portraits include: HM The Queen; HRH Prince Charles; HRH Princess of Wales; HM Queen Mother; Baroness (Margaret) Thatcher; Sir John Major; Prime Ministers of Australia and Fiji; Presidents of Philippines and Iceland; series of musicians inc. Sutherland, Solti, Menuhin, Colin Davis, Mackerras Tippett. Group portraits include: House of Commons in Session; Council of Royal College of Surgeons; House of Representatives, Canberra. Hon DLitt Bath University; Hon.DLitt Loughborough

University; AO(Australia); lectures; TV, also Hon. Doctor of Open Univ. *Recreations*: music, theatre, travel. *Address*: 34 Inner Pk. Rd., London SW19 6DD. *Email*: june@junemendoza.co.uk *Website*: www.junemendoza.co.uk *Signs work*: "MENDOZA"

MENZIES, Gordon William, DA; Josef Sekalski Award for Printmaking; Head of Pottery Dept., Community Centre, Edinburgh; established Iona Gallery and Pottery, 1982 (Workshop/Gallery) with own ceramics, engravings, landscapes; specialising in paintings of Iona - Early 20th Century to Contemporary. *Medium*: etching, ceramics, watercolour, pastel. *b*: Motherwell, Scotland, 9 Jan 1950. *s of*: David M. Menzies, storekeeper. *m*: Fiona Menzies. one *s*. *Educ*: Dalziel High School, Motherwell. *Studied*: Duncan of Jordanstone College of Art, Dundee (1969-73) under Sheila Green, Ron Stenberg; Atelier 17, Paris (1974) under S. W. Hayter. *Exhib*: Edinburgh, Printmakers Workshop, Compass Gallery, Glasgow, Montpelier Art Institute, France, RSA, SSA, Edinburgh, City Art Centre, Edinburgh, many others within Edinburgh and surrounding area; Dundas St. Gallery, Edinburgh: 100 years of Iona Paintings (2002), Hebridean Odyssey (2003), Iona & The West (2004), An Eye for Iona (2006). *Publications*: books illustrated mainly within Children's Educational area. *Address*: Lorne Cottage, Isle of Iona, Argyll PA76 6SJ. *Email*: menzies@ionagallery.com *Website*: www.ionagallery.com

MEO de, P. (Pamela Synge): see DE MEO, P. (Pamela Synge).

MEREDITH, Julian Nelson, artist and printmaker. *b*: Bath, 4 Mar 1952. *s of*: Bernard Nelson Meredith, MA, ARIBA. *m*: Jane. three *d*. *Educ*: Clifton College. *Studied*: Exeter College of Art (1972, 1974). *Exhib*: RA Summer Exhbn. (1989), Henry Brett Galleries (1989), Natural History Museum London (1995), Cartwright Hall (1993), Mead Gallery (1984). *Works in collections*: V&A Museum, London, Birmingham University, Teesside Airport, Deutsche Bank. *Commissions*: RVI Hospital Newcastle, Ross-on-Wye Hospital. *Address*: Avondale House, Polmont, Falkirk FK2 0YF. *Signs work*: "J.Meredith."

MEREDITH, Norman, ARCA; illustrator; tutor University of Aberystwyth (1935) and St. Martin's School of Art; war service M. of A.P. (Farnborough). *s of*: Jane Ann Meredith. *m*: Violet Mary Brant. *Studied*: Liverpool College of Art and RCA; travelling scholar. *Exhib*: frequently at Chris Beetles Gallery, London SW1, since 1984. *Works in collections*: HRH The Duke of Gloucester, etc. Textiles for Moygashel, Crowson Fabrics; designs for Metal Box Co., greetings cards, gift wraps, nursery pictures for Brunott of Holland; nursery china. *Works Reproduced*: in Punch, Tatler, Bystander; books illus. most British publishers, strip cartoonist. *Misc:* Hobbies: Recording piano music, photography, travel, (two world tours). *Address*: The Elders, Epsom Rd., Ewell, Surrey KT17 1JT. *Signs work*: "NORMAN MEREDITH."

MERRICK, Tony, DipAD Fine Art (1st Hons); HDA (Chelsea); provisional member of Royal institute of Oil Painters. *Medium*: Oil; drawing; pastels. *b*: Castleford, Yorkshire, 18 Mar 1948. *Partner*: Homera Jennings. three *d*. *Educ*: Castleford Grammar School. *Studied*: Hull College of Art, DipAD Fine Art (1st Hons) (1970); Chelsea School of Art (1972-74); HDA (1974) (head of painting - Ian Stephenson). *Exhib*: Young Contemporaries, Whitworth Art Gallery, Manchester (1972); Whitechapel Gallery (1973); Museum of Modern Art, Oxford (1974); Hawker Gallery, Amersham; ROI Mall Galleries; Pastel Society, Mall Galleries. *Works in collections*: Private/corporate (including Gretchen Nail, Georgia, USA); The late Leo Crawley (novelist); Hayley Mills (actress). *Official Purchasers*: Cambridge Econometrics Board. *Principal Works*: Oils, elected provisional member of ROI (2008). *Recreations*: Demonstrates at 'Art in Action', Waterperry, Oxford. *Misc*: Demonstrates for art societies/residential painting centres (Pear Tree Farm, Derbyshire). *Address*: 5 Norwood Close, Twickenham TW2 5EX. *Email*: anthony.merrick@yahoo.com *Website*: www.tonymerrick.com *Signs work*: "M".

MERRILLS, David, NDD, ATD, DAE, RCA (Royal Cambrian Academy, 1997). *b*: Rotherham, Yorks, 9 Feb 1933. *s of*: Gilbert Merrills. *m*: Rona. two *s*. *Studied*: Rotherham/Sheffield/Cardiff Colleges of Art (1973). *Represented by*: Royal Cambrian Academy. *Exhib*: throughout North Wales: Denbigh, Rhyl, Llanbedwrog, Theatre Clwyd Mold, Llangollen; St. David's Cardiff. *Works in collections*: in France, Australia, America, UK. *Address*: Ty Isaf, Bodfari, Denbigh, Denbighshire LL16 4DD.

MERRYLEES, Andrew, RSA, B.Arch, DipTP, RIBA, FRIAS, FCSD, FRSA, hon. Prof. of Arch. University of Dundee; architect, Hypostyle Architects. *b*: 13 Oct 1933. *m*: Maie. two *s*. one *d*. *Studied*: Glasgow. *Commissions*: University Bldgs. at Edinburgh, Heriot-Watt, Dublin, Liverpool, Newcastle and Aston, Birmingham, Scottish HQ for Automobile Association, sorting office for Post Office, National Library of Scotland, British Golf Museum at St. Andrews, Motherwell Heritage Centre, and Dundee Science Centre. *Clubs*: Scottish Arts. *Misc*: Awards: Student Senior Prize, Student Life Drawing Prize, R.I.B.A. Bronze Medal, Saltire Award, Civic Trust Award, Art in Architecture Award, R.S.A. Gold Medal, Concrete Award, Sconul Award. *Address*: 204 Bonkle Rd., Newmaws, Lanarkshire ML2 9AA. *Email*: amer@hypostyle.co.uk

MESSER, Peter John Easton, Chichester Art Prize (1997). *Medium*: tempera. *b*: Brighton, E.Sussex, 28 Feb 1954. *s of*: John & Patricia Messer. *m*: Margaret Pethick. two *s-s*. *Educ*: Purley County Grammar School; Lewes Priory School. *Studied*: Brighton Polytechnic Faculty of Art and Design (now Univ. of Brighton). *Exhib*: RA; NEAC; Hunting Prizes; Garrick Milne; Star Gallery, Lewes. *Works in collections*: University of Brighton; House of Lords. *Commissions*: various mural commissions for East Sussex Hospitals; 'The Book of Sussex Revelations' - 12 paintings for handmade book. *Publications*: 'The Book of Sussex Revelations' (published to accompany the above); 'On the Way to Work' - The Lewes Paintings of Peter Messer. *Official Purchasers*: House of Lords; University of Brighton. *Recreations*: playing guitar, growing vegetables. *Clubs*: Commercial Square Bonfire Society (CSBS). *Address*: 5 Market Lane, Lewes, E.Sussex BN7 2NT. *Email*: peter.messer1@btinternet.com *Signs work*: 'Peter Messer'.

MICHAEL, Colin, BA (Hons), NS, UA; D&AD Award (1986); Winner Aya Broughton Award (2004); The London Group - Albert Irvin RA Award (2009). Hon. Treasurer for National Society of Painters, Sculptors and Printmakers. *Medium*: mixed media. *b*: Bulawayo, 6 Nov 1959. *s of*: Eric Alfred Fuller. *Educ*: Churchill School. *Studied*: Ravensbourne College of Art (1977-81); Slade Post-graduate (1993-99). *Represented by*: londonart.co.uk. *Exhib*: Gallery 47, London (solo, 1994, 95, 97, 98); Candid Arts (1998, 99); Gallery 17, Beckenham (1998-2007); Blackheath Gallery (2004, 2006); RA Summer Exhbn (selected 1994); Oxo Tower (2005); The Art Connection, Eton (2005); Stark Gallery (2005); Picture Room, Dulwich (2005-08); Menier Gallery (2006-2014); London Underground (2009). *Works in collections*: private collections - Karen Squibb-Williams (Barrister), Viscount Francois Dumonteil-Lagreze, Andrew Scott (Architect), Doctor Laura Gallo. *Commissions*: BP, Canon, Matra-Marconi, Amdahl, Midland Bank, Bromley Arts Council, Dulwich Life magazine. *Clubs*: Friends of the Royal Academy, National Society, The Arts Club London. *Address*: 161 Village Way, Beckenham, Kent, BR3 3NL. *Email*: colinmichael@btconnect.com *Website*: www.colinmichael.wix.com/colinmichael *Signs work*: 'Colin Michael'.

MICHIE, David Alan Redpath, OBE (1997); painter; Prof. Emeritus, Heriot Watt University (1991); Head, School of Drawing and Painting, Edinburgh College of Art (1982-90); Appointed Honorary Fellow Edinburgh College of Art (2009). *b*: St. Raphael, Var, France, 30 Nov 1928. *s of*: James Michie. *m*: Eileen Michie (decd). two *d*. *Educ*: Hawick High School. *Studied*: painting: Edinburgh College of Art (1946-1953), Italy (1953-1954). *Exhib*: one-man shows, Mercury Gallery, London (9 exhibitions 1967-1999), Mercury

Gallery, Edinburgh (1986), Lothian Region Chambers (1977), The Scottish Gallery, Edinburgh (1980, 1994, 1998, 2003, 2009), Kasteel de Hooge Vuursche, Netherlands (1991); Scott Gallery, Hawick (2009); Scottish Art Club, Edinburgh (2010); Michie Family, Scottish Gallery (2012); The Border Boys, Tweeddale Gallery, Peebles (2013). *Works in collections*: HM The Queen, Scottish National Gallery of Modern Art, Royal Scottish Academy, Royal West of England Academy, Fleming Collection. *Misc*: music, gardening. *Address*: 17 Gilmour Rd., Edinburgh EH16 5NS. *Signs work*: "David Michie."

MIDDLETON, Michael, ARWS (2013), ARE (1981), RE (1986), DipAD (1971), HDA.(1974); lecturer/painter/printmaker in oil, water-colour, etching, woodcut; teaches printmaking, art history, Colchester Inst. School of Art and Design. *Medium*: acrylic, oil, etching, watercolour. *b*: Louth, Lincs., 25 Jun 1950. *s of*: Roy Middleton. *Partner*: Debbie Ayles. four *s*. *Educ*: Heron Wood, Aldershot. *Studied*: Farnham School of Art (1966-68), Sheffield Polytechnic (1968-71), Chelsea School of Art (1973-74). *Exhib*: RA, RE, and several one-man shows. *Works in collections*: Harlow Town Corp., RE, Ashmolean Museum Oxford, Fitzwilliam Museum Cambridge. *Commissions*: Print Collectors Club. *Works Reproduced*: Printmakers The Directory, Printmakers Secrets, Printmaking Today. *Address*: 18 Woodfield Drive, West Mersea, Colchester, Essex, CO5 8PX. *Email*: mike.middleton@btinternet.com *Website*: www.mikemiddletonartist.co.uk *Signs work*: "M. Middleton."

MIDDLETON, Nicholas. *Medium*: oil, etching. *b*: London, 10 Mar 1975. *s of*: Michael Middleton. *Educ*: Wanstead High School. *Studied*: London Guildhall University; Winchester School of Art . *Exhib*: RA Summer Exhbns (2000, 01, 02, 05, 07, 08, 09); BP Portrait Award (2004, 05); John Moores 23, John Moores 24, Walker Art Gallery (2004, 2006); Discerning Eye 2004, The Mall Galleries; Defining the Times, Milton Keynes Gallery (2000); Oil and Silver, Hoopers Gallery (2007); Space Invaders, Liquid Gallery (2008); Originals '09, Mall Galleries. *Commissions*: numerous paintings for Royal Caribbean Cruise Liners 'Eagle' series (1998-2003). *Works Reproduced*: John Moores 23 Exhibition Catalogue (2004); BP Portrait Award Catalogue (2004 & 05); John Moores 24 Exhibition Catalogue (2006). *Address*: 53 Montague Road, Hackney, London E8 2HN. *Email*: info@nicholasmiddleton.co.uk *Website*: www.nicholasmiddleton.co.uk *Signs work*: infrequently as possible.

MIDGLEY, Julia, RE (2005), DipAD (1969); Manchester Academy of Fine Arts (Vice President, 1994-96); Reader, Liverpool School Art & Design (1997-2013 ret'd). *Medium*: drawing, printmaking, reportage. *b*: 1948. *m*: J. Godfrey. two *s*. *Studied*: Northwich School of Art (1965-66), Manchester College of Art and Design (1966-69). *Exhib*: Manchester Academy annually since 1979, RA (1983, 1986, 1987, 1997, 2005, 2009, 2010, 2013), Business A.Gs. (1981, 1982, 1983, 1985), New Academy (1987-94), Chelsea Arts Club; RE, Bankside Gallery, London, annually since 1990. *Works in collections*: national, international, public and private. *Commissions*: corporate and public. *Publications*: 'Drawn from Experience', 'Granada Sketchbook', 'Blackpool Pleasure Beach - A Palette of Life', 'Amphitheatre'. *Official Purchasers*: Collections inc: Museum Science and Industry; Wellcome Trust; Royal College Surgeons; Whitworth Art Gallery; University of Liverpool. *Recreations*: tennis. *Clubs*: Chelsea Arts. *Misc*: member: Artists & Archaeology; Reportager, RE. *Address*: 79 School Lane, Hartford, Cheshire, CW8 IPG. *Email*: julia@juliamidgley.co.uk *Website*: www.juliamidgley.co.uk *Signs work*: "Julia Midgley."

MIERS, Christopher John Penrose, RBA (1986); artist in oil and tempera; Secretary, The Arts Club (1986-90); Trustee, RBA (1999-2005). *b*: 26 Sep 1941. *s of*: Lt. Col. P R.P. Miers, RA and Mrs M.T. Miers. *m*: Liza. one *s*. one *d*. *Educ*: Wellington College and R.M.A. Sandhurst. *Exhib*: RA, RBA, NEAC, The Minories, Colchester (1964), Ansdell Gallery, Kensington (1967, 1968), Fortescue Swann, Brompton Rd. (1976), C.D. Soar & Son,

Launceston Pl. (1986, 1988), Sally Hunter Fine Art (1990, 1993, 1995), Mall Galleries (1991), Jerram Gallery (1994, 1996), Grosvenor House (1996), Tryon & Swann Gallery (1998), Rafael Valls Ltd (2000, 2002, 2004, 2006, 2008) Oakham Contemporary 2010. *Works in collections*: Imperial War Museum, House of Commons, Sultan of Oman, Provost of Eden. *Clubs*: Arts, Chelsea Arts, Fadeaways. *Address*: 114 Bishop's Mans., Bishop's Park Rd., Fulham, London SW6 6DY. *Website*: www.christopher-miers.co.uk *Signs work*: "C. MIERS."

MILBURN, Elizabeth Mary. *Medium*: acrylics, oil, watercolour, drawing, prints. *b*: Southport, 25 Apr 1962. *m*: David. one *s*. one *d*. *Studied*: BSc (Eng) Electrical Engineering, Imperial College, London (1980-83). *Exhib*: Solo exhibitions: "French Life", Corn Exchange, Newbury; various collective exhibitions & galleries including Newbury Open Studios (2005, 06, 08, 09, 10, 12); Bath Society Exhibition (102nd). *Works in collections*: West Berkshire Community Hospital (Cafe in the Old Town, Cafe in the Shaded Corner). *Commissions*: various. *Misc*: known as Liz Milburn, largely self-taught, influenced by Mitch Waite at Maison des Arts while living in France (2001-03). *Address*: "Timberscombe", Burdens Heath, Upper Bucklebury, Reading RG7 6SX. *Email*: liz@lizmilburn.co.uk *Website*: www.lizmilburn.co.uk *Signs work*: "LM".

MILES, Arran Elizabeth, BA (Hons) 1973; artist in charcoal, pastel and inks (drawings). *b*: Southampton, 28 Mar 1951. *m*: Steve Tapper. one *s*. one *d*. *Studied*: Leicester School of Art (1969-70), St. Martin's School of Art (1970-73). *Exhib*: regularly with Jelly Leg'd Chicken, Reading; Wine Street Gallery Devizes; SWA Westminster Gallery; Marlborough Festival Open Studios; Newbury Open Studios; Corn Exchange, Newbury; Mosaic Gallery, Buxton, Mall Galleries, London. *Works Reproduced*: greetings cards, postcards, life drawings at Pennyhill Park Hotel, Bagshot. *Address*: 5 Forge Cottages, Froxfield, Marlborough, Wilts. SN8 3LE. *Email*: arranmiles28@yahoo.co.uk *Signs work*: "AEMiles".

MILLER, Andrew Peter, SIAD. *Medium*: oil, watercolour, drawing. *b*: Totnes, Devon, 26 Apr 1958. one *s*. *Studied*: Eastbourne College of Art (1978-80). *Represented by*: Brownstone Gallery, Modbury, Devon. *Exhib*: D'Art Gallery, Dartmouth; Walker Gallery, Honiton; Cove's Quay, Salcombe. *Commissions*: Royal Marines: Stone House, Plymouth; Lymstone, 30 Commando, 40 Commando, 45 Commando; Scots Dragoon Guards; London Scottish. *Publications*: Herrick 14 - Delivering the Offer - Royal Marines. *Works Reproduced*: Military paintings reproduced - Royal Marines. *Recreations*: tennis, gardening. *Clubs*: Avon Vale Tennis Club. *Address*: 6 Fore Street, Ugborough, Nr. Ivybridge, Devon PL21 0NP. *Email*: artistandrewmiller@gmail.com *Website*: www.andrewmillerartist.com *Signs work*: "Andrew Miller".

MILLER, Colin James, ARBS. *Medium*: sculpture in marble, stone, bronze, olive wood; oil, drawing. *b*: Simla, India, 9 Oct 1943. *s of*: Bunty Miller (painter). *m*: Diana. one *s*. one *d*. *Educ*: Nautical College, Pangbourne. *Studied*: self-taught. *Exhib*: one-man: Lasson Gallery; Kunsthandel Ina Broerse, Amsterdam; British Council, Athens (1979-81); Phoenix Gallery, Lavenham, Suffolk (1988); Gallery Bonneland Odder Denmark (1994, 2000). Group: RA Summer Exhbn (1973, '74, '82); Le Salon Societe des Artists Francais, Paris; Gallery Madison 90, New York (1985). *Works in collections*: The Froehlich Foundation, and many private collections around the world. *Commissions*: Property Partnerships plc; Allied Lyons; Norwich Union; Wyndham Investments; Jersey Museum; Bedford Maternity and Paediatric Hospital. *Publications*: Oakham School, Rutland. *Recreations*: diving, travelling. *Clubs*: RBS. *Address*: Sea Grass, Saxlingham Road, Blakeney, Holt, Norfolk NR25 7PB . *Email*: colin@colin-miller.co.uk *Website*: www.colin-miller.co.uk *Signs work*: 'COLIN MILLER'.

MILLER, David, RBA (1994), NDD (1958); artist in oil; ILEA Head of Dept. for Art in AEI (1971-87). *b*: Belfast, 25 Feb 1931. divorced. one *s*. one *d*. *Educ*: Trinity College,

Glenalmond, Perthshire. *Studied*: Polytechnic School of Art, Regent St. London (1954-60, Norman Blamey, RA, Sir Lawrence Gowing CBE, RA). *Exhib*: RA, RBA, RP, New Soc. of Portrait Painters, and other mixed exhbns. *Works in collections*: private collections. *Commissions*: many portrait commissions. *Address*: First Floor Flat, 76 Auckland Hill, West Norwood, London SE27 9QQ. *Email*: dmillerrba@aol.com *Signs work*: "DAVID MILLER."

MILLER, Ingrid, printmaker, painter in oil, etching, drypoint, acrylic, water-colour. *b*: Copenhagen, 1940. *d of*: William Tougaard. *m*: R.G. Miller, printmaker. *Educ*: Copenhagen University. *Studied*: Malmö Printmaking School. *Exhib*: RA, RSA, Mall Galleries, Leighton House Gallery, Guildhall Gallery, RA Copenhagen, National Museum Gdansk, Wainö Aaltonen Museum Finland, Liljevalchs Stockholm, Print Triennales Malmö and Gothenburg. International Print Biennales: Cracow, Ljubljana, Rockford, Horgen, Cadaques, Varna, Maastrich, Biella, Berlin, Fredrikstad; Museums: Kalmar, Eksjö, Kristianstad, Vetlanda, Växjö; Gallery Loftet, St.Petersburg; Bornholm Museum, Vejle Museum. *Works in collections*: Cabo Frio, Brazil; Swedish States Arts Council; Kalmar Museum; Vetlanda Museum. *Publications*: 'Ronald and I'; 'Mountains'. *Clubs*: Swedish and Danish Federations of Printmakers, G.S., D.G. and K.R.O., S.K., K.K.S., F.S.K., Grant Swedish State. *Address*: Bolmen, 34194 Ljungby, Sweden. *Email*: bolmen.grafik@telia.com *Website*: millerkonst.se *Signs work*: "Ingrid Miller."

MILLER, Michael John, John Laing Calendar Award. *Medium*: oil, watercolour, acrylic. *b*: Kingston, 14 Nov 1940. *s of*: Leonard Miller. *m*: Sheila Mary (Lawlor). one *s*. one *d*. *Studied*: Epsom School of Art; St.Martin's, London. *Exhib*: Royal Academy; Mall Galleries; NEAC; Royal Society of Oil Painters; John Neville Gallery, Canterbury. *Works in collections*: John Laing (private collection). *Commissions*: Cricket mural-Royal Marsden Hospital, Surrey. *Publications*: RA Summer Exhbn Catalogue. *Official Purchasers*: John Laing (calendar). *Works Reproduced*: RA; Surrey Life Magazine. *Recreations*: musician: banjo and guitar player. *Address*: 22 Court Farm Avenue, Ewell, Surrey KT19 0HF. *Signs work*: 'M.Miller'

MILLER, Ronald George, printmaker, painter in etching, mezzotint, engraving, acrylic; sculptor in wood. *b*: London, 1938. *s of*: George Frederick Miller. *m*: Ingrid Miller, printmaker. *Educ*: Haverstock Hill Secondary School. *Studied*: Ingrid Miller's Print Workshop, Ljungby, Sweden. *Exhib*: RA, RSA Edinburgh, International Print Biennales in Ljubljana, Krakow, Grenoble, Cadaques, Varna, Biella, Maastrich, Majdanek, Frechen, Berlin, Fredrikstad; museums in Kristianstad Vetlanda, Kalmar, Växjö, Liljevalchs, 4th National Exhbn. of British Prints, Grundy Gallery, Blackpool; Royal Academy of Art, Stockholm, Xylon, France. *Works in collections*: Majdanek Museum Poland, Museums in Växjö, Vetlanda, Swedish Arts Council. *Clubs*: Federation of Swedish Printmakers, G.S., K.R.O., S.K., Grant Swedish State. *Address*: Bolmen, 34194 Ljungby, Sweden. *Email*: bolmen.grafik@telia.com *Website*: ronaldmiller.se *Signs work*: "Ronald Miller."

MILLER, Rosemary, SWA; winner, Anthony J Lester Art Critic Award (SWA, 2005); winner, Derwent Artist Award (2005, 2007); Rosemary & Co Award (SWA, 2011). *Medium*: watercolour. *b*: Leicester. *m*: Colin John Miller. one *s*. one *d*. *Educ*: Ranelagh Grammar School, Bracknell. *Studied*: self taught. *Exhib*: RSMA, RI, SWA. *Works in collections*: internationally. *Clubs*: Maritime Art Group. *Address*: 1 Pilgrims Cottages, Wood Lane, Sale, Farnham, GU10 1HS. *Email*: rosemarym-art@tiscali.co.uk *Signs work*: 'Rosemary Miller'.

MILLER, Roy Cooper, SEA; AAEA (American Academy of Equine Art); Presidents Medal SEA (2005). *Medium*: oil, drawing, prints, sculpture. *b*: Manchester, 8 Sep 1938. *s of*: Tom & Alice Miller. *m*: Judy. two *d*. *Educ*: St.Margaret's Central School, Manchester. *Studied*: Manchester Regional College of Art (4 years, 3 evenings a week); began work at

14 in commercial art studio, Manchester. *Represented by*: Equestrian Art Ltd; Sally Mitchell Fine Art; Obsidian Gallery; Lawrie Art; self. *Exhib*: One-man exhibitions: London, USA, Canada, Australia; SEA, Mall Galleries, London; AAEA Kentucky, USA. *Works in collections*: many paintings in private collections worldwide. *Commissions*: Lester Piggott gates, Epsom Racecourse; paintings, Royal Hong Kong Jockey Club; Kempton Park; Coaching Club of Great Britain; Canadian Jockey Club; Victoria Racing Club. *Official Purchasers*: as above. *Works Reproduced*: several famous racehorses and jockeys. *Principal Works*: Commissions for owners, breeders, trainers, jockeys, worldwide. *Recreations*: golf, travel, eating out, visiting galleries, theatre. *Address*: 11 Vaughan Avenue, Tonbridge, Kent, TN10 4EB. *Signs work*: "Roy Miller"

MILLER, Shannon, Rural career awards (1999), Cosmopolitan Woman of the Year award, National Acrylic Painters Assoc. member, Equestrian Society honorary member. *Medium*: acrylic. *b*: Redruth, Cornwall, 1963. *d of*: Patti Slee and Frank Miller. *Educ*: Queen Elizabeth College, Crediton, Devon. *Represented by*: Womens Rural Workshop; Duncan Keith; President of Grasslands Assoc., John Vincent MA, Timney D Fowler Mills Photographer. *Exhib*: Radar Galleries Washington USA, 'Quo Vadis' Phillipines (resident artist); Blue Pineapple, Florida; The Plough Art Centre; Queen's Theatre Barnstaple; Burton Gallery Devon; St Ives Tate, Cornwall; works on 2 year tour for Royal Agricultural Society 'Celebration of the Farmyard'; "Dog Dancer" touring show of lifesize dog portraits (2014). *Works in collections*: of Rebecca Bernt (Germany), Elsa Bennatar (London); Custance International; Bank Chambers, Geneva; Min Gita, Japan. *Commissions*: National Farmers Union and Royal Agricultural College; Salar Hatherleigh and Torrington Town Councils. *Publications*: 'Celebration of the Farmyard' (2001); Shan Miller Dotcom; 'Portrait of Torrington'. *Official Purchasers*: Timney D'Fowler-Mills, Noel Edmunds, the Le Bons, Jean Lethbridge, National Botanical Society, Tracy Merrifield, Women's Rural Workshop. *Works Reproduced*: 'The Farmyard', 'Charolais Bull'. *Principal Works*: 'The Diner', 'The Hand that Feeds', 'Soho' reworked, as 'Yr Place or mine' 2000, 'Everything I've E ver Done', 'Jumpin' Jack'. *Clubs*: Lepa Club, Taddiport Torrington, Country Club UK, St. James Club London, Chapelles. *Address*: Loft Studios, Limers Hill, Torrington, Devon, EX38 8AX. *Website*: www.shanmiller.com *Signs work*: S F Miller.

MILLINGTON, Terence, painter/printmaker in oil, water-colour, etching. *b*: B'ham, 20 Oct 1942. *s of*: George Millington. *m*: Patricia. one *s*. *Educ*: Moseley Secondary School of Art. *Studied*: painting: B'ham College of Art (1958-63), and printmaking at Manchester College of Art (1965-66). *Exhib*: many group and one-man exhbns. throughout Europe and the USA. *Works in collections*: various private and public including Tate Gallery, and V&A. *Commissions*: Royal Mail stamp commission 1997 (100th Anniversary of sub post offices). *Publications*: Editions of etchings regularly published by CCA London and Behr-Thyssen Ltd. New York. *Address*: c/o GPC, Unit 16, Griffin Mill, Thrupp, Nr. Stroud GL5 2AZ. *Website*: www.terencemillington.net *Signs work*: "Terence Millington.".

MILLIS, Susan M., SWA (1987), SEA (1995), ARMS (1997), MASF (1998); BA Hons First Class 2002; pyrographic artist specializing in wildlife, equestrian and pictorial subjects on hand turned wooden paper-weights, pomanders, plaques, jewellery, paper and blowtorch fire paintings, also works in other media. *b*: Tidworth, Hants., 14 Nov 1953. *d of*: Major W.G. Lemon, ARCM psm, RE (decd.). *m*: Gareth Hughes Millis. one *s*. one *d*. *Studied*: De Montfort University Lincoln, conservation and restoration; PhD student 2005-at BCUC. *Exhib*: RMS, SWA, SEA, MASF annually. Work in private collections worldwide. *Publications*: A Burning Art (Popular Crafts, May 1989); Pyrography: A Guide (SSCR Journal, Nov.2004). *Clubs*: Fellow of the Royal Society for the encouragement of Arts Manufacturers and Commerce, member of Institute for Conservation of Historic and Artistic works. *Address*: 26 Doglands Farm, Newtoft, Market Rasen Lincs. LN8 3NG. *Email*: smmillis@hotmail.com *Signs work*: "S.M. Millis."

MILLMORE, Mark Alexander, RE, BA (Hons) Fine Art; artist in etching, painter in oil and water-colour - computer art. *b*: Shanklin, I.O.W., 13 Jan 1956. *Studied*: Falmouth School of Art (1977-80, Prof. Lionel Miskin). *Exhib*: CCA Galleries, and around the UK (1990-95); mixed shows: Japan, USA, Sweden, Taiwan, Australia, Spain, Canada, Kenya and the UK. *Works in collections*: Ashmolean Museum, Habikino City Hall Japan, Crown Court, Bristol, Victoria A.G. Bath, Kanagawa Prefectural Gallery Japan, Auburn University Contemporary Art Collection USA, International Centre for Wildlife Art Gloucester. *Publications*: 1990: 'Working with Etching' Artists& Illustrators Magazine; 1992: 'Ideas for Images' The Magazine for The International Collector of Water-colours, Drawings & Prints; 1996: 'Medi8or Magic' Pc Answers, 'Birds, Beasts & Fish' Multimedia Cd Rom, 'From Paint to Pixels' Pc Answers; 1997 & 98: Monthly column in Web Masters (Paragon Publishing); Editor of 'Printworks Magazine', Mark Millmore's Ancient Egypt, www.discoveringegypt.com. *Works Reproduced*: 2001-Discovering Ancient Egypt CD ROM; 2003-The Ancient Egyptian Print Studio. *Clubs*: Fellow, Royal Soc. of Painter-Printmakers. *Misc*: Theatre designer: Stinkfoot, a comic opera by Vivian Stanshall (Bristol 1985, London 1988); Rawlinson Dogends, starring Vivian Stanshall (London 1991), Global Art Director for Microgystics Inc (2000), Director for Eyelid Productions Ltd (2002). *Address*: Turvey House, Coldwells Road, Holmer, Hereford HR1 1LH. *Email*: mark@markmillmore.com *Website*: www.eyelidproductions.co.uk *Signs work*: "Millmore."

MILLNER, Etienne Henry de la Fargue, FRBS; President, SPS. *Medium*: figurative sculptor in plaster and clay for bronze. *b*: Penang, Malaysia, 15 Jan 1954. *m*: Mary Castle. one *s*. two *d*. *Educ*: Stowe School. *Studied*: Goldsmiths' College (Ivor Roberts-Jones, CBE, RA), RA Schools. *Represented by*: Fine Art Commissions Ltd, Portraits, Inc., Cadogan Contemporary. *Exhib*: RA Summer Shows (1979, 1982, 1984, 1985, 1986, 1988), NPG 'New Faces' (1987), Chelsea Harbour (1993), Cadogan Gallery Summer Show (1993); one-man show Cadogan Contemporary (1994). SPS Annual Exhbn. (1995-2012), People's Portraits (April 2000 - July 2001). *Works in collections*: NPG, Wellington College, Harris Manchester College, Oxford, Goodwood House, Longford Castle, Holdenby House, Daily Mail Newspapers, Chester Music, The Museum of Negev, Israel, Ealing Borough Council, Arsenal Football Club. *Commissions*: Field Marshal Sir Claude Auchinleck for Wellington College (1992), Capt. Charles Harris, M.C., Statue for Harris Manchester College, Oxford (1997), Rumer Godden (1996), Lord Thurlow (1996), Sir Derek Alun-Jones (1997), Lord Settrington (1999), Count Jules Dembinski (2000), Oliver Mould (2002), Mr Garry Weston, Lord Balfour of Inchrye, Lord Allenby, The family of Viscount Folkestone, Arsene Wenger. *Publications*: Editor, Society of Portrait Sculptor's Annual Exhibtion Catalogue. *Official Purchasers*: Trustees of The National Portrait Gallery, British Embassy, Tel Aviv. *Principal Works*: Charles Harris, M.C. at Harris Manchester College, Oxford; Lord Allenby (Museum of Negev, Israel). *Clubs*: Chelsea Arts. *Address*: 5 Priory Grove, London SW8 2PD. *Email*: etienne.millner@btinternet.com *Website*: www.etiennemillner.com

MILLS, Clive, BA Hons. (1987); painter in oil on canvas. *b*: Shoreham, Sussex, 7 Mar 1964. *s of*: G.Mills, builder. *Educ*: Portslade College. *Studied*: Brighton Polytechnic (1984-87), R.A. Schools (1987-90). *Exhib*: Mall Galleries (group show 1988; Post Grad. show 1989), R.A. Summer Exhbn. (1989). *Works in collections*: South East Arts and private collections including Switzerland. *Address*: 22 Easthill Drive, Portslade, Brighton, E. Sussex BN4 2FO. *Signs work*: "Clive Mills.".

MILLS, Glynis, BA (Illustration), SEA. *Medium*: oil, watercolour, drawing, prints, sculpture, china trophies, etchings, woodcut. *b*: Tadcaster, 12 Aug 1952. *d of*: Iorwerth Lloyd Mills. *Educ*: Tadcaster Grammar School. *Studied*: York College of Art (Foundation); Leicester Polytechnic (BA). *Exhib*: Tyron Gallery, Mall Galleries, local galleries. *Works in collections*: UK, USA, France, Spain. *Commissions*: too many to list. *Works Reproduced*: various equestrian paintings as cards. *Principal Works*: equestrian and hound paintings.

Recreations: dressage to high level; listed judge; keen gardener. *Clubs*: British Dressage. *Address*: 41 Wharfedale Crescent, Tadcaster, N.Yorks LS24 9JH. *Email*: glynismills@btinternet.com *Website*: www.equestrianartists.co.uk *Signs work*: 'G.Mills'.

MILLS, John W., ARCA, FRBS; sculptor in bronze; Hon.MA, UCN. *b*: London, 4 Mar 1933. *s of*: William Samuel Mills. *m*: Josephine Demarne. one *s*. one *d*. *Educ*: Bec School, Tooting. *Studied*: Hammersmith School of Art (1947-54), RCA (1956-60, John Skeaping). *Exhib*: Arts Council, RA, Alwin Gallery London, Simsar Gallery Michigan. *Works in collections*: Wellcome Foundation, Chicago Inst. of Fine Art, University of Cambridge, University of Michigan, Orient Express, City of London, British Museum. *Commissions*: Memorials to William Blake and National Firefighter, plus various Royal Mint coins and medals; Monument to the women of WWII, Whitehall. *Publications*: 8 books on sculpture techniques, recent - Encyclopedia of Sculpture Technique. *Clubs*: Chelsea Arts. *Address*: Hinxworth Pl., Hinxworth, Baldock, Herts. SG7 5HB. *Email*: mail@johnwmills.com *Website*: johnwmills.com *Signs work*: "John W. Mills.".

MILLS, Teresa Ann, ARBS; BA (Hons) Mixed Media Arts; Millennium Award, Champions for Change (2003); Awards for All (2004, 2006, 2008); Norwich County Council Award (1999); Texaco Award (1998). *Medium*: sculpture, drawing, film/conceptual/installation. *b*: Hitchin, Herts, 12 Apr 1948. *d of*: Charles Mills & Vera Victoria Miller. *m*: divorced. one *s*. one *d*. *Educ*: West Thames College (1991-92). *Studied*: Art Foundation, Sir John Cass (1992-3); University of Westminster (1993-96); work placements with Antony Gormley, and the late Helen Chadwick. *Exhib*: selected exhibitions: Mall Galleries (1996); Brixton Art Gallery (2002); RBS Annual Open (2003); Art house, Hants (2004); UEL Docklands (2006); Kowalsky Gallery, Great Sutton St. (2007-08); solo show, West Reservoir Stoke Newington (2003); Shoreditch Town Hall (Basement). Curator of "The Sublime", "Love Religion - Exposures", "Love, Warmth and Waterlilies", "A Gothic Story", "An Orchestra of Strings". *Publications*: Essays by: Kathy Fawcett, Rachael Fijalkowska, Martin Holman, Dr. Emmanuel Minne; Westminster Alumni (1998). *Recreations*: High soprano singer. *Clubs*: "Eccentric Club". *Misc*: Founder of Artram Arts Organisation. *Address*: 23A Chesholm Road, Stoke Newington, London N16 0DP. *Email*: teresamills00:yahoo.co.uk *Website*: www.teresamills.blogspot.com *Signs work*: "Teresa Mills".

MILLWARD, Michael, MA, AMA; museum curator; Curator and Museum Manager, Blackburn Museum and Art Gallery. *b*: Oldham, 9 Nov 1944. *s of*: Alan Millward, solicitor. *m*: Dorothy. one *s*. one *d*. *Educ*: King George V Grammar School, Southport; St. John's College, Cambridge. *Publications*: Victorian Townscape (with Brian Coe) 1974. *Address*: Blackburn Museum and Art Gallery, Museum St., Blackburn, Lancs. BB1 7AJ.

MILNE, Judith Erica, SGFA (2008), NDD (1965), ATD (1966); painter of botanical, landscape and garden scenes in water-colour; writer; tutor. *Medium*: watercolour, pen, ink & wash, acrylic. *b*: Malvern, 30 Oct 1943. *d of*: E.G. Knight, head teacher. *m*: J.A.S. Milne. one *s*. one *d*. *Educ*: St. Mary's Convent, Worcester. *Studied*: B'ham College of Art and Crafts. *Exhib*: London and various galleries in British Isles. *Works in collections*: nationally and internationally. *Commissions*: taken. *Publications*: Flowers in Water-colour (B.T. Batsford); Wildflowers in Water-colour (B. T. Batsford, 1995); greetings cards and prints, regular articles for Leisure Painter magazine; 'Judith Milne's 'Drawings and Watercolours' (self-publication, 2009). *Works Reproduced*: many landscapes and florals. *Recreations*: Theatre, music, reading. *Clubs*: Chairman Society of Floral Painters (1997-2012). *Misc*: School Governor (retired). *Address*: Miart, 20 Colemansmoor Rd., Woodley, Reading, RG5 4DL. *Email*: judith.milne1971@gmail.com *Website*: www.miart.org.uk *Signs work*: "Judith Milne."

MILNER, Judy, BA (Hons) Fine Art; MA. *Medium*: Drawings; sculpture; photographs. *b*: Birmingham, 9 Mar 1957. *m*: Jon Davis. one *s*. one *d*. *Studied*: Middlesex Polytechnic

(1976-79); Royal College of Art (1979-82). *Exhib*: Royal Academy Summer Exhibition (2006, 2007, 2013); Hugon Gallery, London (1999); London Institute (1999); Galerie Athanor, Marseilles, France (1994); Galerie Samia Saouma, Paris (1998); Cartier Foundation, Paris (1988); Arca, Marseilles, France (1982); Christie's, London (1982). *Works in collections*: Private (USA and Europe). Public: Cartier Foundation, Paris; FRAC Franche Comte and Provence Alpes, Cotes d'Azur, France. *Works Reproduced*: Royal Academy Catalogue (2007). *Principal Works*: Ascenseur (1987); Dissimulateur (1987(; Virtual Reality. *Address*: 47 Ivanhoe Road, London SE5 8DH. *Email*: judydmilner@gmail.com *Website*: www.judydmilner.com *Signs work*: "JUDY MILNER".

MILO-GRAY, Marcelle Jane, BA (Hons) Art. *Medium*: *Oil*. b: Devon, 1 Apr 1954. two *s*. *Studied*: University of Essex (1971-74); Exeter College of Art and Design (1967-77). *Represented by*: Hybrid, Honiton. *Exhib*: Usual mixed shows: RP; RA; SWA. *Works in collections*: Private; corporate. *Address*: Garden Cottage, North Street, Denbury TQ12 6DJ. *Email*: studio@milo-gray.co.uk *Website*: www.milo-gray.co.uk *Signs work*: "MJMG".

MINERS, Neil, artist in oil, water-colour. *b*: Redruth, Cornwall, 19 Jun 1931. *s of*: Charles Arthur Miners. *m*: Wendy Noak. two *d*. *Studied*: Falmouth School of Art under Jack Chalker (1948) drawing only. *Exhib*: RI, ROI, and Britain in Water-colours; one-man shows and various in Cornwall. *Works in collections*: RNLI, Trinity House and HRH Prince Charles. Official designs and medals, illustrated book and Flags for Tall Ships start from Falmouth (1966). *Address*: 6 Chy Nampara Trevethan Rd., Falmouth, Cornwall TR11 2AH.

MINTER, Lynda Maria, BA Hons Sculpture. *Medium*: oil painter. *b*: Liverpool, 24 Mar 1952. *m*: Christopher Minter. *Studied*: St. Martins School of Art (1980-84). *Represented by*: Lacy Road Gallery, Putney, London. *Exhib*: Piers Feetham, Chelsea Arts Club, Arts Club, Gallery Tresco, RA Summer Exhbn (2005/6), Discerning Eye (2005), Belgravia Gallery (2002), Aylesbury Museum, Thompson Gallery, The Royal Society of British Artists, The Chelsea Arts Society, The Painters' Fine Art Society. One-man shows: Winchester College, Angulus Gallery (2012); River and Rowing Museum, Henley (Sept. 2013). *Works in collections*: Mr John Skuse, Tresco Estate, Lord Alpine, River and Rowing Museum Henley. *Commissions*: Comtesse de la Rochefoucauld. *Publications*: Discerning Eye newsletter (2006); LLoyds Review (2004, 2006, 2008). *Works Reproduced*: Arts Club cover (Spring 2006). *Recreations*: travel, collecting art books, tennis. *Clubs*: Chelsea Arts Club, Hurlingham Club. *Address*: 115 Hurlingham Road, London SW6 3NJ. *Email*: lynda@lyndaminter.com *Website*: www.lyndaminter.com *Signs work*: "L Minter".

MIRECKI, Wladyslaw, self-taught painter in water-colour; co-Proprietor of Chappel Galleries. *b*: Chelmsford, 1956 of Polish parents. *m*: Edna Church, née Battye. *Educ*: Kingston Polytechnic (B.Sc. Applied Sciences, 1975-78). *Exhib*: NEAC (1988/07), Epping Forest District Museum 'Artists in Essex' (1989), Beecroft Art Gallery, Essex: awarded prize and Shirley Robson Bowl 2007 (1989, 1997, 2007); Chappel Galleries, Essex (solo: 1990, 96, 98, 99, 2003, 06, 09, 12); Foyles Art Gallery, London (solo 1991); Dept of Transport Art Competition, London (1992); Deuxième Salon Biennale de L'Aquarelle, Hirson, France (1992); Chelmsford 1993; Sunday Times Watercolour Competition, London: 3rd Prize 2007; 2nd prize 2010 (1997, 2007, 08, 10, 11); Jiangsu Provincial Art Gallery, Nanjing, China (solo, 1999); RA Summer Exhibition, London (2004); RWS, London (2007); RI, London (2007, 10); RBS, London: winner of Edward Wesson Award (2007); Lynn Painter Stainers, London: 3rd prize 2008 (2007, 08, 09, 12); Chichester Open Art Exhibition (2007); RWA, Bristol (2007); Eastern Open, Norfolk (2010); Duncan Campbell Fine Art, London (solo, 2010); Discerning Eye, London (2011); Piers Fettham Gallery, London (solo, 2012); Norwich Castle Open Art Show (2012); Chelmsford Borough Museum: joint exhibition with Paul Rumsey (2013). *Works in collections*: Essex County Council, Jiangsu Province Art Museum/Jiangsu Province Department of Culture, People's

Republic of China; Chelmsford Museums, Essex; Ipswich Borough Council Museums & Gallery, and Art Galleries, Suffolk. *Publications*: Jiangsu Art Monthly (2000); Artists & Illustators Magazine (2000); 'Southwold: An Earthly Paradise' by Geoffrey Munn (2006); BBC TV: 'Seven Man-made Wonders of the East' - interview with Mirecki and his paintings of Chappel Viaduct; The Spectator: Reviews by Andrew Lambirth (2009/12); Jackdaw magazine 'Easel Words'/New: That Beckham Tattoo' (2009/12); The Artist magazine 'Masterclass' (2009); Pratique des Arts, France (2009); 'On My Doorstep' Introduction by Laura Gascoigne publ. Chappel Galleries (2009); 'Closely Observed' Landscape: Introduction by Andrew Wilton publ. Piers Feetham gallery (2012). *Address*: 15 Colchester Rd., Chappel, Essex CO6 2DE. *Email*: info@chappelgalleries.co.uk *Website*: www.chappelgalleries.co.uk *Signs work*: "Mirecki."

MISTRY, Dhruva, Hon.CBE (2001), RA, MA (1981), MS University, MA (RCA 1983), FRBS (1993); artist in Residence, Kettle's Yard, Cambridge (1984-85); sculptor in plaster, bronze, stone; Prof. of Sculpture, Faculty of Fine Arts, MS University of Baroda (1999); Hon. Doctor of the Uni, Birmingham City University (2007). *Medium*: stainless steel, bronze, stone, plaster. *b*: Kanjari (Gujarat) India, 1 Jan 1957. *Exhib*: over 20 one-man shows worldwide, U.K., India, Japan. *Works in collections*: Tate Gallery, National Museum of Wales, Fukuoka Art Museum, British Council, etc. *Commissions*: Hunterian Art Gallery, Glasgow (1990), the City Council of Birmingham (1991), National Museum of Wales, Cardiff (1998), Tamano City Project, Uno, Japan (2002), LNG Petronet (2004). *Publications*: exhbn. catalogues: Kettle's Yard (1985), Nigel Greenwood Gallery (1990), Fukuoka Art Museum (1994), Anthony Wilkinsons Fine Art (1995), Gallery Espace (1999), Sakshi Gallery (2001), Bodhi Art (2007), Harmony Art (2008). *Recreations*: drawing, painting, reading. *Clubs*: London Arts Club. *Address*: c/o Royal Academy, Burlington House, Piccadilly, London W1V 0DS. *Email*: dhruva@dhruvamistry.com *Website*: www.dhruvamistry.com *Signs work*: "Dhruva Mistry" or "D.M."

MITCHELL, Brian, RSMA. *Medium*: oil, watercolour, acrylic. *b*: St. Ives, Cornwall, 12 Oct 1937. *s of*: Edward Matthew and Lily Mitchell. *m*: Marion Louise Scott Mitchell. one *s*. *Educ*: Penzance Grammar School. *Studied*: Penzance (1958-60, Bouverie Hoyton), Falmouth (1960-62), Inst. of Educ. London University (1962-63). *Exhib*: RWA, RWS, RI, RBA, RSMA, Grand Prix International de la Peinture a l'Eau, (2002). *Address*: Little Hendra, Boskerris Road, Carbis Bay, St. Ives, Cornwall TR26 2NQ. *Email*: little.hendra@tiscali.co.uk *Signs work*: "MITCHELL.", "B.MITCHELL RSMA".

MITCHELL, Enid G. D., FRBS; Dip.A.D. (Ceramics), Visual Arts Diploma, London University (Ghilchrist Prize); sculptor of portraits and figures cast in bronze, ceramics in porcelain and stoneware. *Medium*: bronze & ceramic. *b*: London. *d of*: R. J. Mitchell, BA Hons, Lond., J.P. one *s*. two *d*. *Educ*: Lady Eleanor Holles School, Hampton, Middx. *Studied*: Ealing School of Art (sculpture tutors, Tom Bailey and Robert Thomas, A.R.C.A.), Chelsea School of Art (ceramics). *Exhib*: RBS London and regional shows; one man shows London and Bristol; RWA Bristol etc. *Works in collections*: Leamington Spa Permanent Collection, various Primary Schools. Private collections: England, Holland, Israel, Denmark, U.S.A., Brunai (ceramics). *Commissions*: Nigerian High Commission for Memorial Park Lagos; portrait heads small figures and relief portraits, ceramics, etc. *Official Purchasers*: as above. *Recreations*: drawing, horticulture. *Clubs*: Royal Society of British Sculptors. *Address*: 'Medmenham 2', 32 Stanier St., Swindon, Wilts. SN1 5QX. *Signs work*: "MITCHELL" or "Enid G. D. Mitchell."

MITCHELL, Gordon, DA (Edin), RSA, RSW, RGI; many national awards. Full time painter since 1989. *Medium*: oil. *b*: Edinburgh, 16 Nov 1952. *m*: Deirdre. one *s*. three *d*. *Studied*: Edinburgh College of Art. *Represented by*: Roger Billcliffe Gallery, Glasgow; Portland Gallery, London. *Exhib*: many solo shows include: Open Eye Gallery (7), Roger

Billcliffe Gallery (10), Albemarle Gallery, London (2), Portland Gallery, London (3). *Works in collections*: include: Alliance & Leicester, Arthur Anderson Diageo Distillers, Kansas City Art Inst., Macfarlane Group, Nat West Bank, Pears Soap, Royal Bank of Scotland, Scottish Arts Council, Scottish Brewars, Teachers Whisky, The Knesset, Israel, University of Edin., Edin. Coll. of Art . *Works Reproduced*: limited edition prints of many works (damgoodimages.com). *Recreations*: golf. *Clubs*: Past President, Scottish Arts Club. *Address*: 6 Learmonth Terrace, Edinburgh EH4 1PQ. *Email*: gordon@gordonmitchell.co.uk *Website*: www.gordonmitchell.co.uk www.gordonmitchell.net *Signs work*: "MITCHELL".

MITCHELL, Janet Elizabeth, BA Hons Fine Art (Reading Univ. 1964). *Medium*: Watercolour and collage. *b*: Yorkshire, 2 Jun 1942. *m*: David. one *s*. one *d*. *Educ*: Reading University, School of the Museum of Fine Art, Boston USA. *Studied*: assemblage with Jesseca Ferguson USA, painting with Claude Rogers and Terry Frost UK. *Represented by*: artspaces. *Exhib*: Royal Academy, Mall Galleries, Society of Wood Engravers, Orleans House Twickenham, Riverside Gallery Richmond, Boston, Cambridge, Albany USA, Braintree Museum, Essex, Sherborne House Dorset, Turnpike Gallery Manchester, Brighton University Gallery, Thelma Hulbert Gallery Honiton; Flavel Dartmouth; Oxford University Club Oxford; Royal West of England Academy, Bristol; Royal Watercolour Society, London. *Works in collections*: UK, Europe, Australia, USA. *Publications*: Printmaking Today. *Official Purchasers*: Boston University, Print Club of Albany USA, Braintree Museum, Essex, UK. *Works Reproduced*: cover of 'Network'. *Misc*: Committee member Totnes and Dartington Open Studios. *Address*: Leechwell Cottage, Leechwell Street, Totnes, Devon, TQ9 5SY. *Email*: janet@artifex.freeserve.co.uk *Website*: www.janetmitchell.co.uk *Signs work*: "JM".

MITCHELL, John, RSW, Mem. SSA; lecturer and writer; works in all media. *b*: Glasgow, 21 Dec 1937. *Partner*: Sue. two *s*. one *d*. *Educ*: Glasgow Academy, Royal High School. *Studied*: Edinburgh College of Art, The Open University. *Exhib*: Royal Scottish Academy, Royal Scottish Soc. of Painters in Water-colours, Royal Glasgow Fine Arts Inst., Soc. of Scottish Artists, many one person and group exhbns. *Works in collections*: Fife Council; University of Dundee. *Publications*: illustrated: 'Scottish Hill and Mountain Names', 'The Bothy Brew', 'The Cairngorms Scene and Unseen'. *Address*: West Gowanbrae, 4 The Temple, Lower Largo, Fife KY8 6JH. *Signs work*: "John Mitchell."

MITCHELL, Lewis John. *Medium*: Oil. *b*: Penzance, 25. Jul 1938. *m*: Jennifer. one *s*. *Educ*: Secondary Modern. *Studied*: Self-taught Cornish artist. *Represented by*: Rainyday; Little Picture Gallery. *Exhib*: Throughout the UK and Denmark; David Cross Gallery, Bristol (20 years); Rainyday, Penzance (six one-mans); Demarco Gallery, Edinburgh; Stubtoft, Copenhagen. *Works in collections*: All over UK and abroad. *Publications*: 20th Century British Primitives, Innocent Eye, ABNA 2012. *Works reproduced*: 20. *Recreations*: Modern jazz; real ale; rugby; history. *Address*: 40 Heabrook Parc, Penzance, Cornwall TR18 3QR. *Email*: lewismitchell337@gmail.com *Website*: www.rainydaygallery.co.uk Lewis Mitchell Artist. *Signs work*: "LEWIS".

MITCHELL, Shuna Patricia. *Medium*: oil, watercolour, Chinese pen and ink. *b*: Bedford, 16 Dec 1959. *d of*: Gordon Hinchcliff & Agnes Patricia Mitchell. *Educ*: Bedford High School. *Studied*: Slade School of Fine Art; Ruskin University, Cambridge. *Represented by*: Barbara Vanderbilt, Nantucket, USA. *Exhib*: RA Summer Exhbn.; Hohenberger Gallery, Houston, USA (2005); Leicestershire County Schools; Bedford School Solo, 1998; Art for Life benefit charity shows; Christies Auctioneers; Kintyre, Scotland (2008). *Works in collections*: UK, USA, Paraguay, China. *Publications*: currently writing an illustrated book on world travels. *Recreations*: outdoors, riding, travel. *Clubs*: Chelsea Arts Club. *Misc*: President: University College London, Womens Dining Club (2007-2010). *Address*: 33-34 Devonshire Street, London W1G 6PY. *Email*: sp.mitchell@yahoo.co.uk *Website*: www.shoosal.com *Signs work*: '-Shuna'.

MOCKFORD, Harold, self taught artist. *Medium*: oil. *b*: 25 Jan 1932. *m*: Margaret. three *s*. one *d*. *Exhib*: one-man shows: Towner A.G. (1970, 1987), Hove Museum (1980, 1985), Thackeray Gallery, London (1978); RA Summer Exhbns., London Group, Newport (Gwent) A.G. (1995), Star Gallery, Lewes (1999, 2000, 2002, 2005), Retrospective, Towner (2012). *Works in collections*: Tate Gallery, Chantry Bequest, Towner Gallery, Hove Museum of Art, Government Art Collection. *Publications*: Harold Mockford. *Address*: 45 Hillcrest Rd., Newhaven BN9 9EE. *Signs work*: "H. Mockford" on back of board.

MOFFAT, Alexander, OBE, RSA. *Medium*: painting. *b*: Dunfermline 23 Mar 1943. *Studied*: Edinburgh College of Art (1960-64). *Exhib*: Royal Scottish Academy; Open Eye Gallery, Edinburgh. *Works in collections*: Scottish National Portrait Gallery; Scottish National Gallery of Modern Art; Yale Center for British Art, Newhaven, USA. *Commissions*: portraits of: Hugh MacDiarmid (Scottish Arts Council), Muriel Spark (Scottish National Portrait Gallery). *Publications*: Seven Poets, Third Eye Centre, Glasgow. *Works Reproduced*: "Scottish Art" by Murdo MacDonald (Thames & Hudson). *Principal Works*: Poet's Pub (Scottish National Portrait Gallery). *Clubs*: The Glasgow Art Club. *Address*: 20 Haddington Place, Edinburgh, EH7 4AF. *Email*: sandysmoffat@btinternet.com *Signs work*: "MOFFAT"

MOGER, Jill, RMS (2009), SWA (2001), SWLA. (1999); ceramic sculptor (wildlife) in stoneware, porcelain; Council mem. SWLA (1999-), Hon Sec. SWLA (2004-2009): editor SWLA bi-annual newsletter (2000-2007, 2009-2011), Vice-President RMS (2009-2013); Awards: SWA President's and Vice Presidents' Award 2001 (Best in Exbn.); Anthony J. Lester Art Critic Award (SWA 2006); Bidder & Bourne Sculpture Award (RMS 2009, 2012); Gold Bowl Hon Mention (RMS 2009, 2011, 2012). *b*: London, 10 Aug 1946. *m*: Dr. Philip Moger. two *s*. two *d*. *Educ*: Ursuline High School, Ilford, and Saffron Walden County High. *Represented by*: Llewellyn Alexander, Waterloo, London; Blake Gallery, York; House of Bruar, Perthshire. *Exhib*: Llewellyn Alexander, London; 'Nature in Art' Wallsworth Hall; Wildlife A.G. Lavenham; Slimbridge WWT; Blake Gallery, York; Bonham's "Art of Living World", Singapore; Yorkshire Sculpture Park; SWA, SWLA and RMS, Mall Galleries, London. *Works in collections*: Stoke on Trent City Museum and A.G., Nature in Art Museum, Wallsworth Hall, Gloucester. *Commissions*: Leeds Playhouse, Yorkshire Museum of Farming. *Publications*: included in 'Drawn to the Forest' by Robert Burton and the S.W.L.A., 'Bugs Britannica' by Peter Marren & Richard Mabey; 'Reptile to Reef' Ceramic Sculpture by Jill Moger, pub Langford Press 2014. *Address*: The Studio, 75 Millfield Lane, Nether Poppleton, York YO26 6NA. *Email*: jill_moger@hotmail.com *Website*: www.jillmogersculptures.co.uk *Signs work*: "Jill Moger" (and date) etched into clay.

MONCHER-DUNKLEY, Anthea, SBA, SFP; scientific illustrator (botanical and geological) in oil; University illustrator/cartographer and muralist and botanical painter. *Medium*: oil painter. *b*: Isle of Wight, 10 Oct 1945. *m*: Arthur James Dunkley. *Educ*: private school. *Studied*: Southampton College of art (part-time). *Exhib*: commissioned paintings: Dept. of Geology, Southampton University, and educational establishments; commissioned work in private collections: England, Egypt, Japan, India, Syria, USA, France and Australia. *Works in collections*: varied. *Commissions*: private collections worldwide. *Publications*: scientific journal illustrator. *Official Purchasers*: varied. *Works Reproduced*: Botanical painting greeting cards. *Principal Works*: Botanical painting. *Recreations*: music. *Address*: 'Trees', Hamstead Road, Cranmore, IOW PO41 0XP. *Signs work*: "Anthea Moncher Dunkley" or monogram of "AMD".

MONROE, Chuck, BA (Hons) Fine Art. *Medium*: oil, watercolour, drawing, objects. *b*: Frankfurt, 16 Sep 1950. *Educ*: Grammar School (Ancient Languages). *Studied*: Academy of Arts, Kassel (Fine Art). *Represented by*: Chuck Monroe Art, London. *Exhib*: London; Royal Academy Summer Shows, Mall Galleries, Royal Society of Oil Painters, Chelsea Art

Society; Bankside Gallery, Affordable Art Fair, Llewellyn Alexander and many more. Also Hamburg, Munich, Frankfurt and Paris. *Works in collections*: private collections in England, USA, Germany, Switzerland, Italy, Spain. *Publications:* Richmond Magazine (2002); Arts & Crafts Magazine (2002). *Works Reproduced*: Marilyn in Art (Roger Taylor, 2006). *Clubs*: United Society of Artists; DACS (Design and Artists Copyright Society). *Address*: 26 Albany Road, London E17 8DA. *Email*: info@chuckmonroeart.com *Website*: www.chuckmonroeart.com *Signs work*: 'Chuck Monroe', '-Monroe'.

MONTAGUE, Lucile Christine, LCAD (1974); Byam Shaw Diploma. *b*: London, 9 May 1950. *d of*: Gen.Sir Allan Taylor, KBE, MC. *Partner*: David Greene. one *s*. *Educ*: Fyling Hall School, Yorks. *Studied*: Plymouth College of Art (1967-69), Byam Shaw School of Art (1971-74). *Exhib*: Pastel Society, Royal West of England Academy, RA, Whitechapel Open, London Group, Spirit of London, South Bank Show, Thumb Gallery; group shows: Artsquare, London, kon Gallery touring, 'Ways of Telling' Mostyn Gallery, Llandudno, 'Subjective City' touring, 'Witnesses and Dreamers' touring; 'A Century of Art' Herbert Museum, Coventry; one-man shows, Mario Fletcher Gallery, London; Clayton Gallery, Newcastle; The Studio Gallery, London; Riverside Studios, London; Signatures Gallery, London (2005); Pastels Today (2005). *Works in collections*: Bankers Trust, Coopers and Lybrand, Herbert Museum and A.G., Coventry Museum and Art Gallery. *Address*: 47 Hargrave Pk., London N19 5JW. *Email*: lucearts@hotmail.com *Website*: www.axisartists.org.uk *Signs work*: "L.C. Montague.".

MONTGOMERY, Iona Allison Eleanor, BFA(Hons) (1987), Post.Grad. DFA (1988), RSW (1991); numerous awards including Alexander Graham Munro travel award, Lauder Award, Sir William Gillies Award. *Medium*: painting and printmaking. *b*: Glasgow, 14 Apr 1965. *d of*: Hamish & Isabella Montgomery. *Educ*: Boclair Academy, Bearsden, Glasgow. *Studied*: Glasgow School of Art, Tamarind Inst., Albuquerque, U.S.A. *Exhib*: one-man shows including Galerie Seghaier, Vienna, State University of West Georgia USA, Ancrum Gallery, Edinburgh Gallery, Lillie Art Gallery, various group shows including RSA, RSW, RGI, GPS, Consument Art, also USA, Europe, USSR, and Japan. *Works in collections*: Lillie Art Gallery, Milngavie, BBC, Hilton Hotels, etc. *Clubs*: RSW, GPS, GSWA, SAC. *Misc*: Various teaching including part-time lecturer Edinburgh College of Art. *Address*: 13 Avon Avenue, Bearspen, Glasgow G61 2PS. *Signs work*: "Iona A.E. Montgomery."

MONTGOMERY, James Alexander, artist in water-colour, pen and ink, oil; Leader of Complex of Rehabilitation Units, including Art Therapy. *b*: Glasgow, 3 Oct 1928. *s of*: James Montgomery. *m*: Isabelle, artist. two *s*. one *d*. *Educ*: Woodside School, Glasgow. *Studied*: Glasgow School of Art (David Donaldson, Edward Powell), apprenticed to industrial artist. *Exhib*: numerous one person shows including Columbus City Museum, U.S.A., Carrollton Nova Lomason A.G., Atlanta, Lillie Art Gallery and Glasgow University Chapel. Exhibited widely in group shows in UK and Europe. *Works in collections*: in UK and USA. *Clubs*: Glasgow Art. *Address*: 13 Avon Ave., Bearsden, Glasgow G61 2PS. *Signs work*: "Hamish Montgomery."

MONTGOMERY, Kate, BFA (Oxon) 1988, MA Fine Art (1992); painter in casein. *b*: Wokingham, 5 Nov 1965. *m*: Jonathan Warner. two *d*. *Educ*: Oxford High School for Girls. *Studied*: Ruskin School of Drawing and Fine Art (1985-88), RCA (1990-92, Prof. Keith Critchlow). *Exhib*: Cadogan Contemporary London, Piccadilly Gallery London, RA Summer Show, The Discerning Eye. *Works in collections*: internationally including HRH The Prince of Wales. *Publications*: illustrations for children's book 'Razia, Queen of India' (Hood Hood Books). *Clubs*: London Group. *Address*: 18 Farm Rd., Hove, East Sussex BN3 1FB. *Email*: kate@3-w.net *Signs work*: "Kate Montgomery" on back of work.

MOOD, Kenneth, BA (Hons); artist/writer, actor (equity member), teacher. *b*: Gateshead, 24 Nov 1950. *m*: Margaret. one *s*. one *d*. *Educ*: Gateshead. *Studied*: Sunderland Art College.

Works in collections: Arts Council, Whitney Museum (NY), sixty-five UK art galleries and museums; 100 Pastel Portraits at Gateshead Baltic International Art Gallery; Drawings at San Francisco Art Gallery and Museum USA; Arts Museum, TX, USA; Hepworth Wakefield; Folkestone Museum & Art Gallery; Modern Art Oxford; Atkinson Gallery Southport; Bristol Museum & Art Gallery; Hull Ferens Gallery; Tate Liverpool; Mimi Middlesbrough; Oldham Art Gallery; Huddersfield Art Gallery; Wolverhampton Art Gallery; National Portrait Gallery Sydney Australia; Art Gallery of Ontario, Canada. *Address*: 1 Burns Cres., Swalwell, Tyne and Wear NE16 3JE.

MOON, Liz, BA./MA Oxon. (Engineering) 1964, SWA (1987); painter in acrylic, watercolour; Artist Residency, John Innes Centre, Norwich (1997-98), Downing College Cambridge (1999-2000), St Hugh's College Oxford (2002). *b*: India, 4 Oct 1941. *d of*: Lt.-Col. L. Montague-Jones. *Educ*: Sherborne Girls' School; St. Hugh's College, Oxford; Redlands College, Bristol. *Studied*: San Francisco Art Inst. *Exhib*: RSMA, RWA, RBA, RI; solo shows: Barbican Level 5 West, Royal Opera House, Covent Gdn., John Russell Gallery, Ipswich, and Clare Hall, Cambridge. "Liz Moon paints the world she knows with amused intensity. Her everyday scenes of people in action are infused with energy and humour." *Works in collections*: John Innes Centre, Norwich; Downing College and Clare Hall, Cambridge, St Hugh's College Oxford. *Commissions*: Private Commissions, Parties, Weddings, playing music and sport. *Publications*: article in The Artist (1987). *Address*: 21 Bermuda Terr., Cambridge CB4 3LD.

MOON, Michael, First prize, John Moores Liverpool Exhbn. (1980), print award, Gulbenkian (1984); painter in mixed media. *b*: Edinburgh, 9 Nov 1937. *s of*: Donald Moon, Lt.Col. *m*: Anjum Moon. two *s*. *Educ*: Shoreham Grammar School, Sussex. *Studied*: Chelsea School of Art (1958-62), R.C.A. (1963). *Exhib*: one-man shows in U.K., Australia and U.S.A. including Tate Gallery (1976); numerous group exhbns. worldwide. *Works in collections*: Tate Gallery, Arts Council, Saatchi Collection, provincial and overseas. *Address*: 10 Bowood Rd., London SW11 6PE. *Signs work*: "Mick Moon."

MOONEY, Eddie, HRHA. *Medium*: oil paintings, mixed media, drawings, pastels, etc. *b*: 31 Jul 1940. one *s*. one *d*. *Studied*: National College of Art, Dublin, Ireland. *Represented by*: Royal Hibernian Academy. *Exhib*: all major exhibitions in Ireland. *Works in collections*: most important collections in Ireland. *Official Purchasers*: publicised in most art publications in Ireland. *Address*: 18 Waterloo Road, Ballsbridge, Dublin 4. *Signs work*: 'Ed. Mooney'.

MOORE, Bridget, RAS.Dip., RBA, NEAC, Greenshield Foundation (1985); De Laszlo Medal Winner (2010). *Medium*: Painter in oil, gouache and mixed media. *b*: Whitstable, 2 Aug 1960. *d of*: Keith Charles Moore. *m*: Alistair Milne. one *s*. one *d*. *Educ*: The Sir William Nottidge School, Whitstable. *Studied*: Medway College of Design, Epsom School of Art, R.A. Schools. *Exhib*: RA, RBA, NEAC, numerous mixed shows, London; Enid Lawson Gallery, Neville Gallery, Cedar House Gallery, Red Biddy Gallery, Milne & Moller, Business Art Gallery, New Academy Gallery, Red Rag Gallery, Lynne Strover Gallery, Denise Yapp Contemporary Art, Bankside Gallery. *Address*: 'Old Laundry Cottage', 18, Cotmandene, Dorking, Surrey RH4 2BT. *Email*: bridget_milne@yahoo.co.uk *Signs work*: "BRIDGET MOORE" on back.

MOORE, Cleland Randolph, BA, MFA; Artist in Residence Royal Academy of Arts 'Starr Scholar'. *Medium*: oil. *b*: Richmond, Virginia, USA, 28 Sep 1964. *s of*: John Williamson Moore III. *m*: Mark Patrick Murray-Threipland. one *s*. one *d*. *Studied*: College of Charleston, SC, USA (1987, BA); School of Visual Arts, New York, USA (1995, MFA); RA Schools (1996-98). *Exhib*: RA Summer Exhbn (1998, 2001); Visual Arts Gallery, New York (1995); City Gallery/Halsey Gallery, Charleston, South Carolina (1993). *Works in collections*: Linklaters and Paines. *Works Reproduced*: Summer Academy Illustrated (2001) (curated by Peter Blake). *Clubs*: Alumni Assoc. RA. *Address*: 7 Pier Head, Wapping, London E1W 1PN. *Email*: cleland@freeola.com *Website*: www.clelandmoore.co.uk *Signs work*: 'Cleland R.Moore'.

MOORE, Gabrielle Kaye, Chadwyck Healey Painting Prize (1981); Rodney Burn Drawing Prize (1981); Richard Ford Travel (1983); Wimbledon Centenary poster (1986). *Medium*: oil, etching, sculpting. *b*: Worcs, 6 Feb 1949. *m*: David Lewis - Architect. *Educ*: Manor House Convent, London. *Studied*: Byam Shaw; City & Guilds of London Art School; RA Schools. *Exhib*: Contemporary Artists in Camden (1981); NPG BP Portrait Awards (1981,1982); NEAC (1981, 2001); Agnews (1983); RPPS (1984); one-man show Spink & Son (1991); Charleston Sussex (1992); 'Making a Mark' Mall Galleries (1993); RWEA (1995); Glyndebourne Opera (1999, 2002, 2007); frequently at the RA Summer Exhbn; Sculpting Artist in Residence, Glyndebourne Opera House 2010 season; many one-man exhibition Ahmadebad India 2012; many one-man and mixed exhbns. *Works in collections*: Lloyds of London. *Commissions*: Zamana Gallery, London; Museum of Jerusalem; Alhambra, Grenada; Glyndebourne - six aquatints. *Recreations*: raising chickens. *Misc*: taught life drawing and trompe l'oeil painting under Roger de Grey at City & Guilds Art School for fourteen years. *Address*: 1 Poundfield Cottages, Chalvington, E.Sussex BN27 3TG. *Email*: gaby@macdream.net *Website*: www.gabymoore.co.uk *Signs work*: 'G.M.' 'Gaby Moore'.

MOORE, Gerald John, NDD (1958), ATC, ATD (Manc) (1959), BA (Hons.Theol.) (1969), FRSA (1985); traditional painter in water-colour and oil: landscapes, animals, birds, buildings, historical genre and portraits. *Medium*: oil and watercolour. *b*: Ratby, Leics., 21 Aug 1938. *s of*: Gilbert Moore. *Educ*: Broom Leys School, Leics. *Studied*: Loughborough (1955-58), Manchester Regional College of Art (1958-59), University of Exeter (Theology 1966-69; History of Art 1974-75). *Exhib*: Teignmouth, Tiverton, Taunton, Widecombe-in-the-Moor, Braunton, Bournemouth, Salisbury and Bristol. *Works in collections*: Private Collections in Australia, Italy, France. Sweden, Germany and Britain. *Works Reproduced*: Harvest Time at Plush, Dorsetshire, Afternoon: Double Lock Inn on the Exeter Canal, Sunday Evening: the River Parrett, The Cloud: West Sedgemoor. *Principal Works*: Portrait: Boy with violin, oil on canvas 36" x 28"; Summer Storms: Mawddach, oil on canvas 42" x 54". *Misc*: Work may be seen at my home during Somerset Art Weeks and at other times by Appointment. *Address*: Lower Huntham Farm, Stoke St. Gregory, Taunton, Som. TA3 6EY. *Signs work*: "G.J.M." or "G.J. MOORE."

MOORE, Sally, BA, Fine Art (1984), MA Fine Art (1987); Welsh Artist of the Year (2005) prizewinner, Discerning Eye, Mall Galleries, London (1996), Abbey Memorial Scholarship at British School in Rome (1992-1993), Residency at Delfina Studios Trust (1988-1990), Prizewinner, National Eisteddfod of Wales (1994); painter in oil, self-employed artist. *b*: Barry, S. Wales, 7 Apr 1962. *Studied*: South Glamorgan Institute, Cardiff (1980-1981), Ruskin School of Drawing and Fine Art (1981-1984), City of Birmingham Polytechnic (1986-1987). *Represented by*: Martin Tinney Gallery, Cardiff. *Exhib*: solo exhibs. include Martin Tinney Gallery (1995, 1997, 2000, 2003, 2005, 2007, 2010), Long and Ryle Art International, London (1991); group exhibs. include RA Summer Exhib. (2000, 2001), Art London with Martin Tinney Gallery (1994-2012), Oriel Tegfryn Gallery, Menai Bridge. *Works in collections*: National Museum of Wales, Cardiff; National Library of Wales; Newport Museum and Art Galleries, Wales; Contemporary Art Society U.K.; Contemporary Art Society, Wales; Sunderland Art Gallery; South East Wales Art Association; St. John's College, Oxford; private collections worldwide. *Address*: c/o Martin Tinney Gallery, 18 St. Andrew's Crescent, Cardiff CF10 3DD. *Email*: mtg@artwales.com *Website*: www.artwales.com *Signs work*: "Sally Moore.".

MOORE, Tom. *Medium*: oil. *b*: Sunderland, 5 May 1951. *s of*: Stanley Moore/ Eileen Pitt. *m*: Linda Maddison. *Educ*: Bede Grammar School, Sunderland. *Studied*: Northumbria

University at Newcastle-upon-Tyne; Newcastle-upon-Tyne University. *Exhib*: Chatton Gallery, Northumberland; Globe Gallery, North Tyneside; VANE, Newcastle; New British Artists-AAF London; Art London (2004, 2005); Sheridan Russell, London; solo exhbns: Customs House, South Shields; Henshelwood Gallery, Newcastle; Red Box Gallery, Newcastle. *Works in collections*: Herwood Collection. *Commissions*: private and business UK. *Publications*: 'Finding A Language' (catalogue, Red Box Gallery); 'Brief Encounters' (catalogue, Henshelwood Gallery) . *Address*: 33 Clayton Road, Jesmond, Newcastle-upon-Tyne NE2 4QR. *Signs work*: 'TOM MOORE' on verso.

MORAN, Carolyne Sandra Anne, DipAD, ATC (Fine Art); formerly head of Art: Queensmount Bournemouth, and Knighton House, Durweston; C21 First Prize Award (2005, 2010). *Medium*: gouache, oil. *b*: Trowbridge, Wilts., 27 Dec 1946. *d of*: John Henry Parsons OBE, FRCVS. *m*: James. two *s*. *Educ*: Bruton School for Girls, Sunny Hill, Bruton, Somerset. *Studied*: Bournemouth College of Art, Exeter College of Art, Cardiff Post. Grad. College of Art Educ. *Exhib*: 1989 onwards: RWS, C21, Bankside Gallery, London (Open), RI, Mall Galleries, London (Open), Jerram Gallery, Salisbury, Four Seasons Gallery, Wimborne, The New English Art Club Open, Mall Galleries, London (1995 onwards), Josephine Harpur, Bury St Edmunds. *Commissions*: Sir Michael and Lady Angus; Sir Edward and Lady Hulse (Breamore House, Fordingbridge). *Publications*: The Encyclopedia of Water-colour Techniques-Painting Solutions; Houses and Buildings Texture; How to Paint It, How To Draw It, Painting and Drawing Magazine; Water-colour Still Life, The Art of Drawing and Painting, A Compendium of Water-colour Techniques; 'Step by Step' Paintings for Dorling Kindersley Publications/Eaglemoss Publications; The Watercolour Artist Bible; The Artist Magazine. *Address*: Cleohill Cottage, 27 Blandford Rd., Corfe Mullen, Wimborne, Dorset BH21 3HD. *Email*: carolyne@carolynemoran.com *Website*: www.carolynemoran.com *Signs work*: 'Carolyne Moran'.

MORENO, Michel. *Medium*: oil, watercolour, drawing, sculpture. *b*: St.Etienne du Rouvray, 26 Nov 1945. *s of*: Jules Moreno. *m*: Christiane. *Studied*: Ecole d'Arte Technique, Paris. *Exhib*: Galerie Marcel Bernheim (1973); Galerie de Lucia (1974); Galerie Miromesnil (1994) Salon Independent (1987), Salon Leonard de Vinci (1988), Paris; 2008 Exposition International Art Fair, Guangzhou, China; 2009 American International Fine Art Fair, Miami, USA. *Works in collections*: Petit Palais, Genève. *Publications*: Benezit, Mayer, Annual des Arte, Artprice. *Official Purchasers*: Ville de Paris. *Works Reproduced*: catalogues *Principal Works*: Parabole de la vie (1991). *Recreations*: marathon. *Address*: 11 Mont Thabor, Paris 75001, France. *Email*: renogaou@free.fr *Website*: http://www.michelmoreno.com *Signs work*: 'Michel Moreno'.

MORESCHI, Maria, ABA, FPS; art teacher, portrait artist in oil, pastel and water-colour; art teacher The American School, Cobham. *b*: Florence, 18 Jul 1949. married. *d of*: Galliano Taddey, Col. in The King's Cavalry. one *s*. two *d*. *Educ*: SS. Ma. Annunziata. *Studied*: Academia delle Belle Arti; taught portraiture by Annigoni in Florence. *Exhib*: America, Italy, Holland, England, Paris. *Works in collections*: La Loggia, Oxshott, Walton, Epsom, Studio 54 Cobham, The Investment Gallery, private collections: Galerie Jacques, Galerie L'Oeil de Boeue, Galleria St Croce, Il Nerone, La Cantina, Turelli, Il Toro, La Studente, Vallerini. *Commissions*: private portraits. *Publications*: in the process of illustrating an animal and wildlife drawing book. *Official Purchasers*: ACS. *Recreations*: travel, cooking, theatre, photography, animals, music, hiking. *Clubs*: Epsom, Oxshott, Walton, Mosley, Cobham, London, Ferndown, Ringwood. *Address*: A.C.S. Middle School, Heywood, Portsmouth Rd., Cobham, Surrey. *Signs work*: "M. Moreschi."

MORETON, Nicolas, BA (Hons) (1985), ARBS (1995). *Medium*: fine art sculptor in English stones, bronze, pencil drawing. *b*: Watford, Herts., 22 Oct 1961. *s of*: Cecil Peter Moreton, PhF, FRICS, FCBSI. *m*: Julie Rose Bills. one *s*. *Educ*: Weston Favell Upper

School, Northampton. *Studied*: Nene College, Northampton (1981-82, Frank Cryer), Wolverhampton Polytechnic (1982-85, John Paddison, RCA). *Exhib*: The Discerning Eye; Young Sculptors, Beaux Arts; British Art Fair ('95-2001); Conversation, Milton Keynes Gallery; Sherborne Festival; one-man shows: Mall Galleries (1989, 1991), Lamont Gallery (1992), Hunt Jennings (1993), Goldmark Gallery (1995, 1997, 1999), Peter Gwyther Gallery (2001), Longleat House (2002), Hutson Gallery (2004), 'Transition', national tour (2004-2006). *Commissions*: Double public commission, Milton Keynes (1995), Millenium Sculpture, University College Northampton (2001), Cefn Henllan, Monmouthshire (2005). *Address*: 4 West Lodge Cottages, London Rd., Courteenhall, Northampton NN7 2QA. *Website*: www.nicholasmoreton.com *Signs work*: drawing "Nicolas Moreton".

MOREY de MORAND, C. FRGS; LG; Greater London Arts Grant (1979); Arts Council GB (1980); Elephant Trust Grant (1983); Europe Prize for Painting, Ostend (Bronze Medal, 1986); British Council Grant (1988); Leighton Foundation, Alberta Canada (1991); Arts Council England Award (2006). *Medium*: abstract contemporary painter. *b*: Paris, France. *Represented by*: Palette Contemporary, Albuquerque; Poussin Gallery, London. *Exhib*: Solo exhbns include: Lalin Museum, Spain (2011); Poussin (2010); Milchhof, Berlin (2007), Palette Contemporary, Albuquerque (2005, 2008). Group: Hunting Prize Exhbn, RCA (2001, 05), Santorino Biennale (2012); RA Summer Exhbn (2000, 01, 04, 09, 2012); London Group; Flowers East (2003, 06, 09); Denizli City Art Centre, Turkey (1998); Museo Municipal Orense, Spain (1997); Riverside Studios, London (1996); Discerning Eye; major retrospective Dean Clough Gallery (2002). *Works in collections*: public and private collections worldwide. *Commissions*: Time Out building; installation, Oakmayne Building. *Address*: 61d Oxford Gardens, London W10 5UJ. *Email*: colettemoreydemorand@yahoo.co.uk *Website*: www.cmoreydemorand.co.uk

MORGAN, Geri, painter in oil; part time teacher at Hornsey College of Art (1958-1968), Camberwell College of Art (1962-1970), Principal of Byam Shaw School of Art (1970-1991). *b*: London, 19 Mar 1926. three *d*. *Educ*: The Bec School, Tooting, London. *Studied*: St. Martin's School of Art (1944), Camberwell School of Art (1948-1951). *Exhib*: R.A. Summer Exhibs. regularly since mid 1960s; recent solo exhibs., Duncan Campbell Gallery (1998, 1999), Collins and Hastie (2002), Millinery Works Gallery (2009). *Works in collections*: private collections in UK, USA, and Canada. *Commissions*: portrait of President of Institution of Civil Engineers (1991). *Publications*: 'Getting it Right' William Packer, Collins and Hastie (2002). *Clubs*: Chelsea Arts. *Address*: 7 Mildmay Grove North, London N1 4RH. *Signs work*: "GERI MORGAN" on verso.

MORGAN, Glyn. *Medium*: painter in oil, water-colour, collage. *b*: Pontypridd, 16 Jul 1926. *s of*: H I Morgan. *m*: Jean Bullworthy. *Educ*: Pontypridd Grammar School. *Studied*: Cardiff School of Art (1942-44, Ceri Richards), Camberwell School of Art (1947), East Anglian School (1944-82, Cedric Morris). *Exhib*: one-man shows: Gilbert Parr, London (1978, 1980), Alwin, London (1982, 1983), Richard Demarco Gallery, Edinburgh (1973), Minories, Colchester (1971, 1981), Archway Gallery, Houston, Texas, Chappel Gallery, Essex (1991, 1996, 2001, 2006), Rhondda Heritage Park, Y Tabernacl, Wales (1997), John Russell Gallery, Ipswich (1998); organised 'The Benton End Circle' exhbn. of work by pupils of Cedric Morris and Lett Haines, Bury St. Edmunds Gallery (1985), 'Glyn Morgan at Eighty' National Library of Wales (2006). *Works in collections*: Auckland and Brisbane A.Gs, Derbyshire, Monmouthshire, Oxford and West Riding Educ. Coms., Welsh Arts Council, Contemporary Art Soc. for Wales, Ipswich Borough Museum and A.G., Newport Museum and A.G., National Museum of Wales, Brecknock Museum, Nat. Library of Wales, Glynn Vivian Art Gallery, Swansea. *Publications*: 'A Vision of Landscape', The Art of Glyn Morgan (Chappel Galleries), 'Glyn Morgan at Eighty', John Sansom. *Address*: Hunters, 120 High St., Hadleigh, Suffolk IP7 5EL. *Signs work*: "MORGAN."

MORGAN, Helena Frances, Dip. in Textiles (1985), FFPS (1997), LCGI (1992); fibre artist; Gold Medal, Hungary. *Medium*: fibre art. *b*: Mountain Ash, Mid Glam., 11 Feb 1938. *m*: Hugh. one *s*. two *d*. *Educ*: Mountain Ash Grammar School. *Studied*: Glos.College of Art (1957-61); Regent St. Polytechnic (1963-64); London College of Furniture (1983-85). *Exhib*: group shows in France, Hong Kong, Hungary, London, and throughout Britain. *Works in collections*: Work in private collections. *Address*: Lansbury, 51a High St., Langford, Beds. SG18 9RU. *Email*: handhfmorgan@googlemail.com *Signs work*: "Helena Morgan."

MORGAN, Howard James, MFA, RP; painter in oil, water-colour, casein. *b*: 21 Apr 1949. *s of*: Thomas James Morgan, teacher. *m*: Susan Ann (divorced); Sarah Jane Morgan (2004). four *s*. two *d*. *Educ*: Fairfax High School. *Studied*: Newcastle-upon-Tyne University (Ralph Holland, Charles Leonard Evetts). *Exhib*: Anthony Mould, Claridges, Agnews (2011), Richmond Gallery, Eaton Gallery, Sarah Stewart, Messums, Masterpiece (2011). *Works in collections*: NPG. *Commissions*: numerous Royal and private commissions. *Official Purchasers*: various universities etc. *Works Reproduced*: in various newspapers and books. *Clubs*: Chelsea Arts, Beefsteak. *Misc*: (studio) 401½ Wandsworth Rd., London SW8. *Address*: 12 Rectory Grove, Clapham, London SW4. *Email*: howard@howard-morgan.co.uk *Website*: howard-morgan.co.uk *Signs work*: roman numerals of month, followed by arabic year and surname, i.e. "MORGAN II 98."

MORGAN, Jennifer Frances, RSMA (2009); NDD (1962). 'Classic Boat' Art Prize (RSMA, 2007); Winner of 'Derek Gardner Deep Seas' Award (RSMA 2011). Freelance artist-painter, mostly in oil/gouache, specializing in marine painting, ships, sailing craft, etc. *b*: Woolwich, London, 22 Jun 1942. *Educ*: boarding school. *Studied*: Camberwell School of Art (1960-64, Robert Medley). *Exhib*: throughout UK and overseas,including RSMA, Mall Galleries (2007); Ferens Gallery, Hull; National Maritime Museum, Falmouth; Royal Cornwall Polytechnic Society, Falmouth; solo shows: Grimsby (1995), Waterman Fine Art, London (1998), Coach House Gallery, Guernsey (2004, 2008); Myton Gallery, Hull; The Wykeham Gallery, Stockbridge, Hants; also shows regularly at Mall Galleries, London, and work sold regularly through Gallerie Marin, Appledore, Devon; Kendall's Fine Art, Cowes, Isle of Wight. *Works in collections*: private collections overseas and UK. *Commissions*: many private commissions over years, including works in Australia, Switzerland, Ireland, USA and major oil corporation; large public art commission (2009) for NHS Medical Practice. *Publications*: catalogues, book illustrations, calendar publications, Ltd. Ed. prints. Sotheby's Catalogues. *Works Reproduced*: Allan & Bertram corporate 'Marine Artists' calendars. *Address*: The Nest, Highgate lane, Sutton-on-sea, nr. Mablethorpe, Lincs. LN12 2LH. *Email*: jenny.morgan802@gmail.com *Signs work*: "J.F.MORGAN".

MORGAN, Mark Andrew, BA (Hons) Fine Art/Sculpture (2003); HND Fine Art (Distinctions, 2001); Salon Culinaire de Londres, Hotel Olympia Silver Medal (1996)/Cert.Merit (1998). *Medium*: sculpture, drawing, prints. *b*: Kensington, London, 21 Apr 1965. *s of*: David Richard Morgan, Dublin. one *s*, Conor. one *d*, Whitney. *Educ*: Lampton Secondary School, Middx (1982); Brighton Tech. Coll. (1985). *Studied*: Northbrook College, W.Sussex (1997-2003). *Exhib*: RA Summer Show (2001); Worthing Artists & Makers Festival (2004, 05); 'Fresh Art' Fair, Battersea (2003); Northbrook College (2000, 2003); Worthing Museum & Gallery Open Art Comp. (1991); Salon Culinaire, Earls Court Olympia (1986, 96, 98); Royal Hibernian Academy, Dublin, Summer Show (2006); 'Elementals' Exhibition, Pyramid Gallery, Silver Springs, MD, USA (2011); Elementals Exhibition, Richard F. Brush Gallery, Canton, USA (2011); Firsty Birthday Show, Rabbit Rooms, Bangor, Co. Down NI (2011); Bangor Castle Walled Garden Sculpture Exhibition, Ward House, Bangor, NI (2012). *Works in collections*: permanent siting of Sculpture, Devils Dyke, Sussex (National Trust, 2000). *Works Reproduced*: works photographed for British Airways Flight Magazine (1986). *Principal Works*: 'Earth Egg (A

Glimmer of Hope)' selected for Sonia Lawson's Summer Show Gallery, RA (2001), 'Seed from the Tree of Life', RHA Dublin 2006. *Misc*: calligraphy work selected for presentation to H.R.H. The Queen Mother (1980). *Address*: 24 Southwell Road, Bangor, Co. Down BT20 3AQ. *Email*: markasculptor@hotmail.com *Website*: www.marksculptor.com *Signs work*: 'M.A.Morgan'.

MORGAN, Ronald, RBA (1984), ROI (1984); draughtsman, painter in water-colour, black and white, oil and pastel, illustrator, teacher; Mem. Chelsea Art Soc.; winner of numerous awards for painting. *b*: Landywood, Staffs., 28 Feb 1936. *s of*: J. Morgan. *Educ*: Landywood Junior School, Great Wyrley Secondary School, Staffs. *Studied*: Walsall School of Art (1951-53). *Exhib*: RA, RI, RBA, NEAC, SGA, RWA, RBSA, RSMA, ROI, Paris Salon, Britain in Water-colours and touring exhbns., etc. *Works in collections*: London Boroughs of Islington, and Tower Hamlets, Graves A.G., Sheffield, Sultan of Oman. *Works Reproduced*: in Leisure Painter, La Revue Moderne (Paris, 1963, 1965), Royal Academy Illustrated. *Address*: 8 Marina Ct., Alfred St., Bow, London E3 2BH. *Signs work*: "R. MORGAN. 1990."

MORGAN, Tina, SWA (2003), LSIAD SWAc (2006); painter in oil; art director (1973-1983); Awards: Silver Award, Cannes Film Festival (1980), Campaign Press Award (1980), two awards London Designers and Art Directors Assoc. Gold Award, Cannes (1981), Irish Advertising Award, British Television Award (1982); Winsor and Newton Prize (2003); Daler Rowney Award (2005); voted onto SWA Committee (2004); invited onto Selection Committee SWAc (2009). *b*: Linton, Devon, 9 Jan 1952. *m*: Roger. three *s*. *Studied*: Cornwall College of Art and Design. *Exhib*: RWA, RSMA, RBA, SWA, Southwest Academy, Discerning Eye, Exeter University; solo exhibs. at Albemarle Gallery, Marine House at Beer Gallery, Priory Gallery, Fowey River Gallery, Sarah Samuels Fine Art. *Works in collections*: national and international. *Commissions*: MBNA Bank, Madrid Branch. *Publications*: Leisure Painter Magazine 2002, International Artist Magazine 2004. *Address*: Woodside, Farringdon, Exeter, Devon EX5 2JA. *Email*: ART@eclipse.co.uk *Signs work*: "Tina Morgan."

MORLEY, John, SWE; wood engraver and painter in oil and pastel. *b*: Beckenham, Kent, 12 Sep 1942. *m*: Diana. one *d*. *Studied*: Beckenham Art School, Ravensbourne College of Art, RA Schools. *Exhib*: RA Summer Exhibs. (1962-2011 inclusive), Piccadilly Gallery (1977-2003), Brotherhood of Ruralists, International Art Fair, Basle, Cologne, Dusseldorf, London. *Works in collections*: Museum of Modern Art, Wales, Arts Council of Great Britain, Ashmolean Museum, Glasgow City Art Gallery, National Trust, V&A Museum, British Museum. *Publications*: numerous. *Official Purchasers*: see above. *Clubs*: Soc. of Wood Engravers, Art Workers Guild. *Address*: North Green Only, Stoven, Beccles, Norfolk NR34 8DG. *Website*: www.johnmorley.info *Signs work*: "John Morley."

MORPETH, Vivienne Helen Bland, (née Totty), BA Hons Fine Art (1984), AMA (Art) (1990); curator/fine art; Fine Arts Officer, Middlesbrough Art Gallery (1985-88), Exhbns. Officer, Scunthorpe Museum (1989-92), County Arts and Museums Officer, Cleveland C.C. (1992-95), freelance curator (1995-). *b*: Edinburgh, 16 Feb 1962. *d of*: Alan Bland Totty, MBE, BA. *Educ*: The Rudolph Steiner School, Edinburgh. *Studied*: history of art and architecture: University of E. Anglia, Norwich (1981-84). *Exhib*: curated numerous exhbns. at Middlesbrough A.G. and Scunthorpe Museums, local, national, international art and artists tours. *Publications*: exhbn. catalogues. *Address*: 28 Westfield Rd., Barton-upon-Humber, South Humberside DN18 5AB.

MORRELL, Peter John, NDD 1st Hons (Painting, 1956), ARCA 1st Hons (Painting, 1959), Prix de Rome in Painting (1959), RWS (1973), Mem. London Group (1990); Arts Council Prize (1959); painter in oil and water-colour, lecturer. *b*: Newton Abbot, 28 Feb 1931. *s of*: Arthur Markham, MA. *m*: divorced. one *s*. one *d*. *Educ*: Worthing High School for Boys. *Studied*: Kingston-upon-Thames College of Art (1952-56), RCA (1956-59, Ruskin Spear, Carel Weight, John Minton, Colin Hayes). *Exhib*: RA, John Moores, Grabowski Gallery, New Art Centre, London Group, Beaux Arts Gallery, Arnolfini Gallery, Six Young Painters, Gimpel Fils, RWS, Arts Council Touring Exhbns., Gallery Appunto Rome; RWA Bristol. *Works in collections*: Arts Council, LCC, Charterhouse Boys' School, Science Museum, worldwide. *Commissions*: P&O Shipping. *Publications*: 'Face to Face' (pub. Piano Nobile), 'The Watercolour Expert' (pub. RWS). *Address*: 19 Tremeadow Terrace, Hayle, Cornwall TR27 4AF. *Email*: peterjmorrell@gmail.com *Website*: petermorrell.co.uk *Signs work*: "MORRELL."

MORRIS, Anthony, RP, NDD (1958), RAS (1961), NEAC (1995); painter/ illustrator in oil and water-colour. *b*: Oxford, 2 Aug 1938. *s of*: Francis Morris. *m*: Aileen. *Studied*: Oxford School of Art, RA Schools (Peter Greenham). *Exhib*: RA, RP, Medici Gallery. *Works in collections*: Bodleian Library, Open University, King's College Hospital. *Publications*: BBC and major publishers. *Address*: Church House, Cloduck, Longtown, Herefordshire HR2 0NY. *Signs work*: "MORRIS."

MORRIS, Elizabeth, NDD (1953), ATC (1955), Coley & Tiley Prize RBSA (1999). *Medium*: oils, watercolour, etchings. *b*: Bristol, 20 Jul 1932. *d of*: Captain George Villar RN. *m*: Bill Morris FRIBA FRSA. one *s*. two *d*. *Educ*: St. Stephens College, Broadstairs. *Studied*: Southern College of Art, Bournemouth (1949-53), Goldsmiths College (1954-55), Central School (1953-54, part-time), Morley College (1975-77, part-time). *Exhib*: RA 'Originals', Mall Galleries, The Barbican, National Theatre, Eastern Open. Solo shows: Bircham Gallery, Holt (2001), John Russell, Ipswich (2004), Haylett's, Maldon (2004, 2006, 2009, 2013), Univ. of Essex (2004), Geedon Gallery, Finginghoe. *Works in collections*: Chelsea and Westminster Hospital; Colchester Castle; 'Graphotek' Berlin; House of Lords; various LEA Collections. *Commissions*: 2 editions of etchings commissioned for the P&O cruiser 'Oriana' (1993); mural, Langley Primary School (1956); edition of Jubilee Alphabet for 2012 Regatta West Mersea. *Publications*: illustrations for: 'Oysters & Ale' by Heather Howard; 'Barbeque Cookers' by Maggie Black. *Official Purchasers*: etchings for House of Lords; Ministry of Defence; Chelsea and Westminster Hospital. *Works Reproduced*: in 'Water Marks' by Ian Collins; in 'Wildlife in Printmaking' by Carrie Akroyd; Aldeburgh, A Song of the Sea; The Coach House in Gainsborough's Garden. *Recreations*: boating, gardening, and DIY on island home in West Cork. *Misc*: Featured in Anglia TV series 'Coastal Inspirations' (2006). Founder Member of Greenwich Printmakers Association & Chair for 2 years. Member from 1979-2002. *Address*: Stone House, 112 Coast Road, Mersea Island, Essex, CO5 8NA. *Email*: liz@elizabethmorrisprints.co.uk *Website*: www.elizabethmorrisprints.co.uk *Signs work*: "Elizabeth Morris" (prints), "E.M." (oil paintings).

MORRIS, John, Mem., Water-colour Soc. of Wales; painter in water-colour. *b*: Deiniolen, N. Wales, 27 Sep 1922. *s of*: Robert Morris, boot and shoe retailer. *m*: Eluned Mary. one *s*. one *d*. *Educ*: Brynrefail County School, Bangor Normal College. *Studied*: Bangor Normal (1955-57, H. Douglas Williams), Press Art School, London (1958-60, Percy V. Bradshaw). *Exhib*: Williamson A.G. Birkenhead, Oriel Theatre Clwyd Mold, Wrexham Arts Centre, Albany Gallery Cardiff, R.I., N.S., Royal National Eisteddfod of Wales, Water-colour Soc. of Wales. *Works in collections*: Royal Welsh Agricultural Soc., National Library of Wales, Midland Bank Ltd., Burnley Building Soc., Clwyd C.C., Shotton Paper Co. *Publications*: Newid Aelwyd, Newid Bro. *Address*: Elidir, 46 Bryn Awelon, Yr Wyddgrug (Mold), Clwyd CH7 1LU, N. Wales. *Signs work*: "John Morris."

MORRIS, John Meirion, NDD (1959), ATD (1961), M.Phil (1989), RCA (2000), MOMA Glyndwr Award (2001); Lecturer: Kumasi University, Ghana. Aberystwyth University (1968-1981), Bangor University (1985-1990). *Medium*: sculptor in bronze &

wood mainly. *b*: Wales, 14 Mar 1936. *m*: Gwawr. two *s*. one *d*. *Educ*: Bala Boys Grammar School. *Studied*: Liverpool College of Art (1955-1961), University of Liverpool (1961-62),University of Bangor (1985-1990). *Exhib*: Piccadilly Gallery, Cork St., London, National Museum Galleries of Wales, Cardiff (1999). Solo at. MOMA Tabernacle, Wales (2000). solo exhibition at the Royal Cambrian Academy (2005). Maquette for a Tryweryn Monument, exhibited at British Embassy, New York (2004-2007). Retrospective exhibition at the Gregynog Gallery, National Library of Wales. *Works in collections*: Many of my sculptures are in private collections, 'Tryweryn' sculpture in The National Museum of Wales, Cardiff, and 11 bronze portraits of famous people at the National Library of Wales, Cardiff. *Commissions*: Memorial bronze bust of the Celtic scholar Edward Llwyd outside the University of Wales Centre for Celtic Studies, Aberystwyth. Designed a cross to commemorate R.S. Thomas, the poet, at Porthmadog Church. *Publications*: The Celtic Vision by John Meirion Morris, Lolfa (2002); 'John Meirion Morris, artist' with Professor Gwyn Thomas (2011). *Principal Works*: Bronze bust of Edward Llwyd (see commissions). Bronze portrait of the poet 'Gwenallt' and the dramatist Saunders Lewis. *Address*: Cae Blanc, Llanuwchlyn, Bala, Gwynedd LL23 7TT. *Email*: johnmeirion@btinternet.com *Website*: john meirion morris *Signs work*: "J.M.M."

MORRIS, Mali, RA (elected 2010); BA, MFA; Awards: Lorne, Daiwa, Arts Council, British Council, research awards, Prizewinner Creekside Open 2007. *Medium*: acrylic, canvas, paper, print. *b*: North Wales, 1945. *Partner*: Stephen Lewis. *Studied*: University of Newcastle upon Tyne (1963-68), University of Reading (1968-70). *Exhib*: 30 solo shows since 1979, including Ikon Gallery, Serpentine Gallery, Mostyn Gallery; many group shows worldwide; solo shows in Tokyo and New York. *Works in collections*: ACGB, British Council, Contemporary Arts Soc., Eastern Arts Assoc., Government Art Collection, Lloyds of London, National Museum of Wales, Cardiff, Royal Collection, Whitworth Gallery, Manchester, etc., many private collections. *Commissions*: Ledbury Poetry Festival (2009). *Publications*: Mali Morris ('92) (by Stuart Bradshaw) ISBN 1 873215 606; Mali Morris ('94) (by Martha Kapos) ISBN 1 899535 004; Mali Morris ('02) (by David Ryan) ISBN 0 905634 543; Turps Banana Issue 7 (by Peter Suchin), Issue 8 (on Robert Welch) and Issue 12 (on Geoff Rigden), RA Magazine, Spring 2014 (on Matisse). *Address*: Apt Studios, Harold Wharf, 6 Creekside, London SE8 4SA. *Email*: malimorris@talktalk.net *Website*: www.malimorris.co.uk *Signs work*: "Mali Morris."

MORRIS, Nigel William, B.Des (Hons), Cert.Ed. *Medium*: oil, acrylic, mixed, watercolour. *b*: Wirral, 24 Oct 1957. *s of*: R W Morris. *Partner*: J E Fish. *Studied*: Liverpool Hope University. *Exhib*: Mall Galleries, Manchester Aerospace Museum, Bury Art Gallery, Mariners Gallery, DLI Gallery Durham, Westminster Gallery, Carisbrooke Gallery, Royal Cambrian Academy, Grosvenor Museum and Gallery, Williamson Art Gallery, RAF Cosford Aerospace Museum, Red Bill Gallery, Deeside, Obsidian Gallery, Buckinghamshire. *Works in collections*: Chester Grosvenor Museum and Gallery; many private collections. *Commissions*: British Aerospace, Royal Air Force Association, many private commissions. *Official Purchasers*: Chester City Council. *Works Reproduced*: numerous. *Clubs*: Deeside Art Group mem, Irby Artists Asociation, Wallasey Arts Society. *Misc*: NAPA, Associate of GAvA. *Address*: 1 Headington Road, Saughall, Massie, Wirral, CH49 4GG. *Signs work*: Nigel W.Morris.

MORRIS, Suzi, Currently undertaking a Professional Doctorate at University of East London (UEL). MA in Fine Art. *Medium:* Oil. b: Ayr, Scotland. *Studied:* City and Guilds of London Art School. *Exhib:* Affordable Art Fair (2013), The Other Art Fair (2013), Henley Festival of Arts (2013). *Works in collections:* Private/corporations. *Publications:* Parallels of the Sublime, ISBN 5060 15 1960 191. *Misc:* Art director in film. Worked on Shady Lady, a 2013 Academy Award contender. *Email:* suzi@suzimorrisart.com *Website:* www.suzimorrisart.com *Signs work:* "Suzi Morris Loraine".

MORRIS-JONES, Muriel (Moo), (nee TURNER), RDS Hons; no formal art education; City & Guilds 'Post graduate' painting prize, prizes for water-colours, drawings and prints; Judged Winner of 'Inspired By' exhibited at V&A Museum (2011) sculpture 'Finding a Voice'. Royal Navy 30 years. *Medium*: oil, acrylic, scuplture and most others. *b*: London, 4 Nov 1928. one *s*. one *d*. *Educ*: Private. *Exhib*: USA (1963-69), Belgium, London. Invited to submit for 'Drawmore' at the Rootstein Hopkins Drawing Exhibition (2011). *Works in collections*: USA, Belgium. *Commissions*: bronze bust of Princess Diana at Gt. Ormond Street Hospital. Intellectual Property, patents granted USA and UK. *Publications*: cartoons 'Women Draw 84' and Sunday Times; 'Science and Public Affairs' (Christmas 1999). *Principal Works*: Bronze bust Princess Diana; 'In the Beginning' acrylic. *Address*: 26 Old Gloucester St., Bloomsbury, London WC1N 3AF. *Email*: moosideas@hotmail.com *Signs work*: early work: "MURIEL TURNER," now "M. Morris-Jones.", "M" or "MOO".

MORRISON, James, RSA, RSW, D.Univ., DA.; painter in oil and water-colour; paints extensively in the High Arctic, France. *b*: Glasgow, 11 Apr 1932, married. one *s*. one *d*. *Educ*: Hillhead High School, Glasgow School of Art. *Represented by*: The Scottish Gallery, 16 Dundas St., Edinburgh EH3 6HZ tel: 0131 558 1200. *Exhib*: Edinburgh, London, Glasgow, New York, Toronto, Florence, Dusseldorf, The Hague, Johannesburg, Tokyo, Hong Kong, Dublin. *Works in collections*: Glasgow, Dundee and Aberdeen Art galleries, Arts Council, Argyll, Dundee and Edinburgh Educ. Committees, Glasgow, Edinburgh, Strathclyde and Stirling Universities, H.R.H. the Duke of Edinburgh, Dept. of the Environment, various embassies, Kingsway Technical College, Vaughan College, Leicester, Municipality of the Hague, Earls of Dalhousie, Moray, Airlie, Robert Fleming, Merchant Bankers, BBC, Grampian Television, General Accident, Scottish Amicable, Life Assoc. of Scotland; Banks: Royal, Scotland, Clydesdale, T.S.B. *Commissions*: numerous private and public. *Publications*: author, Aff the Squerr; Paris in Winter. *Works Reproduced*: From Balgove, 1996; Montrose, 1995. *Misc*: Chamber Music Group. *Address*: Craigview House, Usan, Montrose, Angus DD10 9SD. *Signs work*: "Morrison" and date.

MORRISON, Les (Leslie Howard), BSc (Eng), BA (Arch), M.Arch, RIBA. CEPHD. Best Commercial Facade, City of London (1990). Arguenteuil Award for Architecture 2009. *Medium*: 3D Animation, Illustration, Parametric Design. *grandson of*: Thomas Walter Morrison. *m*: Keiko Hayama. *Studied*: Chartered Engineer, Exeter College (1972-75); Chartered Architect, Brooks College, Oxford (RIBA 1986); Certified Passivhaus Designer, BRE/PHI Darmstadt (2010), BREEAM International AP, Deloittes Paris (2011). *Represented by*: Philip Kucharski & Keiko Hayama. *Exhib*: Royal Academy 1989 (Fitzroy Robinson), Royal Academy, London (2002), Musee D'Orsay, Paris (2003), UENO Museum of Art, Tokyo (2007). *Works in collections*: Facade to King William Street, City of London; School of Music, Lyon; Kenzo Birdstair, Shinjuku, Tokyo. *Commissions*: IPE, London (1992), Cipieres Planning Strategy (1994), Furniture of Classicium, Mitsui (1995), Gigouzac, MTV & Musique Bibliotheque (2002-2010), Bordeau Centre. *Publications*: Rural Buildings of the South West of England, OUP, Revit for Architects (New Riders). *Works Reproduced*: King William Street, Birdstair, Conservatoire de Musique de Lyon. *Principal Works*: MTV European, 'Yet to come'. *Recreations*: President of Improvise Records. *Clubs*: 606, London. *Misc*: Major works - the Continuing Evolution of Classical Architecture & Design through Modern Technology; Passivhaus - a means to reduce energy use in buildings. BIM (Building Information Modelling). BREEAM International AP. *Address*: 41 Manchuria Road, London SW11 6AF. *Email*: les@lesmorrison.co.uk *Website*: www.lesmorrison.co.uk *Signs work*: "Les Morrison"

MORROCCO, Jack Bernard, DA (1974) Post Diploma (Highly Commended) (1975); Farquhar Reid Travelling Scholarship (1975). *Medium*: oil, watercolour. *b*: Edinburgh, 27 May 1953. *s of*: Valentino Morrocco ARIBA & Rozelle Morrocco, artist. *m*: Fiona Morrocco. one *s*. one *d*. *Educ*: Madras College, St.Andrews. *Studied*: Duncan of Jordanstone

College of Art, Dundee. *Exhib*: solo exhbns: Thompson's Gallery, London; Richmond Hill Gallery, London; Leith Gallery, Edinburgh; Henshelwood Gallery, Newcastle; Broadway Modern, Cotswolds; Solo Gallery, Edinburgh; Rendezvous Gallery, Aberdeen; Eduardo Alessandro Gallery, Dundee; Open Eye Gallery, Edinburgh; group exhbns include: RSA, RGI, Compass Gallery, Glasgow; 6 Scottish Colourists, St.Andrews; Falle Fine Art, Jersey; Forbes Gallery, New York; Gallerie Azur, St. Paul de Vence; CFAG, Eton. *Works Reproduced*: various signed editions by 'Rosenstiels'. *Address*: Cairnie House, By Colinsburgh, Fife, Scotland KY9 1JX. *Email*: jack@jackmorrocco.com *Website*: www.jackmorrocco.com *Signs work*: 'MORROCCO'.

MORROCCO, Leon, DA (Edin), ARSA, RGI; painter in oil and mixed media. *b*: Edinburgh, 4 Apr 1942. *m*: Jean Elizabeth Selby. two *s*. *Educ*: Harris Academy, Dundee. *Studied*: Duncan of Jordanstone College of Art, Dundee (1960, Alberto Morrocco, RSA), Slade School of Fine Art (1960-61, Sir William Coldstream), Edinburgh College of Art (1961-65, Sir Robin Philipson, RSA). *Represented by*: John Martin Galleries, London; Open Eye Gallery, Edinburgh. *Exhib*: 20 one-man shows since 1966, Scotland, London, Melbourne, Sydney. *Works in collections*: USA, Britain, Australia, etc. *Commissions*: mural, John Lewis Partnership, Glasgow (2000); 3 paintings aboard P&O's 'Arcadia' (2004). *Publications*: 'Journeys and Observations' monograph (1999) . *Clubs*: Chelsea Arts. *Address*: c/o Royal Scottish Academy, The Mound, Edinburgh EH2 2EL. *Signs work*: "Leon Morrocco."

MORROW, Gary Thomas, BSc (Hons) (not art related). *Medium*: Oil; drawing. *b*: Glasgow, 29 Jul 1974. *Studied*: Strathclyde University (not art related); Academy of Realist Art, Toronto, Summer 2006; mostly self-taught. *Represented by*: Morningside Gallery, Greens and Blues Gallery, Red Rag Bath. *Exhib*: The Contemporary Fine Art Gallery, Eton; By Distinction Art, Glasgow; Harkirk Gallery, Liverpool; Art in the City, Glasgow; Glasgow Art Club; Edinburgh Art Fair; The Blythswood Gallery. *Commissions*: Numerous private, mostly portraiture. *Publications*: Portrait used for advertising campaign for McTears Auctioneers (tv), Scotsman magazine and Scottish Field gallery advertising. Works Reproduced: 'Black and White', 'At the Exhibition'. *Clubs*: Glasgow Art Club. *Address*: 6b Montgomery Square, Eaglesham, Glasgow G76 0AB. *Email*: gary@garymorrowart.com *Website*: www.garymorrowart.com *Signs work*: "GM".

MORSE, Colin Benjamin Scale, DipAD (1982); illustrator in water-colour and mixed media. *b*: Pembrokeshire, 6 Aug 1942. *m*: Joan, Ellen. one *s-s*. two *s-d*. *Educ*: Haverfordwest Grammar School. *Studied*: Dyfed College of Art, Carmarthen (1978-82); work on display in various commercial galleries throughout UK. *Publications*: limited edition prints – images of the coast, countryside and people of Wales. *Address*: Beudy Bach Penfeidr, Castlemorris Haverfordwest Pembrokeshire, SA62 5EN. *Website*: www.bestofruralwales.co.uk www.welshpictures.co.uk *Signs work*: "Colin Morse".

MORSMAN, Phil, Northern Arts Awards 1986, 87, 89, 92, 97; Oppenheim-Downes 1989; Cumbria Visual Arts Award 1996; Eden Arts Bursary 1996; Cultural Business Award 2000. *Medium*: acrylic, gouache, mixed media, prints. *b*: London, 30 Jan 1946. *m*: Jean. two *d*. *Studied*: Epsom School of Art (1962-63), Wimbledon School of Art (1963-65), Sheffield College of Art (1965-67). *Exhib*: Abbot Hall Gallery, Kendal; Northern Centre for Contemporary Art, Sunderland; Salt House Gallery, St. Ives; Collins Gallery, Glasgow; The View, Liverpool; Broughton House Gallery, Cambridge; Lady Margaret Hall, Oxford; Storey Gallery, Lancaster; Tullie House, Carlisle; McLellan Galleries, Glasgow; RFH, London; Lamec, Vicenza, Italy; Irma Stern Museum, Capetown. *Works in collections*: Tullie House Museum, Carlisle; Penrith Museum, Fitzwilliam Museum (prints), Darlington Borough Council, North Tyneside Council, Cumbria County Council, Durham City Council, Cumberland Infirmary, Lancaster Royal Infirmary, University of Newcastle-upon-Tyne,

Marriott Hotel Group. *Address*: St.Michaels, Bongate, Appleby, Cumbria, CA16 6UR. *Email*: philmorsman@beeb.net *Signs work*: "MORSMAN".

MORTIMER, Justin Roger, BA Fine Art (1992); painter in oil. *b*: UK, 6 Apr 1970. *Partner*: Kathy Dalwood. *Educ*: Wells Cathedral School. *Studied*: Slade School (1988-1992). *Exhib*: solo exhibs., Beaux Arts, Bath (1993), Blue Gallery, London (1995, 1997, 1998), Lefevre Contemporary (2000), Bertin Toublanc, Paris (2006); Pippy Houldsworth, London (2007); Five Hundred Dollars, London (2009); Master Piper, London (2010). *Works in collections*: National Portrait Gallery, NatWest Collection, Henley River & Rowing Museum, Royal Collection, RSA, MCC Lords, FA. *Commissions*: portraits of Harold Pinter (NPG 1992), David Bowie & Iman (1994), H.M. The Queen Elizabeth (RSA 1998), Lord Chamberlain (Airlie, RCA 1998), Steve Redgrave (1998), Brian Lara (MCC, 2006); Glenn MacGrath (MCC, 2010). *Clubs*: Ivy Colony Room Club. *Address*: 165 Victoria Rd., London NW6 6TE. *Email*: justin@justinmortimer.co.uk *Website*: justinmortimer.co.uk *Signs work*: "J Mortimer."

MORTIMER, Martin Christopher Fortescue, Consultant, Delomosne & Son Ltd. Specialist in English Porcelain, English and Irish Glass, particularly English glass lighting fittings, and articles on these subjects in various art journals. *b*: London, 4 Jul 1928. *s of*: George Mortimer (British Aluminium Co.). *m*: Sara Ann Proctor. *Educ*: Shrewsbury School. *Publications*: author, The English Glass Chandelier (Antique Collectors' Club, 2000). *Address*: Court Close, North Wraxall, Chippenham, Wiltshire SN14 7AD.

MORTON, Gina, RMS, HS, SLm; Awards: RMS Gold Memorial Bowl (2005); Llewellyn Alexander Subject Miniature Award (RMS, 2003), SLm 'Chairman's Choice' (2004 & 2011); Llewellyn Alexander Masters Award (2005); RMS Group Award (2005); Mary Scott-Kestin Award (HS, 2005); Peter Charles Booth Memorial Award (RMS, 2006); winner, 'Saunders Waterford Postcard Competition' (2006); Best Flora & Fauna - World Federation of Miniaturists (2008); President's Special Commendation (RMS, 2008), Country Club UK Award (2009); Winner 'Sennelier 2011 Watercolour Painting Competition'; Anthony J Lester Art Critic Award (RMS 2012); Prince of Wales Award (RMS 2013); Anita Emmerich Presentation Award (RMS 2013). *Medium*: watercolour. *b*: Darlington, 26 Apr 1951. *Educ*: Branksome School, Darlington. *Exhib*: solo exhbns: County Durham and North Yorkshire; group exhbns: Mall Galleries, Llewellyn Alexander Gallery, and others. *Works in collections*: Darlington Borough Council. *Principal Works*: traditional loose watercolours and detailed miniatures. *Clubs*: Hon.Sec. Darlington Society of Arts (1977-2007). *Address*: 37 Westbourne Grove, Darlington, Co.Durham, DL3 8HT. *Email*: georginamorton@btinternet.com *Website*: www.ga-morton.co.uk *Signs work*: 'G MORTON'.

MOSELEY, Malcolm, BA (1969), MA (1973); RCA Travel Award; RCA Alumni (2011); painter. *Medium*: mixed media on canvas and paper, and drawing. *b*: Birmingham, 2 Feb 1947. one *s*. one *d*. *Studied*: Birmingham College of Art (1965), Winchester School of Art (1966-69), Central School of Art (1969-70), RCA (1970-73). *Exhib*: RA, RSW, London Group, Mall Galleries, Barbican, Eastern Open, New English, Laing Landscape, Suffolk Group, Suffolk Showcase, Snape Maltings. *Works in collections*: Ipswich Museums, P&O, McDonalds, Hammersmith and Fulham Council, private collections. *Publications*: How Artists See.. Nature (Green Pebble Publications, Beccles). *Recreations*: walking, reading, cinema, music, theatre. *Clubs*: Ipswich Art Soc., Suffolk Group. *Address*: 133 Norwich Rd., Ipswich, Suffolk IP1 2PP. *Email*: moseleymalcolm@yahoo.co.uk *Website*: www.malcolmmoseley.com *Signs work*: "M.M."

MOSS, Zoë, BA Hons Fine Art, Dip AD. *Medium*: oil, drawing. *b*: London, 19 Sep 1981. *d of*: Layn & Stuart Moss. *Studied*: Chelsea College of Art and Design (200-01, Foundation); University of Central Lancashire (2002-05). *Exhib*: Curwen and New Academy Gallery (2005), Cork Street Gallery (2008), Chichester Open Art Competition (2008), Royal

Academy Summer Exhibition (2008, 2009). *Commissions*: over 40 private commissions, consisting of drawings and oil paintings. *Publications*: Artists and Illustrators magazine (2008), The Big Issue (Jul/Aug 2008). *Official Purchasers*: various private purchases, commissioned through website. *Works Reproduced*: 'Mireille' oil painting 2007. *Principal Works*: 'Mireille' oil painting 2007, 'Silver Horse' oil painting 2009, 'Ephemera, Animals' 2005. *Misc*: I am currently illustrating a childrens book I have written, and putting together a solo show. *Address*: 12A Hervey Close, Finchley, London N3 2HD. *Email*: zoemoss@hotmail.com *Website*: www.zoemoss.com *Signs work*: "Zoë Moss".

MOTT, Miranda J. M. *Medium*: oil, acrylic and watercolour, etching, lino, wood engraving, intaglio and relief prints, artist's books. *b*: London, 6 Jul 1934. *d of*: Helga and Tom Mott. *m*: John Hoskyns. two *s*. one *d*. *Educ*: Eothen, Caterham, Surrey. *Studied*: Byam Shaw; Royal Academy Schools. *Exhib*: Royal Academy, Portrait Painters, Society of Wood Engravers, Barbican, National Theatre, sixteen solo exhibitions, numerous group exhibitions in UK and abroad. *Works in collections*: public and private collections in UK, Germany, USA, South Africa. *Commissions*: portraits and murals, various others and publishers. *Publications*: book illustration for Faber, Michael Joseph, MacMillan, Folio Society, Penguin; 'When the Wind Blew' written and illustrated, Miranda Hoskyns; 'The Coach house in Gainsborough's Garden' (Editor) pub. Oct 2012. *Works Reproduced*: as above. *Recreations*: writing, gardening. *Misc*: Gainsborough's House Print Workshop (Chairman 1979-82), Printmakers Council (1981-6), 12PM (twelve printmakers) (1996), Gainsborough Printmakers (1979); Member, Society of Wood Engravers (1991-2009). *Address*: Windrush, Great Waldingfield, Sudbury, Suffolk, CO10 0RZ. *Email*: mj_mott@hotmail.co.uk *Website*: www.mjmott.co.uk *Signs work*: "M.J.MOTT".

MOUNTFORD, Derylie Anne, BA Hons, SWA (1988); artist in pencil, etching, oil and water-colour. *b*: London, 17 Jun 1943. *d of*: Alfred Hobson, FRCS. *m*: Malcolm Mountford, B.A.(Oxon.). two *s*. *Educ*: Montessori, Wimbledon. *Studied*: Byam Shaw School of Art (1960-62, Peter Greenham, Bernard Dunstan), St. Martin's School of Art (1963), University of Brighton (B.A. Hons. History of Design, 1998). *Exhib*: RA, RBA, RMS, SWA, NSPS, CDS; one-man shows: Japan (1986, 1988), Lyric Theatre, Hammersmith (1990), Cambridge (1988); group shows: Cambridge, Ely, Saffron Walden, Salisbury, London, Sussex, etc., Brighton Festival, Sussex Open. *Works in collections*: Addenbrookes Hospital Trust. *Commissions*: various. *Address*: 3 Belle Vue Gdns., Brighton, Sussex BN2 2AA. *Email*: derrymountford@hotmail.com *Signs work*: "Derylie Mountford" (etchings), "D. Mountford" (paintings).

MOUNTJOY, Robert William, Trustee and Member of the South West Academy of Fine and Applied Arts (SWAc); Arts Council Painting Award (1981); Mail Marketing International Prize (2002); Lynn Painter Stainer Shortlist (2005). *Medium*: watercolour. *b*: Bideford, 13 Dec 1950. *s of*: Gordon Henry Mountjoy. *m*: Sian Mountjoy. two *d*. *Educ*: Bideford Grammar School, St. Pauls', Cheltenham. *Studied*: Bristol University BEd (Hons). *Represented by*: Elford Fine Art, Faraway Islands. *Exhib*: Cheltenham Group (1972-1984); RWA (1979-2008); SWAc (2000-2012); RSMA (2005); Lynn Painter Stainer Mall (2005). Solo Shows: Rookesmoor (1983); Delahaye (1984); Mayflower (1990); Artframe, Plymouth (2006); Beaux Arts (2006). *Works in collections*: Cheltenham Borough Council (1980); private. *Works Reproduced*: ln 'Art in Devon' Summer Edition (2006); 'A Picture of Devon' R. Balkwill, Halsgrove (2008). *Recreations*: fishing. *Address*: 12 Morley Drive, Crapstone, Devon, PL20 7UY. *Email*: robertmountjoy@mac.com *Website*: mountjoy-rw.com *Signs work*: "R.W.MOUNTJOY".

MOWAT, Jane Catherine, BA (Hons) History of Art, PGCE (Art); artist/printmaker in woodcuts. *b*: Stamford, Lincs., 5 Apr 1956. *Partner*: Johnny Mars, musician. one *s*. one *d*. *Studied*: Courtauld Inst.of Art - Art History (1975-78, Anita Brookner, George Zarnecki).

Exhib: many Open Exhbns. in South West, including RWEA and Spike Island in Bristol, Royal Academy, Curwen Gallery, Air Gallery, National Print at Mall Galleries in London. *Commissions*: Screen for Russell-Cotes Museum, Bournemouth; carving for Hestercombe Gardens (National Trust), Taunton, Somerset; prints for Musgrove Park Hospital, Taunton. *Publications*: illustrated: You and Your Child's Behaviour (Birmingham and Redditch Health Authority, 1984). *Clubs*: Somerset Printmakers, Hurstone Studios, Swiss Artists UK. *Address*: 5 Palmerston Rd., Taunton Somerset TA1 1ES. *Email*: janemowat@eclipse.co.uk *Signs work*: "Jane Mowat."

MOWLL, Benjamin Nicholas Bullen, LLB Solicitor; RSMA; St Cuthberts Mill Award (2006); Buzzacott Award (2011). *Medium*: Oil, watercolour, drawing. *b*: Yorkshire, 16 Mar 1967. *m*: Annabel. two *d*. *Educ*: The Kings School, Canterbury. *Represented by*: Kendalls Fine Art, Windrush Gallery. *Exhib*: since 2004 Royal Society of Marine Artist, Mall Galleries, London. Since 1996 annual solo exhibition at home. Kendalls Fine Art, Cowes, Isle of Wight; Windrush Gallery, Windrush, Burford, Oxfordshire OX18 4TU. *Works in collections*: Private; corporate. *Publications*: The Artist magazine, article published in Summer issue 2014. Cover illustration for 'Operation Red Jericho' (winner of Poppy Red Award for innovation in childrens books at the British Book Trade Awards). Spine illustrations for 'Operation Typhoon Shore' and 'Operation Storm City' (known collectively as the Guild Trilogy). Author Joshua Mowll. All published by Walker Books. *Recreations*: Guitar. *Misc*: RSMA council member. *Address*: Sandbanks Court, Sandbanks Lane, Graveney, Faversham ME13 9DH. *Email*: themowlls@hotmail.com *Signs work*: "BENJAMIN MOWLL".

MOXLEY, Ann Barbara, (nee March); RWA, FRIBA; chartered architect. *Medium*: pen and ink, watercolours, oils. *b*: Shanghai, 2 Feb 1933. *d of*: Ewart March. *m*: Ray Moxley. three *d*. *Studied*: Royal West of England Academy School of Architecture. *Exhib*: annual exhibits at RWA Bristol. *Works in collections*: mainly private. *Address*: March House, Cargreen, Cornwall, PL12 6PA. *Signs work*: "ANN SCAMPTON", "A.S." or "A. Scampton."

MOXLEY, Ray, FRIBA, RWA, FRSA, Hon. F.(W.Eng.). *b*: 28 Jun 1923. *s of*: Rev. H.R. Moxley. *m*: Ann. one *s*. two *d*. *Educ*: Caterham. *Studied*: architecture: Oxford (1940-42 and 1946-49). *Exhib*: RWA annual 1960 onwards, ACA Salons at the Royal Academy (1982, 1984, 1986). *Commissions*: architect of Chelsea Harbour and Excel Exhibition Centre, London; Vice-president RIBA (1971-74), President ACA (1974-76). *Publications*: Building Construction (Batsford), Fee Negotiations (AP), Architects Eye (GPC), Building Management by Professionals (Butterworth). *Works Reproduced*: Pics of Excel and Chelsea Harbour frequently reproduced. *Recreations*: sailing, classical piano. *Clubs*: Royal West of England Yacht Club, Cargreen Yacht Club Cornwall, RIBA, ACA, WCCA. *Address*: March House, Cargreen, Saltash, Cornwall, PL12 6PA. *Signs work*: "Ray Moxley."

MOXLEY, Susan, Diploma in Fine Art, Postgraduate Printmaking. *Medium*: oil, drawing, prints and stained glass. *b*: South Africa, 17 May 1955. *d of*: Peter Moxley. *m*: Korky Paul. one *s*. one *d*. *Educ*: matriculation. *Studied*: Durban School of Art, South Africa (1974-77); Croydon College of Art (1978-79). *Exhib*: mixed and private, Print Show Barbican, Mall Galleries, Affordable Art Fair. *Commissions*: Stained glass panel for Reading Museum of Rural Life, SSI Philip & James School Oxford. *Official Purchasers*: Art in Hospitals, Foreign Office. *Address*: 43 Oakthorpe Road, Summertown, Oxford, OX2 7BD. *Website*: www.susanmoxley.co.uk *Signs work*: "Susan Moxley".

MUIR, Jane, artist, in mosaic, etching and water-colour. *b*: 11 Apr 1929. *d of*: H. Pinches, MD. *m*: A. W. E. Muir. two *s*. *Educ*: Rye St. Antony School. *Studied*: Oxford University, Teesside College of Art. MA Oxon (1950), Dip. Architectural Decoration (1969), FCSD (1974). *Exhib*: numerous. Founder Mem. International Assoc. of Contemporary Mosaic Artists, UK exhibitor Ravenna (1980), Trier (1984), Louvain (1986), Tokyo (1994), Alexandria (1996), Exeter (1999), Touring Anglo-Italian Mosaic Exhbn. (2000). Patron,

British Assoc. for Modern Mosaic, 'Sounding Image', Buckinghamshire Art Gallery (2003); 'Soundings', St.Anne's College Oxford (2005). *Works in collections*: Public: Oxon County Museum, Buckinghamshire County Museum, Glynn Vivian A.G., Open University, St. Anne's College, Oxford; Ruskin Gallery, Sheffield; Corning Museum, USA Major Commissions: St. Anne's College Oxford; Open University; Princes Sq., Glasgow; Longmarket, Canterbury; Becket's Well, Northampton; Doha, Arabian Gulf. *Commissions*: numerous. *Publications*: videos: 'Mosaic as Art', 'New Directions in Mosaic'. *Official Purchasers*: Picture of Health Ltd. *Clubs*: Art Workers' Guild; Guild of St.George. *Address*: Butcher's Orchard, Weston Turville, Aylesbury, Bucks. HP22 5RL. *Email*: forestfool99@gmail.com *Website*: www.janemuir.com *Signs work*: "Muir."

MUIRDEN, Philip, David Murray Student, NDD, ATD; Lecturer, Mansfield College of Art (1965-72), Senior lecturer, Newport College of Art (1975-). *b*: Milford Haven, 23 Oct 1932. one *s*. *Educ*: Haverfordwest Grammar School. *Studied*: Cardiff College of Art, Cardiff University. *Represented by*: Agents: Janet Martin, GPF Gallery, Newport, Gwent; www.seapicturesgallery.com. *Exhib*: RA (5 yrs.), Sunday Times Water-colour of the Year (3 yrs.), Hunting Group - Britain in Water-colour; one-man shows include Newport Gallery (2); Welsh Drawing Biennale (2). *Works in collections*: Arts Council of Wales, Contemporary Art Soc., Mold Council, Newport Museum, Newport Council S. Glam., International Drawing Biennale 1999, one man show Newport, Gwent 2003. *Publications*: Poems; TV BBC Wales, and Swap Shop National BBC; articles for Art News and Review; films: River Patrol S4C 2000, 30 minute film Nigerian TV 2003. *Clubs*: The Welsh Group. *Address*: 6 Lower Hill St., Hakin, Milford Haven SA73 3LP. *Signs work*: "PHILIP MUIRDEN" or "MUIRDEN."

MULCAHY, Bruce, Member, Royal Society of Marine Artists (2007); BA (Hons) Fine Art; Hamer Award (1991); Sykes Award (1995, 1997, 2000); Laing Competition Guests Award (1995, 1997); Calder Graphics Prize (2003). *Medium*: painter in gouache, oil, acrylic. *b*: Dewsbury, 1955. *Educ*: Wheelwright Grammar School, Dewsbury. *Studied*: University of Newcastle-upon-Tyne (1974-78) Fine Art (Prof. Kenneth Rowntree). *Represented by*: Trattles and Geall, Whitby; Myton Gallery, Hull; Look Gallery, Helmsley; Staithes Gallery. *Exhib*: Mall Galleries, London; Singer and Friedlander/Sunday Times Watercolour Competition; Manchester Academy of Fine Arts; many group and one-man shows in UK. *Works in collections*: work in many private collections in UK and fourteen other countries to date. *Clubs*: Fylingdales Group of Artists; Huddersfield Art Society; Dewsbury Art Group. *Misc*: part-time private art tutor/demonstrator. *Address*: 44 Barber Walk, Eightlands, Dewsbury, W Yorks, WF13 2PN. *Email*: bruce.mulcahy@virginmedia.com *Website*: www.brucemulcahy.co.uk *Signs work*: 'B. MULCAHY' (and date).

MULES, Joanna Mary, B.Ed (1977), ARUA (1990). *Medium*: Mixed. many and various. *b*: Hants., 4 Sep 1949. *d of*: Mary Watson & Nicholas Marwood Mules. *m*: Marcus Patton. three *s*. *Educ*: Elmhurst Ballet School, Camberley, Surrey (1957-63), Londonderry High School (1963-66). *Studied*: Belfast College of Art and Design (1966-68); Stranmillis College of Education, Belfast (1973-77). *Exhib*: Royal Ulster Academy, Bell Gallery, Arts Club, QUB Common Room, Linehall Library, Ulster Museum, Flowerfield Arts Centre Portstewart. *Works in collections*: DOE, but mainly private collections. *Commissions*: National Self-portrait Collection, Limerick, portraits, landscapes, Still life, design for operas at Zezerearts. *Publications*: covers for Gape Row, Night of the Big Wind (1st and 2nd Edition). *Works Reproduced*: RUA catalogues; History of RUA. *Recreations*: singing, reading, gardening, wildlife. *Clubs*: R.U.A. *Address*: Ingledene, 1 Sans Souci Lane, Belfast BT9 5QY. *Email*: joanna.patton@virgin.net

MULLEN, Kay, SWA (1993), SBA (1995), ARMS (1998); self taught painter; Winner of Alexander Gallery Award, SWA (1999). *Medium*: watercolour, pastel, mixed media *b*: Mottingham, Kent, 3 Sep 1959. one *d*. *Educ*: Nonsuch High School for Girls, Cheam, Surrey. *Studied*: City and Guilds, - teaching of adults in further education. *Exhib*: SWA, SBA and RMS at Westminster Central Halls, many mixed exhbns. *Commissions*: numerous for private collections. *Works Reproduced*: Medici, The Paper House Group and Quatro Publishing. *Address*: 1b Parkhurst, Epsom, Surrey KT19 8QZ. *Email*: kaymullen51@yahoo.com *Website*: www.epsomartcourses.co.uk *Signs work*: 'K.Mullen'.

MULLETT, Vivien, ARMS (1992), HS (1990), BA Fine Art (1974); artist in watercolour, graphic designer. *b*: Oxford, 1952. *Educ*: Milham Ford School, Oxford. *Studied*: Reading University (1970-74). *Exhib*: RA Summer Show, RMS, HS, MAS-F. *Publications*: illustrated The Night Watchman - collection of stories. *Address*: 111 Penwith Rd., Earlsfield, London SW18 4PY. *Signs work*: "VM."

MULLINGS, Pam, freelance artist of British wildlife in gouache. *b*: Littlehampton, 18 Jan 1940. *m*: Maurice. one *s*. one *d*. *Exhib*: London and West Country. *Clubs*: H.S., A.R.M.S. *Address*: 'Rough Close', 13 Park Lane, Seend Cleeve, Melksham SN12 6PT. *Signs work*: "Pam Mullings."

MULLINS, Edwin Brandt, BA, MA (Hons.) Oxford University (1957); writer and film-maker, mainly on art subjects. *b*: London, 1933. *m*: Gillian Brydone (d. 1982). one *s*. two *d*.; Anne Kelleher (1984). *Educ*: Midhurst Grammar School and Oxford University. *Publications*: numerous books and over 200 television films. *Misc*: son of Claud Mullins. *Address*: 25 The Crescent, Barnes, London SW13 0NN.

MULROY, Alison, ASWA, SWA Committe Member; Winsor & Newton Young Artist Award (SWA, 2006). *Medium*: oil on canvas. *b*: Aylesbury, Bucks, 23 Oct 1978. *Studied*: self taught. *Exhib*: Mall Galleries. *Address*: Flat 4, 145A Balham Hill, London SW12 9LD. *Email*: alison_mulroy@yahoo.co.uk *Website*: www.alisonmulroy.com *Signs work*: 'A J Mulroy'.

MUMBERSON, Stephen Leonard, RE (1995), MA (1981), BA (Hons.) (1977); Reader in Fine Art Printmaking - Associate Professor (2014); Grand Prize Winner International Cartoon Contest China (2005); Special Prize Winner Bird 05 China, Master Cup Silver Medal China (2011); Gold Panda Silver Medal China (2012); Gold Panda Copper Medal China (2014). *Medium*: printer/ painter/ sculptor/ 3D printer/ cartoonist/ digital artist. *b*: Beaconsfield, 16 Feb 1955. *Educ*: Secondary Modern School, Bucks. *Studied*: Brighton Polytechnic (1977-78), RCA (1978-81, Prof. Grant, Prof.Chris. Orr), Cité des Arts, Paris (1980). *Exhib*: RE, Bankside London, Art Now London, PMC - Print Makers Council. *Works in collections*: V&A, USA, Japan, S. America, Europe, Canada, Zambia, Zimbabwe, China. *Publications*: 'Printmaking on a Budget' A&C Black. *Recreations*: travel, photography. *Address*: Fine Art Programme, Middlesex University, The Grove Building, The Burroughs, Hendon NW4 4BT. *Email*: s.mumberson@mdx.ac.uk *Website*: ADRI *Signs work*: "Stephen Mumberson" or "S. Mumberson.".

MUNDY, William Percy, RMS, MAA, MASF, HS, SLm; self taught artist, miniaturist, portrait and Trompe l'oeil painter; Awarded "Exhibit of the Year" at 1980 and 1982 RA Summer Exhbns; Silver medal, Paris Salon (1982); Gold Memorial Bowl, RMS (1986); Bell Award (1987); Best of Show MASF (USA) (1997); Bell Award (1996, 2000, 2009); Best of Show HS (2001); Best Portrait MASF (USA) (2004). *Medium*: watercolour, pencil, oil. *b*: Wokingham, 30 Oct 1936. *s of*: P. W. Mundy. *Educ*: Forest School, Berks. *Exhib*: RA, RMS, RP. *Works in collections*: HM The Queen; HRH The Duke of Edinburgh; HM King Bhumipol Aduladej of Thailand; The Yang di Pertuan Agong of Malaysia; HRH The Sultan of Johor; HRH The Sultan of Oman; V&A, London; Cincinatti Museum of Art, USA. *Publications*: 'Portrait Miniatures', 'Portrait Miniatures 2', 'Portrait Miniatures - Oriental'. Autobiography: 'A Brush with Life'. *Recreations*: boating, photography. *Clubs*: Tanglin, Singapore; Phyllis Court, Henley. *Address*: 2 Marsh Mills, Wargrave Rd., Henley-on-

Thames, Oxon. RG9 3JD. *Email*: WPMundy@aol.com *Website*: www.billmundy.co.uk *Signs work*: "W. P. Mundy."

MUNOZ, Andrew, Royal West of England Academician (RWA). *Medium*: oil, drawing, print. *b*: London, 10 May 1967. one *s*. one *d*. *Studied*: Plymouth College of Art (1995-97); Falmouth College of Art (1997-2000). *Exhib*: Solo exhibitions: Lane Gallery, Plymouth (2000); Flying Colours Gallery, London (2002); Red Propeller Gallery, Devon (2008); Andipa Contemporary, London (2012). Group exhibitions: Royal College of Art, London (2001); ART2002, London (2002); AAF, Commonwealth Centre, London (2003); Phoenix Arts Centre, Exeter (2004); Royal Albert Museum, Exeter (2005); Atkinson Gallery, Liverpool (2005); RWA, Bristol (2006); Mivart Studios, Bristol (2006); Southbank Arts, Bristol (2007); Plymouth College of Art (2008); VINEspace, London (2009); RWA, Bristol (2009, 2010, 2011); Andipa Contemporary (2012); Academician's Selection Show, RWA, Bristol (2013); Contemporary British Painters, London (2013); Swindon Museum and Art Gallery (2014). *Works in Collections*: Swindon Art Gallery and Museum, Wiltshire; Lakeland Arts Trust, Abbots Hall, Cumbria; Royal West of England Academy, Bristol; Madison Museum of Fine Art, Georgia, Atlanta, USA. *Publications*: PROOF magazine (Apr 2008); Evolver magazine (2014). *Principal Works*: 'Das Kind'; 'The Bather'; 'All Good Dogs go to Heaven'. *Misc*: Member of British Contemporary Painters Group. *Address*: 11 Cromer Road, Bristol BS5 6JU. *Email*: munozandrew@hotmail.com *Website*: www.andrewmunoz.co.uk *Signs work*: "A Munoz".

MUNRO, Barbara, BScHons Botany; PGCE; Cert Exol & Cons; Dip SBA (Distinction); made full member SBA (2013); made fellow of Sheffield Florilegium Society; awarded cert. of bot. merit at SBA exhibition (2011). *Medium*: watercolour, drawing. *b*: Keighley, 22 May 1948. *m*: Iain. one *s*. one *d*. *Studied*: Durham; Beckenham College of Art; distance learning for SBA. *Exhib*: S.E. London Institute of Botany; Bromley Library; SBA Open Exhibition at Westminster Central Hall (2009-2014); Thorlesby Gallery, Notts; Harley Gallery, Notts; John Noot Gallery, Broadway; Palmengarten, Frankfurt; Luton Hoo 'Ars Butanica'. *Works in collections*: 7 works accepted by archive at Sheffield Botanical Gardens. *Commissions*: Illustration for 'Handbook of Plant Forms for Botanical Artists' by Ernest E Clark and Margaret Stevens. *Recreations*: Photography, travel. *Clubs*: Sheffield Florilegium; BSBI (Bot Soc of BL); Scientific Exploration Society. *Address*: Tundy Leas, Main Street, Flintham, Newark, Notts NG23 5LS. *Email*: barbara.munro5@gmail.com *Website*: botanicalart-barbaramunro.co.uk *Signs work*: "BARBARA MUNRO".

MUNSLOW, Angela E., HNC, Grad.RIC, BEd.Hons.; sculptor in bronze, resin, terracotta, ceramic, cement and plaster, glass; figurative painter in oil, water-colour and pastel. *b*: Sandbach, Ches. *m*: Peter. two *s*. *Educ*: Ravenscroft Hall School, Cheshire; N.Staffs. Polytechnic (now Staffs. University); Crewe and Alsager CHE (now Manchester University). *Studied*: sculpture: Sir Henry Doulton School of Sculpture. *Exhib*: Expo '92 Seville; group shows: St. Martin in the Fields, Mall Galleries, Westminster Gallery, and galleries in the North-West and Midland regions. *Works in collections*: Stapeley Water Gdns., Nantwich Ches., private collections. *Commissions*: 'Discovery' for British Pavilion at Expo 92, Seville, Spain; 'Harmony' (Stapeley Water Gdns.); 'Heredities'; Garden Sculpture - a series of fairies. Private and religious commissions including St. Francis of Assisi for Franciscan order, and portraits. *Publications*: featured in Royal Doulton literature. *Clubs*: Cheshire Artist Network, Soc. of Staffordshire Artists. *Address*: Mayfield Studio, 65 Station Rd., Alsager, Stoke-on-Trent ST7 2PD. *Email*: am@figurativeart.co.uk *Website*: www.figurativeart.co.uk *Signs work*: "A.E. Munslow".

MURISON, Neil, ATD (1951), RWA (1979); painter in oil and acrylic; Head, Dept. of Foundation Studies, Bristol Polytechnic (1961-87); previously art master, Queen Elizabeth's Hospital, Bristol (1952-61). *b*: Bath, 10 Oct 1930. *s of*: William Murison, MPS, PhC.

m: (1) Valerie Elizabeth John. one *s*. one *d*.; (2) Sheila May Tilling (1985). *Educ*: Bristol Grammar School. *Studied*: West of England College of Art (1946-51). *Works in collections*: Nuffield, Wills Tobacco Co., Bank of America, Skopje Modern Art Museum, Yugoslavia, Trumans Breweries, Bridgwater Public Library, Bristol, Devon, Leeds, Herts., Hull, Leics., Liverpool, Surrey and West Riding of Yorks, Educ. Authorities, The Fleming Collection. *Clubs*: Bath Society of Artists; President, Clevedon Arts Club. *Address*: The Grange, 53 High Street, Wick, S.Glos BS30 5QQ. *Signs work*: "Murison."

MURLEY, Lawrence Mario. *Medium*: sculpture. *b*: Wickrath, W.Germany, 2 Mar 1962. Cornish. Parents working abroad. *m*: Carah. one *s*. one *d*. *Educ*: Penzance Humphry Davy Grammar School. *Studied*: Geevor Tin Mine, Pendeen (1981-85); Building, scaffolding, rigging, fishing. Penzance (1986-1995); Self taught sculpting. San Francisco and Penzance (1992-present). *Exhib*: Market House, Marazion; Customs House, Porthleven; Trelowarren, Helston; New Craftsmen, St .Ives; Trelissick Feock, Cotehole; Coach House, Guernsey; Courcoux & Courcoux, Stockbridge. *Comissions*: many. *Recreations*: surfing, Shotokan karate, running, weight training. *Address*: Bosulval Farm Cottage, Bosulval, Newmill, Penzance, Cornwall TR20 8XA. *Email*: lawrence@gulval.fslife.co.uk *Website*: lawrencemurley.co.uk *Signs work*: "LM", Year, Item number in Roman numerals and bind rune.

MURPHY, Richard, BA (Hons), Dip.Arch, FRSA, FRIAS, ARSA, RIBA; architect; recipient of 14 RIBA awards. *b*: Cheshire, 24 Apr 1955. *Educ*: Newcastle and Edinburgh Universities. *Commissions*: Fruitmarket Gallery; Dundee Contemporary Arts; Stirling Tolbooth Arts Centre; John Muir Visitor Centre, Dunbar; The Eastgate Theatre, Peerles; Galeri Enterprise Centre, Caernarfon; New Medical Centre, The University of East London. *Publications*: The Works of Richard Murphy Architects (1977), two books on Carlo Scarpa; Richard Murphy Architects - Ten Years of Practice. *Address*: Richard Murphy Architects Ltd. The Breakfast Mission, 15 Old Fishmarket Close, Edinburgh EH1 1RW. *Email*: mail@richardmurphyarchitects.com *Website*: www.richardmurphyarchitects.com *Signs work*: "Richard Murphy."

MURRAY, Dawson Robertson, DA (1965); Post-grad (1966); RSW (1988); RGI (1995); Head of Art and Design, Boclair Academy (1976-94); President, Glasgow Group of Artists (1990-94); Vice President, RSW (1993-96); painter in water-colour, acrylic, etching; atmospheric abstractions of garden themes. *b*: Glasgow, 25 Jun 1944. *s of*: Dawson Murray, engineer and gardener. *m*: Liz Murray. two *d*. *Studied*: Glasgow School of Art (1961-66), L'Accademia delle Belle Arti, Venice (1966). *Exhib*: Solo shows: 1999 Roger Billcliffe Gallery, Glasgow; 1997 Nancy Smillie Gallery, Glasgow; 1990 Richard Demarco Gallery, Edinburgh, 2006 Pittenweem Festival, Invited Artist. Group shows: 2007 Scottish Printmaking, Glasgow Print Studio, 2005/6 Mini Print International tour, 2003 Sanctuary/Amnesty, Gallery of Modern Art, Glasgow; 2002 "Beyond Conflict", European Parliament, Brussels: 2000 "Beuys in Scotland", Matthew Gallery, Edinburgh School of Architecture; 1999 Maritime Museum, Vittoria, Malta; 1998 Lord Provost's Prize, Gallery of Modern Art, Glasgow; 1994 Encuentro Acuarela, Santa Cruz, Canaries. *Works in collections*: McManus Galleries Dundee; BBC Scotland; SAC. *Commissions*: Buchanan Galleries, Glasgow. *Address*: The Old Post Office, Kilmany, Cupar, Fife KY15 4PT. *Signs work*: "Dawson Murray."

MURRAY, Donald, BA, DA; artist and designer in calligraphy, water-colour and acrylic; formerly Head of Art, Robert Gordon's College, Aberdeen. *b*: Edinburgh, 1940. *s of*: James Murray. *m*: Mary F. Low. two *s*. *Educ*: George Heriot's School, Edinburgh. *Studied*: Edinburgh College of Art (1958-63). *Exhib*: RSW, SSA, Pitlochry Festival Theatre, Aberdeen Artists' Society. *Works in collections*: Edinburgh District Council, Heriot-Watt University, Moray House College of Education, Edinburgh Merchant Company, HRH The

Princess Royal. *Commissions*: Illuminated scrolls and miscellaneous formal calligraphy: Aberdeen City Council; Orkney Islands Council, University of Aberdeen, Robert Gordon University. *Publications*: Growing up in the Church, Christian Symbols, Ancient and Modern, An Leabhar Mor, Amra Choluim Chille, Calligraphic Styles. *Works Reproduced*: Growing up in the Church, Christian Symbols Ancient and Modern, An Leabhar Mor, Amra Choluim Chille, Calligraphic Styles. *Address*: Manorlea, Commerce St., Insch, Aberdeenshire AB52 6JB. *Email*: donaldmurrayda@btopenworld.com *Website*: www.donaldmurrayda.co.uk *Signs work*: "Donald Murray".

MURRAY, George Alexander, NDD (Kingston School of Art 1956); Des RCA (1961). *Medium*: Oil; watercolour, drawing. *b*: Stockton on Tees, 22 Feb 1938. *m*: Elsbeth. four *s*. one *d*. *Educ*: Middlesborough Junior Tech. *Studied*: Kingston School of Art (1954-57); Royal College of Art (1957-61). *Exhib*: Roseberry Homes Ltd sponsored watercolour exhibition at Bankside (2005); The Spirit of London one man show (2005); The Fountain Gallery, East Molesey, watercolours and drawings (2006); regular exhibitions at 'Art in Action', Waterperry House as demonstrator in watercolour and practical classes teacher (1977-2007). *Works in collections*: A considerable number of works in private collections. *Commissions*: Presentation Perspectives a speciality for architects/engineers/developers, ongoing clients included M&S, Sainsburys, Arup Associates, Taylor Woodrow, Sir R McAlpine, Rendel Palmer and Tritton, Freeman Fox Engineers. *Works Reproduced*: Illustrated for Collins Publishers, 'View of the Thames', 'Christian England', 'Offshore' (1980-1990s).. *Recreations*: Walking and sketching; student of philosophy and economics in London. *Clubs*: Member of Twickenham Art Circle. *Misc*: Currently taking portrait commissions locally. Note all records of exhibitions have been destroyed in recent move. *Address*: 235 Percy Road, Twickenham TW2 6JL. *Email*: gamurray2011@live.co.uk *Website*: www.george-murray.co.uk

MURRAY, Howard, NDD; Cert RA Schools; RA Bronze Medal; David Murray Prizes. *Medium*: oil, sculpture. *b*: London, 23 Mar 1937. *m*: Gillian Mary. two *s*. *Educ*: Academic Art School; Walthamstow School of Art. *Studied*: RA Schools. *Exhib*: RA; Burlington Fine Art Gallery. *Recreations*: photography. *Clubs*: The East India Club; The Thunderers Dining Club. *Misc*: worked extensively in theatre and film; Founder Member of the Props and Sets company MDM. *Address*: 11 The Crescent, Independent Place, London E8 2HE. *Email*: howardmurraydalston.m@ukonline.co.uk

MURRAY, Liz, DA (1965), SSA (1991), RSW (1992); painter in mixed media - collage including stitched and moulded paper. *b*: Aberdeen, 21 May 1943. *m*: Dawson Murray. two *d*. *Studied*: Duncan of Jordanstone College of Art, Dundee (1961-65). *Exhib*: regularly at RSA, RSW, SSA, RGI, SAAC; work featured in many touring exhbns. in Scotland, and selected for group exhbns. in Italy, Poland, Germany, Bosnia and Canaries. *Works in collections*: Scottish Arts Council, Renfrewshire Educ. Authority, Lanarkshire Educ. Authority, Hamilton District Libraries, City Art Space, plc., Angus Council. *Address*: The Old Post Office, Kilmany, Cupar, Fife, KY15 4PT. *Email*: liz@kilmany.plus.com *Signs work*: "Eliz Murray." or "E.M.".

MUSGRAVE, Olivia Mirabel, BA in Sculpture; Vice president of the Society of Portrait Sculptors. *Medium*: bronze sculpture. *b*: Dublin, 30 Nov 1958. *d of*: Richard and Lady Musgrave. *m*: John Gardiner. *Educ*: Newtown School, Waterford, Ireland. *Studied*: City and Guilds of London Art School. *Represented by*: John Martin of London, 38 Albemarle St., London W1X 3FB; Jorgensen Fine Art, 29 Molesworth Street, Dublin 2; Everard Read Gallery, 6 Jellicoe Ave, Rosebank, Johannesburg, S. Africa. *Exhib*: Royal Academy, (1992, 94), Royal Hibernian Academy, Dublin (1997, 02), Discerning Eye, Mall Galleries (1989, 2002), John Martin of London, Christopher Hull Gallery, Jorgensen Fine Art Dublin. *Works in collections*: Boots plc, The National Bank of Greece, The National Self-Portrait

Collection of Ireland, Oxford University, Irish Guide Dogs for the Blind. *Commissions*: Oxford University, Irish Guide Dogs, Boots plc. *Principal Works*: Life-size Ox for Oxford University; life-size figure and dog for Irish Guide Dogs. *Recreations*: antique collecting, tapestry. *Clubs*: Chelsea Arts Club. *Address*: Flat 1, 163 Sussex Gardens, London W2 2RH. *Email*: olivia@oliviamusgrave.com *Website*: www.jmlondon.com *Signs work*: Musgrave.

MUSGRAVE, Sally Ann, Dip AD Fine Art; Slade Higher Dip. in Fine Art; Arts Council Award; Boise travelling scholarship. *Medium*: oil, drawing, prints, objects (gesso wood). *b*: Hampstead, London, 1959. *Studied*: Central School of Art; Slade School of Art; University of London. *Represented by*: Kapil Jariwala Gallery, New Burlington St., London W1. *Exhib*: RA Summer Show (2004); 'Modern Tantra', New Burlington Street; 'British Abstract Art' LA, USA; Flowers West; Flowers Central. *Works in collections*: private and public. *Publications*: catalogue; 'Surface' by Stephen Bann. *Address*: 12a Approach Road, London E2 9LY. *Website*: www.kapiljariwalagallery.co.uk *Signs work*: 'Sally Musgrave'.

MUSKER, Alison Awdry Chalmers, Member Royal Watercolour Society (2000, elected Council Member 2006), Chelsea Art Society (1980), Small Paintings Group (2000) The Painters Fine Art Society; Agnes Reeve Award (1989 & 1991); won the William-Powlett prize; award International Watercolour Biennale, Mexico; Royal Society of British Artists, Mall Galleries; Leslie Orriss. *Medium*: watercolour and gouache. *b*: Southampton, 9 Sep 1938. *m*: Roger. one *s*. two *d*. *Educ*: Sherborne. *Studied*: in Paris, at the Ecole des Beaux Arts under Edward Wesson. *Exhib*: solo exhbns. include: Richmond Gallery in Cork Street, King Street Gallery, St. James's, Brotherton Gallery, Walton Street and Royal Geographical Soc., London; group exhibitions include ROI (1958), RA Summer Exhibition (1999, 2002, 2003, 2005, 2006), RWS, RI, NEAC, Singer and Friedlander (1998, 1999, 2000), Ebury Galleries, WH Patterson & Select Seven Exhibitions Watercolour & Drawing Fair; Friends of the City Churches, London; Leslie Orris, Reading College of Art; Painswick Garden Exhibition; Travellers' Survival Kit, Reading Guild of Artists. *Works in collections*: The Late Elizabeth, Queen Mother; HRH The Prince of Wales, Peter Boizot, Martin Vandersteen, John Julius, Norwich; Barry Munn; Lady Dashwood; Timothy Yorath; Save Britain's Heritage; Sir Hugh Casson PPRA; Creative Watercolour Techniques, and others. Collections abroad. *Commissions*: Whitehall Palace watercolour, Agnes Reeve Memorial Prize. Watercolour Pennant auctioned for Red Cross Appeal for the Gulf War; Koestler Award Trust. *Publications*: Artist's Manual (Collins); Creative Watercolour Techniques (Collins); Light and Color Techniques in Watercolour (North Light Books, Ohio); The Watercolour Expert / Watercolour Masters(Cassell); 'Textile Design' Jacqueline Groag; The Artist Magazine - article on India; The Enchanted River by Simon Fenwick; Dictionary of International Biography, Melrose Press, Cambridge; Complete Guide to Drawing and Painting, Readers Digest; Illustrated demonstration articles, Eaglemoss Publications. *Works Reproduced*: 'Music In Country Churches' charity, Nadfas Tours poster of Petra, Jordan. *Principal Works*: watercolour painting. *Recreations*: painting and taking painting courses. *Clubs*: Freeman of the Worshipful Company of London Painter-Stainers. *Misc*: Awards: Rotary Club. Watercolour donated to Hampshire Hospital. *Address*: Rose Cottage, Beech Hill, Reading RG7 2AZ. *Email*: alisoncmusker@btinternet.com *Signs work*: "A.C.Musker."

MYERS, Chris, RBA; BA (DipAD Hons). *Medium*: watercolour. *b*: London, 5 Oct 1949. *m*: Lynda Jane Myers. two *s*. one *d*. *Educ*: William Morris School, Walthamstow. *Studied*: Maidstone College of Art. *Exhib*: RI, RWS, RBA, Kent Painters Group, Singer & Friedlander/Sunday Times Competition; Gascoigne Gallery (Harrogate), Curwen Gallery, Goodwood Revival/Festival of Speed. *Publications*: feature articles in 'The Artist' (June 2004); 'Octane' (Dec 2005); Classic and Sports Car (Oct 2004) . *Recreations*: music/ guitar. *Clubs*: Royal Society of British Artists. *Address*: Woodside Cottage, Wadhurst Road, Frant, Tunbridge Wells, TN3 9EH. *Email*: chris.Frant@virgin.net *Website*: www.chrismyersart.com *Signs work*: "CHRIS MYERS".

MYERS, Emily Margaret, BA (Hons) Ceramics. *Medium*: Ceramics. *b*: Stogumber, 5 Mar 1965. *m*: Matthew Somerville. one *s*. two *d*. *Educ*: King Alfred School, North London. *Studied*: Bristol Polytechnic (1983-87). *Represented by*: Contemporary Ceramics. *Exhib*: Solo: Beaux Arts, Bath (2001, 2003, 2005); Contemporary Ceramics, London (2002); The Art Stable, Dorset (2011). Also: Tel Aviv, Paris, Hamburg. *Works in collections*: Liverpool City Art Gallery; Aberystwyth Arts Centre. *Commissions*: Private commissions. *Publications*: Article in Ceramic Review (1997) about Emily Myers; work in various books on ceramics including 'The Complete Potter's Companion' by Tony Birks. *Misc*: Pots bought for the Guggenheim Museum shop. *Address*: 2 Chalkpit Cottages, Tangley SP11 0RX. *Email*: emily@emilymyers.com *Website*: www.emilymyers.com *Signs work*: Potter's mark is a V screw head slotted.

MYERS, Mark Richard, BA (Hons), RSMA (1975), President RSMA (1993-1998), ASMA (1978), Fellow, ASMA (1979); marine artist. *Medium*: watercolours, oils, acrylics, inks, lithography, etching. *b*: San Mateo, Calif., USA, 19 Nov 1945. *s of*: Jackson Sandine Myers, airline pilot. *m*: Peternella Bouquet. one *s*. two *d*. *Educ*: Pomona College, Calif. *Exhib*: RSMA, ASMA, New York, London, Seattle. *Works in collections*: National Maritime Museum, Greenwich, San Francisco Maritime Museum, N. Devon Maritime Museum. *Publications*: various maritime books illustrated. *Address*: The Old Forge, Woolley, Bude, Cornwall EX23 9PP. *Email*: mark@myers67.freeserve.co.uk *Signs work*: "Mark Myers," "Mark Richard Myers" or "Myers."

MYERSCOUGH, Ishbel, BA, Post Dip. & Distinction; painter in oil. *b*: London, 5 Nov 1968. *m*: Cormac Alexander. *Educ*: Highbury Hill High School, City of London Girls School. *Studied*: Glasgow School of Art (1987-1991), Slade (1993-1995). *Exhib*: three solo exhibs., Anthony Mould Contemporary, London (1992, 1996, 2001), BP Portrait Award, National Portrait Gallery (1990, 1991, 1992, 1993, 1995); various group exhibs. including Flowers East and National Portrait Gallery. *Works in collections*: Natwest Bank, Christies, National Portrait Gallery, MCC. *Commissions*: Helen Mirren for National Portrait Gallery, Graham Gooch for MCC, private and public paintings and portraits. *Publications*: catalogues for solo exhibs., 'British Sporting Heroes', National Portrait Gallery, 'British Figurative Art Part 1', Flowers East, 'Die Kraft Der Builder', Berlin, 'Treasures from the National Portrait Gallery,' Japan. *Address*: 81B St. Peter's St., London N1 8JR. *Signs work*: "I M" or "I Myerscough" on verso.

MYERSON, Ingrid, BA, MBA (1986), UA. *Medium*: sculptor in bronze, stone, stainless steel, perspex, marble. *b*: 30 Jun 1960. two *s*. one *d*. *Studied*: University of Witwatersrand, Hampstead Institute. *Exhib*: Business Design Centre, Mall Galleries, Westminster Gallery, Expo Geneva, Les Hirondelles Geneva, McHardy Sculpture Gallery, London, Cato Gallery, London, Affordable Art Fair, Phillips Ltd, London. *Commissions*: private and business: England, Switzerland, S. Africa, USA, Australia. *Clubs*: U.A. *Address*: 22 Maresfield Gardens, Hampstead, London NW3 5SX. *Email*: ingrid@ingridmyerson.com *Signs work*: "IMyerson".

MYINT, Khin, MSc; MA (Ed); PGCE (secondary); CIM (Chartered Institute of Marketing) Adv Cert. *Medium*: Oil; watercolour; drawing; mixed media. *b*: Burma, 6 Nov 1952. *m*: S A Weinman. two *s*. *Studied*: Rangoon University, Burma; St Mary's College, Twickenham; University of Surrey. *Represented by*: Oc-Eo Gallery (2010-11); McNeill Gallery. *Exhib*: United Society of Artists UA annual/satellite exhibitions; Russian, Eastern and Oriental Fine Art Fair; Oc-Eo Gallery, Islington, London; Chelsea Art Fair; McNeill Gallery, Radlett; The Menier Gallery; The Bankside Gallery (2013). *Works in collections*: Private collections in UK, USA, Canada, France, Germany, Norway, Russia, Japan, Italy and Burma. *Commissions*: By Melissa Cosgrove Childrens Foundation for charity auction; Prospect Burma for charity auction; Burma Art Festival for charity auction. *Official*

Purchasers: Rangoon University (Library); UNICEF Office, Burma. *Misc*: Member of United Society of Artists. *Address*: 24 Townfield, Rickmansworth, Herts WD3 7DD. *Email*: khinmyint@khinmyint.co.uk *Website*: www.khinmyint.co.uk *Signs work*: "Khin".

MYLES, Noel, Artist in Residence for ITN (1995/6), Shaftesbury PLC (1995), Rowe & Mann (1994); 1984 London Group Prizewinner; 1987 National Museum Photography Film & TV Prizewinner; 2007 Discerning Eye Prizewinner. *Medium*: fine photography; platinum printing. *b*: London, 19 Oct 1947. *Studied*: Hornsey and Walthamstow Schools of Art (1966-70). *Represented by*: Chappel Galleries; Art Contact; Byard Art. *Exhib*: RA Summer Exhbn (1989, 90, 92, 93, 99, 2000, 01, 03); Contemporary Art Society (2002, 03); Inside Space (2002, 03); Discerning Eye (2007); Royal Photographic Society (1995-6), and extensively in Europe, UK and Japan. Selected solo exhbns: NPG (1986); The Gallery in Cork Street (1995); Gainsborough's House (1999), L'Oeil Ecoute, Limoges (1995, 1999); Zelda Cheatle Gallery (2001); Stephanie Hoppen Gallery (2003). *Works in collections*: Stonehart Publications; Contemporary Arts Society; Sir William Halcrow & Ptnrs; Paintings in Hospitals; Dept. of the Environment; National Westminster Bank; Paintings in Churches; V&A (etching, cyanotype); Rank Xerox; Camden Council; St. Thomas' Hospital; MORI; Rowe & Maw; Bradstocks; L'Oeil Ecoute, Limoges; Fondation D'Art Contemporain du Limousin; V&A; Platinum Printa; Roche Pharmaceuticals; Coutts Bank; Bostick & Sullivan. *Commissions*: NPG (1986); MORI (1987); Rowe & Maw (1988/9, 1994); Shaftesbury Plc (1995); ITN (1995, 96); Nationale Woningraad, Netherlands (1997-8), Roche Pharmaceuticals (2007), etc. *Official Purchasers*: Contemporary Art Soc.; V&A (2); Fondation D'Art Contemporain, Limousin; Dept. of Environment. *Works Reproduced*: reviews: Sing Tao Daily; The Observer (full page colour); Daily Telegraph; Daily Express; Evening Standard; British Journal of Photography; Amateur Photographer (5 page feature); Artists & Illustrators; Creative Review; Independent on Sunday (double page colour); The Times; Boardroom; The Lawyer; Siyu Times (front cover Feb.1996, feature Mar 1996); Foto, Germany. *Address*: 51 Newton Croft, Sudbury, CO10 2RW. *Email*: noelmylesphoto@hotmail.co.uk

MYLIUS (MASSIE), (Frances) Jill, Dip Art (Edin, 1959), Teachers Cert (1970), BA Hons (1983); Prize for Painting, GLC 'Spirit of London' (1983). *Medium*: oil, watercolour, etching. *b*: Coventry, 27 Nov 1938. *d of*: Charles & Ellen Sweetman. *m*: Peter Massie. two *s*. two *grand-d*. *Educ*: St.Michael's Convent, Stoneleigh; Croft School, Stratford-on-Avon; Abbotsford School, Kenilworth. *Studied*: Edinburgh College of Art (1955-59), Sidney Webb, London (1968-70), Birkbeck College (1979-83). English Etching, Morley College, Central School of Art. *Exhib*: RA (1975-81); Royal Society of Watercolours, Mall Galleries (2005); Pool on the Park, Southwark (2006-2013); one woman shows: Scottish Art Council, Edinburgh (1975,2004); Dryden St., London (1979), Senior Common Room, Bristol (1982). *Works in collections*: Fine Art Dept., Seoul National University, South Korea; Scottish Arts Council. *Recreations*: Involved in Birkbeck Poetry workshop. *Address*: 85 Camberwell Grove, London SE5 8JE. *Signs work*: "Jill Mylius" (Massie).

MYNOTT, Gerald P., FSSI; landscape artist, printmaker and calligrapher. *Medium*: oil, watercolour, pastel. *b*: London, 2 Mar 1957. *s of*: Derek Mynott, RBA, NEAC, and Patricia Mynott, artist. *Studied*: Reigate College of Art; College of Arms, London; Vienna Kunstlerhaus, Austria. *Exhib*: Francis Kyle Gallery, London, continuously from 1980, New York (1984), Bath Festival (1983), Arts Club, London (1987), Lincoln Centre, New York (1991), Hong Kong (1992), National Theatre (2001), 'Discerning Eye' Mall Gallery, London (2002). *Works in collections*: V&A, Tate Gallery (Curwen Archive), The Savoy Group, Chevening Estate, USA, Tokyo. Lloyds Printmakers Award (1981), King's Foundation, London, St Catherines, Oxford. *Commissions*: Antony Lambton 'The Lunette' Cetinale, Italy, 1989. *Works Reproduced*: in The Times, The Observer, Tatler, Radio Times, Weidenfeld and Nicolson, Penguin Books, V&A Publications, The Field, BBC, OUP.

Clubs: Arts. *Address*: 3 Belgrave House, 157 Marine Parade, Brighton, Sussex. *Signs work*: Gerald Mynott.

MYNOTT, Katherine S., BA; illustrator/printmaker in gouache, line and lino. *b*: London, 1962. *d of*: Derek Mynott, NEAC, and Patricia Mynott, artist. one *s*. *Studied*: Heatherley School of Art, Central School of Art and St. Martin's School of Art. *Works Reproduced*: in Vogue, Radio Times, Daily Telegraph, Tatler, Harpers and Queen, B.B.C., Palace Pictures, Cosmopolitan, Time Out, Over 21, 19, The Observer, The Listener, I.P.C., New Society, Economist, etc. *Address*: 23 Mount Park Rd., London W5. *Signs work*: "K. Mynott."

MYNOTT, Lawrence, MA (RCA), AOI; portrait painter, illustrator in water-colour, oil, line and gouache; lecturer and art writer. *b*: London, 1954. *s of*: Derek Mynott, NEAC, and Patricia Mynott, artist. *Studied*: Chelsea School of Art (1972-76), Royal College of Art (1976-79). *Exhib*: RA, European Illustrators, Folio Soc., Thames Television; two one-man shows of portraits at Cale Art, Chelsea. *Works in collections*: NPG, National Gallery of Wales, Hull A.G., Arts Council. Awarded D&AD silver award (1985). Lecturer at V&A, 'The Sitwells as Patrons', Neo-Romanticism, The Rococo Revival. *Works Reproduced*: in Radio Times, Vogue, Tatler, Harpers and Queen, The Observer, Penguin Books, Macmillans, Hamish Hamilton, etc. *Clubs*: Chelsea Arts. *Address*: c/o "The Organisation", 69 Caledonian Rd., London N1. *Signs work*: "Lawrence Mynott," "Mynott" or monogram "L.M."

N

NAGL, Hazel Anna, RSW (1988), RGI (2000); painter in mixed media of still life and landscape, mainly Scottish gardens and castles; Convener of RGI, PAI (2010) *Medium*: mixed media. *b*: Glasgow, 2 Nov 1953. *Partner*: David Greenock. one *d*. *Educ*: North Kelvinside Senior Secondary School. *Studied*: Glasgow School of Art under Donaldson, Robertson, Shanks. *Exhib*: RSW, RGI, RSA Thomsons, London, Roger Billcliff; solo exhibs, Open Eye, Stenton, GAC. *Works in collections*: Royal Bank of Scotland, Glasgow University, Fleming Collection, Arthur Anderson, Scottish and Newcastle Breweries. *Recreations*: archaeology, walking, history. *Clubs*: Glasgow Art Club. *Address*: Lawmarnock House, 2 Troon Drive, Bridge of Weir, Renfrewshire PA11 3HF. *Signs work*: "NAGL."

NAPP, David, Dip. CSD, Elizabeth Greenshields Foundation award (1986, 1990); artist in chalk, pastel, oil and water-colour; sessional lecturer, Kent Inst. of Art and Design. *b*: London, 5 Mar 1964. *Educ*: Queen Elizabeth's School, Faversham. *Studied*: Canterbury College of Art (1981-85). *Exhib*: Bourne Gallery, Reigate (1987-) Art London (1989, 1990, 1991), Walker Galleries, RWS, RBA, PS, Napier Gallery Jersey. *Publications*: illustrations: Encyclopaedia of Pastel Techniques (Headline); Colour: How to see it, how to paint it; How to Paint Trees, Flowers and Foliage; Pastels Workshop. *Address*: Windmill Cottage, Mill La., Barham, Canterbury, Kent CT4 6HH. *Signs work*: "David Napp" and date.

NAPPER, Helen, BA (1980), MFA (1983), PGCE (1985); painter in oil on board. *b*: Wivenhoe, 29 Mar 1958. *d of*: Peter Napper. *Educ*: Friends School, Saffron Walden; Colchester County High School for Girls. *Studied*: Colchester Art School, Wimbledon Art School (Maggi Hambling, Colin Cina), Reading University (Adrian Heath, Terry Frost), London University Central School of Art (Norman Ackroyd, Bernard Cheese). *Exhib*: Sue Rankin Gallery (1989-91), LA Contemporary Art Fair (1989, 1990), Olympia Art, London (1990, 1991) with Sue Rankin Gallery, Tatistcheff and Co., NY and LA (1992, 1993). *Works in collections*: Citicorp Bank, London. *Address*: 5 Castle Hill, Orford, Suffolk. *Signs work*: "Helen Napper."

NASH, David, OBE (2004), RA (1999), BA (Hons.) Fine Art (1967); artist/sculptor in wood; Hon. Doc. Kingston University; Research Fellow, University of Northumbria. *b*: Esher, Surrey, 14 Nov 1945. *m*: Claire Langdown. two *s*. *Studied*: Kingston College of Art

Foundation Course (1963-64), Brighton College of Art (1964-65, painting), Kingston College of Art (1965-67, sculpture), Chelsea College of Art (1969-70, post-grad.). *Exhib*: Forest of Dean, Sculpture Trail, Walker Art Centre, Minneapolis, USA, Nagoya City Museum, Japan, Guggenheim Museum, NY, Muhka Antwerp, Kröller Müller Museum, Holland. *Works in collections*: Tate Gallery, London, Guggenheim Museum NY, British Council. *Commissions*: "Eighteen Thousand Tides" Eastbourne, public sculpture (1996), "Divided Oaks" and "Turning Pines" (planted sculptures) Ottorlo, Netherlands (1985), "Seven Vessels" Cincinnatti. *Publications*: The Sculpture of David Nash by Julian Andrews; Forms into Time (with essay by Marina Warner); Black and Light (essay by Dr. Judith Collins), "Pyramids Rise, Spheres Turn, Cubes Stay Still" (essay Ian Barker). *Address*: Capel Rhiw, Blaenau Ffestiniog, Gwynedd LL41 3NT.

NASH, Elizabeth, DipAD, B.Ed. *Medium*: mixed media, textiles, prints. *b*: London, 4 Nov 1947. *d of*: Richard & Joan Nash. *m*: Michael Shearman. *Educ*: St.Michael"s Petworth. *Studied*: West Sussex College of Art (1965-66), West of England College of Art (1966-69), Redland College. *Represented by*: The First Gallery, Southampton. *Exhib*: various galleries, incl. Basingstoke, Bath, Bristol, Dorchester, Glasgow, Farnham, Frome, Gloucester, Guernsey, London, Salisbury, Winchester. RWA Autumn Exhbitions, Bristol; National Open Print, London; Society of Wildlife Artists, London; Yewtree 2006 Salisbury. *Works in collections*: Artcare, Salisbury District Hospital. *Commissions*: "In Praise of Trees" Salisbury Festival 2002 - 2 silk hangings for Cathedral; Newbury Spring Festival 2003 - 14 silk hangings for St. Nicholas Church, Newbury. *Works Reproduced*: "In Praise of Trees" (2002), Art in Nature, Search Press (1996). *Recreations*: plays flute, member of "Musica Rustica" ensemble. *Misc*: Community Art, Silk Paintings and Print Projects for Artcare. Broughton Banners, Millennium Project. Projects for "The Making" and "Making Space". *Address*: Doves, Vicarage Road, Tisbury, Wilts, SP3 6HY. *Email*: lizjnash@live.co.uk *Website*: www.elizabethnash.co.uk *Signs work*: "ELIZABETH NASH".

NASON, Kristine, SEA, SWA; portrait painter, equestrian artist. *Medium*: watercolour, pencil, oils, acrylic. *b*: Matlock, Derbyshire. *d of*: Denis Nason and Anna Oswell-Jones. *m*: L.B.Giwa. one *s*. one *d*. *Educ*: Basingstoke High School. *Studied*: Portsmouth College of Art and Design. *Exhib*: Mall Galleries, London: Society of Equestrian Artists, Society of Women Artists, etc.; and various group exhibs. and galleries throughout UK. *Works in collections*: private collections worldwide. *Commissions*: UK and international clients. *Works Reproduced*: over 230 images produced as limited-edition prints. *Clubs*: S.A.A. Professional Associate. *Address*: 1 Savory Walk, Foxley Fields, Binfield, Berks. RG42 4LP. *Email*: kristinenason@btinternet.com *Website*: www.kristinenason.com *Signs work*: "Kristine Nason.".

NAUMANN, Anuk Danuta Katarzyna, BSc Hons, Dip Arch. *Medium*: watercolour, paintings in mixed media. *b*: Bristol, 18 May 1951. *d of*: Danuta & Teodor Chmielinski. *m*: Roger. one *s*. one *d*. *Studied*: Bartlett School of Architecture UCL (1969-74). *Exhib*: from 1990 to present: RWA Open, New Gallery RWA (Bristol); Verandah, Oxford; John Davies Gallery, Stow on the Wold; Gallery 41, Edinburgh; Parkfields Gallery, Ross on Wye; Jerdans Gallery, Crail, Fife; Ingleby Gallery, Derbyshire; Stour Gallery, Shipston on Stour; Anderson Gallery, Burford (also solo shows in studio). *Works in collections*: private collections in UK, USA & Europe. *Publications*: Harper Collins Art Books: Artists Problem Solver & Rescue Tactics; articles for The Artist magazine. *Works Reproduced*: prints by Kelix Rosensteil Widow & Son. *Recreations*: walking, reading, music, dancing. *Address*: The Shrubbery, The Tewer, Gt. Rollright, Oxon OX7 5RG. *Email*: anuk@anuknaumann.co.uk *Website*: www.anuknaumann.co.uk *Signs work*: "ANUK NAUMANN".

NEAL, Arthur Richard, DipAD; painter/printmaker in oil, water-colour and etching. *b*: Chatham, 15 Mar 1951. *m*: Jane. one *s*. one *d*. *Educ*: Reeds School. *Studied*: Camberwell

School of Art. *Exhib*: RA Summer Shows, Cadogan Contemporary, Lynne Strover, New English Art Club. *Publications*: Illustrated Poems of Edward Thomas. *Clubs*: N.E.A.C. *Address*: 32 Duke St., Deal, Kent CT14 6DT. *Email*: arthur.r.neal@googlemail.com *Website*: www.arthurneal.co.uk *Signs work*: "ARN" or "ARNEAL" or not at all.

NEAL, Charles William, BSc Hons (1980); Contemporary British Impressionist, and Alter Realist painter. *Medium*: painter in oil. *b*: Carshalton, 27 Nov 1951. *m*: Susan Ann (painter - Susan Lane). one *s*. *Educ*: Highview High School/City of London University. *Studied*: initially private tuition with Malcolm Domingo and Francis Lane-Mason; later self taught to perfect style and technique. *Exhib*: Omell Gallery (1982); RBA: Omell Gallery (1983), Godalming Gallery (1984), Harrods Picture Gallery (1985); annual, national, international exhbns.: Campbell's of London and Astley House Fine Art, Glos., The Jersey Gallery at Osterley Park with the National Trust (1996, 2000); Museum of Garden History, London (1994); The Royal Horticultural Hall in support of the RHS (1998); The River and Rowing Museum (2006); The Museum in Docklands, London (2006); In Support of the English Speaking Union, New York (2010); First Alter Realist Exhibition, London (2010). *Works in collections*: one royal and many private and commercial collections both national and international. *Misc*: Gallery affiliation: Astley House Fine Art, Moreton-in-Marsh, Glos., GL56 0LL; Wally Findlay Galleries International Inc, Palm Beach, New York, Barcelona. *Address*: Woodside Cottage, 4 Cotswold Park, Woodmancote, Cirencester, Glos. GL7 7EL. *Website*: www.charlesnealartworks.co.uk *Signs work*: C. Neal.".

NEAL, Trevor, self taught artist in all media. *b*: York, 15 Oct 1947. *s of*: Reginald and Anne Neal. *m*: Sharon. one *d*. *Exhib*: Graves A.G. (1972-75, 1977), White Rose Gallery Bradford (1974), RA (1975, 1980, 1981, 1992), Art Centre St. Petersburg, U.S.A. (1980, 1982), Anderson Marsh Galleries St. Petersburg (1983), Ginnel Gallery Manchester (1988), Evander Preston Gallery St. Petersburg (1988, 1989, 1991), S. Yorks. Open Cooper A.G. Barnsley (1989), Ferens A.G., Hull (1995, 1996, 1997), Roy Miles, London (1994, 1995), Art Miami, Florida (1998), Leighton House, London (2001), Not The Turner Prize (2003), Mall Galleries London; Cooper Gallery, Barnsley: Retrospective, 2004; Derwent-Wye Fine Art (2009); Leeds Artist Show, Leeds City Art Gallery (2009). *Works in collections*: UK, USA, France, Germany, Israel, Mexico. *Commissions*: UK, USA, Germany, Italy. *Publications*: "Dreams" (The Bridgewater Book Co., 1996). *Clubs*: Member of the Guild of Motoring Artists. *Address*: Fossdale Towers, 23 Fossdale Rd., Sheffield S7 2DA. *Email*: painter@trevorneal.co.uk *Website*: www.trevorneal.co.uk

NEALE, John, self taught landscape and seascape painter in oil and water-colour. *b*: 13 Sep 1944. divorced. two *s*. two *d*. *Studied*: self taught, but privately helped by Edward Seago. *Exhib*: Omell Galleries, Quantas Galleries, Frost and Reed, Bristol, John Noott, Broadway, Chime Gallery, NY, etc. *Works in collections*: in Europe and USA. *Address*: Maple Leaf House, 59 Maidenhead Rd., Stratford-on-Avon CV37 6XU. *Signs work*: "John Neale."

NEEDHAM, Timothy, BA (Hons); R.a.t.h. Dip AT; various awards. *Medium*: oil, watercolour, drawing, printmaking, acrylic. *b*: Doncaster, 28 Feb 1961. *s of*: Arther and Joan Needham. *m*: Helen Claire Needham. two *s*. one *d*. *Studied*: Winchester School of Art (1982); Sheffield University (1986). *Exhib*: RA (2003, 05, 08); various regional galleries. *Works in collections*: various UK and abroad (private), public and private collections. *Official Purchasers*: NHS. *Recreations*: travel, sailing. *Address*: Chadwell, 15 Caistor Road, Barton on Humberside, Lincs. DN18 6AH. *Email*: timneedham@hotmail.co.uk *Signs work*: "T.Needham", "TN", "Tim Needham".

NEILAND, Brendan, RA (1992), DipAD (1966), MA (1969), Silver Medal RCA (1969); painter in acrylic on canvas, printmaker in silkscreen, lithography; Prof. of Painting, University of Brighton (1996); Visiting Prof., Loughborough University (1998); Keeper,

Royal Academy of Arts (1998), resigned Keepership (2004), ex-RA (2005). *b*: Lichfield, 23 Oct 1941. *m*: Hilary. two *d*. *Educ*: St. Philip's G.S., B'ham; St. Augustine's Seminary, Ireland. *Studied*: B'ham College of Art (1962-66, William Gear, John Walker, Ivor Abrahams), RCA (1966-69, Carel Weight, Roger de Grey). *Represented by*: Redfern Gallery; Turlej Gallery, Poland. *Exhib*: Angela Flowers Gallery, Fischer Fine Art, Redfern Gallery. *Works in collections*: Tate Gallery, V&A, British Council, Arts Council. *Commissions*: National Bank of Dubai (1997), Rolls Royce Engines, Pidemco Singapore. *Publications*: "Brendan Neiland on Reflection" (Motivate Publishing, Oct. 1997). *Clubs*: Chelsea Arts. *Misc*: alternative address: Crepe, La Greve sur Mignon, Courcon 17170, France. *Address*: 2 Granard Rd., London SW12 8UL. *Email*: neilands@talktalk.net *Website*: www.brendanneiland.com *Signs work*: "Brendan Neiland" on all prints and paper work; "NEILAND" stencilled onto back of canvas on stretcher.

NEILL, Errol James, LL.B. (Lond.), Paris Salon: Silver Medallist (1980), Gold Medallist (1981); solicitor; artist in oil and pastel. *b*: Doune, Perthshire, 15 Aug 1941. *s of*: James Francis O'Neill. *m*: Audrey Bradbury. one *s*. two *d*. *Educ*: Christ Church, Preston. *Exhib*: RBA, ROI, RSMA, NEAC, UA, SEA, RSA, RGI, Lancashire Art, Société des Artistes Francais, Paris, Deauville, NY, Melbourne, Australia. *Works in collections*: Britain, France, Eire, USA, Dominican Republic Aberdeen Asset Management PLC. *Publications*: Travelling the Turf 1987 to 1992. *Clubs*: Law Soc. Art Group. *Address*: Bridge House, 217 Chapel La., New Longton, Preston, Lancs. PR4 4AD. *Email*: errolneill@neillfineart.co.uk *Website*: www.neillfineart.co.uk *Signs work*: "ERROL NEILL."

NEILL, Keith Thomas, *Medium*: Oil; watercolour; drawing. *b*: New Longton, Preston, 9 Jul 1969. *Educ*: Priory High School, Penwortham, Preston. *Studied*: Central St Martins. *Exhib*: RA; RSA; RGI. *Works in collections*: Britain; Australia; Canada; USA. *Recreations*: Film making; cycling; music. *Address*: Bridge House, 217 Chapel Lane, New Longton, Preston PR4 4AD. *Email*: keithneill@neillfineart.co.uk *Signs work*: "Neill" or "K. Neill".

NEILL, William Andrew Knight, DipAD (Fine Art) Leeds (1966), ATC Goldsmiths' (1967), SWLA (1990); wildlife and landscape artist in water-colour. *b*: Middlewich, Ches., 22 Aug 1943. *Educ*: Sandbach School. *Studied*: Leeds College of Art, Goldsmiths' College. *Exhib*: annually with SWLA, Oban, Taigh Chearasbhagh, Lochmaddy. *Works in collections*: Nature in Art, Wallsworth Hall. *Commissions*: Scottish Natural Heritage, and The Western Isles Health Board. *Publications*: illustrations in: British Birds, Scottish Birds, etc.; illustrated, Scottish Wildlife Trust, Discovery Book of Western Isles. *Address*: Rannachan, Askernish, South Uist., Western Isles HS8 5SY. *Email*: bill_neill@hotmail.com *Website*: www.william-neill.co.uk

NELSON, Kathleen, RMS (1984), HSF (1982); Hon. Men. Gold Memorial Bowl award RMS (1985, 1994), Drummond award RMS (1984), Llewellyn Alexander subject miniature award RMS (1996); Llewellyn Alexander Masters award (1997), Presidents award Hilliard Soc. (1998); wildlife, natural history artist in water-colour and oil. *b*: Durham City, 12 Mar 1956. *Educ*: Durham Wearside. *Exhib*: RMS, HS, Medici Gallery, Llewellyn Alexander Gallery; solo shows: Darlington A.G., Durham A.G. *Works in collections*: Darlington A.G., Diploma Collection, RMS. *Publications*: chapter with illustrations, The Techniques of Painting Miniatures by S. Burton (B.T. Batsford Ltd., 1995). *Address*: 18 Beverley Gdns., Chester-le-Street, Co. Durham DH3 3NB. *Signs work*: "Kathleen Nelson."

NESBITT, Mark Alexander, MA (Distinction) Visual Communication through Cartooning; Awards: Guardian Cartoon Competition (1985), Botswana Press Trust Award (1990). *Medium*: pen and ink, finished on AppleMac and delivered by email. *b*: Dublin, Ireland, 1 May 1961. *Studied*: Trinity College Dublin (1980-5), University of Central England (1995-6). *Exhib*: since 1994 at international cartoon festivals and exhibitions in

Rathdrum (Ireland), Holland, France, Scotland, Turkey and the UK. *Works in collections*: private and corporate collections. *Commissions*: The Financial Times, The Daily Telegraph, The Press Association, The Times Higher Education Supplement, The Evening Standard, The Irish Times, The Sunday Business Post, and many others. *Publications*: see commissions. *Works Reproduced*: Children's Picture Book "The Toy That Got Away" ISBN 0 222 77451 5 (2000). *Clubs*: BCA, PCO, PCS, CCGB. *Misc*: works as cartoonist and caricaturist principally for the national press in UK and Ireland. *Address*: Greencroft, Hartland, Devon, EX39 6AE. *Email*: info@CaricaturesByLukeWarm.co.uk *Website*: www.CaricaturesByLukeWarm.co.uk *Signs work*: "Luke Warm".

NEVE, Margaret, painter in oil on wood panels. *b*: Wolverhampton, 29 Mar 1929. *d of*: John Neve, solicitor. *m*: James Sutton. two *s*. *Educ*: privately. *Studied*: Birmingham College of Art (1946-49), RA Schools (1949-55, B. Fleetwood Walker). *Represented by*: Brian Sinfield Gallery, 127 The Hill, Burford, Oxfordshire OX18 4RE. *Exhib*: Hamilton Gallery (1967), Marjorie Parr Gallery (1976), Gilbert Parr Gallery (1977, 1979), New Grafton Gallery (1981), Montpelier Studio (1987, 1990, 1994), Montpelier Sandelson Gallery (1998), St.John the Baptist Church, Burford (2001), Robert Sandelson Gallery (2002, 2006), Brian Sinfield Gallery, Burford (2010). *Works in collections*: Birmingham City Art Gallery; private collections in England and abroad. Hull, West Riding, Hertfordshire, Derbyshire & Glamorgan Local Authorities; Pictures for Hospitals Scheme. *Publications*: monograph: Margaret Neve (Montpelier Sandelson, 1998). *Works Reproduced*: Sister Wendy Beckett on Art and The Sacred Rider Books. Images of Earth and Spirit (2003) Resurgence Art Anthology. *Address*: 18 Greville Pl., London NW6 5JH. *Signs work*: "M. Neve."

NEVETZ: see COX, Stephen B.

NEW, Terry, FRBS (1996); DipAD; MA; RCA; Jack Goldhill Prize for Sculpture, RA (1992, 2002). *Medium*: sculpture, drawing, prints. *b*: Prest, 6 Oct 1945. *s of*: John New. *Partner*: Vicki Reynolds. three *d*. *Studied*: Wimbledon School of Art (1963-65); Hornsey College of Art (1965-68); RCA (1968-71). *Exhib*: RA Summer Show (1987-05); RWA (2003); RBS (2003); Air Gallery; group shows in Australia, UAE, Italy, France, Switzerland, and across UK; selected solo shows: Serpentine Gallery (1974); Studio Exhbn, Tabernacle Street (1982, 85); Windsor Workshop, London (1996); GEC Building (1998). *Works in collections*: The Art Gallery of Western Australia; Visual Arts Board of Australia; Freemantle AG, W. Australia; Artbank, Australia; Merck, Sharp & Dohme, UK; Sharjah Art Museum. *Commissions*: St. Peter's Hospital, Chertsey; WAIT, Western Australia; Intasun, Bromley; Robert Nabarro, Whitchurch; Day, Leigh and Co., UK; Keith Benham. *Publications*: "Modern British Sculpture" by Guy Portelli. *Works Reproduced*: "Germinations II", "Unfold", "Nidus", "Flayed Landscape II", "Undercurrents II", "Lunar Manouevres", "Moya", "Fetter", "Spinifex Spectrum". *Recreations*: gardening, chess, reading, swimming. *Misc*: Head of Sculpture at RA Schools since 1986; Head of Fine Art at RA Schools since 2001. *Address*: 74 Florence Road, Newcross, London SE14 6QL. *Email*: terry.new@royalacademy.org.uk

NEWBERRY, Angela, ARCA; Vogue Talent Contest; Earthwatch Art Fellowship. *Medium*: printmaking. *b*: Surrey, 17 Oct 1934. three *s*. one *d*. *Studied*: Art Schools: Kingston/Wimbledon/Royal College of Art (1953-57). *Represented by*: Joshua McLelland Print Room, Melbourne; Solander Gallery; Framed Gal. Darwin. *Exhib*: solo: Rebecca Hossack, London; Royal Exchange, Manchester; Valerie Cohen, Sydney; Joshua McLelland, Melbourne; Framed Gallery, Darwin; Gippsland Regional Gallery; group shows: RA, RWA, RSMA; SWLA; National Print Open; Print Fairs, Hamburg, Bremen, USA, London, Paris etc. *Works in collections*: Manchester City Art Gallery; St.Mary's Hospital Collection; MoD; Royal Veterinary College; Gulbenkian Trust; St.Thomas' Hospital; National Gallery of Australia, Canberra; Olivia Newton John Wellbeing Centre. *Commissions*: Sunday Express newspapers; Ian Sinnamon Collection. *Publications*: Printmaking Today; Australian Artist Magazine; Arts Review; Bridgeman Art Library. *Official Purchasers*: House of Lords; MoD; Customs House, Darwin; Hospitals; Libraries. *Works Reproduced*: Wentworth Wooden Jigsaws; publishers USA/Australia. *Principal Works*: limited edition linocuts/screenprints on handmade paper from Nepal, India and Japan. *Misc*: international artist, studios England and Australia. *Address*: Old Forge House, 4 Cannon Street, Lydd, Romney Marsh TN29 9AS. *Email*: newberry.angela@gmail.com *Website*: www.angela-newberry.co.uk *Signs work*: "Angela Newberry"

NEWBERRY, John Coverdale, RWS (1995), BA Dunelm (1960), MA Oxon. (1989); Water-colour Foundation prize RWS (1990); painter of landscapes in water-colour and figure compositions in oil; tutor, Ruskin School of Drawing, Oxford (1963-89), Acting Head of Department (1988-89). *b*: Horsham, 8 May 1934. *s of*: G.W. Newberry, MA. *Partner*: B.G. Kelly. *Educ*: Kingswood School, Bath; School of Architecture, Cambridge. *Studied*: King's College, Newcastle upon Tyne (1957-60, Lawrence Gowing, Victor Pasmore). *Exhib*: RWS, OAS, RA, RI, NEAC, Singer & Friedlander, numerous one-man shows mostly in Oxford: Ashmolean (1978), Chris Beetles (1990, 1991), Duncan Campbell (1993-2007), Christ Church Picture Gallery, Oxford (2002), Sadler Street Gallery, Wells (2007). *Commissions*: P&O cruise liners "Aurora" (1999), "Azura" (2010). *Address*: 2 Churchway Close, Curry Rivel, Langport, Somerset TA10 0ED. *Email*: newberryandkelly@gmail.com *Signs work*: "Newberry."

NEWCOMB, Tessa, BA (Hons.) Fine Art 1976; painter in oil. *b*: Suffolk, 20 May 1955. *d of*: Mary Newcomb. *Partner*: Telfer Stokes. one *s*. one *d*. *Studied*: Bath Academy of Art (1973-76), Wimbledon School of Art (1977). *Represented by*: Crane Kalman Gallery. *Exhib*: Royal Academy, Crane Kalman, Messum's, Lena Boyle Fine Art and many regional galleries. *Works in collections*: Bradford Metropolitan Museum, Whitworth Art Gallery, Manchester; The Chelsea & Westminster Hospital Collection; Archant, Norwich. *Commissions*: many commissions for paintings, ceramics and furniture. *Publications*: jacket illustrations for Julia Blackburn's "Daisy in the Desert" (Secker & Warburg, 1994),and "The Emperor"s Last Island" Minerva Paperback edn., 1994; "Line Dancing" (Black Dog Books, 2003); 'Tessa Newcomb' by Philip Vann (Sansom & Company 2010); 'An Artist in the Garden' by Jason Gathorne-Hardy (Full Circle Editions (2012); 'The Adorable Plot' by Tessa Newcomb (Sansom & Company 2012). *Works Reproduced*: Lithographs and etchings made with Curwin Press and Cawfold Gallery. Cards by Green Pebble, Canns Down Press and Artists Cards. *Address*: Driftwood, Back Rd., Wenhaston, Halesworth, Suffolk, IP19 9EB. *Email*: tessanewcomb@hotmail.co.uk *Signs work*: "TN" joined.

NEWELL, Robert Alan, BA Hons (1977), MA (1984), PGCE Art (1981), PhD (2005); artist in water-colour, oil, drawing, lecturer; Associate lecturer, in Fine Art, Swansea Inst HE. *b*: 4 Dec 1952. *m*: Eileen Valerie Newell. *Studied*: Wimbledon School of Art (1973-77), University of Reading, School of Educ. (1980-81), Goldsmiths' College (1982-84), Swansea Institute of Higher Education (1999-2005). *Exhib*: RA Summer Show, Royal Cambrian Academy, Glynn Vivian A.G., other galleries in Wales, London, Dusseldorf, etc. *Works in collections*: Brecknock Museum and Art Gallery. *Official Purchasers*: Brecknock Museum and Art Gallery. *Address*: Bryneira, Talley Road, Llandeilo Carmarthenshire SA19 7HS.

NEWMAN, Ros, *b*: London, 29 Mar 1939. *m*: Chris Wade. one *d*. *Educ*: Private school. *Studied*: Chelsea School of Art (1955-57); Hammersmith College of Art (1968-69). *Represented by*: Alwin Gallery, London (1971-1989). *Exhib*: Alwin Gallery, London (1971, 1973, 1978, 1981, 1983, 1985, 1987); PanPan Gallery, Taipei (1991); Alwin Gallery, Tunbridge Wells (1997, 1999). *Works in collections*: Numerous. *Commissions*: Large flight of birds for Norfolk and Norwich University Hospital (2005). *Recreations*: Cooking; gardening. *Clubs*: Norfolk Contemporary Arts Society; Norwich Twenty Group. *Address*:

Chiltern House, 1a Cecil Road, Norwich NR1 2QL. *Email*: rosanewman@ntlworld.com *Website*: www.rosnewman.com *Signs work*: "RN".

NEWSOME, Peter Martin, FRBS (2014), RBA; Batchelor of Technology, PhD, RBA Survival Memorial Award (2007). *Medium*: sculpture. *b*: Isleworth, Middx. *s of*: Henry Albert Newsome. *Educ*: Little Ealing School; Acton Tech. College (1948-61). *Studied*: Brunel University (1961-5,1972-5); Sutton College Liberal Arts (1970 - 2007). *Represented by*: Gallery Different, Mine Gallery, Garden Gallery. *Exhib*: Mall Gallery, London; DFN Gallery, New York; International Sculpture, Guernsey; RBS, London; Cynthia Corbett Gallery. London, Art Hamptons USA and Chicago art fairs. *Works in collections*: private collections, UK, USA, Australasia. *Commissions*: for Hilton Hotels, Peter Gabriel, Leasing Group, Watersheds, Roffey Park, Royal Caribbean. *Publications*: "Peter Newsome - Sculptures in Glass" (2006), "Light and Form" (2009), 'British Sculptors of the 20th Century' by A. Windor (2008), 'Light Vision & Transformation' (co-author 2003), 'A Need for Transparency' (2003). *Official Purchasers*: Cambridge University. *Principal Works*: "If"; "In Concert Series", watercolour-glass sculptures for cruise ship "Oasis of the Seas". *Recreations*: oil painting. *Misc*: since 1993 specialised in constructivist glass sculpture, exploring light and form. *Address*: The Limes, 20A York Road, Cheam, Surrey, SM2 6HH. *Email*: Peter@Newsome.com *Website*: www.peter.newsome.com *Signs work*: "PETER NEWSOME".

NEWSOME, Victor George, artist in egg tempera. *b*: Leeds, 16 Jun 1935. one *s*. one *d*. *Studied*: Leeds School of Art, British School at Rome. *Exhib*: A. d'Offay, Anne Berthoud, Marlborough Fine Art, Grosvenor Gallery. *Works in collections*: Arts Council, Contemporary Arts Soc., British Council, Ferens Art Gallery, Whitworth Art Gallery. *Address*: 4 Elizabeth Mews, London NW3 4TL.

NEWTON, Joanna Dawson, Dip. in Art (1982); artist in oil on canvas, charcoal drawing. *b*: Oxford, 24 Apr 1958. *d of*: Dr. G. F. Newton. *Educ*: Headington School, Oxford. *Studied*: Byam Shaw School of Art (1979-82, P. Gopal-Chowdhuny, N. Volley). *Exhib*: Whitechapel Open, NPG, John Player award, RA Summer Exhbn., Picture Brokers Exhbn. *Clubs*: Chelsea Arts. *Address*: 60 St. Dionis Rd., Fulham, London SW6. *Signs work*: "Joanna D. Newton."

NEWTON, William Alexander, sculptor, specialising in lost wax casting in bronze and silver, mainly animals; creator of The Derby Trophies, Epsom (1998-2008). *b*: Alford, Somerset, 1959. *m*: Sharon. one *s*. one *d*. *Represented by*: Jonathan Cooper, Park Walk Gallery, London SW10. *Exhib*: solo exhibs. at Park Walk Gallery (1995, 1997, 2000), and other group exhibs. *Principal Works*: One-third life size "Lester Piggott Start to Finish", Haydock Park; Life size Lord Oaksey, Lambourn. *Recreations*: Gardening. *Address*: The Rosary, West Hill, Wincanton, Somerset BA9 9BY. *Email*: wnewton@live.co.uk *Website*: williamnewtonsculptor.com *Signs work*: "Newton" or "W. Newton."

NGUYEN, Tân-Phuoc, Mem. Confédération Internationale des Associations des Experts et du Conseils auprès du Conseil Economique et Social de l'Onu Cidadec.; Président Asia-Africa Museum (fondé en 1961); Président de la Chambre Internationale de Commerce Vietnam-Suisse; art expert on Asiatic archaeology and Africa Art, specialised in the founding of Fine Art Collections and Museums, historian, writer. *b*: Saigon, S.Vietnam, 11 Oct 1932. *s of*: Thierry & Florian Nguyen. *m*: Hélène Gerber. two *s*. *Educ*: Saigon, S. Vietnam, and Paris. *Studied*: l'Institut Hautes, Etudes Indochinoises, and Ecole du Louvre. *Represented by*: Asia-Africa Museum, 30 Grande Rue, CH-1204-Geneve. Tel: 4122 311 71 90. *Publications*: Archéologie asiatique, Netzuke, La Culture de Ban-Chiang (Siam) 7.000-5.000 ans, Fouilles archéologiques à Ban-Chiang. Conférencier invité à Davos Symposium (from 1985 during 10 years) by W.E.F. *Recreations*: tennis, golf. *Clubs*: Musée d'Ethnographie, Musée des Collections Baur-Duret, Union Internationale des Experts, Croix Rouge Suisse, Intérêt de Genève, Kiwanis International, Président, Asia-Africa Museum (GVA) (1993), Chevalier du Tastevin, Expert membre C.I.D.A.D.E.C., O.N.U., Tennis Club Geneva. *Misc*: President Asia-Africa Museum: expose en permanence ses collections d'antiquites selectionees de grande qualite, 30 Grand Rue, CH-1204-Geneve. Tel: 4122 311 71 90, Fax: 4122 735 89 04. *Address*: 30 Grand Rue, CH-Genève 1204, Switzerland.

NICE, Derek Vernon, NDD Painting and Ceramics; ATD Teacher Training; Postgraduate Design. *Medium*: oil, sculpture. *b*: London, 25 May 1933. *s of*: Emily & Robert Nice. *m*: Mary Nice. one *s*. one *d*. *Educ*: Municipal College, Southend, Essex. *Studied*: Southend School of Art; Central School of Art; London University Inst. of Education . *Exhib*: group exhbns: Victoria Art Gallery, Bath; solo shows: Fermoy Arts Centre, Kings Lynn; Kings School, Worcester; Chelsea and Westminster Hospital; Piers Feetham Gallery, London and Aldeburgh; Yew Tree Gallery, Cornwall; St. James Centre for Creativity, Valletta, Malta; The Cut, Halesworth, Suffolk; Sladers Yard, West Bay, Bridport, Dorset; Aldeburgh Festival; Messums Gallery, London. *Publications*: catalogues (various); Derek Nice Images (1997/2007). *Official Purchasers*: Shirley Conran O.B.E.; Chelsea Westminster Hospital. *Works Reproduced*: Bridgeman Library. *Principal Works*: Viking Longship Sculpture for Tusenfryd Park, Oslo. *Recreations*: travel, films and music (various). *Misc*: particular interest in marine archaeology and associated historical graffiti. *Address*: The Stable, Poplar Farm, Stanton Prior, Bath BA2 9HX. *Email*: stablesp@gmail.com *Signs work*: "D.N.", "Derek Nice".

NICHOLLS, Paul Edward, Diploma in Art and Design (DipAD), ATC (Art Teachers' Cert). *Medium*: acrylic, water-colour, pastels. *b*: Colchester, Essex, 1 Apr 1948. *s of*: Robert James Nicholls, architect and surveyor. *m*: Jennifer. nine *s*. one *d*. *Educ*: Epsom College of Art 1966-67, Portsmouth College of Art (1967-69), Brighton College of Art, Dept. Ed. Studies (1969-70). *Studied*: Painting and Ceramics. *Represented by*: Lander Gallery, Lemon Street, Truro. *Exhib*: Newlyn, St. Ives, Birmingham, Taunton, Pont Aven, Torquay, Wadebridge, Truro, RWA Bristol, Guildford. *Works in collections*: UK, Israel, Ireland, USA, France, Canada, Australia. *Commissions*: Mural: Our Lady of Lourdes R.C. Church, Portmouth, Redruth Operatic HQ, Leedstown Village Hall, private swimming pool, Truro, and two primary school (library projects), Jack's Cows Project, Hall for Cornwall. *Publications*: Drawing Towards the End of a Century (Newlyn Society); Paintings in Public Ownership Cornwall and Isles of Scilly; 100 Years in Newlyn. *Official Purchasers*: see mural projects, also Royal Cornwall Museum. *Works Reproduced*: history books and covers, cartoonist. *Principal Works*: Action figures (surf paintings), landscape and still life. *Clubs*: Newlyn Society of Artists (1973-). *Address*: South Barn, Mithian, St.Agnes, Cornwall, TR5 0QH. *Email*: south_barn@yahoo.co.uk *Website:* www.paulnichollsartwork.com *Signs work*: "P.Nicholls".

NICHOLS, Patricia Mary, RMS, SWA; portrait painter in miniature and full-size portrait drawings in sanguine, chalk; Mem. Royal Society of Miniature Painters; and Soc. of Women Artists; taught miniature painting at the West Norfolk Art Centre for 12 years, and Art at Glebe Horne Pre. School, Hunstanton, Norfolk for 14 years. *Medium*: watercolours, oils, sanguine chalk. *b*: Berkshire, 1923. *d of*: W/Cdr. E. T. Carpenter, AFC, RAF. *m*: Dr. F.D.P. Shaw. one *s*. one *d*. *Educ*: innumerable private schools. *Studied*: Central School of Arts and Crafts London. *Exhib*: RI, Mall Galleries, Westminster Gallery and many others. *Commissions*: has undertaken many important, including royal, commissions. *Publications*: "Dictionary of Miniature Painters 1870-1970" Atrui Phillips. *Works Reproduced*: in The Artist, Illustrated county magazines and newspapers. "R.M.S. One Hundred Years". *Address*: Sealand, Wodehouse Rd., Old Hunstanton, Norfolk PE36 6JD. *Signs work*: "Patricia Nichols."

NICHOLSON, Alison Mary, BA Hons, ATD. *Medium*: pastels, acrylics, mixed media, oil, watercolour, drawing. *b*: Carlisle, 12 Nov 1949. *m*: Nicholas Francis Crowhurst. *Educ*: Gillespies (Edinburgh), Harwich County High School (Dovercourt). *Studied*: Colchester College of Art & Technology (1968-69), Norwich School of Art (1969-72), Liverpool University (1973-74). *Represented by*: Kennetts Fine Art. *Exhib*: Royal Academy Summer Exhibition. Mall Galleries: Royal Society of British Artists, Royal Institute of Painters in Watercolour, Pastel Society; Rye Society of Artists, Affordable Art Fair Battersea, Red Leaf Gallery. *Works in collections*: USA, Canada, Belgium, France, Germany, Holland, Switzerland & throughout the UK. *Commissions*: private. *Official Purchasers*: Norwich School of Art (1972). *Misc*: Art Tutor in schools (1974-94); Art Lecturer Hastings College of Art & Technology (1997-2002); Art Lecturer Southampton University (1997-98). *Address*: Kennets Cottage, Wittersham Road, Peasmarsh, E.Sussex, TN31. *Email*: kennetsfineart@btinternet.com. *Signs work*: "ALISON NICHOLSON" or initialled "AMN".

NICKERSON, Dee. *Medium*: narrative paintings, acrylic or pastel. *b*: Wymondham, 10 Jun 1957. *d of*: Colin F. Lord. *Partner*: Richard Hunter. one *d*. *Studied*: Great Yarmouth College of Art and Design (1982-84). *Exhib*: since 1998: The Cork Brick Gallery, Bungay; The Harleston Gallery; The Halesworth Cut Open (2007/8); The Southwold Gallery (2008-); Primavera, Cambridge; Norwich Castle Museum; Hintlesham Hall, Long Gallery (2008) guest of Suffolk Coastal Group, Walberswick (2009), The Fry Art Gallery, Essex (Annual sale); The Lion House Gallery, Lavenham (2010); Wymondham Art Centre and The Steeple End Gallery (2012), The Assemnly House, Norwich (2011 Prizewinner). *Works in collections*: private. *Commissions*: private. *Publications*: Green Pebble Magazine and 'Artist in our Midst Vol. 2', Eastern Daily Press, Norfolk Magazine "Artist of the Month" April 2009. *Works Reproduced*: Green Pebble Cards. *Misc*: member of Harleston and Waveney Art Trail (2005-). Work can be seen on www.southwoldgallery.co.uk www.hwat.org.uk www.bungay-suffolk.co.uk/cork-brick www.greenpebble.co.uk @dEEN1cKersOn twitter. *Address*: The Van, Park Farm, Foxes Lane, Mendham, Harleston, IP20 0PE. *Signs work*: "dee nickerson".

NICKOLLS, Deborah, BA (Hons) First Class: Fine Art; MA Fine Art (RAS). *Medium*: acrylic. *b*: Watford, 31 Aug 1976. *m*: Joe Fletcher. one *s*. one *d*. *Educ*: Aylesbury High School. *Studied*: Central St.Martins College of Art and Design; RA Schools. *Exhib*: RA Exhbns; New Academy Gallery (solo show); "Earth Songs" A.T.Kearney; Paton Gallery; Rebecca Hossack Gallery; East 73rd Gallery; The Barbican Centre; Royal Festival Hall; Sotheby's Auction Shows: Tel Aviv and Chicago; Maiden Bridge Gallery. *Works in collections*: London Institute; private collections. *Commissions*: private. *Recreations*: mountain walking, rock-climbing, independent travel. *Misc*: works based on rock-forms and other elements of the landscape, predominantly paintings in acrylic. *Address*: 20 Lound Street, Kendal, Cumbria LA9 7EA. *Email*: info@deborahnickolls.com *Website*: www.deborahnickolls.com *Signs work*: "D Nickolls", "Deborah Nickolls".

NIEKERK, Sarah Compton Van: see VAN NIEKERK, Sarah Compton.

NIJMAN, Christina Maria, SWA; LOCN. *Medium*: Prints; artist printmaker. *b*: Amsterdam, 12 Jun 1954. *Educ*: Rietveld Academy, Amsterdam. *Studied*: Morley College, London; Kensington and Chelsea, London. *Exhib*: Society of Women Artists; Society of Wildlife Artists; Oxfordshire Artweek (2013); Printmakers Council and in other group shows. *Works in collections*: Private and corporate. *Publications*: International Contemporary Artists, Vol IV. *Clubs*: West Oxt Art Centre. *Address*: The Barns at Manor Farm, Maugersbury, Glos GL54 1HT. *Email*: tiny@tinynijmanart.com *Website*: www.tinynijmanart.com *Signs work*: "Tiny".

NINNES, Lesley Marian, HNC Art And Design (Illustration); member of Art Space Gallery co-operative, St. Ives. *Medium*: watercolour, gouache, acrylic, oil. *b*: Cornwall,

1953. two *d. Educ*: St. Ives School. *Studied*: Cornwall College. *Represented by*: Art Space Gallery; Mariners Gallery; Crypt Gallery; St. Ives Society of Artists; online galleries. *Exhib*: group exhibs. Cornwall, Devon, Scotland, York, Cirencester and France, RWS Annual Open (2008, 2009), Bath Soc. of Artists Annual Open (2011, 2012, 2013). *Works in collections*: private collections in U.K. and abroad. *Publications*: colour illus. for "The Endemic Plants of St. Helena" and pen and ink illus. for F.A.O. pub. on Inland Fisheries, pen and ink illustrations for series of Distance Learning Work Books. *Works Reproduced*: Millers Pictures Price Guide (2003); "St. Ives 1975-2005, Art Colony in Transition" by Peter Davies; "Bath Society of Artists, A History" by Peter Davies. *Clubs*: St. Ives Arts Club, Penwith Soc. of Artists - assoc. member, St. Ives Society of Artists. *Address*: 8 St. Johns Walk, St. Ives, Cornwall TR26 2JJ. *Email*: ninnes@btinternet.com *Website*: www.picturesfromstives.com *Signs work*: "Lesley Ninnes." or "LN" date.

NOAD, Julie Ann, BA Hons Fine Art (1978); painter in oil; figurative painter of interiors and views through windows preoccupied by light and colour. *b*: Essex, 29 Oct 1955. *Partner*: Miles Fairhurst. one *s*. *Studied*: Camberwell School of Art (1975-1978), under Antony Eyton RA. *Exhib*: NEAC, SWA, Mall Galleries; John Russell Gallery, Chappel Galleries, South London Gallery. *Works in collections*: private collections, UK, Europe, America. *Publications*: illustrations for Agenda, PN Review. *Address*: Turkey Hall, Metfield, Suffolk IP20 0JX. *Email*: julienoad@btinternet.com *Signs work*: "J Noad."

NOAD, Timothy Martin, MA, BA (Hons) in History of Art (London), Herald Painter at HM College of Arms, London; HSDAD (Higher Surrey Diploma in Art and Design), FSSI, FCLAS. *Medium*: Heraldry and Calligraphy in gouache and watercolour on vellum, miniatures and illumination. *b*: 3 Jul 1966. *m*: Alice Clark. one *d. Educ*: Bishop Ramsey C of E School, Ruislip. *Studied*: Reigate School of Art and Design: calligraphy, heraldry and illumination (1986). *Exhib*: Llewellyn Alexander Gallery (best miniature in show) (1996), RMS Annual Exhibition, various exhbns with SSI and CLAS; Bedlam Gallery, Brunel University (2001), Art in Action (1995-7). *Commissions*: College of Arms, Chapel Royal St. James Palace (ceiling panels), Royal Mint (Jubilee medal and Gold sovereign), Brunel University, Northern Ireland Assembly. *Publications*: The Art of Illuminated Letters, Mastering Calligraphy. *Works Reproduced*: British Library Companion to Calligraphy, Illumination and Heraldry (2001). *Recreations*: concerts, exhibitions, travel, gardening. *Address*: 23a Parkfield Road, Ickenham, Uxbridge, Middlesex, UB10 8LN. *Email*: teanoad@aol.com *Signs work*: T.Noad, Tim Noad, Timothy Noad.

NOAKES, Michael, PPROI, RP, CPS, HonNS, HonUA, Cert. RAS, NDD; landscape and portrait painter (subjects include the Queen, other members royal family, Pope Benedict XVI, Margaret Thatcher, Bill Clinton,etc.); Chairman (1971) Contemporary Portrait Society; Pres. Royal Institute of Oil Painters (1972-78); art correspondent (1964-68), BBC Television. *b*: Brighton, 28 Oct 1933. *m*: Dr.Vivien Noakes MA DPhil FRSL (decd). two *s*. one *d. Educ*: Downside. *Studied*: Reigate School of Art and R.A. Schools. *Exhib*: RA, ROI, RP, RBA, NS, etc. *Works in collections*: The Queen, The Prince of Wales, BM, National Portrait Gallery, etc. *Commissions*: London portrait sittings can be held at studio in Prince Albert Road, NW8, overlooking Regent's Park. *Publications*: A Professional Approach to Oil Painting (Pitmans, 1968); The Daily Life of The Queen: an Artist's Diary (illustrated) (Random House/Ebury Press, 2001) by Vivien Noakes. *Recreations*: idling. *Clubs*: Garrick. *Misc*: Tel:01684 575530. *Address*: Eaton Heights, Eaton Road, Malvern, Worcs. WR14 4PE. *Website*: www.michael-noakes.co.uk *Signs work*: "Michael Noakes," with date underneath.

NOBLE, Guy, BDA; LCAD; National Portrait Award; Singer & Freidlander/Sunday Times Watercolour Competition. *Medium*: oil, watercolour, drawing, prints. *b*: Kent, 1959 *s of*: Reginald Noble. *m*: Nicola. two *s*. *Educ*: Byam Shaw School of Art. *Represented by*: Peter Müller (GR) Germany; Joao Ferreira Gallery, Cape Town, S. Africa; Gallery Miralli,

Viterbo, Italy. *Exhib*: NPG; John Moores Liverpool; Whitechapel Gallery; Chisenhale; Manchester City Art Galleries; Raw Space, London. *Works in collections*: numerous corporate and private collections in UK and abroad. *Commissions*: BAA, Clyde Petroleum, Christopher Firmstone, numerous corporate and private commissions. *Publications*: has written for "Art Review" - Professor Stephen Bann - The True Vine; 16 minute video by Bill Long "Victims". *Works Reproduced*: widely. *Recreations*: sailing/skiing. *Address*: 66 Hornsey Lane, Highgate, London N6 5LU. *Email*: guy@guynoble.com *Website*: www.guynoble.com *Signs work*: "Guy Noble".

NOBLE, Jean, RI, SWA, BA Hons (Fashion & Textile Design); RSA Design Competition Winner; Abstract Painting Award, Hertford Art Soc. (2002); Lady Laming Award for Abstract Art (2007); The John Goss Prize (2011). *Medium*: acrylic, oil, mixed media. *b*: 1949. *m*: John. two *s*. *Educ*: Kingston Polytechnic. *Studied*: Loughborough College of Art; Central St.Martins (short courses); Slade Summer Schools. *Exhib*: RA Summer Exhbn (2005, 2006); RI, Mall Galleries; Discerning Eye; SWA; RWS 21st Century Open, Bankside; many galleries across UK. *Works in collections*: private collections. *Commissions*: private, in UK and abroad. *Publications*: websites - Green Pebble. *Works Reproduced*: postcards, notelets. *Principal Works*: abstract paintings. *Recreations*: garden, theatre. *Clubs*: Chelsea Art Society, Cambridge Drawing Society, Society of Women Artists, Royal Institute of Painters in Watercolour. *Address*: Brooklands, Clavering, Saffron Walden, Essex, CB11 4QW. *Email*: mail@jeannoble.com *Website*: www.jeannoble.com *Signs work*: "JNoble".

NOELLE: see SIMPSON, Noelle.

NOOTT, Edward John, BA, RBSA (2001); painter in oil. *b*: W. Midlands, 4 Oct 1965. *s of*: John Noott, Fine Art Dealer. one *s*. one *d*. *Educ*: Cheltenham College. *Studied*: Gloucestershire College of Art, Cheltenham, Trent Polytechnic College, Nottingham, State University of NY. *Exhib*: John Noott Galleries, RBSA, ROI, RWA. *Works in collections*: University of Wales. *Works Reproduced*: by The Art Group, Robertson Collection. *Address*: Broadway Modern, 10 The Green, Broadway, Worcs WR12 7AA. *Signs work*: "Edward Noott.".

NORBURY, Ian, BA (1979); sculptor in wood, metal, semi precious stones. *b*: Sheffield, 21 Aug 1948. *s of*: Kenneth Peter Norbury. *m*: Betty Ann. two *s*. one *d*. *Educ*: Andover Grammar; St. Paul's College, Cheltenham. *Studied*: St. Paul's College, Cheltenham (Harold Sayer, RE, RWA, ARCA). *Exhib*: one-man exhibitions as and when collection allows. *Works in collections*: Tower of London, Fine Art Museum of the South of Mobile, USA, Nature in Art, many private collections. *Publications*: Techniques of Creative Woodcarving, Projects for Creative Woodcarving, Relief Woodcarving and Lettering, Fundamentals of Figure Carving, Carving Facial Expressions, Carving Classic Female Faces, Carving Classic Female Figures, The Art of Ian Norbury. *Address*: Ballycommare, Tournafulla, Co. Limerick, Eire. *Signs work*: "IAN NORBURY," "I. NORBURY" or "I.N.".

NORLAND (NEUSCHUL), Khalil, MA Physics (Oxon.); artist-painter in mixed media. *b*: Aussig (Usti), Czechoslovakia, 25 Mar 1934. *s of*: Ernest Neuschul-Norland, artist-painter. *m*: Layla Shamash (decd). three *s*. *Educ*: Merton College, Oxford. *Studied*: Ruskin College of Art, Oxford (1953-57), Slade School of Art London University (1959-60). *Exhib*: Artist House, Jerusalem (1959), Woodstock Gallery, London (1961), Gallerie Lambert, Paris (1964), Camden Arts Centre, London (1987), Queen Elizabeth House, Oxford (1987), Loggia Gallery, London (1988), Haus am Lützowplatz, Berlin (1991), Linacre College, Oxford (2006). *Address*: 25 Southmoor Rd., Oxford OX2 6RF. *Email*: khalilnorland@gmail.com

NORMAN, Barbara, Paris Salon bronze medal (1975), silver medal (1976); glass engraver in diamond point, flexible drive drill. *b*: London. *d of*: Augustus Arthur Norman.

Studied: Stanhope Institute and glass engraving at Morley College under Mary Stevens. *Exhib*: Bourne Hall, Ewell, New Ashgate Gallery, Farnham, Florida Gulf Coast Art Center, Clearwater, Florida, Tampa Bay Art Center, Florida. *Publications*: Engraving and Decorating Glass (David and Charles 1972, McGraw Hill, U.S.A. 1972); Glass Engraving (David and Charles 1981, ARCO, U.S.A. 1981, A. H. & A. W. Reed, Australia 1981). *Address*: 9 Downs Lodge Court, Church St., Epsom, Surrey KT17 4QG. *Signs work*: "Barbara Norman."

NORMAN, Michael Radford, RSMA (1975); artist in pen and water-colour, often of river and coastal scenes, mixed media architectural subjects; Award of Excellence - Mystic Maritime Museum (1982). *b*: Ipswich, 20 Aug 1933. *s of*: Frank Norman 1869-1958. two *d*. *Educ*: Woodbridge School. *Studied*: Bournemouth School of Art, Regent St. Polytechnic. *Exhib*: RI, RSMA; one-man shows, Colchester, Ipswich, Norwich, London. *Works in collections*: water-colour at DoE. *Commissions*: numerous. *Publications*: illustrated, The Suffolk Essex Border by John Salmon. *Works Reproduced*: 'R. Orwell - Various Crafts Lying About' and 'Shipping Lying Ipswich Dockside' in 'A Celebration of Marine Art - 60 Years of RSMA'. *Recreations*: reading, gardening, cricket, ornithology, serious music. *Clubs*: Royal Harwich Yacht Club. *Address*: The Studio, Woolverstone, Ipswich, Suffolk IP9 1AX. *Signs work*: "Michael Norman" usually in black ink.

NORMAN, Richard, DA (1978), RSW (1994); Cargill award RGI (1991), Travelling Scholarship, Venice (1995); artist in water-colour and oil; teacher. *b*: Glasgow, 15 Jun 1956. *Studied*: Glasgow School of Art (1974-78, Dr. David Donaldson, James Robertson, Leon Morrocco). *Exhib*: regularly at RGI, RSA and RSW; one-man shows 1990-92: Kelly Gallery, Glasgow, Blythswood Gallery, Glasgow. One-man shows: Artbank, Glasgow 1995, Glasgow Art Club 1999, Theatre Royal Glasgow 2002, Glasgow Film Theatre 2003; various galleries in England, France, Netherlands, Hong Kong. *Principal Works*: "Preparation Time", "Baksheesh". *Recreations*: travel, classical music, history. *Clubs*: Glasgow Art. *Address*: c/o Ms. P. Herman-Smith, B-R, 45 Bentinck St., Glasgow G3 7TS. *Signs work*: "Richard Norman."

NORRINGTON, Claire, Whitbread Award, Wessex Artists, Salisbury; P&O Award, Chichester; BAHons Fine Art; Diana Wood Prize, The Mall Galleries, London. *Medium*: Drawing, sculpture. *b*: Bromley, London, 21 Feb 1969. *m*: Mr M Butson. two *s*. one *d*. *Studied*: Winchester School of Art (1989-91); North East Essex School of Art (1987-88). *Represented by*: Ian Courcoux, Thompsons, Leslie Pratt, Phillip Collier. *Exhib*: Courcoux & Courcoux, Stockbridge, Hants; Thirteen, Langton Street, London; Thompsons, London and Aldeburgh; Brian Sinfield, Oxon; Newby Hall Sculpture Park. *Works in collections*: Nor Systems Ltd, Harwich Dock Company, Albert Goodman. *Commissions*: "Eve" life size bronze figurine; "Walking Man" Andover; "Wild Deer Leaping" Chewton Glen Country Club. *Publications*: Modern British Sculpture by Guy Portelli, Sculpture in the South East - Arts Council, Britain. *Principle Works*: "Wild Deer Leaping", "Boxing Hares", "Eve". *Address*: The Old Gables, East Wellow, Romsey, SO51 6DR. *Email*: claire@clairenorrington.com *Signs work*: "Claire Norrington".

NORRIS, David, Cert. RAS, FRBS: sculptor; Vice-Pres. Royal Soc. of British Sculptors; Awarded the Sir Otto Beit Medal. *Medium*: bronze and stainless steel. *b*: São Paulo, Brazil, 26 Sep 1940. *s of*: Sir Alfred Norris, KBE. *m*: Carol. three *d*. *Educ*: Millfield. *Studied*: Guildford School of Art and Royal Academy Schools (1963-66). *Exhib*: Mall Galleries, Royal Mint, RA Summer Exhibition and many provincial galleries. *Works in collections*: "Women and Doves" Stevenage Town Park; "Britannia" for the Falklands Monument; "Mother and Child" Portland Hospital; Sir Barnes Wallis, RAF Museum Hendon; "Spindrift" 3.5m. high stainless steel spiral with bronze gulls for P&O liner Royal Princess; two life-size bronzes for Royal Caribbean Cruise Line; group of "flying flamingos", Arndale

Centre, Luton; bronze portrait of Maria Callas for the Royal Opera House, London; bronze relief portrait of General Sir David Fraser, Grenadier Guards; bronze "Birds of Prey" for the Middle East. *Commissions*: Life-size figures of Presidents Lincoln and Washington for Star Cruises, Sacred Heart. *Official Purchasers*: Ministry of Defence, Royal Mint. *Clubs*: RASA. *Address*: 15 Danemere Street, London SW15 1LT. *Email*: david@davidnorris.co.uk *Website*: www.davidnorris.co.uk *Signs work*: "David Norris.".

NORRIS, Linda, BA (Hons) Visual Art (1982); artist in mixed media. *b*: Chichester, 22 Jun 1960. *m*: Denbeigh Vaughan. one *d*. *Studied*: UCW Aberystwyth. *Exhib*: selected: 1998: New Academy Gallery, London, Martin Tinney Gallery, Cardiff; 1999: Attic Gallery, Swansea, Six Chapel Row Gallery, Bath; 2000: New Academy Gallery, London; 2000-2001: Adam Gallery, Bath; ongoing galleries in artist's home. *Works in collections*: Chevron U.K., General Medical Council. *Commissions*: Llandough Hospital, Penarth, Urdd Llangrannog. *Address*: The Manse, Trefgarn Owen, Haverfordwest SA62 6NE. *Email*: linda@linda-norris.com *Website*: www.linda-norris.com

NOSWORTHY, Ann Louise, NDD (1952), ATD (1953); painter in oil, gouache, pastel and charcoal. *b*: Stonehaven, Scotland, 24 Aug 1929. *d of*: Col. J. M. Savege, RAMC. *m*: T. C. Nosworthy. one *s*. *Educ*: private. *Studied*: Harrogate Art School, Leeds College of Art. *Exhib*: one-man shows: Redcar, Yorks. (1968), Castle de Vide, Portugal (1966), Egton Surgery, Whitby (2005); with Pickering Art Club (2009, 2010, 2011). *Works in collections*: Municipal Art Gallery, Port Allegre, Portugal, private collection J Dalgleish. *Works Reproduced*: 2 prints on canvas, print on paper. *Principal Works*: Green Still Life, Blue Nude in Dales Landscape. *Recreations*: reading, crosswords, music. *Clubs*: Pickering Art Club. *Address*: Brackengarth, Lealholm, Whitby, Yorks. YO21 2AE. *Signs work*: "A. L. Nosworthy."

NOT, Philip James, self taught artist in oil; proprietor of Galerie Not. *b*: 28 Feb 1938. *m*: Violet Vidot 'Une Belle Seychelleoise'. one *s*. two *d*. *Educ*: Holloway Grammar School. *Works in collections*: Etablisement de Reu (Arras, France), Lloyds Bank Plc. (Hampstead Village Branch). *Misc*: Noted for legal still life and local West Hampstead and Hampstead landscapes. *Address*: 37 Narcissus Road, West Hampstead, London NW6 1TL. *Signs work*: "P.J. Not" or "PJN".

NOYES, Margot, NDD (1960). *Medium*: mostly oil paintings, but also other media. *b*: London, 17 Aug 1939; divorced. *d of*: Frederick Henry Noyes and Margaret Jane Noyes. one *s*. one *d*. *Educ*: Fulham County Grammar School. *Studied*: Camberwell School of Arts and Crafts (1956-60, Robert Medley, Anthony Eyton, Richard Lee, Michael Salaman, Richard Eurich, Henry Inlander). *Exhib*: Many solo shows and mixed shows nationwide and overseas. *Works in collections*: private. *Commissions*: many portrait commissions and paintings for feature films, including "Last Judgment" church painting for the film "A Month in the Country". *Publications*: 'Camberwell School of Arts & Crafts - Its Students & Teachers 1943-1960' by Geoff Hassel; 'Artists at Walberswick - East Anglian Interludes 1880-2000' by Richard Scott. *Misc*: A founder member of the Suffolk Group. *Address*: 51 London Rd., Halesworth, Suffolk IP19 8LS. *Website*: www.thesuffolkgroup.co.uk *Signs work*: "M. Noyes," very small works initials only.

NUGENT, Lesley. *Medium*: watercolour, prints, acrylic. *b*: Manchester, 25 Aug 1957. *m*: David Nugent. two *d*. *Represented by*: ABNA (Association of British Naive Artists); The Acorn Gallery. *Exhib*: Association of British Naive Artists, Mariners Gallery, St. Ives; The Acorn Gallery, Pocklington, Yorkshire; Churchtown Art Club Annual Exhibition. *Commissions*: various private commissions using themselves and their pets and homes within my imaginary Nuggleton by the Sea series. *Official Purchasers*: various galleries in the UK and abroad. *Principal Works*: Nuggleton by the Sea series. *Clubs*: Churchtown Art Club. *Misc*: A self taught artist living in a coastal area, whose intricately detailed mixed media paintings have a growing number of followers from around the world. *Address*: 12 Holmdale Avenue, Crossens, Southport PR9 8PS. *Email*: lesleynugent258@btinternet.com *Website*: www.nuggletonart.co.uk *Signs work*: "Lesley Nugent".

O

O'AIVAZIAN, Edman, RSMA, ROI; prizes - 1st prize Iranian Contemp. Artists (1956), 1st prize Iranian Ministry of Culture Competition (1958), George Grimm prize R.O.I. (1998), Windsor and Newton Award R.O.I. (2000). painter in oil, water-colour and acrylic; designer. *b*: Tehran,10 Aug 1932. *m*: Thelma. two *s*. *Educ*: Tehran, Rome and London. *Exhib*: since 1948; Tehran, Venice (Biennale), New York, Boston, Jeddah, Yerevan, London - ROI, RSMA, NEAC. *Works in collections*: Museums - San Lazaro, Venice; Aram Khachaturian, Yerevan; Aivazovski, Crimea; Armenian National Gallery, Yerevan; Modern Art, Yerevan. Private collections - Saudi Arabia, Oman, Tehran. *Commissions*: Boston, New York, Los Angeles, London; portraits for Saudi Royals, and Sultan Qaboos, Oman; Murals in Armenian churches; calligraphy and design of Grand Mosque, Riyadh; mural for Jeddah airport; designs for King Fahed Int. Airport Mosque; mosaic design for Sultan Qaboos Mosque, Muscat; mural for Nat. Museum, Riyadh. *Publications*: illus. Armenian Village (1984), Portraits of Poets (1970); Poems of Toumanian (1970); Komitas (1998); illus. "Edman" Book of Painting (Iran, 2004). *Clubs*: Wapping Group of Artists. *Misc*: 2001 design of Armenian exhibition, British Library; 2009 Armenian Festival, Moncton, New Brunswick, Canada. *Address*: 61a Fulham High St., London SW6 3JJ. *Email*: edman@lineone.net *Website*: www.edmano.com *Signs work*: "EDMAN".

O'BRIEN, Emer, BA (Hons); MA; The Art of the Stitch, Embroiderers Guild, Student Award; Fujifilm Professional, Student Gold Award. *Medium*: Photography; film. *b*: Dublin, 9 Oct 1974. *Studied*: Goldsmiths MA (2003); The London Consortium MRES (2006-08). *Represented by*: Self. *Exhib*: Wapping Project; RA; 4 Corners; International Biennale of Contemporary Art (Narondni Balerie V Praze); The Whitechapel Gallery; VTO Gallery; Dutch Textile Museum; Chelsea College of Art and Design. *Works in collections*: City University; London University of the Arts; many private collections. *Commissions*: City University School of the Arts Commission (2009). *Publications*: Include: Royal Academy Illustrated 2008, Exhibition Catalogue, RA (2008); Journeys into a Bright World, Exhibition Catalogue, Ferreira Projects, London (2008); East Academy, Exhibition Catalogue, The Whitechapel Gallery, London (2004). *Works Reproduced*: Where the Wild Things Are (2004); The Listed Screen (2007). *Principal Works*: Storm 2007. *Misc*: Visiting lecturer at Sotheby's Institute, City University. *Address*: The Former Lilian, Baylis School, Lollard Street, London SW11 6PY. *Email*: lime@madasafish.com *Website*: www.emerobrien.com *Signs work*: "emer o'brien".

O'CARROLL, John Patrick, South West Arts Dip., graduated distinction, painting. *Medium*: painting, sculpture, books. *b*: Bedfordshire, 17 Mar 1958. *s of*: Shirley Finch, John F.O'Carroll. *Partner*: A. El Najjar. *Studied*: Cornwall College of Art and Design; Lamar University, TX, USA. *Represented by*: Galerie Roger Katwijk, Amsterdam; Contemporary Art Gallery, UK. *Exhib*: Holly Solomon, NYC (1985); Galerie Charlotte Daneel, Amsterdam (1994-97); L'Atelier, Alexandria, Egypt (1995); Pulitzer Gallery, Amsterdam; British Council, Cairo, Egypt (1996); Contempo, Rotterdam (1996); Kunst RAI, Amsterdam (1984-2003); Art Fare, Rotterdam; PBS, Houston, Texas; Akzo Nobel, Arnhem, NL.(1997); British Embassy, Cairo (2001); Galerie Le Besset/parc de scultures, France (2003); Galerie Pimm van der Donk, Hamburg (2004); Kunst RAI Hamburg (2004, 2005); International Biennale, Alexandria Library, Egypt (2005); 'Groen en Haut', Haarlem, Netherlands (2005); DL13, Amsterdam (2008); Galerie Roger Katwijk, Amsterdam (2008); Art Amsterdam, solo (2009). *Works in collections*: Pulitzer Art Collection, Amsterdam; Royal Collection, The Hague, Akzo-Nobel Art Collection, Arnhem, NCM Headquarters, Cardiff, AMC

Amsterdam. Private collections worldwide. *Commissions*: Akzo-Nobel - Garden of Time and Desert Poems. *Publications*: 'John O'Carroll - Art Works 1998-2008' ISBN 978-0-9560308-0-1; Proof of Principle (Akzo Nobel) (2003), illustrations for Island of Blessed by Harry Thurston (Cairo Times), Ai Ahram Weekly, De Welt. *Official Purchasers*: The Royal Collection, Den Hague, Pulitzer Art Collection, Amsterdam, AMC, Amsterdam, NCM Headquarters, Cardiff. *Principal Works*: NCM Cardiff, Desert Tracks; Akzo Nobel Garden of Time and Desert Poem. *Recreations*: archaeological, travel, fieldwork. *Clubs*: Dakhleh Oasis Project, Egypt. *Misc*: studios in Egypt, Amsterdam, Cornwall. Abstractions of place, landscape, time and space. *Address*: Pell Allema, Rosenannon, St.Wenn, Cornwall, PL30 5PJ. *Email*: info@johnocarroll.co.uk *Website*: www.johnocarroll.co.uk

O'CONNELL, Richard Marcus, DipAD (Hons) Norwich (1969), Cert. FA (Oxon. 1972); figurative painter in oil, acrylic, water-colour, poet. *b*: Mumbles, Swansea, 19 Jul 1947. two *d*. *Educ*: Swansea College of Art (1965-66), Ruskin School of Drawing, Norwich School of Art (1966-69), University of Oxford (1971-72). *Exhib*: one-man shows: Marlborough Fine Art, London (1974), St. David's Hall, Cardiff (1989, 1996), National Museum of Wales, Turner House, Penarth (1994), Washington Gallery, Penarth (2001, 2002, 2006). *Works in collections*: Balliol College-Oxford University, National Museum of Wales, Cardiff, Vale of Glamorgan Council, Barry. *Publications*: poetry book: 'Cardiff, my Cardiff' (Inika Press, Penarth, 1997); 'I Remember Swansea' (1999). *Clubs*: Vale of Glamorgan Artists. *Address*: 26 Coronation Terrace, Penarth, Vale of Glamorgan, Wales CF64 1HN. *Signs work*: "Richard O'Connell".

O'CONNOR, Marcel, BA (Hons) Fine Art; artist/teacher in oil and wax encaustic painting. *b*: Lurgan, Co. Armagh, 19 Nov 1958. *Educ*: St. Michael's High School, Lurgan. *Studied*: Liverpool Polytechnic (1977-78), Brighton Polytechnic (1978-81), Cyprus College of Art (1983-84). *Exhib*: Scotland, Ireland, England, Cyprus, Hungary, Germany. *Works in collections*: City Arts Centre, Edinburgh. *Publications*: catalogues: 'Boundaries' in Edinburgh and Belfast; 4 Artists in Hungary; 'Europe 24' in Hungary; 'Europe 24 no.2' in Germany, bookcover artwork 'Scotland and Ulster'. *Address*: 5 Main Street, Hillend, Fife KY11 9ND. *Signs work*: "Marcel O'Connor".

O'CONNOR, Martin Simon, BA Hons (1973-76); RA Post Grad (1977-80); C&G of London Inst. - Adv. masonry distns (1992); C & G Art School- Dip. in Conservation & Rest. (1993-95); conservator. *Medium*: sculptor in stone, wood, plaster, bronze, etc. Draughtsman (mixed media on paper and canvas). *b*: London, 2 Jan 1953. *m*: divorced. Angelica Bornhausen (prima ballerina). one *s*. *Educ*: Salvatorian College, Harrow Weald, London. *Studied*: Harrow School of Art (1972-73), Canterbury College of Art (1973-76), RA Schools (1977-80). *Exhib*: Maidstone, Falmouth, Canterbury, RA Dip. Gallery. Germany: Freiburg, Kassel, Hamburg. *Works in collections*: all private. *Commissions*: all private. *Publications*: appears in The Dictionary of Artists in Britain since 1945. *Clubs*: Reynolds Club (RA). *Address*: 10 Woodcroft Ave, Mill Hill, London NW7 2AG. *Email*: martin_oconnor@hotmail.co.uk *Signs work*: "M.O'CONNOR".

O'DONOGHUE, Declan, MCSD (1986), FSC-D (1991), M.InstPI (1991), MSDI (1991); designer and furniture maker in wood, metal, stone, glass; Director, Wilcogold Ltd. (1985), Adviser, Connemara West plc. (1992), Owner, S.F. Furniture (1980), Principal visiting tutor, Furn. Coll. Letterfrack (1988). *b*: Cork, 18 Oct 1960. *s of*: Dr R.F. O'Donoghue FRCS FRCOS. *m*: Fiona Mary Curry. two *d*. *Educ*: St. Vincent's College, Castleknock, Dublin. *Studied*: Parnham College (1978-80, R. Ingham). *Exhib*: National Theatre, Barbican, Camden Arts Centre, Mall Galleries, Bath Festival, Kilkenny Design Dublin, British Crafts Centre, British Crafts, Cheltenham; ORGATEC, Cologne; Bonhams, London: Create Cork. *Commissions*: National Gallery, Dublin, Guildhall, London. *Publications*: numerous exhbn. catalogues, articles, book features, B.B.C. (1981), H.T.V. (1992-93). Freeman City of

London (1994), Liveryman Worshipful Co. of Furn. Makers (1994), Furniture for 21st Century (Norbury); Celebration of Excellence (WCFM). *Clubs*: Royal Cork Yacht, Exe Sailing Club, London City Livery Yacht Club. *Address*: Street Farm, Acton Turville, Badminton, Glos. GL9 1HH. *Email*: declan@sffurniture.co.uk *Website*: www.sffurniture.co.uk

O'FARRELL, Bartholomew Patrick, BEd.Hons (Wales), DipAD; landscape painter; Lecturer in Illustration, Faculty of Art, W.G.I.H.E., Swansea (1981-85). *Medium*: acrylic and water-colour. *b*: Ogilvie, Mid-Glamorgan, 11 Aug 1941. *Educ*: Caerphilly Grammar School. *Studied*: Cardiff College of Art (1959-62), Polytechnic of Wales, Barry (1974-78). *Exhib*: Cornwall and S. Wales; annual one-man shows in Cornwall from 1986 onwards at Trelowarren, Helston Folk Museum, Camborne School of Mines Museum and Gallery, St. Austell Arts Centre, Falmouth A.G.; selected: National Museum of Wales, Albany Gallery, Cardiff; Celtic Art, Falmouth; Manor House Fine Arts; 3 Spires, Truro; Royal Cornwall Museum, Truro. *Works in collections*: National Library of Wales, Lloyds TSB Bank plc. *Works Reproduced*: in The Encyclopedia of Acrylic Techniques; The Best of Acrylic Painting; Inspirational Portraits; Encyclopedia of Water-colour Landscape Painting; Water, How to paint it; Acrylic School; The Acrylic Artists Bible. *Recreations*: dowsing. *Address*: Treleague Farm, St. Keverne, Helston, Cornwall TR12 6PQ. *Signs work*: "Bart O'Farrell".

O'GORMAN, Linda Helen, BA Hons, graphics/illustration; artist and framer in monoprint and mixed media. *b*: Woodend, Staffs., 8 Jul 1948. *m*: Tom O'Gorman. one *s*. four *d*. *Studied*: Gwent College of Art, Nuneaton School of Art and Bath Spa University. *Exhib*: Royal West of England Autumn open, Cheltenham open, Battersea Art Fair, Bath Society of Artists, Atrium Gallery Spring show, Society of Graphic Fine Artists, Bath Visual Arts Exhibition. *Clubs*: member Bath Area Network of Artists, Society of Graphic Fine Artists. *Address*: 2 Beech View, Bath BA2 6DX. *Email*: lindaogorman@hotmail.com *Signs work*: "L H O'Gorman".

O'HARA, D. Patrick, FLS; botanical sculptor (original works in porcelain, engraving and enamelling on crystal); botanical water-colours. *b*: Windsor, 17 Jun 1936. *m*: Anna O'Hara, landscape painter (decd 2013). one *s*. one *d*. *Educ*: Haileybury and Reading University. *Studied*: Malvern Art School (1969-71). *Exhib*: Cartier, NY (1972), Tryon and Moorland Gallery (1973), Chicago Flower Show (1975), Wexford Festival (1976), Victor Zelli (1978), RHS (1979), Bank of Ireland (1980), Meister Gallery, Zurich (1980, 1981), Chester Beatty Library, Dublin (1984), United Nations (1984), EXPO, Osaka (1990), Royal Bot. Gdns. (1994), Huntington, California (1998), Ulster Museum, Belfast (2001), National Botanical Gardens, Dublin (2002), Fota House, Cork (2004), Amoco, CA & Santa Barbara Botanic Garden (2008), University College Cork (2011). *Works in collections*: Lewis Ginter Botanical Gdn., Richmond, Va.; Flagler Museum, Florida; Jones Museum, Maine; International Museum of Wildlife Art, Gloucester; Chicago Horticultural Soc.; Gloucester City Museum; Adachi Inst., Tokyo; Smithkline Beecham Corp., Sumitomo Group; Jefferson Smurfit Foundation; Molecular Nature Ltd., National Museum of Ireland; American Museum of Ceramic Art, Pomona, CA; California Academy of Sciences; HRH Prince Charles; National Bank of Dubai; Santa Barbara Botanic Garden. *Commissions*: ongoing commission: collection of watercolours of California wildflowers for Santa Barbara Botanic Garden. *Publications*: 'Botanical Sculpture - A Lifesaving Alternative' (Biological Collections & Diversity, Linnean Soc/Westbury). *Address*: Manor House, Currabinny, Carrigaline, Co. Cork, Eire. *Email*: patrick@oharasculpture.com *Website*: www.ohara-art.com *Signs work*: "Patrick O'Hara".

O'KEEFE, Kevin, Diploma in Art and Design, Painting. *Medium*: prints, acrylic. *b*: West Kirby. nr. Liverpool, 10 May 1950. *s of*: John and Mary O'Keefe. *Partner*: Jane Tanner.

one *d*. *Studied*: Chester School of Art (Pre-Dip, 1968-69); Camberwell School of Arts & Crafts (1969-72). *Represented by*: The Black Hat Gallery. *Exhib*: Il Bordelo Arts Club, Bristol (solo), Widcombe Studios, Bath (mixed), Coningsby Gallery, London (solo), Black Hat Gallery, London (solo), successive Royal Academy Summer Shows. *Works Reproduced*: numerous magazines, Daler Rowney Screenprinting Manual. *Principal Works*: '69 Camberwell, Or So It Seemed', 'Domestic Airport'. *Recreations*: music, film, food and drink, swimming. *Address*: 40 Osborne Road, Bristol, BS3 1PW. *Email*: jokevanoke@blueyonder.co.uk *Website*: www.kevinokeefe-art.com *Signs work*: "KEVIN O'KEEFE".

O'NEILL, Junko, MA; BAHons; Stephen Heffer Memorial Award (2008). *Medium*: Oil, acrylic. *b*: Tokyo, 25 Jun 1961. *m*: Derek. two *d*. *Studied*: Rikkyo University, Tokyo (1981-85); Winchester School of Art (2004-2009). *Exhib*: The Link Gallery, Winchester (2010); The Lloyd Gill Gallery, Weston-Super-Mare (2011); Fairfields Arts Centre, Basingstoke (2009, 2010, 2012); Debut Contemporary, London (2012); The Other Art Fair, London (2012, 2013); GV Art, London (2013); Galleria Via Larga, Florence (2013); Espacio Gallery, London (2014); Eagl Gallery, Berlin (2014). *Publications*: "Hidden Treasure Art Magazine Yearbook 2014 (HT Art Magazine Publishing). *Principal Works*: Winter Veil (2009); Without Wings (2009); Dissolved (2011); The Intervals (2013). *Address*: Bicton, Sleepers Hill, Winchester, Hampshire SO22 4NB. *Email*: info@junkooneill.com *Website*: www.junkooneill.com *Signs work*: "Junko O'Neill".

O'REILLY, Faith, NDD, Dip RA, ATC; oil and water-colourist. *b*: Boston, Mass., USA, 6 Aug 1938. *d of*: Eileen O'Reilly. *Partner*: Sandra Freeman, playwright. *Educ*: in USA and England. *Studied*: Berkshire College of Art, Royal Academy Schools, Hornsey and University of London. *Exhib*: group and solo shows: Midland Group Gallery; 273 Gallery, London; shows in Universities, Surrey, Sussex, Montpellier, Paris and Dieppe. *Works in collections*: USA, France, Australia, Singapore, Britain. *Commissions*: 'Roman' Mosaic, Moorgate, London. *Publications*: Snoopy's Guide to Computors, Btn. Poly, Mag. *Clubs*: N.A.A., Reynolds Club, R.A. London. *Misc*: Helped to found Stanley Spencer Gallery, Cookham, Berkshire. Studios: Le Vernet, Zamalou les Bains, 34240 France; Kemptown, Brighton BN2 2EB. *Address*: 13 Walpole Terr., Kemptown, Brighton, Sussex BN2 2EB. *Signs work*: "F.O.R." and "Faith O'Reilly." Returned to "O'Reilly" from adoptive name "Gibbon" in 1975.

O'REILLY, Joseph, 1st Class Hons, Fine Art; Awards: Hunting Art Prize; Edward Oldham Prize, Manchester Academy. *b*: Yorkshire, 1957. *Educ*: Batley School of Art and Design. *Studied*: Sheffield Polytechnic of Art and Design. *Represented by*: Bruton Gallery Ltd., and others. *Exhib*: Discerning Eye, Mall Galleries, London; RCA; Olympia; Hunting Art Prize, RCA; public galleries in Dean Clough, Leeds, Bradford, Liverpool, Huddersfield, Halifax, Manchester; France and Holland. *Works in collections*: Boston, USA; Calderdale Art Gallery; Kirklees Art Gallery; Duke of Devonshire; private collections, UK & USA. *Principal Works*: Still Life. *Address*: c/o Bruton Gallery Ltd., P O Box 145, Holmfirth, Yorks, HD9 1YU. *Signs work*: "Joseph O'Reilly".

O'REILLY, Oran, MA (RCA). *Medium*: digital media, drawing, prints. *b*: Stockport, 27 Jun 1975. *Studied*: RCA (1999-2001). *Represented by*: Keith Talent Gallery, London; Toomey-Tourel, San Francisco. *Exhib*: Cynthia Broan Gallery, New York (2005); Keith Talent Gallery, London (2003-05); Toomey-Tourel Gallery, San Francisco (2003); RA Summer Show (2003, 2005); Nickle Arts Museum, Calgary (2002). *Works in collections*: Thomas Dane (London); Royal College of Art; University of Lincoln. *Publications*: Miser and Now Magazine 'Eighty six Occurences'. *Address*: c/o Keith Talent Gallery, 2-4 Tudor Road, London E9 7SN. *Email*: mail@oranoreilly.co.uk *Website*: www.oranoreilly.co.uk *Signs work*: 'Oran O'Reilly'.

O'REILLY, Richard, FPS; artist in oil, water-colour, ink, wood. *b*: London, 11 May 1932. *m*: P. Turner. two *s*. one *d*. *Educ*: Avondale School, Cheadle Heath, Ches. *Studied*: under William Redgrave, sculptor-draughtsman 'One to One'. *Exhib*: Guildhall London, Ragley Hall, Foyles's King's College, Vienna 9th International, PS, Tattershall Castle, Cambridge Union, University of Essex, House of Commons, BAC, St. Martin-in-the-Fields, London. *Works in collections*: Loggia Gallery, The Investment Gallery, Paris, Berlin, Vienna, NY. *Works Reproduced*: Arts Review. *Address*: 12 Acanthus Rd., Battersea, London SW11 5TY. *Signs work*: "O'Reilly".

O'RORKE, Robert Ashley, MARCA. *Medium*: oil, watercolour, drawing. *b*: London, 21 Sep 1945. *s of*: H C A O'Rorke. *Partner*: Julia Brown. *Educ*: Eton College. *Studied*: Byam Shaw School of Art (1963-66); Royal College of Art (1966-69). *Exhib*: Piers Feetham Gallery (2008); Garsington Opera Artist-in-Residence (2006). *Works in collections*: Nottingham Council; Lindblad Travel Inc. *Commissions*: 2 large oils of Rufford Abbey for the new Council Chamber at Nottingham (2003). *Works Reproduced*: The White Cat, 'Cats in Art' (Studio Editions); Fishing Boat at Beesands; 'Practical Watercolours' (Dorling Kindersley); Garden at la Mortola 'History of Italian Gardens', Francis Lincoln. *Clubs*: Chelsea Arts Club, Art Workers Guild. *Address*: 109 Portland Road, London W11 4LN. *Email*: robert@robert-ororke.com *Website*: www.robert-ororke.com *Signs work*: "ROBERT O'RORKE".

OATHAM, Richard, BSc (Chemistry). *Medium*: oil, watercolour, prints. *b*: Ruislip, Middx, 21 Aug 1942. *s of*: Robert Oatham. *m*: Catherine Oatham. *Studied*: Reading University. *Exhib*: RA Summer Exhbn; Orleans Gallery, Twickenham. *Works in collections*: etchings: London Borough of Richmond upon Thames. *Recreations*: golf, bridge, walking, reading, gardening. *Address*: 58 Marina Place, Hampton Wick, Kingston-upon-Thames, Surrey, KT1 4BH. *Email*: oatham@hotmail.com *Signs work*: 'Richard Oatham'.

OCEAN, Humphrey, RA (2004); winner Imperial Tobacco Award (1982); Professor of Perspective, Royal Academy of Arts 2013-; Hon. Doctorate, Canterbury Christ Church University 2012. *b*: Pulborough, 22 Jun 1951. *s of*: Capt. M.E. Butler-Bowdon, O.B.E., R.N. *m*: Miranda Argyle. two *d*. *Educ*: Ampleforth. *Studied*: Tunbridge Wells Art School (1967-69), Brighton College of Art (1969-70), Canterbury College of Art (1970-73). *Exhib*: RA, Haus der Kunst Munich, British Council; one-man shows: NPG (1984), Ferens A.G. Hull (1987), Whitechapel A.G.,and Tate Gallery, Liverpool (1991), Whitworth A.G., Manchester, 'Painter's Eye' NPG (1999), Dulwich Picture Gallery (2003), Sidney Cooper Gallery, Canterbury Christ Church University (2009), 'A handbook of modern life' NPG (2013). *Works in collections*: NPG, Imperial War Museum, Ferens A.G., Scottish NPG, V&A Museum, Royal Library, South London Gallery Collection, Wolverhampton A.G., National Maritime Museum, Bruges-Zeebrugge Port Authority; British Council; Christ Church, Oxford; The Whitworth Art Gallery, University of Manchester; Pallant House Gallery, Chichester. *Publications*: The Ocean View (Plexus 1982), Big Mouth (Fourth Estate 1990, and Brown Trout, San Francisco 1994), 'Zeebrugge' (M.B.Z. Belgium 2002); 'A handbook of modern life' (Lecturis, Eindhoven, 2012). *Address*: 22 Marmora Rd., London SE22 0RX.

OCKENDEN, John Richard, B.Ed (Hons) (1978); artist in water-colour and acrylic; Vice Chairman, Deeside Art Group. *b*: Cheltenham, 6 Aug 1946. one *d*. *Educ*: Alsager CHE, Chester CHE. *Exhib*: one-man shows: Theatr Clwyd Gallery since 1988; many mixed shows in England and Wales, including International Spring Fair, NEC B'ham. *Publications*: limited editions. *Address*: 29 Marksway, Pensby, Wirral L61 9PB. *Signs work*: "John R. Ockenden".

ODA, Mari-Ruth, MA/ BA (Hons); Keith Godwin Award for Sculpture. *b*: Papua New Guinea, 10 Jan 1974. *d of*: Nobuaki & Taeko Oda. *Studied*: University of Wolverhampton,

Wolverhampton (1996-7); Manchester Metropolitan University, Manchester (1993-6). *Exhib*: RA Summer Show, London (2007); Touch Me, Victoria and Albert Museum, London (2005); City of Carouge Prize 2003, Musee de Carouge, Geneva, Switzerland (2003); Object Gallery, Sydney, Australia (2001). *Works in collections*: Manchester Gallery 'Sit-able Sculpture'; Shigaraki Ceramic Cultural Park 'Fossilised Bone Form'. *Commissions*: various public and private. *Publications*: 'Raku, Investigation into Fire' by David Jones. *Address*: 90 Humphrey Road, Manchester, M16 9DF. *Email*: mari@mari-ruthoda.com *Website*: www.mari-ruthoda.com *Signs work*: "MARI".

OFFEN, John, BA (Hons); designer and author; The Observer Mace (1969); partner Ken Moore Design Associates. *b*: 15 Mar 1951. *s of*: Raymond Offen. *Educ*: University of Exeter. Positions held: British Council, UNESCO, OECD Attache, British Embassy, Tunis; Director, Queen Alexandra's House, Kensington. *Publications*: A History of Irish Lace, Thoroughbred Style. *Address*: 13 McLeods Mews, London SW7 4HP.

OGDEN, Catherine, ARBSA (1992), RMS (1993), SWA (1988); miniature seascape painter, flower pastelist; acrylic landscapes. *b*: London, 10 Apr 1951. *Educ*: Plashet Secondary Modern, Kingsway College. *Exhib*: RMS, SWA, RI, RBSA, RWS, Mid 'Art' 86 Dudley, Laing Art collection competition, John Noott Gallery, Llewellyn Alexander Gallery. *Address*: 26 Robins Meadow, Evesham, Worcs., WR11 4RN. *Signs work*: "C. Ogden".

OGILVY, Susan Pamela, RHS Silver Gilt Medal (1995), RHS Gold Medal (1997); botanical illustrator. *Medium*: water colour, pen and ink, pencil. *b*: Bromley, Kent, 22 Mar 1948. *m*: A.R.W. Ogilvy. three *s*. *Educ*: Park School, Yeovil and St. Loyes School of Occupational Therapy, Exeter. *Studied*: Luton School of Art. *Exhib*: six solo exhibs. at Park Walk Gallery and group exhibs. at Tryon Gallery and R.H.S. *Works in collections*: Dr. Shirley Sherwood; The Hunt Institute, USA; The Highgrove Florilegium; The Sutton Collection, USA. *Commissions*: national. *Publications*: "Overleaf" by Richard Ogilvy and Susan Ogilvy (pub. Kew Publishing, 2013). *Address*: Orchard End, East Lambrook, South Petherton Somerset TA13 5HN. *Email*: spogilvy@hotmail.com *Signs work*: "Susan Ogilvy" or a monogram of an S within an O.

OLIN, Leon, NDD (1962), ATD (1963); artist and illustrator. *Medium*: oil, water-colour, ink. *b*: 28 May 1939. *m*: Sylvia Gainsford. one *s*. *Studied*: Leicester and Brighton Colleges of Art. *Exhib*: Numerous. *Works in collections*: Portsmouth Civic Gallery, Kallis Foundation, Beverly Hills. *Commissions*: numerous. *Publications*: Pembrokeshire Architecture (Rosedale Pub.), Wildlife of St. James' Park (Brick by Brick L.H.A.G.), Food from the Countryside, Where have all the Cowslips gone, Out of This World (Bishopsgate Press), The Country Kitchen (Bell and Hyman), A Strange Way to Make a Living (Pembrokeshire Press) 319 pages, includes 49 colour plates of artists' work - reviewed on Amazon.co.uk. *Works Reproduced*: Limited edition prints by Buckingham Fine Art Publishers Ltd. *Misc*: old agricultural landscapes, traditional marine subjects. *Address*: Fron Haul, Rhos-y-Caerau, Goodwick, Pembrokeshire SA64 0LB. *Signs work*: "LEON OLIN".

OLINER, Sheila. *Medium*: oil/canvas, drawing, etching. *b*: London. one *s*. two *d*. *Studied*: Slade and City & Guilds. Printmaking - Dorothea Wight Studio Prints. *Represented by*: Penwith Gallery, St. Ives; Plumbline Gallery, St. Ives; Willshane Gallery, St. Ives. *Exhib*: solo: London, St. Ives, Tokyo, Hiroshima, Osaka. *Works in collections*: private collections. *Publications*: 'Artists in their Workplace', '22 Painters' (M.Whybrow), 'Art and Artists-Contemporary Cornwall' (Tom Cross), 'Drawing Towards the End of the Century' - NSA 'Art NSA 2002', 'St.Ives 1975-2005 Art Colony in Transition' (Peter Davies, 2007). *Recreations*: walking, reading, music. *Clubs*: Penwith Society. *Address*: Studio 7, Penwith Galleries, Porthmeor Rd, St.Ives TR26. *Email*: sheilaoliner@yahoo.co.uk *Website*: http://www.org/artist/sheilaoliner

OLIVER, Dawn Nicola, HS (1999), MAS-F (1999); artist in water-colour, art tutor. *b*: High Wycombe, 14 Apr 1959. *Exhib*: RMS Westminster, HS Wells, MAS-F, Royal Soc. of Painters in Watercolour, Mall Galleries, etc. Work in collections internationally. *Clubs*: Chilterns Art Group. *Address*: 20 Elmhurst Road, Aylesbury Bucks. HP20 2EA. *Email*: dawnoliver2@hotmail.com

ONIANS, Richard (Dick) Lathbury, MA (Cantab), ARBS (1989); City and Guilds Art School Cert. of Merit (1968); lecturer; Senior Carving Tutor, City and Guilds of London Art School; President of the City & Guilds Institute's Award for Teaching (2003). *Medium*: sculptor in wood and stone. *b*: Chalfont St. Giles, 19 May 1940. *s of*: Prof. R.B. Onians, MA, PhD. *m*: Frances Clare Critchley. *Educ*: Merchant Taylors' School, Northwood; Trinity College, Cambridge. *Studied*: City and Guilds of London Art School (1966-68). *Exhib*: Mall Galleries, Marjorie Parr Gallery, Century Galleries, Henley-on-Thames, Galleria Renata, Chicago, Clementi House Gallery, Edith Grove Gallery, Bow House Gallery, London, Pashley Manor Gardens, Woburn Abbey Gardens. *Works in collections*: The Newton Institute for Mathematical Sciences, Cambridge University. *Commissions*: 'The Family' outdoor wood sculpture for S.Oxhey, Watford, 2001; "The Still Centre of the Turning World" stainless steel sculpture for New Capital Quay, Greenwich Riverside, London (2014). *Publications*: Essential Woodcarving Techniques: (G.M.C. Publications Ltd., 1997); Carving The Human Figure: (G.M.C. Publications Ltd., 2001). *Address*: Woodside, Commonwood, King's Langley, Herts. WD4 9BA. *Email*: dick.onians@talk21.com *Website*: www.dickonianssculptor.co.uk *Signs work*: "R.L.O".

ONO, Takumasa, Award for Excellence, Salon des Beaux Arts international Arts Exchange Exhibition, New York (1988). *Medium*: watercolour, "sumi-e" Japanese ink painting. *b*: Tokyo, Japan, 20 Oct 1959. *m*: Mari. one *s*. Exhib: "HENRO" Exhibition, National Trust properties (2001-2014); Art in Action (2009, 2010, 2014); Nature in Art Museum (2006, 2009-2011); Calre Hall, Cambridge (2006); Japanese Embassy (2004); plus many others across the UK and worldwide. Selected artist at: Triennial Frechen International Print Exhibition, Germany (1990); New Zealand Print Exhibition (1989); Le Solban Grand Prix, Nippan Kai Print Exhibition (1989); Contemporary Japanese Art Expo, LA, USA (1988). *Works in collections*: Tosa washi Museum, Japan; National Trust, UK. *Commissions*: Wales Millennium Centre, Cardiff; Toyota Motor Corporation, Japan; National Trust. Publications: "The Simple Art of Sumi-e" (Cico Books). *Works Reproduced*: National Trust prints. *Address*: c/o Teikyo Foundation, Framewood Road, Wexham, Bucks SL2 4QS. *Email*: takumasaono@hotmail.co.uk *Website*: www.takumasaono.co.uk *Signs work*: "Takumasa Ono".

OOZEERALLY, Barbara, BA Hons Architecture; botanical artist in water-colour. *b*: Poland, 18 Dec 1953. *m*: Shahood. one *s*. *Educ*: Warsaw Politechnik. *Exhib*: SBA, SFP, RHS, Chelsea Flower Show, United States Boatanica Gardens in Washington, New York Horticultural Society, Kirstenbosh Botanica Garden in Cape Town, Hunt Institute of Botanical Documentation (Pittsburgh, USA). *Works in collections*: Dr Shirley Sherwood, UK, and Mrs Barbara Macklowe, New York, Lindley Library Collection (RHS), Hunt Institute of Botanical Documentation (Pittsburgh, USA). *Publications*: book to be pub. 2003. *Works Reproduced*: A Passion for Plants' Dr. Shirley Sherwood. *Address*: 45 Manor Close, London NW9 9HD. *Email*: barbara@barbaraoozeerally.co.uk *Website*: www.barbaraoozeerally.co.uk *Signs work*: "B Oozeerally".

ORAM, Ann Alexandra, BA (Hons) 1980, Post Grad. Dip. in Fine Art (1981), RSW (1986); painter in water-colour, mixed media and oil. *b*: London, 3 May 1956. *d of*: Thomas Alexander Oram. *m*: David Cemery. one *s*. *Educ*: Grantown Grammar School, Inverness Royal Academy. *Studied*: Edinburgh College of Art/Heriot Watt University (1976-82). *Exhib*: one-man shows include: Thackeray Gallery, Scottish Gallery, Portland Gallery,

Loomshop and Macauley Gallery; group shows: RSA, RSW, RGI, RA, Stowell's Trophy, Royal Overseas League, Compass Gallery - New Generation, Corrymelia Scott, Duncan Miller Fine Art, Roger Billcliffe, STV Student Show. Air Fairs Bath, London, Manchester, New York. *Works in collections*: Britain and abroad. *Address*: Logie East, Crossford, Fife KY12 8QN *Signs work*: "Ann Oram".

ORCHARD, Alison, BA (Hons) Illustration; Ordinary Surrey Diploma (Pre BA foundation); Scott, Brownrigg & Turner Art Award. *Medium*: Oil; drawing; acrylic; mixed media. *b*: Wimbledon, 13 Jul 1971. *m*: Simon Hart. two *d*. *Educ*: George Abbott Secondary School and 6th Form, Guildford, Surrey. *Studied*: Harrow College (University of Westminster) (1990-93); Epsom School of Art and Design (UCA) (1989-90); St. Ives School of Art - various courses. *Represented by*: Gallery One, Grayshott. *Exhib*: Gallery One, Grayshott, Surrey - solo exhibition 'Arvor' (2009); Affordable Art Fairs, Battersea and Hampstead Heath; London Art Fair (2012); Corte Real Gallery, Portugal; McAllister Thomas Gallery; Cambridge Art Fair (2010); Art Agency, Esher; Wey Gallery, Godalming. *Works in collections*: Private. *Commissions*: Private commissions - various. *Publications*: Illustration work published in Daily Telegraph. *Clubs*: Founder of 'The Drawing Room' group. Teaches Art and Life Drawing. *Misc*: Illustration published in Virgin Atlantic and V&A playing card competition. Married name 'Hart' but paints under maiden name. *Address*: Colton, Clovelly Road, Beacon Hill, Hindhead GU26 6RW. *Email*: info@alisonorchard.com *Website*: www.alisonorchard.com *Signs work*: "AO".

ORCHARD, Colin, RBA (2007). *Medium*: oil. *b*: Ewell, Surrey, 7 Jul 1935. *s of*: Thomas Seth Orchard. *m*: Celia Mary. two *s*. two *d*. *Educ*: state education (Secondary Modern). *Studied*: self-taught. Full-time painter since 1990; typographer/graphic designer 1952-90. *Represented by*: The New Craftsman Gallery, St. Ives. *Exhib*: Royal Academy Summer Exhibitions (1993-98 inclusive), New Grafton Gallery, David Messum, Brian Sinfield, Walker Galleries, Ainscough, Rowley, City Gallery, Thompson's, Langham Fine Art, Hagen Aria, Penhaven (St. Ives); Medici Gallery RBA Annual Exhbns (2006-2012). *Works in collections*: Falmouth Art Gallery. *Commissions*: 1957-75, produced humorous illustrations for 'The Times', Shell, ICI, WHSmith, RTZ, Sony and many leading publications. *Publications*: Dictionary of Artists in Britain since 1945; St. Ives 1883-1993 - Portrait of an Art Colony, by Marion Whybrow; designer and co-publisher with Janet Axten 'Gasworks to Gallery- Story of St. Ives'; co-author of 'Art About St.Ives' with Cyril Gilbert and Roy Ray. *Recreations*: classical music, opera, films (cinema). *Address*: Manor House, Ayr, St. Ives, Cornwall, TR26 1DU. *Email*: cocostives@btinternet.com *Signs work*: monogram of 'C' inside 'O'.

ORGAN, Robert, DFA (Lond), RWA; painter in oil, water-colour, sometimes tempera; Arts Council Award (2005). *b*: Hutton, Som., 27 Jan 1933. *s of*: Edward Organ, architect. *m*: Valerie Barden. one *s*. three *d*. *Studied*: West of England College of Art, Slade School. *Exhib*: Beaux Arts, Bath (1983-95), Browse & Darby (1981-2007), RWA (1995). *Works in collections*: Brighton and Hove A.G., Exeter Royal Albert Museum, Devon Educ. Com., Cornwall Educ. Com., RWA Collection, Somerset CC, SWA Collection, Universities: Edinburgh, Exeter, Reading, Dorset County Hospital, Dorchester, Hereford County Hospital; Godolphin House, Cornwall. *Publications*: By the Look of Things (biography) Jenny Pery, Redcliffe Press 2003; various articles, art and architectural journals. *Address*: 4 South Parade, Penzance, Cornwall TR18 4DJ. *Signs work*: "Robert Organ" usually on back.

ORMELL, Christopher Peter, FRSA; FIMA; BLitt; MA. *Medium*: watercolour and acrylic. *b*: Coventry, 24 Dec 1929. *s of*: Dr. R.L.Wormell. *m*: (1) Iris Bennett (1958-90); (2) Sheila Rosemary Richards (1995-). one *d*. *Educ*: King Henry VIII School, Coventry (1938-48) (Senior Painting Prize 1946, 47). *Studied*: Magdalen College, Oxford. *Exhib*: RA Summer Exhbn (2003); Blackheath Conservatoire (2002-07); Blackheath Art Society (2005,

2006). *Publications*: 'After Descartes' (Ingleside-Ashby, 2000). *Official Purchasers*: painting in RA Summer Exhbn 2003 sold. *Principal Works*: Madrid from the Viaduct (2002); Landscape Peak District (2003); A Visitor from the Past, Broadstairs (2005). *Recreations*: writing, walking. *Clubs*: Royal Overseas League. *Misc*: painting was my favourite activity at school. It was suggested that I should go to Slade School of Art, however, I chose an academic career. Since 2002 I have returned to painting. *Address*: 3 Ingleside Grove, Blackheath, London SE3 7PH. *Email*: chrisormell@aol.com *Website*: www.philosophyforeducation.co.uk *Signs work*: 'Chris Ormell'.

ORR, Chris, MBE (for Services to the Arts, 2008); MA (1967), RA (1995); artist in painting, etching, lithography; Professor of Printmaking, Royal College of Art; Professor Emeritus (2008). *Medium*: artist, printmaker, writer. *b*: London, 8 Apr 1943. *m*: Catherine Terris. one *s*. one *d*. *Educ*: Beckenham & Penge Grammar School. *Studied*: RCA (1964-67). *Exhib*: RA Summer Exhbn.; one-man shows: London, America, Australia, France, Japan, Canada, Jill George Gallery, London. *Works in collections*: V&A, British Council, Arts Council, Science Museum, Royal Academy of Arts, Government Art Collection, British Museum, Tate Gallery. *Publications*: John Ruskin (1976), Arthur (1977), Many Mansions (1990), The Small Titanic (1994), Happy Days (1999), Semi-Antics (2001), The Disguise Factory (2003), Cities of Holy Dreams (2007), The Multitude Diaries (RA, 2008), Chris Orr: The Making of Things (RA, 2012). *Clubs*: Chelsea Arts Club. *Address*: 5 Anhalt Road, Battersea, London SW11 4NZ. *Email*: chrisorr@aol.com *Website*: www.chrisorr-ra.com *Signs work*: "Chris Orr".

ORR, Jacqueline Elizabeth, RSW (Elected Member); RGI (Elected Member); BA (Hons); Charles Rennie Mackintosh Residency 2013, Collioure; RSW Riverside Award (2009), PAI Joe Hargan Award (2009), RSW Alexander Graham Munro Award (2008), RGI Armour Award (1996), James Torrance Memorial Award (1995), GSA Armour Prize (1983). *Medium*: oil, watercolour, acrylic, mixed media, drawing. *b*: Glasgow, 6 Jan 1961. *Studied*: Glasgow School of Art (1979-1983). *Exhib*: Royal Glasgow Institute of the Fine Arts, Royal Scottish Academy, Royal Scottish Society of Painters in Watercolour, Paisley Art Institute. *Works in Collections*: Mairie de Collioure. *Misc*: Facebook page (www.facebook.com/JacquelineOrrRSW). Images of work can be seen on website and Facebook page. *Address*: 36 Gray Street, Prestwick, Ayrshire KA9 1LX. *Email*: info@jacquelineorr.com *Website*: www.jacquelineorr.com *Signs work*: "JACQUELINE ORR".

ORR, James, Royal College of Surgeons and Physicians award R.G.I. (1997); artist in acrylic. *b*: Glasgow, 29 Jun 1961. *m*: the late Elizabeth Inglis. one *d*. *Studied*: part time, Glasgow School of Art (1970-78). *Exhib*: RSA, RGI, RWA, PAI. *Works in collections*: Royal College of Surgeons and Physicians, London and Glasgow; HRH The Duke of Edinburgh; Ayr Civic Collection. *Address*: 36 Gray St., Prestwick, Ayrshire KA9 1LX. *Email*: jamesorrart1st@gmail.com *Signs work*: "Orr".

ORWIN, Carol, SWA, SSS, CAS; Falle Fine Art Bronze Award. *Medium*: sculptor. *b*: Herts, 8 Dec 1950. *d of*: Cyril William Orwin. one *s*. *Studied*: High Wycombe School of Art; St.Martins School of Art. *Represented by*: Leslie Frontl. *Exhib*: Mall Galleries; SWA; RHS Wisley Borde Hill Savill Garden, Painshill Park, Petworth; Polesden Lacey, Chelsea; Fire Iron Gallery; Beaulieu; Birtley House; Kinghall Lodge; Guildford Cathedral; Hidcote Manor Garden. *Works in collections*: in Israel, America, Canada, Australia, New Zealand, Europe. *Commissions*: University of Surrey, ZSL, London Zoo. *Address*: 26 Barrack Road, Guildford, Surrey, GU2 9RU. *Email*: carole@orwin554.orangehome.co.uk *Website*: www.orwinsculptures.com *Signs work*: 'Carol Orwin'.

OSBORNE, Mark, BA (Hons); MARCA. *Medium*: Oil; watercolour; acrylic. *b*: Ashford, 9 Sep 1949. *m*: Judy White. *Educ*: Abingdon School. *Studied*: Oxford Polytechnic; Chelsea

School of Art; Royal College of Art. *Exhib*: Chichester Open; Broughton House; Cambridge; Highgate Gallery. *Works in collections*: Many private. *Principal Works*: Abstracts and Venetian oilscapes. *Recreations*: Watching Chelsea Football Club. *Misc*: Lives and works in London and Venice. *Address*: 80 Norbury Crescent, London SW16 4LA. *Email*: osbo@btinternet.com *Website*: www.markosborneart.com *Signs work*: "Mark Osborne".

OSBORNE, Roy. Turner Medal of Colour Group GB (2003); MA (Lond.) (1994), BA (Hons) (1970). *Medium*: painter, author, educator, historian. *b*: Bristol, 15 Jul 1948. *Studied*: Inst. of Education (1992-94), Brighton Polytechnic (1966-71). *Exhib*: UK and USA (since 1970). *Works in collections*: Brighton Museums, RCA (London), private collections (UK and abroad). *Publications*: Morato On the Signification of Colours (2013), Books on Colour since 1500 (2013), Don Pavey, Life & Work (2009), Color Influencing Form (2004), From Prism to Paintbox (exhbn. cat. 1989), Lights and Pigments (1980), and contributions to Colour Concepts (Pavey, 2014), Colour Design (Best, 2012), Colour Engrained in the Mind (Pavey 2010), Colour Symbolism (Pavey, 2009), Colour and Humanism (Pavey, 2003), The Color Compendium (Hope, 1989). *Official Purchasers*: University of Newcastle (2002). *Principal Works*: Bends, Heraldic, Compass, and Chromotopia Series. *Recreations*: writing, music. *Misc*: lectured at 200 art schools worldwide (1978-2008). *Address*: 17 Hepplestone Close, London SW15 5DE. *Email*: art.school@virgin.net *Website*: www.coloracademy.co.uk

OSLER, Anthony John. *Medium*: watercolour, gouache, oil. *b*: Ipswich, 5 Jan 1938. *m*: Gillian Osler. two *d*. *Educ*: Northgate Grammar School, Ipswich; Royal Agricultural College, Cirencester. *Studied*: Southampton University. *Represented by*: Francis Iles, Rochester; The Southwold Gallery; Alexander Miles Gallery, London. *Exhib*: Mall Galleries (with EAGMA, 7 times; with RSMA twice); Spencer Coleman Galleries, Stamford and Lincoln; Caxton Gallery, Frinton on Sea, Essex; Sea Pictures, Clare, Suffolk; The Chrome Gallery, Norwich; Snape Matlings, Suffolk; Thoresby Exhibition Centre, Nottinghamshire; work always in stock in these galleries. *Works in collections*: work in private collections worldwide. *Commissions*: many commissions for yachts and traditional craft. *Publications*: Yachts and Yachting Illustrations (1970s); author of book about a sailing barge skipper "Whe're Yer For" (Chaffcutter Books, 2006). *Works Reproduced*: Yachting Magazines (see above); The Artist. *Recreations*: yachting (own boat). *Clubs*: Society of East Anglian Watercolourists. *Misc*: Founder Member (1979), East Anglian Group of Marine Artists; President of Felixstowe Art Society. *Address*: Cambria Cottage, 20 The Street, North Lopham, Diss, Norfolk, IP22 2NB. *Email*: oslers@camcot.fsnet.co.uk *Website*: www.anthonyoslermarineartist.co.uk *Signs work*: "ANTHONY OSLER".

OTTEY, Piers Ronald Edward Campbell, BA (Hons); painter in oil on canvas and panel, lecturer. *b*: London, 27 Sep 1955. *s of*: Ronald Harry Ottey, FSCA. *m*: divorced. two *s*. one *d*. *Educ*: King's College School, Wimbledon. *Studied*: Chelsea School of Art (1974-78, the late Patrick Symons, Myles Murphy). *Exhib*: RA, Bath Contemporary Arts Fair, London, Sussex, Paris; one-man shows: Brighton (1988), Midhurst (1991), Stansted House (1994), Seaford College (1994), The Mill Studio, Sussex (1996, 2003, 2004, 2005), Bates Gallery, London (1996, 1998), Sheridan Russell Gallery, London (2000, 2001), Weil am Rhein, Germany (2006), West Stoke House (2006), Zimmer Stewart Gallery (2008, 2009, 2011, 2012), Medici Gallery, Cork St. London (2011, 2012), The Gallery, Shoreditch (2013). *Works in collections*: Exxon UK, National Health Service Trust, Worthing Museum, Portsmouth Museum & Art Gallery, Pallant House Gallery, Bath University. England, France, Denmark, Canada. *Commissions*: Grant Thornton, Chichester Hospital. *Publications*: Exhibit 'A' Magazine, 4 page feature (2000), Norbert Lynton Essay (2000). *Address*: The Mill Studio, Newhouse Farm Barns, Ford Lane, Arundel, W. Sussex BN18 0EF. *Website*: www.piersottey.co.uk *Signs work*: "Ottey".

OULTON, Therese. BA Hons (Fine Art), MA (RCA); painter in oil. *b*: Shrewsbury, Salop, 20 Apr 1953. *m*: Peter Gidal. *Studied*: St. Martin's and Royal College of Art. *Represented by*: Marlborough Fine Art, London. *Exhib*: twenty five solo exhibs. since 1984 in London, New York, Los Angeles, Vienna, Berlin, Munich, Museum of Modern Art, Oxford etc., as well as group exhibs. Venice Biennale, Turner Prize at The Tate, Mellon Centre, Yale, Stockholm etc. *Works in collections*: Tate, Metropolitan, National Gallery of Australia, Harris Museum, Museum of Fine Art, Boston, British Museum, Leeds City Art Museum, V&A, St. Louis Art Museum, Missouri, Broadgate, Hoffman Collection, Berlin etc. *Publications*: monograph catalogues include Marlborough, London, Andrew Benjamin in 'Journal of Philosophy and the Visual Arts', Stuart Morgan's essay and interview in 'What the Butler Saw', Angela Moorjani's chapter in 'Loss and Lestness' (Palgrave), and Jacqueline Rose 'Women in Dark Times' Bloomsbury (2014). *Works Reproduced*: Paul Crowther: Critical Aesthetics and Post-Modernism (OUP); Martin Kemp: Oxford History of Western Art; Richard Cork: Interviews with Artists (Tate Publ. 2014). *Address*: 28 1/2 Lansdowne Crescent London W11 2NS. *Email*: thereseoulton@btinternet.com *Website*: Tate, Marlborough & "therese oulton" *Signs work*: "Therese Oulton".

OUTRAM, Steven, RBA. *Medium*: pastel, oil. *b*: Kent, 22 Jul 1953. *Studied*: Medway College of Art (1969-73). *Represented by*: Fairfax Gallery; Llewellyn Alexander (Fine Paintings) Ltd; Linda Blackstone Gallery; John Allen Fine Art; Red Rag Gallery. *Exhib*: solo: Seen Galleries, London (1979, 1981, 1983, 1985); King Street Gallery, London (1986); Gloucester City Museum and AG (1992); group shows inc. New York Art Expo, Seen Galleries Seattle, The Private Collector Cork & Dublin; Mall Galleries; NEAC; ROI; PS; RBA; Christie's Contemporary Arts, Bath & Cambridge; Liverpool Royal Liver Building; Glasgow Kelvingrove Museum & AG; The Affordable Art Fair New York; Discerning Eye 2010. *Address*: Mission Hall, Forge Hill, Lydbrook, Glos GL17 9QS. *Email*: steve_outram@hotmail.com *Website*: www.stevenoutram.com *Signs work*: 'Outram'.

OVERTON, Alan, artist in acrylic, pastel and print-maker. *b*: Salisbury, Wilts., 27 Nov 1946. *m*: Petula (decd 2013). one *d*, Melissa. *Educ*: St. Thomas' School, Salisbury. *Exhib*: RA Summer Show, RWA, Royal Bath and West Show, NAPA (The Artist award Wales, 1999), S.W. Academy of Fine and Applied Arts, Exeter, Oexmann Art Awards Competitions, Devizes (3rd prize 1992), Black Swan Arts Open Painting Competitions, Frome, Bath Society of Artists Open Exhibition; Britain's Painters '89, Mall Galleries, London. *Works in collections*: Lord Bath, many private collections. *Clubs*: Frome Art Soc., Bruton Art Society. *Address*: 21 Orchard Close, Frome, Somerset, BA11 4EA. *Email*: alanovertonartist@ymail.com *Website*: www.fromecreativenetwork.org.uk *Signs work*: "A. Overton".

OWEN, Glynis, BA Fine Art, ATC, FRBS (1990); *Medium*: stone, metals, glass, prints. *b*: Kent, 1945. m: Dr. Robert John Owen FRCP. two *s*. one *d*. *Educ*: Portsmouth High School, GPDST. *Studied*: Portsmouth College of Art (1962-66), Goldsmiths' College (1966-67). *Represented by*: Royal Society of British Sculptors, Fine Art Consultancy, Printmakers Council. *Exhib*: RIBA (1991), Glyndebourne Festival Opera (1996), R.A.Summer Exhibition (2003), AAF New York (2003), Chichester Cathedral, Sussex (2009), Verge NYC (2012), AAF NYC (2012), Verge Art Fair New York, AAF Hampstead London (2013), AAF Singapore (2014). *Works in collections*: Portrait of Jacqueline du Pre, St. Hilda's College, Oxford; Tate Modern, Resource. *Commissions*: Teaching Awards trophy (2000), established by Lord Puttnam C.B.E. Relief Sculpture, Stafford (2003), Covent Garden Commemorative Bronze Relief, Piazza, London (2006), Aluminium relief sculpture, Architectural Practice, Camden, London (2011). *Publications*: Carving Techniques by Glynis Beecroft (Batsford 1976), Casting Techniques by Glynis Beecroft (Batsford 1979). *Official Purchasers*: Tate Modern, Teaching Awards Trust, The Worshipful Company of Fruiterers. *Works Reproduced*: Open Air Sculpture in Britain, W.J. Strachan, Zwemmer, Tate Gallery. *Recreations*: walking.

Address: Hampstead, London. *Email*: info@glynisowensculptor.co.uk *Website*: www.glynisowensculptor.co.uk *Signs work*: "Glynis Owen", "Glynis Jones Owen".

OWEN, Muriel Sylvia, NDD, ATD, SWA, FRSA; painter in water-colour, lecturer; Head of Art and Deputy Principal, Dixon and Wolfe, Tutors, London SW1 (1969-82); Vice-Pres., Soc. of Women Artists; runs painting holidays worldwide – under the name "Muriel Owen Painting Holidays". *Medium*: mainly watercolour. *b*: Welwyn Garden City. *d of*: Arthur Tremlett Cuss. *m*: Edward Eardley Owen, M.A. three *s*. by previous marriage. *Educ*: Welwyn Garden City Grammar School. *Studied*: St. Albans School of Art (1946-50 under Gwen White and Christopher Sanders, RP, RA), London University (1951). *Exhib*: RI, SWA, UA, Llewellyn Alexander Gallery, London; ten one-man shows, London, Fairfield Halls, Croydon, Yarmouth Castle, IOW official galleries, Italy, permanent exhibition at Osborne House, Isle of Wight. *Works in collections*: 38 paintings English Heritage, IOW Arts Council, Bank of England, Queen Elizabeth Military Hospital, Woolwich, Atomic Energy Commission, London. *Commissions*: English Heritage. *Publications*: 'Artist in Residence' (new book of Painting). *Official Purchasers*: Bank of England, English Heritage. *Works Reproduced*: St. Paul's, Westminster, floral, (Henry Ling), calendars and 32 cards (IoW County Press), series of 4 art teaching videos, articles in major newspapers. *Principal Works*: Westminster Cathedral, Bank of England, Guildhall, etc. *Address*: Briarwood House, Church Hill, Totland, I.O.W. PO39 0EU. *Email*: muriel@po39eu.freeserve.co.uk *Signs work*: "Muriel Owen".

OXENBURY, Helen Gillian, illustrator/writer in water-colour; Kate Greenaway medal (1969), Smarties award (1989), Boston Globe award, Kurt Maschler award (1985). *b*: 2 Jun 1938. *m*: John M. Burningham. one *s*. two *d*. *Studied*: Ipswich School of Art and Central School of Arts and Crafts, London. *Publications*: illustrated: The Three Little Wolves and the Big Bad Pig (1993), Farmer Duck (1991), We're Going on a Bear Hunt (1989), Alice's Adventures in Wonderland (1999), Franny B. Kranny (2001), Big Momma Makes the World (2002). *Address*: c/o Walker Books, 87 Vauxhall Walk, London SE11 5HJ. *Signs work*: "Helen Oxenbury".

OXLADE, Roy, MA, RCA; painter. *b*: 1929. *s of*: William Oxlade, engineer. *m*: Rose Wylie. one *s*. two *d*. *Studied*: Bromley College of Art and with David Bomberg. *Represented by*: Art Space Gallery, London. *Exhib*: Young Contemporaries (1952-54), Borough Bottega Group (1954, 1955), Winnipeg Biennial (1st prize drawing, 1960), John Moores (1963, 1991), Hayward Annual (1982), Norwich Gallery 'Rocks and Flesh' (1985), Cleveland International (1989), Norwich Gallery, 'EAST' (1991, 1994), Velan, Turin (2000); one person shows: Vancouver A.G. (1963), New Metropole, Folkestone (1983), AIR Gallery (1983), Odette Gilbert Gallery (1985, 1987, 1988), Gardner Centre, University of Sussex (1990), Reed's Wharf Gallery, London (1993), Art Space Gallery, London (2001, 2004); two person show: Wrexham & Aberystwyth Arts Centres (1999). Korn/Ferry R.A. Picture of the Year (1997). *Works in collections*: South East Arts, Railtrack London, Deal Dallas, University College Oxford, J.C.R. *Publications*: David Bomberg (R.C.A. Papers 3 1981), Art & Instinct 2010. *Clubs*: Chelsea Arts Club. *Address*: Forge Cottage, Newnham, Kent, ME9 0LQ.

OXLEY, Brian, MA, ATC, NDD. *Medium*: oil, watercolour. *b*: Croydon, 25 May 1943. *m*: Jennifer Deirdre. two *s*. *Educ*: Southlands School. *Studied*: Folkestone School of Art (Int. 1958-61); Canterbury College of Art (1961-63); Goldsmiths' College (1965-66); Kent Inst of Art & Design (MA, 1994-96). *Exhib*: RA Summer Exhibition (1987); Oriel Gallery, Dublin (1990); New Metropole Art Centre (1961-99); Hampshire Open (2005); Hunter Gallery, Long Melford, Suffolk (2001); Horsebridge, Whitstable (2008); Llewelyn Alexander (2010); SE Open Studios (2004-2014); One-man shows: The Talent Store, Belgravia (1972); Sandgate Gallery (1998); Retrospective, The Cube Gallery, Folkestone (opened by Dr. Fred Cuming RA, 2010); Hastings Arts Forum, E. Sussex (2011). *Works in collections*: private collections in Canada, USA, Australia, Germany, Italy, France, Eire and throughout UK. *Commissions*: Saga Rose (two murals for the cruise liner, 1995); Six portraits for the Imos Foundation (2011). *Publications*: 'Artists in Britain since 1945', David Buckman; 'A Celebration of Romney Marsh' (catalogue created by Brian Oxley, 1995); Demonstrator for the 'Artist Magazine'. *Works Reproduced*: in several mixed exhibition catalogues. *Recreations*: travel in GB and Europe, tennis, cooking, restoration of paintings. *Clubs*: Hon. Mem. FAS/HAS. *Misc*: Head of Art at three schools: Morehall, Pent Valley, Brockhill. Also taught life drawing for over 40 years in Adult Education, and part-time Drawing courses at KIAD. *Address*: Wayfield House, St Mary's Road, West Hythe, Kent CT21 4NU. *Email*: brianoxley2@aol.com *Signs work*: "B E Oxley".

OXLEY, Valerie Mary, Cert.Ed. (1969), ANEA. (1983), SBA (1987), FHEA, SFP; self taught botanical illustrator in pencil, water-colour, pen and ink; Tutor, botanical illustration, AEC. *b*: Manchester, 26 Sep 1947. *m*: Michael Oxley, M.Sc., C.Eng. one *d*. *Educ*: Abbeydale Girls' Grammar School, Sheffield; Hereford College of Educ. *Exhib*: SBA, RHS, Linnean Soc., Portico Gallery, Manchester, Durham A.G., Museum of Garden History, London. *Works in collections*: The Florilegium Society at Sheffield Botanical Gardens Archive. *Publications*: Art Editor 'Wild Flowers of the Peak District' published by the Hallamshire Press, Sheffield; author 'Botanical Illustration', Crowood Press (2008). *Clubs*: Chairman: Florilegium Society at Sheffield Botanical Gardens. *Address*: Brookside, Firbeck, Worksop, Notts. S81 8JZ. *Signs work*: "Valerie Oxley".

P

PACE, Nicholas, BA Hons; NOAC South of England Prize 2011; Elizabeth T Greenshields Award (1982). *Medium*: oil. *b*: Bristol, 31 Mar 1957. *s of*: Dennis Pace. *m*: Kim Pace. *Studied*: Gloucestershire College of Art & Design (1976-79); University of London (1980-81). *Exhib*: RA (2009); Partridge Fine Art Summer Show (2008); Threadneedle Art Prize, Mall Galleries (2008); Society of Wildlife Artists, Mall Galleries (2006); Jerwood Drawing Prize Exhibition (2005); Thinking the Unthinkable, Northern Gallery for Contemporary Art (2005); National Open Art Competition, Pallant House (South of England Prize, 2011); Store Street Gallery, London 'Wunderkabinett; (2012); East Sussex Open; Towner Art Gallery (2013); Wimbledon Space, 'Self-made Worlds' (2013); NOI; RCA (2014). *Works in collections*: Butterfields Club, Hong Kong; various private collections. *Commissions*: private/corporate commissions. *Address*: 22 Cromwell Court, Cromwell Road, Hove, BN3 3EF. *Email*: pacenicholas@hotmail.com *Website*: nicholaspace.info

PACE, Shirley, sculptor and artist in bronze, charcoal, pen and ink, conté, monochrome, representational. *b*: Worthing, Sussex, 16 Feb 1933. *d of*: Arthur Blasdale, musician, writer, artist. *m*: Roy Pace. two *d*. *Educ*: Worthing Convent. *Studied*: Worthing School of Art (1948-51). *Exhib*: Mall Galleries, Alwin Gallery, many provincial and overseas galleries. *Works in collections*: Life and a quarter dray-horse, London; private collections: Britain, U.S.A., Bermuda, New Zealand, Australia, Hong Kong. *Commissions*: bronze works from life of specific horses including one of 'Lloyds Bank' horse. 2nd bronze dray horse, 1¼ life size for Brewery Square, Dorchester (2012). *Works Reproduced*: most, in limited editions. *Clubs*: Chichester Art Soc. *Misc*: specialising in dynamic power of movement. Representational. *Address*: Quinnings Barn, Mill Road, West Ashling, Chichester, W.Sussex PO18 8EA. *Email*: royandshirleypace@googlemail.com *Signs work*: "Shirley Pace".

PACKER, Neil Martin, SIAD; DipAD. *Medium*: watercolour, drawing. *b*: Sutton Coldfield, 7 Aug 1961. *s of*: Judith & John Packer. *Partner*: Emily Bickerton. one *s*. *Studied*: Colchester School of Art (1977-81). *Represented by*: Hugo Wienberg, 32 Place St. George, Paris. *Exhib*: Royal Academy; Portal Gallery, London; Medici Gallery, London; Chris

Beetles; British Museum; British Library. *Works in collections*: several hundred in The Hoffman Collection, Atlanta, Georgia, USA; many in private collections in the UK. *Commissions*: Atlanta Historic Society, numerous private and commercial commissions. *Publications*: various advertising campaigns in UK/USA; wide variety of books including eight for the Folio Society. *Works Reproduced*: several prints reproduced by Cheyne Walk Publications as well as many illustrated books. *Recreations*: walking, drinking, opera. *Clubs*: Brave Club. *Address*: 129 Rossmore Court, Park Road, London NW1 6XZ. *Email*: arvokimchi@yahoo.co.uk *Signs work*: 'Neil Packer'.

PACKER, William John, NDD (Painting), NEAC, Hon FRCA, Hon RBA; painter in oil and water-colour; Art Critic, The Financial Times (since 1974). *b*: Birmingham, 19 Aug 1940. *s of*: Rex Packer. *m*: Clare Winn. three *d*. *Educ*: Windsor Grammar School; Wimbledon School of Art (1959-63), Brighton College of Art (1963-64). *Represented by*: Piers Feetham Gallery. *Exhib*: RA; solo shows at Piers Feetham Gallery (1996, 2001, 2004), two-man show (with William Feaver) (2005); group exhbns.: Angela Flowers, Cadogan Contemporary , Ian Potts (2007), and many other galleries. *Works in collections*: private collections. *Publications*: The Art of Vogue Covers (Octopus, 1980), Fashion Drawing in Vogue (Thames & Hudson, 1983), Henry Moore (with Gemma Levine) (Weidenfeld & Nicolson, 1985); John Houston (Lund Humphries, 2003), Tai-Shan Schierenberg (Flowers East, 2005). *Clubs*: Chelsea Arts, The Academy, Garrick. *Address*: 60 Trinity Gardens, Brixton, London SW9 8DR. *Signs work*: "W.P." or "W. PACKER".

PACKHAM, John Leslie (Les), MBE. *Medium*: watercolour, oil, acrylic. *b*: Keighley, 9 Feb 1945. *m*: Judith. one *s*. one *d*. *Studied*: self-taught. *Exhib*: Mall Galleries, London; House of Commons; University Womens' Club, London; Ferens, Hull; Mercer, Harrogate; Smith Galleries, Winston-Salem NC, USA. *Works in collections*: National Trust; Barnsley M.D. Council; Halifax BS (HBOS), Arla. *Commissions*: National Trust; Archant Life Magazines; 'Emmerdale', Yorkshire TV. *Publications*: Yorkshire Life Magazine, Dalesman Magazine, Judges Calendars, Yorkshire Ridings Magazine. *Recreations*: motorcycling. *Clubs*: Fylingdales Group of Artists. *Address*: Holly House, 104 Lennox Drive, Wakefield, W.Yorks, WF2 8LF. *Email*: les.packham@btinternet.com *Website*: www.lespackham.co.uk *Signs work*: 'P A C K H A M'.

PAES, Rui, MA, RCA (1988), Dip. ESBAP (1976-81); painter in oil and water-based media. *b*: Pemba, Mozambique, 13 Jul 1957. *m*: divorced. one *s*. *Educ*: Escola de Belas Artes do Porto, Portugal (1976-81), Royal College of Art, London (1986-88); Calouste Gulbenkian Scholarship (1986-1988) and the Beal Foundation Grant. *Exhib*: England, Germany, Portugal and Spain. *Works in collections*: Museu de Arte Moderna, Oporto, Portugal, The Beal collection, USA, the Royal College of Art Permanent collection; John Studzinski; Durazzo Pallavicini, Genoa; Madonna. *Commissions*: Mural painting in Egypt, England, France, Germany, Norway, Portugal, Lebanon and Italy. *Publications*: illustrations for "....do tempo inutil" by Gloria de Sant'anna (1975); illustrations for 'Lotsa de Casha' by Madonna (2005). *Clubs*: Chelsea Arts. *Address*: Studio 4, 381 King's Road, London SW10 0LP. *Email*: paes.rui@gmail.com

PAGE, Dione, RWA; RWA Watercolour Award (1983, 1988); Essex Open Exhibition Award (1994, 1995); East of England Art Exhibitions Award (1995, 1996); Graphic Designer, Adult Education Art Tutor. *Medium*: mixed media - wax pastels, gouache and lumograph pencil 8B. *b*: London, 10 Jul 1930. *m*: Nelson Blowers (decd 2010). two *s*. one *d*. *Studied*: Colchester School of Art. *Exhib*: RA; RWA (1984-present); Fermoy Gallery, Kings Lynn; Heffer Gallery, Cambridge; Fishguard/ Cardiff, South Wales; Aldeburgh Festival; Merrick Gallery; Patricia Wells Gallery, Bristol; 5D Gallery, Chepstow; Clifton Gallery, Bristol; John Russell Gallery, Ipswich; Hayletts, Colchester, Maldon; The Minories, Colchester; Chappel Galleries, Essex. *Publications*: The Artist (Nov '04). *Official*

Purchasers: National Library of Wales; Nuffield Foundation; Guiness plc; Waterworks, Bristol; Essex County Council; Chelmsford and Essex Museum; Suffolk Education Committee; Glamorgan Education Committee; Faculty of Design, Bristol; The Minories, Colchester. *Recreations*: gardening, travelling, collecting ceramics. *Address*: Dale Brow, Thorpe Road, Weeley, Clacton, CO16 9JL. *Signs work*: 'D Page R.W.A'.

PAGE, Susan Claire. *Medium*: sculpture. *b*: Northampton, 7 Jan 1952. one *s*. *Studied*: Stamford, Lincs (2006/7); Bolton, Lancs (2007). *Represented by*: Imagine Gallery; Workshop Wales. *Exhib*: Art in Action (2014); Sculpture Lounge, Holmfirth. *Misc*: studio: The Sculpture Lounge, Bottoms Hill, Woodhead Road, Holmfirth HD9 2PX. *Address*: 14 Cortex Close, Spalding, Lincs PE11 2GT. *Email*: sueclairepage@gmail.com *Signs work*: "SCP" each letter encased in joined boxes.

PAGE, Warren Lee, UK finalist, Lexmark European Art Prize (2003). *Medium*: acrylic on aluminium; acrylic on canvas. *b*: Shoeburyness, Essex, 5 Mar 1979. *Studied*: self-taught. *Exhib*: Lexmark European Art Prize, Eyestorm Gallery, London (2003). *Principal Works*: Angelina on Mars; Second Coming Advent Calendar (series); Read My Lips (series). *Address*: 80a Southwold Crescent, Benfleet, Essex. *Email*: warren@pagenw.fsnet.co.uk. *Signs work*: WLP (on reverse).

PAGE-ROBERTS, James, painter in oil and pastel, sculptor, and writer. *b*: Silchester, 5 Feb 1925. *m*: Margaretha Klees. two *s*. *Educ*: Wellington College, and Taft, USA. *Studied*: Central School of Arts. *Exhib*: one-man shows at Galerie de Seine, Reid Gallery, Kintetsu Gallery, Osaka, Qantas Gallery, Cambridge, Mayor Gallery. *Works in collections*: National Art Collection. *Publications*: Writer of over 700 articles on vines and wines, and author/illustrator of 14 books on vines, wines, cooking, docklands, household management and travel. *Clubs*: MCC. *Misc*: paintings sold Christie's 2006 - £33,600. *Address*: 37 St. Peter's Grove, London W6 9AY. *Email*: jpageroberts@gmail.com *Website*: www.webpageroberts.blogspot.com *Signs work*: "P R" and "PAGEROBERTS".

PAINE, Ken, PS, SPF; portrait artist in pastel, oil, water-colour; Master Pastellist of France. *b*: 2 Nov 1926. *Partner*: Penelope Lee (artist). one *s*. two *d*. *Studied*: Worked with R.Q. Dunlop, RA; studied at Twickenham College of Art. *Exhib*: annually at Mall Galleries; at various Society exhibitions including PS, RP, ROI, RI; widely exhib. in and around London, USA, France (with La Societe des Pastillistes de France - awarded coveted title of "Master Pastelist" and Past VP), Canada, Germany; solo exhbns. include Frost & Reed in St. James's, Llewellyn Alexander Gallery, London; Edward Day Gallery, Ontario, Canada, Holburne Museum of Art, Bath; L'Abbaye de Flaran, nr. Toulouse, France. *Works in collections*: La Collection Simonow. *Commissions*: many which include Sir David Atkinson Air Marshal, Trevor McDonald broadcaster, Joss Ackland actor, Lord Anthony Lester QC. *Publications*: (Biography) "Ken Paine - His Life and Work" by Michael Simonow; (Biography) "Ken Paine - Nowhere to Hide" by Penelope Lee (2014). *Works Reproduced*: television programme 'Ken Paine, Painting Faces' for Sky Arts. *Address*: 8 Spring Gdns., E. Molesey, Surrey KT8 0JA. *Email*: pennyart@hotmail.co.uk *Signs work*: "PAINE".

PAINTER, Jen, National Diploma in Design - Painting & Etching (1961). *Medium*: oil, drawing. *b*: London, 3 Oct 1938. *d of*: N & E Beales. one *s*. two *d*. *Educ*: Grammar School, Art College. *Studied*: Hornsey College of Art, London (1958-1961). *Exhib*: Mall Galleries - Society of Women Artists (2007, 2008); Royal Academy Summer Exhibition (2008); National Open Art Competition Exhibition, Chichester (2007), Red Biddy Gallery, Shelford, nr. Guildford, Surrey (2009). *Official Purchasers*: Royal Academy Summer Exhibition 2008. *Principal Works*: portraiture, figure and landscape. *Address*: 1 Castledown Avenue, Hastings, East Sussex, TN34 3RJ. *Email*: jenpainter@hastings01.orangehome.co.uk *Signs work*: "Jen Painter".

PALLISER, Anthony, *Medium*: oil, watercolour, drawing. *b*: Brussels, 5 May 1949. *m*: Diane. *Educ*: Downside School, New College Oxford. *Studied*: self-taught. *Exhib*: see website. *Publications*: 'Palliser' by Adrian Dannatt (Ed. du Regard, France). *Official Purchasers*: Graham Greene, National Portrait Gallery; Pamela Harriman, American Embassy, Paris; Lord Ashdown, Parliamentary Art Collection; Sir Michael Howard, King's College, London. *Address*: 108 Rue Du Bac, 75007 Paris, France. *Email*: anthony@anthonypalliser.com *Website*: www.anthonypalliser.com *Signs work*: "Palliser".

PALMER, Jean C., BA (Hons) Fine Art; painter in oil; part-time Tutor - Adult College, Lancaster. *b*: Southport, 1961. *m*: Peter Layzell. one *s*. one *d*. *Studied*: Southport College of Art (1977-79), University of Central Lancs. (1979-82). *Exhib*: RA Summer Shows (1992-99), Society of Women Artists, Mall Galleries, London (2007); various North West and London exhbns. *Works in collections*: Manchester City A.G., NatWest Coll., Warrington Arts Council, Jerwood Foundation. *Address*: 72 Vale Rd., Lancaster LA1 2JL. *Signs work*: "J.Palmer" on reverse.

PALMER, John Frederick, RWA.(1991); Cornelissen prize RWA annual exhbn. (1985); graphic designer; artist in oil, water-colour, gouache; PP, Bristol Savages. *b*: Bristol, 11 Aug 1939. *s of*: Robert Palmer. *Educ*: Carlton Park, Bristol. *Studied*: West of England College of Art (1955-56, J. Arnold). *Exhib*: Bristol Artists, Arnolfini, RWA, Mall Gallery, First Sight. *Works in collections*: Bristol Savages, Leeds Bldg. Soc., NatWest Assurance, British Aerospace, Atomic Energy Authority, Wessex Collection, Block Busters, International Duty Free, private collectors. *Publications*: Drawing & Sketching (1993), Watercolour Landscape (1994. *Clubs*: Bristol Savages. *Address*: 18 Haverstock Rd., Knowle, Bristol BS4 2BZ. *Signs work*: "J.F. Palmer".

PALMER, Juliette, RBA (2001), NDD (1950), ATD (1951); painter in watercolour, illustrator, author; Finalist in Hunting, Singer & Friedlander/Sunday Times National Art Competitions, prizewinner Laing Painting Competition (1996); travel prize RWS (1996); St.Cuthberts Mill Prize, Royal West of England Academy (2000); Discerning Eye; Lynn Painter-Stainers. *b*: Romford, 18 May 1930. *d of*: Sidney Bernard Woolley. *m*: Dennis Palmer BSc (Eng), DIC MICE. one *d*. *Educ*: Brentwood County High School. *Studied*: S.E. Essex School of Art (1946-50). *Exhib*: RA, RBA, RI, NEAC, RWS, RWA; many commercial group gallery shows; one-man shows, S. Australia, Tokyo, Cambridge, Chipping Norton, Cookham. *Works in collections*: Barking Library, Leicestershire Educ. Com. *Commissions*: numerous house portraits. *Publications*: 60 children's books illustrated; author/illustrator, 6 children's picture/information books (Macmillan). *Works Reproduced*: magazines: Artists & Illustrators, International Artist; books: 'A Complete Watercolour Course' by Michael Whittlesea; 'Encyclopedia of Watercolour Techniques' by Hazel Harrison; 'Watercolour Techniques of 23 International Artists' by International Artist magazine. *Clubs*: Hon. Bucks Art Society. *Address*: Melmott Lodge, The Pound, Cookham, Maidenhead, Berks. SL6 9QD. *Website*: www.royalsocietyofbritishartists.org.uk *Signs work*: "Juliette Palmer".

PALMER, Margaret, PS, ATD, NS; Member of Pastel Society since 1960; portrait painter in oil and pastel, animal and genre painter, book illustrator. *b*: London, 10 Sep 1922. *d of*: R.E.A. Palmer. *m*: R.G.W. Garrett. two *d*. *Studied*: Hornsey School of Art (1938-39), Salisbury School of Art (1939-41), Bournemouth College of Art (1941-42). *Exhib*: RP, ROI, etc.; one-man shows in London, Guildford, Farnham, Leatherhead, works in worldwide collections. *Works in collections*: Guildford Borough Council. *Commissions*: Lord Howell, Lord Nugent, Sir David Rowe-Ham, Sir Richard Nichols, Sir Greville Spratt, Mother Teresa, Sandy Gall, Susan Hampshire, etc. *Publications*: written and illustrated, Honeypot and Buzz; also illustrated books published by Harrap, Heinemann, etc. *Address*: Robins Oak, Wonersh Common Rd, Wonersh, Guildford, Surrey GU5 0PR. *Website*: Pastel Society. *Signs work*: "Margaret Palmer".

PALTENGHI, Julian Celeste, BFA; Winner 1993 Hunting/Observer art prizes: Travel award - Australia; painter in oil, sculptor in plaster and bronze. *b*: London, 28 Aug 1955. *s of*: David Celeste, ballet dancer/film director. *m*: Angela. one *d*. *Educ*: Stowe, Bucks. *Studied*: Cambridge (1976-77), Loughborough College of Art (1978-81). *Exhib*: 'Critic's Choice' Clare Henry: Cooling Gallery, Beaux Arts Galleries, London and Bath, Swiss Artists in Britain: October Galleries, Stephen Bartley, Chelsea, Camden Annual, G.L.C. Spirit of London Festival Hall, Centre Georges Pompidou, Paris, Royal West of England Academy, (purchased by) Christie's Cooperate Collection, Cassian de Vere Cole 'Paintings from Zanzibar'. *Clubs*: Chelsea Arts, Colony Rooms. *Address*: 38 Rue Charles Demery, 13150 Tarascon, France. *Signs work*: "PALTENGHI".

PANCHAL, Shanti, Artist Prize, Bankside Gallery (2010); 1st prize winner Singer and Friedlander/Sunday Times Watercolour Competition (2001); MA Bombay (1977), Byam Shaw, London (1980); painter; resident artist, Harris Museum, Preston, British Museum (1994), W&N art factory (2000). *b*: Mesar, India. three *s*. *Studied*: Byam Shaw, London. *Exhib*: over 25 solo exhibitions worldwide. *Works in collections*: Arts Council, British Museum, Birmingham Museum, Walker Art Gallery, Liverpool. *Commissions*: Imperial War Museum (1989), De Beers (1996), B. Arunkumar, Mumbai (2006). *Publications*: exhib. catalogues, 'Earthen Shades', Cartwright Hall, Bradford; Castlefield Gallery, Manchester (1998); 'Windows of the Soul', Angel Row Gallery, Nottingham (1997); 'Private Myths', Pitshanger Manor Museum and Gallery, London (2000), 'A Personal Journey' British Council, Jehangir Art Gallery and Cymroza Art Gallery, Mumbai (2003), 'Rigard and Ritual', Ben Uri Gallery, London Jewish Museum (2007). *Address*: 11a Graham Road Harrow, Middx. HA3 5RP. *Email*: shantipanchal@yahoo.co.uk *Website*: www.shantipanchal.com *Signs work*: "Shanti Panchal" or in Gujarati.

PANKHURST, Alvin Ernest, Diploma Graphic Design (Hons); Benson & Hedges Art Award Winner (1974). *Medium*: oil, silk screen art, prints. *b*: New Zealand, 16 Nov 1949. *m*: Ephra. two *s*. *Studied*: Wellington School of Design. *Represented by*: Real Gallery, Auckland, NZ (Director). *Exhib*: RA Summer Exhbn; Apunto Gallery, Amsterdam; Real Gallery, Auckland, NZ; public galleries throughout NZ. *Works in collections*: London University; Te Papa National Art Gallery; Christchurch, Dunedin and Southland Public Art Galleries. *Commissions*: Equestrian Hotel, Christchurch; Fox Glacier Hotel, Westland National Park (50 paintings). *Publications*: 100 New Zealand Paintings; Art New Zealand Today. *Official Purchasers*: Parliament Buildings, Wellington: Te Papa, Dunedin, Southland Public Art Gallery. *Works Reproduced*: Treasures of the Dunedin Public Art Gallery. *Principal Works*: NZ Art - A Modern Perspective. *Address*: 78 Gurney Court Road, St.Albans, Herts AL1 4RJ. *Email*: alvin@pankhurst.co.nz *Website*: www.alvinpankhurst.com *Signs work*: 'Alvin Pankhurst'.

PANNETT, Denis Richard Dalton, Hon. Freeman Painter Stainers Company; Fellow of the Guild of Aviation Artists; Winner, Hawker Siddeley Trophy (five times, for aviation art); Awarded The Order of Merit for Fine Art in Brazil; President, Wapping Group of Artists; Past President, Arun Art Society; Chairman, The Chiltern Painters. *Medium*: watercolour and oils. *b*: Hove, Sussex, 7 Sep 1939. *s of*: Major M R D Pannett & Juliet Pannett MBE (portrait painter). *m*: Valerie. one *s*. two *d*. *Educ*: Uppingham School, Rutland. *Studied*: taught by my mother, Juliet Pannett MBE. *Exhib*: RI, RSMA, City of London Art Exhbn.; Guild of Aviation Artists; Painter Stainers Company; Wapping Group; Singer & Friedlander/Sunday Times Watercolour Competition; plus many private exhibitions including Hong Kong & USA. *Commissions*: The official Christmas cards for Sandringham, St.George's Chapel Windsor, St.Paul's Cathedral, Canterbury Cathedral, Salisbury Cathedral and the House of Commons. *Works Reproduced*: illustrations and covers for many books, calendars and cards; over 300 prints of golf courses. *Principal Works*: mainly landscape, marine, aviation and golf. *Recreations*: tennis, collecting militaria. *Address*:

1 Woodlands Drive, Beaconsfield, Bucks HP9 1JY. *Email*: info@denispannett.co.uk *Website*: www.denispannett.co.uk *Signs work*: 'Denis Pannett'.

PAPADOPOLOUS, George, MA, Glass & Ceramics; Bombay Sapphire Prize (Short-listed). *b*: Cyprus, 28 Oct 1969. *s of*: R E Nos. *Studied*: RCA (1997-99). *Exhib*: The Hub, Sleaford (2006); 50 Bank Street, Canary Wharf (solo, 2006); Gallery in Cork Street (solo, 2004); 'Rosenthal: New Routes, New Destinations', Frankfurt, Milan; many others in UK and abroad. *Works in collections*: British Airways Art Collection. *Commissions*: Cunard - MV Queen Victoria (2004); Vima Dance Studio, San Francisco (2005); Pied à Terre Restaurant (2006). *Publications*: 'Lamination', George Papadopolous (A&C Black, 2004). *Principal Works*: Architectural Glass Art. *Address*: 31 Tower Gardens Road, London N17 7PS. *Email*: george@yorgosglass.com *Website*: www.yorgosglass.com

PARDUE, Prudence, NDD (Painting); ATD; College Painting and Drawing Prizes. *Medium*: oil, drawing. *b*: Witney, Oxon, 1940. *m*: widow. one *s*. *Educ*: Witney Grammar School. *Studied*: Oxford School of Art, Cardiff College of Art, RA Schools London; pupil of Evelyn Dunbar, war artist. *Exhib*: RA Summer Exhbn; NEAC Mall Galleries; The Gallery, Cork Street; Merriscourt Gallery, Oxon; Central Gallery, Oxford; Oxford University Said Business School Gallery; The Northwall, Oxford. *Misc*: worked as a textile designer for Manchester Studios and textile firm 'Cohn Hall Marx' New York; freelance illustrator for Pergammon Press; Head of Art, Mandeville School, Bucks; painting tutor (part-time) College of Education, Oxford; Prue Pardue Painting and Pictorial Composition Classes for ex-Art Graduates, Oxford; tutor, Meridian TV programme 'Summer Painting'. *Address*: 14 Chaucer Road, Heine Hill, London SE24 0NU. *Email*: prupardue@tiscali.co.uk *Website*: www.pruepardue.com

PARFITT, David Granville, ARCA, NEAC; David Murray Landscape Award 1963, Anstruther Award 1964, RCA Life Painting Prize 1964, J. Milner Kite Award 1966, Hugh Dunn Memorial Award 1966, Abbey Minor Scholarship 1966. *Medium*: oil painting, watercolours, drawing. *b*: Pontypool, Gwent 13 Jan 1943. *s of*: Sidney Parfitt. *m*: Sara Paton MA, FSA. one *d*. *Educ*: Abersychan Grammar School 1954-55, Monmouth School 1955-59. *Studied*: Newport College of Art 1959-63, Royal College of Art 1963-66 1st Class Hons Painting; Art History. *Represented by*: Messum's, 8 Cork Street, London W15 3LJ. *Exhib*: RA Summer Exhbns (1991-2003), NEAC (1997-2013), Royal Society of Portrait Painters (1998-2013), Discerning Eye (1996, 1999); Messum's (2010, 2012). *Works in collections*: private collections worldwide. *Commissions*: many commissions, mostly portraits. *Works Reproduced*: catalogues: Discerning Eye (1996), New English at Sotheby's (2002), The View (2003). The Artists Magazine (2003, Feb.), Artists' Kew (2006), The Magic and Poetry of Everyday Life, Messum's (2010). *Recreations*: gardening, jazz piano. *Clubs*: Chelsea Arts Club. *Misc*: Senior Tutor, Royal Academy Schools (1987-90). *Address*: 20 Strand on the Green London W4 3PH. *Website*: www.newenglishartclub.co.uk www.messums.com

PARFITT, James Roderick, BA (2nd class Hons), RAS Post Grad Cert; GCE Bretton Hall, Leeds University; RHS General Cert. in Hort.; landscape and portrait painter. *Medium*: painting. *b*: 5 Aug 1951. *Educ*: King's School, Ely. *Studied*: The Heatherley School of Art, Walthamstow Polytechnic, St.Martin's School of Art, Royal Academy Schools. *Represented by*: Gallery 44, Lauderdale House. *Exhib*: Edith Grove Galleries, Trinity Arts and Crafts Guild. *Clubs*: RASAA, London Sketch Club, CAS, Trinity Arts and Crafts Guild. *Misc*: also studied etching. *Address*: 45c Roland Gardens, London SW7 3PQ.

PARKER, Cornelia, OBE, RA; Honorary Doctorates: University of Gloucestershire (2008); University of Birmingham (2005); University of Wolverhampton (2000). Nominated for Turner Prize, (1997). *Medium*: sculpture, installation, drawing, photography, video. *b*: Cheshire, 14 Jul 1956. *m*: Jeff McMillan. one *d*. *Studied*: Reading University (MFA, 1980-82). *Represented by*: Frith Street Gallery, London; Gallery Guy Bärtschi,

Geneva; Galeria Carles Taché, Barcelona. *Exhib*: Selected solo: Baltic Centre for Contemporary Art, Gateshead (2010); Frith Street Gallery, London (2008); Ikon Birmingham/Museo De Arte de Lima Peru (touring, 2007-2008); Selected group: 16th Biennale of Sydney (2008); 8th Sharjah Biennial, Sharjah UEA (2007). *Works in collections*: include: Arts Council of Great Britian; British Museum; Deutsche Bank; Fundacio La Caixa, Barcelona; ICA Boston; MOMA, New York; Tate Gallery; V&A; Various private collections in Europe and the USA. *Commissions*: (Selected): Folkstone Triennial (2011); Jupiter Artland, Edinburgh (2010); Commissioned sculpture for new British Galleries V&A, London (2001). *Address*: 3 South Villas, Camden, London NW1 9BS. *Email*: corneliaparker@mac.com. *Website*: www.frithstreetgallery.com/artists/bio/cornelia_parker. *Signs work*: "Cornelia Parker".

PARKER, Gill, SEA (1987); winner President's Medal SEA (1992); sculptress in bronze. *Medium*: bronze. *b*: Amesbury. *Educ*: South Wilts. Grammar School. *Studied*: self-taught. *Exhib*: solo shows: Sladmore Gallery, London (1984, 1987, 1989), SEA (1984-96), National Horse Racing Museum, Newmarket (1991), Chute Standen (1992), Robert Bowman Ltd, London (Dec. 1999, June 2000), Kevin Anderson Gallery, Los Angeles (Nov. 2000), Robert Bowman Ltd., London (Nov. 2002); Compton Cassey Gallery (2009); Osbourne Gallery, London (2011); Whittington Fine Art, Henley-on-Thames (2011). *Works in collections*: National Horse Racing Museum, Newmarket, World Wildlife Art Museum, Jackson Hole, Wyoming. *Commissions*: Habibti, Mrs. Moss, Precocious, Rainbow Quest, Sir Wattie, Dancing Brave, Middleroad, Motivator (Lifesize) Ascot Racecourse. *Recreations*: breeding and showing American quarter horses. *Address*: Mill Lodge, Mill Lane, Lowbands, Redmarley, Glos. GL19 3SH. *Email*: bronze@gillparker.com *Website*: www.gillparker.com *Signs work*: "G. Parker" or "Gill Parker".

PARKIN, Ione. Royal West of England Academician; BA (Hons). *Medium*: painting and printmaking. *b*: Henley-on-Thames, 19 Oct 1965. *m*: David Madison Metcalfe. two *s*. *Studied*: Winchester School of Art (1985-88). *Represented by*: Cube Gallery, Bristol; Byard Art, Cambridge; Adam Gallery, Bath; Original Print Gallery, Dublin. *Exhib*: Art First, Cork St (1995/96/98); Adam Gallery (2006); Northcote Gallery, Chelsea (2005); Rosenberg & Kaufman, New York (1998); Gomez Gallery, USA (1998); Stour Gallery, Warkwickshire (2004/05/07); Crane Kalman (1996/97); RWA (2001/03/04/06); Anthony Hepworth Fine Art (1993/95); exhibited extensively since 1991. *Works in collections*: Taylor Vinters Solicitors (Cambridge); Reuters HQ (London); Duchas Heritage Service; Premier Steel; Caceis Financial Services; Kindle Banking Systems; Knightsley Ltd.; Alliance Corporate Ireland plc (Dublin); Vera Forsyth Chartered Architects; G&D Services, Bath; RWA (Bristol); West Wiltshire Primary Care Trust; Mullis & Peake, Essex. *Publications*: 'Collecting Original Prints' Rosemary Simmons (A&C Black, London, 2005); 'Fred Cuming RA & Ione Parkin RWA' (Adam Gallery, 2006); '50 Wessex Artists' (Evolver, 2006); Exhibition catalogue, Six Chapel Row, Bath (2004). *Clubs*: Bath Area Network for Artists (BANA). *Address*: 15 Kensington Gardens, Bath, BA1 6LH. *Email*: ione@ioneparkin.fsnet.co.uk *Website*: www.ioneparkin.co.uk *Signs work*: 'Ione Parkin RWA'.

PARKIN, Jane Maureen, SEA., SWA; numerous awards with SEA. *Medium*: oil and pastel. *b*: Sheffield, 29 Aug 1936. *m*: Frank. one *d*. *Educ*: Wath Grammar School, S. Yorks. *Studied*: mainly self taught with five years tuition by P K C Jackson, ARCA. *Exhib*: Mall Galleries: SEA.,SWA; Westminster Gallery, Christie's, Carisbrooke Gallery, every year since 1997 with the Society of Women Artists at Westminster Gallery, American Academy of Equine Art, Kentucky. *Publications*: Limited edn. prints and Open prints by Rosensteils London/New York. *Address*: 104 Howden Road, Silsden, W. Yorks. BD20 0JB. *Email*: frank.parkin@totalise.co.uk *Signs work*: "Jane M. Parkin".

PARKIN, Michael Robert, art dealer; chairman/managing director, Michael Parkin Fine Art. *b*: London, 1 Dec 1931. *s of*: Frank Robert Parkin. *m*: Diana Mary Frances. three *d*.

Educ: Mill Hill and St. George's Schools; Magdalen College, Oxford. *Exhib*: at Michael Parkin Gallery, 11 Motcomb St., SW1. Cover British Art 1850-1950, have included The Cafe Royalists, Four for Whistler, The Fitzrovians, Claude Flight, A Salute to Marcel Boulestin and J. E. Lâboureur, Jean Cocteau, Cecil Beaton Memorial Exhbn., Artists of the Yellow Book, Nina Hamnett, Walter Sickert, Walter Greaves, Rex Whistler and Stephen Tennant, Walter Bayes, Jaques Emile Blanche, Artists of Corsham, Sylvia Gosse, Therese Lessore, the 7 & 5 Society, Paul Stevenson and John Pawle, Hermione Hammond, Gwyneth Johnstone, Roland Collins, Philip Jones, Damian O'Brien. *Publications*: Old Chelsea (Newson, London 1975), Louis Wain's Cats (Thames & Hudson, London 1983), Louis Wain's Edwardian Cats (Thames & Hudson, New York 1983); in preparation: Modern British Art 1860-1960; Walter Greaves. *Clubs*: Beefsteak, B.A.F.T.A., Chelsea Arts, Garrick. *Address*: Gunton Hall, Hanworth, Norfolk NR11 7HL. *Email*: michael@parkinfineart.co.uk *Website*: parkinfineart.co.uk

PARKINSON, Richard Henry, Dip. A/D (1967); painter in oil on canvas/board, restorer, critic, designer, frame maker; Prop./MD The Studio, judge at Royal College for Parkinson/Henderson Prize since 1988, and Cheltenham Correspondence College. *b*: Epsom, 23 Mar 1947. *s of*: Freddy Parkinson (decd) art director and publisher, Principal, Heatherleys Art School. *m*: Susan Sanders. one *s*. one *d*. *Educ*: Ewell Castle, Epsom. *Studied*: Folkestone School of Art (1963-67), Heatherleys School of Art (1968-71). *Exhib*: RA 1967 Resigned: nothing to do with RA since 2000; Wye, Henley, Wimbledon, RWA, Mall Galleries, R.B.A., Stockbridge, etc. *Works in collections*: Woolworth Holdings, various Boardrooms. *Commissions*: portraits various, restorer to Canterbury Cathedral, clocks, items of fine art etc. *Publications*: Introductory Art (Pitman), Mounting Water-colours (The Artist). *Recreations*: Tutor for Cheltenham College since 1970. *Clubs*: Life mem. Chelsea Arts Club. *Misc*: Past Sheriff (2004-2005) Canterbury, Kent, UK. *Address*: Restorer's Cottage, 13 St. Peter's Lane, Canterbury, Kent CT1 2BP. *Email*: arty4best@hotmail.co.uk *Website*: www.richardparkinson.co.uk *Signs work*: "R.H.P." or "Richard Parkinson".

PARR, Elizabeth, painter in water-colour and oil; paints the Lake District, Cornwall and teddy bears. *b*: Horsham, W. Sussex. *m*: Douglas Ashley (1999), (previously widowed in 1996). one *s*. two *d*. *Educ*: St Christophers, Horsham. *Studied*: Horsham School of Art and ICS under Patrick Barclay. *Exhib*: eighteen solo exhibs. in Cornwall and The Cotswolds; group exhibs. at Mall Galleries and Westminster Galleries, London; work accepted by "Britain's Painters" for four consecutive years. *Works in collections*: various national and international collections incl. St Ives Gallery. *Publications*: greeting cards and prints. *Address*: The Beach House, Coverack, Nr. Helston, Cornwall TR12 6TE. *Signs work*: "Elizabeth Parr".

PARRISH, Kevin Alun, First Prize, Kenilworth Arts Festival (2011). *Medium*: Colour and monochrome oils. *b*: Birmingham, 9 Oct 1953. *s of*: Mr & Mrs V. Parrish. one *d*. *Educ*: GCE O level Art and HNC Structures (1976). *Studied*: Birmingham Polytechnic; Sutton Coldfield Collete; Warwickshire College. *Represented by*: Mitchell Gallery, Warwick, UK. *Exhib*: Mitchell Gallery, Warwick, Warwick Studios, Leamington Spa, Jane Powell Art Studio, Kenilworth, Royal Birmingham Society of Artists. *Works in collections*: UK and overseas; Birmingham Council House, Warwick School, Tornado Locomotive, Country Collection (Grays of Shenstone Ltd). *Commissions*: Warwick Castle, Warwick School, Warwick Court House. *Publications*: Emotions of Railway art book; Buckingham Fine Arts; Newcomers Gallery Ltd.; Flying Scotsman Collectors Print; Legends Who's Who Jigsaw Puzzle (Doctor Who). *Official Purchasers*: Mitchell Gallery, Bradford Exchange, London. *Works Reproduced*: CD cover painting for musician Paul Bliss. *Principal Works*: Warwick School, Kings High School, Warwick. *Recreations*: Tennis and rambling. *Clubs*: Guild of Railway Artists. *Misc*: Portrait montages of famous luminaries painted in oils. *Address*: 54 Coniston Road, Leamington Spa, CV32 6PG. *Email*: parrish@quicknetuk.com *Website*: www.kevinparrish.co.uk *Signs work*: "Parrish".

PARROTT, Denis William, NDD (Painting) (1953), ATC (1958), PhD (1993), Fulbright Scholar, USA (1970-71), FRSA (1977), FSAE (1980); painter, printmaker; lecturer, University of Northampton. *b*: Dewsbury, Yorks., 22 Mar 1931. *s of*: Ernest and Edith Parrott. *m*: Kathleen Hendry. one *s*. *Educ*: Dewsbury Technical College. *Studied*: Dewsbury and Batley School of Art (1948-51), Camberwell School of Art (1951-53), Leeds College of Art (1957-58). *Exhib*: RA, Mall Gallery, USA, Centre International d'Art Contemporain de Paris and Galerie Salammbo, Paris. *Works in collections*: England, Europe and USA. *Publications*: author for Schools Council. *Address*: 37 Bowling Green Rd., Kettering, Northants. NN15 7QN. *Signs work*: "Denis W. Parrott".

PARRY, Alan, NDD, *Medium*: Acrylic. *b*: Stock, Essex, 29 Oct 1940. *m*: Linda. three *s*. *Studied*: Willesden School of Art (1953-55); Hornsey School of Art (1955-60). *Represented by*: Catto Gallery, London. *Exhib*: Montpellier Gallery, Stratford-upon-Avon (three one man shows); Catto Gallery, London (two one man shows plus a shared show); Marine House at Beer; Iona Gallery, Woodstock; John Noott Gallery, Broadway. *Works in collections*: Hurlingham Club. *Commissions*: Numerous. *Works Reproduced*: Aquarelle Publishing. *Address*: Hillside, Mill Lane, Cleeve Prior, Evesham WR11 8JZ. *Email*: parryartstudio@btinternet.com *Website*: www.alanparryart.com *Signs work*: "ALAN PARRY".

PARRY, David, SWLA, NDD, CSD. *Medium*: watercolour, oil, pencil. *b*: Liverpool, 23 Jun 1942. *m*: Patricia Parry. *Educ*: in Tunbridge Wells. *Studied*: Tunbridge Wells School of Art, Central School of Art, London. *Exhib*: Mall Galleries, Walton Street Gallery; one-man shows, Brasted, Kent, Lanhydrock House, Cornwall PL22 0JN. *Commissions*: many bird paintings for The Sultan of Oman and other private collectors. *Publications*: Bird and animal books for Salmon Publications. *Works Reproduced*: limited edition prints. *Principal Works*: paintings and drawings of African Wildlife. *Recreations*: birding, sailing. *Clubs*: RFYC (Official Artist). *Address*: Holly Hall, Milton Lilbourne, Pewsey, Wilts, SN9 5LQ. *Website*: www.davidparryart.com *Signs work*: "David Parry".

PARTINGTON, Peter Norman, NDD, ATC, SWLA; painter in water-colour, oil, drypoint etching, art lecturer; Com. mem. SWLA. *b*: Cambridge, 29 Sep 1941. *m*: Josephine. two *s*. one *d*. *Educ*: Poole Grammar School. *Studied*: Bournemouth College of Art and Design (1960-66), Middlesex Polytechnic (1967-68). *Exhib*: various galleries in London including Tryon Gallery, Glos., Wilts. *Works in collections*: Nature in Art Museum. *Publications*: illustrations, 'Down the River' H.E. Bates (Gollancz 1987), 'Painting Birds in Watercolour' (Collins 1989), 'A Floating World' own poetry and illustration, 'Learn to Draw' 'Birds', 'Wildlife', 'Farm Animals' (Harper Collins, 1998). *Address*: The Hall, Kettlebaston, Suffolk IP7 7QA. *Signs work*: "Peter Partington".

PASCOE, Jane, BA (Hons) Fine Art (1977), ATC (1978), RWA (1988); painter/ sculptor/ printmaker, teacher (Head of Art Dept.). *b*: Bristol, 9 May 1955. *d of*: Ernest Pascoe, DFA (Lond), FRBS, RWA. one *s*. *Educ*: The Redmaids School, Bristol (Bristol Foundation Scholarship 1966-73). *Studied*: Bristol Polytechnic Faculty of Art and Design, Dept. of Fine Art (1974-77), Brighton Polytechnic School of Art Education (1977-78). *Exhib*: RWA, Eye Gallery, Bristol, Parkin Fine Art, Mall Galleries, London, Salisbury Arts Centre, Swindon Museum and A.G., Victoria Gallery, Beaux Arts Gallery Bath. *Works in collections*: RWA, Avon County Art Collection, Cheltenham and Gloucester Bldg. Soc. Art Collection. *Address*: Honeysuckle Cottage, Charmus Rd, Old Calmore, Southampton SO40 2RG. *Signs work*: "Jane Pascoe".

PASKETT, David, PRWS (2009), VPRWS (2007), RWS (2001), BA (1966), ATD (1967), Queens Award (1965); resident artist, Pitt Rivers Museum, Oxford (1993). *Medium*: watercolour, oil, tempera. *b*: Potters Bar, 3 Jun 1944. *m*: Sally. two *d*. *Educ*: Mountgrace Comprehensive School, Potters Bar. *Studied*: Hornsey and Exeter Colleges of Art, teacher training at Liverpool College of Art. *Exhib*: Singer Friedlander Sunday Times Watercolour Competition (1992-2001), prizewinner (1992); Highly Commended, Hunting Observer Competition, RWA; Pitt Rivers Museum; Oxford University (1993); Pastel Society (1994); RWS Open prizewinner (1994, 1999); Catto Gallery (1997), Bankside Gallery (2001-2007), Kew Gardens (2006), Watercolour & Drawings Fair, Burlington House (2004-07), New Grafton Gallery (2007), Picture This Gallery, Hong Kong (2006, 07); Royal Academy (2007, 2009); The Bond Shanghai (2008); Hilton Beijing (2008); Gallery du Monde (HK, 2003); The China Club (1999); Salmagundi Club, Fifth Avenue, New York (1997); Blackfriars Bridge, London (2009-2010). *Works in collections*: Philip Morris, Kerry International, Honeywell, Shell, World Bank, Chase Manhattan, Jardines, Freshfields, Lord and Lady Wilson, Standard Chartered Bank, Hutchison Wampoa, Royal Collection, British Museum. *Commissions*: H.R.H. The Queen Mother's 100th Birthday Celebration, Hong Kong Jockey Club, Hong Kong Tourist Assoc., Time Life, Chinese University of Hong Kong. *Publications*: book: 'A Vision of China, The Paintings of David Paskett', boxed silk bound book, pub. Hutchison Whampoa. *Official Purchasers*: Hutchison Whampoa UK, Standard Chartered Bank, Shanghai. *Works Reproduced*: Networtk Rail. *Misc*: 1986 to present day, paintings inspired by annual visits to China. *Address*: 50 Bickerton Rd., Headington, Oxford OX3 7LS. *Email*: info@davidpaskett.co.uk *Website*: www.davidpaskett.co.uk *Signs work*: "PASKETT".

PASS, Donald James, NDD, RAS; portrait and landscape painter in oil, pastel and water-colour; noted for works of a visionary nature; Silver Medal RA (1953), 1st Prize, Art of Imagination Society (1999). *Medium*: watercolour, mixed media, contè, crayon. *b*: Congleton, Ches., 9 Sep 1930. *s of*: Arthur James Pass, master builder & Alice Pass. *m*: Anne Jacqueline Whitelegge. two *s*. three *d*. *Educ*: Macclesfield Kings School. *Studied*: Macclesfield School of Art, Stoke-on-Trent Regional College of Art, RA Schools (silver medal). *Represented by*: Henry Boxer Gallery, Richmond. *Exhib*: Drian Gallery - New Art Centre, Premio Lissone, Milan, Royal Soc. Portrait Painters, Royal Inst. Painters in Water-colours, Royal Water-colour Soc., Soc. of Art of the Imagination (1999) First Prize at Mall Galleries, also in 2000 adjudicator, 2001 Outsider Art Exhibition, New York, The Attic Gallery, Nashville, Tennessee, Art of Imagination Cork Street London 2002-3, New York 2002-10, Orleans House 2008, Private Worlds Exhibition London 2001, Eloquent Obsessions 2008. *Works in collections*: Gdansk National Museum, Poland, Stoke-on-Trent A.G., Yorkshire Educ. Com., Gallery of Contemporary Art Skopje, Yugoslavia, Gallery of Art Lissone, Milan, University of Keele, Church of St. Mary the Virgin, Elmley Castle, Worcs., Graves A.G., Sheffield, Sir John Rothenstein, American Museum of Visionary Art, Baltimore, USA, HRH Duke of Edinburgh, Prince Edward (1991, 2001), Museum of Everything Permanent Collection (2009). *Commissions*: portraits: Sir Compton Mackenzie, Brigadier Sir Alex Stanier, Bt., DSO, MC, Lt. Col. Sir John Miller, GCVO, DSO, MC. *Publications*: Apollo Magazine article by Sir John Rothenstein, Quarto Press, work included in Encyclopedia of Water-colour Techniques, Raw Vision Magazine and others, Art Visionary Australia Time Out 2001, Private Worlds Raw Vision Magazine 2005, New York Arts Magazine Vol 13 2009, article Iliana McCloud. *Official Purchasers*: Museum of Everything, American Museum of Visionary Art, Baltimore, USA. *Works Reproduced*: Quarto Press Raw Vision, New Statesmen. *Recreations*: birds and wildlife. *Clubs*: Reynolds. *Misc*: Dealer, Henry Boxer, Henry Boxer Gallery, 98 Stuart Court, Richmond, London; Dance Theatre Production 'Awakenings' based on Pass's visionary paintings, music composed by Marcus Davidson, performances in Norwich Cathedral and Dorchester Abbey, Oxon. Animated film shown in Planetarium with music by Marcus Davidson 2009 designed by Harfiyah Haleem. *Address*: 6 Fullers Field, Great Milton, Oxford, OX44 7PJ. *Email*: donald.jacqueline@btinternet.com *Website*: www.donaldpass.com *Signs work*: "D. Pass" or "DONALD PASS".

PATERSON, Donald M., DA; artist in water-colour, teacher; elected Mem. Royal Scottish Soc. of Painters in Water-colour. *b*: Kyleakin, Isle of Skye, 28 Nov 1950.

m: Alexandra. two *s*. *Educ*: Portree High School. *Studied*: Glasgow School of Art (1969-73). *Exhib*: one-man show: Fair Maids Gallery, Perth; mixed shows: 'Artists under 30' Third Eye Centre, Glasgow, Glasgow Herald Exhbn. Collins Gallery, Strathclyde University, RSA Annual, GI Annual. *Address*: Blaven, Torr Rd., Bridge of Weir, Renfrewshire PA11 3BE. *Signs work*: "D.M. Paterson".

PATON, Anne Elizabeth, London Diploma in Art and Design. *Medium*: oil, watercolour, drawing, prints, sculpture, mixed media. *d of*: Christopher Paton. *Educ*: St.Agnes & St.Michaels' School, East Grinstead, Sussex. *Studied*: Chelsea School of Art (1975-78). *Exhib*: NEAC, RA Summer Exhbn., Leighton House, Peter Pears Gallery, Chappell Galleries; solo exhbns: Chappel Galleries, 2007; Walberswick annually since 1992; Shape Maltings, Southwold Gallery, The Cut, Halesworth, The Castle Museum, Norwich. *Works in collections*: London Borough of Kensington and Chelsea; Guinness; private collections worldwide. *Commissions*: for architects and private collectors. *Publications*: 'Artists at Walberswick 1880-2000'; Artists & Illustrators Magazine, 'Artists in Britain since 1945' David Buckman (2006). *Works Reproduced*: Richard Scott's book : 'Artists at Walberswick 1880-2000'. *Recreations*: listening to opera, playing the paino, travelling, interior design. *Clubs*: Chelsea Arts Club. *Misc*: Artworks Group. *Address*: Close Cottage, Manor Close, Walberswick, Suffolk IP18 6UQ. *Email*: annpannie@tiscali.co.uk *Website*: www.annepaton.com *Signs work*: 'Anne Paton'.

PATRICK, Emily (Katherine Emily). *Medium*: oil. *b*: Hawkhurst, 4 Oct 1959. *m*: Michael Perry. one *s*. two *d*. *Studied*: Faculty of Architecture, Cambridge University (1979-82). *Represented by*: Independent. *Exhib*: Sarah Long (1985); Thos Agnew & Sons, Bond Street (1986, 1989, 1992, 1995); King Street Gallery (1985); Lefevre Gallery (1997); National Portrait Gallery (1988); RP (1989); Hanover Square Gallery, New York (1997); Independent (1997, 2000, 2002, 2005, 2007, 2010, 1013). *Works in collections*: Farringdon Collection; New Hall Art Collection; Christie's, King Street; Cour de justice de I'UE; many private collections in UK, USA, Australia, Hong Kong and France. *Commissions*: Portraits: Frank Cabot (1982), Sir Murray Stuart-Smith (1984), Emma Hope (1984), Victor de Waal (1984), Lord Cottesloe (1984), Lord Strathcone (1986), Diana, Princess of Wales (1987), Tatiana Nikolayeva (1988), Sir James Gowans (1987), Sir Alistair Horne (1999), Professor Griffith Edwards CBE (1999), Adam Lowe (2002), Professor John Cox (2003), Robert Hasell McCosh (2005), Don Justo Gallego (2007), Sir Konrad Schiemann (2013). *Works Reproduced*: see Bridgeman Art Library. *Recreations*: painting. *Email*: info@emilypatrick.com *Website*: www.emilypatrick.com *Signs work*: "Emily Patrick" or "EP".

PATTERSON, Janet, Slade Dip., Churchill Fellow (1987), MA (1993); painter/printmaker, art lecturer; Vice President, London Group (1991-92), Vice Chairman, Chelsea Arts Club (1996-97); Awards: French Government Scholarship (1964), RWS award (1984), Winston Churchill Travel award (1987), Norwegian Travel Scholarship (1989), major prizewinner Hunting Art Prizes (2000); MA (2008) Art & Media Practice. *Medium*: paintings, prints, installations *b*: 13 Feb 1941. *d of*: John & Agnes Patterson. *Partner*: Angus McLeish. one *s*. one *d*. *Studied*: Slade School of Fine Art (1960-64). *Represented by*: Workhouse Gallery; Pilgrim Gallery; The Walk Gallery. *Exhib*: 'Natural Elements' University Sussex tour, 'Dreamtime' Talbot Rice, Edinburgh, London Group, RA, RAC Club, Deutsche Bank, Clifford Chance RCA, Freud Museum. *Works in collections*: Scottish Arts Council, Unilever, Texaco, ICI, NatWest, Ciba-Geigy, Coopers & Lybrand, Astra Zeneca, Freud Museum, London. *Commissions*: Dresdner Kleinwort Benson. *Publications*: 'Dreamtime' catalogue; Britart Directory; The London Group; Out of the Box, Dreams catalogue. *Clubs*: Chelsea Arts. *Address*: Studio @ 66 Strahan Road, Bow, London E3 5DB. *Email*: janetpatterson_arts@hotmail.com *Website*: www.janetpatterson.co.uk *Signs work*: "J.P".

PATTERSON, Linda, BA Hons, SBA, SFP, Dip. Eur. Hum. (Open) 1999; painter in pastel, oil, acrylic, teacher, lecturer; Chairman, Christchurch and District Arts Council; President, Christchurch Arts Guild. *b*: London, 3 Dec 1942. *m*: David. one *s*. one *d*. *Studied*: London and Bournemouth. *Exhib*: Westminster Central Hall, London, Bournemouth, Christchurch, Salisbury, Romsey, Sofiero Castle, Sweden (1998), Société Jersiaise, Jersey (1999), St. Lo, France, Compton Acres, Poole; Forest Arts, Lyndhurst; Work in collections internationally. *Works Reproduced*: cards for Medici; published in 'Pastel Artist International' magazine; published works in "How to Create Light in your Paintings" by Tony Paul. *Clubs*: Soc. of Botanical Artists, Soc. of Floral Painters, Christchurch Arts Guild, Romsey Art Group, Wessex Artists, Southbourne Art Society. *Address*: 24 Solent Road., Southbourne, Dorset BH6 4BP. *Email*: lindapatterson@hotmail.com *Signs work*: "L. PATTERSON".

PATTON, Marcus, OBE, BSc, DipArch, ARUA; architect/illustrator in ink, water-colour, screen printing; Trustee of 'In You We Trust' (artists' residency), and past chairman Belfast Print Workshop. *b*: Enniskillen, Co. Fermanagh, 23 Aug 1948. *m*: Joanna Mules. three *s*. *Exhib*: various. *Works in collections*: BBC, Arts Council of N. Ireland, Ulster Television, Belfast City Council, Down Museum, etc. *Commissions*: BBC, UTV, etc. numerous posters. *Publications*: 'Ireland', 'Scotland', 'South West Ireland', 'Bugs, Bites and Bowels' (all Cadogan Press), etc. *Works Reproduced*: in 'The Opera Hat of Sir Hamilton Harty' (Grand Piano Press, 2003). *Clubs*: Tonk's. *Address*: Ingledene, Sans Souci Park, Belfast BT9 5BZ. *Website*: www.operahat.co.uk *Signs work*: signature usually hidden in a maze of lines.

PAUL, Celia Magdalen, RE; BA 1st. Hons. Fine Art (1981); First Prize, The Ruth Borchard Self-portriat Award 2011; painter in oil and etcher. *b*: Trivandrum, India, 11 Nov 1959. one *s*. *Educ*: Edgehill College, Bideford, Devon. *Studied*: Slade School (1976-1981) under Prof. Lawrence Gowing. *Represented by*: Marlborough Fine Art, London. *Exhib*: Bernard Jacobson (1986), Marlborough Fine Art (1991, 1995, 1999, 2006, 2011), Israel Museum (Bacon to Bevan) (1991), Musée Maillol, Paris (1998), Charlottenborg, Copenhagen (2003), Abbot Hall Kendal (2004), Graves Art Gallery, Sheffield (2005), University of Nurthumbria, Newcastle (2010), Veneklasen/Werner Gallery, Berlin (2010). *Works in collections*: Saatchi Collection, British Museum, Metropolitan Museum, New York, Fitzwilliam Museum, Cambridge, Abbot Hall, Kendal; Carlsburg Foundation, Denmark; V&A; Yale Center for British Art, Newhaven; National Portrait Gallery, London; Herzog Ulrich Gallery, Germany. *Publications*: School of London - Alistair Hicks, Marlborough Fine Art catalogues; Rowan Williams: Modern Painters (Summer 2004); William Feaver: Abbott Hall Catalogue (2004); Catherine Lampert: Graves Catalogue (2005) & Marlborough Catalogue (2011). *Address*: 50 Great Russell St., London WC1B 3BA. *Signs work*: "Celia Paul".

PAUL, John, President, London Sketch Club (1999, 2000); Treasurer, Small Paintings Group. *Medium*: oil. *b*: Chelsea, London 19 Jan 1940. *m*: Beatrix. two *s*. one *d*. *Educ*: Henry Compton Boys School (1951-56). *Studied*: Camberwell School of Art (1956-59). *Exhib*: Piers Feetham Gallery (1996-2014); Russel Gallery (2007, 2009, 2011, 2013); Mall Galleries (1992. 94); St.James Gallery (2003); Park Lane Fine Arts (2006-08); Hamstead Gallery (2004); The Cinema Gallery (2006); Bartley Drew (1999); Carlyle Gallery (1994); Duncan Miller Fine Arts (2006); Hawker Gallery (2002); Red Leaf Gallery (1994); Chappel Gallery (2006, 2008); Falle Gallery (2010); Highgate Contemporary Art (2010, 2011); Red Rag Gallery (2011, 2013); Josephine Harpur (2012). *Works in collections*: private collections in the UK and Continental Europe; The Stiefsohn Trust, Austria. *Commissions*: Daiichi Jitsugyo Co Ltd, Tokyo; H.Genthner, Commerzbank Frankfurt; James Dingeman QC; London Borough of Hammersmith & Fulham; John and Elizabeth Miles; James and Emma Farquharsons. *Publications*: The Art Pack (aimed at people with disabilities, LBHF, MENCAP, SHAPE). Listed in Dictionary of Biographical Centre. *Clubs*: Small Paintings

Group, Fulham Artists and Potters, Chelsea Art Society, London Sketch Club, Chelsea Arts Club, Artist in Residence at All Saints Primary School, London. *Address*: 65 Shorrolds Road, Fulham, London SW6 7TU. *Email*: ja.paul@btinternet.com *Signs work*: 'JOHN PAUL'.

PAUL, Sylvia. *Medium*: oil, acrylic, collage, pastel, mixed media. *b*: Maldon, Essex, 11 Aug 1956. *m*: Geoffrey Alan Catchpole. two *s*. *Studied*: Colchester School of Art, Hockeril College of Education. *Exhib*: PS, SWA, ROI, Laing Landscape Exhibition, RI, Royal Academy Summer Exhibition 2009. *Works in collections*: internationally. *Address*: Shobita's Ship, 21 Empire Road, Dovercourt, Harwich, CO12 3QA. *Email*: sylvialouisepaul@hotmail.com *Website*: www.sylviapaul.com *Signs work*: 'SYLVIA PAUL'.

PAVEY, Don, FRSA, ARCA; lecturer in art & design, Kingston (1950-83), co-founder, National Art Education Archive, Wakefield (1983), director, Micro Academy, London (1986), Freedom of the City of London (1987), Newton Medal (Colour Group, 1997), originator, ProMICAD System for Enpowerment (1998, 2003). *Publications*: Methuen Handbook of Colour (1963, 1968, 1983), Art-based Gales (1979), Color (1980), The Artists' Colourmen's Story (1985), Colour and Humanism (2003, 2009), Thylesius on Colour 1528 (2003), Colour Symbolism (2009), Buddhist Colour (2009), Colour Engrained in the Mind (2010). *Address*: Studio House, 30 Wayside, Sheen, London SW14 7LN. *Email*: studio@coloracademy.co.uk *Website*: www.coloracademy.co.uk

PAVITT, Dianna: see GOODWIN, Dianna.

PAVLENKO, Sergei, potrait artist. *Medium*: oil, drawing. *b*: St. Petersburg, Russia, 26 Oct 1953. *m*: Tatiana Radko. one *s*. one *d*. *Studied*: Painting Dept. of the Academy of Fine Arts, St.Petersburg (6 years). *Represented by*: Fine Arts Commissions, London; Andreeva Gallery, Santa Fe, NM, USA. *Exhib*: solo shows: Russian Embassy, London (2004); British Embassy, Moscow (2004); group exhbns: RA Summer Show (1996, 97), RP (1992-2007), ROI (1989, 93, 2006), Discerning Eye, Mall Galleries, Art London, Andean Gallery, RWA, Los Angeles Art Expo, Kertesz Gallery San Francisco. *Works in collections*: HRH the Prince of Wales; HRH Prince of Hanover; Prince Nikolas Romanoff; Lee Bass; Drapers Company; Brown University, Cambridge University, Cazenove Group plc, plus many others worldwide. *Commissions*: many distinguished names worldwide; Worshipful Company of Drapers: portrait of HM Queen Elizabeth II (2000); Royal Military Academy, Sandhurst: The Royal Family Group Portrait (The Queen, Prince Philip, Prince Charles, Duchess of Cornwall, Prince William, Prince Harry). *Works Reproduced*: postage stamp of the Queen's Portrait; The Guardian; Daily Mail; The Telegraph; The Times, and all British main newspapers; Hello Magazine; many in Russia; a film on Channel 4 about Sergei and his portraits. *Principal Works*: portrait of HM The Queen, Duke of Marlborough, Michael Stone, Hawila children; Group portrait of the Royal Family at Sandhurst Military Academy. *Recreations*: tennis. *Clubs*: Chelsea Arts Club. *Address*: 51 Heathwood Gardens, London SE7 8ES. *Email*: sergei@spavlenko.demon.co.uk *Website*: www.spavlenko.demon.co.uk *Signs work*: 'Sergei Pavlenko'.

PAYNE, David, RWS (elected 2012); ARWS (2009); NDD, ATC (1954); painter in oil and water-colour (triptychs); formerly senior lecturer in painting, Bedford College of Educ. *b*: Dover, 29 Jul 1928. *m*: Iris. one *s*. one *d*. *Studied*: Canterbury, Farnham and Brighton Colleges of Art, London University, Institute of Education Department, until 1954, RA Schools (1980-81) (Guest student/Peter Greenham). *Exhib*: RA (40 paintings hung), Singer & Friedlander, NEAC, RWS, Portal Gallery, Laing Gallery, Ellingham Mill, Ash Barn Gallery, Sotheby's; The Gallery, Wellingborough, New Ashgate Gallery, Farnham, Discerning Eye. *Works in collections*: Beds. Educ. Loan Service, Bedford Hospital Trust (two paintings), University of Central England Archive 'David Payne Collection' Childrens Work; and private collections. *Publications*: reviews, ITV (1982), BBC2 (1983), Academy

Illustrated (1983, 1984, 1991), Royal Academy Exhibitors (1971-89); RA German TV film (ARD, 1999). *Address*: 25 Willmers Cl., Bedford MK41 8DX. *Signs work*: "David Payne".

PAYNE, Mandy, BA (Hons) Fine Art (First Class), HND Fine Art, MDentSci, BDS. Awards: Emerging Artist, South Yorkshire Open (2012); Judges Prize, Harley Open Exhibition, Worksop (2013). *Medium*: oil, drawing, print, mixed media. *b*: Pontypool, 3 Mar 1964. *m*: Martin. one *s*. one *d*. *Studied*: Nottingham University (Fine Art Degree, 2011-13), Sheffield College (HND, 2007-2010), Leeds University (MA in Dental Science, 1992-1995), Manchester University (Dentristy, 1982-86). *Represented by*: Tarpey Gallery, Castle Donnington, DE74 2PQ. *Exhib*: Solo show: Tarpey Gallery, Castle Donnington (2014); Selected for: RA Summer Show (2014), John Moores Painting Prize, Walker Art Gallery, Liverpool (2014), Threadneedle Prize for Painting and Sculpture, Mall Galleries (2013). Group shows include: Midlands Open, Tarpey Gallery; Wirksworth Festival Artists Trail, Derbyshire (2013), Cooper Gallery, Barnsley (2013), Millennium Gallery, Sheffield (2013), Harley Gallery, Worksop (2013), Derby Museum and Art Gallery (2012). *Works in collections*: private collections in UK and overseas. *Commissions*: several private commissions undertaken. *Publications*: review of solo exhibition at Tarpey Gallery in Guardian Guide (3.5.14) http://www.theguardian.com/.../03/this-weeks-new-exhibitions *Address*: 24 Moorside, Lodge Moor, Sheffield S10 4LN. *Email*: mandypayne24@googlemail.com *Website*: www.mandypayneart.com *Signs work*: "A J PAYNE".

PAYNE, Margaret A., NDD (1959), ATC (1960), BA (Hons) History of Art (1981), MA (Art Educ.) (1983), RE (1975); graphic artist including computer graphics, painter in oil, etcher; Currently researching children's learning in NC Art at KS1 & 2. *b*: Southampton, 14 Apr 1937. *d of*: G E B Payne, MD, DPH. *Educ*: St. Helen's School, Northwood, Middx. *Studied*: Harrow School of Art (1955-59), Goldsmiths' College (1959-60), Birkbeck College (Lond Univ) (1977-1981), Institute of Educ (London Univ) (1981-1983). *Exhib*: RA, RE, Paris Salon, Society of Women Artists, Young Contemporaries, RI. *Works in collections*: Sheffield and Nottinghamshire CC, Pictures for Schools circulation. *Publications*: in Journal of Art and Design Education (1993), Froebelian Principles and the Art National Curriculum. *Address*: 11a Wallorton Gdns., London SW14 8DX.

PAYNE, Michael Gustavius, BA Hons Fine Art (1996); PGCE (2012). *Medium*: oil, drawing. *b*: 25 Jun 1969. *Partner*: Janine Lewis. two *s*. one *d*. *Studied*: Cheltenham & Gloucester College of Higher Education (BA Hons); Mid Glamorgan Centre of Art and Design Technology; Athens School of Fine Arts, Greece (ERASMUS). *Represented by*: Ffin-y-Parc, Llanrwst. *Exhib*: MoMA, Wales; West Wales Art Centre; Washington Gallery, Penarth; Undercurrents Gallery, Deptford, London; Water Street Gallery, Todmorden; Art Central, Barry; Y Galeri, Caerphilly; Galeri, Betws y Coed; Raw Gallery, Tower Bridge, London; Old Library, Cardiff: Norwegian Church Arts Centre, Cardiff; Kilvert Gallery, Hay on Wye; Dylan Thomas Centre, Swansea; Ffin-y-Parc. *Works in collections*: University of South Wales; The Tabernacle Collection, MoMA; Cheltenham & Gloucester Building Society; University of Gloucestershire. *Publications*: Edited; All Roads Lead to Merthyr; Merthyr Writing; Never Mind the White Socks. *Official Purchasers*: Museum of Modern Art, Wales. *Works Reproduced*: Music CD covers and poetry collection covers including: Red Poets; Barkin! by Mike Jenkins; Tynnu Sylw by The Joy Formidable; The Barking Thing by Suzanne batty; Jamie Bevan a'r Gweddillion; plus others. *Misc*: Member of The Welsh Group (Art collective established in 1948). *Address*: 32 Heol Balaclafa, Dowlais, Merthyr Tydfil, CF48 3BS. *Email*: art@mgpayne.com *Website*: mgpayne.com *Signs work*: "MGP" or "MG Payne".

PAYNE, Tom, BA (Hons) Ceramics. *Medium*: ceramics, high grog crank. *b*: Camberwell, 24 Apr 1978. *s of*: Alasdair and Elizabeth Payne. *Studied*: KIAD Rochester (Kent Institute of Art and Design). *Represented by*: Start Space, 150 Columbia Road, London E2 7RG. *Exhib*: UK (London, Surrey, Eton, Glasgow, Winchester, Birmingham), Ireland. *Works in collections*: of Greg Dyke, and private collections in UK, Ireland and USA. *Commissions*: Whipps Cross NHS Trust; Dino Dig at the Natural History Museum, London; Bolton Council. *Works Reproduced*: figurative works up to lifesize. *Principal Works*: small figurines, smoke fired, and larger stone carving inspired pieces. *Address*: c/o Eduardo Sant'Anna, Start Space, 150 Columbia Road, London E2 7RG. *Email*: contact@startspace.co.uk *Website*: www.startspace.co.uk *Signs work*: monogram of 'TP'.

PAYNTER, Hilary, NDD (1964), ATC (1965), MA (Psych.Ed., 1982), ARE (1984), MSc (1988), FRSA (1986); wood engraver; Chairman SWE. *b*: Dunfermline, 16 Jun 1943. *d of*: Comdr. E.V.K. Paynter, RN. *m*: Gerry Bradley. one *s*. one *d*. *Studied*: Portsmouth College of Art (Gerry Tucker). *Exhib*: SWE, RE, Xylon, Switzerland. *Works in collections*: Hereford, Birmingham, Portsmouth and Durham City AGs, Ashmolean Museum, V&A, Fitzwilliam Museum; Laing Art Gallery. *Commissions*: Newcastle-upon-Tyne Central Station Station Metro mural. *Publications*: Fragments from the Satyricon (1999), The Story of Poetry (1992), Legal London Engraved (1998), The Engraver's Cut (1996), Goblin Market (2003). *Address*: Torridge House, Torridge Hill, Bideford, Devon EX39 2AZ. *Email*: hilarypaynter@yahoo.com *Signs work*: "Hilary Paynter".

PAYNTON, Colin Frank: see SEE-PAYNTON, Colin Frank.

PEARCE, Antony, BA (Exeter) (1963), FRSA (1990), ANS (1991); teacher/full time artist in water-colour and acrylic since 1980. *b*: Leigh, Essex, 21 Jul 1933. *Educ*: Mayfield College, Sussex. *Studied*: self taught, but inspired principally by Rowland Hilder and Edward Seago. *Exhib*: Edwin Pollard Gallery, Wimbledon (annually), numerous one-man shows. *Publications*: by Sharpe's, Castlebar Graphics, Kingsmead Publications. *Clubs*: R.S.A. *Address*: 16 Sandra House, Hansler Gr., E. Molesey, Surrey KT8 9JL. *Signs work*: "Antony Pearce".

PEARSON, Bruce Edward, BA Fine Art (1973), SWLA (1978); printmaker, and painter in water-colour and oil; President, Soc. of Wildlife Artists (1994-2004); GMAC Commercial Mortgage Europe Art Award (2005). *b*: Newmarket, Suffolk, 20 Sep 1950. *m*: Sara Oldfield. two *d*. *Studied*: pre-Dip.: Gt. Yarmouth College of Art and Design (1969-70); BA Fine Art: Leicester Polytechnic (1970-73). *Exhib*: many solo exhbns. in U.K., and group shows in USA, Holland; Ministère de L'Environment, France; Natural History Museum, London. *Commissions*: Sultan of Oman, Natural History Museum, Royal Caribbean Cruise Line. *Publications*: chapter with illustrations in 20th Century Wildlife Artists, Nick Hammond (Croom Helm, 1981); author and illustrator: An Artist on Migration (Harper Collins, 1991). Author and illustrator: In a New Light (Wildlife Art Gallery 2003); author & illustrator: Troubled Waters. Trailing the Albatross, An Artist's Journey (Langford Press, 2012). *Recreations*: playing music (guitar) in jazz/funk band. *Address*: 5 Marshall Road, Cambridge CB1 7TY. *Email*: bep@brucepearson.net *Website*: www.brucepearson.net *Signs work*: "B.P." (on some illustrative work), "BRUCE PEARSON" (on all other work).

PEARSON, Yvette L., BA Hons; freelance graphic designer in oil and water-colour, fashion designer; visiting lecturer, South Devon College of Art and Design. *b*: 16 May 1962. *Studied*: South Devon College and Ravensbourne College of Art and Communication (1985). *Exhib*: South Devon. *Misc*: Work manufactured: Kirtle, Jester Dress. *Address*: 22 Central Ave., Paignton, S. Devon.

PEART, Tony, BA (Hons) (1983), MA (1986); painter in oil; associate lecturer, Cumbria College of Art and Design. *b*: Darlington, 23 Jun 1961. *m*: Sharyn Brown. one *d*. *Educ*: Eastbourne School. *Studied*: Cheltenham College of Art, Leeds Polytechnic, Newcastle Polytechnic. *Exhib*: Piccadilly Gallery (1988-). *Works in collections*: Carlisle A.G.,

Darlington A.G., Government Painting Coll., Rank Xerox, Newcastle University, Northern Arts. *Address*: 4 Beanley Ave., Lemington, Newcastle upon Tyne NE15 8SP. *Signs work*: "Tony Peart" always on reverse.

PEBWORTH, Pam, RWA; Certificate of Education; Diploma in Visual Arts. *Medium*: wood engraving. *b*: Altrincham, 28 Jan 1931. *Educ*: Withington Girls' School, Manchester (1942-47). *Studied*: Bath Academy of Art (1951-54). *Exhib*: Royal West of England Academy, Bristol; South West Academy of Fine and Applied Arts, Exeter; Society of Wood Engravers. *Works in collections*: Royal Albert Memorial Museum, Exeter; Tiverton and Mid-Devon Museum, Tiverton. *Commissions*: Brook Gallery, Budleigh Salterton. *Publications*: examples of work included in Simon Brett's 'Engravers two (1992)/ Engravers' Globe (1992); Hilary Paynter's 'Engraved Gardens (2001); 'Art in Devon' magazine no.5 Summer 2006 (article by Hilary Paynter about wood engraving, entitled 'Touch Wood' with my work of that title illustrating it); 'Devon Life' magazine (article by Jenny Pery 'World within World', a short biography illustrated with nine of my wood engravings). *Address*: Dovetail, Lower Town, Sampford Peverell, Tiverton, Devon, EX16 7EG.

PECKHAM, Barry Arthur, SEA (1984), ROI, ARSMA; Awards: Royle prize (1984), Cuneo medal (1989), Crossgate Gallery award (1989), Pastel award (1990), Champagne Mumm Marine Artist (1990), Cuneo medal (2002), Winner, The Menena Joy Schwabe Memorial Fund Award (2009); landscape, marine and equestrian artist. *Medium*: oil, water-colour, pastels, etching. *b*: New Forest, Hants., 30 Dec 1945. *s of*: Arthur & Doris Peckham. *m*: Sarah Peckham. three *d*. *Educ*: Bartley School. *Studied*: Southampton College of Art. *Exhib*: RA, RI, ROI, PS, RSMA, SEA, NEAC, Royal West of England Academy. *Works in collections*: Royal Marines, Poole. *Publications*: Barry Peckham's New Forest (Barry Peckham-paintings and text, Barry Miles-text), pub. Halsgrove 2001; Seasons of the Forest (paintings and text by Barry Peckham) pub. Red Post Books 2005. *Clubs*: member: Royal Institute of Oil Painters, Society of Equestrian Artists, Associate - Royal Society of Marine Artists. *Address*: Fletchwood Cottage, 15 Busketts Way, Ashurst, Southampton, Hants. SO40 7AE. *Email*: barry@barrypeckham.wanadoo.co.uk *Website*: www.barrypeckham.co.uk *Signs work*: "B.A. PECKHAM".

PEGLITSIS, Nicolas, painter in oil, water-colour, pastel; awards: (1990, 1993) Beecroft Gallery Trustees Award for best painting in Essex open exhib., by public vote, (1993) short listed for the Bank of Cyprus (London) Ltd. Art Award, (2001) awarded prize for Best Landscape, Essex Open exhib. *b*: Larnaka, Cyprus, 9 Oct 1938. *m*: Jacqueline Taylor. two *d*. *Educ*: Southend High School. *Studied*: Goldsmith's College, London. *Exhib*: RA; RWS; Minories, Colchester; Beecroft Gallery, Westcliff; Crome Gallery, Norwich; Furneaux Gallery, London; Chartwell Gallery, Southend; Melford Fine Arts, Suffolk. *Works in collections*: private collections in UK, USA, Canada, Australia, New Zealand, Germany, Denmark, Holland, France, Spain, Cyprus; public collections, Municipal Gallery, Larnaka, Cyprus. *Commissions*: many private commissions, various subjects, important commission for The Moneo Company, Tokyo, Japan. *Publications*: Monograph: 'As John Constable Saw it'. *Address*: 25 Bridgwater Drive, Westcliff-on-Sea, Essex SS0 0DJ. *Email*: nicolas.peglitsis@btinternet.com *Website*: www.nicolaspeglitsis.com *Signs work*: "Peglitsis" with date.

PELHAM, Mary Catherine, SWA. *Medium*: watercolour, pastel, collage. *b*: Harrow, 30 Sep 1936. *d of*: Alan & Florence Henderson. *m*: Rodney Pelham. one *s*. two *d*. *Educ*: North London Collegiate School (1948-54). *Studied*: Maria Grey College, London University (1954-57). *Exhib*: SWA; RSMA (1994-); Mall Galleries; Central Hall Westminster; St. Breock Gallery, Wadebridge, Cornwall; Cowes, Isle of Wight; John Lewis, London; Holt, Norfolk; Bristol. *Commissions*: Northwood Prep School; Merchant Taylors School. *Works Reproduced*: Medici greeting cards. *Recreations*: yoga and badminton. *Misc*:

taught art at Northwood Prep School for 25 years; marine subjects of particular interest. *Address*: 4 Chester Road, Northwood, Middx HA6 1BQ. *Signs work*: 'Mary Pelham'.

PELLING, John Arthur, ARCA; painter in oil on canvas; retired clergyman of the Church of England, now Catholic, and member of the Ordinariate. *b*: Hove, 9 Aug 1930. divorced. *s of*: Arthur Robert Pelling. four *s*. *Educ*: Brighton, Hove and Sussex Grammar School. *Studied*: Brighton College of Art (1946-49) and Royal College of Art (1951-55), Chichester Theological College (1955-58). *Exhib*: nine one-man shows: Drian Gallery, London, Sussex University, Manchester, and including two latest exhbns., Air Gallery, Dover St., London. 'The Splitting Image' - Dilemma of Women as Priests (1998) and 'Double Exposure' (2001). *Works in collections*: National Collection of Modern Art, Gdansk, Poland, Nuffield Foundation, Vittorio 'de Sica private collection, Italy. 14 'Stations of the Cross', The Church of St. Thomas, Hanwell, London. At present full time painter in France and London. *Commissions*: 'Annunciation' Altar Piece for Lady Chapel, St Gabriel's, Acton, London. *Clubs*: Chelsea Arts. *Address*: 44 Redcliffe Rd., London SW10 9NJ. *Signs work*: "PELLING" (on paintings), "John Pelling" (on drawings).

PELLY, Frances, RSA, DA; sculptor in wood, stone, clay, paper. *b*: Edinburgh, 1947. *d of*: Russell Steele Pelly, forester. *Educ*: Morrisons Academy, Crieff. *Studied*: Duncan of Jordanstone, Dundee (1965-71, Scott Sutherland, Alistair Smart). *Exhib*: RSA, SSA, RGI; solo show: 'Nousts', travelling exhbn. in Highland Region and Norway (1992-93), St. Magnus Festival, Orkney; Shetland and Norway in 2003; Scottish Lettercutters, Edinburgh (2004), Perthshire (2007), West Dean, Sussex. *Works in collections*: Fine Art Soc., Scottish Arts Council, Dundee, BBC Glasgow, Perth, Orkney, Aberdeen, Royal Concerthall Glasgow, Banff, City Halls Glasgow and Fort William, Edinburgh, Kirkwall, RSA. *Commissions*: North Inch Perth, Orkney Art Soc., Parcelforce Glasgow, Mobil North Sea Banff, Strathclyde Regional Council Glasgow, Highland Regional Council Fort William, Orkney Arts Soc., Kirkwall, Museum of Scotland, Edinburgh, Wick. *Address*: Quoyblackie, Rendall, Orkney KW17 2HA. *Signs work*: Never signs work.

PELZ, Peter, MA (Cantab) (1968); artist in oil, tempera, water-colour, drawing and etching. *b*: Oxford, 18 Sep 1945. *Educ*: King's College, Cambridge. *Studied*: Wigan, Lancs. (1957-63, Theodore Major). *Exhib*: Rebecca Hossack Gallery, London. *Works in collections*: on commission (chief works): triptych at St. James's, Piccadilly; mural at St. Peter's, Morden. *Publications*: Prayer for the Day (Cairns). *Address*: 28 Victoria Rd., Cirencester, Glos. GL7 1ES. *Signs work*: "Peter Pelz" and date.

PENDERED, Susan Marjorie Anne, MCSP, Hon. Retired Member RI; painter in water based medium; Winner of the Winsor & Newton RI Award (1988). *b*: London, 15 Jun 1925. *d of*: Robert. *m*: John H. Pendered, GP, MBE, MB, BS (decd). one *s*. two *d*. *Educ*: Lillesden School for Girls, Hawkhurst, Kent. *Studied*: part-time at Brighton Polytechnic (1975-82, Norma Weller). *Exhib*: Mall Galleries, RI, RA Summer Exhbn., RWA, Bristol, participated in travelling exhbn. to Vancouver, Canada and Seattle, USA (1986). *Works in collections*: work purchased by Hertford Education Authority. *Address*: Littleway, West Furlong La., Hurstpierpoint, W. Sussex BN6 9RH. *Signs work*: "S. Pendered".

PENDERY, Carroll, SWA (1997); artist in pastel, water-colour, oil. *b*: Leicester, 30 Dec 1935. *m*: Terence Pendery, BSc. two *s*. *Educ*: Gateway Girls School, Leicester. *Exhib*: by selection in Yorkshire, Birmingham, Peterborough, Leicestershire, Norfolk and London. *Recreations*: gardening. *Clubs*: Founder Member Leicester Pastel Society, Kirby Bellans Art Group. *Address*: 17a Broadwalk, Buxton, Derbyshire, SK17 6JR. *Signs work*: "C. Pendery" or "Carroll Pendery".

PENKETH SIMPSON, Barbara, FRSA, RMS, PPSWA; Mundy Sovereign portrait award (1989), RMS President's Special Commendation (1996), RMS Gold Memorial Bowl

(1997), RMS Presidents special commendation (1999); Hon.Sec. RMS (2002- 2009), President SWA (2005-2011); self taught artist and miniaturist, larger oils and portraiture. *Medium*: oil. *b*: Crewe, Ches. *d of*: George & Gwendoline Penketh. *m*: F.W. Simpson. one *s*. one *d*. *Exhib*: HS, SWA, RMS. *Works in collections*: Britain and abroad. *Publications*: featured on flyer for, and included in, Royal Society of Miniature Painters, Sculptors and Gravers '100 Years of Miniatures', Artists & Illustrators Magazine (A&I). *Address*: The Cottage, 22 St. Agnes Road, Conwy, LL32 8RY. *Email*: bsimpson1@btconnect.com *Website*: www.penketh-simpson.co.uk

PEPYS, Sandra, BA (Hons) London University; artist, art historian, exhibition curator. *Medium*: oil, watercolour. *b*: Cape Town, 1942. one *s*. one *d*. *Educ*: South Hampstead, SOAS, University of London. *Studied*: Slade School of Art, also studied with Ruszkowski. *Exhib*: Solo shows include: London: Hampstead Art Cellar (1962, 1973-76), Studio 36 (annually from 1966-76), Duncan Campbell (1994, 1996, 1998, 2000); Paris: Galerie Tedesco (1962); Italy: Sperlonga (1962, 1965, 1999); group shows: London: Society of Landscape Painters, annually from 1989 at W.H. Patterson and Duncan Miller Fine Arts. "Venice in Peril", annually from 1992 at W.H. Patterson. "Images of Italy", Accademia Italiana, London. Arts Club Dover St. Florentine Artists Assoc. Soc. of Landscape Painters Rotunda Gallery Hong Kong (1995). R.A. Summer Exhbn. (frequently from 1973 to present) . *Works in collections*: University of London, Municipality of Jerusalem, Brown Forman, Yeo Valley Organic. *Commissions*: mural paintings, London University (1966), British Railways (1967). Portraits include: Professor Sir Ernst Gombrich, OM, Lady Alexander Fleming, Dr. Arnold Miles FCCP, FACP, Vineyards and Vintners Fattoria Castellina Capraia. *Publications*: Contributor: Artists and Illustrators Magazine, The Art of Drawing and Painting, Former Editor: Arts Club Journal, Dover Street Arts Club. *Works Reproduced*: The Art of Painting and Drawing. *Clubs*: Chelsea Arts Club. *Misc*: Founder and Chairman, Society of Landscape Painters; Founder and Vice President, Small Painters Group; 1st Prize University of London Exhbn. (1966); Co-ordinator Soil Association Arts Project. *Address*: 36 Ferncroft Ave., London NW3 7PE. *Signs work*: "Sandra Pepys".

PERKINS, Marion, FRSA; MIL (London, 1963); SBA (2001); Margaret Stevens Award for Work which reflects concern for the environment (2009); Certificate of Botanical Merit (2007); Director of Society of Botanical Artists (2006-2013); Sennelier Watercolour Award (2005). *Medium*: watercolours, gouache, egg tempera. *b*: London, 25 Feb 1943. *m*: Carl. two *d*. *Educ*: Wembley County Grammar School. *Studied*: University of Westminster; Harrow School of Art; St.Albans College of Art; Chelsea Physic Garden. *Exhib*: Westminster Gallery (1999-2002, 2004-14); RA Summer Exhbn (1975), Palmengarten, Frankfurt (2010, 2014); galleries in the London area. *Works in collections*: private collections. *Commissions*: mostly landscape, private collectors. *Publications*: entries in 'The Art of Botanical Painting' (Collins, 2004); 'The Botanical Palette' (Collins, 2007). Author and Illustrator of childrens book 'The Stone Cat' (Book Guild 2009). *Works Reproduced*: Greeting cards, self-published and for Ling's. *Principal Works*: rosa 'Crazy for You'; Lilium orientalis covers for SBA Catalogue and publicity. 'The Rainforest, Series I, II, III. *Recreations*: music, gardening, writing. *Address*: Red Lion Cottage, Bovingdon Green, Bovingdon, Hemel Hempstead, HP3 0LF. *Email*: marionperkinswatercolours@msn.com *Website*: www.soc-botanical-artists.org *Signs work*: 'Marion Perkins'.

PERKINS, Shelly Louise, BA Hons Illustration. *Medium*: Mixed media illustration, traditional and digital techniques. *b*: Worcester, 2 Nov 1984. *Partner*: Stuart Hendren. *Studied*: Stourbridge College of Art and Design (2003-04); The University of the West of England (2004-2007). *Exhib*: Society of Wildlife Artists (2012); David Shepherd Wildlife Artist of the Year Exhibition (2013). *Works in collections*: Nature in Art Gloucestershire. *Commissions*: BBC Wildlife Magazine; RSPB; National Trust. *Publications*: BBC Wildlife Magazine, The Radio Times. *Principal Works*: "The Obelisk Opportunists", "Vulpes

Homage", "Great Malvern". *Address*: The Stepps, Neen Stollars, Nr. Kidderminster, Worcestershire DY14 0AN. *Email*: artbyshelly@gmail.com. *Website*: www.shellyperkins.co.uk *Signs work*: "Shelly Perkins".

PERKINS, Stuart M.G., RMS (1991), MAA (1990), ATD, NDD 1st Class Hons. (1956), MPSG, MAS-F; landscape miniaturist in water-colour and gouache with occasional still life; trained as a sculptor, and practised as a Studio Potter (1976-85). *b*: Leicester, 4 Jul 1935. *s of*: Frederick G. Perkins & Audrey H.Harris. *m*: Joan Chatterley, ATD. three *d*. *Educ*: Alderman Newton Boys G.S., Leicester. *Studied*: Leicester College of Art (1952-56, Albert Pountney). *Exhib*: RMS, RWA, RWS Summer Show, WAC; many mixed exhbns. in England and Wales, miniature exhbns. in UK, Canada, USA, Australia and Japan. *Works in collections*: MAS-F, MPSG & Washington. Works mainly held in private collections in Canada, France, USA. *Address*: The Old School, Scowles, Coleford, Glos. GL16 8QT. *Email*: sperkins@freeuk.com *Signs work*: "S. PERKINS, R.M.S, M.A.A.," (dated), "Stuart Perkins".

PERRIN, Brian, ARCA, Rome Scholar (1954); painter/etcher; Head of Printmaking Dept., Wimbledon School of Art (1964-97); Mem. CNAA Fine Art Board (1978-90). *b*: 19 Aug 1932. *s of*: Charles Perrin. *m*: Jane Lisle. two *s*. *Educ*: Whitgift Middle School. *Studied*: Croydon School of Art (1948-51), RCA (1951-54). *Exhib*: extensively in Europe and USA, including international print Biennales, National Museums of Art Barcelona and Madrid. *Works in collections*: Library of Congress, Washington, V&A, Arts Council, British Council; Museums of Art: Metropolitan NY, Perth, Jerusalem, Boston, Cincinatti, Glasgow, Ashmolean Museum Oxford, British Government Art Collection. *Address*: 293 Kings Rd., Kingston-upon-Thames, Surrey KT2 5JJ. *Signs work*: "Brian Perrin".

PERRIN, Sally Jane. *Medium*: water-colour and oil. *b*: Hoddesdon, 1964. *d of*: Eric James Clark. *m*: Graham Russell Perrin. one *s*. one *d*. *Represented by*: The Society of Botanical Artists. *Exhib*: Westminster Gallery with SBA annually, Mall Galleries with RSMA, Medici, Naze Tower Gallery, Walton on the Naze; solo show: Tudor House Gallery, Aldeburgh; solo show: Wimpole Hall, Arrington, Royston, Cambs. *Works Reproduced*: greetings cards for RHS. *Recreations*: camping, genealogy. *Misc*: Descendant of victorian artist Samuel James Clark. *Address*: 25 The Roundings, Hertford Heath, Herts. SG13 7PX. *Email*: sally_jane.perrin@btinternet.com *Website*: www.saa.co.uk/arts/sallyjaneperrin *Signs work*: "SJP" with the J crossing horizontally above S and P and looping below S, or "S J PERRIN".

PERRY, Jayne, ABNA. *Medium*: acrylic. *b*: Buckinghamshire, 22 May 1959. *m*: Philip. two *d*. *Exhib*: usual, mixed and solo. *Works in collections*: private collections. *Address*: The Studio, Riverside Road, Dittisham, Devon TQ6 0HS. *Email*: jaynecperry@gmail.com *Website*: www.jaynecperry.com *Signs work*: "JAYNE".

PERRY, Julian, BA Hons Fine Art; British Council Exhibition award; Arts Council Major Individual Award. *Medium*: oil. *b*: Worcester, England, 19 Jan 1960. *Studied*: Berkshire College of Art & Design (1977-78); Bristol Polytechnic (BA Hons Fine Art, 1978-81). *Represented by*: Austin Desmond Fine Art, London. *Exhib*: solo shows: Tom Allen Centre, Stratford (1987), Bristol City Museum & Art Gallery (1998), Wysing Arts, Cambridgeshire (2003), Guildhall Art Gallery, London (2004), Austin Desmond (1995, 1997, 2001, 2007). Selected group shows include: Discerning Eye (2001, 02, 06), Hunting Art Prize (2002, 03, 06), RA Summer Exhibition (2006). *Works in collections*: Bristol City Museum & Art Gallery, Museum of London, London Transport Museum, London Guildhall Art Gallery, Prince of Wales Collection, Forbes Collection, USA. *Publications*: Julian Perry 'Testament' pub. London Guildhamm; 'A Common Treasury' (2007, ADFA). *Works Reproduced*: London in Paint (pub. Museum of London, 1997), 'Modern Painters', Autumn Issue 2001. *Principal Works*: Shed 54 & Rhubarb, Collection of Museum of London (purch.2008). *Misc*:

Studio - Britannia Works, Bow, East London; I am Member of Faculty, The Prince's Drawing School. *Address*: Leyton, East London. *Email*: gallery@austindesmond.com *Website*: www.austindesmond.com *Signs work*: "JP" and date.

PERRY, Roy, RI (1978); painter in oil, water-colour and acrylic; awarded RI Medal (1978), RI Council (1979). *b*: Liverpool, 1935. *s of*: Sydney Perry, chartered accountant. *m*: Sallie Charlton. one *s*. one *d*. *Educ*: John Lyon School, Harrow and Southampton University. *Exhib*: RA, RI, RBA, RSMA, etc.; one-man shows, Oxford, Guildford, London, Henley and Cambridge. *Works in collections*: many large business corporations; The Fleet Air Arm Museum; HRH The Duke of Edinburgh and other private collections throughout the world. *Works Reproduced*: Lithographs, New York, Industrial Reviews and Laings Calendar. *Address*: The Mill House, Donhead St. Mary, Shaftesbury, Dorset SP7 9DS. *Signs work*: "Roy Perry".

PERRYMAN, Margot, MA; painter; tutor at Goldsmiths, Portsmouth, Ravensbourne, and Winchester Colleges of Art (1967-1974); By-Fellowship - Churchill College, Artist in Residence Cambridge University (2002-2003). *b*: Plymouth, 26 Mar 1938. *m*: Luc Delfanne. three *s*. *Studied*: Harrow School of Art and The Slade. *Exhib*: numerous solo and group exhibs. *Works in collections*: Tate Gallery, Arts Council GB, Govt. Art Collection UK, BBC, Leicestershire County Education Authority, Moller Centre, Cambs., Fitzwilliam Museum, Cambs.; Cambridge University; University of Natal, S.Africa. *Commissions*: various private commissions. *Works Reproduced*: Tate Women Artists (2004). *Address*: 26 Leighville Dr., Herne Bay, Kent CT6 8UJ. *Email*: info@margot-perryman.co.uk *Website*: www.margot-perryman.co.uk www.arttolivewith.co.uk *Signs work*: "Perryman." (on reverse of canvases).

PERSEY, Robert, B.Ed, Diploma in Advanced Studies Sculpture. *Medium*: Sculpture. *b*: London, 15 Sep 1951. *m*: Katherine Gili. one *s*. *Studied*: Bulmershe College, Reading (1971-75); St. Martin's School of Art (1976-77). *Exhib*: Lanchester Gallery (solo, 1993); New Contemporaries, RA (1977); Tate Gallery (1984); Cartwright Hall (1985); Royal Northern College of Music (1986); International Contemporary Art Fair, Olympia (1986); Conde Duque Centre, Madrid (1988); Milton Keynes Gallery (1994); Pride of the Valley Sculpture Park (2002-); Blok Sculpture Festival, Canterbury (2004); 20th Century British & Irish Art, Sotheby's (2006, 2007). *Works in collections*: Private collections in United Kingdom and USA. *Commissions*: Berkshire County Council. *Misc*: Director of Studies, Blake College, London (1995-2006). *Address*: 7 The Mall, Faversham, Kent ME13 8JL. *Email*: robert@persey.plus.com *Website*: www.robertpersey.com *Signs work*: most works signed with monograph.

PESKETT, Tessa, BA (Hons.) Fine Art (1979), PGCE (1982), H.Postgrad.Dip.Painting (1992), ROI (1994); Chadwick Healey prize for painting (1992), Anne LeClerc Fowle medal (1993); artist in oil, charcoal. *b*: Three Bridges, Sussex, 25 Apr 1957. *m*: Nigel Cox. *Educ*: Beaumont School, St. Albans. *Studied*: Reading University (1975-79), City & Guilds of London Art School (1992). *Exhib*: RA Summer Shows, RBA, ROI, Linda Blackstone Gallery, Mall Galleries, Trinity A.G. Arundel, Parkview, Bristol, Laing Art Competition, London (1994-97), Atrium Gallery, Bournemouth University, solo show (1996), Albemarle Gallery, London (1996-97), Paris (1996), New York (NYAD 2000), Four Seasons Gallery, Wimborne (2001, 2003), Discerning Eye Mall Galleries 2002, ROI Annual Exhibition Mall Galleries 2002, The Gallery Upstairs (Henley-in-Arden) 2003, The Orange Tree Galerie, Seillans, South of France - Artist in Residence (2004-). *Commissions*: numerous. *Publications*: Positive Health, Dorset Magazine, Living France. *Misc:* Has own studio and gallery in Var region of Southern France (see website). *Address*: The Orange Tree, Route de Bargemon, 83440 Seillans, France. *Email*: tessapeskett@hotmail.com *Website*: www.theorangetreegalerie.com *Signs work*: "Tessa D. Peskett" and "T.P".

PETERSEN, David Thomas, NDD (1965), ATC Lond. (1966), R.C.A.; sculptor; Head of Sculpture, Harrow School of Art (1967-1970), lecturer in Fine Art (1972-1974), senior lecturer in Fine Art (1974-1978), head of Sculpture and 3D, Dyfed College of Art (1978-1982); now full time sculptor; director of First Internat. Festival of Iron, Cardiff (1989); visiting prof. at Makina Inst., St. Petersburg; visiting lecturer to World Congress in Aachen, Germany, ABANA conference, Birmingham, Alabama, and to Penland, North Carolina, USA. *b*: Cardiff, 25 Feb 1944. *m*: Bronwen. three *s*. one *d*. *Educ*: Taunton School. *Studied*: Newport College of Art (1961-1965), London University, Inst. of Educ. (1965-1966). *Exhib*: numerous from 1963 onwards. *Works in collections*: Dyfed County Council, Cardiff City Council, London Borough of Harrow. *Commissions*: Cardiff City Council H.Q. building (1989), Mametz Wood Dragon, Somme, France (1987), Trinity College (1990), Millennium Beacon for Wales (2000). *Clubs*: past chairman of B.A.B.A. *Address*: Efail Y Tyddyn, San Clêr, Sir Gaerfyrddin SA33 4EJ. *Email*: davidtpetersen@aol.com *Signs work*: "David Petersen".

PETERSON, Peter Charles, NDD, PPRBA, RBA (1978); mem. Landscape Soc. (1989), Vice Chairman, Soc. of Landscape Painters; Daler Rowney Prize (1983), First Prize (1988), De Laszlo medal (1994); artist in oil, water-colour and gouache; lecturer, Visual Research Dept. Chesterfield College of Art; senior lecturer, Fine Art Dept. Epsom College of Art; visiting lecturer, Falmouth College of Art (1986). two *d*. *Studied*: Hornsey College of Art. *Exhib*: RA Summer Exhbn. since 1968, RBA since 1978, Falmouth A.G., Hallam Gallery, NEAC, Crossgate Gallery, USA; one-man shows, Portal Gallery, Highgate, Southwell-Brown Gallery, Richmond, Gt.Yarmouth Museum; group shows, Odette Gilbert Gallery (1983-84), Southwell-Brown Gallery, Richmond, Alexander Gallery London. *Clubs*: Dover Street Arts Club, Penzance Arts Club. *Address*: Waratah House, 11 The Praze, Penryn, Cornwall TR10 8DH. *Signs work*: "Peter Peterson".

PETHERS, Ian Peter Andrew, SBA(1989), RMS(2006), HS; Winner of Llewelyn Alexander Masters Award 2003, RMS Gold Bowl Honourable Mention 2007; Suzanne Lucas Botanical Award 2012. *Medium*: watercolour, oil, ink & wash, botanical, marine, architectural , still life inc. miniatures. *b*: London, 23 Jan 1956. *m*: Marylou. *Educ*: Langley County School, Slough (under Thomas McCabe, 1967-73). *Studied*: Marlow Community College under Jenny Riley (1983-1986). *Exhib*: SBA Westminster Gallery since 1987, RMS Westminster Gallery since 1999, Llewellyn Alexander Gallery, Waterloo since 2002. Hilliard Society, Wells; Mall Galleries, London. *Commissions*: Two miniature paintings - Sue Lee Collections. *Publications*: 'Visions of Glastonbury'. *Works Reproduced*: illustrated Travel Guides by Kingsley Media (1996-99), jacket cover designs for various publishers, wrote and illustrated 'Visions of Glastonbury', Bossiney Books (2001). *Recreations*: model making. *Address*: Glenrock Studio, Drakewalls, Gunnislake Station, Cornwall PL18 9EE. *Email*: glenrockstudio@yahoo.co.uk *Website*: www.glenrockstudio.co.uk *Signs work*: "Ian Pethers".

PETLEY, Roy, self taught. *Medium*: oil, watercolours, pastels, pencil. *b*: Grantham, Lincs, 3 Apr 1951. *s of*: Ernest Petley. one *s*. *Studied*: Brighton School of Art. *Represented by*: Petley Fine Art; David Messum Gallery; Petley Fine Art (Monte Carlo). *Exhib*: Bell Gallery, Belfast (1968), Liberty's Gallery London (1970), Heals Gallery London (1972-85), Open Air Art Show, Green Park London (1973), Crome Gallery, Norwich (1975), Travelling Show, East Anglian Marine Artists (1978-80), Century Gallery, Henley-on-Thames (1979-86, 2001), Fine Art Trade Guild Gallery (1987-89), David Messum (1993-95, 97-01), Jorgensen Fine Art, Dublin (1995-2002), and extensively in UK and abroad. *Works in collections*: Her Late Majesty Queen Elizabeth the Queen Mother, HRH the Duke of Edinburgh, HRH The Prince of Wales, HRH The Duchess of Kent, Her Grace the Duchess of Norfolk, Sultan of Brunei, Durban Museum, Ulster Museum, The High Lane Municipal Gallery, Dublin, Harvard University, Lord Hanson, Frederick Forsyth, Mr. & Mrs. RK

Black, Susan George, Timothy Dalton, Philip and Dorothy Solomon, Michael Jaye. *Commissions*: Her Late Majesty Queen Elizabeth the Queen Mother, Duchess of Kent, Duchess of Norfolk, The Salbanchi family, Lord Hanson. *Publications*: Roy Petley by Brian Sewell. *Principal Works*: oil paintings in the figurative manner, portraiture (landscape), beach scenes and the nude. *Recreations*: chess, classical music. *Address*: 9 Cork Street, London W1S 3LL. *Email*: info@petleyfineart.com *Website*: www.petleyfineart.com *Signs work*: Roy Petley.

PETRITOLI, Alvaro, BA (Hons) Italian Literature; BA Fine Art. *Medium*: Ink drawings. *b*; Rome, Italy, 10 Sep 1967. *Studied*: Central St. Martins, London (1998-2003); University "La Sapienza", Rome, Italy (1986-92). *Represented by*: Full Circle Art Consultancy - First Sight Gallery (Hastings). *Exhib*: Coutts & Co Bank; Affordable Art Fair (2008, 2009, 2010, 2011); Hart Gallery; Heathfield Art & Books; Salon des Arts, London; Riverside Gallery, Lewes; Coastal Current '10, Hastings; Artwave 2011, Lewes. *Works in collections*: TDR Capital, London; Barbarini & Foglia, Rome; hundreds of pieces in private collections around the world. *Principal Works*: 54 series of ink miniatures. *Misc*: Video of my Art Practice: http://vimeo.com/1637264 Address: 29 Baldslow Road, Hastings TN34 2EZ. *Email*: alvaro.petritoli@gmail.com *Website*: www.alvaropetritoli.com

PETRY, Nancy Virginie, Batchelor of Fine Arts (1952); Canada Council for the Arts: Grants 1969, '71, '78, '81; Ministere des Affaires Culturelles du Quebec: Grant 1965. *Medium*: acrylic, oil, watercolour, drawing, prints, Interventions, Happenings, dance, film, photography. *b*: Montreal, Quebec, Canada, 10 Apr 1931. *d of*: Elizabeth & Howard Petry. *Studied*: McGill University, Montral (Fine Arts 1948-52); L'Academie Julien, Paris (1954); L'Academie de la Grand Chaumiere (Henri Goetz) Paris (1955-58); L'Atelier 17 (W.S. Hayter) Paris (1956); Slade School of Fine Art (Stanley Jones) London (1968); The Print Workshop (Birgit Skiold) London (1972-74); London Film-makers Co-op, London (1978). *Represented by*: Beaux-arts des Ameriques, Montreal. *Exhib*: Solo: Galerie Voyelles, Paris (1956); Galerie Agnes Lefort, Montreal (1959, '61, '63); National Gallery of Canada, Ottawa - Touring Exhibition in Western Canada (1963); Anthony Tooth Gallery, London (1966); Commonwealth Institute, London (1969); Galerie Godard-Lefort, Montreal (1969); Nancy Poole's Studio, Toronto (1974, '76); Vehicule Art, Montreal (1976, '78, '79); Galerie Esparanza, Montreal (1985); Musée des Beaux-arts de Mont-Saint-Hilaire, Quebec (Retrospective, 2008); Beaux-arts des Ameriques, Montreal (2014); Group exhibitions since 1957 in Canada, France, USA, Italy, Sweden, Switzerland and the UK. *Works in collections*: many private and public collections in USA, Canada, England, France and Italy. *Publications*: 'Identité - artist's book (Limited edition, 1984); 'Tre Giorni' Geiger limited editions; 'Island', deluxe edition of lithographs and poems (Print Workshop, London 1973). *Official Purchasers*: Bibiothèque National du Québec, Montreal; Canada Council Art Bank, Ottawa; Confederation Art Gallery, Charlottetown, PEI; Musée d'Art Contemporain, Montreal; National Library of Canada, Ottawa. *Works Reproduced*: "Vie des Arts" (2006, '08); The Gazette, Montreal (2000); Le Devoir (1985); Parallelogramme (1979); Ateliers, Musee d'art Contemporain, Montreal (1975). *Misc*: Vêhicule Art, Montreal. Delegate to L'Arte Fiera, Bologna, Italy (1988-'78). Member of Board of Directors, Vice-Chairman and Gallery. *Address*: 97 King Henry's Road, London NW3 3QX. *Email*: nancypetry@yahoo.com *Website*: www.nancypetry.com *Signs work*: "Petry".

PETTERSON, Melvyn Lawrence, NEAC, RE (1991), BA (1986); painter/printmaker in oil, etching, water-colour; partner, Artichoke Print Workshop. *b*: Cleethorpes, 7 Jul 1947. *m*: Glynis. one *d*, Sara. *Educ*: Cleethorpes-Beacon Hill Sec. Modern. *Studied*: Grimsby Art School (Peter Todd, Alf Ludlam, Nev Tipper), Camberwell School of Art (Graham Giles, Francis Hoyland, Anthony Eyton, R.A., Ben Levene, R.A.). *Represented by*: NEAC, RE, RBA, SPG. *Exhib*: RA, NEAC, ROI, Bankside Gallery, museums and galleries in USA, France, Russia, China, Spain, Sweden, Finland, Monte Carlo. *Works in collections*: Oxford, Leicester, British Museum, galleries in USA. *Publications*: British Painters/Sculptors,

Painting and Drawing, Art Review, Drawing and Painting the Landscape (Collins-Brown). *Address*: c/o Artichoke, Unit 51, 245a Coldharbour Lane London SE9 8RR. *Website*: www.melvynpetterson.com *Signs work*: "M.L. Petterson" or "M.L.P".

PEVERALL, Adrienne, B.Ed, DipAD; printmaker of etchings and monoprint landscapes; ceramics tutor (1979-1982). *b*: London, 15 Oct 1939. *m*: Ronald Peverall. two *s*. *Educ*: Southgate Grammar School. *Studied*: King Alfred's College, Winchester (1974-1978), Falmouth College of Art (1990-1992). *Exhib*: Regular exhibitions through the year at the Mariners Gallery (St. Ives Society of Artists). *Works in collections*: Penlee House, Penzance, Cornwall. *Publications*: 'Ten Penwith Printmakers' (pub. Penwith Printmakers). *Address*: Kerrow Lodge, Bosullow, Penzance, Cornwall TR20 8NR. *Website*: www.stisa.co.uk *Signs work*: "A Peverall".

PHILIP, Jackie, BA (Hons), MA; Italian gov. Scholarship, Andre de Sezonaz Scholarship, British Institute Award, Mary Amour Award, RSA Hospitalfield Residency, Russel Trust Award, VAS; John Cunningham Award RGI; Hunting Art Prize Exhibition; Garyvald Residency, Lewis; artist/lecturer. *Medium*: raw pigment/oil. *b*: Edinburgh, 3 Jan 1961. *Studied*: Gray's School of Art, Aberdeen, Wimbledon School of Art, Royal Academy Schools, London. *Exhib*: UK, Caribbean, Hong Kong, Australasia. *Works in collections*: corporate and private. *Clubs*: RASAA, VAS, RGI, PAI. *Address*: 5 Great King Street, Edinburgh, EH3 6QW. *Email*: philipjackie@hotmail.com

PHILIPPS, Nicola Jane, artist in oil. *b*: London, 27 Aug 1964. *Studied*: City & Guilds; apprentice to Studio Cecil Graves, Florence (1986-88). *Exhib*: Malcolm Innes Gallery (3) including solo shows (1995, 1997); Arndean Gallery (solo, 2001, 2003, 2004); BP Portrait Exhbn, NPG (2005); Garrick Club: Garrick/Milne Exhbn. *Commissions*: Scottish and Newcastle Breweries, The Irish Guards, Freemasons Hall, Grocers Livery Company, Ken Follett (author), Baltic Exchange, Lord Mayor 1999. *Clubs*: Chelsea Arts Club. *Address*: c/o Fine Art Commission Ltd., 79 Walton St., London SW3 2HP. *Signs work*: "Nicola J. Philipps".

PHILLIPS, Anna, (formerly BRAIN, Ann). BA Fine Art: ATC London; Maltese Biennale Special Distinction Award (1995). *Medium*: oil, printmaking. *b*: Coventry, 20 Feb 1944. *Educ*: Rugby High School for Girls. *Studied*: Coventry College of Art; London University Institute of Education. *Represented by*: Bridgeman Art Library. *Exhib*: RA (1986, 92, 93, 94, 96, 97, 2004, 06, 08); Rugby Art Gallery and Museum (2 exhbns); Mall Galleries; Artifex, Sutton Coldfield; Maltese Biennale (1995); Cygnet Gallery, Toronto; Anna-Mei Chadwick, London; Llewellyn Alexander, London. *Works in collections*: Rugby Borough Council, private collections in UK, Europe and USA. *Commissions*: many private. *Official Purchasers*: Warwickshire C.C., Rugby B.C. *Works Reproduced*: various works reproduced as cards, CD covers, book jackets. *Recreations*: walking, reading, music, gardening, meals with friends. *Clubs*; The Tantalus Project; Rugby District Art Society; Rugby Artists' Group. *Address*: 8 Dun Cow Close, Brinklow, Warwickshire CV23 0NZ. *Email*: annapaws@hotmail.co.uk *Website*: www.annbrain.co.uk *Signs work*: 'Anna Phillips', 'AB' or 'PAB'.

PHILLIPS, Francis Douglas, painter and illustrator in water-colour, oil, acrylic, pastel, ink. *b*: Dundee, 19 Dec 1926. *s of*: James Phillips, engineer. *m*: Margaret Parkinson. one *d*. *Educ*: Dundee. *Studied*: Dundee College of Art (J. Milne Purvis). *Exhib*: RSA, RSW, RGI, RI; 'Grampian' T.V. appearances (Feb. and July 1987, Aug 1991) 'Tayside Artist'. Radio Tay broadcast 1995. *Works in collections*: National Trust for Scotland, English Speaking Union, Northern College of Educ., Aberdeenshire Health Board, Glasgow Port Authority; private collections worldwide. *Works Reproduced*: Limited Edn. Prints; illustrated over 100 books; covers on British and French Reader's Digest, The Artist Magazine, International Artist Magazine, Scots Magazine March 2001, Artists and Illustrators Magazine Feb 2007; Over

1160 covers for People's Friend magazine (previously). *Address*: 278 Strathmore Ave., Dundee DD3 6SJ. *Signs work*: "Phillips".

PHILLIPS, John Edward, NDD (Sculpture) 1958, ATC (Lond.) 1961; full-time sculptor and Artist in Residence. *b*: Ealing, London, 28 Jun 1937. *s of*: William Francis Phillips. *m*: Valerie Maughan. one *s*. one *d*. *Educ*: Ealing College. *Studied*: Ealing School of Art (1953-58), Hornsey College of Art (1960-61). *Exhib*: various galleries, art centres, libraries, schools in London, Southern England and France. *Works in collections*: Hillingdon Civic Centre, Uxbridge Library and various schools in the London area, Bucks., Herts. and Oxford. *Address*: Lanhael, Hedgerley Hill, Hedgerley, nr. Slough SL2 3RW. *Signs work*: "John Phillips".

PHILLIPS, Karen E., SGFA; artist in pencil - graphite and colour, pastel, photography and tattoo art; wildlife, portraits and fantasy; Karisma prize for drawing, Born Free Foundation Auctions. *b*: Bromley, Kent, 7 Sep 1966. *Studied*: self taught from life and nature. *Exhib*: SWLA, SGFA, Wildlife Art Soc., and various exhibs. throughout UK. *Works in collections*: private collections in UK, USA, and Australia. *Commissions*: nationally and internationally. *Publications*: Absolute Press. *Clubs*: B.F.P. *Address*: 1 Brambleacres Cl., Sutton, Surrey SM2 6NJ. *Signs work*: 'K E Phillips".

PHILLIPS, Karen Erica, DATEC (1982), BAHons. (1985), MFA (1987); painter in oil, ink, charcoal, acrylic. *b*: Kidderminster, 1 Nov 1962. *d of*: Alan Neville Phillips, NDD, SDAS. *Educ*: Franche Middle School, Kidderminster; Ilfracombe Comprehensive. *Studied*: North Devon College (1979-82, Robin Wiggins), Bristol Polytechnic (1982-85, Ernest Pascoe), Newcastle University (1985-87, Norman Adams). *Exhib*: New Theatre Gallery, Barnstaple (shared exhbn. with father), Zetland Studios, Bristol, Burton A.G., Bideford, Jigsaw, Barnstaple, Long Gallery, Newcastle, RWA, RA, Vicarage Cottage Gallery, North Shields. *Address*: 6 Laburnum Ct., Guidepost, Northumberland. *Signs work*: "K. Phillips".

PHILLIPS, Rex, Cdr. RN (retd); marine and landscape artist. *Medium*: oil and water-colour. *b*: March, Cambs., 19 Jul 1931. *m*: Shirley Chadwick. one *s*. two *d*. *Educ*: Nautical College, Pangbourne. *Exhib*: RSMA, AFAS, and various one-man shows. *Works in collections*: Royal Naval, Royal Marines and Fleet Air Arm Museums, London and provincial galleries; private collections in U.K. and abroad, naval ships and establishments, RNLI and other institutions. *Commissions*: Royal Navy, RNLI, various. *Publications*: various. *Address*: 15 Westbourne Ave., Emsworth, Hants. PO10 7QT. *Email*: rex.phillips7@ntlworld.com *Website*: www.rex-phillips.co.uk *Signs work*: "Rex Phillips".

PHILLIPS, Tom, CBE, RA (1988), RE, MA (Oxon), NDD; artist in oil, water-colour, book productions, television director (A TV Dante, etc.). *b*: London, 25 May 1937. *m*: Fiona Maddocks, 1995. one *s*. one *d*. *Educ*: St. Catherine's, Oxford. *Studied*: Camberwell School of Art (Frank Auerbach). *Exhib*: Royal Academy of Arts, Yale Centre for British Art, Victoria & Albert Museum. *Works in collections*: Tate Gallery, BM, V&A, MoMA, NY, etc. Gallery (Graphics) www.57talfourd.com *Publications*: A Humument (etc). *Clubs*: S.C.C.C., Groucho. *Address*: 57 Talfourd Rd., London SE15 5NN. *Email*: tom@tomphillips.co.uk *Website*: www.tomphillips.co.uk *Signs work*: "Tom Phillips".

PHIPPS, Howard, BA (Hons) Fine Art (1975), RWA (1979), SWE(1985); wood engraver and painter; Three Awards (National Print Exhibition); Contemporary Print Award, RA Summer Exhbn (1985); The Rachel Reckitt Wood Engraving Prize (2008). *b*: Colwyn Bay, 1954. *s of*: Eric and Margaret Phipps. *Studied*: Cheltenham Art College and Brighton Polytechnic. *Exhib*: RWA, SWE, and R.A. Summer Exhbns.; one-man exhbns. include Dorset County Museum (1993, 1998, 2004), Salisbury Museum, Victoria Gallery, Bath (1994, 2001), Cassian de Vere Cole Fine Art, London, '20th Century Wood Engraving' Exeter Museums (1996/7) Cheltenham Art Gallery (1997), Lymington Museum (2001,

2008), Bircham Gallery (2006), Sladers Yard, Bridport (2011). *Works in collections*: British Museum, Ashmolean Museum; Cheltenham, Salisbury, Exeter and Dorset County museums, RWA Bristol. *Publications*: illustrated books for: Bloomsbury, Century, Perdix, Folio Soc., Fleece Press, and Whittington Press who published the artist's own books: Interiors, Further Interiors, and Ebble Valley. *Works Reproduced*: 3 catalogues of work; 'An Engraver's Globe' (S.Brett, 2001). *Address*: Hilfield, Homington Rd., Coombe Bissett, Salisbury SP5 4ND.

PHIPPS, Jemma Louise Rose. *Medium*: oil (mainly portraits), drawing. *b*: Edinburgh, 21 Jul 1977. *d of*: Susan Crawford. *m*: Dr. William Fenton. *Educ*: Sherborne School for Girls, Dorset. *Studied*: Charles Cecil Studios, Florence, Italy (1995-1999). *Exhib*: Summerleaze Gallery, Wiltshire (2003), Mall Galleries (2003, 2006). *Commissions*: HM The Queen, HRH Prince of Wales, Duke of Devonshire, Lord Rothermere, HH Prince Khalid Abdullah, Prince Philip Duke of Edinburgh. *Recreations*: travel, walking my dog, galleries, churches, Italy. *Address*: 22 Rowena Crescent, London SW11 2PT. *Email*: jlrphipps@hotmail.co.uk *Website*: www.jemmaphipps.com *Signs work*: "Jemma Phipps".

PICHÉ, Roland, 1st Class NDD, ARCA, FRBS, Medal for Work of Distinction, RCA; many awards since 1961, most recently: The Julian Trevelyan Award for Prints, 'Originals' (2007); sculptor in resin, fibreglass, stainless steel, stone and bronze; lecturer in sculpture; Principal Lecturer, Canterbury College of Art. *b*: London, 21 Nov 1938. one *s*. two *d*. *Educ*: Romsey College, Embley Park, Hants. *Studied*: Hornsey College of Art (Mr. C. Anderson, ARCA, 1956-60), Royal College of Art (Mr. B. Meadows, ARCA, 1960-64). *Exhib*: Recent Exhibitions: Sculpture in the Garden, Botanic Garden, Leicester (solo, 2006), RA Summer Exhbn (1994-98), 'Originals' Print Exhibition, Mall Galleries (2007), Bridehall Garden Exhibition, Herts (2007), Chichester 'Sculpture in Paradise' (2007), Arts Council Collection Sculpture at McLaren Technology Centre, Working, Surrey (2007-08). *Works in collections*: The Arts Council of Great Britain and Wales, São Paulo Museum, Gothenburg Museum, Sweden, National Gallery of Western Australia, MoMA New York, Aberdeen Scotland, Nene College, Northampton, and many more. *Commissions*: two sculptures for Lovells, Paris (2004). *Publications*: Private View (B. Robertson and T. Armstrong-Jones), Dada, Surrealism (W. S. Rubin). *Address*: Victoria Studios, Tollesbury, Essex CM9 8RG. *Website*: www.rolandpiche.com

PICK, Wayne Erich, National Diploma in Graphic Design (Distinctions: drawing, sculpture, printing). *b*: Johannesburg, South Africa, 6 Dec 1970. *s of*: Wolfgang and Nadalina Pick. *Partner*: Kin Pick (writer). one *d*. *Educ*: Edenvale High School, Johannesburg (1984-88) Bronze medal: Painting (highest distinction). *Studied*: Witwatersrand Technicon, Johannesburg (1989-91). *Represented by*: Start Space, 150 Columbia Road, London E2 7RG. *Exhib*: London, New York, Miami, Chicago. *Works in collections*: Price (Waterhouse) Forbes, Anchor, Presidential Medical, Display Concepts International, University of the Witwatersrand, African Eagle Insurance; Private collections in the UK, USA, South Africa, Germany. *Principal Works*: 'Somebody Else's Boy', 'Getting Some Colour'. *Address*: c/o Eduardo Sant'Anna, Start Space, 150 Columbia Road, London E2 7RG. *Email*: contact@startspace.co.uk *Website*: www.startspace.co.uk *Signs work*: 'Pick'.

PICKEN, Mollie, NDD (1963), ATC (1964); freelance artist in illustration, embroidery and fabric collage. *b*: 13 Oct 1940. *Studied*: Goldsmiths' College School of Art (1959-64) under Constance Howard and Betty Swanwick. *Works in collections*: Education Authorities, Sibford Village Panels (1999 community project). *Publications*: Illustrated books by Constance Howard; collaborated with Christine Bloxham to produce Love and Marriage (Pub. date: Feb. 1990). Art work for Oxfordshire Museum Services, Embroiderers Guild. *Clubs*: S.D.C.; Embroiderers' Guild, Assoc. of Illustrators. *Address*: The Old Post Office, Sibford Gower, Banbury, Oxon. OX15 5RT.

PICKERING, J. Robin H., BA (Hons); First Prize, Thelma Hulbert Gallery Open Exhbn (2005). *Medium*: pastel, oil. *b*: Exeter, 5 Oct 1945. *s of*: Major Jim Pickering, Royal Warks. Regiment. two *s*. *Educ*: St. Lawrence College (Ramsgate), Queen's College (Taunton); Exeter University (1964-68). *Studied*: self-taught. *Exhib*: South West Academy; Pastel Society; AAF; solo shows: Exeter University (1995-2002); Inspires Gallery, Oxford (2004, 2009, 2010); Rostra Gallery (1995, 1999); Troubadour Gallery, Manchester (2007); Rhapsody House Gallery, Tunbridge Wells (2007); mixed/group shows: Art Connection, Eton; Bohemia Galleries; Llewellyn Alexander; Marine House at Beer; No. 5 Gallery; Red Rag Gallery; Art House Gallery, St. Ives. *Works in collections*: University of Exeter permanent collection; private collections in the UK, USA and Australia. *Commissions*: private and business. *Works Reproduced*: signed limited editions: Solomon & Whitehead; Buckingham Fine Art. *Misc*: specialises in Venice, Tuscany, St. Ives. *Address*: 1 Tipton Lodge, Tipton St.John, Sidmouth, Devon EX10 0AW. *Email*: robin_pickering@hotmail.com *Website*: www.robinpickering.co.uk *Signs work*: monogram R with reverse P.

PICKING, John, NDD (1960), DA Edin (1962), ATD (1966); painter and lecturer; Mem. Manchester Academy; ex Senior Lecturer in Fine Art, Manchester Polytechnic. *Studied*: Wigan School of Art, 1956-60 (Governors Medal); Edinburgh College of Art, 1960-63 (Postgrad. Scholarship); Scholarship to Spain 1963-64; Goldsmiths' College, London, 1965-66. *Exhib*: Scottish Gallery, Edinburgh, Colin Jellicoe Gallery, Manchester, Mercury Gallery, London, La Barcaccia galleries in Rome, Naples, Palermo etc.; since 1989 exclusive with Telemarket (Brescia) with galleries in Milan, Rome, Bologna etc.; many group exhibitions including Royal Academy, London and Galleria Borghese, Rome. *Works in collections*: Salford and Manchester Universities, Edinburgh Corp., Palermo Museo Regionale, private collections over the world. Work reflects interest in mixing painting languages, mythology, geology. Since 1979 painting full-time. Studios in Brescia and Sicily. *Address*: c/o Colin Jellicoe Gallery, 82 Portland St., Manchester M1 4QX.

PICKLES, Cherry, BA Hons Painting (First Class), Slade School Higher Diploma; Part-time Senior Lecturer, Cardiff Art School (Howard Gardens); painter. *b*: Bridgend, Wales. *Studied*: Ulster University (BSc Mathematics); Chelsea Art School; Slade School. *Represented by*: Piano Nobile, London; Jill Yakas Gallery, Kifissia, Athens. *Exhib*: recent solo shows: Dylan Thomas Centre, Swansea, Wales (2010); Jill Yakas Gallery, Athens (2009, 2006); Altos de Chavon, Dominican Republic (2009); Piano Nobile, London (2008, 2005); Bay Art, Cardiff (joint show with Carol Robertson, 2007). *Clubs*: Chelsea Arts Club. *Address*: Pembrokeshire. *Email*: cherrypickles *Signs work*: "CHERRY PICKLES" (only signs on reverse of works).

PIDOUX, Janet Anne, SWA (1992), SOFA (1997). *Medium*: pastel. *b*: High Wycombe, Bucks., 2 Sep 1950. *m*: Derek. one *s*. one *d*. *Educ*: Wellesbourne. *Exhib*: SWA, SWLA, PS, SOFA. *Works in collections*: private collections: England, America and Canada. *Works Reproduced*: greetings cards, limited edition prints, Cat World publication, Essential Cattitude book. *Address*: 29 Holloway, Malmesbury, Wiltshire SN16 9BB. *Email*: janetpidoux@mac.com *Website*: www.janepidoux.co.uk *Signs work*: "JANET PIDOUX".

PIER, Catherine Julie, Fellow Royal Society of Arts; BSc (Hons). *Medium*: oils, pastel, watercolour. *b*: Shurdington, 8 Jun 1956. *d of*: John Farrar. *m*: Michael Pier. two *s*. *Studied*: Birmingham University (1974-77). *Represented by*: Artgallery.co.uk, Londonart.co.uk. local art galleries. *Exhib*: one-man shows, Wiltshire. Regular exhibitor in Wiltshire Group exhibitions. Regular invited artist in charity fundraising exhibitions; Edinburgh Macmillan Art Show; Marlborough Summer Exhibition; Art West. *Works in collections*: Sultan of Oman; numerous private collections around the world. *Commissions*: several for Oman Royal Estates; Pear Tree Hotel, Purton; St. Mary's School, Purton; Ridgway Hospital, Wroughton; private commissions including country houses and pet portraits. *Works*

Reproduced: Limited Edition prints of original art works. *Principal Works*: Landscape paintings of the Wiltshire countryside. *Recreations*: walking. *Clubs*: Marlborough Art Society (Exhibition Sec.); Faringdon Art Society (Hon Mem); Highworth Art Society; Purton Artists. *Misc*: regular demonstrator to art groups, and workshop tutor. *Address*: 16 Birdbrook Rd., Kingsdown, Swindon, SN2 7RY. *Email*: catherine-pier@yahoo.co.uk *Website*: www.catherinepier.com *Signs work*: "CATHERINE J. PIER".

PIERCY, Rob, RCA; painter in water-colour and mixed media. *b*: Porthmadog, Wales, 22 Jan 1946. *m*: Enid. three *s*. *Studied*: Bangor under Selwyn Jones. *Exhib*: regularly in Singer and Friedlander/Sunday Times Watercolour; shortlisted in Garrick Milne Art Prize (2000), Wales Artist of the Year 2002. *Address*: Rob Piercy Gallery, Porthmadog, Gwynedd LL49 9BT. *Email*: gallery@robpiercy.com *Website*: www.robpiercy.com *Signs work*: "Rob Piercy".

PIERCY, Sioban, MA, National Dip.; painter, printmaker, lecturer in Fine Art, Galway and Mayo Inst. of Technology. *b*: Rutland, 6 Jan 1957. *m*: Gerard O'Brien. *Studied*: Ravensbourne College of Art, Kent; Crawford College of Art, Cork; Royal College of Art . *Exhib*: International Print exhbns. Norway, Brazil, Germany, Poland, Slovenia, Japan, Spain, Taiwan; numerous including one and two person shows in Ireland and UK. *Works in collections*: private and public: UK, USA and Ireland. *Publications*: 'Profile 4 - Sioban Piercy' (Gandon Edns., 1997). *Clubs*: Artists Assoc. of Ireland. *Address*: Rahard, Athenry, Co. Galway, Eire. *Email*: spgob@eircom.net *Signs work*: "SIOBAN PIERCY".

PIERSE, Simon, RWS (2003); VPRWS (2009-2012); BA (London, 1979); MA (Essex, 1992), PhD (Wales, 2009). *Medium*: painter in oils and watercolour. *b*: 18 Sep 1956. *m*: Alison Hall. one *d*. *Educ*: Haberdashers' Aske's School, Hatcham. *Studied*: Slade School of Fine Art (1975-9); Essex University (1991-2). *Exhib*: RA, RWS, RI; Singer Friedlander/Sunday Times Competition; Barbican Art Centre; Commonwealth Institute; Oxford Gallery; National Library of Wales; ICIA Mumbai; MOMA Wales; Treeline Gallery, Michigan; Taiwan International Watercolor Exhibition. *Works in collections*: Royal Collection, Slade School of Art, London University, La Trobe University Melbourne, Aberystwyth University, Alpine Club, MoMA Wales, Dunmoochin Foundation, Heritage Malta. *Publications*: The Watercolour Expert (Cassell Illustrated, 2004); Watercolour Masters Then and Now (Cassell Illustrated, 2006-with other RWS members); Artists of the Alpine Club (Ernest Press/Alpine Club, 2007); Watercolour Secrets (Bloomsbury, 2014). *Clubs*: Alpine Club. *Address*: Corlan, North Road, Aberystwyth, SY23 2EE. *Email*: srp@aber.ac.uk *Website*: www.simonpierse.co.uk *Signs work*: 'PIERSE'.

PIERSON, Rosalind, landscape miniaturist in water-colour. *b*: Tavistock, Devon, 14 Sep 1954. *d of*: L.G. Pierson, MA. *Educ*: St. Audries School, West Quantoxhead, Som. *Studied*: Ruskin School of Drawing and Fine Art (John Newberry). *Exhib*: RA, Paris Salon, Silver Medal (1978), Gold Medal (1981); RMS Drummond Award (1987), Twice Hon. Mention for Gold Bowl; Bilan de l'Art Contemporain, New York (1982), Silver Medal; Florida Miniature Art Society (1996), Best in Exhibition; Hilliard Soc. of Miniaturists, Co-founder (1981); MAA; MPSG Washington DC; MASF. *Works in collections*: Miniature Art Soc., Florida, Hilliard Soc. of Miniaturists, Wells, Som. *Address*: Brangwyn House, Kilworthy Hill, Tavistock, Devon PL19 0EP. *Signs work*: "R. Pierson".

PIESOWOCKI, Leon, painter and printmaker in oil, water-colour and silkscreen; Prizewinner: International Print Biennale (Bradford, 1968; Krakow, 1972; Copernice & Sapense, 2nd prize and distinction; Fridrikstad/Norway, 1974, distinction); Prix Jean Forey, Salon d'Hiver, Lyon (2009). *b*: Poznan, Poland, 9 Dec 1925. two *d*. *Studied*: painting: Academy in Rome (1946-47), graphics: Sir John Cass College of Art, London (1949-52). *Exhib*: International Biennale of Graphis, Bradford, Krakow Poland, Frechen Germany, Biella Italy, Fredrikstad Norway; Gorner & Millard Gallery, London; Compendium Gallery,

Birmingham; Crest (France) Espace Liberte; Gallery Everarts Paris, Galerie Arrivage 10000 Troyes; Salon de Montelimar (2nd Prize). *Works in collections*: V&A, Nuffield Foundation, National Museum Warsaw, Stedelijk Museum Netherlands, Boymans van Beunigen Netherlands, Arts Council, British Council, Dudley Museum and A.G., Northampton Central Museum, National Museum Poznan. *Publications*: 'Modern Prints' by Pat Gilmour (Studio Vista, 1970); Life & Work of Leon Piesowocki, by Krzysztof Kittel (University of Torun, 2004). *Clubs*: International Prizewinners Club, Krakow, ex-mem. Printmakers Council. *Address*: 65 rue Haute, 26160 Manas, France. *Email*: galerie@leonpiesowocki.net *Website*: www.leonpiesowocki.net

PIG, Christopher Maximillian, BAHons; MA. *Medium*: prints. *b*: Hemel Hempstead, 23 Mar 1965. *Partner*: Pandora. two *s*. one *d*. *Studied*: St Albans (foundation); Exeter (BAHons); Barcelona/Winchester (MA). *Represented by*: Vinsonart, Art at Wharepuke, Ninety Four Columbia Road, E2. *Exhib*: Victoria Gallery, Bath; Bankside Gallery; Freud Museum; Hemingway Art, Oxford; Ian Rastrick Fine Art; High Roller Society; Pie Factory, Margate; The Forge, Shoreditch; Mall Galleries; Royal Western Academy; The Station, Richmond, Yorkshire; Sussex Art Club; Vinson Gallery, Atlanta; Vincent Gallery, Exeter; Arte 21, Cordoba, Spain; British Institute, Barcelona, Spain; Impact 8 Dundee; Douro Bienale. *Works in collections*: Victoria and Albert Museum; Ashmolean Museum; Guang Dong Museum of Art. *Publications*: Ambit Magazine (2007-2012). I Couldn't Paint Golden Angels. Non-toxic Printmaking. *Official Purchasers*: Guang Dong Museum of Art; Ashmolean Museum. *Works Reproduced*. 'Life is Very Sweet Brother', 'Madame Emilia Never Lies', 'Ghost', 'Name Your Price', 'Champagne Charlie'. *Principal Works*: Noble Diggers; Shot; Ghost; Surabaya Johnny; Over London by Rail; Will's Fear of Pipes. *Recreations*: Food, drink, friends, garden. *Clubs*: Society of Wood Engravers, East London Printmakers. *Address*: 2 Sophia Road, London E10 5AX. *Email*: christophermaxpig@yahoo.com *Website*: chrispig.com vinsonart.com *Signs work*: "CM PIG" as monogram.

PIKE, Celia, SWA, HS, SFA; BA; artist in gouache and oil. *b*: Surrey, 24 May 1952. *m*: Richard Morris. two *s*. *Studied*: Central College of Art and Design, St. Martin's School of Art, RA Schools post.grad. *Exhib*: RA, Whitechapel, Mall Galleries. Work in collections internationally. *Works Reproduced*: prints, calendars, greetings cards. *Address*: 51 Estcourt Rd., Woodside, London SE25 4SE. *Signs work*: "CELIA PIKE".

PIKE, Jonathan, BA (1971); First Prize, RWS/Sunday Times Watercolour Competition 2009; painter in water-colour and oil. *b*: Leatherhead, 17 Jan 1949. two *d*. *Studied*: Central School of Art and Design, Falmouth School of Art. *Exhib*: one-man shows: London; mixed shows: throughout England and USA. *Works in collections*: Ashmolean Museum. *Commissions*: Oxford University Press, The Clothworkers' Company, City of London Corporation. *Recreations*: open water swimming. *Address*: 26 Manor Lane Terr., London SE13 5QL. *Email*: jonathan.pike@hotmail.co.uk *Website*: www.jonathanpike.co.uk *Signs work*: "JONATHAN PIKE".

PIKE, Mark Walter, painter in oil, water-colour and acrylic. *b*: Wilts., 22 Sep 1938. *m*: Lesley-Jean. *Exhib*: worldwide. *Works in collections*: private and corporate: worldwide. *Commissions*: best known for development of "Dark 2" dual reality paintings. *Clubs*: N.A.A., Fine Art Guild, N.A.P.A. *Address*: Langley Studio, Rake, Liss, Hants. GU33 7JL. *Signs work*: "MARK PIKE," "PIKE" , "M.P." or "P".

PIKE, Septimus: see WATTS, Michael Gorse.

PIKESLEY, Richard Leslie, NEAC, Dip.AD (1973), ATC (1974); finalist, Hunting Group Prize (1981 and 1989), winner, E.F. Hutton Prize (1987), W.H. Patterson Prize (1988); painter in oil and water-colour. *b*: London, 8 Jan 1951. *s of*: Leonard Leslie Pikesley.

m: Susan Margaret Stone. *Studied*: Harrow School of Art (1969-70), Canterbury College of Art (1970-73). *Exhib*: RA, ROI, RWA, RI; one-man shows include New Grafton Gallery London (1990), Linfield Gallery, Bradford-on-Avon (1986), St. James's Gallery, Bath Festival (1986). *Clubs*: N.E.A.C. *Address*: Middlehill Farm, Marrowbone Lane, Bothenhampton, Bridport, Dorset. *Signs work*: "Richard Pikesley".

PILKINGTON, Ruth Jane, ROI (1976), Hon SWA (1985; painter in oil. *b*: Manchester, 2 May 1924. *d of*: Sir Leonard Behrens. *m*: Eric W. L. Pilkington (decd). one *s*. (decd). one *d*. (decd). *Educ*: Ladybarn House School, Manchester and Maltman's Green, Gerrard's Cross. *Studied*: Johannesburg Technical College (1957-58), Macclesfield CFE (1962-65). *Exhib*: RBA, ROI, Paris Salon, Manchester Academy, etc., other groups exhbns., one-man show in Channel Islands (1976). *Works in collections*: Barreau A.G., Société Jersiaise, Jersey States. *Address*: 97 Rose Mews, L'Hermitage Gardens, St. Peter, Jersey JE3 7HF, C.I. *Email*: vjpilk@gmail.com *Signs work*: "Ruth J. Pilkington".

PILLKAHN, Lorna Mary, Awards: Special Recognition, "Nature 2013 Art Competition", Light Space & Time Gallery. *Medium*: acrylic, inks, pastel. *b*: Puerto La Cruz, Venezuela, 8 Oct 1983. *m*: Carlos Torres. one *d*. *Studied*: London Art College; private classes in Venezuela with Geraldine Gabasa and Zulmira Ortega. *Represented by*: Dot-Art Gallery. *Exhib*: Liverpool Independents Biennial (2014); Madelaina's Art Gallery, Liverpool (2010, 2011); Williamson Art Gallery & Museum (2010); Liverpool Academy of Arts (2008, 2009). *Works in collections*: private collections. *Commissions*: private commissions. *Address*: Flat 14, White Court, 48a Nelson Street, Liverpool L1 5DN. *Email*: thiff832@hotmail.com *Website*: www.kristelpillkahn.co.uk *Signs work*: "Kristel Pillkahn".

PILLOW, Lorna Mary Carol, ARCA; Sir Frank Warner Memorial Medal; freelance textile, exhibition and graphic designer; taught, Croydon and Berkshire Colleges of Art; senior lecturer, West Surrey College of Art and Design (retd). *b*: Cork, Eire. widow of Peter John Palmer. *d of*: W. Farquhar Pillow. one *s*. *Educ*: Wolverhampton and Leeds. *Studied*: Leeds, Hull and the Royal Colleges of Art. *Exhib*: Beverley Art Gallery, Ferens Art Gallery, Guildhall, RWS Galleries, Mall Galleries, London, WSCAD Gallery, Farnham, RSA Travelling Exhibition, Design Centre, London. *Publications*: International Textiles; illustrated Geography of Flowering Plants. *Address*: 33 Havelock Rd., Maidenhead, Berks. SL6 5BJ. *Signs work*: "Lorna Pillow".

PIMLOTT, Geoffrey, RWS (2009); MA Fine Art, Painting (2004); Cert Ed. (1975); Dip AD (1968); Nina Hosali Award (2nd Prize, 1991); Rome Study Bursary (1992); RWS Award (2005). *Medium*: watercolour, acrylic, oil. *b*: Croydon, 1 Jul 1946. *m*: Lorraine. two *d*. *Studied*: Reigate School of Art and Design (1965-8); Wimbledon School of Art (2001-4). *Represented by*: RWS. *Exhib*: solo: Thorndyke Theatre (1972); Garnett College (1975); Arts 38 Gallery (1976-79); Centre Gallery (1981, 1996); Loggia Gallery (1997, 99, 2000); The Bettie Morton Gallery (2000-2002); Bankside Gallery (2005-14); Bar des Arts, Guildford (2012). Opens: The Ludlow Summer Exhibition of Centemporary Art; Canterbury Art (2009, 2010); Marziart International Gallery, Hamburg (2014). *Works in collections*: RWS Diploma Collection; Queen's Collection; UK, USA. *Works Reproduced*: 'Encyclopedias of Techniques (Quarto Books); The Acrylic Artists' Bible (Chartwell Books); Artist Magazine article (Mar 07). *Principal Works*: watercolours on paper as abstract visual compositions. *Misc*: taught in UK 2006, and Papua New Guinea. *Address*: 16 Church Court, Monks Walk, Reigate RH2 0DS. *Website*: http://www.1clikpic.com/geoffreypimlottarws/ *Signs work*: 'PIMLOTT'.

PINCUS, Helen Frances, BA Hons (1982), MFPS (1984), MSDC (1993), Adult Educ. Dip. (1979); fibre and textile artist, designer, embroiderer in fibres, yarns, aluminium mesh, wood, piano wire and pure silk; freelance lecturer, writer and musician. *b*: London, 22 Oct 1938. *Educ*: Haberdashers' Aske's Acton Girls' School; Arts Educational Schools. *Studied*:

Nottingham University; Loughborough College of Art and Design. *Exhib*: numerous one-man shows and mixed exhbns. both in the UK and abroad including Commonwealth Inst. A.G., Cork St. Fine Arts, Leighton House, Savaria Muzeum (Hungary), Galeria Bellas Artes (Spain), University of Surrey, Loggia Gallery, Contemporary Arts (Hong Kong), Hampton Court Palace, Guild Gallery, Bloomsbury Gallery, Vincent A.G. (Australia), Cecilia Colman Gallery, Metro Toronto Convention Centre (Canada), Del Bello A.G. (Canada), Strathclyde University, Barbican Centre, The Rotunda Gallery Hong Kong, dfn Gall., Manhattan NYC, Tidedancers, Easton, Md. USA, Mall Galleries, Sheridan Russell Gallery, London. *Works in collections*: Savaria Muzeum, Hungary, Embroiderers' Guild Collection, Hampton Court Palace, The World Bank, U.S.A. *Clubs*: F.P.S., Soc. of Designer Craftsmen, The Colour Group (G.B.), Embroiderers' Guild, Cornwall Crafts Assoc., New Embroidery Group, Registered with the Crafts Council. *Address*: MoonGates, 9 Castle Heights, Tintagel, N. Cornwall PL34 0ED. *Signs work*: occasionally embroiders initials and year.

PINE, Diana, Assoc. Sussex Artists (1974, Hon. Sec. 1978-83); artist in water-colour, pastel and oil; documentary film director, Crown Film Unit, Wessex, etc. BBC; part-time teacher, Mole Valley AEC and Day Centre. *b*: London. *d of*: Charles F.R. and E.M. Gubbins. *Educ*: Jersey, France, London, PNEU. *Studied*: Regent St. Polytechnic (1936-37) under Clifford Ellis, Chelsea Art School under H.S. Williamson, Central School; apprentice Edward Carrick for Art Direction, Films (-1940), Ernest Savage, Aubrey Sykes (1968-75). *Exhib*: RI, PS, SWA (1976-86), Assoc. Sussex Artists, Horsham, Barns Green, Dorking Group. *Address*: 2 Lodge Close, North Holmwood, Dorking, Surrey RH5 4JU. *Signs work*: "D. Pine".

PINKETT, Neil Anthony, SIAD (Society of Industrial Artists and Designers). *Medium*: oil. *b*: Penzance, 27 Jan 1958. *s of*: Mr. & Mrs. J.B.Pinkett. *m*: divorced. one *d*. *Educ*: as designer and illustrator. *Studied*: Cornwall College. *Exhib*: many galleries including: Great Atlantic Mapworks Gallery, St. Just, Cornwall; Beside the Wave Gallery, Falmouth; Thompson's Gallery, London; Innocent Fine Art, Bristol; Lemon Street Gallery, Truro. *Works in collections*: many. *Commissions*: one of several artists asked to provide work for ocean liner Queen Mary II. *Publications*: small books of collected paintings. *Official Purchasers*: limited edition prints produced through Great Atlantic Mapworks Gallery, St. Just. *Address*: 18 Belgravia Street, Penzance, Cornwall, TR18 2BJ. *Email*: neilpinkett@blue-earth.co.uk

PINKNEY, Richard, NDD, ATD; painter, sculptor and printmaker in oil, acrylic, gouache, intaglio, etc.; teacher, Ipswich, Colchester and St. Martin's Schools of Art, and Kingsway College; Director, Lady Lodge Arts Centre, Peterborough, Open College of the Arts. *b*: 22 Jul 1938. *m*: Judith Foster, ARCA. two *s*. *Educ*: Ipswich School. *Studied*: Ipswich Civic College, School of Art; West of England College of Art, Bristol. Represented by: Peppermint Shed; Trivia Press. *Exhib*: solo shows: AIA Gallery, London; Traverse Theatre, Edinburgh; Paperback Bookshop, Edinburgh; St. Martin's Schools of Art, London; Lady Lodge Arts Centre, Peterborough; Manor School of Ballet, Edinburgh; University College Suffolk; Christchurch Mansion, Ipswich; Sans Walk Gallery, London; Gainsborough's House, Sudbury; group shows: graphics and mailart widely, UK, Europe, USA, Japan, S. America. *Works in collections*: Tate Gallery, V&A, BM G.A.C.,Yale Centre for British Art; public and private collections UK and worldwide. *Publications*: Circle, Tetrad, Trivia & Bad Presses. *Clubs*: Suffolk Group, Ipswich Arts Soc. *Misc*: Gallery: Peppermint Shed, Sproughton, Suffolk. *Address*: 10 The Street, Bramford, Ipswich, Suffolk IP8 4EA. *Email*: noredtram@btinternet.com *Signs work*: "R.P.," "R. Pinkney," "Richard Pinkney".

PINSCHOF, Maria Flora, MA Philosophy and Psychology. *Medium*: oil, watercolour, drawing, mixed media. *b*: Vienna, 2 Apr 1936. *Studied*: St Andrews University; Cubertous, SW France. *Exhib*: SW France in the 1970s/80s; London, Heifer Gallery, Islington (1990s); Meeting House Gallery, Ilminster, Somerset; Collyer Bristow Gallery; The Florence Trust;

Highgate Gallery; Kings Place, London and from her London studio. *Works in collections*: yes. *Address*: 87 Northchurch Road, London N1 3NU. *Email*: pinschof@metronet.co.uk *Website*: pinschofpaintinggallery.com *Signs work*: "Maria Pinschof".

PINSKY, Michael, Doctorate in Fine Art, MA (RCA), BA (Hons) Fine Art (1991); artist in photography, sculpture, site-specific installation. *b*: Scotland, 24 Nov 1967. *Educ*: James Gillespies High School. *Studied*: Manchester Polytechnic (1987-88), Brighton Polytechnic (1988-91, Bill Beach), RCA (1993-95), University of East London (1998-2001). *Exhib*: one-man shows: Collective Gallery Edinburgh, The Warehouse Amsterdam, Open Eye Gallery Liverpool, Viewpoint Gallery Manchester, Quay Arts Centre, IOW, Gatwick Airport, Metropole A.G. Folkestone, Dean Clough A.G. Halifax, Towner A.G. Eastbourne, Photofusion, London, Duncan of Jordanstone A.G. Dundee, Delfina London, Bonnington Gallery Nottingham, Leeds City A.G., Watershed, Cymar, Wiemar, Germany, Economist Gallery, London, East London Gallery; group shows worldwide, including ICA London, Cornerhouse, Manchester, Armory Centre of the Arts, Los Angeles, Contemporary Art Forum, Canada, Rotterdam International Architectural Biennale; CCC, Tours, France; Le Parvis, France. *Commissions*: British Waterways, Nexus, Commissions East, NHS, Arts Council England, Sustrans. *Publications*: Transparent Room, Catalogue, pub. Skelton-Forster ISBN 09525098 14; Pinsky Projections, catalogue (pub. Chelmsford Council ISBN 095185 63 16). *Address*: Studio, 88 Gifford Street, Islington, London N1 0DE *Email*: michael@michaelpinsky.com *Website*: www.michaelpinsky.com

PIPER, Ian Leslie, PWS (1999), EAGMA (2009). *Medium*: oil, watercolour, drawing, prints. *b*: Ipswich, Suffolk, 12 Jun 1941. *s of*: Leslie Charles Piper. *Studied*: Slade School of Art (1988); Norwich School of Art (1989-96). *Represented by*: Mandells Gallery, Elm Hill, Norwich, NR3 1HN. *Exhib*: Royal Academy, Royal West of England Academy, Royal Cambrian Academy, Paisley Art Institute, The Mall Galleries London, Rizet Gallery Kristiansand Norway, Connal Gallery Glasgow, Kranenburg Fine Art Oban, Mandells Gallery Norwich, Mandells Gallery Jersey, The Catto Gallery, London, Wentworth Gallery Sydney, Swann Gallery Woodstock, Thompsons Gallery, Aldeburgh, Swann Gallery, London. *Works in collections*: in Europe, North America, Australia. *Recreations*: sailing. *Address*: 4 Cecil Road, Norwich, NR1 2QL. *Email*: ian@bamboo.co.uk *Signs work*: "IAN PIPER".

PIPER, John S., have painted and exhibited since mid 1960s. Paintings are always in oil and either on canvas or board. Images based on the Cornish Landscape, in particular that of West Penwith. *b*: Salisbury, 27 Aug 1946. *Exhib*: major one-man shows in recent years: St. Ives (Penwith Gallery), London (Northcote Gallery), Antwerp (Capela Arte Falco). *Clubs*: Penwith Society, Newlyn Society of Artists. *Misc*: Mowhay, Trebehor, St.Levan, Penzance TR19 6LY.

PITTAWAY, Neil John, RWS, RE, RAP, G.DIP, MA, BA (Hons). *Medium*: painter and printmaker. *b*: Wakefield, Yorks, 14 Aug 1973. *Studied*: RA Schools (Norman Adams, 1998-2001), University of Bradford (1996-98), Gloucestershire University (1992-96), Huddersfield University (2004). *Exhib*: nationally and internationally including India, USA, Kenya, Taiwan, Malta, Italy, and throughout UK. *Works in collections*: Ashmolean Museum, Royal Collection, V & A, St. Paul's Cathedral, Guild Hall (London), Gloucestershire University, DH Lawrence Museum (Nottingham), Dover Street Arts Club London. *Commissions*: DH Lawrence Museum (painting). *Publications*: drawings for 'London in Poetry and Prose' ed. Anna Adams, Enitharm Press, London, 2003. *Clubs*: hon. artist mem. Dover Street Arts Club, London. *Misc*: featured in Channel 5 TV 'Great Artists' series. *Address*: 1 Glenfields, Netherton, Wakefield, WF4 4SH. *Email*: njpittaway@hotmail.com *Website*: www.njpittaway.co.uk

PLATT, Theo, BA (Hons). *Medium*: oil, watercolour, egg tempera, drawing. *b*: York, 26 Aug 1960. *s of*: Russell Platt, ARCA & Margaret Mackay, ARCA. *m*: Louise. two *s*.

Studied: York College of Art (1979-80), St.Martin's School of Art (1980-83). *Exhib*: National Portrait Gallery, Royal Society of Portrait Painters. One-man shows: Jon Wylder Gallery, Belgravia (1996); Air Gallery, Mayfair (2000, 2004); The Gallery in Cork Street (2008, 2012). *Works in collections*: Stirling Castle, National Hospital of Neurology, Inner Temple, National Portrait Gallery, Scotland. *Commissions*: portraits: HRH The Princess of Wales; HRH The Countess of Wessex; Chief of Defence Staff, Sir Jock Stirrup; James Garfunkel; Sir Jackie Stewart, OBE. *Address*: 62 Grove Road, Harpenden, Hertfordshire AL5 1ES. *Email*: theoplatt@hotmail.com *Website*: www.theoplatt.com *Signs work*: "THEO PLATT".

PLINCKE, J. Richard, RI, AFAS; 1997 St Cuthberts Watercolour Prize, Royal West of England Academy; 2000 AIM International Exhibition Award, Vancouver; 2002 L. Blackstone RI Prize for Most Innovative Work; 2004 Allan Edwards Award 'Painting on the Edge' Exhbn, Federation of Canadian Artists; Painter Stainers Prize, Mall Galleries (2014). *Medium*: watercolour and mixed media; work includes designs for tapestries and stained glass. *b*: Woldingham, Surrey, 29 Oct 1928. *s of*: John Plincke. *m*: Rosemary D. Ball. two *d*. *Educ*: Stowe, Bucks. *Studied*: art: Southampton Inst. of Higher Educ., gaining Higher Cert. (Distinction); architecture: Architectural Assoc. School of Architecture, London. *Represented by*: Linda Blackstone Gallery. *Exhib*: RA, RWA, RI, RSMA; Manor House Gallery, Chipping Norton; Linda Blackstone Gallery, Rickmansworth; Minster Gallery, Winchester; also USA, Canada, Germany, France and Jersey. *Works in collections*: Work included in a number of private collections. *Publications*: 'Watercolour Innovations' by Jackie Simmonds (Harper Collins); 'Painting Workshop' by Doreen Roberts (Harper Collins); 'Pastels Workshop' by Jackie Simmonds (Harper Collins). *Address*: Portway, St. Marybourne, Andover, Hants., SP11 6BL. *Email*: roseplincke@btinternet.com *Signs work*: "R.P".

PLUME, Anita Frances, BA Hons, Fine Art (1993-2000); painter in oil, water-colour, acrylic, pastel. *b*: 11 May 1947. *m*: David. one *d*. *Educ*: Glendale Grammar School, N. London. *Studied*: Falmouth College of Arts. *Exhib*: Mariners Gallery, St. Ives; Norway Gallery, St. Ives Soc. of Artists; Vitreous Contemporary Gallery, Mitchell Hill, Truro, Estuary Estates, Trebetherick. *Clubs*: St. Ives Society of Artists, Porthmeor Group St. Ives. *Misc*: regular attendee of the St. Ives School of Painting. *Address*: 3 Sarah's Meadow, Padstow, Cornwall PL28 8LX. *Email*: dplume9705@aol.com *Signs work*: "Anita Plume" or "AP".

PLUMLEY, Richard Harry, interior designer, painter in oil, water-colour and gouache, early sculpture, stage and theatre design, consultant; co-Director, Personal Choice Interiors. *b*: Harrow, Middx., 5 Mar 1944. *m*: Snezana Nikolic. one *s*. one *d*. *Educ*: Orange Hill, Edgware. *Studied*: Harrow College of Art (1962). *Exhib*: one-man shows: George St. London (1969, 1972), Isle of Man (1994); mixed shows: Windsor (1976), Douglas (1984), artfulhand (2000) Castletown (2006); retrospective exhbn. (1998); Arts & Antique Gallery Permanent Exhibition. *Works in collections*: London, Chicago, Spain, Isle of Man, Gallery artfulhand I.o.Man, private and corporate collections. *Commissions*: Interiors Avon Castle, Ringwood, Creek Peel. *Publications*: Manx Life, Isle of Man Examiner and Courier. *Principal Works*: London River Studies, People & Places, Venice, Set Designs Isle of Man. *Clubs*: Legion Players, Dramatic Personae. *Misc*: Recent return to stage design and painting on large scale. *Address*: Seaforth House, 4 Crown St., Peel, I.O.M. IM5 1AJ. *Email*: plumleyr@hotmail.com *Signs work*: "R.H. Plumley" or "R.P." or monogram with year.

PLUMMER, Brian. *Medium*: acrylic relief panels, watercolour, drawing. *b*: London, 1934. *m*: Sheila. two *d*. *Studied*: Hornsey College of Art, R.A. Schools. *Exhib*: RA Summer Exhibition, Expo Montreal, Barcelona Biennale (prizewinner), Toronto, Abbot Hall, Kendal, Lucy Milton, Galerie van Hulsen, Amsterdam, Rex Irwin Sydney, Sloane St. Gallery, Audun Gallery, Macquarie Galleries, Sydney, Gallerie St. Pierre, Bordeaux, Piano Nobile, London. *Works in collections*: DOE, St. Thomas' Hospital, Power Collection Sydney, Ministero

Cultura Madrid, Mobil Oil Co., Lancaster University, Abbot Hall, Kendal. Armidale NSW. *Commissions*: mural: London Office, Western Asset, Pasadena, USA. *Publications*: Brian Plummer - Landscape & Perception, text by Norbert Lynton & Susan King (University of Westminster). *Clubs*: The Arts Club. *Address*: 89 Palmerston Rd., London N22 8QS. *Signs work*: "BRIAN PLUMMER" on acrylics, hand written on water-colours.

POCKLEY, Jenepher Ruth, BA (Hons) Fine Art; PG Dip Fine Art. *Medium*: oil. *b*: Felsted, Essex, 26 Mar 1972. *d of*: Tom and Jane Pockley. *m*: Nicholas Archer. one *s*. one *d*. *Educ*: Chelsford County High School for Girls. *Studied*: Kent Institute of Art and Design at Canterbury; RA Schools. *Represented by*: Sarah Myerscough Fine Art, London. *Exhib*: Royal Academy of Arts; Sarah Myerscough Fine Art; Gibsone Jessop Gallery, Toronto, Canada. *Commissions*: various private commissions, London, Scotland and UK. *Publications*: article in 'The Independent'. *Address*: High Meadow, Friarshill, Guestling, E.Sussex TN35 4EP. *Email*: jennypockley@hotmail.com *Signs work*: 'J.Pockley'.

POCOCK, Heather, BA (Hons) (1976), ATC (1978). *Medium*: oil, acrylic, mixed media. *b*: London, 5 May 1954. *Studied*: St. Albans and Sheffield Colleges of Art (1972-76), University of London (1977-78), British Council Travelling Bursary Italy (1978). *Represented by*: Francis Kyle Gallery (since 1994). *Exhib*: Malcolm Innes Gallery, Edinburgh; Royal Glasgow Institute; Royal Scottish Academy, Edinburgh; Royal Academy, London; Francis Kyle Gallery, London - group shows, and one person shows. *Works in collections*: private and corporate. *Publications*: Arts Review 1999 (Art & Artists in Argyll and Bute). *Address*: c/o Francis Kyle Gallery, 9 Maddox Street, London W1S 2QE. *Email*: info@franciskylegallery.com *Website*: www.franciskylegallery.com *Signs work*: "Heather Pocock" (on back of painting).

PODBERY, Neil, BA Hons, Illustration. *Medium*: oil, drawing. *b*: Oxford, 12 Dec 1979. *s of*: Roger & Jan Podbery. *m*: Sarah Podbery. two *s*. *Educ*: Buckland Primary C of E School, Cokethorpe School. *Studied*: Oxford Brookes University, Swindon College/Cranfield University. *Represented by*: Horton's. *Exhib*: Retromobile, Paris; Amelia Island Concour d'Elegance USA; Techao Classica Essen; Goodwood Festival of Speed; Pebble Beach "Concourse D'Elegance". *Works in collections*: throughout UK, Europe and USA. *Clubs*: member of the Guild of Railway Artists. *Address*: Gable Cottage, 22 High Street, Meyseyhampton, Cirencester, Gloucestershire, GL7 5JT. *Email*: neilpodbery@yahoo.co.uk *Website*: www.neilpodberyfineart.co.uk *Signs work*: "Neil Podbery".

PODESTA, Anthony Andrew, *Medium*: pastel, watercolour, oil. *b*: Leek, Staffordshire, 31 Mar 1936. two *s*. *Educ*: Leek High School. *Exhib*: With Staffordshire Artists for 18 years; Annual exhibition, The Rudyard Activity Centre (8 solo exhibitions). *Work in collections*: The Potteries Federation; The MEB (now NPower). *Commissions*: The Potteries Federation in Stoke-on-Trent; The MEB (now NPower). *Principal Works*: Landscapes in Scotland, Wales and local; portriats. *Recreations*: reading, gardening. *Address*: The Laurels, Reacliffe Road, Rudyard, Nr. Leek, Staffs ST13 8RS. *Email*: aapodesta@googlemail.com *Website*: https://sites.google.com/site/aapodesta/ *Signs work*: "A Podesta" with a flourish around A.

POLAINE, Peter David, NDD, FCSD, FRSA. *Medium*: painter in oil, printmaker and stained glass artist. *b*: London, 30 Apr 1937. *m*: Betty. two *s*. *Educ*: Harlow College. *Studied*: Walthamstow School of Art (1954-1959). *Represented by*: Sudbourne Park Printmakers (member). *Exhib*: RA, and other London and East Anglian galleries. *Commissions*: private worldwide. *Works Reproduced*: Printmaking Today. *Address*: Gardener's Cottage, Broke Hall Park, Nacton, Suffolk IP10 0ET. *Email*: peter@polaine.com *Website*: www.peterpolaine.com *Signs work*: "PETER POLAINE" or monogram or both.

POLLARD, Brian, *Medium*: Acrylic. *b*: Walsall, 25 Aug 1946. *m*: Jane. two *s*. *Studied*: Studied medicine at Birmingham University. Qualified 1977. *Exhib*: Barbican Gallery,

Plymouth; Mid-Cornwall and Newlyn Galleries; Greenwich Theatre Gallery, London; Colonnade, London; The Old School Gallery, Bleddfa, Wales; Delamore House, Debon; Kaya Gallery, Plymouth. *Works in collections*: 29th Commando Royal Artillery, The Citadel, Plymouth. *Commissions*: The National Trust; RNLI; The Royal Navy; Plymouth City Council; South Hams Council; 29th Commando Regiment, Royal Artillery. *Publications*: The Association of British Naive Artists. *Works Reproduced*: Worldwide publication of over thirty images by London publishers, Rosenstiels. *Misc*: Self taught member of the Association of British Naive Artists. *Address*: 5 Kingsland Gardens Cl, Mannamead, Plymouth PL3 5NR. *Email*: brian.pollard46@btinternet.com *Website*: www.brianpollard.co.uk *Signs work*: "Pollard".

POLLARD, Michael Vincent, DipAD (1970), SBA (1988); freelance artist, designer and model maker in oils, acrylics, water-colour, gouache and crayon; visiting tutor to junior and secondary schools. *b*: Cambridge, 6 May 1948. *s of*: Vincent Samuel Pollard. *Educ*: Harpur Secondary School, Bedford. *Studied*: Luton School of Art (1966-70). *Exhib*: Westminster Gallery, London, 'Flora', Sevenoaks, Rackhams, Birmingham and New York. Work in private collections worldwide. *Commissions*: over 200 postage stamps designed for British Crown colonies and dependencies, worldwide. *Publications*: books illustrated: Fairytales and romance. *Works Reproduced*: greetings cards, jigsaw puzzles and calendars. *Recreations*: gardening. *Clubs*: Hasselblad Forum. *Misc*: Architectural models, sculpture, photography. *Address*: Tara House, Dychurch Lane, Bozeat, Northants. NN29 7JP. *Signs work*: 'Michael Pollard' or 'M.V.P'.

POLLOCK, Sir George F., Bt., MA (Cantab), Hon. FRPS, , Hon. PAGB, FRSA, EFIAP, MPAGB; artist-photographer, a-v producer; past President, Royal Photographic Society. *b*: Paris, 13 Aug 1928. *s of*: Sir John Pollock, Bt., Officer Legion of Honour (etc.). one *s*. two *d*. *Educ*: Eton College and Trinity College, Cambridge. *Exhib*: numerous. *Works in collections*: British Council, RPS, National Gallery of Victoria, Musée de Photographie, Bièvres, Towner A.G., Eastbourne, Texas University, University of Surrey, National Media Museum. *Commissions*: murals for Lloyds Bank, British Petroleum, Metals Research. *Publications*: numerous articles on photography; "The Limits of Photography" - Prizewining essay. *Works Reproduced*: Focal Encyclopedia of Photography; Concise History of Photography by H & A Gernsheim. *Address*: 83 Minster Way, Bath BA2 6RL. *Website*: www.georgepollock.co.uk *Signs work*: "George F. Pollock".

POMEROY-MATTHEWS, Barbara, awarded place at Birmingham College of Art (1940s). *Medium*: watercolour, drawing. *b*: Warwickshire, 21 Mar 1930. *m*: Vincent (decd). one *s*. *Educ*: private, Warwickshire and Oxfordshire. *Studied*: Birmingham College of Art (1945-47). *Exhib*: mainly West Country (45 years). *Works in collections*: private. *Commissions*: private commissions - Holland, Germany, USA, Canada, Columbia, England, etc. *Principal Works*: Birds, butterflies, waterfowl, flora, or the Moor. *Clubs*: Tavistock Group of Artists (in existence for 52 years). *Misc*: Resided in Cornwall for 40 years, and since 1988 has lived on Dartmoor. *Address*: 'Horndon Cottage', Horndon, Peter Tavy, Tavistock, Devon PL19 9RQ. *Signs work*: "Barbara Pomeroy-Matthews".

PONSONBY, Caroline Christine, BA Hons Humanities. *Medium*: oil painter. *b*: Scarborough, 29 Nov 1953. *d of*: Brigadier W.M.Ponsonby. *m*: John F. Molony. two *d*. *Educ*: Sherborne School for Girls, Dorset. *Studied*: Thames Polytechnic, Woolwich (1974-76); self-taught. *Exhib*: Eastern Open (2000); RBA (2000, 2010); W.H. Patterson (2001-03); Albemarle Gallery (2001); Eaton Gallery (2003-05); Llewellyn Alexander (2004-08, 2009, 2011); NEAC (2006, 2007, 2008); Fairfax Gallery, Burnham Market (2007-2011); Discerning Eye (2008, 2009, 2010, 2013); Chelsea Art Society (2010, 2011); Frost & Reed (2011); Downhill Only Ski Club, Wengen, Switzerland (2013); Not the Royal Academy, llewellyn Alexander (2014). *Works in collections*: Korn Ferry International; The Late Lord

Alexander of Weedon; Anthony Mould Esq. *Recreations*: tennis, amateur dramatics, good conversation, skiing, scrabble, Tai Chi. *Address*: Clematis Cottage, 30 St.Ann's Lane, Godmanchester, Huntingdon, PE29 2TE. *Email*: caroline.molony@talk21.com *Signs work*: "Caroline Ponsonby".

POOK, Graham Arthur, *Medium*: oil. *b*: Gravesend, 28 Oct 1952. one *d*. *Educ*: Gravesend School for Boys. *Studied*: self-taught. *Exhib*: Leith Gallery, Edinburgh; EA Studios, Broughty Ferry; Boath House, Auldearn; Still Life Gallery, Aberlour; Mall Galleries, London; The Worshipful Company of Painter-Stainers, London; Francis Iles, Rochester; Rendezvous Gallery, Aberdeen; Tore Gallery, Inverness. *Works in collections*: The Royal Collection; numerous private. *Address*: Garden Cottage, Arndilly House, Craigellachie, Banffshire AB38 9QS. *Email*: grahampook@btinternet.com *Website*: grahampook.co.uk *Signs work*: "POOK".

POOLE, David James, RP (1969), ARCA; artist; President, Royal Soc. of Portrait Painters (1983-91); Senior lecturer in Painting and Drawing, Wimbledon School of Art (1962-77). *b*: 5 Jun 1931. *s of*: Thomas Herbert Poole. *m*: Iris Mary Toomer. three *s*. *Educ*: Stoneleigh Secondary School. *Studied*: Wimbledon School of Art, RCA. *Exhib*: one-man shows: Zurich and London. Portraits include: HM The Queen, HRH The Duke of Edinburgh, HM The Queen Mother, HRH Prince Charles, HRH Princess Anne, HRH Princess Margaret, Earl Mountbatten of Burma, The Duke of Kent Sir Alan Lascelles, Sir Michael Adeane, Sir Martin Charteris, Sir Philip Moore, Sir William Heseltine, Sir Robert Fellowes, Sir Robert Janvrin; also distinguished members of govt., industry, commerce, medicine, the academic and legal professions. *Works in collections*: HM The Queen and HRH The Duke of Edinburgh; and in Australia, S. Africa, Bermuda, France, W. Germany, Switzerland, Saudi Arabia, USA. *Address*: Trinity Flint Barn, Weston Lane, Weston, Petersfield, Hants. GU32 3NN.

POOLE, Greg, BSc Zoology (1983); Mem. SWLA; artist/illustrator in printmaking and collage. *b*: Bristol, 26 Oct 1960. *Studied*: Foundation Course, Manchester Polytechnic (1989-90). *Exhib*: many mixed exhbns., annually with SWLA. *Works in collections*: Nature in Art Museums, Glos. Many private collections. *Publications*: At present working on a book for Editions Gallimard based on the Cote d'Azur. *Works Reproduced*: Book covers for Blackwells, CUP and Reed International, many magazine illustrations. *Misc*: Participant in Artists for Nature Foundation Projects on the Loire Estuary, France, and Bandavgarh, India. Recent Residences in France, Ireland and Barbados. *Address*: 1 Eagle Tap, Eagle Lane, Kingscliffe, nr. Peterborough PE8 6XD. *Email*: greg.poole@virgin.net *Website*: http://homepage.virgin.net/greg.poole

POOLE, Jonathan, City & Guilds Diploma (Sculpture); exhibition organiser and designer; sculptor; wildlife artist. After leaving school, organised a Tour of the work of Royal Academicians. Organised exhibitions for numerous artists and musicians including Ronnie Wood, John Lennon, John Illsley (Dire Straits), Miles Davis, Judy Collings, Anthony Hopkins, Tico Torres (Bon Jovi) and others. Organised a World Tour of Contemporary Russian Sculpture in the early 90s. *b*: London, 20 Sep 1947. *s of*: Rozelle & Harold Poole. *m*: Virginia. two *s*. one *d*. *Educ*: Kings School, Ely. *Studied*: Hertford College of Design; City and Guilds of London Art School (Sculpture Degree). Worked in the studio of Madame Tussauds. Studio Assistant to James Butler RA, and Robert Mitchell. *Represented by*: Galleries ini New York, London, Woodstock and Compton Cassey. *Exhib*: Royal Academy, London; Majlis Gallery, Dubai; Numerous Galleries in the UK, USA, Rissia, Europe, Capw Town, Singapore and The Middle East. *Works in collections*: many private collections worldwide. *Commissions*: Commissioned by the Dubai Royal Family to paint their birds of prey. Many portrait commissions of dogs and humans. *Publications*: Four works illustrated in the "Tusk Foundation" book. *Recreations*: fishing, shooting. *Clubs*: Sloane Club, London.

Misc: Brought up in Rhodesia until the age of thirteen. Working full-time as an artist in Glos. *Address*: Compton Cassey House, nr. Withington, Cheltenham, Glos. GL54 4DE. *Email*: jonathan@jonathanpoole.demon.co.uk *Website*: www.jonathanpoole.co.uk *Signs work*: 'Jonathan Poole'.

POOLEY, Vanessa, FRBS; BA Hons; PG Dip. *Medium*: sculpture. *b*: Norwich, 7 May 1958. *d of*: Mr W.B. & E.M. Pooley. *m*: Tobias Arnup. two *s*. *Studied*: Norwich School of Art (1977/8, 1978/81); City and Guilds of London Art School (1982/3). *Represented by*: Bircham Contemporary Artists. *Exhib*: RA Summer Show (2002); Bircham Contemporary Art, Norfolk (1999, 2002, 2004); Chelsea Flower Show (2004); Thompsons Gallery, London (2002); Keele Gallery, Keele University (2001); ART '92, '94, '95, '97, '98, 2001; City AG, London (2000); Aldeburgh Festival (1997); The Castle Art Show, Norwich (1995); solo show: The Orangery, Holland Park, London (1994); RCA (1993); Beaux Arts Gallery, Bath; Discerning Eye; Sotheby's; Art Fair, Ghent, Belgium; and many others in UK. *Works Reproduced*: various books. *Recreations*: masters swimming. *Address*: 9 The Crescent, Norwich, Norfolk, NR2 1SA. *Email*: vanessapooley@onetel.com *Website*: www.vanessapooley.com *Signs work*: 'VMP'.

POPE, Annabel, *Medium*: watercolour, drawing. *b*: Norfolk, 25 Oct 1974. *Studied*: Cambridge Arts Tutorial, Heatherley, London, Oxford Brookes University (BSc). *Represented by*: Pattersons Gallery, Cricket Fine Art, The Sloane Club, Iona House Gallery. *Exhib*: Oakham Gallery, Ackerman & Johnson, Air Gallery, Christie's St. James, Patrick Mauros, Studio Gallery, Lavender Hill, Battersea, London. *Commissions*: Please see website. *Address*: 29 Sussex Street, London SW1V 4RN. *Email*: art@annabelpope.com *Website*: www.annabelpope.com *Signs work*: "Annabel Pope".

PORTELLI, Guy Anthony, FRBS, RBA; UBS Sculpture Award; Scott, Goodman, Harris Award; Elizabeth Frink School Award; sculptor; specialises in large corporate commissions. *Medium*: bronze, mosaic, stainless steel and glass. *b*: Durban, S. Africa, 13 Jun 1957. one *d*. *Educ*: Hugh Christie School, Tonbridge. *Studied*: Medway College of Art (1974-1978). *Represented by*: Robert Bowman Modern, Bill Clarke, Manchester. *Exhib*: various in UK, London, Manchester, Edinburgh, Guernsey & USA. *Works in collections*: Porsche Collection, Paris, Ringo Starr. *Commissions*: Sainsburys, Eagle Gates, Guernsey, Commomwealth Inst., London Pavillion, Piccadilly, Trafford Park, Manchester, Rowland Hill Monument. *Publications*: 'Modern British Sculpture'. *Address*: The Studio, 125 St. Mary's Rd., Tonbridge, Kent TN9 2NL. *Email*: guyportelli@hotmail.com *Website*: www.portelli.sculptor.co.uk *Signs work*: "Guy Portelli" and date.

PORTSMOUTH, Delia, painter of landscapes, portraits, flowers, birds, wildlife in oils. *b*: Mottram, Ches., 6 Aug 1939. *d of*: Edward Ford, farmer. *m*: A.C. Portsmouth. four *d*. *Educ*: Hyde and Bala Grammar Schools. *Studied*: self taught. *Exhib*: ROI, Hesketh Hubbard, Flower Painters' Summer Salon; one-man shows: Chester, Lampeter, Bala, Brantwood, St. Davids, Usher Gallery, Lincoln, Public Gallery, Oldham. *Works in collections*: National Library of Wales, National Museum of Wales, Liverpool Corp. and numerous private collections worldwide. *Clubs*: founder member, Modern Millais Association. *Address*: 14 Saffron Park, Kingsbridge, Devon TQ7 1RL. *Signs work*: "Delia Portsmouth".

PORWOL, Steven, painter in watercolour on paper; specializes in natural history painting, predominantly birds. *b*: Ilford, London, 14 Feb 1973. *Educ*: Ilford County High Grammar School. *Studied*: self taught. *Represented by*: Jonathan Cooper, Park Walker Gallery: jonathancooper.co.uk. *Exhib*: Singer and Friedlander Watercolour Exhib., Art and Antiques Fair, Olympia (2001-2003), Park Walk Gallery (2001-2003), Natural History Museum, Vienna (2001). *Commissions*: numerous in UK and Europe. *Email*: mail@stevenporwol.co.uk *Website*: www.stevenporwol.co.uk *Signs work*: "Steven Porwol" or "S.Porwol".

POTTER, David. *Medium*: oil, pastel, acrylic, collage. *b*: Hillingdon, 28 Jun 1939. *s of*: F S & G O Potter. three *d*. *Educ*: St. Clement Danes Grammar School, London. *Studied*: bibliography and librarianship, Ealing. *Exhib*: Alpha Gallery, Swanage; Bettles Gallery, Ringwood; Blue Lias Gallery, Lyme Regis; Allsop Gallery, Bridport; John Davies Gallery, Stow-on-the-Wold. *Works in collections*: UK, Europe, USA. *Recreations*: painting. *Address*: 37 Gallwey Road, Weymouth, Dorset, DT4 9AJ. *Email*: davidpotter@no46.fslife.co.uk

POTTER, George, RHA (2006); BFA Rhode Island School of Design (1962); Fulbright Fellowship, Berlin (1967-68) and many other awards. *Medium*: oil, drawing. *b*: Washington DC, USA, 28 Jan 1941. *s of*: George Potter Sr. *Studied*: Rhode Island School of Design; Hochschule fur Bildende Kunst, Berlin (1968-71). *Represented by*: Taylor Galleries, 16 Kildare Street, Dublin 2. *Exhib*: solo shows at Taylor Galleries since 1982; Project Arts Centre (1973), Tom Caldwell Gallery, Dublin (1976, 78); United Arts Club, Dublin (1974, 75, 77, 79, 80, 81); many group shows including RHA Annual since 1990, United Arts Club, Dublin (1975-83); across Ireland, in USA and Germany. *Works in collections*: in Ireland, England, France, Italy, Germany, Philippines, USA; some Irish collections include: Trinity College Dublin, Bank of Ireland Dublin, St.Patrick's Hospital Dublin, GPA Group Shannon, Imperial Hotel Cork, Nissan (Ireland). *Commissions*: many commissioned portraits over the years. *Publications*: The Irish Times (reviews and profiles since 1973); The Sunday Independent (numerous profiles). *Official Purchasers*: Bank of Ireland, Trinity College, Jury's Hotel Group, St. Patricks Hospital, GPA Group, Shannon, Nissan (Ireland), Office of Public Works. *Works Reproduced*: Art in Ireland (1982). *Recreations*: walking, antiques, cooking. *Clubs*: United Arts Club. *Misc*: moved to Dublin (1971); part-time lecturer NCAD (1975-2000); served in US Army Germany (1963-65). *Address*: 2 Clarinda Manor, Clarinda Park East, Dun Laoghaire, Co.Dublin Ireland. *Signs work*: 'Potter'.

POTTINGER, Frank DA Sculpture (1963), RSA (1991); sculptor in bronze, stone, wood, clay. *b*: Edinburgh, 1 Oct 1932. *s of*: William Pottinger, stone mason. *m*: Dr. Norah Smith, 1991. one *s*-s. two *s*-d. *Educ*: Boroughmuir School. *Studied*: Edinburgh College of Art (1958-63). *Exhib*: Richard Demarco Gallery, Yorkshire Sculpture Park, Landmark Scottish Sculpture Trust, Camden Arts Centre, Pier Arts Centre Orkney, Kildrummy Castle, S.S.W. Open, Royal Scottish Academy. *Works in collections*: Heriot Watt University, Hunterian Museum, IBM, Scottish Development Agency, Leeds Educ. Authority, Scottish Arts Council, Paisley Museum; Europos Parkas, Lithuania; private collections, UK and abroad. *Commissions*: LASMO, The Woodland Trust, Motherwell District Council, Ellon Development, Aberdeenshire, Dundee University, Royal Mail, Western Isles Health Board, Scottish Parliament. *Clubs*: Scottish Arts Club. *Address*: 30/5 Elbe St., Edinburgh EH6 7HW.

POTTS, David, FBSP (1999), NAPA, winner of British Society of Painters 'Old Masters Award' (2001). *Medium*: oil, acrylic. *b*: Maltby, South Yorkshire, 13 Apr 1945. *s of*: John Reginal Potts. *m*: Patricia. two *s*. *Educ*: Rotherham, South Yorks. *Studied*: self-taught. *Exhib*: widely throughout Midlands and North of England, and with Societies inc. Royal Birmingham Society of Artists (RBSA). *Works in collections*: work in many private collections in UK, Europe and Australasia. *Clubs*: British Society of Painters (fellow), NAPA (full member). *Address*: 20 Packington Road, Doncaster, S Yorks, DN4 6TZ. *Email*: pottshq@talktalk.net *Website*: www.davidpottspaintings.com *Signs work*: "Potts" (or monogram "DP" for works on paper).

POTTS, Ian N., NDD, RAS Cert.; artist in water-colour; retd. Dept. Head, School of Art, University of Brighton. *b*: 11 Apr 1936. *m*: Helen B. Bewick. one *s*. two *d*. *Studied*: Sunderland College of Art (1956-59), RA Schools (1959-63, H. Rushbury). *Exhib*: Barbican London, RA Summer Show, Brighton Museum, Amalgam Art London, Coombes Gallery London, SCR Bath, Centro Modigliani, Florence. *Works in collections*: V&A, Arts Council,

British Council, Towner A.G. Eastbourne, University of Kent, The Aldrich Collection at the University of Brighton. *Commissions*: Brighton Festival, Daystar, Contemporary Sundials, Windsor Castle, St. George's House. *Publications*: Water-colours and Landscapes (Bridgewater Press). *Works Reproduced*: Royal Academy Summer Exhibition. *Address*: 12 Southdown Ave., Lewes, Sussex BN7 1EL.

POTTS, Kenneth Arthur, ARBS; Dip AD, BA; BoWS. *Medium*: sculptor in bronze and ceramic. *b*: Macclesfield, 16 Mar 1949. *s of*: Reginald Potts. one *s*. one *d*. *Studied*: Stafford College of Art (1969), Stoke-on-Trent College of Art (1972). *Exhib*: RA Summer Show, Festival Hall, Sladmore Gallery, Art Expo NY, RBS West of England Academy, Tokyo, Hakone Sculpture Park and Museum, Japan, Sausmarez Manor, Guernsey etc. *Works in collections*: Dyson Perrins Museum, Raphael Djanogly Trust. *Commissions*: National Memorial Sir Edward Elgar, Worcester; A.E. Housman, bronze statue, Bromsgrove; R J Mitchell Memorial, Longton, Stoke on Trent; Cassidy Memorial, Tamside Metropolitan Borough; The Craftsman, Poole; Bull Entry & Worcester Black Pear, Crown Estate, Worcester; Sir Douglas Bader Memorial, bronze statue, Goodwood airfield; National Destroyer Memorial, Chatham Historic Dockyard; Battle of Worcester Memorial, Worcester (in progress). *Address*: Langholme House, 50 Albert Road North, Malvern, Worcestershire WR14 2TL. *Email*: langholme@tiscali.co.uk *Signs work*: "Kenneth Potts".

POUNTNEY, Monica, (née Brailey), SEIFAS Cup for Oils (1976); freelance artist in oil, water-colour, acrylic, pastel, etc. *b*: London. *m*: D. H. Pountney. one *s*. *Studied*: Hammersmith School of Arts and Crafts (Carel Weight and Ruskin Spear), Central School (John Farleigh). *Exhib*: Federation of British Artists, UA, SWA, RI, NS, and various mixed exhbns. *Works in collections*: landscapes in London, Moscow and USA. *Commissions*: various. *Principal Works*: books illustrated for Heinemann, Blackie and others. *Clubs*: U.A., L.A.G., Essex A.C. *Address*: 3 Thickwood House, Bedford Rd., S. Woodford, London E18 2AH. *Signs work*: "M.P." or full name.

POUNTNEY, Robert, BA Fine Art (Painting). *Medium*: drawing. *b*: Nottingham, 11 Feb 1952. *m*: widower. one *s*. one *d*. *Studied*: Nottingham Trent University (Foundation Art & Design, 1970-71); Loughborough School of Art & Design (1971-74). *Exhib*: Solo exhibitions include: The Dorset County Museum (2000); Salisbury & South Wiltshire Museum (2004); Macclesfield Silk Museum (2006); Study of Modern Art, Poole (2006); Wiltshire Museum, Devizes (2007). "Three Artists" (David Gunning, David Inshaw, Rob Pountney), Wiltshire Museum, Devizes (2011), Salisbury & South Wiltshire Museum (2012), The Dorset County Museum (2012). *Works in collections*: Yorkshire Arts Association, Bedfordshire Education Authority, The Dorset County Museum, Wiltshire Museum, Devizes. *Commissions*: numerous private drawing commissions. *Publications*: The Thomas Hardy Society Journal (Feb 2001, Oct 2003, Autumn 2008, Summer 2012). *Principal Works*: drawings. *Clubs*: Member of the Thomas Hardy Society. *Address*: 31 Maythorn Close, West Bridgford, Nottingham NG2 7TE. *Email*: robpountney@hotmail.co.uk *Signs work*: "Rob Pountney".

POVER, Lesley, RBA; sculptor (largely figurative and portraiture) in bronze, plaster, cement. *b*: Plymouth, 1 Apr 1950. two *s*. *Educ*: Devonport High, St. John's, Singapore. *Studied*: New College of Speech and Drama. *Exhib*: numerous provincial galleries, Woodlands, RA , Mall Galleries, Islington Art Fair. *Works in collections*: life-sized bronze Lambeth Palace; Pegasus & Boy, Mervyn Peake Library, Eltham College; various private collections. *Commissions*: Eric Liddell Sports Centre, Edinburgh University; Life-sized statue of Nelson sited on the Thames at Greenwich. *Recreations*: dance. *Address*: 34 Guibal Road, Lee, London SE12 9LX. *Email*: lesley.pover@gmail.com. *Signs work*: "L. Pover" or "Pover".

POVEY, Edward, B.Ed (1978), RCA. *Medium*: artist in oil, and bronze. *b*: London, 1 May 1951. *s of*: Edward Povey. two *s*. *Educ*: Crown Woods Comprehensive School, Eltham. *Studied*: Eastbourne College of Art and Design (1972-73), University of Wales (1974-78, Selwyn Jones). *Represented by*: Hanson Gallery, New Orleans; Kooywood Gallery, Cardiff. *Exhib*: Martin Tinney Gallery, Cardiff; Jan de Maere Galleries, Brussels; Gallery Gerard, The Hague; Midtown Payson Galleries, N.Y.; Hanson Gallery, New Orleans and San Francisco. *Works in collections*: University of Wales at Bangor, Laguna Gloria Museum in Austin, Texas, The National Library of Wales, Aberystwyth, Wales; National Museum of Wales, Cardiff, Wales; Glynn Vivien Art Museum, Swansea, Wales; J.P.Morgan Inc., New York; Goldman Sachs, London; Anglesey Museum of Art Collection, Wales; Mastercard Europe, Belgium; Procter and Gamble, Venezuela, 3M Art Collection, USA. *Publications*: chapters and photographs in: Painting The Town by Cooper and Sargent (Phaidon Press 1979), Wales on Canvas by Hywel Harries (Lolfa Press 1983), Gwynedd by Ian Skidmore (Robert Hale 1987), The University of Wales (1839-1939) by J. Gwynn Williams (University of Wales Press 1997). *Address*: The Studio, Meirion Rd., Bangor, Gwynedd LL5 2BY. *Email*: artist@edwardpovey.com *Website*: www.edwardpovey.com *Signs work*: "Edward Povey" or "Povey".

POWELL, Adela Margaret, DipAD. *Medium*: ceramics. *b*: Birkenhead, 14 Aug 1945. *m*: John. three *s*. *Studied*: Liverpool University (1963-65); College of Art & Design, Plymouth (1975-77). *Represented by*: Badcocks Gallery, Penzance; Artmill Gallery, Plymouth. *Exhib*: Extensively in the South West, inc. Serenade Arts, Plymouth; Ceramica, An International Festival of Clay, St Ives International; Badcocks, Newlyn; Cornwall Crafts Association, Trelowarren and Art in the Garden Trelissick; Cornwall Ceramics and Glass Group Exhibitions; Delamore Arts, Devon; Contemporary Crafts, Bovey Tracy; Artmill Gallery, Plymouth; Affordable Art Fairs (2001-2014) Battersea and Hammersmith (Courtesy of Badcocks Gallery); Art in Clay, Hatfield. 2014. *Works in collections*: Trewithen House, Truro, and private collections. *Principal Works*: Large ceramic vessels (Coastline series); torsos/metamorphic figures. *Recreations*: Gardening, walking, drawing/painting. *Clubs*: Cornwall Ceramics; Glass Group. *Address*: Harewood House West, Harewood, Calstock, Cornwall PL18 9SQ. *Email*: adelapowellceramics@yahoo.co.uk *Website*: www.adelapowell.co.uk *Signs work*: "A P" (letters overlaid).

POWELL, Andy, BA Hons; IFPO, EMCD, Fellow of Agora Gallery, Broadway, New York, founder of Artists Ratpac and Ratpac TV. *Medium*: tempera, oil, watercolour, drawing, prints, mixed media; also works in cast metals for sculpture and one-off jewellery. *b*: Ipswich, Suffolk, 1 Nov 1957. *s of*: George Andrew Shove & Reneé Abrahams. *Educ*: Alton Park School, Clacton-on-Sea; Colbains High, Clacton-on-Sea. *Studied*: Ipswich College of Art (1995) as mature student, but painting and exhibiting for 40 years. BA Hons (London Road School, Clacton-on-Sea) Mavis Baker School of Music, Clacton-on-Sea. *Represented by*: self and Saatchi Gallery, London. Contacts Saatchi Gallery or McClean Fine Art or Andy Powell. *Exhib*: from 1968, including: Tel-Aviv Central Gallery; St. Matthews, Norwich; The Gallery, Bury St. Edmunds; St. Matthews Ipswich; Theatre Royal, Norwich; Dale Res Gallery, Ipswich; Ipswich Library; St. Stevens, Ipswich; Butter Market Ipswich; Norwich Cathedral; Corn Exchange Ipswich; Stoke Gallery; Saffron Walden; Plus 31; RA Summer Exhibition (1997); many others. *Works in collections*: private collections various celebrities and Royals worldwide and McClean Fine Art London. *Commissions*: ongoing, and welcome by post, email or by appointment for viewings (private). *Publications*: on website since 1994; National News UK; National News USA; various others: see internet - listed on over 25,000 sites, and Bard Poetry; Who's Who in Art; Who's Who in the World. *Official Purchasers*: McClean Fine Art London and Saatchi Gallery, Chelsea, London. *Works Reproduced*: private print run Limited Editions, last 2000 limited to 500 "Babyface". *Principal Works*: Time Dimensional Vortex montage (oil, ink); Baby Face. *Recreations*: music, history, writing, events, socialising. *Misc*: Born Andrew Shove, known only as Andy Powell. Contact direct on artistandypowell@gmail.com Phone number on request only. *Address*: 59 Scott Ellis Gardens, Grove End Road, St.John's Wood, London NW8 9HE. *Email*: artistandypowell@gmail.com *Website*: under construction, see saatchigallery.com. *Signs work*: "Baron".

POWELL, Christopher Alan, LL.B. (1957), BA (2000); former journalist; painter mainly in oil with occasional water-colour and tempera of landscapes, seascapes, city scenes, still life and flower studies; former sub-editor on The Times (1968-92). *b*: Newcastle upon Tyne, 11 Jul 1935. *s of*: Alan Powell, consulting engineer. *Educ*: Queen Elizabeth Grammar, Hexham. *Studied*: part time at City Literary Inst., London (Cecil Collins). Studied Law at King's College, Newcastle upon Tyne, Arts with Open University. *Exhib*: Mall Galleries, Leighton House, various art societies in London. *Works in collections*: UK, USA, Japan. *Address*: Flat A7, Sloane Ave. Mans., Chelsea, London SW3 3JF. *Email*: powell7st@aol.com *Signs work*: "C.A. POWELL".

POWELL, Joanne, RBSA (2007), SWA (2009), Art College Scholarship to Italy (1962), RBSA Prize Exhibition Award (2005), SWA President and Vice-President Award (2010). *Medium*: pastel, oil, watercolour, drawing. *b*: Cumbria, 25 Apr 1943. *m*: Michael. one *s*. one *d*. *Studied*: Carlisle College of Art (1959-63). *Exhib*: RBSA, Birmingham, Mall Gallerie: ROI, SWA, Pastel Society; Picture Craft Gallery, Norfolk; No9 Gallery, Birmingham; The Art Room, Ludlow; Shell House Gallery, Ledbury; Gallery No8 Pershore; The Cathedral, Worcester, Harbour Gallery, Cumbria. *Works in collections*: private and corporate; RBSA Archives. *Publications*: The Public Catalogue Foundation; Oil Paintings in Public Ownership; Birmingham BBC; Your Paintings, bbc.com *Clubs*: Art Societies throughout the West Midlands and Worcestershire. *Misc*: Curator, Museum & Art Galleries West Bromwich (1965-71), Denman College tutor, New College Worcs tutor. *Address*: Roanoake, Tanwood Lane, Chaddesley Corbett, Worcestershire DY10 4NR. *Email*: joannepowellart@gmail.com *Website*: joannepowellart.co.uk *Signs work*: "JOANNE POWELL".

POWELL, Roy Owen, NDD (1956), ATD (1959); landscape figure and still life artist in oil on canvas, charcoal and pencil drawings; retd. art teacher. *b*: Chepstow, 3 Dec 1934. *s of*: Ivor Powell, primitive painter (decd). *Partner*: Jenni Rule. *Educ*: Monmouth School and West Mon School, Pontypool. *Studied*: Cardiff College of Art (1952-56, Eric Malthouse, J.C. Tarr). *Exhib*: National Gallery of Wales, 1996 (with the work of my father - 1906-85 - a primitive painter); one-man shows: Brecknock Museum (1994), International Pavilion, Llangollen, Washington Gallery, Theatre Brecheiniog; various group shows in England, Wales and Scotland including Celtic Vision. *Works in collections*: Brecknock Museum, National Library of Wales, private collections. *Publications*: articles for 'Planet' magazine. *Official Purchasers*: Contemporary Art Society for Wales. *Works Reproduced*: 'Planet' front covers. *Clubs*: The Welsh Group; Watercolour Society of Wales. *Address*: 10 Mill St., Brecon, Powys LD3 9BD. *Signs work*: "R.O. Powell".

PRAED, Michael, NDD, ATD. *Medium*: oils, mixed media. *b*: 29 Nov 1941. one *s*. two *d*. *Educ*: Falmouth and Brighton Colleges of Art. *Studied*: etching and engraving, oil painting two and three dimensional. *Represented by*: Praed Gallery, Marazion, Penzance, Cornwall TR17 0AR. *Exhib*: Cornwall: Praed Gallery, Marazion; Penwith Society; London: mixed exhbns. and one-man; Brittany, S. France, Holland, Germany, Sweden. *Works in collections*: United Nations, New York. *Commissions*: many private. *Publications*: Cornish Magazine and TV programmes, recently Grenadas 'Landscapes'. *Works Reproduced*: Twenty Paintings. *Principal Works*: Large Semi-abstract Cornish Cliff Scenes. *Recreations*: photography, gardening, bowls. *Clubs*: Bowls Club. *Address*: c/o Summerhouse Gallery, Market Place, Marazion, Cornwall TR17 0AR. *Website*: www.michaelpraed.co.uk *Signs work*: MJ Praed.

PRAGNELL, Hubert John, MA, ATD, NDD. Taught at: Stonyhurst College, Lancs (Art), The Kings School, Canterbury (History of Art), Oxford University for Continuing Education (part-time tutor, History of Art & Architecture). *Medium*: pastel, watercolour, drawing in pen and wash. *b*: 20 Jul 1942. *s of*: Laurence & Mary Pragnell. *m*: Dorothea. one *s*. one *d*. *Studied*: Goldsmiths' College School of Art (1959-60), Ruskin School of Drawing & Fine Art, Oxford (1960-63), Univ. Reading (1963-64), Univ. Kent (1982-85). *Exhib*: Royal Soc. of Painter Etchers; Royal Institute of Painters in Watercolour. *Works in collections*: Univ. Kent; City of London commercial companies; private collections in Europe & America. *Commissions*: Weidenfeld & Nicolson; Norfolk & Norwich Tourist Board, Canterbury Cathedral, National Trust, Contemporary Watercolours. *Publications*: 'Styles of English Architecture', Batsford (1984); 'Short Walks in English Towns' Weidenfeld & Nicolson (1988); 'Britain: A Guide to Architectural Styles' Batsford (1995); Industrial Britain, an Architectural History, Batsford (2000); Architectural Britain', National Trust (2007); 'Oxford Sketchbook', Spire Books (2011); 'Portrait of British Schools' (contributor); Contemporary Watercolours (2012)l; 'Architecture in York; An Artists View' Jeremy Mills (2014). *Recreations*: local & railway history, travel, classical music, biographies, architecture. *Address*: 12 Meadow Road, Canterbury, Kent, CT2 8EU. *Email*: hubert_pragnell@yahoo.co.uk *Signs work*: "Hubert Pragnell".

PRENTICE, Dinah, NDD (1956), ATD (1957), textile artist. *Medium*: silk, drawing & printmaking. *b*: Beckenham, Kent, 9 Sep 1935. *m*: David Prentice. four *d*. *Educ*: Haberdashers Askes, Wyggeston G.S., Leicester. *Studied*: Birmingham College of Art, Royal Academy Schools. *Represented by*: Number Nine, The Gallery, Birmingham. *Exhib*: Objects of Our Time, Crafts Council London & New York (1996-8); Revelation, London (touring), 7 MOMA Kyoto Japan (1997-8); Take 4, Whitworth (touring) (1998); Ikon 40th Anniversary Exhibition (2004); Quilts 1700-2010, Victoria and Albert Museum (2010); Installation 'Fragments' No.9 The Gallery, Birmingham (2009); Ruskin Museum, Lancaster University (2007); solo: Worcester Museum (2002). *Works in collections*: private and public including V&A, Shipley Art Gallery. *Commissions*: BDF TESA, Milton Keynes. *Publications*: '88 Leading Quiltmakers of the World', Nihon Press; 'Fragments' (2010). *Principal Works*: 'Persephone Rising', 'Giotto's Flying Footballer', 'The Everyday Life of Lou Andres-Salome'. *Clubs*: RASAA. *Misc*: co-founded Ikon Gallery Birmingham (1963). *Address*: 9 Hanley Terrace, Malvern, Wells, Worcs WR14 4PF. *Email*: d.prentice40@btinternet.com. *Email*: d.prentice40@btinternet.com *Signs work*: "DINAH PRENTICE".

PRESLEY-ROY, Michael: see ROY, Michael Presley-.

PRESS, Eugène, RSPA (Road Safety) Art Award (1950); Best Art on Gospel Music Album (1980). *Medium*: oil, watercolour, drawing. *b*: Sutton-on -Trent, 14 Jan 1936. *s of*: Thomas James Press. *m*: Jo (Joan). three *d*. *Studied*: part-time, London; St.Martins Central and Northampton; privately under Graham Sutherland, James Fitton, influence of Charles Mahoney. *Exhib*: Royal Academy; Woodstock Gallery; Brixton; Clapham; Sevenoaks; Folkestone; Tunbridge Wells. *Works in collections*: private: London, Bath and throughout Britain, Italy, France, Canada, USA. *Commissions*: mural at Borough Green; Turner Society: portrait of Turner; Thames Wildlife and Plants; Thames Dockland Old Buildings Record; National Gallery, 1982 Extension Proposal; Turner's Birthplace Trust-New Building Proposal. *Works Reproduced*: Art Magazines, News Print, journals, cards, prints, books. *Recreations*: music, art and antiquities. *Address*: Old Pond House, Forest Way, Tunbridge Wells, Kent TN2 5HA. *Signs work*: 'Eugène Press' or 'EP'.

PREST, Kathy, Best Visual Artist (London Art, Art of Love, Oxo Tower); Best Figurative Artist (SWA, Mall Galleries); Sculpture Award (Chelsea Art Society). *Medium*: clay, plaster, bronze, stainless steel, polystyrene. *b*: London. *d of*: Mr & Mrs Wall. one *s*. two *d*.

Represented by: Jack Fine Art, Ballon Rouge Art. *Exhib*: Affordable Art Fair, Art London, Christie's, Richmond Riverside Gallery, RSBA, SW Academy of Fine Art; Mall Galleries, 20/21 RCA. *Works in collections*: private collections. *Commissions*: Mayfair Properties (2005); Intuitive Systems (2001); private commissions. *Works Reproduced*: in 'Artist & Illustrators Magazine' (Sept 07); Hertfordshire Magazine (2001). *Principal Works*: figurative sculpture, contemporary and classical. *Misc*: Register of Sculptors, RBS. *Address*: 145 St.Albans Road, Barnet, Herts, EN5 4LD. *Email*: kathy@kathyprest.co.uk *Website*: www.kathyprest.co.uk *Signs work*: 'Kp' or 'Kathy Prest'.

PRESTON-GODDARD, John, Professional painter. *Medium*: oil, water-colour, gouache. *b*: Liverpool, 5 May 1928. *m*: Kathleen Preston-Goddard, art gallery owner. *Educ*: private. *Studied*: Croydon College of Art 1946-50. *Exhib*: foremost London galleries, Moscow and Croydon. *Works in collections*: Britain, USA, Europe, Australia, Japan and S.Africa. *Commissions*: numerous and ongoing. *Publications*: numerous. *Official Purchasers*: Oxford University, Leicester Education Authority, Surrey EA. *Principal Works*: located in Surrey UK and Arkansas US. *Address*: Studio House, Selborne Rd., Croydon CR0 5JQ. *Signs work*: "PRESTON GODDARD".

PRICE, Christopher Francis, BA Hons Hull University. *Medium*: Black & white and colour illustration and paintings. *b*: Birmingham, 17 Aug 1947. *s of*: Rex Price and Anne Grogan (of Tipperary). *m*: Delisia Howard. one *s*. *Studied*: The Design Studio, Cadbury Bros, Bourneville (1964-5), Hull University (1966-69). *Represented by*: Debut Gallery, 30 Tottenham Street, London W1. *Exhib*: (Mel Calmans) Workshop Gallery, Lambs Conduit St. (one-man show, 1973), South Bank Picture Show (1991), Salon des Arts (1998), Smiths Gallery, Covent Garden (1987), Libby Edwards Gallery, Sydney, Australia (2006), London Transport Museum (2009) A view of London. *Works in collections*: Brighton Museum and Art Gallery (portrait of Barbara Hulaniki and Steven Fitzimon), Maxwells, Covent Garden, The Rank Organisation (Jumpin Jaks Clubs, 1997). *Commissions*: BBC, Observer, Sunday Times, Daily Mail, Financial Times, Radio Times, etc. *Publications*: most newspapers and magazines, many books and publications - 30 years of freelance illustration - Erotic Review, Harpers Bazaar, TES, OUP, Harper Collins, Pan Picador, Heinemann, Hamish Hamilton etc., Radio Times, GQ. *Works Reproduced*: Association of Illustrators 10th Annual, AKJ Erotica, Harpers Bazaar Big Red Book. Annual: in Biba, Sin Biba, Boogie Woogie Book. *Recreations*: publishing, music, cabaret, poetry, theatre (passions not recreations). *Clubs*: London Sketch Club, Dilke St, Chelsea. *Misc*: regularly performs in clubs and festivals as Hazard Arts Theatre. *Address*: The New House, 46 Marlborough Place, St. John's Wood, London NW8 0PL. *Email*: priceart@btinternet.com *Website*: www.BibaBook.com *Signs work*: "CHRIS PRICE" (sometimes with Delisia Howard).

PRICE, Harry, NDD, ATD, MA, RI; RI Award (2005); Winsor & Newton Award, Patchings Open (2003, 2005). *Medium*: watercolour, oil, acrylic. *b*: Kington, Herefordshire, 1933. *s of*: I.W & M.E Price. *m*: Yvonne. one *s*. one *d*. *Educ*: Kington Grammar School, Herefordshire. *Studied*: Hereford College of Art; West of England College of Art, Bristol; Middlesex University. *Represented by*: Linda Blackstone Gallery, Pinner; Broadway Modern, Worcs. *Exhib*: RWA; RI; Mall Galleries; AAF London; Watercolour and Drawing Fair, Park Lane Hotel, London; Chichester Open; Broadway Modern, Worcs; Linda Blackstone, Pinner; Hillier Gallery, Stratford on Avon; Sunday Times/Smith Williamson Exhibition. *Works in collections*: private collections in England, USA and Australia. *Publications*: International Artist (Feb/Mar 2007); The Artist (April 2009); Practique des Arts (Nov 2012). *Address*: 49 Station Road, Balsall Common, Coventry CV7 7FN. *Email*: harry@49rowan.googlemail.com *Website*: www.harrypriceart.co.uk *Signs work*: 'Harry Price'.

PRICE, Richard Evan, AROI (2009); BA Hons; Teaching Cert.; Winner, Charles Pears Memorial Award; Non-Member ROI Prize; Manya Igel Prize; The Cedar House Gallery

Prize, ROI Portrait Event Prize. *Medium*: oil. *b*: Upminster, Essex, 30 Aug 1962. *s of*: D F Price. *Partner*: Lucy Best. *Studied*: Portsmouth Polytechnic (1980-83, BA Hons Degree in Fine Art: Painting). *Represented by*: Manya Igel Fine Arts. *Exhib*: RA, RWA, RBA, ROI, RSMA, NEAC, LPS, 20/21 British Art Fair, Lapada, Chelsea Art Fair; Open Studios Exhibitions 2006, 2008, 2010. *Works in collections*: private. *Commissions*: private. *Publications*: 'The Artist' (Dec '07, "In Conversation"); Artist & Illustrator; The Wessex Muse. *Clubs*: Bournemouth Arts Club; Southern Contemporaries. *Address*: Flat 5, 52 Southcote Road, Bournemouth, Dorset, BH1 3SS. *Email*: richard.price10@virgin.net *Website*: www.manyaigelfinearts.com *Signs work*: "RICHARD PRICE".

PRICE, Stephen Jon, MA, FMA; former Head of Museums and Art Gallery, Bristol. *b*: Birmingham, 15 Feb 1949. *Educ*: University of Exeter 1967-70 (BA). *Studied*: University of Birmingham 1970-71 (MA) History and Archaeology. *Publications*: various on museums and visitor attractions. *Address*: 75 London Road, Worcester WR5 2DU.

PRICE, Trevor, BA Hons; artist/printmaker; RE Royal Society of Painter-Printmakers; Printmaking Today Award (1997); Julian Trevelyan Outstanding Printmaking Award (2002), Printfest 'Printmaker of the Year 2012'. *b*: Cornwall, 18 Jul 1966. two *d*. *Studied*: Falmouth School of Art (1984-85), Winchester School of Art (1985-88). *Exhib*: various including: National Print Exhibitions, Royal Academy of Arts Summer Exhibitions, Royal West of England Academy. *Works in collections*: Bank of England, Yale University, USA, University of Wales, Ashmolean Museum (Oxford), Guangdong Museum of Art (China). *Commissions*: various including P&O, Marriott Hotels, John Lewis plc. etc. *Address*: 23 Blue Anchor Lane, London SE16 3UL. *Email*: trevor@trevorprice.co.uk *Website*: www.trevorprice.co.uk *Signs work*: "Trevor Price".

PRIESTNER, Stephen Miles, artist in oil, pastel, water-colour, collages; life-guard, film projectionist, sign draughtsman, waiter. *b*: Altrincham, Ches., 1 May 1954. *s of*: Arthur Priestner. *m*: Ann (nee Warburton). *Educ*: Dodoma School, Tanzania (1959-61), Ellesmere College, Salop. (1967-70), Blackpool College of Art (1971-72), Manchester Polytechnic (1972-74). *Studied*: Polytechnic (1972-74, B. Neiland), École des Beaux Arts, Paris (1978). *Exhib*: Olympian Arts, London (1993), Salford Museum (1988), New York City, Art Competition Winner (1994), Nice, Milan, Venice, Barcelona (1998). *Works in collections*: Ghent Museum, Belgium; British Museum London; Bradford Art Gallery, Tate Gallery. *Publications*: Flash Art Directory (1995). *Works Reproduced*: The Artist, Apollo Magazine, New York Post, Contemporary Art, N.Y., etc.; book: New Art International, N.Y., Art News, Art Monthly, Modern Painters, Granada TV interview, work shown (1989). *Address*: 20 Sandpiper Drive Stockport, Cheshire SK3 8UL. *Signs work*: "Stephen M. Priestner".

PRING MacSWEENEY, Dale Louisiana, Dip.AD. *Medium*: oil on linen and water-colour on paper. *b*: London, 17 Apr 1949. *d of*: Percy Pring. *m*: divorced Dr. D. MacSweeney. *Educ*: Burlington Grammar, W. London; Greycourt School, Ham, Surrey, Kingston School of Art. *Studied*: Wimbledon School of Art (1966), Waltham Forest College (1967-70). *Represented by*: Jorgensen, Dublin; Thompson's UK. *Exhib*: RA, NEAC, Piccadilly Gallery, London; Hammer Galleries, NY; Montgomery Gallery, San Francisco; Gerald Peters Gallery, Santa Fe, New Mexico; Riverside Museum, Calif.; Louis Newman Galleries, Beverly Hills; Thompson's Galleries, UK; Jorgensen Fine Art, Dublin. *Works in collections*: HM Ministry of Arts, London; Chelsea Arts Club, London; Dallas Museum of Art, Texas; D'Management Milan; Inland Revenue and Customs and Excise U.K., private collectors. *Commissions*: Princess Cruise Lines; private galleries; private collectors. *Publications*: American Artists Magazine; Art Scene USA; Galleries UK. *Works Reproduced*: www.rainbowzebra.net/dale_pring_macsweeney/ *Principal Works*: Interiors and Still Life. *Recreations*: music, concerts mainly classical and operas; dancing; cooking. *Clubs*: Chelsea Arts. *Address*: 2 Benhall Lodge, Benhall, Saxmundham, Suffolk IP17 1JD. *Email*:

dale.macsweeney@onetel.com *Website*: www.rainbowzebra.net/dale_pring_macsweeney/ www.dalepringmacsweeney.com *Signs work*: "Dale Pring MacSweeney" or "DPMac S".

PRITCHARD, Marion Ruth, SWA (1987), SOFA (1994); painter and illustrator. *Medium*: oil, water-colour. *b*: London, 10 Nov 1934. *d of*: Albert Henry Latter. *m*: Ronald Pritchard. two *s*. one *d*. *Educ*: Minchenden Grammar School. *Studied*: Hornsey College of Art and Crafts (1951-56, graphic design). *Exhib*: RA Summer Exhibition (1987, 1988, 1991, 1993, 1997, 2000, 2005, 2006, 2009), RBA, RI, ROI, SWA, SWLA, SGA, SBA, RMS, SOFA; mixed exhbns. throughout London; Discerning Eye (2005). *Works Reproduced*: greetings cards and calendars for Medici, Royle, Bucentaur, Camden Graphics, Hallmark. *Recreations*: gardening, reading. *Address*: 50 Arnos Grove, Southgate, London N14 7AR. *Signs work*: "Marion Pritchard".

PROCTER, Alison, SBA. *Medium*: oil and watercolour. *b*: Hertford, 17 Dec 1935. *d of*: Dr M & Dr M E Thomson. *m*: Tony. one *s*. one *d*. *Educ*: Westcliff (Weston-Super-Mare). *Studied*: no formal training. *Exhib*: SBA, North Somerset Art, various local exhibitions and RHS garden Rosemoor. *Works in collections*: private collections in the UK, Japan, Holland and Australia. *Commissions*: various. *Publications*: two books on making flowers in sugarcraft: 'Flowers for Cakes', 'Simplifying Sugar Flowers'. *Works Reproduced*: by Woodmansterne card and notelets. *Recreations*: painting, family and gardening. *Clubs*: Clevedon Art Club. *Address*: Treelands, Hillside Road, Bleadon, Weston-Super-Mare, N.Somerset, BS24 0AA. *Email*: tony.procter123@btinternet.com *Website*: www.alisonprocter.co.uk *Signs work*: 'ALISON PROCTER' or 'ALISON M.PROCTER', on oils: 'A.P'.

PROCTER, Brenda, BA (Hons) Fine Art, 1970, PGCE Art Education, 1971. *Medium*: mixed media, prints, PVA. *b*: Manchester, 9 Jun 1948. *d of*: Frank & Elizabeth Cuttle. *m*: John W. Procter. two *d*. *Studied*: Dept. of Fine Art, University of Newcastle-upon-Tyne (1966-70), Dept. of Education, University of Newcastle-upon-Tyne (1970-71). *Represented by*: Colin Jellicoe Gallery, Portland Street, Manchester. *Exhib*: Haworth Art Gallery, Accrington; Laing Art Gallery; Hatton Gallery, Newcastle; Robert Burns Centre, Dumfries (one-man); Old Well Theatre, Moffat; Portfolio Gallery, Lincolnshire (one-man); Lockerbie Ice Rink; Gracefield Arts Centre, Dumfries; Colin Jellicoe Gallery, Manchester. *Works in collections*: private collections. *Commissions*: "Tried and Tested" Art and Design School Syllabus. *Recreations*: reading, music. *Misc*: I am intrigued by metamorphosis and the beauty of the covering and assimilation by nature of rejected man-made objects. My work grows by accretion in the same way. *Address*: Gilmartin, Waterbeck, Lockerbie, DG11 3HL. *Email*: procterjb@btinternet.com *Website*: www.brendaprocter.webeden.co.uk *Signs work*: "BRENDA PROCTER".

PROUD, Alastair Colm, artist in oil and water-colour, specialising in wildlife and landscape. *b*: Dublin, Rep. of Ireland, 2 Oct 1954. *m*: Jill Paula. one *s*. one *d*. *Educ*: St. Andrews College, Dublin. *Studied*: West Wales School of Art. *Exhib*: 'Birds in Art' Leigh Yawkey Museum of Art, USA, Mall Galleries, London, Combridge Fine Art, Dublin. *Works in collections*: Sultan of Oman. *Publications*: illustrator: Birds of Prey of British Isles; Wildfowl of British Isles and North West Europe. *Clubs*: S.WL.A. *Address*: Plas Bach, Newchurch, Carmarthen, SA33 6EJ. *Email*: alastair.proud@btinternet.com *Website*: alastairproud.com

PROWSE, Alexander Reginald, PS. *Medium*: artist, illustrator in acrylic, oil, watercolour and pastel. *b*: London, 23 Jun 1949. *m*: Janet Prowse. *Studied*: Harrow School of Art (Christopher Sanders, RA). *Exhib*: one-man shows: London, Mexico, Venezuela; NEAC, PS, RSMA, RP, RI, RMS, RWA - Christie's. *Works in collections*: Lord & Lady Sainsbury, Hotel de Ville, Paris, Sadlers Wells Theatre, Chaitanya Jyoti Museum, India. *Publications*: illustrator: Love All Serve All; book covers for Gerald Durrell and Jennings series. *Official Purchasers*: Linbury Trust. *Address*: 25 Bitham Mill Court Yard, Westbury,

Wiltshire, BA13 3DB. *Email*: alex@alexprowse.co.uk *Website*: www.alexprowse.co.uk *Signs work*: "Alex Prowse."

PRYSE: see SPENCER PRYSE, Tessa.

PUGH, Tim, RCA; awarded 'Creative Connections' Grant by the Arts Council of Wales for personal research (2004); awarded travel grants to Tasmania (2000) and Switzerland (2005) for Environmental Art residencies, by Arts Council of Wales. *Medium*: drawing, environmental art and mixed media. *b*: 10 Dec 1965. *s of*: Christopher Alan Pugh. *Studied*: Wrexham and Edinburgh College of Art: OND, HND, BA (Hons) Ceramics. *Exhib*: Elbe-Ejter, Germany (2011); 125th Summer Exhibition at the RCA in Conwy (2007); Welsh National Eisteddfod, Felinheli, Gwynedd (2005); Muhlberg, Germany; Summer Show, Galerie Wandlebar, Gstaad, Switzerland; Botanical Gardens of Wales, Carmarthen (2003); Lorient, Brittany, France; Hobart, Tasmania (1999), and many other venues. *Works in collections*: private collections in the UK and worldwide. *Commissions*: 'Storyteller's Seat' for schools in Conwy, North Wales; large outdoor sculpture for Alyn Waters Country Park. *Publications*: many gallery catalogues. *Address*: 61 Mancot Way, Mancot, Deeside, Flintshire CH5 2AW. *Email*: timpugh.artist@gmail.com *Website*: www.timpugh.co.uk *Signs work*: 'Tim Pugh'.

PULLAN, Tessa, SEA (1988), FRBS (2001); sculptor in wood, stone, bronze. *b*: London, 20 Dec 1953. one *s*. one *d*. *Educ*: Tudor Hall. *Studied*: apprenticeship John Skeaping, RA (1971-74), City & Guilds (1974-77), RA Schools (1977-80). *Exhib*: RA Summer Shows, Cork St. Fine Arts, Ackermann (London and NY), SEA, Christies, London Contemporary Art Fair, Bruton St. Gallery, etc.; solo shows: Quinton Green Fine Arts, London, John Hunt Gallery, Frank T. Sabin, London. *Works in collections*: NPG, National Horse Racing Museum, Newmarket, Yale Center for British Art, Clare College, Cambridge, Virginia Museum of Fine Art, Virginia Historical Soc., Fitzwilliam Museum. *Address*: Granby House, Kings Lane, Barrowden, Rutland LE15 8EF. *Email*: tessapullan@btinternet.com *Website*: www.tessapullan.co.uk *Signs work*: "Tessa Pullan" and monogram.

PULLÉE, Michael Edward, Des.RCA, FCSD, NEAC, FRSA; artist in oil, designer and educational consultant; former H.M. Inspector of Schools. *Medium*: oil. *b*: London, 8 Sep 1936. *s of*: Edward and Margaret Pullee. *m*: Sheila Mary Threadgill. two *d*. *Educ*: Bootham School, York. *Studied*: Leeds College of Art (1955-57), RCA (1959-62). *Exhib*: New English Annual, Pattersons, RA Summer Exhbn., Bankside, Lloyds TSB Private Banking, Alresford Gallery, Sheen Gallery, Cedar House Gallery, Cross Gate Gallery (Kentucky USA). *Works in collections*: various private. *Works Reproduced*: in 'The New English' by Kenneth McConkey (Royal Academy Publications) and New English Annual Exhibition illustrated catalogue. *Clubs*: N.E.A.C.; Penn Club. *Address*: White Gables, 48 Wray Common Rd., Reigate, Surrey RH2 0ND. *Signs work*: "Michael E. Pullée".

PULLEN, William, MA (Hons) 1st Class; 1st Prize, Hunting Art Prizes, 1987; John Kinross Scholarship, RSA (1984). *Medium*: egg tempera, oil, watercolour. *b*: Alton, Hants., 17 Feb 1961. *s of*: Brian Pullen. *m*: Brenda. one *s*. *Educ*: Midhurst Grammar School, W. Sussex. *Studied*: University of Edinburgh; Edinburgh College of Art (1979-84). *Exhib*: RA, Christie's, RCA, Piccadilly Gallery, RP, RBA, Belgrave Gallery, St. Ives, Beatrice Royal Gallery Eastleigh, Russell Gallery, London and others in Scotland, England and France. *Works in collections*: Edinburgh College of Art. *Commissions*: painter of architectural landscape subjects, occasional portrait, including commissions. *Recreations*: garden design. *Address*: 6 The Mead, Petersfield, Hants. GU32 3LG. *Signs work*: 'W.P.' or 'William Pullen'.

PURNELL, John, PhD, MA, BAHons, FRGS, FRSA, FHEA, FBPA, ARPS, ABIPP, ABAPA, LCGI, DSPE; Vice-Chancellor's Staff Award for Excellence (2007, 2009); art and photography tutor. *b*: Birmingham, 8 Jan 1954. *Studied*: Bournville College of Art and Design; University of Wales. *Clubs*: Mensa. *Address*: Flat 13, 132 Newport Road, Roath, Cardiff, CF24 1DJ.

PURSER, Keith. *Medium*: oil, collage, gouache, watercolour, pastel, woodcut, 3D. *b*: Bromley, Kent, 20 Jun 1944. *s of*: Eric Purser, Doris Tidy. *m*: Mhaire McLean. one *s*. one *d*. *Studied*: Sidcup School of Art (1960-62, Graphic Design). *Represented by*: Jonathan Clark Ltd., 18 Park Walk, London SW10 0AQ. *Exhib*: frequent one-man exhbns Jonathan Clark from 1989; numerous group exhbns. *Works in collections*: corporate and private. *Publications*: 20th Century Painters and Sculptors by Francis Spalding, Jonathan Clark Exhibition catalogues. *Recreations*: music. *Address*: c/o Jonathan Clark Fine Art, 18 Park Walk, London SW10 0AQ. *Email*: jclark@jc-art.com *Website*: www.jc-art.com

PUTMAN, Salliann, BA (Hons) Fine Art, RWS, NEAC; painter in oil and water-colour. *b*: London, 20 Apr 1937. *m*: Michael. one *s*. one *d*. *Studied*: West Surrey College of Art and Design, Farnham (1988-93). *Exhib*: one and two-man shows: London, Windsor, Stockbridge, USA; RA, Mall Galleries, NEAC, RBA, ROI, RI, PS, Bankside Gallery, WH Pattersons Gallery, New Grafton Gallery, Oakham Gallery, Rowley Gallery, Alresford Gallery, Russell Gallery. *Address*: 3 Pinecote Drive, Sunningdale, Berks. SL5 9PS. *Email*: salliann_putman@onetel.net.uk *Signs work*: water-colours: "Salliann Putman," oils: "S.P."

PYBUS, Michelle Christine. *Medium*: oil, watercolour. *b*: Whitby, 3 May 1954. *d of*: William & Patricia. *Educ*: Whitby Primary and Secondary Schools; York Technical College. *Studied*: self-taught. *Represented by*: Turnstone Gallery, Sandsend; Zillah Bell, Thirsk; Russell Gallery, Putney. *Exhib*: Royal Academy; Royal Institute of Oil Painters; Royal Society of Marine Artists; Henley Regatta; Eton College. *Publications*: 'Leisure Painter' articles. *Principal Works*: marine/landscape oils. *Recreations*: travel. *Clubs*: The Fylingdales Group of Artists. *Misc*: Paints throughout Europe, Russia, Australia and New Zealand. Owned a gallery in Whitby from 1998-2007. *Address*: 1 Newlands Avenue, Whitby, N.Yorkshire YO21 3DX. *Email*: christine.pybus@btinternet.com *Website*: www.pybusfinearts.co.uk *Signs work*: 'M.C.Pybus', 'C.PYBUS'.

PYE, Chris, MCA. *Medium*: woodcarver. *b*: Co. Durham, 24 Jan 1952. two *s*. *Address*: Linden, Brilley, Whitney-on-Wye, Hereford, HR3 6JZ. *Email*: chris@chrispye-woodcarving.com *Website*: www.chrispye-woodcarving.com

PYE, Patrick, Mem. of Aosdána and RHA; NCAD; DPhil (Hon. Causa, Maynooth) (2005); painter in tempera and oil, stained glass artist, etcher - an artist of the sacred theme. *Medium*: oil and alkelyne. *b*: Winchester,10 Apr 1929. *s of*: Dorothy & Edmund Pye. *m*: Noirin Kennedy. two *d*. *Educ*: St. Columba's College, Dublin 14. *Studied*: National College of Art, Dublin (1951-54), Jan van Eyck Akad., Maastricht (1957-58). *Represented by*: Jorgensen Fine Art, Hibernian Way, D2. *Exhib*: many one-man shows, (Jorgensen Fine Art); Dublin, RHA Annual (since 1990), Retrospective: Triptychs & Related Works, March 1997 at RHA Gallery, Ely Pl., Dublin 2 (catalogue available), Major Works Exhibition: Oct 2003, Jorgensen Fine Art; Irish Living Art (1960s-1980s); David Hendricks Gallery, Dublin (pre-1980). *Works in collections*: Ulster Museum; Hyde Lane Municipal Gallery; Crawford, Cork; Boyle Civic Museum. *Commissions*: Stations of the Cross, Killarney; Wall Hanging, The Transfiguration, Maynooth University and church commissions throughout Ireland including St. Thomas More, and Dulwich. *Publications*: author: Apples and Angels; The Time Gatherer (on El Greco) publ. by Veritas (1981) & Four Courts Press (1991) respectively. *Official Purchasers*: Municipal Hugh Lane Gallery, Parnell Sq.; Crawford Gallery, Cork; St. Thomas' University, St. Paul, MN, USA. *Works Reproduced*: Allied Irish Bank Coll.; Bank of Ireland Coll; various catalogues. *Principal Works*: 'The Glory Fortold', 'Theologian in his Garden', 'Transfiguration' (Maynooth), 'Woman and Serpent' (Bank of Ireland HQ, 1982). *Misc*: converted to Roman Catholicism (1963); accepts William Blake's valuation of imagination in processes of art, and Coleridge's distinction between fantasy and imagination; second cousin of William Pye, sculptor. *Address*: c/o Roisin Alexander-Pye, Friarstoen Upper, Bohernabreena, Dublin 24, Eire. *Signs work*: "P.Pye" and "TI".

PYE, William, ARCA, FRBS, HonFRIBA; sculptor. *b*: 16 Jul 1938. *s of*: Sir David Pye, MA, ScD, FRS, CB. *m*: Susan. one *s.* two *d. Educ*: Charterhouse. *Studied*: Wimbledon School of Art (1958-61) under Freda Skinner, RCA Sculpture School (1961) under Prof. B. Meadows. *Works in collections*: Arts Council, Museum of Modern Art, NY, Contemporary Art Soc., Szépmúvészeti Muzeum, Budapest, National Museum of Wales, National Portrait Gallery, London. *Commissions*: Water Wall, British Pavilion Expo '92, Seville; Slipstream and Jetstream, Gatwick Airport; Chalice, London WC1; Cristos, St. Christopher's Place, London; Derby Cascade; British Embassy Oman; Antony House, Cornwall; Cader Idris, Central Sq., Cardiff; Aquarena, Millennium Sq. Bristol; Jubilee Fountain, Lincoln's Inn, London; Charybdis, Seaham Hall, Sunderland; eight water sculptures for Serpent Garden, Alnwick, Northumberland; Mount Parnitha, Greece; Three water sculptures for Marinsky Concert Hall, St. Petersburg. *Recreations*: playing the flute. *Clubs*: Chelsea Arts Club. *Address*: 43 Hambalt Rd., Clapham, London SW4 9EQ. *Website*: www.williampye.com *Signs work*: 'William Pye' or 'W.Pye'.

PYNE, Kenneth John, CCGB Cartoonist of the Year (1981); Strip Cartoonist of the Year, Cartoonist Art Trust Awards (2001); Caricaturist of the Year, Cartoonist Art Trust Awards (2006); several international awards. *b*: London, 30 Apr 1951. *s of*: John and Maud Pyne. *Partner*: Pamela Todd. *Studied*: Holloway County School, London. *Exhib*: Burgh House, Hampstead; Cartoonist Gallery, London; Barbican Centre, London; Cartoon Museum, London. *Works in collections*: V & A, British Museum, Cartoon Art Trust, Brunswick Centre, Salon International du Pessin et d'Humour, Switzerland, Cartoon Museum, London. *Commissions*: The Times, Private Eye, Punch, The Independent, The People, London Evening Standard, The Observer, Hampstead and Highgate Express, The Guardian. *Publications*: The Oldie, Reader's Digest, Which?, Sunday Times, Today, Marketing Week, Stern etc., plus 30 books. *Official Purchasers*: see commissions and publications. *Recreations*: walking, drawing, drinking and reading. *Clubs*: British Cartoonist Association. *Address*: 15 Well Walk, Hampstead Village, London NW3 1BY. *Email*: pyne9@hotmail.com *Website*: www.kenpyne.com *Signs work*: 'Ken Pyne'.

PYTEL, Walenty, NDD (1961), ARBS; Crown Estates Award, SWLA, Mall Galleries; Coventry Design Award 2001 Conservation area - bridge - 'Wings over Water'. *Medium*: bronze and mild steel. *b*: Poland, 10 Feb 1941. *m*: Janet Mary. one *s.* one *d. Studied*: Hereford College of Art (1956-61). *Exhib*: worldwide. *Works in collections*: Hereford, Worcester and Stockport County Library and Art Galleries; J. Bamford, Uttoxeter (JCB) etc. *Commissions*: Silver Jubilee Fountain, New Palace Yard Westminster, B'ham International Airport, JCB Uttoxeter, Gracemount Developments Ltd. Royal Caribbean Cruiseline; Lloyds Bank Trophy; Lloyds of London; Colin Grazier Memorial, Tamworth; 10 Millenium Planet Walk Sculptures - Tamworth Borough Council, bronze War Memorial - Ludlow branch of British Legion, H.P. Bulmer, Hereford; Yamazaki Mazak - Europe Corporation; Royal National College for the Blind 'Futuristic Runner', 3 flying buzzards, Malvern - for Queen's Diamond Jubilee. *Publications*: Debrett's Distinguished People of Today -2012. *Works Reproduced*: bronze limited editions. *Recreations*: shooting, fishing and sailing. *Misc*: Ambassador for Herefordshire. *Address*: Hartleton, Bromsash, Ross-on-Wye HR9 7SB. *Email*: info@wyebridge.com *Website*: www.wyebridge.com *Signs work*: "WALENTY PYTEL," "W. Pytel" or "W.P."

Q

QUANTRILL, David James. *Medium*: most media. *b*: Lowestoft, 11 Jul 1938. *m*: Angela. one *s. one d. Studied*: Lowestoft College (part-time). *Represented by*: various galleries East Anglia (John Russell Gallery, Ipswich, King of Hearts, Norwich). *Exhib*: since 1985 Mall Galleries London, PS, NEAC, RMS; Sudbury Open Exhibition, Gainsborough's House, Fermoy Centre, Kings Lynn Eastern Open. Work on tour, Eastern Open Exhibition 1988. *Works in collections*: Norwich Castle; James Paget Healthcare Trust; private collections UK, USA, Europe. *Misc*: Born in Suffolk where he still lives, a natural artist in most media and subject matter which gives way to feelings, atmospheres and textural surfaces. *Address*: 18 Carlton Sq., Lowestoft, Suffolk NR33 8JL. *Signs work*: "Quantrill."

QUARTLEY, Freddie, LCP Distinction typography; Diploma Calligraphy/Lettering; Associate Fellowship of GGE; Christopher Russell engraved lettering prize (2000); International Festival of Glass Sourbridge Best lettering award (2008). *Medium*: glass engraving and calligraphy. *b*: Cambridge, 27 May 1946. *m*: Nicholas Quartley. two *s*. *Educ*: Cambridge St. Mary's Convent. *Studied*: Cambridge College of Art & Technology Pre-Diploma; Wolverhampton College of Art; London College of Printing & Hampstead Garden Suburb Institute. *Exhib*: Annually with Guild of Glass Engravers; Art in Action (3 times); Solo exhibition, Pennsylvania USA; SSI; CLAS. *Commissions*: Churches, colleges, schools, private commissions (see website). *Principal Works*: Birmingham Oratory; St. Mary's, Goudhurst; St. Gregory & St. Augustine, Oxford. *Recreations*: Ashtanga Yoga, gardening, flower arranging. *Address*: 45 Bainton Road, Oxford OX2 7AG. *Email*: freddiequartley@gmail.com *Website*: www.freddiequartley.com

QUEMBY, Sigrid, Slade Dip.Fine Art; Nettleship Prize (1964); Boise Travelling Scholarship (1964-5); prizewinner, Open Exhibition, Mall Galleries (2001). *Medium*: painter/printmaker, textile designer, oil, watercolour, drawing. *b*: London, 8 Jan 1942. *d of*: Arthur and Maryann Quemby. *Studied*: Ealing School of Art (1958-62); Slade School of Fine Art (1962-64). *Exhib*: RA; V&A; Mall Galleries; The Morley Gallery; Bankside Gallery, London; Pryzmat Gallery, Krakow; Morandi Museum, Bologna. *Commissions*: Heals; Fidelis; Bernard Wardle; Sanderson's Textiles. *Publications*: Treasury of Embroidery Designs (pub. Bell & Hyman, 1985). *Works Reproduced*: 20th Century Pattern Design-Textile and Wallpaper Pioneers (pub. Mitchell Beazley, 2001); Stone Lithography (pub.A&C Black, 2001). *Misc*: teacher of printmaking, Ealing School of Art (1965-73), Wimbledon School of Art (1972-2002). *Address*: 32 Bushwood Road, Kew Gardens, Surrey TW9 3BQ. *Email*: sigrid.q.@tesco.net *Signs work*: 'S.Quemby'.

QUIGLEY, Thomas Antony Gerard. *Medium*: acrylic (collage), oil, watercolour, drawing, sculpture, collage. *b*: Cregan, Armagh, N.Ireland, Dec 1935. *s of*: Peter and Theresa Quigley (nee Murphy). *Educ*: Killkerley. *Studied*: Technical School, Dundalk, Ireland (painting and drawing); mostly self-taught, including picture conservation and restoration. *Represented by*: Mary Quigley, Newtown, Ballegan, Dundalk, County Louth, Ireland. *Exhib*: RA Summer Exhbn; invited painter, Discerning Eye, Mall Galleries; Art for Life, Cancer UK at Christie's; Hammersmith Open; The Atrium, Hammersmith Town Hall. *Works in collections*: private collections in England, Ireland and USA including the collections of Sir Peter Blake, Noel Sheridan, Jean Kenney Smith, Victoria Chaplin, Willie Nelson, President Clinton, Professor Eileen Joyce. *Publications*: Bare Facts Fulham Gazette. *Principal Works*: 'Latter Day Aesthete'; 'Pingo Corner' series. *Clubs*: RA Friends Membership. *Misc*: Artist in Residence, Atrium Festival (2006); invited to curate and exhibit at Hammersmith & Fulham Festival, 2006, by Mayor Charlie Treloggan. Exhibition opened by Sir Peter Blake and Deputy Mayor Michael Cartwright. *Address*: 3 River Side Gardens, Hammersmith, London W6 9LE. *Website*: www.tomquigleyshowcase.co.uk *Signs work*: 'Tom Quigley'.

QUIGLEY, Vlad, artist and portraitist in monochrome, linear, Art Nouveau; Pop Art; Baroque; works in collaboration with celebrity Hollywood supermodels, Playboy models, porn stars, Hollywood actresses, Page 3 models, Gothic and Fetish models. *Studied*:

Southampton Inst. of Art and Design, Northbrook College, Joe Orlando (E.C. Comics). *Exhib*: Pop Art Nouveau portraits of Viola D'Amour, Fairfield Halls, Vampyria, Hippodrome, Big Draw, Alfresco, Vampire Viola, Frogpond, The 100 (100 years of comic art), A.D. 2000, Shock, Anglo-French Aubrey Beardsley Centenary. *Commissions*: private portraits for clients, models, actresses, model agencies. Book illustrations, Pop Art exhbns. *Publications*: too numerous to list. *Address*: 5 Southcourt Close, Rustington, Little Hampton, W.Sussex, BN12 3JD. *Email*: happyvlad2002@yahoo.co.uk *Website*: www.vladquigley.com

QUINN, Máire Catherine, BA Hons Fine Art (1984); National Portrait Gallery award finalist (1988), RWS Elizabeth Scott Moore prize winner (2001); artist in oil, water-colour, printmaking, sculpture, textile. *b*: Armagh City, N. Ireland, 4 Aug 1961. *Studied*: University of Ulster. *Exhib*: NPG, Whitechapel Gallery, South London Gallery, Bankside Gallery, Museum of London, plus solo and group exhibs. in UK and abroad. *Commissions*: private, national and international. *Address*: Eliot Lodge, 295 Hither Green Lane, London SE13 6TH. *Signs work*: "Máire Quinn."

QUINN, Mary P., (née McLAUGHGLIN), Hons. sculpture (1986); sculptor in bronze portrait busts and statues. *b*: Co. Down, N.I., 26 May 1943. three *d*. *Educ*: St. Dominic's High School, Belfast. *Studied*: Richmond Adult College (1982-89). *Exhib*: many group shows since 1985. *Works in collections*: many bronze busts and statues in Ireland, England and USA including life-size statue of John Wesley in Virginia Wesleyan College, Virginia, USA. *Commissions*: Frank Sinatra, Frankie Dettori (bronze busts). *Clubs*: F.P.S., S.C.A. *Address*: 1 Exeter Rd., Hanworth, Feltham, Middx. TW13 5PE. *Email*: mary@maryquinnsculptor.com *Website*: www.maryquinnsculptor.com *Signs work*: "Mary Quinn."

QUIRKE, Michael Patrick, Fine Arts Diploma. *Medium*: oil, acrylic and pastel on canvas, board, paper. *b*: Hampstead, London, 19 Apr 1946. *s of*: David Quirke. *m*: Geraldine. two *s*. *Educ*: St.James', London. *Studied*: St. Martin's School of Art, and with Maurice Feild (Prof. Art at Slade). *Represented by*: Simpson Fine Art, London; Highgate Fine Art, London; Webb's Gallery. *Exhib*: New York, Spain, Germany, France, Italy. Since 1982: 14 one-man shows and 12 group shows. *Works in collections*: Paul Hillman Collection; private collections all over the world. *Commissions*: Spar Group plc; Marks and Spencer Group plc. *Publications*: British Artists from 1945. *Principal Works*: London scenes, fairgrounds and musicians. *Recreations*: music. *Clubs*: St. Ives Art Club, President of Arts Club 2000-2002. *Address*: 'Half Moon Gallery', 12 St. Andrew's St., St. Ives, Cornwall, TR26 1AH. *Signs work*: "M.Q." (in red paint).

R

RAE, Barbara, CBE, RA, RSA, RSW, RGI; DArts, FRSE, Napier University Edinburgh (1999), Hon. Fellowship, Royal College of Art, London (2003), D.Litt. University of Aberdeen (2003); painter and printmaker. *b*: Falkirk, Scotland, 10 Dec 1943. *m*: Gareth Ward-Rae. one *s*. *Educ*: Morrisons Academy, Crieff. *Studied*: Edinburgh College of Art. *Exhib*: Rae has solo painting and printmaking exhibitions in major cities of the USA, Norway, Ireland, Europe and the United Kingdom. Most recently the Adam Gallery London and Bath, Royal Academy, London; Edinburgh International Festival. Her artworks, including tapestries, are held in private and public collections worldwide. *Publications*: "Barbara Rae" (Lund Humphries) 2007; "Barbara Rae - Prints" (Royal Academy) 2009; "Barbara Rae - Sketchbooks" (Royal Academy) 2011. *Recreations*: travel. *Clubs*: Glasgow Art Club. *Address*: The Studio, 6 Northumberland Street, South East Lane, Edinburgh EH3 6LP. *Email*: barbararaera@aol.com *Website*: www.barbararae.com *Email*: barbararaera@aol.com. *Website*: www.barbararae.com. *Signs work*: "Barbara Rae."

RAE, John, Formerly RIBA & RTPI; works in mixed media and watercolour, and draws in conté, pencil and ink. Formerly a lecturer in Architecture at University College London, the Architectural Association, and Principal Lecturer at Hornsey College of Art. He has travelled and painted in Australasia, Africa, and the New World. *b*: Exeter, 1931. *Educ*: Blundells. *Studied*: University College London. *Exhib*: Royal Academy and other galleries world-wide. *Publications*: Sketch Book of the World (ISBN 0-9524557-0-6); William Lyons-Wilson 1892-1981 (ISBN 0-9524557-1-4); The Hedgers (ISBN 0-9524557-3-0, coloured paperback). *Address*: 14 Orchard St., St. Albans, Herts AL3 4HL. *Website*: johnraeartist.wordpress.com *Signs work*: "John Rae."

RAE, Robin, ARCA (1953). *Medium*: oil, prints, sculpture. *b*: London, 24 Nov 1928. *m*: Catherine. two *d*. *Educ*: Colet Court, Peter Symonds' Winchester. *Studied*: Ealing School of Art (1945-48); Royal College of Art (1949-1953). *Exhib*: RA, RSA, London Group, Liverpool Academy. 2 one-man shows at Little Gallery, Piccadilly (1949-50); one-man show at Dorset County Museum (1995). Group or two-man exhibitions at: Ashmolean Museum, Oxford; Aitken Dott, Edinburgh; Bridport Art Centre; Belgrave Gallery; Camden Gallery; Old Warehouse Gallery, Dorchester; Thomas Henry Fine Art, Nantucket, USA. Retrospective Exhibition: Sladers Yard, West Bay, Dorset (2008). *Works in collections*: Walker Art Gallery, Liverpool; many private collections. *Publications*: amongst many, 'Re-inventing the Landscape', Vivian Light. *Official Purchasers*: Pictures for Schools. *Works Reproduced*: 'Liverpool Seen' by Peter Davies. *Misc*: Taught at Edinburgh College of Art and Liverpool College of Art. *Address*: 4 Tunis Terrace, Bradpole, Bridport, Dorset DT6 3ET. *Email*: kate@tunis.fsnet.co.uk *Website*: www.robinraepaintings.co.uk *Signs work*: "Robin Rae".

RAEBURN, Kenneth Alexander, DA (Edin) (1966); Post Grad. Scholarship (1966-67). *Medium*: figurative sculptor (preferred medium is wood), works in a range of materials. *b*: Haddington, E. Lothian, 9 Jun 1942. *s of*: Francis James Raeburn. *m*: Helen Raeburn. one *s*. one *d*. *Educ*: Trinity Academy, Edinburgh. *Studied*: School of Sculpture, Edinburgh College of Art under Eric Schilsky. *Exhib*: RSA, SSA, various group exhbns. in Scotland, Salon des Nations Exhbn., Paris (1983); one-man show, Metropolis Galerie d'Art, Geneva (1985). *Works in collections*: having undertaken public and private commissions, the sculptor now concentrates on free-standing figures (up to life-size). *Misc*: "I have always drawn inspiration from the human figure, concentrating on a certain stillness, rather than gesture or excessive movement. The content of the work is intensely personal: the human figure 'Out of Time'". *Address*: Edingreine, Middle Terrace, Kingussie, Inverness-shire PH21 1EY. *Email*: helen.raeburn@hotmail.co.uk *Signs work*: "Raeburn."

RAGGETT, Mark Andrew, ARWS; BA Fine Art. *Medium*: acrylic/mixed media, watercolour, drawing. *b*: Pembrokeshire, 4 Dec 1953. *s of*: Jean & Paul Raggett. *Partner*: Neesh Ruben. two *s*. *Educ*: Haverfordwest Grammar School. *Studied*: Reading University. *Represented by*: ARC Prints, London; RWS, Bankside Gallery, London. *Exhib*: RA Summer Exhbns (1999, 2005); Fountain Gallery, Llandeilo; National Eisteddfod Exhbn; Stow Gallery, Shipston on Stour; East West Gallery, London; Arc Prints, London; West Wales Art Centre, Fishguard; New Leaf Gallery, Monmouth; Tenby Museum & Art Gallery, Pembrokeshire; Bankside Gallery, London. *Address*: 4 Wallingford Avenue, London W10 6QB. *Email*: markraggett@aol.com *Signs work*: 'MR'.

RAISON, Jennifer Mary. *Medium*: oil, acrylic. *b*: London, 31 Mar 1933. *d of*: Harold Sutcliffe. *m*: John Raison. two *s*: one *d*: *Educ*: 4 years at Crofton Grange Buntingford, Herts. Home tutored otherwise. *Studied*: OCA 3 years, no formal art training; BA (OU) Humanities. *Exhib*: Aldeburgh Gallery, Suffolk; Mariners Gallery, ABNA St Ives; Mall Galleries London (Art for Youth); Hintlesham Hall, Suffolk (Cobbold & Judd); Ass. International Naive Artists, Verneuil-sur-Aivre, nr. Paris; Thompson's Gallery Aldeburgh;

Royal College of Art (Art for Youth). *Works in collections*: private collections. *Publications*: in ABNA book of Naive Artists 2012. *Recreations*: painting, writing. *Address*: The Old Rectory, Theberton, Nr. Leiston, Suffolk, IP16 4RY. *Email*: johnraison@supanet.com *Website*: with ABNA (Association of British Naive Artists). *Signs work*: "JR" or "Jen Raison" (on some recent works).

RAKE, Charles Robert, NEAC; Surrey Diploma Hons. Painting Printmaking. *Medium*: oil, drawing. *b*: Crickhowell, 29 Oct 1946. *s of*: Peter Edward Tudor. *m*: Maria José. two *d*. *Educ*: The Reading Blue Coat School, Sonning on Thames, Berks. *Studied*: Farnham School of Art, Farnham, Surrey. *Exhib*: RA, NEAC, RBA, many galleries in UK, USA and Spain. One man Russell Gallery, Putney (2011, 2014). *Works in collections*: University of Surrey, Guildford; Merchant Bank of America; Their Royal Highnesses the King and Queen of Spain. *Misc*: Elected member of New English Art Club (2013). *Address*: 9 Avington Close, London Road, Guildford, Surrey, GU1 1SL. *Email*: charlesrake@hotmail.co.uk *Website*: www.charlesrake.co.uk *Signs work*: "Charles Rake".

RAMOS, Theodore S.de P., RAS Dip. (1954); RAS Silver Medal. *Medium*: oil. *b*: Oporto (Portugal), 30 Oct 1928. *m*: Julia. four *s* (one decd). *Educ*: Colegio Araújo Lima. *Studied*: Royal Academy Schools (1949-54). *Exhib*: Royal Academy of Arts, Royal Society of Portrait Painters, Portraits, Inc. (New York), Chatsworth Collection, The Guards Museum. *Works in collections*: National Portrait Gallery (Anita Leslie, Lord Thorneycroft), Royal Academy of Arts, Government House, Western Australia, The Guards Museum, Chatsworth, Valderrama Golf Club, Louisiana University, several other institutions. *Commissions*: numerous Royal and civil commissions including 'The Transfiguration'- a mural painted for number 20 St.James' Square (a famous Robert Adam house). *Publications*: illustrated for Penguin Books: 'Monumental Brasses' by Sir James Mann; 'Chinese Art' (two vols.) by William Willetts, etc. *Works Reproduced*: H.M. The Queen, H.R.H. The Duke of Edinburgh, H.R.H. Prince Charles, H.M. Queen Elizabeth the Queen Mother, The Grand Duke of Luxembourg, The Duke of Devonshire, group portraits of The Irish Guards, 'The Transfiguration'. *Clubs*: East India Club, Marylebone Cricket Club. *Misc*: Freedom and Livery of the Worshipful Company of Painter-Stainers, and the Worshipful Company of Founders. *Address*: Studio 3, Chelsea Farm House, Milmans St., London SW10 0DA. *Signs work*: Ramos.

RAMSAY, Alexander, DipAD (Hons), 1968, HDA (1969); artist in oil paint and drawing media; Senior lecturer in Fine Art, Central/St. Martin's School of Art. *b*: London, 23 Mar 1947. *m*: Tricia Gillman. two *s*. one *d*. *Studied*: Chelsea School of Art (1964-69). *Exhib*: one-man shows: Hatton Gallery Newcastle, Newcastle Polytechnic Gallery, Creaser Gallery London, Castlefield Gallery Manchester, South Square Gallery Bradford. *Clubs*: London Group. *Address*: 149 Algernon Rd., London SE13 7AP. *Signs work*: "Alex Ramsay."

RAMSBOTHAM, Meredith, BA (1965). *Medium*: oil, watercolour. *b*: Haifa, Palestine, 30 Oct 1943. *d of*: Brian & Kay Jones. *m*: Oliver. three *s*. *Educ*: Cranborne Chase School. *Studied*: The Slade (1961-65). *Represented by*: Madeleine Ponsonby, Sally Hunter, Piers Feetham. *Exhib*: New Art Centre, London; Sally Hunter Fine Art, Halkin Arcade, London; Piers Feetham Gallery, London; Minories, Ipswich; Parkin Gallery, London; The Playhouse, Salisbury; Contemporary Arts Fair, London; Ken Spelmans, York. *Works in collections*: Courtalds Collection, Arts Council of Great Britain, New College Oxford, Pilkington Glass Collection, IBM Collection, University of Melbourne. *Commissions*: Lord Rothschild. *Publications*: entry in 'Dictionary of Artists in Britain since 1945', David Buckman. *Address*: 7 Museum Chambers, Bury Place, London WC1A 2LD. *Email*: meredithramsbotham@yahoo.co.uk *Website*: www.meredithramsbotham.com *Signs work*: "MEREDITH RAMSBOTHAM".

RANASINGHE, Tissa, FRCA (1991); Dip. Tropical Agriculture (1946); Dip. Painting (1952); Dip.Sculpture (1958); Awarded first Unesco Scholarship allocated to Sri Lanka

(1958); 'Bunka Prize, '98' (Japan/Sri Lanka Friendship Cultural Fund (1998); 7th Sao Paolo Biennale 'Honourable Mention Plaque for bronze 'Brazil'. *Medium*: sculpture. *b*: Sri Lanka, 2 Nov 1925. *m*: Sally Anne. one *s*. one *d*. *Studied*: Government College of Fine Arts, Colombo, Sri Lanka; Chelsea School of Arts; RCA (bronze casting). *Exhib*: RA Summer Exhbn (since 1955 and 1974, 75, 81, 88, 89, 90, 1998); Sao Paolo Biennale (7th, 9th); 43 Group Exhbn, Royal Festival Hall (1964, 85, 87); Expo '67, Montreal Canada; solo exhbns: Lionel Wendt Gallery, Colombo, Sri Lanka (1959, 1971, 1994); RSBA; SPS; plus many galleries and exhbns in UK and worldwide. *Works in collections*: Government of Sri Lanka; MOMA, Sweden; London CC Art Collection; private collections in Sri Lanka, Germany, UK, Greece, USA, France, and Australia. *Commissions*: bronze panel for International Court of Justice, The Hague; Professor Gananath Obeyeskere, Princeton, USA; bronze statues for Sri Lankan Government; many private and corporate commissions. *Official Purchasers*: Govt. of Sri Lanka; former London CC; Museum, Malmo, Sweden. *Recreations*: reading, travel. *Address*: 7 Woodlands Rd, Isleworth, Middx TW7 6NR. *Signs work*: 'Tissa'.

RANCE, Victoria, BA Hons, MA, Fellow of the Higher Education Academy, Member of The London Group. *Medium*: sculpture, photography & installation, drawing. *b*: Wallingford, Berkshire, 5 Oct 1959. *d of*: Janet Maxtone Graham, Patrick Rance. *Partner*: Alex Pemberton. two *s*. one *d*. *Studied*: Banbury School of Art, University of Newcastle upon Tyne, Kingston University, Mexico & Bolivia (1983-4). *Exhib*: solo: The Mark Tanner Award, Stand Point Gallery, Hoxton (2004), The Economist Plaza (2000). Group: Jerwood (2007), APT Gallery (2008), Canary Wharf - 1 Canada Square (2006), New Art Centre (1993-2005), Sculpture at Goodwood (1998-2000), Yokohama Japan residency (2003), Noordbrabant Museum, Holland (1998), Kunsthalle Mannheim, Germany (1999). *Works in collections*: London School of Economics, Institute of Child Health, Hammerson plc, St.John's Waterloo, Housing 21, Banque AIG. *Commissions*: Warneford Hospital, Oxford; St. Laurence, Catford; St. Andrews, Waterloo; Mumford Mill, Deptford; Church of the Holy Family, RAF Halton; Diana Payne Myers. *Publications*: FE_2 05, Darlington Arts Centre, Sculpture at Goodwood 99/00, 98/99. *Principal Works*: Spire, St.Georges, Tooting; Wheat Spire, Mumford Mill; Bridge, Warneford Hospital. *Misc*: extensive collaborations with Clare Whistler, director and choreographer; designer for Glyndebourne Youth Opera (2002-07). *Address*: 4 Lizban Street, London SE3 8SS. *Email*: victoriarance@btinternet.com *Website*: www.victoriarance.com

RANDALL, Carl, BA Hons in Fine Art (Slade School), MA in Drawing (The Princes Drawing School) RBA; Prizes and awards: John Adams Fine Art Award, The Mall Galleries, London; 1st prize, 1998 Singer and Freidlander Water-colour Competition; 2nd prize, William Coldstream Painting Competition, The Slade School of Art; The Slade School of Art Travel Scholarship; painter in oil, and water-colour, sculptor in wood and mixed media, draughtsman in pencil and charcoal. *b*: South Shields, 26 Jul 1975. *Studied*: Slade School of Fine Art, University College, London (1995-99), The Princes Drawing School, The Princes Foundation, London (2002-03). *Exhib*: National Portrait Gallery, Royal Academy of Arts, Mall Galleries, London. *Works in collections*: Singer and Friedlander Bank, Railtrack Plc., Forbes Finances Ltd. *Address*: 22 Ryton Court, South Shields, Tyne and Wear NE33 4HS. *Email*: info@carlrandall.com *Website*: www.carlrandall.com *Signs work*: "CARL RANDALL."

RANDALL-PAGE, Peter, BA (Hons) 1977, Hon Dr of Arts, University of Plymouth (1999), Hon Dr of Letters (University of Bath 2013, University of Exeter 2010, York St John University 2009); FRSA, FRWA, FRBS; Marsh Award for Public Sculpture (2006). *b*: Rochford, Essex, 2 Jul 1954. *m*: Charlotte Eve Randall-Page. one *s*. one *d*. *Studied*: Bath Academy of Arts (1973-77). *Exhib*: 'New Sculpture and Works on Paper', Pen Arts & PCMAG, Plymouth (2014); 'Peter Randall-Page at the Yorkshire Sculpture Park' (2009-10);

'Stones, Sunlight and Shadows', New Art Centre (2008-9); 'Rock Music Rock Art', Pangolin London Gallery (2008); Gwangje Biennale, Korea (2004); 'Sculpture and Drawings 1980-1992' Leeds City AF (1992). *Works in collections*: Tate Gallery, British Museum, etc. *Commissions*: University of Music, Karlsruhe (2013); Eskisehir, Turkey (2011); University of Iowa (2011); Jerwood Foundation (2008); Eden Project (2006). *Publications*: New Sculpture and Works on Paper (2014); Peter Randall-Page at the YSP (2009); Sculpture and Drawings (1977-1992). *Address*: P.O. Box 5, Drewsteignton, Exeter, Devon EX6 6YG. *Email*: contact@peterrandall-page.com *Website*: www.peterrandall-page.com

RANDLE, Susan Ann, Dip.HE; Associate Member Guild of Railway Artists; painter. *Medium*: oil painter. *b*: Portsmouth, 16 Jun 1936. *d of*: Harry Wilson, director. *m*: Dave Randle, writer. one *s*. one *d*. *Educ*: Dominican Convent, Harare, Zimbabwe. *Studied*: Dartington College of Art, Totnes (1978-80, Chris Crickmay, John Gridley). *Exhib*: Carlos Gallery, London, Arnolfini, Bristol; one-man show: Bruyas Gallery, Torquay, Wrotham Art Festival, Salon des Paintres-Ile de Re, France; South East Open Studios. *Clubs*: Forge Arts, Romney Marsh Art Society. Weald of Kent Art Group, Folkestone Art Society. *Address*: 26 High Street, Lydd, Romney Marsh, Kent. *Email*: suerandle@aol.com *Signs work*: "Sue Randle."

RANK-BROADLEY, Ian, HDFA (Lond.) (1976), Boise scholar (1976), FRBS (1994), AWG (1995). *b*: Walton-on-Thames, 4 Sep 1952. *s of*: John Kenneth Broadley. *Studied*: Epsom School of Art (1970-74), Slade School of Fine Art (1974-76). *Works in collections*: British Museum, Fitzwilliam Museum, Cambridge, Staatliche Museen, Berlin, Rijksmuseum, Leiden, NPG London, Royal Swedish Coin Cabinet, Royal Mint, Goldsmiths' Hall, London, Imperial War Museum, Ashmolean Museum, Oxford. *Commissions*: effigy of H.M.Queen on UK coinage from 1998, effigy of H.M. Queen for Golden Jubilee crown & medal; Armed Forces Memorial (2005); H.M. Queen for the Supreme Court of the United Kingdom (2009); statue of St. Matthew for St. Matthews, Northampton (2009). *Misc*: Freeman of the Goldsmiths' Company (Liveryman, 2009); Granted Freedom of City of London (1996). *Address*: Green Farm, Nastend, Stonehouse, Glos., GL10 3RS. *Email*: irb@ianrank-broadley.co.uk *Website*: www.ianrank-broadley.co.uk

RASKIN, Philip, *Medium*: acrylic. *b*: Glasgow, 11 May 1947. *m*: Barbara. one *s*. two *d*. *Educ*: High School of Glasgow. *Studied*: Glasgow School of Art (1966-68). *Represented by*: The Jerdan Gallery, Crail; Ealain Gallery, Drymen. *Exhib*: The Jerdan Gallery, Crail; Ealain Gallery, Drymen; Affordable Art Fair, London & Bristol; Alpha Art, Edinburgh; Art Exposure Gallery, Glasgow; Art Fairs: Edinburgh, Glagow, Chelsea, Aberdeen; Steam Gallery, Devon; Fotheringham Gallery, Bridge of Allan; Susan Lemond Gallery, Glasgow; Glasgow Art Club. *Publications*: Front cover 'Artists & Illustrators' (2008); Front cover 'Picture Business' (2008). *Works Reproduced*: by Demontfort Fine Art, who place work throughout the UK (originals and limited editions). *Recreations*: playing piano. *Clubs*: Glasgow Art Club (Council Member). *Address*: 4 Baird Gardens, Strathaven, South Lanarkshire ML10 6FD. *Email*: philip_raskin@hotmail.com *Signs work*: "PHILIP RASKIN".

RASMUSSEN Peter Ole, BA Fine Art Painting. *Medium*: Oil, drawing, prints. *b*: London, 26 Jun 1954. *Partner*: Ms Sigune Hamann. *Studied*: Chelsea School of Art (1972-1977). *Represented by*: Emma Hill Eagle Fine Art, London. *Exhib*: Selected solo: Kulturhaus Standau, Berlin (191); Galerie Clara Zetkin 90, Berlin (1992, 93, 95); Geo Galerie, Berlin (1997); Eagle Gallery, London (2006, 09); Campden Gallery, Gloucs (2008, 10); Raumx, London (2013). Selected group: Kirsten Kjaers Museum, Denmark (2005); London Original Print Fair, RA (2007, 11, 13); Flowers East, London (2008); Jerwood

Drawing Prize, London (2010); RA Summer (2008, 10); London Group Open (2011); Bite Print, Mall Galleries (2012); RE London (2013). *Works in collections*: Delvina Studio Award, Spain (1992, 93); Fundación Valparaiso, Spain (1999); Cill Riaug Project, Ireland (2001); Vermont Studio Center, USA (2002); Kirsten Kjaers Museum, Denmark (2005); Bite Artists Making Print, RE Award (2012). *Commissions*: Senat Berlin (Berlin Arts Council (1991-96, 1998)). *Misc*: Has lived and worked in Scotland, Berlin, Madrid and Barcelona where he taught on the international MA of Winchester School of Art (1994-95). *Address*: 22b Thurlow Hill, London SE2 8JN. *Email*: peter@peterrasmussen.co.uk *Website*: peterrasmussenpainting.co.uk peterrasmussenportraits.co.uk *Signs work*: "P.RASMUSSEN".

RAVEN, Shane. *Medium*: limewood. *b*: Farnborough, 14 Oct 1959. *s of*: James & Kathleen Raven. *m*: Alexandra L. Raven. three *d*. *Exhib*: Battersea Fine Arts and Antiques Fair; Fergus Cochrane Antiques, Kings Rd., Chelsea; Old World Antiques, Kings Rd, Chelsea. *Works in collections*: Guild of Master Carpenters; Throgmorton Ave; Shepperton Studios; Susan Schrieburg Interior Designs. *Commissions*: Susan Schrieburg, Valerie Foster, Shepperton Studios, Maggie Charpentier, Louise Higgs (Anthemion). *Publications*: Sunday Telegraph, Appolo, Home & Gardens, Country Life, Wood Carving Magazine. *Principal Works*: Augustus Panel, English Country Gardens. *Clubs*: Assoc. Mem. Guild of Master Carvers. *Address*: 16 Thorndon Close, Orpington, Kent, BR5 2SJ. *Email*: corvuscarvings@hotmail.co.uk *Signs work*: "S. Raven".

RAWLINGS, Bryan John, BA Hons, SHA; First Class BA Honours Degree in Ceramic Sculpture; Member of Society of Heraldic Arts. *Medium*: sculpture, specialising in Heraldic Sculpture. *b*: Keynsham, 31 Mar 1949. *s of*: Graham & Joy Rawlings. *Partner*: Anne-Mary Rawlings. one *s*. one *d*. *Studied*: Somerset College of Art Foundation Course 1967-68; Stoke-on-Trent College of Art (changed to North Staffs Polytechnic mid-course); Diploma in Art and Design converted to BA Hons. *Commissions*: Eagle Star Insurance (sculpture of eagle); BAe sculptural relief bronze plaque; Bishop of Paterson, relief sculptural coat of arms; Worshipful Company of Cutlers, relief sculptural coat of arms; Worshipful Company of Girdlers, relief sculptural coat of arms. *Official Purchasers*: Manchester Magistrates Court; Ceredigion DC for Welsh Assembly Building, Aberystwyth; Port Talbot Council; Gwynedd County Council; Kenyan National Intelligence Service - all Coats of Arms (plus many more). *Works Reproduced*: my sculptural relief Royal Coat of Arms for courts, embassies, and other government buildings. *Principal Works*: 3 metre wide eagle sculpture on Eagle Star entrance, St Mary Axe; Set of London Regimental badges in the London Guildhall. *Recreations*: inventing, flying. *Clubs*: South West Inventors Club, Bristol & Wessex Flying Club. *Address*: 45 Nunney Close, Keynsham, Bristol, BS31 1XG. *Email*: bryan@bryanrawlings.com *Website*: www.bryanrawlings.com *Signs work*: "Bryan Rawlings".

RAWLINGS, Raymond, commercial artist in water-colour (retd). *b*: Windsor, 26 Apr 1934. *m*: Frances. three *d*. *Studied*: apprenticed to major art studio (London) producing artwork for major multi national companies (1951). *Exhib*: Oxford, RWA. Work in collections worldwide. *Clubs*: Oxford Art Soc. *Address*: 1 Chestnut Close, Fawley, nr. Wantage, Oxon. OX12 9YW. *Email*: ray.rawlings@tiscali.co.uk *Website*: www.rayrawlings.co.uk

RAWLINS, Janet, NDD (Illustration), ATD, book illustration, fabric collage, gouache, water-colour. *b*: Horsforth, Leeds, 3 May 1931. *d of*: E. J. Rawlins. *m*: Kenneth Parfitt d. 1971; John G. Leyland, FCA d. 2010. one *s*. *Educ*: Gt. Moreton Hall, Ches. *Studied*: Leeds College of Art. *Exhib*: RA, northern galleries. *Works in collections*: Northern galleries. 5 education committees. *Commissions*: Fabric collage for the Bishop of Ripon and Leeds (2013). *Publications*: children's books; compiled and illustrated A Dales Countryside Cookbook (1993); A Grass Rope to Catch a Unicorn; Wensleydale Wild Flowers and other illustrations (2014). *Address*: Unicorn House Bainbridge Via Leyburn N. Yorks. DL8 3EH. *Email*: jleyland@freeuk.com *Signs work*: "Janet Rawlins."

RAY, Karen, painter in oil, water-colour, pencil, coloured pencil, lecturer. *b*: Queensland, Australia, 8 Dec 1931. *m*: Stuart Ray (decd). three *s*. *Studied*: Walthamstow School of Art (Stuart Ray, John Tichell, Fred Cuming); RA Schools (Peter Greenham). *Exhib*: many times in the RA Summer Exhbn. *Address*: 91 Mountview Rd., London N4 4JA. *Signs work*: "K. Ray."

RAYMENT, Brenda, ARMS (1991); artist in oil on ivorine. *b*: Paddock Wood, Kent, 5 May 1951. *m*: Laurence Rayment. one *s*. one *d*. *Educ*: Kidbrooke School. *Studied*: Bexley AEC (1980-90, Barry Shiraishi, RMS). *Exhib*: SWA, RMS. *Address*: Willow Cottage, Main Street, Northiam, E.Sussex TN31 6LE.

RAYNOR, Trevor Samuel, former Mem. Associé, Société des Artistes Français (1977) (resigned); textile designer, artist in oil and water-colour and floral subjects in gouache. *b*: Oldham, 13 May 1929. *s of*: William Ernest Raynor, produce merchant. *m*: Margaret Joyce Marwood (decd). one *s*. *Educ*: Werneth Council School. *Studied*: Oldham School of Art (1942-45), Manchester School of Art (1945-49). *Exhib*: Paris Salon (1975, 1976, 1977); one-man shows, Salford City A.G., Swinton Memorial A.G. Work in private collections. *Works Reproduced*: prints of floral work. *Address*: 1 Hollin Cres., Greenfield, Oldham OL3 7LW. *Signs work*: "RAYNOR" or "T.S. RAYNOR."

READ, Sue, RI (1985), NDD (1963), ATD (1964); artist in water-colour. *b*: Slough, 1941. *d of*: John Melia (decd). *m*: Robert Read (divorced). three *s*. *Educ*: Aylesbury Grammar School. *Studied*: High Wycombe School of Art (1959-63), Royal West of England College of Art (1963-64). *Exhib*: Mall Galleries, RA Summer Exhbn., RWS, NEAC, Thompson's Gallery, Aldeburgh. *Publications*: International Artist Magazine; Artists & Illustrators; Watercolour: A Step-by-Step Guide, by Angela Gair. *Address*: 26 Rectory Street, Halesworth, Suffolk IP19 8AE. *Email*: susanread41@btinternet.com *Signs work*: "S.R."

READING, Peter William, MSIA (1957); painter in oil, acrylic, pastel, water-colour and etcher; design consultant, (retired 1990). *b*: London, 3 Aug 1933. *m*: Doreen Rita. two *d*. *Educ*: Edmonton County Grammar School. *Studied*: Hornsey and London School of Printing (part time). *Exhib*: London, Henley-on-Thames, Bournemouth, Gloucester, Plymouth, Penzance, St. Ives, Brest, France, Minneapolis, USA; two solo exhibs. annually, Mariners Gallery, St. Ives. *Works in collections*: various private collections in UK and USA, and St. Ives Gallery. *Clubs*: St. Ives Soc. of Artists. *Address*: 5 Higher Tamar Terr., Gunnislake, Cornwall PL18 9LP. *Email*: enq@peter-reading.co.uk *Website*: www.peter-reading.com *Signs work*: "Peter Reading" and date.

REAL, Jacqueline, FFPS (1992); contemporary painter in acrylic, collage and mixed media. *b*: Zürich, 5 Oct 1931. *d of*: Fred Berger, architect. *m*: Christopher Butler. one *s*. one *d*. *Studied*: in Zürich (1975-78), Academy of Modern Art, Masterclass, Salzburg (1979), Painting Course in Meran (1980). *Represented by*: International Art Consultants, London, Gallery One, London, Artizan Editions, Hove, Penhaven Gallery, St. Ives, Galerie Elfi Bohrer, Bonstetten (Zürich), Galerie Ruth Schwarzer, Illnau (Zürich), Galleria Borgo, Ascona (CH). *Exhib*: solo and group shows: Switzerland, England, USA and Germany. *Works in collections*: Switzerland, England, USA, Germany, including Oerlikon Contraves, Zürich, Mark Rich Switzerland, Union Bank of Switzerland Zürich and London, Zürich Insurance, Credit Swiss Bank Zürich, British Government, Johnson & Johnson, Tokai Bank, Bank of Austria, Crown Court Truro. *Publications*: New Visions, St. Ives Painters. *Clubs*: F.P.S., Soc. of Swiss Painters, Sculptors and Architects, Eastbourne Group of Artists. *Address*: 7 Bath Court, Kings Esplanade, Hove BN3 2WP. *Signs work*: "J. Real."

REAY, Ferelith, B Tech in Printmaking. *Medium*: printmaking, watercolour or oils. *b*: 12 Feb 1931. *m*: Lt. Gen. Sir Alan Reay KBE. two *s*. two *d*. *Studied*: London School of

Printmaking. *Exhib*: Chelsea Art Society, Royal Academy Summer Exhibition, Westminster Art, Printmakers Council, Hesketh Hubbard, Nine Elms, Armed Forces Art Society. *Works in collections*: many collections. *Principal Works*: Printmaking, woodcut. *Recreations*: birdwatching. *Clubs*: RSM. *Address*: 63 Madrid Road, Barnes, London SW13 9PQ. *Signs work*: "FHR".

REDEMER, Roberta, 2nd Prize, Eli Lilly "Oncology on Canvas" (2006, World-wide Comeptition, now on tour world-wide). *Medium*: acrylic, pastel, charcoal, watercolour, drawing. *b*: London, 30 Jan 1937. *d of*: Robert Mortimer. one *s*. *Educ*: Tiffins Girls School, Kingston. *Studied*: Kingston School of Art. *Exhib*: annually at Wokingham & District Art Group Exhibition, Berkshire; "Paws" Exhibition, Hertfordshire. *Works in collections*: various trading establishments in Bracknell, Berks.; private. *Works Reproduced*: copies of works on canvas in The Ambassador Hotel, 12 Upper Woburn Place, London WC1H 0HX. *Recreations*: bridge, gardening. *Clubs*: Wokingham & District Art Group; Great Hollands Art Group. *Address*: 54 Wheatley, Great Hollands, Bracknell, Berks., RG12 8UG. *Email*: roberta.redemer@ntlworld.com *Website*: www.bracknellartgallery.org.uk *Signs work*: "BREDEMER".

REDFERN, June, DA (1972); prizewinner, Scottish Young Contemporaries; Artist in Residence, National Gallery (1985); painter in oil and water-colour. *b*: St. Andrews, Fife, 16 Jun 1951. one *d*. *Educ*: Dunfermline High School, Fife. *Studied*: Edinburgh College of Art (1968-73, Robin Philipson, David Michie, Elizabeth Blackadder, John Houston). *Exhib*: many throughout Britain and USA including National Gallery, London (1985). *Works in collections*: SNGMA, National Gallery London, BBC Television, Robert Fleming plc, Arthur Andersen, Texaco, Hiscox Holdings, etc. *Commissions*: many private; corporate: Scottish Equitable. *Recreations*: opera. *Address*: 12 Lawley St., London E5 0RJ. *Website*: www.juneredfern.com *Signs work*: "June Redfern" on reverse of oils only.

REDINGTON, Simon, BA (Fine Art), Postgrad.Dip. in Art Therapy, Cert. of Advanced Printmaking; artist/printmaker in etching, woodcuts, letterpress, painting, mixed media. *b*: London, 28 Sep 1958. *Educ*: Pimlico School. *Studied*: Goldsmiths' College, Hertfordshire College of Art, Central St. Martin's College of Art. *Exhib*: NPG, RA Summer Show, Slaughterhouse Gallery, Southbank Picture Show, Royal Festival Hall, Bankside Gallery. *Works in collections*: V&A, Theatre Museum, Ashmolean Museum, N.Y. Public Library, Harvard University, Yale Center for British Art, Museum of London, Newberry Library, Chicago. *Commissions*: Peter O'Toole as Jeffery Bernard, Shaftesbury Theatre, London. *Publications*: see website. *Clubs*: R.E. *Address*: c/o 10 Maunsel Street, London SW1P 2QL. *Website*: www.kamikazepress.com *Signs work*: "S. Redington."

REES, Darren, BSc (Hons) (1983), SWLA (1985); self taught artist in water-colour of natural history particularly birds. *b*: Andover, Hants., 15 Mar 1961. *m*: Gwynneth Jane Rees (Kenny). one *s*. one *d*. *Educ*: Southampton University. *Exhib*: SWLA, Artists for Nature Foundation, Holland, Sweden, Poland, USA. *Works in collections*: Lloyds, Les Ecrins National Park, Leigh Yawkey Museum Wisconsin, Stirling Council. *Commissions*: Awards: B.B.C., R.S.P.B., Lloyds. *Publications*: Bird Impressions, Portrait of Wildlife on a Hill Farm, Birds by Character. *Misc*: Awards: R.S.P.B. Fine Art Award, Natural World Award, Young European Bird Artist Award. *Address*: New East Frew, Thornhill, Stirling FK8 3QX. *Signs work*: "Darren Rees" or "DR".

REES (HARRIS), Delphine Valerie. *Medium*: watercolour. *b*: Lucknow, India 3 Sep 1931. *d of*: Reginald Desbrosses, Dorcas Burns. *m*: Hugh Rees (decd); Patrick Harris. one *s*. three *d*. *Educ*: La Martiniere, Lucknow, India; Stratford House School, Kent. *Studied*: self-taught. *Exhib*: two RBSA Summer Exhibitions, Royal Academy Summer Exhibition (2008), Royal Botanical Gardens, Birmingham, Cotswold Galleries. *Misc*: studied at City of Birmingham College as mature student. Teacher specialising in teaching less able and disruptive pupils. *Address*: 12 Chestnut Walk, Stratford on Avon, Warks., CV37 6HQ. *Email*: del.rees@googlemail.com *Website*: www.delreeswatercolours.com *Signs work*: "Del Rees".

REES-DAVIES, Kay, ALCM (1976), SBA (1994), Cert. Botanical Merit, SBA (1994 and 2003); RHS Gold Medals (1996, 1998, 2003, 2010). *Medium*: watercolour. *b*: Brighton, 17 Jun 1936. *d of*: Rev. G R Myers BA BD. *m*: John Rees-Davies. one *s*. one *d*. *Educ*: Bretton Hall College (1954-56), Adult Study Centre, Gwynedd (1988-89). *Exhib*: SBA, London; RHS; North Wales Society of Fine Art; Oriel Ynys Mon, Anglesey; Oriel Ffin-y-Parc, Wales. *Works in collections*: RHS Lindley Library; Hunt Inst. for Botanical Documentation, Carnegie Mellon University, Pittsburgh USA; Library, RBG, Kew; Shirley Sherwood Collection; Chelsea Physic Garden Florilegium; Highgrove Florilegium. *Publications*: 'Plantas Endemicas e Avores Indigenas de Cabo Verde'; 'Contemporary Botanical Artists' Shirley Sherwood Collection; 'Fine Botanical Paintings' – Gordon Craig Gallery; 'Arte y Botanica' SBA; 'The Art of Botanical Painting' SBA (2004); 'Flower Painting from the Apothecaries' Garden', Andrew Brown, 'The Botanical Palette'; 'Plant Forms' (2013). *Recreations*: music, drama. *Clubs*: North Wales Society of Fine Art, Botanical Artists of Ness Gardens. *Address*: 6 Balmoral, The Promenade, Llanfairfechan, N.Wales LL33 0BU. *Email*: kreesd@outlook.com *Website*: www.kay-rees-davies.co.uk *Signs work*: 'Kay Rees-Davies'.

REEVE, Michael John, NDD (1959); Wedgewood Scholarship (1955, 1957). *Medium*: oil, watercolour, drawing, prints, sculpture. *b*: Kensington, 22 Apr 1939. *s of*: R.D.H. Reeve, Art Director . *m*: Liliane. two *d*. *Studied*: Camberwell School of Art, London (1952-59). *Represented by*: Michael Parkin Fine Art. *Exhib*: London. *Works in collections*: private. *Recreations*: art, design, music. *Misc*: Brother of Geoffrey R Reeve ARCA. *Address*: c/o Michael Parkin Fine Art, Studio 4 Sedding Street, 1-6 Sloan Square, London SW1. *Signs work*: "MICHAEL REEVE" or "MJR".

REEVES, Philip Thomas Langford, ARCA (1954), RE (1963), RSW (1959), ARSA (1971), RSA (1976), RGI (1981); painter-etcher; Founder member of the Edinburgh Printmakers Workshop (1967); Founder Member of the Glasgow Print Studio (1972). *b*: Cheltenham, 7 Jul 1931. *s of*: Herbert John Reeves, printer. *m*: Christine MacLaren (decd). one *d*. *Educ*: Naunton Park Senior Secondary School, Cheltenham. *Studied*: Cheltenham School of Art (1945-49), Royal College of Art (1951-54). *Represented by*: Fine Art Society, London, Open Eye Gallery, Edinburgh, Glasgow Print Studio, Glasgow, Cyril Gerber Fine Art, Glasgow, Hughson Gallery, Glasgow. *Works in collections*: Arts Council of Gt. Britain, V&A, Contemporary Art Soc., Gallery of Modern Art, Edinburgh, Glasgow A.G., Glasgow University Print Collection, Aberdeen A.G., Paisley A.G., Milngavie A.G., Dundee A.G., Edinburgh University, Stirling University, Dept. of the Environment, British Government Art Collection, Edinburgh City Art Collection; The Fleming-Wyfold Art Foundation; Royal Scottish Academy. *Address*: 13 Hamilton Drive, Clyde, Glasgow, G12 8DN. *Signs work*: "Philip Reeves."

REGO, Paula, FRCA; painter in various mediums; D. Litt. (Honoris Causa) University of St. Andrews, Scotland, and University of East Anglia; The London Institute; Oxford University; Roehampton University and Rhode Island School of Design, USA; Fellow of Murray Edwards College, Cambridge; created Dame of the British Empire in 2010. *b*: Lisbon, Portugal, 26 Jan 1935. *m*: Victor Willing (decd). one *s*. two *d*. *Educ*: St. Julian's, Portugal. *Studied*: Slade School of Fine Art. *Works in collections*: Gulbenkian Foundation, Lisbon; National Gallery, London; Tate Gallery, London; Saatchi Collection, London. *Commissions*: National Gallery, Sainsbury Wing Brasserie, mural. *Publications*: Paula Rego by John McEwen (Phaidon Press), Peter Pan (Folio Soc.), Nursery Rhymes (Thames & Hudson), Pendle Witches (Enitharmon Press). *Address*: c/o Marlborough Fine Art, 6 Albemarle St., London W1X 4BY.

REID, Paul John, MA (Hons.) Fine Art: painter in oil. *b*: Perth, 21 Apr 1975. *m*: Heather Reid. *Studied*: Duncan of Jordanstone College of Art, Dundee (1994-98). *Exhib*: Rendezvous Gallery, Aberdeen; Scottish Gallery, Edinburgh; 108 Fine Art, Harrogate. *Works in collections*: Flemings of London, Perth Museum and Art Gallery, Duke and Duchess of Roxburgh, HRH The Prince of Wales. *Publications*: Art Tomorrow-Edward Lucie Smith-Terrail, Paris (2002); A History of Scottish Art-Selina Skipwith/Bill Smith-Merrel, London (2003). *Address*: 6 Ash Grove, Scone, Perth PH2 6NU. *Signs work*: "REID."

REILLY, Kevin Patrick, FIGA (1994); painter in oil, water-colour and pastel; tutor, lecturer, founder of Hermes Galleries; studied humanities, Open University (1979-1984). *b*: Lancs., 1949. *m*: Diane. one *s*. one *d*. *Educ*: Sts. John Fisher and Thomas More, Lancs. *Studied*: Wirral Art College (1978) under Philip Smith. *Exhib*: IGA, British Soc. Oil Painters, Watercolour, Pastels, Liverpool Academy; solo exhibs. Laing, Manchester, and in Cumbria, Liverpool, Wirral, Ireland, Portico Manchester (solo) (2002), Midland Museum, Texas USA (2002), Liverpool Academy, Spectacular (2003), Glasgow (2003), Liverpool University Gallery (2003), Liverpool Artists Club (2003), Royal Cambrian Academy Open (2005). *Works in collections*: various private collections in UK, Eire, USA, Australia, Spain, Italy. *Commissions*: National and international, Artist and Illustrator Magazine, Wet Day in Dublin, (Feb. 1996), various articles in MAM magazine 2002-3. *Publications*: magazine articles, national and international, Hermes publications, prints, gift cards, postcards, limited editions, Cheshire Life. *Clubs*: Liver Sketching Club 1989. *Address*: 6 Cromarty Rd., Wallasey, Wirral, Merseyside CH44 2BH. *Signs work*: "Kevin Reilly."

REILLY-DEAS, Anne, business studies, qualified for "Mensa"; self taught artist; accounting executive; Eclipse Award 2004, Woman of the Year 2004/2005 USA, Woman of Achievement Award 2005 USA. *b*: Mullingar, 28 Nov 1950. *Educ*: Loreto, Bloomfield, Rosse, Christie Colleges. *Exhib*: Tullynally Castle, RHA, Westmeath County Library, Alliance Francaise, Longford Library, Granard Library, Caley House, Orchard House, Allen Manor, Cheltenham Show, selected for New York Prestige Artists Debut 2000, National Irish Bank, dfn Gallery NY, Christie Wild Int., Florida, Athlone Agricultural Show, invited to exhibit: Irish Council Against Blood Sport Exhbn., Art US Exhbn., International Lions Club Art Auction, Townley Hall, Art Horizons NY, International Artexpo NY, International Artexpo San Fransisco, Art 54 Gallery NY, Special Olympics World Games Art Exhbn., Mullingar Arts Centre, Rogallery NY. *Publications*: Who's Who in Art UK, Dictionary of International Biography UK, Great Women of 21st Century USA, Contemporary Who's Who of Professionals USA, European City Guide Spain, Cambridge Blue Book UK. *Works Reproduced*: catalogues, articles, exhbns. *Address*: "Greenville", Dublin Rd., Castlepollard, Co. Westmeath, Eire. *Signs work* "Anne Deas", "Reilly-Deas."

REIS, Klari, BA; MFA; Associate Research Fellowship, City and Guild of London Art School; Signpost New Graduate Competition. *Medium*: mixed media painting. *b*: Denver, USA, 4 Oct 1977. *d of*: Ron and Barbara Reis. *Educ*: Masters in Painting. *Studied*: City and Guilds of London Art School; University of California at Davis. *Represented by*: Cynthia Corbett Gallery; Beverley Knowles Fine Art; Steps Gallery, Florence Fine Art, Themes and Variations. *Exhib*: solo shows in London and Bristol; group shows: AAF New York/Bristol; ArtLondon; Cynthia Corbett Gallery, London; in the USA, UK, Italy and Spain. *Works in collections*: many international collections. *Commissions*: public: Standard Life, 10 Piccadilly, London; Matt Roberts Center, 16 Berkeley Street, London; The Guardian; The Independent; Financial Times Magazine; A-N Magazine; RA Magazine. *Email*: klarireis@hotmail.com *Website*: www.klarireis.com *Signs work*: 'Klari Reis'.

REITER, Laura, BA (Hons) (1986), MA (1989); painter in oil, acrylic and water-colour, printmaker mainly in silkscreen/linocut; PGCE, tutor/lecturer. *Medium*: mixed media/acrylics/watercolour. *b*: London, 25 Aug 1950. *m*: Steve Reiter. three *d*. *Educ*: Brondesbury and Kilburn High School. *Studied*: Kingston School of Art (1983-86), Wimbledon School of Art (1986-89), Middlesex University (1991-92). *Exhib*: Bankside Gallery, Barbican, London, Manchester Royal Exchange Theatre Gallery, Brunel University Gallery, Mall Galleries, Tavistock Gallery, Espacio Group Gallery, Llewelyn Alexander Gallery London. *Commissions*: book covers, magazine illustrations. *Publications*: 'Learn to Paint Abstracts' (Harper Collins, 2006); article, 'The Artist Magazine' (various); 'Painting Accessible Abstracts' (Batsford Books, 2010). *Address*: 5 Norman Crescent, Pinner, Middx. HA5 3QQ. *Email*: laura.reiter@btinternet.com *Website*: laurareiter.com *Signs work*: "Laura Reiter."

RELF, James Alan. *Medium*: oil, drawing, prints. *b*: Carlisle, Cumbria, 15 May 1982. *Studied*: De Montfort University (2000-01), Lincoln School of Art (2002-04); mainly self-taught. *Represented by*: www.jamesrelf.com and various galleries. *Exhib*: The City Art House, Lincoln (2006, 2007 - group shows), Gallery on the Strait (2004, 2005, 2006 - group shows), The Burrows Gallery (2007 - solo exhibition), Spencer Arts (2007 - group show), British Contemporary Art, Hong Kong (2008 - group show), Burgh House London (2009 - group show), Three Roses Gallery, Arundel (2008 - group show), The Buttermarket, Newark on Trent (2009 - solo exhibition). *Works in collections*: private/corporate. *Commissions*: private/corporate. *Publications*: Art of England, Bailgate Independant, Lincolnshire Pride, Lincolnshire Echo, The Journal, Life & Style Magazine. *Works Reproduced*: signed limited editions of 75 or under. *Address*: 14 Coningsby Crescent, Lincoln, LN4 2JL. *Email*: info@jamesrelf.com *Signs work*: "JR" or "JRELF".

RELFE, Elizabeth Anne Harvey (Liz): see SEWARD RELFE, Elizabeth Anne Harvey (Liz).

RELTON, Christine, BA (Hons) Fine Art. *Medium*: acrylic painting. *b*: Penrith, UK, 25 Apr 1959. *Partner*: Tom Marine. *Studied*: Jacob Kramer, Leeds (1977-78); Lancaster (1978-82). *Represented by*: Galleries throughout the UK. *Exhib*: many exhibitions and art fairs in UK and Europe, Asia and USA. *Works in collections*: 5 paintings in House of Lords, London. *Commissions*: many: both private and corporate. *Publications*: 'Artists in Britain since 1945' (2006 edition). *Official Purchasers*: House of Lords, July 2011. *Works Reproduced*: prints through Winn Devon, USA; International Graphics, Germany. *Principal Works*: Landscapes, still life and travel based paintings. *Recreations*: travel. *Misc*: Paints in collaboration with Tom Marine since 1996. They run the gallery 'Colourbox' as well as painting together. *Address*: 9 Carr Bank, Otley, W. Yorkshire LS21 2AE. *Email*: colourbox.reltonmarine@btinternet.com *website*: www.reltonmarine.com *Signs work*: "C.RELTON & T. MARINE" on reverse of canvas.

RELTON, Maxine, RWA; BA Hons 1st Class Sculpture; MA Sculpture; Richard Briganshaw Prize, Sculpture (London, 1975); F&L Warren Award, Farnham (1989); UWE Drawing Prize, RWA (2000); Tibbatts Associates Prize, RBSA (2004). *Medium*: works on paper (drawings, paintings, prints). *b*: Weybridge, Surrey. *Educ*: Shute School, Devon. *Studied*: Camberwell College of Art (1971-75), Slade (1975-77). *Represented by*: Maxine Relton Studio Gallery, Gloucestershire. *Exhib*: Whitechapel Gallery; Genie de la Bastille, Paris; National Museum of Women in the Arts, Washington DC; RWA; RA Summer Exhbn; Hunting/Observer, Mall Galleries; RBSA; SWE; Llewellyn Alexander Gallery; London Print W'shop; Art-in-Action; Off Centre Gallery, Bristol; Royal National Theatre, London; Guest Artist Glos. Guild of Craftsmen; Arnolfini Gallery; Spike Island, Bristol; SBA; Victoria Art Gallery, Bath; Greenwich Arts Festival, London; Solo touring show of West Africa. *Works in collections*: RWA Permanent Collection. *Commissions*: TV documentary 'Frieze Frame' (1997). *Works Reproduced*: 'Relief Printmaking' (AC Black); 'The Spirit of Trees' by F. Hagenaden (Gaia International Journal, 1990). *Misc*: Visiting Lecturer, numerous US Universities (1990-2001). *Address*: 5 The Street, Horsley, Stroud, GL6 0PU. *Email*: maxine.relton@tiscali.co.uk *Website*: www.maxinerelton.com *Signs work*: 'M Relton'.

REMFRY, David, MBE; RWS; painter in oil and water-colour. *b*: Sussex, 30 Jul 1942. *Studied*: Hull College of Art (1959-64). *Exhib*: solo shows: Mercury, London (1978/80/82/84/86/88/90/92/94/97), Edinburgh (1983), New Grafton Gallery (1973), Editions Graphiques (1974), Old Fire Engine House, Ely (1975/77/79/81/83/86/90/92/94), Ferens A.G., Hull (1975, 2005), New Art Centre, Folkestone (1976), Ankrum Gallery, Los Angeles (1980/81/83/85/87), Bohun Gallery, Henley (1978/81/83/85/87/89/91/93/96), Galerie de Beerenburght, Holland (1979/80/83/86), Middlesbrough A.G. (1981), Zack Shuster Gallery, Florida (1986/88/90), Margaret Lipworth Fine Art, Florida (1992/93/97), NPG (1992), Portal Gallery, Bremen, Germany (1993/95), Tatistcheff Gallery, NY (1996), Elaine Baker Gallery, Florida (1999, 2002), Boca Raton Museum of Art (1999, 2002), Neuhoff Gallery, NY (1999, 2001, 2004), PSI Contemporary Art Center, Museum & Modern Art NY Affiliate (2001). *Works in collections*: N.P.G., V. & A., Middlesbrough A.G., Minneapolis Museum of Art, U.S.A., Swarthmore College, Pennsylvania, U.S.A., Museo Rayo, Colombia, South America, Boca Raton Museum of Art, Florida, U.S.A., Royal Collection, England, Whitworth Art Gallery, Manchester, Contemporary Art Society, Butler Institute of American Art, Fitzwilliam Museum Cambridge . *Clubs*: Chelsea Arts, Groucho, Colony, Soho House. *Address*: 19 Palace Gate, London W8 5LS. *Email*: info@davidremfry.com *Website*: www.davidremfry.com *Signs work*: "David Remfry."

RENTON, Joan Forrest, DA, RSW; Moray House Teacher's Training Diploma; Ann Redpath Award (SAAC Special Award twice), RSW Betty Davies Award; painter and teacher. *Medium*: oil & water-colour, mixed media. *b*: 1935. *m*: Professor R. S. Renton. two *s*. one *d*. *Educ*: Dumfries Academy and Hawick High School. *Studied*: Edinburgh College of Art, Post.Dip. Travelling Scholarship for one year. *Exhib*: RSA, RSW, SSA, SAAC, RGI, RA and many private galleries in UK, Europe and USA. *Works in collections*: HRH the Duke of Edinburgh, Yorkshire Educ. Dept., Scottish Hospitals, Lothian Region Collection, Royal College of Physicians, Paintings in Hospitals and Jean Watson Trust; private collections in Europe, UK, USA and NZ. *Commissions*: Ferniehurst Castle for Lady Lothian. *Publications*: 'Scottish Watercolours' by Jack B. Firth. *Works Reproduced*: Trinity at Night, Stargazer, RSW, Edinburgh Gallery. *Clubs*: Member of RSW, VAS societies. *Address*: Holmcroft, 4 Tweeddale Ave., Gifford, E. Lothian EH41 4QN. *Signs work*: "Joan Renton."

RENTON, Margaret Mary, prizewinner, Artist Magazine (1976); finalist Laing Landscape Competition. *Medium*: oil. *b*: Ireland, 6 Nov 1931. one *s*. *Educ*: Convent education. *Studied*: Maynooth, Ireland; Epsom School of Art (1973-76). *Exhib*: RA (1977, 78, 81, 82, 84, 86, 2001); NEAC, RBA; ROI, RWA, RHA,; Stock Exchange, London; Paris (awarded Diploma, 1979); Spirit of London, Festival Hall; Walker Gallery, Camden Town; Pictures for Schools; National Museum of Wales; Gloucester Museum. *Works in collections*: in Europe, USA, Japan, Canada, Australia; solo exhbns: The New Gallery, Sutton; Art Centre, Christ Hospital, Horsham (1979). *Commissions*: The Histon Gallery, Cambridge; Bourne Hallewell, private commissions. *Publications*: local newspapers, magazines. *Official Purchasers*: Canadian Ambassador. *Works Reproduced*: 'The Signal Box, Epsom, Surrey'. *Recreations*: reading, gardening, walking, entertaining friends, visiting galleries. *Misc*: trained nurse. *Address*: 12 Dirdene Gdns, Epsom, Surrey KT17 4AX. *Signs work*: 'M Renton'.

RHIND, Margaret Scott, DA, RSW; Shell Award in Aberdeen Artists' Exhibition. *Medium*: watercolour and oil. *b*: Strichen, Aberdeenshire, 23 Feb 1935. *d of*: John H. Taylor. *m*: David Gordon Rhind. one *s*. one *d*. *Educ*: Fraserburgh Academy, Aberdeenshire. *Studied*:

Gray's School of Art, Robert Gordon's College (now Univ.) Aberdeen: sculpture and drawing - specialisation within four year course. *Exhib*: regularly, annually, in RSW, RSA, RGI exhibitions, and in several galleries throughout Scotland: The Edinburgh Gallery, John Green Fine Art, Glasgow & Tolquhon Gallery, Tarves, Aberdeenshire; solo exhibitions: Randolph Gallery, Edinburgh (1997), The River Room, Pitlochry Theatre, Pitlochry (2003). *Works in collections*: several private collections. *Commissions*: private commissions. *Recreations*: curling, bridge, walking and gardening. *Clubs*: Aberfeldy Breadalbane. *Address*: Rannoch Lea, Taybridge Road, Aberfeldy, Perthshire, Scotland, PH15 2BH. *Signs work*: Margaret S. Rhind.

RHOADES, Peter G., CFA Oxon (1958), NDD Painting (1959), MA Cardiff (1992), RE (1989); artist/lecturer in printmaking, drawing, photography; Tutor in Art, Christ Church College, Oxford, Visiting Tutor in Drawing, Ruskin School of Drawing, University of Oxford, Lecturer, Abingdon College. *b*: Watford, 6 May 1938. *m*: Jane Harrison. one *s*. three *d*. *Educ*: Bryanston School. *Studied*: Ruskin School of Drawing (1955-59, Percy Horton), Central School of Art and Crafts (1960-61, William Turnbull, Alan Davie), Cardiff Inst. of Higher Educ. (1990-92, John Gingell). *Exhib*: periodic one-man shows, numerous selected exhbns. in Britain, Europe and USA. *Works in collections*: Ashmolean Museum Oxford, John Radcliffe Hospital Oxford, Art in Hospitals, The Museum, Trondheim, Norway. *Address*: Seven Stars, Spurt St., Cuddington, Aylesbury, Bucks. HP18 0BB. *Signs work*: "PETER RHOADES" or "P.G.R."

RHYS-JAMES, Shani, MBE (2006); RCamA; BA Hons; Hunting/Observer First Prize (1993), Gold medal, Eisteddfod (1992), BP Portrait prize (1994), BBC Wales Visual Artist of the Year (1994); Jerwood Painting Prize (2003); Creative Wales Award (2006); Glyndwr Award (2007); Hon.Fellowship, UWIC, Hereford College. *Medium*: oil on linen, canvas, automata. *b*: Melbourne, Australia, 2 May 1953. *d of*: Harold Marcus Rhys-James. *m*: Stephen West, artist and curator. two *s*. *Educ*: Parliament Hill Girls' School. *Studied*: Loughborough (1972-73), St. Martin's (1973-76). *Represented by*: Martin Tinney Gallery, Cardiff; Connaught Brown, London. *Exhib*: mixed shows: Disclosures, Mostyn, Llandudno and Barcelona; Reclaiming the Madonna, Lincoln, Intimate Portraits Glyn Vivian, In the Looking Glass, Usher, Jerwood Painting Prize, Kunstlerhaus, Dortmund; The Black Cot (2004), Discerning Eye (2004); Towards Addiction, Tactile Bosch, Cardiff (2007); solo shows: Blood Ties Touring (1993), Beaux Arts Bath (1992), Martin Tinney, Cardiff (1993-2013) Facing the Self, Mostyn Llandudno, touring (1997), Stephen Lacey London (2000), Aberystwyth Tour (2004); Connaught Brown (2008-2012); The Rivalry of Flowers Aberystwyth tour London/Newcastle (2014). *Works in collections*: National Museum of Wales, Contemporary Art Soc., Glyn Vivian, Swansea, B.B.C., Usher Lincoln, Birmingham Museum, Wolverhampton Art Gallery, National Library of Wales, GoMA Glasgow, Arts Council of England, New Hall College, Cambridge, Jerwood Foundation, Hastings, Ruth Borchard Collection. *Commissions*: Florilingua, an installation collaborating with 7 prets, commissioned by Aberystwth Arts Centre. *Publications*: Art Today Edward Lucie-Smith (Phaidon); Facing the Self, Welsh Artists Talking, Tony Curtis; The Black Cot (Gomer Press, 2003); Imagining the Imagination (Seren Books), Cassandra's Rant, The Rivalry of Flowers (Seren Press 2013), Florilingua (Seren Press 2013). *Clubs*: Royal Cambrian Academy. *Address*: Dolpebyll, Llangadfan, Powys SY21 0PU, Wales. *Email*: shanirhysjames@btinternet.com *Website*: www.axisweb.org/secvpg.aspxartistID67 *Signs work*: "Shani Rhys-James."

RICE, Brian Wilfrid, NDD, ATC; Arnolfini Open (1963); Westward TV Print Prize (1971); Millfield Open (2003), Evolver Prize (2007). *Medium*: mixed media, oil, drawing, prints. *b*: Yeovil, Somerset, 12 Aug 1936. *s of*: Wilfrid Harry Rice. *Partner*: Jacy Wall. *Educ*: Yeovil Grammar School. *Studied*: Yeovil School of Art; Goldsmiths College; London University. *Represented by*: Belgrave Gallery, St. Ives; Redfern Gallery, London; The Art

Stable, Dorset; Gwen Hughes, London. *Exhib*: NVC London (1964, 65); London Arts Gallery, Detroit (1968); Verona, Padua, Milan (1970); Clytie Jessop, London (1970); Paperpoint Gallery, London (1979); touring exhbn. Bridgwater, Torrington, Plymouth univ. (1997); Retrospective (2001-2003); Messum's, London (2001); Atkinson Gallery, Millfield, Som. (2003), Atrium Gallery, Univ.of Bournemouth (2004); Bridport Art Centre (2006); Westbrook Gallery, London (2007); Redfern Gallery, London (2014); Belgrave Gallery, St. Ives (2014). *Works in collections*: Tate Gallery, V&A, British Council, Government Art Collection, over 60 public collections in UK and USA. *Publications*: 'The English Sunrise' (1972); 'A Pictorial History of Santa Claus' (1995); 'Brian Rice: Retrospective' (2001); 'Brian Rice Catalogue Raisonné of Prints: 1953-2013' (2013). *Recreations*: archaeology, music. *Address*: New House, Hewood, Chard, Somerset TA20 4NP. *Email*: jacy.wall@btinternet.com *Website*: brianrice.info *Signs work*: 'Brian Rice' or 'RICE'.

RICE, Cecil, BA (Hons) Fine Art (1983), PGCE (1989); artist in water-colour and oil. *b*: Nottingham, 3 Mar 1961. *m*: Linda. one *s*. *Studied*: Brighton College of Art (1979-83). *Exhib*: Brighton, London, Suffolk, Norfolk; one-man shows: Red Pot Gallery London, Clairmonte Galleries Brighton, Ropner Gallery, London. Work in collections internationally. *Works Reproduced*: fine art screen prints (Chapel Green Prints). *Address*: 14 Granville Rd., Hove, E. Sussex BN3 1TG.

RICE, Elizabeth Helen, RHS Gold Medal; botanical painter in water-colour; illustrator. *b*: Canterbury, 4 Apr 1947. *d of*: Patrick Arthur Rice, FRSA, farmer retd. *Educ*: Ashford School, Kent. *Studied*: Exeter College of Art (1963-65), bursary to study wallpaper design with Arthur Sanderson & Sons (1965-70). *Exhib*: Mall Galleries, Medici Gallery, Pawsey & Payne, St. James's, Jersey Wildlife Preservation Trust, C.I., McEwan Gallery, Scotland, Hunt Institute, USA, etc. *Works in collections*: HRH The Princess of Wales, Hunt Institute for Botanical Documentation USA, Bridgeman Art Library. *Commissions*: Sultan of Oman, Sissinghurst Castle Kent, Medici Society, etc. *Publications*: contributor to Collins Fieldguide to Crops of Britain and Europe, Reader's Digest Fieldguide to Butterflies, Collins Gem Guide to Herbs, etc. *Address*: Flat F, 22 Bassett Road, London W10 6JJ. *Signs work*: "Elizabeth H. Rice."

RICH, Graham Denton, BA Hons, PGCE (Distinction), MA (Distinction). *Medium*: mixed media. *b*: Kingswood, Surrey, 23 Feb 1945. *s of*: L.A & B.E Rich. *m*: Lesley Kerman. one *s*. one *d*. *Studied*: Foundation (Bursary Award), BA Hons, Exeter College of Art (1963/1967), PGCE, Bristol University (Distinction, 1967/1968), MA Exeter University (Distinction 1987/89). *Represented by*: The Fine Art Society, 148 New Bond Street, London W1S 2JT. *Exhib*: Artist with Gordon Hepworth Fine Art (1990-2006), 'The Sea, The Sea' Ingleby Gallery, Edinburgh (1999), 'Ian Hamilton Finlay and Friends' Pittenwheem (2002), 'Time and Tide' Margaret Mellis and Graham Rich, The Hub, Ingleby Gallery, 'Greenwaters' Pier Gallery, Stromness, Orkney (1998), 'Beyond Stereotypes' Tibilisi, Georgia (2005), 'Spike Open', Spike Island, Bristol (2005), Vannabe Museum, Endhoven (2006), Cairn Gallery, Nailsworth (1988-91, 1996, 97, 99). Artist with the Fine Art Society 2006. 'Monochrome 1' 2006, 'Private Keep Out' (solo exhibition) 2007, 'Monochromed 2' 2007, 'Trying to Reach the Sea', Bourne Fine Art, Edinburgh (solo, 2008), 'Hut' The Fine Art Society, London (2008/9); 'Open Sea' The Belgrave Gallery St. Ives (2011); 'Crossing Lyme Bay' The Fine Art Society, London, 'Things that I love at the Fine Art Society' curated by Sir Peter Blake (2013). *Works in collections*: Victoria and Albert Museum. *Publications*: "Green Waters" ed. Alec Finlay (pub. Morning Star), 'Open Sea' pub The Belgrave Gallery St. Ives (2011); 'HUT' The Fine Art Society (2008); 'Trying to Reach the Sea' pub Bourne Fine Art Edinburgh (2008); 'Private Keep Out' The Fine Art Society (2007); 'Monochromed' FAS (2006); 'Sea Level' October Foundation Eindhoven Holland; 'Sea Dreams' Victoria Gallery Bath (1998); 'Graham Rich - A Memoir' Little Silver (1997); 'Open Sea' Thomas A Clark, pub The Cairn Gallery, Nailsworth. *Works Reproduced*: "Two

Painters", works by Alfred Wallis and James Dixon, Irish Museum of Modern Art, Tate Gallery St. Ives, Merrell Holberton. *Address*: 13, Riverside Road, Topsham, Devon EX3 0LR. *Email*: graham.d.rich@btinternet.com. *Website*: www.faslondon.com. *Signs work*: "GRAHAM RICH", "GRAHAM D. RICH" or boat.

RICHARDS, Patricia, NDD; freelance display artist, art tutor with Adult Educ. including art for the handicapped, pre-school toddlers and paper sculpture for primary school children; diversional therapist for the elderly (retired), Clare House Nursing Home, Walton, Surrey; artist in oil, water-colour, pencil and pen work; demonstrator of varied crafts; private art tutor for the over 60s. *b*: New Malden, Surrey, 9 Nov 1935. divorced. *d of*: Harold Richards. one *s*. one *d*. *Educ*: Wimbledon County Grammar School. *Studied*: Kingston Art School (1950-55, Reginald Brill). *Exhib*: Graphic Artists (1984), Heritage '84 (National Trust), RA (1984), Mall Galleries, Festival Hall, London, Guildford House, Blaydon Gallery, Parkshot Gallery, Richmond, Garden Gallery, Kew, Boathouse Gallery, Walton; one-man show, Trends (FPS) and Esher. Work in private collections. *Misc*: art tutor for the over 50s, Walton Day Centre, Walton, Surrey. *Address*: 39 Woodlands, Meadowlands Pk., Weybridge Rd., Addlestone, Surrey KT15 2RQ. *Signs work*: "P. Richards" or "P.RICHARDS."

RICHARDSON, Barbara E., BA (Hons), RBA (1996); elected member of Small Paintings Group (2006); de Laszlo Medal Winner at RBA (2008). *Medium*: oils, watercolour/gouache. *b*: 29 Jun 1944. two *s*. *Studied*: Chelsea School of Art (1975-79). *Exhib*: NPG Portrait Competition, RA, NEAC, London Group Open, Discerning Eye, ROI, RP, RBA, RWS, Singer & Friedlander/Sunday Times. *Address*: 71 Engadine St London SW18 5BZ. *Email*: barbara.richardson@btconnect.com *Signs work*: "B.R." (oils), "Barbara Richardson" (water-colours).

RICHARDSON, Fran, BA (Hons) Fine Art (2005); MA Fine Art (2006). *Medium*: Oil; drawing. *b*: Dewsbury, 1974. *Studied*: City & Guilds of London Art School, London. *Exhib*: Aspex, Portsmouth (2008, 2009); Bristol Drawing School; Pallant House Gallery, Chichester; The Bristol Gallery; 20/21 British Art Fair; The Kowalsky Gallery; RWA Bristol; Mall Galleries, London; London Art Fair (2007, 2008, 2010); Sartorial Contemporary Art; Beverley Knowles Fine Art; Boundary Gallery; Pastel Society; National Open Art Competition. *Works in collections*: Public and private. *Publications*: Manifest International Drawing Annual 4. *Clubs*: Chelsea Arts Club. *Misc*: 2007 to present, visiting lecturer, City & Guilds of London Art School, London. *Address*: Chichester, West Sussex. *Email*: mail@franrichardson.com *Website*: www.franrichardson.com *Signs work*: "FRAN RICHARDSON".

RICHARDSON, Geoffrey Philip, landscape artist in oil, water-colour, etching, drypoint. *b*: Woodbridge, 15 Apr 1928. *s of*: Philip John Richardson, cabinet maker. *Educ*: Woodbridge Elementary School. *Studied*: Ipswich School of Art (1942-46) under A. Ward, ARCA, A W Bellis, ARCA, Miss E. Wood, ARCA. *Exhib*: RI, NS, Summer Salon; one-man shows, Haste Gallery, Ipswich, Deben Gallery, Woodbridge; and various group shows. *Works in collections*: England, America, Germany, Turkey, New Zealand. Drypoint prints in permanent collection Woodbridge Museum. *Works Reproduced*: A film of artists' life and work shown on YouTube and on DVD. *Address*: 21 Jubilee House, Seckford Alms Houses, Seckford Street, Woodbridge IP12 4NB. *Signs work*: "G. Richardson", followed by date and monogram, paintings, and "G" engraved in etchings and drypoint.

RICHARDSON, Ilana, DipAD (1968); painter in water-colour and oils, screen printer. *b*: Haifa, Israel, 1946. *m*: Crispin Ellison. two *d*. *Studied*: Betzalel Academy of Art, Jerusalem (1963-67), Hornsey College of Art (1967-68). *Exhib*: CCA Galleries London, Oxford, Bath, Window Gallery Brighton, RA, Catto Gallery, Tidal Wave Gallery, Hereford, Brighton Festival, Roynee Fine Art and many exhbns. abroad. *Commissions*: St. John's College, Oxford; McDonalds International; Taylor's Port, Portugal; Crofts, Portugal; many private commissions. *Publications*: participated as artist in The New Guide to Screen Printing by Brad Faine. Prints published by CCA since 1982 printed at Coriander Studio London. Posters published by the art group and Ikea. Gicleé prints published by the Artist. *Clubs*: Member, Sussex Watercolour Society. *Address:* 66 Langdale Gardens, Hove, East Sussex BN3 4HH. *Email*: art@ilana-richardson.com *Website*: www.ilana-richardson.com *Signs work*: "Ilana Richardson."

RICHARDSON, Michael Peter. *Medium*: painter in watercolours and oils. *b*: Hendon, 7 Mar 1943. *m*: Catherine. *Educ*: Ipswich School. *Studied*: Ipswich School of Art, under Bernard Reynolds and John Green. *Exhib*: RI, RSMA (Mall Galleries), many galleries London and Home Counties. *Commissions*: Korean Air, Han Jin Shipping, Hutchison Ports, Kingsmead Publications. *Clubs*: Wapping Group of Artists, Chelsea Art Society. *Address*: 17 Esmonde Drive, Manston, Kent, CT12 5LY. *Email*: michprich@aol.com *Website*: www.michaelrichardsonfineart.com *Signs work*: "Richardson", or "MR".

RICHARDSON, Philip David, BA (Hons.) 1974 (Painting). *Medium*: oil and watercolour. *b*: Harpenden, 11 Oct 1951. *Studied*: St. Albans School of Art (1970-71), Liverpool College of Art (1971-74). *Exhib*: recent solo shows include: Highgate Contemporary Fine Art, London (2001, 2003, 2005, 2008, 2010, 2012), Enid Lawson Gallery, London (2002, 2004, 2006); has particpated in group shows at the above plus: The Lime Tree Gallery, Long Melford and Bristol, Morningside Gallery Edinburgh, Pantiles Edge Gallery Tunbridge Wells, New Grafton Gallery London, Star Gallery Lewes, Rowley Gallery London. *Address*: Studio 1, The Round House, Angley Park, Cranbrook, Kent TN17 2PN. *Website*: philip-richardson.com

RICHARDSON, Ray, BA (Hons) 1987; artist in oil and printmaking. *b*: London, 3 Nov 1964. *m*: Gila. two *s*. *Studied*: St. Martin's School of Art (1983-84), Goldsmiths' College (1984-87). *Exhib*: Boycott Gallery, Brussels (1989, 1992, 1995, 1998, 2000, 2001, 2002, 2005), Galerie 31, Lille (1990), Gallery Aoyama, Tokyo (1999, 2002), Galerie Alain Blondel, Paris (1994, 1996, 1998, 2000, 2003), Beaux Arts, London (1994, 1996, 1999), Mendenhall/Sobieski Gallery, LA (1998, 2005), Gallery Fabien Fryns, Marbella (2002, 2004), Advanced Graphics, London (2002, 2004, 2006), New Arts Gallery Connecticut USA (2005), Gallery 11 London (2006). *Works in collections*: de Beers, J.P Morgan, NPG London, Kasen-Summer, NY, Tama University, Tokyo, RCA London, V. & A. Museum, London, Ashmolean Museum Oxford, Arnold Collection Connecticut. *Commissions*: Sir Matt Busby (commemoration sculpture), Lennox Lewis (portrait), paintings for the RSC. *Publications*: Ray Richardson: 'One Man on a Trip', 'Oil on Canvas', 'British Figurative Painting', 'British Sporting Heroes'; TV: Oil on Canvas (BBC2), Titian National Gallery Films, Sampled LWT; radio: Radio 3 Artists on Music, BBC London various interviews. *Official Purchasers*: Telegraph Magazine. *Clubs*: Royal Brussels British F.C., Old Roan F.C., King Vic F.C., Old Tennisonians FC. *Address*: 58 The Hall London SE3 9BG. *Website*: www.rayrichardson.co.uk *Signs work*: "RAY RICHARDSON."

RICHES, Lizzie. *Medium*: oil and pastel. *b*: London, 1950. one *s*. one *d*. *Educ*: Chingford Grammar School. *Studied*: Camberwell School of Art. *Represented by*: Portal Gallery, 15 New Cavendish Street, London W1G 9UB. *Exhib*: Chicago, Paris, Holland, Germany, London. *Works in collections*: P&O, Sainsbury, Prudential, Accenture. *Commissions*: London Underground, Leopold Joseph, Websters Publishing. *Works Reproduced*: Livre de Poche (France), Garsington Opera, London Underground. *Recreations*: wine, books, travel, friends. *Address*: Fairhurst Gallery, Bedford Street, Norwich, NR2 1AR. *Signs work*: Lizzie Riches.

RICHMOND, Robin, BA, MA; artist in water-colour, pastel, mixed media, oil; writer and broadcaster. *b*: Philadelphia, USA, 7 Nov 1951. *d of*: Patricia Cooper Richmond, M.A. *m*: Dr. James Hampton. one *s*. one *d*. *Educ*: St. George's English School, Rome. *Studied*:

Chelsea School of Art (1969-74). *Exhib*: (selected) Mercury Gallery (1989, 1990, 1992), Barbican Centre (1992); group shows: (selected) Cleveland Biennale (1990), Southwestern Arts, Dallas (1993), etc. *Works in collections*: San Francisco Fine Art Museum, Middlesbrough A.G., MoMA (NY). *Publications*: (selected) illustrated: The Magic Flute (Faber); author: Michelangelo and the Creation of the Sistine Chapel (Barrie and Jenkins, 1992), Introducing Michelangelo (Little Brown, 1992), Story in a Picture, Vols. I, II (Ideals, 1992, 1993), Frida Kahlo in Mexico (Pomegranate, 1993). *Address*: c/o Rebecca Hossack Gallery, 35 Windmill St., London W1. *Signs work*: "Robin Richmond."

RICKETT, Michael, BA Hons English; Foundation Degree in Fine Art; BA Hons, MA Creative Practice. Awards: Women's Hospital Purchase Prize (2010), Highly Commended: Hope University Alumni Exhibition (2011). Founder Member of the Liverpool School art movement (2013). *Medium*: print, acrylics on canvas, wood reliefs, woodcuts. *b*: Liverpool, 12 Dec 1942. *m*: divorced. one *s*. one *d*. *Studied*: University of Liverpool (1960-63); Liverpool Hope University (2009-2013). *Exhib*: Liverpool Anglican Cathedral (Liverpool School launch exhibition, 2013); Arteology Galery, Hulme, Lancashire (2013); Liverpool Clove Hitch Gallery (2013); RBS (2012); Liverpool CUC Gallery (2012). *Works in collections*: Liverpool Women's Hospital. *Address*: 25 Coventry Road, Liverpool L15 9HR. *Email*: mikerickett007@yahoo.co.uk *Website*: www.dot-art.co.uk/artist/mike-rickett *Signs work*: "Mike Rickett".

RICKETTS, Jean, RHS Gold Medal, RHS Silver Medal. *Medium*: watercolour. *b*: Wigston, 14 Apr 1929. *m*: widowed. one *s*. one *d*. *Principal Works*: Proteas, Western Cape, South Africa; Dahlias, Types of. *Clubs*: West Wickham Art Club. *Address*: 48 Camden Park Road, Chislehurst, Kent BR7 5HF. *Email*: jeanandleslie@aol.com *Signs work*: "Jean Ricketts".

RIDLER, Valerie, ASWA. *Medium*: mixed media and oil. *b*: Bristol, 29 Oct 1940. *m*: Mr C Ridler. one *s*. two *d*. *Studied*: Bath College of Art. *Exhib*: Mall Galleries, London; Bath College of Art; The Guild, Bristol. *Clubs*: South Cotswold Art Society (Chairlady); Thornbury Art Society; Winterbourne Art Society. *Address*: 10 Mill Close, Frampton Cotterell, South Gloucestershire, BS36 2RJ. *Signs work*: 'VAL RIDLER'.

RIDLEY, Annabel, Member, Chelsea Art Society; Craft Member Guild of Glass Engravers; mem. Army Arts Society; National Society of Painters, Sculptors and Printmakers. *Medium*: oil and watercolour; diamond point and drill glass engraving. *b*: London, 27 Aug 1940. *m*: Adam. one *s*. two *d*. *Educ*: Hatherop Castle. *Studied*: South Thames College. *Exhib*: Cork Street; Mall Galleries; Sotheby's; NEAC; Kuga Gallery. *Works in collections*: HRH Prince of Wales; HRH Duchess of York. *Commissions*: BBC; RICS; Sultanate of Oman; British Council, Yemen; Winchester College; Yehudi Menuhin School; Radio Times; Law Society. *Official Purchasers*: Richmond Borough Council. *Works Reproduced*: Glass engraving. *Principal Works*: 12 x 17ft mural for hotel in Mexico. *Recreations*: tennis, swimming. *Address*: 29 Richmond Hill, Richmond, Surrey, TW10 6RE. *Email*: a.ridley@btinternet.com *Website*: www.annabelridley.co.uk

RIDLEY, Martin Friedrich, HND; artist and wildlife illustrator. *b*: Liverpool, 9 Aug 1967. *Educ*: Calday Grange Grammar School, Wirral. *Studied*: Carmarthenshire College of Technology and Art (1985-88). *Exhib*: 'Birds in Art' Leigh Yawkey Woodson Art Museum, Wausau, Wisconsin, USA, Nigel Stacy-Marks Gallery, Perth, Scotland, The Wildlife A.G, Lavenham, Suffolk, SWLA, 'Wild in de Natur' Enschede, Holland, Theatre in the Forest, The Grizedale Soc. Cumbria, St. Helier Gallery, Jersey, John Noott Galleries, Carousel Gallery, 'Nature in Art' Wallsworth Hall, Glos. *Publications*: The Best of Wildlife Art (North-light Books, 1997). *Address*: c/o John Noott Galleries, 14 Cotswold Ct., Broadway, Worcs. WR12 7AA. *Signs work*: "Martin Ridley."

RIDLEY, Philip, BA (Hons); artist in oil and charcoal. *b*: London, 29 Dec 1962. *Educ*: St. Martin's School of Art. *Exhib*: The Vinegar Blossoms. *Address*: c/o Lamont Gallery, 65 Roman Rd., Bethnal Green, London E2 0GN. *Signs work*: "Philip Ridley."

RIDLEY, Virginia. *Medium*: oil. *b*: London, 13 May 1933. *d of*: Count Cosimo de Bosdari. *m*: Simon Ridley. one *s*. two *d*. *Educ*: private and at Arts Educational School as a dancer. *Studied*: Heatherley Art School (life drawing, 1950s). *Exhib*: RA Summer Exhbn (several times); Mall Galleries; Wykeham Gallery; Barnes Gall.; Scotland, Jersey, etc. and regularly in Rye. *Works in collections*: private collections. *Commissions*: many oils of children. *Works Reproduced*: for Medici. *Recreations*: gardening, tapestry, tennis, bridge. *Address*: Oxney House, Wittersham, Tenterden, Kent TN30 7ED. *Email*: VRidley@btinternet.com *Website*: http://www.VirginiaRidley.co.uk *Signs work*: 'V.Ridley'.

RIGDEN, Geoffrey, NDD (1963), ARCA (1966); painter/sculptor in acrylic, oil, canvas, wood; visiting artist, Cyprus College of Art. *b*: Cheltenham, 22 Jul 1943. *s of*: John S. Rigden. *Educ*: King's School, Gloucester, Grammar School, Weston-super-Mare. *Studied*: Somerset College of Art, Taunton (1960-63, Terence Murphy), R.C.A. (1963-66). *Exhib*: John Moores Liverpool (prize, 1965), Tolly Cobbold (prize, 1977), Hayward Annual (1980-82); one-man shows: Francis Graham-Dixon Gallery (1988, 1990, 1993, 1995). *Works in collections*: Arts Council, Contemporary Art Soc., Eastern Arts Assoc. *Address*: 57 Reardon House, Reardon Street, London E1 9QJ. *Signs work*: "Rigden."

RIGGS, Clive, BA (Hons) SGFA, PGCE, Dip. Eng. Language Studies (Open) MIfL. *Medium*: oils, watercolour, pencil, relief and intaglio print, mezzotint engraving. *b*: Bournemouth, 19 Aug 1964. *s of*: Mr & Mrs F Riggs. *Educ*: The King's School, Ely. *Studied*: Duncan of Jordanstone College of Art and Design (1995-99), The Open University (2008-10). *Represented by*: The Lawson Gallery, Cambridge. *Exhib*: The Leith Gallery, Edinburgh (1999, 2000, 2001); Compass Gallery, Glasgow (1999); Cambridge Open Studios (2005, 06); Society of Graphic Fine Art (2003, 04, 07, 08, 10, 11, 12), RK Burt Paper 2012. *Works in collections*: private collections UK; University of Dundee. *Commissions*: The King's School Ely Swimming Pool Appeal design. *Clubs*: Parachute Regiment Ass. Cambridge '85 branch. *Misc*: Professional Associate for the Society for All Artists, Cambs. Cricket Umpires and Scorers Association Education Officer; Curriculum Development Manager, Cambridgeshire Adult Learning & Skills. *Address*: 12 Station Road, Swaffham Prior, Cambridge, CB25 0LG. *Email*: clive.riggs@talk21.com *Website*: www.saa.co.uk/art/cliveriggs *Signs work*: "CLIVE RIGGS".

RILEY, Bridget, CBE (1972), ARCA; 1st English painter to win the major Painting Prize at Venice Biennale (1968); painter. *b*: London, 1931. *Studied*: Goldsmiths' College of Art; Royal College of Art. *Works in collections*: Arts Council, Tate Gallery, V&A, British Council, Museum of Modern Art, New York, Albright Knox Gallery, Buffalo, Gulbenkian Foundation, Art Gallery of Victoria, Melbourne, Stuyvesant Foundation, Chicago Institute, Whitworth A.G., Manchester, Power Gallery of Contemporary Art, Sydney, Walker A.G., Liverpool, Dept. of the Environment, Fitzwilliam Museum, Cambridge, Scottish National Gallery of Modern Art, Edinburgh, Ulster Museum, Belfast, Museum Boymans van Beuningen, Rotterdam, Stedilijk Museum, Amsterdam, Ohara Museum, Okayama-Ken, National Gallery of Australia, Canberra. *Address*: Karsten Schubert Ltd., 41-42 Foley St., London W1P 7LD.

RILEY, James Ingham, NDD. *Medium*: watercolour. *b*: Oswaldtwisle, Lancs, 15 Sep 1928. *m*: Marion Bradley. *Studied*: Accrington School of Art (1942-47, 1949-50). *Exhib*: many galleries in N.W. England, both mixed and with Marion Bradley mostly at Wolf House Gallery, Silverdale, Lancs. *Works in collections*: many private and corporate collections here and abroad. *Principal Works*: mountain landscapes. *Recreations*: climbing, walking, biking. Semi-retired now. *Clubs*: Lake Artists Society (1982), Ambleside Art Society, Lancaster Art

Society. *Address*: Gale House Villa, Low Gale, Ambleside LA22 0BB. *Signs work*: "J Ingham Riley".

RIMMINGTON, Eric, artist in oil and charcoal. *b*: Portsmouth, 14 Jun 1926. one *d*. *Studied*: Slade School of Fine Art. *Represented by*: Bohun Gallery. *Exhib*: many mixed exhbns. in public and private galleries since 1963, R.A., Mercury Gallery (1983-99), Bohun Gallery, Henley-on-Thames (1999-present), Millinery Works Gallery, London (2000-present). *Works in collections*: Bradford City A.G., Gulbenkian Foundation, Scarborough A.G., Museum of London, Imperial War Museum, Reading Museum. *Address*: c/o Bohun Gallery, 15 Reading Road, Henley-on-Thames, Oxon, RG9 1AB. *Signs work*: "E.R." "Eric Rimmington" or not at all.

RISOE, Paul Schjelderup, DipAD (Painting) (1968), ATC (1972). *Medium*: Figurative painter, oil and acrylic. *b*: Calcutta, 19 Mar 1945. *m*: Clare Perry. two *s*. one *d*. *Educ*: Christ College, Brecon. *Studied*: Epsom (1963-65, Leslie Worth), Chelsea (1965-68, Brian Young, Jeremy Moon). *Exhib*: Young Contemporaries, RA; one-man shows, London, Middlesbrough, Newbury; various mixed exhbns including Discerning Eye, and Sunday Times Watercolour Competition. *Works in collections*: International, Leicester Educ. Authority etc. *Address*: 3 Tower Hill Court, Kingsclere, Newbury, Berks. RG20 5SS. *Email*: paulrisoe@hotmail.co.uk *Website*: www.paulrisoe.com *Signs work*: "Paul Risoe."

RITCHIE, Ian, CBE (2000); RA (1998); Professor of Architecture RA Schools (2004). *Medium*: etching, stainless steel sculptures, light sculptures. *b*: Hove, 24 Jun 1947. *s of*: Christopher Charles Ritchie. *Partner*: Jocelyne van den Bossche. one *s*. *Educ*: Varndean G.S. *Studied*: Liverpool and Univ. Westminster. *Exhib*: Royal Academy; Reina Sofia Museum of Modern Art; Lodz Municipal Art Gallery; Venice Biennale; numerous UK and overseas exhibitions. *Works in collections*: Royal Academy, Renia Sofia Museum of Modern Art, Lodz Municipal Art Gallery, Hugh Lane Gallery (Dublin). *Commissions*: The Spire, Dublin; Alba de Milano sculpture, Milan; 'S' Seat, Turville Sun, Log, Fountain. *Publications*: 'The Biggest Glass Palace in the World' (Ellipsis 1997), Plymouth Theatre Royal Production Centre (Categorical Books, 2003), 'The Spire', Ian Ritchie Architects (Categorical Books, 2004), 'The RSC Courtyard Theatre' (Categorical Books, 2007), 'The Leipzig Book of Drawings' (RA, 2007), 'Lines' (Royal Academy 2010), 'Being an Architect' (Royal Academy 2013). *Works Reproduced*: etchings of architectural projects with poems. *Principal Works*: etchings. *Recreations*: writing, reading, thinking. *Clubs*: Arts. *Address*: 14 Garford Street, London E14 8JG. *Email*: ian@rvdbvr.co.uk *Website*: www.ianritchiearchitects.co.uk *Signs work*: "Ian Ritchie".

RITCHIE, Paul Stephen, DipAD (1972); painter, etcher and intaglio printmaker; formerly ran Manchester Etching Workshop; formerly ran, Two Rivers Paper Co. (1984-88). *b*: Chatham, 29 Oct 1948. *Educ*: Taunton School. *Studied*: Somerset College of Art, Manchester College of Art and Design (Norman Adams, Brendan Neiland), Croydon College of Art. *Exhib*: RA, RSA, SAC, MAFA, Whitworth A.G. *Works in collections*: Arts Council, SAC, Johnsonian, SNGMA, Hunterian, Aberdeen A.G., Salford A.G., Bradford A.G., Oldham A.G., Rochdale A.G. *Publications*: in conjunction with V&A and BM: facsimile edition of William Blake's Songs of Innocence and of Experience (1983). *Address*: Seaview, Collieston, Ellon, Aberdeenshire AB41 8RS. *Website*: www.ritchieart.co.uk *Signs work*: "Paul Ritchie."

RITMAN, Lieke, Interior Design Diploma. *Medium*: mixed media painting on board. *b*: Holland, 23 Apr 1942. *Educ*: Royal Melbourne Institute of Technology Australia. *Studied*: Interior Design (5 year course). *Exhib*: DeMarco Edinburgh, Marjorie Park London, Dublin, Shipston-on-Stour, Penwith Gallery, St. Ives, New Craftsman St. Ives, Plumbline Gallery, St. Ives, Penzance, Truro, Brittany. *Recreations*: walking, cycling, foreign travel. *Clubs*: Penwith Society of Arts (mem.). *Address*: 6 Bowling Green Terrace, St. Ives, Cornwall, TR26 1JS. *Email*: lieke.ritman@tesco.net

RIZVI, Jacqueline Lesley, RBA (1992), RWS (1986), ARWS (1983), NEAC (1982), DipAD (1966); painter. *b*: Dewsbury, Yorks., 25 Jun 1944. *d of*: Fred Haigh Sterry, FCA, AACCA. *m*: Syed Muzaffar Rizvi. one *d*. *Educ*: Whitley Bay Grammar School. *Studied*: The Polytechnic, Regent St. (1962-63), Chelsea School of Art (1963-66, Patrick Symons, RA, Norman Blamey, RA). *Exhib*: RA, RI, RSMA, NEAC, RWS, RBA, ICAF; Bath Festival; London Chamber of Commerce; Sothebys; World of Watercolours, Park Lane; Lineart, Ghent; 20th Century British Art Fair; Minton Fine Art Toronto; Ruthven Gallery, Ohio; Glyndebourne; The Upstairs Gallery, R.A.; New Grafton Gallery; The New Academy Gallery; Agnews, National Trust Foundation for Art; Fosse Gallery; Patterson Gallery; Milne and Moller; Tokyo; St. James' Art Group; The Arts Club; The Hague; Castle Museum, Norwich; Catto Gallery; Waterman Fine Art; Exchange Quay, Manchester; Visions of Venice; SAVE, The Heart of the City; Duncan Miller; Albany Gallery, Cardiff; Malcolm Innes, Edinburgh; Bilbao; Seville; Barcelona; Gorstella Gallery, Chester; City Gallery; Duncan Cambell; Thompsons Gallery; Whittington Gallery, Amersham; Discerning Eye; County Gallery, Maidstone; Piers Feetham; Mexico City; Crown Estates Millenium, New Academy/Curwen; Vaila Fine Art, Shetland; Royal Cornwall Museum; six one-man shows: The Sallyport Tower, Newcastle-upon-Tyne, Cale Art, Chelsea, New Grafton Gallery, The Upstairs Gallery, RA, The New Academy Gallery. *Works in collections*: murals for The Medical School, St. Mary's Hospital, Paddington; London Underground Ltd., London Clubs Ltd., Shell, Amoco, Davy Corporation. *Commissions*: three murals for The Medical School, St. Mary's Hospital, Paddington; London Underground Ltd.; London Clubs Ltd. *Clubs*: The Arts, Dover Street. *Address*: c/o Whittington Fine Art, 26 Hart Street, Henley-on-Thames, Oxon RG9 2AU. *Signs work*: "J.L.R." and year.

ROBERT, Mary, MA RCA (1985), BA (1973); photographer/artist in photographic and mixed media; Professor of Lens Media at Richmond International University, London; Tutor in Photography, Royal College of Art; Fellow, Royal College of Art. *b*: Atlanta, Georgia, 11 Dec 1951. *d of*: R.R. Robert, Engineers. *m*: Dr. John Dickerson. *Educ*: Miami University, Oxford, Ohio; University of Akron, Akron, Ohio; R.C.A., London. *Represented by*: Axiom, Lebrecht. *Exhib*: USA, UK, France, Japan, Mexico, Australia. *Works in collections*: Bibliothéque Nationale, Paris, NPG London, Indianapolis Museum, USA, and private collections in USA, Britain, Europe, Asia. *Commissions*: many, especially in the areas of classical music and portraiture. *Misc*: UK Board Member: Young Photographer's Alliance. *Address*: 47 Creffield Rd., London W5 3RR. *Email*: robertm@richmond.ac.uk *Signs work*: "Mary Robert."

ROBERTS, Gladys Gregory, RCA; artist in oil and acrylic. *b*: Rhyl. *d of*: C. Wesley Haslam, surveyor. *m*: Prof. E. J. Roberts, MA, MSc (decd). one *d*. *Educ*: Pendre Private School, Prestatyn. *Studied*: Bangor Technical College (1959-63). *Exhib*: Royal Cambrian Academy of Art, Tegfryn Gall., Menai Bridge, Anglesey. *Address*: "Bryn Llinos", Victoria Drive, Bangor LL57 2EY. *Signs work*: "G. Roberts."

ROBERTS, Marguerite Hazel: see HARRISON, Marguerite Hazel.

ROBERTS, Richard Travers, BA Hons Fine Art Sculpture. *Medium*: sculpture - bronze, glass. *b*: Little Horwood, Bucks, 11 Oct 1956. *s of*: Keith Roberts & Betty (nee) Travers. *Partner*: Michael Glasson. *Educ*: St.Martins, Northwood, Middlesex; Zambia, South Africa; Royal Latin School, Bucks. *Studied*: Norwich School of Art; studying MA Applied Art & Design, glass - Wolverhampton University. *Exhib*: Mall Galleries, Bruton Street Gallery; Sheridan Russell Gallery, London; Artifex, Birmingham; Wildlife Art Gallery, Lavenham; Walsall New Art Gallery; Brian Sinfield Gallery, Burford; Lion Street Gallery, Hay-on-Wye; Buckenham Gallery, Southwold. *Commissions*: private commissions in the UK including portraits. *Works Reproduced*: primarily birds and animals in bronze, also portraits. Glass blowing, kiln cast glass, sand cast glass. *Principal Works*: Series of male figures.

Recreations: walking, bird watching, swimming, classical music, opera, water polo. *Clubs*: GOC (Gay Outdoor Club). *Address*: 52 Buchanan Road, Walsall, W.Midlands WS4 2EN. *Email*: richard.roberts1@homecall.co.uk *Website*: www.richardrobertsbronzes.com *Signs work*: RTR.

ROBERTS, Simon, Fellow of the Royal Photographic Society; Grants from Arts Council & John Kobal Foundation. *Medium*: photography. *b*: Croydon, 5 Feb 1974. *s of*: John & Maureen Roberts. *m*: Sarah Fishburn Roberts. two *d*. *Studied*: University of Sheffield (1993-1996 BA (Hons) Human Geography 1st Class); Sheffield College (1997) Diploma in Photography. *Represented by*: Klompching Gallery, New York. *Exhib*: National Media Museum, Bradford (Mar-Sep 2010); Klompching Gallery, New York (2009); The Photographers Gallery, London (2009); Royal Academy Summer Exhibition (2008, 2009); Museum of Contemporary Art, Shanghai (2008). *Works in collections*: Deutsche Borse Art Collection (Frankfurt); Natural Media Museum (Bradford); Wilson Centre for Photography (London); Birmingham Central Library; several private collections. *Commissions*: Bursary from National Media Museum for 'We English' (2008); Artist in Residence, Merrill Lynch Financial Centre, London (2008). *Publications*: 'We English' (Chris Boot Publishing, Sept 2009); 'Motherland' (Chris Boot Publishing, Sept 2007). *Principal Works*: 'We English' (2007-2008); 'Motherland' (2004-2006). *Recreations*: running, tennis, cinema, galleries. *Address*: 26 Montgomery Street, Hove, E. Sussex, BN3 5BF. *Email*: mail@simonroberts.com *Website*: www.simonroberts.com *Signs work*: "Simon Roberts".

ROBERTSON, Anderson Bain, DA (1955), ATC (1956), BA Hons (1982); painter in oil and water-colour; formerly Principal Art Master, Prestwick Academy. *b*: Bristol, 22 Oct 1929. *s of*: Mungo Robertson. *m*: Mary M.M. Christie (decd). two *s*. *Educ*: Ardrossan Academy, Ayrshire. *Studied*: Gray's School of Art, Aberdeen (1951-52, Robert Sivell), Glasgow School of Art (1952-55, 1981-82, David A. Donaldson, William Armour, Jack Knox). *Exhib*: RSA, RSW, RGI, SSA, RP, VAS, RI. *Works in collections*: Many private collections. *Clubs*: Glasgow Art (Elected Professional Member 1982). *Misc*: Elected professional member of Visual Arts Scotland (1996). *Address*: "Window Rock", Sandy Beach, Innellan, Argyll PA23 7TR. *Email*: kiowa@dsl.pipex.com *Signs work*: "Anderson B. Robertson."

ROBERTSON, Barbara Janette, DA (1970), SSA (1974), Lily MacDougall, SSWA (1975); printmaker in linoprint, part-time lecturer. *Medium*: linocut. *b*: Broughty Ferry, Dundee, 16 Aug 1945. *d of*: James Fleming Robertson, inn-keeper. *Educ*: Blairgowrie High School. *Studied*: Duncan of Jordanstone College of Art, Dundee (1965-71) under Ron Stenberg, Josef Sekalski. *Exhib*: Aberdeen Art Centre, Print Exchange, Galerie Tendenz; Contributor RSA (1973-75), Prints in Folios of Compass Gallery, Glasgow, Glasgow Print Workshop, Strathearn Gallery Crieff. *Works in collections*: Leeds, Aberdeen, Glasgow, Stirling, Angus. *Publications*: illustrated The Cuckoo's Nest by Carl McDougall; The Oath Takers, Sea Green Ribbons, by Naomi Mitchison. *Clubs*: Artists Lunch. *Address*: 10 The Row, Douglastown, Forfar DD8 1TL, Scotland. *Signs work*: "Barbara Robertson."

ROBERTSON, Saul, BA (Hons) Fine Art; Hunting Art Prizes, Young Artist of the Year (2001); Prizewinner, BP Portrait Prize (2005); Elizabeth Greenshields Foundation Award (2006/2011); Armour, Cargill, City of Glasgow Prize at RGI (2003-11). *Medium*: oil, drawing. *b*: Glasgow, 21 Aug 1978. *m*: Jennifer Robertson. two *d*. *Studied*: Duncan of Jordanstone College of Art & Design (1996-2000). *Represented by*: The Contemporary Fine Art Gallery, Eton; The Stafford Gallery, London. *Exhib*: solo: The Lillie Art Gallery (2010), Thompsons Gallery, London (2005, 2008), Roger Billcliffe Fine Art Glagow (2006), The Lamb Gallery, University of Dundee (2014). Group: RA Summer Show (2007, 2010), 'Divided Selves - The Scottish Self Portrait from 17th Century to Present, Talbot Rice Gallery & The Fleming Collection (2006). *Works in collections*: Glasgow Museums,

Lillie Art Gallery, Univeristy of Dundee Museum Collections, Tayside NHS, Walter Scott Investment, Edinburgh. *Address*: 180 Churchill Drive, Broomhill, Glasgow G11 7HA. *Email*: saulrobertson@saulrobertson.com *Website*: www.saulrobertson.com *Signs work*: "S.R."

ROBINSON, Barbara, Prize for Portrait, Marlborough Fine Art, Prize and Medal, City of Monaco/Medal, City of Rodez; Medaille de l'Assemblie Nationale; painter in oil, gouache, pencil. *b*: London, 7 Mar 1928. *d of*: Major William Lloyd Jones, D.S.O. *m*: Walter Robinson (decd). two *s*. *Educ*: Lycée Français du Royaume Uni, Kensington High School. *Studied*: Slade and Ruskin Schools (1943-45, Prof. Randolph Schwabe), Ruskin School of Drawing (1945-47, Albert Rutherston). *Exhib*: New Art Centre, London (1959-83), French, Swiss and American Galleries (1975-94), Nîmes (1987), Sommières (1994), Bruton St. Gallery, London (1999, 2000). *Works in collections*: Contemporary Art Soc. London; City Halls Monaco, Sommières, Rodez and Pamiers; Museums de Vieux/de la Rochelle, Nimes, St. Annes College, Oxford, BP, Shell, The Daily Express, British North Sea Oil Corp., St. Hilda's College, Oxford, Students Union London Univ., Girton College, Cambridge, British Library, Society of Performing Arts, National Gallery Western Australia; Westminster School, London; Musée de Laverune (Herault). *Publications*: Lumières du Barbara Robinson by Geneviève Conte (1985), D'Autres Lumières du Barbara Robinson by Marc Moulin (1997), Let There Be Light! Que La Lumiere Soit! *Official Purchasers*: see Works in collections, and St. Anne's College Oxford, British Petroleum. *Recreations*: sudoku, crosswords. *Address*: Chemin de la Tuilerie, 30260 Vic-le-Fesq (Gard), France. *Email*: robarbara@wanadoo.fr *Website*: www.barbararobinsonpaintings.com *Signs work*: 'Barbara Robinson'.

ROBINSON, Dr. Hilary, BA (Hons) (1979), MA (RCA) (1987), PhD (1999), FRSA; Dean, College of Fine Arts, Carnegie Mellon University Pittsburgh (2005-); previously senior lecturer, research co-ordinator, University of Ulster. *b*: UK, 25 Jun 1956. *Educ*: John Mason School, Abingdon. *Studied*: University of Newcastle upon Tyne (1975-79, Prof. Kenneth Rowntree), RCA (1985-87, Prof. Christopher Frayling), University of Leeds (1993-1999, Prof. Geiselda Pollock). *Publications*: author: Reading Art, Reading Irigaray: The Politics of Art by Women (I.B.Tauris, 2006); Feminism-Art-Theory 1968-2000 (Blackwells, 2001), Visibly Female: Feminism and Art Today (Camden Press 1987, Universe (N.Y.) 1988), The Rough Guide to Venice (1989, 1993); many catalogue essays including: Mothers, Ikon Gallery, Birmingham (1990), Sounding the Depths, I.M.M.A., Dublin (1992), Louise Bourgeois, M.O.M.A. Oxford (1996); Editor, Alba (1990-92). *Address*: College of Fine Arts, Carnegie Mellon University, 5000 Forbes Avenue, Pittsburgh, PA 15213, USA.

ROBINSON, Gillian, MA (1984), PhD (1989); Isis Gallery award best contemporary work, Artists in Essex award winner; Emeritus Reader. *Medium*: mixed media, oil on paper, artists books. *b*: 30 Jun 1944. *m*: John Robinson. three *s*. one *d*. *Studied*: University of London. *Exhib*: Bloomsbury Gallery London, Elizabeth Soderberg Gallery Israel, Sabae Contemporary Art Centre, Japan, Residence Gallery, Herzliya, Israel, RA Summer Exhibition, London. *Works in collections*: Epping Forest Museum, Archive of the Karelian Republic Art Museum, Petravodska, Russia; and private collections. *Publications*: Sketchbooks: Explore and Store (Hodder & Stoughton, 1995, Think Inside the Sketchbook (Harper Collins 2011). *Address*: Coolmore Lodge, High St., Thorpe-le-Soken, Essex CO16 0EG. *Email*: gill.robinson@anglia.ac.uk *Signs work*: "Gillian Robinson."

ROBINSON, Kay, BA (Hons), AFAS; Fine Art Degree, John Moores University; Wirral Metropolitan Print Fellowship Award (1998-99). *Medium*: fine art printer-painter. *b*: Warrington, 18 Mar 1945. *d of*: John & Priscilla I Robinson. *Educ*: Warrington Collegiate. *Studied*: Wirral Metropolitan College. *Exhib*: AFAS, Mall Galleries (2003, 04, 07); NS (1999-2004); RA Summer Exhbn (2000); National Print, Mall Galleries (2000); Christie-

Wild International NYAD 2000, dfn Gallery, New York; MAFA (2001, 02, 04); Printmakers Council, Falmouth (1999, 2000); Mercury Music Prize (Finalist), Mayfair, London (1997); Discerning Eye, Mall Galleries (2006); Cancer Research, Christie's, London (2002-05, 07); Chester CC Artists, Sens, France (1999); Senigalia, Italy (2005); Museum am Burghof, Lorrach, Germany (2006); 7th British International Mini Print Exhibition (2009); Mini Print International of Cadaques, Barcelona (2008, 09, 10, 11); Lessedra World Art Print Annual, Bulgaria (2011); International Miniature Print Exhibition, Centre for Contemporary Printmaking, Connecticut, USA (2011). *Works in collections*: Manchester Art Galleries Patrons Loan Collection; Warrington Museum and Art Gallery. *Publications*: Dictionary of International Biography 2010. *Clubs*: Cheshire Artists Network. *Address*: 15 Parkland Close, Appleton Thorn, Warrington, WA4 4RH. *Email*: kay.robinson54@yahoo.co.uk *Website*: www.c-a-n.co.uk *Signs work*: "K ROBINSON".

ROBINSON, Leslie Ernest, BA (Hons) 1968, Post Grad. (1969); painter in water-colour, acrylic, pen and ink; Artists' Manager, Art Exhbn. Promoter. *b*: Consett, Co. Durham, 3 Sep 1947. *m*: Jill Robinson. *Studied*: Sunderland College of Art and Design, Manchester University. *Exhib*: numerous worldwide. *Works in collections*: UK, Europe, Australia and Gulf States. *Publications*: wrote, photographed and published 'The Materials of the Artist' - a visual 15 series course. *Clubs*: Falmouth Arts Soc., Royal Cornwall Polytechnic Soc. *Address*: Lemon Court, Carclew, Perranarworthal, Truro, Cornwall TR3 7PB. *Email*: lescornwallart@aol.com

ROBINSON, Paul Roy Wills, RIBA Chartered Architect. *Medium*: watercolour, drawing, prints. *b*: Teignmouth, Devon, 25 Feb 1942. *m*: Wendy Jelbert SWA. five *g-s*. two *d*. *Educ*: Kings College, Taunton, Somerset. *Studied*: Portsmouth School of Architecture (1960-64) & art college. Final exams and qualification at RIBA London. *Exhib*: Romsey Art Group, twice annually. *Commissions*: 9 house portraits. *Official Purchasers*: two doctor's surgeries. *Recreations*: Military history. *Clubs*: Army Art Society, Romsey Art Group. *Misc*: Demonstrations in 20 town in Central South England. *Address*: 25 Richmond Lane, Romsey, Hampshire SO51 7LB. *Signs work*: "Paul Robinson".

ROBINSON, Peter Lyell, BA (Hons) (Geog. Geol.); sculptor in clay, plaster, bronze, stone. *b*: Melbourne, Australia, 12 Apr 1962. *m*: Kate MacNab. two *s*. one *d*. *Educ*: King's School, Bruton. *Studied*: Durham University. Apprenticed to sculptor John Robinson (1987-90). *Exhib*: London: Alwin Gallery, Harrods F.A. Gallery, McHardy Sculpture Co., Art Scene; Arlesford Gallery Hants., Beaver Galleries, Australia, McHardy Sculpture Company at Butler's Wharf, The Garden Door at Ladbroke Sq., Alwin Gallery at Tunbridge Wells. *Address*: Fennel House, Beryl Lane, Wells, Somerset BA5 3AD. *Signs work*: "LYELL."

ROBINSON, Virginia Susanne Douglas, artist in pastel, oil, acrylic. *b*: London, 27 Jul 1933. *d of*: Douglas Stannus Gray, RP. *m*: Lowther. *Educ*: privately. *Studied*: Brighton College of Art, RAS. *Exhib*: RA, Bradford, York, Cheltenham, Gottingen, Annecy. *Address*: 49 The Green, Southwick, Brighton BN42 4FY. *Signs work*: "Virginia S.D. Robinson."

ROBINSON, Wayne, BA Hons, Fine Art (1981), MA Fine Print (1991); painter, printmaker-woodcut; Head of Painting, St. Helens College of Art. *Medium*: painter printmaker. *b*: Peterborough, 19 May 1959. *m*: Amy. one *d*. *Studied*: Cambridge College of Art, Loughborough College of Art and Design, Manchester Metropolitan University. *Exhib*: widely throughout Britain and Europe. *Works in collections*: Malta, USA, Germany, Poland, GB, Cyprus, France. *Address*: 254 Dentons Green Lane, St. Helens, Merseyside WA10 6RY. *Email*: wayne.robinson@talk21.com *Website*: www.waynejrobinson.com *Signs work*: "W Robinson."

ROBOZ, Zsuzsi, mem. Pastel Society, Fellow of Royal Society of Arts. *Medium*: painter in oils, acrylics, pencil, charcoal and pastel, photo collage. *b*: Budapest. married. *Studied*:

Regent St. Polytechnic, R.A. under Peter Greenham, and in Florence under Annigoni. *Represented by*: Messum's, Cork St., London. *Exhib*: solo shows include 'Revudeville' at Theatre Museum (1978) at V&A, London, Lincoln Centre NY (1989), David Messum, Cork St. (1995, 1997, 1999, 2000, 2002, 2005, 2008). *Works in collections*: Museum of Fine Arts, Budapest, National Portrait Gallery, Tate Gallery, V&A, Royal Festival Hall, London, Bradford Museum, Graves A.G., Sheffield, Cambridge University. *Publications*: Women and Men's Daughters, Chichester 10 - Portrait of a Decade, British Ballet To-day, British Art Now with E. Lucie-Smith (1993); 'Roboz, A Painter's Paradox' by John Russell Taylor (2005). *Clubs*: Chelsea Arts, Arts Club, Dover St. *Address*: The Studio, 76 Eccleston Sq. Mews, London SW1V 19N. *Signs work*: "Roboz."

ROBSON, Hugh Mather, artist in oil, gouache, pen and ink. *b*: Hinckley, Leics, 28 Jun 1929. *m*: Barbara Ann Mills. four *d*. *Educ*: Hinckley Grammar School. *Studied*: Fine art: St. Martins School of Art (1945-49, William Craig, Russell Hall); Slade School of Art (1949-53, Lucien Freud, Sam Carter, tutor). *Exhib*: Arthur Jeffress, Trafford Gallery, Windsor Fine Arts, King St. Gallery, Mallets at Bourdon House, Colefax and Fowler, Nina Campbell's and Stphanie Hoppens Gallery. Murals include Crockfords, Park Lane Hotel, Belfry Club, Capital Hotel, 45 Park Lane, Croix des Gardes and many private houses. Visuals of gardens for Peter Coats; visuals of interiors for Interior decorators including John Siddley, Nina Campbell and Colefax and Fowler. Fabric designs for Nina Campbell. Bookplates, letterheads and tile designs. A series of Genre Singerie water-colours (96 to date), also a series of 20 military pansy figures (signed EWL). *Publications*: articles in House and Garden, Country Life, Connaissance des Arts, World of Interiors, Harpers, Southern Accents, etc. *Address*: 47 Loraine Road, London N7 6HB. *Signs work*: "Hugh Robson." or "H.M. Robson."

ROCHE, Helen, DA (Edin); painter in acrylic and mixed media; theme of work includes abstract and semi abstractions based on natural and man made objects. *b*: Limavady, Co. Derry, 23 Mar 1945. *m*: Laurence Roche, DA (Edin). *Studied*: Edinburgh College of Art (1963-67). *Exhib*: RSA, RWA, SSA, RSW, SSWA, and numerous other exhbns. *Works in collections*: private collections in Britain and abroad. *Address*: 67 Valley View Rd., Stroud, Glos. GL5 1HW. *Email*: helen@hroche.orangehome.co.uk *Signs work*: "Helen R."

ROCHE, Joan, RAS; lecturer. *Medium*: oil, watercolour, acrylic, mixed media. one *s*. one *d*. *Studied*: Royal Academy Schools. *Exhib*: Modigliani Centre, Florence (2002), Discerning Eye (2001). *Works in collections*: private collections. *Publications*: Footprint-animals, insects, flowers, trees, illustrations . *Clubs*: RASAA. *Address*: 12 Grand Union Walk, Kentish Town Road, Camden, London NW1 9LF. *Email*: joan@roche.demon.co.uk

ROCHE, Laurence, NDD, DA(Edin.), (Art Teachers Certificate). *Medium*: oil and acrylic (marine, landscape, industrial subjects, etc.). *b*: Goodwick, Pembs., 1 May 1944. *m*: Helen Roche, D.A.(Edin.). *Educ*: Fishguard County Secondary School. *Studied*: Swansea College of Art (1961-65), Edinburgh College of Art (1965-68, Postgrad. scholarship); Moray House College of Educ., Edinburgh (1969-70). *Exhib*: Many group and one-man exhbns. *Works in collections*: in UK and abroad, corporate and private. *Commissions*: several for the steel and construction industry. *Recreations*: walking-standing,staring,observing-painting. *Address*: 67 Valley View Rd., Stroud, Glos. GL5 1HW. *Email*: helen@hroche.orangehome.co.uk *Signs work*: "Laurence Roche."

ROCHFORT, William, BA (Hons) Fine Art. *Medium*: oil, drawing. *b*: Southamptom, 12 Dec 1985. *Studied*: Kingston University (2005-2008); Bournemouth Arts Institute: (2004-2005). *Represented by*: Forest Gallery, Guildford; Lyndhurst Gallery; Coastal Gallery, Lymington. *Exhib*: Forest Gallery, Guildford; Lyndhurst Gallery; Coastal Gallery, Lymington; Battersea Art Fair (2010); Affordable Art Fair Battersea (2011); Terminal 5 Expo Fine Art Gallery; Henley Regatta (2009-2012); London City Hall; Canadian Embassy;

The Fountain Gallery, Hampton. *Works in collections*; private/corporate. Olympic Exhibition, Terminal 5 Expo Fine Art Gallery. *Commissions*: several in support of the 2012 London Olympics. *Publications*: Artists & Illustrators magazine, (June 2010, May 2009, May 2008); Picture Business (July/August 2009). *Principal Works*: 'The Waiting Room', 'Shutterbugs', 'Ticket Booth'. *Misc*: Worked as an official artist for the 2012 London Olympics from 2008-2010. *Address*: 3 Clockhouse, Tatchbury Mount, Calmore SO40 2RN. *Email*: willrochfort@aol.com *Website*: www.williamrochfort.com *Signs work*: "Will Rochfort" or "W".

ROCK, Jill Elizabeth, NDD; BEd Hons London; Hygeia Dip. Colour; Fellow Royal Geographic Society; Wilfred Sirrell Award; Westminster Arts Council. *Medium*: bri-collage, performance, oil, watercolour. *b*: Twickenham, UK, 9 Sep 1942. *d of*: Frank & Marie Barron. *m*: John Rock (decd). one *s*. one *d*. *Educ*: St.Catherine's Convent School, Twickenham. *Studied*: Twickenham Art School (1959-63); Maria Grey College (1970-74); studied under: Karen Jonzen (1970-74), Brian McCann (1994-98). *Exhib*: solo shows since 2000: Sheridan Russell Gallery WC1 (2000); Brantwood, Cumbria (2004); The Foundry, EC1 (2007); Macond EC1 (2008). Group shows include: ICA London; Liverpool Bi-Annual (2004/6/8); Curwen Gallery W1; Lancaster University; SOAS; Kew Gardens; Isola Della Poesia, Venice Biennale 2005; Lab Gallery, New York; Texas; Sao Paolo; Mam Chile; Santiago; Valparaiso; Montevideo; Beirut; Berlin; Turin; Milan; Naples; Rome; Perugia; Sardinia; Graz, Austria; Holland; Hong Kong; Dublin. *Works in collections*: Fondacion Neruda, Chile; Mam Chile, OCA Sao Paolo, Brazil; Westminster Arts Council; Paintings in Hospitals; NHS Trusts. *Publications*: catalogues and newspapers: UK, Berlin, Beirut, Chile. *Principal Works*: Gaia, Homage to Rimbaud, Fragments, Constructions. *Recreations*: walking, travelling. *Misc*: Instigated and curated shows involving over 200 artists worldwide: Guten Morgen Her Schwitters, Brantwood; Museum of Erotic Misery, Museuman, Liverpool; In Arcadia, Stables Gallery, Twickenham; $E=MC^2$, Institute of Physics; Berliner Kunstsalon; Brompton Cemetery. *Address*: 96 Edith Grove, World's End, London SW10 0NH. *Email*: jill.e.rock@gmail.com *Website*: www.galleryartist.com/JillRock *Signs work*: "ROCK".

RÖDER, Endre Zoltán Eugene, painter in oil on canvas and acrylic on paper; formerly art gallery educ. officer, senior lecturer (Art History). *b*: Budapest, 17 Aug 1933. *s of*: Pál Röder, journalist (decd). *m*: Carole. one *s*. *Educ*: St. John's College, Southsea. *Studied*: School of Art, Malta; College of Art, Portsmouth; Sheffield College of Art (1956-60, W.S. Taylor, Eric Jones). *Exhib*: ROI, various Open Shows (provinces), but generally in private galleries in England, Scotland, USA and France. *Works in collections*: Sheffield City A.Gs., Sheffield University, etc. *Publications*: Book 'Endre Roder' by John Basford published by Derwent-Wye. *Address*: c/o Quarr Gallery, 17 High Street, Swanage, Dorset BH19 2LP. *Signs work*: "RÖDER."

RODGER, Willie, RSA (2006), ARSA (1989), RGI (1994); artist in lino and woodcuts; Hon. Degree of Doctor of the University of Stirling (1999); Saltire Awards for Art in Architecture (1984-87). *b*: Kirkintilloch, 3 Mar 1930. *s of*: Robert Gilmour Rodger, pawnbroker. *m*: Anne Henry, illustrator. two *s*. two *d*. *Educ*: Lenzie Academy. *Studied*: Glasgow School of Art (1948-53, Lennox Paterson). *Exhib*: many one-man since 1964, also group in U.K. and abroad, including RSA, RA, SSA, RGIFA, Glasgow Group, 'In Between the Lines' retrospective, Collins Gallery, Glasgow (1986); now exhibits mainly 'The Open Eye Gallery' Edinburgh, transparencies of paintings, Bridgeman Art Library, London. *Works in collections*: V&A, SAC, Flemings, Scottish Parliament, numerous public collections in UK. *Commissions*: Enamel mural, Exhibition Station, Glasgow, (Scot Rail, 1987); illustrations and mural, Dallas DHU Distillery, Forres (Historic Scotland, 1987-88); designs, stained glass windows, St. Mary's Parish Church, Kirkintilloch (1987-93); street banners, 200th Anniversary, Union St., Aberdeen (1994), edition of linocut prints P & O Ferries

(2000), linocut illustrations "Finding Alba', Scottish Television (2000). *Publications*: Scottish Historical Playing Cards (1975); illustrated, The Field of Thistles (1983); Willie Rodger, Open Eye Gallery, Edinburgh (1996, 2000); Willie Winkie, Strathpride Universality Ltd., Glasgow (1997); Willie Rodger 'On the Other Hand' Open Eye Gallery, Edin. 2003; Lino and Woodcut Prints accompanying book of poems - 'The Colour of Black and White' by Liz Lochhead, 2003; Media Matters Education Consultancy Ltd. *Misc*: Artist in Residence, University of Sussex (1971). *Address*: Stenton, 16 Bellevue Rd., Kirkintilloch G66 1AP. *Signs work*: "Willie Rodger."

RODULFO, Peter, Barony of Fulwood Award (2003). *Medium*: oil, watercolour, drawing, prints, sculpture. *b*: Washington DC, USA, 6 Feb 1958. *s of*: Monty & Mary Rodulfo. one *d*. *Educ*: Glebe House, Hunstanton; Framlingham College, Suffolk. *Studied*: Norwich School of Art (1975-79). *Represented by*: Doric Art, Holt UK. *Exhib*: RA; Hong Kong Museum; Norwich Museum; Margaret Fisher Gallery, London; diverse galleries in Switzerland, Asia, Miami USA, New York USA, London, Brazil, Venezuela. *Works in collections*: Norfolk Museums Service Collection. *Commissions*: Lloyds 'Lutine' commission. *Address*: 95 Connaught Road, Norwich, Norfolk NR2 3BS. *Email*: peterrodulfo@fsmail.com *Website*: www.rodulfo.deviantart.com *Signs work*: 'Rodulfo' also sometimes monogram 'R'.

RODWELL, Charles, Slade Diploma. *Medium*: oil, watercolour, drawing, prints. *b*: Nairobi, Kenya, 1955. *s of*: R.M.H. Rodwell. *m*: Diana. two *d*. *Educ*: Marlborough College. *Studied*: Slade School of Art 1974-78 (Sir William Coldstrea, Patrick George, Phillip Sutton. *Represented by*: self. *Exhib*: RA, RWA, RWS; mixed and regular one-man shows. *Works in collections*: private, national and international. *Commissions*: private. *Clubs*: Chelsea Arts Club. *Address*: Leasview Cottage, Charlcott, Calne, Wiltshire, SN11 9HH. *Email*: charles@charlesrodwellarts.com *Website*: charlesrodwellarts.com *Signs work*: "C.R." and "Charles Rodwell".

ROGERS, Carol Ann, UA (2003); artist and tutor, water-colourist and printmaker, clay sculptor. *Medium*: watercolour/mixed media/acrylic/clay/oils. *b*: Enfield, 12 Dec 1944. *m*: Dennis. one *s*. *Studied*: West Herts. College, Harrow Arts Centre. *Exhib*: UA regularly, London and Herts. *Works in collections*: in France, Germany and Switzerland. *Commissions*: 'St. Mary's Parish Church, Watford' for Mayor of Watford as gift for twin town of Mainz, Germany, 2003; 'Almshouses, Watford' for twin town of Pesaro, Italy, 2003. *Publications*: 'Optima', 'Hertfordshire Countryside' (magazines). *Official Purchasers*: Mayor of Watford for Watford Council. *Principal Works*: painting/sculpting/runs workshops. *Recreations*: photography, gardening, bird watching, walking. *Clubs*: U.A., Herts. Visual Arts Forum, Watford Area Arts Forum, Society for All Artists. *Misc*: demonstrator to art societies. *Address*: Oxhey Hall Cottage, Hampermill Lane, Oxhey, Watford, Herts. WD19 4NU. *Email*: rogerscd@talktalk.net *Website*: www.hvaf.org.uk/carol-rogers/gallery *Signs work*: C A Rogers.

ROGERS, John Rowland, painter, mainly landscapes, in water-colour and oil; Art Com., WAC, Mem. WCSW. *b*: Cardiff, 28 May 1939. *s of*: Ronald Edwin Rogers. *m*: De (Diane). three *s*. *Studied*: Cardiff (John Roberts, Phil Jennings, David Tinker). *Exhib*: RSMA, ICA, WAC (touring); Pascoe Gallery, Winnipeg; Mostyn Gallery, Wales; 'Journey in Morocco' (1983), Cardiff; Edwin Pollard Gallery, London; John Rogers' Retrospective (touring) (1991); Royal Society of Arts, London (1999). Solo exhibition 'From Africa to Iceland', National Library of Wales (Spring 2008). *Works in collections*: Haverfordwest County Museum, West Wales Arts, WAC, Museum and A.G., Newport, Gwent, National Library of Wales, Aberystwyth, Contemporary Art Soc. for Wales, The Museum of Modern Art, Wales. *Publications*: 'Magic Islands', Gomer Press 2002, BBC Wales, 'From Africa to Iceland', John Rogers, with an essay by Alistair Crawford (hardback, Gomer Press, 2007). *Works*

Reproduced: Numerous: photo, litho and giclée. *Address*: Peter's Lane, St. Davids, Pembrokeshire, Wales, SA62 6NT. *Website*: www.johnrogersartist.co.uk *Signs work*: "John Rogers."

ROGERS, Lord Richard George (Rogers of Riverside), Baron 1996 (Life Peer), Kt. 1991; M.Arch., RIBA; Richard Rogers Partnership, Rogers P.A. Technical and Science Centre; Piano and Rogers, France. *b*: 23 Jul 1933. *m*: Ruth Elias (1973). four *s*. *Educ*: Architectural Assoc. (graduate, Dip.); Yale Univ. (Fulbright, Edward D. Stone, and Yale Scholar, M.Arch), RIBA Chairman, Tate Gallery (1984); Royal Gold Medal for Architecture (1985); Royal Academician; Hon. Fellow Royal Academy of the Hague; Hon. Fellow American Institute of Architects; Saarinen Professor Yale University (1985); Mem. United Nations Architects Committee; IBM Fellow; Mem. RIBA Council; Visiting Lecturer/Professor: UCLA, Princeton, Harvard, Berkeley, Cornell USA, McGill Canada, Hong Kong University, Aachen Germany, Cambridge University England. *Publications*: incl. contribs. to Architectural Design, Global Arch. and Arch. and Urbanism. Monograph. G.A. Beaubourg. *Address*: (offices and studios) Thames Wharf, Rainville Rd., London W6 9HA.

ROGERSON, Joyce, RMS (1986); SWA (1986), wildlife artist and miniaturist in watercolour, for miniatures vellum; Vice Pres. SWA (1997-2005); RMS Group of Paintings Award (2003); Peter Charles Booth Memorial Award RMS (2009); SBA (2010); President's Award (RMS, 2011); HRSWA (2011); Llewellyn Alexander Subject Miniature Award RMS (2012). *Medium*: Watercolour miniatures on vellum. *b*: Yorkshire. *m*: Ronald Rogerson, AMRAeS, I.Eng.Cei., retd. aeronautical engineer. one *s*. one *d*. *Educ*: Mayfield Girls School, Walton-on-Thames. *Studied*: self-taught. *Exhib*: RMS, SWA, HS, MAS-F (USA), GMAS (USA), USM (Ulster), Mall Galleries, Westminster Gallery, Medici Gallery, Llewellyn Alexander Gallery, Soc. of Wildlife Art of the Nations, SBA. *Commissions*: worldwide, and designs for greetings cards. *Publications*: Included in: Technique of Painting Miniatures, Royal Miniature Society 100 Years, Magic of Miniatures. *Works Reproduced*: 'Swallow', 'Tawny Owl', 6 miniatures. *Principal Works*: Miniatures Botanical. *Address*: 84 Cobham Rd., Fetcham, Surrey KT22 9JS. *Signs work*: "Joyce Rogerson.", "JOYCE ROGERSON".

ROMAIN, Ricky Stuart, Major Purchase Award (South West Arts, 1982). *Medium*: oil. *b*: London, 25 Mar 1948. *Partner*: Heather Fallows. one *d*. *Studied*: self taught. *Exhib*: Selected solo exhibitions: The Marle Gallery, Axminster, Devon (2013); The Gallery, Burgh Halls, Linlithgow, Scotland (2013); David West Gallery, Lyme Regis (2012); Ricky Romain at Matrix Chambers, London (2012); White Space Gallery, Axminster (2009, 2011); Douvres la Delivrande, France (2010); Weston College, Bath Spa University (2008); Amnesty International, International Secretariat, London (2007); Tooks Chambers, The Chambers of Michael Mansfield QC (2006). *Works in collections*: Amnesty International, United Nations, Arts Council South West, The Liberal Jewish Synagogue St. John's Wood, London, Pierian Centre Bristol, John Fowles, Sir Neville Mariner, Richard Harvey, Prof. Françoise Hampson, Joel Bennathan QC. *Publications*: in 'The Bible in 20th Century Art' (pub. Pagoda Books, 1987). *Works Reproduced*: Redress Annual report (2012-13) also www.redress.org website (2013), 'Book of Disposition' by Clara Janes (cover, pub. Delit Editions, 2010), 'Human Security and Non-Citizens' by Alice Edwards & Carla Ferstman (cover, pub. CUP, 2009), Annual Reports, Bail for Immigration Detainees (covers, 2006/7); 'Art in Devon Magazine' (cover for first edition in 2005). *Misc*: Work used to illustrate Channel 4 documentary 'A Sense of Belonging', which examined Jewish identity and also explored the artist's own spiritual journey through Judaism. Series was screened at the National Film Theatre (1990) and broadcast June-July 1991. *Address*: Flat 1A, Milton's Yard, West Street, Axminster, Devon EX13 5FE. *Email*: rickyheatherduende@tiscali.co.uk *Website*: www.rickyromain.com *Signs work*: "Ricky Romain".

ROMER, Philippa Maynard, portrait painter in oil. *b*: Hitchin, Herts. *d of*: Maynard Tomson, MC, FRICS. *Studied*: Cambridge School of Art and R.A. Schools. *Exhib*: RA, RP,

RBA, NEAC. *Clubs*: RASA. *Address*: North End Farm, Littlebury, Saffron Walden, Essex CB11 4TW. *Signs work*: "Philippa Romer."

RONA. *Medium*: oil. *b*: Ontario, Canada, 22 Apr 1965. *m*: Dr. Philip Marsden. one *s*. one *d*. Studied: Nova Scotia College of Art & Design. *Exhib*: Solo exhibitions in London, Oxford, Tokyo, Toronto and Ottawa. Group exhibitions: Japan, Canada and across the UK. *Works in collections*: Japan, New York, Paris, Toronto, Oxford, London. *Works Reproduced*: Bullingdon Painting - Giclee prints (edition of 12). *Address*: 26 Norreys Road, Oxford OX2 9PT. *Email*: rona.inc@virgin.net *Website*: www.ronapainting.com *Signs work*: "Rona".

RONALDSON, David Bruce, BA (Hons), PGCE; NADFAS Lecturer, OCA Tutor; freelance art historian. *Medium*: oil, water-colour and egg tempera. *b*: Felsted, 20 Jan 1950. *m*: Dorothy Ronaldson.one *s*. one *d*. *Studied*: Newcastle University. *Works in collections*: UK, Europe, USA. *Address*: Limelight, School Road, Wickham St Paul, Halstead, Essex CO9 2PR. *Email*: bruce.ronaldson@btinternet.com. *Signs work*: 'Bruce Ronaldson'.

RONN: see HILL, Ronald James.

ROONEY, Michael John, RA (1991), RE (2001), NDD (1964), ARCA, MA (1967); painter in gouache, water-colour, tempera, oil; printmaking in etching, collographs, drypoint, monoprint. *b*: Epsom, 1944. *s of*: John Rooney, steel fixer (decd). *m*: (1) Patricia Anne (decd); one *s*. one *d*. (2) Alexandra. one *s*. *Educ*: Sutton School of Art (1959-62), Wimbledon School of Art (1962-64), RCA (1964-67), British School at Rome (1967-68; Rome Scholar). *Exhib*: Royal Academy, Mercury Gallery (London), Portal Gallery (London), Arts Council Touring 'Fragments against Ruins' (1981), 'Headhunters' (1984), 'After Ausschwitz' (London, Manchester, Sunderland, Dresden, 1995), De Vreeze Gallery (Amsterdam), Seasons Gallery (The Hague). Ten years retrospective 1980-1990 (Folkestone, Eastbourne, Hastings). Art Fairs: Chicago, New York, Basle, London, Bath, Galerie Franziskanergasse (Salzburg, 1999), Broderick Gallery, Portland (Oregon, U.S.) (1999/2001). *Works in collections*: Hove Museum, Towner (Eastbourne), Rye A.G., University of Aston, Museo Ralli (Uruguay), De Beers (London), Bolton Museum, Ambro Bank (Amsterdam), Tullie House (Carlisle). *Commissions*: 'Annunciation' (mosaic, Franciscan Basilica, Nazareth, 1968), Gulbenkian Foundation Printmakers' Award (1984), Financial Times centenary (1988), 'Brick Lane' (London Underground Poster, 1991), 'Aesop's Fables' (tapestry for T.S.B. HQ in Birmingham, 1991). *Publications*: Country Life - P. Kitchen 'A Vision for Europe' (1991). *Clubs*: Chelsea Arts. *Misc*: Artist in Residence, Towner Art Gallery, Eastbourne (1984), Korn Ferry Premium Award (R.A., 1990). *Address*: The Old Sorting House, 19 Alder Rd., Mortlake, London SW14 8ER. *Email*: mick.rooney@ukgateway.net *Signs work*: "M.R." joined, from 1996.

ROOT, Malcolm Trevor, self taught, FGRA. *Medium*: oil, drawing, prints. *b*: Colchester, 12 Sep 1950. *s of*: George and Barbara Root. *m*: Marilyn. two *d*. *Educ*: Halstead Secondary School. *Studied*: Printing College, NEETC, Colchester. *Exhib*: Grimes House Gallery, Moreton-in-the-Marsh, Gloucestershire; Bressingham Steam Museum, Guild of Railway Artists (various). *Works in collections*: Colchester Castle Museum, HRH The Duke of Edinburgh (Royal Train), Shanes Castle, Antrim. *Commissions*: various including BT Phone Book covers. *Publications*: 4 books (colour, each containing 60+ full page images. *Works Reproduced*: various as prints, cards, collectors plates, calendars, etc. *Principal Works*: Painting of Halstead town commissioned for Millennium. *Recreations*: local history, cycling, watching football. *Clubs*: CAMRA (Real Ale). *Address*: 38 Churchill Avenue, Halstead, Essex, CO9 2BE. *Email*: meryl_malc@hotmail.com *Signs work*: "R..+".

ROOUM, Denise, ARMS; BA. *Medium*: oil, watercolour, drawing. *b*: Bradford, 26 Dec 1929. *d of*: Fred Rooum and Sarah Taylor Rooum. *m*: Brian John Vale. two *d*. *Educ*: Hanson Girls High School, Bradford; Darlington Training College. *Studied*: evening classes

Bradford and Canterbury, mostly self-taught. *Exhib*: Royal Academy; Leeds Art Gallery; Sheffield Art Gallery; most Yorkshire galleries; Cartwright Hall, Bradford. *Works in collections*: Middlesborough Art Gallery, Keighley Cliff Castle, many private collections. *Publications*: 'Stories of the Stars'; 'Hurdy Gurdy Figurines'. *Clubs*: Bradford Arts Club. *Address*: Westmoorside, 90 Smith Lane, Daisy Hill, Bradford BD9 6DQ. *Signs work*: 'Denise R.' or 'Denise Rooum' or 'Denise Rooum Vale'.

ROPER, Geoffrey John, painter in oils and water-colours, illustrator. *b*: Nottingham, 30 Jul 1942. *s of*: Tom Roper, OBE, political agent. *Educ*: Nottingham Sec. Art School. *Studied*: Nottingham College of Art (1958-60); Edinburgh College of Art (1960-63) under Sir Robin Philipson, PRSA. *Exhib*: William St. Gallery, Edinburgh (1964, 1965, 1966), Silver Coin Gallery, Harrogate (1965, 1966), Douglas Foulis Gallery, Edinburgh (1967), Middlesbrough Civic A.G. (1968), King St. Gallery, Dublin (1967-8), David Letham, Edinburgh (1967, 1968, 1969), Great King St. Gallery, Edinburgh (1970, 1971, 1972), Fine Art Society (1972, 1974, 1975, 1977, 1980, 1988), Teesside A.G. (1972), Paullencroix des Garges, Cannes (1979), Figurehead Gallery, Edinburgh (1992), Murray Motor Co., Edinburgh (1994), Loomshop Gallery (1997), Open Eye Gallery, Edinburgh (1995, 1997-99, 2001-03). *Works in collections*: works in public and private collections throughout Europe. *Publications*: illustrated books, poems - Sydney Goodsir-Smith; Stanley. R. Green; Suburn of Belsen; mainstream pub. 'Destiny's Daughter; Newhall House, illustrations; McDonald Press, 100 life paintings. *Address*: Whinstane Cottage, Pumpherstone Farm, Mid Calder, Scotland EH53 0HR.

ROPER, June Morgan, mural painter in oil and acrylic. *b*: Kirkaldy, Fife, 7 Jun 1940. *m*: Geoffrey John Roper. *Studied*: Edinburgh College of Art (1958-62, Sir Robin Philipson, Sir William Gillies, John Maxwell). *Exhib*: Douglas & Foulis, Torrance Gallery, Loomshop Gallery, Kilbarchan Gallery, The Edinburgh Gallery. *Commissions*: A. Fletcher of Saltoun, Travel Scotland Ltd., H. Cathie, Sangster Distillers Jamaica, Dr. Melvin of Edinburgh, Mr. & Mrs. D. Workman of Edinburgh, Hunter Carson Co. Ltd., Torphichen, M. Ladzow, W. Lothian, Mr & Mrs J Duncan, Edinburgh. *Address*: Whinstane Cottage, Pumpherston Farm, Mid Calder, Scotland EH 53 0HR.

ROSCINI, Count M., FRSA (1967), MFPS (1985), BA (1960); sculptor in bronze. *b*: Rome, 22 Dec 1933. *m*: divorced. one *d*. *Educ*: Rome and Cambridge University. *Studied*: Accademia dell'Art Rome. *Exhib*: Hamilton Gallery, Drian Gallery, Loggia Gallery, Salon de Provence, Grenoble, Tevere Expo Rome. *Works in collections*: Morristown N.J., Manilla, Lambeth Palace. *Publications*: Sounds of the Cross by David Owen. *Address*: 19a Annandale Rd., Greenwich, London SE10 0DD. *Signs work*: "Roscini."

ROSE, Christopher Andrew, SWLA; Biology BSc Hons. (1981); artist in acrylic and oils. *b*: Uganda, 27 Aug 1959. *Educ*: Rydens County Secondary School, Hersham, Surrey; Nottingham University. *Exhib*: Wildlife A.G., Lavenham, annually at Society of Wildlife Artists, London; many mixed exhbns. in UK, France, Holland, Spain, USA, Japan, Singapore. *Publications*: Swallows and Martins of the World (Christopher Helm, 1989), Complete Book of British Birds (RSPB and AA, 1988), Handbook of the Birds of the World (Lynx Edicions), In A Natural Light-The Wildlife of Chris Rose (Langford Press, 2005); and many other publications. *Address*: 6 Whitelee Cottages, Newtown St. Boswells, Melrose, Scotland TD6 0SH. *Email*: chris@chrisrose-artist.co.uk *Website*: www.chrisrose-artist.co.uk *Signs work*: "Chris Rose."

ROSE, Juliet Sarah, MA Fine Art; BA (Hons) Ceramics. *Medium*: Oil, acrylic. *b*: London, 25 Jan 1964. *m*: Kevin Smith. *Studied*: University of Westminster (1995-98); City & Guilds of London Art School (2004-5). *Exhib*: Solo shows: Pearlfisher, London (2004); Centrespace, Bristol (2005); Etz Chayim Gallery (2007); The Palmerston, London. Steps Gallery Group Show, Bristol (2004); Affordable Art Fair, Bristol (2005); Life Squared

(2005); IAF, London (2005); Magnetix Installation, London; AAF, Steps Gallery (2006); 20/20 Beverley Knowles, London (2006); 2121 Glasgow (2006); 2006 Art, Santa Fe; Los Angeles Art Show (2006); Armosfear, London; Glasgow Art Fair; Art Now, New York; Art Miami, Florida, USA; Art DC, Washington USA. *Commissions*: Daily Telegraph Portrait for Axa 'Jim'. *Principal Works*: Remembering Memory Series. *Misc*: Works at Wimbledon Art Studios. *Address*: 63b Overhill Road, East Dulwich, London SE22 0PQ. *Email*: rockpoolrose@googlemail.com *Website*: www.juliet-rose.com *Signs work*: "JULIET ROSE".

ROSE, Tim Simon, BA Hons Fine Art. *Medium*: oil, watercolour. *b*: London, 8 Mar 1953. *Studied*: Watford School of Art (1971-72); Sheffield Polytechnic (1972-75). *Represented by*: Ingleby Gallery, Derbyshire. *Represented by*: Ingleby Gallery, Derbyshire. *Exhib*: Royal Watercolour Society Open; Royal Institute of Watercolourists Open; Ingleby Gallery, Gallery 93 Derby, St Pauls Cathedral (2000) and many group shows. *Works in collections*: Barclays Bank, Marks & Clerk, Institute of Economic Affairs. *Commissions*: portrait of Headquarters of Barclays Bank Plc, London Patent Office. *Publications*: International Artist magazine. *Works Reproduced*: cards and prints, Solomon & Whitehead, Royal Doulton. *Principal Works*: Architectural studies of cathedrals. *Recreations*: music, good food and good company. *Address*: 17 Plymouth Road, Sheffield, South Yorks., S7 2DE. *Email*: tim@timrose.co.uk *Website*: www.timroseartist.com Signs work: "*Tim Rose*".

ROSEN, Hilary, BA (1976), MA (1980); painter in water-colour; part-time art lecturer. *b*: London, 3 Sep 1953. married. one *s*. one *d*. *Educ*: JFS Comprehensive School, London. *Studied*: Trent Polytechnic (1973-76, Derek Carruthers), RCA (1978-80, Peter de Francia). *Exhib*: solo shows: Royal National Theatre, Galerie Rose Hamburg, Strausberg Galerie Berlin, Galerie Fischinger Stuttgart; mixed shows: RA, Singer and Friedlander, Arthur Andersen, Boundary Gallery, London. *Works in collections*: Neville Burston Coll., Zeiss, Hamburg, Imperial College; private and public collections in Munich, Hamburg, New York, Paris, Arthur Andersen, BT, British Gas, Liberty, Brown Part Works Publisher, Brompton Hospital. *Publications*: Dorling Kindersely: Water-colour Still Lives. *Clubs*: Chelsea Arts. *Address*: Chisenhale Studios, 64-84 Chisenhale Rd., London E3. *Signs work*: "H. Rosen."

ROSENBLOOM, Paul, BA (Hons); HDipAD. *Medium*: Painting; drawing. *b*: Manchester, 25 Mar 1949. *m*: Jan. one *d*. *Studied*: Lanchester Polytechnic (1967-8); Leeds Polytechnic (1968-71); Birmingham Polytechnic (1971-72); Fellowship in Painting, Glos College of Art and Design (1972-3). *Exhib*: Solo: National Museum of Wales, Cardiff (2008); Natural History Museum of Oslo, Norway (2004); Sedgwick Museum of Earth Sciences, Cambridge (2003); Natural History Museum, London (2002); Smyrnios Gallery, Melbourne (2001); Spacex Gallery, Exeter (1994); 70 Arden Street Gallery, Melbourne (1986); Nicola Jacobs Gallery, London (1982). Selected Group: Lion and Lamb (2014); Worcester Cathedral (2012); Unearthed, London (2012); 'Art at the Rockface', Norwich Castle Museum and Arts Gallery (2006); Jerwood Drawing Prize (2004); 'British Drawing', Hayward Gallery (1982); 'British Painting', Hayward Gallery (1974). *Works in collections*: Private, UK and abroad; Victoria & Albert Museum. *Publications*: Exhibition reviews; Studio International (1973-75). *Official Purchasers*: V&A, from '40 Artists - 40 Drawings', Drawing Gallery, London (2005). *Address*: 17 Lansdowne Road, Walthamstow, London E17 8QT. *Email*: paulrg@macunlimited.net *Signs work*: "PAUL ROSENBLOOM".

ROSKELL, Susan Kim, SWA (1998); BA Hons in Furniture Design. *Medium*: prints, acrylic on canvas. *b*: Preston, Lancs, 5 Apr 1960. *d of*: George and Ann Roskell. *Partner*: Jackie Grisley. *Studied*: W.R. Tuson College, Preston; Harris Art College, Preston; Nottingham Polytechnic. *Represented by*: Picturecraft Gallery, Holt, Norfolk; The Hunter Gallery, Suffolk. *Exhib*: SWA Annual Exhbns at Mall Galleries, London; Aubergé du lac Restaurant, Herts; Sheene Mill, Cambs.; Redcoats Restaurant, Herts. *Works in collections*:

many private collections including Mr. David Jackson. *Clubs*: Hertford Art Society. *Misc*: paintings are in modern impressionistic style with a particular love of man-made structures within nature. *Address*: 2 Cheapside Cottages, Anstey, Buntingford, Herts SG9 0BL. *Email*: kimroskell@aol.com *Website*: www.kimroskell.co.uk *Signs work*: 'KIM ROSKELL'.

ROSMAR: see BOOTH, Rosa-Maria.

ROSS, Alastair Robertson, C.St.J., FRBS, RSA, RGI; sculptor; DA (1965), Post-grad. (1966), FRSA (1966), FSA Scot. (1971), ARBS (1968), FRBS (1975), ARSA (1980), Mem. of Council, SSA (1972-75), Scottish Mem. of Council, RBS (1972-92), Vice Pres., RBS (1988-90), Hon. FRIAS (1992), Mem. of Council, Royal Scottish Academy (1998-2000); Hon. Doctorate of Arts (University of Abertay Dundee, 2003), RGI (2004), RSA (2005); Awards: Dickson Prize (1962), Holokrome Award (1962), SED Travelling Scholarship (1963), RSA Chalmers Bursary (1964), RSA Carnegie Travelling Scholarship (1965), Duncan of Drumfork Scholarship (1965), SED Post-grad. Scholarship (1965-66), bronze and silver medallist Paris SalonGillies Award of RSA (1989); Sir Otto Beit Medal of RBS (1989); Freeman of the City of London (1989); Librarian, RSA (2005- 09); Assessor, Scottish Drawing Competition (2009). *b*: Perth, Scotland, 8 Aug 1941. *s of*: Alastair J. Ross, FSA Scot. *m*: Kathryn Wilson. one *d*. *Educ*: St. Mary's Episcopal School, Dunblane, McLaren High School, Callander. *Studied*: Duncan of Jordanstone College of Art, Dundee. *Works in collections*: numerous collections in this country and abroad. *Clubs*: Puffins, Edinburgh. *Address*: Ravenscourt, 28 Albany Terr., Dundee DD3 6HS.

ROSS, Annie, BA Fine Art (Slade), MA Fine Art (Slade), MA Royal College of Art. *Medium*: mixed media including glass. *b*: Birmingham, 29 Jul 1951. *d of*: Solange & Charles Ross. *Partner*: variable. one *s*. *Studied*: Slade School of Fine Art (1975-1980), Royal College of Art (1980-). *Exhib*: see website. *Works in collections*: Arts Council Collections, private collections. *Commissions*: glass commissions - Margate Hospital; public glass works nationally and internationally. *Official Purchasers*: Arts Council of Great Britain. *Misc*: Teaching - lecturer at KIAD (now University College for the Creative Arts). *Address*: 19 Wordsworth Road, Maidstone, Kent, ME14 2HH. *Email*: info@annieross.com *Website*: www.annieross.com *Signs work*: "AR" (previously "ARD").

ROSS, John, MA (RCA); US Bicentennial Fellowship (1978-79); Sunday Times Illustration Award, First Prize (1974); Berger Painting Award (1975); BAFTA Nomination, Best Animated Film category (1998). *Medium*: oil, drawing, prints. *b*: Leicester, 27 May 1949. *m*: Anne Dalley, landscape architect. two *s*. *Studied*: Northampton School of Art (1967-69); Leeds Fine Art (1969-72); RCA (1972-75). *Exhib*: 18 solo exhbns in Britain, France, Germany, Malta and USA, inc. 'The New Fossils' J. Walter Thomson (1975); 'Watch Out Son, This is Cougar Country' UCLA Gallery, California (1978); 'Skating on Thin Ice', Norwich Gallery (1995); 'Dog Years' Volksbank Gallery, Tubingen, Germany (2001); group shows: British Painting and Drawing, Angela Flowers (1972); Leeds Kids Rule, ICA (1973). *Works in collections*: including V&A, Imperial War Museum, Leeds City Art Gallery, Leicester City Museum, Vancouver City Museum, J. Walter Thompson, the late Sir Stephen Spender, the late Elizabeth Frank. *Commissions*: The Times, Sunday Times, Guardian, New York Times, Het Parool, Aardman Animation, Frankfurter Allgemeiner, Jackdaw, Royal Corp. of Transport, etc. *Publications*: Monogram: Words and Pictures - or As Quiet as an Eel in a Barrel of Tripe' (Arcturus Pub., 1996); The Biggin Hill Frescoes (Lion & Unicorn Press, 1975). *Works Reproduced*: creative review - article 'Class Struggle' Oct 1996. *Recreations*: the politics of the environment and lobbyist, cartoonist, etc. *Misc*: a graphic artist who now concentrates on oil painting. Has worked as an illustrator, cartoonist, scriptwriter and educationalist. *Address*: Gloom Hall, 44 Beaumont Park Road, Huddersfield, W.Yorks HD4 5JS. *Email*: annedalley.la@virgin.net *Website*: www.axisweb.org/artist/johnross *Signs work*: 'Ross'.

ROSS, Michèlle, SBA (1987), BA (1985) Illustration and Applied Drawing; freelance illustrator/artist in water-colour. *b*: Morpeth, Northumberland, 9 Mar 1964. *Educ*: Hustler Comprehensive, Middlesbrough. *Studied*: Cleveland College of Art (1980-82), Harrow School of Art (1982-85). *Exhib*: solo show: Talent Store Gallery, Belgravia, London (1988), SBA Open Exhibitions, The Mall Galleries, London, Westminster Halls, London, The Dover Prize, Darlington, Co. Durham. *Works Reproduced*: illustrated numerous books for adults and children, including Dorling Kindersley Eye-Witness Guides, greetings cards, calendars, posters and packaging. *Recreations*: playing a Celtic harp, walking, travelling. *Address*: The Conifers, Moorsholm, Saltburn-by-the-Sea, Cleveland TS12 3JH. *Website*: http://www.michelleross.org.uk *Signs work*: "Michèlle Ross."

ROSS, Rachel, BA (Hons); RGI Art Exposure Gallery Award (2012); Lynn Painter-Stainers Prize Runner Up (2012). *Medium*: painter. *b*: Edinburgh, 23 Nov 1965. three *s*. *Studied*: Central St. Martin's College of Art & Design (1983-87). *Exhib*: Group shows at Mall Galleries, London; Royal Glasgow Institute of the Fine Arts; Royal Scottish Society of Painters in Watercolour; Royal Scottish Academy; plus solo and group shows throughout the UK including Hybrid Gallery, Devon. *Works in collections*: Private collections in UK and abroad. *Address*: 15 Dudley Terrace, Edinburgh EH6 4QQ. *Email*: rachel@rachelross.co.uk *Website*: www.rachelross.co.uk *Signs work*: "Rachel Ross".

ROSSER, Jennifer C., BA Hons (Fine Art Painting) 1973; art tutor, partner in printing business, home educator; artist. *Medium*: oil, watercolour, mixed media, photography, video, sound. *b*: Reading, Berkshire, 28 Aug 1950. *m*: A.P. Hill. two *d*. *Educ*: Alfred Sutton School. *Studied*: Falmouth School of Art, Royal Academy Schools. *Exhib*: mixed: ICA Mall Galleries, RA Schools, Centro Modigliani Florence. *Publications*: Calligraphy for Juniper Press. *Clubs*: RASAA. *Address*: 25 Lark Hill Rise, Winchester, SO22 4LX. *Email*: jenniferrosser@yahoo.co.uk

ROSSER, John, NDD (1952); painter. *b*: London, 8 Jun 1931. *s of*: Edward John Rosser. *m*: Margaret Rosser. *Studied*: Regent St. Polytechnic and Watford School of Art (1947-52) under A. J. B. Sutherland. *Represented by*: Ebury Gallery, 200 Ebury Street, London SW1. *Exhib*: RA, RBA, NEAC, RI, Young Contemporaries, Medici Gallery, Compton Gallery, Windsor, Neville Gallery, Sandford Gallery, Paris Salon; one-man shows: Brian Sinfield Gallery, Burford (1987), Hallam Gallery, SW14 (1989); finalist in the Hunting Group art prizes (1981); Chelsea Library (1992), Radisson Hotel, Brussels (1997); Retrospective Exhibition at John Adams Fine Art, Ebury Galleries, London (2009); Affordable Art Fair, Battersea Park, London (2009). *Works in collections*: Watford Museum. *Works Reproduced*: print: 'One Day by the River' (Sloane Graphics); Elgin Court, Simon and Schuster, Australia, Foyles Books, Rosenstiels, Medici. Print: 'Serenade in Venice' Limited Editions 2012. *Recreations*: tennis. *Misc*: National Service: army 1952-54. *Address*: 4 Beachview, 91 Banks Rd., Sandbanks, Poole, Dorset BH13 7QQ. *Email*: john.rosser1931@googlemail.com *Signs work*: capital R.

ROSSETTI, Mary Christina, SWE. *Medium*: oil, pastel, drawing, prints. *b*: Kingsbridge, S. Devon, 8 Oct 1946. *d of*: Oliver Gabriel Rossetti. *m*: Lionel Rutterford. two *d*. *Studied*: self taught with occasional assistance. *Exhib*: SWE Annual (Touring) Exhbns (1998, 2002-07); '500 Cats Exhbn' (2002); South Africa (2003); also small exhbns in Somerset, Dorset and Univ. of Surrey in 1990s. *Commissions*: private commissions for wood engravings, pastel and oil paintings. *Publications*: SWE Catalogue (2003). *Recreations*: sketching etc., reading, gardening, visiting exhibitions, listening to baroque music, pottery. *Address*: The Red House, Waterloo Lane, Stourton Caundle, Sturminster Newton DT10 2JF. *Email*: rossetti@rutterford.eclipse.co.uk *Signs work*: 'MCR', 'MRR' (Mary Christina Rossetti, Mary Rossetti Rutterford).

ROSSIE, Kay, DipFA, A.Dip., FFPS; abstract painter/sculptor in acrylic, water-colour, oil, wood, metal constructions. *b*: Porthcawl, 1940. one *s*. *Studied*: Croydon College of Art (1983-86), one year advanced sculpture (1986-87). *Exhib*: one-man show, Loggia Gallery, London; many mixed exhbns. of painting and sculpture, including Trends, Phillips, GEC Management College, Business Design Centre, Royal Society of Birmingham Artists, NYAD 2000 Manhattan, New York; Cotton's Atrium, City of London; Blythe Gallery, Manchester; Bankside Gallery, London; Osterley Park House Gallery, London. *Works in collections*: Croydon College, Price Waterhouse. *Commissions*: Kenetic Sculpture for First Light Ltd. *Publications*: included in international biographies, and The Cambridge Blue Book. *Clubs*: F.P.S., London, Reigate Soc. of Artists. *Address*: 12 Brokes Cres., Reigate, Surrey RH2 9PS. *Signs work*: "Kay Rossie."

ROUSE, Laura, Young Marine Artist of the Year (1st Prize, 2007, RSMA). *Medium*: gouache, drawing ink. *b*: Hampstead, 4 Mar 1989. *Studied*: Newnham College, Cambridge University (2007-10). *Exhib*: Bankside Gallery, London; Mall Galleries, London. *Address*: 57 Roe Lane, Kingsbury, London NW9 9BB. *Email*: lau7uk@hotmail.com *Signs work*: "L. Rouse".

ROWAN, David Paul, RBA (1979), RA. Schools Post. Grad. Cert. (1972-75), Dip.AD (Painting, 1969-72); artist in acrylic. *b*: Colne, Lancs., 28 Apr 1950. *s of*: William Rowan, careers officer. *Studied*: Maidstone College of Art (1969-72, D. Winfield, RBA, W. Bowyer, RA), RA Schools (1972-75, P.Greenham, CBE, RA, Margaret Green, John Holden). *Exhib*: RBA, Mid-Pennine Arts, Colne. *Works in collections*: F. Kobler, London; A. Whalley, Windsor. *Address*: 1 Sandown Rd., London SE25 4XD. *Signs work*: "DAVID ROWAN" or "D.P. Rowan."

ROWBOTHAM, Mark A., DipAD, PS (1992); painter in oil and pastels; Mem. Pastel Soc., winner Patterson Award. *b*: Sarawak, Borneo, 1959. *m*: Sherree E. Valentine-Daines. one *s*. two *d*. *Studied*: Epsom School of Art (1977-81). *Exhib*: RBA, ROI, RWS, RP, NEAC, PS. *Address*: St. Michael's House, Dell Close, Mickleham, Dorking, Surrey RH5 6EE. *Signs work*: "M.A.R."

ROWBOTTOM, Georgina Marian, (née HUDSON); NDD, City & Guilds in Embroidery 1958. *Medium*: acrylic. *b*: Crayford, Kent, 30 Sep 1938. *d of*: George Jones Hudson. *Educ*: Our Lady's High School (Dartford); Bexley Technical School. *Studied*: Bournemouth College of Art (1954-58). *Exhib*: RA Summer Exhibition (2009), Will & Em Gallery, Furzey Gardens, Minstead, New Forest (one month, annually), The Pine Walk, Bournemouth (annually), Peppercorns Gallery, Sopley. *Works in collections*: many commissions and sales. *Commissions*: 2 Medieval panels for Mrs H. De Winton (Ringwood, Hampshire), a Marvin Gaye painting for Mr. S. Richardson (Bournemouth), 2 abstract paintings for Mr. Ennis (Canada), 'Mostly Red' (exhibited at RA, sold to London buyer). *Recreations*: keeping and riding horses. *Clubs*: Chirstchurch Arts Guild, Hengist Group of Artists. *Address*: 212 Stony Lane, Burton, Christchurch, Dorset BH23 7LB.

ROWE, Julian, MA. *Medium*: sculpture, installation, assemblage. *b*: King's Lynn, 28 Feb 1951. *Studied*: Cambridge Art School; Open University; UCA Canterbury. *Represented by*: Invisible Print Studio. *Exhib*: Otter Gallery, Chichester; Rochester Art Gallery; Hastings Museum; Art Vaults, Southampton; Quay Arts, Newport, IOW; 20/21 Visual Arts Centre, Scunthorpe; Chichester Open; Nordart 2011, Budelsdorf, Germany; Parfitt Gallery, Croydon; Discerning Eye, London. *Works in collections*: public and private including Kent County Council; Tunbridge Wells Museum; University Coll. Chichester. *Publications*; 'Capriccio' (Chrome Green Pubns. 2012). *Address*: Campers, School Hill, Lamberhurst, Kent TN3 8DF. *Email*: julian@julianrowe.co.uk *Website*: www.julianrowe.co.uk *Signs work*: rarely signs work.

ROWLAND, Dawn, Fellow Royal British Society of Sculptors; member RBS and MAFA. MAFA Awards - Joes Davies Award, Addleshaw & Latham Award, National Westminster Bank Award, Coopers & Lybrand Award. *Medium*: Sculptor in stone and bronze. Drawings and stone lithography. *b*: London, 24 Sep 1944. *m*: Prof. Malcolm Rowland. two *d*. *Educ*: Orange Hill Girls' Grammar School. *Exhib*: Chelsea Harbour Sculpture (1993), Chichester Festival (1994), Konishi Gallery Kyoto, RA Summer Show, Salford A.G., Hannah Peschar Sculpture Garden, Davies & Tooth (Air Gallery), London (2000), Newby Hall Sculpture Park, Renishaw Sculpture Garden, Salford Art Gallery, Ben Uri Gallery, London, The Casson Gallery London, Stockport Art Gallery, McLennan Galleries, Glasgow, Blackheath Gallery, Portico Library AG, Manchester, Royal Society of British Sculptors, Wendy J Levy Contemporary Art, Kings Place, London. *Works in collections*: Nicola Horlick, Lord Archer, Lord Turnberg. *Commissions*: Nicola Horlick. *Address*: 54C Belsize Avenue, London NW3 4AE. *Email*: sculpture@dawnrowland.com *Website*: www.dawnrowland.com www.dawnrowland.co.uk *Signs work*: "DAWN" in semicircle with date under.

ROWLAND, Robert John, SNR Dip. Art & Design. *Medium*: oil, watercolour, acrylic. *b*: Chesterfield, 17 Sep 1946. *m*: Althea. *Studied*: Nottingham College of Art (1963); Gloucester College of Art & Technology (1980, 1982). *Exhib*: various galleries UK, and with Gloucestershire Society of Artists, and Guild of Railway Artists. *Works in collections*: private and corporate. *Commissions*: private and corporate. *Recreations*: plays trumpet - jazz. *Misc*: Themes of work include: 19c and early 20c Social History, Industrial Heritage and Landscape. *Address*: 54 Henry Road, Gloucester, GL1 3DY. *Signs work*: "ROB ROWLAND".

ROWLETT, George Goldie. *Medium*: painter of land and seascapes, portrait and figure in oil. *b*: Troon, Ayrshire, 29 June, 1941. *m*: Marion Sneller. two *s*. *Educ*: De Aston Grammar, Market Rasen. *Studied*: Grimsby School of Art (1960-62), Camberwell School of Art (1962-65), R.A. Schools (1965-68). *Represented by*: Michael Richardson Contemporary Art. *Exhib*: one-man shows: Grimsby Museum (1962), Greenwich Theatre Gallery (1975), Woodlands Gallery (1982), Zur Torkel Zehn, Konstanz (1985, 1986, 1987, 1991), D.M. Gallery (1987), Everard Read Gallery, Johannesburg (1987, 1988, 1990, 1992), Smith-Jariwala Gallery (1989), Cleveland Bridge Gallery, Bath (1989), Albemarle Gallery (1990, 1992, 1995), Art Space Gallery (1993,'95,'97,'99, 2001,'03,'05), Belloc Lowndes, Chicago (1995), Grant Fine Art, Newcastle, N. Ireland (1996), Abergavenny (2005), Maidstone & Rochester Galleries (2002), Canterbury Christchurch University (2000); mixed shows: R.A., Whitechapel Open, Cleveland Drawing Biennale, N.P.G., Hayward Annual 'A Singular Vision', Hunting Group, Spirit of London, South Bank Picture Show, London Group, Druce-Constable, Zur Torkel Zehn, Read Stremmel San Antonio, Everard Read, Architectural Arts Co. Dallas, Elizabeth Gordon Durban, Cleveland Bridge, Albemarle, Henry Wyndam, National Trust Centenary - Christies, Grant Fine Art, Belloc Lowndes, Art Space Gallery, Chicago Art Fair, Glasgow Art Fair, Discerning Eye, Canterbury Museum. *Works in collections*: Grimsby Museum, Northern Arts, Cleveland Museum Service, Nuffield Foundation, Baring Bros., Manny Davidson Discretionary Trust, Equitable Real Estate Investment, Atlanta, Ga., Kelmac Group, Price Forbes Ltd., Auto & General Ltd., Innovative Marketing Ltd., Ken Solomon Ltd., African Salt Works Ltd., Weedon Minerals, Anglo American Ltd., A.G. Diamond Cutters, Mesquite Investments, Philip Loot's Assoc., Stephen Fauke Interiors, Altron Ltd., Charles Glass Soc., Rose Gardens Ltd., Nedfin Bank Ltd., Momentum Components, Grinrod Unicorn Group Ltd., Voicevale Ltd.; Hiscox plc; Prudential Corporate plc; Berardo Foundation, Lisbon; Medway Council; British Council. *Misc*: Gallery: Art Space Gallery, 84 St. Peter's St, London N1 8JS. *Address*: c/o Art Space Gallery, Michael Richardson Contemporary Art, 84 St. Peter's Street, London N1 8JS. *Signs work*: "George Rowlett."

ROWSELL, Joyce, History of Art Degree (London). Membership of the following Societies: Royal Society of Miniature Painters, Sculptors & Gravers; Miniature Artists of America; Miniature Art Society of Florida; Hilliard Society Founder Member; Miniature Painters Sculptors and Gravers Washington DC; Cider Painters of America; New Mexico Miniature Art Society; 94 International Awards for Miniature Painting. *Medium*: oil. *b*: S. Wales, 20 Nov 1928. *d of*: William and Floss Gwyther. *m*: Geoffrey N. Rowsell. two *s*. *Educ*: Coborn School, Bow; Bishop Fox's School, Taunton. *Represented by*: Llewellyn Alexander Gallery, London; Francesca Anderson Fine Art, Lexington Mass. *Exhib*: London, Wells, Bristol, Tavistock, Exeter, Windsor, Bath, Birmingham (in UK); New York, Philadelphia, New Mexico, New Jersey, North Carolina, Oregon, Alabama, Tasmania. Permanent exhibition at Spring Grove. *Works in collections*: Hilliard Society, Miniature Art Society of Florida, Dutch Foundation of Miniature Art, Miniature Artists of America. Private collections. *Commissions*: portraits, landscapes, events. *Works Reproduced*: Somerset Magazine, May 2001; West Country Life, June 16th 2001 & 2010; The Artist Magazine, Nov 2001; 'Countryman' Magazine April 2005; book jacket designs, illustrations, limited edition prints. *Address*: Spring Grove Farm, Milverton, Som. TA4 1NW. *Email*: joycerowsell@btinternet.com *Website*: www.joycerowsell.com *Signs work*: "Joyce Rowsell" or "JR".

ROWSON, Hugh Thomas, BA, DA, RSW; former Educ. Officer, Aberdeen A.G.; former VP, Aberdeen Artists Soc., mem. Peacock Visual Arts, Aberdeen, mem. Royal Scottish Soc. of Painters in Water-colour, Edinburgh (since 1980). *Medium*: water-colour, acrylic, pen and ink. *b*: Aberdeen, 4 Aug 1946. *m*: Lesley. two *s*. *Studied*: Fine Art Diploma/ Post Diploma Study, Travel Scholarships to Europe and UK, Grays School of Art, The Robert Gordon University (1965-70, Alexander Fraser, Ian Fleming), Certificate in Art Education, Aberdeen College of Education (1970-71), Batchelor of Arts Degree in Humanities, Open University (1972-76). *Exhib*: RSW Exhibitions from 2002-10 in Scotland each year, Aberdeen University, Aberdeen Arts Centre, Peacock Visual Arts, Aberdeen (1997-2003), Riverside Gallery, Stonehaven (1999, 2007), Queens Road Gallery, Aberdeen (2000). *Works in collections*: Grampian Hospitals Art Trust, The Robert Gordon University, Aberdeen, Gray's School of Art, Aberdeen, private collections. *Publications*: Children's Guide to Aberdeen Art Gallery. *Address*: 276 Union Grove, (Ground Floor Flat East), Aberdeen, AB10 6TQ. *Email*: hughrowson107@btinternet.com *Signs work*: "Hugh T. Rowson" or "H.T.R."

ROWSON, Martin George Edmund, MA (Cantab) 1983; Cartoon Arts Trust Political Cartoonist of the Year (2000, 2003); Political Cartoon Society Cartoon of the Year (2002). *b*: London, 15 Feb 1959. *s of*: K E K Rowson. *m*: Anna Clarke. one *s*. one *d*. *Educ*: Merchant Taylors', Northwood; Pembroke College, Cambridge; no formal artistic training. *Exhib*: Gekoski's Bookshop and Gallery (1996); Politico's Bookshop and Gallery (1998, 2000, 2002); Tate Britain (2001, 2003). *Works in collections*: British Museum; Saatchi Collection; countless private collections. *Commissions*: regularly from newspapers and periodicals, including The Guardian, The Times, Daily Mirror, Independent on Sunday, Scotsman, etc., etc. *Publications*: 'Scenes from the Lives of Great Socialists' (Grapheme 1983); 'Lower than Vermin: An Anatomy of Thatcher's Britain' (Arrow 1986); 'The Waste Land' (Penguin 1990); 'The Nodland Express' (Macmillan 1994); 'Imperial Exits' (Macmillan 1995); 'Tristram Shandy' (Picador 1996); 'The Sweet Smell of Psychosis' (with Will Self, Bloomsbury 1996); 'Purple Homicide' (with John Sweeney 1997). *Recreations*: zoo administration. *Clubs*: Chelsea Arts Club, Soho House, Zoological Club, British Cartoonists' Association (Chairman). *Misc*: Vice-President and Council member of Zoological Society of London; appointed first 'Cartoonist Laureate' for London by Ken Livingstone. *Address*: 46 Vicars Hill, London SE13 7JL. *Email*: ye46@dial.pipex.com *Signs work*: Martin Rowson.

ROXBY, Brian, ROI (1993); Honorary Senior Member ROI (2012); painter in oil, acrylic and water-colour. *b*: 25 Oct 1934. *s of*: Thomas Roxby (decd). *m*: Christina Mary (decd); Iris Irene. one *s*. two *d*. *Educ*: St. Cuthbert's Grammar School, Newcastle upon Tyne. *Studied*: Sunderland College of Art (1951-55, Harry Thubron), RCA (1955-58, Leonard Rosoman, Robert Buhler). *Exhib*: RBA, NEAC, RI, ROI, Contemporary British Painters, Wildenstein (1958); one-man shows: Queen's Hall Gallery, Hexham (1988), Trevelyan College, Durham (1989), Zillah Bell, Thirsk (1998), Gallery 5 Lincoln (2001), Hawker Gallery, Amersham (2002, 2004, 2006, 2008). *Works in collections*: National Gallery of Wales and Government Art Collection. *Address*: The Chestnuts, 21 High St., Walcott, Lincoln LN4 3SN. *Email*: broxby@gmail.com *Signs work*: "B. Roxby."

ROY, Michael Presley-, ATC (1970) Reading University, DAE (1976) London University; professional artist (drawing, painting) landscapes, religious themes, flower-pieces, abstract motifs; art lecturer; ABI/IBC World Forums St John's College, Cambridge (2010) and St Catherine's College, Oxford (2012); Distinction (Reading Univ); Lifetime Achievement for Excellence in Created Artworks UCC (USA 2010); Diploma (International Section) Visual Poetry Biennial, Mexico City (1995). *Medium*: multi-media. *b*: London, 20 Apr 1928. *Educ*: Upton Grammar, Berks (1939-44); gained Oxford School Certificate (credits). *Studied*: Newland Park College (1967-70), Post Grad Centre, Hornsey College of Art (1973-76). *Exhib*: Reading A.G., Southampton Civic A.G. *Works in collections*: private and public, U.K. and abroad. *Publications*: Author: "The Rôle of the Art Teacher" (1976); "The Art Lark" (1992). Profile p.182 "International Panorama of Contemporary Art" (Verona, Italy 1998); p.61 "British Contemporary Art" (Gagliardi, London 1993); "Dictionary of International Biography" (Cambridge, 2008), pps 214/215 "2000 Outstanding Artists & Designers of the 20th Century" (Cambridge, I.B.C., 2001); Biopic in "Cambridge Blue Book" (2008). *Works Reproduced*: 'Art Lark' monoprint series (from original works by Michael Roy). *Principal Works*: oil paintings: 'Flight of Holy Family', Allington Castle, Kent; 'Mary Magdalene', Crowmarsh Church, Oxon; 'Carisbrooke Halt', Castle Museum, Carisbrooke, IoW; 'Road to Calvary' (1967), Parish Church, Windsor, Berkshire; 'Crucifixion', 'Madonna and Child Jesus' (1970), 'Sailing into New Millennium, 2000AD', Gosport Parish Church of Holy Trinity, Hants (www.holytrinitygosport.co.uk). *Address*: Flat 73, Homefort House, 82 Stoke Road Gosport, Hants. PO12 1QQ. *Signs work*: "Michael Roy" with symbol of small spider and date.

ROZELAAR GREEN, Alfred: see GREEN, Alfred Rozelaar.

RUBIRA, Sue (Susan Debra), BA (1st Class Hons), MA (RCA) Royal College of Art; Winner, Daily Mail 'Portrait of the Queen' Competition (2006), Second Prize, Sunday Times/Singer & Friedlander Watercolour competition (2006); 1st Prize, Daler Rowney, RWS 21st Century Open Exhibition (2007); Anthony J. Lester Art Critic Award, SWA Annual Exhibition (2007). *Medium*: oil, watercolour, drawing. *b*: Brentwood, Essex, 10 May 1959. *m*: Carlos. two *s*. one *d*. *Studied*: Banbury School of Art (1976-77); University of West of England (1977-80); Royal College of Art, London (1980-83). *Represented by*: Roman Black Gallery. *Exhib*: RP, ROI, RWS, Mall Galleries, London Art Fair (2007), Southampton City Art Gallery (006), 'Slave Market Gallery', Lagos, Portugal (1983-94), and others. *Works in collections*: June New Hall Art Collection, Cambridge University; "Geoff" Singer & Friedlander (Kaupthing) Collection. *Commissions*: 'Engraving' for Granada Televisions' 'Jewel in the Crown (1982). *Publications*: The Art of Watercolour magazine June 2010; 500 Portraits (BP Award). *Address*: 2 Pretoria Road, Hedge End, Southampton, Hants, SO30 0BS. *Email*: info@suerubira.co.uk *Website*: www.suerubira.co.uk *Signs work*: "S. RUBIRA" or "S.R." (hidden on some portraits).

RUDD, Bob, BA (1973), RI (1995); Turner Watercolour Award (2010); painter in water-colour and oil. *b*: Ipswich, Suffolk, 18 Jan 1944. *m*: Jennifer Cuff. two *s*. *Studied*: Ipswich

Art School (1960-63), Bath Academy of Art (1969-73, Adrian Heath). *Exhib*: RA, RI, RWA and many mixed exhbns. and one-man shows in London and Edinburgh. *Works in collections*: 15 works in the permanent collection of the Houses of Parliament. *Address*: 38 The Causeway, Chippenham, Wilts. SN15 3DB. *Email*: bob.rudd@icloud.com *Website*: www.bobrudd.com

RUDDUCK, Ron, FFPS (1990), Mem. SSS (1997), LRBS (1999), ARBS; sculptor in steel, copper and bronze. *b*: 1 Apr 1932. *m*: Annette. two *d*. *Educ*: Chiswick School. *Studied*: Richmond and Kingston Colleges, Middlesex Polytechnic. *Exhib*: 'Age of Shakespeare' British Council, Athawes Gallery W. London, Loggia Gallery W1, RSBA, Boxfield Gallery, Stevenage, Bettina Fine Art, London. *Works in collections*: FPS, London, Belfast, USA. *Address*: 53 Axbridge, Forest Park, Bracknell, Berks. RG12 0XB. *Email*: ronald.ruddock@ntlworld.com. *Website*: www.rbs.org.uk www.sculpturesales.fsnet.co.uk

RUDDY, Austin, NDD. *Medium*: oil, watercolour, drawing, prints, etching. *b*: Harrogate, Yorks, 13 May 1942. *s of*: Austin Ruddy & Edith Smith. *m*: Stephanie Jane Percy-Ruddy. two *s*. one *d*. *Studied*: Harrow School of Art. *Represented by*: Zillah Bell (Thirsk); Godfrey & Watt (Harrogate). *Exhib*: RA Summer Exhbn; Royal Watercolour Society; Royal Institute of Watercolour Painters; John Laing Landscape; Harrogate Open; Zillah Bell and various galleries in North of England. *Works in collections*: Harrogate Permanent Public Collection, mainly private collections in Europe, Australia, N. America. *Commissions*: taken. *Official Purchasers*: Mercer Gallery, Harrogate Permanent Collection. *Recreations*: Art History, walking, archery. *Clubs*: Laithwaites Wine Club. *Misc*: formerly Senior Designer BBC Television, retd. 1990 to take up painting full-time. *Address*: Yorebank Studio, Mickley, Ripon, N.Yorks HG4 3JE. *Website*: c/o www.art-connections.org.uk *Signs work*: 'A.RUDDY' or 'RUDDY' or 'AUSTIN RUDDY' or 'AR' (A and R joined).

RUNAGALL, Alan Trevor, RSMA, marine artist in water-colour; worked for thirty five years with Port of London Authority in India and Tilbury Docks; St.Cuthberts Mill Watercolour Award-RSMA Exhbn. 2002. *b*: Rochford, Essex, 26 May 1941. *m*: Carol. two *d*. *Educ*: Southend High School. *Studied*: self taught. *Exhib*: various solo and group exhibs. throughout UK and USA. *Works in collections*: Southend Museums Service, various shipping companies. *Commissions*: Port of London Authority, Port of Tilbury London Ltd. *Works Reproduced*: (1) A Celebration of Marine Art - 60 Years of the Royal Society of Marine Artists (2005 ed.); (2) The Wapping Group of Artists - 60 Years of Painting by the Thames. *Clubs*: Wapping Group of Artists., East Anglian Group of Marine Artists. *Address*: 7 Albany Rd., Rayleigh, Essex, SS6 8TE. *Email*: alan.runagall@tesco.net *Signs work*: "Alan Runagall."

RUNAYKER, Irene, NDD (1958); painter. *b*: London, 11 May 1937. *m*: decd. two *s*. *Educ*: Sarah Bonnell Grammar School, London. *Studied*: Camberwell School of Art (1954-58), Drawing with Merlyn Evans, Central School (1960-61). *Exhib*: Towner AG, Eastbourne; Brighton Art Fair; Bonhams Auction NNAH, Britart Gallery, W1; Art in Health, Eastbourne DGH; Thebe's Gallery, Lewes; NYAD2K Show, British Artists in New York (2000), Sussex Open '98; Brighton AG; Standard Cable & Wireless plc (1996/7); Musee Jeu de Paume, Albert, France; Stadtiches Museum, Gelsenkirchen, Germany (curated by Anne-Lise Knorr); London Borough of Camden 'Abstraction and Allusion'; University of East London; Morley College Gallery, SE1 'Laithwaites Gyroscopes'; curator: 'Sources of Humanity' Show, Conway Hall WC1; Portobello Fitness Centre 'Art & Sport', London W11; 4 Over 50, Thebe's Gallery, Lewes; 3rd Age Arts, Sussex. *Works in collections*: London Borough of Camden Permanent Collection; University of Technology, Sydney, Australia; Our Lady of Dolours, London; Hallfield School, London. Private collections Australia, Barbados, Canada, Cuba, Mexico, South Africa, Europe and USA. *Publications*: ref. in: Camberwell Students and Teachers 1943-1960 (by Geoff Hassell pub.Antique

Collectors, Woodbridge, 1995), Edgell Rickword by Charles Hobday (Carcarnet Press); Femmes Artists International, Paris (interview with Laurence Morechand); 'Dictionary of International Biography (Cambridge); Blue Book, International Biography (Cambridge); 'East' magazine interview with Adam Lloyd-Monaghan. *Official Purchasers*: London Borough of Camden. *Works Reproduced*: Camberwell School, it's Students and Tutors; 'East' magazine March and September 2005; Artwave video, Lewes (1998); Education Through Art (professional development programme, 1999). *Clubs*: IAA; INIVA. *Misc*: niece of Frank Runacres, RA (1904-1974); Talks: Artists Talk, Arts Council, Claremont, Hastings; Nomadic Lines in Becoming a Woman Artist' Brit. Sociology Annual Conference (University of E. London). *Address*: 1/68 Terminus Road Eastbourne BN21 3LX. *Email*: runayker@aol.com *Website*: www.runayker.com *Signs work*: "Runayker"; before 1982 "Runacre."

RUSH, Maureen Elizabeth, freelance artist in water-colour and pastel; Adult Educ. teacher; mem. Yorkshire Water-colour Soc. *b*: Surrey, 1938. *m*: Christopher John Rush. three *s*. *Educ*: Roseberry County Grammar School, Epsom. *Studied*: primarily self taught, influenced by Edward Wesson and the English Water-colour Impressionist School. *Exhib*: many joint and solo shows. *Works in collections*: Royal Tunbridge Wells A.G. *Address*: Weaver's Cottage, 3 New Row, Birstwith, Harrogate, N.Yorks. HG3 2NH. *Signs work*: "Maureen Rush."

RUSHBURY, Julia, Royal Academy Gold Medallist (1950), Landseer prize for Painting (1950), Edward Stott travelling scholarship. *Medium*: oil, watercolour, tempera, pencil. *b*: Stoke-by-Nayland, Suffolk, 8 Oct 1930. *d of*: Sir Henry Rushbury, RA. four *s*. *Educ*: Langford Grove School, Maldon, Essex. *Studied*: Chelsea School of Art; Royal Academy Schools (1947-51); studied fresco painting in Italy. *Exhib*: RA Summer Exhbns., British and Arts Council exhbns., Young Contemporaries, Redfern Gallery, Southover Gallery, AIA Gallery. *Works in collections*: private collections. *Commissions*: major mural projects at Lewes: for Asa Briggs; Mrs. Stewart-Roberts; Lord Lieutenant of East Sussex; mural panels at: St. Augustine's Church, Scaynes Hill, Sussex, The Old Bridge, Huntingdon, Cambs. The Hon. Julian Fane, Anthony Smith, President of Magdalene College, Oxford, Richards Sachs. *Publications*: article on murals 'Word of Interiors' 1988; Architectur & Wohnen 1992. *Principal Works*: mural commissions as above. *Recreations*: walking, talking. *Clubs*: RASAA. *Address*: 39A Southover High Street, Lewes, Sussex, BN7 1HX.

RUSHMER, Gordon, landscape and war artist; Rowland Hilder Award, RI.. *Medium*: oils and water-colours. *b*: Petersfield, 12 Jul 1946. one *s*. one *d*. *Educ*: Petersfield School. *Studied*: Farnham School of Art (1962-67). *Exhib*: Tate Britain, Furneaux Gallery, Edwin Pollard Gallery, Ceri Richards Gallery, R.I., Ashbarn Gallery, New Ashgate Gallery, Peter Hedley Gallery, Dragon St. Gallery, Gallery East, N.Y., David Curzon Gallery, Francis Iles Gallery, Weald & Downland Museum, Royal Marines Museum, Mariniers Museum Rotterdam, Lincoln Joyce Fine Art, Oriel Ynys Mon, Wykeham Gallery, Albany Gallery, 'A Decade of Conflict' - Hampshire Museums, Allen Gallery, Imperial War Museum, The Museum of Army Flying, Oxmarket Gallery, J.Morton Lee Fine Watercolours, John Creasey Gallery, Haslemere Museum. *Works in collections*: Her Majesty The Queen, Royal Logistics Corps, Special Boat Service, National Library of Wales, ICI, Nelson Mandela, Royal Marines, Royal Netherlands Marine Corps., HM Foreign and Commonwealth Office, Princess of Wales' Royal Regiment, Royal Marines Museum, Mariniers Museum, House of Lords, Japanese Govt., Lincoln's Inn, Royal Navy, Royal Artillery. *Commissions*: British Embassy Warsaw, Series on Conflicts in Bosnia, Cambodia, Kosovo, Eritrea, Afghanistan 2002 & 2007,and Iraq, Palace of Westminster. *Publications*: Art Business News USA, Artists and Illustrators Magazine, Globe and Laurel, Korps Mariniers Magazine, Hampshire the County Magazine, Sunday Times Magazine, The Imperial War Museum sound archive, 'The Road to Kandahar'. *Official Purchasers*: British Government, Royal Navy, Royal

Army, Dutch Goverment. *Works Reproduced*: Felix Rosenstiels, Hamlyn Group, Champaign Publishing. *Recreations*: cycling, hill walking. *Clubs*: Royal Naval Club, Royal Albert Yacht Club. *Misc*: interviews: BBC World Service, BBC Radio Solent. *Address*: Katimavik, Durfold Wood, Plaistow, West Sussex RH14 0PL. *Email*: gordonrushmer123@gmail.com. *Website*: www.gordonrushmer.com. *Signs work*: "Gordon Rushmer."

RUSHTON, James, ARCA, RWS, NEAC; artist in oil and water-colours; principal lecturer (ret'd). *b*: Newcastle-u-Lyme, 15 Jan 1928. widower. one *s*. one *d*. *Studied*: Burlem School of Art; Royal College of Art. *Exhib*: RA, RWS and NEAC annual exhbns. Work in private collections. *Works in collections*: portraits: Dr. Derek Ferrington, Mrs. Bette Pyatt, Mrs J. Barrow, The Earl of Belmore. *Publications*: illustrations for, Maxwells Ghost, On a Shoe String to Coorg, Archaeology Publications (Quality Book Club, London). *Address*: 17 Gower St., Newcastle-u-Lyme, Staffs. ST5 1JQ. *Signs work*: "J Rushton."

RUSPOLI, Francesco Mario Robert, Silver Medal, Rome & Villeneuve (1985), Silver Medal, French Institute (1986), Eugene Fromentin Award (1987), Gold Medal, French Institute (1988), Knight of the Art, Italy (1998), Bronze Medal, Paris (1991); Gold Medal, Beijing Olympic Fine Art (2008); MA theatre designer of set and costumes - (St. Martin, London). *Medium*: oil. *b*: Paris, 11 Dec 1958. *Studied*: Central St. Martin, London. *Represented by*: Katherine Maginnis; Galerie Ludwig Trossaert. *Exhib*: America, China and Europe. *Works in collections*: Gauguin Museum, Tahiti, French Polynesia; International Museum of Cupramontana, Italy; Museum of Art of Chianciano, Italy. *Publications*: Exhibit A Magazine, The Observer Magazine, Absolut Magazine, Contemporary Famous Artists, Art in Vogue, Gallery and Studio Magazine, Art Spectrum Magazine. *Address*: 54 Chestnut Gr., London SW12 8JJ. *Email*: francesco.ruspoli@ntlworld.com *Website*: www.francesco-ruspoli.com *Signs work*: "Ruspoli."

RUSSELL, Caroline, BA (Hons) 1989, ARBS; sculptor, work cast in foundry bronze and bronze resin. *b*: London,12 Jun 1968. *m*: Howard Granville. one *s*. one *d*. *Studied*: privately under Patricia Finch, FRBS. *Exhib*: Air Gallery, Gallery 27 London; Belgravia Gallery. *Works in collections*: various private collections. *Commissions*: large sculpture - Lehmann Communications plc. Entrance Hall. *Address*: Russell Sculptures, 50 The Drive, Edgware, Middx. HA8 8PT. *Email*: caroline@russellsculptures.com *Website*: www.russellsculptures.com *Signs work*: "C. RUSSELL."

RUSSELL, Christine Gillian, SWA; self taught professional artist specialising in pastel still life and other subject matter; SWA President & Vice-Presidents Award (2003). *Medium*: pastel, oils, watercolour, acrylics. *b*: London, 4 Apr 1952. *m*: Sidney Stephen Russell. one *s*. one *d*. *Educ*: Tollington Park School, London. *Exhib*: SWA, UA, PS, RBSA; Bourne Gallery, Reigate, Alexander Gallery, Bristol, John Noott Galleries, Broadway, Century Gallery, Datchet, Royall Gallery, Tunbridge Wells, Thornbury Castle, South Glos., Webbs Country Gallery, Battersea; Artifex Gallery, Sutton Coldfield; Peter Hedley Gallery, Dorset; Llewellyn Alexander, London; Figura Gallery, Windsor; Fine Art UK, Ledbury. *Works in collections*: private collections. *Commissions*: private commissions. *Publications*: entry in S.W.A. Exhibitors 1855-1996, work illustrated in 'Masterstrokes: Pastel' and 'Painting Great Pictures from Photographs' , 'International Artist' Magazine, 'Pastel Artist International' magazine and 'The Artist's Sketchbook' , 'The Collins Artist's Sketchbook'. *Works Reproduced*: 3 limited edition, 5 open edition prints; greetings cards. *Misc*: Tutors painting holidays: Spain, Italy, UK, Morocco (2008), Marlborough College Summer School. Workshops: own studio and Art Societies. *Address*: The Laurels Studio, Stone, Nr.Berkeley, Glos GL13 9LD. *Email*: christinerussell@gmx.co.uk *Website*: www.art-christinerussell.co.uk *Signs work*: "C.G. Russell" (originals) "Christine Russell" (prints).

RUSSELL, Edwin John Cumming, FRBS, Cert. RAS, RA Gold Medal for sculpture; Sir Otto Beit Medal for sculpture (1991); sculptor in bronze, stone, wood. *b*: Heathfield, 4 May

1939. *m*: Lorne McKean, sculptor. two *d*. *Studied*: Brighton College of Art and Crafts (1955-59), Royal Academy Schools (1959-63). *Works in collections*: Crucifix, and St. Michael, St. Paul's Cathedral; Bishop, Wells Cathedral; Dolphin Sundial, Greenwich; Sundials for Oman University and Dubai Parliament Sq.; Mad Hatters Tea Party, Warrington; Lion and Lamb, best shopping centre (1987); Alice and White Rabbit, Guildford; Panda, W.W.F., H.Q.; Forecourt Sculpture, Rank Xerox U.K., H.Q. *Address*: Lethendry, Hindhead, Surrey GU26 6BE. *Signs work*: "E.R."

RUSSELL, Jim, RBA; painter and illustrator in oil and water-colour. *b*: Walsall, Staffs., 30 Jun 1933. *m*: Becky. one *s*. one *d*. *Educ*: Royal School, Wolverhampton. *Studied*: Birmingham College of Art. *Exhib*: RA, John Moores, RBA, FBA, Bankside, Laing, Singer & Friedlander, Hunting, etc.; one-man shows: Amalgam, Drian London, Alpha House Sherborne, Boxfield Stevenage. *Works in collections*: Liverpool University, various LEAs. *Commissions*: various theatre rehearsal drawings, Wine Soc. *Works Reproduced*: Radio Times, Punch, newspapers, theatres, etc. *Address*: 10 Milton Rd., London SE24 0NP.

RUSSON, Bobbie Jane, BA Hons, MA (RCA); Florence Trust Residency Award (1997). *Medium*: oil, drawing. *b*: Birmingham, 27 Jan 1966. *m*: Robert Cleveland. one *s*. two *d*. *Studied*: Bournville School of Art, Birmingham (Foundation 1982-84); St. Martins School of Art (BA Hons, 1984-87); RCA (MA, 1988-90). *Represented by*: Bo-lee Gallery. *Exhib*: Solo: Merz Contemporary Art (1994), Bo-lee Gallery, Bath (2011); Mixed include: Whitworth Young Contemporaries (1987); South Bank Picture Show (1991); Young Contemporaries (Frost & Reed 1992, Roy Miles Gallery 1995); Hunting Art Prizes (1996); AAF Parris (2010); London Art Fair (2011, 2012). *Works in collections*: private. *Address*: 111 Stillingfleet Road, Barnes, London SW13 9AF. *Email*: bobbierusson@btinternet.com *Website*: axis, and Facebook 'Bobbie Russon's Art Page'. *Signs work*: "B.J.RUSSON".

RUST, Graham Redgrave, artist (muralist, illustrator and botanical painter) in water-colour and water-based paints; Artist-in-Residence, Woodberry Forest School, Virginia (1967-1968). *b*: Hatfield, 17 Feb 1942. *Studied*: Polytechnic School of Art, Regent St. (1958-60), Central School of Arts and Crafts (1960-61), under Sir Lawrence Gowing, and Norman Blamey, RA, National Academy of Art, NY (1962). *Exhib*: First exhib. RA (1965), over 30 one-man exhbns. since 1964. *Commissions*: Private mural commissions in various country houses in England. Largest work, the South staircase, Ragley Hall, Warwickshire for the Marquess of Hertford (1969-83). Public mural commission, The Theatre, Chipping Norton, Oxon. (1996), The Theatre, Espelkamp, Germany (2002) with Rui Paes. *Publications*: The Painted House (1988), Decorative Designs (1996), Needlepoint Designs (1998), The Painted Ceiling (2001), Revisiting the Painted House (2005). *Clubs*: Brooks's; Art Workers Guild. *Address*: The Old Rectory, Somerton, Suffolk, IP29 4ND. Website: www.grahamrust-murals.com *Signs work*: "GRAHAM RUST" or "G.R. Rust."

RUSTON, Sandra, SBA (Society of Botanical Artists). *Medium*: Watercolour, drawing. *b*: Walton-on-Naze, 11 Jan 1943. two *s*. two *d*. *Studied*: Colchester School of Art, Essex (1950/60s); St. Martins School of Art (1960s). *Exhib*: Westminster Hall, London; local exhibitions in Essex and Suffolk; Spain Living Design, Albox. *Commissions*: Local people in Suffolk. *Works Reproduced*: Prints of paintings by NIS Art. *Address*: Bells Corner, Martens Lane, Polstead CO6 5AG. *Email*: sandra.ruston@hotmail.co.uk *Signs work*: "S A Ruston".

RUTHERFORD, Iain, MA, DipAD, ATC. *Medium*: oil, watercolour, oil and soft pastel, gouache, acrylic, prints. *b*: Hitchin, Herts, 28 Jun 1953. *s of*: George (John) Rutherford. one *d*. *Educ*: Rainham, Kent, New Milton, Hants (comprehensives); Southampton Technical College. *Studied*: Winchester School of Art (1970-71); GoldsmithsCollege (1971-74) (1976-77) (1978-80). *Represented by*: Harlequin Gallery, London www.studio-pots.com. *Exhib*: one-person exhbns: Art Space Gallery, London (1986); L'Artiste Assoiffé Restaurant,

London (1993); Harlequin Gallery, London (2002, 04); Group exhbns: ICA; Heatherly Gallery; City of London University; Camden Arts Centre; Whitechapel Open; Leicester Exhibition for Schools and Colleges; Air Gallery; Greenwich Citizens Gallery; Woodlands Gallery; The Gallery at Architecture Ltd.; Barbican Centre; RCA; RA Summer Exhbn; Berkeley Square Gallery; Business Design Centre; Tudor Barn Art Gallery; Harlequin Gallery; The French House Soho; Belgrave Gallery, St. Ives; 'Sharing a View' exhbns (including the late Denis Bowen) at Huddersfield Art Gallery; Derby Museum and Art Gallery; Quarr Gallery, Swanage, Dorset; APT Gallery, London; Burton Art Gallery and Museum, Bideford, Devon; Dimbola Lodge Museum (Julia Margaret Cameron Trust), Isle of Wight. *Works in collections*: The Leicester Collection for Schools and Colleges; Huddersfield Art Gallery; Dimbola Lodge Museum (Julia Margaret Cameron Trust), Isle of Wight; many private collections in UK and abroad. *Publications*: Directory of Artists, Space Open Studios (London, 1975); Hampstead and Highgate Express; The Hill Magazine; The Guardian; Dictionary of Artists in Britain since 1945; St. Ives Times and Echo, and Hayle Times; The Huddersfield Daily Examiner; Derby Evening Telegraph; 'Sharing a View' catalogues; 'St. Ives 1975-2005, Art Colony in Transition' by Peter Davies. *Works Reproduced*: Directory of Artists, Space Open Studios (London, 1975); The Hill Magazine; Derby Evening Telegraph; 'Sharing a View' Catalogues. *Address*: 83 Riverdale Road, Plumstead, London SE18 1PD. *Email*: iain@iainrutherford.com *Website*: www.iainrutherford.com *Signs work*: 'Iain Rutherford'.

RUTT, Loraine, BA (Hons) Ceramics, HND Surveying and Cartography; Winston Churchill Memorial Trust Travelling Fellowship (1996). *Medium*: ceramics. *b*: Wimbledon, 29 Aug 1962. *m*: Stephen Tomkinson. *Educ*: Maidstone Girls' Grammar School. *Studied*: Central St.Martins (1990), Southbank University (1983). *Exhib*: Michael Simpson Fine Art, London; Ice House Holland Park (2 solo exhbns); Gainsboroughs House, Suffolk; Mall Galleries, London; A.T.Kearney, London; USA: New York, Miami; Byard Art, Cambridge. *Works in collections*: NHS Trust South London and Maudsley, Wooden Spoon House Panels, private collections in the UK and USA. *Commissions*: Bellenden Map Terrace: Bellenden Renewal Scheme, London; Fred Clarke Memorial Map of Jersey: Le Masuriers, Jersey; Fairacre, Roehampton. *Publications*: 'Porcelain' Caroline Whyman (Batsford, 1994). *Works Reproduced*: ceramics, wall panels. *Clubs*: Society of Designer Craftsmen. *Misc*: research studio ceramics in public art and architecture. *Address*: Arch 191, Blenheim Court, 48 Blenheim Grove, London SE15 4QL. *Email*: info@lorainerutt.net *Website*: www.lorainerutt.net *Signs work*: Loraine Rutt.

RUTTER & BENNETT, Christopher & Evelyn, *CR*: MA, Dip, ARBS; *EB*: MA (RCA), BA, ARBS; McColl Foundation Bursary, Southeast Arts Major and Travel Awards, Arts Council Grant, Leonardo da Vinci Fellowship to Cyprus; Merit Award, Beijing Olympics Sculpture Competition. *Medium*: sculpture, mixed media, drawing. *b*: *CR*: Catterick; *EB*; Gosport. one *s*. *Educ*: *CR*: Maidstone, Wimbledon, City & Guilds of London, East London Uni. Architecture School; *EB*: Portsmouth, Worthing, Winchester, Royal College of Art. *Studied*: Winchester Royal College of Art. *Represented by*: 'Sculpture at Goodwood'; 'Plan Art'. *Exhib*: 'Sculpture at Goodwood', De Lawarr Pavilion, Bexhill; Rochester City Art Gallery; Rollo Contemporary Art, London; Aspex Gallery, Portsmouth; Turner Contemporary, Margate; Beijing Olympics Touring Exhibition in China. *Works in collections*: Sculpture at Goodwood, Dame Stephanie Shirley, various private collections. *Commissions*: Sculpture at Goodwood; Royal Caribbean Cruises; Chichester, Hastings and Swindon hospitals; Lovells Developers. *Publications*: British Sculptors of the 20th Century; Ten Years of Sculpture at Goodwood. *Misc*: Christopher Rutter and Evelyn Bennett have worked in partnership for 15 years. *Address*: 2 Queens Road, Faversham, Kent, ME13 8RJ. *Email*: rutterandbennett@yahoo.com *Website*: www.rbs.org.uk rutterandbennett.com *Signs work*: 'rb'.

RYAN, Thomas, KCHS (Knight Commander Equestrian Order of the Holy Sepulchre of Jerusalem); KLJ (Knight Hospitalier Order of St. Lazarus of Jerusalem); PPRHA, D.Litt., ANCAD, Hon.RA, Hon.RSA; painter in oil, water-colour, pastel, red chalk, coin, postage stamp and medal designer; President, United Arts Club, Dublin, and Limerick Art Soc.; Council mem. Stamp Design Com. An Post; Freeman of Limerick. *b*: Limerick, Ireland, 16 Sep 1929. *d of*: John and Mary Ryan (nee Ryan). *m*: Mary Joyce. four *s*. two *d*. *Educ*: Christian Brothers School, Limerick. *Studied*: Limerick School of Art (Richard Butcher, ARCA), National College of Art, Dublin (Seän Keating, Maurice McGonigle). *Exhib*: many one-man and mixed shows in Ireland, GB, Ukraine, USA, Latvia. *Works in collections*: Mostly portrait and figure subjects: National Gallery of Ireland, President of Ireland official residence, Cardinal's residence Armagh, European Court, EEC, Brussels, St. Patrick's College, Maynooth, Kings Inns, Dublin, Royal College of Surgeons, Trinity College Dublin, University College, Dublin, University College, Galway, Limerick University, State Apartments Dublin Castle, Leinster House (Dáil Eireann), National University of Ireland, Royal Hibernian Academy, Archbishop of Cashel, McKee Barracks (Chiefs of Staff), Government Buildings (Taoiseachs Office), Pro-Cathedral, Christ Church Cathedral, NCEA; Office Public Works, Pontificial Irish College, Rome, Episcopal Residence, Limerick, Derry, Irish Management Institute, Irish Embassies abroad. *Commissions*: 2002-2003: Hon. Mr. Justice Ronan Keane, Chief Justice, His Eminence, Desmond, Cardinal Connell, Archbishop of Dublin; for National Gallery, Dr. Ken Whittakee; John Hume; Eamon de Valera; 24 portraits of eminent citizens for Limerick Civil Trust. *Publications*: 'Thomas Ryan, Oil Paintings' (2009); 'Dublin and thereabouts' (2011). *Official Purchasers*: see above. *Principal Works*: 'The Crucifixion', 'Flight of the Earls', 'GPO 1916'. *Clubs*: Arts Dublin, Friendly Brothers of St. Patrick, Dublin. *Address*: Robertstown Lodge, Robertstown, Ashbourne, Co. Meath, Eire. *Signs work*: "Thomas Ryan."

RYDER, Brian Leonard, ROI, IEA; Full Member of Royal Institute of Oil Painters and Institute of East Anglian Artists. *Medium*: oil, watercolour, drawing. *b*: Freeland, Oxfordshire, 1 Dec 1944. *Partner*: Linda Burn. two *d*. *Studied*: Holloway, North London. *Exhib*: Frasers in Glasgow; Llewelyn Alexander Gallery, London (one person show); Kendals IOW; Thompsons Gallery, Suffolk; Cambridge Contemporary Art; ROI, Mall Galleries; USA, Spain, France and Malta and many galleries in Norfolk in mixed exhibitions. *Works in collections*: Harvard and Yale Universities, USA; Moina Gallery, Malta. *Publications*: 'Beyond Realism' and 'Watercolours with Confidence' (David & Charles); 'Norfolk and Beyond' (Halstar); six DVDs by Town House Films. *Misc*: President IEA - formed with three other East Anglian Artists in 2012. *Address*: 9 Mill Court, Wells-next-the-Sea, Norfolk NR23 1HF. *Email*: info@brianryder.org *Website*: www.brianryder.org *Signs work*: "B.RYDER".

RYDER, Susan, RP (1992), NEAC (1980), NDD (1964), David Murray Travel scholarship (1964); Vice President RP 2002-2008; NEAC Critics prize (1990, 1993), Barney Wilkinson prize (1990), Alexon Portrait Competition (1991). *Medium*: oil. *b*: Windsor, 14 Mar 1944. *d of*: Capt. Robert Ryder, RN, VC. *m*: Martin Bates. one *s*. one *d*. *Studied*: Byam Shaw School of Painting (1960-64, Maurice de Sausmarez, ARA, Bernard Dunstan, RA). *Exhib*: RA, Portrait Painters, NEAC; one-man shows, Haste Gallery, Ipswich (2), W.H. Patterson, Albemarle St., W1. (1989, 1995, 1999), Oakham Gallery, Bury St., St.James (2004), Ackermann, 27 Lowndes St. SW1 (2009). *Works in collections*: "Miss Pears 1984" Pears Collection, Imperial College, London, Clare College Cambridge, Royal Automobile Club. *Commissions*: HRH The Princess of Wales (1982); HM The Queen (1997). *Address*: 17 Queen's Gate Place, London SW7 5NY. *Email*: susanryder.paintings@virgin.net *Website*: www.susanryder.co.uk *Signs work*: "Ryder."

RYLAND, Christopher, BA Fine Art (1972), ATC (1975), SBA (1995); Winner of SBA President's Award 2001, St.Cuthbert's Mill Award 2007; artist specialising in flower painting in water-colour, also runs art courses from his studio. *b*: Eastbourne, Sussex, 2 Feb

1951. *m*: Pamela Ryland. *Studied*: Goldsmiths' College School of Art, University of London. *Exhib*: The Barbican, London, Antony Dawson Fine Art, London, Medici Galleries, London, RBA, Mall Galleries, London, recently two solo exhbns. at John Russell Gallery, Ipswich, Exhibitions John Russell Gallery, Ipswich (Feb 2006, Sept 2008), The Wildlife Gallery, Lavenham (Aug 2010). *Commissions*: Wedgewood, Royal Doulton. *Publications*: articles in Country Life, International Artist, Leisure Painter. *Address*: 35 Gainsborough St., Sudbury, Suffolk CO10 2EU *Website*: www.christopherryland.co.uk *Signs work*: "Ryland" or "RYLAND."

RYRIE, Jennie, RBSA; MA Fine Art; Kate Fryer Prize, RBSA (2010). *Medium*: watercolour, acrylics, mixed media. *b*: Lincolnshire, 8 Sep 1957. *m*: Philip Brockley (decd). one *d*. *Studied*: Edinburgh College of Art, University of Edinburgh (1975-80). *Represented by*: Belgrave St. Ives; Wendy J. Levy Contemporary Art, Manchester; Bridgegate Gallery, Holt. *Exhib*:Thackeray Gallery, London (1990-03); The Spectator National Painting Competition, Barbican Centre, London (1992); Oriel Gallery, Theatr Clwyd (1994); Ekaterinburg Museum of Fine Art, Russia (1997); Kingfisher Gallery, Edinburgh (1994-2000); Canyon Road Contemporary Art, Santa Fe, New Mexico, USA (1994-2008); Wendy J. Levy Contemporary Art, Manchester (2001-13); Castle Street Gallery, Hay-on-Wye (2004-06); Grosvenor Museum, Chester (2006); Galerie Englische Kirche, Meiringen, Switzerland (2009); Moray Art Centre, Inverness (2010); Roger Billcliffe, Glasgow (2001/13); Porthminster Gallery, St. Ives (2013); Belgrave St. Ives (2012-14). *Works in collections*: Grosvenor Museum, Chester; Natural History Museum; Sultanate of Oman; University of Durham; Brown-Forman Corporation, USA; L.I.M.E. Hospital Trust; British Midlands Airline; Burke Ford Insurance, Liverpool. *Commissions*: East Cheshire Hospital Trust; Grosvenor Museum, Chester. *Publications*: "Picturesque Chester, The City In Art", Peter Boughton (1997); "Dictionary of Artists In Britain Since 1945", David Buckman (1998); "The Brit Art Directory", Henry Mayhew (2001); "Miller's Picture Price Guide 2005"; "Twelve Women Artists In The North West", Judy Rose and Wendy J. Levy (2006); Flora Iranica; Flora of Arabia. *Official Purchasers*: Grosvenor Museum, Chester. *Principal Works*: "Ocean Music", "Dream of The Yellow Horse", "Daybreak Symphony", "Jazz Nights", "Red Ocean". *Clubs*: Member of CHART (North West Artists Collective). *Misc*: 'Musical Abstracts', featured artists, 2005 BBC Radio 2 Jazz Awards. *Address*: 55 Hermitage Road, Saughall, Chester CH1 6AQ. *Email*: jenny_ryrie@hotmail.com *Website*: www.jennyryrie.com *Signs work*: "J.A.Ryrie" or "J.R."

RYVES, Ann Catherine, NS; Awarded Silver Cup twice by FBA (1973, 1985); President, Thames Valley Arts Club. *Medium*: Palette Knife painter, oil. *b*: Lambeth, London, 22 Sep 1929. *d of*: J. Bertram Roberts, Chartered Accountant. *m*: Bruno Ryves, Nuclear Physicist. three *s*. one *d*. *Educ*: Queenswood School for Girls. *Studied*: Kingston School of Art under Reginald Brill (Fine Art, Pottery, 1947-1952). *Represented by*: NS, ROI (The Mall), Alpine Gal. South Audley St., UA. *Exhib*: Paris Salon (1987); Mernier Gallery, Southwark, London (2006-2008); Smiths Gallery, Covent Garden - Westminster Hall (1994-2003); 4-woman show, Fulham (2007); Antrim Gallery, Queensway; solo exhibition Woodstock Gallery, London (1960); Llewellyn Alexander Gallery (2008-2009). *Works in collections*: many private collections in USA, Denmark, Germany, France, UK. *Official Purchasers*: St. Hilda's College, Oxford. *Clubs*: United Artists, National Society; Art Societies: Ridley, Richmond, Thames Valley. *Address*: 48 Galsworthy Road, Kingston Hill, Surrey, KT2 7BS. *Signs work*: "ANN RYVES"

S

SAHAI, Virendra, OBE, DipTP, RIBA; painter in oil and water-colours, and illustrator. *b*: Shahjehanpur, India, 25 Jun 1933. *s of*: Girwar Sahai. *m*: Ingrid Clara Marie. one *s*. *Educ*: trained as an architect and townplanner. *Studied*: painting: Central School of Art, London.

Exhib: one-man shows: New Vision Centre and Biggins Gallery, London (1961), Commonwealth Institute, London (1966), Galerie Suzanne de Coninck, Paris (1967), Bear Lane Gallery, Oxford (1967), Horizon Gallery, London (1991); group and mixed exhbns: Redfern Gallery, London, Commonwealth Biennale of Abstract Art (1961-67), Kettle's Yard, Cambridge (1996), Reading Museum, Bradford Museum, Brighton Museum, Beaune Gallery, Paris, Cambridge Book and Print Gallery, Wimpole Hall, Cambridge (2003) and others. *Works in collections*: Bradford Museum, Councils for Art Education, Leicester, Oxford and Cambridge University; private collections in England, Nigeria, USA, Canada, Germany, Hong Kong and Spain. *Commissions*: Illustrations for Cambridge Street Names (CUP). *Publications*: Guardian, Art International, Discovering an Historic City - Cambridge. *Misc*: represented India at Commonwealth Biennales. *Address*: 39 New Rd., Barton, Cambs. CB23 7AY. *Signs work*: "Virendra Sahai".

SALAMAN, Christopher, artist in oil, bronze and resin bronze. *b*: Dorking, 4 Nov 1939. married. *s of*: Easton Salaman, ARIBA. one *s*. *Educ*: Bedales School. *Studied*: Camberwell School of Art and Crafts under Karel Vogel. *Exhib*: Woodstock Gallery, Upper Street Gallery, Mall Galleries, Margaret Fisher Gallery. *Address*: West Park Lodge, High Ongar, Essex. *Signs work*: "Christopher Salaman."

SALARZA-GRANT, Chito, British Institution Award - RA Summer Exhibition (2004). *Medium*: mixed media, hat sculptures, oil, watercolour, drawing, prints, sculpture. *b*: Philippines, 15 Apr 1965. *s of*: Gloria & Escolastico Salarza. *Partner*: Gerald Grant (decd). *Educ*: Minoanao State University, Philippines. *Studied*: Westminster College, London (2001); Central St.Martins (2002); Morley College (2003-). *Exhib*: Affordable Art Fair, Battersea Park, London (1999); Royal College of Art (2000); Air Gallery, London (1999); Royal Academy Summer Show (2004); V&A Museum of Childhood (Inspired By, 2009). *Works in collections*: private collectors. *Works Reproduced*: Featured on BBC live coverage of the Royal Wedding (live interview). *Misc*: Married name Chito Salarza-Grant, aka The Hatman of London. *Address*: 349 Queenstown Road, London SW8 4LH. *Email*: csalarzagrant@yahoo.com *Website*: www.chitosalarza.com *Signs work*: "-Chito-".

SALMON, Antonia. *Medium*: ceramic sculpture. *b*: London, 17 Apr 1959. one *s*. *Studied*: Harrow School of art (1982-84); Middlesex University (2005-2011). *Represented by*: Beaux Arts; Contemporary Ceramic Centre; Porthminster Gallery; Garden Gallery. *Exhib*: Selected solo shows: Cecilia Colman Gallery, London (1990, 1995, 2010); Hart Gallery, London (1997, 1999, 2001, 2003, 2004); Studio Contemporary Ceramics, Devon (2005); Stour Gallery, Warwickshire (2008); Beaux Arts, Bath (2009, 2013). Selected Group shows include: Pangolin Gallery, Glos (2006); Bluecoat Gallery, Liverpool (2008); The New School Gallery, York (2010); Porthminster Gallery, St. Ives (2012, 2013, 2104); Art in Action, Waterperry House (1986-2014); SOFA Chicago (2001-03); V&A (2005-08); Ceramic Art London, RCA (2005-2014); Oxford Ceramics Fair (2010, 2011, 2014). *Publications*: include: "Smoke Fired Pottery" Jane Perryman (A&C Black, 1995, 2007); "Modern Pots, The Lisa Sainsbury Collection" Cyril Frankel (Thames&Hudson, 2001); "Raku: Investigations into Fire" David Jones (Crowood Press, 2000). *Recreations*: walking, gardening, tennis, reading. *Misc*: Also works as a psychotherapist. *Address*: 20 Adelaide Road, Sheffield S7 1SQ. *Email*: antoniasalmon.sheffield@googlemail.com *Website*: www.antoniasalmon.co.uk *Signs work*: potters mark.

SALMON, Martin, illustrator in watercolour and gouache; designer (Advertising). *b*: Barnehurst, Kent, 19 Apr 1950. *m*: Janice. *Educ*: Dartford Technical School. *Exhib*: Lincoln Joyce Gallery, Limpsfield Watercolours, Westcott Gallery, Bourne Gallery, Linda Blackstone Gallery. *Works in collections*: Hong Kong, NZ, Italy, N. America, Switzerland, Kuwait, Spain, etc. *Works Reproduced*: Greeting cards, tablemats, etc. *Address*: Dome Hill, Caterham, Surrey CR3 6EE. *Signs work*: "Martin Salmon."

SALTER, Anthony, graphic designer and printmaker in etching. *b*: London, 2 Mar 1949. *Studied*: Goldsmiths' College School of Art (1966-69). *Exhib*: RA, RSPEE, PMC. *Works in collections*: Rank Zerox, London Borough of Greenwich. *Address*: 34 Lizban St., London SE3 8SS. *Signs work*: "ANTHONY SALTER."

SALTER, Rebecca, BA Art and Design; artist in acrylic on canvas, works on paper, woodcut prints. *b*: Sussex, 24 Feb 1955. *m*: Geoffrey Winston. *Educ*: Bristol Polytechnic (1974-77). *Exhib*: extensively in Britain and Japan; solo shows: Jill George Gallery (1994, 1996), New York (1997). *Works in collections*: Tate Gallery, British Museum, Portland Museum and San Francisco Museums of Modern Art, Library of Congress, Washington, British Council. *Publications*: Exhibition catalogue (1996, 1998, 1999). *Address*: c/o Jill George Gallery, 38 Lexington St., London W1R 3HR. *Signs work*: "REBECCA SALTER."

SAMUEL, Alison, Cert.Ed., BSc (Hons) Psych. (Open). *Medium*: Works on canvas or board, framed and unframed, in oils and acrylics. *b*: Leamington Spa, 17 Dec 1951. *m*: Philip. two *s*. *Educ*: Truro High School (1960-70), Bedford College of PE (1970-73), Open University (1996-2000). *Studied*: Physical Education and Art (dissertation on Printing). *Exhib*: Market St. Mews Gallery, Trelowarren, Lander Gallery, Wavelength Gallery, Crantock Forge Gallery, Falmouth Arts Centre. Prints and cards at Navigator Gallery, Ottakars, Gluvian Gallery, Gallery Tresco, Round House and Capstan Gallery, Children's Royal Academy, London. *Commissions*: A. Scales, H. Mulcahy, P. Christian (NZ). *Principal Works*: seascapes (Scilly Isles) and wave forms, enlarged plant forms, abstract work. *Recreations*: sailing, walking. *Address*: Bithek House, Budock Vean Lane, Mawnan Smith, Falmouth, Cornwall, TR11 5LH. *Email*: alisam5@aol.com

SAMUELSON, Becky, SWA, HS; marine and landscape artist in pastel and gouache; teacher, Adult Educ. IOW. *b*: Oxon, 13 Jul 1959. *m*: Colin. one *s*. one *d*. *Educ*: self taught. *Represented by*: DDFA Licencing. *Exhib*: London (various), Kendall's Fine Art Cowes, Turnpike Gallery Petersfield, Bembridge Gallery IOW, HS, Century Gallery, Datchet, Alexander Gallery, Bristol; Fine Art UK, Ledbury; Seaview Arts. *Works in collections*: private. *Commissions*: marine and landscape paintings in pastel, acrylic and gouache/watercolour. *Publications*: contributor to Leisure Painter Magazine. *Works Reproduced*: greetings cards, prints for Shanklin Chine, Sailing Clubs, Appuldurcombe House, Priory Hotel, calendar and local cards, prints through 'Art Marketing'. *Recreations*: sailing, gardening. *Clubs*: Bembridge Sailing Club, Brading Haven Yacht Club. *Address*: Kempsford, Hilbre Rd., St. Helens, Ryde, I.O.W. PO33 1TJ. *Email*: becky@beckysamuelsonfinearts.co.uk *Website*: www.beckysamuelsonfinearts.co.uk *Signs work*: "B. SAMUELSON."

SANDERS, Rosanne Diana, SBA; botanical painter in water-colour and printmaker; five RHS gold medals, RA miniature award. *b*: Stoke Poges, Bucks., 21 Jun 1944. one *s*. *Educ*: Roedean. *Studied*: High Wycombe College of Art. *Represented by*: Jonathan Cooper, London. *Exhib*: Hunt Institute, USA, SBA, Westminster, Tryon & Swann Gallery, London, RHS, Devon Guild, and various galleries in Britain; solo exhib., Hortus, London, Jonathan Cooper, Park Walk Gallery. *Works in collections*: Dr. Shirley Sherwood, V&A Museum, First National Bank, Johannesburg, S. Africa. *Commissions*: stamps - commemorative plates for HM Queen Elizabeth and the Queen Mother. *Publications*: The English Apple, Phaidon Press; Portrait of a Country Garden, Aurum Press; Painting The Secret Life of Nature, Search Press; A Little Book of Old Roses, Appletree Press; The Art of Making Wine, Aurum Press; The Apple Book - Frances Lincoln, 2010. *Address*: c/o Jonathan Cooper, Park Walk Gallery, 20 Park Walk, London SW10 0AQ. *Email*: info@rosiesanders.com *Website*: www.rosiesanders.com *Signs work*: "RS" and on prints "Rosie Sanders."

SANDERS, Susan Mary, DFA (1968), RA Schools Post Grad. Cert. (1971); painter in oil, water-colour, pencil, gouache; *b*: Haslemere, 11 Aug 1946. *d of*: Air Commodore P.J.

Sanders, DFC. *m*: Richard Henry Parkinson. one *s*. one *d*. *Educ*: St. Mary's School, Baldslow Hastings. *Studied*: Byam Shaw School (1964-68), RA Schools (1968-71). *Exhib*: RA Summer Exhbn. (1971-98), RWA, (1983-88), Mall Galleries (1986-89), Bath, Bristol. *Address*: Restorers Cottage, 13 St. Peter's Lane, Canterbury, Kent CT1 2BP. *Email*: sue.parky@hotmail.co.uk *Website*: richartparkingson.co.uk *Signs work*: "S. Sanders," "Susan Sanders," or "S.S."

SANDERSLEY, Deborah, PG Cert in Glass and Architecture; PG Cert in Glass and Fine Art; William de Morgan Travel Award (2002); Chase Charity Award (2003)p; Kiln Formed Glass BTEC HNC (2000) and Intermediate Studio Glass (1998). *Medium*: Glass; photography; print. *b*: London, 6 Oct 1968. one *d*. *Studied*: Central Saint Martins School of Art and Design (2001-3); Westminster Adult Ed Services (WAES). *Represented by*: Sable Fox, UK. *Exhib*: 'British Glass Biennale' (2012, 2004) Stourbridge; 'Buildings to Burlesque' (solo) Clare Hall Gallery, Cambridge (2011); 'The Glass Canvas' Glass Museum, Glazenhuis, Belgium (2011); Cafe Jello; Affordable Art Fair, London (2011, 2006, 2005); Candid Gallery, London (2006); The Windows Gallery (solo) (2006); New London Glass at Designersblock, London (2005); East London Design Show, London (2005). *Work in collections*: Private and corporate collections, France, Belguim, UK, Australia and USA. *Commissions*: Worshipful Company of Information Technologists, London; Hotel Murano, Tacoma, Washington, USA; Starbucks, Kings Cross, London. *Publications*: 'Contemporary Glass' Blackdog Publishing; '50 Distinguished Contemporary Artists in Glass', 'The Intelligent Laymen', 'Stained and Art Glass', Il Publishing; 'Glass at Central', Malvert Arts Press. *Principal Works*: Commissions for architectural panels combining photography and glass. *Clubs*: Contemporary Glass Society; Craft Central. *Misc*: Worked as freelance portrait and reportage photographer (1991-2003). *Address*: Flat C, 38-44 Broadway Market, London E8 4QT. *Email*: info@deborahsandersley.com *Website*: www.deborahsandersley.com *Signs work*: "DEBORAH SANDERSLEY".

SANDERSON, C. J., 1st Prize Corfu Landscapes (1967); Dip. d'Honneur Salon International Biarritz (1974); artist in oil, acrylic, water-colour, pastel, gouache, pencil, etching, Indian ink, stone, clay and wood. *b*: London, 18 Aug 1949. *s of*: James Comber Sanderson, printer. *Educ*: Millfield. *Studied*: Byam Shaw School of Art (1967-71) under Maurice de Saumarez and Ruskin Spear, RA. *Exhib*: one-man shows: Woodstock Gallery (1974), Gallery Vallombreuse (1974), Gallery Mouffe (1974), Drian Gallery (1979); mixed shows: John Neville (1974), Ashgate Gallery (1973, 1974), Paris Salon (1974), R.A. (1970, 1972, 1973, 1983-86, 2006), Wylma Wayne Gallery (1983), Roy Miles Gallery (1995), Grosvenor Gallery (1995), Bruton St. Gallery (1995), Highgate Fine Art (1999), Cornelius Gallery (1999-2001), Finalot Fine Art (2001), Guildford House Gallery (2007); Galerie Tamenega, Paris, and 2 websites: artdirectukltd and finalotgal and other mixed shows London and abroad. *Works in collections*: D. J. Redwood White, Warsaw Art Gallery Poland, London, and Paris. *Publications*: 1995 Critics Choice Sunday Telegraph, Arts Review, La Revue Moderne. *Official Purchasers*: Warsaw Art Gallery (1980); Guildhall Gallery (2005). *Recreations*: gardening, music, cooking. *Clubs*: The Organ, The Arts Club. *Address*: 7 Gordon Pl., London W8 4JD. *Signs work*: "C.J. Sanderson."

SANDERSON, Philip James. *Medium*: oil, watercolour. *b*: Malaysia, 13 Jan 1935. *s of*: James Sanderson. *Partner*: Mary Aitken. one *s*. one *d*. *Studied*: London University. *Exhib*: Highgate Fine Art, Highgate, London; Barry Keene, Henley on Thames; Llewellyn Alexander, London. *Works in collections*: LB Camden, numerous private. *Commissions*: several privately. *Address*: 17 Gilbey House, 38 Jamestown Road, London NW1 7BY. *Email*: drpjsanderson@yahoo.co.uk *Signs work*: "Philip Sanderson".

SANDERSON, Roger, NDD (1951), SGFA (1985-96), AOI (1980), SCA (1986); painter in water-colour, illustrator, designer (landscapes, figurative, humorous); Senior tutor,

Linguaphone Institute's Paris School of Art (1982-94). *b*: London, 23 Nov 1923. *s of*: Herbert Arthur Sanderson, banker. *m*: Hilde Kokorz. one *s*. three *d*. *Educ*: Dulwich College. *Studied*: Croydon and Epsom Art Schools (Barbara Jones, Michael Cadman, Leslie Worth, Ray Evans). *Exhib*: RI, RWS Open, RBA, PS, UA, etc. H.W. Peel prizewinner - drawing SGFA (1992). Private and corporate collections. *Publications*: illustrations for leading publishers. *Address*: Bucklers Lodge, St. Ives, Ringwood, Hants. BH24 2NY. *Signs work*: "ROGER SANDERSON".

SANDLE, Michael Leonard, RA, FRBS, DFA (Lond.); artist in water-colour and ink, sculptor in bronze; Prof. at The Academy for Visual Arts, Karlsruhe, W. Germany. *b*: Weymouth, 18 May 1936. divorced. *s of*: Charles Edward Sandle, CPO, RN. *m*: Demelza Spargo, 1988. one *s*. *Educ*: Douglas High School. *Studied*: Douglas School of Art, I.O.M. (1951-54), Slade School of Fine Art (1956-59). *Exhib*: group: Young Contemporaries (1957-59), Grabowski Gallery, London (1964, 1966), British Sculptors '72, RA (1972), Hayward Annual (1978), Träume vom Frieden, Recklinghausen (1982), etc.; one-man: Drian Gallery (1963), Haus am Lützowplatz, Berlin (1975), Allen Gallery, Vancouver (1975), Fischer Fine Art (1981, 1985), Wilhelm Lehmbruck Museum (1984), Whitechapel (1988), Württembergischer Kunstverein, Stuttgart (1989), Ernst Museum, Budapest (1990), etc. *Works in collections*: Arts Council, British Council, BM, Imperial War Museum, Leics. A.G., Leics. Educ. Authority, Metropolitan Museum, NY, Museum des 20. Jahrhunderts, Vienna, Neuberger Museum of Modern Art, USA, Neue Sammlung, Munich, National-Galerie, Warsaw, Preston Art Museum, Tate Gallery, V&A, W. German Government, etc. *Address*: 22a Avonmore Road London W14 8RR. *Signs work*: "Michael Sandle."

SANN, Tin Tin, Council Member of United Society of Artists. *Medium*: all. *b*: Thayet Myo, Myamar, 20 Oct 1944. *s of*: Dr Ba Khet and Daw May Yu. *m*: Dr. M. Salman Raschid. *Educ*: BSc (Hons), MSc, MCAM. *Studied*: Rangoon Arts and Science University, Martran College (Marketing and Communications) under well known Burmese and Chinese artists. *Represented by*: ASC Studios, Camberwell, SE5 0UH. *Exhib*: Participated in more than 60 exhibitions in Burma, USA, UK - Mall, Menier, Bankside Galleries etc. *Works in collections*: Rangoon Arts and Science University, UNESCO, Paris, private collections all over the world - Burma, Nepal, UK, USA, Germany, Norway, Australia, Russia. *Commissions*: 3R Exhibtion in Myanmar (Burma) early '70s, private commissions for portraits, landscapes and seascapes. *Official Purchasers*: Rangoon Arts and Science University, UNESCO during 3R Exhbn. in Burma. *Recreations*: going to art exhbns, concerts, theatre, opera, pilates, gym, swimming, walking. *Clubs*: BBC Art Club and Life Style Club, UA. *Misc*: one of the pioneers of Young Avant-Garde Art Movement in Burma (Myanmar). *Address*: 15 Hillfield Mansions, Hampstead, London NW3 4ZR. *Email*: tintinsann@yahoo.co.uk *Website*: www.tintinsann.com *Signs work*: Tin Tin Sann.

SAPIEHA, Christine, SWA, APA; painter in acrylic, portraits, sculpture; therapist. *b*: Vienna, 5 May 1934. *m*: Adam Fremantle. two *s*. *Educ*: The Brearley, NYC, Georgetown University, Washington DC. *Studied*: Abbott School of Art, Washington DC (1951-52), Parsons School of Design, NYC (1952-56). *Exhib*: Mall Galleries, Spirit of London, RA Summer Show, Francis Kyle, Stable Gallery, Ice House, Bush House, Beach Thomas Gallery, Burford, Gallery East, NY, Westminster Gallery. *Works in collections*: Sheldon Weisfeld, Brownsville, Tex., WASL. *Publications*: illustrated science and fiction for children, local press. *Address*: 20 Macduff Rd., Battersea, London SW11 4DA.

SAPP, Prudence Eugenie, (née Williams), School Cert. with Hons. in Art and English (1945); painter in oil. *b*: London, 11 Mar 1928. *m*: Reginald Walter. *Educ*: Wycombe Abbey; Benenden School, Kent; English School of Languages, Chateau d'Oex, Switzerland. *Studied*: CFE Bognor Regis (1964), portraiture at Epsom AEC (1974, Reg Sapp). *Exhib*: one-man shows: Hyde Park Gallery (1992, 1993); two-man shows: Barnes Gallery, SW13

(1994, 1995); Mall Galleries since 1974; RA Summer Exhbn. (1987, 1992-95, 2004, 2005), Llewellyn Alexander Autumn Exhibitions (2000, 2001, 2003). *Works in collections*: America, Sweden, Japan. *Commissions*: portraits undertaken. *Clubs*: Chelsea Art Soc. *Address*: 19 Waterer Gdns., Tadworth, Surrey KT20 5PB. *Signs work*: "Prue Sapp."

SAUMAREZ SMITH, Romilly, Fellow of Designer Bookbinders; bookbinder. *b*: London, 10 Feb 1954. *m*: Charles Saumarez Smith. two *s*. *Studied*: Camberwell School of Art and Crafts (1975-78). *Exhib*: many bookbinding exhbns. since 1982. *Works in collections*: Crafts Council, V&A, NY Public Library, HRC, Austin Texas, British Museum. *Publications*: reviews and articles for Crafts Magazine. *Address*: 133-135 Mile End Road, London E1 4AQ.

SAUNDERS, Anthony James, Award of Distinction, 'Horizons of Flight Exhibition', Dallas, Fort Worth. *Medium*: oil. *b*: Chelmsford, 30 Apr 1964. *s of*: D.R. Saunders. *m*: Bernadette. one *s*. one *d*. *Represented by*: The Military Gallery, 32 High St., Wendover. *Exhib*: Cranston Fine Arts Gallery, Scotland; The Military Gallery, Wendover; The Mall Galleries, London. *Works in collections*: Peter Jackson Collection, New Zealand. *Commissions*: as above. *Works Reproduced*: over fifty limited edition prints. *Principal Works*: Naval: Napoleonic to WWII. *Recreations*: languages. *Clubs*: Associate Member, Guild of Aviation Artists. *Address*: The Old Manor House, Cambridge Street, Godmanchester, Cambs., PE29 2AT. *Email*: anthonyjsaunders@aol.com *Website*: www.militarygallery.com *Signs work*: "T. Saunders".

SAUNDERS, Jutta Gabrielle, Slade Dip.; painter in oil and water-colour, portrait sculptor; tutor. *b*: 10 Jul 1929. *d of*: Felix Callman, LDS, RCS. *Partner*: Laurie Hollands artist Slade DFA. one *s*. one *d*. *Educ*: The Hall School, Somerset, St. Maurs, Weybridge. *Studied*: Kingston School of Art (1945-48), Slade School of Fine Art (1948-51) under William Coldstream, John Piper; sculpture under F.E. McWilliam. *Exhib*: RA, RWA, Leicester, Chichester, London and provincial galleries. *Works in collections*: in England, USA, Brazil, Germany, France, Sweden and Canada. *Commissions*: National Trust, and portraits. *Official Purchasers*: Elmbridge Museum, Weybridge, The National Trust. *Works Reproduced*: In the series, 'Oil Painting in Public Ownership' editions 'London the Slade and UCL' and 'Surrey'. *Clubs*: New Park Artists. *Address*: Flint House, Oatlands Mere, Weybridge, Surrey KT13 9PD. *Email*: juttagabrielle@aol.co.uk *Signs work*: "J.S." or "J.G.S." or "J. Saunders."

SAVAGE, Judith, LDAD; artist in oil on canvas; Specialises in colour: therapeutic, psychological, symbolic aspects. Studies in art therapy, psychology, sociology (1991-92). Guest Lecturer Chelsea College of Art. Currently working St. Bernards Psychicatric Hospital, Ealing. *b*: Sydney, Australia. one *s*. *Educ*: Australia. *Studied*: Interior Design and Decoration and Mural Design, Chelsea College of Art (1977-80). *Exhib*: London: Loggia Gallery, Leighton House, CWAC, etc. *Address*: c/o Art Psychotherapy, West London Mental Health Trust, Uxbridge Road, Southall, London UB1 3EU. *Signs work*: "J. Savage."

SAVAGE, Nicolette Jane, SWA; Society of Feline Artists; NDD; ATC. *Medium*: ceramics, watercolour, drawing, prints. *b*: London, 2 Feb 1943. *d of*: Ernest Savage PVPPS (decd). *m*: Tom Jaffray. *Educ*: Plaistow Grammar School. *Studied*: Goldsmiths College, School of Art (1961-66); Guildhall School of Music and Drama (Opera Singing) (1970-72). *Exhib*: etchings and paintings: RA Summer Exhbn (2003, 04, 05); SWA; Assoc. of Sussex Artists; Llewellyn Alexander; Peter Hedley Gallery; annual one-man show Bromley; ceramics: Chelsea Flower Show; Petworth House; Bettles Gallery. *Works in collections*: many private collections inc. Lord Sterling; Herb Adler (USA). *Commissions*: private commissions of etchings, paintings and garden ceramics. *Works Reproduced*: greeting card designs, Woodmansterne; RA postcard (2004). *Principal Works*: 'First Flight', etching ed. 150 (sold entire edition RA 2004). *Recreations*: gardening, singing, animal welfare. *Misc*:

Head of Art Dept., Blackheath High School (1966-70); Bromley Adult Education tutor in printmaking and pottery (1972-99). *Address*: 145 Goodhart Way, West Wickham, Kent BR4 0EU. *Email*: nicolettesavage@aol.com *Signs work*: 'Nicolette Savage'.

SAVIC, Nikola Voin, BA Fine Art; MA Fine Art; Award: Atkinson Gallery, Somerset (selected as one of best 30 Post-graduates in Fine Art from all UK Universities). *Medium*: acrylic on canvas. *b*: Belgrade, Serbia, 19 Feb 1973. *s of*: Voin Savic (composer), M.Ruza Savic (architect). *m*: Tanja Savic (shoe designer). one *s*. *Studied*: Belgrade Academy of Art (1992-97); Central St.Martins College of Art & Design, London (1998-99). *Represented by*: Flora Fairburn, London; Gallery Zvono, Belgrade. *Exhib*: RA Summer Exhbn (2004); Contemporary Art Society 'Art Futures' (2003, 2004, 2005); Museum of Contemporary Art, Belgrade (2005); Contemporary Art Auction, Marine Stewardship, Billingsgate Market, London (Damien Hirst, Tracy Emin, Cathy Demonchioux, etc.); October Salon, Belgrade; Muzel de Arta Timisoara, paintings, Romania (2008); Gallery Zvono "The Best Of" Paintings (2009); Flora Fairbairn Projects ('At Home', 'Heriscourt', 2009) solo exhibition, Museum of Contemporary Art, Belgrade (2008). *Works in collections*: Museum of Contemporary Art, Belgrade, Serbia; The Bank of America, London; European Diamonds plc, London; Shimuzu Japan; Mulva Collection, Austin, Texas, USA; Gallery Rollo Contemporary, London; private collections USA, UK and Europe. *Commissions*: FIFA World Cup 2010 - painting. *Publications*: Catalogue written by Barry Schwabsky, 2008 "Love is Patient, Love is Kind", 2008 (pub. MOCA Belgrade, Serbia). *Works Reproduced*: Soen Magazine, Tokyo; Royal Summer Exhibition Illustrated, London; The Times, Play Supplement; MOCA Belgrade Catalogue; Politika Newspapers, Belgrade; Blic Newspapers, Belgrade; Independent Newspapers. *Address*: Flat 3, 71 Haverstock Hill, London NW3 4SL. *Email*: rittermansavic@hotmail.com.*Website*: www.artnet.com *Signs work*: 'NIKOLA VOIN SAVIC'.

SAVINE, Gerald, NDD Commercial Design; Guild of Railway Artists (full member). *Medium*: oil, watercolour, gouache, drawing, prints. *b*: London, 30 Oct 1945. *Educ*: Mora Road School/ John Kelly School, Cricklewood, London 1950-59. *Studied*: Harrow School of Art (1959-65). *Represented by*: self. *Exhib*: Kenith Kendal Gallery, Cowes; Buckleshard, Eastleigh, Southampton; Verkehrshaus, Luzern, Switzerland; Newmarket, Derby, Bristol, Mirfield, City of London. *Works in collections*: private collections, Group 4 Security. *Commissions*: Hag Model Railway Engineers, Switzerland; Planet Three Publishing; Club San Gottardo, Switzerland; private commissions. *Publications*: British Steam Railways, Swiss Express, Yachts on Canvas, Emotions of Railway Art, Railway Art, Japan; Fantasy Art, China. *Principal Works*: marine, Swiss and British railways. *Recreations*: member local Baptist church. *Clubs*: Swiss Railway Society; Professional Member, Society of All Artists (SAA). *Misc*: operates 6 art classes based at studio/monthly workshops. Demonstrations to art groups and societies. *Address*: The Studio, Bridge House, Waterside, Upton-on-Severn, WR8 0HG. *Email*: geraldsavine@btconnect.com *Website*: geraldsavine.co.uk *Signs work*: "G. Savine".

SAWYER, David James, RBA (2005); Katherine William-Powlett Memorial Award for Watercolour, Chelsea Arts Society (1997); Education Purchase Prize awarded, RBA (2006); RBA, De Laszlo Medal (2013). *Medium*: oil, watercolour, drawing. *b*: London, 19 Jul 1961. *s of*: James & Cynthia Sawyer. *m*: Stefanina Sawyer. *Studied*: Canterbury College of Art. *Represented by*: Panter & Hall, London; The Wykeham Gallery, Stockbridge; Thompson's Gallery; Crossgate Gallery, Kentucky, USA. *Works in collections*: private collections worldwide. *Commissions*: 3 oil paintings for the State Rooms of the Cunard Liner 'Queen Mary II' (26 limited edition prints of each painting, 2003); "Skylines for Boardrooms", views from the 8th floor of the Friedfrank building, City Rd, London EC1 (2006-07). *Address*: 10 Corsehill St., London SW16 6NF. *Email*: djsawyerrba@talktalk.net *Website*: http:davidsawyerrba.artweb.com *Signs work*: 'David Sawyer', 'D.Sawyer', 'DJS'.

SAWYERS, David Robert, ATC (1964), ARE (1964), MA (1983); topographical draughtsman in pen and ink with water-colour washes. *Medium*: Watercolour, black and white line drawings. *b*: Brighton, 29 Apr 1941. married. one *s*. one *d*. *Educ*: Varndean Grammar School, Brighton. *Studied*: Brighton College of Arts and Crafts (1959-64), University of Sussex (1982-83). *Exhib*: Gardner Centre, Bankside Gallery, Corn Exchange and Gallery, Brighton Museum and Library. *Works in collections*: held by Leoframes, 70 North Rd., Brighton. *Recreations*: all year round sea bathing. *Address*: 34 Kensington Place, Brighton BN1 4EJ. *Signs work*: "D.R. Sawyers."

SAYERS, Brian, BA (1978); painter in oil on canvas. *b*: Bromley, Kent, 3 Oct 1954. one *s*. two *d*. *Educ*: St Olave's Grammar School, Kent. *Studied*: Slade School of Fine Art (1974-78, Jeffery Camp, Patrick George). *Exhib*: RA, NPG, Long & Ryle, Hohental & Littler, Munich, Discerning Eye, Mall Galleries (1st Prize). *Address*: 27a Walterton Rd., London W9 3PE. *Email*: b.sayers@homecall.co.uk *Signs work*: "Brian Sayers" on reverse.

SCALES, Terry, National Diploma Fine Art; Arts Council Award (1972, 1983); President of Blackheath Art Society, 2011 onwards. *Medium*: oil, watercolour, drawing. *b*: Rotherhithe, London, 16 Nov 1932. *s of*: Sidney Jacob Scales & Elizabeth Driscoll. one *s*. one *d*. *Educ*: Sir Walter Trevelian, Seaton, Devon. *Studied*: Camberwell School of Art (1946-52). *Represented by*: Duncan Campbell. *Exhib*: RA (1976, 83, 84, 85); London Group (1960, 64); Scottish Arts Council (1972); Ikon Gallery, (1976); Arts Council (1987); Belgrave Gallery (1988); Austin Desmond (1989); Michael Parkin Gallery (1995, 96); retrospective, Guildhall Art Gallery (2003); One person shows: Duncan Campbell Gallery (2009); Paul McPherson Gallery (2011); Old Royal Naval College (2011). *Works in collections*: South London Gallery, Guildhall Art Gallery, Boroughs of Southwark and Lambeth; Landmark Trust; Tate & Lyle. *Commissions*: National Maritime Museum, Civil Service, Tate & Lyle, Scruttons plc, and many private commissions. *Publications*: 'Bermondsey Boys' (1999); 'Visions of Greenwich Reach' (2000); 'To Seaton With Love'. *Official Purchasers*: City of London Guildhall Art Gallery; Civil Service; Borough of Southwark & Lambeth. *Works Reproduced*: Countryman Magazine (1972); BBC1 TV Royal Academy Review (1984); London Magazine (1995); British Satellite News; BBC1 Newsnight interview. *Principal Works*: Thames landscapes, Classical musicians. *Recreations*: classical music, jazz. *Address*: 12 Prior Street, Greenwich, London SE10 8SF. *Signs work*: 'Terence Scales'.

SCARLAND, John, RWS (Royal Watercolour Society); Daler Award. *Medium*: Oil; watercolour; drawing; gouache. *b*: Redhill, 5 May 1947. *m*: Ruth Elizabeth. one *s*. one *d*. *Represented by*: Redleaf (Tunbridge Wells); Francis Iles (Rochester). *Exhib*: Wykham Galleries, Barnes; Royal Watercolour Society (prizewinner); Mall Gallery; Harrods; Bourne Gallery, Reigate; Kentmere House, York; Cider House, Blechingley; Fire and Iron, Leatherhead. *Works in collections*: Private and commercial. *Commissions*: Tokai Bank via Cider House Gallery. *Recreations*: Gardening; walking. *Address*: Farm Field, Park Road, East Grinstead RH19 1DW. *Email*: john@scarland.co.uk *Website*: www.scarland.co.uk *Signs work*: "SCARLAND".

SCHAVERIEN, Pat, BA in Fine Art, Slade Higher Diploma in Fine Art. *Medium*: Prints. *b*: London, 12 Oct 1951. *m*: Charles Frydman. *Studied*: Middlesex Polytechnic (1970-74) Slade School of Fine Art (1974-76). *Represented by*: For Art's Sake, London; Bowie Gallery, Hay on Wye; Courtyard Gallery, Appleby. *Exhib*: The Queens Terrace Cafe, London (2012); 7th International Mini Print ex. Travelling Show (2009); Wrexham Print International (2007); Images in the City, Geffrey Museum, London. *Works in collections*: Victoria & Albert Museum; Museum of London; Guildhall Library; Guys and St Thomas's Hospital, London. *Commissions*: Henderson Bldg., Broadgate, London; Bracken House, (in the city of London). *Publications*: Illustrated a book 'Weep Not For Me' by Constance

Jenkins, also 'Naming and Blessing' a book of names by Andrew Tawn both published by Souvenir Press. *Clubs*: On committee of the National Society for Painting, Sculpting and Printmakers. *Address*: 12 Frognal Lane, London NW3 7DU. *Email*: pat.schaverien@btopenworld.com *Website*: www.printmakers3.com

SCHETNEV, Leonid, SWE (2006); Artists Union of Russia (1982); Awards: The Sign on the Ministry of the Russian Federation "For Achievements in Culture" (2002). *b*: Sokol, Vologda, 1942. one *s*. two *d*. *Studied*: Graphic Arts Faculty, Kostroma Pedagogical Institute (graduated 1981). *Exhib*: A participant of numerous national and foreign exhibitions, about ten solo, the most recent being Vologda (1997), and the Museum of Bookplate, Moscow (1999). Participated in the International Ex Libris Congresses in Austria (1980), St. Petersburg (1998), USA (2000), Denmark (2002). *Works in collections*: many in State museums and picture galleries, also in private collections around the world. *Works Reproduced*: Has created more than 400 bookplates, 80 easel engravings, and over 30 complimentary postcards. *Address*: PO Box 30, Vologda, 160000, Russia. *Email*: leonschet@yandex.ru *Website*: www.cultinfo.ru/schetnev

SCHILDERMAN, Pamela, First Prize '15 Anniversary Show' Cupola Art Gallery; prizewinner, 'Re-Worked Exhbn', Oriel Washington Gallery; prizewinner, '3-D Show', Surface Gallery; Development Arts Council Grant. *Medium*: painting, drawing, installation. *b*: 4 Feb 1982. *d of*: Theo Schilderman. *Studied*: Goldsmiths University (BA Hons, 2004). *Exhib*: St. Martins, Birmingham, St.Andrews, Rugby; St. Pancras, London; Red Gallery, Hull; Stroud Gallery; Artworks-MK; Oriel Wrecsam; Banbury Museum; Bury Gallery; Burgerweeshuis, Netherlands; Camac, France; Surface Gallery, Nottingham; Mall Galleries, London; Discovery Centre, Winchester; Harley Gallery, Welbeck; Warwick Museum. *Publications*: SSA 109th Annual Exhibition 2006 (Woods of Perth Ltd.); 'Art of Recycling' (Washington Gallery Education publication, Dalton Printers, 2006); Discerning Eye Exhbn (2004); 'Precious' Hove Museum & Gallery, Gemini Press (2010); 'Check Mate/Human Sciences', Professor Matos, Saint Mary College Publication (2010). *Works Reproduced*: 'Punctum', 'Allusions', 'Miniatures 30', 'Void'. *Principal Works*: 'Bula Matari', 'Oculto', 'Self-portrait'. *Address*: 3 Main Street, Clifton-upon-Dunsmore, Rugby, CV23 0BH. *Email*: pamela.schilderman@btinternet.com *Website*: www.pamelaschilderman.com *Signs work*: 'PAMELA SCHILDERMAN'.

SCHLEE, Nick, MA (Oxon). *Medium*: painter in oil. *b*: 17 Jul 1931. *m*: Ann Acheson Schlee. one *s*. three *d*. *Educ*: Rugby School (1942-47), Oxford (1952-55). *Studied*: Evening Classes, Art Students League New York, Central School London, Morley College, Putney Art School, Slade. *Exhib*: one-man, Flying Colours Gallery, Edinburgh (1992), Barbican Centre, University of Liverpool (1994), Christchurch Picture Gallery, Oxford (1996, 2003), Gallery 27, London (1998, 2000, 2002, 2004, 2006, 2008, 2010, 2012), River and Rowing Museum (2002, 2010); Modern Artists Gallery, Berkshire (2012); National Trust, Basildon Park (2013); Gallery 8, London (2014). *Works in collections*: Guildhall Art Gallery, London; Hampshire County Council; Oxfordshire Museums; Portsmouth University; John Creasey Collection, Salisbury; Swindon Art Gallery, Reading Art Gallery, River and Rowing Museum, Henley; Southampton City Art Gallery, Liverpool University, Wessex Collection, Longleat; West Berkshire Museum; Gallery Oldham. *Publications*: 'Nick Schlee, Paintings from 1987-2008' Academy Press (BN2 1AU); 'Nick Schlee. Drawings from 1958-2010' Academy Press, BN2 1JB (2012). *Address*: Galvey, Upper Basildon, Reading RG8 8LU. *Website*: www.nickschlee.co.uk

SCHOFIELD, David Owain, BA (Hons); Latimer Award, Royal Scottish Academy; N.S. Macfarlane Award; The David Cargill Award; James Torrance Award (all RGI); City of Glasgow Award (RGI). *Medium*: oil. *b*: Wrexham, 12 Jan 1972. *s of*: Gerry Schofield & Mary Rogers. *Partner*: Bragela Hornal. one *d*. *Educ*: Nairn Academy. *Studied*: Duncan of

Jordanstone College of Art Dundee (1989-93). *Represented by*: Open Eye Gallery, Edinburgh. *Exhib*: various group shows: RGI, RSA; solo shows: Henshelwood Gallery, Newcastle; Open Eye Gallery, Edinburgh; Rendezvous Gallery, Aberdeen. *Works in collections*: private collections. *Commissions*: private. *Address*: Fla 2, 27 Learmonth Crescent, Edinburgh EH4 1DD. *Email*: tigercalmdown@hotmail.com *Website*: www.david-schofield.com *Signs work*: 'D.S.' or 'D.Schofield'.

SCHOFIELD, Sara Anne, FSBA (1986); RHS Gold medal (1987, 1991); artist, primarily botanical, also animals, birds, landscape, seascape, still-life. *Medium*: water-colour, chromacolour, pastel. *b*: London, 21 May 1937. *m*: John Schofield. one *s*. one *d*. *Educ*: Ashford County Grammar School. *Studied*: Twickenham College of Art. *Exhib*: solo shows: London (3); solo and group shows: RWS, RBA, RI, SBA and around the UK regularly. *Works in collections*: Hunt Inst. of Botanical Documentation; Carnegie Mellon University, Pittsburgh; The Shirley Sherwood Collection of Contemporary Botanical Artists, and many private collections worldwide. *Commissions*: numerous series of collectors plates, several of them Royal commemoratives. *Publications*: 'The Artist' magazine. *Works Reproduced*: in books of collections, reference, and in Society of Botanical Artists; Fine Art prints and cards. *Clubs*: Founder mem. S.B.A. *Misc*: artists, Sara M. & R. Francis Sutton. *Address*: 40 Grove Wood Hill, Coulsdon, Surrey CR5 2EL. *Email*: sara@saraschofield.co.uk *Website*: www.saraschofield.co.uk *Signs work*: "SARA ANNE SCHOFIELD" or "S.A.S."

SCHUTT, Gisela, *Medium*: Mixed media. *Studied*: Mainly self-taught. *Represented by*: Association of British Naive Artists. *Exhib*: Wales; London; Hamburg. *Works in collections*: Private collections in Hamburg, London, Australia. *Commissions*: Several private. *Publications*: The Association of British Naive Artists. *Address*: Flat 2, 40 Oaklands Park Avenue, Ilford IG1 1TG. *Email*: geselaschutt6@gmail.com *Website*: www.britishnaives.co.uk *Signs work*: "Gisela Schutt".

SCOTT, Celia Maxwell, BSc; DipArch, RIBA, FRSA. *Medium*: sculpture: bronze, iron, plaster, oil paint. *b*: Bristol, 5 Apr 1947. *d of*: John Moffatt Cuthbert Scott. *m*: Prof. Robert Maxwell. *Educ*: Cambridgeshire High School for Girls. *Studied*: Corsham, Bath Academy of Art, Bartlett School of Architecture, UCL. *Exhib*: Royal Academy, London; John Nichols Gallery, New York; Museum of Modern Art, Ostend, Belgium, and others. *Works in collections*: HRH The Prince of Wales; Scottish National Portrait Gallery; National Trust for Scotland; British Library; Clare College, Cambridge. *Commissions*: portraits: Mies van der Rohe, Sir Eduardo Paolozzi; Sir James Stirling; Prof. Sir Colin St. John Wilson; Sir Terry Farrell; Richard Meier; Peter Eisenman; John Miller; Edward Jones; Michael Graves; Leon Krier, David Attenborough, Richard Portes. *Publications*: Book: Celia Scott (Black Dog Publishing, 2008). *Official Purchasers*: Scottish National Portrait Gallery. *Principal Works*: portraits of Sir James Stirling, Sir Eduardo Paolozzi, Sir Terry Farrell, Leon Krier, David Attenborough OM CH FRS. *Address*: 3 Mall Studios, Tasker Road, London NW3 2YS. *Email*: cs@celiascott.com *Website*: www.celiascott.com *Signs work*: 'Celia Scott' or 'Celia Maxwell Scott'.

SCOTT, Dafila Kathleen, SWLA (1991), MA (1975), PhD (1978); painter. *Medium*: oil, water-colour, pastel, acrylic. *b*: London, 9 Jun 1952. *m*: Tim Clutton-Brock. one *s*. one *d*. *Educ*: Badminton School, Millfield School, Oxford University, Cambridge University. *Studied*: in the studios of Peter Scott (during childhood), Robin Child. *Publications*: illustrated 'Antarctica: A Guide to the Wildlife' by Tony Soper (Bradt Publications, 1994). *Address*: White Roses, The Hythe, Reach, Cambs. CB5 0JQ. *Email*: dafilascott@yahoo.co.uk. *Website*: www.dafilascott.co.uk. *Signs work*: "Dafila Scott" or "DKS."

SCOTT, I. Borg, Associate, Société des Artistes Français, FRSA; artist in oil and sanguine chalk. *b*: 4 Feb 1940. *Studied*: under Leonard Boden, RP, and F. Wyatt, VPSWA,

RMS. *Exhib*: Salon des Artistes, France; Salon Sony, Osaka, Japan; European Art, Auckland, NZ; Roy Miles, London; group shows: Westminster Gallery; Gagliardi Gallery, etc. *Address*: 8 Colinwood, Colinwood Rd., Farnham Common, Berks. SL2 3LN. *Signs work*: "I. Borg Scott."

SCOTT, Jac, ARBS; BA (Hons) Design Crafts; Artist-in-Residence, University of Central Lancashire (2012); University of Surrey (2014). *Medium*: sculpture. *b*: Bournemouth, 12 May 1959. *m*: Michael Slaney. two *s*. *Studied*: University of Cumbria (1991-96). *Exhib*: throughout UK including: Commonwealth Institute, London (1995); Whitworth Art Gallery, Manchester (1995); Edinburgh City Arts Centre (1999); Tullie House, Carlisle (2001); Oxo Peugeut Design Awards (Shortlisted, 2001); V&A Museum (2002-3); Sheffield Millennium Galleries (2004); Royal Hospital, Chelsea (2006); Brewery Arts Centre, Kendal (2006), Collins Gallery, Glasgow (2009); Open West, Gloucester (2012). *Works in collections*: Bowes Museum, Tullie House Museum. *Commissions*: Feather Brooksbank (corporate); Bowes Museum; Tullie House Museum (public); Whitehaven Civic Centre (public); Pennington School (public); Ness Gardens, Chester (public); Walney School (public). *Publications*: Artist author of 'Textile Perspectives in Mixed-Media Sculpture' (Crowood Press, 2003); Artist author of 'The Language of Mixed-Media Sculpture' (Crowood Press, 2014). *Address*: Studio, Swallow Cottage, Broughton Beck, Ulverston, Cumbria, LA12 7PR. *Email*: studio@jacscott.com *Website*: www.jacscott.com *Signs work*: 'Jac Scott'.

SCOTT, Malcolm, First Prize for Outstanding Work, Arcade Gallery (1983); Money Prize for Outstanding Work, The Harrogate Open, 2005. *Medium*: oil, watercolour, drawing, prints. *b*: Sudbury, Suffolk, 18 Apr 1935. *s of*: F.G. Longbottom. two *d*. *Works in collections*: Leeds City Municipal Collection at the City Art Gallery; Harrogate Borough Council Museums and Arts Collection, Mercer Art Gallery. *Publications*: DVDs and films (see YouTube for paintings Nature and The Bomb). *Official Purchasers*: Leeds City & Harrogate Council. Many works sold at auction over the years, including Bonhams Leeds, 'The White Horse' £720, Andrew Hartley, Ilkley, Yorkshire, Keighley Station (oil) £700, Tennents Layburn 'A Lighthouse on Mull' (oil) £650. *Principal Works*: George Mallery and Andy Irvin on the 1924 Everest Expedition; Trying to Sketch Crows in the Snow. *Address*: 63 Eastville Terrace, Ripon Road, Harrogate, HG1 3HJ. *Email*: malcolm.scott74@ntlworld.co *Website*: YouTube (Painting Nature and The Bomb)/Google Malcolm Scott Artist *Signs work*: "MALCOLM".

SCOTT, Richard Ridsdale, National Diploma in Design (Sculpture). *Medium*: oil. *b*: Bromley, Kent, 5 May 1938. *s of*: Eric & Marjorie Scott. *m*: Lesley Scott. two *d*. *Educ*: Cranbrook School, Kent. *Studied*: Lowestoft School of Art (1954-56, Intermediate), Camberwell School of Art & Crafts (NDD, 1956-58), (post-NDD year 1960-61). *Exhib*: solo: Chappel Galleries, Essex (1999, 2007); Ipswich Borough Council, Christchurch Mansion (2002). Mixed: RA (1984); Suffolk Group (since formation in 1991); NEAC (frequently from 1992). *Works in collections*: Ipswich Borough Council Museums and Galleries. *Commissions*: many private commissions. *Publications*: Author of "Artists at Walberswick: East Anglian Interludes 1880-2000" (Art Dictionaries Ltd., 2002); "The Walberswick Enigma" (Ipswich Borough Council Museums and Galleries, 1994); Contributing author: "Southwold: Portraits of an English Seaside Town" (Phillimore, 1999), "Painting at the Edge" (Sansom, 2005). *Works Reproduced*: in: 'Making Waves', Ian Collins (Black Dog Books, 2005), 'Southwold: An Earthly Paradise' by Geoffrey Munn (Antique Collectors Club), 'Artists at Walberswick' (see above). *Recreations*: writing. *Clubs*: Founder Member, The Suffolk Group, Life Member, Ipswich Art Society. *Address*: Samphire Cottage, The Green, Walberswick, Suffolk, IP18 6TX. *Email*: rrs38@btinternet.com *Website*: www.thesuffolkgroup.co.uk *Signs work*: "R.R.SCOTT"

SCOTT, Sally, painter in oil, pastel, drawing and lithography, glass engraver in sandblasting and engraving on flat architectural glass; Partnership with David Peace, Peace and Scott (1986-2002). *b*: London, 28 Jan 1939. *d of*: Sir Hilary & Lady Scott. *m*: widowed. one *s*. one *d*. *Educ*: Benenden School, Kent. *Studied*: Croydon College of Art (1957-59), R.A. Schools (1959-62). *Works in collections*: glass work in Norwich, Leicester, Llandaff, St. Albans, Ripon Cathedrals, Westminster Abbey, Lancaster, Sheffield, Oxford and Cambridge Universities, Birmingham Museum; private collections in France, England and USA. *Commissions*: Ripon Cathedral glass in Nanthex (2012); Glass screen at R.C. National Shrine Church to Our Lady, Walsingham, Norfolk (2010). *Publications*: contributed to Drawing, Seeing and Observing by Ian Simpson (1992), co-author, Engraved Glass in Architecture (Peace and Scott, 1995). Included in 'Modern and Contemporary Prints' by Phoebe Phillips and Tom Robb. 'Engraved Glass - International Contemporary Artists' by Tom & Marilyn Goodearl. Antique Collector's Club 2001. *Clubs*: A.W.G., Fellow, Guild of Glass Engravers, C.A.S. *Address*: The Cottage, Cambalt Rd., London SW15 6EW. *Email*: sallyscott.guy@btopenworld.com *Website*: www.sallyscottartist.co.uk *Signs work*: "Sally Scott."

SCOTT BOLTON, Tim. *Medium*: oil, watercolour. *b*: Shrewsbury, 29 Mar 1947. *m*: Patricia Scott Bolton. one *s*. three *d*. *Educ*: Bromsgrove, London University. *Studied*: Heatherley. *Represented by*: Summerleaze Gallery. *Exhib*: Tryon Gallery; Summerleaze Gallery; Malcolm Innes Gallery; Mathaf Gallery. *Works in collections*: National Trust, Richard Branson, Sultan of Oman, HRH The Prince of Wales. *Commissions*: HM The Queen, the late Duke of Devonshire, Duke of Wellington. *Works Reproduced*: Whitbread Calendar of Trees. *Recreations*: travel, history. *Clubs*: Chelsea Arts Club. *Misc*: teaches and takes art tours to India and Romania, helps run the Summerleaze Gallery; artist-in-residence Garsington Opera (2004). *Address*: Summerleaze House, East Knoyle, Salisbury, Wiltshire SP3 6BY. *Website*: timscottbolton.co.uk *Signs work*: 'Tim Scott Bolton'.

SCOTT-KESTIN, Colin, SEA (2003); painter in oil, water-colour and gouache of landscapes, equestrian and other animal subjects; Commendation of Excellence, Llewelyn Alexander Fine Art (1995, 2001); Honourable Mention in Oil, Miniature Art Society of Florida (2002). *b*: Sidcup, Kent, 14 Jan 1921. *m*: Mary Widdows. *Educ*: St. Giles School, St. Leonards-on-Sea. *Studied*: Beckenham School of Art (1938-39, Henry Carr, RP). *Exhib*: RMS, HS, SEA, MAS-F, Llewellyn Alexander (Fine Art). Regular exhibitor at above until retired - now exhibits locally. *Works in collections*: war sketches, Royal Signals Museum, Blandford. *Commissions*: for equestrian painting. *Works Reproduced*: by The Medici Society. *Clubs*: Civil Service Club. *Misc*: R.M.S. (2005, retired); H.S. (2004, retired); MASF (2003 retired). *Address*: Strapp Cottage, Skillgate La., Chiselborough, Som. TA14 6TP. *Signs work*: "C. SCOTT-KESTIN."

SCOTT-MILLER, Melissa Emma, BA Hons, RP; painter in oil. *b*: London, 17 Jul 1959. *Partner*: Frank Walsh. one *s*. one *d*. *Educ*: Queens College, London. *Studied*: Slade School of Fine Art (1977-1981). *Represented by*: Mark Jason Fine Art. *Exhib*: RA, BP Portrait Awards, National Gallery; Albemarle Gallery (1989), Grosvenor Gallery (1995), Mark Jason Fine Art (2002), Oakham Gallery (2004), Acquarella Gallery, NY. *Works in collections*: the late Stanley Kubrick, David Gray, Sir Simon Rattle, Royal Bank of Scotland, John Lewis. *Clubs*: NEAC, RP. *Address*: Flat G, 5 Lonsdale Sq., London N1 1EN. *Email*: melissascottmiller@yahoo.co.uk *Signs work*: "Melissa Scott-Miller."

SCOULLER, Glen, DA (1972), PGDip (1973); RGI (1989), RSW (1997); artist in oil and water-colour. *b*: Glasgow, 24 Apr 1950. *m*: Carol Alison Marsh. two *d*. *Educ*: Garthamlock Secondary, Glasgow. *Studied*: Glasgow School of Art (1968-73, David Donaldson). *Exhib*: solo shows: John D. Kelly Gallery, Glasgow (1977), The Scottish Gallery, Edinburgh (1980), Fine Art Soc., Glasgow (1985, 1988), Harbour Arts Centre, Irvine (1986), Fine Art Soc., Edinburgh (1989), Portland Gallery, London (1989, 1992, 1994, 1998, 2011),

Macauley Gallery, Stenton (1990, 1993, 1996), French Inst., Edinburgh (1990), Open Eye Gallery, Edinburgh (1992, 1994, 1997, 2000, 2002, 2007, 2012), Roger Billcliffe Fine Art, Glasgow (1992, 1995), Everard Read Gallery, Johannesburg (1997, 2001, 2006, 2007), Roger Billcliffe Gallery, Glasgow (1998, 2003, 2007, 2010) Corrymella Scott Gallery, Newcastle upon Tyne (1999), Everard Read Gallery, Capetown (2000, 2008), Lemon Street Gallery, Truro (2002), The John Davies Gallery, Stow-on-the-Wold (2004); Red Box Gallery, Newcastle-upon-Tyne (2005), Henshelwood Gallery (2005); Thompson's Marylebone, London (2006); John Davies Gallery, Moreton-in-Marsh (2008); Inverarity, Glasgow (2010); Lemond Gallery, Glasgow (2011); Rowallan Castle, Ayrshire (2012). Regular exhibitor: Royal Scottish Academy, Edinburgh, RGI, RSW. *Works in collections*: Works in numerous private and corporate collections worldwide. *Publications*: Italian Sketchbook/W. Gordon Smith; Who's Who in Scotland (1999), Kilmarnock/J.A.Mackay (1992); Dictionary of Art in Britain since 1945/D.Buckman; The Dictionary of Scottish Painters 1600 to the Present (1998). *Address*: East Loudoun Hill Farm, Darvel, Ayrshire KA17 0LU. *Email*: glen.scouller@btinternet.com *Website*: www.glenscouller.com *Signs work*: "SCOULLER."

SCOULLER, Kim, Awarded Anna Miller Trust Scholarship (2007); Winner of The Aspect Prize (2005). *Medium*: oil, drawing. *b*: Glasgow, 1980. *d of*: Glen Scouller, Artist. *Studied*: Duncan of Jordanstone College of Art, Dundee (1999-2003); MA in Drawing, Prince's Drawing School, London (2007-2008). *Exhib*: BP Portrait Award, NPG (2003), Royal Institute of Oil Painters, Mall Galleries, London (2003), Aspect Prize Exhibition, Thompson's Gallery (2005), Royal Society of Portrait Painters, Mall Galleries (2005), Paisley Art Institute (2004-2007). *Works in collections*: Aspect Capital, London; Clyde Property, Glasgow. *Commissions*: several private portrait commissions. *Address*: East Loudoun, Hill Farm, Darvel, Ayrshire, Scotland, KA17 0LU. *Email*: kim.scouller@btinternet.com *Website*: www.kimscouller.com *Signs work*: "K SCOULLER".

SCOULLER, Lara, BA Hons Fine Art; RSA Landscape Painting Prize (2006); RSA John Kinross Scholarship (2006); Sponsored by Robert Innes, Millers City Art Shop Prize (2007), The Elizabeth Greenshields Foundation Award (2008), Dundee Visual Artists Award (2009), The James Torrance Memorial Award (2010), The Wates Foundation, Diana Brooks Prize (2011), Art Hire, The Artists Frame Shop Award (2011). *Medium*: painter in pastels and water-based media. *b*: Glasgow, 28 Nov 1983. *d of*: Glen Scouller RSW, RGI. *Educ*: Loudon Academy (1996-2001). *Studied*: Duncan of Jordanstone, Dundee (2002-2006). *Exhib*: RSA Edinburgh, Wade Gallery Elie, RSA Student Exhibition, John Davies Gallery, The Green Gallery, The Compass gallery, McGill Duncan Gallery. *Works in collections*: RSA, Edinburgh, Museum Services Art Collection, University of Dundee, VRC Centre for Artists' Books. *Publications*: Royal Scottish Academy, John Kinross Scholars. *Address*: 246F Blackness Road, Dundee DD2 1RR. *Email*: lara.scouller@btinternet.com *Website*: www.larascouller.com *Signs work*: "Lara Scouller".

SCRIVENER, Tony (Anthony Graham Roux), BA (Hons) Open First Class. *Medium*: mixed media, oil. *b*: London, 3 Jan 1944. *s of*: Kenneth & Stella Scrivener. *m*: Eleanor Margaret. one *s*. one *d*. *Educ*: Carshalton Technical College. *Studied*: Bournemouth and Poole College of Art. *Exhib*: regularly at Royal Academy Summer Exhbn; widely in London and throughout the UK. *Recreations*: reading, travel. *Clubs*: International Ambassador Club. *Misc*: began painting after business career, professionally since 1993. *Address*: 'Crandel', 28 Beaufoys Avenue, Ferndown, Dorset BH22 9RH. *Email*: tony@scrivenerart.com *Signs work*: 'TONY SCRIVENER'.

SCRYMGEOUR WEDDERBURN, Janet, FRBS (1980), RSA Ottillie Helen Wallace Scholarship (1972), RSA Benno Schotz Prize (1973), Paris Salon bronze medal, silver medal; sculptor in clay and bronze, stained glass window designer. *b*: Winchester, 14 Aug 1941. *d of*: Lt. Col. the Hon. David Scrymgeour Wedderburn, DSO. *m*: Mervyn Fox-Pitt. one *s*. two *d*. *Educ*: Kilgraston, Convent of the Sacred Heart, Bridge of Earn, Perthshire. *Studied*: with Alastair Ross, FRBS (1970-71). *Exhib*: RSA (1971-76, sculpture); Paris Salon (1972, 1973, sculpture). *Works in collections*: East Window of the Episcopal Church of St. James the Great, Cupar, Fife; West Window the Chapel Royal, Falkland Palace; Meditation Window Bedale Church, Yorks.; Victory and Freedom Windows, RAF Leuchars, St. Paul's Church (1993), Sir Nicholas Fairbairn, MP (Scottish National Portrait Gallery), (posthumous) The Marquis of Bute, National Museum of Scotland. *Commissions*: St. Columba 1997 (Diocese of Dunkeld), Admiral Lord Duncan, 1997 (Camperdown Trust), Dundee Sea Gate (seven foot high), The Cosmic Christ (crucifix 8ft.) Carnoustie (1998), The Stobhall Madonna (6ft. bronze) Stobhall, Perthshire (1998), The Annunciation (3ft. bronze figures) (1999), Dancing Girl (4ft bronze) Stobhall (2002), Skipping Girl (4ft Bronze), Easter Dunboy (2000), stained glass doors St. Mathews RC Church, Auchtermuchty (2004). *Principal Works*: The Stations of the Cross, Aberfeldy Perthshire (2005). *Clubs*: Boisdale. *Address*: Grange Scrymgeour, Cupar, Fife. KY15 4QH. *Signs work*: "J.S.W."

SCULL. Paul Harvey, BA Hons (1975), HDFA (1978), RE (1986), MEd (1988); artist; Senior Lecturer in fine art, University of Wolverhampton. *b*: London, 21 Jun 1953. *m*: Dawn. *Educ*: Kimbolton School, Cambs. *Studied*: Northampton School of Art (1971-72), Maidstone College of Art (1972-75), Slade School of Fine Art (1976-78), University of Wales, Cardiff (1984-88). *Exhib*: Whitworth A.G., Manchester; Museum of Modern Art, Wales; Manchester City A.G.; University of Keele Gallery; Taipei Museum of Fine Art, Taiwan. *Works in collections*: Rank Xerox; Oxigen Foundation, Hungary; Xantos Janos Museum, Gyor; Mappin A.G., Sheffield; H.M.K. (Fine Arts) New York; West Midlands Arts. *Address*: Fair View, Brockhampton, Hereford HR1 4SQ. *Signs work*: "Paul Scull."

SCULLARD, Susan Diane, SWE, BA (Hons), MA; freelance illustrator in wood engraving, pen and ink, water-colour. *b*: Chatham, 20 Apr 1958. *m*: Jeremy Duncombe. one *s*. *Educ*: Chatham Grammar School. *Studied*: Camberwell School of Art (John Lawrence), RCA (Yvonne Skargon). *Exhib*: regularly with SWE, RA Summer Show (1999), Open Eye Gallery Edinburgh, Watergate St. Gallery Chester, The Gallery at Waterperry nr. Oxford, West End House Gallery, Smarden, Lion House Gallery, Lavenham; Avocet Gallery, Rye; Heathfield Art & Books, Heathfield; Singing Soul Gallery, Cranbrook; Henry Paddon Art, Eastbourne; Zillah Bell Gallery, Thirsk. *Publications*: illustrations for Folio Soc. books, Canterbury Tales, Shakespeare, The Lives of the Later Caesars; children's books: The Great Round the World Balloon Race, and Miss Fanshawe and the Great Dragon Adventure, Freya and the Magic Cloak by Nanna Aida Svensden (USA only), The Nutcracker pop-up book with Nick Denchfield, The Flyaway Pantaloons, 'Lark Rise to Candleford' by Flora Thompson (Folio Society Book). *Address*: Beech Hill Cottage, Glassenbury Rd., Cranbrook, Kent TN17 2QJ. *Email*: sue@suescullard.co.uk *Website*: www.suescullard.co.uk *Signs work*: "Sue Scullard."

SCULLION, Anthony Kevin, BA Hons, Painting; painter in oil: Garrick-Milne Prize 2005 (2nd Prize). *b*: East Kilbride, 3 Jun 1967. *m*: Fiona Stewart. one *s*. *Educ*: St. Bride's High School, East Kilbride. *Studied*: Glasgow School of Art (1988-1992). *Exhib*: solo and group exhibs. in S. Africa (1995-1998), solo exhib., Flying Colours Gallery, London (2000, 2002, 2004, 2006, 2010). *Address*: c/o Flying Colours Gallery, 6 Burnsall St., London SW3 3ST. *Email*: art@flyingcoloursgallery.com *Signs work*: "A S" on verso.

SEAGER, Harry Abram, ATD (Birm., 1955); sculptor in glass and mixed media, cast and constructed metals; Senior Lecturer, College of Art, Stourbridge, W. Midlands. *b*: Birmingham, 9 May 1931. *s of*: Maurice Seager. *m*: Marie. one *s*. one *d*. *Educ*: Holly Lodge Grammar School, Smethwick, Warley, W. Midlands. *Studied*: College of Art, Birmingham. *Exhib*: Gimpel Fils London, Rotterdamse Kunstkring, Camden Art Centre,

Fondation Maeght, S. France, Middleheim Park Antwerp, Perth, Economist Bldg London; Retrospective Broadfield House Glass Museum, W. Midlands. *Works in collections*: City Art Gallery, Leeds, CAS, London, Joseph H. Hirshorne Coll., USA, DOE London, V&A, W. Midlands Arts; private collections in Canada, UK, USA, Holland, Italy, Broadfield House Glass Museum. *Commissions*: London Hilton Park Lane, Hilton, Mauritius, 'Arcadia' P&O, AJEX Memorial Alrewas National Memorial Park. *Publications*: Open Air Sculpture in Britain, W. Strachan Tate Gallery (A. Zwemmer Ltd); International Modern Glass, Geoffrey Beard Barrie & Jenkins, London; Public Sculpture of Birmingham, George Noszlopy, Liverpool University Press. *Address*: 1 Baylie St., Stourbridge, W.Midlands DY8 1AZ. *Email*: info@harryseagersculptor.com *Website*: www.harryseagersculptor.com

SEAWARD, Tommy, BA (Joint Hons), MA; three-dimensional, wall mounted work in mixed media. *b*: 1967. *Studied*: Reading University (1986-1990); Winchester School of Art (1993-1994). *Exhib*: usual, mixed and private, mostly in London and Barcelona. *Works in collections*: private/corporate, mostly in UK and Spain. *Misc*: 2006 elected member of The London Group and has served as its Honorary Secretary since 2008. *Address*: c/o The London Group, PO Box 61045, London SE1 8RN. *Email*: tom@tommyseaward.com *Website*: www.tommyseaward.com *Signs work*: only by way of an individual serial number on the back of each piece.

SEDDON, Joyce, SWA (1988). *Medium*: oil: small still-life subjects on wood panels. *b*: Horwich, 26 Dec 1933. *m*: Dr. G.B.Seddon MBChB, DA. one s. two *d*. *Studied*: self-taught. *Exhib*: RA Summer Exhbns (1977, 79, 82, 84, 87, 92, 2006, 2010); SWA since 1988; RBSA; Toronto International Exhibition, Canada; Birmingham and Midland Medical Art Society; galleries in London, Stratford-upon-Avon, and Ledbury. *Address*: Garden House, Homefield, 34 High Street, Little Eversden, Cambridge CB23 1HE. *Signs work*: 'J.Seddon'.

SEDDON, Richard Harding, PRWS, ARCA, PhD; painter in oil and water-colour, and writer on art. *Educ*: King Edward VII School and Reading University. *Studied*: Sheffield College of Art (1932-36); Royal College of Art (1936-39). *Exhib*: RA, RWS. *Works in collections*: HM The Queen, V&A, Imperial War Museum, Sheffield, Leeds, Derby, Southport, Reading, Philadelphia (USA), Neufchatel (France). *Publications*: The Academic Technique of Oil Painting (1960), A Hand Uplifted (War Artist Memoirs) (1963), Art Collecting for Amateurs (1965), A Dictionary of Art Terms (1982) (with K. Reynolds), The Artist's Studio Book (1983); art criticism in The Guardian and most art journals; London art critic of Birmingham Post (1961-70); of Yorkshire Post since 1974. *Address*: 6 Arlesey Cl., London SW15 2EX.

SEDLECKA, Irene, FRBS; SPS; Prize of the City of Prague (1953), State Prize of Czechoslovakia (1953). *Medium*: sculpture. *b*: Czech Republic, 7 Sep 1928. *Studied*: Academy of Art, Prague. *Works in collections*: private collections in the UK, USA, Germany and the Czech Republic; life-size statues of Sir Arthur Conan Doyle and Sherlock Holmes (for publisher Felix Dennis). *Commissions*: commissioned portraits include: Lord Lichfield, Bobby Charlton CBE, Donald Sinden, Lord Laurence Olivier, Magnus Magnusson, Lord Chilver (for Granfield Institute of Technology), Sir Frank Whittle (for Institute of Mechanical Engineers), Duncan Goodhew, Paul Eddington, Nigel Hawthorn, Jackie Stewart OBE, Kenneth Kendall, Nicholas Parsons, Raymond Baxter, Richard Briers, Kenneth Williams, David Bellamy, Gordon Kay, Ken Dodd, Andrew Gardner, Jimmy Edwards, Ted Moult, William Lyne (for Wigmore Hall), Peter Brown (for British Academy), Vernon Ellis (for English National Opera) and many others. Most recent public work monument to Freddie Mercury in Montreux and Beau Brummell in London. *Official Purchasers*: public works include monument to the victims of Fascism at Velke Mezirici in Moravia, Julius Fucik in Pilsen and relief on public buildings in Prague. *Address*: 4 The Green, Sutton Courtenay, Oxfordshire. OX14 4AE.

SEE-PAYNTON, Colin Frank, RCA (1993), RE (1986), SWLA (1986), SWE (1984), ARE (1983); painter, etcher and engraver in water-colour, etching and wood engraving. *b*: 8 Jul 1946. *s of*: Frederick Paynton. *m*: Susie See (decd). *Educ*: Bedford. *Studied*: Northampton School of Art (1963-65, Henry Bird). *Represented by*: Bankside Gallery, London. *Exhib*: RA, RE, RWS, SWE, SWLA. *Works in collections*: V&A London, Ashmolean Museum Oxford, Beecroft A.G., Southend, Bedford CC, Fremantle Museum, Australia, National Museum of Wales, National Library of Wales, SWAN, and others. *Publications*: illustrations in many private press and commercial publications, The Incisive Eye - Colin See-Paynton Wood Engravings 1980-1996 (Scolar Press, 1996), Of a Feather (Gwasg Gregynog, 2007), Of a Feather -An Avian Alphabet (National Library of Wales, 2007). *Recreations*: walking and working. *Address*: Oerle Hall, Berriew, Powys, Wales SY21 8QX. *Email*: info@see-paynton.co.uk *Website*: www.see-paynton.co.uk

SEELEY, Eric Charles, BA Hons (1973), Cert RAS (1976), ATC (1977); British Inst. Fund Award in Fine Art, Armitage Prize (silver medal) for painting, Landseer Prize (bronze medal) for painting, Arthur Hacker Prize (silver medal) for portrait painting, Laing Art Show winner (1977, 1993). *Medium*: painter, printmaker; oil watercolour, drawing. *b*: Luton, 2 Dec 1951. *m*: Su Kiteley. two *d*. *Studied*: Luton School of Art (1968-1970), Kingston Polytechnic (1970-1973), RA Schools (1973-1976), under Ruskin Spear, David Tindle, Gertrude Hermes, Peter Greenham, London University, Goldsmiths (1976-1977). *Exhib*: RA, John Player Awards, National Gallery, Marryat Gallery, Leighton House, Famagusta, Cyprus, Cambridge Contemporary Arts, Centro Modigliani, Florence, Russell Gallery, Martins Gallery, Burlington Fine Art, Eagle Gallery Bedford. *Works in collections*: Cecil Higgins Art Gallery, Bedford; Bedford BC; Bedford Art Loan Collection; private collections home and abroad. *Publications*: illustrations for 'Sketches of Academe; by Trevor Whittock; cover illustration 'The Interpreter's House' (2000); 'Face to Face', Artists & Illustrators (Dec 2000). *Works Reproduced*: Royal Academy Illustrated (1979, 1990). *Clubs*: (Reynolds Club), RASA. *Address*: 4 Irwin Rd., Bedford, Beds. MK40 3UL. *Email*: susan.seeley@btinternet.com *Website*: www.rasalumni.org *Signs work*: "Eric Seeley" and year.

SEGELMAN, Frances Rosaline, FRSA; ARBS; Liveryman of the Painters-Stainer's Company. *Medium*: sculpture in terracotta, bronze and polished steel; prints, oil, drawing. *b*: Leeds, Yorkshire, 10 Feb 1949. *d of*: Sonia & Stanley Segelman. *Partner*: Jack Petchey OBE. one *s*. one *d*. *Educ*: Gateways High School, Harewood, Yorkshire. *Exhib*: many since 1986 including: Harewood House, Yorkshire (1986), Leeds Art Fair (1986), Walkers Art Gallery, Harrogate (1987), Burgh House, Hampstead (1997), Painters' Hall (1998, 1999, 2004, 2006, annually), Coutts Bank, The Strand (1998), House of Commons (2002), Chelsea Arts Society (2002), Fine Arts Gallery, Bond Street (2005), HM The Queen and HRH The Duke of Edinburgh, Buckingham Palace (2009), Portcullis House (2009). *Commissions*: HM The Queen, Duke of Edinburgh (Buckingham Palace), Ronald Walker (Australia), Arnold Ziff, OBE (Merrion Centre, Leeds), Billy Bremner (Leeds Utd FC), Raymond Burton (Jewish Museum, Camden), HM The Queen (2007/09); also many other commissions of well known people. *Publications*: in numerous magazines and newspapers throughout career. *Official Purchasers*: many. *Works Reproduced*: Limited Editions of various sculptures reproduced for clients and for sale. *Principal Works*: H.M.The Queen (unveiled 2007); Duke of Edinburgh, Buckingham Palace; Billy Bremner (at Leeds Utd. FC). *Address*: 5 The Pierhead, Wapping, London E1W 9PN. *Email*: jpfspier@aol.com *Website*: www.segelman.com *Signs work*: "FRANCES SEGELMAN".

SEGRAVE, Lydia. *Medium*: sculpture in bronze. *b*: London, 10 Jun 1945. *d of*: Edmond & Desirée Segrave. *m*: Dr I M D Little (decd). one *s*. one *d*. *Studied*: Maidstone College of Art. *Works in collections*: private collections and sculpture parks. *Works Reproduced*: Edition number is usually seven per sculpture. *Address*: Hedgerows, Pyrton, Watlington,

Oxon, OX49 5AP. *Email*: lydiasegrave@hotmail.com *Website*: www.lydiasegrave.com *Signs work*: monogram of "LS" with edition no.

SEIJO, Armando. *Medium*: oil on board, watercolour on paper. *b*: Spain, Sep 1971. *Studied*: University of Seville 'Santa Isabel de Hungria' (91-96), Central St.Martins (1996), Chelsea School of Arts (1996-7). *Exhib*: BP Portrait Award (NPG), Royal Society of Portrait Painters, Glasgow, Aberdeen, Bristol, London; Miami, USA; Sevilla, Utrera, Spain. *Works in collections*: several private and corporate collections in UK and abroad. *Commissions*: private. *Address*: Studio 300-305, 566 Cable Street, London E1W 3HB. *Website*: http://armandoseijo.blogspot.com/ *Signs work*: seijo.

SELBY, William, RBA (1989), RWS (1992), ROI (1982), NEAC (1994), RSW (1998); Prizes: Christina Leger award ROI (1985, 1987), Chris Beetle award (1986), L. Cornelissen & Son award ROI (1988), Le Clerc Fowle medal ROI (1994), Granada award, Mancaster Academy NS (1995), Macfarlane award RGI (1995), Llewellyn Alexander award NEAC (1995), Menena Joy Schwabe Memorial Award (2004); painter. *b*: Fitzwilliam, nr. Pontefract, Yorks., 26 Dec 1933. *s of*: Henry Selby, miner. *m*: Mary. *Educ*: Fitzwilliam Secondary Modern. *Exhib*: RA Summer Exhbns. from 1972; solo shows: Adam Gallery, Bath (1995, 1997, 1999, 2001, 2003, 2005), Thomsons Gallery, Dover St., London (1997, 1999), City Gallery (1998, 2000, 2002), Thompsons Marylebone Gallery (2003, 2005). *Works in collections*: Mapin Gallery, Sheffield. *Clubs*: Leeds Fine Art. *Address*: 2 Broad Steps, Middle Street, Brixham, S. Devon TQ5 8EW. *Signs work*: "SELBY" or "WILLIAM SELBY."

SELIGMAN, Lincoln David Madron. *Medium*: Acrylic, oil, watercolour, sculpture, designs for ballet (Covent Garden 2013, Sadlers Wells 2012/2014). *b*: London, 15 Feb 1950. *m*: Patricia. one *s*. two *d*. *Educ*: Harrow School. *Studied*: Balliol College, Oxford (1969-1972) Jurisprudence. *Represented by*: Belgravia Gallery; Quantum; Osborne Studio; Gerald Bland, New York. *Exhib*: V&A Museum; Royal Academy; Belgravia Gallery; Osborne Studio; Gerald Bland, New York; Grosvenor House. *Works in collections*: NY Public Library; Swires; European Parliament; Standard Chartered Bank; Flemings; Tiffany; Laurent Perrier; Chanel. *Commissions*: Swires; Royal Carribean; Chinese Government (China Resources); Cathay Pacific; Temasek (Singapore); British Land; New English Ballet Theatre. *Works Reproduced*: via Bridgeman Art Library. *Recreations*: Skiing, tennis, travel, work. *Clubs*: Chelsea Arts Club: *Misc*: One time selector 'Discerning Eye'. *Address*: 22 Ravenscourt Park, London W6 0TG. *Email*: lincoln.seligman@gmail.com *Website*: www.lincolnseligman.co.uk *Signs work*: "Lincoln Seligman".

SELWAY, John Henry, artist in mixed media; lecturer. *b*: Askern, Yorks., 11 Jul 1938. *m*: Alison. one *s*. one *d*. *Studied*: Abertyleri Technical School, Newport School of Art, RCA. *Exhib*: one-man shows: Roland, Browse & Delbanco, Browse Darby, Christopher Hull, Jeffrie Museum, Piccadilly Gallery, Washington Gallery Penarth, Queens Galleries Narberth; Retrospective, Newport City Gallery; Richard Demarco, Edinburgh. *Works in collections*: ACGB, Welsh Arts Council, National Museum Wales, Leeds City A.G., Ferens Gallery Hull, Glynn Vivian, Johannesburg A.G., Nuffield Foundation, de Beers; private: USA, GB, USSR, Europe. *Address*: Park View, Roseheyworth Rd., Abertyleri, Blaenau, Gwent NP3 1SB.

SELWYN, William, RCA; artist in water-colour, mixed media. *b*: 4 Dec 1933. *m*: Mary Ann Jones. one *s*. one *d*. *Educ*: Bangor Normal College. *Works in collections*: National Library of Wales, Gwynedd CC, Anglesey CC, University of N. Wales, Bangor. *Misc*: Award: Welsh Artist of the Year (2001). *Address*: Bron Eryri, Aelygarth, Caernarfon, Gwynedd LL55 1HA.

SEMMENS, Jennifer Anne, BA (Hons) (1986). *Medium*: mixed media on paper, and oil painting on board/canvas. *b*: Penzance, 12 Jan 1964. *d of*: Peter Semmens. *m*: Roger Asbury.

one *s*. two *d*. *Educ*: in Penzance, Cornwall. *Studied*: Falmouth School of Art (1982-83), Gloucestershire College of Arts and Technology, Cheltenham (1983-86). *Exhib*: Alpha Gallery, Sherborne; Candover Gallery, Alresford; Penwith Gallery and New Craftsman, St. Ives; Rainyday Gallery, Penzance. *Works in collections*: George & Ann Dannatt, Truro School. *Publications*: 'Twenty-Two Painters (who happen to be women) St. Ives' by Marion Whybrow; 'Drawing Towards the End of the Century' by Newlyn Society of Artists. *Clubs*: Penwith Soc. of Artists - currently vice chairman. *Address*: Higher Barn, Bone Farm, Bone Valley, Heamoor, Penzance, Cornwall TR20 8UJ. *Email*: higherbarn@tiscali.co.uk *Website*: www.jennifersemmens.co.uk *Signs work*: "J. Semmens."

SEMPLE, Kate, *Medium*: Sculpture. *b*: Kent, 16 Aug 1966. *Partner*: Fay Goodridge. *Educ*: St Georges, Broadstairs, Kent. *Studied*: Medway College of Art and Design, Rochester (1982-86); West Surrey College of Art and Design, Farnham (1986-89). *Exhib*: Doddington House, Lincolnshire; Delamore Arts, Devon; Bishop's Palace, Wells, Somerset; Murrhardt, W Germany; Navigator Gallery, Cornwall; Moncrieff Bray Gallery, Sussex; Black Swan Gallery, Frome; Chateau Gontier, France. *Commissions*: Millennium Garden, Frome; Somerset PCT Hospital Grounds sculpture; multiple commissions for Elstone Hayes Art Agents; Claire Cooke, Somerset; Selwood Manor, Somerset. *Principal Works*: 'Interlocking Notes', Selwood Manor, Frome; 'New Era', Stanbridge Hall, Banbury. *Recreations*: Print-making; growing veg; opera. *Clubs*: Secretary of Frome Film Club. *Address*: 15 Catherine Hill, Frome, Somerset BA11 1BZ. *Email*: kate.semple@gmail.com *Website*: www.katesemplesculpture.co.uk *Signs work*: "KATE SEMPLE SCULPTURE".

SEMPLE, Patricia Frances, SSA (1980), RSW (1987); painter of expressionist landscape in water-colour, ink, oil, charcoal; tutor, Open College of the Arts. *b*: Kintyre, Argyll, 3 Jul 1939. *d of*: Neil Thompson Semple, merchant naval officer. *Educ*: Lasswade Grammar. *Studied*: Edinburgh College of Art (1958-63), post. grad. (1963-64). *Exhib*: Stirling Gallery, Art Space Aberdeen, Edinburgh University, Aberdeen University, Dundee College of Art, Open Eye Gallery Edinburgh, regularly with RSA, SSA, RSW; group shows: Glasgow Group, Scottish Gallery, Compass Gallery, Arts Council Travelling Exhbn. Scotland and Yugoslavia. *Works in collections*: SAC, Aberdeen A.G., BBC, Globus, Gateway Inc. NY, Educ. Inst. of Scotland, Grampian TV, Aberdeen Hospitals, Shell UK. *Address*: Tigh-Nan-Uiseagan, By Drumnadrochit, Inverness-shire. *Signs work*: "Pat Semple."

SENFT, Nadin, ARBS (1980), City and Guilds DFA (1968); Award: First Prize Winner W. Mid. Arts Open Exhibition (1999); sculptor in bronze, stone, wood, perspex and stainless steel. *b*: London, 8 Mar 1932. *d of*: Basil Andreanoff, B.Sc. *m*: Dr. Paul Senft (decd). *Educ*: St. Mary's Abbey, London; Eversley, Lymington, Hants. *Studied*: Leicester College of Art; City and Guilds of London College of Art, Kennington. *Exhib*: RA, Alwin Gallery, Royal Exchange, Jordan Gallery, Annely Juda Fine A.G., Hertford Museum, Sutton College of Art, Natalie Stern Gallery, Richard Demarco Gallery, Edinburgh, Scone Palace, Perth, Herbert Museum and A.G. Coventry, Aim Gallery, Milton Keynes, Nature in Art, Glos., Broomhill Sculpture Gardens, Barnstaple, Devon, Art Lounge, Birmingham, steel sculpture, Druidstone Wildlife Park, Blean, Kent, Artparks International, Guernsey, C.I., Natural History Museum, Cromwell Road, London. *Works in collections*: Nature in Art Museum, Twigworth, Glos., and private collections worldwide. *Commissions*: 'St. George and the Dragon', St. George's Centre, Preston; 'Seated Bronze Figures' Guildhall Sq., Portsmouth; Royal Inst. of Chartered Surveyors Trophy (sculpture of Logo in perspex for annual presentation); The Fasson Trophy (6 aluminium sculptures); Bronze Crucifixion, St. Gregory's, Tredington; Madonna and Child, painted wood carving, St. George's, Brailes, steel sculpture fountain, Alveston, Warks; 2 competition trophies for Wildlife Photographer of the Year (for Natural History Museum). *Publications*: Sixteen Stories as they Happened by Michael Bullock. *Address*: Willowbrook, Cotswold Cl., Tredington, Warwicks. CV36 4NR. *Email*: nadin.senft@hotmail.co.uk *Website*: www.nadinsenft.co.uk *Signs work*: "Nadin Senft".

SENIOR, Bryan, painter of figures, streets, landscape, still-life in oils and acrylic; Prizes include: GLC 'Spirit of London'; Druce Competition. *b*: Bolton, 10 Jun 1935. *Represented by*: www.courtgallery.com. *Exhib*: one-man shows include: Crane Kalman Gallery, London (1965, 1968, 1971), Demarco, Edinburgh (1970, 1973), Vaccarino, Florence (1968, 1970, 1975), Pucker-Safrai, Boston, USA (1968), Bolton A.G. (1961), Fieldborne Galleries, London (1972), Ashgate Gallery, Farnham (1973), Exeter Museum (1974), Exeter University (1975), Galleria Acropoli, Milan (1976), Lad Lane Gallery, Dublin (1977), Architectural Assoc., London (1982), Hampstead Museum (1983), Manor House, Finchley (1989), Tricycle Gallery, London (1990), Tunbridge Wells Museum (1998, 2000), Sevenoaks Library Gallery (2004), Trinity Gallery, Tunbridge Wells (2007). *Address*: 134 Upper Grosvenor Rd., Tunbridge Wells, Kent TN1 2EX. *Website*: www.civicsociety.org/gallery.html

SEPPLE, Rosa, RI SWA; The Herring Award (RI, 2003); The Elizabeth Scott-Moore Award (RWS, 2003); Debra Manifold Award (RI, 2004); Daler-Rowney Award (RWS, 2003, 2005); Freshfields Brackaus Deringer Award (RWS 2006); Andrew Hillier Award (SWA, 2008). *Medium*: watercolour, mixed media. *b*: London, 7 Sep 1951. *d of*: James & Luciana Wright. *m*: Ted. two *s*. *Educ*: Collegio S.Liberale, TV, Venezia, Italy. *Studied*: St. Angela's Convent, London. *Represented by*: Linda Blackstone Gallery; Enid Lawson Gallery, London; Albany Gallery, Cardiff; Sheen Gallery, London; Fine Art UK, Ledbury; David Curzon Gallery, London; Blackheath Gallery, London; St. Giles Street Gallery, Norwich; Dart Gallery Dartmouth; Jamandic Fine Art. *Exhib*: Mall Galleries; Linda Blackstone Gallery; Bankside Gallery (RWS); RCA; Sheen Gallery; Shell House; David Curzon Gallery; Blackheath Gallery; Singer & Friedlander/Sunday Times; Enid Lawson Gallery; Albany Gallery; Fine Art UK; Orange Street; Royal Academy, London; Jamandic Fine Art, Chester; Plas Glynn-y-Weddw, Wales. *Works in collections*: private collections in UK, Italy, France, India and USA. *Commissions*: J.D.Wetherspoons. *Address*: 33 Hacton Lane, Hornchurch, Essex RM12 6PH. *Email*: tedsepple@clara.co.uk *Signs work*: 'Rosa Sepple'.

SERGEANT, Emma, BA Fine Art; Winner of the National Portrait Gallery Portrait Painting Award 1981. *b*: 9 Dec 1959. *d of*: Sir Patrick Sergeant. *m*: Count Adam Zamoyski. *Educ*: Channing (1965-76), Camden School for Girls (1976-78), Holmes Road Institute (1978), Camberwell Foundation (1978-79). *Studied*: Slade (1979-83). *Represented by*: The Fine Art Society (1996-2003, next show November 2004). *Exhib*: Agnews (1984-96), Fine Art Society, The New House Gallery New York (1996), Brian Sinfield (2002) (Oxfordshire), Green and Stone Chelsea, The Prince's Foundation, The Royal Hibernian, Dublin. *Works in collections*: The Queen's Collection, Prince Charles, Duke of York, Earl of Radnor, Sting and Trudie Styler, National Portrait Gallery, Lord Olivier, Lord David Cecil and Sir Christopher Cockerell. *Commissions*: Paul Dacre, Sir Rocco Forte, Jeremy Pazman, Michael Portillo. *Publications*: 'Dottie's Diary' (illustrated and written by Emma Sergeant, pub. Harper Collins). *Principal Works*: every picture feels like a principal work. *Recreations*: riding. *Address*: 12 Avenue Studios, Sydney Close, London SW3 6HW. *Website*: www.emmasergeant.com *Signs work*: 'ES'.

SEROTA, Sir Nicholas Andrew, Director, Tate (since 1988); Hon. Fellow, Queen Mary and Westfield College; Univ. of London (1988), Hon DArts, London Guildhall (1990), Hon DLitt. City University (1990), Hon FRIBA(1992), Hon DLitt. Plymouth University (1993), Hon DLitt. Keele University (1994), Hon. Fel. Goldsmiths (1994), Hon DLitt. South Bank University (1996), Sen. Fel. RCA(1996), Hon DUniv.,University of Surrey (Wimbledon School of Art, 1997), Hon DLitt. Exeter (2000), Hon DLitt. London Institute (2001), Hon.Fellow Christ's College, Cambridge (2001). Regional Art Officer and Exhbn. Organiser, Arts Council of GB (1970-73); Director, Museum of Modern Art, Oxford (1973-76); Director, Whitechapel A.G. (1976-88). Mem., Fine Art Advisory Com., British Council (1976-), Chairman 1992; Trustee, Public Art Development Trust (1983-87); Trustee,

Architecture Foundation (1992-99). Selector 'A New Spirit in Painting', RA (1981), Carnegie International, Carnegie Museum of Art, Pittsburgh (1985,1988); Commissioner, Commission for Architecture and the Built Environment (1999-2006); Member, Olympic Delivery Authority (2006). *b*: 27 Apr 1946. *s of*: Stanley & Beatrice Serota. *m*: Angela Mary Beveridge (marr. diss. 1995); two *d.* m Teresa Gleadowe (1997). *Educ*: Haberdashers' Askes School, Hampstead and Elstree; Christ's College, Cambridge (BA). *Studied*: Courtauld Inst. of Art, London (M.A.). *Publications*: Experience or Interpretation: The Dilemma of Museums of Modern Art 1996 (Neurath Lecture, National Gallery, 1996). *Address*: Tate, Millbank, London SW1P 4RG.

SETCH, Terry, RA, RWA; DFA (Lond, 1959); Bryan Robertson Trust Award (2009); painter. *b*: London, 11 Mar 1936. *m*: Dianne Shaw. one *d*. *Educ*: Sutton and Cheam School. *Studied*: Sutton School of Art (1950-54), Slade School of Fine Art (1956-60). *Represented by*: Flowers, London. *Exhib*: Solo exhibitions include: 70th Birthday Display, Tate Gallery, London (2006); Art Space Gallery, London (2008-2010); Art Centre, Barry, South Wales (2011); Terry Setch: Recent Works, Flowers, Cork St. London (2012); Terry Setch, Theatr Clwyd, Mold (2012); Group exhibitions include: Tate Gallery, London (2003); RWA (2007); National Museum of Wales, Cardiff (2010, 2012); Royal Academy Summer Exhibition, London (2010-2012); Seongnam Art Centre, Korea (2010). *Works in collections*: Tate Gallery, Arts Council of GB, Welsh Arts Council, Aberystwyth University, Contemporary Arts Soc. of Wales, V&A, University College, London, Gallery of Modern Art, Lodz, Poland, Swansea University, British Council, National Museum of Wales, Contemporary Arts Soc., Coleg Harlech, Wakefield City A.G., Glynn Vivian Museum and A.G., Northampton A.G., Rugby Borough Council, Leicestershire Educ. Authority, Cardiff C.C., Glamorgan Educ. Authority, Normal College Bangor, Royal Academy, Royal Collection. *Commissions*: National Museum and Galleries of Wales, painting for the restaurant, Cardiff. *Publications*: New Work by Terry Setch, pub. Welsh Arts Council, National Museum of Wales, Camden Arts Centre (1992); Terry Setch a Retrospective, pub. University of Wales Institute, Cardiff (2001); Terry Setch, by Martin Holman published by Lund Humphries in association with Broken Glass 2009. *Clubs*: Chelsea Arts Club; The Arts Club, London. *Address*: 111 Plymouth Rd., Penarth, Vale of Glamorgan CF64 5DF, S. Wales. *Website*: www.terrysetch.co.uk *Signs work*: "Terry Setch."

SETFORD, Derek Lawrence, Diploma of Fine Art (London), Art Teachers Certificate. *Medium*: oils, gouache, wood-engraving, etching. *b*: Liverpool, 1 Mar 1936. *s of*: Harry and Catherine Setford. *m*: Eirlys. two *d*. *Educ*: Leeds College of Art, Slade School of Fine Art. *Studied*: drawing, painting, print-making. *Exhib*: Manchester Academy, Society of Wood Engravers Annual Exhbns, Society of Botanical Artists Open Exhbns. *Recreations*: the countryside, gardening. *Clubs*: Society of Wood Engravers. *Address*: 1 Oakbank Drive, Sharples, Bolton, Lancs, BL1 7DG.

SEWARD, Prue, ARCA, Hon. Retd. ARE, RWS, Rome Scholar, Dip. in Paper Conservation; artist in pen and ink, water-colour, etching and lithography, and ceramics. *Medium*: ceramic. *Exhib*: RA, Bankside Gallery, Curwen Gallery, Barbican, London, Flitcroft Gallery, London, Oliver Contemporary, London, Fine Art Society (ceramics). *Works in collections*: Mr. & Mrs. A. Walsh, Mr & Mrs Mark Mason and Bankside Gallery, Mrs. Paul Anthony, Gaynor Thompson, Robert Cooper. *Publications*: children's books, cookery books, Radio Times. *Address*: 30 Sekforde St., London EC1R 0HH. *Signs work*: "P. Seward" or "Prue Seward".

SEWARD RELFE, Elizabeth Anne Harvey (Liz), SFP (2000), SWA (1993), FETC (1980); painter in water-colour and pastel, teacher; lecturer in drawing, water-colour and mixed media: Surrey Adult and Continuing Educ. Service (retired). *Medium*: all water-soluble media and drawing media. *b*: Harrow, Middx., 21 Dec 1943. *m*: Gerald (Gerry)

Seward (decd). two *d. Educ*: Paddington and Maida Vale High School for Girls. *Studied*: with John Kingsley Sutton (1972-75), Edward Wesson (1977-82). *Exhib*: SWA, SFP, numerous mixed and solo shows in London and around United Kingdom. *Works in collections*: Surrey Heath Museum, Chertsey Museum. *Publications*: five teaching videos; The Artists' Sketch Book, 'Watercolour Plus'; regular contributor to 'The Artist Magazine', 'Dynamic Acrylics'. *Recreations*: choral singing. *Address*: 12 Riverside Ave., Lightwater, Surrey GU18 5RU. *Email*: liz@sewardart.co.uk *Website*: www.sewardart.co.uk *Signs work*: "Liz Seward Relfe" or "L.S.R."

SEXTON, Anthony John, (known as John Sexton), NDD Special Level, MA Fine Art, Churchill Fellowship. *Medium*: drawing, prints, sculpture, digital imaging. *b*: London, 16 Feb 1944. *m*: Ute Kreyman. *Educ*: Woolverston Hall, Suffolk. *Studied*: Hammersmith College of Art (1962-67); Goldsmiths College (1980-82). *Exhib*: solo shows: 'Transit London Durchreise', Berlin (1995); Janus Avivson, London (1991, 1995); Gymnasium Project Space, Goldsmiths College (1989); Mario Flecha, London (1989), Artworks Space, London (1986). Selected Group exhibitions: Millennium Monument, Paris (2000); Whitechapel Open (1996); 'On Site', Abbey St., London (1992); 'Attention au Vide', Nantes (1990); 'Three London Artists', New York (1987). *Works in collections*: Henry Moore Foundation; Victoria and Albert Museum; various private collections. *Publications*: 'Reports of Worldwide Visual Diseases', Hausmeister . *Misc*: Taught at City Lit, London (1981-2006). *Address*: 90 Lynmouth Road, Walthamstow, London E17 8AQ. *Email*: john@johnsexton.myzen.co.uk *Website*: www.jsexton.eu *Signs work*: "JOHN SEXTON".

SEYMOUR, Jack, NDD (1954), Ad.Cert.Ed. (1962); painter of landscapes, interiors and portraits in oil, pencil and water-colour. *b*: London, 23 Apr 1928. *s of*: Clive Seymour. one *s*. two *d*. *Educ*: Southall Technical School. *Studied*: Harrow School of Art (1948-52, C. Sanders, T. Ward), Gloucester College of Art (1952-54, R S.G Dent), St. Paul's College, Cheltenham (1960-62, H.W. Sayer). *Exhib*: RBA, RP, RA, RWA; one-man show, Stroud, Gloucs.; provincial galleries, travelling exhbns. and abroad. *Works in collections*: Britain and abroad. *Works Reproduced*: RA Illustrated, An Introduction to Painting Portraits. *Address*: 3 Holeground, School Hill, Wookey Hole, Som. BA5 1BU. *Email*: jackseymour30@yahoo.co.uk *Signs work*: "SEYMOUR" and year.

SHACKLETON, Keith Hope, Past President RSMA & SWLA.; LL.D. (Birmingham); oil painter, writer, naturalist, TV. *Medium*: oil. *b*: Weybridge, 16 Jan 1923. *s of*: W.S.Shackleton. *m*: Jacqueline Tate. two *s*. one *d* (d. May 2003). *Educ*: Grimwade House, Melbourne, Australia; Oundle, UK. *Exhib*: RSMA, SWLA, RA. *Works in collections*: RSMA Maritime Museum, Greenwich, Birkenhead, Belfast A.G., LYW Art Museum Wisconsin, USA. *Commissions*: Royal Marines; Shell; BP; Whitbread. *Publications*: Wake, Tidelines, Wild Animals in Britain, Ship in the Wilderness, Wildlife and Wilderness, Keith Shackleton: An Autobiography in Paintings, Shakewell Afloat. *Works Reproduced*: limited edition prints by Millpond Press Inc., Florida. *Recreations*: field work. *Clubs*: Itchenor Sailing Club, Royal Geographical Society. *Address*: 39 Holmead Walk, Poundbury, Dorchester, Dorset, DT1 3GE. *Website*: sarahspackman.com

SHAKESPEARE, Francesca, muralist in London for 15 years before becoming full-time painter. *Medium*: gouache, fresco techniques, oil, watercolour, drawing. *b*: Oxford, 20 Aug 1961. *m*: Christopher Shakespeare. one *s*. two *d*. *Studied*: Exeter University/College of Art; Rome and Florence (fine art and Italian). *Represented by*: The New Grafton Gallery, London. *Exhib*: Discerning Eye (2001); Oxford Arts Society; Merriscourt Gallery; Rowley Gallery, Modern Art Oxford. *Commissions*: US Naval Headquarters. *Principal Works*: conceived and produced "Spoon Race", Modern Art Oxford (Sept 2007), www.spoonrace.co.uk Gold Silver and Bronze at The Ashmolean Museum 2012. *Address*: 1 Oakthorpe Road, Oxford OX2 7BD. *Email*: francesca@francescashakespeare.com *Website*: www.francescashakespeare.com

SHANKS, Duncan Faichney, DA, ARSA (1972), RGI (1983), RSW (1987), RSA (1990); artist in oil; Provost's prize for contemporary art (GOMA) 1996. *b*: Airdrie, 30 Aug 1937. *s of*: Duncan Faichney, DA. *m*: Una Brown Gordon. *Studied*: Glasgow School of Art. *Exhib*: Art Spectrum, Contemporary Art from Scotland (1981-82), Five Glasgow Painters, Scottish Painting - Toulouse, About Landscape - Edinburgh Festival, Scottish Painting - Rio de Janeiro, Ten Scottish Painters - London, Scottish Painting - Wales, Bath, Basle, London Art Fairs; one-man shows: Stirling University, Scottish Gallery, Fine Art Soc. - Glasgow and Edinburgh, Talbot Rice Gallery, Edinburgh (cat.), Crawford Centre, St. Andrews, Maclaurin Gallery, Ayr, Glasgow A.G. (1990), Touring Exhbn. Wales (1991-92) (Cat.), Billcliffe Fine Art (1992, 2006), Scottish Gallery (1997, 2000, 2004, 2007), London (2002). *Works in collections*: ACGB, Scottish Art Council, Glasgow, Dundee and Swansea A.Gs., Hunterian Museum, Edinburgh University, City Art Centre, Edinburgh, Lillie A.G., Government Art Collection, Scottish TV., 'Talking Pictures', STV film. *Recreations*: music. *Address*: Davingill House, Crossford By Carluke, Clyde Valley ML8 5RA. *Signs work*: "SHANKS."

SHANKS, Una Brown, DA (Textiles) (1962), RSW (1988); Awards: Alexander Stone RGI (1990, 1991), Betty Davies RSW (1993); artist in water-colour, pen and ink. *b*: Hartwood, 9 Jun 1940. *d of*: Lawrence Gordon. *m*: D.F. Shanks. *Educ*: Wishaw High School. *Studied*: Glasgow School of Art (1958-62). *Exhib*: Scottish Artists Shop (1987), Fine Art Soc. (1988, 1989, 1993). *Address*: Davingill House, Crossford By Carluke, Clyde Valley ML8 5RA. *Signs work*: "Una B. Shanks."

SHARMA, Alli, BA Fine Art. *Medium*: Oil. *b*: South Shields. *Studied*: Central St Martins College of Art (2007). *Represented by*: Transition Gallery, London. *Exhib*: John Moores Painting Prize (2014); Walker Art Gallery, Liverpool (2014); H-Project Space, Bankok (2014); Weekend Gallery, Los Angeles (2014); London Art Fair (2014); Transition Gallery (2013); Wintergarden, Sutton House, London (2013); Sluice Art Fair, London (2013); Huntergather, London (2013); Laing Art Gallery, Newcastle (2013); Galerie d'YS, Brussels (2013); A-side B-side Gallery, London (2013). *Works in collections*: Central St Martins College Contemporary Collection, London; Artists Book Collection, Victoria and Albert Museum, London. *Publications*: 'Painting Past Present' ISBN 978-0-9565433-6-3; 'About Painting' ISBN 0-9568814-0-3; Trends 09-10' ISBN 978-1-906388-22-5; 'Arty' ISSN 1750-0400; 'Garageland' ISSN 1749-9267. *Address*: Transition Gallery, 25a Regent Studios, 12 Andrews Road, London E8 4QN. *Email*: alli.sharma@hotmail.com *Website*: www.allisharma.com *Signs work*: "Alli Sharma".

SHARP, Elizabeth, SEA (1988), ASEA (1984), SWA (1986), BHSAI (1969); artist in oil and acrylic, China and silk painting, also sculptor specializing in golfing, animal and equestrian subjects, presentation items and trophies, in hand painted porcelain. *b*: 7 Jan 1947. *d of*: H.S. Sharp (decd). *Educ*: Kesteven and Grantham Girls' High School. *Studied*: Leicester College of Art and Design (1965-66), Stoke Rochford College (1966-70). *Represented by*: Stanton Graphics, and Artworks. *Exhib*: regularly with SEA and SWA in London; occasionally one-man shows, Napier Gallery, St. Helier, Jersey, Newmarket, Melton Mowbray, Mkt. Harborough, Cheltenham Sporting Gallery @ Tetbury. *Works in collections*: sculpture in Victoria Centre, Sydney, Australia; Flying Horse Centre, Nottingham; Reindeer Court, Worcester. Numerous private collections internationally, Duke of Rutland. *Commissions*: Lords Cricket Club, Hunt committees, societies, corporations. *Publications*: Osprey Historical Books. *Works Reproduced*: numerous prints and cards, and limited edition prints. *Clubs*: B.C.P.A.A., British Horse Soc., SWA, SEA. *Misc*: Breeds American Morgan horses, avid golfer. *Address*: Stanton Court, Denton, Grantham, Lincs. NG32 1JT. *Email*: stantongraphics@btinternet.com *Website*: www.stantongraphics.co.uk *Signs work*: "Elizabeth Sharp."

SHAVE, Terry, BA (Hons), HDFA (Slade); artist in oil, acrylic on canvas, etching; lecturer; Head of Painting, Staffordshire Polytechnic; Professor of Fine Art (1998). *b*: 8 Jun

1952. *m*: Helena. three *s*. one *d*. *Studied*: Loughborough College of Art (1972-75), Slade School of Fine Art (1975-77). *Exhib*: Anderson O'Day Gallery, John Moores Liverpool Exhbn. (Prizewinner), Ikon Gallery Birmingham, City Gallery Stoke. *Works in collections*: ACGB, Unilever, B'ham City Museum and A.G., Stoke Museum and A.G. *Address*: 19 Park Ave., Wolstanton, Staffs. ST5 8AY. *Signs work*: "Terry Shave."

SHAW, Andrew Stuart Dunlap, BSc Architecture; DipArch; James Clerk Maxwell Prize for Science. *Medium*: architectural design, drawing, prints. *b*: Edinburgh, 2 Dec 1977. *s of*: Drs TRD & MPL Shaw. *Educ*: The Edinburgh Academy. *Studied*: The Bartlett School of Architecture; University College London. *Represented by*: Clarke Mulder Purdie Public Relations. *Exhib*: RA, London; Beyond Media, Florence; Biennale, Rotterdam; Venice Biennale; University of Technology, Tokyo. *Works in collections*: The Cooper Foundation. *Commissions*: Aberdeen Futures. *Principal Works*: Casa Lenta; The Hiker. *Recreations*: film, music, sky-diving, whisky. *Clubs*: The Duck Fund Club (President). *Address*: 16 Wigmore Place London W1U 2LX. *Email*: andyabides@mac.com *Website*: www.oio.nu *Signs work*: 'Andy Shaw'.

SHAW, Philip Trevor, Associate Professor Middlesex University, PhD, MA (RCA), BAHons Fine Art. *Medium*: Sculpture, short animated films. *b*: Huddersfield, 27 Jul 1950. *m*: Susan Light. one *s*. one *d*. *Studied*: Huddersfield School of Art (1968); Leeds Polytechnic (1974-77); Royal College of Art (1977-80); Middlesex University (1994-2000). *Represented by*: Rebecca Hossack Gallery, London and New York. *Exhib*: Solo shows: Rebecca Hossack Gallery (New York 2011, London (2010); Museum of Garden History, London (1997); Leeds University Gallery (1976). Retrospective show: The Artworks 1830 Gallery, Halifax (2014). Also Royal Academy Summer Show (2012, 13, 14); National Open Art Exhibition, Royal College of Art/The Minerva Theatre (2013); Discerning Eye, Mall Galleries, London (2001); Angela Flowers Gallery, London (1983); Northern Young Contemporaries, Whitworth Gallery, Manchester (1975); Mirandy Gallery, London (1976); Ecole des Beaux Arts, Valence, France (1978); New Contempories ICA, London (1978); Whitechapel Open, London (1981, 82). *Works in collections*: Government Art Collection; The Lunder Art Gallery; Colby College, Maine, USA; Barings ING, London and many private collections in the UK, USA, the Far East and Australia. *Commissions*: 'The Group of Eight' an edition of 10 prints commissioned by the Prime Minister of the UK and presented to the 8 world leaders attending the G8 Summit in Lough Erne, Northern Ireland June 2013. *Publications*: Works have appeared in several publications including Les Levres Nues (Belgium); The Ethical Record (UK); In New York (USA); Sancti Clandestini - Undercover Saints (poems by Maggie Butt); 'Londinium: A London Pageant' (text by A N Wilson and Matthew Sturgis); Eclipse Journal (USA); GQ; World of Interiors and House and Garden. Academic articles include: Phytochromography - Screenprinting with Plants: Research into Alternative Ink Technology Leonardo Vol 32 No 1 (1999) Fruit and Veg or Growing Your Own Ink Printmaking Today Vol 4 No 4 ISSN09609253 London, UK (1995/7) Grow Your Own Inks Appropriate Technology Vol 22 No 2 (1995). *Official Purchasers*: UK Government Art Collection; Barings ING Purchase prize. *Principal Works*: The 'Fiction' and 'Friction' series of prints, 'Londinensi Subterraneis' suite of 10 prints celebrating the 150th anniversary of the London Underground. *Recreations*: Drums, guitar, harmonica and singing Rhythm and Blues. *Address*: Rebecca Hossack Gallery, 2A Conway Street, London W1T 6BA. *Email*: philshaw775@btinternet.com *Website*: www.rebeccahossack.com www.philshawonline.com *Signs work*: "Phil Shaw".

SHAW, Tim, 1st Class Honours Degree: Sculpture (Fine Art); Distinction Award: Foundation Diploma; Awards include: The Kenneth Armitage Fellowship (2006); The Mullan Prize (RUA, 2005); First Prize, Millfield Open (2003); prizewinner, Discerning Eye (1997). *Medium*: sculpture, installations. *b*: Belfast, 7 Aug 1964. *Educ*: Manchester Polytechnic (1984-85). *Studied*: Falmouth School of Art (1985-89). *Represented by*:

Goldfish Fine Art. *Exhib*: solo shows: Albemarle Gallery (1992), Duncan Campbell (1995, 1997), Falmouth Art Gallery (1999), Truro Cathedral (2005), Goldfish Fine Art (2006, 2007); selected group exhibitions: London Art Fair (2005, 2006), Discerning Eye (1997), Lemon Street Gallery, Truro (2000-2004), SWA Open (2003, 2004), many more across UK. *Works in collections*: David Roberts; Eden Project; Delfina Andalucia. *Commissions*: Eden Project, Cornwall; portrait bust Seamus Heaney, and other private commissions. *Principal Works*: The Middle World (1989-95); La Corrida - Dreams in Red (1996-9); The Rites of Dionysus (2000-4). *Recreations*: cattle herding and karate. *Clubs*: Newlyn Society of Artists. *Address*: 22a Avonmore Road, London W14 8RR. *Email*: timshawsculptor@btinternet.com *Website*: www.timshawsculptor.com

SHEARD, Rosalind Elizabeth Allaway, (nee MOIR); ARMS, HS, AUA; artist in oil and water-colour; Daler Rowney Choice Award (2005). *b*: Penzance, 9 Sep 1940. *m*: Michael (decd). two *s*. one *d*. *Educ*: Chiswick County Grammar School. *Studied*: Webber Douglas Academy of Dramatic Art. *Exhib*: RA, Medici Gallery, Llewellyn Alexander Gallery; 'Discerning Eye' Mall Galleries; RMS, HS, SWA, UA, SLm, Chichester, Tunbridge Wells, Leeds, Aberdeen, London, Inside Art Gallery, Ryde, Kendalls Fine Arts, Cowes, Alchemist Gallery, Yarmouth, Ryde Gallery, Saltgrass Gallery, Lymington. *Commissions*: Quay Arts, Newport, IOW - postcard. Various private. *Clubs*: I.O.W. Art Club, A.P.K. Group. *Address*: c/o The Sea Chest, 9 Westfield Park, Ryde, I.O.W. PO33 3AB. *Email*: rossheard@btinternet.com *Website*: www.londonart.co.uk *Signs work*: "ROS SHEARD."

SHEATH, Janet, RMS (1998), SWA (1995), HS (1992); self taught artist in miniatures, water-colour, dry mediums and egg tempera; Llewelyn Alexander Masters Award (2001); Fairman Members' Subject Miniature Award, RMS (2001). *b*: Portsmouth, 1952. *m*: Robert J.C. Sheath. two *d*. *Educ*: Cowplain Secondary Modern School for Girls. *Exhib*: RA, RMS, SWA, SBA, HS, Llewellyn Alexander, Medici, Fine Art UK. *Address*: 4 Cupressus Ave., Winford, Sandown, I.O.W. PO36 0LA. *Signs work*: "Janet Sheath" or "J. SHEATH."

SHEDLEY JORDAN, Tessa, DipAD. *Medium*: Watercolour. *b*: London, 30 Jul 1948. *m*: Roy. one *d*. *Educ*: Christs Hospital. *Studied*: Camberwell School of Arts and Crafts (1965-69). *Represented by*: Llewellyn Alexander Gallery, London; Hunter Gallery, Long Melford. *Exhib*: Royal Watercolour Society Open (2012, 2011, 2010, 2009); Geedon Gallery (2010); Society of East Anglian Watercolourists (2012, 2011, 2010, 2009, 2008); Sunday Times Watercolour Comp (2011, 2010, 2009, 2008); osborne Studio Gallery (2009, 2008); Llewellyn Alexander Gallery (2012, 2011, 2010, 2009, 2008, 2007, 2006); Society of Women Artists (2012); Hunter Gallery (2012, 2011, 2010, 2009, 2008, 2007, 2006, 2005). *Works in collections*: Private/corporate. *Address*: 7 The Glebe, Alpheton, Sudbury, Suffolk CO10 9BS. *Email*: tessashedleyjordan@gmail.com *Website*: www.tshedleyjordan.co.uk *Signs as*: "T SHEDLEY JORDAN".

SHEINMAN, Sally, BA Fine Art and History of Art; MA Program. Awards: Arts Council of England Grants for the Arts Award (2000, 2004, 2010, 2012). *Medium*: acrylic painting, installations, digital art. *b*: USA, 16 May 1949. *m*: John. one *s*. *Studied*: State University of New York, Albany (1967-71); Hunter College, NYC (1971-73). *Exhib*: Touring exhibitions: National Trust (2010-2012); East Midlands Airport, The Richard Attenborough Centre, Sudbury Hall, The National Trust Museum of Childhood (2008-09); ARTNAOS (five London hospitals, The Collection, Lincoln 2007); "Wishing Ceremony" (with University of Hertfordshire, Leicester City Council & mac Birmingham 2004-05). *Works in collections*: National Gallery of Slovenia; Northampton Museum. Many private collections in Europe and USA. *Commissions*: National Trust's Mottisfont Abbey; Towner Art Gallery, Eastborune; firstsite @ The Minories Art Gallery, Colchester; BBC Birmingham at the Mailbox; South and East Belfast Trust; Arts Council England. *Publications*: "Lets Celebrate" (2011); "Artnaos" (2007); "The Wishing Ceremony" (2005); "Sacred Vessels"

(2004); "Days" (2002). *Principal Works*: "What Makes You, You?"; "Let's Celebrate"; "Artnaos"; "Wishing Ceremony"; "Days". *Misc*: Advisor to the Institute of Physics in the artists in residency program, Former Chair of air, Founding Member of Artists Union England, Steering Group member of Emvan, Artist advisor to The Artists Fund. *Address*: Middle Court House, 6 North Street, Rothersthorpe, Northamptonshire NN7 3JB. *Email*: sallysheinman@gmail.com *Website*: www.sallysheinman.co.uk www.wmyy.co.uk *Signs work*: "Artist Sally Sheinman".

SHELBOURNE, Anita, RHA (2002); Diploma History of Eurpoean Painting; painter in oil, water-colour, acrylic, mixed media; Art Flight, Irish Arts Council Aer Lingus Travel Award, De Veres Award for a Work of Distinction, R.H.A., Oireachtas, Landscape Award. *b*: 17 Jul 1948. *Educ*: Holy Faith Convent, Dublin. *Studied*: Trinity College, Dublin. *Represented by*: Royal Hibernian Academy, Gallagher Gallery, 15 Ely Place, Dublin 2, Eire. *Exhib*: solo: Solomon Gallery (1987), Pantheon Gallery (1993), Ashford Gallery, RHA Gallagher Gallery (2000). Group: RHA, Oireachtas, Pyms Gallery London (1997), Art for Omagh (1998), Ashford Gallery , RHA Gallagher Gallery (1999-2002), Wexford Festival (1999-2002), RHA Gala Show (2002) etc. *Works in collections*: Irish Arts Council, Irish Embassies, Greece and Japan, Bank of Ireland, Ulster Bank, Trinity College, Dublin, Jefferson Smurfit Group, University College, Dublin, Embassy of The Republic of Korea, Haverty Trust, Norma Smurfitt Collection and collections in Milan, Rome, Sardinia. *Publications*: Irish Woman Artists, Dorothy Walker (1987), The Female Vision, Brian Fallon (1990), Irish Arts Review Year Book (1998), Dictionary of Living Artists by Robert O'Byrne, The National Self-Portrait Collection of Ireland Vol 2 by William Gallagher, Photographs RHA 2009 by Amelia Stern. *Recreations*: music, theatre, poetry. *Clubs*: United Arts Club. *Address*: 76 Willowfield, Park Ave., Sandymount, Dublin 4, Eire. *Signs work*: "ANITA SHELBOURNE."

SHELLEY, John David, NDD 1957. *Medium*: oil. *b*: Margate, 23 Feb 1938. *s of*: W.E.G. & M.Shelley. *Partner*: Angela Williams. *Educ*: Sutton East County Sec. *Studied*: Wimbledon School of Art (1953-58); Slade School of Art (1958). *Exhib*: RA Summer Exhbn (1968-1980, 1988, 1992). One-man shows: Trafford Gallery (1970-75). Tate Gallery 'Art of the Garden' (2004). *Works in collections*: Tate Britain, Contemporary Art Society. Private collections in England, America. *Publications*: 'Garden Painters', Ariel Luke (2009). *Works Reproduced*: Tate Diary 2005. *Address*: 16 Warren Park, Warlingham, Surrey, CR6 9LD. *Signs work*: "JOHN SHELLEY".

SHEPHERD, Eve, ARBS, SPS; Commendation for Tiranti Prize, & Pangolin Prize for Best Newcomer (2002). *Medium*: bronze, silver and resin sculpture. *b*: Sheffield, 12 May 1976. *Studied*: Chelsea College of Art and Design. *Exhib*: Sotheby's Artlink 2001, New York; Face Portrait Awards, Cork St., London (2002, 04, 06); Blake Gallery, York (ongoing); The Biscuit Factory, Newcastle (ongoing); The Hatton Gallery, Newcastle (2006); The Calder Gallery, Hebdonbridge (ongoing). *Works in collections*: private collections. *Commissions*: private portrait commissions; Sheffield Woustead Woodlands; Stephen Hawking, Cambridge University. *Principal Works*: "Stephen Hawking", "Dignified", "Silent Circle". *Address*: 46 Downland Road, Woodingdean, Brighton, E.Sussex, BN2 6DJ. *Email*: info@eveshepherd.com *Website*: www.eveshepherd.com *Signs work*: "E.SHEPHERD".

SHEPHERD, Gerald, FFPS (1990); painter and graphic artist in oil, acrylic, ink and pencils; sculptor in metal & found materials. *b*: Salisbury, 17 Feb 1955. *m*: June Taylor. one *s-d*. *Exhib*: solo and group exhbns. in London and south of England, including Loggia Gallery, London. *Works in collections*: Surrey University, Stevenage Art and Leisure Centre; private collections. *Publications*: edited, Ion Exchange Magazine; Editor, FPS Newsletter. *Recreations*: wildlife conservation and gardening. *Clubs*: Founded: Ionist Art Group,

Modern Wiltshire Artists & Artists for Animals. *Misc*: Coined terms 'Ionist' and 'Meditative Process Art'. *Address*: 56 Mylen Rd., Andover, Hants. SP10 3HG. *Email*: geraldshepherd@ionistart.com *Website*: www.ionistart.com www.ionistart.co.uk wwwlionstart.me.uk wwwlgeraldshepherd.co.uk *Signs work*: usually "G.S." occasionally "GERALD SHEPHERD"; signature often incorporated into composition.

SHEPHERD, Philip, RWS (1977); Gold medal Paris Salon (1976); artist in water-colour, oil, wood engraving. *b*: London, 4 May 1927. two *d*. *Studied*: Harrow College of Arts and Crafts (1941-45), Birmingham College of Arts and Crafts (1948-50). *Exhib*: RWS. *Works in collections*: Fitzwilliam Museum Cambridge, Whitworth A.G. Manchester (wood engravings). *Address*: 52 Aston Cantlow Rd., Wilmcote, Stratford-upon-Avon, Warwickshire CV37 9XZ. *Signs work*: "Philip Shepherd, R.W.S."

SHEPHERD, Valerie Mary, SWA (1987), Cert.AD; graphic artist, sculptor and printmaker, paints in water-colour, oil and mixed media. *b*: Orpington, Kent, 5 Feb 1941. *d of*: John Freed, consulting electrical engineer. *m*: Norman Shepherd, dental surgeon Ret. one *s*. two *d*. *Educ*: St. Philomena's Convent. *Studied*: Gyula Sajo Atelier; Brighton Polytechnic. *Clubs*: S.W.A., W. Sussex Art, Arun Art Soc., Assoc. of Sussex Artists, President of Worthing Art Club. *Address*: Bacon Hall, Poling, nr. Arundel, Sussex BN18 9PU. *Email*: vmshepherd99@yahoo.co.uk *Signs work*: "Valerie Shepherd."

SHEPPARD, Liz, Intermediate in Arts Crafts (1953), NDD Painting (1955), ATD (Lond. 1956), Scholarship Pratt bequest (1956, to Italy); painter, printmaker in etching. *b*: Tonbridge, 20 Dec 1933. *d of*: D O Pearce. *m*: Clive Sheppard, sculptor (decd). two *s*. one *d*. *Educ*: St. Albans Girls Grammar School. *Studied*: St. Albans School of Art (1950-52), St. Martin's College of Art (1952-55), London University Institute (1955-56). *Exhib*: Digswell House, Bear Lane Gallery, Oxford, City Gallery, Milton Keynes, R.A. Summer Exhbn. (1977, 1978), Cartoon (1978), Wavendon Festival (1979), Margaret Fischer (1980), Bedford School (1990), Leighton Buzzard Arts Centre (1990), Milton Keynes Exhbn. Gallery (1991), Bromham Mill Gallery, Bedford (1992), Art in Milton Keynes (1993), New Studio Gallery Olney (2001). *Works in collections*: HRH The Princess Margaret; John Dankworth and Cleo Laine; The Open University; Milton Keynes Development Corp.; M.K. Hospital; Anglian Water, Huntingdon; Bedford Art Loan Collection; Bedfordshire Library; Leicester Royal Infirmary; Ernst and Young, etc. *Publications*: writes for Printmaking Today since 1994. *Clubs*: Friends of Royal Academy. *Misc*: Millenium Artist in Residence, Woburn Schools Cluster (2001). *Address*: 6 Leighton St., Woburn, Milton Keynes MK17 9PJ. *Signs work*: "Liz Sheppard."

SHEPPARD, Maurice, PPRWS, NEAC, MA (RCA), DipAD; professional painter in oil and water-colour. *b*: Llangwm, Pembrokeshire, 25 Feb 1947. *s of*: the late W. E. & F.H. Sheppard. *Educ*: Haverfordwest Grammar School. *Studied*: Loughborough College of Art; Kingston College of Art under Alfred Heyworth; RCA under Hamilton-Fraser, Buhler, Spear, Weight. *Exhib*: London and abroad. *Works in collections*: V&A, National Museum of Wales, Cardiff, B'ham Museum and A.G., BM, National Library of Wales, Aberystwyth, Tullie House, Carlisle, Towner - Eastbourne, Bedford Museum, Maidstone Museum. *Commissions*: 'The Golden Valley' image for 'Shadowlands' movie: Lord Attenborough. *Publications*: Old Water-colour Soc. Club Annual Vol. 59. *Misc*: Gifted 'Private Collection' to The National Library of Wales Aberystwyth 2007. *Address*: 33 St. Martin's Pk., Crow Hill, Haverfordwest, Pembrokeshire SA61 2HP, Wales. *Signs work*: "Maurice Sheppard."

SHEPPERSON, Patricia Ann, artist in pastel and oils, wildlife, still life and landscape; recent works in coloured charcoal pencils. *Medium*: Derwent Coloured Pencils. *b*: London, 2 Oct 1929. *d of*: Robert and Doris Apps. *m*: Desmond Vereker (decd). one *s*. one *d*. *Educ*: Holy Trinity Convent, Bromley. *Studied*: Heatherley School of Art (1959-62, Patrick

Larking, ROI), Sir John Cass School of Art (1963-67), studied drama at Guildhall School of Music and Drama (1946-49). *Exhib*: one-man shows, London, Norwich and The Hague, mixed exhbns., RA, Mall Galleries. *Works in collections*: UK and abroad. *Publications*: Medici Cards. *Recreations*: piano, play reading. *Clubs*: U3A Norwich. *Address*: 2 Grange Rd., Norwich, Norfolk NR2 3NH. Email: gaia@p.shepperson.co.uk *Signs work*: "Patricia Shepperson."

SHERLOCK, Siriol Ann, BA Hons (1977), SBA (1988); Former President, Society of Floral Painters; RHS Gold Medal (1993, 1994, 1995, 1999); textile designer, water-colour painter, botanical artist. *b*: Nantwich, 28 Aug 1954. *d of*: Dr. Alexander Cattanach. *m*: Stephen Paul Sherlock. two *d*. *Educ*: Fernhill Manor School; Brockenhurst College. *Studied*: Winchester School of Art (1973-77). *Exhib*: many galleries in south of England, The Hillier Gdns. and Arboretum (1990, 1993, 1996), Kew Gdns. Gallery (1992), Sweden (1998), Jersey (1999). *Works in collections*: The Hunt Inst., Pittsburgh, USA, The Hillier Gdns. and Arboretum, Romsey, The Royal Horticultural Soc, The Shirley Sherwood Collection. *Commissions*: RHS 'Chelsea Flower Show Plate' (1999). *Publications*: Exploring Flowers in Water-colour by Siriol Sherlock (B.T. Batsford, 1998), Botanical Illustration by Siriol Sherlock (B.T. Batsford, 2004). *Works Reproduced*: in The Kew Magazine, The New Plantsman, Contemporary Botanical Artists, Treasures of Botanical Art. *Address*: Woodside, Embley Lane, East Wellow, Romsey, Hants. SO51 6DN. *Signs work*: "Siriol Sherlock."

SHERRATT, Matt, First BAHons Ceramics; MA Ceramics and Glass. *Medium*: Ceramic Sculpture. *b*: Wolverhampton, 12 Aug 1969. *m*: Antoinette Sandbach. one *d*. *Studied*: Loughborough College of Art Design; Royal College of Art. *Represented by*: Ashley Gray Modern and Contemporary Art. *Exhib*: London Art Fair (2014); Denbigh Library (2013-14); Strand on the Green (solo show 2013); 20/21 International Art Fair (2013); The Decorative Art Fair (2013); Ruthin Craft Centre (2012-13). *Commissions*: Mehta Group, Mumbai, India. *Address*: Hendre, Llangernyw, Abergele LL22 8UB. *Email*: mattrsherratt@gmail.com *Website*: www.mattsherratt.com

SHETLAND, Ilric, Hornsey Dip.; painter. *b*: London, 24 Oct 1946. *s of*: John Preston. *Partner*: Sally Sules. *Educ*: Forest Hill Comprehensive School. *Studied*: Hornsey College of Art (1966-69), Goldsmiths' College of Art. *Represented by*: Thomas Corman Arts. *Exhib*: International Cultural Centre, Antwerp, Gamstyl, Brussels, Basle, Serpentine Gallery, London, Treadwell Gallery, London, Patrick Seale Gallery, London, Angela Flowers, RA Hunting Prize. *Publications*: The Male Nude by Edward Lucie Smith. *Clubs*: Space Studios Arts Service Grants Ltd. *Address*: 76a Lauriston Rd., London E9 7HA. *Signs work*: "Ilric Shetland."

SHIELDS, Christopher Ronald, DipAD (1973); artist in water-colour, gouache, acrylic and oils. *b*: Sale, Ches., 7 Jun 1954. divorced. *s of*: Ronald Brian Shields, AMIP. one *d*. *Studied*: Northwich College of Art and Design (1970-73). *Exhib*: Warrington Museum and A.G., Wildfowl Trust Martin Mere, Towneley Hall A.G. and Museum, Burnley, Stockport A.G., The Art House, Shanghai, China, Stock Exchange, Shanghai, China; Shanghai International Art Fair, and The Mall Galleries London. *Works in collections*: Trafford Borough Council's Art Archives, City of Wakefield Educ. Resource Service Collection, Shanghai Insect Museum. *Publications*: published in Gt. Britain, Europe, N. America and Japan. Illustrated over 300 books including Collins Guide - Seashore of Britain and Europe, Collins New Generation Guide - Collins Mushroom Guide - Pond Life, Tracks and Signs of the Birds of Britain and Europe (A & C Black Publishing); City Birds (A & C Black Publishing); plus commissions for BBC publications, the RSPB and the Field Studies Council. *Address*: 2 Bramble Walk, Sale, Ches. M33 5LL. *Email*: chris@chris-shields.com *Website*: www.chris-shields.com *Signs work*: "Chris Shields" - always includes moth or butterfly in every work.

SHIELDS, Mark, BA (1985), PGCE (1989), ARUA; painter in acrylic, oils and watercolour. *b*: Co. Down, N. Ireland, 22 Feb 1963. *Educ*: Regent House School, Newtownards, Co. Down. *Studied*: University of Ulster (1981-1985 & 1988-1989). *Exhib*: RA, RI, ROI, NPG, Florence Biennale; 'Inhabitants of the Dream Courtyard', 'Pilgrimage', and 'Paintings and Drawings' Grosvenor Gallery, London; Art Basel. *Works in collections*: National Gallery of Ireland, Ulster Museum, Arts Council for Northern Ireland, National Self-Portrait Collection of Ireland. *Commissions*: portrait of Prince Charles for Royal Gurkha Regiment. *Address*: c/o Grosvenor Gallery 21 Ryder Street, London SW1Y 6PX. *Email*: art@grosvenorgallery.com *Website*: www.grosvenorgallery.com *Signs work*: "MS" monogram.

SHIRAISHI, Barry Toshio, teacher (painting and sculpture); Vice Pres. Royal Soc. of Miniature Painters, Sculptors and Gravers. *b*: Woolwich, London, 5 May 1938. *m*: Colleen Powell. two *s*. three *d*. *Studied*: Woolwich Polytechnic School of Arts (1950-54, Heber Matthews). *Exhib*: Geneva, Frankfurt, Paris and London. *Works in collections*: Franklin Mint Museum, Philadelphia. *Commissions*: Channel Tunnel Products and Franklin Mint. *Address*: 34 Paget Rise, Plumstead, London SE18 3QQ.

SHIRLEY, Rachel, BA Hons (1986); animal, landscape and figures in oil; Daler Rowney art prizewinner (Spring 1995 and Autumn 1998), winner of Best Professional Abstract Painting in the SAA Competition (2001). *b*: Nuneaton, 26 May 1965. *d of*: Sidney Raymond Shirley. *Partner*: Keith Busby. one *s*. one *d*. *Studied*: Kingston Polytechnic School of Fine Art (1983-86); PCET Teaching Qualification, Warwick University (2010). *Exhib*: one-man shows around Warwickshire, Leics and London. *Works in collections*: Midland private collections. *Commissions*: Cow Parade, London (2002), Cow Parade, Manchester (2002). *Publications*: 'Oil Paintings from your Garden'; 'Oil Paintings from the Landscape' (Guild of Master Craftsman Publications); 'Why Do My Clouds Look Like Cotton Wool?'; 'How Can I Inspire My Painting Class?' (Oil Painting Medic); Children's picture books 'Katie's Magic Teapot' and 'Ben's Little Big Adventure'. *Works Reproduced*: Rosenstiels Fine Art Ltd., The Guild of Master Craftsmen Publications Ltd., Oil Painting Medic. *Address*: 65 Gipsy Lane, Whitestone, Nuneaton, Warwickshire CV11 4SH. *Website*: oil painting medic *Signs work*: "Rachel Shirley."

SHIRLEY, Sidney Raymond, Médaille d'Argent (Paris Salon, 1981); still life artist in oil. *b*: Coventry, 27 Nov 1930. *s of*: the late Horace James Shirley. *m*: Sylvia Denise Elizabeth. six *d*. *Studied*: privately. *Represented by*: Claire Galleries, Birmingham. *Exhib*: one-man shows, Museum and A.G., Nuneaton (1968, 1974, 1982, 1993); group shows, RA, NEAC, RBA, ROI, RBSA, New King's Rd., and 20th Century Galleries, London. *Works in collections*: Australia, NZ, France, Austria, UK. *Publications*: Brimstone Design and Print, Nuneaton, Warwickshire. *Works Reproduced*: R.A. Illustrated, La Revue Moderne, Le Monde, etc. Work reviewed BBC-CWR (1993). *Clubs*: Membre Associé, Société des Artistes Français, Founder mem, Bedworth Civic and Arts Soc. (1969). Misc: WW1 and social history contributions to 'The Armourer', 'The Countryman', 'This England', 'The Field'. Personal albums 'Basin to Junction' photos of the Coventry canal, 'Victorian Paintings' a car boot collections. *Address*: 65 Gipsy Lane, Whitestone, Nuneaton, Warwickshire CV11 4SH. *Signs work*: "R. SHIRLEY" or "R.S".

SHIRLEY SMITH, Richard Francis, Slade Diploma. *Medium*: wood engraving, acrylic painting, mural decorations. *b*: Hampstead, 1935. three *s*. one *d*. *Educ*: Harrow School, Slade School of Fine Art. *Studied*: Rome (1961-62). *Exhib*: over 25 solo shows including: Aldeburgh Festival, Holburne Museum, Bath, The Maas Gallery, Chris Beetles Gallery. a 50th birthday Retrospective at the Ashmolean Museum, Oxford. *Works in collections*: British Museum, V&A, Sir Roy Strong, Ashmolean Museum Print Room (hold all the engravings). *Commissions*: illustrations: The Limited Editions Club of New York, The Folio

Society, etc.; murals: Grey's Court, Princes Gate, Kensington Palace Gdns, The Kindersley Centre, etc. *Publications*: The Wood Engravings of Richard Shirley Smith (Silent Books, 1992); Richard Shirley Smith, The Paintings & Collages (John Murray, 2002); The Bookplates of Richard Shirley Smith (The Fleece Press, 2005). *Recreations*: music. *Misc*: Photographic expeditions to the villas of Veneto (1970), The Roman Baroque (1972), and Antiquities of Asia Minor (1996). *Address*: Studio House, Elcot Lane, Marlborough, Wilts, SN8 2BA. *Website*: www.richardshirleysmith.co.uk *Signs work*: 'Richard Shirley Smith'.

SHIRREFF, Jack Robert, NDD, ATD, ARE; artist in intaglio; Lecturer, Bath Academy of Art (1965-85); Director of 107 Workshop; Currently engaged in producing and publishing work by Howard Hodgkin, Joe Tilson, Jim Dine, Oleg Kudryashov, David Inshaw, Gillian Ayres, Patrick Hughes, Mark Vaux, Tony Fry, Tony Eyton, Craig Aitcheson, Michael Heindorff, Tom Hopkins, William Kendridge. *b*: Sri Lanka, 11 Jul 1943. *m*: Patricia. *Educ*: Sutton Valence. *Studied*: Brighton Polytechnic. *Publications*: S.W. Hayter: Eluard; S.W. Hayter: Death of Hektor; produced The Way We Live Now: Hodgkin/Sonntag; 'Evermore' (Hodgkin/Barnes). *Recreations*: flying: aerobatics. *Address*: 107 Workshop, The Courtyard, Bath Rd., Shaw, nr. Melksham, Wilts. SN12 8EF. *Signs work*: "J. Shirreff."

SHOA, Nahem, RSPP winner Carol Foundation, Mall Galleries (1992), BP National Portrait award NPG (1993), Elizabeth Greenshield award (1994). *Medium*: oil on canvas. *b*: 4 Oct 1968. *Educ*: Holland Park Comprehensive. *Studied*: London College of Printing (1987-88), BA, Manchester School of Art (1988-91), Post Graduate, Prince of Wales Drawing School (2003-04), Trained with R O Lenkievicz (1986-1999). *Exhib*: RA Summer Show (1992, 1993), Discerning Eye (1992), The Sacred Body, James Colman Fine Art (1996), Modern British Show, RCA (1996,1997), Art 98-99 Business Design Centre . One-man shows: Montpelier Sunlesom's, London (1999); Walton Gallery, London (2002). 'Youth Culture' Plymouth City Museum and Art Gallery (2004); 'Giant Heads' (2004), 'Uncompromising Study' (2006) Hartlepool City Art Gallery; 'Facing Yourself' Bury City Art Gallery (2006) 'We Are Here' (2005), 'True to Life' (2007) The Herbert, Coventry (2007), The Other Art Fair (2010), Threadneedle (2009), Drawing Vernaculer, House of the Noble Man (2013), Face to Face (2014). *Works in collections*: regional galleries, Manchester, Hartlepool, Bury, Plymouth, Kew Gardens, Royal Albert Memorial Museum, Exeter (RAMM). *Commissions*: Peter Mandelson, MP, Dr. Mary Cowling, Lady Kate Douglas, Lord Queensbury. *Publications*: The Amazing Aventures of Nahem Shoa, Montpelier Sandleson (1999). *Misc*: Member Contemporary Arts Panel, RAMM, Exeter (2012 ongoing). *Address*: 69 Princes Sq., London W2 4NY. *Email*: nahem.shoa@virgin.net *Website*: http://www.nahemshoa.co.uk *Signs work*: "N. Shoa."

SHORES, Margot, painter in oil and acrylic; lecturer in painting, University of Newcastle upon Tyne (1985-90); visiting lecturer, RA Schools (1987-88). *b*: 1961. *Exhib*: 'Young Masters' Solomon Gallery (1985), R.A. Summer Show (1986-87), Cleveland Drawing Biennale (1989). *Address*: 70 On the Hill, Old Whittington, Chesterfield, Derbyshire S41 9HA. *Signs work*: "Margot Shores."

SHORT, Andy M., BA (Hons) Painting (1977). *Medium*: acrylic, watercolour, oil, pencil, etc. *b*: London, 10 Nov 1954. *m*: Bernadette. one *s*. two *d*. *Educ*: Blackpool and Loughborough Colleges of Art. *Represented by*: Sandpiper Gallery, NAPA. *Exhib*: numerous individual and group exhbns including Daybook Exhibition and Tour, Cleveland International Drawing and Biennial Show, John Moores Liverpool Exhibition, RA Summer Show, NAPA-Birmingham Society of Artists. *Works in collections*: Jones Art Ltd, Leics CC, Blackpool Borough Council. *Publications*: exhbn catalogus: Cleveland International Drawing Biennial; John Moores 10. Natural History Southport. *Works Reproduced*: Art Review. *Clubs*: NAPA (1990). *Address*: 14 Leyburn Avenue, Norbreck, Blackpool, FY2 9AQ.

SHORT, Susan, MA Fine Art (print); First Prize, The Bread & Roses Competition (2004); KR Burt Paper Prizes (1999, 2000). *Medium*: painting, etching, woodcut. *b*: Yeovil, 10 Sep 1955. *Studied*: Wimbledon School of Art (Univ. of Surrey); London College of Printing; Goldsmiths College. *Represented by*: Southbank Printmakers Gallery, London SE1 9PP. *Exhib*: RA (2002, 2004, 2011); 5th British International Miniature Print Exhbn. (2003-05); Mall Galleries; Chamber of Commerce and Industry; John Moore's; Morley Gallery, SE1; Beldam Gallery, Brunel Univ.; Riverside Studios, W6; The Tannery, SE1; BHF Bank, Queen St., London. *Works in collections*: BP/AMACO, private collections. *Publications*: 2009 'Printmaking Today', Winter, Vol 18 no 4; 2004 'Printmaking Today Magazine', Summer, Vol 13 no.2; 'The Instant Printmaker' by Melvyn Petterson & Colin Gale (pub.Chrysalis, 2003); 'Screen Printing: The Complete Water-based System' by Robert Adam & Carol Robertson (pub. Tahmes & Hudson). *Works Reproduced*: 'Canary Wharf, E14' (woodcut, reproduced on postcard). *Address*: 35 Ring House, Sage St., London E1 0BZ. *Email*: susan.short1@yahoo.co.uk *Website*: www.susan-short.co.uk. *Signs work*: 'S.Short'.

SHOWELL, Billy, BA; SBA; SFP; Certificate of Botanical Merit, SBA (2001-04, 2006-07); Silver Gilt RHS. *Medium*: watercolour and oil. *b*: 7 Aug 1966. *Partner*: Simon J. Cook. two *s*. *Studied*: St. Martins School of Art; Epsom Art School (Diploma and BA in Fashion Design and Illustration). *Exhib*: Westminster Central Hall; Tunbridge Wells Art Gallery; Cranbrook Art Show; Jersey; Isle of Wight; Lincoln Art. *Works in collections*: UK and internationally. *Publications*: Watercolour Flower Portraits, & Watercolour Fruits and Vegetables (Search Press); The Art of Botanical Illustration by Margaret Stevens. *Official Purchasers*: Hunt Institute USA, RHS Lindley Library. *Works Reproduced*: images sold for cards/books. *Recreations*: cartoon/portraits. *Misc*: private classes ongoing. *Address*: 41 Bayham Road, Tunbridge Wells, Kent, TN2 5HU. *Email*: billyshowell@live.co.uk *Website*: www.billyshowell.co.uk *Signs work*: 'Billy Showell'.

SHRAGER, Ann Jessica, NEAC (1975); artist in oil and water-colour; Arts Club Prize (2001); Travel Prize (2004). *b*: London, 9 Jan 1948. *m*: Martin Anderson. two *s*. *Studied*: Byam Shaw (1967-70, Maurice De Saumarez), RA (1970-73, Peter Greenham). *Represented by*: Manya Igel, Claudia Wolfers, Rowley Gallery. *Exhib*: mixed: RA, NEAC, New Grafton, Erica Bourne, British Art at Auction, Bilan de L'Art Contemporian, Paris; one-man: Michael Parkin (1976, 1978, 1979, 1996), New Grafton Gallery (2004, 2005), Olympia, James Huntington-Whiteley; two-man show: New Grafton Gallery (April 2002). *Works in collections*: Sir Brinsley Ford, Mitsubishi Japan, De Beers. *Publications*: book cover design for Remember Your Gramer! (Winged Lion Publishers). *Clubs*: Arts Club. *Address*: 3 Maids of Honour Row, The Green, Richmond, Surrey TW9 1NY. *Signs work*: "A.J.S."

SHUKMAN, Barbara Benita, Jacox Students Painting Prize, Edmonton, Canada (1968), John Radcliffe Purchase Prize, Oxford (1983); painter in acrylic on paper and canvas, and inks on silk, and printmaker, etchings, etc. *b*: London, 25 Nov 1934. *d of*: Denys King-Farlow, MBE. *m*: (1) Harold Jacobs. one *s*. two *d*. (2) Harold Shukman. *Educ*: USA primary schools; Queen's College, London. *Studied*: University Saskatchewan, Regina, Canada (1963-65), University Alberta, Edmonton, Canada (1966-70). *Exhib*: group shows: Canada, UK, Spain; solo shows: UK, USA. *Works in collections*: USA: Solomon Guggenheim Museum, NY; Georgia Museum of Art; New Orleans Museum. Turkey: Sheraton Voyager, Antalya. Barbados: Sandy Lane Hotel. UK: Sedgwick Group; British and Commonwealth; Sarm Film Studios; Bain and Co.; Jardine and Co.; Strutt and Parker; Chartwell Land: Christiana Bank; Booz Allen, (all London). John Radcliffe Hospital Oxford. *Address*: 11 Cunliffe Cl., Oxford OX2 7BJ. *Signs work*: "Barbara Shukman."

SHURROCK, Christopher, Art Advisor, University Settlement, Bristol. Cardiff College of Art, Foundation Dept., 1962-91 (Senior Lecturer/Director). Practising artist. *Medium*: painting, sculpture, print, constructions. *b*: Bristol, 1939. *Studied*: West of England College of Art Bristol Painting School, Postgraduate Cardiff, ATD (Dist.). *Exhib*: 'Some Small Works', Old Hall Gallery, Cowbridge (1994), 'Cabinet' Howard Gardens Gallery, Cardiff (2007), group exhibitions internationally 'Drawing mmx2 Surface Language' Howard Gardens Gallery (2012). *Works in collections*: National Gallery of Slovakia, Bratislava, National Museum/Gallery of Wales, University of Wales, Bristol City Museum & Art Gallery, etc. *Publications*: 'Do You Feel Surrounded by Things.' (1974); Studio International (June, 1966) D'Ars Agency N36-37 (1967), Art and Artists (Jan. 1969), Art in Britain, 1969-70 (Dent), Studio International 991/2 (1981), Art in Wales 1850-1980. *Official Purchasers*; ACW, CASW. *Clubs*: member: 56 Group Wales; Royal West of England Academician. *Address*: 9 Min-y-Nant, Rhiwbina, Cardiff CF14 6JR. *Website*: www.rwa.org.uk www.56groupwalesart.co.uk

SHUTT, David Richard Walter, BA 1st Class Hons Fine Art; HDip (Post Grad); mem. London Group. *Medium*: oil, watercolour, drawing, prints. *b*: West Kirby, UK, 30 Jan 1945. *s of*: Arthur Shutt. *Partner*: Sarah Snell. one *d*. *Studied*: graduate and postgraduate study in painting, Leeds University, Slade School of Art UCL. *Represented by*: Kapil Jariwala Gallery (UK); Jill Yakas Gallery (Greece). *Exhib*: UK, USA, Greece, Ireland, Italy. *Works in collections*: Leeds University; Arts Council of Wales; museums on Merseyside; Emmanuel College Cambridge; private: USA, Australia, Japan & UK. *Commissions*: not accepted. *Publications*: 'David Shutt, A Retrospective (Andrew Lambirth, 1999 ISBN 1 898 669 21 X); 'David Shutt, The Greek Paintings' (Kapil Jariwala, 2002, ISBN 1 899 253 114); 'David Shutt, Sacred Sites' (Augustine Zenakos, 2005, ISBN 1 898 669 23 6). *Official Purchasers*: as in collections. *Works Reproduced*: various newspapers, catalogues (solo and group exhbns), magazines. *Misc*: mem. London Group. *Address*: c/o Kapil Jariwala Gallery, 2 Talfourd Place, London SE15 5NW. *Email*: shuttdavid@yahoo.co.uk *Website*: www.shuttpaintings.com *Signs work*: 'David RW Shutt'.

SIDOLI, Dawn Frances, RWA (1987), NEAC (1990); Awards: NEAC: Critic's Prize (1988, 2004), Drawing Prize (2000); 1st Prize Winner: Laing National Painting Competition (1988); Teacher's Cert. (1956); Finalist, Laing '85, '86; Hunting Group '86, '87, '89, Inveresk, Singer and Friedlander Comp., RWA Excellence Award 2003, RWA Award (2012). *Medium*: oils, prints. *b*: Gosport, Hants., 24 Nov 1933. *d of*: Patrick Thompson, accountant. *m*: Frank Sidoli. two *s*. one *d*. *Educ*: Wigton High School, Cumbria; Notre Dame Convent, Northampton. *Studied*: Northampton Art School (1949-52). *Exhib*: RA from 1977-2011, Annually: RWA, NEAC; Discerning Eye Comp. (1997, 2002). Mixed exhbn: Red Rag Gallery, Fosse Gallery, Stow-on-the-Wold; NEAC Mall Galleries; Rowley Cont.Art, London; Lynne Strover, Cambridge; solo exhbns: New Gallery, RWA (Bristol 2000, 2004), Cube Gallery, Bristol (2008). *Works in collections*: RWA, West Glamorgan CC, Cardiff School of Economics (Schools Art, Avon, Cardiff, Salisbury), Hewlett Packard, The Royal Collections, London (2013). *Clubs*: Clifton Arts. *Address*: Grafton Lodge, Battery Lane, Portishead, Bristol BS20 7JD. *Website*: RWA & NEAC. *Signs work*: "Dawn Sidoli" or "SIDOLI."

SIEVEWRIGHT, Dionne Lesley, B.Des (Hons) Illustration and Printmaking degree; Livewire Young Business Award, Crighton Bequest-Travel Scholarship. *Medium*: painter and illustrator in mixed media, watercolour and printmaker. *b*: Perth, Scotland, 24 Jul 1973. *d of*: Alan and Lesley Abel. *Partner*: David Wiltshire. one *s*. *Educ*: Perth Grammar School. *Studied*: Duncan of Jordanstone, Dundee University, Scotland (graduated 1997). *Exhib*: Clifton Gallery, Bristol (2003); Leith Gallery, Edinburgh (2003); The Art Shop, Abergavenny (2001-08); Broadway Modern (2003); The Strathearn Gallery, Crieff (1997, 2003), D.Art, Dartmouth (2003-08); The Albany Gallery, Cardiff (2005-12); The Waterford Gallery, Manchester (2005-08); Scottish Art Portfolio (2003-12); Portland Gallery (2012) Richmond; McAuley Fine Art, Edinburgh (2012); AAF Bristol (2003-12). *Commissions*: Woodmansternes, Hallmark, Ling Design, Carlton, Gibsons, Marks & Spencer, Waitrose, Barnardo's, Tesco, and for private clients. *Address*: 'Dunvegan' Wern-y-Cwrt', nr. Raglan,

Monmouthshire, NP15 2JG. *Email*: info@dionnesievewright.co.uk *Website*: www.dionnesievewright.co.uk *Signs work*: 'Dionne Sievewright', or 'DS'.

SILBER, Evelyn Ann, PhD (Cantab), MA (Cantab), MA (University of Pennsylvania), FMA; art historian and museum curator; Director, Leeds Museums and Galleries (1995-2001); Director, Hunterian Museum and Art Gallery, University of Glasgow (2001-6); Chairman, Charles Rennie Mackintosh Society; heritage and museums consultant; lecturer. *b*: Welwyn Garden City, 22 May 1949. *d of*: Martin Silber, MSc. *Educ*: Hatfield Girls' Grammar School. *Studied*: history of art: New Hall, Cambridge (1968-72), University of Pennsylvania (1972-73), Clare Hall, Cambridge (1975-78). *Exhib*: organised: Jacob Epstein, Sculpture and Drawings, Leeds City A.G., and Whitechapel A.G. (1987). *Publications*: The Sculpture of Jacob Epstein (Phaidon, 1986), Gaudier - Brzeska: Life and Art (Thames and Hudson, 1996); catalogues, articles, lectures. *Clubs*: Royal Overseas League. *Address*: Hon. Prof. Research Fellow. Dept. of Art History, University of Glasgow, Glasgow G12 8QQ. *Email*: evelyn.silber@glasgow.ac.uk

SILVERMAN, Lisa Nicole, BA (Hons) 1991, PGCE (1997); painter in oil and acrylic, printmaker, art teacher. *b*: London, 26 Jun 1968. *Studied*: Exeter College of Art (1987-91), Ecole des Beaux Arts, Toulouse (1989-90). *Exhib*: London: Mall Galleries, Barbican Centre, Battersea Arts Centre, Suburb Gallery, Railings Gallery, International A.G., Smith's Galleries, Ben Uri Gallery (The London Jewish Museum), Business Design Centre. *Works in collections*: Apthorp Fund for Young Artists. *Address*: 2 Danescroft, 21 Torrington Park, London N12 9AG.

SILVERTON, Norma, MA, NS, HND, FETC; artist/printmaker in etching, lithograph, silkscreen, 2D and 3D. *Medium*: printmaking/sculpture. *b*: Birmingham, 1941. married. one *s*. two *d*. *Educ*: in Birmingham. *Studied*: Byam Shaw School of Art, Camberwell College of Art (MA). *Exhib*: solo shows: Tel Aviv, Israel and London; and continually in group shows in UK and abroad. Curated print exhbns. between UK, Israel and Germany. *Works in collections*: Scarborough Municipal A.G., Ben Uri Museum Collection. *Commissions*: private commissions and corporate. *Publications*: Eye Music - a collection of nine lithographs, Unspoken Poems - a collection of ten etchings. *Clubs*: Printmakers Council, N.S.P.S. *Address*: Apt. 11, Allingham Court, 44 The Bishops Avenue, London N2 0BA. *Email*: norma@silverton.co.uk *Website*: www.normasilverton.com *Signs work*: "Norma Silverton."

SIMCOCK, Jack. *Medium*: painter in oils. *b*: Biddulph, Staffs., 6 Jun 1929. one *s*. one *d*. *Exhib*: over 50 one-man shows, England and abroad. Work in many public art galleries and private collections at home and abroad. Major retrospective, Potteries Museum and Art Gallery (2001). *Publications*: Simcock, Mow Cop, autobiography (1975), Midnight Till Three, volume of poems (1975). *Address*: 13 Primitive St., Mow Cop, Stoke-on-Trent ST7 3NH. *Signs work*: "SIMCOCK." and date of printing.

SIMMONDS, Colin Dennis, NDD, ARBSA. *Medium*: oil, watercolour, pastel, drawing. *b*: Birmingham, 25 Oct 1940. *s of*: Charles & Lilian Simmonds. *Partner*: Christine McNaught. two *s*. *Educ*: Moseley School of Art (1953-56). *Studied*: Birmingham Collge of Art (1956-60); Birmingham School of Art Education (1973-74). *Represented by*: Broadway Modern. *Exhib*: The Europe Salon, Brussels; The John Moores Exhibition, Liverpool; The Hurlingham Gallery, London; Royal Society of Portrait Painters; Royal West of England Academy; Royal Institute of Oil Painters; Royal Birmingham Society of Artists; The John Davies, Stow-on-the-Wold; Malvern Festival; hArt, Herefordshire. *Works in collections*: Arts Council, Worcester University; numerous private collections in Germany, France, America, New Zealand. *Commissions*: various portrait and landscape commissions. *Official Purchasers*: West Midland Arts Council. *Clubs*: member of Birmingham and West Midlands Pastel Society. *Address*: Nethercourt, Stoke Lacy, Herefordshire, HR7 4HJ. *Email*: c.simmonds687@btinternet.com *Signs work*: "CDSimmonds".

SIMMONDS, Jackie, HND; artist in pastel and all other media; First Prize 'Art in Nature' (1992), Pastel Society Award (1989). *b*: Oxford, 27 Dec 1944. *m*: Geoffrey Simmonds. two *d*. *Educ*: Preston Manor Grammar. *Studied*: Harrow School of Art (1978-82). *Exhib*: PS, RI, RWA, RSBA, RWEA, BPS, Britain's Painters (1992), several one-man exhbns in London; numerous UK galleries inc. Kelvingrove Museum, Glasgow; Art Expo, NY, USA; Smart Gallery, Florida. *Works in collections*: Guernsey Museum, Middlesex Hospital, Chesterfield Hospital, Bristol. *Publications*: Pastels Workshop (Harper Collins, 1994), Pastels Workbook (David & Charles), Learn to Paint Gardens (Harper Collins), You Can Sketch (Harper Collins), 6 videos for 'Teaching Art', Watercolour Innovations (Collins, 2005). *Works Reproduced*: many works reproduced as prints and sold world-wide. *Misc*: signature member of The Pastel Society of America. *Address*: 23 Linksway, Northwood, Middx. HA6 2XA. *Email*: jackiesimmonds@aol.com *Website*: www.jackiesimmond.co.uk *Signs work*: "Jackie Simmonds.PSA".

SIMMONS, Fay, NDD (1959), Cert.RA (1963), Leverhulme Scholarship (1963), ARBS (1976); sculptor in bronze or gesso composition with mixed media; VSO Business/Social Development, Uganda. *b*: New Zealand, 12 Jul 1938. *d of*: Eric Simmons, MRCVS. *m*: Sean Mullaney (decd). *Educ*: Stella Maris Convent, Bideford. *Studied*: Bideford School of Art; Hammersmith College of Art; RA Schools. *Exhib*: RA, Nicholas Treadwell Gallery, AIA, Alec Mann Birmingham, XVIII Gallery Knightsbridge, Jersey, Guernsey, Gallery Oste Hamburg, New York, Washington. *Clubs*: R.B.S. *Misc*: First woman awarded the President's Prize for Sculpture, R.A. Schools (1963). *Address*: 54 Coburg Cl., Greencoat Pl., London SW1P 1DP. *Signs work*: "F.S."

SIMMONS, Rosemary, NDD (1955), Hon RE (1990); artist in relief printmaking, water-colour; writer; Founder Editor, Printmaking Today, now retired as editor. *b*: Brighton, 19 Oct 1932. *d of*: Alys & Donald Simmons. *m*: Anthony Christie, MA, FSA (decd). *Studied*: Chelsea School of Art (1951-55). *Exhib*: International Gdn. Festival (1984), Museum of Gdn. History (1985), St. John's, Smith Sq. (1987). *Works in collections*: Tate Gallery print collection. *Publications*: Collecting Original Prints (1980), Complete Manual of Relief Printmaking with Katie Clemson (1988), Dictionary of Printmaking Terms (2002), Collecting and Understanding Original Prints (2005). *Address*: 12 Greendown Place, Combe Down, Bath BA2 5DD. *Email*: rosyprint@care4free.net *Signs work*: "Simmons."

SIMONDS, Gillian Betty, NDD (1956); artist in acrylic. *b*: London, 8 Jun 1935. *m*: Brian Simonds. one *d*. *Educ*: Henley Grammar School. *Studied*: Folkestone and Dover Art Schools (1952-54), Canterbury College of Art (1954-56), Folkestone Arts Centre (1979-85, Beryl Bell). *Exhib*: Shepway Show, Folkestone; with NAPA: Newcastle-under-Lyme, Ludlow, RBSA Gallery B'ham, Westminster Gallery, London, Durham Art Gallery, Rooksmoor Gallery, Bath, Mariners Gallery, St. Ives, two-man exhbn, The Nevill Gallery, Canterbury; one-man exhbn: Shaftesbury Arts Centre; Obsidian Gallery, Stoke Mandeville, Williamson Art Gallery, Wirral. *Commissions*: Mr. A. Hobbs, Mrs. M. Eason, Mrs. M. Pender. *Publications*: illustrated: From My Reading to Yours (Prometheus Trust), pencil drawings; 'One Pair of Boots'; 'Not All Little Angels' by Tony Hobbs (Logaston Press 2000, 2009), pen & ink drawings. *Clubs*: N.A.P.A. *Address*: 8 Home Farm, Iwerne Minster, Blandford Forum, DT11 8LB. *Signs work*: "Simonds."

SIMPSON, Alan John, RSMA; marine and landscape artist in oil, water-colour, pastel. *b*: Basingstoke, 22 Jul 1941. *s of*: Arthur James Simpson. *m*: Denise. two *s*. *Studied*: informal training at College of Art, Bournemouth. *Exhib*: RSMA, ROI, RI, Britain in Water-colour, Mystic, Seaport, USA, Linda Blackstone Gallery, Lincoln Joyce Fine Art, Kendalls Fine Art, Peter Hedley Gallery. *Address*: 24 Waltham Rd., Bournemouth BH7 6PE. *Email*: alansimpsonrsma@lineone.net *Signs work*: "Alan Simpson."

SIMPSON, Catherine Anne, *Medium*: Watercolour. *b*: Kingston on Hull, 15 Nov 1959. *Studied*: St Martins School of Art (Ian Ribbons (1984-86); University of Central England (1996-8); Swindon College (2006-7). *Represented by*: Weekend Gallery, Hastings. *Exhib*: Royal Institute of Painters in Watercolour; RBSA; Society of Women Artists; Society of Wildlife Artists; Society of Botanical Artists; Royal Miniature Society; Association of Illustrators; Shrewsbury Cartoon Festival; various exhibitions in the USA. *Works in collections*: RBSA; Viscountess Cobham; Duke of Gloucester; other private collections. *Publications*: Many illustrated books. *Address*: Flat 1, 89 Marina, St Leonards on Sea TN28 0BL. *Email*: casartist@o2.co.uk *Website*: www.cathysimpsonillustration.com *Signs work*: "CAS".

SIMPSON, Cathy, BA (Hons), ARBSA, RMS, HS; freelance illustrator in water-colour and gouache; PG Cert; PG Diploma. *b*: Kingston on Hull, 15 Nov 1959. *Educ*: Christ's Hospital Girls' School, Hertford; Leicester University; Birmingham University. *Studied*: Central St. Martin's School of Art, Swindon College/University of Bath. *Exhib*: RI, SWLA, SWA, SBA, RMS, HS, RBSA, MAS-F, MAS-G, SAMAP. *Address*: 23 The Dock, Catshill, Bromsgrove, Worcs. B61 0NJ. *Email*: casartist@ukonline.co.uk *Signs work*: 'with monogram'.

SIMPSON, Charles, BA (Hons); Chairman's Purchase Award 'The Discerning Eye' (2003) (invited artist). *Medium*: Oil. *b*: Scotland, 17 Nov 1952. *m*. Mary. *Educ*: Alloa Academy, Alloa. *Studied*: Glasgow School of Art (1970-75). *Represented by*: Bourne Fine Art, Edinburgh; Panter & Hall, London. *Exhib*: Bourne Fine Art; Panter & Hall; John Davies Gallery. *Works in collections*: Royal Bank of Scotland; M&G; Arisaig Partners. *Publications*: Article in 'The Artist' Dec 2011. *Recreations*: Making bread. *Address*: Inglecraig, Bowland Road, Clovenfords, Selkirkshire TD1 3ND. *Email*: inglecraig@btinternet.com *Website*: www.csimpson-art.co.uk *Signs work*: "Simpson".

SIMPSON, Leslie, FRSA (1985); portrait artist in oil and water-colour working to commission on all subjects; Director, Soc. of Miniaturists, British Water-colour Soc., British Soc. of Painters; Founder, Yorkshire Artists Exhbn. (1981); Principal, International Guild of Artists; inventor of 'Whimseycollie' collection of humorous paintings. *b*: Horsforth, 28 May 1930. *s of*: Sidney Arthur Simpson (decd). *m*: Margaret. one *s*. *Educ*: Bridlington School. *Studied*: Hull College of Art. *Works in collections*: portrait of the full Wakefield City Council (1974); portraits of the Lady Lord Mayors of Leeds, Bradford, Sheffield and London; 'The Winning Throw' portrait of Tessa Sanderson, Los Angeles Olympics (1984). Descendant of James Simpson (1791-1864) leading non-conformist architect in the North, and John Simpson official portrait artist to Queen Donna Marie II of Portugal (1837). *Address*: c/o Sutcliffe Galleries, 6 Montpellier Street, Harrogate, N. Yorks HG1 2TQ. *Email*: info@britpaint.co.uk *Website*: www.britpaint.co.uk www.britpaint.com *Signs work*: "Leslie Simpson."

SIMPSON, Noelle, painter, colourist of joyous landscapes, nudes, interiors and portraits in oil on canvas, original limited edition prints. *b*: Auckland, NZ, 10 Aug 1950. *d of*: Noel Simpson, racehorse breeder. one *d*. *Educ*: Chatelard, Switzerland; Moreton Hall, Shropshire. *Studied*: under Philip Sutton, RA, and Frederick Deane, RP (1985), Van Wieringen, Bali (1986-90). *Exhib*: J. Weston Gallery, London (1985), Symon Gallery, Bali (1987), Bowmoore Gallery, London (1991), Hilton International, Bali (1992), Gagliardi Gallery, London (1992, 1994), Pacific Rim Gallery, San Diego (1993), Los Angeles (1995-97), Auckland, N.Z. (1998-99). *Works in collections*: Agung Rai Museum, Bali. *Publications*: Then Till Now - Noelle Simpson. *Address*: 18 Cottesmore Gdns., London W8 5PR.

SIMPSON, Sarah, BA Hons Fine Art Painting (1974), Post Graduate Cert. Ed. (1995). *Medium*: Oil. *b*: Crosby, Liverpool, 18 Feb 1951. *Studied*: Liverpool College of Art (Foundation - Maurice Cockrill); Chelsea School of Art; Brighton University. *Represented* *by*: Will's Art Warehouse Gallery, London. *Exhib*: London Galleries, Art Fairs, Affordable Art Fair London. *Works in collections*: private collections - national and international. *Works Reproduced*: Paintings published as prints by Rosenstiel's Fine Art Prints. *Misc*: known as Sarah Simpson - uses middle name initial (Ann) in signature. *Address*: c/o Will's Art Warehouse Gallery, 180 Lower Richmond Rd., London SW15 1LY. *Email*: sarahsimpson@itpmail.com *Signs work*: "SAS".

SIMS, Anna, Southampton Institute of Higher Education Certificate in Painting (1986). *Medium*: oil, watercolour, drawing. *b*: Ringwood, Hants, 29 Mar 1953. *Partner*: Lally Sims (sculptor). two *s*. *Studied*: Southampton College of Fine Art, part-time, but mainly self-taught. *Represented by*: The Hunter Simmons Gallery, Westbourne, Bournemouth. *Exhib*: RA (2000); Llewellyn Alexander; Royal Society of Painters in Watercolours; Mall Galleries; 'Not the Turner Prize' (2003). *Works in collections*: Margaret Ziegler. *Commissions*: portrait, pastel: Mrs Lawrie McMenemy; Dr. Adam Sawyer and his three children. *Publications*: International Artist Magazine (article, Sept 2005); 100 Ways to Paint People and Figures (pub. by International Artist). *Works Reproduced*: 'Untitled Lady', 'Waldolf Castle' published by the above. *Clubs*: CAD Arts, Christchurch, Dorset. *Address*: 25 Millhams Street, Christchurch, Dorset BH23 1DN. *Email*: anna@annasims.co.uk anna.sims@ntlworld.com *Website*: www.annasims.co.uk *Signs work*: 'Anna Sims'.

SIMS, Ronald Ivan, Painting BA; RA Schools MA; Hayward Gallery Prizewinner Award; Gloucestershire College of Art Fellowship, £1000 Wyss Foundation Painting Award 2012. *Medium*: acrylic paintings, prints. *b*: Burnham-on-Crouch, Essex, 25 May 1944. *s of*: Frank & Irene Sims. *m*: Wendy Cruickshank. two *d*. *Studied*: RA Schools; Manchester College of Art; Colchester Art School. *Represented by*: Minories Art Gallery Colchester. *Exhib*: RA Summer Shows; Chappel Galleries, Colchester; Hayward Gallery, Young Contemporaries at RA; Hayletts Gallery, Maldon - solo; Minories Art Gallery - solo retrospective; NEAC. *Works in collections*: Portsmouth College of Education; Essex and Suffolk Museums Print Collection; Chappel Galleries. *Commissions*: Essex Churches; Russian Orthodox, Manchester; Ancoats Junior School Mural. *Publications*: 'British Artists since 1945' (Buckman); *Official Purchasers*: Essex and Suffolk Museums. *Works Reproduced*: RA Illustrated; RSA 'Brush with Words'; RASA 'Serious Pleasure'; Connoiseur Magazine; Country Life. *Principal Works*: 'Arise, the Equinox Ram and Sun'; 'Blue Paolozzi'. *Recreations*: Italian holidays. *Clubs*: Colchester Art Society (President); Gainsborough's House Print Workshop; Art Workers Guild; RASA East. *Misc*: art criticism, 'a-n Magazine'; 'Art Expo' Essex County Standard *Address*: Bugle Cottage, 123, Tilkey Road, Coggeshall, Essex CO6 1QN. *Email*: simsrw@hotmail.co.uk *Website*: ronsimsart.com *Signs work*: 'R.I.Sims' (on reverse of painting) e.g. R.I.Sims '05.

SINCLAIR, David Mackenzie, RSW (2001) elected to Council (2002); Post Diploma Glasgow School of Art (Highly Commended), DA. *Medium*: painting oil/watercolour; printing craft (etching and wood engraving). *b*: Glasgow, 9 Oct 1937. *s of*: David Sinclair and Jessie McLennan. *m*: Anitra Rushbrook. two *s*. *Educ*: Allan Glen's School, Glasgow. *Studied*: Glasgow School of Art. *Represented by*: Ewan Mundy Fine Art (Glasgow); Randolph Gallery (Edinburgh); Tom Dean's Gallery (Atlanta, USA). *Exhib*: London: Duncan Campbell, Piano Nobile, Mall Galleries, Islington Art Fairs; Edinburgh: Bourne Fine Art, Open Eye, Randolph, RSA, RSW, Printmakers; Glasgow: Ewan Mundy, Gerber, Compass, Kelly Gallery, Art Fairs, RGI; Tom Dean's, Atlanta, USA. *Works in collections*: Paintings in Hospitals Scheme, Scotland; Gracefield Art Centre, Dumfriesshire; Hunterian Collection Glasgow; various private collections Britain/USA. *Commissions*: various private commissions. *Official Purchasers*: Paintings in Hospitals, Gracefield Art Centre, Hunterian Collection, Royal Bank of Scotland. *Works Reproduced*: winning portrait for Morrison Portrait Award RSA (1997). *Address*: Rosebank, Paxton, Berwick-on-Tweed, TD15 1TE. *Email*: anitrasinclair@onetel.com

SINCLAIR, Elizabeth, NDD (1954), ATD (1958), Visual Arts Dip.(1969), Dip. in History of Art (1972); painter in oil, pastel, acrylic and water-colour. *b*: Glasgow, 18 Jan 1933. *d of*: Surgeon Captain, A.D. Sinclair, MB, ChB, FFA, RCS. *Educ*: 'Wings', Charlton Pk., Wilts. *Studied*: Plymouth School of Art, Bath Academy of Art, London University. *Exhib*: one-man shows: Hong Kong, Italy; group shows: Hong Kong, Germany, Plymouth, London, Reigate, etc., Surrey Open Studios. *Works in collections*: Plymouth A.G. *Clubs*: Reigate Soc. of Artists, North Weald Group, Free Painters and Sculptors, Society of Feline Artists. *Address*: 10 Cockshot Hill, Reigate, Surrey RH2 8AE. *Signs work*: "E. Sinclair."

SINCLAIR, Helen, BFA (Hons) (1976); sculptor in cast stone and metal. *b*: S.Wales, 27 Feb 1954. *d of*: Noël Sinclair, electrical engineer. *m*: Terry Ryall, sculptor. *Educ*: Llanelli Girls' Grammar School. *Studied*: Dyfed School of Art, Wimbledon School of Art (1973-76, Peter Startup, Jim Turner). *Exhib*: Online Gallery, Southampton, Fairfax Gallery, Tunbridge Wells, Fairfax Gallery, Chelsea & Norfolk; Garden Architecture, Fulham; Hannah Peschar Sculpture Garden, Surrey. *Works in collections*: Bultarbo Estate, Sweden, Gary Rhodes. *Commissions*: Trophy for W. Wales Tec Management Awards; Wall Reliefs, Castle Square, Swansea; Award Trophy for Shelter Cymru; 'Mother & Child' for churchyard, All Saints, Fulham; circle of figures for St. Mary's Hospital, Chichester; seated figure for 'Rhodes 24' restaurant. *Misc*: half-hour TV programme in 'Jigsaw' Arts Series (Aug 2003). *Address*: Rhossili Farmhouse, Rhossili, Gower, Swansea SA3 1PL. *Email*: helen@sculptureculture.co.uk *Signs work*: "Helen Sinclair" or "H.S."

SINCLAIR, N. T. MA, FMA; Senior Curator. *Address*: Museum and Art Gallery, Borough Rd., Sunderland SR1 1PP.

SINGLETON, Alex, BA, PGCE, Post Grad Cert, C.E.L.T.A. *Medium*: oil, watercolour, drawing, prints, sculpture. *b*: Amersham, 16 Jan 1972. *s of*: R K L Singleton. *Partner*: Verity-Ross-Smith. *Educ*: Frensham Heights School, Surrey; Junior English School, Rome. *Studied*: Central St. Martins College of Art & Design, London 1991-94; University of Sydney, NSW, 2001; Thames Valley University, Reading 2005; Oxford and Cherwell Valley College - CELTA 2010. *Exhib*: John Radcliffe Hospital, Oxford (1999); The Maclay Museum, NSW (2001); Broad Canvas Art Shop, Oxford (2005); Oxford Science Park (2006); Greens Cafe, Oxford (2009), Ark-T-Centre (1998, 2004), Rye St. Anthony School (1998), 1+2 Studios, NSW (2001), The James Harvey Gallery, NSW (2001), East Oxford Community Centre, Oxford (2003), Oxford Art Society (2005, 2006), The Taurus Gallery (2006), Royal Academy Summer Show (2006), Modern Art Oxford (2008), Chris Whites Studio, Oxford (2009), Art Jericho 'Pause' (July 2009), Greens Cafe 'Nativity' (Dec 2010), Edinburgh Festival - 2d and 3d Craft Stall (Summer 2011), Llewellyn Alexander Gallery - Not the Royal Academy - 'First Time Flyers' wood block paintings (2011, 2012). *Commissions*: Caroline Milhouse, Richmond 'H5 N1 Resurrection P1' (oil on wood); Thomas Griem, Temple, London 'H5 N1 Resurrection P2' (oil on wood). *Publications*: 'Underworld' Katherine Sutherland & Alex Singleton (Lulu Publishing) . *Principal Works*: 'Kouri from the Outback - Arriving in Sydney Olympics' 2000 (oil). *Misc*: Group exhibition catalogues: Royal Academy of Arts Summer Exhibition 2006; The Oxford Open List of Works - Modern Art Oxford 2008. *Address*: 20 Marlborough Close, Littlemore, Oxford, OX4 4PH. *Email*: singletonalex@hotmail.com *Website*: www.saatchionline.co/profile/2533 www.artgallery.co.uk/artist/alex_singleton_2 *Signs work*: "A.G.Singleton"

SINNOTT, Kevin, MA (RCA); artist in oil on canvas. *b*: Wales, 1947. *m*: Susan. three *s*. one *d*. *Studied*: Cardiff College of Art (1967-68), Gloucester College of Art (1968-71), RCA (1971-74). *Exhib*: one-man shows: Ikon Gallery (1980), Blond Fine Art (1982, 1984), Chapter Arts Centre, Cardiff (1984), Bernard Jacobson Gallery (1986, 1987, 1988, 1990), Flowers East (1992, 1994, 1996, 1998, 2012, 2014), Caldwell/Snyder NY (2000, 2001, 2002), Martin Tinney, (2001, 2003. 2005, 2007. 2009, 2011, 2013). *Works in collections*: British Council,

BM, ACGB, RCA, Whitworth Manchester, Wolverhampton City Gallery, Unilever, Deutsche Bank A.G. London, Metropolitan Museum of Art, NY, National Museum of Wales, Ashmolean, Oxford. *Publications*: autobiography 'Behind the Canvas' pub. Nov 2008. *Clubs*: Chelsea Arts. *Address*: Ty'r Santes Fair, Pont-y-Rhyl, Bridgend CF32 8LJ. *Email*: mail@kevinsinnott.co.uk *Website*: kevinsinnott.co.uk *Signs work*: initials right hand corner.

SKARGON, Yvonne. *Medium*: wood engraving, botanical watercolours. *b*: Dovercourt, 1 May 1931. *m*: John Commander. *Educ*: Colchester School of Art (Blair Hughs Stanton, John O'Connor). *Studied*: wood engraving and design. *Exhib*: Society of Wood Engravers, numerous mixed exhibitions, International Exhibition of Botanical Art and Illustration, Pittsburgh. *Works in collections*: V & A, Hunt Institute for Botanical Documentation, Pittsburgh. *Commissions*: many books for most major publishers, Royal Mail Commemorative Stamps, Roses (1991). *Publications*: Author/Compiler/Illustrator: The Importance of Being Oscar (1988); Lily and Hodge & Dr. Johnson (1991); A Garden of My Own (1996); Concatenation (2000); Watermarks (2003). *Address*: 44 Prentice Street, Lavenham, Suffolk, CO10 9RD.

SKEA, Janet, RI (2002); BFA (1968); RI Members Award (2004); RI Arts Club Award (2006). *Medium*: water-colour, tempera and oils. *b*: Johannesburg, S. Africa, 15 Sep 1947. *Educ*: Parktown Girls' High, Johannesburg. *Studied*: Stellenbosch University (1965-68, Prof. Otto Schröder). *Exhib*: Moved to France in 2007 and now exhibits mainly at the RI Annual Exhibition, Mall Galleries, London; Manya Igel Fine Arts, London and Ham; Lincoln Joyce Fine Arts; Little Picture Gallery, Mousehole. Also works on commission. Solos: Museum of Garden History (1985), Heifer (1994), Southwark Festival (1996), Dick the Dog, Penzance (2001 & 2002). Exhibitor and demonstrator at Art in Action, Waterperry House (2006). *Works in collections*: Hertfordshire CC. *Publications*: Artists and Illustrators (January 1996, March 2002). *Works Reproduced*: 'Watercolour Workshop' (Harper Collins, 1995); 'Artists' Kew' (Kew Gardens, 2006). *Address*: Le Bourg, 24300 St. Front la Riviere, France. *Signs work*: "Janet Skea" dated on reverse.

SKINNER, John, BA (Hons) Fine Art (Painting); artist in oil painting. *b*: Kent, 19 Aug 1953. *m*: Mary Skinner. one *s*. *Educ*: Brighton Polytechnic (1973-76). *Exhib*: Foyer de Compagne, Poussan, France (2008); Paint Image Beauty, Abbotsbury, England (2005); Art Connexion, Lille, France (2004); Study Gallery, Poole, England (2002). *Works in collections*: Dorset Education Authority; Novi Nordisk; New Look. *Publications*: "Switch off the Light and Let Me Try on your Dress", Sara Hudson and John Skinner (Agre Books, 2002). *Works Reproduced*: Painting and Drawing People, A Fresh Approach, by Emily Ball (2009). *Address*: 31 Quai Docteur Scheydt, 34200 Sete, France. *Signs work*: www.johnskinner.me.uk

SLASKI, Peter, Dip Arch; FRIBA; DipTP London; Building Diploma. *Medium*: watercolours, oils, acrylic, pastels. *b*: 28 Jun 1925. *s of*: C.Slaski. one *s*. one *d*. *Studied*: Regent Street Polytechnic. *Represented by*: Chelsea Art Society; Langham Sketching Club; Merton Art Society. *Exhib*: Chelsea Art Society; Langham Sketching Club; FAAS (Architects Artists Society); My Studio; Polish Cultural Society; France (Forces); Hurlingham Club. *Commissions*: portraits, landscapes. *Principal Works*: landscapes. *Recreations*: painting, reading, music, theatre. *Clubs*: Hurlingham Tennis. *Address*: 18 Homefield Road, London SW19 4QF. *Signs work*: 'Peter Slaski'.

SLATER, Georgeanne, . *Medium*: acrylic, watercolour, oil, sculpture. *b*: Newcastle upon Tyne, 3 Jan 1940. *d of*: George & Ria Marr. *m*: Ken Slater (decd). one *s*. one *d*. *Exhib*: RA (sculpture in Thassos marble); Kensington & Chelsea Art Show (painting); Chelsea Art Society Show, Chelsea Old Town Hall (paintings). *Works in collections*: sculpture in private collection (sold by RA). *Address*: 21a Redcliffe Gardens, Chelsea, London SW10 9BG. *Email*: GeorgeanneSlater@aol.com *Signs work*: "GeorgeAnne".

SLATER, Paul, MA; many and various design awards; D&AD Glenfiddich, National Library Illustration Award. *Medium*: acrylic, oil, drawing, prints. *b*: Burnley, Lancs.,7 Aug 1953. *s of*: Clayton & Marie Slater. *m*: Sophie. one *d*. *Studied*: Burnley College of Art (1969-71); Royal College of Art (1975-78). *Exhib*: regular one-man shows (annually) London and Florida, USA. *Commissions*: illustrated 'The Times' Saturday Magazine 'Restaurant Review' since 1990; work regularly appears in 'Radio Times' and 'The Week'. *Clubs*: The United Arts Club, Dublin; patron AOI. *Address*: 22 Partridge Close, Chesham, Bucks HP5 3LH. *Email*: paulslater@btinternet.com *Website*: www.paulslaterbugle.com *Signs work*: 'P.SLATER'.

SLATTER, Alexander John, BA (Hons) Graphic Design; Best Collection - Great North Art Show, Ripon Cathedral (2007). *Medium*: oil. *b*: Harrogate, 9 Feb 1970. *s of*: Mervyn Slatter. two *d*. *Educ*: Head Chorister, Durham Cathedral Choir (1978-83); Bishop Wordsworth Grammar School, Salisbury (1986-88). *Studied*: Salisbury College of Art, Exeter College of Art (1989-92). *Represented by*: Kendalls Fine Art, Cowes; Webbs Fine Art, London; Sheldon Fine Art, Rhode Island. *Exhib*: Kendalls Fine Art, Cowes (2003-2012); Webbs Fine Art, London (2007-2012); Sheldon Fine Art, Rhode Island (2004, 2012); Affordable Art Fair, Battersea (2004-2012); Brighton Art Fair (2005-2012); Battersea Contemporary Art Fair (2006, 2007, 2008); Serena Hall Gallery, Southwold (2009, 2011, 2012); Great North Art Fair, Ripon Cathedral (2003-2009). *Works in collections*: Forge - Provence; Smithson - Sydney; David - London; Chan - Hong Kong. *Commissions*: Stoke Hall Mural (2010); Cliff Road (2011); Fisk (2008); Gale (2007); Gregory (2008); Gullen (2009); Honour (2007); Randall (2011); Hove (2007); Payne (2006); Shaw (2005); Surridge (2006). *Publications*: 'Waves, trees and beaches', A Selection of Paintings by Alexander Slatter (2011). *Official Purchasers*: Brighton & Hove Hospital Trust (5 pieces). *Works Reproduced*: The Art Group London; Pyramid International; John Lewis. *Misc*: Full time artist for 10 years. *Address*: 1 Catton Grove Road, Norwich, Norfolk NR3 3NJ. *Email*: alexanderslatter@yahoo.co.uk *Website*: www.alexanderslatter.co.uk *Signs work*: "SLATTER".

SLATTERY, Nicola, BA (Hons) Fine Art (2986). *b*: 1963. *Studied*: Coventry Art School. *Exhib*: The John Russell Gallery, Ipswich (1996-2006); The Grapevine, Norwich (2004-05); The Rona Gallery, Mayfair, London (2004-2009); The Hallward, Dublin, Ireland (2006-2009); Cambridge Contemporary Art (2006-2009); The Royal Society of British Artists, Mall Galleries (2006-07); The Castle Gallery, Inverness, Scotland (2007-2009). *Works in collections*: Public: Bedford County Council, Leicestershire Collection for Schools, South Norfolk District Council, Norfolk Contemporary Art Society, North Kesteven District Council, Queen Elizabeth II Law Courts, Birmingham. Corporate: JD Wetherspoons Plc, Barlow, Lyde & Gilbert, London. *Publications*: Artists and Illustrators; The Artist; Art of England; Galleries Magazine; BBC Homes and Antiques. *Address*: North Barn, Mill Road, Alburgh, Harleston, Norfolk, IP20 0DS. *Email*: artpeople@btopenworld.com *Website*: www.nicolaslattery.com *Signs work*: "NICOLA SLATTERY".

SLOAN, Bob, RUA, DA, ATD; Mont Kavanagh award (1983), RUA medals: Silver (1983), gold (1988, 1999); sculptor in mixed media; Lecturer in Fine Art, University of Ulster. *b*: Belfast, 10 Apr 1940. *m*: Veronica. one *s*. one *d*. *Studied*: Belfast College of Art (1959-63), Central Schools, London (1963-64). *Exhib*: Belfast, London, Liverpool, Dublin, NY, Kassel Germany. *Works in collections*: Ulster Museum, N.I. Arts Council, Arts Council of Ireland, National Self-Portrait Collection; private collections in Ireland, England, America. *Commissions*: Northern Bank, Strabane District Council, N.I. Tourist Board, Belfast Newsletter, Diocese of Derry, N.I. Housing Executive. *Address*: 58 Upper Mealough Rd., Belfast BT8 8LR, Northern Ireland. *Signs work*: "R.W. Sloan".

SLOAN, Joseph, Best Sculpture, Kilkenny Festival (1990); Gold Medal Salon d'Art, Cavaillon (1996); Silver Medal, Salon d'Art, Chateau-Arnoux (1996-2002); Prix du Public,

Cavaillon (1998). *Medium*: Sculpture; wood-engraving; relief printing. *b*: Warrenpoint, Co Down, 25 Jan 1940. *Partner*: Monica Brain. *Educ*: Self taught sculptor and bronze caster. *Studied*: Heatherley's School of Art, London - part time courses in print-making and drawing. *Represented by*: Kilcock Art, Ireland; Kenny Gallery, Ireland. *Exhib*: Include: Invited artist Royal Ulster Academy (2009). Group shows inc: Royal Hibernian Academy, Dublin; Royal Academy Summer Exhibition; Printmakers Council Miniprint Exhibitions; Royal Society of Engravers and Etchers, London; Camden Arts Centre, London. *Works in collections*: Worldwide including National Concert Hall, Dublin; Mairie de Sorgue Municipal Collection; Office of Public Works; Bank of Ireland; Maryland Bank; Ulster TV. *Commissions*: ONE Air Corps Memorial, Baldonnel Airport, Ireland; private and corporate collections including DHL/AIB Export Awards; Europaws TV drama. *Publications*: 'AIB Art - 1985-1995'; Art in State Buildings 1995; OPW 1979. *Official Purchasers*: Office of Public Works, Ireland; ESB Ireland; Bolton Museum and Art Gallery; Ulster TV. *Principal Works*: Thematically, works influenced by music. The Aran Islands, Galway, Ireland have also featured strongly. *Recreations*: Cycling; yoga. *Clubs*: Visual Artists, Ireland; Trevisian International Art. *Misc*: Film 'Ulster TV: The Collection' (2002); teaching wood-engraving Camden Arts Centre; Exploring Sculpture, Ateliers Fourwinds, Provence. *Address*: 73 Rathdown Park, Terenure, Dublin 6W, Eire. *Email*: artyjoe.mobrain@neuf.fr *Website*: www.artvitae.com/sloan *Signs work*: "JS"; "JSLOAN"; Sloan with J over the top for last fifteen years.

SLOAN, Sarah Elizabeth, ABNA. *Medium*: water based paint (mixed medium), previously oil. *b*: Woking, Surrey, 6 Feb 1952. two *s*. *Studied*: self taught. *Represented by*: self. *Exhib*: solo: Stark Gallery, London (2002); Burgh House Museum, Hampstead (2003). Group shows include: AAF Battersea (2002, 2004); The Art on Paper Fair, RCA (2004); DACS 20th Anniversary Exhibition, Mall Galleries, London (invited (2004); ABNA: Mariners Gallery, St. Ives (2006, 2009, 2013), France (2008), Crypt Gallery, St. Ives (2010, 2011); Gt. Glemham, Suffolk (2006, 207, 2011); The Plough Arts Centre, Torrington (2012); Little Picture Gallery, Mousehole, Cornwall (2012); Suffolk Show (2007, 2009, 2014) plus many others across UK. *Commissions*: ongoing. *Publication*: ABNA book, and magazines. *Works Reproduced*: Magazine front covers: Blackheath & Greenwich Gazette (Dec '90/Jan '90), Putney Wimbledon & Wandsworth Time & Leisure (March 2003); two pictures in ABNA book. *Principal Works*: Sea Greens; Mousehole Jug; Mariners, St. Ives; Mevagissey Breeze. *Recreations*: playing guitar, singing, sketching, painting, cooking for friends. *Clubs*: Member of DACS. *Misc*: Started in textile design, worked for a card and giftwrap company, also designed stage sets. Qualified nurse: SRN, RMN. *Address*: Orchard House, Gosbeck, Nr. Ipswich, Suffolk IP6 9RX. *Signs work*: 'Sloan' and full signature on verso. Early works 'S' and full signature on verso.

SLOAN, Victor, MBE, DA, FRPS, ATC, RUA, FRSA; visual artist/lecturer - photography, video, printmaking, painting and drawing; Awards: British Council, Arts Council of N. Ireland, Dept. of Foreign Affairs (Ireland), An Chomhairle Ealaion, Arts Council of Ireland, Culture Ireland, Gold Medal Print Award and Connor Prize (RUA). *b*: Dungannon, Co. Tyrone, 16 Jul 1945. *s of*: Isaac & Margaret Sloan. *m*: Katherine Joyce Sloan (nee McCrum). two *s*. *Studied*: Belfast and Leeds Colleges of Art - Fine Art Painting (1963-69). *Exhib*: Exhibited widely throughout Europe, North America, South America and Asia. *Works in collections*: Imperial War Museum; National Photographic Archives; State Art Collection, Ireland; Department of Finance and Personnel, Northern Ireland; Dublin City University; Arts Council; National Self-Portrait Collection of Ireland; North West Arts Trust; British Telecommunications; National Museum of Photography, Film and Television; Ulster Museum; also public and private collections in U.S.A., Canada, Europe, Australia, Asia. *Publications*: 'Marking the North - The Work of Victor Sloan' (England); 'Walls' (Northern Ireland); 'Borne Sulinowo' (Poland); 'Stadium' (Germany); 'Acts of Faith' (Ireland); 'Victor Sloan: Selected Works 1980-2000' (Northern Ireland)., 'Victor Sloan:

Walk' (Germany); 'Luxus' (Northern Ireland). *Address*: Rosedale House, 10 Church Rd., Portadown, Co. Armagh BT63 5HT. *Email*: mail@victorsloan.com *Website*: www.victorsloan.com *Signs work*: "VICTOR SLOAN."

SMAIL, Elizabeth Ann, FLS (1991), FSBA (1985); Cert. of Botanical Merit (SBA Exhbn. 1993 & 2000); botanical artist; Personnel Officer, Council Mem. (Ex-officio), Soc. of Botanical Artists (1988-95). *Medium*: watercolour. *b*: Ross-on-Wye, 5 Mar 1942. *d of*: Robert and Joan Ollis. *Educ*: Ross-on-Wye. *Studied*: Hereford College of Art (1958-62). *Exhib*: Mall Galleries (1986, 1987), Westminster Gallery (annually since 1988), Hereford Museum and A.G. (1991), Kent Painters Group since 1992, Sevenoaks Reserve annually since 1994; 21 other centres worldwide since 1984. *Works in collections*: Hunt Inst. of Botanical Documentation, Pittsburg; Marine Soc., London; private collections throughout the world. *Commissions*: Wildfowl and Wetlands Trust (designs for stationery and giftware). *Publications*: contributions to 'Arte y Botanica (Banco de Madrid); Encyclopedia of Flower Painting Techniques; The Art of Botanical Painting. *Works Reproduced*: illustrations for articles in various publications; designs for reproduction on greetings cards and ceramics. *Recreations*: music, cinema, dandelions. *Misc*: teaches botanical illustration at centres in Kent and Dorset; tutor/assessor for SBA Distant Learning Diploma Course. *Address*: 25 Walton Rd., Tonbridge, Kent TN10 4EF. *Signs work* "Elizabeth Smail."

SMAIL, Janice Ann, UA; Council mem. UA (1995-98), Teacher's Cert. (1962), C&G Fashion (1980); painter in oil, pastel, and water-colour. *b*: Bury St. Edmunds, Suffolk, 23 Feb 1939. *m*: Peter. one *s*. one *d*. *Educ*: Whitelands College, Putney. *Studied*: University of London Inst. of Educ., Reigate College of Art. *Exhib*: Westminster Gallery, London with UA; solo shows: Surrey and Cambs. Castle Gallery, Rothesay, Isle of Bute. *Works in collections*: internationally. *Clubs*: U.A., Cambridge Drawing Society, Barn Art Society, Cambridge Open Studios. *Address*: Woodlands, 24 North Rd., Whittlesford, Cambs CB2 4NZ. Email: janice.smail1@btinternet.com *Signs work*: "Jan Smail."

SMITH, Barry Edward Jervis, BA; artist/illustrator in water-colour. *b*: Sydney, Australia, 27 Apr 1943. *Educ*: Coburg High School; University of Melbourne (1961-66). *Exhib*: group shows in London; one-man shows: Nantes, Edinburgh, Sweden and Australia. *Publications*: written and illustrated 15 children's books. *Address*: Flat 15, Colonnades Apartments, 35 Sylvester Road, London E8 1EP. *Email*: bejsmithart@gmail.com *Website*: barrysmithwork.co.uk *Signs work*: "B. Smith" , "B.E.J.Smith" or "Barry Smith."

SMITH, C. Philip, MBE (for services to art) (2000); ARCA (1st Class) (1954), MDE (1970), Hon.Fellow and Past President (1977-79) Designer Bookbinders; Presidium of Honour (Czech) (1989); several international Gold, Silver Medals; book artist, bookbinder, painter, author, inventor (Patents: maril, lap-back book-structure); Editor, The New Bookbinder (1980-95); British Museum team Florence flood 1966-67; Hon, Fellow of Designer Bookbinders (2012). *Medium*: book-art making (physical objects). *b*: Southport, Merseyside, 10 Jun 1928. *m*: Dorothy M. Weighill, artist. three *s*. *Educ*: Ackworth School, Yorks. *Studied*: Southport School of Art (1949-51), RCA (1951-54, Roger Powell); Sydney Cockerell bindery (1957-61). *Represented by*: British Library National Sound Archive, Life Story Collection (2004). *Exhib*: several solo UK and abroad, over 150 book-art, binding exhbns. UK, USA, France, Germany, Holland, Belgium, Luxembourg, Spain, Norway, Czechoslovakia, S. America, Canada, Japan, S. Africa, etc.; painting exhbns. include John Moores, RBA, etc. *Works in collections*: V&A, BM (BL), Royal Collection, Bibliothèque Historique, Paris, Royal Library Holland, and other major public collections UK, USA, Spain and around the world including Municipal Library Collection, Johannesburg, SA; Humanities Research Centre, Texas; Lilly Library, Indiana. *Publications*: The Lord of the Rings and Other Bookbindings, (1970); New Directions in Bookbinding (London and N.Y. 1975); The Book: Art & Object (1982); The Book as Art in prep.; numerous exhbn.

catalogues, articles and reviews internationally. *Official Purchasers*: Man Booker Prize Author's Presentation Bindings, 1991-present. *Principal Works*: book-walls: notably for Lord of the Rings, Vesalius: De Humani Corporis Fabrica (BL), Macbeth (BL), King Lear (USA), 5-vol English Bible (V&A). *Recreations*: philosophy, table tennis. *Clubs*: Designer Bookbinders, Meister der Einbandkunst, Canadian G. of B.B.A., Soc. of Bookbinders, Center for Book Arts, N.Y., Hon. Fellow Soc. of Czech Bookbinders. *Address*: The Book House, Yatton Keynell, Wilts. SN14 7BH. *Email*: philipsmithbookart@gmail.com *Website*: philipsmithbookart.com *Signs work*: "Philip Smith."

SMITH, Caryl, SBA (1997); mainly self taught artist, mostly flowers and gardens. *Medium*: pastel and water-colour. *b*: Wiltshire, 21 Oct 1943. *m*: V. J. Smith. two *s*. *Exhib*: galleries in the Cotswolds, Wiltshire and Sussex. *Publications*: greetings cards. *Clubs*: SFP. *Address*: 16 Elm Avenue, East Peston, W. Sussex, BN16 1HJ. *Email*: carylsmith@onetel.com *Signs work*: paintings "CARYL."

SMITH, Colin Hilton, BA (Hons), MA (RCA); Harkness Fellow (Yale University), Royal Overseas League joint first prizewinner; painter in oil on canvas, acrylic etc. on paper; associate lecturer, Loughborough University. *b*: Harpenden, Herts., 21 Feb 1953. divorced. *s of*: Reginald Walter Smith, headmaster. one *s*. *Educ*: Hitchin Boys Grammar School. *Studied*: St. Albans School of Art (1971-72), Falmouth School of Art (1972-75), RCA (1975-79), Yale (1983-85). *Exhib*: solo shows: Adair Margo Gallery, El Paso, Texas USA (1999), Musikpaviljongen, Grenadjarstaden, Örebro, Sweden (1999), British Council Art Centre, Buenos Aires (1998), 6 Chapel Row Contemporary Arts, Bath (1998), VIP Lounge, Virgin Airways, Heathrow Airport (1997), Galleri M, Stockholm (1997), Arte.X.Arte, Buenos Aires (1996), Wilmer, Cutler and Pickering, Berlin (1995), University of Northumbria Gallery, Newcastle-upon-Tyne (1995), Chelsea Arts Club, London (1995), Galleri M, Stockholm (1995), Big Paintings for the Barbican, London (1993), Gallery Three Zero. N.Y. (1993), Kunst Europa, Kunstverein Freiburg, Germany (1991), Anderson O'Day Gallery (1991), Ruth Siegal, N.Y. (1986), Art Iteinera '83, Volterra, Italy (1983), Nicola Jacobs Gallery, London (1982, 1984, 1987, 1989). *Works in collections*: Tate Gallery, London, British Council, Buenos Aires, NatWest Group, London, Royal Palm Hotel, Phoenix, Arizona, Scottish Equitable, Edinburgh, Museum of Modern Art, Tel Aviv (Herrmann's Bequest), Virgin Communications, London, Wilmer, Cutler and Pickering, Berlin, BML Corporate Management, Frankfurt, Arthur Anderson, Newcastle, Amerivox Scandinavia, Stockholm, Duke and Duchess of Westminster, Coopers Lybrand, London, Hunting Group Plc., British Airways, Kettering A.G. and Museum, Kettering, Arthur Andersen, London, EMI Worldwide, London, British Standards Inst., London, Pearl Development, London, Contemporary Art Soc., London, Pepsi Cola, London, Prudential Holborn, London, ACGB, Unilever, London, Royal College of Art, London. *Clubs*: Chelsea Arts. *Address*: 27 Orsman Rd., London N1 5RA. *Signs work*: "Colin Smith."

SMITH, David Henry, M.Art, RCA (1971), Hugh Dunn Plaque (1971); artist in oil and water-colour. *b*: Cleethorpes, 29 Oct 1947. *s of*: Henry Smith. *m*: Irena Ewa Flynn. *Educ*: Elliston Secondary Modern School, Cleethorpes. *Studied*: Grimsby School of Art (1965-68); R.C.A. (1968-71). *Exhib*: one-man shows, New Art Centre, London (1970-72), Fischer Fine Art, London (1974, 1976, 1978, 1981), Vienna (1976), W. Germany (1976), Sweden (1979). *Works in collections*: Arts Council, Contemporary Art Soc. *Address*: Hall Lodge, Holton-cum-Beckering, Wragby, Lincoln. *Signs work*: "D. H. Smith."

SMITH, Edward John Milton, ATD (1952), NDD 2nd Cl. Hons. (1951), FSAE; artist in lettering, writing and illumination; Principal Lecturer, Subject Leader (Art) PGCE Course, Leeds Polytechnic 1963-85 (now retd); art teacher, West Monmouth School, Pontypool (1952-62); visiting lecturer, Newport College of Art (1954-62); President NSAE (1972). *b*: Stonehouse, Glos., 3 May 1922. *s of*: Edward Milton Smith. one *s*. two *d*. *Educ*: Central

School, Stroud, Glos. *Studied*: Stroud School of Art (1936-38), Gloucester College of Art (1939-40), Leeds College of Art (1946-52). *Address*: c/o 58 Mountbatten Avenue, Sandal, Wakefield, W. Yorks WF2 6HD.

SMITH, Elizabeth Anne, RSMA (President). *Medium*: pastel. *b*: 1950. *Studied*: Winchester School of Art; Bournemouth and Poole College of Art. *Exhib*: RSMA, PS, RBSA. *Commissions*: BASF; National Power; BP; South Tees Health Authority. *Address*: 43 The Rydes, Bodicote, Banbury, Oxfordshire OX15 4EJ. *Website*: www.elizabethasmith.co.uk *Signs work*: 'Elizabeth A.Smith'.

SMITH, Graham, NDD; Samuel Jones Post Graduate Award (1961-62); Committee Member, Printmakers Council. *Medium*: drawing, prints, artists books. *b*: Exeter, 4 Feb 1941. *s of*: F.C. Smith & Jane Coakley. *m*: Susanna King. two *s*. one *d*. *Educ*: Roan Grammar School (1952-57). *Studied*: Camberwell School of Arts & Crafts (1957-61). *Exhib*: Print shown: 'Originals 05', 10, Mall Galleries; Lessedra Mini Print Exhibition (2003, 04, 05); Major Show of Prints, Stark Gallery (2005); Exhibitor, Artists Books Show, ICA (2006); various book fairs (2007-14). Solo show Deco Galleries, Whitstable (2008). Work shown with Printmakers Council exhibitions (2003-2014). *Works in collections*: various private collections. *Publications*: illustrated article, "Mangle to Printing Press", Printmaking Today (2004); Featured in 'In Praise of Beautiful Book' published by BNC Books (2014). *Works Reproduced*: Linocut print in 'Showcase' feature, 'Computer Arts Projects' (Feb 2007). *Clubs*: Phoenix AWC. *Address*: 51 Murillo Street, London SE13 5QG. *Email*: gs.prints@virgin.net *Website*: www.gfsmith.net *Signs work*: "G.F.SMITH".

SMITH, Gregor, RSW, DA (1966), Post-grad. scholarship (1967); artist in oil and water-colour. *b*: Renton, Dunbartonshire, 15 Jul 1944. *s of*: Rev. Henry Smith, MA (decd). *m*: Elizabeth. *Educ*: Wishaw High School. *Studied*: Edinburgh College of Art (1962-67). *Exhib*: RSA, RSW, RI, Compass Gallery, Glasgow, numerous group and one-man shows. *Works in collections*: HRH The Duke of Edinburgh, SAC, numerous educ. authorities and district councils. *Address*: 'Waveney', Argyll Rd, Kilcreggan, Helensburgh, Dunbartonshire G84 0JR. *Signs work*: "Gregor Smith."

SMITH, Ivor Stanley, MA, LL.D., RIBA, AA Dip.; consultant architect; educational consultant, Professor Emeritus. *b*: Leigh-on-Sea, Essex. *s of*: H.S. Smith, MA. *m*: Audrey. one *s*. three *d*. *Studied*: Southend School of Art; Bartlett, Cambridge; AA Schools of Architecture. *Address*: 28 Victoria Park, Cambridge, CB4 3EL. *Email*: ivor.arch@btinternet.com *Signs work*: "Ivor Smith."

SMITH, Jenny, SSA; BA (Hons) Drawing & Painting (1st Class), MA Print; Awards include: Royal Scottish Academy Award for Painting; Farquar Reid Scholarship; Scottish Arts Council Creative Development Award. *Medium*: drawing, prints, artists books, painting, film. *b*: Leicester, 14 Jul 1965. *d of*: Brian & Marjorie Smith. *Studied*: Duncan of Jordanstone College of Art, Dundee (1990-1993); University of the West of England (2005-2007). *Exhib*: (selected): Royal Academy; Royal Scottish Academy; RWA; National Galleries of Scotland; Open Eye Gallery, Edinburgh; Cupar Arts; Apex Hotels; RGI. *Works in collections*: National Galleries of Scotland, Tate, Scottish Amicable, Gracefields Arts Centre - Dumfries, University of Dundee, New Hall Collection - Cambridge, Western General Edinburgh; British Midland Airways, Royal Bank of Scotland, Ask Plc, LEEL, Chhaap Print Trust, India, ECA, Edinburgh City Libraries. *Commissions*: Personal Group Holdings Plc. *Publications*: Jenny Smith: Drawings & Paintings & Prints, In Praise of Beautiful Books, momentum, What is the Best Advice You've Been Given?, What is the Most Important Decision You Have Made?. *Works Reproduced*: Art Review, AN, Scotsman, Glasgow Herald, Fife Herald, Fife Courier. *Clubs*: Professional member of Society of Scottish Artists. *Address*: Studio 10, Bonnington Mill, 72 Newhaven Road, Edinburgh, EH6 5QG. *Email*: jenny@jennysmith.org.uk *Website*: www.jennysmith.org.uk *Signs work*: "Jenny Smith" on reverse.

SMITH, Jesse, BA (Hons) 1988, Postgrad. Dip. (1992); artist in mixed media, visiting lecturer. *b*: London, 5 Aug 1966. *m*: Sharon Purves. one *d*. *Studied*: Norwich School of Art (1985-88), RA Schools (1989-92). *Exhib*: solo shows: One Gallery, Brick Lane, London (1999), Ozten Zeki Gallery, Walton St. London (1997-98); group shows: Bow Wow, Holland Pk. (1999), Clink St. Gallery, London Bridge (1999), R.A. Summer Show (1999), Studio 3 Gallery, Old St. London (1995-98). *Address*: 67 Whipps Cross Rd., Leytonstone, London E11 1NJ.

SMITH, Joan, MA (Hons) (1987), Postgrad. Dip. in Painting (1988), MFA (1989); artist in acrylic, oil and mixed media on canvas and paper, lithography; Lecturer in Drawing and Painting, Edinburgh College of Art. *b*: Dundee, 28 Jun 1964. *Educ*: Monifieth High School, Dundee. *Studied*: Edinburgh University (1982-87, Prof. Fernie), Edinburgh College of Art (1982-89, Prof. David Michie). *Exhib*: solo shows: Collective Gallery, Edinburgh (1992), Crawford Art Centre, St. Andrews (1993); many group shows, Pier Art Centre, Orkney (1994), Christopher Boyd Gallery, Galasheils (1995). *Works in collections*: RSA, Edinburgh College of Art, Edinburgh City Art Centre, Heriot Watt University, Glasgow Museums and Art Galleries. *Publications*: Drawing Comparisons (1997). *Address*: 14 Coillesdene Gdns., Edinburgh EH15 2JS. *Signs work*: "Joan Smith."

SMITH, Jonathan, DA; PGCE (A&D); Alexander Barker Award (1979). *Medium*: oil, acrylic, ,drawing. *b*: Aberdeen, 16 Feb 1958. *s of*: D J Smith DA; J B Smith DA. *m*: Catherine Smith BSc Hon, MA Dist. two *s*. *Educ*: Ellon Academy, Aberdeen; Nicolson Inst., Stornoway. *Studied*: Grays School of Art, Aberdeen (1976-80). *Represented by*: The Barry Keene Gallery, Henley-on-Thames; Will's Art Warehouse, London SW. *Exhib*: RBA (2006, 2014); Barry Keene Gallery; Fairfax Gallery Tunbridge Wells; RA (2004); RCA (2005); AAF London; Brighton Festival (various); Maltby Contemporary Art, Winchester; Henley Festival; Brighton Art Fair; Will's Art Warehouse; New York, San Francisco. *Works in collections*: private collections UK, USA, Europe and Far East. *Official Purchasers*: East Sussex CC; Art and Museum Service; Art for Hospitals. *Principal Works*: 'Old Boat' (exhib. RA 2004); 'Boat Shed, St. Ives' (RCA, 2005), 'Hebridean Beach' (RBA Henley 2007), 'Field, North Norfolk' (RBA 2014). *Recreations*: music, walking. *Misc*: Head of Art, Varndean College, Brighton. *Address*: 24 South Way, Lewes, East Sussex BN7 1LU. *Email*: jonathansmithart@googlemail.com. *Website*: www.jonathansmithart.co.uk *Signs work*: 'Jonathan Smith'.

SMITH, Keir, BA Fine Art (1973); artist and teacher. *b*: Gravesend, Kent, 1950. *m*: Clare. *Studied*: University of Newcastle upon Tyne (1969-73), postgraduate study, Chelsea School of Art (1973-75). *Exhib*: selected solo shows: 'Mark/Meaning' AIR Gallery, London (1977); 'Like Nimrod's Tower' Acme Gallery, London (1980); 'Sailing Ancient Seas' Ceolfrith Gallery and Ikon Gallery (1982); 'Navigator' Rochdale A.G. and nautical tour (1984); 'The Dreaming Track' Laing Gallery, Newcastle upon Tyne and Wolverhampton A.G. (1989); 'Flint Sepulchre' Mead Gallery and Bury St. Edmunds A.G. (1994); 'Ognissanti' Concourse Gallery, Barbican Centre (1998), Enclosed Garden, Lincoln Cathedral (2001). *Commissions*: 'The Iron Road' Forest of Dean (1986); 'The Way of Clouds' Usher Gallery, Lincoln (1990); 'From the Dark Cave' Henrietta House, London (1992); 'Stefano' - Enabled by Sculpture at Goodwood (1997). *Publications*: 'Ognissanti. Essays by Keir Smith, William Furlong and Ann Elliott' (1998); 'Towards the Eremitani'. Essay by Keir Smith (2000); 'Enclosed Garden'. Essay by Keir Smith (2001). All titles available on request from address below. *Address*: 19 Florence Rd., New Cross, London SE14 6TW.

SMITH, Ken. *Medium*: sculpture and printmaking. *b*: Manchester, 1944. *Educ*: Carpentry apprenticeship. *Studied*: Walthamstow College of Art; Bristol College of Art. *Represented by*: Bruton Gallery Ltd., and others. *Exhib*: Royal Academy, London; Royal West of England Academy; Manchester City Art Gallery; Cardiff City Art Gallery; Leighton House, London;

Cork Street, London; Bath, Bristol, Leeds, etc. *Works in collections*: University of Vienna; Phillips Collections; private collections. *Commissions*: Large Scale commission in Majorca (2003). *Principal Works*: Stone carved figures and groups. *Address*: c/o Bruton Gallery, P O Box 145, Holmfirth, Yorks., HD9 1YU.

SMITH, Leo Illesley Gibbons, PUA; Pres. United Society of Artists, past mem. of Executive Council, Federation of British Artists, past Vice-Pres. Soc. of Graphic Fine Arts, past Pres. Herts. Visual Arts Forum; painter in water-colour, pastel, acrylic, landscape, portrait, works of the imagination; Art Director in publishing and advertising, illustrator, typographer; latterly art editorial, Radio Times. *b*: Cobham, Surrey. *s of*: Cecil Arthur Smith, engineer, and Ethel Illesley Smith. *m*: Constance Hilda (decd). one *d*. *Educ*: Queen Elizabeth's Grammar School Kingston. *Studied*: Hornsey College of Art (1945-49). *Exhib*: Mall Galleries, RBA, RI, RP, PS, NEAC, RWS; several one-man shows. *Works in collections*: Ealing Educ. Com. *Publications*: UA News and Views. *Address*: 207 Sunnybank Rd., Potters Bar, Herts. EN6 2NH. *Signs work*: "Leo Gibbons Smith" or "L.I.G.S."

SMITH, Marion, BA Hons (1991), ARSA (1998), RSA (2005); 2000 Sir William Gillies Bequest, RSA; 2003 Thyne Scholarship, English Speaking Union; 2010 Sir William Gillies Bequest. *Medium*: Sculpture in stone, wood, metal, mixed media; printmaking and bookmaking. *b*: St. Andrews, 14 Feb 1969. *Studied*: Grays School of Art, Aberdeen (1987-1991). *Exhib*: solo exhib: Park Gallery, Falkirk (2009), Patriothall Gallery, Edinburgh (2005), Bonhoga Gallery, Shetland (2004), Crawford Arts Centre, St. Andrews (1997); Group Exhibitions: Iwate Art Festival, Japan (1998); Scandex, Stavanger, Norway (1995); Lulea, Sweden; Kemi, Finland. *Works in collections*: Royal Scottish Academy, St. Andrews University, Scottish Poetry Library, Edinburgh, University of Dundee. *Commissions*: Lock Leven (2014), Lancastria Memorial, Clydebank (2011), The Plough and Reaper, Austruther, Fife (2009), Panmure Passage, Dundee (2009), Loch Leven (2008), Fine Ball, Linlithgow (2007). *Address*: Royal Scottish Academy, The Mound, Edinburgh, RH2 2EL. *Email*: info@marionsmithsculpture.co.uk *Website*: marionsmithsculptor.co.uk *Signs work*: "Marion W Smith."

SMITH, Peter Macdonald, Fine Arts Hons Degree; oil painting - both figurative and abstract, pencil; seascapes worked mostly out in front of the subject or from drawings and memory; also abstract in oil plus acrylic collages since the mid 80s. *b*: Hinckley, Leics, 6 Oct 1945. *s of*: Joan and Harry Smith. *Educ*: Secondary Modern, Hinckley, Leics. *Studied*: Falmouth College of Art. *Exhib*: Newlyn Society of Artists, Penwith Society of Artists, various St. Ives galleries, plus gallery mixed shows in Bristol, Cheltenham, Basingstoke, Cambridge and Mall Galleries, London, 'Webbs Road Fine Art', Battersea, London. *Publications*: 'Drawings to the End of the Century', 'Newlyn Society of Artists'. *Recreations*: gardening, sailing, listening to music, collecting contemporary ceramics. *Clubs*: Sailing Club, St. Mary's. *Misc*: love ceramics which I also made at college - I buy other peoples now. *Address*: The Bungalow, Rocky Hill, St. Mary's, Isles of Scilly, TR21 0NE. *Website*: www.petermacdonaldsmith.co.uk. *Signs work*: Peter Smith.

SMITH Richard Michael BA (Hons) (1993); winner, Carroll Foundation award (RP); painter in oil on canvas, pastel, pencil . *b*: Warlingham, Surrey, 15 Jun 1957. three *s*. one *d*. *Educ*: Caterham School. *Studied*: Coventry Art School (1977-80, Colin Saxton, Harry Weinberger), and in studio of John Ward, RA. *Exhib*: RA Summer Exhbns., RP, Brian Sinfield Gallery, Burford, Portland Gallery, London, David Messum Gallery, London. *Works in collections*: GLC. *Commissions*: Dr. Robert Runcie, Past Archbishop of Canterbury; Lord Plumb, Past President of European Parliament; Mr. Justice Owen; Mr. John Fenwick. *Address*: Flat 5, Stangrave Hall, Godstone, Surrey RH9 8NB. *Email*: richardsmith.gallery@btinternet.co.uk *Website*: www.richardsmith.gallery.btinternet.co.uk *Signs work*: "Richard Smith," "R.S." or "R.M.S."

SMITH, Rita, BA (Hons) (1978), HDFA (Lond.) (1980); Winner of The Guinness Award for best first-time exhibitor at Royal Academy of Art Summer Exhibition, 1993; artist in water-colour, oil and etching. *b*: London, 9 Mar 1946. two *s*. *Educ*: Collingwood School for Girls. *Studied*: Camberwell School of Art (1974-78), Slade School of Fine Art (1978-80), Boise Travelling Scholarship (1980). *Represented by*: Art Mill Gallery, Plymouth. *Exhib*: The Townmill Galleries, Lyme Regis; Thelma Hulbert Gallery, Honiton; Chapel Gallery, Saltram House, Devon; Plymouth Arts Centre; University of Surrey; Royal Academy of Arts Summer Exhibition (1993, 1997, 1998, 2003); Singer and Friedlander/Sunday Times Watercolour Competition (1995, 1997, 1998, 2000); SW Academy Open (2001-2005). *Works in collections*: National Trust, Guinness plc, University College London, University of Surrey. *Address*: 1 Gnaton Terr., Albaston, nr. Gunnislake, Cornwall PL18 9AG. *Email*: smithandarcher@aol.com *Website*: www.ritasmith.org.uk *Signs work*: "RITA SMITH."

SMITH, Ronald F., RGI (1999), RSW (2008). PAI (2012); David Cargill Award (RGI, 1997); John Cunningham Award (RGI, 2001); Inverarity Travel Award (RGI, 2008); House for an Art Lover Award (PAI, 2010); Rendezvous Gallery Award (RSW, 2012); University of the West of Scotland Award (Paisley Art institute Annual Exhibition 2013). *Medium*: oil on canvas, gouache on board. *b*: Glasgow, 1946. *Partner*: Yvonne. *Educ*: Hillhead High School. *Studied*: Glasgow School of Art: graduated in Drawing and Painting (1969). *Exhib*: RGI; RSA (Festival Exhbn), PAI; Ainscough Contemporary Art, London; Portland Gallery; Thompson's Gallery, London; Edgar Modern Art, Bath; Lemon Street Gallery, Truro; RSW; Billcliffe Gallery, Glasgow. *Works in collections*: internationally. *Commissions*: Cunard: Queen Mary II. *Publications*: BBC Your Paintings website (Public Catalogue Foundation). *Official Purchasers*: Glasgow City Council; Leeds Education Authority; Lanarkshire Education Authority; Walter Scott & Partners. *Recreations*: squash; eating. *Clubs*: Glasgow Art Club. *Address*: c/o Glasgow Art Club, 185 Bath Street, Glasgow G2 4HU. *Email*: r.smith33@virginmedia.com *Website*: gallery websites *Signs work*: 'SMITH' (on paintings): 'RONALD F SMITH' (on back).

SMITH, Simon, ARBS; Member, Master Carvers Association; Graduate, City & Guilds Institute; Member, Art Workers Guild. *Medium*: stone, marble, clay, brick, bronze. *b*: 18 Nov 1964. *s of*: Jeremy & Mary Smith. *Partner*: Isabel Graham-Yooll. one *d*. *Studied*: City and Guilds of London Art School, London. *Exhib*: Geedon Gallery, Colchester, Essex. *Commissions*: public and private commissions. *Principal Works*: statue of Sir Hans Sloane, Duke of York Square, London; Cherubs and Cartouche, UCS School, London. *Address*: Unit 3, Fishers Court, Besson Street, London SE14 5AS. *Email*: stonecarving@simonsmith.plus.com *Website*: www.simonsmith.plus.com *Signs work*: "SIMON SMITH".

SMITH POLYBLANK, Emily Elizabeth. *Medium*: woodcuts & lino. *b*: Whitstable, 1 Mar 1968. *d of*: Tony Ronald Smith RA & Linda Clarke-Smith. *m*: Julian Polyblank. one *s*. one *d*. *Educ*: Rudolf Steiner, Chartham, Kent. *Studied*: Maidstone Art College (Foundation, 1987-88); Farnham College of Art and Design (1988-91). *Exhib*: Royal Academy Summer Exhibition (1996, 2009); Mall Galleries (2003, 2008); Chapel Gallery, Saltrum House, Devon (2000); Affordable Arts Fair, Battersea; The Whibley Galleries Contemporary Prints (1997). *Commissions*: Amanda Cottrell (Sheriff of Kent & Justice of the Peace); Moira Anderson. *Principal Works*: Long Dog", "Oblivious", "Its an Animals Life". *Recreations*: walking dogs, sketching, gardening, swimming. *Address*: Old Church School, The Street, Shadoxhurst, Ashford, Kent TN26 1LU. *Email*: print@emilysmithpolyblank.co.uk *Website*: www.emilysmithpolyblank.co.uk

SNOW Graham DipAD (1968), H.Dip (1972); Mombusho scholar, Japan (1974-77), Artist in Residence, Cambridge University (1977-81); artist in oil and water-colour; *b*: Exeter, 28 Oct 1948. *Educ*: Colfox School, Dorset. *Studied*: Bournemouth College of Art

(1966-68), Hornsey College of Art (1968-70), Slade School of Fine Art (1970-72). *Exhib*: one-man shows in London, New York and Tokyo. *Works in collections*: Arts Council, Chase Manhattan Bank, Texaco, etc. *Address*: c/o Grob Gallery, 20 Dering St., London W1R 9AA. *Signs work*: "G. SNOW."

SNOWDEN, Matthew, BA Hons (1993, Industrial Design); Wirral Society Arts National Open, Joint First Prize Winner 2006, Award Winner 2007. *Medium*: acrylic, palette knife. *b*: Heswall, 7 Nov 1969. *s of*: David A. Snowden & Diana M. Brown. *Studied*: Withens Lane Art College (1989); Teesside University (1990-93). *Represented by*: Galleri Betws-y-Coed; Gorstella Gallery, Chester; McAllister Thomas, Godalming; Kooywood Gallery, Cardiff. *Exhib*: One-man shows: Over 20 Clwyd Theatre Cymru, North Wales; Hanover Gallery, Liverpool; Magenta Gallery; Dee Fine Arts; Gallery Betws-y-Coed; Kooywood Gallery, Cardiff; Gorstella Gallery. Group exhibitions: British Watercolour Society; Williamson Art Gallery; RCA; RI, London; RSMA; RWS Open; View Two Gallery, Liverpool; RI, Mayfair; Gorstella Gallery, Chester; Oriel Tegfryn, Anglesey; Oriel Kyffin Williams; Oriel Plas Glyn-y-Weddw, N.Wales; Artroom; Wirral Society of Arts; McAllister Thomas; Galerie Archange, Paris; Oriel-yns-Mon. *Works in collections*: Williamson Art Gallery & Museum; National Library of Wales. *Official Purchasers*: Williamson Art Gallery & Museum; National Library of Wales. *Works Reproduced*: 12. *Address*: 'Carrick', 63 Hillside Road, Heswall, Wirral, CH60 0BL. *Email*: matthewsnowden@hotmail.com *Website*: www.matthewsnowden.co.uk *Signs work*: "MATTHEW SNOWDEN".

SNOWDEN, Richard Connal, *b*: Harewood, Leeds, 11 May 1950. *Partner*: Claire Thomas. one *s*. one *d*. *Educ*: Fylingham School, Robin Hood's Bay, Whitby. *Studied*: Cirencester (1969-71). *Represented by*: The Packhouse Gallery, Harewood; Zillah Bell, Thirsk; Colourbox. *Exhib*: Includes solo: Vernon Gallery, Preston (1969-70); Victoria Gallery, Harrogate (1969-75, 1978-79); Aquarius Gallery, Harrogate (1978); Zillah Bell Gallery; The Packhouse Gallery, Leeds. Group: The ICI Gallery, Middlesborough (1970); The Delahaye Gallery, Cirencester (1974); Walker Art Gallery, Liverpool (1985); The Laing Collection Exhibition, Harrogate Art Gallery (1991); Leeds City Art Gallery (2003, 2004); Affordable Art Fair, London (2007-14). *Works in collections*: Private and corporate. *Clubs*; North Yorkshire Open Studios. *Address*: Wharfedale Grange, Harrowgate Road, Harewood, Leeds LW17 9LW. *Email*: richard@wharfedalegrange.co.uk *Website*: www.richardsnowden.co.uk *Signs work*: "SNOWDEN".

SOAN, Hazel Penelope, BA Hons; Awards: Holbrook Trust Prize (1976), SAA Book & Video of the Year (1999). *Medium*: painter. *b*: UK, 1 Aug 1954, married. one *s*. *Educ*: Camberwell & Leicester (1972-76). *Represented by*: self, and M1 Fine Art, London. *Exhib*: include Royal Academy; Midland Open; Barbican; Mall Galleries; CCA Gallery, Tokyo; London Contemporary Art, USA; British Council Museo de Bellas Artes, Caracas, Venezuela; EU Embassy, Namibia; Zimbabwe Embassy, London; Anna Mei. *Works in collections*: including: Chadwick, London; M1 Fine Art, London; National Portrait Gallery; BBC; Trowbridge Museum & Art Gallery; BP; Chelsea & Westminster. *Commissions*: inc. The Ritz Hotel, London; The Durban Hilton. Numerous portraits, EU, Namibian Embassy. *Publications*: Artists' Stories, Artist Magazine, Kunst for Alle (Norway). Author of 12 books on Watercolour (Harper Collins, Batsford, Search Press). *Official Purchasers*: BP, The Ritz Club, The Churchill, The Lister, Conrad Hilton, The EU. *Works Reproduced*: by CCA Galleries, London Contemporary Art, Rosentiels, Athena, De Montfort Fine Art. *Principal Works*: Murals Durban Hilton, Nazareth House Cape Town, Red & Blue Ele, EU Namibia. *Clubs*: Chelsea Arts Club, Hurlingham. *Misc*: TV: Art Expert on 'Watercolour Challenge' (Ch4, 2000, 01, 02); own two series' 'Splash of Colour' (Anglia TV, 1996, 97), 'Great Picture Chase' (BBC). Studios in London and Cape Town. *Address*: Soan Studio, Crookham Road, London SW6 4EG. *Email*: hsoan@iafrica.com *Website*: www.hazelsoan.com *Signs work*: "Hazel Soan".

SOAR, John Richardson, MA (1966), BSc (1952), ARMS (1996), HS (1989); landscape painter in pastel (from miniature to large size pastel paintings); Principal, Swindon Technical College and School of Art (retd 1984); Inspector of Further Education for Essex CC (1965-70). *b*: London, 30 May 1927. *s of*: John C. Soar (decd). *m*: Miriam Theresa. one *s*. one *d*. *Educ*: West Ham Municipal College; King's College, London. *Exhib*: UA (annually), Westminster Gallery; Hilliard Soc. of Miniaturists (annually), Wells; RMS Westminster Gallery (annually); World Exhbn. of Miniatures (1995); regular contributor to Medici Gallery and Llewellyn Alexander Gallery, London. *Works in collections*: mostly in West of England, USA, Canada and various European countries. *Clubs*: Guild of Wiltshire Artists (President). *Address*: 81 Chestnut Springs, Lydiard Millicent, Swindon, Wilts. SN5 3NB. *Signs work*: "JOHN SOAR."

SOBIEN, Inka, (aka STEVEN, Inka); Grand Prix Humanitaire de France avec Medaille d'Argent (1977), La Palme D'or, Belgo-Hispanique (1977); artist; lecturer, Hornsey College of Art and Central Academy of Film, Art and Drama, London (1963-66), St. Martin's School of Art (1963-67). *b*: 25 Feb 1939. *d of*: Prof. Sobieniewski Zdzislaw. *m*: Stewart Steven (decd). one *s*. *Studied*: St. Martin's School of Art (1959-63). *Exhib*: one-man shows: Upper St. Gallery, London (1974), Gallerie Raymond Duncan, Paris (1975), New Jersey (1975), Ligoa Duncan, NY (1975), Philadelphia (1975), Florida (1976), Festival International de Peinture et d'Art Graphico-Plastique de St. Germain-des-Pres, Paris (1976), Scribes Writers' Club, London (1978), Little Palace, Warsaw (1979), BWA Gallery, Cracow (1979), Avant Garde Gallery, Wroclaw (1979), Barbican Centre (1985), Budapest (1985), Camden Arts Centre (1989); mixed shows: Grande Palais Paris; London: Marjorie Parr Gallery, Gallery XVIII, Annely Juda Fine Art, Leinster Fine Art, Salomon Gallery, Inka's Extravaganza ('97, '98, 2001), 'Inka's Story' Cork Street Gallery, London (2003). *Works in collections*: National Museum, Warsaw and Cracow, Museum of Modern Art, Budapest. *Address*: 15 Charlwood House, Strand Drive, Kew, Surrey, TW9 4DP. *Email*: inkasteven@btinternet.com *Signs work*: "Inka Sobien."

SOFILAS, Mark Peter, *Medium*: oil. *b*: Australia, 24 Mar 1961. *s of*: Peter & Rose Marie Sofilas. *Partner*: Katherine Newman. two *d*. *Studied*: Perth (Western Australia) Technical College (Diploma in Graphic Design); The School of Self-taught. *Represented by*: The Pepper Gallery, London, and all galleries listed in 'Exhibited'. *Exhib*: The Biscuit Factory, Newcastle; Harrison Lord Gallery, Brighouse; Zillah Bell Gallery, Thirsk; Art in the Mill, Knaresborough; Look Gallery, Helmsley; Artsbank, Saltburn-by-the-Sea; Affordable Art Fair, London; Leeds Gallery, Leeds. *Works in collections*: The Wiley Group Private Collection (Perth, Australia); Limited Edition book in the Permanent Library of The White House, Washington DC. *Commissions*: The Wiley Group, Perth, Australia. *Address*: 18 Oakwood Drive, Oakwood, Leeds, West Yorkshire LS8 2AE. *Email*: mark@marksofilasart.com *Website*: www.marksofilasart.com *Signs work*: "M.SOFILAS".

SOLOWAY, Louise Joanne, BA Fine Art; Baroda Scholarship. *Medium*: watercolour, drawing. *b*: London 27 Feb 1962. *d of*: Audrey & Alan Soloway. *m*: Reynold Chan. one *s*. *Studied*: Bath Academy of Fine Art, Corsham; Harrow College of FE. *Exhib*: Whitechapel Open; BP Portrait Awards; Museum of London Transport; exhbn. of drawings at Spitalfields Health Centre (sponsored by Whitechapel Gal.); Hillside Gallery, Edinburgh; Gallery 7, Hong Kong; China Club, Hong Kong. *Works in collections*: British Council, Bombay; Timothy Hyman; Homerton Hospital; Hackney Museum of London Transport; Whitechapel Library; Airport Authority Hong Kong. *Commissions*: London International Financial Futures Exchange; Oxford House Community Centre; Salomon Brothers Hong Kong Chek Lapkok Airport; Smithkline Beecham; Royal Bank of Scotland; new station wall reliefs for MTR Hong Kong. *Address*: c/o Derwent Cottage, 1060 High Road, Whetstone, London N20 0QP. *Email*: lou_@hotmail.com

SONGHURST, Anne. *Medium*: oil. *b*: Ashford, Kent, 19 Jan 1946. *m*: Peter. two *d*. *Represented by*: Wren Gallery, Burford; Norton Way Gallery, Letchworth; The Marylebone Gallery, London. *Exhib*: Mall Galleries, W H Patterson (2005), Hitchin Museum and Art Gallery, Chapel Gallery, Riseley (2000-2007), Royal Academy (2009), Llewelyn Alexander Gallery (2002-2009. *Works in collections*: private and public. *Address*: 7 Stotfold Road, Hitchin, Herts, SG4 0QN. *Email*: anne.songhurst@ntlworld.com *Website*: www.annesonghurst.co.uk *Signs work*: "A SONGHURST".

SOPHIA-WHITE, Elizabeth Mary. *Medium*: oil, acrylic, pastel. Sculpture in clay, plaster, bronze. *b*: Hatfield, 26 Apr 1948. *d of*: Alexander Sturrock. *Studied*: 5 years with Jean Gibson, Royal College of Art; 5 years with Karin Jonzen, Associate Academician. *Represented by*: Pangolin. *Exhib*: Gloucester Cathedral, Eastnor Castle, Royal Academy. *Works in collections*: private. *Commissions*: private portrait sculpture. *Principal Works*: 'Broody', 'Warrior', 'Masai', 'Islamic Woman', 'Arriving at Alayrac'. *Clubs*: The Landsdowne *Address*: Brookhill Cottage, Upper Mitchell, Ledbury, HR8 1JF. *Email*: sohiawhite85@btinternet.com *Website*: elizabethsophiawhite.com *Signs work*: "Elizabeth White", "Elizabeth Sturrock", "E.M.S."

SOREL, Agathe, RWS, RE, Churchill Fellow (1967), Fellow, Printmakers Council; printmaker, sculptor, lecturer. *Medium*: sculpture, prints, watercolours, artist's books. *b*: Budapest, 1935. *m*: G. Sitkey. one *s*. *Studied*: Academy of Fine Art, and Academy of Applied Art, Budapest; Camberwell School of Art and Crafts; Atelier 17, Paris. *Represented by*: RWS, RE and Sandra Higgins. *Works in collections*: in 43 major museums including BM, Tate Gallery, Los Angeles Museum of Art, Philadelphia Museum of Art, Chicago Art Inst., National Gallery, Washington. *Publications*: illustrated: Jean Genet, Le Balcon, 'Catalana Blanca' in collaboration with Lorand Gaspar; 'The Book of Sand' in collaboration with David Gascoyne, Text Messages (2007). *Official Purchasers*: DCMS Government Art Collections, British Library, British Museum. *Works Reproduced*: Printmaking Today, Print Quarterly, Art & Metier du Livre, The Tamarind Papers. *Address*: Dorrell Hall, 43 London Rd., London SE23 3TY. *Email*: agathe@sorel.eclipse.co.uk *Website*: www.agathesorel.co.uk *Signs work*: "Agathe Sorel."

SORRELL, Julia, RI, RBA; BA, Post-Grad RA Schools; artist/tutor. *Medium*: painter in all media. *b*: Westcliff-on-Sea, 4 Aug 1955. *d of*: Alan & Elizabeth Sorrell. *m*: Ian Sanders. two *s*. *Studied*: Southend College of Art (1972-73); Goldsmiths College (1973-76); RA Schools (1978-81). *Exhib*: RA Summer Exhbns, New Grafton Gallery, RBA, NEAC, Singer & Friedlander, RWS Open Shows, National Portrait Gallery, RI, Waterhouse & Dodd, Russell Gallery, Chappel Gallery, Maas Gallery (one-woman show), various exhbns nationwide. *Works in collections*: Chelmsford Museum and Art Gallery, Reading Museum Schools Service, National Portrait Gallery, Beecroft Art Gallery, Prof. Philip Rieff, Pennsylvania, various UK, USA and Europe. *Commissions*: Baron Ramsay of Canterbury, National Portrait Gallery, portrait commissions. *Publications*: 'The Artist' (2007, 2011), 'Tree News' (2006); Living Woods (2012); British Archaeology (2012). *Recreations*: textiles, travelling, walking. *Clubs*: RASAA. *Misc*: keen to uphold the importance of drawing. *Address*: Manor Farm, Wash Lane, Snetterton, Norfolk, NR16 2LG. *Email*: juliasorrell@ukartists.com *Website*: www.juliasorrell.ukartists.com

SORRELL, Richard, PPRWS; DipAD (1969), RA Schools Post. Grad. Cert. (1972), RWS (1978), RBA (1989), NEAC (1995); Past President, the Royal Watercolour Society. *Medium*: oil, water-colour and acrylic. *b*: Thundersley, Essex, 24 Sep 1948. *s of*: Alan and Elizabeth Sorrell, artists. *m*: Doreen Burke (divorced). *Partner*: Sue Ross. two *s*. *Educ*: Eton House School, Thorpe Bay, Essex. *Studied*: Walthamstow Art School (1965-66), Kingston College of Art (1966-69), RA Schools (1969-72). *Exhib*: RA, RWS, NEAC, Agnews, Leamington Art Gallery, Galleries Sternberg, Chicago, Russell Gallery, Porthminster

Gallery, St. Ives. *Works in collections*: V&A, Museum of London, National Trust. *Publications*: The Artist, Country Life. 'Alan Sorrell' ISBN 978-1-908326-37-9. *Clubs*: Art Workers Guild, Chelsea Arts Club. *Address*: Higher Hellangove Farm, Badgers Cross, Gulval, Penzance, Cornwall, TR20 8XD. *Email*: SorrellR@aol.com *Website*: www.richardsorrell.co.uk *Signs work*: "Richard Sorrell."

SOSNER, Robert, BAHons Fine Art; MA Design for Interactive Media; Bursary, Pollock Krasner Foundation, New York; Spanish Government Scholarship. *Medium*: Acrylic painting. *b*: London, 7 May 1958. *Studied*: Chelsea School of Art (1977-1980); Middlesex University (1997-1998). *Exhib*: RA Summer Show; Cadogan Contemporary; Surrey University; London Art Fair. *Commissions*: Numerous commissions over the past eight years for private residential spaces in Central London. *Address*: Flat 9, Arundel House, 22 The Drive, Hove BN3 3JD. *Email*: robert43uk@hotmail.com *Website*: www.robertsosner.com *Signs work*: "Robert Sosner".

SOUTHEY, Marilyn Sylvia April. *Medium*: oil, watercolour, drawing, prints. *b*: Zambia (N.Rhodesia) 17 Apr 1942. *d of*: Douglas & Sylvia MacKendrick. *m*: Verner Southey. one *s*. one *d*. *Educ*: Chaplin School, Gwelo, Zimbabwe (S.Rhodesia). *Studied*: Hornsey College of Art; Regent St. Polytechnic . *Exhib*: ROI, RWS, RI, RA Summer Exhbn; National Print Exhbn 'Originals '05'; Zimbabwe National Gallery; in France, and in International Print exhibitions. *Works in collections*: Royal Free Hospital; private collections. *Recreations*: gardening, reading, film, ballroom dancing. *Clubs*: SASA. *Address*: Flat 10, Southgrove House, South Grove, Highgate, London N6 6LP. *Email*: marilynsouthey@aol.com *Website*: www.marilynsoutheyshowcase.com *Signs work*: 'Marilyn Southey'.

SOWDEN, Trevor, ATD, NDD, Adv.Dip.Ceramics (Goldsmiths); Taught in Newham, London (1957-92), finally as Head of Faculty of Design and Technology, Snr. Assessor MREB (1983-87). *Medium*: relief printmaking, small sculpture, painting. *b*: Cardiff, 7 Apr 1933. *s of*: Reginald & Muriel Sowden. *m*: Madeleine Chabloz. one *s*. *Educ*: Hereford High School; Cathays High School, Cardiff. *Studied*: Cardiff College of Art (1950-54); Royal Navy (1954-56); University of Wales (1956-57); Goldsmiths (1979-80). *Represented by*: Bircham Gallery, Holt; Gainsborough's House, Sudbury; Seapictures Gallery; Lime Tree Gallery, Bristol and Long Melford. *Exhib*: Mall Galleries, London; Mandell's Gallery, Norwich; Westcliffe Gallery, Sheringham; Gainsborough's House, Sudbury; Rooksmoor Gallery, Bath; Peter Hedley Gallery, Wareham; Lime Tree Gallery, Bristol. *Works in collections*: Palace of Westminster; private collections in Europe and America. *Commissions*: numerous private commissions for sculpture, paintings and illustrations. *Official Purchasers*: Palace of Westminster Print Collection. *Recreations*: reading and working. *Clubs*: Member and ex-Chair, Gainsborough's House Printmakers; Elected Member and Past Secretary, East Anglian Group of Marine Artists. *Address*: 10 Harefield, Long Melford, Sudbury, Suffolk CO10 9DE. *Email*: tbsowden@btinternet.com *Signs work*: "Trevor Sowden".

SPACKMAN, Sarah, BA (1981); painter in oil, water-colour, gouache, charcoal. *b*: Reading, Berks., 19 Feb 1958. *Educ*: Abbey School, Reading. *Studied*: Byam Shaw School of Art (1977-78), Camberwell School of Art (1979-81). *Represented by*: Sarah Wiseman Gallery, Oxford; New Ashgate Gallery, Farnham; Campden Gallery, Chipping Campden, Glos; Josie Eastwood Fine Art, Hants; Jerram Gallery, Dorset. *Exhib*: Austin Desmond Fine Art, Cadogan Contemporary, New Ashgate Gallery, Farnham, Solomon Gallery, Dublin, Mitchell Gallery, Toronto, Canada; Het Cleyne Huys, Den Haag, The Netherlands; Sarah Wiseman Gallery, Oxford; Campden Gallery, Chipping Campden, Glos; Jerram Gallery, Sherborne, Dorset; Josie Eastwood Fine Art, Hants. *Works in collections*: Contemporary Art Collection, Allied Irish Bank, many private collections worldwide. *Commissions*: portraits, landscapes and still lives. *Publications*: Millers Guide; c20 Painters and Sculptors, ed. Frances Spalding. *Works Reproduced*: several paintings as posters and cards by The Art Group. *Address*: 12 Henley St., Oxford OX4 1ER. *Email*: spackmansarah@hotmail.com *Website*: sarahspackman.com *Signs work*: "S.S."

SPAFFORD, Iola Margaret, DFA (1953), RCA (1984), mem. MAFA.; artist in oil, pen and ink, water-colour, etching. *b*: Cambridge, 24 Aug 1930. *d of*: B.L. Hallward, MA. *m*: George Spafford (decd). one *s*. one *d*. *Educ*: Queen Anne's, Caversham. *Studied*: Bristol Art School (1947), Nottingham Art School (1948-50), Slade School of Fine Art (1950-54). *Exhib*: 8 one-man shows, Tib Lane Gallery, Manchester; Tegfryn Art Gallery, Menai Bridge, Anglesey; Snape Art Gallery, Suffolk; One-man show: Bebb & Seckers, Alderley Edge, Cheshire (April 23-May 8, 2012). *Works in collections*: Manchester A.G. (Rutherston Collection), Salford A.G., and many private collections here and abroad. *Recreations*: music, travel. *Address*: 57 Hawthorn La., Wilmslow, Ches. SK9 5DQ. *Signs work*: "Iola Spafford."

SPANKIE, Will, BA, MA. *Medium*: sculpture: stone and wood. *b*: Kent, 1967; married. two *d*. *Studied*: Degree in History, MA in Social Work; Sir John Cass School of Art, Whitechapel (1987-9); Central St. Martins School of Art (1989-91). *Exhib*: Garden Gallery; Moncrieff Bray Gallery; Penwith Gallery (Associate Member); The Stone Wall Gallery, Kaleidoscope Arts; Market House Gallery. *Commissions*: public and private commissions. *Publications*: Garden Gallery Collection. *Principal Works*: sculpture, lettering, garden ornamental. *Email*: will@willspankie.com *Website*: www.willspankie.com

SPARE, Richard John, BA. *Medium*: glass, prints. *b*: Chelmsford, Essex, 16 Apr 1951. *s of*: Charles & Phyllis Spare. *m*: Kay Greendale. two *s*. *Educ*: Billericay School. *Studied*: Thurrock Technical College (Foundation); Maidstone School of Art (BA). *Exhib*: frequent exhibitor at RA Summer Exhbn; invited exhibitor 'Discerning Eye', Mall Galleries; 'The Art on Paper Fair', RCA; National Print Exhbn; has exhibited widely throughout Japan, Australia, and UK. Solo shows in: Tokyo, Fukuoka, Osaka, Yokohama, Hiroshima, Matsuyama, Nara (Japan), Melbourne, London. *Works in collections*: Trevelyan College, University of Durham, Aston University. *Works Reproduced*: by The Art Group; 'Etching, A Guide to Traditional Techniques' (Alan Smith, pub. Crowood); 'Galerie d'Amour' (John Powls), Canns Down Press, Art Press Publishing Ltd; Museums and Galleries Marketing Ltd. *Recreations*: travel, visiting museums. *Address*: 72 Ravensbourne Park, London SE6 4XZ. *Email*: kayart@globalnet.co.uk *Website*: www.richardspare-kayspare.com *Signs work*: 'Richard Spare'.

SPELLER, Michael Phillip. *Medium*: sculpture. *b*: Romford, Essex, 20 Feb 1958. *s of*: Keith & Olive Speller. *m*: Sarah Speller. one *s*. *Studied*: Chelsea School of Art. *Exhib*: Kings Road Gallery, Woolff Gallery, Biscuit Factory, Art London, Affordable Art Fair, London Art Fair, The Gallery Cork Street, Fairfax Gallery, Gallery One, Expo Gallery T5 Heathrow. *Works in collections*: private and public, UK and worldwide. *Commissions*: "Equity" - Newham Health Authority; Loch Lomond Golf Club, Scotland; Drexel University, Philadelphi USA; Mougins School, South of France; Wing Tai Properties, Hong Kong. *Publications*: "At Home with Art" Tiddy Rowan Quadrille. *Principal Works*: Supportive Brothers; Family Tree; Secure; Balance; Commitment; Harmony; Momentum. *Address*: 42 Beaconsfield Road, Blackheath, London SE3 7LZ. *Email*: speller@sculpture2000.fsnet.co.uk *Website*: www.spellersculptures.com *Signs work*: "MS" or "MICHAEL SPELLER".

SPENCE, Leslie James Arthur, painter in oil. *b*: Wallasea, 30 Sep 1934. *m*: Mary. two *s*. one *d*. *Educ*: Leeds. *Studied*: under Prof. George McTaque. *Exhib*: RSMA, RBA, Royal Society, Birmingham Artists; solo exhibs. throughout UK. *Works in collections*: Westward TV, Rowntrees of York. *Commissions*: RN Devonport, Norwegian Royal Navy, Rowntrees of York, Arndale Developments, Royal Marines, Plymouth Sound Radio, Leeds Regional

Hospital Board, Chandos Records, Kunstanstalten May A.G., Germany, Lloyds Bank plc. *Publications*: reproductions published by Northern Editions, Solomon and Whitehead and others. *Clubs*: St. Ives Soc. of Artists, ECSofA. *Address*: Clifton Farmhouse, Landulph, Saltash, E. Cornwall PL12 6QG . *Signs work*: "L J A Spence."

SPENCER, Claire, NDD (1958), ARCA (1963), ATD (1973), RBSA (1980), PS (1985); painter in oil, water-colour and pastel. *b*: Kingsbury, Middx., 17 May 1937. one *s*. *Educ*: Harrow County School for Girls. *Studied*: Hornsey College of Art (1954-58), RCA (1960-63), Accademia di Belle Arti, Perugia (1966). Numerous individual and group exhbns. *Represented by*: Bridgeman Art Library for reproduction. *Exhib*: Major Retrospective, RBSA Galleries (2007). *Works in collections*: Nuffield Collection, West Midlands Arts Collection. *Publications*: contributor to The Artist Magazine, A Life with a View (Retrospective catalogue 2007). *Address*: 10 Sandbourne Drive, Bewdley, Worcs. DY12 1BN. *Email*: cpostins@gotadsl.co.uk *Signs work*: "Claire Spencer".

SPENCER, Gwen, NS; painter in oil, pastel and water-colour; member of the National Soc. of Painters, Sculptors and Printmakers since 1980. *b*: Argentine, 2 Oct 1927. *d of*: Edwin Arthur Conran, engineer. *m*: Christopher Spencer, FCA. two *s*. one *d*. *Educ*: St. Hilda's College, Buenos Aires. *Studied*: Atelier Josse, Buenos Aires, and Putney School of Art. *Exhib*: NS, ROI, PS, Ridley Soc., County Hall Westminster; Pump House, Battersea; Medici Gallery; Central Gallery, Great Yarmouth; Chelmsford Museum; Poole Art Centre; The Versicherungskammer, Bayern-Munich; The Menier Gallery, and others. *Works in collections*: UK, N.and S.America, Italy, Holland, Denmark, India and Australia. *Works Reproduced*: Medici Soc. *Misc*: member: Thames Valley Arts Society, Richmond Art Society. *Address*: 122 Copse Hill, Wimbledon, London SW20 0NL. *Signs work*: "Gwen Spencer" or "G. Spencer."

SPENCER, Liam David, BA; artist in oil paint. *b*: Burnley, 16 Apr 1964. *m*: Heather Walker. two *s*. *Educ*: Manchester Polytechnic (1983-86). *Represented by*: Clark Art, Hale, Cheshire. *Exhib*: touring exhbns. "Windows on the City" (1996-97), "The Mancunian Way" (1997-98), "Painting from Life: Twenty Years and Counting" (2010-2012), "Urban Panoramas" (2000) – The Lowry, Salford; "Manchester to Shanghai" (2006), Manchester Art Gallery; "Lasting Impressions" Adolphe Valette and Liam Spencer (2011). *Works in collections*: Towneley Hall A.G. and Museum, Burnley, Manchester City A.G., Readers Digest, NY, Touchstones, Rochdale, Salford Museum and Art Gallery. *Commissions*: Price Waterhouse, Manchester, Addleshaw, Booth & Co., Eversheds. *Publications*: 'Article of Faith' Richard Kendal Art Review (Oct. 1996), 'Landscape Next Door' Laura Gascoigne Artists and Illustrators (Sept. 1997), 'Urban Panoramas' David Sweet (2000), 'Liam Spencer - Painting from Life' (pub. Wendy J. Levy, Contemporary Art Ltd., 2004). *Recreations*: fly fishing, music. *Address*: Higher Bridge Clough Farm, Coal Pit Lane, Waterfoot, Rossendale BB4 9SB. *Email*: liam@liamspencer.demon.co.uk. *Website*: www.liamspencer.co.uk. *Signs work*: paintings signed on reverse.

SPENCER, Sarah, BA (Hons.) (1988), Post. Dip.RA.Schools (1991); painter in oil, charcoal, pastel; Elizabeth Greenshields Painting Awards & others. *Medium*: oils. *b*: Sevenoaks, 26 Sep 1965. *m*: Andrew Malone. one *s*. two *d*. *Educ*: Tonbridge Grammar School, West Kent College of FE. *Studied*: Camberwell School of Art and Crafts (1985-88), RA Schools (1988-91). *Exhib*: solo shows: New Grafton Gallery, Waterman's Fine Art, Russell Gallery, London; many mixed shows. *Works in collections*: West Wales Arts Council. *Publications*: 'Pure Gold' FBA; '500 Portraits' National Portrait Gallery. *Address*: 9 Cromwell Road, Whitstable, Kent CT5 1NW. *Email*: sarah@smalone2006.wanadoo.co.uk *Website*: www.sarah_spencer.co.uk *Signs work*: full signature on reverse of works, sometimes "S.S." on front.

SPENCER PRYSE, Tessa, RBA (1986); painter of portraits, landscapes and interiors in oil, water-colour, lithography. *b*: Highcliff on Sea, 28 Sep 1939. *d of*: Capt. Gerald Spencer Pryse, artist and lithographer. *m*: E.D.A. Cameron. one *s*. one *d*. *Educ*: France and Switzerland. *Studied*: Byam Shaw School of Art (1960-64, Peter Greenham, Bernard Dunstan). *Exhib*: RA, RP, RBA, NEAC, RSA, RWS; one-man shows: Phoenix Gallery, Lavenham, Hayletts Gallery, Colchester, Alpine Gallery, London, John Russell, Ipswich, Arthur Andersen, London, Llewellyn Alexander, London, Davies and Tooth, London, Wykeham Gallery, Stockbridge. *Works in collections*: Essex Museum. *Address*: 12 Alma St., Wivenhoe, Colchester, Essex CO7 9DL. *Signs work*: "PRYSE."

SPOWERS, Antonia Caroline. *Medium*: Drawing, sculpture. *b*: Knaresborough, 29 Jun 1934. three *s*. *Educ*: School in Hertfordshire. *Studied*: Paris (1950) Ateliers Souverbie and Anre Lhote; Adult Education, Camberley, Surrey (1971-1981). *Represented by*: Jagged Art, Devonshire Street, London. *Exhib*: Solo: Pumphouse Gallery and Subtropical Garden, Battersea Park (1995); Schumacher College, Devon (1996); Allen Gallery, Alton (1998); Brecknock Museum, Brecon (2000); Beatrice Royal Gallery, Eastleigh (2002); Tabernacle Gallery, MoMA Wales, Machynlleth (2005); Washington Gallery, Penarth (2006); Newport Museum and Gallery (2009); The Muse at 269, London (2012). *Works in collections*: Brecknock Museum and Gallery; Elgee Park Sculpture, nr Melbourne, Australia. *Commissions*: Mrs B Hunt, Baillieu Myer (Australia); Forestry Commission, Garwnant; NICP Holding, Royston. *Publications*: Landscape and Art Network Journal (2000); Resurgence (1996). *Official Purchasers*: Brecon Museum and Gallery; Elgee Park Scupture near Melbourne, Australia. *Works Reproduced*: Glass Mountain, RBS calendar. *Principal Works*: Kite, Ring, Dancing, Forming, Keeping, Watching, Phaganx, Glass Mountain; Not Quite Cloned; Trojan Horse; The Golden Gates. *Recreations*: Music, walking, gardening, travel. *Misc*: 18 @ 108 talk at RBS on glass (2007); Finalist Big Art Challenge, Channel 5 tv (2004); The Welsh Group at 60, ITV Wales. *Address*: 24 The Village, Clyro, Hereford HR3 5SF. *Email*: antonia.spowers@gmail.com *Website*: antoniaspowers.co.uk *Signs work*: "A.S."

SPRAKES, John, ROI, RBA; Andrew Grant scholarship, DA (Edin) post grad.; Prizewinner, Singer Friedlander/Sunday Times water-colour (1992), Manchester Academy (prize 85), Barclays Bank award (1986, 1991), P/P award (1989), The Le Clerc Fowle Gold Medal (ROI); DAS Award, The Stanley Grimm Prize; The Menena Joy Schwabe Award; UBS Award, Nationwide Building Society. *Medium*: oils, acrylic and watercolour. *b*: 17 Oct 1936. *s of*: T.B. Sprakes. *m*: Barbara Ann. three *s*. *Studied*: Doncaster College of Art, Edinburgh College of Art (1955-57). *Exhib*: RA; group and one-man shows. Work in public and private collections. *Works in collections*: Manchester City Art Gallery, UBS Collection, Singer Friedlander, Nationwide. *Works Reproduced*: several images reproduced in Books and Art magazine. *Clubs*: Mem. of The Manchester Academy, ROI, RBA. *Misc*: Agent Patrick Sprakes. *Address*: 39 Douglas Rd., Long Eaton, Notts NG10 4BH. *Website*: johnsprakes.com *Signs work*: "John Sprakes" or "J. Sprakes."

SPRINGS, John, American Society of Illustrators. *Medium*: ink, oil on canvas, acrylic. *b*: Leeds, Yorkshire 6 Feb 1960. *Educ*: Moorlands School, Leeds; Lawnswood School, Leeds. *Studied*: Park Lane College of Further Education. *Exhib*: Sally Hunter Gallery, Motcomb Street (1993); Rebecca Hossack Gallery, London (1998); Cartoon Gallery, London (1995). *Works in collections*: V & A, Chelsea Arts Club, Travellers' Club, private collections. *Commissions*: book illustrations, magazines (UK and USA). *Publications*: 'The Isles of the Sea' (Collins, 1983), The Spectator, Telegraph etc. *Official Purchasers*: private portraiture. *Recreations*: bodybuilding, motor sport. *Clubs*: Chelsea Arts Club, Travellers' Club, Savage Club. *Address*: 53/55 Dovehouse Street, London SW3 6JY. *Email*: john.springs@ft.com *Signs work*: Springs.

SPROULE, Lin, DES RCA; 1st & Silver Medal. *Medium*: goldwork, sculpture, oil painting, drawing. *b*: Oxford, 26 Feb 1942. *d of*: Donald Sproule, physicist & Elizabeth

Irving Watson, artist. one *s*. one *d*. *Educ*: Monkton Wylde School, Dorset. *Studied*: Colchester School of Art, Central School of Arts & Crafts; Royal College of Art; Slade School of Fine Art. *Represented by*: David Thomas, 65 Pimlico Road, London SW1W 8NE. *Exhib*: RA Summer Exhbns; Bear Lane Gallery, Oxford; Arnolfini Gallery, Bristol; V&A; Goldsmiths Hall, London, The Worshipful Company of Goldsmiths' Gold: Power and Allure; and New York; Metropolitan Museum, New York, USA; Oxford Art Society. *Works in collections*: Goldsmiths Hall, London; Norman Parkinson; Noma Copley, New York, USA; John Aspinal, Michael Severne. *Commissions*: Norman Parkinson: to make gold tiara for Princess Anne to be photographed in for her 21st birthday celebrations; Norman Parkinson: Gold tiara for his wife Wendell; Michael Severne: Gold grass stem and pomegranate pill box. Bronze and 18ct gold branch for Nina Campbell. *Publications*: 'Treasures of the 20th Century', 'The World of Interiors'. *Recreations*: work, friends, food, dancing, sun, reading, film, music. *Address*: 8 Castle Street, Totnes, Devon TQ9 5NU. *Email*: lin.sproule@virgin.net *Signs work*: 'Lin Sproule' or 'LS'.

ST. JOHN ROSSE, Nicholas David, figurative artist in oil, pencil, pastel, gouache, tempera; twice Elizabeth Greenshields Foundation. *b*: London, 18 Sep 1945. *m*: Chantale. one *s*. one *d*. *Educ*: University College School. *Studied*: under Pietro Annigoni, Florence, and at the Scuola del Nudo of the Florence Academy, early 60s. *Exhib*: regular one-man shows and group shows London, nationwide and the Continent. *Works in collections*: E. Greenshields Foundation, Montreal, Britannia Royal Navy College, Dartmouth, Lord St. Levan, St. Michael's Mount. *Commissions*: portrait/figure, religious, houses. *Publications*: series of illustrated articles on egg tempera painting 'Artist' magazine (1980) and article 'From the Seashore to the Studio' Artist Magazine (2014). *Works Reproduced*: privately and by leading publishers. *Principal Works*: 'Last Supper' St. Paul's Catholic Church, Tintagel. *Recreations*: plays clarinet. *Clubs*: Full Member of Royal Society of Marine Artists. *Address*: St. Adwen, Trethevy, Tintagel, Cornwall PL34 0BE. *Email*: nicholas@nstjohnrosse.com *Website*: www.nstjohnrosse.com *Signs work*: "N. St. John Rosse."

STACK. Sharon Rachel, BTEC Cert. in Fine Arts. *Medium*: mixed media, oil, watercolour, drawing, prints. *b*: Penbury, Kent, 28 May 1973. *d of*: Sander & Bill Stack. *Partner*: Peter. *Studied*: Coleg Ceredigion (2005-2007). *Exhib*: Aberystwyth Arts Centre, Ceredigion Arts Society, Aberystwyth Museum, Morlan Centre. Museum of Modern Art Wales. *Works in collections*: private collections in Wales and England. *Commissions*: private. *Principal Works*: semi abstract, and abstract. *Recreations*: fashion and interior designer. *Clubs*: Ceredigion Arts Society. *Address*: c/o Maes-y-Deri, Cribyn, Lampeter, Ceredigion, SA48 7NP. *Email*: stack.sharon@ymail.com *Signs work*: "S.Stack".

STAFFORD, C. Carolyn, PMC, NS, NDD, DA (Manc) (1955), Dip. Fine Art (1957); First Prize Life Painting & Life Drawing, Still Life & Plant Drawing. Steer Landscape Prize - oil; 3 travelling scholarships to Paris; painter in oil and water-colour, printmaker in etching, woodcut, lino; tutor. *b*: Bolton, 9 Aug 1935. *d of*: Stanley & Elizabeth Stafford. *m*: Gordon Clough, broadcaster (decd). one *s*. three *d*. *Educ*: Bolton School Girls Division. *Studied*: Bolton School of Art, Manchester College of Art (Ralph Downing, Ian Grant), Slade School of Fine Art (William Coldstream, Claude Rogers, Anthony Gross), Esmond Scholar British Inst. in Paris, etching with S.W. Hayter (1957-58). *Exhib*: John Moores, Liverpool, RA, Bankside Open Prints, London Group, Arts Council tours, RI, RBA, Printmakers Council, Malta, Art Olympia, Pump House, Northern School (Pelter-Sands and touring exhbn.), Lvov, New Academy Gallery, Paris, Universities of Bristol, Cambridge, London, Oxford and Surrey, Tel Aviv, Ben Uri Gallery, Curwen, Munich, North-South Printmakers Barbican, Yehudi Menuhin School, National Society; New Zealand, France and Germany; National Society; Royal Academy; Retrospective Exhibition Menier Gallery London (2014). *Works in collections*: Slade School, Bolton School (Girls Div.), Bolton A.G., Lvov A.G., Landau

A.G., Scarborough A.G., Government Art Collection. *Commissions*: paintings for cruise ship "Musica", private commissions. *Publications*: Arts Review, A Northern School (Peter Davies). *Works Reproduced*: UCL & Slade Catalogue Foundation (2007); Government Art Collection (2008). *Recreations*: singing. *Address*: 52 Ellerton Rd., London SW18 3NN. *Email*: c.carolyn.stafford@gmail.com *Signs work*: "Carolyn Stafford," "Carolyn Stafford Clough" or "C. STAFFORD."

STAFFORD, Simeon. *Medium*: oil, plaster, wood, bronze. *b*: Dukinfield, 1 Jul 1956. *Represented by*: Oliver Contemporary, 17 Bellevue Road, London SW17 7EG. *Exhib*: Oliver Contemporary, London (2003, 2005, 2006, 2007); Sancreed House Sculpture Garden, Cornwall (2005); Shire Hall Museum, Bodmin, Cornwall (2005, 2006); Falmouth Art Gallery & Museum, Cornwall (2006); Musée de l'Art en Marche, Hauterives, nr. Lyon, France (2006); Badcocks, Newlyn, Cornwall (2006, 2007); Retrospective 2008; McAllister Thomas Fine Art, Godalming, Surrey (2009 solo show); Royal Cornwall Museum Truro (solo show 2008); Bill Clark Art, Cheshire; Thompsons Gallery, Marylebone (2013); Astley Cheethams Gallery, Thameside. *Works in collections*: HM The Queen. *Publications*: St. Ives - Art Colony in Transition, by Peter Davies (pub. 2007); Simeon Stafford by Jonathan Riley (pub. 2010). *Misc*: Made a member of Penwith Society of Artists, St. Ives, Cornwall. *Address*: Island View, Beachfield Cottages, Long Rock, Penzance, Cornwall TR20 8JF.

STAGE, Ruth, BA Hons, PGDip, NEAC; painter in egg tempera. *b*: 8 Jan 1969. *m*: Benet Spencer (painter). *Educ*: Blakeston Comprehensive. *Studied*: Newcastle University, RA Schools. *Exhib*: 4 solo exhibs., New Grafton Gallery. *Works in collections*: A T Kearney, Charing Cross Hospital, Durham University, Hiscox Plc. *Commissions*: Chevron U.K. Calendar. *Clubs*: NEAC. *Address*: 13a Wyneham Rd., London SE24 9NT. *Signs work*: "R Stage."

STAHL, Andrew, painter; Head of Undergraduate Painting, Slade School of Fine Art. *b*: London, 4 Jul 1954. *m*: Kumiko Stahl. one *s*. three *d*. *Studied*: Slade School of Fine Art. *Exhib*: many one-man and group shows in U.K. and abroad. *Works in collections*: Arts Council, British Council, British Museum, Contemporary Arts Soc., City Museum Peterborough, Leics. Educ. Authority, Metropolitan Museum of Art, New York, Government Art Collection. *Publications*: Numerous art reviews, catalogues and press reviews. *Misc*: Ex Rome Scholar and Wingate Scholar and other artists residencies. *Email*: andrewstahl@hotmail.com *Signs work*: back of work usually "ANDREW STAHL" or "A. STAHL."

STAINTON, Frances: see EASTON, Frances.

STALLARD, Michael James, ARBS; NDD; ATD; Cert.Ed. *Medium*: sculpture: carving in marble. *b*: Stourport-on-Severn, 20 Nov 1944. two *d*. *Educ*: Adams Grammar School, Newport, Salop. *Studied*: High Wycombe College of Art; Camberwell School of Arts and Crafts 1963-65; Bristol School of Art Education (West of England College of Art/Bristol University). *Exhib*: RA (1985-1996); Festival of London Sculpture Exhbn, Alexandra Palace; New Academy Gallery; Ewan Phillips Gallery. *Works in collections*: HRH Sultan of Brunei; many private collections in Britain and the USA. *Commissions*: Hiram Walker International; Wapping Arts Trust; Homerton Hospital; Sun Life of Canada. *Publications*: founder of 'The Art and Design Directory' (pub. AVEC Designs Ltd., 1991). *Principal Works*: 'Scribble' (1993); 'Random One' (1988); 'Sidestep' (1995); 'Around Zero' (1988). *Recreations*: drawing in pencil and charcoal. *Misc*: member of Spike Island Artists Studios (1986-98). See 'British Sculptors of the 20th Century' by Alan Winsor (Ashgate Pubs.). *Address*: 5 South Road, Redland, Bristol BS6 6QP. *Email*: mike.stallard@blueyonder.co.uk *Signs work*: marble sculpture not signed.

STANDAERT, Dora. *Medium*: ceramics, sculpture. *b*: Antwerp, Belgium, 2 Feb 1944. *d of*: Achilles Standaert & Isabel Deroeck. *m*: Paul Gelissen. one *s*. *Studied*: Royal Academy,

Antwerp. *Exhib*: various exhbns in Belgium, Holland and Paris; selected by the Royal Academy of Arts, London for the Summer Exhibition 2002. *Works in collections*: private collections in Belgium, Holland, USA, Australia, Great Britain. *Works Reproduced*: in several catalogues. *Recreations*: exhibitions, gardening, expressive dancing, tango, theatre, film. *Address*: Herentalsebaan 1, Ranst, Belgium 2520. *Email*: ceramics@dorastandaert.be. *Signs work*: monogram.

STANDEN, Peter, DA (Edin); works in oil, acrylic, etching: subjects allegorical, subtle humour, imaginary future ruins, merpeople and cats; Mem. Edinburgh Printmakers Workshop; Scottish Art Council Awards incl. 'Artist in Industry' Ferranti plc (1987). *b*: Carshalton, 3 Apr 1936. *s of*: Charles Standen and Isabel (née) Ogier. *m*: Helen. one *s*. one *d*. *Educ*: Epping Secondary. *Studied*: Nottingham College of Art (1954-56), Edinburgh College of Art (1956-59). *Exhib*: one-man shows: 'Up the Nile' Commonwealth Inst., Edinburgh (1965), 'Paintings' New 57 Gallery, Edinburgh (1977), 'Mr. Cat' Traverse Theatre Club, Edinburgh (1985), 'Looking Back to the Future' PMW Edinburgh (1988); group shows: 'Art into Landscape' I and III Serpentine Gallery, London (1974, 1979), ' 5 Scottish Printmakers' selected by Peter Fuller, PMW Edinburgh Festival (1983), 'Ljubljana Biennial' Yugoslavia (1987). *Works in collections*: HM The Queen, Windsor Castle, Hamilton A.G., Ontario, City of Edinburgh, Moray House College Edinburgh, Eastern General Hospital Edinburgh, The University of Edinburgh, Royal Bank of Scotland, Durham University Collection. *Publications*: etchings included in "Edinburgh Suite" (1992) and "The Sea, the Sea" portfolios (Pub. by EPMW, Edinburgh). *Address*: 5 Lee Cres., Portobello, Edinburgh EH15 1LW. *Email*: peterstanden@edinburghetchings.com *Website*: www.reubensutton.com *Signs work*: prints: "P. Standen" (pencil signature); paintings: "P. STANDEN."

STANDIGE, Ramon Gary, DipAD (Hon), MA (RCA), Sanderson Scholarship from RCA. *Medium*: watercolour, drawing, prints. *b*: Blackpool, 11 Mar 1946. *s of*: Raymond Standige. two *s*. *Studied*: Stoke-on-Trent College of Art (1964-67); Royal College of Art, Kensington (1967-70). *Represented by*: throughout this country and abroad. *Works in collections*: Victoria & Albert Museum, London; Ulster Museum, Belfast. *Recreations*: music, sailing. *Address*: Yew Tree Barn, Windermere Road, Lindale, Cumbria LA11 6LB. *Email*: garystandige@btinternet.com *Signs work*: "GS", G above S enclosed in a box.

STANFORD, Dee, Diploma in Photography; Winner Best of Show prize, Cork Street Open Art Exhibition (2013); Winner Best Sculpture award ING Discerning Eye Exhibition (2013); Winner Best Sculpture prize SWA Exhibition (2014). *Medium*: Sculpture. *b*: UK, 30 Apr 1969. one *s*. *Studied*: Paddington College, London. *Represented by*: Panther and Hall, Pall Mall; Go Figurative, Hampstead. *Exhib*: York and Albany, London (2012); LAFY Show (2012, 2013); Cork Street Open Art Exhibition (2013); ING Discerning Eye Exhibition (2013); Winter pride exhibition (2014); Office Session exhibition (2014); RBA exhibition (2014); AAF Hampstead (2014); SWA exhibition (2014). *Works in collections*: MOMA, Cyprus (2013); Museum of Michael and Loukia Zampelas, Cyprus. *Commissions*: Private and corporate. *Official Purchasers*: Private and corporate. *Misc*: Spent most of my adult life in Cape Town RSA. Works sold private and corporate inc wine farms across SA. *Address*: Hydeaway, Lower Road, East Farleigh, Kent ME14 0JL. *Email*: deestanford@live.co.za *Website*: www.deestanford.com *Signs work*: "D. Stanford".

STANSFIELD, David Paul, Awarded City & Guilds of London in printing, printing science and lithographic printing. *Medium*: Acrylic. *b*: Lancashire, 19 Feb 1963. *m*: Elizabeth. one *s*. three *d*. *Studied*: Blackburn College of Art and Design (1978-82). *Represented by*: The New Craftsman, St Ives; Lander Gallery, Truro; Newquay Fine Art; The Picture House Galleries, Cornwall; Zeath Gallery, Polzeath, Cornwall; Haddon Galleries, Torquay, Devon. *Exhib*: Usual mixed and private. *Publications*: Published by

Haddon Gallerys, Torquay and self-published. *Works Reproduced*: By Haddon Galleries, Torquay. *Principal Works*: Paints in acrylics on reclaimed timber and wood. Very quirky ships, boats, vehicles and Fab lollies. *Recreations*: Committed Christian. *Address*: Moonfleet Cottage, St Newlyn East, Cornwall TR8 5HA. *Email*: thestansfieldfamily@msn.com *Website*: www.davidstansfieldartist.co.uk *Signs work*: "DAVID STANSFIELD".

STAPLETON, Rose, WCSI (Watercolour Society of Ireland); BA Fine Art; James Adams Salesrooms Award (RHA), NCAD College Prize, Fergus O'Ryan Memorial Prize (RHA). *Medium*: painter in oils, watercolour; printmaking. *b*: Dublin, 27 Oct 1951. *d of*: Frank Stapleton. *m*: John C. Brobbel, RBA. three *s*. *Studied*: National College of Art and Design, Dublin (1995-99). *Represented by*: Soloman Gallery, Dublin; James Wray, Belfast. *Exhib*: Jorgensen Fine Art, Dublin; Lavit Gallery, Cork; Petley Fine Art, London; Wren Gallery, London; Royal Ulster Academy, Belfast; Royal Hibernian Academy Annual Exhibition; Royal Hibernian Academy Banquet Exhibition, Dublin. *Works in collections*: AXA Insurance; Bank of Ireland; Bank of Montreal; Maynooth College, Co. Kildare, Ireland; O'Flaherty Holdings; United Arts Club, Dublin; Watercolour Society of Ireland Collection (at University of Limerick, Ireland). *Publications*: 'Thought Lines' (2000). *Address*: 14, Lansdowne Park, Ballsbridge, Dublin 4 Eire. *Email*: rosemaryannestapleton@yahoo.com *Signs work*: "ROSE STAPLETON" since 1997, "ROSE CONNOLLY" prior to 1997.

STARK, Christine Anne, BA Hons (painting). *Medium*: mixed media (painting). *b*: Derby, 3 Dec 1962. *Studied*: Chelsea College of Art. *Exhib*: RA Summer Exhbn; Contemporary Art Society (Art Future), London; The New Ashgate Gallery, Farnham; RCA. *Works in collections*: many private collections. *Recreations*: travel, cinema, theatre, golf. *Address*: Basement Flat, 9 Dartmouth Park Road, London NW5 1SU. *Email*: starkbat@hotmail.com

STARR, Marion, artist in oil. *b*: Hitchin, Herts., 19 Apr 1937. *d of*: Walter Starr. *m*: Christopher Fielder. two *d*. *Educ*: various Grammar Schools in UK and abroad. *Studied*: Chinese brush painting and the Sogetsu School discipline of flower arrangement while in the Far East. *Exhib*: RA Summer Exhbn. (since 1979), RWA, ROI, RBA, NEAC, Laing, Spirit of London, Rye Soc. of Artists, Chichester City of Culture Open Art Exhbn., 'A Celebration of the Romney Marsh' at Sassoon Gallery, Folkestone and Marsh Gallery, New Romney; New Grafton Gallery, Easton Rooms and Stormont Studio, Rye, Neville Gallery, Canterbury, Attendi Gallery, Chiswick, Talents Fine Arts, Malton; Bank Street Gallery, Sevenoaks; Stables Gallery, Old Town Hasings. *Works in collections*: Exhall Specialist School & Science College - Your Paintings - The Nations Art Collection (BBC). *Misc*: Major winner, Laing Landscape Painting competition (1994). *Address*: Flat 2, 31 Cornwallis Gardens, Hastings, TN34 1LR. *Email*: marionestarr@aol.co.uk *Signs work*: "M.S." or "Marion Starr."

STATTER, David Harold, NDD, ATD. *Medium*: acrylic, oil, watercolour, drawing, sculpture. *b*: St. Helens, Lancs., 13 Dec 1942. *s of*: Braithwaite Statter. *m*: Kay. three *s*. *Studied*: Liverpool College of Art (1960-1965). *Exhib*: One-man, Two-man and group exhibitions at various galleries in South East London, East End and Kent. Mall Galleries: SWA (1994); RSMA (1997, 1999, 2000, 2001, 2002, 2003, 2005); Lynn Painter-Stainers Prize Exhibition & WH Patterson Gallery (2012); RBA (2014); Lynn Painter-Stainers Award (2014). *Works in collections*: various private collections; Mall Galleries. *Commissions*: Illustrations: Lilac Tree Press, Michael Joseph, Peuple Libre. Drawings of London: Dane & Co., Trio. Bible Illustrations: 'Project It!'. *Publications*: Arts Review' International Artist Magazine 2nd Prize Seascapes (Oct/nov 2012); Masterclass: The Artist Magazine (June 2013). *Works Reproduced*: 'Dancing Ledge No 1', 'Bull Point No 1, North Devon', 'Canary Wharf Excalators', 'The Listener, Speakers Corner', 'HSBC Queue, Canary Wharf',

'Afternoon Sunlight, Toledo'. *Principal Works*: Coastal Series, Canary Wharf Reflections, Brief Encounters ongoing. *Misc*: Taught Painting and Sculpture in London schools (1966-1983), Design Technology (1983-1992). *Address*: 33 Hinstock Road, Plumstead, London SE18 2TQ. *Email*: davidstatter@talktalk.net *Website*: www.davidstatter.com *Signs work*: "D. STATTER".

STEAD, David Thomas Kirby, BA (Hons); artist in oil on canvas, and watercolour. *b*: Ripon, Yorks., 14 Apr 1959. *m*: Rebecca Susan. one *s*. three *d*. *Studied*: Harrogate and Wimbledon. *Exhib*: Ariel Centre, Devon, Henry Brett Gallery, Stow, Coves Quay Gallery Salcombe, Thompson Gal. Stow., Art Co. Leeds, etc. Work in collections internationally. *Works in collections*: UK, America, Europe, Far East. *Commissions*: album covers for 'Just Music' records. *Address*: 34 Kirkgate, Ripon, HG4 1PB.

STEEL, Hilary, BA Hons (1985), DipArch (1988); draughtsman in pen and pencil; freelance architectural illustrator; specialises in architectural elevational drawings. *b*: Carshalton, 17 Mar 1964. *m*: Adrian Odey. one *s*. *Studied*: Brighton University School of Architecture. *Exhib*: RA Summer Exhib. (2000-2001), RA Summer Exhbn prize runner-up (2002). *Commissions*: Medici Gallery Cards (2001). *Principal Works*: Kensington Trio, Big Ben, St. Pancras Details. *Address*: 132 Lower Church Rd., Burgess Hill, W. Sussex RH15 9AB. *Email*: h.steel@btclick.com *Signs work*: "Hilary Steel."

STEELE, Jeffrey, *b*: Cardiff, 3 Jul 1931. one *s*. two *d*. *Represented by*: Osborne Samuel, 23a Bruton Street, London W1J 6QJ. *Misc*: Attended art schools in Cardiff and Newport in the late 1940s but found himself in disagreement with the official criteria for art education which prevailed at the time. Maintained a studio in Cardiff and experimented with a wide range of approaches to painting throughout the 1950s. Awarded a French Governemnt Scholarship to study in Paris (1959). Took up a teaching position in Portsmouth (1968). Organised the SYSTEEMISYSTEM exhibition in Helsinki (1969). *Address*: 11a Eastern Villas Road, Portsmouth PO4 0SU. Signs work: "Jeffrey Steele".

STEPHENS, Ian, NDD (1961), RE (1984), SWE (1984) (Chairman 1992-95); artist in wood engraving, water-colours. *b*: Gt. Linford, Bucks., 19 May 1940. *s of*: the late A.B. Stephens. *m*: Valerie. two *s*. *Educ*: Wolverton Technical School. *Studied*: Northampton School of Art (1956-61). *Exhib*: RE (1975 onwards), Fremantle, Jeune Gravure Contemporaine, Paris, Humberside (1985); one-man show Daventry (1989, 1993), British Miniature Print International, Bristol (1989, 1997), Cadaqués (1991, onwards), National Print Exhibition, London (1996-2001), Aylesbury (2001), Harlech (2000), Society of Wood Engravers (1984 onwards). *Works in collections*: Northants CC, Notts.CC, Surrey CC, Warwicks. Museums, Kettering BC, Daventry DC, Fremantle Arts Centre, Ashmolean Museum Oxford, Northampton Central Museum and A.G., Adogi Cadaqués. *Publications*: The Engravers Cut, Primrose Academy (2001). *Works Reproduced*: The Engravers Globe (ed. Simon Brett), Primrose Hill Press Ltd. (2002). *Recreations*: walking, music, reading, natural history. *Address*: 46 Yardley Drive, Northampton NN2 8PE. *Signs work*: "I. Stephens" or "Ian Stephens."

STEPHENS, Nicholas Anthony, NDD (1960), ARCA (1963), Harkness Fellowship, USA (1963-65), Arts Council Major award (1977), ARBS (1981); sculptor in bronze; Principal Lecturer in Fine Art, Glos. College of Art and Technology; visiting teaching: U.C. Davis, California (1971), Victoria College, Prahran, Australia (1983). *b*: Nottingham, 6 Jun 1939. *s of*: R.S. Stephens. *m*: Jenifer Beesley (divorced 1984). two *s*. *Educ*: Nottingham High School. *Studied*: Central School (Wm. Turnbull), RCA (1960-63, Lord Queensbury), Pratt Inst., NY (1964), San Francisco Art Inst. (1965, James Melchert). *Exhib*: Davis Cal. (1971), SW Arts (1978), The State of Clay (1978-80), RA (1980, 1981, 1983, 1984), RBS Scone Palace (1983), Park Gallery Cheltenham (1982, 1985), St. Donat's

Castle, Wales (1983), Nicholas Tredwell Gallery (1985), Air Gallery, Harkness Arts (1985), St. David's Hall, Cardiff (1988). *Address*: The Red House, Bredon, Tewkesbury, Glos. GL20 7LM. *Signs work*: "N.A. STEPHENS."

STEPHENS, Roger Madoc, City & Guilds Architectural Stonecarving (Distinction); Prizes: Millfield Open Exhibition.; Wiltshire Open Exhibition; Onyx Environmental Trust Award; Lady Radnor Award, Salisbury Civic Society; "Best Street Furniture" award, South of England in Bloom. *Medium*: sculpture. *b*: London, 27 May 1944. *Educ*: Grenvill College, Bideford, Devon. *Studied*: Salisbury College of Art; Weymouth College. *Represented by*: Cadogan Contemporary, London; The Garden Gallery, Broughton, Hants. *Exhib*: Millfield Summer Show (1996, 2004); Henley Arts Festival (2001); Discerning Eye(2002); Sir Harold Hillier Gardens, Romsey (2003,04,06); Grapevine Gallery, Norwich (2004); Artsway Open, Sway (2005); Kelly Ross Fine Art, Child Okeford (2006,07); Wiltshire Open, Salisbury (2006); Morgan Boyce, Marlborough (2008,09); "Liminality" Salisbury Cathedral (2010); The Art House Gallery, Bournemouth (2010); "Sculpture in Paradise" Chichester (2011); Bloomsbury Art Fair (2011); "Figures in a Landscape", Winchester (2011); The Cartshed Gallery, Dorset, (2012); Avebury Manor, Avebury (2012); Red Orb, Dorset (2012); Cadogan Contemporary, London (2013); "Stewards of the Earth", Salisbury (2013); Royal West of England Academy, Bristol (2013); Mompesson House, Salisbury (2014); West Lavington Manor, Wiltshire (2014); The Garden Gallery, Broughton, Hants(1999-2014). *Works in collections*: private/corporate. *Commissions*: Wayside seating, Broughton Hants. Cartouche, Taylors Almshouse, Salisbury, Wilts. Sundial and seat, St Mary's Church, Broughton, Hants. Commemorative Sculpture, St Peters School, Winchester, Hants. Seats for The Porter's Garden, HM Naval Base, Portsmouth. Sandstone sculpture and seat, Hants. Carved Panel, Longford Castle, Salisbury. Stone Memorial, Salisbury. Sandstone Acorns, Eastliegh, Hants. Memorial Seat, Church of St Cross, Winchester. *Publications*: "Material Connections Across the Ages". Contemporary Sculpture & Mompesson House; "The Figure in the Landscape" Winchester Discovery Centre; "Liminality, Toward the Unknown Region", Salisbury Cathedral; Hampshire Chronicle; Yew Tree, New Work; Sculpture Techniques Bible; The Garden Gallery, Rachel Bebb and John Garfield; Art Loan Collection, University of Winchester. *Official Purchasers*: Wayside Seats, Broughton Parish Council; Three granite seats, The Porter's Garden, Historic Dockyard, HM Naval Base, Portsmouth; Sandstone Acorns, Fair Oak & Horton Heath Parish Council Hants; University of London. *Recreations*: music, sport. *Address*: 34 Wyndham Road, Salisbury SP1 3AB. *Email*: rogmar@waitrose.com *Website*: rs-sculpture.net *Signs work*: "Roger Stephens".

STEPHENSON, Christine Frances, NDD (1957), ATD (1958), SBA (1997), RHS Silver Medal (1996), Gold Medal (1997), Cert. of Botanical Merit SBA (1999); botanical artist. *Medium*: watercolour. *b*: Winchester, 3 Apr 1937. *m*: Jack Stephenson, portrait painter. two *s*. *Educ*: St. Swithun's School, Winchester. *Studied*: Bournemouth College of Art (1953-58); University of London Goldsmiths College (1984). *Exhib*: Capel Manor Gallery, Enfield (1993); Thompson's Gallery, Aldeburgh, Suffolk (1994); Royal Horticultural Society, London (1995, 96); Society of Botanical Artists (1993-99); Open Studios Galleries, Suffolk (1997, 98); Lucy B. Campbell Gallery, London (1996-2005); Gordon Craig Gallery, Knightsbridge (1999); Chelsea Flower Show (2000); The Hunt Institute of Botanical Documentation, Pittsbugh, USA (2000); Hindlesham Hall Gallery, Suffolk (2001, 04); Scanlons Court Museum, Poole, Dorset (2004); Cobbold and Judd, Hindlesham Hall, Suffolk (2001-); Julia Gooch Pictures, Aldeburgh, Suffolk (2004-). *Works in collections*: Hunt Institute for Botanical Documentation, Pittsburgh, USA and private collections worldwide. *Publications*: "Woottens of Wenhaston" Handbook 1994-2004; Country Living magazine (May 2004); Detuin Exclusif (March 2004). *Address*: 3 Causeway Cottages, Middleton, nr. Saxmundham, Suffolk IP17 3NH. *Email*: christine@paintingsofplants.com *Website*: www.paintingsofplants.com *Signs work*: "C.F.S."

STEPHENSON, Daphne Eulalia Beatrix Feliciam ABNA; Chairman, ABNA (2003-2013). Primitive naive art specialist. Designer of Lovelight lamps (present). Previously: designer and enameller for Halcyon Days, designer of ties and scarves for Victor Sumner. *Medium*: oils, acrylic and mixed media. *b*: Holland, 17 Jul 1959. one *d*. *Educ*: Convent of Sacred Heart, Tunbridge Wells & Wokingham. *Studied*: University of Angewartekunst, Vienna (metalwork). *Represented by*: Lacy Road Gallery, Putney. *Exhib*: Royal Academy Summer Exhibition; ING Bank City, 29 Cork Street, Piccadilly; 9 Langton Street; Lacy Road Gallery, Putney; Masterworks Museum, Bermuda; ABNA Mariners Gallery, St. Ives; Paragon Gallery, Cheltenham; Festival of Naives, Verneuil, France; John Martin Gallery, Agora Gallery, Soho, New York. *Works in collections*: Masterworks Museum, Bermuda, Debby Brice, Lyford Cay, Bahamas; Queen Beatrix of the Netherlands. *Commissions*: J. John Evangelist; Debby Brice; Sir Andrew & Lady Usher; Sir John & Lady Stewart-Clark, and many more. *Publications*: The Association of Britsh Naive Artists coffee table book. *Works Reproduced*: Greenpebble Greetings Cards. *Principal Works*: Island and tropical exotic scenes, leopard tryptychs and other Primitive Naive art. *Recreations*: dancing, painting, designing, galleries, travel. *Clubs*: ABNA. *Address*: c/o 15 Ivory house, Plantation Wharf, Battersea, London SW11 3TN. *Email*: daphnestephenson@aol.com *Website*: www.daphnestephenson.com *Signs work*: "D. Stephenson".

STEPHENSON, Jack, BA Fine Art; Post Graduate Diploma. *Medium*: oil, drawing. *b*: Lincolnshire, 27 May 1945. *s of*: Ernest and Felicity. *m*: Christine Frances. two *s*. one *d*. *Educ*: East Ham Grammar School. *Studied*: Walthamstow School of Art (1963-64); Hornsey College of Art (1964-67, BA Fine Art); Goldsmiths' (1983-84, P.G.Dip). *Exhib*: Royal Academy Summer Exhibition; Peter Pears Gallery, Aldeburgh; Buckenham House Gallery; Aldeburgh Gallery. *Works in collections*: private collections. *Commissions*: Christ's Hospital (portrait of Headmaster, with two senior Grecians); Bancroft's School (portrait of Headmaster, with two senior Grecians). *Publications*: Dictionary of Artists 1945 to Present. *Clubs*: President of Southwold Art Society; Treasurer of Suffolk Group. *Misc*: Committee Member, Blythe Valley Chamber Music Society. *Address*: 3 Causeway Cottages, Middleton, Saxmundham, IP17 3NH. *Email*: jackstephenson@metronet.co.uk *Website*: www.portraitsfromlife.co.uk *Signs work*: "J.Stephenson".

STEVENS, Chris, BA (Hons.) Fine Art; Awards: Southern Arts Award for Painting (1981); South West Arts Award for Painting (1982); Calouste Gulbenkian Foundation Award (1985); BP Portrait Award (1990); Painted Faces prizewinner, Saatchi Online (2013). *b*: Basingstoke, 1956. *Studied*: University of Reading (1974-78). *Exhib*: one-man shows: U.K., London and Holland; group shows: London, Spain, Germany and USA shows with Sue Williams, London. *Works in collections*: Calouste Gulbenkian Foundation, London; Museo Municipal Lalin, Spain; National Gallery of Wales; Nat Kramer, New York; North Street Films, Los Angeles; Northern Arts; Mercury Films, Los Angeles; Galerija Portreta, Tuzla, Bosnia & Herzegovena; Standard Chartered Bank; Unilever; University of Durham; Victoria & Albert Museum. Private collections UK, USA, South Africa, Europe. *Commissions*: Standard Chartered Bank, London; Cheltenham Music Festival; North Street Films; Mercury Films. *Publications*: "Reality, Modern & Contemporary British Painting" (East Publishing); "Painted Faces" (ROAR, 2014); "The Quietly Surreal Paintings of Chris Stevens" by Danny Olda (2014); Roves and Roams, issue 5, 2012 (digital); "500 Portraits" (NPG, 2011); "BP Portrait Award" (NPG, 2001); exhibition catalogues. *Email*: chrispstevens@mac.com *Website*: www.chrisstevens.co *Signs work*: "Chris Stevens".

STEVENS, Helen M., SWA (1989); artist in pure silk hand embroidery, writer. *b*: Belmont, Surrey, 2 Oct 1959. *m*: Brian Rayner. *Educ*: Bury St. Edmunds County Grammar School. *Exhib*: SWA, Soc. of Wildlife Art in Nature; numerous solo shows every two years. *Works in collections*: Palace of Westminster. *Publications*: author and illustrator: 'The Embroiderers Countryside', 'The Embroiderers Country Album'; 'The Timeless Art of

Embroidery' and 'The Myth and Magic of Embroidery' (David & Charles). *Address*: 3 The Green, Flempton, Bury St. Edmunds, Suffolk IP28 6EL. *Signs work*: "Helen M. Stevens."

STEVENS, Margaret, PSBA (2005-2010), VPBSA (1997-2005); RHS Silver Gilt Lindley Medal (1989); Gold Cert. Botanical Merit, SBA (1998); Adult Class Tutor at two ARCA colleges for number of years: Course Director: Distance Learning Diploma Course (DLDC) in Botanical Painting (2004-2010), now acts as mentor to budding botanical painters. *Medium*: watercolour. *b*: Brixham, Devon, 14 Oct 1937. *m*: Derek Stevens (decd). *Educ*: Dartmouth Grammar School. *Exhib*: solo shows: Penrhyn Castle, National Trust; Mixed exhibitions: SBA, Westminster; Llewellyn Alexander Gallery; RMS - all regularly. *Works in collections*: Hunt Institute for Botanical Documentation, Pittsburgh; numerous private collections worldwide. *Commissions*: large collection of old roses for private buyer, Fine Art prints, greetings cards, etc., Chelsea plate (1993, Franklin Mint), Royal British Legion plates (Bradford Exchange). *Publications*: "An Introduction to Drawing Flowers" (1994); "The Art of Botanical Painting" (2004); "The Botanical Palette" (2007); "Botanical Sketch Book" with Mary Ann Scott (2010); "Handbook of Plant Forms" with Ernest E Clark (2013). *Recreations*: reading, music, opera and ballet. *Clubs*: Founder Member SBA. *Misc*: Continues to paint for private clients in her retirement. *Address*: 1 Hen Gapel, Gerlan, Bethesda, Gwynedd LL57 3ST. *Signs work*: "Margaret Stevens".

STEVENSON, David John, painter in egg tempera and oil; 2007, Dunelm Prize, Leicester Open; 2009 shortlisted, Attenborough Prize, Leicester Open; 2009 shortlisted, Regional Prize, Discerning Eye; 2010 shortlisted, Attenborough Prize, Leicester Open. *b*: Leicester, 26 Nov 1956. *s of*: Samuel Stevenson. *m*: Alison Wilkins. two *s*. *Educ*: Guthlaxton College, Leicester. *Exhib*: RA; Leicester Museum; Loseby Gallery, Leicester; Tettenhall Gallery; City Gallery, Leicester; Gallery 3, Leicester; Catmose Gallery, Oakham; Discerning Eye, Mall Galleries, London; Lynn Painter Stainers, Mall Galleries & WH Patterson Gallery, London. *Address*: High Brinks, 107 Lubenham Hill, Market Harborough, Leics., LE16 9DG. *Email*: stevenson@highbrinks.fsnet.co.uk *Signs work*: "D. Stevenson."

STEVENSON, Richard Lee, printmaker, intaglio, relief printing, oils. *b*: Penzance, 9 Apr 1955. *Studied*: Falmouth School of Art, North Staffs. University, Penzance School of Art (Sue Lewington). *Exhib*: RWA Mall Galleries, Victoria Galleries, Bath, The St. Ives Society of Artists, The Cornwall Crafts Association, The Great Atlantic Map Works Galleries. *Commissions*: Linocut cover design for the 18th International Celtic Film And Television Festival catalogue. *Publications*: Ten Penwith Printmakers (1998). *Clubs*: St. Ives Soc. of Artists, Cornwall Crafts Assoc., Penwith Printmakers. *Address*: Little Trevarrack, Brandy Lane, Rosudgeon, Penzance, Cornwall TR20 9QB. *Email*: lee@littletrev.fsnet.co.uk *Signs work*: "Lee Stevenson."

STEVENTON, Brian Thomas, RBSA, MBA, BA Hons. *Medium*: oil, watercolour, acrylic, mixed media, pen & wash, pastel, gouache. *b*: Ladymoor, Bilston, 20 Jul 1948. *s of*: Ethel Pearl Steventon. *m*: Valerie Steventon. *Educ*: Engineering Design & Management and IT. *Studied*: self taught artist, tutor for "Authentic Adventures" art groups. *Represented by*: Bircham Gallery, Bridgegate Gallery, Ferrers Gallery, Bevere Gallery. *Exhib*: Bircham Gallery, Bridgegate Gallery, Ferrers Gallery, Martins Gallery, AAF London, RBSA Gallery, Albany Gallery, Buckenham Gallery, Mall Galleries, The Old Chapel Gallery, Gallery Top, The Upstairs Gallery, on-site artist at Black Country Living Museum (2001). Solo exhibition: Ferrers Gallery, RBSA Gallery, Granary Gallery. *Works in collections*: private and corporate. *Commissions*: various. *Publications*: The Art of England, The Limner (both 2006), The Magazine, How Artists See 'Places' - Green Pebble. *Works Reproduced*: landscapes, genre, still life, figurative. *Recreations*: walking, music, history. *Clubs*: Royal Birmingham Society of Artists, Easel Club, Birmingham Art Circle, BWS, Southwold Art Circle. *Address*: 6 Rookery Rise, Wombourne, Staffs, WV5 0NP. *Email*: briansteventon@tiscali.co.uk *Website*: briansteventon.co.uk. *Signs work*: "B Steventon".

STEWART, Alan, BA Hons, PG Dip. *Medium*: oil, watercolour, drawing. *b*: 23 May 1970. *m*: Zoe. *Studied*: Edinburgh College of Art (1992-96); London Guildhall University (1997-98). *Exhib*: Waterhouse & Dodd (2007, 2009), Royal Academy (2008), Catto Contemporary (2003), Royal Scottish Society of Painters in Watercolour (2002, 1996), Spit2 (2001), BP Portrait Award (2000), Maclaurin Art Gallery (1997), Noble Grossart (1996), Brave Art (1996), Threadneedle (2013). *Works in collections*: Stirling Smith Art Gallery & Museum, Ministry of Justice. *Address*: Flat 2, 3 Larkstone Close, Ilfracombe EX34 9PJ. *Email*: agstewart1@gmail.com *Website*: www.alanstewart.org.uk *Signs work*: "STEWART".

STEWART, David, Diploma in Photography, BAFTA Nomination Best Short Film, 'The Independent' Top 10 Photographers 2002. *Medium*: photographer. *b*: Lancaster, 4 Jan 1958. *s of*: Geoff and Margaret. *m*: Angela. two *s*. one *d*. *Studied*: Blackpool and Fylde College. *Exhib*: In Camera, New York; Brenda Taylor Gallery, New York; Camandona Art Gallery, Alba, Italy; SS Robin Gallery, London; Art Hotel, Milan, Italy; Gallery Sand Groningan, Netherlands; Fotografica Bogota 2009; Fotomuseuo Bogota Columbia, RA Summer Show 2008. *Works in collections*: V&A Museum, London; Ingalls Library, Cleveland Museum of Art, Cleveland, USA; Harvard Business School, Boston, USA. *Commissions*: V&A London Surreal Things Exhibition poster. *Publications*: 'Fogeys' (2001), 'Thrice Removed' (2009). *Works Reproduced*: National Portrait Gallery Photo Prize (1995-2008, 10 works). *Principal Works*: Fogeys, Cabbage, Thrice Removed, In-Decision. *Address*: 39 Featherstone Street, London EC1Y 8RE. *Email*: david@davidstewwwart.com *Website*: davidstewwwart.com *Signs work*: "David Stewart".

STEWART, Hannah, 2000 Alec Tiranti Prize for Young Portrait Sculptors; 1999 Manchester Academy of Fine Arts Major Award; 1998 Second Prize Sefton Open Exhibition. *Medium*: sculpts in clay and casts in bronze. *b*: Horsham, 19 Jan 1976. *m*: Dr. Simon Stewart. *Studied*: City & Guilds of London Art School, Kennington, London. *Commissions*: many private commissions, also 3m long bronze Iguanodon, Southwater (Miller Construction & Horsham District Council); human-sized bronze of 'The St. Leonards Forest Dragon' (Horsham in Bloom Committee). *Email*: hannah@hannahstewartsculpture.co.uk *Website*: www.hannahstewartsculpture.co.uk *Signs work*: "Hannah Stewart".

STEYN, Carole, sculptor, painter, pastellist and engraver - abstract, pop art and figurative. *Medium*: oils, watercolour, pastels, etchings drypoint, aquatint and arte povera media. *b*: Manchester, 20 Sep 1938. two *s*. *Educ*: Wycombe Abbey. *Studied*: Académie Julian, Paris (1954), St. Martin's School of Art (1955-57). *Represented by*: Noel Oddy, Highgate Fine Art, N1; Richard Chapman, Sheridan Russell Gallery, W1. *Exhib*: eight solo shows: Drian Galleries (1971, 1975, 1981 (First Retrospective Exhbn.), 1985), Jablonsky Galleries, London (1987), Galerie Harounoff, London (1991); 30+ group shows: all in London (1968-97); Lauderdale House (1997), Sheridan Russell Gallery (-2005); current mixed exhibitions in London, Harlequin Gallery, London SE10. *Works in collections*: National Museum, Warsaw, Poland (Nalecz Collection), Sheffield City Museum, National Museum, Gdansk, Poland, Ben Uri Collection, National Gallery of Art, Bosnia, Herzogovina. *Commissions*: British Telecom (1985). *Works Reproduced*: Catalogue of Art Auction for Medical Foundation (victims of torture); in Apollo "The Select Few" (1975), Arts Review (1975, 1981); Radio broadcast BBC (1971), Open House (1975) and BBC Manchester (1985). Television BBC1 (1971) and BBC2 (1989), inclusion of brochures, letters and photographs in both archive and library of Tate Britain; The Feminine Eye by Halina Nalecz; Bonhams Catalogue; British Contemporary Art; le Benezit (1999). *Address*: c/o The Director, Noel Oddy Highgate Fine Art 26 Highgate High Street London N6 5JG. *Signs work*: "C. Steyn."

STIEGER, Jacqueline, FRSA (1986); Royal Scottish Academy Award (1959); 1st Prize, Revival of the Medal, Paris (1974); Freeman of the Worshipful Company of Goldsmiths

(1985); 1st Prize Medal Design, Goldsmiths Crafts Council (2000). *Medium*: sculpture, jewellery, medals - lost wax technique, casting, bronze and precious metals. *b*: London, 26 Jan 1936. *s of*: H. J. Stieger, FRAeS. *m*: Alfred Gruber. two *s-s*. *Educ*: Bedales, Hants; The Mount School, York. *Studied*: Edinburgh College of Art (1952-58) under W. Gillies. *Exhib*: Goldsmiths' Hall, Galerie Riehentor, Basel; Beverley Art Gallery Retrospective Exhibition (2011). *Works in collections*: Eidgenosische Kunstkommission, Bern Ch; Museum of Medallic Art, Cracow, Poland; Goldsmiths' Hall Collection; BM. *Commissions*: Plaque to commemorate Second World War, The Reform Club, London (1995), Bronze Sculpture, St. Clare's Oxford (1997); Bronze font, St. Martins in the Bullring, Birmingham (2000); Bronze cross, Scots Kink, Paris (2003); Medallion, University of Edinburgh Benefactors (2005). *Address*: Melton Hill Farm, South Lawn Way, North Ferriby, East Yorkshire HU14 3BL. *Email*: ja@gruberstieger.karoo.co.uk *Signs work*: "J. Stieger."

STILLMAN, John, The Frank Herring Award, ROI; marine, town, landscape painter. *Medium*: oil, pencil, watercolour. *b*: Carshalton, 6 Jun 1968. *s of*: Peter Stillman. *Studied*: self-taught artist. *Exhib*: RSMA, ROI, RA, London. *Works in collections*: London Borough of Sutton and private collections in America, France, Anatolia and the UK. *Publications*: Author of 'The Paintings of John Stillman'. *Principal Works*: The Rainbow, Carshalton Ponds. *Recreations*: music, travelling, circus, photography. *Clubs*: Croydon Arts Society, Chelsea Arts Society, The Wapping Group of Artists. *Address*: 196 Stanley Park Road, Carshalton, Surrey, SM5 3JP. *Email*: info@johnstillman.co.uk *Website*: www.johnstillman.co.uk *Signs work*: 'JOHN STILLMAN', or 'J.STILLMAN'.

STJERNSWARD, Philippa, BA Hons; Dupree Painting Award for a Woman Artist, Royal Academy (2003). *Medium*: oil, mixed media on canvas board. *b*: Kenya, 7 Jun 1952. *Studied*: St. Martins College of Art (1981); Ravensbourne College of Art (1982-85). *Exhib*: Royal Academy; Diorama; Barbacan; Stephen Lacey; Reeds Wharf Gallery; London Group; Art First; Discerning Eye. *Works in collections*: many private collections. *Recreations*: travel, reading, exhibitions, cinema, gardening. *Clubs*: London Group. *Address*: 181b Lavender Hill, London SW11 5TE. *Email*: philippastjernsward@yahoo.co.uk *Website*: www.philippastjernsward.com

STOBART, Jane, Fellow, Royal Society of Painter-Printmakers; artist printmaker; lecturer at West Dean College; 'Printmaking Today' magazine prize (2013). *b*: S. Shields, Tyne and Wear, 10 Nov 1949. *d of*: Robert William & Edith Stobart. *m*: Mustafa Sidki. *Educ*: S.E. Essex Technical School, Dagenham. *Studied*: Hornsey College, Central School and Angela Ruskin University. *Represented by*: Bankside Gallery; Axisweb. *Exhib*: UK, USA, Australia, Kenya, Russia, the Netherlands, India. *Works in collections*: British Museum, Ashmolean Museum, Museum of London, Smithsonian Inst., U.S.A., Fitzwilliam Museum; Draifflessen, Germany 2010; University Centre Harlow 2011. *Commissions*: National Grid (1995), Smithsonian Inst., U.S.A. (1996), Florence Nightingale Health Centre, Harlow (1997), University Centre, Harlow (2011). *Publications*: 'Printmaking for Beginners' (A&C Black), 'Drawing Matters (A&C Black); 'Extraordinary Sketchbooks' (A&C Black) 2011. *Clubs*: Wynkyn de Worde Society. *Address*: 47 Potter St., Harlow, Essex CM17 9AE. *Email*: janestobart@btinternet.com

STOCK, Andrew Nicholas, RE, PPSWLA; Richard Richardson award for bird illustration (1980); PJC award for individual merit (1990), prizewinner in Natural World fine art awards (1989, 1990), runner-up in BBC World Magazine's Wildlife Artist of the Year (1991); Bird Illustrator of the Year (1995); Council mem. S.WL.A. (1992-94), secretary (1995-2004), President (2004- 2009); Governor F.B.A. (1997-2003), Council Member RE (2003-2005); self taught painter in water-colour, etching, oil, pen and ink. *Medium*: oil, watercolour, etching. *b*: Germany, 1960. *s of*: Lt. Col. Peter William Stock, M.B.E., M.A. *m*: Melanie Vass (divorced 1995). one *d*. *Educ*: Sherborne School, Dorset.

Represented by: Frost & Reed, St. James's, London. *Exhib*: SWLA, Tyron Gallery, Royal Academy, etc.; one-man shows: Malcolm Innes Gallery, London (4), Alpine Club Gallery, London (2), Gallery in Cork St., London (1), The Mall Galleries (5), Edinburgh and Cerne Abbas, Dorset (2), Frost & Reed, London. *Works in collections*: 29 Commando RA, The Sultan of Oman, RACAL. *Commissions*: MAFF, RSPB. *Publications*: illustrated Driven Game Shooting by D. Bingham (Unwin Hyman, 1989). *Address*: The Old School House, Ryme Intrinseca, Sherborne, Dorset DT9 6JX. *Email*: AndrewNStock@aol.com *Website*: www.andrewstock.co.uk *Signs work*: "Andrew Stock."

STOCKHAM, Alfred Francis, ARCA (1966), Rome Scholar (1967), Granada Arts Fellow (1968), RWA (1992); painter in oil. *b*: London, 1 Jan 1933. *m*: Catherine Bellohoubek. *Studied*: Camberwell School of Art (1960-63, Robert Medley), RCA (1963-66, C. Weight), Rome Scholar (1966-67). *Exhib*: Il Capittello, Rome, Munster, Germany, Arts Fair, New York, RA, RWA. *Works in collections*: Bradford City Museum, Bristol City Museum, GLC, MoW, Arts Council (NI), York City A.G. *Address*: 75 Woodhill Rd., Portishead, Bristol BS20 9HA. *Signs work*: "A.S." front; "Alfred Stockham" back.

STOCKWELL, Susan, RBS; MA RCA, BA (Hons). *Medium*: sculpture, installation, drawing. *b*: Manchester, 19 Aug 1962. *d of*: Peter & Peggy Stockwell. *m*: Mr. Michael Roberts. *Studied*: Royal College of Art (1991-93, MA Fine Art/Sculpture); Sheffield Hallam University (1985-88, BA (Hons) Fine Art/Sculpture). *Exhib*: 2009 - Florence Nightingale Museum, London; Katonah Museum of Art, NY, USA; Incheon Womens Biennale, Korea; Peel Gallery, Houston, Texas. 2008 - Royal Academy Summer Show, Beijing Biennale, China; Miami Art Fair; Patrick Heide Contemporary Art, London; British Trade and Culture Offices, Taipei, Taiwan. Tag Fine Art, London; Manchester City Art Gallery; London Transport Museum (2012); Berardo Museum, Lisbon, Portugal - "Mappamundi" touring to Hotel des Artes, Toulon (2013). *Works in collections*: V&A, London; Binghampton Museum, New York; Finesilver Gallery, San Antonio; British Embassy, Taipei; Florence Nightingale Museum, London; London Transport Museum. *Commissions*: Royal Geographic Society, London, V&A, Florence Nightingale Museum, London Transport Museum, Bedfordshire University. *Publications*: Crafts Magazine (2006), 'The Map as Art: Contemporary Artists Explore Cartography' by Kitty Harmon (Tributary Books, 2009). *Works Reproduced*: The Guardian, Taipei Times, The Independent, Crafts Magazine, The New York Times, see website. *Misc*: 'Visiting Arts' residency - Taipei, Taiwan (Sept-Dec 2007). Installations 2010 - York City Museums. *Address*: 44 Effra Parade, London SW2 1PZ. *Email*: susanstockwell7@gmail.com *Website*: www.susanstockwell.co.uk

STOKER, Richard, FRAM (1973); artist in oils, pen, pencil; film actor, composer, author. *b*: Castleford, Yorks., 8 Nov 1938. *m*: Dr. Gillian Stoker. *Studied*: Huddersfield Art School under Sugden and Napier (1954-58), Paris with Nadia Boulanger (1962-63) (Mendelsohn Scholarship). *Exhib*: Lawrence House , Lewisham Soc. of Arts(1992), Tudor Barn, Eltham (1990), Blackheath Art Soc.(1989, 1990, 1991), Lewisham Festival (1990, 1992). Private collections. *Publications*: Open Window - Open Door (Regency); Words Without Music (Outposts); Tanglewood (Merlin); Diva (Minerva); Collected Short Stories (Minerva). *Official Purchasers*: Trinity College. *Works Reproduced*: on CD covers. *Clubs*: The Garrick, Blackheath Art Soc. (1988), Lewisham Arts Soc. (1990), International PEN (1996), Atlantic Council (1993), Euro-Atlantic Group (1993), RSL (1997), BASCA (1962). *Misc*: Painted by John Bratby, RA (1983) and David Weeks (2012). Treasurer, Lewisham Arts Festival (1990, 1992). Nominated: 'Man of the Year 1997', three Editors Awards: National Library USA. *Address*: 22A Leyland Road, Lee, London SE12 8DT. *Email*: r_stoker@btinternet.com *Website*: www.richardstoker.co.uk and facebook *Signs work*: Richard Stoker.

STOKES, Jayne Emma, BA (Hons) Fine Art; MA European Fine Art. *Medium*: Watercolour; sculpture; installation. *b*: Shropshire, 1 Feb 1973. *m*: Benjamin Mack. one *s*.

one *d*. *Studied*: Edinburgh College of Art (1992-96); Winchester School of Art (1997-98). *Represented by*: Cameron Contemporary Art and The Found Gallery, Dunbar. *Exhib*: Affordable Art Fair, Battersea, London (2011, 2012, 2013, 2014); Howden Park Centre, Livingston, Scotland; Royal Glasgow Institute, Mitchell Library, Scotland (2009-2011); Art4Aid, International Modern Art, Amsterdam (2007); New Contemporaries, Beconsfield Gallery, London (1999). *Works in collections*: Grizedale Sculpture Park; Edinburgh College of Art. *Commissions*: Morgan Williams, Hanover Square, London. *Publications*: New Contemporaries ISBN 9870951555682; Artists and Illustrators (Mar 2013). *Works Reproduced*: 'Homeology' A Mobile Museum, New Contemporaries. *Address*: 5 York Road, North Berwick, EH39 4LX. *Email*: jaynestokesuk@yahoo.co.uk *Website*: www.jaynestokes.com *Signs work*: "JAYNE STOKES".

STOKES, Tina Yvette, SWA (2004); BA Hons Sculpture (1984); Post Graduate in Publishing (1985); Picture Restoration (1987); President & Vice President Award (SWA) for Best Art Work (2005); Winsor & Newton First Prize (SWA) 2007. *Medium*: oil, acrylic. *b*: Willenhall, 8 Feb 1964. *d of*: George, Henry Stokes. *Studied*: Walsall College of Art (1980); Exeter College of Art and Design (1981-85); Billington - Picture Restoration. *Represented by*: Marine House at Beer, Devon. *Exhib*: International AAF: London (2008-2014), Bristol (2008-2014), Bath, Dublin, Edinburgh (2000-07, 2011); Singapore (2011-2014); Hong Kong (2014); SWA Westminster Hall, Mall Galleries (2001-14); Marine House at Beer (2000-14); South West Academy (2005); Webbs Fine Art, London (2004-14); The Flint Gallery, Blakeny, Norfolk (2010-2014). *Works in collections*: private collections worldwide (Hong Kong, Canada, USA, Germany, France, Belgium, etc.). *Commissions*: Netherton Hall, Honiton, Devon; Palace of Westminster. *Publications*: Country Life, Devon Life, Devon Today, and catalogues. *Official Purchasers*: Princess Michael of Kent. *Works Reproduced*: series of limited edition prints (limited to 150). *Recreations*: travel, photography, people. *Clubs*: Branscombe, Emouth, Seaton. *Misc*: paintings predominantly marine landscape of a calm impressionistic nature, with an expansive use of sky and water. *Address*: Watch House, Quay Lane, Lympstone Devon, EX8 5HA. *Email*: stokes.tina@sky.com *Signs work*: 'Tina Stokes'.

STOKES, Vincent, BA (Hons) Photography and Semiotics; designer/photographer; art director. *b*: 9 Jan 1964. *s of*: Vincent Stokes. *Studied*: London College of Printing (1986-89, Ann Williams, Peter Osborn). *Exhib*: Camera Work UK, Camera Work San Francisco, Photographers Gallery, Arnolfini Bristol, New Orleans, Buffalo, Vancouver, NY. *Address*: 14 Beckley House, Hamlets Way, London E3 4SZ.

STOKOE, Michael Arthur, NDD (1957); painter; ex-senior lecturer, Ravensbourne College of Design. *b*: London, 30 Sep 1933. *s of*: Dr. Neville Stokoe, MA. *m*: Gillian Stacey. one *s*. one *d*. *Educ*: King's School, Bruton. *Studied*: St. Martin's School of Art (1953-57). *Exhib*: RA, RBA, ROI, RSOPP, Young Contemporaries, Arts Council, Belfast, Piccadilly Gallery, Arnolfini Gallery, Hamilton Gallery, John Moores, New Gallery, Belfast etc.; one-man shows: Temple Gallery, Drian Galleries, Bear Lane Gallery, Nottingham City A.G., Oxford Gallery, Anna Mei Chadwick Gallery, Zella Gallery. *Works in collections*: Arts Council of N. Ireland, V&A, WAG, Ferens A.G., Hull, Leeds City A.G., ICI, etc., and 20 educational authorities. Bibliotheque National. *Publications*: prints with editions Alecto, Collectors Guild, Anely Juda Fine Art. *Recreations*: sailing. *Address*: The Bough House, 43-45 High Street, Robertsbridge, TN32 5AL. *Signs work*: "STOKOE."

STONE, Adam, BA Fine Art, Post Graduate Diploma Royal Academy School, Edna Rose Weiss Figurative Painting Travel Award Brinsley Ford, Vincent Harris Painting Prize. *Medium*: oil, drawing, prints. *b*: Leeds, 11 Oct 1969. *m*: Gail Stone. one *s*. two *d*. *Studied*: Staffordshire University (BA, 1990-93), Royal Academy Schools (Leonard McComb, Brendan Neiland, PGDip, 1996-99), Huddersfield University (2002-04). *Represented by*:

Sarah Wiseman Gallery, Oxford. *Exhib*: Royal Academy (1997, 1998, 1999); 'Award Winners', Air Gallery, London (1998); Group shows: The Gallery, Cork Street (1998), Dean Clough, Halifax (2000), Bruton Street Gallery, London (2000), Kunst Darm Henry Peacock Gallery (2001), Catto Contemporary, London (2001), Design Centre, Islington, London (2002), RA Summer Show (2009). *Commissions*: Rover Group. *Publications*: 'The Exhibitionist' (Where is) Painting Now? - Chris Taylor (2000); 'New Talent' catalogue, Bruton Street Gallery, London. *Official Purchasers*: Rover Group. *Address*: 10 Cockridge Drive, Leeds, LS16 7LT. *Email*: adam.stone2@ntlworld.com *Website*: adamstoneart.com *Signs work*: "A. STONE".

STONE, Pamela Ann, Silver Cup for Best Artist in Cheltenham Club. *Medium*: oil, watercolour, pastels. *b*: Fletton, Hunts., 10 Apr 1938. *d of*: Francis Henry Clayson. *m*: Jeffrey Stone. one *s*. one *d*. *Educ*: State educated. Profession - nurse (1954). *Studied*: self taught artist. Studied in West Africa (1961). Taught Art in Cheltenham (2000) and Glasgow (2000). Teaching Art Swindon Art Club (2013-2014). *Exhib*: Mall Galleries; Lloyds TSB Private Banking, Cheltenham (2005); Singer & Friedlander/Sunday Times Competition (2005); RSMA (2006, 2011); SWA (2007-2012); SWLA (2007); RI (2008, 2011); Solo exhibition: Garden Gallery, Cheltenham (2008-2012); Fosseway Artists (2009-2011); Cheltenham Artists (2010, 2011, 2012). RI 2 paintings sold (2011), SWA 2 paintings shown (2011, 20112), RSMA shown (2011, 2012, 2013), Parker & Harris Sunday Times 1 sold (2012), RI shown (2013, 2014), Fossway Artists (2012, 2013, 2014). Solo exhibition Garden Gallery (Aug 2014). *Commissions*: many commissions including: SWA; Richard and Judy (portraits); Christian Furr, Toyah, Paul O'Grady, Canon Edward Eweing, Steve Bennett, Gems TV - Noushka Williams presenter, and many others. TV Gems Sarah Bennett (2013), Mall Gallery 2 pics, Barry Wiggins Gems and many more. 7 for Queens Hotel Cheltenham, 10 ordered 3 more to paint. *Publications*: Every year since 2005, The Cheltenham Echo. *Clubs*: Cheltenham Art Club; Swindon Art Club; Tewkesbury Art Club; Fosseway Artists. *Address*: Leith House, Tewkesbury Road, Coombe Hill, GL19 4AW. *Email*: pam.stone@hotmail.co.uk *Website*: www.pamstone-artist.co.uk *Signs work*: "Pamela A Stone" or monogram "PSA".

STONES, Alan. *Medium*: oil, drawing, prints. *b*: Manchester, 29 Dec 1947. *Partner*: Rebecca Payn. two *s*. one *d*. *Educ*: St. Martin's School of Art, London (1967-71). *Exhib*: Carlisle Museum & Art Gallery (1996); one-man touring: Falkland Islands (1995), Carlisle Museum & Art Gallery (1986-87) Lady Lodge Arts Centre Peterborough (1985-86). Competitions: Ruth Corchard Self Portrait (2011), Wrexham Print International 2011, Jerwood Drawing Prize (2008, 2003), Cheltenham Drawing Open (1999, 1998), Tolly Cobbold (1981, 1979), Brantwood, Cumbria (2014). *Works in collections*: includes: Portsmouth City Council, Gulbenkian Foundation, Universities of Aberystwyth, Sheffield, Liverpool & Imperial College, Darlington Museum, Bolton Museum & Art Gallery, Derbyshire Museum Service, Eden District Council. *Commissions*: include: Falkland Island Government, National Science Museum London, Eden District Council Cumbria, Copeland Borough Council, Dista Products Ltd, Eden District Council. *Clubs*: Chelse Arts Club. *Address*: Glen Cottage, Blencarm, Penrith, Cumbria CA10 1TX. *Email*: alan@alanstones.co.uk *Website*: www.alanstones.co.uk *Signs work*: "Alan Stones".

STONES, Anthony, FRBS (1992), President the Society of Portrait Sculptors (1998-2004), FRSA; sculptor in clay for bronze; Visiting Professor: Tsinghua University, Beijing, China & Nanjing University, Nanjing, China 2004-2008. *b*: Glossop, Derby., 8 Feb 1934. *s of*: Arnold Stones, dyer. *m*: Lily Feng-Stones. *Educ*: St. Bede's College, Manchester. *Studied*: Manchester Regional College of Art (1950-51), Auckland Teacher's College 1959-61. *Works in collections*: bronze portrait heads: John Piper in Reading City Art Gallery; Prof. Dorothy Hodgkin, OM, Somerville College, Oxford; Sir Ronald Syme, OM, and Sir Isaiah Berlin, OM, Wolfson College, Oxford; Liam Ó Flaherty, National Gallery of Ireland; Sean

Ó Faolin, Irish Writers Museum, Dublin, John Wain CBE, Philip Larkin & Seamus Heaney at St. John's College Oxford; Sir S.Y. Chung, The University of Science & Technology, Hong Kong; Bruce Mason, Downstage Theatre, Wellington, New Zealand; Han Meilin, sculptor, private coll. Beijing. *Commissions*: commemorative bronze figures: The Hon. Peter Fraser, Wellington, NZ; Lord Freyberg, VC, Auckland, NZ; Jean Batten, Auckland International Airport; Victorian Navvy (1992), Gerrards Cross Railway Station; Seven Pacific Explorers for New Zealand Pavilion Expo 92 Seville; Captain James Cook, Gisborne, New Zealand (1994); The Pioneer Wine Maker, Waitakere City, New Zealand (1995); equestrian statue of "Bonnie Prince Charlie", Derby (1995); Captain James Cook, National Maritime Museum, Greenwich (1997); Blair 'Paddy' Mayne, Newtownards, Northern Ireland (1997); 'King' and 'Queen', 'Orpheus and Eurydice', four bronze statuettes for Royal Caribbean Cruise Line A/S (1997), John Northwood, Merry Hill Birmingham, Abel Tasman, Nelson, New Zealand, Arthur Brooke, Manchester, The Emperor Nerva, equestrian statue, Gloucester, Prince Potemkin, equestrian statue, private collection UK: 'The Young Shakespeare' 2004, 'Migrant Family Group' 2005 Nelson, NZ, 'Michelangelo', Nanjing Museum, China, 'Prof. Tu Chang Wang', China Meteorological Administration HQ, Beijing, China; 'Brunel', Brunel University UK (2006); 'Gustav Holst', Cheltenham, UK (2007). *Publications*: edited: Celebration (Penguin Books, 1984); wrote and illustrated: Bill and the Ghost of Grimley Grange (Wolfhound Press, 1988; Puffin Books, 1994), Bill and the Maze at Grimley Grange (Wolfhound Press, 1990); 'Venus and Cupid': a relief carving by Michelangelo? papers of The British School at Rome Vol. LXI (1993). *Clubs*: Commonwealth. *Address*: 2 Kent Place Lechlade-on-Thames GL7 3AW. *Email*: fengstones@hotmail.com *Website*: www.sculptor.co.nz *Signs work*: "Anthony Stones."

STONES, Leslie W. *Medium*: oil. *b*: May 1957. *m*: Brenda Carol Stones. two *d*. *Educ*: Yorkshire. *Studied*: self taught. *Represented by*: Talents Fine Art (Yorkshire); Bourne Gallery (Surrey). *Exhib*: ROI, RSMA (Mall Galleries); Ferens Gallery, Hull; Leeds City Art Gallery; Llewellyn Alexander Gallery, London; Cooper Gallery, Yorkshire; Doncaster Museum & Art Gallery; D'arcy Foyle Exhibition (Brisbane, Australia). *Commissions*: Medici, Woodmansterne, private clients, Otterhouse Ltd, Hallmark, Simon Elvin, Camden Graphics. *Publications*: The Artist Magazine, limited edition prints. *Works Reproduced*: Art licenced to many publishers/manufacturers, and limited edition prints in collection of the Rare Breeds Survival Trust. *Principal Works*: Farm livestock, British countryside scenes. *Recreations*: wildlife, history. *Address*: Fernleigh, West End Road, Norton, Doncaster, DN6 9DH. *Email*: lesliestonesart@aol.com *Website*: www.lesliestones.co.uk *Signs work*: "Leslie W. Stones".

STONYER, Andrew Allan, RWA, RBS; BA (1966), AA Dip. Arch. (1974), PhD (1978); sculptor; Prof. in Fine Art, University of Gloucestershire. *b*: Sibbertoft, Leics., 11 Oct 1944. *m*: Linda. one *s*. one *d*. *Studied*: Northampton School of Art (1960-63), Loughborough College of Art and Design (1963-67), Architectural Assoc. (1970-72), Leicester Polytechnic/Slade School of Fine Art (1975-78). *Exhib*: RA, Ikon Gallery, Cairn Gallery, Barbican Centre, Art 45 and Terre des Hommes, Montreal. *Works in collections*: Ottawa, Hague, Leicester, etc. *Commissions*: Leicester City Council, Cheltenham Racecourse, Ottawa City Council, Laval - Montreal, Newcastle Metro, Cumberland Infirmary, Gloucester Docks, etc. *Publications*: Leonardo Vol.18. No.3, The Structurist No.27/28. *Clubs*: Chelsea Arts. *Address*: Eastmead, Watery Lane, Newent, Glos. GL18 1QA.

STOREY, Terence, PPRSMA, RBSA, FRSA; marine and landscape artist in oils and water-colour. *b*: Sunderland, 17 Apr 1923. *Educ*: Sunderland Art School and Derby College of Art. *Exhib*: NS, RBA, RSMA, ROI, NEAC,SWLA and RBSA. *Works in collections*: HRH the Prince of Wales, RSMA Diploma Collection, Derby A.G., The Picture collection of the Port of London Authority, and private collections in USA, Canada, Australia, New Zealand,

Germany and the UK. *Commissions*: Sultan of Oman, The Royal Eagles Club, The Royal Burnham Yacht Club, The Forth Ports - Tall Ships Gathering - Leith. *Works Reproduced*: Rolls-Royce Ltd., Medici Soc., Royles, Winsor and Newtons, 20th Century British Marine Art, Square Rigged Sailing Ships, Marine Painting, A Celebration of Marine Art, International Artist Mag.,and numerous shipping lines. *Address*: Merlewood, 6 Queensway, Derby DE22 3BE.

STRAFFORD, Judy, artist in oil and water-colour. *b*: Hove, 6 Mar 1932. *m*: Thomas Strafford (Earl of Strafford). one *s*. two *d*. *Studied*: Brighton College of Art. *Exhib*: solo and group shows: London, Paris, New Dehli, Alresford, Bristol, etc. Work in collections internationally. *Works in collections*: private. *Publications*: illustrated: The Green Home by Karen Christensen. Wrote and illustrated 'An Indian Journal', 'Pig Tales' etc. *Works Reproduced*: 1993 Good Hotel Guide, greetings cards, Limited Edn. prints. *Recreations*: travelling, gardening, cooking, wine. *Misc*: Workshops in water-colour, oil and mixed media in England, Italy, Spain, Turkey & Canada. *Address*: Apple Tree Cottage, Easton, Winchester, Hants SO21 1EF. *Email*: painting@judystrafford.co.uk *Website*: www.judystrafford.co.uk *Signs work*: 'Judy Strafford'.

STRANG, Michael, DipAD (Hons). *Medium*: oil, watercolour, drawing. *b*: Datchet, 24 Oct 1942. *s of*: Christopher John & Margaret Ann Strang. four *d*. *Educ*: Surrey and Windsor, Berks. *Studied*: Wimbledon School of Art (1968-70); Camberwell School of Art (1970-73). *Represented by*: Cry of Gulls Gall., Fowey; Oriel Pen y Fan Gall., Brecon; Elder Fine Art, North Carolina; Great Atlantic Galls, St. Just, Falmouth, Monmouth. *Exhib*: RA; Tate St. Ives (over 50 works shown 1995); Medici, Bond St.; St. Martins-in-the-Fields Church, London; Curr St. Galls., London; Brecknock Museum, Wales; George Frederick Watts Museum & Gallery; Truro Museum, Cornwall; Chelsea Arts Club; Frost & Reed, Bristol; Cornwall Education Coll.; Thomsons Gall., London; Chomé, Bath; Guardian Exh Gall., USA, and many others. *Works in collections*: Penlee House Museum, Penzance; C&G Building Society Collection; Brecknock Museum Coll.; Cornwall County Educ. Coll.; Mandells, Norwich; USA galleries. *Commissions*: many commissions including Bryan Forbes, Nanette Newman, Frank Muir, a number of portrait commissions. *Publications*: Guardian, Arts Review, Western Morning News, Cornishmen, etc. *Official Purchasers*: Brecknock Museum, Wales. *Principal Works*: recent retrospective Brecknock Museum 'The Welsh Collection', unique coll. of Llanelly Hill Brynmawr in 1970s - last mining years in Valleys, 3 works bought for collection; works sold at Christie's. *Clubs*: Chelsea Arts Club. *Misc*: painting of St. Martins-in-the-Fields, Trafalgar Square, London 'Easter Symphony' in the church to help promote £34 million restoration project. Documentary film being made. Studio at: 299 Stroude Road, Virginia Water, Surrey, GU25 4DE. *Address*: 1, Ridgeo Mill, Gulval, nr.Penzance, Cornwall TR18 3BX. *Email*: michaeljstrang@tiscali.co.uk *Website*: www.michaelstrang.com *Signs work*: 'M J Strang'.

STRANGELOVE, Nikolas Alexander, BA (Hons); Awards: Creative Skills; Arts Council Grants; Kodak Bursary; University of London Laurel; Guardian/NUS Photographer of the Year; Finalist, Guardian/Penguin Book Cover; Finalist, Seeds of Change/Observer, Best of the Southwest Prize, National Open Art Competition. *Medium*: photography. *b*: London, 9 Apr 1970. *Studied*: University of Westminster; Northbrook College of Technology. *Represented by*: Michael Wood Fine Art, Plymouth; Stoneman Gallery, Cornwall. *Exhib*: Festival Internazionale Di Roma, Italy; Falmouth Art Gallery, Penlee House, Cornwall; RWA, Bristol. *Works in collections*: The National Portrait Gallery. *Commissions*: BBC, The Progressive (USA), Prima Records, Tate Enterprises Ltd., Kneehigh Theatre, ES Magazine, DJ Magazine, The Wire Magazine. *Publications*: "PZ" self-published book. *Principal Works*: B&W/colour hand printed photography. *Clubs*: Newlyn Society of Arts. *Misc*: Selected for: Discerning Eye, Mall Galleries, & Festival Internazionale Di Roma, Italy: National Open Art Competition. *Address*: The Flat, Trevelyan House, 16 Chapel Street,

Penzance, Cornwall, TR18 4AW. *Email*: nik@nikstrangelove.com *Website*: www.nikstrangelove.com. *Signs work*: "NIK STRANGELOVE".

STREET, Clare, SHA; HEA; Freeman of the Goldsmiths' Company; currently Chair of SHA. *Medium*: Watercolour; prints; sculpture; designer; jeweller; hand engraver and die-sinker. *b*: Isle of Wight, 27 Oct 1942. *m*: Divorced. *Educ*: Frensham Heights School, Farnham, Surrey; Seale Hayne Agricultural Colege. *Studied*: John Cass School of Art (line and seal engraving, classical diamond setting and v-mounting). *Exhib*: Includes: Goldsmiths Hall: 'On the Cuff' (2005); 'Bridal Style'/'Love Story' (2003); 'Celebration' (2002); Goldsmiths Fair for 18 years (1092-2003). Goldsmiths Hall Annual Exhibition of Winning Competition Entries. 'Loot' (Goldsmiths' Co) London & Leeds (1977); Minneapolis, USA (1978). *Commissions*: Two from Prime Warden of the Goldsmiths' Co and two from clerk of same. Several from HRH The Princess Royal. *Official Purchasers*: Goldsmiths' Co (2005) handmade 18ct gold certificate line engraved; Heraldic Achievement of the Goldsmiths' Company. *Works Reproduced*: illustrations of my work in a few books in addition to exhibition catalogues. *Recreations*: Walking; seeing exhibitions of painting and other arts and crafts; visiting National Trust houses and collections and similar non NT houses, collections and churches. *Clubs*: Ramblers Association. *Address*: Little Orchard, 11 Woodcut Road, Wrecclesham, Farnham GU10 4QF. *Email*: clare@seal-engraving.com *Website*: www.handengravers.co.uk/clarestreet www.heraldic-arts.com/clarestreet *Signs work*: "CLARE STREET" or "G. CLARE STREET".

STREETHER, Lila Pauline. SFP, SBA Diploma. *Medium*: watercolour, drawing, mixed media, prints, collage, acrylic. *b*: Cardiff, 17 Aug 1950. *d of*: Audrey Gajewski. *m*: Nigel Streether. three *d*. *Educ*: Cardiff; Bristol. *Studied*: trained by Angie Girling; courses and workshops in botanical painting; two year course with the Society of Botanical Artists. *Exhib*: Exhibitions in the South-West; Old Bakery Artists Art Trails and Exhibitions; Bath Society of Botanical Artists exhibitions in England and Ireland. One-woman exhibitions, Clevedon 2010; Bristol 2011; Cam Valley Art Trail; 'Swans of Wells' charity project. Society of Floral Painters Exhibitions at Stourhead, Chichester and Basingstoke. *Works in collections*: private collections in America, Australia and Europe. *Publications*: local newspapers, i.e. Bath Chronicle; BSBA calendars. *Works Reproduced*: for prints, cards and gift items. *Principal Works*: Botanical paintings for Augustine Henry exhibition in Dublin, 2009. *Recreations*: photography, collecting Moorcroft pottery, Vintage Car Club (with spouse), walking. *Clubs*: Bath Society of Botanical Artists; Timsbury Art Group; Society of Floral Painters; Society of Botanical Artists. *Address*: Lyndhurst, Green Lane, White Cross, Hallatrow, BS39 6ER. *Email*: n.streether@sky.com *Website*: www.bsba.co.uk/lilastreether *Signs work*: "L.Streether" or "Lila Streether" or "LS".

STREVENS, Bridget Julia, MA (Cantab., 1979); artist and illustrator in oil, water-colour, line, and digital pen. *b*: Ongar, Essex, 24 Sep 1956. *d of*: John Strevens, painter. *m*: (1) Stephen Romer. one *s*. (2) Michael Finch. one *d*. *Educ*: King's College, Cambridge University. *Studied*: Ecole Nationale Superieure des Beaux Arts, Paris. *Exhib*: London, Paris, Society of Illustrators, New York. *Works in collections*: Epping Forest District Museum. *Publications*: 'Toto's Travels' (Little, Brown & Co.), 'Kiss, Kiss!' (Little Hare, Simon & Schuster US, Bayard, France), The Big Book for Little Hands (Tate UK, Harper Collins US). *Address*: 59 Rue de Meaux, 60300 Senlis, France. *Email*: b@bridgetstrevens.com *Website*: www.bridgetstrevens.com *Signs work*: "B. Strevens" or "Biddy Strevens." or B.Strevens.Marzo.

STRICKLAND, David Robert. *Medium*: sculpture, drawing. *b*: Saltburn, 12 Oct 1965. *Studied*: Cleveland College of Art, Middlesbrough (Ceramics and Fine Art); Stafford College & Stafford University (HND, Figurative Sculpture). *Exhib*: Woodbine Contemporary Arts; The Frazer Gallery, Albemarle St.; The Maddox Gallery, Maddox St.;

The Air Gallery, Dover St,; Dover St Arts Club; La Galleria, Pall Mall; Gallery Kaleidescope, Kilburn, London. *Commissions*: Various portrait busts. Statuette of Charles Bronson, Creatures Unlimited. *Works Reproduced*: The First Wish/The Third Wish - bronze statuettes. *Email*: DavidStrickland041@gmail.com *Website*: www.stricklandsculpting.co.uk

STRINGER, Simon Kenneth, MA Royal Academy Schools (1985); Vice-President of Royal Society of British Sculptors. *Medium*: sculptor. *b*: Bovey Tracey, 3 Feb 1960. *m*: Barbara. one *d*. *Studied*: Royal Academy. *Exhib*: various one-man and group shows from 1985. *Works in collections*: Tate Modern Education Department; The Sculpture Park, Churt. *Commissions*: Hackney Council, Gloucester City Council, Foulton Group Ellesmere Port, Holte Birmingham. *Clubs*: Fellow of Royal Society of British Sculptors, RASAA. *Address*: Rear Studio, 24 Englefield Rd, London N1 4ET. *Email*: simonstringer@blueyonder.com *Website*: simonstringer.com

STRONG, Sir Roy, PhD Fellow Ferens (1976), Prof. of Fine Art (1972), Hon DLitt (Leeds) (1983), Hon.D.Litt. (Keele) (1984); writer and historian; Director, Victoria and Albert Museum (till Dec. 1987); Fellow, Royal Society of Literature (1999). *b*: London, 23 Aug 1935. *s of*: G.E.C. Strong. *m*: Dr. Julia Trevelyan Oman (1971). *Educ*: Edmonton County Grammar School; Queen Mary College, London; Warburg Inst., London. *Commissions*: Occasionally acts as garden consultant. In this capacity he has designed and aided H.R.H. Prince of Wales, Gianni Versace and Sir Elton John with their gardens. *Publications*: author: Portraits of Queen Elizabeth I (1963), Holbein - Henry VIII (1967), Tudor - Jacobean Portraits (1969), The English Icon: English - Jacobean Portraiture (1969), Van Dyck: Charles on Horseback (1972), The Cult of Elizabeth: Elizabethan Portraiture - Pageantry (1977), And When Did You Last See Your Father? (1978), The Renaissance Garden in England (1979), Gloriana, Portraits of Queen Elizabeth I (1987), Cecil Beaton, The Royal Portraits (1988), The Story of Britain (1996), The Roy Strong Diaries 1967-1987 (1997), The Spirit of Britain (1999), The Artist and the Garden (2000), Feast, A History of Grand Eating (2002), The Laskett, The Story of a Garden (2003), Coronation (2005); 'A Little History of the English Country Church' (2007); Visions of England (2011), Self-portrait of a Young Man (2013); contributor to numerous books and learned journals. *Clubs*: Garrick. *Misc*: Serving or has served on numerous public committees including: Chevening House, the Council of the Royal College of Art, Fine Arts Advisory Committee of the British Council, Arts Council and South Bank Board. In 2000 became High Bailiff and Searcher of the Sanctuary of Westminster Abbey, one of the institution's two great lay offices. *Address*: The Laskett, Much Birch, Herefordshire HR2 8HZ

STUART, Gordon Thomas, RCA (2000), WSW (1995); painter in oil, water-colour and draughtsman; lecturer, Heatherleys School of Art, Dyfed College of Art (1975-1982); artist in residence, UK Year of Literature (1995); artist in residence, Dylan Thomas Centre (since 1996); Second Prize, Welsh Painter of the Year (2005). *b*: Toronto, Canada, 30 May 1924. *m*: Mair Jenkins. *Educ*: Toronto Schools (1931-1946). *Studied*: Central Technical College, Toronto, Ontario College of Art, St. Martin's London, University of London. *Exhib*: numerous, Toronto, Vancouver, England, Wales. National Library of Wales, Aberystwyth honoured artist with exhibition on his 80th birthday; St. David's Centre Cardiff, 2005: 30 portraits by artist for 50 Years Cardiff as Capital celebration. *Works in collections*: HRH Prince of Wales, Contemporary Art Soc., Wales, Canadian High Commission, London, National Portrait Gallery, Ontario College of Art, Buffalo University, New York, National Library of Wales, Glynn Vivian Art Gallery, Swansea; National Gallery, Canada. *Commnissions*: numerous over 70 years. *Publications*: Dylan Thomas Trail, illustration, Dylan the Bard, Sinclair, illustration. *Works Reproduced*: numerous. *Principal Works*: Portraits of Literary worthies. *Recreations*: music, books. *Signs work*: "Gordon Stuart".

STUART, Henrietta Margaret Mercedes, BAHons Fine Art (1st). *Medium*: Oil, drawing. *b*: London, 21 Mar 1965. *m*: Mr David Richardson. *Studied*: Newcastle upon Tyne

University. *Represented by*: Nicholas Bowlby. *Exhib*: the Art Agency, Esher; AAF Battersea (2010-2014); AAF Hampstead (2013, 2014); Chelsea Art Society (2012, 13, 14); NRA Llewellyn Alexander (2012, 13, 14); Box Galleries (2013, 14). Mixed shows in London, Paris, Marseilles. Solo shows in London, Marseilles, St Ives. Ithaka. *Works in collections*: Private collections in New York, Houston, Vancouver, Sydney, Perth, Melbourne, Paris and UK. *Address*: Studio 109, Wimbledon Art Studios, Riverside Road, SW17 0BB. *Email*: hstuartart@gmail.com *Website*: www.henriettastuart.com *Signs work*: "STUART".

STUART, Robert, BA; MSc. *Medium*: Oil, drawing. *b*: London. *m*: Emma. *Educ*: self taught. *Studied*: Princes Drawing School (2012-13). *Exhib*: Juried events - Art at the Court House (2012); The Other Art Fair (spring and autumn 2013, spring 2014); Wycombe Museum (2014). *Works in collections*: Private. *Commissions*: Various private commissions. *Misc*: Signature and date are usually on the back of work, the front may be initialled RAS. *Address*: Unit 4, 1st Floor, Block A, Commercial Square, Leigh Street, High Wycombe HP11 2RH. *Email*: robert@robertstuartart.com *Website*: www.robertstuartart.com *Signs work*: "Robert A Stuart".

STUART-SMITH, Susanna J., BMus, DipEcol, Gold medal (RHS); botanical artist in water-colour, pencil, ink; freelance botanical illustrator working at RBG Kew; experienced in fieldwork abroad (Oman), orchid illustration; botanical illustration tutor. *b*: B'ham, 26 May 1943. *m*: Richard Clymo, ecologist. *Educ*: Universities of London, Cambridge, Kent. *Studied*: trained: RBG Edinburgh (1984), RBG Kew (1993). *Exhib*: RHS London; RBG Edinburgh; RBG Kew; Linnean Soc. London; Hunt Inst.,USA; World Orchid Conference, Glasgow. *Works in collections*: RBG Edinburgh, RBG Kew, Highgrove Florilegium. *Publications*: illustrated: 'Plants of Dhofar, Southern Region of Oman', Miller and Morris (Sultanate of Oman 1988); 'The New RHS Dictionary of Gardening' (Macmillan Press Ref. Books 1992); 'The Orchids of Belize' (1996), 'Orchids of Bhutan', 'Orchids of Borneo'; reference books and scientific publications. *Address*: 49 High St., Robertsbridge, E. Sussex TN32 5AL. *Signs work*: "Susanna Stuart-Smith" or "S.S.S."

STUBBS, Michael, BA (Hons) Fine Art, MA (Fine Art), Phd (Fine Art). *Medium*: oil based mixed media on MDF. *b*: Rustington, West Sussex, 1 Sep 1961. *Studied*: Bath Academy of Art (1984-87), Goldsmiths College (1988-90, 1999-03). *Represented by*: Laurent Delaye Gallery; Hollenbach Gallery, Stuttgart; Oscar Cruz Gallery, São Paulo. *Exhib*: solo: Nicola Jacobs Gallery (1991); Bipasha Ghosh, London (1993); Curtain Road Arts, London (1995); Lotta Hammer Gallery, London (1996); Concourse Gallery, Byam Shaw School of Art (1997); Duncan Cargill Gallery, London (1998); Entwistle Gallery, London (2002); Marella Contemporary Art, Milan (2005); Hollenbach Gallery, Stuttgart (2006); Barocruz Gallery, Sao Paulo (2007); Rob Barton Gallery, London (2009); Laurent Delaye Gallery, London (2009, '10, '11); Cass Gallery, London Metropolitan University (2013); The Avenue, London; Hollenbach Gallery, Stuttgart (2014). *Works in collections*: Government Art Collection, British Council, Gibraltar Bank, Kreditanstalt fur Wiederaufbau; BHP Oils, Texas Pacific, Marsh, Slough Estates and numerous international private and corporate. *Email*: momentum@dircon.co.uk *Website*: www.michaelstubbs.org *Signs work*: 'Michael Stubbs'.

STULTIENS, Jeff, DipAD (1966), RP (1990); First Prize - The Portrait Award, National Portrait Gallery (1985); Hon Sec RSPP; Senior Lecturer at Hertfordshire College of Art and Design (1974-1987); painter in oil. *b*: Blackpool, 12 Sep 1944. *s of*: Thomas Stultiens. *m*: Catherine Knowelden. *Educ*: Hutton and Tiffin Schools. *Studied*: Kingston School of Art under Alfred Heyworth and Camberwell School of Art under Robert Medley R.A. (1961-1966). *Exhib*: John Player Portrait Award - NPG, British Portraiture 1980-85, Drawings for All, RSPP, Hunting/Observer, Nikkei Exhbn. - Tokyo, The Portrait Award 1980-89. *Works in collections*: NPG, Merton and Oriel Colleges - Oxford, National Heart and Lung Inst.,

RNLI, Royal Medical Foundation, RAM. Many other public and private commissions. *Address*: 26 St. George's Cl., Toddington, Beds. LU5 6AT. *Signs work*: "Stultiens."

STUMMEL, Henning Friedrich, Dip-Ing.Architect, RIBA, RIBA Award, RIBA Housing Award. *Medium*: architecture. *b*: Frankfurt, 9 Jun 1966. *m*: Alice Dawson. one *d*. *Educ*: Deutsche Schule, London; Rokeby Prep; Gutenberg Gymnasium, Wiesbaden. *Studied*: TH. Darmstadt; ETH Zurich; worked with N. Foster (1993), and D. Chipperfield (1993-2000). *Exhib*: RA Summer Exhbn; RIBA. *Publications*: RIBA Journal (Feb 2003), Casa Bella (Oct 2009), Hauser (Jun 2009), Intelligente Architektur (Oct 2013). *Works Reproduced*: The Workshop, Camden. *Principal Works*: extension to Georgian townhouse, Marylebone; Mews house, Alba Place, Notting Hill. *Address*: c/o Henning Stummel Architects Ltd, The Workshop, 183 Royal College Street, Camden, London NW1 0SG. *Email*: mail@henningstummelarchitects.co.uk *Website*: www.henningstummelarchitects.co.uk

STYLES, (Elizabeth) Caroline, DipAD, PG Cert. *Medium*: pastels, oil, pencil, charcoal. *b*: Paulton, Bristol, 27 Nov 1947. *s of*: Harry & Betty Styles. *Partner*: Stephen Middleton. two *s*. two *d*. *Educ*: King Edward's School, Witley, Surrey. *Studied*: Chelsea School of Art (1965-72); Royal Academy Schools (1969-72). *Exhib*: Grabowski Gallery, Bowmoore Gallery, Whitechapel Open, Space Open, Fish Island Events, Burlington Fine Art, Arts Unwrapped, Royal Academy Summer Exhibitions. *Works in collections*: private collections. *Commissions*: portraits and landscapes for private clients. *Works Reproduced*: 2006 RA Summer Exhibition Catalogue. *Principal Works*: 'Still Dying', series of still lives evoking roadside flower shrines. *Recreations*: gardens, concerts, theatre. *Clubs*: Chelsea Arts Club. *Misc*: taught at The Working Men's College, Mornington Crescent, and various adult colleges and secondary schools. *Address*: 14 Byron Road, London E10 5DT. *Email*: caroline_styles@hotmail.com *Website*: www.carolinestyles.com *Signs work*: "Caroline Styles" or "CS".

STYLIANOU, Lorraine, BA (Hons) European Literature with Norwegian Major. *Medium*: acrylic. *b*: N. Ireland, 25 Jan 1965. *m*: Chris Stylianou. one *s*. one *d*. *Studied*: University of East Anglia, Norwich (1986-90) (University of Oslo 1988-89); self taught artist. *Represented by*: ABNA. *Exhib*: Little Picture Gallery, Mousehole; Society of Naive Artists, St Ives. *Works in collections*: private. *Commissions*: many private commissinos (greeting cards, portraits). *Works Reproduced*: as greetings cards, stationery, colouring books (Amazon). *Recreations*: painting, travel. *Clubs*: KPI Business Forum, Ladder Club. *Address*: 7 Ilex Close, Colchester CO2 9QB. *Email*: lorraine@lorrainestylianou.com *Website*: lorrainestylianou.com *Signs work*: "Lorraine Stylianou".

SULLIVAN, Benjamin Christian, RP, NEAC; BA (Hons) degree in Painting (2000). *Medium*: painter in oil and printmaker. *b*: Grimsby, 10 May 1977. *Educ*: Priestlands School, Lymington. *Studied*: Edinburgh College of Art (1997-2000). *Exhib*: Royal Academy, Royal Scottish Academy, National Portriat Gallery, Mall Galleries, etc. *Works in collections*: Royal Scottish Academy, Edinburgh; Parliament House Portraits, Edinburgh; University College, Oxford; Girton College, Cambridge; Institute of Civil Engineers, London. *Commissions*: Faculty of Advocates, private commissions. *Clubs*: NEAC, RP. *Address*: 8 Duddery Road, Havershill, Suffolk, CB9 8EA. *Email*: benjaminsullivanrp@yahoo.com *Website*: www.benjaminsullivan.com

SULLIVAN, Jason, BA (1979); painter in oil. *b*: Poole, Dorset, 31 Mar 1958. *s of*: Michael Sullivan. *m*: Una. one *s*. *Educ*: Queen Elizabeth Grammar School, Horncastle, Lincolnshire. *Studied*: Grimsby College of Art (1974-76, Mr. Todd), Sheffield College of Art (1976-79, Mr. Peacock). Numerous exhbns. *Address*: 19 Meersbrook Pk. Rd., Sheffield, S. Yorks.

SULLIVAN, Wendy, poet, painter; Winner: Brixton Open. *b*: London, 18 May 1938. *Educ*: Notre Dame High School, Battersea; attended Sir John Cass and Goldsmiths' Colleges; life drawing Leonard McComb, RA; anatomy (UCH) .*Exhib*: RA Summer Shows,

Galerie Dagmar, Portobello Open, South Bank Show, Cooltans, Paperworks IV, Brixton Gallery, W. Norwood Library, First Sight Gallery, Bristol, The Ritzy, Brixton Library, The Village Hall, Brixton, Brixton Open, Jacaranda, Brixton, Bettie Morton Gallery, Gems of Lambeth Archives; Carnegie Library; Art in Brixton; Dulwich Lodge; Boqueria Tapas (SW2); Brixton Library. *Works in collections*: on loan/and collections: Galerie Dagmar, Breast Screening Clinic Camberwell, St, John's Church, Brixton, Lambeth Archives, Movement for Justice, St. Marks Centre, Deptford. *Publications*: Interviewd CD and DVD. *Works Reproduced*: www.bbc.co.uk/yourpaintings. *Misc*: Artist-in-Residence, A.S.C. Studios, Brixton (2000/2001). *Address*: 127 Crescent La., London SW4 8EA. *Email*: draw2day@hotmail.co.uk *Website*: www.wendysullivanartist.com *Signs work*: "Wendy Sullivan".

SUMMERFIELD, Angela Mary, BA (Hons); MA; PhD; British Government Scholarship, British Academy (PhD research 1994-97); Art Critic for The Spectator (2000-); elected member of AICA (International Association of Art Critics) (1995). *Medium*: Oil, watercolour, printmaker. *b*: London, 5 Apr 1970. *Studied*: University of Leeds (1988-92); Courtauld Institute of Art, University of London (1992-92); City University, London (1993-97). *Exhib*: Include: 'Discerning Eye' Mall Galleries, London (2002); Singer Friedlander/The Sunday Times Watercolour Competition, Mall Galleries, London (2004); Southwark Open CGP London Cafe Gallery (2007); Cork Street Open, London (2009); solo show, Chelsea and Westminster Hospital (2010); Winchcombe Art Trail (2014); Broadway Festival (2014). *Works in collections*: Private collections in UK, Canada, Germany and USA. *Recreations*: Creating an artist's garden; short story writing. *Misc*: Curator: thememorycollective.co.uk Senior Curator Royal Academy of Arts, London (2002-02). Published 100+ articles, catalogue essays etc. *Address*: Bandon House, Church Lane, Toddington, Cheltenham GL54 5DQ. *Email*: amsummerfield@btinternet.com *Website*: www.angelasummerfield.com *Signs work*: "AMS" or unsigned.

SUMMERFIELD, Janette, BA (Hons) (1985); Post Graduate Diploma in History of Art and Design (1992). *Medium*: Oil; pastel. *b*: Birmingham, 5 Aug 1963. *Studied*: Birmingham Institute of Art and Design (1981-85). *Exhib*: Mall Galleries, London; RBSA Gallery, Birmingham; Ludlow Castle; O3 Gallery, Oxford; Fine Art UK Gallery, Ledbury; Number 8 Arts Centre, Pershore; Gateway Arts Centre, Shrewsbury; The Cowleigh Gallery, Malvern; Art Materials Live, NEC, Birmingham; Art in Action, Waterperry; The Gallery at Ridware Arts, Ridware. *Works in collections*: Private. *Publications*: 'The Artists and Illustrators' August 2009 edition - Artist of the Year competition - runner up, landscape section. *Clubs*: Elected full member of Royal Birmingham Society of Artists (2010); Elected full member of SWA (2009). *Misc*: Exhibitor with Birmingham and Midland Pastel Society. *Address*: 120 Billesley Lane, Moseley, Birmingham B13 9RD. *Email*: summerfield.artist@gmail.com *Website*: www.jls-artist.com *Signs work*: "jls".

SUMMERS, Haidee-Jo, BA (Hons) Graphic Design & Illustration; Awards: Artist of the Year, SAA (2012); First Prize, ROI Portrait evening (2012); Young Artist Award, ROI (1997, 1998). At The Artist/Patchings Award Exhibition: Royal Talens Award (2013), The Artist Purchase Award Pro Arte Award (2012, 2014), The Artist Exhibition Award (2014). *Medium*: oil, watercolour. *b*: Great Yarmouth, 16 Nov 1971. *m*: Tim Hewitt. one *s*. one *d*. *Studied*: York College of Arts & Technology (1990-1991); Leicester De Montfort University (1991-1994). *Represented by*: The Russell Gallery, Putney; The Harbour Gallery, Portscatho; The Little Picture Gallery, Mousehole; Peter Barker Fine Art, Uppingham. *Exhib*: Royal Institute of Oil Painters (1997, 1998, 2005, 2006, 2012, 2013); Royal Society of Marine Artists (2013); Society of Women Artists (2013, 2014); Lincolnshire open studios (2007-2010). Over 12 solo shows, and many other mixed exhibitions. *Works in collections*: Private collections UK, USA, Canada, France, Holland, Belgium, Ireland. *Commissions*: BBC (to paint the Queen's Diamond Jubilee river pageant 2012). *Publications*: "The Encyclopaedia of Watercolour Techniques" (pub. 1999, contributor). Many feature articles in The Artist magazine 2012 - ongoing. Feature articles and front cover in the Artists and Illustrators magazine (1997-99). *Misc*: In 2013 the only international artist invited to participate in Florida's 'Forgotten Coast' plein air event. Has blog at www.haideejo.blogspot.com *Address*: 3 Long Meadow, Sudbrook, Grantham, Lincolnshire NG32 3SR. *Email*: thedrawingroomgallery@gmail.com *Website*: www.haideejo.com *Signs work*: "Haidee-Jo Summers".

SUMMERS, Rosalind, SEqA; SWA; GSWA; DA; Daler-Rowney Award (SWA, 2003); Winsor & Newton Award, (SAA, 1998); SAA Artist of the Year (Best Professional, 1998); SAA International Art Event (Best Professional, 2000); Barclay Lennie Award 2010 (Lillie Gallery). *Medium*: oil, watercolour, pastel. *b*: Irvine, Ayrshire, 2 Apr 1951. *d of*: Charles Summers (ex-Provost of Troon). *Partner*: John McKerrell, artist. *Educ*: Marr College, Troon. *Studied*: The Glasgow School of Art; Jordanhill College of Education, Glasgow . *Exhib*: Scotland: Maclaurin Galleries, Ayr; Kelly Gallery, Glasgow Art Club, Lillie Gallery. England: Carisbrooke Gallery; Christies; Westminster Gallery; Mall Galleries. USA: Arlington Park. *Commissions*: STV (King Hussein's daughter's stallion); James Patch's racehorse 'Killycally' (USA) winning at Arlington Park; Ayr Gold Cup Runner 'Ho Leng'; Ayr Silver Cup Runner 'Gift of Gold'. *Works Reproduced*: The Medici Society; The British Horse Society. *Principal Works*: equestrian. *Recreations*: ex-horse trials competitor. *Address*: 36 Main Street, Symington, Ayrshire KA1 5QF. *Email*: equineart@btintnert.com *Website*: ispyart www.artistsandillustrators.co.uk/rosalindsummers *Signs work*: 'Rosalind Summers'.

SUMNER, Emma Elizabeth, MA (with merit) Art History and Curating; Arts & Humanities Studentship Award (MA). *Medium*: mixed media, painting and textiles. *b*: Whiston, 24 Oct 1985. *Studied*: Liverpool Hope University (2010-2012); The University of Salford (2005-2008). *Exhib*: Warrington Art Gallery (2013); Metal (2011); Tate Liverpool, Blackburn House (2010); Ladyfest Manchester, The University of Salford (2008); Bankley Studio Gallery (2007). *Works in collections*: private. *Clubs*: Castlefield Gallery Associate Member. *Address*: 95 Cronton Lane, Widnes, Cheshire WA8 5AP. *Email*: hello@emmasumner.com *Website*: www.emmasumner.com *Signs work*: "EMMA SUMNER" (on reverse).

SUMNER, Josephine Louise, HND Graphic Design (1986); Winner of St Cuthberts Mill Award, SWLA (2009). *Medium*: Drawing; prints. *b*: Oxford, 4 Nov 1964. *m*: Chris Amor. *Educ*: Gosford Hill Comprehensive, Kidlington, Oxford. *Studied*: Banbury School of Art (1983-84); Nene College, Northampton (1984-86). *Exhib*: Selected shows: City Hall, London; SAA Illustrations Awards (2006); Royal Academy, London (2007); Victoria Art Gallery, Bath (2008); Mall Galleries, London, SWLA and originals (2008-09); RWA Bristol, Open Print (2009); Bankside Gallery, London; St Barbe Museum and Art Gallery, Hants; Art Jericho, Oxford, SWE (2009-10); Royal Academy, London (2010). *Works in collections*: Private. *Commissions*: Various illustration commissions including 'The Nation's Favourite Children's Poems' BBC Worldwide (2001). *Principal Works*: Blue Monkey (2006); Silverback (2009); Mandrill (2010). *Recreations*: Archaeology; dance. *Clubs*: Association of Illustrators; Oxford Printmakers Co-operative. *Misc*: Professional Illustrator since 1988. *Address*: 16 Nursteed Road, Devizes SN10 3AH. *Email*: print@josephinesumner.com *Website*: www.josephinesumner.com *Signs work*: "J.L. SUMNER" or "JOSEPHINE SUMNER".

SUMSION, Peter Whitton, ARCA (1955); painter in oil and printmaker in relief and mono prints, drawing, lecturer; Lecturer, Glasgow School of Art (retd 1995). *b*: Gloucester, 23 Aug 1930. *s of*: Dr. H. W. Sumsion, CBE, composer and cathedral organist. *m*: Sarah Noble. two *s*. two *d*. *Educ*: St. George's Choir School, Windsor, St. Thomas' Choir School,

New York City, Rendcomb College, Glos. *Studied*: Cheltenham School of Art (1949), Chelsea School of Art (1950-52), RCA (1952-55, Carel Weight, John Minton, Robert Buhler). *Exhib*: one-man, Drawing Schools Gallery, Eton College (1960, 1978), Bury St. Edmunds Gallery; group shows, RP, RGI. *Works in collections*: Brewhouse Gallery, Eton College. *Address*: Bachie Bhan House, Cairndow, Argyll PA26 8BE. *Signs work*: "Peter Sumsion."

SURREY, Kit, DipAD (Theatre design, 1968); theatre designer and artist in several media, mainly pastel and charcoal drawing; Winner of Drawing Prize, SGFA (2002, 2003, 2005, 2006, 2009). *b*: B'ham, 23 Jun 1946. *m*: Meg Surrey (née Grealey). one *s*. one *d*. *Educ*: Tauntons Grammar School, Southampton. *Studied*: Southampton College of Art (1963-65), Wimbledon School of Art (1965-68). *Exhib*: RA Summer Exhbn. (1993, 2002, 2004), International Drawing Biennale Cleveland (1991), Cheltenham International Open (1994), S. W. Academy of Fine Art (2000-03), Soc. of British Theatre Designers (1976, 1978, 1983, 1999, 2003), International Organisation of Scenographers, Berlin (1981), Moscow (1982). *Works in collections*: RSC Coll., Stratford, The Alpine Club, London, many private collections. *Publications*: included in British Theatre Design - The Modern Age, 'Time & Space', Design for Performance 1995-1999. *Recreations*: mountain walking and climbing. *Clubs*: mem. Society of British Theatre Designers; mem. Society of Graphic Fine Art; Assoc. Mem., The Alpine Club. *Address*: Rock Cottage, Balls Farm Rd., Alphington, Exeter, Devon EX2 9HZ. *Email*: kit.surrey@btinternet.com *Signs work*: "KIT SURREY" or not at all.

SURRIDGE, Mark Steven, BA Hons Graphic Design, Maidstone College of Art (1984); MA Fine Art, Falmouth University (2009); part-time lecturer in Fine Art at Falmouth University; prizewinner Hunting Art Prizes (2001). *Medium*: mixed media; oil. *b*: Walthamstow, 6 Aug 1963. *s of*: Terrance & Joyce Surridge. *m*: Lisa Wright. two *s*. *Studied*: Maidstone College of Art (1981-1984). *Represented by*: Beardsmore Gallery; The New Millennium Gallery. *Exhib*: Beardsmore Gallery, London, solo exhibitions (2000-2012), Millennium Gallery, St. Ives, solo exhibitions (2001-2014), many open exhibitions: National Open Competition, London, Chichester, ING Discerning Eye Exhibition, Mall Galleries (2012), Art Now Cornwall, Tate St Ives, RA Summer Exhibitions (2002, 2003, 2005), 20/21 British Art Fair, Art London, The Newlyn Gallery. *Works in collections*: Private collections, UK, Europe and USA. *Commissions*: three editions of lithographic prints for Club Quarter, London (2000, 2004), and two editions of lithographic prints New York. *Publications*: Guardian 'Living on the Edge'; catalogues for solo exhibitions (2000-2014); Grand Designs Magazine. *Recreations*: guitar, walking, nature, cycling, archaeology. *Clubs*: Newlyn Soc. of Artists. *Address*: Chapel House, Crelly, Helston, Cornwall TR13 0EY. *Email*: art@marksurridge.co.uk *Website*: www.marksurridge.co.uk *Signs work*: "Mark Surridge".

SUTHERLAND, Carol Ann, BA Hons. (1973); artist in water based mixed media oil. *b*: Greenock, Scotland, 16 Mar 1952. *d of*: James Sutherland. three *s*. *Educ*: St. Columba School for Girls, Kilmacolm, Renfrewshire. *Studied*: Glasgow School of Art (1969-73, Donaldson, Goudie, Grant, Robertson). *Exhib*: Mercury Gallery. *Works in collections*: McNay Museum, San Antonio, Tex., Middlesbrough A.G., Paintings in Hospitals. *Publications*: Leafy and Adam at the Seaside (handmade artist's book). *Address*: c/o Mercury Gallery, 26 Cork St., London W1X 1HB. *Signs work*: "Carol Ann Sutherland" or "C.A.S."

SUTHERLAND, Dianne, SBA; BSc (Hons) Biology; Dip Botanical Art (Dist.); Cert Botanical Merit (SBA, 2010); RHS Silver Medals (2006, 2008, 2012, 2014). *Medium*: watercolour, drawing. *b*: Staffordshire, 12 Mar 1964. two *d*. *Studied*: University of Aberdeen (2004-2006); Society of Botanical Artists (2009-2011). *Exhib*: Society of

Botanical Artists, Westminster Halls (2003, 2004, 2008, 2010, 2011); Hunt Institute of Botanical Illustration, Pittsburgh, USA (2007); Anthony Woodd Gallery, Edinburgh (2012); McEwen Gallery, Ballater, Scotland since 1990s. *Works in collections*: Hunt Institute of Botanical Documentation; Aberdeenshire Council Arts & Heritage Collections. *Commissions*: private and commercial illustrations and artwork. *Publications*: Handbook of Plant Form for Botanical Artists (Ernest E. Clark, ed. Margaret Stevens SBA, pub. Batsford, 2013). *Principal Works*: botanical. *Clubs*: Fully Elected Member of Society of Botanical Artists (2012), Society of Staffordshire Artists (2012), Sydney Royal Botanic Garden Florilegium Member (2013). *Address*: 12 Fulmer Place, Meir Park, Longton, Stoke-on-Trent ST3 7QF. *Email*: diannesutherland@btinternet.com *Website*: www.diannesutherland.com *Signs work*: "DIANNE SUTHERLAND" and "DIANNE SUTHERLAND BALL".

SUTTON, Jake, BA (Hons) Fine Art - Painting. *Medium*: Watercolour; drawing; prints. *b*: Manchester, 2 Aug 1947. *m*. Kim Sutton. two *s*. one *d*. *Studied*: St Martins School of Art. *Represented by*: Kim Sutton. *Exhib*: 20 one-man shows in Cork St, London. Many exhibitions including: Petworth House; Royal Opera House; Bath Festival; Royal Society of Portrait Painters. *Work in collections*: V&A, London; Palace of Westminster/House of Commons. *Commissions*: Royal Mail stamps; London Underground poster. *Publications*: 'The Importance of Drawing from Life'. *Works Reproduced*: Many. *Address*: Kim Sutton Gallery, 10 High Street, Fairford, Glos GL7 4AD. *Email*: jakesutton@btinternet.com *Website*: www.jakesuttonprints.com *Signs work*: "JAKE SUTTON".

SUTTON, Jilly Bazeley, SRN, BA, ARBS. *Medium*: sculpture - mainly wood, some cast in bronze. *b*: Whitminster, Glos., 3 Mar 1948. *d of*: Bonham & Phylis Bazeley. *m*: Peter Sutton, Architect. two *s*. one *d*. *Educ*: Malvern Girls College; Westminster Hospital; Exeter College of Art. *Studied*: Exeter University (1988). *Represented by*: Rebecca Hossack Gallery, London. *Exhib*: Rebecca Hossack Gallery, London; Bourne Fine Art, Edinburgh; Holly Snapp Gallery, Venice; Galerie het Vifde Huis, Antwerp, Belgium; Coombe Gallery, Devon; various sculpture gardens. *Works in collections*: National Portrait Gallery, London; Museum of Liverpool Life, Liverpool. *Commissions*: portrait of Poet Laureate; Swan Centre, Leatherhead; P&O Cruise Ship 'Ventura'; Bulgari family; Mary Wesley; Nicholas Evans; HSP Architects, and many more. *Publications*: Modern British Sculpture by Guy Portelli; many magazines and broadsheets. *Works Reproduced*: many wood carvings are cast in bronze, including bronze of Andrew Motion for Portsmouth Grammar School. *Principal Works*: wooden portrait of Andrew Motion, Poet Laureate, for NPG in 2000. *Recreations*: rowing on River Dart. *Clubs*: Chelsea Arts Club. *Misc*: known for large grain bleached wooden heads. *Address*: Whitestone Farmhouse, Cornworthy, Totnes, Devon TQ9 7HF. *Email*: info@jillysutton.com *Website*: www.jillysutton.com *Signs work*: 'JS' on wooden sculpture.

SUTTON, Linda Olive, MA (RCA) (1974); painter in oil on canvas, etching, water-colour, books; Double Painting Prize, Winchester School of Art (1968); prizewinner, Royal Festival Hall (1979, 80, 81); prizewinner, NPG (1982); prizewinner, RA (1987). *Medium*: oils, acrylic, etching, all drawing media. *b*: Southend-on-Sea, 14 Dec 1947. *Educ*: Southend College of Technology. *Studied*: Winchester School of Art (1967-70), Royal College of Art (1971-74). *Exhib*: see website www.lindasutton.com *Works in collections*: Royal Academy of Arts, Chantrey Bequest for Tate, Longleat House, Liverpool University. *Commissions*: 100 murals commissioned by Royal College of Art (1972). *Publications*: Limited Edition of etchings and poems in collaboration with Brian Patten (1996), Limited Edition Books of paintings and text of Shakespeare's "The Tempest" (1999), Ovid's Metamorphoses I and II (2000, 2001) Secret Language of Birds Tarot 2011 (published by Schiffer). *Recreations*: reading, opera, wine. *Clubs*: Chelsea Arts. *Address*: 192 Battersea Bridge Rd., London SW11 3AE. *Website*: www.lindasutton.com *Signs work*: "Linda Sutton."

SUTTON, Philip, RA (1976); artist in oil and water-colour. *b*: Poole, Dorset, 20 Oct 1928. *s of*: Louis & Ann Sutton. *m*: Heather. one *s*. three *d*. *Studied*: The Slade School of Fine Art. *Exhib*: Roland, Browse & Delbanco (1954-79), Australia, S. Africa and USA, Berkeley Square Gallery, London, Piano Nobile, London; Richmond Hill Gallery, Richmond. *Works in collections*: Tate Gallery, etc. *Commissions*: Post Office, stamps design. *Publications*: Philip Sutton 'Life and Work' (RA, 2008); Philip Sutton - 'An Artist View' (2009). *Address*: 3 Morfa Terr., Manorbier, Tenby, Pembrokeshire SA70 7TH. *Signs work*: "Philip Sutton."

SWALE, Suzan Georgina, DipAD (Hons) 1969, MA (RCA) Painting (1972); Artists Union (1983), IAA (UK) (1979-86), London Group - mem. Working Party and Selection Com. (1984), RCA Soc. (1993) artist/lecturer in paint, photo media, text, print, performance; Lecturer, Central/St. Martin's School of Art (1992-2002); Tutor, Morley College. *b*: Nottingham, 30 Apr 1946. *m*: Robert Coward. one *s*. one *d*. *Studied*: Pre-Dip. Derby (1965-66), Bristol Polytechnic (1966-69), RCA (1969-72). *Exhib*: 'A Catalogue of Fear' retrospective Gardner Arts Centre, Brighton (1998); Grabowski Collection, Sztuki Muzeum, Lodz, Poland; 'Swinging London' Exhibition (2007), 'Pop Art in Europe' Balkhof Museum, Nijmegen, Holland (2012-13). Exhibits widely solo and group shows. *Works in collections*: public and private, UK and abroad. *Publications*: 'A Catalogue of Fear' Collective Works - Suzan Swale ISBN 09533977 01. *Works Reproduced*: catalogue 'Swinging London' Sztuki Museum 2007 etc. *Address*: 217 Brecknock Rd., Tufnell Park, London N19 5AA. *Email*: susanswale@hotmail.co.uk *Website*: www.susanswale.co.uk www.thelondongroup.com *Signs work*: "Suzan Swale." (or "Sue Swale" pre-1973).

SWAN, Ann, SBA, SGFA; RHS Silver-gilt medal (1990), Gold medal (1991, 1993, 1997), Joint Gold (1999); botanical artist in pencil, coloured pencil, oil pastel, water-colour, drypoint engraving. *b*: England, 7 Apr 1949. *Educ*: Gravesend Grammar School for Girls. *Studied*: Manchester College of Art and Design. *Exhib*: RHS Hampton Ct. International Flower Show (1990, 1991, 1994-97), SBA (1991, 1992, 1994-97), RHS (1990, 1991, 1993, 1997), Century Gallery Henley (1991), Lyric Theatre Hammersmith (1992), RBG, Kew (1994), Hunt Inst. of Botanical Documentation, Pittsburgh, USA (1996), RHS Chelsea Flower Show (1998-99). *Works in collections*: The Shirley Sherwood Collection, National Collection of Lycastes, Beckenham, Kent. *Works Reproduced*: limited edns. prints, and greetings cards. *Address*: 55 Railway Rd., Teddington, Middx. TW11 8SD. *Email*: ann@annswan.co.uk *Website*: www.annswan.co.uk *Signs work*: "Ann Swan."

SWAN, Martin BA (Hons) Philosophy; RSMA. *Medium*: oil, watercolour, drawing. *b*: Newport, Isle of Wight, 14 Apr 1951. *s of*: Mr & Mrs E.N. Swan. *m*: Melanie. *Educ*: Carisbrooke Grammar School (Newport, IoW); University College of Wales (Aberystwyth). *Studied*: self-taught. *Exhib*: Mall Galleries (RSMA); National Maritime Museum (RSMA); Portsmouth Cathedral (RSMA); Jonathan Grant Gallery, Auckland, New Zealand; St. David's Hall, Cardiff (RSMA); Les Artistes et la Mer, St. Malo; Bankside, London; Quay Arts, Newport, IOW; various local galleries. *Works in collections*: Isle of Wight Archive; Quay Art Archive; various private collection. *Commissions*: Royal Estates of Oman, numerous private commissions. *Official Purchasers*: Healing Arts. *Works Reproduced*: limited ed. Marine Paintings reproduced 2005 (Artists Harbour, Portsmouth). *Recreations*: walking, reading, music, food, drink, rugby, cricket. *Address*: 124 Carisbrooke Road, Newport, Isle of Wight PO30 1DF. *Email*: swanmartin@hotmail.com *Website*: www.martinswan.com *Signs work*: 'Martin Swan'.

SWAN, Peter John, RWA, NDD, ATD. *Medium*: painter in oil. *b*: London, 28 Sep 1936. *s of*: John Thomas Swan. *m*: Janet. two *s*. three *d*. *Educ*: Dr. Morgan's Grammar School, Bridgewater, Somerset 1947-53. *Studied*: Somerset College of Art, Taunton 1953-55; St. Martin's School of Art, London 1955-57 NDD Painting; Institute of London University 1958-59 ATD. *Exhib*: solo: Arnolfini Gallery, Bristol 1961, 62, 66; Barrow Court 1979; Group: AIA

Galleries, London, John Moore's Liverpool, Ben Lane Gallery, Oxford, RWA Bristol. *Works in collections*: private collections in England, Jersey CI, Australia, America, France, Abu Dhabi DAE. *Commissions*: two murals for Yateley Comprehensive School, Hampshire. *Clubs*: RWA. *Misc*: retired full-time lecturer Faculty of Fine Art, Bristol Polytechnic. *Address*: 23 Cornwallis Crescent, Clifton, Bristol, BS8 4PJ. *Signs work*: Peter Swan.

SWANBOROUGH, Patsy & Janet, both studied Illustration at Medway College of Design, Rochester, Kent (both 1st Class passes). Patsy mem. Society of Feline Artists. *Medium*: watercolour, drawing, prints, soft sculpture, egg tempera, acrylics. *b*: Maidstone, Kent. *d of*: Pam & Alan Swanborough. *Studied*: Medway College of Design (1972-76). *Represented by*: Rosehill Studio, St.Mary's, Isles of Scilly. *Exhib*: 'Cats in Windows' exhibited at RA Summer Exhibitions (1992, 1993, 2000) - the only living twins to have exhibited in the same year. Have been exhibiting since 1977, including Llewellyn Alexander (SOFA-Patsy only). *Works in collections*: private collections. *Commissions*: Roy Mitchell; Robert Dorrien-Smith; The Isles of Scilly Tourism Association; Jeremy Mills (for BBC TV); Michael Galsworthy. *Publications*: latest series of 'Cats in Windows' published by Hockin & Roberts Ltd; 'Cats in Windows' Calendar 2006 by Judges Ltd. *Works Reproduced*: available as prints, giftware from our gallery or by mail order. *Clubs*: SOFA. *Address*: The Swanborough Twins, Gallery, Rosehill Studio, Rosehill, St.Mary's, Isles of Scilly, Cornwall TR21 0NE. *Email*: patsyjanetswanborough@btinternet.com *Website*: www.rosehillstudio.co.uk

SWANN, Marilyn, Fellow of Free Painters and Sculptors; painter; Women's Art Library, Fulham. *Medium*: water-colour, oils, acrylic. *b*: Kent, 16 Apr 1932. *d of*: H.H. Whiddett and C.W. Swann. *Studied*: Woolwich Poly. (1945-50), Central, Chelsea and Sidcup (evenings and Adult Education). *Exhib*: Trends (Mall, Wieghouse, Barbican, Bloomsbury Galleries, etc.), F.P.S. shows since 1973, St. Martin's Crypt, Trafalgar Sq.; solo shows, Brangwyn Studio (1976/7), Univ. of Surrey, Old Bull, Barnet (1978), Loggia Gallery (1984), Holland Park Orangery (1987), Hall Place and various other venues in Bexley and Cheltenham. *Works in collections*: Univ. of Surrey, Wilfred Sirrel Collection, Westminster Arts Council, Queen Mary's Hospital, Sidcup. *Official Purchasers*: Westminster Arts Council. *Recreations*: writing, and studying history. *Clubs*: CPS Artists. *Address*: Fairview Street Cheltenham GL52 2JJ. *Signs work*: "SWANN."

SWEENEY, Deborah, BA Hons Fine Art; PGCE. *Medium*: oil, watercolour, drawing, prints. *b*: Halifax, W.Yorks., 18 Jun 1956. one *d*. *Educ*: Highlands Grammar, Halifax. *Studied*: Sheffield Polytechnic College of Art; Bretton Hall. *Represented by*: Bull Yard Gallery, Southwell, Notts. *Exhib*: Royal Academy Summer Exhbns (2003, 2004, 2005); Mappin Art Gallery, Sheffield; Sheffield Colourists (2002). *Commissions*: various. *Works Reproduced*: some works available as prints. *Misc*: established 'The Westhorpe School of Art' in 1997, teaches young people and adults. *Address*: Long Barn, Westhorpe, Southwell NG25 0NG. *Email*: deborah@westhorpeart.demon.co.uk *Signs work*: 'Deborah Sweeney'.

SWEENEY, Kevin Michael. *Medium*: sculpture. *b*: Maldon, Essex, 28 Jan 1965. *s of*: Michael & Jackie Sweeney. *m*: divorced. one *s*. one *d*. *Studied*: studied spraying at all levels since leaving school, including water born, electro c static, 2pack. *Exhib*: RA Summer Exhibition (first two pieces) (2007), Flitch Gallery, Gt. Dunmow. *Works in collections*: private and corporate. *Commissions*: waiting list. *Publications*: Royal Academy Illustrated 2007 (Summer Exhibition). *Works Reproduced*: none. *Misc*: Spent 3 years at E15 Acting School. *Address*: 17th Floor, 69 Old Broad Street, London EC2M 1QS. *Email*: kevin@sweeney.org.uk *Website*: www.abstractsculptures.co.uk *Signs work*: initials: 'K.M.S".

SWEENEY, Maureen, NSPS; MNS; BA Hons (Fine Art); PGCE; Anya Broughton Award, NSPS (Best Painting, 2005); Roberson Award for Best Figurative Painting (1974).

b: London. *d of*: Patrick & Anne Sweeney. *m*: Christopher Lewis Ruffley. one *s*. one *d*. *Educ*: Notredame High School for Girls. *Studied*: Wimbledon School of Art (1973-77), under previous name Williams; Roehampton University. *Represented by*: Southbank Printmakers, Gabriels Wharf, Lambeth, London; Greenwich Printmakers Gallery, Greenwich. *Exhib*: RA Summer Exhbn; RWS; NEAC; Llewellyn Alexander (2002-09); Salon de Graphique; Curwen Gallery; Natural History Museum (under M. Williams); Southbank Printmakers, London; Oxo Gallery, London; Menier Chocolate Factory, London; Business Design Centre, Islington; Paris, Germany, Norway & Russia; National Theatre; Affordable Art Fair; Villa Steccius, Landau, Rheinlandpfalz, Germany (1993, 2007, 2009). *Works in collections*: private and public, home and abroad. *Commissions*: private commissions for portraits, landscapes and seascapes. *Official Purchasers*: Kunstverein, Landau, Germany; Merton Local Authority. *Recreations*: travel, reading, theatre. *Clubs*: Southbank Printmakers; Greenwich Printmakers. *Address*: 13 Burntwood Grange Road, Wandsworth, London SW18 3JY. *Email*: mosweeney2003@yahoo.co.uk *Signs work*: 'Sweeney'.

SWINFEN EADY, Katherine Anne, BA (Hons); William and Mary Armour Award PAI (2007). *Medium*: Oil; watercolour; drawing; prints. *b*: Guildford, 18 May 1966. *m*: Gareth Davies. *Studied*: Edinburgh College of Art (1986-89). *Represented by*: The Jerram Gallery, Sherborne. *Exhib*: Solo shows since 2005: Wren Gallery (2005, 2006, 2008; Walker Gallery (2007); Jerram Gallery (2009, 2011, 2013); Manor Farm Gallery (2014); Langham Fine Art; The Mall Galleries; The Jerram Gallery; The Wren Gallery; The Wykeham Gallery; Whitespace Gallery; The Splinter Group; Paisley Art Institute; Oakham Contemporary; Lime Tree Gallery; The Walker Gallery; The Royal Glasgow Institute; Panter and Hall Gallery; Quidding Fine Art, all major art fairs. *Works in collections*: Private/corporate. Numerous private collections inc UK, Beijing China, USA, France, Spain, Italy, Russia and Australia *Commissions*: Numerous private commissions, Chelsea Harbour Hotel (1990). *Misc*: Trustee of The Swinfen Charitable Trust, specialising in Telemedicine in the Developing World; Studying for an MA in First World War Studies, Wolverhampton University. *Address*: The Red House, 4 Townsend, Chitterne, Warminster, BA12 0UF. *Website*: www.katherineswinfeneady.com *Signs work*: "Katherine Swinfen Eady".

SWINGLER, Brian Victor, NDD, ATD, RBSA (1986); artist in water-colour and acrylics; part time teacher at Birmingham, Hereford and Worcester. *b*: Birmingham, 8 Jul 1939. divorced. *s of*: Ernest Swingler. two *s*. *Educ*: Yardley Grammar School. *Studied*: Birmingham Art School (1962-65, Gilbert Mason, Roy Abell). *Exhib*: mainly at Potter Clarke Gallery, St. Ives, also at Compendium Gallery, Ombersley Gallery, RBSA, Timaeus Gallery, Helios Gallery, Cedric Chivers Gallery, Pictures, Henry-Brett Gallery, Richard Hagen Gallery, New Gallery, Moseley Gallery, Bankside, Frames, Noott Gallery. *Works in collections*: RBSA Gallery. *Commissions*: many public and private portrait commissions. *Works Reproduced*: Artist Magazine and Leisure Painter. *Clubs*: V.P.R.B.S.A. *Address*: 17 Beverley Rd., Rubery, Birmingham B45 9JG. *Signs work*: "B.V. Swingler."

SYKES, Barbara, BA (Hons.) Fine Art (1993); MA Printmaking (2005); painter in water based paint on paper, and charcoal; textile designer (1962-75). *b*: Doncaster, 4 Mar 1944. *d of*: Richard and Ada Johnson. *m*: Jeffrey Howard Sykes. two *s*. one *d*. *Studied*: Bretton Hall, University of Leeds (1990-93, Tom Wood), Bradford College, MA Printmaking (2003-2005). *Exhib*: Mall Galleries, RA Summer Show, Discerning Eye; RWA; Djanogley Gallery (Nottingham University), Logos London, Dean Clough, Halifax, Huddersfield Art Gallery, Peterborough Museum and Gallery, Bury Art Gallery, DFN New York, North West House Brussels, Bradford University, Hastings Museum and Art Gallery, Cleveland Gallery Middlesborough, Derby Art Gallery, Buxton Art Gallery, Oldham Art Gallery etc. *Works in collections*: Studio: Dean Clough, Halifax, Provident Financial Group, Bretton Hall. Private collections: UK, USA, France, Slovenia. *Commissions*: private commissions. *Works Reproduced*: magazines, cards, etc. *Principal Works*: 'Concerning Senses';

'Intergenerational'; 'Human Condition'. *Recreations*: reading, gardening, jazz. *Clubs*: MAFA, SGFA, NAPA. *Misc*: studio holder at Dean Clough Galleries, Halifax. *Address*: The Hollows, Shore Edge, Shaw, Oldham, Lancs. OL2 8LJ. *Email*: enquiries@barbarasykes.com *Website*: www.barbarasykes.com *Signs work*: "Barbara Sykes" (on request.).

SYKES, Thelma Kathryn, BA Hons (1962), SWLA (2001). *Medium*: artist printmaker, linocut and woodcut. *b*: Heckmondwike, Yorks., 29 Apr 1940. *Educ*: Durham University. *Represented by*: Birdscapes Gallery, Manor Farm Barns, Glandford, Holt, NR25 7JP; Pinkfoot Gallery, High Street, Cley-next-the-Sea, Norfolk, NR25 7RB; Emma Mason British Prints, 3 Cornfield Terrace, Eastbourne, BN21 4NN. *Exhib*: SWLA, Mall Galleries, London, Royal National Theatre (2001), Soc. of Wood Engravers, Internat. Festival of Printmaking, Chong Qing, China (2000), English Nature Touring Exhbn (2004-2005), Cheng-Kim Loke Gallery, Slimbridge (2000, 2014). *Works in collections*: Nature in Art, Wallsworth Hall, Gloucester; Grosvenor Museum, Chester, Powergen, Bristol University. *Publications*: European Atlas of Breeding Birds, Academic Press (1997), New Atlas of Breeding Birds, Wildlife in Printmaking, Langford Press 2011, The Natural Eye - Art Book One (2013), The Wildlife Artist's Handbook (2013) and many publications for British Trust for Ornithology. *Address*: Blue Neb Studios, 18 Newcroft, Saughall, Chester CH1 6EL. *Email*: thelmasykes@tiscali.co.uk *Signs work*: "Thelma K Sykes' or book illustrations, "TKS."

SYMINGTON, Christy Mary, ARBS elected 2002; Board Member (2003-07), Royal British Society of Sculptors; Head of Sculpture, The Art Academy, London (2013). *Medium*: sculpture and drawing. *b*: Northampton, 10 Nov 1962. *m*: José Antonio 'Tontxi' Vazquez. two *s-d*. *Educ*: Wycombe Abbey School, Bucks. *Studied*: Les Atelier Beaux Arts, Paris, France (1996-7); New York Studio School, NYC, USA (1997-2001); Byam Shaw School of Art, University of the Arts, London (2001-02); PDCE in Education. *Exhib*: Pangolin London (2011); ZSL London Zoo (2013); Marist College, NY, USA (2012), Society of Portrait Sculptors (2002, 04, 07); University of Leicester "Sculpture in the Garden" (2005, 06); RWA (2003, 04, 08); USA: National Arts Club, New York (Paul Manship Award, 2001); Taller Boricua, New York (2001); Angel Orensanz Foundation Center for the Arts, New York (1999). *Works in collections*: Angel Orensanz Foundation, New York. *Misc*: originator of Sculpture Bridge Park across the River Thames. *Address*: 23 Brockley Grove, London SE4 1QX. *Email*: christysym@aol.com *Website*: www.christysymington.com *Signs work*: "Christy" (with paw mark).

SYMONDS, Peter John, BA; painter in oil of landscape architectural and marine subjects. *Medium*: oil on canvas. *b*: Woking, 15 Jan 1964. *m*: Vanessa. one *s*. one *d*. *Studied*: Leicester University. *Exhib*: Bourne Gallery, Reigate; Clifton Gallery, Clifton; Beckstones nr. Penrith; four solo shows SE England, mixed shows nationwide. *Commissions*: Lloyds Bldg. London, numerous private commissions home and abroad. *Works Reproduced*: Limited Edn. prints (Solomon & Whitehead). *Recreations*: trekking, sport, travel. *Address*: Magpies, Vicarage Lane, Send, Woking, Surrey GU23 7JN. *Signs work*: "Peter Symonds".

SYNGE Pamela: see de MEO, P.

SYVERSON, Judith, RMS. *Medium*: traditional miniature paintings in oil and acrylic. *b*: Merrill, Wisconsin, 20 Sep 1944. *m*: Richard F. Syverson. one *s*. two *d*. *Educ*: BS Wisconsin State University, River Falls. *Studied*: Sergei Bongart School of Painting/Marke Ogle/Joe Abbreccia/Jean Hamilton/Joan Willies RMS. *Exhib*: London, UK; USA: Colorado, California, Florida, Montana, Minnesota, Washington DC-Smithsonian, Connecticut, Wyoming. *Works in collections*: corporate and private individuals worldwide. *Commissions*: corporate and private individuals across the US. *Publications*: 'Royal Society of Miniature Painters, Sculptors and Gravers: One Hundred Years' (pub. 1995). *Works Reproduced*: 'Story Time'; 'The Eccles Farm'; 'Mountain Homestead'; 'High Mountain Monarch'; 'The

Ol' Dortch Place' . *Recreations*: gardening, hiking the mountains of the North-West. *Clubs*: Montana Professional Artists Assoc.; Royal Miniature Society, London. *Misc*: noted for her delicate portrayal in miniature of a wide range of subjects. Inspired by her great-grandparents' stories of ranching in Montana, she especially enjoys portraying homesteads of the West. Many of her pieces are documented. *Address*: 136 Lake Hills Drive, Bigfork, Montana 59911 USA. *Website*: www.MontanaProfessionalArtistsAssoc.com *Signs work*: 'Judith Syverson RMS.

T

TABB, Barrington Moore, RWA (1999); self taught painter in oil. *b*: Almondsbury, Glos., 25 Apr 1934. *m*: Grace Pearn. two *d*. *Educ*: All Saints School, Bristol. *Represented by*: Cube Gallery, Bristol; Anthony Hepworth Fine Art, Bath. *Exhib*: Olympia Fair, London (4 yrs.), Wimbledon Gallery (1980), Christopher Hull Gallery (1982), Neville Gallery, Bath (1986), Cleveland Bridge Gallery (1990), Black Swan Gallery, Frome (1997), RWA (1998 onwards), Cube Gallery, Bristol (2002-2007), St. David's Hall Cardiff (2002), Albany Gallery Cardiff (2002), Rob Whittle Gallery (2002), Gormleys Gallery (Belfast, 2007). *Works in collections*: 14 paintings Wessex Collection Longleat House. *Publications*: 'Pictures' with forewords by Anthony Hepworth and Charles Hall; 'Passion for Paint' by Jonathan Bennington. *Recreations*: painting! *Address*: 10 Frys Hill, Brislington, Bristol BS4 4JW. *Signs work*: "B.M.T." , "Barrington M Tabb", or "BT."

TABER, A. Lincoln, artist. *b*: Colchester, 1970. *Studied*: City and Guilds School of Art (1989-92). *Exhib*: RA Summer Show, New Grafton Gallery. *Commissions*: murals, portraits. *Clubs*: Chelsea Arts. *Address*: 6 Hermes House, Arodene Rd., London SW2.

TABER, Jacqueline, Hon RBA (2013); artist and picture restorer. *Medium*: oil. *b*: London, 1 Sep 1946. *m*: the late A. Lincoln Taber, painter. one *s*. *Educ*: Heathfield School; Paris (one year). *Studied*: Florence (Signorina Simi), Gabinetto del Restauro, Uffizi Museum. *Represented by*: Russell Gallery; Geedon Gallery. *Exhib*: RA Summer Exhbn (1999-2008), RBA (2005, 2007), New Grafton Gallery, Discerning Eye (2000, 2003, 2006), Hayletts Gallery (two solo exhbns), Lennox Gallery, Russell Gallery (solo exhibition), Mall Galleries. *Works in collections*: Sir Bob Worcester. *Commissions*: 'Tulips'. *Publications*: A Bit of Trompe - The Art of Lincoln Taber. *Principal Works*: 'Still Lives'. *Recreations*: reading, painting, projects. *Clubs*: Chelsea Arts, Colchester Art Society, Art Workers Guild. *Misc*: Made RBA (hon) (2013). *Address*: Jaggers, Fingringhoe, Colchester, Essex CO5 7DN. *Email*: jataber@aol.com *Website*: www.jacquelinetaber.co.uk *Signs work*: 'J.A.Taber'.

TAHERIAN, Christine, SWA; a number of awards from art societies. *Medium*: oil, acrylic, mixed media. *b*: Cardiff, 14 Dec 1960. *m*: Dr. Alireza Taherian. two *s*. one *d*. *Educ*: Art. *Studied*: Glasgow University. *Exhib*: SWA, ROI; Yvonne Arnaud; Guildford & Woking Art Society. *Works in collections*: internationally. *Commissions*: no. *Works Reproduced*: Limited editions in print. *Principal Works*: Impressionism. *Clubs*: Guildford Art Society, Woking Art Society. *Address*: Gralyn, Sylvan Close, Woking, Surrey, GU22 7DD. *Email*: christine@wambrook.com *Website*: www.society-women-artists.org.uk www.christinetaherian.com *Signs work*: 'C.TAHERIAN'.

TAIT, Renny, painter. *b*: Perth, Scotland, 27 Jun 1965. *m*: Valerie Anderson. one *d*. *Studied*: Edinburgh College of Art, Royal College of Art. *Exhib*: regularly with Flowers East, London. *Address*: c/o Flowers Gallery, 21 Cork Street, London W1S 3LZ. *Signs work*: "Renny J. Tait" on back of painting.

TAIT, Wendy Ann, SFP, SBA; water-colour artist and demonstrator. *Medium*: watercolour, oils, acrylic. *b*: Derby, 19 Apr 1939. *d of*: W.G. & K. Kirk. *m*: H.D.L. Tait (decd). two *s*. two *d*. *Studied*: Joseph Wright School of Art, Derby (1952-55), Adult Educ.

(1974-78, Roy Berry). *Exhib*: Derbyshire and Westminster, London galleries. Residential courses and Dayschools, Midlands and Yorkshire area. *Commissions*: 'Autumn Flowers' (1999), 'Winter Flowers' (2003), 'Summer Flowers' (2007), 'Spring Flowers', Government of Jersey Philatelic Bureau. *Publications*: 'Watercolour Flowers' (Search Press & video), 'Wild Flowers in Watercolour' (Search Press & video), 'Ready to Paint' (Search Press & video). *Works Reproduced*: greetings cards by Robertson Collection. *Clubs*: Amber Art Group, Belper Art Group, Matlock Society of Artists, Society of Botanical Artists, Society of Flower Painters. *Address*: 24 Duffield Court, Chapel St., Duffield, Derbyshire DE56 4EQ. *Email*: wendytait@gmail.com *Website*: www.wendytait.com *Signs work*: "W.A. Tait."

TALBOT KELLY, Chloë Elizabeth. MCSD (1968), SWLA (1964), MBOU (1960); freelance bird artist/illustrator in water-colour, gouache, oil, and black and white. *b*: Hampstead, 15 Jul 1927. *d of*: the late Major R. B. Talbot Kelly (Richard Barrett), M.B.E., M.C., SWLA, RI. one *s*. *Educ*: St. George's School for Girls, Convent of the Sacred Heart; adviser, father and Bird Room, BMNH. *Exhib*: SWLA and provincial galleries in UK, Australia and Canada. *Commissions*: various. *Commissions*: various. *Works Reproduced*: Field Guides to Birds N.Z, Seychelles, Fiji, Tonga and Samoa; contributor to New Dictionary of Birds, African Handbook of Birds, Collins Handguide to Birds of New Zealand, etc. *Clubs*: Leicestershire and Rutland Ornithological Society. *Address*: 22 St. Philip's Rd., Leicester LE5 5TQ. *Email*: cetk@btinternet.com *Signs work*: "C.E. Talbot Kelly" semi printed in paint or written, or initials only.

TALKS, David, Received Gold Medal in Rouen (2001) for services to French culture; Former mem. Coventry and Warwickshire Society of Artists; Past President, Rugby and District Art Society; President, Norfolk and Norwich Art Circle (2007-09); East Anglian Group of Marine Artists. *Medium*: watercolour. *b*: Wimbledon, 10 Nov 1937. *m*: Audrey. four *s*. *Educ*: Mercers School, London (1946-56); Worcester College, Oxford (1958-63); MA (French and Russian); M.Litt (French). *Exhib*: RI (1988-92, 94, 95); RSMA (1992); EAGMA, Mall Galleries (1998, 2000, '02, '04, '06, '08); Thompson's Gallery, London (1996); Westcliffe Gallery, Sheringham; Mandell's Gallery, Norwich; La Galerie Lespinasse, Rouen (1998-2008); Crome Gallery, Norwich. *Commissions*: Norwich Cathedral, Rugby School, plus many private commissions. *Recreations*: walking, bird-watching. *Misc*: Reserve Decoration for service as Lieutenant-Commander in the Royal Navy Reserve (1958-1986). *Address*: 20, The Close, Norwich, NR1 4DZ. *Signs work*: 'DAVID TALKS'.

TAMPLIN, Heather, MFPS (1984); artist in oil, digital images, installations in response to the North Norfolk landscape. *Medium*: oil & acrylic. *b*: Caterham, 4 Aug 1950. one *s*. one *d*. *Studied*: Wimbledon College of Art (1967). *Exhib*: Loggia Gallery / Barbican / Letchworth Museum with FPS. Mall Galleries / Battersea Contemporary Art Fair / Tanner & Lawson, London. sfn Gallery Broadway NY. Fermoy Art Centre King's Lynn. The Forum / Anteros Arts and 18/21 Gallery, Norwich. The Upstairs Gallery Beccles. Salthouse Norfolk 05/08/10. CO3 Gallery Colchester. *Commissions*: 34 digital images for The Raven music Alison Burns Words Tony Bonning Scottish Arts Council Funded. Wind Harp, Sound and Light landscape installation funded Awards for All. *Publications*: How Artists See; East Anglian Places. *Misc*: Founder Member NOVA, committee for Salthouse Annual Exhibition 2000-2003. *Address*: Orchard House, The Green, Aldborough, Norfolk NR11 7AA. *Email*: h.tamplin@btinternet.com *Website*: www.heathertamplin.co.uk *Signs work*: "H. TAMPLIN."

TANDY, Bonita Marilyn, BA Fine Art, Painting & Printmaking. *Medium*: oil, watercolour. *b*: London 9 Mar 1946. *d of*: Herbert Mortimer Lewis. *m*: divorced. one *s*. *Studied*: Camberwell School of Art (1963-68). *Exhib*: RA Summer Shows, Whitechapel Open, Royal Overseas League, Mall Galleries, Cardiff Museum, Trinity Art, Woodlands

Gallery, Lynn Stern Associates, Llewellyn Alexander; Southwark Open, Battersea Contemporary Art, Zella Gallery, Highgate Fine Art, British Society of Graduate Artists, Lynn Painter-Stainers, Blackheath Art Society. *Works in collections*: Paintings in Hospitals. *Address*: 56 Upland Road, East Dulwich, London SE22 0DB. *Email*: bonnietandy@talktalk.net *Website*: www.theinternetartshop.com *Signs work*: 'BT'.

TANG, George, Associate, Society of Botanical Artists. *Medium*: rice paper/silk. *b*: Hong Kong, 30 Aug 1948. *m*: Dr. Wai Yuk Chun Veronica. three *s*. *Educ*: Lai Ching Art Institute (1957-66). *Studied*: University of Hong Kong (1968-71), B.Soc. Sc., Solicitor of England and Wales (1978). *Exhib*: Hong Kong, London, Toronto, Singapore, China. *Commissions*: Hong Kong Post: Hong Kong stamps "Flowers of Hong Kong" (2008). *Publications*: 'The Artworks of George Tang' (2005). *Official Purchasers*: Hong Kong Post (Hong Kong Government SAR). *Recreations*: calligraphy. *Address*: 43 Stubbs Road, D1 3/F, Evergreen Villa, Hong Kong. *Email*: gkwtang@hotmail.com *Website*: www.georgetang.com.hk *Signs work*: "Tang Kwok Wing".

TARR, Michael, Prizewinner 'Excellence in Watercolour' RWA (2009). *Medium*: acrylic, oil, watercolour, drawing. *b*: Bridgwater, 11 Jun 1946. *m*: Anne-Marie. one *s*. one *d*. *Studied*: Somerset College of Art, Taunton (1962-65). *Exhib*: one-man shows include: Brewhouse, Taunton; Bridgwater Arts Centre; mixed shows - RA Summer; RWA Autumn; SWAc Annual Show Exeter; Millfield Open Art (Prizewinner 2008); Royal Institute of Watercolour Painters, Mall Galleries; Llewelyn Alexander, Waterloo and others. *Works in collections*: Somerset County Cricket Club, Somerset Cricket Museum and many private collections in UK, Italy and USA. *Commissions*: numerous from Somerset County Cricket Club, inc. many portraits, Hampshire CCC. *Works Reproduced*: numerous cricket book publications, RA Summer Exhibition catalogue (2013). *Recreations*: tennis, Italy. *Misc*: known for cricket paintings and illustrations up to 2000. *Address*: Pitch View, Howleigh, Blagdon Hill, Taunton, Somerset, TA3 7SR. *Email*: tarrart@tiscali.co.uk *Website*: www.michaeltarr.co.uk *Signs work*: "TARR".

TARRANT, Peter Rex, FNDD; artist in oil and mixed media. *b*: Shropshire, 1943. *Educ*: Morville School. *Studied*: Shrewsbury Art School. *Works in collections*: Birmingham City Museum and A.G. *Address*: 10 Lower Bromdon, Wheathill, Burwarton, nr. Bridgnorth, Salop. WV16 6QT. *Email*: ptarrant@btinternet.com.uk

TARRANT, Terence Richard, FRCOphth. (Hon); MSC (Hon); FMAA; medical artist; ophthalmic artist Theodore Hamblin Ltd. (1945-48); ophthalmic artist Queen Alexandra's Military Hospital, Millbank (1948-50); medical artist at Inst. of Ophthalmology, London (1950-84). *b*: London, 7 Jan 1930. *s of*: R. J. Tarrant. *m*: Susan. one *s*. two *d*. *Educ*: London. *Studied*: Camberwell School of Arts and Crafts. *Works in collections*: Moorfields Eye Hospital, Bristol Eye Hospital. *Publications*: Stallard's Eye Surgery, Roper-Hall; Clinical Ophthalmology, J.J. Kanski; System of Ophthalmology, Duke-Elder; Management of Vitreoretinal Disease, Chignell and Wong; Contact Lens Complications, N. Efron. *Address*: 'Woodlands', Rectory Lane, Child Okeford, Blandford Forum, Dorset DT11 8DT. *Signs work*: "TARRANT" with tops of the Ts joined.

TAULBUT, John Maurice, RWA; Jack Goldhill award for sculpture R.A. (1987); sculptor in stone, wood and bronze, teacher. *b*: Gosport, 19 Jan 1934. *s of*: Patrick John Taulbut (decd). *m*: Janet Marian Rickards. three *s*. *Educ*: Portsmouth College of Art, Highbury Technical College. *Studied*: Eaton Hall College of Educ., Retford. *Exhib*: RA, RBA, RWA, S.WL.A., RSMA., Sotheby's, Southampton A.G., Swindon A.G., Oxford Soc., Cheltenham Soc., 3D Gallery, Bristol, Rooksmoor Gallery, Bath, Ceri Richards Gallery, Swansea, Ash Barn, Petersfield, Swansea Arts Workshop, Barry Keene Gallery, Henley on Thames, The McHardy Sculpture Co. *Works in collections*: Royal West of England Academy, Grand Pavilion, Porthcawl, and private collections. *Commissions*: Madonna and

Child, Parish Church, Llansteffan; bronze plaque, St. Anthony's Well, Llansteffan; major conch form, St. Anthony's Well, Llansteffan. *Address*: 40 Crawte Ave., Holbury, Southampton SO45 2GQ. *Email*: johntaulbut@btinternet.com *Signs work*: "John Taulbut."

TAUNTON, Adrian, MA (Cantab). *Medium*: watercolour, oil, some pastel/gouache. *b*: Norwich, 9 Mar 1939. *s of*: John Taunton. *m*: Juliet Taunton. one *s*. one *d*. *Educ*: Norwich School, Gonville & Caius College, Cambridge. *Exhib*: Mall Galleries (RI, RSMA, EAGMA); Thompson's Gallery, Aldeburgh/London; Century Gallery, Henley-on-Thames; Mandell's Gallery, Norwich; Westcliffe Gallery, Sheringham; Peter Hedley Gallery, Wareham; Hunter Gallery, Long Melford; Geedon Gallery, Colchester; Sarah Samuels, Rossett. *Works in collections*: Mr.S.B. Witt, Richmond, Virginia, USA; Miss Shama Habiballah, Bombay, India; Mr Ralph Lauren, New York; Miss Helene Cox, Sussex. *Commissions*: Mr Ralph Lauren, New York. *Recreations*: music, sailing, good food, rowing. *Clubs*: East Anglian Group of Marine Artists; Brancaster Staithe Sailing Club. *Address*: The Old Barn House, Kelling, Holt, NR25 7EF. *Email*: j.taunton112@btinternet.com *Signs work*: 'Adrian Taunton'.

TAYLOR, Alan, NDD (1954), ARCA (1957); artist in water-colour, gouache, ink, chalks; TV Designer/Art Director; retd. from TV, painting full time, now producing computer art and writing novels. *b*: India, 5 Jun 1930. s-s of Vladimir Shibayev, Prof. of Languages, Delhi University. *m*: Rachel Taylor. *Studied*: RCA (Prof. John Skeaping, Leon Underwood). *Exhib*: one-man shows: three in Wales, one in Holland; mixed shows: Wales, England, France, Holland and USA; one-man show in computer art: Newport (Nov., 1997). *Works in collections*: University of Wales, Bangor, University of Wales, Cardiff, BBC, Welsh Tourist Board. *Commissions*: Computer landscape and portrait commissions (private), computer images for TV Channel S4C; designed book covers for the last two years: see website. *Publications*: illustrated Song of the Harp (Christopher Davies); illustrations for BBC TV and HTV. Listed in Welsh Arts Council and Axis slide libraries, published novel 2001 'One Day as a Tiger' set in India - published by Authors on Line and Amazon Kindle. 3 books of short stories on Amazon Kindle (2012). *Recreations*: writing, reading, cooking, eating. *Address*: 75 Preston Ave., Newport, S. Wales NP20 4JD. *Email*: a.taylor6@ntlworld.com *Website*: www.supercovers.co.uk

TAYLOR, Alan, BA (Hons)(1973), ATC (1974). *Medium*: acrylic on canvas. *b*: Wembley, Middx., 1942. *s of*: John and Constance Taylor. *m*: Josephine. one *d*. *Educ*: Hornchurch Grammar School. *Studied*: Colchester School of Art (1963-65, drawing: John Nash), Stourbridge College of Art (1965-68 and 1972-73), University of Sussex Art Teachers' Certificate (1973-74). *Represented by*: http://www.artgallery.co.uk/artisan/alan_taylor *Exhib*: Midland Young Contemporaries, London, Trends in Modern Art, Corning Museum, N.Y., numerous mixed and one-man shows Birmingham, London, Colchester, Wivenhoe, Exeter, Chudleigh, Sidmouth, Normandy. *Works in collections*: UK, France, Middle East, Australia, USA. *Commissions*: Commissions welcomed. *Address*: La Chapelle, Foulognes, 14240 Caumont L'Evente, Calvados, Normandie, France. *Email*: alan.f.taylor@orange.fr *Website*: www.paintingstore.net *Signs work*: "ALAN TAYLOR." + date (year)

TAYLOR, Anita, BA (Hons), MA (RCA), RWA (Academician); Professor University of Surrey/Wimbledon School of Art; Hunting Art Prize (2000); Hunting Art Prize (Drawing) (1999); Cheltenham Open Drawing (1999); Malvern Award, Drawing (1993). *Medium*: oil, drawing. *b*: Cheshire, 3 Dec 1961. *m*: Paul Thomas MA (RCA), RWA. *Studied*: Gloucestershire College of Art (1981-84); Royal College of Art (1985-87). *Exhib*: Agnew's, London (2007); The Drawing Gallery, London (2004); Mall Galleries, London; NAS Sydney, Australia; Sherborne House, Dorset; Artsway, Hampshire; NCCA, Sunderland; Durham Museum and Art Gallery; Berkeley Square Gallery, London; RWA, Bristol; Lanchester Gallery, Coventry; Kunstlerhaus, Gottingen, Germany. *Works in collections*: V&A, London; Jerwood Foundation, London/Oxford; RWA; NAS, Australia; Universities of Gloucestershire/Sunderland; Leicestershire Collection; Leeds Education. *Commissions*: Project Director, Jerwood Drawing Prize (1994-present). *Publications*: Drawing, Cassell Illustrated (2003); Jerwood Drawing Prize Catalogues (2001-2007); Drawing Breath (2007). *Works Reproduced*: Drawing, Cassell Illustrated; Hunting Art Prize: 25 Years. *Address*: Old Methodist Chapel, The Street, Leonard Stanley, GL10 3NR. *Email*: a.p.taylor@wimbledon.arts.ac.uk *Signs work*: 'Taylor' and year completed.

TAYLOR, John Russell, BA (Cantab, 1956), MA (Cantab, 1959); writer; Art Critic, The Times since 1978. *b*: Dover, 19 Jun 1935. *s of*: Arthur Russell Taylor. *Partner*: Ying Yeung Li. *Educ*: Jesus College, Cambridge; Courtauld Inst. of Art, London. *Publications*: The Art Nouveau Book in Britain; The Art Dealers; Impressionism; Edward Wolfe; Bernard Meninsky; Impressionist Dreams; Ricardo Cinalli; Muriel Pemberton; Claude Monet: Impressions of France; Bill Jacklin; The Sun is God: The Life and Work of Cyril Mann; Roberto Bernardi; Peter Coker, RA; Philip Sutton, Printmaker; Roboz; Adrian George: Luxe, Calme et Volupté; The Art of Michael Parkes; Carl Laubin: Paintings; The Art of Jeremy Ramsey; The Glamour of the Gods; Phillip Sutton: Life and Work; La "Risurrezione" di Ricardo Cenelli; Exactitude; Hyperrealist Art Today; Kurt Jackson; etc. *Address*: The Times, 1 Pennington St., London E1 9XN. *Signs work*: "JOHN RUSSELL TAYLOR".

TAYLOR, Krista Louise, BTEC Dip G.AD, MC SD. *Medium*: painter. *b*: Lancashire, 2 Feb 1967. *d of*: Mr & Mrs G Taylor. *m*: Rob Maynard. two *s*. *Educ*: Falmouth College of Arts. *Exhib*: Great Atlantic Gallery, Falmouth. *Works Reproduced*: Wisdom of the Psyche series, Goddess series, Lifelines series, Swanpool series. *Principal Works*: current 2005: Swanpool series. *Address*: 34 Wood Lane, Falmouth, Cornwall. *Email*: krista@kristataylor.com *Website*: www.kristataylor.com *Signs work*: Krista Taylor.

TAYLOR, Martin, BA (Hons) (1975), ATD (1976); Awards: Chris Beetles Open Exhbn. (1988), Jeffrey Archer Award RWS (1989); artist, etcher. *Medium*: water-colour, pencil, oil. *b*: Hayes, Middx., 10 May 1954. *m*: Marianne Read. one *s*. one *d*. *Studied*: Ealing School of Art, Wimbledon School of Art, Goldsmiths' College. *Represented by*: Catto Gallery, 100 Heath Street, Hampstead, London. *Exhib*: Bankside Gallery (1986-2002), Contemporary British Water-colours (1983-93), Mercury Gallery, Cork St., Catto Gallery, Hampstead, London, Edwin Pollard Gallery, Wimbledon, Linda Blackstone Gallery Pinner, Savage Fine Art, Northampton, RA Exhbns. (1982, 1985), Singer & Friedlander/Sunday Times water-colour exhbns. (1987-97), RWS Open Exhibitions (1986-2002), Wold Galleries, Bourton, Glos., World of W/C Fair, Park Lane (1990-2002), Chris Beetles Gallery, London (1991, 1993), Compton Cassey Gallery, Glos. (1996). *Works in collections*: The Prudential, The Fuller Collection. *Publications*: contributor to: Encyclopaedia of Water-colour Techniques (Quarto), Buildings (Quarto), Acrylics Masterclass (Quarto), Encyclopaedia of Drawing Techniques (Quarto); articles in The Artist magazine; Watercolour Artists Bible (Quarto). *Address*: 13 St. Georges Ave., Northampton NN2 6JA. *Email*: martintaylorartist@hotmail.com *Website*: www.martintaylor.org *Signs work*: "Martin Taylor."

TAYLOR, Michael John, Dip.Arch. (1953), ARIBA (1955), Hon SGFA; architectural illustrator in water-colour, gouache, linocuts; Commended & Master's Awards "Million Brushstrokes" Llewellyn Alexander Gallery. *b*: Scarborough, 22 Sep 1930. *s of*: H S P Taylor, artist. *m*: Molly Crowther, textile artist. one *s*. one *d*. *Educ*: Scarborough Boys High School. *Studied*: Leeds College of Art, School of Architecture (1948-53). *Exhib*: RA, RI, RSMA, SGFA, UA, "Not the RA" Llewellyn Alexander Gallery, Laing, Singer and Friedlander and Hunting competitions; one-man shows: Bath, Canterbury, Harrogate, Russell Gallery Putney, Discerning Eye Exhibition, Mall Galleries. *Works in collections*: RAC Pall Mall, Hertfordshire CC Museums Service, private collections France and USA. *Commissions*: Aoke Soletanche (Jubilee Line Extension), RAC Pall Mall. *Publications*:

book jackets for Foyle, Hodder and Stoughton. *Works Reproduced*: Artist & Illustrators. *Address*: 4 Sewell Ave., Wokingham, Berks. RG41 1NS. *Signs work*: "Michael J. Taylor".

TAYLOR, Michael Ryan, RP (2001), BA Hons(Lond); Awards: Changing Faces Prize (winner 2002), Holburne Contemporary Portrait Prize (winner 2002), Royal West of England Academy Lark Trust Award (2005), NPG John Player Award (1983). *Medium*: oil. *b*: Worthing, 17 Feb 1952. *s of*: Patrick Taylor. *m*: Caroline. one *s*. one *d*. *Educ*: Worthing High School for Boys. *Studied*: Goldsmiths' School of Art (1970-73). *Represented by*: Waterhouse & Dodd, London. *Exhib*: Morley Gallery, Millfield Open (winner 1989), Hunting Group Art Prize (3rd prize 1989), RA, Worthing Art Gallery, Quay Arts Centre, IOW, Beaux Arts, Bath, and Beaux Arts, London (1993, 1997), Royal Society of Portrait Painters; Waterhouse & Dodd, London (2006, 2010). *Works in collections*: NPG, Christchurch Hall, Oxford, Robinson College, Cambridge, Holburne Museum of Art, Bath, House of Lords, Westminster, Scheringa Museum, Netherlands. *Commissions*: Julian Bream (NPG, 1984); P D James (NPG, 1996), Sir John Tavener (NPG, 2001), Andy Sheppard (Holburne Museum of Art, 2003), Lord Falconer - Lord Chancellor (House of Lords, 2007); 'Boy with Apple' commissioned by Wes Anderson for his 2014 film 'The Grand Budapest Hotel'. *Misc*: member: Royal Society of Portrait Painters. *Address*: 1 Upper St., Child Okeford, Blandford Forum, Dorset DT11 8EF. *Email*: michael@mrtaylor.co.uk *Website*: www.mrtaylor.co.uk

TAYLOR, Pam, ARBS (1980), SPS (1975); Chelmsford Borough Council Civic Award for services to the Arts (1998). *Medium*: sculptor in bronze. *b*: Pontypridd, 13 May 1929. *d of*: the late W.G. Archer. *m*: Peter William Taylor. two *s*. *Educ*: South Shields and Wick High Schools. *Studied*: Sir John Cass College School of Art (1947-50). *Exhib*: Mall Galleries, Guildhall, Royal Exchange. *Works in collections*: Principal works: RAF and Allied Air Forces WW2 Monument, Plymouth Hoe; RAF, Battle of Britain and Bomber Command Museums, Hendon; Shakespeareplatz, Berlin; Colgate-Palmolive Head Office; Bancrofts School; Georgetown Guyana; bronze bust of Shakespeare in Shakespeare's Globe Theatre, London; RAF North Coates Strike Wing Memorial; Hordle Walhampton School – child figures, Garden of Heroes, Dorsington. *Commissions*: All the above were commissions as well as numerous portrait commissions. *Clubs*: Royal Soc. of British Sculptors, Society of Portrait Sculptors. *Address*: Merrydown, 88 Haltwhistle Rd., S. Woodham Ferrers, Chelmsford, Essex CM3 5ZF. *Email*: pam.petetaylor@tiscali.co.uk *Signs work*: "Pam Taylor".

TAYLOR, Sean, Hon DFA (1982), MAFA (1983), FFA (1989); sculptor in mixed media; Course Director, Sculpture and Combined Media, Limerick School of Art and Design, Ireland; mem. Sculptors Society of Ireland. *b*: Cork, 16 Aug 1959. *m*: Annette Moloney. one *d*. *Educ*: Presentation Brothers College, Cork. *Studied*: Crawford College of Art and Design, Cork (1979-82), University of Ulster, Belfast, N.I. (1982-83), Kunstenacademie, Rotterdam (1988-89). *Exhib*: 29 one-man shows since 1983 worldwide. *Works in collections*: museums in Poland, Ireland, Mexico. *Commissions*: in Glasgow and Ireland. *Publications*: 34 catalogues; 5 CD, CD Roms: Bliain le Baisteach, Coisir an Tsionann; articles for Circa Art Magazine. *Misc*: Work on: axis website (UK) http://www.lmu.ac.uk/ces/axis also www.the-artists.org *Address*: The Old School, Brackile, Pallasgreen, Co. Limerick, Rep. of Ireland. *Email*: seantaylor@eircom.net *Website*: www.softday.ie *Signs work*: "Sean Taylor."

TAYLOR, Wendy Ann, CBE (1988); sculptor; Mem. Royal Fine Art Commission (1981-99); Specialist Adviser, Com. for Arts Design (1988-91); Mem. Advisory Group PCFC (1989-90); FZS (1989-); Mem. Design Advisory Panel, London Docklands Development Corp. (1989-98); Trustee, LAMA (1993-2010), FQMW (1993-), FRBS (1994-) Council Mem. (1999-2000); FRSA (2004-). *b*: 29 Jul 1945. *d of*: Edward Philip Taylor and Lilian Maude Wright. *m*: 1982, Bruce Robertson. one *s*. *Educ*: St. Martin's School of Art, LDAD

(1st Dist.). *Exhib*: thirteen one-man shows: (1970-2009); over 100 group exhbns. (1964-82). *Works in collections*: GB, USA, Eire, NZ, Germany, Sweden, Qatar, Switzerland, Seychelles. *Commissions*: Major commissions: over seventy throughout the UK. *Publications*: 'Wendy Taylor' monograph by Edward Lucie-Smith (1992). *Address*: 73 Bow Rd., London E3 2AN. *Email*: wendy-taylor@fsmail.net *Website*: www.wendytaylorsculpture.co.uk

TAYLOR, Mrs. M.: see BRIDGE, Muriel Elisabeth.

TAYLOR WILSON, Joanne, MA Fine Art (Edin 1977), ATC Goldsmiths' College (1978), RA Schools Post. Grad. Cert. (1981), Elizabeth Greenshields Scholarship (1981-82); still life, landscape and portrait painter; Mem. of Manchester Academy of Arts (1985). *Medium*: watercolour, gouache, oils *b*: Bolton, Lancs., 12 Sep 1953. *d of*: James Spencer Taylor, A.R.C.A. *m*: Ivan Wilson, RIBA. one *s*. one *d*. *Educ*: Canon Slade Grammar School, Bolton. *Studied*: Edinburgh College of Art, Edinburgh University (1972-77), RA Schools (1978-81, Peter Greenham, RA). *Exhib*: Royal Scottish Academy (1975, 1987), RA (1979, 1980, 1982, 1983, 1986, 1987), RBA (1980), Manchester Academy (1979-83, 1985-97), Manchester; one-man show, Bolton A.G. (1979), Howarth A.G., Accrington (1991), Towneley Hall, Burnley (1999). *Works in collections*: Bolton A.G., West Midlands College of Education, Howarth Art Gallery, Accrington & many private collections. *Address*: 4 Beechwood Ave., Clitheroe, Lancs. BB7 1EZ. *Signs work*: "J. TAYLOR WILSON" or "J.T.W."

TEBBS, Margaret, Freelance botanical illustrator in ink and water-colour; freelance artist: RBG Kew, Natural History Museum, New Plantsman, etc. *b*: 5 Sep 1948. *Educ*: Manor School, Ruislip. *Studied*: Ealing College of Art. *Exhib*: Westminster Gallery, London, Everard Read Gallery, South Africa. *Publications*: numerous illustrations for Kew Bulletin, Flora of Arabia, B.S.B.I. Publications, Wild Flowers of Europe (New Holland), Flora Zambesiaca, Flora of Bhutan, Flora of Egypt. *Address*: c/o Royal Botanic Gdns, Kew, Richmond, Surrey TW9 3AB. *Signs work*: "M. Tebbs."

TENGBERG, Violet, City of Gothenburg award for cultural achievement (1966), Bronze Medal, Europe Prize for painting (1971), Ostende, Belgium; Accademico Tiberino, Rome, Il Premio Adelaide Ristori, Rome (1984); City of Gothenburg Hon. Award (1987); Swedish Artists Foundation (1995); artist in oil and graphic work, and enamels on iron; poet, has published poetry books, 'Vision of the World Egg' (1996, 1997), 'Poetish Inspiration' (1999), 'Studies and Whisperings' (2004), 'Microcosmos - Macrocosmos' A book of oil and enamel paintings with 180 colour ill. and poem. *b*: Munktorp, Sweden, 21 Feb 1920. *s of*: A. Englund, master builder. *m*: J G A Tengberg, DHS (decd). one *s*. one *d*. *Educ*: Dipl. Academy of Fine Arts, "Valand" (1958-63), BA in Art History, Gothenburg University (1997). Religion, Science and History, Gothenburg University. *Exhib*: 19 one-man shows, Stockholm, Helsinki, London, Brussels, Paris, Rome, Viterbo, etc.; nearly 200 group shows all over Europe; Riksutställningar travelling exhbn.; 2nd Enamel Triennial, Trondheim, Norway (1993); group exhbn.: Enamel Artists from the Northern Countries, Kecskemet (1993); Szegred, Budapest, Hungary; Vienna, Austria; Germany (1994); 3rd International and enamel ausstellung, Coburg, Germany (1995). Official invite to exhibit in India, New Delhi and The Government Museum of Chandigarh (1997). *Works in collections*: Museums and official collections in Sweden including: Modern Art Museum, Stockholm, Kalmar Art Museum; Institut Tessin, Paris; Musée de Pau and Musée de Caen, France; Bibliothèque Nationale, Paris; Musée Vatican, Italy; Tate Gallery, London; Museo Nationale, Gdansk, Poland; Galleria Nationale, Varsavia, Poland; Museo di Viterbo, Italy; National Gallery of Modern Art, New Delhi, The Government Museum of Chandigarh, India, Dos Ehamil Museum, Coburg, Germany. *Publications*: Swedish Art Lexicon, part V, Allhem; Enciclopedia Universale "SEDA" della Pittura Moderna, Milano, etc. (colour ill.); "Violet Tengberg - Paintings, drawings, graphics and poems" (1982) in three languages and with 45 colour reproductions; Creative Mysticism - a Psychological Study of Violet Tengberg's religious visions and artistic creations by Prof. Antoon Geels (University of Lund, 1989). Essays by (Prof.) J.P. Hodin, Teddy Brunius (Prof. art History, University of Copenhagen) and Benkt-Erik Benktson (Prof. University of Gothenburg); Violet Tengberg: paper on William Blake's poem "The Tygor" of "Songs of Innocence and of Experience" (Gothenburg University of Art Dept. 1994), M.A. paper on William Blake's "World of Ideas" (1997). *Clubs*: A.I.A., W.I.A.C., F.P.S., K.R.O. *Address*: Götabergsgatan 22, 41134 Gothenburg, Sweden. *Website*: www.violettengberg.com *Signs work*: "VT," "Violet Tengberg."

TERRY, John Quinlan, FRIBA (1962); architect, artist in pen and ink, water-colour, linocut. *b*: London, 24 Jul 1937. *s of*: Philip Terry, solicitor. *m*: Christine. one *s*. four *d*. *Educ*: Bryanston School. *Studied*: architecture: Architectural Assoc., London. *Exhib*: RA Summer Show since 1962, Biennale in Venice (1980), San Francisco (1982), Paris (1981), Real Architecture Building Centre (1987); one-man shows: Rye A.G. (1980), Architectural Design (1981), Anthony Mould Gallery (1986), Judd St. Gallery (1987), Vision of Europe, Bologna (1992). *Publications*: The Kingswalden Notes, Pentagram Design, Pentagram Papers 16; 'Quinlan Terry, The Revival of Architecture' by Clive Aslet (Viking Penguin, 1986); Quinlan Terry, Selected Works. Architectural Monographs 27 (Academy Editions, 1993); 'Radical Classicism, the Architecture of Quinlan Terry' by David Watkin (Rizzoli New York, 2006); 'Architects Anonymous' by Quinlan Terry (Academy Editions, 1994). *Recreations*: The Pauline Epistles. *Address*: Old Exchange, Dedham, Colchester, Essex CO7 6HA.

TERRY, Karl Elliott, Winner of Winsor & Newton Oil Painting Prize, Patchings Art Fair (2009); Red Rag Award, Royal Society of British Artists; member of Wapping Group. *Medium*: oil, drawing. *b*: Ashford, Kent, 12 Nov 1967. *s of*: Phillip & Hazel Terry. *m*: Joanna Terry. one *s*. one *d*. *Educ*: The Norton Knatchbull School for Boys, Ashford, Kent (1980-84). *Studied*: mentoring by Chris Paynes. *Represented by*: Enid Lawson Fine Art, London: Royall Fine Art, Tunbridge Wells; Great Atlantic Art, Falmouth. *Exhib*: Turtle Fine Art, Rye; Galerie Gabrie, Pasadena, USA; Rye Society of Artists; Kent Art Fair; Battersea & Bristol Affordable Art Fairs; Royal Academy Summer Show (2008); RSMA (2009); Discerning Eye, Mall Galleries (2008); Richard Schmid Art Auction, Colorado, USA (2009); Hampshire, Cambridge & North of England Art Fairs; Patchings Art Exhibition; Wapping Group of Artists, Mall Galleries; RSMA; Red Rag Gallery, Stow on the Wold, Plein Air, Easton (2011). *Works in collections*: Jeff Beck, Sir Donald Sinden, Heather Mills, Sir Paul McCartney, Haralampi Oroschocoff. *Publications*: The Artist Magazine, Artists & Illustrator, Cornwall Today. *Recreations*: painting, travel, scuba diving, skiing. *Clubs*: Wapping Group of Artists, Plein Air Brotherhood. *Misc*: featured on BBC2 'Show Me the Monet'. *Address*: The Glyndes, 15 The Street, Wittersham, Tenterden, Kent, TN30 7EA. *Email*: karlterry1@btconnect.com *Website*: www.karlterry.co.uk *Signs work*: "Karl Terry".

TESIC, Biljana, FdA University of the Arts 2003; Kew Studio Prize for Outstanding London-based etcher, Originals 2009; Prize for Application & Progress in Life Drawing, Westminter Kingsway College 2001; Member of ULUS (The Association of Fine Artists in Serbia). *Medium*: artist in printmaking (etcher), photography, mixed media/textiles, watercolour, oil. *b*: Sarajevo, ex. Yugoslavia, 17 Jan 1952. *d of*: Dragan and Emilija Tesic. *Studied*: University of Belgrade, Faculty of Philology (1970-74); University of the Arts, London (Foundation Degree in Arts, 2001-2003); Morley College London Printmaking (2004-2009); Morley College: C&G Teacher Training Certificate, Level 3 in Visual Arts. *Exhib*: Group exhib: Royal Academy of Arts (2005, 2008, 2011, 2012); Art Pavilion "Cvijeta Zuzoric" (ULUS), Belgrade, Republic of Serbia (2013); "A Month of Serbian Culture in London", Queen Victoria Gallery, London (2013); Mall Galleries (2005, 2006 - UK Youth); Originals, Mall Galleries (2006, 2008, 2009); Mall Galleries BITE 2011; Morley College (2005-2009); South of England Show: Norfolk Pavilion (2007). Solo shows: Pozega (2005); Uzice (2008) Republic of Serbia. *Works in collections*: private. *Commissions*: various private. *Works Reproduced*: Etchings: Limited edition - 20 each. *Principal Works*: Photo Etching & etching. *Recreations*: photography, music, theatre, reading, travel. *Clubs*: The Royal Photographic Society. *Misc*: The outstanding facilities at Morley College and the University of Arts have been instrumental in my artistic development and achievements. *Address*: 10b Leopold Road, London W5 3PB. *Email*: info@biljanatesic.com *Website*: biljanatesic.com *Signs work*: "Biljana" or "Biljana Tesic".

TESKEY, Donald, RHA (2003); awards from Arts Council of Ireland, EV&A Limerick, ESB, RHA, Vermont Studio Centre - Fellowship. Ballinglen Arts Foundation Fellowship, Josef Albers Foundation Award, Centre Culturel Irlandais Paris Award. Elected member of Aosdana. *Medium*: oil, acrylic, drawing. *b*: Co. Limerick, Ireland, 1956. one *s*. one *d*. *Educ*: Diploma in Fine Art. *Studied*: Limerick School of Art and Design. *Represented by*: Art First, London; Oliver Sears Gallery, Dublin; Dolan Maxwell Gallery, Philadelphia, USA. *Exhib*: Rubicon Gallery, Dublin (1993, 95, 97, 99, 2001, 04, 05. 07, 09); Art First, London (1998, 2000, 2002, 2003, 2006, 2011); Oliver Sears Gallery (2013) also in Canada, USA, Germany, France, Finland, UK and in group and curated shows. *Works in collections*: Arts Council of Ireland, Allied Irish Bank, Barings Assett Management London, Contemporary Irish Art Society, Royal Victoria Hospitals, KPMG Dublin, Irish Museum of Modern Art, National Gallery of Ireland. *Commissions*: The Electricity Supply Board (ESB); Irish Agricultural Wholesalers Society (IAWS); Crampton Builders. *Publications*: 'Profile: Donald Teskey' (Gandon Editions, pub. 2005); 'Donald teskey - a Connemara Folio' (Occasional Press 2011); 'The Idea of Islands' (pub Occasional Press 2010); 'Conversation in the Mountains' (pub Gallery Press 2008). *Address*: c/o Oliver Sears Gallery, 29 Molesworth Street, Dublin 2, Eire. *Email*: donaldteskey@eircom.net *Website*: donaldteskey.com *Signs work*: "DONALD TESKEY RHA".

THICKE, Thelma Gwendoline, NDD, ATD, DipHE, MFPS; dealer in fine art, restorer and painter in oil and water-colour; principal: Thicke Gallery, and Swansea Antique Club; retd. lecturer, Faculty of Art and Design, W. Glamorgan Inst. of Higher Educ., Swansea, also Swansea University, Faculty of Educ. *b*: 20 Aug 1921. *Educ*: St. Leonards-on-Sea. *Studied*: Hastings School of Art (Vincent Lines), West of England College of Art, Bristol University, B'ham University (1966-67). *Exhib*: RA, RBA, NEAC, FPS, RWS etc. *Works in collections*: many private collections. *Clubs*: Royal Overseas League, LAPADA. *Misc*: Valuations and restoration of oils, water-colours and prints. *Address*: 24 Masefield Way, Parc Beck, Sketty, Swansea SA2 9FF. *Signs work*: "T.G. Thicke."

THISTLETHWAITE, Ann, NDD painting; artist, landscape painter in oil, pastel and charcoal. *Medium*: oil, pastels. *b*: Birmingham, 22 Oct 1944. *d of*: C E D Thistlethwaite, dental surgeon. *Educ*: Edgbaston Church of England College. *Studied*: Birmingham College of Art and Design (1961-66) under Gilbert Mason and Mr. Francis, Mr. Hawes Principal. *Exhib*: one-man shows: London, Birmingham, Worcester, Tunbridge Wells, Malvern, RBA, ROI, RSMA, PS, Contemporary Art, Melbourne, Australia (Royal Overseas Commonwealth Art 1st Prize (1969) presented to H.M. the Queen). *Works in collections*: J. M. Beaul, Michigan, Bank of England. *Recreations*: loves countryside, wild flowers, birdsong, wildlife. *Address*: 4 King George Ave., Droitwich, Worcs. WR9 7BP. *Signs work*: "Ann Thistlethwaite."

THOMAS, Chris, BA Fine Art (1969); Diploma in Art Therapy (1972). *Medium*: Oil; watercolour; drawing. *b*: Bradford, 31 May 1947. *m*: Rosalind. two *s*. one *d*. *Studied*: Reading University; St Albans School of Art. *Represented by*: Brian Sinfield. *Exhib*: Brian Sinfield (2006, 2008, 2010); Cadogan Gallery (2010); Sarah Adams, Padstow Studio (2006-). *Works in collections*: Private and corporate. *Official Purchasers*: Cornwall Partnership Trust. *Works Reproduced*: Three catalogues from Brian Sinfield. *Principal Works*: The

Derelict Social Hall at Davidstow (2008). *Address*: Rose Cottage, Trevalga, Boscastle, Cornwall PL35 0DZ. *Email*: thomascj@btinternet.com *Website*: www.christhomas.info *Signs work*: "Chris Thomas".

THOMAS, Glynn David Laurie, LSIA (1967), RE (1975); freelance artist in etching; taught printmaking, Ipswich Art School (1967-79). *b*: Cambridge, 7 Apr 1946. *m*: Pearl. two *s*. *Studied*: Cambridge College of Art (1962-67). *Exhib*: mixed and one-man shows incl. RA, National Print Exhbn. Pall Mall Gal., Barbican, Cambridge Contemporary Art, John Russell, Ipswich, Printworks, Colchester, Royal Exchange, Manchester, Lyric, Hammersmith, Aldephi, New York, Toronto, Hong Kong, Birhcam Gallery, Snape Maltings. *Works in collections*: Museum of London, Ashmolean and Ipswich Museum. *Commissions*: Christies Contemporary Art. *Publications*: Victorian Cambridge, Illustrated Journal of Nepal. *Address*: Lodge Cottage, Bluegate Lane, Capel St. Mary, Ipswich IP9 2JX. *Email*: studio@glynnthomas.com *Website*: www.glynnthomas.com

THOMAS, Jean, DipAD Fine Art (Bristol, 1974); painter/printmaker in oil on canvas. *b*: Haverfordwest, 1950. *m*: Paul Preston, goldsmith. one *s*. one *d*. *Educ*: Taskers, Haverfordwest. *Studied*: Newport College of Art (1969-71), Bristol Polytechnic (1971-74). *Exhib*: Welsh National Eisteddfod, RSPP, RSBA, RSPM, Galerie d'Or Hamburg, Fountain Fine Art Llandeilo, Manor House Cardiff; and numerous exhbns. GBH, Germany, Austria. *Commissions*: portraits for: Earl of Halifax, Lady Brooksbank, Judge Haworth, plus commissions for Christie's, and Northallerton Council for Duke and Duchess of York. Recently worked on large mural and now flag/banner sculpture. *Address*: The Old Smithy, Llandeilo, Haverfordwest, Pembrokshire SA62 6LD.

THOMAS, Lex, BA Hons; PG Dip Fine Art. *Medium*: oil, drawing, collage. *b*: London, 3 Jan 1972. *Studied*: Greenwich University (1991-94), University of the West of England (1995-98); Chelsea College of Art & Design (2007). *Exhib*: 2012: Woolgather Art Prize, Leeds; Rising Start Art Prize, Farnham; Lynn Painter-Stainers Prize, London. 2011: Young Masters @ Sphinx, London; Future Proof (solo show), Opus Gallery, Newcastle; Great Brampton House, Hereford. 2010: Orleand House Gallery. 2009: Scope, Miami, USA; Galeria Espacio, Valencia, Spain; Royal Academy Summer Exhibition, London; Scope, Basel, Switzerland; Bridge, New York, USA; Grimestown Gallery, London; Opus Gallery, Newcastle upon Tyne; Sage Centre, Newcastle upon Tyne. 2008: Truman Brewery, London; Guerilla Gallery, London; Salon Gallery, London. *Works in collections*: private collections UK, Europe & USA. *Address*: Dalston Underground Studios, 28 Shacklewell Lane, London E8 2EZ. *Email*: lexland@hotmail.com *Website*: www.lexthomas.co.uk *Signs work*: "LEX Thomas".

THOMAS, Margaret, RWA, RBA (1947), NEAC (1951); De Lazlo Medal (RBA, 1971); Hunting Group Award (Oil Painting of the Year, 1981). *Medium*: oil. *b*: London 26 Sep 1916. *d of*: Francis Stewart Thomas & Grace Whetherley. *Educ*: private. *Studied*: Slade School (1936-38), R.A. Schools under Thomas Monninston and Ernest Jackson (1938-39). *Exhib*: RA (since 1943), annually RWA, and RSA; one-man exhbns. include Leicester Galleries (1949 and 1950); Aitkin Dott's Edinburgh (1952, 1955 and 1966); Canaletto Gallery (1961); Howard Roberts, Cardiff (1963); Minories, Colchester (1964); Queen's University, Belfast (1967); Mall Galleries (1972); Octagon, Belfast (1973); Scottish Gallery, Edinburgh (1982); Sally Hunter Gallery, London (1988, 1991, 1995, 1998); Royal West of England Academy (1992); Messum's Gallery, London (Sept. 2001, Dec 2003), several solo shows at Strand Gallery, Aldeburgh. *Works in collections*: HRH Duke of Edinburgh; Chantrey Bequest; Arts Council; Tate Britain; Exeter College, Oxford; Min. of Educ.; Min. of Works; Paisley, Hull and Carlisle Art Galleries; GLC; Edinburgh City Corporation; Steel Company of Wales; Financial Times; Nuffield Foundation Trust; Scottish National Orchestra; Robert Fleming; Lloyds of London; Warburg Group. *Commissions*: National

Library of Wales (portrait of Sir Kyffin Williams RA). *Works Reproduced*: in 'Country Life', 'Eastern Daily Press'. *Recreations*: dogs, gardens. *Address*: Ellingham Mill, Bungay, Suffolk NR35 2EP.

THOMAS, Robin, SGFA; Cert.Ed.; Certificate of Fine Art; The Coghill Prize for Landscape Painting, Oxford (1973). *Medium*: oils, watercolour, bodycolour. *b*: Nuneaton, 8 Jul 1948. *m*: Pamela. one *s*. one *d*. *Educ*: Yallet Hall, Staffs; Whittlebury School, Northants. *Studied*: The Ruskin School of Drawing, Oxford (1973); Glos. College of Art (1967). *Exhib*: Ashmolean Museum, Oxford (1973); Museum of Modern Art, Oxford (1973); Bodleian Library, Oxford - London (with SGFA) from 2001; also Bath, Cheltenham, South Molton, Dartington, Totnes, Widecombe and other South Devon galleries. *Works in collections*: international collections, private British collections; National Trust; Lord Lichfield Collection; Royal Navy. *Commissions*: The Wordsworth Trust; The National Trust; private and corporate commissions, Midas Construction. *Publications*: prints and cards. *Official Purchasers*: The National Trust; Wordsworth Trust; Royal Navy. *Works Reproduced*: over 50 NT properties - prints, notecards, postcards. *Principal Works*: English cottages; Genre landscapes and farming scenes from 1950s in watercolour & oils. *Recreations*: music, country pursuits, gardens & painting. *Misc*: runs classes, clubs, holidays etc. (private and local authority) for artists. Now includes talks, lectures etc on British Art. *Address*: 'Mynwy', 25 Biltor Road, Ipplepen, Newton Abbott, Devon, TQ12 5QL. *Email*: robinthomasart@btinternet.com *Website*: www.robinthomasart.co.uk *Signs work*: "R.D.Thomas".

THOMAS, Shanti, artist in oil, pastel and charcoal, teacher; Artist in Residence, Gatwick Airport (1993). *b*: London, 3 Dec 1949. *Studied*: School of Signa Simi (1965), Academy of Fine Arts, Florence (1965-67), Camberwell School of Art and Crafts (1971-73, Sargy Mann). *Exhib*: Commonwealth Inst. (1987), Ikon touring (1984, 1989), Whitechapel Open (1987, 1989), Athena Arts Award Open, Barbican (1987), 'Critical Realism' Nottingham, Camden Arts Centre (1988), 'Black Art, Plotting the Course' Oldham (1988), 'The Artist Abroad' Usher Gallery, Lincoln (1989). *Works in collections*: ACGB, Leicester Schools, and private collections. *Publications*: Birthday Book, Women's Artist Diary (1988), catalogues, Critical Realism, Black Art, The Artist Abroad, etc. *Address*: 18 Cornwall Rd., London N4 4PH. *Signs work*: "Shanti Thomas."

THOMPSON, Christopher, PGDip. Painting, RA Schools 1997; The Noel Spencer Award for Painting, Norwich School of Art (1994), George Isted Prize for Portrait Painting, RA Schools (1996), Armitage Prize for Painting, RA Schools (1997), Villiers David Prize, shortlisted (2003). *Medium*: painter in oil on canvas. *b*: Grimsby, 4 Aug 1969. one *s*. *Studied*: Grimsby School of Art (1988-90), Norwich School of Art (1991-94), Royal Academy Schools (1994-97). *Represented by*: Albemarle Gallery. *Exhib*: over 30 solo and mixed exhibitions in UK and abroad since 1993, including: RA Summer Exhbn (1996, 1997), Royal Society of Portrait Painters, Mall Galleries (1999, 2002), BP Portrait Award, NPG (2002), Young Contemporaries, Albemarle Gallery (2002, 2003), DFN Gallery New York (2002), Eleanor Ettinger Gallery, New York (2005). *Works in collections*: National Portrait Gallery, London. *Address*: 17 Crystal Drive, Peterborough, Cambridgeshire, PE2 9RJ. *Signs work*: 'C.Thompson'.

THOMPSON, George, PS; ATD, NDD. *Medium*: oils, watercolours, pastels and acrylics. *b*: Wigan, Lancs, 26 Jul 1934. *s of*: George and Annie Thompson. *Educ*: Chester College School. *Studied*: Chester School of Art (1950-54), Liverpool College of Art (1955). *Exhib*: one-man shows: Chester (annually), Melbourne Australia, Vancouver Canada, Tokyo Japan (on two occasions). Mixed shows: Pastel Society, Mall Galleries, Solomon Gallery Dublin, Wirral Society of Arts; Retrospective Exhibition, Williamson Gallery, Birkenhead (2004), Grosvenor Museum Art Gallery, Chester (2007). *Publications*: Three instructional videos of my work published by Far Meadow Arts, from 2001 to 2005. *Works Reproduced*: Twenty five limited edition prints published by The Brentwood Gallery, Stockton Heath, Cheshire. *Address*: 3 Deefords House, Sandy Lane, Chester CH3 5UN. *Signs work*: 'George Thompson'.

THOMPSON, Hilli, BA Hons (1967), MPhil (1971), PGCE (1977); artist/botanical illustrator in linocut, etching, pen, pastel, acrylic, stained glass. *b*: London, 3 Apr 1946. *Educ*: Brondesbury and Kilburn Grammar School; Universities of Newcastle (1964-67), Ulster (1968-71), Leeds (1976-77). *Exhib*: frequently at botanical socs. of British Isles, SBA; solo shows: Ipswich/E. Anglia. *Works in collections*: Norwich City Museum. *Publications*: The New Flora of British Isles by C.A. Stale (C.U.P.). *Recreations*: music, gardening. *Address*: 42 Dover Rd., Ipswich, Suffolk IP3 8JQ. *Signs work*: "Hilli."

THOMPSON, Kathleen M., BA Hons Fine Art; MA Fine Art; BA Hons Philosophy; David Murray Award, RA; South East Arts Research Grant. *Medium*: painting and drawing, oil. *b*: London, 26 Jun 1948. *d of*: Charles Thompson & Myra Love. *m*: Brian Watterson. *Educ*: Blackwell County, Harrow, London. *Studied*: Harrow School of Art; Sheffield College of Art; Chelsea School of Art; London University Birkbeck College. *Exhib*: RA Summer Exhbns; Cheltenham Art Gallery (2002); 8th Mostyn Open, Llandudno, Wales (1997); Maidstone Museum & Art Gallery (1996), EAST Norwich, Radcliffe & Newlands, London (2012) etc. *Works in collections*: Department of the Environment, London; Kings College, London University; Kings College Hospital; private collections England and abroad. *Publications*: exhibition catalogues, Blunter Edge; Drawings 2009. *Works Reproduced*: 'Empedocles', 'Zoogony', 'Yellow Car'. *Principal Works*: paintings and drawings. *Address*: 3 Haynes Cottages, High Street, Brasted, Westerham, Kent TN16 1HS. *Email*: kmtartist@hotmail.com *Website*: Flickr and Saatchi online *Signs work*: 'K.T.' or 'Kathleen Thompson'.

THOMPSON, Kevin Barry, EAGMA; Professional East Anglian landscape and marine artist since 1989. *Medium*: oil, acrylic, water-colour. *b*: Dorking, Surrey, 11 Mar 1950. *s of*: Brian P. Thompson & Hilda M.Goff. *m*: Vanessa Jane. one *s*, Spencer. one *d*, Carrie. *Educ*: Roman Hill School, Lowestoft; studied general design at Lowestoft College (1985-87). *Studied*: self taught artist. *Exhib*: ROI, RSMA, Mall Galleries, London; one-man shows: Assembly House, Norwich (1982), Reades Gallery, Aldeburgh (1986), Conservative Hall, Southwold (1989), Toll House Gallery, Gt. Yarmouth (1991, 2003, 2004, 2005, 2006, 2008), Ferini Gallery, Lowestoft (2002); Assembly House, Norwich (2009, 2010). Exhibits Chrome Gallery, Norfolk; Ferini Gallery, Suffolk; also throughout UK with EAGMA and NNAC. *Works in collections*: Many works are held in private collections, both in Gt. Britain and abroad. *Publications*: "How Artists See Places", "How Artists See People", "How Artists See Nature" all published by Green Pebble. *Clubs*: Norfolk and Norwich Art Circle (NNAC), East Anglian Group of Marine Artists (EAGMA). *Address*: 24 Pound Farm Drive, Lowestoft, Suffolk, NR32 4RQ. *Signs work*: "KEVIN.B. THOMPSON." or "K.B.THOMPSON".

THOMPSON, Liam, BA Hons (1978); self employed artist in water-colour and oil; Adult Educ. tutor, creative studies curriculum leader. *b*: Larne, Co. Antrim, 20 Nov 1956. *Educ*: Campbell College, Belfast. *Studied*: Newcastle College of Art and Design (1974-75), Chelsea School of Art (1975-78), City and Guilds of London Art School (1978-79, Peter Coker, RA). *Exhib*: RA Summer Shows (1983-97). *Works in collections*: National Trust, UTV Collection. *Commissions*: National Trust, Storm Damage at Nymans, Sussex, Mount Stewart House, Co. Down. *Works Reproduced*: Leisure Painter Magazine (1990-97). *Address*: Stone Cottage, Hogbens Hill, Selling, Faversham, Kent ME13 9QU. *Signs work*: water-colours and oils: signed on back.

THOMSON, Diana, (née Golding), BA, FRBS; sculptor in bronze, terracotta, wood, resin. *b*: Manchester, 1939. *m*: Alex Thomson BSC, Cinematographer. one *d*. *Educ*:

Cheltenham Ladies' College. *Studied*: Kingston Polytechnic Sculpture Dept. (1976-79). *Exhib*: RA, RWA, New College, Oxford, Margam Park, S. Wales, and various group shows including "Free Range" Simmons Gallery, London WC1. *Commissions*: 'Woking Market' bronze plaque 7'3" x 4'6" at Network House, Bradfield Cl., Woking; 'Father and Child' bronze over life-size at Central House, off New St., Basingstoke; 'The Swanmaster' 7' bronze at Fairfield Ave., Staines; 'The Hurdler' bronze life-size, at APC International, The Lodge, Harmondsworth, Middx.; 'The Inheritors' bronze life-size group; 'Portrait of Yvonne de Galais and her daughter' life-size group; 'The Bargemaster' 7' bronze at Data-General Tower, Brentford, Middx.; 'Portrait of D.H. Lawrence' bronze life-size, at Nottingham University; 'The First Cinematographer' bronze life-size homage to William Friese-Greene, sited at Shepperton Studios, Middx.; Pinewood Studios, Bucks; Panavision U.K. Ltd., Greenford, Middx.; and Panavision, L.A., Calif., U.S.A.; Bronze homage to DH Lawrence at Nottingham Castle Museum and Art Gallery (2007). *Address*: The Summerhouse, 64 Mincing La., Chobham, Surrey GU24 8RT. *Email*: dianathomsonsculptor@intamail.com *Website*: dianathomsonsculptor.co.uk *Signs work*: "D.C. Thomson" or "D.C.T." and the year.

THOMSON, Harry Ross, Diploma of Art (Edinburgh) Graphics; over 100 International Cartoon Prizes and Awards. *Medium*: cartoonist. *b*: Hawick, 5 Oct 1938. *m*: Glenda Charnley. one *s*. one *d*. *Educ*: George Watson's College, Edinburgh. *Studied*: Edinburgh College of Art. *Exhib*: Ankara, Turkey (2002), Zenum, Subotica, Novi Sad, Serbia (2003), Daejeon, S.Korea (2005), Gabrovo, Bulgaria (2006), European Cartoon Centre, Kruishautem, Belgium (2012), Marostica, Italy (2013). *Publications*: How to Draw and Sell Cartoons (Apple Press). *Clubs*: FECO, British Cartoonists Assoc. *Address*: 'Portus', Haywards Heath Road, Balcombe, Sussex, RH17 6PG. *Email*: rossglenn@rosscartoons.com *Signs work*: roSS.

THORESBY, Valerie Cecilia, second year MA Painting, Wimbledon. *Medium*: acrylic, oil, watercolour, drawing, mixed media. *b*: Suffolk, 3 Feb 1941. *d of*: June Vyvyan. *m*: Henry Thoresby. two *s*. *Educ*: CLC, Cheltenham. *Studied*: Byam Shaw School of Art; Wimbledon School of Art; Cecil Collins City Lit. (1982-84). *Represented by*: Wills Art Warehouse, London SW15 1LY. *Exhib*: Royal College of Art; New Grafton Gallery; RA Summer Exhbn; Art League of Daytona, USA; Jacksonville Watercolour Society (USA). *Works in collections*: Royal Museum, Canterbury; De Beers, London; Merrill Lynch, Florida. *Commissions*: Nicholas Byam Shaw. *Publications*: The Public Catalogue Foundation. *Official Purchasers*: oil paintings in public ownership in Kent. *Principal Works*: Towards Reculver (Thoresby Valeria). *Clubs*: University of the Arts, 40 Dover St, London W1. *Address*: 6 Granville Road, Walmer, Kent CT14 7LU. *Email*: studio@valeriethoresby.co.uk *Website*: www.valeriethoresby.co.uk *Signs work*: 'Valerie C.Thoresby'.

THORN, Richard Charles. *Medium*: Acrylic, Pastel, watercolour. *b*: Torbay, 7 Mar 1952. *Partner*: Sue-Ellen Johnson. two *d*. *Studied*: Newton Abbot School of Art (1968-70); Torquay Technical College (Graphic Art and Design) (1984-86). *Exhib*: Solo shows: John Robertson, Bourne Gallery, John Davies Gallery, Alexander Gallery, Bristol & Bath; Beside the Wave Gallery, Falmouth; Portugese Embassy; Mapworks, Cornwall; Torre Abbey. Group shows include: RI Open; Panter & Hall; Davidson Fine Art. *Works in collections*: Various private collections in the UK and USA. *Commission*: Various private commissions. *Publications*: The Artist magazine Masterclass editorial (Aug 2011); Devon Today magazine Devon Arts (2008); A Picture of Devon, various artists, Halsgove Pubs. *Official Purchasers*: Princess Michael of Kent; Portugese Ambassador. *Works Reproduced*: Large body of limited edition prints (Haddon Galleries, Torquay). *Principal Works*: Landscapes; seascapes; cityscapes. *Recreations*: Composing and playing jazz; reading; travel. *Clubs*: SWAc (Academician); Devon Arts Society member; International Watercolour Society judge. *Address*: 25 Teign Village, Newton Abbott, Devon TQ5 9JY. *Email*: thornart2@bmail.com *Website*: www.richardthornart.co.uk *Signs work*: "RICHARD THORN".

THORNBERY, Mary, painter in oil. *b*: Bredhurst, Kent, 23 May 1921. *m*: Michael Dobson, FRAM. one *s*. one *s-d*. *Studied*: painting: London, Florence, Rome. *Exhib*: RA, London Group, New English Art Club. *Works in collections*: West of England Academy, Bristol B8; Imperial War Museum, London SE1; West Wales General Hospital, Carmarthen, SA31. *Official Purchasers*: West of England Academy, Bristol. *Address*: 20 Hafan Tywi, The Parade, Carmarthen, S. Wales SA31 1LW. *Signs work*: "MARY THORNBERY."

THORNE, Trevor John. *Medium*: painter of figurative subjects mainly set in the 1920s and 1930s in watercolour, gouache, pen and ink, and pastel. *b*: Southampton, 8 May 1961. *m*: Marriam. *Educ*: Wyvern School, Hampshire. *Studied*: engineering at Southampton College of Technology 1977-81, and Politics and Economics at the Open University. *Exhib*: London and provincial shows including the Wykeham Galleries, Peter Hedley Gallery, Century Gallery, Dragon Gallery, WH Patterson Ltd., James Purdey & Son Ltd., Whitgift Gallery and The Phoenix Gallery. *Commissions*: various private commissions. *Recreations*: walking, reading and listening to music. *Address*: 4 Masefield Close, Eastleigh, Hants, SO50 9EH. *Email*: trevorthorne.art@btinternet.com *Signs work*: "T J Thorne" or "Trevor Thorne".

THORNTON, Leslie, ARCA (1951). *Medium*: sculpture. *b*: Skipton, 1925. *Studied*: Leeds College of Art (1945-48), R.C.A. (1948-51). *Exhib*: One-man shows, Gimpels Fils (1957, 1960, 1969); Retrospective, Manchester (1981); ICA (1955); Berne (1955); British Council Young Sculptors Exhbn. (Germany, 1955-56), Sweden (1956-57); São Paolo Biennal (1957); Holland Park (1957); CAS Religious Theme Exhbn., Tate Gallery; British Embassy, Brussels (1958); Middelheim Biennial, Antwerp (1959); Royal Academy (1974, 76, 78, 79, 1987); 100 Years Sculpture, Leeds (2004). *Works in collections*: Museum of Modern Art, New York; Arts Council of Gt. Britain; Leeds Art Gallery; Felton Bequest, Australia; Albright Museum; Fogg Art Gallery; National Gallery of Scotland; Peggy Guggenheim, Venice; private: UK, Europe, USA and S. America. *Commissions*: Daily Mirror Building; Crucifix: St. Louis Priory Missouri, and St. Ignatious College, London. *Address*: Stable Cottage, Chatsworth Pl., Harrogate HG1 5HR. *Email*: thornton-dl@sky.com *Website*: www.leslie-thornton.net

THORPE, Hilary, BA (Hons) Woven Textiles; marine and landscape painter in acrylic. *b*: Elsecar, Yorks., 9 Apr 1959. *Studied*: West Surrey College of Art and Design. *Exhib*: solo shows: Cowes, Camelford and London. *Works in collections*: Cowes Maritime Museum. *Commissions*: marine paintings: various locations UK, Bermuda. *Works Reproduced*: several limited edition prints available. *Misc*: Hilary Thorpe paints primarily 'on location'. *Address*: 58 Nelson Drive, Cowes, I.O.W. PO31 8QY. *Email*: hilary@hilarythorpe.co.uk *Website*: www.hilarythorpe.co.uk

THURGOOD, Gwyneth, NDD (1958), ATD (1959), FNSEAD (1970); Woman of Achievement 2007 Award; artist/teacher in painting, etching, stained glass; Ambassador of Knowledge, University of Cambridge (2010). *b*: Swansea, 2 Apr 1938. *m*: Anthony Thurgood (decd). one *s*. *Educ*: Neath Girls' Grammar School. *Studied*: Swansea College of Art, B'ham College of Art. *Exhib*: nine solo shows: art/science (1987-2001) including BA Meeting (1993), Science Museum, London (1995); Annual Exhibition of Microscopy, Natural History Museum, London, various including 2005, 2006, 2007 (sciart images) 2011, 2012, 2013. *Works in collections*: Universities of Surrey, Manchester, Kent and Warwick, Maidstone Hospital. *Commissions*: University of Warwick. *Publications*: illustrated: papers - three international journals, catalogues; Meridian Television The Gallery (1994, 1995), Meridian Tonight, interview (1997); included in: Dictionary of International Biography 32nd Ed. (2004); The Cambridge Blue Book (2005); Woman of the Year 2006, Great Women of the 21st Century 2007, Great Minds of the 21st Century 2005/6 Edition, American Biographical Institute, International Profiles of Accomplished Leaders 2007, International Who's Who of Professional and Business Women 2009, World Who's Who of

Women 15th Edition 2009, Dictionary of International Biography, 37th Edition 2014, 2000 Outstanding Intellectuals of the 21st Century 8th Edition 2014, Outstanding People in the Arts Today 2014. *Official Purchasers*: University of Warwick. *Works Reproduced*: in journals. *Principal Works*: Images invisible to the naked eye - micro crystals, etc., drawings, paintings, etchings. *Recreations*: tennis, badminton. *Clubs*: Quekett Microscopical. *Address*: Starling Steps, Old Ashford Road, Lenham, Maidstone, Kent ME17 2PX. *Email*: gwynethmthurgood@btinternet.com *Website*: www.micro-art.co.uk *Signs work*: "Gwyneth Thurgood" or "Thurgood."

THYNN, Alexander (7th Marquess of Bath), BA, MA (Oxon); painter in oil, novelist. *b*: London, 6 May 1932. *s of*: Henry Thynne (6th Marquess of Bath). *m*: Anna Gael. one *s*. one *d*. *Educ*: Eton and Christchurch, Oxford. *Studied*: Paris: Grande Chaumiere (Henri Goetz), Academie Julian (Andre Planson), Academie Ranson (Roger Chastel). *Works in collections*: murals at Longleat House. *Publications*: Lord Weymouth's Murals by Alexander Thynn; novels, The Carry-Cot (W. H. Allen 1972), The King is Dead (Longleat Press 1976), Pillars of the Establishment (Hutchinson 1981), The New World Order of Alexander Thynn (Starhaven 2000), Strictly Private (an autobiography). *Address*: Longleat House, Warminster, Wilts. BA12 7NN. *Email*: lordbath@btinternet.com *Website*: www.lordbath.co.uk

TIDNAM, Nicholas Rye, RBA (2001), NDD (1961); illustrator, lecturer; visiting lecturer, Kent Institute of Art & Design; De Laszlo Medal 2013. *Medium*: painter in oil and water-colour. *b*: Oadby, Leics., 13 May 1941. *s of*: Albert Arthur Tidnam. *m*: Ruth Murray. three *s*. one *d*. *Educ*: Kings Park, Eltham. *Studied*: Camberwell School of Art (1957-61) (Michael Rothenstein RA, Frank Martin, Henry Inlander, Richard Lee, Bernard Dunstan RA, Peter Weaver RI, RBA). *Exhib*: Mercury Gallery, London, RA, NEAC, RBA, Drew Gallery, Canterbury, The Peter Hedley Gallery, Wareham, The Fry Gallery, Saffron Walden, ROI, Laing Landscape and Seascape, Teriade Museum, Greece; All India Fine Arts, New Delhi; Randolph Gallery, Edinburgh; The Scottish Arts Club, Edinburgh; Caxton Contemporary, Whitstable; Discerning Eye; Piers Feetham Gallery, Geedon Gallery, Russell Gallery. *Works in collections*: Unilever, Leics., Notts. and W. Riding Educ. authorities and numerous private collections in UK., USA, France, Germany, Greece, India. *Publications*: 'Oils and Acrylics' (Cassell). *Works Reproduced*: magazine and book illustrations. *Recreations*: walking, gardening, travel, theatre, music. *Clubs*: Savage, The London Sketch Club. *Address*: 16 Roebuck Rd., Rochester, Kent ME1 1UD. *Email*: nicktidnam@hotmail.com. *Website*: www.tidnam.com. *Signs work*: "Nick Tidnam" or "N.T."

TIERNEY, James Richard Patrick, DipAD (1966), Postgrad. Dip. in Printmaking (1967); artist in all painting and printmaking media; principal lecturer. *b*: Newcastle upon Tyne, 23 May 1945. *m*: Janet Rosemary. one *d*. *Educ*: The Royal Grammar School, Newcastle. *Studied*: Sunderland Polytechnic (1961-66, David Gormley), Brighton Polytechnic (1966-67, Jennifer Dickson). *Address*: Maple Cottage, Holt End La., Bentworth, Nr. Alton, Hampshire GU34 5LF.

TIERNEY, Sadie, MA, RCA (1997); Basil Alkazzi Travel Award (1996); Printmakers Council Award (1997); The Abraham and Lillian Rosenberg Foundation (1997); Arts Council England Grants for Individuals Awards (2006, 2007). *Medium*: acrylic, watercolour, drawing, prints, film. *b*: London, 4 Oct 1971. *d of*: John & Ingrid Tierney. *m*: Neal Layton. two *d*. *Studied*: Newcastle University (1990-4); RCA (1995-7). *Exhib*: Flowers East, Flowers Ireland, Eton College, Oxford Gallery, Rivington Gallery, Clifford Chance, RCA, Christie's, Peterborough Museum and Art Gallery, 39, Rabley Contemporary Drawing Centre; ICA, Millais Gallery, Transition, Aspex Gallery. *Works in collections*: Sir Michael Hopkins, Albert Irvin, Roger Evans, Eton College, Clifford Chance, Baker & MacKenzie, Angela Flowers. *Commissions*: Chichester Harbour Conservancy; RCA; MOD. *Works*

Reproduced: Sunday Times, Basil H. Alkazzi Foundation Catalogue. *Address*: 37 Hunter Road, Southsea PO4 9AU. *Email*: sadie@sadietierney.co.uk *Website*: www.sadietierney.co.uk *Signs work*: 'Sadie Tierney'.

TIFFIN, Sheila, self-taught. *Medium*: oil on canvas/board. *b*: Essex, 11 Feb 1952. *Studied*: self-taught. *Represented by*: Tony Sanders. *Exhib*: Royal Portrait Society's Exhibition at the Mall Galleries; John Noot; Tony Sanders, Penzance. *Address*: 28 Union Street, Camborne, Cornwall, TR14 8HG.

TIHOV, Yanko, BA Printmaking and Fine Arts; Robertson Award ROI at Mall Galleries (2004); Ex Libris Award, Argentina (2001), and others; The Discerning Eye Drawing Bursary runner up award (2009). *Medium*: oil, prints. *b*: Burgas, Bulgaria, 30 Aug 1977. *s of*: Georgy Tihov. *Partner*: Nadia Tsakova. *Studied*: National Art Academy, Sofia. *Represented by*: Jack Fine Art. *Exhib*: ROI (2004); PS (2004); RA Summer Exhbn (2003, 2006); RP (2003, 2006, 09, 10); Mall Galleries; Ex Libris, Ville d'issy, les Molineaux, France (2001); 21st Mini Print Biennial, Cadaques, Spain (2001). *Works in collections*: Biblioteca Comunale di Lomazzo, Italy; Rotary Club Acqui Terme, Italy; Internationale Ex Libris Center, Sint-Niklas, Belgium. *Commissions*: The Culture Society in Buenos Aires for Ex Libris: small print of 'Gral.S.Martin' Argentina. *Publications*: UK Press; 'Kensington News'; The Mill Magazine, London. *Official Purchasers*: Tim Guinness, MF Husain. *Address*: 81 Wadloes Road, Cambridge CB5 8PF. *Email*: yankotihov@hotmail.co.uk *Website*: www.yankotihov.co.uk *Signs work*: Yanko Tihov (in cyrmic or latin).

TILL, Michael John, SGFA; artist in graphic, engraving, etching, pastel; Insurance Broker. *b*: Sri Lanka, 23 Mar 1939. *m*: Kathleen Margaret. one *s* (decd). two *d*. *Educ*: St. George's College, Weybridge. *Studied*: City and Guilds (1970-72 part-time). *Exhib*: SGFA. *Clubs*: Bosham S.C., R.C.Y.C., Royal London Y.C. *Address*: 57 Southway, Carshalton Beeches, Surrey SM5 4HP.

TILLEY, Nicola Jane, (née FISHER), painter in watercolour; tutor and demonstrator. *b*: Ismailia, Egypt, 31 Jan 1956. *d of*: Peter Fisher. *m*: Peter George. two *s*: Robin, Roo. one *d*: Rosie. *Educ*: Maidstone Grammar School for Girls. *Studied*: Penzance Art School, under Colin Scott. *Exhib*: various in Cornwall, Exeter, Mall Galleries, London, St. Ives Soc. of Artists, South West Academy of Fine and Applied Arts, Exeter (2002, 2003). *Works in collections*: many private collections at home and abroad. *Commissions*: National Trust, Godolphin Estate-front cover illustration for guide. *Publications*: articles in Artists and Illustrators magazine (Sept. 2001, Aug 2002). *Clubs*: St. Ives Soc. of Artists. *Address*: Evergreen Cott., Townshend, Hayle, Cornwall TR27 6AQ. *Signs work*: "Nicola Tilley."

TILLYER, William, artist in acrylic on canvas and panel, water-colour, print; French Government Scholarship (1962); Artist in Residence, Melbourne University (1981-82); residence Co. Kerry, Ireland (2001); residence, City of Cadiz (2006). *b*: Middlesbrough, 25 Sep 1938. *m*: Judith. one *s*. one *d*. *Studied*: Slade School of Fine Art (1960-62, William Coldstream, Anthony Gross), Atelier 17, Paris (1962, gravure under William Hayter). *Exhib*: one-man shows: Bernard Jacobson Gallery (1978-80, 1983, 1984, 1987, 1989, 1991), Wildenstein & Co. (1991, 1994), Andre Emmerich, NY (1994), Whitworth A.G., Manchester (1996), Eton College (2007), Jacobson Howard, New York (2008). *Works in collections*: V&A, ACGB, Tate Gallery, MOMA (NY), Brooklyn Art Museum, British Council. *Commissions*: Broadgate Development; stained glass window, Northumberland. *Publications*: illustrations for A Rebours by J.K. Huysmans, 'William Tillyer: Against the Grain' monograph by Prof. Norbert Lynton, published October 2000 by 21 Publishing, 'Hardware Variations on a Theme of Encounter' by W. Tillyer (2002), pub. 21. *Clubs*: Chelsea Arts Club, FRSA. *Address*: c/o Bernard Jacobson Gallery, 6 Cork Street, London W1S 3EE. *Email*: William@Tillyer.com *Website*: www.jacobsongallery.com www.tillyer.com *Signs work*: surname on back.

TILMOUTH, Sheila, DipAD (Hons), ATC. *Medium*: oil on gesso panel: non toxic print. *b*: London, 25 Sep 1949. two *s*. one *d*. *Educ*: Latymer Grammar School, London. *Studied*: Hornsey College of Art (1969-72, Jack Smith, Nigel Hall, Norman Stevens), Byam Shaw School (1974-75, Bill Jacklin), Finnish Academy, Helsinki (1973). *Exhib*: RA Summer Exhbn., Alresford Gallery, Hants., Resident Dean Clough Artist; Soil Association Exhibitions including tour from Low Luckens Organic Farm. Residency, Cumbria as broadcast on Radio 4 and BBC1 (Shared Earth with Dylan Winters, and Countryfile with John Craven). *Works in collections*: Calder Museums, Halifax Courts. *Commissions*: Samaritans. *Publications*: Limited Edn. prints (Buckingham Fine Arts, and Contemporary Arts Group). *Address*: 2 Bethel Terrace Hebden Bridge, W. Yorks. HX7 8HT. *Email*: sheila@sheilatilmouth.co.uk *Signs work*: "ST 2002" "ST 2004".

TILSON, Joe, RA, ARCA; painter, sculptor. *b*: London, 24 Aug 1928. *s of*: Frederick A.E. Tilson. *m*: Joslyn. one *s*. two *d*. *Studied*: St. Martin's School of Art (1949-52), RCA (1952-55), Accademia Britannica Rome 1955-57. *Represented by*: Alan Cristea Gallery, Marlborough Fine Art. *Exhib*: Venice Biennale (1964), Marlborough Gallery (1960-77), since 1977 Waddington Galleries, internationally since 1961. *Works in collections*: major museums in Gt. Britain, USA, Italy, S. America, Australia, Germany, Holland, Denmark, Belgium, NZ, etc. *Address*: 93 Bourne St., London SW1W 8HF. *Signs work*: "Joe Tilson."

TIMMIS, Rosemarie, Diploma in Drawing and Painting Byam Shaw. *Medium*: oil, drawing. *b*: Staffordshire, 9 Feb 1946. *d of*: A.M Timmis. *Educ*: Lowther College. *Studied*: Byam Shaw School of Art. *Exhib*: RA Summer Exhbn, Royal Society of Portrait Painters, Society of Women Painters. *Works in collections*: Harrow School, The Admiralty, Sweden, Sir Tim Rice, Lady Antonia Fraser, portrait of the Master, University College, Oxford. *Commissions*: H.M. Sultan of Oman, Lord Butler of Brockwell, Lord Guthrie of Craigie Bank, family of William Cash MP. *Address*: 9 Douro Place, London W8 5PH. *Website*: www.rosemarietimmis.co.uk *Signs work*: Rosemarie Timmis.

TINDLE, David, RA (1979), Hon.FRCA (1984), MA (Oxon.) (1985); painter in egg tempera; Ruskin Master of Drawing, University of Oxford (1985-87), Hon. Fellow at St. Edmund Hall, Oxford; Hon. RBSA. *b*: Huddersfield, 29 Apr 1932. *Studied*: Coventry School of Art (1945-47). *Represented by*: Redfern Gallery, Cork St., London. *Exhib*: Fischer Fine Art since 1985, Piccadilly Gallery (1954-83), Galerie XX, Hamburg (1974, 1977, 1980), Redfern Gallery (1994). *Works in collections*: Tate Gallery, Manchester City Art Gallery, Wakefield, Coventry & Whitworth Art Galleries, Bradford, Huddersfield, RA, NPG, London Museum, Government Art Collection, National Portrait Gallery. *Clubs*: Arts Club, Dover St. *Address*: c/o Redfern Gallery 20 Cork Street, London W1S 3HL. *Signs work*: "David Tindle" or "D.T."

TINGLE, Michael, BA Fine Art. *Medium*: acrylic, drawing, etching, painted copper relief. *b*: Skegness, 12 Oct 1954. *s of*: Peter Tingle. *m*: Val. three *d*. *Studied*: Bath Academy of Art, Corsham (1973-76). *Represented by*: Devon Guild of Craftsmen. *Exhib*: one-man shows: inc. Heffer Gallery, Cambridge; Printworks, Colchester; Gainsboroughs House Museum, Sudbury; Market Cross Gallery, Bury St.Edmunds, Suffolk; mixed shows include: Royal Academy; North House Gallery, Manningtree; Allen Art Gallery, Singapore; Devon Guild Summer Shows, Bovey Tracey; Black Swan, Frome. *Works in collections*: Met. Office, Exeter; Christchurch Mansion, Ipswich; Manor House Museum, Bury St. Edmunds, Metropolitan Museum, New York. *Publications*: 'Drawings from the Attic' (Nosuch Press, 2005). *Works Reproduced*: 'Elemental Insight' catalogue; 4th, 5th, 6th, 7th and 8th British International Miniature Print Catalogue; Wrexham Print International Catalogue. *Recreations*: walking (between country pubs). *Address*: 29 Applegarth Avenue, Newton Abbott, Devon TQ12 1RP. *Website*: www.mike-tingle.com *Signs work*: 'M.Tingle' or 'MT' (monogram).

TINSLEY, Francis, MA (1971); lecturer, painter in oil, etching, woodcut; Sen. lecturer, Camberwell College of Arts. *b*: Liverpool, 30 Mar 1947. *m*: Jennifer. *Studied*: Camberwell College of Arts (1967-70), Chelsea College of Art (1970-71). *Exhib*: one-man and mixed shows in London. *Works in collections*: Flyde Museum, Blackpool, Hereford Museum, and Liverpool. *Publications*: Practical Printmaking. *Clubs*: Chelsea Arts. *Address*: 28 Ewell Court Ave, Epsom Surrey KT19 0DZ. *Signs work*: "FRANCIS TINSLEY."

TIPPETT, Jane, freelance artist in water-colour, tempera, also lithography, and teacher. *b*: London, 25 Feb 1949. *d of*: George Thomas Tippett. *Studied*: Gloucestershire College of Art and Design, R.A. Schools (1977-80). Artist in Residence, Oundle School (1980-82). *Exhib*: RA Summer Exhbn. (1978-90), Agnew's Albermarle St. Gallery (1982), Church St. Gallery, Saffron Walden (1983, 1984, 1986); 14 lithographs made at the Curwen Studio. *Address*: 11 Cantelupe Rd., Haslingfield, Cambridge CB3 7LU. *Signs work*: "Jt."

TITCOMBE, Cedric Anthony, NDD (1962); painter and screen-printer in charcoal, oil, screen prints. *Medium*: stone carving; painted cardboard sculptures; giclée prints. *b*: Gloucester, 11 Dec 1940. divorced. two *s*. two *d*. *Educ*: Crypt Grammar School, Gloucester. *Studied*: Gloucester College of Art (1959-63, James Tucker, John Whiskerd, Gordon Ward). *Exhib*: RA, RWA, and numerous mixed shows. *Works in collections*: Trevor Barnes, etc. *Address*: 72 Priory Rd., Gloucester GL1 2RF. *Website*: www.bigartweb.net *Signs work*: "TITCOMBE."

TITHERLEY, Hazel M., RCA (1985), ATC, ATD (Manc); painter in oil, acrylic and water-colour. *b*: Little Singleton, Lancs., 4 Mar 1935. *d of*: Tom C. Burgoyne. *m*: Philip Titherley, FRIBA, MRTPI (decd). one *s*. *Educ*: Queen Mary School, Lytham. *Studied*: Blackpool School of Art (1953-58), Manchester Regional College of Art (1958-59). *Exhib*: over 30 solo, many open and groups shows. Exhibits with New Longton Artists & Central Lancashire Fine Art Fair. *Works in collections*: Salford A.G. and private collections in Europe, USA, and Far East. *Clubs*: Founded New Longton Artists (1969). *Address*: Woodside, Woodside Ave., New Longton, Preston, Lancs. PR4 4YD. *Signs work*: "Hazel Titherley."

TO, Frank, MA Fine Art; BA (Hons) Fine Art Painting and Drawing. *b*: Falkirk, 10 Mar 1982. *Studied*: Duncan of Jordanstone Art College; University of Huddersfield. *Represented by*: Witmer Fine Art, New York City, USA. *Exhib*: Albemarle Gallery, London (2007); Queens Gallery, Dundee (2006-07); Beaux Arts Gallery, Bath (2006); Modern Artist Gallery, Pangbourne (2007); Mansfield Park Gallery, Glasgow (2006); Leith Gallery, Edinburgh (2006); Gallery 23, Glasgow (2006); Gascoigne Gallery, Harrogate (2002, 2003); Fairfax Gallery, London (2005-07). *Works in collections*: Patrick Stewart O.B.E. *Commissions*: Louise Chapman, Texas, USA. *Address*: Studio 200, WASPS Factory, 77 Hanson Street, Glasgow, G31 2HF. *Email*: frank_to_artist@hotmail.com *Signs work*: 'FRANK TO'.

TOBOLEWSKI, Marek, BA (Hons) Painting; awards: Pollock-Krasner Foundation, USA (1989); 1st Prize, 'East Midlands Artist of the Year' Printing Section (1993) Smiths Wallers, London. *Medium*: oil, watercolour, drawing, prints. *b*: Bishops Stortford, 16 Aug 1964. *s of*: Helena & Mieczyslaw Tobolewski. *m*: Beatrice. one *s*. one *d*. *Studied*: Brighton Polytechnic (1986). *Exhib*: 11 solo exhbns in UK and abroad, inc. Angel Row Gallery; Galerie Oz, Paris (1991, 92, 94); selected group exhbns: RA Summer Exhbn (2000); Silverstein Gallery, NY, USA (1995); Air Gallery, London (1996); Angel Row Gallery, Nottingham (2004). *Works in collections*: Warwick Arts Trust, London; Nottingham City Council; Nottingham Trent University; Nottingham Law School; Eversheds Solicitors UK HQ; Pharmaceuticals Profiles UK HQ. *Commissions*: Derby Dance Centre (1997); Nottingham City Council (2001). *Works Reproduced*: exhibtion catalogues Angel Row Gallery (1994, 2004). *Address*: 16 Drummond Road, Ilkeston, Derbyshire DE7 5HA. *Email*: marek.tobolewski@ntlworld.com *Signs work*: 'M. TOBOLEWSKI'.

TODD, Anthony (Tony) John, DipAD. *Medium*: acrylic, watercolour, drawing. *b*: London, 29 Feb 1940. *m*: Iris. one *s*. one *d*. *Studied*: Guildford School of Art (1954-58); Harrow School of Art (1979-1980); St.Martins School of Art (1981-82). *Represented by*: Red Rag Gallery; Getty Images; The Bridgeman Art Library. *Exhib*: Mall Gallery, London; Llewellyn Alexander Gallery, London; Forest Gallery, Guildford; Red Biddy Gallery, Guildford; Denbies Art Centre, Dorking; Showcase Gallery, Bramley; Guildford House Gallery; Obsidian Gallery, Buckinghamshire; Cranleigh Arts Centre, Surrey; Red Rag Gallery, Riverside Gallery, Life the Gallery. *Works in collections*: Hillingdon Borough Council. *Commissions*: Sir Emmanuel, CBE & Lady Elizabeth Kaye (commissioned seven paintings including one for HM Queen and Prince Philip). *Works Reproduced*: many works reproduced and published throughout the world. *Principal Works*: nineteen large paintings - Dylan Thomas's 'Under Milk Wood'; twelve large paintings - Gerald Durrell's 'My Family and Other Animals'. *Clubs*: National Acrylic Painters Association; International Association of Two and Three Dimensional Artists (IATTDA); Guildford Art Society; Dorking Group of Artists (DGA); Cranleigh Art Society. *Address*: Christmas Cottage, 65 New Road, Chilworth, Guildford, Surrey, GU4 8LP. *Email*: sales@tony-todd.co.uk *Website*: www.tony-todd.co.uk *Signs work*: "ANTHONY TODD", "TONY TODD", "TODD".

TODD, Daphne Jane, OBE, PPRP, NEAC, FRSA, Hon. SWA, HDFA (Lond.); awards: 2nd prize John Player award (1983), GLC prize (1984), 1st prize Hunting Group (1984), Ondaatje prize for Portraiture & Gold Medal (2001); President R.P. (1994-2000); Governor, Heatherley School of Art (1986-); Governor, Federation of British Art (1995-2000); Worshipful Co. of Painter Stainers (Hon. Liveryman, 2004); Freedom, City of London (1997), Hon. Doctorate of Arts, DMU (1998); 1st Prize BP Award 2010. *b*: York, 27 Mar 1947. *d of*: Frank Todd. *m*: Lt.Col. P.R.T. Driscoll. one *d*. *Educ*: Simon Langton Grammar School, Canterbury. *Studied*: Slade School (1965-71). *Represented by*: Messum's Gallery, 8 Cork Street, London; Royal Society of Portrait Painters. *Exhib*: RA, RP, NEAC, Patterson Gallery; Retrospective Morley Gallery (1989). *Works in collections*: Chantrey Bequest; University College, London; Royal Holloway A.G. and Museum; HQ Irish Guards; Pembroke College, Cambridge; Lady Margaret Hall, Oxford; St. David's University; NPG; St. Catharine's College, Cambridge; Science Museum; De Montfort University; NUMAST; Institution of Civil Engineers; Bishop's Palace, Hereford; University College, Oxford; Science Museum; National Portrait Gallery; HM The Queen, HRH the Prince of Wales. *Clubs*: Chelsea Arts, The Arts. *Address*: Salters Green Farm, Mayfield, E. Sussex TN20 6NP. *Email*: daphne.todd@btinternet.com *Website*: daphnetodd.com *Signs work*: "D. Todd."

TODD, James Gilbert, MA (1965), MFA (1970), RE (1997); visiting art residencies: China (1984), Russia (1985), Lithuania (1997), Slovakia and Austria (1998); artist in painting and wood relief printmaking; Prof. Emeritus of Art and Humanities, University of Montana. *Medium*: painting and printmaking. *b*: Minneapolis, Minn., 12 Oct 1937. *s of*: James and Doris Todd. *m*: Julia Katherina Brozio. three *s*. *Educ*: Chicago Art Inst., College of Great Falls (1958-63), University of Montana (1964-70, Rudy Antio, Donald Bunse, James Dew). *Represented by*: Royal Society of Painter-Printmakers; Society of Wood-Engravers; Annex Galleries. *Exhib*: North and South America, England, Europe, Russia, Asia. *Works in collections*: North America, England, Europe, Asia. *Commissions*: murals: Univ. of MT. (1973); AmerFed. of Labor (1076), wall relief sculpture MT. *Publications*: numerous articles on art theory, and six books illustrated. *Official Purchasers*: Honolulu Academy of Art; Gonzaga Univ.; Missoula Museum of Art; Rendsburg Sparkasse; Yellowstone Art Center. *Works Reproduced*: 'Berlin Wall'; 'Angel over Berlin'; 'Easter at Hussman's'; 'Evacuation of Phnom Penh'; 'Julia and Seamus'. *Recreations*: martial arts, billiards, reading, walking. *Clubs*: Society of Wood Engravers, Royal Society of Painter-Printmakers (Eng), Jean Chieze Assoc (France). *Address*: 6917 Siesta Drive, Missoula, Montana 59802, USA. *Email*: masuria@mtwi.net *Signs work*: "James G. Todd", "JR" or "TODD."

TODD WARMOTH, Pip, BA (Hons), MA; artist in oil. *b*: 5 Oct 1962. *Educ*: Caistor Grammar School. *Studied*: Grimsby, Camberwell, RA Schools. *Exhib*: Catto Gallery, New Grafton, Bellock-Lowndes, Chicago, Albemarle, LKF Gallery, Hong Kong, China Club, Hong Kong, CAC; group shows: RA, Bonhams, Ice Gallery, NY. *Works in collections*: Franklin Trust, Kingston Lacey, Montacute - National Trust, London Transport, Standard Chartered Bank, Abn Ambro, HRH Prince of Wales. *Commissions*: poster for London Underground, Crown Trust. *Works Reproduced*: Country Life, House and Garden, Evening Standard, South China Morning Post, Hong Kong Standard, Artist Illustrators, Art Review. *Clubs*: Dover St. Arts, Chelsea Arts. *Misc*: B.B.C. Breakfast Show, H.K. Radio 4 and 5, C.B.S., News International. *Address*: 396 Brixton Rd., London SW9 7AW. *Signs work*: "Pip T.W."

TOLLEY, Elinor, BA, MA, Lic, MSc. *Medium*: Oil, watercolour, paper mosaics. *b*: Bryn Mawr, PA, USA, 12 Jan 1934. *m*: Dr Bruce Tolley. *Studied*: Columbia University, USA; Royal Institute of Chemistry, University of Oxford. *Exhib*: Several exhibitions at Green College, Gallery 47 in London, Brian Sinfield in Burford and several submissions in the Oxford Art Society exhibitions. *Clubs*: Oxford Art Society. *Address*: The Fields, East End, North Leigh OX29 6PZ. *Email*: elinortolley@tiscali.co.uk *Website*: elinortolleygallery.co.uk *Signs work*: "Elinor Tilley".

TOLLEY, Sheila, RWA (Royal West of England Academy); artist in all media; Twice winner of the Cornelissen Prize for Painting. *b*: Birmingham, 28 Jun 1939. *d of*: Ernest Saville Atkins. *Educ*: Richard C. Thomas School for Girls, Staffs. *Studied*: Bournemouth and Poole College of Art (1972-74, Edward Darcy Lister, RCA). *Exhib*: RA Summer Exhbns. (1978-2004), RWA (1976-2005). *Works in collections*: UK and abroad. *Address*: Flat 16 Hollybush House, 3 Wollstonecraft Rd., Boscombe Manor, Bournemouth, Dorset BH5 1JQ. *Signs work*: "sheila tolley".

TOLSTOY, Carolinda. *Medium*: faience ceramic, 22 carat gold, lustre, mixed media. *b*: London. two *s*. one *d*. *Studied*: Sir John Cass, and apprenticed for 7 years at Chelsea Pottery. *Represented by*: Cigdem Simavi- Istanbul, Viktor Wynd Fine Art - UK, The Arts Club- London, XVA - Dubai. *Exhib*: worldwide. *Works in collections*: The Watts Gallery, School of Oriental and African Studies, London. *Publications*: Carolinda Tolstoy Ceramics by Ernst J. Grube (ADI); Sources of Inspiration by Caroline Genders (A&C Black); Three Journeys in the Levant by Shusha Guppy (Starcrest); The Golden Age of Persian Art by Sheila Canby (British Museum Press), Dream Homes by Andreas Einsiedel (Merrell), Arabesque by Claudia Rhoden (Michael Joseph). *Clubs*: Chelsea Arts Club; The Arts Club, London. *Address*: 8 Orlando Road, London SW4 0LF. *Email*: carolinda@carolinda-tolstoy.co.uk *Website*: www.carolinda-tolstoy.co.uk

TOMALIN, Peter John, RIBA Dip.Arch. (Leics. 1964), FSAI (1978), UA (1978); first prize in BBC Christmas painting competition (1977); self employed architectural illustrator and water-colour artist. *b*: Kettering, 18 Oct 1937. *s of*: Sidney Tomalin. *m*: Marjorie Elizabeth. two *s*. *Educ*: Kettering Technical College, Leicester School of Architecture. *Studied*: Northampton School of Art (1976-79, Peter Atkin, Frank Cryer). *Exhib*: Mall Galleries, UA, RI, Grosvenor Gallery, Hitchin, Northampton A.G. *Clubs*: Northampton Town and County Art Soc., S.A.I. *Address*: 170 Sywell Rd., Overstone, Northampton NN6 0AG. *Signs work*: "Peter Tomalin."

TOMBS, Sarah Jane, BA (Hons) 1983, MA (RCA) 1987; sculptor in welded steel, stone; Sculpture Fellow, Keele University. *b*: Herts., 17 Nov 1961. *Studied*: Wimbledon School of Art (1981-83, Glynn Williams), Chelsea School of Art (1983-84), RCA (1984-87). *Exhib*: Cannizaro Pk. Wimbledon (1981-84), Christopher Hull Gallery, Berkeley Sq. Gallery, Mall Galleries, Margam Pk. Glamorgan, RCA, Keele University, etc. *Works in collections*: Government Art Collection, Christie's Contemporary Collection, Linklater & Paines.

Commissions: 'The Man at the Fire' National Gdn. Festival, Stoke on Trent and British Steel (1986); 'Sailing by Stars' Basingstoke Railway Station (1990); 'Breath of Life' Hammersmith Hospital (1993); 'Beths Arch' Black Country Route, Wolverhampton (1996), etc. *Address*: 80a Nightingale Lane, Balham, London SW12 8NR.

TOMLINSON, Greta, DipFA, NAPA; Awards: Daler Rowney, Chris Beetles, Jo Aicheson, St. Cuthberts Mill (1st Prize, RWS). *Medium*: water-colour, acrylic, oil, mixed media. *b*: Burnley, 30 Jan 1927. *m*: Richard Edwards (decd). one *d*. *Educ*: privately. *Studied*: Burnley School of Art (Harold Thornton), Slade School, Oxford and London (Prof. Schwabe). *Exhib*: regularly with RI, RWS, RWE and London Galleries. Fosse Gallery, Stow on the Wold. *Works in collections*: Southport A.G. *Commissions*: Hamilton Barnes, Interiors, private, London Metropole hotel. *Publications*: Eagle Magazine for Boys, 'Dan Dare' (1950-54). *Works Reproduced*: fine art prints, cards, USA. *Recreations*: travel, interior design. *Clubs*: Farnham Art Soc. *Address*: South Dunrozel, Farnham Lane, Haslemere, Surrey GU27 1HD. *Signs work*: "G. TOMLINSON." or "Greta Tomlinson".

TOMS, Peter Edward, ARSMA (1997), RMS (1995), ARMS (1991), HS (1991); marine and landscape painter, principal designer, British Aerospace, to 1982; full time painter since then. *b*: Hayes, Middx., 28 May 1940. *s of*: Edward James Toms, athlete. *m*: Patricia Mary Toms. five *s*. two *d*. *Educ*: Mellow Lane School, Hayes. *Studied*: engineering and design: Southall Technical College (1956-63). *Exhib*: RSMA, RI, RMS, RBA, NS, UA, numerous London and provincial one-man and other exhbns. including Alpine Club, Century, Edwin Pollard, Oliver Swann, Omell, Skipwith, Solent and Wykeham Galleries. *Works in collections*: P&O "SS Canberra", Royal Hampshire Regt., Royal Navy (HMS "Osprey"), NV Amev Group (Utrecht), HM Land Registry, Astrid Trust and many other corporate and private collections. *Publications*: biographical notes in: RMS. Centenary Book '100 Years', 'Celebration of Marine Art (Sixty Years of the RSMA)'. *Clubs*: Dorchester (past President 1991-98). *Address*: 20 Egdon Glen, Crossways, Dorchester, Dorset DT2 8BQ. *Signs work*: "Peter Toms."

TONG, Belinda Josephine, VPSWA; painter in oil, pastel, water-colour and acrylic. *b*: Woodford, Essex, 7 Sep 1937. *m*: Bernard Tong. two *s*. one *d*. *Educ*: Loughton County High School for Girls, Havering College. *Studied*: Open College of the Arts. *Represented by*: Picturecraft Gallery, Holt, Norfolk. *Exhib*: ROI, SBA, SWA, Essex Art Club, local galleries and societies. *Works in collections*: private collections in UK and abroad. *Commissions*: animal portraits in pastel, houses and gardens. *Recreations*: Golf - President Essex Ladies County Golf Association. *Clubs*: Chigwell G.C., Essex Art Club. *Address*: 57 Theydon Grove, Epping, Essex, CM16 4PX. *Signs work*: "B. Tong" (oil, acrylic), "Belinda Tong" (watercolour and pastel).

TOOP, Bill, RI (1979), MCSD (1971); artist and illustrator in water-colour, line and wash, line, with own gallery in Broadmayne, Dorchester. *Medium*: watercolour. *b*: Bere Regis, Dorset, 27 May 1943. *s of*: Richard & Jean Toop. *m*: Elizabeth Thurstans. one *s*. one *d*. *Educ*: Weymouth Grammar School, Blandford Grammar School. *Studied*: Bath Academy of Art (1961-63, Robyn Denny, Howard Hodgkin), Southampton College of Art (1964-66, Peter Folkes), Bristol Polytechnic Art Faculty (1967-68, Derek Crowe). *Represented by*: DDFA for greetings cards and various other. *Exhib*: RI, RWA, numerous one-man shows. *Works in collections*: The Sultan of Oman, Northern Telecom, British Gas, Whitbread Inns, Coutts & Co., The Sedgwick Group, NFU Mutual and Avon Insurance, Royal School of Signals, Atomic Energy Authority, Inst. of Directors, etc. *Commissions*: BBC TV, British Gas, National Westminster Bank, The Duke of Edinburgh's Royal Regiment, The Piscatorial Society, MacFisheries, Rexel Cumberland Ltd, UKLF Wilton, Southern Cathedrals Festival, Mr & Mrs Leslie Thomas, Costain UK Engineering & Construction Ltd., Robert Key MP, etc. *Publications*: illustrated Portrait of Wiltshire (Pamela Street), National Gardens Scheme

Handbook, etc. *Official Purchasers*: Lloyds Bank, Nat Westminster Bank, Southern Tourist Board, West Country Tourist Board etc. *Works Reproduced*: very many! *Address*: Bill Toop Gallery & Studios, Easter Cottage, 5 Knighton Lane, Broadmayne, Dorchester Dorset DT2 8EZ. *Email*: bill@billtoop.com *Website*: www.billtoop.com *Signs work*: "Bill Toop."

TOPHAM, John, FPS, IAA, Assoc. Internationale des Arts Plastiques; painter. *b*: Hampstead, London. *m*: Hazel Grimsey, painter. two *s*. *Studied*: Melbourne, Australia; Harrow and Ealing Schools of Art. *Exhib*: RWA, RBA, FPS, RSBA, UA, HAC, Camden Art Centre, Allsop Gallery, Anglo-French Exhbn., Poole Art Centre, Seldown Gallery, Hambledon Gallery, Archer Gallery, Minstrel Gallery, Colne Group, Parkway Gallery, Questers Gallery, Swiss Cottage Library, Olympus Gallery, Upton House Gallery, Poole Art Centre Open Exhbn. *Works in collections*: Nuffield Foundation, Camden Council; private collections in UK and USA. *Clubs*: F.P.S., life mem. I.A.A., Assoc. Internationale des Arts Plastiques. *Address*: Holmstoke, West Milton, Bridport, Dorset DT6 3SJ. *Signs work*: "Topham."

TOVEY, David Charles Wilson, BA (1999), MA (1976); Solicitor (1979), since 1999 working as independent art historian specialising in Cornish art; author, curator for various exhibitions including 'Dawn of a Colony: St. Ives 1811-1888' (Tate St. Ives 2008); 'Lyrical Light: St. Ives (1889-1914) (Penzance 2008); 'Creating a Splash - the St. Ives Society of Artists 1927-52' (2003-4), also Penzance, Lincoln, Doncaster, Hereford, Sunderland, Newport; NADFAS lecturer, contributor to Dictionary of National Biography. *b*: Bristol, 4 Jul 1953. *s of*: Gordon Tovey, founder of Tockington Manor School. *m*: Sherry. *Educ*: Clifton College Bristol (1967-71); Pembroke College, Oxford (MA in Jurisprudence 1976). *Studied*: University of Warwick (BA in History of Art, 1999). *Publications*: St. Ives Art pre-1890 (2008); Pioneers of St. Ives Art at Home and Abroad (2008); St. Ives 1860-1930 - The Artists and the Community - A Social History (2009); Sea Change - Art in St. Ives 1914-1930 (2010). *Recreations*: walking and photography. *Address*: Mill Avon House, 11.13 Millbank, Tewkesbury, Glos GL20 5SD. *Email*: dwt4@talktalk.ne. *Website*: www.stivesart.info

TOWNSEND, Christopher Leonard, BA (Hons). *Medium*: Sculpture. *b*: Moreton-in-Marsh, 28 Nov 1973. *m*: Emma. one *s*. *Studied*; Liverpool University (graduated 1996). *Represented by*: Fire and Iron Gallery, Surrey; John Noott Gallery, Broadway. *Exhib*: Tatton Park Flower Show (2007, 2008, 2009); Hampton Court Flower Show (2008); Affordable Art Fair, London (2010, 11, 12); John Noott Gallery; Edinburgh Art Fair; Ginny Grey Gallery; Chelsea Art Fair (2012). *Works in collections*: Private collections in UK, USA, Australia and New Zealand. *Commissions*: P&O Cruise Ship Azura, sculptures for the glass house (2009). *Recreations*: Tai Chi; walking. *Misc*: Also represented by The Waterperry Gallery, Thame, Oxford and The Taurus Gallery, Oxford. *Address*: The Loft Gallery, Crown Farm, Ascott-under-Wychwood OX7 6AB. *Email*: info@christophertownsend.co.uk *Website*: www.christophertownsend.co.uk *Signs work*: "CT".

TOWNSEND, Storm Diana, NDD (Sculpture) (1960), ATC (1962); Resident Fellowships: Siswa Lokantara Fdn, Indonesia (1960-61), Huntington Hartford Fdn, Calif. (1963), Wurlitzer Fdn. Taos, NM, USA (1964); sculptor. *Medium*: plastilina, plaster, wax, fibreglass, concrete and bronze. *b*: London, 31 Aug 1937. *d of*: Douglas & Winifred Townsend. *Educ*: Sacred Heart Convent, Hammersmith, London (1947-55). *Studied*: London University, Goldsmiths' College (1955-60, Harold S. Parker, Ivor Roberts-Jones). *Exhib*: throughout USA, LA, New York, Santa Fe (New Mexico, USA). *Works in collections*: Museum of New Mexico, Santa Fe and the City of Albuquerque, public works, many private collections. *Commissions*: over life-size bronze "To Serve and Protect" commissioned by City of Albuquerque and others, N.M. (1984); "Bronze Trophy" for P.G.A. 'Charlie Pride International Senior Golf Classic' Albuquerque (1987); Three figure bronze

'Tres Culturas del Rio Grande' commissioned by Sunwest Bank, Albuquerque, N.M. (1988). *Publications*: many and various articles and interviews in local and national publications. *Official Purchasers*: many. *Misc*: sculpture instructor: The College of Santa Fe, NM (1974-75), University of Albuquerque, NM (1976-83), University of New Mexico in Albuquerque (1980-93); Associate sculptor, Alcazar Corp., Albuquerque (1988-99); contract sculptor: New Mexico Museum of Natural History (1987-1991). *Address*: P.O. Box 1165, Corrales, New Mexico 87048, USA. *Website*: by name 'Storm Townsend' *Signs work*: "STORM."

TOWSEY, Mary, TD; Stock Exchange Award (1971-72); SBA Honourable Mention, Exhibit of the Year, Alton 1984; Josephine Majella Award, Petersfield 1986; Best Collection of Work 'Ville d'Epone' 2000; landscape artist, oils. *b*: Epsom, 24 Jul 1936. *d of*: G.T.N. Prideaux & Mrs. F.D. Prideaux. three *d*. *Studied*: Goldsmiths' College University of London (1955-57), Epsom College of Art (1960-67). *Exhib*: Wintershall Gallery Bramley, Hallam Gallery London, Edwin Pollard Gallery, Ebury Gallery London, Wykeham Gallery London, Jonleigh Gallery Wonersh, Llewellyn Alexander Gallery, London, Galerie de Vétheuil, France, RBA, ROI, NEAC, RWS, SWA, SBA BBC2 television series 'Painters', winner - Best Collection Paintings "Au Bout du Monde" Êpone, France, Gallery 60, Giverny. *Works in collections*: Marie de Vétheuil - France, Government Art Collection, King's College School, Wimbledon. *Commissions*: The Great Hall, King's College, Wimbledon, private collections. *Publications*: 'Mary Towsey - Vétheuil and other Passions. *Works Reproduced*: Ropley Station, The Great Hall, Kings College Wimbledon. *Recreations*: gardening, interior decoration, reading. *Misc*: TV demonstration BBC2 "Painters". *Address*: 9 Wheatsheaf Cottages, Arford Road, Headley, Hampshire GU35 8AN. *Email*: mary.towsey@btopenworld.com *Website*: www.marytowsey.com *Signs work*: "Mary Towsey."

TRANT, Carolyn, DFA (Lond) (1973); David Murray Landscape Scholarship; artists books under imprint 'Parvenu Press'; First Prize for 'Gawain', Soc. of Bookbinders; Chichester Prize for Painting (2001). *Medium*: painter-printmaker. *b*: Middx., 29 Oct 1950. *d of*: Brian Trant, musician. two *s*. one *d*. *Educ*: North London Collegiate School. *Studied*: Slade School of Fine Art (1969-73). *Exhib*: New Grafton Gallery, Brighton Festival, London Artists Bookfair - ICA, RA Summer Shows, Oxford Fine Press Fair, West Dean College, St. Brides Printing Library. *Works in collections*: RA, National Art Library (V&A). *Commissions*: ESCC/SE Arts commission: 'Rituals and Relics' - Earthworks on the Downs, National Theatre - poster 'Blood Wedding' (Lorca). *Publications*: Art for Life: Biography of Peggy Angus (Incline Press 2004). *Official Purchasers*: Library Collections across USA, British Library - Modern British Collection. *Works Reproduced*: Illustration Magazine - Spring 2006, Parenthesis 14, bound & lettered, Vol.7.2. *Principal Works*: Gawain, Lorca's Sonnets of Dark Love, The Garden of Earthly Delights, Beauty and the Beast, Winterreise, The Falcon Bride, Bluebeards Castle. *Address*: 17 St. Anne's Cres., Lewes, E. Sussex BN7 1SB. *Website*: http://carolyntrantparvenu.blogspot.com *Signs work*: "Carolyn Trant".

TRATT, Richard, SWLA (1981), SBA (1987); painter in oil; First prize winner of national competition - 'Nature in Art', 2009 BBC Wildlife Artist of the Year - British Category Winner. *b*: Enfield, 19 Oct 1953. *s of*: Robert Tratt. *m*: Hilary Wastnage. two *d*. *Educ*: Crewe Grammar School. *Studied*: Northwich College of Art (1970-72), Dartington College of Arts (1972-74). *Exhib*: RA, Mall Galleries, Robert Perera Fine Arts, Alresford Gallery, New Forest Fine Art, Peter Hedley Gallery, Isetan Gallery, Tokyo; thirty eight one-man shows. *Works in collections*: Nature-in-Art, Royal Palace of Oman. *Works Reproduced*: Reynard Fine Art, Royles, McDonald, Rosenstiel's, Langford Press. *Address*: 10 Sharpley Cl., Fordingbridge, Hants. SP6 1LG. *Email*: rtratt@btinternet.com *Website*: www.richardtratt.co.uk *Signs work*: "TRATT."

TRAVERS SMITH, Linda Mary, SWA, AFAS; Awards: 'Paint a Wildlife Subject': Best in Show and Best Watercolour. *Medium*: watercolour, collage. *b*: London, 24 Jan 1949.

m: Ian. two *d*. *Educ*: Raines Foundation. *Exhib*: Royal Institute of Watercolour, Society of Women Artists, Laing Exhibition. *Recreations*: gardening, photography. *Clubs*: Armed Forces Art Society, Society of Women Artists, West Wycombe Art Group, Visual Images Group. *Address*: 319 Tring Road, Aylesbury, Bucks HP20 1PJ. *Email*: travsart@gmail.com *Website*: www.travsart.net *Signs work*: "TRAVERS SMITH".

TRAYHORNE, Rex, RMS (1988); artist in water-colour and gouache; art teacher, demonstrator and writer. *Medium*: watercolour. *b*: 13 Oct 1931. *m*: Geraldine. two *s*. (one *s-s*), two *d*. (one *s-d*). one *s*. one *d*. *Educ*: Newbury Grammar School. *Studied*: Reading College (1958). *Exhib*: RI, RMS, RWS, local art societies, Wessex Artists Exhbns., etc. *Works in collections*: Lord Romsey (now known as Lord Brabourne), also Jeffrey Archer (MP). *Publications*: 'Adventure into Watercolour' (an instructional video). *Clubs*: Romsey Art Group, Ringwood Art Soc. *Address*: Stable House Studio, Newton Lane, Romsey, Hants. SO51 8GZ. *Email*: rex.trayhorne@btinternet.com *Website*: www.rextrayhorne.co.uk *Signs work*: "Rex Trayhorne" R.M.S.

TRAYNOR, Mary, JP. *Medium*: water-colour, oils, drawing, mixed media. *b*: Hong Kong, 23 Mar 1934. *d of*: Rev. A.F. Griffiths. *m*: Brian Traynor (decd). one *s*. two *d*. *Educ*: Walthamstow Hall, Sevenoaks. *Studied*: Goldsmiths, Birmingham College of Art and Crafts, Theatre Design: Findlay James, Roy Mason. *Represented by*: Albany Gallery, Cardiff. *Exhib*: National Museum of Wales, Welsh National Eisteddfod; Washington Gallery, Penarth (2001, 2004), Llanover Hall Arts Centre (2005), Waterloo Gardens Teahouse, Cardiff (2009), Albany Gallery, Cardiff (2010), Washing Gallery, Penarth (2011). *Works in collections*: National Museum of Wales, Cardiff Magistrates, Professional Offices, County of Cardiff, Gwent Health Authority, University of Wales, St. James's Palace, private collections. *Commissions*: public and private inc. CADW, University of Wales, Cardiff, Welsh Development Agency, Welsh Rugby Union. *Publications*: illustrated: Wales Tourist Board, Western Mail, National Museum of Wales, Cardiff City Council, C.A.D.W.; book: "Temples of Faith: Cardiff's Places of Worship" (2001). *Official Purchasers*: National Museum of Wales, Cardiff University; Cardiff Magistrates. *Works Reproduced*: Various. *Principal Works*: Millennium Stadium, Senydd & Pierhead, City Hall, University and Cardiff Castle. *Recreations*: travel, reading, language study. *Clubs*: The Victorian Soc., Cardiff Architectural Heritage Soc., Cardiff Civic Soc. *Address*: 72a Kimberly Rd., Penylan, Cardiff CF23 5DN. *Email*: mary_traynor@btinternet.com *Signs work*: "Mary Traynor."

TREANOR, Frances, PS (1978), ATC (1967), NDD (1966); L'Artiste Assoifee awards winner (1975), Diplome d'Honneur, Salon d'Antony, France (1975), George Rowney award (1982), Frank Herring award (merit) (1984), Conté (UK) award (1986), Government Print Purchase (1987); 'Woman of the Year 2006' (nominated by ABI). *b*: Penzance, Cornwall. *d of*: George Treanor, musician. *m*: (1) Frank Elliott, (2) Anthony Taylor (divorced). one *d*. *Educ*: Assumption Convent, Kensington; Sacred Heart Convent, Hammersmith. *Studied*: Goldsmiths' College (1962-66), Hornsey College of Art (1966-67). *Exhib*: London, Paris, Yugoslavia, Berlin. Stage set design commission 'As You Like It' OUDS Summer Tour (Japan, USA, UK) 1988. *Works in collections*: Embassy of Ireland (2009). *Commissions*: Broomfield Hospital NHS Trust 2002; Royal Parks Greenwich First Artist-in-Residence (2005-06). *Publications*: Vibrant Flower Painting (David & Charles). *Clubs*: London Press Club. *Address*: 121 Royal Hill, London SE10 8SS. *Website*: www.francestreanor.com *Signs work*: "Treanor" or "F.T."

TREASURE, Paul. *Medium*: Oil. *b*: Gloucester, 21 Jul 1961. one *s*. one *d*. *Educ*: Bellmont Abbey School, Hereford. *Studied*: Cheltenham Art College (1979-80). *Represented by*: Courcoux & Courcoux; Enid Lawson Gallery, Galleryone; Josie Eastwood. *Exhib*: Courcoux & Courcoux; Enid Lawson Gallery; Galleryone; Josie Eastwood; Affordable Art Fair, London, Edinburgh, Milan, Bristol; London Art Fair. Solo shows at

Courcoux & Courcoux and Galleryone. *Commissions*: Numerous private. *Address*: Longwood House, Parkstone Road, Ropley, Hants SO24 0EW. *Email*: paul.treasure1@btinternet.com *Website*: www.paultreasurepaintings.co.uk

TRELOAR, Janet Quintrell, MA Oxford, Past Vice President RWS, FRGS. *Medium*: watercolour and work on paper, oil on board. *b*: West Cornwall,12 Feb 1940. *d of*: Arthur and Doris Treloar. *m*: John Hale-White. two *s*. two *d*. *Educ*: David Manzur Atelier, Bogota. *Studied*: Burleighfield House, High Wycombe (Patrick Reyntiens); Stavanger (Stanislas Dombronsky). *Represented by*: Royal Watercolour Society; Chelsea Art Society. *Exhib*: London: R.A. Summer Exhibition; R. Watercolour Society; Chelsea Art Society; Chelsea Arts Club; Piers Feetham Gallery; Russian Embassy; Nehru Centre; Pushkin House; Square One Gallery; Nine Elms Group; Rainy Day Gallery; Trereife House and Cornwall Contemporary, Penzance; Lander Gallery, Truro; R. West of England Academy; Scotland-Russia Forum, Edinburgh; Galitzine Library and Society of Russian Watercolourists, St. Petersburg; Kunstforegning; Stavanger and Bergen; Indian Art Trust, Mumbai; British Council, Dubrovnic; Downside Abbey; Norwich Cathedral. *Works in collections*: Kunstforening Bergen; Stavanger, Norway; Richard Demarco Foundation, Edinburgh; RWS Archive; Malta Art Archives; Zagreb Museum; Anna Akhmatova Museum, St Petersburg. *Commissions*: private commissions in UK; Viyella UK; Croatian Embassy; Russian Embassy. *Publications*: Illustrated Catalogues: The Romanesque Arch in Europe; Russia's Hero Cities; Anna Akhmatova Defending the Countryside. Illustrated articles in: Watercolour Masters Then and Now (RWS, 2006); St. Ives Revisited, 1975-2005, by Peter Davies (2007); The Artist (magazine, March 2005/October 2009). *Official Purchasers*: Croatian Embassy, London; Lipik Town Hall, Croatia; Rogaland Kommune, Norway; Bergen Kunstforening, Dubrovnik City. *Principal Works*: 3 series on (1) Romanesque Arch in Europe: (2) Russia's Hero Cities; (3) Anna Akhmatova at the Fountain House. *Recreations*: looking, walking, thinking, cinema. *Clubs*: Chelsea Arts Club. *Misc*: Eleanor of Aquitaine; Pilgrimage to Santiago de Compostela (Russian History). *Address*: 3 Cornell Square (Flat 106), London SW8 2ES. *Email*: hale.treloar@homechoice.co.uk *Website*: Royal Watercolour Society Members page & Chelsea Art Society Members page *Signs work*: "J.Q.TRELOAR" or "J.Q.T."

TREMLETT, Phillippa Mary, HS(1994), RMS (2002), Llewellyn Alexander award HS (1998); self taught miniaturist following a stroke in 1988. *Medium*: watercolour on vellum. *b*: London, 21 Sep 1947. *m*: Peter Ian (decd). *Educ*: London. *Studied*: dress-making and design at Risinghill Comprehensive (1962-64). *Exhib*: annually RMS and HS, London and Wells, locally. *Works in collections*: private: London, Home Counties, Jersey, USA, E. Anglia, NZ. *Commissions*: from £250. *Recreations*: reading, dogs, computers, all music genres, writing short stories. Practising Christian, letter writing to prisoners. *Misc*: teaches miniature painting, lectures and talks with demonstrations. *Address*: 4 Paddock Cl., Ropsley, Grantham, Lincs. NG33 4BJ. *Email*: phillippa.tremlett@btopenworld.com *Signs work*: monogram.

TRESS, David, painter in mixed media, graphite, acrylic. *b*: London, 11 Apr 1955. *Educ*: Latymer Upper School, Hammersmith. *Studied*: Harrow College of Art (1972-73), Trent Polytechnic, Nottingham (1973-76). *Exhib*: regularly in Wales, England, Ireland. *Works in collections*: National Museum of Wales, National Library of Wales, CASW, Glynn Vivian Art Gallery, Guildhall Art Gallery, London. *Commissions*: Royal Mail, one of their millennium stamps (1999). *Publications*: Exhbn. catalogues: Boundary Gallery, London, West Wales Arts Centre, Brian Sinfield Gallery. Monograph: 'David Tress', Gomer Press, 2003. *Address*: c/o West Wales Arts Centre 16 West Street Fishguard Pembrokeshire SA65 9AE. *Signs work*: "David Tress."

TREVENA, Shirley, RI (1994); Winsor and Newton Award (1995); Llewelyn Prize (1996); self taught artist. *Medium*: watercolour. *b*: London, 11 Sep 1934. *m*: Michael

Pickerill. *Educ*: Drayton Manor Grammar School, Middx. *Exhib*: RI Mall Galleries, RWS Bank St. Gallery; Nicholas Bowlby Gallery, Tunbridge Wells; Orange Street Gallery, Uppingham. *Publications*: 'Taking Risks with Watercolours', Vibrant Watercolours; author of 2 books, and numerous articles and reviews; examples of work in several books on water-colour painting and drawing. *Address*: Flat 3, 4 Medina Villas, Hove, E.Sussex, BN3 2JR. *Email*: shirley@shirleytrevena.com *Website*: shirleytrevena.com *Signs work*: "S. Trevena."

TRINDER, Wendy, FSBA (founder member); SWA; BSc (Botany) and PG Cert. in Education. *Medium*: acrylic, watercolour, drawing, prints. *b*: Oswestry, Shropshire, 12 Sep 1942. *m*: divorced. one *s*. one *d*. *Educ*: Twickenham County Grammar School (1954-61). *Studied*: University of Hull (1961-65). No formal art training but attended courses run by Edward Wesson, Moira Huntly, Tom Coates, John Yardley, Ken Paine, John Blockley. *Exhib*: SBA, SWA; galleries across UK; Marlborough Open Studios. *Commissions*: Bishopsgate School, Englefield Green, Surrey; Guards Polo Club, Windsor Great Park. *Publications*: illustrated 'Teddy Bear Quotations', 'Teddy Lovers Address Book', 'Teddy Bears - A Celebration' (Exley Publications, 1990). *Works Reproduced*: limited edition prints: 'Pottering at Urchfont' (2000); 'Roses' (2007); 'Back Door Step' (2007), 'Misty Morning' (2008); greeting cards (Woodmansterne Ltd.). *Clubs*: Virginia Water Art Society; Lawrence Society, Devizes. *Address*: 5 Canada Rise, Market Lavington, Devizes SN10 4AD. *Email*: wendytrinder@waitrose.com *Signs work*: 'Wendy Trinder' (watercolours); monogram on acrylics and drawings.

TROITZKY, Nina, MA Fine Art, BA Hons, Professional Development Diploma; painter, installations & mixed media. *d of*: Rev. Nicanor Troitzky, Archimanderite, Russian Orthodox Church in Exile. *m*: Philip Richardson. *Studied*: The City Lit London, London Guildhall University, University College Chichester, Brighton University and West Dean College. *Exhib*: Mall Galleries, London Contemporary Art Fair, British Painters, Discerning Eye, Llewellyn Alexander, London, Chelsea Arts Club, SWAN Sydney, Australia, Mountbatten Gallery, Portsmouth, University College Chichester, Brighton University Gallery, Hotbath Gallery Bath, Stroud Gallery, Phoenix Gallery Brighton, Cheltenham & Gloucester Open, Hereford College of Art & Design, St. Mary Woolnoth Church, London, Ox Market Gallery, Chichester, Havant Art Centre, Oceanography Centre, Southampton, Chichester Museum, Brighton Festival, Brighton Museum & Art Gallery,and many provincial and European galleries, selected Exhbn. 1999 in Dostoyevsky Museum, St. Petersburg, Russia. *Works in collections*: V. & A. Museum, London, St. Richard's Hospital, Chichester, California State University of Long Beach, U.S.A., University College, Chichester. *Works Reproduced*: Medici card. *Clubs*: Chelsea Arts. *Misc*: Mem. of 'Catalyst' Women, Arts and Science Group, Artel Studio Trust, East & West Cultural Artists Club. *Address*: 10 Henty Gardens, Chichester, W. Sussex PO19 3DL. *Email*: troitzsky@btinternet.com *Website*: www.artel.org.uk *Signs work*: "N.T."

TROTH, Miriam, BA Hons (1983); fine artist. *Medium*: mixed media. *b*: Edgbaston, 1 Oct 1951. *Studied*: W. Surrey College of Art (1980-83) . *Exhib*: Barbican, British Commonwealth Inst., Swansea A.G., Coleridge Piccadilly, Bristol A.G., R.A., Bankside, Royal Soc. of Artists, Salisbury Museum, Windsor Arts Centre, Christchurch Museum, Bournemouth University, London Contemporary Art, Waterloo Gallery, Brunei Gallery, CCA Glasgow, Kube Gallery Poole, Southampton AG, CBK Leiden, Spandow G. Berlin, National Trust, Artsway, Pallant House. *Works in collections*: London, Sydney, Detroit, Frankfurt, Wiltshire C.C., Bournemouth CC. *Commissions*: Russell Cotes Museum, Bournemouth. *Official Purchasers*: Wiltshire C.C., Bournemouth C.C. *Address*: 31, Overcombe Court, 22 St. John's Road, Boscombe Spa Village, Bournemouth BH5 1EW. *Signs work*: "Miriam Troth."

TROWELL, Jonathan Ernest Laverick, NDD (1959), RAS Dip (1962), FRSA (1983), NEAC (1986); painter in oil, pastel and water-colour. *b*: Easington Village, Co. Durham,

1938. *m*: Dorothea May Howard. *Educ*: Robert Richardson School. *Studied*: Sunderland College of Art, RA Schools. *Exhib*: New Bauhaus Cologne, Young Contemporaries, John Moores, RA, Lee Nordnes NY, Bilan de Contemporain Paris, RBA, NEAC; one-man shows, Brod Gallery London, Century Gallery, Culham College Oxford, Richard Stone-Reeves New York, Osborne Gallery London, Stern Galleries Australia. *Works in collections*: Bank of Japan; Culham College, Oxford; de Beers (Diamond Co.); Oriental Diamond Co.; Ciba-Geigy; Imperial College of Science; RCA; BP. *Clubs*: Chelsea Arts. *Address*: Carr Farm, Old Buckenham, Attleborough, Norfolk NR17 1NN. *Signs work*: "TROWELL."

TRUZZI-FRANCONI, Jane, BA (1977); Angeloni prize (1979), Discerning Eye prize (1990); sculptor in bronze; Supervisor, Fiorini Fine Art Foundry. *b*: London, 26 Jul 1955. one *d*. *Educ*: Sydenham School . *Studied*: Goldsmiths' College of Art (1973-74), Ravensbourne College of Art (1974-77), RCA (1978-79). *Exhib*: RA, Mall Galleries, many mixed shows in London, E. Anglia, Kent and Surrey. *Address*: 4 Wolsey Cottages, Strickland Manor Hill, Yoxford, Suffolk IP17 3JE. *Signs work*: "J.E.T.F."

TUBB, Stephen David. *Medium*: pastel, oils, drawing, prints. *b*: Chippenham, 7 Jun 1959. *s of*: A.A. Tubb & D.M. Cornwell. *Studied*: self-taught. *Exhib*: various. *Works in collections*: British Racing Drivers Club, Silverstone. Various private collections in USA, UK and Australia. *Works Reproduced*: prints. *Principal Works*: motoring, motorcycle, portrait. *Recreations*: motorcycling. *Address*: 86 New Road, Wootton Bassett, Swindon, Wilts., SN4 7AW. *Email*: steve.tubb7@btinternet.com *Website*: www.tubbart.co.uk *Signs work*: "Steve Tubb", "Stephen Tubb", or "Tubb".

TUCKER, Alistair, RBSA; BA (Hons) Fine Art, PGCE Art & Design; Winner, Liverpool Open (2013). *Medium*: oil, watercolour, drawing, print. *b*: Whitchurch, Hampshire, 2 Jun 1970. *m*: Zoe Tucker. one *s*. one *d*. *Studied*: Bristol Polytechnic; Middlesex Polytechnic. *Represented by*: Castlegate House Gallery, Cockermouth; Zillah Bell Gallery, Thirsk; Editions Ltd, Livepool. *Exhib*: RBSA, Birmingham; RWA, Bristol; Castlegate House Gallery, Cockermouth; Zillah Bell Gallery, Thirsk; Editions Ltd, Liverpool; Denbigh Arts Centre; Wrexham International Print Exhibition; Lichfield Festival; The Tabernacle (MoMA) Machynlleth; The Architects Gallery, London. *Works in collections*: Grosvenor Museum, Chester; IOWA biennial exhibition of Miniature prints. *Address*: 5 Edward Manton Close, Higher Bebington, Wirral CH63 8PU. *Email*: alistair@alistairtucker.com *Website*: www.alistairtucker.com *Signs work*: "Alistair Tucker".

TUCKER, Patricia Rosa, (née Madden), NDD (1950), ATD (1951); oil and water-colour painter, art teacher; Chairman, Bromley Art Soc.; Visual Arts Officer, Bromley Arts Council (1970-87); Sec. Chelsea Open Air Art Exhbn. (1967-87). *b*: London, 2 Jan 1927. *d of*: Michael and Rosa Madden. *m*: L. Tucker. two *s*. one *d*. *Educ*: Mayfield, Putney, St. Catherines, Swindon. *Studied*: Swindon School of Art, West of England College of Art. *Exhib*: RA, Bankside, Mall, etc.; one-man shows, London, Blackheath, Greenwich, Bromley, Chelsea, Gloucester and Denmark. *Works in collections*: Bromley, Gloucestershire, Kensington and Chelsea, Swindon. *Commissions*: portraiture, architectural landscapes, floral work, illustration. *Publications*: illustrations, Parenting Plus, The Infighter's Guide to Divorce by Richard Marsden. *Official Purchasers*: Bromley Education Authority. *Recreations*: Theatre, travel, architecture history. *Clubs*: Croydon, Blackheath, Bromley, SEFAS, UA. *Address*: 5 Bromley Ave., Bromley, Kent BR1 4BG. *Signs work*: "Patricia Tucker."

TUDBALL, Ruthanne Amelia, BA (Hons) English Lit and Lang; Post Graduate Diploma (Commendation) Ceramics, PGCE. *Medium*: Ceramics. *b*: Sierra Madre, California, 16 Aug 1948. *d of*: Helen Marie Thomas / Edwin Gage Meyer. *m*: David. one *s*. one *d*. *Studied*: University of Reading (1971-97, 1984-85); Goldsmiths College, University of London (1987-89). *Exhib*: Gallery Roola, Nagoya, Japan (2012); Shozandd Gallery, Fukuora, Japan

(2012); Contemporary Applied Art, London (2011); Centre de Creation, La Borne, France (2009); Grapevine, Burnham Market, Norfolk (2009); Bourbon Bottles in Bluegrass, Kentucky, USA (2007); Bettles Gallery, Hampshire (2006) Shanghai City Museum, Shanghai, China (2006); Contemporary Ceramics, London (2005); Yingge County Ceramics Museum (2002); Bykuarn Hantuerk, Enkopeng, Sweden (2001). *Works in collections*: Yingge County Ceramics Museum, Taipei; Aberystwyth University; Ashmolean Museum, Oxford; Brown Forman Collection, Kentucky, USA; Museum der Stadt, Landshut, Germany; Norwich Castle Museum, Norfolk; Waismay Collection, York Museum; South London Gallery Collection; Western Illinois Univeristy; Jan Van Houdt Collection, Institut Pietre Breughel, NL. *Publications*: Soda Glazing pub 1995 by A&C Black. *Official Purchasers*: Ashmolean Museum, Oxford; Yingge County Ceramics Museum, Taipei; Castle Museum, Norwich; Aberystwyth University, Wales. *Recreations*: Walking; music; reading; drawing; gardening. *Clubs*: Fellow Craft Potters Association; Norfolk Contemporary Craft Society; International Academy of Ceramics. *Address*: Solomon's Temple, Welborne, Dereham, Norfolk NR20 3LD. *Email*: ruthanne.tudball@btopenworld.com *Website*: www.ruthannetudball.com *Signs work*: "Ruthanne Tudball".

TUFF, Richard, BA Hons (Textile Design). *Medium*: gouache. *b*: Cheshire, 3 Dec 1965. *s of*: Mr & Mrs Tuff. *m*: Sara Tuff. one *d*. *Educ*: Winchester School of Art (1985-88). *Studied*: textile design. *Represented by*: Beside the Wave Gallery, CCA Galleries. *Exhib*: Royal West of England Society of Art (1990-92), various. *Publications*: silkscreen prints published regularly from 1992 (CCA Galleries). *Works Reproduced*: approx. 20 images over 12 years (Art Group). *Address*: Beside the Wave, 8-10 Arwenack Street, Falmouth, Cornwall, TR11 3JA. *Signs work*: Richard Tuff (lower case letters).

TULLY, Joyce Mary, UA (1978); teacher; speaker at local societies; teaches calligraphy and exhibits examples of work. *Medium*: oil, watercolour, acrylic. *b*: Wooler, Northumberland. *d of*: Walter Tully. *Educ*: Duchess Grammar School, Alnwick. *Studied*: Hammersmith Art College (part-time) and private tuition with Mr. Harold Workman, ROI, RBA, RSMA. *Exhib*: Paris Salon, ROI, RBA, Chelsea Artists, NS, UA, Ridley Soc. and in Australia, British Painting in 1979, Paxton House, Berwickshire, participates in Northumberland Art Tour. *Works in collections*: Copeland Castle, and private collections in England, Europe and America. *Publications*: entry in Marshall Hall's 'The Artists of Northumbria' . *Address*: Kia-ora, 26 Tenter Hill, Wooler, Northumberland NE71 6DG. *Signs work*: "J. M. Tully."

TUMELTY, Marian, SBA, RMS, SWA; Cert. of Botanical Merit; RHS Silver Gilt Medal, Llewelyn Alexander Masters Award, Fairman Members Subject award (2nd, RMS), Llewelyn ALexander Prize for a Subject Miniature (RMS). *Medium*: watercolour. *b*: Norwich, 3 Feb 1944. *d of*: Alfred and Gladys Michette. *m*: Peter Tumelty. one *s*. one *d*. *Educ*: Blyth Grammar School, Norwich. *Studied*: Bath Academy of Art. *Exhib*: The Westminster Gallery, The Mall Galleries, Chelsea Flower Show, Hampton Court Flower Show, Chris Beetles Gallery, Hitchin Museum; The Everard Read Gallery, Johannesburg; Sevenoaks Wildlife Reserve, Kent; The Barbican Centre, Burlington House, The Beecroft Art Gallery, Essex, The Garden Festival of Wales. *Works in collections*: many private collections at home and abroad. *Commissions*: many private commissions. Also worked for 3 years as design artist for H. Bronnley & Co. Ltd. *Publications*: "The Tree" (Woodland Trust). *Works Reproduced*: "Tiger Lilies", "Poppies", "Helleborus", "Rose", "Freesias". *Recreations*: ceramics and grandchildren! *Address*: 37 Woodland Way, Stevenage, Herts, SG2 8BU. *Email*: mariantumelty@ntlworld.com *Signs work*: "Marian Tumelty" or "MT".

TURNBULL, Alan, BA (Hons) Fine Art (1977), MA (1978); painter in oil, printmaker (etching), lecturer; Boise Scholar; numerous Arts Council Awards. *b*: Co. Durham, 3 Oct 1954. one *s*. *Studied*: Newcastle University, Chelsea School of Art. *Exhib*: selected one-man shows: Emory University, Atlanta (2010); Vladimir Nabokov Museum, St. Petersburg (2005, 2008); North House Gallery (2007); Hatton Gallery (2007); Liteyny Studios, St Petersburg (2003); York City Art Gallery (2001); Marlowe Centre, Canterbury; State Theatre Dresden, Cathedrals of Durham, Ripon, Newcastle, Norwich. Selected group shows: RA London, Scottish Royal Academy, Society of Scottish Artists Edinburgh, Canterbury Museum, 7th Mostyn Open, Compass Gallery Glasgow, Mappin Art Gallery Sheffield, Ketterer Kunst Hamburg, Museum of Fine Arts Ekaterinberg. *Works in collections*: City of Dresden, London University, Northern Arts, Nabokov Museum St. Petersburg, Harvard University, Arts Council England, Woodland Trust; private collections worldwide. *Publications*: 'Etchings after Van Gogh' Liteyny Print, St. Petersburg. *Works Reproduced*: RA Summer Exhibition Catalogues 2001/2004, 'Aspects of Drawing', Canterbury Museum, 'Waterlog' Literary Journal, Autumn 2001. *Address*: The Cottage, Moor Rd., Bellerby, Leyburn, N.Yorks. DL8 5QX. *Email*: turnbull.fineart@virgin.net *Signs work*: "Alan Turnbull."

TURNBULL, Andrew, Fellowship Royal Academy Schools (2002-05); MA (RCA) Printmaking (2000-02); First Class Honours Fine Art: Printmaking, Loughborough University; The Tim Mara Printmaking Award. *Medium*: prints. *b*: Hastings, 12 May 1978. *Studied*: HCAT, Loughborough University, Royal Academy Schools, Royal College of Art . *Exhib*: solo shows: RA (2005); New Academy Gallery, London (2004); Case-1 Gallery, London (2004); many group exhbns inc. Workplace Art, London (2004), RA Summer Exhbn (2003, 04); Metropolis, Mark Jason Gallery, London (2002). *Works in collections*: V&A; Churchills College, Cambridge; RCA; Loughborough University; many private collections. *Commissions*: Cable & Wireless (Red Lion Square, London, 2005); R3 (London, 2003). *Principal Works*: 'Water Arch' (2004); 'Canary Construct' (2004); 'Middle Town' (2003). *Website*: www.akturnbull.com *Signs work*: 'A.Turnbull'.

TURNER, Alan, Image Liberation Front (ILF). *Medium*: various. *b*: Farnham, Surrey, 2 Feb 1942. *s of*: Helen & Harold Turner. *m*: Janet Barbara. one *s*. two *d*. *Educ*: Grammar School, Bexhill-on-Sea. *Studied*: Hornsey School of Art (1962-65); Camden Institute (1965-70). *Represented by*: England & Co. *Exhib*: London Group, Tolly Cobbold, Eastern Art National Exhibition, Discerning Eye, Alternative Arts, England & Co., Haringey Arts Council, Aberystwyth Printmaker, Cambria Arts. *Works in collections*: various private international. *Publications*: Leonardo, Pergamon Press, Printmaking Today, Raw Vision. *Misc*: It is the duty of the artist to engage with the issues of the day. Involved in Mail-Art since 1992. *Address*: Penarth, Pennant, Llanon, Ceredigion, SY23 5JP. *Signs work*: "ALAN TURNER".

TURNER, Anthony Hugh, RBS; BA (Hons) Social Studies. *Medium*: sculpture: stone and bronze. *b*: Nairobi, Kenya, 20 Apr 1959. *s of*: Pilly Turner. one *s*. one *d*. *Educ*: Marlborough College (1971-76). *Studied*: Exeter University (1977-80); 4 year apprenticeship with Peter Randall-Page. *Represented by*: Sladmore Contemporary, London; On Form Sculpture, Oxford. *Works in collections*: mainly private. *Commissions*: mainly private, also seating for Barratt's Homes and East Cumbria Countryside Project; gatepost finials for Asthall Manor, Oxfordshire. *Address*: Burnt Cottage, Lower Ashton, Exeter, Devon EX6 7QW. *Email*: at@anthonyturner.net *Website*: www.anthonyturner.net

TURNER, Derek, Xeron Painting Competition First Prize; East/West Contemporary Art Online Competition. *Medium*: acrylic and mixed media. *b*: London, 27 Aug 1934. *Partner*: Joyce. *Studied*: Beckenham School of Art (National Diploma in Design). *Exhib*: Gallery Circus Circus, Osaka, Japan; Gallery Le Deco, Paris; Stanley Picker Gallery, Kingston upon Thames; Mariners Gallery St. Ives; Bankside Gallery, London; A la Galerie E-Space, Paris; Battersea Arts Centre, London; Royal Society of Arts, London; Menier Gallery, London; Rooksmoor Gallery, Bath; Gallery Le Deco, Tokyo, Japan; Atrium Gallery, London; Robern

Phillips Gallery, Walton on Thames; Foyles Gallery, London; View Two Gallery, Liverpool; Gallery Kiku, Osaka, Japan. *Works in collections*: Hounslow & Spetthorne Trust; Hillingdon Hospital; West Middlesex Hospital. *Address*: 45 Templemere, Oatlands Drive, Weybridge, Surrey, KT13 9PA. *Email*: joyce553@btinternet.com *Signs work*: "DEREK TURNER".

TURNER, Helen Louise, BA Hons. *Medium*: oil, watercolour, acrylic, mixed media, drawing, prints. *b*: Bromley, 23 Jun 1964. *Studied*: Canterbury College of Art (1982-86). *Represented by*: HQ Gallery, Lewes, East Sussex. *Exhib*: one person shows: HQ Gallery, Lewes (2008), 'Artist of the Day', Flowers Central, Cork Street (2006), Trinity Arts Centre, Tunbridge Wells (2005), Rochester Art Gallery (2005). Group exhibitions: Olympia Art Fair (2004), John Moores 22 The Walker Art Gallery, Liverpool Biennale (2002), Sussex Arts Club, Brighton (1997), Brighton Museum and Art Gallery (1994), Smiths Gallery, Covent Garden, London (1992). *Works in collections*: private and corporate. *Address*: 14 Castle Ditch Lane, Lewes, East Sussex, BN7 1YJ. *Signs work*: "H Turner".

TURNER, Helen Margaret Fordyce, (née REID), DA Edin.; Daler-Rowney Painting Award (MAFA, 2000); Still Life Award (RI, 2003); Bessie Scott Award (2006) Paisley Art Institute Annual Open Exhbn. *Medium*: oil, watercolour. *b*: Torphins, Aberdeenshire, 21 Apr 1950. *d of*: William Reid. *m*: Clive D.R.Turner. two *s*. *Educ*: Ross High School, Tranent, East Lothian. *Studied*: Edinburgh College of Art (1967-71); Moray House College of Education (Edin.) (1971-72). *Represented by*: Walker Gallery, Harrogate. *Exhib*: in open exhbns with: RBSA; MAFA; RSA; RSW; RGI; RWS; Royal Institute of Painters in Watercolour; Singer & Friedlander/Sunday Times Watercolour Competition; Lake Artist Society Annual Exhbns; various gallery mixed exhbns. *Publications*: feature in 'The Lake Artists Society - A Centenary Celebration' (pub.2004). *Works Reproduced*: RWS/RGI catalogues. *Principal Works*: still life, landscape. *Clubs*: elected member Lake Artists Society. *Address*: 4 Yeats Close, Kendal, Cumbria LA9 5HY. *Signs work*: 'H.M.F.TURNER'.

TURNER, Jacquie, BA; painting in mixed media on paper. *b*: Kent, 27 Mar 1959. *m*: Nigel Wheeler. three *s*. one *d*. *Educ*: Rickmansworth School, Herts. *Studied*: Winchester School of Art (1979-81). *Exhib*: Linda Blackstone Gallery, Pinner, Middlesex. *Works in collections*: Leics. Coll. for schools and colleges, Norsk Hydro Oslo, Adam Bank London, Shangri La Hong Kong. *Publications*: The Encyclopaedia of Acrylic Techniques by Hazel Harrison (Headline), How to Capture Movement in Your Paintings by Julia Cassels (Northlight Books), Artists Manual (Collins), Mixed Media Pocket Palette by Ian Sidaway (Northlight Books), Israel at 50 (Linda Blackstone Gallery). *Address*: Fairview House, Chinnor Rd., Bledlow Ridge, Bucks. HP14 4AJ. *Email*: jacquieturner@o2.co.uk *Website*: www.jacquieturner.com *Signs work*: "Jacquie Turner."

TURNER, Lynette, Hons.BSc (Zoology, 1968), HNDD (Graphic design, 1970); printmaker in coloured etchings using zinc. *b*: London, 28 May 1945. *d of*: Engineer Rear-Admiral A. Turner. *Educ*: Hall School, Wincanton, Som., Manchester University. *Studied*: Brighton Art School (1963), City and Guilds Art School (1969, etching), Manchester Art School. *Exhib*: Century Gallery, Henley (1976), Margaret Fisher Gallery (1976), RA (1977), SE London Art Group, YMCA, Gt. Russell St., WC1. (1983), RA Summer Show (1987), December 1989 exhbn. in Crypt of St. Martin-in-the-Fields, (etchings and water-colours), writing and illustrating comic strip adventures. *Clubs*: Falmouth's Royal Cornwall Polytechnic Soc. *Address*: 2 Doctors Hill, St. Keverne, Cornwall TR12 6UX. *Signs work*: "Lynette Turner."

TURNER, Martin William, NDD (1961), ROI (1974), NS (1975); painter in oil, acrylic and water-colour, printmaker. *b*: Reading, 3 Oct 1940. *s of*: William Alexander Turner. *Educ*: Gravesend Technical School. *Studied*: Medway College of Art under David Graham, C. Stanley Hayes. *Exhib*: RA, ROI, RBA, NS, RSMA, RE. *Works in collections*: Abbot Hall

Gallery, Swansea University, Cardiff Museum, Glamorgan Educ. Com., Liverpool A.G. *Works Reproduced*: articles for Leisure Painter. *Clubs*: RI, NSPS, Hampstead Artists' Council. *Address*: 24 Marshall Rd., Rainham, Kent ME8 0AP. *Signs work*: "Martin Turner."

TURNER, Nicholas James, RWA (2003); BA Hons Fine Art. *Medium*: oil. *b*: London, 23 Jun 1972. *Studied*: UWE, Bristol. *Exhib*: solo shows: RWA (2003, 2007, 2010); Thompson's London (2004); Parkview Paintings (1998, 2000); group exhbns: Redrag Gallery, Cotswolds; Musee Beaux Arts, Bordeaux, France (1998); RWA Autumn Shows since 1994; Art Ireland, Manchester Fair (2006), Rowley Contemporary (2007); Foss Fine Art, London (2008, 2010). *Works in collections*: RWA Permanent Collection; Marquess of Bath; Law Society; Lady Heseltine; Gerrard Investments. *Commissions*: Unite Plc. *Works Reproduced*: Rembrandt's Hat; Signature series art cards; 'Pictures in an Academy' (Redcliffe Press). *Principal Works*: landscapes Bristol and hillsides of Spain (imaginary and observed). *Recreations*: jazz drummer. *Misc*: intimate semi-romantic oil on cardboard panels of small scale, elements of pointilism and post-impressionism. *Address*: 2 Algiers Street, Windmill Hill, Bristol BS3 4LP. *Email*: nicknak4654@hotmail.com *Signs work*: 'Nicholas Turner'.

TURNER, Prudence, freelance artist in oil on canvas; Scottish landscape painter specifically since 1966; plus portraiture, seascapes and dream-fantasies. *b*: 15 Mar., 1930. *d of*: Colonel C EWindle, OBE, MC (ret). *Studied*: in India, Egypt, France and England, learning from artists already famous. Nationally recognized in England in 1934. Fine Art Publication copyrights purchased from 1967 onwards by well-established publishers and given international circulation, including limited editions of signed prints. *Works in collections*: UK, and Overseas. *Commissions*: Professional: constant, including royalty. *Address*: 49 Romulus Ct., Justin Cl., Brentford Dock Marina, Brentford, Middx. TW8 8QW. *Signs work*: "Prudence Turner."

TURNER, Roger. *Medium*: acrylic, pastels, mixed media, oil, watercolour, drawing. *b*: Great Bridge, 6 Jun 1956. *Studied*: self taught. *Works in collections*: private collections. *Commissions*: WH Smiths. *Publications*: Artist & Illustrators (Jul 2014). *Works Reproduced*: "Polperro Harbour at Low Tide" as jigsaw for WH Smiths. *Address*: 9 Freshwater Drive, Lakeside, Brierley Hill, West Midlands, DY5 3TP. *Email*: roger@rogerturnerart.com *Website*: www.rogerturnerart.com *Signs work*: "R N Turner".

TURNER, Silvie, publisher, writer, artist, curator, book/internet based projects. *b*: 19 Oct 1946. two *d*. *Studied*: Corsham (1965-68), University of Brighton (Post grad., 1968-70). Work in permanent collections worldwide. *Publications*: about 25 on various print, paper, book subjects. *Clubs*: Chelsea Arts. *Address*: 204 St. Albans Ave., London W4 5JU. *Signs work*: "Silvie Turner."

TURNER-ALDRIDGE, Gillian, RBSA; BWS (2000); ARBSA (2001); RBSA (2002); Laing Finalist (1993), Laing National Finalist (1994); First Prize, RCamA; Major Award Birmingham Watercolour Society Centenary Exhibition (2007); Hon. BWS (2012). *Medium*: acrylic, oil, watercolour, pastel. *d of*: Mr & Mrs George Henry Turner. *Studied*: Solihull College; Birmingham College of Art. *Exhib*: Mixed exhibitions include: Laing (1993-present); Dudley Mid-Art (1994); Llewelyn Alexander (1994, 1997, 1998); RBSA High Commendation (1994); John Noott, Broadway (1996, 2001), Royal Cambrian Academy (1997); RBSA (1997-present); RCA (1998); SWA (1999); Royal Bath & West of England Show (1999); Gloucester Cathedral, St. Ives Society Mariners Galleries Cornwall (1999); Woodbridge Gallery (1996); Royal Birmingham Society of Artists. Solo shows include: Royal Shakespeare Company (1996, 2002); Pendrell Hall and RBSA. *Works in collections*: RBSA; private collections nationally and internationally. *Clubs*: BWS; Birmingham Art Circle. *Misc*: Demonstrates and lectures, Visiting Tutor/Lecturer. *Address*: 721 Old Lode Lane, Solihull, West Midlands, B92 8JD. *Signs work*: monogram initials 'GTA' within diamond lozenge.

TURPIN, Louis, DipAd (Hons) Fine Art (1971); painter in oil on canvas; South East Arts Major Award. *b*: 25 Apr 1947. *s of*: Digby Denis Turpin, film director. *m*: Davida Smith. two *s*. *Educ*: Alleyns, Dulwich; Sunbury Grammar School, Sunbury-on-Thames. *Studied*: Guildford School of Art (1967-68), Falmouth Art School (1968-71). *Exhib*: Beaux Arts, Bath, NPG, Bohun Gallery, Henley-on-Thames, Rye A.G., RA, RSPP, Rona Gallery, London, Fosse Gallery, Stow-on-the-Wold, Langham Gallery London. *Works in collections*: Rye A.G., South East Arts, Towner A.G., Bath University, John Radcliffe Hospital, Oxford, Nat.West Bank, Dame Stephanie Shirley Collection, Sir Paul McCartney, Dr. Bolling Feild, Fred Olsen. *Commissions*: Miss Pears, Bedruthan Steps Hotel, Priors Court School. *Publications*: The Painted Garden by Huxley, The Art of Priors Court School. *Clubs*: Rye Soc. of Artists. *Address*: 19 Udimore Rd., Rye, E. Sussex TN31 7DS. *Email*: louisturpinartist@hotmail.com *Website*: www.louisturpin.com *Signs work*: "Louis Turpin."

TUTE, George William, NDD Illustration, NDD Painting, RACert., MA (RCA), RE, RWA; Landseer and David Murray Scholarships, silver and bronze medals for Drawing and Mural Painting; artist in oil, water-colour, printmaking; freelance graphic designer, wood engraving. *Medium*: oil, watercolour, wood engraving. ceramic. *m*: Iris Stoltenberg-Lerche (decd 2009). two *s*. *Studied*: Blackpool School of Art (1951-54); Royal Academy Schools (1954-59); Regent St.Polytechnic (part-time, 1954-56); Royal College of Art (1981-88); Central Schools (part-time, 1959-60), Courtauld Institute (part-time, 1956-57); Royal West of England Academy. *Exhib*: RA, RWA, RE; private and public galleries. Exhibits prints and paintings, book illustration and general illustration for commissions, wood engraved illustrations and autographic prints. *Works in collections*: private/public. *Commissions*: advertising, book illustration. *Publications*: various illustrated: Shakespeare, Rob Roy, The Monk, The Professor, Chris Marlow, etc. *Official Purchasers*: Royal West of England Academy, etc. *Works Reproduced*: RWA, website C.V. *Principal Works*: oil paintings of landscape, figures, autographic prints. Freelance graphic designer/painter. *Recreations*: travel, gardening, collecting 20th century English paintings and engravings. *Clubs*: Society of Wood Engravers (former chairman). *Misc*: lecturer York School of Art (1961-63), ret. principal lecturer Graphic Design Univ. of W. of England (1963-85). *Address*: 46 Eastfield, Westbury-on-Trym, Bristol BS9 4BE. *Email*: georgetute@talktalk.net *Website*: www.georgetute.com *Signs work*: "G. W. Tute."

TUTTIETT, Dora, NDD; David Murray Award RA; RA Cert.; Tutor Fine Art. *Medium*: painter in oil. *b*: Bromley, Kent, 29 Nov 1935. *Educ*: Charterhouse Secondary Modern, Chelsfield, Kent. *Studied*: Bromley College of Art, Royal Academy, Goldsmiths College of Art. *Exhib*: RA, RA West of England, Mall Galleries, Burlington Fine Arts, Bedales, etc. 21 one-man shows. *Works in collections*: Los Angeles, Holland, Scotland, England. *Commissions*: Holland and Scotland, and Bromley portrait. *Publications*: Golden Hands Illustrator, British Medical Association, Illustrations Bristol University Biochemical Dept. Medical Artist. *Clubs*: RA Alumni Association Club; Royal Academy; Blackheath A.S., Bromley A.S.; Bexley Arts Council; Bromley Arts Council. *Address*: 63a Queensway, Petts Wood, Kent, BR5 1DQ. *Website*: www.dorat.yourprivatespace.com www.axisartists.org.uk.

TWEED, Jill, FRBS, Slade BA.; sculptor in bronze. *b*: U.K., 7 Dec 1931. *m*: Philip Hicks. one *s*. one *d*. *Studied*: Slade School of Art (F. E. McWilliam). *Represented by*: Messums, Cork St., London. *Exhib*: London, Caen, France, Dorset, Gloucesteshire, New York USA, Dublin. *Works in collections*: HM The Queen; Corps of the Royal Military Police, Chichester; Royal Engineers, Mill Hill, London; Austin Reed Ltd., London; Picker Collection, Kingston-upon-Thames, Guernsey Museum C.I. Numerous private collectors. *Commissions*: Large public sculptures commissioned by: Hampshire CC; Amec UK Ltd., London; Conseil Regionale de Normandie, Caen, France; KCC; Oxon.CC; Gosport DC; Herts.CC; Kent CC, Millennium Sculpture, Ware, Herts, Cirencester Shopping Centre, Glos. *Official Purchasers*: Hampshire CC; Kent CC; Oxfordshire CC; Ware Millennium.

Principal Works: The Pegasus Bridge, Caen - D-Day memorial bronze h. 4m. *Address*: Royal Society of British Sculptors, 108 Old Brompton Rd., London SW7 3RA. *Email*: jill.tweed@zen.co.uk *Website*: www.jilltweed.com *Signs work*: "Jill Tweed."

TWOMBLEY, Peter Angus, BA Fine Art (Hons); Goldsmiths Company Travel Scholarship (1984). *Medium*: stone sculptures, drawing, mixed media acrylic and pastel pieces. *b*: Leicester, 31 Dec 1940. *m*: Jenny. two *s*. one *d*. *Studied*: Durham University (Newcastle Annexe, 1959-64); Kings College (Victor Pasmore, Richard Hamilton). *Exhib*: Leicester City Art Gallery; Charnwood Arts; Sidi Bou Said Town Hall, Tunisia; Wayside Studio Gallery 1993, 95, 97 (Bi-annual shows); Stables Art Gallery, Renishaw Hall, Derbyshire (invited to exhibit for HRH Prince Charles); Yewtree Gallery, Stroud; Gallery 18, Loughborough. *Works in collections*: private/corporate (Bowes Museum Schools Collection), Astra-Zeneca Collection, Loughborough. *Commissions*: Brussels Airport Executive Lounge; Bradgate Bakeries, Leicester; Scoles Manor Gardens, Dorset. *Address*: 'Wayside', 2 Main Street, Rempstone, Loughborough, LE12 6RH. *Email*: peter@twombley.info *Signs work*: "Twombley".

TYDEMAN, Naomi, RI (2004); BEd (Hons); Welsh Artist of the Year - Watercolour Award; Frank Herring Award (2005), John Blockley Award (2008); Winsor & Newton Prize (2010); self taught water-colourist, gallery owner. *b*: Taiping, Malaysia, 5 Jun 1957. *Studied*: Trinity College, Carmarthen (B.Ed Hons). *Exhib*: Naomi Tydeman Gallery, Mall Galleries (RI), Bankside Gallery (RWS); Fine Art Gallery, Ledbury; Albany Gallery, Cardiff; Denise Yapp Contemporary Art, Monmouth; Fountain Fine Art, Llandeilo; Affordable Art Fairs (since 2004) etc. *Works in collections*: Tenby Museum. *Publications*: "Different Strokes" (author), pub. Walter Foster; several watercolour instruction books. *Address*: Naomi Tydeman Gallery, Cobbs Lane, Tenby, Pembrokeshire, SA70 7AR. *Email*: naomi@naomitydeman.co.uk *Website*: www.naomitydeman.co.uk *Signs work*: "Naomi Tydeman."

TYLER, Carol, BA (Hons) Fine Art, MA Fine Art; Emma Phipps Award MA Studies, two awards Yorkshire Arts. *Medium*: oil, drawing, mixed media. *b*: Sunderland, 4 Jan 1941. one *s*. *Studied*: Wolverhampton Polytechnic (BA, 1983-86); Birmingham Insitute Art & Design (MA, 1989/90). *Exhib*: Zillah Bell Gallery, Thirsk, N.Yorks, Brick Lane Gallery London (2012). *Works in collections*: private. *Commissions*: Grizedale Forest Residency, workshops and exhibitions in hospitals at Birmingham and Dudley, Artist-in-Residence, North Yorkshire Moors Music Festival 2009-2012, Swaledale Festival. *Publications*: Grizedale catalogue (1995) "Natural Order", Wills Art Warehouse catalogues 2000-06, North Yorkshire Moors Chamber Music Festival brochure 2009-2012. *Recreations*: walking, archaeology. *Misc*: currently fascinated by medieval ruins, wall paintings, tiles. Quantity of work stolen in 1995 after Grizedale Residnecy. *Address*: 2 Mill Fosse, The Bridge, Hawes, N.Yorks, DL8 3QF. *Email*: carol.tyler227@btinternet.com *Website*: www.caroltylerpaintings.com *Signs work*: "CAROL TYLER".

TYLER, Neil, Daler Rowney Art Paper Prize (1999). *Medium*: oil, watercolour. *b*: London, 14 Jun 1945. *s of*: James Tyler. *m*: Catherine Rhoda Tyler (nee Pethybridge). *Studied*: 1966-72, tutored in Life Drawing and Portraiture by Haydn Mackey (1881-1979). *Represented by*: The Spa Galleries, TN2 5TN. *Exhib*: CAS (1973-4, 1992 onwards); Paris Salon (1974-5); ROI (1971, 88, 89); A Taste of Brighton at Dieppe Town Hall (1992); Chateau Derchigny-Graincourt (1994); Envermeu Town Hall (1994, 2002); Sussex Open, Brighton (2003). *Works in collections*: internationally. *Commissions*: various townscapes in Normandy; landscapes and still life in UK. *Works Reproduced*: The Daler Rowney Art Paper (1999). *Clubs*: Chelsea Art Society (resigned 2011), Scarborough Art Society (SAS). *Address*: 16 Westbourne Park, Scarborough, Yorkshire YO12 4AT. *Signs work*: 'NEIL TYLER', 'N.TYLER'.

TYSON EDWARDS, Marian, DFA; sculptor in bronze, cement fondu, terracotta. *b*: Manchester, 2 Oct 1937. *d of*: Henry Tyson Edwards, civil servant. *m*: John T. Sharples. one *s*. one *d*. *Studied*: Liverpool College of Art and High Wycombe College of Art. *Exhib*: Mall Galleries, galleries in Henley, Birmingham, Chalfont, etc. *Works in collections*: Windsor and Eton Fine Art. *Address*: Wispington House, Worster Rd., Cookham, Berks. SL6 9JG. *Signs work*: "M. Tyson Edwards."

U

UGLOW, Ruth, RE; BA Fine Art: Printmaking, MA Fine Art: Printmaking. *Medium*: print, drawing. *b*: Plymouth, Devon, 1 Oct 1975. *m*: Douglas Burton. two *s*. *Studied*: Royal College of Art, London; Winchester School of Art and Design. *Exhib*: Royal Society of Painter-Printmakers Annual Exhibition, London (2011, 2013, 2014); RE Open (2012); 6th International Kyoto Hanga, International Print Exhibition Japan/UK (2012); Bite, Mall Galleries (2012); The Architeccts Gallery, London (2010); RA Summer Exhibition (2010); 14th International Print Exhibition, National Museum of Fine Arts, Taiwan (2010). *Works in collections*: Clifford Chance; Aberystwyth Museum, Wales; Ashmolean Museum, Oxford; The Plains Art Museum, North Dakota. *Commissions*: The Royal Free Hospital (10 drawings to celebrate their research into infectious diseases, viruses and stem cells). *Address*: Littleton Cottage, Hele Bay, Ilfracombe, Devon EX34 9RL. *Email*: ruglow@hotmail.com *Website*: www.ruthuglow.com *Signs work*: "Ruth Uglow".

UNDERWOOD, George, painter in oil. *b*: Bromley, Kent, 5 Feb 1947. *m*: Birgit. one *s*. one *d*. *Educ*: Bromley Technical High School. *Studied*: Beckenham Art School (1963), Ravensbourne College of Art (1964-1965). *Exhib*: solo exhib., About Face, London (1997), group exhibs. in Japan, Copenhagen, Spain, UK, RA Summer Exhibs. (1998, 2001, 2006, 2008, 2009, 2013). *Works in collections*: David Bowie Collection (15 works). *Commissions*: Helena Bonham Carter, David Bowie, Mike Leigh (Topsy-Turvy film poster 1999). *Publications*: illustrated many book covers, authors include, Julian Barnes, John Fowles, William Styron, Russell Hoban, William S. Burroughs. *Address*: The White House, Limes Lane, Buxted, Uckfield, East Sussex TN22 4PB. *Email*: underwood.george@gmail.com *Website*: www.georgeunderwood.com *Signs work*: "george underwood".

UNDERWOOD, Keith Alfred, Leverhulme Research Award in Fine Art (France, 1957-58); realist painter in oil and water-colour; sculptor, restorer, designer. *b*: Portsmouth, 21 Jun 1934. *s of*: A. T. Underwood, BEM, RE. *Educ*: Monmouth School (1946-53). *Studied*: Newport College of Art (1953-57) under the late Tom Rathmell, ARCA, and the late Hubert Dalwood; West of England College of Art (1960-61), Diploma in Education. *Exhib*: Welsh Arts Council, Pictures for Schools, British Art for Moscow, Young Contemporaries, Mall Galleries, Chepstow locale. *Works in collections*: Margaret Cleyton Memorial restoration (St. Mary's, Chepstow 1984), Onitsha Cathedral, Nigeria (portrait bronze 1985), Earl of Worcester armorial sculpture (Chepstow Town Gate 1988); large historical mural, Drill Hall, Chepstow, and town map (1991); Caldicot town map (1994); twelve stained glass cartoons for windows in SS. Richard and Alexander, Bootle (1994); Illuminated vellums for Ivor Waters, Harry Warren and (2011) the Rifles Regiment; paintings in private collections: U.K., U.S.A., Australia, S. Africa and Netherlands, Portskewett & Sudbrook Map 2002. *Recreations*: local history. *Clubs*: Monmouthshire Antiquarian Association. *Misc*: since 1983 involved in heraldic, set and prop design for the pageants and son et lumiere productions of the Chepstow Biennial Festival in Chepstow Castle and Tintern Abbey; costume/prop design Usk Castle Pageant (2005). *Address*: 1 Madocke Rd., Sedbury, nr. Chepstow, Monmouthshire NP16 7AY. *Signs work*: "KAU" until c1974, "K. Underwood" and "Keith Underwood" thereafter.

UNWIN, Dr. Bren, PRE, NSA; BA (Hons) Fine Art; MA (Research) Fine Art; PhD; Gewn May award, RE; President, Royal Society of Painter-Printmakers (RE). *Medium*:

printmaking, film, paint, drawing. *b*: Kent, 1 Sep 1956. *d of*: Leslie & Irene Hall. *m*: Stephen Unwin. two *s*. *Educ*: Presdales Girls School, Ware. *Studied*: University of Hertfordshire. *Represented by*: Cornwall Contemporary Gallery, Great Atlantic Galleries. *Exhib*: Newlyn Art Gallery, Cornwall; Bankside Gallery, London; Lemon St. Gallery, Truro; Mall Galleries, London; Gallery Tresco, Isles of Scilly, Exchange Gallery, Penzance. *Works in collections*: Ashmolean Museum; various private collections. *Publications*: 'Bren Unwin' ISBN 1 898543 860. *Principal Works*: films: 'Line', 'Length'; prints: Palimpsest Series; 'Chiasm: Cage Series'. *Recreations*: walking, reading. *Address*: 24 Bosorne Road, St. Just in Penwith, Penzance, Cornwall, TR19 7JJ. *Email*: brenunwin@btopenworld.com *Website*: www.brenunwin.com *Signs work*: 'Unwin'.

UPSON, (Rosalie) Anne, NDD, RMS, Hon. Fellow Inst. RVAP. *Medium*: oil, watercolour, enamel on copper. *b*: Wigan, 20 Apr 1938. *d of*: Rev. E.A. Marsh. *m*: Peter Norman Upson. one *s*. one *d*. *Educ*: Slepe Hall (St. Ives, Huntingdon); Maidstone Tech. for Girls. *Studied*: Maidstone Art College. *Exhib*: Royal Miniature Society. *Works in collections*: Royal Miniature Collection. *Commissions*: special commission animals on enamel. *Official Purchasers*: Halcyon Days Ltd. Special Commissions. *Recreations*: equine, canine. *Clubs*: Member of Royal Miniature Society. *Misc*: animal physiotherapist since 1976. *Address*: 1 New Barn Cottages, Loughborough Lane, Lyminge, Folkestone CT18 8DG. *Signs work*: 'RA Upson', 'A', 'R.Anne Upson' and monogram.

UPTON, Mark Lundy. *Medium*: oil, watercolour, drawing, prints. *b*: Marlborough, 9 Dec 1964. *s of*: Roger and Jean Upton. *m*: Rachelle Upton. one *s*. one *d*. *Studied*: St. John's, Marlborough; Swindon College of Art. *Exhib*: The Osborne Studio Gallery, London; Mathaf Gallery, London; Rocham Gallery, Jeddah, Saudi Arabia; The Park Grosvenor Gallery, London; William Marler Gallery, Cirencester; The Gallery, Cirencester; The McEwan Gallery, Aberdeenshire; The Lee Gallery, Cork, Ireland; Callaghan Gallery, Shrewsbury. *Works in collections*: The Late Queen Elizabeth the Queen Mother; most of the Middle Eastern Royal families. *Commissions*: Injured Jockeys Fund; Spinal Injuries Association; British Horseracing Board; Countryside Alliance; Fahad Bin Sultan Falconry Centre, Riyadh. *Recreations*: falconry, hunting, racing. *Address*: Plough Cottage, Bath Road, Marlborough Wilts SN8 1PT. *Email*: mark@markupton.com *Website*: www.markupton.com *Signs work*: 'M.L.UPTON'.

URQUHART, Anne, MA, RCA. *Medium*: painting/oil. *b*: Chorley, Lancs, 29 Oct 1962. *Educ*: Royal College of Art. *Represented by*: Benjamin C. Hargreaves Contemporary Art, 90 Kenyon Street, Fulham, London SW6 6LB. *Exhib*: British Consulate, New York USA (2002), Montserrat Gallery (2002), 'Works on Paper' Royal College of Art (2002). *Works in collections*: Karen Burke USA; Stephenson Harwood London; Shannon Smith USA; British Airports Authority. *Clubs*: Chelsea Arts Club. *Address*: 147a Bermondsey Street, London SE1 3UW. *Email*: anne@home147a.demon.co.uk *Website*: www.nonsafety.co.uk/pauk.html

USHER, Jean, BA (Hons) Fine Art, MA Fine Art. *Medium*: Oil; drawing; acrylic; mixed media; installation work. *b*: UK, 9 Dec 1941. three *d*. *Studied*: Sheffield Hallam University. *Represented by*: Penley Art, Sheffield; Cupola Gallery, Sheffield; Christine Bowen Gallery, Ireland; The Oratory, Ireland. *Exhib*: UK and Ireland. *Recreations*: Walking; gardening; stitching. *Address*: Tullig, Waterville, Co. Kerry, Ireland. *Email*: jean@jeanusher.com. *Website*: www.jeanusher.com. *Signs work*: "Usher".

V

VAHEY, Lorna, NEAC; BA Fine Art (1967); Cecil Jospe Award, Chichester Open; Lynn Painter-Stainer Prize, Runner Up; narrative and autobiographical painter. *Medium*: oil, watercolour. *b*: Pett, Sussex, 22 Apr 1946. two *d*. *Educ*: Rye Grammar School. *Studied*: Brighton College of Arts and Crafts (1962-1967). *Exhib*: RA, RSA, NEAC; Cross Gate

Gallery, Kentucky, USA; Brighton Museum, Hastings Museum, Rye Art Gallery; Bankside, London; Mall Gallery, London. *Works in collections*: Hastings Museum, private collections. *Recreations*: more work. *Clubs*: Hastings Against War. *Misc*: daughter of Fred and Zoe Vahey (artists). *Address*: 145 Emmanuel Rd, Hastings, E. Sussex TN34 3LE. *Email*: lvahey@hotmail.com *Website*: www.neac.co.uk *Signs work*: "L. VAHEY."

VAIZEY, Marina (Lady Vaizey), BA Radcliffe, MA (Cantab.); Art Critic, Sunday Times (1974-91); Editor, NACF (1991-94), Editorial Consultant, NACF (1994-98); Art Critic, Financial Times (1970-74); Past Trustee, National Museums and Galleries on Merseyside, Imperial War Museum, South Bank Centre, London Open House, Geffrye Museum, National Army Museum; Friends of the Victoria & Albert Museum. *b*: New York City, 16 Jan 1938. *m*: Lord Vaizey (decd 1984). two *s.* one *d. Publications*: 100 Masterpieces of Art (1979); Andrew Wyeth (1980); Artist as Photographer (1982); Peter Blake (1985); Christo (1990); Christiane Kubrick (1990); organised Critic's Choice, Tooth's (1974); Painter as Photographer, Arts Council (1982-85); Shining Through (Crafts Council, 1995), Sutton Taylor (1999), Art the Critics Choice (1999); Women Collectors (1999); The British Museum Smile (2002); Tracy Emin (2012); David Hockney (2012); Lucien Freud (2012); Rooms of Dreams (2012); Andrew Logan (2010). *Address*: 41 Brackley Road., Chiswick, London W4 2HW

VALENTINE, Barbara, NDD (Illustration), RMS, MAS-F, SLM; miniaturist in oil and water-colour, art tutor; over 20 international and national awards. *Medium*: oil on ivorine. *b*: London, 1943. *m*: Louis Dodd, marine artist (decd). one *s.* one *d. Studied*: Goldsmiths' College (1960-64, Betty Swanwick). *Exhib*: RA Summer Exhbns (1989-99); RMS; annual miniature shows at Llewellyn Alexander Galleries. *Works in collections*: private collections internationally. *Publications*: featured in 'How to Paint Miniatures', 'Miniature Painting', etc. *Works Reproduced*: articles in art magazines, books on miniatures, fine art prints. *Recreations*: rose growing. *Clubs*: R.M.S., M.A.S.-F. *Misc*: teaches adult education leisure classes, and puts on two or three exhbns a year of her students work. *Address*: Mountfield Pk. Farmhouse, Mountfield, Robertsbridge, E.Sussex TN32 5LE. *Email*: barbara.valentine@mypostoffice.co.uk *Signs work*: "B.V."

VALENTINE, Dennis Robert, NDD (1953), ATD (1956), Advanced Diploma in Educational Studies - Cambridge Inst. of Ed. (1980); professional artist in oil, pen and ink, charcoal, water-colour. *b*: Leicester, 12 Jan 1935. *s of*: Robert and Olive Valentine. *m*: Anne Valentine. two *s.* two *d. Studied*: Leicester College of Art (D.W.P. Carrington), Plymouth College of Art. *Exhib*: Lincolnshire Artist Soc. regularly since 1966, Spectrum (Arts Council) 1971, Corby Glen Gallery, Lincs.: one-man show (1999): John Laing Art Competition Mall Galleries (1989), Singer and Friedlander/Sunday Times W/c competition (2002). *Works in collections*: private collections. *Commissions*: portrait of Miss Butcher, one-time principal of Bishop Grosseteste College, Lincoln (1990). *Clubs*: Lincolnshire Artists Soc. *Address*: Wheelwright Barn, 6 East Rd., Navenby, Lincoln LN5 0EP.

VALENTINE-DAINES, Sherree E., DipAD, UA (1983), SWA; painter in oil. *b*: Effingham, 1956. *d of*: Rose & Ralph Valentine-Daines, master builder and stone mason. *m*: Mark Alun Rowbotham. two *s.* three *d. Studied*: Epsom School of Art and Design (1976-80, Leslie Worth, Peter Petersen). *Exhib*: RBA, RA, Tate Gallery, ROI, RWS, RP, Royal Overseas League, NEAC, UA, PS, Olympic Games Exhbn., Royal Festival Hall, Barbican, Laing Landscape, NSPS. *Commissions*: include Test Cricket, 5 Nations Rugby, Royal Ascot, Henley Royal Regatta. *Address*: Park Lane Fine Arts, 102 The Street, Ashtead, Surrey KT21 1AW. *Email*: lorna@parklanefinearts.com *Website*: www.parklanefinearts.co.uk *Signs work*: "S.E.V.D."

VAN BIERVLIET, Emmie, BA Applied Arts; Diana Brookes Award (2010). *Medium*: Painting; mixed media. *b*: Oxford, 1983. *Educ*: D'Overbroecks College (1997-2001).

Studied: Oxford Brookes University Arts Foundation (2002-03); Nottingham Trent University (2003-06). *Represented by*: Quantum Gallery, Battersea; Wiseman Gallery, Oxford; Jerram Gallery, Dorset. *Exhib*: Affordable Art Fair, Battersea, New York (2012); 20/21st Century, RA (2012); Art, Palm Beach, Florida (2012); The Jerram Gallery (2011, 2010); Affordable Art Fair, Singapore (2011); Halcyon Gallery, London (2011); Wiseman Gallery, Oxford (2011); Affordable Art Fair, New York (2011); Art, Chicago (2011); Inspires Gallery, Oxford (2010); The RCA (2010); Waterperry Gallery (2010). *Works in collections*: Lady Goodhart, Patron of the Arts. *Commissions*: 'Amara's Journey', a commission for 'Apprentice' runner up Saira Kahn to create a piece for her adopted daughter to explain her story from Karachi to Oxford. Created for BBC documentary (16 Sep 2011). *Publications*: 'The Oxford Children's A-Z of Art' (OUP, 1999). *Works Reproduced*: 'No Time to Stand and Stare'; 'Honeycombe'; 'Istanbul Ark'; 'Amber Light on Broad Street'. *Principal Works*: 'The Istanbul Ark' a piece used to publicise a national charity exhibition. *Misc*: Artist in residence for the charity 'The Art Room' (2009/10). *Email*: emmievb@hotmail.com *Website*: www.emmievb.com *Signs work*: Below, "EMMIEVB".

van DOORSSELAERE, Joyce. *Medium*: oil, watercolour, drawing. one *d. Educ*: Royal Navy School, Regents Park Central, Sondes Place County Secondary, Surrey (left with A's in Art, English and Maths, B's History and Geography). *Studied*: City Literary Institute (St.Martins in the Fields) (1962); Pitmans College (1950s). *Exhib*: Royal Academy (1997, 2001, 2006); The Mall; 'Not the Royal Academy'; New York Gallery (2001); Art for Life, St. James' (2002); New Gallery, Store St,.WC1. *Works in collections*: Jordanian Royal Palace Collection; Michel Grunberg, architect; Peter Letts; Lady Margaret Thatcher; Great Ormond Street Hospital, etc. *Recreations*: cycling, reading, writing, music, theatre, film world. *Address*: 11 High Street, West Moseley, Surrey KT8 2NA. *Signs work*: 'Joyce van Doorsselaere'

VAN DUYN, Jeroen, SWE. *Medium*: wood engraving, linocut, watercolour. *b*: The Hague, Holland, 31 May 1952. *Partner*: Cecile Bonnet. *Studied*: Vrije Akademie, Psychopolis, The Hague (1969-73). *Exhib*: Galerie Edison, The Hague; since 1989 regular contributions to the SWE Annual Exhibition; The Line Gallery, Linlithgow. *Works in collections*: Roberto Peccolo, Livorno, Italy. *Commissions*: illustrations for 'Tien Verzen Voor Een Doode', Avalon Pers Woubrugge. *Publications*: 3 volumes of privately printed linocut illustrated poetry. *Works Reproduced*: Engravers III; An Engravers Globe. *Address*: Coffray, Flety 58170, France. *Signs work*: 'JEROEN VAN DUYN'

VAN GROUW, Katrina, SWLA; MA (RCA) Natural History Illustration; BA (Hons) Fine Art; Birdwatch Artist of the Year Award: Category Winner 1996, Overall Winner 1997. *Medium*: large graphite landscape drawings; drypoints; bird anatomical drawings. *b*: UK, 13 Oct 1965. *d of*: unknown Welsh and Italian. *m*: Hein van Grouw (m. 2009). *Studied*: The Royal College of Art; University of Plymouth (Exeter College of Art and Design). *Exhib*: SWLA (annually, since 1987); solo shows: Bonhoga Gallery, Shetland; Plumbline Gallery, St. Ives, Cornwall; Royal Albert Memorial Museum, Exeter; The Walter Rothschild Zoological Museum, Tring; British Birdwatching Fair (annually, since 1995). *Works in collections*: Royal Albert Memorial Museum, Exeter; Nature in Art, Twigworth, Glos. *Commissions*: Aig an Oir Art Residency; Artist in Residence, Oceanwide Expeditions. *Publications*: Author of 'Birds' (Quercus Publications, 2007) - a history of birds in art. Anatomical drawings awaiting publication 2011. *Official Purchasers*: Kent Kingdon Trust, Royal Albert Memorial Museum, Exeter. *Works Reproduced*: John Busby 'Drawing Birds' (2nd ed.); Nicholas Hammond 'Modern Wildlife Painting'. *Principal Works*: Albatross. *Recreations*: ornithology; taxidermy; history of natural history art. *Clubs*: Society of Wildlife Artists. *Misc*: employed as Bird Curator at The Natural History Museum. *Address*: 36 Northern Road, Aylesbury, Bucks HP19 9QY *Email*: katrinavangrouw@aol.co.uk *Signs work*: 'Katrina Cook' now 'Katrina van Grouw'.

VAN INGEN, Jennifer Anne, NDD (1962). *Medium*: acrylic, mixed media, oil, drawing. *b*: Wormley, nr.Witley, Surrey, 12 Mar 1942. *d of*: Mr & Mrs C.L.Vincent. *m*: John. one *s.* one *d. Educ*: Convent of the Sacred Heart, Barnes. *Studied*: Ealing School of Art. *Represented by*: The Bruton Street Gallery, London. *Exhib*: RA Summer Exhbn (1996); RBA, RGI, NEAC, RSA, The Bruton Street Gallery (1997, 2001 solo/1998, 1999, 2002 mixed); Drian Galleries, London (1969-88); Black Swan Arts, Frome, Somerset (solo, 2003); Sue Rankin Gallery, London (1993); 238 Gallery, Dorking, Surrey (1995, 2006 mixed exhibition). *Commissions*: The Royal Caribbean Cruise Lines (1997, London Contemporary Art). *Publications*: The Artist Magazine, article on mixed media (1993, 2001). *Works Reproduced*: The Artist Magazine. *Recreations*: music, theatre, swimming. *Clubs*: National Art Fund, NADFAS, Kingston, Surrey. *Address*: 131 Ember Lane, Esher, Surrey KT10 8EH. *Email*: johnvaningen@tiscali.co.uk *Signs work*: 'Mrs Jenny Van Ingen'

VAN NIEKERK, Sarah Compton, RE (1976), SWE (1974), RWA (1992), HonRBSA; wood engraver; Tutor, City and Guilds of London Art School (1978-2000), RA Schools (1976-86), West Dean College. *Medium*: wood engraving. *b*:London, 16 Jan 1934. *d of*: D.J. Hall, writer. *m*: Chris van Niekerk. one *s.* two *d. Educ*: Bedales. *Studied*: Central School of Art, Slade School of Fine Art. *Represented by*: Bankside Gallery, Society of Wood Engravers. *Exhib*: RA, USA, RWA, RBSA, Royal Cambrian Academy, Victoria Gallery, National Print, etc. *Works in collections*: V&A, Fitzwilliam, Ashmolean, National Museum of Wales, National Library of Wales, UCLA, USSR, Fremantle Arts Centre, Graves, Hereford Museum. *Commissions*: illustrator for: Folio Soc., Gregynog, OUP, Readers Digest, Pavilion, Virago, Rider. *Publications*: The Engraver's Cut. Sarah van Niekerk (Primrose Academy Press). 'A Being More Intense' Jenny Pery. *Recreations*: gardening, reading, cooking. *Address*: 1 Portland Place, Frampton-on-Severn, Glos. GL2 7ET. *Email*: s.vanniekerk@btinternet.com "Sarah van Niekerk" in pencil.

van ZWANENBERG, Miki, NDD Hornsley College of Art (1966) Fine Art; previously Production Designer in film, tv and theatre (1968-97), Cannes Film Festival (1989) for 'Distant Voices/Still Lives' by Terence Davies. *Medium*: painting and sculpture. *b*: London, 23 May 1945. *d of*: Claude Kahn and Andree Weiss. *m*: William van Zwanenberg. two *s. Educ*: Woodhouse Grammar School, London. *Studied*: Motley Design School (1968). *Represented by*: Andrew Coningsby Gallery. *Exhib*: Affordable Art Fair (2002-06), Andrew Coningsby (2004); Catherine Hodgekinson (2004); Works on Paper 2005, Tricycle Theatre Gallery; Form (Benjamin Hargreaves, 2006); Artefact: Fitzrovia (2008/9); Oxgate Gallery, Chichester (2008/9); Chelsea & Westminster Hospital (2009); Andrew Coningsby (2012). *Works in collections*: portraits: Vanessa (as Hecuba) & Corin (as Tynan) Redgrave in performance - Theatre Museum (2006). *Commissions*: mural (Graeme Garden, 1998); sculpture (Ruth Nissim, 2000); garden sculpture commissioned by Peter Bramley (2005). *Official Purchasers*: paintings (Julia Goodman) 1998-2012, paintings (Ben Daniels) 2000-2011. *Recreations*: travel. *Address*: 12 Georges' Mansions, Causton Street, London SW1P 4RZ. *Email*: mikivz@hotmail.com *Website*: www.mikivanzwanenberg.co.uk *Signs work*: "Miki van Zwanenberg"

VANDER HEUL, Yvonne Christine, BA Fine Art (1980); Daily and Sunday Telegraph 'Best Display of British Fashion' (National and London Trophy, 1962); London Trophy (1965). *Medium*: painting, oil, watercolour, drawing, sculpture. *b*: South Africa, 8 Sep 1939. *d of*: Winnefred & Piet Vander Heul. *Studied*: Hammersmith College of Art and Building; Regent St.Polytechnic; Michaelis School of Fine Art; University of Cape Town. *Exhib*: RA Summer Exhbn (1997); Royal College of Music (1998); London South African Embassy (1993); Fox Theatre, Atlanta, USA; World Congress Centre (1990); Nico Malan Opera House foyer, Cape Town (1983); Museo Nationale Bellas Artes, Rio de Janeiro (1982); Coliseum (2007); Bruton Street Gallery (1995); Holy Trinity Church, Sloane Street (2007). *Commissions*: Swiss Embassy, London (1999); private. *Publications*: 'Dictionary of Art and

Artists' Esmé Berman (Everaad Reed Gallery, S.Africa, 1980). *Official Purchasers*: RA Summer Exhbn sold £1200. *Works Reproduced*: Chelsea Festival Program (1997-2007). *Principal Works*: ballet, orchestral. *Recreations*: swimming, dance, travel, water related yoga. *Clubs*: Trinity Arts and Crafts Guild, Sloane Street. *Misc*:work produced en situ, during performance, Royal Opera House, Cadogan Hall, Coliseum. *Address*: 49 Draycott Place, Flat 3, London SW3 3DB. *Email*: heul39@yahoo.co.uk *Website*: www.drawingwaterworks.net *Signs work*: "Y.Vander Heul", or "YVDH"

VANGO, David, self taught artist in oil and mixed media; early work mostly perceptual reductionism. Since 1994 large metamorphic abstract constructions; recent work: creating a convincing, deceptive sensation of 3D real space and form on a 2D surface: Illusionism. *b*: London, 18 Feb 1950. one *s*. *Studied*: private studies Witt Library, and galleries and museums U.K. and abroad. *Exhib*: 6 one-man shows: Vidal Gallery, Barcelona; Picture Workshop; Gallery Three, City Art House, Lincoln; Loggia Gallery; 23 group shows, including: FPS Gagliardi Gallery, Kings Rd.; Paxhaven Studio; Foresters Court; Black Horse Chambers, Sam Scorer Gallery, Drury Lane, Gallery on the Strait, Lincoln; Artworld at the NEC; Manchester Art Show, IMEX. *Works in collections*: Japan, France, Spain, Germany, Italy, Australia, America, etc. *Commissions*: Large abstract construction (Nicron 1) for number, 10. (Lincoln), portrait Colin McFarlane (actor). *Publications*: contributor to British Contemporary Art (1993), The BritArt Directory (2000), Dictionary of International Biography (IBC, Cambridge, 2004). *Address*: 68 Alexander Terr., Lincoln LN1 1JE. *Email*: rosie.ritchie@btinternet.com *Signs work*: "VANGO" with V, A and N forming monogram.

VARELA, Armando, Gold Medal, ENBA (1960); French Government Scholarship (1963); First Prize National Award of Sculpture, Peru (1963); Malta Biennale Award (1999). *Medium*: sculptor. *b*: Lima, Peru, 2 Oct 1933. *s of*: Alberto Varela. *m*: Maria Varela. two *s*. *Educ*: ENBA (Escuela Nacional de Bellas Artes) Peru (1952-60). *Studied*: L'Ecole de Beaux Arts, Paris (1963-64); St. Martin's School of Art, London (1972-73). *Exhib*: National Society (2000-07); Instituto de Arte Contemporaneo, Lima, Peru; Museo de Arte, Lima, Peru; Tesoros Del Peru, Mexico; Galeria Lirdlay, Argentina; Festival of London, Barnet Borough Arts, Brent Arts Council; The Stables Gallery; RA Summer Exhbn; Espace Latino American Paris; Contemporary Art Medals, British Art Medal Soc. London; Shamballa Gallery, Copenhagen. *Works in collections*: Museo De La Nacion, Lima, Peru; Burghley Sculpture Garden; The Pride of the Valley Sculpture Park; private collections internationally. *Commissions*: Collection of Latin American Art, University of Essex (2004). *Misc*: paintings, drawing, and ceramic. *Address*:151 Elmstead Avenue, Wembley Park, Middlesex, HA9 8NU. *Email*: varela@maria35fsnet.co.uk *Website*: www.armandovarela.net *Signs work*: 'Armando Varela'.

VASIONIS, Gintautas Augustinas, SFP; Awarded Art Creator Status by the Lithuanian Ministry of Culture; award 05 ARS Nova Suisse; Miggy & Gordon Bath Award for Oil Painting, SFP (White Roses, 2007). *Medium*: oil. *b*: Kaunas, Lithuania, 29 Aug 1930. *s of*: Vasionis Augustinas. *m*: Vasioniene Kitija Anda. one *s*. two *d*. *Educ*: engineer, Dr. of Sciences. *Studied*: Studio 'Palete' under Rimas Biciunas since 1991. *Represented by*: ARS Nova Suisse; Saatchi Gallery; Gallery Dailininku Mene, Vilnius, Lithuania. *Exhib*: 16 Solo exhibitions including: Parliament Gallery, 2003; History Muzeum of Neringa Town, 2008; Gallery of Klaipeda, 2009; Regional Museum of Rokiskis Town, 2009; Samogitian Art Museum, 2011; 79 group exhibitions in Lithuania, Poland, Great Britain. *Works in collections*: History Museum of Neringa Town, Regional Museum of Rokiskis Town, Samogitian Art Museum. *Publications*: 33 publications including 10 catalogues. *Clubs*: Society of Floral Painters; The Club of Artist "Pleksne" in Vilnius. *Address*: Mieziu 18-6, Vilnius, LT-04816, Lithuania. *Email*: gintautas@vasionis.eu *Signs work*: "VG" or "Vasionis".

VEALE, Anthony McKenzie, self taught painter in oil and acrylic, sculptor (surrealist and figurative work) in bronze, wood, marble and stone; also abstract painting and minimalist work. *b*: Tonbridge, 20 Oct 1941. *m*: Susan. one *s*. two *d*. *Educ*: Sevenoaks School. *Exhib*: Tryon Gallery (1979), 20th Century Gallery (1985), Mall Galleries (1992), Delamore, Devon (2011), Ashcombe Towers, Devon (2012). Permanent exhbn. of bronzes in sculpture garden at Buckstone House; Worthing Museum & Art Gallery (2010). *Works in collections*: "Pointless" bronze (1993), "Dust" bronze (1990). *Commissions*: "In Unison", bronze (2013). *Publications*: cartoon illustrations: 'Hippo, Potta and Muss' (Chatto, Boyd & Oliver U.K., 1969), 'A Lemon Yellow Elephant called Trunk' (Harvey House Inc. U.S.A., 1970), 'The Orchard': A Novel (Snowball Press, ISBN 0-9547733-1-4) (paperback - Imprint Academic ISBN 1-845-400585); 'Bamboo Chicken': A Novel (Snowball Press, 2012, ISBN 9780954773328). *Principal Works*: please refer to website www.anthonyveale.com *Recreations*: poetry & music compositions, www.libralibretto.com *Clubs*: Star Cross Dining Club. *Address*: Buckstone House, Upton Hellions, Crediton, Devon EX17 4AE. *Email*: info@anthonyveale.com *Website*: www.anthonyveale.com *Signs work*: "Tony Veale," "Anthony Veale" or "A.V."

VELAZQUEZ, Fernando, Winner of the Dorchester Open (2013), Marshwood Vale Arts Award Exhibition (2014). *Medium*: oil. *b*: Seville, 1966. *m*: Ellen Velazquez. two *d*. *Studied*: self taught. *Represented by*: Rosenberg & Kaufman Gallery, New York; Biondetta Gallery, Madrid; E1 Gallery, London. *Exhib*: Solo include: Dorchester Arts, Dorset (2014); Harris Interiors Gallery, Poole, Dorset (2008, 2011); Hillfield Manor Gallery, Sherborne (2011); Rosenberg & Kaufman, New York (2003); E1 Gallery, London (2000); Woodlands Gallery, London (1999); Madelaine Pearson Gallery, ISlington Arts Facory, London (1997),Muralla Bizantina Gallery, Cartagena, Spain (1994). Group shows UK, Spain and USA since 1988 include: RWA (2014); Biondetta Art Gallery Madrid (2010, 2011); Harris Interiors Gallery, Poole (2006, 2008, 2009, 2010); Galeria Punto-Arte, Barcelona (2009); Rosenberg & Kaufman Gallery, New York (2001, 2004, 2005); Contemporary Art Fair, London (2000); Focus Foundation, Seville, Spain (1996); Expo 92, Seville, Spain (1991). *Works in collections*: Hotel Arts Contemporary Art Collection, Barcelona; Universal Records, London; Stephen Rosenberg, New York; Biondetta Art Gallery, Madrid; Galeria Punto, Barcelona; Editorial La Muralla, Madrid; Solterra, Burgos, Spain. *Commissions*: Rosenberg & Kaufman; Thalia Nimoy Theatre, New York; ICE, Chicago (to celebrate the 80th birthday of American composer George Crumb); "Bueliau" - large painting on glass as part of an architectural project in the New Forest. *Publications*: "The Dictionary of Art in Britain since 1945" by David Buckman (2001/2011); "Art on Demand. Art and Antiques in America" by Margaret Littman (2004); The Sunday Times, New York Times, Dorset Echo, Evolver Magazine, The Telegraph, Marshwood Vale Magazine, etc. Catalogues from E1 Gallery, London; Rosenberg & Kaufman, New York; Olivert Holt Gallery, Sherborne. *Email*: f.velazquez@hotmail.co.uk *Website*: www.fernandovelazquez.co.uk *Signs work*: "Fernando Velazquez".

VERITY, Charlotte Eleanor, DipFA (1977); Slade Prize; Fellowship Bath Academy of Art; Boise Travelling Scholarship, Italy. *Medium*: oil on canvas, watercolour, monoprint, etching. *b*: Germany, 1 Jun 1954. *d of*: Hugh B.Verity. *m*: Christopher Le Brun, RA. two *s*. one *d*. *Educ*: Downe House. *Studied*: Slade School of Fine Art UCL (1973-77). *Represented by*: Browse & Darby. *Exhib*: solo shows: Garden Museum, London (2011), Anne Berthoud Gallery (1984, 1988, 1990), Browse & Darby (1998, 2002, 2007); John Moores, Liverpool (1980, 87); Harris Museum, Preston (1985); L.A. Lower Gallery, USA (1988); many mixed shows including RA Summer Exhbn (1999, 2007, 2009, 2012); Singer & Friedlander Watercolour Competition (1993); Discerning Eye (2003, 2007, 2013); Tate Modern (2005). *Works in collections*: Arts Council; East of England Arts; Deutsche Bank; Electra Investment; Paintings in Hospitals; Stanhope Properties; Tate Modern Education Dept.; UCL , CAS, San Diego MOCA, Westminster School, Garden Museum. *Commissions*: Soane

Museum. *Works Reproduced*: Exhibition catalogues 1990; 1998; 2002; 2007., 2011 *Address*: 8 Love Walk, London SE5 8AD. *Email*: info@charlotteverity.co.uk *Website*: www.charlotteverity.co.uk *Signs work*: "Verity."

VERRALL, Nicholas Andrew, AROI (2009); RBA (2010); NDD (1965); artist in oil, pastel, water-colour, etching and litho. *b*: Northampton, 4 Jan 1945. *s of*: R.E. Verrall, civil servant.one *s*. one *d*. *Studied*: Northampton College of Art (1960-65). Full-time artist since 1970. Prizes: R.W.S. Barcham Green Prize for Water-colour, Royal Horticultural Grenfell Medal, R.A. Committee Prize from B.A.T. *Exhib*: RA, RWS, RE, RBA, RP, and NEAC; mixed shows: Tryon Gallery, RA Upstairs Gallery, Abbott & Holder, Gallery 10; one-man shows: Upper Grosvenor, Langton Gallery Chelsea, Catto Gallery, Hampstead, Art Obsession Inc., Tokyo, and Brian Sinfield, Oxfordshire. *Works in collections*: City of London, B.A.T. Coll., Crown Life, Painshill Park Trust, Coys of Kensington. Private collections in Britain, France, America and Japan. *Publications*: 'Colour and Light in Oils' by Nicholas Verrell, 'Painting Still Life' by Peter Graham; entry in 'Forty Years at Curwen Studios'. *Address*: The Orchard, Ivy La., Woking, Surrey GU22 7BY. *Signs work* "Nicholas Verrall."

VIBERT, Elizabeth. *Medium*: Oil; collage. *b*: Bristol, 24 Oct 1937. *Partner*: Philip Sweeney. *Studied*: Self-taught. *Exhib*: The Portal Gallery, Rooksmoor Gallery, Bristol; Sweetwaters Gallery, London; Museum of Rural Life, Somerset (1992); RA Summer Exhibitions (1984, 1997, 2009); West Wales Workshop, Fishguard (2009-11); RWA Bristol Autumn Exhibition (1991-1997, 2000-2009, 2011); Primavera Gallery, Cambridge; RWA New Gallery; South West Academy of Fine and Applied Art (2001-2005); West Bristol Art Trail (2009-11). *Works in collections*: Private collections France, Great Britain. *Works Reproduced*: Art cards of Cornwall. *Recreations*: WEA classes studying Shakespeare, gardening, cooking, theatre. *Misc*: Earlier career as a novelist. *Address*: 71 Lower Redland Road, Redland, Bristol BS6 6SP. *Email*: lizvibert@blueyonder.co.uk *Signs work*: "E. VIBERT".

VICARI, Andrew, artist, official painter to: King and Govt. of Saudi Arabia, Interpol, CRS; European Parl and Cncl of Europe Beaux arts Prize; Freeman City of London; Chevalier Order of Merit (Monaco). *b*: Port Talbot, UK, 20 Apr 1938. *s of*: Cavaliere Vittorio Vicari. *Educ*: Neath Grammar School for Boys. *Studied*: Slade School of Fine Art, London. *Exhib*: Major exhibitions in London include: New Burlington Galleries (1955), Redfern Gallery (1956), Obelisk Gallery (1956), RBA (1957), United Society of Artists (1957). Contemporary Art Soc of GB Vicari Retrospective (UC Wales, 1963); many overseas including Rome, Beirut, Riyadh, Basle, Washington DC, Monte Carlo, Geneva, Paris, Lyons, Monaco, Versailes, Beijing, Sardinia, Malta, Minorca, Dubai. *Works in collections*: incl: Nat. Library of Wales, Tate Gallery, many private and corporate worldwide. *Commissions*: The Children of Ty Morfa, four panels for Galmorgan Educ. Authority (1956); National Eisteddfod of Wales (1964); Bath Festival Exhibition (1964); Millennium Stadium (2002); Manchester United Carrington Training Ground (2003). *Publications*: Triumph of the Bedouin (1978), Ghazi A Al Ghosaibi: From the Orient and the Desert (illustrations, 1984), The Mystery of Memory: The Truth is not Enough (Vol 1 of autobiography, 2007). *Clubs*: MCC, East India and Public Schools, Cardiff and County, Bristol Channel Yacht. *Address*: Le Shakespeare, 12 Boulevard Princesse, Charlotte, MC 98000, Monaco. *Email*: a.vicari@andrew-vicari.com *Website*: www.andrew-vicari.com *Signs work*: "Andrew Vicari".

VINCENT, John, BAHons Fine Art, MA Fine Art, Fellow Digswell Arts Trust (2012-present); Creekside Open Winner (2011); Apthorp prizewinner (2011). *Medium*: Oil, video and photographic. *b*: Hitchin, 15 Nov 1975. *Studied*: Middlesex University (1996-1999); University of East London (2002-2014). *Exhib*: Fenners Project Space, Digswell Arts Trust (2013, 2014). Solo shows: Westminster Reference Library, London (2013); Fondazione

Patrizio Patelli, Locarno, Switzerland (2007); The Residence, London (2006). *Works in collections*: Private collections. *Commissions*: Vision of Utopia Public Programme - Dystopian Vision, Letchworth Garden City Heritage Foundation (2014); various private painting and digital commissions (2004-present). *Principal Works*: 'The Big Glass (aka This Time Hubby Gets It)' oil on canvas (2009). *Address*: 43 Lytton Avenue, Letchworth Garden City, Hertfordshire SG6 3HY. *Email*: jv@johnvincent.co.uk *Website*: www.johnvincent.co.uk *Signs work*: "J" and year.

VINCENT, Michael John, CertEd (Dist) 1973, BEd (Hons) 1974, MA (1979), DipEd (1983); landscape and seascape artist in gouache and oil, pencil and ink. *b*: Bury St. Edmunds, Suffolk, 9 Feb 1949. *m*: Kaisa (decd). one *d*. *Studied*: Chelsea School of Art (1968-69), London University (1970-74), Inst. of Educ. (1977-79). *Exhib*: throughout UK, Finland, NZ. Work in collections worldwide. *Official Purchasers*: Somerset County Council; H.M.S. Somerset (Royal Navy). *Works Reproduced*: The Guardian, T.E.S., Artist and Illustrators Magazine, Countryman, The Somerset Magazine. *Clubs*: U.A. *Address*: 79 Northload Street, Glastonbury, Somerset BA6 9JR. *Email*: artvincent@onetel.com *Signs work*: "M. VINCENT."

VINE, Edward, landscape/still life artist in acrylic, water-colour, oil, pastel. *b*: Weymouth, Dorset, 10 May 1943. *Exhib*: exhibited regularly with Royal Society of Marine Artists at the Mall Galleries, London. *Works in collections*: Work in private and corporate collections worldwide. Commissions welcome. Studio visits by appointment. *Publications*: 'Edward Vine's Dorset', 120 colour reproductions in hardback, published by Halsgrove, Tiverton, Devon. ISBN 84114 1992 (2002). *Address*: 90 Easton St., Portland, Dorset DT5 IBT. *Email*: dogloom90@fsmail.net *Signs work*: "Edward Vine."

VISOCCHI, Michael, BA (Hons) Fine Art – Sculpture; Royal Scottish Academician (nominated 2004); Jerwood Sculpture Prize (2009); Royal Society of British Sculptors Bursary Award (2003); Scottish Arts Council Assistance Grants (2002 & 2005). *Medium*: sculpture and photography. *b*: UK, 10 May 1977. *Partner*: Julia Carson. *Studied*: Glasgow School of Art (1997-2001). *Exhib*: Royal Scottish Academy, Edinburgh; Peacock Visual Arts, Aberdeen; Jerwood Space, London; Muzuel National, Sibiu, Romania; Royal Society of British Sculptors, London; Glasgow Print Studio. *Works in collections*: Royal Scottish Academy; Italian Cultural Institute; Glasgow Art Galleries and Museums; Art in Healthcare, Edinburgh Demarco European Foundation. *Commissions*: The Merchants House of Glasgow; The Saltire Society; Channel 4; The City of London; BBC4 World Cinema Awards; West Lothian Council; East Ayrshire Council; Clackmannanshire Council. *Works Reproduced*: Why Scottish Literature Matters by Carla Sassi (published by The Saltire Society). *Principal Works*: The Guilt of Cain, Memorial to the Bicentenary of the Transatlantic Slave Trade - The City of London. *Address*: The Old School House, Carroch, By Kirriemuir DD8 4RN. *Email*: info@michaelvisocchi.com *Website*: www.michaelvisocchi.com *Signs work*: 'MICHAEL VISOCCHI' OR 'M VISOCCHI'

VIZE, Susan Linda (Sue), SBA (Society of Botanical Artists); Derwent Award (2012); Art of the Midlands Award (2011, 2008, 2007, 2006). *Medium*: Watercolour, drawing. *b*: Hull, 20 Feb 1955. *m*: Stuart. *Represented by*: The Little Red Gallery, Lincoln. *Exhib*: Society of Botanical Artists, (2007, 2008, 2009, 2010, 2011, 2012, 2013); Cumberland Lodge, Windsor Park (2010); Hunt Institute, Pittsburgh, USA, 13th International (2010); Newby Hall (2011); Art of the Midlands (2006, 2007, 2008, 2011); Indigenous Arts (2008, 2009). *Works in collections*: Nottingham University Plant Sciences Division; RHS Lindley Library; Hunt Institute, Pittsburgh, USA. *Commissions*: Corporate and private. *Official Purchasers*: Nottingham University, RHS Lindley Library, Hunt Institute. *Misc*: Botanical artist and illustrator. *Address*: 34 Norfolk Avenue, Toton, Nottingham NG9 6GP. *Email*: suevizesba@gmail.com *Website*: www.suevize.com Signs work: "Sue Vize".

VLITOS, Roger, BA English with Hons; Dip AD Art & Design. *Medium*: watercolour, drawing, prints, photography. *b*: New York, 15 Dec 1950. *s of*: Prof. A.J. Vlitos. *Studied*: Central School of Art and Design, Hornsey School of Art and Design, Bristol University, Greenwich University. *Exhib*: New York, London, Bristol, Cardiff, Swansea, Venice, Athens, Bath, Swindon. *Works in collections*: National Trust, English Heritage. *Commissions*: Thorn/EMI: The Seasons (film), HTV, National Maritime Museum, British Museum, Natural History Museum. *Publications*: contributed to over 90 books and magazines worldwide. *Works Reproduced*: extensively. *Principal Works*: This Foreign Land (Travelling Exhibition); Reflections of Venice (Travelling Exhibition). *Recreations*: walking, reading, films, travel. *Address*: 110 High Street, Avebury, Wilts, SN8 1RF. *Email*: rogervlitos@hotmail.com *Signs work*: "R.G.Vlitos".

VOGEL, Paul Sidney, BA Hons. *Medium*: textile design - wovens. *b*: London, 6 May 1966. *s of*: Peter & Juliette Vogel. *m*: Samatha Denny Hodson. three *s*. *Educ*: Mill Hill School; Foundation at Harrow College. *Studied*: Nottingham Trent University. *Represented by*: Antony Brown, Los Angeles, USA. *Exhib*: most major textile exhibitions: Indigo, Paris; Surtex, NYC; Directions, NYC; Heimtex, Frankfurt, Germany. *Works in collections*: US Clients: Abercrombie & Fitch; Calvin Klein; Donna Karran; Kate Spade; Martha Stewart; Old Navy; Gap; Ralph Lauren; Stussy; Victoria's Secret; UK: Oasis, M&S, Mothercare; Timberland; Levi Strauss UK; Missioni; Warehouse; Monsoon; Top Shop; Debenhams; East; Liberty; Ted Baker. *Commissions*: Uniqco, Japan; Timberland, UK; Alfred Dunhill; Levi Strauss; Boden; Warren Noronita. *Publications*: Vogue, Elle, Hello, OK Magazine, Sunday Express Magazine. *Misc*: lecturer at Royal College of Art, Central St. Martins, Winchester School of Art, Nottingham Trent University. *Address*: Packway Farm, Halesworth Road, Chediston, Suffolk IP19 0AE. *Email*: paul@paulvogel.com *Website*: www.paulvogel.com

VOGEL, Suzi, SBA, SWA; self taught botanical and landscape artist in oil on panel. *b*: Kent, 1950. one *s*. *Exhib*: regularly with SBA and SWA. Suzi Vogel paints to celebrate the beauty of the natural world. She belongs to a long established Kentish family of passionate writers, gardeners and horticulturalists. Now living and working in Dorset and working only in oils, she uses the finest traditional methods and materials, following in the footsteps of the Dutch and French masters of the sixteenth and seventeenth centuries. Her paintings combine the classically decorative with the botanically accurate and are appreciated and collected by connoisseurs of fine representational oil painting. *Publications*: example of work, picture and caption on page nine of "Drawing Flowers" by Margaret Stevens. *Address*: Flat 1, 22 Victoria Grove, Bridport, Dorset DT6 3AA.

VOJDAEVA, Olga Alexseevna, artist in acrylic and oil. *b*: Crimea, Kerch, USSR, May 1972. *m*: Nathaniel James Giles. *Studied*: Art School, St, Petersburg (1983-88). *Exhib*: Beechfield House, Corsham, The Gallery Cirencester, Royal Inst. of Artists Birmingham, The Highgate Gallery, London (1999), Westminster Gallery, London (1999). *Works in collections*: Lord Bath, Longleat House. *Commissions*: Gleeson Homes, Pizza Hut (U.K.) Ltd. *Clubs*: N.AP.A. *Address*: 29a Bath Rd., Wootton Bassett, Wilts. SN4 7DF. *Signs work*: "Olga Vojdaeva."

VOLLER, Peter Robert, painter in oils, acrylic polymer, painted wood and paper collage, *b*: Fleet, Hants., 26 Sep 1943. *m*: Tessa Philpot. two *s*. one *d*. *Studied*: Farnham School of Art. *Exhib*: mostly in London, including R.A., Discerning Eye, and nationally. *Works in collections*: America, Australia, Germany, Hong Kong and UK. *Address*: 53 The Street, Wrecclesham, Farnham, Surrey GU10 4QS. *Signs work*: "Voller" or "Peter Voller."

von HARTMANN, Sylvia, DA (Edin.) (1965), Post.Dip (1966), RSW (1983); artist in wax. *b*: Hamburg, Germany, 8 Dec 1942. *d of*: Wolf von Hartmann, merchant. *m*: Hamish Dewar. one *s*. one *d*. *Educ*: Walddoerfer Schule, Hamburg-Volksdorf. *Studied*:

Werkkunstschule, Hamburg (1961-63), Edinburgh College of Art (1963-66), Royal College of Art, London. *Exhib*: RA, RSA Edinburgh, RSW, RGIFA, The Scottish Gallery, Edinburgh, National Trust of Scotland, Grosvenor Gallery, London, Open Eye Gallery, Edinburgh, City Art Centre, Edinburgh; Roger Billcliffe Gallery, Glasgow, etc. *Works in collections*: Scottish Arts Council, Scottish National Gallery of Modern Art, City of Edinburgh Art Collection, Dundee Museum and Art Galleries, National Westminster Bank, Edinburgh, The Royal Infirmary, Edinburgh, HM The Queen, St. John's Hospital, Livingstone, Aberdeen Art Gallery, Moray House College, Edin., Royal Bank of Scotland, Playhouse Theatre, Edin., Scottish Provident. *Publications*: Living Light, Books II and III (Holmes McDougall), The Scots Magazine (June, 1984), The Green Book Press Ltd., Bath, Botanical Illustrations in: Sales, F. & Hedge, I.C. 2003, Apiaceae (Umbelliferae) in: Flore de Madagascar et des Comores 157 Museum National d'Histoire Naturelle, Paris. *Works Reproduced*: Waterstones, Stirling Gallery Publications, Kunstkartendruck Vontobel Feldmeilen (Zurich). *Address*: Rhododendron House, 5 Whitehorse Cl., Canongate, Edinburgh EH8 8BU. *Signs work*: "Sylvia von Hartmann."

VON STROPP. *Medium*: oil, watercolour, drawing. *b*: London, 1962. *m*: Fiona. *Represented by*: Henry Boxer Gallery. *Exhib*: American Visionary Art Museum, Baltimore; Orleans House Gallery, Twickenham; Collection de L'Art Brut, Lausanne; Whitechapel Art Gallery, London; England and Co., London; New York Outside Art Fair (1999-2006). *Works in collections*: American Visionary Art Museum (Baltimore), Collection de l'Art Brut (Lausanne), Outsider Archive (London). *Official Purchasers*: Bethlem Royal Museum Collection 'Oestrum' (1980, acrylic on board). *Works Reproduced*: Whitechapel Art Gallery 'Inner Worlds Outside'. *Principal Works*: 'Vision' (c.1982), 'Transvextion' (1979, mixed media on board). *Misc*: self taught visionary artist. *Address*: 98 Stuart Court, Richmond Hill, TW10 6RJ. *Website*: www.outsiderart.co.uk *Signs work*: "VON STRÖPP".

VON STUMM, Johannes, President of Oxford Art Society (2014-); Past President of the Royal British Society of Sculptors (2009-2012); Member of Deutscher Künstlerbund; Founding Member of 'Sculpture Network' (2003); Diploma in Sculpture. *Medium*: sculpture. *b*: Munich, Germany, 27 Jul 1959. *m*: Carolyn. one *s.* one *d. Educ*: Ettal, Benedictine Monastery; OVM Gymnasium, Munich. *Studied*: Academy of Fine Arts, Munich (1985-89). *Represented by*: Robert Bowman Modern. *Exhib*: RBS (2003); Cass Sculpture Foundation (2004); RA (2005); German Embassy, London (2005); Hannah Peschar Sculpture Garden (2006); Robert Bowman Modern Gallery (2007); Thompson Gallery (2008); Fitzwilliam Museum (2009); Museum fur Konkrete Kunst, Greiburg, Germany (2009); Pulse Miami (2010); Fine Art Asia, Hong Kong, China (2011); Bowman Sculpture (2013), EWAEE Kyoto, Japan. *Commissions*: 'Couple' Vale of the White Horse District for Grove; 'Couple in Conversation' for the town of Newbury, 'Welcome Figure', Greenham. *Publications*: Johannes von Stumm (2000, ISBN 0 95303 43 48); Modern British Sculpture (2005, ISBN 0-7643-2111-0). *Clubs*:Chelsea Arts Club. *Address*: Wellhill House, South Fawley, Wantage OX12 9NL. *Email*: vonstumm@aol.com *Website*: www.vonstumm.co.uk *Signs work*: "Johannes von Stumm"

VOROBYEV, Alexander, RWS. *Medium*: oil, acrylics, mixed media. *b*: 63 Lyham Road. *s of*: Leonid Vorobyev. *m*: Oksana Vorobyev. one *s. Studied*: Almaty Art College (Almaty, Kazakhstan). *Represented by*: Bankside Gallery, *Exhib*: Bankside Gallery; The Mall Galleries; White Knights Gallery; Michael Wood Fine Art Gallery; Modern Art Gallery (Moscow); Paul Costello Art & Fashion Charity Show (London), *Official Purchasers*: Victoria & Albert Museum. *Works Reproduced*: in 'Royal Watercolour Society Masters - Then and Now'. *Principal Works*: 'Red Drummer', 'Construction of a Dream', 'The City of Jerusalem'. *Address*: 3 Ashby Mews, Clapham Park, London SW2 5EP. *Email*: alexander_vorobyev@yahoo.co.uk *Website*: www.alexandervorobyev.com *Signs work*: 'Alexander Vorobyev'

W

WADDELL, Heather, MA St. Andrews (1972), DFA (1976), Cert. Ed. London (1977); author, artist, art critic. *Medium*: paintings, etchings, drawings, photography (b & w). *b*: Scotland, 1950. *Partner*: Roger Wilson (1974-78, decd 1999). *Studied*: Byam Shaw School of Art, London (1972-76); St. Andrews University (1968-72). *Exhib*: NSW House A.G., (1980), ACME Studio (1977-80), Battersea Arts Centre (1979), Morley Gallery (1984). *Works in collections*: National Portrait Gallery Photography Collection (photo portraits of David Hockney, and others). *Publications*: Articles on art: Artnews, Art and Australia, The Artist, Art Monthly, Glasgow Herald (1978-94), London correspondent, Vie des Arts (1979-89), The Independent, The European (arts editor, 1990-'91), The Times (1994, 2011); author/photographer: London Art and Artists Guide (11th edn. 2012); The London Art World 1979-99 (2000); co-author, The Artists Directory (3rd edn. 1988); photographer: Glasgow Arts Guide; National Portrait Gallery, London. *Official Purchasers*: National Portrait Gallery. *Clubs*: IAA (1978-84) , AICA (1980-); Society of Authors (1998-). *Email*: hw.artlondon1@virginmedia.com *Website*: www.hwlondonartandartistsguide.com *Signs work*: 'Heather Waddell'.

WADDINGTON, Geri, DFA, ATC, SWE. *Medium*: wood engraver. *b*: Chatham, Kent, 20 Sep 1953. *m*: David Wilson. *Studied*: Slade School of Fine Art (1972-76). *Exhib*: Royal Academy Summer Exhibition, Society of Wood Engravers, RBSA, RWA, National Print Exhibition, Originals, International Miniprint Exhibition. *Works in collections*: Ashmolean Museum, Georgetown University Library, Washington DC, Bristol City Museum and Art Gallery, Hunt Institute for Botanical Documentation, Pittsburgh. *Commissions*: Ashmolean Museum, Oxford; Bristol City Museum and Art Gallery; The Edward Thomas Society; Tobinson College, Cambridge; The Peak Prints Project. *Publications*: illustrated books: "The Five Senses" (Incline Press 1999), Hans Andersen's "The Storks" (Ken Ferguson, 2002), "My Father Made Toys" (Incline Press, 2006), "Aeroplane" (Oundle Festival of Literature Press, 2007). *Works Reproduced*: 'Engraved Gardens' (2001), 'An Engraver's Globe' (2002), both by Primrose Hill Press, "Two by Two" (Society of Wood Engravers 2004), 'Wood Engraving and Linocutting' (Crowood Press 2008). *Clubs*: Society of Wood Engravers (General Secretary). *Address*: 51 Sunningdale, Orton Waterville, Peterborough, Northants PE2 5UB. *Email*: geri@geriwaddington.com *Website*: www.geriwaddington.com

WADE, Jonathan Armigel, MA St. Andrews (1983); painter in oil and water-colour (mentioned in despatches (1991) - British Army, Captain RHF). *b*: Virginia, USA, 12 May 1960. *m*: Marie-Louise Maze. one *s*. one *d*. *Educ*: Lancing. *Exhib*: Paris Salon (1991), Cognac (1991, 1992), Clarges Gallery, London (1993, 1994, 1996, 2000, 2004), Sutton, Sussex (1995), Haddo House, Aberdeenshire (1995), Grimsby (1996, 1997), Arundel (1997), Alchemy Gallery, London (1998), Glasgow (1998), Elsham Hall (2004), Lincoln (2006), Sherwin Gallery (2007), Arndean Gallery London (2008). *Works in collections*: National Army Museum (several sketches and paintings of Gulf Campaign, Bosnia and Northern Ireland), RMA Sandhurst (water-colours), and many private. *Commissions*: 117 completed including a Bosnian triptych for A&N Club. Commissioned to paint in Iraq 2004. *Works Reproduced*: many works reproduced as prints and cards. *Recreations*: shooting, playing accordion and violin, sea fishing, tree growing. *Clubs*: Ex A&N. *Misc*: painted in India (1979), Pakistan (1982 and 1993), Turkey (1980 and 1983), Bosnia (1994), Iraq (2004). *Address*: Walk House, Walk Lane, Irby, N.E. Lincs DN37 7JU. *Email*: wadezx@hotmail.com *Website*: www.jonathanwade.co.uk *Signs work*: "JONATHAN WADE," "J. Wade," J.A. Wade" or "Armigel Wade.".

WAGER, Sandy, ABNA; Awards include: winner, The Technicolour Abstract Award (2011); winner, The Darkness Falls Challenge (2012); winner, The Award Tree (2012); runner up, The Road Ahead Challenge (2012). *Medium*: acrylic, mixed media, watercolour, drawing. *b*: Colchester, Essex, 20 Jun 1953. *m*: Allan Paul Wager. one *s*. *Studied*: self taught. *Represented by*: ABNA; Plymouth Flameworks; Samuel Radloff Gallery, Cambridge; The Evelyn Gallery, Northampton; TheLittle Picture Gallery, Mousehole. *Exhib*: selected exhibitions include: Gornerstones Art Centre, Didcot, Oxon (2010, 2011), The Crypt Gallery, St. Ives (2010, 2011, 2012); Broadwalk Arts, Bristol (2011); The Noah's Ark, Mousehole (2012); The Gloss Art Gallery, Exeter (2013); The Art Gallery, Liverpool (2013); The Mariners Gallery, St. Ives, Cornwall (2013). Solo exhibition: Plymouth BAS7 Fringe (2011). *Works in collections*: UK and abroad. *Commissions*: UK and Europe. *Publications*: "Zooz, the Boy from Space" (Oct 2014). The Guardian(2012), ABNA book (2012); British and Irish Artists of the 20th Century Artists Biographies (2013); local and regional newspapers. *Recreations*: Illustrator for children's books, clay work. *Clubs*: British Women Artists, Association of British Naive Artists, Plymouth Flameworks, Devon Artsts Network. *Misc*: Founder of Whitleigh Arts, Plymouth, Devon. UK representative of www.naivepainters.com *Address*: 94 Lancaster Gardens, Plymouth PL5 4AE. *Email*: artbysandywager@gmail.com *Website*: http://artbysandywager.weebly.com *Signs work*: "Sandy Wager".

WAGH, Ibrahim, PGDip Ceramics (1989); Silver medal and cash prize in Bombay Art Society Annual Exhibition (1961); First prize in the final year of studies at the Sir JJ School of Art Annual Exhibition; Post Graduate Diploma in Ceramics (1989); Awarded the Sir Mark Turner Scholarship to attend Banff Art Centre, Canada as artist-in-residence (1990). *Medium*: Oil; sculpture; paper ceramics. *b*: Bombay, India, 1 Nov 1932. *Studied*: Sir JJ School of Art, Bombay; Central School of Art, London; London College of Printing and Graphic Art; John Cass School of Art; Goldsmiths College. *Exhib*: Solo shows include: Jehanqier Art Gallery, Bombay (1961); Richmond Hill Art Gallery (1971); The Other Gallery, Banff, Canada (1990); Windsor Art Gallery (1993, 1995); Radlett Art Gallery (1998, 2000, 2002). Group shows include: India House, London (1964); Mandeer Gallery, London (1974); Herbert Art Gallery and Museum, Coventry (1990); Affordable Art Fair, Battersea (2002, 2003). *Works in collections*: Herefordshire County Collection; International Ceramic Art, Tokoname, Japan; Banff Art Centre, Banff, Canada; Meghraj Bank, London. *Publications*: Includes: 'Amazing Paperclay' by Rosette Gault; Ceramic Review; Art Review; 'Humanoid', Beyond Frontiers (Saffron Publications). *Misc*: Developed paper ceramics during two years of research at Goldsmiths College in the late 1980s; Established IAUK Art Centre, London (1980-82); Organised and co-ordinated several exhibitions in the UK (1979-82). *Address*: 1 Strawberry Crescent, Napsbury Park, London Colney AL2 1US. *Email*: wagh1@btinternet.com

WAITE, Andrew Jon. *Medium*: Oil. *b*: Buckinghamshire, 7 Sep 1954. *Partner*: Karin Suhrbier. two *s*. one *d*. *Educ*: Sherborne, Dorset (1967-73). *Studied*: West Sussex College of Art and Design (1974-77). *Represented by*: Self. *Exhib*: Many galleries, UK. Annual open house exhibition at home, August, since 1989. *Works in collections*: Private. *Address*: 54 Tarrant Street, Arundel, West Sussex BN18 9DN. *Email*: andywaite@tiscali.co.uk *Website*: www.andywaite.net *Signs work*: "ANDY WAITE".

WAKEFIELD, Nicole, RCamA; BA (Hons) Fine Art (1983), PGCE (1991); artist in oil, pastel, acrylic, clay; teacher. Member of the Royal Cambrian Academy. Art teacher in school for special education needs 1992+. *b*: Manchester, 27 Oct 1960. *Studied*: Wolverhampton (1980-83), Blackburn (1979-80), Bangor (1991-92). *Exhib*: RCamA, Royal Cambrian Academy, Penrhyn Castle and locally. *Clubs*: local mountain clubs, drama groups. *Address*: 2 Tan y Bonc,. Valley Rd., Llanfairfechan, Conwy LL33 0ET. *Email*: nicolewakefield@btinternet.com Website: www.nicolewakefield.co.uk *Signs work*: "Nicole."

WALCH, Kenneth Charles Crosby, NDD (1955); artist in oil, garden design; former AE art tutor with ILEA Hounslow, Bognor. *Medium*: oil, mainly. *b*: Wimbledon, 16 Sep 1927.

m: Olive Winifred (decd). *Educ*: Bradfield College. *Studied*: National Gallery Art School, Melbourne (1952-53, Murray Griffin), St. Martin's School of Art (1953-55, Bateson Mason, F. Gore). *Exhib*: Belgium (Hof de Bist), London, Germany (Unna), Hong Kong (Nishiki), Dublin; John Batten Gallery, Hong Kong. *Works in collections*: Hof de Bist, Antwerp, Chichester Centre of Arts; private collections in U.K., Europe, America, Australia, Quaker International Centre, Byng Place, London, Nuffield Hospital, Chichester, St. Winifreds Hospice, Chichester. *Official Purchasers*: Agent John Stocks, Horsham. *Works Reproduced*: drawing of Rothesay Church N.B.-End Papers, Hong Kong Dairy, The Milky Way. *Principal Works*: 4 Views from Pallant House; Historical Time Chart. *Recreations*: essays and letters. *Clubs*: Chichester Centre of Arts, Friends of Pallant Ho. *Address*: 193 Oving Rd., Chichester, W. Sussex PO19 4ER. *Signs work*: in block letters with pencil into wet paint, or scratched or black marker. Future signature "K.WILMOT WALCH".

WALCOTT-YATES, Yvonne Veronica, painter in oil and alkyd on canvas, pastel on paper. *b*: Lincoln, 2 Oct 1954. *d of*: Windell Oliver Walcott, RAF Civil Service retd, now Clr Conservative. *m*: David Yates. *Educ*: St. John's School, Episkopi, Cyprus. *Exhib*: Mall Galleries, FPS, Loggia Gallery, NSPS (1982), Manchester Academy, Commonwealth Inst; one-man shows: Bagazzo Gallery Marlborough, Loggia Gallery, etc. *Works in collections*: Bath Rd. Gallery, Old Town, Swindon and numerous private collections including Jamaica, Canada and Japan. *Address*: The New House, Ascott, Shipston-on-Stour, Warwickshire CV36 5PP. *Signs work*: "Habgood". (paintings signed as Habgood).

WALDEN, Lynne. *Medium*: Watercolour; pastels. *b*: Lewisham, 13 Nov 1938. two *s*. one *d*. *Exhib*: Gravesend Art Group Annual Exhibition at St Andrews Art Centre; Mariners Gallery, St. Ives. *Publications*: My Life in Naive Art and Poetry. *Clubs*: Life member of Gravesend Art Group; life member of ABNA. *Address*: 3 Mead Road, Gravesend, Kent DA11 7PP. *Website*: www.britishnaives.co.uk

WALDING, Barry Jeffrey, Former full member of The Guild of Railway Artists. *Medium*: oil, acrylic, gouache, drawing, prints. *b*: N. Bristol, 23 Dec 1945. *m*: Margaret Jean. *Educ*: Apprentice draughtsman, Rolls-Royce, Bristol; Mechanical Engineering Technicians Course (Aero, Bristol), later Graphic Design Artist & Illustrator. *Studied*: self-taught artist. *Exhib*: GRA York (NRM), Bury Museum, Bristol (Wildlife Art Society); 3 major one-man exhibitions, Slimbridge, Wildfowl Wetlands Trust; Artist-in-Residence, Nature in Art Museum, Glos., on three occasions. *Works in collections*: RNAS Station, Yeovilton; Rolls-Royce Museum, R-R Bristol; Bristol Aero collection; private USA collection, Dallas, Texas & private collectors. *Commissions*: 501 Squadron, Brize Norton; Battle of Britain Memorial Flight x2, 100s of private commissions including landscape and portraiture. *Publications*: illustrations for books & book jackets. *Official Purchasers*: raising monies for RAF Benevolent Fund; some architectural work. *Works Reproduced*: wildlife, landscape, aircraft, steam locomotive. *Principal Works*: as above inc. portraiture. *Recreations*: painting en-plein-air, music, walking, aero modelling. *Misc*: exhibited at Slimbridge (July 2010) "Wildlife & Landscape", further invitation to be Artist-in-Residence NIA Glos 2012. *Address*: 36 Cherry Orchard, Wotton-under-Edge, Gloucester GL12 7HT. *Signs work*: "Barry Walding".

WALDRON, Dylan Thomas, RBSA; BA Hons Art & Design. *Medium*: artist in egg tempera, acrylic, pencil, silverpoint, watercolour and gouache. *b*: Newcastle-under-Lyme, 21 Aug 1953. *s of*: the late Jack L. Waldron, sculptor and lecturer in fine art. *m*: Susan Dorothy Ann Waldron. *Educ*: King Edward VI Grammar School, Stourbridge. *Studied*: Stourbridge College of Art (1971-72), Wolverhampton Polytechnic, Faculty of Art and Design (1972-76). *Represented by*: Goldmark Gallery. *Exhib*: RA Summer Exhbn. (1983-2013), Piccadilly Gallery, Cork St., London (1981-96), Mall Galleries, London (1988-2003), Goldmark Gallery (1986-2014). *Works in collections*: West Midlands Arts, Basildon Arts Trust, University of

Leicster, RBSA Permanent Collection. Private collections worldwide. *Publications*: Buckman Directory of British Artists Since 1945, The Public Catalogue Foundation. *Works Reproduced*: The Public Catalogue Foundation, oil paintings in public ownership, Essex. *Recreations*: country walking, running, cycling, gardening, music, literature, theatre. *Clubs*: Royal Birmingham Society of Artists, Leicester Soc. of Artists. *Address*: 2 Hallaton Rd., Slawston, nr. Market Harborough, Leics LE16 7UA. *Email*: dylan.waldron1@hotmail.co.uk *Website*: www.dylanwaldronartist.co.uk www.dylanwaldron.co.uk *Signs work*: "Dylan Waldron" paintings initialled "D.W."

WALES, Patricia Ann, SWA (1995), SFP (1997); artist in water-colour - flower paintings. *b*: Hamilton, Ontario, 27 Feb 1933. *m*: Graham Wales. two *s*. *Exhib*: London, Paris, Sweden and Wessex Region. *Works in collections*: paintings in private collections in Australia, Americas and Western Europe. *Works Reproduced*: greetings cards. *Clubs*: Lymington Art Group, Lyndhurst Art Group, Lymington Palette. *Address*: Willowbank, Widden Close, Sway, Hants SO41 6AX.

WALKDEN, Paul, Hon. Lay Member SWLA (2009); Founder Member of Nature in Art; Art Consultant to Wildfowl and Wetlands Trust; Art Adviser to Wildfowl and Wetlands Trust, and British Association of Shooting & Conservation (BASC), Elected Vice President BASC 2012; Art Adviser to Wildlife Habitat Trust. UK duck Stamp programme 1993 to date. *Medium*: consultant/adviser. *b*: Huddersfield, 3 Nov 1952. *m*: Suzanne Dorothy. one *s*. one *d*. *Publications*: Book: "Wild Geese of the Newgrounds" (about Peter Scott & WWT, 2009); Peter Scott's bibliographer, & wrote biography for DNB; Book 'Countrywise - The Language of the Countryside' with John Dryden (2010); various articles on Wildlife Art & Conservation; TV Presenter (Country Matters). *Misc*: Exhibitions organised: Terence Lambert Retrospective exhibition 1999 (Oriel Ynys Mon, Anglesey; MoMA Machynlleth; Wildfowl & Wetlands Trust, Llanelli); SWLA Founder Members Show to celebrate its 40 years; Nature in Art, 2003 (Gloucester). *Address*: 4 Watts Close, Station Road, Berkeley, Glos. GL13 9EQ. *Email*: paul_walkden@hotmail.com

WALKER, Edward Donald, marine artist, publisher; owner, Sumar Publications. *Medium*: oils, watercolour. *b*: 2 Aug 1937. *s of*: A.E. Walker, ship constructor. *m*: Susan. one *s*. one *d*. *Educ*: Warbreck School, Liverpool. *Studied*: Liverpool College of Art (1950-56). *Exhib*: RSMA, Paris Salon, Talbot Gallery, Ethos Gallery, Lancs., Harrods London, Fulmar Gallery, N. Wales, McEwan Gallery, Ballater, Scotland and galleries throughout USA. Major one-man exhibition at Williamson Art Gallery & Museum, Birkenhead, Wirral. *Works in collections*: Liverpool Museum; private and public collections worldwide. *Commissions*: from Cunard Steamship co., Royal Mail, Museum Science and Industry Chicago USA, Merseyside Maritime Museum. Official Artist for RMS Titanic Touring Artefacts Exhbn. *Publications*: "Sea Liverpool", "Titanic". *Official Purchasers*: Cunard. *Address*: 1 Richmond Grove, Lydiate, Merseyside L31 0BL. *Email*: info@edwalkermarine.com *Website*: www.edwalkermarine.com *Signs work*: "E.D. Walker."

WALKER, Leigh Diane, BA (1st Class Hons), MFA; Royal Scottish Academy Latimer Award (2006), The Derwent Award (2005), Hope Scott Trust Award (2005), Andrew Grant Bequest (2004), Ken Cowley Award (1999), Australian Sunday Mail Commended (1998), Great Universal Stores Award (1998), Macallan Award (1997). *Medium:* acrylics, drawing, prints. *b:* Irvine, Scotland, 23 Sep 1974. *d of:* William & Elise Walker. *m:* Roger Scott Barnes. one *d. Studied:* Edinburgh College of Art (1993-97, 2004-06), Ecole des Beaux Arts, Strasbourg (1996). *Exhib:* Contemporary Scottish Art, The Chambers Gallery, London (2006); RSA 180th Annual Exhibition (2006); Atkinson Gallery, Somerset (2006); RSA Open (2004, 2005); Society of Graphic Fine Art (2005, 2006); Singer & Friedlander/Sunday Times Watercolour Competition (2005); Edinburgh College of Art Degree Show (1997, 2005, 2006); RSA Student Exhibition (1996, 2005); 'Fromage et Frottage', Evolution

House, Edinburgh (2005); Talbot Rice Gallery, University of Edinburgh (2004); Manchester Academy of Fine Arts (2004); Philips Gallery, Manchester (2003, 2004); Orleans House Gallery, Twickenham (2004); 'Art London 2003'; BP Portrait Award (2000, 2001); The Scottish Gallery, Edinburgh (2002); Compass Gallery (2002/2003), Scottish Portrait Exhibition, RSA (1997); Affordable Art Fair, New York (2002). *Works in collections:* Scottish Equitable, South Ayrshire Council, Livingstone, Batnes & Cunninghame Construction. *Commissions:* South Ayrshire Council; Philips Gallery, Manchester; Satow, Edinburgh; MacDonnel/De Laszlo, London; Simmons, London. *Official Purchasers:* Scottish Equitable, South Ayrshire Council. *Principal Works:* 'The Brides' acrylic on canvas; 'Bye' acrylic on canvas, landscape diptych. *Recreations:* walking, reading, yoga. *Address:* 39 Letham Rise, Dalgety Bay, Fife, Scotland KY11 9FW. *Email:* leighdwalker@hotmail.com *Signs work:* "LEIGH D.WALKER".

WALKER, Roy, ARE (1975); painter/etcher; Director, Print Workshop, Penwith Society of Arts, St. Ives, Cornwall. *b:* Welling, Kent, 25 Aug 1936. *s of:* Edwin James Walker. *m:* Margaret Anne Walker. two *s.* one *d. Studied:* Gravesend School of Art (1951-52), Regent St. Polytechnic (1952-54); Central School of Art (1957-60). *Exhib:* one-man shows: Camel Gallery, Wadebridge, Orion Gallery, Penzance, Plymouth Art Centre; three-man show: Marlborough Graphics; joint shows: Penwith Society of Arts, Wills Lane Gallery, St. Ives, Newlyn Gallery. *Works in collections:* Print Room, V&A. *Misc:* Studio: 6 Porthmeor Studios, Back Rd. West, St. Ives. *Address:* Warwick House, Sea View Terr., St. Ives, Cornwall. *Signs work:* "Roy Walker.".

WALKER, Sandra, RI; artist in water-colour. *b:* Washington DC, USA. two *s.* one *d. Exhib:* many mixed and one-man shows: Singer & Friendlander (1st Prize); RI, RWS, RBA, Galerie Mensch, Hamburg; Bourne Gallery; Mall Galleries; Watermans, London; Gallery Henoch, NY, USA, Franz Bader Gallery, Wash. DC, Corcoran Gallery, Wash. DC, Smithsonian Inst., Wash. DC, National Geographic, Wash. DC, Tregastel Salon International de la Peinture a l'Eau, France, Curzon Gallery, Wimbledon. *Works in collections:* John Le Carré, Senator Edward M. Kennedy, Senator George McGovern, Wall St. Journal; National Geographic Soc., Washington DC, Baroness Thatcher. *Commissions:* Baroness Thatcher: print of Parliament. *Publications:* work illustrated in: "Water-colour Step by Step" (Harper Collins, 1993), "How to Draw and Paint Texture" (Harper Collins, 1993), "Collins Complete Painting Course" (Harper Collins, 1993), "Shapes and Edges" (Sandstone Books, 1996), "Houses and Buildings" (Cassells Press, 1991). *Clubs:* Arts Club, London. *Misc:* Designer of President's Medal of Freedom honouring Simon Weisenthal (U.S. Mint). *Address:* 39 Stewkley Rd., Wing, Leighton Buzzard, Beds. LU7 0NJ.

WALKLIN, Carol, MA, RCA (1953), RE (1986); graphic artist and printmaker. *Medium:* wood and lino-cuts - etching. *b:* 10 Jun 1930. *m:* Colin, ARCA, co-Director 'Mullet Press'; tutor-lecturer in printmaking. *Studied:* Beckenham School of Art and Royal College of Art (Graphic Design. *Exhib:* widely in UK including Bankside Gallery and Mall Galleries, London, Royal Academy Summer Exhibition. *Works in collections:* National Portrait Gallery, London; UK, USA and Europe. *Commissions:* BBC TV 'Jackanory', Post Office UK (stamp designs and air letters). *Clubs:* Senior Fellow, Royal Soc. of Painter-Printmakers. *Address:* 2 Thornton Dene, Beckenham, Kent BR3 3ND. *Email:* colinwalklin@btinternet.com *Signs work:* "Walklin."

WALL, Jacy, BA Constructed Textiles, MA Multi-disciplinary Printmaking; Theo Moorman Trust for Weavers Award (1994, 2008); Arts Council England G4A Award 'The Nature of Mending' (2012). *Medium*: woven tapestry. *b*: London, 28 Aug 1952. *m*: Brian Rice. *Educ*: Bedales School. *Studied*: Middlesex Polytechnic (BA 1976/9); UWE, Bristol (MA, 1999-2002). *Represented by*: Own studio. *Exhib*:University Gallery, Leeds (2001); 'Footsteps' Walford Mill, Dorset & National Tour (2004/6); Black Swan Arts, Frome (2006,

2009); Atrium Gallery, Bournemouth University (2008); Stroud International Textile Festival (2009); Impact Print Conference, Bristol (2009); Walford Mill 'The Journey Exploring the Nature of Mending' (2013); Barrington Court 'Make the Most' (2013). *Works in collections*: private. *Commissions*: NMB Bank, Amsterdam; National Grid Plc; Somerset Health Authority; private clients. *Official Purchasers*: Somerset Health Authority 1998. *Works Reproduced*: 'A Legacy in Weaving' ISBN 1874331 26X. *Recreations*: walking, reading. *Misc*: 1992-8: developed 'Art for Life', Musgrove Park Hospital, Taunton; Trustee Thoe Moorman Trust for Weavers (2014-). *Address*: Newhouse, Hewood, Chard TA20 4NP. *Email*: jacy.wall@btinternet.com *Website*: www.jacywall.co.uk *Signs work*: "JACY WALL".

WALLACE, Donald Ian Mackenzie, SWLA: GCE: A (Art), BA (Economics, Law), Cantab.; artist in pencil, ink, gouache; author. *b:* Gt. Yarmouth, 14 Dec 1933. *m:* Wendy. three *d. Educ:* Loretto School; Clare College, Cambridge. *Exhib:* SWLA (annually). *Commissions:* several annually; roughs supplied free. *Publications:* Birds of the Western Palearctic (Field Characters, plates); six other books, including 'Beguiled by Birds' (2004); many papers. *Recreations:* natural history; wilderness; R&B. *Address:* Mount Pleasant Farm, Main Rd., Anslow, Burton-on-Trent, E. Staffs. DE13 9QE. *Email:* wcwallace@hotmail.co.uk *Signs work:* "dim wallace."

WALLER, Jonathan Neil, BA (Hons), MA (Painting). *Medium:* mixed media. *b:* Stratford upon Avon, 16 Apr 1956. two *d. Studied:* Nene College, Northampton (1979-80), Coventry (Lanchester) Polytechnic (1980-83), Chelsea School of Art (1984-85). *Exhib:* one-man shows: Paton Gallery, London (1986, 1988), Flowers East, London (1990, 1992, 1993, 1994), New End Gallery, London (1997), Axiom, Cheltenham (1998), Lancaster Gallery, Coventry (2003), Jonathan Waller's True Adventures, National Maritime Museum, Cornwall (2005), touring to Arlington Gallery, London (2006); group shows: 1984: New Contemporaries, I.C.A. London, Midland View 3 (major prizewinner), 1988: London, Glasgow, N.Y., Metropolitan Museum, N.Y., New British Painting, Cincinnati (touring), 1991: Kunst Europa, Karlsruhe, Germany. *Works in collections:* Tate Gallery, London; Metropolitan Museum, N.Y. *Commissions:* Art on the Underground (1994), Heathrow Airport (1995). *Publications:* Jonathan Waller (Flowers East, 1990); Jonathan Waller's True Adventures (NMMC, 2005). *Address:* 35 Campbell Road, Walthamstow, London E17 6RR. *Email:* j.waller@coventry.ac.uk *Website:* www.geocites.com/jonathanwalleruk *Signs work:* "J.W.2001."

WALLIS, Linda Joyce, SWA (1994), SBA, (1999); artist in oil. *b:* 20 Sep 1940. *m:* Howard. one *s.* two *d. Studied:* largely self taught, local evening class, and Verrochio Art Centre, Casole d'Elsa. *Exhib:* Guildhall, Royal Exchange, Westminster Gallery, Mall Galleries and many provincial galleries. *Works in collections:* America, Canada, Japan. *Works Reproduced:* CD covers, Limited Edn. prints, Medici cards. *Clubs:* Epsom and Ewell Art Group, Croydon Art Soc., Carshalton and Wallington, Oxshott. *Address:* 25 Langton Ave., Ewell, Surrey KT17 1LD. *Email:* lindawallisart@yahoo.co.uk *Signs work:* "WALLIS."

WALTER, Stephen, MA RCA Fine Art Print, Jerwood Drawing Prize (2nd) (2004); Tim Mara Charitable Trust (RCA) (2001); Daler Rowney Drawing Prize (RCA) (2001). *Medium:* drawing, prints, photography and painting. *b:* London, 7 Oct 1975. *Educ:* Queen Elizabeth's Boys School, Barnet. *Studied:* Middlesex University; Manchester Met. University; RCA. *Exhib:* selected shows: RA Summer Exhbn (2005); Foster Art Summer Show (2005); The Lab, San Francisco, USA (2005); solo shows: Vertigo Gallery, The Drawing Gallery. *Works in collections:* The British Museum, Deutsche Bank (London), The Houses of Parliament Museums; Trussardi Foundation (Milan). *Commissions:* Queen Elizabeth's School for Boys, Barnet. *Publications:* RA Summer Exhibition Illustrated Catalogue (2005); Jerwood Drawing Prize Catalogue (2004). *Works Reproduced:* RA

Summer Exhibition Illustrated Catalogue (2005). *Principal Works:* Throw Away After Use (A London Town), 2002-2004. *Recreations:* music (guitar, DJ-ing), golf, football. *Address:* 144 Brooke Road, Stoke Newington, London N16 7RR. *Email:* contact@stephenwalter.net *Website:* www.stephenwalter.net *Signs work:* 'Stephen Walter'

WALTERS, Juliet, NC Ceramic Design; HNC Ceramic Design. *Medium*: Ceramic Sculpture. *b*: Redhill, Surrey, 18 Aug 1962. *m*: Mark Philip Walters. one *s*. one *d*. *Educ*: Dunottar School, Reigate. *Studied*: South Thames College. *Exhib*: Ceramic art shows include: Art in Clay, Hatfield; Art in Clay, Farnham; Rutford: Earth & Fire; Art in Action, Waterperry House. *Commissions*: private commissions. *Publications*: Ceramic Review, Marie Claire, Homes & Gardens, London Potters Newsletter, Contemporary Potters Association magazine. *Address*: Studio 4N5, Phoenix Brighton, 10-14 Waterloo Place, Brighton BN2 9NB. *Email*: mail@julietwalters.co.uk *Website*: www.julietwalters.co.uk *Signs work*: "JW" as monogram inside square.

WALTERS, Kate, BA (Hons) Fine Art 2:1; two awards from ACE for development of practice; one award from Juliet Gomperts Trust. *Medium:* drawings in watercolour and oil paintings. *b:* London, 1958. one *s*. *Educ*: Byam Shaw, London (1976-77). *Studied:* Brighton College of Art (1978-81), Falmouth College of Art (1966-2000). *Represented by*: Millenium, New Schoolhouse Gallery and Arusha Gallery. *Exhib:* ICA, Raw Art, Millfield, Laing, Beatrice Royal, Goldfish Fine Art, Discerning Eye, Jerwood Drawing Prize (2003, 2008), Sefton Open, The Exchange & Newlyn Art Galleries, Penzance; Kube, Poole (2010), Truro Cathedral (2010), solo show (2012/13) Newlyn Art Gallery, Cornwall. *Works in collections:* private: UK and Europe. *Publications:* several catalogues; essay by Prof. Penny Florence entitled 'Becoming Sanguine'; review by Laura Gascoigne in 'Galleries' 2008. *Recreations:* walking in Italy, wild places. *Clubs*: member Newlyn Society of Artists. *Address:* 6 Tremenheere Road, Penzance, Cornwall, TR18 2AH. *Email:* kate.horse@tiscali.co.uk *Website:* www.katewalters.co.uk

WALTON, Barbara Louise, MFA (Hons.) (1981), Post.Grad. Dip. Painting and Drawing (1982); painter in oil and acrylic paint on canvas and paper. *b:* Bishop Auckland, 30 Dec 1955. *d of:* Martin and Mavis Walton, teachers. *m:* Dursun Cilingir, doctor. *Educ:* Queen Anne Grammar School. *Studied:* Edinburgh University/College of Art (Elizabeth Blackadder, David Michie). *Exhib:* York University (1982), Gloucester College of Art (1983), Paisley Art Inst. drawing competition (1987), N.P.G. portrait competition (1987, 1989), Mall Galleries Open (1989); solo shows: Mercury Gallery (1988, 1993), Grape Lane Gallery, York (1989); regular exhib. with Mercury Gallery since 1986. *Address:* 31 St. John's Rd., Exeter EX1 2HR. *Signs work:* "B.L. Walton".

WALTON, John, DFA (Lond. 1949), RP (1976); portrait painter in oil and tempera; Principal, Heatherley School of Fine Art, London; Governor, Federation of British Artists, Mem., Royal Soc of Portrait Painters. *b:* Birkenhead, 5 Dec 1925. *s of:* Eric Walton. *m:* (1) Annette d'Exéa. two *s*. one *d*. (2) Alice Low. *Educ:* Birkenhead School, Edge Grove School, Aldenham School. *Studied:* Ruskin School of Fine Art (1944-45, Albert Rutherston), Slade School of Fine Art (1945-49, Randolph Schwabe). *Represented by*: Royal Society of Portrait Painters; www.therp.co.uk/rpartists/artistjohnwalton. *Exhib:* RA, RP, Paris Salon (Hon. mention), Academie des Beaux Arts, Institut de France. *Clubs:* Chelsea Arts. *Address:* 30 Park Rd., Radlett, Herts. WD7 8EQ. *Email*: johnwalton.rp@internet.com *Website*: www.therp.co.uk/rpartists/artistjohnwalton *Signs work:* "John Walton."

WANG, Elizabeth, FSBA (1987); Founder mem. Soc. of Botanical Artists, Medalife Art award (1990); artist in water-colour, oil, pencil, writer. *b:* Slough, 24 Aug 1942. *m:* M.K. Wang. two *s*. one *d*. *Educ:* Dr. Challoner's Grammar School, Amersham. *Studied:* part-time at St. Albans College of Art. *Exhib:* FBA Mall Galleries; mixed shows: still-life and botanical works: SBA, RA, RI, Fine Art (Solihull); solo shows: recent religious works: Harpenden, Westminster Cathedral, Bar Convent Museum, York, St. Paul's Conference Rooms, Westminster, The French Church, London (Leicester Square). *Works in collections:* numerous private collections. *Commissions:* numerous private commissions until approx. 1993 when I decided only to do my own themes, and to halt all sales. *Publications:* illustrated: The Way of the Cross (Collins Liturgical 1988); written and illustrated: Teachings in Prayer, Vols. 1-4 (Radiant Light, 1999), My Priests are Sacred (Radiant Light, 1999), How to Pray (Radiant Light, 1999). *Works Reproduced:* by The Bridgeman Art Library, USA. *Principal Works:* The Mass Paintings. *Address:* 25 Rothamsted Ave., Harpenden, Herts. AL5 2DN. *Email:* mail@radiantlight.org.uk *Website:* www.radiantlight.org.uk *Signs work:* "Wang" or "E.W."

WANLESS, Tom, NDD (1957), DAE (1970), M.Ed. (1974), ROI (1996), RBA (1997); Prizes: Cornelissen Award (ROI,1994), Charles Pears Award (RSMA,1994), Roberson Award (ROI,1996), Sir William Ramsay Award (RBA 2002/2006); artist/printmaker in oil, water-colour and etching. *b:* Philadelphia, Co. Durham, 19 Jul 1929. *m:* Marjorie. one *d.* *Studied:* Bede College (1946-48), Sunderland College of Art (1952-57), Bristol University (1970-74, post graduate). *Exhib:* regular exhibitor in London and regional galleries; one-man/ group shows: Zillah Bell Gallery (Thirsk); Russell Gallery (London); Walker Gallery (Harrogate); Blake Gallery (York); Red Rag Gallery (Stow). *Works in collections:* UK, Europe, N. America and Australia. *Publications:* illustrated educational books for Collins, Schofield & Sims, and Harraps (1958-89). Featured artist in 'The Artist' (1997), 'International Artist' (2005). *Official Purchasers:* Provident Financial plc, MBNA, Paintings in Hospitals, Brighton West Pier Trust; Scarborough Art Gallery; Leeds City Council. *Clubs:* ROI, RBA. *Address:* 41 Badgerwood Glade, Wetherby, W. Yorks. LS22 7XR. *Email:* t.b.wanless@btinternet.com *Website:* www.t.b.wanless.btinternet.co.uk *Signs work:* "T. Wanless.".

WARD, Benjamin Gordon Tobias, NEAC; Richard Ford Award. *Medium*: oil, watercolour, pastel, drawing. *b*: Ashford, Kent, 12 Nov 1965. *m*: Alison Ward. two *s*. one *d*. *Educ*: Kings School, Canterbury; RMA Sandhurst. *Studied*: City & Guilds of London Art School 1992-1996. *Represented by*: Catto Gallery; Fine Art Commissions Ltd. *Exhib*: Ardean Gallery, Catto Gallery, New English Art Club, Discerning Eye, Royal Museum Canterbury. *Works in collections*; Royal Collection, Royal Academy, Brindsley Ford, National Trust, Royal Opera House, Athenaeum Club, Merlers' Company. *Commissions*: portraits: HRH Duke of Edinburgh; Lord Rothermere; Sir Sydney Kentridge. Drawings: Record the rebuild of The Royal Opera House, renewal of St-Martin-in-the-Fields. *Publications*: Illustrated "Shooting Leave" and "Sabres on the Steppes" (pub. Constable & Robinson). *Official Purchasers*: National Army Museum, City & Guilds Institute. *Principal Works*: Giro II, King of the Hill. *Recreations*: cycling, European travel. *Clubs*: New English Art Club, Garrick Club. *Address*: Westward House, Hartley Road, Cranbrook TN17 3QP. *Email*: toby@tobyward.net *Website*: www.tobyward.net *Signs work*: "Toby Ward".

WARD. Claire Kathleen, SBA; SBA DLDC Distinction. *Medium*: watercolour, pastel, gouache, drawing. *b*: Johannesburg, SA, 1969. *m*: Dominic. two *s*. *Studied*: SBA - Society of Botanical Artists Distance Learning Diploma. *Exhib*: MoMA Wales, Machynlleth (mixed exhibition); Central Hall Westminster, London (SBA). *Address*: Llanafan, Aberystwyth, Ceredigion SY23 5AY. *Email*: ckbotanica@googlemail.com *Website*: www.claireward.net

WARD, Eric Thomas. *Medium:* oil, watercolour, drawing, prints. *b:* St.Ives, Cornwall, 20 Nov 1945. *s of:* Tom Ward. *m:* Karen Ward. two *s*. *Educ:* Hayle Grammar School, Cornwall. *Studied:* St. Ives School of Painting (1986-90). *Represented by:* New Gallery, Portscatho, Cornwall. *Exhib:* solo: MONMA Gallery, Japan (2009), Waterside Gallery (2006), Coves Quay Gallery, Salcombe (2003-6), Fowey River Gallery (2004), Belgrave

Gallery, St. Ives (2004), Glasshouse Gallery, Truro (2002), Out of the Blue, Marazion (2001), Tregony Gallery (1999), The One Below Gallery, London (1998), Mid Cornwall Galleries, St. Austell (1997), Sims Gallery, St. Ives (1994), Hallam Gallery, London (1989). Mixed exhibitions across UK and Europe. *Works in collections:* Penlee House Museum, Penzance; Grey College, Durham University; Westfield Grant Maintained School; Royal Cornwall Museum. *Commissions:* numerous. *Publications:* "Eric Ward, St. Ives from His Studio and Beyond" (Halsgrove Press, 2003); "Eric Ward, Painting in Cornwall and across the Tamar" (2013). *Clubs:* Chelsea Arts Club, London. *Misc:* Joined RNLI as St. Ives Lifeboatman in 1964, promoted to Coxwain in 1989, retired after 34 years of service in 2000. *Address:* 5 Ocean View Terrace, St.Ives, Cornwall, TR26 1RQ. *Email:* wardthp@aol.com *Website:* www.ericward.org *Signs work:* "ERIC WARD".

WARD, Gordon, DFA Lond., RWA; artist in all mediums; formerly Head of Painting, Gloucestershire College of Arts and Technology. *b:* N. Walsham, Norfolk, 1932. *s of:* William Ward. *m:* Maureen Liddell. one *s.* two *d. Educ:* Paston Grammar School, N. Walsham, Norfolk. *Studied:* Norwich School of Art (1949-53), Slade School of U.C.L. (1955-57). *Works in collections:* Royal West of England Academy, Robert Fleming Holdings, The Royal Bank of Scotland, Prudential Assurance and various private collections in Europe, America and Australia. *Address:* Prospect House, Oakridge Lynch, Stroud, Glos. GL6 7NZ. *Signs work:* "GORDON WARD" and date.

WARD, Michael Lawrence, 1st Class Hons Fine Art Painting, HDFA Lond. *Medium:* mixed media, oil. *b:* Barrow-in-Furness, 9 Feb 1952. *s of:* Clifford and Marjorie. *Partner:* Rosemarie Hayden. two *s.* one *d. Studied:* Manchester Polytechnic, Ravensbourne, Slade School. *Exhib:* Oriel Cardiff, Battersea Arts Centre, Fitzwilliam Museum Cambridge; White Space, London; Leeds City Gallery; Talbot Rice, Edinburgh; MoMA Oxford; Royal Academy, London; Walker Liverpool. *Works in collections:* Weisman Foundation Los Angeles, USA; Simkin Estate, San Diego; Science Museum, London. *Works Reproduced:* Pandemonium; Bandits. *Recreations:* horse racing, snooker, physics. *Address:* 121 Tooting Bec Road, London SW17 8BW. *Email:* michaellward@btinternet.com *Website:* www.michaelwardstuff.com *Signs work:* 'M.Ward' or monogram.

WARD, Nicholas, DipAD (1971), RA Schools (1974), RE (1992); David Murray Landscape Scolarship (1972), Eric Kennington Award (1973), Duff Greet Silver Medal (1973); Clark Consultancy Award (1988). *Medium:* etching, pencil, pen and ink, watercolour. *b:* Gt. Yarmouth, 10 Jan 1950. *m:* Elizabeth Somerville. one *s. Educ:* Lowestoft County Grammar School. *Studied:* Lowestoft School of Art (1967-68), St. Martin's School of Art (1968-71, Alan Cooper, James Stroudley), R.A. Schools (1971-74, Denis Lucas, Peter Greenham. *Exhib:* RA Summer Shows (1982, 1984-87, 1990, 1994), RE Annual (1988-2003), British Miniature Print (1989, 1994, 1997), Bradford Print Biennale (1990), National Print Exhbn. (1995-2003); one-man shows 1974-97. Triennale Mondiale D'Estampes Petit Format (1994), Bircham Gallery, Holt, Norfolk (1991-). *Works in collections:* Norfolk Museums, Ipswich Museum, British Railways Board. *Publications:* BP Petroleum Development Ltd. (1987, 88, 89), Print Collectors Club (1991), National Grid (1994). *Address:* 38 Bulmer La., Winterton-on-Sea, Gt. Yarmouth, Norfolk NR29 4AF. *Signs work:* "N. Ward."

WARDEN, Peter Campbell, ARBA (1982), RBA (1994), DA (1976), Post. Dip. (1977); award, Robert Colquhoun (1976); 1st prize Devon and Cornwall Figurative Art competition (1992); painter in oil, water-colour, pen, pencil. *b*: Vancouver, Canada, 19 Mar 1950. *s of:* Jack & Doreen Warden. one *d. Educ:* Lancing College. *Studied:* Glasgow School of Art (1972-77). *Exhib:* RA, RBA, RSA, RGI, RSW, NEAC, RWA, RBSA; one-man shows: Malaga, Marbella, Dumfries, Sterts. *Works in collections:* Kilmarnock and Loudon D.C.; Sociedad Economica, Malaga. *Works Reproduced:* various art magazines, books on techniques. *Address:* 62 St. Anne's Drive, Llantwit Fardre, Pontypridd, Mid Glam., CF38 2PD. *Email:* peterwardenpear@yahoo.com *Signs work:* "Peter C. Warden" and date.

WARDLE, Ralph Lewis, Diploma in Fine Art (London University 1960); Robert Ross Scholarship, Slade School; First Prize, Sunday Pictorial National Exhibition of Childrens' Art (1956). *Medium:* oil, prints. *b:* Doncaster, 17 May 1939. *m:* Ann. two *s. Studied:* Doncaster College of Art (1955); Slade School of Fine Art (1956). *Exhib:* Special Art Exhibition under Maurice de Sausmarez (1956); Royal Academy Summer Exhibitions; NEAC; The Lake Artists Society Summer Exhibition (member); Young Contemporaries (1957); Mall FBA Gallery. Artists Making Prints BITE (2011). *Works in collections:* Cooper Gallery, Barnsley - Exhibition of woodcuts; Graves Art Gallery, Sheffield; Cheshire Education Authority; Yorkshire Arts Association. *Publications:* 1956 Arts Reviews cover, lead article; 1989 Royal Academy Illustrated. *Principal Works:* woodcuts, paintings drawing. *Recreations:* music, football (Liverpool). *Address:* 20B Quarry Close, Kirkby Stephen, Cumbria, CA17 4SS.

WARMAN, Sylvia (Mrs.), Ass. des A. Francais; portrait sculptor and painter; Wells Prize in Fine Art Reading University (1952); Owen Ridley Prize in Fine Art Reading University (1954); Bronze Medal (Sculpture) Paris Salon (1969); Silver Medal (Sculpture) Paris Salon (1973); Gold Medal Accademia Italia (1981); Hon. Sec. National Society Painters, Sculptors Printmakers (1978-83) Vice-President (1984/5). *b:* St. Leonards on Sea, Sussex. *m:* J. Royce Warman. three *d. Studied:* Reading University (1947-54). *Exhib:* various including RA, London, and West of England RA, five times Paris Salon. *Commissions:* various. *Address:* 1 Chester St., Caversham, Reading RG4 8JH.

WARNER, Robert, artist in oil and water-colour. *b:* Colchester, 14 Sep 1947. *s of:* Harold Warner. *Studied:* Colchester Art School (1964-71, John Nash, Peter Coker). *Exhib:* ROI, NEAC, RI, RA Summer Exhibitions (1974-84, 1986, 1988, 1991, 1992, 1993, 2000, 2001, 2006, 2008), Athena Art Awards (1987), Hunting Group (1988), Sunday Times W/c Exhbns. (1988, 1990, 1996-99), Laing Art Competition (1990, 1991,1994, 1996), Discerning Eye (2003) Mall Galleries, prizewinner 32nd Essex Open 35th best water-colour; one-man shows: Minories, Colchester (1973), Mercury Theatre (1972, 1980, 1985), Chappel Gallery, Essex (2000). *Works in collections:* Epping Museum, private collections in Britain and America. *Works Reproduced:* RA Illustrated (1980, 1988, 2000). *Principal Works:* 'Yearly Excitement' (oil painting for which I had a postcard made to sell in the R.A. shop 2006-8). *Clubs:* Colchester Art. Soc. *Address:* St. Elmer, Queens Rd., W. Bergholt, Colchester, Essex CO6 3HE. *Signs work:* "R. Warner."

WARNER, Zheni. *Medium*: Oil and light features. *b*: Bourgas, Bulgaria, 21 Apr 1954. *m*: Tony Warner. one *s.* one *d. Studied*: Norwich School of Art (1967-7, 1978-81). *Represented by*: Galerie Last (Zurich); Jill Bishop Contemporary Art. *Exhib*: Royal Academy (2009); Thompson Gallery (2008); Grapevine Gallery, Norwich (solo 2007); Galerie Last, Zurich (2004); Centre d'Art Contemporaire, Reuen (1990); Espace Gambetta, Carcassonne (solo 1988); Cahill & Grebler, London (solo 1988); Manfred Schuler, Zurich (solo 1983); Marzia Frozen, Berlin (2014); Nordart 2012 (2013). *Works in collections*: National Gallery, Sofia; Addenbrooke's Hospital, Cambridge; Norwich and Norfolk Hospital. *Address*: 7 Abinger Way, Norwich NR4 6NA. *Email*: twarner@paston.co.uk *Website*: www.zheni.co.uk *Signs work*: "Zheni".

WARNES, Robin, PS; BA (Hons), RA Schools Cert. (Postgrad.); painter in oil, charcoal, pastel, acrylic, pencil; David Murray Studentship, Turner Gold medal for Landscape Painting (1980), regional prizewinner, Laing Landscape Exhbn. (1990); Artist in Residence, Ipswich Museums and Galleries (1989-90); Elected Member of Pastel Society 2012. *b:* Ipswich, 13 Mar 1952. *m:* Vanessa. two *s.* one *d. Studied:* Ipswich School of Art (1972-

74, Colin Moss), Canterbury College of Art (1974-77, Tom Watt), R.A. Schools (Peter Greenham, CBE, RA). *Exhib:* RA, Federation of British Artists, Laing Landscape, John Russell Gallery Ipswich, Cadogan Gallery London, Chappel Gallery Colchester. *Works in collections:* Ipswich Borough Council, Suffolk CC. *Commissions:* Richard Ellis Drawing commission. *Clubs:* Royal Academy Schools, Alumni Association. *Address:* 77 Rosehill Rd., Ipswich, Suffolk IP3 8ET. *Email:* robin@rwarnes.freeserve.co.uk *Signs work:* "R. Warnes" or "R.W.".

WARREN, Barbara, RHA (1989), Aosdana (1990); Certificate for South Kensington Drawing Exams, honours in all subjects (1941), Diploma in History of European Painting - Trinity College, Dublin (1955). *Medium*: oil painting, pastel, and gouache studies (previously lithography, etching). *b:* Dublin, 28 Aug 1925. *d of:* John Warren. *m:* William Carron, ARHA. one *d. Studied:* National College of Art, Dublin, Regent St. Polytechnic, London (with Norman Blaney, RA). Also in 1950s studied over a period of time with Andre L'Hote in Paris. *Represented by:* RHA, Taylor Galleries, 16 Dawson Street, Dublin. *Exhib:* solo: Dublin Painters Gallery (two shows, 1950s), Dawson Gallery, Dublin (1957, 1976, 1982, 1992), Taylor Galleries Dublin (3 shows). Many group shows in Ireland, England and Scotland. *Works in collections:* Ulster Museum, Irish Museum of Modern Art (Gordon Lambert Collection), Royal Bank of Scotland, National Self-Portrait Collection Limerick University, Haverty Trust, Boyle Civic Collection, Co. Roscommon. *Commissions:* Mosaic: St. Philip & St. James Church, Mt. Merrion, Black Rock, Co. Dublin. *Publications:* listed in succeeding catalogues Royal Hibernian Academy Dublin 2002, A Retrospective with essay by Dr. Julian Campbell (catalogue). *Works Reproduced:* Art of the State Exhibition, New Direction 1970-85 (Office of Public Works, 1998); Florence Biennale Italy Certificate and Medal (catalogue, 1999). *Recreations:* reading, gardening, photography. *Clubs:* RHA, Arts Club. *Misc:* over many years I have returned to work in the West of Ireland - all landscape studies. *Address:* Matakana, Gray's Lane, Howth, Co. Dublin, Eire. *Signs work:* 'B.Warren'.

WARREN, Michael John, NDD (1958), SWLA (1971). *b:* Wolverhampton, 26 Oct 1938. *s of:* Herbert Leslie Warren. *m:* Kathryne. one *s.* one *d. Educ:* Wolverhampton Grammar School. *Studied:* Wolverhampton College of Art (1954-58). *Exhib:* (recent): Wildlife Art Gallery, Lavenham, Suffolk, (2001/2003/2007/2010); Auditorium Sa Maniga, Cala Millor, Mallorca (2000), Conservatoire du Patrimoine Naturel de Savoie, Le Prieure, Le-Bourget-du Lac, France (2001), Casa da Cultura, Alpera, Albacete, Spain (2001), WWT London Wetland Centre (2002), Artists for Nature Foundation, Holland; Scottish Ornithologists'Club, Aberlady, East Lothian (2010); WWT Slimbridge, Glos (2011). *Works in collections:* Nature in Art. *Commissions:* 1985-87 Unicover Corporation USA, paintings from 50 States; 1990-92 Unicover / Ducks Unlimited USA, 50 paintings North American Wildfowl; Tarmac Calendar 1995-2001; work for RSPB. *Publications:* 1984: 'Shorelines', Hodder & Stoughton, London & Times Books, N.Y.; 1998: 'Field Sketches', Arlequin Press, Chelmsford, England; 1999: 'Langford Lowfields 1989-99', Arlequin Press, Chelmsford, England; 2001: 'Le Lac du Bourget' Gallimard, Conservatoire du Littoral, Paris, France; 2007: 'Images from Birding', Langford Press; 2012: 'USA Birding Sketchbook', Langford Press. *Recreations:* chess. *Clubs* Nottinghamshire Birdwatchers (President); Society of Wildlife Artists (treasurer). *Misc:* postage stamp designs: waterbirds – British Post Office (1980); Native & migratory birds, Republic of Marshall Islands (1990-92); conservation stamp designs: National Audubon Society, U.S.A. (1984-1997, 2001); U.K. Habitat Stamp (1996). *Address:* The Laurels, The Green, Winthorpe, Notts. NG24 2NR. *Email:* mike.warren@tiscali.co.uk *Website:* www.mikewarren.co.uk *Signs work:* "warren" (paintings), "Michael Warren" (prints).

WARREN, Valerie Florence, RBA, SWA, FSAI, SGFA (PP); BA (Hons) English Language & Literature. Diplomas in: Art & Architecture (University Prize), History of Art, Drama. *Medium*: watercolour, drawing, prints. *b*: London, 10 Aug 1929. *m*: David. one *d. Educ*: Minchenden Grammar. *Studied*: Bedford College for Women (London University).

Exhib: with RWS, PS, RBA, SWA, SAI, SGFA, Blackheath Art Society. At: Mall Galleries, Llewellyn Alexander Gallery, Blackheath Halls, Greenwich Theatre Gallery, Sadlers Wells Theatre, the Barbican Gallery, the National Theatre; Headcorn Gallery, Kent; Montepulciano Arte, Tuscany, Italy; Holt, Norfolk; Wareham, Dorset and Ledbury, Herefordshire. *Publications*: Illustrated "Country Walks" series by JBH Peel in The Daily Telegraph, and subsequent books "Another Country Walk" and "Off the Beaten Track". Illustrated articles in South East London Mercury, and publications by London Tourist Board, Civic Trust and Government Publications. *Recreations*: reading, travel, photography, jewellery making (for BIBA), play-reading. *Misc*: Career: Secretary to the publisher, OUP; taught English Language and Literature, Queensmount School, Bournemouth; Ladies' College, Guernsey; Teachers' College of Education, Worcester (now Worcester University College); and Art at Morden College, Blackheath. Blue Badge Guide, London. Has Certificate in Egyptology (London). *Address*: 34 South Row, London SE3 0RY. *Email*: valerie-david@tiscali.co.uk *Signs work*: "Valerie Warren".

WARREN, Vaughan, BA Hons 1st Class Fine Art, Royal Academy Schools, MA Postgraduate Diploma Fine Art, Royal Academy Schools. *b:* Watford, Herts, 22 Jan 1959. *s of:* Frank and Grace Warren. *m:* Dr. Sandra Warren (divorced). *Educ:* English Lit./Art A level, Grange Park Boys School. *Studied:* Royal Academy Schools, Piccadilly, London (1978-84). *Represented by:* Burlington Fine Art, London, Padstow Contemporary Art Gallery and Camelford Gallery, Cornwall. *Exhib:* National Portrait Gallery, RA, Royal Overseas League, Royal Festival Hall, Cork Street Galleries, various exhbns in London and Cornwall. *Works in collections:* Fort Worth, Texas. Private collections in Finland. *Commissions:* undertaken, various private portrait commissions. *Publications:* 'Found' Painting. A Statement of Intent (2002); 'Fragmentations of Light' (2005). *Works Reproduced:* A Marazion Moment (Melanie) (2003), limited edition print. *Principal Works:* Empty Harbour (2002), Grand Slipway (2002), Fragmentations of Light Series (2005). *Recreations:* teaching and surfing. *Misc:* Co-created The Penzance Art Gallery, 1 East Terrace, Penzance, Cornwall, TR18 2TD. *Address:* c/o Padstow Gallery, 3A Parnell Court, Padstow, Cornwall PL28 8BH. *Email:* pzartgallery@btconnect.com *Website:* www.thepenzanceartgallery.com

WATERFIELD, Ken, SWLA (1972); landscape and wildlife artist; 'Natural World' Wildlife Art Award (1995, 1998); Accademia Nazionale D'Arte Antica e Modena -Culture (2000) 'Lifetime Achievement'. *Medium:* oils, acrylic. *b:* Watford, 7 Nov 1927. *s of:* George Waterfield. *m:* Enid. two *s.* two *d. Studied:* Watford School of Art (1940-43). *Exhib:* Mall Galleries, Medici, Guildhall London, Southern Regional Galleries; major one-man show, Winchester City Gallery (1979), 'Nature in Art' Gloucester (2000), Rome Biennale (2001), Blacksheep Gallery, Hawarden (2001), Culture 2000, 2nd International Animals in Contemporary Art Turin, Barcelona, London (2002-03), Pierrepoint Gallery, Bridport Dorset - Retrospective (2005), Pierrepoint Gallery (2008); Uploders Chapel (2009). *Works in collections:* Oxford CC, King Alfred's College, Winchester, 'Nature in Art', Wallsworth Hall, Twigworth, Gloucester, Public Catalogue Foundation - Oil Paintings in Public Ownership. *Commissions:* Oystercatchers @ E. Quantoxhead, Through the Blackthorn, Winternight on Eggardon, Mrs. P. Coombs. *Publications:* Illustrated Review, Bridport News (2009). *Works Reproduced:* Tiger Rag I; Fisher King; illus. profiles, RSPB Magazine 'Birds' (Autumn, 1978); Oxford Mail (28 Oct., 1976); Entry Dictionary of International Biography (1999), Dorset Art Weeks Dictionary (2002), Dorset Life (Oct 2005). *Principal Works:* Nine Day Wonders; Pond; Green Man; River Osprey; Fisher King; Suns of Prague. *Recreations:* walking. *Address:* Plaintiles, Uploders, Bridport, Dorset DT6 4NU. *Signs work:* "Waterfield." Later work displays strong abstract characteristics.

WATERS, Jefferson, A level Art, Art History; Hons Degree in Interior Design. *Medium*: Oil, watercolour, drawing, sculpture. *b*: London, 24 Dec 1969. *Studied*: Goldsmiths College,

London. *Represented by*: Dot Art, Carling Gallery, Saatchi Online (under American pseudonym 'Jefferson Blood'). *Exhib*: Burgh House Art Fair, Hampstead, London (2010, 2011, 2012); Liverpool Art Fair (2014); Dot Art featured artist (Jul/Aug 2014). *Works in collections*: Italian Embassy, London. *Commissions*: Numerous private individuals, approximately 20 commissions over the last five years. *Recreations*: Collecting African art. *Address*: Flat 3, 24 Upper Parliament Street, Liverpool L8 1TE. *Email*: jeffwaters@live.co.uk *Website*: www.dot-art.co.uk *Signs work*: "JEFFERSON WATERS".

WATERS, Katherine Mary, MA Fine Art. *Medium*: Sculpture. *b*: Sutton Coldfield, 8 Feb 1963. *Partner*: Don Henderson. one *d*. *Studied*: Foundation in Art and Design at Stafford College of Art (1981-82); studied sculpture under Stuart Osbourne at Stafford College of Art HND Sculpture (1982-85); Staffordshire University MA Fine Art (2001-03). *Represented by*: Corpus Gallery. *Exhib*: The Barber Institute of Fine Arts, Birmingham, UK, solo exhibition (2008); The Pump Rooms, Leamington Spa, UK (2010) 'Looking in Wonderland' a joint exhibition with Sir John Tenniel, a contemporary artist's response to the Alice books; Chiesa di Santa Maria in Cammuccia, Todi, Umbria, Italy (2007) solo exhibition; Lichfield Garrick Galleries, Lichfield, UK (2004) solo exhibition. *Works in collections*: The estate of Lord Patrick Lichfield; James Perkins, Aynoe Park; Uri Geller; Naseem Hamed; Frank Warren. *Commissions*: Banbury Town Council, marketplace commission (2012); Mr Peter Schwartz, Wooden Ships (2009); Lichfield City Council, David Garrick Memorial Commission, Lichfield Garrick (2003). *Clubs*: Art Professionals Worldwide. *Address*: 33 Slang Lane, Cannock Wood, Staffordshire WS15 4RY. *Website*: www.corpusgallery.com *Signs work*: "KATHERINE M WATERS".

WATLING, Gareth. *Medium*: acrylic. *b*: Doncaster, 28 Sep 1964. *Studied*: Doncaster Church View Art College (1971-83). *Exhib*: Solo show: The Ingleby Gallery, Derbyshire (2010); Art in Action (2014). *Commissions*: many private across the UK. *Publications*: "British Garden Birds" Vol. 1 & 2 (pub. Seven Hills Press, c.2009). *Works Reproduced*: Several images reproduced by Heath McCabe Ltd. (ceramics). *Clubs*: Kirk Sandall Art Group (Chairman). *Misc*: works solely on images of British birds. *Address*: Mary Gray House, 9 Latham Square, Kirk Sandall, Doncaster DN3 1PA. *Email*: garethwatling@yahoo.com *Website*: www.gwbirdpaintings.co.uk *Signs work*: "G.WATLING".

WATSON, Alan, DA, Post Diploma; Royal Scottish Academy Carnegie Travelling Scholarship and Latimer Award. *Medium*: acrylic, mixed media, drawing. *b*: St. Andrews, 1957. *m*: Pat. one *s*. two *d*. *Studied*: Duncan of Jordanstone College of Art, Dundee (1976-81). *Exhib*: solo exhibitions: 369 Gallery, Edinburgh (1982, 85, 86, 89, 90 & 91); McLean Museum, Greenock (1987); Kirkcaldy Museum (1987, 2001); Barbican Centre, London (1989); Pittenweem Festival (1989, 1996); Crawford Art Centre, St. Andrews (1989, 1990); An Lantair, Stornoway (1989, 2003); Scottish Gallery, Edinburgh (1993); Q2, Dundee (2004). *Works in collections*: McManus gallery Dundee, Kirkcaldy Museum, City Art Centre Edinburgh, BBC Edinburgh, Fife Council, Design Council London, Stirling University, Dundee University, British Rail, Forth Rail Bridge Centenery Trust, private collections UK, USA, France, Spain & Russia. *Commissions*: British Rail. *Publications*; Artwork, 'The Sea King's Daughter' by George McKay Brown (pub. Balnain Books, 1991). *Works Reproduced*: 'Glimmer of Cold Brine' (1986); Scottish Sea Anthology (AUP 1988). *Principal Works*: Listening for Herring (1986); Hunting the Big Fish Whaling Drawings; Oil Rig Series, East Neuk Fishing Painting, St. Kilda Bird Men; Voyage St Brendan. *Address*: 61 Sandylands Road, Cupar, Fife KY15 5JP. *Email*: enquiries@alanwatsonartist.com *Website*: www.alanwatsonartist.com *Signs work*: "ALAN WATSON" ("ALAN G.D.WATSON" early 1990s).

WATSON, Alfred Colin, BA (Hons) Fine Art; Ireland Fund of Great Britain Award; Don Niccolo D'Ardio Carracciolo Medal and Award; De Veres Award; RUA Most Popular

Painting Award; ARUA Diploma. *Medium:* oil, drawing, casein tempera. *b:* Belfast, 28 Jun 1966. *s of:* Lorenzo & Mary Watson. *m*: Karima. one *d*. *Studied:* University of Ulster (1984-88). *Represented by:* John Martin, Mayfair, London; Dickon Hall, Belfast. *Exhib:* solo exhbns: Pyms Gallery, London; Simon Dickonson, London; Ava Gallery, N Ireland; Dickon Hall Ltd, Belfast: Lawrence Arnott, Marrakech; Jorgenssen Fine Art, Dublin. mixed: National Portrait Gallery, London; RA; RHA; Discerning Eye, Mall Galleries; Gallery Revel, New York, USA; Ava Gallery, N.Ireland; Albemarle Gallery, London. *Works in collections:* Royal Geographical Society, London; Northern Ireland Office; Arts Council of Northern Ireland; National Self-Portrait Collection of Ireland; Royal Collection, London - HRH Prince of Wales, HRH Duchess of Cornwall; King Mohamed VI of Morocco; Ulster Museum. *Publications*: exhibition catalogues; Modern Masters (2005); Works on Paper 1800-Present Day (2005). *Official Purchasers*: Royal Collection - HRH Prince of Wales - King Mohamed VI of Morocco. *Recreations*: travel. *Address*: 34 Cherryvale Gardens, Belfast, N.Ireland. BT5 6PQ. *Email*: alfredcolinwatson@hotmail.com *Signs work*: 'CW' or 'C.WATSON'.

WATSON, Arthur James, PRSA, HRHA, DA; sculptor/printmaker; Senior Lecturer Fine Art, Duncan of Jordanstone College of Art and Design, University of Dundee; The Highland Society Prize (2001), Edinburgh; The Chicago Prize (2004). *b:* Aberdeen, 24 Jun 1951. *Educ:* Aberdeen Grammar School. *Studied:* Grays School of Art, Aberdeen (1969-74). *Exhib:* Venice Biennale (1990), New Directions, Sarajevo (1988), 'Singing for Dead Singers' 5 Exhbns, Aberdeen (2000), Leaving Jericho, Chicago (2003), Art on the Borders of Art, Venice & Wroclaw (2003); Towards Double Diablerie, Nagoya (2010). *Works in collections:* Aberdeen A.G. and Museum, Arts Council of England; The Robert Gordon University. *Commissions:* University of Aberdeen, Monklands District Council, Sabhal Morostaig, Skye, Cairngorm Mountain. *Publications:* Singing for Dead Singers (Aberdeen City Council); Leaving Jericho (John David Mooney Foundation, Chicago); 101 Dialogues: Richard Demarco, Scotland and the European Avant Garde, with Euan McArthur (Royal Scottish Academy). *Address:* 5B Melville Street, Perth PH1 5PY. *Email*: a.j.watson@dundee.ac.uk *Signs work:* 'A.J.Watson'.

WATSON, Howard, abstract painter. *Medium:* oil on canvas and soft pastel. *b:* 13 Oct 1930. *m:* Patricia. one *s.* two *d. Educ:* Grammar School. *Studied:* Coventry School of Art. *Exhib:* Plumbline Gallery St. Ives, Penwith Gallery, St. Ives, Number Nine The Gallery, Brindley Place, Birmingham (www.numberninethegallery.com). *Works in collections:* South Warwickshire Hospital Trust, Stratford-on-Avon & Warwick Hospitals; County Library, Warwick. *Commissions:* BMW Group Financial Services, Pizza Express Albangate, Charlotte St. London, Maidenhead, New Delhi, Walton-on-Thames, Cambridge, British Telecom HQ London. *Official Purchasers:* Art Consultants. *Principal Works:* Radiant Abstraction, multi-forms, minimalism. *Recreations:* music, cycling, swimming, cinema. *Clubs:* Penwith Soc. of Arts (Associate), St. Ives, Cornwall. *Address:* 2 The Cedars, Telegraph Street, Shipston-on-Stour CV36 4DA. *Signs work:* "Howard Watson" and initials on verso.

WATSON, Janet, RWA. *Medium:* oil and mixed media painting. *b:* Harrogate, 12 Feb 1953. *m:* Peter. one *s.* one *d. Exhib:* RWA; Crane Kalman, London; Schoolhouse Gallery, Bath; Black Swan Guild, Frome. *Works in collections:* private and corporate, RWA Permanent Collection. *Address:* 50 Devonshire Bldgs, Bath, BA2 4SU. *Signs work:* 'Janet Watson' or 'J.W.', often on verso.

WATSON, Thomas Jude (Tomas), BA (Hons) Fine Art (1994), 3rd prize Stoves Exhibition (1991), Robert Ross Scholarship (1994), Greek Govt. Scholarship (1994-96), Gavin Graham Gallery award (1997), BP Portrait Award (1998). *Medium:* oil on canvas, charcoal etc. *b:* Shoreham-by-Sea, Sussex, 6 Jun 1971. *m:* Ornella Mammoliti. *Studied:*

Slade School of Fine Art (1990-94). *Represented by:* Jill George Gallery, Soho, London. *Exhib:* solo exhbns in London and Greece; group exhbns in USA, Canada, UK, Greece. *Works in collections:* National Portrait Gallery, Clare College Cambridge, University College London. *Commissions:* portrait of John Fowles for NPG, portrait of Bob Hepple (Master of Clare College, Cambridge). *Publications:* exhib. catalogue - 'Shadow and Light' 2003 - intro. by John Russell Taylor; 'Aspects' 2005 - intro. by Jane Carter. *Address:* Stenies Village, Andros, Greece. *Website:* www.jillgeorgegallery.co.uk

WATSON STEWART, Lady Avril Veronica, (née GIBB); DGSJ (1997), FRSA (1969), Hon.FBID (1979), Hon.MAustSC (1983); artist/calligrapher/lettering designer on vellum, glass, metals, stone; worldwide lecturer with humour; The Gilbert Inner Award (Glasgow School of Art). *b:* Glasgow. *m:* Sir James Watson Stewart, Bt. (decd 1988). *Educ:* Glasgow High School for Girls, Glasgow and West of Scotland College of Commerce (now University of Strathclyde). *Studied:* Glasgow School of Art (1950, Prof. Colin Horsmann). *Exhib:* California, Norfolk, Va., St. Andrews, Dunfermline, Greenock A.G., National Library of Scotland, Australia. *Works in collections:* V&A, Paul Getty, Royal Family, Glasgow School of Art Archive, and private collections. *Commissions:* glass doors in churches, all forms of architectural lettering or illuminated panels, calligraphy heraldry worldwide. *Recreations:* caring for sick and injured birds. Known as Bird Woman of area. *Misc:* Lecturer aboard 'Royal Princess', 'QE2', and for GMC London. Now confined to travelling in Scotland. Lectures: 'Illuminating Thoughts by a Designing Woman', 'A Calligrapher Goes West' (own art in USA), 'The Birds and The Bees' (Illuminated Mss. and own contemporary designs, i.e. from monks to modern. 11th Year as Hon. President 'Variations', 50 members of Choral Society, Largs; Donating Lecturer 15 medical societies and Drogowan Hospice, etc., etc. *Address:* 36 Brisbane Road, Largs, Ayrshire, Scotland, KA30 8NH. *Signs work:* owl followed by maiden name.

WATSON-GANDY, Basia, BA Hons, SWA, IPA, Grollo d'Ora Silver Medal (1980), Gold Medal (1981); painter on china, porcelain and ceramics using glazes, lustres, goldwork; lecturer and researcher in the Industry; lecturer. Founder Com. mem. and past president, BCPAA. Commissioned work in private collections throughout the world. *Publications:* many magazine articles; appearances on TV and radio. *Clubs:* S.W.A., Confraternity of Polish Artists, Virginia Water Art Soc. *Address:* Squirrel Court Studio, Hare La., Little Kingshill, Gt. Missenden, Bucks. HP16 0EF.

WATT, James, RGI (2002), SSA (1965); DA Drawing and Painting (1954); Royal Bank of Scotland Award RGI (1997). *Medium:* oil painting. *b:* Port Glasgow, 17 Nov 1931. *s of:* Alexander Watt. *m:* Nancy Sinclair (decd). one *s.* three *d. Educ:* Greenock. *Studied:* Glasgow School of Art (1950-54). *Represented by:* Cyril Gerber Fine Art, Glasgow; Leith Gallery, Edinburgh. *Exhib:* RSA, RGI, SSA, RSMA, Greenock Art Gallery, Aberdeen Art Gallery, Perth Art Gallery, Strathclyde University, Paisley Art Gallery, Leith Gallery, Cyril Gerber Fine Art, AIA Gallery, T.R.Annan Gallery, Scottish Gallery Hong Kong, Torshavn Smidjanilitluvik. *Works in collections:* HM The Queen, HRH The Princess Royal, HRH Prince Phillip; Scottish Arts Council; BBC, Clydeport, IBM, Yarrow Shipbuilders Ltd., Royal Bank of Scotland, United Distillers, WD & HO Wills; Danish Embassy Ivory Coast, Clyde Shipping Co., Britoil, GEM Shipping Co., Greenock Art Gallery, Scottish Education Authorities, Glasgow Museums, Hunterian Museum, J&J Denholm, Paisley Art Gallery. *Publications:* The Artist, Scots Magazine, Scottish Field, Maritime Life and Traditions, Biography: 'The Clyde, An Artist's River'. *Works Reproduced:* 'The Clyde' Canniesburn Hospital, Glasgow. *Principal Works:* Industrial shipping on River Clyde; Faroe Islands; landscape. *Clubs:* Glasgow Art Club. *Misc:* Founder Member, Glasgow Group (1957). *Address:* 5 Boathouse Drive, Largs, Ayrshire, KA30 8NX. *Signs work:* "Watt".

WATTS, Brenda Mary, NDD (1951), Cert. in Educ. (1973), SBA (1998), CBM (2002); Joyce Cummings Award (1999), GM (2001); botanical artist in water-colour, retd. Teacher.

b: Ilford, Essex, 29 Jul 1932. *m:* Michael Watts. two *s.* *Educ:* S.E. Essex (1948-51). *Exhib:* annually SBA and RHS, Pashley Manor, Florum. *Works in collections:* Dr. Shirley Sherwood and Lindley Library. *Commissions:* private. *Address:* Barrohill, Horsell Rise, Woking, Surrey GU21 4AY. *Signs work:* "B.W." in a lozenge.

WATTS, Michael Gorse, (otherwise PIKE, Septimus - cartoonist), ARIBA (1965), MFPS (1989); artist, cartoonist, illustrator, in ink, acrylic, water-colour. *b:* Stepney, London, 3 Dec 1934. *s of:* the late George Watts, OBE. *m:* Meg Wattson Dean. three *s.* one *d.* by first marriage. *Educ:* St. Edward's School. *Studied:* Oxford School of Technology and Art (1951-54), S.W. Essex School of Art (1960-62). *Exhib:* Group, solo, etc., in Gt. Britain and the USA. Work in private collections at home and on four continents. *Commissions:* pair of Trompe l'Oeil doorways in 14th century house, Shropshire, portraits, book illustrations, church furniture design. *Works Reproduced:* numerous articles, cartoons and illustrations. *Clubs:* ELAND. *Address:* Trinity Cottage, School Road, Egmond, Shropshire TF10 8LB. *Email:* megwump@btinternet.com *Signs work*: "MW" as monogram.

WATTS, Richard, LLb Barrister, BVSc, MRCVS, HS. *Medium:* watercolour portraits and caricatures, and animation. *b:* Birmingham, UK, 17 Mar 1955. *s of:* George & Nora Watts. *m:* Joanne. two *s.* two *d.* *Educ:* King Edwards School, Birmingham. *Studied:* Birmingham University, Liverpool University. *Exhib:* HS; Birmingham Botanical Gardens. *Address:* 16 Hollister Drive, Harborne, Birmingham, B32 3XG. *Email:* richardwatts21@hotmail.com *Signs work:* 'RICHARD WATTS'.

WATTS, Terry, RBA; awards: Buzzacott Defries Memorial Prize, RI (2007); Guest Prize, Laing Landscape Competition (2002); First Prize, City Airport Competition (2002, 2003). *Medium:* acrylic. *b:* London, 4 Aug 1946. *s of:* KE & G Watts. *m:* Jennifer Watts (née Precious). *Studied:* Camberwell School of Art, Hammersmith College of Art, Open University. *Exhib:* Sunday Times Watercolour Competition; Discerning Eye; galleries: Beaux Art (Bath), Bell (Winchester), Blackheath, Bloxham, Hunter, John Noott, Francis Iles, Llewellyn Alexander, Redleaf, Piers Feetham, Stark, Mall - RSMA, RI, RBA, plus many other London and provincial galleries. *Works in collections:* Wiltshire County Council, Transco Plc. *Commissions:* London Docklands Development Corporation; Soviet Weekly; L.B. of Merton; Aldeburgh Festival. *Publications:* Pratique des Arts, Spring 2006, My Room, Quistgard, Anderson et al. *Works Reproduced:* Blackheath Guide: n paradoxa. *Address:* 8 Rainton Road, Charlton, London SE7 7QZ. *Signs work:* "TW" (or monogram of TW).

WATTSON DEAN, Meg, HS, MAS-F, MPSG, SLM, GGE; specialist in miniatures and glass engraving; artist/sculptor. *b:* Luton, 11 Nov 1929. *m:* Michael Watts. one *s.* one *d.* *Educ:* Bedford High School. *Studied:* Rolle College, Exmouth (1968-70). *Exhib:* with RMS (1989-2004), Hilliard Soc., 'A Million Brushstrokes' at Llewellyn Alexander Gallery, Florida & Washington Miniature Art Socs. (1991-2005), Guild of Glass Engravers, Westminster Arts Council, 3rd World Exhibition Fine Art in Miniature, Smithsonian Institute, Washington DC (2004); 4th World Miniature Art Exhibition (Australia 2008); one-person exhibitions Oxmarket Centre of Arts, Chichester. *Works in collections:* Chelsea and Westminster Hospital, private collections U.K., U.S.A. and Australia. *Commissions:* Millennium window Edmond Church. *Clubs:* Guild of Glass Engravers. *Address:* 27 Sutherland St., London SW1V 4JU. *Email:* megwattsondean@btinternet.com *Signs work:* uncial cipher of MWD, W and D attached to base of M either side, or "Meg Wattson Dean".

WAUGH, Eric, ARCA (1953), RI (1990); artist in water-colour. *b:* London, 15 Dec 1929. two *s.* two *d.* *Studied:* Croydon School of Art (1946-50), R.C.A. (1950-53). *Exhib:* Ashgate Gallery, Farnham (1965-67), Geffrye Museum (1968), Roland, Browse & Delbanco (1971), Arte Benimarco, Spain (1980), Galeria de Arte Denia, Spain (1981), Galeria de Arte Javea, Spain (1982), RA, RI, RBA, London Group, Sport in the Fine Arts, Madrid; various galleries in Devon and Cornwall; View Gallery, Bristol. *Works in collections:* Mexico, USA, Australia, Spain, UK. *Commissions:* 100ft x 7ft mural - tactile for West of England School for the Partially Sighted. *Publications:* articles written for various magazines; Painting in Acrylics - A Correspondence Course (Pitmans); "Face to Face" British Self Portraits in the 20th Century. *Address:* Pen-an-Vrea, Leeches, St. Kew Highway, Bodmin, Cornwall PL30 3EG. *Signs work*: "Eric Waugh.".

WEALLEANS, Jon, MA (RCA) Distinction; FRCA; FCSD. *Medium*: oil, watercolour. *b:* Yorkshire, 10 Feb 1946. *m:* Natalie Gibson MBE. *Studied:* Royal College of Art (1967-70). *Represented by:* Francis Kyle Gallery, Maddox St, London W1. *Exhib:* Royal Academy Summer Shows; Francis Kyle Gallery. *Works in collections:* all private. *Recreations:* architecture and design. *Address:* 9 Grange Walk, London SE1 3DT. *Email:* jonwealleans@btinternet.com *Website:* www.jonwealleans.co.uk *Signs work:* JW (monogram within circle).

WEAVER, Felicity, NDD City & Guilds; printmaker in etching and drawing. *b*: Leeds, 11 Feb 1930. *m*: Peter Weaver. one *d. Exhib*: B'ham Museum and A.G., Greenwich Printmakers Gallery, LWT Terrace Gallery; group shows: RE, RWA, RBSA, RP, RBA, Curwen Gallery, Barbican, CPS, PS, etc., also Moscow, Paris, Landau, Belize, Belfast, 54 The Gallery. *Works in collections*: B'ham Museum and A.G., Scarborough Archives, Victoria and Albert Museum, Lewisham Council, and private collections in England, Germany, America, New Zealand and Australia. *Clubs*: Printmakers Council, N.S. *Address*: 2 Brookside Cottages, Ismays Road, Ivy Hatch, Kent TN15 0NY. *Signs work*: "FELICITY WEAVER".

WEAVER, Peter Malcolm, RI, RBA, ARBS, Slade Dip.; painter in water-colour, sculptor in mixed media; Founder mem. Printmakers Council; teacher of drawing and lithography: Camberwell School of Art and Crafts (1957-87). *b:* London, 10 Jun 1927. *s of:* P.R. Weaver. *m:* Felicity Rachel. one *d. Studied:* St. Martin's School of Art and Camberwell Schools of Art, Slade School of Fine Art, UCL. *Represented by:* Mall Gallery. *Exhib:* galleries: Grosvenor Gallery, Nicholas Treadwell, Sloane St., Ikon, Primavera Gallery, Alresford Gallery, ICA, Whitechapel Gallery, Shell House Gallery, Manor House Gallery; Open exhbns: RA, RWS, RBA, RWA, NEAC, RI, PMC, London Group, Birmingham Museums and Art Gallery, 54 The Gallery. *Works in collections:* V&A, Birmingham Museum and AG, also private collections in UK, Japan, Sweden and America. *Publications:* The Technique of Lithography; Printmaking - A Medium for Basic Design. *Works Reproduced:* 'The Artist' Magazine; 'British Sculpture' by Guy Portelli; 'International Artist'. *Clubs:* The Arts Club, Dover St.; Chelsea Arts Club. *Address:* 2 Brookside Cottages, Ismay Road, Ivy Hatch, Kent TN15 0NY. *Signs work:* "P. WEAVER, RI, RBA".

WEBB, Barbara, etcher; teacher for ILEA. *b:* London, 18 Dec 1933. *m:* T.R. Webb (sculptor). one *d. Educ:* South Hampstead High School. *Studied:* Cass School, Whitechapel, London, Corcoran School of Art, Washington, DC, USA. *Represented by:* Camden Printmakers co.uk - Founder of Camden Printmakers with Annette Lewin. *Exhib:* R.A. Summer Exhbns, St. John's Smith Sq., Print Exhbn Mall Gallery; Contemporary Art Fair; invited to demonstrate etching at Art in Action, Oxon, July 2009. *Works in collections:* Government Art Collection, Camden Council. *Commissions:* etchings of wedding ceremonies, and houses and gardens. Received commission for 2 different etchings of ancient farming instruments and tackle. Etchings of Woodchester Mansion and set of etchings for the Royal Free Hospital of the operating theatre. *Address:* 39b Rosslyn Hill, London NW3 5UJ. *Email:* randbwebb@oz.co.uk *Website:* www.camdenprintmakers.co.uk *Signs work:* "Barbara Webb."

WEBB, Elizabeth, ARCM, (1953), GRSM (London) (1955); artist in oil on canvas or board; music teacher. *b:* Fakenham, 7 Sep 1931. *m:* (1) Frank Rayer (decd). (2) Graham

Webb (decd). two *s. Educ:* The Park School, Yeovil; Royal College of Music, London. *Studied:* Evening Classes with Mary Bairds (1989-93). *Exhib:* RA, Paris Salon, Meridian International Center, Washington, Sui Loung Gallery, Hong Kong. *Address:* La Guelle, Guelles Rd., St. Peter Port, Guernsey, C.I. GY1 2DE. *Signs work:* "Elizabeth Webb".

WEBB, Gwendoline E., RAS Cert (1954), London University Extra-Mural Diploma History of Art (1975); picture conservator (retired), painter. *Medium:* painter in oil, some watercolour. *b:* Bromley, Kent, 8 Jul 1929. *Educ:* Kingston School of Art, NDD Painting 1949. *Studied:* Royal Academy Schools 1950-54. *Exhib:* RA Summer Exhibitions, NEAC, Society of Women Artists, Lord Mayors Art Award Exhibition, SEA Pictures for Schools. Shared: Fairfield Halls, Croydon; Old Bankhouse Watlington; Phoenix Gallery, Lavenham; Century Galleries, Sonning. *Works in collections:* private collections and SEA Schools. *Commissions:* portraits (private). *Publications:* Encyclopedia Britannica, section on picture conservation. *Recreations:* visiting exhibitions, National Trust, etc. *Clubs:* RASAA. *Address:* 7 Parkfields, Shirley, Surrey, CRO 8DH. *Signs work:* 'GW'.

WEBB, Kenneth, NDD, ATD Hons, NS, FRSA, RWA; Head of Painting School, Ulster College of Art (1953-60). *Medium*: oil, acrylic. *b:* London, 21 Jan 1927. *s of:* William George Webb and Mabel Melissa Webb. *m:* Joan Burch. two *s.* two *d. Educ:* Bristol Grammar School; Lydney Grammar School and School of Art. *Studied:* Gloucester College of Art and University College, Swansea. *Exhib:* one-man shows 1954 to 2012: Verhoff Washington DC, Arts Council Belfast, Walker Galleries London, Toronto, San Francisco, Ritchie Hendricks Dublin, Kenny Galleries, Alexander Gallery Bristol, Geneva, Solomon, James Gallery, W.H. Patterson London, worldwide. *Commissions*: murals Bangor Abbey, Trust House Forte, Grand Metropolitan, African Sarari Hotels, galleries UK & Ireland. *Publications:* Kenneth Webb (Shenval Press, London), Profile of an Artist by Thomas Kenny (1990), 'A Life in Colour' (Antique Collectors Club, UK, 2003), British Flower Painters 1650-1950 (two entries), also video 'A Life in Colour'. *Works Reproduced:* landscape prints, Paul Hamlyn, Prints for Pleasure, and Quality Prints. *Clubs:* Bel-Air Equestrian Club. *Address:* Portland House, Chagford, Devon TQ13 8AR. *Signs work:* figurative work: "Kenneth Webb," non figurative work: "Webb."

WEBB, Sarah Ann, BA (Hons) (1978), SWA (1994); Best of Show (1987) and Athena award (1992) Central South Art competition (U.S.A.); artist in oil. *b:* Nashville, TN, 19 Feb 1948. *m:* Gary A. Webb, attorney. *Educ:* University of Tennessee. *Studied:* University of Tennessee and Vanderbilt University. *Exhib:* regular exhib. SWA and Central South Art competition (USA), winner American Artists National Art competition, Grand Central Gallery (NY 1985), Tennessee All State competition, numerous national and international group and solo shows; PBS Television (USA 1994, 1995), Radio (USA 1985), Nashville Arts Comn (USA, 1994); Belmont Univ. (USA 1999). *Works in collections:* corporate and private collections worldwide. *Publications:* Who's Who in American Art. *Address:* P.O. Box 50134, Nashville, TN 37205, USA. *Website:* www.sarahwebb.com *Signs work:* "Sarah Webb."

WEBSTER, John Morrison, RSMA (2001); marine and landscape painter in oil, pastel, water-colour; 40 years in Royal Navy; Chairman, Armed Forces Art Society (1990-96), mem. Board of Governors FBA (2002-2008). *b:* Sri Lanka, 3 Nov 1932. *m:* (decd). two *d. Studied:* No formal art training. *Exhib:* one-man shows: Art Gallery of Nova Scotia (1976), London since 1980, Tryon and Swann, Cork St. (1996, 1999), Tryon, Bury St. (2002, 2004, 2007, 2009, 2011); NEAC, ROI, RI, RSMA, Alresford Gallery, Alresford; Wykeham Gallery, Stockbridge; Jerram Gallery, Sherborne. *Works in collections:* HM The Queen, HRH The Prince of Wales, Corporation of Trinity House, Naval establishments, HM Ships, and private collections in Canada, Australia, New Zealand, Holland, UK. *Commissions:* Royal Cruising Club, Trinity House, many private. *Works Reproduced:* numerous. *Principal*

Works: 'HMY Britannia on Decommissioning Day' Collection, H.M. The Queen; 'International Fleet Review 2005' Collection, Trinity House; 'Silver Jubilee Fleet Review 1977' Diploma Collection RSMA. *Address:* Old School House, Soberton, Southampton SO32 3PF. *Website:* www.johnwebster.org.uk *Signs work:* "JOHN WEBSTER."

WEBSTER, Norman, RWS, RE, ARCA; painter etcher. *b:* Southend-on-Sea, 6 May 1924. *s of:* George W. Webster. *m:* Joan W. Simpson, ARCA. three *s. Educ:* Dover Grammar School; Tunbridge Wells School of Art (1940-43, E. Owen Jennings, RWS); Royal Navy (1943-46); RCA School of Engraving (1946-49, Malcolm Osborne, CBE, RA, Robert Austin, RA). *Studied:* School of Engraving, Royal College of Art (1946-49). *Exhib:* Painter Etchers, RWS, RA, Yorkshire Artists at Leeds, Bradford, Wakefield and Hull City A.G.s., with Yorkshire Printmakers in Britain, USA, Israel and Canada. *Works in collections:* Ashmolean Museum; Salford University; Leeds City A.G. and Arts Council of GB. *Address:* 48 The Drive, Cross Gates, Leeds. LS15 8EP. *Signs work:* "Norman Webster."

WEEKS, John Lawrence Macdonald, LRMS (1984), ARMS (1987), FNCM (1984); artist in oil and water-colour; private music teacher and organist. *b:* Chelmsford, 28 Apr 1954. *Educ:* Moulsham High School, Chelmsford. *Studied:* Colchester Inst. of HE (1973-74, John Buhler). *Exhib:* RMS annual, Medici Gallery and one-man shows. *Address:* 49, Prescott, Hanworth, Bracknell, Berks. RG12 7RE. *Signs work:* name followed by date and device.

WEERDMEESTER, Neil Jackson, BA (Hons) Fine Art (1986), MA Fine Art (1994); artist in painting and photography. *b:* London, 21 Feb 1960. one *d. Studied:* Dartington College; Reading University; Winchester School of Art. *Exhib:* London, Barcelona, Antwerp. *Clubs:* London Group. *Address:* 99 Manor Park, London SE13 5RQ. *Email:* neilweerdmeester@hotmail.com

WEGMULLER-PATON, Ann, BA (Hons) Fine Art, RSW, RWS; Freshfields Bruckhaus Deringer Prize, Bankside Gallery (2002), Scottish Arts Club Award, RSW (1996), Macdonald Orr Ltd. Purchase Prize SAAC (1994), James Torrence Memorial Award, RGI (1989), RSW Council Award (2009). *Medium*: oil, gouache and watercolour. *b*: Gourock, Inverclyde, 3 May 1941. *d of*: William Bayne Paton & Isabella Forbes Paterson. *m*: Alfred Wegmuller. two *s*. *Educ*: Greenock Academy, Renfrewshire, Scotland. *Studied*: Duncan of Jordanstone College of Art Dundee (1981-85). *Represented by*: Bankside Gallery, London; Gallery Heinzel, Aberdeen; Lost Gallery, Strathdon, Aberdeenshire. *Exhib*: Royal Scottish Academy, Royal Glasgow Institute, Aberdeen Artists Society, Royal Scottish Society Painters in Watercolour; Gallery Wollebrandshof, Cullemborg, Holland. Solo and group shows Scotland, England, Holland, Switzerland. *Works in collections*: Mobile North Sea Ltd. Aberdeen, Delaitte & Touche, Aberdeen, various private collections worldwide. *Publications*: 'The Watercolour Expert' (RWS, Cassell Illustrated); Watercolour Masters Then and Now (RSW, Cassell). *Works Reproduced*: Lallans magazine, Chapman magazine. *Recreations*: reading poetry, Scottish Country Dancing. *Clubs*: Aberdeen Artist Society (Professional Member), SSA (Ordinary Member), RGI (Ordinary Member). *Misc*: lived for ten years in Zurich, Switzerland (1961-71). *Address*: Kirk House, Main Road, Aberuthven, Perthshire. PH3 1HE Scotland. *Email*: annwegmuller@hotmail.co.uk *Signs work*: 'Ann Wegmuller'.

WEGNER, Fritz James, MCSD, Mem. Art Workers' Guild; freelance artist, retired lecturer, St. Martin's School of Art. *b*: Vienna, 15 Sep 1924. *m*: Janet Wegner. two *s*. one *d*. *Studied*: St. Martin's School of Art. *Represented by*: John Huddy of Olympia Fine Art. *Works in collections*: private. *Official Purchasers*: bookjackets and illustrations for British, American and Continental publishers; cover designs and illustrations for magazines; educational publications; G.P.O. Christmas and Anniversaries sets of stamps. Examples of work reproduced in several manuals on illustration. *Clubs*: Chelsea Arts, Double Crown Club. *Address*: 14 Swains Lane, London N6 6QS. *Signs work*: "Wegner."

WEIR, Linda Mary, BA Hons Fine Art, MA Hons Fine Art Painting, MA Counselling & Psychotherapy, PGCE Art Education. *Medium*: oil, watercolour, drawing. *b*: Manchester, 12 May 1949. *Partner:* Andrew Stewart. two *s*. *Educ:* St. Pius X RC Secondary. *Studied:* Manchester University 1986, Manchester Polytechnic 1979-1983, Nottingham Trent University 1984-86, University of Nottingham 1984-86. *Represented by:* Graham Baizley, Lanes Fine Art. *Exhib:* Oldham Art Gallery, Stockport, Mappin, Harris Galleries, Blackfriars Boston, Djainogly Gallery, Lemon Street Gallery, New Craftsman St. Ives, Rainy Day Gallery Penzance, Castlefield Gallery Manchester, Manchester City Art Gallery, Worcester Art Gallery, Royal Academy 1986-1988, Bonnington Art Gallery, Bonhams Knightsbridge, Lanes Fine Art Exhibitions, BBC Manchester Granada M/cr. *Works in collections:* America, Nigeria, N. Ireland, Europe. *Publications:* 'Plasticity and Permission: the Creation of the Self and the Self Creating' University of Nottingham, Advanced Study Dept. of Education. *Principal Works:* 'St. Ives Harbour', 'Still Life with St. Ives', Flower panel, 'Still Life Manchester'. *Recreations:* American Literature, Social Psychology. *Clubs:* MAFA. *Misc:* mother, teacher, grandmother, artist, ecology, animal welfare. *Address:* 15 Tregenna Terrace, St. Ives, Cornwall, TR26 2DL. *Email:* espaceblue@btopenworld.com *Website:* www.lindaweir.com *Signs work:* "Linda Weir".

WEISS, Edna Sheila, (Née ROSE); Landseer Scholar, Royal Academy of Arts, silver and bronze medals, portrait painter, and writer of letters to newspapers. *Medium:* painter in oils. *b:* London, 10 Dec 1927. *m:* Willard Weiss. one *d. Educ:* Skinners' Company School. *Studied:* St.Martins, Royal Academy Schools (1946-51). *Exhib:* RP & RA. *Works in collections:* private collections and Arts Club. *Commissions:* private collections. *Works Reproduced:* in 'Daily Telegraph' and 'Builders' Magazine'. *Recreations:* gardening, swimming, tennis. *Clubs:* Arts Club, RASAA. *Misc:* worked in animation film studio of Halas & Batchelor; fax no: 0208-455-0788. *Address:* 3 Maurice Walk, London NW11 6JX.

WELCH, Robert Joseph, BA (1979), MA (1981); painter in oil and acrylic on canvas. *b*: 22 Feb 1956. *s of*: V.R. Welch. *Educ*: Regis Comprehensive, Wolverhampton. *Studied*: Hull CHE (1976-79, John Clarke), Manchester Polytechnic (1980-81, David Sweet). *Exhib*: Castlefield Gallery, Manchester, Showroom Gallery, London, Winchester School of Art, Mall Galleries; one-man shows: Patricia Brown, Dulwich, Smith-Jariwala, London. *Address*: APT, 6 Creekside, Deptford, London SE8 4SA. *Signs work*: "Welch, R.J.W."

WELCH, Rosemary Sarah. SEA, AAEA. *Medium*: oil, pastel. *b*: 24 May 1943. *m*: Anthony Crockford. *Educ*: private school Bournemouth, American High School, NY. *Studied*: St. Ives School of Painting (Leonard Fuller, RA, ROI). *Exhib*: Belfast, Mall Galleries, Omells, John Davies, St. Ives Soc. of Artists, American Academy Equine Art. *Works in collections*: Russell-Cotes Museum, Bournemouth. *Works Reproduced*: Limited Edition prints, Sally Mitchell Fine Art. *Recreations*: riding, walking. *Address*: Meadow keep, Main Road, Chillerton, Newport, Isle of Wight PO30 3EZ. *Email*: rosie.welch21@googlemail.com *Website*: rosemarywelch.info *Signs work*: "Rosemary Sarah Welch."

WELLINGS, Tricia, self taught artist in gouache, charcoal and ink and gouache. *b*: Guildford, 20 Mar 1959. *Educ*: Horsham High School. *Exhib*: Painters Hall, London EC2, Mall Galleries, London SW1, Edith Grove Gallery, London SW10, Wattis Fine Art, Hong Kong, Ramsay Galleries, Honolulu, Hawaii, Ropner Gallery, London SW6, Bartley Drey Gallery, London SW3. *Works in collections*: USA, Australia, Mexico, UK, Hong Kong, Ireland (Eire). *Clubs*: The Nine Elms Group of Artist. *Address*: 5a Pentland Gdns., Wandsworth, London SW18 2AN. *Signs work*: "T. Wellings."

WELTON, Peter, BA; artist in water-colour; Emeritus Prof. of Fine Art, De Montfort University, Leicester. *b*: Barnetby, Lincs., 15 Mar 1933. *m*: Liza. two *s*. *Studied*: King's College, Newcastle (Gowing, Pasmore and Hamilton). *Exhib*: Keele University (1997),

Laing Gallery, Newcastle, Bar Convent Museum, York, Buxton Art Gallery, Jersey Arts Centre, Unicorn Gallery, London, The Royal Academy. *Works in collections*: Wimbledon 1997 "The New No. 1 Court", HM The Queen "Moored Boat" (1992), Peter Ogden: "The Jethou Suite" (1997), National Art Archive (London Transport), The Duke of Gloucester "Kimbolton School", Lady Conyngham "Udaipur 2001". *Publications*: "See What I Mean" with John Morgan (Edward Arnold, London, 1986), "Paint in Water-colour" (Patchings Farm, Nottingham). *Works Reproduced*: in Illustrated London News, The Artists Magazine; "Peter Welton's Sketch Diary 1999". *Misc*: DVD "Peter Welton's Way with Water-colour" (1997). *Address*: Orchard Cottage, Arnesby, Leics. LE8 5WG. *Email*: peter@peterwelton.com *Website*: www.peterwelton.com *Signs work*: "Peter Welton."

WERGE-HARTLEY, Alan, NDD (Leeds) 1952, ATD; painter in oil, pen and wash of marine landscapes, lecturer; senior lecturer Dept. of Education, Portsmouth Polytechnic (1962-90). *b*: Leeds, 1931. *m*: Jeanne Werge-Hartley. two *d*. *Studied*: Leeds College of Art (1947-53) under Maurice de Sausmarez and E. E. Pullée; Hornsey College of Art (1972-73) (sabbatical). *Exhib*: in group exhbns. and one-man shows in Hampshire from 1962. *Works in collections*: Portsmouth City Gallery and numerous private collections in England and abroad. *Address*: 5 Maisemore Gdns., Emsworth, Hants. PO10 7JU. *Email*: werge068@virginmedia.com

WERGE-HARTLEY, Jeanne, NDD, FSDC, FRSA; designer/jeweller/goldsmith; Founder Mem., Chairman, Designer Jewellers Group; Vice-President and past Chairman, Soc. of Designer Craftsmen, member of the Association for Contemporary Jewellery. *b*: Leeds, 26 Aug 1931. *d of*: Edgar Vauvelle. *m*: Alan Werge-Hartley. two *d*. *Educ*: Leeds Girls' High School. *Studied*: Leeds College of Art (1948-52). *Exhib*: nationally and internationally. *Works in collections*: City of Portsmouth University, Portsmouth County Council, private collections in UK and abroad. *Commissions*: UK, USA, Europe, New Zealand, Japan. Freeman of the Worshipful Company of Goldsmiths and the City of London (1986). Included on Craft Council Index and BBC Domesday Project. *Publications*: 'Enamelling on Precious Metals'. *Address*: 5 Maisemore Gdns., Emsworth, Hants. PO10 7JU. *Email*: jeanne@werge.go-plus.net

WESSELMAN, Frans, RE (1986); painter, etcher, stained glass artist. *b*: The Hague, Holland, 1953. one *s*. *Studied*: printmaking and photography at Groningen College of Art (1976-78). Work concerned with the human figure, emotions and interactions. Sometimes literary sources (Shakespeare) are a starting point, from where my paintings develop into valid graphic, pictorial statements with strong colours and compositions. *Exhib*: RE, RA, RWS, RWA, and widely in the UK, Holland, Ireland, Germany. *Works in collections*: Fitzwilliam, Ashmolean Museum; private collections in USA, Japan, Australia. *Commissions*: limited edition print for Shropshire County Council, limited edition print for Galerie Inkt., Holland, commissions of paintings for private collectors. *Address*: 5 Green Mount, Cunnery Rd., Church Stretton. SY6 6AQ.

WEST, Johe, Diploma in Art and Design; Master of Arts Degree. *Medium*: oil. *b*: West Wickham, 9 Oct 1948. *s of*: Mr. Peter West & Mrs. B. La Trobe-West. *Educ*: Fan Court School, Surrey; Boxhill School, Surrey. *Studied*: London College of Printing (1966-68); Chelsea School of Art (1968-69); Brighton (1969-72); Royal College of Art (1972-74). *Represented by*: Chameleon Gallery, Brighton. *Exhib*: solo exhibitions since 1975 including: Queensland House Gallery, London (1989, 1992, 1997); Joyce Grenfell Centre, Claremont, Esher, Surrey (1990, 1991, 1993); Room for Art, Cobham, Surrey (2005); group exhibitions in UK and Australia since 1975 including: RA Summer Exhibition (1975); Huntingtower, Melbourne, Australia (1976, 1987, 2003); Llewellyn Alexander (1999); Chameleon Gallery, Brighton (2007, 2008); Foyles Bookshop, Charing Cross Road, London (2009); Susan Scates Fine Art (2014). *Works in collections*: Cheney Best, California, USA; Maneval,

Munich, Germany; Perrot, Lyon, Tymlock & Keyser Architects, Melbourne; Graphics Allsorts, Southfield, London. *Commissions*: Lady Baillieu, Melbourne. *Publications*: Guardian, Arts Review, Financial Times. *Works Reproduced*: Financial Times, Design Magazine, Arts Review, London Guide, TNT. *Principal Works*: Pastoral. *Recreations*: writing, music. *Misc*: Landscape design. *Address*: 16 Roundhill Way, Cobham, Surrey, KT11 2EX. *Email*: johewest@gmail.com *Website*: see Chameleon Gallery *Signs work*: "Johe West".

WEST, Keith. *Medium*: oil, drawing. *b*: Warwickshire, 26 Sep 1947. *Studied*: Coventry College of Art (CCA). *Exhib*: numerous group and one-man shows including LBH, Chelmsford; Minories, Colchester; Kettles Yard, Cambs; Curwen, London; Ikon, B'ham; Shaw Theatre, Gallery 47, London; St. Albans Cathedral; St. Martin-in-the-Fields; St. James, Piccadilly; The Actors Church, Covent Garden; St. Margarets; Westminster Abbey. *Works in collections*: Sir Alastair McAlpine, Russell Harty Estate, Dame Janet Baker, Wayne Sleep. *Commissions*: Dame Janet Baker, Wayne Sleep. *Publications*: Tate Gallery Archive: Memoir of CCA and Barbara Reise. *Principal Works*: 'The Passion Suite' touring exhibition. *Address*: 58 Union Street, Barnet, Herts. EN5 4HZ. *Email*: Keithfwest@btinternet.com *Website*: art-sacredprofane.com *Signs work*: "K West", usually on back.

WEST, Steve, DipAD (1969), RAS Higher Cert. (1972), Prix de Rome (1972), ARBS (1992); sculptor in bronze, and a variety of media. *b*: Warrington, 6 Apr 1948. *m*: Jenny. one *s*. one *d*. *Studied*: Liverpool College of Art and Design (1965-69), RA Schools (1969-72, Willi Soukop). *Represented by*: Plus Fine Art Limited, 161/163 Seymour Place, London W1H 4PS. *Exhib*: Crescent Gallery Scarborough, Oldknows Gallery Nottingham, Lanchester Gallery Coventry, Tabor Gallery Canterbury, Woodlands Gallery Blackheath, Prediger Schwabisch Gmund, Hart Gallery London, Derby Museum and Art Gallery, Doncaster Museum and Art Gallery, Buckenham Galleries Southwold, Wolverhampton Art Gallery. *Address*: 17 Swift St., Barnsley, S. Yorks. S75 2SN. *Signs work*: "Steve West."

WESTERGAARD, Hanne, Individual Craft Award, Yorkshire Arts (1986, 1996, 1999). *Medium*: Ceramic. *b*: Denmark. *m*: I H Westergaard (decd). one *s*. one *d*. *Studied*: Kunsthaandværkerskolen, København, Denmark (1960-64). *Exhib*: Cupola Contemporary Arts, Sheffield; Art in the Garden, Sir Harold Hillier Garden; Derby City Open Exhibition; Oriel Wrexham; Oriel Davies; New Town, The Biscuit Factory, Newcastle; Piece Hall Art Gallery, Halifax; Ruskin Gallery, Sheffield; Royal Danish Embassy, London; Wallsworth Hall, Gloucester. *Works in collections*: Sheffield Museum and Gallery Trust; Pinchen Collection; City Museum and Art Gallery, Stoke on Trent. *Recreations*: Walks in the countryside and coastal areas. *Address*: Studio 18, Yorkshire Artspace, 21 Brown Street, S1 2BS. *Email*: hannewestergaard@gmail.com *Website*: hannewestergaard.co.uk *Signs work*: "HW".

WESTON, David J., BA (Hons.) Fine Art, RMS, MAA, HS, MASF, MPSG, FRSA; seascape and landscape painter in water-colour; miniaturist. *Medium*: watercolour. *b*: 21 Sep 1936. *m*: Ann. two *s*. one *d*. *Studied*: St. Albans School of Art and Design (University of Hertfordshire). *Exhib*: one-man shows: Clare Hall Cambridge, Grosvenor Gallery, Old Fire Engine House Ely and Conservatory Gallery. Has exhibited at New Academy, Llewellyn Alexander and Medici galleries; with UA, RMS, RSMA, RBA, RI, NEAC and HS at Mall and Westminster Galleries, also with BWS and BSM at Ilkley. Overseas with MAS-F, MPGS and WFH. *Address*: Little Glebe, 11 Longcroft Ave., Harpenden, Herts. AL5 2RD. *Email*: david.weston3@ntlworld.com *Website*: www.artisticactivities.co.uk *Signs work*: "DAVID J. WESTON" or "D.J.W." (miniatures and small works). More recently "David Weston" or "DW".

WESTON, Neville Edward, NDD, ATD, DFA (Lond), MEd. (Manc), PhD (Adelaide, Aus). *Medium*: watercolour, drawing, print, oil. *b*: Birmingham, UK, 26 Jun 1936. *s of*: D C

Weston. one *s*. *Educ*: King Edward VI, Stourbridge. *Studied*: Stourbridge School of Art; Slade School, Universities of Birmingham, Manchester and Adelaide. *Represented by*: BMG Art, Adelaide. *Exhib*: Royal Academy (1972, 2006); Lynn Painter Stainers Prize (2008, 2009); Threadneedle Prize (2012). Solo exhibitions: Picton Castle, Adelaide Festival Gallery; Australian Embassy, Paris (1995); Copenhagen University (1995); BMG Art; Robin Gibson, Sydney; Inverness Museum & Art Gallery etc. *Works in collections*: UCL, V&A Print Collection; Bolton Art Gallery, Bowes Museum, Art Bank, Australia; War Memorial Collection, Canberra; Australian National University; Art Gallery of Western Australia; Granada Art Collection. *Commissions*: Many private and public works through BMG. *Publications*: Kaleidoscope of Modern Art (Harrap); The Reach of Modern Art (Harper & Row); Lawrence Daws, Sydney; Frank Kempf, Wakefield Press; In the Public Eye, VAB Australia. *Official Purchasers*: Liverpool Centre of the Creative Universe (Tate Liverpool, 2007); Ill Starred Captains; Royal Academy Illustrated (2006); New Art Four, Germaine Encyclopedia of Australian Art. *Address*: The Reading Rooms, Station Road, Clynderwen, Pembs. SA66 7NF. *Email*: neville@nevilleweston.co.uk *Website*: www.nevilleweston.co.uk *Signs work*: "WESTON".

WHALLEY, Ann Penelope, NDD, ATD, ATC, SWA; artist in oils, water-colour, acrylic and pastel; tutor and organiser for painting holidays abroad. *b*: Yorks., 1 Apr 1933. *d of*: Dr G.M. Mayhall, MD, FRCS. *m*: Theo Whalley, NDD, ATD, ATC. four *s*. *Educ*: Pontefract Girls' High School. *Studied*: Leeds College of Art (1950-55, Mr. Pullé). *Exhib*: one-man shows: Albany Gallery, Cardiff, Fountain Gallery Llandeilo, Library Hall, Haverfordwest annually since 1981, Workshop, Wales (1983), Bloomfield Hall (1986), Coachhouse (1987), Henry Thomas Gallery, Carmarthen, Patricia Wells Gallery (1987), Art Matters, Tenby; group shows: St. Ives Gallery (1984), B.W.S. (1986), Laing Comp. (1987), S.W.A. (1987), R.I. (1986), Albany Gallery, Cardiff, Century Gallery, Henley-on-Thames, Bromley Gallery, Kent, Fountain Gallery, Llandeilo, Wold Gallery, Bourton on the Water. *Publications*: illustrated, About Pembrokeshire; author, Painting under a Blue Sky; author, Painting Water in Water-colour (Batsfords); articles for Artist and Illustrator, and Leisure Painter. *Recreations*: gardening, travel, teaching abroad. *Address*: Haroldston House, Haverfordwest, Pembs. SA61 1UH. *Signs work*: "Ann Whalley."

WHALLEY, Stella. *Medium*: fine artist. *b*: Lichfield, 4 Jul 1958. *Studied*: Central School of Art (1981) Postgraduate. *Exhib*: 'Tokorode', Visions Gallery, Tokyo (2008), book launch 'Tokyo Tales', Whitechapel Gallery (2007); Royal Academy Summer Exhibition (2004, 2003); Jerwood Drawing Prize (2004); Project A4 Kunstverket Gallery, Oslo, Norway (2003); Digital Responses, V&A (2002); Williamson Gallery, Birkenhead (2000); Installation, Waterloo Bridge Exhibition (2000). *Works in collections*: British Embassy, Moscow; Kunstverket, Oslo; Metropolitan Museum, New York; Grundy Art Gallery, Lancs. *Commissions*: London Print Gallery, and Birmingham Museums & Art Galleries; Colville Gallery, London. *Publications*: 'Tokyo Tales' (2007); 'Bodysnatcher' (1999); Artist Newsletter Review (2003). *Works Reproduced*: in Art Worlds 2002 Vol.213 Korean Publication. 'Body of Evidence' 1999 Make magazine, review of 'Bodysnatchers'. *Address*: 19 Alexandra Grove, London N4 2LQ. *Email*: stellawhalley@talktalk.net *Website*: www.stellawhalley.com

WHEELER, Colin, SGFA (1986); graphic artist, illustrator and cartographer in ink, pencil and pastel. *b*: Amersham, Bucks., 4 Jul 1946. *s of*: Arthur Wheeler, retd. industrial engineer. *Educ*: Alleyne's Grammar School, Stevenage. *Studied*: privately. *Exhib*: SGFA, various one-man shows including Fermoy Gallery, King's Lynn, Lion Yard, Cambridge, Theatre Royal, Norwich, Denington Gallery, Stevenage. *Works in collections*: B.Ae., Stevenage and N. Herts. Museum. *Commissions*: 'Discover Hertford'; Stevenage Museum, Stevenage Borough Council. *Publications*: travel and tourist brochures. *Clubs*: Artists' Co-operative. *Address*: 39 Plash Drive, Stevenage SG1 1LN. *Signs work*: "Colin Wheeler."

WHEELER, Fiona, SBA, SFP. *Medium*: watercolour. *b*: Surrey, 14 Jun 1965. *m*: Nigel. *Studied*: Epsom School of Art & Design (1983-87). *Exhib*: Methodist Central Hall, Westminster, London; Mottisford Abbey, Hampshire; The Oxmarket, Chichester, West Sussex; The Savill Garden, Englefield Green, Surrey (2014). *Works in collections*: private. *Address*: Milestone Cottage, Coldharbour Lane, Woking, Surrey GU22 8SL. *Email*: fiona@botanical-artist.com *Website*: www.botanical-artist.com *Signs work*: "FW".

WHELAN, Diana, ARBS (1992). *Medium*: sculpture: bronze, resin, terracotta. *b*: Sussex, 9 Jul 1931. *d of*: James Drawbell (Editor) & Marjorie Drawbell (FRBS). *m*: 1: Dennis Whelan; 2: Peter Held. three *d*. *Educ*: Bedales. *Studied*: Goldsmiths' College School of Art (1950-53); Adult Education Colleges; City & Guilds Further Education Teaching Cert (1974). *Exhib*: Artparks International; RBS; SPS; SWA; RBA; two-sculptor show in Orangery, Holland Park, London. *Works in collections*: UK, USA, Italy, Holland, Germany, Switzerland, Portugal, France. *Commissions*: St. Thomas' Hospital; Keele University; Heinrich Stahl Housing Association; Albourne Church Sussex. *Clubs*: Chelsea Art Society. *Address*: 13 Princedale Road, London W11 4NW. *Signs work*: 'WHELAN'.

WHIDBORNE, Timothy Charles Plunket, artist in oil, tempera, sanguine, lithography, sculptor. *b*: Hughenden, Bucks., 25 Jul 1927. *s of*: Charles Whidborne. *m*: Wendy. *Educ*: Stowe School. *Studied*: St. Martin's Art School (1944), with Mervyn Peake, Chelsea (1945) and Pietro Annigoni, Florence (1949). *Exhib*: RA, RP, SPS, etc.; Kent Painters Group, East Kent Art Society; one-man show: Upper Grosvenor Galleries (1969). *Works in collections*: portrait of HM The Queen, HQ Irish Guards, London; St. Katherine of Alexandria, Worshipful Company of Haberdashers, London; HM The Queen Mother, the Inspection of the In-Pensioners Founder's Day at the Royal Hospital, Chelsea, 1991; The Duke of Devonshire, Proprietor of Pratt's Club, 1994; collection of the late Sir Paul Getty, KBE and Lady Getty; St. Jude, 2000 Pheasantry Studios. *Publications*: various poems illustrated. *Clubs*: Chelsea Arts. *Address*: The Studio. 30 Albert Rd., Deal, Kent CT14 9RE. *Signs work*: "T. Whidborne" or "T.W."

WHIGHT, Janet Beryl, BA Hons (Fine Art). *Medium*: oil/monoprints. *b*: Redhill, 5 Jun 1953. *d of*: Mr & Mrs Whight. *Studied*: Reigate School of Art (1994-96); Sir John Cass School of Art; London Guildhall University (1996-2001) (now London Metropolitan University). *Exhib*: The Guildhall Art Gallery (SEIFAS) 1985; The Mall Galleries (RSMA) 1998, 2003; various local exhibitions. *Works in collections*: private: UK & Switzerland. *Recreations*: sailing, gardening, walking. *Clubs*: Weir Wood Sailing Club. *Address*: 10 Chaldon Way, Coulsdon, Surrey, CR5 1DB. *Email*: janetbw@talktalk.net *Signs work*: "J.B.Whight" (& year).

WHISHAW, Anthony, RA, RWA, ARCA (1955), Travelling Scholarship, RCA, Spanish Government Scholarship, Abbey Premier Scholarship (1982), Lorne Scholarship (1982-83), John Moores minor prize. *b*: 22 May 1930. two *d*. *Exhib*: one-man shows: Madrid (1956), Roland, Browse and Delbanco (1960, 1961, 1963, 1965, 1968), I.C.A. (1971), New Art Centre (1972), Hoya (1974), Nicola Jacobs (1981, 1983, 1984), Mappin A.G. (1985), Barbican Centre (1994). Mixed: RWA (1993); ArtSpace (1994, 1995); Art First (1997); Stephen Lacey (2000); Osborne Samuel (2007); Fine Art Society, King's Place Gallery (2011). *Works in collections*: National Gallery, Melbourne, Australia, Seattle Museum, Arts Council, Coventry Museum, Leicester Museum, Chantrey Bequest, Bolton A.G., Bayer Pharm., Western Australia A.G., Museo de Bahia, Brazil, Power A.G., European Parliament, Ferens A.G., Tate Gallery, Graves A.G. Sheffield. *Address*: 7a Albert Pl., Victoria Rd., London W8 5PD. *Email*: anthony.whishaw@btinternet.com *Website*: www.anthonywishaw.com

WHISKERD, Jennifer, BA Hons. Fine Art Painting; travel illustrator, Central Asia, Armenia, Syria, Eastern Europe, Islamic Africa. *b*: Gloucester, 23 Mar 1962. *d of*: John

Whiskerd, artist. *Exhib*: international and national. Work in public and private collections. Fine Art tutor. *Commissions*: Gulfoil, Terrapin International. *Address*: c/o School of Art & Design, University of Gloucestershire, St. Paul's Road, Cheltenham GL50 4BS. *Signs work*: "J.H. Whiskerd."

WHITAKER, Rita Elizabeth, RMS, HS, MAS-F, MAA; Top awards, Royal Miniature Soc., Llewellyn Alexander Gallery, London, and Florida Miniature Art Soc. in America; Awards: Llewelyn Alexander Master Award, RMS Group Award, Fairman Subject Award; professional artist. *Medium*: oil on copper. *b*: 3 Sep 1936. *d of*: Mr & Mrs W.J. Pedley. *m*: C.J. Field. two *s*. *Educ*: Sion Convent, Worthing. *Studied*: Worthing Art College; Regent St. Polytechnic under Stuart Tresilian. *Exhib*: Royal Miniature Soc., RA, Medici's, Hilliard Soc., Llewellyn Alexander, Assoc. of Sussex Artists, Miniature Art Soc. of Florida and various galleries throughout England, Wales and USA. *Works in collections*: Royal Miniature Soc., Baltic Exchange, London, Florida Miniature Society; private collections throughout the world. *Commissions*: Baltic Exchange, private houses and animals. *Works Reproduced*: Medici cards. *Recreations*: gardening, walking, sketching and croquet. *Clubs*: Sidmouth Croquet Club. *Address*: 3 Roswell Court, 8 Douglas Avenue, Exmouth EX8 2FA. *Email*: ritaefield@icloud.com *Signs work*: "R. E. Whitaker."

WHITAKER, Vivien, ARBS; MSc BA Art & Design (First Class). *Medium*: directly carving the last of the English alabaster. *Represented by*: Celia Lendis Gallery, Moreton -on-the-Marsh. *Exhib*: Bankside Gallery, London (2007); Transparent Rock Gallery, Henley (2008), Peinmore Gallery, Skye (2009); Burnham Market (2009); Buckenham Galleries, Southwold (2009); Mitchell Gallery, Warwick (2010); Galeria Oberlichtsaal, Sindelfingden, Germany (2011); Millenium Galleries, Sheffield (2013). *Works in collections*: Lawrence Batley Theatre, Huddersfield; Dartington Hall, Devon; Weston Park Museum, Sheffield; The University of Hull Art Collection; Sheffield Business School; Towneley Hall, Burnley; Woodbrooke, Birmingham; Hill House, Brixham; St. Lawrence's Church, Barlow. Private collectors include: E. Auzan, Geneva; Interlogos, Brussels; S J Aravelo, California; P. Ratcliff, Virginia Water; Dr. V. James, Sheffield; R. Shaw, Ripley; N Macindoe, London. *Commissions*: Silent Art Auction for Music in the Round, Sheffield (2013). *Principal Works*: First retrospective: 'Source of Inspiration', Townley Art Gallery, Burnley (2013). *Address*: Studio Vie, 16 Rutland Terrace, Barlow, Dronfield, S18 7SS. *Email*: enquiries@vivienwhitakersculpture.com *Website*: www.vivienwhitakersculpture.com

WHITCOMBE, Susan Anne Clare, painter in oil and water-colour of equestrian portraits and landscapes, and bronzes. *b*: London, 17 Jun 1957. *d of*: Philip Whitcombe. two *s*. *Educ*: N. Foreland Lodge, Hants. *Studied*: Heatherley School of Fine Art (John Walton, Bernard Hailstone). *Exhib*: SEA., NEAC (2004, 2005, 2006); one-man shows: London (1981, 1988, 1993, 2003, 2009), Tokyo (1985, 1987), Melbourne (1982). *Address*: Redwood Cottage, West Meon, Hants. GU32 1JU. *Website*: www.susiewhitcombe.com. *Signs work*: "S. WHITCOMBE".

WHITE, Amanda, LSIAD. *Medium*: acrylic, collage, drawing, prints. *b*: London, 9 Apr 1952. two *d*. *Studied*: Croydon College of Art 1969-74 (Theatre Design) (Pamela Howard, Ralph Adron). *Exhib*: usual - mixed and solo, UK, Spain, New York. *Works in collections*: Private; corporate: Manchester City Art Gallery (Rutherston Collection); Prints & cards of writers' houses. *Commissions*: collages in UK museums and retail outlets. *Recreations*: reading, procrastinating, weeding, filling sketchbooks. *Clubs*: member Association of British Naive Artists. *Address*: Camino Carrasco 20, La Costa, Pto Cruz, 38400 Canary Islands, Spain. *Email*: amanda.awhite@yahoo.co.uk *Website*: amandawhite-contemporarynaiveart.com *Signs work*: Initials/monogram - A above W with a line between the two letters.

WHITE, Donna, BA Fine Arts, Higher Education Diploma. *Medium*: oil, gloss paint. *b*: South Africa, 5 Mar 1953. *m*: Peter Snyman. three *s*. *Studied*: University of Natal Pietersmaritzburg, South Africa (1970-76); Johannesburg Art Foundation (1982). *Exhib*: Art South Africa Today (1975), Natal Society of Arts (1978), South African Contemporary Realism, Pretoria Art Gallery (1983), Volkskas Atelier (1988, 1990), Artists of the Eighties, Gencor Gallery Rand Afrikaans University (1990), Crake Gallery (1984-1995), Strack van Schyndel Gallery (1987), Elizabeth Gordon Gallery (1987), Gallery 709 (1991-94), Royal Society of Portrait Painters, Mall Galleries (2005, 2007); Royal West of England Academy Autumn Show (2006), Royal Academy Summer Show (2009). *Works in collections*: private/corporate collections. *Commissions*: Polana Hotel, Inhaca Island Lodge (entire hotel); portrait of Mandela - Escom. Various corporate commissions. *Publications*: 'Looking at South African Art' by Frieda Harmsen. *Misc*: relocated with family to the UK in 2000. *Address*: 84 Portlock Road, Maidenhead, SL6 6DZ. *Email*: donna@donnawhite.co.uk *Website*: www.donnawhite.co.uk *Signs work*: "DONNA WHITE".

WHITE, Helen Elizabeth, RMS (2002), HSDAD (1986), MA (2007); calligrapher, illuminator and miniaturist in watercolour and gold; also ceramics (handmade tiles). *b*: Amersham, 26 Jul 1965. *Educ*: Chesham High School. *Studied*: Reigate School of Art and Design (1984-86), The Prince's School of Traditional Arts (2005-2007). *Exhib*: annually with RMS at the Mall Galleries: Llewellyn Alexander Gallery - A Million Brushstrokes; RA Summer Show (1997). *Commissions*: Plaque of hand painted tiles for Leighton House, London to commemorate the visit of HRH The Prince of Wales in 2010. *Address*: 115 Vale Rd., Chesham, Bucks. HP5 3HP. *Website*: www.helen-white.co.uk *Signs work*: "H.W." sometimes "H.E.W."

WHITE, John Norman, NDD (1951); painter, illustrator, oil, gouache, and water-colour. *b*: Chipperfield, Herts., 27 Mar 1932. *s of*: John Eugene White. *m*: Irene White, potter. two *s*. *Educ*: Belmont Senior Modern School. *Studied*: Harrow School of Art (1945-51). *Exhib*: RA, Young Contemporaries. *Works in collections*: Municipal collection Borken Germany. *Address*: Northwood Lodge, Bullockstone Rd., Herne, Herne Bay, Kent CT6 7NR. *Email*: john.nwhite@btopenworld.com *Signs work*: "JOHN - WHITE."

WHITE, Josephine Helen, 3 Distinctions in City & Guilds Design & Decoration of Flour Confectionary; Assoc. SBA. *Medium*: oil/wax pencil. *b*: Malvern, Worcs., 1 Sep 1951. *m*: Keith. two *s*. *Educ*: with various recognised artists, aiming to elevate and promote oil/wax pencil internationally. *Exhib*: SBA, Westminster Hall, London (2013, 2014); Palmengarten, Frankfurt, Germany (2014); private gallery, The Lodge, Temple Cloud. *Commissions*: too many to list. *Works Reproduced*: Over 27 Limited Edition Giclee prints. *Principal Works*: Old Crunchy, Black Calla Lilies, Ode to Autumn, Roses for Valentine, Emily's Bouquet, Jenny's Apple Blossom, Raising the Flag, Pineapple. *Address*: The Lodge, Eastcourt Road, Temple Cloud, Nr. Bath BS39 5BU. *Email*: jowhite@homecall.co.uk *Website*: josiewhiteart.co.uk *Signs work*: "J.H. WHITE".

WHITE, Judy, BA Hons (Cant). *Medium*: oils, watercolour, drawing, prints. *b*: Eastry, Kent, 2 Feb 1945. *d of*: Rev. Gordon White. *m*: Mark Osborne, MA, MSIAD, FRSA. *Educ*: Stroud High School for Girls, Stroud. *Studied*: Cheltenham College of Art (1962-4); Canterbury College of Art (1964-8). *Exhib*: RA Summer Exhbn; Morley Gallery, London; Jerwood Open Drawing Exhbn, Cheltenham, Berlin, Geneva; Pastel Society Centenary Exhbn; Highgate Gallery, London. *Principal Works*: Specialising in the figure. *Address*: 80 Norbury Crescent, London SW16 4LA. *Email*: whitejudy@btinternet.com *Signs work*: 'JUDY WHITE'.

WHITE, Karyn, BA (Hons) Art. *Medium*: painter/printmaker. *b*: Australia, 16 Aug 1956. *d of*: John & Patricia White. one *d*. *Educ*: Melbourne State College, Victoria Australia (Fine Art/Craft). *Represented by*: Benjamin Hargreaves, London SW6. *Exhib*: Gryphon Gallery,

Australia; Camberwell Press, London; Square Gallery, London; Business Art Gallery, London; Roar Gallery, Australia; Republique Gallery, Australia; Contemporary Art Fairs, Islington (91-95), Benjamin Hargreaves, Lennox Gallery London. *Works in collections*: private collections. *Commissions*: World Wildlife Fund Portfolio, Camberwell Press. *Works Reproduced*: exhibition catalogues. *Recreations*: music, opera, horseriding, cooking. *Address*: 58 Shacklewell Lane, London E8 2EY. *Signs work*: KWhite.

WHITE, Laura, BA (Hons); sculptor in stone, wood and bronze. *b*: Worcester, 10 Mar 1968. *Educ*: Alice Ottley School, Worcester. *Studied*: Worcester Art College, Loughborough College of Art and Design. *Exhib*: various mixed and solo shows in UK. *Works in collections*: Art Scene London, Gallery Shurini London. *Address*: c/o Cubitt Studio, 8 Angel Mews, London SE8 4SA. *Signs work*: "LAURA WHITE" or not at all.

WHITE, Lucy Annette, painter in egg tempera, oil, with prelim. sketches in conté crayon; modernist, landscapes, people, nature, usually combined, including design styles of 1950s. *b*: Perth, Australia, 29 Oct 1960. *Educ*: Perth Technical College. *Studied*: self taught. *Address*: Room 11, Everton Court, Milford Rd., Everton, Hants. SO41 0JG. *Website*: www.cornwallhumanists.org.uk *Signs work*: "LAW."

WHITE, Michael B., painter in oil, water-colour; also etcher, serigrapher, lithographer; unique monoprints, trichoprints, bronze, charcoal, pastel. *b*: Hythe, Kent, 2 Jul 1958. *Partner*: Sarah E. Charles. *Educ*: Sevenoaks School, Kent. *Studied*: Hastings College of Art and Design (1972-1974), Ravensbourne College of Art and Design (1974-1976), Brighton Polytechnic (1979-1981). *Exhib*: various including, RA Summer Exhib., BP National Portrait Gallery, Internat. Contemporary Arts Fair, Bath Arts Festival, NEAC, Not the Royal Academy, London Group, Hildt Gallery, Chicago, Printmakers Council, national open prize winner, Hunting Group, Singer & Friedlander. *Works in collections*: Foundation Wood, Fontenay, France; Stena, Oslo, Norway; Hildt Corpn., Chicago; Kidd Collection; New Zealand. *Commissions*: Eyre Estate, J.&J. Allen, Cochrane Co., Dewars. *Recreations*: big game, fishing, vintage motorbikes and travelling. *Clubs*: Chelsea Arts, RNC, RAYC, Blue Bird. *Address*: 143 Old Church St., London SW3 6EB. *Website*: m.b.white@artcreative.com *Signs work*: "M B White"or "M B W."

WHITE, Philippa. *Medium*: watercolour, pastel and oils. *b*: Aberdeen, Scotland, 18 Jun 1944. *Partner*: Jeremy. two *s*. *Educ*: Lycée Francais, London & Ancaster House, Sussex. *Studied*: largely self-taught, studied briefly in Paris and Chelsea. *Exhib*: Chelsea Art Society (2001-); Art Westminster (2002); St. Martin's-in-the-Field Gallery. *Commissions*: private. *Recreations*: sailing; skiing. *Clubs*: Itchenor Sailing Club. *Address*: No 4, 36 Buckingham Gate, London SW1E 6PR. *Email*: philippa_white@hotmail.com *Website*: www.chelseaartsociety.org.uk *Signs work*: "Philippa White".

WHITE, Robert Edward, BA (Hons) Fine Art, Post Grad Diploma, Royal Academy Schools; BBC4/Meritcafe Trust Award (2002), Greenshields Foundation, Lucie Morison Prize ROSL. *Medium*: oils on canvas, prints, watercolour, mixed media. *b*: Westminster, London, 17 Oct 1963. *s of*: Mr E T and Mrs A M White. *m*: Susannah Beasley-Murray. one *d*. *Educ*: Royal Academy Schools, Norwich School of Art, Medway College of Art and Design. *Studied*: Fine Art (painting). *Exhib*: Lexmark Art Prize, Eyestorm Gallery, London; Neuropop A & D Gallery, London; Hunting Group, Royal College of Art, solo shows at Royal Overseas League, London and Edinburgh; BP Portrait Award, National Portrait Gallery, Discerning Eye, Mall Galleries, London Art Fairs Art 98 and Art 97, Business Design Centre, London; The Collection - Lawrence Graham, London (2006); One Love - The Lowry, Manchester (2006-7). *Works in collections*: Royal Overseas League, London; Scottish Equitable, Edinburgh; Paintings in Hospitals, London; Prudential Corporate Collection; Norwich School of Art. *Commissions*: Sir Geoffrey Ellerton, Royal Overseas League, The Prudential Collection. *Publications*: The First Harlech Biennale (ISBN 0 9524147911).

Works Reproduced: Arts Review, The Guardian, The Times, The Sunday Telegraph, RA Magazine; The Observer. *Recreations*: cooking, travelling. *Misc*: Travel Scholarship to Barcelona (Norwich School of Art, 1985). *Address*: 26 Shaftesbury Road, London E7 8PD. *Email*: robert@robertwhite.info. *Website*: www.robertwhite.info. *Signs work*: Robert White.

WHITE, Victoria, BA Hons, Art Foundation. *Medium*: photography, prints, gouache. *b*: London, 24 Nov 1972. *d of*: Mr & Mrs White. *Studied*: Chelsea College of Art (1997), Camberwell College of Art (2000). *Represented by*: Trowbridge Gallery, 555 Kings Road, Chelsea. *Exhib*: Royal Academy of Art (2009); The Affordable Art Fair, London (2002); RCA (2003). Solo exhibitions include: Trowbridge Gallery (2008, 2009); Rooms Eleven, Belgravia (2005). *Works in collections*: Joely Richardson, Prince Albert II of Monaco, Vanessa Redgrave. *Commissions*: Prince Albert II of Monaco, Joely Richardson, Kensington & Chelsea Libraries. *Publications*: Tatler, The Sunday Telegraph, The Daily Mail, Vanity Fair. *Works Reproduced*: portraits of Joely Richardson, and Prince Albert II of Monaco. *Clubs*: Chelsea Art Club. *Address*: 46 Starfield Road, London W12 9SW. *Email*: info@victoriawhite.com *Website*: www.victoriawhite.co.uk *Signs work*: "Victoria White".

WHITE-OAKES, Sue, MCSD; metal sculptor in copper and bronze. *Medium*: sculpture. *b*: 26 May 1939. *m*: Roger Oakes. two *s*. *Educ*: St. Martin's High School, London. *Studied*: Central School of Art. *Represented by*: The Lost Gallery, Aldachuie, Strathdon, Aberdeenshire, AB36 8UJ. *Exhib*: Edinburgh, Glasgow, St. Andrews, London, Scottish Borders, Aberdeenshire and Ireland. *Works in collections*: many private collections. *Commissions*: not taken. *Publications*: articles: Craftsman Magazine and The Scotsman colour supplement. 'Sculpting in Copper' by Jim Pratt and Sue White-Oakes (pub Bloomsbury 2013). *Recreations*: archaeology, photography. *Clubs*: C.S.D., FSA (Scot.). *Address*: Reivers Retreat, Deansfoot Road, West Linton, Peeblesshire EH46 7BD. *Signs work*: "Sue White-Oakes."

WHITEFORD, Joan, NDD (1963), ATD (1964); artist in etching and wood engraving. *b*: St. John, Cornwall, 5 May 1942. *d of*: Francis Kinsmund Doidge. *m*: David Whiteford. *Educ*: Grammar School, Tavistock, Devon. *Studied*: Plymouth College of Art (1958-63, William Mann, Jeff. Clements), Bournemouth College of Art (1963-64). *Exhib*: RA, RE, NS, SWA, NEAC, RI, Mall Print. *Address*: Meadowside, Cockwells, Penzance, Cornwall TR20 8DB. *Signs work*: "J. Whiteford."

WHITEFORD, Kate, DipAD (1973), DipFA (1976) History of Art; Sargant Fellow, British School at Rome (1993-94); artist in oil on gesso, also land drawings. *b*: Glasgow, 9 Mar 1952. *m*: Alex Graham. *Educ*: Glasgow High School. *Studied*: Glasgow School of Art (1969-73), Glasgow University (1974-76, History of Art, Prof. Martin Kemp). *Exhib*: Institute of Contemporary Art (1983), Riverside Studios (1986), Whitechapel A.G. (1988), Glasgow Museum and A.G. (1990). *Works in collections*: Tate Gallery, British Council, CAS, ACGB, National Gallery of Modern Art Edinburgh, SAC, Glasgow Museum and A.G. *Publications*: artists books published by Whitechapel A.G. (1988), Tetra Press and Advanced Graphics (1992), Cairn Gallery (1992), Sitelines (1992), Graeme Murray Gallery (1992). *Address*: c/o Frith St. Gallery, 60 Frith St., London W1V 5TA. *Signs work*: "Whiteford" or "Kate Whiteford."

WHITEHEAD, Steve, twice won the Wales Open Exhibition. *b*: Coventry, 1960. *m*: Paula Zimmerman. *Studied*: UCW Aberystwyth, Coutrauld Institute of Art. *Represented by*: Panter & Hall, London. *Exhib*: Panter & Hall, London. *Works in collections*: Contemporary Art Society of Wales; Prudential Corporate Collection; The Royal Bank of Scotland. *Publications*: 'Steve Whitehead: Realist Painter' by michael Paraskos; Exactitude: Hyperrealist Art Today. *Address*: c/o Panter & Hall, 11-12 Pall Mall, London SW1Y 5LU. *Email*: enquiries@panterandhall.com *Website*: www.panterandhall.com *Signs work*: 'Steve Whitehead' (on reverse only).

WHITFORD, Christopher, artist in water-colour and acrylic. *b*: Malvern, Worcs., 18 Feb 1952. *m*: Filippa. two *d*. *Studied*: Malvern. *Exhib*: RMS, John Noott, Broadway. *Address*: c/o John Noott Twentieth Century, 14 Cotswold Ct., Broadway, Worcs. WR12 7DP. *Signs work*: "C. Whitford" or "C.W."

WHITFORD, Filippa, artist in water-colour. *b*: Italy, 22 Jan 1951. *m*: Christopher Whitford. two *d*. *Exhib*: RMS, RWS, John Noott, Broadway. *Address*: c/o John Noott Twentieth Century, 14 Cotswold Ct., Broadway, Worcs. WR12 7DP. *Signs work*: "Filippa Whitford."

WHITING, David Geoffrey, BA (Hons); AICA; FRSA; art critic, writer and curator; Appointments: Trustee of the Anthony Shaw Collection at York Art Gallery; External Examiner, BA Ceramics, University of Wales Institute, Cardiff (2002-05); Awards Examiner Dip HE Ceramics, City Lit. London 2004-08; Editorial Board, 'Interpreting Ceramics' Electronic Journal (2004); External Examiner, MA Ceramics, University of Wales Institute, Cardiff (2009-12). *b*: Bromsgrove, 14 Feb 1963. *s of*: Geoffrey Whiting, artist potter. *Studied*: Oxford Brookes University (1982-85). *Publications*: numerous books, publications and exhibition catalogues. Writes for various magazines and for 'The Guardian'; contributor 'Oxford Dictionary of National Biography' (OUP); contributor 'Redaktion Allegemaines Kunstlerlexicon', Leipzig. *Misc*: Exhibitions curated include: 'Pandora's Box and the Tradition of Clay' Crafts Council, London (1995); 'Ewen Henderson Paintings' London Institute Gallery (2001); 'Functional Form Now' Galerie Besson, London (2005); Annie Turner 'River' RBSA Gallery, Birmingham (2007); 'Pots for Light', Galerie Besson, London (2009). *Address*: Crossways, Hampton Lovett, Droitwich Spa, Worcs. WR9 0LU.

WHITING, Philip John, Dip AD (Hons) (1969); PG Dip University College of Falmouth (2002); ARD Cert Ed, Leicester University (1974); Eastern Arts Association Award (1981). *Medium*: Oil; prints; water-based medium. *b*: London, 18 Apr 1948. *m*. Emma. two *s*. two *d*. *Represented by*: Belgrave, St Ives. *Exhib*: solos include: The Camden Gallery (2005); Rainyday Gallery (2005, 06, 08); European Parliament Building, Brussels (2006); Royal Cornwall Museum (2008); Bay Art Gallery, Cardiff (2008); Truro Cathedral (2008, 2012); Stuart House Museum (2009); Oxford University (2009); Belgrave, St Ives (2012); Kings School, Worcester (2013). *Works in collections*: Oxford University; Royal Cornwall Museum; Stuart House Museum; Monmouth School; Truro School; Truro Cathedral; Chancellor Goerge Osborne MP. *Commissions*: The Guardian; English Heritage; Fund for Refugees in Slovenia; Amnesty International. *Official Purchasers*: Royal Cornwall Museum; Stuart House Museum; Monmouth School; Truro School. *Works Reproduced*: The Guardian (2006); Galleries Mag (2007); many other publications. *Principal Works*: 'Places of Mourning in the Western World'. *Clubs*: acting chairman Newlyn Society of Artists (2007). *Address*: 57 Courtland Road, Oxford OX4 4HZ. *Email*: philwhitinglezerea@hotmail.co.uk *Website*: www.axisartists.org/artistid/9453 *Signs work*: "PHIL WHITING".

WHITMAN, Rosalind Marion, MA, HDFA, PGCE, BA Hons; Peabody Trust Millennium Commission Fellowship (2000). *Medium*: oils, tempera, etching, relief, prints. *b*: London, 16 May 1949). *m*: Ignatius F. Mascarenhas. one *d*. *Educ*: Italia Conti Stage School, London. *Studied*: Prince's School of Traditional Arts, London (2006-08); Greenwich University (1998-99); Slade School of Art (1973-75); Sheffield School of Art & Design (1970-73). *Exhib*: Solo shows: Ghadir Gallery, Kuwait (1987); Valparaiso School of Law, Indiana (1988); The Brontë Parsonage Museum, Yorkshire (2003); Group exhibitions: Wells Cathedral, Somerset (2012); Anna Freud Museum, London (2011); London (inc. Royal Academy, Royal National Theatre, Mall Galleries), and throughout the UK, Europe, Indonesia and the Middle East (1985-2012). *Works in collections*: Anne Dinsdale, Brontë Parsonage Museum, Prince's Trust. *Commissions*: The Sultan of Oman and various private individuals. *Publications*: 'A Very Special House', E. Whitman (London, 1994, ISBN 0-9521-751-0-X). *Official Purchasers*: Southwark College, London; British Indonesian Artists Association. *Works Reproduced*: Printmaking Today, Volume 12, No 1, Spring 2003; Brontë Studies, the Journal of the Brontë Society, Volume 28, November 2003. *Principal Works*: Arab world; Indonesian Temples and Antiquities; Wuthering Heights; etchings and paintings. *Recreations*: Reading, concerts, gallery visits, travel. *Clubs*: East London Printmakers (ELP); Greenwich Printmakers Association (GPA). *Misc*: Currently studying for a PhD at Prince's School of Traditional Arts. *Address*: 66 Amhurst Road, London E8 1JH. *Email*: rosalindwhitman@aol.com *Website*: www.rosalindwhitman.com *Signs work*: "Rosalind Whitman".

WHITTAKER, Lucianna, BA; MA; Shortlisted for Visual Arts Prize, Brighton Festival Fringe (2006). *Medium*: oil. *b*: Aldershot, 22 Dec 1979. *m*: Ben Whittaker. *Studied*: University of Brighton (2002-2003, MA Cultural and Critical Theory); Bath Spa University (1998-2001 BA Fine Art Painting). *Exhib*: Friese Green Gallery, Brighton Media Centre; Friends Meeting House, Brighton; Open Houses, Brighton & Hove; Art in Mind, Hoxton, London; Universities of Brighton and Bath. *Principal Works*: The New Sublime: Be Found, Believe, Be Held, Behold (2m x 1.4m oil paintings, 2006-07). *Clubs*: Founding Member of 'See This' (2005-06). *Address*: Flat 2, 71 Staubyns, Hove, BN3 2TL. *Email*: info@luciannawhittaker.com *Website*: www.luciannawhittaker.com *Signs work*: "LUCIANNA WHITTAKER".

WHITTEN, B. Janice E., Dip.Bact. (1960), FRSH (1990); bacteriologist and freelance artist in oil. *b*: Middx., 15 Jul 1937. *m*: Don Whitten, designer (decd). two *d*. *Educ*: Torquay Girls' Grammar School, Greenford Grammar School. *Studied*: Regent St., Chelsea, Harrow School of Art. *Exhib*: RI Gallery, mixed exhbns., Devon County Show, Royal Bath and West, Thelma Hulbert Gallery. *Publications*: illustrated: Modern Cereal Chemistry; Countryside Commission: The East Devon Way; Science of Bread; catalogues, articles. *Works Reproduced*: "Ryalls Court circa 1830s", cover jacket. *Address*: 1 Boundary Park, Seaton, E. Devon EX12 2UN. *Signs work*: capital W supporting initials.

WHITTEN, Jonathan Philip, BA Hons (1977), PGCE (1978); teacher and potter in ceramic; Head of Art, Sir James Smith's School, Camelford; Chairman: Cornwall Ceramics and Glass Group. *b*: Eastbourne, 23 Sep 1954. *s of*: Philip Whitten, ARCA. *m*: Sally Bowler. two *s*. *Educ*: Eastbourne Grammar School. *Studied*: Eastbourne College of Art and Design (1972-73, Geoffrey Flint, ARCA), University of E. Anglia (1974-77, Prof. Andrew Martindale), University of London (1977-78, William Newland); apprentice potter to Michael Leach (1978-79) and Roger Cockram (1980-81). *Exhib*: Brewhouse Gallery, Taunton (1979), Devon Guild of Craftsmen (1981), Leics. Guild of Craftsmen (1983-87), Cornwall (1990-05), etc. *Address*: Hale Farmhouse, St. Kew, Bodmin, Cornwall PL30 3HE. *Email*: whitten@stkew.eclipse.co.uk *Website*: www.stkewpottery.co.uk

WHITTEN, Miranda M.A., BSc (Hons) (1994), PhD (2001), MRSH (1994), FRSA (1998), MI Biol, C Biol (2001); biologist, artist/illustrator in acrylic, pencil, ink; nature artist commissioned by E. Devon District Council; Post-Doctoral research assistant (immunology); Member of Guild of Natural Science Illustrators (2006). *b*: London, 25 Sep 1972. *m*: Jef Walker. *Educ*: Colyton Grammar School; Aston University; Swansea University. *Exhib*: mixed shows: Christie's, Devon County Show, Bath and West, Thelma Hulbert Gallery. *Publications*: illustrated: Countryside Commission: The East Devon Way; Nature in East Devon; Elefriends Recipe Book; catalogues, posterwork. *Address*: 232 Langdon Road, Swansea SA1 8RB. *Email*: mwhitten@vegemail.com *Signs work*: "M. Whitten."

WHITTEN-LOCKE, Helena M.J. freelance artist in pen and ink, water-colour; scientific proof reader. *b*: London, 9 Oct 1970. *m*: Tony Locke. one *s*. one *d*. *Educ*: Colyton

Grammar School. *Exhib*: mixed shows: Devon County Show, Royal Bath and West; exhbn. designer: The Business Shop Agency. *Commissions*: sign writing, various house and pub exteriors in pen and ink. *Publications*: illustrated: Countryside Commission: The East Devon Way; catalogues, articles, posterwork. *Address*: 'The Rosary', Godford Cross, Awliscombe, E. Devon EX14 3PP. *Signs work*: "H.W.," "H.L." or "H. LOCKE."

WHITTINGHAM, Dr. Selby, BA (1964), MA, PhD (1975); art historian; founded Turner Soc. 1975 (Hon. Sec. 1975-76, 1980-84; Vice Chairman 1984-85); and Watteau Soc. 1984 (Sec. General and Editor); and J.M.W. Turner, RA (Co-Editor), 1988; and Donor Watch, 1995. *b*: Batu Gajah, Malaya, 8 Aug 1941. *s of*: H.R. Oppenheim, FCA. *m*: Joanna Dodds. *Educ*: Shrewsbury School; Universities of Oxford and Manchester. *Publications*: An Historical Account of the Will of J.M.W. Turner, R.A. (1989, 1996); The Fallacy of Mediocrity: The Need for a Proper Turner Gallery (1992); World Directory of Artists' Museums (1995). *Address*: Turner House, 153 Cromwell Rd., London SW5 0TQ.

WHITTLE, Janet, SBA, SFP, CBM; Teaching Cert.; Founder Pres. Award SBA; Chairman's Trophy SFP 2011. *Medium*: watercolour. *b*: 22 Apr 1948. *m*: Barry. two *s*. *Studied*: self-taught. *Represented by*: Portfolio Select. *Exhib*: Westminster Galleries; Mottisfort Abbey; various. *Works in collections*: Australia, Sweden, USA. *Publications*: Ready to Paint Roses; How to Draw Wild Flowers; How to Draw Exotic Flowers; Painting Flowers and Plants; Janet Whittle's Watercolour Flowers; Draw and Sketch Landscapes; How to Draw Flowers; DVDs: 'Painting Flowers and Plants', 'The Magic of Flowers in Watercolour'. *Works Reproduced*: De Montfort Fine Art; Solomon & Whitehead. *Address*: 5 Manor Road, Barrowby, Grantham, Lincs. NG32 1BB. *Email*: janet@janetwhittle.co.uk *Website*: www.janetwhittle.co.uk *Signs work*: 'JANET WHITTLE SBA SFP'.

WHITTLESEA, Michael, RWS (1985), NEAC; painter; prizewinner, Singer Friedlander/Sunday Times Water-colour Competition. *b*: London, 6 Jun 1938. *s of*: Sydney Charles Whittlesea. *m*: Jill. *Studied*: Harrow School of Art. *Publications*: The Complete Watercolour Course (1987). *Clubs*: Chelsea Arts. *Address*: 98 Defoe House, Barbican, London EC2Y 8ND. *Email*: whittlesea@waitrose.com *Signs work*: "Michael Whittlesea."

WHITTON, Judi, BSc (Hons) Physics (1966), MSc, Radiobiology (1967); painter in water-colour, teacher and demonstrator in water-colour; President, Palette Club. *b*: St. Helens, 24 Nov 1944. *m*: Peter. three *d*. *Exhib*: solo shows: Painswick Town Hall (1995-00, 2005), St. George's Church, Upper Cam (1994, 1998). Work in collections internationally. *Publications*: Book of Paintings (1999); Limited Edn. prints for Radio Times. Regular contributor to 'The Artist' magazine, including in 'The Artists Problem Solver' (watercolour), pub. Collins (2003), author of 'Loosen Up Your Watercolours' (Collins, 2005). *Clubs*: Fosseway Artists, Thornbury Art, Tetbury Art, Palette Club. *Misc*: appeared on BBC1 'Countryfile', painting Upper Cam Church (Sept, 2005). *Address*: Street Farm, Upper Cam, Dursley, Glos. GL11 5PG. *Email*: judi@watercolour.co.uk *Website*: www.watercolour.co.uk

WIGGILL, Karyn, ARMS, MASSA. Awards include: Highly Commended & Best in Show (MASSA); "Best Work by Young Artist", First Prizes for Human Figure & Drawing & Pastel (MASF); First Prize, Elizabeth Specht Memorial Exhibition, California, USA; Honourable Mention (MPSGS). Obtained Associate Membership of the Royal Society of Miniaturists (2013). *Medium*: watercolour, drawing. *b*: Johannesburg, 31 Dec 1974. *m*: Leon Bell. one *s*. one *d*. *Studied*: University of Natal, Pietermaritzburg (Batchelor of Social Science); Rand Afrikaans University, Johannesburg (Advanced Diploma in Labour Law). *Exhib*: Miniature Art Society of Florida (2011, 2013, 2014); Miniature Painters, Sculptors & Gravers Society of Washington DC (2013); Elizabeth Sprecht Memorial Miniature Show (2012); RMS (2012, 2013); Miniature Art Society of SA (2009-2013). *Works in collections*:

Llewellyn Alexander Gallery. *Publications*: Included in "Strokes of Genius 5, The Best of Drawing" (North Light Books). *Recreations*: reading, road running. *Clubs*: MASSA, ARMS. *Misc*: Wiggill is her maiden name, used to sign her work. *Address*: 27 Beukes Avenue, Highway Gardens, Johannesburg 1609, South Africa. *Email*: karynleon@mweb.co.za *Signs work*: "Karyn Wiggill".

WIGGINS, Toby, RP; BA Hons Fine Art, Royal Academy Diploma in Painting, BP Travel Award 2006, Changing Faces Award 2005, Princes Drawing Prize 2005, Lynn Painter Stainer Prize 2009. *Medium*: oil, watercolour, drawing, prints. *b*: Swanage, Dorset, 29 Mar 1972. *s of*: Wendy & Tim Wiggins. *Studied*: RA Schools (1996-99); Falmouth College of Art (1991-94). *Represented by*: Royal Society of Portrait Painters. *Exhib*: BP Portrait Award, National Portrait Gallery, Royal Society of Portrait Painters, Mall Galleries, RA Summer Exhbn, Jerwood Drawing Prize, Royal West of England Academy, New English Art Club, Discerning Eye. *Works in collections*: Somerset County Council, Falmouth College of Art, University of Wales, Girton College Cambridge, Imperial College London, Worshipful Company Painter-Stainers, and numerous private. *Publications*: Times Magazine (Saturday 9th June 2007). *Clubs*: Poole Printmakers. *Address*: 4 Alexandra Terrace, Cowleaze, Swanage, Dorset BH19 2QQ. *Email*: tobywiggins@hotmail.com *Website*: www.tobywiggins.co.uk *Signs work*: "TMW".

WILCOX, Joan Celia. *Medium*: watercolour, some lino-printing. *b*: Meldreth, Cambs, 19 Jan 1939. *Educ*: Cambridge Technical College. *Studied*: Cambridge School of Art (1955-59). *Exhib*: Laing (Cambridge & London); Royal West of England, Bristol; Royal Institute of Painters in Watercolour, Mall Gallery; Pastel Society, Mall Gallery; Wooburn Festival Visual Art Exhibition; Open Studio during Buckinghamshire Art Weeks; RWS Hawker Gallery Old Amersham. *Works in collections*: Director of Flatford Mill. *Commissions*: various local gardens - paintings. *Publications*: Local press. *Recreations*: music making, garden, and walking. *Clubs*: Bucks. Art Society. *Address*: 69 Wycombe Lane, Wooburn Green, Bucks, HP10 0HD. *Email*: foxglove60@hotmail.co.uk *Signs work*: "Joan Wilcox".

WILD, David Paul, DFA Slade (1955), Abbey Major Scholarship to Rome (1955); artist in oil and water-colour; Founder Chairman, Friends of the Weavers Triangle. *b*: Burnley, 14 Apr 1931. *s of*: Benjamin Wild. *Educ*: Burnley Grammar School. *Studied*: Burnley School of Art; Slade School of Fine Art; Academia Britannica, Rome. *Exhib*: extensively in the north of England since 1957; Woodstock Gallery (1965), John Moores (1965, 1970), RA (1972-74), Arts Council 'Drawings of People' Serpentine Gallery. *Works in collections*: Manchester City A.G., Rutherston Coll., Granada TV, Arts Council of G.B., Walker A.G., Liverpool. *Principal Works*: 'Landscape' Walker A.G.; 'Landscape' Towneley Hall, Burnley; View of Towneley Hall, Burnley (2009). *Address*: 66 Rosehill Rd., Burnley BB11 2QX. *Signs work*: "D. Wild."

WILDE-LATHAM, H.V., EAWLS Award, Nairobi (1991); specialised in African subjects 1988-2001. *Medium*: oil, acrylic, on canvas, landscape/wildlife. *b*: Worcester, 15 Apr 1931. *Educ*: Worcester High School. *Studied*: Victoria Institute Worcester (Harry Adams, RA), evening classes. *Represented by*: Galerie Kornye West, Fort Worth, Texas, USA. *Exhib*: Mall Galleries, London (1989); Whaletail Exhbn. Niarobi (1991); Harrods Gallery, London; First Texas Council of Campfire (1998-03); CISAC (2002); DACS Exhbn, Lyttleton Gallery Malvern; many provincial galleries since 1969. *Works in collections*: 'The Adoption' Oserian Dev. Co. Kenya, and private collections internationally. *Commissions*: 'After the Rain', Ludlow (2000), Millennium Trust Fund (2003). *Publications*: exhibition catalogues, 'Campfire' USA. *Works Reproduced*: 'After the Rain' Ludlow (2000), Mill Trust Fund; 'Elephants in the City of Ghosts' (1987). *Recreations*: research into lost knowledge, walking. *Clubs*: EVP Soc., DH Soc., EAWLS, DACS. *Address*: 2A Church Street, Ludlow, Shropshire, SY8 1AP. *Signs work*: 'wilde-latham'.

WILEMAN, Peter, FROI, RSMA, EAGMA, FRSA; Frank Herring Award, Cornelissen & Son Award, Clerc Fowle Gold Medal, DAS Prize, Charles Pears Award. *Medium*: oil, watercolour. *b*: Greenford, Middlesex, 10 Dec 1946. *m*: Joanne Wileman. four *s*. three *d*. *Studied*: self taught. *Exhib*: solo and mixed exhibitions including John Noott, WH Patterson, Walker Galleries, Whittington Fine Art, Mall Galleries, Lime Tree Gallery, The Hawker Gallery, Pinkfoot Gallery. *Works in collections*: private and corporate worldwide. *Commissions*: Scottish Solar Power. *Publications*: 'Painting Light in Oil' by Peter Wileman; Painting the Light in Oils DVD (Town House Films); Inspirational Oil Landscapes DVD (Town House Films). *Clubs*: Past President, Royal Institute of Oil Painters; Royal Society of Marine Artists; Fellow, Royal Society of Arts, East Anglian Group of Marine Artists. *Address*: 53 Belle Baulk, Towcester, Northants NN12 6YE. *Email*: pj.wileman@tiscali.co.uk *Website*: peterwilemanartist.co.uk *Signs work*: "Wileman".

WILHIDE, Carol Louise, BA (Hons), PGCE. *Medium*: prints. *b*: 12 Sep 1959. *Studied*: Brighton Polytechnic (Art & Design Foundation 1978-79); Newcastle Polytechnic (BA Hons Graphic Design, 1980-83); London Institute of Education, London University (PGCE). *Exhib*: solo shows: Floral Hall (1991), Gallery 47 (1993), Grey's Inn (2000); mixed: (1983) St.Martins School of Art; (1986) Tricycle Theatre; (1987) Summer Exhibition Royal Academy; (1987) National Theatre Southbank D&AD; (1993) Piers Fleetham Gallery; (1994) Liberty Print Room; (1997) Chalk Farm Gallery; (1997) Abbott & Holder; (1997) Southwark Arts Festival; (1999) Greenwich Village. *Misc*: also known as CAROL JUSTIN (married name). *Address*: 7 Seymour Road, London N3 2NG. *Email*: caroljustin@hotmail.com *Signs work*: prints: using maiden name "CAROL WILHIDE".

WILKES, Lynne, BA Hons Fine Art/English (1969); Dip. Advanced Fine Art (Distinction, 1997). *Medium*: mixed media. *b*: Leeds, 23 Mar 1948. *m*: Adrian. two *s*. one *d*. *Studied*: Leeds University under Quentin Bell and Sir Lawrence Gowing; Bournemouth Arts Institute. *Exhib*: Royal Academy; RWEA; NEAC; Mall Galleries; Alpha Gallery, Dorset; Bettles Gallery, Hampshire; Thompsons Gallery, London/Stow-on-the-Wold; Cambridge Contemporary Art; Leith Gallery, Edinburgh; Firbob and Peacock, Cheshire; Study Gallery, Poole. *Works in collections*: RNLI Headquarters, Poole; other private collections here and abroad; Art Loan Collection (2003 & 2007); Bournemouth University. *Commissions*: several small private commissions. *Publications*: 'Fifty Wessex Artists' (Evolver Books), 'Ex Chaos' (Renscombe Press). *Clubs*: Bournemouth Art Club. *Address*: 58 Elms Avenue, Poole, Dorset. BH14 8EF. *Email*: adrwilkes@aol.com. *Signs work*: 'Lynne Wilkes'.

WILKIE, Kim, MA Modern History, Oxford; MLA Landscape Architecture, University of California, Berkeley. *Medium*: watercolour, drawing, models, earth forms. *b*: Malaysia, 30 Oct 1955. *Partner*: Pip Morrison. *Commissions*: Earth/Sculptural Land Forms, V&A Museum; Boughton Park, Hyde Park Corner, Heveningham Hall, Shawford Park. *Publications*: Led by the Land (2012). *Address*: Franklin Farm, Dean Lane, Bishop's Waltham SO32 1FX. *Email*: kim@kimwilkie.com *Website*: www.kimwilkie.com

WILKINS, William Powell, ARCA; artist in oil, lecturer and consultant. *b*: Kersey, Suffolk, 4 Apr 1938. *m*: Lynne Brantly. two *d*. *Educ*: Malvern College. *Studied*: Swansea and Royal College of Art. *Represented by*: Martin Tinney Gallery, Wales. *Exhib*: London, New York, San Francisco, Swansea, Cardiff. *Works in collections*: National Museum of Wales, Glynn Vivian Museum Swansea, Hirshorn Museum Washington DC. *Publications*: 'William Wilkins' pub GRAFFEG Oct 2014. *Address*: Carreg Cennen, Llandeilo, Carmarthenshire SA19 6TL. *Website*: williamwilkins.co.uk

WILKINSON, Chris, OBE, RA, DipArch RIBA, HonFAIA, FCSG; Elected to Royal Academy 2006. *Medium*: watercolour, drawing, acrylic, sculpture. *b*: Amersham, 1 Jul 1945. *s of*: Edward Anthony Wilkinson. *m*: Diana Wilkinson. one *s*. one *d*. *Studied*: Regent St Polytechnic School of Architecture (1964-70). *Exhib*: RA Summer Exhibition (2012); 10x10

Drawing the City (2011). *Commissions*: Courtyard Sculpture, RA Summer Exhibition 2012. *Publications*: Exploring Boundaries. *Principal Works*: Architecture, sculpture, painting. *Clubs*: Chelsea Arts Club. *Misc*: Director of Wilkinson Eyre Architects. *Address*: 52 Park Hall, London SE21 8BW. *Email*: c.wilkinson@wilkinsoneyre.com *Signs work*: "CHRIS WILKINSON RA".

WILKINSON, John Charles, RBA, certificate in Decoration (University College London), certificate Royal Academy Schools; artist in oil, water-colour, pastel, and all drawing mediums. *b*: Barnes, London, 20 Jul 1929. *m*: Sarah Goodwin, artist. one *s*. one *d*. *Educ*: Bradfield College. *Studied*: Decoration, Bartlett School of Architecture, University College London (1949-52); Drawing and Painting, RA Schools (1954-59). *Exhib*: two one-man shows, numerous mixed exhbns. *Works in collections*: UK, France, Italy, Germany, Switzerland, Greece, Australia, Japan, USA. *Commissions*: portrait, figure and decorative arts compositions. *Principal Works*: portrait, figure and landscape. *Recreations*: reading (classical novels), Artists biographical data. *Address*: Orchard House, Alderholt Rd., Sandleheath, Fordingbridge, Hampshire SP6 1PT. *Signs work*: "J.C.W." and on back of work signs full name.

WILKS, Paul John, NDD (1961), RASC (1965); researcher and lecturer Visual Perception and Comparative media; University of London CIT (1975-91). *Medium*: painter in oil, draughtsman. *b*: York, 12 Aug 1941. *m*: Kay. two *s*. *Educ*: Danesmead School, York. *Studied*: York School of Art (1956-61), Royal Academy Painting Schools (1961-65). *Works in collections*: University of Birmingham, City University, Kettering Art Gallery, Municipa Gallery Brazilia. *Publications*: correspondant 'Jackdaw' Artists Newsletter. *Clubs*: RASAA. *Address*: 10 Peak Hill, Forest Hill, London SE26 4LR.

WILLAN, Maeve, BA Hons; NS; Hesketh Hubbard Art Society 'Best Figurative Painting Prize' Mall Galleries (2007) and HH 'Best Portrait Prize' Mall Galleries (2007); N.S. 'The Aya Broughton Painting Prize' Highly Commended (2001) and 'The Aya broughton Best Oil Painting Prize' (2009). *Medium*: figurative painter mainly oil, also watercolour and pastel. *b*: Ireland. *m*: Peter James Willan, Hon RCM. *Educ*: Salesian Convent School, Limerick, Ireland. *Studied*: Limerick School of Art (1963-68), Slade School of Art masterclasses (1989-2002) and Open University Degree in Art History. *Exhib*: Group Exhbns: Mall Galleries Reopening Celebration (2007) and annually at Open and other exhibitions; RA Private Event (2000); Regularly in London/home counties with NS, Hesketh Hubbard Art Society and Richmond Art Society. Other group exhibitions have included SWA, Trinity Arts and Crafts Guild, and Galsworthy Group. Galleries include Mall, Westminster, Menier, Whiteleys, Osterley House, Lauderdale House and the Embassy of Japan, London (FBA) and ARCIF 50th Anniversary Fontainbleau (2012). *Works in collections*: Johathan Ross. *Recreations*: music and reading. *Address*: 7 The Green, Richmond, Surrey, TW9 1PL. *Email*: willan829@btinternet.com *Signs work*: "Maeve Willan".

WILLIAMS, Alex, NDD, ATD; artist in oil on canvas. *b*: Reading, 22 Jul 1942. *s of*: Sqn. Ldr. Albert George Williams. *m*: Celia. one *s*. two *d*. *Educ*: St. Peter's School, Cambs. *Studied*: St. Martin's School of Art (1962-66, Frdk. Gore, Peter Blake, Peter de Francia, David Tindle). *Represented by*: Fosse Gallery Stow on the Wold. *Exhib*: Helen Greenberg Gallery, Los Angeles (1977, 1982), Retrospective Hereford City Museum (1987), Fosse Gallery Stow on the Wold. *Works in collections*: National Library of Wales, National Trust, Hurst Newspapers, Los Angeles International Airport, Hereford, Brecon and Worcester City Museums; public and private collections in the USA, Australia and the UK. *Commissions*: designed flags, passports etc. for The Independent Kingdom of Hay (1977), numerous country house portraits, restaurant designs and many book illustrations. *Publications*: illustrated The Bird who Couldn't Fly (Hodder & Stoughton, 1988); 2009, My America, blurb.com; many prints and reproductions, greetings cards and book covers. Over 100 fine bone china designs distributed worldwide. *Recreations*: boating and pond yachts. *Address*: 13 St.Philip's Street, Leckhampton, Cheltenham, Glos. GL50 2BP. *Email*: thealexwilliams@googlemail.com *Website*: www.alexwilliams.net *Signs work*: "Alex Williams '98." now signs 'AW'o5'.

WILLIAMS, Angela Elizabeth, SGFA; artist in drawing, water-colour, oil; college tutor. *b*: Belfast, 15 Jul 1948. *Partner*: John Shelley. *Studied*: Wimbledon School of Art. *Exhib*: London and UK including RA Summer Exhib., SBA, SGFA, NEAC. *Works in collections*: UK and abroad. *Publications*: magazine articles, greetings cards, limited edition prints. *Address*: 16 Warren Park, Warlingham, Surrey CR6 9LD. *Email*: angelawilliams@ukgateway.net *Signs work*: "A E Williams."

WILLIAMS, Annie, RBA (2011), RWS (2003); RE (2005); Chris Beetles Prize (1984); Collins & Brown Award (1996); Abbot and Holder Travel Award (1998); Baker Tilly Award (2001); The Artist Magazine Award (RBA exhbn, 2004), Purcell Paper Award, Originals 06 (Mall Galleries); RWS Turner Watercolour Award (2009); Originals 10 Aberystwyth University Prize; Edward Wesson Award (2011, 2014). *b*: London, 6 May 1942. *d of*: Ivor Williams. *m*: Ron Bayliss. one *s*. one *d*. *Studied*: City & Guilds (1966-69). *Represented by*: Bankside Gallery, 48 Hopton Street, London SE1. *Exhib*: Royal Academy Summer Exhbns; RWS Opens at Bankside Gallery; Original Print Exhbns; Discerning Eye/Singer & Friedlander/The Laing (Mall Galleries); Whitechapel Gallery, and many small galleries around the country. *Works in collections*: private collections worldwide. *Works Reproduced*: in books, magazines, posters and cards, the most recent being 'The Watercolour Expert' for the RWS, and 'Printmakers Secrets' 2009. *Misc*: demonstrated at Art in Action (2003, 2005, 2008). *Address*: 31 Ellington Street, London N7 8PN. *Email*: annienwilliams@btinternet.com

WILLIAMS, Antony Mack, Still Life Prize, Discerning Eye (1998); Carroll Award (1991, 1995); Arts Club Prize (2004); Ondaatje Prize (1995). *Medium*: egg tempera. *b*: Kingston-upon-Thames, 23 Jun 1964. *s of*: Mrs Jean Williams. *Partner*: Caroline Bays. *Studied*: North West Surrey College of Art; Portsmouth University. *Exhib*: solo exhbns: Albemarle Gallery, London (1997); Sala Parés, Barcelona (1999); Messum Gallery, London (2000); Galeria Leandro Navarro, Madrid (2001), Petley Fine Art, London (2004). *Works in collections*: National Portrait Gallery; Royal Society of Portrait Painters, The Queen's College, Oxford. *Commissions*: HRH The Queen, Sir Alan Budd, Amartya Sen. *Publications*: The School of London and their Friends: The Collection of Elaine and Melvin Merians (Herlin Press); The Portrait Now: The 21st Century (NPG Publications). *Recreations*: swimming, walking. *Address*: The Cottage, 8E Windsor Street, Chertsey. KT16 8AS. *Signs work*: 'Antony Williams'.

WILLIAMS, Brigitte, BA (Hons) 2004, MFA (2006), Caitlin Art Prize - AHRC Award for Research. *Medium*: artist in mixed media, print. *m*: Graham. three *s*. *Studied*: Surrey Institute of Art and Design (1999/2004); Slade School of Art (2005/2006). *Exhib*: Royal Academy Summer Show (2006, 2007); Art Amsterdam (2007); The Empire (2007); Catlin Art Prize (2007); Northern Print Biennale (2009); Woburn Studios, London (2009). *Works in collections*: Erasmus University (Netherlands), Land Securities, Penguin Books, Catlin, Eversheds, Clifford Chance, NHS. *Commissions*: ARUP (2009). *Address*: Rushdene House, Dene Road, Ashtead KT21 1EE. *Email*: brigitte_williams@mac.com *Website*: www.brigittewilliams.co.uk *Signs work*: "Brigitte Williams".

WILLIAMS, Charles, BA (Hons) (1989), MA (RAS) (1992); Prize for Anatomical Drawing (1991), Creswick Prize, Silver Medal for Painting, British Institute Fund Award, Landseer Scholarship and Richard Ford Award for Study in Spain (1992), Countess Driscoll-Spalietti Watercolour Prize (1993), Bursary from SEArts and NEAC/Marks and Spencer Young Artists (2nd prize 1994), Travel Bursary, ROSL (1995), Sir Ernst Cassel Education

Fund Prize, ROSL (1997), 'The Real Turner Prize' (2000, 02). *Medium*: oil painter, watercolour painter, sculptor. *b*: Evanston, Ill., USA, 16 Mar 1965. *Partner*: Anna Latham, Latham & Neve Jewellery. *Studied*: Maidstone College of Art (1986-89, Mike Upton, Peter Morrell, John Titchell), R.A. Schools (1989-92, Norman Adams, Mick Rooney, Roderic Barrett, David Parfitt). *Exhib*: Star Gallery Lewes, Coombs Contemporary, C.A.S., Mercury Gallery, NEAC, RA, ROSL, NPG, Beaux Arts, Bath, The Bakersfield Museum of Art, California (2004), Cadogan Contemporary, Thomsons Gallery, Marylebone High Street. *Works in collections*: HSBC, TVS, Chevron UK, KIAD, British High Commission in Nairobi, Hammersmith Hospital Trust, Lily Savage, British Design Council, Alan Howarth MP and many private collections. *Publications*: Art Review (Sept., 1999). *Clubs*: Reynold's, NEAC, Stuckists, Barbican Arts Group, RWS. *Address*: 21 Warneford St. London E9 7NG. *Email*: swiftcharles2002@yahoo.co.uk *Website*: www.unclecharles.co.uk *Signs work*: "C.W." or "VERSO.".

WILLIAMS, Emrys, BA Fine Art (1980); painter in acrylic and oil; Lecturer in art and design, Coleg Menai, Bangor. *b*: Liverpool, 18 Jan 1958. *Partner*: Nathalie Camus. one *s*. *Studied*: Slade School of Fine Art (1976-80). *Exhib*: Benjamin Rhodes Gallery (1989, 1991, 1994), touring shows: 'Sunny Spells' Oriel Mostyn, Llandudno (1995), 'Various Fictions' Collins Gallery, Glasgow (1998). *Works in collections*: Metropolitan Museum of Art, N.Y., Arts Council of England, Government Art Collection. *Commissions*: National Museum of Wales. *Address*: First Floor Flat, 10 Whitehall Road, Rhos on Sea LL28 4HW.

WILLIAMS, Fran, GNVQ Art and Design (Distinction); BA (Hons) General Illustration (1st). *Medium*: Oil; drawing; mixed media; acrylic. *b*: Swansea, 13 Oct 1980. *Studied*: Swansea College (1997-1999); Swansea University (2005-2008). *Represented by*: View Gallery. *Exhib*: Northern Lights Gallery (2003); Swansea Uni Met Solo Show (2006); Artist in Residence Show Swansea Met (2008); Tunnadine Fine Art (2009); View Gallery (2010); Dreweatt's Contemporary Art Auction (2010); Bo.lee Gallery (2010); View Gallery (2010); Red Propeller - guests artists (2010). Solo shows: Bo.lee (2011); The Knifesmith Gallery (2009); Elysium Gallery (2009). *Works in collections*: Private collection of David James (England goalkeeper); private collection of painter Guy Denning; private collections throughout UK, Europe and US. *Misc*: 'The Last Forever' sold at Dreweatts Auction (Apr 2010) for twice estimate. Artist in residence at Swansea University for one year. *Address*: 47 Hen-Llys, Wind Street, Swansea SA1 1DP. *Email*: franwilliams1310@hotmail.co.uk *Website*: www.franwilliams1310.com *Signs work*: "FRAN WILLIAMS".

WILLIAMS, Glynn, sculptor in stone and bronze; Prof. of Sculpture, RCA, Head of the School of Fine Art, retired 2009. Awarded Emeritus Professor of Sculpture RCA. *b*: Shrewsbury, 30 Mar 1939. *s of*: Idris & Muriel Williams (decd). *Partner*: Diana Charnley. two *d*. *Educ*: Wolverhampton Grammar School. *Studied*: Wolverhampton College of Art (1955-60, 1960-61 Post Dip.); Rome Scholarship in Sculpture (1961-63). *Exhib*: one-man shows: including Blond Fine A.G. (1982), Bernard Jacobson Gallery (1985, 1986, 1988, 1991, 1994, 2000), Artsite Gallery, Bath (1987), Retrospective exhbn. at Margam Park, S. Wales (1992), Atkinson Gallery, Millfield (1997). *Works in collections*: ACE, Hakone Open Air Museum, Japan, V&A, Tate Gallery, NPG, Henry Moore Centre for Sculpture, Leeds; Cube Gallery, Bournemouth; Atkinson Gallery. *Commissions*: Henry Purcell Memorial, City of Westminster (1996), "Gateways of Hands", Chelsea Harbour, memorial to Lloyd George in Parliament Square unveiled in 2008. *Recreations*: music, cooking, crosswords. *Clubs*: Chelsea Arts. *Address*: Follyfield, Shrewton, Salisbury, Wilts, SP3 4JL. *Email*: glynn.williams@rca.ac.uk *Website*: www.glynnwilliams.co.uk *Signs work*: "G.W."

WILLIAMS, Graham Richard, ARBS (2001), SWE (1982). *Medium*: sculptor in metal and stone. *b*: Bromley, Kent, 21 Feb 1940. *m*: Nina. one *s*. one *d*. *Educ*: Beckenham Grammar School. *Studied*: Day release from Grammar School to Beckenham Art School, also in evenings. *Represented by*: Annely Juda Fine Art, 23 Dering Street, London W1S 1AW. *Exhib*: One man shows: West End House Gallery, Smarden (2006), Konstruktiv Tendens, Stockholm (1998, 2001), Annely Juda Fine Art, London (1995, 2000, 2004), Sassen Galerie, Berlin (1992), Galerie Walzinger, Saarlouis (1991), Alex Gerard Fine Art, Battle (1985). *Works in collections*: private and corporate. *Commissions*: all private. *Publications*: illustrated exhibition catalogues. Has written several essays on Naum Gabo. *Works Reproduced*: Roxtec 1990-2000 pub. Roxtec International AB (2000) , 40 Nudes, pub. Silent Books (1988), Engraver Two pub. Silent Books (1992), A Forest of Sculpture, pub. Collection Simon Spierer (2008). *Clubs*: Society of Wood Engravers, Brother of the Art Workers Guild, Patron of the Gabo Trust. *Address*: Vent House, Stalisfield Road, Charing, Kent, TN27 0HH. *Email*: grw@grahamwilliams.co.uk *Website*: www.grahamwilliams.co.uk

WILLIAMS, Jacqueline E. E., NEAC; BA (Hons.) (1985), Advanced Dip. (R.A.) (1988); artist in oil. *b*: Lincoln, 2 Nov 1962. *Educ*: Downlands School, Hassocks. *Studied*: Glos. College of Arts and Technology (1982-85), R.A. Schools (1985-88). *Exhib*: New Grafton Gallery, Barnes; solo show: Brian Sinfield Gallery; mixed shows: NEAC, RWA, RA, Adam Gallery, Bath; Russell Gallery, Putney, London. *Works in collections*: Cheltenham and Gloucester Bldg. Soc. HQ, Contemporary Arts Soc. for Wales. *Clubs*: CGA, NEAC. *Address*: Garden Flat, 73 Bath Rd., Cheltenham, Glos. GL53 7LH. *Website*: www.jacquelinewilliams.co.uk *Signs work*: "J.W."

WILLIAMS, Jane Harker, 1993 Saunders Waterford Prize at Royal Watercolour Society Open exhbn; 2007 Rugby Fine & Decorative Arts Society Award at Rugby Open. *Medium*: watercolour, acrylic, drawing, collage, pastel. *b*: Monxton, Hants., 28 Sep 1942. *d of*: Capt. & Mrs. John Smallwood. *m*: Charles Williams. one *s*. one *d*. *Studied*: Coventry School of Art; Birmingham Institute of Art and Design. *Exhib*: Manor House Gallery, Chipping Norton; The Whibley Gallery, Worthing; Castle Gallery, Kenilworth; Park View Gallery, Edgbaston; The Stour Gallery, Shipston on Stour; Open exhbns: RI, RWS, RBSA, Coventry, Cheltenham, Leamington. *Works in collections*: private collections in Great Britain, Australia, Singapore, France, USA. *Commissions*: Warwick School Recital Room (2004). *Publications*: Warwickshire Life Sept 2006; Artspace (no 31). *Clubs*: Association of Midland Artists. *Misc*: Artist in Residence, Leamington Music. *Address*: 17 Binswood Avenue, Leamington Spa, Warwickshire. CV32 5SE. *Email*: janeh.williams17@gmail.com *Website*: www.janewilliamsartist.co.uk *Signs work*: 'JW'.

WILLIAMS, John, NDD, ATC. *Medium*: photography. *b*: Bury St.Edmunds, 17 May 1941. *s of*: George Barnacle Calvert. two *d*. *Educ*: Silver Jubilee Secondary School for Boys. *Studied*: Cambridge School of Art (1956-61), University of South Wales (1969-70), Leeds and Leicester Polytechnics p/t MPhil (1974-76, not completed). *Exhib*: extensively in UK and Europe, including solo show for London Undergrounds 'Platform for Art' (82 portraits) Piccadilly Circus (2003); Jelly-Legged Chicken Gallery, Reading (2004); 20/21 Gallery Scunthorpe (2005); Royal Photographic Society International Touring Exhbn (2004/5); Peter Piers Gallery/Sudbury Quay, Bury St. Edmunds (2005); Brighton Art Fair (2005); Brighton Photo Biennial Fringe (2006); Hellenic Photographic Society (2006); Suffolk Open (2006); Christopher Gull Brighton (2006); East London Photo-Feast (2006); Bow Arts East London (2007); Ickworth Round House, National Trust (2007); Simultaneous Portraits at National Stroke Headquarters London and Edinburgh Scotland (2007); Et.Cetera Gallery, London (2007); Islington Photography and Design Fair (2007). *Recreations*: have sailed a board for 20 years, then took up skate boarding. *Clubs*: F6 foto-group. *Address*: 92 Kings Road, Bury St.Edmunds, Suffolk IP33 3DT. *Email*: info@freeformphoto.co.uk *Website*: www.freeformphoto.co.uk

WILLIAMS, Martin, BAHons. *Medium*: Sculpture. *b*: London, 22 Jun 1954. *Partner*: Helen John. one *d*. *Educ*: Penlan Comprehensive, Swansea. *Studied*: Swansea College of Art

(1972); Staffordshire University (1973-1976); University of London, Institute of Education (1977). *Exhib*: Glynn Vivian, Swansea (1985); Leo Gallery, Swansea (1988); Mission Gallery, Swansea (1985); National Eisteddford, Wales (1989); Taliesin, Swansea University (2014). *Works in collections*: Glynn Vivian Gallery, Swansea. *Commissions*: Smallpox Immunisation Monument, Geneva, Switzerland and Collegeville, Pennsylvania, USA (2010/12); Slimbridge Entrance Sculpture in stone, Gloucestershire (2012); Nelson Roundabout Sculpture in portland stone, Nelson, South Wales (2007); North Leicestershire Probation Service, Clipsham limestone, Leicester (2006); Tony Allcock, bronze, Thurmaston, Leicestershire (2005); Bridgend Sculptural Railings and seating in steel, Bridgend, South Wales (2004); Steamwheel, sculpture in steel, Mold, North Wales (2002); Sporting Success, bronze, City of Leicester (1998); Lutterworth Ceramic Tower, Lutterworth, Leicestershire (1997); Gilfach Goch, BBC documentary (1995); Canal Park Entrance in steel and ceramic, Cardiff (1995); The Bay Panels, 12 relief panels, Cardiff Bay, Cardiff (1994); Woolwich Arsenal Workers, wall relief, Woolwich Arsenal Station, Woolwich, London (1993); Copper Flame, stone, ceramic and copper seaside monument, Maritime Quarter, Swansea (1988). *Publications*: 'The Furnished Landscape', 'Immortals in British Sport'. *Official Purchasers*: Pfizer, Collegeville, Pennsylvania, USA. *Works Reproduced*: Smallpox Immunisation monument; Sporting Success; Tony Allcock; Woolwich Arsenal Workers; Gilfach Goch, BBC documentary; Copper Flame. *Principal Works*: Smallpox Immunisation monument; Nelson roundabout sculpture; Sporting Success; Woolwich Arsenal Workers; Copper Flame. *Address*: 10 Kimberley Road, Sketty, Swansea SA2 9DL. *Email*: swanseajack47@yahoo.co.uk *Website*: www.sculpturaldesignltd.co.uk *Signs work*: "MW".

WILLIAMS, Michael Antony Ellis, BA Modern History. *Medium*: watercolour, pen and ink, graphite. *b*: Patna, India, 11 Nov 1936. *Partner*: Naomi Brandel. two *s*. *Studied*: University College, Oxford. *Exhib*: London Group; John Moores, Liverpool; RA Summer Exhbn; Singer & Friedlander/Sunday Times Watercolour Comp. (commended 2007); 56 Group Wales, inc. exhbns in Prague and Bratislava; Christie's, London (National Trust Centenary); MoMA Dublin; Austin Desmond Fine Art (solo shows 1988, 1991); Aegean Centre, Paros, Greece; Bay Art, Cardiff; Silk Top Hat, Ludlow; Slader's Yard, West Bay. *Commissions*: many private commissions for landscape. *Publications*: Francis Spalding: Dictionary of British Art, Vol.6, 20th century; David Buckman: Dictionary of Artists in Britain since 1945. *Recreations*: some writing, e.g. catalogue introductions. *Misc*: extensive teaching career. *Address*: The Hawthorns, Middle Road, Thrupp, Stroud, Glos. GL5 2DL. *Email*: maewilliams2005@yahoo.co.uk *Signs work*: 'MAEW'.

WILLIAMS, Nicholas Charles, figurative painter in oil on canvas; Hunting art Prize 2001. *b*: UK, 1961. one *d*. *Studied*. Richmond College (1977-79). *Represented by*: Fine Art Management. *Exhib*: Brian Sewell's A Critic's Choice, Cooling Gallery, London; The Spectator Awards, Christie's, London; Hunting/Observer Awards, Mall Galleries, London; Bayer art prize, London; Garrick Milne Exhibition, London; Royal Cornwall Museum; Russell-Cotes Museum and Gallery; Liverpool Cathedral, European Capital of Culture. *Works in collections*: Hunting plc, Bluestone, Bournemouth Central Library. *Works Reproduced*: cover of Steven Berkoff's Collected Plays, volume one. *Principal Works*: Searching III, Adoration of the Sea, Desideratum. *Recreations*: surfing. *Address*: Old Lifeboat Station, Towan Headland, Newquay, Cornwall TR7 1HS. *Website*: www.nicholascharleswilliams.co.uk *Signs work*: "Nicholas Charles Williams."

WILLIAMS, Simon, SBA; Silver Gilt Medal (RHS); Certificate of Botanical Merit (SBA, 2001, 2003); Course Director for the Society of Botanical Artists. *Medium*: gouache, watercolour, acrylic. *b*: Poole, 26 Nov 1979. *s of*: Rona & Roger Williams. Partner: *Hayley* Davis. two *d*. *Studied*: The Arts Institute, Bournemouth (1996-2000, HND in Natural History Illustration). *Exhib*: SBA Annual Exhbn; RHS shows for Botanical Art; National

Orchid Show. *Works in collections*: internationally. *Commissions*: private commissions and illustration work undertaken. *Publications*: Gouache Painting Step-by-Step chapter 'The Art of Botanical Painting'; 'Wildflowers and Flora of the World'; '3D Viewer on Ocean Life'. *Official Purchasers*: Anness Publishing, Cowley Robinson Publishing. *Works Reproduced*: in 'The Art of Botanical Painting' (see Publications). *Address*: S.W. Illustrations, 7a Aldridge Road, Kinson, Bournemouth BH10 5NW. *Email*: simon@swillustrations.com *Website*: www.swillustrations.com

WILLIAMS, Sue, MA (Oxon); SBA; Fellow Chelsea Physic Garden Florilegium Society; RHS Silver Gilt Medal (2006); RHS Gold Medal (2008). *Medium*: botanical watercolours. *b*: Murree, Pakistan, 10 May 1942. *d of*: AM & MJ Dent. *m*: Martin John. two *s*. *Studied*: St. Hughs College, Oxford (Modern Languages). *Exhib*: Harare Botanical Gardens (1998); Adam Art Gallery, Wellington, NZ (1999); RHS; SBA London; Florum Kent Painters Group; Tasmania; Shirley Sherwood Gallery, Kew Gardens & Brooklyn Botanical Gardens, USA (with Chelsea Physic Garden Florilegium Society); St. Hugh's College Oxford; Palmengarten, Frankfurt. *Works in collections*: The Girdlers Company; Chelsea Physic Garden; Pitcairn Philatelic Bureau; RHS Lindley Library; Hunt Institute for Botanical Documentation, Pittsburg USA; Shirley Sherwood Collection. *Commissions*: Definitive Stamp Issue (2000); botanical, Pitcairn and stamp designs of shells and beekeeping (1991-2001). *Publications*: 'Flower Painting from the Apothecaries' Garden' (Andrew Brown). *Recreations*: Theatre, literature, travel. *Address*: Russet House, Lughorse Lane, Yalding, Kent. ME18 6EG. *Email*: sueandmartin@tiscali.co.uk *Signs work*: 'Sue J Williams' or 'SJW'.

WILLIAMS, Susan, RA Schools Dip.; artist in oil and water-colour. *b*: Lichfield, Staffs., 23 Jul 1944. *m*: Ben Levene. one *s*. *Educ*: Lichfield Central School. *Studied*: Stafford Art School, Byam Shaw School, R.A. Schools. *Exhib*: regularly at RA Summer Exhbn., Spirit of London (prizewinner), Ogle Gallery, Cheltenham, Hintlesham Hall Pictures, Ipswich, The Gallery Southwark Park, Bermondsey, Duncan Campbell Gallery, Waterman Gallery, London. Work in private collections. *Recreations*: gardening, cooking. *Address*: 26 Netherby Rd., London SE23 3AN. *Signs work*: "S.W."

WILLIAMS-ELLIS, Bronwyn Mary, RCA (2001), BA (1973), MA (1983). *Medium*: drawing and colour in 2D ceramics, sculpture, tiles; also on paper; ceramicist. *b*: 20 Jan 1953. *Partner*: Louis Hodgkin. *Studied*: Cardiff College of Art (1971-1973), SGIHE, Cardiff (1982-1983), MA. *Exhib*: regularly, including, 1000 Years of Tiles (1991-1993), Ceramic Series, Aberwsytwyth Arts Centre, Tremayne, St. Ives, Oriel Plas Gly-y-Weddw, Royal Cambrian Academy, Victoria Art Gallery, Bath. *Works in collections*: Aberwsytwyth Arts Centre, private collections. *Commissions*: majority tile work. *Publications*: work appears in Decorating With Tiles, Elizabeth Hilliard; Ceramics and Print, Paul Scott; Practical Solutions for Potters, Gill Bliss; 20th Century Decorative British Tiles, C. Blanchett, 5000 Years of Tiles - British Museum, Hans Van Lemmen. *Address*: Old Orchard, 89a Walcot Street, Bath BA1 5BD. *Website*: www.handmade-tiles.co.uk *Signs work*: "B W-Ellis", "BRON" or "B W-E."

WILLIAMS-ELLIS, David Hugo Martyn, RCA (1993), ARBS (1992); sculptor in clay for bronze and terracotta. *b*: Ireland, 6 Apr 1959. *m*: Serena Stapleton. two *s*. two *d*. (one decd). *Educ*: Headfort School, Ireland; Stowe School. *Studied*: in Florence (1977-78, Signorina Nerina Simi), Carrara (1979-80), Sir John Cass (1981-83). *Represented by*: Robert Bowman Gallery, London. *Exhib*: London, Belfast, Paris, USA, Japan, Argentina, South Africa. Many portrait busts and figures in private and public collections. *Clubs*: Chelsea Arts. *Address*: Lazonby Manor, Lazonby, Penrith, Cumbria. CA10 1BA. *Email*: david@dwe.com *Website*: www.DWE.com *Signs work*: "D.W.E." dated with signet ring eagle on larger pieces.

WILLIAMSON, Geraldine Mooring, PSC (1980), HNDipAD (1994). *Medium*:acrylic, mixed media. *b*: Poole, Dorset, 29 Sep 1960. three *d*. *Studied*: Chelsea College of Art & Design; St.Ives School of Art; with Paul Riley, Devon (2002), and Jenny Wheatley, France (2007). *Represented by*: Imagination Gallery, St.Ives; Gallery@96, Topsham; Azure, Sidmouth; Panoratia, Topsham; Gloss Gallery, Exeter. *Exhib*: RIBA, London; International Festival of Naive Art, Poland; Ealing Art Group; Art Shed, New Milton; ABNA exhibitions at: Crypt Gallery, Mariners Gallery, St.Ives Society of Artists Gallery, St.Ives; Little Picture Gallery, Mousehole; Gloss Gallery, Exeter; Exeter Central Library; Art in the Mill, Harrogate; Delamore Arts, Cornwood; Art for Life, Torrington; Devon Guild of Craftsmen, Bovey Tracey; various, Bournemouth, Poole. *Works in collections*: private worldwide. *Commissions*: private commissions. *Publications*: ABNA book. *Official Purchasers*: Bodyshop (South West region) UK. *Works Reproduced*: in ABNA book, cards, limited edition prints. *Principal Works*: "Naive" still life. *Clubs*: Ealing Art Group, ABNA, Associate Member Penwith Society. *Address*: 13 School Lane, Exeter, Devon, EX2 6LB. *Email*: clive15williamson@btinternet.com *Website*: www.britishnaives.co.uk *Signs work*: "GMW" and/or "Geraldine Williamson".

WILLIS, Lucy, RWA (1993); BP Portrait Award. *Medium*: water-colour, oil, printmaking. *b*: 15 Dec 1954. *m*: Anthony Anderson. one *s*. one *d*. *Educ*: Badminton School, Bristol. *Studied*: Ruskin School of Drawing and Fine Art, Oxford (1972-75). *Represented by*: Curwen & New Academy Gallery, London W1. *Exhib*: eight solo shows at Chris Beetles, London since 1986; RA, RWA, NPG, BP Portrait award (1st prize 1992), Mall Galleries, RWS, RE, Curwen Gallery, London: eight solo shows (2000-2012). *Works in collections*: NPG, RWA. *Commissions*: 'Year of the Artist' murals in Portland Prison (2000); NPG, oil portrait of Lord & Lady Longford (1993); Badminton School (2012). *Publications*: 'Light, How to See it, How to Paint it'; 'Excursions in the Real World' by William Trevor (illustrations); Light in Water-colour (1997); Travels with Watercolour (2003). *Official Purchasers*: Exeter Health Care Arts, National Portrait Gallery, RWA. *Works Reproduced*: numerous works as prints and cards. *Principal Works*: 'Her Majesty's Pleasure' (oil on canvas, BP Portrait Award, 1992). *Address*: Moorland House, Burrowbridge, Bridgwater, Som. TA7 0RG. *Email*: info@lucywillis.com *Website*: www.lucywillis.com *Signs work*: "Lucy Willis."

WILLIS, Victor, MA Fine Art (1985); artist in oil. *b*: London, 2 Aug 1934. *m*: Mary. two *d*. *Educ*: Dulwich College. *Studied*: Camberwell College of Art (1974), City & Guilds (1978), Goldsmiths' College (1985). *Works in collections*: London and abroad. *Commissions*: Swan Hellenic, British Rail, Anna Bornholt Assoc. *Publications*: articles illustrated: 'The Thames at Night', 'Light on Landscape'. *Clubs*: Chelsea Arts. *Address*: Studio: Unit 8, Shakespeare Business Centre, 245 Coldharbour Lane, London SW9 8RR. *Signs work*: "Victor Willis."

WILLOW, Hannah. *Medium*: Drawing; prints; acrylic; silver. *b*: Aldershot, 5 Oct 1964. *m*: Philip Holmes. one *d*. *Studied*: Art Foundation Basingstoke Technical College (1980-81); Printmaking, Southhill Park, Berkshire and West Dean, Hampshire. *Represented by*: Campbell Wilson, London and Aberdeen. *Exhib*: Gallery Eight, Glastonbury; Obsidian Gallery, Stoke Mandeville; Twenty Twenty Gallery, Much Wenlock; Bluestone Gallery, Devizes; Trelyon Gallery, St Ives; Lion House Gallery; Lavenham; Oriel-y-Park, St Davids; Haymakers, Hay on Wye; Blue Ginger, Cradley, Worcs. *Works in collections*: many private, worldwide. *Commissions*: Various and many. *Works Reproduced*: In Earth Pathways Diary; Wiltshire Life, in "Spirit of the Hare" by K Cater. *Misc*: Sisterhood of Ruralists with three other artists. *Address*: Home Farm, Cholderton, Salisbury SP4 0DR. *Email*: willowhannah@gmail.com *Website*: www.hannahwillow.com *Signs work*: "H.WILLOW".

WILLS, Richard Allin, NDD, AUA; painter in oil and water-colour, etc.; art tutor; visiting lecturer. *b*: Monmouth, 11 Sep 1939. *s of*: W.L.J. Wills. *m*: Vera Elizabeth. one *s*.

two *d*. *Educ*: King Henry VIII Grammar, Abergavenny. *Studied*: Newport College of Art (1956-61, Thomas Rathmell). *Exhib*: RA, RWA, Welsh Young Contemporaries, RSPP, UA, WCSW, PS, RWS, RI. *Works in collections*: British Steel Corp., Welsh Div. British Steel, Rank Xerox, Lloyds TSB, International Rugby Board, Electronic Art, National Museum of Wales, University of Wales. *Commissions*: Welsh Office, Whitehall; Guildhall School of Music, London; Polytechnic of Wales; Yamazaki Mazak Europe; Royal Monmouthshire Royal Engineers; Royal Regiment of Wales Contemporary Art Society. *Publications*: Collins: Complete Drawing Course, Watercolour Workshop; Headline: Encyclopedia of W/C Techniques. *Address*: The Studio, Mansard House, Vine Acre, Monmouth, Gwent NP25 3HW. *Signs work*: "Richard A. Wills."

WILSON, Arnold, MA, FSA, FMA; former Chairman of Trustees, Holburne of Menstrie Museum, Bath, and serves on numerous other Coms.; formerly Director, City Art Gallery, Bristol. *b*: Dulwich, 1932. twice married. two *d*. by first marriage. *s of*: Robert Arthur Wilson, artist. *Educ*: Selwyn College, Cambridge, and Courtauld Inst. of Art. *Publications*: author: Dictionary of British Marine Painters (3 eds.); Dictionary of British Military Painters; Exploring Museums: South West England; numerous articles for Burlington Magazine, Apollo, Connoisseur, Country Life, etc. *Address*: 2 Sydney Lawn, Sydney Place, Bath BA2 6BW.

WILSON, Chris, BA (Hons) (1982), MA (1985); artist in oil and collage. *b*: Belfast, 27 Dec 1959. *m*: Cindy Friers. one *s*. *Educ*: Belfast Royal Academy. *Studied*: Brighton College of Art (1979-82), University of Ulster (1984-85). *Exhib*: 'Shocks to the System' ACGB (1991), 'On the Balcony of the Nation' touring USA (1991-92), 'Shadows of Light' one-man touring Romania (1992), Bulgaria (1993). *Works in collections*: ACGB, Arts Council of Ireland, Aer Rianta Dublin, Queens University Belfast; private collections in Ireland, England, Germany, USA. *Address*: 44 Victoria Rd., Bangor, Co. Down BT20 5EX. *Signs work*: "CHRIS WILSON" or "C. WILSON" with date.

WILSON, Conor John. *Medium*: Oil painter, watercolour painter, acrylic painter, airbrush muralist. *b*: Tarrangau, Papua New Guinea, 26 Jul 1973. *Educ*: Dover College, Dover, Kent. *Studied*: Aston Uni (1992-93); Birmingham Uni (1993-94). *Represented by*: Driftwood Gallery, Ilfracombe; Drang, Padstow. *Exhib*: Custard Factory, Birmingham (1996); Blue Groove, Croyde, N. Devon (2001-2012). *Works in collections*: Uri Geller - private collection. *Commissions*: Gillette, Levis Jeans, Red Bull, Saltrock Surf Co., Wrigleys Gum, and many private individuals. *Recreations*: surfing, travel, nature. *Clubs*: Member of 'The Devon 11' Plein Air Painters. *Address*: 15 Church Street, Braunton, North Devon EX33 2EL. *Email*: conor@conorwilson.co.uk *Website*: www.conorwilson.co.uk *Signs work*: "C.J.WILSON".

WILSON, David, BA (Hons) (Open) (2000); painter in oil, acrylic, water-colour, gouache, etching, linocut. *b*: Gillingham, Kent, 23 May 1936. *s of*: Jack Wilson, RN. *m*: Sheila. two *s*. two *d*. *Educ*: Sir Joseph Williamson's Mathematical School, Rochester; Joint Services School of Linguists. *Studied*: Heatherley's (Evening classes 1976-77, Terry Shave). *Exhib*: RA, RBA, Royal National Eisteddfod, RWA, The Discerning Eye, NEAC, SGA, RCamA, FPS, and elsewhere in UK, France and Ireland. *Works in collections*: National Library of Wales, Aberystwyth. *Address*: Treleddyn Isaf, Bridell, Cardigan SA43 3DQ. *Email*: david@david-wilson.net *Website*: www.david-wilson.net *Signs work*: "David Wilson Bridell."

WILSON, Douglas, RCA, DFA, FRSA; painter in oil and water-colour. *b*: 8 Nov 1936. *s of*: George William Wilson. *m*: Heather Hildersley Brown. one *s*. *Studied*: Oxford University (1959-62, Percy Horton, Richard Naish, Geoffrey Rhodes). *Represented by*: Highgate Fine Art, London. *Exhib*: RA, RBA, ROI, RCA (2008, 2009), Vis Art I (prizewinner), Edinburgh Festival, National Library of Wales, New Grafton Gallery,

Piccadilly Gallery, Thackeray Gallery, Jablonski Gallery, Waterman Fine Art, St. James's, London; one-man shows: Bluecoat Gallery, Williamson A.G. (1981, 1983), King St. Galleries, St. James's (1983, 1986, 1991), Metropolis International Galerie d'Art Geneva (1985), Phoenix Gallery, Lavenham (1987, 1989), Phoenix Gallery, Kingston upon Thames (1987), Anthony Dawson Artists at the Barbican (1987, 1990), Outwood Gallery (1987), Newburgh St. Gallery (1988), Highgate Fine Art, London (2001, 2004, 2008, 2010, 2012), Distinguished Landscapes 1 (2003). *Works in collections*: Lord Wandsworth College, Williamson A.G, Shire Hall Gallery, Stafford, numerous collections in Britain and abroad. *Publications*: author, 'Wirral Visions'. *Official Purchasers*: Williamson AG, Staffordshire Arts and Museums Service. *Works Reproduced*: The Public Catalogue Foundation - The National Inventory of Oil Paintings in Public Ownership. *Clubs*: Royal Over-seas League. *Address*: 123 Masons Pl., Newport, Salop. TF10 7J. *Website*: www.highgateart.com *Signs work*: "Douglas Wilson."

WILSON, Helen, BA (FA) 1995 (Uni.SA); painter in oils; administrator at Somerset Art Week Ltd. *b*: Surrey, 1 Sep 1948. *m*: Mua Wilson. two *s*. *Studied*: City and Guilds of London Art School (1987-88), University of South Africa (1990-95). *Exhib*: solo show at National Art Gallery of Namibia (1996), SBA (1997), Brewhouse Theatre and Arts Centre, Taunton (1999). *Works in collections*: Telecoms Namibia. *Publications*: article in "De Arte" (1994). *Clubs*: Greenpeace. *Address*: Orchard Cottage, Hare Lane, Buckland St Mary, Chard, Somerset TA20 3JS. *Email*: helen@orchardstudio.freeserve.co.uk *Signs work*: "HW" joined.

WILSON, Helen Frances, DA (1975), RGI (1984), RSW (1998), PAI (2005); artist in oil, water-colour, mixed media. *b*: Paisley, Scotland, 25 Jul 1954. one *d*. *Educ*: John Neilson High School, Paisley. *Studied*: Glasgow School of Art (1971-76); Hospitalfield (1973). *Exhib*: RGI, RSA, RSW, etc. and various galleries in Britain and USA. *Works in collections*: Glasgow A.G., Kelvingrove; Scottish Arts Council; Royal College of Physicians, Edinburgh; Paisley A.G. *Commissions*: portraits: Royal College of Ophthalmologists, Royal College of Physicians, Garrick Club, London, etc. also private commissions. *Address*: 1 Partickhill Rd., Glasgow G11 5BL.

WILSON, Lorna Yvette, BA Hons (1989), DipFA - RA Schools (1992); artist in oil and gouache. *b*: Jamaica, 6 Jul 1967. *Studied*: Kingston University (1986-89, Derek Hirst), RA Schools (1989-92, Prof. Norman Adams, RA). *Exhib*: many mixed exhbns. in London. Currently doing series of prints for CCA Galleries. *Address*: 8 Petherick House, 79 Stanley Rd., Hounslow, Middx. TW3 1YU.

WILSON, Marion Veronica, SBA, Dip.SBA (Dist). *Medium*: gouache, watercolour, drawing. *b*: Gillingham, Kent, 2 Jul 1944. *m*: John. two *d*. *Exhib*: Society of Botanical Artists, London; Palmengarten, Frankfurt; Marvejois, France; Lake Artists Society, Grasmere; Carlisle, Keswick, Milnthorpe, Gosforth, Eskdale. *Address*: Treetops, Ullock, Workington, Cumbria CA14 4TP. *Email*: marion.wilson575@btinternet.com *Signs work*: "Marion V. Wilson".

WILSON, Peter Reid, DA; artist in oil paint on canvas. *b*: Glasgow, 4 Sep 1940. married. one *s*, Damien. one *d*, Galia. *Partner*: Dr. Joy Schaverien. *Studied*: Glasgow School of Art (1960-64). *Works in collections*: Contemporary Arts Soc., ACGB, SAC, Sheffield City A.G., Ferens A.G. Hull, Nottingham Castle Museum and A.G., Leicester Museum and A.G., Glasgow A.G., Kelvingrove, Stoke-on-Trent Museum and A.G., Kettles Yard, Cambridge, Museum of Modern Art, Glasgow, Loyola Marymount University, Los Angeles. *Publications*: Peter Wilson - Paintings 1979-1985 (Third Eye, Glasgow, 1985), Dacapo - Drawings (Arc Publications, 1989). *Works Reproduced*: Bridgeman Art Library. *Clubs*: Chelsea Arts. *Address*: 5 The Square. South Luffenham, Oakham, Rutland LE15 8NS. *Email*: peewee.wilson@virgin.net *Website*: peterwilson-artist.com *Signs work*: c within a circle "Peter Wilson" and date.

WILSON, Susan, BFA, DipRA Schools; Richard Ford Award to Spain (1986); Italian Government Borso di Studio (1985); British School at Rome (Abbey Award) 1993; artist in oil on canvas. *b*: Dunedin, NZ. *d of*: Rev. C.R. Wilson, BA. *m*: Edward Gretton. *Studied*: Camberwell School of Art (1978-82), RA Schools (1982-85). *Represented by*: Browse & Darby, 19 Cork Street, London W1. *Exhib*: 2000, 2005, 2009. *Works in collections*: National Trust, HRH The Prince of Wales, Usher Gallery, Rochdale A.G., Auckland Museum, Contemporary Art Soc., Tauranga Art Gallery (NZ), Aigantighe Art Gallery (NZ), Bishop Suter Gallery, Nelson (NZ). Collection Focus - Abengoa Seville Spain, Whangarei Art Gallery (NZ), Auckland Art Gallery (NZ). *Commissions*: portrait of Baroness Helena Kennedy QC for Oxford Brookes Univ. *Publications*: illustrated: Katherine Mansfield's Short Stories (Folio Soc., 2000), Balancing Acts (Virago), Gillett: The Mind and Its Discontents (OUP, 1999), Catalogues to Touring Shows (co-curator), Reclaiming the Madonna (1993) and In the Looking Glass (1997 - Usher Gallery Publications). *Official Purchasers*: Usher Gallery, Lincoln; Rochdale Art Gallery and Museum; Contemporary Art Society; National Trust, Auckland Art Gallery NZ; Oxford Brookes University. *Email*: susanruddwilson@sky.com *Website*: www.susanwilsonartist.com

WILSON, Timothy Hugh, MA, MPhil, FSA (1989), HonRE (1991), Fellow of Balliol (1990); Barrie and Deedee Wigmore Research Keeper, Department of Western Art, Ashmolean Museum, Oxford (since 2013); Professor of the Arts of the Renaissance, University of Oxford (2010). *b*: Godalming, 8 Apr 1950. *m*: Jane Lott. two *s*. one *d*. *Educ*: Winchester College; Mercersburg Academy, USA; Corpus Christi College, Oxford; Warburg Inst. (London University); Dept. of Museum Studies (University of Leicester). *Publications*: books and articles chiefly on Italian maiolica and Renaissance applied arts. *Address*: Balliol College,. Oxford OX1 3BJ. *Website*: www.ashmolean.org/contact/staffpages/?pid=386

WILSON, Vincent John, ATD, Mem. Penwith Soc. of Arts, Devon Guild of Craftsmen (prints); painter and etcher. *Medium*: various. *b*: Mold, Flintshire, 24 Nov 1933. *s of*: J. Wilson. *m*: Sheila Richards. one *d*. *Educ*: Alun Grammar School, Mold. *Studied*: Chester School of Art (1950-54), Liverpool College of Art (1954-55). *Exhib*: RA, RWA, RCA, Piccadilly, Thackeray, Gagliardi, Penwith Galleries, Celle, W. Germany, Welsh Arts Council (1958, 1974, 1981), Cornwall Now (Sussex 1986), Cornwall in the Eighties (Chichester 1987); one-man shows: Exeter University (1966), Newlyn (1971, 1972, 1980), Plymouth (1979), Taunton (1981), Guernsey (1990), St. Ives (1992), St. Ives Artists (Dublin, 1998), four-man exhibition, Minster Fine Art, York (2005), regularly at Porthminster Gallery, St. Ives. *Works in collections*: Plymouth A.G., Devon C.C., Surrey Educ. Com., Royal Cambrian Academy, Celle, British Foreign and Commonwealth Office (etchings), V & A Museum (prints). *Works Reproduced*: in 'Devon Life', 'Inside Cornwall', 'Drawing Towards the End of a Century' (Newlyn SA), 'St. Ives 1975-2005', 'Arts Review'. *Recreations*: music (singing). *Address*: 3 Drakefield Drive, Saltash, Cornwall PL12 6BU. *Signs work*: "V. Wilson."

WILSON-DICK, Ian, Higher National Certificate Mechanical Engineering, Chartered Engineer, MRAeS, GAvA; landscape, marine and aviation artist. *Medium*: oil. *b*: London, 16 Nov 1927. *s of*: Hugh Wilson Dick, artist & pharmacist. *Educ*: Tottenham County School (1939-44). *Studied*: Enfield Technical College (1948-50); S.W.Essex Technical College (1950-51); self taught artist. *Represented by*: self. *Exhib*: Lockheed California (In House); Guild of Aviation Artists (Mall Galleries, London 2000-2009; Yeovil 2001); Rolls Royce Centenary Exhibition (2005). *Works in collections*: private clients UK & USA. *Commissions*: UK & USA private clients. *Works Reproduced*: "Go Concorde", "City of London's Front Door", "The Finishee" (book cover). *Principal Works*: "31 Sqn at Work" (paintings). *Recreations*: painting, swimming, travel. *Address*: 49 Hither Chantlers, Langton Green, Tunbridge Wells, TN3 0BL. *Email*: ian.wilson-dick@virgin.net *Website*: ianwilson-dick.com *Signs work*: "I. WILSON-DICK".

WILTON, Andrew, MA, FSA, FRSA, Hon.RWS; museum curator; Keeper of British Art, Tate Gallery (1989-1998); Keeper and Senior Research Fellow, Tate Gallery (1998-2002); Visiting Research Fellow, Tate Gallery (2003-); Curator, Turner Collection, Clore Gallery (1985-89), Curator of Prints and Drawings, Yale Center for British Art (1976-80), Asst. Keeper, Dept. of Prints and Drawings, British Museum (1967-76, 1981-84). *b*: Farnham, Surrey, 7 Feb 1942. *Educ*: Dulwich College; Trinity College, Cambridge. *Publications*: British Watercolours 1750-1850 (1977); The Life and Work of J.M.W. Turner (1979); Turner and the Sublime (1980); Turner in his Time (1987); Five Hundred Years of British Painting: Holbein to Hodgkin 2002; Turner as Draughtsman (2006) and numerous exhbn. catalogues, articles and reviews. *Clubs*: Athenaeum, Chelsea Arts Club. *Address*: Tate Gallery, London SW1P 4RG. *Signs work*: "Andrew Wilton".

WINDSOR, Alan, BA (Lond), Dip.FA (Lond), NDD, DA (Manc). *Medium*: acrylics, watercolour, drawing, prints. *b*: Fleetwood, Lancs., 10 Jul 1931. *s of*: Major G V Windsor, MC, MBE. *m*: Elfriede Windsor. one *s*. two *d*. *Educ*: Audenshaw Grammar School. *Studied*: Regional College of Art, Manchester (1949-54); Slade School, University College (1954-56); Universities of Paris and Aix (1956-57); Courtauld Institute, London University (1967-69). *Exhib*: Young Contemporaries, London Group, Gimpel Fils, Roland, Browse & Delbanco, Pollock, Toronto, New Ashgate, Farnham; Conningsby Gallery, London (with Camden Printmakers); Surrey University. *Works in collections*: University of Surrey, University of Reading. *Commissions*: Wine Traders Club, London; Carmelite Convent, Blackburn. *Publications*: Peter Behrens, 1868-1940, Architect and Designer (Architectural Press, 1981); Handbook of Modern British Painting, 1900-1980 (Scolar Press, 1992); British Sculptors of the Twentieth Century (Ashgate, 2003). *Works Reproduced*: in: "Oil Paintings in Public Ownership: Surrey" (The Public Catalogue Foundation, 2006). *Clubs*: member of Camden Printmakers. *Address*: 5 Gussiford Lane, Exmouth, Devon EX8 2SD. *Email*: alan.windsor@tiscali.co.uk *Website*: www.alanwindsor.eu *Signs work*: "Alan Windsor."

WINER, Zalmon, RBA (1984); painter in oil, pastel, acrylic, water-colour; designer, etcher and lithographer. *b*: Gateshead, Co. Durham, 21 Nov 1934. married. *s of*: Louis Winer. one *s*. two *d*. *Educ*: Gateshead Grammar School. *Studied*: art and architecture at Durham University; etching at Central School of Art and Design. *Exhib*: RA, RBA, PS, UA, NS, Ben Uri Gallery (The London Jewish Museum), CPS, Safrai Gallery, Jerusalem, Discerning Eye Exhbn. at Mall Galleries (1990), etc. *Works in collections*: Shipley A.G., Oundle Public School Gallery. *Publications*: illustrated Haggadah for the Exilarchs Foundation. *Address*: 53 Shirehall Park, London NW4 2QN.

WINKELMAN, Joseph William, BA (1964), CFA (1971), RE (1982), RWA (1989), Hon RWS (1996); Prizes: International Print Shows: Spain '82, Korea '82, New York '98, Connecticut 2001 & 2003; artist and printmaker; Past President, Royal Soc. of Painter-Printmakers; Artist-in-Residence, St. John's College, Oxford (2004). *Medium*: etching. *b*: Keokuk, Iowa, USA, 20 Sep 1941. *s of*: George Winkelman, BA. *m*: Harriet Lowell Belin. two *d*. *Educ*: University of the South, University of Pennsylvania, University of Oxford. *Studied*: University of Oxford, Ruskin School of Drawing (1968-71). *Exhib*: New Grafton, Royal Academy, Bohun, Lumley Cazalet, Graffiti, Anthony Dawson, Oxford Gallery, MoMA Oxford, Matsuya Ginza, Tokyo, Space Gallery, Seoul, Connecticut Graphic Arts Centre, Taller Galeria Fort, Barcelona. *Works in collections*: Ashmolean, The Museum of London, The Royal Collection, Fitzwilliam, National Museum of Wales, Science Museum London, Tate Gallery, V&A. *Commissions*: Balliol, St. Antony's, Christ Church, St.John's College, Oxford; Keeper of the Royal Collection, Lady Berlin. *Publications*: 'Sewanee Poems', with Richard Tillinghast. *Official Purchasers*: Lord Sainsbury. *Clubs*: Oxford University Yacht Club. *Address*: 69 Old High St., Headington, Oxford OX3 9HT. *Email*: joe@winkelman.co.uk *Website*: www.winkelman.co.uk *Signs work*: "J. W. Winkelman."

WINNER, Tolleck, ARBS. *Medium*: mixed media. *b*: Russia, 30 Jul 1959. *m*: Angela. two *s*. one *d*. *Educ*: Russia, Israel, United Kingdom. *Represented by*: mixture of galleries. *Exhib*: solo: Diorama Gallery (2003), Charity Fair, Business Design Centre (2003), Fresh Art (2003), Alon Zakaim Gallery Cork Street, London (2007); group: The Art Engine Gallery (2004), ICI, Manchester Square, London (2004/5), Beldam Gallery Brunel University (2005), Brunei Gallery Russell Square London (2005), Millais Gallery, Southampton University (2006), Alon Zakaim Gallery Cork Street, London (2006, 2007); DAC'S London (2007); ArtParks International, Guernsey (2007); Chichester Cathedral (2008); Artsparks International (2008, 2009); Novas Gallery, Liverpool (2009); Russian Art Fair, London (2010); RBA Annual Exhibition, Mall Galleries (2011); Gallery Diffrent, London (2011); Albemarle Gallery, London (2014). *Works in collections*: Private hands and institutions throughout the world. *Commissions*: Octavia Hill Museum, Peterborough; BUPA Insurance, Holland Park, London; Peterborough Sculpture Park, Peterborough; Octavia Housing (Miranda House), Holland Park, London. *Clubs*: Designer and Artist Copyright Society; Association of Independent Museums. *Address*: 31 Fencepiece Road, Barkingside, Ilford, Essex, IG6 2LY. *Email*: tolleck@yahoo.com *Website*: www.tolleck.com www.tolleckwinner.com www.artlandfoundation.org.uk *Signs work*: "Tolleck Winner".

WINSTANLEY, Paul. *Medium*: oil, watercolour, drawing, prints. *b*: Manchester, 15 Jun 1954. *m*: Carrie. two *d*. *Studied*: Cardiff College of Art (1973-76); Slade School of Fine Art (1976-78). *Represented by*: Kerlin Gallery, Dublin; Mitchell-Innes Nash, New York; Vera Munro, Hamburg; 1301PE, Los Angeles; Alan Cristea, London. *Works in collections*: Tate Gallery, MoMA New York, MoCA Los Angeles, Southampton City Art Gallery; private, corporate. *Publications*: 'Archive - Complete Paintings 1989-2000', 'Paul Winstanley. Threshold'. *Address*: 130 Oglander Rd, London SE15 4DB. *Email*: mail@paulwinstanley.com *Website*: www.paulwinstanley.com *Signs work*: "WINSTANLEY".

WINSTANLEY, Roy, CertEd (Hons) 1961, BA (Hons) 1973, Dip. (1986); painter in water-colour, acrylic, oil, mixed media. *b*: Wakefield, 31 Mar 1940. *m*: Jean. two *s*. *Studied*: Westminster College, Oxford (1959-61), University of Leek (1970-73), Goldsmiths' College (1986). *Exhib*: RI, RWS, John Laing Landscape, Images of Dorset, Poole, Honiton Festival, Thomas Hardy Conference Dorchester, Twin Tracks Bridport, Modern British Painting Exeter, Battersea Contemporary Art Fair. *Works in collections*: Sheffield City A.G. *Commissions*: series of paintings: Capital Interiors, London for a Royal Villa in Rabat, Morocco (1998); water-colours: The Constable Wing of Colchester General Hospital (1998). *Address*: Fig Tree Cottage, Preston, Weymouth, Dorset DT3 6DD. *Signs work*: "Winstanley."

WINTER, Faith, FRBS, Feodora Gleichen Sculpture Award, FRBS, Silver Medal Open Award (1984), Bronze, William Crabtree Memorial Award (1993), Bronze; sculptor in stone, wood, and bronze. *b*: Richmond, Surrey, 1927. *d of*: J.F.Ashe, architect. *m*: Col. F.M.S. Winter, MBE, FRSA. two *s*. one *d*. *Educ*: Oak Hall. *Studied*: Guildford and Chelsea Schools of Art. *Exhib*: RA, RBA, RWS, Glasgow Academy of Fine Art, Covent Garden and elsewhere in the UK; International Centre of Contemporary Art, Paris; Malaysia and Singapore. *Works in collections*: Earl of Mansfield, Scone Palace. Sir Reresby & Lady Penelope, Renishaw Hall etc. *Commissions*: include: "The Soldiers" Catterick Camp; "Compassion" Hambro Foundation; Falklands Islands Memorial relief; The Mysteries of the Rosary, Church of Our Lady Queen of Peace, East Sheen; John Ray statue, Braintree; Air Chief Marshal Lord Dowding and Marshal of the Royal Air Force Sir Arthur "Bomber" Harris statues, The Strand, London; Lennard standing figure 'The Spirit of Youth', Ontario, Canada; Salters' Hall Coat-of-arms, London; Archbishop George Abbot, Guildford; HRH The Princess Royal, The President of Kenya, Jeffrey Archer, Maria Callas and the late Kamal Jumblatt; David Devant, Magic Circle; memorial relief Mulberry Harbour, Arromanches, Normandy; General Sikorski, Portland Place, London; Sir Frank Whittle

(1½ life size, Coventry 2007). *Address*: Venzers Barn & Studio, The Street, Puttenham, Guildford, Surrey GU3 1AU. *Email*: Faith@FaithWinter.co.uk *Website*: www.FaithWinter.co.uk *Signs work*: "Faith Winter" (formerly "Faith Ashe.")

WINTERINGHAM, Claude Richard Graham, Dip.Arch., FRIBA, RBSA; Architect; RNVR Fleet Air Arm Lt. (1942-46), chairman, Solihull Round Table (1956-57), founder mem. and vice chairman, Solihull Civic Soc. (1958-62), president, B'ham Architecture Assoc. (1971-72); chairman, Sir Barry Jackson Trust (1982-96), Trustee (1996-); Awards: Mason Court Civic Trust (1969), Lichfield City Hall, Civic Soc. Commendation (1976), Lench's Close, Moseley, DOE Housing Design (1983), B'ham Repertory Theatre Architecture (1972). *b*: Louth, Lincs., 2 Mar 1923. *s of*: Francis Winteringham, MBE (decd). *m*: Lesley Patricia. two *s*. one *d*. *Clubs:* Edgbaston Priory. *Address*: 7 Sir Harry's Rd., Edgbaston, Birmingham B15 2UY.

WINTERS, Susan, NDD. *Medium*: illustration, oil, drawing. *b*: Birmingham, 14 Jan 1942. *d of*: William Winters, MIMechE. *Educ*: The Kingsley School, Leamington Spa. *Studied*: Leamington Spa School of Art; Goldsmiths College (Betty Swanwick 1960-63, Bernard Cheese, Sam Rabin), Richard Bawden. *Exhib*: RWA, RHS, National Trust, South West Academy, Wren Gallery, Burford, Chomé Fine Art, Bath, The Thelma Hulbert Gallery, Honiton. *Publications*: illustrations for Pergamon Press, BBC, John Lewis plc. *Works Reproduced*: Limited Edition prints. *Recreations*: walking, live music. *Address*: 1 Bellevue Terrace, Crewkerne, Somerset, TA18 8HD. *Signs work*: "SMW" (monogram), or "SWINTERS" on reverse.

WISE, Gillian. *Medium*: traditional & industrial materials and video. *b*: London, 1936. *d of*: Arthur & Elsie Holden Wise. one *s*. *Educ*: Sir William Perkins Grammar School for Girls, Chertsey, London. *Studied*: Wimbledon School of Art (1953-57); post-graduate, Repin Inst., Leningrad (1969-70); Unesco Fellowship, Prague (1968); Fellow, CAVS (MIT) 1981-82; Research Fellow, Open University, UK (1983). Awards: ACGB (1976); Research Grant, International Communication Agency (1981); Graham Foundation, Chicago (1983). *Represented by*: Alan Fowler - see Wikipedia. *Exhib*: London, Paris, Chicago, Liverpool, Japan, Germany, New York, Finland, Switzerland. *Works in collections*: see website. *Commissions*: Steel wall relief: Nottingham University Hospital (1975); Relief panel in wood: Unilever House (1982); painting/relief: Barbican Arts Centre (1982); three wall relief: Open University (1984). *Publications*: 'Low Frequency', Paris 2003; '20 Works and the Alice Walls at the Barbican' (both books in Tate Gallery Library). *Official Purchasers*: see website. *Works Reproduced*: in 'English Constructed Art' by Alastair Grieve (Yale Univ. Press, 2005). *Principal Works*: Barbican murals. *Address*: 26 Square de Clignancourt, Montmartre, Paris 75018, France. *Website*: www.gillianwise.com *Signs work*: "Gillian Wise."

WISZNIEWSKI, Adrian, painter, sculptor, interior designer. *b*: Glasgow, 31 Mar., 1958. *m*: Diane. two *s*. one *d*. *Studied*: Mackintosh School of Architecture, Glasgow School of Art. *Works in collections*: Tate, MOMA New York, Setegaya, Tokyo. *Commissions*: Liverpool Cathedral. *Publications*: exhib. catalogues and historical books. *Address*: Calder House, Main St., Lochwinnoch, Renfrewshire PA12 4AH. *Email*: awiszniewski@btclick.com *Signs work*: "A. Wiszniewski."

WITHINGTON, Roger, DipAD (Graphics) (1966), ATD (1967), ARE (Hon. retd.); artist/designer at Bank of England (1983-93), designed new series of banknotes known as Series E. *Medium*: pencil, watercolour, etching. *b*: Prestwich, 4 Oct 1943. *m*: Rose-Marie Edna Cobley. one *s*. one *d*. *Educ*: Barry Grammar/Technical School, S. Glam. *Studied*: Cardiff College of Art (1962-63, etching: Philip Jennings, ARE), Newport (Gwent) College of Art (1963-66, illustration: John Wright). *Exhib*: RE Galleries, Bankside Galleries. *Publications*: designed/part author series of booklets to accompany new banknotes. Limited

Editions of prints from selected pieces of artwork for series E banknotes issued 1990-94; limited edition print of St. Paul's Cathedral and Thames Riverside that featured on reverse of £50D note issued in 1981. *Address*: Hedge-Rose, Goodleigh, Barnstaple, N. Devon EX32 7NP. *Signs work*: "R. Withington" or "R.W."

WNEK-WEBB, Ewa, NDD; artist. *b*: Przemysl, Poland, 7 Jan 1940. *m*: Michael Robert Webb. two *s*. one *d*. *Studied*: St. Martin's School of Art (1958-61), Regent St. Polytechnic School of Art, and Chelsea College of Art (1961-63), London College of Printing. *Exhib*: ROI, UA, SWA, Mall Galleries, RA Summer Show; solo shows: Gallery 47 London, Terrace Gallery Worthing, Ropner Gallery London, Heifer Gallery London, St. Rafael Gallery London, Thomson Gallery-Aldborough, Suffolk, Hunter Gallery, Long Melford, Suffolk, Chase Gallery, Wadebridge, Cornwall, National Physical Laboratories, Teddington. *Clubs*: Assoc. of Polish Artists in G.B., Teddington Artists. *Address*: 8 King Edward's Gr., Teddington, Middx. TW11 9LU. *Email*: ewawebb@connectfree.co.uk *Website*: www.wnek-webb.co.uk

WOLKERS, Joan Elizabeth Margaret, NDD (Painting,1948), Abbey Scholarship (1949), RA Silver Medals (1951, 52, 53); Diploma of Association of Occupational Therapists; retd. Teacher. *Medium*: oils, watercolours. *b*: Tunbridge Wells, 28 Aug 1928. *d of*: M. E. Ransome. *m*: G.L. Wolkers (decd). one *s*. *Educ*: Lawnside, Malvern. *Studied*: Malvern School of Art under Victor Hume Moody (1945-50) and RA Schools under Henry Rushbury, Fleetwood Walker and William Dring (1950-54); State Academy, Amsterdam (1954-58). *Exhib*: RA, RBSA, RP, RSPP, NEAC, Brighton A.G., Worcester A.G., Malvern Art Club, Art Society, Exeter. Specialises in portraiture. *Commissions*: portraits/landscapes. *Address*: 37 Powderham Cres., Exeter EX4 6BZ. *Signs work*: "J.E.M. Wolkers."

WOLSTENHOLME, Jonathan, artist/illustrator in water-colour, oil, pen and ink. *b*: London, 22 Nov 1950. *m*: Margaret. one *s*. one *d*. *Educ*: Purley Grammar School. *Studied*: Croydon College of Art (1969-72). *Exhib*: several one-man shows in London, others in Paris, Brussels and New York. *Works in collections*: private and corporate collections internationally. *Commissions*: many. *Misc*: Gallery affiliation: Campbell's of Walton St. Ltd., 1-5 Exhibition Rd, London SW7 2HE. *Address*: c/o Campbell's of Walton St. Ltd., 164 Walton St., London SW3 2JL. *Signs work*: "Jonathan Wolstenholme."

WOLVERSON, Margaret Elizabeth, NDD, ATD, elected ARMS (1977); painter of living landscape, portraits and miniatures (in oils); formerly lectured Hornsea Inst. of Further Education and Stourbridge College of Art. *b*: 1937. *d of*: Charles Lloynes Smith. *m*: 1961. one *s*. (div. 1985); *m* 1987, S. Jones-Robinson. *Studied*: Dudley School of Art, Wolverhampton College of Art, Leicester College of Art. *Exhib*: RMS, Mall Galleries, Cheltenham Group, Britain's Painters; one-man show Dean Heritage Centre, Workshop Gallery, Chepstow, Taurus Gallery (1999). *Works in collections*: East Riding Collection for Schools, Ferens A.G.; private collections in UK, USA. *Commissions*: numerous. *Clubs*: Forest Artists Network, Hon. Mem. Hornsea Art Society, Glos, Guild of Weavers, Spinners and Dyers. *Misc*: Hand spun, dyed and woven, felted, or knitted-tapestries, bags, clothes to own design. *Address*: Sunny Bank, Pope's Hill. Newnham-on-Severn, Glos. GL14 1JX.

WOLVERSON, Martin, FRBS (1971), FRSA (1976); RBS Silver medal (1971), Trident Television Fine Art Fellow (1977-78), Fulbright Prof. Kansas City Art Inst. (1985); sculptor in wood, stone, metal, lecturer. *b*: Wolverhampton, 26 May 1939. *s of*: Cyril Wolverson, accountant. *m*: (1) Margaret Smith; one *s*. (2) Sandra Tipper. *Educ*: Wednesbury Boys High School. *Studied*: Wolverhampton School of Art (1956-60, Tom Wright, John Paddison), Goldsmiths' College, London University (1960-61). *Exhib*: widely in the North, London and in the USA. *Works in collections*: Ferens A.G., Hull, Usher A.G., Lincoln, Yorkshire Television, NCB, Ecclesiastic Insurance Co. Ltd., Lincolnshire and Humberside Arts, Humberside CC, Leeds City A.G., and numerous private collections. *Commissions*: National

Coal Board - Safety Trophy, for the Nation's safest mine; Caedmon School, Whitby - 'Caedmon Cross'; St. Mary's Church, Whitby - 'Altar Cross'; Hull Maternity Hospital, Hull - bronze relief to celebrate its centenary; Tivoli House, Hull - bronze portrait head and installation commemorating 'Old Mother Riley' (Arthur Lucan); Presentation 'Aussohnung' a collage presented to Klever Cathedral as an act of reconciliation for war damage between Whitby and Klever. *Recreations*: jazz piano. *Address*: Alexandra Lodge, Mount Pleasant East, Robin Hoods Bay, Whitby, N. Yorks. YO22 4RF. *Signs work*: "M. Wolverson."

WONNACOTT, John Henry, CBE; Slade Dip. (1962); Hon. RP. *b*: London, 1940. *s of*: John Alfred Wonnacott, ARIBA. *m*: Anne Rozalie Wesolowska, B.Sc. one *s*. two *d*. *Educ*: University College School. *Studied*: Slade School (1958-63). *Exhib*: Hayward (1974), RA Jubilee (1952-77), Marlborough (1981), Marlborough, NY (1983), Tate Gallery (1984), The Foudation Veranneman (1986-87), The Pursuit of the Real, Barbican (1990); one-man shows, Minories, Colchester (1972), Rochdale (1978); touring, Marlborough (1980-81, 1985, 1988), Scottish National Portrait Gallery (1986-87), Agnews (93, 97, 2000), Hirschl & Alder, NY (2000), NPG (2000), NMM (2001). *Works in collections*: Nat. Art Collection, Arts Council, Rochdale A.G., Norwich Castle Museum, Tate Gallery, Scottish National Portrait Gallery, NMM, IWM, Met. Mus. York, Brit. Council. *Commissions*: Sir Adam Thomson (NPG), Rt. Hon. John Major (NPG), Lord Lewin (Nat. Mar. Mus.), Royal Family (2000). *Official Purchasers*: Arts Council, Tate, NMM, IWM, Norwich, Ipswich, British Council, SNPG, NPG, Gov. Art Coll., House of Commons. *Address*: 5 Cliff Gdns., Leigh-on-Sea, Essex. *Signs work*: "C.B.E."

WOOD, Andy, DipAD (1970), ARBA (1980), RI (1981), RBA (1999), Honorary Secretary RI (2009); painter in acrylic, oil and water-colour. *b*: Porlock, Som., 1947. *s of*: H.E. Wood. *m*: Katrina Wood. one *s*. two *d* (one decd). *Educ*: schools in Walton-on-Thames, Hersham and Dorking. *Studied*: Croydon and Newport Colleges of Art (1965-70). *Exhib*: RI, RBA, Thackeray Gallery, etc. *Works in collections*: Sultan of Oman; Duke University, NC, USA; Central Carolina Bank, NC, USA; Lyme Regis Museum. *Commissions*: Sultan of Oman; British Telecom; Southern Gas. *Publications*: Dictionary of 20th Century British Painters, Sculptors and other artists (Antique Collectors Club Ltd). *Clubs*: Chelsea Arts. *Address*: Rafters, Old Brick Yard, Rye, E.Sussex TN31 7EE. *Email*: andy@andywoodgallery.com *Website*: www.andywoodgallery.com *Signs work*: "Andy Wood" or "A. Wood."

WOOD, Christopher Malcolm Fayrer, RSW (2006), PPSSA, VAS/Glasgow Art Club Fellowship (2005); BA Hons (Edinburgh); James Torrance Memorial Award (RGI , 1993); Nancy Graham Memorial Award (1994); The Scottish Arts Club Award (SAAC, 1994); The Armour Award (RGI, 1994); SSWA Special Award for Painting (1997). *Medium*: oils, acrylics, mixed media. *b*: Leeds, 9 Jul 1962. *s of*: Sheila & Dr.Eric A M Wood. *m*: Jane. one *s*. one *d*. *Educ*: George Watsons Boys College, James Gillespies High School (both Edinburgh). *Studied*: Edinburgh College of Art (1980-84). *Represented by*: The Scottish Gallery, Edinburgh. *Exhib*: RSA, RGI, RSW, SSA, SAAC, VAS, The Scottish Gallery, The Manor House Gallery, Thompson's Gallery, The Hart Gallery, The Richmond Hill Gallery. *Works in collections*: HRH Prince Charles, The Duke of Rothsay, Bank of Scotland, United Distillers, Edinburgh University, The Demarco European Foundation, Macroberts Solicitors, Premier Property Group. *Publications*: The Glasgow Art Club Fellowship Exhibtion Catalogue ISBN 0 9554121 0 2. *Misc*: President of the Society of Scottish Artists 2009-2011. *Address*: Port Lodge, 7 High Street, Dunbar, EH42 1EN. *Email*: mail@christopherwood.co.uk *Website*: www.christopherwood.co.uk *Signs work*: 'Wood'.

WOOD, Christopher Paul, BA Hons (1984), MA (1986); painter in oil on canvas. *b*: Leeds, 10 Jun 1961. *s of*: Peter Liddle Wood. *m*: Simone Abel. two *d*. *Educ*: Leeds. *Studied*: Jacob Kramer School of Art (1980-81), Leeds Polytechnic (1981-84), Chelsea

School of Art (1985-86). *Exhib*: one-man shows: Oldham City A.G. (1986), Sue Williams Gallery, London (1989, 1990, 1992, 1994), Rebecca Hossack Gallery, London (1996, 1997, 1999), Newark Park, Glos. (1998); retrospective exhibition Mercer Gallery Harrogate (1999), Michael Carr Gallery, Sydney Australia (2000), Picidilly Gallery (2002); mixed shows include Festival Hall (1986), New Contemporaries (1986), New Generation (1991), Hunting Prize (2000) R.C.A. *Publications*: 'Echo Moment' Mercer Gallery (1999). *Address*: 1 Norfok Pl., Chapel Allerton, Leeds LS7 4PT. *Signs work*: full signature on back of canvas; initialled on front of paintings - "C.P.W." and date.

WOOD, Duncan, BA Hons Fine Art, PGCE, Art and Design Education, MA Fine Art; Artist in Residence: National Trust (1997-99); visiting tutor in Fine Art London University (2000-01). *Medium*: oil, water-colour, charcoal/chalk. *b*: London, 14 Nov 1960. *s of*: Mr E.C. and Mrs. M.A. Wood. *Educ*: Brockhurst School, Berks., Kingham Hill School, Oxfordshire. *Studied*: Gloucestershire College of Art (1980-81), Sheffield College of Art (1981-84), The Institute of Education, London University (1996-97),City & Guilds of London Art School, (2001-03). *Exhib*: RCA, RA, City art galleries: Sheffield, Glasgow, Nottingham; galleries: Cardiff, Edinburgh, Birkenhead, London, Fosse Gallery, Stow-on-the-Wold; also exhib. at 'Discerning Eye Exhbns.' (work chosen by Glynn Williams, Prof. of Fine Art at RCA 1992, and by Sir Brinsley Ford former Chairman of National Art Collections Fund 1991, William Packer, art critic Financial Times, and Martin Gayford, writer and art critic of the Daily Telegraph and Modern Painters 1996), National Trust (1997-99). *Works in collections*: London, throughout the UK and in the USA, Germany and Japan; public collections: The Finnish Embassy, Sheffield University, The Duke of Devonshire and the Trustees of the Chatsworth House Settlement. *Clubs*: N.E.A.C. (1991), mem. Com., N.E.A.C. School of Drawing (1995-). *Misc*: delivered lectures on 'The Understanding of Contemporary Art' at 'The Affordable Art Fair' London (1999). *Address*: York House, Baslow, Derbyshire DE45 1RY. *Signs work*: "Duncan Wood."

WOOD, Juliet Anne, Slade Diploma in Fine Art. *Medium:* painter in oil. *b*: London, 4 Jun 1939. *d of*: Dr.Paul Wood OBE. *m*: Simon Brett. three *s*. two *d*. *Educ*: Arts Educational Schools, London and Tring. *Studied*: St. Albans School of Art (1955-7), Slade School of Fine Art (1957-60), British School in Rome (1960-61). *Represented by*: New Grafton Portrait Centre. *Exhib*: RA, Swindon Museum, RP, New Grafton Gallery. *Works in collections*: Scottish National Portrait Gallery; Royal Society of Edinburgh; Stirling University, Heriot Watt University; St. Cross and Hertford Colleges, Oxford. *Commissions*: portraits include: Sir Michael Atiyah, Sir Peter Ramsbotham, Lord Balfour of Burleigh, Sir Walter Bodmer, Judge Monier Williams, and numerous public and private commissions. *Official Purchasers*: British Cardiac Society, Dr. Paul Wood, OBE. *Works Reproduced*: Rosalind Cuthbert - An Introduction to Painting Portraits (Leo in Red, Emily Brett). *Principal Works*: Sir Michael Atiyah; Dr. Doris Littljohn; Sir Walter Bodmer. *Recreations*: gardening, music, dancing. *Misc*: Lecturer in Fine Art, Swindon College 1978-95. *Address*: 12 Blowhorn Street, Marlborough, Wilts, SN8 1BT. *Email*: julietwood39@googlemail.com *Website*: www.julietwood.co.uk *Signs work*: Juliet Wood, or J Wood.

WOOD, Nigel, Dip. (wildlife illustration) 1984; painter in oil, pastel and acrylic. *b*: Reading, 26 Dec 1960. one *s*. one *d*. *Studied*: Dyfed College of Art (1980-84). *Exhib*: solo and group shows including NPG, RCA, Aberdeen A.G., Glyn Vivian Gallery, Ceri Richards Gallery, Mall Galleries, Martin Tinney Gallery, Oriel Myrddin, Fountain Fine Art and Edith Grove Gallery. *Works in collections*: Carmarthenshire County Collection. *Address*: Jaqsalton, Llangrannog, Llandysul, Ceredigion, SA44 6SE. *Email*: info@nigel-wood.co.uk *Website*: www.nigel-wood.co.uk *Signs work*: "NIGEL WOOD."

WOOD, Sarah Diane, Dip SBA; SBA; Rennies Arts and Crafts Award (2008); Barbie Coates Trophy (2009, 10, 13); Schmincke Award (2014); Margaret Granger Memorial

Award (2014). *Medium*: Watercolour. *b*: Eastham, Wirral, 9 Jan 1959. *m*: Mike Wood. one *s*. one *d*. *Exhib*: Society of Botanical Artists, Westminster Central Hall (2010, 11, 12, 13, 14); Royal Institute of Painters in Watercolours, Mall Galleries (2013, 14); NEC Birmingham (2010, 11, 12); Wirral Society of Arts, Williamson Art Gallery (2007-2013); WSA Pannet Gallery, Whitby (2009); Irby Artists, Wirral (2003-2014). *Commissions*: Private. *Publications*: 'Leisure Painter' (2014); 'International Artist' (2010, 12); 'Paint' (2009). *Clubs*: Irby Artists, Wirral Society of Artists. *Address*: 5 Dutton Drive, Bebington, Wirral CH63 9AE. *Email*: sarahdiwood@gmail.com *Website*: www.sarahwoodart.com *Signs work*: "SARAH WOOD".

WOOD, Tom, painter in oil, printmaker, lecturer; Hon. Fellow, Sheffield Hallam University (1989). *b*: Dar es Salaam, Tanzania, 1955. *m*: Elaine Barraclough. three *d*. *Studied*: Batley School of Art (1975), Sheffield School of Art (1976-78). *Exhib*: solo shows: Huddersfield A.G., Leeds City A.G., Schloss Cappengberg, Kreissunna, Germany, Hart Gallery London and Nottingham. *Works in collections*: HRH The Prince of Wales, NPG, Yale University, Provident Financial Group. *Commissions*: portraits: Arthur Haigh and W.T. Oliver (1984); HRH The Prince of Wales (1987); Alan Bennett (1990); Prof. Lord Winston for the National Gallery (1999). *Publications*: Man and Measure - The Painting of Tom Wood by Duncan Robinson (Hart Gallery Pub.). *Misc*: Studio: Dean Clough, Halifax. *Address*: 4 Westfield Ave., Lightcliffe, Halifax, W. Yorks HX3 8AP. *Signs work*: "TOM WOOD."

WOOD, Annette (Mrs.): see GARDNER, Annette.

WOODFINE, Sarah, BA; Post Graduate RA Schools; Jerwood Drawing Prize (Winner, 2004); Gold Medal, Royal Academy Schools (1985). *Medium*: drawing, prints. *b*: Poole, Dorset, 27 Sep 1968. *d of*: Alan Woodfine (photographer). *m*: Mujeeb Bhatti (graphic artist). *Studied*: Sir John Moores University (BA Sculpture, 1989-91); RA Schools (Post-graduate, 1992-95). *Represented by*: Danielle Arnaud Contemporary Art. *Exhib*: Compton Verney, Sheffield Millennium Gallery, Middlesbrough Art Gallery (MIMA), Maritime Museum Portsmouth, Museum of Garden History; in Norway: Galleri F15, Ha Gamle Prestegard, Haugersund Art Museum; Outline, Amsterdam. *Works in collections*: Middlesbrough Art Gallery; Ha Gamle Prestegard (Norway). *Publications*: 'The Drawing Book' (Sarah Simblet); 'Drawing' (Paul Thomas & Anita Taylor). *Misc*: only works in monotone (pencil on paper and lithographs). *Address*: Flat D, 23 Gloucester Street, London SW1V 2DB. *Email*: sarah.woodfine@virgin.net *Website*: www.daniellearnaud.com *Signs work*: 'Sarah Woodfine' (always on back of works).

WOODFORD, David, NDD, ATC with distinction, Cert. RAS; painter in oil and water-colour; Royal Cambrian Academician. *b*: Rawmarsh, Yorks., 1 May 1938. *m*: June. two *s*. *Educ*: Lancing College. *Studied*: West Sussex College of Art (1955-59), Leeds College of Art (1959-60), Royal Academy Schools (1965-68). He lives by his painting. *Works in collections*: British Arts Council; Welsh Arts Council; National Museum of Wales; National Library of Wales. *Address*: Ffrancon House, Ty'n-Y-Maes, Bethesda, Bangor, Gwynedd LL57 3LX. *Signs work*: "David Woodford."

WOODMAN, Jim, Full member of The National Society of Painters, Sculptors and Engravers. *Medium*: Oil, watercolour. *b*: Newbury, 15 Jul 1944. *m*: Liz. two *d*, one *s-d*. *Educ*: self taught. *Represented by*: John Iddon Fine Art. *Exhib*: Galleries: Greens and Blues, North Berwick; The Wey Gallery, Godalming; MacKenzie Gallery, Teddington; Dandelion Designs, Isle of Skye; Fountain Gallery, East Molesey. Annual solo exhibition at Gallery AnTalla Dearg, Isle of Skye. *Works in collections*: Private collections in UK, USA, Canada, Germany, France and Spain. *Commissions*: Richmond Upon Thames Environment Trust Nov 2010. *Publications*: Featured in 'The Acrylic Artist's guide to Exceptional Colour' by Lexi Sundell. *Works Reproduced*: A comprehensive range of Giclee prints. *Principal Works*:

Scottish landscapes and cityscapes. *Recreations*: Walking, reading and golf. *Clubs*: Richmond Art Society (Vice President); National Society of Painters Sculptors and Engravers. *Address*: 41 Arlington Road, Teddington, TW11 8NL. *Email*: jimwoodman@hotmail.com *Website*: www.jimwoodman.co.uk *Signs work*: "JIM WOODMAN".

WOODROW, Bill (William Robert), RA (2002); finalist Turner Prize (1986); winner Anne Gerber Award, Seattle (1988). *Medium*: sculpture, drawing, prints. *b*: near Henley-on-Thames, 1 Nov 1948. *m*: Pauline Rowley. one *s*. one *d*. *Educ*: Barton Peveril Grammar School, Eastleigh, Hants. *Studied*: Winchester School of Art, Winchester; St.Martin's School of Art; Chelsea School of Art. *Represented by*: Waddington Galleries, Cork Street, London. *Exhib*: since 1972, 70 plus solo exhbns in UK, Europe, Australia, N.America, including: Duveen Galleries,Tate Gallery; 'Regardless of History' for the fourth plinth, Trafalgar Square; London/Mappin Art Gallery, Sheffield; Glynn Vivian Art Gallery, Swansea; many group exhbns around the world. *Works in collections*: Arts Council of England, British Council, British Library, BM, Imperial War Museum, Government Art Collection, Tate Gallery, Cecil Higgins AG & Museum, Scottish National Gallery of Modern Art, Leeds City Art Galleries, Henry Moore Inst., Southampton AG, University of Warwick; major museums and art galleries worldwide. *Commissions*: 'Regardless of History' for the fourth plinth, Trafalgar Square. *Publications*: Bill Woodrow, Sculpture 1980-86 (Fruitmarket Gallery, Edinburgh, catalogue); A Quiet Revolution-British Sculpture since 1965 (Thames & Hudson, 1987); Bill Woodrow, About This Axis, Drawings 1990-95 (Camden Arts Centre, 1995); Fools Gold (Tate Gallery, 1996); Sculptures 1981-1997 (Mestne Galerija, Ljubljana, Slovenia (1997). *Misc*: trustee of the Tate Gallery 1996-2001; trustee of the Imperial War Museum (2003-); governor of the University of the Arts London (2003-). *Email*: bill@billwoodrow.com *Website*: www.billwoodrow.com

WOODRUFF, Bronte Elizabeth. *Medium*: watercolour, pigments, acrylic, collage; rural subjects. *b*: Woking, Surrey, 17 Jan 1959. *m*: divorced. two *s*. one *d*. *Studied*: Self-taught. *Exhib*: prolific artist exhibiting throughout Herefordshire, Shropshire, Welsh Borders, including Radnorshire Museum, Llandrindod Wells (Wayfaring) (2008), St. Andrew's Art Show, Presteigne (2007, 2008); Ludlow Assembly Rooms (Land Meets Sky) (2012); Showborough House, Glos. (2008-2012); Blue Ginger Gallery, Cradley (2009-2012); Pontypool Museum (Treescapes) (2010); Palace Art-fest, Hereford (2010-2014); Wyeside Arts Centre, Builth Wells 2012 (Sightlines); art@thegranary, Lingen (2010-14); Herefordshire Art Week (2004-2014); Oriel Cric, Crickhowell (2012); Dore Abbey Residency (2008/2013). *Works in collections*: private collections worldwide. *Recreations*: walking, music, plants. *Misc*: Curated: 'Art for Your Sake', Macmillan at The Colloquy (2008, 2010); Help for Heroes, Lemore Manor (2008); The Maggie's Spring Art Show, Lyde Arundel (2011); Art at No. 10, The Struet, Brecon (2008-2014); h-Art Steering Group (2009-2014); Out of Nature, Newport House (2013). *Address*: Marsh Cottage, Yatton, Leominster, Herefordshire, HR6 9TP. *Email*: bronte@woodruffsworld.co.uk *Website*: www.h-art.org.uk *Signs work*: "BW".

WOODS, Alistair. *Medium*: Mixed media, photography, collage, sculpture. *b*: Guildford, 25 June 1991. *Studied*: UCA Farnham (2010); Leeds Metropolitan University (2013). *Exhib*: Flash Show, Broadcasting Place, Leeds (2011); Enjoy, Leeds (2012); Basement Arts, Leeds (2012, 13); Unit 12, Melbourne Street, Leeds (2012); Leeds Metropolitan University Degree Show, Broadcasting Place, Leeds (2013); Northern Graduates Exhibition, The Curwen Gallery, London (2013); Harvey Gallery, Guildford (2013); Basement Arts, Leeds (2014 - two week residency and solo show). *Works in collections*: Work in Basement Arts Projects collection. *Address*: 20 Old Glebe, Fernhurst, Haslemere, Surrey, GU27 3HS. *Email*: alistairwoods01@gmail.com *Website*: www.alistairwoods.co.uk *Signs work*: "Alistair Woods"

WOODS, Brian, DipAD (Hons), MAFA, shared 1st Prize Painting (Manchester Academy, 1986); Edward Oldham Trust Bursary (Venice, 1995 and 2001); Siemens Figure Painting Award (1997); RWS Award 21st Century Watercolours (2008). *Medium*: acrylic, watercolour, drawing, prints. *b*: Loughborough, 22 Mar 1938. *s of*: C.L.& E Woods. *m*: June M.Woods. one *s*. one *d*. *Educ*: Loughborough College School (1949-54), GPO Telephones, Youth in Training (1954-56), RAF National Service, SAC (1956-58), GPO Telephones Engineer (1958-63). *Studied*: Loughborough College of Art (1963-67). *Represented by*: Wendy Levy Gallery, Didsbury, Manchester. *Exhib*: solo exhbns: Rochdale Art Gallery, Bury Art Gallery (x2), Portico Gallery, Manchester; mixed exhbns: RA Summer Exbhns; Singer & Friedlander/Sunday Times Competition (2003-07); Manchester Academy Annual Open Exhbns; Contemporary British Watercolours, Bankside Gallery, London; British Print Open Exhbn; West of England Academy; House of Commons, London with Rochdale Sculptors Group; RWS 21st Century Watercolours Exhibition (2008-09); RWS/Sunday Times Competition (2008-09). *Works in collections*: Manchester City Art Gallery, Bury Art Gallery, Rochdale Art Gallery. *Commissions*: Wetherspoons. *Official Purchasers*: Manchester, Bury and Rochdale Art Galleries; Wetherspoons. *Recreations*: things Italian. *Clubs*: elected member MAFA (1989); member of Rochdale Sculptors Group (late 60s early 70s). *Misc*: lecturer (drawing and painting) Rochdale College of Art, then Hopwood Hall College (1967-92); occasional host on SAGA painting holidays (1996-2005). *Address*: 7 North Court, Thornton-Cleveleys, Lancashire FY5 1JA. *Signs work*: 'Brian Woods' or 'BW'.

WOODS, Michael John, Slade Diploma in Fine Art. *Medium*: ceramics, oil, watercolour, drawing, prints. *b*: Norwich, 6 Dec 1933. *s of*: Reginald Woods MBE. *m*: Jacqueline. one *s*. two *d*. *Educ*: Norwich School under John Marshall. *Studied*: Norwich School of Art under Noel Spencer; Slade School of Fine Art under Sir William Coldstream; Farnham School of Art (Ceramics) under Paul Barron. *Exhib*: RA, London galleries, Manchester, Norfolk, Surrey and Sussex; ceramics: British Crafts Centre. *Works in collections*: Nuffield Foundation; The National Trust; City of Norwich Castle Museum; private collections in UK, USA and Australia. *Commissions*: The Bishop of Norwich; academic portraits; Memorial at Dachau for The International Committee; Historic Map for the Godalming Trust; illustrator of ten books; Ceramic Fountain for RHS Chelsea. *Publications*: nine books on the process of drawing and painting for Batsford and Dryad Press. *Official Purchasers*: City of Norwich. *Works Reproduced*: 20 books; articles for art magazines. *Recreations*: walking. *Misc*: taught at Charterhouse from 1957, Director of Art 1970-94. *Address*: 2 Alan Road, King Street, Norwich. NR1 2BX. *Website*: www.michaelwoods.me.uk *Signs work*: 'MICHAEL WOODS'.

WOODSIDE, Christine A., DA (1968), Post Dip. (1969), RSW (1993), RGI (1999); artist in water-colour and mixed media. *b*: Aberdeen, 24 Apr 1946. *Partner*: Charles T.K. Macqueen, RSW, RGI. one *s*. one *d*. *Educ*: Aberdeen High School for Girls. *Studied*: Gray's School of Art, Aberdeen (1964-69, Ian Fleming, Robert Henderson Blythe). *Exhib*: numerous including RSA, RSW, RGI. *Works in collections*: Saltire Soc., RSA, Perth Museum. *Commissions*: 2 paintings for Queen Victoria Cunard Liner. *Clubs*: The Scottish Arts Club. *Address*: Tower View, 1 Back Dykes, Auchtermuchty, Fife KY14 7AB. *Email*: christinewoodside@hotmail.com *Signs work*: "Woodside".

WOODWARD, Justine, HS (1998); MASF, SLM. *Medium*: watercolour, pastels and oil, specialising in miniatures of children. *b*: Beckenham, 23 Feb 1944. divorced. *d of*: George Woodward. one *s*. one *d*. *Educ*: Columbia University. *Studied*: self-taught. *Exhib*: RMS, Hilliard Society, Miniature Art Society of Florida. *Commissions*: completed many commissions of children. *Publications*: Leisure Painters article. *Works Reproduced*: Louis de Grandpre (1790-1810). *Recreations*: gardening, reading, travelling. *Clubs*: art societies; Runnymede, Virginia Water. *Address*: Fauns Glen, The Friary, Old Windsor, Berks. SL4 2NR. *Email*: jwofow@onetel.net.uk *Website*: Hilliard Society website

WOOLF-NELLIST, Meg, BA, ATD, FSDC; awarded Exhibition, RCA (1949); formerly lecturer in art, Rachel McMillan College of Educ., Director, Bermuda Art Assoc. School (1950-52); artist in stone, wood, calligrapher. *b*: Isle of Thanet, 10 Dec 1923. *d of*: Dr. E. A. Woolf, D.Litt. *m*: Anthony Nellist (decd). one *s*. three *d*. *Educ*: Couvent des Oiseaux. *Studied*: Ravensbourne College of Art, Brighton College of Art (1939-42). *Exhib*: Roland, Browse and Delbanco, AIA, RBA, RA, V&A, Russell Cotes, Hove A.G. (one-man, 1948); with Designer Craftsmen (1968-69), Hornchurch A.G. (1986, 1987, 1989, 1991, 1993, 1994, 1998, 1999), Oxford Scribes (2000). *Works in collections*: Canada, USA, Germany, Australia. *Works Reproduced*: Studio. *Address*: 84 Front Lane, Cranham, Essex RM14 1XW.

WORMELL, Christopher, Graphics Prize, Bologna for 'An Alphabet of Animals' International Children's Book Fair (1991); Bronze Medal, Smarties Award, for 'Two Frogs'(2003); New York Times Book Review - Best Illustrated Children's Book for 'Teeth, Tails and Tentacles'. *Medium*: wood engraving, lino cut, watercolour, commercial artist. *b*: Gainsborough, Lincs., 1 Sep 1955. *s of*: John Wormell (now L.J.W. Linsey). *m*: Mary Carroll. one *s*. two *d*. *Represented by*: The Artworks, 40 Frith Street, London W1D 5LN (Illustration Agency). *Exhib*: many shows in UK and US. *Works in collections*: Victoria and Albert Museum. *Commissions*: numerous since 1983. *Publications*: many children's picture books. *Works Reproduced*: all work is for reproduction. *Address*: 34 Brownlow Rd, New Southgate, London N11 2DE. *Email*: chriswormell@blueyonder.co.uk

WORTH, Philip, MA, LL.B, Hon Sec FPS; self taught artist in acrylic. *b*: Gillingham, 23 Jun 1933. *s of*: Lloyd Worth, Major (RE). *m*: Jennifer Louise. two *d*. *Educ*: Royal High School, Edinburgh, Edinburgh University. *Exhib*: many one-man and group shows throughout U.K. since 1984. *Address*: The White House, 282 St. John's Rd., Boxmoor, Hemel Hempstead, Herts. HP1 1QG. *Signs work*: "P. WORTH."

WOUDA, Marjan Petra, ARBS, BA (Hons.) Fine Art (1987), MA Fine Art/Sculpture (1988); sculptor in clay/bronze. *Medium*: bronze, clay, welded steel. *b*: Aduard, The Netherlands, 20 Feb 1960. *m*: Immy Deshmukh. two *s*. one *d*. *Studied*: N.E. London Polytechnic, Manchester Polytechnic. *Represented by*: Curwen Gallery, London; Broomhill, Barnstaple, Devon; Pride of the Valley Sculpture Park, Farnham, Surrey; Cloud Gallery, Chester, Worthing and Brighton; Linto Court gallery, Settle. *Exhib*: Art Fair, Islington, London (1997, 1998), Affordable Art Fair, London (2003, 2010), Edinburgh Festival (2005), Chelsea Flower Show, London (2009, 2011-2014), Beelden in Gees, the Netherlands (2014). *Works in collections*: Provident Financial Head Office, Bradford, Bury Art Gallery and Museum, Blackburn Museum and Art Gallery, and private collection of Felix Dennis, publisher. *Commissions*: London Dockland Development Corp.; Groundwork Trust, Wigan; Arcades Shopping Centre, Ashton-under-Lyne: major bronze sculpture at centre of development; drawings for British Consulate, Hong Kong, River Lune Millenium Park, Lancashire, Mustique, West Indies (first public sculpture on island), United Utilities - Entwhistle Reservoir; Sustrans - way of the Roses, Bentham. *Clubs*: R.B.S., M.A.F.A., R.Cam.A. *Address*: Whitehall, Queen's Rd., Darwen, Lancashire BB3 2LN. *Email*: marjan@marjanwouda.co.uk *Website*: www.marjanwouda.co.uk *Signs work*: "Marjan" or "M.W." joined.

WRAGG, John, RA, ARCA, RIS; sculptor. *b*: York, 20 Oct 1937. one *s*. *Studied*: York School of Art (1954-56), Royal College of Art (1956-60). Awards: Sainsbury Award (1960), Winner of Sainsbury Sculpture Competition (1966), Arts Council (1977), Chantrey Bequest (1981). *Exhib*: solo shows: (1963-97), include; Hanover Gallery, Gallerie Alexandre Iolas Paris, York Festival, Devizes Museum Gallery, L'Art Abstrait London, Monumental '96 Belguim; Courcoux, etc.; group shows (1959-93): Bradford A.G., Gimpel Hanover Galerie Zurich, L'Art Vivant, Bath Festival Gallery, Quinton Green Fine Art London, Connaught Brown, etc. *Works in collections*: Sainsbury Centre, University of E. Anglia; Israel Museum,

Jerusalem; Tate Gallery, London; ACGB; Arts Council of N.I.; Contemporary Art Soc.; Wellington A.G., NZ; National Gallery of Modern Art, Edinburgh. *Publications*: Neue Dimensionen der Plastic (Undo Kutterman), British Sculpture in the 20th Century (1981), etc. *Address*: 6 Castle Lane, Devizes, Wilts. SN10 1HJ. *Email*: johnwragg.ra@virgin.net

WRAITH, Edwin. *Medium*: oil, watercolour, drawing. *b*: Sheffield, 29 Aug 1927. *m*: Betty Wraith. *Educ*: local school. *Studied*: self taught artist - started painting at 52 years old. *Exhib*: Edward Mayor Gallery, Sheffield; Earl Marshall School, Sheffield; Rotherham Library and Art Gallery; Wath on Dearn Library; Sheffield Octagon (for 11 years); Clifton Park Museum, Rotherham; The Old Market, Westgate Gallery, Rotherham; A one Man Show of 80 Paintings. *Commissions*: portraits, landscapes, animals. *Address*: 121 Pringle Road, Brinsworth, Rotherham, S60 5AZ. *Email*: edwinwraith@yahoo.co.uk *Website*: www.edwinraith.com *Signs work*: "E Wraith".

WRAITH, Robert, RP; painter in oil, water-colour, drawing, etching. *m*: Tina. one *s*. two *d*. *Educ*: Stowe. *Studied*: Florence (Pietro Annigoni). *Exhib*: twenty-seven one man shows, also NPG, RA, RP etc. *Works in collections*: HM The Queen, HRH The Prince of Wales, Chatsworth, The Vatican, MCC, National Trust, Oxford University, fresco in the Church of Ponte Buggianese, Italy, etc. *Commissions*: Many portrait commissions, including HM The Queen, The Duke and Duchess of Devonshire. *Clubs*: Arts. *Misc*: Invited by H.R.H. The Prince of Wales to accompany him on his visit to South Africa as travelling artist, 1997. *Address*: The Old School House, The Green, Holton, Oxon. OX33 1PS. *Email*: robbie@robbiewraith.com *Website*: www.robbiewraith.com *Signs work*: "WRAITH" or "Robbie Wraith."

WRAY, Peter, RE (1991), MA (1992), PGDipAD (1984), Cert.Ed. (1972); Senior lecturer in Printmaking, University of York St. John (1987-2001). *Medium*: printmaking/painting. *b*: Sedgefield, Co. Durham, 27 Oct., 1950. two *d*. *Educ*: St. Mary's School, Darlington. *Studied*: St. Mary's College, Strawberry Hill, Twickenham (1969-72), Goldsmiths' College (1983-84, John Rogers, Peter Mackarrell, Trevor Allen), Leeds Polytechnic (1990-92, Geoff Teasdale). *Represented by*: Cornwall Contemporary, Penzance; Bankside Gallery, London. *Exhib*: RE, International Print Biennale, New Academy Gallery, Curwen Gallery, etc. *Works in collections*: Price-Waterhouse, Sainsbury, Intel UK, St. Thomas's Hospital, Bank of England, Royal Hospital Trust, Art Committee PTT, Netherlands. *Clubs*: Royal Society of Painter/Printmakers (R.E.), Penwith Society of Artists. *Address*: c/o Trewidden Studios, Trewidden Garden, Buryas Bridge, Penzance, Cornwall TR20 8TT. *Email*: peterwrayre@aol.com *Website*: www.peterwrayre.com www.handprintstudio.co.uk *Signs work*: "P. Wray."

WRIGHT, Anne, RBA, NDD, RA Dip.; portrait painter in oil and pastel; Mem. Chelsea Art Soc., and President of The Small Paintings Group. Elected Member of the Royal Society of British Artists (2012). *b*: Nottingham, 28 Mar 1935. *m*: Henry Brett. two *d*. *Studied*: Nottingham College of Art (1952-54), RA Schools (1954-59, Peter Greenham). *Represented by*: commissionaportrait.com. *Exhib*: Coach House Gallery, Guernsey, Carlyle Gallery, London, Piers Feetham Gallery, London; Llewellyn Alexander Gallery, London; Russell Gallery, London. *Works in collections*: Candie Museum, Guernsey. *Commissions*: murals: McAlpine and General Dental Council. *Clubs*: Chelsea Arts. *Address*: 55 Englewood Rd., London SW12 9PB. *Email*: annewright.brett@gmail.com *Website*: www.annewrightart.co.uk *Signs work*: "A" above "W".

WRIGHT, Bert, PPRSMA, FRSA; Past President, Royal Society of Marine Artists; President, Wapping Group of Artists; President Ealing Art Group; Prizewinner Sunday Times/Singer Friedlander Water-colour competition; marine and landscape painter of contemporary subjects, plein air painter on location worldwide, also paints architectural subjects. *Medium*: watercolour, oils. *b*: 1930. *m*: Marjorie Wright. one *s*. two *d*. *Studied*:

Nottingham College of Art. *Represented by*: Mall Galleries, London; Frances Iles Galleries, Rochester. *Exhib*: RA, and regularly at major galleries in the London area and in the USA. One-man show, Mall Galleries (2005). Audience with Her Majesty the Queen and Duke of Edinburgh (2005). *Works in collections*: UK, USA, Far East and the Middle East. *Commissions*: New York Yacht Club, Sultan of Oman, Daily Express, Standard Chartered Bank, British American Tobacco, Mullard Electronics, Beecham Group, Lloyds, Allied Dunbar, P&O. *Publications*: listed in '20th Century Marine Art', articles for 'Artist' magazine. *Recreations*: music (piano). *Clubs*: Arts Club. *Address*: 19 Carew Rd., Ealing, London W13 9QL. *Email*: bert.wright@virgin.net *Website*: www.bertwright.com

WRIGHT, Bill, RSW (1974), RGI (1990), PAI (1996); painter in water-colour and acrylic; President, Scottish Artists' Benevolent Soc. *b*: Glasgow, 1 Sep 1931. *m*: Annie. three *d*. *Studied*: Glasgow School of Art. *Exhib*: many solo and national exhbns. *Works in collections*: several public collections including HRH The Duke of Edinburgh. *Clubs*: Glasgow Art. *Address*: Old Lagalgarve Cottage, Bellochantuy, Argyll PA28 6QE.

WRIGHT, Brian Howell, ARCA; Chelsea Diploma of Painting. *Medium*: oil, watercolour, drawing. *b*: London, 8 Feb 1937. *m*: Julia Chandler (decd). one *s*. one *d*. *Educ*: Emanuel School. *Studied*: Chelsea College of Art under Edward Middleditch, Derek Greaves, Jack Smith (1956-60); RCA under Carel Weight, Roger de Grey, Julian Trevelyan (1960-63). *Exhib*: London, Japan. *Works in collections*: in UK, USA, Canada, Belgium, Poland, Israel, Japan. *Commissions*: paintings, sundials. *Misc*: demonstrator and organiser painting section 'Art in Action'. *Address*: 33 Park Place, Ealing, London W5 5NQ. *Email*: bhowellwright@aol.com *Signs work*: 'WRIGHT'.

WRIGHT, Jennifer May, DipAd; ASEA. *Medium*: Oil; drawing; gouache, pastel. *b*: Wembley, 10 Apr 1948. *m*: Edmond Bain. one *s*. one *d*. *Studied*: St Martins School of Art, London (1965-69). *Exhib*: RA Summer Exhibition (1976); Society of Equestrian Artists (1986, 87, 88, 89); ROI (1988); RBA (1989); NEAC (2998, 2009); Society Women Artists (2011). *Works in collections*: Private; Rathbones Bank, London; Southampton University Hospital. *Recreations*: Horse riding; sailing. *Address*: Hatchgate Farm, Dennypot Lane, Chobham, Surrey GU24 8DL. *Email*: wbain@hatchgate.eclipse.co.uk *Website*: www.wrightfineart.co.uk *Signs work*: "JENNIFER M. WRIGHT".

WRIGHT, Lisa, BA Hons 1st Class, MA Fine Art; Threadneedle Prize Winner (2013); Royal Academician RWA (2012); NOAC 2009 (1st Prize), Lynne Painter Stainers (2009 Prizewinner), NOAC 2008 (2nd Prize), Sovereign European Art Prize (2006), Hunting Art Prize 2003 (1st Prize). *Medium*: oil. *b*: Kent, 3 Jan1965. *m*: Mark Surridge. two *s*. *Studied*: Maidstone College of Art (1983-1987), Royal Academy Schools (1990-1993). *Represented by*: Beardsmore Gallery. *Exhib*: Beardsmore Gallery, (1999-2010); Lemon Street Gallery (2003, 2006); Millennium Gallery (2011, 2013); Hunting Art Prizes (2000-2004); The Royal Overseas League (1993, 1994, 1996); RA Summer Ex (1991-2012 inclusive). *Works in collections*: Jerwood, Linklaters,Unilever, Guinness, BUPA, Astra Zeneca, Royal Shakespeare Co. *Commissions*: Artist-in-Residance with Royal Shakespeare Company (2006-2008). *Publications*: catalogues for solo exhibs. (1994-2013). *Clubs*: Royal Academician RWA. *Address*: Chapel House, Crelly, Helston, Cornwall TR13 0EY. *Email*: wright65@me.com *Website*: lisawrightartist.co.uk *Signs work*: "Lisa Wright."

WRIGHT, Liz, BA Art and Design. *Medium*: oil, watercolour, drawing, prints. *b*: Wembley, London, 14 Dec 1950. *d of*: George Wright. *Educ*: St. Bernards Convent School. *Studied*: St. Martins College of Art (1968-69); West of England College of Art (1969-72, under David Inshaw and Alfred Stockham). *Exhib*: in UK and USA. *Works in collections*: Wessex Collection, Lord Bath, Longleat, Wiltshire. *Publications*: illustrations 'Chocolate' (Pavillion Books). *Works Reproduced*: many with the Bridgeman Art Library; book covers, CD covers, cards, prints. *Recreations*: walking, swimming. *Clubs*: Chelsea

Arts Club. *Address*: 8 Higher Lane, Portland, Dorset DT5 1AT. *Email*: lizonportland@btinternet.com *Website*: www.wrightfineart.co.uk *Signs work*: 'Liz Wright'.

WRIGHT, Roy, PS; NDD (Post Dip); RA Summer Exhibition Drawing Prize (2001); Cross Gate Gallery Award, Kentucky USA (1999); Willie Hoffmann-Guth Award (PS, 2002); 'Arcadia in the City' Exhibition Award (2002); Anthony J.Lester Art Critic Award (PS, 2009); Graphic Artist of the Year 1987 & 1988 (British Press Awards), Daler Rowney Award 2011. *Medium*: charcoal, watercolour. *b*: Hornsea, E.Yorks, 4 Jul 1945. *s of*: Ken & Olive Wright. *m*: Jennifer. one *s*. one *d*. *Educ*: Hornsea Secondary School. *Studied*: Hull College of Art (1961-66). *Represented by*: Henry Boxer Gallery; Roman Black Gallery, Rebecca Hossack Gallery. *Exhib*: RA Summer Exhbns; Cheltenham Open Drawing; Hunting Art Prizes; 20/21 British Art Fair; Pastel Society; Art London; Singer & Friedlander Watercolour; Affordable Art Fair; Laing Landscape; Roman Black Gallery; Messum's; London Art Fair; NEAC; AA Fair NYC; Art on Paper Fair; Kew Gardens Gallery; Southampton City Art Gallery; Rebecca Hossack, London/New York. *Works in collections*: The Open University; Liberty Syndication; Harrogate Borough Arts Council; Richmond & Twickenham Arts Council; Merrill Lynch; BHF Charterhouse CCF; Peggy & Herschel Post MBE; Cath Kidston MBE; Terry Gilliam; Charlie Mayfield; Chairman John Lewis Partnership; Richard Todd QC; Stephen Wiener CEO Cineworld Cinemas. *Commissions*: private and business: Louise Bradley Interior Designs; Parker Harris Partnership; Catherine Pooley Home Interiors; McGraw Hill; Jane Houghton Interiors. *Publications*: The Times T2 2004; London Topographical Society (2002); Anglo-Spanish Society Review (2001); catalogues: RA Summer Exhibition catalogues (2001, 04); 20/21 British Art Fair catalogues; AAF (2002) / Books: "The View" (2003), "Artists' Kew" (2006), Mail on Sunday (2011). *Works Reproduced*: 'Oak Tree, Spring' on greeting cards sold through RA shops; 'You Can Never Hold Back Spring' on postcards sold through RA shops. *Address*: 4 Rosemont Road, Richmond, Surrey TW10 6QL. *Email*: roywrightart@hotmail.com *Website*: roywright.co.uk *Signs work*: 'Roy Wright' or 'Wright'.

WRIGHT, Sally Diane, SBA; artist in water-colour and pencil. *b*: London, 21 Oct 1952. *m*: Robert Wright. one *s*. one *d*. *Exhib*: Westminster Gallery, London, Brighton Festival. *Publications*: work published by Medici. *Address*: Holly Cottage, Elven Lane, East Dean, E. Sussex BN20 0LG.

WRIGHT, Steve, BA Hons, MFA; Lecturer at Morley College, London (2011-date); Visiting Lecturer, Staffordshire University (2014); Visiting Lecturer, Newcastle University (2002). *Medium*: oil. *b*: Bath, Somerset, 20 Aug 1975. *Partner*: Rev. Geoffrey Farrar. *Studied*: Wimbledon School of Art (1995-98); Newcastle University (1999-2001). *Exhib*: Atkinson Gallery, Millfield (2001); Shire Gallery, Alnwick (2003); National Glass Centre, Sunderland (2007); Berwick Gymnasium Gallery (2007); Elysium Gallery, Swansea (2009); Lit & Phil, Newcastle (2010); Morley Gallery, London (2011); St. Barnabas Gallery, Cambridge (2012); Museum of St. Albans (2013); Roller Gallery (2013). *Works in collections*: University of Surrey; BHF Bank, London; Dept of Animal Anatomy, University of Cambridge. *Commissions*: various private; 'Steeling Skies', Rednile Projects Ltd., Sheffield. *Publications*: a-n Magazine, August 2006. *Recreations*: plays the piano. *Address*: 33 Bushey Mill Lane, Watford, Hertfordshire WD24 7QU. *Email*: wright2steve@yahoo.co.uk *Website*: www.stevewrightart.com *Signs work*: "Steve Wright".

WRIGHT, Stuart Pearson R., Awards include: John Moore's Prize, Walker Art Gallery, Liverpool (2008); Singer and Friedlander/Sunday Times Watercolour Comp. (1998, 1999 - third prize, 2004 - first Prize); Garrick/Milne Prize (2000 - Third Prize, 2005 - First Prize). *Medium*: painter in oil, printmaker, sculptor, video artist, curator, set-designer. *b*: Northampton, 11 Oct 1975. *s of*: Penelop Wright (painter). *m*: Polly Bowman. one *s*. *Studied*: Slade School of Fine Art (1995-1999), BA Fine Art, Prince's Drawing School

(2002-03). *Represented by*: Riflemaker. *Exhib*: see awards, also Jerwood Space London, National Portrait Gallery London, National Portrait Gallery Washington, Solyanka State Gallery Moscow, Aberdeen Art Gallery, General Assembly New York, National Theatre London, University Art Gallery Aberystwyth, St James' Palace London, Chatsworth Derbyshire, Agnews London, Riflemaker, Galerie Huebner, Frankfurt. *Works in collections*: National Portrait Gallery, British Academy, Ashmolean Oxford, Garrick Club, University of Aberystwyth, Rhode Island School of Design Museum (US), Aberdeen Art Gallery, House of Commons, British Museum. *Commissions*: John Hurt, The Six Presidents of the British Academy, Prince Philip, Diane Abbott MP, Mike Leigh, J K Rowling – NPG, Sachin Tendulkar. *Publications*: Most People are Other People - Saveloy Press, I Remember You - Riflemaker, Together in Electric Dreams - Saveloy Press, Painting Today - Tony Godfrey, Phaidon Publications, Love & Death - Riflemaker. *Works Reproduced*: front cover for 'The League of Gentlemen' Script Book for BBC, Front cover 'What Happens Now?' Jeremy Dyson, front cover 'The Late Hector Kipling' David Thewlis, 'Modern Man is Quick' - Gavin Wright. *Recreations*: fencing. *Misc*: Curated exhibitions: 2009 Kunskog, Five Hundred Dollars, Vyner Street, London; 2009 Anopseudononymous, Five Hundred Dollars, Vyner Street, London. *Website*: www.stewartpearsonwright.com *Signs work*: "SPW".

WRIGHT, Valerie Margaret, B.Ed.Hons (1977), SWA (1986), SBA (1987); landscape, botanical and wildlife painter in water-colour. *b*: Manchester, 6 Jan 1934. *d of*: Sydney Wainwright Musgrove. *m*: Norman Wright. one *s*. two *d*. *Educ*: Peterborough High School, Hendon Polytechnic, Coloma College of Educ. London University. *Studied*: Coloma College (Constance Stubbs, Norma Jameson). *Exhib*: RI, SWA, SBA, Portico Gallery, Manchester, Manchester Academy, BWS. Gorstella Gallery; one-man shows: Chester, Warrington, Bolton Octagon Theatre, Frodsham Arts Centre, Norton Priory. *Address*: Appletree Cottage, 55 Rushgreen Rd., Lymm, Ches. WA13 9PS. *Signs work*: "Valerie Wright."

WYATT, Joyce (Mrs Derek Wraith), RMS, VPSWA, Hon.UA, FRSA; Prix Rowland and Mention Honorable (Paris Salon, 1963); Médaille D'Argent (Paris Salon, 1965); Médaille D'Or (Paris Salon, 1969); Member of La Société des Artistes Français (1969); portrait painter in oil, water-colour, etc. *b*: London. *d of*: Francis W. Wyatt, company director. *m*: Dr. Derek Greenway Wraith. one *s*. one *d*. *Exhib*: RA, RP, RMS, RBA, Société des Artistes Français, UA, SWA, etc.; one-man shows: Federation British Artists, Edinburgh Festival Exhbn., Rutland Sq., Edinburgh, La Galerie Mouffe, Paris. *Works in collections*: Fresco (Christ Consoling the Women) Italy; St. Andrew's Church, Totteridge (The Nativity). *Commissions*: include portraits for HRH Prince Michael of Kent. *Address*: Archgate, North Stoke, nr. Wallingford, OX10 6BL. *Signs work*: "WYATT."

WYER, Annraoi, BA Hons. Fine Art (1986), Dip. Design Hons. (1985); Greenshield Foundation award, Montreal (1988), President's Gold medal (1987); Prof. of Art, Blackrock College; painter, printmaker, illustrator. *Medium*: print. *b*: Dublin, 7 Sep 1963. *s of*: Henry A. Wyer. *m*: Sheila. one *s*. *Educ*: Blackrock College. *Studied*: National College of Art and Design, Dublin, Dublin Inst. of Technology (1981-84, Alice Hanratty, Patrick Graham). *Exhib*: Ljubljana (1987, 1989), Varna (1989, 1991), Taipei (1988), various national exhbns. Work in corporate and private collections. *Works in collections*: national and international. *Publications*: 'Blackrock College 1860-1995'. *Clubs*: Assoc. of Artists in Ireland, Black Church Print Studio. *Address*: 3 Ardmore Wood, Herbert Rd., Bray Co., Wicklow, Eire. *Signs work*: "Annraoi Wyer."

WYLES, June, BA (Hons) Fine Art, MA Printmaking; painter/printmaker in oil, charcoal - landscape and the human form; lecturer of art, Berkshire College of Art and Design. *b*: Berks., 1955. *Studied*: St. Martin's School of Art. *Exhib*: one-man shows: Dusseldörf, London. *Address*: 14a Eldon Rd., Reading, Berks. RG1 4DL. *Signs work*: "June Wyles."

WYLIE, Rose Forrest, MA, RCA; Dupree Award (R.A. 1999); painter. *b*: 14 Oct 1934. *d of*: Alexander Forrest Wylie, OBE, Director of Ordnance, India. *Studied*: Folkestone and Dover School of Art, RCA. *Exhib*: Stadtiche Galerie, Wolfsberg (2014); Tate Britain (2013); Haugar Art Museum, Tonsberg (2013); Jerwood Gallery, Hastings (2012); Rosenwald Wolf Gallery, University of the Arts, Philadelphia (2012); National Museum of Women in the Arts, Washington (2010). And at: Union Gallery London/Cologne; Michael Janssen Gallery, Berlin; Thomas Erben Gallery NY; Regina Gallery, Moscow; Vous Etes Ici, Amsterdam; Kate McGarry, London; The Approach, London; Timothy Taylor Gallery, London. *Works in collections*: Arts Council of England; University College, Oxford; York City Art Gallery; Norwich Gallery print collection; Royal College of Art print collection; Tate Britain; Jerwood Foundation; Stadtiche Galerie, Wolfsberg; National Museum of Women in the Arts, Washington DC. *Publications*: Twink and Ivy, and other Paintings; Rose Wylie Some Drawings; Rose Wylie, Big Boys Sit in the Front; Rose Wylie Rosemount; Picture on the Wall....Rose Wylie; Rose Wylie Hauger/Skira. *Address*: Forge Cottage, Newnham, Sittingbourne, ME9 0LQ.

Y

YALLUP, Pat, RWA; DipAdSA (1956), SIAD, ATD (1963); artist in water-colour (landscapes and abstracts), oil (portraits); Pat Yallup Studio/Gallery, Llandogo, Gwent, (teacher own School). *Medium*: watercolour, oil, pastel. *b*: Johannesburg, S. Africa, 29 Sep 1929. *d of*: Hugh Astley Treadwell, accountant. *m*: R W Yallup. three *s*. *Studied*: Witwatersrand, Johannesburg; Twickenham. *Exhib*: 35 one-man shows, six in London (1984-94); New York (1996). *Commissions*: Expressionist Abstracts, S. Africa, Canada, Germany, America, Australia and New Zealand. *Publications*: many portraits, landscapes and places. *Official Purchasers*: "Creative Imagination". Current and permanent display of paintings to poetry "Creative Imagination" (paintings by Pat Yallup, poems John Birch) now on 4th publication. *Works Reproduced*: Calendars, Limited Prints, Postcards, Gift Cards. *Principal Works*: St. Oudoseus Church, Llandogo Church. *Clubs*: Wye Valley Art Society; RWA Bristol. *Address*: Gallery House, Llandogo, nr. Monmouth, Monmouthshire NP25 4TJ. *Email*: patyallup-artist@yahoo.co.uk *Website*: www.patyallup.com *Signs work*: "Pat Yallup" (water-colours and abstracts).

YARDLEY, Bruce Christopher, AROI (2000); painter in oil. *b*: Reigate, Surrey, 18 Jul 1962. *m*: Caroline Rosier. *Educ*: Reigate Grammar School, Bristol University, Worcester College, Oxford. *Exhib*: ROI, biannual solo exhibs. at various galleries in UK. *Address*: 22 Somers Rd., Reigate, Surrey RH2 9DZ. *Signs work*: "Bruce Yardley."

YARDLEY, John Keith, RI (1990); painter, particularly interior and street subjects, in oil and water-colour; Water-colour Foundation prize RI (1990), and various individual gallery prizes at RI Annual Exhbns. *b*: Beverley, Yorks., 11 Mar 1933. *s of*: R.E. Yardley. *m*: Brenda. two *s*. one *d*. *Educ*: Hastings Grammar School. *Exhib*: RI, RWS, NEAC, numerous one-man shows. *Works in collections*: Merrill Lynch, C.T. Bowring, APV, and private collections. *Publications*: 'Water-colour - A Personal View'; 'The Art of John Yardley' by R. Ranson; 'Water-colour Impressionists' by R. Ranson; 'John Yardley' by Susanne Haines; 'As I See It' by Steve Hall; videos: 'Sunlight in Water-colour' , 'Water-colour in Venice' and 'Variety in Water-colour'. DVD: 'Watercolour Moments'. *Address*: 5 Evesham Rd., Reigate, Surrey RH2 9DF. *Email*: johnyardley@tiscali.co.uk *Signs work*: "John Yardley" in script.

YASMIN, Robina, BA Hons, Postgraduate (Commended). *Medium*: oil on canvas. *b*: Sanwell, Pakistan, 17 Sep 1968. *d of*: Mr & Mrs Rashid. *m*: Jan Morgan. one *s*. *Studied*: Birmingham Institute of Art and Design; Glasgow School of Art. *Represented by*: Ingo Fincke Gallery, 24 Battersea Rise, London SW11. *Exhib*: Ingo Fincke Gallery, London; Fairfax Gallery, Tunbridge Wells; New Designers BDC, Tiley House Carlisle; Worcester Art

Gallery; Birmingham Museum and Art Gallery; Paperleaf Art Fair, Affordable Art Fair, Chelsea Art Fair, Art Ireland, Glasgow Art Fair, Art 2003 Islington, Contemporary Fine Art Gallery, Eton. *Works in collections*: private collections. *Commissions*: numerous private. *Publications*: Art Review, Living etc., SW Magazine, The Index, Living South. *Misc*: subjects constantly changing, currently studying giraffes, reflections, swimmers, people. *Address*: Kira Fincke, Ingo Fincke Gallery, 24 Battersea Rise, London SW11 1EE. *Signs work*: R.Yasmin.

YATES, Alan, ARBS, FSCD, FRSA; sculptor in cast bronze. *b*: Bishop Auckland, 30 Nov 1947. *Educ*: Leeholme School; Bishop Auckland Grammar School. *Studied*: Bede College, Durham University (1966-69). *Exhib*: RA, RSA, RGI, RWA, Paris Salon, Durham University, York, Grantham, Darlington, Perth, Newcastle Polytechnic, Edinburgh, Swansea University, Stratford, Northern Open Touring Exhbn., Chelsea Harbour, Manchester Academy, Mall Galleries London, Kowalsky Gallery London, NEC Birmingham, Tatton Park, Windsor Park. *Commissions*: St. James' Youth Centre, Coundon; Grey College, Durham University. *Publications*: entries in: 'Artists in Britain since 1945' by David Buckman; 'Artists of Northumbria' by Marshall Hall. *Address*: Leaside, Frosterley, Bishop Auckland, Co. Durham DL13 2RH. *Email*: enquiries@sculpturestudio-alanyates.com *Website*: www.alanyates-sculpture.com *Signs work*: "A. YATES."

YATES, Anthony, RBSA (2002); RBA (2005); major awards: Kate Fryer Award, RBSA (2002); Davison Award, RBA (2005); TNT Award, RBSA Prize Exhibition (2005). *Medium*: oil. *b*: Birmingham, 18 Sep 1957. *s of*: Clifford and Lily Yates. *m*: Janice Yates (nee Mills). one *d*. *Studied*: Bourneville College of Art. *Represented by*: Fosse Gallery Fine Art, Stow-on-the-Wold, Gloucestershire. *Exhib*: Driffold (1998, 99); Anderson (1999); Park View (1999, 2000, 2001); Galerie "De Herkening" Amsterdam, Holland (1999); Cowleigh (2001); The Stables, Birmingham (2002); Ombersley (2003, 04); Chomé, Bath (2005); Claire Galleries (2006); Fosse Gallery (2006-2012); Society Exhibitions: RBSA (1995-2012); RWA (1996, 97, 2004); Pastel Society (1998); NEAC (2004); RBA (2003-12). *Works in collections*: RBSA Permanent Collection. *Commissions*: private commissions only. *Publications*: featured in "Miller's Pictures Price Guide 2003", and "West Midlands Public Foundation Catalogue 2007". *Principal Works*: 'Nude in the Bathroom', 'Wet day at the Seaside'. *Misc*: type of work: figurative, landscape, still life, domestic size. *Address*: 495 Harborne Park Road, Harborne, Birmingham, B17 0PS. *Signs work*: "A.Yates."

YATES, Jeremy, RCA (Royal Cambrian Academy). *Medium*: watercolour, acrylic, oils (landscape and figure). *b*: Wolverhampton, 14 Mar 1947. *m*: Christine (decd). two *s*. *Educ*: Brewood Grammar School, Staffordshire. *Studied*: Stafford (1963-65); Brighton College of Art (1965-68); Chelsea School of Art (1968-69). *Exhib*: Summer Shows: RI & RWS; Royal Cambrian Academy of Art. *Works in collections*: various private collections - UK, Canada, Moscow, University of Wales, Bangor. *Publications*: author of 'Frank Brangwyn RA (1967-1956)': The Bangor Collection (2006). *Misc*: Tutor with Univ. Wales Bangor & WEA/Coleg Harlech; Yale Center for British Art, Research Fellowship (1994). *Address*: Y Fron, Cilfodan, Bethesda, Gwynedd LL57 3SL. *Email*: jslyates@tiscali.co.uk *Signs work*: 'Yates.'

YATES, Kate (Katherine). *Medium*: oil, drawing. *b*: New York, 11 Nov 1937. *m*: Dr.Michael Yates MA, MB, BChir. (decd) one *s*. one *d*. *Studied*: JR College New York State (Harry Guggenheimer); Accademia dei Belle Arte, Florence, Italy (Primo Conti); Art Students League, NYC (Julian Levy, Harry Sternberg: graphics/Robert Hale: life drawing/anatomy). *Exhib*: RA, NEAC, CAS (group shows); London, Dakha, France (solo shows). *Works in collections*: many private collections in England, USA, France, Italy, Bangladesh, Switzerland. *Commissions*: (NYC) murals, portraits. *Publications*: via Bridgeman. *Works Reproduced*: Bridgeman Library. *Recreations*: skiing, golf, tennis for sport, theatre, food. *Clubs*: Arts Club, Dover Street, London (resigned). *Misc*: observes passing moments in life with a lean towards caricature. *Address*: 25 Bloomfield Terrace, London SW1W 8PQ. *Email*: kateyates@mac.com *Signs work*: 'Kate Yates.'

YATES, Marie, BA Hons (1971); artist. *b*: Lancashire, 9 Aug 1940. *Studied*: Manchester and Hornsey. *Exhib*: Arts Council, British Council, Arnolfini. *Works in collections*: Arts Council, Arnolfini Trust, Cornwall Educ. Com., Plymouth City A.G. *Publications*: A Re-Evaluation of a Proposed Publication (1978). *Address*: 17 Victoria Rd., London N22. *Signs work*: "Marie Yates."

YEOMAN, Martin, RP, NEAC; artist in oil, pencil, pen and ink, silver point, pastel, etching, clay. *b*: Egham Hythe, 21 Jul 1953. *s of*: Arthur John Yeoman. *m*: Anne Louise. one *s*. *Studied*: RA Schools (Peter Greenham). *Exhib*: Agnews, New Grafton Gallery, RA, NPG, Mallett, Waterman Fine Art, Hampton Court Palace, National Gallery, Yemen. *Works in collections*: HM The Queen, HRH The Prince of Wales, NPG, Sir Brinsley Ford, National Trust, Barings Bank. *Commissions*: The Queen's Grandchildren; The Royal Household. *Publications*: National Trust Foundation for Art, catalogue; British Council, catalogue; Ford Collection (The Walpole Soc.); illustrated: Yemen Travels in Dictionary Land by T. MacIntosh Smith. *Clubs*: R.P., N.E.A.C. *Address*: 101 West Street, Warminster, Wilts. BA12 8JZ. *Signs work*: "Yeoman."

YHAP, Laetitia, DFA (Lond) (1965); artist. *b*: St. Albans, 1 May 1941. *d of*: Dr. L.N. Yhap. one *s*. *Educ*: Fulham County Grammar School. *Studied*: Camberwell School of Art (1958-62, Euan Uglow, Frank Auerbach), Slade School of Fine Art (1963-65, Harold Cohen, Anthony Green). *Exhib*: solo shows, Piccadilly Gallery (1968-73), Serpentine Gallery (1979), Air Gallery (1984), 'Life at the Edge' Charleston Farmhouse (1993); 'The Business of the Beach' 1988-89 Touring show organised by Laing A.G., Newcastle-upon-Tyne, 'Bound by the Sea', The Berwick Gymnasium (1994), Maritime Counterpoint (1996), Boundary Gallery, London, 'Being in the Picture' A Retrospective (2002), Piers Feetham Gallery, London; 'The Catch', Memorial Art Gallery, Hastings (2009). *Works in collections*: Tate Gallery, Unilever House, Hove A.G., Hastings Museum, Rugby Museum, Portsmouth City A.G., British Council, Contemporary Art Soc., New Hall Cambridge, S. East Arts Coll., University College London, Walker A.G., Liverpool, Nuffield Foundation, DOE, Arthur Anderson Coll., Yorkshire, Leicestershire Educ. *Recreations*: badminton, concert going, singing. *Signs work*: "Laetitia Yhap."

YOSHIMOTO, Eiko, PS, SWA, SBA, SPF; artist in pastel, conte, charcoal, oil. *b*: Japan, 5 Jul 1937. *Educ*: Notre Dame Sacred Heart School, Japan; Diploma from Drama School of Toho Film Company, Tokyo. *Studied*: City & Guilds of London Art School (part-time, 1994-96, Eric Morby), École de Société des Pastellistes de France (Jean Pierre Merat). *Exhib*: PS (1986-), SBA (1986-), SWA (1987-), Glyndebourne Opera House (1989, 1991), RA (1993, 1994, 1997), NEAC (1986-), Royal Opera House (1992); solo shows: SPF Paris (1992, 1993, 1995, 1996, 1997). *Address*: "Hermitage Lodge", The Hermitage, Richmond, Surrey TW10 6SH. *Signs work*: "Eiko Yoshimoto."

YOUNG, April, BA (Hons) Literature, specialising in Scottish Lit; BA (Hons) Fine Art. *Medium*: Oil; drawing; sculpture. *b*: Barrow-in-Furness, 10 Apr 1972. *Studied*: Glasgow (1999); Loughborough (2009). *Represented by*: Tallantyre Gallery, Morpeth; Gormley Fine Art, NI; Greenstage Gallery, Herts; Artparks, Guernsey. *Exhib*: British Embassy, New Dehli, India (2010); Brighton Art Fair (2011, 2010); Mall Galleries (2011); Black Swan Arts, Frome (2011); Glasgow Art Fair; Royal South West Academy; RBSA Open; Animal Art Fair (2011). *Works in collections*: Total Oil. *Commissions*: Total Oil; Treasure Pilgrim; Morgan Stanley. *Works reproduced*: Warhorse; Clockwork Elephant, 'Courage', 'Dynamism', 'Spirit', Minoan Bull. *Principal Works*: 'Horses in Motion' series, Carousel Horses. *Clubs*: Society of Equestrian Artists. *Address*: Studio 1.3, Bank's Mill, 71 Bridge Street, Derby DE1 3LB. *Email*: info@aprilyoung.co.uk *Website*: www.aprilyoung.co.uk

YOUNG, Emily. *Medium*: stone. *b*: London, 13 Mar 1951. *d of*: Lord & Lady Kennet. one *s*. *Educ*: varied. *Studied*: Chelsea School of Art, St.Martins School of Art, Stonybrook University, NY, USA. *Represented by*: Fine Art Society. *Exhib*: RA, London; Thackeray Gallery, Fine Art Society, Berkeley Square Gallery, Ingleby Gallery, Royal Botanical Gdns Kew, and many others. *Works in collections*: worldwide. *Commissions*: La Defense Paris, London St. Pauls Churchyard, Gateshead (public), Salisbury Cathedral, numerous private commissions. *Publications*: Emily Young (Ingleby Gallery, 2003); 'Time in the Stone' (Tacit Hill Editions, 2007). *Principal Works*: Wounded Angel I, Royal Botanical Gdns Kew; Golden Angel, Gateshead; 5 Angels for St. Paul's Churchyard; Lunar Disc, Salisbury Cathedral. *Recreations*: singing. *Clubs*: Chelsea Arts Club, Academy Club, Frontline Club, Electric House. *Address*: 47 Blenheim Cres. London W11 2EF. *Email*: info@emilyyoung.com *Website*: www.emilyyoung.com *Signs work*: 'Emily Young', but does not normally sign.

YOUNG, Pippa, BA Hons Fine Art (First Class). *Medium*: oil, drawing. *m*: David Mankin. two *s*. *Studied*: Falmouth (2010-2012). *Exhib*: Medici Gallery, Cork Street; Beaux Arts, Bath; Coombe Gallery, Dartmouth; Belgrave, St. Ives; Cornwall Contemporary. *Works in collections*: private. *Clubs*: Member of Newlyn Society of Artists. *Address*: Churchtown House, Perranuthnoe, Penzance, TR20 9NR. *Email*: pippa@spydesign.co.uk *Website*: www.pippayoung.co.uk *Signs work*: "Pippa Young" or "PS YOUNG".

YOUNGER, Elspeth Chalmers, DA (1957), Post Dip. (1958); embroiderer, painter in inks, water-colour, gouache. *b*: Paisley. *d of*: William Younger. *m*: John Gardiner Crawford. one *s*. one *d*. *Educ*: Camphill Secondary School, Paisley. *Studied*: Glasgow School of Art (1953-58, Kathleen Whyte); National Wool Textile Award (1957), Travelling Scholarship, Paris (1958). *Exhib*: solo shows: 57 Gallery, Edinburgh (1965), Lane Gallery, Bradford (1965), Civic Arts Centre, Aberdeen (1969, 1971), University of Aberdeen (1971), Cornerstone Gallery, Dunblane (1983, 1984, 1988, 1989), Haddo House, Aberdeen (1988), McEwan & Ritchie Fine Art, Dundee (1990), Tolquhon Gallery, Tarves (1992), Cottage Gallery, Newtyle (1993, 1995, 1997, 1999); group shows include Glasgow School of Art, SAC, SSA, Scottish Gallery, RSW, etc. *Works in collections*: Aberdeenshire Educ. Authority, Tayside Educ. Authority, North British Hotel, Dundee A.G., and private collections throughout Britain, and Norway, Holland, Germany, France, Australia, Canada, USA. *Publications*: in various publications, and in "20th Century Embroidery in Gt. Britain", Vols. 2, 3, 4, by Constance Howard. *Address*: 34 Strachan St., Arbroath, Angus DD11 1UA, Scotland. *Signs work*: "ELSPETH YOUNGER" and date, embroidery unsigned, label on reverse.

YOUNGMAN, Erica, HS, ARMS; HND in Natural History and Technical Illustration; 'Honorable Mention' (HS, 2004); Suzanne Lucas Award (Hilliard Society, 2008); RMS Group Award (for best set of 5 or more works, RMS). *Medium*: watercolour. *b*: Skelmersdale, 27 Sep 1972. *m*: Mark. *Studied*: Bournemouth and Poole College of Art and Design. *Exhib*: Mall Galleries (1994, 2008, 2009); The Town Hall, Wells, Somerset; HS. *Works in collections*: Fine Art of all sizes, and miniature fine art; landscapes, floral, animal portraits, human portraits (large and miniature). *Publications*: book illustrations for Dorling Kindersley, and OUP. *Works Reproduced*: many as greeting cards. *Address*: 15 Cutlers Place, Colehill, Wimborne, Dorset BH21 2HN. *Email*: ericayoungman5@yahoo.co.uk *Signs work*: 'E.Youngman.'

YOUNSON, Sydna, BA (Hons) Painting; City & Guilds Calligraphy; Artist-in-Residence, St.John-at-Hackney (1991-95). *Medium*: oil, watercolour. *b*: London, 5 Jan 1968. *d of*: George & Sylvia Younson. *Studied*: Central St.Martins College of Art & Design. *Represented by*: Beverley Knowles Fine Art. *Exhib*: selected exhbns: Beverley Knowles Fine Art (Bedale Gallery, Bevington Street, Art London, Affordable Art Fair); Discerning

Eye (Mall Galleries); Fordham Gallery (1999-); Paul Smith Flagship Store; Roger Evans College; Hat on Wall; Transition Gallery; Quantum Contemporary Art; Tabernacle; Lethaby; Smiths; Ing Bank; solo shows at Fordham, Lyndons Fine Art, Antics, Dreiflessen Collection, Germany. *Works in collections*: various private collections worldwide. *Commissions*: Topshop; Topman; Dreiflessen Collection, Germany. *Works Reproduced*: 'World of Interiors'; 'London Evening Standard'. *Misc*: Also resides in Cordoba, Argentina.*Address*: Flat 2, 40 Thurlow Park Road, London SE2 8JA. *Email*: sydna@younson.com *Website*: www.younson.com *Signs work*: "SY".

YULE, (Duncan) Ainslie, DA (1963); sculptor/teacher; Head of Sculpture, Kingston University 1982- (Reader 1987-). *b*: North Berwick, 1941. *s of*: Edward Campbell Yule & Elizabeth Morgan Yule. *m*: (1) Patricia Carlos (m dissolved). one *d*. (2) 1982, Mary Johnson. *Educ*: Edinburgh College of Art. *Exhib*: regular solo and group exhbns. including Whitechapel A.G. (1973), Gubbio Biennale (1973), Silver Jubilee Exhbn. Battersea Park (1977), Fruitmarket Gallery and travelling (1977-79), Angela Flowers (1986-99), Scottish Gallery (1989-91), Talbot Rice (1999). *Works in collections*: include Aberdeen A.G., ACGB, Dundee A.G., Leeds City A.G., SAC University of Leeds, Gregory Fellow (1974-75). *Clubs*: Chelsea Arts. *Address*: 11 Chiswick Staithe, Hartington Rd., London W4 3TP. *Signs work*: "Ainslie Yule."

Z

ZACRON, NDD Painting (Special Level), RA School Diploma; founder member of the Psychedelic Surrealist Movement (late '60s), and of 'The New Visionaries' school (1978). *Medium*: multi-media artist, photography, poetry, journalism, writing. *b*: Surrey, 29 Sep 1943. *Studied*: Studio 35, Surbiton (1957-60), Kingston College of Art (1961-64), Royal Academy Schools (1964-67). Lectured in Visual Studies at Leeds College of Art (1967-70). *Represented by*: Number Nine the Gallery, Birmingham; The Grapevine Gallery, Norwich; The Lantern Gallery, S.Norfolk; BBC Radio Norfolk. *Exhib*: Royal Academy, Leeds College of Art, widely throughout the UK including East Anglia, the Midlands and London West End galleries, Also travelling exhibitions in the USA; recent one-man shows include: 'Art is Human Ecology', BBC Norwich; 'Zacron Past and Present', The Warehouse, Lowestoft; 'Zacron at the Grapevine Gallery', Norwich. Permanent exhibition at the Lantern Gallery. *Works in collections*: include: Christie's Contemporary Art, Ordnance Survey, Halifax Pemanent Collection, V&A Museum, extensive private collections worldwide. *Commissions*: Brian Epstein, Leyland Cars, Alginate Industries, Led Zeppelin, Fancy the Supergroup, Legs & Co., Whatman Paper, Daler Rowney, Longford and Hill, Mo Faster, numerous private commissions. *Publications*: Graphics World, Graphics, Creative Review, The Artists' & Illustrators Magazine, 'New Visionaries' (pub. Zacron Studios), East Anglian Daily Times, Eastern Daily Press; hundreds of articles and reviews. *Official Purchasers*: Led Zeppelin III album cover (1970). *Principal Works*: 'Between Heaven and Earth' (fine art print, Ordnance Survey, 1978); 'A Window on London' (painting & collage, 1964); Media Exposure - 300 works; 250 works for Daler Rowney-Media Research; Reflections of Paris (2007). *Recreations*: Astronomy, Ancient History, ancient language, extra-terrestrial research, arts collecting. expanding arts and film libraries. *Clubs*: Chelsea Arts Club, Royal Academy ex-students. *Misc*: Widely regarded as an ambassador for the arts, campaigning for freedom in the arts, art as human ecology and as a humanity in education. Zacron combats elitism and insularity in post-modernism. He supports the right of all to their legacy of historic knowledge and their right of access to all skills and processes - established and progressive. Regular contributor to BBC Radio Norfolk and other regional media networks. *Email*: enquire@zacron.com. *Website*: www.zacron.com. *Signs work*: "Zacron."

ZALMON: see WINER, Zalmon.

ZELIN, Linda, SWA; Frank Herring Award, RI Exhibition (Mall Galleries, 2012); awards for painting and sculpture at various exhibitions. *Medium*: oil, watercolour, acrylic, sculpture. *b*: London, 1 Sep 1940. *d of*: Rose & Harry Alton. *m*: Bernard Zelin. two *s*. *Educ*: Hendon County. *Studied*: Harrow College of Further Education (painting); Hampstead Institute (sculpture). *Exhib*: Mall Galleries; Westminster Gallery; John Noot Gallery; Linda Blackstone Gallery; Russell Sheriden Gallery. *Works in collections*: in Spain, Switzerland and USA. *Clubs*: Pinner Sketch Club, Law Society Art Group, Harrow Art Society, Medical Art Society, Society of Women Artists. *Address*: 42 Batchworth Lane, Northwood, Middx. HA6 3DT. *Email*: bernzelin@yahoo.co.uk *Signs work*: 'L.Z.', 'L.'

ZENIN, Eugene, PhD degree, professional painter, graphic designer and book illustrator; gold medal of the University of St. Petersburg. *Medium*: painting, oil on canvas. *b*: Khodjent, USSR, 27 Nov 1946. *s of*: Emilia and Mikhael Zenin. *m*: divorced. one *d*. *Educ*: PhD degree University of St.Petersburg, Russia; State Art School, Tashkent, USSR. *Represented by*: Artistic Licence Gallery, London NW3 3AJ. *Exhib*: many solo and group exhibitions in Denmark, France, England, USA, Russia. *Publications*: 'Angels My Beloved', (pub.A Seraphim Book, Copenhagen 2002); V.Sosnora 'Ajojib Parvoz', 'Sovet Uzbekistoni Sanati' Nr.8.1985 p.17-18; S.Spirikhin 'From Here to Eternity', 'Young Generation' Nr.2 (44) 1990 p.26-27; Affordable Art Fair catalogue, London, October 2003, and 17 other catalogues; 'Dansk kunst 96', 'Danst kunst 99', Forlaget Soeren Fogtdal, 1996 p.67, 1999 p.72; Dictionary of International Biography, 32nd Edition, Cambridge, 2005/06. *Works Reproduced*: in the book 'Angels My Beloved'; 2 articles in magazines, 27 articles in newspapers, 42 postcards (pub. 'Go-Card'), also in the Affordable Art Fair catalogue 2003, and 17 other catalogues. *Principal Works*: 'The Annunciation' (75x110cm) 1996; Madonna and Child (128x85cm) 1996. *Address*: Perlestikkervej 11, 2400 København NV, Denmark. *Email*: ezenin@sol.dk. *Website*: www.zenin.dk. *Signs work*: 'eZenin.'

ZESCHIN, Elizabeth Anne, MA (1978); New York Art Directors Club Awards; Association of Photographers Merit Awards. *Medium*: photography. *b*: Los Angeles, California. *m*: Hugh Gilbert. *Educ*: Boston College A.B. (1976); North Tern University, Chicago (1978). *Represented by*: Arden Anstruther Gallery, Petworth, UK. *Exhib*: National Portrait Gallery (2003, 2005, and Schweppes Photographic Portrait Prize 2008); Taylor Wessing Photographic Portrait Prize Shows; RA Summer Show (2009); Arden Anstruther Gallery Shows (2007, 2009), Chelsea Arts Club Solo and Group Shows (1990-2012); Vision Gallery, York. *Works in collections*: various private collections. *Publications*: American Photography, The Graphis Annual, Eros, The Association Awards Books (Lowern). *Recreations*: cello playing. *Clubs*: Chairman, Chelsea Arts Club; London Cello Society. *Address*: Hurston Studio, Hurston Lane, Pulborough, West Sussex, RH20 2EW. *Email*: zeschin@zen.co.uk. *Website*: www.zeschin.com. *Signs work*: "Elizabeth Zeschin."

ZGORZALEK, Jerzy. *Medium*: oil. *b*: Rowne, 8 May 1944. *s of*: Aleksander Wladyslawa. *m*: Monika Zgorzalek. one *d*. *Studied*: Prof. of the Painter's Artist Jerzy Baurski, Leon Kustrzynski - Title of Painter's Artist from Min. of Culture and Art, Poland (1983). *Exhib*: include: The Akademy of Art, Erewas, Armenia (1977), National Railway Museum, Warsaw (2008). Since 1973 has exhibited in Poland, mainly Warsaw. A member of the Guild of Railway Artists, with whom he exhibited in 2008 & 2009. *Works in collections*: Museums, Polish Foreign Office, private collections in Poland and worldwide. *Publications*: 'Wolsztyn in Painting Jerzy Zgorzalek', biography in Who's Who in Polish (Hubners Publishing). *Recreations*: horsemanship, literature, walks after work with dogs. *Clubs*: Guild of Railway Artists. *Misc*: interviews, broadcsts, reports from exhibitions on TV and radio. TV documentary about his artistic life 'Jerzy Zgorzalek - History of Sure Painting' (46 minutes). *Address*: Jantarowy szlak 2 m 39, Warsaw 03 982, Poland. *Email*: jerzy@artgallery-reklama.com.pl. *Website*: www.artgallery-reklama.com.pl. *Signs work*: "Jerzy Zgorzalek."

ZWART, Valerie. *Medium*: Oil, drawing, digital photography. *b*: Toronto, Canada, 21 Oct 1967. *Studied*: University of Toronto (1986-1990); Ontario College of Art and Design University (1992-1996). *Exhib*: Solo: Artsite Gallery, NL (2007); Gibson Jessop, Toronto, CA (2004, 05, 05); ZW/art projects, NL (2009, 2012). Group: Twente Biennale (2011) NL; Dreamscapes International, NO (2012); Artsite Gallery (2009); Gallery Zoete Broodjes, Amsterdam (2007); Canvas Gallery, Toronto, CA (2005). *Works in collections*: Private/corporate/cultural foundations. *Commissions*: private/corporate. *Publications*: Daily Constitutional (2008); The Artery Show Newspaper (2012). *Clubs*: East Street Arts, Axisweb a-n. *Misc*: Taught at Falmouth Art Guild, Massachusetts, USA (1996-7). Curator of: The Artery Show (Tetem Artspace, NL); Chromophobia (zw/artprojects, NL); Fresh Art to Go (Tetem Artspace, NL) 2012. *Address*: Studio 26, Patrick Studios, St Mary's Street, Leeds LS9 7DP. *Email*: info@valeriezwart.com. *Website*: www.valeriezwart.com. *Signs work*: "V.ZWART".

ZWOLINSKA-BRZESKI, Teresa, RIBA, NS, SWA, SFP, FRSA, Cyril Flisher Prize, Charles Morris Award (2006), Barbare Spreadley Rose Bowl Award (2000). *Medium*: acrylic. *b*: Poland, 17 Jun 1934. *d of*: Konstancia Zwolinska. *m*: Zygmuni Brzeski. *Educ*: Iran, Lebanon and England. *Studied*: at Bournemouth College of Art, Architectural Association School, Brixton School of Building. *Exhib*: one-man exhbns: Krakow and Warszawa, Polish Cultural Inst. London, TZB Southbourne Gallery; mixed exhbns: Priory House Art Gallery, Red House Museum, St. Barbe Museum, Mottisfont Abbey, Sofiero Castle, Westminster Gallery, Highcliffe Castle, Jersey, Austria, RWA Bristol, Bankside, Mall Galleries, Sir Harold Hillier Gardens. *Works in collections*: Canada, Austria, Poland, Spain, USA, England, NZ, Ukraine. *Publications*: Who's Who in Art and Antiques, Dziehnik Polski, The Sticks, Daily Echo, Who's Who Polonia, book: How to Paint from Photographs, SWA catalogues. *Works Reproduced*: poster for Southbourne in Bloom, greeting cards, calendars NZ/UK, book by T.Paul, Who's Who Polonia, Dorset Art Week, Daily Echo, SWA catalogues, Dorset Life. *Recreations*: photography, classical music. *Clubs*: RHS, CAG, HAF, SAS. *Address*: TZB Southbourne Gallery, 2 Carbery Row, Southbourne Road, Bournemouth, BH6 3QR. *Website*: www.theartshopper.com.

NOTES

NOTES

APPENDIX I

OBITUARY

2011
JOHNSON, Diana Victoria, b. 20 Mar 1944, d. 11 Dec 2011
LAING, Gerald FRBS, b. 11 Feb 1936, d. 23 Nov 2011
SIMPSON, Ian, b. 12 Nov 1933, d. 4 Dec 2011
THURSBY, Peter PPRWA, b. 23 Dec 1930, d. Jan 2011

2012
ARDIZZONE, Charlotte RWA, NEAC, b. 24 Oct 1943, d. Dec 2012
CARRICK, Desmond RHA, b. 18 Dec 1928, d. 2012
CLARK, Kenneth Inman Carr MBE, b. 31 Jul 1922, d. 10 Jun 2012
DE FRANCIA, Peter, b. 25 Jan 1921, d. Jan 2012
GILLESPIE, Michael Norman ARBS, d. Feb 2012
HENTY-CREER, Deirdre FRSA, d. 2012
HOLISTER, Frederick Darnton RIBA, b. 14 Aug 1927, d. 10 Aug 2012
IND, John William Charles FRSA,b. 9 Oct 1927, d. 2012
JONES, Trevor, b. 15 Jul 1931, d. 2012
LE GRICE, Jeremy Day, b. 17 Sep 1936, d. 9 Aug 2012
TARRANT, Olwen FROI, b. 1927, d. 29 Oct 2012
TURNBULL, William, b. 11 Jan 1922, d. Nov 2012
WYNNE, Althea FRBS, b. 6 Oct 1936, d. 24 Jan 2012

2013
ASHMORE, Lady Patricia PS, b. 13 Jul 1929, d. 18 Apr 2013
BARROW, Julian PPCAS, b. 28 Aug 1939, d. 3 Sep 2013
BELLANY, John CBE, HRSA, RA, LLD, b. 18 Jun 1942, d. 28 Aug 2013
CARO, Sir Antony CBE, Kt., OM, RA, b. 8 Mar 1924, d. 23 Oct 2013
DANIELS, Harvey Hon RE, b. 17 Jun 1936, d. 23 Aug 2013
DAWSON, Patricia Vaughan, b. Jan 1925, d. 2013
DEWBURY, Brian, b. 25 Jun 1935, d. 3 Oct 2013
FAIRMAN, Sheila RMS, SWA, FSBA, b. 18 Aug 1924, d. 29 Jan 2013
GOODAY, Leslie OBE, RI, FRIBA, FCSD, FRSA, b. 1921, d. Mar 2013
GREEN, Alfred Rozelaar RWA, b. 14 Jul 1917, d. Sep 2013
HOPE, Polly, b. 21 Jun 1933, d. 20 Nov 2013
KENDALL, Kay Thetford RMS, SWA, d. Jan 2013
LOIZOU, Renos, b. 24 Jan 1948, d. 2013
MOSELEY, Austin Frank RBSA, CAS, b. 25 Apr 1930, d. Oct 2013
OWEN, Don RBA, WSW, b. 7 Dec 1929, d. 2013
RAND, Keith ARBS, ARSA, b. 25 Oct 1956, d. Apr 2013
REYNOLDS, Arthur Graham CVO, OBE, FBA, b. 10 Jan 1914, d. 6 Oct 2013
SCOTT, Judy, b. 7 Nov 1939, d. 2013
SLOWE, Vikki RE, b. 24 May 1947, d. 3 Jun 2013
TOVEY, Robert Lawton, b. 3 Apr 1924 d. 2013
WELLS, Peter MFPS, b. 12 Jan 1919, d. 16 Sep 2013
WHEELER, Sir H. Anthony Kt., OBE, PPRSA, PPRIAS, FRIBA, MRTPI, Hon RA, Hon RGI, Hon RBS, b. 7 Nov 1919, d. 19 Dec 2013
WRIGHT, David ASFGA, LSIAD, MSTD, b. 17 Jan 1948, d. 2013
ZAO, Wou Ki, b. 1 Feb 1921, d. 9 Apr 2013

2014
BANEY, Ralph FRBS, b. 22 Sep 1929, d. 21 Jan 2014
BUCKMASTER, Ann Devereaux MSIA, b. 27 Mar 1924, d. Jan 2014
DOWSON, Sir Philip Manning CBE, PPRA, RIBA, FCSD, Hon.FRCA, b. 16 Aug 1924, d. 22 Aug 2014
HICKS, Jerry MBE, RWA, b. 12 Jun 1927, d. 1 Feb 2014
HUNTER, Alexis, b. 4 Nov 1948, d. 24 Feb 2014
JOHNSON, Carl, b. 5 Dec 1946, d. 24 Feb 2014
KEMPSHALL, Kim RBSA, b. 1934, d. Jul 2014
MANNES-ABBOTT, Sheila FSBA, d. 23 Jan 2014
McCANN, Brian FRBS, b. 2 Jul 1952, d. 3 Mar 2014
PRENTICE, David, b. 4 Jul 1936, d. 7 May 2014
TOLSON, Roger Nicholas, b. 2 Dec 1958, d. 11 Feb 2014
WILES, Gillian ARBS, b. 25 Sep 1940, d. 20 Jan 2014

OTHER
DE GOEDE, Julien ARBS, b. 20 May 1937, d. 19 Sep 2007
DE LA FOUGERE, Lucette ROI, RBA, b. 4 Oct 1921, d.
GALVANI, Patrick, b. 11 Sep 1922, d.
HOMESHAW, Arthur Howard RWA, b. 27 Nov 1933, d.
HUBBARD, Deirdre ARBS, FRBS, b. 28 Oct 1935, d. Oct 2009
LEEDS, Caroline (Lady Hobart), b. 17 May 1931, d. 2005
MAER, Stephen FSCD, b. 1933, d. 7 Jan 2007
OSMOND, Edward MSIA, d.
PACKARD, Gillian, Des.RCA, FSDC, FRSA, FCSD, b. 16 Mar 1938, d. 1997
PERRY, Jeffrey NAPA, b. 10 Jan 1935, d. 2007
PRETSELL, Peter, b. 25 Sep 1942, d.
RAVERA, John PPRBS, FRSA, b. 27 Feb 1941, d.,2006
STUBLEY, Trevor Hugh RP, RSW, RBA, RWS, b. 27 Mar 1932, d.
WHITTEN, Philip John FRSA, b. 19 Jun 1922, d.
WISHART, Sylvia RSA, b. 11 Feb 1936, d. 2008
ZIAR, Elizabeth Rosemary, d.

APPENDIX II
QUALIFICATIONS AND GENERAL ABBREVIATIONS

In using this list of abbreviations care should be taken to split up any compound abbreviation into its constituent parts, e.g., "FRS" should be broken into "F" and "RS" the equivalents of these letters being found under "F" and "RS" respectively.

A.	Associate
AA	Architectural Association; Automobile Association.
AAA	Allied Artists of America; Australian Academy of Art.
AAH	Association of Art Historians.
AAI	Association of Art Institutions.
AAL	Academy of Art and Literature.
AAPL	American Artists Professional League.
AAS	Aberdeen Art Society.
ABPR	Association of British Picture Restorers.
ACA	Association of Consultant Architects; Atlanta College of Art.
ACAVA	Association for Cultural Advancement through Visual Art
ACGB	Arts Council of Great Britain.
ACW	Art Council of Wales (formerly WAC).
ADAE	Advanced Diploma in Art Education.
ADB	Associate of the Drama Board.
AEA	American Academy of Equine Art.
AEC	Adult Education Centre.
AFAS	Armed Forces Art Society
AGBI	Artists' General Benevolent Institution.
AGI	Artistes Graphiques Internationales.
AGMS	Art Gallery and Museum Services.
AI	Auctioneers' Institute.
AIA	Academy of Irish Art; American Institute of Architecture.
AIAL	Association of International Institute of Art and Letters.
AI Archts.(Scot.).	Association of the Incorporation of Architects in Scotland.
AICA	Association Internationale des Critiques d'Art.
AM	Air Ministry; Member of Order of Australia.
AMA	Associate of the Museums Association.
AMC	Art Masters' Certificate.
AMTC	Art Masters' Teaching Certificate.
ANA	American National Academy.
AO	Officer, Order of Australia
AOI	Association of Illustrators.
AOSDANA	Aosdana is an affiliation of artists engaged in literature, music and visual arts in Ireland.
APA	Association of Polish Artists.
APS	American Portrait Society.
ARCA	Associate of the Royal College of Art.
ASA	American Society of Artists Inc.
ASBA	American Society of Botanical Artists.
ATC	Art Teachers' Certificate.
ATD	Art Teachers' Diploma.
AUC	Anno Urbis Conditæ (from the foundation of the city).
AVAW	Association of Visual Artists in Wales.
Ave.	Avenue.

AWG	Art Workers' Guild.
AWI	Australian Water-colour Institute.
b.	born.
BA	Bachelor of Arts; British Airways.
BAAT	British Association of Art Therapists.
BBC	British Broadcasting Corporation.
BCC	British Craft Centre.
B.Ed	Bachelor of Education; Board of Education.
BFA	Batchelor of Fine Arts.
B'ham.	Birmingham.
BIAT	British Institute of Architectural Technicians.
BIIA	British Institute of Industrial Art.
BIID	British Institute of Interior Design.
BL	Barrister-at-Law.
Bldg.	Building.
BLitt.	Bachelor of Letters.
Blvd.	Boulevard.
BM	British Museum.
BPD	British Society of Posters Designers.
BPS	British Psychological Society; Birmingham Pastel Society.
BSc.	Bachelor of Science.
BSI	British Standards Institution.
BSMGP	British Society of Master Glass Painters.
Bt.	Baronet.
BWS	British Water-colour Society.
CAC	Chertsey Art Club.
CASW	Contemporary Art Society for Wales.
Cav.	Cavalière (Knight).
CAVS.	Center for Advanced Visual Studies.
CB	Companion of the Bath.
CBE	Commander Order of the British Empire.
CC	County Council
Cert.	Certificate.
CertAD.	Certificate in Art and Design.
CertFA	Certificate in Fine Art.
CFE	College of Further Education.
CGA	Cheltenham Group of Artists.
CHE	College of Higher Education.
CI	Channel Isles.
CIAD	Central Institute for Art and Design.
CIE	Companion of the Order of the Indian Empire.
CLAS	Calligraphy and Lettering Art Society.
CMG.	Companion of St. Michael and St. George.
Col.	Colonel.
Comdr.	Commander.
CPA	Craft Potters Association.
CPS	Contemporary Portrait Society.
CSD	The Chartered Society of Designers (formerly Society of Industrial Artists and Designers).
CSI	Companion of the Order of the Star of India.
CSMA	Cornish Society of Marine Artists.
CVO	Commander of the Royal Victorian Order.
CWAC	City of Westminster Arts Council.

d.	daughter.
DA	Diploma of Art; Diploma of Edinburgh College of Art; Doctor of Arts.
DACS	Design and Artists Copyright Society
DAE	Diploma in Art Education.
DBE	Dame Grand Cross Order of the British Empire.
DC	District of Columbia.
DCM	Distinguished Conduct Medal.
decd.	deceased.
Des.RCA	Designer of the Royal College of Art.
DFA	Diploma of Fine Art.
DipAD	Diploma in Art and Design.
DipFA	Diploma in Fine Art.
DipHE	Diploma in Higher Education.
DLitt.	Doctor of Letters.
DNB	Dictionary of National Biography.
DOE	Department of the Environment.
DSc	Doctor of Science.
DSLU	Association of the Slovene plastic artists.
DSO	Companion of the Distinguished Service Order.
DStJ	Dame of Honour, Order of St. John of Jerusalem.
E.	East.
EAGMA	East Anglian Group of Marine Artists.
ECIA	European Committee of Interior Architects.
Educ.	Educated; Education.
Exhbn.	Exhibition.
Exhib.	Exhibited.
F.	Fellow; Foreign Member.
(F)	Founder Member (usually following Society initials)
FATG	Fine Art Trade Guild.
FBA	Fellow of the British Academy.
FCA	Federation of Canadian Artists.
FdA	Foundation Degree in Arts.
FECO	Federation of Cartoon Organisations
FETC	Further Education Teacher's Certificate.
FGCL	Fellow, Goldsmiths' College, London.
FGE	Fellow of the Guild of Glass Engravers.
FIAL	Fellow of the International Institute of Arts and Letters.
FLS	Fellow, Linnean Society of London.
FPS	Free Painters and Sculptors.
FSI	Fellow of the Surveyors' Institute.
FSS	Federation of Scottish Sculptors.
FTDA	Fellow of the Theatrical Designers and Craftsmen's Association.
GBE	Knight Grand Cross Order of the British Empire.
GCB	Knight Grand Cross of the Bath.
GCMG	Knight Grand Cross of St. Michael and St. George.
GCSI	Knight Grand Commander of the Star of India.
g-d.	grand-daughter.
GLC	Guild of Lettering Craftsmen; Greater London Council.
GMAS	Miniature Art Society of Georgia.
GMC	Guild of Memorial Craftsmen.
GNVQ	General National Vocational Qualification
GPS	Glasgow Printmaking Society.
GRA	Guild of Railway Artists.

g-s.	grandson.
GS	Geological Society.
GSA	Glasgow School of Art.
GSWA	Glasgow Society of Women Artists.
Gt.	Great.
Hon. D'Art	Honorary Doctorate of Art
H.	Hon. Member.
HDFA	Higher Diploma in Fine Art.
HDipAD	Higher Diploma in Art and Design.
HM	His Majesty; Her Majesty.
HMI	H.M. Inspector of Schools.
HMSO	Her Majesty's Stationery Office.
HND	Higher National Diploma
HRH	His Royal Highness; Her Royal Highness.
HS	Hilliard Society.
IAA	International Association of Art.
IAAS	Incorporated Association of Architects and Surveyors.
IAASBA	International Associate, American Society of Botanical Artists.
IAL	International Institute of Arts and Letters.
IAS	Incorporated Association of Surveyors; Irish Art Society.
IBD	Institute of British Decorators and Interior Designers.
IBIA	Institute of British Industrial Art.
ICA	Institute of Contemporary Arts.
ICE	Institute of Civil Engineers.
ICOGRADA.	International Council of Graphic Design Association.
ICSID	International Council of Societies of Industrial Design.
ID	Institute of Directors; Institute of Decorators.
IED	Institution of Engineer Designers.
IEE	Institute of Electrical Engineers.
IFA	Incorporated Faculty of Arts.
IFI	International Federation of Interior Architects/Designers.
IGA	International Guild of Artists.
IIC	International Institute for Conservation of Paintings.
ILEA	Inner London Education Authority.
IMCE	Institute of Mechanical and Civil Engineers.
IME	Institute of Mechanical Engineers; Institute of Engineers.
Inst.	Institute; Institution.
IOM	Isle of Man.
IOW	Isle of Wight.
IPD	Institute of Professional Designers.
IPG	Independent Painters Group; Industrial Painters Group.
ISCA	International Society of Catholic Artists.
ISMP	International Society of Marine Painters.
ISO	Imperial Service Order.
ITD	Institute of Training and Development.
KBE	Knight Commander Order of the British Empire.
KC	King's Counsel.
KCB	Knight Commander of the Bath.
KCMG	Knight Commander of St. Michael and St. George.
KCSG	Knight Commander of St. Gregory the Great.
KCSI	Knight Commander of the Star of India.
KCVO	Knight Commander of the Royal Victorian Order.
KG	Knight of the Order of the Garter.

KIAD	Kent Institute of Art and Design.
Kt.	Knight.
L.	Licentiate.
LAA	Liverpool Academy of Arts.
LAMDA	London Academy of Music and Dramatic Art.
Lancs.	Lancashire.
LCAD	London Certificate in Art and Design.
LCC	London County Council.
LDAD	London Diploma of Art and Design.
LI	Landscape Institute.
Lieut.	Lieutenant.
LIFA	Licentiate of International Faculty of Arts.
LLD	Doctor of Laws.
LLM	Master of Laws.
LS	Linnean Society.
LSIA	Licentiate of the Society of Industrial Artists.
Ltd.	Limited.
M.	Member; Ministry; Monsieur.
m.	married; metre.
MA	Master of Arts.
MAA	Medical Artists' Association; Miniature Artists of America.
MAFA	Manchester Academy of Fine Arts.
MAI	Master of Fine Arts International.
MAS-F	Miniature Art Society/Florida.
MAS-NJ	Miniature Art Society/New Jersey.
MAS-W	Miniature Art Society/Washington.
MBE	Member of the Order of the British Empire.
MC	Military Cross.
MD	Doctor of Medicine; Managing Director.
Mem.	Member.
MFA	Master of Fine Art.
MGP	Master Glass Painters.
MIT	Massachusetts Institute of Technology.
ML	Licentiate in Medicine.
MLitt	Master of Letters.
MoD	Ministry of Defence.
MOMA	Museum of Modern Art.
MPSG	Miniature Painters, Sculptors and Gravers Society of Washington DC
MS	Society of Miniaturists; Motor Ship.
MSc.	Master of Science.
MSM	Meritorious Service Medal.
MVO	Member of the Royal Victorian Order.
NA	National Academy of Design (New York).
NAA	National Artists Association.
NACF	National Art Collection Fund.
NADFAS	National Association of Decorative and Fine Arts Societies.
NAMM	National Association of Master Masons.
NAOW	Naïve Artists of Wales.
NAPA	National Acrylic Painters' Association.
NCAC	New Chertsey Art Club.
NCDAD	National Council for Diplomas in Art and Design.
NDD	National Diploma in Design.
NEAC	New English Art Club.

NFT	National Film Theatre.
NFU	National Froebel Union/ National Farmers Union
NGA	National Gallery of Australia.
NI	Northern Ireland.
NMGM	National Museums and Galleries on Merseyside.
NPG	National Portrait Gallery.
NPS	National Portrait Society.
NS	National Society.
NSA	New Society of Artists; Natal Society of Artists; Newlyn Society of Artists.
NSAE	National Society for Art Education.
NSMP	National Society of Mural Painters.
NSPS	National Society of Painters, Sculptors and Printmakers.
NSW	New South Wales.
NWAB	North West Art Board.
NYC	New York City.
NZ	New Zealand.
OAS	Oxford Society of Artists.
OBE	Officer, Order of the British Empire.
OC	Order of Canada (Officer).
OCS	Oriental Ceramic Society.
ODF	Ouvrier de France
OLJ	Officer Companion of Order of St. Lazarus of Jerusalem.
O.Ont.	Order of Ontario.
OSA	Ontario Society of Arts.
OSB	Order of St. Benedict.
O.St.J.	Officer of the Most Venerable Order of the Hospital of St. John of Jerusalem.
OUP	Oxford University Press.
Oxon.	Oxford/Oxfordshire
P.	President.
PAI	Paisley Art Institute.
PGCE	Post Graduate Certificate of Education.
PhB	Bachelor of Philosophy.
PhD	Doctor of Philosophy.
Phil.	Philosophy.
PI	Portrait Institute.
PIH	Pictures in Hospitals.
Pk.	Park.
Pl.	Place.
P&O	Peninsular and Oriental Steam Navigation Co., Ltd.
Pres.	President.
Prof.	Professor.
PS	Pastel Society.
QC	Queen's Counsel.
QEH	Queen Elizabeth's Hospital School.
RA	Royal Academician; Royal Academy.
RAA	Runnymede Association of Arts.
RAAS	Royal Amateur Art Society.
RAF	Royal Air Force.
RAI	Royal Anthropological Institute.
RAM	Royal Academy of Music.
RAMC	Royal Army Medical Corps.

RAS	Royal Astronomical Society; Royal Asiatic Society; Richmond Art Society; Ridley Art Society.
RBA	Royal Society of British Artists.
RBS	Royal Society of British Sculptors.
RBSA	Royal Birmingham Society of Artists.
RCA	Royal College of Art; Royal Canadian Academy; Royal Cambrian Academician.
RCamA	Royal Cambrian Academy.
RCGP	Royal College of General Practitioners.
RCHS	Royal Caledonian Horticultural Society.
RCM	Royal College of Music.
RCP	Royal College of Physicians.
RCS	Royal College of Surgeons.
RCSE	Royal College of Surgeons, Edinburgh.
RDI	Royal Designer of Industry.
RDS	Royal Drawing Society.
RE	Royal Society of Painter-Printmakers (formerly Royal Society of Painter-Etchers and Engravers); Royal Engineers.
Regt.	Regiment.
Retd.	Retired.
Rev.	Reverend.
RFA	Royal Field Artillery.
RGA	Royal Garrison Artillery.
RGI	Royal Glasgow Institute.
RGS	Royal Geographical Society; Royal Graphic Society.
RHA	Royal Hibernian Academy.
RHS	Royal Horticultural Society.
RHistS	Royal Historical Society.
RI	Royal Institute of Painters in Water-colours.
RIA	Royal Irish Academy.
RIAI	Royal Institute of Architects in Ireland.
RIAS	Royal Institute of Architects in Scotland.
RIBA	Royal Institute of British Architects.
RICS	Royal Institution of Chartered Surveyors.
RM	Royal Marines.
RMS	Royal Society of Miniature Painters.
RN	Royal Navy.
RNIB	Royal National Institute for the Blind.
RNLI	Royal National Lifeboat Institution.
RNR	Royal Naval Reserve.
RNVR	Royal Naval Volunteer Reserve.
ROI	Royal Institute of Oil Painters.
RP	Royal Society of Portrait Painters and Member.
RPS	Royal Photographic Society.
RSA	Royal Scottish Academy; Royal Society of Arts.
RSAI	Royal Society of Antiquaries of Ireland.
RSMA	Royal Society of Marine Arts.
RSPB	Royal Society for the Protection of Birds.
RSW	Royal Scottish Water-colour Society or Royal Scottish Society of Painters in Water-colours.
Rt.	Right.
RUA	Royal Ulster Academy of Painting, Sculpture and Architecture; Royal Ulster Academician.

RWA	Royal West of England Academician; Royal West of England Academy.
RWS	Royal Watercolour Society (formerly Royal Society of Painters in Water-colours).
S.	South.
s.	son; sons.
SA	Society of Antiquaries; Society of Apothecaries.
SAA	Society of Aviation Artists; Society of All Artists
SAAC	Society of Scottish Artists and Artist Craftsmen (renamed 'Visual Arts Scotland').
SABA	Scottish Artists' Benevolent Association.
SAC	Scottish Arts Council.
SAE	Society of American Etchers; Society of Automobile Engineers (American).
SAF	Société des Artistes Français.
SAGA	Society of American Graphic Artists.
SAI	Scottish Arts Institute; Society of Architectural Illustrators.
SAII	Society of Architectural and Industrial Illustrators.
Salop.	Shropshire.
SAM	National Society of Art Masters.
SAP	Society of Artist Printmakers.
SBA	Society of Botanical Artists.
s-d.	step daughter.
SDC	Society of Designer Craftsmen and Craft Centre (formerly Arts and Crafts Exhibition Society).
SEA	Society for Education in Art; Society of Equestrian Artists (see SEqA).
Sec.	Secretary.
SEFAS	South Eastern Federation of Art Societies.
SEqA	Society of Equestrian Artists (formerly SEA).
SFP	Society of Floral Painters.
SGA	Society of Graphic Art.
SGE	Society of Glass Engravers.
SGFA	Society of Graphic Fine Art (formerly Society of Graphic Art).
SGP	Society of Graver Printers.
SGT	Society of Glass Technology.
SHA	Society of Heraldic Art.
SI	Surveyors' Institute.
SIAD	(see CSD)
SID	Society of Industrial Designers of USA; Mem. Swedish Industrial Designers.
SLm.	Society of Limners.
SM	Society of Miniaturists.
SMOM	Knight of Magisterial Grace of the Sovereign Military Order of Malta.
SMP	Society of Mural Painters.
SNAD	Society of Numismatic Artists and Designers.
SNGMA	Scottish National Gallery of Modern Art.
SNPG	Scottish National Portrait Gallery.
Soc.	Société; Society.
Socs.	Societies.
SOFA	Society of Feline Artists.
SPF	Société des Pastellistes de France.
SPS	Society of Portrait Sculptors.
SPSAS	Swiss Society of Painters, Sculptors and Architects.

Sq.	Square.
s-s.	step son.
SSA	Society of Scottish Artists.
SSI	Society of Scribes and Illuminators.
SSMCE	Society of Sculptors Medal and Coin Engravers.
SSN	Societaire de la Société Nationale des Beaux Arts.
SSWA	Scottish Society of Women Artists.
St.	Saint; Street.
STD	Society of Typographical Designers.
SWA	Society of Women Artists.
SWAc	South West Academy of Fine and Applied Art Academician
SWAS	Society of Women Artists of Scotland.
SWE	Society of Wood Engravers.
SWLA	Society of Wildlife Artists.
TCD	Trinity College, Dublin.
TCM	Trinity College of Music.
TPI	Town Planning Institute.
TWASI	The Wildlife Art Society International
UA	United Society of Artists.
UAE	United Arab Emirates.
UCH	University College Hospital.
UCL	University College, London.
USA	United States of America.
USM	Ulster Society of Miniaturists.
USWA	Ulster Society of Women Artists.
UWA	Ulster Women Artists.
UWP	University of Wales Press.
UWS	Ulster Water-colour Society.
V.	Vice.
v.	versus.
V&A	Victoria and Albert Museum.
VC	Victoria Cross.
VD	Volunteer Officers' Decoration; Victorian Decoration.
Vol.	Volume.
VP	Vice-President.
W.	West.
WAC	Welsh Arts Council (see ACW).
WAG	Walker Art Gallery.
WCSI	Water-colour Society of Ireland.
WSW	Water-colour Society of Wales.
WGA	Wapping Group of Artists
WIAA	Women's International Arts Association.
WIAC	Women's International Art Club.
WIAS	Women's International Art Society.
WWF	World Wildlife Fund.
ZS	Zoological Society.

NOTES

NOTES

NOTES

NOTES

NOTES

NOTES

NOTES